# Eastern Europe

Tom Masters

Brett Atkinson, Greg Bloom, Peter Dragicevich, Lisa Dunford, Steve Fallon, Steve Kokker, Patrick Horton, Vesna Maric, Jeanne Oliver, Leif Pettersen, Robert Reid, Tim Richards, Wendy Taylor

**ST PETERSBURG (p718)**
The greatest repository of art and culture in the region, Russia's imperial capital is enchanting

**KYIV (p865)**
The spirit of rebellion is contagious in Ukraine's fun-loving post-revolutionary capital

**RĪGA (p417)**
Baltic beauty delights with its stunningly diverse Old Town, delicious art nouveau and seething nightlife

**VILNIUS (p443)**
Europe's largest Old Town is an intoxicating maze of cobbled streets and baroque churches

**SPIŠSKÝ HRAD (p809)**
The vast 11th- to 14th-century castle ruin rambles a top a 200m-high hill, and is one of the largest in eastern europe

**KRAKÓW (p561)**
The former royal capital of Poland, a blend of splendid historic architecture and vibrant nightlife

**SAAREMAA (p343)**
Gorgeous stretches of juniper groves, deserted coastlines and an ancient landscape

**OLOMOUC (p300)**
The Czech Republic's travel secret blends a stunning Old Town with a buzzing student lifestyle

**CHISINAU (p506)**
Take a wine tour at one of Moldova's famous vineyards, and party in the clubs of Chisinau

**BRASOV (p640)**
Transylvania's hub has an incredible wealth of medieval architecture in it's gothic heart

**VELIKO TÂRNOVO (p162)**
Bulgaria's stunning ancient capital and main university town, one of the most beautiful cities in Eastern Europe

**BUDAPEST (p356)**
Party on the Danube, soak in historik spas, feast on culture and goulash

**NOVI SAD (p762)**
Europe-famous EXIT music festival held annually in the city's ancient fortress

**LAKE OHRID (p481)**
This ancient lake is a place of dramatic beauty and the spiritual heart of Macedonia

**BLED (p838)**
A castle overlooking an island in a placid lake - it just can't get more picture perfect

**MOSTAR (p116)**
Mostar's new Old Bridge once more attracts tourist and daring young men who plunge off it for cash

**DUBROVNIK (p233)**
George Bernard Shaw's 'paradise on earth' is Croatia's most alluring town

**KOTOR (p533)**
Montenegro's medieval walled city at the head of a brooding Wagnerian fjord

# Destination Eastern Europe

Eastern Europe buckles under the sheer strain of being forced together for descriptive purposes. Never has a region been so slippery for those trying to grasp it, pin it down and define it. The region's strangely unifying factor is, paradoxically, its incredible contrasts, particularly in the face of recurrent clichés that stereotype it as grey, poor and backward. Even the most superficial glance will tell you that nothing could be further from the truth, whether you're using wi-fi in Tallinn or trying fusion cuisine in Sarajevo.

The geographic, cultural, linguistic and culinary sweep of Eastern Europe is simply enormous – from Mediterranean Albania to Baltic St Petersburg, from EU-approved transparency to bureaucratic peat bog, from Latin to Cyrillic and from blinis to goulash. Experiencing and living Eastern Europe is the way to go (merely seeing it will never do) and independent travel is definitely the best way to do this. Beautiful baroque cathedrals in Poland, peasant hospitality in the Balkans or just the sheer black comedy of daily life in Belarus will leave enduring impressions on any visitor's mind long after the majesty of the region's great cities, beaches or mountain ranges has faded.

It helps to be a surrealist, of course. Two decades after the region changed beyond recognition from the grey, uniform communist states immortalised by TV images of bread queues in the 1980s, going to Eastern Europe remains a trip through the looking glass when coming from the relatively predictable certainties of the West. Look no further for adventure; come to Eastern Europe to be confounded, bemused, amazed and amused. You have nothing to lose but your preconceptions!

# Urban Grooves & Café Society

Live tunes and packed-out underground bars rock Bucharest's budding nightlife scene (p632), Romania

RICHARD I'ANSON

JONATHAN SMITH

Sample some local õlu (beer) and soak up the laid-back vibe of Tallinn's hip bars and clubs (p329), Estonia

Terrace dining, coffee-drinking dens and sweet smelling bakeries are all part of the charm of eating in Sarajevo (p112), Bosnia and Hercegovina

DOUG MCKINLAY

# Architectural Treasures

JONATHAN SMITH

Visit the sombre Soviet WWII memorial of Brest Fortress (p90), Belarus

JONATHAN SMITH

The colourful domes of the Church on Spilled Blood (p725) adorn St Petersburg's skyline, Russia

Make like the ancient Romans and see a show at Plovdiv's 2nd-century Philippopolis theatre (p153), Bulgaria

PAUL GREENWAY

*Opposite*: Soak up the old, the new and some sun in Prague's Staré Město Square (p264), Czech Republic

IZZET KERIBAR

See local lads plunge off Mostar's Stari Most (Old Bridge; p118), Bosnia and Hercegovina

WITOLD SKRYPCZAK

# Beaches & Islands

The dramatic Crimean mountains meet the sparkling Black Sea at Yalta (p895), Ukraine

Laze away some days along the sapphire-blue coast near Budva (p532), Montenegro

Escape the bustle of Riga at Majori beach (p427), Latvia

Row across Bled's spectacular lake to visit its fairytale-like church (p839), Slovenia

WAYNE WALTON

Explore the peaceful villages, azure waters and pine-covered slopes of Hvar Island (p228), Croatia

Find the twitcher within while bird-spotting on the rich, marshy wetlands of Romania's World Heritage Danube Delta (p682)

DIANA MAYFIELD

Crystalline waters lap the pristine, isolated shore of Dhërmi beach (p65), Albania

RAFAEL ESTEFANIA

# Great Outdoors

Carve up the snow-covered slopes of Slovakia's Tatra Mountains (p801)

The legendary vineyard of Cricova (p513), Moldova

The spectacular Pravčická Brána
natural arch, Bohemian Switzerland National Park (p282), Czech Republic

TOM COCKREM

The festive ski town of Bansko (p150) nestles beneath the Pirin Mountains, Bulgaria

MARTIN MOOS

© TIIT VEERMÄE/ALAMY

Hike, bike or canoe your way around the enchanting Lahemaa National Park (p331), Estonia

Turquoise streams carve through steep forested hills in the Plitvice Lakes National Park (p221), Croatia

The picturesque rewards of a day of hiking in the Tatra Mountains (p574), Poland

WAYNE WALTON

# Diverse Cultures

RICHARD NEBESKY

Colourful, handmade folk crafts on sale in Budapest (p356), Hungary

Traditional folk wear, Lithuania (p439)

Women in traditional costume, Serbia (p747)

JONATHAN SMITH

LEE

The Orthodox frescoes of Sveta Bogorodica Bolnička church, Ohrid (p481), Macedonia

PAUL DAVID HELLANDER

# Contents

**16** CONTENTS

## Regional Map Contents

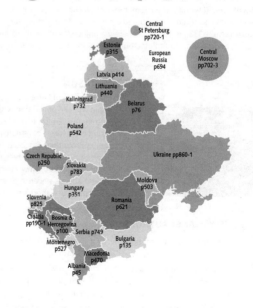

Central
St Petersburg
pp720-1

Estonia
p315

European
Russia
p694

Central
Moscow
pp702-3

Latvia p414

Lithuania
p440

Kaliningrad
p732

Belarus
p76

Poland
p542

Czech Republic
p250

Slovakia
p783

Ukraine pp860-1

Moldova
p503

Hungary
p351

Romania
p621

Slovenia
p825

Croatia
pp190-1

Bosnia &
Hercegovina
p100

Serbia p749

Montenegro
p527

Bulgaria
p135

Macedonia
p470

Albania
p45

# The Authors

## TOM MASTERS

Tom first visited Eastern Europe at the age of 14 when he went to stay with family friends in Bulgaria just as communism was crumbling there. He has had a love affair with the once-obscure region since he can remember, and aged 15 travelled around a newly democratic Eastern Europe by train with his mother (an experience not unlike a Graham Greene novel). At 18 Tom finally got to see Russia, his true passion, while studying the language at university. A decade later and he still doesn't claim to truly understand the country, but thinks he's got a better idea than most. More of his writing can be seen at www.mastersmafia.com.

**My Favourite Trip**

In summer 2005 I found myself retracing the route of the Nazi invasion of the Soviet Union for a TV documentary I was working on. Starting in Gdańsk (p597), where WWII started, we headed through the beautiful Polish countryside of the Great Masurian Lakes (p608), stopping to see Hitler's wartime HQ, the Wolf's Lair (p610), where our flesh was stripped from our bones by swarms of mosquitoes deep in the forest. We then went on to Kaunas (p455), where we got drunk with students in Lithuania's biggest university town, visited the chilling Ninth Fort (p457) and continued to Rīga (p417), where we enjoyed the amazing architecture and hung out with Latvia's biggest boyband, BrainStorm. (I wonder if each member of Westlife speaks three languages and could give a guided architectural tour of their home town?) After this we visited university town Tartu (p333), in Estonia, where we enjoyed the beer halls and midnight sun, before crossing into Russia and arriving in St Petersburg (p718) in time for the summer solstice. Magical.

## BRETT ATKINSON

Brett's first experiences of Eastern Europe were Bulgaria and Yugoslavia, when the Iron Curtain was still pulled tightly shut. He's since returned to write about Hungary's communist legacy, island hopped in Croatia and honeymooned in Sarajevo. During eight weeks of research in the Czech Republic, he furthered his hobby of beer appreciation, especially while watching Friday night ice hockey at the local *pivnice* (pub). When he's not travelling for Lonely Planet, Brett lives with Carol in Auckland, New Zealand, about as far from Eastern Europe as is possible. He advises never to drive a Skoda Fabia across a narrow castle drawbridge – especially if there's no room to turn around on the other side.

## GREG BLOOM

While living in Ukraine from 1997 to 2002, Greg used to visit Latvia annually for the ultimate Frisbee tournament in Jūrmala. Back then you could still find a $10 hotel room, bribe a traffic cop, and hail Ladas in lieu of cabs. Rīga was an undiscovered jewel. Returning to the Baltics for the first time in years, Greg reports that a) Rīga is no longer undiscovered; and b) apparently, you can no longer bribe Baltic traffic cops. The cops are nicer, though, and speeding tickets not too expensive. Formerly the editor of the *Kyiv Post*, Greg is now based in Manila.

## PETER DRAGICEVICH

Over the course of a dozen years working for newspapers and magazines in both his native New Zealand and Australia, Peter's covered everything from honeymooning in Verona to gay resorts in Fiji. He finally gave in to Kiwi wanderlust, giving up staff jobs to chase his typically diverse antipodean roots around much of Europe – spending time in his grandparents' villages in Croatia, Scotland and northern England. While it's family ties that first drew him to the Balkans, it's the history, natural beauty, convoluted politics, cheap *rakija* (Macedonian firewater) and, most importantly, the intriguing people that keep bringing him back.

## LISA DUNFORD

A fascination with Eastern Europe gripped Lisa from childhood, probably because her grandfather came from the Carpathian region that was Hungary, then Czechoslovakia and is now in the Ukraine. She studied in Budapest for her junior year and arrived in Bratislava, Slovakia, after graduation looking for work; various projects led to a job at the US Agency for International Development. She danced with the country as it became an independent nation, learned the language and made life-long friends. Lisa now lives in Houston, Texas, but projects and travel take her back to the region often; she always makes sure she spends as much time as possible on the trip in Slovakia. It still feels like home.

## STEVE FALLON

Steve has been travelling to Slovenia since the early 1990s, when a well-known publishing company refused his proposal to write a guidebook to the country because of 'the war going on' (it had ended two years earlier) and an influential American daily newspaper told him that their readers weren't interested in 'Slovakia'. Never mind, it was his own little secret for a good 10 years. Though he still hasn't reached the top of Mt Triglav, Steve considers at least part of his soul Slovenian and returns to the country as often as he can for a glimpse of the Julian Alps in the sun, and a dribble of *bučno olje* (pumpkinseed oil).

## PATRICK HORTON

Born with restless feet, Patrick's journeys have taken him to the more arcane areas of the world, especially those with current or former communist leanings. North Korea, Cuba, the old USSR, the old Yugoslavia and Nicaragua come to mind. Donning his author disguise of sunnies, fedora and trench coat, Patrick prowled around Serbia, Montenegro and Bosnia and Hercegovina to unearth the traveller hot spots. Patrick has been a contributing author and photographer for many Lonely Planet guides.

## STEVE KOKKER

Steve has long found life in Eastern Europe more thrilling and full of exciting possibilities than back in his otherwise-great hometown of Montreal. A frequent visitor to the region since 1992, he has spent most of his time in Estonia, Russia and elsewhere in Eastern Europe since 1996. He's now living in Tallinn, where his father was born, thereby completing a karmic circle of sorts.

## VESNA MARIC

Vesna loved researching Hungary in below-zero January temperatures, spending a lot of time warming her bones in thermal baths, eating hot goulash, drinking wine and dancing in smoky clubs. Her first visit to Hungary was some years ago: after an overnight train from Sarajevo, she emerged into a springtime Budapest so full of beans and birds and bees, and she kept longing to go back for more. Vesna will never forget the joy of skating on a frozen lake, along with residents of a whole Hungarian village.

## JEANNE OLIVER

Jeanne arrived in Croatia in 1996 just as the country was getting back on its feet and she has returned every year since. Enchanted by the coastline and fascinated by the ever-evolving political scene, Jeanne spends her vacations in Croatia between writing every Lonely Planet guide to the country. As well as turning out newspaper and magazine articles, Jeanne has launched a Croatia travel website, www.croatiatraveller.com.

## LEIF PETTERSEN

In 2003, Leif's 'unhinged contempt for reality' spurred him to abandon an idiot-proof career with the Federal Reserve in America and embark on a homeless odyssey of travel writing. Despite having no leads or training – and a dubious grasp on grammar – he achieved modest success by deluging hapless editors with material so raw and protracted that a trilingual international support group was formed to deal with it. Leif's weakness for pretty girls brought him to Romania in 2004, where the low cost of living compelled him to stay. Speaking the language, having an apartment and owning a 1990 Dacia 1310, it's said that Leif need only learn how to distill *ţuica* to gain honorary Romanian citizenship.

## ROBERT REID

Somewhere between an Oklahoma tornado and a Rambo movie, little Robert's sense of rebellion led him to old *Soviet Life* mags, and on to the Bulgarian-created Cyrillic alphabet and travels in lands where sickles aren't just a convenient rhyme for pickles. After studying Russian in college ('nearly a minor!'), he spent a couple of summers roaming Eastern Europe. He maintains a disproportionate attraction to planned cities made to impress Soviet dignitaries, clunky '70s hotels with drastically floral carpets, and grey housing blocks – but he likes the pretty parts too. He updated two of his favourites for this guide, Bulgaria and Romania. He lives in Brooklyn.

## TIM RICHARDS

Tim spent a year teaching English in Kraków, Poland, in 1994–95, having transferred with an international teaching organisation from a two-year stint in Egypt. He was fascinated by the massive post-communism transition affecting every aspect of Polish life, and by surviving remnants of the Cold War days. As a result, he jumped at the chance to return for this assignment more than a decade later, and was delighted by his intense reacquaintance with this beautiful, complex country. When he's not on the road for Lonely Planet, Tim is a freelancer living in Melbourne, Australia, writing on topics such as travel, lifestyle, the arts, technology and pets.

## WENDY TAYLOR

Wendy Taylor is a 35-year-old *luftmensch* whose affinity for vast snowy landscapes started at an early age when she toddled around Anchorage, Alaska, looking for a carrot for her snowman's nose. But it wasn't until the 1990s, when her humour had sufficiently blackened, that she fulfilled all requirements for the perfect Slavophile. With a degree from UC Berkeley in Slavic Languages and Literatures she set off for big bad Moscow in 1994. She has since teetered back and forth between California and the former USSR, steered by the ups and downs of her love/hate relationship with the place. She recently spent six months in Belarus writing, editing and participating in anti-Lukashenko activities.

# Getting Started

You've bought this book, you've doubtless got lots of places you'd like to see, but what to do now? Whether you plan your trip from start to finish before leaving home or prefer to wait and see how you feel each morning before deciding what to do, there are some things you should definitely take into account beforehand. While Eastern Europe is a joy to travel round these days compared to how it was just a decade ago, you'll still find a number of bureaucratic hurdles, largely manifesting themselves more clearly the further east you go.

Visas remain an issue – not only getting them but also registering them. Questions of dual or multientry visa and timing create problems. Planning ahead is the simple answer. For example, two decades after *perestroika* and you still find all sorts of visa headaches when visiting Russia, the *bête noire* of the region's independent travellers. You still need to get an official invitation to visit Russia or Belarus before you'll be granted a visa!

## WHEN TO GO

Balancing the good weather against the huge summer crowds is the major concern when deciding when to go. If you plan to go to the 'big three' of Prague, Budapest or Kraków it's a good idea to avoid July and August when these cities can be unbearably crowded, although this is not such a problem elsewhere if you're getting off the beaten path. Eastern Europe has a surprisingly consistent weather pattern for a region its size. High season runs from May until September; in July and August you'll find the above cities and anywhere beachy teeming with backpackers and coach tours. The best time to visit is either side of the summer peak – May, June and September stand out, as it's not too hot, too crowded or overbooked anywhere.

See Climate Charts (p911) for more information.

Travelling out of season can result in some real bargains in accommodation; however, many places where tourism is the main industry all but close down during the low season. Also, bear in mind that Russia, the Baltics, Belarus and Ukraine have very cold winters, with -20°C not being unusual between November and February, although average temperatures are far less extreme. Winter is cold everywhere, but the further south you get the milder it is – Albania's average winter temperature is a relatively mild 9°C.

## COSTS AND MONEY

Along with EU expansion have come inevitable price rises. It truly is risible when people think they can go east and live like kings for peanuts (yet a surprising number of people seem to expect this in the region's less-visited corners). While this was once true, things have changed a lot, much to the horror of locals who in many cases cannot afford to live well in their own countries. Generally speaking it's still true that Eastern Europe is cheaper than Western Europe, but buy a cappuccino in Moscow or pay for a hotel room in Prague and you may find yourself lamenting the advance of the free market. Even in the least touristy niches of the region such as Belarus or Albania, locals are well aware of travellers' spending power and price things accordingly.

Trying to give daily budgets for such a huge region is hard indeed. Backpackers staying in hostels and eating cheaply can expect to spend around €30 to €40 per day, probably more in cities such as Moscow, Prague and Budapest. Those wanting to have a more comfortable trip (staying in mid-range accommodation and eating in decent restaurants most of the time) will need to spend between €60 and €70 per day. These are very much ballpark figures; in the countryside you'll be able to get by on far less, while if you're in bigger cities during high season and visiting lots of museums and sights, you'll find you need more than that.

Unthinkable as it would have been just 10 years ago, these days as long as you have an ATM card, you need not worry about obtaining money in any major Eastern European city.

All major credit and debit cards are accepted by ATMs, including those on the Cirrus/Maestro system. However, always have a back-up plan, so if an ATM is not working or your card is stolen you won't be stranded. Most major banks will do cash advances on credit cards (you'll need to bring your passport) and, of course, exchange travellers cheques.

Travellers cheques are the safest way to carry large sums of money – they can be replaced if lost or stolen, and when stolen, cannot be cashed by the thief. However, they are a pain in the proverbial sometimes too, and should never be relied upon outside major towns.

Cash is the easiest way to carry money, of course, but lose it all and you're screwed. The euro and US dollar are the currencies most easily exchanged. In many places you can even pay for hotel accommodation in euros, although never assume this to be the case. The days of currency controls in Eastern Europe are gone, so there's no need to fear converting your 'hard' currency and being unable to re-exchange it before leaving the country. However, many countries' currencies are difficult to exchange elsewhere. In most cases it's best to change any currency into either euros, dollars or the currency of your next destination before leaving, even if this means getting bad exchange rates at the border.

XE (www.xe.com/ucc) is an up-to-the-second online currency-exchange calculator. Find out the rates for all Eastern European currencies, and see exactly how much your trip is going to cost you.

## READING UP
### Books

There are a huge number of books about the region. While the most pertinent titles for each country are listed in the individual country directories of this book, the following books provide an interesting introduction to the complexities and idiosyncrasies of Eastern Europe as a region.

One classic of travel writing is *Black Lamb and Grey Falcon,* a huge unclassifiable look at the Balkans on the eve of WWII through the eyes of Brit Rebecca West as she makes her way through Bosnia, Serbia, Kosovo, Albania and Croatia in 1937. Her pro-Serbian sentiment has made the book unfashionable since the area's recent ethnic cleansing, although her dark assertion that 'the whole world is a vast Kosovo, an abominable blood-logged plain' seems to have rung true some 50 years after she wrote it. This is a magnificent, poetic and fascinating account.

A more recent Balkan odyssey is Robert Kaplan's *Balkan Ghosts.* Kaplan, who roamed Yugoslavia, Romania, Greece and Bulgaria in the 1980s and 1990s, recorded the stories of people he met on his way, and produced an engaging read.

*Stalin's Nose,* Rory Maclean's much-loved account of travelling from Berlin to Moscow via Romania in the period immediately following the fall of the Berlin Wall, is a travelogue set during a unique time in history. Crossing the remnants of the Eastern Bloc with his aunt and her pet pig in a Trabant, Maclean draws an engaging and moving portrait of a region in turmoil.

Jason Godwin's *On Foot to the Golden Horn* is set at a similar time and details a walk from Gdańsk to Istanbul in the early 1990s. Mainly concerned with Poland and Romania, the book is entertaining and encyclopaedic, jumping from the fears of locals as democracy arrives to local history and getting along with his fellow walker and girlfriend, Kate.

An unconventional travel guide and Lonely Planet send-up, *Molvania: A Land Untouched by Modern Dentistry* (Santo Cilauro et al) creates a fictitious land in Eastern Europe that's the 'next big thing'. A good laugh for anyone travelling in the region and sick of guidebooks like this one!

## TOP FIVE MUST-READS

Eastern Europe's creative wealth is immense, nowhere more so than in its ever-challenging, ever-innovative literary production. The list below barely scrapes the surface, but these titles are warmly recommended by the authors of this book and will make great companions on any trip.

- *The Joke* (Milan Kundera) An insight into Czech society during the communist era. In a moment of anger, Ludvik sends his girlfriend a postcard with the message 'Optimism is the opium of the people! A healthy atmosphere stinks of stupidity! Long live Trotsky!' It's a joke, meant to shock her, but instead, she reports him to the party, and a downward spiral of persecution and paranoia begins.

- *Death and the Penguin* (Andrei Kurkov) A charming novel about life and loneliness in post-Soviet Ukraine. Unsuccessful writer Viktor adopts Misha the penguin from Kyiv Zoo when it runs out of money to buy the animals food. Together they have many curious adventures in the magical Ukrainian capital, although they soon become embroiled in something far darker than Viktor ever imagined.

- *The Notebook* (Agota Kristof) The first book in a trilogy about war-torn Hungary, this coldly narrated, simple novel follows inseparable twins sent to live with their evil grandmother during WWII. The brutalising effects of the war, their grandmother's hatred and a lack of love turn them into true monsters before the reader's eyes. Watch out for the shock ending!

- *The Concert* (Ismail Kadare) History dissected by Albania's greatest living writer. Set during the break between President Enver Hoxha and China in the 1970s, this book follows the lives of the party elite and those who seek to join their ranks. A fascinating account of a hidden time.

- *Sarajevo Marlboro* (Miljenko Jergovic) This collection of short stories from Bosnian journalist Jergovic has established itself as a classic in just a few years. Within its pages, life rather than death is extolled, and while the dark events of the war in Bosnia are always present, the warmth and humanity of the stories are the overwhelming impression left with the reader.

*My War Gone By, I Miss It So,* by Anthony Lloyd, is a brilliant memoir of the Bosnian war by a heroin-addicted war correspondent, which was mildly controversial due to him not blaming the Serbs exclusively for the war.

Eastern Europe's culturally rich and sad Roma people are explored in Isabel Fonseca's *Bury Me Standing,* a history, travelogue, cultural guide and deeply moving account of Roma trying to retain their culture in postcommunist, nationalist Eastern Europe.

Bruce Benderson's *The Romanian* is a haunting memoir of his own love affair with a Romanian hustler he meets in Hungary. Falling into unrequited love, Benderson follows the object of his affection back to Romania where they live for a time, during which Benderson becomes fascinated by Romanian history and art. A bleak insight into the realities of Eastern European life.

A more light-hearted read is British TV comedian Griff Rhys Jones' *To the Baltic with Bob,* an account of sailing from the UK to St Petersburg via the canals of Eastern Europe. It's eccentric and grumpy but good fun.

## Websites

There's a huge amount of up-to-date information on the web and, whether you're planning a weekend in Prague or a two-month odyssey through the entire region, you'll find the internet an invaluable tool.

**Euromost** (www.euromost.com) A chaotic (have these guys heard of spell check?) but interesting and useful site gathering news and information about the entire region.

**Flycheapo** (www.flycheapo.com) This brilliant website saves you the hassle of checking every budget airline's website for routes to wherever you want to go. Flycheapo monitors the flights of all these airlines and tells you who flies to where you want to go.

**Hostels.com** (www.hostels.com/en/easterneurope.html) This site has a list of most hostels and budget accommodation in Eastern Europe, organised by country. There are plenty of photos so you get an idea of what you are letting yourself in for!

**In Your Pocket** (www.inyourpocket.com) This Vilnius-based desktop-publishing company has enjoyed incredible success. The formula is simple: it produces frequently updated booklets about scores of destinations within Eastern Europe, which are financially supported by advertising. You can download a huge amount of information in PDF form from the website – all for free!

**Rail Europe** (www.raileurope.com) Gives lots of information on timetables, routes and prices for most of the region (but not the former Soviet Union). For detailed information about the entire former Soviet Union's trains, check out www.poezda.net.

**Thorn Tree** (http://thorntree.lonelyplanet.com) The Lonely Planet interactive travellers' message board. There's a dedicated section for posts relating to Eastern Europe and a huge number of travellers able to give up-to-the-minute advice.

## MUST-SEE MODERN MOVIES

There's no better way to whet your appetite for travel than by seeing films about the region. Mention Eastern European film to most people and they'll think of slow-paced psychological dramas in black and white, a stereotype that couldn't be less true these days. Against all odds, Eastern Europe has a small but creatively dynamic film industry, as well as a long history of classic (erm, slow-paced, black-and-white) films.

- *Lost and Found* (2005) Six short films produced in Estonia, Bulgaria, Bosnia and Hercegovina, Hungary, Romania and Serbia and Montenegro. All offer poignant peeks into the hearts and minds of young Eastern Europeans in the generation since the fall of the Berlin Wall.

- *Ya Lyublyu Tebya* (You I Love; 2004) A quirky Moscow-based romp featuring a romantic threesome between a gorgeous newsreader, an introspective advertising exec and a Mongolian zookeeper. Russia's first 'gay-friendly' film, it offers an interesting slant on old versus new in the Russian capital.

- *Cesky Sen* (Czech Dream; 2004) A 2004 documentary about two students who undertake the hoax of launching a huge new supermarket. A clever and compelling film full of observations on consumer society in the Czech Republic after the fall of communism.

- *Grbavica* (2006) Set in the area of Sarajevo of the same name, *Grbavica* is a Bosnian film about the realities of Serb rape camps during the Bosnian War. It's a harrowing story, which has broken the final taboo of Bosnian society as well as outraging Serbs who dispute its accusations. It won a Golden Bear for best film at the Berlin Film Festival in 2006.

- *Parrullat* (Slogans; 2001) This ponderous and poignant film about 1980s Stalinist Albania depicts life in a small village as seen through the eyes of a young teacher arriving to take up his first post. A love story interwoven with the denouncement of a social misfit, *Slogans* is a touching and lovely film.

## TOP FIVE FESTIVALS

Once limited to folk dancing and classic music, there's a huge range of great festivals every year in Eastern Europe. Some of our favourites:

**EXIT Festival, Novi Sad, Serbia** (www.exitfest.org) Eastern Europe's answer to Glastonbury! Novi Sad's historic Petrovaradin Fortress hosts this excellent annual festival in July, with five or more stages shaking to the best in rock, hip-hop and techno. The event is hugely popular and attracts people from all over the region. Tickets are around €70.

**Prague Spring, Czech Republic** (www.festival.cz) Held in mid-May to early June, this is one of Europe's biggest festivals of classical music, inspired by Czech composer Bedřich Smetana, kicks

One of the best films about the Bosnian war, *No Man's Land,* sees a Serb and a Bosnian soldier trapped in the same trench. More complications occur when the media and the UN blunder in.

Encumbered with plaudits such as 'greatest film of all time', Eisenstein's masterpiece *Battleship Potemkin* has influenced most film directors since it was released. The famous scene of the massacre on the Odesa steps with a baby's pram tumbling to destruction should be familiar to all. The Pet Shop Boys recently composed a new score for the film.

---

**DON'T LEAVE HOME WITHOUT...**

Eastern Europe can supply pretty much everything you need on the road today, although when visiting places like Albania, Moldova, Belarus and Russia it's advisable to leave as little as possible to chance. Medicines and toiletries are generally well supplied, although it's probably easier to bring birth control, tampons and any prescription medicine with you. EU citizens should bring their European Health Insurance Card with them to receive free treatment within the EU, and of course everyone should have full medical insurance for serious situations.

Flip flops/thongs are useful all over Eastern Europe as it's generally not done to wear outdoor shoes inside. Backpacks are the easiest way to carry luggage for those on a long trip, although shoulder bags and suitcases with wheels are also fine for the majority of trips. A Swiss Army knife, a torch, ear plugs, plug adaptors and a towel are other things that will more than repay their weight in your backpack.

---

off the summer. The festival begins with a parade from his grave at Vyšehrad to the Smetana Hall, where his *Má vlast* is performed.

**Karlovy Vary Film Festival, Czech Republic** (www.kviff.com) This is Eastern Europe's most important film festival and it's perfectly timed for travellers visiting the charming spa town of Karlovy Vary each summer in late June to early July. Getting tickets is easy – all films are open to the public, and over seven days around 240 films are shown.

**Kazantip, Ukraine** (www.kazantip.com) Kazantip isn't just a festival, it's a Republic, or at least that's according to its organisers. Held for a whole month over July and August, this piece of Crimea hosts thousands of ravers from all over the former Soviet Union. Nudity, camping, dancing on the beach and free love are the main ingredients. Just don't try to do drugs, this is still Ukraine.

**Sziget Festival, Budapest, Hungary** (www.sziget.hu/festival_english) A week-long world-music bash held in late July to early Aug on Óbudai Island. People come from all over Europe to camp and party. There are more than 1000 acts with bands from around the world playing at more than 60 venues.

> Eastern Europe's cities get intolerably crowded in peak season. Traffic congestion on the roads is a major problem, and visitors will do themselves and residents a favour if they forgo driving and use public transport.

## RESPONSIBLE TRAVEL

In Eastern Europe's nature reserves and national parks, be sure to follow the local code of ethics and common decency and pack up your litter. Minimise the waste you must carry out by taking less packaging and no more food than you will need. Don't use detergents or toothpaste (even if they are biodegradable) in or near natural water sources. When camping in the wild (checking first to see that it's allowed), bury human waste in holes at least 15cm deep and at least 100m from any nearby water. Avoid driving as much as you can – the cities of Eastern Europe are already choked with traffic and public transport is fantastic nearly everywhere. Consider offsetting your carbon emissions used when flying to the region by using websites such as www.climatecare.org and www.carbonneutral.com.

Local charities that would benefit massively from donations include the Chernobyl Children's Project (www.chernobyl-international.com), the Relief Fund for Romania (www.relieffundforromania.co.uk) and Healthprom (www.healthprom.org), all of whom work for some of the neediest people in the region and all of whom accept online donations. If you'd like to sponsor an Eastern European child, try SOS children's villages (www.soschildrensvillages.org.uk), the world's largest child sponsoring charity, which operates in 15 Eastern European countries.

# Itineraries

## CLASSIC ROUTES

### THE BIG FIVE
**Four Weeks**

Begin your trip in magical **Prague** (p256), spending several days absorbing the city and nearby towns, such as beer-lovers' mecca **Plzeň** (p286) and beautiful **Kutná Hora** (p278). Head into Poland to stunning **Kraków** (p561) with its gobsmacking Old Town. This is a great base for visiting the beautiful **Tatra Mountains** (p574) and the harrowing trip to **Oświęcim** (Auschwitz; p570). From Poland head to Slovakia, where you can enjoy magnificent scenery in the **High Tatras** (Vysoké Tatry; p801) before pursuing more urban activities in delightful **Bratislava** (p786). Next to stunning **Budapest** (p356) where you can enjoy the vibrant city. From here visit the picturesque Hungarian countryside – try the baroque city of **Eger** (p400) with its ancient castle and **Pécs** (p391), stuffed full of relics from the Turkish occupation. Now plunge into Romania. Use **Cluj-Napoca** (p653) as your base for visiting the medieval region of **Maramureş** (p663) and stunning **Braşov** (p640) and try to get to **Timişoara** (p659), Romania's coolest city, before heading on to imposing **Bucharest** (p625), where you can drink in the monolithic architecture. End up on the Black Sea coast where you can join partying Romanians in summer at a beach resort around **Constanţa** (p675).

This is a great trip for any first-time visitor to Eastern Europe, taking in five of the most popular and accessible countries in the region.
It begins in the Czech Republic and wends its way through Poland, Slovakia, Hungary and Romania, providing a fantastic introduction to a region in transition.

## THE BALKAN SHUFFLE                                          Four Weeks

Begin in lively little Slovenia with a cheap flight to charming **Ljubljana** (p827). Enjoy superb scenery and adrenaline-rush mountain sports in the magnificent **Julian Alps** (p838) before heading south to the Croatian coast and working your way through **Dalmatia** (p218) and its gorgeous beaches to delightful **Dubrovnik** (p233). Enjoy the stunning Old Town and explore the surrounding islands. Take the opportunity to see Bosnia from Dubrovnik – perhaps a day trip to **Mostar** (p116) to see the newly reconstructed bridge or a night or two in picturesque, bustling **Sarajevo** (p106) – before continuing south into dynamic Montenegro, Europe's youngest country. Spend some time enjoying the fantastic scenery, stay a night or two in historic **Kotor** (p533) and see its charming walled city, then enjoy some of the country's beautiful beaches around **Budva** (p532) before heading over into once-mysterious Albania. From the northern city of **Shkodra** (p58) take a bus straight on to **Tirana** (p51), a mountain-shrouded, ramshackle capital on the rise. Enjoy a day or two here and make an excursion to **Kruja** (p59) and gorgeous **Berat** (p62) before taking a bus through the stunning mountains into little-explored Macedonia, ending up in **Ohrid** (p481). Spend at least two days here – enjoy its multitude of sights and swim in the beautiful eponymous lake. Make your way to **Skopje** (p474), Macedonia's fun capital, from where you can head overland through Serbia to the booming post-Milošević metropolis of **Belgrade** (p752).

This wonderful trip – unthinkable a decade ago – takes you through some of Europe's youngest countries and down the spectacular coastline of the former Yugoslav states and Albania. Beginning in Ljubljana the route snakes through six more Balkan states to bring you back to where you started.

# EAST OF EAST TOUR
**Three to Four Weeks**

Begin in bustling **Warsaw** (p547) where you can see the reconstructed Old Town and learn about its dark history. From here, head by train to **Lviv** (p874), Ukraine's most beautiful city, and spend a few days here before crossing the country to graceful **Kyiv** (p865), the Jerusalem of East Slavonic culture. You'll need a couple of days in the capital to enjoy its sights before taking the sleeper train to monolithic **Moscow** (p700), Europe's biggest city and a place of the most striking extremes. A visit to the **Golden Ring** (p716) is also highly recommended, to get a sense of Russian life outside big cities. **St Petersburg** (p718) is next on the agenda – staggeringly beautiful and full of cultural life, you can easily spend three or four days in the city itself, although there are abundant sights outside the city, such as the tsarist palace at **Petrodvorets** (p731). Exiting Russia to Estonia, you'll love charming medieval **Tallinn** (p320) and you can visit **Saaremaa** (p343) for some rural delights. Next up is **Rīga** (p417), an exceptional city with a huge wealth of Art-Nouveau architecture that is generally considered Europe's finest. Make sure you don't ignore Latvia's other highlights such as the medieval castles and caves of **Sigulda** (p428) and the breathtaking **coastline** (p432). Unsung Baltic gem Lithuania is next. Enjoy charming **Vilnius** (p443) and the amazing **Curonian Spit** (p463) on the Baltic Sea before re-entering Poland and heading back to Warsaw.

The nitty-gritty of Eastern Europe – this trip is fascinating, but involves some visa planning for Russia. It takes you in a circle from Poland, through Ukraine and Russia to the lovely and largely undiscovered Baltic countries.

# ROADS LESS TRAVELLED

## ON THE EDGE: UKRAINE & AROUND                                    Three Weeks
Begin with a cheap flight from Western Europe to **Timişoara** (p659), the best budget gateway city for the far reaches of Eastern Europe. Spend a day here before heading overland for medieval **Braşov** (p640) and charming **Iaşi** (p667) near the Moldovan border. Here the real adventure starts – cross into Europe's poorest and most corrupt country and head for the entertaining capital, **Chişinău** (p506) where partying is a way of life and wine is plentiful and cheap as it's made in the local **vineyards** (p513). Travel into **Transdniestr** (p515), a country that doesn't officially exist, and go back in time in **Tiraspol** (p517) before heading into post-revolutionary Ukraine. Make a beeline for ethnic melting pot **Odesa** (p885) and enjoy the relaxed pace of the Black Sea before heading for **Kyiv** (p865), which demands several days' attention. Be one of the few people in the world who has made the grim but fascinating trip to **Pripyat** (p864), the abandoned town next to the Chernobyl reactor. From here, head to gorgeous, crumbling **Lviv** (p874), a place for which the moniker 'the new Prague' might not be too far from the truth. After a few days here, Belarus, Europe's last bastion of repression, is your next stop – although after Transdniestr it may not look so Soviet. Check out amazingly monolithic **Minsk** (p80) and see the ultimate Soviet War memorial at **Brest Fortress** (p90) before crossing into Poland from where cheap flights back to Western Europe abound.

Take advantage of the fact that once totally Soviet Ukraine is now a visa-free zone for most. Enjoy its fascinating cities, beautiful scenery and the wealth of interesting off-the-beaten-track neighbouring countries such as Moldova and Belarus. Not a simple trip, but a world away from the crowds of Prague!

# THE IONIAN TO THE BALTIC                     Four Weeks

Arriving in Albania at **Saranda** (p66), stay the night and try to see the glorious ruins of **Butrint** (p66) before travelling either up the beautiful **coastline** (p65) or via historic **Gjirokastra** (p67) to **Tirana** (p51), where you can spend a day or two before taking the bus to **Prishtina** (p772) in Kosovo. From Kosovo head north to **Belgrade** (p752), a city that has been rejuvenated since Milošević's time and one of the most interesting places in the Balkans. Head north to **Novi Sad** (p762) – if you come in July you might catch the **EXIT Festival** (p763), held annually in the city's historic hilltop fortress. From Serbia cross into Hungary at pretty **Szeged** (p397) and head for **Lake Balaton** (p385). Keep surging north and into Slovakia, aiming for **Bratislava** (p786) before going on to the incredible **Slovenský Raj** (p811) with its wonderful scenery. Crossing the **Tatra Mountains** (p574) into Poland, travel via gorgeous **Kraków** (p561) to unsung gem **Wrocław** (p584), spending a few days in both before dropping in on beautifully restored **Poznań** (p589). From here, the Baltic is yours – try any of the relatively undeveloped towns along the coast, **Hel** (p604) and **Łeba** (p604) are both highly recommended for beaches, wildlife and watersports, while you shouldn't miss **Malbork** (p605), famed for Europe's biggest Gothic castle, or historic and thriving **Gdańsk** (p597). Finally, for true adventure (and that's just getting your Russian visa) head for **Kaliningrad** (p732) – about as far from the beaten track as anyone can get in Europe!

**A paradoxical way to begin perhaps – get a cheap flight to package-tourist destination Corfu, and take the daily ferry just 27km into a different world. Beginning on Albania's magnificent and as yet totally undeveloped coastline, weave your way north through the continent to Poland's equally neglected Baltic coast.**

# TAILORED TRIPS

## WORLD HERITAGE–LISTED SIGHTS
One Month

Begin this most cultured of trips in Moscow to see the **Kremlin** (p707) and **Red Square** (p705) with day trips to Sergiev Posad for the **Troitse-Sergieva Lavra** (Trinity Monastery of St Sergius; p717), and **Suzdal** (p716) and **Vladimir** (p716). Head west through Belarus, stopping at **Mir Castle** (p89) and the fabulous **Belavezhskaja Pushcha National Park** (p92) before entering Poland. Stop in medieval **Zamość** (p581) before heading to **Kraków** (p561) where you can see

Auschwitz (p570) in a day trip before carrying on to see the historic centres of **Prague** (p256), **Kutná Hora** (p278), **Český Krumlov** (p291), **Telč** (p303) and the Vila Tugendhat in **Brno** (p296). Cross into Slovakia and stop at **Spiš Castle** (p809), then on to **Bardejov** (p812). Press on into Hungary and stop off to explore the wine-producing region of **Tokaj** (p403) before steaming on to sumptuous **Budapest** (p356) with its Castle District. Head south via **Pécs** (p391) for the early Christian cemetery before crossing into Croatia. Stunning sights here include the **Plitvice Lakes National Park** (p221), **Split's old centre** (p223), the centre of **Trogir** (p228) and finally, the jewel in Croatia's glittering crown, sublime **Dubrovnik** (p233).

## JEWISH HERITAGE TRIP
Two to Three Weeks

Begin in Rīga and learn about the deportation of Latvia's Jewish population at the **Jews in Latvia Museum** (p422), then visit the haunting memorial to the **Salaspils Concentration Camp** (p426) before going south to Lithuania. Vilnius has plenty of interest including the **Vilna Gaon Jewish State Museum of Lithuania** (p448). Nearby there's **Trakai** (p453), still home to some 360 Karaite Jews, a fascinating example of cultural continuity. Stop in Kaunas for a visit to the chilling **Ninth Fort** (p457) and the **Sugihara House & Foundation** (p457), home to Japanese consul and sometime Schindler of Lithuania, Chiune Sugihara. Next to Poland; head straight for **Warsaw** (p547), taking in the wealth of museums, memorials and other sights associated with the ghetto and the holocaust. Stopping first at **Lublin** (p578), where you can walk the Jewish

heritage trail, head for **Kraków** (p561), where there are a number of fascinating sights, including the 15th-century Old Synagogue, remarkable for having survived WWII. Make the harrowing trip to **Auschwitz** (p570) and **Birkenau** (p570) for a shocking first-hand glimpse of human evil. From here carry on to Prague's **Staré Město** (p264) to visit Josefov, the Prague Jewish Museum, and the Old-New Synagogue – the continent's oldest Jewish house of worship. End in **Budapest** (p356) where you'll find a flourishing Jewish population of 80,000 and some 25 active synagogues, including Europe's largest, the 1859 Great Synagogue, a hopeful and positive end to a sometimes harrowing trip.

# Snapshots

## RECENT HISTORY

Eastern Europe, a huge, diverse area and the fastest-changing part of this extraordinary continent, may sometimes seem to have more differences than similarities when individual nations are pitched together. What does ultramodern, superclean Estonia have in common with chaotic and somewhat backward Albania? How can swaggering behemoth Russia, the world's largest country and Eastern Europe's most powerful nation, be grouped with tiny Slovenia, the region's answer to Switzerland? Why are Greece and Finland – far more easterly lying than the Czech Republic – never included among these countries?

These questions are totally valid and the simple answer – 20th century history – at once belies and underlies the complexity of these 19 countries and their national identities, outlooks and respective fates.

*Blessed is the mother who gives birth to a brewer – Czech proverb.*

## THE SOVIET UNION

It has been said that the Russian Revolution of 1917 was the single most important event of the 20th century, and without it, it's certain that Eastern Europe would be a very different place today. Following victory in a bloody civil war, the Bolshevik government formed a vast conglomerate of nations from the remains of the Russian Empire, which became the Union of Soviet Socialist Republics, the world's first communist state.

Brutally industrialised by Josef Stalin in the 1930s, during which new benchmarks in terror and political oppression were carved, the Soviet Union had become a huge economic and military power by the time of WWII. Initially in a nonaggression pact with Hitler, the USSR was forced into the war against its will in 1941 when Germany shocked the world by invading its erstwhile friend. This insane act of German aggression marked the beginning of the agonisingly slow end for the Third Reich, and during the siege of Leningrad, and at battles in Stalingrad, Moscow, Kursk and Sevastopol, literally millions of Soviets died.

*Despite most people connecting the Cyrillic alphabet with Russia, it was invented by two Bulgarian monks, Cyril and Methodius, in the 9th century and is a huge source of national pride to the Bulgarians.*

When Stalin, Churchill and Roosevelt met in Yalta in 1945 as the Third Reich finally crumbled and Soviet troops advanced on Berlin, the agreement hammered out between them effectively created the delineation we still use today between East and West. The Iron Curtain between the Soviet and US 'spheres of influence', which fell in the aftermath of the war, is still how most people understand and approach the region today: the Soviet Union annexed the three Baltic States of Estonia, Latvia and Lithuania, which became republics within the USSR, while Poland, Czechoslovakia, Hungary, Romania and Bulgaria were deemed to be in the Soviet Unions' 'sphere of influence'. Countries such as Greece and Finland, parts of Eastern Europe by anyone's reckoning – just look at a map – remained outside Stalin's reach. Yugoslavia and Albania were the only two countries that became communist of their own will, meaning they were never as subject to Moscow's control as other Eastern European countries, but to all intents and purposes were thought of as being in the same Eastern 'bloc'.

*During the reign of Albania's dictator Enver Hoxha, half a million defensive bunkers were installed throughout the country to protect it in the event of an invasion. Many have now been dismantled, but they're still plentiful.*

With the exception of Albania and Yugoslavia, for 40 years all the Eastern bloc countries were satellite states to Moscow, with imposed communist governments that denied freedom of speech, foreign travel and free assembly to their inhabitants. Those Cold War years can be characterised by economic backwardness (many wealthy countries before WWII, such as Romania and Hungary, became poor countries postwar due to centralised economies run on communist principles), political repression and the formation of underground opposition movements. Revolts against the Soviet Union's regional leadership were not tolerated: in 1956 Soviet tanks quelled an uprising in Budapest, and in 1968 the 'Prague Spring' of Alexander Dubček was brutally brought to an end in the same way. When Josip Tito's Yugoslavia and Enver Hoxha's Albania broke with the Soviet Union in 1948 and 1956, respectively, it was probably only the lack of a border between them and the USSR that prevented an invasion to impose a pro-Soviet government.

A Bulgarian cinematic classic (no, really), *The Goat Horn* is set during the Turkish occupation. A young girl avenges her mother's rape and murder by tracking down three of the four culprits and killing them with a goat's horn. Before she kills the fourth, more tragedy strikes.

## CRACKS IN THE IRON CURTAIN

While a vast array of opinion can now be found in Eastern Europe about the second half of the 20th century, it's no exaggeration to say that when the communist system suddenly began to collapse in the late 1980s, the vast majority of the local populations were delighted and threw out the communist governments with great enthusiasm.

The beginning of the end came with the 1985 appointment of Mikhail Gorbachev as General Secretary of the Communist Party in the Soviet Union, the country's most important post. A young reformer in a country whose once relatively strong economy had slipped into a period known as the stagnation under Leonid Brezhnev during the 1970s, Gorbachev was determined to make changes to a system he had realised needed fundamental reform.

Gorbachev's twin policies of *glasnost* (openness) and *perestroika* (restructuring) brought relatively free speech to the Soviet Union for the first time in 70 years, in the hope that through debate the Soviet people would support Gorbachev's economic restructuring, being held up by the all-powerful apparatchiks, senior party officials who had total control over the centralised (and desperately inadequately run) economy.

Awaking from their decades of dutiful slumber, the Soviet people responded in a way that was not quite what Gorbachev had in mind, and this response manifested itself in scandal after scandal as information about the high crimes and misdemeanours of the Communist Party reached a previously ignorant population. Whether it was the true extent of Stalin's brutal purges, the gory details of the gulag, corruption in the present-day leadership or the food shortages and bad housing that were a reality for millions but had never been discussed openly before, the new freedoms allowed people to talk about far more than economic restructuring.

## DEMOCRACY

At the same time, change throughout Eastern Europe – where similar policies to those begun in the USSR had been enacted – was outpacing the politicians. The year of revolutions was 1989: Lech Walesa's Solidarity Movement came to power in Poland; the Velvet Revolution saw the peaceful overthrow of communism in Czechoslovakia; Hungary instituted democracy and allowed its citizens to travel abroad freely; the Berlin Wall came down; and in Romania a violent revolution overthrew the particularly repugnant regime of Nicolae Ceauşescu, who was later executed with his wife on national TV.

Gorbachev somehow managed to keep the Soviet Union together until 1991, despite total economic meltdown and the loss of its European empire. Plucky Lithuania declared itself independent of the USSR in 1990, and despite Soviet forces brutally trying to quell the revolt well into 1991, it eventually accepted the inevitable and Lithuania became the first former Soviet state. Later that year, amid mass nationalist movements throughout its vast expanse, the Soviet leadership bowed to fate and lowered the famous hammer and sickle flag over the Kremlin for the last time on 31 December 1991.

Since 1989, the peoples of the region have largely gone their own way, despite sharing a number of the same economic and social problems. In general the transfer of nationalised commodities into private hands in the early 1990s benefited the very few (usually 'communists' with good connections) at the expense of the many. Entire industries worth billions were sold off for a fraction of their true worth. This rampant feeding frenzy gave rise to organised crime, which was particularly strong in the former Soviet Union, but a factor everywhere. The various 'mafias' so often associated with the region have in most cases become far less important in daily life, but there's an entire class of oligarchs (mainly in Russia) who made billions out of communism's collapse and still broker considerable power today.

In many cases, former communists have rebranded themselves as democrats and have retained positions of power in postcommunist Eastern Europe. Most obviously, both Boris Yeltsin, Russian president from 1991 to 1999, and his successor Vladimir Putin (2000–present) are from staunch communist backgrounds, Putin having once been head of the KGB's successor organisation, the creepy FSB.

The 1990s was a frenetic time of 'shock therapy' economics for the region. Most countries responded positively to this despite much hardship – economic miracles have well and truly occurred in the Baltics and to a

*Did you know six out of the first seven countries in the world to send a human into space were in Eastern Europe?*

## RELIVING THE COMMUNIST PAST

All over Eastern Europe you can find bars, cafés and restaurants that hark back to the 'good old days' of the USSR: central planning and bad food. These can be very good fun, but why pay extra to relive the past? Below, the authors of this book have selected their favourite surviving buildings, monuments and other sights that will fascinate anyone interested in the communist era.

**Lenin's Mausoleum & Red Square, Moscow, Russia** – Communist ground zero. The man who started it all still lies embalmed on the Moscow square where the USSR annually showed off its military might to the world in huge choreographed parades.

**Szobor Park, Budapest, Hungary** – See the incredible collection of communist statues, (unwanted Lenins, broken Marx and forgotten Engels) collected together here in Szobor (Statue) Park, a short journey from central Budapest.

**Palace of Culture & Science, Warsaw, Poland** – Stalin's 'gift' to Warsaw after WWII dominates the city's skyline and is generally cited as being Europe's ultimate Stalinist structure. Loathed by many during communist times, the building is now treated more fondly by locals and is still the city's tallest structure.

**Former Enver Hoxha Museum, Tirana, Albania** – Designed by the dictator's daughter, this astonishingly ugly complex (usually known as the Pyramid) is now a disco, but its eerie shape and general feel make you wonder how dead the past is.

**Minsk, Belarus** – Few entire cities can be described as communist monuments, but Minsk certainly can. Totally destroyed in WWII and rebuilt under Stalin, this gloomy, monolithic city should be on any nostalgic communist's itinerary.

**Brest Fortress, Brest, Belarus** – Sweeping, sombre made-for-the-movies orchestral music is blasted over loudspeakers, and men and women in period uniforms march around Belarus' vast memorial to the fallen of WWII.

**Palace of the People, Bucharest, Romania** – Ceauşescu's monstrous palace still dominates this part of his capital, as does the eerie Blvd Unirii, 6m longer than the Champs Elysées in Paris. Now housing the Romanian deputies' offices, it still retains its grotesque Cold War aura.

**Creators of the Bulgarian State Monument, Shumen, Bulgaria** – Looming above the provincial town of Shumen is this incredible concrete block commemorating Bulgarian independence.

**Ninth Fort, Kaunas, Lithuania** – The Soviet monument commemorating the murdered at this former German concentration camp has to be one of the most astonishing pieces of monolithic art in the region.

**Transdniestr** – Forget Minsk, a mere communist city, Transdniestr is a self-proclaimed country devoted to communism, even though the rest of the world doesn't recognise its existence. The communists are still in power here, taking photographs will usually land you in trouble and locals are afraid to have anything to do with you. Fun!

lesser extent in the Czech Republic, Slovakia and Hungary. However, some countries became basket cases, such as tiny, isolated Albania, and, of course, Yugoslavia, the tragedy of which deserves its own discussion.

## THE COLLAPSE OF YUGOSLAVIA

That the USSR had dissolved itself with such a small loss of life was a miracle. Sadly the pattern didn't repeat itself and the region's second-largest conglomerate nation, Yugoslavia, descended into a series of wars and a period of genocide and ethnic cleansing not seen in Europe since WWII. The scars of these atrocities are still all too visible today when visiting the six countries the nation gradually became.

Post-WWII Yugoslavia is synonymous with one of the giants of postwar European politics, Josip Broz Tito, leader of the anti-German partisans, president of the Socialist Federation of Yugoslavia and the only communist leader to openly defy Stalin. Yugoslavia broke with the Soviet Union in 1948, causing a rift that would never be properly repaired. Tito had the power to hold together an ethnically and religiously disparate society. Following his death in 1980, the country's ethnic strife threatened to blow up immediately. At this time the Serbian communist party boss, Slobodan Milošević, consolidated his power base by exploiting tensions between Serbs and Kosovar Albanians in the Serbian province of Kosovo, eventually becoming Serbian president in 1989.

By 1991 the collapse of Yugoslavia seemed inevitable in the wake of the changes throughout Eastern Europe. Pro-democracy, pro-independence forces controlled regional capitals, while authoritarian federalist Milošević held sway in Belgrade. Slovenia declared independence in 1991 and, after a short war, became an independent nation. Croatia and Macedonia followed suit, but it was Bosnia and Hercegovina's declaration the same year that made bloodshed inevitable, as Bosnia's population, divided between Bosniaks, Serbs and Croats saw their future in different places. The Bosnian War (1992–95) cost more than 200,000 lives and saw the worst genocide in Europe since WWII, as 'ethnic cleansing' became a tool used to ensure ethnic uniformity and thus a common direction. Meanwhile in the remains of Yugoslavia (Serbia and Montenegro) hyperinflation saw prices rise by five quadrillion percent (that's 5000 *trillion*), the highest in history, and the general collapse of the economy.

As if the region hadn't experienced enough horror, in 1996 a guerrilla campaign by Kosovar Albanians against Serbs in Kosovo marked the beginning of another long and bloody conflict, which resulted in the bombing of Belgrade by NATO in 1999 and UN control of the region ever since. While Milošević was forced from power in 2001, both Kosovo and Macedonia remain an ethnic tinderbox and could easily slip back into ethnic conflict in the future.

## NEW EUROPE

Eastern Europe was comprehensively divided in two in May 2004 when eight of the region's most economically progressive countries joined the EU. To say that this changed the regional dynamic would be a massive understatement – to put it into historical perspective, just a decade and a half before most of these countries had been members of Comecon (the communist version of the EU), grey and undemocratic Moscow satellites with little or no self-determination. Since 2004, for better or for worse (and you'll be given a massive breadth of opinion by locals on your travels) they have been part of a huge European superstate where the market economy is king, trade barriers and borders no longer exist, and democracy and human rights are

---

You might hear *Wind of Change* by German rockers the Scorpions during your visit to Eastern Europe – it's still got a special place in many people's hearts there as it became the unofficial anthem of freedom and democracy when it was released in 1990.

*Russian Ark*, the ponderous yet incredible 2002 Alexander Sokurov film, was the first feature length movie to be made with one continuous tracking shot. Sokurov got it on the second take.

For a bizarre and satirical 'first-person' view of Josip Tito's life, see the late Yugoslav leader's 'homepage' at www .titoville.com – pictures, anecdotes, jokes and general partisan sniping await.

enshrined as sacrosanct. At the time of writing Romania and Bulgaria were due to join the EU in 2007 and 2008, respectively, with Croatia, Macedonia, Bosnia and Hercegovina, Albania and Serbia hoping to join them some time after 2010.

Mountainous Slovenia is the homeland of the first married couple to scale Mt Everest together. Andrej and Mariga Stremfelj reached the summit on 7 October, 1990.

The eagerness with which the EU has embraced its new members has been viewed with great suspicion by Russia, which feels its traditional 'sphere of influence' has been breached and is gently fuming at its impotence to do anything about it. The EU accession countries, however, all clearly see their destiny as being part of Europe and view the idea that they are somehow in Russia's 'sphere of influence' as a vaguely humorous hangover from the long-gone days of communism.

Almost without exception Eastern European countries have centre-right democratically elected governments whose priorities have been economic stability and development. The obvious exception to this rule is Belarus where, to many people's utter amazement, the dictatorship of Alexander Lukashenko continues to fester while the country slips further and further behind its neighbours economically. Russia is another conundrum. Despite the extraordinary laissez-faire capitalism of the 1990s, the country has reverted to an austere regime under Vladimir Putin. While the country seeks to make itself the world's undisputed energy superpower due to its massive oil and gas resources, press freedom and transparency have suffered enormously. With Putin's departure from office scheduled for 2008 (he's unable to seek a third term as president without changing the constitution), what lies beyond that date for Russia is anyone's guess, although most commentators believe he'll seek to install a loyal and trusted friend as his successor.

*The Death of Mr Lazarescu* (2005) by Romanian director Cristi Puiu has been hailed as one of the country's greatest-ever films, winning prizes at film festivals around the world. The film concerns the fate of the eponymous pensioner, shuffled from one Bucharest hospital to another in search of medical treatment – a dark, comedic commentary on modern Romania.

## RECENT EVENTS

Eastern Europe saw more considerable change in 2006, including the sudden death of Slobodan Milošević during his trial in the Hague for crimes against humanity. Milošević's death from a heart attack robbed thousands of his victims of justice, but it also went some way to confining the brutal bloodshed and ethnic hatreds of the 1990s to the past. Two other war criminals, Radovan

---

### STAGS AND HENS ROAMING THE REGION

As if anything were needed to further illustrate Eastern Europe's transformation from buttoned-down autocracy to hedonistic playland, visit Bratislava on a Saturday night. Groups of men in specially printed T-shirts being sick, fighting locals, shouting and swearing, inebriated gangs of women crawling from one bar to the next in unfeasibly high heels and sporting plastic breasts; welcome to stag and hen culture, Eastern Europe style.

The rise of the cheap airline industry has meant that Eastern European cities are often flooded at weekends with gangs of male and female friends celebrating stag and hen nights (bachelor and bachelorette parties). While these events can be fun, there's nothing quite like a gang of 20 drunk men vomiting in public to ruin your romantic weekend in an otherwise lovely Eastern European city.

Cities that are particularly notorious include Bratislava, Rīga, Tallinn, Ljubljana, Budapest, Kraków, Prague and Vilnius. If you're keen to avoid this proud (mainly British) tradition, the simplest thing to do is avoid the above cities over the weekends. If you can't do this, check with your hotel that they don't accept stag groups (most decent hotels won't) and staying outside of the Old Town is usually a good bet.

There are usually certain bars associated with stag groups, so for example in Bratislava avoid the Dubliner or Slovak pubs (p793) at the weekend if you want to avoid a close encounter. Think of it as wildlife-watching and it can be fairly amusing.

Karadžić and Ratko Mladić, remain at large in the Balkans and their capture is still a priority as their ethnic cleansing still casts a long shadow over the shattered nations of the former Yugoslavia.

A far more positive development was the final dismantling of the trans national compromise that was Yugoslavia, when Montenegro voted in a 2006 referendum to leave its union with Serbia, thus creating two newly independent countries. To many people's surprise, Serbia shrugged and accepted the decision stoically.

Did you know Belarus has the highest number of US green-card lottery winners in the world?

Not all development has been positive. The 'brain drain' is an inescapable reality in countries that have recently joined the EU: Estonian IT specialists have been absorbed by countries throughout the EU, while Poland has seen a massive number of people leaving to work in the service and construction industries in the UK. Likewise, Latvia and Lithuania have seen huge numbers of young professionals relocate to Ireland. Further flows into the west are expected when Germany and Austria relax their immigration rules for the new members in the next few years.

Despite this exodus, there's palpable excitement in the air in Eastern Europe today. Even where the political system remains miserable and democracy seems a long way off, there's a new spirit of hope. Belarus is case in point; since the mass antigovernment protests following the rigged elections of 2006, and despite the failure of protestors to dislodge the government, there's a very definite feeling that things can't go on like this for much longer. As democracy and transparency become ever more Eastern European traits the future looks extremely bright for this once benighted region.

# Albania

Awaking Sleeping Beauty–like in the 1990s from her hardline communist isolation, Albania was a stranger from another time. Her cities weren't choked by car fumes, her beaches were unspoilt by mass tourism, her long-suffering people were a little dazed and confused.

While things have changed a lot since then, this ancient land still offers something increasingly rare in Europe these days – a glance into a culture that is all its own. Raised on a diet of separation and hardship, Albania is distinctly Albanian.

You'll continue to find beautiful pristine beaches, fascinating classical sites and dramatic mountain citadels, but the mad traffic of Tirana is symptomatic of a bustling, bright city shrugging off its Stalinist grey patina. Squat toilets are no longer the norm and you can even sip cocktails at hip bars while listening to rock bands.

Not just the preserve of the adventurous, Albania is a warm and sincerely hospitable country – with enough rough edges to keep it interesting.

## FAST FACTS

- **Area** 28,748 sq km
- **Capital** Tirana
- **Currency** lekë; €1 = 123 lekë; US$1 = 97.04 lekë; UK£1 = 182.15 lekë; A$1 = 72.94 lekë; ¥100 = 82.59 lekë; NZ$1 = 63.45 lekë
- **Famous for** international diaspora, concrete bunkers, cool flag
- **Official Language** Albanian
- **Phrases** *tungjatjeta* (hello), *lamtumirë* (goodbye), *ju lutem* (please), *ju falem nderit* (thank you)
- **Population** 3,582,205
- **Telephone Codes** country code ☎ 355; international access code ☎ 00
- **Visas** no visa needed for citizens of the EU, Australia, New Zealand, the US and Canada; see p71

**ALBANIA**

## HIGHLIGHTS

- Visit beautiful **Berat** (p62), a living museum of Ottoman houses, elegant mosques and an ancient citadel.
- Indulge your *Lord of the Rings* fantasies at Shkodra's dramatic **Rozafa Fortress** (p58).
- Touring Albania's colourful capital **Tirana** (p51) reveals tantalising glimpses of its recent communist past.
- Travel down the high mountain pass to the olive groves framing isolated white beaches; the crystalline **Ionian Coast** (p65) is nothing short of spectacular.
- Travel back in time to the ruins of **Butrint** (p66), hidden in the depths of the forest in a serene lakeside setting.

## ITINERARIES

- **Three days** With two nights in Tirana, spend one day exploring the city and then take a day trip to Kruja. On day three make an early start for Berat, leaving the afternoon free for the sights of this fascinating town.
- **One week** Leaving Berat stop off at Fier to explore the ruins of Apollonia, before heading on to Vlora for the night. Catch the bus over the stunning Llogoraja Pass and spend the rest of the day lazing around Dhërmi beach. The next day continue to Saranda for two nights, making sure you visit the tranquil ruins of Butrint and beautiful Ksamili beach.

## CLIMATE & WHEN TO GO

Coastal Albania has a pleasant Mediterranean climate. Summer is the peak tourist season, when people from the sweltering interior escape temperatures that can reach the high 30s in July. In Tirana and other inland towns on the plains there is plenty of rainfall during the winter, but temperatures below freezing are rare. The high mountains often experience heavy snow between November and March. The best time to visit Albania is spring or autumn.

## HISTORY

Albanians call their country Shqipëria, and trace their roots to the ancient Illyrian tribes. Their language is descended from Illyrian, making it a rare survivor of the Roman and Slavic influxes and a European linguistic oddity on a par with Basque. The Illyrians occupied the western Balkans during the 2nd

---

**HOW MUCH?**

- **Bottle of excellent Albanian wine** 650 lekë
- **English translation of an Ismail Kadare novel** 1800 lekë
- **Basic pizza** 300 lekë
- **Cocktail in a swanky bar** 600 lekë
- **Cappuccino** 120 lekë

**LONELY PLANET INDEX**

- **Litre of petrol** 130 lekë
- **Litre of bottled water** 50 lekë
- **Tirana beer** 200 lekë
- **Souvenir T-shirt** 1800 lekë
- **Street snack (byrek)** 30 lekë

---

millennium BC. They built substantial fortified cities, mastered silver and copper mining and became adept at sailing the Mediterranean. The Greeks arrived in the 7th century BC to establish self-governing colonies at Epidamnos (now Durrës), Apollonia and Butrint. They traded peacefully with the Illyrians, who formed tribal states in the 4th century BC.

Inevitably the expanding Illyrian kingdom of the Ardiaei, based at Shkodra, came into conflict with Rome, which sent a fleet of 200 vessels against Queen Teuta in 229 BC. A long war resulted in the extension of Roman control over the entire Balkan area by 167 BC.

Under the Romans, Illyria enjoyed peace and prosperity, though the large agricultural estates were worked by slaves. Like the Greeks, the Illyrians preserved their own language and traditions despite centuries of Roman rule. Over time the populace slowly replaced their old gods with the new Christian faith championed by Emperor Constantine. The main trade route between Rome and Constantinople, the Via Egnatia, ran from the port at Durrës.

When the Roman Empire was divided in AD 395, Illyria fell within the Eastern Empire, later known as the Byzantine Empire. Three early Byzantine emperors (Anastasius I, Justin I and Justinian I) were of Illyrian origin. Invasions by migrating peoples (Visigoths, Huns, Ostrogoths and Slavs) continued through the 5th and 6th centuries.

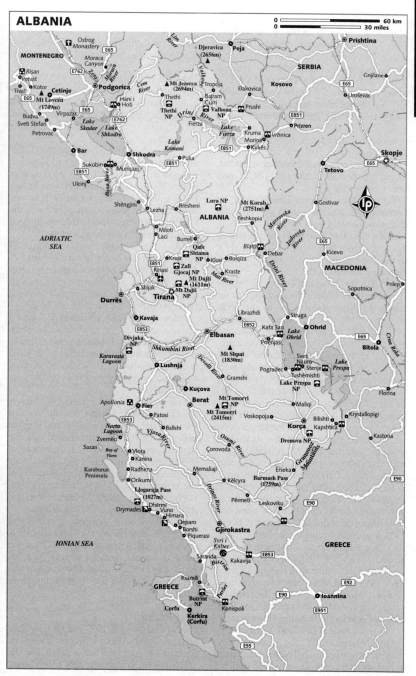

# ALBANIA

0          60 km
0          30 miles

ALBANIA

In 1344 Albania was annexed by Serbia, but after the defeat of Serbia by the Turks in 1389 the whole region was open to Ottoman attack. The Venetians occupied some coastal towns, and from 1443 to 1468 the national hero Skanderbeg (Gjergj Kastrioti) led Albanian resistance to the Turks from his castle at Kruja. Skanderbeg won all 25 battles he fought against the Turks, and even Sultan Mehmet-Fatih, the conqueror of Constantinople, could not take Kruja. After Skanderbeg's death it was only a matter of time before the Ottomans overwhelmed Albanian resistance, taking control of the country in 1479, 26 years after Constantinople fell.

For more than 400 years Albania was under Ottoman rule. Muslim citizens were favoured and were exempted from the Janissary system, whereby Christian households had to give up one of their sons to convert to Islam and serve in the army. Consequently many Albanians embraced the new faith.

In 1878 the Albanian League at Prizren (in present-day Kosovo) began a struggle for autonomy that was put down by the Turkish army in 1881. Further uprisings between 1910 and 1912 culminated in a proclamation of independence and the formation of a provisional government led by Ismail Qemali at Vlora in 1912. These achievements were severely compromised when Kosovo, roughly one-third of Albania, was ceded to Serbia in 1913. The Great Powers tried to install a young German prince, Wilhelm of Weld, as ruler of the rump of Albania, but he was never accepted and returned home after six months. With the outbreak of WWI, Albania was occupied in succession by the armies of Greece, Serbia, France, Italy and Austria-Hungary.

In 1920 the capital city was moved from Durrës to less vulnerable Tirana. A republican government under the Orthodox priest Fan Noli helped to stabilise the country, but in 1924 it was overthrown by the interior minister, Ahmed Bey Zogu. A northern warlord, he declared himself King Zogu I in 1928, but his close collaboration with Italy backfired in April 1939 when Mussolini ordered an invasion of Albania. Zogu fled to Britain with his young wife Geraldine and newborn son Leka, and used gold looted from the Albanian treasury to rent a floor at London's Ritz Hotel.

On 8 November 1941 the Albanian Communist Party was founded with Enver Hoxha as first secretary, a position he held until his death in April 1985. The communists led the resistance against the Italians and, after 1943, against the Germans, ultimately tying down 15 combined German-Italian divisions.

## The Rise of Communism

After the fighting had died down, the communists consolidated power. In January 1946 the People's Republic of Albania was proclaimed, with Hoxha as president and 'Supreme Comrade'.

In September 1948 Albania broke off relations with Yugoslavia, which had hoped to incorporate the country into the Yugoslav Federation. Instead, it allied itself with Stalin's USSR and put into effect a series of Soviet-style economic plans – rising the ire of the USA and Britain, which made an ill-fated attempt to overthrow the government.

Albania collaborated closely with the USSR until 1960, when a heavy-handed Khrushchev demanded that a submarine base be set up at Vlora. Breaking off diplomatic relations with the USSR in 1961, the country reoriented itself towards the People's Republic of China.

From 1966 to 1967 Albania experienced a Chinese-style cultural revolution. Administrative workers were suddenly transferred to remote areas and younger cadres were placed in leading positions. The collectivisation of agriculture was completed and organised religion banned.

Following the Soviet invasion of Czechoslovakia in 1968, Albania left the Warsaw Pact and embarked on a self-reliant defence policy. Some 700,000 igloo-shaped concrete bunkers (see opposite) serve as a reminder of this policy. The communist authorities made progress in draining the malarial swamps of the central coastal plains, building hydro-electric schemes, raising the literacy level and laying down the country's railway lines.

With the death of Mao Zedong in 1976 and the changes that followed in China after 1978, Albania's unique relationship with China also came to an end, and the country was left isolated and without allies. The economy was devastated and food shortages became more common.

## Post-Hoxha

Hoxha died in April 1985 and his long-time associate Ramiz Alia took over the leadership. Restrictions loosened half a notch, but the whole system was increasingly falling apart.

## BUNKER LOVE

On the hillsides, beaches, people's front gardens and generally most surfaces in Albania, you will notice small concrete domes gazing at you through their rectangular slits. Meet the bunkers: Enver Hoxha's concrete legacy, built from 1950 to 1985. Weighing in at five tonnes of concrete and iron, these little mushrooms are almost impossible to destroy, as they were built to repel an invasion and can resist full tank assault – a fact proved by their chief engineer, who had to vouch for his creation's strength by standing inside one while it was bombarded by a tank. The shell-shocked engineer emerged unscathed and an estimated 700,000 bunkers were built. Today, apart from being an indestructible reminder of a cruel regime, they serve no real purpose, and as they are impossible to move, the locals sometimes try to decorate them with pot plants or a coat of paint. They do have one modern use – quite a few Albanians will admit to losing their virginity in the security of a bunker. It puts a whole new spin on practising safe sex!

People were no longer bothering to work on the collective farms, leading to food shortages in the cities, and industries began to fail as spare parts ran out. The party leadership promised reform, but remained paralysed.

In June 1990, inspired by the changes that were occurring elsewhere in Eastern Europe, around 4500 Albanians took refuge in Western embassies in Tirana. After a brief confrontation with the police and the Sigurimi (secret police) these people were allowed to board ships for Brindisi in Italy, where they were granted political asylum.

After student demonstrations in December 1990, the government agreed to allow opposition parties. The Democratic Party, led by heart surgeon Sali Berisha, was formed. Further demonstrations produced new concessions, including the promise of free elections and independent trade unions. The government announced a reform programme and party hardliners were purged.

In early March 1991, as the election date approached, some 20,000 Albanians fled the country's crumbling economy and nonexistent infrastructure, seeking a 'better life' abroad. They set out from Vlora to Brindisi by ship, creating a crisis for the Italian government, which had begun to view them as economic refugees. Most were eventually allowed to stay.

The March 1992 elections ended 47 years of communist rule. After the resignation of Alia, parliament elected Sali Berisha president in April. In September 1992 former president Alia was placed under house arrest after he wrote articles critical of the Democratic government. In August 1993 the leader of the Socialist Party, Fatos Nano, was also arrested on corruption charges.

During this time Albania switched from a tightly controlled communist regime to a rambunctious free-market free-for-all. A huge smuggling racket sprang up, bringing stolen Mercedes-Benzes into the country, and some former collective farms were converted into marijuana plantations. The port of Vlora became a major crossing point for illegal immigrants from Asia and the Middle East into Italy. A huge population shift took place as collective farms were broken up and reclaimed by former landowners, pushing the peasants off the land. Tirana's population tripled as people, now able to freely move to the city, joined internal exiles driven off the old collective farms.

A severe crisis developed in late 1996 when private pyramid-investment schemes – widely thought to have been supported by the government – inevitably collapsed. Around 70% of Albanians lost their savings (in total more than US$1 billion), resulting in nationwide disturbances and riots. New elections were called, and the victorious Socialist Party under Nano – who had been freed from prison by the rampaging mob – was able to restore some degree of security and investor confidence. But the new wave of violence destroyed many of the remaining industries still left from the communist era. Towns where the whole working population was employed by one mine or factory were left destitute as the economy collapsed again.

In spring 1999 Albania faced a crisis of a different sort. This time it was the influx of 465,000 refugees from neighbouring Kosovo during the Serbian ethnic-cleansing campaign. While this put a tremendous strain on resources, the net effect has in fact been positive. Substantial amounts of international aid money have poured in, the service sector has grown and inflation has declined to single digits.

Since 2002 the country has found itself in a kind of miniboom with much money being poured into construction projects and infrastructure renewal.

The general election of 2005 saw a return of Berisha's Democratic Party to government. Albanian politics and the economy have been stable, but work still has to be done to ensure that there is an end to electricity shortages and other infrastructure deficiencies that plague the country. Hopes are high that NATO membership will be achieved by 2008, while an invitation to the EU club remains an elusive goal.

## PEOPLE

In July 2003 the population was estimated to be 3,582,205, of which approximately 95% is Albanian, 3% Greek and 2% 'other' – comprising Vlachs, Roma, Serbs and Bulgarians. The Vlach are an old ethnic group in the Balkans, and descendants of a people Romanised during the days of the Empire.

The Albanian people are generally kind, warm and unquestioningly generous. If you ask for directions, don't be surprised if you're guided all the way to your destination. While it's common to see young men walking around arm and arm, don't mistake this for an expression of gay culture – Albanian society is staunchly homophobic.

The Shkumbin River forms a boundary between the Gheg cultural region of the north and the Tosk region in the south. The people in these regions vary slightly in dialect, musical culture and traditional dress.

## RELIGION

Religion was banned during communism and Albania was the world's only officially atheist state from 1967 to 1990. Despite the fact that the people are now free to practise their faith, Albania remains a very secular society and it is impossible to assess how many followers each faith has, since the 2001 census didn't include a question on religion. Albania's population was traditionally split into 70% Muslim, 20% Orthodox and 10% Catholic, but in most cases this is merely nominal. Many remain fervently atheist, while Protestant fundamentalists (and other groups such as the Mormons and Jehovah's Witnesses) have aggressively sought to make inroads into the country.

The majority of Albania's Muslims are Sunni, but there is a substantial minority of adherents to Bektashism. Similar to Sufism, Bektashism has had its world headquarters in Albania since 1925, when this dervish order was expelled during Turkey's attempts at 'modernisation'. The Bektashi followers worship at *teqe* (templelike buildings without a minaret) rather than mosques.

The Albanian Orthodox Church was founded in Boston, USA in 1908 and has been recognised as autocephalous (self-governing) since 1937.

## ARTS
### Literature

When it comes to Albanian writers, all others pale under the shadow of Ismail Kadare (b 1936). His books have been translated into dozens of languages and are widely available in English. A former nominee for the Nobel Prize for Literature, he won the inaugural Man Booker International Prize in 2005 for his wistful look at a nation in transition in *Spring Flowers, Spring Frost*. His latest novel is even better. *The Successor* (2005) is an entertaining take on Albanian political machinations under Hoxha – essential reading for anyone visiting Tirana.

Kadare's books are not only enriching literary works, they are also a great source of information on Albanian traditions, history and social events. They exquisitely capture the atmosphere of daily life during difficult times, such as the lyrical descriptions of Kadare's birthplace, Gjirokastra, in *Chronicle in Stone* (1971), where wartime experiences are seen through the eyes of a boy. *Broken April* (1990), set in the northern highlands before the 1939 Italian invasion, follows the doomed footsteps of a young man who is next in line in the desperate cycle of blood vendettas. In *The Concert* (1988) we get an insight into the communist way of life around the time of Albania's break in relations with China.

There is no substantial body of Albanian literature before the 19th century as the Ottomans banned the teaching of Albanian in schools, fearing the spread of anti-Turkish propaganda. The adoption of a standardised orthography in 1908 coincided with the rise of the Albanian nationalist movement.

A group of romantic patriotic writers, such as Migjeni (1911–38) and Martin Çamaj (1925–92), wrote epics and historical novels.

## Cinema

During Albania's isolationist years the local film industry had a captive audience, hungry for anything to break the cultural tedium. While much of its output was propagandist, by the 1980s this little country was turning out an extraordinary 14 films a year. Despite a general lack of funds, two recent movies have gone on to win awards at international film festivals. Gjergj Xhuvani's comedy *Slogans* (2001), is a warm and touching account of life during communist times. This was followed in 2002 by *Tirana Year Zero*, Fatmir Koci's bleak look at the pressures on the young to emigrate.

Another film worth seeing is *Lamerica* (1995), a brilliant and stark look at Albanian postcommunist culture. Woven loosely around a plot about a couple of Italian scam artists, and Albanians seeking to escape to Italy, the essence of the film is the unshakable dignity of the ordinary Albanian in the face of adversity.

## Music

You can't go anywhere in Albania without hearing the local pop music. Incredibly catchy and melodic, traditional instruments such as clarinets combine with contemporary beats. A particularly popular young star is Mariola. Switch on the TV and you won't escape the accompanying videos, which inevitably involve a hunky lad in traditional costume chasing after some coy village lass. Hilarious. Albanian rap is also surprisingly good.

Polyphony, the blending of several independent vocal or instrumental parts, is a southern Albanian tradition dating from Illyrian times. Peasant choirs perform in a variety of styles, and the songs, usually with an epic-lyrical or historical theme, may be dramatic to the point of yodelling, or slow and sober, with alternate male and female voices combining in harmony. Instrumental polyphonic *kabas* (a sedate style, led by a clarinet or violin alongside accordions and lutes) are played by small Roma ensembles.

## Visual Arts

The art scene in Albania is slowly on the rise. One of the first 'signs of art' that will strike you are the multicoloured buildings of Tirana, a project organised by the capital's mayor Edi Rama, himself a painter. One of his paintings can be found in Tirana at the National Art Gallery (p53). An up-and-coming artist is Norway-based Anri Sala, whose video installations are a modern account of Albanian life.

There are still plenty of remnants of socialist realism, with paintings and sculptures adorning the walls and gardens of galleries and museums, although many were destroyed after the fall of the communist government as a reflex against the old regime. The massive public sculptures honouring the partisans (not including Enver Hoxha) were largely left intact.

One of the most delicious Albanian art treats is to be found in Berat's Muzeu Onufri (p63). Onufri was the most outstanding Albanian icon painter of the 16th and 17th centuries and his work is noted for its unique intensity of colour, using natural dyes that are as fresh now as the day he painted them.

## ENVIRONMENT
### The Land

Albania has three main zones: a coastal plain, a mountainous region and an interior plain. The coastal plain extends approximately 200km from north to south and up to 50km inland. The forested mountain spine takes up three-quarters of the country, stretching its entire length and peaking at Mt Korab (2751m). The interior plain is alluvial, with seasonal precipitation. It is poorly drained and therefore alternately arid or flooded and is often as inhospitable as the mountains.

The longest river in Albania is the Drini (285km), which runs from Lake Ohrid into the Buna River, which connects Lake Shkodra to the sea. Albania has suffered some devastating earthquakes, including the one that struck in 1979, leaving at least 100,000 people homeless.

### Wildlife

In the lower regions the flora is rich with beech trees, oak and patches of rare Macedonian pine *(Pinus peuce)*. Birch, pine and fir cover the mountain sides to an altitude of 2000m, after which all is barren. Forests cover an estimated 36% of the country, much of it in the isolated northern highlands and close to the Greek border. Bears, deer and wild boar inhabit these isolated forests, but they have been pushed out of regions closer to settlements by widespread summer grazing and by the Albanian penchant for hunting.

The endangered loggerhead turtle nests on isolated beaches on the Ionian Coast and on the Karaburun peninsula, where Mediterranean

**ALBANIA**

monk seals also have colonies. The fauna of World Heritage–listed Lake Ohrid is a relic of an earlier era, including the endangered *koran* trout, the European eel and a genus of snail dating back 30 million years.

There are several wetland sites at the mouths of the Buna, Drini and Mati Rivers in the north and at the Karavasta Lagoon south of Durrës, with many interesting and rare birds (white pelicans and white-headed ducks, among others).

## National Parks

Albania has 13 protected areas, covering only 3.9% of the country (34,550 hectares): Thethi, Valbona and Lura in the north; Qafe Shtama and Zall Gjocaj near Kruja; Mt Dajti (p57) near Tirana; Divjaka near Lushnja; Mt Tomorri near Berat; Llogaraja (p65) on the Ionian Coast; Drenova and Lake Prespa near Korça; and Bredhi i Hotoves and Butrint (p66), also a World Heritage site, in the south.

Most of Albania's national parks are not really protected by anything but their remoteness, and tree cutting and hunting still take place. There are no hiking maps of the parks and very few hotels or camping grounds. Mt Dajti, Mt Tomorri and Llogaraja are the most accessible for hikers. Independent camping is not advisable because the mountains are almost completely uninhabited and have no mobile-phone coverage; help, in case of an injury, would be impossible to find.

## Environmental Issues

With the collapse of communism, before which there were only around 2000 cars in the country, the number of roaring automobiles has risen drastically to something around 500,000 – many of which are very old. In March 2004, reports claimed that Tirana was now considered to be the most polluted capital in Europe.

Illegal logging and fishing reached epidemic proportions during the 1990s, but the authorities are clamping down on this problem. This hasn't stopped the fishing of the rare *koran* trout from Lake Ohrid.

The decrepit oil pumps in the central plains around Fier constantly leak black sludge into the rivers and down to the sea, creating health problems for the local populace. Pollution in the water around Durrës resulted in an outbreak of skin infections recently.

There is also a disturbing amount of rubbish littering roadsides, beaches, picnic spots,

remote valleys – just about everywhere. Under communism, plastic wasn't widely used and most refuse was biodegradable or recycled. Now blue plastic bags are as much a feature of the landscape as the bunkers, clogging rivers and getting caught in trees in even the most remote places. Riverbanks appear to be a favourite dumping ground for domestic waste. Even rubbish that does make its way to a designated tip site is burnt, releasing toxins into the air.

In short, Albania is quickly turning into an environmental disaster zone, with little hope for improvement in sight. One organisation trying to make a difference is the **Organic Agriculture Association** ( ☎ 04-250 575; www.organic.org .al). It successfully campaigned to stop US 'aid' shipments of genetically modified maize and soy, and its members have been involved in a campaign to prevent a US company building an oil pipeline straight through the beautiful Bay of Vlora.

## FOOD & DRINK

Albanian cuisine is mainly dominated by roast lamb in the mountains and fresh seafood near the coast. The local ingredients tend to be organic by default – few farmers can afford pesticides. Tomatoes, in particular, are very tasty. A simple slice of bruschetta can be quite extraordinary.

Offal, veal escalopes, *biftek* (beef loin), *qebaps* (kebabs) and *qoftë* (meat balls) are very popular. *Fërgesë Tiranë* is a traditional Tirana dish of offal, eggs and tomatoes cooked in an earthenware pot. Don't order the *koran* trout as it's endangered. You will find *byrek* stands all over the place; it's the Balkan alternative to fast food and a delicious budget option at that. *Byrek* comes in many forms: filled with cheese, tomato, meat, or spinach, layered between thin slices of filo pastry.

If you're taking a journey by *furgon* (minibus) or bus, chances are you'll stop at a roadside restaurant. The typical dish on offer is a greasy lamb soup – best viewed as an anthropological rather than culinary treat. This is the basic worker's meal and also serves as breakfast. Breakfasts in hotels are nearly always terrible, consisting of a couple of dry slices of toast and packet jam. Cafés don't generally serve food. If you ask for a croissant, it'll be a stale thing out of a bag. You're better to look for a bakery or *byrek* shop, or buy some fresh fruit.

If you are a vegetarian, your best bet will be Italian restaurants, of which there are plenty. There are also some delicious Turkish-style vegetable dishes to be had, such as roast peppers and aubergines.

Albanians do not eat dessert after their meal, but they do drink a shot of raki before they tuck into their food. There are two main types of raki to be had in Albania: grape raki (the most common one) and *mani* raki (mulberry, an Albanian type). If raki is not your cup of tea, try Rilindja wine – either a sweet white (Tokai) or a medium-bodied red (Merlot). Wine aficionados should seek out the native red varietal Kallmet. Skënderbeu *Konjak* (Cognac) is the national aperitif, and it's very good indeed, even though fancy bars will try to serve you a French brand.

# TIRANA

☎ 04 / pop 700,000

Lively, colourful Tirana has changed beyond belief in the last decade from the dull, grey city it once was. It's amazing what a lick of paint can do – covering one ugly tower block with horizontal orange and red stripes, another with concentric pink and purple circles and planting perspective-fooling cubes on its neighbour.

Trendy Blloku buzzes with the well-dressed nouvelle bourgeoisie hanging out in bars or zipping between boutiques. Quite where their money comes from is the subject of much speculation in this economically deprived nation, but thankfully you don't need much of it to have a fun night out in the city's many bars and clubs.

The city's grand central boulevards are lined with fascinating relics of its Ottoman, Italian and communist past – from delicate minarets to socialist murals – guarded by bored-looking soldiers with serious automatic weaponry. The traffic does daily battle with both itself and pedestrians in a constant scene of unmitigated chaos. On any given day half the roads seem to be dug up, although it can be hard to tell where the roadwork ends and the potholes begin.

Loud, crazy, colourful, dirty – Tirana is simply fascinating.

## ORIENTATION

Tirana revolves around the busy Sheshi Skënderbej (Skanderbeg Sq), from where various streets and boulevards radiate like the spokes

**TIRANA IN TWO DAYS**

Check out the **National Art Gallery** (p53), the **National Museum of History** (p54) and the **Et'hem Bey Mosque** (p54). Walk back the length of Bulevardi Dëshmorët e Kombit, stopping to take in the view at **Sky Club Panoramic Bar** (p56). Head to **Efendy** (p55) for an Ottoman banquet, then party in trendy **Blloku** (p53).

On day two take the **Postcommunist Walking Tour** (p54) through the centre of the city. Catch a cab to the **Martyrs' Cemetery** (p53) before heading to **Prince Park** (p56) for a fine Italian meal.

of a wheel. Running south to the university and park-covered hill beyond is shady Bulevardi Dëshmorët e Kombit. Running north, Bulevardi Zogu I leads to the busy train and bus station. The Lana River is like a large culvert, cutting the city in two below Sheshi Skënderbej. Mt Dajti (1612m) rises to the east.

## INFORMATION
### Bookshops
**Adrion International Bookshop** ( ☎ 235 242; Palace of Culture, Sheshi Skënderbej; 8.30am-9.30pm) Stocks magazines and newspapers from around the world and a selection of English-language books with a great Albanian section.

### Internet Access
Both the following have new computers, fast connections and charge 100 lekë per hour.
**Center Internet** (Rr Brigada e VIII; 24hr) Look for the yellow sign down a laneway.
**Internet: Point** (Rr Dëshmorët e 4 Shkurtit 7; 24hr)

### Laundry
**Drycleaner & Laundry** ( ☎ 068-216-8268; Rr Hoxha Tahsim; 8am-10pm Mon-Sat, 9am-1pm Sun) Laundering of trousers/shirts costs 200 lekë.

### Medical Services
**ABC Family Health Center** ( ☎ 234 105; Rr Qemal Stafa 360; 8am-4pm Mon-Fri) Run by the Baptists, with English-speaking doctors, ABC offers a range of services including regular (US$60) and emergency (US$72) consultations (discounts for missionaries!). This is the best place to go for consultations but there are no trauma facilities. If you're in an accident, the ambulance will take you to the Military Hospital where treatment is rudimentary.

# TIRANA

0 _____ 500 m
0 _____ 0.3 miles

To Mt Dajti (25km)

To Airport (26km); Kruja (32km); Durrës (38km)

To Durrës (38km); Berati (122km)

To Martyrs' Cemetery & Former Palace of King Zogu (400m); Mother of Albania Statue (400m); Elbasan (54km); Pogradec (140km)

To Diplomat Fashion Hotel (300m)

To Plan B (200m)

Rr Don Bosko

Train Station

Rr Arben Broci

Bul Zogu I

Rr Barrikadave

Rr Mine Peza

Rr Durrësit

Rr Mihal Duri

Rr Myslym Shyri

Rr Skënderbej

Rr Naim Frashëri

Rr Muhamet Gjollesha

Rr Bajram Curri

Rr Siri Kodra

Rr Dibrës

Rr Qemal Stafa

Rr Qemal Guranjaku

Rr Abdi Toptani

Rr Murat Toptani

Rr Lek Dukagjini

Rr Mujo Ulqinaku

Rr Ded Gjo Luli

Rr Ismail Qemali

Rr Pjeter Bogdani

Rr Gjergj Fishta

Bul Bajram Curri

Bul Gjergj Fishta

Rr Deshmoret e 4 Shkurtit

Rr Vaso Pasha

Rr Sami Frashëri

Rr Islam Alla

Rr Sulejman Delvina

Bul Dëshmorët e Kombit

Rr Asim Zeneli

Rr Elbasanit

Lana River

Lumi i Tiranës

Sheshi Avni Rustemi

Sheshi Skënderbej

Sheshi Italie

Parku Rinia

Parku Kombëtar

Palace of Culture

Selman Stërmasi Stadium

Blloku

Unaza

## Money

Tirana has plenty of ATMs connected to international networks. The main chains are Tirana Bank, Pro Credit Bank, Raiffeisen Bank and American Bank of Albania. Independent moneychangers operate directly in front of the main post office and on Sheshi Skënderbej, offering the same rates as the banks. Changing money is not illegal or dangerous, but do count the money you receive before handing yours over. It's nearly impossible to exchange travellers cheques outside Tirana, so if you're relying on them (our advice is, don't) try one of the following banks:

**American Bank of Albania** ( ☎ 276 000; Rr Ismail Qemali 27; ☷ 9.30am-3.30pm Mon-Fri) A reliable, secure place to cash your travellers cheques (2% commission). Also an Amex representative.

**National Savings Bank** ( ☎ 235 035; Blvd Dëshmorët e Kombit; ☷ 10.30am-5pm Mon-Fri) Located in the Rogner Hotel Europapark Tirana, it offers MasterCard advances, cashes US dollar, euro and sterling travellers cheques for 1% commission and exchanges cash.

## Post

**Main post office & telephone centre** ( ☎ 228 262; Sheshi Çameria; ☷ 8am-8pm Mon-Fri) There is an additional post office branch on Rruga Mohamet Gjollesha.

**Telephone centre** (Bul Zogu I; ☷ 7.30am-6.30pm)

## Tourist Information

Tirana does not have an official tourist office. Useful references include *Tirana in Your Pocket* (www.inyourpocket.com; 400 lekë) and *Tirana: The Practical Guide and Map of Tirana* (200 lekë), available from the main bookshops and hotels.

## Travel Agencies

**Albania Travel & Tours** ( ☎ 232 983; albaniatraveland tours@yahoo.com; Rr Durrësit 102; ☷ 8am-8pm Mon-Fri, 8am-2pm Sat & Sun) A central agency that books flights, ferries and private rooms.

**Outdoor Albania** ( ☎ 272 075; www.outdooralbania .com) Excellent trailblazing adventure-tour agency offering all manner of specialist tours, including hiking, mountain biking and village stays – with a strong commitment to ecotourism.

## DANGERS & ANNOYANCES

Tirana is a very safe city with little petty crime. The streets are badly lit and full of cavernous potholes, so mind your step and arm yourself with a pocket torch at night to light your way. There are occasional power cuts in the city so the torch idea stretches further. Crossing the street is not for the faint-hearted and you need to adopt a love for adrenaline-fuelled high-risk activities before you attempt this.

## SIGHTS

Running south from **Sheshi Skënderbej** the spacious, tree-lined, fascist-designed, pothole-covered **Bulevardi Dëshmorët e Kombit** houses most of the government buildings, recognisable by their Italianate columns and heat-packing military guards. Further along the street the **National Art Gallery** (admission 100 lekë; ☷ 9am-7pm) has a wonderful collection ranging from 13th-century icons to modern art, but most interesting are the large socialist-realist canvases. Note the central role of women in this work – from the breastfeeding mother with a shotgun slung over her lap in *Lokja* (1983), to the manager giving instructions in *Giant of Metallurgy*.

Further down the boulevard, across the bridge, the **Council Of Ministers building** still has an impressive socialist relief, along with the 2nd-floor balcony where Enver Hoxha and cronies would stand and view military parades. In the forecourt of **Tirana University**, which abuts the boulevard, is a lovely **statue of Mother Teresa** with arms outstretched as if to give you a big hug.

Beyond the university, the lush **Parku Kombëtar**, with its serene artificial lake, stretches up to the **former palace of King Zogu** (Rr Elbasanit). At the top of the hill, on the other side of the road, lies the **Martyrs' Cemetery**, where some 900 partisans who died in WWII are buried. The views over the city and surrounding mountains are excellent. Many still come here, clutching laurel sprigs to pay their respects under the shadow of the immense, beautiful and strangely androgynous **Mother Albania statue** (1972). Hoxha was buried here in 1985, but was exhumed in 1992 and interred in an ordinary graveyard on the other side of town.

Nestled between the park, the boulevard and the river is the once totally forbidden but now totally trendy **Blloku**, the former exclusive Communist Party neighbourhood. When the area was opened to the general public in 1991, Albanians flocked to see the style in which their proletarian leaders lived. Judging by the three-storey pastel-coloured house that was the **former residence of Enver Hoxha** (cnr Rr Deshmorët e 4 Shkurtit & Ismail Qemali), they lived a much simpler life than their comrades in Romania, for example.

Along Rruga Murat Toptani are the 6m-high walls of the **Fortress of Justinian**, the last remnants of a Byzantine-era castle.

## WALKING TOUR: POSTCOMMUNIST TIRANA

The rapid pace of change in Albania is nowhere more pronounced than in its capital. The most obvious symbol of this is the wackily painted tower blocks throughout the city – a surprisingly effective means of shaking off its recent grey past.

Start your walk at the Orthodox **Church of the Holy Evangelist** ( ☎ 235 095; Rr e Kavajës 151), set back from Rruga e Kavajës in a laneway nearly opposite the Macedonian embassy. In the mid-1960s the infamous atheism campaign resulted in many churches and mosques being bulldozed or converted into public buildings. On this church's steeple you can clearly see where the cross-shaped holes in the brickwork were once covered over. While the reinstatement of this church has been accomplished quite tastefully, the same can't be said of the Catholic **Church of St Marie** (Rr e Kavajës) just along the road. The hilariously garish photorealistic images painted over the communist whitewash have to be seen to be believed – particularly the scenes to the left of the altar, with the Magdalene in billowing scarlet robes.

Continue along the road until you reach **Sheshi Skënderbej**, the bustling heart of the city. Until it was pulled down by the angry mob on 20 February 1991 a 10m-high gold-leaf-covered statue of Enver Hoxha stood here, watching over a mainly carless square. Now only the **equestrian statue of Skanderbeg** remains, deaf to the cacophony of screeching horns, as cars four lanes deep try to shove their way through the battlefield below.

Follow the lead of the locals and walk blindly into the mass of traffic to one of the central islands to get a good view of the wonderful socialist-realist *Albania* mosaic on the front of the **National Museum of History** (admission 300 lekë; ☺ 9am-1pm & 5-7pm Tue-Sat, 9am-noon & 5-7pm Sun). It still shows proud Albanians marching through history, only now the flag is missing its communist star. Inside are many of this ancient land's archaeological treasures, dating back as far as 100,000 BC. The extensive partisan-communist section has been retained (unfortunately without English translations),

but it now ends with a large memorial exhibit to victims of Hoxha's regime.

As you leave the museum the white stone building to your left is the **Palace of Culture**. Construction began as a gift from the Soviets in 1960 although it was delayed by the 1961 Soviet–Albanian split. Past this monolith, a delicate minaret marks out a true survivor. The exquisite 18th-century **Et'hem Bey Mosque** escaped destruction during the battle for the liberation of the city near the end of WWII, and went on to survive the state's atheism campaign due to its sheer beauty. Take off your shoes and look inside at the beautifully painted dome of this once-again functioning mosque.

When you exit, turn right. At the next intersection the socialist-realist **Statue of the Unknown Partisan** seems to be aiming his weapons at the **Parliament** building (1924) down the road. At the foot of the statue day-labourers wait for work, some with their own jackhammers – a fitting image of the precarious position of the postcommunist Albanian worker.

Veer right and follow the road to the oversized dirty drain that is the **Lana River**. Under the old regime, Tirana was rated as one of the cleanest cities in Europe. Turn right and you'll soon come to another example of religious revival, **St Paul's Catholic Cathedral** (Bul Zhan D'Ark). This massive edifice looks a bit like a hotel from the outside, while inside it has all the ambience of a hotel lobby. There are some interesting stained-glass windows, particularly the one featuring John Paul II and Mother Teresa to the left of the front door.

Continue to the bridge and cross to the sloping white-marble and glass walls of the **Pyramid** (cnr Bul Bajram Curri & Dëshmorët e Kombit) – also known as the former Enver Hoxha Museum (1988) – designed by Hoxha's daughter and son-in-law. In a hilarious twist of fate the building, which once housed a grandiose statue of the ruler, is now home to a disco called the Mummy. In front of the Pyramid the **Bell of Peace** is a touching little memorial to the country's difficult postcommunist years, forged from bullet cases collected by Albanian schoolchildren during the anarchy of 1997.

## SLEEPING
### Budget

**Tirana Backpacker Hostel** ( ☎ 272 075, 069-218 8845; tiranabackpacker@hotmail.com; Rr Elbasanit 85; dm €12) The young crew that runs this place is your ticket to a good time in Tirana. This large villa has 13 beds in three rooms and two shared bathrooms, although at the time of research the downstairs floor was being converted into more rooms and a bar. It has big balconies, a garden, a kitchen and a laundry for guests to use. Winter power cuts are usually brief, but they do tend to affect the water supply.

**Hotel Endri** ( ☎ 244 168, 069-227 2522; Rr Vaso Pasha 27, entrance 3, apt 30; s/d €20/30; ✖ ) Not really a hotel at all, the Endri consists of seven sparkling-clean rooms housed in two communist-era housing blocks next door to the owner's apartment. It's great value and located where all the action is. Call in advance as you'll never find this place on your own.

**Hotel Kruja** ( ☎ 238 106; fax 238 108; Rr Mine Peza; s/d/tr €35/50/75; ✖ ) Only 300m from the main square on a less-frantic side street, Hotel Kruja has a relaxed vibe. While the exterior looks like a 1960s motel, the rooms are bright, airy and clean.

**Hotel Lugano** ( ☎ /fax 222 023; Rr Mihal Duri 34; s/d €40/50; ✖ ) This handsome little hotel in a quiet side street, a few minutes from the main square, has pleasant, light-flooded rooms with small balconies and some kitsch fake marble bathrooms.

## Midrange

**Vila Tafaj** ( ☎ 227 581; www.tafaj.com; Rr Mine Peza 86; s €40-50, d €60-70; P ✖ ) This fine-looking boutique hotel, in an ornate 1930s villa, has a lovely large garden where you can enjoy breakfast under a canopy of wisteria, while canaries twitter in cages.

**Firenze Hotel** ( ☎ 249 099; firenzehotel@albmail.com; Bul Zogu I 72; s/d €50/70; P ✖ ) Sporting king-sized beds and new bathrooms, this cheerfully coloured little hotel is conveniently located between the railway station and the main square.

**Hotel Nirvana** ( ☎ /fax 235 270; Rr e Kavajës 96/2; s/d €60/80; P ✖ ) With its ostentatious marble

staircase and walls dripping in art, this hotel may have delusions of grandeur but thankfully the price remains reasonably humble and the staff friendly and helpful.

**Diplomat Fashion Hotel** ( ☎ 235 090; www.diplomat fashion.com; Bul Bajram Curri; s €85-110, d €130-160) While its name is a misnomer (fashionable diplomats?), this zany boutique hotel has the most stylish interiors in town, with each level themed around the world's great centres of fashion. You can even work on that fashionable waistline in the exercise room in the basement, complete with Jacuzzi, steam room and sauna.

**Hotel Mondial** ( ☎ 232 372; www.hotelmondial .al; Rr Muhamet Gjollesha; s/d/ste €90/110/130; P ✖ ✖ ) It's quite a hike from the centre of town but the Mondial has a reputation for good service, along with an attractive rooftop pool that has views over the city.

## Top End

**Sheraton Tirana Hotel & Towers** ( ☎ 274 707; www.shera ton.com; Sheshi Italia; r €180, ste €273-384; P ✖ ✖ ✖ ) This is hands-down the most impressive hotel in town, offering a choice of indoor or outdoor swimming pools, an extensive gym and several good restaurants.

# EATING

Tirana has no shortage of restaurants – some fantastic and some absolutely dire, but most perfectly acceptable. Cafés don't tend to serve food, and breakfast options are sadly lacking.

**Buke dhe Embelsira Franceze** (Rr Dëshmorët e 4 Shkur-tit 1; breakfasts 210 lekë; ✖ 7.30am-10.30pm) One of the few good breakfast spots in Tirana, where you can stop for a coffee and croissant or take away a delicious *pain au chocolat*.

**Plan B** (Rr Sami Frasheri; mains 500 lekë; ✖ noon-4.30pm & 7-11.30pm) This fantastic pasta place is tucked

---

**AUTHOR'S CHOICE**

**Efendy** ( ☎ 274 949; Rr Sami Frashëri; mains 1000-1500 lekë; ✖ midday-midnight) Foodies alert! Housed in an inconspicuous building in Blloku is an authentic Ottoman dining experience that is as much a history lesson as a sublime culinary one. Chef Ahmet Dursun hails from Turkey, where he studied at one of the world's finest Ottoman restaurants, extracting recipes from the old chefs and researching their collection of documents. He ended up in Albania 12 years ago (as an opera singer – it's a long story), and he's since travelled throughout the Balkans ('from Croatia to Bulgaria') collecting dishes along the way. Let him lead you through his seasonal delicacies and you won't be disappointed. He'll even regale you with stories about the origins of the dishes if you're so inclined.

underneath the equally great bar (open 7am to 4am) of the same name. It's a good option for vegetarians as it doesn't operate by a set menu and the staff are happy to cook to your request with deliciously fresh ingredients.

**Era** ( ☎ 274 949; Rr Ismail Qemali; mains 600 lekë; 🕙 10am-11pm) Traditional Albanian fare in the heart of Blloku. There are some vegetarian choices on the menu, but check first – there may well be mince lurking in your stuffed vegetables.

**Prince Park** (Rr e Elbasanit; mains 300-1000 lekë; 🕙 11am-midnight) Tucked into the top of the city park, this upmarket restaurant is like a hunting lodge with an open fire in winter, and wooden interiors and antlers on the walls. The cuisine is Italian, with some vegetarian pasta options.

**Piazza** ( ☎ 247 706; Rr Ded Gjon Luli; mains 550-1500 lekë; 🕙 noon-6pm & 7-11pm) Sit back and enjoy the stylish interior of the large dining room, while impeccably dressed waiters buzz about serving fine Italian cuisine (including some vegetarian pasta options).

## DRINKING

**Sky Club Panoramic Bar & Restaurant** ( ☎ 221 666; Sky Tower, Rr Dëshmorët e 4 Shkurtit; 🕙 8am-midnight) It may seem wrong to make a bar your first stop in Tirana, but a visit to this rotating tower is the best way to orient yourself, offering spectacular views over the entire city. Not recommended for a night on the turps – the rotation is a bit jerky and may leave you slightly seasick.

**Living Room** ( ☎ 274 837; Rr Punetoret e Rilindjes 16; 🕙 7.30pm til late) This is the hippest place to drink and dance in Tirana – with eclectic DJs, a good crowd, cool lampshades and '70s sofas for you to lounge on when you're danced (or drunk) off your feet.

Tirana's vibrant and fast-changing bar scene is easily accessed by strolling the streets of fashionable Blloku:

**Buda-bar** (Rr Ismail Qemali; 🕙 4.30pm-late) This place has subdued lighting, with the supreme being smiling serenely over the super-groovy crowd.

**Charl's** (Rr Pjeter Bogdani 5; 🕙 8am-late) At the opposite extreme, this rocking student pub has a great beer garden and a constant roster of bands playing live on the weekends.

## ENTERTAINMENT

There is a good range of entertainment options in Tirana, in the form of bars, clubs,

cinema, performances and exhibitions. For the lowdown check out the monthly leaflet *ARTirana* (a free supplement to *Gazeta Shqiptare*), which contains English summaries of current cultural events.

**Theatre of Opera and Ballet** ( ☎ 224 753; Palace of Culture, Sheshi Skënderbej; tickets around 500 lekë) Check the posters outside for performances ranging from folk-dancing to the state ballet, opera and orchestras.

**Academy of Arts** ( ☎ 257 237; Sheshi Nënë Tereza) Classical music and other performances take place throughout the year in either the large indoor theatre or the small open-air faux-classical amphitheatre; both are part of the university. Prices vary according to the programme.

**Kinema Millenium 2** ( ☎ 253 654; Rr Murat Toptani; tickets 200-500 lekë) Screens recent box-office hits (usually in English with Albanian subtitles) and boasts a lovely garden bar.

Next to the university, Qemal Stafa Stadium often hosts pop concerts and other musical events (look out for street advertising). Football matches are held here every Saturday and Sunday afternoon.

## SHOPPING

Blloku is a boutique-shopper's paradise.

**Natyral & Organik** ( ☎ 250 575; Rr Vaso Pasha) This wonderful store in Blloku not only supports small village producers by stocking organic olive oil, honey, herbs, tea, eggs, spices, raki and cognac (they make great gifts, but be aware of customs regulations in the countries you're travelling through), it's also a centre for environmental activism.

There are a few good souvenir shops on Rruga Durrësit, Bulevardi Zogu I and around Sheshi Skënderbej. Most of them sell the same things: Albanian flags, carved wooden plates, T-shirts and traditional textiles.

## GETTING THERE & AWAY
### Air

Nënë Tereza International Airport is at Rinas, 26km from the city. For a list of airlines flying from here to other parts of Eastern Europe, see p72.

### Bus

Getting out of Tirana can be extremely confusing, as much for locals as anybody else. You have the option of buses or *furgons* (see p73), which leave from several hubs on the outskirts of the city that are prone to move from time to time. Travelling times are totally dependent on what degree of 'crazy' the traffic out of town is currently operating at.

At the time of writing, *furgons* going north leave from the chaotic Zogu i Zi roundabout – Kruja to the right (150 lekë, 45 minutes, 32km) and Shkodra to the left (300 lekë, two hours, 116km). Keep asking until someone points you in the right direction.

You can catch a *furgon* to Fier (400 lekë, 2½ hours, 122km), Vlora (400 lekë, three hours, 161km) and Gjirokastra (1000 lekë, five hours, 244km) from Rruga e Kavajës, and there are also buses to Fier (300 lekë).

*Furgons* towards Macedonia (Elbasan and Pogradec) leave from a stand by Qemal Stafa Stadium. Macedonia-bound buses going through Struga (€10, six hours, 197km, six per week) and on to Tetovo, leave from the patch of mud in front of the train station. *Furgons* and buses for Durrës (bus 100 lekë, *furgon* 150 lekë, 45 minutes, 38km) also leave from here.

Buses for Prishtina (€30, 10 hours, 343km, three daily) leave from behind the museum near Sheshi Skënderbej.

If all else fails, get in a taxi and say *'furgon per* [destination], *ju falem nderit'*. It may not be great Albanian, but your taxi driver should understand and they should know the latest departure points.

## Train

The run-down train station is at the northern end of Bulevardi Zogu I. Albania's trains range from sort-of OK to very decrepit. Trains go to Durrës (55 lekë, one hour, eight daily), Elbasan (160 lekë, four hours, three daily), Pogradec (245 lekë, seven hours, twice daily), Shkodra (120 lekë, 3½ hours, twice daily) and Vlora (210 lekë, 5½ hours, twice daily).

## GETTING AROUND
### To/From the Airport

Hertz operates a shuttle bus service that will take you from the airport to Sheshi Skënderbej for 500 lekë. Your other options are taxis (agree on a price before you travel – about €20) or the infrequent buses that leave from the carpark (€20). Given the state of Tirana's traffic, allow plenty of time to get to the airport.

## Car & Motorcycle

Our advice would be DON'T DO IT. Tirana's roads, and drivers, are insane. For the foolhardy, here are some car-hire agencies in Tirana:

**Avis** ( ☎ 235 011; Rogner Hotel Europapark Tirana, Bul Dëshmorët e Kombit)
**Hertz** ( ☎ 255 028; Tirana International Hotel, Sheshi Skënderbej)
**Sixt** ( ☎ 259 020; Rr e Kavajës 116)

Some of the major hotels offer guarded parking; others have parking available out the front.

## Taxi

Taxi stands dot the city and charge 400 lekë for a ride inside Tirana (600 lekë at night). Make sure you reach an agreement with the driver before setting off. **Radio Taxi** ( ☎ 377 777), with 24-hour service, is particularly reliable.

## AROUND TIRANA
### Mt Dajti National Park

Mt Dajti (1612m) is visible from Tirana, 25km to the east. It is the most accessible mountain in the country and many Tiranans go there on the weekends to escape the city rush and have a spit-roast lamb lunch. There is a checkpoint about 15km from Tirana that levies an admission fee into the national park of 100 lekë for cars with up to three passengers, or 200 lekë for four or more passengers. Put your sturdy shoes on for a gentle hike in the lovely, shady beech and pine forests and have a coffee and enjoy the spectacular views from the wide terrace of the **Panorama Restaurant** ( ☎ 361 124; meals 800 lekë; ☽ 9am-11pm), the most popular spot on Dajti.

There is no public transport. A cab from the city takes about 45 minutes, whereupon you can arrange to phone the driver to pick you up when you want to go back. It shouldn't set you back more than 600 to 700 lekë each way. If you're driving, the road to Dajti starts on Rruga Qemal Stafa past the Chateau Linza Hotel.

# NORTHERN ALBANIA

Notions of Albania as a wild frontier of bleak mountains and villages that time forgot have their roots in the north. The northern Albanian landscape is a mixture of rich wildlife, swamps and lagoons around Shkodra and the Adriatic Coast, and high, unforgiving mountains, Bjeshkët e Namuna (Accursed

**ALBANIA**

Mountains), in the northeast. Visits to these mountainous regions still involve some element of risk due to the revival of traditional blood feuds and the rise of organised crime. Tourists are unlikely to get caught up in this, but incidents, such as the shoot-out on a bus in early 2006, occasionally happen. The lowlands, including Shkodra and the main road corridor from Tirana to Montenegro, are perfectly safe.

## SHKODRA

☎ 022 / pop 91,300

With its dramatic setting by the shores of the Balkan's largest lake and backed by imposing mountains, Shkodra was once the most powerful city in the region and is still the centre of Gheg culture and Albanian Catholicism. It's now a little down-at-heel and suffers from terrible power blackouts in winter. Still, its smattering of fascinating sights makes for a good half-day introduction to Albania for those entering from Montenegro.

By 500 BC an Illyrian fortress already guarded the strategic crossing just west of the city where the rivers meet, through which all traffic moving up the coast from Greece to Italy must pass. Queen Teuta's Illyrian kingdom was based here in the 3rd-century BC, until the last Illyrian king was taken by the Romans in Rozafa fortress in 168 BC. Later the region passed through the hands of the Byzantines, Slavs and Venetians, who held Rozafa against Suleiman Pasha in 1473, only to lose it to Mehmet Pasha in 1479. The Ottomans lost 14,000 men in the first siege and 30,000 in the second.

As the Ottoman Empire declined in the late 18th century, Shkodra became the centre of a semi-independent pashalik – a region governed by a pasha (an Ottoman high official) – which led to a blossoming of commerce and crafts. In 1913 Montenegro attempted to annex Shkodra (it succeeded in taking Ulcinj), and the town changed hands often during WWI. Badly damaged by the 1979 earthquake, Shkodra was subsequently repaired and now is Albania's fourth-largest town.

The centre has some atmospheric laneways with great old buildings in varying states of decay. The massive Catholic cathedral is gradually recovering from its tenure as a volleyball court during the state ban on religion. Its side altar displays the photos of 40 local clerics martyred at this time.

### Sights

Two kilometres southwest of Shkodra, near the southern end of Lake Shkodra, is **Rozafa Fortress** (admission 200 lekë), founded by the Illyrians in antiquity and rebuilt much later by the Venetians and Ottomans. The fortress derives its name from a woman named Rozafa, who was allegedly walled into the ramparts as an offering to the gods so that the construction would stand. The story goes that Rozafa asked for two holes to be left in the stonework so that she could continue to suckle her baby. Nursing women still come to the fortress to smear their breasts with milky water taken from a spring here. Bring a torch and indulge your Dungeons & Dragons fantasies, poking around the entryways to

---

**FAMILY FEUD WITH BLOOD AS THE PRIZE**

The *Kanun* (Code) was formalised in the 15th century by powerful northern chieftain Lekë Dukagjin. It consists of 1262 articles covering every aspect of daily life: work, marriage, family, property, hospitality, economy and so on. Although the *Kanun* was suppressed by the communists, there has been a disturbing revival of its strict precepts in northern Albania. How much so is uncertain, as dramatic incidents may have been overplayed by the media.

According to the *Kanun*, the most important things in life are honour and hospitality. If a member of a family (or one of their guests) is murdered, it becomes the duty of the male members of that clan to claim their blood debt by murdering a male member of the murderer's clan. This sparks an endless cycle of killing that doesn't end until either all the male members of one of the families are dead, or reconciliation is brokered through respected village elders.

Hospitality is so important in these parts of Albania that the guest takes on a godlike status. There are 38 articles giving instructions on how to treat a guest – an abundance of food, drink and comfort is at his or her disposal, and it is also the host's duty to avenge the murder of his guest, should this happen during their visit.

tunnels leading to subterranean chambers. There are marvellous views from the highest point.

In the roundabout in the centre of town stands **5 Heroes**, one of Albania's best examples of socialist-realist sculpture. Fans of the work of gay artist Tom of Finland will see similarities with this superbly homoerotic bronze of five ruggedly handsome men, some holding hands, gazing steely-eyed and square-jawed down the five streets that make up this intersection.

Hidden inside a building that looks like a block of flats, the **Fototeke Marubi** (Muhamet Gjollesha; admission €1; ⏰ 8am-3pm Mon-Fri) boasts fantastic photography by the Marubi 'dynasty', Albania's first and foremost photographers. The first-ever photograph taken in Albania is here, and dates from 1858. The exhibition shows fascinating portraits, places and events, including that of a young Enver Hoxha giving a speech while still in local government in Gjirokastra. To get there, from 5 Heroes take the next street to the left after the one leading to Rozafa. Turn right at the first street. On the left you will see a metal grille gate about 10m past a jeweller. Enter and follow the path around and you will eventually find the sign. Knock if the door isn't open.

### Sleeping & Eating

**Hotel Mondial** ( ☎ 40 194; www.freewebs.com/mondial shkodra; cnr Rr Vasil Shanto & 13 Dhjetori; s/d €50/60, ste €80-110; 🛜 ) This new hotel above a popular restaurant has clean, comfortable rooms with balconies and a large suite with two bedrooms, two bathrooms, a living room and a spa!

### Getting There & Away

Frequent *furgons* depart from the main road near Rozafa Castle for Tirana (300 lekë, two hours, 116km) and three daily buses leave from the 5 Heroes roundabout. The train is the cheapest but slowest option (120 lekë, 3½ hours).

There are regular minibuses between Shkodra and Ulcinj ('Ulqini' in Albanian) in Montenegro (€8, 40 minutes), crossing the border at Muriqani. By taxi it's €10 to the border and US$10 from there to Ulcinj. The road to Han i Hotit on the way to Podgorica is in poorer shape. A taxi to this border costs about €15.

# CENTRAL ALBANIA

## KRUJA

☎ 0511 / pop 17,400

Kruja's impressive beauty starts from the journey itself, up the winding road into the grey, rocky mountains. The fields stretch around you, and soon you can start making out the houses seated in the lap of the mountain, and the ancient castle jutting out on one side. Kruja is a magnificent day trip from Tirana and the best place for souvenir shopping in the country. The bazaar hides antique coins and medals along with quality traditional ware, such as beautifully embroidered tablecloths, copper coffee pots and handwoven rugs.

As you get off the *furgon* a statue of Skanderbeg (George Kastrioti; 1405–68) wielding his mighty sword greets you, with the sharp mountain edges as his backdrop. The hilltop town attained its greatest fame between 1443 and 1468 when this national hero made Kruja his seat of government. At a young age, Kastrioti, son of an Albanian prince, was handed over as a hostage to the Turks, who converted him to Islam and gave him a military education. There he became known as Iskander (after Alexander the Great) and Sultan Murat II promoted him to the rank of *bey* (governor), thus the name Skanderbeg.

In 1443 the Turks suffered a defeat at the hands of the Hungarians at Niš in present-day Serbia, which gave Skanderbeg the opportunity he had been waiting for to abandon the Ottoman army and Islam, and rally his fellow Albanians against the Turks. Among the 13 Turkish invasions he subsequently repulsed was that led by his former commander Murat II in 1450. Pope Calixtus III named Skanderbeg the 'captain general of the Holy See' and Venice formed an alliance with him. The Turks besieged Kruja four times, finally taking it in 1478 (after Skanderbeg's death) and Albanian resistance was suppressed.

### Sights

The main sight in Kruja is the still-inhabited **castle** (admission 100 lekë) and its rather retro-modernistic **Skanderbeg Museum** (admission 200 lekë; ⏰ 9am-1pm & 3-6pm, Tue-Sun). Designed by Enver Hoxha's daughter and son-in-law, it displays mainly replicas of armour and paintings depicting Skanderbeg's struggle against the Ottomans – along with a socialist-themed stained-glass window at the end.

The **Ethnographic Museum** ( ☎ 22 225; admission 300 lekë; ⏰ 8am-1pm & 3-8pm) is certainly one of the most interesting experiences in Kruja. Set in an original 19th-century house (opposite the Skanderbeg Museum) that once belonged to an affluent Albanian family, the museum shows the level of luxury and self-sufficiency maintained in the household with the production of food, drink, leather, weapons etc, including its very own steam bath. The English-speaking guide hardly stops for breath and will explain everything in minute detail; it's polite to give him a tip of 100 to 200 lekë.

Wander around the old streets, with kids racing around and turkeys being walked like dogs, but beware that you'll probably be set upon by old women trying to sell you some of their craft. Near the lowest part of the walls you will find the remains of a small **hamam** (Turkish bathhouse). Take a torch to look around inside. Nearby sits the **Dollma Teqe**, a small place of worship for the Bektashi branch of Islam (see p48), maintained by successive generations of the Dollma family since 1789. It was resurrected after the fall of the Hoxha regime and is now functioning again. Just to the left of the Teqe complex is a **tunnel** that leads through the walls to a terrace on the side of the cliff, where you can sit among the olive trees and enjoy the panorama.

Kruja is 10km off the main road between Tirana and Lezha. A return journey from Tirana by cab with two hours' waiting time will cost around 4000 lekë, but your best option is to take a *furgon* (150 lekë, 45 minutes, 32km). *Furgons* also run the 45km route from Durrës.

## DURRËS
☎ 052 / pop 112,000

With miles of coast and its proximity to Tirana, Durrës should be a seaside resort par excellence. In reality it's dirty and polluted, and you can't swim without risking skin infections. It's a sad reminder of how far the country has slipped since the beach resorts were built here in communist times.

However, the city has an ancient history, the remnants of which make for a fascinating visit. If you believe the sign in the museum it was founded by 'Greek colons' in 627 BC and named Epidamnos. Local political unrest

played a part in sparking the Peloponnesian war that pitted the Greek states against each other from 431 to 404 BC. For a brief period it became part of an Illyrian kingdom before being taken by the Romans in 228 BC and renamed Dyrrachium. War once again touched it in 48 BC when Julius Caesar and Pompey did battle nearby during the Roman Civil War.

Despite all the bloodshed, the town itself was sacred to Aphrodite (Venus), the goddess of love, whose images fill the museum. Since Aphrodite's decline, Durrës has changed hands between the Bulgarians, Byzantines, Argevins, Serbs, Venetians, Ottomans and German Prince Wilhelm of Weld, before briefly becoming the capital of an independent Albania between 1918 and 1920.

### Orientation
The town is easily covered on foot. In the centre, the Great Mosque on Shesi i Lirisë serves as a point of orientation; the archaeological attractions are immediately around it, the city beach to the south. The harbour, immediately to the east, cuts the town off from the Plazhi i Durrësit stretch of beach and hotels.

### Information
There are plenty of ATMs around town.
**American Bank of Albania** (Sheshi Mujo Ulqinaku) Has an ATM.
**Dea Lines** ( ☎ 30 386; www.dealines.com; Rr Tregtare 102; ⏰ 9am-8pm) A trustworthy travel agency in the middle of town with staff who speak excellent English and can help you with hotel, air and boat bookings, as well as give bus information.
**Galaxy Internet** (Rr Taulantia; per hr 200 lekë)
**Post office** ( ☎ 35 522; Rr Prokop Meksi)

### Sights
The **Muzeu Arkeologjik** (Rr Taulantia; admission 200 lekë; ⏰ 8am-4pm Tue-Sun) has an impressive collection of artefacts from the city's Greek, Illryian and Roman periods, as well as a statue-graveyard (including some fallen communists) scattered around the grounds.

Beyond the museum are the 6th-century **Byzantine city walls**, begun after the Visigoth invasion of AD 481 and supplemented by round Venetian towers in the 14th century.

The impressive **Roman amphitheatre** (admission 200 lekë; ⏰ 10am-5pm Mon-Sat) was built on the hill side just inside the city walls between the 1st and 2nd centuries AD. In its prime

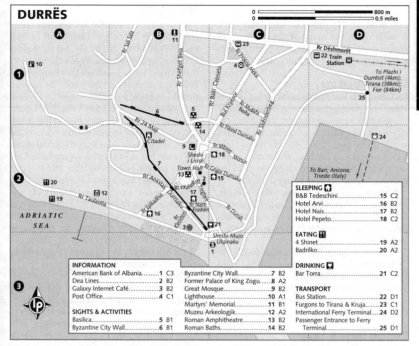

**DURRËS**

**INFORMATION**
American Bank of Albania..........1 C3
Dea Lines....................................2 B2
Galaxy Internet Café..................3 B2
Post Office..................................4 C1

**SIGHTS & ACTIVITIES**
Basilica......................................5 B1
Byzantine City Wall...................6 B1

Byzantine City Wall...................7 B2
Former Palace of King Zogu......8 A2
Great Mosque............................9 B2
Lighthouse...............................10 A1
Martyrs' Memorial....................11 B1
Muzeu Arkeologjik....................12 B2
Roman Amphitheatre...............13 B2
Roman Baths............................14 B2

**SLEEPING**
B&B Tedeschini.......................15 C2
Hotel Arvi................................16 B2
Hotel Nais...............................17 B2
Hotel Pepeto...........................18 C2

**EATING**
4 Shinet..................................19 A2
Badrilko..................................20 A2

**DRINKING**
Bar Torra................................21 C2

**TRANSPORT**
Bus Station.............................22 D1
Furgons to Tirana & Kruja.......23 C1
International Ferry Terminal.....24 D2
Passenger Entrance to Ferry
    Terminal.............................25 D1

it had the capacity to seat 15,000 spectators. While poking around in the well-preserved vaults, keep an eye out for the mosaics belonging to a small Byzantine chapel, built into the structure after bloodsports fell out of fashion. There's also a massive tunnel, which originally ran for 500m towards the current town centre to enable the aristocracy to arrive in their carriages. Beware the savage dog chained in one of the pits at the far side of the complex.

Dating from the same period, the ruins of the **Roman baths** can be found just off the main square at the back of the Alexsandër Moisiu Theatre. Just across the road a large circular **basilica** still has some columns standing.

Durrës' attractions are not all ancient. There are some fine socialist-realist monuments, including the **Martyrs' Memorial** (Rr Shefget Beja) and a couple of dramatic statues down by the waterfront.

On the hill top west of the amphitheatre stands the **former palace of King Zogu**. A **lighthouse** stands on the next hill, where you can enjoy the royal views and check out the bunker constellation (see p47). It's a 1.5km walk,

but the views of the bay make it well worth the climb.

## Sleeping

These establishments are in the city itself, but many more line the Plazhi i Durrësit.

**B&B Tedeschini** ( ☎ 24 343, 068-224 6303; ipmcrsp@icc .al.eu.org; Dom Nikoll Kaçorri 5; r per person €15) This homely B&B, occupying the former 19th-century Italian then Austrian consulate, has airy rooms with antique furniture, watched over by portraits of former consuls. From the square fronting the mosque, walk down the alley to the left of the town hall; take the first left then a quick right.

**Hotel Nais** ( ☎ 30 375; hotel_nais@yahoo.it; Rr Naim Frashëri 46; s €25, d €30-40, tr €60; 🔀 ) Perched by the city walls, this 1930s building has been smartly refurbished although the rooms are tiny.

**Hotel Pepeto** ( ☎ /fax 24 190; Rr Mbreti Monun 3; s €25-30, d €40; 🔀 ) A well-run guesthouse, just off the square fronting the mosque. The rooms are decent and quiet, with good showers, minibars and balconies. One is like a suite and has an exercise bike.

**Hotel Arvi** ( ☎ 30 403; www.hotelarvi.com; Rr Taulantia; d €60, ste €80-100; ☒ ) This new multistorey block is fairly drab, but many of the rooms have amazing sea views. The large open-plan suites have bathtubs and small balconies.

## Eating & Drinking

**Bar Torra** (Sheshi Mujo Ulqinaku; paninis 100 lekë; ☯ 8am-11pm) This wonderful place is housed inside the fortified Venetian tower at the base of the city walls. The antique brick interior forms a gentle dome that echoes the curves of Hoxha's omnipresent bunkers, and there's a roof terrace for cheap alfresco eating, or drinking coffee, cocktails or beer under the stars.

**Badriklo** ( ☎ 25 650; Rr Taulantia; mains 250-600 lekë; ☯ 9am-11pm) This restaurant on the landward side of Rruga Taulantia may lack sea views but it has the best pizzas in Durrës, good service and a lively terrace bar.

**4 Shinet** ( ☎ 35 389; Rr Taulantia; mains 350-1250 lekë; ☯ 9am-11pm) The large terrace reaches right to the sea at this popular upmarket eatery. Seafood predictably dominates the menu, which also contains the usual mix of grilled meat, pasta and pizza.

## Getting There & Away

Albania's 720km railway network centres on Durrës, with trains heading to Tirana (55 lekë, 1½ hours, eight daily), Shkodra (150 lekë, 3½ hours, two daily), Pogradec (245 lekë, 6¾ hours, two daily) and Vlora (210 lekë, five hours, two daily) via Fier.

Buses to Tirana (100 lekë, 38km, 45 minutes) leave from the bus station whenever they're full. There are also two daily buses to Berat. In summer, buses from Tirana to Fier, Vlora, Gjirokastra and Saranda (two daily) stop here as well, but off-season they bypass the town and stop at the intersection at the end of Plazhi i Durrësit, to the far east of the harbour. You'll need to get a taxi to the bus stop (500 lekë).

*Furgons* to Berat (400 lekë, 93km, two hours) also leave from this intersection. For Tirana (150 lekë, 38km, 45 minutes) and Kruja they leave from Rruga e Dëshmorët, between the bus station and the Martyrs' Memorial.

Numerous travel agencies handle ferry bookings for Bari, Ancona and Trieste. All offer much the same service (see p931). International ferries leave from the terminal south of the bus station.

## APOLLONIA

The ruined city of ancient **Apollonia** (Pojan; admission 700 lekë; ☯ 9am-5pm) is 12km west of Fier, itself 89km south of Durrës. Set on rolling hills among olive groves, Apollonia has views that expand for miles across the plains below. Enjoy the panoramas from one of the cafés on the site or bring a picnic.

Apollonia was founded by Corinthian Greeks in 588 BC and quickly grew into an important city-state, minting its own currency. Under the Romans the city became a great cultural centre with a famous school of philosophy. Julius Caesar rewarded Apollonia with the title 'free city' for supporting him against Pompey the Great during the civil war in the 1st century BC, and sent his nephew Octavius, the future Emperor Augustus, to complete his studies there. After a series of military disasters, the population moved southward into present-day Vlora, and by the 5th century only a small village with its own bishop remained at the site.

The picturesque ruins include a small theatre and the elegant pillars on the restored façade of the city's 2nd-century AD administrative centre. Much of the site remains to be excavated. The Byzantine monastery of St Mary has fascinating gargoyles on the outside pillars. Since the restoration of religion, seats have been raided from a cinema to serve as pews. Ancient statues are displayed in the church garden.

Apollonia is best visited on a day trip from Tirana, Durrës, Vlora or Berat, as there's nothing of interest in nearby Fier. The lack of public transport to the site means that you will have to get a bus, *furgon* or train to Fier. The bus from Durrës will cost 200 lekë (1½ hours), and it's 300 lekë from Tirana (two hours). A *furgon* will take about an hour from Berat (200 lekë, 50km) or Vlora (150 lekë, 39km). The train from Tirana (175 lekë, 4½ hours) comes via Durrës. Once in Fier, find a taxi. You should expect to be charged around 2500 lekë for a return journey (30 minutes each way) and an hour's waiting time.

## BERAT

☎ 062 / pop 47,700

A highlight of any trip to Albania, Berat is one of the country's most beautiful towns, having been preserved as a museum city by the communist government. Its most striking feature is the collection of white Ottoman houses climbing up the hill to the castle, earning it the title 'town of a thousand windows'. Its rugged mountain setting is archetypically Albanian, and particularly evocative when the clouds swirl around the tops of the minarets and battlements.

In the 3rd century BC an Illyrian fortress called Antipatria was built here on the site of an earlier settlement. The Byzantines strengthened the hilltop fortifications in the 5th and 6th centuries, as did the Bulgarians 400 years later. The Serbs, who occupied the citadel in 1345, renamed it Beligrad (White City) and there is speculation that this is where the town's name comes from. In 1450 the Ottomans took Berat, and after a period of decline it began to thrive in the 18th and 19th centuries as a crafts centre, specialising in woodcarving. For a brief time in 1944 Berat was the capital of liberated Albania.

Berat suffers terribly from power cuts in the winter, and generators are not widely used. While the Osum River that divides the town is fairly dirty, the streets are mostly free of the rubbish that blankets the country. We even saw a team of street cleaners on our last visit! There are several ATMs and an internet café on the main strip.

## Sights
There is plenty to see in this small town and the best place to start is to take the hard slog up to the impressive 14th-century **Kala** (admission 100 lekë; 24hr), built on ancient Illyrian foundations along a ridge high above the gorge. Built in a traditionally Christian neighbourhood, the citadel is still inhabited and has a dozen surviving churches within its 10 hectares. The **Muzeu Onufri** ( 32 258; admission 200 lekë; 9am-2pm Mon-Fri) is housed in one of these, displaying artistically important icons, some rare tapestries and a beautiful gilded iconostasis. A torch will come in handy to peer into the Tolkienesque depths of the **Inner Fortress**; ruined stairs lead to a vast cavernous water reservoir.

The houses below the castle form the traditionally Muslim **Mangalem** quarter. The **Muzeu Etnografik** ( 32 224; admission 200 lekë; 9am-4pm Mon-Fri) is based in a fine 18th-century Ottoman villa just off the road up to the citadel. Check out the *mafil*, a kind of mezzanine looking into the lounge, where the women could watch the male guests being entertained.

At the foot of the hill the 14th-century **Sultan's Mosque** (Xhamië e Mbretit) is one of the oldest in Albania. There is a **Helveti teqe** next to the mosque with a richly decorated prayer hall. The Helveti, like the Bektashi, are a Dervish order of Muslim mystics. Next door is the office of the **Institute of Cultural Monuments** ( 32 300; www.beratmonument.org.al; 9am-4pm Mon-Fri), which can arrange guides and help with keys to locked sites. The big mosque on the town square is the 16th-century **Leaden Mosque** (Xhamië e Plumbit), so named because of the lead coating its domes. The 19th-century **Bachelors' Mosque** (Xhamië e Beqarëvet) is by the river, with enchanting paintings on the external walls.

A new footbridge and a seven-arched stone bridge (1780) lead to **Gorica**, another Christian quarter, where you can visit the old **Monastery of St Spyridon** and the little church of **St Thomas** (Shen Tomi). If you feel energetic you can climb up to the remains of another old **Illyrian fortress** in the woods above.

## Sleeping & Eating
**Hotel Mangalemi** ( 32 093; hotelmangalemi _tomi@yahoo.it; Rr e Kalasë; s/d/tr 1500/2500/3000 lekë) Situated in a sprawling Ottoman house, this is the best budget B&B in Albania. Run by the affable Tomi Mio and his family, the hotel has a great bar and restaurant on the ground floor and a clutch of warm, cosy rooms upstairs, plus a terrace with great views across Berat over to Mt Tomorri. Mangalemi even provides the rarest of Albanian services – a decent breakfast. The dinner menu is an offal-lovers paradise (order by the organ).

**Hotel Berati** ( 36 953; Rr Veli Zaloshnja; s/d €18/30) This traditional-style building is just off the main strip, not far from the post office. The hotel offers 10 tidy rooms and a cosy restaurant (mains 250 to 660 lekë) with a fantastic carved wooden ceiling.

## Getting There & Away
Buses depart from the station next to the big new Orthodox church for Tirana (250 lekë, three hours, 131km, every half hour from 4.30am to 3pm), Durrës (two daily), Fier (six daily), Vlora (250 lekë, two hours, 89km, nine daily) and Gjirokastra (one daily at 7am).

*Furgons* leave across the square from the buses and travel frequently to Tirana. For

Vlora you'll need to head first to Fier (200 lekë, one hour, 50km) and change *furgons* (150 lekë, one hour, 39km).

# SOUTHERN ALBANIA

With snow-capped mountains squeezing up against sparkling white beaches and the azure water of the Ionian, southern Albania is the most visually arresting part of the country. It's also the least populated and therefore the least spoiled – perhaps the last pristine stretch of Europe's Mediterranean coastline.

## VLORA

☎ 033 / pop 71,200

Nestled in the broad bay where the Adriatic meets the Ionian, the port city of Vlora is a much more attractive summer destination than its dirty northern sister Durrës. You can actually swim here in the crystal waters of the beaches, which stretch south from the harbour. Many see this beautiful bay as Albania's best hope for developing tourism. It's no wonder that the locals are fighting so hard to sink the plans of a US company to run an oil pipeline straight through it.

A grand palm-tree-lined avenue stretches through town, although the poverty is palpable just a block away on either side. Daily winter blackouts bring everything to a standstill. This was one of the most lawless towns at the end of the 1990s and, owing to its proximity to Italy, has been a hub of mafia activity, including the trafficking of drugs and slaves.

Vlora's main claim to fame is that it was the place where Albanian independence was proclaimed in 1912.

## Information

Everything you'll need in Vlora is on the broad main avenue, Sadik Zotaj, including several ATMs, the post office and telephone centre. By far the best place to get online is **Internet Café Studenti** ( ☎ 33 250; 2 Kullat Skele; per hr 200 lekë; ☺ 8am-10pm), at the bottom of a new white tower complex just past the turnoff to Plazhi i Ri. **Colombo Travel & Tours** ( ☎ 27 659; www .colomboalb.com; Hotel Sazani, Sheshi i Flamurit; ☺ 8am-noon & 4-10pm Mon-Sat) is a helpful travel agency on the ground floor of the Hotel Sazani, which sells ferry tickets for Brindisi.

## Sights

Start at **Sheshi i Flamurit** (Flag Square), near the top of Sadik Zotaj. The magnificently socialist-realist **Independence Monument** stands proud against the sky, representing the key figures in the movement for Albania's sovereignty, as the flag bearer hoists the double-headed eagle into the blue. Near the base of the monument lies the **grave of Ismail Qemali**, the country's first prime minister.

On the other side of the avenue is the **Muzeu Historik** (admission 100 lekë; ☺ 8am-2pm & 5-8pm Mon-Sat), and, opposite, behind an inconspicuous grey metal gate, is the **Ethnographic Museum** (admission 100 lekë; ☺ 9am-2pm Mon-Sat).

Walk down towards the 16th-century **Muradi Mosque**, a small elegant structure made of red and white stone and with a modest minaret; its exquisite design is attributed to one of the greatest Ottoman architects, Albanian-born Sinan Pasha. Further down by the harbour, the **Museum of Independence** (admission 100 lekë; ☺ 9am-noon & 5-8pm) is housed in the lovely little villa that became the headquarters of Albania's first government in 1912. All of the signs are in Albanian, but the preserved offices and historic photographs make it an interesting place for a short visit.

Vlora's **main beaches** stretch south from the harbour and the further you go, the better they get. Turn left before the harbour to reach **Plazhi i Ri**, a long sandy space that can get quite crowded. A good 2km walk away, **Uji i Ftohtë** is the best beach by far, with open-air bars and discos during summer. Municipal buses run from Sadik Zotaj to the Uji i Ftohtë post office (20 lekë, 10 minutes, every 20 minutes from 8am to 6pm).

## Sleeping & Eating

**Hotel Tozo** ( ☎ 23 819; Rr Sadik Zotaj; s/d 2500/3500 lekë; ☒ ) You can forgive broken showerheads and ill-fitting drapes when your hotel is the only place for blocks with electricity during Vlora's frequent winter power cuts. This midsized hotel is set back from the main strip behind a cute little park, about halfway between the bus station and the port.

**Hotel New York** ( ☎ 24 648; fax 24 649; Uji I Ftohtë beach; s/d €30/50, ste €60-120; ℙ ☒ ☎ ) With a gravity-defying terrace jutting clear across the road, this hotel has great views across the Bay of Vlora to Sazan Island. The tiled rooms are airy and tidy and there's a bright, modern restaurant with Italian meals for around 1300 lekë. It's situated at Uji i Ftohtë beach, 500m past where the bus terminates.

**Hotel Primavera** ( ☎ /fax 29 664; Plazhi i Ri; s/d/tr €40/40/45; 🛏 ) Looking more like a cheap 1990s apartment block than a hotel, the three-storey Primavera has 18 rooms with balconies and is located just across from the town's main beach.

**Xhokla** (Plazhi i Ri; mains 200-1000 lekë) With a sunny terrace facing the beach, this wonderful Italian seafood restaurant and bar is the best in town.

### Getting There & Away

In Vlora the bus and *furgon* terminus is easily spotted by the Muradi Mosque. Getting to Vlora from Tirana and Durrës is easy, with buses (300 lekë, three hours, 161km) and *furgons* (400 lekë) whizzing back and forth in the morning hours. There are also buses to Berat (250 lekë, two hours, 89km, nine daily), or you can catch a *furgon* to Fier (150 lekë, one hour, 39km) and change there (200 lekë, one hour, 50km). Buses to Gjirokastra (700 lekë, 5½ hours) and on to Saranda leave at 6am, 7am, 1pm and 2pm.

The bus to Qeparo will get you to Dhërmi and Himara. It stops on the main road near the terminus before continuing through Plazhi i Ri and Uji i Ftohtë. It takes 90 minutes to climb the Llogaraja Pass, where it often stops for a breather before commencing the 40-minute trip down to Dhërmi (300 lekë).

Trains head from Tirana (210 lekë, 5½ hours, twice daily) via Durrës (210 lekë, five hours). There are also ferries from Vlora to Brindisi, Italy (€40, four to seven hours depending on the boat, 13 weekly).

## IONIAN COAST
### Llogaraja Pass

The road going south from Vlora climbs up to the Llogaraja Pass, more than 1000m high, for some of Albania's most spectacular scenery. After the road passes shepherds on the plains guiding their herds, and thick forests where deer, wild boar and wolves roam, the view opens out onto the intense blue of the Ionian, looking out to the Greek island of Corfu. In winter, when snow blankets the ground, it's particularly dazzling. The road winds down a number of hairpin turns before reaching Dhërmi, although the views continue to be breathtaking all the way to Himara.

### Dhërmi & Drymades Beaches

Surely there are no more deserted shores in Mediterranean Europe than this wonderfully isolated stretch of coast. Apart from the ever-present bunkers, this landscape is largely unchanged since the ancient Greeks wandered these shores. If you're arriving by bus (from Vlora 300 lekë, 2½ hours, 55km) ask to be let off by the turnoff for the *plazhi* (beach), just past the town. From here it's an easy 15-minute walk downhill through the olive groves to the beautiful long beach at the foot of the snow-capped mountains.

In Dhërmi the best place to stay and eat at is the little **Hotel Luçiano** ( ☎ 069-209 1431; per person 1000 lekë; 🛏 ), consisting of an assortment of rooms above a popular seafood restaurant. The water's only metres away and the views are sublime. During winter blackouts the hotel's generator makes it a beacon for locals and visitors alike. The restaurant quickly fills up with people sitting out the surrounding darkness over a drink or a meal.

Even more deserted is Drymades. Leave the road going down into Dhërmi at the sign pointing right, indicating 1200m to the beach. After a good 45-minute walk along a dirt road winding through the olive groves, the path opens out onto a long, wide, sandy beach. This little slice of paradise is disturbed only by more bunkers and a character-filled beach bar with a straw roof. **Drymades Hotel** ( ☎ 068-228 5637; bungalows 4000 lekë) is a constellation of bungalows under the shade of the pine trees, each housing two or three people in fairly basic conditions.

### Himara

This sleepy town has tremendous potential as a holiday spot, with fine beaches, a couple of Greek tavernas and an attractive newly built seaside promenade. Unfortunately, the standard of accommodation is pretty dismal and half the beach is marred by half-demolished concrete buildings and a disturbing amount of litter. Strolling past rusting car wrecks and a tidal line of plastic isn't quite what you'd hope for in a beach. If you're still keen to stay here, your best bet is to find one of the friendly locals with a private room to rent.

Buses and ferries run between Saranda, Himara and Vlora daily and there are some *furgons,* but you'll probably have to get up early. Ask a local for the times. The trip from Dhërmi is stunning and takes 75 minutes by bus (100 lekë). It's a further two hours to Saranda.

# SARANDA

☎ 0852 / pop 32,000

With the most attractive waterfront in Albania, Saranda is a charming little town. Its houses fan over the hillsides, small boats bob on the blue sea and people stroll up and down the waterfront promenade, enjoying the 290 sunny days per year. Ayii Saranda, an early Christian monastery dedicated to 40 saints gave the town its name. Saranda is a stone's throw from the Greek island of Corfu (12.5 km) and a good point to cross between the two countries.

Most of Saranda's attractions are a little outside of the town itself. Nearby is the mesmerising ancient archaeological site of Butrint, the hypnotic Syri i Katterc (Blue Eye Spring), and some lovely beaches at Ksamili village, where you can dip and refresh after a day of exploring.

## Information

There are plenty of ATMs, cardphones and a **post office** ( ☎ 23 45; Rr Skënderbeu) in the centre of town. The incredibly helpful **Tourist Information Office** ( ☎ 23 80; bashkiasarande@yahoo.com; Rr Skënderbeu; ⏰ 8am-4pm Mon-Fri) on the 1st floor of the town hall can assist you with transport or information about sights.

## Sleeping & Eating

**Kaonia** ( ☎ 26 00; fax 26 08; Rr 1 Maji; s/d €20/40; ✗ ) A lovely midsized hotel positioned on Saranda's seafront boasting great beds, power showers and fabulously kitsch 1950s-style patterned awnings on the balconies looking over the sea.

**Hotel Delfini** ( ☎ 60 72; Rr Sarandë-Butrint; r €40; ✗ ) There's something of the spaceship about the large round bar anchoring one corner of this new construction, with the water beckoning at the bottom of the stairs.

**Hotel Butrinti** ( ☎ 55 92; www.butrintihotel.com; Rr Sarandë-Butrint; s €70-110, d €80-125, ste €120-270; P ✗ ⌨ ) This hotel is the swankiest place on the entire coast, even if it doesn't quite live up to its five-star delusions.

**Kalaja e Lëkurësit** ( ☎ 55 32; Lëkurës; mains 250-1200 lekë) Perched high above the town in an old castle, this excellent eatery boasts breathtaking views over the town, Corfu and the Butrint lagoon.

## Getting There & Away

There are regular buses to Butrint (100 lekë, 45 minutes, seven daily) via Ksamili (35 minutes), which leave from the street just below the **bus station** (Rr 8 Nëntori).

Buses to Gjirokastra (300 lekë, 1½ hours, 70km) leave from Saranda's bus station each hour from 5.30am up to 1pm. Some go on to Tirana (1000 lekë, eight hours, 314km) and Durrës (900 lekë, seven hours, 276km). There are also *furgons* to Gjirokastra, Tirana and Vlora (via Himara), usually leaving between 7am and 9.30am. Some smaller buses also take the coastal route to Vlora via Himara and Dhërmi.

There's a daily boat (more in summer) from Saranda to Corfu (€17.50, one hour, 27km). A taxi to the Greek border at Kakavija will cost 3500 lekë, while a cab to the border near Konispoli will cost around 3000 lekë (30 minutes).

# AROUND SARANDA
## Butrint

The ancient ruins of **Butrint** ( ☎ 0732-46 00; admission 700 lekë; ⏰ 8am-7.30pm), 24km south of Saranda, are a truly remarkable experience. Set at the foot of a lagoon in a 29-sq-km national park, the ruins of antiquity reveal themselves gradually. You will need at least three hours to lose yourself among the lovely forest paths. Bring water and snacks with you, as there are no eating and drinking facilities.

The poet Virgil (70–19 BC) claimed that the Trojans founded Buthrotum (Butrint), but no evidence of this has been found. Although the site had been inhabited long before, Greeks from Corfu settled on the hill in Butrint in the 6th century BC. Within a century Butrint had become a fortified trading city with an acropolis. The lower town began to develop in the 3rd century BC and many large stone buildings had already been built by the time the Romans took over in 167 BC. Butrint's prosperity continued throughout the Roman period and the Byzantines made it an ecclesiastical centre. The city subsequently went into decline, and it was almost abandoned by 1927 when Italian archaeologists arrived.

As you enter the site the path leads to the right to the 3rd-century BC **Greek theatre**, secluded in the forest below the acropolis. It could seat about 2500 people and was sacred to Ascelpius, the god of healing, whose **temple** can be seen on the slopes slightly to the left. Close by are the small **public baths**, with geometric mosaics that are unfortunately buried

---

**WORTH A TRIP**

Like something from a vampire movie, it's hard to imagine a creepier setting than the stone city of **Gjirokastra**, shrouded in cloud on its rocky perch, and surrounded by savage mountains. Above it all a gloomy, dark castle with a blood-chilling history watches over everything, perpetually guarded by black crows. It's the sort of place where dictators are raised (Enver Hoxha) and young boys dream up dramatic stories and become famous writers (Ismail Kadare, whose *Chronicle in Stone* is set here). In short, it's a thrilling place to spend a day absorbing the life of its steep cobbled streets, where the pace is slow and suspended in the past.

For an authentic experience of Ottoman Albania, stay at the **Hotel Kalemi** ( ☎ 63724; draguak@yahoo .com; Lagjia Palorto; r 4000 lekë), a cross between a hotel and an ethnographic museum, with original carved wooden ceilings and stone fireplaces.

Located 70km northeast of Saranda, the bus takes 90 minutes and costs 300 lekë.

---

under the sand and cannot be seen. You are allowed to make a small hole to peek at the mosaics, but don't touch them, and do cover it up again.

Deeper in the forest is a wall covered with crisp Greek inscriptions, and a 6th-century palaeo-Christian **baptistry** decorated with colourful mosaics of animals and birds, again under the sand. Beyond are the impressive arches of the 6th-century **basilica** built over many years. A massive **Cyclopean wall**, dating back to the 4th century BC, is further on. Over one gate is a splendid relief of a lion killing a bull, plundered from an earlier temple to reduce the height of the gate and make it easier to defend. Just inside the gate is a perfectly preserved **well** with its endearing Greek inscription, 'Junia Rufina, friend of nymphs'.

The top of the hill is where the **acropolis** once was; there's now a castle here with a museum displaying artefacts found at the site. From the courtyard you can enjoy the views over the site and the lagoon.

There are regular buses between Butrint and Saranda (100 lekë, 45 minutes, seven daily), or a one-way cab will cost around 800 lekë.

### Ksamill Beach

A better bathing alternative to Saranda's beaches is this sandy spot 17km south, with four small dreamy islands within swimming distance. The village was only founded in 1973 as a model communist collective. Enjoy its relative seclusion now, as developers have big plans for Ksamili. A couple of hotels were being built at the time of writing.

It's easy to get here on the bus from Saranda to Butrint. A cab will cost about 700 lekë.

### Syri i Kalter

The Blue Eye Spring, about 15km east of Saranda, is a hypnotic spring of deep blue water surrounded by electric blue edges like the iris of an eye. It feeds the Bistrica River and its depth is still unknown. This is the perfect picnic spot, under the shade of the oak trees.

There is no public transport, so unless you are driving you will have to get a taxi. A return journey to Syri i Kalter will cost around 2000 lekë, with half an hour's waiting time. You get a tantalising glimpse of it en route to Gjirokastra.

# ALBANIA DIRECTORY

## ACCOMMODATION

Albania's budget accommodation (singles €12 to €40) is usually decent and clean with TVs and private bathrooms. Most of the available options fall into the midrange category, with prices ranging widely (singles €40 to €100) and the most expensive being in Tirana. Rooms usually have direct-dial telephones, minibars and air-conditioning. Top-end establishments on a par with leading European hotels are to be found in mainly in Tirana. Room prices start at €150 and head up to the ridiculous.

Accommodation has undergone a rapid transformation in Albania, with many custom-built private hotels replacing the run-down state ones (usually named Hotel Tourism or Hotel Grand). Breakfast is often included in the price but it's usually absolutely awful. Don't take it for granted that credit cards will be accepted.

Most of the country suffers from lengthy blackouts during winter, so it pays to check

ALBANIA

if your hotel has a generator. Tirana is the exception, as power cuts don't tend to last long. When the power goes out the water doesn't pump, unless a gravity-driven tank system has been installed.

You can often find unofficial accommodation in private homes by asking around. Camping is possible in the southern region and sometimes on deserted beaches.

## ACTIVITIES

Swimming is great along the Adriatic and Ionian Coasts, except for the polluted section from Durrës to Fier. You can go bird-watching around Lezha and hiking in the national parks (p50). Adventure tourism is in its infancy in Albania, and the national leaders are the enthusiastic young team at **Outdoor Albania** ( ☎ 04 272 075; www.outdooralbania.com; Tirana).

## BOOKS

For a helpful list of Albanian words and phrases check out the *Eastern Europe Phrasebook* from Lonely Planet.

*Biografi* (1993), by New Zealander Lloyd Jones, is an arresting semifictional account of the writer's quest in the early 1990s for the alleged double of former dictator Enver Hoxha.

*The Albanians: A Modern History* (1999), by Miranda Vickers, is a comprehensive and very readable history of Albania from the time of Ottoman rule to the restoration of democracy after 1990.

*Albania: From Anarchy to a Balkan Identity* (1999), by Miranda Vickers and James Pettifer, covers the tumultuous 1990s in great detail.

*The Best of Albanian Cooking* (1999), by Klementina Hysa and R John Hysa, is one of scant few books on the subject of Albanian cuisine and contains a wide range of family recipes.

*High Albania* (published in 1909 and reprinted in 2000), by Albania's 'honorary citizen' Edith Durham, recounts the author's travels in northern Albania in the early 20th century.

*Rumpalla: Rummaging through Albania* (2002), by Peter Lucas, is a personal account by an Albanian-American journalist detailing several visits to Albania before and after the revolution.

*Albania: The Bradt Travel Guide* (2004), by Gillian Gloyer, is a thorough guide to the whole country.

James Pettifer's *Albania and Kosovo Blue Guide* (2001) is an informed source for answering any questions on Albanian history and a good guide to sights.

## BUSINESS HOURS

Most offices open at 8am and close around 5pm. Shops usually open at 8am and close around 7pm, though some close for a siesta from noon to 4pm, opening again from 4pm to 8pm. Banking hours are shorter (generally 9am to 2.30pm). Restaurants are normally open from 8.30am to 11pm, and bars from 8.30am to midnight or later.

## COURSES

The **University of Tirana** ( ☎ 04-228 402; pages.albania online.net/ut/unitirana_en/default_en.htm; Sheshi Nënë Tereza) runs a summer-school programme in Albanian language and culture.

## DANGERS & ANNOYANCES

Many prejudices surround Albania, but the country is now safe for travel. In fact, despite poor street lighting, the level of petty crime is much less than in most Western countries. You should not feel unduly concerned passing groups of young men on the streets at night. There isn't a hardcore drinking culture, so it's almost unheard of to be attacked by drunks after dark.

That said, the mountainous regions of the north still involve some element of risk due to the revival of ancient blood feuds and the rise of organised crime – the latter is also a problem in Vlora. Tourists are unlikely to get caught up in this, but incidents occasionally happen. There are reports of people being held up at gunpoint in isolated corners of northern Albania, though these events are becoming rare. There may still be landmines near the northern border with Kosovo around Bajram Curri.

Take the usual precautions about avoiding rowdy political demonstrations, not flashing money around and being aware of pickpockets in crowded places.

The most serious risk to safety is on the roads. Most people have been driving for less than 10 years, and this inexperience, combined with the terrible state of the roads and a typically Balkan disregard for traffic laws, make for a high accident rate. Other dangers to pedestrians include gaping holes in pavements, missing manhole covers and treacherous black ice in winter.

As Albania was closed for so long, black and Asian travellers may encounter some curious stares; in fact most visitors to Albania, male or female, can expect to encounter such stares! Studiously ignoring the man sitting next to you on a *furgon*, as he bores holes into the side of your head, will have no effect, so you may as well get used to it.

Do not drink the tap water; locals jokingly refer to it as Hoxha's revenge. Plenty of bottled water is available. Also, don't swim in the water at Durrës – you may end up with a nasty skin infection. The standard of health care in Albania is quite poor. Local hospitals and clinics are under-resourced.

## DISABLED TRAVELLERS

There are few special facilities for travellers in wheelchairs. Public transport and access to sights, shops and hotels will all prove to be extremely problematic. Only the very top hotels in Tirana have properly designed wheelchair-accessible rooms.

## EMBASSIES & CONSULATES
### Albanian Embassies & Consulates

Following are some of the main addresses for Albanian embassies. There's a full list on the website of the **Albanian Ministry of Foreign Affairs** (www.mfa.gov.al).

**Canada** ( ☎ 613-2363 0953; embassyrepublicofalbania@ on.albn.com; 130 Albert St, Ste 302, ON K1P 5G4, Ottawa)

**France** ( ☎ 01 47 23 31 00; ambasade.albanie@wanadoo .fr; 57 avenue Marceau, Paris 75116)

**Germany** ( ☎ 030-259 30 40; kanzlei@botschaft-albanien .de; Friedrichstrasse 231, D-10 969, Berlin)

**Greece** Athens ( ☎ 2106 876 200; albem@ath.forthner .gr; Vekiareli 7, Filothei); Ioannina ( ☎ 2651 021 330; algefeer@panafonet.gr; Str Foti Tzavella 2); Thessaloniki ( ☎ 31 547 4494; fax 31 546 656; Odysseos Str 6)

**Italy** Rome ( ☎ 686 22 41 20; fax 686 21 60 05; Via Asmara 5); Bari ( ☎ 805 72 76 47; fax 805 28 33 35; Via Cafelati 7)

**Kosovo** ( ☎ 038-548 3689; fax 038-548 209; Lagjja Pejton, rr Hekurudha, Nr 1 Prishtina)

**Macedonia** ( ☎ 022-614 636; ambshqip@mt.net.mk; ul HT Karpoš 94a)

**Netherlands** ( ☎ 0704 27 21 01; embalba@xs4all.nl; Anna Paulownastraat 109b, 2518 BD, The Hague)

**Serbia** ( ☎ 11-306 5350; fax 11-665 439; Bulevar Mira 25A, Belgrade)

**UK** ( ☎ 020-7828 8897; amblonder@hotmail.com; 2nd fl, 24 Buckingham Gate, London SW1 E6LB)

**USA** ( ☎ 202-223 4942; albaniaemb@aol.com; 2100 S St NW, Washington DC 20008)

## Embassies & Consulates in Albania

Following are some embassies in Tirana:

**France** ( ☎ 04-234 250; ambcrtir@mail.adanet.com.al; Rr Skënderbej 14)

**Germany** ( ☎ 04-232 048; www.tirana.diplo.de; Rr Skënderbej 8)

**Greece** ( ☎ 04-223 959; grembtir@albnet.net; Rr Frederik Shiroka 3)

**Italy** ( ☎ 04-234 045; www.ambitalia-tirana.com; Rr Lek Dukagjini)

**Macedonia** ( ☎ 04-233 036; makambas@albnet.net; cnr Rr Skënderbej & Rr e Kavajës)

**Netherlands** ( ☎ 04-240 828; www.netherlandsembassy tirana.com; Rr Asim Zeneli 10)

**Serbia** ( ☎ 04-223 042; ambatira@icc-al.org; Rr Skënderbej Pall. 8/3 Shk. 2)

**UK** ( ☎ 04-234 973; www.uk.al; Rr Skënderbej 12)

**USA** ( ☎ 04-247 285; www.usemb-tirana.rpo.at; Rr Elbasanit 103)

## GAY & LESBIAN TRAVELLERS

Early in 1995 homosexuality in Albania was decriminalised, with the age of consent set at 18 for sex between women or between men, four years higher than for male–female sexual acts.

Like many Eastern European nations, this change came about not through a transformation of societal attitudes, but more from a desire to comply with the EU and fall into step with the West. Unfortunately, prejudice against gays and lesbians in Albania is as strong as ever. There are no venues and the community that exists is so far underground it's inaccessible to travellers.

## HOLIDAYS

**New Year's Day** 1-2 January
**Orthodox Christmas** 7 January (not a public holiday, but shops may shut in Orthodox areas)
**Summer Day** 14 March
**Nevruz** 22 March (Bektashi feast day)
**May Day** 1 May
**Mother Teresa Day** 19 October
**Independence Day** 28 November
**Liberation Day** 29 November
**Catholic Christmas** 25 December

The following movable religious feast days are also public holidays:

**Catholic Easter** March/April/May
**Orthodox Easter** March/April/May
**Bajram i Madh** Currently around October (end of Ramadan)
**Bajram i Vogël** Currently around December

ALBANIA

# LANGUAGE

Albanian (Shqip) is a descendant of ancient Illyrian, with a number of Turkish, Latin, Slavonic and (modern) Greek words, although it constitutes a linguistic branch of its own. It has 36 characters (including nine diagraphs or double letters, eg dh and ll). It shares certain grammatical features with Romance languages (particularly Romanian), but it's fair to say the Albanian language is a world unto itself.

Most Albanian place names have two forms as the definite article is a suffix. An example of this is *bulevardi* (the boulevard), as opposed to *bulevard* (a boulevard). The capital city's name is Tirana, which is the definite form of the name, meaning 'the Tirana', as opposed to Tiranë, which can mean 'to Tirana', in its indefinite form. In this chapter, for place names we have used the spelling most commonly used in English ie Tirana, Durrës.

Many Albanians speak Italian, thanks to Italian TV broadcasts, which can be picked up along the coast. Quite a few people in the south also speak Greek, and younger people are learning English.

See the Language chapter, p944, for pronunciation guidelines and useful words and phrases.

# MEDIA
## Newspapers

A diverse range of newspapers is printed in Tirana and the independent daily *Koha Jonë* is the paper with the widest readership. Newspapers are often directly owned by political organisations and sensationalism is often the norm in the print media. Dependence on external funding tends to limit objectivity.

The *Albanian Daily News* is a fairly dry English-language publication that has useful information on happenings around Albania. It's generally available from major hotels for 300 lekë, or you can read it online at www.albaniannews.com.

Foreign newspapers and magazines are sold at most major hotels, and at some central street kiosks, though they tend to be a few days old.

## Radio

The BBC World Service can be picked up in and around Tirana on 103.9FM, while the Voice of America's mainly music programme is on 107.4FM. Some of the most popular Albanian radio stations are: Albanian Radio

and TV (RTSh), a public broadcaster; Radio Tirana, an external service run by RTSh, with programmes in eight languages including English. The private station Top Radio is the hippest in the country, pumping out a colourful mix of hip-hop, Turkish pop, techno and rock.

## TV

There are many TV channels available in Albania including the state TV service TVSH, the private station TVA and, among others, Eurosport, several Italian channels and even a couple of French ones.

# MONEY
## ATMs

In just the last year or so ATMs connected to the major international networks have appeared in towns and cities everywhere, which makes travel here much easier. The main networks are Raiffeisen Bank, American Bank of Albania, Pro Credit Bank and Tirana Bank.

## Credit Cards

Only the larger hotels and travel agencies accept credit cards, and in only a handful of establishments outside Tirana. Major banks can offer credit-card advances.

## Currency

Albanian notes come in denominations of 100, 200, 500 and 1000 lekë. There are five, 10, 20 and 50 lekë coins. Since 1997, all notes issued are smaller and contain a sophisticated watermark to prevent forgery. In 1964 the currency was revalued; prices on occasion may still be quoted at the old rate (3000 lekë instead of 300).

Everything in Albania can be paid for with lekë but most hotel prices are quoted in euro, which is readily accepted as an alternative currency.

## Moneychangers

Every town has its currency market, which usually operates on the street in front of the main post office or state bank. Such transactions are not dangerous or illegal and it all takes place quite openly, but do make sure you count the money twice before tendering yours. The advantages are that you get a good rate and avoid the 1% bank commission. There are currency exchange businesses in major towns, usually open 8am to 6pm, and closed on Sundays.

The euro and the US dollars are the favourite foreign currencies. You will not be able to change Albanian lekë outside the country, so exchange them or spend them before you leave.

### Travellers' Cheques

These are about as practical here as a dead albatross, though you can change them at the National Savings Bank (p53) and at major banks in Tirana. Travellers cheques (euro and US dollar) can be used at a few top-end hotels, but cash is preferred everywhere.

## POST

Outside main towns there are few public mail boxes but there is an increasing number of post offices springing up. Sending an international postcard costs around 40 lekë, while a letter costs 80 lekë to 160 lekë. The postal system does not enjoy a reputation for efficiency. Don't rely on sending or receiving parcels through Albapost.

## RESPONSIBLE TRAVEL

Ohrid Lake trout is almost extinct and in 2004 the Macedonian government issued a seven-year ban on catching it. No such ban exists on the Albanian side, and you'll see people selling it on the roadside around the lake, and on menus from Korça through to Tirana under the name *koran*. Resist the urge to order it.

Plastic wasn't widely used during the old regime and most refuse was biodegradable or recycled. Now blue plastic bags are everywhere. An interesting game is to see how long you can go refusing bags from shopkeepers. If you fail, the penalty is to fill it up with rubbish and dispose of it properly. The disappointing thing is that most of the rubbish collected will be burnt anyway, causing further damage to the environment. If you're really hardcore, take your recyclables with you when you leave the country.

## TELEPHONE & FAX

Long-distance telephone calls made from main post offices are cheap, costing about 90 lekë a minute to Italy. Calls to the USA cost 230 lekë per minute. Calls from private phone offices are horribly expensive – 800 lekë per minute to Australia. Unfortunately there aren't any cheap internet phone centres, or at least none

---

### EMERGENCY NUMBERS

- Police ☎ 129
- Ambulance ☎ 127
- Fire ☎ 128

---

where you can hear the person at the other end of the line. Hopefully this will change soon. Faxing can be done from the main post office in Tirana for the same cost as phone calls, or from major hotels, though they will charge more. Several important local numbers are Domestic directory enquiries ☎ 124 and International directory assistance ☎ 12.

### Mobile Phone

There are two established mobile-phone providers (Vodafone and AMC); a third company, Eagle Mobile, has been granted a licence. Nearly all areas of the country are covered, though the networks can become congested and, after all, it is a mountainous nation. The tariffs are quite high. Check that a roaming agreement exists with your home service provider. Mobile numbers begin with ☎ 068 or ☎ 069 (Eagle Mobile's prefix is not yet known).

## TOILETS

Squat toilets were the norm until very recently, and you'll still find them in some hotels, restaurants and private homes. This is especially true in more remote areas, making a toilet stop en route something of an adventure. Where there is no running water a large jar or bucket will usually take the place of the flush. It's not a bad idea to carry some toilet paper with you, and a packet of premoistened wipes for cleaning your hands. None of the hotels listed in this chapter have squat toilets.

## VISAS

No visa is required by citizens of EU countries, Australia, Canada, Japan, New Zealand, Norway, Switzerland or the USA. South Africans will need to apply for a visa from the Albanian embassy in Rome or London (€25). Travellers from other countries can check visa requirements at www.mfa.gov.al. Citizens of all countries – even those entering visa-free – will be required to pay an 'entry tax' at the border. The entry tax for all visitors (apart from Czechs and Poles; they get in for free) is €10.

**ALBANIA**

## WOMEN TRAVELLERS

Albania is quite a safe country for women travellers, but it is important to be aware of the fact that outside Tirana it is mainly men who go out and sit in bars and cafés, whereas the women generally stay at home. It may feel strange to be the only woman in a bar, so it is advisable to travel in pairs if possible, and dress conservatively. Staring seems to be a national pastime, and both men and women will find themselves on the receiving end. It's usually not intended to be threatening. While Albania has developed a reputation as a centre for people trafficking, the unfortunate victims are mostly ensnared in poverty-stricken Eastern European countries, and tourists don't seem to be targets.

# TRANSPORT IN ALBANIA

This section covers transport connections between Albania and the other countries in this book. For information on getting to Albania from further afield, see p925.

## GETTING THERE & AWAY
### Air

Albania's only international airport is **Nënë Tereza International Airport** (also known as Mother Theresa and, more commonly, Rinas airport), which is located 26km northwest of Tirana. There are no domestic flights within Albania.

### AIRLINES

**Adria Airways** (code JP; ☎ 04-228 483; www.adria.si, Ljubljana)

**Albanian Airlines** (code LV; ☎ 04-235 162; www.albanianairlines.com.al; Prishtina)

**Hemus Air** (code DU; ☎ 04-230 410; www.hemusair.bg; Sofia)

**JAT Airways** (code JU; ☎ 04-251 033; www.jat.com; Belgrade)

**Malév Hungarian Airlines** (code MA; ☎ 04-234 163; www.malev.hu; Budapest)

---

#### DEPARTURE TAX

No matter how you enter Albania you will have to pay a €10 charge. On leaving the country, there is another standard €10 fee. There is also a €1 daily tariff on vehicles, payable upon crossing the border out of the country.

---

### Land
#### BUS

From Tirana, buses for Prishtina (€30, 10 hours, 343km, three daily) leave from behind the museum near Sheshi Skënderbej. Buses for Sofia (€40, 17 hours) leave from **Albtransport** ( ☎ 223 026; Rr Mine Peza, Tirana; ☺ 8am-4pm Mon-Fri).

Macedonia-bound buses, going via Struga (€10, six hours, 197km, six per week) and on to Tetovo, leave from the muddy patch in front of the train station. Get tickets from the nearby **Pollogu travel agency** ( ☎ 04-23 500; 069-209 4906; Pall. 103, Bul Zogu I). It's a little hard to find, upstairs in a modern apartment building; the entrance is next to a bright orange café, Pause.

#### CAR & MOTORCYCLE

You will need a Green Card endorsed for Albania to bring a car into the country. You'll find that many insurers and hire companies will not cover you. For further information on driving around Albania see opposite.

#### BORDER CROSSINGS

Albania has land borders with Greece, Macedonia, Montenegro and the UN-monitored territory of Kosovo. Access to/from all neighbouring states is generally trouble-free and unrestricted.

#### Greece

There are border crossings between Korça and Florina at Kapshtica/Krystallopigi, between Ioannina and Gjirokastra at Kakavija/Kakavia, between Ioannina and Përmeti, and north of the Greek port of Igoumenitsa at Konispoli/Sagiada.

#### Macedonia

There are four border crossings with Macedonia. The two main ones are on either side of Lake Ohrid: Qafa e Thanës–Kafa San, 65km east of Elbasan; and Tushëmishti–Sveti Naum, 5km east of Pogradec. The latter is normally crossed on foot, as taxis from Pogradec will drop you off just before the Macedonian border. You can then wait for the bus to Ohrid (80MKD, 50 minutes, 29km, four daily) on the Macedonian side. There are two smaller crossings at Blato, 5km northwest of Debar, and at Stenje on the western shore of Lake Prespa.

#### Montenegro

There are currently two border crossings. There are regular minibuses between Shkodra and Ulcinj (€8, 40 minutes), crossing the border at Muriqani. By taxi it's €10 to the border and US$10 from there to Ulcinj. The road to Han i Hotit on the way to Podgorica is in poorer shape. A taxi to this border crossing costs about €15.

### Kosovo
The best crossing for travellers is at Morina/Vrbnica between Kukës and Prizren, though there is another rather isolated one at Prushi. There are still occasional reports of trouble in the border area, though nothing like as bad it as once was. Travellers on buses through to Prishtina should have no problems.

## GETTING AROUND
### Bicycle
Although many Albanians cycle short distances, cycling through the country is not recommended, especially if you are not familiar with the abysmal driving on Albanian roads. Furthermore, many roads are not paved and there are no cycling paths anywhere in the country.

### Bus
Most Albanians travel around their country in buses or *furgons,* which are nine- to 12-seater vans. Buses to Tirana depart from towns all around Albania at the crack of dawn. Pay the conductor on board; the fares are low (eg Tirana–Durrës is 100 lekë). Tickets are rarely issued.

Both buses and *furgons* are privately owned and don't follow a timetable – they leave when they've got enough passengers to make it worth their while. The *furgon* and bus drivers seem to take it in turns to strike, each looking for some concession from the government to restrict the activities of the other. At the time of writing it was the bus drivers' turn, some of whom were on hunger strike. Clearly neither group make much money from the meagre fares charged.

The *furgon* system can seem daunting at first, but it actually works really well. There are always more *furgons* running in the mornings and the last departure is usually in plenty of time to enable the driver (they're always men) to reach his destination before nightfall.

### Car & Motorcycle
Albania has only recently acquired an official road traffic code and most motorists have only learned to drive in the last 10 years. During the communist era car ownership required a permit from the government, which in 45 years issued only two to nonparty members. As a result, the government found it unnecessary to invest in new roads. Nowadays the road infrastructure is improving but it's still more akin to India than Europe. There are decent roads from the Macedonian border to Tirana and Durrës, and north from these cities to Shkodra, but the main roads leading south are still being expanded. The coastal road from Vlora to Saranda is particularly treacherous. Highway signage is bad and there are a lot of road works going on to accommodate the explosive growth in vehicle numbers. In short, it's a really, really hard place to drive, and local driving habits are best described as free-spirited. Off the main routes a 4WD is a necessity. Driving at night is particularly hazardous and driving on mountain 'roads' in winter is an extreme sport. There is no national automobile association in Albania as yet.

### DRIVING LICENCE
Foreign driving licences are permitted but it is recommended to have an International Driving Permit as well. Car-hire agencies usually require that you have held a full licence for one year.

### FUEL & SPARE PARTS
There are plenty of petrol stations in the cities and increasing numbers in the country. Unleaded fuel is widely available along all major highways, but fill up before driving into the mountainous regions. A litre of unleaded petrol costs 130 lekë. There isn't yet a highly developed network of mechanics and repair shops capable of sourcing parts for all types of vehicles.

### HIRE
Car hire is fairly new to Albania, but given the driving conditions we wouldn't recommend it unless you have a lot of experience of similar conditions.

### ROAD RULES
Drinking and driving is forbidden, and there is zero tolerance for blood-alcohol readings. Both motorcyclists and their passengers must wear helmets. Speed limits are as low as 30km/h to 35km/h in built-up areas and 35km/h to 40km/h on the edges of built-up areas.

## Train

Before 1948 Albania had no passenger railways, but the communists built up a limited north–south rail network. Today, however, nobody who can afford other types of transport takes the train, even though fares are seriously cheap. The reason will be obvious once you board: the decrepit carriages typically have broken windows, no toilets and are agonisingly slow. That said, they are something of an adventure and some of the routes are quite scenic.

For timetable and fare information, refer to the official website of Hekurudha e Shqipërise (Hsh; Albanian Railways) at www.hsh.com.al.

# Belarus Беларусь

Few people consider venturing into this hermetically sealed Soviet time capsule, notoriously ruled with an iron fist by its moustachioed megalomaniac, Alexander Lukashenko.

But that's exactly why you *should* visit. Only in Belarus – where the KGB still listens in to phone calls and people keep their politics to a low whisper – will you feel as if the Cold War never ended. Although getting a visa isn't a problem, the government isn't crazy about foreign influences and encourages xenophobia with all-pervasive propaganda. Westerners cool enough to come here are living, breathing examples that the world outside Belarus is not going to hell in a hand basket – at least not in the near future, anyway.

The capital city of Minsk – with its staunch, Stalinist buildings and orderly streets – is a testament to Soviet ideology, but sprouting up like stubborn weeds in the cracks of communism you'll find enough chic boutiques, cafés and nightclubs to keep you entertained and get you connected with the lovable locals, who are shy at first but intrigued and flattered by foreign visitors.

With almost no street crime, you are probably safer here than anywhere else in Eastern Europe, and foreign tourists are untouched the government's repressive ways. So why waste a visa application on a country that's trying to be like yours anyway? If you were born post-*perestroika* or never got to visit before the Wall came crumbling down, now's your chance to be back in the USSR. Until then, you won't know how lucky you are.

## FAST FACTS

- **Area** 207,600 sq km
- **Capital** Minsk
- **Currency** Belarusian rouble (BR); A$1 = BR1639; €1 = BR2759; ¥100 = BR1930; NZ$1 = BR1379; UK£1 = BR4040; US$1 = BR2156
- **Famous for** dictatorial president Lukashenko, bearing the brunt of Chernobyl, Soviet time capsule, supermodel breeding farm
- **Official Languages** Belarusian and Russian
- **Phrases** *dobry dzyen* (hello), *kalee laska* (please), *dzyahkooee* (thanks)
- **Population** 10 million
- **Telephone Codes** country code ☎ 375; international access code ☎ 810
- **Visa** invitations/vouchers (US$30 to US$75), visas (US$100 to US$200) and proof of medical insurance required of most visitors (see p95)

## HIGHLIGHTS

- Gawk at grandiose Stalinist architecture, and settle into the cosy cafés of **Minsk** (p80).
- Stroll through the mellow pedestrian streets to the epic WWII memorial of **Brest Fortress** (p90).
- Spot an endangered zoobr (European bison) on a trip to the primeval forests of the **Belavezhskaja Pushcha National Park** (p92).

## ITINERARIES

Belarusian cities and towns are not packed with tourist attractions, so you can count on each of these itineraries feeling rather leisurely.

- **Three days** Give Minsk two days and then take a day trip to Dudutki.
- **One week** Follow the three-day itinerary, then add a day in Brest (spend a couple of hours at the Brest Fortress) and an overnight visit to Belavezhskaja Pushcha National Park before you return to the capital.

## CLIMATE & WHEN TO GO

Belarus has a continental climate. Average January temperatures are between -4°C and -8°C, with frosts experienced for five to six months of the year. The warmest month is July, when temperatures can reach up to 30°C, but the average temperature is 18°C. June and August are the wettest months.

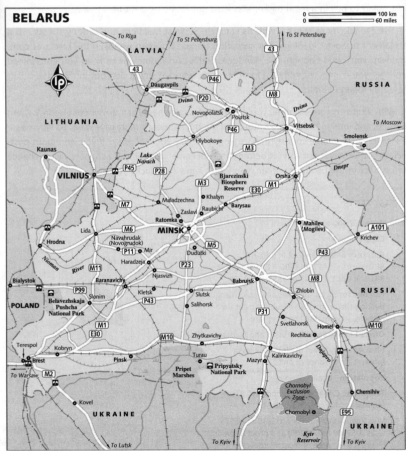

Since Belarus is not visited by many tourists, you won't have to worry about when to go to beat the crowds. If you don't mind cold weather, the snowy winters can be very pretty, especially on sunny days.

## HISTORY

Once part of Kyivan Rus, Belarus was gradually taken over by Lithuania in the 14th century and became part of the Polish–Lithuanian Grand Duchy. It was to be 400 years before Belarus came under Russian control, a period during which Belarusians became linguistically and culturally differentiated from the Russians to the east and the Ukrainians to the south.

At this time, trade was controlled by Poles and Jews, and most Belarusians remained peasants – poor and illiterate. After the Partitions of Poland (1772, 1793 and 1795–96), Belarus was absorbed into Russia and faced intense Russification policies.

During the 19th century Belarus was part of the Pale of Settlement, the area where Jews in the Russian Empire were required to settle, so Jews formed the majority in many cities and towns.

### World Wars & the Soviet Union

In March 1918, under German occupation during WWI, a short-lived independent Belarusian Democratic Republic was declared, but the land was soon under the control of the Red Army, and the Belarusian Soviet Socialist Republic (BSSR) was formed. The 1921 Treaty of Rīga allotted roughly the western half of modern Belarus to Poland, which launched a program of Polonisation that provoked armed resistance by Belarusians. The eastern half was left to the Bolsheviks, and the redeclared BSSR was a founding member of the USSR in 1922.

The Soviet regime in the 1920s encouraged Belarusian literature and culture, but in the 1930s under Stalin, nationalism and the Belarusian language were discouraged and their proponents ruthlessly persecuted. The 1930s also saw industrialisation, agricultural collectivisation, and purges in which hundreds of thousands were executed – most in the Kurapaty Forest, outside Minsk.

In September 1939 western Belarus was seized from Poland by the Red Army. When Nazi Germany invaded Russia in 1941, Belarus was on the front line and suffered greatly.

---

**HOW MUCH?**

- **Half-litre of Belavezhskaja (herbal firewater)** US$3
- **Bottle of Belarus Sineokaja vodka (750mL)** US$6.75
- **Straw doll** US$3-6
- **Plate of *draniki* (potato pancakes)** US$1.50-3
- **Milavitsa brassiere** US$9 (average)

**LONELY PLANET INDEX**

- **Litre of petrol** US$8
- **Litre of bottled water** US$0.25
- **Half-litre of bottled Krynitsa beer** US$0.56
- **Souvenir Lukashenko poster (size A2)** US$0.51
- **Street snack (hot dog)** US$0.70

---

German occupation was savage and partisan resistance widespread until the Red Army drove the Germans out in 1944, with massive destruction on both sides. Hundreds of villages were decimated, and barely a stone was left standing in Minsk. At least 25% of the Belarusian population (over two million people) died between 1939 and 1945. Many of them, Jews and others, died in 200-plus concentration camps; the third-largest Nazi concentration camp was set up at Maly Trostenets, outside Minsk, where over 200,000 people were executed.

Western Belarus remained in Soviet hands at the end of the war, with Minsk developing into the industrial hub of the western USSR and Belarus becoming one of the Soviet Union's most prosperous republics.

### Modern History

The 1986 Chornobyl (spelt Chernobyl in Russian) disaster left about a quarter of the country seriously contaminated, and its effects are still felt today, particularly in the southeastern regions of the country. See p864 for more information on Chornobyl.

On 27 July 1990, the republic issued a declaration of sovereignty within the USSR. On 25 August 1991 a declaration of full national independence was issued. With no history

BELARUS

whatsoever as a politically or economically
independent entity, the country of Belarus
was one of the oddest products of the disin-
tegration of the USSR.

Since July 1994 Belarus has been governed
by Alexander Lukashenko, a former collec-
tive-farm director, from which his derogatory
nickname, *kolkhozni* (a member of a collective farm owned by the communist state), is
derived; his favourite nickname is *bat'ka*
(papa). His presidential style has been autocratic and authoritarian, and the country
was declaimed an 'outpost of tyranny' by
US Secretary of State Condoleeza Rice. Lukashenko has on several occasions altered
the constitution (using referenda widely regarded in the West as illegitimate), render-
ing the parliament essentially toothless and
extending both his term and the number of
times he can campaign for president. He
has almost complete control of the media,
and attempts at independently produced
publications are easily quashed as media
distribution is handled by the state. Online
publications are all that is left for independent Belarusian media, and even those are on
shaky ground.

There have long been talks of political and
economic unification between Belarus and
Russia. It's widely believed that Lukashenko
and Russian President Vladimir Putin can't
stand each other personally, and although
Putin publicly supports Lukashenko's regime, he has also given serious consideration
to cutting off the huge Russian gas subsi-
dies that have long kept Belarus' command
economy afloat. If he goes ahead with this,
merging with Russia (and therefore being

able to buy Russian gas at domestic prices)
could be the only way the country would
survive economically.

On 19 March 2006, Lukashenko officially
won another five-year term as president,
with an unbelievable 83% of the vote and an
even more unbelievable 98% voter turnout.
(His opponents – the most popular being
mild-mannered, European-styled Alyak-
sandr Milinkevich – were harassed and
deprived of public venues throughout the
campaign.) On the night of the 19th, thousands of protesters turned out on the city's
main square for what was being termed as
the Denim Revolution – a 'mini-*maydan*'
echoing what happened in Kyiv 1½ years
earlier. A peaceful tent city started, and hundreds of people, mostly students, withstood
freezing temperatures for almost a week.
But once international media left the scene
to cover Ukrainian parliamentary elections,
the riot police stormed in, arresting and allegedly beating everyone still on the square.
Throughout the election process and as we
go to press, thousands have been arrested –
including Milinkevich and other political
opponents. If you get a chance to make good
friends in the capital city, you'll soon realise
that a surprising number of Minskers have
had a friend or family member jailed for
political reasons.

For inside coverage of the fight against Lukashenko, check out www.charter97.org.

BELARUS

---

**VOX POP**

*Name, age, occupation?* Inna Bukshtynovich, 26, civil-society worker.

*Dreams for your country?* It's sad, but Belarus is a forgotten country. Ironically, in Spielberg's *The Terminal*, a close-up shows Tom Hanks' character has a Belarusian driver's license. But the movie's supposed to take place in an imaginary Eastern European country that ceases to exist after a war. I hope Belarus has a different future, that it opens up its borders and gets more than a dozen pages in Lonely Planet.

*Favourite night-time hang-out?* London coffee shop, sipping mint tea with honey or enjoying live music at Graffiti.

*What would make you leave Belarus?* Another -25C° winter! Actually it is the impossibility of self-realisation that is wearing me down.

*How has Lukashenko's reign affected your life?* He basically ruined my friendships. My best friends left the country because they did not see any future in Belarus. They are happier to live in Moscow, Boston, Capetown, Bournemouth, Warsaw, Rimini, but not in Belarus.

*Best and worst moments of the 2006 protests?* Best: marching along the streets with other protesters and waving at the honking cars. Police were giving fines to the honkers, but that didn't stop them. Worst: the moment when I received a text message at 3am saying that police raided the tent city and arrested its inhabitants.

---

# PEOPLE

There are approximately 10 million people in Belarus, of which 81.2% are Belarusian, 11.4% Russian, 4% Polish and 2.4% Ukrainian, with the remaining 1% consisting of other groups. This results in a rather homogeneous population. Prior to WWII 10% of the national population was Jewish, and in cities like Minsk, Hrodna and Brest Jews made up between one-third and three-quarters of the population. They now make up about 0.3% of the country's population.

Generally speaking, Belarusians are quiet, polite and reserved people. Because they tend to be shy, they seem less approachable than Russians and Ukrainians, but they are just as friendly and generous (probably more so) once introductions are made.

# RELIGION

Atheism is widespread. Of believers, 80% are Eastern Orthodox and 20% are Roman Catholic (about 15% of the Catholics are ethnic Poles). During the early 1990s the Uniate Church (an Orthodox sect that looks to Rome, not Moscow) was re-established and now it has a following of over 100,000 members. There's also a small Protestant minority, the remnant of a once-large German population.

# ARTS

The hero of early Belarusian literary achievement was Francysk Skaryna. Born in Polatsk but educated in Poland and Italy, the scientist, doctor, writer and humanist became the first person to translate the Bible into Belarusian. In the late 16th century the philosopher and humanist Symon Budny printed a number of works in Belarusian. The 19th century saw the beginning of modern Belarusian literature with works by writers and poets such as Maxim Bohdanovich, Janka Kupala and Jakub Kolas.

The Belarusian ballet is one of the most talented in all of Eastern Europe. See p86 for information on how to attend a performance.

The band Pesnyary have been extremely popular since the 1960s for putting a modern twist on traditional Belarusian folk music. Acclaimed Belarusian rock bands (now banned by the regime) include **Lyapis Trubetskoi** (www.lyapis.com) and **NRM** (www.nrm.by.com). See opposite for information on how to obtain banned Belarusian music and p87 for where to catch live performances by unsanctioned groups.

# ENVIRONMENT

Belarus has an area of 207,600 sq km. It's a flat country, consisting of low ridges dividing broad, often marshy lowlands with more than 11,000 small lakes. In the south are the Pripet Marshes, Europe's largest marsh area. The marshland area known as Polesye, in the south of the country, is dubbed locally the 'lungs of Europe', because as air currents passing over it are re-oxygenated and purified by the swamps. Around 6.4% of Belarusian land is protected.

Because of the vast expanses of primeval forests and marshes, Belarusian fauna abounds. The most celebrated animal is the *zoobr* (European bison), the continent's largest land mammal. They were hunted almost to extinction by 1919, but were fortunately bred back into existence from 52 animals that had survived in zoos. Now several hundred exist, mainly in the **Belavezhskaja Pushcha National Park** ( ☎ 01631-56 122, 56 132), a Unesco World Heritage Site. It is the oldest wildlife refuge in Europe, the pride of Belarus and the most famous of the country's five national parks. The *pushcha* (wild forest) went from obscurity to the front page in late 1991 as the presidents of Belarus, Russia and Ukraine signed the death certificate of the USSR – a document creating the Commonwealth of Independent States (CIS) – at the Viskuli dacha (p93) here.

Trips to Belarusian national parks and biosphere reserves, including arranged activities and camping or hotel stays, are possible; contact a tourist agency in Minsk for all but the Belavezhskaja, which is best arranged with Brest agencies (p90). Also, try www.belarus .ecotour.ru or www.belintourist.by.

The 1986 disaster at Chornobyl has been the defining event for the Belarusian environment. The dangers of exposure to radiation for the casual tourist, particularly in the areas covered in this guide, are negligible. For more about Chornobyl, see p864.

## FOOD & DRINK

Belarusian cuisine rarely differs from Russian cuisine (see above), although there are a few uniquely Belarusian dishes. *Draniki* are the Belarusian version of Russian *olad'i* (potato pancakes); *kolduni* are delicious, thick potato dumplings stuffed with meat; and *kletsky* are dumplings stuffed with mushrooms, cheese or potato. *Manchanka* are pancakes served with a thick meat gravy.

*Belavezhskaja* is a bitter herbal alcoholic drink. Of the Belarusian vodkas, Charodei is probably the most esteemed (but can be hard to find). Other popular souvenir-quality vodkas are Belarus Sineokaja and Minskaja.

Although the cuisine is largely meat-based, and although the concept of vegetarianism (let alone veganism) is not exactly widespread, it is possible to find some dishes without meat, although eating vegan will be considerably more difficult. Restaurants with a decent choice of vegetarian options are listed in this chapter.

# MINSK МІНСК

☎ 017 / pop 1.78 million

Hands down, there is no city on earth like Minsk. Where else can you dine on sushi, dose up on *sake* and then cross the street to chuck a snowball at the KGB headquarters? All right, that last part is not recommended – but it's theoretically possible, and that's Minsk in a nutshell.

There's a palpable pride about the capital of Belarus: the pride of a survivor. In WWII, barely a stone was left standing, and half the city's people perished, including almost the entire population of 50,000 Jews. Stalin had the city rebuilt from scratch, and to this day the architecture and ambience reflects his grandiose aesthetic more than any other place in the former USSR. Today, President Lukashenko runs a tight ship, and you'll see the evidence of it in Minsk. The wide streets are clear of litter and low on chaos – you're unlikely to see even a jaywalker.

If it all seems just a little too perfect and ordered for you, don't worry. After spending the day in the shadows of Soviet architecture, you can spend all night in the strobe lights, text messaging the hotties on the dance floor.

## ORIENTATION

Minsk's main thoroughfare, praspekt Nezalezhnastsi, stretches over 11km from the train station to the outer city limits. The most interesting section is between the stubbornly austere and huge ploshcha Nezalezhnastsi and ploshcha Peramohi.

---

**MINSK IN TWO DAYS**

Take a walk down Soviet memory lane, praspekt Nezalezhnastsi, stopping to take a guided tour of the **Museum of the Great Patriotic War** (p83). Finish your walk at **Lido** (p85) with a big cafeteria-style lunch. Next, pay a visit to the **Island of Tears** (p84) monument and the **Traetskae Pradmestse** (p83). Have dinner (make reservations at) **Strawnya Talaka** (p85), then cross the street to **Rakovsky Brovar** (p86) for some killer home-brews.

Take a day trip to **Dudutki** (p88) for its open-air interactive museum and traditional meals.

# MINSK

0 — 1 km
0 — 0.5 miles

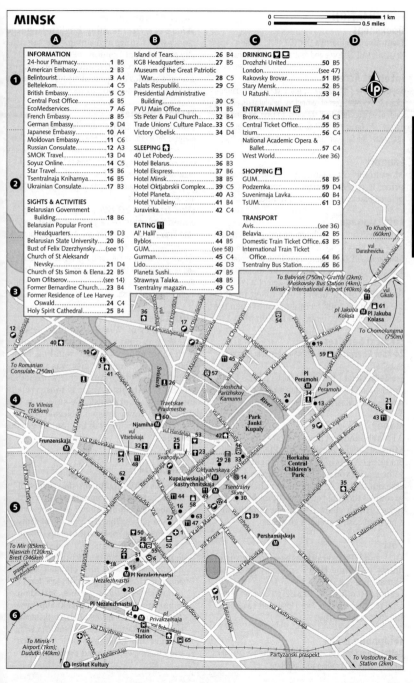

### INFORMATION
24-hour Pharmacy.................1 B5
American Embassy.................2 B3
Belintourist.........................3 A4
Beltelekom..........................4 C5
British Embassy....................5 C5
Central Post Office................6 B5
EcoMedservices...................7 A6
French Embassy....................8 B5
German Embassy...................9 D4
Japanese Embassy...............10 A4
Moldovan Embassy..............11 C6
Russian Consulate................12 A3
SMOK Travel.......................13 D4
Soyuz Online......................14 C5
Star Travel..........................15 B6
Tsentralnaja Kniharnya..........16 B5
Ukrainian Consulate.............17 B3

### SIGHTS & ACTIVITIES
Belarusian Government
   Building.........................18 B6
Belarusian Popular Front
   Headquarters..................19 D3
Belarusian State University.....20 B6
Bust of Felix Dzerzhinsky.....(see 1)
Church of St Aleksandr
   Nevsky..........................21 D4
Church of Sts Simon & Elena..22 B5
Dom Ofitserov.................(see 14)
Former Bernardine Church.....23 B4
Former Residence of Lee Harvey
   Oswald...........................24 C4
Holy Spirit Cathedral............25 B4

Island of Tears.....................26 B4
KGB Headquarters................27 B5
Museum of the Great Patriotic
   War..............................28 C5
Palats Respubliki..................29 C5
Presidential Administrative
   Building.........................30 C5
PVU Main Office..................31 B5
Sts Peter & Paul Church........32 B4
Trade Unions' Culture Palace..33 C5
Victory Obelisk....................34 D4

### SLEEPING
40 Let Pobedy.....................35 D5
Hotel Belarus......................36 B3
Hotel Ekspress.....................37 B6
Hotel Minsk........................38 B5
Hotel Oktjabrskii Complex......39 C5
Hotel Planeta......................40 A3
Hotel Yubileiny...................41 B4
Juravinka............................42 C4

### EATING
Al' Halil'.............................43 D4
Byblos................................44 B5
GUM...............................(see 58)
Gurman..............................45 C4
Lido...................................46 D3
Planeta Sushi.......................47 B5
Strawnya Talaka...................48 B5
Tsentralny magazin...............49 C5

### DRINKING
Drozhzhi United...................50 B5
London............................(see 47)
Rakovsky Brovar...................51 B5
Stary Mensk........................52 B5
U Ratushi............................53 B4

### ENTERTAINMENT
Bronx.................................54 C3
Central Ticket Office..............55 B5
Izium.................................56 C4
National Academic Opera &
   Ballet............................57 C4
West World......................(see 36)

### SHOPPING
GUM.................................58 B5
Podzemka..........................59 D4
Suvenirnaja Lavka................60 B4
TsUM.................................61 D3

### TRANSPORT
Avis................................(see 36)
Belavia...............................62 B5
Domestic Train Ticket Office..63 B5
International Train Ticket
   Office............................64 B6
Tsentralny Bus Station............65 B6

BELARUS

## INFORMATION

### Bookshops
**Tsentralnaja Kniharnya** ( ☎ 227 4918; praspekt Nezalezhnastsi 19) Large and central (hence the name).

### Internet Access
**Soyuz Online** ( ☎ 226 0279; 2nd fl, vulitsa Krasnaarmejskaja 3; ✌ 24hr) Lots of computers, helpful staff, all kinds of services (printing, scanning, gaming, etc) and a decent café. Go up the steps to the Dom Ofitserov (opposite); enter the far door, near the tank monument.

### Laundry
Most hotels offer laundry services for a fair price; if you're renting an apartment only pricier places will have a machine.

### Left Luggage
Hotels will hold your baggage for several hours after you check out. Downstairs at the **train station** (lockers US$0.25, luggage room US$0.50; ✌ 24hr) is a well-signed place. To use the lockers, put your stuff in an empty one, select a code on the inside of the door, put a token in, shut the door. Use your second token to open the locker again (see the boxed text on p84).

### Medical Services
**24-hour Pharmacy** ( ☎ 227 4844; praspekt Nezalezhnastsi 16)

**EcoMedservices** ( ☎ 207 7474; vulitsa Tolstoho 4; ✌ 8am-9pm) The closest thing to a reliable, Western-style clinic. Dental services are here too.

### Money
ATMs abound, but there's often a small queue. Minskers really linger on the PIN pad. Many but not all ATMs offer US dollars or euros, if for some reason you need foreign currency (don't take out dollars or euros just to change them to roubles though; you'll pay the exchange rate twice). Hotels all have exchange bureaus, and a handful cash traveller's cheques.

### Post
DHL and UPS have offices based in the major hotels, including Hotel Yubileiny (p85) and Oktjabrskii (p85).

**Central post office** ( ☎ 227 8492; praspekt Nezalezhnastsi 10; ☎ phone office 7am-11pm) There's an Express Mail office on the 2nd floor.

### Telephone & Fax
**Beltelekom** ( ☎ 236 7124; vulitsa Enhelsa 14; ✌ 24hr) Another convenient calling and fax centre.

### Tourist Information
*Where* is a free monthly English-language glossy with listings and a map. You can usually get a copy at London (p86).

There are no tourist information centres. Travel agencies can provide information but of course want to book tours.

### Travel Agencies
**Belintourist** ( ☎ 226 9971; www.belintourist.by; praspekt Peramozhtsau 19A; ✌ 8am-1pm & 2-8pm Mon-Sat, 9am-5pm Sun & holidays) The state-run tourist agency does visa support, city tours and trips to Mir, Dudutki, Njazvizh and Belavezhskaja Pushcha National Park – as well as to the Stalin Line open-air museum of 1930s military fortifications.

**SMOK Travel** ( ☎ 233 9569; www.smoktravel.com; praspekt Nezalezhnastsi 40) A good option for visa support.

**Star Travel** ( ☎ 226 5882; www.startravel.by; praspekt Nezalezhnastsi 6) It looks like STA travel and acts like STA travel (deals with ISIC cards and student airfares) and sounds like STA travel. But it's not STA travel. The agency does provide free plane-ticket delivery and staff members speak English.

## SIGHTS
The ravages of WWII absolutely levelled Minsk, meaning very few buildings older than about 60 years remain standing. However, after the war the city was promptly rebuilt with a victorious, fiercely proud Soviet flair, and this is what is most visually interesting about Minsk. Be sure to take a slow walk down praspekt Nezalezhnastsi, using the following walking tour to get the full effect.

---

**CIRCLE 16**

There is little graffiti on the streets of Minsk, but you may come across the circled number '16' spray-painted in somewhat obscure places. This is a sign of solidarity with Belarusian political prisoners, disappeared oppositionists and independent journalists. At 8pm on the 16th of each month, participants turn off their lights and put a candle in their window for 15 minutes. Sometimes people, including journalist-turned-activist **Irina Khalip** (www .time.com/time/europe/hero2005/khalip.html), turn up on Kastrychnitskaja ploshcha with a candle and stand there until the police shoo them away or round them up.

**BELARUS**

---

**WHERE AM I?**

Between the Soviet, post-Soviet Russian, and nationalist Belarusian names for streets and places in Minsk, things can get confusing.

To honour the great Belarusian renaissance man, the main thoroughfare was once called praspekt Francyska Skaryny (prospekt Frantsiska Skoriny in Russian), but Lukashenko had enough of that nationalism and in 2005 changed it to 'Independence Prospect': praspekt Nezalezhnastsi (prospekt Nezavisimosti in Russian). All variations are used colloquially.

Metro stop and town square ploschad Lenina also goes by its post-Soviet name, which switches out 'Lenin' for 'Independence': ploshcha Nezalezhnastsi (ploshcha Nezavisimosti in Russian).

Metro stop and main town square Oktyabrskaya ploschad (its Soviet, Russian name) is sometimes called Kastrychnitskaja ploshcha (Belarusian).

Ploshcha Peramohi (Victory Square) is often referred to as its Russian variant, ploshchad Pobedy.

And just to make sure everyone was thoroughly puzzled, since 2005 vulitsa Varvasheni has been renamed praspket Masherava, and what was praspekt Masherava is now praspekt Peramozhtsau (prospekt Pobeditelei in Russian).

In this book, we've gone with the Belarusian names, as we'd like to support the nationalist cause, and as streets are usually posted in Belarusian, even though most people in Minsk speak Russian. Go figure.

---

## Walking Tour of Soviet Ideology

After it was obliterated in WWII, Minsk was rebuilt from the ground up, under the direction of Stalin. A walk down praspekt Nezalezhnastsi is a testament to the grandiose monumentalism the Soviets were so famous for.

**Ploshcha Nezalezhnastsi** (also called ploshcha Lenina) is dominated by the **Belarusian Government Building** (behind the Lenin statue) on its northern side, and the equally proletarian **Belarusian State University** on the south side.

Many of Minsk's main shops and cafés are northeast of the main square, ploshcha Nezalezhnastsi, including Soviet **GUM** (Government All-Purpose Store; see p87). An entire block at No 17 is occupied by a yellow neoclassical building with an ominous, temple–like Corinthian portal – the **KGB headquarters**. On the other side of the street is a long narrow park with a **bust of Felix Dzerzhynsky**, the founder of the KGB's predecessor (the Cheka) and a native of Belarus.

Between vulitsa Enhelsa and vulitsa Janki Kupaly is a square that is still referred to by its Russian name, Oktyabrskaya ploshchad (in Belarusian, it's ploshcha Kastrychnitskaja). This is where opposition groups gather to protest against Lukashenko from time to time, and it's where they attempted the Denim Revolution in March 2006. Here you'll find the impressive, severe **Palats Respubliki** (Palace of the Republic), a concert hall. Also on this square is the classical, multi-columned **Trade Unions' Culture Palace**, and next to this, the recommended Museum of the Great Patriotic War (below).

Across the street is Tsentralny Skver (Central Square), a small park on the site of a 19th-century marketplace. The dark-grey building is **Dom Ofitserov** (Officer's Building), which has a tank memorial in front, devoted to the soldiers who freed Minsk from the Nazis. Beyond this is the lifeless-looking, seriously guarded **Presidential Administrative Building**, where Lukashenko practises his bully routine.

Further north on praspekt Nezalezhnastsi is ploshcha Peramohi, marked by a giant **Victory Obelisk** and its eternal flame.

## Other Sights

Don't leave town without visiting the **Museum of the Great Patriotic War** ( ☎ 277 5611; praspekt Nezalezhnastsi 25A; admission US$2; ⏰ 10am-6pm Tue-Sun), where Belarus' horrors and heroism during WWII are exhibited in photographs, huge dioramas and other media. Particularly harrowing are the photographs of partisans being executed in recognisable central Minsk locations. The big sign above the building (ПОДВИГУ НАРОДА ЖИТЬ В ВЕКАХ) means 'The Feats of Mankind Will Live On for Centuries'.

The faux Old Town, called **Traetskae Pradmestse**, is worth strolling through for its little cafés, restaurants and shops. At the end of a little footbridge nearby is the evocative

---

**QUIRKY MINSK**

Just across the bridge over the Svislach River, on the west bank, is the **former residence of Lee Harvey Oswald** (vulitsa Kamunistychnaja 4); it's the bottom left apartment. The alleged assassin of former US president John F Kennedy lived here for a couple of years in his early 20s. He arrived in Minsk in January 1960 after leaving the US Marines and defecting to the USSR. Once here, he truly went native: he got a job in a radio factory, married a Minsk woman, had a child – and even changed his name to Alek. But soon he returned to the United States and…you know the rest.

Lovers of **old coins** should stop in at the train station's left luggage area, where there are lockers that (surprise, surprise) date back to the Soviet days – and they still only work with Soviet coins. Pay BR550 and get in exchange two locker 'tokens' –15-kopek coins from the USSR, some dating back to the 1960s.

Exerting complete control over a nation takes a lot of energy, so even an omnipotent dictator like Lukashenko needs to refuel after a hard morning at work. Every afternoon, around 1pm, he heads out from his offices to tuck into a meal. If you want to see the speeding, **black armoured-car procession** slam through the city streets, hang out around the McDonald's on praspekt Nezalezhnasti around that time. He usually heads down vulitsa Lenina.

---

Afghan war memorial, **Island of Tears**. Standing on a small island connected by a walking bridge, it's built in the form of a tiny church, with four entrances, and is surrounded by towering gaunt statues of sorrowful mothers and sisters of Belarusian soldiers who perished in the war between Russia and Afghanistan (1979–89). Look for the small statue of the crying angel, off to the side – it is the guardian angel of Belarus.

Breaking the theme of Soviet classicism that dominates ploshcha Svabody is the red-brick Catholic **Church of Sts Simon & Elena** (ploshcha Nezalezhnastsi), built in 1910. Its tall, gabled bell tower and attractive detailing are reminiscent of many brick churches in the former Teutonic north of Poland.

The baroque, twin-towered orthodox **Holy Spirit Cathedral** (ploshcha Svabody), built in 1642, stands confidently on a small hill. It was once part of a Polish Bernardine convent, along with the **former Bernardine Church** next door, which now houses city archives.

Across the vulitsa Lenina overpass is the attractively restored 17th-century **Sts Peter & Paul Church** (vulitsa Rakovskaja 4), the city's oldest church (built in 1613, looted by Cossacks in 1707 and restored in 1871). Now it is awkwardly dwarfed by the surrounding morose concrete structures.

Another red-brick one is the **Church of St Aleksandr Nevsky** (vulitsa Kazlova 11). Built in 1898, it was closed by the Bolsheviks, opened by the Nazis, closed by the Soviets and now it's open again. It's said that during WWII, a bomb crashed through the roof and

landed plum in front of the altar, but never detonated.

## SLEEPING

If you're staying more than a few days, it could be a good idea to consider renting an apartment. There are only a few online agencies that can help you; the best option is **Belarus Rent** (www.belarusrent.com). Rates range from US$38 to US$58. Another option is **Belarus Apartment** (www.belarusapartment.com). Stay in a hotel at least one night for visa-registration purposes. For upmarket, more Western-style apartments, contact **Valentin** (☎ 029 656 4010; rent2002@mail.ru). His remodelled, central flats range from US$40 to US$100.

### Budget

**Moskovsky Bus Station Dorms** (☎ 219 3627; vulitsa Filimonava 63; d with shared bath BR46,000) Out the back of the station, these are clean, quiet and watched over by a very serious babushka. However, they cannot register visas; you'll have to stay a night elsewhere to do that.

**Hotel Ekspress** (☎ 225 6463; ploshcha Privakzalnaja 3; d without shower from US$29) Dark and cheerless, the only things the Ekspress has going for it are the cheap prices and convenient location, smack bang between the central bus station and the train station. There are decent renovated rooms with shower, but they are way too overpriced.

**40 Let Pobedy** (☎ 236 7963; vulitsa Azgura 3; s/d US$28/43) The name of this small hotel, which means '40 Years of Victory', is dated (it's now been 60 years since the end of WWII, which is what 'victory' always refers to in Belarus). The surprise is that it's actually kind of pleasant here. Staff is warm and helpful to foreigners, despite the Lukashenko portrait on display at the front desk.

## Midrange

**Hotel Yubileiny** ( ☎ 226 9024; fax 226 9171; praspekt Peramozhtsau 19; s US$43-64, d US$58-83; ⊠ ) Because there's a sports stadium right across the street, Yubileiny keeps busy. Who knows, you might be able to have a drink at the hotel's bar with a foreign hockey player who has been paid to play against Lukashenko himself. It's been known to happen. The rooms are comparable to Hotel Planeta's.

**Hotel Planeta** ( ☎ 226 7855; www.hotelplaneta.by; praspekt Peramozhtsau 31; s US$57-82, d US$62-88; ⊠ ) Despite the photographs of Lukashenko displayed at the front desk, the staff at Planeta seem more West-oriented, attractive and cheery than the employees at other midrange hotels. The economy rooms have remodelled bathrooms, which makes them a good deal.

**Hotel Belarus** ( ☎ 209 7693; belarus@hotel.minsk.by; vulitsa Starazhouskaga 15; s US$56-96, d US$76-111) It's just one of many monolithic Soviet-era hotels, but Belarus is clearly the most well known. Rooms are run-of-the-mill *sovok* (Soviet-style), and the echoing old marble lobby, where guests sit in old leather chairs, seems like a weigh station for lost souls. Breakfast is served on the top floor, where there are panoramic views.

**Hotel Oktjabrskii Complex** ( ☎ 222 3289; oktyabr@tut .by; vulitsa Enhelsa 13; s/d/ste US$54/91/115) The Oktjabrskii is time-capsule Soviet, and you may luck out and get a nice young person at the front desk, who can share with you a sense of humour about it all. It's a little overpriced for its category, but if you like the spooky, tense feeling you get from being right across from Lukashenko's high-security workplace, you couldn't pick a better spot.

## Top End

**Juravinka** ( ☎ 206 6900; minselko@tut.by; vulitsa Janki Kupaly 25; s/d/ste US$119/167/877; P ⊠ 🖳 🖳 ) The high-quality rooms at sweet lil' Zhuravinka give Hotel Minsk a run for its money, but book in advance: there are only 18 possible vacancies. It has a bowling alley on site (as well as a fitness centre and fancy restaurant), and it seems to be a hot spot for Belarusian elite, so it has a sort of bubbly, party feel to it. The presidential suite is ginormous and has its own swimming pool.

**Hotel Minsk** ( ☎ 209 9074; www.hotelminsk.by; vulitsa Nezalezhnastsi 11; s US$144-185, d US$185-206, ste US$237-370; ⊠ ⊠ 🖳 ) If you want no surprises and no hassles, you won't be disappointed with four-star Hotel Minsk, which has Western-standard, but not posh, chain-style rooms that are a bit on the small side. Service is everything it should be (polite and convenient), but nothing more.

## EATING

On weekend nights, many places are full, so consider booking ahead. There are some good, obvious places on or near Kastrychnitskaja ploshcha.

### Regional

**Lido** ( ☎ 284 8264; praspekt Nezalezhnastsi 49/1; mains US$2-6) There are several cafeteria-style restaurants similar to Latvian-run Lido (see the boxed text on p424), but none are nearly as good. All food (a giant selection of Eastern European dishes) is on display, so it's easy for non-Russian speakers: just point at what you want. Lunchtime is packed, but staff will help you find a seat.

**Gurman** ( ☎ 290 6774; vulitsa Kamynistychnaja 7; mains US$3-12) With its locally famous *pelmeni* (Russian-style meat dumplings) and its wide selection of Italian-style pastas, Gurman is worth the long (though pleasant) walk from the metro.

**Strawnya Talaka** ( ☎ 203 2794; vulitsa Rakovskaja 18; mains US$7-25) This small Belarusian eatery is suitable for a romantic, intimate dinner amid sophisticated Slavic décor, although it can get a little smoky, depending on the other diners. It's a stone's throw from Rakovsky Brovar (see p86), if you are up for something a bit rowdier afterward. Reservations are required.

### International

**Al' Halil'** ( ☎ 285 2780; vulitsa Kazlova 14; mains US$2-5) Don't let the hole-in-the-wall aspect of this Palestinian joint freak you – here you'll chow down on hot fresh *lavash* (soft flatbread) and all kinds of Middle Eastern treats: *dolma, baba ganoush* and several meat dishes. Note that what's on the menu isn't everything, and that some of what is on the menu is prepared in a 'Russianised' way (think mayonnaise). But talk to the staff members (they speak a little English) and let them know what you want. They're eager to please.

BELARUS

**Byblos** ( ☎ 289 1218; vulitsa Internatsjanalnaja 21; mains US$3-6) This popular, inexpensive joint near the *ratusha* (town hall) serves up tasty Lebanese meat dishes and a soul-warming spinach-lentil soup.

**Chomolungma** ( ☎ 266 5388; vulitsa Gikalo 17; mains US$4-20) Wow. A huge menu with a wide range of prices and cuisines: Nepalese, Tibetan, sushi and Indian. There is only one tofu dish, but there is plenty more for vegetarians. It's well worth the 10-minute walk from metro Yakuba Kolasa.

**Planeta Sushi** ( ☎ 210 5645; praspekt Nezalezhnasti 18; mains US$5-30) Sushi? In Belarus? You bet. In fact there are now several choices for a bowl of *miso* and a plate of *nigiri*. Other Japanese dishes (*udon, tempura* etc) are offered as well. The place seems to have a surprisingly decent connection for fresh fish, but it could use a new avocado supplier.

### Self-Catering
**Tsentralny magazin** ( ☎ 227 8876; 2nd fl, praspekt Nezalezhnasti 23) A large, Western-style grocery store with plenty of fresh stuff for self-caterers.

## DRINKING
Be careful about drinking alcohol in public. You'll see other people doing it, but it's technically illegal and therefore you could be asking for trouble.

**Rakovsky Brovar** ( ☎ 206 6404; vulitsa Vitsebskaja 10) This jolly two-storey brewery is the most popular of its kind in Minsk. It's known for its good cheer and not its food, which is not bad but a little pricey. The huge menu of Belarusian and other European cuisine will at least help keep you from getting too drunk. There are often roving accordionists.

---

#### TOP FIVE PLACES TO TIE ONE ON

▪ Graffiti (opposite) – cheap beer and underground bands.

▪ Stary Mensk (right) – try the honey-sweet *krambambulia*.

▪ Rakovsky Brovar (above) – a selection of home-brews in a rowdy atmosphere.

▪ Bronx (right) – favourite haunt of the beautiful people.

▪ U Ratushi (right) – multilevel bar with live bands and a let-loose crowd.

---

**U Ratushi** ( ☎ 226 0643; vulitsa Gertsena 1; ☺ 10-2am) Formerly called 'Nul Pyat', referring to the standard serving of beer (a half-litre), this multilevel pub-style restaurant, right across from the *ratusha,* is packed with a raucous, fun-loving crowd on weekends (there is often a small cover charge for live bands). Book ahead for weekends, or come really early.

**Drozhzhi United** ( ☎ 200 5456; vulitsa Sverdlova 2; ☺ 9-2am) It's a strange name (*drozhzhi* means 'yeast') and a strange location, but once inside, this Irish-style pub is all familiar.

The hippest cafés are the itsy-bitsy **Stary Mensk** ( ☎ 289 1400; praspekt Nezalezhnasti 14; ☺ 10am-11pm) and its teeny-weeny cousin, **London** ( ☎ 289 1529; praspekt Nezalezhnasti 18; ☺ 10am-11pm). They both serve coffees and fresh teas, and whip up a mean hot chocolate. London has an upstairs area, but you'll have to order an alcoholic beverage to sit there. In summer, Stary Mensk puts on *batlejka* (traditional Belarusian puppet shows) – very nationalistic, and all right across from the KGB headquarters.

## ENTERTAINMENT
### Performing Arts
Just like they were during the Soviet Union, the performing arts here are of very good quality, and tickets are priced to make them accessible to the proletariat. Opera performances are held at 7pm on Thursday, Saturday and Sunday. Ballet performances are at 7pm on Tuesday, Wednesday, Friday and Sunday.

To buy advance tickets or to find out what's on, head to the **central ticket office** (praspekt Nezalezhnasti 18; ☺ 9am-7pm). There are more places for tickets in the underground crossing in the centre. Same-day tickets are sometimes available only from the venues.

**National Academic Opera & Ballet Theatre** ( ☎ 234 8074; ploshcha Parizhskoy Kamunni 1; tickets ☺ 9am-1pm & 2-6pm Mon-Fri) The ballet here has a highly respected reputation; some think it better than Moscow's Bolshoi. Performances start at 7pm. There are several different operas performed each month.

### Nightclubs
If you read Russian, a great website for clubs and events is www.mixtura.org/minsk/clubs .html.

**Bronx** ( ☎ 288 1061; www.bronx.by; praspekt Masherava 17/1; cover free or US$8-18; ☺ noon-5am Thu-Sat, noon-2am

**BELARUS**

---

**AUTHOR'S CHOICE**

The place to go if you want to hear the latest Belarusian musicians or to see some live theatre is **Graffiti** ( ☎ 266 0154; www .graffiti.avilink.net/afisha.html; per Kalinina 16; cover US$3-5; ☺ noon-midnight Mon-Sat). The underground club is small (get there early if you want in) and not conveniently located (best take a taxi), but the bands and the troupes are often on Lukashenko's shit-list, and this is the only venue in town where they get away with performing (at least most of the time). Bar snacks and beer are tasty and super cheap (a big draft beer for under $1.50!).

---

Sun-Wed) Without a doubt, the Bronx is the hippest nightclub in town. Special guest bands and DJs from abroad show up at the sleek, ultramodern warehouse-style space, where there are billiards, dance floors and fashion shows.

**Izium** ( ☎ 206 6618; praspekt Nezalezhnastsi 25; cover US$3-8; ☺ noon-2am Sun-Wed, to 6am Thu-Sat) Splashy and chic, Izium has a high-tech design, fusion food and live music nights. Apart from the dance area, there are two dining halls – one is particularly fancy, the other is just hip. Flat-screen TVs at many tables show music videos, if that gives you any idea of what to expect. Service is gracious but slow.

**Babylon** ( ☎ 8-029 677 0445; vulitsa Tolbukhina 4; ☺ 10pm-6am Tue-Sun) The city's main gay-friendly locale, and probably the least pretentious and most fun-spirited club in town. Here people of all persuasions gather just to have a down-to-earth good time. It's on the 3rd floor of a commercial building – just walk in the open door and follow the music.

**West World** ( ☎ 239 1798; vulitsa Starazhouskaja 15a; cover US$4-8; ☺ 1pm-5am) Because of its circular shape, locals call this place *shaiba* (hockey puck). It's quite a scene, with erotic dancing, flashy nouveau riche, Eurotrash wannabes and prostitutes aplenty, as well as visiting Turks, Azeris and Georgians. Sometimes 'face control' is exercised, so shy away from wearing jeans and trainers, just in case.

## SHOPPING

Because of a dearth of tourism, you won't be blown away by what's offered as Belarusian mementos. One favourite purchase is a pho-

tographic portrait of Lukashenko, available in Tsentralnaja Kniharnya (see p82). At many grocery shops you'll find candies with old-fashioned wrappers steeped in nostalgia for a Soviet childhood – check out the tabletops at Stary Mensk (see opposite) to see some favourites.

Belarus is also known for its straw crafts, which include dolls and wooden boxes intricately ornamented with geometric patterns of the stuff. Linens and other woven textiles unique to Belarus are also popular handicrafts. These are easily found in city department stores, hotel lobbies and in some museum kiosks.

**Suvenirnaja Lavka** ( ☎ 234 5451; vulitsa Maxima Bahdanovicha 9; ☺ 10am-7pm Mon-Fri, 10am-6pm Sat) Excellent quality, and helpful and patient service here; staff speak some English. You'll find straw crafts, wooden boxes, lots of beautifully embroidered linens and Belarusian vodka – as well as Belavezhskaja.

**Podzemka** ( ☎ 288 2036; www.podzemka.org; praspekt Nezalezhnastsi 43; ☺ 10am-8pm Mon-Sat, 10am-6pm Sun) This underground bohemian shop-cum-art-gallery sells all sorts of goodies you be hard-pressed to find anywhere else; for example, 'Women of the War' calendars, funky artistic pieces, photographs and handmade jewellery.

The Belarusian company **Milavitsa** (www .milavitsa.com.by) sells stylish lingerie for a fraction of what Westerners pay. Check the department stores, such as **GUM** ( ☎ 226 1048; praspekt Nezalezhnastsi 21) and **TsUM** ( ☎ 284 8164; praspekt Nezalezhnastsi 54) for souvenirs and Milavitsa products. There are no dressing rooms.

## GETTING THERE & AWAY
### Air
International flights entering and departing Belarus do so at the **Minsk-2 international airport** ( ☎ 006, 279 1300), about 40km east of Minsk. Some domestic flights as well as those to Kyiv, Kaliningrad and Moscow depart from the smaller **Minsk-1 airport** ( ☎ 006; vulitsa Chkalova 38), only a few kilometres from the city centre.

### Bus
There are three main bus stations, and you can buy tickets for anywhere at any of them. You'll probably only be leaving from the Tsentralny (Central) station, but to be sure, ask which station you're departing from (v ka-*kom* av-toh-vak-*za*-le ot-prav-*lye*-ni-ye?).

**Moskovsky** ( ☎ 219 3622; vulitsa Filimonava 63) Near Maskouskaja metro station.

**Tsentralny** ( ☎ international 227 0473, CIS destinations 227 4083; vulitsa Bobrujskaje 6; Ⓜ Ploshcha Lenina) By the train station.

**Vostochny** ( ☎ 248 0882; vulitsa Vaneeva 34) To get here from the train station (or metro Ploshcha Lenina), take bus 8 or trolley 20 or 30; get off at 'Avtovokzal Vostochny'.

## Train

The Minsk train station is relatively modern and safe. Food and left-luggage services are available here. Nothing is in English yet, but there are picture-signs. You can buy tickets at the train station, but the ticket offices have shorter lines. At the station, there are ATMs and exchange offices, but the lines are often long.

**Domestic train ticket office** ( ☎ 225 6124; praspekt Nezalezhnastsi 18; ⏱ 9am-8pm Mon-Fri, 9am-7pm Sat & Sun) Tickets for domestic and CIS destinations.

**International train ticket office** ( ☎ 213 1719; vulitsa Babrujskaja 4; ⏱ 9am-8pm) Advance tickets for non-CIS destinations; located to the right of the train station.

**Minsk train station** ( ☎ 005, 596 5410) Domestic and CIS tickets.

## GETTING AROUND

See p97 for information on car rentals.

### To/from the Airport & Train Station

From Minsk-2 airport, a 40-minute taxi ride into town should cost $25, but you'll be lucky to get it for under $40. There are buses ($1.30, 90 minutes, hourly) that bring you to the Tsentralny bus station, not far from the centre and metro station Ploshcha Lenina. There are also about eight daily minibuses that make the trip in a little over an hour and cost $2. From Minsk-1 airport, take bus 100 to the centre; it goes along praspekt Nezalezhnastsi.

If you arrive by train, you're already in the centre, at a metro station even (Ploshcha Nezalezhnastsi).

### Public Transport

Minsk's metro is simple – just two lines with one transfer point – and operates until just after midnight. One token (*zheton*) costs $0.25.

Buses, trams, trolleybuses and the metro cost $0.25 per ride and operate from 5.30am to 1am. Minibuses (*marshrutki*) cost about

$0.50 and are a quicker way to get around once you know their routes. Popular Bus 100 comes every five to 15 minutes and plies praspekt Nezalezhnastsi as far as Moskovsky bus station. You can buy a ticket from the person on board wearing a bright vest. Once you get the ticket, punch it at one of the red buttons placed at eyelevel on poles.

For taxis, ☎ 081 is the state service and almost always has cars available, while ☎ 007 is private, the cheapest and has the best service (less likely to rip off foreigners) but cars are sometimes not available during peak times. You can also hail one from the street. Private cars don't stop for passengers.

## AROUND MINSK

If you're going to be in Minsk for more than 48 hours, a day trip to an outlying town is in order. On a road trip out of the busy capital city, you'll take in barely undulating plains as far as the eye can see and pretty clutches of birch forests. You'll hum by worn wooden houses and catch glimpses of old women riding bicycles and old men chopping wood. Getting a taste of pastoral Belarus helps to correctly balance the visitor's image of the country – after all, only one-fifth of the population lives in Minsk, where anti-Lukashenko sentiments are strongest.

If you have extra time, consider trying out Valeria's (of Dudutki) association of B&Bs. It's a somewhat new operation but already has dozens of homes on offer, throughout the country. Visit www.ruralbelarus.by.

If you do decide to get to these places using public transport, keep in mind that Sunday evenings are often booked in advance for the return trip to Minsk, as people are returning from their country homes.

### Dudutki Дудуткі
☎ 01713

Tasting delicious farm-made sausages, cheese and bread is only a small part of the experience of a visit to the **open-air interactive museum** of Dudutki, located 40km south of Minsk. This completely self-sufficient farm offers horseback riding, sleigh rides, demonstrations of ceramic-making and blacksmithing and more. You'll be offered fresh *salo* (tallow) with garlic, salt and rye bread; pickles dipped in honey; and homemade moonshine – even the ficklest eater should try them. All are scrumptious.

There are three daily buses (one hour, $1.50 each way) to/from Dudutki from Minsk's Tsentralny bus station; they leave at 10am, 12.35pm and 5pm and return at 11.15am, 1.50pm and 6.05pm. Otherwise, contact Valeria's **Dudutki Tur** ( ☎ 251 0076; dudutki@telecom.by; vulitsa Dunina Martsinkevicha 6, Minsk).

## Njasvizh Нясвіж
☎ 01770 / pop 15,000

Njasvizh, 120km southwest of Minsk, is one of the oldest sites in the country, dating from the 13th century. It reached its zenith in the mid-16th century while owned by the mighty Radziwill magnates.

The **Farny Polish Roman Catholic Church** was built between 1584 and 1593 in early baroque style and features a splendidly proportioned façade. Just beyond the church is the red-brick arcaded **Castle Gate Tower**. Constructed in the 16th century, the tower was originally part of a wall and gateway controlling the passage between the palace and the town. Here there's an **excursion bureau** ( ☎ 54 145; vulitsa Leninskaja 19; ⏰ 8am-5pm Mon-Fri) where you pay to enter the fortress grounds ($4.50). **Guided tours** ( ☎ 53 132; vulitsa Geysika; US$22.50; ⏰ tours 8am-5pm) for one to 25 people last about 1½ hours and are available in either Russian or Belarusian ($19).

Further on is a causeway leading to the **Radziwill Palace Fortress** (1583), the main sight in Njasvizh. In Soviet times it was, unfortunately, turned into a sanatorium. Although nothing was under way during research, it's said the building is being renovated.

From Minsk's Tsentralny bus station, there are five to six daily buses to/from Njasvizh ($4.50, 2½ hours).

## Mir Mip
☎ 01596 / pop 2500

About 85km southwest of Minsk is the small town of Mir, where the 16th-century **Mir Castle** sits overlooking a pond. It was once owned by the powerful Radziwill princes and has been under Unesco protection since 1994. Today the castle is under restoration, but one tower is already open as an **archaeological museum** ( ☎ 23 610; admission US$5, guided tour in Russian for 1-10 people US$9.50; ⏰ 10am-5pm Wed-Sun). The tight, steep, stone spiral stairwell that carries you from floor to floor is the most thrilling part of visiting the museum, which is otherwise a little dull.

The small, friendly **Hotel Mir** ( ☎ 23 851; ploshchad 17ogo Sentybrya 2; s/d/ste US$36/28/48) is the only place in town. Suites can theoretically sleep four. You'll find it in the town centre, across the way from the bus station.

From Minsk's Tsentralny bus station, buses to Navahrudak (Novogrudok in Russian), Lida, Svitsiaz and Zel'va stop in Mir ($4, 2½ hours, 10 daily).

## Khatyn Хатынь
☎ 01774

The hamlet of Khatyn, 60km north of Minsk, was one of many villages that was burned to the ground by Nazis on 22 March 1943. Of a population of 149 (including 85 children), only one man, Yuzif Kaminsky, survived. The site is now a sobering **memorial** ( ☎ tours in Russian 55 787; ⏰ 9am-5pm Tue-Sat). More information can be found at www.khatyn.by.

There's no public transport to Khatyn from Minsk, but a taxi will cost around $33 for the return journey. Pricey trips are organised by Belintourist (p82).

# BREST БРЭСТ

☎ 0162 / pop 290,000

You'd never believe that with its laid-back vibe, colourful wooden houses and quiet, pedestrian-only streets, Brest is home to one of the busiest border points in Eastern Europe. Right up at the influential edge of Poland, the city and its outgoing locals have a sort of breezy charm that's easy to enjoy. You can visit Brest just to enjoy the quaintness of it all, but don't leave without visiting the Brest Fortress, a moving WWII memorial. And if you have time, pay a visit to the nearby primeval forests of Belavezhskaja Pushcha National Park – maybe you'll spot an endangered zoobr (European bison).

## ORIENTATION

Central Brest fans out southeast from the train station to the Mukhavets River. Vulitsa Savetskaja is the main drag and has several pedestrian sections. Brest Fortress lies where the Buh and Mukhavets Rivers meet, about 2km southwest of the centre down praspekt Masherava.

## INFORMATION

**24-hour pharmacy** ( ☎ 23 80 28; vulitsa Hoholja 32)
**Belarusbank** (ploshcha Lenina) Currency exchange, Western Union and a nearby ATM.

BELARUS

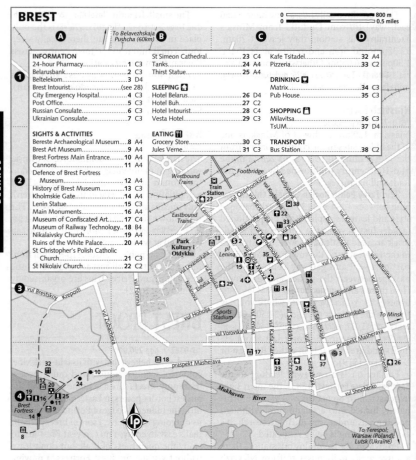

**BREST**

0 ————— 800 m
0 ————— 0.5 miles

**Beltelekom** ( ☎ 22 13 15; praspekt Masherava 21; per hr US$1; ☼ 7am-10.30pm) Internet access and long-distance calls.

**Brest Intourist** ( ☎ 22 19 00; www.brest-intourist.com; praspekt Masherava 15; ☼ 9am-6pm Mon-Fri) Inside Hotel Intourist; the super-friendly and English-, Polish- and German-speaking staff can arrange city tours (including 'Jewish Brest') and trips to national parks, including over-night hotel stays or camping trips in Belavezhskaja Pushcha.

**City Emergency Hospital** ( ☎ 23 58 38; vulitsa Lenina 15)

**Post office** (ploshcha Lenina)

## SIGHTS
### Brest Fortress

If you are going to see only one Soviet WWII memorial in your life, make it **Brest Fortress** (Brestskaja krepost; ☎ 20 03 65; praspekt Masherava;

admission free). It's at the western end of praspekt Masherava (which is lined with Soviet monuments and plaques), about a 20-minute walk (3km) from the centre; the hourly bus 17 travels between here and Hotel Intourist.

The fortress was built between 1838 and 1842, but by WWII it was used mainly for housing soldiers. Two regiments bunking here when Germans invaded in 1941 defended the fort for an astounding month.

The **Brest Fortress main entrance** has a sombre sound presentation, and as you leave a short tunnel, on the left and past a small hill, you'll see some **tanks** and, straight ahead, the stone **Thirst statue**. After you cross a small bridge, to your right are the brick ruins of the **White Palace**, where the 1918 Treaty of

Brest-Litovsk – which marked Russia's exit from WWI – was signed. Further to the right is the **Defence of Brest Fortress Museum** ( ☎ 20 03 65; admission US$3; 9.30am-5pm Tue-Sun). Its extensive and dramatic exhibits demonstrate the plight of the defenders. Near this museum is Kafe Tsitadel (p92).

On the other side of the fortress, you'll see a collection of **cannons**, which kids like to climb on (makes for cute pictures). Behind this area is the entrance to the new **Brest Art Museum** ( ☎ 20 08 26; admission US$1; 10am-6pm Wed-Sun), which holds art done by Brest citizens and some local crafts.

Heading to the **main monuments** – a stone soldier's head projecting from a massive rock, entitled Valour, and a sky-scraping obelisk – you'll see an eternal flame and stones bearing the names of those who died (several are marked 'unknown'). Sombre orchestral music is pumped into the area, and there are often men and women in period military uniforms marching to the music.

Behind the Valour rock is the attractive, recently renovated Byzantine **Nikalaivsky Church**, the oldest church in the city, which dates from when the town centre occupied the fortress site. It holds regular services.

To the south is **Kholmskie Gate**; its bricks are decorated with crenulated turrets and its outer face is riddled with hundreds of bullet and shrapnel holes. Beyond the Kholmskie Gate is the **Bereste Archaeological Museum** ( ☎ 20 55 54; admission US$2; 9.30am-6pm Tue-Sun), which has several old log cabins found on nearby land.

### Other Sights

Arguably the most interesting museum in town is the **Museum of Confiscated Art** ( ☎ 20 41 95; vulitsa Lenina 39; admission US$1.50; 10am-5pm Wed-Sun). The collection of once-stolen icons and other precious items is unlike anything else you'll see in the country – the smugglers definitely went for the cream of the crop.

New on the scene is the **Museum of Railway Technology** ( ☎ 27 47 64; praspekt Masherava 2; admission US$2.50; 9am-5pm Wed-Sun). Tours are only in Russian, and it is pricey, but train buffs will love it even if they don't understand the guide. If that fails, just walking by and seeing the trains through the cast-iron fence is interesting enough.

With its gold cupolas and yellow-and-blue façades shining gaily in the sunlight,

the breathtakingly detailed 200-year-old Orthodox **St Nikolaiv Church** (cnr vulitsa Savetskaja & vulitsa Mitskevicha) is one of many lovely churches in Brest. On ploshcha Lenina, a **Lenin statue** points east towards Moscow, but it appears more to be pointing across the street accusingly at the 1856 **St Christopher's Polish Catholic Church** (ploshcha Lenina). The peach-and-green **St Simeon Cathedral** (cnr praspekt Masherava & vulitsa Karla Marxa) was built in 1865 in Russian-Byzantine style (the gold on the cupolas was added in 1997).

In a pretty white building, the two-storey **History of Brest Museum** ( ☎ 23 17 65; vulitsa Levaneiskaha 3; admission US$1.25; 10am-5pm Wed-Sun) has a small exhibit on the city in its different guises throughout history.

### SLEEPING

**Hotel Buh** ( ☎ 23 64 17; vulitsa Lenina 2; s/d/tr US$26/40/58) It's on the dreary side, but the rooms are spacious and the building is interesting. If your room faces the main street, it'll be noisy. Because renovations are scheduled for autumn 2006, it may be temporarily closed.

**Hotel Belarus** ( ☎ 22 16 48; bresttourist@tut.by; bulvar Shevchenko 6; s US$36-41, d US$51-62, ste US$90) Yes, it's a Soviet-style hotel, but staff are smiling and helpful. All rooms have modernised bathrooms and a good amount of floor space. A great-smelling bakery and restaurant are on the premises.

**Hotel Intourist** ( ☎ 20 20 82; www.brest-intourist.com; praspekt Masherava 15; s/d US$42/69) Similar to Hotel Belarus but less modern and less friendly at the front desk. Brest Intourist (opposite) is in the building – and they're friendly and English-speaking. Rooms are remodelled very well – in the economy rooms, only the bathroom hasn't been redone yet.

**Vesta Hotel** ( ☎ 23 71 69; hotelvesta@tut.by; vulitsa Krupskoi 16; s/d US$49/74, ste US$94-186) Privately owned Vesta is peaceful, cosy and small. It has cheerful, helpful service (apart from the upstairs café), a well-manicured lawn and sunny rooms done up in tan and gold. Some singles have an additional fold-out couch, so it's possible to share the room for an extra fee.

### EATING

For self-caterers, there is a decent **grocery store** (vulitsa Savetskaja 48; 8am-8pm Mon-Sat, 10am-8pm Sun) in the centre. Along the pedestrian-only part of vulitsa Savetskaja, there are lots of little cafés that serve hot, inexpensive food.

**BELARUS**

BELARUS

**Kafe Tsitadel** (Brest Fortress; mains US$2-4) If you're starving and stuck at the fortress, Kafe Tsitadel is your only hope. Surly staff tosses *pelmeni* (dumplings) and chicken Kiev in your general direction, but it would be better to stick to the Snickers or crisps sold behind the bar.

**Pizzeria** (vulitsa Pushkinskaja 20; pizzas US$2-6) It's not well signed, but you can pretty much follow your nose into the building and down the stairs. Really yummy thin-crust pizzas are made to order – try the 'Mexican'. Salads and fries are available as well.

**Jules Verne** ( ☎ 23 67 17; vulitsa Hoholja; mains US$4-14; ☻ noon-midnight) This is a true anomaly. The focus is on seafood, but there are also Indian, Thai and vegetarian dishes – apparently a sort of *Around the World in 80 Days* theme. Ironically, your bill is delivered in a miniature treasure chest.

## DRINKING

**Pub House** ( ☎ 21 93 46; vulitsa Hoholja; ☻ 9am-11pm) Small and smoky, with a sort of faux wood and faux brick interior, ye olde Pub House offers 12 tap beers and plenty more in bottles, served up with a smile from the cute young women behind the bar.

**Matrix** ( ☎ 23 82 39; vulitsa Savetskaja 73; ☻ noon-midnight) Bowling, billiards, bars and babes – it's all here. There's dancing too. The cover ranges from US$4 to $7.

## SHOPPING

Souvenirs can be bought in a pinch on the 1st floor of the city's **TsUM** ( ☎ 20 57 44; praspekt Masherava 17), although there's not tons of goodies to choose from. Just in case you missed your bra-purchasing opportunity in Minsk, there's a branch of **Milavitsa** ( ☎ 26 64 69; www.milavitsa.com.by; vulitsa Pushkinskaja 21) in Brest as well.

## GETTING THERE & AROUND

The **train station** ( ☎ 005) has on-site customs. Trains leave for Minsk (1st-/2nd-class US$10/7, four hours) several times daily. When taking a train from Brest, note that the platform nearest the city centre is for eastbound trains; the next one is for trains heading west. To get to the city from the train station, you'll have to mount a steep flight of steps from the platform; once you're up, go right on the overpass. If you're exhausted or have a lot of luggage, a taxi into town should be no more than $2.50.

The **bus station** ( ☎ 004) is in the centre of town. There is at least one daily bus between Minsk and Brest (US$7 to US$10, five hours).

To get to Belavezhskaja Pushcha on your own, you can take a minibus from the bus station (US$2, three daily except Wednesday). They are marked 'Kamjanjuky'.

What's covered here is all walkable. For a taxi, call ☎ 061 or have your hotel call for you.

## AROUND BREST
### Belavezhskaja Pushcha National Park

A Unesco World Heritage site some 60km north of Brest, **Belavezhskaja Pushcha National Park** ( ☎ 01631-56 122, 56 132; admission US$10) is the oldest wildlife refuge in Europe and the pride of Belarus. The park is co-administered by Poland, where the other half of the park's territory lies.

Some 1300 sq km of primeval forest survives here. It's all that remains of a canopy that eight centuries ago covered northern Europe. Some oak trees here are over 600 years old and some pines at least 300 years old.

At least 55 mammal species, including deer, lynx, boars, wild horses, wolves, elks, ermines, badgers, martens, otters, mink and beavers, call this park home, but the area is most celebrated for its 300 or so European bison, the continent's largest land mammal. These free-range zoobr – slightly smaller than their American cousins – were driven to near extinction (the last one living in the wild was shot by a hunter in 1919) and then bred back from 52 animals that had survived in zoos. Now a total of about 2000 exist, most of them in and around western Belarus, Lithuania, Poland and Ukraine.

There's a nature museum and *volerei* (enclosures), where you can view bison, deer, boars and other animals (including the rare hybrid Tarpan horse, a crossbreed of a species that was also shot into near extinction).

### SLEEPING & EATING

There are a few different options for overnight stays, all of which are best arranged through Brest Intourist (see p90). Camping requires permission but costs only about €5 per person. Indoor options include **Kamjanjuky** (s/d US$24/28) in the eponymous village just outside the national park (rooms are remodelled, have bathrooms and include breakfast) and

**Dom Grafa Tushkevicha** (5-/9-person accommodation US$85/280), a guesthouse better for families or other small groups. For a little history (p80) choose the **Viskuli Hotel** (s US$48-72, d US$52-76). Meals can be arranged.

### GETTING THERE & AWAY
The national park rarely sees individual tourists, but Brest Intourist (see p90) says it's entirely possible to do so, although a bit more difficult if you don't use their help – especially if you don't speak Russian. However, you can take a *marshrutka* there (US$2). They leave at least four times a day from Brest's bus station (the destination is Kamjanjuky). A guided group tour costs from US$50 to US$100 for up to 40 people. They'll include visits to historical spots along the way to the park, and can fix a summer picnic in a lovely area, as well as arrange overnight accommodation in the park itself.

# BELARUS DIRECTORY

## ACCOMMODATION
Farmers and villagers are generally generous about allowing campers to pitch a tent on their lot for an evening. Outside national parks you may camp in forests and the like, provided you don't make too much of a ruckus. Camping in or near a city is asking for trouble from the police.

While budget and midrange accommodation standards in Belarus tend to be lower than in the West, they are still generally acceptable and often better than in Russia or Ukraine. Top-end places, of which there are few, are for the most part equal to what you would expect from a top-end place in the West. Prices are elevated as much as five times higher for non-CIS citizens.

A fledgling B&B association was started by the woman who runs **Dudutki** (p89; www .ruralbelarus.by).

## ACTIVITIES
In winter, Kastrychnitskaja ploshcha is turned into a public ice-skating rink, and you can rent skates for under US$5 (bring your passport).

Belarus is flat, but it's not so flat that you can't find some places to enjoy skiing. About 20km from Minsk is the Raubichy Olympic Sports Complex, where you can enjoy some great cross-country skiing, while downhill

skiing and snowboarding is possible at **Logoisk** ( ☎ 0177453758, 53 000; www.logoisk.by, not in English) and the newer **Silichy** ( ☎ 0177450285; www.silichy.by, not in English), both about 30km from Minsk. Belintourist (p82) does skiing and other activity-related tours.

## BUSINESS HOURS
Lunch is usually for an hour and anytime between noon and 2pm. Offices are generally open 9am to 6pm during the work week, with banks closing at 5pm. Shops are open from about 9am or 10am to about 9pm Monday to Saturday, closing on Sunday around 6pm (if they're open at all that day). Restaurants and bars usually open around 10am and, with unfortunately few exceptions, close between 10pm and midnight.

## EMBASSIES & CONSULATES
### Belarusian Embassies & Consulates
Belarusian embassies abroad include the following (if your country doesn't have a Belarusian mission, contact the nearest one to you). If you are trying to get a visa in a neighbouring country, see that country's chapter in this book for Belarus embassy information.

**Canada** ( ☎ 613-233 9994; canada@belembassy.org; 130 Albert St, ste 600, Ottawa, Ontario K1P 5G4)

**France** ( ☎ 01 44 14 69 79; www.france.belembassy .org/; 38 blvd Suchet, 75016 Paris)

**Germany** Berlin ( ☎ 030-536 359 0; www.belarus -botschaft.de; Am Treptower Park 31, 12435); Bonn ( ☎ 0228-20 113 10; www.belarus-botschaft.de; Fritz-Schaeffer Str 20, 53113)

**Japan** ( ☎ 813-34 48 16 23; www.belarus.jp; 4-14-12 Shirogane, Shirogane K House, Minato-ku 108 0072, Tokyo)

**Latvia** Riga ( ☎ 371 732 3411; fax 371 732 2891; latvia@belembassy.org; Jezusbaznicas iela 12, 1050); Daugavpils ( ☎ 371 541 0086; fax 371 541 0883; email latvia@belembassy.org; 18th November street 44, 5403)

**Lithuania** ( ☎ 370 5 213 2255; fax 370 5 233 0626; consulate@belarus.lt; ul Muitines 41, 03113 Vilnius)

**Poland** Warsaw ( ☎ 48 22 742 0710; fax 48 22 842 4341; poland@belembassy.org; ul Wiertnicza 58, 02-952, Warsaw); Bialystok ( ☎ 48 85 744 5501; fax 48 85 744 6661; konsulatblrbialystok@sitech.pl; ul Elektryczna 9, 15-080); Gdansk ( ☎ 48 58 341 0026, 341 8088; fax 48 58 341 4026; gdansk@belembassy.org; ul Waly Piastowski 1, pok 905, 80-958)

**Russia** Moscow ( ☎ 7 095 624 7095; fax 7 095 628 7813; consular@embassybel.ru; Armyanskii per., dom 6, 101990); St Petersburg ( ☎ 7 812 273 0078; fax 7 812 273

BELARUS

4164; st_petersburg@belembassy.org; 8/46 Naberezhnaya Robespiera, kv 66)
**South Africa** ( ☎ 2712-430 76 64; sa@belembassy.org; 327 Hill St, Arcadia, Pretoria 0083)
**Sweden** ( ☎ 8-731 5744; www.belembassy.org/sweden; Herserudsvagen 5, 4 tr. 181 34 Lidingö/Stockholm)
**The Netherlands** ( ☎ 070-3631566; www.witrusland .com; Anna Paulownastraat 34, 2518 BE, Den Haag)
**UK** ( ☎ 020-7938 3677; www.belembassy.org/uk; 6 Kensington Court, London W8 5DL)
**Ukraine** ( ☎ 38 044 537 5203; www.belembassy.org.ua; ulitsa M Kotsyubinskogo, dom 3, 01031, Kyiv)
**USA** ( ☎ 212-682-5392; www.belarusconsul.org; 708 Third Ave, 21st fl, New York, NY 10017)

### Embassies & Consulates in Belarus

There is no representation for Canada, Australia, New Zealand or The Netherlands. Unless otherwise indicated, the listed missions are in Minsk.
**France** ( ☎ 017-210 2868; www.ambafrance-by.org; ploshcha Svabody 11)
**Germany** ( ☎ 017-217 5900; www.minsk.diplo.de; vulitsa Zakharava 26)
**Japan** ( ☎ 017-203 6037; fax 210 2169; 7th fl, praspekt Peramozhtsau 1)
**Moldova** ( ☎ 017-289 1441; vulitsa Belarusskaja 2)
**Romania** ( ☎ 017-203 8097; pereulok Moskvina 4)
**Russia** Minsk ( ☎ 017-222 4985; fax 250 3664; vulitsa Gvardeiskaja 5a); Brest ( ☎ 0162-23 78 42; fax 0162-22 2473; brestcons@brest.by; vulitsa Pushkinskaja 10)
**UK** ( ☎ 017-210 5920; www.britishembassy.gov.uk /belarus; vulitsa Karla Marxa 37)
**Ukraine** Minsk ( ☎ /fax 017-283 1958; vulitsa Staravilenskaja 51); Brest ( ☎ 0162-23 75 26; vulitsa Pushkinskaja 16/1)
**USA** ( ☎ 017-210 1283; http://minsk.usembassy.gov; vulitsa Staravilenskaja 46)

### FESTIVALS & EVENTS

The night of 6 July is a celebration with pagan roots called **Kupalye**, when young girls gather flowers and throw them into a river as a method of fortune-telling, and everyone else sits by lake or riverside fires drinking beer.

Another festival worth checking out is **Bely Zamak** (White Castle; alterego@tut.by), usually held at the end of March in Maladzechna, 80km from Minsk. It's a medieval-themed festival, where costumed folk engage in tournaments and contests.

### GAY & LESBIAN TRAVELLERS

Homosexuality is not tolerated in Belarus. Officially, the government retains a confron-
tational and intolerant attitude towards gays and lesbians; Belarusian state TV even uses the image of two men kissing as part of its repertoire of 'scare' tactics to encourage xenophobia. There are a few gay-friendly clubs such as Babylon (p86), but no official ones. Gay websites have been blocked on Belarusian servers, and most people keep their orientation largely a secret.

### HOLIDAYS

**New Year's Day** 1 January
**Orthodox Christmas** 7 January
**International Women's Day** 8 March
**Constitution Day** 15 March
**Catholic & Orthodox Easter** March/April
**Labour Day** (May Day) 1 May
**Victory Day** 9 May
**Independence Day** 3 July
**Dzyady** (Day of the Dead) 2 November
**Day of the October Revolution** 7 November
**Catholic Christmas** 25 December

Note that Independence Day is the date Minsk was liberated from the Nazis, not the date of independence from the USSR, which is not celebrated.

### INSURANCE

All visitors to Belarus are required to possess medical insurance from an approved company to cover the entire period of their stay. It is probably unlikely you will ever be asked for it. If your coverage is not accepted, insurance is also sold at entry points and is relatively cheap; see www.belarusconsul.org for costs and details. Note that medical coverage is not required for holders of transit visas (see opposite).

### LANGUAGE

Belarusian is closely related to both Russian and Ukrainian. Today Russian dominates nearly all aspects of social life and has been the second official language since 1995. There is little state support for keeping Belarusian alive and flourishing. While much of the signage is in Belarusian (street signs, inside train and bus stations), usage is indiscriminate, and speaking it in public attracts attention. There is a small but strong and growing group of student nationalists who are working to support the use of Belarusian, and it is now considered to be the country's language of the intellectual elite.

## MONEY

Belarusian roubles are sometimes dotingly referred to as *zaichiki* (rabbits), as the one-rouble note, first issued in 1992, featured a leaping rabbit. The bunny money's wide spectrum of bill denominations is overwhelming to the newcomer (there are 10s, 20s, 50s, 100s, 500s, 1000s, 5000s, 10,000s, 20,000s and 50,000s). Thank god there are no coins.

ATMs and currency-exchange offices are not hard to find in Belrusian cities. Major credit cards are accepted at many of the nicer hotels, restaurants, and supermarkets in Minsk, but travellers cheques are not worth the effort. Some businesses quote prices in euros or US dollars (using the abbreviation YE), but payment is only accepted in BR.

## POST

The word for post office is *pashtamt*. Posting a 20g letter within Belarus costs US$0.08, to Russia US$0.17 and to any other country US$0.28. Airmail costs US$0.42. The best way to mail important, time-sensitive items is with the Express Mail Service (EMS), offered at most main post offices.

## TELEPHONE & FAX

Although many if not most businesses here use mobile numbers for contact with the public, numbers listed here are land phones; if a mobile number is given, you'll see the three digits listed before the main number.

Avoid using payphones in Belarus; they require special phonecards and are a hassle. It's better to find the local Beltelekom, a state-run company that opens late. You can access the internet, place international and domestic calls, and send and receive faxes at these offices. Domestic calls cost less than US$0.01 per minute within a city, and about US$0.03 per minute to elsewhere in the country. International calls are much cheaper after 9pm and on weekends and holidays (to the UK it's US$0.28 per minute, to the USA US$0.32, and to Canada US$0.39).

To dial a Minsk land-line number from a Minsk land line number, just dial the number;

**EMERGENCY NUMBERS**

- Ambulance ☎ 03
- Fire brigade ☎ 01
- Police ☎ 02

from a local mobile phone, press £ or ☎ 8 017 or ☎ +375 17 and then dial the number.

To dial from one Minsk mobile number to another, dial ☎ 8 029 for Velcom, MTS and Diallog (the most common providers) or ☎ 8 025 for BeST.

To make an intercity call from a land phone, dial ☎ 8 (wait for the tone), the city's area code (including the 0) and the number; from a mobile, do the same, and if it doesn't work, try dialling ☎ +375 and the area code without the 0, then the number.

To make an international call from a land phone, dial 8 (wait for the tone) 10, then the country code, area code and number; from a mobile, press + then dial the country code, area code and number.

If your local mobile phone is on roaming, call a Belarusian land line by dialling ☎ +375 and the area code without the 0; to call a Belarusian mobile, dial ☎ +375 29 and the number (or ☎ +375 25 for calls to BeST phones).

To phone Belarus from abroad, dial ☎ 375 followed by the city code (without the first zero) and number.

For operator inquiries, call ☎ 085 (it's serviced 24 hours); a few of the staff speak English.

It's not possible to get a prepaid SIM card – probably just another way to keep the flow of information in Lukashenko's hands – just a contract one. To get a contract, you need to bring your passport and visa registration to the provider. Some foreigners have a Belarusian friend get the SIM card for them to avoid getting their passport involved. There are now a few providers in Belarus, but by far the most common is **Velcom** ( ☎ 222 4901; www .velcom.by; Melnikayte 14; ☻ 9am-9pm). A basic package starts at about US$3.50 a month after a one-time US$7 activation fee; local calls cost US$0.05 to US$0.20 per minute.

## VISAS

Belarusian visa regulations *change frequently,* so check with your embassy first. The Belarusian US embassy website, at www.belarusembassy.org, stays pretty up to date.

### Who Needs One

All Western visitors need a visa, and arranging one before you arrive is essential. Point-of-entry visas are only issued at the Minsk-2 international airport, but you still need to get an invitation in advance. (People do it

**BELARUS**

---

**AT YOUR OWN RISK**

As we went to press, there was effectively no border between Russia and Belarus. In theory, it's possible to enter Belarus by train and leave it for Russia – or go to Russia and back from Belarus – without going through passport control, and therefore without needing a visa for the country you're sneaking into. However, a hotel won't take you without a visa, so you'd have to stay with friends or rent an apartment, and if your visa-less documents are checked on the street (unlikely unless you're a trouble-maker or a person of colour), you will be deported.

---

this way, usually without trouble, but if the authorities decide to deny your application, what then? Better to do it in advance.)

Citizens of 13 countries, including UK, Canada and South Africa, do not need an invitation to receive a tourist visa; they merely need to complete an application and submit a photo at a Belarusian embassy or consulate (visit www .belarusembassy.org for more details).

## Applications

To get a visa, you will need a photograph, an invitation from a private person or a business, or a confirmation of reservation from a hotel, and your passport. There are three main types of visas: tourist, issued if you have a tourist invitation or hotel reservation voucher; visitor (guest), if your invitation comes from an individual; and business, if your invitation is from a business. There are also transit visas, if you are passing through and won't be in the country for more than 48 hours. Visitor and tourist visas are issued for 30 days (tourist visas can be multi-entry); business visas are for 90 days and can also be multi-entry.

By far the simplest – although the most expensive – way to get a visa is to apply through a travel agency. Alternatively, you can take a faxed confirmation from your hotel to the nearest Belarusian embassy and apply for one yourself.

Tallinn, Rīga and Vilnius have numerous travel agencies specialising in Belarusian visas. In Vilnius, the most convenient point to jump off, try **Viliota** ( ☎ 370 5-265 2238; www.viliota.lt, in Lithuanian; Basanaviciaus gatvė 15), where you can get

a visa hassle-free with a photo of yourself and between US$50 and US$100.

Getting an invitation from an individual can be a long, complex process. Your friend in Belarus needs a *zaprashenne* (official invitation) form from their local passport and visa office and should then send it to you. With this, you apply at the nearest Belarusian embassy.

Visa costs vary depending on the embassy you apply at and your citizenship. Americans pay more, but typically single-entry visas cost about US$50 for five working-days service and US$90 for next-day service; double-entry visas usually cost double that. Business visas are more expensive than tourist visas. Transit visas typically cost from US$20 to US$35.

## Registration

If you are staying in the country for more than 72 hours, you must have your visa officially registered. Hotels do this automatically, sometimes for a small fee. They'll give you small pieces of paper with stamps on them, which you keep to show to customs agents upon departure if asked. In theory you'll be fined if you don't provide proof of registration for every day of your stay; in practice, proof of one day is good enough.

If you've received a personal invitation, you'll need to find the nearest *passportno-vizovoye upravleniye* (passport and visa department; PVU, formerly OVIR) or try to convince hotel staff to register your visa for the cost of one night's stay. The **PVU main office** ( ☎ 017-231 9174; vulitsa Nezalezhnastsi 8) is in Minsk.

## Transit Visas

All persons passing through Belarusian territory are required to possess a transit visa, which can be obtained at any Belarusian consulate upon presentation of travel tickets clearly showing the final destination as being outside of Belarus. The possession of a valid Russian

---

**HIDE THIS BOOK**

Lonely Planet's coverage of Belarusian politics has been honest and ongoing enough to warrant attention from the authorities. Before letting you go on your way, customs officials may politely take your LP guidebook from you if they happen to see it. Just keep it out of sight, and for Pyotr's sake, don't list it on your customs form.

visa is not enough to serve as a transit visa. Transit visas are not available at the border.

# TRANSPORT IN BELARUS

## GETTING THERE & AWAY
### Air
There is no departure tax in Belarus. See p87 for information Minsk airport. In Eastern Europe, Belarus' national airline **Belavia** (code B2; ☎ 210 4100; www.belavia.by; vulitsa Njamiha 14).

The following are the main international airlines with offices in Minsk.

**Aeroflot** (code SU; ☎ 017-227 2887; www.aeroflot.com /eng)

**Austrian Airlines** (code OS; ☎ 017-289 1970; www .austrianair.com)

**El Al** (code LY; ☎ 017-279 1939; www.elal.co.il)

**LOT Polish Airlines** (code LO; ☎ 017-226 6628; www .lot.com)

**Lufthansa** (code LH; ☎ 017-284 7129; www.lufthansa .com)

### Land
#### TRAIN
Train is usually a more comfortable way to travel than bus; to Vilnius, the *electrichka* (electric train) to Vilnius is cheap and quick ($7, four hours).

#### BORDER CROSSINGS
Long queues at border crossings are not uncommon. The most frequently used bus crossings are those on the quick four-hour trip between Vilnius (Lithuania) and Minsk, and the seven-hour trip between Minsk and Bialystok (Poland). Buses stop at the border for customs and passport controls.

#### CAR & MOTORCYCLE
If you're driving your own vehicle, there are 10 main road routes into Belarus via border stations, through which foreigners can pass. International driving permits are recognised in Belarus. Roads in Belarus are predictably bad, but main highways are decent. On intercity road trips, fill up when existing the city; fuel stations may be scant before you hit the next big town.

## GETTING AROUND
There are no flights between Brest and Minsk.

**Avis** ( ☎ 017-234 7990; belideal@avis.solo.by; vulitsa Staravilenskaja 15, Minsk) rents cars and even drivers for between US$60 and US$120 per day from Hotel Belarus (p85) in Minsk; English is spoken.

Hitching is practiced by young locals quite a bit. But it's never entirely safe in any country in the world, and Lonely Planet doesn't recommend it.

The Brest–Minsk highway (Brestskoye shosse; E30/M1) is an excellent two-laner, but have a supply of new US$1 bills for the frequent tollbooths (they only charge cars with foreign licence plates).

With spare parts rare, road conditions rugged and getting lost inevitable, driving or riding in Belarus is undeniably problematic, but is always an adventure and the best way to really see the country. Know that signs are almost always in Cyrillic.

Drivers from the USA or EU can use their own country's driving licence for six months. Cars drive in the right-hand lane, children 12 and under must sit in a back seat, and your blood-alcohol should be no higher than 0%. Fuel is usually not hard to find, but try to keep your tank full, and it would even be wise to keep some spare fuel as well.

You will be instructed by signs to slow down when approaching GAI (road police) stations, and not doing so is a sure-fire way to get a substantial fine. You may see GAI signs in Russian (ГАИ) or in Belarusian (ДАЙ).

BELARUS

# Bosnia & Hercegovina

Once known for tragic reasons, Bosnia and Hercegovina now features in travel plans as people realise what this country has to offer: age-old cultures, stunning mountain landscapes, access to the great outdoors and a sense of adventure. This most easterly point of the West and the most westerly point of the East bears the imprint of two great empires. Five hundred years of domination, first by the Turks and then briefly by the Austria-Hungarians, have inexorably influenced the culture and architecture of this land.

In Sarajevo, minarets, onion-shaped domes and campaniles jostle for the sky in a town where Muslims, Jews, Orthodox Christians and Catholics once lived in harmony. Alluring Baščaršija is a jumble of cobbled laneways spanning centuries of activity. Here workshops for ancient crafts are mixed in with cafés, souvenir shops, and trendy bars. There's also plenty to lure visitors away from the capital. Mostar's Old Bridge has been rebuilt and daring young men now plunge from its heights to amuse the tourists. Small Jajce delights with its medieval citadel and waterfall while Međugorje attracts thousands to its Virgin Mary apparition site.

Most likely it'll be in adventure sports where Bosnia and Hercegovina will make its name. Already its major rivers are rafted and kayaked and its mountains are skied, climbed and hiked over, and as more out-of-the-way areas are made safe this country could easily become the year-round adventure centre of Eastern Europe.

**BOSNIA & HERCEGOVINA**

## FAST FACTS

- **Area** 51,129 sq km
- **Capital** Sarajevo
- **Currency** convertible mark (KM); A$1 = 1.16KM; €1 = 1.96KM; ¥100 = 1.38KM; NZ$1 = 0.96KM; UK£1 = 2.84KM; US$1= 1.55KM
- **Famous for** the bridge at Mostar, 1984 Winter Olympics
- **Official Languages** Bosniak, Croatian and Serbian
- **Phrases** *zdravo* (hello), *hvala* (thanks), *molim* (please), *dovidjenja* (goodbye)
- **Population** 3.85 million (2003 estimate)
- **Telephone Codes** country code ☎ 387; international access code ☎ 00
- **Visas** none required for citizens of the EU, Australia, Canada, Croatia, Japan, South Korea, New Zealand, Norway, Russia, Serbia, Montenegro, Switzerland and the USA; see p130

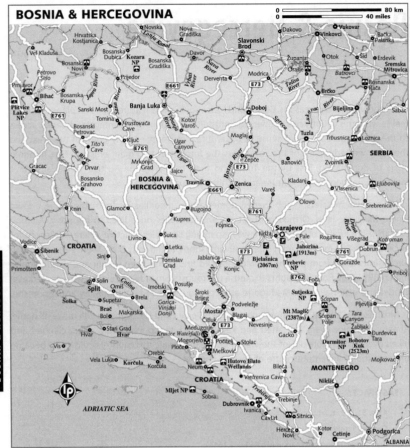

## HIGHLIGHTS

- Take coffee with the locals in the old Turkish quarter of **Sarajevo** (p109).
- Watch the locals jump off Mostar's **Stari Most** (p119).
- Window-gaze on the **train** (p121) from Mostar to Sarajevo as it climbs the mountains via tunnels, viaducts and switchbacks.
- Raft the rolling Una River through gorges near **Bihać** (p127).
- Witness the pilgrims to **Medugorje** (p122), site of the Virgin Mary apparitions.

## ITINERARIES

- **One week** Arrive in Mostar from coastal Croatia, roam the old town and take a side trip to Medugorje before heading north to Sarajevo. Visitors often linger in Sarajevo, which could push this itinerary to 10 days.
- **Two weeks** As above, but stay longer in Sarajevo, taking an organised tour into the mountains and visiting Travnik and Jajce on day tours. Bihać should certainly be on the itinerary for some rafting. Continue on to Serbia and Montenegro via Banja Luka or by train from Sarajevo to Budapest.

## CLIMATE & WHEN TO GO

Bosnia and Hercegovina has a mix of Mediterranean and central European climates: it gets hot in summer but quite chilly in winter,

---

**WARNING: LAND MINES**

Hundreds of thousands of mines and unexploded ordnance make for danger wherever there were lines of confrontation, be it countryside or suburb. There is a continuing programme to clear away all these dangers but it will take many years.

The golden rules are: don't enter war-damaged and abandoned buildings; stay away from taped-off areas; keep away from places not used by local people; and use guides or go on organised tours when walking in the countryside.

What's safe? With the exception of war-damaged buildings, all highly populated areas, national parks and any area where there's strong evidence of people activity.

Only the experts have a full idea of where danger areas might be. If in doubt, contact Sarajevo's **Mine Action Centre** ( ☎ 033-253 800; www.bhmac.org; Zmaja od Bosne 8, Sarajevo; ☷ 8am-4pm Mon-Fri).

---

especially at elevations where snowfall can last until April.

The best time to visit is from May to September; skiers should come between December and February. Sarajevo temperatures range from minus 2°C in winter up to 27°C in July and August. Temperatures in the south will be several degrees warmer.

## HISTORY

Bosnia has been a cultural cocktail from the beginning. People from all over the world – including Italy, Spain, Africa, Asia Minor, Syria, Egypt and Palestine – have at various times populated the areas of Dalmatia and Bosnia and Hercegovina. The region's ancient inhabitants were Illyrians, followed by the Romans who settled around the mineral springs at Ilidža near Sarajevo in AD 9. When the Roman Empire was divided in AD 395, the Drina River, today the border with Serbia, became the line dividing the Western Roman Empire from Byzantium.

The Slavs arrived in the late 6th and early 7th centuries. In 960 the region became independent of Serbia, only to pass through the hands of other conquerors: Croatia, Byzantium, Duklja (modern-day Montenegro) and Hungary. Bosnia's medieval history is a much-debated subject, mainly because different groups have tried to claim authenticity and territorial rights on the basis of their interpretation of the country's religious make-up before the arrival of the Turks. During this period (1180–1463) Bosnia and Hercegovina became one of the most powerful states in the Western Balkans. The most significant event was the expansion of the Bosnian state under Stephen Kotromanić who conquered large parts of the Dalmatian coast and in 1326 annexed the southern province of Hercegovina.

The country thus became Bosnia and Hercegovina for the first time.

The first Turkish raids came in 1383 and by 1463 Bosnia was a Turkish province with Sarajevo as its capital. Hercegovina is named after Herceg (Duke) Stjepan Vukčić, who ruled the southern part of the present republic from his mountain-top castle at Blagaj, near Mostar, until the Turkish conquest in 1482.

Bosnia and Hercegovina was assimilated into the Ottoman Empire during the 400 years of Turkish rule. Islamicisation largely took place during the initial 150 years of Turkish rule and it's generally held that people converted voluntarily. Orthodox and Catholic Christians continued to practise their religions although under certain constraints.

As the Ottoman Empire declined elsewhere in the 16th and 17th centuries, the Turks strengthened their hold on Bosnia and Hercegovina as a bulwark against attack. Sparked

**BOSNIA & HERCEGOVINA**

**HOW MUCH?**

- **Short taxi ride** 5KM
- **Internet access** 3KM per hour
- **Coffee** 1KM
- **Slug of šlivovica** 1.50KM
- **Movie ticket** 3.50KM

**LONELY PLANET INDEX**

- **Litre of petrol** 1.79KM
- **Litre of water** 2KM
- **Half-litre of beer** 2KM
- **Souvenir T-shirt** from 12KM
- **Street snack (burek)** 1.50KM

by the newly born idea of nationhood, the South Slavs rose against their Turkish occupiers in 1875–6.

In 1878 Russia inflicted a crushing defeat on Turkey in a war over Bulgaria and at the subsequent Congress of Berlin it was determined that Austria-Hungary would occupy Bosnia and Hercegovina despite the population's wish for autonomy.

The Austria-Hungarians pushed Bosnia and Hercegovina into the modern age with industrialisation, the development of coal mining and the building of railways and infrastructure. Ivo Andrić's *Bridge over the Drina* succinctly describes these changes in the town of Višegrad.

But political unrest was on the rise. Previously, Bosnian Muslims, Catholics and Orthodox Christians had only differentiated themselves from each other in terms of religion. But with the rise of nationalism in the mid-19th century, Bosnia's Catholic and Orthodox population started to identify themselves with neighbouring Croatia or Serbia respectively. At the same time, resentment against foreign occupation intensified and young people across the sectarian divide started cooperating with each other and working against the Austria-Hungarians, thus giving birth to the idea of 'Yugoslavism' (land of the southern Slavs).

Resentment against occupation intensified in 1908 when Austria annexed Bosnia and Hercegovina outright. The assassination of the Habsburg heir Archduke Franz Ferdinand by a Bosnian Serb, Gavrilo Princip, in Sarajevo on 28 June 1914 led Austria to declare war on Serbia. Russia and France supported Serbia, and Germany backed Austria, and soon the world was at war. These alliances still resonate today, with the Russians and French being seen as pro-Serb, and Austrians and Germans as pro-Croat.

Following WWI Bosnia and Hercegovina was absorbed into the Serb-dominated Kingdom of the Serbs, Croats and Slovenes, which was renamed Yugoslavia in 1929.

After Yugoslavia's capitulation to Germany in 1941, Bosnia and Hercegovina was annexed by the newly created fascist Croatian state. The Croatian *Ustaše* (fascists), who ruled for the Nazis, mimicked their masters in persecuting and murdering Croatia's and Bosnia's Jewish population, and persecuting the Serbs.

The Serbs responded with two resistance movements: the *Četniks* led by the royalist Dražva Mihajlovič and the communist 'Partisans' headed by Josip Broz Tito. The two groups managed to put up quite an effective resistance to the Germans, but long-term cooperation was impossible due to conflicting ideologies.

After WWII Bosnia and Hercegovina was granted republic status within Tito's Yugoslavia. After Tito fell out with the USSR in 1954 and the country cofounded the 'nonaligned movement', constraints on religious practices were eased but the problem of nationality remained. Bosnia's Muslims had to declare themselves as either Serbs or Croats until 1971, when 'Muslim' was declared to be a distinct nationality.

In the republic's first free elections in November 1990, the communists were easily defeated by nationalist Serb and Croat parties and a predominantly Muslim party favouring a multiethnic country. The Croat and Muslim parties joined forces against Serb nationalists, and independence from Yugoslavia was declared on 15 October 1991. The Serb parliamentarians withdrew and set up their own government at Pale, 20km east of Sarajevo. Bosnia and Hercegovina was recognised internationally and admitted to the UN, but talks between the parties broke down.

## The War

War commenced in April 1992. Bosnian Serbs began seizing territory aided by their inheritance of most of the Yugoslav National Army's weapons, and Sarajevo came under siege by Serb irregulars on 5 April 1992. Bosnian Serbian forces then began a campaign of brutal 'ethnic cleansing', expelling Muslims from northern and eastern Bosnia and Hercegovina to create a 300km corridor joining Serb ethnic areas in the west with Serbia.

The West's reaction to the increasingly bloody war in Bosnia was confused and erratic. The pictures of victims found in concentration camps in northern Bosnia in August 1992 finally brought home the extent to which Bosnian Muslims in particular were being mistreated.

In June 1992 the UN authorised the use of force to ensure the delivery of humanitarian aid; 7500 UN troops were sent but this UN Protection Force (Unprofor) proved notoriously impotent.

Ethnic partition seemed increasingly probable. The Croats wanted their own share and in early 1993 fighting erupted between the Muslims and Croats; the latter instigated a deadly siege of the Muslim quarter of Mostar, culminating in the destruction of Mostar's historic bridge in 1993.

Even as fighting between Muslims and Croats intensified, NATO finally began to take action against the Bosnian Serbs. A Serbian mortar attack on a Sarajevo market in February 1994 left 68 dead, and US fighters belatedly began enforcing a no-fly zone over Bosnia and Hercegovina by shooting down four Serb aircraft.

Meanwhile the USA pressured the Bosnian government to join the Bosnian Croats in a federation. Soon after, Croatia joined the offensive against the Serbs, overrunning Croatian Serb positions and towns in Croatia in 1995. With Croatia now heavily involved, a pan-Balkan war seemed closer than ever.

Again, Bosnian Serb tanks and artillery attacked Sarajevo. When NATO air strikes to protect Bosnian 'safe areas' were finally authorised, the Serbs captured 300 Unprofor peacekeepers and chained them to potential targets to keep the planes away.

In July 1995 Unprofor's impotence was highlighted when Bosnian Serbs attacked the safe area of Srebrenica, slaughtering an estimated 7500 Muslim men as they fled through the forest. This horrendous massacre was only publicly acknowledged by Bosnian Serbs in 2004.

The end of Bosnian Serb military dominance was near as European leaders loudly called for action. Croatia renewed its own internal offensive, expelling at least 150,000 Serbs from the Krajina region of Croatia.

With Bosnian Serbs battered by two weeks of NATO air strikes in September 1995, US President Bill Clinton's proposal for a peace conference in Dayton, Ohio, USA was accepted.

### The Dayton Agreement

The Dayton Agreement stipulated that the country would retain its pre-war external boundaries, but be composed of two parts. The Federation of Bosnia and Hercegovina (the Muslim and Croat portion) would administer 51% of the country, which included Sarajevo, while the Serb Republic, Republika Srpska (RS), would administer the other 49%.

The agreement emphasised the rights of refugees (1.2 million in other countries, and one million displaced within Bosnia and Hercegovina itself) to return to their pre-war homes. A NATO-led peace implementation force became the Stabilisation Force (SFOR), which was replaced by Eufor (an EU force) in 2005.

### After Dayton

Threatened sanctions forced Radovan Karadžić to step down from the RS presidency in July 1996 and Biljana Plavsić, his successor, split from his hardline policy and moved the capital to Banja Luka in January 1998.

A relatively liberal Bosnian Serb prime minister Milorad Dodik pushed several Dayton-compliant measures through the RS parliament, including common passports, car licence plates and a new currency called the convertible mark (KM). Dodik lasted until November 2000, when he failed to be re-elected to power.

Recent EU and American policy has been to centralise government, which is a development away from the separate powers concept of the Dayton Agreement. A result is that Bosnia and Hercegovina now has a unified army; meanwhile in the RS the Serb socialist party has taken power and booted out the nationalist politicians.

The Dayton Agreement also emphasised the powers of the Hague-based International Court of Justice and authorised the arrest of indicted war criminals. Minor players have

**THE TWO ENTITIES OF BOSNIA & HERCEGOVINA**

Republika Srpska (Serbs)

Federation of Bosnia & Hercegovina (Muslims & Croats)

Prijedor · Posavina Corridor

Bihać · Sanski Most · Banja Luka · Brčko

SERBIA

Tuzla

Jajce

Travnik

CROATIA

SARAJEVO · Pale

Goražde

Split

Mostar · Medugorje

MONTENEGRO

A D R I A T I C   S E A

Dubrovnik

ALBANIA

BOSNIA & HERCEGOVINA

---

**MEETING & GREETING**

Removing your shoes is usual in Muslim households and your host will offer you slippers. When greeting acquaintances in Sarajevo or elsewhere in the Federation, it is customary to plant one kiss on each cheek. In the RS, three kisses (one-one-one) is the norm.

---

been arrested but the two most-wanted – Bosnian Serb leader Radovan Karadžić and his military henchman Ratko Mladić – remain at large. Several hunts for them have ended in embarrassing failure, allegedly because of tip-offs.

Bosnia and Hercegovina still remains divided along ethnic lines, but tensions have ebbed. More people are now crossing between the RS and the Federation and more refugees are returning home.

## PEOPLE

According to the 1991 census, Bosnia and Hercegovina's pre-war population was around 4.5 million. Today it's estimated at less than 4 million. No subsequent census has been taken and massive population shifts have changed the size of many cities. The population of Banja Luka grew by over 100,000 through absorbing many Croatian Serb refugees, and initially Sarajevo and Mostar shrank, although the former has been growing again.

Serbs, Croats and Bosnian Muslims are all of the same ethnic stock and physically indistinguishable. The pre-war population was incredibly mixed with intermarriage common, but ethnic cleansing has concentrated Croats in Hercegovina (to the south and west), Muslims in Sarajevo and central Bosnia and Hercegovina, and Serbs in the north and east.

Inhabitants are known as Bosnian Serbs, Bosnian Croats or Bosniaks (Muslims).

## RELIGION

The division of Europe between Catholicism and Orthodoxy placed a fracture line straight through Bosnia and Hercegovina. The west fell under the aegis of Rome and became Roman Catholic while the east looked to Constantinople and the Orthodox Church.

In between was the home-grown Bosnian Church that prospered in the early Middle Ages; when the Ottoman Turks invaded, many of these adherents converted to Islam, probably in a trade-off to retain civil privileges.

At the end of the 15th century Spain and Portugal evicted its Jews, who were offered a home by the Turks in Bosnia and Hercegovina, thus adding a fourth religion.

Today, about 40% of the population is Muslim, 31% is Orthodox, 15% Roman Catholic, 4% Protestant and 10% other religions. Most Bosnian Serbs are Orthodox and most Bosnian Croats are Catholic.

Across Bosnia and Hercegovina churches and mosques are being built (or rebuilt) at lightning speed. Many mosques have been funded by Saudi Arabia and there are local concerns that extreme (and alien) forms of Islam are being introduced into what is a generally secular Muslim society.

## ARTS

Sarajevo, in the old Yugoslavia, was the cultural capital of the federation. The wars put an end to that with participants fleeing back to their home republics or emigrating, and, consequently, the arts scene is taking time to recover.

Bosnia's best-known writer is Ivo Andrić (1892–1975), winner of the 1961 Nobel Prize for Literature. His novels *The Travnik Chronicles* and *Bridge over the Drina* are fictional histories dealing with the intermingling of Islamic and Orthodox societies in the small Bosnian towns of Travnik and Višegrad.

Bosnia and Hercegovina has excelled in film. Danis Tanović won an Oscar in 2002 for his film *No Man's Land* portraying the relationship between two soldiers, one Serbian, the other Muslim, caught alone in the same trench while Sarajevo was under siege. The early films of Sarajevo-born Emir Kusturica, such as *When Father was Away on Business* and *Do You Remember Dolly Bell?* deal with fraught family life in 1980s Bosnia, and rank among the director's best. The recent prize-winning *Set Free the Bears* and the comedic *Karaula* (Border Post) are well worth watching.

Jasmila Zbanic's *Grbavica* explores the trauma of a young girl discovering that her father was not a war martyr as she thought, but that she was conceived in a rape camp and how confrontation with that fact provides the first step in reconciliation with her mother. The film won the golden bear award at the 2006 Berlin Film Festival.

---

**PYRAMID SELLING**

An amateur Bosnian archaeologist, Semir Osmanagic, has amazed the world with claims that an ancient step pyramid lies beneath a Visočica hill 32km northwest of Sarajevo.

The 250m hill in question is evenly shaped, with 45-degree slopes and has corners facing north, east, south and west. Initial excavations have revealed a paved entrance patio, tunnel entrances and large stone slabs. Osmanagic says that his claims have been backed by aerial and satellite images and by an Egyptian expert in pyramid constructions.

If a pyramid is discovered, early European history could be rewritten as currently the only known pyramids are in Egypt and Latin America. Learned opponents claim that there was no civilisation around in prehistory with the skills to accurately shape a hill and then cover it with stone slabs. Regardless of the outcome, the shopkeepers of nearby Visoko are enjoying a small economic boom selling T-shirts, triangular pizzas and pyramid-shaped clocks.

---

Traditional Bosnian music is called *sevdah* and is often described as the 'Bosnian blues'. Sung in a heart-wrenching style, the lyrics are always about unhappy love. Pop and rock music have always been successful as has folk and, more recently, hip hop. Jazz is also highly popular with an annual festival in Sarajevo (p111).

The craft industry is well developed with artisans fashioning ornamental or practical items from copper and brass, and jewellery in gold and silver. All these items can be found in the lanes of Kujundžiluk (p118) in Mostar, and Baščaršija (p115) in Sarajevo.

## ENVIRONMENT

Bosnia and Hercegovina is a mountainous country of 51,129 sq km with only 8% of its land below 150m and with 30 mountain peaks between 1700m and 2386m; Mt Maglič, the highest, is on the border with Serbia. Just a toe of land connects it to the sea through Croatia.

The dry and arid south gives way to a central mountainous core before descending to green rolling hills and the northeast flatlands that form the edge of the Hungarian plain.

Limestone forms much of the uplands creating distinctive scenery with light-grey craggy hills, and caves. The rivers shine green and possess a clarity that's seldom seen elsewhere in Europe; with their potential for electricity generation they form part of the country's wealth. Most of them flow north into the Sava – only the Neretva cuts south from Jablanica through the Dinaric Alps to Ploče on the Adriatic Sea.

There are two main national parks. Unesco-protected Sutjeska still has remnants of a primeval forest going back 20,000 years,

while the Hutovo Blato wetlands are a prime sanctuary for migratory birds. About half the country, mostly the north, is forest, with beech at lower altitude giving way to fir trees higher up. Wildlife is found mainly in these forests: rabbits, foxes, weasels, otters, wild sheep, ibex, deer, lynxes, eagles, hawks and vultures. Bears and wolves are at higher altitudes.

Mines and unexploded ordnance put much of the country around the former battle zones out of reach, but visits with local guides are quite feasible. These leftovers from war, the infrastructure damage, air pollution from metallurgical plants and rubbish disposal are significant environmental problems for Bosnia and Hercegovina. Small organisations such as **Green Visions** (www.greenvisions.ba/gv/) battle to bring environmental issues into the public consciousness, but apathy, corruption and political pressures make this task very difficult.

## FOOD & DRINK
### Staples & Specialities

Bosnia's Turkish heritage is savoured in grilled meats such as *ćevapčići* (minced lamb or beef), *šnicla* (steak) and *kotleti* (rack of veal).

Stews are popular, often cooked slowly over an open fire, with favourites such as *bosanski lonac* (cabbage and meat stew) or *dinstana teletina sa povrćem* (veal and vegetable stew).

*Burek*, which is sold in *pekara* (bakery shops), is a substitute for a missed breakfast and comes filled either with *sir* (cheese), *meso* (meat) or *krompiruša* (potato). Snacks for vegetarians include *sirnica* (cheese pie) and *zeljanica* (spinach pie), and for full-blown meals there are stewed bean dishes and stuffed peppers or zucchini dishes.

The ubiquitous pizza and pasta props up the national cuisine and fish is readily available,

**BOSNIA & HERCEGOVINA**

especially trout from various fish farms on the nation's rivers.

For syrup-soaked desserts, try baklava or *tufahije* (an apple cake topped with walnuts and whipped cream). Many towns and villages produce their own type of cheese with the feta-like Travnik cheese being particularly well known.

A shot of *šlivovica* (plum brandy) or *loza* (grape brandy) makes a good aperitif or end to a meal.

The best wines come from Hercegovina and include Žilavka (white) and Blatina (red).

## Where to Eat & Drink

Cafés and restaurants offering traditional Bosnian food are plentiful, and in Mostar's old town and Sarajevo's Baščaršija you just have to follow your nose to find the nearest place offering *ćevapčići*. Bus stations are always good places for cheap snacks.

Alcohol is readily available even in Muslim areas and there are enough bars to constitute a good pub crawl in Mostar and Sarajevo.

Coffee is, however, the main social lubricant; people, mostly men, meet to sip their Bosnian coffee, smoke, play cards or just talk the world into some sort of order. The coffee is served in a long-handled small brass pot from which the precious black liquid is carefully decanted into thimble-sized cups. Two lumps of sugar are usually added or the lump is held in the teeth and the coffee sipped through it. A piece of Turkish delight completes the ritual.

## Vegetarians & Vegans

The emphasis on meat in the diet means that vegetarians and vegans are hard done by. However, traditional and top-end restaurants will have several vegetarian dishes, although a pure vegan might be challenged when eating trying to eat out.

# SARAJEVO

☎ 033 / pop 737,000

How can a people that has suffered so much produce a city of such vitality? This is a question you'll ask yourself time and time again as you explore Sarajevo. In the 1990s this was a city and people on the edge of annihilation, but today it has become a favourite traveller destination.

Sarajevo is a living museum of history. And boy, is there a lot of it! Mosques, churches, cathedrals and fine municipal buildings built by the Ottoman Turks and Austria-Hungarians; a bridge where world history took a fateful turn; and the Tunnel Museum, the yellow Holiday Inn, and the artillery-scarred Library as reminders of recent tragedy.

Sarajevo has charm: rattly old trams circle a city centre containing the Baščaršija bazaar, an ancient trading place with artisans' workshops, coffee drinking dens, restaurants, cosy bars and endless souvenir choices. Further west the Ottoman traces disappear and the city takes on its other guise of a proud Austro-Hungarian colonial capital.

There's a big-village atmosphere here making you immediately feel comfortable and part of what's going on from the outset; it's that elusive sense of belonging somewhere. So expect your travel plans to become *mañana* as a couple of days slip into a week or more.

You don't need to invest much energy in appreciating Sarajevo; it's a city that's easily covered on foot, and it has good public transport. Being a very open city there's a lot to see, and sitting down at a café in Baščaršija gives you a ringside seat on a rich theatre of life.

## HISTORY

While the region had its attractions for those who populated prehistory, it wasn't until the Romans arrived that Sarajevo gained a significant mention on the pages of history. Their legions, always on the lookout for a new bathhouse for 'R and R', founded the settlement Aquae Sulphurae around the sulphur springs at Ilidža.

Sarajevo then slipped back into obscurity until the Turks arrived in the mid-15th century and their governors set up house and stayed until 1878. The city then became an important market on the east–west trading routes, and during this time acquired its name, which originates from the Turkish *saraj* (palace).

The 'on the go' Austro-Hungarians, who replaced the fading Ottoman Empire, built railways that connected Sarajevo with the West. Sarajevo even had street lighting before Vienna – there were doubts about the safety of electricity and it was deemed wiser to first test it in the colonies. In 1914, Austro-Hungarian rule was effectively given notice on the Latin Bridge by the fatal pistol shot that killed Archduke Franz Ferdinand.

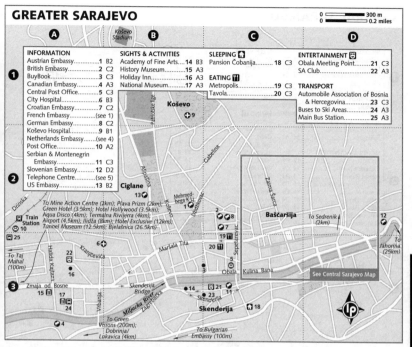

**GREATER SARAJEVO**

| INFORMATION | | SIGHTS & ACTIVITIES | | SLEEPING | | ENTERTAINMENT | |
|---|---|---|---|---|---|---|---|
| Austrian Embassy............1 B2 | | Academy of Fine Arts....14 B3 | | Pansion Čobanija.......... 18 C3 | | Obala Meeting Point........21 C3 | |
| British Embassy.................2 C2 | | History Museum...........15 A3 | | | | SA Club...........................22 A3 | |
| BuyBook.........................3 C3 | | Holiday Inn..................16 A3 | | EATING | | | |
| Canadian Embassy...........4 A3 | | National Museum..........17 A3 | | Metropolis....................19 C3 | | TRANSPORT | |
| Central Post Office...........5 C3 | | | | Tavola.........................20 C3 | | Automobile Association of Bosnia | |
| City Hospital...................6 B3 | | | | | | & Hercegovina..............23 C3 | |
| Croatian Embassy.............7 C2 | | | | | | Buses to Ski Areas...........24 A3 | |
| French Embassy.............(see 1) | | | | | | Main Bus Station............25 A3 | |
| German Embassy...............8 C2 | | | | | | | |
| Koševo Hospital...............9 B1 | | | | | | | |
| Netherlands Embassy.......(see 4) | | | | | | | |
| Post Office....................10 A2 | | | | | | | |
| Serbian & Montenegrin | | | | | | | |
| Embassy...................11 C3 | | | | | | | |
| Slovenian Embassy......... 12 D2 | | | | | | | |
| Telephone Centre...........(see 5) | | | | | | | |
| US Embassy....................13 B2 | | | | | | | |

Seventy years later, in 1984, Sarajevo again attracted world attention by hosting the 14th Winter Olympic Games. Then from 1992 to 1995 the infamous siege of the city grabbed the headlines and horrified the world. Ratko Mladić, the Bosnian Serb commander, is reported as having said, 'Shoot at slow intervals until I order you to stop. Shell them until they can't sleep, don't stop until they are on the edge of madness.'

Sarajevo's heritage of six centuries was pounded into rubble and the only access to the outside world was via a 1km tunnel under the airport. Over 10,500 Sarajevans died and 50,000 were wounded by Bosnian Serb sniper fire and shelling. The endless new graveyards near Koševo stadium are a silent record of those terrible years.

## ORIENTATION
Sarajevo is wedged into a valley created by the Miljacka River and flanked to the south by the mountains of Jahorina and Bjelašnica, host of the 1984 Winter Olympics.

From the airport, 6.5km southwest, the main road runs up to the suburb of Ilidža,

and then swings east through Novo Sarajevo. In doing so it passes the yellow Holiday Inn, home to journalists during the war, and becomes the section of road that gained notoriety as 'sniper alley'. The bus and train stations are to the north. Towards the town centre the road runs alongside the shallow Miljacka River, before leaving it at Baščaršija in the eastern end of town to swing around in a loop back towards the west.

Sedrenik, up on the northeastern side, gives a fine view of the city and mountains behind.

## INFORMATION
### Bookshops
**BuyBook** (www.buybook.ba) Radić eva (Map p107; ☎ 716 450; Radićeva 4; ◷ 9am-10pm Mon-Sat, 10am-6pm Sun); Zelenih Beretki (Map pp108-9; ☎ 712 000; Zelenih Beretki 8; ◷ 9am-11pm Mon-Sat, 10am-6pm Sun) Art, Balkans and coffee-table books, English-language newspapers and magazines, CDs and in-house cafés.

**Šahinpašić** (Map pp108-9; ☎ 220 111; Mula Mustafe Bašeskije 1; ◷ 9am-8pm Mon-Sat, 10am-2pm Sun) English-language newspapers, magazines, cheap English classics, maps and a stack of Lonely Planet guidebooks.

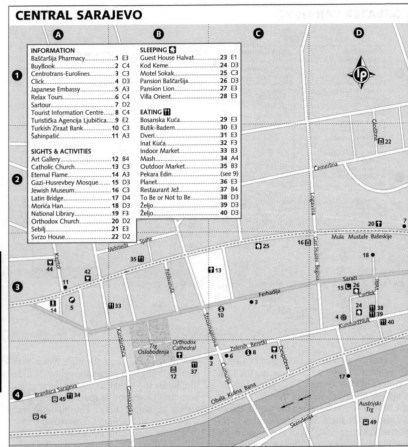

## CENTRAL SARAJEVO

**INFORMATION**
| | |
|---|---|
| Baščaršija Pharmacy | 1 E3 |
| BuyBook | 2 C4 |
| Centrotrans-Eurolines | 3 C3 |
| Click | 4 D3 |
| Japanese Embassy | 5 A3 |
| Relax Tours | 6 C4 |
| Sartour | 7 D2 |
| Tourist Information Centre | 8 C4 |
| Turistička Agencija Ljubičica | 9 E2 |
| Turkish Ziraat Bank | 10 C3 |
| Šahinpašić | 11 A3 |

**SIGHTS & ACTIVITIES**
| | |
|---|---|
| Art Gallery | 12 B4 |
| Catholic Church | 13 C3 |
| Eternal Flame | 14 A3 |
| Gazi-Husrevbey Mosque | 15 D3 |
| Jewish Museum | 16 C3 |
| Latin Bridge | 17 D4 |
| Morića Han | 18 D3 |
| National Library | 19 F3 |
| Orthodox Church | 20 D2 |
| Sebilj | 21 E3 |
| Svrzo House | 22 D2 |

**SLEEPING**
| | |
|---|---|
| Guest House Halvat | 23 E1 |
| Kod Keme | 24 D3 |
| Motel Sokak | 25 C3 |
| Pansion Baščaršija | 26 D3 |
| Pansion Lion | 27 E3 |
| Villa Orient | 28 E3 |

**EATING**
| | |
|---|---|
| Bosanska Kuća | 29 E3 |
| Butik-Badem | 30 E3 |
| Dveri | 31 E3 |
| Inat Kuća | 32 F3 |
| Indoor Market | 33 B3 |
| Mash | 34 A4 |
| Outdoor Market | 35 B3 |
| Pekara Edin | (see 9) |
| Planet | 36 E3 |
| Restaurant Jež | 37 B4 |
| To Be or Not to Be | 38 D3 |
| Željo | 39 D3 |
| Željo | 40 D3 |

## Internet Access
**Click** (Map pp108-9; ☎ 236 914; Kundurdžiluk 1; per hr 3KM; ☻ 9am-11pm) Nonsmoking.

## Laundry
**Turistička Agencija Ljubičica** (Map pp108-9; ☎ 232 109; Mula Mustafe Bašeskije 65; ☻ 8am-10pm Oct-Apr, 7am-11pm May-Sep)

## Left Luggage
**Main bus station** (Map p107; Put Života 8; 1st hr 2KM, then per hr 1KM) Useful while you go into town to look for accommodation.

## Medical Services
Ask your embassy for a list of private doctors or in an emergency try the following:

**Baščaršija Pharmacy** (Map pp108-9; ☎ 272 301; Obala Kulina Bana 40; ☻ 24hr)
**City Hospital** (Map p107; ☎ 291 100; Kranjčevića 12)
**Koševo Hospital** (Map p107; ☎ 445 522; Gradska Bolnička 25)

## Money
ATMs are sprinkled all over the city centre, accepting all varieties of debit cards. There's nowhere to change money at the bus or train station, but there is a Visa ATM outside the bus station. Come with some euros in your pocket.

**Airport Money Exchange** ( ☻ 10am-5pm) ATM, cashes travellers cheques, money transfers and credit card-cash advances. A financial lifesaver when banks are closed on Sundays.

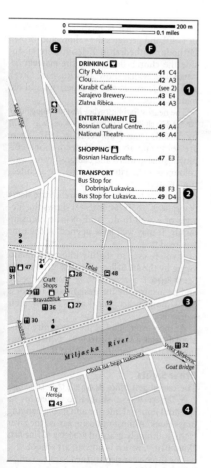

**Post office** ( ☎ 723 422; 🕐 7am-10pm Mon-Sat) Gives MasterCard and Visa cash advances.
**Turkish Ziraat Bank** (Map pp108-9; ☎ 720 209; Ferhadija 10; 🕐 8.30am-8pm Mon-Fri, 9am-3pm Sat) ATM; travellers cheques cashed.

## Post & Telephone
**Central post office** (Map p107; ☎ 252 252; Obala Kulina Bana 8; 🕐 7am-8pm Mon-Sat) Queue at counter 17 for post. There's also a telephone centre here.

## Tourist Information
**Tourist Information Centre** (Map pp108-9; ☎ 220 724, 220 721; www.sarajevo-tourism.com; Zelenih Beretki 22a; 🕐 9am-6pm Mon-Fri, 9am-3pm Sat, 9am-3pm Sun) A most helpful place with books, maps, brochures and ready answers for those awkward tourist questions. It can also provide information on the rest of the country.

## Travel Agencies
**Centrotrans-Eurolines** (Map pp108-9; ☎ 205 481; www.centrotrans.com; Ferhadija 16; 🕐 8.30am-8.30pm Mon-Fri, 9am-3pm Sat) As part of the Eurolines trans-Europe bus network, it books international bus tickets; also plane and ferry ticketing.
**Relax Tours** (Map pp108-9; ☎ /fax 263 330; www.relaxtours.com; Zelenih Beretki 22; 🕐 9am-7pm Mon-Fri, 9am-5pm Sat) Books airline and ferry tickets.

## SIGHTS
### Baščaršija & Around
A labyrinth of cobbled laneways makes up Baščaršija, the bustling old Turkish Quarter where, behind the tourist panache, Sarajevo keeps its soul. Lose yourself among the small shops, watch craftsmen at work, bargain for jewellery and then rest your legs at a coffee shop over a thimbleful of the strong black stuff.

The central open space of Baščaršija, known as Pigeon Square because of the many birds, revolves around the **sebilj** (Map pp108–9). This fountain, looking like an enclosed Oriental gazebo, is not original and only dates from 1891. From the square a series of parallel lanes, cross alleys and open courtyards strike off in all directions to the National Library (east) and the Gazi-Husrevbey Mosque (west).

The stylish Austro-Hungarian **National Library** (Map pp108–9), decorated with Moorish flourishes, was targeted by the Serbs as a repository of Bosnian books and manuscripts, and therefore an entire people's culture. An incendiary shell on 25 August 1992 wiped out a heritage; restoration work is slow and many books may be irreplaceable.

Austrian Archduke Franz Ferdinand and his wife Sophie paused at the National Library

**BOSNIA & HERCEGOVINA**

**SARAJEVO IN TWO DAYS**
Hop on a tram and rattle up to Ilidža and back to see what's what. Wander into and get lost in **Baščaršija**, grab a *ćevapčić* at **Željo** (p113) and walk over the river to check out the **Sarajevo Brewery** (p114).

Wake up with breakfast at **Mash** (p113). Take a city tour and get ready for a night out starting at the **Zlatna Ribica** (p114), then aim for the **City Pub** (p114) and finish at the **Club** (p114).

BOSNIA & HERCEGOVINA

---

**STREET ADDRESSES**

Addresses sometimes have the letters 'bb' instead of a street number. This is shorthand for *bez broja* (without a number) and is mostly used by businesses or other non-residential institutions, indicating that it's an official place without a street number.

---

(then the town hall) on that fateful day in 1914. Despite an earlier unsuccessful assassination attempt that day, they rode west along the riverside in an open car to the **Latin Bridge** (Map pp108–9). It was here that Gavrilo Princip stepped forward to fire his pistol, killing them both and sparking off war between Austria-Hungary and Serbia. Thanks to a series of European alliances, this escalated into WWI.

The elegant stone Latin Bridge has been repaired and it is intended that the plaque bearing the footprints of the assassin be replaced, along with the bust of the archduke. The plaque was ripped from the pavement during the recent war because Princip was a Bosnian Serb. There are also plans to open a museum on the north side of the bridge.

Look for the infamous **Sarajevo roses** on the pavements in central Sarajevo. These are flower shape indentations where a shell has exploded and some have been symbolically filled in with red cement.

**Morića Han** (Map pp108-9; near Saraći 73) was a tavern when Sarajevo was a caravan stopover on the ancient trading route between East and West. Wicker chairs for coffee drinkers have now replaced plain benches for weary travellers and a carpet shop with waist-high stacks of rugs fills the former stables. The *han* (tavern) has been burnt down several times, with the latest reincarnation dating from the 1970s.

As a measure of their tolerant and multicultural history, Sarajevans are proud to point out that four religions and their places of worship share one city block. Close together are the neo-Gothic 1889 **Catholic church** (Map pp108-9; Ferhadija bb) and the old synagogue (1581, last rebuilt in 1821), which is now the **Jewish Museum** (Map pp108-9; ☎ 215 532; Mula Mustafe Bašveskije; admission 2KM; ☺ 10am-6pm Tue-Fri, 10am-6pm Sun) with revealing explanations of a Jewish society in Sarajevo that almost ended with the genocides of WWII.

In the same road is the old **Orthodox Church** (Map pp108-9; ☎ 571 065; Mula Mustafe Bašeskije 59;

☺ 8am-5pm), which is medieval (last rebuilt in 1740) and predates the yellow-and-brown Orthodox cathedral in Zelenih Beretki. Inside the church don't miss the **museum** (admission 1KM), which showcases Russian, Greek and local icons, as well as tapestries and old manuscripts.

The nearby **Gazi-Husrevbey Mosque** (Map pp108-9; ☎ 534 375; off Veliki Savači; ☺ 9am-noon) was built by masons from Dubrovnik in 1531. There are some superb internal decorations employing line, pattern and calligraphy in pastel colours to delineate every separate architectural feature.

Closed at the time of research, **Svrzo House** (Map pp108-9; ☎ 535 264; Glodžina 8) shows the lifestyle of a well-to-do, 18th-century Muslim family. It may well have opened by the time you read this.

If you're ever so slightly interested in art, swing by the **Art Gallery** (Map pp108-9; ☎ 266 550; Zelenih Beretki 8; admission 2KM; ☺ noon-2pm Tue-Sat) and be inspired by the designs and boldness of its modern art. Local artists show their work here.

At the western end of the city centre is the **eternal flame** (Map pp108–9), which commemorates the sacrifices of WWII.

## Other Sights

The **central post office** (Map p107; Obala Kulina Bana 8; ☺ 7am-8pm Mon-Sat) should be visited for its splendid imperial interior and its big hanging brass clock. Almost opposite across the river is the stunningly graceful **Academy of Fine Arts** (Map p107), which is now an art school.

The three-year siege turned Sarajevo into a killing field. The road in from the airport was dubbed 'sniper alley' because Serbian snipers in surrounding hills could pick off civilians as they ran from shelter to shelter along the road. In the middle of this stood the bright yellow **Holiday Inn** (Map p107) that, as the

---

**THEFT WARNING**

There are regular reports about thefts on the overnight Sarajevo to Budapest train. Keep your doors locked and check on who wants to enter your compartment. Being with other travellers or in compartments with families helps reduce your potential as a target and, of course, lock up your valuables.

---

last functioning hotel, became the home of journalists covering the war. The side facing sniper alley was heavily damaged, but the hotel has since been given a facelift.

The best exhibition in the **National Museum** (Map p107; ☎ 668 026; www.zemaljskimuzej.ba; Zmaja od Bosne 3; admission 5KM; ⏲ 10am-2pm Tue-Fri & Sun) is the Ethnology section with its fine display on Bosnian music and instruments, well explained in English. The Natural History section has its share of stuffed birds and beasts but the Prehistory section is empty due to impending building repairs.

The adjacent **History Museum** (Map p107; ☎ 210 418; Zmaja od Bosne 5; admission 1KM; ⏲ 9am-4pm Mon-Fri, 9am-1pm Sat & Sun) is essentially one room of archive material, mostly photographs, covering WWII up to the Srebrenica massacre.

The tunnel that saved Sarajevo! Most of the 800m-stretch under the airport has collapsed, but the **Tunnel Museum** (☎ 628 591; Tuneli 1; admission 5KM; ⏲ 9am-4pm Oct-Apr, 9am-7pm May-Sep), on the southwestern side of the airport, gives visitors just a glimpse of its hopes and horrors: the hopes of people surviving with the food it brought in and of the injured it took out, and the horrors from the pounding overhead artillery and sniper fire during the long hours of waiting to go through.

The house in which the tunnel entrance was secreted has a small but image-provoking collection of construction equipment, photos and a video.

A small road leads alongside the Miljacka River, eastwards from the National Library, to an old Turkish bridge, **Goat Bridge**, several kilometres upstream. It's pleasant for a walk or a cycle.

## ACTIVITIES

Sarajevo can get stinking hot in the height of summer. What better place to cool off than at the water park, **Termalna Rivijera** (☎ 771 000; Butmirska Cesta bb, Ilidža; day admission adult/child 11/8KM; ⏲ 9am-10pm), with its indoor and outdoor pools (open May to September) and water slides? There's also a restaurant here.

## TOURS

The Tourist Information Centre has a list of city tour guides.

**Green Visions** (☎ 717 290; Radnička bb; www.greenvisions.ba; ⏲ 9am-5pm Mon-Fri) An active ecotourism organisation that promotes and lobbies for the preservation of the country's pristine upland environment. It runs hiking treks, (snowshoes in winter), mountain biking and rafting events as well as visits to traditional Bosnian villages. It takes zero risks with mines and operates in places that were never areas of conflict.

**Sarajevo Discovery** (☎ 061 190 591; www.sarajevo-discovery.com) Conducts city tours.

**Sartour** (Map pp108-9; ☎ 238 680; Mula Mustafe Bašeskije 63; ⏲ 9am-7pm) Conducts city tours.

**Turistička Agencija Ljubičica** (Map pp108-9; ☎ 232 109, 061 131 813; www.hostelljubicica.net; Mula Mustafe Bašeskije 65; ⏲ 8am-10pm Oct-Apr, 7am-11pm May-Sep) Conducts city tours.

## FESTIVALS & EVENTS

The Tourist Information Centre has a monthly *Programme of Cultural Events*; check www.sarajevoarts.ba as well.

**Baščaršija Noči** (Nights of Baščaršija; www.bascarsijskenoci.ba) Basically an excuse to put on and enjoy a whole range of international events in July covering dance, music and street theatre.

**Sarajevo Film Festival** (☎ 209 411; www.sff.ba; Zelenih Beretki 12/1) Presents new commercial releases and art-house movies at a globally acclaimed festival in August.

**International Jazz Festival** (www.jazzfest.ba) Week-long event in November showcasing the best in jazz from international and local performers.

## SLEEPING

There is an increasing number of private homeowners prepared to rent out rooms or apartments of varying sizes and quality. Always look before you 'buy', making sure the renter gives you a receipt and registers you with the police.

### Budget

**Turistička Agencija Ljubičica** (Map pp108-9; ☎ 232 109, 061 131 813; www.hostelljubicica.net; Mule Mustafe Bašeskije 65; dm/r/apt from €8/12.50/16.50; ⏲ 5.30am-11pm Nov-Apr, 24hr May-Oct) This helpful and hospitable ('Would you like a coffee?') agency has nearby hostels (one with a women-only room) and can arrange private rooms and apartments. By arrangement, agency staff can collect from the airport or stations. The train station reception (☎/fax 222 783, open 5am–10pm) has luggage storage and bicycle hire.

**Kod Keme** (Map pp108-9; ☎ 531 140; Ćirčiluk Mala 15; www.hostel.co.ba; r €20) Location, location, location. Right in the heart of Baščaršija, this small guesthouse run by a friendly Bosnian-Australian is just the haven for the party animal who wants to roam Sarajevo's nightlife.

**Pansion Lion** (Map pp108-9; ☎ 236 137; http://lion
.bih.net; Bravadžiluk 30; s/d/t with shared bathroom €25/50/60)
A fresco-adorned lobby, hand-decorated
wardrobes, bed linen that matches colour,
and mother of pearl and dolphin-patterned
lavatory seats – the owners of the Pansion
Lion certainly want your stay to be colourful.
Centrally situated in Baščaršija, the Lion is
within crawling distance of all the sights and
bars. Breakfast isn't provided but there are
plenty of eating joints nearby. The owners
speak English, French and Italian, are very
friendly and will do your laundry for you.

**Pansion Baščaršija** (Map pp108-9; ☎ 232 185; Veliki
Čurčiluk 41; s/d 60/100KM) Also recommended, for
its cosy atmosphere, is this central *pansion*.

## Midrange

**Pansion Čobanija** (Map p107; ☎ 441 749; fax 203 937;
Čobanija 29; s/d 80/120KM) A home-away-from-
home guesthouse with character. Light, fresh
and airy rooms come in all shapes and sizes,
from the attic to the ground floor. Downstairs
the lobby flows out on to a small quiet 'beer
at dusk' terrace. The centrepiece is the big
first-floor wood-beamed sitting room with
collapse-into leather armchairs. Suitable for
solo women travellers.

**Guest House Halvat** (Map pp108-9; ☎ /fax 237
714; www.halvat.com.ba; Kasima Dobrače 5; s/d 99/138KM;
Ⓟ 🖳) A suitable choice for a family visiting
Sarajevo as children are welcome and those
under 13 stay free. There are four doubles
and one single, so families should book in
advance. Downstairs there's a cosy lounge
and breakfast area.

**Hotel Hecco** (Map p107; ☎ 273 730; info@hotel-hec
co.net; Medresa 1; s 80KM, d 110-130KM, t 150KM, apt 150-
160KM; Ⓟ 🔀 🖳) An arty boutique hotel de-
signed by a local architect who has a bit of a
thing for Mondrian and cubism. Proximity to
Baščaršija, parking and good-value rates make
it popular with those with a bit of business in
town, or travellers wanting fluffier pillows.

**Green Hotel** ( ☎ 639 701; www.green.co.ba; Ustanička
bb, Ilidža; s/d/tr €22/34/51; Ⓟ) Tired and jaded from
so much travelling, or just overweight from
all those traditional Bosnian meals? Come,
stay and work out here at this tidy cheapie,
which comes with a free, fully equipped gym
and sauna. The tram terminus is a 150m jog
away and it's a 20-minute ride into Baščaršija.
Or you could run all the way.

**Motel Sokak** (Map pp108-9; ☎ 570 355; Mula Mustafe
Bašeskije 24; s/d/tr €37/68/93; 🔀 ⓰) Despite the
name, this is a straightforward no-frills hotel.
Its advantage is centrality and good value in
a city centre that's short of midrange price
accommodation. The Sokak has 11 compact
doubles with cable TV; breakfast is continental but being in the thick of Baščaršija there's
plenty of cafés to top up at. Free internet is
available at reception.

## Top End

**Villa Orient** (Map pp108-9; ☎ 232 754; orient@bih.net.ba;
Oprkanj 6; s/d/tr 153/206/256KM; Ⓟ 🔀 🖳) Architecturally it's a Turkish delight, with a traditional
Balkan exterior and a burgundy-and-cream
colour scheme inside. The Villa is a boutique
hotel with most angles covered: there's a free
fitness centre, internet (3KM per hour) and
a coffee bar open until midnight.

Also recommended is the **Hotel Exclusive**
( ☎ 580 000; www.hotel-exclusive.ba; Zabrđe 5b; s 120-
160KM, d 180KM, apt 200-300KM; Ⓟ 🔀 🔀 🖳 ⓰),
about 12km out of town but compensated
for by value, luxury and a free shuttle service; and **Hotel Hollywood** ( ☎ 773 100; www.hotel
-hollywood.com.ba; Dr Pintola 23; s/d/tr/apt 75/120/160/
180KM; Ⓟ 🔀 🖳 ⓰) in Ilidža.

## EATING

The eating scene is well established in Sarajevo. For a snack or quick lunch there are
*ćevabdžinicas* (cafés that make and sell
*ćevapčići*) and *pekara* (bakeries). For bigger
bites there's a good selection of cheap restaurants, most offering traditional Bosnian
cuisine and some adding a little international
selection. The top-notch restaurants attract
the expense-account foreign clientele with
global menus prepared by chefs who know
their sauces. The majority of eateries are in
the centre, in Baščaršija, and up from the river
on the south side.

### Restaurants

**Dveri** (Map pp108-9; ☎ 537 020; Prote Baković 12; mains
5-12KM; 🕚 11am-4pm & 7-11pm; 🔀 ⓰ ) A tiny
restaurant-in-hiding, which could just pass
as someone's kitchen laid out to receive family
guests. Try one of their home-made brandies
(quince, walnut?) while you watch the cook
prepare your meal in surroundings hung with
strings of garlic, chillies and corncobs.

**To Be or Not to Be** (Map pp108-9; ☎ 233 265, 061
545 846; Čizmedžiluk 5; mains 8-16KM; ⓰ ) Somewhat
similar in style to the Dveri, To Be or Not
to Be offers grills, generous salads and tangy

seafood dishes in its cosy dining room. We ended up with a whale of a fish and more veggies on one plate than we've ever seen in a Balkan restaurant. If you look at the signboard outside you'll notice that the words 'or not' have been crossed out; this alteration was made during the siege when the owners wanted to present a far more positive message.

**Restaurant Jež** (Map pp108-9; ☎ 650 312; Zelenih Beretki 14; mains 16-20KM; ⏰ 5pm-late) A mood of intimacy is felt from the moment you walk into the warmly lit antiques arcade leading into this basement restaurant. Bring the love of your life for that 'heads together, rest of the world doesn't exist' meal. If solo, then fill those noneating moments checking the grandmother clocks on the wall – how many tell the correct time? The cuisine is typical Bosnian tinged with international extras. Our waiter offered a surprise meal, which revealed itself as steak à la chef, served on a wooden platter surrounded by a dam of mash potato to retain the Camembert sauce.

**Taj Mahal** ( ☎ 658724; Paromlinska 48a; ⏰ 10am-11pm Mon-Sat, 5-11pm Sun; ⑆ ) For those missing their spices, the dishes here range from the innocuous to a throat-searing application of chillies. There are plenty of vegetarian dishes plus lots of Sarajevo beer to extinguish any fire.

**Inat Kuća** (Spite House; Map pp108-9; ☎ 447 867; Velika Alifakovac 1; mains 7-18KM) The restaurant was once on the other side of the river, but when the authorities wanted to demolish this traditional Bosnian house to build the town hall the owner insisted it be reconstructed

---

**AUTHOR'S CHOICE**

**Tavola** (Map p107; ☎ 222 207; Maršala Tita 50; dishes 9-12KM; ⏰ 11am-11pm Mon-Sat, 2-11pm Sun) A simple, elegant, old-fashioned restaurant where frequent customers are greeted like old friends. Voices here will tend to be non-Bosnian as it's popular with expats, who have the time and networks to discover the best a town has to offer. Parting guests have left messages written on muslin pieces, which have been framed, backlit and hung on the wall. If you're on the lower level, you can see right into the kitchen and watch your meal as a work in progress. Superb pasta, especially the salmon, but memo to the chef: a little less salt please.

---

here – hence the name. Offerings range from snacks, a sticky baklava, a bowl of chips and beer to a full-blown grill. In warm weather the riverside terrace is the spot for a bit of afternoon relaxation and reading. The service is a bit casual, so keep them on their toes.

**Plava Prizm** ( ☎ 471 514; Džemala Bijedića 185; dishes 10-25KM; ⑆ ⑆ ⑆ ) Got two hours for lunch? That's how long it takes the world to turn around you on this 15th-floor revolving restaurant, atop the gleaming glass Avaz Business centre. We recommend the mushroom stew that comes with a baked pastry top.

## Cafés

**Mash** (Map pp108-9; ☎ 063 489 033; Branilaca Sarajeva bb; mains 6-12KM; ⏰ 7.30-1am Mon-Thu, 7.30-3am Fri, 9-3am Sat, 10am-midnight Sun) Cool, suave place with sofas for a late-night or early-morning collapse, and bar stools for coffee- and snackgrabbers. Sandwiches, snacks and a few veggie dishes (eg fajitas) feature on the menu.

**Bosanska Kuća** (Map pp108-9; ☎ 237 320; Bravadžiluk 3; mains 6-9KM; ⏰ 24hr) 'Come eat,' says the waiter in national costume, inviting you into a restaurant promoting Bosnian tradition in food and setting. This snappy joint makes choosing easier with its colour-picture menu – maybe a kebab, some grilled fish, or stuffed peppers or aubergines for vegetarians.

## Quick Eats

### SNACKS

**Pekara Edin** (Map pp108-9; Mula Mustafe Bašeskije 69; ⏰ 24hr) An always-open bakery selling pizza slices, pastries and *burek*. The *krompiruša* (spicy potato *burek*) provides just the wake-up call for a sleepy palette.

**Butik-Badem** (Map pp108-9; ☎ 533 135; Abadžiluk 12) Nibbles from this health-food shop include yummy chocolate-coated pistachios, fruit bars and nuts.

**Žjelo** (Map pp108-9; ☎ 441 200; Kundurdžiluk 19 & 20) Having two branches on the same street says something about the popularity of this *ćevabdžinica*.

### CAKE SHOPS

Bosnia and Hercegovina produces wonderful (but dreadfully bad for you) cakes.

**Planet** (Map pp108-9; ☎ 447 447; Bravadžiluk bb) For an afternoon treat take the corner table by the window, devour your 'chosen with difficulty' cake, then sip your coffee and watch the world go by.

**Metropolis** (Map p107; ☎ 203 315; 21 Maršala Tita) A big restaurant with a large display of eat-me cakes that's popular with everyone who loves those delicious creamy things.

## Self-Catering

**Outdoor market** (Map pp108-9; Mula Mustafe Bašeskije; ◐ 7am-5pm) Near the cathedral, this market overflows with fruit and vegetables.

**Indoor market** (Map pp108-9; Mula Mustafe Bašeskije 4a; ◐ 7am-5pm Mon-Sat, 7am-2pm Sun) In a remarkable neoclassical building, it sells dairy products and meat.

## DRINKING

Pubs, clubs and bars are mostly concentrated in and to the west of Baščaršija, all within staggering distance.

**City Pub** (Map pp108-9; ☎ 299 916; Despićeva bb; mains 6-9KM; ◐ 8am-late) It's easy to let this place become your daytime address: a kick-back café-bar that turns into a big music and drinking venue at night. This pub swings, and even the bouncers smile.

**Club** (Map pp108-9; ☎ 550 550; Maršala Tita 7; ◐ 10am-late) This sassy basement joint grooves to DJ music or local bands on weekends. Different rooms cater for drinking, dancing or just chatting up others under the seductive lighting. Out the back a restaurant cooks up sizzling pizzas (12KM to 25KM). It's a bit difficult to find. There's no sign, as the management prefers recommendations by word of mouth. Take the first door on the left after the entrance and then go down the stairs. Note, there's a smart-dress code.

**Zlatna Ribica** (Map pp108-9; ☎ 215 369; Kaptol 5; ◐ 9am-late) A collision of aesthetics as baroque, fin-de-siècle Paris and Vienna, and Art Deco crash together in this warmly lit bar. Nature abhors a vacuum and so does the owner who has filled every nook and cranny with period knick-knacks; it's a visual feast. Drinks come with complimentary nuts and dried figs, and the music is blues and early rock'n'roll.

**Karabit Café** (Map pp108-9; ☎ 712 000; Zelenih Beretki 8; ◐ 9am-10pm Mon-Sat, 10am-6pm Sun) This is often the place to go when others are closed, you've had enough of them, or you're out of ideas. Buy a book, read a magazine, allow your thoughts to drift and let the coffee or booze edge you back into life.

**Sarajevo Brewery** (Map pp108-9; ☎ 239 740; Franjevacka 15; ◐ 10am-1am; ☒ ) Above the river on the south bank stands a large red-and-cream edifice with fat copper drainpipes, this is Sarajevo's famous brewery. Part of it has been converted into a cavernous bar, all dark stained wood and brass railings, serving the brewery's draft draught plus a very pleasant dark beer that slips down easily. Meals are also available (mains 8KM to 18KM).

**Clou** (Map pp108-9; ☎ 061 203 984; Mula Mustafe Bašeskije 5; ◐ 10pm-late) A smoky underground den that revs up late at night and then cruises on regardless of the dawn arriving. It's a favourite with locals, expats and travellers in the know, who come for the atmosphere and the free flowing R'n'B and jazz. The club can be difficult to find: enter the fancy doorway, go through the passageway and turn left, then left again down some steps.

## ENTERTAINMENT

The Tourist Information Centre is always well up on what's on in town.

## Cinemas

Check the daily cinema listings under the 'Kina' column in Sarajevo's daily paper, Oslobođendje.

**Bosnian Cultural Centre** (Map pp108-9; ☎ 668 186; Branilaca Sarajeva 24; movie admission 5KM) Domestic films, plus concerts and cultural events.

**Obala Meeting Point** (Map p107; ☎ 668 186; Hamdije Kreševljakovića 13; movie admission 4KM) A comfortable cinema in Skenderija showing films in English, with subtitles for the locals.

## Gay & Lesbian Venues

There is no visible gay and lesbian scene in Sarajevo but a chat with the friendly staff at Karabit Café (left) may reveal something.

## Live Music

**SA Club** ( ☎ 211 911; Kranjceviceva bb; admission 3-6KM; ◐ 10pm-6am) Tucked in behind the Holiday Inn, the club is a spacey venue for rock, disco, house, Latino and live music.

Live music is also performed at City Pub (left), Club (left), Clou (above), Bosnian Cultural Centre (above) and the Aqua Disco (below).

## Nightclubs

**Aqua Disco** ( ☎ 625 500; Mali Kiseljak 8; admission 10KM; ◐ 9pm-3am Fri & Sat) A big-stage disco with DJs and live music. It's part of a swimming-pool complex, where some like to mix swimming and dancing.

## Theatre

**National Theatre** (Map pp108–9; ☎ 663 647; Obala Kulina Bana 9) Stages concerts, ballets and plays.

# SHOPPING

This city has enough souvenirs to fill your luggage and exhaust your budget! Baščaršija is the shopping magnet, with small craft shops specialising in enamelled and sculptured copper and brassware, jewellery, clothes and carpets. Be adventurous and bargain. Don't miss the *Survival Map* (17KM), a cartoon-like map of wartime Sarajevo, available in bookshops.

**Bosnian Handicrafts** (Map pp108–9; ☎ 551 535; www.bhcrafts.org; Culhan 1; ☻ 8am-8pm Mon-Sat, 10am-4pm Sun) A nonprofit organisation working with refugees who produce colourful woven items.

# GETTING THERE & AWAY
## Air

For flights servicing Sarajevo see p130.

## Bus

Sarajevo is blessed with two bus stations. Buses to Republika Srpska, Serbia and Montenegro go from the Lukavica bus station in the Dobrinja suburb near the airport.

In winter buses for the ski fields leave from near the National Museum at 9am and return at 3.30pm (fare from 7KM).

Bus schedules change so check with the Tourist Information Centre, which has current schedules.

**MAIN BUS STATION**

Daily services from this **station** (Map p107; ☎ 213 100; Put Života 8) go to Banja Luka (29.50KM, five hours, 9.15am, 2.30pm and 3.30pm), Bihać (39.50KM, 6½ hours, 7.30am, 1.30am and 10pm), Jajce (23KM, 3½ hours, five buses), Međugorje (20KM, 3½ hours, 2.30pm and 4.45pm) and Mostar (13.50KM, 2½ hours, 15 buses).

Centrotrans-Eurolines runs buses to Dubrovnik (44KM, seven hours, 7.15am), Split (36KM, eight hours, 10am, 2.30pm and 9pm), Zagreb (54KM, eight hours, 6.30am, 12.30pm and 10pm) and Herceg Novi (34KM, seven hours, 11am, 7pm and 10.30pm). For services to Western Europe, see www.centrotrans.com.

**DOBRINJA/LUKAVICA BUS STATION**

This **station** (☎ 057-317 377; Nikole Tesle bb) has seven daily buses to Belgrade (28KM, eight hours),

four to Podgorica (25KM, eight hours), three to Novi Sad (28KM, nine hours) and hourly buses to Banja Luka (18.50KM, five hours).

For the Lukavica terminus take either trolleybus 103 from Austrijski Trg or bus 31e, from the bus stop behind the town hall, to the last stop and walk 150m straight ahead.

## Train

Services from the **train station** (☎ 655 330; Žtrava Genocida u Srebenicica) run to Mostar (10KM), Banja Luka (22KM), Zagreb (46KM) and Budapest (90KM). See p131 for times.

# GETTING AROUND
## To/From the Airport

Taxi (20KM) is the quickest way to town, but a cheaper alternative is to take the taxi to Ilidža (5KM) and transfer to tram 3 for Baščaršija.

## Car & Motorcycle

Much of Baščaršija is pedestrianised and the rest is narrow, making parking either illegal or impossible. The best option is to park to the west and use the tram.

Rental agencies include **Budget** (☎ 766 670), **Dollar & Thrifty** (☎ 289 272), **Europcar** (☎ 289 273) and **National** (☎ 267 591). **Lami Rent a Car** (☎ 061 260 609) charges from €33 a day.

## Public Transport

A rattly but efficient tram network runs east–west between Baščaršija and Ilidža. Tram 4 from Baščaršija goes to the bus and train stations; tram 1 goes between the bus and train stations and Ilidža; and tram 3 runs between Ilidža and Baščaršija. Buy tickets (1.60KM) from kiosks near tram stations or from the driver (1.80KM); a daily ticket (5.30KM) can be bought from a kiosk. Validate your ticket in the machine once on board as inspectors can fine you for not doing so. Bus and trolleybus tickets work the same way.

## Taxi

All of Sarajevo's taxis have meters that begin at 2KM and charge about 1KM per kilometre. Call **Radio Taxi** (☎ 1515) or **Samir i Emir** (☎ 1516).

# AROUND SARAJEVO

Jahorina and Bjelašnica hosted the 1984 Winter Olympics and now offer some of Europe's best-value skiing. In winter, hotels and *pansions* (pensions) generally only accept guests staying for a whole week starting on Saturday. All accommodation offers a choice of B&B, half-board or full board.

## Jahorina

☎ 057

In the Republika Srpska, 25km southeast of Sarajevo, lie the challenging slopes of Mt Jahorina, with 20km of runs for alpine and Nordic skiing. In summer there's mountain biking and hiking. The following hotels are open all year.

The grey-and-black Gothic exterior of **Termag** ( ☎ 270 422; www.termaghotel.com; r per person from 132KM Dec-Mar, 96KM Apr-Nov; P ✕ ☐ ☒ ) doesn't really prepare you for the well-designed interior that employs grey-stained wood, stone-slab walls and cow hide–covered seating that's, well, rather Argentinean. It scores on facilities such as a big open sit-around fire in the bar, a fitness centre and a swimming pool plus a sauna, ski rental and skiing lessons. Guests can stay for less than seven days in winter, if there's space, and there's a handy weekend special – check in Friday, check out Sunday at 5pm – outside the ski season.

**Hotel Košuta** ( ☎ 270 401; fax 270 400; r per person from 53KM Dec-Mar, 38KM Apr-Nov; P ) is a big, made-for-the-Olympics hotel just a handy 50m from the ski lift. Guests can stay for less than a week in the snow season. Some rooms have balconies while those at the back have the best views.

**Hotel Kristal** ( ☎ 270 430; s/d B&B 86/152KM, half-board 98/172KM; P ☐ ) is an enlarged mountain hut of a hotel; the rooms here are comfortable, although not spacious. It can be booked out for winter as early as August.

## Bjelašnica

☎ 033

A more compact area than Jahorina, Bjelašnica is undergoing some massive development that in future years will provide rental accommodation, shops, restaurants and skiing services. In mind is another Winter Olympics, but at the moment there's just one hotel within minutes of some exciting skiing action.

**Hotel Maršal** ( ☎ 279 100; fax 279 149; per person B&B/half-board €26/31 Apr-Nov, €33/38 Dec-Mar; P ☐ ) is a well-equipped hotel of several storeys, with commanding views over the nearby ski slopes. Guests can stay for less than seven days in winter but there's a surcharge for doing so. Added attractions include a disco

with bands in the winter season, excursions out to old Bosnian villages and transport to Igoman, a small nearby skiing field with a lift and ski jump. Ski-equipment rental and lessons are available.

# SOUTHERN BOSNIA & HERCEGOVINA

## MOSTAR

☎ 036 / pop 110,000

The slim, elegant Stari Most (Old Bridge), which arches over the swirling Neretva River, provides this ancient town with its icon and name: Mostar meaning 'keeper of the bridge'. The rebuilt bridge was reopened on 22 July 2004 with fine words of reconciliation and hope.

Flanking the bridge is the old cobbled Ottoman Quarter, a haven for the city's artists and craftsmen, along with 16th-century mosques, old Turkish houses and endless cafés. On the western side restaurant terraces hug the steep rocky riverbanks jostling for perfect views of the Old Bridge and its river.

Some magnificent buildings, such as the Gymnasium and City Baths, remain from Austro-Hungarian times, giving an added grandeur. While many grand buildings were destroyed in the war, with only their shells remaining, others are gradually being brought back to life.

## History

Mostar grew from a simple crossing point on the Neretva River to an important crossroads settlement and provincial capital in the Ottoman Empire. Ottoman governors liked to set their stamp on their cities through monumental architecture, usually grand mosques but in the case of Mostar, the Stari Most.

The Austria-Hungarians further developed Mostar with a planned city on the western banks where the Gymnasium and City Baths are good examples of their fine architecture.

During the 1980s Mostar became an important tourist attraction centred on the old bridge and the preserved Ottoman quarter. Visitors from all over Yugoslavia flocked here in summer, especially for the July diving competition.

Mostar suffered greatly during the inter-ethnic wars from 1992 to 1995 that resulted from the collapse of Yugoslavia. Initially a Serbian force shelled the city from the eastern hills killing thousands and forcing even more from their homes. Croats and Muslims combined to expel the Serbs but shortly afterwards became adversaries. The Croat forces took over the western bank expelling Muslims and the city became divided along the river.

The Stari Most was a favoured target for Croat artillery based in the western hills, and on November 9 1993 a direct hit collapsed the bridge into the river.

The Dayton Agreement established a unified city corporation, which concentrated on rebuilding the city centre and culminated in the reopening of the new Stari Most in July 2004.

## Orientation

The Neretva River running north to south bisects the town into a Croatian west and Bosnian east section. The Ottoman Quarter spans both sides of the river around the Stari Most. You'll find maps at most kiosks and tourist agencies.

## Information

### BOOKSHOP

**Buybook** ( ☎ 558 810; Onešćukova 24; ✆ 9am-9pm Mon-Sat, 11am-7pm Sun) For an array of books, CDs and guidebooks.

### INTERNET ACCESS

**Barbados** ( ☎ 558 525; Braće Fejića 26; per hr 2KM; ✆ 9am-11pm)

BOSNIA & HERCEGOVINA

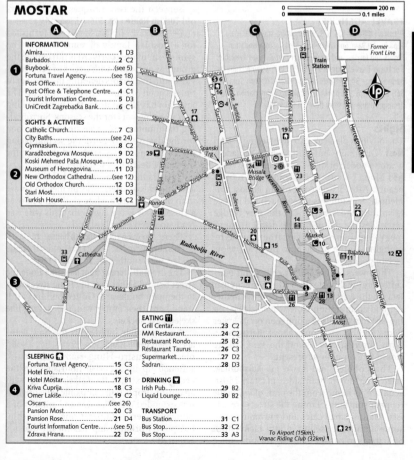

**MOSTAR**

0 ———— 200 m
0 ———— 0.1 miles

| INFORMATION | |
| --- | --- |
| Almira............................................**1** | D3 |
| Barbados.......................................**2** | C2 |
| Buybook......................................(see 5) | |
| Fortuna Travel Agency...............(see 18) | |
| Post Office...................................**3** | C2 |
| Post Office & Telephone Centre....**4** | C1 |
| Tourist Information Centre...........**5** | D3 |
| UniCredit Zagrebačka Bank..........**6** | C1 |

| SIGHTS & ACTIVITIES | |
| --- | --- |
| Catholic Church............................**7** | C3 |
| City Baths..................................(see 24) | |
| Gymnasium..................................**8** | C2 |
| Karadžozbegova Mosque............. **9** | D2 |
| Koski Mehmed Paša Mosque.......**10** | D3 |
| Museum of Hercegovina..............**11** | D3 |
| New Orthodox Cathedral..........(see 12) | |
| Old Orthodox Church...................**12** | D3 |
| Stari Most....................................**13** | D3 |
| Turkish House..............................**14** | C2 |

| EATING 🍴 | |
| --- | --- |
| Grill Centar.................................**23** | C2 |
| MM Restaurant............................**24** | C2 |
| Restaurant Rondo.......................**25** | B2 |
| Restaurant Taurus.......................**26** | C3 |
| Supermarket................................**27** | D2 |
| Šadran.........................................**28** | D3 |

| SLEEPING 🏠 | |
| --- | --- |
| Fortuna Travel Agency...............**15** | C3 |
| Hotel Ero.....................................**16** | C1 |
| Hotel Mostar...............................**17** | B1 |
| Kriva Ćuprija...............................**18** | C3 |
| Omer Lakiše............................... **19** | C2 |
| Oscars......................................(see 26) | |
| Pansion Most...............................**20** | C3 |
| Pansion Rose...............................**21** | D4 |
| Tourist Information Centre........(see 5) | |
| Zdrava Hrana...............................**22** | D2 |

| DRINKING 🍷 | |
| --- | --- |
| Irish Pub.....................................**29** | B2 |
| Liquid Lounge............................**30** | B2 |

| TRANSPORT | |
| --- | --- |
| Bus Station.................................**31** | C1 |
| Bus Stop.....................................**32** | C2 |
| Bus Stop.....................................**33** | A3 |

Former Front Line

Train Station

Musala Bridge

Market

Lucki Most

To Airport (15km); Vranac Riding Club (32km)

**MONEY**

**UniCredit-Zagrebačka Bank** ( ☎ 312 112; Kardinala Stepinca 18; 🕑 8am-2.30pm Mon-Fri, 8am-noon Sat) Cashes travellers cheques; ATM.

**POST & TELEPHONE**

**Post office & Telephone Centre** ( ☎ 328 362; Dr Ante Starčevića bb; 🕑 Telephone centre 7am-7pm Mon-Sat & 8am-noon Sun) Poste restante; bureau de change.

**Post office** ( ☎ 576 513; Braće Fejića bb; 🕑 8am-8pm Mon-Sat, 9am-noon Sun) ATM outside.

**TOURIST INFORMATION**

**Tourist Information Centre** ( ☎ 580 275; www.herce govina.ba; Onešćukova bb; 🕑 9am-9pm) A useful one-stop shop with erratic hours outside May to September. Sells maps, guidebooks and postcards, and books accommodation, buses, planes and trains.

**TRAVEL AGENCIES**

**Almira** ( ☎ /fax 551 873; www.almira-travel.ba; Mala Tepa 9; 🕑 9am-6pm Mon-Sat) Books accommodation, flights and ferries, and arranges car rental; maps available.

**Fortuna Travel Agency** ( ☎ 552 197; www.fortuna.ba; Rade Bitange 34; 🕑 8am-4.30pm Mon-Fri, 9am-1pm Sat) Sells maps and booklets, books accommodation, and arranges plane and ferry tickets and car hire.

## Sights

The obvious place to start sightseeing is **Stari Most**. Originally built in 1556 to replace a nearby wooden bridge, it was named the Petrified Moon because of its slender and refined beauty. After its destruction an almost immediate decision was taken to rebuild it once hostilities had ceased, and the new bridge resembles the old in minute detail. In summer young men earn a living from tourists by plunging off the bridge into the river below (see opposite).

The towers of Tara and Helebija stand as architectural anchors to the bridge. Semicircular **Tara**, on the west bank, used to be the gunpowder and ammunition store while **Helebija**, on the east bank, housed a dungeon on its lower floors and a guardhouse above. **Herceguša**, a third tower, stands behind the Tara. All are closed to the public at present.

The cobbled old town of **Kujundžiluk**, stretching down both sides of Stari Most, acquired its name from the craft of *kujunžije* (copper smithing). Lining the streets are artists' studios, small cafés and souvenir shops, some admittedly selling pretty tacky stuff. Still, items to consider buying include coffee sets and embossed plates, all created by copper smiths wielding little hammers. The 'tap tap tap' you can hear as you wander these streets is the sound of these craftsmen at work.

Along the eastern side is the 1618 **Koski Mehmed Paša Mosque** (mosque/mosque & minaret €1/2.50; 🕑 9am-6pm) with a commanding view of Stari Most from its minaret. Within the mosque, lit by an immense chandelier plus natural light filtered through coloured glass, is some beautiful linear design work outlining the interior architectural shapes and mihrab.

Nearby is the slightly older 1557 **Karadžozbegova Mosque** (admission mosque/mosque & minaret €1/2.50; 🕑 9am-7.30pm), the most famous mosque in Mostar. At the moment it is more plainly decorated than the Paša mosque because of considerable rebuilding after the war.

Between the two mosques is a 350-year-old **Turkish House** ( ☎ 550 677; Bišoevića 13; admission €1; 🕑 9am-3pm Nov-Feb, 8am-8pm Mar-Oct) furnished for a Bosnian family of some stature. The symbolism of the courtyard is intriguing: the ground is decorated with circles of pebbles divided into five sectors denoting the number of times a good Muslim must pray each day. The fountain has 12 spouts for the months, filling four watering pots for the seasons. Surrounding the fountain are three stone globes, one for the day we were born, the second facing Mecca for the life we lead, and the third for inevitable death that will greet us.

Upstairs the rooms are divided into men's and women's quarters. Muslim men had more than one wife and a white cloth draped over a closed door was a signal that this wife was ready to receive her husband.

There's an even older **Turkish house** ( ☎ 550 913; Gaše Ilića 21; admission 2KM; 🕑 8am-8pm), older than the bridge, with another fascinating interior.

The dramatic **former front line** runs along the street behind Hotel Ero, then one street west to the main boulevard. Gutted buildings still stand here, their empty windows gaping like skeletal eye sockets.

A once-stately building is the now damaged 1896 **Gymnasium** (School; Spanski Trg), a solid piece of Austro-Hungarian architecture softened up by Moorish flourishes. In the background stands the **Catholic Church**, with an out-of-proportion campanile. The original was extended after the war and smacks of a campanile-versus-minaret one-upmanship, but poor workmanship has meant that it's acquired a lean.

---

**HIGH JUMP**

The annual diving competition at the end of July is quite an adrenaline rush. Young men from all over the country and abroad (including world diving champions) gather to dive off the bridge into the river 21m below. Most jump, however, as diving is rather dangerous. Before the war these testosterone-charged divers were known as 'the Icaruses of Mostar' and their displays of masculinity had a certain pulling power with the girls of the town.

Now that the bridge has been rebuilt, Mostar's young divers are re-embracing the tradition with a particular frenzy, and have a clubhouse in the Tara tower. While once they dived for cigarettes or a girl's attention, now they're after cold hard cash. A group can expect to pay €50, individuals can bargain for €35 and for a dive it's about €300.

---

The **Museum of Hercegovina** ( ☎ 551 602; Bajatova 4; admission 1.5KM; ⏲ 9am-2pm Mon-Fri, 10am-noon Sat) is the former house of Džemal Bijedić, who was the ex-head of the Yugoslav government and died in mysterious circumstances in 1978. Now a small museum, that's dedicated more to Mostar than him, it has as its prize exhibit a 10-minute film on how Mostar used, before 1990, the bridge-jumping competition and the actual destruction of the bridge.

At the bottom of the hill is a telling graveyard where all headstones share the same date of death. Further up Bajatova, after the road passes under Udame Divizije, is a large mound of rubble. This was the **New Orthodox church**, hit by Croatian shelling in 1993. Behind this rubble, and protected in a depression, is the **Old Orthodox church**, which survives but cannot be entered.

## Activities

**Badžo-Raft** ( ☎ 061 719 577; www.badzoraft.com) is a rafting company based at Konjic, 83km north of Mostar.

**Vranac Riding Club** ( ☎ 036-806 575; www.villa-rustica.ba; Villa Rustica Čaplinja) is a horse-riding school, 34km south of Mostar, which can accommodate people with disabilities.

Enjoy a swim at the beautiful **City Baths** ( ☎ 551 023; Trg Republike 5; ⏲ 10am-5pm), an Austro-Hungarian place dating from 1912.

## Sleeping

Both **Fortuna Travel Agency** ( ☎ 552 197; www.fortuna.ba; Trg Ivana Krndelja 1; r per person 20-50KM; ⏲ 8am-4.30pm Mon-Fri, 9am-1pm Sat) and the **Tourist Information Centre** ( ☎ 397 350; www.hercegovina.ba; Onešćukova bb; ⏲ 9am-9pm) book private accommodation.

**Omer Lakiše** ( ☎ 551 627; Mladena Balorde 21a; bed with shared bathroom 25KM) Look for the brown metal gate. Omer is a kindly retired professor, who has a smattering of English and lets out rooms in his private house. There are eight beds in two rooms and homeliness compensates for the shared bathroom and bed-cluttered rooms.

**Zdrava Hrana** ( ☎ /fax 551 444; Alikalfića 5; r per person from 30KM; ⓟ ☒ ) A short leg-stretch uphill on the east side will take you to this quiet place that is suitable for small groups. There are some apartments with a basic kitchen but no cooking facilities. Breakfast costs 5KM.

**Pansion Most** ( ☎ 552 528; www.pansionmost.dzaba.com; Adema Buća 100; s/d from 45/72KM; ⓟ ☒ ▣ ) An eight-room guesthouse, 150m from Stari Most, that's a cheery spic-and-span place. A small café fronts the *pansion* and services here include currency exchange, maps and brochures, and a laundry room.

**Pansion Rose** ( ☎ 578 300; www.pansion-rose.ba; Bulevar bb; s/d/tr 42/84/90KM; ⓟ ☒ ▣ ♿ ) A city-fringe guesthouse run by a friendly family. Rooms are small to cosy but well equipped with comfy beds, fluffy duvets and cable TV. Off-road parking makes this ideal for car-roaming folk.

**Kriva Ćuprija** (Crooked Bridge; ☎ 550 953; www.motel-mostar.de; Kiva Ćuprija br 2; s/apt from €25/50; ☒ ) For those who like the soothing sounds of rushing water, this guesthouse created out of a former mill, with imported furniture and all mod cons. The epitome of European taste, and sited by one of the tributaries to the main river, the accommodation is as near to the Stari Most and the Ottoman Quarter as you can get.

**Hotel Ero** ( ☎ 386 777; www.ero.ba; Dr Ante Starčevića bb; s/d/apt €51/85/110; ⓟ ☒ ▣ ♿ ) Take a war-damaged hotel and apply money to attract the business guest. The glitzy glass-and-gilt lobby with yellow-spotted green armchairs is the opening statement. Upstairs a peachy-cream décor that's warm and friendly extends into the light and airy bedrooms. The beds

BOSNIA & HERCEGOVINA

are properly made, too, with white duvets; none of the 'make your bed from a pile of folded sheets and blankets' stuff common in cheaper hotels.

Also recommended are **Oscars** ( ☎ 061 823 649; Oneščukova 33; per person €10), a cosy *pansion* just off the western side of the Stari Most, and the unexceptional but cheap **Hotel Mostar** ( ☎ 322 679; www.hotel-mostar.com; Kneza Domagoja bb; s/d €32.50/55, apt from €65; P ⊠ ).

## Eating & Drinking

Cafés and restaurants with divine views of the river cluster along the western riverbank near Stari Most. Sit in the shade during the day, or under a starlit sky at night, to enjoy a *ćevapčiči* or grilled fresh local trout. There's a cluster of café-bars on Kralja Tomislava.

**Grill Centar** ( ☎ 061 198 111; Braće Fejića 13; grills 3.50-4.50KM; &) Cooking aromas lead you by the nose to this little noshing place full of happy customers. The local recommendation is *ćevapčiči* with *kajmak* (salted cream turned to cheese) accompanied by a round lump of *lepinon* (bread).

**MM Restaurant** ( ☎ 558 900; Mostarskog Bataljona 11; meals 6-12KM; ✆ 8am-10pm Mon-Sat) Buffet presentation makes this a visitor-friendly feeding station. The food's lip-smackingly good with some veg options, and there's a ham and eggs breakfast for 3KM.

**Restaurant Rondo** ( ☎ 322 100; cnr Kraljice Katerine & Save Kovačevića; mains 8-18KM; P ⊠ &) This place is right by the roundabout, hence its name. Snack on the *zelzanica stagana* (spinach pie) for 3KM, or revel in a *San Pietro all Cartoccio* (a fish fillet baked in foil with a wine sauce, mushrooms, shrimps and mussels) for 16KM.

**Šadran** ( ☎ 579 057; Jusovina 11, dishes €4-12) Just before the western entrance to Stari Most this courtyard restaurant has trestle tables set under the spreading tentacles of a kiwi-fruit vine. Service is prompt and there's a good variety of meals to appease a meat, vegetarian or fish appetite.

**Restaurant Taurus** ( ☎ 061 212 617; off Oneščukova; mains 8-20KM) In an old mill down below Oneščukova, the Taurus comes with ancient smoke-stained beams and a large log fire for winter; a roofed terrace looks out onto the river. Risotto is a good test of a restaurant's capabilities; too often it comes as a tasteless sludge but not here, where our tasty seafood dinner came in a 'shouldn't have had lunch' portion.

**Supermarket** ( ☎ 551 984; Maršala Tita bb; ✆ 7am-10pm) This supermarket has plenty of different food goodies for the self-caterers.

**Irish Pub** ( ☎ 315 338; Kralja Zvonimira 15b; ✆ 8am-11pm Sun-Thu, 8am-1am Fri & Sat) A try-hard Irish pub, decorated with a few reproduction Irish knick-knacks, serving Guinness and Kilkenny Bitter. A large outdoor video screen shows sports etc, in silence, so it doesn't compete with the music in the pub.

**Liquid Lounge** ( ☎ 063 444 414; SPC, Rondo 66; ✆ 8am-late) Ultracool hang-out bar decorated in mauves, blues and greens to sink you into an ocean of languor. When you can't focus on the fish swimming along the front of the bar (it's an aquarium), you've had too many of their 150 cocktails on offer. Appropriately they play lounge music during the day but swing into house and R'n'B when guest DJs spin the discs at the weekends.

## Getting There & Away

### AIR

BH Airlines flies from **Mostar airport** ( ☎ 350 992) to Zagreb and Istanbul.

### BUS

The following companies have office in the **bus station** ( ☎ 552 025; Trg Ivana Krndelja).

**Autoprevoz-bus** ( ☎ 551 900) services include Zagreb (43KM, 9½ hours, 9am) and 14 buses to Sarajevo (13.50KM, 2½ hours, 6am to 7.55pm). Its ticket office sells tickets for other lines except Prevoz Vučić and Globtour.

Centrotrans-Eurolines runs to Herceg Novi in Montenegro (€9, 4½ hours, 2.30pm).

**Prevoz Vučić** ( ☎ 552 690) has services to Belgrade (34KM, 10 hours, 7.30pm) and Banja Luka (20KM, six hours, 1.30pm).

**Globtour** ( ☎ 377 292, 550 065; www.globtour.com) runs to Vienna (€50, 15 hours, 8.30am) and Belgrade (35KM, 11 hours, 9pm), Sarajevo (13KM, three hours, 6.30am, 8.30am and 4pm) and Herceg Novi (43KM, 5½ hours, 7am) via Dubrovnik (25KM, 3½ hours) and Split (20KM, 3½ hours, 7am).

Bus 48 goes from the bus stop on Biskupa Čule to Međugorje (3KM, 45 minutes, seven buses 6.30am to 7.40pm Monday to Friday, and 6.30am, 11.30am and 6.10pm Saturday).

### TRAIN

The **train station** ( ☎ 550 608) is upstairs from the bus station. Two trains run from Mostar to Sarajevo (10KM); the morning train goes

---

### THE PLEASURE OF TRAINS

Travellers going to Sarajevo from Mostar should consider the twice-daily train that starts its day at Ploče on the coast. The best train leaves Mostar's neglected station at 8.04am.

Don't expect a big train – maybe just a loco and three carriages – and perhaps you'll get a compartment to yourself. There may be a buffet service of sorts; in 2004 there was a range of spirits or coffee offered, but this time nothing materialised, so come armed with an espresso from Mostar station.

This is a formidable journey for the train. The first part involves running alongside the pea-green Neretva River, which, nicely situated in a gorge, has been dammed for electricity. If you ate trout in Mostar, likely as not it came from one of the fish farms here. Leaving the gorge the train executes a massive U-turn and then, through a series of loops, switchbacks, tunnels and viaducts, climbs slowly over the Bjelašnica Mountains to Sarajevo.

Another useful train, where poor patronage works to the traveller's advantage, is the overnight Banja Luka to Belgrade service. While the service is marginally cheaper than the bus, it takes longer. But which would you prefer? Arriving in Belgrade in the early hours in a cramped bus seat? Or by train in your own compartment and seating that allows you to stretch right out?

---

onto Zagreb (58KM) and the evening train travels overnight to Budapest (101KM). See p131 for timetable information.

### Getting Around

**Mostar Bus** ( ☎ 552 250) operates an extensive bus service. From Spanski Trg bus 10 goes to and from Blagaj (3KM, 30 minutes, seven buses from 6.30am to 7.40pm, three buses Saturday), and Bus 51 goes to the airport (3KM, 30 minutes, five buses from 6.45am to 3.30pm Monday to Saturday and 7.30am, 2pm and 3.30pm Sunday).

## AROUND MOSTAR

About 15km southeast of Mostar is the village of **Blagaj**. Here, perching under a cliff at the point where the Buna River gushes out of a gaping cave, is a 16th-century **Tekija** (Dervish monastery; ☎ 573 221; admission 2KM; ☉ 8am-9pm) where Dervishes gather every May. Two wooden tombs in an upper room house the bodies of two Tajik dervishes, who arrived with the Turks at the end of the 15th century. Downstairs, among the souvenirs, you might find a fez in your size.

## MEĐUGORJE

☎ 036 / pop 4,500

Međugorje is a remarkable place – a religious tourist resort attracting Catholics worldwide – and when the Irish are in town there's plenty of *craic* (and Guinness) to be had. Whether you come as a sceptic or as a pilgrim, you'll be amazed by this conjunction of belief and commercialism.

On 24 June 1981 six teenagers in this once dirt-poor village claimed they'd seen a miraculous apparition of the Virgin Mary, and Međugorje's cash registers began to ring out. Now Međugorje is awash with pilgrims, tour buses and tacky souvenir shops.

The Catholic Church hasn't officially acknowledged the apparitions (the first in Europe since Lourdes, France, in 1858 and Fatima, Portugal, in 1917). Three of the original six still claim to see the vision daily, while the Virgin Mary only appears to the others on special days.

The crowds swell around Easter for the Walk of Peace celebrating the anniversary of the first appearance in 1981, the Assumption of the Virgin (15 August) and the Nativity of the Virgin (first Sunday after 8 September). Međugorje can be visited as a day trip from Mostar.

### Orientation

A town without street names or numbers! The Mostar road turns southwest at the post office and becomes the main strip ending at St James' Church 500m away. Most of the shops, restaurants, banks and travel agencies are on this strip. There are also some guesthouses, but most are spread alongside lanes reaching out into the fields and vineyards. Southwest, behind the church, is Mt Križevac, while Apparition Hill is to the south. Nearly any shop can provide a map.

### Information

The euro is the favoured currency and used in most pricing.

BOSNIA & HERCEGOVINA

**Globtour** ( ☎ 651 393; www.globtour.com; ◷ 8.30am-4.30pm) Books ferries and flights, and runs its own buses.
**Paddy Travel** ( ☎ /fax 651 482; paddy@tel.net.ba; ◷ 9am-3pm Mon-Sat Nov-Mar, 9am-6pm Mon-Sat Apr-Oct) Books accommodation, changes travellers cheques and organises day trips.
**Post office** ( ☎ 651 510; ◷ 7am-8pm Mon-Sat, 10am-5pm Sun) Telephone, postal services and cash advances on credit cards.
**UniCredit Zagrebačka Bank** ( ☎ 650 862; ◷ 8am-2.30pm Mon-Fri, 8am-noon Sat) Cashes travellers cheques; has an ATM.
**Ured Informacije** ( ☎ 651 988; www.medjugorje.hr; ◷ 9am-5pm) Church schedules and Virgin Mary monthly message.

## Sights & Activities

Completed in 1969, **St James' Church** is the hub of daily religious activity with services in many languages. Some 200m behind the church is the **Resurrected Saviour**, also known as the Weeping Knee statue, because this gaunt metallic figure of Christ on the Cross oozes liquid at the knee. Pilgrims bring their rosaries, medallions and small bottles and hold them up to capture the supposedly holy fluid. A watery substance does indeed ooze from a fissure but whether this is a miracle or some internal plumbing problem is for the devout or sceptic to decide.

**Apparition Hill**, where the Virgin was first seen on 24 June 1981, rises above Podbrdo hamlet, southwest of town. A rocky, well-worn path leads uphill, with the rocks shining from the polishing by thousands of passing feet, many barefoot in acts of penitence. The clamber uphill to the statue of the Virgin that marks the place of apparition is punctuated by 10 Stations of the Cross where pilgrims stop to pray.

**Mt Križevac** (Cross Mountain) rises up about 2.5km southwest of town. The 45-minute hike to the top via 14 Stations of the Cross leads to a white cross planted in 1934 to commemorate the 1900th anniversary of Christ's death. Millions of passing feet have worn away the soil leaving a cheese-grater surface of sharp-edged rocks, so wear sturdy shoes unless you're doing it the hard way in bare feet. Remedial cold beers are available from the several café-bars at the bottom of the hike.

## Sleeping

Unless the Virgin walks down the main street, Međugorje's 17,000 rooms (and increasing)

can cope with most accommodation demands, but if you're visiting at Christmas or Easter then it's best to book.

Most *pansion* rooms are similar although they are most expensive around the church. Proprietors usually offer the choice of B&B, half-board or full board with homemade meals usually complemented with a bottle of *domaći vino* (homemade wine).

**Paddy Travel** ( ☎ /fax 651482; paddy@tel.net.ba; private/hotel r from €10/20; ◷ 9am-3pm Mon-Sat Nov-Mar, 9am-6pm Mon-Sat Apr-Oct) This friendly, helpful Irish-Croatian outfit can book private and hotel accommodation.

**Vox Tours** ( ☎ /fax 650 771; per person half-board/full board from €20/26; ◷ 9am-5.30pm Mon-Fri, 9am-2pm Sat) Over the road from Paddy Travel, Vox Tours deals with most of the *pansions* in town.

**Pansion Zemo** ( ☎ /fax 651 878; www.medjugorjetravel .com/zemo; Kozine district; camp site per person & tent €3, B&B/half-board €9/14; Ⓟ ) Away from the town bustle, this camping ground and *pansion* lies about 1km southeast of the church in village fields. Rooms are available for noncampers.

**Pansion Stanko Vasilj** ( ☎ 651 042; per person B&B/half-board/full board €15/20/25; Ⓟ ) This ivy-covered tavern and *pansion* with a vineyard nicely mixes the two local earners, religion and wine. Downstairs is a wonderfully atmospheric bar with a stone-flagged floor, wooden beams and a rack of wine barrels – you could be in any period pre-WWI. The *pansion* is 200m southeast from the bottom of the Mt Križevac trail; it's popular so book early.

**Pansion Park** ( ☎ 651 155; fax 651 494; r with B&B/half-board/full board €20/25/28; Ⓟ ) Fronted by a big landscaped garden, these two large Swiss chalet–style houses are set back from the main street. Rooms are big and spacious, and downstairs there's a large restaurant to cater for those who have half- or full board.

## Eating

Many people opt for half-board or full board at their hotels and *pansions*. Nevertheless there are several good restaurants not only for food but also for a knees-up.

**Pizzeria Colombo** (pizzas €4-6; Ⓖ ) Hail Mary! There's Guinness here, and the dispensing font on the bar is protected with a rosary to ensure a continual flow of the elixir. One of the town's popular eateries, just by the church, it serves up decent pasta, pizza and salads.

**Gardens** ( ☎ 650 499; dishes €6-15) A ceiling with winsome cherubs plucking lyres greets customers in this classy place, where pilgrims come to party after doing penitence. They keep a plate of fresh-eyed fish on ice to tempt you into choosing one of their signature fish dishes.

**Dubrovnik** (☎ 651 472; mains €4-10; ♿) Good for a hearty cooked breakfast but it mainly scores on desserts: try the walnut pancake. Guinness is on tap and it's not unknown for an impromptu accordion band to strike up a few jigs and have the Irish dancing.

### Shopping

The biblical phrase 'money lenders in the temple' comes to mind as you prowl through the shops selling kitsch religious knick-knacks and souvenirs. Crosses, medallions, candles, rosaries, jigsaws of the Virgin Mary, statues, Christs in snow domes, and vestments; take your pick. One hundred euro will buy the vestments to hold your own mass while €2500 buys a 1.5m statue of the Virgin Mary.

These aside, a few stalls sell exquisitely sewn lacework, homemade wine and big chunky woollen sweaters. As there is no specific commandment against copyright piracy, there are a number of shops selling very cheap CDs.

### Getting There & Around

**Globtour** (☎ /fax 651 393, 651 593) runs buses to Zagreb (42KM, nine hours, 7.30am), Dubrovnik (25KM, 4½ hours, 6.10am) and Sarajevo (17.50KM, 3½ hours, 9am). Local buses run to Mostar (3KM, 40 minutes, 3.50pm, 5.30pm and 7.45pm).

Taxis charge a flat fee of €5 to anywhere in town.

**Duga Gift Shop** (☎ 063 403 614; 🕑 10am-10pm) rents out bicycles/scooters €10/50 per day.

# CENTRAL & NORTHERN BOSNIA & HERCEGOVINA

## TRAVNIK

☎ 030 / pop 33,000

With its impressive hillside medieval castle dominating the town and its birthplace association with famous author Ivo Andrić, Travnik is an ideal day trip from Sarajevo or a stop en route to Jajce.

Tucked into a narrow wooded valley only 90km northwest of Sarajevo, Travnik was the seat of Turkish viziers who ruled Bosnia and Hercegovina from 1699 to 1851. The town became an international crossroads, with France and Austria opening embassies here, and their diplomatic lives were the inspiration for Andrić's *The Travnik Chronicles*.

### Orientation & Information

Travnik's main street, Bosanska, runs east-west. The bus station is off Bosanska on the western end of town, within sight of the **post office** (☎ 547 102; Prnjavor), which can issue MasterCard advances.

### Sights

The **medieval castle** (☎ 518 140; admission 2KM; 🕑 10am-6pm Apr-Nov) was built in the 15th century to hold the Turks at bay. It never proved itself, as the Bosnian state was already collapsing and, when tested, the defenders surrendered without a fight. The Turks strengthened the fortifications and it remains largely unchanged today, except that the tower is being turned into a city museum.

If the castle is closed, the key is held by the anthropological and archaeological **museum** (☎ 518 140; admission 2KM; 🕑 9am-3pm Mon-Fri, 10am-2pm Sat & Sun), off Bosanska, which presents an eclectic variety of fossils, minerals, stuffed fauna and interesting artefacts from the Turkish period.

The museum also has the key, if needed, to the **Ivo Andrić museum** (☎ 518 140; Mustafa Kundić; admission 2KM; 🕑 9am-3pm Mon-Fri, 10am-2pm Sat & Sun), which is the 'birthplace' of the Bosnian author of *Bridge over the Drina* and *The Travnik Chronicles*. You will find Andrić's texts here in many languages, photos of his 1961 Nobel Prize ceremony, and, in case you never go, a photograph of the actual bridge over the Drina at Višegrad. Don't be fooled though, this museum is not the place where the author was born but a replica built in 1974.

Given Andrić's fame it's most surprising that Travnik has no street or building named after him. Town council please note!

At the eastern end of Bosanska is the famous **Many-Coloured Mosque**, which allegedly contains hairs from the prophet Mohammed's beard. Built in 1851 on the site of the burnt-down original (1757), it has an eastern rather than a western minaret and the exterior has some rather fine decoration – hence the name. Underneath the mosque is a bazaar.

**Plava Voda** (Blue Water), across the main highway, is a favourite summer spot for idling by the side of a rushing mountain stream. Stalls sell touristy knick-knacks and a few restaurants serve up local trout.

Viziers' **turbes** (tombs) in the town reflect the importance of Travnik as the capital of Bosnia in the 18th and 19th centuries. There are a couple on Bosanska, near the Hotel Lipa, with explanatory boards in English providing a historical background to the town.

## Sleeping & Eating

**Pansion Oniks** ( ☎ 512 182; Žitarnica bb; s/d/tr 35/60/80KM) A cheery option with reasonable rooms behind the café of the same name, and near the Many-Coloured Mosque. Breakfast is in the cosy downstairs café, which is a good place for other meals as well.

**Hotel Lipa** ( ☎ 511 604; Lažajeva 116; s/d/tr 52/84/121KM; P &) A plain but renovated hotel; everybody's friendly although not much English is spoken.

**Restoran Konoba** (Plava Voda; dishes 6-12KM; P) Local trout provides this restaurant with its signature dish, one of the best trout you'll taste with veggies that don't normally turn up on Bosnian plates (such as carrots and corn). Finish with baklava and a Bosnian coffee as you gaze at the tumbling river to the side of your terrace table.

## Getting There & Away

Buses go from the **bus station** ( ☎ 792 761) to Sarajevo (14KM, two hours, almost hourly), Jajce (13KM, 1½ hours, five daily) and Bihać (30KM, four hours, six daily).

## JAJCE

☎ 030 / pop 30,000

Not many towns can boast of their own waterfall, but Jajce can. Not only that, but with medieval catacombs, defensive towers and a hilltop citadel, a prehistoric temple, a massive polystyrene statue of Tito and some exceptionally beautiful lakes there's enough to please the most jaded traveller. As a bonus, there's one of Bosnia and Hercegovina's better hotels to stay in.

## Orientation & Information

The old town of Jajce is tiny. It's protected on one side by a ravine formed by the Vrbas River and on the others by sturdy city walls. The only road in passes through the Travnik gate and leaves 200m later by the Banja Luka gate. The waterfalls, the crescendo to the Pliva

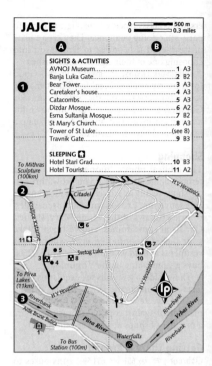

River, crash 21m down to join the Vrbas below the Travnik gate. They can be reached through a little park just before that gate.

The bus station is on the other side of the Pliva.

## Sights

Put on your walking legs – most of Jajce's attractions can be seen in a two-hour ramble, starting from the lane between the Hotel Stari Grad and the **Esma Sultanija Mosque**. As you go, look out for the information plates in English.

First stop is the roofless ruin of the medieval **St Mary's Church** with an adjacent campanile, **Tower of St Luke**. The bones of St Luke were reputedly kept in the church until the town fell to the Turks in 1459, when they were transferred to Venice, and then Padua. The church became a mosque and the tower a handy minaret until fire destroyed the church in 1832.

Beyond the church looms the **Bear Tower**, so called because of its size and strength. The lower walls are some 6m thick and, until WWII, when a ground entrance was added, the only entry was through the top-storey gateway. A quickly removable ladder made access impossible to an enemy.

By the tower is a small **caretaker's house** (☎ 659 231; ☿ 9am-dusk), the home of Alida and her husband, who hold the keys for access to the tower, the adjacent catacombs, the citadel and the Roman relief sculpture of Mithras. For 1KM per person per site, they will open doors for you and provide an English or German commentary.

The **catacombs** were built around 1400 by the powerful Duke Hrvoje as an underground church-mausoleum for his family. There are unoccupied crypts, an altar for funeral ceremonies, and, decorating the interior, sculpted double crosses, suns and crescent moons symbolising death, life after death and eternal sleep.

Opposite St Mary's church, steps lead to the **citadel** via the small **Dizdar Mosque** (Women's Mosque), which has a dome concealed beneath its angled roof. The **citadel walls** crown the egg-shaped hill upon which they sit, giving Jajce its name, 'little egg'. The interior contains little except a powder magazine, which the Turks converted into a school, but a walk on the walls gives a good view of the town. As you leave the entrance and walk anticlockwise around the walls, look at the sculpted relief by the entrance – it is the coat of arms of the Bosnian king, Stjepan. Walk around the citadel, down ulitsa Kralje Katerine and then turn right to find ulitsa Mitrasova. At the end is a stone building containing a Roman-era **sculpture** depicting the god Mithras and a bull-slaughter ritual.

In 1943 Jajce hosted the second congress of AVNOJ (Antifascist Council of the People's Liberation of Yugoslavia), which formulated the postwar socialist constitution of Yugoslavia. The actual building in the park opposite the Pliva falls is now a small **AVNOJ museum** (admission 2KM; ☿ 10am-2pm & 4-7pm). In the corner is a large brooding statue of partisan Tito, carved from polystyrene and painted gold. On the floor of the hall are the seats and benches where the delegates sat, and flanking them are contemporary photographs of the congress. Tito's comfy armchair is there in the front row under a beady-eyed photograph of Marx, but his comrades had to make do with hardback benches. Many of the artefacts were looted in the last war but it's still worth a visit.

The upper reaches of the Pliva River are damned into a series of **lakes** that make for a superb relaxation spot: boating, fishing and swimming are all possible. Between the lakes is a line of small wooden **mills** that were built in Ottoman times to grind wheat.

## Sleeping & Eating

There are two hotels in town, which also serve up food.

**Hotel Stari Grad** (☎ 654 006; Svetog Luke 3; s/d/apt 55/80/160KM; P ✗ ☖) The immediate eye-catcher is the glass-covered 3m gaping pit in the floor of the reception and restaurant-bar. As you step around it, gingerly for the first time, you'll see an old wall of an ancient Turkish hammam that was unearthed during reconstruction. It's a most pleasant hotel that looks old although it isn't, with well-furnished comfortable rooms, saunas and helpful staff who speak good English. The good restaurant serves up tasty traditional Bosnian food plus some Italian dishes.

**Hotel Tourist** (☎ 658 151; Kraljice Katerine bb; s/d/tr 47/74/96KM; P ✗ ☖) A straightforward business-conference hotel that's perfectly acceptable when the more atmospheric Stari Grad is full.

## Getting There & Away

Buses go from the **bus station** (☎ 659-202) to Sarajevo (22KM, 3½ hours, six daily), Banja Luka (10KM, 1½ hours, seven daily) and Banja Luka (10KM, two hours, six daily).

## BANJA LUKA

☎ 051 / pop 232,000

There's little to attract visitors to the Republika Srpska capital. The only reasons for stopping are to take a breather en route to Belgrade, Zagreb or Sarajevo, or for the rafting.

Banja Luka was never much of a tourist centre. A 1969 earthquake destroyed about 80% of the town and in 1993 local Serbs updated the damage by blowing up the city's mosques, including the famous 1580 Ferhadija. In 2001 a bussed-in nationalist mob stoned an attempt to lay a new foundation stone

## Orientation & Information

The bus station and adjacent train station are about 3km northeast of the centre. There's now a city **tourist office** (☎ 349 910; www.banjaluka-tourism.com; Bana Lazarevića 6; ☿ 8am-6pm Mon-Fri, 9am-2pm Sat).

BOSNIA & HERCEGOVINA

## Sights & Activities

The walls of a large 16th-century **castle** of Roman origin now enclose parkland, and the castle is host to a summer-long festival of music, dance and theatre.

The Vrbas River is a big centre for rafting; contact **Kanjon Rafting Club** ( ☎ 065 420 000; www.kanjonraft.com) or the tourist office for details.

## Sleeping & Eating

Veselina Maslaše, parallel to Kralja Petra but one block east, is a long strip of cafés, bars, pastry shops and ice-cream vendors. Take your choice.

**Hotel Bosna** ( ☎ 215 775; www.hotelbosna.com; Kralja Petra 9; old s/d 67/104KM, renovated s/d 102/144KM; **P** ) A grand hotel right in the heart of matters with some perfectly adequate and cheap un-renovated rooms – some are big enough for a party. A big restaurant, bar and shops augment this city hotel.

**Kod Muje** ( ☎ 358 492; snacks 3-6KM; ☺ 7am-11pm; ☺ ) Take the lane beside No 34 Veselina Maslaše and discover the best in old-fashioned cheap eateries. It's a wooden cabin with a big front garden that quickly fills in fine weather. Whether it's a ćevapčići or a grill you're after, you will be treated like a guest of the family.

**Master** ( ☎ 317 444; Sime Šolaje 7; mains 6-15KM; ☺ 10am-midnight; ☺ ) Jaded by all that grilled meat? Then try Mexican; the locals have certainly warmed to enchiladas, fajitas and a Corona beer or two.

## Getting There & Away

The **bus station** ( ☎ 315 355; Prote N. Kostića bb) has hourly buses to Belgrade (29KM, seven hours), six to Sarajevo (23KM, five hours), and services to Zagreb (24KM, seven hours, 8.45am, 9.10am, 4.10pm and 5.30pm) and Bihać (16KM, three hours, 5.30am, 7.30am, 1pm and 2pm).

The **train station** ( ☎ 301 229; Prote N. Kostića bb) has international connections with Belgrade, coastal Croatia and Zagreb; see p131 for more information.

A taxi from the centre to the train station should cost 6KM.

## BIHAĆ

☎ 037 / pop 80,000

Tucked up in northwest Bosnia and Hercegovina, Bihać is earning a reputation as one of the country's more outdoors-oriented towns.

---

> **WARNING**
>
> The Bihać area was mined extensively during the war and while much de-mining has been carried out there are still dangers in the countryside. While tour operators in the area will know what's safe, if you're intending doing any off-road adventuring then check with the local tourist office or, better still, Sarajevo's Mine Action Centre (p101).

---

The attraction is the tumbling rapids of the sapphire-coloured Una River, which make it a kayaking and rafting playground. The Una Regatta in the last week of July is three glorious days of messing about in boats.

## Orientation

The Una River splits the town into two. The western side contains the town centre while the eastern side has some riverside hotels (where you're paying for the riverside location) and restaurants. From here Bihaćkih Branilaca leads out of town northwards to the Croatian border and Put V Korpusa leads south past the bus station on to Sarajevo.

## Information

**Centar** (Put V Korpusa 5; per hr 2KM; ☺ 7am-10pm) Internet access.

**Post office** ( ☎ 332 332; Bosanska 2; ☺ 7am-8pm) Exchange office and MasterCard cash advances.

**Raiffeisen Bank** ( ☎ 329 000; Dana Državnosti 5; ☺ 8am-6pm Mon-Fri, 8am-2pm Sat) Cashes travellers cheques; ATM.

**Telephone office** ( ☎ 310 055; Bosanska 3; ☺ 7am-9pm Mon-Sat, 9am-noon Sun)

**Tourist office** ( ☎ 222 777; Dr Irfana Ljubijankića 13; ☺ 8am-4pm Mon-Fri) A clued-up organisation with its finger on the pulse of river activities and accommodation possibilities. It also has a kiosk (open in summer) at the junction of Bosanska and Put V Korpusa.

## Sights

The lofty, stone **captain's tower** on the western side of the river dates from the early 16th century. It was a prison from 1878 to 1959, but now holds a nifty multilevel **museum** ( ☎ 223 214; admission 1KM; ☺ 10am-2pm & 4-8pm Mon-Fri), featuring sarcophagi from the Bihać area and displays on the history of the town.

Behind the tower are the remains of the **Church of St Anthony**, destroyed in WWII. The original St Anthony is now the **Fethya Mosque** at the other end of the town, and was converted by the Turks in the 1530s. At the end of the 17th century the Croats ousted the Turks and built a new St Anthony's, but it was never completed and WWII damage left just a bell tower.

Adjacent is a Muslim **turbe** containing the bodies of two martyrs.

## Activities

The rafting season usually runs from March to October, and there are two outfits providing the thrills and spills. Both need a minimum of six but it's always possible to join up with another group. Prices depend on the length and complexity of the trip and they can cater for both the nervous and hard cases. Both owners will collect by arrangement from the bus station.

**Una Kiro Rafting** ( ☎ /fax 223 760, 061 192 338; www.una-kiro-rafting.com; Golubic bb) is based at Golubic, 6km from Bihać. These rafters offer kayak lessons (€50 per day) and rafting (€20 to €40 per person). B&B is available at €26 per person, camping from €5 per person and there's a free kayak available for just messing around in.

**Una Rafting** (Sport Bjeli; ☎ 388 555, 061 138 853; raftbeli@bih.net.ba; Klokot Pecikovići bb) is based about 12km away from Bihać. It offers rafting (from €22), kayaking (two/five days €47/100), mountain biking and climbing. B&B accommodation costs €15.

For more specialised activities **Club Extreme Sport Limit** ( ☎ 061 144 248; lipa3@bih.net.ba; Dzanica Mahala bb) offers guided mountain climbing,

hiking and biking from April to October, plus canyoning and caving.

For information on fishing, ask at the tourist office.

## Sleeping

If the following are full ask at the tourist kiosk for alternatives, but note that the hotels in town, down on the river, are expensive.

**Hut Aduna** ( ☎ 314 304; Put V Korpusa bb; per person 6KM; P ) An under-the-trees camping ground about 5km out of town, between the Una River and the Ada Hotel. Sites are powered, there's a toilet and shower block, and a shared kitchen.

**Villa Una** ( ☎ /fax 311 393, 061 919 303; Bihaćkih Branilaca 20; s/d 50/60KM; P ) Centrally placed near the river and good value for a sparkling-clean private home with well-equipped rooms.

**Hotel Park** ( ☎ 226 394; www.aduna.ba; Put V Korpusa bb; s/d/apt €28/48/65; P ⚿ ) The town's big hotel has reasonable prices for recently renovated rooms. Singles are a bit shoebox, the doubles have more space and the apartments (three people) are even better. A coffee shop, restaurant and pretty good pizzeria complete the picture.

## Eating

**Express** ( ☎ 332 380; Bosanska 5; mains 3-6.50KM; ⏱ 7am-10pm) It's express by name and express by nature at this choose-point-and-buy cafeteria near the post office. There's a large video screen here for sports broadcasts.

**Biffe Mlin** ( ☎ 061 144 200; Put V Korpusa bb; dishes 5-12KM; ♿ ) Sitting-out weather? OK, arrive before sunset and bag the table on the small island in the river; it's all right, there's a causeway. Quaff a beer or three while the sun goes down and watch the light planes buzz round the sports aerodrome over the river. After five or six beers you might try the plate of pig knuckles garnished with a bunch of spring onions, otherwise there are more usual items on the menu.

**Sunce** ( ☎ 310 487; Put V Korpusa bb; mains 8-15KM) If you don't want to travel so far, then this restaurant is just off the southeastern side of the bridge. Go for a table on the terrace or by the large picture windows giving a marvellous view of the Una rushing by. Go for the house speciality, *Plata Una* (30KM for two), an antipasto dish with nearly everything on it.

**River Una** ( ☎ 310 014; Džemala Bijedića 12; mains 8-15KM; ⏱ 7am-11pm) Sedate downstairs dining, drinks on the river terrace with the water

---

**WORTH A TRIP**

Bosnia and Hercegovina's second-most famous bridge spans the Drina at **Višgrad**. The **Mehmed-Pasha Sokolovic** bridge is the star of Ivo Andrić's *Bridge over the Drina*. A multi-arched graceful structure, it's still the same bridge, albeit with repairs, as built in the 16th century.

Up in the hills, 5km from Višgrad, **Vilina Vlas** ( ☎ 058-620 311; vvlas@teol.net; Višgrad; s/d full board with treatment 48/80KM) is a thermal-waters resort specialising in post-surgery recovery, gynaecological problems, stroke recovery and back troubles. Visitors can come for a three-day relax and tune up, but serious treatment requires 10 to 28 days.

lapping at your feet, or snug tables among the wooden beams upstairs – take your pick. The succulent trout is first choice with a fall-back of traditional Bosnian grills.

**Samoposluga** ( ☎ 312 601; Bihaćkih Branilaca bb; ☯ 7.30am-10pm Mon-Sat, 8am-3pm Sun) A sizable supermarket next to Villa Una for feed-yourself requirements.

### Getting There & Away

Useful services from the **bus station** ( ☎ 311 939; Put V Korpusa bb) go to Banja Luka (16KM, three hours, 5.30am, 7.30am, 1pm and 3pm), Sarajevo (39.50KM, seven hours, 12.45am, 7.30am, 2.30pm and 10pm) and Zagreb (21KM, 2½ hours, 4.45am, 10.20am, 2pm and 4.45pm).

For adventurous rail travellers there's a train to Zagreb (21KM, 10¾ hours, 9am), which involves a five-hour wait and change of trains in Novi Grad.

# BOSNIA & HERCEGOVINA DIRECTORY

## ACCOMMODATION

Private accommodation is easy to arrange in Sarajevo and is possible in Mostar; most likely you'll be approached at the bus or train station. Staying in a home is not only cheaper but also usually very pleasant. Likely as not, your hosts will ply you with coffee, pull out old pictures of Tito (depending on their age and politics) and regale you with many tales of old Yugoslavia's glorious past.

Sarajevo is well blessed with budget accommodation and most towns have *pansions* (pensions) that are generally slightly humbler, though more personable, than the hotels. Some hotels have not changed since the days of state ownership while others have been privatised and modernised.

Unless otherwise mentioned, breakfast is included but not usually with private accommodation, and all rooms have bathrooms. The prices quoted are for the high season.

## ACTIVITIES

Bosnia and Hercegovina has a huge potential for outdoor activities that will be fully realised once de-mining is completed. Water activities are obviously safe, as are activities in national parks and those led by local guides. Skiing is available at Jahorina (p116) and Bjelašnica (p116); rafting and kayaking at Bihać (p127), Banja Luka (p126) and near Mostar (p119); and mountain climbing and canyoning from Bihać (p127).

Popular with expat workers, **Green Visions** ( ☎ 717 290; www.greenvisions.ba; Radnička bb; ☯ 9am-5pm Mon-Fri) is a Sarajevo ecotourism agency that runs outdoors trips; they also return a portion of their proceeds to local communities (see p111).

## BOOKS

Rebecca West's mammoth *Black Lamb & Grey Falcon* (published in 1941) remains a classic piece of travel writing, although its 1937 ending is of no help in understanding more recent history. Noel Malcolm's *Bosnia: A Short History* is a good country-specific complement that brings history up to date.

Misha Glenny's *The Balkans, Nationalism, War, and the Great Powers, 1804-1999* has some telling pages on the background to the recent war. *Balkan Babel* by Sabrina Ramet is an engaging look at Yugoslavia from Tito to Milošević.

*Forgotten Beauty, a Hiker's Guide to Bosnia and Hercegovina's 2000m Peaks* by Matias Gomez is a very useful publication for hikers.

## BUSINESS HOURS

Business hours are 8am to 4pm Monday to Friday; banks open Saturday morning. Shops are open longer hours and many open on Sunday.

## DANGERS & ANNOYANCES

Bosnia and Herzegovina's greatest danger is mines and unexploded ordnance; see p101. Nationalism runs strong in some parts of the country (notably the RS and Croatian areas to the south and west), but this should not affect travellers, who can expect a warm welcome almost everywhere.

## DISABLED TRAVELLERS

There has been much effort to make things easier for travellers with disabilities, especially those with wheelchairs. This is partly in response to those who have been disabled through war and also through rebuilding to Western standards. Smaller hotels don't have lifts and disabled toilets are still rare.

## EMBASSIES & CONSULATES
### Bosnian Embassies & Consulates

Bosnia and Hercegovina has embassies and/or consulates in the following countries; check www.mvp.gov.ba for further listings.

**Australia** ( ☎ 02-6232 4646; www.bosnia.webone.com .au; 6 Beale Crescent, Deakin, ACT 2600)

**Canada** ( ☎ 613-236 0028; fax 613-236 8557; 130 Albert St, Suite 805, Ottawa, Ontario K1P 5G4)

**Croatia** ( ☎ 01-46 83761; 01-46 83764; Torbarova 9, PP27, 10001 Zagreb)

**France** ( ☎ 01 42 67 34 22; fax 01 40 53 85 22; 174 Rue de Courcelles, 75017 Paris)

**Germany** ( ☎ 030-814 712 33/4/5; www.botschaftbh.de; Ibsenstrasse 14, D-10439)

**Netherlands** ( ☎ 70-358 85 05; fax 70-358 43 67; Bezuidenhoutseweg 223, 2594 AL Den Haag)

**Slovenia** ( ☎ 01-23 43 250; fax 01-23 43 261; Kolarjeva 26, 1000 Ljubljana)

**UK** ( ☎ 020-7373 0867; fax 020-7373 0871; 5-7 Lexham Gardens, London W1R 3BF)

**USA** ( ☎ 202-337-1500; www.bhembassy.org; 2109 E St NW, Washington, DC 20037)

### Embassies & Consulates in Bosnia & Hercegovina

The nearest embassies for Australia, Ireland and New Zealand are found in Vienna, Ljubljana and Rome respectively. These countries have representation in Sarajevo:

**Austria** (Map p107; ☎ 033-279 400; fax 033-668 339; Džidžikovac 7)

**Bulgaria** ( ☎ 033-668 191; fax 033-668 182; Soukbunar 5)

**Canada** (Map p107; ☎ 033-222 033; fax 033-222 004; Grbavička 4/2)

**Croatia** (Map p107; ☎ 033-444 331; fax 033-472 434; Mehmeda Spahe 16)

**France** (Map p107; ☎ 033-282 050; fax 033-212 186; Mehmed-bega K Lj 18)

**Germany** (Map p107; ☎ 033-275 000; fax 033-652 978; Mejtaš Buka 11-13)

**Japan** (Map pp108-9; ☎ 033-209 580; fax 033-209 583; MM Bašeskije 2)

**Netherlands** (Map p107; ☎ 033-562 600; fax 033-223 413; Grbavička 4/1)

---

**EMERGENCY SERVICES**

- Ambulance ☎ 124
- Fire ☎ 123
- Police ☎ 122
- Roadside emergency ☎ 1282, 1288

---

**Serbia** (Map p107; ☎ 033-260 080; fax 033-221 469; Obala Maka Dizdara 3a)

**Slovenia** (Map p107; ☎ 033-271 251; fax 033-271 270; Bentbaša 7)

**UK** (Map p107; ☎ 033-282 200; fax 033-282 203; Tina Ujevića 8)

**USA** (Map p107; ☎ 033-445 700; fax 033-659 722; Alipašina 43)

## GAY & LESBIAN TRAVELLERS

Attitudes to homosexuality are very conservative with no open displays of affection between same-sex couples and there are no openly gay places to meet. Same-sex couples are not likely to encounter difficulties booking a room.

The staff at the BuyBook (p107) store in Sarajevo may be able to put you in contact with the Q Association, a gay and lesbian organisation.

## HOLIDAYS

Bajram, a twice-yearly Muslim holiday (February and November or December), is observed in parts of the Federation. Easter and Christmas are observed but Orthodox and Catholic dates may not coincide.

**New Year's Day** 1 January
**Independence Day** 1 March
**May Day** 1 May
**National Statehood Day** 25 November

## INTERNET RESOURCES

**Bosnia & Hercegovina** (www.bhtourism.ba) Useful tourist information.

**Bosnian Institute** (www.bosnia.org.uk) Deals with Bosnian culture.

**Grad Sarajevo** (www.sarajevo.ba)

**Hidden Bosnia** (www.hiddenbosnia.com) Useful tourist information.

**InsideBosnia** (www.insidebosnia.com) Has news on events and other interesting links.

**Ministry of Foreign Affairs of Bosnia and Hercegovina** (www.mvp.gov.ba) Has details on embassies and visas.

**Office of the High Representative** (www.ohr.int) A good source of news.

## LANGUAGE

The people of Bosnia and Hercegovina basically speak the same language, but it's referred to as 'Bosniak' in the Muslim parts of the Federation, 'Croatian' in Croat-controlled parts and 'Serbian' in the RS.

The Federation uses the Latin alphabet; the RS uses Cyrillic. See the Croatian and Serbian section of the Language chapter (p947).

## MAPS

Freytag & Berndt produces a good 1:250,000 road map of Bosnia and Hercegovina. Maps of Mostar, Sarajevo and Banja Luka are readily available from bookshops, kiosks or tourist information centres.

## MONEY

### ATMs

ATMs taking credit and debit cards are common in towns and cities.

### Credit Cards

Visa, MasterCard and Diners Club are readily accepted by larger establishments all over the country.

### Currency

The convertible mark (KM; *ki*-em) is Bosnia and Hercegovina's official currency. It's tied to the euro – 1KM equals €0.51129, but in effect 2KM equals 1€. Many establishments (especially hotels) accept euros (notes only) and sometimes list prices in euros.

Aim to finish your visit with no convertible marks as the currency is difficult to exchange outside the country.

### Travellers Cheques

Travellers cheques can be readily changed at Raiffeisen and Zagrebačka banks but they impose a low monthly exchange limit. We were asked at one bank to show a receipt for our original purchase.

## POST

Post and telephone offices are usually combined. Poste restante service is available at all cities included in this book; letters should be addressed to the person at 'Poste Restante, [postcode], Bosnia and Hercegovina'. Useful postcodes:

**Bihać** 77000
**Međugorje** 88266
**Mostar (Zapadni)** 88000
**Sarajevo** 71000

## TELEPHONE

Phonecards, for local or short international calls at public phones, can be bought at post offices or street kiosks for 2KM or 5KM. Unfortunately, cards issued in the Serbian, Croatian or Bosnian parts of the country are not interchangeable. It's cheaper to use the telephone section of post offices for longer calls.

Public telephones have a button labelled 'language' to give you instructions in English. Dial ☎ 1201 for the international operator and ☎ 1182 for local directory information.

### Mobile Phones

Mobile (cell) phone starter kits can be bought at kiosks for 29.50KM, including a SIM card and 10KM of credit. The numbers with the best coverage start with ☎ 061 or ☎ 062.

## VISAS

Citizens of the EU, Australia, Canada, Croatia, Japan, South Korea, New Zealand, Norway, Russia, Serbia, Montenegro, Switzerland and the USA do not require a visa.

Citizens of all other countries must apply for a visa; forms can be obtained from Bosnia and Hercegovina consular offices. An application for a private-visit visa must be accompanied by a letter of invitation from a citizen of the country, while a tourist-visa application must be accompanied by a voucher from the tourist agency organising the visit.

The cost of a single entry visa is €31. For a full list and application requirements check the government website www.mvp.gov.ba.

# TRANSPORT IN BOSNIA & HERCEGOVINA

## GETTING THERE & AWAY

### Air

Bosnia and Hercegovina's main airport is located at Sarajevo, with others at Mostar and Banja Luka.

European airlines such as Austrian Airlines, Czech Airlines and Lufthansa operate out of intercontinental hubs such as London, Frankfurt, Prague and Vienna. No discount airlines fly into Bosnia and Hercegovina yet, but a cheap flight to Zagreb or Dubrovnik and a bus trip could be an option.

The following airlines (Sarajevo numbers) serve **Sarajevo airport** ( ☎ 289 120; www.sarajevo -airport.ba; Kurta Schorka bb):

**Adria Airways** (code JP; ☎ 232 125; www.adria-air ways.com)
**Alitalia** (code AZ; ☎ 556 565; www.alitalia.com)
**Austrian Airlines** (code OS; ☎ 474 444; www.aua.com)
**BH Airlines** (code JA; ☎ 550 125; www.airbosna.ba)
**Croatia Airlines** (code OU; ☎ 666 123; www.croatiaair lines.hr)

**ČSA** (Czech Airlines; code OK; ☎ 289 250; www.csa.cz)
**JAT** (code JU; ☎ 259 750; www.jat.com)
**Lufthansa** (code LH; ☎ 474 444; www.lufthansa.com)
**Malév Hungarian Airlines** (code MA; ☎ 473 200; www.malev.hu)
**Turkish Airlines** (code TK; ☎ 666 092; www.turkishairlines.com)

BH Airlines serves **Mostar airport** ( ☎ 350 992) with international flights.

## Land
### BUS
Well-established bus routes link Bosnia and Hercegovina with its neighbours and Western Europe.

Međugorje, Mostar, Sarajevo and Bihać have bus connections with Split and Dubrovnik on the coast, and Zagreb in Croatia. Sarajevo and Banja Luka have services to Belgrade and Podgorica in Serbia and Montenegro.

### CAR & MOTORCYCLE
Drivers will need Green Card insurance for their vehicle, and an International Driving Permit. Fuel is readily available in towns but it's sensible not to let your tank get too low, especially at night when stations may be closed. Spares for European-made cars should be readily available, and there'll be mechanics in all largish towns.

### TRAIN
A daily service connects Ploče (on the Croatian coast) with Zagreb via Mostar, Sarajevo and Banja Luka; another connects Ploče and Budapest via Mostar and Sarajevo.

| Ploče | Mostar | Sarajevo | Banja Luka | Zagreb | Budapest |
|---|---|---|---|---|---|
| 6.40am | 8.04am | 10.18am | 3.34pm 7.47pm | - | - |
| 10.22am | | 8.50am | 6.25am (next day) | | 5.45pm |
| 4.20pm | 5.56pm | 8.32pm | | | 8.48am (next day) |
| 11.06pm | | 8.40pm | 6.18pm 8.57am | 1.11pm | |

A 1st-/2nd-class seat from Sarajevo to Budapest costs 90/131KM, and a 2nd-class seat from Banja Luka to Zagreb costs 22KM. An overnight service goes from Banja Luka to Belgrade (24KM, 6½ hours, 9.55pm).

## GETTING AROUND
### Bicycle
Only adventurous foreigners cycle out into the countryside, where the roads can be very hilly. Do not venture off established concrete or asphalt surfaces because of the risk of mines. There is a core of cyclists in Sarajevo but, again, they tend to be foreigners.

### Bus
Bosnia and Hercegovina's bus network is comprehensive and reliable, although some buses verge on the decrepit. Some services between distant towns may be limited. As in other matters, the Federation and RS run separate services. Stowing luggage usually costs up to 2KM per item, depending on the route. Buses usually run on time, although they are slow due to winding roads and occasional stops for drivers and passengers to eat and smoke.

Sample fares are 13.50KM for Mostar to Sarajevo, 23KM for Sarajevo to Jajce and 16KM from Banja Luka to Bihać. Generally, reservations aren't really necessary except on international buses or on infrequent long-distance services during holiday times.

### Car & Motorcycle
Narrow roads, hills and bends in the countryside slow down car driving and make for challenging motorcycling. Some drivers believe they're immortal and drive like maniacs, overtaking on sharp curves, but vigilant roadside police with speed cameras often catch them.

#### AUTOMOBILE ASSOCIATIONS
The **Automobile Association of Bosnia & Hercegovina** (Map p107; ☎ 033-212 771; www.bihamk.ba; Skenderija 23, 71000 Sarajevo) offers road assistance and towing services for members. A membership costs 25KM per year.

#### HIRE
Car rental is available in the bigger cities with prices from €40/250 for one day/week with unlimited mileage. In Sarajevo **Lami Rent a Car** ( ☎ 061 260 609) charges from €33 a day. There's no problem with driving hire cars between the country's different entities.

#### ROAD RULES
Driving is on the right, seat belts must be worn and the tolerated level of alcohol in the blood is 0.05. Speed limits are 60km/h for urban roads and 80km/h for rural roads.

BOSNIA & HERCEGOVINA

# Bulgaria България

Hurry. Eastern Europe's last stop to the south, Bulgaria, is changing fast. Now part of the EU and with 'New Bulgarians' (aka middle-aged Brits) buying up beach and mountain villas, Bulgaria is having a change-forever moment. Its 'big four' – bustling modern capital Sofia, laid-back hill town Veliko Târnovo, lively Black Sea city Varna, and cobbled Roman-rooted Plovdiv – dominate most itineraries. They're worthy, but it's worth digging deeper, where you'll find whitewashed gingerbread taverns to bunk in, old guys whispering baby goats to sleep on trains, locals bragging about 'hangover-free' wine and hikes to huts on Alp-like peaks with ski runs weaving down them. Bulgaria's reputation as a budget ski and beach destination is starting to wear out: its chief beach resort, Sunny Beach, has three times the hotel capacity than its beach can fit. Once a quiet ski base, Bansko is building itself up to make a case for the 2014 Winter Olympics.

All is far, far from lost though. DIY explorations through the culturally rich Stara Planina or Rodopi Mountains take in traditional villages – including some Turkish ones where Bulgarian phrases are met with confused shrugs. Strong links to Bulgaria's distant history are being uncovered with gusto, as just-discovered Thracian sites – particularly around Kazanlâk – are opening to visitors. Up in Belogradchik, medieval walls surround animated bluffs so lifelike you wonder if Medusa had her way with a tea party of giants.

Many visitors use guides such as this one to 'check the Bulgaria box' with a couple of days in Sofia, then move on. It's kinda sad – but all the better for those capitalising on areas that see fewer folk.

## FAST FACTS

- **Area** 110,910 sq km
- **Capital** Sofia
- **Currency** leva (lv); A$1 = 1.20; €1 = 1.96lv; ¥100 = 1.39; NZ$1 = 1.07; UK£1 = 2.85lv; US$1 = 1.64lv
- **Famous for** Black Sea beaches, monasteries, yogurt
- **Official Language** Bulgarian
- **Phrases** *zdrasti* (hello), *blagodarya* (thank you), *imati li?* (do you have?), *kolko struva?* (how much?), *oshte bira molya* (another beer please)
- **Population** 8 million
- **Telephone Codes** country code ☎ 359; international access code ☎ 00
- **Visa** no visa required for citizens of Australia, Canada, the EU, New Zealand, USA and several other nations; see p186 for details

BULGARIA

## HIGHLIGHTS

- Look across a river gorge and up to the tsar-sized citadel that was once home to a royal court at hilly **Veliko Târnovo** (p162).
- Visit the Black Sea's busiest hub, **Varna** (p170) where the museums, open-air discos and sailor caps would be worth visiting even without the sea.
- Don your hiking boots to explore the mountainous topography of beautiful **Rila and Pirin** (p147) and **Rodopi** (p151) ranges.
- Channel *The Lord of the Rings* in the animated peaks that surround **Belogradchik** (p182), a medieval fort in Bulgaria's northwest pinkie.
- Check out Roman theatres and revival-era taverns in **Plovdiv** (p151), Bulgaria's most relaxing city.

## ITINERARIES

- **One week** Stop off at Veliko Târnovo for a couple days, then bus to Plovdiv for Roman ruins or Varna for the disco nights on the beach. Finish with a wander around the centre in bustling Sofia.
- **Two weeks** Start off in Sofia for a couple of days, then head south to Rila Monastery for a night, and spend another in Melnik for some of the country's best wine. Go, via Sofia, to Plovdiv for two days, and then travel east to Kazanlâk for a peek in a Thracian tomb. Head to the beach – walk the cobbled core of Sozopol, then hit the beach bars at Varna. Finish with two or three days in Veliko Târnovo.

### HOW MUCH?

- Night in Sofia hostel 20lv
- Sofia–Plovdiv bus ticket 10lv
- Museum admission 2lv to 10lv
- Varna city map 3lv
- Day rental car 30lv to 50lv

### LONELY PLANET INDEX

- Litre of petrol 1.60lv
- Litre of bottled water 0.60lv
- Kamenitza beer 0.80lv
- Souvenir T-shirt 3lv to 5lv
- Street snack – banitsa 0.50lv

## CLIMATE & WHEN TO GO

Bulgaria has a temperate climate with cold, damp winters and hot, dry summers. See Climate Charts (p911) for more. From mid-July to August, Bulgaria swarms with tourists, particularly at Black Sea resorts. For beaches in the hot sun, a better time is September – the off-season is too quiet as almost everything's closed from October to March. The ski slopes fill from mid-December to March or mid-April, while much of the country's attractions trim their hours.

If you're not beach-bumming or skiing, spring or autumn are great times (particularly May) as there are very few tourists, and theatres and other cultural venues awake from hibernation.

## HISTORY
### Becoming Bulgaria

Thracians moved into the area in the 4th millennium BC, and by AD 100 Romans controlled the lands. The first Slavs migrated here from the north in the 5th century, and the First Bulgarian State was formed in 681.

The fierce Turkic Bulgars – whose name later became Bulgaria – first reached these areas from their expansive territories between the Caspian and Black Seas. By the time the Byzantine Empire conquered Bulgaria in 1014 (after blinding 15,000 Bulgarian troops in one bloody poke-fest), the first state had created a language, the Cyrillic alphabet, a church and – spurred on by enforced conversion to Christianity – a people (a mix of Slavs, Proto-Bulgarians and a few Thracians).

Bulgaria's second kingdom, based in Veliko Târnovo, began in 1185 and saw much warfare with Serbs, Hungarians and the Ottoman army, who took control in 1396.

### Life with the Ottomans

The next 500 years were spent living 'under the yoke' of Ottoman rule. The Orthodox church persevered by quietly holing up in monasteries. Higher taxes for Christians saw many convert to Islam.

During the 18th and 19th centuries, many butt-kicking 'awakeners' are credited with reviving Bulgarian culture. By the 1860s several revolutionaries (including Georgi Rakovski, Vasil Levski and Hristo Botev) organised *cheti* (rebels) bands for the (failed) April Uprising of 1870. With Russia stepping in, the

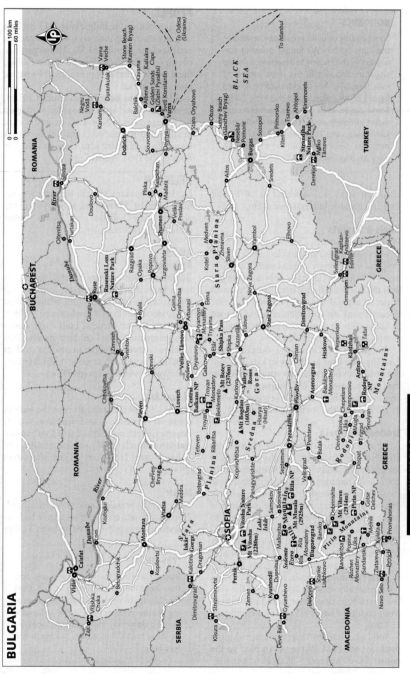

BULGARIA

---

**BOGOMILS**

These cuddly celibate vegetarian hermits of the 10th century AD fought growing corruption in the church by rejecting *anything* visual as dripping in the most satanic of evils. Naturally, they quickly became revered heroes of their day, called the 'Holy Ones'. Some argue their hermitic complacency didn't stimulate a much-needed intellectual awakening, and Bogomils slowly died off in all but street names around the country. *Vivos los Bogomilos!*

---

Ottoman army was defeated in 1878, and Bulgaria became independent again.

### Nazis & Soviets

With eyes on lost Macedonia, and following a series of painful Balkan wars (including WWI), Bulgaria surprisingly aligned with Nazi Germany in WWII – Germany only just won out over the USSR for Bulgaria's allegiance – with hopes to expand its borders. Famously, Tsar Boris III said 'no' to Hitler, refusing to send Bulgaria's Jewish population to concentration camps, sparing up to 50,000 lives.

As the war drew to a close, Bulgaria did a final flip-flop over to the Soviet side, but that did little to smooth relations with the West or the USSR following WWII. Bulgaria embraced communism wholeheartedly (even proposing in 1973 to join the Soviet republics).

### Modern Bulgaria

After making friends with the USA (there are US military bases outside Burgas), NATO saying 'yep' to Bulgaria in 2004 and the EU in 2007, Bulgarians are a little more upbeat these days. However, considering average monthly salaries linger around €165, one local joke is more pessimistic: 'We were little brother to the Ottoman Empire for 500 years; they collapsed. Then the Nazis and Soviets, and they collapsed. NATO, USA and EU, watch out!'

Real estate has become a giant money-making revenue for locals, as property values have generally shot up by 200% in the past few years. Run-down homes and new beachfront condos start at €15,000 and climb past €50,000.

Sofia and Bansko together are making a pitch for the 2014 Winter Olympics, so the construction business is likely to boom, too.

## PEOPLE

The population of Bulgaria is 7.45 million (slightly shrinking recently), with Bulgarians and Slavs constituting 83.5%. The largest minorities are Turks (9.5%) and Roma (4.6%); there are also smaller populations of Russians, Jews and Greeks.

A few famous Bulgarians include Christo, an environmental artist famous for putting up the orange gates in New York's Central Park in 2005; and Hristo Stoichkov, the country's favourite footballer, who won the Golden Boot in the 1994 World Cup.

## RELIGION

During the communist era Bulgaria was officially atheist. These days, about 84% of the population are Orthodox and 12% are Muslim (almost all are Sunni).

## ARTS
### Architecture

Bulgaria's 19th-century revival saw many town makeovers with quaint, traditionally styled *kâshta* buildings (with whitewashed walls, wood shutters, wood-carved ceilings and hand-woven carpets) built close alongside (sometimes over) cobbled streets. This massive source of Bulgarian pride is evident in many towns, such as Koprivshtitsa (p159) and Plovdiv's Old Town (p153).

### Visual Arts

Bulgaria's most treasured art is on the walls of medieval monasteries and churches, such as Boyana Church near Sofia (p147), Arbanasi's Nativity Church (p166) and the paintings by Zahari Zograf (1810–53) at Rila Monastery (p148).

### Music

The currently popular and controversial 'wedding music', aka *chalga*, is a vaguely Indian-sounding synth-pop (picked up from Turkey

---

**'YES OR NO?'**

Bulgarians shake their head 'yes' and nod their head 'no'. It's confusing at first, then fun. Just try to think that a shake is sweeping the floor clean ('yes, come in') and a nod is a slamming shut a garage door ('no, go away fool!'). If in doubt, ask '*da ili ne?*' (yes or no?).

---

**YOU'VE NOT BEEN TO BULGARIA UNTIL YOU...**

There are just some things you have to do to really *be* in Bulgaria:

■ Try *banitsa* (cheese-filled pastry), *boza* (ill-tasting fermented soft drink) and *rakiya* (brandy).

■ Visit a 19th-century revival-era *kâshta* house; Plovdiv and Koprivshtitsa have heaps.

■ Learn Cyrillic: it was made here (not Russia, dammit) and takes an hour and a beer to figure out.

■ Fill a bottle with mineral water; springs are everywhere and it's a ritual for many Bulgarians.

■ Do the 'yes' horizontal head shake.

■ Put some ketchup on that pizza slice, amigo!

■ Listen to the sexually ambiguous pop of Azis (opposite) and deny liking it.

---

and Serbia) with less-than-intellectual lyrics. (One sample: 'We win, we lose…either way we get drunk, we're Bulgarians!') Essentially no-one in the country admits to liking Azis, a seriously flamboyant, sexually ambiguous *chalga* performer, who sells more CDs than nearly any Bulgarian artist.

Traditional music – played with *gaida* (bagpipes), *tambura* (four-stringed lute) and *tâppan* (drum) – is widespread. Turn on a TV and you'll see it on several channels nightly. Schools in Plovdiv (p154), Shiroka Lâka (p158) and Kotel (p162) stage recitals and offer classes.

## ENVIRONMENT
### The Land
Bulgaria lies in the heart of the Balkan Peninsula, stretching 502km from the Serbian border to the Black Sea.

Bulgaria is one-third mountains. The Stara Planina (also known as the Balkan Mountains) stretch across central Bulgaria. In the southwest are three higher ranges: the Rila Mountains, south of Sofia (home to the country's highest point, Mt Musala, 2925m); the Pirin Mountains, just to the south, which reach Greece; and the Rodopi Mountains to the east.

### Wildlife
Although Bulgaria has some 56,000 kinds of living creature – including one of Europe's largest bear populations – most visitors see little wildlife, unless venturing deep into the thickets and mountains.

### National Parks
Bulgaria has four national parks (Rila, Pirin, Rodopi and Central Balkans) and 10 nature parks, all of which offer some protection to the environment (and tourist potential).

## FOOD & DRINK
### Staples & Specialities
There are two kinds of Bulgarian food: Bulgarian food and pizza. The former comprises many light dishes, with Turkish or Greek influences. Salads – such as the everywhere-you-look *shopska* (tomatoes, onions, cucumbers and cheese) – start most meals. Main dishes are mostly grilled beef, pork, lamb and chicken – such as the *kebabche* (spicy meat sausages) – or heavier stews such as *kavarma*. Side dishes (such as boiled potatoes or cheese-covered chips) are ordered separately.

Vegetarians are not at a loss. Aside from salads, most restaurants have yogurt- or vegetable-based soups and several egg dishes. Well-made pizza, served by slice or whole, is everywhere.

Breakfast for most Bulgarians is espresso, cigarettes (plural intended) and a hot cheese-filled *banitsa* pastry, available at small bakeries (often named *zakuska*, 'breakfast').

Wine is super in Bulgaria, particularly Melnik's red. Says one local: 'Our wine is as good as France's, and their worst is worse than our worst.'

---

**SHOPSKA'S A FAKE!**

Horrors! Bulgaria's famous, tasty *shopska*, the 'traditional' meal starter that woos even hardened hearts across this fine land, is something of the 'Spice Girls of salads'. Its nomenclature is actually a 1970s, Balkantourist creation – something to help tourists stomach something distinctly *Bulgarian*. It spread like rabbits with locals though; hardly a meal here gets started without it.

---

BULGARIA

## Where to Eat & Drink

Evocative Bulgarian *krâshta* restaurants, it must be said, don't differ from one another much. A 10% tip is expected at sit-down restaurants, though sometimes it's included with the *smetka* (bill).

Cafés also act as de facto bars, serving local beer, wine and brandies. Many towns you'll come across have more standard beer houses (*birarias*).

# SOFIA СОФИЯ

☎ 02 / pop 1.11 million

OK, in comparison with Eastern European capitals to the north, Sofia is something of a Novosibirsk, an urban mass without any serious standout attractions, or even a clear central square or street. But that's just the first impression – and it's not at all fair. The whole Bulgarian world twirls around Sofia, and its shady gold-brick streets and parks give it energy and confidence that lures some travellers into its artier nooks for (on occasion) weeks. Also, Sofia has a huge mountain in Mt Vitosha, about 10km south, with skiing and hiking options waiting all year.

## HISTORY

Settled perhaps 7000 years ago by a Thracian tribe (eying the area's springs), and later named Serdica by Romans, Sofia is – despite the years – young. It was an outpost of 1200 residents when it became the nation's unlikely fourth capital in 1879 for its geographical location (ie proximity to ever-sought Macedonia). In the decades thereafter, much planned or aesthetic development was curbed by war and communism.

---

**SOFIA IN TWO DAYS**

Walk! Start at the **Aleksander Nevski Church** (p140) and nearby souvenir stands, and make 'Ministry of Silly Walks' jokes at the **changing of the guards** (p141). Wander south on side streets – lunch at **Divaka** (p144) – and make your way to **NDK** (p142) for deck views. Head back along bul Vitosha to **Sveta Nedelya Cathedral** (p142) to fill up your bottle at the **spring wells** (p142) and wander the **Ladies Market** (p145). A second day is well spent hiking or skiing at **Vitosha** (p147).

---

The name (changed from Serdica in the 15th century) comes from the Greek word for wisdom, not from an Italian.

## ORIENTATION

Sofia's main bus and train station are across bul Maria Luisa from each other, about 500m north of the start of the centre. Thoroughfares bul Maria Luisa and Vitosha meet at pl Sveta Nedelya, which is crossed by ul Tsar Osvoboditel, which leads past government buildings. City maps with transport routes are widely available.

## INFORMATION

For directory assistance call ☎ 144, or check http://db.infotel.bg:8889 for an online Bulgarian-language Sofia directory.

### Bookshops

**Book market** (pl Slaveikov) This daily open-air market sells some English secondhand novels and is open during daylight hours.

**Dom na Knigata** ( ☎ 981 7897; ul Graf Ignatiev, pasazh No 1; ☺ 10am-7pm) Book nuts' best haven in Bulgaria is found on ul Graf Ignatiev, across from pl Slavekiov. Messy racks of paperbacks in English, French, German, Spanish and Italian.

### Emergency

For police matters between 8am and 6pm, you (allegedly) can reach an English-speaking operator at ☎ 988 5239, or a French-speaking one at ☎ 982 3028. Otherwise, call ☎ 166. Presently you call ☎ 150 for an ambulance and ☎ 160 for the fire department.

### Internet Access

**BTC** (ul General Gurko; per hr 2lv; ☺ 8am-8pm) Eleven internet computers. Likely to be open 24 hours in future.

**Garibaldi** (ul Graf Ignatiev; per hr 2lv; ☺ 24hr)

**Site** (bul Vitosha 45; per hr 2lv; ☺ 24hr) Also makes international calls for 0.22lv per minute.

### Laundry

It's a problem, here and throughout Bulgaria. Hostels can help, otherwise you may have to wash it yourself.

### Left Luggage

**Central Bus Station** (per bag per day 5lv; ☺ 8am-midnight)

**Train Station** (per bag per day 2lv; ☺ 6am-11pm) At the south end of the main floor; electronic lockers (2lv per day) are in the basement.

**STS KIRIL & METODII**

The two brothers Kiril (Cyril) and Metodii (Methodius) were born in Thessaloniki in the early 9th century to a noble Byzantine family of Slavic-Bulgarian origins. Both were scholars and monks who studied and worked throughout the Balkans.

They are revered in Bulgaria for developing in 863 the first Bulgarian alphabet, called Glagolic, which was later simplified by one of their disciples, Clement, and became known as the Cyrillic alphabet. But, more importantly, they helped spread Orthodox Christianity throughout the Balkans by promoting the use of Slavic as the fourth accepted language of the Church (after Latin, Greek and Hebrew).

The Cyrillic alphabet is now used in Bulgaria, Russia, Macedonia, Ukraine, Belarus, Serbia and Mongolia. Bulgarians even celebrate Cyrillic Alphabet Day (also known as the Day of Bulgarian Culture) on 24 May.

## Media

*Sofia Echo* is an English-language paper, with entertainment listings, that comes out Friday (2.40lv). A few freebie publications list restaurants and bars: the quarterly *Sofia Inside & Out*, the monthly *Sofia City* (www.sofiacityguide.com) and the weekly *Programata* (in Bulgarian only; its website www.programata.bg has an English version).

## Medical Services

**Poliklinika Torax** ( ☎ 988 5259, 980 5791; bul Stamboliyski 57; ☽ 24hr) Good private clinic with English-language doctors west of the centre.

**Pirogov Hospital** ( ☎ 915 4111; bul General Totleben 21; ☽ 24hr) English is a crap-shoot.

## Money

Most foreign-exchange booths along bul Vitosha, bul Maria Luisa and bul Stamboliyski run nonstop.

**Bulbank** (ul Lavele & ul Todor Alexandrov; ☽ 8.30am-5pm Mon-Fri) Changes travellers cheques for 0.2% commission (minimum €1). There's an additional €0.50 charge for euro cheques, and £0.25 charge for British-pound cheques. You may need to show your cheque receipts.

**Central Cooperative Bank** (ul Dondukov 7B; ☽ 8.30am-5pm Mon-Fri) Charges 0.75% fee on travellers cheques (minimum €3).

## Telephone

**BTC** (ul General Gurko; ☽ 24hr) Snazzy phone booths. It's 0.36lv per minute for international calls, 0.72lv if calling a mobile phone. Domestic long-distance calls are 0.25lv for the first minute, then 0.18lv per minute.

## Tourist Information

**National Tourism Information & Advertising Centre** ( ☎ 987 9778; www.bulgariatravel.org; ul Sveta Sofia; ☽ 9am-5.30pm Mon-Fri) Has national brochures. English-speaking staff are nice, but have little information to share.

## Travel Agencies

**EBP Tours** ( ☎ 0888 922 916; Traffic Market, office 61; ☽ 6.30am-6.30pm Mon-Fri, 6.30am-2pm Sat & Sun) Bus station agent books tickets and helps with accommodation (€10 per person); they also have an office in the train station basement.

**Usit Colours** ( ☎ 937 3175; ul Vasil Levski 35; ☽ 9.30am-6.30pm Mon-Fri) Sells ISIC cards (10lv) and offers discounted air fares for students.

**Zig Zag** ( ☎ 980 5102; www.zigzagbg.com; bul Stamboliyski 20V; ☽ 8.30am-7.30pm Mon-Fri, daily in summer) Super-helpful English-language staff charge a 5lv consultation fee to book rooms, and give advice on hikes and activities around the country. Check its website for organised tours (hiking, kayaking and horse riding) that individuals can join. Zig Zag works with Odysseia-In, a national agency. Enter from ul Lavele.

## Visas

**Immigration Office** ( ☎ 982 3316; bul Maria Luisa 48; ☽ foreigner services 1am-noon Mon-Thu) This hectic office (in an unmarked entrance of the 'MBP' building) can extend visas.

## DANGERS & ANNOYANCES

Pickpockets (including some well-dressed mum-and-kid teams) sometimes troll bul Vitosha, particularly around Sveta Nedelya Cathedral, as well as outside the train station. Note that if you are carrying a big backpack or bulky luggage on public transport you will need to punch an extra ticket for it (some travellers have been fined about 5lv from officials).

Cab drivers often con travellers by charging exorbitant amounts.

BULGARIA

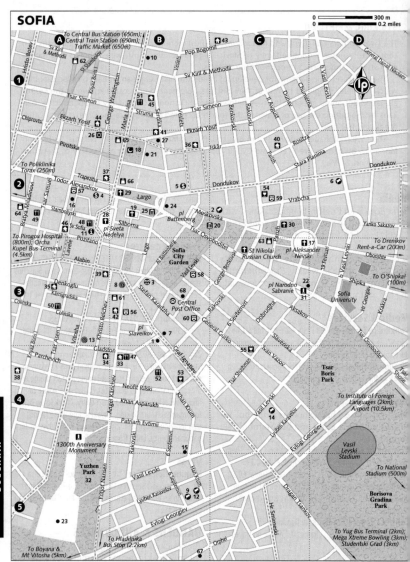

## SIGHTS

See Sofia at its best by roaming its atmospheric streets, particularly the tight lanes between ul Graf Ignatiev and bul Vitosha north of the NDK, Borisova Gradina Park (with its giant monuments and leafy grounds) and Studentski Grad. Also see the Around Sofia section (p147).

## Around Ploshad Aleksander Nevski

Gold-domed and massive, Sofia's premier focal point is the deliberately Russian-style **Aleksander Nevski Church** (pl Aleksander Nevski; admission free; 7am-7pm), constructed between 1892 and 1912. It's named after a Swedish-born Russian warrior in honour of the Russian liberators (including the 200,000 who died fighting the Ottomans). Inside the church are giant brass chandeliers hanging from the smoky ceilings high above. This and the Russian **Tsar Osvoboditel statue**, two blocks south, sandwich the Bulgarian **National Assembly**, something that gets some Bulgarians to eye-roll over.

On the church's northwestern corner, a door leads down to the **Aleksander Nevski Crypt** (☎ 981 5775; adult/student 4/2lv; ⏱ 10.30am-6.30pm Tue-Sun). It's a wide, well-lit space containing many national icons stretching back to the 5th century.

To the west (with an eternal flame burning outside), **Sveta Sofia Church** (admission free; ⏱ 7am-7pm summer, 7am-6pm winter) dates from the 5th century and inspired the name of the city. You can see earthquake-battered mosaics under the stone floor.

---

**STYLIN' COPS**

Watch for Porsche, Mercedes and Audi convertible 'police cars'. Sofia's home to a handful of luxury cars that have been 'confiscated' (for whatever reasons) and converted into the world's most slick police fleet.

---

## Around Sofia City Garden

This fountain-filled park a couple of blocks southwest of pl Aleksander Nevski is lined with cafés in good weather and surrounded by a gold-brick road.

To the north is the former Royal Palace, now home to two museums. The better of the two is the **Ethnographical Museum** (☎ 988 1974; ul Tsar Osvoboditel; adult 3lv; ⏱ 10am-6pm Tue-Sun Apr-Nov, 10am-4pm Tue-Sun Dec-Mar). It's palatial, but its dozen rooms (with lots of English signs) give a greater regional context to the whys and whats of traditional Bulgarian costumes and customs than you'll find in most such museums in the country.

Also in the palace, the **National Art Gallery** (☎ 980 0093; ul Tsar Osvoboditel; adult/student 4/2lv; ⏱ 10am-6pm Tue, Wed & Fri-Sun, 10am-7.30pm Thu) is a squeaky-floored 10-hall museum, with often changing exhibits dedicated to Bulgarian art.

Across from the giant white **Party House** (closed to the public) is the **President's Building** (also closed to the public), the site of the **changing of the guards**, where three feather-capped guys ceremoniously slap boot soles on the pavement (on the hour during daylight hours).

**BULGARIA**

The walkway the soldiers come from leads to the courtyard home of the small red-brick **Church of St George**, which dates from the 3rd century. It was much damaged in WWII, but you can see fragments of murals inside that date from the 12th century.

## Around Ploshad Sveta Nedelya

In the heart of pl Sveta Nedelya (a big block west of the President's Building) is well-lit, ornate **Sveta Nedelya Cathedral** (admission free; ☺ 7am-7pm), built between 1856 and 1863. Colourful murals line the inside top of the dome (if you can see through the candle smoke). Communists bombed the church in 1925 to kill Tsar Boris III, but failed.

Just north, accessed via an underpass, the **Sveta Petka Samardjiska Church** (adult 2lv; ☺ 8am-7pm) is a small church that pokes up its 14th-century steeple from the underpass amid a sea of traffic.

North on bul Maria Luisa are the ornate red-and-gold **mineral baths** (aka Turkish Baths), which have long been closed but at research time were, supposedly, due to reopen as a 'city museum' and 'spa'. If not, you can get an idea of its interiors from the renovated Tsentralni Khali (a mall across the street, which dates from 1909), or see mineral water in action just across ul Ekzarh Yosi, where locals fill bottles from modern **spring wells**.

Nearby is the unmistakable 16th-century **Banya Bashi Mosque** (admission free; ☺ dawn-dusk).

A block west is the **Sofia Synagogue** (ul Ekzarh Yosif 16; ☺ approx 10am-3.30pm Mon-Sat, closed to public during prayers), the largest Sephardic synagogue in Europe.

To the south, ritzy bul Vitosha faces its far-off namesake, Mt Vitosha. South of pl Sveta Nedelya 1km is **Yuzhen Park**, home to a falling-apart monument and the gigantic 'viva-1981!' **NDK** (Palace of Culture) complex, with cafés, shops, cinema and some events. On most days, its viewing deck is open.

## Studentski Grad

A few kilometres closer to Mt Vitosha (south of the centre), Student Town is an enclave of college students living in a spread-out neighbourhood of drab communist-era apartments booming with life at all hours (except the summer break). One resident said: 'Nightlife leads to day life. We party all the time'.

The Grad is home to an ever-changing selection of busy new cafés and bars at the base of the housing blocks – a fascinating mix. Bowl big and beyond limits at **Mega Xtreme Bowling** (☎ 969 2600; ul Stefanov; per game 5lv; ☺ 10am-4am), about 500m north of the minibus terminus. There's also a pool, a bar (beer from 1.2lv, cocktails 2lv to 3lv) and captive audiences for rock shows at 11pm Saturday (and other times).

Take minibus 7 from bul Maria Luisa or minibus 8 along ul Rakovski (1.5lv one way). City bus 94 comes here from ul Tsarigradsko Shose, across from Sofia University. From the last stop, walk back toward the centre to find the bulk of activity.

# COURSES

The **Institute of Foreign Languages** (☎ 710 069; www.deo.uni-sofia.bg; ul Kosta Loulchev 27) offers Bulgarian-language courses (the three-week class costs €220) as well as song and dance classes.

# SLEEPING
## Budget

Many hostels will offer pick-up service from the bus or train station if you reserve ahead. Prices drop by a couple of euro off-season.

**Sofia Hostel** (☎ 989 8582; www.hostelsofia.com; ul Pozitano 16; dm incl breakfast €10) Bulgaria's first hostel has family decorations giving the small place a kindergarten feel (in a good way). Staff speak English. Two dorm rooms sleep 16 and have themes – the 'traditional' one has witches on the 'stone' wallpapered walls; the 'gallery' has reprints of Bulgarian masterpieces (and a balcony with mountain views). There's a kitchen (with laundry) and free internet. Only one bathroom though.

**Hostel Mostel** (☎ 0889-223 296; www.hostelmostel.com; ul Denkoglu 2; dm/s/d incl breakfast €10/25/30; ☐) Lovingly run by a Bulgarian couple, who speak English and give rides back from the train station, the Mostel was in the process of moving to a new, bigger location at research time. The new spot, just off bul Maria Luisa, occupies two floors, with balconies and views of Banyi Bashi Mosque and Mt Vitosha; again it's more spacious than other hostels – with a giant sitting area planned. Staff are superb, gush with information and strive to keep things quiet after 11pm. There's a full kitchen to use and laundry service.

**Art Hostel** (☎ 987 0545; www.art-hostel.com; ul Angel Kânchev 21a; dm incl breakfast €10) This laid-back, nook-and-cranny hostel gets its subtitle, which is 'Usually we spend our time in the garden', for its leafy courtyard out back. Past guests have helped transform small spaces – such as the wee kitchen and cool hang-out area inside – into a cosy scene where travellers mix with arty locals, who sometimes stage exhibitions. Things keep going late.

**Sofia Backpacker's Inn** ( ☎ 983 1672; www.sofiabackpackersinn.dir.bg; ul Struma 6; dm/r incl breakfast 18/48lv; 🖳 ) Down an alley from busy ul Maria Luisa, this three-room, Japanese-owned inn has two pretty bare dorm rooms and lone double. The TV room has TV and VHS player, a guitar, and free internet.

Other hostel choices:

**Kervan Hostel** ( ☎ 983 9428; www.kervanhostel.com; ul Rositza 3; dm incl breakfast €10) Homely and quite clean – it feels a bit like a B&B – Kervan's a bit removed. It has antique radios, a small 'Spanish' tiled kitchen and bikes to rent.

**Internet Hostel** ( ☎ 989 9419; interhostel@yahoo.co.uk; 2nd fl, ul Alabin 50; dm €8-10; 🖳 ) Small hostel with four rooms, an windowless cramped sitting area and lone shared bathroom.

**Oriental Express** (ul Khristo Belchev 8A) In the planning at time of research; owned by the Red Star crowd.

**Red Star Hostel** ( ☎ 986 3341; 3rd fl, ul Angel Kânchev; dm incl breakfast €8-10, s €18-20, d €24-28; 🖳 ) Internet's nicer cousin, the Red Star again packs in the beds – the computer is in the dorm room – but has a nicer setting.

## Midrange

New hotels pop up frequently in Sofia. We've focused on nonchains, all within walking distance of the main sights around town.

Homestays are also an option to consider. Run by friendly ladies (who speak a bit of English and chain-smoke in front of a wall-sized map of Sofia), **Markela Accommodation Agency** ( ☎ 980 4925; markela@mail.bg; room 103, ul Ekzarh Yosif 35; ⏱ 8.30am-7.30pm Mon-Fri, 9.30am-4.30pm Sat & Sun) can hook you up with private, clean single rooms for 26lv to 33lv or doubles for 34lv to 40lv. Full apartments start at 45lv. It has a photo book to see what you're getting. Art Hostel (opposite) rents nice, private apartments in great locations (from €45 for a double). There's also an accommodation agency on the train station's ground floor that seems never to be open, and EBP Tours (p139) can find rooms near the station.

**Hotel Maya** ( ☎ 980 2796; ul Trapezitsa 4; s/d 30/40lv) Clean and homy, this central guesthouse has 12 rooms on either side of a rooftop courtyard overlooking TsUM shopping centre. Unfortunately all but one of the tiny private bathrooms are down the hall. No English is spoken and most furnishings predate communism's fall.

**Rooms** ( ☎ 983 3508; the roomshostel@yahoo.com; ul Pop Bogomil 10; r 40lv) A purple-and-gold house on a grey street, the six-room guesthouse offers tidy but tiny themed rooms. A few antique pieces – an old bedside stand, a painted headboard – add some flair. No TVs. Singles are sometimes available for 20lv.

**Hotel Iskâr** ( ☎ 986 6750; ul Iskâr 11; r 40-53lv; 🅿 ) For a simple but welcoming midrange deal, the Iskâr's 11 rooms are tough to beat. They're a bit small, and a few have private bathrooms across the hall, but views overlook a small patch of trees. Most staff light up for chats in English. Breakfast is 4lv in the small café downstairs.

**Scotty's Boutique** ( ☎ 983 6777; www.geocities.com/scottysboutiquehotel; ul Ekzarkh Iossif 11; s €45, d €55-85; 🅿 🖳 ) In a former Jewish apartment, across from the Sofia Synagogue, this splash of modernity is a welcome site for those looking for a break from grubby communist leftovers, or tackier 'modern' hotels. Each of the 16 terrific rooms are named for cities – 'Paris' is particularly bright and welcoming – and have TV, internet access, original wooden floorboards and low mattress frames. Scotty's is gay friendly, and staff often wears all-black outfits with Adidas shoes. Yes, it's hip.

**Hotel Niky** ( ☎ 952 3058; www.hotel-niky.com; ul Neofit Rilski 16; s/d incl breakfast from €30/35; 🅿 🖳 ) It's chiefly about business travellers, but an English-speaking staff keeps it cheerful. The 22 rooms aren't huge but are super clean, with a hint of the modern (blue carpet, headboards running along the wall and coffee makers). Room 203 has a big balcony. The back restaurant's great.

## Top End

**Art O'tel** ( ☎ 980 6000; www.artotel.biz; ul Gladston 44; r incl breakfast €95-100; 🅿 🖳 ) This side-street boutique – owned by the Barcelona football team owner! – is a flashy spot, from the lobby's marble-pillar fireplace and sunken dining room looking over a garden area to 22 colour-themed rooms (some with balconies). Prices drop by €15 or €20 at weekends.

## EATING

Sofia has the country's most dynamic and stylin' dining. Appealing new places are popping up constantly – try between bul Vitosha and ul Rakovski.

## Bulgarian

**Trops Kâshta** (ul Maria Luisa 26; salads 1lv, mains 1.50-3lv; ⊗ 8am-8.30pm) For cheap, fast, point-and-eat cafeteria-style food, Trops is your new comrade. It's half price after 8pm.

**Happy Bar & Grill** (pl Sveta Nedelya; grills 1-7lv; ⊗ 24hr) This chain institution is Bulgaria's 'American grill', something like a Hard Rock Cafe (guitars, trombones and BB King photos line the walls) with a crew of miniskirted waitresses serving rather un-American fare. The photo menu helps. Breakfast is served from 8am to 11am.

**Krâchme Sam Doidokh** (I Came Alone; ul Tsar Samuel 73; dishes 1.50-3lv; ⊗ 11am-11pm Mon-Sat) Like a timeless social club of sorts; you'll feel like you're in a *National Geographic* article from 1976. Old-timers often pluck on guitars and eat traditional goodies (rabbit, pigs legs, fish, pickled onion) and drink…a lot. A sign reads 'tull sobriety leads to instant death' (in Bulgarian). Not for everyone.

**Divaka** ( ☎ 989 9543; ul Gladston 54; grills 1.20-10lv, mains 1.90-10lv; ⊗ 24hr) This sprawling, modern four-room restaurant fills daily with happy Bulgarians chomping on low-cost traditional fare – grilled meats, fish fillets and cheese-covered chips. The chicken *divashki* is smothered in dill, garlic and lemon (3.60lv). Several vegetarian options.

**Pri Yafata** ( ☎ 980 1727; ul Colinska 28; mains 5-12.50lv; ⊗ 10am-midnight) An excellent introduction to Bulgarian cuisine (and traditional costumes), this chain restaurant (forgivably trite) packs in locals and tourists for its grilled meats (chicken *mehanzhuki* is a tasty pork and mushroom–filled fillet for 6.90lv). Plenty of vegetarian options.

## Fast Food & Self-Catering

**Familiya Supermarket** (bul Maria Luisa; ⊗ 8.30am-8.30pm) On north side of TsUM shopping centre.

**Tsentralni Khali** (cnr bul Maria Luisa & ul Ekzarh Yosif; ⊗ 7am-midnight) This refurbished covered market dates from 1909 and has three floors busy with locals seeking fresh produce, sausage, Swiss chocolate, beer, ice cream and cheap meals for 2lv or 3lv.

## Pizza

**O'Shipka!** ( ☎ 944 1288; ul Shipka 11; pizza 2-6.70lv; ⊗ 24hr) This lively three-storey restaurant-bar fills with students. The pizzas are tasty, and there's live music most nights

in the cavernous basement bar (often 3lv to get in). The cramped upstairs room is nonsmoking.

**Ugo** (ul Khan Krum 2; pizza 2-7lv; ⊗ 24hr) Twenty-something couples date and meet up at this slick, modern chain. It's location is great, with soft hanging lights and seats looking out on a quiet side street. If you're pizza'd out (this *is* Bulgaria after all), there's couscous (4.90lv) and plenty of pasta dishes.

## Vegetarian

**Dream House** (ul Alabin 50A; mains 2.10-3.70lv; ⊗ 11am-10pm) Sofia's seen a welcome splash of vegetarian eateries in recent years, but we still go for Dream for meatless dining. This cool-mint restaurant, upstairs from the tram lines, fills its tables for most meals. Loads of inspired options (including Thai noodle dishes and 18 vegan choices!), plus a Sunday buffet from noon to 7pm for 5lv.

## DRINKING

Look for *Programata*'s free annual *Club Guide* for listings in English. Studentski Grad has many good bars, too.

**Poison's** (ul Tsar Shushman 22; ⊗ 10am-2am) This place has a nice, leafy outdoor space and pavement standing spots, which fill with 20-something locals.

**Opera** (ul Rakovski 113; ⊗ 9am-midnight) Below the neoclassical opera house, this bar adds serious chic to royal past (modern covers drape ornate, antique chandeliers).

**Khambara** (ul 6 Sevtemvri 22; ⊗ 8pm-late) Located in a century-old grain storage building, where a WWII antifascist (thus illegal) press was based, this low-key, candle-lit place is unsigned, and down a dark path (watch out for the fanged gnomes). Jazzy music is kept low.

## ENTERTAINMENT
### Cinemas

**Dom na Kinoto** ( ☎ 980 7838; ul Ekzarh Iosif 37; tickets 4lv) alternates three or four films on its screen, while **United Cinema Multiplex** ( ☎ 951 5101; NDK; tickets 4-6lv) is a more modern theatre.

### Nightclubs

Sofia's big kids' favourite disco is **Escape** ( ☎ 0887-468 005; ul Angel Kânchev 1; cover 3-5lv; ⊗ 8.30pm-late). **Exit Club** ( ☎ 0887-965 026; ul Lavele 16; ⊗ 8pm-late) is a gay-friendly club with house music and food.

## Live Music

**O'Shipka!** ( ☎ 944 1288; ul Shipka 11; ☼ 24hr) The basement club of this pizza place has a very welcoming vibe and interesting rock shows or arty slide deals (entry free to 3lv) on weekdays only.

**Viad** ( ☎ 934 4004; cnr ul General Gurko & ul Rakovski; admission 3-10lv; ☼ 9pm-late) In the if-you-can't-beat-'em-join-'em column, Bulgaria's infamous *chalga* music lights up this cheesy basement supper club (with stars such as Azis and Malina) playing most nights but Sunday and Monday.

**National Opera House** ( ☎ 987 1366; www.geobiz.com /sfopera; ul Vrabcha 1) Opera is taken seriously in this country and this place features Sofia's best.

## Sport

**Levski** ( ☎ 989 2156) and **CSKA** ( ☎ 963 3477) are Sofia's most popular football teams. **National Stadium** ( ☎ 988 5030; Borisova Gradina) is the main venue.

## Theatre

**Ivan Vazov National Theatre** ( ☎ 986 2252; www.national theatre.bg; cnr uls Dyakon Ignatii & Vasil Levski) Great if you know Bulgarian.

## SHOPPING

The cheapest souvenirs (T-shirts, 'CCCP' stuff) are found in the underground shops, just next to TsUM. Those wanting something more upmarket should try bul Vitosha's boutique ghetto. Sidewalk vendors on pl Aleksander Nevski sell antiques from the communist era, icons and traditional crafts. A lot of it's fake, but some of the Soviet cameras (10lv and up) are the real deal.

**Souvenir shop** (ul Tsar Osvoboditel; ☼ 10am-6pm) At the Ethnographical Museum, this (pricey) shop is your quick-need-Bulgarian-gift saviour.

**Cohort** (ul Denkoglu 40; ☼ 11am-7pm Mon-Fri) Particularly good communist-era antiques.

**Stenata** ( ☎ 980 5491; ul www.stenata.com; ul Bratya Miladinovi 5; ☼ 10am-7pm Mon-Fri, 10am-6pm Sat) Bulgaria's best outfitter for the woods-bound. The two-floor shop has knowledgeable staff and plenty of big names (Patagonia and a dozen others) for whatever rock-climbing, hiking or camping gear you need. It hopes to start renting gear at some point.

**Ladies Market** (ul St Stambolov; ☼ dawn-dusk) A lively, messy market (mostly food) a couple of blocks west of bul Maria Luisa.

**TsUM** (ul Maria Luisa; ☼ 10am-9pm Mon-Sat, 11am-8pm Sun) Uniformed door attendants open the door to an ex-communist mall, now filled

---

### SQUAT SHOPS

In the can-do capitalist fervour that followed the fall of communism, Sofia saw an outbreak of the *klek* (squat shop), a basement-level window that sells coffee, beer, snacks and the like. These days Western-style boutiques are everywhere, but these legacies of the transition – when expanding a basement window was cheaper and quicker than overhauling a ground-floor apartment – are everywhere. Just look for Sofians bent over and holding their backs in pain.

---

with the Swiss Army and a comrade named Tommy Hilfilger.

## GETTING THERE & AWAY

### Air

Hemus Air flies daily to Varna (€65/100 one way/return), with extra flights in summer, when there are also more flights to Burgas. Travel agents book flights (see p139).

The airport's departures terminal has an **information booth** ( ☎ 937 2211; www.sofia-airport.bg) and there's an ATM outside, across from the arrivals hall, where you'll find car-rental agencies, a couple of ATMs and foreign-exchange offices.

See p186 for more information on airlines and international routes.

### Bus

#### DOMESTIC BUSES

Modern and highly efficient, Sofia's **Central Bus Station** ( ☎ 813 3232; www.centralnaavtogara.bg; bul Maria Luisa; ☼ 24hr), next to the train station, has a 24-hour English-speaking information centre to help you find the next bus leaving from **Traffic Market**, a confusing array of bus-ticket stands outside the train station. The upstairs mezzanine has eating areas, and the OK Taxi stand out front is dependable.

One reader found the bus station's two-attendant bathrooms (token needed) helped spur on a 'blissful bowel movement'. Considering a chipped floor tile and waits at the broken turnstile we found it a bit overpriced at 50 stotinki. It's not bad for a 0.20lv tinkle though.

Following are sample bus fares. All go from the central bus station and times are frequent – generally every hour – unless otherwise noted.

**Bansko** 10lv, three hours, four daily (also from Zapad)
**Belogradchik** 10lv, four hours, one daily (Traffic Market)
**Blagoevgrad** 6lv to 7lv, two hours
**Burgas** 17lv to 18lv, 5½ hours
**Kârdzhali** 12lv to 13lv, four hours
**Kazanlâk** 10lv, three hours
**Koprivshtitsa** 6lv, two hours, twice daily
**Melnik** 10lv, three hours, once daily
**Plovdiv** 8lv, two hours
**Ruse** 14lv, 4½ hours
**Shumen** 20lv, five hours
**Sliven** 13lv to 4lv, four hours
**Smolyan** 116lv to 17lv, 4½ hours, seven daily
**Troyan** 10lv, four hours, four daily
**Varna** 22lv to 24lv, six hours
**Veliko Târnovo** 12lv to 13lv, 3½ hours
**Vidin** 15lv, 4½ hours

In summer direct services link Sofia to popular Black Sea destinations such as Nesebâr and Sozopol.

Those heading to Borovets must transfer in Samokov. Minibuses leave for Samokov (4lv, 1½ hours) from Sofia's **Yug Bus Terminal** ( ☎ 722 345) half-hourly between 7am and 8pm. Ongoing metro construction has blocked the bus link there; take a taxi.

From the **Ovcha Kupel Bus Terminal** (aka Zapad; ☎ 955 5362; bul Tsar Boris III) there are a couple of daily buses to Rila town (6lv, two hours) – important if you're planning to visit Rila Monastery by public transport. There are also frequent buses to Bansko (10lv) from about 7am to 5pm. Reach the station by tram 5 from pl Makedonia, west of the centre on ul Alabin (it's a 20-minute ride).

### INTERNATIONAL BUSES
Many bus companies sell tickets to bordering countries and beyond. Ticket prices can vary, so ask around at Traffic Market. **Matpu** ( ☎ 981 5653; www.matpu.com; office 58, Traffic Market) is a good agency.

Sample fares:
**Athens** 98lv, 12 to 13 hours, one or two daily (Tuesday to Sunday)
**Belgrade** 35lv to 59lv, nine hours, two daily
**Istanbul** 34lv to 40lv, eight to 10 hours, eight daily
**Skopje** 20lv to 24lv, six hours, three or four daily
**Thessaloniki** 43lv, six to seven hours, a couple daily

### Train
Sofia's **Central Train Station** ( ☎ 931 1111; www.bdz .bg; bul Maria Luisa) is a bit confusing, though departures and arrivals are listed in English

on a large computer screen on the main floor, where there's an information booth (but usually no English). You buy same-day tickets for Vidin, Ruse and Varna on the main floor, and all other domestic destinations downstairs. Advance tickets are available at another office downstairs. Finding the right platform isn't always a breeze; ask a few people.

International tickets can be purchased at the **Rila Bureau** ( ☎ 932 3346; 🕑 24hr) in the northern part of the main floor, or at its **centre office** ( ☎ 987 0777; ul General Gurko 5; 🕑 7am-6.30pm Mon-Sat).

Sample train fares:
**Athens** seat/sleeper 64/84lv, 12½ hours, three daily
**Belgrade** 26lv, 7½ hours, two daily
**Blagoevgrad** 5.50lv, 2½ to three hours, five daily
**Bucharest** seat/sleeper 36/54lv, 10½ hours, two daily
**Burgas** 14.30lv, 6½ to 7½ hours, five daily
**Gorna Oryahovitsa** (near Veliko Târnovo) 10.70lv, 4½ hours, 10 daily
**Koprivshtitsa** 3.50lv, two to 2½ hours, five daily
**Istanbul** 36.50lv, 14½ hours, one daily
**Plovdiv** 8.80lv, 2½ hours, 12 daily
**Ruse** 14.30lv, seven hours, four daily
**Varna** 18.70lv, 7½ to 8½ hours, six daily
**Vidin** 11.20lv, 5½ hours, three daily

Trams 1 and 7 connect the station with pl Sveta Nedelya.

## GETTING AROUND
### To/From the Airport
An **OK Taxi** ( ☎ 973 2121) booth in the arrivals hall arranges metered cabs to the centre (about 7lv or 8lv). Outside is a bus stop, where bus 84 leaves for a stop along bul Vasil Levski, near Sofia University. Minibus 30 travels between bul Maria Luisa and the airport.

### Car & Motorcycle
Parking is a problem in Sofia, but signed parking garages are available (1lv per hour, 6lv to 7lv overnight). Watch for speed traps if entering Sofia from the east.

Most travel agents rent out cars. The big names are here, but you'll save by going with local companies. **Drenikov Rent-a-Car** ( ☎ 944 9532; www.drenikov.com; ul Oborishte 55; 🕑 9am-6pm Mon-Fri, 10am-2pm Sat & Sun) has several classes of cars from €15 per day – tax is waived if you pay in cash. **Penguin Travel** ( ☎ 400 1051; ul Orphei 9) will deliver cars (from €19 per day) and free drop-off in Plovdiv's often possible.

## Public Transport

Sofia's trams, buses and metro line run from 5.30am to 11pm and use the same ticket system. A single ride is 0.50lv and a day pass 2.25lv. There are no transfers. Blue ticket booths are near most stops, and many newsstands sell tickets too. Single-ride tickets must be validated once you board; disguised officials charge a 5lv fine if you're caught without one.

Minibuses ply many useful city routes at 1.50lv per ride.

Sofia's relatively new metro line reaches western suburbs but is little use to travellers. A new line, going southeast, was under construction at research time.

## Taxi

Sofia's taxis have a reputation for overcharging foreigners. Chances are less likely if you call for a cab. **OK Taxi** ( ☎ 973 2121) runs on the meter.

## AROUND SOFIA
### Boyana Бояна

Once a separate village (now officially a part of Sofia), hillside Boyana has a couple of prime-time attractions. The capital's best museum, the **National Historical Museum** ( ☎ 955 4280; www .historymuseum.org; bul Okolovrusten Pat; adult/student 10/7lv, guide 10lv; 9.30am-6pm Apr-Oct, 9am-5.30pm Nov-Mar) didn't do itself a favour by moving from its previous grand locale on bul Vitosha. Now housed in a 1970s presidential palace, it boasts some of the nation's most treasured pieces, such as the world's oldest gold (4th millennium BC) and remarkable Thracian horse decorations.

Built between the 11th and 19th centuries, the inside walls of the **Boyana Church** ( ☎ 959 0939; adult/student 10/5lv, guide 5lv; 9.30am-5.30pm Apr-Dec, 9am-5pm Jan-Mar), 1.5km south of the museum, feature some 90 medieval frescoes, most dating from 1259. They are certainly among Bulgaria's finest.

Take tram 9 down ul Khristo Botev to Hladnika bus stop (the name means 'refrigerator'), where bus 64 goes past the museum to the east then within 200m of the church.

### Vitosha Витоша

The feather in Sofia's cap is this 23km by 13km mountain range (part of Vitosha Nature Park), just south of the city. At summer weekends, many Sofians come to hike, picnic and berry-pick.

It's worth paying 5lv for the Cyrillic trail map *Vitosha Turisticheska Karta* (1:50,000), available in Sofia.

### CHAIRLIFTS

A popular way to get high up quickly is from a couple of lift stations at the mountain's base. When operating, both lifts run from about 9am to 5pm. Hours vary; in some months lifts run only Thursday to Sunday, or just weekends.

The cheaper of the two, **Dragalevtsi** ( ☎ 961 2189) is 2km up from the Dragalevtsi village bus stop (walk up next to the creek). It's actually two lifts – one to Bai Krâstyo, and a second lift to Goli Vrâh (1837m).

**Simeonovo** sends six-person gondolas to the peaks. It costs 5lv to Aleko, a popular base for hikes and more ski lifts.

It's a 30-minute hike between the top of the two lifts.

### HIKES

Dozens of well-marked trails await your boot tread. Popular ones include the steep 90-minute trip up Mt Cherni Vrâh (2290m) from Aleko; a three-hour trek east of Mt Sredets (1969m) from Aleko past Goli Vrâh to Zlatni Mostove; and a three-hour hike from Boyana Church past a waterfall to Zlatni Mostove.

### SKIING

Cheaper than other Bulgarian slopes (lift tickets 22lv; night skiing 12lv), Vitosha's ski season runs from mid-December to April. There are 29km of ski runs (including one 5km stretch) ranging from easy to very difficult. Rental equipment is available.

### GETTING THERE & AWAY

About 2km south of NDK in Sofia, the useful **Hladilnika bus stop** (ul Srebârna), just east of bul Cherni Vrâh, has several Vitosha-bound buses. Bus 122 leads directly to the Simeonovo chairlift. Bus 64 goes to Dragalevtsi centre and on to Boyana. Get to Hladilnika bus stop by tram 9, just east of NDK.

# RILA & PIRIN MOUNTAINS

The two Alp-like mountain chains (also national parks) between Sofia and the Greek border are made of serious rocky-topped peaks brimming with rewarding and strenuous hiking paths, clear streams rushing past

BULGARIA

monasteries and some appealing towns. It's here that one of Bulgaria's most famous sites, Rila Monastery, stands guarded by mountains. Other access points include Samokov, Bansko and Melnik.

## Hiking

Most paths are well signed. For Rila hikes, the monastery is a possible starting point, with four trails meeting others higher up. Day hikes are certainly possible and *hizhas* (mountain huts) are spaced three to nine hours apart; you can reserve ahead through Zig Zag in Sofia (p139). For longer hikes, it's best to start up at Maliovitsa (southwest from Samokov), where you can reach the monastery (mostly downhill) on a one- or two-night trip via Sedemte Ezera (Seven Lakes).

Pirin hikes are generally tougher than Rila ones, with more abrupt slopes. In summer it's better to end in (not start from) Melnik, as the steep climbs aren't fun in the particularly hot climate there.

Drop by Zig Zag for tips or tour info. Be sure to get the *Rila* and/or *Pirin* maps (1:55,000) by Kartografia if you're venturing out (each are 5lv). Get more information on these at www.rilanationalpark.org and www.pirin-np.com.

## RILA MONASTERY
### РИЛСКИ МАНАСТИР
☎ 07054

Bulgaria's most famous **monastery** (admission free; ☾ 6am-9pm or 10pm), set in a towering forested valley 120km south of Sofia, is a popular destination for day-trippers on tours from around the region. The Unesco World Heritage site is gorgeous. It drips with history and is near excellent hikes, but for some travellers an hour here is enough.

Day trips to Rila from Sofia (widely available around the country) range from about €20 to €50 or more. Seeing Rila by public transport is tough (though possible) in a day. Try to avoid crowded summer weekends.

First built in 927, and heavily restored in 1469, the monastery helped keep Bulgarian culture and language alive during Ottoman rule. A fire engulfed most buildings in 1833, but they were rebuilt shortly thereafter.

The entrance to the monastery is from the west at Dupnitsa Gate, and around the east side at Samokov Gate. **Rila village**, 21km away, has a fine hotel and ATM, plus an informa-

tion centre that helps with accommodation (if open!).

## Sights

The 300 monks cells fill four levels of colourful balconies overlooking the large misshapen courtyard. The **Nativity Church**, built in the 1830s, contains 1200 magnificent murals – the ones outside more easily viewed. **Tsar Boris III's tomb** – actually his heart only – is to the right when you enter; it's believed he was poisoned by the Nazis after clamouring to save Bulgaria's Jewish population during WWII. Nearby, the 23m stone **Hrelyu Tower** is all that remains from the 14th century.

The two-storey **Ethnographic Museum** (adult/student 5/3lv; ☾ 8.30am-4.30pm) houses many ornate woodwork pieces (it's a cross frenzy); museum pride soars over its double-sided Rila Cross, with 140 tiny biblical scenes.

If you have time, hike up the **Tomb of St Ivan** (Grobyat na Sv Ivan Rilski). To reach the start of the 15-minute hike up the clearly marked trail, walk about 3.7km east on the road, behind the monastery.

## Sleeping

There are a couple of hotels, camping grounds and restaurants outside Samokov Gate. You can stay in the **monastery's rooms** ( ☎ 2208; r with private/shared bathroom €15/10); the attendant often leaves midafternoon. A great spot is **Zodiak** ( ☎ 088-216 527; s/d incl breakfast 20/40lv, camp sites 10lv), a string of bungalows by the stream, nearly 2km past the monastery.

The nearest *hizha* is about a six-hour walk up.

## Getting There & Away

At the time of research there were no direct buses from Sofia to the monastery, but a lone one (at 3pm) back to Sofia. You can take a bus from Sofia's Ovcha Kupel to Rila village (6lv, two hours) at 10.20am in time for the 12.40pm bus to the monastery. The last bus out is to Dupnitsa (4lv, 90 minutes) at 5.10pm. These times likely will change. If you have a car, you can see Rila then reach Melnik in a single day.

## MELNIK МЕЛНИК
☎ 07437 / pop 275

Amid the jutting, 'sand pyramid' part of the Pirins only 15km from Greece, little quiet Melnik is home to unique whitewashed, stone-walled revival buildings and, frankly, the country's best wine, which is sold in plastic jugs (2L is 6lv) and served from giant wood barrels. Best yet, many locals swear the wine here is 'hangover free'. Selfless research methods back up their claim.

From the bus stop, roads run on either side of a (mostly dry) creek into town. About 150m up, on the northern side, is a post office, 24-hour ATM and pay phone. There's no bank or internet access.

## Sights

**Mitko Manolev Winery** (Shestaka; admission incl tasting 1lv; ☺ approx 10am-dusk) overlooks town from the hill on the town's east side; follow the road (and handpainted signs) about 350m east of the post office. This 250-year-old winery – carved out of the hill – serves its wines in a nice locale with log stools, looking over the hills.

Located to the south is **Kordopulov House** (admission 3lv; ☺ 10am-9pm summer, 10am-5pm winter), a giant revival-period home with high-ceilinged rooms. Past the winery to the north are the battered remains of the 10th-century **Bolyaskata Kâshta**.

**Church ruins** are everywhere. Head 300m up the big hill to the south (opposite the post office) to see some atop a ridge overlooking town.

The hilltop **Rozhen Monastery** (suggested donation 2lv; ☺ 7am-9pm), 10km east of town by road, was originally built in 1217, but most of what remains was redone in the mid-18th century. It's an atmospheric place, with woodcarvings and a mural-filled church, but best is the **hiking trail** that leads 3km between Melnik and the site; it takes about an hour downhill.

The best option is to bus up to Rozhen village from Melnik (1lv, 20 minutes, four daily), walk 800m up to the hilltop site, then walk back to Melnik (signs point west, going behind the monastery). Some parts of the trail can be slippery; don't chance it during rain.

## Sleeping

Most of the traditional-style private homes let out simple rooms with shared bathroom for roughly 15lv per person. Try the homes on the hillsides.

**Mekhana Megdana** ( ☎ 088 866 6047; r incl breakfast 25-30lv) Just before the post office, the Megdana has six plain but clean rooms and a busy restaurant.

**Hotel Despot Slav** ( ☎ 248; s/d incl breakfast 48/60lv) On the main strip heading towards the win-

ery, this hotel has nice, modern rooms with wood floors and TV.

**Litova Kâshta** ( ☎ 313; www.litovakushta.com; r incl breakfast 70-100lv) Behind the museum, this 10-room modern hotel has an enviable, quiet location – its modern rooms are decorated traditionally and its restaurant spills onto private decks outside. You can ride horses here for 20lv.

## Eating

Pretty much anywhere here you'll pay a little more for your *shopska* salad. A couple of shops sell grocery items. A popular restaurant is **Mencheva Kâshta** (dishes 5-12lv; ☺ 8am-10 or 11pm) is a homy tavern with a few rooms and small deck, halfway to the winery. It serves an egg, cheese and ham 'Melnik Pyramid' for 5lv; save space for sheep yogurt and fresh figs for dessert.

## Getting There & Away

One daily bus connects Melnik with Sofia (10lv, four hours) and the pleasant college town Blagoevgrad (4lv, two hours); its bus station is next to the train station (a couple of kilometres west of the centre) and has connections to Rila village and Bansko.

There are also five daily buses to highway town Sandanski (2lv, 30 minutes), where Spartacus was born (some connecting buses are 200m south of bus station, past pedestrian mall ul Makedonia).

## SAMOKOV САМОКОВ
☎ 0722 / pop 26,500
This scruffy but personable town serves as Borovets' ski-slope hub. It's an ideal place for independent travellers looking for a cheaper base.

The central bus station is off the main street, ul Târgovska, just west of administrative buildings where you'll find a bank, 24-hour ATM and cinema. A block north of ul Târgovska is **Internet Zala** (per hr 1lv; ☺ 8am-10pm). Facing it is the two-storey gold **History Museum** ( ☎ 66712; admission 1lv; ☺ 8am-5pm), with a mill model that (noisily) turns when clicked on plus exhibits of local journo Konstantin Fotinov (museum attendant: 'The first and greatest of Bulgarian journalists').

Some skiers avoid Borovets' lines at **Maliovitsa**, 25km southwest, which is also a good hiking hub in summer.

The best hotel is the sprightly, four-room **Relax Hotel** ( ☎ 24284; www.relaxhotel-bg.com; d incl breakfast 50lv), across from the museum. A block

BULGARIA

west is the scrappier but cheaper **Hotel Koala** ( ☎ 0899-411 378; ul Mikail Koneb 25; s/d 30/36lv), with a downstairs restaurant; it's about 300m from the station.

Samokov's **bus station** ( ☎ 66540) sends frequent buses from 7.30am to 7pm to Borovets (1.20lv) and from 6am to 7pm to Sofia (4lv, 1½ hours). There are four daily buses to Maliovitsa (3lv, one hour) and Plovdiv (7lv, three hours).

## BOROVETS БОРОВЕЦ

The ski slopes of Bulgaria's first ski resort, in the central-north Rila mountains about 70km southeast of Sofia, boom between December and April. Its 23 ski runs (which are better than Mt Vitosha's) include Bulgaria's longest. Ski equipment is on hand (about 20lv or 25lv daily); the 50lv lift pass drops to 30lv on weekends, when locals pour in. There are many resorts here that cater to package tours.

Half-hourly minibuses go to Samokov. A taxi costs about 10lv to/from Samokov.

## BANSKO БАНСКО

☎ 07443 / pop 8910

Far more than the ski town it's known to be, friendly Bansko – at the base of Mt Vihren (2914m) and the Pirin mountains – probably has the country's best *mekhanas* (festive tavern restaurants), with rollicking folk bands playing many nights all year. It's aiming for the 2014 Olympics though, and development is running rampant. A couple of years ago all souvenir signs were in Bulgarian – now they're in English. Still, it's a fun base for skiing and summer hikes.

### Orientation

Buses and trains stop about 300m north of the central pl Nikola Vaptsarov, reached along ul Todor Aleksandrov. From the square ul Pirin goes south to pl Vûzhrazhdane and on to the ski lifts and, 2km further, the Pirin National Park entrance. West of pl Nikola Vaptsarov is the short pedestrian mall, ul Tsar Simeon.

### Information

The **tourist information centre** (pl Nikola Vaptsarov) is generally closed and of no use. Aside from the many foreign-exchange offices, try **DSK Bank** (ul Tsar Simeon; ♥ 8am-noon & 1.30-4.30pm Mon-Fri), with an ATM. **Internet Club Zonata** (ul Bulgaria 22; per hr 1lv; ♥ 8am-10pm), a block north, is one of the few places to get online.

### Sights

The **Kâshta-Museum of Nikola Vaptsarov** ( ☎ 8304; pl Nikola Vaptsarov; admission 2lv; ♥ 8am-5 or 5.30pm) is dedicated to an appealing local poet who lived here at a time when words could get you shot. (And did.) Arrested for antifascist poems written during WWII, Vaptsarov was executed in 1942 at the same age as Jesus, a fact not lost on the curators here. Ask to hear the tape in English.

The **Sveta Troitsa Church** (pl Vûzhrazhdane; ♥ 7.30am-5 or 6pm) is particularly striking for its wood-carved interior and gloomy, faded murals.

**Kâshta-Museum of Neofit Rilski** ( ☎ 8272; ul Pirin 17; admission 3lv; ♥ 9am-noon & 2-5pm), behind the church, has five revival-style rooms.

### Activities

#### HIKING

Paths to the Pirin Mountains are accessed just south of town. In summer minibuses go to Banderitsa (about 4lv, three daily) to access trails to lakes and *hizhas*.

#### SKIING

The ski season in Bansko lasts from mid-December to April. And it's good skiing. There are two major mountains – the lower Chalin Valog and the bigger Shiligarnika, higher up – with 26km of runs (7km of night skiing, too). A lift pass for all four lifts is 50/30lv for a full/half day; rentals are about 18lv to 30lv. If you like old-school lifts, and shorter lines, consider bussing 6km east to **Dobrinishte**.

### Festivals & Events

The **Pirin Sings Folk Festival** is staged nearby in August in odd-numbered years, as is the **International Jazz Festival**.

### Sleeping

A hotel boom is happening as Bansko braces for the potential Olympics – most are medium-sized ski centres. Prices generally drop by 20% in summer.

**Hotel Tipik** ( ☎ 8185; ul Tudo Aleksandrov 15; s/d 20/40lv) A nice budget hotel with small but clean rooms a block south of the stations.

**Alpin Hotel** ( ☎ 8075; ul Neofit Rilski 6; s/d incl breakfast 34/47lv) With 17 older but clean rooms on an atmospheric lane, this is ski central – with equipment, lessons, rides to the lift – and afterwards a spell in the sauna for 5lv.

**Dvata Smarcha** ( ☎ 2632; ul Velyan Ognev 2; s/d incl breakfast 36/72lv) One of many *mekhanas* that offer rooms, this one is 50m southeast of pl Vûzhrazhdane and has eight gorgeous rooms and a garden sitting area.

**Star Pod Naem** ( ☎ 3998; bul Bulgaria 33; d/tr €20/30) An alpine-style guesthouse run by a sweet English-speaking mum-and-daughter team. There's a basement kitchen with TV to use, and the rooms are spotless, with TVs. Prices drop by €6 or €7 off season. It's a block north of the bank.

## Eating
In ski season, most life is on ul Pirin, in the (more modern) blocks south of pl Vuzhrazhdane (and the old district) towards the lifts. But the most appealing *mekhanas* – with wood-beamed ceilings, hanging vines and live bands – are on the cobbled lanes north of the square. **Kasapinova Kâshta** (ul Yane Sandanski 4; dishes from 7lv; ☾ noon-midnight) is a slightly touristy one; waiters sit with you when ordering. It's good, but there are dozens more to choose from.

## Getting There & Away
From the **bus station** ( ☎ 8420; ul Patriarh Evtimii), buses go to Sofia (10lv, three hours, frequent), Blagoevgrad (5lv, one hour, 10 daily) and Plovdiv (9lv, 3½ hours, two daily).

Bansko is on the wonderful narrow-gauge railway through mountains to Septemvri (on the Sofia–Plovdiv line). The **train station** (ul Akad Yordan Ivanov) is next to the bus station. The train (4lv, five hours, three daily) goes slowly, but offers great glimpses of local life both out the window and in the train carriage. If bored, count tunnels and stops (at last tally, tunnels beat stops 31 to 18).

# PLOVDIV & RODOPI MOUNTAINS

Bulgaria's second city, Plovdiv, lies just within the cusp of the Thracian plain, with the deeply forested Rodopi Mountains (with culturally rich villages) looming to the south. Plovdiv is the easiest gateway to Smolyan (the key Rodopi hub) and Pamporovo ski resort, but less frequent buses (with changes) do connect the Pirin mountains to the west.

## Hiking
Shiroka Lâka, 24km northwest of Smolyan, is a good base for hikes (with more day-

hike potential than the Rila or Pirin ranges). A popular one is the five-hour hike south to Golyam Perelik (where there's a *hizha*) or there's a two-day hike from Shiroka to Trigrad via Mugla (a mountain village with accommodation). A shorter hike connects Trigrad with Yagodina Cave in less than three hours. The international trail E8 plies the Rodopis.

Trail maps (5lv each) split the Rodopis into the western and eastern ranges.

Ask at one of the Smolyan tourist offices for hiking tips, or drop by Zig Zag in Sofia (p139).

## PLOVDIV ПЛОВДИВ
☎ 032 / pop 341,500
Probably Bulgaria's most appealing city, Plovdiv has it all – Roman walls and theatre seats spilling out under walkways and aside hills, and a compact, cobbled 19th-century revival-era district with open-air cafés frequented by the city's students. Bulgarians love it, some foreigners give it a shrug after a day, but any Bulgarian site in the hunt for 'country's best' must reckon with The Plov.

Known as Philippopolis to the Romans in the 3rd century AD, but settled thousands of years before by Thracians, Plovdiv has several plump hills – mounds really – that look like burps from the Rodopi mountains southwest.

## Orientation
Plovdiv's train station and (main) Yug Bus Terminal are about 600m southwest of the central pl Tsentralen. From the square, the main pedestrian mall, ul Knyaz Aleksandâr, stretches 500m north to pl Dzhumaya. East from pl Dzhumaya, via ul Sâborna, is Old Town, which is easily explored by foot. The centre's northern border is the reed-filled Maritsa River.

## Information
Plovdiv sorely lacks an official tourist information centre. Foreign-exchange offices and ATMs abound along the pedestrian mall (ul Knyaz Aleksandâr) and also on ul Ivan Vazov.

### BOOKSHOPS
**Litera** (pl Dzhumaya; ☾ 8.30am-7.30pm Mon-Fri, 10am-6pm Sat) Bookshop with some English-language titles and maps.

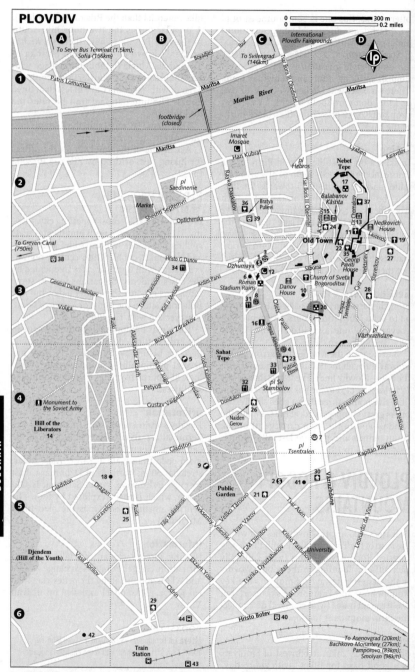

# PLOVDIV

To Sever Bus Terminal (1.5km);
Sofia (156km)

Patris Lomumba

Boyadjiev

To Svilengrad
(146km)

International
Plovdiv Fairgrounds

Maritsa River

footbridge
(closed)

Maritsa

Imaret
Mosque

Han Kubrat

pl
Hebros

Nebet
Tepe

pl
Saedinenie

Rayko Daskalov

Shesti Septemvri

Market

Opālchenska

Bratya
Pulievi

Balabanov
Kāshta

Nedkovich
House

Old Town

Hristo G Danov

pl
Dzhumaya

Danov
House

Georgi
Pavliti
House

General Danail Nikolaev

Roman
Stadium Ruins

Church of Sveta
Bogoroditsa

Volga

To Greven Canal
(750m)

Sahat
Tepe

pl
Vāzhrazhdane

Monument to
the Soviet Army

Hill of the
Liberators
14

pl Sv
Stambolov

Patriah
Efimii

Gladston

pl
Tsentralen

Naiden
Gerov

Public
Garden

Djendem
(Hill of the Youth)

University

Hristo Botev

Train
Station

To Asenovgrad (20km);
Bachkovo Monastery (27km);
Pamporovo (83km);
Smolyan (98km)

**BULGARIA**

0                300 m
0               0.2 miles

## INTERNET ACCESS
**Fantasy Internet Club** (1st fl, ul Kynaz
Aleksandâr 31; per hr 0.80lv;
🕑 24hr)

**Speed** (ul Kynaz Aleksandâr 10; per hr 0.60lv;
🕑 24hr) Also offers international calls for 0.12lv per
minute.

## LEFT LUGGAGE
The train station has 24-hour luggage storage
(2lv per piece per day); the Yug bus station
holds small bags (only) for 0.50lv per day.

## MONEY
**Bank DCK** (ul Rayko Daskalov; 🕑 8am-5pm Mon-Fri)
**Bulbank** (ul Ivan Vazov 4; 🕑 8am-6pm Mon-Fri)

## POST
**Main post office** (pl Tsentralen; 🕑 7am-7pm Mon-Sat,
7am-11am Sun)

## TELEPHONE
**Call Centre** (ul Balkan; international calls per min 0.15lv;
🕑 9.30am-11pm Mon-Sat, noon-8pm Sun)

## TRAVEL AGENCIES
**Inter Jet Tours** ( ☎ 635 001; www.interjet-bg.com;
2nd fl, ul Knyaz Aleksandâr 35; 🕑 10am-6pm Mon-Fri)
Arranges treks and rents cars (from €15 per day, with free
drop-off in Sofia).

# Sights
Plovdivniks sure love their hills – don't leave
without climbing at least one. **Hill of the Liberators** (Bunardjika Park) is the most prominent;
the lonely bloke up top is 'Alyosha', a Russian
soldier.

## OLD TOWN
Revival-era wood-shuttered homes lean over
wee cobbled lanes (and antique shops – some
of Bulgaria's better souvenir shops actually) in
this hilly neighbourhood, which is practically
a free, living museum.

Seeing the 22 rooms inside the Old Town's
most striking building (built in 1847) is an
added bonus to the country's finest **Ethnographical Museum** ( ☎ 625 654; ul Dr Chomakov 2;
admission 4lv; 🕑 9am-noon & 2-5 or 5.30pm). It has
many traditional outfits upstairs, including
the masked *kukeri* costumes from the Rodopi
region with pointed noses and bell-belts.

A handful of other 'baroque' homes are
open to visit, including **Hindliyan Kâshta** ( ☎ 628
998; ul Artin Gidikov 4; adult/student 3/1lv; 🕑 9am-5pm
Mon-Fri), an 1835 two-storey home that really
evokes the period. Its basement cellar doubles
as a **wine museum** ( ☎ 635 376; three wine tastings 5lv;
🕑 10am-5.30pm Mon-Fri).

One of the country's most impressive
Roman ruins, the **Theatre of Ancient Philippopolis**
(admission 3lv; 🕑 9am-5.30pm summer, 9am-5.30pm Wed-
Sun winter), is easily seen from outside the gates,

BULGARIA

but entry lets you tread on worn steps approaching their 2000th birthday. The theatre holds various events from June to October.

Tucked behind walls, the **Church of St Constantine & Elena** (ul Sâborna 24; admission free; ☉ dawn-dusk) dates from the 4th century AD, though much of what you see was rebuilt in 1832.

The **Ruins of Eumolpias** (ul Dr Chomakov; admission free; ☉ 24hr), scattered upon Nebet Tepe hilltop, date from a Thracian settlement from about 5000 BC. Look for a green-and-white smokestack of the Kamenitza brewery (Plovdiv's so-so beer) to the southeast. Some of the stuff gets drunk up here too.

Be sure to poke around the back streets: the ones down the hill to the east are less commercial. Here you can see the walled **Sveta Nedelya Church** (ul Slaveikov 40), which originally dates from 1578 and has a frickin' dragon-slaying mural inside.

### OTHER SIGHTS

The **Dzhumaya Mosque** (Friday mosque; pl Dzhumaya; admission free; ☉ dawn-dusk) originally dates from 1368 – the first in Balkan Europe – but was renovated after a 1928 earthquake (note the cracks inside).

The nation's biggest canal, the impressive 2.5km river-fed **Green Canal**, is an interesting detour, about 1km west of the centre. Bulgaria's last communist-built project features rowing races and is surrounded by jogging paths and shady Loven Park. Take bus 10 west as far as it goes on ul Sheshti Septemvri, then walk 200m northwest.

Don't laugh, but the **Excelsior** (ul Knyaz Aleksândar 24; ☉ 10am-8pm Mon-Fri, 11am-8pm) is a 'neo-Roman' mall with some (allegedly) real ruins to see in its basement, and nice views from the roof.

## Courses

A number of foreigners have taken classes in traditional Bulgarian instruments or folk singing at Plovdiv's **Art Academy** ( ☎ 679 218; www .artacademyplovdiv.com, ul Todor Samoudomov 2), near the Roman theatre.

## Sleeping

Many visitors to Plovdiv opt for a private room – there are plenty of options. If a cuddly tout doesn't find you on arrival, a reliable agency is **Esperansa** ( ☎ 260 653, 0897-944 951; ul Ivan Vazov 14; s/d 20/30lv, s/d apt from 40/50lv), a nine-minute walk from the main stations. It

arranges rooms in homes or private apartments. It's in the back of the building.

### BUDGET

**Hiker's Hostel** ( ☎ 0885-194 553, www.hikers-hostel.org; ul Sâborna 53; dm/d incl breakfast 20/48lv; ☐ ) Plovdiv's top backpacker stop is this little house in Old Town. The staff is plenty laid-back. (The hostel car, toaster, washing machine and door knob were out of service at last pass; one attendant said, 'I rarely go into town' – about a 100m walk downhill!) The eight-bunk dorm room is kept clean, while the cramped private room is really a converted storage space. There's free internet, frequent parties (music: Doors, Marley) and a big sitting space with views.

**Tourist's House** (Turisicheska Kâshta; ☎ 635 115; ul Slaveikov 5; dm 20lv) Just down the back side of Old Town's hill (but still feeling a part of it), this 19th-century, three-storey 'hostel' (briefly closed at last pass, but reopening) has cheap beds in a traditional building. High wood-carved ceilings loom over rooms. Some rooms are let as private rooms.

**PBI Hostel** ( ☎ 326 384; www.pbihostel.com; ul Naiden Gerov 13; dm/r €10/15; ☐ ) Maybe PBI means 'problems being in', as the staff *frequently* aren't around to let travellers in. It's lacking much charm. Three dorm rooms and a lone private room.

### MIDRANGE

**Trakiya Hotel** ( ☎ 622 355; ul Ivan Vazov 84; s/d 30/60lv) This cheerful place is near the train and main bus stations. Double-glazed windows and thick curtains keeps out noise and light from after-hours activity nearby. The 10 comfy rooms have fans, and at least one a German football blanket.

**Rooms** ( ☎ 665 177; ul Tsanko Alavrenov 14; r 40-50lv) Three simple rooms in an Old Town home, across from Svetya Nedelya church.

**Hotel Leipzig** ( ☎ 632 250; www.leipzig.bg; bul Ruski 70; s/d incl breakfast from 40/50lv; ☐ ) West of the centre and standing a dozen storeys in its (faded) salmon-and-blue colour scheme, this 120-room hotel's East German name gives an idea of when it was built. Bright blue carpets keep rooms a little fresh. The higher floors have great views.

### TOP END

**Hotel Hebros** ( ☎ 260 180; www.hebros-hotel.com; ul Stoilov 51; s/d incl breakfast €79/95; ☒ ) Those looking for a classic Old Town sleep should opt for this inviting 10-room inn. There's a back courtyard, spa and sauna. Each of the 10 big rooms is done up in lush 19th-century design, with varying looks. The restaurant on premises (right) is one of Plovdiv's best.

**Hotel Bulgaria** ( ☎ 633 599; www.hotelbulgaria.net; ul Patriah Etimii 13; s/d incl breakfast from €39/61 Fri-Sun, €44/68 Mon-Thu; ✖ ▣ ) It's location, right off the pedestrian crawl, makes this 59-room hotel worth considering, even though the standard rooms show some wear and tear (peeling wall paint and some carpet stains) and the bathrooms are small.

**Trimontium Princess Hotel** ( ☎ 605 000; reservation@trimontium-princess.com; pl Tsentralen; s/d incl breakfast from 128/178lv Fri-Sun, 167/217lv Mon-Thu; Ⓟ ✖ ▣ ) A made-up relic to the palatial from less bourgeois times, the Princess' 158 rooms are comfy, though not quite reaching the five-star standard they flag (there are nicks on some of the side tables). Pay 20lv extra to get the spa rooms, with separate TV room and newer carpets.

## Eating

Most of the pedestrian-mall spots are drinks-oriented, with a menu as an afterthought. Kebab and pizza stands (for 1lv or 1.50lv) are everywhere, particularly north of pl Dzhumaya on ul Rayko Daskalov. King of both, however, is alley-hub **Alaeddin** (ul Kynaz Aleksandâr; two doner kebabs 1lv, pizza slices 1.50lv; ✖ 24hr), which draws lines all day.

**Orientalska Cladkarnitsa Dzhumyata** (ul Blakan; baklava 2lv; ✖ 7.30am-9pm Mon-Sat, 7.30am-8pm Sun) Built right into the 14th-century mosque, this pastry shop serves Plovdiv's best fresh, flaky baklava.

**Liliya** (ul Kiril u Metodii 2; dishes 1-2lv; ✖ 7am-8pm Mon-Fri, 8am-6pm Sat) A bustling pick-and-point cafeteria that's less fluorescent bulb than most. Prices drop by 20% after 4pm.

**Dayana** (ul Dondukov; grills from 2.20lv; ✖ 24hr) Aside the rocky walls of Sahat Tepe hill are several great choices, including this sprawling spot with the usual Bulgarian grill items plus ham'n'egg plates all day (1.70lv) and a host of vegetarian options (3.20lv) on the English photo menu. Inside there's traditional seating in a sprawling dining room with lots of windows to look out on the (preferable) leafy courtyard.

**Dreams** (pl Sv Stambolov; sandwiches 2.10-2.40lv; ✖ 9am-11pm) Set up like a fast-food café, Dreams serves good hot sandwiches, plus plenty of desserts and cocktails. In summer, it takes over a good chunk of the square. Plus there's a Coke and coffee combo for 2lv – dreams do come true, sometimes.

**Hotel Hebros** ( ☎ 260 180; ul Stoilov 51; mains 12-21lv; ✖ 11am-midnight) Even if you can't spring for the rooms, Hebros' cosy basement (and courtyard) is one of Old Town's best dining spots. Live music is held nightly, and the menu changes frequently, with superbly prepared 'European' dishes such as rabbit with plums (12lv), salmon in mustard sauce (21lv) and a few vegetarian options (9lv).

## Drinking

**Rahap Tepe** (ul Dr Chomakov; snacks 1.20-4lv; ✖ 10am-midnight Apr-Oct) Near Old Town's highest point, this open-air bar has nice views west – enjoyed by many a midday and late-day beer sipper.

**Marmalad** (ul Bratya Pulievi 3; cocktails 3lv; ✖ 9am-2am) On a side lane, the ultramod Marmalad has cream leather booths and stools on old wooden floors. The music is kept chat-encouraging soft – until the basement night-

---

**QUIRKY-IRKY PLOVDIV**

**Hug the 'Great Gossiper'**

The big-eared statue in the central steps of the pedestrian mall honours Milyu, the great gossiper of Plovdiv in the 1980s and '90s, who won fans for his unsubtle listenings-in of passers-by. Near the **Milyu Statue** in summer a speaker sometimes pipes out old Milyu sayings in Bulgarian.

**Do hills have ghosts?**

Proudly a seven-hill town (like Rome), Plovdiv up and lost one during the communist era, when city authorities broke it down to rubble to provide stone steps around Old Town. Pay tribute to the site – with a tear in a beer, or over a *banitsa* – at the walled-off, gaping-hole **seventh hill site**, 100m south of the Hill of the Liberators.

club gets going after 9pm or so. DJs get nods on weekend nights and there are rock shows on Thursday.

**King's Stable** (ul Sâborna; cocktails 3.40lv; ⏲ 8.30am-2am Apr-Oct) This great open-air bar – behind a host of Old Town buildings – serves drinks and snacks at a leisurely pace.

## Entertainment
Look around for club, restaurant and cinema listings in Bulgarian-language publications: *Programata*, *Navigator* and *Plovdiv Guide* (all free).

### NIGHTCLUBS
**Infinity Club** ( ☎ 0888-281 431; ul Bratya Pulievi 4; ⏲ 10pm-late Mon-Sat) is a long-popular disco in the centre, while **Plazma** ( ☎ 624 761; bul Hristo Botev 82; ⏲ 10pm-8am Wed-Sat) sees body-to-body dancing under the unnerving charms of the disco ball.

### CINEMAS
**Flamingo Cinema** ( ☎ 644 004; ul Sheshti Septemvri 128; tickets 3lv) Foreign films are shown at several venues, including this four-screen theatre.

## Getting There & Away
### BUS
Plovdiv has three bus stations. The main **Yug Bus Terminal** ( ☎ 626 916; ul Hristo Botev), 100m northeast of the train station, gets the honours for Sofia-bound buses. Just south of the train station (reached by underground passageway), the new **Rodopi Bus Terminal** ( ☎ 765 160) sends buses south and to Kazanlâk and Shumen. The third, 1½ km north of the river, **Sever Bus Terminal** ( ☎ 935 705) has services to Veliko Târnovo and Koprivshtitsa.

Sample fares follow; buses leave/arrive at Yug unless otherwise noted:

**Athens** (via Sofia) 108lv, 15 hours, one to three daily
**Bansko** 9lv, four hours, one daily (at 3pm)
**Blagoevgrad** 10lv, four hours, one daily
**Burgas** 14lv, four hours, two daily
**Istanbul** 25lv to 30lv, six hours, 10 daily
**Kazanlâk** 6.50lv, two hours, three daily (Sever)
**Koprivshtitsa** 5lv, two hours, one daily (Sever)
**Pamporovo** 7lv, two hours, hourly 6am to 7pm or 8pm except noon (Rodopi)
**Ruse** 14lv, seven hours, one daily (Sever)
**Shumen** 15lv, 5½ hours, one daily (Rodopi)
**Sliven** 8lv, 2½ hours, six daily
**Smolyan** 7.50lv, 2½ hours, hourly 6am to 7pm or 8pm except noon (Rodopi)

**Sofia** 9lv to 10lv, two hours, every 30 minutes or hour 6am to 8pm
**Thessaloniki** 32lv, nine hours, two daily
**Troyan** 7lv, 3½ hours, one daily (Sever)
**Varna** 9.20lv, seven hours, two daily (Yug or Sever)
**Veliko Târnovo** 10lv, 4½ hours, three daily (Sever)

International tickets only can be purchased from **MTT** ( ☎ 624 274; pl Tsntralen). **Medilien** ( ☎ 632 095; Yug bus station) handles tickets for Black Sea destinations.

### TRAIN
Direct trains from Plovdiv's **train station** ( ☎ 622 729; bul Hristo Botev) include the following (prices are for 1st-class seats; 2nd-class tickets save 1lv to 2lv):

**Belgrade** 35lv, 7½ hours, one daily
**Burgas** 12.80lv, five hours, three daily
**Istanbul** 35/48lv seat/sleeper, 11 hours, one daily
**Septemvri** 4.90lv, 45 minutes, frequent
**Sofia** 6.50, 2½ hours, frequent
**Varna** 16.70lv, six hours, three daily
**Veliko Târnovo** 8.90lv, six hours, at least one daily

For international tickets, go to **Rila Bureau** ( ☎ 643 120; bul Hristo Botev 31a; ⏲ 8am-6pm Mon-Fri, 8am-2pm Sat).

## Getting Around
It's easy to get around Plovdiv's centre by foot. On arrival, take bus 7, 20 or 26 in front of the train station (0.60lv) and exit on ul Tsar III Obedinitel past the tunnel to reach Old Town.

## AROUND PLOVDIV
Plovdiv is a bit too stranded in the Thracian plain to catch much Rodopi action by day. The closest and most rewarding trip is 20km south to **Asenovgrad**, a modest town at the start of the hills, with an 11th-century **fortress** with great views atop the hills. Smolyan-bound buses stop here.

Another 7km south (past the Chepelarska Gorge), **Backhovo Monastery** (admission free; ⏲ 6am-10pm) is Bulgaria's second biggest and is a nice stop-off, particularly if you have your own wheels and are heading deeper into the Rodopi. Founded in 1083 and restored in the 17th century, Bachkovo's central courtyard is filled with a 12th-century **Archangel Church** and a larger 17th-century **Church of the Assumption of Our Lady**. Buses bound for Smolyan will let you off here, at the southern end of the village.

# PAMPOROVO ПАМПОРОВО

☎ 3021

This popular ski resort 83km south of Plovdiv has eight ski runs and 25km of cross-country trails in a pine-thick mountain-top location. Rental equipment is about 30lv and a lift ticket 48lv. A bus connects the centre (near the T-junction of the roads to Smolyan, Plovdiv and Shiroka Lâka/Devin, where the bus stop is) to the lifts. It's quiet off-season, though you can hike up **Mt Perelik** (2190m) from here.

Most people book tours, or book way ahead, to stay in resort hotels sprinkled along the roads around the lifts. Talk to the **information centre** ( ☎ 8442) about hotels, or contact the Smolyan information centres. One good-value one, 6km from the lifts, is **Raikovski Livadi** ( ☎ 0301-35683; s/d 30/46lv).

Buses travelling between Plovdiv and Smolyan stop here.

# SMOLYAN СМОЛЯН

☎ 0301 / pop 32,100

With its setting in a sweeping valley between sky-scraping Rodopi peaks of mixed greens, Smolyan could be Bulgaria's most beautiful city. But on the streets, which are spread out and 'lacking harmony with nature', as one local complains, it feels a bit lacklustre. That said, the location (near Pamporovo's ski runs) wins out and Smolyan swings its own swagger with remarkably good attractions.

## Orientation & Information

Buses arrive near the west end of long bul Bulgaria (at the 'old centre'). About 250m east it becomes a pedestrian mall, where you'll find a **tourist office** ( ☎ 65 448; bul Bulgaria 80; ☺ 9am-1pm & 2-6pm Mon-Fri). About 200m further is **Access Internet Club** (per hr 1lv; ☺ 24hr), then the **Telephone Centre** (per min 0.36lv; ☺ 9.30am-6.30pm) 150m further still. After the pedestrian mall ends, you'll find a **Bulbank** ( ☺ 8.30am-4.30pm Mon-Fri) with an ATM.

Another 1km east on bul Bulgaria, near the museums, is another (much more helpful) **tourist office** ( ☎ 62 530; www.smolyan.com; bul Bulgaria 5; ☺ 9am-noon & 12.30-5.30pm Mon-Fri), with great handouts on hikes and accommodation.

## Sights

The **Historical Museum** ( ☎ 62 727; pl Bulgaria 3; adult/student 5/3lv; ☺ 9am-noon & 1-5pm Tue-Sun), a five-minute walk up steps (just east of the tourist office in the new centre), is one of the nation's best, with numerous English signs on three floors outlining Bulgaria's ethnographical past. Highlights include an artful display of hanging bells and full-bodied *kukeri* costumes (think *Star Wars* bar scene plus chicken feet).

The **Art Gallery** ( ☎ 62 328; adult/student 5/1lv; ☺ 9am-noon & 1-5pm), across from the Historical Museum, has seven halls of modern art (mostly Bulgarian), much of which is rather derivative.

The **Planetarium** ( ☎ 23 074; admission 5lv, minimum 3 visitors; ☺ English shows 2pm), open since 1975, features a domed-ceiling show of outer space (about 40 minutes, also in French and German) that conjures the age of cosmonauts despite its updated soundtrack. The best part is watching the stars for real via the mega-telescope at 6.30pm Wednesday if the sky's clear (admission 2lv). The show in Bulgarian is 3lv.

## Sleeping

The tourist office has a partial list of private accommodation available (about 8lv per person). A lot of new hotels are being built.

**Three Fir-Tree House** ( ☎ 64 281; dreliannen_h@yahoo.com; ul Srednogorec 1; s/d 30/40lv) The motherly owner of this lovely hotel is an absolute gem – as proud of her homemade meals (giant breakfast is 5lv, four-course dinner about 15lv) and namesake trees outside as of ensuring homely comfort in her nicely furnished rooms (with hair dryer, iron, free water, sheepskin blankets and balconies). She speaks German and English, and can arrange hikes and visits to Bulgarian bagpipe workshops. It's 250m from the bus station, down the steps at the start of bul Bulgaria's pedestrian mall.

**Hotel Smolyan** ( ☎ 62 053; www.hotelsmolyan.com; bul Bulgaria 3; s/d incl breakfast 25/42lv; ☒ ☒ ) This Balkantourist hotel, near the museums in the 'new centre', is trying to keep up with the recent hotel boom – its reduced prices for its fine but older rooms help. There's a pool in summer.

## Eating

Smolyan's pedestrian mall has surprisingly few options for diners. **Pizzeria Luchiya** (pizza 5-6lv; ☺ 7am-11pm) is a slightly older spot with good pies. Even nonguests can opt for a superb dinner at Three Fir-Tree House.

## Getting There & Around

Hourly buses leave Smolyan's **bus station** ( ☎ 63 104) north to Plovdiv (7.50lv), stopping in Pamporovo (2lv). Smolyan has important,

BULGARIA

but infrequent, links into the mountains. At time of research five daily buses left for Shiroka Lâka (2.80lv, 40 minutes). Buses for Kârdzhali leave from Ustov, in Smolyan's eastern reaches.

City buses 1 and 2 go from the bus station past the pedestrian mall and museums. Bus 1 goes to Ustov.

## SHIROKA LÂKA ШИРОКА ЛЪКА
☎ 03030 / pop 1501

Cute Shiroka Lâka, 24km west of Smolyan, is a stream-side town of Roman bridges and 19th-century whitewashed villas, which give a very other-era vibe (maybe it's the dung heaps). The best time to visit is early March, when locals adorn full-bodied animal-like costumes during the *kukeri* festival.

Of all things, there are two good tourist information centres; one **tourist office** ( ☎ 226; www .shirokaluka.com; ul Kapitan Petrko Voivoda 48; ◷ 8.30am-5pm Tue-Sat) is 100m east of the bus stop.

Hikes – overnight or day – loom in the green forested hills. One goes a few hours up to **Gela village**, which has held a bagpipe festival in August in the past. Another goes up **Mt Perelik**.

It's possible to study traditional music (or sit in on a recital) at the revered **Folk Music & Instruments High School** ( ☎ 333; nufi_shirokaluka@ abv.bg) across the water; it's closed July to mid-September.

The small, family-run **Hotel Kalina** ( ☎ 675; r incl breakfast summer/winter 15/20lv) is by the centre.

Buses between Devin and Smolyan stop here; it's easy to hail a group taxi for about 2lv or 3lv, too.

## KÂRDZHALI & AROUND КЪДЖАЛИ
☎ 0361 / pop 45,400

Linked to 17th-century Turkish general Kârdzhi Ali by name, and still retaining a large Turkish population (unusual for Bulgarian cities), friendly Kârdzhali looms in a broad valley of the eastern Rodopis, a few curvy hours east of Smolyan by road. It's fairly industrial – a lot of coal is plucked from the mountains nearby – but is near some thrilling archaeological sites and still feels off the tourist circuit.

Housed in a 1930s one-time Muslim school, the artful and well-arranged **Regional History Museum** ( ☎ 63 584; ul Renublikanska 4; admission 2lv; ◷ 9am-noon & 1-5pm Tue-Sun) has rewarding collections of Thracian and Roman sites in the area – all signed in English.

The main reason to venture here is the recently rediscovered site of **Perperikon**, about 20km east of town (brown signs lead the way, if driving). Atop a rocky bluff (a 45-minute walk up) are stunning indications of Thracian (and later Roman) life – dug-out water tanks and grooves where doors were pivoted open, supposedly part of the Temple of Dionysus – are up to 7000 years old.

About 27km southwest (east of Momchilgrad town) is **Tatul**, a battered Thracian ruins reached by a short dung-splattered trail (there are lots of shepherds here).

The drives along the **Kârdzhali Dam**, just west of the city, take in Turkish villages such as Enchets and Dâzhdovnitsa.

Across from the bus station, about 1km south of the centre, **Hotel Kârdzhali** ( ☎ 82 354; www.hotel-kardjali.com; bul Belomorski 68; s/d 34/55lv; ⊠ ) has simple, modern rooms and friendly staff.

Getting to the sites will require lots of planning, a car or a taxi. Kârdzhali is connected to Smolyan and Plovdiv by bus. Infrequent buses go to villages mentioned here.

# CENTRAL BALKANS

This broad swipe of lovely and surprisingly high mountains – called the Stara Planina (Old Mountain, or Balkans) locally – occupies much of Bulgaria's belly. The area is dotted with towns in 19th-century revival style (Veliko Târnovo, Koprivshtitsa, Tryavna and Kotel are standouts). Some of the many hiking paths through the broad Central Balkans National Park can also be cross-country skied or cycled. The international E3 hiking trail crosses here. Other windswept hubs (Kazanlâk, Sliven and Shumen) are more off the beaten track. Check www.staraplanina.org for more information.

Some travellers find themselves changing trains or buses in the Stara Planina's outer reaches at Stara Zagora, where there's a nice central garden and little else to see.

## KOPRIVSHTITSA КОПРИВЩИЦА
☎ 07184 / pop 2645

Popular with Bulgarian travellers seeking peace and quiet (or cooler temperatures in summer), historical Koprivshtitsa (say it three times fast) offers a glimpse of 19th-century life with its 400 lovely revival-era buildings where you can sleep, eat and get drunk. A babbling creek runs through town, and green

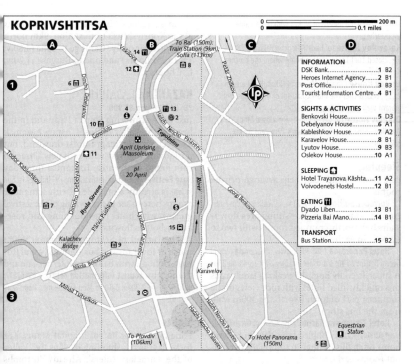

**KOPRIVSHTITSA**

| INFORMATION | |
| --- | --- |
| DSK Bank | 1 B2 |
| Heroes Internet Agency | 2 B1 |
| Post Office | 3 B3 |
| Tourist Information Centre | 4 B1 |

| SIGHTS & ACTIVITIES | |
| --- | --- |
| Benkovski House | 5 D3 |
| Debelyanov House | 6 A1 |
| Kableshkov House | 7 A2 |
| Karavelov House | 8 B1 |
| Lyutov House | 9 B3 |
| Oslekov House | 10 A1 |

| SLEEPING | |
| --- | --- |
| Hotel Trayanova Kâshta | 11 A2 |
| Voivodenets Hostel | 12 B1 |

| EATING | |
| --- | --- |
| Dyado Liben | 13 B1 |
| Pizzeria Bai Mano | 14 B1 |

| TRANSPORT | |
| --- | --- |
| Bus Station | 15 B2 |

hills with trails surrounding it. It's a great place to kick back.

Koprivshtitsa was the setting for a key early revolt against the Turks: the 20 April 1876 Uprising. Its re-enactment (actually held on 1 May or 2 May) along with the **Folklore Days Festival** (mid-August) are popular annual events.

## Orientation

The town spreads north–south for 1km along a small creek and is walkable. The bus stop is about 100m south of the centre, which is at pl 20 April. The train station (Gara Koprivshtitsa) is 9km north of town.

## Information

The **tourist information centre** ( ☎ 2191; www.koprivshtitsa.com; pl 20 April; ☼ 9am-7pm summer, 9am-6pm winter) has helpful English-speaking staff that can arrange private stays (usually 20lv to 25lv) and horse-riding trips, rent out bikes (2lv per hour) and sell town maps with hiking information (3.50lv).

The **DSK Bank** ( ☼ 8am-4pm Mon-Fri), next to the bus station, has a 24-hour ATM and exchanges money. The gold **post office** (Lyuben Karavelov;

☼ 7.30am-noon & 1-4.30pm Mon-Fri) has telephone services.

**Heroes Internet Agency** (ul Hadzhi Nencho Palaveev 49; per hr 1.2lv; ☼ 9am-midnight) offers unheroic speeds for its Web connection.

## Sights

If you visit a traditional home only once in Bulgaria, make it here. Six of Koprivshtitsa's traditional homes are now 'house museums', and a super-value combo ticket (adult/student 5/2lv) will get you into them all; otherwise it's 2/1lv each. All have signs in English and keep the same hours (9am to 5.30pm summer, 9am to 5pm winter), but alternate Monday or Tuesday off (see listings). The six pack is:

**Benkovski House** (ul Georgi Benkovski 5; ☼ closed Tue) Exhibits on the cavalier who continued the 1876 uprising in surrounding areas; it's near an impressive equestrian statue 400m southeast of the centre.

**Debelyanov House** (ul Dimcho Debelyanov 6; ☼ closed Mon) The 'tender poet' who lived here was not as short as the ceiling suggests (the floors were raised for renovation).

**Kableshkov House** (ul Todor Kableshkov 8; ☼ closed Mon) The home of the intriguing chairman of the revolutionary committee, this house has a wavy trifaçade

BULGARIA

and must-see old photos of blokes with remarkable moustaches.

**Karavelov House** (ul Hadzhi Nencho Palaveev 39; ☒ closed Tue) Three-section home where the brothers Karavelov grew up.

**Lyutov House** (Topalov House; ul Nikola Belovezhdov 2; ☒ closed Tue) The most colourful of the homes, with vibrant walls and ceilings.

**Oskelov House** (ul Gereniloto 4; ☒ closed Mon) Detailed home of one of the town's 19th-century tax collectors.

## Sleeping

The tourist office can help arrange private rooms.

**Voivodenets Hostel** ( ☎ 2145; ul Vekilova 5; dm 7-8lv) An old home with a nice sitting area downstairs but mostly cramped rooms with two to 10 beds in each.

**Hotel Panorama** ( ☎ 2035; www.panoramata.com; ul Georgi Benkovski 40; s/d/tr/apt incl breakfast 36/48/60/80lv) A super-friendly English-speaking family runs this quickly filled hotel with nice views of the southern part of town (worth the 300m walk from the bus stop).

**Hotel Trayanova Kâshta** ( ☎ 3057; ul Gereniloto 5; r/apt 40/80lv) Off a cobbled lane, this four-room home often fills its huge, traditionally decked-out rooms early.

**Rai** ( ☎ 2637; ul Dyado Liben 8; d summer/winter 40/50lv) A nice 11-room hotel in an old building just north of the centre.

## Eating

Traditional *kâshtas* are found on side streets, some keeping seasonal hours.

**Dyado Liben** ( ☎ 2109; ul Hadzhi Nencho Palaveev; dishes 7.50-10lv, grills 2.50-10lv; ☒ 10am-midnight) This good *kâshta* is set in a lushly kept revival-era home. There are four dining rooms upstairs; the courtyard fills up in summer. Save room for yogurt with blueberries (3lv) for dessert. The two-man band travels the musical highway between Stevie Wonder and *Dr Zhivago*.

**Pizzeria Bai Mano** (ul Hadzhi Nencho Palaveev) For those in need of Bulgaria's other food.

## Getting There & Away

The **bus station** ( ☎ 3044) sends a few buses daily to Sofia's central or Poduene bus station (6lv, 2½ hours); at research time, buses left for Sofia at 6.45am, 8.50am, 12.50pm and 4.55pm. A 6.30am bus (2pm on Sunday) left for Plovdiv (6lv, 2½ hours).

Taxis and local buses meet incoming trains at the Koprivshtitsa train station, 9km north of town. Four or five trains go to Sofia (4.60lv, 1¾ to 2½ hours) and one to Burgas (11.20lv, five hours).

# KAZANLÂK КАЗАНЛЪК
☎ 0431 / pop 51,900

Just below towering Shipka Pass, and in the heart of the Valley of Roses, happy Kazanlâk isn't yet a mainstream tourist drawcard, but it's moving that way with each new Thracian ruin found in the area. Its annual three-day **Rose Festival** (www.rose-festival.com; ☒ finishes 1st Sun in Jun) is already a huge deal (with some tour groups here to see the crowning of the festival queen), with hotel rates doubling and rose-liquor bottles flowing.

The central pl Sevtopolis is about 400m north of the train and bus stations (via ul Rozova Dolina), with banks, an internet café and the nearby **tourist information centre** ( ☎ 62817; ul Iskra 4; ☒ 8.30am-5.30pm Mon-Fri summer, hours vary winter).

## Sights

Long famous for its 'rose capital' status, Kaz these days is refashioning itself as the 'Valley of the Thracian Rulers'. Already 40 tombs have been found.

The go-to place for Thracian tomb information is a couple of blocks north of pl Sevtopolis at the **Iskra Museum & Art Gallery** ( ☎ 63741; ul Slaveikov 8; admission 2lv; ☒ 9am-5pm). It has plenty of Bulgarian art, and lots of Thracian and Roman pieces (including a copy of the 5th-century golden mask, believed to be King Sevt III's likeness, found in 2004).

Kazanlâk's **Tyulbe Park** (about 300m northeast of the centre) houses the small, 3rd- or 4th-century **Tomb of Kazanlâk** (admission 20lv; ☒ 9am-6pm Apr-Oct), a remarkably well-preserved Unesco World Heritage site with paintings and a nice echo. You can get the idea at the far cheaper **tomb copy** ( ☎ 64750; admission 3lv; ☒ approx 9am-5pm).

More rewarding is the energetically run **Kosmatka** (admission 3lv; ☒ 9am-5pm), just south of the pleasant town of Shipka (about 10km north, reached by hourly bus 6). The illuminated-at-night mound (which you can climb) has three chambers where the 5th-century tomb of Sevt III was found in 2004.

Near Tyulbe Park, **Kulata Ethnological Complex** ( ☎ 21733; admission 3lv; ☒ 8am-6pm May-Oct, by arrangement Nov-Apr) is a revival-style 'village' with rose-liquor tastings and (often) live music.

## Sleeping

**Hadzhi Eminova Kâshta** ( ☎ 62595; bul Nikola Petkov 22; r 25lv, apt 40 & 50lv) Next to the Kulata complex, this place has four good-value rooms in an 180-year-old building.

**Grand Hotel** ( ☎ 63440; www.hotelkazanlak-bg.com; pl Sevtopolis 1; s/d 35/44lv; ☒ ) A former Balkantourist hotel has refashioned itself for modern times – new furnishings and balconies hanging over the square surely help.

## Eating

Pl Sevtopolis might as well be 'Little America', with restaurants and clubs named for Hollywood and Manhattan. Kaz's favourite pizzeria is **New York Bar & Grill** (pl Sevtopolis; pizza from 3lv; grills 3-5lv; ☒ 10am-midnight), featuring salads named for all New York's boroughs but Staten Island.

## Getting There & Away

Daily bus services include four buses to Plovdiv (10lv, 2½ hours), four to Veliko Târnovo (6lv, three hours), five or six to Sofia (20lv, three hours) and two to Burgas (12lv, three hours).

A few daily trains head to Sofia (8.30lv, 3½ hours) and Burgas (8.30lv, three hours).

## SLIVEN СЛИВЕН
☎ 044 / pop 96,000

Where plains meet 1000m craggy peaks (and the rare tourist), Sliven – known as Bulgaria's 'windy city' and home to a big Roma population – is often overlooked, but it can hold its own for a half-day or longer.

Central pl Hadzhi Dimitâr is reached by the street of the same name from the train and bus stations, 500m and 750m south respectively. The street curves before hitting a long pedestrian mall, ul Tsar Osvoboditel. Nearby, the golden clock tower houses city hall, a tourist office (open irregular hours), a gallery and a good bookshop.

### Sights

Sliven's top attractions are the views and trails up the **blue rocks** (*sinite skali*), reached by **chairlift** (one way/return 6/10lv; ☒ supposedly 8.30am-3pm). Take bus 116 from the market (facing pl Hadzhi Dimitâr, near Hotel Sliven) to the end of the line, where it's a 20-minute walk.

In town, the **Hadzhi Dimitâr Museum** ( ☎ 622496; ul Asenova 2; admission 2lv; ☒ approx 9am-noon & 2-5pm Mon-

Fri), over the river west of Hotel Sliven, brings to life the local 19th-century revolutionary hero.

### Sleeping

**Hotel Sliven** ( ☎ 624056; pl Hadzhi Dimitâr, s/d incl breakfast from 25/34lv) A classic communist-era high-rise with dodgy plumbing, 1980s décor and shockingly helpful staff.

**Hotel Kredo** ( ☎ 625080; ul Predel 1; r incl breakfast 59lv; ☒ ) On an alley just west of ul Hadzhi Dimitâr (just past the Billa supermarket), this blue-and-gold hotel is Sliven's best midrange value, with cable TV and small balconies.

### Eating

There's plenty to eat and drink along ul Tsar Osvoboditel. A long-time favourite is **Restaurant Maki** (ul Tsar Osbvoboditel; pizza 3-5.40lv, dishes 3.50-5.50lv; ☒ 7am-1am), with a fake McDonald's logo and photo menu.

### Getting There & Away

The **bus station** ( ☎ 626629) has frequent connections to Burgas (7lv, two hours), Plovdiv (8lv, three hours), Kotel (4lv to 5lv, 1½ hours) and Sofia (14lv). There's also a daily bus to Veliko Târnovo (8lv).

Most trains on the Sofia–Burgas line stop at the Sliven **train station** ( ☎ 636614).

## KOTEL КОТЕЛ
☎ 0453 / pop 6700

Seen by a smattering of Sunny Beach day-trippers in tour buses, Kotel (*Ko*-tel) is a traditional carpet-making centre filled with 19th-century revival-era homes in the Stara Planina's eastern reaches, about 50km north-east of Sliven.

From the bus station walk up a few blocks to the centre, where you'll find an ATM behind the pink city hall. Extending west, ul Izvorska leads past the **Information Business Centre** ( ☎ 2334; ul Izvorska 14; ☒ 9am-7pm Mon-Fri), which gives out brochures including a hiking map and has internet access (also try www.kotel.bg). The road curves left, past a carpet-making factory you can visit, and comes out on a main road, where a trellis-covered pedestrian lane, ul Khrum Petrob, leads eventually to Izvorite Park.

### Sights

Kotel has several museums. Its best is the dramatic **History Museum** (National Revival Kotel Enlighteners; ☎ 2549; admission 1.60lv; ☒ 8am-noon & 1-5pm) in the blob-like 1981 building facing the

**BULGARIA**

city hall. In four halls, English signs tell how Kotel boys made a big impact on Bulgarian culture and history. The main attraction is the mausoleum for Georgi Rakovski, a 19th-century warrior hero.

About 500m west, **Izvorite Park** is filled with folkloric statues and the mysterious source of the Kamcha River (known locally as 'crazy river').

Hikes in the hills include the two-hour walk to ultra-gingerbread village **Zherevna**, and walks to waterfalls north of the nearby town **Medven**. Ask at the information centre.

### Courses

Bulgaria's famous **Philip Kotev School** ( ☎ 2215; smu_k_l@mail.bg; ul Georgi Zahariev 2) offers *gaida* and other traditional music classes in July and August. Occasionally you can catch students' recitals, particularly in April and May.

### Sleeping & Eating

**Starata Vodenitsa** ( ☎ 2360; r 40lv) Near the entrance to Izvorite Park, this 'old mill' features seven dark-wood rooms decked richly in Bulgarian crafts, including locally made rugs. The rooms (with cable TV!) are some of the country's best deals, and the restaurant is one of Kotel's best.

### Getting There & Away

The decrepit **bus station** ( ☎ 2052) has regular services to Sliven (4lv to 5lv, 1½ hours), a lone bus to Shumen (5.50lv, 2½ hours) and a couple to Burgas (7lv). A couple of buses go to/from Zherevna and Medven daily.

## TROYAN & AROUND ТРОЯН

☎ 0670 / pop 22,460

Hilly Troyan's biggest claims to fame are its proximity to the Troyan Monastery and the Central Balkans National Park (with hiking paths and downhill skiing at Beklemeto). Several spa towns are in the mountains to the west, including Ribaritsa (with villas for rent).

About 1km south of Troyan's bus and train stations is a **tourist information centre** ( ☎ 60 964; www.troyan.bg; ul Vasil Levski 133; ☼ 10am-6pm Mon-Fri). Banks and internet access are found along ul Vasil Levski.

There are a couple of hotels, including the recently renovated, hilltop **Kâpina Hotel** ( ☎ 62 930; hotelkapina@abv.bg; r from €20), 800m south of the bus station (and just up to the right).

One of Bulgaria's most popular monasteries, 10km away, the **Troyan Monastery** (admission

free; ☼ 6am-10pm) was established in the 1500s and is famed for Zahari Zograf's apocalyptic murals (painted in the 1840s) inside and outside the Church of the Holy Virgin. The small **museum** (admission 3lv; ☼ 8am-7pm) dedicated to Vasil Levski, who spent time during the rebellion here, is for fanatics only. Simple **rooms** ( ☎ 069-522 866; r per person 10-12lv) are available.

Troyan is reached by bus from Sofia, Pleven and Karlovo. About a dozen buses bounce between town and the monastery on weekdays, and five a day at weekends (about 1lv, 20 minutes). A taxi to the monastery costs 5lv or so.

## VELIKO TÂRNOVO ВЕЛИКО ТЪРНОВО

☎ 062 / pop 66,200

Off the Bucharest–Istanbul track, on a sharp S-shaped gorge split by a snaking river and home to the best damn ruined citadel in the country, Veliko is not only good to look at but is also near hill towns, hill hikes, hill cycling and hill climbs, all of which make excellent day-trip fodder. A medieval capital of one of Bulgaria's past lives (1185–1393), Veliko is chiefly a lively student town these days, as one in six residents is a student.

March 22 is Veliko's (and a certain LP author's) birthday, when a big festival is staged around town.

### Orientation

Sloping ul Hristo Botev leads north from the Yug Bus Terminal to pl Maika Bulgaria, where ul Vasil Levski heads west and the main crawl, ul Nezavisimost, heads east for 1km. This street looms way over the gorge, with (slightly confusing) side streets and stairways weaving down to the water.

Note that signs pointing to attractions in town are often turned to point in the wrong direction. Damn kids.

### Information

The main streets winding through town have many foreign-exchange offices. Veliko earns a special place in our heart for having *several* laundry services, something foreign to much of Bulgaria.

**Main post office** (ul Nezavisimost) There is also a telephone centre.

**Navigator** (ul Nezavisimost 3; per hr 0.50-0.80lv; ☼ 24hr) Has 90 computers and offers international calls for 0.19lv per minute. There's a laundry service next door (open 8am to 9.30pm).

**Plino** (ul Baba Moto 10; per load about 3lv; ⊕ 10am-6pm Mon-Fri, 10am-4pm Sat) Quick drop-off laundry service.

**Real Matrix** (ul Nezavisimost; international calls per min 0.25lv; ⊕ 24hr) Telephone and internet services.

**Tourist Information Centre** ( ☎ 22 148; www .velikotarnovo.info; ul Hristo Botev; ⊕ 9am-6pm Mon-Sat Apr-Oct, 9am-6pm Mon-Fri Nov-Mar) Remarkably helpful

centre with English-speaking staff who can arrange private accommodation, book rental cars for 30lv daily, sell regional maps (4lv) and offer tips on seeing the region.

**United Bulgarian Bank** (ul Hristo Botev; ⊕ 8.30am-4.30pm Mon-Fri) Cashes travellers cheques, but its ATM is inside.

**USIT Colours** ( ☎ 601 751; pl Slaveikov 7; ⊕ 9.30am-6.30pm Mon-Fri) Sells student cards for 10lv.

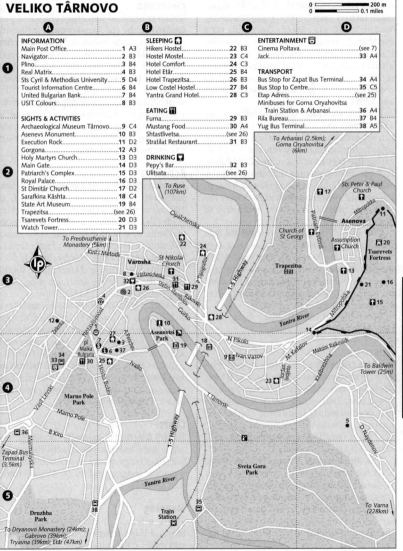

## VELIKO TÂRNOVO

| INFORMATION | | |
|---|---|---|
| Main Post Office | 1 | A3 |
| Navigator | 2 | B3 |
| Plino | 3 | B4 |
| Real Matrix | 4 | B3 |
| Sts Cyril & Methodius University | 5 | D4 |
| Tourist Information Centre | 6 | B4 |
| United Bulgarian Bank | 7 | B4 |
| USIT Colours | 8 | B3 |

| SIGHTS & ACTIVITIES | | |
|---|---|---|
| Archaeological Museum Târnovo | 9 | C4 |
| Asenevs Monument | 10 | B3 |
| Execution Rock | 11 | D2 |
| Gorgona | 12 | A3 |
| Holy Martyrs Church | 13 | D3 |
| Main Gate | 14 | D3 |
| Patriarch's Complex | 15 | D3 |
| Royal Palace | 16 | D3 |
| St Dimitâr Church | 17 | D2 |
| Sarafkina Kâshta | 18 | C4 |
| State Art Museum | 19 | B4 |
| Trapezitsa | (see 26) | |
| Tsarevets Fortress | 20 | D3 |
| Watch Tower | 21 | D3 |

| SLEEPING | | |
|---|---|---|
| Hikers Hostel | 22 | B3 |
| Hostel Mostel | 23 | C4 |
| Hotel Comfort | 24 | C3 |
| Hotel Etâr | 25 | B4 |
| Hotel Trapezitsa | 26 | B3 |
| Low Costel Hostel | 27 | B4 |
| Yantra Grand Hotel | 28 | C3 |

| EATING | | |
|---|---|---|
| Furna | 29 | B3 |
| Mustang Food | 30 | A4 |
| Shtastlivetsa | (see 26) | |
| Stratilal Restaurant | 31 | B3 |

| DRINKING | | |
|---|---|---|
| Pepy's Bar | 32 | B3 |
| Ulitsata | (see 26) | |

| ENTERTAINMENT | | |
|---|---|---|
| Cinema Poltava | (see 7) | |
| Jack | 33 | A4 |

| TRANSPORT | | |
|---|---|---|
| Bus Stop for Zapat Bus Terminal | 34 | A4 |
| Bus Stop to Centre | 35 | C5 |
| Etap Adress | (see 25) | |
| Minibuses for Gorna Oryahovitsa Train Station & Arbanasi | 36 | A4 |
| Rila Bureau | 37 | B4 |
| Yug Bus Terminal | 38 | A5 |

**BULGARIA**

## Sights

English- and Bulgarian-language signs explain many historic sites, churches and houses around town, making for good DIY exploration. Be sure to walk along **ul Gurko**, Veliko's best-preserved street that cobbles its way along the gorge.

### TSAREVETS FORTRESS

About a kilometre from the centre, this mammoth **fortress** (admission 4lv; ☺ 8am-7pm Apr-Sep, 9am-5pm Oct-Mar) sits stoically, sprawling on a site shared over the centuries by Thracians, Romans and Byzantines. What's seen now – a triangular, high-walled fortress with the remains of more than 400 houses and 18 churches – was largely built between the 5th and 12th centuries.

From the **main gate**, follow the left wall past a **watch tower** to the northern end where you can see **execution rock**, from where convicted souls were pushed. Back south, the giant Bulgarian flag flies from the ruined **Royal Palace**. Its high-up neighbour is the renovated **patriarch's complex**. Inside are surprisingly modern murals and a suspended altar. Back near the main gate, you can follow the south wall to **Baldwin Tower**.

The after-dark, 40-minute **sound and light show** (☎ 636 828; admission 12lv) takes place over the scene – once 30 tourists have paid. Ask at the gate if a show's on. Or, as one local said, 'When the tourists come and pay for the show, the whole town watches from outside for free.' Generally it's held every Saturday.

Buses 20, 400 and 110 make the trip between the centre and the site.

### MUSEUMS

**Sarafkina Kâshta** ( ☎ 635 802; ul Gurko 88; adult/student 4/2lv; ☺ 9am-5pm Mon-Fri Dec-Mar, 9am-noon & 1-6pm Mon-Fri Apr-Nov) is a two-storey former banker's home from 1861 with a sitting room set up upstairs, including traditional objects and interesting photos that a matter-of-fact guide may point out ('It is rich women, it is 1910 scene, it is very rich man…').

The **Archaeological Museum Târnovo** ( ☎ 601 528; ul Ivan Vazov; admission 4lv; ☺ 8am-noon & 1-6pm Tue-Sun Apr-Oct, 9am-5pm Tue-Sun Nov-Mar), just up the zigzag road from Sarafkina Kâshta, was closed for renovation at last pass. You can see Roman ruins laying amok outside, and the recently discovered tomb of King Kaloyan inside.

The **State Art Museum** ( ☎ 638 941; admission 3lv; ☺ 10am-6pm Tue-Sun, free Thu) has an interesting collection of (mostly) communist-era art. It's worth reaching (at least) for the spot outside the huge 1985 **Asenevs Monument** (aka Four Bulgarian Kings Monument, for Assen, Petâr, Ivan Shishman and Kaloyan), which faces town from across the river.

### CHURCHES

Veliko is home to numerous churches, particularly in the old Asenova quarter (including the Byzantine-influenced **St Dimitâr Church**, Veliko's oldest), reached across a wood-plank pedestrian bridge from the fortress. Many churches, however, keep inconsistent hours and some charge about 4lv to enter. At research time, the riverside **Holy Martyrs Church** – where King Kaloyan's tomb was discovered in 2004 – was wrapping up a long renovation and planning to open as a museum. Call ☎ 638 841 for more information.

## Activities

**Trapezitsa** ( ☎ 635 823; www.trapezitca1902.com; ul Stefan Stambolov 79; ☺ 9am-6pm Mon-Fri), which dates from 1902, arranges **rock-climbing** trips, sells a climbing guide (2lv), offers advice and can sometimes set up climbs on a huge indoor wall at the Palace of Culture and Sport, the site of international climbing competitions. Nearby climbs include St Trinity Monastery and Usteto (2km south). Check the website for information on week-long hut-to-hut hikes and bike trips.

**Gorgona** ( ☎ 601 400; www.gorgona-shop.com, in Bulgarian; ul Zelenka 2; ☺ 10am-1pm & 2-7pm Mon-Fri, 10am-2pm Sat) rents out mountain bikes (10lv per day) and can point you to good trails. Head up the steps across ul Nezavisimost from the post office.

Ask at the tourist centre about **horse riding** and **hiking** in the area. One lovely hike goes 5km north on and up-and-down, two-hour hike to **Preobruzhenie Monastery**.

## Courses

**Sts Cyril & Methodius University** ( ☎ 639 869; www.cet-vtu.com; ul Teodosi Tarnovski 2) holds three-week Bulgarian language classes in August for €550 including lodging and meals. Private tutors cost 8lv or 9lv per hour.

## Sleeping

Touts offering abundant private rooms (around 15lv per person) usually await buses and trains at the stations.

## BUDGET

**Low Costel Hostel** ( ☎ 0885-726 733; lowcostel@hotmail.com; ul Assen Ruskov 6; dm incl breakfast 16-20lv; 🖳 ) Nearly open at research time, this British-run hostel is closest to the stations – and the cheapest. It has a simple layout in a 1950s building, with three dorm rooms on one floor and a sitting area and kitchen upstairs. Laundry is 4lv.

**Hikers Hostel** ( ☎ 0889-691 661; www.hikers-hostel.org; l Rezevoarska 91; dm/r incl breakfast €10/26; 🖳 ) Up (way up) a cobbled path, this nice, smallish hostel is a hike to reach but has superb views – the upstairs terrace looks at the fortress' light show. Staff are friendly, though at times their friends can take over the common area. The two-tiered front deck sets up 'camp' spots at peak time; it's a bit busy for the two showers. Reserve ahead for (the crucial) pick-up from stations.

**Hostel Mostel** ( ☎ 0897-859 359; www.hostelmostel.com; l Iordan Indjeto 10; dm incl breakfast from €10; 🖳 ) Just getting set up at last pass, Sofia's Mostel folks were looking to take over Veliko's hostel scene with a big house three minutes from the fortress' entrance. Pluses include a barbecue area, huge balcony, big sitting area inside and – get ready – a stone-walled 'wine cellar' downstairs. Three dorm rooms and three private ones.

## MIDRANGE

**Hotel Trapezitsa** ( ☎ 635 823; ul Stefan Stambolov 79; dm 15-20lv; s/d apt 30/40/55lv) This central, cheap hotel has 40 rooms. It's slightly old (eg manifesto-brown carpet) but attracts youthful guests. Make sure you have a room at the back; they have ridiculously great gorge views. The two apartments (only) have TVs plus small balconies.

**Hotel Etâr** ( ☎ 621 838; www.etar.veliko.info; ul Ivailo ; s/d incl breakfast 40/60lv, with air con 60/80lv; 🍴 ) This old commie-era tower hotel has clean but stuffy rooms (about 80 in all); higher ones have fortress views.

**Hotel Comfort** ( ☎ 628 728; ul P Tipografov 5; s/d 55/65lv; 🍴 ) Many of the Comfort's dozen rooms have full-frontal views of the fortress and the light show – a few have balconies. Some private bathrooms are across the hall.

## TOP END

**Yantra Grand Hotel** ( ☎ 958 2843; www.yantrabg.com; pl Velchovazavera; s/d incl breakfast from 90/120lv; 🍴 🖳 🍷 ) Off Veliko's main strip, this new 71-room, eight-floor hotel has big rooms with earthy tones and a health club with a small pool. Half the rooms look over the fortress (definitely spring for the view: it's an extra 13lv).

## Eating

**Furna** (Samovodska Charshiya; banitsa 0.60lv; ☯ 7am-5pm) A fresh bakery on the site of the old market.

**Stratilat Restaurant** (ul Rakovski 11; sandwiches & pizza from 1.60lv; ☯ 8am-midnight) Named 'the lucky one', perhaps because it's hard to get a seat at the outside tables. Most popular for cakes (1.90lv to 3lv), coffee and drinks.

**Mustang Food** (ul Maika Bulgaria; mains 2-5lv; ☯ 24hr) For a lapse into the West, this Americanised diner serves a full breakfast of eggs, bacon, hash browns and toast all day.

**Shtastlivetsa** ( ☎ 600 656; ul Stefan Stambulov 79; mains 5-11lv; ☯ 10am-11pm) If you're into detail, allow an hour to look over the two giant menus (for Bulgarian or Italian food) in the two-storey spot that's long been Veliko's most popular (and best) eating place. There are nine 'diet pizzas' made of rye flour and 20lv family-sized 'Gypsy' meals, plus 82 salads including the tasty carrot-and-apple salad with honey (2.60lv).

## Drinking

**Pepy's Bar** (ul Veneta Boteva 5; ☯ 8am-11pm) A laid-back, softly lit bar with mixed ages, a grab-bag décor (Jackie O photos, Bulgarian 78s) and an emphasis on chatting, not loud music.

**Ulitsata** (ul Stefan Stambolov 79; draft beer 0.80lv; ☯ 7am-late) A local *birraria* with a couple of seats facing the gorge and some metal on the stereo.

**Jack** (ul Magistralna 5; beer 1.50lv; ☯ 9am-2 or 3am) As in Daniels, Jack blares dance music when bands aren't splaying on this (sometimes) student-filled 2nd-floor club with big leather sofas.

## Entertainment

**Cinema Poltava** ( ☎ 620 542; tickets 2-4lv; ul Nezavisimost 3) Plays foreign movies with Bulgarian subtitles.

## Getting There & Away

### BUS

Private buses leave from the **Yug Bus Terminal** (ul Hristo Botev), a 15-minute walk downhill from the centre. Hourly (if not more frequent) buses en route to Sofia (9lv to 13lv, three hours) and Varna (9lv to 13lv, three hours) stop here and at the more convenient location of **Etap Adress** ( ☎ 630 564; Hotel Etâr). Yug also sends buses to Istanbul (30lv).

The quiet, public **Zapad Bus Terminal** ( ☎ 640 908), 4km west of the centre, sends eight buses daily to Ruse (6lv, two hours), three to Plovdiv (12lv, four hours), four to Kazanlâk (6lv, two hours) and four to Burgas (12lv, four hours), and a couple of buses weekly to Troyan (7lv,

BULGARIA

two hours). There are also buses to nearby Elena and Gabrovo. Bus 10, among others, heads west to the terminal from ul Vasil Levski.

#### CAR

The tourist information centre can arrange rental cars for 30lv per day.

#### TRAIN

Veliko's small **train station** (☎ 620 065) sends about six trains a day to Ruse (4.30lv, 2½ to 3½ hours) and eight to Tryavna (2.90lv, one hour). A much busier station is just 8.5km north at Gorna Oryahovitsa, a stop on the Sofia–Varna line. Two trains from there go to Bucharest (seat/sleeper 25/41lv) and there's a daily train to Istanbul (35/62lv). Minibuses along ul Vasil Levski, or bus 10 east from the centre, head there every 10 or 15 minutes (1lv).

There's a walkway from the train platform (away from station) that connects to an underpass leading to ul Hristo Botev, near the bus station. Catch bus 4, 5, 13, 30 or 70 heading south from outside the station to reach the centre.

Buy international tickets at **Rila Bureau** (☎ 622 2042; ul Tsar Kolyan; 🕑 8am-noon & 1-4.30pm Mon-Fri), in the alley behind the information centre.

## AROUND VELIKO TÂRNOVO

Much of the following can be seen in a day if you have (motorised) wheels. Contact Trapezitsa (p164) for a week-long guided hike from Veliko to the historic hill town of **Elena**.

### Arbanasi Арбанаси

**☎ 062 / pop 1500**

Five kilometres from Veliko Târnovo, high-on-a-hill Arbanasi is a collection of spread-out old walled churches and villas, some of which serve as classy *mekhanas* or hotels. It can feel a bit exclusive, with walled villas and upmarket restaurants (some run, it's whispered, by mafia). The town never was a real town, but rather served as quarters for much of the king's royal entourage. Still, many a blissful beer-soaked afternoon has been spent watching Veliko turn gold, pink or purple in the setting sun.

Worth getting lost to find, the 16th-century **Nativity Church** (☎ 604 323; adult/student 4/2lv; 🕑 9am-6pm Apr-Oct, 9am-5pm Nov-Mar), 200m west of the bus stop, is a shock to enter. It was built ho-hum and low to obscure the building's purpose from the Ottomans. Inside, it bursts with colourful, ceiling-to-floor murals depicting 2000 scenes, including the evocative 'wheel of life'.

**Panorama** (☎ 623 421; d 35lv; Ⓟ) is a friendly simple, daringly nontraditional hillside hotel about 400m west of the bus stop (towards the end of the road). It has a few rooms and is expanding. Its outdoor café serves hilariously large ice-cream portions.

A more traditional budget option is **Falkite** (The Torches; ☎ 604 496; s/d 16/32lv), about 150m northwest from the bus stop.

It's about 3lv or 4lv to reach Arbanasi by taxi from Veliko. Some Gorna Oryahovitsa-bound minibuses from ul Vasil Levski in Veliko stop in Arbanasi (all come within a 700m walk of the centre). Nine minibuses ply the journey daily (0.50lv).

### Dryanovo Monastery

Дряновски Манастир

Top-heavy cliffs stoop over this charming stream-side **monastery** (☎ 0676-2389; admission free; 🕑 7am-10pm), 24km south of Veliko. Built in the 12th century, the monastery's been destroyed a time or two, and was last rebuilt in the early 18th century. The priest here is quite chatty.

It's possible to stay in the simple rooms (9lv to 15lv per person with shared bathroom). There are bungalows and a small hotel nearby and along the river a leafy open-air *mekhana* serving Bulgarian food. Gabrovo-bound buses will stop at the turn-off (if requested), about 5km south of the town Dryanovo, where it's a 1.5km walk to the monastery.

### Etâr Етър

Played up by travel agents and tour operators, **Etâr Ethnographic Village Museum** (☎ 066-801 838; www.etar.hit.bg; adult/student 4/1lv; 🕑 8.30am-6pm May-Sep, 9am-4.30pm Oct-Apr) is an open-air museum with shops and workshops recreating Bulgaria's revival period of the 19th century. A nice 3km walk uphill is the pleasant **Sokolski Monastery**.

**Hotel Perla** (☎ 066-801 984; r 38lv) – just before the Etâr gate – has six huge, very inviting rooms.

To get here by public transport, take a bus to the large town of Gabrovo, 8km north of Etar, and take blue-and-white city bus 8 to the gate, or bus 1 or 7 to near Hotel Perla; buses run every half hour. A taxi to Gabrovo from Etar is about 5lv.

### Tryavna Трявна

**☎ 0677 / pop 10,500**

As Bulgaria's woodcarving capital – with an old town centre and revival-era shopfronts – Tryavna is an Arbanasi without the tourists or an Etâr without the ticket price. It's good for a day visit, but it's even more evocative when the whitewashed buildings glow under moonlight and the locals' laughter pours out of small *mekhanas*.

### ORIENTATION & INFORMATION

Tryavna is 39km south of Veliko. Its bus and train stations are opposite each other on the north side of town. Follow ul Angel Kânchev (just east of the stations), or the road along the tracks, 400m south (over the creek) to the centre.

The **tourist office** ( ☎ 2247; www.tryavna.bg; ul Angel Kânchev 22; ☼ 9am-noon & 2-5pm Mon-Fri), next to the post office, was closed for renovation at last pass. In the past it's offered help on local hikes and even rented camping equipment. There's an ATM next door.

### SIGHTS

Tryavna has about a dozen museums and churches. All museums are allegedly open 9am to 6pm daily April to October (8am to 5pm other times); admission is 2/1lv for adults/students.

West of the tourist office is **Shkolo** ( ☎ 2278), a school-turned–art museum with 500 regional artists' works. Across the street is **St Archangel Michael Church** (admission 1lv), with a two-storey collection of icons.

Over the arched bridge to ul Slaveikov, you will pass several workshops with artisans chipping away at wood blocks. Around 150m further is the **Daskalov House** (1808; ul Slaveikov 27), Bulgaria's lone woodcarving museum.

### SLEEPING & EATING

**Trevnenski Kât** ( ☎ 2033; ul Kânchev 8; s/d from 30/40lv) It's simple, but the best place to stay – a classic 19th-century tavern-style guesthouse on the main square with a buzzing *mekhana* downstairs. It fills on weekends.

**Zograf** ( ☎ 4970; zograf@mbox.digsys.bg; ul Slaveikov 1; s/d 32/46lv) Has rooms next to the old bridge, with a huge courtyard restaurant.

**Starata Loza** (ul Slaveikov 44; mains 2.80-7.50lv; ☼ 8am-midnight) Across from the Daskalov House, Starata Loza serves tasty Bulgarian fare.

### GETTING THERE & AWAY

Tryavna has half-hourly bus connections with Gabrovo (13km east), but nowhere else. Nine trains a day go to/from Veliko Târnovo (2.90lv, one hour).

## Shipka Pass Шипченски проход

The scene of an important Russian–Turkish battle in 1877, Shipka Pass (about 60km south of Veliko) is accented by the bare-top, 1326m-high Mt Stoletov and the six-storey **Freedom Monument** (admission 2lv; ☼ 9am-5pm summer, 9am-5pm Sat & Sun winter) with displays on the battles and, up top, 360-degree views of the Stara Planina and Valley of Roses below (hey kids, it's Kazanlâk!).

It's a Shipka tradition to finish a visit with **buffalo yoghurt** (birosko mlyako; cups 1.3lv) at the stands below.

Hourly buses between Kazanlâk and Gabrovo will drop you off at the pass, where you can hail the next bus. Shipka town is 13km to the south.

## SHUMEN ШУМЕН

☎ 054 / pop 86,800

Set along a long sweeping mountain halfway between Varna and Ruse, Shumen lacks the quaint cobbled-lane punch of some historical towns, but its neighbours (forts, monuments and ancient capitals) and Shumensko beer make it an appealing stop-off. Its historic core is tied to Bulgaria's beginnings in the sweet 7th century.

The name Shumen may be from a word for 'leaves', or a version of Tsar Simeon's name – it doesn't mean the town is full of male cobblers.

### Orientation & Information

The main square, pl Osvobozhdenie, is about 1km west of the neighbouring bus and train stations on bul Slavyanksi. About halfway between them is a **Bulbank** (bul Slavyanski; ☼ 8.45am-5.40pm Mon-Fri) with an ATM. Across from the post office and Hotel Madara on pl Osvobozhdenie is the **International Call Centre** (bul Slavyanski; ☼ 8am-11pm), with internet access (1.20lv per hr) and calls abroad for 0.20lv per minute. In the city office building is a **tourist information centre** ( ☎ 853 773; bul Slavyanski 17; ☼ 8.30am-5pm Mon-Fri).

### Sights

From afar it's an enigmatic slab of grey overlooking town, but up close the super **Creators of the Bulgarian State Monument** (admission 2lv; ☼ 24hr) welcomes those who climb the 1300m up the obvious steps from the centre (or cheat and take a taxi) with incredible cubist-style horseback figures peering down from between crevices like stone Don Quixotes. The monument was built in 1981 to commemorate Bulgaria's 1300th birthday. Those into communist-era statements shouldn't miss it; you can sometimes get in for half price or even free.

On a hilltop 6km west of the centre, the **Shumen Fortress** (admission 3lv; ☉ approx 8am-5pm) is a spread-out site dating from the early Iron Age. Thracians, Romans and Byzantines have left their mark as well. A taxi to the fortress is about 3lv or 4lv. It's possible to walk between the monument and fort, but the path isn't always clear.

Everything in the impressive 18th-century (and still active) **Tombul Mosque** (ul Doiran; admission 2lv; ☉ 9am-6pm), 500m southwest of pl Osvobozhdenie, is original – much of the paint has been atmospherically lost to the ages.

## Sleeping

The information centre *may* be able to find private accommodation.

**Hotel Madara** ( ☎ 57451; pl Osvobozhdenie; s/d 34/48lv) is an OK ex-Balkantourist hotel that divvies its space between rooms and local businesses.

**Zamâka** ( ☎ 800 049; www.zamak-bg.com; ul Vasil Levski 17; s/d/apt 35/55/85lv; ⊠ ) Definitely the best deal in town, the 12-room hotel (100m west of Hotel Madara) has a good restaurant downstairs and a courtyard in the back.

**Hotel Pazara** (aka Stivest; ☎ 292 756; ul Maritsa 15; r 40lv) A bit out of the centre, this 13-room, simple hotel is four blocks north of the start of the pedestrian mall.

## Eating

Zamâka's restaurant is super. On the pedestrian mall, **Pizzeria Elit** (bul Slavyanski; pizza about 2lv) is a funny half–basement bar, half–teen pool hall with good pizza in a smoky room that looks like it's from 1984.

## Getting There & Away

Numerous buses en route to Sofia (20lv, five hours) and Varna (5lv, 1½ hours) stop in Shumen. Also, at least six buses daily go to Ruse (6lv, 2½ hours) and Veliko Târnovo (6lv, two hours).

Around nine or 10 daily trains leave for Varna (4.90lv, two hours) and Ruse (4.90lv, two hours), five for Sofia (15lv, 6½ hours) and one to Plovdiv (13.70lv, six hours).

## MADARA МАДАРА

Home to the cute horseman that brands all of Bulgaria's stotinki coins, the superb

**Madara National Historical & Archaeological Reserve** ( ☎ 05313-2095; admission 4lv; ☉ 8am-6.30pm summer, 8am-5pm winter), 16km east of Shumen, is a lovely area with a mountain-top fort, open-air cave wall, intriguing rock chapel and, most importantly, the horseman – a bas-relief carved in a viva-Bulgaria fever onto the 100m cliff-side in the 8th century. The reserve is a 2km uphill walk from the village (the sign read 'Madara Konnik'). At research time **NBDN** ( ☎ 800 629; www.travelbg.org; ul Tsar Osvoboditel 130, Shumen) was setting up hang-gliding trips from Madara.

About 100m before the entrance are some cosy cabins and a sign pointing to a camping-bungalow area. The cabins are at **Motel Magarski** ( ☎ 05313-2063; motel_madarskikonnik@abv.bg; r/apt 30/40lv).

Some Varna-bound trains stop in Madara, but no buses make the trip. A taxi from Shumen is 15lv or 20lv one way.

## RUSE РУСЕ

☎ 082 / pop 158,200

Chipper for a border town, with leafy streets and a buzzing central square, Ruse (aka Rousse) isn't a bad introduction or 'so long' to Bulgaria for travellers heading between Bulgaria and Romania, across the Danube. Attractions often sit behind locked doors, but Ruse (Roo-*say*) is definitely the busiest Danube town in Bulgaria (or Romania), and nearby Rusenski Lom Nature Park provides appealing overnight or day-trip rural adventures.

Ruse's **March Days Music Festival** is held in the last two weeks of March.

## Orientation

From the bus and train station, ul Borisova leads 2km north to the central pl Svoboda, from where the busy pedestrian mall ul Aleksandrovska extends northeast and southwest. The Danube is several blocks further north from pl Svoboda.

## Information

**Bulbank** (pl Sveta Troitsa; ☉ 8.30am-4.30pm) Just southeast of pl Svoboda (next to the red opera house); 24-hour ATM.
**Central post office** (pl Svoboda)
**Interphone** ( ☎ 440 368; ul Vidin 35; per hr 0.40lv; ☉ 24hr) Internet access, a couple blocks north of pl Svoboda. Calls overseas cost about 0.40lv per min.
**Left Luggage** (train station; per day 2lv; ☉ 24hr)
**Tourist Information Centre** ( ☎ 824 704; ul Aleksandrovska; ☉ 9.30am-12.30pm & 1-6pm Mon-Fri) Stocks

brochures and finds private accommodation. Just northeast of pl Svoboda.

**Telephone centre** (ul Panov 14; international calls per min 0.40lv; ☽ 8am-midnight) A block south of pl Svoboda, to the left as you enter the pedestrian mall from the south.

## Sights

Ruse's attractions seem to find a way to be closed when we're in town. The best thing to do is walk. Head from central pl Svoboda along the pedestrian mall, ul Aleksandrovska, about 400m northeast to the largely untouched **Soviet Army Monument**, at the start of the **Youth Park**, which is filled with open-air cafés and 1.50lv rides (in good weather).

Much of Ruse seems to turn its back to the Danube (or Romania), but there is a **promenade** that gets views of both, and you can access the shore at various points. There are many lovely historic buildings to wander around too. The river is about five blocks northwest of pl Svoboda.

Facing the grey hulk of the communist-era Riga Hotel is the (sometimes open, we hear) **Museum of the Urban Lifestyle in Ruse** ( ☎ 820 997; ul Tsar Ferdinand 39; adult/student 4/1lv; ☽ 9am-noon & 1-5.30pm Mon-Sat), a revival-era home filled with period crafts and furniture.

About halfway between the train station and centre is the small **Rousse Art Gallery** ( ☎ 221 494; ul Borisova 39; admission 0.50lv; ☽ 9am-1pm & 2-6pm Tue-Sun), a scruffy, modern space with edgier exhibits than in most Bulgarian art museums, and – hey – it's open at weekends.

About 200m east of pl Svoboda, via ul Petko, the gold-domed **Pantheon of the National Revival** (ul Tsar Osvoboditel), dedicated to those who fought the Ottomans in 1878, is usually closed. Just outside is **Paniot Ivanov Kitov's tomb**. He was apparently a remarkably moustached man.

## Sleeping

The office of **Dunav Tours** ( ☎ 825 048; dtbktu@ dunavtours.bg; pl Khan Kubrat 5; s/d €8/15; ☽ 9am-5.30pm Mon-Fri), two blocks southwest of pl Svoboda, can book private rooms.

**Hotel Ruse** ( ☎ 823 255; ul Borisova 69; s/d 26/32lv; ⚇ ) It's tacky as a Vegas knock-off, but this 10-room job is Ruse's best-deal budget hotel. It has thin walls, TVs and some balconies. It's midway between the train station and the centre. Hopefully prices won't rise.

**Evropa Hotel** ( ☎ 875 599; autogara; s/d 72/84lv; ⚇ ) The 20 new rooms are perfumed, garish and overpriced but convenient and clean. It's attached to the bus station.

**Anna Palace** ( ☎ 825 005; www.annapalace.com; ul Kniajeska 4; s incl breakfast 88-108lv, d 117-137lv; ⚇ ) This back-street splurge has high-ceilinged, stylish rooms in a 25-room makeover of an historic building near the river. It's several blocks west of the centre.

## Eating

There are plenty of open-air cafés and snacks to find on ul Aleksandrovska. For groceries, head northwest on ul Aleksandrovska 200m from pl Svoboda to **Gradski Hali** (ul Aleksandrovska 93; ☽ 8am-10pm). Just behind it to the north is residential street ul Omurtag, which leads four blocks to a couple of open-air restaurants with river views. A good one is **Chineshla** ( ☎ 826 682; bul Prdumuski 50; mains 5-10lv; ☽ 11am-11pm), serving 'all kinds of food' (meaning Bulgarian grills and salads).

**Chiplika** ( ☎ 828 222; ul Aleksandrovska 1; mains 4-10lv; ☽ 11am-2am) Ruse's top Bulgarian restaurant has richly traditional rooms and a stone-floor mezzanine for tasty local fare in a buzzing spot. Follow ul Aleksandrovska southwest from pl Svoboda and turn left on ul Otets Paicii (near a small square).

## Getting There & Away

Ruse's **Yug Bus Terminal** (ul Pristanishtna) has frequent daily buses heading to Sofia (12lv to 14lv, five hours) and Veliko Târnovo (5lv to 7lv, two hours). There are also a few buses to Varna (10lv, 3½ hours) and one daily bus to Plovdiv (15lv, 2½ hours). A couple of companies send buses to Istanbul (30lv, 13 hours); **Ozbatu** ( ☎ 874 777) is one. There are four minibuses going daily to Bucharest (€14); call ☎ 821 964 for information on these.

Three daily buses to Cherven and Ivanovo in Rusenski Lom Nature Park leave from **Iztok Bus Terminal** ( ☎ 845 064), 4.5km east of the centre. City buses 2 and 13 go there from ul Skobelev, near the roundabout four blocks east of ul Borisova.

The **train station** ( ☎ 820 222), next to Yug, has three daily trains to Sofia (14.70lv, seven hours), four to Veliko Târnovo (5.50lv, 2½ to 3½ hours), two to Varna (8.90lv, four hours) and three to Bucharest (15lv, three hours), which spend half the duration stopped for border checks. In the station, **Rila Bureau** ( ☎ 828 016; ☽ 9-noon & 1-5.30pm Mon-Fri) sells international train tickets.

**BULGARIA**

## RUSENSKI LOM NATURE PARK
ПРИРОДЕН ПАРК РУСЕНСКИ ЛОМ

Starting just southwest of Ruse, this 32.6-sq-km park is home to winding rivers, other-era villages wedged between cliffs, hiking paths, rock-climbing sites, and cave and rock monasteries. In summer nearly 200 bird species flock here.

It's best to access the western part of the park – with the town of Ivanovo and the more appealing Koshov and Cherven. Another, Nisovo, is further east. Before setting out, drop by the **Rusenski Lom Nature Park Office** ( ☎ 872 397; www.lomea.org; ul Gen Skobelev 7; ☼ 9am-5pm Mon-Fri) in Ruse. Helpful staff can point out camping grounds and where to hike along the river, and sell maps (3lv). Look for the official sign and walk in (enter from ul Tinka Dzhein).

The **Ivanovo Rock Monastery** (admission 3lv; ☼ 9am-noon & 1-6pm Tue-Sun) is 4km east of Ivanovo: a centuries-old sanctuary cut into cliffs with colourful, remarkably well-preserved murals from the 14th century. Opening hours seem iffily adhered to. For a guide – and some certainty that it's open – contact the so-called **History Museum** ( ☎ 925 006; pl Battemberg) in Ruse.

In Cherven, the spread-out remains of the 6th-century **citadel** (admission 3lv when attendant is present, free otherwise) sit atop a cliff at a sharp bend in the river.

Rooms in traditional homes are available in Cherven and Koshov if you ask around.

Buses from Ruse's Iztok bus terminal go a few times a day to Cherven via Ivanovo and Koshov. It's feasible to enter at one town and hike to the next – ask (and get a map) at the Ruse park office.

# BLACK SEA COAST

For many travellers, the blue-green water and golden beaches along the Black Sea coast *are* Bulgaria. The gateway towns – beach-clubbing Varna and grittier Burgas – and resortburgs Sunny Beach, Golden Sands and Albena sizzle with bodies in summer. Also popular are cobbled Sozopol and Nesebâr: inviting seaside towns with long histories. Stretches south of Sozopol and north of Varna are more popular with locals, but have some of the most tempting options.

Most hotels raise their rates in June and again in July and August, then drop them back a bit in September. At many other times

of year, as one local said, 'It's just you and the dogs.'

Before taking a splash, take a moment to reflect on this body of water, which is landlocked and long a treasure for a grab-bag of non-Western peoples (Muslims, Roma and communists). It's changing though. From afar, formerly quiet Sunny Beach now looks like a city, and its neighbours are being subjected to (seemingly) unplanned development of side-by-side hotels surrounded by dirt paths and makeshift fences that catch debris in the wind. You wonder if the Black Sea, in parts at least, is slowly dying.

## VARNA ВАРНА
☎ 052 / pop 312,000

Even without the Black Sea at its lip, Varna would be a Bulgarian highlight. Big for Bulgaria, it has one of the country's most rewarding museums, heaps of exposed Roman-wall ruins and, of course, the water. From Varna, there are easy pops north and south to beaches, and the town beaches aren't bad either. If you're looking for Black Sea nightlife, Varna's beach lights up with open-air clubs all summer – it's definitely *the* party place on the beach.

Varna was briefly called 'Stalin' after WWII. Long before, Thracians lived in the area from 4000 BC, and Greek sailors re-founded it as Odessos in the sixth century BC. You still see plenty of sailor outfits about these days, too.

### Information

Find entertainment listings in the free weekly Bulgarian-language *Programata* and the annual English-language *Varna Guide*.

**Bulbank** (ul Slivinitsa; ☼ 8am-6pm Mon-Fri)

**Frag** (pl Nezavisimost; per hr 1lv; ☼ 24hr) Get online down the spiral stairs from a back door of the Dramatic Theatre building; it has beer and 59 computers.

**Global Tours** ( ☎ 601 085; www.globaltours-bg.com; ul Kynaz Boris I 67; ☼ 8am-10pm Jun-Sep, 9am-7pm Mon-Fri Oct-May) Excellent travel agency books cars (from €16 per day) and private accommodation (from €20) and offers guided day trips to Balchik and Kaliakra Cape for €17.

**International Phone Booths** (ul Batenberg 44; long-distance calls per min 0.23lv; ☼ 9am-10pm)

**Left Luggage** (main bus terminal; bul Vladislav Varenchik; per day 4lv; ☼ 7am-10pm)

**Main post office** (ul Sâborna 36)

**Municipal Tourist Information Centre** (ul Batenberg; ☼ approx 10am-6pm Mon-Fri)

**Peralnya** (ul Voden; per load 4.60lv; ☼ 9am-7pm Mon-Sat) Drop-off laundry service.

# VARNA

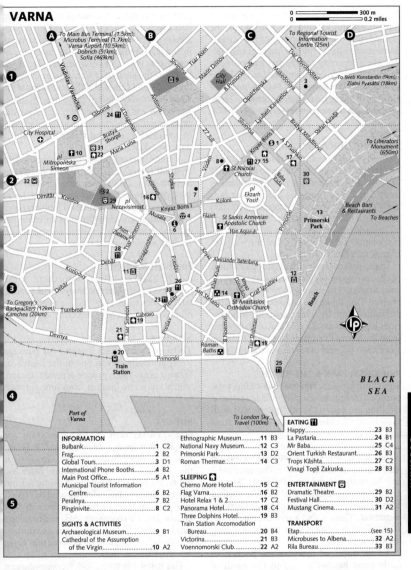

**Pinginivite** (ul 27 Juli 13; ☽ 9am-7pm Mon-Fri, 10am-6pm Sat & Sun) This bookshop stocks maps and some English-language titles.

**Regional Tourist Information Centre** ( ☎ 602 907; tourism@tourexpo.bg; bul Tsar Osvoboditel 36; ☽ 9am-7pm Mon-Fri, 9am-1pm Sat) Helpful English-speaking staff can arrange car rental (from €25 per day) and apartments (from 50lv) and help with trips around the Black Sea coast.

**Sea Shadow** ( ☎ 0887-364 711; www.guide-bg.com) One-man operation of Patrick Perev, who leads various trips up and down the coast; a day at Kaliakra Cape and Balchik costs €18 per person (with three going).

## Dangers & Annoyances

Nothing to panic about, but Varna has one of the worst reputations for rip-offs in

Bulgaria. Kids in packs sometimes storm tourists around the open-air market and the Cathedral of the Assumption of the Virgin. Some readers have reported lost bags and wallets when departing microbuses from Golden Sands at the microbus terminal. Taxis in Varna commonly overcharge: one Brit we met paid 60lv for the 8km ride from the airport! To be safe, call one of the companies listed on p174.

## Sights

### ARCHAEOLOGICAL MUSEUM

Housed in a grand old two-storey building (a former girls' school), this large **museum** ( ☎ 681 030; ul Maria Luisa 41; adult/student 5/2lv; ✆ 10am-5pm Tue-Sun Apr-Sep, 10am-5pm Tue-Sat Oct-Mar) is up for Bulgaria's best. It's filled with more than 100,000 pieces from some 6000 years of local history, all remarkably well explained in English. No place better helps contextualise the waves of change this fine land has faced.

In the first room, a wall display posts finds of chronological periods (Stone Age, Bronze Age, Roman, Ottoman etc) to show how art evolved. Don't miss the sculpted goatee on the 3rd millennium BC Thracian tomb. More serious highlights are the gold and copper pieces from the Varna Eneolithic Necropolis, dating from 4500 BC and excavated in the 1970s.

### PRIMORSKI PARK & THE BEACH

Stretching for 8km, **Primorski Park** claims to be Europe's largest seaside park, and is a popular strolling ground for locals. It's freckled with museums, a kiddie ride park, heroic statues and numerous popcorn vendors.

At its southern end, the outside ships, planes and canyons of the **National Navy Museum** (bul Primorski 2; adult/student 4/1lv; ✆ 10am-5pm Mon-Fri) can be easily viewed over the gate. (Sample cannon graffiti: 'chaos punx!') To the north, a 1km shaded promenade leads to the **Liberators Monument**. There's also a monument for the 10,000 British soldiers who died here during the Crimean War.

To the south of the park are pockets of fairly good **beaches** in and to the north of Primorski Park, as there are up north (just east of the Liberators Monument), plus the peak of Varna's club action.

### OTHER SIGHTS

Wedged impossibly between the St Anastasios Orthodox Church and more modern apartment buildings, the leftovers of the 2nd century AD **Roman Thermae** (ul Khan Krum & ul San Stefano; adult/student 3/2lv; ✆ 10am-5pm May-Oct, 10am-5pm Tue-Sat Nov-Apr) comprise the largest ruins in Bulgaria. Frankly, there's not much to see inside that you can't see from outside.

Inside the greatest of Varna's churches, the onion-domed **Cathedral of the Assumption of the Virgin** (pl Mitropolitska Simeon; admission free; ✆ 7.30am-7pm summer, 7.30am-5.30pm winter), you'll hear the crackle of offering candles in a massive room of colourful murals and stained glass with a dark-wood altar.

Varna's second-best museum, housed in an 1860 revival building, is the **Ethnographic Museum** ( ☎ 630 588; ul Panagyurishte 22; adult/student 4/2lv; ✆ 10am-5pm Tue-Sun Apr-Sep, 10am-5pm Tue-Sat Oct-Mar), a complex of traditional buildings on a rising pedestrian alley. On show are examples of local dress nicely arranged by region and healthy servings of old tools.

## Festivals & Events

You're likely to witness something of the renowned **Varna Summer International Festival**, which dates from 1926 and features all sorts of music between May and October.

## Sleeping

Those without plush budgets (or package trips) generally stay in one of the hostels or arrange great-value private accommodation, which knows no bounds from June through September.

### BUDGET

**Gregory's Backpackers** ( ☎ 379 909; www.hostelvarna .com; 82 Fenix St, Zvezditsa; dm incl breakfast €10; 🖳 🖳 ) Run by a young British couple, Gregory's is the best kick-back hostel base the Black Sea offers. It's in a small village 15 minutes from Varna's discos; staff offer one daily drop-off and pick-up ride; or bus 36 makes its way hourly. The TV room with sofas and beanbags gets busy with its DVD catalogue and the bar, plus there's a small wading pool outside. Open April to October only.

**Flag Hostel** ( ☎ 089 656 4679; flagvarna@yahoo.com; 2nd fl, ul Sheinovo 2; dm/r incl breakfast €8/25) The first Flag was traded for a yacht in 2006, but a Brit grabbed the reins at this location, which opened after our last pass through town. Its central location is good for the disco-oriented.

**Victorina** ( ☎ 603 541; http://victorina.borsabg.com; Tsar Simeon 36; s/d with family 22/30lv, s/d in private apt 30/40lv; ✆ 7am-9pm Jun-Sep, 10am-6pm Mon-Fri Oct-May)

Working all year (bless their hearts), this window bureau helps find private apartments or rooms with families around Varna. They 'always have a room'. From the station, exit and go through the underpass.

Campers can venture about 20km south of Varna at the delta of the Kamchea River to **Kamchea**, a protected area of mangroves and sandy beach. Locals love it, there are bungalows to rent (from 10lv per person) and endless spots to pitch tents. A sign points the way, 3km from the highway.

Other agencies that can help with homestays:

**Global Tours** ( ☎ 601 085; www.globaltours-bg.com; ul Kynaz Boris I 67; ✆ 8am-10pm Jun-Sep, 9am-7pm Mon-Fri Oct-May)

**Main Bus Terminal Accommodation Bureau** ( ☎ 505 747; www.accommodatebg.com; s/d with family from 15/25lv, s/d with private apt from 24/30lv)

**Train Station Accommodation Bureau** ( ☎ 602 318) Some travellers have reported an extra '25% charge'.

**MIDRANGE**

**Hotel Relax 1 & 2** (s/d 35/40lv; ✖ ) No 1 ( ☎ 607 847; www.hotelrelax1.com); No 2 ( ☎ 361 586; ul Stefan Karadzha 22) This odd-ball complex of two Relaxes is a good, cheap beat. No 1, in the back, has more modern and smaller rooms, looking like a *2001* interpretation of 1976 Novosibirsk. No 2, in a century-old house, has four mix-and-match rooms with the hilarious addition of a 130-year-old piano in one.

**Voennomorski Club** ( ☎ 617 965; vmkvarna@varna.net; ul Vladislav Varenchik 2; s/d 31/46lv; ✖ ) Filling the top two floors of the sky-blue building, rooms at the 'BNK' can be a little musty and the staff grumpy. Rooms are set around a great unintentionally retro TV lounge. Staff devoutly guarded summer prices, so expect the leva count to be higher than posted here.

**Cherno More Hotel** ( ☎ 612 243; www.chernomorebg .com; bul Slivinitsa 33; s/d from 35/40lv, with air con from 50lv; ✖ ) It gets mocked, and no doubt this Balkantourist beaut, rising like a Karl Marx beacon, has seen its best days. But it's smack-bang in the centre, and a minimal renovation (new carpets, some furnishings) has helped soften (or hide) the smudges. All rooms have balconies with superb ocean views. Ask for the '02' line for corner views.

**Three Dolphins Hotel** ( ☎ 600 911; three_dolphins@ abv.bg; ul Gabrovo 27; s incl breakfast 42-51lv, d 50-60lv; ✖ ) Most of the 10 rooms at this friendly hotel, on a leafy side street near the train station, spout off a recent, highly successful renovation that reflects the owners' love of keeping things interesting. The 'retro' room goes all-out Victorian, while the nautical-blue 'dolphin' features translucent dolphin toilet seats. Rates rise 10% in summer.

**TOP END**

**Panorama Hotel** ( ☎ 687 300; www.panoramabg.com; bul Primorski 31; s/d incl breakfast 128/164lv; ✖ ⬛ ) For the swank set, this 57-room hotel – right across from the pier road and the start of Varna's beach – has Varna's nicest rooms for the best (relative) price. Rooms have internet connection, and there's a fitness centre.

## Eating

In summer, try the outdoor seats and front bar-restaurants along ul Knyaz Boris I and (a bit more upmarket) bul Slivnitsa, leading to Primorski Park, where at least a couple of waterfront bars keep hours in winter. This is a good place to try a beer with fried *tsatsa* fish.

**Vinagi Topli Zakuska** (cnr ul Tsar Simeon & ul Debâr; banitsas 0.60lv; ✆ 6am-7pm Mon-Fri, 6am-2pm Sat & Sun) The walk-up stand – its name means 'always warm breakfast' – draws lines for some of the country's best *banitsas,* plus chocolate- or fruit-filled rolls.

**Trops Kâshta** (bul Knyaz Boris I 48; dishes 2-3lv; ✆ 8.30am-9pm) This bright pick-and-point chain offers fresh, cheap and fast Bulgarian staples. Prices drop by 30% after 8pm.

**Happy** (ul Preslav 11; dishes from 3lv; ✆ 8am-midnight) Bow your head at this holy site, mortal travellers; here in 1994 Bulgaria's enormously popular 'American' chain (a mix of TGIF's and Hooters) began. It mostly offers Bulgarian grill items.

**Orient Turkish Restaurant** ( ☎ 602 380; ul Tsaribrod 1; dishes 3-6lv; ✆ 10am-midnight) Chicken hearts and lamb heads are part of the (photo) menu, so watch what you order at this well-priced, atmospheric Turkish restaurant with traditional wooden bench seats.

**La Pastaria** ( ☎ 622 060; ul Dragoman 25; pastas 4.20-6.50lv; ✆ 11am-11pm Mon-Sat, 5-11pm Sun) This real-deal Italian place delivers with well-prepared salads and house-made pastas. There are eight pizzas, served on wooden platters. It's one of a few slightly upmarket eateries on Dragoman.

**Mr Baba** ( ☎ 614 629; ul Primorski at ferry road; fish dishes 6-19lv; ✆ 8am-midnight) Moored at the south end of the beach, the goofy novelty pirate-ship setting probably beats the uninspired food…

'Hold on, you feckin' landlubber – I'll keelhaul you,' declares the irate ghost of Mr Baba, a 17th-century pirate from nearby Kavarna. 'On me boat we swag the decks slip'ry, give the mates deck seats, and sea bass and red mullets comes just gutted like.' (Translation: the place is clean, there's open-air seating and the seafood is fresh and tasty.)

## Drinking

Now on to business. In summer, beach night-clubs/discos/bars open their doors along the beach and rattle locals' windows pretty much all hours. Some, such as **Las Playas**, incorporate the water, with inflatable chairs to float in. If you don't like what you see, move on; only a few charge an entry fee. Other stalwarts include **Pench's** (Guinness World Record holder for the biggest cocktail list, apparently), **Exit** and **Planetar**. Some open 'inland' locations off-season around town. Locations vary slightly season to season.

## Entertainment

Varna's great opera hits the stage at **Dramatic Theatre** (Opera House; ☎ 650 555; www.operavarna.bg; pl Nezavisimost). The screens at **Festival Hall** (☎ 685 000; bul Slivnitsa; tickets 3-4lv) show many English-language movies, or try **Mustang Cinema** (☎ 610 333; ul Bratya Shorpil 33; tickets 3-4lv).

## Getting There & Away

### AIR

**Varna airport** (☎ 650 835), 10.5km west of the centre, booms with charter-flight action from mid-April to October; all year there's a daily flight to/from Sofia (about €65/100 one way/return). Bus 409 waddles there, past the bus station from the centre; a taxi ride costs about 25lv.

### BOAT

There's no ferry service to Istanbul, but the curiously named **London Sky Travel** (☎ 601 330; www.lstravel.com.ua; Morska Gara) runs a weekly service to Odessa from May to September.

### BUS

The **main bus terminal** (☎ 433 162; bul Vladislav Varenchik) is 2km northwest of the city centre. Buses 409 and 148 stop near the main cathedral, as at Slivinitska and Knyaz Boris I. Tickets for private buses can be bought at agencies in town, such as **Etap** (☎ 604 674; ul Slivnitsa 33; ⏰ 9am-8pm) at Hotel Cherno More.

Direct buses:

**Athens** 137lv, 26 hours, one weekly (presently Sunday)
**Balchik** 3lv, 50 minutes, five daily
**Burgas** 8lv, 2½ hours, every 30 or 40 minutes (by microbus)
**Istanbul** 40lv, 10 hours, three daily
**Odessa** 88lv, 20 hours, one weekly (presently Saturday)
**Plovdiv** 17lv, six hours, two daily
**Ruse** 10lv, four hours, four daily
**Shumen** 8lv, 1½ hours, four daily (plus Sofia buses)
**Sofia** 22lv, seven to eight hours, every 45 minutes
**Veliko Târnovo** 13lv, four hours, every 45 minutes

### MICROBUS

The **microbus terminal** (Avtogara Mladost; ☎ 500 039; ul Knyaz Cherkazki), 200m west of the bus station (cross the street via an underpass and go left – towards the centre – 50m, then right for a block), sends little buses hourly to Burgas from 7am to 6pm (8lv), and to Albena and Balchik (4lv) from 6.30am to 6.30pm. Less frequent services go to Nesebâr (via Sunny Beach) and Shumen. Note that some readers have complained about pickpockets here.

Microbuses also leave for Albena (4lv) from the more convenient stop at ul Maria Luisa.

### TRAIN

Direct train services from the **main train station** (☎ 630 444; bul Primorski) link Varna to Sofia (18.70lv, 7½ to 8½ hours, at least six daily), Plovdiv (13.70lv, 6½ hours, three daily), Ruse (8.90lv, 3¾ hours, one or two daily) and Shumen (4.90lv, 1½ hours, six to eight daily).

Direct trains to Bucharest (50lv, 21 hours) are available from mid-June to mid-September only. international tickets must be purchased at Rila Bureau (☎ 632 348; ul Preslav 13; ⏰ 8am-5.30pm Mon-Fri, 8am-3.30pm Sat), a few minutes' walk from the station.

## Getting Around

Local bus routes are listed on the Domino city map; tickets cost 0.60lv per ride. Some taxi drivers are prone to overcharging foreign travellers – make sure the meter is on. A couple of taxi services with clean(er) records include **Chaika Taxi** (☎ 644 444) and **Omega** (☎ 388 888).

Global Tours (p170) rents out cars from €16 per day.

## NORTH OF VARNA

Just north of Varna are several upmarket beach resorts that cater to rich foreigners on package tours, and further up are spots with more street cred. All can be visited on day trips from Varna or Balchik. It's possible to walk across the Romania border at **Vama Veche**; taxis here go to Balchik for about €30 and minibuses across the border go on to Mangalia, Romania.

## Sveti Konstantin Свети Константин

Just 9km north of Varna, this small resort has several hotels along a pretty beach. The tiny **Sv Konstantin & Sv Elena Monastery** (admission free; 🕙 dawn to dusk, except Sun morning) is just off Post Office Lane. Take bus 8 from ul Maria Luisa in Varna to the end of the line.

## Golden Sands Златни Пясъци

Bulgaria's second-largest resort, 18km northeast of Varna, Golden Sands (Zlatni Pyasâtsi) has a 4km-long beach. The **Aladzha Monastery** ( ☎ 052-355 460; admission 4lv; 🕙 9am-4pm) is a bizarre rock monastery. Stairs lead to and around the caves, whose heyday was in the 13th and 14th centuries. To get there on foot, head past the post office, cross the main highway and follow the signs to 'Kloster Aladja'.

Buses 109, 209, 309 and 409 connect Golden Sands with Varna about every 15 minutes between 6am and 11pm.

## Albena Албена

Possibly the best beach north of Sunny Beach (it's shallow enough to wade out 150m), Albena is a popular beach resort. Located behind the bus station, **Gorska Feia** ( ☎ 057-962 961) has camp sites and bungalows in a wooded setting about 500m from the beach.

Microbuses leave hourly for Albena from Varna (3lv, 30 minutes), continuing on to Balchik.

## Balchik Балчик

☎ 0579 / pop 12,400

Wedged between a rocky shoreline and white-chalk bluffs, Balchik – a 'real' town, after all the commercialised resorts – is a good alternative base for northern beaches.

The bus stop is 1km above the historic centre, by the water. Near the centre is a **DCK Bank** ( 🕙 8.30am-4.30pm Mon-Fri) with an ATM. A **tourist information centre** ( ☎ 5797 2034; ul Ribarski) is open in summer.

In the 1920s, when the region was part of Romania, King Ferdinand built the (pricey) **Summer Palace Queen Marie & Botanical Gardens** (Dvoretsa; admission 10lv; 🕙 8am-8pm summer, 8am-7pm winter) for his wife because she wanted something 'small and romantic' (as a guide tells it).

The palace shows off Marie's eccentric tastes, mixing Islamic and Bulgarian revival styles. It's set near the water below lush gardens. It's a nice 2km walk south from the centre along the promenade.

In summer, accommodation agencies open their doors in the port area. **Esparansa** ( ☎ 75 148; ul Cherno More 16; s/d with shared bathroom 15/20lv), about 150m up from the port, is a four-room hotel open seasonally. It's a step into a past world, with lace tablecloths and overflowing bookcases dressing up four very eclectic rooms.

The more standard **Balchik Hotel** ( ☎ 72 809; www.hotel-balchik.com; s/d €15/25) faces quiet pl Nezavisimost, 400m up from the port.

In summer, buses wind down the coast hourly to Varna (3lv, one hour) stopping at beach resorts. They run less frequently off season.

## Kaliakra Cape Нос Калуакра

This 2km-long headland – its name meaning 'beautiful' – pokes out into the Black Sea about 30km northeast of Balchik. It's a popular boat and/or bus day trip for resort folk to the south, but is worth the effort. Plus you can see dolphins offshore. Most of the cape is part of the **Kaliakra Nature Reserve** (admission 3lv; 🕙 24hr), where you can witness the ruins of an 8th-century citadel being defecated on by 300 species of birds.

No public transport goes here. From Balchik, you can take a bus to Kavarna and then take a taxi, or walk 6km from the last bus stop at Bâlgarevo. Locals (with cars) like to stop off at **Midena Ferma** (Mussels Farm), between Balchik and Kavarna, for shellfish meals in a remote setting.

## Kamen Bryag (Stone Beach) & Around Камен Бряг

About 18km north (by road) from Kaliakra Cape, this rocky cliff 'beach' is popular with rock-climbers who scale the rocks 4km north (at Tulenovo) rope-free, tumbling safely into the water. It's also possible to arrange scuba-diving trips. You'll need your own transport to make it here. Check agencies in Varna (p170) for trips that make it to this quiet but up-and-coming place.

## NESEBÂR НЕСЕБЪР

☎ 0554 / pop 9360

About 35km north of Burgas, historic and touristy Nesebâr sits on a small rocky isthmus on the south end of the wide (and just about perfect) bay that's home to Sunny Beach a couple of kilometres away. A Unesco World Heritage site, Nesebâr is a tad nicer than Sozopol and flaunts its centuries, back to 3000 BC when Thracians settled Mesembria here. A lot of tourists come for that flaunting in summer.

**Biochim Commercial Bank** (ul Mesembria; 8.30am-12.15pm & 1-5.30pm Mon-Fri) cashes travellers cheques and has an ATM. The **tourist information centre** ( ☎ 42611; www.nessebarinfo.com; ul Mesembria 10; 10am-6pm Mon-Fri) wryly confessed to not yet having any tourist information at last pass; hopefully its role will someday reflect its name. Internet access is available in summer at the **White House Hotel** (ul Tsar Simeon 2) and in Nesebâr's new town (about 1km west) all year. The town **post office** ( 8am-8pm Tue-Sat) is located on ul Mesembria.

## Sights
### CHURCHES

Even the churched-out should stroll by Nesebâr's Byzantine-influenced beauties (or ruins of their former shining selves), all built between the 6th and 14th centuries and once numbering about 80. Most are free and some close in the off-season.

Now in ruins, the towering frame of the 6th-century **Basilica** (ul Mitropolitska) juts over the town's historic centre. One of the best-preserved churches is **Pantrokrator Church** (ul Mesembria), built in the 14th century with a bell tower that now houses an art gallery. Most churches are jealous of the lookout spot facing the water of earthquake-battered (and busted) **St John Aliturgetos Church** (ul Mena).

### OTHER SIGHTS

There are a couple of museums in town, including the **Archaeological Museum** ( ☎ 46 012; ul Mesembria 2; admission 2.50lv; 9am-8pm summer, 9am-noon & 12.30-5pm Mon-Sat winter), which sees a daily tide of quick-look visitors in summer for its Thracian tombs and Roman tablets.

## Sleeping

Many lodgings are part of the package-trip loop, and even private rooms can book out. The following hotels are open all year.

**Hotel Toni** ( ☎ 42 403; ul Kraybrezhna; r 35-40lv; ) This friendly family hotel (just past the St

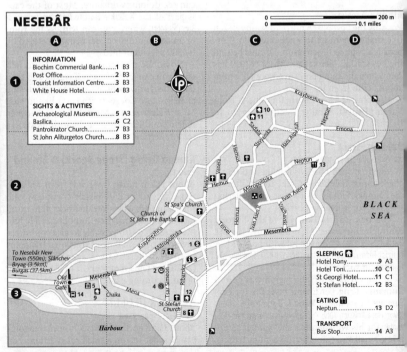

## NESEBÂR

```
0 _____ 200 m
0 _____ 0.1 miles
```

**INFORMATION**
Biochim Commercial Bank........1 B3
Post Office.............................2 B3
Tourist Information Centre......3 B3
White House Hotel..................4 B3

**SIGHTS & ACTIVITIES**
Archaeological Museum...........5 A3
Basilica.................................6 C2
Pantrokrator Church..............7 B3
St John Aliturgetos Church......8 B3

**SLEEPING**
Hotel Rony....................9 A3
Hotel Toni....................10 C1
St Georgi Hotel............11 C1
St Stefan Hotel...........12 B3

**EATING**
Neptun.......................13 D2

**TRANSPORT**
Bus Stop....................14 A3

Georgi) is unsigned. It has 12 quiet, cosy rooms, some with seriously great balconies overlooking Sunny Beach.

**Hotel Rony** ( ☎ 44 001; ul Chaika 1; s/d incl breakfast summer 49/65lv, winter 34/45lv; ❄ ) This budget hotel, just past the town gate, has 11 clean, basic rooms.

**St Georgi Hotel** ( ☎ 44 045; www.gsk.5u.com; ul Sadala 10; r from 50lv) Stylish St Georgi, facing Sunny Beach, has a dozen rooms often full of package tourists.

**St Stefan Hotel** ( ☎ 43 603; st_stefan@infotour.org; ul Ribarska 11; r summer 105lv; ❄ ) This classier 17-room hotel has balconies and overlooks its namesake church.

### Eating

**Neptun** (ul Neptun; mains from 5lv; ☟ 10am-11pm) One of several fish restaurants at the end of the main drag, Neptune has vine-covered outside tables on either side of the walkway. Splurge for grilled bluefish snagged offshore (about 15lv).

### Getting There & Away

Not all Varna–Burgas buses along the coast leave the main highway, 2km to the west. Nesebâr-bound buses stop in the new town, 1km west, and (usually) at the old town gate. From the old gate, up to half a dozen daily buses (more in summer) head north to Varna (8lv, two hours) and more often to Burgas (3lv, 40 minutes). Buses go to Sunny Beach every 15 or 30 minutes, or it's a 30-minute walk.

## SUNNY BEACH СЛЪНЧЕВ БРЯГ

Built for tourism, Nesebâr's famous neighbour, Sunny Beach (Slânchev Bryag), is a long strip of fine beach speckled with hotels marking (clearly) the eras they came from. It's said the beach has the capacity for 30,000 bums, while the hotels can fit 100,000! Over-development has already taken away a lot of Sunny Beach's charm, but you can enjoy its setting on a day trip from Burgas. The centre is near the fading Hotel Kuban, with ATMs, internet cafés and lots of places to eat lining the 300m walkway to the water.

See the bus information for Burgas (p179), Nesebâr (above) and Varna (p174) for details on how to get here.

## BURGAS БУРГАС

☎ 056 / pop 189,500

A little ugly and a little unloved, the industrial port town of Burgas carries its own charm once you get down into it. Its beach can't

rival the best (or even Varna's), but open-air cafés, a more relaxed air, easy day-trip links to Sozopol and Nesebâr, and recently added flights on Wizz Air make it a pretty good beach-hopping base.

Hilariously, the rivalry between Varna and Burgas led the Varna-bred founder of national chain Happy Bar & Grill to ban expansion here.

### Information

Many sites and hotels have information at www.bourgas.net.

**Bulbank** (ul Aleksandrovka; ☟ 8am-6pm Mon-Fri) ATM.

**ENet Internet** (ul Tsar Boris; per hr 1.20lv; ☟ 24hr)

**Helikon Bookshop** ( ☎ 800 231; pl Troikata 4; ☟ 9am-7.30pm Mon-Sat, 10am-7.30pm Sun) Near the university, this place has a great selection of maps and a few guidebooks.

**Internet Klub** (cnr ul Slavyanska & Bogoridi; per hr 1lv; ☟ 24hr)

**Left Luggage** (per bag 2lv; ☟ 6am-10pm) Outside the train station.

**Post Office** (ul Tsar Petâr)

**Telephone Booths** (ul Bogoridi 36; per min to UK or USA 0.30lv, to Australia 0.39lv; ☟ 9am-midnight) Calls are cheaper with a prepaid card.

**Tourist Service Agency** (Hotel Bulgaria, ☎ 840 601; Hotel Bulgaria, ul Aleksandrovka 21; ☟ 7.30am-7pm Mon-Fri, 7.30am-5pm Sat & Sun) Very helpful English-speaking staff can book bus tickets or help with rental cars (via TS Travel; see p179).

### Sights

Burgas' **beach** has a 2km-long strip of sand, and its long concrete pier sees a lot of strolling. It's not five-star lovely, but it doesn't get the Sunny Beach crowds either, plus its bars and clubs give Burgas a bolt of life on summer nights. Running alongside the beach is the pleasant, if a bit decaying, **Maritime Park**.

The museums in town aren't knockouts. Probably the best is the **Ethnographical Museum** ( ☎ 842 586; ul Slavyanska 69; adult/student 2/1lv; ☟ 8am-5pm Mon-Fri mid-Sep–mid-Jun, 9am-6pm Mon-Fri & 10am-6pm Sat mid-Jun–mid-Sep), with two floors of hundred-year-old traditional clothing.

On the main mall, the pink **Archaeological Museum** ( ☎ 843 541; ul Bogoridi 21; admission 2/1lv; ☟ 8am-5pm Mon-Fri mid-Sep–mid-Jun, 9am-6pm Mon-Fri & 10am-6pm Sat mid-Jun–mid-Sep) has Thracian and Roman pieces, some of which are visible from outside. Ask for the leaflets, in various languages, to get more out of the museum.

Housed in a former synagogue, the **Art Gallery** ( ☎ 842 169; ul Mitropolit Simeon 24; admission

**BULGARIA**

2lv; 🕑 9am-noon & 2-6pm Mon-Fri) has three floors of icons and modern Bulgarian art.

The towering Hotel Bulgaria (rooms not recommended) has a nice indoor **swimming pool** (pl Svoboda; admission 5lv; 🕑 9am-10pm) with a spa and a full bar; you can get smashed before you cannonball.

## Sleeping
### BUDGET

**Dim-ant** ( ☎ 840 779; dimant91@abv.bg; ul Tsar Simeon 15; per person from 9lv; 🕑 8am-9 or 10pm summer, 8am-5.30pm Mon-Fri winter) finds homestay rooms in Burgas and along the coast. You can also try **Primorets Travel** ( ☎ 842 727; ul Ivan Vazov; per person 12lv; 🕑 7am-7pm summer, 9.30am-5.30pm Mon-Fri winter) opposite the train station.

### MIDRANGE

**Fotinov Guest House** ( ☎ 579 018; ul K Fotinov 22; r 40-45lv; 🔀 ) This fairly new 11-room boutique-inspired hotel has chic, rust-coloured shagpile carpet, colourful bedspreads, small work desks and TVs.

**Hotel Elite** ( ☎ 845 780; ul Morska 35; s/d incl breakfast 45/50lv) In a pleasant location off ul Bogodini, the Elite has nice new rooms – some with balcony, all with phone. Avoid the cramped attic room.

**Luxor** ( ☎ 847 670; www.luxor-bg.com; ul Bulair 27; s/d 70/80lv; 🔀 ) This new Egyptian-style hotel is on a busy road a few blocks from the pedestrian mall, but has Burgas' smartest rooms (with safes in the closet and tiled bathrooms) for the price. Prices do not include breakfast.

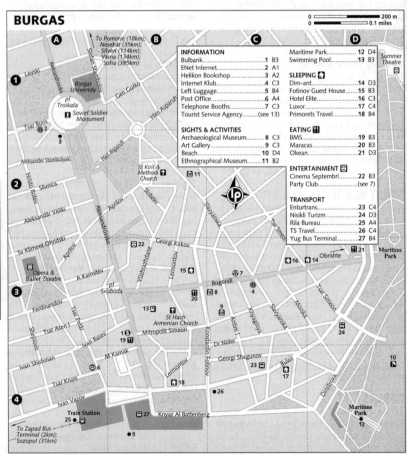

BURGAS

0 ——————— 200 m
0 ——————— 0.1 miles

## Eating

Walk up busy ul Bogoridi or ul Aleksandrovska to find the snack that suits you (big-ass doner kebabs are 3lv).

**BMS** (ul Aleksandrovska; dishes 1.30-2.40lv; 8am-10pm) Fluorescently lit, this is a peppy pick-and-point cafeteria with good Bulgarian food.

**Maracas** (ul Bogoridi 19; mains 3-6lv, desserts 1.89lv; 7am-midnight) The best sit-and-stare spot on the pedestrian mall is great for desserts, coffee and drinks – but you can find better pizza elsewhere.

**Okean** (ul Bogoridi 64; fish dishes 6-19lv; 11am-midnight) A popular place at end of the pedestrian mall, with a huge two-tiered patio and pleasant décor with a nautical vibe. It's known for its fish. The *lefer* (blue fish) is a Black Sea favourite (17lv).

## Entertainment

Ul Bogoridi and ul Aleksandrovska's cafés are de facto bars, with outside drinking buzzing most hours.

The unfortunately named **Party Club** (ul Bogoridi 36; cove 2lv; 11am-late) is a cavernous basement bar that lights up with original/cover rock bands.

**Cinema Septembri** ( 844 226; ul Georgi Kirkov; tickets 3lv) plays Hollywood films.

## Getting There & Away

For information on transport to nearby beach towns, see p181.

### AIR

The airport, 8km north of town, sees many charter flights in summer. From June to September, Wizz Air connects Burgas with Budapest (about €90 return) once weekly, and with London (about £180 return) two or three times weekly. Bus 15 (0.50lv, 15 minutes) heads to/from Yug Bus Terminal every half hour from 6am to 11pm.

### BUS

Most buses and microbuses leave from and arrive at the convenient **Yug Bus Terminal** ( 842 692; near cnr ul Aleksandrovska & ul Bulair). However, Varna-bound buses from central Bulgaria usually drop off Burgas passengers at the **Zapad Bus Terminal** ( 831 429), 2km west of the centre. City bus 4 connects the two.

Buses from Yug connect Burgas with Sofia (17lv to 19lv, six hours, every 30 minutes or hour), Veliko Târnovo (17lv, four hours, two

daily), Kazanlâk (15lv, 2½ hours, three daily) and Plovdiv (14lv to 16lv, four hours, six to nine buses daily). There are also several buses daily to Varna (8lv, 2½ hours, every 30 or 40 minutes) as well as spots along the coast (see p181). A few buses a day go to Kotel from Zapad.

Travel agencies along ul Bulair sell reserved seats for buses. **Enturtrans** ( 844 708; ul Bulair 22; 6.30-1am) handles domestic trips only. Five buses go to Istanbul (35lv, seven hours) daily from **Nisikli Turizm** ( 841 261; ul Bulair).

### CAR

**TS Travel** ( 845 060; www.tstravel.net; ul Bulair 1; 9am-6pm Mon-Sat) rules the car-rental business in Burgas; its high rates (starting at €44 a day) justify making a trip to Varna by bus to rent.

### TRAIN

The **train station** ( 845 022) sells domestic train tickets behind old-school ticket booths. Off-season links include Sofia (14.30lv, seven to eight hours, six daily), Plovdiv (10.70lv, four to five hours, three daily), and stops in Sliven and Kazanlâk. Summer usually sees a couple of extra services.

A train to Bucharest runs in summer only; buy tickets at **Rila Bureau** ( 845 242; 8am-5pm Mon-Fri, 8am-2pm Sat) in the station.

## SOZOPOL СОЗОПОЛ

☎ 0550 / pop 4650

A Nesebâr without the Sunny Beach package-trip beat, Sozopol – with a lovely stone-step centre on a jutting peninsula and two sandy beaches in town – still brings plenty of sun seekers.

The town, 31km southeast of Burgas, has two parts: the peninsular (old) and inland Harmanite (new). The bus terminal is roughly between the two.

In the old town, you'll find several foreign-exchange offices (including one that says 'The best change you can ever made') and a couple of banks including **HVB Bank Biochim** (ul Apolonia 11A; 8.30am-6pm Mon-Fri) with an ATM. There's **Internet** (ul Apolonia) in peak season.

## Sights

Sozopol has two good beaches, though the water can get a little rough. The slightly nicer **town beach**, about 500m long, has umbrellas to rent. The much longer **Harmanite Beach** is lined with cafés. There's calmer waters on the beach 2km to the north.

Just offshore is the 6.6-sq-km **St John's (Ivan) Island**. A 19th-century lighthouse watches over some 13th-century monastery ruins and, at times, 70 species of birds. Sea taxis make the 30-minute trip (5lv to 7lv per person) in summer.

The old town has several churches and museums, all of which tend to be closed in the off season. The pink-and-white **Art Gallery of Sozopol** (ul Kiril & Metodii 70; admission 1.5lv; 10am-7pm Mon-Sat) has enough sea-motif paintings to soothe your inner pirate.

## Sleeping

During summer, an accommodation stand booking private rooms (about 20lv per person and up) operates near the bus stop. All hotels,

sadly, are in the new town. The following are open all year.

**Sasha Khristov's Private Rooms** ( ☎ 0888-759 174; ul Venets 17; r with shared bathroom 21lv) A lovely family homestead in the old town with four homely rooms with terraces and a kitchen to use.

**Hotel Radik** ( ☎ 23 706; ul Republikanska 4; r per person 25-30lv; ☒ ) Just up the hill from the bus stop (one of several options in 'new town'), this bright 15-room hotel has spotless rooms and balconies. It's a good deal, and there's a terrace bar in summer.

**Hotel Dimanti** ( ☎ 22 640; www.hoteldiamanti.com; ul Morski Skali; d/apt 70/100lv) This 20-room modern take on Soz's past sits looking over an empty rocky bluff at the sea. Under renovation at

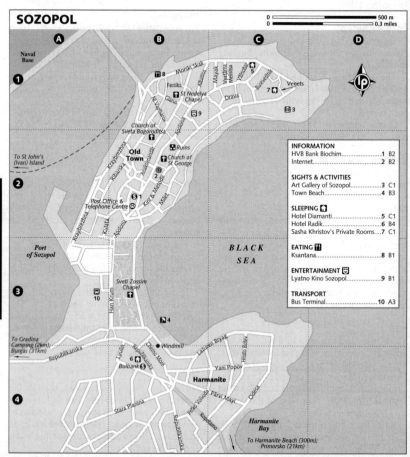

### SOZOPOL

| INFORMATION | |
|---|---|
| HVB Bank Biochim | 1 B2 |
| Internet | 2 B2 |

| SIGHTS & ACTIVITIES | |
|---|---|
| Art Gallery of Sozopol | 3 C1 |
| Town Beach | 4 B3 |

| SLEEPING | |
|---|---|
| Hotel Diamanti | 5 C1 |
| Hotel Radik | 6 B4 |
| Sasha Khristov's Private Rooms | 7 C1 |

| EATING | |
|---|---|
| Ksantana | 8 B1 |

| ENTERTAINMENT | |
|---|---|
| Lyatno Kino Sozopol | 9 B1 |

| TRANSPORT | |
|---|---|
| Bus Terminal | 10 A3 |

last pass, the 22 rooms will have balconies and all mod cons.

**Gradina Camping** has bungalows and lots of tent space near the beach, 2km north of town.

### Eating

A good place to sample fresh cuts of Black Sea fish is at the open-air fish restaurants along the port (open only in summer). Ul Morksi Skali has several *mekhanas* with island views and terrific food, including **Ksantana** (☎ 122 454; ul Morski Skali 7; mains 3.20-12lv; 11am-11pm), which has a huge menu in English.

### Entertainment

**Lyatno Kino Sozopol** (ul Apolonia 50) An outdoor walled space with benches facing the screen for Hollywood's latest at 9pm and 11pm.

### Getting There & Away

Buses and minibuses leave the **bus terminal** (ul Han Krum) for Burgas (3lv, 40 minutes, half-hourly 6am to 9pm) all year. From June to September it's usually possible to take buses south to Primorsko, Kiten, Ahtopol and (possibly) Sinemorets. At other times it's necessary to return to Burgas first.

## SOUTH OF SOZOPOL

The principal towns along this bay-to-bay stretch – Primorsko, Kiten, Ahtopol and far-off Sinemorets – have some nice beaches, though the towns lack the historical charm of Sozopol or Nesebâr. It's possible, with patience and planning, to hop around by public bus; see left. Generally, private rooms aren't hard to find at any of the following.

The bustling resort town of **Primorsko** aspires to be Sunny Beach's little bro, and many Eastern European package trippers come here for the 3km-long sheltered beach, ideal for swimming and boating. **Hotel Stop** (☎ 0888-850 820; r May-Oct 50lv) has 34 nice rooms.

Southbound buses also stop at **Kiten**, 5km south, with hotels and two beaches, where beach bars keep going till 2am or 3am in summer.

About 35km south of Primorsko, and after the road gets bumpy, is the larger town of **Ahtopol**, with a pretty good long beach. At least three daily buses head south from here to Sinemorets.

Bulgaria ends its Black Sea turf with a bang in booming **Sinemorets**, 11km north of the (closed) Turkish border. The town is just scattered new villas and hotels along bumpy dirt roads on a wide, bare bluff that bows toward a bay cupped with lovely golden sand – and another, better one just beyond. This area (and inland west) comprises the wildlife-lush **Strandjha Nature Park**. In town, American-run **Villa Philadelphia** (☎ 0550-66106; www.villaphiladelphia) is a good accommodation choice.

> **GETTING AROUND THE SOUTH COAST**
>
> Bus schedules up and down the coast – from Sunny Beach to Sinemorets – change wildly every summer. At research time, buses left Burgas half-hourly 6am to 8pm for Sozopol (3lv, 40 minutes), Sunny Beach (3lv, 45 minutes) and Nesebâr (3lv, 45 minutes).
>
> More preplanning is suggested for more distant spots; at research time seven buses daily left Burgas for Primorsko (5lv or 6lv, one hour), Kiten (6lv, 1¼ hours) and Ahtopol (7lv to 8lv, 1¾ hours). These usually don't stop in Sozopol.
>
> Taxi drivers cruise for lucrative beach-hopping runs – prices can reach 100lv or more to reach Sinemorets!
>
> The cheapest rental cars are in Varna (p170).

# NORTHWEST BULGARIA

Neglected, even mocked, Bulgaria's little pinkie – wedged between Romania and Serbia – sees few foreign travellers. Vidin is a gateway to Romania by river or to Serbia via bus, and is near Belogradchik's fortress. The train from Sofia goes past impressive **Iskâr Gorge**, south of Mezdra.

In 2006, dead migratory swans infected with the Avian bird flu were found outside Vidin, and some villages were briefly quarantined. No-one was infected, nor were any local birds.

## VIDIN ВИДИН

**☎ 094 / pop 53,500**

If rivers could rank cities, Vidin would score for its locals' misty-eyed devotion to the Danube. While its newly developed riverside park offers Bulgaria's finest spot to hang with the mighty Dan, Vidin is most useful as a link to Belogradchik.

At the main square (pl Bdintsi), two blocks north of the stations, you'll find a bank and ATM.

About 1km north of the centre is the interesting **Baba Vida Museum-Fortress** ( ☎ 601 705; admission 2lv; ☼ 9am-5pm), once a 1st-century Roman citadel, though much of what remains was rebuilt by Turks in the 1600s.

**Hotel Dunav** ( ☎ 600 177; ul Edelvais 3; s/d from 17/24lv) is a decent budget option – some rooms are better than others.

Ten or more daily buses connect Vidin's **bus station** ( ☎ 23179) with Sofia (15lv, four hours), and five or six go to Belogradchik (3.50lv, 1¼ hours), the first at 7.30am. A couple of buses daily head for Nagoutin, Serbia.

The train station, across from the bus station, sees four daily trains en route to/from Sofia (10.20lv, 5½ hours).

Talk of a bridge to Romania is still just that: talk. You supposedly can cross to Calafat, Romania, by passenger ferry (€3) or, when one's not going, on the (when full) car ferry (€10 per car, €3 per passenger) north of town.

## BELOGRADCHIK БЕЛОГРАДЧИК
☎ 0936 / pop 5640

A village sprawling along a rising mountain, remote Belogradchik draws many Bulgarian travellers to see its phenomenal rock formations and stirring craggy red-rock peaks so lifelike they're named for people. It's an amazing sight.

The town has a bank with an ATM on the main road, which starts a block up from the bus station.

Propped upon and between jagged peaks, the huge **Kaleto Fortress** ( ☎ 3001; admission 2.5lv; ☼ 9am-8pm Apr-Oct, 9am-5pm Nov-Mar), a 1km walk up from the main square (follow the signs and veer left at the old mosque), occupies a shocking setting – with Turk-built walls surrounding the peaks. Above the walls on the peaks are smooth spots to sit and listen to sheep bells clang from far-off fields. Romans first built here in the 1st century AD, and the site was later used to fight off Hungarian troops (unsuccessfully) in the 14th century. Ask at the information stand about visits to nearby **caves**.

It's possible to loop back on trails behind the fort to town, via the **Belogradchiski Skali** rock formations (aka 'Bulgaria's Grand Canyon'). The formations are accessible from town, starting about 100m behind (and down from) the main square.

**Hotel St Valentine** ( ☎ 4002; pl Benkovski 1; s/d 20/40lv) pushes it in the romance column, but this eight-room option is clean and central.

In a home that feels like a gingerbread house, **Madona** ( ☎ 5546; www.hotelmadona.hit.bg, in Bulgarian; ul Hristo Botev 26; s/d 35/60lv) is a B&B with small but nice traditional rooms. It's 600m from the main square (follow signs to 'hotel').

A lone daily direct bus leaves Belogradchik for Sofia (10lv, four hours) at 7am; the bus leaves Sofia's Traffic Market at 4pm. A handful of buses go to Vidin, and buses are scheduled to meet trains en route to Sofia at Oroshets station (a crappy town 15km east).

# BULGARIA DIRECTORY

## ACCOMMODATION
Accommodation listings in this guide have been ordered by price from cheapest to most expensive (ie budget to top end). In addition to the following options, most active monasteries have basic rooms for as little as 10lv per night (just no drinking binges, kids).

In the recent past, immigration officials pored over 'registration' forms from hotels where travellers stayed; the practice of form-filling continues, but we haven't heard of officials asking for them. Hold on to them just in case.

### Camping & Huts
Camping is not on the rise in Bulgaria. Generally, 'camping' here refers to rather lifeless areas where bungalows sit side by side in a small thicket of woods. Camp sites can be cheap though (3lv or 5lv). Discreet camping outside the camping ground is, as one local says, 'No problem – just don't have a loud party – and say you have permission if anyone asks.' In other words, it's not technically legal and you probably shouldn't do it.

*Hizhas* (mountain huts) dot the high country and range in quality. Many are now privately run (and cost about €7 to €10 per person); some more remote ones are free. Most Bulgaria maps show these. Some fill in July and August; reserve ahead at an agency such as Zig Zag in Sofia (p139).

### Hostels
Bulgaria's big four – Sofia, Plovdiv, Veliko Târnovo and Varna – are the only places with hostels. Sofia's hostel scene, in particular, is

richly developed. Expect to pay €10 per person in a dorm, including free breakfast and internet use, and often free pick-up from a bus or train station.

## Hotels

Generally hotels have private bathrooms (sometimes down the hall), in-room TV, heating and a fan if not air-conditioned, and about half of them offer free breakfast. All entries in this chapter have private bathrooms and TV unless otherwise noted. Most double rooms have two twin beds. Average rates for a cheapie are around 30lv for a single and 40lv for a double. In some tourist locations this rate can drop by 10lv in the off season. Higher-end hotels – recently built, in more modern style (and with thicker walls) – generally start at 45lv to 60lv for a single.

Many communist-era Balkantourist highrises still plod ahead in these new times. They are often ridiculed, but it's worth staying at one once (those in Varna and Sliven aren't bad choices): they often have good locations, and seeing their interiors (broken mint-and-beige phones, grey-and-brown 1970s curtains and chunky AM radios) feels like stepping into the Cold War era. They won't be there forever.

## Private Rooms

Travellers on a budget should rent private rooms *(stai pod naem)*, often offered by agencies, signed homes or English-speaking touts at train and bus stations. Rates range from 10lv or 15lv per person in smaller towns to 25lv in places such as Sofia, Plovdiv and Varna. Often private rooms mean a shared bathroom in a shared flat with a family; sometimes grandma sleeps in the kitchen.

## ACTIVITIES

Hiking options in the four principal mountain ranges abound (more than 37,000km of trails in all). For hiking tips, see p148, p151 and p158. Kartografia publishes excellent trail maps, available in Sofia and elsewhere. Zig Zag in Sofia (p139) runs guided tours and gives well-informed tips, and Veliko Târnovo's Trapezitsa (p164) leads a week-long hike in the Stara Planina.

Some trails are open to mountain bikes, or can be cross-country skied in winter.

Bulgaria's reputation as a cheap downhill skiing (and snowboarding) destination is outliving its deals. Its three main resorts –

Borovets (p150), Bansko (p150) and Pamporovo (p157) – all charge about 45lv for a one-day lift ticket, with an extra 20lv to 40lv to rent equipment. Mt Vitosha (p147) is cheaper, as are the evocatively older lifts at Maliovitsa (near Borovets) or Dobronishte (near Bansko). The ski season runs mid-December to mid-April. Check www.bulgariaski.com for loads of information plus package deals.

The popularity of rock-climbing is on the rise, with good options all over, including outside Veliko Târnovo as well as on the coast at Kamen Bryag (p175), while Trapezitsa (p164) helps host international events, rents equipment and offers tours.

Caving tours are another draw, such as those near Belogradchik (opposite).

## BOOKS

Lonely Planet's *Bulgaria* offers more comprehensive coverage of the country. For history, RJ Crampton's *A Concise History of Bulgaria* gives a quick (if a little dull) overview from the pre-Thracian era to postcommunism. The communist-era 'KBG' world is uncovered in Alexenia Dimitrova's *The Iron Fist: Inside the Archives of Bulgaria's Secret Police*. Bill Bryson pokes a little fun at Sofia in his 1992 book *Neither Here Nor There: Travels in Europe*.

## BUSINESS HOURS

Banks and most public offices are open Monday to Friday, roughly 8.30am to 5pm or 6pm, sometimes with an hour off for lunch. Many shops and all foreign-exchange booths are open daily, and most internet cafés are open 24 hours, though we've seen 'nonstop' shops with roughly 8am to 11pm hours, too. Many post offices are open daily.

Hours for many Bulgarian museums and shops drift. It can depend on the season (in winter, some museums may close for a few weeks unexpectedly, while summer sees longer hours) or the whim of the guy with the keys ('Oh sorry, Hristo is meeting a cousin in Pleven; come back tomorrow.'). Hours in this chapter reflect the official line, but brace yourself for the occasional hiccup.

'Summer' and 'winter' refer to either side of daylight savings.

## COURSES

It's possible to study Bulgarian language in Sofia (p142) and Veliko Târnovo (p164). You can also learn traditional Bulgarian music or dance at heralded schools in Plovdiv (p154), Kotel (p162) and Shiroka Lâka (p158).

## DANGERS & ANNOYANCES

As long as you don't leave bags unattended at train or bus stations, or wear an unzipped backpack, you're unlikely to have problems in Bulgaria. Pickpocketing is most common in summer in Sofia and Varna. You will be warned by some Bulgarians that Roma will rob you blind (example: 'You'll be lucky to keep your pants'), which is an annoyance in itself.

Smoke is the number-one annoyance for the uninitiated. By law, all restaurants must set aside 'nonsmoking' areas, often a lone table surrounded by 'smoking' ones. Many hotels do not have smoke-free rooms, but the trend is for more to set aside non-smoking rooms.

## DISCOUNT CARDS

Students can save 50% or 75% on admission at most museums, and on airfares from some travel agents. Usit Colours in Sofia (p139) and Veliko Târnovo (p163) can issue student cards for 10lv.

## EMBASSIES & CONSULATES
### Bulgarian Embassies & Consulates

**Australia** ( ☎ 02-9327 7581; fax 02-9327 8067; 4 Carlotta Rd, Double Bay, NSW 2028)

**Canada** ( ☎ 1-613-789 3215; fax 1-613-789 3524; 325 Steward St, Ottawa, ON K1N 6K5)

**France** ( ☎ 01 45 51 85 90; www.bulgaria.com/embassy /france; 1 Ave Rapp, 75007 Paris)

**Germany** ( ☎ 030-201 09 22; bbotscaft@myokay.net; Mauer Strasse 11, Berlin 10117)

**Greece** Athens ( ☎ 30-1-647 8106; fax 30-1-647 8130; 33 Stratigou Kallari St, 15452 Paleo Psychico, Athens); Thessaloniki ( ☎ 031-829 210; Edmundo Abot 1, Thessaloniki)

**Ireland** ( ☎ 0353-1-660 3293; fax 0353-1-660 3915; 22 Burlington Rd, 4 Dublin)

**Israel** ( ☎ 972-3-524 1751; fax 972-3-524 1798; 124 Ibn Gvirol St, 62308 Tel Aviv)

**Macedonia** ( ☎ 03-8991-229 444; fax 03-8991-116 139; 3 Zlatko Shnaider St, Skopje 1000)

**Netherlands** ( ☎ 031-70-350 3051; Duinroosweg 9, 2597 KJ The Hague)

**Romania** ( ☎ 040-1-230 2150; fax 040-1-230 7654; Str Rabat 5, sec 1, Bucharest)

**Serbia** ( ☎ 038-11-64 62 22; fax 038-11-64 10 80; 26 Birchaninova St, Belgrade)

**Turkey** Ankara ( ☎ 090-312-426 7455; Atatürk Buvlari 124, Kavaklidere, Ankara); Istanbul ( ☎ 090-212-281 0115; fax 090-212-264 1011; Ahmet Adnan Saygun Caddesi 44, Ulus-Levent 80600)

**UK** ( ☎ 020-7584 9400; www.bulgarianembassy.org.uk; 186-88 Queen's Gate, London SW7 5HL)

**USA** ( ☎ 1-202-387 0174; www.bulgaria-embassy.org; 1621 22nd St NW, Washington DC 20008)

### Embassies & Consulates in Bulgaria

Designated visiting hours for citizens or those seeking visas are listed. New Zealanders can turn to the UK Embassy for assistance, or contact their **consulate general** ( ☎ 210-6874 701; 268 Kifissias Ave) in Athens. All of the below are in Sofia unless stated:

**Australia** ( ☎ 02-946 1334; ul Trakia 37) Main office in Athens, call for hours.

**Canada** ( ☎ 02-969 9717; ul Moskovska 9)

**Denmark** ( ☎ 02-917 0100; bul Dondukov 54)

**France** ( ☎ 02-965 1100; www.ambafrance-bg.org, in French; ul Oborishte 27-29)

**Germany** ( ☎ 02-918 380; ul Frederic Joliot-Curie 25)

**Greece** ( ☎ 02-946 1750; ul San Stefano 33; ☼ 8.30am-4pm Mon-Fri); I Plovdiv ( ☎ 032-632 003; ul Preslav 10)

**Hungary** ( ☎ 02-963 1135; ul 6 Septemvri 57; ☼ visas 9am-11am Mon, Wed & Fri)

**Ireland** ( ☎ 02-980 0642; bul Stamboliiski 55, fl 4)

**Macedonia** ( ☎ 02-701 560; ul Frederic Joliot-Curie 17; ☼ 10am-1pm Mon-Fri)

**Netherlands** ( ☎ 02-816 0300; www.netherlands embassy.bg; ul Oborishte 15; ☼ 10am-noon Mon-Fri)

**Poland** ( ☎ 02-987 2610, visa info ☎ 02-981 8545; ul Han Krum 46; ☼ visas 9am-1pm Mon-Wed & Fri)

**Romania** ( ☎ 02-971 2858; bul M Eminesku 4; ☼ visas 3-5pm Tue, 10am-noon Wed & Thu) New Zealanders can get visas for Romania in one day for €30.

**Russia** ( ☎ 02-963 0914; www.bulgaria.mid.ru, in Russian; bul Dragan Tskankov 28)

**Turkey** ( ☎ 02-935 5500; bul Vasil Levski 80; ☼ 9.30am-1pm Mon-Fri); Plovdiv ( ☎ 032-632 309; ul Filip Makedonski 10)

**UK** ( ☎ 02-933 9222; www.british-embassy.bg; ul Moskovksa 9)

**USA** ( ☎ 02-937 5100; www.usembassy.bg; ul Kozyak 16)

## FESTIVALS & EVENTS

Bulgaria hosts many fascinating shindigs. City-run music and cultural events happen from spring to autumn. Koprivshtitsa's folk festival is a big one (see p159) and Varna's music festival (p172) spans nearly half a year; others are listed throughout this chapter. Kazanlâk's three-day splash-out for the Rose Festival (p160) ends on the first Sunday in June.

As part of the national custom of Martenitsa in March, most Bulgarians wear red-and-white yarn figures until they see a stork, when they tie the figure to a tree.

Also in March, the *kukeri* festival – famous in Shiroka Lâka (p158) – is held on the first Sunday before Lent, when oddly masked dancers ward off evil spirits.

## GAY & LESBIAN TRAVELLERS

Consensual homosexual sex is legal in Bulgaria. One of the nation's biggest stars, male singer Azis, is purposely sexually ambiguous, but Bulgaria is not yet gay-friendly.

The best source for discos, bars and gay beaches is www.bulgayria.com. **Bulgarian Gay Organization Gemini** (www.bgogemini.org) is a largely political organisation based in Sofia, but can help point out places to go. Sofia has a pretty good range of bars and clubs, but there's almost nothing elsewhere.

## HOLIDAYS

Official public holidays:

**New Year's Day** 1 January
**Liberation Day** (aka National Day); 3 March
**Orthodox Easter Sunday & Monday** March/April; one week after Catholic/Protestant Easter
**St George's Day** 6 May
**Cyrillic Alphabet Day** Our favourite!: 24 May
**Unification** (aka National Day); 6 September
**Bulgarian Independence Day** 22 September
**National Revival Day** 1 November
**Christmas** 25 and 26 December

## INTERNET RESOURCES

In recent years Bulgaria has had an internet boom, with many agencies and attractions setting up sights. A few catch-all sites:

**www.bdz.bg** Train schedule and fares.
**www.bulgariatravel.org** Official tourist site, with detailed background and photos.
**www.centralnaavtogara.bg** Sofia's bus station lists Sofia-based bus routes.
**www.onlinebg.com** News, shopping, links.
**www.sofiacityguide.com** Monthly publication's website, with loads of national information.
**www.sofiaecho.com** English-language paper that has national coverage, travel tips and extensive archives.

## LANGUAGE

Almost everything is written in Cyrillic (even '*kseroks*' for Xerox). Highway signs are written in Roman and Cyrillic. Most Bulgarians in their early 30s and older know a fair bit of Russian, but English is the vogue second-language of choice these days. Remember that Cyrillic is a Bulgarian invention – it's the Russians who borrowed it.

See p945 for a list of useful Bulgarian words and phrases.

## MONEY

In touristy places and upmarket hotels, many prices are quoted in euros. Prices in this chapter reflect quotes given by individual businesses. Many speculate that prices could skyrocket with integration to the EU – meaning the prices in this chapter may woefully undercut the real deal. Aside from this, prices remained roughly the same in the past few years *except* for bus and train fares (which rose by about 25% from 2004 to 2006) – and of course real estate.

### ATMs

ATMs (cash points) are ubiquitous and compatible with foreign cards (ask your bank). Even towns such as Rila, Belogradchik and Melnik have them.

### Cash

The local currency, the lovely leva (lv), comprises 100 stotinki. It's been pegged to the euro (roughly 2:1) since January 2002. In touristy places and upmarket hotels, many prices are quoted in euro. Banknotes come in denominations of one, two, five, 10, 20 and 50 leva, and coins in one, two, five, 10, 20 and 50 stotinki. The little horse guy on the coins is from a bas-relief made in the 8th century at Madara (p168).

### Exchanging Money

It's not a problem changing money in Bulgaria – foreign-exchange offices (many working nonstop) are found in every town. You'll get receipts from these and at banks, but there's no reason to hold onto them. US dollars, UK pounds and euro are the best currencies to carry.

---

**ONE PRICE, ONE WORLD**

In January 2006, the long clung-to, communist-era, dual-pricing scheme where foreigners paid double (or more) for museums and hotels was scrapped. Unfortunately for locals, the change often resulted in simply scrapping the lower price, meaning Bulgarians found themselves paying 'foreign' prices. Some hotels and museums, however, have split the difference.

BULGARIA

### Travellers Cheques

American Express and Thomas Cook cheques can be cashed at nearly all banks; Visa and CitiCorp cheques are also frequently cashed. Bulbank, the country's official bank, often charges the lowest commission rate – 0.2% (minimum €1 per transaction, regardless of how many cheques are cashed). There's a 2% fee to cash cheques into the same currency.

## POST

Sending a postcard or letter to anywhere outside Bulgaria costs 1.40lv. Many post offices in bigger cities are open daily.

## TELEPHONE

In most cities and towns you'll find a Bulgarian Telecommunications Centre (BTC) inside, or next to, the main post office, from where you can make local or international calls (it costs about 0.36lv per minute to call overseas and 0.72lv to call a mobile phone). But when possible, use Net cards (accessed by toll-free numbers from bigger cities) or make international Net calls from internet cafés. Rates are as little as 0.20lv per minute to call the UK, USA or Australia.

Nearly all Mobika and BulFon telephone booths use phonecards *(fonkarta)* for local or international calls. Cards are available from newsstands for 5lv to 25lv. Orange BulFon booths double as free clocks – pick up the receiver to see the time.

The mobile-phone craze has certainly reached Bulgaria. M-tel, Globul and Vivatel are the three operators. Numbers have different codes (eg ☎ 087 and ☎ 088). Costs are substantially more expensive than land lines.

### Area Codes

To ring Bulgaria from abroad, dial the international access code then ☎ 359, followed by the area code (minus the first zero) then the number.

To call direct from Bulgaria, dial ☎ 00 followed by the country code.

## TOURIST INFORMATION

Cities such as Sofia and Plovdiv lack real city-oriented tourist information centres, while smaller places such as Smolyan and Shiroka Lâka have two offices with English-speaking staff and tonnes of brochures. For information, you can always resort to the many travel agents or hotels. Information centres can generally find

---

> **EMERGENCY NUMBERS**
>
> Bulgaria hopes to create a single emergency number ( ☎ 112) by the time this book is published.
>
> ▪ Ambulance ☎ 150
> ▪ Directory Assistance ☎ 144
> ▪ Fire ☎ 160
> ▪ Police ☎ 166

---

private accommodation, help with information on special events and sometimes rent cars at good rates. The best ones even rent bikes.

## TOURS

Though city tours exist, most independent travellers will be OK on their own. Exceptions to consider definitely include hiking tours into rugged mountains, rock-climbing tours and day trips to Rila Monastery from Sofia.

Also see Information sections in the text and Activities, p183.

## VISAS

At the time of research, citizens of the following countries don't require a visa, and are instead issued a free 30-day entry stamp at any Bulgarian border, international airport or seaport: Australia, Canada, Ireland, Israel, Japan, New Zealand, Poland, UK and USA. Citizens of other EU countries will receive 90-day tourist visas. Russians and Turks need to arrange visas.

The easiest way to get an extension on your stay is by leaving the country and returning the same or next day. It may be possible to pay 200lv for an extension at the passport offices in Sofia and Plovdiv, but it's easier to leave the country and return.

# TRANSPORT IN BULGARIA

## GETTING THERE & AWAY

### Air

Bulgaria's three most active airports are in Sofia, Varna and Burgas. **Wizz Air** (www.wizzair.com) flies four times weekly from Budapest to Sofia. **Sky Europe** (www.skyeurope.com) connects Bratislava with Sofia four times weekly. No additional departure tax is levied outside the price of your ticket.

Airlines flying to/from Bulgaria (all addresses are for Sofia):

**Aeroflot** (www.aeroflot.ru; ☎ 02-943 4489)

**Air France** (www.airfrance.com; ☎ 02-939 7010, airport 937 3207; ul Sâborna 5)

**Alitalia** (www.alitalia.it; ☎ 02-981 6702; ul Graf Ignatiev 40)

**Austrian Airlines** (www.aua.com; ☎ 02-980 2323; bul Vitosha 41)

**British Airways** (www.britishairways.com; ☎ 02-945 7000, airport 945 9227)

**Bulgaria Air** (www.air.bg; ☎ 02-937 3243, 02-865 9557; airport)

**ČSA** (Czech Airlines; www.csa.cz/en; ☎ 02-937 3175)

**Hemus Air** (www.hemusair.bg; ☎ 02-981 8330; airport)

**LOT Polish Airlines** (www.lot.com; ☎ 02-987 4562; bul Aleksandâr Stambuliski 27A)

**Lufthansa** (www.lufthansa.com; ☎ 02-937 3141, 02-980 4242; airport)

**KLM** (www.klm.com; ☎ 02-981 9910; ul Patriarh Estimi 36B)

**Malév** (Hungarian Airlines; www.malev.com; ☎ 02-945 9239; airport)

**Turkish Airlines** (www.turkishairlines.com; ☎ 02-945 9145, 02-988 3596)

**Wizz Air** (www.wizzair.com; ☎ 02-960 3888)

## Land
### BORDER CROSSINGS

The most popular entry/exit between Bulgaria and the region is at the Ruse–Giurgiu border with Romania (en route to/from Bucharest); no buses go to Romania, so most travellers go by train, enduring a 60- to 90-minute border check on both sides.

Macedonia-bound buses and trains leave from Sofia (via the Gyueshevo–Deve Bair crossing) and Blagoevgrad (via the Stanke Lischkovo–Delçevo crossing); Belgrade-bound buses and trains from Sofia cross at Kalotina–Dimitrovgrad, Serbia (some travellers have preferred the train on this route). It's also possible to get to Serbia by bus from Vidin, via the Vrâshka Chuka–Zajc crossing.

Bus and train information for links with Greece and Turkey are included in this chapter.

### BUS

International tickets to the region (and beyond) are available at practically any bus station in the country. There's not one set price, so it's worth checking a couple of companies.

---

**SAVING LEVA ON TRAINS**

If you're taking an international train from Bulgaria, you can save 25% or more of the ticket price by purchasing a domestic ticket to the border town (eg Ruse en route to Bucharest), where you can hop off and buy the onward international ticket.

---

### CAR & MOTORCYCLE

Drivers bringing cars into Bulgaria are sometimes asked to pay a 'road fee', based on where you're going. One option is to say you're heading to the nearest big city (eg if crossing from Greece, say 'going to Sofia' and pay €10, rather than €50 for Varna). Allegedly you won't have to show the receipt upon leaving. Drivers must also pay a €3 'disinfection fee'.

### TRAIN

Tickets for international trains can be bought at any government-run **Rila Bureau** (www.bdz-rila.com; ◷ most open weekdays only) or at some stations' dedicated ticket offices (most open daily) at larger stations with international connections.

The daily Trans-Balkan Express (between Budapest and Thessaloniki, Greece) stops at Ruse, Gorna Oryahovitsa (near Veliko Târnovo), Sofia and Sandanski.

A daily train connects Sofia with Belgrade (and good connections to Western and Central Europe) and Istanbul.

The Bulgaria Express (aka 'the Russian train', between Sofia and Moscow) stops in Ruse once weekly (three times in summer). From mid-June to September, trains leave from Varna and Burgas en route to Bucharest, Budapest, Bratislava and Prague. Another summer train also connects Bucharest with Sofia, via Ruse and Gorna Oryahovitsa.

### River

You can ferry across the Danube River from Vidin (p182) or cross by train from Ruse (p168).

## GETTING AROUND

Travelling around Bulgaria is cheap. Prices are the same for foreigners and locals.

### Air

Hemus Air flies between Sofia and Varna daily (about €100 return), with extra flights in summer, when there are also flights to Burgas. See p186 for airline contact information.

## Bicycle

Traffic is relatively light outside the cities, but winding curves in the mountains and/or potholes everywhere can be obstacles.

Bulgaria has few bike-rental options: you can rent wheels at Zig Zag (p139) or Kervan Hostel (p143) in Sofia, in Veliko Târnovo (p164) or the tourist information centre in Koprivshtitsa (p159). Most towns have bike shops that can make repairs or sell some spare parts. You may need to pay an extra fee to take a bike on a train or bus.

## Boat

Sadly there's no regular boat service down the Danube River.

## Bus

Buses (public and private) and minibuses connect all cities and major towns. More popular routes – such as Sofia–Varna – have nice, modern buses; but there are also more ramshackle varieties.

Outside Sofia, centralised information is difficult to find, as stations have a confusing array of private bus booths advertising overlapping destinations; schedules also change frequently. Generally buses leave from 7am to 6pm only. Most bus stations have a left-luggage service with long (but not 24-hour) opening hours.

This chapter lists prices, duration for trips and number of buses daily – *they're changeable, so use them as a gauge only.*

## Car & Motorcycle

Renting a car from a local agent – not an international company, who may charge four or five times the rate – is a great way to beach-hop or visit mountain villages.

A car can be found in bigger cities for €18 to €25 per day, usually with unlimited kilometres and insurance thrown in. Some companies allow free drop-offs in select cities. See individual entries for listings.

To rent, you normally need to be 21 and have a driver's licence from your own country. Some agents drop the 20% VAT (value-added tax) if you pay in cash. In all, agents are pretty reliable. We heard from a British couple who

totalled a car and only lost their €150 deposit due to the company's losses in the time taken to replace the car.

Most road conditions are pretty good and traffic reasonably light. Most roads are well signed in Cyrillic and Roman alphabets. On smaller roads, you may have to negotiate big bumps. If oncoming cars flicks their lights, it's likely a police speed trap is around the corner (the west-bound entry to Sofia is notorious for police traps). Speed limits are well signed: usually 130km/h on main highways and 90km/h on smaller ones. Town speed limits are 50km/h unless otherwise noted.

## Train

Bulgarian trains are fun, as carriage seats expose a bit more local life than you'll get on buses. Trains – all run by the Bulgarian State Railways (BDZh) – are generally cheaper too, but take a little longer than buses. Some offer great views (including the pretty Bansko–Septemvri route). *Ekspresen* (express) and *bârz* (fast) trains way out-speed the slow *pâtnicheski* (passenger) trains.

All prices in the chapter are for 2nd-class seats (with eight seats per cabin); 1st-class seats (only a few leva more) have six seats per cabin, and for some routes see far fewer people.

Most Europe-wide rail passes can be purchased in Bulgaria, but will not be good value for getting around the country.

Bring what food or water you'll need for the trip. Most train stations are signposted in Cyrillic only, and no announcements are made on board.

All train stations have a left-luggage service (about 2lv per bag for 24 hours).

An extra daily train or two runs some routes in summer, particularly serving the Black Sea coast.

---

**BUS & TRAIN SCHEDULES ONLINE**

These websites are huge aids in planning your trip across Bulgaria:

- http://bus.light-bg.com/english/input _engl.html – nationwide bus information
- www.centralnaavtogara.bg – Sofia bus information
- www.bdz.bg – lists times and prices for all train routes

# Croatia

Whether you call it the 'new Greece', the 'new Riviera' or the 'new Tuscany', Croatia has clearly become the latest European 'gotta go' destination for the glitterati. Yachts glide through its island archipelago, a procession of famous faces files through ancient streets and no Mediterranean cruise would be complete without a stop on its shores.

Yet, for all the hype, Croatia's pleasures are more timeless than trendy. Crystalline water laps gently at a 1778km-long coast and no fewer than 1185 islands. In pastel fishing ports children play on cobblestoned streets and family farmers sell their produce in the town square. A millennium of occupiers, from Romans and Venetians to Austrians, Hungarians and Italians, has left Croatia with a unique and slightly schizoid cultural identity. The interior has a strong central-European flavour, evident in the baroque architecture of Zagreb, while the coast could be an extension of Italy. The unifying factor is Croatia's Slavic soul, especially apparent during festivals and celebrations when centuries-old songs, dances and costumes animate towns and villages around the country.

Croatians retain a strong attachment to the land and traditions that nourished the dream of independence for so long. A fierce pride in their natural and cultural heritage has given them strength to hold out against the tide of developers and speculators ready to pave over the coast. Whether the country's natural beauty and traditional lifestyle can endure in the face of overwhelming commercial pressure is an open question. But so far the signs are promising.

## FAST FACTS

- **Area** 56,538 sq km
- **Capital** Zagreb
- **Currency** kuna (KN); A$1=5KN; €1=8.35KN; ¥100=6KN; NZ$1=4.12KN; UK£1=12.45KN; US$1=6.63KN
- **Famous for** neckties, war, Tito
- **Official Language** Croatian
- **Phrases** *bog* (hello), *doviđenja* (goodbye), *hvala* (thanks), *pardon* (sorry)
- **Population** 4.5 million
- **Telephone Codes** country code ☎ 385; international access code ☎ 00
- **Visas** unnecessary for citizens of the EU, USA, Australia, New Zealand and Canada; see p244

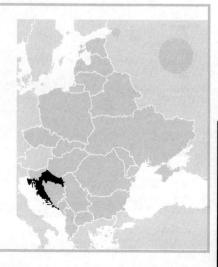

CROATIA

# CROATIA

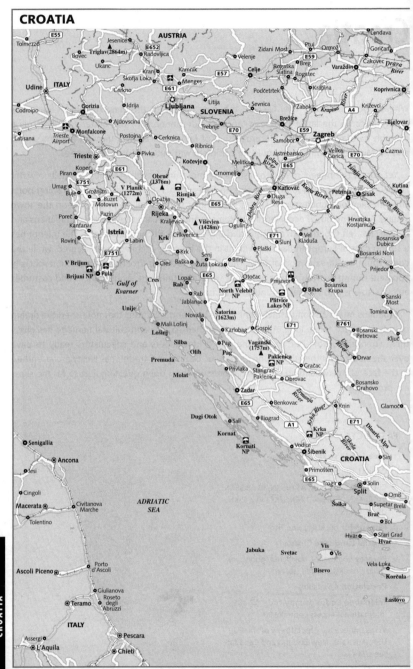

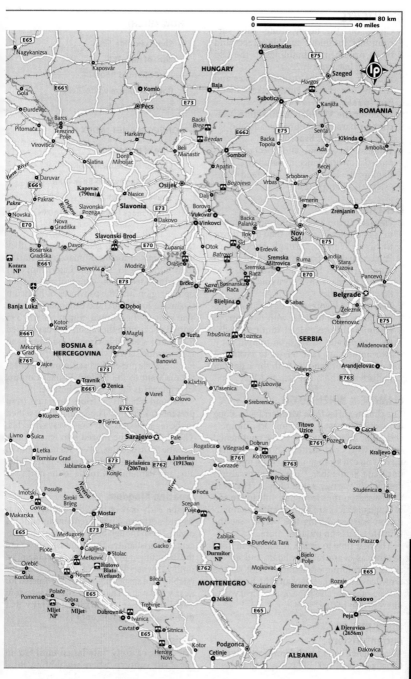

# HIGHLIGHTS

- Check out the heavy stone walls surrounding luminous marble streets and finely ornamented buildings in the Old Town of **Dubrovnik** (p233).
- Wander around the turquoise lakes and rushing waterfalls of **Plitvice Lakes National Park** (p221).
- Discover the Venetian architecture, welcoming harbourside promenade and vibrant nightlife of **Hvar** (p228).
- Witness the colour and spectacle of a *moreška* sword dance in **Korčula** (p230).
- Explore the lakes, coves and island monastery of **Mljet** (p232).

# ITINERARIES

- **One week** Spend a day exploring the museums and cafés of Zagreb, then head down to Split. Wander through Diocletian's Palace, make a trip to Trogir and then take ferries to Hvar and Korčula. End with three days in Dubrovnik, taking a day trip to Mljet.
- **Two weeks** Devote two days to Zagreb and three days to Pula, with day trips to Rovinj and Poreč. Head south to Zadar for a night and then go on to Split for a two-night stay. Take ferries to Hvar and Korčula before ending with three days in Dubrovnik and a day trip to Mljet.

# CLIMATE & WHEN TO GO

The climate varies from Mediterranean along the Adriatic coast – with hot, dry summers and mild, rainy winters – to the continental inland, with cold winters and warm summers. You can swim in the sea from mid-June until late September. Coastal temperatures are slightly warmer south of Split. The peak tourist season runs from mid-July to the end of August. Prices are highest and accommodation scarcest during this period. See the Climate Charts on p911 for more.

The best time to be in Croatia is June. The weather is beautiful, the boats and excursions are running often and it's not yet too crowded. The end of May and the beginning of September are also good, especially if you're interested in hiking.

# HISTORY
## Ancient History

The ancient Illyrians laid claim to what is now Croatia in about 1000 BC as they migrated into

## HOW MUCH?

- **Short taxi ride** 50KN
- **Litre of milk** 7KN
- **Loaf of bread** 3.50KN
- **Bottle of house white** 20KN
- **Newspaper** 5KN

## LONELY PLANET INDEX

- **Litre of petrol** 8KN
- **Litre of bottled water** 6KN
- **33cL of Karlovačko Beer** 10KN
- **Souvenir T-shirt** 75KN
- **Street snack (slice of burek)** 10KN

the region. Although generally warlike, they were no match for the Romans who started their conquest in 229 BC. Later, Emperor Augustus extended the conquest and divvied up the region into the provinces of Illyricum (Dalmatia and Bosnia) and Pannonia (Croatia). The split of the Roman empire in AD 395 caused a schism in the region that has echoed for centuries: Slovenia, Croatia and Bosnia and Hercegovina stayed with the Western Roman Empire, while present Serbia, Kosovo and Macedonia went to the Eastern Roman Empire, later known as the Byzantine Empire.

Around 625, Slavic tribes migrated from present-day Poland. The Serbian tribe settled in the region that is now southwestern Serbia. The Croatian tribe moved into what is now Croatia and occupied two former Roman provinces: Dalmatian Croatia along the Adriatic, and Pannonian Croatia to the north.

## Croatian Kingdom

By the early part of the 9th century Dalmatia and northern Croatia remained politically divided even though both settlements had accepted Christianity. The Frankish north and the Byzantine-influenced south were not united until 925 when the Dalmatian duke Tomislav established a single kingdom that prospered for nearly 200 years. That first Croatian kingdom established a sense of national identity that didn't come to fruition until 1990.

## Division

The spirit of unity only lasted until late in the 11th century when squabbling local leaders weakened the central authority and split the kingdom. From then on, the north-ern and coastal parts of Croatia followed separate paths. The northern Croats united with Hungary in 1102 for protection against the Orthodox Byzantine Empire. Around the same time, the Adriatic coast turned to the Venetians even though Hungary continued to struggle for control of the region. Some Dalmatian cities changed hands repeatedly until Venice imposed its rule on the Adriatic coast in the early 15th century and occupied it for nearly four centuries. Only the Repub-lic of Ragusa (Dubrovnik) maintained its independence.

In the 14th century the Turks began push-ing into the Balkans. The Serbs fell in 1389 and the Hungarians in 1526. With the de-feat of the Hungarian protectors, northern Croatia turned to the Habsburgs of Austria for protection. Their long marriage with Austria began in 1527 and lasted until 1918. Austria also felt threatened by the Turks. To form a buffer against them the Austrians invited Serbs to settle the Vojna Krajina (Military Frontier) north of Zadar in the 16th century. The Serbs in the borderlands had an autonomous administration under Austrian control; these areas were reincorporated into Croatia in 1881 and then attempted to secede in 1991.

## Unity

After Napoleonic France shattered Venice in 1797, the French occupied southern Croatia, abolishing the Republic of Ragusa in 1808. Napoleon merged Dalmatia, Istria and Slov-enia into the 'Illyrian Provinces', but following his defeat at Waterloo in 1815, Austria-Hungary moved in to pick up the pieces along the coast.

A revival of Croatian cultural and political life began in 1835, with leading intellectuals advancing the idea of south-Slavic unity. With the defeat of the Austro-Hungarian empire in WWI, the unity movement gained force across the region. Croatia became part of the Kingdom of Serbs, Croats and Slovenes (called Yugoslavia after 1929), with a central-ised government in Belgrade. But northern Dalmatia remained part of Italy. Italy had been promised control of the Adriatic coast as an incentive to join the war against Austria-Hungary in 1915 and it held much of northern Dalmatia from 1918 to 1943.

## War

After the German invasion of Yugoslavia in March 1941, a puppet government dominated by the fascist Ustaša movement was set up in Croatia and Bosnia and Hercegovina under Ante Pavelić (who fled to Argentina after WWII). At first the Ustaša tried to expel all Serbs from Croatia to Serbia. But when the Germans stopped this because of the problems it was causing, the Ustaša launched an exter-mination campaign that rivalled the Nazis in its brutality. Although there is much contro-versy over the number of victims, estimates indicate that from 60,000 to 600,000 ethnic Serbs, Jews and Roma were murdered.

Not all Croats supported these policies, how-ever. Josip Broz, known as Maršal Tito, was himself of Croat–Slovene parentage and tens of thousands of Croats fought bravely with his partisans. Massacres of Croats conducted by Serbian Četniks in southern Croatia and Bosnia forced almost all antifascist Croats into the communist ranks, where they joined the numerous Serbs trying to defend themselves from the Ustaša. In all, about a million people died violently in a war that was fought mostly in Croatia and Bosnia and Hercegovina.

## The Tito Years

After the war, Maršal Tito became the prime minister of the new Yugoslav Federation and divided it into five republics: Croatia, Serbia, Slovenia, Bosnia and Hercegovina, and Mace-donia. Even with a Stalin-style system of state planning, Croatia and Slovenia moved far ahead of the other republics economically, leading to demands by reformers, intellectu-als and students for greater autonomy. The 'Croatian Spring' of 1971 caused a backlash and purge of the reformers, who were jailed or expelled from the Communist Party.

Tito's habit of borrowing from abroad to flood the country with cheap consumer goods produced an economic crisis after his death in 1980. The sinking economy provoked greater tension among Yugoslavia's ethnic groups, which came to a head when Serbian politician Slobodan Milošević whipped Serbs into a nationalistic frenzy over the aspirations of the Albanian majority in the province of Kosovo.

## Civil War

Fearing a renewal of Serbian hegemony, many Croats felt the time had come to end more than four decades of communist rule and attain complete autonomy into the bargain. In the free elections of April 1990 Franjo Tuđman's Hrvatska Demokratska Zajednica (HDZ; Croatian Democratic Union) easily defeated the old Communist Party. On 22 December 1990 a new Croatian constitution was promulgated, changing the status of Serbs in Croatia to a national minority.

The constitution's failure to guarantee minority rights, and mass dismissals of Serbs from the public service, led the 600,000-strong ethnic Serb community to demand autonomy. When Croatia declared independence from Yugoslavia on 25 June 1991, the Serbian enclave of Krajina proclaimed its independence from Croatia.

Heavy fighting broke out in Krajina (the area around Knin, north of Split), Baranja (the area north of the Drava River opposite Osijek) and Slavonia (the region west of the Danube). The 180,000-member, 2000-tank Yugoslav People's Army, dominated by Serbian communists, began to intervene on its own authority in support of Serbian irregulars, under the pretext of halting ethnic violence.

In the three months following 25 June, a quarter of Croatia fell to Serbian militias and the federal army. In September the Croatian government ordered a blockade of 32 federal military installations in the republic, gaining much-needed military equipment. In response, the Yugoslav navy blockaded the Adriatic coast and laid siege to the strategic town of Vukovar on the Danube.

In early October 1991 the federal army and Montenegrin militia moved against Dubrovnik to protest against the ongoing blockade of their garrisons in Croatia. On 7 October rockets from Yugoslav air force jets hit the presidential palace in Zagreb in an unsuccessful assassination attempt on President Tuđman. Heroic Vukovar finally fell on 19 November when the Yugoslav army ended a bloody three-month siege by concentrating 600 tanks and 30,000 soldiers there. During the six months of fighting in Croatia 10,000 people died, hundreds of thousands fled and tens of thousands of homes were deliberately destroyed.

## Independence

After the Croatian parliament amended its constitution to protect minority and human rights, the European Community (EC), succumbing to strong pressure from Germany, recognised Croatia in January 1992. This was followed three months later by US recognition and in May 1992 Croatia was admitted to the UN. Yet the country remained in turmoil.

In January 1993 the Croatian army suddenly launched an offensive in southern Krajina, pushing the Serbs back as much as 24km in some areas and recapturing strategic points. The Krajina Serbs vowed never to accept rule from Zagreb; in June 1993 they voted overwhelmingly to join the Bosnian Serbs (and eventually Greater Serbia).

The self-proclaimed 'Republic of Serbian Krajina' held elections in December 1993, which no international body recognised as legitimate or fair. Continued 'ethnic cleansing' left only about 900 Croats in Krajina out of an original population of 44,000.

On 1 May 1995 the Croatian army and police entered and occupied western Slavonia, east of Zagreb, causing some 15,000 Serbs to flee the region. At dawn on 4 August 1995 the military launched a massive assault on the rebel Serb capital of Knin. Outnumbered by two to one, the Serb army fled to northern Bosnia, along with about 150,000 civilians whose roots in the Krajina stretched back centuries. The military operation lasted just days, but was followed by months of terror. Widespread looting and burning of Serb villages, as well as attacks on the few remaining elderly Serbs, seemed designed to ensure the permanence of this massive population shift. The actions of the Croatian army in this offensive are the subject of war crimes prosecutions in The Hague.

The Dayton Agreement, signed in Paris in December 1995, recognised Croatia's traditional borders and provided for the return of eastern Slavonia, a transition that was finally completed in January 1998.

Croatia's first president, Franjo Tuđman, died in 1999 after presiding over a regime notable for corruption, cronyism and suppression of dissent. The centre-left coalition that took power in 2000 swiftly made known their desire to enter the European mainstream but was left with serious economic problems. Although the road to privatisation has been bumpy and unemployment remains stubbornly high, the massive influx of tourists has provided an economic lifeline. The country's infrastructure has been much improved. Croatians are especially proud of the new highway linking Zagreb and Split that will eventually extend to Dubrovnik. Croatia is currently involved in negotiations preceding eventual membership in the EU and may join before the end of this decade. A major sticking point remains the return of Serbs who fled during the war. In many cases Croats have occupied their homes, and legal mechanisms to compensate returning refugees have proven cumbersome. Although membership in the EU was highly sought in the late 1990s, public opinion on the subject has become much more nuanced. Most Croatians can see the economic benefits of joining the EU, but there is increasing concern that Croatia's unique culture and way of life will become homogenised to meet EU standards.

## PEOPLE

Croatia has a population of roughly 4.5 million people. Before the war Croatia had a population of nearly five million, of which 78% were Croats and 12% were Serbs. Bosnians, Hungarians, Italians, Czechs, Roma and Albanians made up the remaining 10%. Today Croats constitute 89% of the population, as there was a large influx of Croats from other parts of the former Yugoslavia after the war. Now, slightly less than 5% of the population is Serb, followed by 0.5% Bosnians and about 0.4% each of Hungarians and Italians. Small communities of Czechs, Roma and Albanians complete the mosaic. Most Serbs live in eastern Croatia (Slavonia) where ethnic tensions between the Serbs and Croats run highest. The largest cities in Croatia are Zagreb (780,000), Split (188,700), Rijeka (144,000), Osijek (114,600) and Zadar (72,700).

Croats are united by a common religion, Catholicism, and a common sense of themselves as European. If you ask a Croat what distinguishes Croatian culture from Bosnian or Serbian culture, the answer is likely to be a variant of 'We are Western and they are Eastern'. Even Croats who bear no particular ill will towards other ethnicities will nonetheless note that their former compatriots in Bosnia and Hercegovina, Macedonia, Serbia and Montenegro eat different food, listen to different music, have different customs and, of course, go to different churches.

Although the shelling of Dubrovnik and the atrocities committed in eastern Slavonia and the Krajina have left a bitter taste in those regions, many Croatians are increasingly open to questioning the conduct of the 'Homeland War'. Self-examining books and articles are a staple of the country's intellectual life, but the extradition to The Hague of accused war criminal Ante Gotovina has been highly unpopular.

## RELIGION

Croats are overwhelmingly Roman Catholic, while virtually all Serbs belong to the Eastern Orthodox Church. In addition to doctrinal differences, Orthodox Christians venerate icons, allow priests to marry and do not accept the authority of the Roman Catholic pope. Long suppressed under communism, Catholicism is undergoing a strong resurgence in Croatia and churches have good attendance on Sundays. The Pope has visited Croatia several times and religious holidays are scrupulously observed. Muslims make up 1.2% of the population and Protestants 0.4%, with a tiny Jewish population in Zagreb.

## ARTS

The exhibition pavilion (p202) in Zagreb is a good place to keep up with the latest developments in Croatian art.

### Literature

Croatia's towering literary figure is 20th-century novelist and playwright Miroslav Krleža,who depicted the concerns of a changing Yugoslavia in novels such as *The Return of Philip Latinovicz* (1932). Long ignored by international publishing companies, contemporary Croatian authors are finally seeing their works translated into English. Dubravka Ugresic has written two noteworthy books, *The Ministry of Pain* and *The Museum of Unconditional Surrender,* dealing with the loss experienced by Croatians exiled by the 'Homeland War'. *Croatian Nights* is a lively anthology that mixes narratives by British and Croatian writers to offer a freewheeling look at Croatian life.

### Visual Arts

Vlaho Bukovac (1855–1922) was the most notable Croatian painter in the late-19th century. Important early-20th-century painters include Miroslav Kraljević (1885–1913) and Josip Račić (1885–1908). Post-WWII artists experimented with abstract expressionism but this period is best remembered for the naive art that was typified by Ivan Generalić (1914–92). Recent trends have included minimalism,

CROATIA

conceptual art and pop art. Contemporary artists that are attracting notice include the multimedia works of Andreja Kulunči and the installations of Sandra Sterle.

## Sculpture

The work of sculptor Ivan Meštrović (1883–1962) is seen in town squares throughout Croatia. Besides creating public monuments, Meštrović designed imposing buildings such as the circular Croatian History Museum (p202) in Zagreb. Both his sculptures and architecture display the powerful classical restraint he learnt from Auguste Rodin. Meštrovisč's studio in Zagreb (p202) and his retirement home at Split (p224) have been made into galleries of his work.

## Music & Dance

Croatian folk music has many influences. Roma-style violinists or players of the *tambura,* a three- or five-string mandolin popular throughout the country, accompany the *kolo,* a lively Slavic round dance where men and women alternate in the circle. The measured guitar-playing and rhythmic accordions of Dalmatia have a gentle Italian air.

A recommended recording available locally on CD is *Narodne Pjesme i Plesovi Sjeverne Hrvatske* (Northern Croatian Folk Songs and Dances) by the Croatian folkloric ensemble Lado. The 22 tracks on this album represent nine regions, with everything from haunting Balkan voices reminiscent of Bulgaria to lively Mediterranean dance rhythms. Traditional Croatian music has influenced other musicians, most notable the Croatian-American jazz singer Helen Merrill who recorded Croatian melodies on her album, *Jelena Ana Milcetic a.k.a. Helen Merrill.*

On the radio, you're likely to hear a lot of 'turbofolk': charged-up folk music that is widely popular throughout former Yugoslavia. Split-born Severina Vuckovic enjoys tremendous popularity along with Doris Dragović and Mirakul Gibonni.

## ENVIRONMENT
### The Land

Croatia is half the size of present-day Serbia and Montenegro in area and population. The republic swings around like a boomerang from the Pannonian plains of Slavonia between the Sava, Drava and Danube Rivers, across hilly central Croatia to the Istrian Peninsula, then south through Dalmatia along the rugged Adriatic coast.

The narrow Croatian coastal belt at the foot of the Dinaric Alps is only about 600km long as the crow flies, but it's so indented that the actual length is 1778km. If the 4012km of coastline around the offshore islands is added to the total, the length becomes 5790km. Most of the 'beaches' along this jagged coast consist of slabs of rock sprinkled with naturists. Don't come expecting to find sand, but the waters are sparkling clean, even around large towns.

Croatia's offshore islands are every bit as beautiful as those off the coast of Greece. There are 1185 islands and islets along the tectonically submerged Adriatic coastline, 66 of which are inhabited. The largest are Cres, Krk, Lošinj, Pag and Rab in the north; Dugi Otok in the middle; and Brač, Hvar, Korčula, Mljet and Vis in the south. Most are barren and elongated from northwest to southeast, with high mountains that drop right into the sea.

### National Parks

When the Yugoslav Federation collapsed, eight of its finest national parks ended up in Croatia, occupying nearly 10% of the country. Brijuni near Pula is the most carefully cultivated park, with well-preserved Mediterranean holm-oak forests. The mountainous Risnjak National Park near Delnice, east of Rijeka, is named after one of its inhabitants: the *ris* (lynx).

Dense forests of beech and black pine in the Paklenica National Park near Zadar are home to a number of endemic insects, reptiles and birds. The abundant plant and animal life (including bears, wolves and deer) in the Plitvice Lakes National Park between Zagreb and Zadar has warranted its inclusion on Unesco's list of World Natural Heritage Sites. Both Plitvice Lakes and Krka National Parks (near Šibenik) feature a dramatic series of cascades and incredible turquoise lakes.

The 101 stark and rocky islands of the Kornati Archipelago and National Park make it the largest in the Mediterranean. The island of Mljet near Korčula also contains a forested national park, and the North Velebit National Park includes Croatia's longest mountain range.

### Environmental Issues

The lack of heavy industry in Croatia has left the country largely free of industrial pollution, but its forests are under threat from acid rain from neighbouring countries. The dry summers and brisk *maestral* winds pose substantial fire hazards along the coast. The sea along the Adriatic coast is among the world's cleanest, especially throughout Istria and the southern Adriatic. Waste disposal is a pressing problem in Croatia, with insufficient and poorly regulated disposal sites.

# FOOD & DRINK

Croatian cuisine is one of the high points of a visit. Don't expect fancy sauces or elaborate presentation, although you can find them if you wish. It's the quality of the ingredients that gives each dish a special flavour boost. Most of Croatia's produce is home-grown and the fish is likely to come from local waters.

As you travel throughout the country, you'll notice sharp differences in local taste. Coastal cuisine reflects its Italian heritage with an emphasis on risotto, pasta and fish, usually grilled with a garlic sauce. Up north, the continental climate has induced a reliance on hearty meat and bean dishes.

Whatever your budget it's hard to get a truly bad meal anywhere in Croatia. The price and quality of meals vary little as there is an upper limit to what the local crowd can afford to pay, and a bottom to what they find acceptable. Croatians have little money for dining out, but when they do they expect the food to be worth it, which it usually is.

## Where to Eat & Drink

A *restauracija* or *restoran* (restaurant) is at the top of the food chain, generally presenting a more formal dining experience and an elaborate wine list. A *gostionica* or *konoba* is usually a simple, family-run establishment. The produce may even come from the family garden. A *pivnica* is more like a pub, with a wide choice of beer. Sometimes there's a hot dish or sandwiches available. A *kavana* is a café. The only food you're able to order in a *kavana* is cake and ice cream, but you can nurse your coffee for hours. A *slastičarna* serves ice cream, cakes, strudels and sometimes coffee but you usually have to gobble your food standing up, or take it away. Breakfast is usually consumed at home in Croatia (if it's consumed at all). In this chapter, hotel prices include breakfast, unless stated otherwise.

## Staples & Specialities

Croatian meals often start with a dish of locally smoked ham or Pag cheese with olives. A Zagreb speciality is *štrukli* (boiled cheesecake), served either plain as a starter or sugared as a dessert. In the north you also might begin with a hearty *Zagorska juha od krumpira* (potato soup Zagorje-style) or *manistra od bobića* (beans and fresh maize soup), while coastal folk follow the Italian habit of beginning with a serving of spaghetti or risotto. *Risotto neri* (black risotto) made from squid in its own ink is a particular delicacy.

For a main meal, the Adriatic coast excels in seafood, including scampi (look for *scampi bouzzara*), *prstaci* (shellfish), *lignje* (calamari) and Dalmatian *brodet* (fish stew served with polenta). Istria is known for its *tartufe* (truffles), which frequently appear in risotto or pasta dishes or as a flavouring for meat. In Zagreb and in the north you'll find exquisite spit-roasted goose, duck and lamb. Turkey with *mlinci* (baked noodles) is another Zagrebian wonder.

For fast food you can usually snack on *ćevapčići* (spicy beef or pork meatballs), *ražnjići* (shish kebab), *burek* (a greasy layered pie made with meat) or *sira* (cheese), which is cut on a huge metal tray.

It's customary to have a small glass of brandy before a meal and to accompany the food with one of Croatia's fine wines – there are about 700 to choose from! Croatians often mix their wine with water, calling it *bevanda*. Croatia is also famous for its *šljivovica* (plum brandies), *travarica* (herbal brandies), *vinjak* (cognacs) and liqueurs, such as maraschino (a cherry liqueur made in Zadar) or herbal *pelinkovac*. Italian-style espresso is popular in Croatia.

Zagreb's Ožujsko *pivo* (beer) is very good but Karlovačko *pivo* from Karlovac is even better. You'll probably want to practise saying *živjeli!* (Cheers!)

## Vegetarians & Vegans

Outside of Zagreb, vegetarian restaurants are few and far between but Croatia's vegetables and salads can be quite tasty. *Blitva* (Swiss chard) is a nutritious side dish often served with potatoes. Pasta, risotto and pizza are often made from scratch and lacto-ovo vegetarians will appreciate Croatia's wide variety of cheese. Look for the sharp lamb's-milk cheese from the island of Pag.

CROATIA

# ZAGREB

☎ 01 / pop 780,000

Too often overlooked by tourists making a beeline for the coast, Zagreb is a fascinating destination on its own, combining the best of Eastern and Western Europe. The sober Austro-Hungarian architecture in the town centre houses stylish boutiques, sleek cocktail bars and a smorgasbord of restaurants. The baroque buildings in the upper town are slowly being restored, lending Zagreb's oldest neighbourhood a look that recalls Prague.

Spoiled by a coastline that lies only three hours away, Zagreb's residents have a lively appreciation of the outdoors. Even in winter, the long, refreshing stretch of park that bisects the town centre is rarely empty. With the first breaths of spring, everyone heads to their favourite outdoor café to soak up the sun. On weekends, Maksimir Park in the east is a major destination for bikers, strollers and joggers.

No matter the weather, there's a wealth of diversions in Zagreb. A proper pub-crawl could take weeks; there's an assortment of museums and galleries to explore; regular concerts for the culturally minded; and enough fine shopping to max out a wallet of credit cards.

## HISTORY

Medieval Zagreb developed from the 11th to the 13th centuries in the twin villages of Kaptol and Gradec, which make up the city's hilly Old Town. Kaptol grew around St Stephen's Cathedral (now renamed the Cathedral of the Assumption of the Blessed Virgin Mary) and Gradec centred on St Mark's Church. The two hilltop administrations were bitter and often warring rivals until a common threat in the form of Turkish invaders emerged in the 15th century. The two communities merged and became Zagreb, capital of the small portion of Croatia that hadn't fallen to the Turks in the 16th century. As the Turkish threat receded in the 18th century, the town expanded and the population grew. It was the centre of intellectual and political life under the Austro-Hungarian empire and became capital of the Independent State of Croatia in 1941 after the German invasion. The 'independent state' was in fact a Nazi puppet regime in the hands of Ante Pavelić and the Ustaša movement, even though most Zagrebians supported Tito's partisans.

In postwar Yugoslavia, Zagreb took second place to Belgrade but continued expanding. The area south of the Sava River developed into a new district, Novi Zagreb, replete with the glum residential blocks that were a hallmark of postwar Eastern European architecture. Zagreb has been capital of Croatia since 1991 when the country became independent.

## ORIENTATION

The city is divided into Lower Zagreb, where most shops, restaurants and businesses are located, and Upper Zagreb, defined by the two hills of Kaptol and Gradec. As you come out of the train station, you'll see a series of parks and pavilions directly in front of you and the twin neo-Gothic towers of the cathedral in

---

### STREET NAMES

Particularly in Zagreb and Split, you may notice a discrepancy between the names used in this book and the names you'll actually see on the street.

In Croatian, a street name can be rendered either in the nominative or possessive case. The difference is apparent in the name's ending. Thus, Ulica Ljedevita Gaja (street of Ljudevita Gaja) becomes Gajeva ulica (Gaja's street). The latter version is the one most commonly seen on the street sign and used in everyday conversation. The same principle applies to a square (trg), which can be rendered as Trg Petra Preradovi'ća or Preradovićev trg. Some of the more common names: Trg svetog Marka (Markov trg), Trg Josipa Jurja Strossmayera (Strossmayerov trg), Ulica Andrije Hebranga (Hebrangova), Ulica Pavla Radića (Radićeva), Ulica Augusta Šenoe (Šenoina), Ulica Ivana Tkalčića (Tkalčićeva) and Ulica Nikole Tesle (Teslina). Be aware also that Trg Nikole Šubića Zrinjskog is almost always called Zrinjevac.

Also, at the end of a number of addresses in this chapter, you'll notice the letters 'bb' instead of a street number. This shorthand, which stands for bez broja (without a number), is used by businesses or other nonresidential institutions, indicating that it's an official place without a street number.

---

**ZAGREB IN TWO DAYS**

Start your day with a stroll through **Strossmayerov trg**, Zagreb's oasis of greenery. While you're there, take a look at the **Strossmayer Gallery of Old Masters** (p202) and then walk on to the town centre, Trg Josip Jelačića. Avoiding being hit by a tram as you cross the square, head up to Kaptol for a look at the centre of Zagreb's (and Croatia's) religious life, the **Cathedral of the Assumption of the Blessed Virgin Mary** (p202). As long as you're 'uptown', pick up some fruit at the **Dolac** (p202) fruit and vegetable market or have lunch at **Kaptolska Klet** (p204) and head over to Gradec for a church and museum tour. Don't miss **Meštrović's studio** (p202). Try the nightlife along **Tkalčićeva** (p205) and sup at **Baltazar** (p205).

On the second day, make a tour of the Lower Town museums, reserving a good two hours for the **Museum Mimara** (p203). Have lunch at **Boban** (p204) before tackling the **Archaeological Museum** (p202). Refresh yourself at the museum's outdoor café. Early evening is best at **Bulldog** (p205) before dining at one of the many scrumptious Lower Town restaurants and sampling some of Zagreb's nightlife.

---

Kaptol in the distance. Trg Jelačića, beyond the northern end of the parks, is the main city square of Lower Zagreb. The bus station is 1km east of the train station. Trams 2 and 6 run from the bus station to the train station, with tram 6 continuing to Trg Jelačića.

# INFORMATION

## Bookshops

**Algoritam** (Gajeva; Hotel Dubrovnik) Off Trg Jelačića, Algoritam has a wide selection of books and magazines to choose from in English, French, German, Italian and Croatian.

## Emergency

**Police station** ( ☎ 45 63 311; Petrinjska 30) Assists foreigners with visa problems.

## Internet Access

**Art Net Club** ( ☎ 45 58 471; Preradovićeva 25; per hr 20KN; ⏲ 9am-11pm) Zagreb's flashiest internet café, it frequently hosts concerts and performances.

**Sublink** ( ☎ 48 11 329; Teslina 12; per hr 20KN; ⏲ 9am-10pm Mon-Sat, 3-10pm Sun) It was here first and has a comfortable set up.

## Laundry

If you're staying in private accommodation you can usually arrange with the owner to do your laundry, which would be cheaper than the two options listed below. Five kilograms of laundry will cost about 60KN.

**Petecin** (Kaptol 11; ⏲ 8am-8pm Mon-Fri)

**Predom** (Draškovićeva 31; ⏲ 7am-7pm Mon-Fri)

## Left Luggage

**Garderoba** (per day 10KN; ⏲ 24hr) In the train station.

**Garderoba** (per hr 10KN; ⏲ 5am-10pm Mon-Sat, 6am-10pm Sun) In the bus station.

## Medical Services

**Dental Emergency** ( ☎ 48 28 488; Perkovčeva 3; ⏲ 24hr)

**KBC Rebro** ( ☎ 23 88 888; Kišpatićeva 12; ⏲ 24hr) East of the city, it provides emergency aid.

**Pharmacy** ( ☎ 48 48 450; Jelačića 3; ⏲ 24hr)

## Money

There are ATMs at the bus and train stations and the airport, as well as numerous locations around town. Exchange offices at the bus and train stations change money at the bank rate with 1.5% commission. Both the banks in the train station (open 7am to 9pm) and the bus station (open 6am to 8pm) accept travellers cheques. **Atlas Travel Agency** ( ☎ 48 07 300; Trg Nikole Šubića Zrinjskog 17) is the Amex representative in Zagreb.

## Post

**Main post office** ( ☎ 49 81 300; Branimirova 4; ⏲ 24hr Mon-Sat, 1pm-midnight Sun) Holds poste restante mail. This post office is also the best place to make long-distance telephone calls and send packages.

## Tourist Information

**Main tourist office** ( ☎ 48 14 051; www.zagreb -touristinfo.hr; Trg Jelačića 11; ⏲ 8.30am-8pm Mon-Fri, 9am-5pm Sat, 10am-2pm Sun) Distributes city maps and free leaflets. It also sells the Zagreb Card, which costs 90KN and includes 72 hours of free transport and a 50% discount on entry to museums.

**Marko Polo** ( ☎ 48 15 216; Masarykova 24) Handles information and ticketing for Jadrolinija's coastal ferries.

**National Parks Information Office** ( ☎ 46 13 586; Trg Tomislava 19; ⏲ 8am-4pm Mon-Fri) Has details on Croatia's national parks.

**CROATIA**

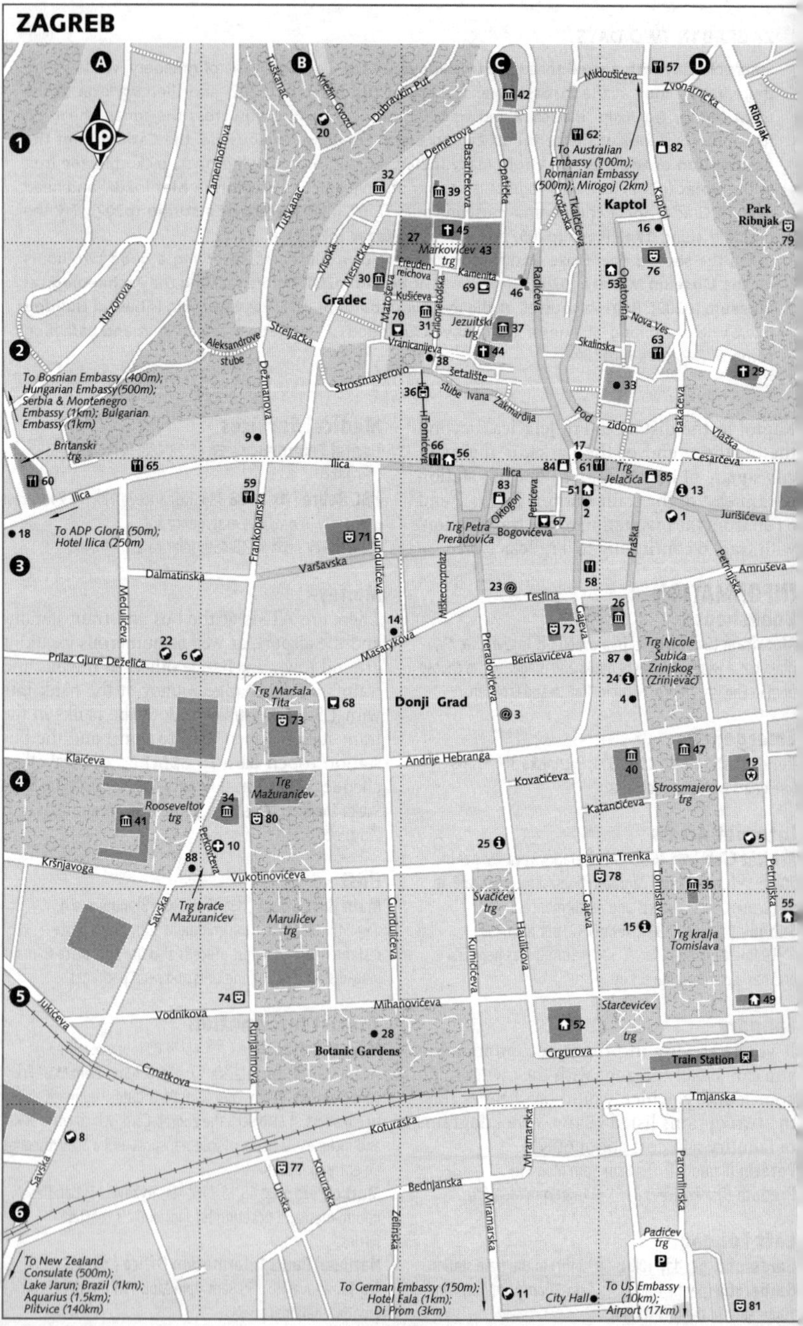

# ZAGREB

Kaptol

Park
Ribnjak

To Australian
Embassy (100m);
Romanian Embassy
(500m); Mirogoj (2km)

Gradec

Markovićev
trg

Freuden-
reichova

Kušlanova

Jezuitski
trg

Vranicanijeva

Šetalište
Ivana Zakmardija

Britanski
trg

To Bosnian Embassy (400m);
Hungarian Embassy (500m);
Serbia & Montenegro
Embassy (1km); Bulgarian
Embassy (1km)

Trg
Jelačića

Trg Petra
Preradovića

Bogovićeva

To ADP Gloria (50m);
Hotel Ilica (250m)

Dalmatinska

Varšavska

Trg Nicole
Šubića
Zrinskog
(Zrinjevac)

Trg Maršala
Tita

Donji Grad

Trg
Mažuranićev

Roosveltov
trg

Strossmayerov
trg

Trg braće
Mažuranićev

Marulićev
trg

Trg kralja
Tomislava

Starčevićev
trg

Botanic Gardens

Train Station

To New Zealand
Consulate (500m);
Lake Jarun; Brazil (1km);
Aquarius (1.5km);
Plitvice (140km)

To German Embassy (150m);
Hotel Fala (1km);
Di Prom (3km)

City Hall

To US Embassy
(10km);
Airport (17km)

Padićev
trg

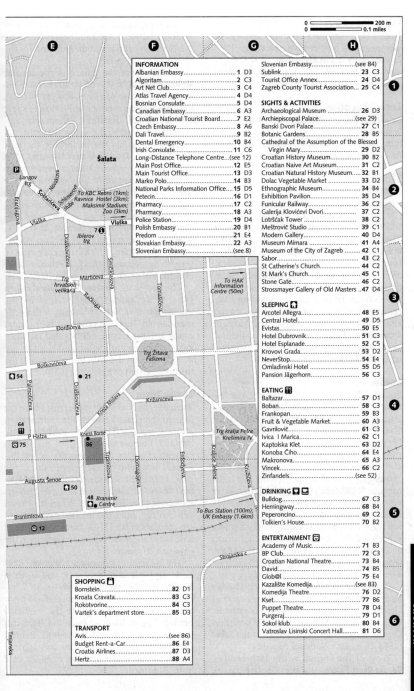

**INFORMATION**

| | | |
|---|---|---|
| Albanian Embassy | **1** | D3 |
| Algoritam | **2** | C3 |
| Art Net Club | **3** | C4 |
| Atlas Travel Agency | **4** | D4 |
| Bosnian Consulate | **5** | D4 |
| Canadian Embassy | **6** | A3 |
| Croatian National Tourist Board | **7** | E2 |
| Czech Embassy | **8** | A6 |
| Dali Travel | **9** | B2 |
| Dental Emergency | **10** | B4 |
| Irish Consulate | **11** | C6 |
| Long-Distance Telephone Centre | (see 12) | |
| Main Post Office | **12** | E5 |
| Main Tourist Office | **13** | D3 |
| Marko Polo | **14** | B3 |
| National Parks Information Office | **15** | D5 |
| Petecin | **16** | D1 |
| Pharmacy | **17** | C2 |
| Pharmacy | **18** | A3 |
| Police Station | **19** | D4 |
| Polish Embassy | **20** | B1 |
| Predom | **21** | C4 |
| Slovakian Embassy | **22** | A3 |
| Slovenian Embassy | (see 8) | |
| Slovenian Embassy | (see 84) | |
| Sublink | **23** | C3 |
| Tourist Office Annex | **24** | D4 |
| Zagreb County Tourist Association | **25** | C4 |

**SIGHTS & ACTIVITIES**

| | | |
|---|---|---|
| Archaeological Museum | **26** | D3 |
| Archiepiscopal Palace | (see 29) | |
| Banski Dvori Palace | **27** | C1 |
| Botanic Gardens | **28** | B5 |
| Cathedral of the Assumption of the Blessed Virgin Mary | **29** | D2 |
| Croatian History Museum | **30** | B2 |
| Croatian Naive Art Museum | **31** | C2 |
| Croatian Natural History Museum | **32** | B1 |
| Dolac Vegetable Market | **33** | D2 |
| Ethnographic Museum | **34** | B4 |
| Exhibition Pavilion | **35** | D4 |
| Funicular Railway | **36** | C2 |
| Galerija Klovićevi Dvori | **37** | C2 |
| Lotrščak Tower | **38** | C2 |
| Meštrović Studio | **39** | C1 |
| Modern Gallery | **40** | D4 |
| Museum Mimara | **41** | A4 |
| Museum of the City of Zagreb | **42** | C1 |
| Sabor | **43** | C1 |
| St Catherine's Church | **44** | C2 |
| St Mark's Church | **45** | C1 |
| Stone Gate | **46** | C2 |
| Strossmayer Gallery of Old Masters | **47** | D4 |

**SLEEPING**

| | | |
|---|---|---|
| Arcotel Allegra | **48** | E5 |
| Central Hotel | **49** | D5 |
| Evistas | **50** | E5 |
| Hotel Dubrovnik | **51** | C3 |
| Hotel Esplanade | **52** | C5 |
| Krovovi Grada | **53** | D2 |
| NeverStop | **54** | B4 |
| Omladinski Hotel | **55** | D5 |
| Pansion Jägerhorn | **56** | C3 |

**EATING**

| | | |
|---|---|---|
| Baltazar | **57** | D1 |
| Boban | **58** | C3 |
| Frankopan | **59** | B3 |
| Fruit & Vegetable Market | **60** | A3 |
| Gavrilović | **61** | C3 |
| Ivica I Marica | **62** | C1 |
| Kaptolska Klet | **63** | D2 |
| Konoba Čiho | **64** | E4 |
| Makronova | **65** | A3 |
| Vincek | **66** | C2 |
| Zinfandels | (see 52) | |

**DRINKING**

| | | |
|---|---|---|
| Bulldog | **67** | C3 |
| Hemingway | **68** | B4 |
| Peperoncino | **69** | C2 |
| Tolkien's House | **70** | B2 |

**ENTERTAINMENT**

| | | |
|---|---|---|
| Academy of Music | **71** | B3 |
| BP Club | **72** | C3 |
| Croatian National Theatre | **73** | B4 |
| David | **74** | B5 |
| Glob@l | **75** | E4 |
| Kazalište Komedija | (see 83) | |
| Komedija Theatre | **76** | D2 |
| Kset | **77** | B6 |
| Puppet Theatre | **78** | D4 |
| Purgeraj | **79** | D1 |
| Sokol klub | **80** | B4 |
| Vatroslav Lisinski Concert Hall | **81** | D6 |

**SHOPPING**

| | | |
|---|---|---|
| Bornstein | **82** | D1 |
| Kroata Cravata | **83** | C3 |
| Rokotvorine | **84** | C3 |
| Vartek's department store | **85** | D3 |

**TRANSPORT**

| | | |
|---|---|---|
| Avis | (see 86) | |
| Budget Rent-a-Car | **86** | E4 |
| Croatia Airlines | **87** | D3 |
| Hertz | **88** | A4 |

CROATIA

**Tourist Office Annex** ( ☎ 49 21 645; Trg Nikole Šubića Zrinjskog 14; ☽ 9am-5pm Mon-Fri) Same services as the main tourist office, but stocks fewer publications.

**Zagreb County Tourist Association** ( ☎ 48 73 665; www.tzzz.hr; Preradovićeva 42; ☽ 8am-4pm Mon-Fri) Has information about attractions in the region outside Zagreb.

## Travel Agencies

**Dali Travel** ( ☎ 48 47 472; travelsection@hfhs.hr; Dežmanova 9; ☽ 9am-5pm Mon-Fri) The travel branch of the Croatian YHA. Can provide information on HI hostels throughout Croatia and make advance bookings.

## SIGHTS
### Kaptol

Zagreb's colourful **Dolac vegetable market** ( ☽ 7am-2pm) is just up the steps from Trg Jelačića and continues north along Opatovina. The twin neo-Gothic spires of the 1899 **Cathedral of the Assumption of the Blessed Virgin Mary** (formerly known as St Stephen's Cathedral) are nearby. Elements of the medieval cathedral on this site (destroyed by an earthquake in 1880) can be seen inside, including 13th-century frescoes, Renaissance pews, marble altars and a baroque pulpit. The baroque **Archiepiscopal Palace** surrounds the cathedral, as do 16th-century fortifications constructed when the Turks threatened Zagreb.

### Gradec

From Ul Radićeva 5, off Trg Jelačića, a pedestrian walkway called stube Ivana Zakmardija leads to the **Lotrščak Tower** ( ☎ 48 51 768; admission 10KN; ☽ 11am-8pm Tue-Sun) and a **funicular railway** (one way 3KN; ☽ 6.30am-9pm) built in 1888, which runs every 10 minutes and connects the lower and upper towns. The tower has a sweeping 360-degree view of the city. To the east is the baroque **St Catherine's Church**, with Jezuitski trg beyond. The **Galerija Klovićevi Dvori** ( ☎ 48 51 926; Jezuitski trg 4; adult/student 40/30KN; ☽ 11am-7pm Tue-Sun) is Zagreb's premier exhibition hall where superb art shows are staged. Further north and to the east is the 13th-century **Stone Gate**, with a painting of the Virgin, which escaped a devastating fire in 1731.

Gothic **St Mark's Church** ( ☎ 48 51 611; Markovićev trg; ☽ 11am-4pm & 5.30-7pm) marks the centre of Gradec. Inside are works by Ivan Meštrović, Croatia's most famous modern sculptor. On the eastern side of St Mark's is the **Sabor** (1908), Croatia's National Assembly.

West of the church is the 18th-century **Banski Dvori Palace**, the presidential palace, with guards at the door in red ceremonial uniform. Between April and September there is a ceremony at noon at the weekend for the changing of the guard.

Not far from the palace is the former **Meštrović Studio** ( ☎ 48 51 123; Mletačka 8; adult/concession 20/10KN; ☽ 10am-6pm Tue-Fri, 10am-2pm Sat & Sun), now housing an excellent collection of some 100 sculptures, drawings, lithographs and furniture created by the renowned artist.

Other museums nearby include the less-than-gripping **Croatian History Museum** ( ☎ 48 51 900; Matoševa 9; temporary exhibitions adult/concession 10/5KN; ☽ 10am-5pm Mon-Fri, 10am-1pm Sat & Sun); the lively and colourful **Croatian Naive Art Museum** ( ☎ 48 51 911; Ćirilometodska 3; adult/concession 10/5KN; ☽ 10am-6pm Tue-Fri, 10am-1pm Sat & Sun); and also the **Croatian Natural History Museum** ( ☎ 48 51 700; Demetrova 1; adult/concession 15/7KN; ☽ 10am-5pm Tue-Fri, 10am-1pm Sat & Sun), which has a collection of prehistoric tools and bones plus exhibits on the evolution of plant and animal life in Croatia.

The best is the **Museum of the City of Zagreb** ( ☎ 48 51 364; Opatička 20; adult/concession 20/10KN; ☽ 10am-6pm Tue-Fri, 10am-1pm Sat & Sun), with a scale model of old Gradec, atmospheric background music and interactive exhibits that fascinate kids. Summaries in English and German are in each room of the museum, which is in the former Convent of St Claire (1650).

### Lower Town

Zagreb really is a city of museums. There are four in the parks between the train station and Trg Jelačića. The yellow **exhibition pavilion** (1897) across the park from the station presents changing contemporary-art exhibitions. The second building north, also in the park, houses the **Strossmayer Gallery of Old Masters** ( ☎ 48 95 117; adult/concession 10/5KN; ☽ 10am-1pm & 5-7pm Tue, 10am-1pm Wed-Sun). When it's closed you can still enter the interior courtyard to see the Baška Slab (1102) from the island of Krk, with one of the oldest inscriptions in the Croatian language.

The fascinating **Archaeological Museum** ( ☎ 48 73 101; Trg Nikole Šubića Zrinjskog 19; adult/concession 20/10KN; ☽ 10am-5pm Tue-Fri, 10am-1pm Sat & Sun) has a wide-ranging display of artefacts from prehistoric times through to the medieval period. The ambient sounds and light can put you in a contemplative mood. Behind the museum is a garden of Roman sculpture that is turned into a pleasant open-air café in the summer.

## West of the Centre

The **Museum Mimara** ( ☎ 48 28 100; Rooseveltov trg 5; adult/concession 20/15KN; ☉ 10am-5pm Tue, Wed, Fri & Sat, 10am-7pm Thu, 10am-2pm Sun) houses a diverse collection amassed by Ante Topić Mimara and donated to Croatia. Housed in a neo-Renaissance palace, the collection includes icons, glassware, sculpture, Oriental art and works by renowned painters such as Rembrandt, Velázquez, Raphael and Degas. The **Modern Gallery** ( ☎ 49 22 368; Andrije Hebrangova 1; adult/concession 20/10KN; 10am-6pm Tue-Fri, 10am-1pm Sat) presents temporary exhibitions that offer an excellent chance to catch up with the latest in Croatian painting. The new permanent exhibition provides a sampling of Croatian art from 1800 to 2000.

The neobaroque **Croatian National Theatre** (Trg Maršala Tita 15) dates from 1895 and has Ivan Meštrović's sculpture *Fountain of Life* (1905) in front. The **Ethnographic Museum** ( ☎ 48 26 220; Trg Mažurani'ćev 14; adult/concession 15/10KN; ☉ 10am-6pm Tue-Thu, 10am-1pm Fri-Sun) has a large collection of Croatian folk costumes, accompanied by English captions. To the south is the Art Nouveau **National Library** ( ☎ 61 64 111; ul Hrvatske bratske zajednice 4) from 1907. The **Botanic Gardens** (Mihanovićeva; admission free; ☉ 9am-7pm Tue-Sun) is attractive for its plants and landscaping, as well as its restful corners that are perfect for a family picnic.

## Out of Town

A 20-minute ride north of the city centre (on bus 106 from the cathedral) takes you to **Mirogoj** (Medvednica; ☉ 6am-10pm), one of the most beautiful cemeteries in Europe. The sculptured and artfully designed tombs lie beyond a majestic arcade topped by a string of cupolas. Don't miss the flower-bedecked tomb of Croatia's last president-dictator, Franjo Tuđman. Some Croats were very sad at his death, some were slightly sad and some wondered if the international community would have paid Croatia as much for his extradition to the war-crimes tribunal at the Hague as they paid Serbia for Milošević.

## TOURS

The main tourist office sells tickets for two-hour walking tours (95KN) and three hour combination walking/bus tours (150KN), which operate daily. The walking tours leave from the front of the tourist office on Trg Jelačića and the combination tours leave from the front of the hotel Arcotel Allegra. Tickets are on sale in tourist offices, travel agencies and most hotels and should be purchased at least one day in advance.

## FESTIVALS & EVENTS

During odd-numbered years in April there's the **Zagreb Biennial of Contemporary Music**, Croatia's most important music event. Zagreb also hosts a **Festival of Animated Films** (www.animafest.hr) during even-numbered years in June and a **Film Festival** (www.zagrebfilmfestival.com) in October. Croatia's largest international fairs are the Zagreb spring (mid-April) and autumn (mid-September) grand trade fairs. In July and August the **Zagreb Summer Festival** presents a cycle of concerts and theatre performances on open stages in the upper town. For a complete listing of Zagreb events, see www.zagreb-convention.hr.

## SLEEPING

The slow progression of tourism in Zagreb has not resulted in a corresponding increase in budget accommodation. Nor is there much in the way of small, centrally located family hotels. An early arrival is recommended, since private room-finding agencies are an attractive alternative and usually refuse telephone bookings. Prices for doubles run from about 250KN to 280KN and apartments start at 380KN per night for a studio. There's usually a surcharge for staying only one night.

### Budget

**Omladinski Hotel** ( ☎ 48 41 261; zagreb@hfhs.hr; Petrinjska 77; per person in 6-/3-bed dm 89/100KN, d 257.50KN) Some say it's a dump. We prefer to call it an auditory and visual challenge with maintenance issues. Checkout is at 9am, which makes sense because the only reason to stay here is if you have an extremely early train to catch.

**Ravnice Hostel** ( ☎ /fax 23 32 325; www.ravnice-youth-hostel.hr; Ravnice 38d; dm 125KN; ▯ ) This is really a delightful option, designed and run by an Australian woman. Comfortable, clean rooms have two, four or 10 beds. Solo female travellers would be most comfortable here. Trams 4, 7, 11 and 12 will bring you here.

**Krovovi Grada** ( ☎ 48 14 189; Opatovina 33; s/d/tr/q 200/300/450/600KN) If you yearn to stay in Zagreb's Upper Town, here's your chance. The restored older house is set back from the street and sleeps eight in two large apartments with shared bathroom. The amenities may be one-star but it's a five-star location within spitting distance of the restaurants and nightlife of Tkalčićeva.

Also recommended:

**Di Prom** ( ☎ 65 50 039; fax 65 50 233; Trnsko 25a; Mon-Sat) is south of the town centre with rooms in Novi Zagreb.

**Evistas** ( ☎ 48 39 554; fax 48 39 543; evistas@zg.t-com .hr; Augusta Šenoe 28; 9am-1.30pm & 3-8pm Mon-Fri, 9.30am-5pm Sat) is closest to the train station.

**NeverStop** ( ☎ 48 87 225; www.nest.hr; Boškovićeva 7; 9am-5pm Mon-Fri) has good deals on apartment rentals for a minimum three-night stay.

## Midrange

**Hotel Ilica** ( ☎ 37 77 522; www.hotel-ilica.hr, in Croatian; Ilica 102; s/d/tw/apt 399/499/599/849KN; P ) Zagreb is short on small hotels but this is a pretty good one for the price. Rooms are of various sizes but all are quiet and there's parking. Trams 6, 11 and 12 stop right outside the entrance.

**Hotel Fala** ( ☎ /fax 61 94 498; www.hotel-fala-zg.hr; Trnjanske ledine 18; s/d 400/541KN; P ) The small rooms have no frills but the price is right and you're not terribly far from the town centre.

**Central Hotel** ( ☎ 48 41 122; www.hotel-central.hr; Branimirova 3; s/d 550/720KN; ) Entirely renovated with modern, plush rooms, this hotel represents good value for money, especially given its location across from the train station. The service is coldly efficient.

**Pansion Jägerhorn** ( ☎ 48 33 877; www.hotel-pansion -jaegerhorn.hr; Ilica 14; s/d/apt 580/680/950KN; ) The downstairs restaurant is known for serving wild game, but there's no wildness in the civilised rooms here. Everything is up-to-date and well maintained.

**Hotel Dubrovnik** ( ☎ 48 73 555; www.hotel-dubrovnik .t-com.hr; Gajeva 1; s/d from 875/1350KN; ) Business travellers love this modern hotel right in the centre of town. Services, rooms and facilities are all first-rate.

## Top End

**Arcotel Allegra** ( ☎ 46 96 000; www.arcotel.at/allegra; Branimirova 29; d 816-1634KN; P ) Billing itself as Zagreb's first 'lifestyle hotel', it's clear that the style of life is quite high here. Your lifestyle, should you choose to accept it, will include ultra-contemporary Mediterranean-inspired décor, and a fitness centre, plus rooms and accoutrements for your business meetings. The hotel is gay-friendly.

**Hotel Esplanade** ( ☎ 45 66 666; www.regenthotels .com; Mihanovićeva 1; s/d 1660/2025KN; P ) This six-storey, 215-room hotel, built in 1924, is an Art Nouveau masterpiece with marble-panelled halls and stately rooms equipped with every comfort. There's also an in-house restaurant, Zinfandels (opposite). It was built next to the train station for the Agatha Christie crowd when simply everyone took the Orient Express, darling.

## EATING

As befits an up-and-coming international city, Zagreb presents a fairly wide array of culinary styles. Exotic spices are not part of the Croatian gastronomic vocabulary, but you can't go wrong with fish, pizza, pasta and roasted meats.

**Boban** ( ☎ 48 11 549; Gajeva 9; mains from 35KN) This Italian restaurant-bar-café offers superb pasta at good prices. It has an outdoor terrace and an indoor lounge with a bar and easy chairs that make it ground zero for after-work socialising. Relax over a drink upstairs and then head downstairs to try the gnocchi made from squid ink and topped with salmon sauce.

**Kaptolska Klet** ( ☎ 48 14 838; Kaptol 5; mains 55-70KN) This huge and inviting space is comfortable for everyone from solo diners to groups of noisy backpackers. Although famous for its Zagreb specialities such as grilled meats, spit-roasted lamb, duck, pork and veal as well as home-made sausages, it turns out a nice platter of grilled vegetables and a vegetable loaf.

**Makronova** ( ☎ 48 47 115; Ilica 72; mains 70KN; Mon-Sat) All very Zen, purely macrobiotic and more than welcome to those of the vegan persuasion. There's also shiatsu treatment, yoga classes and feng-shui courses.

**Ivica I Marica** ( ☎ 48 17 321; Tkalčićeva 70; mains from 40KN) Not exactly veggie, but with a good range of veggie and fish dishes plus meatier fare, this stylish restaurant also serves mouthwatering pastries in its adjoining café.

**Frankopan** ( ☎ 48 48 547; Frankopanska 8; mains 35-85KN) It's a gilt trip with chubby cherubs frolicking on the ceiling while you munch on relatively adventurous dishes. The prices are good because meals are prepared by a hostelry school.

**Konoba Čiho** ( ☎ 48 17 060; P Hatza 15; mains from 55KN; Mon-Sat) Tucked away downstairs, this cosy restaurant turns out a startling assortment of fish and seafood that's grilled, fried and combined in delicious stews.

**Baltazar** ( ☎ 46 66 824; Nova Ves 4; mains from 70KN; ✆ Mon-Sat) Duck, lamb, pork, beef and turkey are cooked to perfection here and served with a good choice of local wines.

**Zinfandels** ( ☎ 456 66 66; Mihanovićeva 1; mains 90-200KN; ✆ Mon-Sat) Here are the tastiest, most creative dishes in town served with polish in the dining room of the Hotel Esplanade, a world-class hotel.

For a simpler but still delicious dining experience, head to **Le Bistro** in the Esplanade. Don't miss the *strukli*. There's a **fruit and vegetable market** (Britanski trg; ✆ 7am-3pm) and you can pick up yummy fresh produce at the Dolac vegetable market (p202), and local cheese, smoked meat and cold cuts at nearby **Gavrilović** ( ✆ Mon-Sat). Slurp up dessert at **Vincek** ( ☎ 45 50 834; Ilica 18), famous for its ice cream.

## DRINKING

The architecture may be sober but the night-life definitely is not, especially as the weather warms up and Zagrebians take to the streets. In the upper town, there's the newly chic Tkalčićeva with a bevy of bars. In the lower town, there's bar-lined Bogovićeva, just south of Trg Jelačića, which turns into prime meet-and-greet territory each evening. Branimir Centre is a large shopping and entertainment complex that has a handful of shadowy bars with soft lighting, sleek furnishings and electronic music. The places listed below open around noon for café society and turn into bars around dinner time.

**Bulldog** ( ☎ 48 17 393; Bogovićeva 6) Belgian beer loosens up a crowd of young execs, sales reps, minor politicos and expats. As soon as the weather edges over the freezing mark, the overflow heads to the outdoor section where the tables and stools have commandeered the entire square.

**Tolkien's House** ( ☎ 48 51 776; Vranicanijeva 8) Get in touch with your inner Frodo at this cosy café-bar decorated in the style of JRR Tolkien's books. The hot chocolate is reputed to be the best in Zagreb.

**Brazil** ( ☎ 091 200 24 81; Veslačka bb) Parked on the Sava River, this bar on a boat refreshes a throng of thirsty revellers and offers occasional live music.

**Peperoncino** ( ☎ 48 51 343; Kamenita 5) After poking around the upper town, stop here to sample one of the excellent Croatian wines on offer.

**Hemingway** ( ☎ 48 34 956; Trg Maršala Tita) The main accoutrements you'll need here are black sunglasses and a mobile phone glued to your ear. Papa (the author, not the owner of this chain of bars) wouldn't be caught dead here but Zagreb's trendies couldn't care less.

## ENTERTAINMENT

Zagreb is a happening city. Its theatres and concert halls present a great variety of programmes throughout the year. Many (but not all) are listed in the monthly brochure *Zagreb Events & Performances*, which is available from the tourist office. Otherwise, drop in at Art Net Club (p199) and peruse the many flyers announcing breaking developments on the music scene.

### Discos & Clubs

The dress code is relaxed in most Zagreb clubs but neatness counts. The cover usually runs to 30KN and the action doesn't heat up until near midnight.

**Aquarius** ( ☎ 36 40 231; Ljubeka bb) On Lake Jarun, this is the night temple of choice for Zagrebians of all ages and styles. The design cleverly includes an open-air terrace on the lake and the sound is usually house. Take tram 17 to the Jarun stop.

**Purgeraj** ( ☎ 48 14 734; Park Ribnjak) A funky, relaxed space to listen to live rock, blues, rock-blues, blues-rock, country rock. You get the idea.

**Sokol klub** ( ☎ 48 28 510; Trg Maršala Tita 6) Across the street from the Ethnographic Museum, Sokol is fashionable without being snooty and the dance floor is always packed.

**BP Club** ( ☎ 48 14 444; Teslina 7; ✆ 5pm-1am) Famous for its high-quality musicians and occasional jam sessions, this is one of Zagreb's classic addresses.

**Kset** ( ☎ 61 29 999; Unska 3; ✆ 8pm-midnight Sun-Fri, 8pm-3am Sat) It's now practically certified as Zagreb's coolest club, running programs that range from cutting-edge jazz to the city's slickest DJs.

### Gay & Lesbian Venues

**David** ( ☎ 091-533 77 57; Marulićev trg 3) This new sauna, bar and video room is a popular spot on Zagreb's gay scene.

**Glob@l** ( ☎ 48 76 146; P Hatza 14) Internet café by day, on Wednesday, Thursday and Friday nights it's transformed into a club with relaxed, friendly vibes.

CROATIA

## Sport

Basketball is popular in Zagreb, and from October to April games take place in a variety of venues around town, usually on the weekend. The tourist office can provide you with the schedule.

Football (soccer) games are held every Sunday afternoon at the **Maksimir Stadium** (Maksimirska 128), on the eastern side of Zagreb; catch tram 4, 7, 11 or 12 to Bukovačka. If you arrive too early for the game, Zagreb's zoo is just across the street.

## Theatre

Rather than going to the individual venue, go to a small office marked 'Kazalište Komedija' in the Oktogon for theatre tickets; it's in the passage connecting Trg Petra Preradovića to Ilica 3.

**Croatian National Theatre** ( ☎ 48 28 532; Trg Maršala Tita 15; ☒ box office 10am-1pm & 5-7.30pm Mon-Fri, 10am-1pm Sat, 30 min before performances Sun) This neobaroque theatre was established in 1895. It stages opera and ballet performances.

**Komedija Theatre** ( ☎ 48 14 566; Kaptol 9) Near the cathedral, the Komedija Theatre stages operettas and musicals.

**Vatroslav Lisinski Concert Hall** ( ☎ ticket office 61 21 166; www.lisinski.fr; Trg Stjepana Radica 4; ☒ 9am-8pm Mon-Fri, 9am-2pm Sat) Just south of the train station, this concert hall is a prestigious venue where symphony concerts are held regularly.

Concerts also take place at the **Academy of Music** ( ☎ 48 30 822; Gundulićeva 6a) off Ilica. Another entertainment option is the **Puppet Theatre** (Baruna Trenka 3; ☒ performances 5pm Sat, noon Sun).

## SHOPPING

Ilica is Zagreb's main shopping street.

**Vartek's department store** (Trg Jelačića) You can get in touch with true Croatian consumerism at this department store.

**Kroata Cravata** (Oktogon) Croatia is the birthplace of the necktie (cravat); Kroata Cravata has locally made silk neckties at prices that run from 175KN to 380KN.

**Rokotvorine** (Trg Jelačića 7) This place sells traditional Croatian handicrafts, such as red-and-white embroidered tablecloths, dolls and pottery.

**Bornstein** ( ☎ 48 12 361; Kaptol 19) If Croatia's wine and spirits have gone to your head, get your fix at Bornstein, which presents an astonishing collection of brandy, wine and gourmet products.

## GETTING THERE & AWAY

### Air

For information about the flights to and from Zagreb, see p244 and p246.

### Bus

Zagreb's big, modern **bus station** ( ☎ 61 57 983; www.akz.hr, in Croatian) has a large, enclosed waiting room and a number of shops, including grocery stores.

The following domestic buses depart from Zagreb:

| Destination | Cost | Duration | Frequency |
| --- | --- | --- | --- |
| Dubrovnik | 170-196KN | 11hr | 7 daily |
| Korčula | 195KN | 12hr | 1 daily |
| Krk | 155KN | 4-5hr | 4 daily |
| Ljubljana | 90KN | 2½hr | 2 daily |
| Osijek | 104-144KN | 4hr | 8 daily |
| Plitvice | 55KN | 2½hr | 19 daily |
| Poreč | 133KN | 5hr | 6 daily |
| Pula | 125-183KN | 4-6hr | 13 daily |
| Rab | 140-166KN | 4½-5hr | 2 daily |
| Rijeka | 97-144KN | 2½-3hr | 21 daily |
| Rovinj | 141-206KN | 5-8hr | 8 daily |
| Split | 90-140KN | 5-9hr | 27 daily |
| Varaždin | 44KN | 1¾hr | 20 daily |
| Zadar | 65-165KN | 3½-5hr | 20 daily |

For international bus connections see p244.

### Train

The following domestic trains depart from **Zagreb train station** ( ☎ 06 03 33 444):

| Destination | Cost | Duration | Frequency |
| --- | --- | --- | --- |
| Osijek | 102KN | 4½hr | 4 daily |
| Pula | 119KN | 5½hr | 2 daily |
| Rijeka | 86KN | 3½hr | 5 daily |
| Split | 152KN | 5½-9hr | 6 daily |
| Varaždin | 50KN | 2½hr | 13 daily |
| Zadar | 143KN | 8hr | 4 daily |

All daily train services to Zadar stop at Knin. Reservations are required on fast InterCity (IC) trains and there's a supplement of 5KN to 15KN for travelling on fast or express trains.

For international train connections see p245.

## GETTING AROUND
### To/From the Airport
The Croatia Airlines bus to Zagreb airport, 17km southeast of the city, leaves from the bus station every half-hour or hour from about 5.30am to 7.30pm, depending on flights, and returns from the airport on about the same schedule (30KN). A taxi costs about 300KN.

### Car
Of the major car-rental companies, you could try **Budget Rent-a-Car** ( ☎ 45 54 936) and **Avis** ( ☎ 46 73 603) in the Hotel Sheraton, and **Hertz** ( ☎ 48 46 777; Vukotinovićeva 1). Prices are around 300KN per day. Zagreb is relatively easy to navigate by car but remember that the streets around Trg Jelačića and up through Kaptol and Gradec are pedestrian only. Watch out for trams sneaking up on you.

**Croatian Auto Club (HAK) Information Centre** ( ☎ 46 40 800; Derenčinova 20) helps motorists in need.

### Public Transport
Public transport is based on an efficient but overcrowded network of trams, though the city centre is compact enough to make them unnecessary. Trams 3 and 8 don't run on weekends. Buy tickets at newspaper kiosks for 6.50KN or from the driver for 8KN. Each ticket must be stamped when you board. You can use your ticket for transfers within 90 minutes but only in one direction.

A *dnevna karta* (day ticket), valid on all public transport until 4am the following day, is 18KN at most Vjesnik or Tisak news outlets. (See Tourist Information on p199 for details of the Zagreb Card.) Controls are frequent on the tram system with fines for not having the proper ticket starting at €30.

### Taxi
Zagreb's taxis ring up 7KN per kilometre after a flag fall of 19KN. On Sunday and from 10pm to 5am there's a 20% surcharge.

# ISTRIA

Sometimes called the 'new Tuscany', Istria (Istra to Croatians) is the heart-shaped 3600 sq km peninsula located just south of Trieste, Italy, with a landscape of green rolling hills, drowned valleys and fertile plains. The rugged and indented coastline is enormously popular with Italian tourists, who are comfortable with the excellent pasta and seafood on the menus of local restaurants and the fact that Italian is a second language for most Istrians.

The pronounced Italian influence dates from the days when the string of Istrian resorts was a part of Italy. Italy seized Istria from Austria-Hungary in 1918, was allowed to keep it in 1920, and then had to give it to Yugoslavia in 1947. Tito wanted Trieste (Trst) as part of Yugoslavia too, but in 1954 the Anglo-American occupiers returned the city to Italy so that it wouldn't fall into the hands of the 'communists'. Today the Koper–Piran strip belongs to Slovenia while the rest is held by Croatia. Visit Piran quickly, then move south to Pula, a perfect base from which to explore Poreč and Rovinj.

## POREČ
☎ 052 / pop 10,450
Sitting on a low, narrow peninsula on the western coast of Istria, Poreč ('Parenzo' in Italian) is the centre of a region dotted with sprawling tourist resorts. Even in the busy summer season, vestiges of the ancient Roman street plan make it well worth a stop. Don't miss the magnificent mosaics in the Euphrasian Basilica, a World Heritage site, before boating out to Sveti Nikola for a refreshing swim.

### History
The Romans called the town Parentium and made it an important administrative base, leaving their mark on the rectangular street plan, which is still evident. After the fall of Rome, Poreč came under the rule of the Byzantines and constructed the famous Euphrasian Basilica. It was later ruled by Venice, then Austria.

### Orientation
The compact old town is squeezed into the peninsula and packed with thousands of shops. The ancient Roman Dekumanus (a Roman longitudinal road) with its polished stones is still the main street, bisected by the latitudinal Cardo. Hotels, travel agencies and excursion boats are on the quay, Obala Maršala Tita, which runs from the small-boat harbour to the tip of the peninsula. The bus station is directly opposite the small-boat harbour just outside the old town.

## Information

### INTERNET ACCESS
**Internet Centre CyberMac** ( ☎ 427 075; Grahalića 1; per hr 42KN) A full-service internet and computer centre.

### LEFT LUGGAGE
**Garderoba** ( ☉ 6am-8pm Mon-Sat, 6am-5pm Sun) At the bus station.

### MEDICAL SERVICES
**Poreč Medical Centre** ( ☎ 451 611; Dr Mauro Gioseffi 2)

### MONEY
You can change money at any of the town's travel agencies. **Istarska Banka** (A Negrija 6) has an ATM.

### POST
**Main post office** (Trg Slobode 14) Has a telephone centre.

### TOURIST INFORMATION
**Tourist office** ( ☎ 451 293; www.istra.com/porec; Zagrebačka 11; ☉ 8am-10pm Mon-Sat year-round, 9am-1pm & 6-10pm Sun Jul & Aug)

### TRAVEL AGENCIES
**Atlas Travel Agency** ( ☎ 434 983; Eufrazijeva 63) Represents Amex.
**Di Tours** ( ☎ 432 100, 452 018; www.di-tours.hr; Prvomajska 2) Also finds private accommodation.
**Fiore Tours** ( ☎ /fax 431 397; fiore@pu.t-com.hr; Mate Vašića 6) Also handles private accommodation.
**Venezia Lines** ( ☎ 422 896; Boze Milanovica 20) Tickets and information for boats to Venice.

## Sights
The main reason to visit Poreč is to visit the 6th-century **Euphrasian Basilica** ( ☎ 431 635; admission free; ☉ 7.30am-8pm Apr-Sep, to 7pm Oct-Mar), which features some wonderfully preserved Byzantine gold mosaics. The sculpture and architecture of the basilica are remarkable survivors of that distant period. For 10KN you may visit the 4th-century mosaic floor of the adjacent early-Christian basilica or visit the baptistry and climb the bell tower for a spectacular view of the region.

The numerous historic sites in the old town include the ruins of two **Roman temples**, between Trg Marafor and the western end of the peninsula. Archaeology and history are featured in the **Regional Museum** ( ☎ 431 585; Dekumanus 9; adult/concession 10/5KN; ☉ 10am-noon & 6-8pm Jul & Aug, 10am-1pm rest of year) in an old

baroque palace. The captions are in German and Italian but there's an explanatory leaflet in English.

From May to mid-October there are passenger boats (20KN return) every half-hour to **Sveti Nikola**, the small island opposite Poreč Harbour that has wonderful swimming. The boats depart from the wharf on Obala Maršala Tita.

## Festivals & Events
Annual events in Poreč include the day-long **Folk Festival** (June) and the **Musical Summer** (May to September). Ask about these at the tourist office.

## Sleeping
All of the travel agencies listed on left find private accommodation. Expect to pay from 215/250KN for a room with shared/private bathroom in the high season, plus a 30% surcharge for stays less than three nights. There are a limited number of rooms available in the old town and it's wise to reserve far in advance for the July to August period.

### BUDGET
Camping grounds are large, well-organised little cities with plenty of activities. Take the 'Zelena Laguna' resort tourist train (20KN), which runs half-hourly or hourly from the town centre between April and October, or the boat shuttle. Prices in high season are about 55KN per person and 80KN for a camp site.

**Autocamp Zelena Laguna** ( ☎ 410 541) Well-equipped for sports, this autocamp can house up to 2700 people.

**Autocamp Bijela Uvala** ( ☎ 410 551) Housing up to 6000 people, the camping ground can be crowded.

### MIDRANGE
**Hotel Poreč** ( ☎ 451 811; www.hotelporec.com; s/d 535/816KN; ✖ ) Near the bus station and an easy walk from the old town, you'll find freshly renovated and comfortable rooms in this hotel.

**Hotel Neptun** ( ☎ 400 800; fax 431 531; Obala Maršala Tita 15; s/d 425/665KN; P ✖ ) This is the best hotel in the town centre, which is an advantage if you want to be in the centre of the action, but it also means being in the centre of a traffic snarl in peak season. The front rooms cost more, but they have an unbeatable harbour view.

**Hotel Hostin** ( ☎ 432112; www.hostin.hr; Rade Končara 4; s/d 710/1015KN; P ✗ ✗ 🖳 ☎ ) One of the newer entries on the hotel scene, this sparkling place is in verdant parkland just behind the bus station. An indoor swimming pool, fitness room and sauna are nice little extras, plus the hotel is only 70m from a pebble beach.

## Eating

**Nono** ( ☎ 435 088; Zagrebačka 4; pizzas 28-35KN) You can tell that Nono serves the best pizzas in town because it's always crowded. With soft, puffy crusts and fresh toppings, these pizzas are actually memorable.

**Konoba Ulixes** ( ☎ 451 132; Dekumanus 2; mains 40-100KN) Truffles are one of Istria's most precious products and you can taste them here in pasta, with beef or fresh tuna.

**Istra** ( ☎ 434 636; Milanovića 30; meals from 80KN) This is where locals go for a special meal. In addition to the usual offerings of grilled fish, spaghetti and calamari there are delicious local specialities such as a mixed seafood starter and *mučkalica*, stewed chicken and vegetables in a spicy sauce. There's a cosy interior and a covered terrace with wooden booths.

There is a large supermarket and department store next to Hotel Poreč, near the bus station.

## Drinking & Entertainment

**Caffe Lapidarium** (Svetog Mauro 10) The sound of Croatian crooners sails forth from the sound system while you relax in a large courtyard or antique-filled inner rooms. Wednesday night is jazz night in the summer when all sorts of groups turn up to play.

**Caffe Bar Torre Rotonda** (Narodni trg 3a) In the historic Round Tower, this upstairs café is a good spot to watch the action on the quays in a soft, jazzy atmosphere.

Most nightlife is out of town at Zelena Laguna where the big hotels host discos and various party nights. The closest party scene is 1km south of town at Gradsko Kupalište where the action centres on **Colonia Iulia Parentium**, an outdoor disco that spins house, ska, pop, rock, acid jazz and any other style that captures the DJ's fancy.

## Getting There & Away

From the **bus station** ( ☎ 432 153; Karla Hugesa 2), buses depart for Rovinj (30KN, one hour, seven daily), Zagreb (175, 4½ hours, six daily), Rijeka (63KN, 1½ hours, eight daily) and Pula (41KN, one hour, 12 daily). Between Poreč and Rovinj the bus runs along the Lim Channel, a drowned valley. To see it clearly, sit on the right-hand side if you're southbound, or the left if you're northbound.

The nearest train station is at Pazin, 30km east, which is connected by bus (26KN, 35 minutes, 12 daily).

For information about bus and boat connections to Italy and Slovenia see p244.

## ROVINJ
☎ 052 / pop 14,200

Despite the tsunami of tourism that threatens to engulf the town, Rovinj ('Rovigno' in Italian) retains shreds of its heritage as a Mediterranean fishing port. You can still watch fishermen haul their catch into the harbour in the early morning, followed by squawking gulls, and mend their nets before lunch. Prayers for a good catch are sent forth at the massive Cathedral of St Euphemia, whose 60m tower punctuates the peninsula. Wooded hills and low-rise luxury hotels surround a town webbed by steep, cobbled streets. The 13 green, offshore islands of the Rovinj archipelago make for pleasant, varied views and you can swim from the rocks in the sparkling water below Hotel Rovinj.

## Orientation & Information

The bus station is in the southeastern corner of the old town and there's an ATM next to the entrance, as well as the Autotrans Travel Agency, which will change money. Boats to Venice leave from the harbour northeast of the old town.

### INTERNET ACCESS

**@-mar(** ☎ 841 211; Carera 26; per hr 20KN) Conveniently located and modern.

### LAUNDRY

**Galax** ( ☎ 814 059; M Benussi; per 5kg 60KN) It may be pricey but at least you can get your clothes washed.

### LEFT LUGGAGE

**Garderoba** ( ⌚ 8am-9pm daily Jun-Sep, 8am-4pm Mon-Fri, 8am-2pm Sat Oct-May) At the bus station.

### MEDICAL SERVICES

**Ambulanta Rovinj** ( ☎ 813-004; Istarska ul bb)

### POST

**Main post office** (M Benussi 4) Across from the bus station, you can also make phone calls here.

## TOURIST INFORMATION

**Tourist office** ( ☎ 811 566; www.tzgrovinj.hr; Obala Pina Budicina 12; ☒ 8am-9pm Mon-Sat, 9am-1pm Sun Jun-Sep, 8am-3pm Mon-Fri, 8am-1pm Sat Oct-May) Just off Trg Maršala Tita, this office is less than a fount of information, and more of a trickle.

## TRAVEL AGENCIES

**Eurostar Travel** ( ☎ 813 144; Obala Pina Budicina 1) Has schedules and tickets for boats to Italy.

**Futura Travel** ( ☎ 817 281; futura-travel@pu.t-com.hr; M Benussi 2)

**Marco Polo** ( ☎ 816 616; www.marcopolo.hr; Istarska 2)

## Sights

The **Cathedral of St Euphemia** ( ☒ 10am-noon & 2-5pm), which completely dominates the town from its hilltop location, was built in 1736 and is the largest baroque building in Istria. It reflects the period during the 18th century when Rovinj was the most populous town in Istria, an important fishing centre and the bulwark of the Venetian fleet.

Inside the cathedral, don't miss the tomb of St Euphemia (martyred in AD 304) behind the right-hand altar. The saint's remains were brought from Constantinople in 800. On the anniversary of her martyrdom (16 September) devotees congregate here. A copper statue of her tops the cathedral's mighty tower.

Take a wander along the winding narrow backstreets below the cathedral, such as **Ul Grisia**, where local artists sell their work. Each year in August Rovinj's painters stage a big open-air art show in town.

Rovinj's **Regional Museum** ( ☎ 816 720; Trg Maršala Tita; adult/concession 15/10KN; ☒ 9am-noon & 7-10pm Tue-Sun mid-Jun–mid-Sep, 9am-1pm Tue-Sat rest of year) contains a collection of Italian painters from the 15th to 19th centuries. Unfortunately, the small size of the museum means that only a small percentage of its collection is on display at any given time.

When you've seen enough of the town, follow the waterfront south past Hotel Park to **Punta Corrente Forest Park**, which was established in 1890 by Baron Hütterodt, an Austrian admiral who kept a villa on Crveni Otok (Red Island). Here you can swim off the rocks, climb a cliff or just sit and admire the offshore islands.

## Activities

Most people hop aboard a boat for serious swimming, snorkelling and sunbathing. A trip to Crveni Otok or Sveti Katarina is easily arranged (see Tours, below). **Divers Sport Center** ( ☎ 816 648; www.diver.hr; Villas Rubin) is 3km south of Rovinj and specialises in wreck diving, especially the wreck of the *Baron Gautsch*, an Austrian passenger-steamer sunk in 1914 by an Austrian mine, causing 177 fatalities. The wreck lies in up to 40m of water and offers plenty of marine life.

## Tours

**Delfin Agency** ( ☎ 813 383), near the ferry dock for Crveni Otok, runs half-day scenic cruises to the Lim Channel for 130KN per person, or you can go with one of the independent operators at the end of Alzo Rismondo that run half-day and full-day boat trips around the region. There's an hourly ferry to the lovely and wooded Crveni Otok (20KN return) and a frequent ferry to nearby Katarina Island (10KN return) from the same landing. Get tickets on the boat or at the nearby kiosk. These boats only operate from May to mid-October.

## Festivals & Events

The city's annual events include the **Rovinj-Pesaro Regatta** (early May), **Rovinj Summer concert series** (July and August) and the **Grisia Art Market** on the 2nd Sunday of August. The tourist office has full details.

## Sleeping

All of the travel agencies listed on left can find private accommodation or you can book directly on www.inforovinj.com. Expect to pay from 215/250KN for a room with shared/private bathroom in the high season, plus a 50% surcharge for stays less than three nights. Guests who stay only one night are punished with a 100% surcharge, but you should be able to bargain the surcharge away outside of July and August. There are few rooms available in the old town however.

**Polari Camping** ( ☎ 800 376; per person/camp site 55/80KN) This spot is about 5km southeast of town and is much larger than Porton Biondi, but it also has more facilities.

**Porton Biondi** ( ☎ 813 557; per person 42.50KN) Less than a 1km from the town (on the Monsena bus route).

**Hotel Adriatic** ( ☎ 815 088; www.maistra.hr; s/d 500/935KN) Rovinj's only hotel right in the town centre is traditional on the outside and hyper-modern inside. The contrast can be jarring but the rooms are certainly comfortable.

**Vila Lili** ( ☎ 840 940; www.cel.hr/vilalili; Mohorovičiča 16; per person 390KN; 🕲 ) The comfort level at this small hotel is excellent, and includes satellite TV, a sauna and bright, modern rooms. It's just a short walk out of town past the marina.

**Hotel Villa Angelo D'Oro** ( ☎ 840 502; hotel.angelo @vip.hr; Via Svalba 38-42; s/d 823/1455KN; 🕲 ) This luxury hotel in a renovated Venetian building has plush, lavishly decorated rooms with satellite TV, minibar, and a free sauna and Jacuzzi room.

## Eating

Most of the fish and spaghetti places along the harbour cater to tourists.

**Kantinon** ( ☎ 811 970; Alzo Rismondo 18; fish mains from 40KN) The lack of an outdoor terrace has kept this local restaurant relatively tourist-free. The interior is enormous and furnished canteen-style, but the fish and seafood are always fresh.

**Veli Jože** ( ☎ 816 337; Sv Križ 1; mains 40-140KN) You can feast on a wide assortment of Istrian delicacies in an interior crammed with knick-knacks or at tables outside.

Picnickers can buy supplies at the supermarket about 25m downhill from the bus station or in one of the kiosks selling *burek* near the vegetable market.

## Getting There & Away

From the **bus station** ( 🕙 811 453; Trg na Lokvi 6), there' are buses to Poreč (30KN, one hour, five daily), Pula (28KN, 40 minutes, 13 daily), Rijeka (90KN, 3½ hours, two daily), Zagreb and Split (295KN, 11¼ hours), and one daily each to Dubrovnik (379KN, 17½ hours) and Ljubljana (155KN, 5½ hours, July and August). Prices and durations vary between different companies and routes.

The closest train station is Kanfanar, 19km away on the Pula–Divača line.

# PULA

☎ 052 / pop 62,400

Pula's star attraction is a remarkably well-preserved amphitheatre, but there is also a wealth of other Roman ruins to explore. Unlike other Istrian destinations, Pula (the ancient Polensium) has an economic life apart from tourism that lends the town an easygoing, small-town appeal. Nearby are some rocky, wooded peninsulas overlooking the clear Adriatic waters, which explain the many resort hotels and camping grounds circling the city. Most residents head out to Verudela Peninsula for the nightlife and swimming coves, but stay in town for one of the many events at the amphitheatre.

## Orientation

The bus station is 500m northeast of the town centre. The centre of town is Giardini, while the harbour is west of the bus station. The train station is near the water, about 500m north of town.

## Information

You can exchange money in travel agencies or at either of the post offices where there are ATMs.

**Atlas Travel Agency** ( ☎ 393 040; atlas.pula@atlas .hr; Starih Statuta 1) Finds private accommodation and organises tours.

**Enigma** ( ☎ 381 615; Kandlerova 19; per hr 20KN) Internet.

**Hospital** ( ☎ 214 433; Zagrebačka 30)

**Jadroagent** ( ☎ 210 431; jadroagent-pula@pu.t-com. hr; Riva 14) Has schedules and tickets for boats connecting Istria with Italy.

**Left luggage** (bus station; per hr 1.30KN)

**Main post office** (Danteov trg 4; 🕙 7am-8pm) You can also make long distance calls.

**Maremonti Travel Agency** ( ☎ 384 000; www .maremonti-istra.hr; bus station) Changes money, finds accommodation and rents cars.

**Tourist Information Centre** ( ☎ 219 197; www .pulainfo.hr; Forum 2; 🕙 9am-8pm Mon-Sat, 10am-6pm Sun) With knowledgeable and friendly staff, this centre provides maps, brochures and schedules of upcoming events in Pula and around Istria.

## Sights

Pula's most imposing sight is the 1st-century **Roman amphitheatre** ( ☎ 219 028; Flavijevska; adult/concession 20/10KN; 🕙 8am-9pm May-Sep, 8.30am-4.30pm Oct-Apr) overlooking the harbour and northeast of the old town. Built entirely from local limestone, the amphitheatre was designed to host gladiatorial contests and could accommodate up to 20,000 spectators. The 30m-high outer wall is almost intact and contains two rows of 72 arches. Around the end of July a Croatian film festival is held in the amphitheatre, and there are pop, jazz and classical events, often with major international stars, throughout summer.

The **Archaeological Museum** ( ☎ 218 603; Cararina 3; adult/concession 12/6KN; 🕙 9am-8pm Mon-Sat, 10am-3pm Sun May-Sep; 9am-3pm Mon-Fri Oct-Apr) is uphill

CROATIA

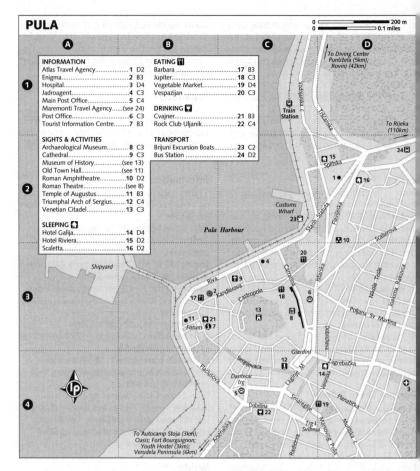

# PULA

0 — 200 m
0 — 0.1 miles

| INFORMATION | | |
|---|---|---|
| Atlas Travel Agency | 1 | D2 |
| Enigma | 2 | B3 |
| Hospital | 3 | D4 |
| Jadroagent | 4 | C3 |
| Main Post Office | 5 | C4 |
| Maremonti Travel Agency | (see 24) | |
| Post Office | 6 | C3 |
| Tourist Information Centre | 7 | B3 |

| SIGHTS & ACTIVITIES | | |
|---|---|---|
| Archaeological Museum | 8 | C3 |
| Cathedral | 9 | C3 |
| Museum of History | (see 13) | |
| Old Town Hall | (see 11) | |
| Roman Amphitheatre | 10 | D2 |
| Roman Theatre | (see 8) | |
| Temple of Augustus | 11 | B3 |
| Triumphal Arch of Sergius | 12 | C4 |
| Venetian Citadel | 13 | C3 |

| SLEEPING | | |
|---|---|---|
| Hotel Galija | 14 | D4 |
| Hotel Riviera | 15 | D2 |
| Scaletta | 16 | D2 |

| EATING | | |
|---|---|---|
| Barbara | 17 | B3 |
| Jupiter | 18 | C3 |
| Vegetable Market | 19 | D4 |
| Vespazijan | 20 | C3 |

| DRINKING | | |
|---|---|---|
| Cvajner | 21 | B3 |
| Rock Club Uljanik | 22 | C4 |

| TRANSPORT | | |
|---|---|---|
| Brijuni Excursion Boats | 23 | C2 |
| Bus Station | 24 | D2 |

To Diving Center
Puntižela (5km);
Rovinj (42km)

To Rijeka
(110km)

Train Station

Customs Wharf

*Pula Harbour*

Shipyard

*Riva*

*Kandlerova*

*Castropola*

*Forum*

*Giardini*

*Danteov trg*

*Dobrilina*

To Autocamp Stoja (3km);
Oasis; Fort Bourguignon;
Youth Hostel (3km);
Verudela Peninsula (6km)

---

from the town centre. Even if you don't visit the museum be sure to visit the large sculpture garden around it, and the **Roman theatre** behind the museum. The garden is entered through 2nd-century twin gates.

Along Istarska are Roman walls that mark the eastern boundary of old Pula. Follow these walls south and continue down Giardini to the **Triumphal Arch of Sergius** (27 BC). The street beyond the arch winds right around old Pula, changing names several times. Follow it to the ancient **Temple of Augustus** and the **old town hall** (1296).

The 17th-century **Venetian Citadel**, on a high hill in the centre of the old town, is worth the climb for the view if not for the meagre exhibits in the tiny **Museum of History** (Kaštel;

admission 7KN; ☷ 8am-7pm Jun-Sep, 9am-5pm Mon-Fri Oct-May) inside.

## Activities

**Diving Center Puntižela** ( ☎ 517 517; www.wreckdiving -croatia.com; Puntižela) offers wreck diving, diving around Brijuni National Park and a variety of other watery adventures.

## Tours

From the Pula waterfront, a number of excursion boats leave for he Brijuni ('Brioni' in Italian) islands, Tito's former summer residence. The islands are highly groomed habitats for exotic animals that Tito received as gifts. Zebras, gazelles and antelope wander through a park planted with some 680 species of plants. You may only visit Brijuni National Park with a group. Instead of booking an excursion with one of the travel agencies in Pula, Rovinj or Poreč, which costs 400KN, you could take a public bus from Pula to Fažana (8km), then sign up for a tour (140KN) at the **Brijuni Tourist Service office** ( ☎ 525 883) near the wharf. It's best to book in advance, especially in summer.

Also check along the Pula waterfront for excursion boats to Brijuni. The two-hour boat trips from Pula to Brijuni (150KN) do not actually visit the islands but only sail around them. Still, it makes a nice excursion.

## Sleeping

The tip of the Verudela Peninsula, about 6km southwest of the city centre, is a vast tourist complex with plenty of sprawling hotels that you can book through **Arena Turist** (www .arenaturist.hr).

The travel agencies listed under Information can find private accommodation, although there is little available in the town centre itself. Count on paying from 110KN per person for a double room and up to 430KN for an apartment.

**Autocamp Stoja** ( ☎ 387 144; fax 387 748; per person/ camp site & car 50/105KN; ⏲ Apr-Oct) Three kilometres southwest of the city centre, Autocamp Stoja is on a shady promontory, with swimming possible off the rocks. There are more camping grounds at Medulin and Premantura, which are coastal resorts southeast of Pula (take the buses heading southeast from town).

**Youth Hostel** ( ☎ 391 133; pula@hfhs.hr; camp sites/ B&B/half-board 72/118/154KN) Only 3km south of central Pula, this hostel overlooks a beach and is near one of the region's largest discos. Take the Verudela bus 2 or 7 to the 'Piramida' stop, walk back to the first street, then turn left and look for the sign. The rate for camping includes breakfast. You can rent tents for 11.25KN, year-round.

**Scaletta** ( ☎ 541 599; www.hotel-scaletta.com; Flavijeska 26; s/d 498/718KN; Ⓟ Ⓧ ) This hotel offers beautifully decorated and thoughtfully arranged rooms with every comfort accounted for. The hotel restaurant is also first rate.

**Hotel Galija** ( ☎ 383 802; www.hotel-galija-pula.com, Epulonova 3; s/d 555/732KN; Ⓟ Ⓧ ) This new and centrally located hotel is comfortably outfitted with modern rooms and facilities that include a sauna, internet access, satellite TV and minibars.

**Hotel Riviera** ( ☎ /fax 211 166; Splitska 1; d 685KN) Neither the service nor the comfort quite justifies the price (which eases in the low season) in this one-star hotel, but there is an undeniably appealing old-world elegance and the rooms are spacious. The front rooms have a view of the water and the wide shady hotel terrace is a relaxing place for a drink.

## Eating

The best local restaurants are out of town but the cheapest places are in the centre and the eating isn't bad. You'll have a number of choices along Kandlerova.

**Jupiter** ( ☎ 214 333; Castropola 38; mains from 28KN) This popular place serves up the best pizza in town and the pasta is good too.

**Vespazijan** ( ☎ 210 016; Amfiteatarska 11; mains from 35KN) This unpretentious spot conjures up yummy risottos and a variety of seafood dishes.

**Barbara** ( ☎ 219 317; Kandlerova 5; fixed-price menu from 40KN) It's your basic calamari and *čevapčići*, but well done and in a great people-watching location.

Self-caterers can pick up vegetables, cold cuts and local cheese at the morning vegetable market.

## Drinking & Entertainment

The streets of Flanatička, Kandlerova and Sergijevaca are lively people-watching spots, and the Forum has several outdoor cafés that fill up in the early evening.

**Cvajner** (Forum) The trendiest café-gallery in town, with a stunning, art-filled interior.

**Rock Club Uljanik** ( ☎ 217 218; Dobrilina 2) It's been around for a while, but is still attracting rockers with its mix of live and recorded music.

Posters around Pula advertise live performances at the amphitheatre or details of rave parties at two venues in Verudela: Oasis and Fort Bourguignon. Take bus 2 or 5 to the Piramida stop for these venues.

## Getting There & Away

### BOAT

For information about ferries to Italy, see Getting There & Away (p245).

### BUS

The buses that travel to Rijeka (61KN to 71KN, 2½ hours, 20 daily) are sometimes crowded, so be sure to reserve a seat in advance. Going from Pula to Rijeka, try to sit on the right-hand side of the bus for a stunning view of the Gulf of Kvarner.

Other destinations you can reach from the **bus station** ( ☎ 502 997; Istarske Brigade bb) include Rovinj (28KN, 40 minutes, nine daily), Poreč (40KN, one hour, 12 daily), Zagreb (152KN to 183KN, five hours, five daily), Zadar (204KN, seven hours, one daily), Split (315KN, 10 hours, one daily) and Dubrovnik (454KN, 15 hours, one daily).

### TRAIN
There are two daily trains to Ljubljana (125KN, four hours) and two to Zagreb (134KN, 6½ hours), but you must board a bus for part of the trip.

## Getting Around
The only city buses of use to visitors are bus 1, which runs to the camping ground at Stoja, and buses 2 and 7 to Verudela, which pass the youth hostel. Frequency varies from every 15 minutes to every 30 minutes, with service from 5am to 11.30pm daily. Tickets are sold at newsstands for 10KN and are good for two trips.

# GULF OF KVARNER

From big cities to islands to forested mountains, the Gulf of Kvarner ('Quarnero' in Italian) offers an incredible range of holiday experiences. Covering 3300 sq km between Rijeka and Pag Island in the south, the region is known for its mild climate and wide range of vegetation as well as a healthy sampling of seaside resorts.

The largest city is the busy commercial port of Rijeka, only a few kilometres from the aristocratic Opatija riviera. The large islands of Krk, Cres, Lošinj and Rab also have their share of admirers, who come for the luxuriant slopes dipping down to the sea.

## RIJEKA
☎ 051 / pop 144,000
Full of boats, cargo, fumes, cranes and the bustling sense of purpose that characterises most port cities, Rijeka ('Fiume' in Italian) has never been on anyone's 'must see' list. Yet, as a hub for the bus, train and ferry network that connects Istria and Dalmatia with

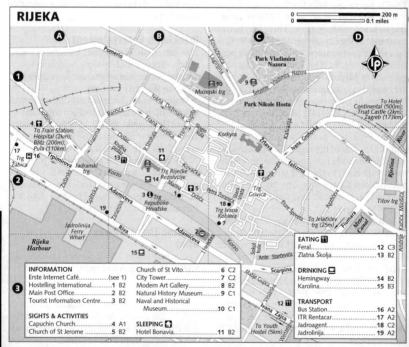

RIJEKA

0 ———— 200 m
0 ———— 0.1 miles

| INFORMATION | |
| --- | --- |
| Erste Internet Café | (see 1) |
| Hostelling International | 1 B2 |
| Main Post Office | 2 B2 |
| Tourist Information Centre | 3 B2 |

| SIGHTS & ACTIVITIES | |
| --- | --- |
| Capuchin Church | 4 A1 |
| Church of St Jerome | 5 B2 |
| Church of St Vito | 6 C2 |
| City Tower | 7 C2 |
| Modern Art Gallery | 8 B2 |
| Natural History Museum | 9 C1 |
| Naval and Historical Museum | 10 C1 |

| SLEEPING | |
| --- | --- |
| Hotel Bonavia | 11 B2 |

| EATING | |
| --- | --- |
| Feral | 12 C3 |
| Zlatna Školja | 13 B2 |

| DRINKING | |
| --- | --- |
| Hemingway | 14 B2 |
| Karolina | 15 B3 |

| TRANSPORT | |
| --- | --- |
| Bus Station | 16 A2 |
| ITR Rentacar | 17 A2 |
| Jadroagent | 18 C2 |
| Jadrolinija | 19 A2 |

Zagreb, Rijeka is nearly impossible to avoid. So enjoy the inevitable. With stately 19th-century buildings, a tree-lined promenade along the harbour and a smattering of museums and restaurants, there's plenty to do during the day and Rijeka's nightlife is about the best on the Croatian coast.

## Orientation

The bus station is south of the Capuchin Church in the centre of town. The Jadrolinija ferry wharf is just a few minutes east of the bus station. Korzo runs in an easterly direction through the city centre towards the fast-moving Rječina River.

## Information

### INTERNET ACCESS

There's free wireless access along Korzo.

**Erste Internet Café** ( ☎ 320 072; Korzo 22; per hr 20KN)

**Hotel Continental** (Andrije Kašića Miočića; per hr 10-15KN) This hotel east of town has a full bank of modern computers.

### LAUNDRY

**Blitz** (Krešimirova 3a; ☼ 7am-8pm Mon-Fri, 7am-1pm Sat) Situated between the bus and train stations, Blitz will do a small load of laundry for 60KN.

### LEFT LUGGAGE

**Garderoba** (per day 15KN; ☼ 5.30am-10.30pm) In the bus station.

**Garderoba** (per day 15KN; ☼ 24hr) In the train station.

### MEDICAL SERVICES

**Hospital** ( ☎ 333 333; Krešimirova 52)

### MONEY

There's an ATM at the train station, and the exchange offices adjacent to the train and bus stations keep long hours. There are a number of ATMs dotted along Korzo, as well as an exchange counter in the main post office.

### POST & TELEPHONE

**Main post office** (Korzo) Opposite the old City Tower, the post office also houses a telephone centre.

### TOURIST INFORMATION

**Hostelling International** ( ☎ 264 176; Korzo 22) Sells HI cards and is a good source of information about Croatian hostels.

**Tourist Information Centre** ( ☎ 335 882; www.tz-rijeka.hr; Korzo 33) Distributes *Rijeka Tourist Route,* a walking-tour guide that is so well produced it makes you actually want to stay and look around.

## Sights

Rijeka's main orientation point is the **City Tower** (Korzo), which was originally one of the main gates to the city, and is one of the few monuments to have survived the earthquake of 1750.

The **Modern Art Gallery** ( ☎ 334 280; Dolac 1; adult/concession 10/5KN; ☼ 10am-1pm & 5-9pm Tue-Sun) is in the upstairs scientific library opposite Hotel Bonavia. The **Naval & Historical Museum** ( ☎ 213 578; Muzejski trg 1; adult/student 10/1KN; ☼ 9am-1pm Tue-Sat) traces the development of sailing, with models and paintings of ships and portraits of the captains. The **Natural History Museum** ( ☎ 334 988; Lorenzov prolaz 1; adult/student 10/5KN; ☼ 9am-7pm Mon-Fri, 9am-2pm Sat) is devoted to regional geology and botany.

Also worth a visit is the 13th-century **Trsat Castle** (admission 15KN; ☼ 9am-11pm Tue-Sun Apr-Nov, 9am-3pm Tue-Sun Dec-Mar), which is on a high ridge overlooking Rijeka and the canyon of the Rječina River. If you have some more time to kill, stroll into some of Rijeka's churches, such as **Church of St Vito** (Trg Grivica 11), **Church of St Jerome** (Trg Riječke Rezolucije) or the ornate **Capuchin Church** (Trg Žabica), all open for Mass only.

## Sleeping

The tourist office can direct you to the few options for private accommodation, most of which are a few kilometres out of town on the road to Opatija. It's just as easy to go on to Opatija, where there are more and better choices for hotels and private accommodation (for details on getting to/from Opatija see p217).

**Youth Hostel** ( ☎ 406 420; rijeka@hfhs.hr; Šetalište XIII divizije 23; s/d/dm 260/342/142KN) Only four bus stops east of the town centre, this new hostel is comfortable and classy. It's in a renovated 19th-century villa and only has 60 beds. Reservations are advisable in the summer.

**Hotel Continental** ( ☎ 372 008; www.jadran-hoteli.hr, in Croatian; Andrije Kašića Miočića; s/d 390/455KN; P 및 ) This old building, northeast of the town centre, has spacious rooms that could use an overhaul.

**Hotel Bonavia** ( ☎ 333 744; www.bonavia.hr; Dolac 4; s/d from 775/965KN; P ✕ ✕ 및 및 ) The Bonavia is about the best four-star hotel in Croatia. It's in the centre of town and has all of the niceties that businesspeople on generous expense accounts find indispensable. Try to get a front room with a view over Rijeka's port.

## Eating

If you get hungry on Sunday, you'll have to head to one of the hotel restaurants, since nearly every restaurant in town will be closed.

**Feral** ( ☎ 212 274; Matije Gupca 5B; mains from 80KN) The marine theme runs strong here with slightly cheaper seafood than Zlatna Školja, but it's still beautifully prepared.

**Zlatna Školja** ( ☎ 213 782; Kružna prolaz 12; mains 100KN) The fetching maritime décor puts you in the mood to savour the astonishingly creative seafood dishes here. The wine list is also notable.

There are several 24-hour grocery stores in and around the bus station.

## Drinking

Ever since Croatia implemented a zero-tolerance approach to drink driving, Rijeka's nightlife has boomed. Young Rijekans used to go to Opatija to drink, but now no-one wants to take the chance of getting stopped on the route back. Bar-hoppers cruise along Riva or Korzo for the liveliest bars and cafés.

**Hemingway** ( ☎ 211 613; Korzo 28) With its wrought-iron chairs outside, this cocktail bar is hard to miss. The comfortable interior is a homage to its namesake, with large photos of The Bearded One on the wall and drinks named 'Hemingway's Tears'.

**Karolina** ( ☎ 330 909; Gar Karoline Riječke) During the day, it's a relaxed place to read a newspaper and have coffee. At night the crowds spill out onto the wharf in a huge outdoor party.

## Getting There & Away
### TO/FROM THE AIRPORT

Rijeka's airport is on Krk Island, 30km from town. For information on international flights to Rijeka see p244. Croatia Airlines' buses meet all flights and leave two hours before flight time from Jelačićev trg. The ticket is 18KN and you can buy it on the bus. A taxi costs about 250KN.

### BOAT

Croatia's national boat carrier **Jadrolinija** ( ☎ 211 444; www.jadrolinija.hr; Riva 16) has tickets for the large coastal ferries that run all year between Rijeka and Dubrovnik. For fares, see p246. For information on all boats to Croatia contact **Jadroagent** ( ☎ 211 276; Trg Ivana Koblera 2).

### BUS

If you fly into Zagreb, note that there is a bus connection directly from Zagreb airport to Rijeka. The bus leaves Zagreb daily at 3.30pm (145KN, two hours) and from Rijeka at 5am.

Other buses departing from Rijeka **bus station** ( ☎ 060 333 444; Trg Žabica) head for the following destinations:

| Destination | Cost | Duration | Frequency |
| --- | --- | --- | --- |
| Baška (Krk Island) | 56KN | 2hr | 2 daily |
| Dubrovnik | 391KN | 13hr | 2 daily |
| Krk | 43KN | 1½hr | 16 daily |
| Poreč | 59-94KN | 4½hr | 7 daily |
| Pula | 61-71KN | 2½hr | 7 daily |
| Rab | 103KN | 3hr | 2 daily |
| Rovinj | 90KN | 3hr | 2 daily |
| Split | 245-259KN | 8hr | 6 daily |
| Trieste | 50KN | 1½hr | 3 daily |
| Zadar | 145KN | 5hr | 6 daily |
| Zagreb | 87-144KN | 2½-3hr | 14 daily |

For international connections see p244.

### CAR

Close to the bus station, **ITR Rent a Car** ( ☎ 337 544; Riva 20) has rental cars for about 300KN per day.

### TRAIN

The **train station** (Ul Krešimirova) is a seven-minute walk west of the bus station. Five trains run daily to Zagreb (86KN, five hours). There's also daily train to Split that changes at Ogulin where you wait for two hours (152KN, 10 hours). Two of the three daily services to Ljubljana (94KN, three hours) require a change of trains at the Slovenian border and again at Bifka or Bistrica in Slovenia, but there is also one direct train. Reservations are compulsory on some *poslovni* (express) trains.

## OPATIJA
☎ 051 / pop 12,719

Fashionable 19th-century aristocrats came to 'take the waters' at Opatija, just a few kilometres due west of Rijeka. Although there are plenty of places to stretch out a towel and take a dip in the sea, Opatija is most famous for its Lungomare, a shady waterfront promenade that stretches for 12km along the

Gulf of Kvarner. And to rest your weary head, there's a wide choice of hotels with baroque exteriors and high-ceilinged plush interiors that offer good value for money.

## Information

There's no left-luggage facility at the bus station, which is in the town centre, but Autotrans Agency at the station will usually watch luggage.

**Atlas Travel Agency** ( ☎ 271 032; Maršala Tita 116) Arranges accommodation and excursions.

**Da Riva** ( ☎ 272 482; www.da-riva.hr; Maršala Tita 162) Finds private accommodation and organises group transfers to regional airports.

**Main post office** (Eugena Kumičića 2; ☺ 8am-7pm Mon-Sat) Behind the market.

**Tourist office** ( ☎ 271 310; www.opatija-tourism.hr; Maršala Tita 101; ☺ 8am-7pm Mon-Sat, 2-6pm Sun Jun-Sep, 9am-noon & 2-4.30pm Mon-Sat Oct-May) Has some information on local events.

## Activities

Opatija is not a museum-gallery kind of place. Come for the swimming in the coves along the Lungomare or just stroll the great seaside promenade. There's also hiking up Mt Učka. Head to the tourist office for details.

## Sleeping & Eating

Private rooms are abundant and reasonably priced. The travel agencies listed under Information have rooms starting at 150KN to 210KN, depending on the amenities.

The hotel scene is competitive and offers good value for money, especially outside of July and August. Most hotels are handled by **Liburnia Hotels** ( ☎ 710 300; www.liburnia.hr).

**Camping Opatija** ( ☎ 704 387; fax 704 112; Liburnjska 46, Ičići; per person/camp site 35/57KN; ☺ May-Sep) Right on the sea and only 5km south of town.

**Hotel Residenz** ( ☎ 271 399; www.liburnia.hr; Maršala Tita 133; s/d from 425/685KN) This place has stodgy but decent rooms in a classic building. You can use the swimming pool at the neighbouring Hotel Kristol and the Residenz is right on the sea. More expensive rooms with balconies are available.

**Hotel Kvarner** ( ☎ 271 233; www.liburnia.hr; s/d from 420/685KN; P ☒ ) This genteel 19th-century establishment has an indoor and outdoor swimming pool and easy access to the sea. The hotel oozes old-fashioned elegance and has more expensive rooms that have sea views and balconies.

Maršala Tita is lined with a number of decent restaurants offering pizza, grilled meat and fish. For a special meal, the best choice is **Bevanda** ( ☎ 712 769; Zert 8; mains from 70KN), located on the port, which has the freshest fish and a good wine list.

## Entertainment

An **open air-cinema** (Park Angiolina) screens films nightly and presents occasional concerts at 9.30pm from May to September. There are some bars around the harbour but Rijeka has a much more dynamic scene.

## Getting There & Away

The **Opatija bus station** (Trg Vladimira Gortana) is in the town centre. Bus 32 stops in front of the train station in Rijeka (11KN, 30 minutes) and runs right along the Opatija Riviera, west of Rijeka, every 20 minutes until late in the evening. If you're looking for accommodation, it's easiest to get off at the first stop and walk downhill, passing hotels and other agencies on the way to the bus station.

## KRK ISLAND

☎ 051 / pop 18,000

Croatia's largest island, Krk ('Veglia' in Italian) has two major attractions: the walled medieval town of Krk and Baška at the island's southern end, which has a 2km-long pebble beach. Krk is somewhat barren and rocky compared with other Croatian islands, but that hasn't stopped tourists from coming in droves. Many Zagreb residents have second homes on Krk and, as host to Rijeka's airport, the island attracts plenty of foreign visitors. Access is easy from the Rijeka airport, lying at the island's northern end.

Tiny Krk town has a compact medieval centre on a scenic port. From the 12th to 15th centuries, Krk town and the surrounding region remained semi-independent under the Frankopan Dukes of Krk, an indigenous Croatian dynasty, at a time when much of the Adriatic was controlled by Venice. This history explains the various medieval sights in Krk town, the ducal seat.

The bus from Baška and Rijeka stops by the harbour, a few minutes' walk from the old town of Krk. There's no left-luggage facility at Krk bus station. The **Turistička Zajednica** ( ☎ /fax 221 414; www.tz-krk.hr, in Croatian; Velika Placa 1; ☺ 8am-3pm Mon-Fri) is in the city wall's Guard Tower and there's a convenient **Tourist**

**Information Centre** (☎ 220 226; Obala Hrvatske Momarice bb; ☧ 9am-8pm Apr-Oct) in the centre of town. You can change money at any travel agency and there's an ATM in the shopping centre near the bus station. For internet surfing, head to **Sistemi** (☎ 222 999) at the bus station. The **hospital** (☎ 221-224) is at Vinogradska bb.

The lovely 14th-century **Frankopan Castle** and 12th-century Romanesque **cathedral** are in the lower town near the harbour. In the upper part of Krk town are three old **monastic churches**. The narrow streets of Krk are worth exploring.

## Sleeping & Eating

There is a range of accommodation in and around Krk, but many places only open during summertime. Private rooms can be organised through **Autotrans** (☎ 222 661; www.autotrans .hr) at the bus station. You can expect to pay from about 140/160KN for a single/double.

**Autocamp Ježevac** (☎ 221 081; per person/camp site 44/53KN; ☧ mid-Apr–mid-Oct) On the coast, a 10-minute walk southwest of Krk town, is this camping ground with easy sea access and merciful shade.

**Veli Jože** (☎ /fax 220 212; www.hfhs.hr; Vitezića 32; dm incl breakfast 145KN) There's nothing shabby at this hostel, located in a spruced-up older building and open year-round. Rooms have three, four or six beds.

**Hotel Dražica** (☎ 655 755; www.hotelikrk.hr; Ružmarinska 6; s/d 585/900KN; ℗ 🐾) A short walk from town along the coastal promenade, this hotel is modern, friendly and well run.

There are a number of restaurants around the harbour, but for something different try **Konobo Nono** (Krčkih iseljenika 8; mains from 45KN), which offers *šurlice* (homemade noodles topped with goulash), as well as grilled fish and meat dishes.

## Baška

At the southern end of Krk Island, Baška is popular for its 2km-long pebble beach set below a dramatic, barren range of mountains. Although crowded in summer, the old town and harbour make a pleasant stroll and there's always that splendid beach. The bus from Krk stops at the top of a hill on the edge of the old town, between the beach and the harbour.

The main street of Baška is Zvonimirova, which overlooks the harbour, while the beach begins at the western end of the harbour, and

continues southwards past a large sprawling hotel complex. The town's **tourist office** (☎ 856 544; www.tz-baska.hr; Zvonimirova 114; ☧ 8am-8pm daily mid-Jun–Sep, 8am-3pm Mon-Fri Oct–mid-Jun) is conveniently located just down the street from Baška's bus stop. To arrange hotels or camping, contact **Hoteli Baška** (☎ 656 801; www.hotelibaska.hr). For private accommodation, there's **Guliver** (☎ 856 004; www.pdm-guliver .hr; Zvonimirova 98).

### Getting There & Away

About five buses a day travel between Rijeka and Krk town (43KN, 1½ hours), and there are seven buses from Krk town to Baška (22KN, up to one hour). To go from Krk to Zadar, take one of the many buses to Kraljevica and then change to a southbound bus.

# DALMATIA

Occupying the central 375km of Croatia's Adriatic coast, Dalmatia offers a matchless combination of hedonism and historical discovery. The jagged coast is speckled with lush offshore islands that are making Dalmatia one of the world's hottest tourist destinations. Roman ruins, spectacular beaches, old fishing ports, medieval architecture and historic cities make a trip to Dalmatia (Dalmacija) unforgettable.

The dramatic coastal scenery is due to the rugged Dinaric Alps, which form a 1500m-long barrier that separates Dalmatia from Bosnia and Hercegovina. After the last Ice Age part of the coastal mountains were flooded, creating the sort of long, high islands seen in the Gulf of Kvarner. The deep, protected passages between these islands are a paradise for sailors and cruisers.'

Split is the largest city in the region and a hub for bus and boat connections along the Adriatic, as well as home to the late Roman Diocletian's Palace. Nearby are the early Roman ruins in Solin. Zadar has yet more Roman ruins and a wealth of churches. The architecture of Hvar and Korčula recalls the days when these places were outposts of the Venetian empire. None can rival majestic Dubrovnik, a cultural and aesthetic jewel.

## ZADAR

☎ 023 / pop 72,700

The main city of northern Dalmatia, Zadar (ancient Zara) is a booming regional centre with an ancient walled town at its core. Outside the massive 16th-century fortifications that shield its marble streets, a busy port receives shipping from Italy. Inside are Roman ruins, medieval churches and several fascinating museums. The town centre is usually crowded with shoppers dashing in and out of stores or relaxing in a café, but the tree-lined promenade along Obala kralja Petra Krešimira IV is perfect for a lazy stroll or a picnic. There are several small beaches east of the old town and a vast over-developed tourist complex crowding around the small beach of Borik, northwest of town.

## History
In the past 2000 years Zadar has escaped few wars; its strategic Adriatic coast position made it a target for the Romans, Byzantines, Venetians, Austro-Hungarians and Italians. Although damaged by Allied bombing in 1943 and 1944, and Yugoslav rockets in 1991, this resilient city has been rebuilt and restored many times. Some old flavour peeks out amid the modern buildings. Don't forget to sample Zadar's famous maraschino cherry liqueur.

## Orientation
The train station and the bus station are adjacent and are 1km southeast of the harbour and old town. From the stations, Zrinsko-Frankopanska ul leads northwest past the main post office to the harbour. Buses marked 'Poluotok' run from the bus station

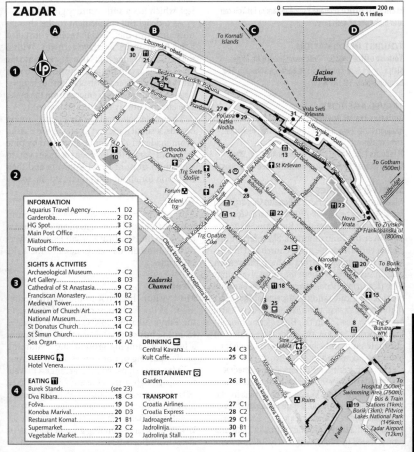

**ZADAR**

0 ———— 200 m
0 ———— 0.1 miles

To Kornati Islands

Jazine Harbour

Orthodox Church

Forum

Zeleni trg

Zadarski Channel

To Gotham (500m)

To Zrinsko-Frankopanska ul (800m)

To Borik Beach

Narodni trg

To Hospital (500m); Swimming Area (750m); Bus & Train Stations (1km); Borik (3km); Plitvice Lakes National Park (145km); Zadar Airport (12km)

**INFORMATION**
| | |
|---|---|
| Aquarius Travel Agency | 1 D2 |
| Garderoba | 2 D2 |
| HG Spot | 3 C3 |
| Main Post Office | 4 C2 |
| Miatours | 5 C2 |
| Tourist Office | 6 D3 |

**SIGHTS & ACTIVITIES**
| | |
|---|---|
| Archaeological Museum | 7 C2 |
| Art Gallery | 8 D3 |
| Cathedral of St Anastasia | 9 C2 |
| Franciscan Monastery | 10 B2 |
| Medieval Tower | 11 D4 |
| Museum of Church Art | 12 C2 |
| National Museum | 13 C2 |
| St Donatus Church | 14 C2 |
| St Šimun Church | 15 D3 |
| Sea Organ | 16 A2 |

**SLEEPING**
| | |
|---|---|
| Hotel Venera | 17 C4 |

**EATING**
| | |
|---|---|
| Burek Stands | (see 23) |
| Dva Ribara | 18 D3 |
| Fošva | 19 D4 |
| Konoba Marival | 20 D3 |
| Restaurant Kornat | 21 B1 |
| Supermarket | 22 C2 |
| Vegetable Market | 23 D2 |

**DRINKING**
| | |
|---|---|
| Central Kavana | 24 C3 |
| Kult Caffe | 25 C3 |

**ENTERTAINMENT**
| | |
|---|---|
| Garden | 26 B1 |

**TRANSPORT**
| | |
|---|---|
| Croatia Airlines | 27 C1 |
| Croatia Express | 28 C2 |
| Jadroagent | 29 C1 |
| Jadrolinija | 30 B1 |
| Jadrolinija Stall | 31 C1 |

CROATIA

to the harbour. Narodni trg is the heart of Zadar.

## Information

### INTERNET ACCESS
**HG Spot** ( ☎ 302 207; Stomorica 8; per hr 30KN)

### LEFT LUGGAGE
**Garderoba** (per day 15KN; ☼ 24hr) At the train station.
**Garderoba** (per day 15KN; ☼ 7am-9pm Mon-Fri) At the bus station.
**Garderoba** (per day 15KN; ☼ 7am-8pm Mon-Fri, 7am-3pm Sat) At the Jadrolinija dock.

### MEDICAL SERVICES
**Hospital** ( ☎ 315 677; Bože Peričića 5)

### POST & TELEPHONE
**Main post office** (Poljana Pape Aleksandra III) You can also make phone calls here.

### TOURIST INFORMATION
**Tourist office** ( ☎ 316 166; www.tzzadar.hr; Mihe Klaića 5; ☼ 8am-8pm Mon-Sat, 8am-1pm Sun Jun-Sep, 8am-6pm Mon-Sat Oct-May)

### TRAVEL AGENCIES
**Aquarius Travel Agency** ( ☎ /fax 212 919; www.jures koaquarius.hr; Nova Vrata bb) Arranges accommodation and excursions.
**Miatours** ( ☎ /fax 212 788; www.miatours.hr; Vrata Sveti Krševana) Arranges accommodation and excursions.

## Sights & Activities

Most attractions are near **St Donatus Church** (Šimuna Kožičića Benje; admission 6KN; ☼ 9.30am-1pm & 4-6pm Mar-Oct), a circular 9th-century Byzantine structure built over the Roman forum. Slabs for the ancient forum are visible in the church and there is a pillar from the Roman era on the northwestern side. In summer ask about the musical evenings here (featuring Renaissance and early baroque music). The outstanding **Museum of Church Art** (Trg Opatice Čike bb; adult/student 20/10KN; ☼ 10am-12.30pm daily, 5-8.30pm Mon-Sat), in the Benedictine monastery opposite St Donatus, offers three floors of elaborate gold and silver reliquaries, religious paintings, icons and local lacework.

The 13th-century Romanesque **Cathedral of St Anastasia** (Trg Svete Stošije) is only open for Mass, and has some fine Venetian carvings in the 15th-century choir stalls. The **Franciscan Monastery** (Zadarscog mira 1358; admission free; ☼ 7.30am-noon & 4.30-6pm) is the oldest Gothic church in Dalmatia (consecrated in 1280), with lovely interior Ren-

aissance features and a large Romanesque cross in the treasury (behind the sacristy).

The most interesting museum is the **Archaeological Museum** (Trg Opatice Čike 1; adult/student 10/5KN; ☼ 9am-1pm & 5-7 Mon-Sat), across from St Donatus, with an extensive collection of artefacts from the Neolithic period and Roman occupation to the development of Croatian culture under the Byzantines. Some captions are in English and you are handed a leaflet in English when you buy your ticket.

Less interesting is the **National Museum** (Poljana Pape Aleksandra III; admission 5KN; ☼ 9am-1pm Mon-Fri, plus 5-7pm Wed), just inside the sea gate, which features photos of Zadar from different periods and old paintings and engravings of many coastal cities. One church worth a visit is **St Šimun Church** (Šime Budinica; ☼ 8am-noon & 6-8pm Jun-Sep), which has a 14th-century gold chest.

As a delightful supplement to the church-museum-ruin diet, Zadar recently installed a **Sea Organ** on its northwestern tip. Within the perforated stone stairs that descend into the sea is a system of pipes and whistles. When the movement of the sea pushes air through pipes, strange, mournful tunes emerge from the holes. The effect is utterly unique and hypnotic.

There's a swimming area with diving boards, a small park and a café on the coastal promenade off Zvonimira. Bordered by pine trees and parks, the promenade takes you to a beach in front of Hotel Kolovare and then winds on for about a kilometre up the coast.

## Tours

Any of the many travel agencies around town can supply information on tourist cruises to the beautiful Kornati Islands, river-rafting and half-day excursions to the Krka waterfalls.

## Sleeping

Most visitors head out to the 'tourist settlement' at Borik, 3km northwest of Zadar, on the Puntamika bus (6KN, every 20 minutes from the bus station). Here there are hotels, a hostel, a camping ground, big swimming pools, sporting opportunities and numerous *sobe* (rooms) signs; you can arrange a private room through a travel agency in town (see left). Expect to pay about 185KN per person for a nice room with a bathroom.

**Autocamp Borik** ( ☎ 332 074; per person/camp site 35/47KN) This large camping ground is just steps away from Borik beach.

**Borik Youth Hostel** ( ☎ 331 145; zadar@hfhs.hr; Obala Kneza Trpimira 76; B&B/half-board 115/150KN) Friendly and well kept, this hostel is near the beach at Borik.

**Hotel Venera** ( ☎ 214 098, 098 330 958; Šime Ljubića 4a; d 300KN) If you want to stay in town, the only choice is this 12-room guesthouse in the heart of town, with small but tidy rooms with bathroom. The price does not include breakfast but there are plenty of cafés around where you can have your morning meal. If you can't reach the owner, the rooms can be reserved through Aquarius Travel Agency (opposite).

You can also try the **Hotel President** ( ☎ 333 464; www.hotel-president.hr; Vladana Desnice 16; s/d 1385/1616KN; P ⊠ 🖳 ) for four-star treatment near Borik beach.

## Eating

**Dva Ribara** (Blaža Jurjeva 1; mains from 45KN) With a wide range of food and an outdoor terrace, Dva Ribara is justifiably popular with the local crowd.

**Konoba Marival** ( ☎ 213 239; Don Ive Prodana 3; mains from 50KN) If your mama married a fisherman, she'd probably dream up the kinds of dishes that are served here. The ambience is also homy and intimate.

**Restaurant Kornat** ( ☎ 254 501; Liburnska obala 6; mains from 60KN) The polished wood floors and spiffy furnishings hint at the sophistication of the menu, which includes truffles from Istria, cheese from Pag and a full range of local and international specialties.

There's a **supermarket** (cnr Široka & Sabora) that is open long hours, and you'll also find a number of *burek* stands around the vegetable market.

## Drinking

In summer the many cafés along Varoška and Klaića place their tables on the street; it's great for people-watching. Elsewhere, **Central Kavana** (Široka) is a spacious café and hang-out with live music at the weekend, while **Kult Caffe** (Stomarica) draws a young crowd that listens to rap music indoors or relaxes on the large shady terrace outside.

## Getting There & Away

### AIR

Zadar's airport, 12km east of the city, receives charter flights and **Croatia Airlines** ( ☎ 250 101; Poljana Natka Nodila 7) flights from Zagreb daily.

A Croatia Airlines bus meets all flights and costs 20KN; a taxi into town costs around 175KN.

### BOAT

The **Jadrolinija** ( ☎ 254 800; Liburnska obala 7) office is on the harbour and has tickets for all local ferries, or you can buy ferry tickets from the Jadrolinija stall on Liburnska obala.

**Jadroagent** ( ☎ 211 447; jadroagent-zadar@zd.t-com .hr; Poljana Natka Nodila 4) is just inside the city walls and has tickets and information for all boats.

For information on boat connections to Italy see p245.

### BUS & TRAIN

Zadar is on the coastal route that goes from Rijeka down to Split and Dubrovnik. There are two fast trains to Zagreb (184KN, seven hours) and three slower trains (134KN, 9¾ hours) that change at Knin. The bus to Zagreb is quicker and many of them stop at Plitvice Lakes National Park (50KN to 70KN, three hours).

**Croatia Express** ( ☎ 250 502; Široka) sells bus tickets to many German cities.

## Around Zadar

### PLITVICE LAKES

**Plitvice Lakes National Park** (adult 55-100KN, student 30-60KN) lies midway between Zagreb and Zadar. The 19.5 hectares of wooded hills enclose 16 turquoise lakes, which are connected by a series of waterfalls and cascades. The mineral-rich waters carve new paths through the rock, depositing tufa (new porous rock) in continually changing formations. Wooden footbridges follow the lakes and streams over, under and across the rumbling water for an exhilaratingly damp 18km. Swimming is not allowed. Your park admission (prices vary by season) is valid for the entire stay and also includes the boats and buses you need to use to see the lakes. There is hotel accommodation only on site, and private accommodation just outside the park. Check the options with the National Parks information office in Zagreb (see p199).

Most buses from Zadar to Zagreb stop at Plitvice (50KN to 70KN, three hours). It is possible to visit Plitvice for the day on the way to or from the coast, but be aware that if they are full buses will not pick up passengers at Plitvice. Luggage can be left at the **tourist information** centres ( ☎ 053-751 015; www.np-plitvice.com; ⊗ 7am-8pm), located at each entrance to the park.

# SPLIT

☎ 021 / pop 188,700

As the largest Croatian city on the Adriatic coast and a major transport hub, Split ('Spalato' in Italian) is more exciting than relaxing. With a massive port sending ferries out to the Dalmatian islands and beyond, Split is a nearly obligatory stop on a Dalmatian visit. Although ringed with apartment-block housing of stupefying ugliness, the remarkable Diocletian's Palace (a World Heritage site) makes a visit to the city more than worthwhile. In the centre of town, within the ancient walls of Diocletian's Palace, rises the majestic cathedral surrounded by a tangle of marble streets containing shops and businesses. The entire western end of town is a vast, wooded mountain park with beaches below and pathways above. A refurbished harbourside promenade lined with cafés makes for a pleasant stroll, and the high coastal mountains set against the blue Adriatic provide a striking frame, best appreciated as your ferry heads into or out of the port.

## History

Split achieved fame when Roman emperor Diocletian (AD 245–313), who was noted for his persecution of the early Christians, had his retirement palace built here from 295 to 305. After his death the great stone palace continued to be used as a retreat by Roman rulers. When the neighbouring colony of Salona was abandoned in the 7th century, many of the Romanised inhabitants fled to Split and barricaded themselves behind the high palace walls, where their descendants continue to live to this day.

## Orientation

The bus, train and ferry terminals are adjacent on the eastern side of the harbour, a short walk from the old town. Obala hrvatskog narodnog preporoda, the waterfront promenade, is your best central reference point in Split.

## Information

### BOOKSHOPS

**Algoritam** (Map p224; Bajamontijeva 2) A good English-language bookshop.

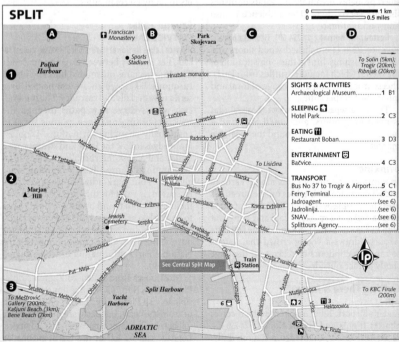

**SPLIT**

0 —————— 1 km
0 —————— 0.5 miles

SIGHTS & ACTIVITIES
Archaeological Museum..............1 B1

SLEEPING 🛏
Hotel Park................................2 C3

EATING 🍴
Restaurant Boban......................3 D3

ENTERTAINMENT 🎭
Bačvice.....................................4 C3

TRANSPORT
Bus No 37 to Trogir & Airport......5 C1
Ferry Terminal............................6 C3
Jadroagent...............................(see 6)
Jadrolinija................................(see 6)
SNAV.......................................(see 6)
Splittours Agency.....................(see 6)

CROATIA

## INTERNET ACCESS
**Mriža** (Map p224; ☎ 321 320; Kružićeva 3; per hr 20KN)

## LEFT LUGGAGE
**Garderoba** ( ⊙ 6am-10pm) At the bus station.
**Garderoba** (Obala Kneza Domagoja 6; ⊙ 7am-9pm)
The train station's left-luggage office is about 50m north of the station.

## MEDICAL SERVICES
**KBC Firule** ( ☎ 556 111; Spinčićeva 1) Split's hospital.

## MONEY
Change money at travel agencies or the post office. You'll find ATMs around the bus and train stations.

## POST & TELEPHONE
**Main post office** (Map p224; Kralja Tomislava 9; ⊙ 7am-9pm Mon-Sat) There's also a telephone centre here.

## TOURIST INFORMATION
**Hostelling International** (Map p224; ☎ 321 614; Domilijina 8) Sells HI cards and is a good source of information about Croatian hostels.
**Internet Games & Books** (Map p224; ☎ 338 548; Obala Kneza Domagoja 3) Luggage storage, information for backpackers, used books and an internet connection for 35KN per hour.
**Turist Biro** (Map p224; ☎ /fax 347 271; turist-biro -split@st.t-com.hr; Obala hrvatskog narodnog preporoda 12) Arranges private accommodation and sells guidebooks and the Split Card.
**Turistička Zajednica** (Map p224; ☎ /fax 345 606; www.visitsplit.com; Peristyle; ⊙ 9am-8.30pm Mon-Sat, 8am-1pm Sun) Has information on Split; sells the Split Card for 60KN, which offers free and discounted admission to Split attractions plus discounts on some car rentals, restaurants and hotels. It's valid for 72 hours.

## TRAVEL AGENCIES
**Atlas Travel Agency** (Map p224; ☎ 343 055; Trg Braće Radića 6) The town's Amex representative.
**Daluma Travel** (Map p224; ☎ /fax 338 484; www .daluma.hr; Obala Kneza Domagoja 1) Finds private accommodation.

## Sights & Activities
### DIOCLETIAN'S PALACE
The old town is a vast open-air museum and the information signs at the important sights explain a great deal of Split's history. **Diocletian's Palace** (Map p224; Obala hrvatskog narodnog preporoda 22), facing the harbour, is one of the most imposing Roman ruins in existence. It

was built as a strong rectangular fortress, with walls measuring 215m from east to west and 181m wide at the southernmost point, reinforced by square corner towers. The imperial residence, mausoleum and temples were south of the main street, now called Krešimirova, connecting the east and west palace gates.

Enter through the central ground floor of the palace. On the left are the excavated **basement halls** (adult/concession 6/3KN; ⊙ 10am-6pm), which are empty but still impressive. Go through the passage to the **peristyle**, a picturesque colonnaded square, with a neo-Romanesque cathedral tower rising above. The **vestibule**, an open dome above the ground-floor passageway at the southern end of the peristyle, is overpoweringly grand and cavernous. A lane off the peristyle opposite the cathedral leads to the **Temple of Jupiter**, which is now a baptistry.

On the eastern side of the peristyle is the **cathedral**, originally Diocletian's mausoleum. The only reminder of Diocletian in the cathedral is a sculpture of his head in a circular stone wreath, below the dome that is directly above the baroque white-marble altar. The Romanesque wooden doors (1214) and stone pulpit are notable. For a small fee you can climb the tower.

In the Middle Ages the nobility and rich merchants built their residences within the old palace walls; the Papalic Palace is now the **town museum** ( ☎ 344 917; Papalićeva ul 5; adult/concession 10/5KN; ⊙ 9am-9pm Tue-Fri, 10am-1pm Sat & Sun Jun-Sep, 9am-5pm Tue-Fri, 10am-1pm Sat & Sun Oct-May). It has a tidy collection of artefacts, paintings, furniture and clothes from Split; captions are in Croatian.

### OUTSIDE THE PALACE WALLS
The east palace gate leads to the market area. The west palace gate opens onto medieval Narodni trg, dominated by the 15th-century Venetian Gothic **old town hall**. The **Ethnographic Museum** (Map p224; ☎ 344 164; Narodni trg; adult/student 10/5KN; ⊙ 10am-1pm Tue-Sun Jun-Sep, 10am-4pm Tue-Fri, 10am-1pm Sat & Sun Oct-May) has a mildly interesting collection of photos of old Split, traditional costumes and memorabilia of important citizens; captions are in Croatian.

Trg Braće Radića, between Narodni trg and the harbour, contains the surviving **north tower** of the 15th-century Venetian garrison castle, which once extended to the water's edge.

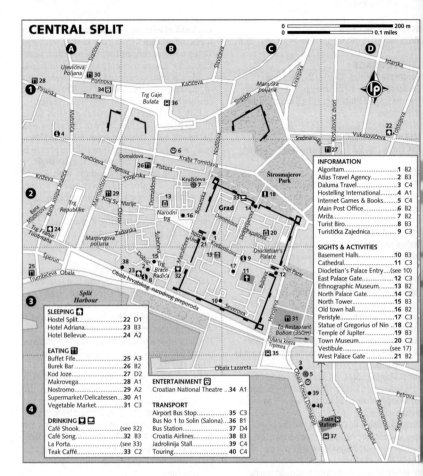

## CENTRAL SPLIT

**INFORMATION**
Algoritam.........................................**1** B2
Atlas Travel Agency...................**2** B3
Daluma Travel..............................**3** C4
Hostelling International............**4** A1
Internet Games & Books...........**5** C4
Main Post Office...........................**6** B2
Mriža.................................................**7** B2
Turist Biro......................................**8** B3
Turistička Zajednica...................**9** C3

**SIGHTS & ACTIVITIES**
Basement Halls...........................**10** B3
Cathedral......................................**11** C3
Diocletian's Palace Entry....(see 10)
East Palace Gate........................**12** C3
Ethnographic Museum.............**13** B2
North Palace Gate......................**14** C2
North Tower.................................**15** B3
Old town hall...............................**16** B2
Peristyle........................................**17** C3
Statue of Gregorius of Nin ...**18** C2
Temple of Jupiter.......................**19** B3
Town Museum.............................**20** C2
Vestibule..................................(see 17)
West Palace Gate ......................**21** B2

**SLEEPING**
Hostel Split...................................**22** D1
Hotel Adriana...............................**23** B3
Hotel Bellevue.............................**24** A2

**EATING**
Buffet Fife......................................**25** A3
Burek Bar.......................................**26** B2
Kod Joze........................................**27** D2
Makrovega.....................................**28** A1
Nostromo.......................................**29** A2
Supermarket/Delicatessen.....**30** A1
Vegetable Market.......................**31** C3

**DRINKING**
Café Shook.............................(see 32)
Café Song......................................**32** B3
La Porta..................................(see 33)
Teak Caffé.....................................**33** C2

**ENTERTAINMENT**
Croatian National Theatre ...**34** A1

**TRANSPORT**
Airport Bus Stop.........................**35** C3
Bus No 1 to Solin (Salona)...**36** B1
Bus Station....................................**37** D4
Croatia Airlines...........................**38** B3
Jadrolinija Stall............................**39** C4
Touring...........................................**40** C4

---

Go through the north palace gate to see Ivan Meštrović's powerful 1929 **statue of Gregorius of Nin**, a 10th-century Slavic religious leader who fought for the right to perform Mass in Croatian. Notice that his big toe has been polished to a shine; it's said that touching it brings you good luck.

### OUTSIDE CENTRAL SPLIT

The **archaeological museum** (Map p222; ☎ 318 720; Zrinsko-Frankopanska 25; adult/student 10/5KN; ☒ 9am-2pm Tue-Fri, 9am-1pm Sat & Sun), north of town, is a fascinating supplement to your walk around Diocletian's Palace and to the site of ancient Salona. The history of Split is traced from Illyrian times to the Middle Ages, in chronological order, with explanations in English.

The finest art museum in Split is **Meštrović Gallery** (Map p222; ☎ 310 800; Šetalište Ivana Meštrovića 46; adult/student 15/10KN; ☒ 9am-9pm Tue-Sun Jun-Sep, 9am-4pm Tue-Sat, 10am-3pm Sun Oct-May). You'll see a comprehensive, well-arranged collection of works by Ivan Meštrović, Croatia's premier modern sculptor, who built the gallery as his home from 1931 to 1939. Although Meštrović intended to retire here, he emigrated to the USA soon after WWII. Bus 12 runs to the gallery from Trg Republike every 40 minutes.

From the Meštrović Gallery it's possible to hike straight up **Marjan Hill**. Go up Ul Tonča Petrasova Marovića on the western side of the gallery and continue straight up the stairway to Put Meja ul. Turn left and walk west to Put Meja 76. The trail begins on the western side of this building. Marjan Hill offers trails through the forest to lookouts and old chapels.

### BEACHES

It's easy to hop on a bus to Omiš or a ferry to Brač, but there are a few bathing opportunities just outside the town centre. Try **Bačvice beach** (Map p222) in front of the entertainment complex (see p226). For less people and concrete, take bus 12 to **Kašjuni beach** at the foot of Marjan hill or go a little further to **Bene beach**, which is surrounded by pines.

## Tours

Atlas Travel Agency (p223) runs excursions to Krka waterfalls and Zlatni Rat beach on the island of Brač, as well as other excursions.

## Festivals & Events

The **Split Summer Festival** (mid-July to mid-August) features open-air opera, ballet, drama and musical concerts. There's also the **Feast of St Dujo** (7 May), a **flower show** (May) and the **Festival of Popular Music** (end of June).

## Sleeping

Private accommodation is the best bet for budget travellers, as hotels in Split are geared towards business travellers with deep pockets. You could go to one of the travel agencies listed on p223, but there are usually packs of women at the bus, train and ferry terminals ready to propose rooms to travellers. Prices rarely exceed 140KN for a room but you'll be sharing the bathroom with the proprietor.

**Hostel Split** (Map p224; ☎ 098 987 13 12; www .hostel-split.com; Vukasoviceva 21; dm 117KN [icon]) Only a short walk from Diocletian's Palace, this friendly, family-run hostel is in an appealing stone building. Check-in is between 2pm and 8pm.

**Hotel Bellevue** (Map p224; ☎ 347 499; www.hotel -bellevue-split.hr; Bana Josipa Jelačića 2; s/d 490/670KN) The Bellevue is an old classic that has seen better days. Rooms on the street side can be noisy, but the location is good and the somewhat faded rooms retain a certain charm. If you take a taxi from the port get ready for a long, meandering ride as the driver navigates the many one-way streets.

**Hotel Adriana** (Map p224; ☎ 340 000; www.hotel -adrianne.com; Obala hrvatskog narodnog preporoda 9; s/d 650/850KN; [icon]) This recent entry on the hotel scene has eight fresh rooms, some of which have a sea view. All are soundproofed.

**Hotel Park** (Map p222; ☎ 406 400; www.hotelpark-split .hr; Hatzeov perivoj 3; s/d 1060/1285KN; [P] [icon] [icon]) Close to the centre, this hotel nonetheless provides a resort experience with a large shady terrace and an easy walk to the beach. Rooms are nicely decorated and quite comfortable, although not large.

## Eating

**Buffet Fife** (Map p224; ☎ 345 223; Obala Ante Trumbića 11; mains from 45KN) Dragomir presides over a motley crew of sailors and misfits who drop in for the simple, savoury home cooking and his own brand of hospitality.

**Kod Joze** (Map p224; ☎ 347 397; Sredmanuška 4; mains from 40KN) A die-hard faction of locals keeps this informal *konoba* (a small, family-owned bistro) alive and kicking. It's Dalmatian all the way – ham, cheese and green tagliatelle with seafood.

**Restaurant Boban** (Map p222; ☎ 543 300; Hekto- rovićeva 49; mains from 60KN) The décor may be sober and traditional but this family-owned restaurant devotes considerable effort to keeping its menu up-to-date. The risotto is perfection and the angler wrapped in bacon, mouth-watering.

**Nostromo** (Map p224; ☎ 091 405 66 66; Kraj Sv Marije 10; mains from 65KN) Marine creatures of all persuasions form a delightful menu in this sweetly decorated spot next to the fish market.

**Makrovega** (Map p224; ☎ 394 440; Plinarska 12; [icon] 9am-7pm Mon-Fri, 9am-4pm Sat) Finally veggies and vegans have a place to call their own, at least for lunches and early dinners.

There's a spiffy **Burek Bar** (Map p224; Domaldova 13) near the main post office, and the vast **supermarket/delicatessen** (Map p224; Svačićeva 1) has a wide selection of meat and cheese for sandwiches. The vegetable market has a wide array of fresh local produce.

## Drinking

The bars, cafés and restaurants of the Bačvice complex (Map p222) are perennially popular food and watering holes for Split clubbers but there are also a few spots in the town centre. Try **Teak Caffé** (Map p224; Majstora Jurja 11) for a drink on the terrace during the day or more intense socialising at night. Le Porta, next door is renowned for its cocktails. Café Song and **Café Shook** (Map p224; Mihovilova Širina) are shoulder to shoulder with young Split-sters at night.

## Entertainment

In summer everyone starts the evening at one of the cafés along Obala hrvatskog narodnog preporoda and finishes up at one of the discos or clubs at Bačvice (Map p222). During winter, see some opera and ballet at the **Croatian National Theatre** (Map p224; Trg Gaje Bulata; best seats about 60KN); tickets for the same night are usually available. Erected in 1891, the theatre was fully restored in 1979 in the original style, and it's worth attending a performance for the architecture alone.

## Getting There & Away

### AIR

**Croatia Airlines** (Map p224; ☎ 362 997; Obala hrvatskog narodnog preporoda 8), runs flights between Zagreb and Split up to four times daily (475KN, one hour). For international flights to Split see p244.

### BOAT

You can buy tickets for passenger ferries at the **Jadrolinija stall** (Map p224; Obala Kneza Domagoja). There are also several agents in the large ferry terminal opposite the bus station that can assist with boat trips from Split: **Jadroagent** (Map p222; ☎ 460 999) represents companies with connec-

tions between Split and Ancona; **Jadrolinija** (Map p222; ☎ 338 333) handles all domestic car ferry services that depart from the docks around the ferry terminal; **Splittours Agency** (Map p222; ☎ 352 553) handles tickets between Ancona, Split and Hvar; and **SNAV** (Map p222; ☎ 322 252) has a four-hour connection to Ancona and Pescara.

For more details on connections to/from Italy see p245.

### BUS

Pre-booked tickets with seat reservations are recommended. Buses run from the main **bus station** (Map p224; ☎ 060 327 327; www.ak-split.hr, in Croatian) to the following destinations:

| Destination | Cost | Duration | Frequency |
| --- | --- | --- | --- |
| Dubrovnik | 118-123KN | 4½hr | 12 daily |
| Međugorje | 66-89KN | 3hr | 4 daily |
| Mostar | 65-95KN | 2-4hr | 8 daily |
| Pula | 315KN | 10hr | 3 daily |
| Rijeka | 245-259KN | 8hr | 14 daily |
| Sarajevo | 112-133KN | 6½hr | 5 daily |
| Zadar | 75-89KN | 3hr | 26 daily |
| Zagreb | 90-140KN | 5-9hr | 27 daily |

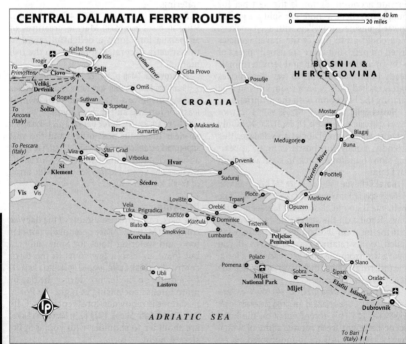

**CENTRAL DALMATIA FERRY ROUTES**

**Touring** (Map p224; ☎ 338 503; Obala Kneza Domagojeva 10), located just near the bus station, represents Deutsche Touring and sells tickets to German cities.

Bus 37 to Solin, Split airport and Trogir leaves from a local bus station on Domovinskog, about 1km northeast of the city centre (see Map p222).

### TRAIN
There are train connections from Split to Zagreb (152KN, 5½ to nine hours, six daily) and Zadar (78KN, six hours, four daily) through Šibenik.

## Getting Around
There's an airport bus stop on Obala Lazareta 3 (Map p224). The bus (30KN, 30 minutes) leaves about 90 minutes before flight times, or you can take bus 37 from the bus station on Domovinskog (11KN for a two-zone ticket).

A one-zone ticket costs 9KN for one trip in Central Split and bus services run approximately every 15 minutes from 5.30am to 11.30pm.

## SOLIN (SALONA)
The ruins of the ancient city of Solin (known as 'Salona' to the Romans), among the vineyards at the foot of mountains 5km northeast of Split, are the most interesting archaeological site in Croatia. Today surrounded by noisy highways and industry, Solina was the capital of the Roman province of Dalmatia from the time Julius Caesar elevated it to the status of colony. Solin held out against the barbarians and was evacuated only in AD 614 when the inhabitants fled to Split and neighbouring islands in the face of Avar and Slav attacks.

## Sights
A good place to begin your visit is at the main entrance, near Caffe Bar Salona. There's a small **museum and information centre** (admission 10KN; ☾ 9am-6pm Mon-Sat Jun-Sep, 9am-1pm Mon-Sat Oct-May) at the entrance, which also provides a helpful map and some literature about the complex.

**Manastirine**, the fenced area behind the car park, was a burial place for early Christian martyrs before the legalisation of Christianity.

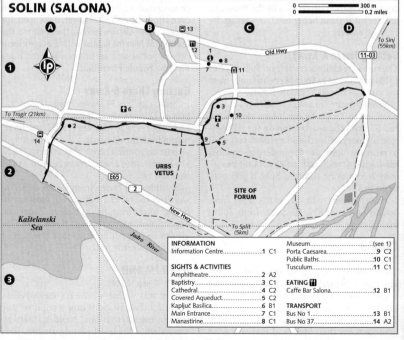

**SOLIN (SALONA)**

CROATIA

Excavated remains of the cemetery and the 5th-century basilica are highlights, although this area was outside the ancient city itself. Overlooking Manastirine is **Tusculum** with interesting sculptures embedded in the walls and in the garden.

The Manastirine-Tusculum complex is part of an archaeological reserve that can be freely entered. A path bordered by cypress trees runs south towards the northern city wall of Solin. Note the **covered aqueduct** along the inside base of the wall. The ruins in front of you as you stand on the wall were the early-Christian cult centre, which include the three-aisled, 5th-century **cathedral** and a small **baptistry** with inner columns. **Public baths** adjoin the cathedral on the eastern side.

Southwest of the cathedral is the 1st-century east city gate, **Porta Caesarea**, later engulfed by the growth of Solin in all directions. Grooves in the stone road left by ancient chariots can still be seen at this gate.

Walk west along the city wall for about 500m to **Kapljuč Basilica** on the right, another martyrs' burial place. At the western end of Solin is the huge 2nd-century **amphitheatre**, destroyed in the 17th century by the Venetians to prevent it from being used as a refuge by Turkish raiders.

### Getting There & Away

The ruins are easily accessible on Split city bus 1 that runs direct to Solin every half hour from the city bus stop at Trg Gaje Bulata.

From the amphitheatre at Solin it's easy to continue to Trogir by catching a westbound bus 37 from the nearby stop on the adjacent new highway. If, on the other hand, you want to return to Split, use the underpass to cross the highway and catch an eastbound bus 37 (buy a four-zone ticket in Split if you plan to do this).

Alternatively, you can catch most Sinj-bound buses (10KN, 10 daily) from Split's main bus station to take you to Solin.

## TROGIR

☎ 021 / pop 600

The profusion of Romanesque and Renaissance architectural styles within 15th-century walls, as well as the magnificent cathedral at the town centre, inspired Unesco to name Trogir a World Heritage site. It's a more manageable town than Split and makes a good

alternative place to stay given its proximity to Split airport.

### Orientation & Information

Trogir occupies a tiny island in the narrow channel lying between Čiovo Island and the mainland, and is just off the coastal highway. The heart of the old town is a few minutes' walk from the bus station. After crossing the small bridge near the station, go through the north gate. Trogir's finest sights are around Narodni trg to the southeast.

**Atlas** ( ☎ 881 374; www.atlas-trogir.com; Zvonimira 10) finds private accommodation, books hotels and runs excursions. There's a **left luggage office** (per day 13KN) in the bus station.

### Sights

The glory of the three-naved Venetian **Cathedral of St Lovro** (Trg Ivana Pavla II; �9.30am-noon year-round, plus 4.30-7pm during summer) is the Romanesque portal of *Adam and Eve* (1240) by Master Radovan, the earliest example of the nude in Dalmatian sculpture. Enter the building via an obscure back door to see the perfect Renaissance Chapel of St Ivan and the choir stalls, pulpit, ciborium (vessel used to hold consecrated wafers) and treasury. You can even climb the cathedral tower, if it's open, for a great view. Also located on the square is the **Church of St John the Baptist** with a magnificent carved portal and an interior showcasing a *Pietá* by Nicola Firentinac.

### Getting There & Away

In Split, city bus 37 leaves from the bus station on Domovinskog. It runs between Trogir and Split every 20 minutes (15KN, one hour) throughout the day, with a short stop at Split airport en route. There's also a ferry (35KN, 1½ hours) once a week from Split to Trogir (but not vice versa).

Southbound buses from Zadar (130km) will drop you off in Trogir, as will most northbound buses from Split going to Zadar and beyond. Getting northbound buses from Trogir can be more difficult, as they often arrive from Split already full.

## HVAR ISLAND

☎ 021 / pop 12,600

First it was yachts – now it's mega-yachts. Beautiful Hvar Island is now a required stop for restless international trend-spotters always alert to the latest island paradise. Hvar deserves the honour, for it is the sunniest and greenest of the Croatian islands. Called the 'Croatian Madeira', Hvar receives 2724 hours of sunshine each year. The stunning interior is a panorama of lavender fields, peaceful villages and pine-covered hills.

Between protective pine-covered slopes and the azure Adriatic, medieval Hvar town exudes more than a whiff of Venice. It was under Venetian rule that Hvar's citizens developed the fine stone-carving skills that resulted in a profusion of beautifully ornamented buildings. Hvar's wide harbour extends its open arms to the sea while a long seaside promenade, dotted with small rocky beaches, stretches from end to end. For more activity, hop on a launch to the Pakleni islands, famous for nude sunbathing.

## Orientation

Car ferries from Split deposit you in Stari Grad but local buses meet most ferries in summer for the trip to Hvar town. The town centre is Trg Sv Stjepana, 100m west of the bus station. Passenger ferries tie up on Riva, the eastern quay, in front of Pelegrini Travel.

## Information

**Atlas Travel Agency** ( ☎ 741 670) On the western side of the harbour.

**Clinic** ( ☎ 741 300; Sv Katarina) About 200m from the town centre, it's past the Hotel Pharos.

**Garderoba** ( ☒ 7am-midnight; 15KN) The left-luggage office is in the bathroom next to the bus station.

**Internet Leon** ( ☎ 741 824; Riva; per hr 30KN) Internet access next to the Hotel Palace.

**Pelegrini Travel** ( ☎ /fax 742 250; www.pelegrini-hvar .hr) Also finds private accommodation.

**Post office** (Riva) You can also make phone calls here.

**Tourist office** ( ☎ /fax 742 977; www.tzhvar.hr; ☒ 8am-1pm & 5-9pm Mon-Sat, 9am-noon Sun Jun-Sep, 8am-2pm Mon-Sat Oct-May) In the arsenal building on the corner of Trg Sv Stjepana.

## Sights & Activities

The full flavour of medieval Hvar is best savoured on the backstreets of the old town. At each end of Hvar is a monastery with a prominent tower. The Dominican **Church of St Marko** at the head of the bay was largely destroyed by Turks in the 16th century, but you can visit the local **archaeological museum** (admission 10KN; ☒ 10am-noon & 8-11pm Jun-Sep) in the ruins. If it is closed you'll still get a good view of the ruins from the road just above, which

leads up to a stone cross on a hill top offering a picture-postcard view of Hvar.

At the southeastern end of Hvar you'll find the 15th-century Renaissance **Franciscan Monastery** ( ☒ 9am-noon & 5-7pm Jun-Sep, Christmas week & Holy Week), with a wonderful collection of Venetian paintings in the church and adjacent **museum** (admission 15KN; ☒ 9am-noon & 5-7pm Mon-Sat Jun-Sep), including *The Last Supper* by Matteo Ingoli.

Smack in the middle of Hvar is the imposing Gothic **Arsenal**, its great arch visible from afar. The local commune's war galley was once kept here. Upstairs off the arsenal terrace is Hvar's prize: the first **municipal theatre** (admission incl entry to art gallery 15KN; ☒ 10am-noon & 5-7pm) in Europe (1612), rebuilt in the 19th century. Hours can vary and you enter through the adjoining **Gallery of Contemporary Croatian Art** (Arsenal; ☒ 10am-noon & 7-11pm Jun-Sep, Christmas week & Holy Week, 10am-noon Oct-May).

On the hill high above Hvar town is a **Venetian fortress** (1551), and it's worth the climb up to appreciate the sweeping panoramic views. The fort was built to defend Hvar from the Turks, who sacked the town in 1539 and 1571.

There is a small town beach next to the Franciscan Monastery, but the best beach is in front of the Hotel Amphora, around the western corner of the cove. Most people take a launch to the offshore islands that include the naturist Pakleni islands of Jerolim and Stipanska and lovely Palmižana.

In front of the Hotel Amphora, **Diving Centar Viking** ( ☎ 742 529; www.viking-diving.com) is a large operation in Podstine that offers a certification course, dives (€30) and hotel packages.

## Sleeping

Accommodation in Hvar is extremely tight in July and August: a reservation is highly recommended. For private accommodation, try Atlas or Pelegrini (left). Expect to pay from 200KN to 375KN per double with private bathroom. At the time of writing, several Hvar hotels were in the process of renovation. See www.suncanihvar.hr for the latest information.

**Jagoda & Ante Bracanović Guesthouse** ( ☎ 741 416, 091 520 37 96; virgilye@yahoo.com; Poviše Škole; s 100-120KN, d 190-220KN) This friendly place is close to the town centre and offers six spacious rooms, each with a bathroom, balcony and kitchen access.

CROATIA

**Hotel Croatia** ( ☎ 742 400; www.hotelcroatia.net; Majerovica bb; s/d from 700/1000KN; P ☐ ) The bright, white rooms are summery and cooled by fans, and the grounds surrounding the hotel are filled with greenery. More expensive rooms have views of the sea.

**Hotel Podstine** ( ☎ 740 000; www.podstine.com; s/d from 410/930KN; P ☒ ) Just 2km southwest of the town centre on the secluded Podstine cove lies this restored hotel with modern and comfortable facilities. If you opt out of one of the pricier rooms with a sea view, you can still enjoy the hotel's private beach.

## Eating

The pizzerias along the harbour offer predictable but inexpensive eating.

**Konoba Menego** ( ☎ 742 036; mains 80KN) Located on the stairway over the Benedictine convent, this eatery is a good choice.

**Bounty** ( ☎ 742 565; fixed-price menu 55KN) This place is a long-time favourite for its succulent fish, pasta and meat dishes at prices geared more to modest local incomes than free-spending tourists.

**Macondo** ( ☎ 742 850; mains from 80KN) Head upstairs from the northern side of Trg Sv Stjepana for mouthwatering seafood.

The **grocery store** (Trg Sv Stjepana) is a viable restaurant alternative and there's a morning market next to the bus station.

## Drinking

Hvar has some of the best nightlife on the Adriatic coast, mostly centred on the harbour.

**Carpe Diem** ( ☎ 717 234; Riva) From a groggy breakfast to late-night cocktails, there is no time of day when this swanky place is dull. The music is smooth, the drinks fruity and expensive, and the sofas more than welcoming.

**Nautika** (Fabrika) Offering cocktails and non-stop dance music, from techno to hip-hop, this place is ground zero for Hvar's explosive nightlife. Just up the street is Kiva Bar, where you can chill out and talk between dance numbers.

## Getting There & Away

The Jadrolinija ferries between Rijeka and Dubrovnik stop in Stari Grad before continuing to Korčula. The **Jadrolinija agency** ( ☎ 741 132; Riva) sells boat tickets.

Car ferries from Split call at Stari Grad (32KN, one hour) three times daily (five daily in July and August) and there's an afternoon passenger boat from Split to Hvar town (23KN, 50 minutes) that goes on to Vela Luka on Korčula Island (22KN, one hour). Even more convenient is the daily passenger boat *Krilo* from Hvar to Split (33KN, 1¼ hour) and Korčula (33KN, 1½ hours). See p245 for information on international connections. Buses meet most ferries that dock at Stari Grad in July and August, but if you come off-season it's best to check at the tourist office or at Pelegrini to make sure the bus is running. A taxi costs from 150KN to 200KN.

There are also between four and 12 car ferries per day making the 30-minute run between Drvenik on the mainland and Sućuraj on Hvar's southeastern tip. No reservations are possible (80KN for car and driver) so show up early, especially in the summer.

It's possible to visit Hvar on a (hectic) day trip from Split by catching the morning Jadrolinija ferry to Stari Grad, a bus to Hvar town, then the last ferry from Stari Grad directly back to Split.

## KORČULA ISLAND
☎ 020 / pop 16,200

Besides the dense woods that led the original Greek settlers to call the island Korkyra Melaina (Black Korčula), Korčula is graced with indented coves, rolling hills and a walled old town that resembles a miniature Dubrovnik. As the largest island in an archipelago of 48, it provides plenty of opportunities for scenic drives, particularly along the southern coast.

Swimming opportunities abound in the many quiet coves and secluded beaches, while the interior produces some of Croatia's finest wine, especially dessert wines made from the *grk* grape cultivated around Lumbarda. Local olive oil is another product worth seeking out.

At the northeastern tip of the island, Korčula town is tucked onto a small hilly peninsula. Within its round defensive towers are red-roofed houses along narrow stone streets designed to protect its inhabitants from the winds swirling around the peninsula. Korčula Island was controlled by Venice from the 14th to the 18th centuries, as is evident from the Venetian coats of arms adorning the official buildings. If you don't stop in Korčula, one look at this unique town from the Jadrolinija ferry will make you regret it.

## Orientation

The big Jadrolinija car ferry drops you off either in the west harbour next to the Hotel Korčula or the east harbour next to Marko Polo Tours. The Old Town lies between the two harbours. The large hotels and main beach lie south of the east harbour, and the residential neighbourhood Sveti Nikola (with a smaller beach) is southwest of the west harbour. The town bus station is 100m south of the Old Town centre.

## Information

There are ATMs in town at HVB Splitska Banka, for one. You can change money there, at the post office or at any of the travel agencies.

**Atlas Travel Agency** ( ☎ 711 060; Plokata 19 travnja 1914 bb) Represents Amex, runs excursions and finds private accommodation.

**Hospital** ( ☎ 711 137; Ul 59, Kalac) It's about 1km past the Hotel Marko Polo.

**Jadrolinija Office** ( ☎ 715 410) About 25m up from the west harbour.

**Marko Polo Tours** ( ☎ 715 400; marko-polo-tours@du .t-com.hr; Biline 5) Finds private accommodation, changes money and organises excursions.

**Post office** Hidden next to the stairway up to the Old Town, the post office also has telephones.

**Rent a Đir** ( ☎ 711 908; www.korcula-rent.com) Next to Marko Polo Tours, it rents autos, scooters and small boats.

**Tino's Internet** ( ☎ 091 509 11 82; Ul Tri Sulara; per hr 25KN) Tino's other outlet is at the ACI Marina; both are open long hours.

**Tourist Office** ( ☎ 715 701; tzg-korcule@du.t-com.hr; Obala Franje Tudjmana bb; ⏱ 8am-3pm & 5-9pm Mon-Sat, 8am-3pm Sun Jun-Sep, 8am-1pm & 5-9pm Mon-Sat Oct-May) An excellent source of information, located on the west harbour.

## Sights

Other than following the circuit of the former city walls or walking along the shore, sightseeing in Korčula centres on Cathedral Square. The Gothic **St Mark's Cathedral** (Katedrala Svetog Marka; ⏱ 10am-noon & 5-7pm Jul & Aug, Mass only during off-season) features two paintings by Tintoretto (*Three Saints* on the altar and *Annunciation* to one side).

The **treasury** ( ☎ 711 049; Trg Sv Marka Statuta; admission 15KN; ⏱ 9am-2pm & 5-8pm May-Oct) in the 14th-century Abbey Palace next to the cathedral is worth a look; even better is the **Town Museum** (Gradski Muzej; ☎ 711 420; Trg Sv Marka Statuta; admission 10KN; ⏱ 10am-1pm Nov-Mar, 10am-2pm Apr-May,

10am-2pm & 7-9pm Jun & Oct, 10am-9pm Jul & Aug) in the 15th-century Gabriellis Palace opposite. The exhibits of Greek pottery, Roman ceramics and home furnishings have English captions. It's said that Marco Polo was born in Korčula in 1254; you can visit what is believed to have been his **house** (admission 10KN; ⏱ 10am-1pm & 5-7pm Mon-Sat Jul & Aug) and climb the tower.

There's also an **Icon Museum** (Trg Svih Svetih; admission 7.50KN; ⏱ 9am-2pm & 5-8pm May-Oct) in the Old Town. It isn't much of a museum, but visitors are let into the beautiful old **All Saints Church**.

In the high-summer season water taxis at the east harbour collect passengers to visit various points on the island, as well as **Badija Island**, which features a 15th-century Franciscan monastery in the process of reconstruction, plus **Orebić** and the nearby village of **Lumbarda**, which both have sandy beaches.

## Tours

Both **Atlas Travel Agency** ( ☎ 711 060) and **Marko Polo Tours** ( ☎ 715 400; marko-polo-tours@du.t-com .hr) offer a variety of boat tours and island excursions.

## Sleeping

The big hotels in Korčula could use a make-over, but there are a wealth of guesthouses that offer clean, attractive rooms and friendly service. Atlas Travel Agency and Marko Polo Tours arrange private rooms, charging from 200KN to 375KN per double with private bathroom. Apartments start at about 450KN. Or you could try one of the following options:

**Autocamp Kalac** ( ☎ 711 182; fax 711 146; per person/ camp site 45/68KN) This attractive camping ground is behind Hotel Bon Repos in a dense pine grove near the beach.

**Depolo** ( ☎ /fax 711 621; tereza.depolo@du.t-com.hr; d with/without sea view 240/200KN; 🅿 ) In the residential neighbourhood close to the Old Town of Sveti Nikola and 100m west of the bus station, this guesthouse has spiffy, modern rooms.

**Pansion Hajduk** ( ☎ 711 267; olga.zec@du.t-com .hr;d with/without breakfast 383/315KN 🅿 ) It's a couple of kilometres from town on the road to Lumbarda, but you get a warm welcome, air-conditioned rooms with TVs, and even a swimming pool.

Other guesthouses nearby for about the same price include **Peručić** ( ☎ /fax 711 458), with great balconies, and the homy **Ojdanić** ( ☎ /fax 711 708; roko-taxi@du.t-com.hr). Local Ratko Ojdanić

CROATIA

also has a water taxi and a lot of experience with fishing trips around the island.

## Eating

**Buffet-Pizzeria Doris** ( ☎ 711 596; Ul Tri Solara; mains from 35KN) Simple but tasty dishes are served up indoors or outdoors on a shaded terrace. The grilled vegetable platter is a welcome vegetarian treat.

**Planjak** ( ☎ 711 015; Plokata 19 Travnja; mains from 50KN) This restaurant-grill, between the supermarket and the Jadrolinija office in town, is popular with a local crowd who appreciate the fresh, Dalmatian dishes as much as the low prices.

**Konoba Maslina** ( ☎ 711 720; Lumbarajska cesta bb; mains from 50KN) It's well worth the walk out here for the authentic Korčulan home cooking. The multi-bean soup is a standout, but all is scrumptious. It's about a kilometre past the Hotel Marko Polo on the road to Lumbarda, but you can often arrange to be picked up or dropped off in town.

There's a supermarket next to Marko Polo Tours.

## Entertainment

Between May and September there's **moreška sword dancing** (tickets 80KN; ☽ 9pm Thu) by the Old Town gate; performances are more frequent during July and August. The clash of swords and the graceful movements of the dancer-fighters make an exciting show. You can purchase tickets from the tourist office and travel agencies.

## Getting There & Away

Transport connections to Korčula are good. There's one bus every day from Dubrovnik (87KN, three hours), one from Zagreb (195KN, 12 hours) and one a week from Sarajevo (152KN, eight hours).

By car from the mainland, take the car ferry from Ploče to Trpanj (103KN, 30 minutes, three or four daily), then drive across the Pelješac peninsula to the car ferry from Orebić to Dominče (58KN, 15 minutes). Prices are for a car and driver.

There's a regular afternoon car ferry between Split and Vela Luka (35KN, three hours), on the island's western end, that stops at Hvar most days. Six daily buses link Korčula town to Vela Luka (28KN, one hour), but services from Vela Luka are reduced at the weekend.

From Orebić, look for the passenger launch (15KN, 15 minutes, at least four times daily year-round), which will drop you off near Hotel Korčula right below the Old Town's towers. There's also a car ferry to Dominče (10KN, 15 minutes) that stops near the Hotel Bon Repos, where you can pick up the bus from Lumbarda or take a water taxi to Korčula town. For international connections see p245.

## OREBIĆ

Orebić, on the southern coast of the Pelješac Peninsula between Korčula and Ploče, offers better beaches than those found at Korčula, 2.5km across the water. The easy access by ferry from Korčula makes it the perfect place to go for the day. The best beach in Orebić is Trstenica cove, a 15-minute walk east along the shore from the port.

## Getting There & Away

In Orebić the ferry terminal and the bus station are adjacent to each other. Korčula buses to Dubrovnik, Zagreb and Sarajevo stop at Orebić. See the Korčula section (left) for additional bus and ferry information.

## MLJET ISLAND

☎ 020 / pop 1111

Magical Mljet ('Meleda' in Italian) would be anyone's idea of an Adriatic island paradise. With 72% of the island covered by forests and the rest dotted by fields, vineyards and small villages, Mljet casts a spell that can be difficult to break. Created in 1960, Mljet National Park occupies the western third of the island and surrounds two saltwater lakes, Malo Jezero and Veliko Jezero.

## Orientation & Information

Tour boats arrive at Pomena wharf at Mljet's western end. Jadrolinija ferries arrive at Sobra on the eastern end and they are met by a local bus for the 1½-hour ride to Pomena and Polače. The *Nona Ana* passenger boat from Dubrovnik docks at Sobra and then the little town of Polače, about 5km from Pomena. You can enter the National Park from either Pomena or Polače. The **tourist office** ( ☎ 744 186; np-mljet@np-mljet.hr; ☽ 8am-1pm & 5-8pm Mon-Fri Oct-May; 8am-8pm Mon-Sat, 8am-1pm Sun Jun-Sep) is in Polače, and the only ATM on the island is at the Odisej hotel in Pomena. The admission price for the national park is 90/30KN adult/concession. The price includes a bus and boat transfer to the Benedictine monastery and there is no park admission price if you stay overnight on the island.

## Sights & Activities

From Pomena it's a 15-minute walk to a jetty on **Veliko Jezero**, the larger of the two lakes. Here you can board a boat to a small lake islet and have lunch at a 12th-century **Benedictine monastery**, which now houses a restaurant.

There's a small landing on the main island opposite the monastery where the boat operator drops off passengers upon request. It's not possible to walk right around Veliko Jezero because there's no bridge over the channel that connects the lakes to the sea.

Mljet is good for cycling; several restaurants along the dock in Polače and the Odisej hotel in Pomena rent bicycles (90KN per half day). If you plan to cycle between Pomena and Polače be aware that a steep mountain separates the two towns. The bike path along Veliko Jezero is an easier pedal, but it doesn't link the two towns.

## Tours

See p231 and p235 in Korčula and Dubrovnik respectively for agencies offering excursions to Mljet. The tours last from 8.30am to 6pm and include the park entry fee. The boat trip from Korčula to Pomena takes at least two hours (less by hydrofoil); from Dubrovnik it takes longer.

## Sleeping

The Polače tourist office (opposite) arranges private accommodation at 220KN per double room in summer, but it is essential to make arrangements before arrival in peak season. There are more *sobe* (private rooms) signs around Pomena than Polače, but practically none at all in Sobra.

There's no camping permitted inside the national park, but there are two grounds outside it.

**Marina** ( ☎ 745 071; per person/camp site 35/35KN; ☺ Jun-Sep) This small camping ground is in Ropa, about 1km from the park.

**Camping Mungos** ( ☎ 745 060; fax 745 125; Babino Polje; per person/camp site 55/35KN; ☺ Jun-Sep) Not very shady, but well located, this camping ground is not far from the beach and the lovely grotto of Odysseus.

The **Hotel Odisej** ( ☎ 744 022; www.hotelodisej.hr; d from 740KN; ☷ ) in Pomena has decent enough rooms and offers a range of activities, but the new, ecofriendly **Soline 6** ( ☎ 744 024; www.soline6 .com; s/d 330/580KN) in Soline is a more interesting choice. It's the only accommodation in the national park and has waterless toilets, solar heating and organic waste composting. You'll have to do without electricity though.

## Eating

**Nine** ( ☎ 744 037; Pomena; mains from 80KN) The Nine, opposite hotel Odisej, is by the sea and, though touristy in high season, turns out succulent seafood.

## Getting There & Away

Most people visit the island on excursions from Korčula or Dubrovnik, but it's possible to take a passenger boat from Dubrovnik or come on the regular car ferry from Dubrovnik (32KN, two hours) or Korčula and stay a few days for hiking, cycling and boating.

The *Nona Ana* is a small boat that makes a run to and from Dubrovnik to Polače daily, leaving in the morning and returning in late afternoon (55KN, 1¾ to 2¾ hours).

Tickets are sold in the **Turistička Zajednica** (Map p234; ☎ 417 983; Obala Papa Ivana Pavla II) in Gruž (Dubrovnik) or on board, but it's wise to buy in advance as the boat fills up quickly.

# DUBROVNIK

☎ 020 / pop 43,770

Lord Byron was not overstating the matter when he proclaimed Dubrovnik 'the pearl of the Adriatic'. Dubrovnik is clearly special. A magnificent curtain of walls surrounds marble streets and baroque buildings that exude a pearly light in the Adriatic sun. The main pedestrian thoroughfare, Placa, is a melange of cafés and shops with outstanding monuments at either end. Churches, monasteries and museums ornamented with finely carved stone recall an eventful history and a vibrant artistic tradition. Beyond the city is a heavenly landscape of beaches, wooded peninsulas and a sea strewn with lush islands.

## History

Founded 1300 years ago by refugees from Epidaurus in Greece, medieval Dubrovnik (Ragusa until 1918) shook off Venetian control in the 14th century, becoming an independent republic and one of Venice's more important maritime rivals, trading with Egypt, Syria, Sicily, Spain, France and later Turkey. The

CROATIA

# DUBROVNIK

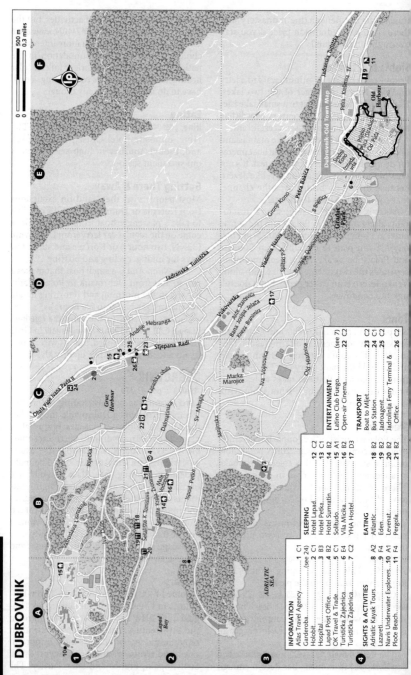

**INFORMATION**
| | |
|---|---|
| Atlas Travel Agency.................... | 1 C1 |
| Garderoba.............................. | (see 24) |
| Holobit................................ | 2 C1 |
| Hospital............................... | 3 B3 |
| Lapad Post Office...................... | 4 B2 |
| OK Travel & Trade..................... | 5 C1 |
| Turistička Zajednica................... | 6 E4 |
| Turistička Zajednica................... | 7 C2 |

**SIGHTS & ACTIVITIES**
| | |
|---|---|
| Adriatic Kayak Tours................... | 8 A2 |
| Lazareti............................... | 9 F4 |
| Navis Underwater Explorers........... | 10 A1 |
| Ploče Beach........................... | 11 F4 |

**SLEEPING**
| | |
|---|---|
| Hotel Lapad........................... | 12 C2 |
| Hotel Petka........................... | 13 C1 |
| Hotel Sumratin........................ | 14 B2 |
| Solitudo.............................. | 15 A1 |
| Vila Micika........................... | 16 B2 |
| YHA Hostel............................ | 17 D3 |

**EATING**
| | |
|---|---|
| Atlantic............................... | 18 B2 |
| Eden.................................. | 19 B2 |
| Levenat............................... | 20 B2 |
| Pergola............................... | 21 B2 |

**ENTERTAINMENT**
| | |
|---|---|
| Latino Club Fuego..................... | (see 7) |
| Open-air Cinema...................... | 22 C2 |

**TRANSPORT**
| | |
|---|---|
| Boat to Mljet......................... | 23 C2 |
| Bus Station........................... | 24 C1 |
| Jadrolinija Ferry Terminal &........... | 25 C2 |
| Office................................ | 26 C2 |

double blow of an earthquake in 1667 and the opening of new trade routes to the east sent Ragusa into a slow decline, ending with Napoleon's conquest of the town in 1806.

The deliberate and militarily pointless shelling of Dubrovnik by the Yugoslav army in 1991 sent shockwaves through the international community but, when the smoke cleared in 1992, traumatised residents cleared the rubble and set about repairing the damage. With substantial international aid, the famous monuments were rebuilt and resculpted, the streets sealed and the clay roofs retiled. Reconstruction has been extraordinarily skilful but you will notice different shades of rose-tiled roofs as you walk around the city walls.

After a steep postwar decline in tourism, visitors are once again flocking to Dubrovnik. It has become a main port of call for Mediterranean cruise ships, whose passengers are sometimes elbow-to-elbow in peak season. Come in June or September if you can, but whatever the time of year the interlay of light and stone is enchanting. Don't miss it.

## Orientation

The Jadrolinija ferry terminal and the bus station are a few hundred metres apart at Gruž, several kilometres northwest of the Old Town, which is closed to cars. The main street in the Old Town is Placa (also called Stradun). Most accommodation is on the leafy Lapad Peninsula, west of the bus station.

## Information

### BOOKSHOPS
**Algoritam** (Map p236; Placa) Has a good selection of English-language books, including guidebooks.

### INTERNET ACCESS
**Dubrovnik Internet Centar** (Map p236; ☎ 311 017; Branitelja Dubrovnika 7; per hr 20KN; ☺ 8am-midnight)
**Holobit** (Map p234; ☎ 352 121; Hotel Kompas, Kralja Zvonimira 56; ☺ 9am-midnight)

### LEFT LUGGAGE
**Garderoba** (Map p234; per day 10KN; ☺ 4.30am-10.30pm) At the bus station.

### MEDICAL SERVICES
**Hospital** (Map p234; ☎ 431 777; Dr. Roka Mišetića)

### MONEY
You can change money at any travel agency or post office. There are numerous ATMs in town, near the bus station and near the ferry terminal.

### POST
**Main post office** (Map p236; cnr Široka & Od Puča)
**Lapad post office** (Map p234; Šetalište Kralja Zvonimira 21)

### TOURIST INFORMATION
**Tourist Information Centar** (Map p236; ☎ 323 350; www.tic-stradun.hr; Placa 1) Across from the Franciscan monastery in the Old Town, it's privately run.
**Turistička Zajednica** (www.tzdubrovnik.hr) Pile gate (Map p234; ☎ 427 591; Dubrovačkih Branitelja 7; ☺ 8am-8pm Mon-Sat, 9am-noon Sun Jan-Sep, 9am-4pm Mon-Fri, 9am-2pm Sat Oct-May); Old Town (Map p236; ☎ 321 561; Placa bb ☺ 8am-8pm); harbour (Map p234; ☎ 417 983; Obala Stepjana Radića 27) Offers maps and the indispensable Dubrovnik Riviera guide. The harbour branch has limited documentation.

### TRAVEL AGENCIES
There's no shortage of travel agencies in Dubrovnik. Most are clustered around the Jadrolinija port. For a full list, see the Dubrovnik Riviera guide or go to www.tzdubrovnik.hr /touristagencies.shtml.

**Atlas Travel Agency** Pile gate (Map p236; ☎ 442 574; Sv Đurđa 1); harbour (Map p236; ☎ 418 001; Obala Papa Ivana Pavla II 1) In convenient locations, this agency is extremely helpful for general information as well as finding private accommodation. Atlas runs all excursions.
**OK Travel & Trade** (Map p234; ☎ 418 950; okt-t@du .htnet.hr; Obala Stjepana Radića 32) Near the Jadrolinija dock.

## Sights & Activities

### OLD TOWN
You will probably begin your visit at the city bus stop outside **Pile Gate** (Map p236). As you enter the city Dubrovnik's wonderful pedestrian promenade, Placa, extends before you all the way to the **clock tower** (Map p236) at the other end of town.

Just inside Pile Gate is the huge **Onofrio Fountain** (Map p236; 1438) and **Franciscan monastery** (Map p236; ☺ 9am-5pm) with a splendid cloister. Each capital over the dual columns is topped by a different figure, portraying human heads, animals and floral arrangements. Further inside you'll find the third-oldest functioning **pharmacy** in Europe; it's been operating since 1391. The pharmacy may have been the first pharmacy in Europe open to the general public. The **monastery museum** (adult/concession 20/10KN)

CROATIA

# DUBROVNIK – OLD TOWN

has a collection of liturgical objects, paintings and pharmacy equipment.

In front of the clock tower at the eastern end of Placa, is the **Orlando Column** (Map p236; 1419) – a favourite meeting place. On opposite sides of Orlando are the 16th-century **Sponza Palace** (Map p236; ☎ 321 032; admission free; ⓨ 8am-3pm Mon-Fri, 8am-1pm Sat), which now houses the State

Archives, and **St Blaise's Church** (Map p236), a lovely Italian baroque building built in 1715 to replace an earlier church destroyed in the 1667 earthquake. At the end of Pred Dvorom, the wide street beside St Blaise, is the baroque **Cathedral of the Assumption of the Virgin** (Map p236). Located between the two churches, the 1441 Gothic **Rector's Palace** (Map p236; adult/

concession 20/7KN; 9am-2pm Mon-Sat Oct-May, 9am-6pm daily Jun-Sep) houses a museum with furnished rooms, baroque paintings and historical exhibits. The elected rector was not permitted to leave the building during his one-month term without the permission of the senate. The narrow street opposite opens onto Gundulićeva Poljana, a bustling **morning market**. Up the stairs at the southern end of the square is the **Jesuit monastery** (Map p236; 1725).

As you proceed up Placa, make a detour to the **Museum of the Orthodox Church** (Map p236; adult/concession 10/5KN; 9am-2pm Mon-Fri) for a look at a fascinating collection of 15th- to 19th-century icons.

By now you'll be ready for a leisurely walk around the **city walls** (Map p236; adult/concession 50/20KN; 10am-3.30pm Oct-Mar, 9am-6.30pm Apr-Sep), which has entrances just inside Pile Gate, across from the Dominican monastery and near **Fort St John**. Built between the 13th and 16th centuries, these powerful walls are the finest in the world and Dubrovnik's main claim to fame. They enclose the entire city in a protective veil over 2km long and up to 25m high, with two round and 14 square towers, two corner fortifications and a large fortress. The views over the town and sea are great – this walk could be the high point of your visit.

Whichever way you go, you'll notice the 14th-century **Dominican monastery** (Map p236; adult/concession 15/7.50KN; 9am-5pm) in the north-eastern corner of the city, whose forbidding fortress-like exterior shelters a rich trove of paintings from Dubrovnik's finest 15th- and 16th-century artists.

Dubrovnik has many other sights, such as the unmarked **synagogue** (Map p236; Ul Žudioska 5; admission 10KN; 10am-3pm Mon-Fri) near the clock tower, which is the second oldest synagogue in Europe. The uppermost streets of the Old Town below the north and south walls are pleasant to wander along.

### BEACHES

**Ploče** (Map p234), the closest beach to the old city, is just beyond the 17th-century **Lazareti** (Map p234; a former quarantine station) outside Ploče Gate. There are also hotel beaches along the Lapad Peninsula, which you are able to use without a problem. The largest is outside the Hotel Kompas.

An even better option is to take the ferry that shuttles half-hourly in summer to lush **Lokrum Island** (return 80KN), a national park

with a rocky nudist beach (marked 'FKK'), a botanical garden and the ruins of a medieval Benedictine monastery.

### ACTIVITIES

Whether you're just dipping into the sport or are an experienced kayaker, **Adriatic Sea Kayaking** (Map p234; 098-438 888; www.adriatic-sea-kayak .com; Masarykov put 9) has a kayak tour for you.

Get certified or explore the 1943 wreck of the *Taranto* off nearby Grebeni Island with **Navis Underwater Explorers** (Map p234; 099-350 27 73; www.navisdubrovnik.com; Copacabana beach).

### Tours

Atlas Travel Agency (p235) offers full-day tours to Mostar (€48.50), Međugorje (€43), the Elafiti Islands (€38) and Mljet (€58), among other destinations. Its tour to Montenegro (€51.50) is a good alternative to taking the morning bus to Montenegro, since the bus schedules make a day trip there impractical.

### Festivals & Events

The **Dubrovnik Summer Festival** (mid-July to mid-August) is a major cultural event, with over 100 performances at different venues in the Old Town. The **Feast of St Blaise** (3 February) and **carnival** (February) are also celebrated.

### Sleeping

Private accommodation is generally the best option in Dubrovnik, but beware of the scramble of private owners at the bus station or Jadrolinija wharf. Some offer what they say they offer, but others are rip-off artists. If you book online most owners will meet you at the station if you call in advance. Otherwise head to any of the travel agencies or the Turistička Zajednica. Expect to pay about 200KN to 220KN a room in high season.

#### BUDGET
#### Old Town

**Apartments van Bloemen** (Map p236; 323 433, 091-33 24 106; www.karmendu.tk; Bandureva 1; apts 625-1000KN; ) This is Dubrovnik's most personal and original accommodation, with a great location in the Old Town. All four apartments are beautifully decorated with original art; three of them sleep three people comfortably.

#### Outside the Old Town

**Solitudo** (Map p234; 448 200; Iva Dulčića 39; site per person 50KN) This pretty, renovated camping ground is within walking distance of the beach.

**YHA Hostel** (Map p234; ☎ 423 241; dubrovnik@hfhs.hr; Vinka Sagrestana 3; B&B/half-board 129/160KN) It's not exactly restful here, but you'll have a lot of fun as there are a fair number of bars and cafés nearby.

**Vila Micika** (☎ 437 332; www.vilamicika.hr; Mata Vodapica; s/d 215/430KN; **P** ) This is a simple, well-run establishment. The rooms are equipped with TVs and modern baths, there's a pleasant outdoor terrace and it's only 200m to the Lapad beaches. Prices do not include breakfast.

### MIDRANGE
### Old Town
**Hotel Stari Grad** (Map p236; ☎ 322 244; www.hotelstarigrad.com; Od Sigurate 4; s/d 980/1400KN) Staying in the heart of the old town in a lovingly restored stone building is a delightful experience. There are only eight rooms; each one is furnished with taste and a sense of comfort. From the rooftop terrace, you have a marvellous view over the town. Prices stay the same all year.

### Outside the Old Town
**Hotel Sumratin** (Map p234; ☎ 436 333; www.hotels-sumratin.com; Šetalište Kralja Zvonimira 31; s/d 460/760KN; **P** ) About 200m from the water, this calm hotel offers fresh, comfortable rooms.

**Hotel Petka** (Map p234; ☎ 410 500; www.hotelpetka.com; Obala Stjepana Radića 38; s/d from 800/1130KN; **P** **⊠** ) Situated opposite the Jadrolinija ferry landing, Hotel Petka won't bowl you over with charm, but the location is great for getting back and forth to the ferry.

**Hotel Lapad** (Map p234; ☎ 432 922; www.hotel-lapad.hr; Lapadska Obala 37; s/d from 830/1080KN; **⊠** **⊠** ) This hotel is a solid, old limestone structure with simple but cheerful rooms and an outdoor swimming pool.

### TOP END
**Pucić Palace** (Map p236; ☎ 326 222; www.thepucicpalace.com; Od Puća 1; s/d 2530/4000KN; **P** **⊠** ) Right in the heart of the Old Town, these palatial digs have been designed and decorated to the cutting edge of fashion. Warm and cosy it's not, but the countesses and moguls that stay here probably don't care.

## Eating
### OLD TOWN
There are dozens of places to chow down in the Old Town but the menus tend to focus on pizza, pasta, fish and seafood. Restaurants with more exotic flavours are beginning to make inroads, but locals tend to stick with the tried and true.

**Kamenice** (Map p236; ☎ 323 682; Gundulićeva Poljana 8; mains from 40KN) Portions are huge at this convivial hang-out known for its mussels. Its outdoor terrace is on one of Dubrovnik's more scenic squares.

**Dundo Maroje** (Map p236; ☎ 321 021; Kovačka; mains from 55KN) Nothing adventurous here, but everything is cooked exactly as it should be. The menu is varied with an accent on seafood.

**Proto** (Map p236; ☎ 323 234; www.esculap-teo.hr; Široka 1; mains from 80KN) This place has become a blockbuster success largely because the fish and seafood are chosen with care and expertly prepared. There's not a lot of fuss in the preparation, allowing the natural flavours to shine. Vegetarians will enjoy the wonderful Župa Dubrovačka potatoes prepared with rosemary.

### LAPAD
The better dining is in Lapad.

**Atlantic** (Map p234; ☎ 435 726; Kardinala Stepinca 42; mains from 45KN) The homemade pasta and vegetarian lasagne are outstanding here, even if the ambience is not terribly atmospheric.

**Levenat** (Map p234; ☎ 435 352; Šetalište Nika i Meda Pucića 15; mains 55-120KN) The interior at this eatery is classic and the outdoor terrace has a smashing view. The food is superb and there's even a vegetarian plate.

**Pergola** (Map p234; ☎ 436 848; Kralja Tomislava 1; mains from 50KN) This is another consistently satisfying place with an outdoor terrace and good seafood.

**Eden** (Map p234; ☎ 435 133; Kardinala Stepinca 54; mains 55-90KN) The leafy terrace upstairs is an agreeable spot to enjoy meat, pasta or fish dishes.

## Drinking
Bars have sprung up like mushrooms on Bana Josipa Jelačića near the youth hostel, but these days thirsty young singles fill the cafés and terraces on Bunićeva in the Old Town. **Troubadur** (Map p236; ☎ 412 154; Gundulićeva Poljana) is a longtime favourite for jazz; the ambience is joyous, especially when the owner, Marko, plays.

## Entertainment
The summer months are chock-full of concerts and folk dancing. The tourist office has the full schedule.

**Latino Club Fuego** (Map p234; Dubrovačkih Branitelja 2) Despite the name, at this disco you'll find a gamut of dance music that includes techno and pop.

**Open-air cinema** (Map p234; Kumičića) In Lapad, this spot allows you to watch movies, shown in their original language, by starlight.

**Labirint** (Map p236; ☎ 322 222; Svetog Dominika 2) A vast restaurant, nightclub, disco and cabaret complex that caters to high rollers. It can chew through your wallet pretty quickly unless you just come for a romantic cocktail on the roof terrace.

### Getting There & Away

#### AIR
Daily flights to/from Zagreb are operated by **Croatia Airlines** (Map p236; ☎ 413 777; Dubrovačkih Branitelja 9). The fare starts at about 400KN one way (higher in peak season) and the trip takes about an hour.

There are also nonstop flights to Rome, London and Manchester that operate from April to October.

#### BOAT
In addition to the **Jadrolinija** (Map p234; ☎ 418 000; Gruž) coastal ferry north to Hvar, Split, Zadar and Rijeka, there's a local ferry that leaves Dubrovnik for Sobra on Mljet Island (26KN to 32KN, 2½ hours) throughout the year. See also the Central Dalmatia Ferry Routes map on p226.

**Jadroagent** (Map p234; ☎ 419 009; fax 419 029; Obala Pape Ivana Pavla 32) handles ticketing for most international boats from Croatia.

For information on international connections see p245.

#### BUS
Buses from Dubrovnik include the following:

| Destination | Cost | Duration | Frequency |
| --- | --- | --- | --- |
| Korčula | 87KN | 3hr | 1 daily |
| Mostar | 87KN | 3hr | 2 daily |
| Orebić | 87KN | 2½hr | 1 daily |
| Rijeka | 391KN | 12hr | 3 daily |
| Sarajevo | 160KN | 5hr | 1 daily |
| Split | 118-123KN | 4½hr | 14 daily |
| Zadar | 170-210KN | 8hr | 7 daily |
| Zagreb | 170-196KN | 11hr | 7 daily |

There's a daily 11am bus to the Montenegrin border, from where a Montenegro bus takes you to Herceg Novi (60KN, two hours) and on to Kotor (100KN, 2½ hours) and Bar (130KN, three hours). In a busy summer season and at weekends buses out of Dubrovnik can be crowded, so book a ticket well before the scheduled departure time.

### Getting Around
Čilipi international airport is 24km southeast of Dubrovnik. The Croatia Airlines airport buses (30KN, 45 minutes) leave from the main **bus station** (Map p234; ☎ 357 088) 1½ hours before flight times. A taxi costs around 220KN.

Dubrovnik's buses run frequently and generally on time. The fare is 10KN if you buy from the driver but only 8KN if you buy a ticket at a kiosk.

# CROATIA DIRECTORY

## ACCOMMODATION
Accommodation listings in this guide have been ordered by pricing from cheapest to most expensive (ie budget to top end).

Along the Croatian coast accommodation is priced according to three seasons, which tend to vary from place to place. Generally October to May are the cheapest months, June and September are mid-priced, but count on paying top price for the peak season, which runs for a six-week period in July and August. Prices quoted in this chapter are for the peak period and do not include 'residence tax', which runs from about 4KN to 7.50KN depending on the location and season. Prices also assume a three-night stay; count on a 30% surcharge for shorter stays. Deduct about 25% if you come in June, the beginning of July and September; about 35% for May and October; and about 50% for all other times. Note that prices for rooms in Zagreb are pretty much constant all year and that many hotels on the coast close in winter. Some places offer half-board, which is bed and two meals a day: usually breakfast and one other meal. It can be good value if you're not too fussy about what you eat.

### Camping
Nearly 100 camping grounds are scattered along the Croatian coast. Opening times generally run from mid-April to September, give or take a few weeks. The exact times change

from year to year so it's wise to call in advance if you're arriving at either end of the season.

Many camping grounds, especially in Istria, are gigantic 'autocamps' with restaurants, shops and row upon row of caravans. Expect to pay up to 100KN for the camp site at some of the larger establishments but half that at most other camping grounds, in addition to 40KN to 50KN per person.

Nudist camping grounds (marked 'FKK') are among the best because their secluded locations ensure peace and quiet. However, bear in mind that freelance camping is officially prohibited. A good site for camping information and links is www.camping.hr.

## Hostels

The **Croatian YHA** ( ☎ 01-48 47 472; www.hfhs.hr; Dežmanova 9, Zagreb) operates youth hostels in Dubrovnik, Rijeka, Zadar, Zagreb and Pula. Nonmembers pay an additional 10KN per person daily for a stamp on a welcome card; six stamps entitle you to a membership. The Croatian YHA can also provide information about private youth hostels in Krk.

## Hotels

Hotels are ranked from one to five stars with the most in the two- and three-star range. Features such as satellite TV, direct-dial phones, hi-tech bathrooms, minibars and air-con are standard in four- and five-star hotels. Many two- and three-star hotels offer satellite TV but you'll find better décor in the higher categories. Gradually, the 1970s concrete-block hotels built to warehouse package tourists are being transformed into four-star establishments. During peak season some hotels may demand a surcharge for stays of less than four nights but this surcharge is usually waived during the rest of the year, when prices drop steeply.

Breakfast is included in the prices quoted for hotels in this chapter, unless stated otherwise.

## Private Rooms

Private rooms or apartments are the best accommodation in Croatia. Service is excellent and the rooms are usually extremely well kept. You may very well be greeted by offers of *sobe* as you step off your bus and boat, but rooms are most often arranged by travel agencies or the local tourist office. Booking through an agency is somewhat more expensive but

at least you'll know who to complain to if things go wrong.

The most expensive rooms are three-star establishments with private bathrooms in places that resemble small guesthouses. Some of the better ones are listed in this chapter. It's best to call in advance as the owners will often meet you at the bus station or ferry dock. In a two-star room, the bathroom is shared with one other room; in a one-star room, the bathroom is shared with two other rooms or with the owner, who is often an elderly widow. Breakfast is usually not included but can sometimes be arranged for an additional 30KN; be sure to clarify whether the price agreed upon is per person or per room. If you're travelling in a small group it may be worthwhile to get a small apartment with cooking facilities, which are quite widely available along the coast.

It makes little sense to price-shop from agency to agency since prices are fixed by the local tourist association. Whether you deal with the owner directly or book through an agency, you'll pay a 30% surcharge for stays of less than four nights and sometimes 50% or even 100% more for a one-night stay, although you may be able to get them to waive the surcharge if you arrive during the low season. Prices for private rooms in this chapter are for a four-night stay in peak season.

# ACTIVITIES
## Diving

The clear waters and varied underwater life of the Adriatic have led to a flourishing dive industry along the coast. Cave diving is the real speciality in Croatia; night diving and wreck diving are also offered and there are coral reefs in some places, but they are in rather deep water. You must get a permit for a boat dive: go to the harbour captain in any port with your passport, certification card and 100KN. Permission is valid for a year. If you dive with a dive centre, they will take care of the paperwork. Most of the coastal resorts mentioned in this chapter have dive shops. See **Diving Croatia** (www.diving-hrs.hr) for contact information.

## Hiking

Risnjak National Park at Crni Lug, 12km west of Delnice between Zagreb and Rijeka, is a good hiking area in summer. Hiking is advisable only from late spring to early autumn. The steep gorges and beech forests of Paklenica National Park, 40km northeast of Zadar, also offer excellent hiking.

## Kayaking

There are countless possibilities for anyone carrying a folding sea kayak, especially among the Elafiti and Kornati Islands. Lopud makes a good launch point from which to explore the Elafiti Islands – there's a daily ferry from Dubrovnik. Sali on Dugi Otok is close to the Kornati Islands and is connected by daily ferry to Zadar.

## BOOKS

Lonely Planet's *Croatia* is a comprehensive guide to the country. There's also Zoë Brân's *After Yugoslavia,* part of the Lonely Planet *Journeys* series, which recounts the author's return to a troubled region.

As Croatia emerges from the shadow of the former Yugoslavia, several writers of Croatian origin have taken the opportunity to rediscover their roots. *Plum Brandy: Croatian Journeys* by Josip Novakovich is a sensitive exploration of his family's Croatian background. *Croatia: Travels in Undiscovered Country* by Tony Fabijancic recounts the life of rural people in a new Croatia.

For a comprehensive account of the personalities and events surrounding the collapse of the former Yugoslavia, it would be hard to go past *Yugoslavia: Death of a Nation* by Laura Silber and Allan Little, based on the 1995 BBC TV series of the same name. Richard Holbrooke's *To End a War* is a riveting look at the people and events surrounding the Dayton Agreement. *Café Europa* is a series of essays by a Croatian journalist, Slavenka Drakulić, that provides an inside look at life in the country since independence. Her most recent book, *They Would Never Hurt a Fly,* examines the deeds of war criminals prosecuted at The Hague. Rebecca West's travel classic, *Black Lamb & Grey Falcon,* contains a long section on Croatia as part of her trip through Yugoslavia in 1937. Tony White, a British writer, recently retraced her journey and wrote *Another Fool in the Balkans* that manages to ignore nearly all of Croatia's trauma during the 1990s. Marcus Tanner's *Croatia: A Nation Forged in War* provides an excellent overview of Croatia's history.

## BUSINESS HOURS

Banking and post office hours are 7.30am to 7pm on weekdays and 8am to noon on Saturday. Many shops are open 8am to 7pm on weekdays and until 2pm on Saturday. Along the coast life is more relaxed; shops and offices frequently close around noon for an afternoon break and reopen around 4pm. Restaurants are open long hours, often noon to midnight, with Sunday closings outside of peak season. Cafés are generally open from 10am to midnight; bars from 9pm to 2am. Internet cafés are also open long hours, usually seven days a week.

## CUSTOMS

Travellers can bring their personal effects into the country, along with 1L of liquor, 1L of wine, 500g of coffee, 200 cigarettes and 50mL of perfume. The import or export of kuna is limited to 15,000KN per person.

## DISABLED TRAVELLERS

Because of the number of wounded war veterans, more attention is being paid to the needs of disabled travellers. Public toilets at bus stations, train stations, airports and large public venues are usually wheelchair accessible. Large hotels are wheelchair accessible but very little private accommodation is. The bus and train stations in Zagreb, Zadar, Rijeka, Split and Dubrovnik are wheelchair accessible but the local Jadrolinija ferries are not. For further information, get in touch with **Savez Organizacija Invalida Hrvatske** ( ☎ /fax 01-48 29 394; Savska cesta 3, 10000 Zagreb).

## EMBASSIES & CONSULATES
### Croatian Embassies & Consulates

Croatian embassies and consulates abroad include the following:

**Australia** ( ☎ 02-6286 6988; 14 Jindalee Cres, O'Malley, ACT 2601)

**Canada** ( ☎ 613-562 7820; 229 Chapel St, Ottawa, Ontario K1N 7Y6)

**France** ( ☎ 01 5370 0287; 2 Rue de Lubeck, Paris)

**Germany** Berlin ( ☎ 030-219 15 514; Ahornstrasse 4, Berlin 10787); Bonn ( ☎ 022-895 29 20; Rolandstrasse 52, Bonn 53179)

**Ireland** ( ☎ 1 4767 181; Adelaide Chambers, Peter St, Dublin)

**Netherlands** ( ☎ 70 362 36 38; Amaliastraat 16, The Hague)

**New Zealand** ( ☎ 09-836 5581; 131 Lincoln Rd, Henderson, Box 83200, Edmonton, Auckland)

CROATIA

**South Africa** ( ☎ 012-342 1206; 1160 Church St, 0083 Colbyn, Pretoria)
**UK** ( ☎ 020-7387 2022; 21 Conway St, London W1P 5HL)
**USA** ( ☎ 202-588 5899; www.croatiaemb.org; 2343 Massachusetts Ave NW, Washington, DC 20008)

## Embassies & Consulates in Croatia

The following addresses are in Zagreb (area code ☎ 01):

**Albania** ( ☎ 48 10 679; Jurišićeva 2a)
**Australia** ( ☎ 48 91 200; www.auembassy.hr; Kaptol Centar, Nova Ves 11)
**Bosnia and Hercegovina** ( ☎ 48 19 420; Hatzova 3)
**Bulgaria** ( ☎ 46 46 609; Gornje Pekrižje 28)
**Canada** ( ☎ 48 81 200; zagreb@dfait-maeci.gc.ca; Prilaz Gjure Deželića 4)
**Czech Republic** ( ☎ 61 77 239; Savska 41)
**France** ( ☎ 48 93 680; consulat@ambafrance.hr; Hebrangova 2)
**Germany** ( ☎ 61 58 105; www.deutschebotschaft -zagreb.hr, in German; avenija grada Vukovara 64)
**Hungary** ( ☎ 48 90 900; Pantovčak 255-257)
**Ireland** ( ☎ 63 10 025; Miramarska 23)
**Netherlands** ( ☎ 46 84 880; nlgovzag@zg.t-com.hr; Medveščak 56)
**New Zealand** ( ☎ 65 20 888; avenija Dubrovnik 15)
**Poland** ( ☎ 48 99 444; Krležin Gvozd 3)
**Romania** ( ☎ 45 77 550; roamb@zg.t-com.hr; Mlinarska ul 43)
**Serbia and Montenegro** ( ☎ 45 79 067; Pantovčak 245)
**Slovakia** ( ☎ 48 48 941; Prilaz Gjure Deželića 10)
**Slovenia** ( ☎ 63 11 000; Savska 41)
**UK** ( ☎ 60 09 100; I Lučića 4)
**USA** ( ☎ 66 12 200; www.usembassy.hr; Ul Thomasa Jeffersona 2)

## FESTIVALS & EVENTS

In July and August there are **summer festivals** in Dubrovnik, Split, Pula and Zagreb. Dubrovnik's summer **music festival** emphasises classical music with concerts in churches around town, while Pula hosts a variety of pop and classical stars in the Roman amphitheatre and also hosts a **film festival**. **Mardi Gras** celebrations have recently been revived in many towns with attendant parades and festivities, but nowhere is it celebrated with more verve than in Rijeka.

## HOLIDAYS

**New Year's Day** 1 January
**Epiphany** 6 January
**Easter Monday** March/April
**Labour Day** 1 May

**Corpus Christi** 10 June
**Day of Antifascist Resistance** 22 June (marks the outbreak of resistance in 1941)
**Statehood Day** 25 June
**Homeland Thanksgiving Day** 5 August
**Feast of the Assumption** 15 August
**Independence Day** 8 October
**All Saints' Day** 1 November
**Christmas** 25 and 26 December

## INTERNET RESOURCES

**Adriatica.net** (www.adriatica.net) Cumbersome navigation but books rooms, apartments, hotels and lighthouses all along the coast.**Croatia Homepage** (www.hr) Hundreds of links to everything you want to know about Croatia.
**Croatia Traveller** (www.croatiatraveller.com) Practical advice, suggested itineraries, accommodation and up-to-date ferry and flight information.
**Find Croatia** (www.findcroatia.com) More Croatia links, with an emphasis on tourism and outdoor activities.

## MEDIA
### Newspapers & Magazines

After the dark days of the 1990s when Croatian strongman Franjo Tuđman leaned heavily on the media to repress negative coverage, Croatian newspapers and magazines have discovered that fighting for advertisers is not much easier than fighting a dictator. The most respected daily in Croatia is the state-owned *Vjesnik*, which has a loyal but relatively small readership. The two largest private dailies, *Večernji List* and *Jutarnji List*, are trying to lure advertisers with a mix of politics, show biz and scandal, while the glossy newsmagazines *Globus* and *Nacional* struggle for readers. It will be interesting to see how the Croatian edition of *Metro* fares after its launch. American, British and French newspapers and magazines are available in most destinations in this chapter.

### Radio & TV

The two national and two private TV stations fill a lot of their air time with foreign programming, generally American, and always in the original language. The rest of the programming schedule is devoted to sports, quiz shows and soaps. The most popular radio station is Narodni radio, which airs only Croatian music. Croatian Radio broadcasts news in English four times daily (8am, 10am, 2pm and 11pm) on FM frequencies 88.9, 91.3 and 99.3 between June and September.

# MONEY

## Changing Money

Exchange offices may deduct a commission of 1% to change cash or travellers cheques, but some banks do not. Hungarian currency is difficult to change in Croatia and Croatian currency can be difficult to exchange in some neighbouring countries.

## Costs

Accommodation takes the largest chunk of a travel budget, and costs vary widely depending on the season. If you travel in March you'll quite easily find a private room for 100KN per person, but prices climb upward to double that in July and August. Count on 45KN for a meal at a self-service restaurant and 45KN to 60KN for an average intercity bus fare.

## Credit Cards

Amex, MasterCard, Visa and Diners Club cards are widely accepted in large hotels, shops and many restaurants, but don't count on cards to pay for private accommodation or meals in small restaurants. ATMs accepting MasterCard, Maestro, Cirrus, Plus and Visa are available in most bus and train stations, airports, all major cities and most small towns. Many branches of Privredna Banka have ATMs that allow cash withdrawals on an Amex card.

## Currency

The currency is the kuna. Banknotes are in denominations of 500, 200, 100, 50, 20, 10 and 5. Each kuna is divided into 100 lipa in coins of 50, 20 and 10. Many places exchange money, all with similar rates.

## Tax

A 22% VAT is imposed upon most purchases and services, and is included in the price. If your purchases exceed 500KN in one shop you can claim a refund upon leaving the country. Ask the merchant for the paperwork, but don't be surprised if they don't have it.

## Tipping

If you're served well at a restaurant, you should round up the bill, but a service charge is always included. (Don't leave money on the table.) Bar bills and taxi fares can also be rounded up. Tour guides on day excursions expect to be tipped.

# POST

Mail sent to Poste Restante, 10000 Zagreb, Croatia, is held at the **main post office** (Branimirova 4; ☉ 24hr Mon-Sat, 1pm-midnight Sun) next to the Zagreb train station. A good coastal address to use is c/- Poste Restante, Main Post Office, 21000 Split, Croatia. If you have an Amex card, most Atlas travel agencies will hold your mail.

# TELEPHONE

## Mobile Phones

Croatia uses GSM 900/1800 and the two mobile networks are T-Mobile and VIP. If your mobile is compatible, SIM cards are widely available and start at 120KN for a basic package.

## Phone Codes

To call Croatia from abroad, dial your international access code, ☎ 385 (Croatia's country code), the area code (without the initial zero) and the local number. When calling from one region to another within Croatia, use the initial zero. Phone numbers with the prefix 060 are free and numbers that begin with 09 are mobile numbers, which are billed at a much higher rate – figure on about 6KN a minute. When in Croatia, dial ☎ 00 to speak to the international operator.

## Phonecards

To make a phone call from Croatia, go to the town's main post office. You'll need a phonecard to use public telephones, but calls using a phonecard are about 50% more expensive. Phonecards are sold according to *impulsa* (units), and you can buy cards of 25 (15KN), 50 (30KN), 100 (50KN) and 200 (100KN) units. These can be purchased at any post office and most tobacco shops and newspaper kiosks.

# TOURIST INFORMATION

The **Croatian National Tourist Board** ( ☎ 45 56 455; www.htz.hr; Iblerov trg 10, Importanne Gallerija, 10000 Zagreb) is a good source of information. There are regional tourist offices that supervise tourist development, and municipal tourist offices that have free brochures and good information on local events. Some arrange private accommodation.

Tourist information is also dispensed by commercial travel agencies such as **Atlas** (http://atlas-croatia.com), Croatia Express, Generalturist and Kompas, which also arrange private rooms, sightseeing tours and so on. Ask for the schedule for coastal ferries.

Croatian National Tourist Offices abroad include the following:

**UK** ( ☎ 020-8563 7979; info@cnto.freeserve.co.uk; 2 Lanchesters, 162-64 Fulham Palace Rd, London W6 9ER)

**USA** ( ☎ 212-279 8672; cntony@earthlink.net; Suite 4003, 350 Fifth Ave, New York, NY 10118)

## TOURS

An interesting option for sailing enthusiasts is **Katarina Line** ( ☎ 051-272 110; www.katarina-line.hr; Tita 75, Opatija), which offers week-long cruises from Opatija to Krk, Rab, Dugi Otok, Lošinj and Cres, or cruises from Split to Dubrovnik that pass the Kornati Islands. Prices run from €270 to €580 a week per person depending on the season and cabin class, and include half-board. For specific tours in individual regions, see Tours in the destination sections.

## VISAS

Visitors from Australia, Canada, New Zealand, the EU and the USA do not require a visa for stays of less than 90 days. For other nationalities, visas are issued free of charge at Croatian consulates. Croatian authorities require all foreigners to register with the local police when they first arrive in a new area of the country, but this is a routine matter that is normally handled by your hotel, hostel or camping ground, or the agency that organises your private accommodation.

# TRANSPORT IN CROATIA

## GETTING THERE & AWAY
### Air

The major airports in the country are as follows:

**Dubrovnik** ( ☎ 020-773 377; www.airport-dubrovnik.hr)
**Pula** ( ☎ 052-530 105; www.airport-pula.com)
**Rijeka** ( ☎ 051-842 132; www.rijeka-airport.hr)
**Split** ( ☎ 021-203 506; www.split-airport.hr)
**Zadar** ( ☎ 023-313 311; www.zadar-airport.hr)
**Zagreb** ( ☎ 01-62 65 222; www.zagreb-airport.hr)

Split has direct connections to Prague and Rome as well as Zagreb.

**Adria Airways** (code JD; www.adria-airways.com; ☎ 01-48 10 011) Hub Ljubljana.
**Aeroflot** (code SU; www.aeroflot.ru; ☎ 01-48 72 055) Hub Moscow.

**Air Canada** (code AC; www.aircanada.ca; ☎ 01-48 22 033) Hub Toronto.
**Air France** (code AF; www.airfrance.com; ☎ 01-48 37 100) Hub Paris.
**Alitalia** (code AZ; www.alitalia.it; ☎ 01-48 10 413) Hub Milan.
**Austrian Airlines** (code OS; www.aua.com; ☎ 062 65 900) Hub Vienna.
**British Airways** (code BA; www.british-airways.com) Hub London.
**Croatia Airlines** (code OU; ☎ 01-48 19 633; www .croatiaairlines.hr; Zrinjevac 17, Zagreb) Croatia's national carrier; hub Zagreb.
**ČSA** (code OK; www.csa.cz; ☎ 01-48 73 301) Hub Prague.
**Delta Airlines** (code DL; www.delta.com; ☎ 01-48 78 760) Hub Atlanta.
**Easyjet** (code EZY; www.easyjet.com) Hub Luton.
**Germanwings** (code GWI; www.germanwings.com) Hub Cologne.**Hapag Lloyd Express** (code HLX; www.hlx.com) Hub Cologne.
**KLM-Northwest** (code KL; www.klm.com; ☎ 01-48 78 601) Hub Amsterdam.
**LOT Polish Airlines** (code LO; www.lot.com; ☎ 01 48 37 500) Hub Warsaw.
**Lufthansa** (code LH; www.lufthansa.com; ☎ 01-48 73 121) Hub Frankfurt.
**Malév Hungarian Airlines** (code MA; www.malev.hu; ☎ 01-48 36 935) Hub Budapest.
**SNBrussels** (code SN; www.flysn.com) Hub Brussels.
**Turkish Airlines** (code TK; www.turkishairlines.com; ☎ 01-49 21 854) Hub Istanbul.
**Wizzair** (code W6; www.wizzair.com) Hub Luton.

## Land
### BUS
#### Austria

Eurolines runs buses from Vienna to Zagreb (€29, six hours, two daily), Rijeka (€47, 8¼ hours), Split (€51, 15 hours) and Zadar (€43, 13 hours).

#### Bosnia & Hercegovina

There are daily connections from Sarajevo (€22, five hours, daily), Međugorje (€10, three hours) and Mostar (€10, three hours, twice daily) to Dubrovnik; from Sarajevo to Split (€14 to €16, seven hours, five daily), which stop at Mostar; and from Sarajevo to Zagreb (€13, eight hours) and Rijeka (€32, 10 hours).

#### Italy

Trieste is well connected with the Istrian coast. There are around three buses a day to Rijeka (€7.50, two to three hours), plus buses to Rovinj (€10.50, 3½ hours, one daily), Poreč (€8.50, 2¼ hours, one daily) and Pula (€14, 3¾ hours, four daily). There are fewer buses on Sunday. To Dalmatia there's a daily bus that leaves at 5.30pm and stops at Rijeka (€7.50, two to three hours), Zadar (€32, 7½ hours), Split (€35.60, 10½ hours) and Dubrovnik (€64, 15 hours).

There's also a bus from Padua that passes Venice and Trieste, Monday to Saturday, and then goes on to Poreč (€19, 2½ hours), Rovinj (€21, three hours) and Pula (€24, 3¼ hours). For schedules, see www.saf.ud.it.

## Montenegro
Between Croatia and Montenegro there's a daily bus from Kotor to Dubrovnik (100KN, 2½ hours) that starts at Bar and stops at Herceg Novi. Visitors can cross at the Croatia–Montenegro border, and Americans, Australians, Canadians and Brits can enter visa-free.

## Serbia
There are six daily bus services from Zagreb to Belgrade (€19, six hours). At Bajakovo on the border, a Serbian bus takes you on to Belgrade. The Croatia–Serbia border is open to visitors, allowing Americans, Australians, Canadians and Brits to enter the country visa-free.

## Slovenia
Slovenia is also well connected with the Istrian coast. There is one weekday bus between Rovinj and Koper (80KN, three hours) stopping at Piran, Poreč and Portorož (38KN, 1½ hours), as well as a daily bus from Rovinj to Ljubljana (94KN, 5½ hours).

There are also buses from Ljubljana to Zagreb (90KN, three hours, two daily), Rijeka (84KN, 2½ hours, one daily) and Split (299KN, 10½ hours, one daily).

## CAR & MOTORCYCLE
The main highway entry/exit points between Croatia and Hungary are Goričan (between Nagykanisza and Varaždin), Gola (23km east of Koprivnica), Terezino Polje (opposite Barcs) and Donji Miholjac (7km south of Harkány). There are dozens of crossing points to/from Slovenia: too many to list here. There are 23 border crossings into Bosnia and Hercegovina and 10 into Serbia and Montenegro, including the main Zagreb–Belgrade highway. Major destinations in Bosnia and Hercegovina, like Sarajevo, Mostar and Međugorje, are accessible from Zagreb, Split and Dubrovnik.

Motorists require vehicle registration papers and the green insurance card to enter Croatia. Bear in mind that if you rent a car in Italy, many insurance companies will not cover your insurance for a trip into Croatia. Border officials know this and may refuse you entry unless permission to drive into Croatia is clearly marked on the insurance documents. Most car-rental companies in Trieste and Venice are familiar with this requirement and will furnish you with the correct stamp. Otherwise, you must make specific inquiries. See p247 for road rules and further information.

## TRAIN
### Austria
There are two daily and two overnight trains between Vienna and Zagreb (€64, 6½ to 13 hours) and three go on to Rijeka (€74, 11½ to 16½ hours).

### Hungary
There are four daily trains from Zagreb to Budapest (€33, 5½ to 7½ hours).

### Italy
Between Venice and Zagreb (€44, 6½ to 7½ hours) there are two daily direct connections and several more that run through Ljubljana.

### Serbia
There are five daily trains which connect Zagreb with Belgrade (€18, seven hours).

### Slovenia
There are up to eleven trains daily between Zagreb and Ljubljana (€13, 2¼ hours) and four between Rijeka and Ljubljana (€12, three hours).

## Sea
Regular boats from several companies connect Croatia with Italy and Slovenia. Companies and routes arise, change or disappear from season to season; it's important to check information carefully. Many routes are available only in summer and the schedules are usually not available until late spring. All of the boat-company offices in Split are located inside the ferry terminal.

CROATIA

**Jadrolinija** (www.jadrolinija.hr); Rijeka ( ☎ 051-211 444; Riva 16); Ancona ( ☎ 071-20 71 465); Bari ( ☎ 080-52 75 439), Croatia's national boat line, runs car ferries from Ancona to Split (€44, 10 hours) and Zadar (€41, seven hours); a line from Bari to Dubrovnik (€44, eight hours); a year-round ferry from Pescara to Split (€44, 10 hours, twice weekly); and a summer ferry from Pescara to Hvar (€44, nine hours, once weekly). Prices are for deck passage; bringing a car costs an extra €57.50 and a basic couchette is €61.

**SEM** (www.sem-marina.hr); Split ( ☎ 021-338 292; Gat Sv Duje); Ancona ( ☎ 071-20 40 90) connects Ancona with Zadar and Split, continuing on to Stari Grad (Hvar).

**SNAV** (www.snav.com); Ancona ( ☎ 071-20 76 116); Naples ( ☎ 081-76 12 348); Split ( ☎ 021-322 252) has a fast car ferry that links Split with Pescara (€69, 4¾ hours) and Ancona (€63, 4½ hours), and Pescara with Hvar (€80, 3¼ hours). **Sanmar** (www.sanmar.it) handles the same route for a similar price.

**Venezia Lines** ( ☎ 041-52 22 568; www.venezialines .com; Santa Croce 518/A, Venice 30135) runs passenger boats from Venice to the following destinations once, twice or three times weekly, depending on the destination and the month: Pula (€54, three hours), Opatija (€57, four hours), Rovinj (€52, 3¾ hours) and Poreč (€52 2½ hours). The company also covers other Istrian destinations and runs some routes from Rimini and Ravenna.

**Emilia Romagna Lines** (www.emiliaromagnalines.it) is another company that has recently started running summer passenger boats from Italy to the Croatian coast for similar prices. Routes run from Ravenna, Cesenatico, Rimini and Pesaro to Rovinj, Poreč, Pula and Hvar.

In Croatia, contact **Jadroagent** ( ☎ 052-210 431; jadroagent-pula@pu.t-com.hr; Riva 14) in Pula and **Istra Line** ( ☎ 052-451 067; Partizansko 2) in Poreč for information and tickets on boats between Italy and Croatia.

# GETTING AROUND
## Air

Croatia Airlines is the one and only carrier for flights within Croatia. The price of flights depends on the season and you get better deals if you book ahead. Seniors and people aged under 26 get discounts. There are daily flights between Zagreb and Dubrovnik (549KN, one hour), Pula (170KN, 45 minutes), Split (207KN, 45 minutes) and Zadar (341KN, 40 minutes).

## Bicycle

Cycling is a great way to see the islands and bikes are fairly easy to rent in most tourist spots. Many tourist offices have helpful maps of cycling routes. Bike lanes are nearly unknown in Croatia, however; you'll need to exercise extreme caution on the many narrow two-lane roads.

## Boat

Year-round Jadrolinija car ferries operate along the Bari–Rijeka–Dubrovnik coastal route, stopping at Split and the islands of Hvar, Korčula and Mljet. Services are less frequent in winter. The most scenic section is Split to Dubrovnik, which all Jadrolinija ferries cover during the day. Ferries are a lot more comfortable than buses, though somewhat more expensive. From Rijeka to Dubrovnik the deck fare is €21/25 in low/high season, with high season running from about the end of June to the end of August; there's a 20% reduction on the return portion of a return ticket. With a through ticket, deck passengers can stop at any port for up to a week, provided they notify the purser beforehand and have their ticket validated. This is much cheaper than buying individual sector tickets but is only good for one stopover. Cabins should be booked a week ahead, but deck space is usually available on all sailings.

Deck passage on Jadrolinija is just that: *poltrone* (reclining seats) are about €4 extra and four-berth cabins (if available) begin at €38.50/46 in low/high season (Rijeka to Dubrovnik). Cabins can be arranged at the reservation counter aboard ship, but advance bookings are recommended if you want to be sure of a place. You must buy tickets in advance at an agency or Jadrolinija office since they are not sold on board. Bringing a car means checking-in two hours in advance.

Local ferries connect the bigger offshore islands with each other and the mainland. Some of the ferries operate only a couple of times a day, and once the vehicular capacity is reached, the remaining motorists must wait for the next available service. During summer the lines of waiting cars can be long, so it's important to arrive early.

Foot passengers and cyclists should have no problem getting on, but you must buy your tickets at an agency before boarding since they are not sold on board. You should bear in mind that taking a bicycle on these services will incur an extra charge, which depends on the distance.

## Bus

Bus services are excellent and relatively inexpensive. There are often a number of different companies handling each route so prices and trip duration can vary substantially, but the information in this book should give you an idea of what to expect (and unless otherwise noted, all bus prices are for one-way fares). Note that you pay a supplement of 6KN or 7KN for luggage placed under the bus, but not for luggage you take on board with you.

It's generally best to call or visit the bus station to get the complete schedule, but the following companies are among the largest:
**Autotrans** ( ☎ 051-66 03 60; www.autotrans.hr) Based in Rijeka with connections to Istria, Zagreb, Varaždin and Kvarner.
**Brioni Pula** ( ☎ 052-502 997; www.brioni.hr, in Croatian) Based in Pula with connections to Istria, Trieste, Padua, Split and Zagreb.
**Contus** ( ☎ 023-315 315; www.contus.hr) Based in Zadar with connections to Split and Zagreb.

At large stations bus tickets must be purchased at the office; book ahead to be sure of a seat. You must visit the bus station to book as there is no online ticketing available. Tickets for buses that arrive from somewhere else are usually purchased from the conductor. Buy a one-way ticket only or you'll be locked into one company's schedule for the return. Most intercity buses are air-conditioned and make rest stops every two hours or so. Some of the more expensive companies charge extra for a video system that allows you to watch Croatian soap operas during your trip. If you plan to catch a nap, bring earplugs since there's bound to be music playing.

On schedules, *vozi svaki dan* means 'every day' and *ne vozi nedjeljom ni praznikom* means 'not Sunday and public holidays'. Check www.akz.hr, in Croatian, for information on schedules and fares to and from Zagreb.

## Car & Motorcycle

Any valid driving licence is sufficient to legally drive and rent a car; an international driving licence is not necessary. **Hrvatski Autoklub** (HAK; Croatian Auto Club) offers help and advice, plus there's the nationwide **HAK road assistance** (vučna služba; ☎ 987).

Petrol stations are generally open 7am to 7pm and often until 10pm in summer. Petrol is Eurosuper 95, Super 98, normal or diesel. See www.ina.hr for up-to-date fuel prices.

You have to pay tolls on the motorways linking Zagreb with the coast, and to use the Učka tunnel between Rijeka and Istria, the bridge to Krk Island and the road from Rijeka to Delnice. For general news on Croatia's motorways and tolls, see www.hac.hr.

### ROAD RULES

Unless otherwise posted, the speed limits for cars and motorcycles are 50km/h in the built-up areas, 80km/h on main highways and 130km/h on motorways. On any of Croatia's winding two-lane highways, it's illegal to pass long military convoys or a line of cars caught behind a slow-moving truck. The maximum permitted amount of alcohol in the blood is – none at all! It is also forbidden to use a mobile phone while driving and seatbelts are mandatory.

### CAR-RENTAL COMPANIES

The large car-rental chains represented in Croatia are Avis, Budget, Europcar and Hertz. Independent local companies are often much cheaper than the international chains, but the chains have the big advantage of offering one-way rentals that allow you to drop the car off at any one of their many stations in Croatia free of charge.

Prices at local companies begin at around 300KN a day with unlimited kilometres. Shop around as deals vary widely and 'special' discounts and weekend rates are often available. Third-party public liability insurance is included by law, but make sure your quoted price includes full collision insurance, called collision damage waiver (CDW); otherwise your responsibility for damage done to the vehicle is usually determined as a percentage of the car's value. Full CDW begins at 40KN a day extra (compulsory for those aged under 25), theft insurance is 15KN a day and personal accident insurance another 40KN a day.

Sometimes you can get a lower car-rental rate by booking the car from abroad or on-line. **Economy Car Rentals** (www.economycarrentals .com) often has the best deals. Tour companies in Western Europe often have fly-drive packages that include a flight to Croatia and a car (two-person minimum).

CROATIA

## Hitching

Hitching is never entirely safe, and we don't recommend it. Hitchhiking in Croatia is particularly unreliable. You'll have better luck on the islands, but in the interior cars are small and usually full.

## Local Transport

Zagreb has a well-developed tram system as well as local buses, but in the rest of the country you'll find only buses. In major cities such as Rijeka, Split, Zadar and Dubrovnik, buses run about every 20 minutes, though less often on Sunday. Small medieval towns along the coast are generally closed to traffic and have infrequent links to outlying suburbs.

Taxis are available in all cities and towns, but they must be called or boarded at a taxi stand. Prices are rather high (meters start at 25KN).

## Train

Train travel is about 15% cheaper than bus travel and often more comfortable, although slower. The main lines run from Zagreb to Rijeka, Zadar and Split and east to Osijek. There are no trains along the coast. Local trains usually have only unreserved 2nd-class seats. Reservations may be required on express trains. 'Executive' trains have only 1st-class seats and are 40% more expensive than local trains.

On posted timetables in Croatia, the word for arrivals is *dolazak* and for departures it's *odlazak* or *polazak*. For train information check out **Croatian Railway** (www.hznet.hr, in Croatian).

# Czech Republic

For a country that's only been around since 1993, the Czech Republic does a fine job of showcasing a thrilling history. Castles and chateaux abound, illuminating the stories of powerful families and individuals whose influence was felt well beyond the nation's current borders. Unravel the history of Bohemia and Moravia and you're delving into the legacy of Europe itself.

Experience beautifully preserved Renaissance towns, but include a 21st-century spin by sharing a chilled Pilsner lager in street-side cafés with a forthright population confidently taking its place in a united Europe. And if the architectural splendour overwhelms, explore some of Europe's most idiosyncratic landscapes and spectacular forests, which are making a comeback after the industrial sabotage and neglect of the communist era.

The impact of 1989's Velvet Revolution is most obvious in Prague, a stunning melange of high culture, architectural achievement and modern Europe, but spend time in the rest of the country as well. Take in the audacious cliff-top chateau and improbably arcing river at Český Krumlov, the discreetly confident Moravian university town of Olomouc, and the energetic blue-collar Bohemian beer towns of Plzeň and České Budějovice.

You'll soon discover that the Czech Republic is as much about the future as the past.

## FAST FACTS

- **Area** 78,864 sq km
- **Capital** Prague
- **Currency** Czech crown (Kč); A$1 = 16.55Kč; €1 = 28.45Kč; Ą100 = 19.47Kč; NZ$1 = 13.56Kč; UK£1 = 41.48Kč; US$1= 22.29Kč
- **Famous for** beer, ice hockey, Kafka, Dvořák
- **Official Language** Czech
- **Phrases** *Dobrý den/ahoj* (hello/informal), *na shledanou* (goodbye), *děkuji* (thank you), *promiňte* (excuse me)
- **Population** 10.2 million
- **Telephone codes** country code ☎ 420; international access code ☎ 00; there are no telephone codes in the Czech Republic
- **Visas** Citizens of Australia, Canada, Israel, Japan, New Zealand, Switzerland and the USA can stay for up to 90 days without a visa (see p309)

# CZECH REPUBLIC

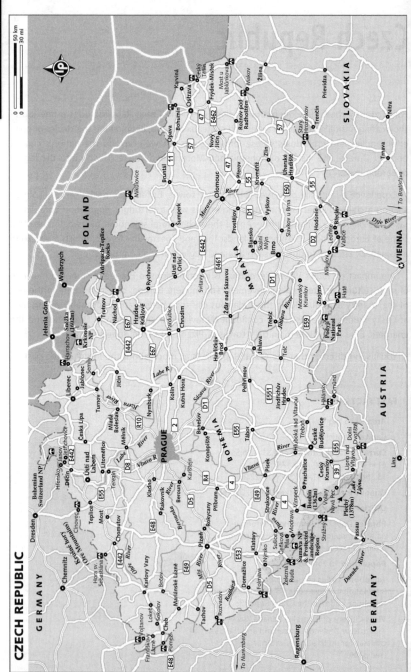

## HIGHLIGHTS

- Tune out the tourist crowds in **Prague** (p256) and immerse yourself in the city's legacy of art, architecture and existential angst.
- Conduct your own taste test of two of the world's finest beers at **Plzeň** (p286) and **České Budějovice** (p289).
- Navigate through the spectacular rock formations and hidden river valleys of the **Bohemian Switzerland National Park** (p282).
- Keep the gorgeous old town square of **Olomouc** (p300) and its relaxed student ambience as your own special secret.

## ITINERARIES

- **One week** Give Prague its best chance to grab your heart – it's worth at least three days. Mix it up with day trips to Kutná Hora and Terezín, and then head south to Český Krumlov for a couple of days riverside R&R.
- **Two weeks** Begin by sampling the spa waters at Karlovy Vary, and then balance the ledger with beer tasting at Plzeň. Continue to Prague and discover it's actually worth at least five days. If you're not all walked out, divert northeast to hike through the Adršpach-Teplice Rocks. More relaxed souls should head south to Český Krumlov for riverside cafés and lazy meandering down the Vltava. Continue east to Telč's Renaissance grandeur and Brno's cosmopolitan galleries and museums. Squeeze in a day trip to the nearby Moravian Karst caves, and continue to underrated Olomouc to admire the Holy Trinity Column.

## CLIMATE & WHEN TO GO

The Czech climate is temperate, with cool, humid winters, warm summers and distinct spring and autumn seasons. While summer has the best weather, July and August are very busy so it's better to visit in May, June or September. Winter has its charms, but Easter, Christmas and New Year are also busy. During the Prague Spring festival (in May), accommodation in Prague can be scarce.

Also see Climate Charts (p911).

## HISTORY

Czech history is the story of a people doing whatever they can to survive occupation, and Czechs are more interested in the stories of their rebels and heretics than they are of the kings, emperors and dictators who oppressed them.

Sited in the middle of Europe, the Czechs have been invaded by the Habsburgs, the Nazis, the Soviets, and now by tour groups. Many see EU membership as just another occupation. The Czechs' location has meant none of their local upheavals has stayed local for long. Their rejection of Catholicism in 1418 resulted in the Hussite Wars. The 1618 revolt against Habsburg rule ignited the Thirty Years' War, and the German annexation of the Sudetenland in 1938 helped fuel WWII. The liberal reforms of 1968's Prague Spring led to tanks rolling in from across the Eastern Bloc, and the peaceful ousting of the government during 1989's Velvet Revolution is a model for freedom-seekers everywhere.

### Bohemian Beginnings

Ringed by hills, the ancient Czech lands of Bohemia and Moravia have formed natural territories since earliest times. A Celtic tribe called the Boii gave Bohemia its name, while Moravia comes from the Morava River, a Germanic name meaning 'marsh water'.

Slavic tribes from the east settled these territories, and they united from 830 to 907 in the Great Moravian Empire. Christianity was adopted after the arrival in 863 of the Thessalonian missionaries Cyril and Methodius, who created the first Slavic (Cyrillic) alphabet.

---

**HOW MUCH?**

- **Night in hostel** 400Kč
- **Double room in pension** 1000Kč
- **Spa Wafer** 5Kč
- **Shot of Becherovka** 45Kč
- **Postcard home** 11Kč

**LONELY PLANET INDEX**

- **Litre of petrol** 30Kč
- **Litre of bottled water** 35Kč
- **Half-litre of beer** 35Kč
- **Souvenir T-shirt** 300Kč
- **Street snack (sausage & mustard)** 15Kč

In the 9th century the first home-grown dynasty, the Přemysls, erected some huts on a hill in what was to become Prague. This dysfunctional clan gave the Czechs their first martyred saints – Ludmila, killed by her daughter-in-law in 874, and her grandson, the pious Prince Václav (or Good 'King' Wenceslas; r 921–29), murdered by his brother Boleslav the Cruel.

The rule of the Přemysls ended in 1306, and in 1310 John of Luxembourg came to the Bohemian throne through marriage, and annexed the kingdom to the German Empire. The reign of his son, Charles IV (1346–78), who became Holy Roman Emperor, saw the first of Bohemia's two 'Golden Ages' – Charles founded Prague's St Vitus Cathedral, built Charles Bridge, and established Charles University. The second was the reign of Rudolf II (1576–1612), who made Prague the capital of the Habsburg Empire and attracted artists, scholars and scientists to his court. Bohemia and Moravia remained under Habsburg dominion for almost four centuries.

## Under the Habsburg Thumb

In 1415 the Protestant religious reformer Jan Hus, rector of Charles University, was burnt at the stake for heresy. Hus led a movement that espoused letting the congregation taste the sacramental wine as well as the host (the Hussites' symbol was the communion chalice). The religious and nationalist Hussite movement, which plunged Bohemia into civil war between 1419 and 1434 was inspired by his ideas.

When the Austrian – and Catholic – Habsburg dynasty ascended the Bohemian throne in 1526, the fury of the Counter-Reformation was unleashed on 23 May 1618 when a group of Protestants threw two Habsburg councillors from a Prague Castle window. The squabble escalated into the Catholic–Protestant Thirty Years' War (1618–48), which devastated much of central Europe and shattered Bohemia's economy.

The defeat of the Protestant uprising at the Battle of White Mountain in 1620 marked the start of a long period of forced re-Catholicisation, Germanisation and oppression of Czech language and culture. The baroque architectural style, which flourished in the 17th and 18th centuries, was the outward symbol of Catholic victory over the Protestant heretics.

## National Reawakening

The Czechs began to rediscover their linguistic and cultural roots at the start of the 19th century, during the so-called Národní obrození (National Revival). Overt political activity was banned, so the revival was culturally based. Important figures of the time included historian Josef Palacký and composer Bedřich Smetana. A distinctive neo-Renaissance architecture emerged, exemplified by Prague's National Theatre and National Museum.

The drive towards an independent Czech and Slovak state was realised after WWI, when the Habsburg Empire's demise saw the creation of the Czechoslovak Republic on 28 October 1918. The first president was Tomáš Garrigue Masaryk. Three-quarters of the Austro-Hungarian empire's industrial power was inherited by Czechoslovakia, as were three million Germans, mostly in the border areas of Bohemia (the pohraniči, known in German as the Sudetenland).

The Czechs' elation was to be short-lived. Under the Munich Pact of September 1938, Britain and France accepted the annexation of the Sudetenland by Nazi Germany, and in March 1939 the Germans occupied the rest of the country (calling it the Protectorate of Bohemia and Moravia).

The rapid occupation ensured the country's historic buildings suffered minimal damage, but most of the Czech intelligentsia and 80,000 Jews died at the hands of the Nazis. When Czech paratroopers assassinated the Nazi governor Reinhardt Heydrich in 1942, the entire town of Lidice was wiped out in revenge.

## Communist Coup

After the war, the Czechoslovak government expelled 2.5 million Sudeten Germans – including antifascists who had fought the Nazis – from the Czech borderlands and confiscated their property. During the forced marches from Czechoslovakia many were interned in concentration camps, and it is estimated that tens of thousands died. In 1997 Czech Prime Minister Václav Klaus and German chancellor Helmut Kohl signed a declaration of mutual apology, but many Sudeten Germans are still campaigning for the restitution of lost land and houses.

In 1947 a power struggle began between the communist and democratic forces, and in early 1948 the Social Democrats withdrew from the postwar coalition. The result was the Soviet-backed coup d'état of 25 February 1948, known as *Vítězný únor* (Victorious February). The new communist-led government established the dictatorship of the proletariat, and communist leader Klement Gottwald became the country's president.

The industrial sector was nationalised and the government's economic policies nearly bankrupted the country. The 1950s were repressive years and thousands of noncommunists fled the country. Many were imprisoned and hundreds were executed or died in labour camps for no more than believing in democracy or religion. A series of Stalinist purges were organised, and many, including top party members, were executed.

## Prague Spring & Velvet Revolution

In April 1968 the new first secretary of the Communist Party, Alexander Dubček, introduced liberalising reforms to create 'socialism with a human face' – known as the 'Prague Spring'. Censorship ended, political prisoners were released and economic decentralisation began. Moscow was not happy, but Dubček refused to buckle. Soviet tanks entered Prague on 20 August 1968, and Czechoslovakia was subsequently occupied by 200,000 Soviet and Warsaw Pact soldiers.

Around 14,000 Communist Party functionaries were expelled, and 500,000 party members lost their jobs after the dictatorship was re-established. Dissidents were summarily imprisoned and educated professionals were made manual labourers.

The 1977 trial of the rock group The Plastic People of the Universe inspired the formation of the human-rights group Charter 77. (The communists saw the musicians as threatening the status quo, but others viewed the trial as an assault on human rights.) Charter 77's group of Prague intellectuals, including the playwright/philosopher Václav Havel, continued their underground opposition throughout the 1980s.

By 1989 Gorbachev's perestroika was sending shock waves through the region and the fall of the Berlin Wall on 9 November raised expectations of change in Czechoslovakia. On 17 November an official student march in Prague was smashed by police. Daily demonstrations followed, and the protests grew to a general strike on 27 November. Dissidents led by Havel formed the anti-Communist

Civic Forum and negotiated the resignation of the Communist government on 3 December.

A 'Government of National Understanding' was formed, with Havel elected president on 29 December. With no casualties, the days after 17 November became known as *Sametová revoluce* (the 'Velvet Revolution').

## Velvet Divorce

Following the dissolution of the communists' central authority, antagonisms between Slovakia and Prague re-emerged. The federal parliament tried to stabilise the situation by granting both the Czech and Slovak Republics full federal status within a Czech and Slovak Federated Republic (ČSFR), but failed to satisfy Slovak nationalists. The Civic Forum split into two factions: the centrist Civic Movement and the Civic Democratic Party (ODS).

Elections in June 1992 sealed Czechoslovakia's fate. Václav Klaus' ODS took 48 seats in the 150-seat federal parliament; while 24 went to the Movement for a Democratic Slovakia (HZDS), a left-leaning Slovak nationalist party led by Vladimír Mečiar.

In July, goaded by Mečiar's rhetoric, the Slovak parliament declared sovereignty. The two leaders could not reach a compromise and splitting the country was seen as the best solution. On 1 January 1993 Czechoslovakia ceased to exist for the second time. Prague became capital of the new Czech Republic, and Havel was elected its first president.

Thanks to booming tourism and a solid industrial base, the Czech Republic started strongly. Unemployment was negligible, shops were full and, by 2003, Prague enjoyed Eastern Europe's highest living standards. Capitalism also meant a lack of affordable housing, rising crime and a deteriorating health system.

In 2003, Václav Havel was replaced by former prime minister Klaus - it took three elections for Czechs to settle on a new president, and the uncharismatic and conservative Klaus is far from the popular leader Havel was. Further government instability followed inconclusive elections in June 2006 that left the Czech Republic's lower house equally divided between the left and the right.

Left-leaning Social Democrat leader Jiri Paroubek finally resigned as Prime Minister in August 2006, and was replaced by right-leaning Civic Democrats leader Mirek

**MIND YOUR MANNERS**

It is customary to say *dobrý den* (good day) when entering a shop, café or quiet bar, and *na shledanou* (goodbye) when leaving. If you are invited to a Czech home, bring fresh flowers and remember to remove your shoes when you enter the house.

Topolanek in an attempt to form a minority government. The country's next general election is planned for 2009, but at the time of writing an early election was looking far more likely due to the impasse in the Czech Republic's lower house.

The Czech Republic became a member of NATO in 1999, and joined the EU on 1 May 2004. With EU membership, greater numbers of younger Czechs are working and studying abroad, seizing opportunities their parents didn't have. The Czech Republic is scheduled to adopt the euro in 2010.

## PEOPLE

The population of the Czech Republic is 10.2 million, and fairly homogeneous: 95% of the population are Czech and 3% are Slovak. Only 150,000 of the three million Sudeten Germans evicted after WWII remain, comprising about 1.5% of the current population. A significant Roma population (0.3%) is subject to hostility and racism, and suffers from poverty and unemployment.

## RELIGION

Most Czechs are either atheist (39.8%) or nominally Roman Catholic (39.2%), but church attendance is low. There are small Protestant (4.6%) and Orthodox (3%) congregations, while the Jewish community (1% of the population in 1918) today numbers only a few thousand. Religious tolerance is accepted and the Catholic Church does not involve itself in politics.

## ARTS
### Literature

Franz Kafka was one of Bohemia's greatest writers, and his circle of German-speaking Jewish writers strongly influenced Prague's literary scene in the early 20th century.

After WWI Jaroslav Hašek devoted himself to lampooning the Habsburg empire and its minions; his folk masterpiece *The Good Sol-*dier *Švejk* is a riotous story of a Czech soldier during WWI.

Bohumil Hrabal (1914–97), one of the finest Czech novelists of the 20th century, wrote *The Little Town Where Time Stood Still*, a gentle portrayal of the machinations of small-town life.

Milan Kundera (b 1929) is the most renowned Czech writer internationally, with his novel *The Unbearable Lightness of Being* having been made into a film. His first work *The Joke* is a penetrating insight into the communist era's paranoia.

An interesting contemporary Czech writer is poet and rock-lyricist Jáchym Topol, whose stream-of-consciousness novel *Sister City Silver* is an exhilarating exploration of post-communist Prague.

### Cinema

*Cesky Sen* (Czech Dream, 2004) is a recent feature documentary showing the hoax launch of a new Czech department store. With a fake marketing campaign, fake advertising and even a massive fake façade to the new hypermarket, *Cesky Sen* is a timely observation of the post-communist expectations of Czech society in the months leading to their entry into the EU.

### Music

Bedřich Smetana (1824–84), the first great Czech composer and an icon of Czech pride, created a national style by incorporating folk songs and dances into his classical compositions. His best-known pieces are the operas *Prodaná Nevěsta* (The Bartered Bride) and *Dalibor a Libuše* (Dalibor and Libuše, named after the two main characters), and the symphonic-poem cycle *Má vlast* (My Homeland). Prague Spring (p307), the country's biggest festival, is dedicated to Smetana and begins with a parade from the composer's grave at Vyšehrad to the Smetana Hall, where *Má vlast* is then performed.

Antonín Dvořák (1841–1904) is perhaps everyone's favourite Czech composer. His most popular works include his symphony *From the New World* (composed in the USA while lecturing there for four years), his *Slavonic Dances* of 1878 and 1881, the operas *The Devil & Kate* and *Rusalka*, and his religious masterpiece *Stabat Mater*.

### Visual Arts

Think Art Nouveau and you're probably thinking Alfons Mucha (1860– 1939). Though he lived mostly in Paris and is associated with the French Art Nouveau movement, Mucha's heart remained at home in Bohemia and much of his work visits and revisits themes of Slavic suffering, courage and cross-nation brotherhood. The most outstanding of his works is a series of 20 large, cinematic canvasses called the *Slav Epic,* which are presently in Moravský Krumlov (p300), and his interior decoration in the Municipal House in Prague (see p264), but his design and print work can be seen all over the Czech Republic.

David Černý (b 1967) is a controversial contemporary Czech sculptor. His work includes the statue of St Wenceslas riding an upside-down horse in Prague's pasáž Lucerna, and the giant babies crawling up the Žižkov TV tower in Prague. See www.davidcerny.cz.

## ENVIRONMENT

The Czech Republic is a landlocked country bordered by Germany, Austria, Slovakia and Poland. The land is made up of two river basins: Bohemia in the west, drained by the Labe (Elbe) River flowing north into Germany; and Moravia in the east, drained by the Morava River flowing southeast into the Danube. Each basin is ringed by low, forest-clad hills, notably the Šumava range along the Bavarian–Austrian border in the southwest, the Krušné hory (Ore Mountains) along the northwestern border with Germany, and the Krkonoše mountains along the Polish border east of Liberec. The country's highest peak, Sněžka (1602m), is in the Krkonoše. In between these ranges are rolling plains mixed with forests and farm land. Forests – mainly spruce, oak and beech – still cover one-third of the country.

The South Bohemian landscape is characterised by a network of hundreds of linked fish ponds and artificial lakes. The biggest lake in the republic, the 4870-hectare Lake Lipno, is also in South Bohemia. East Bohemia is home to the striking 'rock towns' of the Adršpach-Teplice Rocks (p295).

## National Parks

Though numerous areas are set aside as national parks and protected landscape areas, the emphasis is on visitor use as well as species and landscape protection. National parks and protected areas make up approximately 15% of the Czech Republic, including the Bohemian Switzerland (p282)

and Šumava (p294) national parks, as well as the Adršpach-Teplice Protected Landscape Area (p295).

## Environmental Issues

The forests of northern Bohemia and Moravia have been devastated by acid rain created by the burning of poor-quality brown coal at factories and thermal power stations. The most affected region is the eastern Ore Mountains where most of the trees are dead. In recent years sulphur dioxide levels in Prague have declined, while carbon monoxide pollution from cars and trucks has increased. Industrial emissions have been cleaned up in recent years following the entry of the Czech Republic into the EU in 2004. Local industries are being forced to adopt stringent environmental codes which are further alleviating domestic pollution.

Following the entry of the Czech Republic into the EU in 2004, local industries are being forced to adopt EU environmental codes, which should further alleviate domestic pollution.

## FOOD & DRINK

On the surface, Czech food seems very similar to German or Polish food: lots of meat served with *knedlíky* (dumplings) and cabbage. The little differences make the food here special – eat a forkful of *svíčková* (roast beef served with a sour-cream sauce and spices) sopped up with fluffy *knedlíky* and you'll be wondering why you haven't heard more about this cuisine.

## Staples & Specialities

Traditional Czech cuisine is strong on meat, *knedlíky* and gravy, and weak on fresh vegetables; the classic Bohemian dish is *knedlo-zelo-vepřo* – bread dumplings, sauerkraut and roast pork. Other tasty homegrown delicacies to look out for include *cesneková* (garlic soup), *svíčková na smetaně* (roast beef with sour cream sauce and cranberries) and *kapr na kmíní* (fried or baked carp with caraway seed). *Ovocné knedlíky* (fruit dumplings), with whole fruit, are served as a dessert with cottage cheese or crushed poppy seeds and melted butter.

The Czech Republic is a beer-drinker's paradise – where else could you get a 500mL glass of top-quality Pilsner for less than a dollar? One of the first words of Czech you'll

### TOP FIVE BEERS

Czech beer is not just about Pilsner Urquell and Budvar. Watch out for these interesting brews:

- Černá Hora (Black Mountain) Brewery's honey-flavoured Kvasar lager.
- Bernard's special *cerne pivo* (dark beer), which uses five different malts.
- The wheat beer with lemon at Pivnice Pegas in Brno.
- The champagne beer at Pivovarský Dům in Prague.
- Zlatý Bažant (Golden Pheasant) lager from Slovakia.

learn is *pivo* (beer). The Czechs serve their draught beer with a high head of foam.

Bohemian *pivo* is probably the best in the world – the most famous brands are Budvar (see p289) and Pilsner Urquell (p286). The South Moravian vineyards (p304) produce reasonable *bílé víno* (white wines).

Special alcoholic treats include Becherovka (see p282) and *slivovice* (plum brandy). *Grog* is rum with hot water and sugar. *Limonáda* often refers to any soft drink, not just lemonade.

### Where to Eat & Drink

A *bufet* or *samoobsluha* is a self-service, cafeteria-style place with *chlebíčky* (open sandwiches), salads, *klobásy* (spicy sausages), *špekačky* (mild pork sausages), *párky* (frankfurters), *guláš* (goulash) and of course *knedlíky*. Some of these places are tucked to the side of *potraviny* (food shops). A *bageteria* serves made-to-order sandwiches and baguettes.

A *pivnice* is a pub without food, while a *hospoda* or *hostinec* is a pub or beer hall that serves basic meals. A *vinárna* (wine bar) may have anything from snacks to a full-blown menu. The occasional *kavárna* (café) has a full menu but most only serve snacks and desserts. A *restaurace* is any restaurant.

Restaurants start serving as early as 11am and carry on till midnight; some take a break between lunch and dinner. Main dishes may stop being served well before the advertised closing time, with only snacks and drinks after that.

### Vegetarians & Vegans

In Prague and other main cities there is a growing range of vegetarian restaurants, but options in the smaller towns remain more limited. Vegans will find life very difficult. There are a few standard *bezmasá jídla* (meatless dishes) served by most restaurants: the most common are *smažený sýr* (fried cheese) and vegetables cooked with cheese sauce. The pizza joints that you'll find in almost every town make for a good standby option.

### Habits & Customs

Most beer halls have a system of marking everything you eat or drink on a small piece of paper that is left on your table, then totted up when you pay (say *zaplatím, prosím* – I'd like to pay, please). Waiters in all Czech restaurants, including the expensive ones, often whisk away empty plates from under your nose before you manage to swallow the last of your *knedlíky*.

In a pub, always ask if a chair is free before sitting down (*Je tu volno?*). The standard toast involves clinking together first the tops, then the bottoms of glasses, then touching the glass to the table; most people say *Na zdraví* (To health).

# PRAGUE

**pop 1.19 million**

It's the perfect irony of Prague. You are lured there by the past, but compelled to linger by the present and the future. Fill your days with its artistic and architectural heritage – from Gothic and Renaissance to Art Nouveau and Cubist – but after dark move your focus to the here and now in the form of lively bars, cutting-edge galleries and innovative jazz clubs. And if the frantic energy of post-communist Prague and its army of tourists wears thin, that's OK. Just drink a glass of the country's legendary premium Bohemian lager, relax and be reassured that quiet moments still exist in one of Europe's most exciting cities: a private dawn on Charles Bridge; a chilled beer in Letná as you gaze upon the surreal cityscape of Staré Město; or getting reassuringly lost in the intimate streets of Malá Strana. You'll then be ready to dive once more into this thrilling collage of past and future.

## ORIENTATION

Central Prague nestles in a bend of the Vltava River, which separates Hradčany (the medieval castle district) and Malá Strana (Little Quarter) on the west bank from Staré Město (Old Town) and Nové Město (New Town) on the east.

Prague Castle, visible from almost everywhere in the city, overlooks Malá Strana, while the twin Gothic spires of Týn Church dominate the wide open space of Staroměstské nám (Old Town Square). The broad avenue of Václavské nám (Wenceslas Square) stretches southeast from Staré Město towards the National Museum and the main train station.

You can walk from Praha-hlavní nádraží (Prague's main train station) to Staroměstské nám in 10 minutes. From Praha-Holešovice, take the metro (also 10 minutes) to Staroměstské nám. There's a metro station at Florenc bus station too; take Line B (yellow) two stops west to Můstek for the city centre.

### Maps

Lonely Planet's plastic-coated *Prague City Map* is convenient and detailed. Other good maps include Marco Polo's *Praha – centrum* (1:5,000) and SHOCart's GeoClub *Praha – plán města* (1:15,000). PIS offers a free *Welcome to the Czech Republic* pamphlet with a map of the city centre.

## INFORMATION
### Bookshops

**Anagram** (Map pp266-7; ☎ 224 895 737; www.anagram.cz; Týn 4, Staré Město; ☯ 10am-8pm Mon-Sat, 10am-7pm Sun) An excellent range of history and culture books.

**Big Ben Bookshop** (Map pp266-7; ☎ 224 826 565; www.bigbenbookshop.com; Malá Štupartská 5, Staré Město; ☯ 9am-6.30pm Mon-Fri, 10am-5pm Sat & Sun) Prague's biggest range of English-language books, magazines and newspapers.

**Globe** (Map pp266-7; ☎ 224 934 203; www.globebookstore.cz; Pštrossova 6, Nové Město; ☯ 10am-midnight) Has new and secondhand books in English and German, a good range of magazines and Prague's biggest gay and lesbian interest section.

**Kiwi** (Map pp266-7; ☎ 224 948 455; Jungmannova 23, Nové Město; ☯ 9am-6.30pm Mon-Fri, 9am-2pm Sat) A specialist travel bookshop with a huge range of maps and guidebooks.

**Neo Luxor** (Map pp266-7; ☎ 221 111 364; Václavské nám 41, Nové Město; ☯ 8am-8pm Mon-Fri, 9am-7pm Sat, 10am-7pm Sun) Books and magazines in English, German and French and internet access (1Kč per minute).

### Emergencies

If your passport, wallet or other valuables have been stolen, obtain a police report and crime number from the **State Police Station** (Map pp266-7; Vlašská 3, Malá Strana; ☯ 24hr). You will need this to make an insurance claim. Unless you speak Czech, forget about telephoning the police, as you will rarely get through to an English speaker.

### Internet Access

An increasing number of hotels, bars, fast-food restaurants and internet cafés in Prague provide wi-fi hotspots where can use your own laptop.

**Bohemia Bagel** (per min 1.50Kč) Malá Strana (Map pp266-7; ☎ 257 310 694; Újezd 16; ☯ 7am-midnight); Staré Město (Map pp266-7; ☎ 224 812 560; Masná 2; ☯ 7am-midnight). Also provides low-cost international phone calls.

**Globe** (Map pp266-7; ☎ 224 934 203; www.globebookstore.cz; Pštrossova 6, Nové Město; per min 1.50Kč, no minimum; ☯ 10am-midnight) Also has ethernet sockets where you can connect your own laptop (same price; cables provided, 50Kč deposit).

**Mobilarium** (Map pp266-7; ☎ 221 967 327; Rathova Pasaž, Na příkopě 23, Nové Město; per min 1.50Kč; ☯ 10am-8pm Mon-Fri, 11am-8pm Sat & Sun)

**Planeta** (Map pp258-9; ☎ 267 311 182; Vinohradská 102, Vinohrady; per min 0.40-0.80Kč; ☯ 8am-11pm) Cheap rates before 10am and after 8pm Monday to Friday, and 8am to 11pm Saturday and Sunday.

**Praha Bike** (Map pp266-7; ☎ 732 388 880; Dlouhá 24; Staré Město; per min 1Kč; ☯ 9am-7pm Mar-Nov, noon-6pm Oct-Feb) Wi-fi at same cost.

### Internet Resources

**Dopravní podnik** (www.dp-praha.cz) Information about public transport in Prague.

**Prague Information Service** (www.prague-info.cz) Official tourist office site.

**Prague Post** (www.praguepost.cz) Keep up-to-date with news, events and visitor information with this English-language website.

**Prague TV** (www.prague.tv) Highlights Prague's best events, arts and nightlife.

### Laundry

Most self-service laundrettes will charge around 160Kč to wash and dry a 6kg load of laundry.

**Laundry Kings** (Map pp258-9; ☎ 233 343 743; Dejvická 16, Dejvice; ☯ 7am-10pm Mon-Fri, 8am-10pm Sat & Sun)

**CZECH REPUBLIC**

# PRAGUE

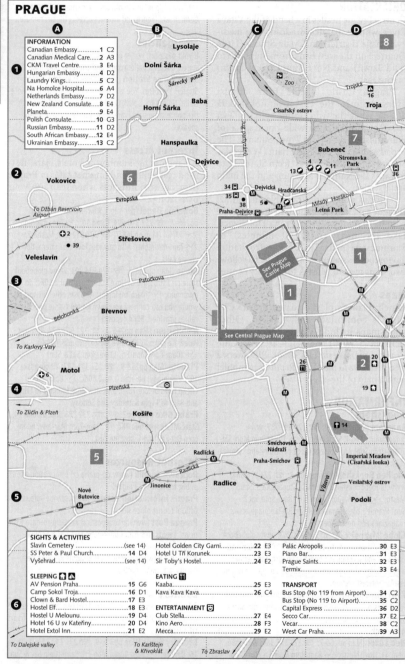

**INFORMATION**

| | |
|---|---|
| Canadian Embassy...............1 | C2 |
| Canadian Medical Care.....2 | A3 |
| CKM Travel Centre...........3 | E4 |
| Hungarian Embassy...........4 | D2 |
| Laundry Kings..................5 | C2 |
| Na Homolce Hospital........6 | A4 |
| Netherlands Embassy.......7 | D2 |
| New Zealand Consulate....8 | E4 |
| Planeta............................9 | E4 |
| Polish Consulate............10 | G3 |
| Russian Embassy.............11 | D2 |
| South African Embassy....12 | E4 |
| Ukrainian Embassy.........13 | C2 |

**SIGHTS & ACTIVITIES**

| | |
|---|---|
| Slavín Cemetery ............................(see 14) | |
| SS Peter & Paul Church..................14 | D4 |
| Vyšehrad.......................................(see 14) | |

**SLEEPING**

| | |
|---|---|
| AV Pension Praha...........................15 | G6 |
| Camp Sokol Troja...........................16 | D1 |
| Clown & Bard Hostel.......................17 | E3 |
| Hostel Elf......................................18 | E3 |
| Hostel U Melounu...........................19 | D4 |
| Hotel 16 U sv Kateřiny ...................20 | D4 |
| Hotel Extol Inn..............................21 | E2 |

**EATING**

| | |
|---|---|
| Kaaba...........................................25 | E3 |
| Kava Kava Kava..............................26 | C4 |

**ENTERTAINMENT**

| | |
|---|---|
| Club Stella.....................................27 | E4 |
| Kino Aero.......................................28 | F3 |
| Mecca............................................29 | E2 |

| | |
|---|---|
| Hotel Golden City Garni..................22 | E3 |
| Hotel U Tří Korunek........................23 | E3 |
| Sir Toby's Hostel............................24 | E2 |

| | |
|---|---|
| Palác Akropolis..............................30 | E3 |
| Piano Bar.......................................31 | E3 |
| Prague Saints.................................32 | E3 |
| Termix...........................................33 | E4 |

**TRANSPORT**

| | |
|---|---|
| Bus Stop (No 119 from Airport)........34 | C2 |
| Bus Stop (No 119 to Airport)...........35 | C2 |
| Capital Express ..............................36 | D2 |
| Secco Car......................................37 | C2 |
| Vecar.............................................38 | C2 |
| West Car Praha..............................39 | A3 |

To Dalejské valley

To Karlštejn & Křivoklát

To Zbraslav

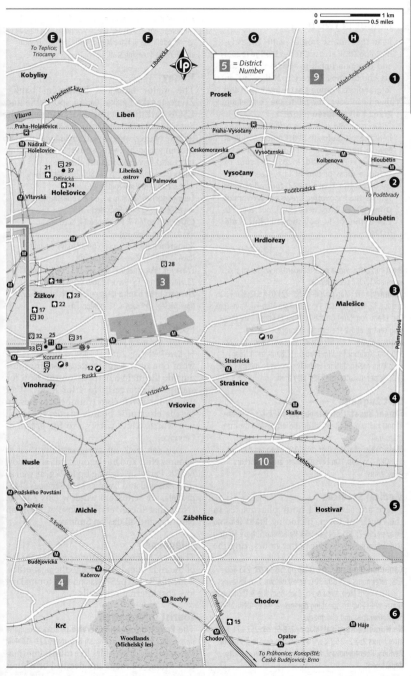

0 — 1 km
0 — 0.5 miles

5 = District Number

**E**
To Teplice;
Triocamp

Kobylisy

V Holešovičkách

Vltava

Praha-Holešovice

Nádraží
Holešovice

21  29
37

Dělnická
24

Vltavská  Holešovice

18

Žižkov  23
22

17
30

32  25
31
33  3
9
27  8
12
Korunní
Ruská

Vinohrady

Nusle

Pražského Povstání
Pankrác
5. května
Michle

Budějovická
Kačerov

4

Krč

Woodlands
(Michelský les)

**F**
Liberecká

Libeň

Libeňský
ostrov
Palmovka

**G**
Prosek

Praha-Vysočany
Českomoravská
Vysočany

Hrdlořezy

28
3

10

Strašnická
Strašnice

Vršovická
Vršovice

10  Švehlova

Zábehlice

15
Chodov
Opatov
To Průhonice; Konopiště;
České Budějovice; Brno

Roztyly
Brněnská

**H**
Mladoboleslavská

9

Kbelská

Vysočanská
Kolbenova  Hloubětín

Podebradská
To Poděbrady

Hloubětín

Malešice

Průmyslová

Skalka

Hostivař

Chodov  Háje

**1**
**2**
**3**
**4**
**5**
**6**

**PRAGUE IN TWO DAYS**

Beat the tourist hordes with an early-morning stroll across **Charles Bridge** (p263) and continue uphill to Hradčany and the eclectic **Strahov Library** (p263). Move on to grandiose **Prague Castle** (opposite) and then head down the hill to the compelling **Franz Kafka Museum** (p263).

On day two continue exploring Kafka's heritage in **Josefov** (p264), Prague's original Jewish quarter, and then visit the hilltop fortress at **Vyšehrad** (p265). Be sure to savour a glass or two of tasty Czech beer: try **U Zlatého Tygra** (p272) for tradition, or sample the innovative brews at **Pivovarský Dům** (p272). After dark check out the jazz vibe at the coolly sophisticated **Dinitz Café** (p271).

Expat-run place with a bulletin board, newspapers and internet (1.50Kč per minute).

**Laundryland** (Map pp266-7; ☎ 221 014 632; Na příkopě 12, Nové Město; ☒ 9am-8pm Mon-Fri, 9am-7pm Sat, 11am-7pm Sun) On the 1st floor of Černá Růže shopping centre, above the Panská entrance.

**Prague Cyber Laundromat** (Map pp258-9; ☎ 222 510 180; Korunní 14, Vinohrady; ☒ 8am-8pm) Near Nám Míru metro station. Friendly place with internet café (1.50Kč per minute) and kids' play area.

## Left Luggage

**Florenc bus station** (per bag per day 25Kč; ☒ 5am-11pm) Halfway up the stairs on the left beyond the main ticket hall.

**Main train station** (per small/large bag per day 15/30Kč; ☒ 24hr) On Level 1. There are also lockers (60Kč coins).

## Medical Services

There are several 24-hour pharmacies in the centre of town, including **Praha lékárna** (Map pp266-7; ☎ 224 946 982; Palackého 5, Nové Město); for emergency service after hours, ring the bell.

**Canadian Medical Care** (Map pp258-9; ☎ 235 360 133, after hours 724 300 301; Veleslavínská 1, Veleslavín; ☒ 8am-6pm Mon, Wed & Fri, 8am-8pm Tue & Thu) Expat centre with English-speaking doctors, 24-hour medical aid, physiotherapist and pharmacy.

**Na Homolce Hospital** (Map pp258-9; ☎ 257 271 111, after hours 257 272 527; www.homolka.cz; 5th fl, Foreign Pavilion, Roentgenova 2, Motol) Prague's main casualty department.

**Polyclinic at Národní** (Map pp266-7; ☎ 222 075 120; 24hr emergencies 720 427 634; www.poliklinika.narodni .cz; Národní třída 9, Nové Město) With English-, French- and German-speaking staff.

## Money

The major banks – Komerční banka, Živnostenská banka, Česká spořitelna and ČSOB – are the best places for changing cash, but using a debit card in an ATM gives a better rate of exchange. Avoid *směnárna* (private exchange booths), which advertise misleading rates and have exorbitant charges.

**Amex** (Map pp266-7; ☎ 222 800 237; Václavské nám 56, Nové Město; ☒ 9am-7pm)

**Česká spořitelna** (Map pp266-7; Václavské nám 16, Nové Město; ☒ 8am-5pm Mon-Fri)

**ČSOB** (Map pp266-7; Na příkopě 14, Nové Město; ☒ 8am-5pm Mon-Fri)

**Komerční banka** (Map pp266-7; Václavské nám 42, Nové Město; ☒ 8am-5pm Mon-Fri)

**Travelex** (Map pp266-7; ☎ 221 105 276; Národní třída 28, Nové Město; ☒ 9am-1.30pm & 2-6.30pm)

**Živnostenská banka** (Map pp266-7; Na příkopě 20, Nové Město; ☒ 8am-4.30pm Mon-Fri)

## Post

To use the **main post office** (Map pp266-7; Jindřišská 14, Nové Město; ☒ 2am-midnight), collect a ticket from one of the automated machines just outside the main hall (press button No 1 for stamps and parcels; No 4 for EMS). Wait until your *lístek číslo* (number) comes up on the electronic boards inside; these tell you which window to go to for *přepážka* (service).

You can pick up poste restante mail at window No 1 and buy phonecards at window No 28. Parcels weighing up to 2kg, as well as international and Express Mail Service (EMS) parcels, are sent from window Nos 7 to 10. (Note that these services close at noon on Saturday and all day on Sunday.)

## Telephone

There's a 24-hour telephone centre to the left of the right-hand entrance to the post office. Bohemia Bagel (p257) has phones for making low-cost international calls.

## Tourist Information

The **Prague Information Service** (Pražská informační služba, PIS; ☎ 12 444, in English & German 221 714 444; www.prague-info.cz) provides free tourist information with good maps and detailed brochures (including accommodation and historical monuments).

There are three PIS offices:

**Main train station** (Praha hlavní nádraží; Map pp266–7; Wilsonova 2, Nové Město; 🕒 9am-7pm Mon-Fri, 9am-6pm Sat & Sun Apr-Oct; 9am-6pm Mon-Fri, 9am-5pm Sat & Sun Nov-Mar)

**Malá Strana Bridge Tower** (Map pp266–7; Charles Bridge; 🕒 10am-6pm Apr-Oct)

**Old Town Hall** (Map pp266–7; Staroměstské nám 5, Staré Město; 🕒 9am-7pm Mon-Fri, to 6pm Sat & Sun Apr-Oct; 9am-6pm Mon-Fri, to 5pm Sat & Sun Nov-Mar)

## Travel Agencies

**Čedok** (Map pp266–7; ☎ 224 197 699, 800 112 112; www.cedok.cz; Na příkopě 18, Nové Město; 🕒 9am-7pm Mon-Fri, 9.30am-1pm Sat) Tour operator and travel agency. Also books accommodation, concert and theatre tickets, rents cars and exchanges money.

**CKM Travel Centre** (Map pp258–9; ☎ 222 721 595; www.ckm.cz; Mánesova 77, Vinohrady; 🕒 10am-6pm Mon-Thu, 10am-4pm Fri) Books air and bus tickets, with discounts for those aged under 26. Sells youth cards.

**Eurolines-Sodeli CZ** (Map pp266–7; ☎ 224 239 318; Senovážné nám 6, Nové Město; 🕒 8am-6pm Mon-Fri) Agent for Eurolines buses.

**GTS International** (Map pp266–7; ☎ 222 211 204; www.gtsint.cz; Ve Smečkách 33, Nové Město; 🕒 8am-8pm Mon-Fri, 11am-4pm Sat) Youth cards and air, bus and train tickets.

## DANGERS & ANNOYANCES

Prague's crime rate is low by Western standards, but beware of pickpockets who regularly work the crowds at the astronomical clock, Prague Castle and Charles Bridge, and on the central metro and tram lines, especially tourists getting on or off crowded trams 9 and 22.

Being ripped off by taxi drivers is another hazard. Most taxi drivers are honest, but a sizable minority who operate from tourist areas greatly overcharge their customers (even Czechs). Try not to take a taxi from Václavské nám, Národní třída and other tourist areas. It's better to phone for a taxi (see p277) or walk a couple of streets before hailing one.

The park outside the main train station is a hang-out for drunks and dodgy types and should be avoided late at night.

### Scams

We've had reports of bogus police approaching tourists and asking to see their money, claiming that they are looking for counterfeit notes. They then run off with the cash. If in doubt, ask the 'policeman' to go with you to the nearest police station; a genuine cop will happily do so.

## SIGHTS

All the main sights are in the city centre, and are easily reached on foot; you can take in the castle, Charles Bridge and Staroměstské nám in a day.

### Prague Castle

#### INFORMATION

Dominating Prague's skyline like a vast, beached battleship is **Prague Castle** (Pražský hrad; Map p262; ☎ 224 373 368; www.hrad.cz; 🕒 9am-5pm Apr-Oct, 9am-4pm Nov-Mar; grounds 5am-midnight Apr-Oct, 6am-11pm Nov-Mar; ♿ ). The biggest castle complex in the world feels more like a small town than a castle. It is the seat of Czech power, both political and symbolic, housing the president's office and the ancient Bohemian crown jewels.

Among many ticket options, **Ticket B** (adult/child 220/110Kč) is the best value, giving access to St Vitus Cathedral (choir, crypt and tower), Old Royal Palace and Golden Lane. **Ticket A** (350/175Kč) includes all of these plus the Basilica of St George, Powder Tower and Story of Prague Castle exhibit. Buy tickets at the **Castle Information Centre** in the Third Courtyard and at the entrance to the main sights. Most areas are wheelchair accessible.

#### SIGHTS

The main entrance is at the western end. The **changing of the guard**, with stylish uniforms created by Theodor Pistek (costume designer for the film *Amadeus*) takes place every hour, on the hour. At noon a band plays from the windows above.

The **Matthias Gate** leads to the second courtyard and the **Chapel of the Holy Cross** (concert tickets on sale here). On the north side is the **Prague Castle Gallery** (adult/child 100/50Kč; 🕒 10am-6pm), with a collection of European baroque art.

The third courtyard is dominated by **St Vitus Cathedral**, a French Gothic structure begun in 1344 by Emperor Charles IV, but not completed until 1929. Colour from stained-glass windows created by early-20th-century Czech artists floods the interior, including one by Alfons Mucha (3rd chapel on the left as you enter the cathedral)

CZECH REPUBLIC

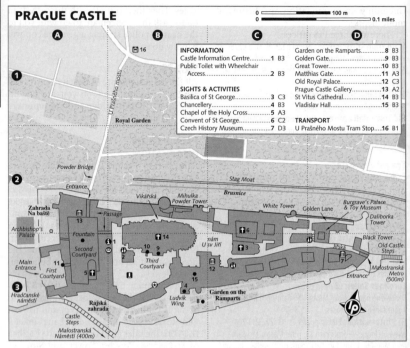

## PRAGUE CASTLE

0 ——— 100 m
0 ——— 0.1 miles

**INFORMATION**
Castle Information Centre...........**1** B3
Public Toilet with Wheelchair
Access.....................................**2** B3

**SIGHTS & ACTIVITIES**
Basilica of St George...................**3** C3
Chancellery.................................**4** B3
Chapel of the Holy Cross............**5** A3
Convent of St George.................**6** C2
Czech History Museum...............**7** D3

Garden on the Ramparts............**8** B3
Golden Gate................................**9** B3
Great Tower...............................**10** B3
Matthias Gate............................**11** A3
Old Royal Palace.......................**12** C3
Prague Castle Gallery................**13** A2
St Vitus Cathedral.....................**14** B3
Vladislav Hall............................**15** B3

**TRANSPORT**
U Prašného Mostu Tram Stop.....**16** B1

featuring SS Cyril and Methodius. In the apse is the massive **tomb of St John of Nepomuk** – two tonnes of baroque silver watched over by hovering cherubs.

The 14th-century chapel on the cathedral's southern side with the black imperial eagle on the door contains the **tomb of St Wenceslas**, the Czechs' patron saint and the Good King Wenceslas of Christmas carol fame. Wenceslas' zeal in spreading Christianity and his submission to the German King Henry I saw him murdered by his brother, Boleslav I. According to legend he was stabbed to death clinging to the Romanesque lion's-head handle that graces the chapel door. The smaller door on the far side, beside the windows, leads to the Bohemian crown jewels (not open to the public).

On the other side of the transept, climb the 287 steps of the **Great Tower** ( 9am-4.15pm Apr-Oct) for views over the city.

On the southern side of the cathedral's exterior is the **Golden Gate** (Zlatá brána) a triple-arched doorway topped by a 14th-century mosaic of the Last Judgment: to the left, the righteous are raised into heaven; to the right, sinners are cast into hell.

Opposite is the entrance to the **Old Royal Palace** with the elegantly vaulted **Vladislav Hall**, built between 1486 and 1502. Horsemen used to ride into the hall up the ramp at the far end for indoor jousts. Two Catholic councillors were thrown out the window of the adjacent **Chancellery** by irate Protestant nobles on 23 May 1618. This infamous Second Defenestration of Prague ignited the Thirty Years' War.

Leaving the palace, the Romanesque **Basilica of St George** (1142) is in front of you, and in the nearby **Convent of St George** (adult/child 100/50Kč; 10am-6pm Tue-Sun) is the National Gallery's collection of Czech art from the 16th to 18th centuries.

Beyond, the crowds surge into Golden Lane, a 16th-century tradesmen's quarter of tiny houses in the castle walls. It's a souvenir-laden tourist trap you can safely miss, though Kafka fans should note his sister's house at No 22, where he lived and wrote in 1916–17.

On the right, before the castle's exit, is the Lobkowitz Palace, housing the **Czech History Museum** (adult/child 40/20Kč; 9am-5pm Tue-Sun). From the castle's eastern end, the Old Castle Steps lead to Malostranská metro station, or turn sharp right to wander back through the lovely **Garden on the Ramparts** (admission free; 10am-6pm Apr-Oct).

Forgoing an uphill hike, get to the castle by tram 22 or 23 from Národní třída on Staré Město's southern edge, Malostranské nám in Malá Strana, or Malostranská metro station to the U Prašného mostu stop. To wander through Hradčany first, stay on the tram until the Pohořelec stop.

## Hradčany

The lanes and stairways of Hradčany are perfect for wandering. The area extending west from Prague Castle is mainly residential, with a single strip of shops and restaurants (Loretánská and Pohořelec). Before it became a borough of Prague in 1598, Hradčany was almost levelled by Hussites and fire. The 17th-century palaces were built on the ruins.

The 18th-century Šternberg Palace outside the castle entrance houses the main branch of the **National Gallery** (Map pp266-7; ☎ 220 514 598; www.ngprague.cz; adult/child 150/70Kč; 10am-6pm Tue-Sun), the country's principal collection of 14th- to 18th-century European art.

A passage at Pohořelec 8 leads to the **Strahov Library** (Map pp266-7; ☎ 233 107 718; www.strahovsky klaster.cz; adult/child 80/50Kč; 9am-noon & 1-5pm), the country's largest monastic library, built in 1679. The Philosophy and Theological Halls feature gorgeous frescoed ceilings. The collection of natural curiosities in the connecting corridor includes books on tree growing bound in the bark of the trees they describe. The long, brown, leathery things beside the model ship are actually whales' penises, despite the prudish attendants claiming they're tanned elephants' trunks.

The exuberantly baroque **Sanctuary of Our Lady of Loreta** (Map pp266-7; ☎ 220 516 789; www .loreta.cz; Loretánské nám 7; adult/child 90/70Kč; 9.15am-12.15pm & 1-4.30pm) is a place of pilgrimage famed for its treasury of precious religious artefacts. The cloister houses a 17th-century replica of the Santa Casa from the Italian town of Loreta, said to be the house of Virgin Mary in Nazareth, miraculously transported to Italy by angels in the 13th century.

## Malá Strana

Head downhill from the castle to the beautifully baroque back streets of Malá Strana (Little Quarter), built in the 17th and 18th centuries by victorious Catholic clerics and nobles on the foundations of their Protestant predecessors' Renaissance palaces. Today it's an upmarket neighbourhood with embassies and government offices.

Near the café-crowded main square of Malostranské nám is **St Nicholas Church** (Map pp266-7; www.psalterium.cz; admission 60/30Kč; 9am-5pm Mar-Oct, 9am-4pm Nov-Feb), one of the city's greatest baroque buildings. If you visit only one church in Prague, this should be it. Take the stairs to the gallery to see the 17th-century *Passion Cycle* paintings and the doodlings of bored 1820s tourists.

To the east, along Tomášská, is the impressive **Wallenstein Palace** (Map pp266-7; Valdštejnský palác; admission free; 10am-4pm Sat & Sun), built in 1630 and home to the Czech Republic's Senate. Albrecht von Wallenstein, a notorious general in the Thirty Years' War, started on the Protestant side but defected to the Catholics, and built this palace with his former comrades' expropriated wealth. In 1634 the Habsburg Emperor Ferdinand II learned that Wallenstein was about to switch sides again and had him assassinated. The ceiling fresco of the palace's baroque hall shows Wallenstein glorified as a chariot-driving warrior.

Enter the adjacent **Wallenstein Gardens** (Map pp266-7; admission free; 10am-4pm Apr-Oct) via the palace or from Letenská, a block to the east. These beautiful gardens boast a giant Renaissance loggia, a fake stalactite grotto full of hidden animals and grotesque faces, bronze (replica) sculptures by Adrian de Vries (the Swedish army looted the originals in 1648 and they're in Stockholm) and a pond full of giant carp.

Malá Strana is linked to Staré Město by the elegant **Charles Bridge** (Karlův most). Built in 1357, and graced by 30 18th-century statues, until 1841 it was the city's only bridge. Stroll leisurely across, but first climb the **Malá Strana bridge tower** (Map pp266-7; adult/child 50/30Kč; 10am-6pm Apr-Nov) for a great view of bridge and city. In the middle of the bridge is a bronze statue (1683) of St John of Nepomuk, a priest thrown to his death from the bridge in 1393 for refusing to reveal the queen's confessions to King Wenceslas IV. Crammed with tourists, jewellery stalls, portrait artists and the odd busker, try and visit the bridge at dawn before the hordes arrive.

North of Charles Bridge is the modern **Franz Kafka Museum** ( ☎ 420 221 333; www.kafkamuseum.cz; Cihelná 2b; adult/child 120/60Kč; 10am-6pm), which

CZECH REPUBLIC

has 'come home' after time in Barcelona and New York. Kafka's diaries, letters and a wonderful collection of first editions provide a poignant balance to the T-shirt cliché the writer has become in tourist shops.

On a hot summer afternoon escape the tourist throngs on the funicular railway (20Kč tram ticket, every 10 to 20 minutes from 9.15am to 8.45pm) from Újezd to the rose gardens on **Petřín Hill**. From here climb up 299 steps to the top of the iron-framed **Petřín Tower** (Map pp266–7; adult/child 50/40Kč; ☑ 10am-7pm Apr-Oct, 10am-5pm Sat & Sun Nov-Mar), built in 1891 in imitation of the Eiffel Tower, for one of the best views of Prague. Behind the tower a staircase leads to picturesque lanes taking you back to Malostranské nám.

## Staré Město

On the Staré Město (Old Town) side of Charles Bridge narrow and crowded Karlova leads east towards **Staroměstské nám**, Prague's Old Town Square, dominated by the twin Gothic steeples of **Týn Church** (Map pp266–7; 1365), the baroque wedding cake of **St Nicholas Church** (Map pp266–7; 1730s), (not to be confused with the more famous St Nicholas Church in Malá Strana; p263) and the Old Town Hall's **clock tower** (Map pp266-7; ☎ 224 228 456; Staroměstské nám 12; adult/child 50/40Kč; ☑ 11am-6pm Mon, 9am-6pm Tue-Sun Apr-Oct, to 5pm Nov-Mar). Climb to the top (or take the lift), and spy on the crowds below watching the **astronomical clock** (Map pp266–7; 1410), which springs to life every hour with its parade of apostles and a bell-ringing skeleton. In the square's centre is the **Jan Hus Monument**, erected in 1915 on the 500th anniversary of the religious reformer's execution.

The shopping street of Celetná leads east from the square to the gorgeous Art Nouveau **Municipal House** (Obecní dům; Map pp266-7; www.obecni-dum .cz; nám Republiky 5; guided tours 150Kč; ☑ 10am-6pm), a cultural centre decorated by the early 20th-century's finest Czech artists. Included in the guided tour are the impressive Smetana Concert Hall and other beautifully decorated rooms.

South of the square is the neoclassical **Estates Theatre** (Stavovské divadlo; Map pp266–7; 1783), where Mozart's *Don Giovanni* was premiered on 29 October 1787 with the maestro himself conducting.

**Josefov**, the area north and northwest of Staroměstské nám, was once Prague's Jewish Quarter. It retains a fascinating variety of monuments, which form the **Prague Jewish Museum** ( ☎ 222 317 191; www.jewishmuseum.cz; adult/ child 300/200Kč; ☑ 9am-6pm Sun-Fri Apr-Oct, to 4.30pm Nov-Mar). The museum's collection of artefacts exists because in 1942 the Nazis gathered objects from 153 Jewish communities in Bohemia and Moravia, planning a 'museum of an extinct race' after completing their extermination programme.

The oldest still-functioning synagogue in Europe, the early Gothic **Old-New Synagogue** (Map pp266-7; Červená 1; 200Kč), dates from 1270. Opposite is the Jewish town hall with its picturesque 16th-century clock tower. The 1694 **Klaus Synagogue** (Map pp266-7; U Starého hřbitova 1) houses an exhibition on Jewish customs and traditions. The **Pinkas Synagogue** (Map pp266-7; Široká 3) is now a holocaust memorial, its interior walls inscribed with the names of 77,297 Czech Jews, including Franz Kafka's three sisters.

The **Old Jewish Cemetery** (entered from the Pinkas Synagogue) is Josefov's most evocative corner. The oldest of its 12,000 graves date from 1439. Use of the cemetery ceased in 1787 as it was becoming so crowded that burials were up to 12 layers deep. Look at the cemetery through an opening in the wall north of the **Museum of Decorative Arts** ( ☎ 224 811 241; 17 listopadu 2; adult/concession 80/40Kč; ☑ 10am-6pm, closed Monday) or from outside the 1st-floor public toilets in the museum.

Tucked away in the northern part of Staré Město's narrow streets is one of Prague's oldest Gothic structures, the magnificent **Convent of St Agnes** (Map pp266-7; ☎ 221 879 111; www.ngprague .cz; U Milosrdných 17; adult/child 100/50Kč; ☑ 10am-6pm Tue-Sun) housing the National Gallery's collection of Bohemian and Central European medieval art, dating from the 13th to the mid-16th centuries.

## Nové Město

Nové Město (New Town) is new only compared with Staré Město, being founded in 1348! The broad, sloping avenue of **Václavské nám** (Map pp266-7; Wenceslas Sq), lined with shops, banks and restaurants, is dominated by a **statue of St Wenceslas** on horseback. Wenceslas Sq has always been a focus for demonstrations and public gatherings. Beneath the statue is a shrine to the victims of communism, including students Jan Palach and Jan Zajíc, both of whom burned themselves alive in 1969 protesting against the Soviet invasion.

At the southeastern end of the square is the imposing, neo-Renaissance **National Museum** (Map pp266-7; ☎ 224 497 111; www.nm.cz; Václavské nám 68; adult/child 100/50Kč; ☼ 10am-6pm May-Sep, 10am-5pm Oct-Apr, closed first Tuesday of every month). The ho-hum collections cover prehistory, mineralogy and stuffed animals (captions in Czech only), but the grand interior is worth seeing for the pantheon of Czech politicians, writers, composers, artists and scientists.

Fans of artist Alfons Mucha, renowned for his Art Nouveau posters of garlanded Slavic maidens, can admire his work at the **Mucha Museum** (Map pp266-7; ☎ 221 451 333; www.mucha.cz; Panská 7; adult/child 120/60Kč; ☼ 10am-6pm), including an interesting video on his life and art. See also Moravský Krumlov (p300).

The **City of Prague Museum** (Map pp266-7; ☎ 224 227 490; www.muzeumprahy.cz; Na Poříčí 52; adult/child 80/30Kč; ☼ 9am-6pm Tue-Sun), housed in a grand, neo-Renaissance building near Florenc metro station, charts Prague's evolution from prehistory to the 19th century, culminating in a huge scale model of Prague in 1826–37. Among the intriguing exhibits are the silk funeral cap and slippers worn by astronomer Tycho Brahe when he was interred in the Týn Church in 1601 (they were removed in 1901).

The **Museum of Communism** (Map pp266-7; ☎ 224 212 966; www.muzeumkomunismu.cz; Na příkopě 10; adult/child 180/140Kč; ☼ 8am-9pm) is tucked ironically behind Prague's biggest McDonald's. The introductory rooms covering communism's origins are a tad wordy, but the exhibition is fascinating through its use of simple everyday objects to illuminate the restrictions of life under communism. The display ends poignantly detailing 1989's Velvet Revolution.

## Vyšehrad

To escape the tourist crowds, pack a picnic and take the metro to the ancient hilltop fortress **Vyšehrad** (Map pp258-9; www.praha-vysehrad.cz; admission free; ☼ 9.30am-6pm Apr-Oct, to 5pm Nov-Mar), perched on a cliff top above the Vltava on Nové Město's southern edge. Dominated by the twin towers of **SS Peter & Paul Church** (Map pp258–9) and founded in the 11th century, Vyšehrad was rebuilt in neo-Gothic style between 1885 and 1903. Don't miss the Art Nouveau murals inside. The **Slavín Cemetery** (Map pp258–9), beside the church, contains the graves of many distinguished Czechs, including the composers Smetana and Dvořák. The view from the citadel's southern battlements is superb.

## TOURS

**City Walks** ( ☎ 608 200 912; www.praguer.com; per person 300-450Kč) Guided walks ranging from 90 minutes to four hours. Tours include a Literary Pub Tour and Ghost Trail.

**Prague Venice** ( ☎ 603 819 947; www.prague-venice .cz; adult/child 270/135Kč; ☼ 10.30am-11pm Jul & Aug, to 8pm Mar-Jun & Sep-Oct, 10.30am-6pm Nov-Feb) Runs 45-minute cruises in small boats under the arches of Charles Bridge and along the Čertovka mill stream in Kampa. Jetties are at the Staré Město end of Charles Bridge, on the Čertovka stream in Malá Strana, and at the west end of Mánes Bridge, near Malostranská metro station.

**Prague Walks** ( ☎ 608 339 099; www.praguewalks .com; per person 300-390Kč) Small group walks ranging from Franz Kafka to micro-breweries to communism.

**Wittman Tours** ( ☎ 603 426 564; www.wittman-tours .com; per person from 500Kč) Specialises in tours of Jewish interest, including day trips to the Museum of the Ghetto (p280) at Terezín.

## FESTIVALS & EVENTS

**Prague Spring** (www.festival.cz) From 12 May to 3 June, classical music kicks off summer.

**United Islands** (www.unitedislands.cz) World music in mid-June.

**Loveplanet** (www.loveplanet.cz) Outdoor rock festival in August.

**Prague Autumn** (www.pragueautumn.cz) Celebrates summer's end from 12 September to 1 October.

**Prague International Jazz Festival** (www.jazzfestival praha.cz) Late October.

**Christmas Market** 1 to 24 December.

**New Year's Eve** *Pivo*-fuelled crowds in Staroměstské nám, and castle fireworks on 31 December.

## SLEEPING

If you're visiting at New Year, Christmas or Easter, or from May to September, book accommodation in advance. Prices quoted are for the high season, generally April to October. These rates can increase up to 15% on certain dates, notably at Christmas, New Year, Easter and weekends during the Prague Spring festival. Some hotels have slightly lower rates in July and August. High season rates normally decrease by 20% to 40% from November to March.

Consider an apartment for stays longer than a couple of nights. Many one- to

# CENTRAL PRAGUE

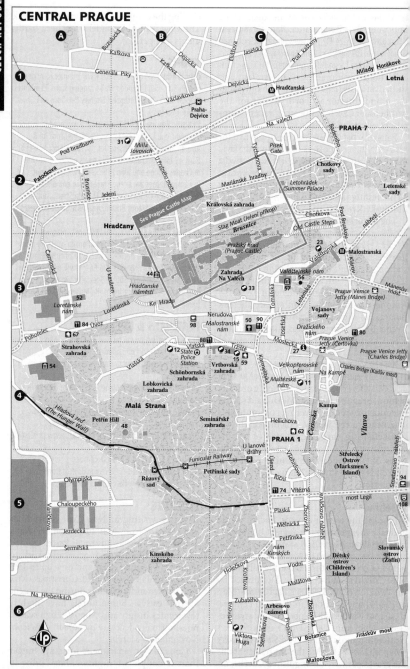

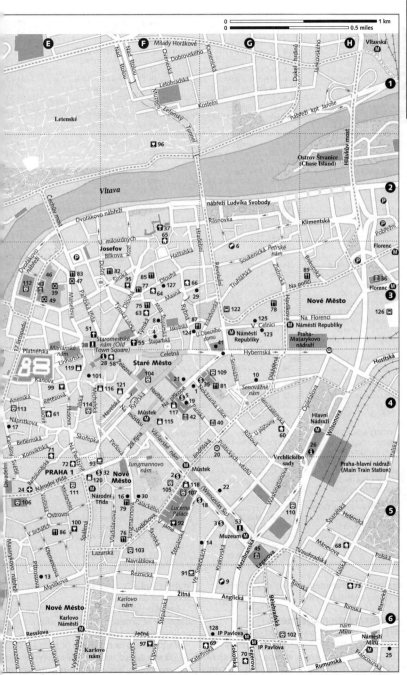

six-person apartments are available for even a single night, offering excellent value.

## Accommodation Agencies

**AVE** ( ☎ 251 551 011; www.avetravel.cz; Praha-hlavní nádraží, Nové Město; ⏰ 6am-11pm) Offices at the airport, main train station and Praha-Holešovice train station. The main train station branch specialises in last-minute accommodation.

**Hostel.cz** ( ☎ 415 658 580; www.hostel.cz) Website database of around 60 hostels, with a secure online booking system.

**Mary's Travel & Tourist Service** (Map pp266-7; ☎ 222 253 510; www.marys.cz; Italská 31, Vinohrady; ⏰ 9am-9pm) Private rooms, hostels, *pensions*, apartments and hotels in Prague and surrounding areas across all price ranges.

**Prague Apartments** ( ☎ 323 641 476; www.prague -apartments.com) Web-based service with a range of smartly furnished flats. Availability displayed online.

**Stop City** (Map pp266-7; 222 521 233; www.stopcity.com; Vinohradská 24, Vinohrady; 🕙 10am-9pm Apr-Oct, 10am-8pm Mon-Sat Nov-Mar) Apartments, private rooms and *pensions* in the city centre, Vinohrady and Žižkov areas.

## Budget

**Clown & Bard Hostel** (Map pp258-9; ☎ 222 716 453; www .clownandbard.com; Bořivojova 102, Žižkov; dm 300-380Kč, d 1000Kč, apt 2400Kč; P 🖳 ) Just maybe Prague's most full-on hostel – party hard in the basement bar, and recharge at the all-you-can-eat breakfast any time until 1pm. The self-catering apartments offer slightly more seclusion.

**Hostel Elf** (Map pp258-9; ☎ 222 540 963; www.hostelelf .com; Husitská 11, Žižkov; dm 320-360Kč, s/d 1000/1200Kč; 🖳 ) Have the best of both worlds at this hip hostel near Žižkov's pub district. Swap travellers' tales in the compact beer garden or grab some quiet time in the nooks and crannies.

**Hostel U Melounu** (Map pp258-9; ☎ 224 918 322; www .hostelumelounu.cz; Ke Karlovu 7, Vinohrady; dm/s/d 390/700/1000Kč; P 🖳 ) An attractive hostel in an historic building on a quiet street, U Melounu also features a sunny barbecue area, and shared kitchen and laundry facilities.

**Sir Toby's Hostel** (Map pp258-9; ☎ 283 870 635; www .sirtobys.com; Dělnická 24, Holešovice; dm 340-400Kč, s/d 1000/1350Kč; P ✗ 🖳 ) In an up-and-coming suburb a quick 10-minute tram ride from the city centre, Sir Toby's is in a refurbished apartment building on a quiet street. The staff are friendly and helpful, and there is a shared kitchen and lounge.

**Hostel Sokol** (Map pp266-7; ☎ 257 007 397; post@sokol -cos.cz; Tyršův dům, Nosticova 2, Malá Strana; dm 390Kč; ✗ ) Set in a converted riverside mansion you can't beat the location, but the dorms can get crowded (and hot) in summer; a worthwhile backup though.

**Hostel Týn** (Map pp266-7; ☎ 224 808 333; www .tyn.prague-hostels.cz; Týnská 19, Staré Město; dm/d/tr 400/1200/1350Kč; ✗ ) In a quiet lane metres from Old Town Square, you'll struggle to find better-value central accommodation. The 14 two–to-six bed rooms are very popular so book ahead

**Camp Sokol Troja** (Map pp258-9; ☎ 233 542 908; www .camp-sokol-troja.cz; Trojská 171a, Troja; camp site per per-

son/car 125/90Kč; P 🖳 ) This riverside camping ground, with kitchen and laundry, is one of six in the suburb of Troja, 15 minutes north of the centre via tram 14 or 17.

## Midrange

**Hotel Extol Inn** (Map pp258-9; ☎ 220 876 541; www .extolinn.cz; Přístavní 2, Holešovice; s/d from 790/1350Kč; P ✗ 🖳 ) The reader-recommended rooms here are all excellent value. The cheapest rooms with shared bathrooms are no-frills but spick and span, while the three-star rooms with private bathroom include use of the sauna and spa. The city centre is just 10 minutes by tram.

**Miss Sophies** (Map pp266-7; ☎ 296 303 530; www.miss -sophies.com; Melounova 3; dm 440Kč, s/d from 1500/1700Kč, apt from 2100Kč) 'Boutique hostel' sums up this tasty spot in a converted apartment building on the southern edge of the New Town. Polished concrete blends with oak flooring and coolly neutral colours, and the basement lounge is all bricks and black leather.

**Pension Březina** (Map pp266-7; ☎ 296 188 888; www .brezina.cz; Legerova 39-41; s/d economy 1100/1300Kč, luxury 2000/2200Kč; P ) A friendly *pension* in a converted Art Nouveau apartment block with a small garden. Ask for a quieter room at the back. The economy rooms are great value for budget travellers.

**Dasha** (Map pp266-7; ☎ 602 210 716; www.accommoda tion-dasha.cz; Jeruzalémská 10; s/d from €30/40, apt €50-110) A restored apartment building 200m from the main train station conceals a variety of private rooms and apartments that can accommodate up to 10 people. With kitchen facilities the apartments are a good choice for larger groups or families. Forward bookings by phone or on the website are essential.

**AV Pension Praha** (Map pp258-9; ☎ 272 951 726; www .pension-praha.cz; Malebná 75, Chodov; d with/without bath- room 2000/1500Kč; P 🐾 ) This garden villa with bright rooms and breakfast on the patio in the southeastern suburbs comes reader recommended. It's a five-minute walk east of Chodov metro station.

**Pension Unitas** (Map pp266-7; ☎ 224 211 020; www .unitas.cz; Bartolomějská 9; dm per person 350-510Kč, s/d 1280/1580Kč; P ✗ ) This former convent has an interesting past – the rooms were once prison cells (ex-president Havel did time here). A generous breakfast is included and bathrooms are shared. Choose between cramped dorms or more spacious *pension* rooms.

**Hotel Golden City Garni** (Map pp258-9; ☎ 222 711 008; www.goldencity.cz; Táboritská 3, Žižkov; s/d/tr

1900/2700/2900Kč; P ✕ ⬛ ) Golden City is a converted 19th-century apartment block with crisp and clean IKEA-furnished rooms, grand buffet breakfasts and easy access to the city centre on tram 5, 9 or 26.

**Dům U Krále Jiřího** (Map pp266-7; ☎ 221 466 100; www.kinggeorge.cz; Liliová 10; s/d 2250/3550Kč) 'King George's House' combines old-world *pension* charm with crisply modern rooms just metres from Old Town Square. The attic rooms (only accessible by steep stairs) are the most attractive with exposed wooden beams.

**Penzión U Medvídků** (Map pp266-7; ☎ 224 211 916; www.umedvidku.cz; Na Perštýně 7, Staré Město; s/d 2300/3500Kč) 'At the Little Bear' is a traditional pub and restaurant with several attractive rooms upstairs. Romantic types should choose an historic attic room with exposed wooden beams. Just mind your head after having a few in the micro-brewery downstairs.

**Hotel 16 U sv Kateřiny** (Map pp258-9; ☎ 224 920 636; www.hotel16.cz; Kateřinská 16, Nové Město; s/d incl breakfast from 2800/3500Kč; P ⬛ ) Near the Botanic Gardens and five minutes' walk from Karlovo nám metro station, you're more likely to wake to birdsong than honking cars at this family-run spot with a quiet garden and cosy bar.

**Hotel U Tří Korunek** (Map pp258-9; ☎ 222 781 112; www.3korunky.cz; Cimburkova 28; Žižkov; s/d from 2480/3380Kč) Rambling across three buildings in Žižkov, the 'Three Crowns' has 78 comfy and clean rooms. It's worth upgrading to a superior room with wooden floors and designer furniture (300Kč extra), and don't be put off by the down-at-heel-looking neighbourhood. It's safe and quiet and the city centre is just a few tram stops away.

**Hotel Antik** (Map pp266-7; ☎ 222 322 288; www .hotelantik.cz; Dlouhá 22; s/d 3590/3990Kč) The Antik shares a 15th-century building (no lift) with a delightfully jumbled antique shop. It's a great area for bars and restaurants, so ask for one of the more quiet back rooms with a balcony. Breakfast is served in a garden courtyard.

**Apostolic Residence** (Map pp266-7; ☎ 221 632 222; www.prague-residence.cz; Staroměstské nám 26; s/d 4600/5700Kč) Right on Old Town Square, this hotel positively reeks understated class with antique furniture and Oriental rugs. Yes, you are paying more for the supercentral location, but it's still good value compared with other more expensive hotels in the city.

## Top End

**Hotel Josef** (Map pp266-7; ☎ 221 700 111; www .hoteljosef.cz; Rybná 20, Staré Město; s/d from €149/173;

P ✕ ⬛ ♿ ) Sleekly modern in old-world Staré Město, this boutique hotel was designed by London-based Czech architect Eva Jiřičná. Descend the playful suspended staircase to surf the web in the lobby's wi-fi hotspot. Two rooms are wheelchair accessible.

**Hotel Casa Marcello** (Map pp266-7; ☎ 222 310 260; www.casa-marcello.cz; Řásnovka 783; d/ste/apt €130/185/215) Housed in two medieval buildings that were once part of the Covent of St Agnes, Casa Marcello is one of Prague's most intimate and romantic hotels. In a quiet but central area near the Old Town Sq, surprise your loved one with room 104 with its king-size bed and preserved medieval archway.

**Hotel Questenberk** (Map pp266-7; ☎ 220 407 600; www.questenberk.cz; Úvoz 5, Hradčany; s/d €160/200; P ✕ ✕ ⬛ ) Spacious and sunny rooms now fill Strahov Monastery's former hospital just minutes from the castle. Old and new blends seamlessly with antique pine furnishings and internet access amid the baroque splendour.

**Aria Hotel** (Map pp266-7; ☎ 225 334 111; www.aria hotel.net; Tržiště 9, Malá Strana; d from €250; P ✕ ⬛ ) Choose your favourite composer or musician and stay in a themed room with a selection of their music. Not at all tacky – just pure five-star class with 21st-century touches like music databanks and flat-screen computers.

## EATING

Prague has restaurants offering all kinds of cuisines and price ranges. Take your pick from good-value Czech beer halls with no-nonsense pork-and-*knedlíky* fare, or enjoy a riverside view in a chic Italian restaurant with a high-flying clientele and prices. In between, there's everything from Afghani to Argentinean, and Thai to Tex-Mex.

Eating in Prague's tourist areas can be pricey, but considerably cheaper eats are available just a block or two away. Pubs offer both snacks and full meals, and there are stands in Václavské nám selling street snacks such as *párek* (hot dog) or *bramborák* (potato pancake).

Prague has an increasing number of vegetarian restaurants, and most restaurants feature at least one or two veggie options. Most restaurants are open from 11am to 11pm.

### Hradčany & Malá Strana

**Bohemia Bagel** (Map pp266-7; ☎ 257 310 694; Újezd 18, Malá Strana; mains 90-270Kč; ⏱ 7am-midnight Mon-Fri, from 8am Sat & Sun) Expat heaven with bagel sandwiches, soups and coffee. There's another Bohemia Bagel at Masná 2 in Staré Město – both are good spots for breakfast.

**Malý Buddha** (Map pp266-7; ☎ 220 513 894; Úvoz 46, Hradčany; mains 60-120Kč; ⊙ noon-10.30pm Tue-Sun) Vietnamese-owned Malý ('Little') Buddha is an incense-infused haven atop Hradčany hill. If the castle's crowds wear you down, restore your chi with restorative wines, healing tea and crab spring rolls. Credit cards are not accepted.

**Hergetova Cihelna** (Map pp266-7; ☎ 257 535 534; Cihelná 2b, Malá Strana; mains 200-550Kč; ⊙ 9am-2am) A restored *cihelná* (brickworks) is now a hip space with a riverside terrace looking back to Charles Bridge and Staré Město. Come for steak, seafood or pizza and linger for the sublime view – 'one more *pivo prosím*'.

Also check out the Moorish flavours (think baklava and spicy *merguez* sausages) at **Shaharazad** (Map pp266-7; ☎ 257 913 046; Vlasská 6, Malá Strana; mains 100-200Kč; ⊙ noon-midnight), and the thoroughly modern **Square** (Map pp266-7; ☎ 257 532 109; Malostranské nám 5, Malá Strana; tapas 3 for 275Kč, 7 for 455Kč; ⊙ 9am-12.30am) with interesting tapas like saffron *arancini* (rice balls).

## Staré Město

**Kolkovna** (Map pp266-7; ☎ 224 819 701; Kolkovně 8; meals 160-400Kč; ⊙ 9am-midnight) This contemporary spin on the traditional Prague beer hall serves up classy versions of heritage Czech dishes like goulash and roast pork. And because it's owned by the Pilsner Urquell brewery, guess what beer accompanies most of the huge meals?

**Country Life** Nové Město (Map pp266-7; ☎ 224 247 280; Jungmannova 1; ⊙ 9.30am-6.30pm Mon-Thu, 9am-6pm Fri); Staré Město (Map pp266-7; ☎ 224 213 366; Melantrichova 15; mains 75-150Kč; ⊙ 9am-8.30pm Mon-Thu, 9am-6pm Fri, 11am-8.30pm Sat & Sun) This all-vegan cafeteria offers inexpensive salads, sandwiches, pizzas, soy drinks, sunflower-seed burgers etc.

**Orange Moon** (Map pp266-7; ☎ 222 325 119; Rámová 5; mains 165-230Kč; ⊙ 11.30am-11.30pm) The world's best beer (no doubt) combines with (probably) the world's best cuisines. Expats and locals are transported to Asia by authentic flavours of Thailand and India.

**Dahab** (Map pp266-7; ☎ 224 837 375; Dlouhá 33; mains 200-400Kč; ⊙ noon-1am) Morocco meets the Middle East amid the softly lit ambience of this North African souk. Relax with a mint tea and a hookah (hubble-bubble pipe). If you've got the munchies there's everything from

baklava to *tagine* (meat and vegetable stew) with couscous.

**Red Hot & Blues** (Map pp266-7; ☎ 222 314 639; Jakubská 12; mains 180-480Kč; ⊙ 8am-midnight) This jumping jive, jazz and jambalaya spot is a long way from 'N'awlins', but the eggplant creole and cajun shrimp have travelled well. There's live jazz night, and breakfast is available until 4pm at the weekend – just maybe the best way to resurrect yourself after a big night.

**Les Moules** (Map pp266-7; ☎ 222 315 022; Pavížská 19; mains 300-500Kč; ⊙ 8.30am-midnight Mon-Fri, 9am-midnight Sat & Sun) Another modern update of a European drinking establishment, Les Moules is a traditional Belgian-style brasserie, dishing up comfort food like *moules* (mussels) with crispy (Belgian!) fries. The Leffe and Hoegaarden on tap prove that Belgian beer travels well – even to the home of Pilsner.

## Nové Město

**Pizzeria Kmotra** (Map pp266-7; ☎ 224 934 100; V Jirchářích 12; pizza 95-145Kč; ⊙ 11am-midnight) More than 30 varieties are on offer at this cellar pizzeria that gets really busy after 8pm. With over 50 additional toppings you can get really creative.

**Kaaba** (Map pp258-9; ☎ 224 254 021; Mánesova 20; snacks 50-80Kč; ⊙ 8am-10pm Mon-Sat, 10am-10pm Sun) Vinohrady's hipsters park themselves on 1950s-style furniture and recharge with snappy espressos, terrific teas and tasty snacks. After dark Belgian beers provide the entrée to nearby clubs.

**Siam Orchid** (Map pp266-7; ☎ 222 319 410; Na poříčí 21; mains 160-280Kč; ⊙ 10am-10pm) The waiter may be from Cambodia, but that doesn't stop the Thai food in this tiny restaurant from being Prague's most authentic Asian cuisine. Try the fiery *laap kai* (spicy chicken salad).

**Café FX** (Map pp266-7; ☎ 224 254 776; Bělehradská 120, Vinohrady; mains 100-200Kč; ⊙ 11.30am-2am) Café FX is shabbily chic, draped in hippy-trippy chiffon, with Prague's best vegetarian flavours from Mexico, India and Thailand. Relax at weekend brunch and lose yourself in the eclectic CD store across the arcade.

**Dinitz Café** (Map pp266-7; ☎ 222 313 308; Na poříčí 14; mains 200-400Kč; ⊙ 9am-3am) Art Deco heaven is this cool homage to 1920s café society. The kitchen delivers elegant Mediterranean-style meals until 2am, and live jazz is dished up every night from 9pm. Try and get a mezzanine table overlooking the stage.

**Kogo** (Map pp266-7; ☎ 224 451 259; Slovanský dům; Na příkopě 22; pizzas 150-250Kč, mains 200-450Kč;

9am-midnight) Prague's business community chooses from a diverse wine list to accompany Kogo's classy pizza, pasta, steak and seafood. There is another stylish branch at Havelská 27.

## DRINKING

Bohemian beer is probably the world's best. The most famous brands are Budvar, Plzeňský Prazdroj (Pilsner Urquell), and Prague's own Staropramen; and there's no shortage of opportunities to imbibe. An increasing number of independent micro-breweries also offer a more unique drinking experience.

Avoid the tourist areas, and you'll find local bars selling half-litres for 30Kč or less (compared with over 65Kč around Malostranské nám and Staroměstské nám). Traditional pubs open from 11am to 11pm. More stylish modern bars open from noon to 1am, and often stay open till 3am or 4am on Friday and Saturday.

If you want to avoid stag parties, stay away from the Irish and English pubs in the Old Town, and the sports bars on and around Ve Smečkách in the New Town.

### Cafés

Before the communist coup Prague had a thriving café scene, and since 1989 it has returned strongly. The summer streets are crammed with outdoor tables, and good-quality tea and coffee are widely available. Keep an eye out for funky teahouses with a diversely global range of brews.

**U zeleného čaje** (Map pp266-7; ☎ 257 530 027; Nerudova 19, Malá Strana; 11am-10pm; ✗ ) Linger at this tiny tea-haven on the way to the castle. There are only four tables so maybe grab a speciality tea to go for the final push up the hill.

**Café Vesmírna** (Map pp266-7; ☎ 222 212 363; Ve Smečkách 5, Nové Město; 9am-10pm Mon-Fri, 1-8pm Sat, closed Sun; ✗ ) The friendly Vesmírna provides training and opportunities for people with special needs. The wait staff are warm and professional, and the menu features healthy snacks like savoury crepes and a 'how do I choose?' selection of teas and coffees. It's a special place making a real difference.

**Káva.Káva.Káva** Nové Město (Map pp266-7; ☎ 224 228 862; Národní třída 37; 7am-10pm Mon-Fri, 9am-10pm Sat & Sun); Smíchov ( ☎ 257 314 277; Lidicka 42; 7am-10pm) Hidden away in the Platýz courtyard, this café offers huge smoothies and tasty nibbles like carrot cake and chocolate brownies. Access the internet (2Kč per minute or 15 minutes

free with a purchase) on their computers or hitch your laptop to their wi-fi hotspot.

**Kavárna Slávia** (Map pp266-7; ☎ 224 220 957; Národní třída 1, Nové Město; mains 130-260Kč; 8am-midnight Mon-Fri, 9am-midnight Sat & Sun) Before or after the theatre savour the cherry wood and onyx Art Deco elegance of Prague's most famous old café.

### Pubs

**U Zlatého Tygra** (Map pp266-7; ☎ 222 221 111; Husova 17, Staré Město; 3-11pm) The 'Golden Tiger' is an authentic Prague pub where President Havel took President Clinton to show him a real Czech *pivnice*. You'll need to be there at opening time for any chance of a seat, but we're sure Václav and Bill had no problems.

**Jáma** (Map pp266-7; ☎ 224 222 383; V jámě 7, Nové Město; 11am-1am) Spot your favourite band on the posters covering the walls of this popular American-themed bar. Expats, tourists and locals come for the burgers'n'Budvar and free wi-fi internet.

**Velryba** (Map pp266-7; ☎ 224 912 484; Opatovická 24, Nové Město; 11am-midnight Sat-Thu, 11am-2am Fri) The 'Whale' is the café-bar that finally fulfils your expectations of 'Bohemian' with smoky and intense conversations between local students and a basement art gallery. Bring your own black polo-neck jumper.

**Kozička** (Map pp266-7; ☎ 224 818 308; Kozí 1, Staré Město; noon-4am Mon-Fri, 6pm-4am Sat & Sun) The 'Little Goat' (look for the iron sculpture outside) rocks in standing-room-only fashion until well after midnight in a buzzing basement bar. Your need for midnight munchies will be answered by the late-night kitchen.

**Pivovarský Dům** (Map pp266-7; ☎ 296 216 666; cnr Ječná & Lipová, Nové Město; 11am-11.30pm) The 'Brewery House' micro-brewery conjures up interesting tipples from a refreshing wheat beer to coffee and banana flavoured styles – even a beer 'champagne' served in champagne flutes. If you're more of a traditionalist, the classic Czech lager is a hops-laden marvel.

**U Medvídků** (Map pp266-7; ☎ 296 216 666; cnr Ječná & Lipová, Nové Město; 11.30am-11pm, beer museum noon-10pm) A microbrewery with the emphasis on 'micro', 'At the Little Bear' specialises in X-Beer, an 11.8% 'knocks-your-socks-off' dark lager. You can't drink too many without falling over, so the usual range of Budvar brews is available to make your evening last longer than a couple of hours.

**Letenské sady** (Map pp266-7; Letna Gardens, Bubeneč) This outdoor garden bar provides sublime views across the river to the Old Town and southwest to the castle. In summer it's packed with young Praguers enjoying cheap beer and grilled sausages. Sometimes the simple things in life are the best.

## ENTERTAINMENT

From clubbing to classical music, puppetry to performance art, there's no shortage of entertainment in Prague. The city has long been a centre of classical music and jazz, and is now also famed for its rock and postrock scenes. The scene changes quickly, and it's possible places listed here will have changed when you arrive. For current listings, see *Culture in Prague* (available from PIS offices; see p260), the 'Night & Day' section of the weekly *Prague Post* (www .praguepost.cz), and the monthly free *Provokátor* magazine (www.provokator.org), from clubs, cafés, arthouse cinemas and backpacker hostels. For online listings see www.prague.tv.

For classical music, opera, ballet, theatre and some rock concerts – even the most 'sold-out' *vyprodáno* (events) – you can often find tickets on sale at the box office around 30 minutes before the performance starts. There are also many ticket agencies selling the same tickets at a high commission.

Although some expensive tickets are set aside for foreigners, non-Czechs normally pay the same price as Czechs at the box office. Tickets can cost as little as 50Kč for standing-room only to over 950Kč for the best seats; the average price is about 550Kč. Be wary of touts selling concert tickets in the street. They often offer good prices, but you may end up sitting on stacking chairs in a cramped hall listening to amateur musicians, rather than the grand concert hall that was implied.

### Ticket Agencies

**FOK Box Office** (Map pp266-7; ☎ 222 002 336; www.fok .cz; U obecního domu 2, Staré Město; ☺ 10am-6pm Mon-Fri) For classical concert tickets.

**Ticketpro** (Map pp266-7; ☎ 296 333 333; www.ticket pro.cz; pasáž Lucerna, Štěpánská 61; Nové Město; ☺ 9am-12.30pm & 1-5pm Mon-Fri) Sells tickets for all kinds of events. Also has branches in PIS offices (see p260).

**Bohemia Ticket International** ( ☎ 224 227 832; www .ticketsbti.cz); Nové Město (Map pp266-7; Na příkopě 16, ☺ 10am-7pm Mon-Fri, 10am-5pm Sat, 10am-3pm Sun); Staré Město (Map pp266-7; Malé nám 13; ☺ 9am-5pm Mon-Fri, 9am-1pm Sat) Sells tickets to all kinds of events.

**Ticketstream** (www.ticketstream.cz) An internet-based agency covering events in Prague and the Czech Republic.

## Classical Music & Performance Arts

Around Prague you'll see fliers advertising concerts and recitals for tourists. It's a good chance to relax in atmospheric old churches and stunning historic buildings, but unfortunately many performances are of mediocre quality. The programme changes weekly, and prices begin around 400Kč.

**Rudolfinum** (Map pp266-7; ☎ 227 059 352; www .rudolfinum.cz; nám Jana Palacha, Staré Město; ☺ box office 10am-12.30pm & 1.20-6pm Mon-Fri plus one hour before performances) One of Prague's main concert venues is the Dvořák Hall in the neo-Renaissance Ruldolfinum, and home to the Czech Philharmonic Orchestra.

**Smetana Hall** (Municipal House; Obecní dům; Map pp266-7; ☎ 222 002 101; www.obecni-dum.cz; nám Republiky 5, Staré Město; ☺ box office 10am-6pm Mon-Fri) Another main concert venue is Smetana Hall in the Art Nouveau Municipal House. A highlight is the opening of the Prague Spring festival.

**Prague State Opera** (Státní opera Praha; Map pp266-7; ☎ 224 227 266; www.opera.cz; Legerova 75, Nové Město; ☺ box office 10am-5.30pm, 10am-noon & 1-5pm Sat & Sun) Opera, ballet and classical drama (in Czech) are performed at this neo-Renaissance theatre.

**National Theatre** (Národní divadlo; Map pp266-7; ☎ 224 901 377; www.narodni-divadlo.cz; Národní třída 2, Nové Město; ☺ box office 10am-6pm) Classical drama, opera and ballet are also performed at the National Theatre.

**Laterna Magika** (Map pp266-7; ☎ 224 931 482; www .laterna.cz; Nová Scéna, Národní třída 4, Nové Město; tickets from 680Kč; ☺ box office 10am-8pm Mon-Sat) Beside the National Theatre is the modern Laterna Magika, a multimedia show combining dance, opera, music and film.

**Estates Theatre** (Stavovské divadlo; Map pp266-7; ☎ 224 902 322; Ovocný trh 1, Staré Město; ☺ box office 10am-6pm) Every night during summer (mid-July to the end of August) **Opera Mozart** ( ☎ 271 741 403; www.mozart-praha.cz) performs *Don Giovanni*. The opera premiered in the same theatre in 1787.

## Clubs & Live Music

**Mecca** (Map pp258-9; ☎ 283 870 522; www.mecca.cz; U Průhonu 3, Holešovice; admission 90-390Kč, free Wed & Thu; ☺ 10pm-6am Wed-Sat) Prague's most fashionable club attracts film stars, fashionistas and fab

**CZECH REPUBLIC**

types attracted by the classy restaurant (11am to 11pm) and the pumping dance floor action.

**Lucerna Music Bar** (Map pp266-7; ☎ 224 217 108; www.muiscbar.cz; Lucerna pasaž, Vodičkova 36, Nové Město; ☾ 8pm-4am) Lucerna features local bands and the occasional up-and-coming international act. Leave your musical snobbery in the cloak room at the popular '80s nights on Friday and Saturday with everything from The Human League to Soft Cell.

**Palác Akropolis** (Map pp258-9; ☎ 296 330 911; www .palacakropolis.cz; Kubelikova 27, Žižkov; ☾ club 7pm-5am) Get lost in the labyrinth of theatre, live music, clubbing, drinking and eating that makes up Prague's coolest venue. Hip-hop, house, reggae and world music – anything goes. Even a few touring acts like the Strokes and the Flaming Lips.

**Club Radost FX** (Map pp266-7; ☎ 224 254 776; www .radostfx.cz; Bělehradská 120, Vinohrady; admission 100-250Kč; ☾ 10pm-6am) Prague's most stylish, self-assured club remains hip for its bohemian-boudoir décor and its popular Thursday hip-hop night FXBounce (www.fxbounce.com).

## Jazz

Prague has dozens of jazz clubs ranging from the traditional to the avant-garde.

**Reduta Jazz Club** (Map pp266-7; ☎ 224 912 246; www .redutajazzclub.cz; Národní třída 20, Nové Město; admission 300Kč; ☾ 9pm-3am) Founded in 1958 and one of the oldest clubs in Europe. Bill Clinton jammed here in 1994.

**USP Jazz Lounge** (Map pp266-7; ☎ 603 551 680; www .jazzlounge.cz; Michalská 9, Staré Město; ☾ 9pm-3am) A less traditional venue with modern (and sometimes uncompromising) live jazz and a DJ session from midnight onwards.

## Theatre

**Black Theatre of Jiří Srnec** (Map pp266-7; ☎ 257 921 835; www.blacktheatresrnec.cz; Reduta Theatre, Národní 20, Nové Město; tickets 490Kč; ☾ box office 3-7pm Mon-Fri) See the uniquely Czech 'black light theatre' shows at various venues. The performances combine mime, ballet, animated film and puppetry. Jiří Srnec's Black Theatre is the original and the best.

**Theatre on the Balustrade** (Divadlo na zábradlí; Map pp266-7; ☎ 222 868 868; www.nazabradli.cz; Anenské nám 5, Staré Město; ☾ box office 2-7pm Mon-Fri, 2 hrs before show Sat & Sun) Plays by former president Václav Havel are often staged (in Czech, of course) here.

**Divadlo Minor** (Map pp266-7; ☎ 222 231 351; www .minor.cz; Vodičkova 6, Nové Město; ☾ box office 9am-

1.30pm & 2.30-8pm Mon-Fri, 11am-6pm Sat & Sun) If the kids are all castled out, consider the puppets'n'pantomime shows at 9.30am and in the afternoon.

## Gay & Lesbian Prague

**Termix** (Map pp258-9; ☎ 222 710 462; www.club-termix .cz; Třebízckého 4A, Vinohrady; ☾ 8pm-5am Wed-Sun) A friendly mixed gay-and-lesbian scene with an industrial/high-tech vibe. You'll need to queue for Thursday's popular techno party.

**Club Stella** (Map pp258-9; ☎ 224 257 869; Lužicka 19, Vinohrady; ☾ 8pm-4pm Mon) A narrow and intimate bar (just wider than a bar stool) opens out into a candlelit lounge filled with armchairs and friendly locals. Ring the doorbell to get in.

**Piano Bar** (Map pp258-9; ☎ 222 727 496; Milešovská 10, Žižkov; ☾ 5pm-midnight or later) This cellar bar, cluttered with bric-a-brac and unpretentious locals, is a good spot for a quiet drink. The background beats usually consist of kitschy '70s and '80s Czech pop.

**Downtown Café Praha** (Map pp266-7; ☎ 724 111 276; Jungmannovo nám 21, Nové Město; ☾ 8.30am-midnight) A Prague institution since 1999, the Downtown Café reopened in April 2006 seemingly even more impossibly hip. Chill until late in the LookBetterNaked Lounge, and then ease into the following day with the all-day breakfast and free wi-fi.

**Prague Saints** (Map pp258-9; ☎ 222 250 326; www .praguesaints.cz; Polska 32) An excellent source of information on Prague's gay scene.

## Cinemas

Most films are screened in their original language with Czech subtitles (*české titulky*), but Hollywood blockbusters are often dubbed into Czech (*dabing*); look for the labels 'tit.' or 'dab.' on listings.

**Kino Aero** (Map pp266-7; ☎ 271 771 349; www.ki noaero.cz; Biskupcova 31, Žižkov) Prague's best-loved art-house cinema, with themed weeks and retrospectives; often with English subtitles.

**Kino Světozor** (Map pp266-7; ☎ 224 946 824; www .kinosvetozor.cz; Vodičkova 41, Nové Město) Your best bet for seeing Czech films with English subtitles, this place is under the same management as Kino Aero but is more central.

**Palace Cinemas** (Map pp266-7; ☎ 257 181 212; www .palacecinemas.cz; Slovanský dům, Na příkopě 22, Nové Město) Central Prague's main popcorn palace – a modern 10-screen multiplex showing first-run Hollywood films.

# SHOPPING

Prague's main shopping streets are in Nové Město – Václavské nám, Na příkopě, 28.října and Národní třída – and there are many tourist-oriented shops on Celetná, Staroměstské nám, Pařížská and Karlova in Staré Město. Prague's souvenir specialities include Bohemian crystal, ceramics, marionettes and garnet jewellery.

**Tesco Department Store** (Map pp266-7; ☎ 222 003 111; Národní třída 26, Nové Město; ☻ 8am-9pm Mon-Fri, 9am-8pm Sat, 10am-7pm Sun) With four floors of clothes, electrical and household goods, plus Prague's best-stocked **supermarket** ( ☻ 7am-10pm Mon-Fri, 8am-8pm Sat, 9am-7pm Sun).

## Crystal

**Moser** (Map pp266-7; ☎ 224 211 293; Na příkopě 12, Nové Město; ☻ 10am-8pm Mon-Fri, 10am-7pm Sat & Sun) Founded in 1857, Moser specialises in top-quality Bohemian crystal.

**Rott Crystal** (Map pp266-7; ☎ 224 229 529; Malé nám 3, Staré Město; ☻ 10am-8pm) Housed in a beautiful neo-Renaissance building, Rott is worth a look even if you're not buying.

## Handicrafts, Antiques & Ceramics

**Manufaktura** (Map pp266-7; ☎ 221 632 480; Melantrichova 17, Staré Město; ☻ 10am-7.30pm) Branches of Manufaktura around the city centre sell traditional Czech handicrafts, wooden toys and handmade cosmetics.

There are good antique and bric-a-brac shops along Týnská and Týnská ulička, near Staroměstské nám. For ceramics in traditional Moravian folk designs, see **Tupesy lidová keramika** (Map pp266-7; ☎ 224 210 728; Havelská 21, Staré Město; ☻ 10am-6pm).

## Music

**Philharmonia** (Map pp266-7; ☎ 224 247 291; Pasáž Alfa, Václavské nám 28; ☻ 10am-7pm Mon-Fri, 11am-6pm Sat) For music by Dvořák, Smetana or Janáček. Also stocks Czech folk music and Jewish music.

**Bontonland** (Map pp266-7; ☎ 224 473 080; Václavské nám 1, Nové Město; ☻ 9am-8pm Mon-Sat, 10am-7pm Sun) A megastore stocking music genres ranging from classical, jazz, folk, rock, metal, dance and Czech pop, Bontonland also sells DVDs and has an internet café and a Playstation arena.

# GETTING THERE & AWAY

See also p309.

## Bus

The main terminal for international and domestic buses is **Florenc Bus Station** (ÚAN Florenc; Map pp266-7; ☎ 12 999; Křižíkova 4, Karlín), 600m northeast of the main train station (ÚAN is short for *Ústřední autobusové nádraží*, or 'central bus station'). Some regional buses depart from near metro stations Anděl, Dejvická, Černý Most, Nádraží Holešovice, Smíchovské Nádraží and Želivského. Find online bus timetables at www.idos.cz.

At Florenc get information at **window No 8** ( ☻ 6am-9pm), or use the touch-screen computer.

Short-haul tickets are sold on the bus. Long-distance domestic tickets are sold at the station from AMS windows 1 to 4 in the central hall or direct from Student Agency. Tickets can be purchased from 10 days to 30 minutes prior to departure.

More buses depart in the mornings. Buses, especially if full, sometimes leave a few minutes early, so be there at least 10 minutes before departure time. If you're not seated five minutes before departure, you may lose your reservation. Many services don't operate at weekends, so trains can often be a better option.

There are direct services from Florenc to Brno (150Kč, 2½ hours, hourly), České Budějovice (125Kč, 2¾ hours, four daily), Karlovy Vary (130Kč, 2¼ hours, eight daily), Litoměřice (61Kč, 1¼ hours, hourly) and Plzeň (80Kč, 1½ hours, hourly).

Most buses from Prague to České Budějovice (120Kč, 2½ hours, 16 daily) and Český Krumlov (140Kč, three hours, seven daily) depart from Ná Knížecí bus station, at Anděl metro's southern entrance, or from outside Roztyly metro station.

Bus companies include the following:

**Capital Express** (Map pp258-9; ☎ 220 870 368; www .capitalexpress.cz; I výstaviště 3, Holešovice; ☻ 8am-6pm Mon-Thu, 8am-5pm Fri) Daily service between London and Prague via Plzeň.

**Eurolines-Bohemia Euroexpress International** (Map pp266-7; ☎ 224 218 680; www.bei.cz; ÚAN Praha Florenc Bus Station, Křižíkova 4-6, Karlín; ☻ 8am-6pm Mon-Fri) Buses to all over Europe.

**Eurolines-Sodeli** (Map pp266-7; ☎ 224 239 318; www.eurolines.cz, in Czech; Senovážné nám 6, Nové Město; ☻ 8am-6pm Mon-Fri) Links Prague with cities in Western and Central Europe. There is another Eurolines office in Florenc.

**Student Agency** Central Prague (Map pp266-7; ☎ 224 999 666; Ječná 37; ☻ 9am-6pm Mon-Fri); Florenc ( ☎ 224

**CZECH REPUBLIC**

894 430; www.studentagency.cz; ⊗ 9am-6pm Mon-Fri) Linking major Czech cities; services throughout Europe.

## Train

Prague's main train station is **Praha-hlavní nádraží** (Map pp266-7; ☎ 221 111 122; Wilsonova, Nové Město). International tickets, domestic and international couchettes and seat reservations are sold on level 2 at even-numbered windows from 10 to 24, to the right of the stairs leading up to level 3. Domestic tickets are sold at the odd-numbered windows from 1 to 23 to the left of the stairs. Note that Praha-hlavní nádraží is undergoing a major redevelopment between 2006 and 2009 and the station layout may alter.

There are three other major train stations in the city. Some international trains stop at Praha-Holešovice station on the northern side of the city, while some domestic services terminate at Praha-Masarykovo in Nové Město, or Praha-Smíchov south of Malá Strana. Study the timetables carefully to find out which station your train departs from or arrives at. Check train timetables online at www.idos.cz.

You can also buy train tickets and get timetable information from the **ČD Centrum** ( ⊗ 6am-7.30pm) at the southern end of Level 2 in Praha-hlavní nádraží, and at the **České drahy** (Czech Railways; Map pp266-7; ☎ 972 223 930; www.cd.cz; V Celnici 6, Nové Město; ⊗ 9am-6pm Mon-Fri, 9am-noon Sat) travel agency.

There are direct trains from Praha-hlavní nádraží to Brno (294Kč, three hours, eight daily), České Budějovice (204Kč, 2½ hours, hourly), Karlovy Vary (274Kč, four hours, three daily), Kutná Hora (98Kč, 55 minutes, seven daily) and Plzeň (140Kč, 1½ hours, eight daily). There are also daily departures to Brno, Bratislava and Vienna from Praha-Holešovice.

## GETTING AROUND
### To/From the Airport

Prague's Ruzyně airport is 17km west of the city centre. To get into town, buy a ticket from the public transport (Dopravní podnik; DPP) desk in arrivals and take bus 119 (20Kč, 20 minutes, every 15 minutes) to the end of the line (Dejvická), then continue by metro into the city centre (another 10 minutes; no new ticket needed). Note that you'll also need a half-fare (10Kč) ticket for your backpack or suitcase (if it's larger than 25cm x 45cm x 70cm).

Alternatively, take a **Cedaz minibus** ( ☎ 220 114 296; www.cedaz.cz) from outside arrivals; buy your ticket from the driver (90Kč, 20 minutes,

every 30 minutes 5.30am to 9.30pm). There are city stops at Dejvická metro and at **Czech Airlines** (Map pp266-7; V Celnici 5) near nám Republiky. You can also get a Cedaz minibus to your hotel or any other address (480Kč for one to four people; 960Kč for five to eight). Phone to book a pick-up for the return trip.

**Airport Cars** ( ☎ 220 113 892) taxi service, with prices regulated by the airport administration, charges 650Kč (20% discount for return trip) into central Prague (a regular taxi fare *from* central Prague should be about 450Kč). Drivers speak some English and accept Visa cards.

## Bicycle Rental

**City Bike** (Map pp266-7; ☎ 776 180 284; www.citybike -prague.com; Královodvorská 5, Staré Město; ⊗ 9am-7pm May-Sep) Two-hour tours cost from 480Kč, departing at 11am, 2pm and 5pm. Rental includes helmet and padlock.
**Praha Bike** (Map pp266-7; ☎ 732 388 880; www.praha bike.cz; Dlouhá 24, Staré Město; 4/8hr 360/500Kč; ⊗ 9am-7pm 15 Mar-15 Nov) Good, new bikes with lock, helmet and map, plus free luggage storage, student discounts and group tours.

## Car & Motorcycle

Driving in Prague is no fun. Challenges include trams, lunatic drivers and pedestrians, one-way streets and police looking for a little handout. Try not to arrive or leave on a Friday or Sunday afternoon or evening, when most of Prague seems to head to and from their weekend houses.

Central Prague has many pedestrian-only streets, marked with Pěší Zóná (Pedestrian Zone) signs, where only service vehicles and taxis are allowed; parking can be a nightmare. Meter time limits range from two to six hours at around 40Kč per hour. Parking in one-way streets is normally only allowed on the right-hand side. Traffic inspectors are strict, and you could be clamped or towed. There are several car parks at the edges of Staré Město, and Park-and-Ride car parks around the outer city (most are marked on city maps), close to metro stations.

## Public Transport

All public transport is operated by **Dopravní podnik hl. m. Prahy** (DPP; ☎ 296 191 817; www.dpp .cz), which has **information desks** ( ⊗ 7am-10pm) at Ruzyně airport and in four metro stations – **Muzeum** ( ⊗ 7am to 9pm), **Můstek** ( ⊗ 7am to 6pm), **Anděl** ( ⊗ 7am to 6pm) and **Nádraží Holešovice**

( ☻ 7am to 6pm) – where you can get tickets, directions, a multilingual system map, a map of *Noční provoz* (night services) and a detailed English-language guide to the whole system.

Buy a ticket before boarding a bus, tram or metro. Tickets are sold from machines at metro stations and major tram stops, at newsstands, Trafiky snack shops, PNS and other tobacco kiosks, hotels, all metro station ticket offices and DPP information offices.

A *jízdenka* (transfer ticket) is valid on tram, metro, bus and the Petřín funicular and costs 20Kč (half-price for six- to 15-year-olds); large suitcases and backpacks (anything larger than 25cm x 45cm x 70cm) also need a 10Kč ticket. Kids under six ride free. Validate (punch) your ticket by sticking it in the little yellow machine in the metro station lobby or on the bus or tram the first time you board; this stamps the time and date on it. Once validated, tickets remain valid for 75 minutes from the time of stamping, if validated between 5am and 8pm on weekdays, and for 90 minutes at other times. Within this period, you can make unlimited transfers between all types of public transport (you don't need to punch the ticket again).

There's also a short-hop 14/7Kč adult/concession ticket, valid for 15 minutes on buses and trams, or for up to five metro stations. No transfers are allowed on these, and they're not valid on the Petřín funicular nor on night trams (51 to 58) or night buses (501 to 512). Being caught without a valid ticket entails a 400Kč on-the-spot fine (50Kč for not having a luggage ticket). The inspectors travel incognito, but will show a badge when they ask for your ticket. A few may demand a higher fine from foreigners and pocket the difference, so insist on a *doklad* (receipt) before paying.

You can also buy tickets valid for 24 hours (80Kč) and three/seven/15 days (200/250/280Kč). Again, these must be validated on first use only; if a ticket is stamped twice, it becomes invalid.

On metro trains and newer trams and buses, an electronic display shows the route number and the name of the next stop, and a recorded voice announces each station or stop. As the train, tram or bus pulls away, it says: *Příští stanice* (or *zastávka*)… meaning 'The next station (or stop) is…', perhaps noting that it's a *přestupní stanice* (transfer station). At metro stations, signs point you towards the *výstup* (exit) or to a *přestup* (transfer to another line).

The metro operates from 5am to midnight daily. There are three lines: Line A runs from the northwestern side of the city at Dejvická to the east at Skalka; line B runs from the southwest at Zličín to the northeast at Černý Most; and line C runs from the north at Nádraží Holešovice to the southeast at Háje. Line A intersects line C at Muzeum, line B intersects line C at Florenc and line A intersects line B at Můstek.

After the metro closes, night trams (51 to 58) and buses (501 to 512) rumble across the city about every 40 minutes. If you're planning a late evening, check if one of these services passes near where you're staying.

## Taxi

Prague taxi drivers are notorious for overcharging tourists – try to avoid getting a taxi in tourist areas such as Václavské nám. To avoid being ripped off, phone a reliable company such as **AAA** ( ☎ 14 014) or **ProfiTaxi** ( ☎ 844 700 800). If you feel you're being overcharged ask for an *účet* (bill). The Prague City Council has a website detailing legitimate fares (http://panda.hyperlink.cz/taxitext/etaxiweb .htm), and has increased the maximum fine for overcharging to one million Kč.

## AROUND PRAGUE

The following places can easily be visited on day trips using public transport.

### Karlštejn

Fairy-tale **Karlštejn Castle** ( ☎ 274 008 154; www .hradkarlstejn.cz; Karlštejn; ☻ 9am-6pm Tue-Sun Jul & Aug; 9am-5pm May, Jun & Sep; 9am-4pm Apr & Oct; 9am-3pm Nov-Mar) perches above the Berounka River, 30km southwest of Prague. Erected by the Emperor Charles IV in the mid-14th century, it crowns a ridge above the village, a 20-minute walk from the train station.

The castle's highlight is the **Chapel of the Holy Rood**, where the Bohemian crown jewels were kept until 1420, with walls covered in 14th-century painted panels and precious stones. The 45-minute guided tours (in English) on Route I cost 200/120Kč for adult/child tickets. Route II, which includes the chapel (June to October only), are 300/150Kč adult/child per person and must be prebooked. Trains from Praha-hlavní nádraží station to Beroun stop at Karlštejn (46Kč, 45 minutes, hourly).

## Konopiště

The assassination in 1914 of the heir to the Austro-Hungarian throne, Archduke Franz Ferdinand d'Este, sparked off WWI. For the last 20 years of his life he avoided the intrigues of the Vienna court, hiding away southeast of Prague in what became his country retreat, **Konopiště Chateau** ( ☎ 274 008 154; www.zamek-konopiste.cz; Benešov; ⏰ 9am-5pm Tue-Sun May-Aug; 9am-4pm Tue-Fri, 9am-5pm Sat & Sun Sep; 9am-3pm Tue-Fri, 9am-4pm Sat & Sun Apr & Oct; 9am-3pm Sat & Sun Nov)

Three guided tours are available. **Tour III** (adult/child 300/200Kč) is the most interesting, visiting the archduke's private apartments, unchanged since the state took over the chateau in 1921. **Tour II** (in English adult/child 180/100Kč) takes in the **Great Armoury**, one of Europe's most impressive collections.

The castle is a testament to the archduke's twin obsessions: hunting and St George. Having renovated the massive Gothic and Renaissance building in the 1890s, and installed all the latest technology (electricity, central heating, flush toilets, showers and a lift), Franz Ferdinand decorated his home with his hunting trophies. His game books record that he shot around 300,000 creatures during his lifetime, from foxes and deer to elephants and tigers. About 100,000 of them adorn the walls, marked with when and where it was killed. The **Trophy Corridor** and antler-clad **Chamois Room** (both on Tour III) are truly bizarre sights.

The archduke's collection of St George related art and artefacts relating is also impressive, with 3750 items, many of which are displayed in the **Muzeum sv Jiří** (adult/child 25/10Kč) at the front of the castle. From June to September weekend concerts are held in the castle's grounds.

There are frequent direct trains from Prague's hlavní nádraží to Benešov u Prahy (64Kč, 1¼ hours, hourly). Buses depart from Florenc and Roztyly metro station to Benešov on a regular basis (37Kč, 1¼ hours)

Konopiště is 2.5km west of Benešov. Local bus 2 (9Kč, six minutes, hourly) runs from a stop on Dukelská, 400m north of the train station (turn left out of the station, then first right on Tyršova and first left) to the castle car park. Otherwise it's a 30-minute walk. Turn left out of the train station, go left across the bridge over the railway, and follow Konopištská street west for 2km.

## Kutná Hora

In the 14th century Kutná Hora rivalled Prague as Bohemia's most important town, growing wealthy on the silver ore that laced the rocks beneath it. The silver *groschen* that were minted here at that time represented the hard currency of Central Europe. The good times ended when the silver ran out. Mining ceased in 1726, leaving the medieval townscape largely unaltered. It's an attractive place with several fascinating and unusual historical attractions, and was added to Unesco's World Heritage List in 1996.

### ORIENTATION & INFORMATION

Kutná Hora hlavní nádraží (the main train station) is 3km northeast of the old town centre. The bus station is more conveniently located on the northeastern edge of the old town.

The easiest way to visit Kutná Hora on a day trip is to arrive on a morning train from Prague, then make the 10-minute walk from Kutná Hora hlavní nádraží to Sedlec Ossuary. From there it's another 2km walk or a five-minute bus ride into town.

The helpful **information centre** ( ☎ 327 512 378; http://infocentrum.kh.cz; Palackého nám 377; ⏰ 9am-6.30pm Apr-Oct; 9am-5pm Sat & Sun, 9am-5pm Mon-Fri Oct-Mar) books accommodation, provides internet access (1Kč per minute), and rents bicycles (220Kč per day).

### SIGHTS

Walk 10-minutes south from Kutná Hora hlavní nádraží to the remarkable **Sedlec Ossuary** (Kostnice; ☎ 327 561 143; adult/child 45/30Kč; ⏰ 8am-6pm Apr-Sep, 9am-noon & 1-5pm Oct, 9am-4pm Nov-Mar). When the Schwarzenberg family purchased Sedlec monastery in 1870 they allowed a local woodcarver to get creative with the bones of 40,000 people, which had lingered in the crypt for centuries. Garlands of skulls and femurs are strung from the vaulted ceiling like macabre Christmas decorations. The central chandelier contains at least one of each bone in the human body. Four giant pyramids of stacked bones squat in the corner chapels, and crosses of bone adorn the altar. There's even a Schwarzenberg coat of arms made from bones.

From Sedlec it's another 2km walk (or five-minute bus ride) to central Kutná Hora. **Palackého nám**, the town's main square is unremarkable, but the interesting old town lies to its south.

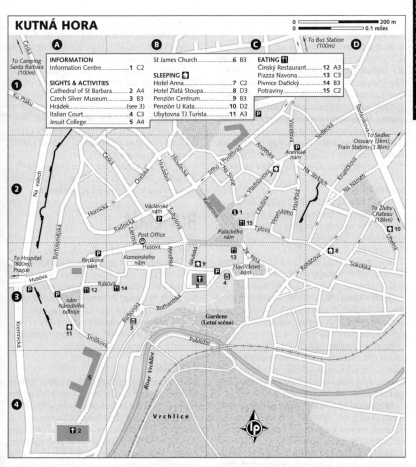

## KUTNÁ HORA

| | | |
|---|---|---|
| **INFORMATION** | St James Church..............**6** B3 | **EATING** |
| Information Centre..............**1** C2 | | Čínsky Restaurant........**12** A3 |
| | **SLEEPING** | Piazza Navona.............**13** C3 |
| **SIGHTS & ACTIVITIES** | Hotel Anna..........................**7** C2 | Pivnice Dačicky.............**14** B3 |
| Cathedral of St Barbara....**2** A4 | Hotel Zlatá Stoupa............**8** D3 | Potraviny....................**15** C2 |
| Czech Silver Museum.........**3** B3 | Penzión Centrum................**9** B3 | |
| Hrádek...........................(see 3) | Penzión U Kata...............**10** D2 | |
| Italian Court...................**4** C3 | Ubytovna TJ Turista.........**11** A3 | |
| Jesuit College..................**5** A4 | | |

---

From the western end of the square a narrow lane called Jakubská leads to **St James Church** (1330), east of which lies the **Italian Court** (Vlašský dvůr; ☎ 327 512 873; Havlíčkovo nám 552; adult/child 80/50Kč; ☼ 9am-6pm Apr-Sep, 10am-5pm Mar & Oct, 10am-4pm Nov-Feb), the former Royal Mint; Florentine craftsmen began stamping silver coins here in 1300. It now houses a mint museum, and a 15th-century **Audience Hall** with two impressive 19th-century murals depicting the election of Vladislav Jagiello as king of Bohemia in 1471 and the Decree of Kutná Hora being proclaimed by Wenceslas IV and Jan Hus in 1409.

From the southern side of St James Church a cobbled lane, Ruthardská, leads to the **Hrádek** (Little Castle), a 15th-century palace housing

the **Czech Silver Museum** (České Muzeum Stříbra; ☎ 327 512 159; www.cms-kh.cz; adult/child 60/30Kč; ☼ 10am-6pm Jul & Aug, 9am-6pm May, Jun & Sep, 9am-5pm Apr & Oct, 10am-4pm Sat & Sun Nov, closed Mon year-round). The exhibits celebrate the mines that made Kutná Hora wealthy, including a huge wooden device used to extricate 1000kg of rock from the 200m-deep shafts. Don a miner's helmet and lamp to join a 45-minute **tour** (adult/child 110/70Kč) through 500m of medieval mine shafts beneath the town.

Beyond the Hrádek is a 17th-century former **Jesuit college**, with a front terrace featuring 13 baroque sculptures of saints, inspired by those on Prague's Charles Bridge. The second one along of a woman holding a chalice with a stone tower at her side, is

St Barbara, the patron saint of miners and Kutná Hora.

At the far end of the terrace is Kutná Hora's greatest monument, the Gothic **Cathedral of St Barbara** ( ☎ 327 512 115; adult/child 30/15Kč; ☉ 9am-5.30pm Tue-Sun May-Sep, 10am-11.30am & 1-4pm Apr & Oct, 10am-11.30am & 2-3.30pm Nov-Mar). Rivalling Prague's St Vitus in magnificence, its soaring nave culminates in elegant, six-petalled ribbed vaulting. The ambulatory chapels preserve original 15th-century frescoes, some showing miners at work. Walk around the outside of the church too; the terrace at the eastern end enjoys fine views.

### SLEEPING

**Camping Santa Barbara** ( ☎ 327 512 051; santabarbara .com@worldonline.cz; camp site per person 100Kč; ☉ Apr-Oct; ℗ ) The nearest camping ground is 800m northwest of the town centre off Česká, near the cemetery.

**Ubytovna TJ Turista** ( ☎ 327 514 961; nám Národního odboje 56; dm 160Kč; ☉ reception 5-6pm; ℗ ) Book ahead at this popular, centrally located hostel.

**Penzión U Kata** ( ☎ 327 515 096; www.ukata.cz; Uhelná 596; s/d 450/600Kč; ℗ ) You won't lose your head over the rates at this great value family hotel called 'The Executioner'.

**Penzión Centrum** ( ☎ 327 514 218; www.centrum .penzion.com; Jakubská 57; d incl breakfast 1000Kč; ℗ ) A quiet, central location with snug rooms – what more could you want? How about pancakes and coffee in the courtyard?

**Hotel Anna** ( ☎ 327 516 315; www.sweb.cz/hotel.anna; Vladislavova 372; s/d 730/1150Kč; ℗ ) The Anna has modern rooms with shower and TV, and a 16th-century cellar restaurant.

**Hotel Zlatá Stoupa** ( ☎ 327 511 540; http://web.tele com.cz/zlatastoupa; Tylova 426; s/d incl breakfast 1220/1950Kč; ℗ ) Treat yourself with an intriguing combination of mahogany period furniture and full-size bottles of wine in the minibar.

### EATING & DRINKING

**Piazza Navona** ( ☎ 327 512 588; Palackého nám 90; mains 100-140Kč; ☉ 9am-midnight May-Sep, 9am-8pm Oct-Apr) Have authentic pizza by an authentic Italian on Kutná Hora's main square. Finish with gelati in summer and hot chocolate in winter.

**Čínský Restaurant** ( ☎ 327 514 151; nám Národního odboje 48; mains 80-220Kč; ☉ closed Mon) The food is Chinese but the stately building is pure Czech. With dishes like rabbit *gung-po*, the menu is still making its mind up. Try the duck with mushrooms.

**Pivnice Dačický** ( ☎ 327 512 248; Rakova 8; mains 80-2200Kč; ☉ 11am-11pm) Try Kutná Hora's dark beer at this traditional beer hall. Rustle up three drinking buddies and order the Gamekeepers Reserve, a huge platter that demands at least a second beer.

There's a **potraviny** (grocery; ☉ 6am-5pm Mon-Fri, 7am-11.30am Sat) on the eastern side of the main square.

### GETTING THERE & AWAY

There are direct trains from Prague's hlavní nádraží to Kutná Hora hlavní nádraží (98Kč, 55 minutes, seven daily).

Buses to Kutná Hora from Prague (64Kč, 1¼ hours, hourly) depart Florenc bus station; services are less frequent at weekends.

# BOHEMIA

The ancient land of Bohemia makes up the western two-thirds of the Czech Republic. The modern term 'bohemian' comes to us via the French, who thought that Roma came from Bohemia; the word *bohémien* was later applied to people living an unconventional lifestyle. The term gained currency in the wake of Puccini's opera *La Bohème* about a community of poverty-stricken artists in Paris.

## TEREZÍN

The massive ramparts of the fortress at Terezín (Theriesenstadt in German) were built by the Habsburgs in the 18th century to repel the Prussian army, but the place is better known as a notorious WWII prison and concentration camp. Around 150,000 men, women and children, mostly Jews, passed through en route to the extermination camps of Auschwitz-Birkenau: 35,000 of them died here of hunger, disease or suicide; only 4000 survived. From 1945 to 1948 the fortress served as an internment camp for the Sudeten Germans who were expelled from Czechoslovakia after the war.

The **Terezín Memorial** ( ☎ 416 782 576; www .pamatnik-terezin.cz) consists of two main parts – the Museum of the Ghetto in the Main Fortress, and the Lesser Fortress, a 10-minute walk east across the Ohře River. Admission to one part costs 160/130Kč; a combined ticket for both (also including the Madeburg Barracks) is 180/140Kč. At the ticket office, ask about the historical films in the museum's cinema.

The **Museum of the Ghetto** (Muzeum ghetta; ☉ 9am-6pm Apr-Oct, 9am-5.30pm Nov-Mar) records daily life in the camp during WWII through moving displays of paintings, letters and personal possessions; the Nazi documents recording the departures of trains to 'the east' chillingly illustrate the banality of evil.

Around 32,000 prisoners, many of them Czech partisans, were incarcerated in the **Lesser Fortress** (Malá pevnost; 8am-6pm Apr-Oct, 8am-4.30pm Nov-Mar). Take the grimly fascinating self-guided tour through the prison barracks, workshops, morgues and mass graves, before arriving at the bleak execution grounds where more than 250 prisoners were shot.

At the **Magdeburg Barracks** (Magdeburská kasárna; cnr Tyršova & Vodárenská), the former base of the Jewish 'government', are exhibits on the rich cultural life – music, theatre, fine arts and literature – that flourished against this backdrop of fear. Most poignant are the magazines containing children's stories and illustrations.

Terezín is northwest of Prague and 3km south of Litoměřice; buses between Prague and Litoměřice stop at both the main square and the Lesser Fortress. There are frequent buses between Litoměřice bus station and Terezín (8Kč, 10 minutes, at least hourly).

## LITOMĚŘICE
**pop 25,100**

The cheerful town of Litoměřice offers relief from the horrors of nearby Terezín. Founded by German colonists in the 13th century, it prospered in the 18th century as a royal seat and bishopric. The old town centre has many picturesque buildings and churches, some designed by the locally born baroque architect Ottavio Broggio.

The old town lies across the road to the west of the train and bus stations, guarded by the remnants of the 14th-century town walls. Walk along Dlouhá to the central square, Mírové nám.

The **information centre** ( 416 732 440; www .litomerice.cz; Mírové nám 15/7; 8am-6pm Mon-Sat, 8am-4pm Sun May-Sep; 8am-4pm Mon-Fri, 8-11am Sat Oct-Apr) in the town hall, books accommodation and run tours from April to October.

## Sights

The main square is lined with Gothic arcades and pastel façades, dominated by the tower of **All Saints Church**, the step-gabled **Old Town Hall** and the distinctive **House at the Chalice** (Dům U Kalicha), housing the present town hall – the green copper artichoke sprouting from

the roof is actually a chalice, the traditional symbol of the Hussite church. The delicate slice of baroque wedding cake at the square's elevated end is the **House of Ottavio Broggio**.

Along Michalská on the square's southwest corner you'll find another of Broggio's designs, the **North Bohemia Fine Arts Gallery** ( 416 732 382; Michalská 7; adult/child 32/18Kč; 9am-noon & 1-6pm Tue-Sun Apr-Sep, 9am-5pm Oct-Mar) with the priceless Renaissance panels of the Litoměřice Altarpiece.

Turn left at the end of Michalská and follow Domská towards tree-lined Domské nám on Cathedral Hill, passing **St Wenceslas Church**, a baroque gem, along a side street to the right. At the top of the hill is the town's oldest church, **St Stephen Cathedral**, from the 11th century.

Follow the arch on the cathedral's left and descend a steep cobbled lane called Máchova. At the foot of the hill turn left then first right, up the zigzag steps to the **old town walls**. Follow the walls to the right as far as the next street, Jezuitská, then turn left back to the square.

## Sleeping & Eating

**Autocamp Slavoj** ( 416 734 481; kemp.litomerice@post .cz; per tent/bungalow 70/200Kč; May-Sep; ) South of the train station, this pleasant camping ground is on an island called Střelecký ostrov (Marksmen Island).

**U Svatého Václava** ( 416 737 500; www.upfront .cz/penzion; Svatovaclavská 12; s/d incl breakfast 600/1000Kč) Beside St Wenceslas Church, this haven has well-equipped rooms, hearty cooked breakfasts, and owners whose English is better than they think.

**Pension Prislin** ( 416 735 833; www.pension.cz; Na Kocandě 12; s/d incl breakfast 700/1200Kč; ) On a busy road near the train station, Pension Prislin conceals a quiet garden with river views.

**Hotel Salva Guarda** ( 416 732 506; www. salva -garda.cz; Mírové nám 12; s/d 990/1450Kč; ) With interesting old maps in reception, it's a shame they keep the lights so low. The spotless rooms, however, are well-lit in this classy hotel that's housed in a *sgraffito* building built in 1566.

**Music Club Viva** ( 606 437 783; Mezibrani; mains 90-220Kč) Shared wooden tables ensures conversation flows as naturally as the drinks in this hip spot in the old town bastion. The posters feature everyone from Frank Sinatra to Bob Marley.

**Radniční sklípek** ( 416 731 142; Mírové nám 21; mains 80-170Kč) Keep your head down in this labyrinth of underground cellars. It should be easy because you'll be tucking into great value grills accompanied by a good wine list.

**Pizzeria Sole** ( ☎ 416 737 150; Na Valech 56; pizza 75Kč) This no-frills Italian café has cheap pizzas and good-value soup, pasta and dessert combos.

**Pekárna Kodys & Hamele** (Novobranská 18) Head here for baked goodies.

## Getting There & Away

Direct buses from Prague to Litoměřice (61Kč, 1L hours, hourly) depart from station No 17 at Florenc bus station (final destination Ustí nad Labem).

## BOHEMIAN SWITZERLAND NATIONAL PARK

The main road and rail route between Prague and Dresden follows the fast-flowing Labe (Elbe) River, gouging a sinuous, steep-sided valley through a sandstone plateau on the border between the Czech Republic and Germany. The landscape of sandstone pinnacles, giddy gorges, dark forests and high meadows that stretches to the east of the river is the **Bohemian Switzerland National Park** (Národní park České Švýcarsko), named after two 19th-century Swiss artists, who liked the landscape so much they settled here.

A few hundred metres south of the German border, **Hřensko** is a cute village of pointy-gabled, half-timbered houses crammed into a narrow sandstone gorge where the Kamenice River flows into the Labe. It's overrun with German day-trippers at summer weekends, but a few minutes' walk upstream peaceful hiking trails begin.

A signposted 16km circular hike takes in the main sights; allow five to six hours. From the eastern end of Hřensko a trail leads via ledges, walkways and tunnels through the mossy chasms of the **Kamenice River Gorge**. There are two sections – **Edmundova Soutěska** (Edmund's Gorge; ☼ 9am-6pm May-Aug; Sat & Sun only Apr, Sep & Oct) and **Divoká Soutěska** (Savage Gorge; ☼ 9am-5pm May-Aug; Sat & Sun only Apr, Sep & Oct) – that have been dammed. Continue by punt, poled along by a ferryman through a canyon 5m wide and 50m to 150m deep. Each ferry trip costs adult/child 50/25Kč.

A kilometre beyond the end of the second boat trip, a blue-marked trail leads uphill to the Hotel Mezní Louka. Across the road, a red-marked trail continues through the forest to the spectacular rock formation **Pravčická Brána** (www.pbrana.cz; adult/child 50/30Kč; ☼ 10am-

6pm Apr-Oct, 10am-4pm Sat & Sun Nov-Mar), the largest natural arch in Europe. In a nook beneath the arch is the **Falcon's Nest**, a 19th-century chateau housing a national park museum and restaurant. From here the red trail descends westward back to Hřensko.

## Sleeping & Eating

**Pension Lugano** ( ☎ 412 554 146; fax 412 554 156; Hřensko; s/d incl breakfast 540/1080Kč; [P] ) A cheerful place in the centre of Hřensko serving terrific breakfasts.

**Restaurace U Raka** ( ☎ 412 554 157; Hřensko 28; mains 100-220Kč; ☼ 10am-9.30pm) Near Pension Lugano is a pretty half-timbered cottage offering Czech specialities. Try the local *pstruh* (trout).

In hills, **Hotel Mezní Louka** ( ☎ 412 554 220; Mezní Louka 71; s/d 700/1050Kč; [P] ) is a 19th-century hiking lodge with a decent restaurant (mains 90Kč to 170Kč). Across the road is **Camp Mezní Louka** ( ☎ 412 554 084; per tent/bungalow 60Kč/450Kč; [P] ).

If you have your own transport, base yourself in the pretty villages of Janov and Jetřichovice. In Janov **Pension Pastis** ( ☎ 142 554 037; www.pastis .cz; Janov 22; s/d incl breakfast 550/1100Kč; [P] ) has an excellent restaurant; in Jetřichovice try **Pension Dřevák** ( ☎ 412 555 015; www.cztour.cz/drevak; s/d incl breakfast 700/1050Kč [P] ), which is housed in a pretty 19th-century wooden building.

## Getting There & Away

There are frequent local trains from Dresden to Schöna (€5.20, 1¼ hour, every half hour), on the German (west) bank of the river opposite Hřensko. From the station, a ferry crosses to Hřensko (€0.85 or 12Kč, three minutes) on demand.

From Prague, take a bus (84Kč, 1¾ hours, five daily) to Děčín, then another to Hřensko (14Kč, 20 minutes, four daily). Alternatively, catch a Dresden-bound train and get off at Bad Schandau (184Kč, two hours, eight daily), then a local train back to Schöna (€1.80, 12 minutes, every half hour).

On weekdays there are three buses a day (year-round) between Hřensko and Mezní Louka (8Kč, 10 minutes), and two a day at weekends (July to September only).

## KARLOVY VARY

pop 60,000

If you've been hiding a designer dog or an ostentatious pair of sunglasses in your backpack, then Karlovy Vary (Karlsbad in German) is

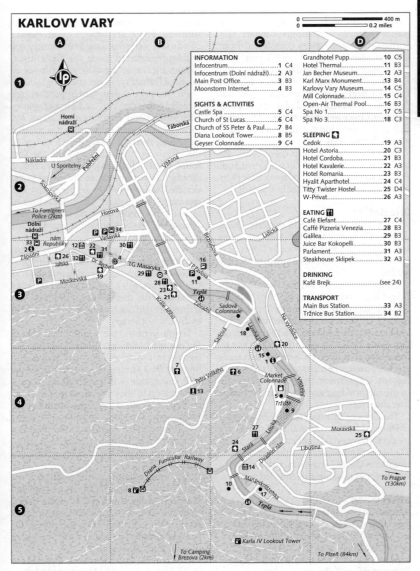

# KARLOVY VARY

| 0 | 400 m |
| 0 | 0.2 miles |

| INFORMATION | |
|---|---|
| Infocentrum | 1 C4 |
| Infocentrum (Dolní nádraží) | 2 A3 |
| Main Post Office | 3 B3 |
| Moonstorm Internet | 4 B3 |

| SIGHTS & ACTIVITIES | |
|---|---|
| Castle Spa | 5 C4 |
| Church of St Lucas | 6 C4 |
| Church of SS Peter & Paul | 7 B4 |
| Diana Lookout Tower | 8 B5 |
| Geyser Colonnade | 9 C4 |

| | |
|---|---|
| Grandhotel Pupp | 10 C5 |
| Hotel Thermal | 11 B3 |
| Jan Becher Museum | 12 A3 |
| Karl Marx Monument | 13 B4 |
| Karlovy Vary Museum | 14 C5 |
| Mill Colonnade | 15 C4 |
| Open-Air Thermal Pool | 16 B3 |
| Spa No 1 | 17 C5 |
| Spa No 3 | 18 C3 |

| SLEEPING | |
|---|---|
| Čedok | 19 A3 |
| Hotel Astoria | 20 C3 |
| Hotel Cordoba | 21 B3 |
| Hotel Kavalerie | 22 A3 |
| Hotel Romania | 23 B3 |
| Hyalit Aparthotel | 24 C4 |
| Titty Twister Hostel | 25 D4 |
| W-Privat | 26 A3 |

| EATING | |
|---|---|
| Café Elefant | 27 C4 |
| Caffé Pizzeria Venezia | 28 B3 |
| Galilea | 29 B3 |
| Juice Bar Kokopelli | 30 B3 |
| Parlament | 31 A3 |
| Steakhouse Sklipek | 32 A3 |

| DRINKING | |
|---|---|
| Kafé Brejk | (see 24) |

| TRANSPORT | |
|---|---|
| Main Bus Station | 33 A3 |
| Trřnice Bus Station | 34 B2 |

your chance to give them both an airing. The fashionable town is the closest the Czech Republic has to a glam resort, but Karlovy Vary is definitely glam with a small 'g'. Well-heeled hypochondriacs from Germany, Austria and Russia make the pilgrimage and try to enjoy courses of lymphatic drainage and hydrocolonotherapy and other such cleansing wonders.

If Russian matrons walking canine 'bling-on-a-string' doesn't appeal, there's good hiking in the surrounding hills, or just have a drink at a riverside café. It will taste infinitely better than the sulphurous spa water everyone else is drinking.

According to legend, Emperor Charles IV discovered the hot springs accidentally in

1350 when one his hunting dogs fell into the waters (Karlovy Vary means 'Charles' Hot Springs). The spa's glory days lasted from the early 18th century until WWI, with royal guests including Tsar Peter the Great and Emperor Franz Josef I. Musical celebrities included Beethoven, Wagner, Chopin and Brahms. Even Tolstoy and Marx came along to foment their leftist doctrines while being slathered in mud and hosed down by a strapping Bohemian lass.

Now the celebrities are more B-list, attending the Karlovy Vary International Film Festival in July, while wondering how their invitation to Cannes got lost in the mail.

## Orientation

Karlovy Vary has two train stations: Dolní nádraží (Lower Station), beside the main bus station, and Horní nádraží (Upper Station), across the Ohře River north of the city centre.

Trains from Prague arrive at Horní nádraží. To get into town, take bus 11, 12 or 13 from the stop across the road to the Tržnice station; 11 continues to Divadelni nám in the spa district. Alternatively, it's 10 minutes on foot: cross the road outside the station and go right, then first left on a footpath that leads downhill under the highway. At its foot, turn right on U Spořitelny, then left at the far end of the big building and head for the bridge over the river.

The Tržnice bus stop is three blocks east of Dolní nádraží, in the middle of the town's modern commercial district. Pedestrianised TG Masaryka leads east to the Teplá River; from here the old spa district stretches upstream for 2km along a steep-sided valley.

## Information

**Infocentrum** Dolni nádraží ( ☎ 353 232 838; www .karlovyvary.cz; Západni; ⏰ 9am-5pm Mon-Fri, 10am-4pm Sat & Sun); Lázeňska ( ☎ 353 224 097; Lázeňska 1; ⏰ 9am-7pm Mon-Fri, 10am-6pm Sat & Sun) Stocks maps, books accommodation and gives transport advice.
**Main post office** (TG Masaryka 1; ⏰ 7.30am-7pm Mon-Fri, 7am-1pm Sat, 7am-noon Sun) Includes a telephone centre.
**Moonstorm Internet** (TG Masaryka 31; per 15 min 12Kč; ⏰ 9am-9pm)

## Sights

At the heart of the old spa district is the neo-classical **Mill Colonnade** (Mlýnská Kolonáda),

where crowds stroll and bands play in the summer. There are several other elegant colonnades and imposing 19th-century spa buildings scattered along the Teplá River, though the 1970s concrete monstrosity of the **Hotel Thermal** spoils the effect slightly.

Pretend to be a spa patient by purchasing a *lázenské pohár* (spa cup) and a box of *oplátky* (spa wafers) and sampling the various hot springs (free); the Infocentrum has a leaflet describing them all. There are 12 springs in the 'drinking cure', ranging from the **Rock Spring** (Skalní Pramen), which dribbles a measly 1.3L per minute, to the robust **Geyser** (Vřídlo), which spurts 2000L per minute in a steaming, 14m-high jet. The latter is housed in the 1970s **Geyser Colonnade** (Vřídelní Kolonáda; admission free; ⏰ 6am-7pm), which also sells spa cups and wafers.

The sulphurous spring waters carry a whiff of rotten eggs. Becherovka, a locally produced herbal liqueur, is famously known as the '13th spring' – a few shots will take away the taste of the spring waters, and leave you feeling sprightlier than a week's worth of hydrocolonotherapy.

If you want to take a look inside one of the old spa buildings without enduring the rigours of *proktologie* and *endoskopie*, nip into **Spa No 3** (Lázně III) just north of the Mill Colonnade – it has a café upstairs, a good reason to stick your nose in. The faded entrance hall offers a glimpse of white-tiled institutional corridors stretching off to either side, lined with the doors to sinister-sounding 'treatment rooms' and echoing to the flip-flopped footsteps of muscular, grim-faced nurses. Shiver.

The most splendid of the traditional spa buildings is the beautifully restored **Spa No 1** (Lázně I) at the south end of town, dating from 1895 and once housing Emperor Franz Josef's private baths. Across the river is the baroque **Grandhotel Pupp**, a former meeting place of European aristocrats.

North of the hotel, a narrow alley leads to the bottom station of the **Diana Funicular Railway** (single/return 36/60Kč; ⏰ 9am-6pm), which climbs 166m to great views from the **Diana Lookout Tower** (admission free). It's a pleasant walk back down through the forest.

If you descend north from Diana towards the **Karl Marx Monument** and Petra Velikého (Peter the Great Street), visit the Russian Orthodox **Church of SS Peter & Paul** (kostel sv Petra a

Pavla; 1897), amid an enclave of elegant villas and spa hotels. Its five golden onion domes and colourful exterior were modelled on the Byzantine Church of the Holy Trinity in Ostankino near Moscow. It and the Anglican **Church of St Lucas** along the road are reminders of the town's once-thriving expat communities.

Rainy-day alternatives include the **Karlovy Vary Museum** (Nová Louka 23; adult/child 30/15Kč; ☻ 9am-noon & 1-5pm Wed-Sun), which has displays on local history, and the **Jan Becher Museum** (☎ 353 170 156; TG Masaryka 57; adult/child 100/50Kč; ☻ 9am-5pm), dedicated to the 18th-century inventor of the local liqueur.

## Activities

Although the surviving traditional *lázně* (spa) centres are basically medical institutions, many of the town's old spa and hotel buildings have been renovated as 'wellness' hotels catering for more hedonistic tastes, with saunas, cosmetic treatments, massages and aromatherapy. **Castle Spa** (Zámecké Lázně; ☎ 353 225 307; Zámechý vrch; basic admission €20; ☻ 7.30am-7.30pm) is a modernised spa centre, complete with a subterranean thermal pool, and retains an atmospheric heritage ambience. Basic admission gets you one hour loafing about in the pool; a four-hour session (€70) adds a full-body massage and spa treatments such as hydro-massage and electro-aerosol inhalation.

If all you want is a quick paddle head for the **open-air thermal pool** (bazén; admission per hr 40Kč; ☻ 8am-8.30pm Mon-Sat, 9am-9.30pm Sun, closed every 3rd Mon) on the cliff above the Hotel Thermal. There's also a sauna (open 10am to 9.30pm) and a fitness club here.

## Festivals & Events

**Karlovy Vary International Film Festival** (www.kviff.com) Early July.

**International Student Film Festival** (www.fresh filmsfest.net) Late August.

**Karlovy Vary Folklore Festival** Early September.

**Jazzfest Karlovy Vary** Early September; international jazz festival.

**Dvořák Autumn** September; classical music festival.

## Sleeping

Accommodation is pricey, and can be tight during weekends and festivals; book ahead. Agencies **Čedok** (☎ 353 227 837; Dr Bechera 21; ☻ 9am-6pm Mon-Fri, 9am-noon Sat) and **W-Privat** (☎ 353 227 768; nám Republiky 5; ☻ 8.30am-5pm Mon-Fri, 9.30am-1pm

Sat) can book private rooms from 400Kč per person. Infocentrum (opposite) can find hostel, *pension* and hotel rooms.

**Camping Březova** (☎ 353 222 665; www.brezovy -haj.cz; tent/bungalow per person 90/150Kč; ☻ Apr-Oct; P ☻ ) Beside a quiet river valley, this camp site is 3km south of town. Catch a bus from Tržnice bus station to the village of Březova.

**Titty Twister Hostel** (☎ 353 239 071; www.hosteltt .cz; Moravská 44; per person from 390Kč) In a town where cheap sleeps aren't bubbling over, this hostel with a silly name rises to the top. Accommodation is in apartments with two, four or six beds; all with separate kitchens.

**Hotel Kavalerie** (☎ 353 229 613; www.kavalerie.cz; TG Masaryka 43; s/d incl breakfast from 950/1225Kč) Friendly staff abound in this cosy spot above a café, located near the bus and train stations, and away from the spa district's high restaurant prices.

**Hotel Romania** (☎ 353 222 822; www.romania.cz; Zahradní 49; s/d incl breakfast 1000/1750Kč; ☻ ) Don't be put off by the ugly Hotel Thermal dominating the views from this good-value, reader-recommended spot. Just squint a little, because the rooms are spacious and the English-speaking staff very helpful.

**Hotel Astoria** (☎ 353 335 111; www.astoria-spa.cz; Vřidelní 92; s/d incl breakfast from €40/80; ☻ ☻ ) A riverside location opposite the Mill Colonnade completes this classy spot offering a full range of treatments. A leafy lobby relaxes you as soon as you walk in.

**Hyalit Aparthotel** (☎ 353 229 638; www.hyalit.cz; Stará Luka 62; d from 1900Kč; P ) With stylish décor and kitchens, these five apartments are recommended for self-caterers. Children under 15 stay free.

**Hotel Cordoba** (☎ 353 200 255; www.hotel-cordoba .com; Zahradní 37; d incl breakfast 1800Kč) A worthwhile backup.

## Eating & Drinking

**Caffe Pizzeria Venezia** (☎ 353 229 721; Zahradní 43; pizza 120Kč) After a strong espresso and tasty pizza, blur your eyes through your designer sunnies, and see if you can spot any gondoliers from this pretty-in-pink spot looking out on the Teplá River.

**Galilea** (☎ 353 221 183; TG Masaryka 3A, Pasáž Alfa; mains 130-180Kč) Try the creamy dips and Turkish bread at this authentic Middle Eastern spot. Downstairs grab a felafel kebab (65Kč) and relax by the river. Both the restaurant and the kebab shop have good vegetarian options.

**Steakhouse Sklipek** ( ☎ 353 229 197; Zeyerova 1; steaks 180Kč) With red-checked tablecloths this place looks like a hangout for Tony Soprano and his mates. The huge steak meals are big enough to feed your entire mob too.

**Parlament** ( ☎ 353 586 155; Zeyerova 5; ☩ closed Sun) With outdoor tables on the edge of the bustling TG Masaryka pedestrian mall, this is a favoured drinking place for locals. And the food's pretty good too.

Also recommended:

**Café Elefant** ( ☎ 353 223 406; Stará Louka 30; coffee 45Kč) Classy old-school spot for coffee and cake.

**Juice Bar Kokopelli** ( ☎ 353 236 254; Bulharská 9; juice & smoothies 20-37Kč) For fruit smoothies that are probably healthier than sulphur-laden spa water.

**Kafé Brejk** (Stará Louka 62; coffee 35Kč, baguettes 50Kč; ☩ 9am-5pm) Trendy new-school spot for takeaway coffees and design-your-own baguettes.

## Getting There & Around

Direct buses to Prague (130Kč, 2¼ hours, eight daily) and Plzeň (76Kč, 1½ hours, hourly) depart from the main bus station beside Dolní nádraží train station.

There are direct (but slow) trains from Karlovy Vary to Prague (274Kč, four hours). Heading west from Karlovy Vary to Nuremberg, Germany (980Kč, three hours, two a day), and beyond, you'll have to change at Cheb (Eger in German). A slow but scenic alternative is a trundle north through the hills and forests to Leipzig (890Kč, 4½ hours, 10 daily); there are several routes, involving two or three changes of train – check the online timetables for these routes at www.idos.cz or www.bahn.de.

Local buses cost 10Kč; there are ticket machines at the main stops. Bus 11 runs hourly from Horní nádraží to Tržnice in the commercial district, and on to Divadelni nám. Bus 2 runs between Tržnice and Grandhotel Pupp (Spa No 1) every half hour or so from 6am to 11pm daily.

## LOKET

Wrapped snugly in a tight bend of the Ohre River, the village of Loket is a pretty little place that has attracted many famous visitors from nearby Karlovy Vary. A plaque on the façade of the Hostinec Bílý Kůň on the chocolate-box town square commemorates Goethe's seven visits. The forbidding **castle**

( ☎ 352 684 104; adult/child with English guide 90/60Kč; with English text 80/45Kč; ☩ 9am-4.30pm May-Oct, 9am-3.30pm Nov-Apr), perched high above the river, houses a museum dedicated to locally produced porcelain, but the village's main attraction is just wandering around admiring the views.

Have lunch at **Pizzeria na Růžka** ( ☎ 606 433 282; cnr TG Masaryka & Kostelni; pizza 110Kč) with a sunny Mediterranean ambience and thin-crust wood-fired pizzas.

You can walk from Karlovy Vary to Loket along a 17km blue-marked trail, starting at the Diana lookout; allow three hours. Otherwise, buses from Karlovy Vary to Sokolov stop at Loket (21Kč, 30 minutes, hourly).

## PLZEŇ

pop 175,000

You'll never forget your first authentic Pilsner beer, and that's why brew aficionados from around the world flock to this city where lager was invented in 1842. Plzeň (Pilsen in German) is the home town of Pilsner Urquell (Plzeňský prazdroj), the world's first lager beer, which is now imitated all around the world. 'Urquell' (in German; *prazdroj* in Czech) means 'original source' or 'fountainhead', and the authentic hoppy marvel concocted by the town's brewery puts all pretenders firmly in the shade.

The capital of West Bohemia is a sprawling industrial city, but at its heart lays an attractive old town wrapped in a halo of tree-lined gardens. Plzeň's industrial heritage includes the massive Škoda Engineering Works. These armament factories were bombed heavily at the end of WWII and now make machinery and locomotives.

These days Plzeň is known as a university town, and the town's many pubs showcase its history as the original fountain of eternal golden froth.

## Orientation

The main bus station is west of the centre on Husova, opposite the Škoda Engineering Works. Plzeň-hlavní nádraží, the main train station, is on the eastern side of town, 10 minutes' walk from nám Republiky, the old town square. Tram 2 goes from the train station to the centre of town and on to the bus station.

There are left-luggage facilities at the **bus station** (per small/large bag 12 Kč/25Kč; ☩ 8am-8pm Mon-

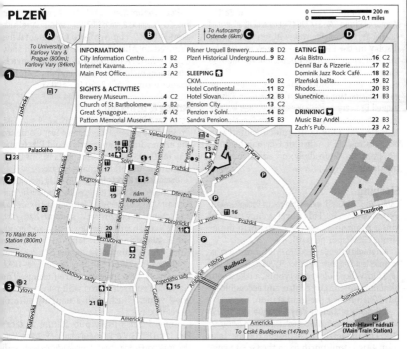

# PLZEŇ

0 ——————— 200 m
0 ——————— 0.1 miles

| INFORMATION | | Pilsner Urquell Brewery............8 D2 | EATING 🍴 | |
|---|---|---|---|---|
| City Information Centre...........1 B2 | | Plzeň Historical Underground...9 B2 | Asia Bistro..............................16 C2 | |
| Internet Kavarna.....................2 A3 | | | Denní Bar & Pizzerie.............17 B2 | |
| Main Post Office.....................3 A2 | | SLEEPING 🛏 | Dominik Jazz Rock Café.........18 B2 | |
| | | CKM...................................10 B2 | Plzeňská bašta.......................19 B2 | |
| SIGHTS & ACTIVITIES | | Hotel Continental..................11 B2 | Rhodos.................................20 B3 | |
| Brewery Museum....................4 C2 | | Hotel Slovan.........................12 B2 | Slunečnice............................21 B3 | |
| Church of St Bartholomew.....5 B2 | | Pension City.........................13 C2 | | |
| Great Synagogue....................6 A2 | | Penzion v Solní......................14 B2 | DRINKING 🍷 | |
| Patton Memorial Museum.......7 A1 | | Sandra Pension......................15 B3 | Music Bar Anděl....................22 B3 | |
| | | | Zach's Pub............................23 A2 | |

Fri) and the **train station** (per small/large bag 12/25Kč; ☒ 24hr).

## Information

**City Information Centre** (www.plzen-city.cz) nám Republiky (městské informační středisko; ☎ 378 035 330; nám Republiky 41; ☒ 9am-6pm); train station (☎ 972 524 313; ☒ 9am-5pm) Charges 1Kč per minute for internet access. **Internet Kavarna** (☎ 377 222 146; Tylova 6, 1st fl; per hr 40Kč; ☒ 8am-10pm Mon-Thu, 8am-7.30pm Fri, noon-8pm Sat & Sun)

**Main post office** (Solní 20; ☒ 7am-7pm Mon-Fri, 8am-1pm Sat, 8am-noon Sun) Includes a telephone centre.

## Sights

In summer people congregate at the outdoor beer bar in nám Republiky, the broad and sunny old town square, beneath the glowering, Gothic **Church of St Bartholomew** (adult/child 20/10Kč; ☒ 10am-6pm Wed-Sat Apr-Sep, 10am-6pm Wed-Fri Oct-Dec). Inside the soaring 13th-century structure there's a Gothic *Madonna* (1390) on the high altar and fine stained-glass windows. On the exterior, around the back, is an iron grille – touch the angel and make a wish. Climb the 102m church **tower** (adult/child 30/10Kč; ☒ 10am-6pm weather dependent), the highest in Bohemia, for great views.

The **Brewery Museum** (☎ 377 235 574; www .prazdroj.cz; Veleslavínova 6; adult/child 80/50Kč, with text 120/60Kč; ☒ 10am-6pm Apr-Dec, 10am-5pm Jan-Mar) is a block east of the square in an authentic medieval malt house. Enjoy a tasty unfiltered beer in the museum's pub.

In previous centuries beer was brewed, stored and served in the tunnels beneath the old town. The earliest were dug in the 14th century and the latest date from the 19th century; some 500m of passages are now open, and you can take a 30-minute guided tour at the **Plzeň Historical Underground** (☎ 377 225 214; Perlová 4; adult/child 45/25Kč; ☒ 9am-5pm Tue-Sun Jul-Sep, Wed-Sun Apr-Jun, Oct & Nov). The temperature is a constant 10°C, so take a jacket.

The **Great Synagogue** (☎ 377 223 346; Sady Pětatřicátníků 11; adult/child 45/30Kč; ☒ 11am-6pm Sun-Fri Apr-Sep, 11am-5pm Sun-Fri Jun, 11am-4pm Sun-Fri Oct, closed Nov-Mar), west of the old town, is the third largest in the world – only those in Jerusalem and Budapest are bigger. It was built in the Moorish style in 1892 by the 2000 Jews who lived here then. English tours cost 50Kč extra.

CZECH REPUBLIC

North of the Great Synagogue is the **Patton Memorial Pilsen** ( ☎ 377 320 414; Podřežni 10; adult/child 45/25Kč; ☺ 9am-5pm Tue-Sun), with an interesting display on the liberation of Plzeň in 1945 by the American army under General George Patton.

Beer fans should make the pilgrimage east across the river to the famous **Pilsner Urquell Brewery** ( ☎ 377 062 888; tour adult/concession 120/50Kč; ☺ 10am-9pm Mon-Sat, 10am-8pm Sun). One-hour guided tours (with beer tasting) in English or German begin at 12.30pm and 2pm daily; no advance booking needed.

## Sleeping

**CKM** ( ☎ 377 236 393; info@ckmplzen.cz; Dominikánská 1; ☺ 9am-6pm Mon-Fri) This travel agency can find you a room in a student hostel in summer (from 225Kč per person).

**Autocamp Ostende** ( ☎ 377 520 194; www.cbox.cz/atc -ostende; tent/bungalow per person 80/200Kč; ☺ May-Sep; **P** ) On Velký Bolevecký rybník, a lake about 6km north of the city centre, and accessible by bus 20 from near the train station.

**University of Karlovy Vary & Prague** ( ☎ 377 259 381; www.webpark.cz/bolevecka; Bolevecká 34; s/d 250/500Kč; **P** ) The university has student rooms. Take tram 4 two stops north from the Great Synagogue. There is a similar operation at Bolevecká 30. Phone ahead.

**Penzion v Solní** ( ☎ 377 236 652; www.volny.cz/pension solni; Solní 8; s/d 600/1020Kč) The best deal in town is this friendly spot sandwiched between a butchery and a clothes shop. With only three rooms, it's essential to book ahead.

**Sandra Pension** ( ☎ 377 325 358; sandra.101@seznam .cz; Kopeckého sady 15; s/d incl breakfast 990/1260Kč; **P** ) This *pension* has three clean rooms above a friendly park-side restaurant with off-street parking. The staff speak good English.

**Pension City** ( ☎ 377 326 069; fax 377 222 976; Sady 5 kvetna 52; s/d incl breakfast 1000/1390Kč; **P** ) On a quiet street near the river, the City is popular with both local and overseas guests. The English-speaking staff are a good source of information.

**Hotel Slovan** ( ☎ 377 227 256; http://hotelslovan.pilsen .cz; Smetanovy sady 1; s/d 1450/2100Kč, s/d with shared bathroom 530/810Kč; **P** ) Centrally located opposite a park, the Slovan's old-world glamour is now faded but the rooms are functional, and it's just a matter of time before it is redeveloped to luxury status. Stay there while you can still afford it.

**Hotel Continental** ( ☎ 377 235 292; www.hotelconti nental.cz; Zbrojnicka 8; s/d 1580/2150Kč, s/d with shared bathroom 860/1460Kč) The Art Deco Continental has survived an Allied bomb in WWII and stays from Gerard Depardieu and John Malkovich. The prices include breakfast and there are also flasher rooms from 2450 to 4500Kč.

## Eating & Drinking

**Denní Bar & Pizzerie** ( ☎ 377 237 965; Solní 9; pizza 75Kč; ☺ 8am-10pm Mon-Fri, 11am-10pm Sat-Sun) Come for the interesting photographs of old Plzeň, and stay for the tasty pizza and pasta in this lively restaurant just off the main square.

**Dominik Jazz Rock Café** ( ☎ 377 323 226; Dominikánská 3; mains 100Kč; ☺ 9am-11pm Mon-Thu, 9am-1am Fri, 3pm-midnight Sat, 3pm-10pm Sun) Get lost in the nooks and crannies of this vast student hangout. There's cool beats all day everyday, and good-value salads and sandwiches at lunchtime. After dark is enjoyably raucous.

**Rhodos** ( ☎ 736 677 344; Bezručova 20; mains 130Kč) Has Greek fare in leafy surroundings. The 'assemble yourself' gyros with pita bread are good value. Finish with a naughty slice of sweet baklava.

Enjoy Plzeň's lively pub culture at **Zach's Pub** ( ☎ 377 223 176; Palackého nám 2; ☺ 1-9pm Mon-Thu, 1pm-2am Fri, 5pm-2am Sat, 5pm-midnight Sun) with live music, tasty food and a suitably student atmosphere, and **Plzeňská bašta** ( ☎ 377 237 262; Riegrova 5) with wooden beams making it a quaint and rustic spot for your first (and maybe your best) Pilsner Urquell.

By day **Music Bar Anděl** ( ☎ 377 323 226; Bezručova 7) is a coolly hip café, but after dark it's a rocking live venue featuring the best of touring Czech bands.

Also recommended:

**Asia Bistro** (Pražská 31; mains 70Kč; ☺ 11am-11pm) Tasty Vietnamese fare including good spring rolls.

**Slunečnice** (Jungmanova 10; baguettes 50Kč; ☺ 7.30am-6pm) For fresh sandwiches on the go.

## Getting There & Away

All international trains travelling from Munich and Nuremberg to Prague stop at Plzeň. There are fast trains that run from Plzeň to Prague (140Kč, 1½ hours, eight daily) and České Budějovice (162Kč, two hours, five daily).

If you're heading for Karlovy Vary, take a bus (76Kč, 1¾ hours, five daily). There are also express buses to Prague (80Kč, 1½ hours, hourly).

# ČESKÉ BUDĚJOVICE

**pop 100,000**

After Plzeň, conduct the ultimate Bohemian beer taste test at České Budějovice (Budweis in German), the home of Budweiser Budvar lager. The regional capital of South Bohemia is also a picturesque medieval city. Arcing from the town square are 18th-century arcades leading to bars that get raffishly rowdy on weekends – all fuelled by the town's prized export of course.

## Orientation

From the adjacent bus and train stations it's a 10-minute walk west down Lannova třída, then Kanovnická, to nám Přemysla Otakara II, the main square.

## Information

**Internet Café Babylon** (5th fl, nám Přemysla Otakara II 30; 10am-10pm Mon-Sat, 1-9pm Sun)

**Kanzelsberger** ( 386 352 584; Hroznová 17) Bookshop with English-language books upstairs.

**Left luggage** (per small/large bag 12/25Kč) bus station ( 7am-7pm Mon-Fri, 7am-2pm Sat); train station ( 2.30am-11pm)

**Municipal Information Centre** (Městské Informační Centrum; 386 801 413; www.c-budejovice.cz; nám Přemysla Otakara II 2; 8.30am-6pm Mon-Fri, 8.30am-5pm Sat, 10am-4pm Sun) Books tickets, tours and accommodation.

## Sights

The broad expanse of **Nám Přemysla Otakara II**, centred on the **Samson Fountain** (1727) and surrounded by 18th-century arcades, is one of the largest town squares in Europe. On the western side stands the baroque **town hall** (1731), topped with allegorical figures of the cardinal virtues: Justice, Wisdom, Courage and Prudence. On the hour a tune rings out from its tower. On the square's opposite corner is the 72m-tall **Black Tower** (adult/child 25/15Kč; 10am-6pm Tue-Sun Apr-Oct), dating from 1553 and providing great views.

The streets around the square, especially Česká, are lined with old burgher houses. West near the river is the former **Dominican monastery** (1265) with another tall tower and a splendid pulpit. Adjacent is the **Motorcycle Museum** ( 723 247 104; Piaristické nám; adult/child 40/20Kč; 10am-6pm Tue-Sun), with its fine collection of Czech Jawas and some wonderful WWII Harley-Davidsons. The **Museum of South Bohemia**

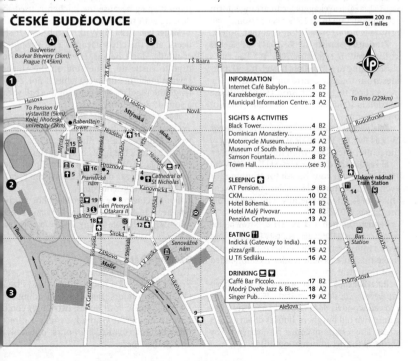

**ČESKÉ BUDĚJOVICE**

| | |
|---|---|
| 0 | 200 m |
| 0 | 0.1 miles |

**INFORMATION**
Internet Café Babylon............1 B2
Kanzelsberger.......................2 B2
Municipal Information Centre..3 A2

**SIGHTS & ACTIVITIES**
Black Tower..........................4 B2
Dominican Monastery............5 A2
Motorcycle Museum...............6 A2
Museum of South Bohemia.....7 B3
Samson Fountain...................8 B2
Town Hall.........................(see 3)

**SLEEPING**
AT Pension............................9 B3
CKM...................................10 D2
Hotel Bohemia.....................11 B2
Hotel Malý Pivovar...............12 B2
Penzión Centrum..................13 A2

**EATING**
Indická (Gateway to India).....14 D2
pizza/grill...........................15 A2
U Tří Sedláků.......................16 A2

**DRINKING**
Caffé Bar Piccolo..................17 B2
Modrý Dveře Jazz & Blues....18 A2
Singer Pub..........................19 A2

(Jihočeské muzeum; ☎ 387 929 328; adult/child 50/20Kč; ۞ 9am-12.30pm & 1-5.30pm Tue-Sun) has an extensive collection on history, books, coins, weapons and wildlife; it's southeast of the centre.

Just as beer from Pilsen (see p286) is called Pilsner, so beer from Budweis is called Budweiser. Indeed, the founders of US brewer Anheuser-Busch chose the brand name Budweiser in 1876 because it was synonymous with good beer. Since the late-19th century, both breweries have used the name, and a legal arm wrestle over the brand continues. There is no debate over which beer is superior: one taste of Budvar and you'll be converted.

The **Budweiser Budvar Brewery** ( ☎ 387 705 341; www.budweiser.cz; cnr Pražská & K Světlé; adult/child 100/50Kč; ۞ 9am-4pm) is 3km north of the main square. Group tours run every day and the 2pm tour (Monday to Friday only) is open to individual travellers; beer tasting costs 22Kč extra. Afterwards taste what all the fuss is about at the brewery's **beer hall** ( ۞ 10am to 10pm).

## Sleeping

The Municipal Information Centre and **CKM** ( ☎ 386 351 270; Lannova třída 63; ۞ 9am-5pm Mon-Thu, 9am-3.30pm Fri) travel agency can arrange dorm accommodation from 150Kč per person. Small private *pensions* are a better deal than hotels.

**Pension U výstaviště** ( ☎ 387 240 148; trpakdl@email .cz; U výzstaviště 17; r per person 270Kč; **P** ) The city's closest thing to a travellers hostel. It's 30 minutes from the city centre on bus 1 from the bus station to the fifth stop (U parku); the *pension* is 100m up the street (Čajkovského) on the right.

**Kolej jihočeské univerzity** ( ☎ 387 774 201; Studentská 13-19; d 440Kč; **P** ) This student block, 2km west of the centre, offers beds from July to September

**AT Pension** ( ☎ 603 441 069; Dukelská 15; s/d 500/800Kč; **P** ) Don't hold your breath for stunning (or even 20th-century) décor, but this convenient spot is mighty friendly with mighty big breakfasts (50Kč).

**Penzión Centrum** ( ☎ 387 311 801; www.penzion centrum.cz; Biskupská 130/3; s/d incl breakfast 900/1200Kč) Huge rooms with queen-size beds and crisp white linen make this an excellent reader-recommended spot right near the main square.

**Hotel Bohemia** ( ☎ 386 354 500; www.hotel-bohemia .cz; Hradební 20; s/d incl breakfast 1490/1790Kč; **P** ) Carved wooden doors open to a restful interior in two old burghers' houses down a quiet street. The restaurant comes recommended by the local tourist information office.

**Hotel Malý Pivovar** ( ☎ 386 360 471; www.malypivo var.cz; Karla IV 8-10; s/d incl breakfast 2300/3300Kč; ☒ ☒ ) With sports trophies and elegant leather sofas, the lobby is like a flash gentleman's club. However, the smartly elegant rooms will please both the men and the ladies, and it's a short stroll to the Budvarka beer hall downstairs (11am to 11pm).

## Eating & Drinking

**pizza/grill** (Panská 17; pizzas 100Kč; ۞ closed Sun) Just maybe where the phrase 'hole-in-the-wall' came from, pizza/grill fits a wood-fired oven, a vintage espresso machine and seating for five diners into a tiny space. Grab takeaway pivo'n'pizza and dine al fresco.

**U Tří Sedláku** ( ☎ 387 222 303; Hroznová 488; mains 100-160Kč) Locals celebrate that nothing much has changed at U Tří Sedláku since opening in 1897. Tasty meat-filled dishes go with the Pilsner Urquell that's constantly being shuffled to busy tables.

**Indická** (Gateway of India; ☎ 386 359 355; 1st fl, Chelčického 11; mains 100-150Kč; ۞ closed Sun) From Chennai to České comes respite for travellers wanting something different. Be sure to request spicy because the kitchen is used to dealing with timid Czech palates.

**Singer Pub** (Česká 55) With Czech and Irish beers, and the city's cheapest and strongest cocktails, don't be surprised if you get the urge to rustle up something on the Singer sewing machines on every table. If not, challenge the regulars to a game of *foosball* with a soundtrack of noisy rock.

**modrý dveře jazz & blues** ( ☎ 386 359 958; Biskupská 1; ۞ 10am-midnight) By day modrý dveře is a welcoming bar–café with vintage pics of Sinatra. At dusk the lights dim for regular jazz piano gigs on Wednesdays (from 7pm) and live blues and jazz on Thursdays (from 8pm). Tell them Frank sent you.

For bracing coffee and decadent hot chocolate head to **Caffé Bar Piccolo** (Ná Mlýnské stoce 9; coffee 35Kč, hot chocolate 40Kč; ۞ 7.30am-7pm Mon-Thu, to 10pm Fri & Sat).

## Getting There & Away

There are fast trains from České Budějovice to Prague (204Kč, 2½ hours, hourly) and Plzeň (162Kč, two hours, five daily). Heading for Vienna (780Kč, four hours, two daily) you'll have to change at Gmünd, or take a direct train to Linz (410Kč, 2¼ hours, one daily) and change there.

**WORTH A TRIP**

It's time to lose the black polo-neck jersey and discover the true meaning of bohemian. Perched on a precarious bluff, the old town of **Tábor** was (and still is) a formidable natural defence to invasion. Six centuries ago, the Hussite religious sect founded Tábor as a military bastion in defiance of Catholic Europe. Based on the biblical concept that 'nothing is mine and nothing is yours, because everyone owns the community equally', all Hussites participated in communal work, and possessions were allocated equally in the town's main square. This exceptional non-conformism gave the word 'bohemian' the connotations we associate with it today. The unconventional Taborites further enhanced the location's natural defences by constructing their town as a maze of narrow lanes and protruding houses; all designed to defeat an enemy attack. Religious structures dating from the 15th century line the town square, and it's possible to visit the 650m stretch of underground tunnels the Hussites used for refuge in times of war.

Now the town square is bordered by lively bars like **Kafe & Bar Havana** ( ☎ 381 253 383; Žižkovo nám 17; mains 60-200Kč). If you're staying overnight, **Penzión Alfa** ( ☎ 381 256 165; www.pensionalfa .zde.cz; Klokotská; s/d/tr 500/800/1200Kč) occupies a cosy corner just metres from the main square. Downstairs you can get your Geronimojo back at the funky Native American–themed café. If that doesn't work there is a groovily hip massage place across the lane that's doing its best to keep the bohemian spirit alive in its original hometown.

The annual **Hussite Festival of Tábor** is held on the second weekend in September. Expect medieval merriment with lots of food, drink and colourfully dressed locals celebrating their Hussite heritage.

Travel to Tábor by bus, either from Prague (80Kč, 1½ hours, 15 daily) or České Budějovice (56Kč, one hour, 18 daily).

The bus to Brno (210Kč, 3½ to 4½ hours, four daily) travels via Telč. Twice a week there's a direct Eurolines bus to Linz (430Kč, 2½ hours) and Salzburg (750Kč, 4½ hours) in Austria.

## HLUBOKÁ NAD VLTAVOU

Hluboká nad Vltavou's neo-Gothic **chateau** ( ☎ 387 843 911; 🕑 9am-6pm Jul & Aug, 9am-5pm Tue-Sun May-Jun, 9am-4.30pm Apr, Sep & Oct), was rebuilt by the Schwarzenberg family in 1841–71 with turrets and crenellations supposedly inspired by England's Windsor Castle; the palace's 144 rooms remained in use right up to WWII. There are two guided tours to choose from. Tour 1 (adult/child with an English-speaking guide 160/80Kč) takes in the main attractions, while Tour 2 (adult/child 150/80Kč) includes the chateau's kitchen. The surrounding park is open throughout the year. The **information centre** ( ☎ 387 966 164; Masarykova 35) can help with accommodation.

Hluboká is 10km north of České Budějovice by local bus (16Kč, 20 minutes, two hourly).

## ČESKÝ KRUMLOV

pop 14,600

Crowned by a spectacular castle, and centred on an elegant old-town square, Český Krumlov is a pocket-sized Prague. Renaissance and Baroque buildings enclose the meandering arc of the Vltava river, housing riverside cafés and bars. Like Prague the town's no stranger to tourists. During summer Český Krumlov may feel like a Middle Europe theme park, but visit a few months either side of July and August and the narrow lanes and footbridges will be (slightly) more subdued and secluded. Winter is an enchanting time to visit with the castle blanketed in snow and pine smoke from chimneys wafting across the river.

The town's original Gothic fortress was rebuilt as an imposing Renaissance chateau in the 16th-century for the lords of Rožmberk, the richest landowners in Bohemia. Since the 18th century the town's appearance is largely unchanged, and careful renovation and restoration has replaced the architectural neglect of the communist era. In 1992 Český Krumlov was added to Unesco's World Heritage List.

### Orientation

The bus station is east of the town centre, but if you're arriving from České Budějovice get off at the Špičák bus stop (the first in the town centre, just after you pass beneath a road bridge). The train station is 1.5km north of the town centre; buses 1, 2 and 3 go from the station to the Špičák bus stop. From the bridge

**LOCAL VOICES**

Olďriška Baloušková's family has lived in Český Krumlov for six generations. Since returning to the town after living in San Francisco for 11 years, she's uniquely qualified to know why living in the town on the Vltava is better than living in the city on the bay.

- 'A feeling of *pohoda*, (peace of mind), permeates Český Krumlov.'
- 'There are no traffic jams – Krumlov is built for people, not for cars.'
- 'We've got a rich history, with buildings over 800 years old.'
- 'We get fog in winter, not in summer.'
- 'It's easier to survive a flood than an earthquake.'

over the main road beside the bus stop, Latrán leads south into town.

Don't take a car into the centre of the old town; use one of the car parks around the perimeter. The one on Chvalšinská, north of the old town, is the most convenient for the castle.

## Information

**Infocentrum** ( ☎ 380 704 622; www.ckrumlov.cz; nám Svornosti 1; ☼ 9am-8pm Jul-Aug; 9am-7pm Jun & Sep; 9am-6pm Apr, May & Oct; 9am-5pm Nov-Mar) Transport and accommodation information, books and maps, plus internet access (5Kč per five minutes).

**Shakespeare & Sons** ( ☎ 380 711 203; Soukenická 44; ☼ 11am-7pm) Good for interesting English-language paperbacks. Cult movies screen in a cinema downstairs, and co-owner Oldřiška Baloušková ( ☎ 737 920 901) conducts interesting walking tours.

**Unios Tourist Service** ( ☎ 380 725 110; tourist. servic@unios.cz; Zámek 57; ☼ 9am-6pm) Tourist information, accommodation booking and internet café with international calls.

## Sights

The old town, almost encircled by the arcing Vltava River, is watched over by **Český Krumlov Castle** ( ☎ 380 704 721; ☼ 9am-6pm Tue-Sun Jun-Aug, 9am-5pm Apr, May, Sep & Oct), and its ornately decorated fairytale **Round Tower** (35/20Kč). Three different guided tours are on offer: Tour I (adult/child 160/80Kč) takes in the lavish Renaissance and baroque apartments that the aristocratic Rožmberk and

Schwarzenberg families once called home Tour II (adult/child 140/70Kč) concentrate: on the Schwarzenbergs and visits the apartments used by the family in the 19th-century and the Theatre Tour (adult/child 180/90Kč explores the chateau's remarkable rococc theatre, complete with original stage machinery. Wandering through the courtyard and gardens is free.

The path beyond the fourth courtyarc leads across the spectacular **Most ná Plášti** tc the castle gardens. A ramp to the right leads tc the **former riding school**, now a restaurant. The relief above the door shows cherubs offering the head and boots of a vanquished Turk – a reference to Adolf von Schwarzenberg, whc conquered the Turkish fortress of Raab in the 16th-century. From here the Italian-style **Zámecká zahrada** (castle gardens) stretch away towards the **Bellarie summer pavilion**.

Across the river is nám Svornosti, the old town square, ringed by pleasant cafés and overlooked by the Gothic **town hall** and a baroque **plague column** (1716). Above the square is the striking Gothic **Church of St Vitus** (1439) and nearby is the **Regional Museum** ( ☎ 380 71 674; Horní 152; adult/child 50/25Kč; ☼ 10am-6pm Jul-Aug 10am-5pm May-Jun & Sep; 9am-4pm Tue-Fri, 1-4pm Sat & Sun Mar-Apr & Oct-Dec), with an interesting collection including an interactive model of the town as it was in 1800.

## Activities

The big attraction in summer is messing about on the river. Rent canoes, rafts and rubber rings from **Maleček** ( ☎ 380 712 508; www.malecek .cz; Rooseveltova 28; ☼ 9am-5pm), where a half-hour splash in a two-person canoe costs 350Kč, or **Vltava Tourist Services** ( ☎ 380 711 988; Kájovská 62; ☼ 9am- 7pm), which also rents bikes (320Kč a day) and arranges horse riding (250Kč an hour). Maleček also has sedate river trips through Český Krumlov on giant wooden rafts seating up to 36 people (45 minutes; 280Kč).

## Festivals & Events

Infocentrum sells tickets to most festivals.

**Five-Petalled Rose Festival** In mid-June; features two days of street performers, parades and medieval games (expect a small admission fee).

**Chamber Music Festival** Late June to early July.

**International Music Festival** (www.czechmusic festival.com) August.

**Jazz at Summer's End Festival** End of August.

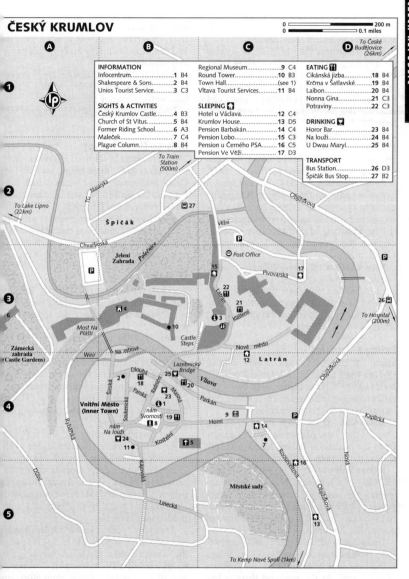

## ČESKÝ KRUMLOV

0 — 200 m
0 — 0.1 miles

To České Budějovice (26km)

**INFORMATION**
Infocentrum...........................1 B4
Shakespeare & Sons.............2 B4
Unios Tourist Service............3 C3

**SIGHTS & ACTIVITIES**
Český Krumlov Castle............4 B3
Church of St Vitus..................5 B4
Former Riding School............6 A3
Maleček..................................7 C4
Plague Column.......................8 B4

Regional Museum...................9 C4
Round Tower..........................10 B3
Town Hall..........................(see 1)
Vltava Tourist Services...........11 B4

**SLEEPING**
Hotel u Václava......................12 C4
Krumlov House.......................13 D5
Pension Barbakán...................14 C4
Pension Lobo.........................15 C3
Pension u Černého PSA..........16 C5
Pension Ve Věži......................17 D3

**EATING**
Cikánská jizba........................18 B4
Krčma v Šatlavské..................19 B4
Laibon....................................20 B4
Nonna Gina............................21 C3
Potraviny................................22 C3

**DRINKING**
Horor Bar...............................23 B4
Na louži.................................24 B4
U Dwau Maryí........................25 B4

**TRANSPORT**
Bus Station............................26 D3
Špičák Bus Stop.....................27 B2

## Sleeping

**Kemp Nové Spolí** ( ☎ 380 728 305; camp site per person 65Kč; ⏳ Jun-Aug; Ⓟ ) Located on the east bank of the Vltava River about 2km south of town, the facilities here are basic but the location is idyllic. Take bus 3 from the train or bus station to the Spolí mat. šk. stop (eight a day on weekdays); it's a half-hour walk from the old town.

**Krumlov House** ( ☎ 380 711 935; www.krumlovhostel .com; Rooseveltova 68; dm/d 300/650Kč) Perched above the river, Krumlov House is friendly and comfortable, and has plenty of books, DVDs and local info to feed your inner backpacker. Lots of fun day trips are also on offer.

**Pension Lobo** ( ☎ 380 713 153; www.pensionlobo.cz; Latrán 73; d incl breakfast 1100Kč) Pension Lobo offers

CZECH REPUBLIC

more than just spotless and central rooms. It also has a convenient laundromat.

**Pension u Černého PSA** ( ☎ 380 712 366; www.pen sion-cerny-pes.cz; Rooseveltova 36; d incl breakfast 1200Kč; **P** ) The name means 'Place of the Black Dog', and the black labrador in the photo outside just begs you to stay. Follow your heart and make the dog happy at this friendly spot with retro '70s furniture.

**Penzión Ve Věži** ( ☎ 380 711 742; www.ckrumlov .cz/pensionvevezi; Pivovarská 28; d incl breakfast 1200Kč; **P** ) Spartan rooms, but where else can you sleep in a Gothic tower with a brewery across the road?

**Pension Barbakán** ( ☎ 380 717 017; www.barbakan .cz; Horní 26; d incl breakfast from 1700Kč; **P** ) Originally the town's gunpowder arsenal, Barbakán now creates fireworks of its own with supercomfy rooms featuring bright and cosy wooden décor. A good restaurant is attached (mains 120Kč to 200Kč).

**Hotel u Václava** ( ☎ 380 715 094; www.uvaclava.cz; Nové Město 25; d 2500Kč; **P** ) Four-poster beds create a romantic atmosphere that's perfect for that first (or second) honeymoon. Not recommended for single travellers, but you won't go wrong with a loved one.

## Eating & Drinking

**Laibon** ( ☎ 728 676 654; Parkán 105; mains 80-160Kč; ☻ 11am-11pm) Candles and vaulted ceilings create a great boho ambience in the best vegetarian teahouse in Bohemia. Try the blueberry dumplings or the tasty couscous.

**Nonna Gina** ( ☎ 380 717 187; Klášteriní ul 52; pizza 110Kč; ☻ 11am-11pm) Authentic Italian flavours from the authentic Italian Massaro family feature in this pizzeria down a quiet lane.

**Krčma v Šatlavské** ( ☎ 380 713 344; Horní 157; mains 100-150Kč; ☻ noon-midnight) Nirvana for meatlovers – this medieval barbecue cellar serves sizzling platters in a funky labyrinth illuminated by candles and the flickering flames of open grills. Be sure to book ahead.

**Cikánská jizba** ( ☎ 380 717 585; Dlouhá 31; mains 100-200Kč; ☻ 3pm-midnight Mon-Sat) The Gypsy Room is the best spot in town to try the flavours of the Roma. At the weekend there is live Roma music.

**Na louži** ( ☎ 380 711 280; Kájovská 66; mains 120-180Kč; ☻ 11am-11pm) Nothing's changed in this woodpanelled *pivo* parlour for almost a century. Locals pack Na louži for tasty dark beer from the local Eggenberg brewery and huge meals.

**U Dwau Maryí** ( ☎ 380 717 228; Parkán 104; mains 80-175Kč; ☻ 11am-midnight) Dive into the authentic

medieval interior and emerge onto a sunn riverside terrace. Inside or outside, the foo and drink go down very easily in this enjoy ably raucous tavern.

**Horor Bar** ( ☎ 728 682 724; Masná 22; ☻ 6pm-late Occasional live gigs surface in this kitsch labyrinth celebrating the (un)dead.

**Potraviny** (supermarket; Latrán 55) For good self catering.

## Getting There & Away

There are direct buses from Prague to Česk Krumlov (140Kč, three hours, six daily) vi České Budějovice; some buses depart from Prague's Ná Knížecí bus station, near Andě metro, others from Florenc.

Local buses (26Kč, 50 minutes, seven daily and trains (46Kč, one hour, eight daily) run t České Budějovice, where you can change fo onward travel to Brno, Plzeň or Austria.

## ŠUMAVA

The Šumava is a range of thickly foreste hills stretching for 125km along the borde with Austria and Germany; the highest sum mit is Plechý (1378m), west of Horní Plan Before 1989 the range was divided by th Iron Curtain: a line of fences, watchtow ers, armed guards and dog patrols betwee Western Europe and the communist Eas many Czechs made a bid for freedom b creeping through the forests at night. Toda the hills are popular for hiking, cycling an cross-country skiing.

The **Povydří trail** along the Vydra (Otter River in the northern Šumava is one of th most popular walks in the park. It's an eas 7km hike along a deep, forested river valle between Čeňkova Pila and Antýgl. Buses ru between Sušice and Modrava, stopping a Čeňkova Pila and Antýgl. Plenty of accom modation is available.

Around the peak of **Boubín** (1362m), the 46 hectare *prales* (virgin forest) is the only part o the Šumava forest that is largely untouched b human activity. The trailhead is 2km north east of the zastávka Zátoň train stop (no Zátoň town train station) at Kaplice, wher there is car parking as well as basic campin facilities. From here it's an easy 2.5km to U pralesa Lake on a blue and green marked trai Remain on the blue trail for a further 7.5km to reach the summit of Boubín. Return b following the trail southwest. The complet loop takes about five hours.

If you'd rather use wheels, the **Šumava Trail** is a week-long ride through dense forests and past mountain streams from Český Krumlov to Domažlice. Top Bicycle (p304) hires out bikes from April to October and also runs organised rides in summer.

If lying in the sun sounds more fun, head to **Lake Lipno**, a 30km-long reservoir south of Český Krumlov. Known as 'the Czech Riviera', it's lined with camping grounds, swimming areas and water-sports centres; there's even a yacht marina at Lipno nad Vltavou.

Infocentrum in Český Krumlov (see p292) has full details.

## Getting There & Away

Up to eight trains a day run from České Budějovice and Český Krumlov to Volary (120Kč, three hours), calling at Horní Planá and Nová Pec on Lake Lipno. From May to September, buses cover a similar route (80Kč, two hours).

From Volary, trains continue north to Strakonice via Zátoň (28Kč, 30 minutes, four daily).

The Povydří trail is best approached from Sušice, which can be reached by direct bus from Prague (105Kč, 2½ hours, two daily). Another bus links Sušice with Čeňkova Pila and Antýgl (44Kč, one hour, two or three daily).

## ADRŠPACH-TEPLICE ROCKS

The Czech Republic's most extraordinary scenery lies near the Polish border, in a protected landscape region known as the Adršpach-Teplice Rocks (Adršpašsko-Teplické skály). Thick layers of stratified sandstone have been eroded and fissured by water and frost to form giant towers and deep, narrow chasms. Discovered by mountaineers in the 19th century, the region is popular with rock climbers and hikers. Sandy trails lead through pine-scented forests, loud with the drumming of woodpeckers, and loop through the pinnacles, assisted occasionally by ladders and stairs.

There are two main formations – **Adršpach Rock Town** (Adršpašské skalní město) and **Teplice Rock Town** (Teplické skalní město). They now comprise a single state nature reserve, about 15km east of Trutnov. At the entrance to each rock town there's a **ticket booth** (adult/child 50/20Kč; 8am-6pm Apr-Nov) where you can pick up a handy 1:25,000 trail map. Outside the official opening hours you can enter for free.

There's a small **information office** (491 586 012; www.skalyadrspach.cz; 8.30am-6pm Apr-Oct) near Adršpach train station. In summer the trails are busy and you should book accommodation at least a week ahead; in winter (snow lingers to mid-April) you'll have this stunning landscape mostly to yourself, though some trails may be closed.

If you're pushed for time, walk the green loop trail (1½ hours), starting at Adršpach and progressing through deep mossy ravines and soaring rock towers to the **Great Lookout** (Velké panorama). Admire the view of pinnacles escalating above the pines, before threading through the **Mouse Hole** (Myší díra), a vast vertical fissure barely a shoulder-width wide.

The blue loop trail (2½ hours), starting at Teplice, passes a metal staircase leading strenuously to **Střmen**, a rock tower once occupied by an outlaw's timber castle, before continuing through the area's most spectacular pinnacles to the chilly ravine of **Siberia** (Sibiř). An excellent day hike (four to five hours), taking in the region's highlights, links the head of the Teplice trail, beyond Sibiř, to Adršpach via the **Wolf Gorge** (Vlčí rokle). Return from Adršpach to Teplice by walking along the road (one hour) or by train (10 minutes).

## Sleeping & Eating

In Teplice nad Metují-Skály the **Hotel Orlík** (491 581 025; www.orlik.hotel-cz.com; s/d incl breakfast 500/1000Kč; ) is a good place to recharge and relax with a popular bar. Nearby **Pension Skály** (491 581 174; www.adrspach-skaly.cz; Střmenské Podhradí 132; s/d incl breakfast 500/1000Kč; ) has cosy rooms for post-hike relaxation.

The modern **Penzion Adršpach** (491 586 102; www.adrspach-skaly.cz; s/d incl breakfast 500/1000Kč; ) in Adršpach overcomes a lack of old-world charm with comfortable rooms, an excellent restaurant and a friendly border collie.

In a quiet setting between Teplice and Adršpach, the **Skalní Mlýn** (491 586 961; www.skalni-mlyn.cz; s/d incl breakfast 580/1060Kč; ) has rustic rooms and more friendly dogs in a restored river mill; it's best if you have your own transport.

## Getting There & Away

There are direct buses from Prague's Černý Most metro station to Trutnov (125Kč, 2¾ hours, hourly).

Single-car trains rattle along from Trutnov to Adršpach (40Kč, one hour) and Teplice nad Metují (46Kč, 1¼ hours, eight daily).

Frequent trains run from Teplice nad Metují station to Týniště nad Orlicí (76Kč, 1½ hours, eight daily), where there is an early evening train to Wrocław in Poland (224Kč, 4¼ hours, one daily).

# MORAVIA

Away from the tourist commotion of Prague and Bohemia, Moravia provides a quietly authentic experience. Olomouc and Telč are two of the country's prettiest towns, and bustling Brno delivers Czech urban ambience, but without the tourists. Active travellers can explore the stunning landscapes of Moravian Karst region, and everyone can celebrate with a good vintage from the Moravian wine country.

## BRNO
**pop 387,200**

Brno, the Czech Republic's second-largest city and the capital of Moravia, might seem a tad buttoned-down after the buzz of Prague. Stay a while though, because that traditional Moravian reserve melts away in the old town's bars and restaurants, and a cosmopolitan array of galleries and museums lets you experience modern Czech life away from the touristy commotion of the capital.

### Orientation

The main train station is at the southern edge of the old town, with a major tram stop outside. Opposite the station is the beginning of Masarykova, which leads north to nám Svobody, the city's main square. The main bus station (Brno ÚAN Zvonařka) is 800m south of the train station, beyond Tesco department store. Go through the pedestrian tunnel under the train tracks, and follow the crowd through the Galerie Vankovka shopping centre. Brno's Tuřany airport is 7.5km southeast of the train station.

### Information

**Geokart** ( ☎ 542 216 561; Vachova 8) Maps and guidebooks.
**Internet Centrum** (Masarykova 22; per hr 40Kč; ☼ 8am-midnight) internet café.
**Knihkupectví Literární Kavárna** ( ☎ 542 217 954; nám Svobody 13; ☼ 10am-7pm) English-language

books with a good café upstairs.**Left luggage** train station (ground fl; per day 26Kč, ☼ closed 11pm-4am); bus station (per day 25Kč; ☼ 5.15am-10.15pm Mon-Fri, 6am-10.15pm Sat & Sun)
**Lékárna Koliště** ( ☎ 545 424 811; Koliště 47) A 24-hour pharmacy.
**Netbox** ( ☎ 542 210 174; Jezuitská 3; per hr 50Kč; ☼ 9am-1am Mon-Sat, 2pm-1am Sun) internet café.
**Tourist information office** (Kulturní a Informační Centrum; KIC; ☎ 542 211 090; www.ticbrno.cz; Radnická 8; ☼ 8am-6pm Mon-Fri, 9am-5.30pm Sat & Sun Apr-Sep; 9am-5pm Sat, 9am-3pm Sun Nov-Mar) Sells maps and books accommodation.
**Tourist police station** ( ☎ 974 626 100; Bartošová 1)
**Úrazová nemocnice** ( ☎ 545 538 111; Ponávka 6) Main hospital.

### Sights & Activities

Heading north on Masarykova from the train station, the second turn on the left leads to the gruesomely compelling **Capuchin Monastery** ( ☎ 542 213 232; Kapucínské nám 5; adult/child 40/20Kč, ☼ 9am-noon & 2-4.30pm Tue-Sat, 11-11.45am & 2-4.30pm Sun, closed Dec & Jan) with a dry, well-ventilated crypt allowing the natural mummification of dead bodies. On display are the desiccated corpses of 18th-century monks, abbots and local notables, from a nameless 12-year-old ministrant to chimney-sweeper Barnabas Orelli, still wearing his boots. In the glass-topped coffin in a separate room is Baron von Trenck – soldier, adventurer, gambler and womaniser, who bequeathed loads of cash to the monastery.

Opposite the monastery, the lane leads into the sloping square of **Zelný trh** (Cabbage Market), the heart of the old town, and where live carp were sold from the baroque **Parnassus Fountain** (1695) at Christmas. The fountain is a symbolic cave encrusted with allegorical figures. Hercules restrains three-headed Cerberus, watchdog of the underworld, and the three female figures represent the ancient empires of Babylon (crown), Persia (cornucopia) and Greece (quiver of arrows). The triumphant lady on top (arrogantly) symbolises Europe.

From the top of the Cabbage Market take Petrská to Petrov Hill, site of the gargantuan **Cathedral of SS Peter & Paul**. Climb the **tower** (adult/child 35/30Kč; ☼ 10am-5pm Tue-Sun) for great views or descend into the **crypt** (adult/child 15/10Kč; ☼ as per tower).

**Nám Svobody**, the city's main square, is rather drab and mostly 19th century but there are a few older monuments. The **plague column** dates

# BRNO

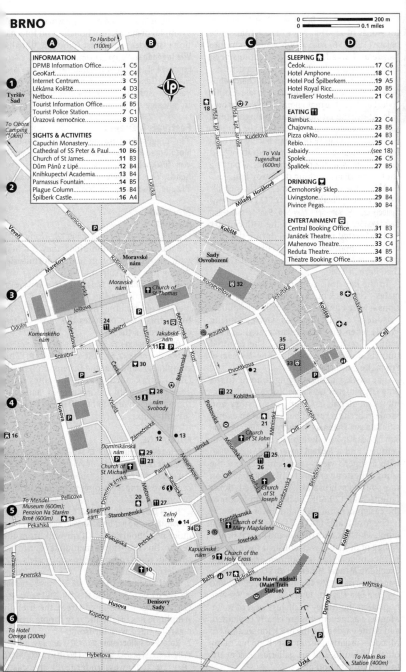

0 — 200 m
0 — 0.1 miles

**INFORMATION**
DPMB Information Office............1 C5
GeoKart.........................................2 C4
Internet Centrum........................3 C5
Lékárna Koliště............................4 D3
Netbox.........................................5 C3
Tourist Information Office............6 B5
Tourist Police Station...................7 C1
Úrazová nemocnice.....................8 D3

**SIGHTS & ACTIVITIES**
Capuchin Monastery....................9 C5
Cathedral of SS Peter & Paul.....10 B6
Church of St James.....................11 B3
Dům Pánů z Lipé........................12 B4
Knihkupectví Academia..............13 B4
Parnassus Fountain.....................14 B5
Plague Column...........................15 B4
Špilberk Castle...........................16 A4

**SLEEPING**
Čedok.........................................17 C6
Hotel Amphone...........................18 C1
Hotel Pod Špilberkem.................19 A5
Hotel Royal Ricc.........................20 B5
Travellers' Hostel........................21 C4

**EATING**
Bambus.......................................22 C4
Čajovna......................................23 B5
Pizza okNo.................................24 B3
Rebio..........................................25 C4
Sabaidy...................................(see 18)
Spolek........................................26 C5
Špaliček......................................27 B5

**DRINKING**
Černohorský Sklep......................28 B4
Livingstone.................................29 B4
Pivnice Pegas.............................30 B4

**ENTERTAINMENT**
Central Booking Office...............31 B3
Janáček Theatre..........................32 C3
Mahenovo Theatre.....................33 C4
Reduta Theatre...........................34 B5
Theatre Booking Office...............35 C3

**CZECH REPUBLIC**

from 1680, and the **Dům Pánů z Lipé** (House of the Lords of Lipá) at No 17 is a Renaissance palace (1589–96) with a 19th-century sgraffito façade and arcaded courtyard that has been converted into a boutique shopping centre.

North of nám Svobody is the **Church of St James** (1473), with a soaring nave in late-Gothic style. However the main point of interest is outside. Above the 1st-floor window on the south side of the tower at the west end of the church, is a tiny stone figure of a man baring his buttocks in the direction of the cathedral. Legend claims this is a disgruntled mason's parting shot to his rivals working on Petrov Hill.

Above the old town looms the sinister silhouette of **Špilberk Castle** ( ☎ 542 215 012; www .spilberk.cz; ☉ 9am-6pm May-Sep, 9am-5pm Oct-Apr, closed Mon Sep-Jun). Founded in the 13th century and converted into a citadel during the 17th century, opponents of the Hapsburgs were imprisoned here until 1855. Baron von Trenck died here in 1749.

In the late-18th century parts of the **casemates** – the brick tunnels within the fortifications – were converted into cells for political prisoners, a role that was revived during WWII when the Nazis incarcerated and executed Czech partisans here. The restored tunnels now house a forbidding **Museum of Prison Life** (adult/child 60/30Kč).

The castle's main building is home to the **Brno City Museum** (adult/child 100/50Kč), with exhibits on Renaissance art, city history and modern architecture. There is also an exquisite **Baroque Pharmacy** (adult/child 20/10Kč; ☉ 9am-6pm Tue-Sun May-Sep), dating from the mid-18th century, and a **lookout tower** (adult/child 20/10Kč) with a superb view – you can pick out the white limestone crags of Mikulov (p305) on the southern horizon. A combined ticket (adult/child 120/60Kč) allows admission to the casemates, museum and tower.

Gregor Mendel (1822–84), the Augustinian monk whose studies of peas and bees at Brno's Abbey of St Thomas established the modern science of genetics, is commemorated in the excellent **Mendel Museum** ( ☎ 543 424 043; www .mendel-museum.org; Mendlovo nám 1; adult/child 80/40Kč; ☉ 10am-6pm May-Oct, 10am-4pm Wed-Sun Nov-Apr), housed in the Abbey itself, just west of town. Mendel's achievements are clearly explained, and in the garden are the brick foundations of Mendel's original greenhouse. Brno has many other museums and art galleries. Ask at the tourist information office.

Fans of modern architecture will love Brno's examples of cubist, functionalist and Internationalist styles. The finest is the functionalis█ **Vila Tugendhat** ( ☎ 545 212 118; www.tugendhat-villa.c█ Černopolni 45; adult/child 120/60Kč; ☉ 10am-6pm Wed█ Sun), northeast of town, and designed by Mie█ van der Rohe in 1930. It's essential to boo█ in advance.

## Festivals & Events

The biggest and noisiest event is August's **Moto Grand Prix** (www.motograndprix.com; admissio█ from 700Kč), when the city packs out with petro█ heads. The race circuit is off the D1 road t█ Prague, 10km west of Brno.

## Sleeping
### BUDGET

**Čedok** ( ☎ 542 321 267; Nádražní 10/12) Along wit█ the tourist information office, they can hel█ with accommodation in student dormitorie█ during July and August.

**Travellers' Hostel** ( ☎ 542 213 573; www.traveller█ .cz; Jánská 22; dm incl breakfast 290Kč; ☉ Jul-Aug) Set i█ a grand old building in the heart of the ol█ town, this place provides the most centra█ cheap beds in the city.

**Obora Camping** ( ☎ 546 223 334; www.autocampobor█ .cz; tent per person 80Kč, dm 200Kč; ☉ May-Sep; P ) Thi█ camping ground is at the Brněnská přehrad█ (Brno dam), northwest of the city centre█ Take tram 1 from the main train station t█ the zoo and change to bus 103. Get off at th█ seventh stop.

### MIDRANGE

**Penzion Na Starém Brně** ( ☎ 543 247 872; www.pension█ -brno.com; Mendlovo nám 1a; s/d incl breakfast 850/1050Kč█ An atmospheric Augustinian monastery conceals five compact rooms that come reader-recommended.

**Hotel Omega** ( ☎ 543 213 876; www.hotelomega.c█ Křídloviská 19b; s/d incl breakfast 890/1350Kč; P ) In a█ quiet neighbourhood, a 1km walk from the█ centre, this tourist information favourite ha█ spacious rooms decorated in cool pastels wit█ modern pine furniture.

**Hotel Amphone** ( ☎ 545 428 310; www.amphone█ .cz; trída kpt Jaroše 29; s/d incl breakfast 990/1490Kč; P █ On an elegant tree-lined street, the friendly█ Amphone has bright and airy rooms around█ a garden filled with birdsong.

**Hotel Pod Špilberkem** ( ☎ 543 235 003; www.hotelpod█ spilberkem.cz; Pekařská 10; s/d incl breakfast 1100/1450Kč█ P ) Tucked away underneath the castle█

...re quiet rooms clustered around a central
courtyard.

**TOP END**
**Hotel Royal Ricc** ( ☎ 542 219 262; www.romantichotels
.cz; Starobrněnská 10; s/d incl breakfast 3500/3900Kč;
✗ ❄ 💻 ) An utterly captivating mix of
traditional and modern, this intimate hotel
with 29 rooms would be right at home in
Paris or Venice.

**Eating**
**Spolek** ( ☎ 542 213 002; Orlí 22; mains 70-100Kč; ☯ 10am-
10pm Mon-Sat) The service is unpretentious at
this coolly bohemian (yes, we are in Moravia)
haven with interesting salads and soups, and
a diverse wine list.

**Sabaidy** ( ☎ 545 428 310; třída kpt Jaroše 29; mains 100-
220Kč; ☯ 5pm-11pm Mon-Fri) With décor incorporating Buddhist statues and a talented Laotian
chef conjuring authentically spicy flavours,
Sabaidy delivers 'ommm…' and 'mmmm…'.

**Rebio** ( ☎ 542 211 110; Orlí 16; mains 60-90Kč; ☯ 8am-
8pm Mon-Fri, 10am-3pm Sat) Who says vegetarian
food can't taste great? Healthy risottos, veggie pies and tasty desserts stand out in this
popular self-service spot.

**Špalíček** ( ☎ 542 215 526; Zelný trh 12; mains 140-300Kč;
☯ 11am-11pm) Brno's oldest (and just maybe its
'meatiest') restaurant sits on the edge of the
Cabbage Market. Ignore the irony and dig into
the huge Moravian meals.

Also recommended:
**Bambus** (Kobližná 13; mains from 70Kč) Tasty Asian
snacks and light meals.
**Chajovna** (Dominikánské nám 6/7; tea 30Kč) Forty differ-
ent types of tea and cruisy world music.
**Haribol** (Lužanecká 4; mains 70Kč; ☯ 11am-4pm Mon-
Fri) Wholesome veggie feasts with Hare Krishna hospitality.
**Pizza okNo** (Solníční 8; pizza by the slice 15Kč) Hole-in-
the-wall and eat-on-the-run pizza.

**Drinking**
**Livingstone** (Dominikánské nám 5; ☯ until 1am) Think
raucous Irish pub meets funky world discoverer
and you're part-way there. There's an adventure
travel agency on hand if you get inspired.

**Pivnice Pegas** (Jakubská 4) *Pivo* melts that old
Moravian reserve as the locals become pleasantly noisy. Try the wheat beer with a slice
of lemon.

**Černohorský Sklep** (nám Svobody 5; ☯ closed Sun)
Try the Black Hill aperitif beer or the honey
infused Kvasar brew at the Black Mountain
Brewery's Brno outpost.

**Entertainment**
Brno has an excellent theatre and classical
music, and you're expected to put your glad
rags on. You can find entertainment listings
(mostly in Czech) in the free monthly *Metropolis*.

**Theatre Booking Office** (předprodej; ☎ 542 321
285; Dvořákova 11; ☯ 8am-5.30pm Mon-Fri, 9am-noon Sat)
Buy tickets for performances at the Reduta,
Mahenovo and Janacek Theatres at this office
behind the Mahenovo Theatre.

**Central Booking Office** (Centrální předprodej; ☎ 542
210 863; Běhounská 17; ☯ 9am-1pm & 2-6pm Mon-Fri)
Tickets to rock, folk and classical concerts at
many venues.

**Janáček Theatre** (Janáčkovo divadlo; Sady Osvobození)
Opera and ballet are performed at the mod-
ern theatre, named after composer Leoš
Janáček.

**Mahenovo Theatre** (Mahenovo divadlo; Dvořákovo
11) The neobaroque Mahenovo Theatre was
designed by the Viennese theatrical architects
Fellner and Hellmer, and presents classical
drama in Czech and operettas.

**Reduta Theatre** (Reduta divadlo; Zelný trh 4) Newly
restored, the Reduta has an emphasis on Mozart's work (he played there in 1767).

**Getting There & Away**
There are frequent buses from Brno to Prague
(130Kč, 2½ hours, hourly), Bratislava (110Kč,
2¼ hours, hourly) and Vienna (200Kč, 2½
hours, two daily). The departure point is either the bus station or near the railway station opposite the Grand Hotel. Check your
ticket.

There are trains to Prague (160Kč, three
hours) every two hours. Direct Eurocity trains
from Brno to Vienna (575Kč, 1¾ hours, five
daily) arrive at Vienna's Südbahnhof.

**ČSA** (www.csa.cz) has scheduled flights to
Prague and **Ryan Air** (www.ryanair.com) flies daily
from London.

**Getting Around**
Buy public transport tickets from tram-stop
vending machines, hotels, newsstands or at
the **DPMB Information Office** ( ☎ 543 174 317; www
.dpmb.cz; Novobranská 18; ☯ 6am-6pm Mon-Fri, 8am-
3.30pm Sat). Tickets are valid for 40/60 minutes,
cost 13/19Kč and allow unlimited transfers;
24-hour tickets are 50Kč. A 10-minute, no-
transfer ticket is 8Kč.

You can order a cab from **City Taxis** ( ☎ 542
321 321).

## Around Brno

### SLAVKOV U BRNA

Slavkov u Brna is better known to history by its Austrian name – **Austerlitz**. On 2 December 1805 the Battle of the Three Emperors was fought over the rolling countryside between Brno and Slavkov, and Napoleon Bonaparte's Grande Armée defeated the combined forces of Emperor Franz I (Austria) and Tsar Alexander I (Russia). The battle was decided at **Pracký kopec**, a hill 12km west of Slavkov, now marked by the **Cairn of Peace** (Mohyla míru; adult/child 75/35Kč; ☯ 9am-6pm Jul-Aug, 9am-5pm May, Jun & Sep, 9am-5pm Tue-Sun Apr, 9am-3.30pm Tue-Sun Oct-Mar) with a museum detailing the horrors of the conflict, which claimed 20,000 lives. Re-enactments of the battle take place annually around December 2.

Pracký kopec is awkward to reach by public transport. Take a local train from Brno to Ponětovice (28Kč, 25 minutes, 10 daily), and walk 3.5km southeast through Prace.

### MORAVIAN KARST

The limestone plateau of the Moravian Karst (Moravský kras), 20km north of Brno, is a speleologist's delight, riddled with caves and canyons carved by the subterranean Punkva River. There's a car park at Skalní Mlýn, at the end of the public road from Blansko, with an information desk and ticket office. A **mini-train** (adult/child 50/40Kč return) travels along the 1.5km between the car park and the cave entrance. You should be able to walk there in 20 minutes.

The first part of the tour through the **Punkva Caves** (Punkevní jeskyně; ☎ 516 418 602; www.cavemk.cz; adult/child 100/50Kč; ☯ 8.20am-3.50pm Apr-Sep; 8.40am-2pm Mon-Fri, 8.40am-3.40pm Sat & Sun Oct; 8.40am-2pm Nov-Mar; ♿) involves an amazing 1km walk through caverns draped with stalactites and stalagmites before you emerge at the bottom of the Macocha Abyss. You then board a small, electric-powered boat to cruise along the underground river back to the entrance.

At weekends, and in July and August, tickets for cave tours can sell out up to a week in advance, so book ahead.

Beyond the Punkva Caves entrance a **cable car** (adult/child 60/50Kč return, combined tourist train and cable-car ticket 90/70Kč) whisks you to the upper rim of the spectacular **Macocha Abyss**, a 140m-deep sinkhole. If you're feeling energetic, hike to the top on the blue-marked trail (2km).

The comfortable **Hotel Skalní Mlýn** ( ☎ 516 418 113; www.smk.cz; s/d 980/1320Kč; ℗ ) and its restaurant (mains 70Kč to 180Kč) is beside the car park. Near the top of the Macocha Abyss is **Chata Macocha** (dm 260Kč), a hikers hostel and restaurant (mains 80Kč); book through Hotel Skalní Mlýn.

From Brno there are frequent trains to Blansko (34Kč, 30 minutes, hourly). Buses depart from Blansko bus station (across the bridge from the train station) to Skalní Mlýn (12Kč, 15 minutes, five daily April to September). Check times at the Tourist Information Office in Brno before setting off. You can also hike an 8km trail from Blansko to Skalní Mlýn (two hours).

### MORAVSKÝ KRUMLOV

If you have been impressed by the works of Art Nouveau artist Alfons Mucha in Prague's Municipal House (p264) and Mucha Museum (p265), then you should visit this obscure town near Brno where his greatest achievement is on display (Mucha was born in the nearby village of Ivančice). The **Slav Epic** (Slovanská epopej; ☎ 515 322 789; adult/child 60/30Kč; ☯ 9am-noon & 1-4pm Tue-Sun Apr-Oct), painted between 1919 and 1926, is housed in a slightly down-at-heel Renaissance chateau 300m off the main square, the only venue big enough to accommodate it. Twenty monumental and cinematic canvases – total area around 1000 sq metres – depict events from Slavic history and mythology. Though different from the Art Nouveau style of the artist's famous Paris posters, these canvases retain the same mythic, romanticised quality, full of wild-eyed priests, medieval pageantry and battlefield carnage, all rendered in symbolic shades. In the artist's own words, 'black is the colour of bondage, blue is the past, yellow the joyous present, orange the glorious future'.

Moravský Krumlov lies 40km southwest of Brno. There are frequent local trains from Brno's hlavní nádraží to Moravský Krumlov (46Kč, 50 minutes, 10 daily); it's a 2.5km walk west from the station to the chateau.

## OLOMOUC

### pop 105,000

As countless tourists embrace the overt charms of Prague and Český Krumlov, Olomouc (pronounced 'Olla-moats'), exudes a subdued charm to emerge as the travellers' equivalent of a special restaurant that is your own little secret. An old town square rivalling Prague for scale and beauty combines with the youthful

# OLOMOUC

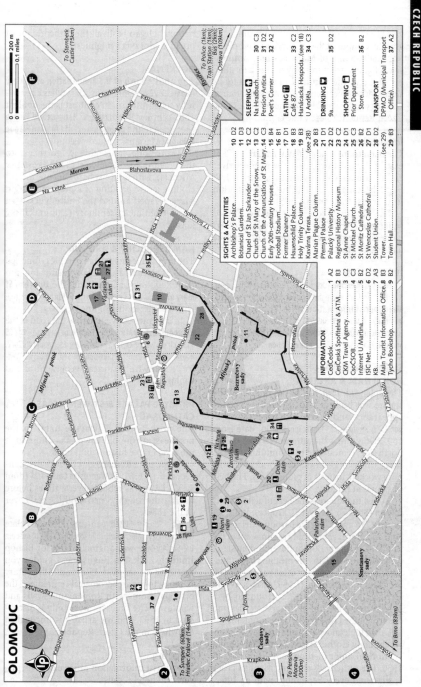

0    200 m
0    0.1 miles

**INFORMATION**

| | |
|---|---|
| CedCedok.......................... | 1  A2 |
| CesCeská Spořitelna & ATM... | 2  B3 |
| CKM Travel Agency............... | 3  C2 |
| CsoČSOB............................ | 4  C3 |
| Internet U Martina................ | 5  B2 |
| ISIC Net............................. | 6  D2 |
| KB................................... | 7  A3 |
| Main Tourist Information Office. | 8  B3 |
| Tycho Bookshop.................. | 9  B2 |

**SIGHTS & ACTIVITIES**

| | |
|---|---|
| Archbishop's Palace.............. | 10  D2 |
| Botanical Gardens................ | 11  D3 |
| Chapel of St Jan Sarkander..... | 12  C2 |
| Church of St Mary of the Snows. | 13  C2 |
| Church of the Annunciation of St Mary. | 14  C3 |
| Early 20th-century Houses...... | 15  B4 |
| Football Stadium.................. | 16  B1 |
| Former Deanery................... | 17  D1 |
| Hauenschild Palace............... | 18  B3 |
| Holy Trinity Column.............. | 19  B3 |
| Kavárna Terasa.................... | (see 28) |
| Marian Plague Column........... | 20  B3 |
| Přemysl Palace.................... | 21  D1 |
| Palacký University................ | 22  D2 |
| Regional History Museum........ | 23  C1 |
| St Anne Chapel.................... | 24  D1 |
| St Michael Church................ | 25  C3 |
| St Moritz Cathedral.............. | 26  B2 |
| St Wenceslas Cathedral......... | 27  D1 |
| Student Union.................... | 28  D2 |
| Tower.............................. | (see 29) |
| Town Hall.......................... | 29  B3 |

vivacity of a modern student town amid the graceful campus of the country's second-oldest university. Some of Moravia's most impressive religious structures play host to a thrilling history, and the youthful population looks ahead with a quiet confidence. And with tourist numbers a mere trickle, Olomouc is one of the Czech Republic's best-value cities.

## Orientation

The main train station (hlavní nádraží) is 2km east of the old town, over the Morava river and its tributary the Bystřice (take tram 1, 2, 5 or 6 heading west). The bus station is 1km further east (take tram 4 or 5).

The old town comprises the two linked squares of Horní (Upper) and Dolní (Lower) nám. The Přemysl Palace is along Ostružinická and třída 1.máje.

## Information

**Internet U Martina** (Ostružnická 29; internet & Skype per min 1Kč; ☉ 9am-midnight) internet and international calls.

**Main tourist information office** (Olomoucká informační služba; ☎ 585 513 385; www.olomouc-tourism.cz; Horní nám; ☉ 9am-7pm) Located in the town hall and sells maps and books accommodation.

## Sights & Activities

### HORNÍ NÁM & AROUND

The splendid, **town hall** in the middle of the square was built in 1378, though its present appearance and needle-like **tower** (věž; admission 15Kč; ☉ tours at 11am & 3pm Mar-Oct) date from 1607. Don't miss the **astronomical clock** on the north side, remodelled in communist style so that each hour is announced by ideologically pure workers instead of pious saints. The best display is at midday.

Across the square is the beautiful **Holy Trinity Column** (Sousoší Nejsvětější trojice). Built between 1716 and 1754, the baroque mélange of gold and grey is remarkably reminiscent of the Buddhist shrine of Borobudur in Indonesia. A delightful nun explains the meaning of the interior sculptures in a variety of languages. In 2000 the column became part of Unesco's World Heritage list. The square's surrounded by a jaw-dropping line-up of historic façades and has two of the city's six baroque fountains.

Down Opletalova is the immense and overwhelmingly Gothic **St Moritz Cathedral** (chrám sv Mořice), built methodically from 1412 to 1530. The cathedral's amazing island of peace is shattered every September with an International Organ Festival (the cathedral's own organ is Moravia's mightiest).

### DOLNÍ NÁM

The 1661 **Church of the Annunciation of St Mary** (kostel Zvěstování Panny Marie) has a beautifully sober interior. In contrast is the opulent 16th-century Renaissance **Hauenschild Palace** (not open to the public), and the **Marian Plague Column** (Mariánský morový sloup).

Picturesque lanes thread northeast to the green-domed **St Michael Church** (kostel sv Michala), with a robust baroque interior, including a rare painting of a pregnant Virgin Mary. Draped around the entire block is an active Dominican seminary (Dominikánský klášter).

### NÁM REPUBLIKY & AROUND

The original Jesuit college complex, founded in 1573, stretched along Universitní and into nám Republiky, and includes the **Church of St Mary of the Snows** (kostel Panny Marie Sněžné), with an interior full of fine frescoes.

In a former convent across the road is the **Regional History Museum** (Vlastivědné muzeum; ☎ 585 515 111; www.vmo.cz; nám Republiky 5; adult/child 40/20Kč, free on Wed; ☉ 9am-6pm Tue-Sun Apr-Sep, 10am-5pm Wed-Sun Oct-Mar) with historical, geographical and zoological displays.

### PŘEMYSL PALACE & ST WENCESLAS CATHEDRAL

The pocket-sized Václavské nám, to the northeast of the old town, has Olomouc's most venerable historic buildings.

Originally a Romanesque basilica first consecrated in 1131, **St Wenceslas Cathedral** (dóm sv Václava) was rebuilt several times before having thoroughly 'neo-Gothic' makeover in the 1880s.

The early 12th-century **Přemysl Palace** (Přemyslovský palác; adult/child 20/10Kč; ☉ 10am-6pm Tue-Sun Apr-Sep), was originally built for Bishop Jindřich Zdík. An English text guides you through a cloister, with 15th- and 16th-century frescoes, to the archaeological centrepiece, the bishops' rooms with Romanesque walls and windows. The quarters were only rediscovered in 1867, and the artistry is unequalled elsewhere in the Czech Republic.

## Sleeping

The tourist information office can book private and hotel rooms.

**Poet's Corner** ( ☎ 777 570 730; www.hostelolomouc
.com; 3rd fl, Sokolská 1; dm/tw 300/800Kč) Aussie owner
Greg is a wealth of local information at this
friendly and well-run hostel. Bicycles can be
hired for 100Kč per day.

**Pension Moravia** ( ☎ 585 416 403; www.pension-moravia
.com; Dvořá kova 37; s/d 500/800Kč; **P** 🖳 ) A 10-minute
walk from the centre, this *pension* provides
good value in a quiet residential street without
the parking hassles of the old town. If arriving
by public transport, catch bus 19 from the
railway station to the Dvořákova stop.

**Na Hradbach** ( ☎ 585 233 243; nahradbach@quick
.cz; Hrnčířská 3; s/d 600/800Kč) On a pretty street
sits Olomuoc's best-value *pension* with two
good restaurants across the lane. Be sure to
book ahead.

## Eating & Drinking

**Café 87** (Denisova 87; chocolate pie 30Kč; coffee 25 Kč;
⏰ 7.30am-8pm) Locals flock to this funky café
beside the Museum of Art for coffee and their
famous chocolate pie. You be the judge – dark
chocolate or white chocolate?

**Hanácacká Hospoda** ( ☎ 582 237 186; Dolní nám 38;
mains 70-100Kč) In the same building as the Hauenschild palace, the menu lists everything in
the local Haná dialect. It's worth persevering
though because the Moravian meals are robust, tasty and supreme value.

**U Anděla** ( ☎ 585 228 755; Hrnčířská 10; mains 130-
395Kč) Have a wander round and look at the
seriously intriguing memorabilia. Don't be
too tardy because the service is prompt and
the Moravian food very good.

**9a** ( ☎ 608 122 993; Nábřeží Premyslovcú 9; ⏰ noon-
midnight Mon-Fri, 3pm-midnight Sat & Sun) Wood and

bricks combine in a spot that's a cut above
Olomouc's other grungier student bars. Try
your hand(s) and feet on the climbing wall.

## Getting There & Away

From Brno, there are about 15 buses (60Kč,
1¼ hours) and five direct fast trains (120Kč,
1½ hours) a day. The best connection from
Prague (294Kč, 3¼ hours) is by fast train from
Praha hlavní nádraží.

## TELČ
### pop 6000

Telč is a quiet town, with a gorgeous old centre
ringed by medieval fish ponds and unspoilt
by modern buildings. It is also a good spot to
unwind with an engrossing book and a glass
of Moravian wine.

The bus and train stations are a few hundred metres apart on the eastern side of town.
A 10-minute walk along Masarykova leads
to nám Zachariáše z Hradce, the old town
square.

The **information office** ( ☎ 567 243 145; www.telc
-etc.cz; nám Zachariáše z Hradce 10; ⏰ 8am-5pm Mon-Fri,
11am-4pm Sat & Sun) is in the town hall; you can
check email here (1Kč per minute).

## Sights

In a country full of picturesque old town
squares, Telč's World Heritage–listed and
cobblestoned **nám Zachariáše z Hradce** outshines
the lot. In the evening, when the tour groups
have gone, the Gothic arcades and elegant
Renaissance façades are a magical setting.

At the square's northwestern end is the
**Water Chateau** ( ☎ 567 243 821; tours in Czech adult/child
70/35Kč, in English adult/child 140/70Kč; ⏰ 9am-11.45am &
1-5pm Tue-Sun May-Aug, 9am-4pm Apr, Sep & Oct), a jewel
of Renaissance architecture. Tour 1 (adult/
concession 80/40Kc, in English 160Kc, one
hour) is through some of the country's loveliest Renaissance halls, while Tour 2 (adult/
concession 70/35Kc, in English 140Kc, 45
minutes) visits the private apartments, inhabited by the aristocratic owners until 1945.

At the castle's entrance gaze into the **Chapel
of All Saints**, where trumpeting angels stand
guard over the tombs of Zacharias of Hradec,
the castle's founder, and his wife. The local
**historical museum** (adult/child 20/10Kč; ⏰ 9am-11.45am
& 1-5pm Tue-Sun May-Aug, 9am-4pm Apr, Sep & Oct), in
the courtyard, has a scale model of Telč from
1895 showing just how little the townscape
has changed.

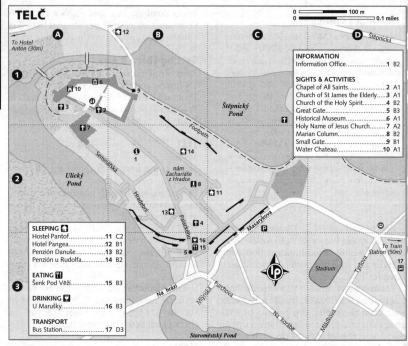

**TELČ**

INFORMATION
Information Office.....................1 B2

SIGHTS & ACTIVITIES
Chapel of All Saints.....................2 A1
Church of St James the Elderly.....3 A1
Church of the Holy Spirit.............4 B2
Great Gate.................................5 B3
Historical Museum.......................6 A1
Holy Name of Jesus Church........7 A2
Marian Column..........................8 B2
Small Gate.................................9 B1
Water Chateau..........................10 A1

SLEEPING
Hostel Pantof...................11 C2
Hotel Pangea...................12 B1
Penzión Danuše.............13 B2
Penzión u Rudolfa...........14 B2

EATING
Šenk Pod Věží..................15 B3

DRINKING
U Marušky......................16 B3

TRANSPORT
Bus Station.....................17 D3

## Sleeping & Eating

**Hostel Pantof** ( ☎ 776 887 466; www.pantof.cz; nám Zachariáše z Hradce 42; dm/d 300/800Kč; ☼ Jul-Aug; P ) A relaxed atmosphere and rooms overlooking the square add up to one of the country's best hostels.

**Penzión u Rudolfa** ( ☎ 567 243 094; www.volny.cz /libuse.javurkova; nám Zachariáše z Hradce 58; s/d 300/600Kč) A pretty merchant's house on the main square conceals a friendly *pension* with shared kitchen facilities.

**Penzión Danuše** ( ☎ 567 213 945; www.telc-etc.cz/cz /privat/danuse; Hradebni 25; s/d 450/900Kč, 4-bed apt 2000Kč; P ) Discreet wrought-iron balconies and wooden window boxes provide a touch of class on this quiet corner just off the main square.

**Hotel Pangea** ( ☎ 567 213 122; www.pangea .cz; Na Baště 450; s/d incl breakfast 1200/1600Kč; P X ⚄ ⌨ ▣ ⚅ ) Huge buffet breakfasts and loads of facilities make this slightly functional spot very good value. Rates drop by up to 30% outside July and August.

**Hotel Anton** ( ☎ 567 223 315; www.hotel-anton.cz; Slavatovská 92; s/d incl breakfast 1350/1800Kč; P ▣ ) Designer furniture and private balconies combine in Telč's best accommodation. This new hotel has been recommended by readers.

**Šenk Pod Věží** ( ☎ 603 526 999; Palackého 116; mains 100-180Kč; ☼ 11am-3pm & 6-9pm Mon-Sat, 11am-4pm Sun) Sizzling grills, tasty pizza and occasional live music are the big drawcards at this cosy restaurant tucked under the tower.

**U Marušky** ( ☎ 605 870 854; Palackého) Telč's hipper younger citizens crowd this buzzy bar for cool jazz and tasty eats.

## Getting There & Away

There are five buses per day from Prague to Telč (120Kč, 2½ hours). Buses between České Budějovice and Brno also stop at Telč (90Kč, two hours, two daily).

# MORAVIAN WINE COUNTRY

If you're heading south from Brno to Vienna, the Moravian wine country lies en route. Bohemian beer is famous worldwide, but until recently the wines of South Moravia were little known internationally.

Czech wine has improved greatly since the fall of communism in 1989, with small producers concentrating on the high-quality end of the market. Czech red wines, such as the local speciality Svatovavřinecké (St Lawrence), are mediocre, but local whites can be very good.

There are lots of *vinné sklepy* (wine cellars), *vinoteky* (wine shops) and *vinárny* (wine bars) to explore, as well as some spectacular chateaux. The Tourist Information Office in Brno (p296) sells maps and guides covering the wine country. The terrain of the wine country is relatively flat, so cycling is a nice and leisurely way to get around.

## Mikulov

The picturesque town of Mikulov lies at the heart of the Moravia's largest wine-growing region, which specialises in dry, fruity whites like Veltlínské Zelené, Vlašský Ryzlink and Müller-Thurgau.

The **tourist information office** ( ☎ 519 510 855; www.mikulov.cz; Nám 30; ◷ 8am-6pm Mon-Fri, 9am-6pm Sat & Sun Jun-Sep, 8.30am-noon & 1-5pm Mon-Fri Oct-May) is on the main square, beneath the impressive Renaissance **chateau** ( ☎ 519 510 255; adult/child 60/30Kč; ◷ 9am-5pm Tue-Sun May-Sep, 9am-5pm Apr & Oct), seat of the Dietrichstein and Liechtenstein families. Bicycles and cycle-touring information are available from **Top Bicycle** ( ☎ 519 513 745; www.topbicycle.com; Nám 24/27).

There are plenty of buses from Brno to Mikulov (52Kč, one hour, 14 daily), and less frequent buses between Mikulov and Vienna (165Kč, two hours, two daily).

## Lednice & Valtice

A few kilometres east of Mikulov, the **Lednice-Valtice Cultural Landscape** consists of 200 sq km of woodland, streams, artificial lakes and tree-lined avenues dotted with baroque, neoclassical and neo-Gothic chateaux. Effectively Europe's biggest landscaped garden, it was created over several centuries by the dukes of Liechtenstein, and is now a Unesco World Heritage site.

The town's main attraction is the massive neo-Gothic pile of **Lednice Chateau** ( ☎ 519 340 128; ◷ 9am-6pm Tue-Sun May-Aug, 9am-5pm Tue-Sun Sep, 9am-4pm Sat & Sun only Apr & Oct), the Liechtensteins' summer palace. Embellished with battlements, pointy pinnacles and dog-shaped gargoyles, it gazes across a vast, island-dotted artificial lake to a minaret-shaped folly. Tour 1 (adult/concession 80/40Kč, 45 minutes) takes you through a selection of the major rooms, while Tour 2 (adult/concession 100/50Kč, 45 minutes) concentrates on the Liechtenstein

apartments. Wander through the gardens for free.

The huge baroque chateau at Valtice houses the **National Wine Salon** (Národní salon vín; ☎ 519 352 072; www.salonvin.cz; Zámek 1; ◷ 9.30am-5pm Tue-Sat), where you can choose from various wine-tasting sessions costing from 99Kč to 399Kč per person (minimum five people). Next door is the **Zámecké vinoteka** ( ◷ 10am-6pm), a wine shop where you can get a free tasting before you buy.

There are five buses a day from Mikulov to Lednice (25Kč, 40 minutes), and one a day from Brno (65Kč, 1¾ hours).

# CZECH REPUBLIC DIRECTORY

## ACCOMMODATION

Accommodation reviews in this chapter are listed in order of price, from cheapest to most expensive. In the Prague section, budget means less than 1200Kč for a double, midrange is 1200Kč to 4000Kč, and top end is more than 4000Kč.

You usually have to show your passport when checking in to accommodation in the Czech Republic; some places might insist on keeping it for the duration of your stay, but you can demand to get it back as soon as your details are registered. If they keep it, don't forget to ask for it before you leave!

There are several hundred camping grounds spread around the Czech Republic; most are open from May to September only and charge around 60Kč to 100Kč per person. Camping on public land is prohibited.

**Klub mladých cestovatelů** (KMC Young Travellers Club; Map pp266-7; ☎ 222 220 347; www.kmc.cz; Karolíny Světlé 30, Prague 1) is the HI affiliate in Prague, and can book hostel accommodation throughout the country. In July and August many student dormitories become temporary hostels, and some in Prague are also year-round backpacker hostels. Prague and Český Krumlov are the only places with a solid choice of backpacker-oriented hostels. Dorm beds costs around 400Kč in Prague and 300Kč to 350Kč elsewhere; it's best to book ahead. An HI-membership card is not usually needed, although it will often get you a reduced rate. An ISIC, ITIC, IYTC or Euro26 card may also get you a discount.

Another category of hostel accommodation is *turistické ubytovny* (tourist hostels), which provide very basic dormitory accommodation (175Kč to 300Kč); rooms can usually be booked through the local tourist information office or KMC branch. Look for signs advertising private rooms (*privát* or *Zimmer frei* – like B&Bs without the breakfast). Most tourist information offices can book them for you. Expect to pay from 300Kč to 500Kč per person outside Prague. Some have a three-night minimum-stay requirement.

*Pensions (penzióny)* are a step up: small, homely, often family-run, but offering rooms with private bathroom, often including breakfast. Rates range from 1000Kč to 1500Kč for a double room (1750Kč to 2500Kč in Prague).

Hotels in central Prague and Brno are expensive, but smaller towns are usually significantly cheaper. Two-star hotels offer reasonable comfort for 800Kč to 1000Kč for a double, or 1000Kč to 1400Kč with private bathroom (50% higher in Prague).

## ACTIVITIES

There is good hiking among the hills of the Šumava (p294) south of Český Krumlov, in the forests around Karlovy Vary (p282), in the Moravian Karst (p300) and in the Adršpach-Teplice Rocks (p295). Climbing is also excellent in the Moravian Karst and the Adršpach-Teplice Rocks. Canoeing and rafting are popular on the Vltava River around Český Krumlov (p291), and the whole country is ideal for cycling and cycle touring. Especially good for cycling are the Sumava region (p294) and the Moravian Wine Country (p304). A recent introduction are beer and wine tours. We do not recommend you combine these with cycling.

The following companies provide activities-based tours:

**Ave Bicycle Tours** ( ☎ 251 551 011; www.bicycle-tours .cz) Cycle touring specialists.

**E-Tours** ( ☎ 572 557 191; www.etours.cz) Nature, wildlife and photography tours.

**Greenways Travel Club** ( ☎ 519 512 603; www.gtc .cz) From cycling and walking to beer and wine, Czech glass and Czech music tours.

## BUSINESS HOURS

Outside Prague, almost everything closes on Saturday afternoon and all day Sunday. Most restaurants are open every day; most museums, castles and chateaus are closed on Mondays year round.

**Banks** 8am to 4.30pm Monday to Friday

**Bars** 11am to midnight daily

**Post offices** 8am to 6pm Monday to Friday, 8am to noon Saturday.

**Restaurants** 11am to 11pm daily.

**Shops** 8.30am to 5pm or 6pm Monday to Friday, 8.30am-noon or 1pm Saturday

## COURSES

The **Institute for Language & Preparatory Studies** (Ústav jazykové a odborné přípravy; ☎ 224 990 411; www.ujop.cuni.cz) runs six-week Czech language courses for foreigners.

The **PCFE Film School** ( ☎ 257 534 013; www.prague -center.cz) runs four-week intensive film-making workshops in summer, covering screenwriting, directing, cinematography, editing and sound design.

The **International Partnership for Service, Learning & Leadership** (www.ipsl.org) provides longer-term (up to one year) opportunities for volunteering in the Czech Republic. Participants stay with local families and combine study with volunteer work. Opportunities for volunteering include teaching English to blind students and working with special-needs children.

## CUSTOMS

Customs officers can be strict about antiques and will confiscate goods that are questionable There is no limit to the amount of Czech or foreign currency that can be taken into or out of the country, but amounts exceeding 500,000Kč must be declared.

## DANGERS & ANNOYANCES

Pickpocketing can be a problem in Prague's tourist zone, and there are occasional reports of robberies on overnight international trains. There is intense racism towards the local Roma population, which occasionally results in verbal abuse (and even assault) directed at darker-skinned visitors.

## DISABLED TRAVELLERS

Ramps for wheelchair users are becoming more common, but cobbled streets, steep hills and stairways often make getting around difficult. Public transport is a major problem as most buses, trains and trams don't have wheelchair access. Major tourist attractions such as Prague Castle do have wheelchair access though – anything described as *bez-barierová* is 'barrier-free'.

**Prague Wheelchair Users Organisation** (Map pp266-7; Pražská organizace vozíčkářů; ☎ 224 827 210; www.pov.cz in Czech; Benediktská 6, Staré Město) can organise a guide and transportation at about half the cost of a taxi, and has a CD-ROM guide to barrier-free Prague in Czech, English and German.

# EMBASSIES & CONSULATES
## Czech Embassies & Consulates
**Australia** ( ☎ 02-6290 1386; www.mzv.cz/canberra; 8 Culgoa Circuit, O'Malley, Canberra ACT 2606)
**Canada** ( ☎ 613-562 3875; www.mzv.cz/ottawa; 251 Cooper St, Ottawa, Ontario K2P 0G2)
**France** ( ☎ 01 40 65 13 00; www.mzv.cz/paris; 15 Ave Charles Floquet, 75007 Paris)
**Germany** ( ☎ 030-22 63 80; www.mzv.cz/berlin; Wilhelmstrasse 44, 10117 Berlin)
**Ireland** ( ☎ 031-668 1135; www.mzv.cz/dublin; 57 Northumberland Rd, Ballsbridge, Dublin 4)
**Netherlands** ( ☎ 070-313 0031; www.mzv.cz/hague; Paleisstraat 4, 2514 JA The Hague)
**New Zealand** ( ☎ 09-522 8736; auckland@honorary.mzv.cz; Level 3, BMW Mini Centre, 11-15 Great South Rd, Newmarket, Auckland) Postal address: PO Box 7488, Auckland.
**UK** ( ☎ 020-7243 1115; www.mzv.cz/london; 26 Kensington Palace Gardens, London W8 4QY)
**USA** ( ☎ 202-274 9100; www.mzv.cz/washington; 3900 Spring of Freedom St NW, Washington, DC 20008)

## Embassies & Consulates in the Czech Republic
Most embassies and consulates are open at least 9am to noon Monday to Friday.
**Australia** (Map pp266-7; ☎ 296 578 350; www.emb assy.gov.au/cz.html; 6th fl, Klimentská 10, Nové Město) Honorary consulate for emergency assistance only; nearest Australian embassy is in Vienna.
**Austria** (Map pp266-7; ☎ 257 090 511; www.austria.cz in German & Czech; Viktora Huga 10, Smíchov)
**Bulgaria** (Map pp266-7; ☎ 222 211 258; bulvelv@mbox.vol.cz; Krakovská 6, Nové Město)
**Canada** (Map pp258-9; ☎ 272 101 800; www.canada.cz; Muchova 6, Bubeneč)
**France** (Map pp266-7; ☎ 251 171 711; www.france.cz in French & Czech; Velkopřerovské nám 2, Malá Strana)
**Germany** (Map pp266-7; ☎ 257 113 111; www.deutsch land.cz in German & Czech; Vlašská 19, Malá Strana)
**Hungary** (Map pp258-9; ☎ 233 324 454; huembprg@vol.cz; Českomalínská 20, Bubeneč)
**Ireland** (Map pp266-7; ☎ 257 530 061; pragueembassy@dfa.ie; Tržiště 13, Malá Strana)

**Netherlands** (Map pp258-9; ☎ 233 015 200; www.netherlandsembassy.cz; Gotthardská 6/27, Bubeneč)
**New Zealand** (Map pp258-9; ☎ 222 514 672; egermayer@nzconsul.cz; Dykova 19, Vinohrady) Honorary consulate providing emergency assistance only (eg stolen passport); the nearest NZ embassy is in Berlin.
**Poland** Consulate (Map pp258-9; ☎ 224 228 722; konspol@mbox.vol.cz; Vúžlabiné 14, Strašnice); Embassy (Map pp266-7; ☎ 257 099 500; www.prague.polemb.net; Valdštejnská 8, Malá Strana) Go to the consular department for visas.
**Russia** (Map pp258-9; ☎ 233 374 100; embrus@tiscali.cz; Pod Kaštany 1, Bubeneč)
**Slovakia** (Map pp266-7; ☎ 233 113 051; www.slovakemb.cz, in Slovak; Pod Hradbami 1, Dejvice)
**South Africa** (Map pp258-9; ☎ 267 311 114; saprague@terminal.cz; Ruská 65, Vršovice)
**Ukraine** (Map pp258-9; ☎ 233 342 000; emb_cz@mfa.gov.ua; Charlese de Gaulla 29, Bubeneč)
**UK** (Map pp266-7; ☎ 257 402 111; www.britain.cz; Thunovská 14, Malá Strana)
**USA** (Map pp266-7; ☎ 257 022 000; www.usembassy.cz; Tržiště 15, Malá Strana)

# FESTIVALS & EVENTS
**Festival of Sacred Music** (www.mhf-brno.cz) Easter; Brno.
**Prague Spring** (www.festival.cz) May; international music festival.
**United Islands** (www.unitedislands.cz) June; world music festival, Prague.
**Five-Petalled Rose Festival** June; medieval festival, Český Krumlov.
**Karlovy Vary International Film Festival** (www.kviff.com) July
**Český Krumlov International Music Festival** (www.auviex.cz) July to August
**Loveplanet** (www.loveplanet.cz) August; rock and hip-hop festival, Prague.
**Dvořák Autumn** September; classical-music festival, Karlovy Vary.
**Prague Autumn** (www.pragueautumn.cz) September; international music festival.

# GAY & LESBIAN TRAVELLERS
**Prague Saints** (www.praguesaints.cz) is the most comprehensive online source for English-language information and has links to gay-friendly accommodation and bars. Homosexuality is legal in the Czech Republic (the age of consent is 15), but Czechs are not yet used to seeing public displays of affection; it's best to be discreet.

# HOLIDAYS
**New Year's Day** 1 January
**Easter Monday** March/April

**Labour Day** 1 May
**Liberation Day** 8 May
**SS Cyril and Methodius Day** 5 July
**Jan Hus Day** 6 July
**Czech Statehood Day** 28 September
**Republic Day** 28 October
**Struggle for Freedom and Democracy Day**
17 November
**Christmas** 24 to 26 December

## INTERNET RESOURCES

**Czech Tourism** (www.czechtourism.com) Official tourist information.

**Czech.cz** (www.czech.cz) Informative government site on travel and tourism, including visa requirements.

**IDOS** (www.idos.cz) Train and bus timetables.

**Mapy** (www.mapy.cz) Online maps.

**Prague Information Service** (www.prague-info.cz) Official tourist site for Prague.

**PragueTV** (www.praguetv.cz) Prague events and entertainment listings.

**Radio Prague** (www.radio.cz) Dedicated to Czech news, language and culture (in English, French, German, Spanish and Russian).

## MONEY
### Currency

The Czech crown (Koruna česká, or Kč), is divided into 100 hellers or *haléřů* (h). Banknotes come in denominations of 20, 50, 100, 200, 500, 1000, 2000 and 5000Kč; coins are of 10, 20 and 50h and one, two, five, 10, 20 and 50Kč.

Keep small change handy for use in public toilets, telephones and tram-ticket machines, and try to keep some small denomination notes for shops, cafés and restaurants – changing the larger notes from ATMs can be a problem.

### Exchanging Money

There is no black market; anyone who offers to change money in the street is a thief.

There's a good network of *bankomaty* (ATMs). The main banks – Komerční banka, ČSOB and Živnostenská banka – are the best places to change cash and travellers cheques or get a cash advance on Visa or MasterCard. Amex and Thomas Cook/Travelex offices change their own cheques without commission. Credit cards are widely accepted in petrol stations, midrange and top-end hotels, restaurants and shops.

Beware of *směnárna* (private exchange offices), especially in Prague – they advertise misleading rates, and often charge exorbitant commissions or 'handling fees'.

## Costs

Food, transport and admission fees are fairly cheap, but accommodation in Prague can be expensive. Staying in hostels and buying food in supermarkets, you can survive on US$20 a day in summer. Staying in private rooms or *pensions,* eating at cheap restaurants and using public transport, count on US$30 to US$35 a day.

Get out of the capital and your costs will drop dramatically. Some businesses quote prices in euros; prices in this chapter conform to quotes of individual businesses.

## Tipping

Tipping in restaurants is optional, but increasingly expected in Prague. If there is no service charge you should certainly round up the bill to the next 10 or 20Kč (5% to 10% is normal in Prague). The same applies to tipping taxi drivers.

## POST

General delivery mail can be addressed to Poste Restante, Pošta 1, in most major cities. For Prague, the address is Poste Restante, Jindřišská 14, 11000 Praha 1, Czech Republic. International postcards cost 11Kč.

## TELEPHONE

All Czech phone numbers have nine digits – you have to dial all nine for any call, local or long distance. Make international calls at main post offices or directly from phonecard booths. The international access code is ☎ 00. The Czech Republic's country code is ☎ 420.

Payphones are widespread, some taking coins and some phonecards. Buy phonecards from post offices, hotels, newsstands and department stores for 150Kč or 1000Kč.

Mobile-phone coverage (GSM 900) is excellent. If you're from Europe, Australia

---

**EMERGENCY NUMBERS**

- Ambulance ☎ 155
- EU-wide Emergency Hotline ☎ 112
- Fire ☎ 150
- Motoring Assistance (ÚAMK) ☎ 1230
- Municipal Police ☎ 156
- State Police ☎ 158

or New Zealand, your own mobile phone should be compatible. It's best to purchase a Czech SIM card from any mobile-phone shop for around 450Kč (including 300Kč of calling credit) and make local calls at local rates. In this case you can't use your existing mobile number.

## TOURIST INFORMATION

**Czech Tourism** (www.czechtourism.com) offices provide information about tourism, culture and business in the Czech Republic.

**Austria** ( ☎ 01-533 2193; info-at@czechtourism.com; Herrengasse 17, 1010 Vienna)

**Canada** ( ☎ 416-363 9928; info-ca@czechtourism.com; Czech Airlines Office, 401 Bay St, Suite 1510, Toronto, Ontario M5H 2Y4)

**France** (info-fr@czechtourism.com; Rrue Bonaparte 18, 75006 Paris)

**Germany** (info-de@czechtourism.com; Friedrichstrasse 206, 10969 Berlin).

**Poland** ( ☎ 22-629 29 16; info-pl@czechtourism.com; Al Róz 16, 00-555 Warsaw)

**UK** ( ☎ information line 207-631-0427; info-uk@czechtourism.com) Office not open to callers.

**USA** ( ☎ 212-288 0830; info-usa@czechtourism.com; 1109 Madison Ave, New York, NY 10028)

## VISAS

Everyone requires a valid passport (or identity card for EU citizens) to enter the Czech Republic.

Citizens of EU and EEA countries do not need a visa for any type of visit. Citizens of Australia, Canada, Israel, Japan, New Zealand, Switzerland and the USA can stay for up to 90 days without a visa; other nationalities do need a visa.

Visas are not available at border crossings or at Prague's Ruzyně airport; you'll be refused entry if you need one and arrive without one.

Note that although the Czech Republic is now part of the EU, the visas issued by the Czech Republic are national and not Schengen visas. When the Czech Republic joined the EU, the country did not become part of the Schengen area. Therefore valid Schengen visas cannot be used for entering the Czech Republic. Note that the reverse of this is also true; Czech visas cannot be used to enter other EU Member States.

Visa regulations change from time to time, so check www.czech.cz or one of the Czech embassy websites listed on p307.

# TRANSPORT IN THE CZECH REPUBLIC

## GETTING THERE & AWAY
### Air

The Czech Republic's main international airport is **Prague-Ruzyně** ( ☎ 220 113 314; www.csl.cz/en). The national carrier, **Czech Airlines** (ČSA; Map pp266-7; ☎ 239 007 007 www.csa.cz; V celnici 5, Nové Město), has direct flights to Prague from many European cities.

The main international airlines serving Prague:

**Aer Lingus** (EI; ☎ 224 815 373; www.aerlingus.ie)
**Aeroflot** (SU; ☎ 227 020 020; www.aeroflot.ru)
**Air France** (AF; ☎ 221 662 662; www.airfrance.com/cz)
**Alitalia** (AZ; ☎ 224 194 150; www.alitalia.com)
**Austrian Airlines** (OS; ☎ 227 231 231; www.aua.com)
**British Airways** (BA; ☎ 239 000 299; www.britishairways.com)
**Croatia Airlines** (OU; ☎ 222 222 235; www.croatiaairlines.hr)
**Czech Airlines** (OK; ☎ 239 007 007; www.csa.cz)
**EasyJet** (EZY; www.easyjet.com)
**El Al** (LY; ☎ 224 226 624; www.elal.co.il)
**FlyGlobespan** (B4; ☎ 220 113 171; www.flyglobespan.com)
**GermanWings** (4U; www.germanwings.com)
**JAT Airways** (JU; ☎ 224 942 654; www.jat.com)
**KLM** (KL; ☎ 233 090 933; www.klm.com)
**LOT** (LO; ☎ 222 317 524; www.lot.com)
**Lufthansa** (LH; ☎ 224 422 911; www.lufthansa.com)
**Malev** (MA; ☎ 220 113 090; www.malev.com)
**SAS** (SK; ☎ 220 116 031; www.sas.se)
**SkyEurope** (NE; ☎ 900 14 15 16; www.skyeurope.com)
**SmartWings** (QS; ☎ 900 166 565; www.smartwings.net)
**SN Brussels Airlines** (SN; ☎ 220 116 352; www.flysn.com)
**Turkish Airlines** (TK; ☎ 234 708 708; www.turkishairlines.com)

### Land
#### BUS

Prague's main international bus terminal is Florenc Bus Station, 600m north of the main train station. The peak season for bus travel is mid-June to the end of September, with daily buses to major European cities; outside this season, frequency falls to two or three a week.

The main international bus operators serving Prague:

**Eurolines-Bohemia Euroexpress International** (Map pp266-7; ☎ 224 218 680; www.bei.cz; ÚAN Praha

Florenc Bus Station, Křižíkova 4-6, Karlín; ⏲ 8am-6pm Mon-Fri) Buses to destinations all over Europe.

**Eurolines-Sodeli** (Map pp266-7; ☎ 224 239 318; www .eurolines.cz, in Czech; Senovážné nám 6, Nové Město; ⏲ 8am-6pm Mon-Fri) Links Prague with cities in Western and Central Europe. There is another Eurolines ticket office in Florenc bus station.

**Capital Express** (Map pp258-9; ☎ 220 870 368; www .capitalexpress.cz; I výstaviště 3. Holešovice; ⏲ 8am-6pm Mon-Thu, 8am-5pm Fri) Daily bus service between London and Prague via Plzeň.

**Student Agency** (www.studentagency.cz) Central Prague (Map pp266-7; ☎ 224 999 666; Ječná 37; ⏲ 9am-6pm Mon-Fri); Florenc bus station (Map pp266-7; ☎ 224 894 430; ⏲ 9am-6pm Mon-Fri) Their big yellow buses link all major Czech cities and provide services to other cities in Western and Central Europe. Also have branches in major Czech cities.

Sample one-way fares from Prague include the following:

**Bratislava** 230Kč, 4¾ hours
**Brno** 130Kč, 2½ hours
**Budapest** 1250Kč, 7¼ hours
**Frankfurt** 1250Kč, 8½ hours
**Salzburg** 930Kč, 7½ hours
**Vienna** 300Kč, five hours
**Warsaw** 820Kč, 10½ hours
**Wrocław** 690Kč, 4¾ hours

### CAR & MOTORCYCLE
Motorists can enter the country at any of the many border crossings marked on most road maps; see the map on p250 for all major 24-hour crossings.

You will need to buy a *nálepka* (motorway tax coupon) – on sale at border crossings, petrol stations and post offices – in order to use Czech motorways (100/200Kč for 10 days/one month).

### TRAIN
International trains arrive at Prague's main train station (Praha-hlavní nádraží, or Praha hl. n.), or the outlying Holešovice (Praha Hol.) and Smíchov (Praha Smv.) stations.

Prague and Brno lie on the main line from Berlin and Dresden to Bratislava and Budapest, and from Hamburg and Berlin to Vienna. Trains from Frankfurt and Munich pass through Nuremberg and Plzeň on the way to Prague. There are also daily express trains between Prague and Warsaw via Wrocław or Katowice.

Sample one-way fares to Prague include the following:

**Berlin** €44, five hours
**Bratislava** €18, 4¾ hours
**Frankfurt** €61, 7½ hours
**Kraków** €28, 8½ hours
**Salzburg** €37, eight hours
**Vienna** €29, 4½ hours
**Warsaw** €36, 9½ hours

You can buy tickets in advance from Czech Railways (České dráhy, or ČD) ticket offices and various travel agencies. Seat reservations are compulsory on international trains. International tickets are valid for two months with unlimited stopovers. Inter-Rail (Zone D) passes are valid in the Czech Republic, but Eurail passes are not.

## GETTING AROUND
### Bicycle
The Czech Republic offers good opportunities for cycle touring. Cyclists should be careful as minor roads are often narrow and potholed. In towns cobblestones and tram tracks can be a dangerous combination, especially after rain. Theft is a problem, especially in Prague and other large cities, so always lock up your bike.

It's fairly easy to transport your bike on Czech trains. First purchase your train ticket and then take it with your bicycle to the railway luggage office. There you fill out a card, which will be attached to your bike; on the card you should write your name, address, departure station and destination.

The cost of transporting a bicycle is 40Kč to 60Kč depending on the length of the journey. You can also transport bicycles on most buses if they are not too crowded and if the bus driver is willing.

### Bus
Within the Czech Republic buses are often faster, cheaper and more convenient than trains, though not as comfortable. Many bus routes have reduced frequency (or none) at weekends. Buses occasionally leave early, so get to the station at least 15 minutes before the official departure time.

Most services are operated by the national bus company **ČSAD** ( ☎ information line 900 144 444; www.csadbus.cz); you can check bus timetables online at www.idos.cz. Ticketing at main bus stations is computerised, so you can often book a seat ahead and be sure of a comfortable trip. Other stations are rarely computerised and you must line up and pay the driver.

The footnotes on printed timetables may drive you crazy. Note the following: crossed hammers means the bus runs on *pracovní dny* (working days; ie Monday to Friday only); a Christian cross means it runs on Sundays and public holidays; and numbers in circles refer to particular days of the week (1 is Monday, 2 Tuesday etc). *Jede* means 'runs', *nejede* means 'doesn't run' and *jede denne* means 'runs daily'. *V* is 'on', *od* is 'from' and *do* is 'to' or 'until'.

Fares are very reasonable; expect to pay around 80Kč for a 100km trip. Prague to Brno costs 130Kč, with Prague to Karlovy Vary around the same.

## Car & Motorcycle

### DRIVING LICENCE

Foreign driving licences are valid for up to 90 days. Strictly speaking, licences that do not include photo identification need an International Driving Permit as well, although this rule is rarely enforced – ordinary UK licences without a photo are normally accepted without comment.

### FUEL

There are plenty of petrol stations, many open 24/7. Leaded petrol is available as *special* (91 octane) and *super* (96 octane), unleaded as *natural* (95 octane) or *natural plus* (98 octane). The Czech for diesel is *nafta* or just *diesel*. *Autoplyn* (LPG gas) is available in every major town but at very few outlets. *Natural* costs around 30Kč per litre and diesel 25Kč.

### HIRE

The main international car-rental chains all have offices in Prague. Small local companies offer better prices, but are less likely to have fluent, English-speaking staff; it's often easier to book by email than by phone. Typical rates for a Škoda Felicia are around 800Kč a day including unlimited kilometres, collision-damage waiver and value-added tax (VAT). Reputable local companies include the following:

**Secco Car** (Map pp258-9; ☎ 220 802 361; www.secco car.cz; Přístavní 39, Holešovice)

**Vecar** (Map pp258-9; ☎ 224 314 361; www.vecar.cz; Svatovítská 7, Dejvice)

**West Car Praha** (Map pp258-9; ☎ 235 365 307; www .westcarpraha.cz, in Czech; Veleslavínská 17, Veleslavín)

## ROAD RULES

Road rules are the same as the rest of Europe. A vehicle must be equipped with a first-aid kit, a red-and-white warning triangle and a nationality sticker on the rear; the use of seat belts is compulsory. Drinking and driving is strictly forbidden – the legal blood alcohol level is zero. Police can hit you with on-the-spot fines of up to 2000Kč for speeding and other traffic offences (be sure to insist on a receipt).

Speed limits are 30km/h or 50km/h in built-up areas, 90km/h on open roads and 130km/h on motorways; motorbikes are limited to 80km/h. At level crossings over railway lines the speed limit is 30km/h. Beware of speed traps.

You need a motorway tax coupon (see opposite) to use the motorways; this is included with most rental cars.

Police often mount checkpoints, stopping vehicles for random checks. They are generally looking for locals driving without insurance or overloaded goods vehicles. If you are stopped, present your licence, passport and insurance or rental documents; as soon as the officer realises you're a tourist, you'll probably be waved on.

## Local Transport

City buses and trams operate from around 4.30am to midnight daily. Tickets must be purchased in advance – they're sold at bus and train stations, newsstands and vending machines – and must be validated in the time-stamping machines found on buses and trams and at the entrance to metro stations. Tickets are hard to find at night, on weekends and out in residential areas, so carry a good supply.

Taxis have meters – ensure they're switched on.

## Train

Czech Railways provides efficient train services to almost every part of the country. Fares are based on distance: one-way, 2nd-class fares cost around 64/120/224/424Kč for 50/100/200/400km. For travel within the Czech Republic only, the Czech Flexipass is available (from US$78 to US$138 for three to eight days travel in a 15-day period). The sales clerks at ticket counters rarely speak English, so write down your destination with the date and time you wish to travel.

Train categories include the following:

**EC** (EuroCity) Fast, comfortable international trains, stopping at main stations only, with 1st- and 2nd-class coaches; supplementary charge of 60Kč, reservations recommended.

**Ex** (express) As for IC (below), but no supplementary charge.

**IC** (InterCity) Long-distance and international trains with 1st- and 2nd-class coaches; supplement of 40Kč, reservations recommended.

**Os** (osobní) Slow trains using older rolling stock that stop in every one-horse town; 2nd-class only.

**R** (rychlík) The main domestic network of fast trains with 1st- and 2nd-class coaches and sleeper services; no supplement except for sleepers; express and rychlík trains are usually marked in red on timetables.

**Sp** (spěšný) Slower and cheaper than rychlík trains; 2nd class only.

If you need to purchase a ticket or pay a supplement on the train, advise the conductor *before* they ask for your ticket or you'll have to pay a fine. Some Czech train conductors may try to intimidate foreigners by pretending there's something wrong with their ticket. Don't pay any 'fine', 'supplement' or 'reservation fee' unless you first get a *doklad* (written receipt).

# Estonia

The secret's out of the Baltic bag: Estonia is one of Europe's coolest destinations (in more respects than one). Since its become a full-fledged member of the EU, ever more tourists have ventured this far northeast…and liked what they saw. They return with images of endless coastline, tales of technology overload and strange ramblings about cheap beer and blood sausages.

The last 100 years has been full of twists and turns for the small country: it went from being a province of the Russian empire to an independent country, then a republic of the Soviet Union, an independent nation once again and now an EU member. Anxious to accent what distinguishes it from the rest of Europe, Estonia's strutting its stuff and waiting to be admired.

Apart from the obvious charms of the capital Tallinn and its enchanting Unesco-protected Old Town, the country boasts a one-two combination of low population and stretches of fabulous nature. That means that despite Estonia's miniature size, you can enjoy its unspoilt seaside or be alone on an island, all while enjoying the comforts of a thoroughly modern e-savvy country.

In Tallinn, brush up on your medieval history while exploring the city's café and bar culture. In Tartu, have fun finding out what 'Tartu spirit' means. In Pärnu, tend to your sunburn all night in beachside discos. On the island of Saaremaa, visit vestiges of WWII and an intact castle. Add a few drops of a strange brew called Vana Tallinn to accompany you on all this, and you're set to experience the new, revamped Estonia – version 5.0 and counting.

**ESTONIA**

## FAST FACTS

- **Area** 45,226 sq km
- **Capital** Tallinn
- **Currency** kroon (EEK); €1 = 15.7EEK; US$1 = 12.3EEK; UK£1 = 23EEK; A$1 = 9.3EEK; ¥100 = 10.5EEK; NZ$1 = 7.9EEK
- **Famous for** Eurovision, Skype & Kazaa, saunas
- **Official Language** Estonian
- **Phrases** *aitäh* (thanks); *Tere!* (Hi!); *Mis on su nimi?* (What's your name?); *Kui palju see maksab?* (How much does this cost?)
- **Population** 1.32 million
- **Telephone Codes** country code ☎ 372; international access code ☎ 00
- **Visa** No visa required for citizens of the EU, USA, Canada and Australia for stays of up to 90 days

## HIGHLIGHTS

- Find medieval bliss hanging out on Tallinn's **Raekoja plats** (p323) and exploring nooks and crannies in the historic **Old Town** (p323).
- Put on your nature lover's cap and head to the **Lahemaa National Park** (p331), where you can scout for beavers, go canoeing or count boulders.
- Head out to lovely **Saaremaa** (p343) to check out a **meteorite crater** (p343) with a bottle of local brew in hand.
- Try a floating sauna, sweating it up atop a raft travelling through bog country in **Soomaa National Park** (p341) for an experience you'll be recounting for years.

## ITINERARIES

- **Five days** Hit Tallinn at a weekend, get your sightseeing, partying and café-bar culture fill, then head out to Lahemaa National Park or west to the islands of Saaremaa and/or Hiiumaa and enjoy nature on an organised tour or on your own. A trip to Pärnu or Tartu will complete the picture.
- **Two weeks** There will be time to explore Tallinn more deeply and take a trip to an island off shore. Saaremaa should be on your agenda, as well as Tartu, from where you can head deep into southern and southeastern Estonia, taking in Suur Munamägi and Setumaa. Or you can opt for fun in the sun in Pärnu, with a venture out to the remote island of Kihnu from there.

## CLIMATE & WHEN TO GO

Between May and September is the best time of the year to travel to Estonia as there's better weather and longer days. 'White nights', when the skies darken slightly for only a few hours each night, peak in late June but the sun rarely sets from mid-May to mid-August. June can still be nippy; the warmest temperatures come in July to August (see Climate Charts p911). Winter is temperate, dark and damp but has a special magic. Slushy, drizzly March is the only really depressing month.

## HISTORY

It's commonly held that in the mid-3rd millennium BC Finno-Ugric tribes came either from the east or south to the territory of modern-day Estonia and parts of Latvia, and mixed with the tribes who had been present from the 8th millennium BC. They were little influenced

---

**HOW MUCH?**

- Espresso in café 15-18EEK
- Bottle of Vana Tallinn 75-85EEK
- Ten-minute taxi ride 75EEK
- Traditional knitted sweater 300-400EEK
- Parking violation 480EEK

**LONELY PLANET INDEX**

- Litre of unleaded petrol (95) 14EEK
- Litre of bottled water 12EEK
- Half-litre of beer 20EEK
- Souvenir T-shirt 225EEK
- Street snack (roasted nuts) 25EEK

---

from outside until German traders and missionaries, followed by knights, were unleashed by Pope Celestinus III's 1193 crusade against the 'northern heathens'. In 1202 the Bishop of Riga established the Knights of the Sword to convert the region by conquest; southern Estonia was soon subjugated, the north fell to Denmark.

After a crushing battle with Alexander Nevsky in 1242 on the border of present-day Estonia and Russia, the Knights of the Sword were subordinated to a second band of German crusaders, the Teutonic Order, which by 1290 ruled the eastern Baltic area as far north as southern Estonia, and most of the Estonian islands. Denmark sold northern Estonia to the Knights in 1346, placing Estonians under servitude to a German nobility that lasted till the early 20th century. Throughout later Swedish and Russian rule, German nobles and land barons maintained great economic and political power. The Hanseatic League (a mercantile league of medieval German towns bound together by trade) encompassed many towns on the routes between Russia and the west and prospered under the Germans, although many Estonians in rural areas were forced into serfdom.

By 1620 Estonia had fallen under Swedish control. The Swedes consolidated Estonian Protestantism and aimed to introduce universal education, however frequent wars were devastating. After the Great Northern War (1700–21), Estonia became part of the Russian Empire. Repressive government from Moscow and economic control by German powers slowly

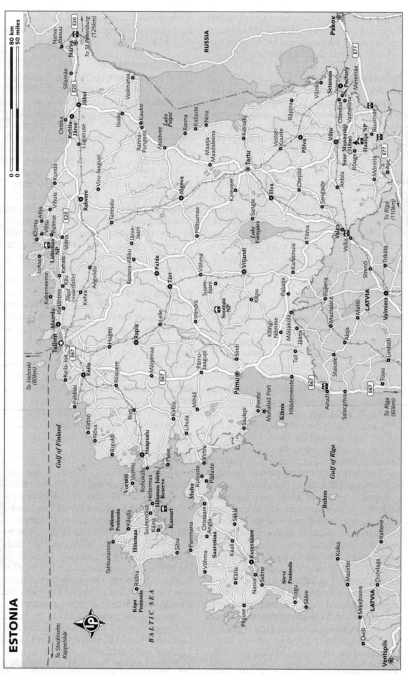

# ESTONIA

**ESTONIA**

forged a national self-awareness among native Estonians. Serfs were freed in the 19th century and improved education and land-ownership rights promoted culture and welfare.

## Independence

The Soviets abandoned the Baltic countries to Germany at the end of WWI with the Treaty of Brest–Litovsk in March 1918. Estonian nationalists had originally declared independence on 24 February. The resulting War of Independence led to the Tartu Peace Treaty on 2 February 1920, in which Russia renounced territorial claims to Estonia, supposedly forever.

Damaged by the war and hampered by a world slump and trade disruptions with the USSR, independent Estonia suffered economically even as it bloomed culturally. Prime Minister Konstantin Päts declared himself President in 1934 and ruled Estonia as a relatively benevolent dictator who also quietly safeguarded the USSR's interests.

## Soviet Rule & WWII

The Molotov-Ribbentrop Pact of 23 August 1939, a nonagression pact between the USSR and Nazi Germany, secretly divided Eastern Europe into Soviet and German spheres of influence. Estonia fell into the Soviet sphere and by August 1940 was under occupation. Estonia was 'accepted' into the USSR after fabricated elections and, within a year, over 10,000 people in Estonia were killed or deported. When Hitler invaded the USSR in 1941, many saw the Germans as liberators, but during their occupation about 5500 people died in concentration camps. Some 40,000 Estonians joined the German army to prevent the Red Army from reconquering Estonia; nearly twice that number fled abroad.

Between 1945 and 1949, with Stalinism back on course, agriculture was collectivised and industry nationalised, and 60,000 more Estonians were killed or deported. An armed resistance lead by the now-legendary *metsavennad* (forest brothers) fought Soviet rule until 1956. With postwar industrialisation, Estonia received an influx of migrant workers from Russia, Ukraine and Belarus, all looking for improved living conditions but with little interest in local language and customs. Resentment among Estonians grew as some of these immigrants received prized new housing and top job allocations. Within the USSR, Estonia had the reputation of being the most

modern and European of all the republics, mainly due to its proximity to Finland, and enjoyed a relatively high standard of living.

## New Independence

On 23 August 1989, on the 50th anniversary of the Molotov-Ribbentrop Pact, an estimated two million people formed a human chain across Estonia, Latvia and Lithuania, calling for secession from the USSR. Independence came suddenly, however, in the aftermath of the Moscow putsch against Gorbachev. Estonia's declaration of complete independence on 20 August 1991 was immediately recognised by the West and by the USSR on 6 September.

In October 1992 Estonia held its first democratic elections, which brought to the presidency the much-loved Lennart Meri, who oversaw the removal of the last Russian troops in 1994. Throughout the 1990s, the government focused on launching radical reform policies and joining the EU and NATO.

The decade since independence, with its sweeping transformations on all levels of society, saw frequent changes of government and no shortage of scandal and corruption charges; this even as the country came to be seen as *the* post-Soviet economic miracle. Today former secretary of the Central Committee of the Communist Party, Arnold Rüütel, is president and Andrus Ansip prime minister. In 2004, Estonia officially entered both NATO and the EU. While there are a large number of Eurosceptics, the majority of Estonians are happy to return to the European fold. Estonia plans to adopt the euro as its currency in 2008.

## PEOPLE

Estonia's population is 68% Estonian, 26% Russian, 2% Ukrainian, 1% Belarusian and 1% Finnish. In 1934 over 90% of the population was native Estonian. Ethnic Russians are concentrated in Tallinn and in the industrial northeast, forming 40% and up to 96% of the respective populations. While much was made of tension between Estonians and Russians in the 1990s, the two communities live together in relative harmony. The youngest generations now mix freely, but in general Estonians and Russians have little to do with each other.

Estonians are closely related to the Finns, and more distantly to the Sámi (indigenous Laplanders) and Hungarians, but not to the Latvians and Lithuanians, who are of Indo-European heritage. Estonians are originally a

### CHARITY

Estonia's **Lastekaitse Liit** ( ☎ 631 1128, www .lastekaitseliit.ee in Estonian, liit@lastekaitseliit.ee) has been involved in dozens of projects since 1988 to promote the interests of and defend the rights of children and teenagers. They hold conferences, provide self-awareness education, have an HIV-prevention campaign and directly aid many underpriviledged children – plus they give them a good time with camps and activities. If you're looking and able to make a donation, this is a good place to channel some funds!

rural people, historically cautious of outsiders and stereotypically most comfortable when left alone. Women are less shy and more approachable than men, though both exude a natural reticence and cool-headed distance in social situations. In general, the younger the Estonian, the more relaxed, open and friendly they'll be. Travellers will find it relatively easy to strike up a conversation and make friends.

## RELIGION

From 1987 to 1990 there was a surge of interest in religion as the state Lutheran Church allied itself to the independence cause. However, that enthusiasm has now waned and many have gone back to their secular ways. There's little sense of Estonia as a religious society. While numerous sects and religious organisations have set up shop in Estonia, these have largely made inroads with Russian-speakers. There are several thousand Muslims in Estonia and some 600 registered Buddhists and 260 Jews.

## ARTS

Most travellers are likely to notice paintings and ceramics of bright pastel colours and fanciful animal compositions as emblematic of contemporary Estonian art, especially works by the one-man industry Navitrolla, whose playful world vision adorns postcards, coffee mugs, posters and café walls. The arts and crafts world in Estonia is much wider than that, however, even though some disciplines have reached a level of excellence (jewellery and ceramics, for example) at the expense of others (art photography is noticeably undeveloped).

### Music

Estonia has a strong and internationally well-respected classical music tradition, most notably its choirs. The Estonian Boys Choir has been acclaimed the world over. Hortus Musicus is Estonia's best-known ensemble, performing Middle Ages and Renaissance music. Composer Arvo Pärt is among the world's most renowned living composers for his haunting sonic blend of tension and beauty, with outwardly simple but highly complex musical structures. The three main Estonian composers of the 20th century are Rudolf Tobias, Mart Saar and Eduard Tubin. Veljo Tormis writes striking music based on old runic chants.

Hard rock thrives in Estonia with groups like Vennaskond, Tuberkuloited and the U2-style Mr Lawrence. The more approachable Ultima Thule and Genialistid are two of the

### LAND OF DREAMS

Estonia is a land of young talent and creative, dynamic entrepreneurs who have already changed the world, or are waiting to do so. Usually, they're well under 25. Two of the biggest success stories are that of Skype and Kazaa, two of the planet's most downloaded programs in history (over 450 million and counting). Both were created by Estonians. The story doesn't end there.

We asked one of these geniuses just why Estonia is so conducive to spawning creative talent and provides the opportunity to realise dream projects. Sten Saar and his company Realister (www .realister.ee) hit upon a simple idea: he developed a new kind of student academic notebook whose look and practicality filled a hole in the marketplace. His first printing was of 1000; 18 months later, he'd received an order for 90,000. Now he's expanding into other countries – when he's not busy creating a program for state TV or participating in swimming competitions.

'Estonia is a tremendously developing country – our economic growth is more than three times bigger than the EU average. Estonia's the best place for entrepreneurs because of its location (between the EU and Russia), very good economic policy (it's easy to establish a company, there are great opportunities for investments) and educated labour force. This business-friendly environment allows me to unleash the entrepreneurial tiger in me...'

country's longest-running and most beloved bands. Jäääär are also at the top, with their album *Tartu-Väike Puust Linn* (Tartu – Small Wooden Town) ranking among the best Estonian albums. Excellent folk bands include Untsakond and Väikeste Lõõtspillide Ühing.

The pop and dance-music scene is strong, exemplified by Estonia's performances in that revered indicator of true art, Eurovision (they hosted the contest in 2002). The tough-girl band Vanilla Ninja has become a hot ticket throughout Europe. Maarja-Liis and Tanel Padar are popular pop singers, while Hedvig Hanson blends jazz and rock with surprising results. Exciting names in electronica are the mesmerizingly talented Paf and house kings Rulers of the Deep.

See the excellent www.estmusic.com for detailed listings and streaming samples of Estonian musicians of all genres.

## Literature

Estonian literature began with the poems and diaries of Kristjan Jaak Peterson, who died when he was but 21 years old in the early 19th century. His lines 'Can the language of this land/carried by the song of the wind/not rise up to heaven/and search for its place in eternity?' are engraved in stone in Tartu and his birthday is celebrated as Mother Tongue Day (14 March).

Until the mid-19th century, Estonian culture was preserved only by way of an oral folk tradition among the peasants. Many of these stories were collected around 1861 to form the national epic *Kalevipoeg* (The Son of Kalev), by Friedrich Reinhold Kreutzwald, inspired by Finland's *Kalevala*. The *Kalevipoeg* relates the adventures of the mythical hero, and ends in his death, his land's conquest by foreigners and a promise to restore freedom. The epic played a major role in fostering the national awakening of the 19th century.

Lydia Koidula (1843–86), the face of the 100EEK note, was the poet of Estonia's national awakening and first lady of literature.

Anton Hansen Tammsaare is considered the greatest Estonian novelist for his *Tõde ja Õigus* (Truth and Justice), written between 1926 and 1933. Eduard Vilde (1865–1933) was a controversial turn-of-the-century novelist and playwright who wrote with sarcasm and irony about parochial mindsets.

Jaan Kross (b 1920) is the best-known Estonian author abroad, and several of his most renowned books, including *The Czar's Madman* and *The Conspiracy and Other Stories*, have been translated into English. Tõnu Õnnepalu and Mati Unt are two main figures in modern Estonian literature.

## Cinema

The first 'moving pictures' were screened in Tallinn in 1896, and the first theatre opened in 1908. The nation's most beloved film is Arvo Kruusement's *Kevade* (Spring; 1969), an adaptation of Oskar Luts' country saga. Grigori Kromanov's *Viimne reliikvia* (The Last Relic; 1969), was a brave, unabashedly anti-Soviet film which has been screened in some 60 countries.

More recently Sulev Keedus' lyrical *Georgica* (1998), about childhood, war, and life on the western islands, and Jaak Kilmi's *Sigade Revolutsioon* (Pigs' Revolution; 2004), about an anti-Soviet uprising at a teenager's summer camp, have made the rounds at international film festivals. René Vilbre, with his *Mat the Cat* (2005), as well as Ivar Heinmaa, with his *Wounds of Afghanistan* (2005), are among the most creative directors in Estonia today.

## Theatre

It is telling of the role theatre has played in Estonia's cultural life that many of the country's theatre houses were built solely from donations collected from private citizens. The Estonia Theatre and the Estonia Drama Theatre in Tallinn, the Vanemuine Theatre in Tartu and others throughout the country were all built on proceeds collected door to door.

Modern theatre is considered to have begun in 1870 in Tartu, where Lydia Koidula's *The Cousin from Saaremaa* became the first Estonian play performed in public.

Experimental theatre and multimedia performances are still in their nascent stages. Fine 5 Dance Theatre (www.fine5.ee) and Nordstar Dance Theatre are two of the finest modern dance and performance troupes in the country, and Vanemuine's Ruslan Stepanov one of the scene's most creative performers and directors.

## SPORT

With over 3700km of coastline, all forms of water sports are popular in Estonia come the summer sun. As Estonia is a flat country, cross-country skiing and bicycling are hugely popular sports. Major bike marathons are held in and around Tartu (p335). Otepää (p336) is

---

### WIFE-CARRYING WORLD CHAMPS

Forget decathlons and cross-country skiing: Estonian wife carriers rule! Since the traditional Finnish sport of wife carrying was revived in 1992 in the northern Finnish village of Sonkajärvi, Estonians have upstaged their Scandinavian cousins by winning several world championships and capturing the world record (yes, there is such a thing).

Men must carry their wives (or a suitable substitute) any way they wish through a 253m-long difficult obstacle course – through water, over barriers. Even Dennis Rodman, visiting the 2005 championships, only managed to do the final 100m of the race, noting that it was too gruelling to complete without practise.

While there are few Estonia-based wife carrying competitions, you may be lucky enough to spot a few couples practising on beaches or stretches of forests during your stay!

---

the country's cross-country (and what passes as downhill) skiing capital. Basketball is the unofficial national sport, and courts small and large are found all over Estonia.

A well-known name in the sports world is Erki Nool, the decathlon gold-medal winner at the 2000 Olympics. Kristina Smigun was the darling of the 2006 Winter Olympics, picking up two gold medals for cross-country skiing.

## ENVIRONMENT

With an area of 45,226 sq km, Estonia is only slightly bigger than Denmark. It is mainly low lying, with extensive bogs and marshes; Suur Munamägi (318m; p337) in the southeast near Võru is the highest point. In Southern Estonia, the regions of Võrumaa and Setumaa (p337) are characterised by attractively rolling, gentle hills. Nearly 50% of the land is forested and 22% is wetlands, with peat bogs 7m deep in places. The 3794km-long coastline is heavily indented. More than 1500 islands make up nearly 10% of Estonian territory and there are over 1400 lakes, the largest of which is Lake Peipsi (3555 sq km), the fourth-largest in Europe.

The Baltic Glint is Estonia's most prominent geological feature. Made up of 60-million-year-old limestone banks that extend 1200km from Sweden to Lake Ladoga in Russia, they form impressive cliffs along Estonia's northern coast, especially in the east – at Ontika the cliffs stand 50m above the coast.

Since independence there have been major 'clean-up' attempts to counter the effects of Soviet-era industrialisation. Toxic emissions in the industrialised northeast of Estonia have been reduced sharply and new environmental-impact legislation aims to minimise the effects of future development. However, heavy oil-shale burning in that area keeps air pollution levels there high.

## National Parks

Most of the population of Estonia's rare or protected species can be found in one of the several national parks, nature reserves and parks. There are beavers, otters, flying squirrels, lynx, wolves and brown bears in these areas. White and black storks are common in southern Estonia.

Estonia's western islands and some areas in national parks boast some of the most unspoilt landscapes in Europe, and air pollution, even in the cities, remains very low by European standards. About 11% of Estonia's lands are protected to some degree as national parks, or as nature, landscape and biosphere reserves. Thus far, the only Unesco World Heritage site is Tallinn's Old Town (p323). Some of the most popular parks are Lahemaa (p331), Soomaa (p341) and the Haanja Nature Park (p337).

## FOOD & DRINK

The conventional excuse for the heaviness of the local cuisine is the northern climate…but that's used as an excuse for many local habits and only goes so far in explaining the proclivity towards fatty and carbohydrate-heavy meals. The Estonian diet relies on *sealiha* (pork), other red meat, *kana* (chicken), *vurst* (sausage), *kapsa* (cabbage) and *kartul* (potato). Sour cream is served with everything but coffee, it seems. *Kala* (fish) appears most often as a smoked or salted starter, most likely *forell* (trout) or *lõhe* (salmon). *Sült* (jellied meat) is likely to be served as a delicacy as well. At Christmas time *verivorst* (blood sausage) is made from fresh blood and wrapped in pig intestine (joy to the world indeed!). Those really in need of a culinary transfusion will find blood sausages, blood bread and blood dumplings available in most traditional Estonian restaurants year-round.

Though the idea that a meal can actually be spicy or vegetarian has taken root, you'll need to hit one of Tallinn's or Tartu's ethnic restaurants for exotic spices or mains that don't include meat. Veganism is completely unknown, except to the local Hare Krishnas. Delicious and inexpensive freshly baked cakes, breads and pastries are available everywhere.

*Restoran* (restaurants) and *kohvik* (cafés) are plentiful and pubs also serve meals. Most Estonians have their main meal at lunch time, and accordingly most establishments have excellent-value set lunches.

*Õlu* (beer) is the favourite alcoholic drink in Estonia and the local product is very much in evidence. The best brands are Saku and A Le Coq, which come in a range of brews. *Viin* (vodka) and *konjak* (brandy) are also popular drinks. Vana Tallinn, a seductively pleasant, sweet and strong (40% to 50% alcohol) liqueur of unknown extraction, is an integral part of any Estonian gift pack. Eesti Kali is the favourite (Estonian) brand of *kvass*, originally made from fermented bread but containing no alcohol.

# TALLINN

**pop 400,000**

Picture a heady mix of medieval church spires, glass-and-chrome skyscrapers, imported DJs spinning tunes in underground clubs, cosy wine cellars inside 15th-century basements, lazy afternoons soaking up sun and beer suds on Raekoja plats, plus bike paths to beaches and forests and yacht rides in a sprawling bay – with a few Soviet monuments thrown in for added spice. That's today's Tallinn, remixing Medieval and cutting-edge and coming up with a new vibe of its own.

The jewel in Tallinn's crown remains the two-tiered Old Town, a 14th- and 15th-century jumble of turrets, spires and winding streets. Most tourists see nothing other than this fabulous, cobble-stoned labyrinth of intertwining streets and picturesque courtyards. Tallinn's relentlessly modern dimension – its new chrome and glass mini-skyscrapers, the wi-fi that bathes much of the city, the sumptuous, hip clubs – are pleasant surprises and harmonious counterbalances to the city's Old World charms.

Whatever your pleasure – fantasising about yesteryear or indulging in the thoroughly modern – Tallinn's seductively laid-back groove is easy to fall for.

## HISTORY

In 1219 the Danes set up a castle and installed a bishop on Toompea ('Tallinn' comes from the Danish *taani linnus*, which means 'Danish castle'). German traders arrived and Tallinn joined the Hanseatic League in 1285, becoming a vital link between east and west. By the mid-14th century, after the Danes had sold northern Estonia to the German knights, Tallinn was a major Hanseatic town. The merchants and artisans in the lower town built a fortified wall to separate themselves from the bishop and knights on Toompea.

Prosperity faded in the 16th century as Swedes, Russians, Poles and Lithuanians all fought over the Baltic region. The city grew in the 19th century and by WWI had a population of 150,000. In 1944 Soviet bombing destroyed several central sectors including a small section on the Old Town's fringes. After WWII, industry developed and Tallinn expanded quickly, with much of its population growth due to immigration from Russia. Politically and economically, Tallinn is the driving force of modern Estonia.

## ORIENTATION

Tallinn fronts a bay on the Gulf of Finland and is defined by Toompea (*tom*-pe-ah), the hill over which it has tumbled since the Middle Ages. Toompea, the upper Old Town, has traditionally been the centre of Tallinn and the medieval seat of power. The lower Old Town spreads around the eastern foot of Toompea, still surrounded by much of its 2.5km defensive wall. Its centre is Raekoja plats (Town Hall Square).

Around the Old Town is a belt of green parks which follows the line of the city's original moat defences, as well as the modern city centre.

## INFORMATION
### Bookshops

**Apollo** ( ☎ 654 8485; Viru tänav 23) Lots of Lonely Planet and travel titles.

**Rahva Raamat** Viru Keskus ( ☎ 644 9444; Viru Väljak 4/6); Old Town ( ☎ 644 3682; Pärnu mnt 10) These shops have the city's largest selection, with good English, art and travel books.

### Internet Access

There are some 300 wireless internet (wi-fi) areas throughout the capital (see www.wifi .ee for a detailed list), so with your laptop in hand, it's never a problem to surf for free.

Otherwise, there are terminals for hire on the 2nd floor of Stockmann department store, as well as pricey ones on the 2nd floor of the Central Post Office.

**Jumping Jacks** (Suur Karja tänav 13; ☎ 11am-9pm; per hr 30EEK) Basement-level, slightly dingy place for internet connection.

**Metro** ( ☎ 610 1515; Viru Väljak 4/6; ☎ 7am-11pm Mon-Fri, 10am-11pm Sat & Sun; per hr 35EEK). Downstairs on the bus terminal level of the Viru Keskas shopping centre (p330), you'll find this flashy, techno-style internet café.

## Laundry

**EcoClean** ( ☎ 646 6193; Roosikrantsi tänav 23; most garments 50-90EEK; ☎ 9am-7pm Mon-Fri, 10am-4pm Sat & Sun) Wide range of dry-cleaning services using environmentally friendly substances.

**Sauberland** ( ☎ 661 2075; Maakri tänav 23; self-wash & dry 5kg 75EEK; ☎ 7.30am-8pm Mon-Fri, 8am-6pm Sat) Wash and wait, or pick-up services in ultra clean surroundings.

## Medical Services

**Aia Apteek** ( ☎ 627 3607; Aia tänav 10; ☎ 8.30am-midnight) One of the many well-stocked pharmacies around town.

**East Tallinn Central Hospital** ( ☎ 620 7015; Ravi tänav 18; ☎ 24hr) Full range of services, including a polyclinic and a 24-hour emergency room.

**Südalinna Arstide** ( ☎ 660 4072; Kaupmehe tänav 4; ☎ 9am-6pm Mon-Fri) This private clinic has ear, nose and throat specialists, gynaecologists, psychologists and other general practitioners on staff.

## Money

Currency exchange is available at all transport terminals, exchange bureaus around the city, the post office and inside all banks and major hotels. ATMs are plentiful. There's a Western Union pickup point at the central post office (see Post).

**Äripank** ( ☎ 668 8000; Vana Viru tänav 7) The Business Bank has some of the city's best rates.

**Estravel** ( ☎ 626 6266; www.estravel.ee; Suur-Karja tänav 15; ☎ 9am-6pm Mon-Fri, 10am-3pm Sat) A travel agent and the official agent for Amex.

**Tavid** ( ☎ 627 9900; Aia tänav 5; ☎ 24hr) This exchange bureau is convenient but has so-so rates unless you change large amounts.

## Post

**Central post office** ( ☎ 625 7300; Narva mnt 1; ☎ 7.30am-8pm Mon-Fri, 8am-6pm Sat) Full postal services, including express mail, fax (send to ☎ 661 6054; 12EEK per page) and telegrams.

**DHL** ( ☎ 680 855; Hobujaama 4; ☎ 9am-5pm Mon-Fri) Express courier services.

## Telephone

If you're one of the odd few not glued to a mobile phone, you can buy 30EEK, 50EEK and 100EEK chip cards from newsstands to use for local and international calls at any one of the blue phone boxes scattered around town. Otherwise, post offices and some newspaper kiosks sell mobile phone starter kits with prepaid SIM cards.

## Tourist Information

**1182** ( ☎ 1182; www.1182.ee) This information service costs 7EEK per minute, but their website is just as useful.

**Infotelefon** ( ☎ 626 1111) This provides free, practical information in English 24 hours a day.

**In Your Pocket** (www.inyourpocket.com) The king of the region's listings guide has up-to-date information on everything to do with arriving, staying and having fun in Tallinn and other cities in Estonia. Its booklets are on sale at bookshops.

**Tallinn Tourist Information Centre** ( ☎ 645 7777; www.tourism.tallinn.ee; Niguliste tänav 2; ☎ 9am-7pm Mon-Fri, 10am-5pm Sat & Sun May-Jun, 9am-8pm Mon-Fri, 10am-6pm Sat & Sun Jul-Aug, 9am-6pm Mon-Fri, 10am-5pm Sat & Sun Sep, 9am-5pm Mon-Fri, 10am-3pm Sat Oct-Apr) This centre offers a full range of services, though it helps if you're very clear with what you're looking for. Here you can purchase the Tallinn Card (130EEK to 450EEK), which offers free rides on public transport, admission to museums, free excursions and discounts at restaurants, valid from six to 72 hours.

## Travel Agencies

**Baltic Tours** ( ☎ 630 0430; www.baltictours.ee; Pikk tänav 31)

---

**TALLINN IN TWO DAYS**

Wander thoroughly around the **Old Town**, climbing **Oleviste Church** (p324) for a great view, stopping at several café's and pubs around the **Raekoja plats** (Town Hall Sqaure). On the second day, do what most tourists don't – step out of the Old Town, explore the **Kadriorg** (p325) region with its old homes, sprawling parks and great museums, and head out to **Pirita** (p325) for a few hours on the beach. Hit a **nightclub** (p329) or go **bar-hopping** (p329) before calling it a day.

---

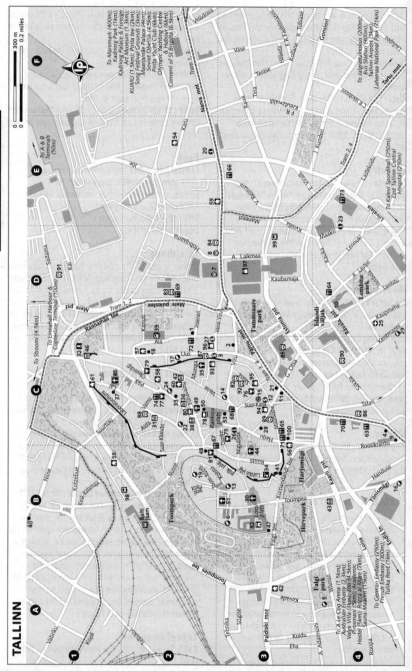

**Estonian Holidays** ( ☎ 627 0520; www.holidays.ee; Rüütli tänav 28/30)

**Union Travel** ( ☎ 627 0627; www.uniontravel.ee; Vana Posti 2) Smaller than most, but friendly, creative and down-to-earth. It can easily arrange visas to Russia and the former USSR.

# SIGHTS
## Old Town
### RAEKOJA PLATS & AROUND

Compact Raekoja plats (Town Hall Square) has been the centre of Tallinn life since markets began here probably in the 11th century. It's dominated by the only surviving Gothic **town hall** ( ☎ 645 7900; adult/student 35/20EEK; ☼ 10am-4pm Mon-Sat Jun-Aug, by appointment Sep-May) in northern Europe (early 14th century, reconstruction 1402–04) and faced by pretty, pastel buildings from the 15th to 17th centuries. Old Thomas, Tallinn's symbol and

guardian, has been keeping watch from his perch on the weathervane atop Town Hall since 1530. You can also climb the building's **tower** (adult/student 25/15EEK; ☼ 11am-6pm Jun-Sep).

The square is Tallinn's pulsing heart: all summer outdoor cafés implore you to sit and people-watch; come Christmas time, a huge pine tree stands in the middle (a tradition some 550 years old). Whether bathed in sunlight or sprinkled with snow, it's always an inviting spot.

The **Raeapteek** (Town Council Pharmacy), on the northern side of Raekoja plats, is another ancient Tallinn institution; there's been a pharmacy or apothecary's shop here since at least 1422, though the present façade is 17th century. Duck through the arch beside it into the charming Saia käik (White Bread Passage), at the far end of which is the lovely 14th-century Gothic **Pühavaimu kirik** (Holy Spirit Church;

☎ 644 1487; ⏰ 10am-3pm). Its colourful clock on the wall outside is the oldest in Tallinn, the lavish carvings inside date from 1684 and the tower bell was cast in 1433.

A medieval merchant's home houses the **Linnamuuseum** (City Museum; ☎ 644 6553; www.linna muuseum.ee; Vene tänav 17; adult/student 35/10EEK; ⏰ 10.30am-6pm Wed-Mon Mar-Oct, to 5pm Wed-Mon Nov-Feb) which traces Tallinn's development from its beginnings through to 1940 with some quirky displays and curious artefacts.

Also on Vene tänav (Estonian for 'Russian', named for the many Russian merchants who lived on the street), in the courtyard at No 18, is the 1844 **Sts Peter & Paul Catholic Church**, whitewashed and looking like it belongs in Spain. A door in the courtyard leads into the **Dominican Monastery** (☎ 644 4606; Vene tänav 16/18; adult/student 45/15EEK; ⏰ 9.30am-6pm mid-May–mid-Sep), founded in 1246 as a base for Scandinavian monks. Today the monastery complex houses Estonia's largest collection of **stone carvings**, which leave an impression on visitors eager to catch a glimpse of medieval-looking life; there are often concerts and medieval-tinged activities and even rituals taking place there.

The majestic 15th-century **Niguliste Church** (☎ 631 4330; Niguliste tänav 3; adult/student 35/20EEK; ⏰ 10am-5pm Wed-Sun), a minute's walk south of Raekoja plats, is now used to stage concerts and serves as a **museum** of medieval church art.

At the foot of the slope below the Niguliste Church is the carefully exposed wreckage of the buildings that stood here before the Soviet bombing of Tallinn on the night of 9 March 1944.

## LOWER TOWN

From Pühavaimu kirik, you can stroll along Pikk tänav, which runs north to the **Great Coast Gate** – the medieval exit to Tallinn's port. Pikk tänav is lined with the 15th-century houses of merchants and gentry as well as buildings of several old Tallinn guilds. In the 1440 building of the **Great Guild**, to which the most important merchants belonged, is the **History Museum** (Ajaloomuuseum; ☎ 641 1630; Pikk tänav 17; adult/student 15/10EEK; ⏰ 11am-6pm Thu-Tue). It features Estonian history up to the 18th century and has ceramics, jewellery and archaeological delights. No 18 is the 1911 **Draakoni art gallery** (☎ 646 4110; ⏰ 10am-6pm Mon-Fri, 10am-5pm Sat & Sun) with its fabulous sculpted façade.

Crane your neck up at Pikk tänav 19 – there's a coy black cat waiting to surprise you. The **Brotherhood of Blackheads** and **St Olaus' Guild** are in adjoining buildings at Pikk tänav 24 and 26. The Blackheads were unmarried, mainly foreign merchants whose patron saint, Mauritius, appears with his head between two lions on the building's façade (dating from 1597).

At the northern end of Pikk tänav stands a chief Tallinn landmark, the gargantuan **Oleviste Church**. Anyone unafraid of a bit of sweat should head up, way up, to the superb **observation deck** (☎ 621 2241; adult/student 20/10EEK; ⏰ 10am-6pm mid-Apr–mid-Oct) halfway up its 124m structure. It offers the city's best views of the Old Town.

First built in the early 13th century, it was once the world's tallest building (it used to tower 159m before several fires and reconstructions brought it down to its present size). The church is dedicated to the 11th-century King Olav II of Norway, but linked in local lore with another Olav (Olaf), the church's architect, who fell to his death from the tower. It's said that a toad and a snake then crawled out of his mouth. The incident is recalled in one of the carvings on the east wall of the 16th-century **Chapel of Our Lady**, which adjoins the church.

Just south of the church is the **former KGB headquarters** (Pikk tänav 59), whose basement windows were sealed to conceal the sounds of interrogations.

The Great Coast Gate is joined to **Paks Margareeta** (Fat Margaret), the rotund 16th-century bastion which protected this entrance to the Old Town. Inside the bastion is the **Maritime Museum** (Meremuuseum; ☎ 641 1408; Pikk tänav 70; adult/student 25/10EEK; ⏰ 10am-6pm Wed-Sun). The exhibits are ho-hum, but there are nice views from the rooftop café.

Just beyond the bastion stands the **broken line monument**, a black, curved slab in memory of victims of the Estonia ferry disaster. In September 1994, 852 people died when the ferry sank en route from Tallinn to Stockholm.

While Pikk was the street of traders, Lai tänav, running roughly parallel, was the street of artisans, whose traditions are recalled in the **Applied Art & Design Museum** (Tarbekunsti ja Desainimuuseum; ☎ 627 4600; Lai tänav 17; adult/student 30/15EEK; ⏰ 11am-6pm Wed-Sun). You'll find an excellent mix of historical and contemporary ceramics, glass, rugs, metal and leatherwork.

Suur-Kloostri tänav leads to the longest-standing stretch of the **Lower Town Wall**, with nine towers along Laboratooriumi tänav.

**ESTONIA**

## TOOMPEA

A regal approach to Toompea is through the red-roofed 1380 **Pikk jalg gate tower** at the western end of Pikk tänav in the lower town, and then uphill along Pikk jalg (Long Leg). The 19th-century Russian Orthodox **Alexander Nevsky Cathedral** (☺ 8am-7pm, also for special religious occasions) greets you at the top. It was built as a part of Alexander III's policy of Russification, and sited strategically across from **Toompea Castle**, Estonia's traditional seat of power. The *riigikogu* (parliament) meets in the pink baroque-style building, an 18th-century addition to the castle. Nothing remains of the original 1219 Danish castle. Still standing are three of the four corner towers of its successor, the Knights of the Sword's Castle. Finest of these towers is the 14th-century **Pikk Hermann** (Tall Hermann) at the southwestern corner, from which the state flag is raised at sunrise and lowered at sunset to the tune of the Estonian anthem. A path leads down from Lossi plats through an opening in the wall to the **Danish King's Courtyard** where, in summer, artists set up their easels.

Nearby **Kiek-in-de-Köök** (☎ 644 6686; Komandanti tee 2; adult/student 25/8EEK; ☺ 10.30am-6pm Tue-Sun), a tall tower built in about 1475, is a museum that holds models of old Tallinn, weapons and a photographic gallery. Its name is Low German for 'Peep into the Kitchen' – from the upper floors of the tower medieval voyeurs could see into Old Town kitchens.

The Lutheran **Toomkirik** (Dome Church; ☎ 644 4140; Toom-Kooli tänav 6; ☺ 9am-4pm Tue-Sun) is Estonia's oldest church. Positioned on the site of a 1219 Danish church, it dates from the 14th century. Inside the impressive, austere and damp church are finely carved tombs and coats of arms. From Toomkirik, follow Kohtu tänav to the city's favourite **lookout** over the Lower Town.

The **Museum of Occupation & Fight for Freedom** (☎ 668 0250; Toompea tänav 8; adult/student 10/5EEK; ☺ 11am-6pm Tue-Sun), just down the hill from Toompea, has a worthwhile display of Estonia's history of occupation, focusing on the most recent Soviet one.

## Kadriorg

To reach the pleasant, wooded **Kadriorg Park** 2km east of the Old Town along Narva maantee, take tram 1 or 3 to the last stop. The park and the 1718–36 Kadriorg Palace were designed for Peter the Great for his wife Catherine I. The **Kadriorg Palace** (☎ 606 6400; Weizenbergi tänav 37; adult/student 45/25EEK; ☺ 10am-5pm Tue-Wed & Fri-Sun, 10am-9pm Thu May-Sep, 10am-5pm Wed-Sun Oct-Apr) and **Foreign Art Museum** (adult/student 15/5EEK; ☺ 10am-5pm Wed-Sun), housed in the same magnificent building, make for a dreamy hour or so – the 17th- and 18th-century foreign art is mainly unabashedly romantic, and the palace unashamedly splendid.

Nearby is the brand new **KUMU** (☎ 602 6000; Weizenbergi tänav 34; adult/student 75/40EEK; ☺ 10am-5pm Tue-Wed & Fri-Sun, 10am-9pm Thu May-Sep, 10am-5pm Wed-Sun Oct-Apr), the country's largest museum by far. A spectacular, massive structure of limestone and green glass, it contains a large amount of Estonian art as well as constantly changing contemporary exhibits.

## Towards Pirita

Jutting north of Kadriorg alongside the sea coast is **Pirita tee**, Tallinn's greatest promenade. Summer sunsets around midnight are particularly romantic from here, and it's the city's nicest biking and rollerblading area. North of Kadriorg you come to the **Lauluväljak**, the Song Festival grounds, an impressive amphitheatre which hosts song festivals and big-name concerts. Under two kilometres north of Lauluväljak, **Maarjamäe Palace** (☎ 601 4535; Pirita tee 56; adult/student 10/8EEK; ☺ 11am-6pm Wed-Sun Mar-Oct, 10am-5pm Wed-Sun Nov-Feb) contains the part of the Estonian History Museum covering the mid-19th century onwards.

Heading further north, you pass the foreboding **Soviet obelisk** locally dubbed 'the Impotent's Dream'. It's the focal point of a 1960 Soviet war memorial that's now more crumbling than inspiring. A small German cemetery is behind it. **Pirita Yacht Club**, some 2km beyond Maarjamäe Palace, and the **Olympic Yachting Centre** were venues for the 1980 Olympic sailing events. International regattas are still held here, and there is the small **Pirita harbour**.

North of the bridge are a beach backed by pine woods and the 15th-century Swedish **Convent of St Brigitta** (☎ 605 5044; Merivälja tee 18; adult/student 20/10EEK; ☺ 9am-7pm Jun-Aug, 10am-6pm Sep, Apr & May, noon-4pm Oct-Mar), ruined by war in 1577. This is an essential Tallinn visit; the labyrinthine ruins are a natural treat for kids too. The long stretch of clean beaches on the other side of Pirita tee is *the* place to shed your clothes in Tallinn summertime. Buses 1, 8 and 34 run between the city centre and Pirita.

## Zoo & Rocca al Mare

About 4.5km southwest from the Old Town, the **Tallinn Zoo** ( ☎ 694 3300; Paldiski mnt 145; adult/child 50/25EEK; ☼ 9am-7pm May-Aug, 9am-5pm Mar-Apr & Sep-Oct, 9am-3pm Nov-Feb) boasts one of the world's largest collections of mountain goats and sheep and 334 different species of animals, birds, reptiles and fish. Opposite the zoo is **Tivoli** ( ☼ 656 0110; Paldiski mnt 100; free admission, pay per ride; ☼ 11am-8pm) a small amusement park for kids.

A kilometre beyond the zoo, Rannamõisa tee turns right towards Rocca al Mare and leads to the **Open Air Museum** ( ☎ 654 9117; Vabaõhumuuseumi tee 12; adult/child 50/30EEK; ☼ 10am-5pm Oct-Apr, buildings 10am-6pm May-Sep, grounds 10am-8pm May-Sep). Most of Estonia's oldest wooden structures (mainly farmhouses as well as a 1699 chapel and a windmill) are preserved here. On Sunday mornings there are folk song-and-dance shows. There's also a **tavern** (mains from 75EEK; ☼ 10am-6pm) serving traditional Estonian meals. Kids will love the entire place – and not only the pony rides. Buses 21 or 21B from the train station stop here, or you can take trolleybuses 6 or 7 then walk the remaining 1.5km along Rocca al Mare tee.

## ACTIVITIES

Waterparks are all the rage in Estonia; the biggest in Tallinn is the **Kalev Spa** ( ☎ 649 3300; www.kalevspa.ee; Aia tänav 18; adult/student from 80/60EEK; ☼ 6.45am-10.30pm Mon-Fri, 8am-10.30pm Sat-Sun). Soon to be dwarfed by competitors, this super-modern water emporium boasts an Olympic-sized pool, several Jacuzzis and slides and other ways to get your skin wrinkled.

Saunas are an Estonian institution and come close to being a religious experience. If you're looking to convert, the best public sauna is **Kalma Saun** ( ☎ 627 1811; Vana-Kalamaja tänav 9A, Tallinn; ☼ 10am-11pm), but you should try **Sauna Maailm** ( ☎ 609 9888; www.saunamaailm.ee; from 400EEK per hr) a makeshift village with four different kinds of saunas, 16km from central Tallinn on the road to Keila & Paldiski.

The most popular beaches are at Pirita and Stroomi. You can rent rowing boats and pedal boats at **Pirita Rowboat Rental** ( ☎ 621 2105; Kloostri tee 6; per hr from 35EEK; ☼ 10am-10pm May-Sep) beside the bridge over the river. For an unforgettable yacht trip out into Tallinn Bay, contact **Emerald** ( ☎ 504 3031; www.spinnaker.ee). It offers three- and four-hour cruises from €120 for 12 persons.

The folks at both Matkad.ee and Reimann Retked (see p344) can organise something more energetic for adventure-seekers.

## FESTIVALS & EVENTS

**Jazzkaar** (www.jazzkaar.ee; mid-Apr) One of Tallinn's hot-ticket events, this brings together jazz greats from around the world in a series of concerts.

**Old Town Days** (www.vanalinnapaevad.ee; early Jun) Usually lasting four days, this sees the Old Town come alive with market stalls, concerts, dancing and medieval-themed merry-making.

**Beer Summer** (www.ollesummer.ee; early Jul) One of the most popular festivals of the year, this beer-guzzling, rock

---

### ISLAND ESCAPE

Who says you can't relive your favourite scenes from *The Blue Lagoon* in Nordic Estonia? Sure, it's no Bora Bora, but the country offers its share of lovely shoreline and remote island landscapes to play around in.

Tiny **Aegna**, just 3 sq km, has been populated for centuries by local fishermen and, from 1689, postal workers who operated mail boats from there to Sweden via Finland. During Soviet times it was an off-limits military base. There are traces of its military past, an old church and cemetery, remains of a medieval village and long stretches of almost-always deserted beaches.

**Naissaar**, much larger at 11km by 4km, has a livelier history and more tourism possibilities. It was off-limits in Soviet times, and there's the remnant of an old army village, bunkers and mine factory to explore. There's a church from 1856 and other attractions, but again, stretches of quiet beach are its largest draws. Just up the hill from the dock is the Nature Park Centre where you can get info, coffee and a meal.

For information about excursions and overnight stays on Naissaar, contact Tiit Koit (tiit.koit@lk .ee). Tallinn's tourist information centre can suggest accommodation on both islands. **MS Monika** ( ☎ 56 638 000; www.saartereisid.ee) runs boats from Pirita's harbour to Aegna (30 minutes; adult/ student/bicycle 100EEK; three times daily Tue-Sun) and to Naissaar (one hour; adult/student/bicycle 125/100/100EEK; twice daily Sat-Sun). It's possible to stay overnight on either island, or just spend about five hours wandering or biking and return to Tallinn the same day.

band–listening extravaganza happens under and around big tents near the Lauluväljak (Song Festival) grounds.

**Dance Festival** (www.saal.ee; Aug) International modern dance troupes usually stage exciting performances.

## SLEEPING

It's not easy to be disappointed in Tallinn's accommodation scene. With a wide array of tasteful, clean, often unique and sumptuous hotels and guesthouses to choose from, your lodging is likely to be a highlight of your visit. Each year the selection gets larger; by 2008, bed spaces in Tallinn will have increased 50% over the 2005 figure, and many of these will be in the upper-budget classes. See www.visit estonia.ee for accommodation of all sorts.

### Apartment Rental

There are dozens of apartments to rent in the capital – a great alternative for those who prefer privacy and self-sufficiency. A good bet is Old House Guesthouse (see right), which has stunning apartments throughout the Old Town.

**Ites Apartments** ( ☎ 631 0637; www.ites.ee; Harju tänav 6) This effective bunch offers several too-good-to-be-true apartments in the Old Town for 1100EEK to 2100EEK per day, with discounts for stays of more than one night.

### Budget

**Hostel Alur** ( ☎ 631 1531; www.alurhostel.com; Rannamäe tee 3; dm/s/tr 235/500/845EEK, d 720-875EEK; P ) Not the liveliest of hostels, but it's clean, friendly, (a bit too) quiet and just a stone's throw from the train station and Old Town. Prices are around 15% cheaper from September to April and there's a 10% discount for ISIC and HI card-holders year-round.

**Old House** ( ☎ 641 1464; www.oldhouse.ee; Uus tänav 26; dm 290EEK, 1-/2-/3-/5-/6-person r 550/650/975/1450/17 40EEK) You won't get a better location than at this refurbished hostel in the Old Town. Sure, the walls are paper-thin, but it's cosy and the breakfast is hearty. There's a 10% discount with ISIC.

**Academic Hostel** ( ☎ 620 2275; www.academichostel .com; Akadeemia tee 11; d 495EEK) Situated on the edge of the Tallinn Technical University campus grounds, this is a bright, happy, freshly done-up hostel with a lively atmosphere. With 108 rooms spread out along five colour-coded floors, it feels more like a modern budget hotel than hostel with a young, vivacious, international clientele. Trolleybus 3 will drop you off at the nearby Keemia stop.

**Old House Guesthouse** ( ☎ 641 1464; www.oldhouse .ee; Uus tänav 22; s/d/tr 450/650/975EEK) Nearly adjacent to the Old House and run by the same people, the guesthouse has the same pros and cons, though the rooms here are more spacious and private. Their sumptuous apartments scattered throughout the Old Town are excellent value (1300EEK to 2500EEK) and can fit four persons.

### Midrange

**Dorell** ( ☎ 626 1200; www.dorell.ee; Karu tänav 39; s 550-700EEK, d 600-800EEK; P ) One of the best deals in this category if being in the centre is important. What it lacks in aesthetic splendour it makes up for with convenience.

**Reval Hotel Central** ( ☎ 633 9800; Narva mnt 7C; s/d/ste from 900/1100/1860EEK; P X X ) One of the best options smack in the centre. Large but friendly, staffed with down-to-earth and helpful people, it offers all the services of a big hotel. Rooms, save for the gorgeous superior doubles and suites, are less than breathtaking, but there are so many other plusses, it hardly matters.

**Unique Stay** ( ☎ 660 0700; www.uniquestay.com; Paldiski mnt 1 & 3; s 1400EEK, d 1500-2120EEK apt 2100-2325EEK; X X ) Here local traditions and folk elements merge with Japanese sparsity, quirky eccentricity and modern furnishings to create one of the most interesting places to lay your head in the city. The pricier 'Zen' doubles are worthwhile for the extra harmony. prices drop around 10% from October to April.

### Top End

**Olevi Residents** ( ☎ 627 7650; www.olevi.ee; Olevimägi tänav 4; s/d/ste from 1100/1600/3500EEK; X X ) Each splendid room has its own character in this Old Town oasis; some with antiques, others

ESTONIA

with arched ceilings and bits of the original medieval building showing through. The suites are worth a splurge. The rooms on the top floor have a sea view.

**Three Sisters Hotel** ( ☎ 630 6300; www.threesisters hotel.com; Pikk tänav 71; s/d/ste from 5320/5790/8140EEK; ☒ ☒ ) Sumptuous luxury in a lovingly refurbished medieval building; original design elements have been preserved alongside hi-tech comforts. Cool your wine in a hole in the centuries-old wall, run a bath in an old-fashioned tub and dream away…

**Schlössle Hotel** ( ☎ 699 7700; www.schlossle-hotels .com; Pühavaimu tänav 13-15; s/d/ste from 4800/5500/7900EEK; ☒ ) These breathtaking rooms in a complex of buildings that have witnessed 600 years of Tallinn life are among the most impressive in the country. All needs are catered for under its five stars, and the cellar restaurant is first-rate.

# EATING

Many ethnic restaurants can be found serving anything from Turkish meze to Thai Kai Phad – though even on exotic dishes, be prepared for an Estonian touch (the sudden appearance of sour cream or cucumbers for example)! Very reasonable lunch specials abound in the city (35EEK to 60EEK), so it's economical to fill up during the daytime. Most of the cafés listed under Drinking also serve food.

## Budget

**Kohvik Narva** ( ☎ 660 1786; Narva mnt 10; mains 35-65EEK) One of the only places left in Tallinn where you can step back into the USSR, this is kitsch without being aware of it. The décor is decidedly brown and faded red, the service dismissive and the menu full of Russian staples from the times of yore. Have fun!

**Kompressor** ( ☎ 646 4210; Rataskaevu tänav 3; mains from 40EEK) Eat one of the enormous, stuffed pancakes and you'll be full for the rest of the day. The large hall and casual atmosphere make it a great hang-out too; the big tables make it easy to chat up locals.

**Peetri Pizza** ( ☎ delivery 656 7567; Pärnu mnt 22 & Mere puiestee 6; pizzas 45-75EEK) This chain opened as soon as Estonia broke free from the USSR and still doles out tasty thin-crusted and pan pizzas.

**Texas Honky Tonk** ( ☎ 631 1755; Pikk tänav 43; mains from 50EEK) No one does Americana quite so well in Tallinn. The menu is mostly Tex-Mex

(the burritos are superb), and the atmosphere lively and yippee-ayo-ta-yay fun.

**Pizza Americano** ( ☎ 644 8837; Müürivahe tänav 2; pizzas from 85EEK) Thick, tasty pizzas of every possible permutation and combination are on offer here, including several vegetarian options.

There are decent fast-food options inside the Viru Keskus shopping centre.

## Midrange

**Bestseller** ( ☎ 610 1397; Viru väjak 4/6, 3rd fl; mains from 55EEK; ⏰ 9am-9pm; ☒ ) Located inside the city's best bookstore, this café is more than a place where beautiful people come to pop open their Apple laptops. Some of the finest food (in delicate, French portions) is served here, delicious, healthy meals and the best *crème brûlée* east of France.

**Café VS** ( ☎ 627 2627; www.cafévs.ee; Pärnu mnt 28; mains from 65EEK) One of the first 'trendy' spots to open in Tallinn, it's still going strong as a bar, club (come evening) and eatery, thanks to some of the city's most stunning Indian meals. Vegetarians head over here! The menu is exhaustive, so there's something for everyone.

**Eesti Maja** ( ☎ 645 5252; www.eestimaja.ee; A Lauteri tänav 1; buffet 75EEK, mains from 100EEK) Here's a good place to sample traditional Estonian fare, in a folksy interior. The weekday lunch buffet is a good deal and lets you try some of the heavy, exotic food without a full-plate commitment.

**Pirosmani** ( ☎ 639 3246; Üliõpilaste tee 1; mains from 55EEK) Worth the hike out here for succulent Georgian food in a lively atmosphere. You can sit outside among the pine trees or inside among the Russians and enjoy mouthwatering delicacies at affordable prices. Take trolleybus 3 (or your bike) to the Ehitajate stop, then south for 300m.

## Top End

**Olde Hansa** ( ☎ 627 9020; Vana turg 1; mains from 175EEK; ☒ ) One of the few touristy places that's truly worth a visit, this Medieval-themed restaurant boasts the friendliest service in the country, delicacies like juniper cheese and exotic dishes like boar and bear, all impeccably presented.

**Gloria** ( ☎ 644 6950; www.gloria.ee; Müürivahe tänav 2; mains 240-380EEK) Voted as one of the world's 100 best restaurants by *Condé Nast*, it's no surprise that this Old World wonder, the *crème de la crème* of Estonia since the 1930s, lives up to all expectations on all levels. For the best wines (and atmosphere) in the city, visit their wine cellar downstairs.

## Self-Catering

Don't wait to be served, get it all yourself at the best supermarkets in the centre: **Toidu-maailm** (Viru väljak 4/6; ☼ 8am-10pm) inside the Viru Keskus shopping centre, the grocery section of **Stockmann** (Liivalaia tänav 53; ☼ 9am-10pm Mon-Fri, 9am-9pm Sat & Sun), and **Rimi** (Aia tänav 7; ☼ 9am-10pm).

## DRINKING

Tallinn without its café and bar culture is simply inconceivable. Even in Soviet times Tallinn was renowned for its cafés. Due to the charm of the surroundings, the Old Town is the obvious place to head to for cellar bars and absurdly cosy cafés.

Note that as of 1 May 2007, an antismoking ban takes effect across Estonia. No one knows how this will change the bar and club landscape yet, but smoking will only be permitted in specially constructed areas, and no service of food or drink will be permitted there.

**Déjà Vu** ( ☎ 645 0044; www.dejavu.ee; Sauna tänav 1) A stylish lounge bar bathed in red is cosier than others of its ilk and boasts a stupendous cocktail menu, plus the largest choice of teas in Estonia. Tasteful live music most evenings adds to the atmosphere.

**Kehrwieder** ( ☎ 644 0818; Saiakäik 1) The city's cosiest café where you can stretch out on a couch, read by lamplight and bump your head on the arched ceilings. Excellent coffees, teas, light meals and ambience galore. A must!

**Maiasmokk** (Sweet-Tooth; ☎ 646 4066; Pikk tänav 16) The city's longest-running café (open since 1884) still draws a (slightly older) crowd who appreciate the classic feel, elaborate ceiling mirror and the pastries (some of which look like they've been there since opening day, but who cares – the atmosphere's great!).

**Hell Hunt** ( ☎ 681 8333; Pikk tänav 39) A trouper on the pub circuit for years, this place boasts an amiable atmosphere and reasonable prices for local-brewed beer and cider (half-litre for 24EEK).

**Von Krahli Teater Baar** ( ☎ 626 9096; Rataskaevu tänav 10/12) One of the city's best bars, it also serves inexpensive meals and sometimes features live bands and fringe plays. A good place to meet interesting locals.

**Levist Väljas** ( ☎ 507 7372; Olevimägi tänav 12) In this cellar bar, it's not only telephones which are 'out of range' (what its name translates to) – so are the clientele! The wobbly seats, cheap booze and draughty interior attracts a refreshingly motley crew of friendly punks, grunge kings, has-beens and anyone else who strays from the well-trodden tourist path.

**Beer House** ( ☎ 627 6520; Dunkri tänav 5) Tallinn's only micro brewery offers up the good stuff in a huge, tavern like space where, come evening, the oompah-pah music can rattle the brain into oblivion. Fun and sometimes raucous, it's for those who have had an overdose of cosy at other venues.

## ENTERTAINMENT

It's a small capital as capitals go and the pace is accordingly slower than in other big cities, but there's lots to keep yourself stimulated, whether in a nightclub, laid-back bar or concert hall. Buy tickets for concerts and main events at **Piletilevi** (www.piletilevi.ee) and its central locations, like inside Viru Keskus. Events are posted on city centre walls and advertised on flyers found in shops and cafés.

### Nightclubs

Most of Tallinn's nightclubs have an entrance fee, ranging from 50EEK to 200EEK, with most under 100EEK. Many clubs are free to enter from Monday to Wednesday.

**Hollywood** ( ☎ 627 4770; www.club-hollywood.ee; Vana-Posti tänav 8) A multilevel emporium of mayhem, this is the one to draw the largest crowds, especially of foreigners.

**Terrarium** ( ☎ 661 4721; Sadama tänav 6) A very down-to-earth club experience is ensured here; prices are lower and there's less attitude than in the posher Old Town clubs. But the DJs still kick out the disco and the twenty-something, mostly Russian crowd laps it up.

**Bon Bon** (661 6080; Mere puistee 6e) This club attracts a 25- to 35-year-old clientele who still want to party; stylish, almost lavish but not elitist, the club plays excellent music and creates an atmosphere hard to leave.

### Gay & Lesbian Venues

**X-Baar** ( ☎ 692 9266; Sauna tänav 1) The only place in the Old Town actually flying the rainbow flag is Tallinn's premier gay bar, whose minuscule dance floor comes alive late at weekends.

**Angel** ( ☎ 641 6880; Sauna tänav 1) Open to all sexes and orientations, this mainly gay club has become one of the liveliest spots in town for fun of all kinds. A heady mix of dark corners, sweat, Madonna impersonators and throbbing beats – amongst other things.

**G-Punkt** ( ☎ 688 0747; Pärnu mnt 23) To see what Eastern European gay clubs were like 15 years ago, head to this underground bar, mainly attracting lesbians, with no sign advertising itself. Retro heaven.

## Theatre

The places listed tend to stage performances in Estonian only, save of course for modern dance shows or the rare show in English or other languages.

**Estonia Theatre & Concert Hall** ( ☎ theatre 626 0215, ☎ concert hall 614 7760; Estonia puiestee 4) The city's biggest concerts and shows are held here. It's Tallinn's main theatre, and also houses the Estonian national opera and ballet.

**Linnateater** (City Theatre; ☎ 665 0800; www.linnat eater.ee; Lai tänav 23) This theatre always stages something memorable – watch for its summer plays on an outdoor stage or different Old Town venues.

**Teater No99** ( ☎ 660 5051; www.no99.ee; Sakala tänav 3) More experimental productions happen here, but definitely come by for the jazz bar downstairs on Friday and Saturday evenings – a true jazz club the likes of which Tallinn has been sorely lacking for years.

**Drugoi Teatr** (The Other Theatre; ☎ 534 15169; Narva mnt 7) This small, grass-roots Russian theatre stages some good, lively productions (mainly performed in Russian), which are mildly alternative.

## Cinemas

Check out what's on at www.superkinod.ee. No dubbing here (this is a civilised country!); all films play in their original languages, subtitled into Estonian and Russian.

There are a few art-house venues in town. **Kinomaja** ( ☎ 646 4510; Uus tänav 3) is your best bet for alternative cinema, and **Sõprus** ( ☎ 644 1919; www.kino.ee; Vana-Posti tänav 8), housed in a magnificent Stalin-era theatre, has an excellent repertoire of European, local and independent productions.

## Sport

**A Le Coq Arena** ( ☎ 627 9940; Asula tänav 4c) About 1.5km southwest of town, this sparkling, newly refurbished arena is home to Tallinn's football team Flora, which is filled with Estonia's toughest, meanest players. Watching a match is great fun.

**Kalevi Sporhidall** ( ☎ 644 5171; Staadioni tänav 8) Basketball is Estonia's most passionately watched game, and the best national tournaments are usually held in this stadium just south of the centre.

## SHOPPING

The Old Town is full of small shops selling Estonian-made handicrafts, costumes, leather-bound books, ceramics, jewellery, silverware, stained-glass and objects carved from limestone. These are traditional Estonian souvenirs – these and a bottle of Vana Tallinn, of course! They are also on sale on the fourth floor of the **Viru Keskus** ( ☎ 610 1400; Viru Väljak 4/6 ☽ 8am-10pm) and other shopping centres. The Draakoni art gallery (p324) sells some lovely handmade glassware. There are also several antique shops selling Soviet memorabilia and Russian icons; there are a few lined up along Aia tänav in the Old Town.

**Domini Canes** ( ☎ 644 5286; Katerina käik) A lovely gallery-workshop where the ancient craft of glassmaking is revived for all to see. There are beautiful stained-glass works.

**Kodukäsitöö** ( ☎ 631 4076; Müürivahe 17) One of the many good places to find locally made handicrafts.

**Ivo Nikkolo** ( ☎ 699 9888; Suur Karja tänav 14) A leading name in the Estonian fashion design world, you'll find trendy and conservative clothes for men and women.

**L & L** ( ☎ 631 3254, Vana Viru 11) Some way-out, super innovative clothes designs.

## GETTING THERE & AWAY
### Air

For detailed information on flights in and out of Tallinn see p347. **Tallinn airport** ( ☎ 605 8888; www.tallinn-airport.ee) is just 3km southeast of the city centre on Tartu maantee. There are helicopter rides throughout the day to Helsinki run by **Copterline** (www.copterline.ee); see also p347.

### Boat

See p347 for information about the many services available between Tallinn and Helsinki and Stockholm. Tallinn's sea-passenger terminal is at the end of Sadama, a short, 1km walk northeast of the Old Town. Tram 1 and 2 and bus 3 and 8 go to the Linnahall stop, five minutes' walk from terminals A, B and C. Terminal D is at the end of Lootsi tänav, better accessed from Ahtri tänav. A taxi

ESTONIA

etween the centre and any of the terminals will cost about 50EEK.

## Bus

Bus services to places within about 40km of Tallinn depart from the platform located next to the train station. You can get information and timetables from **Harju Liinid** ( ☎ 644 801). For detailed bus information and to purchase advance tickets for all other destinations, contact the central bus station **Au-obussijaam** ( ☎ 680 0900, likely to be English speakers available; www.bussireisid.ee; Lastekodu tänav 46), which is southeast of the centre. Trams 2 or 4 will take you there.

## Car & Motorcycle

There are 24-hour petrol stations at strategic spots within the city and along major roads leading to and from Tallinn.

Car rental in Tallinn can often be arranged by your hotel, via these trusted options, or via tes (p327):

**Hertz** ( ☎ 605 8923; www.hertz.ee) At the airport.
**Tulika Rent** ( ☎ 612 0012; www.tulika.ee; Tihase tänav 34)

## Train

Tallinn's **Balti jaam** (Baltic Station; ☎ 615 6851; www edel.ee) is on the northwestern edge of the Old Town, a short walk from Raekoja plats, or three stops on tram 1 or 2 north from the Mere puiestee stop. There are domestic services to many cities and towns throughout Estonia and to/from Russia.

## GETTING AROUND
### To/From the Airport

Bus 2 runs every 20 to 30 minutes between port terminals A and D via Gonsiori tänav in the centre to the airport. From the airport, it's just five bus stops to the centre. A taxi to/from the centre should cost about 60EEK to 70EEK. It's best to order a taxi (right) as the ones stationed at the airport are among the city's most expensive.

## Public Transport

Tallinn has an excellent network of buses, trolleybuses and trams that run from 6am to midnight. *Piletid* (tickets) are sold from street kiosks (adult/student 10/7EEK) or can be purchased from the driver (15EEK). Validate your ticket using the hole punch inside the vehicle. Your Tallinn Card (see

p321) will give you free transport. All public transport timetables are available online at www.tallinn.ee.

## Taxi

Save for some jowly mafia-wannabe drivers at the train station, port, airport and along Viru tänav, drivers are honest and rides metered, costing from 5.50EEK to 9EEK per kilometre. Try **Iks Takso** ( ☎ 638 1381) or **Taxi Marabu** ( ☎ 650 0006). The ecologically sound **Velotakso** ( ☎ 508 8810) offers rides on egg-shaped vehicles run by pedal power and enthusiasm, and charges 35EEK anywhere within central Tallinn.

# NORTHEASTERN ESTONIA

This region has received much less attention by tourists than more popular destinations like Pärnu and Tartu but shows a unique side of Estonia. Directly to the east of Tallinn is a splendidly unspoilt national park and beyond that stretches of impressive, limestone cliff-top views out to sea and historic sites. The vast majority of the population here is Russian-speaking which adds another flavour to the Estonian cultural mosaic, and some places feel like Soviet relics (like Sillamäe, a living museum of Stalin-era architecture). Time to explore!

## LAHEMAA NATIONAL PARK

A rocky stretch of the north coast – encompassing 251 sq km of marine area plus 474 sq km of hinterland with 14 lakes, eight rivers and many waterfalls – forms the lovely Lahemaa National Park, a perfect getaway for a day or more in nature.

## Information

The **Visitors Centre** ( ☎ 329 5555; www.lahemaa.ee; ☯ 9am-7pm May-Aug, to 5pm Sep, to 5pm Mon-Fri Oct-Apr) is located in Palmse, 8km north of Viitna (71km east of Tallinn) in the park's southeast. It's worth getting in touch with them before heading out. For an outstanding personal guide to the park (and to any area in northern Estonia), contact the outgoing and multilingual **Anne Kurepalu** ( ☎ 569 13786; anne@phpalmse.ee).

## Sights & Activities

There is an unlimited amount of sightseeing, hiking, biking and boating to be done here;

remote islands can also be explored. A highlight would be a canoe trip down one of the rivers running through the park; the visitors centre can help organise this. The park has several well-signposted nature trails (a popular one is the Beaver Trail) and cycling paths winding through it. The small coastal towns of **Võsu**, **Käsmu** and **Loksa** are popular seaside spots in summer. Käsmu is a particularly enchanting village, one of Estonia's prettiest. There are also **prehistoric stone barrows** (tombs) at Kahala, Palmse and Vihula, and a **boulder field** on the Käsmu Peninsula.

Lahemaa also features some historic **manor houses**: Kolga, Vihula, Palmse and Sagadi. **Palmse Manor** (adult/student 40/15EEK; ☼ 10am-7pm May-Sep, 10am-1pm Oct-Apr), near the visitors centre, was once a wholly self-contained Baltic-German estate and **Sagadi** was another opulent residence (built in 1749) that now houses the **Forest Museum** ( ☎ 676 7878; www.sagadi.ee; museum & manor adult/student 30/10EEK; ☼ 10am-6pm May-Sep, by arrangement Oct-Apr) and a hotel (see Sleeping & Eating).

### Sleeping & Eating

The visitors centre arranges accommodation to suit every budget and can advise on the best camping spots. Prices are 15 to 20% cheaper from October to April.

**Ojaäärse hostel** ( ☎ 628 1532; puhkus@rmk.ee; dm 200-250EEK; s 300EEK; Ⓟ ) A dream version of a hostel, this is a lushly converted 1855 farmhouse 1.5km southeast of Palmse right by a lake. Dorms have between two and eight beds, toilets are shared, and there's plenty of room to pitch a tent.

**Toomarahva** ( ☎ 325 2511; www.zone.ee/toomarahva; Altja village; camp sites 25EEK; s/d/2-person barn/apt 400/600/500/800EEK; Ⓟ ) 'Rustic' is an cliché, but this lovely guest/farmhouse deserves it. A two-minute walk from the sea in the tiny village of Altja (10km by road east of Võsu). The split-level barn is bucolic heaven. Other meals beside breakfast can be ordered, and there's bike rental.

**Sagadi Hotell** ( ☎ 676 7888; sagadi.hotell@rmk.ee; s/d 700/900EEK; Ⓟ ) Stylishly decorated, splendid rooms are available for rent inside the Sagadi manor itself. The most spacious are rooms 2, 4 and 6. In such perfect surroundings, and with a restaurant downstairs, you'll need little else to keep you happy.

**Vihula Manor** ( ☎ 322 6985; www.vihulamois.ee; s 350-500EEK, d 700-1200EEK, ts 800-900EEK; Ⓟ ) Probably the park's most impressive accommodation option, this manor, 6km east of Sagadi,

has been lovingly restored with wood panelling and a great attention to detail. There's boat and bike rental.

### Getting There & Away

There are about 20 buses daily from Tallinn to Rakvere, which stop at Viitna (40EEK to 60EEK, one hour), and one a day from Tallinn to Võsu (40EEK, 1¼ hours). From Viitna, you can hike or hitchhike to the visitors centre, or call a **taxi** ( ☎ 509 2326) from Võsu to pick you up. You can bring your bikes on the bus.

## NARVA & AROUND
pop 69,000

Estonia's easternmost town is separated only by the thin Narva River from Ivangorod in Russia and is almost entirely populated by Russians. Narva was a Hanseatic League trading point by 1171 and later became embroiled in Russia's border disputes with the German knights and Sweden. Ivan III of Muscovy founded Ivangorod in 1492 and its large castle still menacingly faces Narva's castle, providing a unique and picturesque architectural composition. Narva was almost completely destroyed in WWII.

The **tourist information centre** ( ☎ 356 0184; www.tourism.narva.ee; Puškini tänav 13) is in the city centre. The bus and train stations are located together at Vaksali tänav 2, opposite the Russian Orthodox Voskresensky Cathedral. Walk north up Puškini tänav to the castle (500m) and the centre.

### Sights

Restored after WWII, **Narva Castle**, guarding the Friendship Bridge over the river to Russia, dates from Danish rule in the 13th century. The castle houses the **Town Museum** ( ☎ 359 9230; adult/student 30/10EEK; ☼ 10am-6pm Wed-Sun). Contact the tourist information centre for night-time, candle-light excursions through the castle, usually on the last Friday of the month. In early August, the **Narva Historic Festival** (teadus@narvamuuseum.ee) recreates ancient battles and puts on handicraft displays.

On the square in front of the train station is a **monument** to the Estonians who were loaded into cattle wagons here in 1941 and deported to Siberia. Also worth a visit is the **Kunsti Galerii** ( ☎ 359 2151; Vestervalli 21; ☼ 10am-6pm Wed-Sun), an excellent art gallery some 500m north of the border point.

About 12km north of Narva is the resort of **Narva-Jõesuu**, popular since the 19th century for its long, white, sandy beaches. There are many unique, impressive early-20th-century wooden houses and villas throughout the slightly run-down town.

## Sleeping & Eating

The tourist information centre can recommend guesthouses, hotels and restaurants.

**Hostel Jusian** ( ☎ 356 2656; jusian@hot.ee; Kreenholmi tänav 40; d with shared bathroom 350EEK; **P** ) On the bare-bones side, but perfectly comfortable.

**Mereranna Hostel** ( ☎ 357 2827; Aia tänav 17; dm/s/d 200/350/400EEK; **P** ) Located right by the beach in Narva-Jõesuu, this four-storey complex feels like a mini spa and offers plenty of services.

**Hotel King** ( ☎ 357 2404; www.hotelking.ee; Lavetstrovi tänav 9; s/d/ste from 690/890/1100EEK; **P** ) Just two blocks from the border is your best option in town – a stylish, very comfortable hotel-restaurant (meaty mains from 70EEK).

**Modern** ( ☎ 356 0207; Puškini tänav 12; mains from 40EEK) One of Narva's most welcoming spots, this bar-club-café has simple, decent meals and live music, exhibitions or just lots of activity going on.

**German Pub** ( ☎ 359 1548; Puškini tänav 10; mains from 60EEK) Cosy pub serving great food (lots of sausages!) in cheerful surroundings.

## Getting There & Away

Narva is 210km east of Tallinn on the road to St Petersburg, a further 140km away. From Tallinn there are over 20 buses (95EEK to 120EEK, three to 3½ hours) and a train daily (85EEK, 3½ hours). There are 10 daily buses from Narva to Tartu (85EEK to 110EEK, 3½ hours) and many to nearby cities. Buses go to Narva-Jõesuu throughout the day (10EEK, 20 minutes).

# SOUTHEASTERN ESTONIA

Southeastern Estonia comes as a pleasant shock to anyone who knows only the flat north. South of the historic university city of Tartu, a sprasely-populated, attractive region of gently rolling hills and hundreds of lakes opens up. It's also the traditional land of the Setu people, with their own language and customs.

## TARTU

pop 100,000

Tartu lays claim to being Estonia's spiritual capital. Locals talk about a special Tartu

*vaim,* or Tartu spirit, encompassed by the time-stands-still, 19th-century feel of many of its streets, lined with wooden houses, and by the ethereal beauty of its parks and riverfront.

Small and provincial, with the quietly flowing Emajõgi River running through it, it's also a university town with students making up nearly one-fifth of the population; this injects a boisterous vitality into the leafy, serene and pleasant surroundings. During the Student Days festival at the end of April, carnival-like mayhem erupts throughout the city.

Around the 6th century, there was an Estonian stronghold on Toomemägi Hill. In 1030, Yaroslav the Wise of Kyiv is said to have founded a settlement here called Yuriev. The university, founded in 1632, developed into one of the foremost 19th-century seats of learning. The Estonian nationalist revival in the 19th century had its origins here, and Tartu was the location for the first Estonian Song Festival in 1869.

Tartu provides visitors with a truer glimpse of the Estonian rhythm of life than Tallinn, boasts great museums and is a convenient gateway to exploring southern Estonia. It's also undergoing a delayed construction boom and there's a feeling of a bright future ahead.

## Orientation

Toomemägi Hill and the area of older buildings between it and the Emajõgi River are the focus of 'old' Tartu. At its heart is Raekoja plats (Town Hall Square). Ülikooli tänav and Rüütli tänav are the main shopping streets; ATMs are scattered throughout the centre.

## Information

**Central post office** ( ☎ 744 0600; Vanemuise tänav 7; ⊗ 8am-7pm Mon-Fri, 9am-4pm Sat)

**Estravel** ( ☎ 744 0300; www.estravel.ee; Vallikraavi tänav 2) Official Amex agent; can offer general help.

**Mattiesen** ( ☎ 730 9721; Vallikraavi tänav 4) Bookshop that stocks an extensive range of maps.

**Tourist information centre** ( ☎ /fax 744 2111; www.visittartu.com; Raekoja plats 14; ⊗ 9am-5pm Mon-Fri, 10am-3pm Sat & Sun) This centre has an excellent range of local maps, books and brochures, can book accommodation and tour guides and sells listings guides. They're also the best to recommend excursions outside the city.

**ZumZum** ( ☎ 742 3443; Küüni 2; ⊗ 11am-11pm; 25EEK/hr) If you can't enjoy one of the city's 75 wi-fi hotspots, head to this basement internet café.

ESTONIA

# TARTU

0 —————— 300 m
0 —————— 0.2 miles

**INFORMATION**
Central Post Office.....................**1** C5
Estravel.....................................**2** C5
Mattiesen...............................(see 27)
Tourist Information Centre............**3** C4
ZumZum....................................**4** C5

**SIGHTS & ACTIVITIES**
19th-Century Tartu Citizen's Home
  Museum.................................**5** B4
Cathedral Toomkirik.....................**6** B4
Estonian National Museum............**7** A5
Jaani Kirik..................................**8** C4
KGB Cells...................................**9** B6

Museum of University History......**10** B4
Observatory..............................**11** B5
River Port..................................**12** D5
Student's Lock-Up...................(see 15)
Tartu Art Museum......................**13** C4
Tartu Sports Museum .................**14** C4
Tartu University Art Museum......**15** B4
Town Hall.................................**16** C5
University Building...................(see 15)

**SLEEPING**
Herne......................................**17** A2
Hotel Tähtvere..........................**18** A3
Hotel Tartu...............................**19** D5
London.....................................**20** C4
Pallas......................................**21** C5
Tartu University Guesthousing
  (Pepleri)................................**22** B6
Tartu University Guesthousing
  (Raatuse)...............................**23** D4

**EATING**
Dedi.........................................**24** D5
Püssirohukelder.........................**25** B5
University Café..........................**26** B4

**DRINKING**
Irish Pub..................................**27** C5
Wilde Café, Wine Club...........(see 27)
Zavood....................................**28** C4

**ENTERTAINMENT**
Club Tallinn.............................**29** D4
Rock N Roll..............................**30** A6
Sadamateater...........................**31** D5
Vanemuine Theatre & Concert
  Hall......................................**32** C5
Vanemuine Theatre (small stage).**33** B6

**TRANSPORT**
Bus Station...............................**34** D5

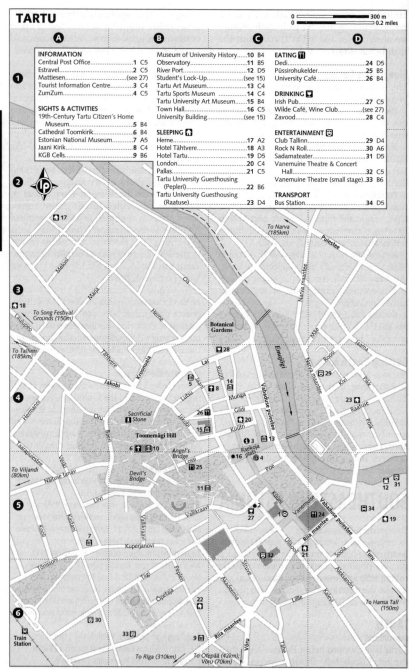

## Sights & Activities

At the town centre on Raekoja plats is the **town hall** (1782–89), topped by a tower and weather vane and fronted by a statue of lovers kissing under an umbrella, an apt, jolly symbol of Tartu. At the other end of the square, the former home of Colonel Barclay de Tolly (1761–1818) is a wonderfully crooked building housing the **Tartu Art Museum** ( ☎ 744 1080; www.tartmus.ee; Raekoja plats 18; adult/student 25/10EEK; ☺ 11am-6pm Wed-Sun).

The main **university building** ( ☎ 737 5100; Ülikooli tänav 18) dates from 1803. It houses the **Tartu University Art Museum** ( ☎ 737 5384; adult/child 8/5EEK; ☺ 11am-5pm Mon-Fri) and **Student's Lock-Up** (adult/child 5/4EEK; ☺ 11am-5pm Mon-Fri), where 19th-century students were held for their misdeeds. Further north, the Gothic brick **Jaani Kirik** (St John's Church; ☎ 744 2229; Jaani tänav 5; free admission), founded in 1330, recently underwent massive reconstruction and boasts its proud collection of some 1000 rare terracotta sculptures surrounding the main portal.

**Tartu Sports Museum** ( ☎ 730 0750; Rüütli tänav 15; adult/student 30/20EEK; ☺ 11am-6pm Wed-Sun) showcases much more than Estonian Olympic excellence. There's a sweet display of the life of a 19th-century postman, and excellent temporary exhibits. Nearby, the **19th-Century Tartu Citizen's Home Museum** ( ☎ 736 1545; Jaani tänav 16; adult/student 8/5EEK; ☺ 10am-4pm Wed-Sun) is worth a peak; inside you can see how a burgher from the 1830s lived – and have a cup of tea.

Rising to the west of Raekoja plats is the splendid Toomemägi Hill, landscaped in the manner of a 19th-century English park and perfect for a leisurely stroll. The 13th-century Gothic **cathedral Toomkirik** at the top was rebuilt in the 15th century, despoiled during the Reformation in 1525, and partly rebuilt in 1804–07 to accommodate the university library, which is now the **Museum of University History** ( ☎ 737 5674; adult/student 20/5EEK; ☺ 11am-5pm Wed-Sun).

Also on Toomemägi Hill are the 1838 **Angel's Bridge** (Inglisild), with a good view of the city; the 1913 **Devil's Bridge** (Kuradisild); and the **observatory** ( ☎ 737 6932), open only by special reservation.

Tartu, as the major repository of Estonia's cultural heritage, has an abundance of first-rate museums. Among them is perhaps the country's best: the **Estonian National Museum** ( ☎ 742 1311; www.erm.ee; Kuperjanovi tänav 9; adult/student 20/14EEK, free Fri; ☺ 11am-6pm Wed-Sun), which

traces the history, life and traditions of the Estonian people. The former KGB headquarters now house the sombre and highly worthwhile **KGB Cells** ( ☎ 746 1717; Riia mnt 15b; adult/student 5/3EEK; ☺ 11am-6pm Tue-Sat).

For information about Emajõgi River **cruises** from Tartu's **river port** (Sadam; ☎ 734 0026; Soola tänav 5), contact **Laevatöö** ( ☎ 734 0025). Services run twice-weekly to the remote island of Piirissaar.

## Festivals & Events

Some of the country's main sporting events happen in and around Tartu, and all of them have the word 'marathon' attached to them. The **Tartu ski marathon**, a 60km cross-country trek from Otepää, involves hundreds of enthusiastic skiers in mid-February; in May both the **Tartu Bicycle Marathon** (a 136km event; a shorter one is held in September) and the **Tartu Running Race** take place. See www.tartumaraton.ee for details.

## Sleeping

### BUDGET & MIDRANGE

**Hotel Tähtvere** ( ☎ 742 1708; Laulupeo puiestee 19; s/d from 125/250EEK; P ) A pleasant 1km walk west from the centre, this run-down but perfectly decent place is by a park and concert stadium. It has comfortable, if nondescript, rooms with TV and private toilet. A great deal for the non-fussy!

**Herne** ( ☎ 744 1959; Herne tänav 59; per person 225EEK) A 1km walk northwest of the city through a traditionally poor neighbourhood of charismatic wooden houses brings you to this lovely B&B with four rooms and a clean, shared bathroom.

**Tartu University Guesthousing** ( ☎ 740 9955; www.kyla.ee; s 250-300EEK; d 400-500EEK; ✗ ) Raatuse (Raatuse tänav 22); Pepleri (Pepleri tänav 14) Two student dorms offer cheap, clean, central accommodation. The Raatuse locale is functional but bathrooms are shared between three rooms and morning noise levels are high; better is the more expensive Pepleri, also modern and spiffy, but each room has private toilet. Advance reservations are a must.

**Hotel Tartu** ( ☎ 731 4300; Soola tänav 3; dm/s/d 300/725/1075EEK; P ✗ ) Being across from the bus station doesn't make for the most charming of locations (or views), but this hotel's recently renovated rooms are sleek and comfy. The dorm rooms hold only three and are spotless. There's an additional 15% student discount.

**TOP END**

**Pallas** ( ☎ 730 1200; www.pallas.ee; Riia mnt 4; s/ste 995/2000EEK, d 1275-1800EEK; P X X ) Named after a local art school, this is among the nicest surprises in the country, with many doubles and all suites featuring original art on the walls and ceilings. The views towards town are superb as well. Worth the extra.

**London** ( ☎ 7305555; www.londonhotel.ee; Rüütli tänav 9; s 1150, d 1630-2300EEK, ste 2500EEK; P X X ) The city's only four-star offering is Zen and luxury rolled into one, with the most peaceful lobbies you could imagine and spacious, elegant rooms for the discerning customer.

## Eating & Drinking

**Dedi** ( ☎ 731 4850; Tartu Kaubamaja, 3rd fl; mains from 35EEK; X X ) A great two-in-one combo – a sleek cafeteria provides great budget meals while the adjacent bar-restaurant (with magnificent terrace overlooking a park) ups the ante with superb food, cocktails and design.

**Püssirohukelder** ( ☎ 730 3555; Lossi tänav 28; mains 40-100EEK) Set majestically in a cavernous old gunpowder cellar, this doubles as a boisterous pub, has hearty meals and the city's largest wine selection.

**Wilde Café, Wine Club & Irish Pub** ( ☎ 730 9764; Vallikraavi tänav 4; mains from 55EEK) One of the city's most pleasant places to relax, no matter your mood – choose grace and elegance in the café/wine club or something more lively at the upstairs pub (with a killer terrace and great menu).

**Hansa Tall** ( ☎ 730 3400; Alexandri tänav 46; mains 70-120EEK) Had enough of slick lounge/bars and want some good old oompah-pah homestyle tradition? Head to this meticulously decked-out tavern. You need not try the chicken gizzards or salted pork fat to enjoy the diverse, hearty menu, live music and even livelier locals.

**Zavood** ( ☎ 744 1321; Lai tänav 30) This low-key bar attracts an alternative, down-to-earth

---

**AUTHOR'S CHOICE**

**University Café** ( ☎ 737 5405; www.kohvik.ut .ee; Ülikooli tänav 20; mains from 35EEK) Some of the most economical meals in town are waiting at the cafeteria-style 1st-floor café while upstairs is a labyrinth of elegantly decorated rooms that create worlds unto themselves, both Old World grand and embracingly cosy. There, delicious, artfully presented dishes are served.

---

crowd with its inexpensive drinks and lack of attitude. It sometimes features a student band.

## Entertainment

**Club Tallinn** ( ☎ 740 3157; Narva mnt 27) This often gets the vote as the best club in Estonia. It shines with top-notch DJs, theme evenings and an enthusiastic and fashionable young crowd.

**Rock N Roll** ( ☎ 53 434 307; www.rocknroll.ee; Tiigi tänav 76A) An antidote to all the stylish clubs is this den of rock, punk, funk, tattoos and sweat. Hyperbolic, down-to-earth and gritty.

**Vanemuine Theatre & Concert Hall** ( ☎ 744 0165, 737 7530; www.vanemuine.ee, www.concert.ee; Vanemuise tänav 6) The first Estonian-language theatre troupe performed here in 1870 and the venue still regularly hosts an array of theatrical and musical performances. It also stages performances at its **small stage** ( ☎ 744 0160; Vanemuise tänav 45A) and **Sadamateater** ( ☎ 734 4248; Soola tänav 5B). The latter has a prime location on the banks of the Emajõgi and tends to stage the most modern, alternative productions.

## Getting There & Away

Some 50 buses a day run to/from Tallinn (65EEK to 100EEK, 2½ to 3¼ hours). There are also three trains daily (85EEK to 125EEK, 3¼ hours). Tartu is the main hub for destinations in south and south eastern Estonia, and has frequent connections with all other towns, including some 20 buses a day to Pärnu (100EEK to 120EEK, 2¾ hours).

## OTEPÄÄ
pop 2200

The small hilltop town of Otepää, 44km south of Tartu, is the centre of a scenic area beloved by Estonians for its hills and lakes – and thus its endless opportunities for sports. The area is dubbed (tongue-in-cheek) as the 'Estonian Alps' as this is where most of the country's skiing activities are centred. There are also well-tended stretches of bike paths.

## Orientation & Information

The centre of town is the triangular main 'square', Lipuväljak, with the bus station just off its eastern corner. There you'll find the **Tourist information centre** ( ☎ 766 1200; www.otepaa .ee; Lipuväljak 13; 9am-6pm Mon-Fri, 10am-3pm Sat & Sun mid-May–mid-Sep, 9am-5pm Mon-Fri, 10am-3pm Sat mid-Sep–mid-May). The post office, bank and main food shop are beside the bus station.

## Sights & Activities

Otepää's pretty little 17th-century **church** is on a hilltop about 300m northeast of the tourist information centre along Tartu maantee. It was in this church in 1884 that the Estonian Students' Society consecrated its new blue, black and white flag, which later became the flag of independent Estonia. The former vicar's residence now houses two museums: **Eesti Lipu Muuseum** (Flag Museum; ☎ 765 5075) and **Suusamuuseum** (Ski Museum; ☎ 766 3670; suusamuuseum@hot.ee). Both can be visited by appointment, or just show up and try your luck.

The tree-covered hill south of the church is the **Linnamägi** (Castle Hill), a major stronghold from the 10th to 12th centuries. There are traces of old fortifications on top, and good views of the surrounding country.

The best views, however, are along the shores of the 3.5km-long **Pühajärv** (Holy Lake) just southwest of town. The lake was blessed by the Dalai Lama and a monument on the eastern shore commemorates his visit in 1992. The lake is the area's main attraction year-round.

It would be a shame to visit and pass by the lovely countryside surrounding the town. To rent bikes, Rollerblades, skis and snowboards, and for fun bike and canoe tours, contact **Fan Sport** ( ☎ 767 7537; www.fansport.ee), which has three offices in Otepää. There's lots to do and see in the **Otepää Nature Park** ( ☎ 765 5876; Kolga tee 28), which incorporates 232 sq km of the region's lakes, forest and very well-marked hiking trails. Activities can be planned by calling them directly or via the tourist information centre.

## Sleeping & Eating

Low season here is April to May and September to November; at this time hotel prices are about 10 to 15% cheaper.

**Edgari** ( ☎ 765 4275; www.hot.ee/karnivoor; Lipuväljak 3; s/d from 200/400EEK) One of the cheapest places to stay right in town, this is a guesthouse that feels like a hostel, with thin walls, a shared kitchenette and communal lounge, all in a pleasant but bland atmosphere.

**Setanta Irish Pub & Hotel** ( ☎ 766 8200; www.setanta.ee; Núpli village; d 500-1500EEK; mains 70-100EEK; P ) Better known for its Irish Pub, this lively place just 3km southeast of Otepää has rooms which boast great views over Lake Pühajärv. On the minus side, their weekend discos are clearly heard in the rooms.

**Pühajärve Spa Hotel** ( ☎ 766 5500; www.pyhajarve.com; Pühajärve village; s/d/ste 700/900/1490EEK; P X X ) Situated right by the lake, this refurbished complex offers a full range of activities, sports and services.

## Getting There & Away

Daily bus services to/from Otepää include Tartu (25EEK to 30EEK, 45 minutes to 1½ hours, 15 daily), Tallinn (100EEK, 3½ hours, three daily) and Võru (30EEK, 1¼ hours, one daily).

## HAANJA NATURE PARK

This 17,000-hectare protected area south of the city of Võru includes some of the nicest scenery in the country and is where several of the best tourist farms in the region are located. The nature park's **headquarters** ( ☎ 782 9090) in the village of Haanja can provide detailed information about the area as well as hiking and skiing opportunities, though you're more likely to get information in English at the **Tourist information centres** in **Tartu** (p333) or **Võru** ( ☎ 782 1881; voru@visitestonia.com). The coolest website devoted to the area is www.haanja kompass.ee.

### Suur Munamägi

Suur Munamägi (literally Great Egg Hill!), 17km south of Võru, is the highest hill in Estonia, Latvia and Lithuania at just over 318m, though it's still easy to miss if you're not on the lookout for it. It's covered in trees, though you can climb to the top and then walk up the 29m **observation tower** ( ☎ 787 8847; adult/student 30/15EEK elevator 60EEK; ☒ 10am-8pm May-Aug, 10am-5pm Sep, 10am-8pm Sat & Sun Oct). On a very clear day you can see Russia, Latvia and lots of lush trees. The summit and tower are a 10-minute climb from the Võru-Ruusmäe road, starting about a kilometre south of the otherwise uninspiring village of Haanja.

## SETUMAA

In the far southeastern part of Estonia is the (politically unrecognised) area of Setumaa. Unlike the rest of Estonia, this part of the country never came under the control of the Teutonic and German tribes, but fell under Novgorod's and later Pskov's subjugation. The Setu people, originally Finno-Ugric, then became Orthodox, not Lutheran. The whole of Setumaa was contained within independent Estonia between 1920 and 1940, but the greater part of it is now in Russia. There are only approximately 4000 Setu left in Estonia (about another 3000 in Russia), half the population of the early 20th century.

Aside from the large, silver breastplate that is worn on the women's national costume, what sets the Setu aside is their singing style, known as *runnoverse:* a phrase is sung by one singer (traditionally the community elder) and then repeated several times by a chorus. There is no musical accompaniment and the overall effect archaic.

Museums worth visiting here include the **Setu House Museum** (adult/student 12/5EEK; ☉ 11am-5pm Tue-Sun May-Oct) in the quaint village of Obinitsa, where there's also a formidable **stone statue** of the Setu Song Mother lording over a small lake, and the **Setu Farm Museum** ( ☎ 505 4673; www.hot.ee/setomuuseum; Pikk tänav 40; adult/student 20/10EEK; ☉ noon-5pm Tue-Sun) in Värska. They host the annual Seto Lace Days in early May, a chance to witness Setu handicraft-making The **tourist information centre** ( ☎ 785 4190; www .hot.ee/setotour) in Obinitsa is a good source of information and can advise on a number of local places to stay, including working farms which are always fun for the kids.

There are six daily buses between Tartu and Värska (70EEK, 1¾ hours), four per day between Tartu and Haanja (55EEK to 70EEK, two to 2½ hours) and one a day between Tartu and Obinitsa (80EEK, 2½ hours).

---

**WORTH THE TRIP**

One of this area's highlights is the **Setomaa Tourist Farm** ( ☎ 50 87 399; info@setotalu.ee) outside the village of Meremäe, some 7km south of Obinitsa (you'll need to travel by car or bike to get there). In glorious surroundings, it's possible to partake in traditional Setu arts and crafts, have a smoke sauna and even stay the night in a log house decorated with natural textiles (with prior reservations; camp site 50EEK, s 440EEK, entire house 2800EEK). The food's great, staff super friendly and you have the impression of partaking in a tradition without feeling touristy. No one leaves disappointed. It's 1.7km from the village of Meremäe towards Vatseliina.

---

# SOUTHWESTERN ESTONIA & THE ISLANDS

## PÄRNU
pop 43,700

Pärnu (*pair*-nu), 127km south of Tallinn on the road to Rīga, is Estonia's leading seaside resort and a magnet for party-loving Estonians and mud cure–seeking Finns. Its name alone is synonymous with fun in the sun. Most of the town, however, is docile, with wide leafy streets and sprawling parks intermingling with grand, turn-of-the-century villas which reflect Pärnu's rich past as a resort capital of the Baltic region.

In the 13th century the Knights of the Sword built a fort here. Pärnu became a Hanseatic port in the 14th century and flourished in the 17th century under Swedish rule. A huge beach and relatively good weather set Pärnu's fate as a resort, and mud baths from the mid-19th century started attracting international visitors. Pärnu is still filled with treatment centres, water parks and of course, watering holes galore.

### Information
The town lies on either side of Pärnu River's estuary, which empties into Pärnu Bay.

**Central post office** ( ☎ 447 1111; Akadeemia tee 7; ☉ 8am-6pm Mon-Fri, 9am-3pm Sat)

**Rüütli Internetipunkt** ( ☎ 443 1552; Rüütli tänav 25; per hr 25EEK; ☉ 9am-9pm Mon-Fri, to 6pm Sat & Sun) You can access the internet here and at the New Art Museum (p340; per hr 30EEK).

**Tourist information centre** ( ☎ 447 3000; www .parnu.ee; Rüütli tänav 16 ☉ 9am-6pm Mon-Fri 10am-4pm Sat & Sun Jun-Aug, 9am-5pm Mon-Fri Sep-May) On the main commercial street in the heart of the Old Town, around 150m southwest of the bus station.

**Ühispank** ( ☎ 447 7100; Rüütli tänav 40A) Behind the bus station; cashes travellers cheques and gives cash advances on credit cards.

### Sights & Activities
The wide, white-sand beach and Ranna puiestee, whose fine buildings date from the early 20th century, are among Pärnu's finest attractions. Note especially the handsome 1927 neoclassical **Mudaravila** ( ☎ 442 5525; Ranna puiestee 1) mud bath cure complex. It is possible to walk west along the coast from here to the 2km stone breakwater that stretches out into the mouth of the river.

# PÄRNU

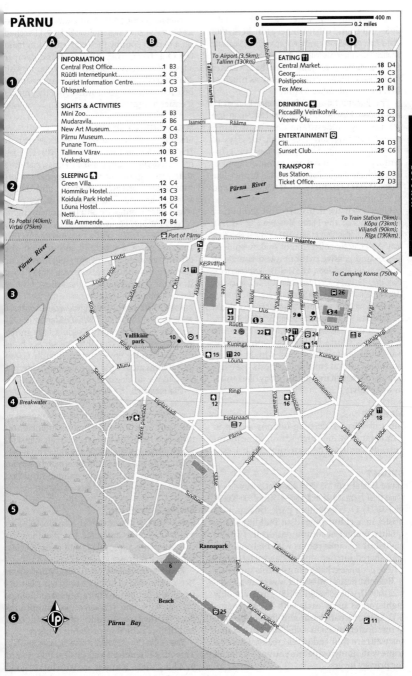

**INFORMATION**
Central Post Office.....................1 B3
Rüütli Internetipunkt...................2 C3
Tourist Information Centre.............3 C3
Ühispank..................................4 D3

**SIGHTS & ACTIVITIES**
Mini Zoo..................................5 B3
Mudaravila................................6 B6
New Art Museum........................7 C4
Pärnu Museum...........................8 D3
Punane Torn.............................9 C3
Tallinna Värav..........................10 B3
Veekeskus..............................11 D6

**SLEEPING**
Green Villa..............................12 C4
Hommiku Hostel.......................13 C3
Koidula Park Hotel....................14 D3
Lõuna Hostel...........................15 C4
Netti.....................................16 C4
Villa Ammende.........................17 B4

**EATING**
Central Market.........................18 D4
Georg....................................19 C3
Poistipoiss..............................20 C4
Tex Mex.................................21 B3

**DRINKING**
Piccadilly Veinikohvik.................22 C3
Veerev Õlu..............................23 C3

**ENTERTAINMENT**
Citi.......................................24 D3
Sunset Club............................25 C6

**TRANSPORT**
Bus Station.............................26 D3
Ticket Office............................27 D3

ESTONIA

To Airport (3,5km);
Tallinn (130km)

To Pootsi (40km);
Virtsü (75km)

To Train Station (5km);
Kõpu (73km);
Viljandi (90km);
Riga (190km)

To Camping Konse (750m)

Pärnu River

Pärnu Bay

Breakwater

Beach

Rannapark

Vallikäär park

A sparkling new water park with pools, slides, tubes and other slippery fun, **Veekeskus** (Water Park; ☎ 445 1166; www.terviseparadiis.ee; Side tänav 14; adult 180-270EEK, student 120-190EEK; ☺ 10am-10pm) is a big draw, especially when bad weather ruins beach plans. Prices dive by as much as 40% from September to May.

The **Punane Torn** (Red Tower; Hommiku tänav 11; adult/student 10/5EEK; ☺ 10am-6pm Mon-Fri, to 3pm Sat), the city's oldest (and despite its name, white) building, survives from the days of the Knights of the Sword. Parts of the 17th-century Swedish moat and ramparts remain in Vallikäär Park, including the tunnel-like **Tallinna Värav** (Tallinn Gate) at the western end of Kuninga tänav.

Check out local history and temporary art exhibits at the **Pärnu Museum** (☎ 443 3231; Rüütli tänav 53; adult/student 30/15EEK; ☺ 10am-6pm Wed-Sun). An eclectic collection of snakes, spiders, geckos and passive pythons await you at the worthwhile **Mini Zoo** (☎ 551 6033; Akadeemia tee 1; adult/child 35/15EEK; ☺ 10am-7pm May-Aug, noon-4pm Mon-Fri, 11am-4pm Sat & Sun Sep-Apr).

The **New Art Museum** (☎ 443 0772; www.chaplin.ee; Esplanaadi tänav 10; adult/student 25/10EEK; ☺ 9am-9pm), southwest of the centre, is among Estonia's cultural highlights, with its café, bookshop and exhibitions which always push the cultural envelope. It hosts the ever-popular **Documentary & Anthropology Film Festival** in early July.

## Sleeping

Most of Pärnu's sleeping options are up to 40% cheaper outside high season (June to August). Prices listed here are summer prices.

### BUDGET

**Lõuna Hostel** (☎ 443 0943; www.hot.ee/hostellouna; Lõuna tänav 2; dm 200-250EEK, s 500-575EEK, d 500-800EEK, ste 1350EEK) Overlooking a park, this spotless hostel in a grand Jugendstil building offers quality budget accommodation in two- to eight-bed spacious rooms with high ceilings. The shared kitchen doubles as social room, where people exchange fun-in-the-sun tales.

**Hommiku Hostel** (☎ 445 1122; www.hot.ee/pav; Hommiku tänav 17; s/d/tr 500/800/1000EEK) There are only eight rooms here, each with a kitchenette, TV, spacious bathroom and fluffy blankets. Wow; hostel Estonian style! The catch is that the walls are thin and pipes creaky. There's a triple with its own separate entrance, a dream for privacy lovers.

**Camping Konse** (☎ 53 435 092; www.konse.ee; Suur-Jõe 44a; tent sites/d/tr from 60/650/850EEK; ℗ ) Perched on a perfect spot by the river only 1km from the Old Town, they offer tent and camper sites and a variety of bright, perky rooms with shared facilities. There's sauna, rowboat and bike rental. It can get crowded, but that makes it easier to meet people.

### MIDRANGE & TOP END

**Green Villa** (☎ 443 6040; www.greenvilla.ee; Vee tänav 21; s/d/tr/ste 600/700-1200/1300/1600EEK; ℗ ) This refurbished villa is impossible to miss, standing stately and grand in all its greenness. Most rooms have private bathrooms and there's a shared kitchen. The décor is eyesore post-Soviet kitsch, but price and location are right!

**Netti** (☎ 516 7958; www.nettihotel.ee; Hospidali tänav 11-1; s/ste 800/1200EEK; ℗ ✽ ) Each room in this amazing place is a suite in and of itself; the price is good for up to four persons. Your vibrant host will make sure you enjoy your stay, and your privacy, to the fullest. One of the best places in the city.

**Koidula Park Hotel** (☎ 447 7030; www.koidulaparkhotell.ee; Kuninga tänav 38; s/d/tr 870/1190/1700EEK Apr-Oct; ℗ ✽ ) Serenely facing the leafy Koidula Park in the town's centre is this humble, full-service hotel which boasts the environment-friendly Green Key. Rooms are snug and on the small side, but the Old World elegance makes up for that.

**Villa Ammende** (☎ 447 3888; www.ammende.ee; Mere puiestee 7; d 1550-3100EEK, ste 4300-6500EEK; ℗ ✽ ✽ ) If money's no object, this is where to spend it. Class and luxury abound in this fabulously refurbished 1905 Russian Art Nouveau mansion, which lords over sprawling grounds. This hotel-restaurant's gorgeous exterior is matched by an elegant lobby, individually antique-furnished rooms and top-notch service. A dream!

## Eating & Drinking

**Georg** (☎ 443 1110; Rüütli tänav 43; mains 30-55EEK) This smoky caféteria-style café has the cheapest eats in town. Soups, salads and daily specials for a quick fill-up.

**Piccadilly Veinikohvik** (☎ 442 0085; Pühavaimu tänav 15; mains from 40EEK) The city's only wine bar offers down-tempo bliss in comfy surroundings, a great wine and tea selection, sumptuous desserts, the largest choice of salads in town and the occasional impromptu concert.

**Veerev Õlu** (☎ 442 9848; Uus tänav 3A; mains 50-85EEK) This wins Friendliest and Cosiest Pub Award by a long shot – a tiny space with lots of good vibes, cheap beer and killer live rock-folk bands. It also serves up decent meals.

**Tex Mex** (☎ 443 0929; Akadeemia tänav 5; mains 50-100EEK) The colourful, cheerful interior is reason enough to chow down here, and the menu boasts a tempting array of first-rate Mexican fare.

**Poistipoiss** (☎ 446 4862; Vee tänav 12; mains 65-200EEK) One of Pärnu's highlights, this converted 17th-century postal house serves scrumptious, memorable Russian meals. Weekend evenings get mighty gleeful after a few vodka shots.

The **central market** (cnr Karja & Suur-Sepa tänav; ❂ 8am-5pm) is southeast of the centre.

## Entertainment

**Sunset Club** (☎ 443 0670; Ranna puiestee 3) Pärnu's biggest and most famous nightclub, set in a grandiose 1939 seafront building. Imported DJs and bands plus a wild young crowd keep things moving until the early hours.

**Citi** (☎ 444 1847; Hommiku tänav 8) By far the liveliest spot downtown, this rustic tavern-style bar/-café gets rowdy and smoky, but it's a friendly place for quick grub and to meet under-35-year-olds.

## Getting There & Away

More than 20 buses daily connect Pärnu with Tallinn (80EEK to 100EEK, two hours). Tickets for a multitude of other destinations, including Rīga and beyond, are available at the Pärnu bus station **ticket office** (☎ 447 1002; Ringi tänav; ❂ 5am-8.30pm), across from the bus station. There are also two daily Tallinn–Pärnu trains (60EEK, 2¾ hours), though the train station is an uncomfortable 5km away from the centre, down Riia maantee.

## KIHNU & RUHNU ISLANDS

Six-kilometre-long Kihnu (population 530), in the Gulf of Rīga 40km southwest of Pärnu, is almost a living museum of Estonian culture. Many of the island's women still wear traditional colourful striped skirts and the community adheres to Orthodox traditions. Transport to and from the island is easy and the number of tourists is increasing every year. Find out more at www.kihnu.ee.

Harder to reach is the remote and tiny Ruhnu (population 100), 100km southwest of Pärnu. For several centuries the island supported a Swedish population of 300, who abandoned it on 6 August 1944 to escape the advancing Red

Army. Traces of the community, including a 1644 **wooden church**, poignantly remain.

**Kihnurand Travel Agency** (☎ 446 9924; kihnurand@kihnu.ee) on Kihnu is the best agency for arranging full-day or longer excursions there.

There are regular ferries operated by **Veeteed** (☎ 443 1069; www.veeteed.ee; Pärnu) from both the port of Pärnu (adult/student/car/bike 70/35/180/25EEK, 2 hours) and from the **Munalaid port** (☎ 449 6312; adult/student/car/bike 30/15/150/10EEK, 1½hrs) in the village of Pootsi, 40km southwest of Pärnu. Tickets can be purchased at both ports. Regular flights to Kihnu (adult/student 120/30EEK, 15 minutes, one to four times daily) and Ruhnu (adult/student 300/200EEK, 25 minutes, three to four times a week) leave from **Pärnu airport** (☎ 447 5000; www.eepu.ee), a 20-minute ride northwest on bus 23 from the central bus station.

## VILJANDI & AROUND
**pop 20,500**

One of Estonia's most charming towns, Viljandi, 90km east of Pärnu, is a relaxed place to stop for a day or more or to use as a base for exploring the country's largest floodplain and bog area (no laughing!). The town itself, settled since the 12th century, has a gentle 19th-century flow to it. The **tourist information office** (☎ 433 0442; Vabaduse väljak 6; ❂ 9am-6pm Mon-Fri, 10am-3pm Sat & Sun) can help with accommodation and tours and has a computer terminal for free internet access.

A highlight is visiting **Lossimäed** (Castle Park), which sprawls out from behind the tourist information office. A picturesque green area with spectacular views over Lake Viljandi, here are the ruins of a 13th- to 15th-century castle founded by the German Knights of the Sword, open for all to muck about in. The excellent **Kondase Keskus** (☎ 433 3968; Pikk tänav 8; adult/student 15/5EEK; ❂ 10am-7pm Wed-Sun) is the country's only art gallery devoted to *art naïf*.

Some 40km west of Viljandi is the **Soomaa National Park** (☎ 445 7164; www.soomaa.com), a rich land of bogs, marsh, crisscrossing rivers and iron-rich black pools of water, perfect for a quick summer dip. Much more interesting than what the word 'bog' implies, this 37,000-hectare park is full of quirky opportunities: from a walk through the unique landscape of swampland, to a single-trunk canoe trip down one of the rivers, or an unforgettable sauna atop a floating raft. Their summertime night canoe expeditions offer a mildly spooky way of exploring swampland.

One of Estonia's most popular festivals takes place here in late July, the **Viljandi Folk Festival** (www.folk.ee), which brings out the flower power in everyone.

### Sleeping & Eating

The folks at Soomaa National Park can set you up with accommodation on their territory. Viljandi is full of nice pub-restaurants, cafés and B&Bs, which the tourist information office can recommend.

**Ingeri** ( ☎ 443 4414; Pikk tänav 2C; s 400, d 500-600EEK; P ✗ ) This small guesthouse inside a health centre on one of Viljandi's most charming streets has spacious rooms. The largest room is worthwhile for its balcony and views onto Castle Park.

**SoSo Juures** ( ☎ 55 665 295; Posti tänav 6; mains from 45EEK) Succulent Armenian cooking in Estonia is found in this unassuming café with outdoor terrace – the *harcho* (spicy lamb and rice soup) and lamb dishes will have you purring.

**Tegelaste Tuba** ( ☎ 433 3944; Pikk täanav 2B; mains from 45EEK) Their terrace overlooking the park is the hit at this tavern-style restaurant – as are the comfy interiors on cold, rainy days.

### Getting There & Away

Viljandi is served by at least 17 daily buses from Tallinn (90EEK to 105EEK, 2½ hours), 14 from Pärnu (75EEK, 1½ hours) and 15 from Tartu (50EEK to 80EEK, one hour). There is no public transport to the Soomaa National Park, but by car, the well-signposted visitors centre is 24km west of the village of Kõpu, itself 17km west of Viljandi. **Unistar Auto** ( ☎ 445 5920; www .unistar-auto.ee; Tehnika tänav 2) in Viljandi has cars for rent from 350EEK a day – a convenient way to explore Soomaa National Park.

## HIIUMAA

pop 10,500

Hiiumaa, Estonia's second-biggest island, is a quiet, sparsely populated haven, rich in bird life, with some delightful stretches of coast. The commercial centre of the island is Kärdla, where you'll find the **tourist information centre** ( ☎ 462 2232; www.hiiumaa.ee; Hiiu tänav 1; ☺ 9am-6pm Mon-Fri, 10am-3pm Sat & Sun May-Sep, 9am-5pm Mon-Fri Oct-Apr) and most of the island's services, including a bank, post office and supermarket. Get great information about the island from http://turism.moonsund.ee.

### Sights

The Hiiumaa headquarters of the **Biosphere Reserve of the West Estonian Archipelago** ( ☎ 462 2101; info@hiiuloodus.ee; Vabriku väljak 1; ☺ 9am-6pm Mon-Fri) and the tourist information centre can organise boat trips (from 200EEK per hour for up to five persons) and advise on other nature tourism opportunities around the Takhuna Peninsula, Käina Bay and Hiiumaa Islets reserve.

Headquartered 3km from Lihula on the mainland, the **Matsalu Nature Reserve** ( ☎ 472 4236; www.matsalu.ee), encompassing coastal areas on both the mainland and on Hiiumaa, is a prime migration stopover and an essential destination for bird enthusiasts.

Other attractions on Hiiumaa are its lighthouses; **Kõpu Peninsula** was the site of an ancient 16th-century lighthouse (although the present one dates from 1845). Another guaranteed memory for life is the walk along the 3km **Sääre Tirp** on the southern coast of Kassari; it's a narrow spit of land and rock which winds ever thinner into the sea.

At **Suuremõisa**, 6km inland from Heltermaa port, you can explore the majestic grounds of the late-baroque **Suuremõisa manor & park** (adult/student 15/5EEK; ☺ 10am-5pm May-Sep).

### Sleeping & Eating

The Kärdla tourist information centre can advise on a range of accommodation options throughout Hiiumaa. Most hotels cut their rates by up to 30% from September to April.

**Allika Guesthouse** ( ☎ 462 9026; www.allika.com; Suuremõisa; s from 500, d 700-1000EEK) Part of the very green, gorgeous Suuremõisa castle complex, this was originally the servant's quarters. The rooms are airy, country-style but vibrantly modern.

**Padu Hotel** ( ☎ 463 3037; Heltermaa mnt 22; s/d/ste 600/750/900EEK; P ) A convenient place in the centre of Kärdla, it boasts older and newer wings, each tastefully decorated, inviting and comfy-cosy.

**Adramadrus** ( ☎ 443 2082; Vabaduse tänav 15, Kärdla; mains from 50EEK) This is the perfect place to try out the locally brewed beers: the old-style tavern feel is warm and inviting, and the menu is varied.

**Vetsi Tall** ( ☎ 462 2550; Kassari; tent space/trailer space/ s/d 50/200/220/440EEK; P ) Located on the road to Orjaku on the sparse, scenic Kassari peninsula in the south of Hiiumaa, this is a camping ground with a sense of humour; the wooden cabins are round, log-shaped. Tiny too!

### Getting There & Away

**SSC** ( ☎ 452 4444; www.laevakompanii.ee) operates ferries between Rohuküla and Heltermaa (adult/student/car 25/12/75EEK, 1½ hours, four to six times daily). Two daily buses from Tallinn travel with the ferry directly to Kärdla or Käina (160EEK, 4¾ hours). **Avies Air** ( ☎ 605 8022; www.avies.ee) flies between Tallinn and Kärdla (adult/student one way 245/215EEK, 30 minutes, once or twice daily).

## SAAREMAA
pop 35,700

Saaremaa (literally 'island land') is synonymous to Estonians with space, spruce, peace, fresh air and killer beer. Tourists would add 'charming, rustic villages, remains of WWII, a meteorite crater and a fairy-tale castle' to the list – plus second the vote for beer! Saaremaa has a long history of beer home-brewing, and even its factory-produced brew has a great reputation. Tuulik and Tehumardi are the most popular (but don't mention that they're now brewed in Tartu). The country's second-biggest beer festival takes place in the end of July.

During the Soviet era, the entire island was off-limits (due to an early-radar system and rocket base). This unwittingly resulted in a minimum of industrial build-up and the protection of the island's rural charm. Estonia's largest island offers idyllic getaways among juniper groves or along poetically deserted stretches of coastline.

### Orientation & Information

To reach Saaremaa you must first cross Muhu, the small island where the ferry from the mainland docks and which is connected to Saaremaa by a 2.5km causeway. Kuressaare, the capital of Saaremaa, on the south coast is a natural base for visitors.

Kuressaare's **tourist information office** ( ☎ 453 3120; www.saaremaa.ee; Tallinna tänav 2; ☽ 9am-7pm Mon-Fri, to 5pm Sat, to 3pm Sun May-Sep, to 5pm Mon-Fri Oct-Apr) can help you make the best of your stay. Internet access is available at **Kultuurikeskus** (Tallinna mnt 6; per hr 20EEK; ☽ 10am-7pm Mon-Fri, 10am-4pm Sat).

You can change money at the bus station or at any of the several banks on Raekoja plats. The **post office** (Torni mnt 1) is north of the town square.

## Sights

The yellow **town hall** in the main Raekoja plats (Town Hall Sq) dates from 1654. Opposite stands the baroque **Weighing House** built in 1663.

The island's most distinctive landmark is the fantastic **Bishop's Castle** (1338–80) at the southern end of the town. It looks plucked from a fairy tale, and now houses the **Saaremaa Regional Museum** ( ☎ 455 6307; adult/child 30/15EEK; ☽ 11am-7pm May-Sep, 11am-7pm Wed-Sun Oct-Apr).

At Angla, 40km from Kuressaare just off the road to the harbour on the Leisi road, is a photogenic group of five **windmills** by the roadside. Two kilometres away, along the road opposite the windmills, is **Karja church**, a striking 13th- to 14th-century German Gothic church.

At Kaali, 18km from Kuressaare on the road towards Muhu, is a 110m-wide, water-filled **crater** formed by a meteorite at least 3000 years ago. In ancient Scandinavian mythology the site was known as 'the sun's grave'. It's Europe's largest and most accessible meteorite crater, but looks mighty tiny up close!

Saaremaa's magic can really be felt along the **Sõrve Peninsula**, jutting out south and west of Kuressaare. This sparsely populated strip of land saw some of the heaviest fighting in WWII. Some bases and antitank defence lines still stand. A bike or car trip along the coastline provides some of the most spectacular sights on the island. Several daily buses from Kuressaare bus station head down the coast of the peninsula. Yet a trip anywhere on this island is likely to be memorable – particularly the sparsely populated, wilder northwestern section.

## Tours

**Arensburg travel agency** ( ☎ 453 3360; abr@tt.ee; Tallinna mnt 25, Kuressaare) This reliable agency offers many tours, specialising in boat trips to remote islands such as Abruka.

**Saaremaa Reisibüroo** ( ☎ 455 5079; Lossi tänav 11, Kuressaare) Another group of winners who can help arrange your excursions.

## Sleeping

The tourist information office can organise beds in private apartments throughout the region. Farm stays are available across the island. Hotel prices are up to 40% cheaper September through April.

ESTONIA

**Kämping Mändjala** ( ☎ 454 4193; www.mandjala.ee; camp site/cabin per person/double 25/160/700EEK ℗ ) ) Just 10km west of Kuressaare is this pleasant, well-organised camping ground, with cabins and separate houses for two to four persons. Buses from Kuressaare to Torgu or Sääre (three per day) go to the Mändjala bus stop. There are water-sporting possibilities.

**Saaremaa School Hostel** ( ☎ 455 4388; www.syg.edu .ee; Kingu tänav 6, Kuressaare; dm 130-145EEK, s/d 250/350EEK) A very cool hostel; being attached to a school, there's a small gym and internet room. A bonus is that dorm rooms hold no more than four persons. On the minus side, there hasn't been much renovation here in ages.

**Lossi Hotel** ( ☎ 453 3633; lossihotell@tt.ee; Lossi tänav 27, Kuressaare; s/d/ste 1090/1350/1750EEK; ⌗ ) Located right on the castle grounds, this dainty little hotel is a nice slice of a dream come true, with an Art Nouveau touch. The main attraction here is the castle and surrounding park right at your doorstep. Mosquitoes love the nearby moat, however, so arm yourself!

**Pädaste Manor** ( ☎ 454 8800; www.padaste.ee; Pädaste village, Muhu; s/d/ste from 1740/2425/4305EEK; ℗ ⌗ ⌗ ) In recent years, this manor has distinguished itself from all others in offering ridiculously beautiful scenery plus a combination of stunningly but humbly furnished rooms, one of the best restaurants in the country, a small spa with alternative therapies and a full menu of activities including horseback riding and fishing.

### Eating & Drinking

**Wildenbergi** ( ☎ 454 5325; Tallinna mnt 1, Kuressaare) The atmosphere is so inviting in this subdued, elegant café/bar, time seems to have stopped within. Some of the island's best coffees, teas and cakes are the main draw.

**Kalaküla** ( ☎ 538 58966; Jõelepa village; mains from 80EEK) You came all the way to Saaremaa; you need to try the fish. This is your best bet – fresh fish served up deliciously in idyllic surroundings. It's 25km north east of Kuressaare on the main road to Muhu and Tallinn.

**Veski** ( ☎ 453 3776; Pärna tänav 19, Kuressaare; meals 45-145EEK; ℗ ) How often can you say you've dined inside a windmill? Without being too touristy, this place keeps both quality and ambience at a premium. There are some vegetarian choices, plus a children's menu.

**La Perla** ( ☎ 453 6910; Lossi tänav 3, Kuressaare; mains 50-120EEK) Right off Raekoja plats, this homy Italian restaurant is the island's gastronomic

saviour – some of the best food in Saaremaa is found here.

### Getting There & Around

A year-round vehicle ferry runs throughout the day from Virtsu on the mainland to the island of Muhu, which is joined by a causeway to Saaremaa. At least eight direct buses daily travel each way between Tallinn and Kuressaare (170EEK to 200EEK, 4½ hours) via the ferry. There are also three daily buses to/from Tartu (205EEK to 225EEK, five hours), and Pärnu (200EEK to 220EEK, five hours). **Avies Air** ( ☎ 605 8022; www.avies.ee) flies from Tallinn to Kuressaare twice per day Monday to Friday and once on Sunday (adult/student one way 350/255EEK, 45 minutes).

# ESTONIA DIRECTORY

## ACCOMMODATION

Finding a decent place to lay your head in Estonia is not a problem; even budget (roughly defined in this chapter as places offering beds for under 350EEK per night) places far afield tend to be tasteful, clean and very orderly. Tallinn has a glut of amazing top-end hotels (defined here as places charging over 1200EEK per double) with full services and luxuries, and a so-so selection of midrange choices, however in smaller towns and villages it shouldn't be a problem finding budget accommodation at a B&B or hostel for under 300EEK per person. HI cards are widely accepted in most hostels. There are a few *kämpingud* (camping grounds; open from mid-May to September) that allow you to pitch a tent, but most consist of permanent wooden cabins, with communal showers and toilets. Places are listed in our Sleeping sections in order of ascending price.

Farms and homestays offer more than a choice of rooms and in many cases meals, sauna and a wide range of activities are on offer. Your best bet would be to book via the regional tourist information centres throughout Estonia. There's a search engine at www .visitestonia.com for all types of accommodation throughout the country.

## ACTIVITIES

Many travel agencies can arrange a variety of activity-based tours of Estonia. A detailed list of companies keeping tourists active can be found at www.turismiweb.ee. **Matkad.ee** ( ☎ 508

7600; www.matkad.ee; Kadaka puistee 31, Tallinn) is an excellent contact. It organises superb rafting, canoe (daytime as well as night) and hiking trips among other things, and can tailor-make an expedition to suit your desired adrenaline levels. **Raeturist** ( ☎ 668 8400; www.raeturist.ee; Narva mnt 13A, Tallinn), offers a nine-day bicycle trip throughout Estonia. **Jalgrattakeskus** ( ☎ 637 6779; Tartu mnt 73, Tallinn), rents bicycles by the hour with deals for long-term rentals.

Cross-country skiing is extremely popular. Head to Otepää (p336) where there are several skiing centres that hire out equipment. See www.otepaa.ee for more information.

The word scuba diving is more associated with Egypt and Thailand than Estonia with its frigid Baltic waters, but the devoted crew at **Maremark** ( ☎ 601 3446; www.maremark.ee; L Koidula 38, Tallinn) offer introductory courses and organises events for amateurs and professionals alike all summer long. Thrilling sea kayaking excursions, as well as other ecofriendly activities are offered by the highly recommended **Reimann Retked** ( ☎ 511 4099; www.retked.ee).

## BUSINESS HOURS

Shops are generally open every day in Estonia, from 9am to 6pm or 7pm Monday to Friday, 10am to 4pm Saturday and Sunday. Food shops and supermarkets are mainly open until 11pm every day. Alcohol can only be sold until 11pm. Restaurants are generally open from 11am to 11pm Sunday to Friday and until 1am or 2am on Friday and Saturday. Cafés often open at 8am and close by 9pm. Clubs are generally open Wednesday to Saturday from 10pm to 5am or 6am. Only exceptions to this general rule are listed in the text.

## CUSTOMS

If arriving from another EU country, the limits for alcohol and tobacco are generous; see www.customs.ee for the latest restrictions. Antique objects made outside Estonia before 1850 or in Estonia before 1945 need special permits to be taken out of the country; these can be obtained from the **National Heritage Board** ( ☎ 640 3050; www.muinas.ee; Uus tänav 18).

## EMBASSIES & CONSULATES

For up-to-date contact details of Estonian diplomatic organisations as well as foreign embassies and consulates in Estonia, contact the **Estonian Foreign Ministry** ( ☎ 637 7000; www.vm.ee; Islandi Väljak 1, Tallinn).

## Estonian Embassies & Consulates

**Australia** ( ☎ 02 9810 7468; estikon@ozemail.com.au; 86 Louisa Rd, Birchgrove, Sydney NSW 2041)
**Canada** ( ☎ 1-613-789 4222; www.estemb.ca; 260 Dalhousie St, Suite 210 Ottawa, Ontario KIN 7E4)
**Finland** ( ☎ 9-622 0260; www.estemb.fi; Itäinen Puistotie 10, 00140 Helsinki)
**France** ( ☎ 01-56 62 22 00; 46, rue Pierre Charron, 75008 Paris)
**Germany** Berlin ( ☎ 30-25 460 600; www.estemb.de; Hildebrandstrasse 5 10785 Berlin); Hamburg ( ☎ 40-450 40 26; Badestrasse 38, 20143 Hamburg)
**Ireland** ( ☎ 1-219 6730; embassy.dublin@mfa.ee; Riversdale House St Ann's, Ailesbury Rd, Dublin)
**Latvia** ( ☎ 781 20 20; www.estemb.lv; Skolas iela 13, Rīga)
**Lithuania** ( ☎ 5-278 0200; www.estemb.lt; Mickeviciaus gatvė 4a, Vilnius)
**Netherlands** ( ☎ 3120-316 5440; embassy.hague@mfa.ee; Snipweg 101, 1118 DP Schiphol)
**Russia** Moscow ( ☎ 495-290 5013; www.estemb.ru; ul Malo Kislovsky 5, 103009 Moscow); St Petersburg ( ☎ 812-702 0920; Bolshaya Monetnaya ul 14, St Petersburg)
**Sweden** ( ☎ 08-5451 2280; www.estemb.se; Tyrgatan 3, Stockholm)
**UK** ( ☎ 020-7589 3428; www.estonia.gov.uk; 16 Hyde Park Gate, London SW7 5DG)
**USA** Washington DC ( ☎ 202-588 0101; www.estemb.org; 2131 Massachusetts Ave, NW, Washington DC 20008); New York ( ☎ 212-883 0636; www.nyc.estemb.org; 600 3rd Ave, 26th fl, New York, NY)

## Embassies & Consulates in Estonia

All embassies and consulates are in Tallinn unless otherwise indicated.
**Australia** ( ☎ 650 9308; mati@standard.ee; Marja tänav 9)
**Canada** ( ☎ 627 3311; tallinn@canada.ee; Toomkooli tänav 13)
**Finland** ( ☎ 610 3200; www.finland.ee; Kohtu tänav 4)
**France** ( ☎ 631 1492; www.ambafrance-ee.org; Toom-Kuninga tänav 20)
**Germany** ( ☎ 627 5300; www.tallinn.diplo.de; Toom-Kuninga tänav 11)
**Ireland** ( ☎ 681 1888; embassytallinn@eircom.net; Vene tänav 2)
**Latvia** ( ☎ 627 7850; embassy.estonia@mfa.gov.lv; Tõnismägi tänav 10)
**Lithuania** ( ☎ 641 2014; www.hot.ee/lietambasada; Uus tänav 15)
**Netherlands** ( ☎ 680 5500; www.netherlandsembassy.ee; Rahukohtu tänav 4-I)
**Russia** Tallinn consulate ( ☎ 646 4146; www.estonia.mid.ru; Lai tänav 18); Narva ( ☎ 356 0652; konsot@narvanet.ee; Kiriku tänav 8)

ESTONIA

**Sweden** ( ☎ 640 5600; www.sweden.ee; Pikk tänav 28)
**UK** ( ☎ 667 4700; www.britishembassy.ee; Wismari tänav 6)
**USA** ( ☎ 668 8100; www.usemb.ee; Kentmanni tänav 20)

## FESTIVALS & EVENTS

Estonia has a busy festival calendar, encompassing all kinds of cultural interests. A good list of upcoming major events throughout Estonia can be found at www.culture.ee.

**All-Estonian Song Festival** (www.laulupidu.ee) Convenes every five years and culminates in a 30,000-strong traditional choir, due in Tallinn in 2009.

**Baltika International Folk Festival** A week of music, dance and displays focusing on Baltic and other folk traditions, this festival is shared between Rīga, Vilnius and Tallinn; the next one will be in Tallinn in June 2007.

**Jaanipäev** (St John's Eve; Jun 23) The biggest occasion in Estonia; a celebration of the pagan Midsummer's Night, best experienced far from the city along a stretch of beach where huge bonfires are lit for all-night parties.

## GAY & LESBIAN TRAVELLERS

While open displays of same-sex affection are infrequent in Estonia, the overall attitude is more of curiosity and openness than antagonism. For more information, you can contact the **Estonian Gay League** ( ☎ 653 4812; gayliit@hotmail .com), or **Mea Culpa** ( ☎ 645 4545; info@meaculpa.ee), both NGOs. A repository of all that is gay in Estonia can be found at www.gay.ee. Tallinn has its own Gay Pride Week in early August (www.pride.ee).

## HOLIDAYS

**New Year's Day** 1 January
**Independence Day** 24 February
**Good Friday & Easter** March/April
**Spring Day** 1 May
**Victory Day** (1919; Battle of Võnnu) 23 June
**Jaanipäev** (St John's Day; Midsummer's Night) 24 June
**Day of Restoration of Independence** (1991) 20 August
**Christmas Day** 25 December
**Boxing Day** 26 December

## LANGUAGE

Like Finnish, Estonian belongs to the Finno-Ugric family of languages. It's a fantastically difficult language to learn, with 14 cases and a lack of gender, double infinitives, articles and even a lack of the future tense. Most every Estonian in Tallinn speaks at least some English, and those under 25 speak it fluently. Elsewhere in the country, people have at least some knowledge of English. Fewer Russians speak English as fluently.

A growing number of Russians in Estonia speak Estonian, and most Estonians speak some Russian.

See the Language chapter at the back of the book for pronunciation guidelines and useful words and phrases.

## MONEY

Estonia introduced its own currency, the kroon (EEK; pronounced krohn) in June 1992; it's now pegged to the euro. The kroon comes in two, five, 10, 25, 50, 100 and 500EEK notes. One kroon is divided into 100 sents, and there are coins of 10, 20 and 50 sents, as well as one- and five-kroon coins. The euro is expected to be introduced as common currency in 2008.

The best foreign currencies to bring into Estonia are euros and US dollars, although all Western currencies are readily exchangeable.

All major credit cards are widely accepted; Visa is the most common, Amex the least. Most banks (but not stores and restaurants) accept travellers cheques, but their commissions can be high. There are frequent student, pensioner and group discounts on transport, in museums and in some shops upon presentation of accredited ID.

The *käibemaks* consumption tax (VAT), levied on most goods and services, is 18%. Tipping in service industries has become the norm, but generally no more than 10% is expected.

## POST

Mail service in and out of Estonia is highly efficient. There is a poste restante bureau, where mail is kept for up to one month, at Tallinn's **central post office** (Narva mnt 1, Tallinn 10101). To post a letter up to 20g to Europe/rest of the world costs 6.50/8EEK.

## TELEPHONE

All telephone numbers in Estonia are written as full seven-digit numbers, the first two of which used to be indicated separately as regional codes. To call Estonia from abroad, dial the country code ☎ 372 followed by the seven digit local number or the seven or eight digit mobile phone number, which always begins with ☎ 5. There is no international operator here: the regular operator (no English spoken) is ☎ 165.

---

**EMERGENCY NUMBERS**

- 24-hour roadside assistance ☎ 1188
- Fire, ambulance and urgent medical advice ☎ 112
- Police ☎ 110
- Tallinn's First Aid hotline ☎ 697 1145 can advise you in English about the nearest treatment centres

---

## VISAS

Ensure your passport will last at least two months more than your travels. Citizens of EU countries, plus Australia, Canada, New Zealand, the USA and many other countries can enter Estonia visa-free for a maximum 90-day stay over a six-month period. South African citizens need a visa to enter, though if they already possess a visa for Latvia or Lithuania they can enter on that visa.

Visa regulations are constantly changing, so check with an Estonian consulate or embassy or directly with the **Estonian Foreign Ministry** (☎ 631 7600; www.vm.ee; Islandi Väljak 1, Tallinn). Note that visas cannot be obtained at the border.

# TRANSPORT IN ESTONIA

## GETTING THERE & AWAY
### Air
The national carrier **Estonian Air** (code OV; ☎ 640 1101; www.estonian-air.ee; Vabaduse väljak 10) links Tallinn with some 20 cities in Europe and Russia, and at reasonable prices. Other airlines serving **Tallinn airport** (www.tallinn-airport .ee), include **Air Baltic** (code BT; ☎ 640 7750; www .airbaltic.com), which has flights to Vilnius and **Finnair** (code AY; ☎ 611 0905; www.finnair.com) , with flights to Helsinki.

**Copterline** (www.copterline.ee) runs pricey helicopter flights between Helsinki and Tallinn's Copterline Terminal, at the Linnahall harbour, nearly hourly from 7am to 7pm weekdays (one way 1395EEK to 3100EEK, 18 minutes).

## Land
### BUS
Buses are the cheapest but least comfortable way of reaching the Baltics. **Eurolines** (☎ 680 0909; www.eurolines.ee; Bus Station, Lastekodu tänav 46, Tallinn) connects Tallinn with several cities in Germany and Poland, and from there to cities throughout Europe. Direct services connect Tallinn to Rīga (200EEK to 230EEK, five to 5½ hours, ten daily) and Vilnius (430EEK, 10½ hours, two daily).

Buses leave Tallinn for St Petersburg five times daily (270EEK to 350EEK, eight hours). There is also one bus from Tallinn to Kaliningrad daily (350EEK, 15 hours).

### CAR & MOTORCYCLE
From Finland, just put your vehicle on a Helsinki–Tallinn ferry. If approaching Estonia from the south or Western Europe, make sure to avoid crossing through Kaliningrad or Belarus – not only will you need hard-to-get visas for these countries, you are likely to face hassles from traffic police and encounter roads in abominable conditions!

### TRAIN
An overnight train runs every evening between Moscow and Tallinn (870/530EEK in 2nd/3rd class, 15½ hours) operated by **GO Rail** (☎ 615 6850; www.gorail.ee). There is currently no train service to St Petersburg.

## Sea
### FINLAND
About 25 ferries, hydrofoils and catamarans cross between Helsinki and Tallinn daily. Ferries make the crossing in 2½ to 3½ hours, hydrofoils in just over an hour. All companies provide concessions, allow pets and bikes (for a fee) and charge higher prices for weekend travel. Expect to pay around the price of an adult ticket extra to take a car. Prices are considerably cheaper for ships operating mid-August through May. There's lots of competition, so check all the companies for their special offers and packages.

**Tallink** (☎ 640 9808; www.tallink.ee) runs up to three ferries and seven catamarans daily. Ferry tickets start from 280EEK and catamaran tickets cost from 390EEK to 670EEK. **Lindaline** (☎ 699 9333; www.lindaliini.ee) makes up to eight hydrofoil crossings each way daily (single/return 450/660EEK), leaving from the Linnahall harbour (behind the huge, monstrous concrete edifice). **Eckerö Line** (☎ 631 8606; www.eckeroline.ee) operates a daily car-carrying catamaran from Terminal B, making the crossing in 3½ hours (single/return 345/380EEK, cabins from 310EEK).

**Nordic Jet Line** (☎ 613 7000; www.njl.ee) has several car-carrying catamarans departing

Terminal C, making the trip in around 1½ hours, seven times a day (single tickets from 420EEK). **Silja Line** ( ☎ 611 6661; www .silja.ee) has ferries and catamarans leaving from terminal A (singles from 520EEK) and offer worthwhile day-trip packages to Helsinki. **Viking Line** ( ☎ 666 3966; www.viking line.ee) operates large car ferries, departing twice daily from Terminal A (single from 735EEK).

### SWEDEN
**Tallink** ( ☎ 640 9808; www.tallink.ee) runs nightly ferries from Tallinn's Terminal D to Stockholm (from 360EEK up to 5740EEK for a luxury suite, 15 hours), as well as daily ferries from Paldiski, 52km west of Tallinn, to Kappelskär near Stockholm (from 375EEK, 12 hours). There are reductions for students and children under 18. Tickets should be booked well in advance in Tallinn or Stockholm's Free Harbour **Frihamnen** ( ☎ 08-667 0001).

## GETTING AROUND
### Air
**Avies Air** ( ☎ 605 8022; www.avies.ee) operates flights from Tallinn to Kuressaare on Saaremaa once or twice daily from Sunday to Friday, and daily flights to Kärdla on Hiiumaa. Flights to the island of Ruhnu leave from **Pärnu airport** ( ☎ 447 5000; www.eepu.ee).

### Bicycle
Estonia is small and predominantly flat with relatively good roads and light traffic – perfect for this green mode of travel. As few locals cycle within main cities, be wary of inconsiderate motorists. However, between cities, cycling has exploded in recent years as a sport and mode of transport. Estonia has some 4000km of well-signed bike trails crisscrossing its territory and is working hard to develop ecotourism. There are Tallinn cycling road maps at www.tallinn.ee, listed under public transport timetables, and on sale at bookstores.

### Bus
Buses are a good option, as they're more frequent, and faster than trains, and cover many destinations not serviced by the limited rail network.

Buses to within about 40km of Tallinn leave from the local bus station beside the train station. Information and timetables can be had via **Harju Liinid** ( ☎ 644 1801; ☾ 24hr). For detailed bus information and advance tickets for all other country destinations, contact the central bus station **Autobussijaam** ( ☎ 680 0900; www.bus sireisid.ee; Lastekodu tänav 46; ☾ 6.30am-9pm).

### Car & Motorcycle
An International Driving Permit (IDP) is necessary, as are your vehicle's registration papers and compulsory accident insurance, which can be bought at border crossings. Fuel and service stations are widely available, though spare parts for sports or luxury cars might be hard to find.

In general, Estonian drivers are reasonably compliant with the laws and quite vigilant for police traps, which are nonetheless relatively few. Speed limits are changed yearly, even seasonally, depending on the previous year's accident record on the respective routes. Intercity speed limits are usually 90 to 100km/h, with some stretches up to 110km/h. Anyone stopped for speeding will have their breath analysed; the blood-alcohol limit is 0.02%. Wearing a seatbelt is compulsory but not strictly enforced. Road conditions between towns tends to be decent to good – most are well-maintained and very safe to drive on; within cities they are not always as good.

### Train
Trains are slower and rarer than buses; the most frequent trains service the suburbs of Tallinn. Regional train schedules are listed at www.edel.ee. The affordable first-class wagon on trains to Tartu make a great alternative to bus travel.

# Hungary

Hungary's uniqueness extends beyond its incomprehensible tongue. Here's your chance to strip down to your swimmers in the midwinter minuses and loll around an open-air thermal spa, while snowy patches glisten around you. Following that, you could go to a smoky bar where a Romani band yelps while a crazed crowd whacks its boot-heels, as commanded by Hungarian tradition. Or go clubbing in an ancient bathhouse, where all dance in swimsuits, waist-deep in healing waters.

If these pursuits don't appeal, check out Roman ruins, ancient castles, Turkish minarets in baroque cities, or experience the rural pleasures of cowboys riding astride five horses, storks nesting on streetlamps, and a sea of apricot trees in bloom.

Cosmopolitan Budapest is a capital to rival any on the continent – with world-class operas, monumental historical buildings, and the Danube River flowing through the middle of it all. Prices here are somewhere in the middle: not nearly as high as Austria or nearly as reasonable as Ukraine. Having established itself as a state in the year 1000, Hungary has a long history, a rich culture and strong folk traditions that are well worth exploring. So go ahead, dive in.

**HUNGARY**

## FAST FACTS

- **Area** 93,000 sq km
- **Capital** Budapest
- **Currency** forint (Ft); €1 = 276Ft; US$1 = 216Ft; UK£1 = 410Ft; A$1 = 164Ft; ¥100 = 185Ft; NZ$1 = 143Ft
- **Famous for** paprika, Bull's Blood and *csárda* music
- **Official Language** Hungarian (Magyar)
- **Phrases** *jo napot kivanok* (good day); *szia* (hi/bye); *köszönöm* (thank you)
- **Population** 10 million
- **Telephone Codes** country code ☎ 36; international access code ☎ 00; intercity access code ☎ 06
- **Visa** no visa required for most countries if you stay less than 90 days; see p408

## HIGHLIGHTS

- Take a bath and ease your soul and your joints in Budapest's **thermal baths** (p364) and throw in a mudpack or water massage to get your blood flowing.
- See the capital city bathed in lights from atop Buda's **Castle Hill** (p363). The gothic Parliament building glows like a birthday cake.
- Taste some of Hungary's greatest wines in the alluring Valley of Beautiful Women in **Eger** (p400) and see the city's wonderful ancient castle and baroque architecture.
- Watch the cowboys ride at Bugac in **Kiskunsági Nemzeti Park** (p397) at the heart of the Hungarian *puszta* (plain) – the stuff of myth and legend.
- Feel a bit Mediterranean in the southern town of **Pécs** (p391), exploring the 16th-century Mosque Church and other Turkish sights.

## ITINERARIES

- **One week** Make sure that you spend at least four days in Budapest, checking out the sights, museums and pavement cafés. On your fifth day take a day trip to a Danube Bend town. See the open-air museum in Szentendre or the cathedral at Esztergom. Day six can be spent getting a morning train to Pécs and seeing the lovely Turkish remains, and checking out the many gal-

leries in town. Let your hair down on day seven and try some local wine in Eger, a baroque town set in red-wine country.

- **Two weeks** If you've already spent a week in Budapest, you still have time to cover a lot of ground, since all the places mentioned in this chapter are no more than five hours by train from the capital. If you are here in the summer, make sure you spend some time exploring the towns around Lake Balaton, or just chill out on the beach by the side of this popular lake. Tihany is a rambling hillside village filled with craftsmen's houses, set on a peninsula that is a protected nature zone. Keszthely is an old town with a great palace in addition to a beach. Alternatively, head south to Pécs and see more of the Great Plain. Szeged is on the Tisza River and Kecskemét is further north. Finish your trip in Eger.

## CLIMATE & WHEN TO GO

Hungary has a temperate continental climate. July and August are the warmest months, and when the thermometer hits 27°C it can feel much hotter, given that most places don't have air-con. Spring is unpredictable, but usually arrives in April. November is already rainy and chilly; January and February are the coldest, dreariest months, with temperatures dropping below 0°C. September, with loads of sunshine, mild temperatures and grape-harvest festivals in the countryside, may be the best time to visit. May, with a profusion of flowers and sunshine, is a close second. See p911 for climate charts.

The busiest tourist season is July and August (Lake Balaton is especially crowded), but hotels quote high-season prices from April to October. In provincial and smaller towns, attractions are often closed, or have reduced hours, from October to May.

## HISTORY
### Pre-Hungarian Hungary

The plains of the Carpathian Basin attracted waves of migration, from both east and west, long before the Magyar tribes decided to settle here. The Celts occupied the area in the 3rd century BC but the Romans conquered and expelled them just before the Christian era. The lands west of the Danube (Transdanubia) in today's Hungary became part of the Roman province of Pannonia, where a Roman legion was stationed at the town of Aquincum (now

---

**HOW MUCH?**

- **Lángos (fried dough snack)** 120-220Ft
- **Hostel bed** 1600-3000Ft
- **Loaf of bread** 160Ft
- **Midrange double room** 8500-14,200Ft
- **Symphony ticket in Budapest** 1200-2500Ft

**LONELY PLANET INDEX**

- **Litre of petrol** 265Ft
- **Litre of bottled water** 150Ft
- **Beer (a bottle from grocery store)** 130Ft
- **Souvenir T-shirt** 900-2500Ft
- **Street snack (gyro)** 500Ft

# HUNGARY

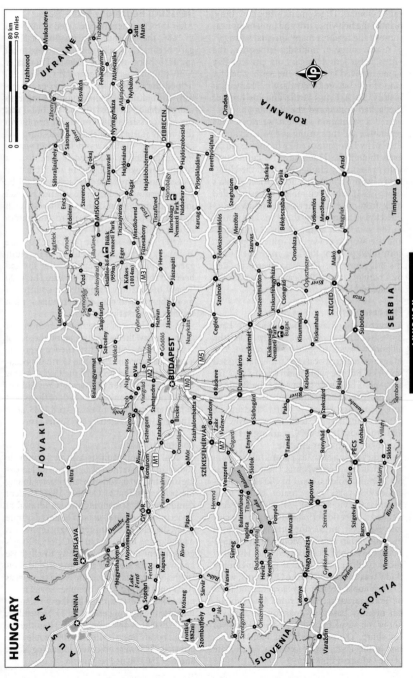

called Óbuda). The Romans brought writing, planted the first vineyards and built baths near some of the region's many thermal springs.

A new surge of nomadic tribesmen, the Huns, who lent Hungary its present-day name, arrived on the scene with a leader who would become legendary in Hungarian history. By AD 441, Attila and his brother Bleda had conquered the Romans and acquired a reputation as great warriors. This reputation still runs strong and you will notice that many Hungarians carry the name Attila, even though the Huns have no connection with present-day Hungarians, and the Huns' short-lived empire did not outlast Attila's death (453), when remaining tribesmen fled back from whence they came. Many tribes filled the vacuum left by the Huns and settled in the area, such as the Goths, Longobards and the Avars, a powerful Turkic people who controlled parts of the area from the 5th to the 8th centuries. The Avars were subdued by Charlemagne in 796, leaving space for the Franks and Slavs to move in.

## The Conquest

Magyar (Hungarian) tribes are said to have moved in around 896, when Árpád led the alliance of seven tribes into the region. The Magyars, a fierce warrior tribe, terrorised much of Europe with raids reaching as far as Spain. They were stopped at the Battle of Augsburg in 955 and subsequently converted to Christianity. Hungary's first king and its patron saint, István (Stephen), was crowned on Christmas Day in 1000, marking the foundation of the Hungarian state.

Medieval Hungary was a powerful kingdom that included Transylvania (now in Romania), Transcarpathia (now in Ukraine), modern-day Slovakia and Croatia. Under King Matthias Corvinus (1458–90), Hungary experienced a brief flowering of Renaissance culture. However, in 1526 the Ottomans defeated the Hungarian army at Mohács and by 1541 Buda Castle had been seized and Hungary sliced in three. The central part, including Buda, was controlled by the Ottomans, while Transdanubia, present-day Slovakia, and parts of Transcarpathia were ruled by Hungarian nobility based in Pozsony (Bratislava) under the auspices of the Austrian House of Habsburg. The principality of Transylvania, east of the Tisza, prospered as a vassal state of the Ottoman Empire.

## Habsburg Hegemony & the Wars

After the Ottomans were evicted from Buda in 1686, the Habsburg domination of Hungary began. The 'enlightened absolutism' of the Habsburg monarchs Maria Theresa (r 1740–80) and her son Joseph II (r 1780–90) helped the country leap forward economically and culturally. Rumblings of Hungarian independence surfaced off and on, but it was the unsuccessful 1848 Hungarian revolution that really started to shake the Habsburg oligarchy. After Austria was defeated in war by Prussia in 1866, a weakened empire struck a compromise with Hungary in 1867, creating a dual monarchy. The two states would be self-governing in domestic affairs, but act jointly in matters of common interest, such as foreign relations. The Austro-Hungarian monarchy lasted until WWI.

After WWI and the collapse of the Habsburg Empire in November 1918, Hungary was proclaimed a republic. But she had been on the losing side of the war. The 1920 Treaty of Trianon stripped the country of more than two-thirds of its territory – a hot topic of conversation to this day.

In 1941 Hungary's attempts to recover lost territories saw the nation in war, on the side of Nazi Germany. When leftists tried to negotiate a separate peace in 1944, the Germans occupied Hungary and brought the fascist Arrow Cross Party to power. The Arrow Cross immediately began deporting hundreds of thousands of Jews to Auschwitz. By early April 1945, all of Hungary was liberated by the Soviet army.

## Communism

By 1947 the communists assumed complete control of the government and began nationalising industry and dividing up large estates among the peasantry. On 23 October 1956, student demonstrators demanding the withdrawal of Soviet troops were fired upon. The next day Imre Nagy, the reformist minister of agriculture, was named prime minister. On 28 October Nagy's government offered an amnesty to all those involved in the violence and promised to abolish the hated secret police, the ÁVH (known as ÁVO until 1949). On 4 November Soviet tanks moved into Budapest, crushing the uprising. By the time the fighting ended on 11 November, some 25,000 people were dead. Then the reprisals began: an estimated 20,000 people were arrested; 2000 were executed, including Nagy; another 250,000 fled to Austria.

By the 1970s Hungary had abandoned strict central economic control in favour of a limited market system, often referred to as 'Goulash Communism'. In June 1987 Károly Grósz took over as premier and Hungary began moving towards full democracy. The huge numbers of East Germans who were able to slip through the Iron Curtain by leaving via Hungary may have contributed to the eventual crumbling of the Berlin Wall.

## The Republic

At their party congress in February 1989 the Hungarian communists agreed to give up their monopoly on power. The Republic of Hungary was proclaimed in October, and democratic elections were scheduled for March 1990. Hungary changed its political system with scarcely a murmur, and the last Soviet troops left the country in June 1991.

The painful transition to a full market economy resulted in declining living standards for most people and a recession in the early 1990s, but the end of the 20th and early years of the 21st century have seen astonishing growth. Hungary became a fully fledged member of NATO in 1999. In a national referendum during April 2003, the Hungarian people voted to join the European Union (EU), and the country became one of the newest members of the EU on 1 May 2004.

The dissolution of intra-European customs controls at airports and borders was immediate, but border restrictions with neighbouring members Austria, Slovakia and Slovenia will not be completely removed any time soon. Hungary aims to adopt the euro by 2010, providing that its high economic deficit is brought within acceptable levels.

In April 2006 the Socialist-led coalition won the parliamentary elections, becoming the first government to win consecutive terms in office since the restoration of democracy in 1990. The new prime minister, Ferenc Gyurcsany, was chosen by the Socialist Party to succeed the former prime minister, Peter Medgyessy. The coalition has been in government since the last elections in 2002.

## PEOPLE

Approximately 10.6 million Magyar people live within the national borders, and another five million Hungarians and their descendants are abroad. The estimated 1.44 million Hungarians in Transylvania constitute the largest ethnic minority in Europe, and there are another 520,000 in Slovakia, 295,000 in Serbia and Montenegro, 157,000 in Ukraine and 40,600 in Austria.

Ethnic Magyars make up approximately 93% of the population. Many minority groups estimate their numbers to be significantly higher than official counts. There are 13 recognised minorities in the country, including Germans (0.6%), Slovaks (0.2%), Croatians (0.1%), Romanians (0.07%), Ukrainians (0.04%) and Rusyns (0.01%). The number of Roma is officially put at 1.9% of the population though some sources place it as high as 4%.

## SPORT

The Formula One Hungarian Grand Prix, held in mid-August, is the year's biggest sporting event. The **Hungaroring** (www.hungaroring.hu) track is 19km north of Budapest, in Mogyórod, but hotels in the capital fill up and prices skyrocket.

---

### TOP FIVE WAYS TO TAKE A BATH

■ Soak in palatial elegance – tiled mosaics, stained-glass skylights – at the **Gellért Fürdő** (p364) in Buda.

■ Bubble up in the jetted central section in one of the expansive outdoor thermal pools at the turn-of-the-century **Széchenyi Fürdő** (p365) in Pest.

■ Float among lilies in the summer, and steam in the winter, at one of Europe's largest thermal lakes, the **Gyógytó** in Hévíz (p390).

■ Go modern at the **Rába Quelle** (p381) thermal spa in Győr: slide down the waterslide and splash under the two-storey waterfall.

■ Take a romantic summer evening swim in the outdoor thermal mineral pool of the **Gyógyfürdő** (p394) in Harkány; the high sulphur content might do you good.

## RELIGION

Of those Hungarians declaring religious affiliation, about 52% are Roman Catholic, 16% Reformed (Calvinist) Protestant, 3% Evangelical (Lutheran) Protestant, 2.5% Greek Catholic, 1% Orthodox and 0.1% Jewish (down from a pre-WWII population of nearly 10 times the current size).

## ARTS

Budapest is Hungary's artistic heart, but the provinces resound with the arts too. The country (and the capital in particular) is known for its traditional culture, with a strong emphasis on the classical – and for good reason. The history of Hungarian arts and literature includes world-renowned composers such as Béla Bartók and Franz Liszt, and the Nobel prize-winning writer Imre Kértesz and his innovative contemporary Peter Esterházy. Hungary's proximity to classically focused Vienna, as well as the legacy of the Soviet regard for the 'proper arts' means that opera, symphony and ballet are high on the entertainment agenda, and even provincial towns have decent companies.

For the more contemporary branches of artistic life, Budapest is the country's queen bee, with many art galleries, theatre and dance companies, as well as folk music and handicrafts that have grown out of village life or minority culture.

## Music

As you will no doubt see from the street names in every Hungarian town and city, the country celebrates and reveres its most influential musician, composer and pianist, Franz (or Ferenc) Liszt (1811–86). The eccentric Liszt described himself as 'part Gypsy', and in his *Hungarian Rhapsodies*, as well as in other works, he does indeed weave Romani motifs into his compositions.

Ferenc Erkel (1810–93) is the father of Hungarian opera, and the stirringly nationalist *Bánk Bán* is a standard at the Hungarian State Opera House in Budapest. Béla Bartók (1881–1945) and Zoltán Kodály (1882–1967) made the first systematic study of Hungarian folk music; both integrated some of their findings into their compositions.

Hungarian folk musicians play violins, zithers, hurdy-gurdies, bagpipes and lutes on a five-tone diatonic scale. Romani (Gypsy) music, found in restaurants in its schmaltzy form (best avoided), has become a fashionable thing among the young, with Romani bands playing 'the real thing' in trendy bars till the wee hours: a dynamic, hopping mix of fiddles, bass and cymbalom (a table-top-like stringed instrument played with sticks). An instrument a Roma band would never be seen without is the tin milk bottle used as a drum, which gives Hungarian Roma music its characteristic sound, reminiscent of traditional Indian music, an influence that perhaps harks back to the Roma's Asian roots. Look out for names such as Kalyi Jag (Black Fire), Ando Drom, Kal, Silvagipsy and Parno Graszt (White Horse). The latter is a folk ensemble of musicians and dancers dedicated to preserving Romani musical traditions, who also borrow from other regional folk styles. (One of their songs sounds quite like a Jewish wedding dance.)

Klezmer music (traditional Eastern European Jewish music) has also made a comeback into the playlists of the young and trendy. Bands like Di Naye, Kapelye and the Odessza Klezmer band are popular.

You can hear classical concerts in Budapest's large, ornate halls, as well as churches, and festivals sometimes bring the music outdoors. Rock, jazz, blues, funk – just about any music you're looking for is on tap at Budapest's many night spots.

### Literature

Hungary has some excellent writers, both of poetry and prose. Sándor Petőfi (1823–49) is Hungary's most celebrated poet. A line from his work *National Song* became the rallying cry for the War of Independence between 1848 and 1849, in which he fought and is commonly thought to have died. His comrade-in-arms, János Arany (1817–82), wrote epic poetry. The prolific novelist and playwright Mór Jókai (1825–1904) gave expression to heroism and honesty in works such as *The Man with the Golden Touch*. Lyric poet Endre Ady (1877–1919) attacked narrow materialism; poet Attila József (1905–37) expresses the alienation felt by individuals in the modern age; and novelist Zsigmond Móricz (1879–1942) examines the harsh reality of peasant life in Hungary.

Contemporary Hungarian writers whose work has been translated into English and are worth a read include Tibor Fischer, Péter Esterházy and Sándor Márai. The most celebrated Hungarian writer is the 2002 Nobel prize-winner, Imre Kertész, whose excellent semi-autobiographical novel *Fateless* describes the ordeal of a teenage boy sent to Nazi death camps at Auschwitz, Buchenwald and Zeitz. Kertész also wrote the screenplay for the film of the same name, directed by Lajos Koltai and nominated for the Golden Bear at the Berlin Film Festival in 2005. It is Hungary's most expensive movie production (it cost US$12 million), and one of its best. Kertész's work has been likened in its power to the writing of Primo Levi. Corvina Books publishes translations and anthologies of the above writers' works.

## Visual Arts

Favourite painters from the 19th century include realist Mihály Munkácsy (1844–1900), the so-called painter of the plains, and Tivadar Kosztka Csontváry (1853–1919). Győző Vásárhelyi (1908–97), who changed his name to Victor Vasarely when he emigrated to Paris, is considered the 'father of op art'. In the 19th and early 20th century, the Zsolnay family created world-renowned decorative art in porcelain. Ceramic artist Margit Kovac (1902–1977), a Hungarian national treasure, produced a large number of statues and ceramic objects during her career. The traditional embroidery, weavings and ceramics of the nation's *népművészet* (folk art) endures and there is at least one handicraft store in every town.

## ENVIRONMENT
### The Land

Hungary occupies the Carpathian Basin to the southwest of the Carpathian Mountains. Water dominates much of the country's geography. The Duna (Danube River) divides the Nagyalföld (Great Plain) in the east from the Dunántúl (Transdanubia) in the west. The Tisza (597km in Hungary) is the country's longest river, and historically has been prone to flooding. Hungary has hundreds of small lakes and is riddled with thermal springs. Lake Balaton (596 sq km, 77km long), in the west, is the largest freshwater lake in Europe outside Scandinavia. Hungary's 'mountains' to the north are merely hills, with the country's highest peak being Kékes (1014m) in the Mátra Range.

## Wildlife

There are plenty of common European animals (deer, wild hare, boar, otter) as well as more rarer species (wild cat, lake bat, Pannonian lizard), but three-quarters of the country's 450 vertebrates are birds, particularly waterfowl. Hungary is a premier European sight for bird-watching. Endangered or vulnerable populations include eastern imperial eagles, saker falcons and the great bustard. An estimated 70,000 cranes pass through every year and a great number of storks arrive in the northern uplands and on the Great Plain every spring.

## National Parks

There are 11 national parks in Hungary. Bükk Nemzeti Park, north of Eger, is a mountainous limestone area of forest and caves. Kiskunsági Nemzeti Park (p397; www.knp.hu) and Bugac (p397), near Kecskemét, and Hortobágy Nemzeti Park (www.hnp.hu) in the Hortobágy Puszta (a World Heritage site), outside Debrecen, protect the unique grassland environment of the plains.

## Environmental Issues

Pollution is a large and costly problem. Harmful emissions from low-grade fuels such as coal and the high numbers of buses and cars, especially in Budapest, affect the air quality. The overuse of nitrate fertilisers in agriculture threatens ground water beneath the plains. However, there has been a marked improvement in air and water quality in recent years as Hungary attempts to conform to EU environmental standards.

## FOOD & DRINK
### Staples & Specialities

The omnipresent seasoning in Hungarian cooking is paprika, a mild red pepper that appears on restaurant tables as a condiment beside the salt and black pepper, as well as in many recipes. *Pörkölt*, a paprika-infused stew, can be made from different meats, including *borju* (veal), and usually it has no vegetables. *Galuska* (small, gnocchi-like dumplings) are a good accompaniment to soak up the sauce. The well-known *paprikas csirke* (chicken paprikash) is stewed chicken in a tomato-cream-paprika sauce (not as common here as in Hungarian restaurants abroad). *Töltött káposzta* (cabbage rolls stuffed with meat and rice) is cooked in a roux made with paprika, and topped with sour cream, as is *székelygulyás* (stewed pork and sour cabbage). Another local favourite is *halászlé* (fisherman's soup), a rich mix of several kinds of poached freshwater fish, tomatoes, green peppers and…paprika.

*Leves* (soup) is the start to any main meal in a Hungarian home; some claim that you will develop stomach disorders if you don't

**HUNGARY**

eat a hot, daily helping. *Gulyás* (goulash), although served as a stew outside Hungary, is a soup here, cooked with beef, onions and tomatoes. Traditional cooking methods are far from health-conscious, but they are tasty. Frying is a nationwide obsession and you'll often find fried turkey, pork and veal schnitzels on the menu.

For dessert you might try the cold *gyümölcs leves* (fruit soup) made with sour cherries and other berries, or *palincsinta* (crepes) filled with jam, sweet cheese or chocolate sauce. A good food-stand snack is *lángos,* fried dough that can be topped with cheese and/or *tejföl* (sour cream).

Two Hungarian wines are known internationally: the sweet, dessert wine Tokaji Aszú and Egri Bikavér (Eger Bull's Blood), the full-bodied red, high in acid and tannin. But the country produces a number of other eminently drinkable wines. Hungarian beers sold nationally include Dreher and Kőbanyai; Borosodi is a decent amber brew. For the harder stuff, try *pálinka,* a strong, firewaterlike brandy distilled from a variety of fruits, but most commonly plums or apricots. Zwack distillery produces Unicum, a bitter aperitif that has been around since 1790; it tastes a bit like the medicine doctors give you to induce vomiting – but it's popular.

## Where to Eat & Drink

An *étterem* is a restaurant with a large selection, formal service and formal prices. A *vendéglő* is smaller, more casual and serves homestyle regional dishes. The overused term *csárda,* which originally meant a rustic country inn with Romani music, can now mean anything – including super-touristy. To keep prices down, look for *étkezde* (a tiny eating place that may have a counter or sit-down service), *önkiszolgáló* (a self-service canteen), *kinai gyorsbüfé* (Chinese fast food), *grill* (which generally serves gyros or kebabs and other grilled meats from the counter) or a *szendvicsbar* (which has open-face sandwiches to go).

There are still a number of stuffy Hungarian restaurants with condescending waiters, formal service and Romani music from another era. For the most part, avoiding places with tuxedoed waiters is a good bet.

Wine has been produced in Hungary for thousands of years and you'll find it available by the glass or bottle everywhere. There are plenty of pseudo British-Irish-Belgian pubs, smoky *sörözö* (a Hungarian pub, often in a cellar, where drinking is taken very seriously), *borozó* (a wine bar, usually a dive) and nightclubs, but the most pleasant place to imbibe a cocktail or coffee may be in a café. A *kávéház* may primarily be an old-world dessert shop, or it may be a bar with an extensive drinks menu; either way they sell alcoholic beverages in addition to coffee. In spring, pavement tables sprout up alongside the new flowers.

## Vegetarians & Vegans

Traditional Hungarian food is heavy and rich. Meat, sour cream and fat abound, and *saláta* generally means a plate of pickles (cucumbers, cabbage, beets and/or carrots). At least in Budapest, other alternatives are available, especially at Italian or Asian restaurants.

Some not-very-light, but widely available dishes for vegetarians to look for are *rántott sajt* (fried cheese), *gombafejek rántva* (fried mushroom caps), *gomba leves* (mushroom soup) and *túrós* or *káposzta csusza* (short, wide pasta with cheese or cabbage). *Bableves* (bean soup) usually contains meat.

## Habits & Customs

The Magyar are a polite people and their language is filled with courtesies. To toast someone's health before drinking, say *egéségére* (egg-eh-shaig-eh-ray), and to wish them a good appetite before eating, *jo étvágat* (yo ate-vad-yaht). If you're invited to someone's home, always bring a bunch of flowers and/or a bottle of good local wine.

# BUDAPEST

☎ 1 / pop 1.8 million

Budapest seductively displays its many cultural influences and historical remains: the sensible Germanic logic of its layout, the decadent opulence of its Turkish baths, the Viennese coffeehouses, the straight lines of the sober Socialist structures, the Habsburg elegance and the silent old Jewish quarter, the Balkan smokiness of its bars, and above all, the unique Magyar spirit.

Budapest can be a summer hotspot – you can walk along the Danube, go drinking and clubbing in the boat bars and get into the boho coffee-house lifestyle. During the chillier months the city transforms into a winter resort with its many bathhouses, where you can be sitting in

---

**BUDAPEST IN TWO DAYS**

The best way to start your day in Budapest is to have an early morning soak al fresco at **Széchenyi Fürdő** (p365). Then stroll through the **Városliget** (City Park; p365) to **Hősök tere** (p365). Depending on your tastes, visit the **Szépmüvészeti Múzeum** (p365), the city's fine art museum, or if contemporary art is more your thing, go to **Műcsarnok** (p365). Stroll down Andrássy út and grab a (very) late breakfast or coffee at **Lukács** (p365), next to the infamous and ever-popular spy museum, the **Terror Háza** (p365). Carry on down, past Oktogon tér, and have lunch in the wonderful **Menza** (p370), then take an afternoon tour around the grand **Magyar Állami Operaház** (Hungarian State Opera House, p365). Have cake at the legendary **Gerbeaud** (p371) before hitting the shops on **Váci utca** (p365). Go dancing at **Cha Cha Cha** (p372) or **Sark** (p371) or have drinks at **Szimpla/Dupla** (p371).

On day two grab breakfast at **Eckermann** (p371) among the city's intellectual crowd, before getting the funicular to **Várhegy** (Castle Hill; p363) in Buda. Wander the old streets and appreciate the views from the pathways along the ancient walls. Tour **Mátyás Templom** (p364) and explore the many museums, including the **Budapesti Történeti Múzeum** (p364), to find out more about the city's history. In the evening, back in Pest, don't forget to take a walk along the waterfront to see Castle Hill lit up. You may want to have a drink or a meal at any of the boat restaurant-pubs and enjoy the scenery before going Hungarian dancing at **Fonó Budai Zeneház** (p372).

---

a steaming outdoor pool while snow glistens around you. Regardless of the season, you can always plunge in and explore Budapest's rich cultural heritage of opulent architecture, fascinating and sometimes bizarre museums, art galleries and Roman ruins. But you don't have to drown yourself in culture – Budapest has some of the more exciting nightlife spots in Eastern Europe, with unusual club nights (such as dancing waist deep in thermal waters), excellent DJs, live Romani and Klezmer music, and more bars than you'll be able to crawl around.

Pest is the city's commercial centre, with culture, restaurants and nightlife, smoky bars and shady gardens, museums, cheap sleeps and high-class hotels. Buda's sleepy green hills are home to the famous Castle Hill and medieval buildings, and its peaceful neighbourhoods house the city's affluent dwellers.

Whatever you choose to sample from the offerings of Budapest, make sure you take time to enjoy it in the city's slow, relaxed pace.

## HISTORY

Strictly speaking, the story of Budapest begins only in 1873 with the administrative union of three cities that had grown together: Buda, west of the Danube; Óbuda (Buda's oldest neighbourhood) to the north; and Pest on the eastern side of the river. But the area had been occupied for thousands of years before Budapest as we know it existed. The Romans built a settlement at Aquincum (Óbuda) during the first centuries of the Christian Era. In the 1500s, the Turks arrived uninvited and stayed for almost 150 years. The Habsburg Austrians helped kick the invaders out, but then made themselves at home for 200 more years.

At the turn of the 20th century, under the dual Austro-Hungarian monarchy, the population of Budapest exploded and many buildings date from that boom. The city suffered some damage in the two world wars and the 1956 revolution left structures pockmarked with bullet holes. Today many of the old buildings have been restored, and Budapest is the sophisticated capital of a proud nation, one of the newest in the EU.

## ORIENTATION

The city's traditional artery, the Danube, is spanned by nine bridges that link hilly, residential Buda with bustling, commercial and very flat Pest. Two ring roads link three of the bridges across the Danube and essentially define central Pest. Important boulevards such as Rákóczi út and leafy Andrássy út fan out from these, creating large squares and circles. The most central square in Pest is Deák tér, where the three metro lines meet. Buda is dominated by Castle and Gellért Hills; the main square is Moszkva tér.

Budapest is divided into 23 kerület (districts). The Roman numeral appearing before each street address signifies the district. Central Buda is district I, central Pest is district V, and fans out to zones VI and VII. You can also tell the district by reading its postal code: the

HUNGARY

# BUDAPEST

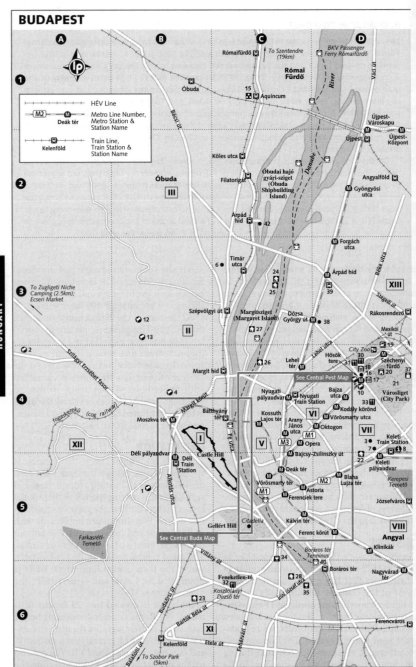

HÉV Line

M2 — Metro Line Number,
Deák tér — Metro Station &
Station Name

Kelenföld — Train Line,
Train Station &
Station Name

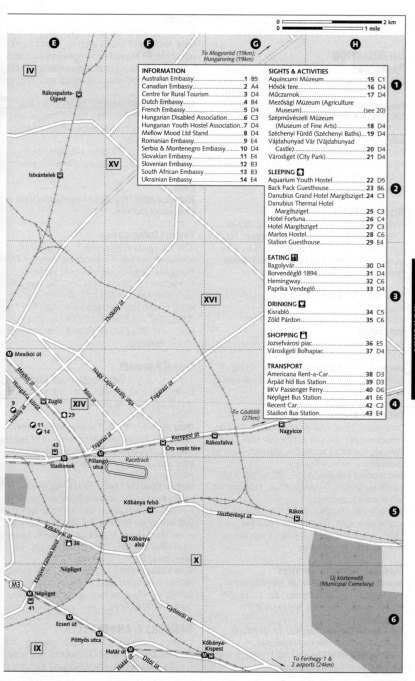

**INFORMATION**
Australian Embassy.....................1 B5
Canadian Embassy......................2 A4
Centre for Rural Tourism.............3 D4
Dutch Embassy..........................4 B4
French Embassy..........................5 D4
Hungarian Disabled Association......6 C3
Hungarian Youth Hostel Association...7 D4
Mellow Mood Ltd Stand..............8 D4
Romanian Embassy.....................9 E4
Serbia & Montenegro Embassy......10 D4
Slovakian Embassy....................11 E4
Slovenian Embassy....................12 B3
South African Embassy...............13 B3
Ukrainian Embassy....................14 E4

**SIGHTS & ACTIVITIES**
Aquincumi Múzeum...................15 C1
Hősök tere..............................16 D4
Műcsarnok.............................17 D4
Mezőgazdasági Múzeum (Agriculture
  Museum)...........................(see 20)
Szépművészeti Múzeum
  (Museum of Fine Arts).............18 D4
Széchenyi Fürdő (Széchenyi Baths)...19 D4
Vájdahunyad Vár (Vájdahunyad
  Castle)..............................20 D4
Városliget (City Park)................21 D4

**SLEEPING**
Aquarium Youth Hostel..............22 D5
Back Pack Guesthouse................23 B6
Danubius Grand Hotel Margitsziget.24 C3
Danubius Thermal Hotel
  Margitsziget.........................25 C3
Hotel Fortuna..........................26 C4
Hotel Margitsziget....................27 C3
Martos Hostel.........................28 C6
Station Guesthouse...................29 E4

**EATING**
Bagolyvár...............................30 D4
Borvendéglő 1894.....................31 D4
Hemingway.............................32 C6
Paprika Vendéglő......................33 D4

**DRINKING**
Kisrabló.................................34 C5
Zöld Párdon............................35 C6

**SHOPPING**
Jozsefvárosi piac......................36 E5
Városligeti Bolhapiac.................37 D4

**TRANSPORT**
Americana Rent-a-Car................38 D3
Árpád híd Bus Station................39 D3
BKV Passenger Ferry..................40 D6
Népliget Bus Station..................41 E6
Recent Car.............................42 C2
Stadion Bus Station...................43 E4

**HUNGARY**

two numbers after the initial one signify the district (ie H-1114 is in the XI district).

# INFORMATION
## Bookshops
**Irók Boltja** (Map p362; ☎ 322 1645; VI Andrássy út 45; ☻ 10am-6pm Mon-Fri, to 3pm Sat) Good selection of Hungarian writers in translation.

**Libri Stúdium** (Map p362; ☎ 318 5680; V Váci utca 22; ☻ 10am-7pm Mon-Fri, to 3pm Sat & Sun) Tons of coffee-table and travel books, many Lonely Planet titles.

**Red Bus Second-hand Bookstore** (Map p362; ☎ 337 7453; V Semmelweiss utca 14; ☻ 10am-6pm Mon-Fri, to 3pm Sat) Sells used English-language books, next door to the hostel.

## Discount Cards
**Budapest Card** (www.budapestinfo.hu; 48/72hr card 5200/6500Ft) Offers free access to many museums; free transport on city trams, buses and metros; and discounts on other services. Buy the card at hotels, travel agencies, large metro station kiosks and some tourist offices.

Also worth considering is the Hungary Card. See p405 for details.

## Emergency
For emergency numbers, see the boxed text, p407.

**District V Police Station** (Map p362; ☎ 373 1000; V Szalay utca 11-13) The most centrally located police station in Pest.

## Internet Access
The majority of year-round hostels offer internet access (free to 250Ft per half hour). Among the most accessible internet cafés in Budapest are the following.

**Ami Internet Coffee** (Map p362; ☎ 267 1644; V Váci utca 40; per hr 700Ft; ☻ 9am-2am) Tons of terminals; it's very central, but superbusy.

**CEU NetPoint** (Map p362; ☎ 328 3506; Oktober 6 utca 14; per hr 400Ft; ☻ 11am-10pm) Quiet and central. There's a dozen terminals, CD writing, fax, webcams and wi-fi connection for your laptop.

## Medical & Dental Services
**American Clinics** (Map p361; ☎ 224 9090; I Hattyú utca 14, 5th fl; ☻ 8.30am-7pm Mon-Thu, 8.30am-6pm Fri, 8am-noon Sat, 10am-2pm Sun) On call 24/7 for emergencies.

**S O S Dental Service** (Map p362; ☎ 322 0602; VI Király utca 14) Around-the-clock dental care.

**Teréz Gyógyszertár** (Map p362; ☎ 311 4439; VI Teréz körút 41) Twenty-four-hour pharmacy.

## Money
ATMs are quite common, especially on the ring roads and main arteries. Most banks have both ATMs and exchange services. Banks have standardised hours nationwide. See p405 for information about opening and closing times.

**American Express** (Map p362; ☎ 235 4330; V Deák Ferenc utca 10; ☻ 9am-5.30pm Mon-Fri, 9am-2pm Sat) Will change its own travellers cheques without commission; not the best rates.

**K&H Bank** (Map p362; V Váci utca 40) Quite central.

**OTP Bank** (Map p362; V Nádor utca 6) Favourable rates.

## Post
**Main post office** (Map p362; V Városház utca 18) Pick up poste restante mail here.

## Tourist Information
The Hungarian National Tourist Board, in conjunction with the Budapest Tourism Office, runs Tourinform offices in Budapest.

**Tourinform** ( ☎ 24hr hotline 06 80 630 800; www.budapestinfo.hu); Main Office (Map p362; ☎ 438 8080; V Sütő utca 2; ☻ 8am-8pm); Liszt Ferenc Square (Map p362; ☎ 322 4098; VI Liszt Ferenc tér 11; ☻ 10am-6pm Mon-Fri); Castle Hill (Map p361; ☎ 488 0475; I Szentháromság tér; ☻ 10am-7pm)

## Travel Agencies
You can get information, book tours and transport, and arrange accommodation at travel agencies in Budapest. They also sell discount cards.

**Ibusz** (Map p362; ☎ 485 2716; www.ibusz.hu; V Ferenciek tere 10; ☻ 9am-5pm Mon-Fri, to 1pm Sat Jul-Aug) The main branch of this national agency has an exchange office, books private rooms and pensions, and sells air and train tickets – the works.

**Mellow Mood Ltd Stand** ( ☎ 413 2062; www.mellowmood.hu; ☻ 7am-8pm) Stands can be found at Keleti (Map pp358-9) and Déli (Map p361) train stations. Staff will help you find hostel and other accommodation, as well as provide info. It's affiliated with the Hungarian Youth Hostel Association and Hostelling International (HI).

**Vista Visitor Centre** (Map p362; ☎ 452 3636; www.vista.hu; VI Paulay Ede utca 2; ☻ 9am-6pm Mon-Fri, 10am-3pm Sat) Book apartments and arrange tours here. There's internet access and a café.

## DANGERS & ANNOYANCES
Overall, Hungary is a very safe country with little violent crime, but scams can be a problem in the capital. Overcharging in taxis is

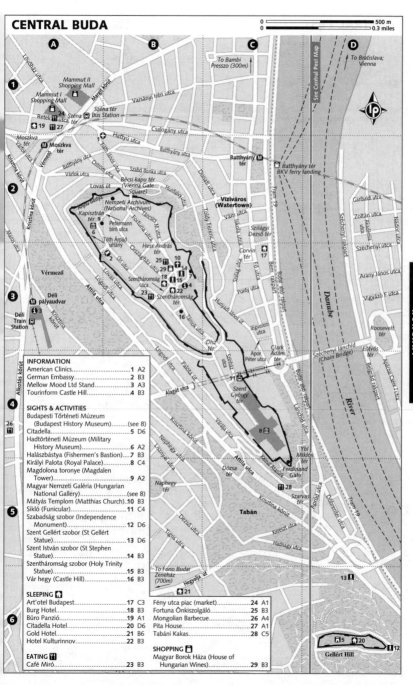

# CENTRAL BUDA

0 ————————— 500 m
0 ————————— 0.3 miles

**INFORMATION**
American Clinics.................................1 A2
German Embassy..............................2 B3
Mellow Mood Ltd Stand..................3 A3
Tourinform Castle Hill......................4 B3

**SIGHTS & ACTIVITIES**
Budapesti Történeti Múzeum
  (Budapest History Museum).........(see 8)
Citadella............................................5 D6
Hadtörténeti Múzeum (Military
  History Museum)...........................6 A2
Halászbástya (Fishermen's Bastion)...7 B3
Királyi Palota (Royal Palace)..............8 C4
Magyar Nemzeti Galéria (Hungarian
  National Gallery)..........................(see 8)
Mátyás Templom (Matthias Church).10 B3
Sikló (Funicular)...............................11 C4
Szabadság szobor (Independence
  Monument).................................12 D6
Szent Gellért szobor (St Gellért
  Statue)........................................13 D6
Szent István szobor (St Stephen
  Statue)........................................14 B3
Szentháromság szobor (Holy Trinity
  Statue)........................................15 B3
Vár hegy (Castle Hill).......................16 B3

**SLEEPING**
Art'otel Budapest............................17 C3
Burg Hotel.......................................18 B3
Büro Panzió.....................................19 A1
Citadella Hotel.................................20 D6
Gold Hotel.......................................21 B6
Hotel Kulturinnov............................22 B3

**EATING**
Café Miró.........................................23 B3

Fény utca piac (market).....................24 A1
Fortuna Önkiszolgáló........................25 B3
Mongolian Barbecue.........................26 A4
Pita House........................................27 A1
Tabáni Kakas.....................................28 C5

**SHOPPING**
Magyar Borok Háza (House of
  Hungarian Wines).........................29 B3

HUNGARY

To Bambi
Presszo (300m)

To Bratislava;
Vienna

See Central Pest Map

Mammut II
Shopping Mall

Mammut I
Shopping Mall

Retek utca
Széna tér
Széna tér Bus Station

Moszkva tér

Varsányi Irén utca
Csalogány utca

Hattyú utca
Batthyány utca
Szabó Ilonka utca

Batthyány tér
Batthyány tér
BKV ferry landing

Bécsi kapu tér
(Vienna Gate Square)

Nemzeti Archivum
(National Archives)

Kapisztrán tér
Petermann bíró utca

Tóth Árpád sétány
Hess András tér

Úri utca

Szentháromság utca

Szentháromság tér

Vérmező

Déli pályaudvar

Déli Train Station

Vízíváros
(Watertown)

Corvin tér

Tram 19

Garibaldi utca
Zoltán utca
Akadémia utca
Széchenyi utca

Arany János utca

Vigyázó F utca

Danube

Roosevelt tér

Dísz tér

Clark Ádám tér

Széchenyi lánchíd
(Chain Bridge)

Eötvös tér

River

Szent György tér

Alagút utca

Szent György tér

Ybl Miklós tér

Ferdinand Gate

Szarvas tér

Tabán

To Fono Budai
Zeneház
(700m)

Naphegy tér

Gellért Hill

# CENTRAL PEST

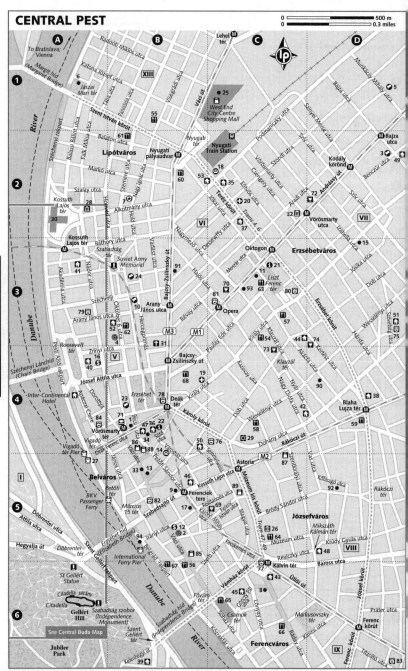

not unknown and we have received reports of unscrupulous waiters stealing credit-card information. Watch out for tricks on the street: the usual pickpocket method is for someone to distract you (by running into you, dropping something etc) while an accomplice makes off with your goods.

Guys should avoid drop-dead gorgeous women who approach them (especially around Váci utca) and offer to take them along to a local nightspot. Disreputable clubs hire these women to lure you in and then charge insane rates for drinks (upwards of €80 a pop) for you and the girls, who order refills adeptly.

There is a small but persistent neo-Nazi presence in Budapest that wants to blame Jews, Roma, Asians or blacks for the ills of the world, but for now their action seems to be limited to the staging of rallies and protests.

## SIGHTS & ACTIVITIES
### Buda
#### CASTLE HILL
Surfacing at the red line metro station of the Socialist-style Moszkva tér, continue left up Várfok utca, or cross the street and board the Vár bus (a minibus with a picture of a castle on the sign) to reach **Várhegy** (Castle Hill; Map p361) where most of Budapest's remaining medieval buildings are clustered. Várhegy is high above the glistening Danube, and wandering the old streets and enjoying the city views is part of the attraction, so get off at the first stop after the Vienna Gate and walk.

**Magdolona toronye** (Magdalen Tower; Map p361; Kapisztrán tér) is all that's left of a Gothic church destroyed here during WWII. The white neoclassical building facing the square is the **Hadtörténeti Múzeum** (Military History Museum; Map p361; ☎ 356 9522; I Tóth Árpád sétány 40; admission free; ☿ 10am-6pm Tue-Sun Apr-Sep, to 4pm Oct-Mar).

For a peek into the life of the Budapest bourgeoisie, check out the mansions of the Buda Hills to the south of the ramparts promenade. Follow the third alleyway to your left and you reach Szentháromság tér and the **Szentháromság szobor** (Holy Trinity Statue; Map p361) at its centre.

Don't miss the gorgeous, neo-Gothic **Mátyás Templom** (Matthias Church; Map p361; ☎ 489 0717; I Szentháromság tér; adult/student 600/300Ft; ☷ 9am-5pm Mon-Sat, 1-5pm Sun), with a colourful tiled roof and lovely murals inside. Franz Liszt's *Hungarian Coronation Mass* was played here for the first time at the coronation of Franz Joseph and Elizabeth in 1867. Classical music concerts are still hosted here some evenings.

Sample the country's varieties of wine at the **Magyar Borok Háza** (House of Hungarian Wines; Map p361; ☎ 212 1031; www.magyarborokhaza.hu; I Szentháromság tér 6; wine tasting 3500Ft; ☷ noon-8pm) across the square, under the gaze of Hungary's first king, the equestrian **Szent István szobor** (St Stephen Statue; Map p361) to the south. Behind the monument, walk along **Halászbástya** (Fishermen's Bastion; Map p361; I Szentháromság tér; adult/student 330/160Ft; ☷ 8.30am-11pm). The fanciful, neo-Gothic arcade built on the fortification wall is prime picture-taking territory with views of the river and the parliament beyond.

Tárnok utca runs southeast to Dísz tér, past which is the entrance for the **Sikló** (Funicular; Map p361; district I Szent György tér; uphill/downhill ticket adult 600/500Ft, child 3-14yr 350Ft; ☷ 7.30am-10pm). The views from the little capsule, across the Danube and over to Pest, are glorious. The Sikló takes you down the hill to Clark Ádám tér. The massive **Királyi Palota** (Royal Palace; Map p361) occupies the far end of Castle Hill; inside are the **Magyar Nemzeti Galéria** (Hungarian National Gallery; ☎ 375 7533; I Szent György tér 6; admission free, special exhibitions adult/child/family 1500/800/3000Ft; ☷ 10am-6pm Tue-Sun) and the **Budapesti Történeti Múzeum** (Budapest History Museum; ☎ 375 7533; I Szent György tér 2; adult/student 900/450Ft; ☷ 10am-6pm daily mid-May–mid-Sep, 10am-4pm Wed-Mon mid-Sep–mid-May).

### GELLÉRT HILL

The 'other peak' overlooking the Danube, south of Castle Hill, is Gellért Hill. The **Szabadság szobor** (Independence Monument), a statue of a gigantic lady with a palm leaf proclaiming freedom throughout the city, sits at its top, and is visible from almost anywhere in town. The monument was erected as a tribute to the Soviet soldiers who died liberating Hungary in 1945, but the victims' names in Cyrillic letters, that used to adorn the plinth, as well as the memorial statues of Soviet soldiers, were removed a decade ago.

West of the monument is the **Citadella** (☎ 365 6076; admission 300Ft; ☷ 8am-10pm). Built by the Habsburgs after the 1848 revolution to 'defend' the city from further Hungarian insurrection, it was never used as a fortress. Excellent views, exhibits, a restaurant and a hotel can be enjoyed in the Citadella. Take tram 19 along the riverfront from Clark Ádám tér and climb the stairs behind the waterfall and **Szent Gellért szobor** (St Gellért Statue), then follow the path through the park opposite the entrance to the Danubius Hotel Gellért. Or take bus 27 which runs almost to the top of the hill from XI Móricz Zsigmond körtér, southwest of the Gellért Hotel (and accessible using tram 19 and 49).

Bellow Gellért Hill is the city's most famous thermal spa, the **Gellért Fürdő** (Gellért Baths; Map p362; ☎ 466 6166; Danubius Hotel Gellért, XI Kelenhegyi út; thermal baths & swimming pool 2700Ft; ☷ 6am-7pm Mon-Fri, to 5pm Sat & Sun May-Sep; baths only Oct-Apr), where majestic domes arch over healing waters. This Art Nouveau palace has dreamy spas where you can soak for hours whilst enjoying its elegant and historic architecture.

### SZOBOR PARK

In Buda's southwest is **Szobor Park** (Statue Park; ☎ 227 7446; www.szoborpark.hu; XXII Szabadkai út; admission 600Ft; ☷ 10am-dusk), a kind of historical dumping ground for Socialist statues deemed unsuitable since the early '90s. It's a major tourist attraction and there is a direct bus from Deák tér in Pest at 11am daily (2450Ft return, including admission). To go independently, take tram 19 from Clark Ádám tér to the XI Etele tér Terminus, then catch a yellow Volán bus to Diósd-Érd.

### AQUINCUMI MÚZEUM

Seven kilometres north of Buda's centre, in Óbuda, is the **Aquincumi Múzeum** (Map pp358-9; ☎ 430 1563; III Szentendre út 139; adult/student 700/300Ft; ☷ 10am-5pm Tue-Sun Oct-Apr, to 6pm May-Sep, grounds 9am) containing the heart of the most complete ruins of a 2nd-century Roman civilian town left in Hungary. Take the HÉV from the Batthyány tér metro stop.

## Pest
### HŐSÖK TERE & AROUND

The leafy Andrássy út, Budapest's own Fifth Ave and Pest's northeastern artery, is the best place to start your sightseeing. At its western end, Andrassy ut turns into Bajcsy-Zsilinszky ut and touches Deak ter. Pest's central square, and its opposite end spills onto the wide, tiled **Hősök tere** (Heroes' Square; Map pp358-9) that bears a sprawling monument constructed to honour the millennial anniversary (1896) of the Magyar conquest of the Carpathian Basin.

Continental Europe's oldest underground – Budapest's M1 yellow line metro, constructed in the 19th century – runs beneath Andrássy út. Start your sightseeing almost at the end of the yellow line at Hősök tere, above the metro station of the same name. The tall green monument on the square showcases statues of important moustachioed tribal leaders, kings and statesmen. Across the street, the **Szépművészeti Múzeum** (Museum of Fine Arts; Map pp358-9; ☎ 469 7100; www2.szepmuveszeti.hu; XIV Hősök tere; admission free, temporary exhibitions adult/child 1200/600Ft; 🕑 10am-5.30pm Tue-Sun) houses a collection of foreign art, including an impressive number of El Grecos. Don't miss the **Műcsarnok** (Map pp358-9; ☎ 460 7000; www.mucsarnok.hu; XIV Hősök tere; adult/student 600/300Ft; 🕑 10am-6pm Tue-Wed & Fri-Sun, noon-8pm Thu), opposite the museum, a large contemporary art gallery that displays the work of Hungarian and international artists.

Adjacent to the oasis of **Városliget** (City Park; Map pp358-9), which has boating on a small lake in the summer, ice skating in winter, and duck-feeding year round. The park's schizophrenic **Vájdahunyad Vár** (Vájdahunyad Castle; Map pp358-9) was built in varied architectural styles typical of historic Hungary, including baroque, Romanesque, Gothic and Tudor. Originally a millennial celebration exhibit hall, the castle now contains the **Mezősági Múzeum** (Agriculture Museum; ☎ 343 0573; XIV Városliget; adult/student 500/200Ft; 🕑 Tue-Fri & Sun 10am-5pm, Sat to 6pm), exciting only for those interested in Hungarian viticulture. In the park's northern corner is **Széchenyi Fürdő** (Széchenyi Baths; Map pp358-9; ☎ 363 3210; XIV Állatkerti út 11; admission 1700Ft; 🕑 6am-7pm Mon-Fri, to 5pm Sat & Sun), its cupola visible from anywhere in the park. Built in 1908, this place has an amazing outdoor pool that is open summer and winter, to cool you down or warm you up. Have a look inside all of the various entrances: the peaceful atmosphere of the indoor thermal baths, saunas and massage area contrasts with the buzzing atmosphere of the outside pool.

Walk southwest from Hősök tere on Andrássy út, to see many grand, World Heritage–listed 19th-century buildings. Stop for coffee

and cake at **Lukács** ( ☎ 302 8747; VI Andrássy út 70; 🕑 9am-8pm Mon-Fri; 10am-8pm Sat & Sun), the old haunt of the dreaded secret police, whose headquarters have now been turned into the **Terror Háza** (Terror House; Map p362; ☎ 374 2600; www.terrorhaza.hu, Hungarian only; VI Andrássy út 60; admission foreigners 3000Ft; 🕑 10am-6pm Tue-Fri, to 7.30pm Sat & Sun), almost next door. The museum specialises in accounts of spying and atrocities, and always attracts a crowd. Although it's an interesting account of Hungary's tough times during WWII and under the Communist regime, the museum has been criticised for its lack of exhibits on the Holocaust.

Further down on Andrássy út, the opulence of the 1884 neo-Renaissance **Magyar Állami Operaház** (Hungarian State Opera House; Map p362; ☎ 332 8197; www.opera.hu; VI Andrássy út 22; tours 1200Ft; 🕑 3pm & 4pm) is a real treat; try to make it to an evening performance here. **Váci utca**, in Pest's touristy centre, is an extensive pedestrian shopping street. It begins at the southwest terminus of the yellow line, Vörösmarty tér. The **Nagycsarnok** (Great Market; Map p362; IX Vámház körút 1-3; 🕑 6am-5pm Mon, to 6pm Tue-Fri, to 2pm Sat) is a vast steel and glass structure. There are produce vendors on the ground floor, souvenirs and snacks on the 1st floor.

## PARLIAMENT & AROUND

Other sights and museums are scattered about Pest. The huge, riverfront **Parlament** (Parliament; Map p362; ☎ 441 4904; www.mkogy.hu; V Kossuth Lajos tér 1-3; adult/student 1700/800Ft; 🕑 8am-6pm Mon-Fri, to 4pm Sat, to 2pm Sun for Hungarian-language tours), apparently modelled on London's Westminster, but with crazy spires, dominates Kossuth Lajos tér. English-language tours are at 10am and 2pm daily.

Across the park is the **Néprajzi Múzeum** (Ethnography Museum; Map p362; ☎ 473 2400; www.hem.hu; V Kossuth Lajos tér 12; adult/student 500/250Ft; 🕑 10am-6pm Tue-Sun), which has an extensive collection of national costumes among the permanent displays on folk life and art. Look for the mummified right hand of St Stephen in the chapel of the colossal **Szent István Bazilika** (Map p362; ☎ 311 0839; V Szent István tér; church admission free, treasury adult/student 200/150Ft, dome 500/400Ft; 🕑 9am-7pm Mon-Sat, 1-4pm Sun) near Bajcsy-Zsilinszky út.

## JEWISH QUARTER

Northeast of the Astoria metro stop is what remains of the Jewish quarter. The twin-towered, 1859 **Nagy Zsinagóga** (Great Synagogue; Map

**HUNGARY**

p362; ☎ 342 8949; VII Dohány utca 2; synagogue & museum adult/child 1000/400Ft; ☼ 10am-5pm Mon-Thu, 10am-2pm Fri & Sun) has a museum with a harrowing exhibit on the Holocaust, and behind the synagogue is a **Holocaust Memorial** in the shape of a weeping willow. Funded by the actor Tony Curtis, it's dedicated to those who perished in the death camps. A few blocks south along the *kis körút* (little ring road) is the **Magyar Nemzeti Múzeum** (Hungarian National Museum; Map p362; ☎ 338 2122; www .hnm.hu; VIII Múzeum körút 14-16; adult/student 800/400Ft; ☼ 10am-6pm Tue-Sun), with its historic relics from archaeological finds to coronation regalia.

### BUDAPEST EYE

For a different view, rise above it all in the **Budapest Eye** (Map p362; ☎ 238 7623; www.budapesteye .hu; VI Váci út 1-3; adult/child 3000/2000Ft, extra to take photos; ☼ 10am-6pm May-Oct), a hot-air balloon tethered to the West End City Centre Shopping Mall.

## TOURS

To tour the Danube, **Mahart PassNave sightseeing cruises** ( ☎ 484 4013; www.mahartpassnave.hu; V Vigadó tér Pier; ☼ Apr-Oct) runs 1½-hour sightseeing cruises (adult/child 1900/950Ft) and lunch and dinner buffet cruises (2800/1400Ft). On Wednesdays and Sundays from May to September, folklore evening cruises (9500Ft) include regional dishes, Romani music and folk dancing. Tickets can be purchased at the pier before departure.

For a fun way to tour the city, day or night, **Yellow Zebra Bikes** (Map p362; ☎ 266 8777; www .yellowzebrabikes.com; V Sütő utca 2, in courtyard; ☼ 8.30am-8pm May-Sep, 10am-6pm Nov-Feb, 9.30am-7.30pm Mar-Apr & Oct) offers bicycle rentals (one day 3000Ft). The office has internet access and is quite the hang-out for English speakers. The same company runs **Absolute Walking Tours** ( ☎ 06 30 211 8861; www.absolutetours.com), and both have tours departing from Deák tér. You could take the entertaining 3½-hour town walking tour (adult/student 4000/3500Ft), but the best tours on offer are the Hammer & Sickle and Pub Crawl (adult/student 5000/4500 Ft) tours, which give you a whiff of life under socialism, and an idea of modern Hungarian drinking habits with a lick of the strong stuff.

## SLEEPING

Accommodation prices and standards are pretty reasonable in Budapest. Many year-round hostels occupy middle floors of old apartment buildings (with or without a lift) in central Pest. Come summer (July to late August), student dormitories at colleges and universities open to travellers. HI-affiliated Mellow Mood Ltd (p360) runs many summer, and a few year-round, hostels in town and has stands at Keleti and Déli train stations. Tourinform and the Hungarian Youth Hostel Association publish a youth-hostel brochure you can pick up in Tourinform's offices and various hostel receptions, or read online (www.youthhostels.hu).

Private rooms assigned by travel agents are plentiful, but not always central. Costs range from 4000Ft to 7500Ft for a single, 9000Ft to 12,000Ft for a double and 12,000Ft to 14,000Ft for a small apartment, with a supplement if you stay fewer than four nights. Ibusz (p360) has the most extensive listings in town (some with photos on its website) and Vista Visitor Centre (p360) is good for apartments. Two other private-room brokers:

**Best Hotel Service** (Map p362; ☎ 318 4848; www .besthotelservice.hu; V Sütő utca 2; ☼ 8am-8pm)

**To-Ma Travel Agency** (Map p362; ☎ 353 0819; www .tomatour.hu/beut/; V Október 6 utca 22; ☼ 9am-noon & 1-8pm Mon-Fri, 9am-5pm Sat & Sun)

### Buda
#### BUDGET

**Zugligeti Niche Camping** ( ☎ 200 8346; www.camping niche.hu; XII Zugligeti út 101; camp sites 1/2 people 1900/ 2800Ft, caravan sites 1/2 people 2800/3700Ft; ☼ May-Oct) An excellent option for mixing a city break with a hiking holiday: the camp's location is in the Buda Hills at the bottom station of a chair lift. The camp is a bit cramped, but has good shade and there's a restaurant nearby. Take bus 158 from Moszkva tér to the terminus.

**Back Pack Guesthouse** (Map pp358-9; ☎ 385 8946; www.backpackbudapest.hu; XI Takács Menyhért utca 33; dm 2500-3000Ft, r 7000Ft; ☒ ⌨ ) A hippy-ish, friendly place with an oasis-of-peace feel. There's a lush garden in the back with a hammock stretched invitingly between two trees. Dorm rooms have five to 11 beds, and there's one small double. Take bus 7 (from Erzsébet híd or Keleti train station in Pest), tram 49 from the *kis körút* in central Pest, or tram 19 from Batthyány tér in Buda.

**Citadella Hotel** (Map p361; ☎ 466 5794; www.citadella .hu; XI Citadella sétány, Gellért Hill; dm/r €10/51; ☒ ) What could be better than sleeping in a historic old fortress? Well, OK, the furniture could be newer, but the place has great views. Solo travellers may prefer somewhere more central, as it's a bit isolated and the disco can get loud.

Take bus 27 from XI Móricz Zsigmond körtér in Buda, then hike.

**Martos Hostel** (Map pp358-9; ☎ 209 4883; reception@hotel.martos.bme.hu; XI Sztoczek utca 5-7; d €32, s/d with shared bathroom €16/20; ✗ ) Primarily student accommodation, Martos is open year-round to all. It's a few minutes' walk from Petőfi Bridge (or take tram 4 or 6).

### MIDRANGE

**Büro Panzió** (Map p361; ☎ 212 2928/29; buro-panzio@axelero.hu; II Dékán utca 3; s 6000-8000Ft, d 10,000-12,000Ft; ✗ ▢ ) Recently revamped and redressed, Büro now wears gleaming white walls, the beds are covered in white linen and small orange lamps light up the rooms. The central Moszkva tér transportation hub – metro stop, tram stations – is barely seconds away.

**Hotel Kulturinnov** (Map p361; ☎ 224 8100; www.mka.hu; I Szentháromság tér 6; s/d €64/80; ✗ ) A small hotel sitting in the belly of the grandiose Hungarian Culture Foundation, with an L-shaped corridor leading to its 16 rooms. The feeling is relaxed and the décor longs for the '80s, but the most impressive are the surroundings: a gorgeous stately building, on top of Castle Hill, and of course the low prices.

**Gold Hotel** (Map p361; ☎ 209 4775; www.goldhotel.hu; I Hegyalja út 14; s €64-84, d €74-94; P ✗ ▢ ▢ ) A rather odd castle-like building at Gellért Hill, with a golden yellow façade and a 'tower feature' at the front, where rooms have extra little seating areas by the window. The rooms are in terracottas and creams, with good, large beds and plenty of light. Take bus 8 from Elizabeth Bridge or bus 78 from Keleti train station in Pest.

**Burg Hotel** (Map p361; ☎ 212 0269; www.burghotel budapest.com; I Szentháromság tér 7-8; s €85-105, d €99-115; ✗ ▢ ▢ ) A fantastic combination of location and price: the affordable Burg is at the centre of Castle Hill. Ask for a room overlooking Mátyás Templom for a truly historic wake-up view. The rooms are simple, with warm peachy walls compensating for a slight lack of light. The reception staff are friendly and informative.

### TOP END

**Danubius Hotel Gellért** (Map p362; ☎ 889 5500; www.danubiusgroup.com/gellert; XI Szent Gellért tér 1; s €66-130, d €150-210; P ✗ ▢ ▢ ) This turn-of-the-(20th)-century grand dame of the Danube is worth peeking into even if you don't choose to stay here. Constructed between 1916 and 1918, its once-legendary elegance is now more on the faded side, and though it's not quite up to

today's luxury standards, staying here guarantees use of big, fluffy bathrobes you can wear on your way to free access to the Gellért Baths (p364). Purr.

**Art'otel Budapest** (Map p361; ☎ 487 9487; www.art otel.hu; I Bem rakpart 16-19; r €198-318; P ✗ ▢ ▢ ) Budapest's supermodern designer hotel, the Art'otel was dreamed up by the American Donald Sultan, and is part of a group of hotel-galleries. The rooms are a sleek mix of red, white and black, with Sultan's artworks adorning each one. The domino and needle-and-thread carpets lead you from the modern glass building through to the four old town houses in the back. Rooms for disabled travellers are available.

## Pest
### BUDGET

**Caterina Hostel** (Map p362; ☎ 269 5990; www.caterina hostel.hu; VI Teréz körút 30, 3rd fl; dm €10, r €27; ✗ ▢ ) A cosy place with a clean and bright interior, excellent for travellers who want to feel at home. The only drawback is that there is no lounge, but the modern, friendly feel and accommodating owners make it a good choice. Rooms have TVs.

**Museum Guest House** (Map p362; ☎ 318 9508; www.budapesthostel.com; VIII Mikszáth Kálmán tér 4, 1st fl; dm 2600-3000Ft; ✗ ▢ ) Wind your way through the maze of rooms. Eclectic décor includes some bunk lofts with blanket curtains and red log bedsteads. No doubles. The building is on a calm square off the main road.

**Aquarium Youth Hostel** (Map pp358-9; ☎ 322 0502; www.budapesthostel.com; VII Alsóerdősor utca 12, 2nd fl; dm/s/d 2800/3900/7800Ft; ▢ ) Associated with the Museum Guest House, but this place has more basic bunk-bed rooms, as well as doubles.

**Red Bus Hostel** (Map p362; ☎ 266 0136; www.redbusbudapest.hu; V Semmelweiss utca 14, 1st fl; dm 3000Ft, r 7900Ft; ✗ ▢ ) Congenial owners are part of the reason that the very central Red Bus has such a faithful following. Spacious rooms with colourful walls and wood floors are another. Next door is an associated English-language used-book store. There's a **Red Bus II** (Map p362; ☎ 321 7100; VI Szövetség utca 35; dm/s/d 2700/6500/7500Ft; ✗ ▢ ) near Keleti train station.

**Garibaldi Guesthouse** (Map p362; ☎ 302 3457; baldi guest@hotmail.com; V Garibaldi utca 5; per person €20-45) This old building belongs to an eccentric, multilingual owner who has many apartments on several floors. Double, triple, quad and five-person guestrooms have shared kitchens and en suite bathrooms and are furnished with crazy deer-in-the-woods tapestries, plush pink draperies and odd antiques. Some small rooms with shared bath (€18) are in the inquisitive owner's flat.

Other recommended hostels:

**Station Guesthouse** (Map pp358-9; ☎ 221 8864; www.stationguesthouse.hu; XIV Mexikói út 36/b; dm 1900-2700Ft, r 6400Ft; ✕ ▣ ) This is a party house: there's a 24-hour bar, pool table and occasional live music. Take red bus 7 from Keleti train station.

**Yellow Submarine Hostel** (Map p362; ☎ 331 9896; www.yellowsubmarinehostel.com; VI Teréz körút 56, 3rd fl; dm/s/d 2800/7000/8000Ft; ✕ ▣ ) Overlooking busy ring road, near Nyugati.

**Best Hostel** (Map p362; ☎ 332 4934; www.best hostel.hu; VI Podmaniczky utca 27, 1st fl; dm/s/d 3000/4200/8400Ft; ✕ ▣ ) Closest to Nyugati train station; not too, too noisy.

**Mellow Mood Central Hostel** (Map p362; ☎ 411 1310; www.mellowmoodhostel.com; V Bécsi utca; dm in 4-/6-/8-bed room 4100/3600/3200Ft, tw 5700Ft; ✕ ▣ )

### MIDRANGE

**Hostel Marco Polo** (Map p362; ☎ 413 2555; www .marcopolohostel.com; VII Nyár utca 6; dm 3800-5800Ft, s 10,800-12,800Ft, d 14,200-17,000Ft; ✕ ▣ ) With telephones and satellite TV in the rooms, and a bar-restaurant in the cellar, this Mellow Mood Ltd hostel is more like a hotel. Pastel greens and yellows colour the nifty rooms. The neighbourhood is not the world's most polished, but it's safe.

**Hotel Queen Mary** (Map p362; ☎ 413 3510; www .hotelqueenmary.hu; district V Kertész utca 34; s €50-70, d €60-85; ✕ ✕ ) Among the trendy bars and cafés of Kertész street, this hotel, in a 19th-century building, has neat rooms with modern furniture and hanging potted plants. If you're travelling in a group, ask about the triples (€75 to €105) and quads (€84 to €112).

**Leo Panzió** (Map p362; ☎ 266 9041; www.leopanzio .hu; V Kossuth Lajos utca 2/A, 2nd fl; s €45-66, d €69-82; ✕ ✕ ) Just steps from Váci utca, the Leo is in the middle of everything. Rooms have an Art Deco-ish flair with cherry-stained beds inset with blonde wood. Some have views of Elizabeth Bridge. The tiny bathrooms sparkle.

**Kálvin Ház** (Map p362; ☎ 216 4635; www.kalvin house.hu; IX Gönczy Pál utca 6; s €55-62, d €65-82; ✕ ▣ ) One of the few historic pensions in town – the Victorian antiques and high ceilings are a standout. Laundry service and internet access are a bonus. The restored 19th-century, coral-colour building is near Kálvin tér metro station and Ráday utca nightlife.

**Radio Inn** (Map p362; ☎ 342 8347; www.radioinn .hu; VI Benczúr utca 19; s €52-70, d €75-86; ✕ ) Spacious apartments with full kitchens, sitting areas and one or two bedrooms are on offer here, and they are perfect if you wish to stay for longer and really feel at home in Budapest. Embassies are your neighbours on the quiet, tree-lined street near Bajza utca metro stop (M1 yellow line).

Other good options:

**Hotel Fortuna** (Map pp358-9; ☎ 288 8100; www .fortunahajo.hu; Szent István Park, waterfront; s with shared bathroom €16-20, d €24-30, tr €32-40; Ⓟ ) Float on a boat (hotel) on the Danube. Doubles with bathroom and satellite TV cost €60 to €80.

**Dunaparts** ( ☎ 225 9003; www.dunaparts.com; apt for 1-2 people €55-60) Perhaps one of the best places for renting apartments, this is an internet booking agency with one- and two-bedroom apartments in central Pest. The friendly staff come and pick you up from the airport, free of charge.

**Hotel Ibis Centrum** (Map p362; ☎ 215 8585; www .ibis-centrum.hu; IX Ráday utca 6; s €59-69, d €85-106; Ⓟ ✕ ✕ ▣ ) So, so near the bar and café scene. The style is chain-hotel modern and modular.

**Hotel Margitsziget** (Map pp358-9; ☎ 329 2949; hotelmargitsziget@axelero.hu; XIII Margitsziget; r 14,500Ft; Ⓟ ✿ ) Good-value budget resort; there are tennis courts, a swimming pool and sauna.

### TOP END

**Corinthia Grand Hotel Royal** (Map p362; ☎ 479 4000; www.corinthiahotels.com; VII Erzsébet körút 43-49; s €140-250, d €160-350; Ⓟ ✕ ✕ ▣ ✿ ) Pest's pride and joy of five-star beauties has been carefully reconstructed in the Austro-Hungarian style of heavy drapes, sparkling chandeliers and large, luxurious ballrooms, and has won prizes for best hotel architecture.

**Danubius Grand Hotel Margitsziget** (Map pp358-9; ☎ 889 4700; www.danubiusgroup.com/grandhotel; XIII Margitsziget; s €131-164, d €150-184; Ⓟ ✕ ✕ ✿ ) The Margaret Island setting is a green oasis in the city, and the 1873 splendour of the hotel contrasts with the contemporary nature of its sister, the **Danubius Thermal Hotel Margitsziget** (Map pp358-9; ☎ 889 4700; www.danubiusgroup .com/thermalhotel; XIII Margitsziget; s €144-174, d €164-194; Ⓟ ✕ ✕ ✿ ). The two are connected via an underground passageway and guests at both enjoy free use of the upscale baths at the Thermal.

**Four Seasons Hotel** (Map p362; ☎ 268 6000; www .fourseasons.com; district V Roosevelt tér 5-6; r €270-700; Ⓟ ✕ ✕ ✿ ) Restored to Dr Seuss–esque elegance with mushroom-shaped windows, whimsical ironwork and glittering gold decorative tiles on the exterior, the Four Seasons inhabits the Art Nouveau Gresham Palace and provides superb views of the Danube through Roosevelt Park.

# EATING

It's becoming more common to find both Hungarian and international cuisines on the streets of Budapest. There are restaurants so modern and trendy that they could sit proudly in the streets of Manhattan, and others that are oblivious to the concept of change, with traditional food and old-fashioned décor. Both types can be equally good (or bad), and there's no guarantee that going posh will result in better nosh. In any case, eating out is affordable in Budapest, and even on the tightest of budgets you should be able to squeeze in one upmarket restaurant.

Fast-food restaurants and take-away windows abound on the ring roads and in pedestrian areas. The train and bus stations all have food stands.

Ráday utca and Liszt Ferenc tér are the two most popular traffic-free streets. The moment the weather warms up, tables and umbrellas spring up on the pavements and the people of Budapest crowd the streets. Both areas have tons of cafés, restaurants, snack shops and bars.

## Buda
### BUDGET
**Fény utca piac** (market; Map p361; II Fény at Retek utca; �־ 6am-5pm Mon-Fri, 6am-2pm Sat) Next to Mammut I Shopping Mall, this market has picnic supplies and produce on the ground level and food stands and butcher shops on the 1st floor.

**Bambi Presszó** ( ☎ 212 3171; II Frankel Leó út 2-4; mains 500-800Ft; �־ 8am-9pm Mon-Fri, 9am-8pm Sat-Sun) Old plastic plants hang above your head here and plastic dominoes whack the plastic tables. This is how the old Communist *presszó* bars used to be and what makes it a cult eatery among young and old Budapestians. The food is basic, but the omelettes and sandwiches taste great. Many come just to have a beer and dream of the old times.

**Fortuna Önkiszolgáló** (Map p361; ☎ 375 2401; I Hess András utca 4, 1st fl; mains 500-900Ft; �־ 11.30am-2.30pm Mon-Fri; ☒ ) For a bite to eat near the castle, climb the passageway stairs to this cafeteria, which serves all the fried favourites.

**Pita House** (Map p361; ☎ 315 1479; II Margit körút 105; mains 500-800Ft; ☒ 8am-midnight; ☒ ) This is an excellent choice if you're in Moszkva tér, with tasty gyros and falafel pitas. A helping from the salad bar costs 410Ft.

### MIDRANGE
**Café Miró** (Map p361; ☎ 375 5458; I Úri utca 30; mains 690-2190Ft; ☒ 9am-midnight) Most restaurants on Castle Hill have surly service and are full of tourists. This arty café is no exception, but the soups and Greek salad are good. For dessert there are plenty of cakes to choose from, and the delicious *erdei gyümölcskremleves* (forest berry soup) is topped with a scoop of vanilla ice cream.

**Tabáni Kakas** (Map p361; ☎ 375 7165; I Attila út 27; mains 1900Ft; ☒ noon-midnight) Everything here is cooked in goose fat, and delicious it is. The place is old-fashioned and dimly lit, and the service friendly. Try the crispy goose leg with juicy, cooked red cabbage and potato and onion mash – absolutely ravishing.

### TOP END
**Hemingway** (Map pp358-9; ☎ 381 0522; XI Kosztolányi Dezső tér 2, Feneketlen-tó; mains 1850-3100Ft; ☒ noon-midnight; ☒ ) A bit of panache: dine on a terrace overlooking the Bottomless Lake. Entrées include lamb cutlet with a blue-cheese mint sauce.

**Mongolian Barbecue** (Map p361; ☎ 353 6363; XII Márvány utca 19/A; mains before/after 5pm 1990/3690Ft; ☒ noon-midnight; ☒ ) Choose your meat and watch as it's grilled in front of you. The all-you-can-eat price includes as much house beer and wine as you can sink, too.

## Pest
### BUDGET
**Frici Papa** (Map p362; ☎ 351 0197; VII Király utca 55; mains 400-700Ft; ☒ 11am-8pm Mon-Sat) A popular place for a basic, hearty, no-frills Hungarian meal where you sit elbow-to-elbow with workers, riff-raff, families and tourists. For the price there's a surprising amount of white-meat chicken in the soup.

**Kisharang** (Map p362; ☎ 269 3861; V Október 6 utca 17; mains 490-850Ft; ☒ 11am-8pm Mon-Fri, 11.30am-4.30pm Sat & Sun) Lantern-like lamps hang low over chequered tablecloths in this wonderful little *étkezde* (canteen). It serves simple dishes that change daily; expect to wait for a table.

**Kis Italia** (Map p362; ☎ 269 3145; V Szemere utca 22; pizzas & pastas 760-990Ft; ☒ 11am-10pm Mon-Sat; ☒ ) Descend into this cellar restaurant for interesting pizza combinations – such as bacon, onion and pickle – at low prices. Just ignore the cheesy synthesizer player in the corner; he's not too loud.

**Ráday Étkezde** (Map p362; ☎ 219 5451; IX Ráday utca 29; mains 420-650Ft; ☒ 6am-4pm Mon-Fri) Of the many takeaway windows and self-service places

HUNGARY

among the cafés and bars on Ráday utca, this is a reliable choice. The *főzelék*, a sort of creamed vegetable stew, is particularly good.

**Nagycsarnok** (Great Market; Map p362; IX Vámház körút 1-3; ☎ 6am-5pm Mon, to 6pm Tue-Fri, to 2pm Sat) This is Budapest's main market, selling fruit and vegetables, deli items, fish and meat. Food stalls on the upper level sell beer, sausage and tasty *lángos* among other quick eats. There's also a cafeteria – a bit of a tourist trap – with a Romani violinist and midrange prices.

Grocery-store chains are everywhere in Pest; Kaiser's has a branch facing Blaha Lujza tér and one opposite Nyugati train station on Nyugati tér.

### MIDRANGE

**Al-Amir** (Map p362; ☎ 352 1422; VII Király utca 17; mains 700-1500Ft; ☎ noon-11pm Mon-Sat; 1-11pm Sun) Good Middle Eastern food is hard to come by in Hungary, but this place is excellent. Pictures of mysterious eyes behind veils and camels in the desert decorate the spacious, otherwise plain space. Order either a meze-type meal, combining the many starters, or try the kebabs and a nice tabbouleh. No alcohol is served.

**Paprika Vendeglö** (Map pp358-9; ☎ 06 70 574 6508; I Dózsa György út 72; mains 950-1600Ft; ☎ 11am-11pm) Step inside what looks like a rustic Hungarian farm house on the very urban street bordering City Park (M1 yellow line, Hősök tere). Good game dishes.

**Angyalok Konyhája** (Map p362; ☎ 412 0427; XIII Visegrádi utca; mains 1080-1480Ft; ☎ 11am-11pm Sun-Thu, to midnight Fri & Sat; ✗ ) Formerly known as Wabisabi, the food here is organic and vegan-friendly, with strong Asian influences – a rarity in meat-

---

**AUTHOR'S CHOICE**

**Menza** (Map p362; ☎ 413 1482; V Liszt Ferenc tér 2; mains 890-1990Ft; ☎ 11am-11pm; ✗ ) Probably the most popular restaurant in Budapest, Menza is a visual and gastronomic delight. The spacious restaurant's design is all retro shapes and colours, futuristic lampshades from the '60s and old plastic-letter wall-hanging menu boards with exquisite offerings such as pumpkin soup garnished with balsamic vinaigrette and toasted pumpkin seeds. One of the best dishes is the roast pork tenderloin with rose lentil purée and roasted potato wedges. The house wine is good. Eat at Menza, we implore you.

---

crazy Hungary. The portions are huge, although not massively delicious. The décor is a mix of Arabic and Japanese, floor seating on cushions and shoes off.

Other recommendations:

**Vista Café** (Map p362; ☎ 268 0888; VI Paulay Ede utca 7; mains 800-1600Ft; ☎ 9am-11pm Mon-Fri, 10am-11pm Sat & Sun) Hungarian, Mediterranean, Italian – a little of everything, including free internet access.

**Kék Rózsa** (Map p362; ☎ 342 8981; VII Wesselényi utca 9; mains 850-1600Ft; ☎ 11am-10pm) Three-course Hungarian menus 1200Ft to 1800Ft.

**Taverna Dionysos** (Map p362; ☎ 318 1222; V Belgrád rakpart 16; mains 1250-2750Ft; ☎ noon-midnight; ✗ ) A bit of Mediterranean sun and juicy *stifado* (a Greek stew with meat, onions and tomato).

### TOP END

**Fatàl** (Map p362; ☎ 266 2607; V Váci utca 67, cnr Pintér utca; mains 1580-2490Ft; ☎ 11.30am-2am) A whimsical menu prefaces the fun at this cellar restaurant with medieval adornment. The homy Hungarian dishes are served in gigantic portions. We've heard comment that waiters can be brusque with foreigners, but that wasn't our experience. Book ahead.

**Bagolyvár** (Owl's Castle; Map pp358-9; ☎ 468 3110; XIV Állatkert út 2; mains 1600-3500Ft; ☎ noon-11pm) Gundel's first sibling, the Owl's Castle, is known for Hungarian classics done impeccably. The hidden courtyard tables are a pleasant surprise.

**Borvendéglö 1894** (Map pp358-9; ☎ 468 4040; XIV Állatkert út 2; mains 1650-2700Ft; ☎ 6-11pm Tue-Sat) This wine cellar is one of the two sister restaurants to the world-famous (and overpriced) Gundel restaurant around the corner. The best things about the place are the choice of wine for tasting and the traditional Hungarian drinking snacks – goose cracklings, steak tartar and *pogacs* (salty, buttery biscuits).

**Múzeum** (Map p362; ☎ 267 0375; VIII Múzeum körút 12; mains 2400-4400Ft; ☎ 10.30am-1.30am) *Fin-de-siècle* ambience, wide lanterns hanging low from the high ceilings, the Múzeum is like an old friend to many of Budapest's diners. The Hungarian food is good and varied, the service is smooth and the place stays open late.

## DRINKING

One of Budapest's ceaseless wonders is the number of bars, cellars, cafés, clubs and general places to drink. The cafés usually serve cakes, and the bars almost always have live music, and, if you can see through the smoke curtains, lovely (or at least interesting) décor.

In the spring and summer months thousands of outdoor pavement tables spring up all over the city. The best places to drink are in Pest (Buda's too sleepy to stay up all night), especially along Liszt Ferenc tér and Radáy utca; the squares are pedestrian-only and have a positively festive feel during the summer.

## Buda

**Kisrabló** (Map pp358-9; ☎ 209 1588; XI Zenta utca 3; ⏰ 11am-2am) The eclectic pub décor here resembles a boat's hull, busty masthead and all. Take tram 19 or 49 one stop past Danubius Hotel Gellért.

**Zöld Párdon** (Map pp358-9; XI Írini József utca at Petöfi híd; Map pp358-9; ⏰ 9am-6am mid-Apr–mid-Sep) College students on a budget flock to the big, seasonal beer garden and disco near Petöfi Bridge.

## Pest

**Sark** (Map p362; ☎ 328 0753; VII Klauzál tér 14; ⏰ 10am-2am Mon-Thu & Sun, 10am-3am Fri & Sat) A small bar on two levels with an airy ground floor and a large photo mural decorating the space. Downstairs is a smoky cellar where a Romani band plays every Tuesday (see p372) and a mix of foreigners, Hungarians and Roma jump around together. During the day it's a quiet place, nice for a coffee, but come evening time, Sark gets packed and the atmosphere is fab.

**Szimpla/Dupla** (Map p362; ☎ 342 8991; VII Kertész utca 48; ⏰ noon-2am) Perhaps it was the espressos that inspired the name ('szimpla' means single and 'dupla' double) of these two excellent places. The café and restaurant are connected by a long, atmospheric cellar bar and make a kind of two-in-one experience. The furniture is distressed, the cutlery and crockery rescued from flea markets, and the crowd super relaxed. There's live jazz on Fridays.

**Eckermann** (Map p362; ☎ 374 4076; VI Andrássy út 24; ⏰ 9am-11pm Mon-Sat; 10am-10pm Sun) Part of the Goethe Institut, this airy café attracts an intellectual crowd that is invariably either reading the newspapers or discussing what they've just read in the newspapers. They are apparently refugees from the now tourist-occupied Müvész across the street. Try the plentiful Viennese coffee, served in bowls, and excellent pastries, perfect for breakfast. In the evenings Eckermann turns out the lights and lights up candles, and the clientele sips wine and discusses tomorrow's news.

**Centrál Kávéház** (Map p362; ☎ 266 4572; V Károlyi Mihály utca 9; ⏰ 7am-1am) Having been closed for a long time, Centrál Kávéház is once again one of the finest coffee houses in the city. The interior has been carefully reconstructed to resemble its original 19th-century décor, with high, engraved ceilings, lace-curtained windows, tall plants, elegant, dainty coffee cups and professional service. You can have an omelette breakfast here, eat a full-on meal, or just sit down with a coffee or beer and enjoy the atmosphere.

For a cup of coffee in exquisite Art Nouveau surroundings, two places are particularly historical: **Gerbeaud** (Map p362; ☎ 429 9000; V Vörösmarty tér 7; ⏰ 9am-9pm; ❌ ✶ ), Budapest's cake-and-coffee-culture king, serving since 1870. Or sit your bum on the same chairs where Hungary's dreaded ÁVO secret police members sat at **Lukács** (Map p362; ☎ 302 8747; VI Andrássy út 70; ⏰ 9am-8pm Mon-Fri, 10am-8pm Sat & Sun), now inside the CIB Bank headquarters.

## ENTERTAINMENT

Budapest has a nightlife that can keep you up for days on end. And we don't mean you trying to get to sleep in your hotel room while the club next door pounds its techno against your walls. There are nightclubs, bars, live concerts – classical and folk – Hungarian traditional dancing nights, opera treats, ballet, DJ bars and random Cinetrip (www.cinetrip.hu) club nights at the thermal spas. Yes, you heard us right. It's you, your swimsuit, your mates and a bunch of strangers, wading waist deep in thermal waters to thumping beats, and it's fantastic.

Ticket prices are quite reasonable by Western European standards, and the venues are often stunning. To find out what's on, contact Tourinform (see p360) or ticket offices, or check out the free, bimonthly *Programme Magazine* (available at tourist spots), and the free, weekly *Pesti Est* (available at restaurants and clubs). The weekly *Budapest Sun* (www.budapestsun.com) has a 10-day event calendar online, and Budapest Week Online (www.budapestweek.com) has events, music and movie listings.

### Gay & Lesbian Venues

**Angyal** (Map p362; ☎ 351 6490; VII Szövetség utca 33; ⏰ 10pm-5am Fri & Sat) Budapest's flagship gay nightclub has three bars and plays some high-energy dance mixes. Men only on Saturday (admission 800Ft).

**Café Eklektika** (Map p362; ☎ 266 3054; V Semmelweiss utca 21; ⏰ noon-midnight Mon-Fri, 5pm-midnight Sat & Sun) The town's only real lesbian venue attracts a mixed, beat generation-type crowd.

## Live Music & Theatre

**Magyar Állami Operaház** (Hungarian State Opera House; Map p362; ☎ 332 8197; www.opera.hu; VI Andrássy út 22) Feel a bit royal and get a box and some binoculars at this amazing, gilt-laden place that was built in 1884. Every opera performance is an event with a capital E. The ballet company performs here as well.

**Liszt Ferenc Zeneakadémia** (Map p362; ☎ 342 0179; www.musicacademy.hu; VI Liszt Ferenc tér 8; ⊙ 10am-2pm Mon-Fri, 2-8pm Sat & Sun for ticket office) You can hear the musicians practising outside this great Art Deco hall, where the 1907 Music Academy hosts excellent classical symphony concerts. Tickets are sold only at the onsite ticket office.

**Kalamajka Táncház** (Map p362; ☎ 354 3400; www.aranytiz.hu, Hungarian only; V Arany János utca 10; ⊙ 9pm-2am Sat) The Kalamajka is an excellent place to hear authentic Hungarian music, especially the Saturday night dance specials where everyone gets up and takes part.

**Fonó Budai Zeneház** ( ☎ 206 5300; www.fono.hu; XI Sztregova utca 3; concerts 700-1000Ft) The best place in Budapest for folk music of any kind, from Hungarian, Transylvanian or Balkan Romani, to Klezmer, tango and even sometimes a didgeridoo night. Check its website for upcoming events.

**Sark** (Map p362; ☎ 328 0753; VII Klauzál tér 14; entry 400Ft; ⊙ 10am-2am Mon-Thu & Sun, to 3am Fri & Sat) For excellent Romani music on Tuesday nights, come here and dance away to Szilvási Gipsy Folk Band (www.szilvasigipsy.hu), a band that has a little following and that gets the crowd doing impressive Hungarian-Romani dances.

Classical concerts are held regularly in the city's churches, including Mátyás Templom (p364) on Castle Hill in Buda.

Useful ticket brokers are **Music Mix** (Map p362; ☎ 266 1655; V Váci utca 33; ⊙ 10am-6pm Mon-Fri, to 3pm Sat) and **Vigadó Jegyiroda** (Map p362; ☎ 327 4322; V Vigadó tér 6; ⊙ 10am-8pm Mon-Fri).

## Nightclubs

Clubbing in Budapest can mean anything from a floor-thumping techno club to a hip place to hang out and listen to jazz. Cover charges range from 200Ft to 1000Ft.

**Cha Cha Cha** (Map p362; V Kálvin tér metro station; ⊙ 11am-5am) Dozens of jeans and corduroy trousers were sacrificed to upholster the furniture in metro station–based Cha Cha Cha, Budapest's hippest bar-club with the city's best DJs playing records until the first morning trains start running, so the punters

can get home. Things don't get started till at least 11pm.

**Gödör Klub** (Map p362; ☎ 06 20 943 5463; V Erzsébet tér; ⊙ 2pm-2am) A large underground club (with a glass ceiling revealing the square above) provides the venue for truly eclectic live music – from world beat to the Doors to jazz – played to a local audience of all ages.

**Trafó Bár Tangó** (Map p362; ☎ 456 2049; IX Lillium utca 41; ⊙ 6pm-1am) An arty crowd makes the scene beneath the eponymous cultural house and exhibit space. Latin, jazz and disco tunes.

## SHOPPING

Apart from the usual folk arts, wines and spirits, food and music, there are a few interesting flea markets and some great young-designer shops. Tons of shops along Váci utca (p365) and stands on the top floor of the Nagycsarnok (p365) sell Hungarian souvenirs, but the real souvenir-shopper's paradise is the old town centre at Szentendre (p374), just 40 minutes away by commuter rail.

**Folkart Kézművesház** (Map p362; ☎ 318 5143; V Régiposta utca 12; ⊙ 10am-7pm Mon-Fri, to 4pm Sat) Some of the most authentic handmade folk crafts available in Budapest. You can buy embroidered folk costumes from Kalocsa, leatherwork horsewhips from the plains, and woven items from across the country.

**Rózsavölgyi Music Shop** (Map p362; ☎ 318 3500; V Szervita tér 5; ⊙ 9.30am-7pm Mon-Fri, 10am-5pm Sat) Classical and folk music CDs and tapes are on sale here.

**Retrock** (Map p362; ☎ 318 1007; www.retrock.com; V Ferenc István utca 28; ⊙ 10.30am-7.30pm Mon-Fri, to 4.30pm Sat) An excellent designer/vintage clothes shop, where a bunch of young Hungarian and international designers produce kitschy, stylish and always unique clothes at affordable prices.

There's an excellent selection of Hungarian wines at the **Magyar Borok Háza** (House of Hungarian Wines; Map p361; ☎ 212 1031; www.magyarborokhaza.hu; I Szentháromság tér 6; ⊙ noon-8pm) in Buda, and of fruit brandies and wine at the **Magyar Palinka Háza** (Map p362; ☎ 235 0488; VIII Rákóczi út 17; ⊙ 9am-7pm Mon-Sat) in Pest.

Three markets take place in Budapest during the week, each a little different from the other. The closest to the city centre is **Városligeti Bolhapiac** (Map pp358-9; ⊙ 7am-2pm Sat & Sun) at Petőfi Csarnok in the City Park. There is junk and antiques, and the best things are to be found early in the morning. The real market mamma though is the **Ecseri** (XIX Nagykőrösi út 156; 8am-4pm Mon-Fri, 7am-3pm Sat), on the western edge of town. International antiques dealers come to scout on Saturdays, so things can get pricey. Take bus 52 from Elizabeth Bridge. **Jozsefvárosi piac** (Map pp358-9; VII Kőbányai út 21-23; 6am-6pm) is a vast Chinese goods market and a world unto itself. Take tram 28 or 37.

## GETTING THERE & AWAY
### Air
The main international carriers fly in and out of Budapest's **Ferihegy 2 airport** (BUD; ☎ 296 9696), 24km southeast of the centre on Hwy 4; low-cost airlines use the older **Ferihegy 1 airport** ( ☎ 296 7000), next door. For carriers flying within Eastern Europe, see p408; for more on getting to Budapest from outside Eastern Europe, see p925.

### Boat
In addition to its hydrofoils that travel internationally to Bratislava and Vienna (p409), **Mahart PassNave** (Map p362; ☎ 484 4005; www .mahartpassnave.hu; Vigadó tér Pier) ferries depart for Szentendre, Visegrád and Esztergom in the Danube Bend daily, April to October.

### Bus
**Volánbusz** ( ☎ 219 8080; www.volanbusz.hu), the national bus line, has an extensive list of destinations from Budapest. All international buses and some buses to/from southern Hungary use **Népliget bus station** (Map pp358-9; ☎ 264 3939; IX Üllői út 131). **Stadion bus station** (Map pp358-9; ☎ 252 4498; XIV Hungária körút 48-52) serves most domestic destinations. Most buses to the northern Danube Bend arrive at and leave from the **Árpád híd bus station** (Map pp358-9; ☎ 329 1450, off XIII Róbert Károly körút). All stations are on metro lines, and all are in Pest. If the ticket office is closed, you can buy your ticket on the bus.

For details of international bus services within Eastern Europe, see p408 and p929.

### Car & Motorcycle
Car rental is not recommended if you are staying in Budapest. The public transportation network is extensive and cheap, whereas parking is scarce and there are more than enough cars and motor emissions on the congested streets already.

If you want to venture into the countryside, travelling by car may be the best way to go. Daily rates start around €40 per day with kilo-

metres included. If an office is not at the airport, the company will usually provide free pick-up and delivery within Budapest or at the airport during office hours. All the major international chains have branches at Ferihegy 2 airport.

**Americana Rent-a-Car** (Map pp358-9; ☎ 350 2542; www.americana.matav.hu; XIII Dózsa György út 65; 8am-6pm Mon-Fri, to noon Sat) Reliable office in the Ibis Volga hotel.

**Recent Car** (Map pp358-9; ☎ 453 0003; www.recent car.hu; III Óbudai hajógyári-sziget 131; 8am-8pm) One of the cheapest.

### Train
The Hungarian State Railways, **MÁV** ( ☎ 461 5400 domestic information, 461 5500 international information; www.elvira.hu) covers the country well and has its schedule online. The **MÁV Ticket Office** (Map p362; ☎ 461 5400; VI Andrássy út 35; 9am-6pm Mon-Fri Apr-Sep, 9am-5pm Mon-Fri Oct-Mar) provides information and sells domestic and international train tickets and seat reservations (you can also buy tickets at the busy stations). To avoid queues go to booths posted 'International Ticket Office' – you can buy domestic tickets here and there might be some English speakers.

The commuter rail, HÉV, begins at Batthyány tér in Buda and travels north through the suburbs. If you have a *turista* pass, you still need a supplemental ticket to get to Szentendre, the northern terminus, and towns outside the city limits.

**Keleti train station** (Eastern; ☎ 333 6342; VIII Kerepesi út 2-4) handles international trains from Vienna and many other points east, plus domestic trains to/from the north and northeast. For some Romanian, German and Slovak destinations, as well as domestic ones to/from the northwest and the Danube Bend, head for **Nyugati train station** (Western; ☎ 349 0115; VI Nyugati tér). For trains bound for Lake Balaton and the south, go to **Déli train station** (Southern; ☎ 375 6293; I Krisztina körút 37). All three train stations are on metro lines.

For details of international trains within Eastern Europe, see p409; for trains travelling to places outside Eastern Europe, see p930.

## GETTING AROUND
### To/From the Airport
The simplest way to get to town is to take the **Airport Minibus** ( ☎ 296 8555; one-way/return 2100/3600Ft; 5am-1am) directly to the place you're staying. Buy tickets at the clearly marked stands in the arrivals halls. The cheapest way is to take the BKV Ferihegy bus (from outside the

HUNGARY

baggage claim at Ferihegy 2, or on the main road outside Ferihegy 1) to the end of its run, the Kőbánya–Kispest stop, which is at the M2 blue line metro terminus. Then ride the metro to your destination. The bus ride takes about 25 minutes, as does the metro ride to the central metro hub (Deák tér). You need a 230Ft ticket, available at newsstands or vending machines, which you can validate on the bus and in the metro. If you want to switch metro lines, you'll need a second ticket.

### Boat

From May to August, the **BKV passenger ferry** (Map pp358-9; ☎ 06 20 955 3782; www.ship-bp.hu, Hungarian only) departs from Boráros tér Terminus beside Petőfi Bridge, south of the centre, and heads to Pünkösdfürdő Terminus north of Aquincum, with many stops along the way. Tickets (adult/child 500/400Ft from end to end) are usually sold on board. The ferry stop closest to the Castle District is Batthyány tér, and Petőfi tér is not far from Vörösmarty tér, a convenient place to pick up the boat on the Pest side.

### Public Transport

Public transport is run by **BKV** ( ☎ 342 2335; www .bkv.hu). The three underground metro lines (M1 yellow, M2 red, M3 blue) meet at Deák tér in Pest. The HÉV above-ground suburban railway runs north from Batthyány tér in Buda. A *turista* transport pass is only good on the HÉV within the city limits (south of the Békásmegyer stop). There's also an extensive network of buses, trams and trolleybuses. Public transport operates from 4.30am until 11.30pm, and 18 night buses (marked with an 'É') run along main roads.

A single ticket for all forms of transport is 140Ft (60 minutes of uninterrupted travel, no metro line changes). A transfer ticket (230Ft) is valid for one trip with one validated transfer within 90 minutes. The three-day *turista* pass (2200Ft) or the seven-day pass (2600Ft) make things easier, allowing unlimited travel inside the city limits. Keep your ticket or pass handy; the fine for 'riding black' is 2000Ft on the spot, or 5500Ft if you pay later at the **BKV Office** (Map p362; ☎ 461 6544; VII Akácfa utca 22; ☒ 6am-8pm Mon-Fri, 8am-2pm Sat).

### Taxi

Overcharging foreigners (rigged meters, detours…) is common. Never get into a taxi that does not have an official yellow licence plate, the logo of the taxi firm, and a visible table of fares. If you have to take a taxi, it's best to call one; this costs less than if you flag one down. Make sure you know the number of the landline phone you're calling from as that's how the dispatcher establishes your address (though you can call from a mobile too). Dispatchers usually speak English. **City** ( ☎ 211 1111), **Fő** ( ☎ 222 2222) and **Rádió** ( ☎ 377 7777) are reliable companies.

# THE DANUBE BEND

North of Budapest, the Danube breaks through the Pilis and Börzsöny Hills in a sharp bend before continuing into Slovakia. Here medieval kings once ruled Hungary from majestic palaces overlooking the river at Esztergom and Visegrád. East of Visegrád the river divides, with Szentendre and Vác on different branches. Today the easy access to historic monuments, rolling green scenery – and tons of souvenir craft shops – lure many day-trippers from Budapest.

## SZENTENDRE

☎ 26 / pop 22,700

Once an artists' colony, now a popular day trip from Budapest (19km north), pretty little Szentendre (*sen*-ten-dreh) has narrow, winding streets and is a favourite with souvenir-shoppers. The charming old centre has plentiful cafés, art and craft galleries, and there are several Orthodox churches that are worth a peek. Expect things to get crowded in summer and at weekends. Outside town is the largest open-air village museum in the country.

### Orientation & Information

From the HÉV train and bus stations, walk under the subway and up Kossuth Lajos utca to Fő tér, the centre of the Old Town. The Duna korzó and the river embankment is a block east of this square. The Mahart ferry pier is about 1km northeast on Czóbel sétány, off Duna korzó. There are no left-luggage offices at the HÉV train or bus stations.

**Tourinform** ( ☎ 317 965; Dumtsa Jenő utca 22; ☒ 9am-6.30pm Mon-Fri, 10am-2pm Sat) has information about the numerous small museums and galleries in town. The **OTP Bank** (Dumtsa Jenő utca 6) is just off Fő tér, and the **main post office** (Kossuth Lajos utca 23-25) is across from the bus and train stations. **Game Planet** ( ☎ 505 068; Petőfi Sándor utca

1; 🕙 10am-10pm) is an internet café with access for 300Ft per hour.

## Sights

Begin your sightseeing at the colourful Fő tér, the town's main square. Here you'll find many buildings from the 18th century, including the **Emlékkereszt** (Memorial Cross; 1763) and the 1752 Serbian Orthodox **Blagoveštenska Templom** (Blagoveštenska Church; ☎ 310 554; Fő tér; admission 200Ft; 🕙 10am-5pm Tue-Sun), which is small but stunning.

All the pedestrian lanes surrounding the square burst with shops, the merchandise spilling out into displays on the streets. Downhill to the east, off a side street on the way to the Danube, is the **Margit Kovács Múzeum** ( ☎ 310 244; Vastagh György utca 1; adult/student 600/400Ft; 🕙 10am-6pm Feb-Oct). Kovács (1902–77) was a ceramicist who combined Hungarian folk, religious and modern themes to create her much beloved figures. Uphill to the northwest, a narrow passageway leads up from between Fő tér 8 and 9 to Várhegy (Castle Hill) and the **Szent Janos Plébánia Templom** (Parish Church of St John; Várhegy), rebuilt in 1710, from where you get great views of the town

and the Danube. Nearby, the tall red tower of the Serbian **Belgradi Székesegyház** (Belgrade Cathedral; Pátriárka utca 5), from 1764, casts its shadow. You can hear beautiful chanting wafting from the open doors during services. The **Szerb Ortodox Egyháztőrnténeti Gyűjtemény** (Serbian Orthodox Ecclesiastical Art Collection; ☎ 312 399; Pátriárka utca 5; adult/student 200/100Ft; 🕙 10am-6pm Wed-Sun mid-Mar–Oct, 10am-4pm Fri-Sun Nov–mid-Mar) is in the courtyard.

Don't miss the extensive **Szabadtéri Néprajzi Múzeum** (Open-Air Ethnographic Museum; ☎ 502 500; adult/student 800/400Ft; 🕙 9am-5pm Tue-Sun Apr-Oct) 3.5km outside town. Walking through the fully furnished ancient wooden and stone homes, churches and working buildings brought here from around the country, you can see what rural life was – and sometimes still is – like in different regions of Hungary. The five reconstructed villages of this *skansen* (village museum) are not close to each other, but you can take a wagon ride (500Ft) between them. In the centre of the park stand Roman-era ruins. Frequent weekend festivals give you a chance to see folk costumes, music and dance, as well as home crafts. To get here, take the bus marked 'Skansen' from stand No 7 (100Ft, 20 minutes, hourly).

HUNGARY

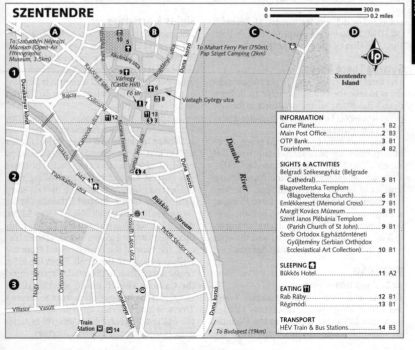

### Sleeping & Eating

Seeing Szentendre on a day trip from Budapest is probably your best bet. The town can be easily covered in a day, even if you spend a couple of hours at the open-air museum. For private rooms in town, head west of the centre around the Dunakanyar körút ring road, and look for *'Zimmer frei'* signs. Being a tourist town, there are plenty of places to sit at an outside table and grab a bite to eat.

**Pap Sziget Camping** (☎ 310 697; www.pap-sziget.hu; camp sites per person €6, caravan sites €15, motel room with shared bathroom €22, 2-bedroom bungalows €32-40; 🕑 May–mid-Oct; P) The grounds have large shady trees, a sandy beach and 120 tent and caravan sites. Bungalows are raised on stilts and there's parking below. Take bus 1, 2 or 3 – it's 2km from north of town on Szentendre Island.

**Bükkös Hotel** (☎ 312 021; Bükkös part 16; s/d €40/45; P) A Maria Theresa yellow exterior and a dark-wood reception hall welcome you to this 16-room hotel in an old building. The location's good, on a stream between the HÉV station and the Old Town.

**Rab Ráby** (☎ 310 819; Pétér Pál utca 1A; mains 700-1200Ft; 🕑 11am-11pm) The locals' favourite for fish.

Crowd-watch on the square at **Régimódi** (☎ 311 105; Dumtsa Jenő utca 2; mains 700-1200Ft; 🕑 11am-11pm), but don't expect very tasty food.

### Getting There & Away

The most convenient way to get to Szentendre is to take the commuter HÉV train from Buda's Batthyány tér metro station to the end of the line (497Ft one-way, 45 minutes, every 10 to 15 minutes).

From mid-May to mid-September, three Mahart PassNave ferries travel daily from Budapest's Vigadó tér Pier to Szentendre (950Ft, 1½ hours) at 9am, 10.30am and 2pm. Return trips are at 12.20pm, 4pm and 5pm. The 9am boat continues on from Szentendre to Visegrád at 10.40am. In April and October, only the daily 9am departure from Budapest (continuing on to Visegrád only on weekends) and the 4pm return to Budapest from Szentendre run.

## VISEGRÁD

☎ 26 / pop 1500

The spectacular views from the ruins of Visegrád's (*vish*-eh-grahd) 13th-century citadel, high on a hill above a curve in the Danube, are what pulls visitors to this sleepy town. The first fortress here was built by the Romans as a border defence in the 4th century. Hungarian kings built a mighty citadel on the hill top, and a lower castle near the river, after the 13th-century Mongol invasions. In the 14th century a royal palace was built on the flood plain at the foot of the hills, and in 1323 King Charles Robert of Anjou, whose claim to the local throne was being fiercely contested in Buda, moved the royal household here. For nearly two centuries Hungarian royalty alternated between Visegrád and Buda.

The destruction of Visegrád came first at the hands of the occupying Turks and then at the hands of the Habsburgs, who destroyed the citadel to prevent Hungarian independence fighters from using it. All trace of the palace was lost until 1934 when archaeologists, by following descriptions in literary sources, uncovered the ruins that you can visit today.

The small town has two distinct areas: one to the north around Mahart ferry pier and another, the main town, about 1km to the south. There's a Tourinform office, and there's also a rather confusing website that discusses the town's history in English (www.visegrad.hu; click on Mûemlékek).

### Sights & Activities

The partial reconstruction of the **Királyi Palota** (Royal Palace; ☎ 398 026; Fő utca 29; adult/student 500/300Ft; 🕑 9am-4.30pm Tue-Sun), 400m south of the Mahart pier, only hints at its former magnificence. Inside, a small museum is devoted to the history of the palace and its excavation and reconstruction.

The palace's original Gothic fountain, along with town-history exhibits, is in the museum at **Salamon Torony** (Solomon's Tower; ☎ 398 233; adult/child 500/300Ft; 🕑 9am-4.30pm Tue-Sun May-Sep), a few hundred metres north of the palace. The tower was part of a lower castle controlling river traffic. From here you can climb the very steep path uphill to the **Visegrád Cittadella** (☎ 398 101; Várhegy; adult/student 800/350Ft; 🕑 9.30am-5.30pm) directly above. While the citadel (1259) ruins themselves are not as spectacular as their history, the view of the Danube Bend from the walls is well worth the climb. From the town centre a trail leads to the citadel from behind the Catholic church on Fő tér; this is less steep than the arduous climb from Solomon's Tower. A local bus runs up to the citadel from the Mahart PassNave ferry pier three times daily (more often in July and August).

## Sleeping & Eating

As with the other towns in the Danube Bend, Visegrád is an easy day trip from Budapest, so it's not necessary to stay over if you don't want to. **Visegrád Tours** ( ☎ 398 160; Rév utca 15; ◷ 8am-5pm), an extremely accommodating travel agency in the town centre, provides information and books private rooms for between 5500Ft and 6500Ft per person, per night.

**Jurta Camping** ( ☎ 398 217; camp sites per adult/child/ tent 650/400/500Ft; ◷ May-Sep; P ) On Mogyoróh-egy (Hazelnut Hill), about 2km northeast of the citadel, this camp sight is pretty and green. There aren't any bungalows, but there are yurt tents for rent with five beds in each. The Kisvillám' bus goes to Jurta Camping from the ferry pier at 9.25am, 12.25pm and 3.25pm, June to August.

**Hotel Honti Panzió** ( ☎ 398 120; hotelhon@axelero.hu; Fő utca 66; s/d pension €30/35, s/d hotel €40/50; P ) Honti is a friendly pension filled with homy rooms. Bigger, more expensive and newer rooms in the adjacent hotel building still have wooden furniture and rose-coloured curtains your aunt might have made.

**Reneszánsz** ( ☎ 398 081; Fő utca 11; mains 1200-2400Ft; ◷ noon-10pm) Eating in a tourist trap can be fun if you go in for men in tights and silly hats. This is the attire at this medieval banquet-style restaurant. A royal feast, with pheasant soup, roast meats and unlimited wine costs a mighty 4000Ft.

Two better, more down-to-earth options are the **Grill Udvar** (Rév utca 6; mains 500-1000Ft; ◷ 11am-11pm), for pizzas and grilled meat; and **Gulyás Csárda** ( ☎ 398 329; Mátyás Király utca; mains 1000-2000Ft; ◷ 11am-10pm). Both are in the town centre and known for reliable Hungarian standards and cymbalom music.

## Getting There & Away

Frequent buses go to Visegrád from Budapest's Árpád híd bus station (423Ft, 1¼ hours, at least hourly), the Szentendre HÉV station (302Ft, 45 minutes, every 45 minutes) and Esztergom (302Ft, 45 minutes, hourly). No trains go to Visegrád.

On weekends in late April and during most of October, a ferry runs from Budapest to Visegrád (per person/car 280/1050Ft, 3½ hours) at 9am (via Szentendre), returning to Budapest from Visegrád at 4pm. From mid-May to mid-September that same ferry runs daily. There is an additional departure at 7.30am from late May to August, which continues on to Esztergom at 10.50am. The return departure from Visegrád to Budapest is at 5.30pm. On weekends from June to August there is also a high-speed hydrofoil service from Budapest to Visegrád (2000Ft, one hour), departing from Budapest at 9.30am and Visegrád at 4.45pm.

## ESZTERGOM

☎ 33 / pop 28,900

A town full of ecclesiastic wonders, Esztergom (*es*-ter-gohm) has been the seat of Roman Catholicism in Hungary since the 19th century. The soaring Esztergom Bazilika is home to the Primate of Hungary and surrounding museums contain many Christian treasures.

The significance of this town reaches far back into history. The 2nd-century Roman emperor-to-be Marcus Aurelius wrote his famous *Meditations* while he camped here. In the 10th century, Stephen I, founder of the Hungarian state, was born and crowned at the cathedral. From the late 10th to the mid-13th centuries Esztergom served as the Hungarian royal seat. In 1543 the Turks ravaged the town and much of it was destroyed only to be rebuilt in the 18th and 19th centuries. Many of the old buildings in the centre date from those centuries.

## Orientation & Information

The train station is on the southern edge of town, about a 10-minute walk south of the bus station. From the train station, walk north on Baross Gábor út, then along Ady Endre utca to Símor János utca, past the bus station to the town centre. Don't be fooled by the run-down buildings along the walk; the town's true character reveals itself once you get to the hill below the cathedral.

**K&H Bank** (Rákóczi tér) does foreign exchange transactions. The **post office** (Arany János utca 2) is just off Széchenyi tér. **Gran Tours** ( ☎ 502 000; Rákóczi tér 25; ◷ 8am-6pm Mon-Fri) is the best source of information in town.

## Sights & Activities

The country's largest church is **Esztergom Bazilika** ( ☎ 411 895; admission free; ◷ 7am-6pm), sitting on a hill above the Danube. The colossal building is easily spotted from the train window en route from Bratislava to Budapest. Reconstructed in the neoclassical style, much of the building dates from the 19th century; the oldest section is the white and red marble **Bakócz Kápolna** (Bakócz Chapel; 1510) that was

HUNGARY

moved here. You can climb up the winding steps to the top of the cupola for 200Ft. The **kincsház** (treasury; adult/student 450/220Ft; 9am-4.30pm mid-Mar–Oct, 11am-3.30pm Mon-Fri & 10am-3pm Sat Nov–mid-Mar) contains priceless objects, including ornate vestments and the 13th-century Hungarian coronation cross. Among those buried in the **altemplom** (crypt; admission 100Ft; 9am-5pm) under the cathedral is the controversial Cardinal Mindszenty, who was imprisoned by the communists for refusing to allow Hungary's Catholic schools to be secularised.

At the southern end of the hill is the **Vár Múzeum** (Castle Museum; 415 986; adult/student 460/240Ft; 10am-6pm Tue-Sun Apr-Oct, to 4pm Nov-Mar), inside the reconstructed remnants of the medieval royal palace (1215), which was built upon previous castles. The earliest excavated sections on the hill date from the 2nd to 3rd centuries.

Southwest of the cathedral along the banks of the Little Danube, narrow streets wind through the **Víziváros** (Watertown) district, home to the **Víziváros Plébánia Templom** (Watertown Parish Church; 1738) at the start of Berényi Zsigmond utca. The **Keresztény Múzeum** (Christian Museum; 413 880; Berényi Zsigmond utca 2; adult/student 400/200Ft; 10am-5.30pm Tue-Sun) is in the adjacent Primate's Palace (1882). The stunning collection of medieval religious art includes a statue of the Virgin Mary from the 11th century.

Cross the bridge south of Watertown Parish Church and about 100m further down is **Mária Valéria Bridge**. Destroyed during WWII, it once again connects Esztergom with Slovakia and the city of Štúrovo. **St István Fürdő** ( 312 249; Bajcsy-Zsilinszky utca 14; adult/child 550/350Ft; 9am-6pm May-Sep, indoor pool only 6am-6pm Mon & Sat, 6am-7pm Tue-Fri, 9am-4pm Sun Oct-Apr) backs up to the Little Danube promenade and has outdoor and indoor thermal baths and pools.

## Sleeping & Eating

Although frequent transportation connections make Esztergom an easy day trip from Budapest, you might want to stop a night if you are going on to Slovakia. Contact Gran Tours (p377) about private rooms, for around 4000Ft per person.

**Gran Camping** ( 411 953; fortanex@alexero.hu; Nagy-Duna sétány 3; camp sites per person 1100Ft, dm/r 1700/6000Ft, bungalows 12,000-16,000Ft; May-Sep; P) For a camping ground this place has quite a

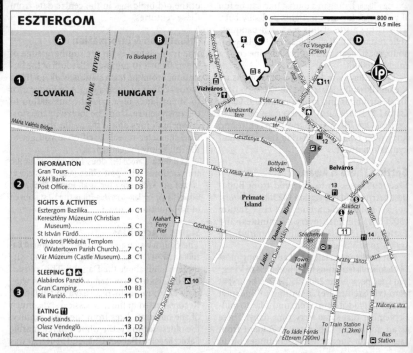

**ESZTERGOM**

0          800 m
0          0.5 miles

To Budapest
To Visegrád (25km)

SLOVAKIA    HUNGARY

Víziváros

Mária Valéria Bridge

Péter utca

Pázmány    Mindszenty tere    József Attila tér

Gesztenye fasor

Táncsics Mihály utca

Bottyán Bridge

Belváros

Primate Island

Mahart Ferry Pier    Gőzhajó utca

Lőrincz utca

Rákóczi tér

Little Danube River    Kis-Duna sétány    Széchenyi tér

Town Hall

Arany János utca

Nagy-Duna sétány

To Jáde Forrás Étterem (200m)

To Train Station (1.2km)

Bus Station

| INFORMATION | |
|---|---|
| Gran Tours | 1 D2 |
| K&H Bank | 2 D2 |
| Post Office | 3 D3 |

| SIGHTS & ACTIVITIES | |
|---|---|
| Esztergom Bazilika | 4 C1 |
| Keresztény Múzeum (Christian Museum) | 5 C1 |
| St István Fürdő | 6 D2 |
| Víziváros Plébánia Templom (Watertown Parish Church) | 7 C1 |
| Vár Múzeum (Castle Museum) | 8 C1 |

| SLEEPING | |
|---|---|
| Alabárdos Panzió | 9 C1 |
| Gran Camping | 10 B3 |
| Ria Panzió | 11 D1 |

| EATING | |
|---|---|
| Food stands | 12 D2 |
| Olasz Vendegló | 13 D2 |
| Piac (market) | 14 D2 |

lot of buildings: elevated bungalows sleep four to six; a dormitory houses about 100 people in four-, five- and eight-bed rooms; and the motel has serviceable doubles. It's a 10-minute walk along the Danube from the cathedral.

**Alabárdos Panzió** ( ☎ 312 640; www.alabardospanzio .hu; Bajcsy-Zsilinszky utca 49; s 7500-9500Ft; d 9500-12,000Ft; **P** ) There are some lovely rooms in Alabárdos and some downright dowdy ones, with motley furnishings: some have iron beds, some modular wood veneer. Look before you choose. The location is great if you want to be close to the cathedral – the hotel is at the base of Castle Hill.

**Ria Panzió** ( ☎ 313 115; www.riapanzio.com; Batthyány Lajos utca 11; s/d €40/48; **P** 🖵 ) Doubles are fresh, with white walls, wood floors and royal-blue linen. Relax on the terrace or arrange an adventure through the family owners – rent a bicycle maybe, or take a water-skiing trip on the Danube in summer.

**Jáde Forrás Étterem** ( ☎ 400 949; Hősök tere 11; mains 600-1400Ft; 🕙 11am-11pm; 🗶 ) Jáde does a mean Hunan chicken and has a reduced-price buffet at lunch. A four-course set menu is 1750Ft.

**Olasz Vendeglő** ( ☎ 312 952; Lőrincz utca 5; pizzas & pastas 700-1000Ft; mains 1000-1400Ft; 🕙 11am-10pm Sun-Thu, to midnight Fri & Sat; 🗶 ) Pizzas and pastas at the originally named Italian restaurant are among the few vegetarian options in town. Mains include dishes such as fruit-stuffed chicken breast.

On the way to the cathedral from the bus station, the **piac** (market; Símor János utca; 🕙 7am-4pm Mon-Fri, to 1pm Sat), north of Arany János utca, has fruit and vegetables, and three **food stands** (Bajcsy-Zsilinszky utca, cnr Szent István fürdő; snacks 200-600Ft; 🕙 8am-8pm) sell burgers, gyros, falafel and the like.

### Getting There & Away

Buses run to/from Budapest's Árpád híd bus station (579Ft, 1½ hours on shortest route) and to/from Visegrád (302Ft, 45 minutes) at least hourly. Two direct buses a day go from Esztergom to Győr (1160Ft, two hours).

The most comfortable way to get to Esztergom from Budapest is by rail: sleek, EC-approved cars run this route. Trains depart from Budapest's Nyugati train station (512Ft, 1½ hours) more than 20 times a day. Cross the Mária Valéria Bridge into Štúrovo, Slovakia and you can catch a train to Bratislava, which is an hour and a half away.

Mahart PassNave ferries depart from Budapest to Esztergom (via Visegrád, 1200Ft,

5½ hours) once a day from late May through August (7.30am). The daily return trip to Budapest departs from Esztergom at 3.20pm. Weekends from June to August there is also a high-speed hydrofoil service between Budapest and Esztergom (2300Ft, 2½ hours), via Visegrád, departing from Budapest at 9.30am and from Esztergom at 3.20pm. From June through August, a ferry service between Esztergom and Visegrád (700Ft, two hours) departs Esztergom at 9am and returns from Visegrád at 3.30pm.

# NORTHWESTERN HUNGARY

The closer you get to the Austrian border, the more prominent the seductive atmosphere of the gilded days of the Austro-Hungarian empire becomes. Northwestern Hungary beyond the Bakony Hills is bounded by the Danube to the east and the Alps to the west. The old quarters of Sopron and Győr are brimming with what were once the residences of prosperous burghers and clerics. Fertőd, outside Sopron, is a magnificent baroque palace and Pannonhalma, outside Győr, is an early Benedictine monastery still in operation.

## GYŐR
☎ 96 / pop 129,500
A sizable pedestrian centre filled with old streets and buildings make riverside Győr (pronounced, impossibly, jyeur) an inviting place for a stroll – even if there isn't one standout attraction. Students hang out at the many pavement cafés in this university town.

Midway between Budapest and Vienna, Győr sits at the point where the Mosoni-Danube, Rábca and Rába Rivers meet. This was the site of a Roman town named Arrabona. In the 11th century, Stephen I established a bishopric here, and in the 16th century a fortress was erected to hold back the Turks.

### Orientation & Information
The large neobaroque City Hall (1898) rises up to block out all other views across from the train station. Baross Gábor utca, which leads to the old town and the rivers, lies diagonally across from City Hall. Much of central Győr is pedestrianised, making parking difficult.

# GYŐR

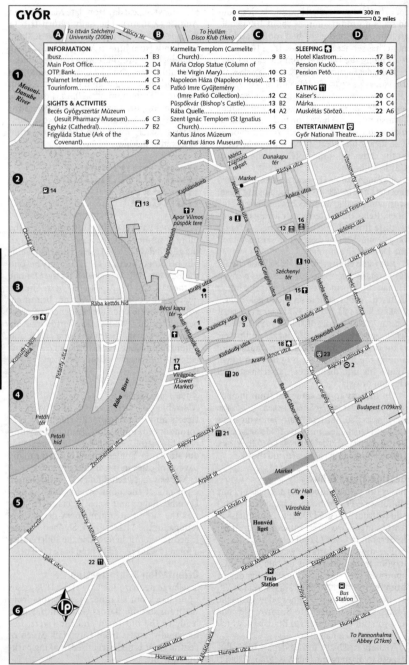

0 — 300 m
0 — 0.2 miles

**INFORMATION**
Ibusz..................................1 B3
Main Post Office..................2 D4
OTP Bank...........................3 C3
Polarnet Internet Café............4 C3
Tourinform..........................5 C4

**SIGHTS & ACTIVITIES**
Becés Gyógyszertár Múzeum
(Jesuit Pharmacy Museum).........6 C3
Egyház (Cathedral)................7 B2
Frigyláda Statue (Ark of the
Covenant)..........................8 C2

Karmelita Templom (Carmelite
Church)............................9 B3
Mária Ozlop Statue (Column of
the Virgin Mary)..................10 C3
Napoleon Háza (Napoleon House)...11 B3
Patkó Imre Gyűjtemény
(Imre Patkó Collection)...........12 C2
Püspökvár (Bishop's Castle).......13 B2
Rába Quelle.......................14 A2
Szent Ignác Templom (St Ignatius
Church)............................15 C3
Xantus János Múzeum
(Xantus János Museum)............16 C3

**SLEEPING**
Hotel Klastrom....................17 B4
Pension Kuckó.....................18 C4
Pension Petö......................19 A3

**EATING**
Kaiser's...........................20 C4
Márka.............................21 C4
Muskétás Söröző..................22 A6

**ENTERTAINMENT**
Győr National Theatre.............23 D4

**Ibusz** ( ☎ 311 700; Kazinczy utca 3; ☺ 8.30am-4pm
Mon-Fri) This travel agency arranges private rooms and
area tours, including to Pannonhalma.
**Main post office** (Bajcsy-Zsilinszky út 46)
**OTP Bank** (Baross Gábor 16)
**Polarnet Internet Café** (Czuczor Gergely utca 6; per
hr 180Ft; ☺ 9am-8pm) Above a clothing shop, with the
entrance around the corner in an alleyway.
**Tourinform** ( ☎ 311 711; Árpád út 32; ☺ 8am-6pm
Mon-Fri, 9am-3pm Sat) Small but helpful; offers currency
exchange.

## Sights & Activities

The enchanting 1725 **Karmelita Templom** (Carmelite
Church; Bécsí kapu tér) and many fine baroque palaces
line riverfront Bécsí kapu tér. On the northwestern side of the square are the fortifications built
in the 16th century to stop the Turks. A short
distance to the east is **Napoleon Háza** (Napoleon House;
Király utca 4), where Bonaparte spent his only night
in Hungary in 1809. Walk around the old streets
and stop in at a pavement café or two.

North up Káptalandomb (Chapter Hill), in
the oldest part of Győr, is the solid baroque
**Egyház** (Cathedral; Apor Vilmos püspök tere; ☺ 10am-noon
& 2-5pm). Situated on the hill, it was originally
Romanesque, but most of what you see inside
dates from the 17th and 18th centuries. Don't
miss the Gothic **Héderváry Chapel** on the southern
side of the cathedral, which contains a glittering
15th- century bust of King (and St) Ladislas.

West of the cathedral, the **Püspökvár** (Bishop's
Castle; ☎ 312 153; adult/student 400/200Ft; ☺ 10am-6pm
Tue-Sun) houses the Diocesan Treasury. The
architecture represents a variety of styles; the
tower was constructed in the 14th century, but
the building saw a major overhaul in the
18th century. At the bottom of the hill on
Jedlik Ányos utca is the **Frigyláda** (Ark of the

Covenant statue) dating from 1731. From here
you can head north to a bridge overlooking
the junction of the city's three rivers.

In Széchenyi tér, the heart of Győr, is the fine
**Szent Ignác Templom** (St Ignatius Church; 1641)
and the **Mária Oszlop statue** (Column of the Virgin
Mary; 1686). Cross the square to the **Xantus János
Múzeum** (Xantus János Museum; ☎ 310 588; Széchenyi tér
5; adult/student 500/250Ft; ☺ 10am-6pm Tue-Sun), built
in 1743, to see exhibits on the city's history.
Next door is the **Patkó Imre Gyűjtemény** (Imre Patkó
Collection; ☎ 310 588; Széchenyi tér 4; adult/child 300/150Ft;
☺ 10am-6pm Tue-Sun), a fine small museum in a
17th-century house. Collections include 20th-
century Asian and African art. Look out for the
highly decorated baroque ceiling at the **Becés
Gyógyszertár Múzeum** (Jesuit Pharmacy Museum; ☎ 320
954; Széchenyi tér 9; admission free; ☺ 7.30am-4pm Mon-Fri).

The water in the pools at thermal bath
**Rába Quelle** ( ☎ 522 646; Fürdő tér 1; adult/student per
day 1600/1000Ft; ☺ 8am-10pm) ranges from 29°C to
38°C. This place is almost an entertainment
complex. One pool has a huge stone-face
waterfall, another a waterslide. There's a restaurant, bar and beauty shop onsite as well as
the requisite massage services.

## Sleeping & Eating

For private rooms ask at Ibusz (left).
**István Széchenyi University** ( ☎ 503 447; Héderváry
út 3; dm 2300Ft) Dormitory accommodation is
available year-round at this huge university
north of the town centre.
**Pension Kuckó** ( ☎ 316 260; fax 312 195; Arany János
utca 33; s/d/apt 5900/7490/9900Ft; ☒ ) An old town
house fitted out with bright modern trim-
mings. The two apartments, with small kitchens, and the café on the ground floor are
especially attractive. Sister property **Pension**

---

**WORTH THE TRIP**

Take half a day and make the short trip to the ancient and impressive **Pannonhalmi Főapátság**
(Pannonhalma Abbey; ☎ 570 191; www.osb.hu, no English; Vár 1; adult/student Hungarian tour 1200/500Ft, adult/
student foreign-language tour 1900/1200Ft; ☺ closed Mon Oct-May), now a Unesco World Heritage site.
Most buildings in the complex date from the 13th to the 18th centuries; highlights include the
Romanesque basilica (1225), the Gothic cloister (1486) and the impressive collection of ancient
texts in the library. Because it's an active monastery, the abbey must be visited with a guide.
From mid-March to mid-November, foreign-language tours in English, Italian, German, French
and Russian are conducted at 11.20am, 1.20pm and 3.20pm.

Pannonhalma is best reached from Győr by bus as the train station is 2km southwest of the abbey.
A direct bus runs daily from the Győr bus station to the abbey (Pannonhalma, vár főkapu stop)
at 8am, 10am and noon (289Ft, 40 minutes), returning at 8.50am, 12.50pm and 5.35pm. Buses go
hourly from Győr to the town of Pannonhalma. The abbey is a 15-minute, uphill walk from there.

**Petö** ( ☎ 313 412; Kossuth Lajos utca 20; s/d 7200/8900Ft; ⊠ ) is not far across the river.

**Hotel Klastrom** ( ☎ 516 910; www.klastrom.hu; Zechmeister utca 1; s/d/tr €55/70/80; P ⊠ 🖳 ) Sleep in a Carmelite friary that is more than 250 years old. Vaulted arch ceilings grace many of the public and guest rooms. Dark modern furniture contrasts appropriately with stark white walls. The interior courtyard looks like a formal garden.

**Márka** ( ☎ 320 800; Bajcsy-Zsilinszky út 30; mains 450-490Ft; ⏲ 11am-3.30pm Mon-Fri) Dine cafeteria-style for lunch. Enter through the pastry shop.

**Muskétás Söröző** ( ☎ 317 627; Munkácsy Mihaly utca 10; mains 630-790Ft; ⏲ 11am-midnight, bar to 1am) Eminently reasonable, this pub and eatery is especially popular with students from the nearby music college. Dine or drink downstairs in the cellar or continue through to the outdoor tables in the courtyard at the rear. The menu includes options such as turkey breast stuffed with a variety of ingredients.

A massive Kaiser's supermarket and department store takes up much of the block at Arany János utca and Aradi vértanúk útja.

## Entertainment

In summer there's a month-long festival of music, theatre and dance from late June. In March, Győr hosts many events in conjunction with Budapest's Spring Festival.

**Győr National Theatre** ( ☎ 314 800; Czuczor Gergely utca 7) The celebrated Győr Ballet and the city's opera company and philharmonic orchestra all perform at the town's main, modern theatre. Tourinform (p381) can help with performance schedules.

**Hullám Disco Klub** ( ☎ 315 275; Héderváry utca 22; ⏲ 6pm-4am Fri & Sat) House music and guest DJs attracts a twenty-something crowd to this disco.

## Getting There & Away

Buses travel to Budapest (1570Ft, two hours, hourly), Pannonhalma (302Ft, 30 minutes, half-hourly), Sopron (1160Ft, two hours, seven daily), Esztergom (1270Ft, two hours, one daily), Balatonfüred (1210Ft, 2½ hours, six daily) and Vienna (3790Ft, two hours, two daily).

Győr is well connected by express train to Budapest's Keleti and Déli train stations (1632Ft, 1½ hours, 15 daily) and to Sopron (1282Ft, 1½ hours, 14 daily). Six daily trains connect Győr with Vienna's Westbahnhof (4750Ft, two hours).

# SOPRON

☎ 99 / pop 55,000

Sopron (*shop*-ron) is one of Hungary's most beautiful towns, with a Gothic town centre enclosed by medieval walls, narrow streets and mysterious passages. Many have called it 'little Prague', and rightly so. Sopron, although much smaller, has something of the charm of the Czech capital. Others see it as a 'dental-holiday' destination, with its surprisingly cheap dentists. Austrian day-trippers in particular come here to fix their dentures and brighten their smiles.

The Mongols and Turks never got this far, so unlike many Hungarian cities, numerous medieval buildings remain in use. The town sits on the Austrian border, only 69km south of Vienna. In 1921 the town's residents voted in a referendum to remain part of Hungary, while the rest of Bürgenland (the region to which Sopron used to belong) went to Austria. The region is known for producing good red wines such as Kékfrancos, which you can sample in local cafés and restaurants.

## Orientation & Information

From the main train station, walk north on Mátyás Király utca, which becomes Várkerület, part of a loop following the line of the former city walls. Előkapu (Front Gate) and Hátsókapu (Back Gate) are the two main entrances in the walls. The bus station is northwest of the old town on Lackner Kristóf utca.

**Internet Centrum Sopron** ( ☎ 310 252; Új utca 3; per hr 400Ft; ⏲ 11am-8pm Mon-Fri, 10am-5pm Sat)

**Main post office** (Széchenyi tér 7-10)

**OTP Bank** (Várkerület 96/a)

**Tourinform** ( ☎ 338 892; www.sopron.hu; Előkapu 11; ⏲ 9am-noon & 1-5pm Mon-Fri, 9am-1pm Sat)

## Sights & Activities

Fő tér is the main square in Sopron; there are several museums, monuments and churches scattered around it. Above the old town's northern gate rises the 60m-high **Tűztorony** (Fire Tower; ☎ 311 327; Fő tér; adult/student 500/250Ft; ⏲ 10am-6pm Tue-Sun), run by the Soproni Múzeum. The building is a true architectural hybrid: the 2m-thick square base, built on a Roman gate, dates from the 12th century, the middle cylindrical and arcaded balcony was built in the 16th century and the baroque spire was added in 1680. You can climb the 154 steps for views of the Alps.

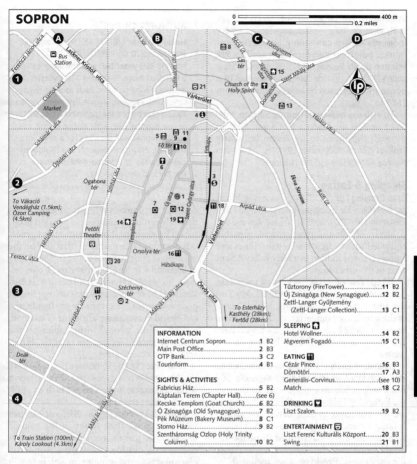

**SOPRON**

| INFORMATION | |
|---|---|
| Internet Centrum Sopron.................1 | B2 |
| Main Post Office............................2 | B3 |
| OTP Bank....................................3 | C2 |
| Tourinform..................................4 | B1 |

| SIGHTS & ACTIVITIES | |
|---|---|
| Fabricius Ház...............................5 | B2 |
| Káptalan Terem (Chapter Hall).......(see 6) | |
| Kecske Templom (Goat Church).......6 | B2 |
| Ó Zsinagóga (Old Synagogue).........7 | B2 |
| Pék Múzeum (Bakery Museum).........8 | C1 |
| Storno Ház..................................9 | B2 |
| Szentháromság Ozlop (Holy Trinity | |
| Column)...................................10 | B2 |

| | |
|---|---|
| Tűztorony (FireTower)....................11 | B2 |
| Új Zsinagóga (New Synagogue).......12 | B2 |
| Zettl-Langer Gyűjtemény | |
| (Zettl-Langer Collection).............13 | C1 |

| SLEEPING | |
|---|---|
| Hotel Wollner..............................14 | B2 |
| Jégverem Fogadó..........................15 | C1 |

| EATING | |
|---|---|
| Cézár Pince.................................16 | B3 |
| Dömötöri....................................17 | A3 |
| Generális-Corvinus.....................(see 10) | |
| Match........................................18 | C2 |

| DRINKING | |
|---|---|
| Liszt Szalon................................19 | B2 |

| ENTERTAINMENT | |
|---|---|
| Liszt Ferenc Kulturális Központ.........20 | B3 |
| Swing........................................21 | B1 |

In the centre of Fő tér is the **Szentháromság Ozlop** (Holy Trinity Column; 1701). On the north side of the square is **Storno Ház** ( ☎ 311 327; Fő tér 8; adult/student 800/400Ft; ☺ 10am-6pm Tue-Sun Apr-Aug, ton2pm Tue-Sun Sep-Mar), where King Mátyás stayed in 1482 while his armies lay siege to Vienna. Today it houses a local history exhibition. Upstairs at **Fabricius Ház** ( ☎ 311 327; Fő tér 6; adult/student 1000/500Ft; ☺ 10am-6pm Tue-Sun Apr-Aug, to 2pm Tue-Sun Sep-Mar) walk through rooms recreated to resemble those in 17th- and 18th-century town homes. In the basement see stone sculptures and other remains from Roman times. The back rooms of the ground floor are dedicated to an archaeology exhibit.

Beyond the square is the 13th-century **Kecske Templom** (Goat Church; Templom utca 1), whose

name comes from the heraldic animal of its chief benefactor. Below the church is the **Káptalan Terem** (Chapter Hall; ☎ 338 843; admission free; ☺ 10am-noon & 2-5pm Tue-Sun May-Sep), part of a 14th-century Franciscan monastery, with frescoes and stone carvings.

The **Új Zsinagóga** (New Synagogue; Új utca 11), built in the 14th century, now houses private residences and offices. The medieval **Ó Zsinagóga** (Old Synagogue; ☎ 311 227; Új utca 22; adult/student 400/200Ft; ☺ 10am-6pm Tue-Sun May-Sep), also built in the 14th century, is in better shape than many scattered around the country and contains a museum of Jewish life.

There are many other small museums in town. Two in the Ikva district, northeast of the centre, are quite interesting: the **Zettl-Langer**

**Gyűjtemény** (Zettl-Langer Collection; ☎ 335 123; Balfi út 11; admission 300Ft; ◷ 10am-noon Tue-Sun Apr-Oct, Fri-Sun only Nov-Mar) containing antiquities, ceramics, paintings and furniture; and the **Pék Múzeum** (Bakery Museum; ☎ 311 327; Bécsí út 5; adult/student 300/150Ft; ◷ 10am-2pm Tue-Sun May-Aug) in a house and shop used by bakers' families from 1686 to 1970.

To visit the hills surrounding Sopron, take bus 1 or 2 to the Szieszta Hotel and hike up through the forest to the 394m-tall **Károly Lookout** (Lóvérek; adult/student 250/150Ft; ◷ 9am-8pm May-Aug, 9am-4pm Sep-Apr) for the view.

## Sleeping & Eating

**Ózon Camping** ( ☎ /fax 331 144; ozoncamping@sopron .hu; Erdei Malom köz 3; camp sites per large tent/small tent/adult/child 1600/800/1200/850Ft; ◷ mid-Apr–mid-Oct) A lovely, 60-site camping ground, superbly equipped with fridges, washing machines and a pool. Ózon is hidden in a leafy valley 4.5km west of the inner town.

**Vákació Vendégház** ( ☎ 338 502; www.szallasinfo.hu /vakaciovendeghaz; Ade Endre út 31; dm 2200Ft; ✗ ) You can't beat the neatness at this hostel. Many of the guests are Hungarian students. Rooms have two to 12 beds each; there's no kitchen. It's about a 15-minute walk west of the centre.

**Esterházy Kastély** ( ☎ 537 640; www.castles.hu/ester hazy; Haydn utca 2, Fertőd; d/tr/q 4900/6400/7200Ft; ✗ ) Book well in advance if you want to sleep in the Esterházy Palace. Even though the rooms are not too royal in their décor, the setting is fantastic and beds go like hot cakes in the summer. Rooms are furnished in period reproductions and a fine courtyard is available for guests only. Breakfast is not included.

**Jégverem Fogadó** ( ☎ 510 113; www.jegverem.hu; Jégverem utca 1; s/d 5000/8000Ft) Citrus yellow walls are a backdrop to plastic plants, and non-

descript furniture in five large rooms belies the 18th-century building this pension occupies. The steaming-hot restaurant has generous portions, with multiple variations on the fried-meat cutlet (mains 850Ft to 1890Ft).

**Dömötöri** ( ☎ 506 624; Széchenyi tér 13; cakes 165-265Ft; ◷ 7am-10pm Mon-Thu, 7am-11pm Fri & Sat, 8am-10pm Sun) On sunny afternoons, a long line of people wait for ice cream-to-go. Inside, the old-world furnishings are quite Victorian; outside, white wrought-iron tables on the umbrella-shaded terrace are brighter. Either way, the cakes are great.

**Cézár Pince** ( ☎ 311 337; Hátsókapu 2; mains 480-890Ft; ◷ 11am-11pm) Wooden platters with a variety of wurst and cheese make a good lunch or snack at this cellar restaurant.

**Generális-Corvinus** ( ☎ 505 035; Fő tér 7-8; mains 990-2100Ft; ◷ 9am-11pm) Right in the middle of the inner town's main square, this café-restaurant's outside tables are a wonderful place in spring and summer for a pizza (650Ft to 1700Ft) and a drink.

For self-catering head for the **Match** (Várkerület 100) supermarket.

**WORTH THE TRIP**

Don't miss **Esterházy Kasthély** ( ☎ 537 640; Haydn utca 2, Fertőd; adult/student 1000/600Ft; ◷ 10am-6pm Tue-Sun mid-Mar–Oct, to 4pm Fri-Sun Nov–mid-Mar), a magnificent, Versailles-style baroque extravaganza 28km outside town in Fertőd. Built in 1766, this 126-room palace was owned by one of the nation's foremost families. You have to put on felt booties and slip around the marble floors under gilt chandeliers with a Hungarian guide, but information sheets in various languages are on hand. From May to October, piano and string quartets perform regularly in the frescoed concert hall where Joseph Haydn worked as court musician to the Esterházys from 1761 to 1790. The Haydn Festival takes place here in early September. The Tourinform in Győr (p381) can help you with performance schedules.

Fertőd is easily accessible from Sopron by bus (348Ft, 45 minutes, hourly); the town is dominated by the palace and its grounds.

## Drinking

**Liszt Szalon** ( ☎ 323 407; Szent György utca 12; drinks 190-490Ft; ☻ 10am-10pm) A wonderful, old-world coffeehouse dedicated to Liszt (of course), with the composer's concert posters from all over the world. Good coffee and Aztec chocolate, spiced with chilli.

## Entertainment

**Liszt Ferenc Kulturális Központ** ( ☎ 517 517; Liszt Ferenc tér 1; ☻ ticket office 9am-5pm Tue-Fri, to noon Sat) A concert hall, café and exhibition space all rolled into one. The information desk has the latest on classical music and other cultural events in town.

**Swing** ( ☎ 06 20 214 8029; Várkerület 15; ☻ 5pm-midnight Sun-Fri, to 2am Sat) Live jazz, country, rock or blues play nightly.

## Getting There & Away

There are four buses a day to Budapest (2660Ft, four hours), nine to Győr (1160Ft, two hours). Trains to Budapest's Keleti train station (3500Ft, 2½ to three hours, eight daily) depart from Sopron, as do trains to Győr (802Ft to 1282Ft, 1½ hours, 14 daily). To get to Vienna's Südbahnhof the best way is to take the train (€12, 1½ hours, 10 daily). You clear border checks before you get on the train.

# LAKE BALATON

The 77km-long Lake Balaton is Hungary's seaside. This, the largest freshwater lake in Europe outside Scandinavia, provides the Hungarians (and foreigners) with fun in both the summer and winter months. During the summer, when the place is at its peak, it's all swimming and outdoor activities, and in winter the locals get their skates on and glide on the frozen lake.

Shallow water, sandy beaches and condominiums attract visitors to the southeastern shore, where the commercialised towns are pretty characterless. More-established towns, trees and rolling hills, deeper water and less sand await on the northwestern shore. Towns on both sides are packed in July and August, and all but deserted from December to February. Many facilities such as museums, pensions and restaurants close for the winter.

Balatonfüred is easily accessed from all points; Tihany peninsula is a nature reserve and a village too cute to be true. Keszthely is really the only town that's a town in its own

right – apart from year-round lake traffic. Nearby Hévíz is a spa centre with a huge thermal *tó* (lake).

# BALATONFÜRED

☎ 87 / pop 13,500

Walking the hillside streets, you catch glimpses of the easy grace that 18th- and 19th-century Balatonfüred (*bal*-ah-tahn fuhr-ed) must have enjoyed. Today many of the old buildings could use a new coat of paint and the renowned curative waters can be taken by prescription only. Stick by the lake, where a tree-filled park leads down to the waterfront, the pier and outdoor cafés. The hotels here are a bit cheaper than those on the neighbouring Tihany peninsula, making this a good base for exploring.

## Orientation & Information

The adjacent bus and train stations are on Dobó István utca, 1km from the lake.
**OTP Bank** (Petőfi Sándor utca 8)
**Post office** (Zsigmond utca 14)
**Tourinform** ( ☎ 580 480; www.balatonfured.hu; Petőfi Sándor utca 68; ☻ 9am-8pm Mon-Fri & to 6pm Sat & Sun Jun-Sep, to 5pm Mon-Fri & to 1pm Sat Mar-May & Oct, to 5pm Mon-Fri Nov-Feb) The main office is inconveniently located 1km northeast of the centre; a second **Tourinform branch** ( ☎ 580 480; Széchenyi utca 47; ☻ 9am-5pm Mon-Fri, to 1pm Sat May-Sep; to 3pm Mon-Fri Oct-Apr) is annoyingly situated about 1.5km to the southwest.

## Sights & Activities

The park along the central lakeshore, near the ferry pier, is worth a promenade. You can take a one-hour **pleasure cruise** ( ☎ 342 230; www.balaton ihajozas.hu; Mahart ferry pier; adult/child 1200/600Ft) at 2pm and 4pm daily, May to August. The **disco hajo** (disco boat; ☎ 342 230; www.balatonihajozas.hu; Mahart ferry pier; cruises 1400Ft), a two-hour cruise with music and drinks, leaves at 9pm Tuesday through Sunday, June to August. **Kisfaludy Strand** (Aranyhíd sétány; adult/student 330/190Ft; ☻ 9am-10pm mid-Jun–mid-Sep), along the footpath 800m northeast of the pier, is a relatively sandy beach. A good way to explore the waterfront is to rent a bike from **Tempo 21** ( ☎ 480 671; Ady Endre utca 52; per hr/day 350/2400Ft; ☻ 9am-5pm Mon-Fri, to 1pm Sat).

North of the pier is the renovated 1846 **Kerek Templom** (Round Church; cnr Jókai Mór & Honvéd utca). **Mór Jókai Múzeum** ( ☎ 343 426; Honvéd utca 1; adult/child 300/150Ft; ☻ 10am-6pm Tue-Sun May-Oct) commemorates the life of the acclaimed novelist in what was once his summer house (1871). The heart of the old spa town is Gyógy tér, where **Kossuth Forrásvíz** (Kossuth Spring, 1853) dispenses slightly sulphurous water that people actually drink for health. Don't stray far from a bathroom afterwards.

## Sleeping & Eating

In peak season (late May to early September) tons of guesthouses and private individuals rent rooms. Tourinform (p385) has a long list of such accommodation on its website, or you might just want to look for signs due south of the train and bus stations on Endrődi Sándor utca. **Ibusz** (www.ibusz.hu) travel agency lists private accommodation in the Balaton area on its website.

The eastern end of Tagore sétány is a strip of pleasant bars and terraced restaurants. You'll find a plethora of food stalls west along the lake and on Zákonyi Ferenc utca.

**Füred Camping** ( ☎ 580 241; cfured@balatontourist.hu; Széchenyi utca 24; camp sites per tent 1860-5300Ft, adult/child 650-1500Ft/550-1100Ft, motel r 5460-19,970Ft, bungalows 6400-19,970Ft; ⊙ Apr–mid-Oct; **P** ) This sprawling beachfront complex 1km west of the centre has water-sport rentals, swimming pools, tennis courts, a restaurant, a convenience

shop and daily programmes. Not all tent and caravan sites have shade; site prices are determined by the size, the month and the number of people; bungalows and motel rooms are for a minimum of three persons.

**Sport Panzió** ( ☎ /fax 340 720; Horváth Mihály utca 35; s/d 3800/7600Ft; **P** ✗ ) Simple and superior. Request one of the two top-floor rooms for views out onto the lake. Honey-coloured wood is the theme in the bedrooms, restaurant and sauna. One hour on the squash court costs 1900Ft.

**Hotel Blaha Lujza** ( ☎ 581 210; www.hotelblaha.hu; Blaha Lujza utca 4; s €37, d €53-58; **P** ) Part of this hotel was once the holiday home of the much-loved 19th-century Hungarian actress-singer Blaha Lujza. Her picture and charming old photos of the lake grace the hallway walls. There's a lot of the contemporary wood and maroon-upholstered furniture in the relatively small rooms, but it looks nice.

**Stéfania Vittorlás Étterem** ( ☎ 343 407; Tagore sétány 1; cakes 110-260Ft; ⊙ 10am-midnight; ✗ ) A touristy place with touristy prices but a great lakeside view. Skip the restaurant and enjoy something from the cake and ice-cream shop in the same location.

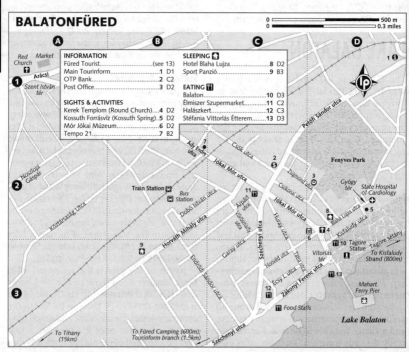

**BALATONFÜRED**

0 ————— 500 m
0 ————— 0.3 miles

**INFORMATION**
Füred Tourist.............................(see 13)
Main Tourinform..........................**1** C2
OTP Bank.....................................**2** C2
Post Office...................................**3** D2

**SIGHTS & ACTIVITIES**
Kerek Templom (Round Church)....**4** D2
Kossuth Forrásvíz (Kossuth Spring)..**5** D2
Mór Jókai Múzeum.......................**6** D2
Tempo 21......................................**7** B2

**SLEEPING**
Hotel Blaha Lujza..........................**8** D2
Sport Panzió..................................**9** B3

**EATING**
Balaton..........................................**10** D3
Élmiszer Szupermarket..................**11** C2
Halászkert.....................................**12** C3
Stéfania Vittorlás Étterem..............**13** D3

**Halászkert** ( ☎ 343 039; Zákonyi Ferenc utca 3; mains 1000-1500Ft; ✲ 11am-10pm Apr-Sep; ✖ ) Come here for the *korhely halászlé* (drunkard's fish soup) and other freshwater fish dishes.

**Balaton** ( ☎ 481 319; Kisfaludy utca 5; mains 1000-2200Ft; ✲ 11am-11pm; ✖ ) In the waterfront park sits a shaded terrace full of rustic tables. This may look like just a beer garden, but Balaton serves a full range of Hungarian specialities. Inside the casual restaurant a dead tree bizarrely sticks out of the floor.

Pack a picnic lunch or dinner with supplies from the **Élmiszer Szupermarket** (Jókai Mór utca 16).

## Getting There & Away

Buses to Tihany (182Ft, 30 minutes) and Veszprém (302Ft, 30 minutes) leave every 15 minutes or so (except at lunch time) throughout the day. For the northwestern lakeshore towns such as Keszthely (810Ft, 1½ hours, nine daily) take the bus, since you have to switch in Tapolca with the train.

Budapest-bound buses (1390Ft) depart from Balatonfüred four times daily and take between two and three hours to get there. Trains take about the same amount of time (1690Ft, 12 daily). There are a number of towns on the train line with 'Balaton' or 'Füred' somewhere in their name, so double-check which station you're getting off at.

From April to September, **Mahart ferries** ( ☎ 342 230; www.balatonihajozas.hu; Mahart ferry pier) ply the water from Balatonfüred to Tihany (660Ft, 20 minutes) and Siófok (on the southeastern shore; 1200Ft, 55 minutes) eight times a day in July and August, six times a day from May to June and in September.

## TIHANY

☎ 87 / pop 1200

The whole Tihany peninsula, jutting 5km into Lake Balaton, is a nature reserve. Many people consider this the most beautiful place on the lake, especially in March when the almond trees are in bloom. The quaint village of the same name sits on the eastern side of the peninsula's high plateau. Ceramics, embroidery and other folk-craft stores fill the bucolic village houses. Prices are a bargain compared to Budapest or Szentendre, and everyone knows it. You can easily shake off the tourist hordes by going hiking – maybe to the Belsőtó (Inner Lake) or the reedy (and almost dried up) Külsőtó (Outer Lake). Bird-watchers, bring your binoculars: the trails have abundant birdlife.

## Orientation & Information

The harbour where ferries to/from Balatonfüred dock is a couple of kilometres downhill from the village of Tihany. Buses pull up in the heart of town, outside the post office on Kossuth Lajos utca.

**Tourinform** ( ☎ 448 804; www.tihany.hu; Kossuth Lajos utca 20; ✲ 9am-7pm Mon-Fri & to 6pm Sat & Sun Jun-Aug, to 5pm Mon-Fri & to 3pm Sat May & Sep, to 3pm Mon-Fri Oct-Apr) sells hiking maps and film, and provides tourist information.

## Sights & Activities

You can spot Tihany's twin-towered **Apátság Templom** (Abbey Church; ☎ 448 405; adult/student 500/250Ft; ✲ 9am-6pm May-Sep, 10am-5pm Apr & Oct, 10am-3pm Nov-Mar), dating from 1754, from a long way off. Entombed in the church's crypt is the abbey's founder, King Andrew I. The Deed of Foundation for the abbey is the earliest existing document that contains Hungarian words (now stored at the Pannonhalma Abbey archives near Győr; see p381). The admission fee includes entry to the attached **Apátsági Múzeum** (Abbey Museum; ☎ 448 405; ✲ 9am-6pm May-Sep, 10am-5pm Apr & Oct, 10am-3pm Nov-Mar). The path behind the church leads to outstanding views; it can be quite windy up there.

Follow the pathway along the ridge north from the church in the village and you pass the tiny **szabadtéri néprajzi múzeum** (open-air ethnographical museum; ☎ 714 960; Pisky sétány 10; adult/student 300/150Ft; ✲ 10am-6pm Tue-Sun May-Sep). It's easy to miss the small cluster of fully outfitted folk houses among all the rest of the old houses that are now shops.

Back at the clearing in front of the church, there's a large hiking map with all the trails marked. Following the green trail northeast of the church for an hour will bring you to an Oroszkút (Russian Well) and the ruins of the Óvár (Old Castle), where the Russian Orthodox monks, brought to Tihany by Andrew I, hollowed out cells in the soft basalt walls.

## Sleeping & Eating

This is an easy day trip from Balatonfüred. The place is pretty small, so there's no reason to stay over unless you're hiking. The Tihany Tourinform website, www.tihany.hu, lists almost 50 houses that rent private rooms, or you could look for a '*Zimmer frei*' sign in one of the windows on the small streets north of the church.

**HUNGARY**

**Erika Hotel** ( ☎ 448 010; fax 448 646; Batthyány utca 6; r €60; ☺ May-Sep; **P** ⌧ ⌦ ) The pink, 16-room inn is right in the centre of the village. The small swimming pool makes for a refreshing surprise; a cocktail from the bar completes the picture.

**Stég Pub** ( ☎ 06 70 503 0208; Kossuth Lajos utca 18; mains 750-980Ft; ☺ 10am-10pm Sun-Thu, to midnight Fri & Sat) Pizzas and salads augment the Hungarian menu at this friendly place. In nice weather, sit in the courtyard.

Of the many touristy eatery options, two have especially good views: the awning-covered back terrace at **Fogas Csárda** ( ☎ 448 658; Kossuth Lajos utca 9; mains 1450-2400Ft; ☺ 11am-11pm May-Oct) overlooks the Inner Lake and the peninsula's interior; and the terrace at the **Rege Café** ( ☎ 448 280; Kossuth Lajos utca 22; cakes 330-520Ft; ☺ 10am-6pm), where you can peer down on Lake Balaton and the harbour.

### Getting There & Away
Buses travel along the 11km of mostly lakefront road between the centre of Tihany village and Balatonfüred's train station (174 Ft, 30 minutes) about 20 times a day. The advantage here is that you don't have to hike up the hill from the harbour, but the bus does stop there too.

Passenger ferries sail between Tihany and Balatonfüred from April to September (660Ft, 20 minutes, six to eight daily). The Abbey Church is high above the pier; you can follow a steep path up to the village from there.

## KESZTHELY
☎ 83 / pop 21,800

Keszthely's amazing Festetics Palace, built in 1745, is a sight worth making the cross-country-and-lake trip for; stroll through the beautifully cultivated lakefront park and it's not long before you find another good reason to be here: a partying public beach. Whether you're seeking history or sun-worshipping hedonism, Keszthely (*kest*-hay) has at least a little of each. The town lies just over 1km northwest of the lake and with the exception of a few guesthouses, almost everything stays open year-round.

### Orientation & Information
The bus and train stations, side by side at the end of Mártírok útja, are fairly close to the ferry pier. Walk northeast on Kazinczy utca and you'll see the water to your right in a few hundred metres. To get to town, turn left and head towards Kossuth Lajos utca.

**Tourinform** ( ☎ 314 144; www.keszthely.hu; Kossuth Lajos utca 28; ☺ 9am-8pm Mon-Fri to 6pm Sat Jul-Aug, to 5pm Mon-Fri & to 1pm Sat Sep-Jun) doles out information on the whole Lake Balaton area. **Keszthely Tourist** ( ☎ 312 031; Kossuth Lajos utca 25; ☺ 9am-5pm Mon-Fri) puts together water-oriented sports and spa packages and represents several private accommodation businesses.

There's a huge **OTP Bank** (Kossuth Lajos utca) facing the park south of the church, and close by is the **main post office** (Kossuth Lajos utca 48).

### Sights & Activities
The glimmering white, 100-room **Festetics Kastély** (Festetics Palace; ☎ 312 190; Kastély utca 1; museum adult/student 1300/700Ft; ☺ 10am-5pm Tue-Sun) was first built in 1745; the wings were extended out from the original building 150 years later. About a dozen rooms in the one-time residence have been turned into a museum. Many of the decorative arts in the gilt salons were imported from England in the mid-1800s. If you can, take one of the evening candlelight tours that are sometimes offered during summer. To reach the palace, follow Kossuth Lajos utca, the long pedestrian street in the centre of the old town. The **Helikon Könyvtár** (Helikon Library), in the baroque south wing, is known for its 900,000 volumes and its handcarved furniture, crafted by a local artisan.

In 1797 Count György Festetics, an uncle of the reformer István Széchenyi, founded Europe's first agricultural institute, the Georgikon, in Keszthely. Part of the original school is now the **Georgikon Major Múzeum** (Georgikon Farm Museum; ☎ 311 563; Bercsényi Miklós utca 67; adult/student 400/200Ft; ☺ 10am-5pm Tue-Sat, 10am-6pm Sun May-Oct).

The lakefront area centres on the long Mahart ferry pier, which has a small café near the ferry landing at the end. From April to September you can take a one-hour **pleasure cruise** ( ☎ 312 093; www.balatonihajozas.hu; Mahart ferry pier; adult/student 1100/500Ft) on the lake at 1pm and 3pm daily. **Városi Strand** (City Beach; Vásár tér; adult/student 500/300Ft; ☺ ticket office 8.30am-7pm, gates to midnight May-Sep) is not far west of the pier, near plenty of beer stands and food booths. There are other beaches you can explore further afield; some hotels have private shore access.

### Sleeping
Like most summer-oriented tourist destinations, prices vary dramatically depending on the month. Private rooms can cost a bit more here than in the non-resort areas of Hungary;

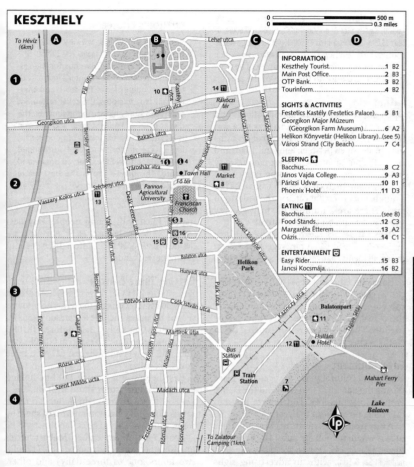

# KESZTHELY

**INFORMATION**
Keszthely Tourist.................................1 B2
Main Post Office................................2 B3
OTP Bank..........................................3 B2
Tourinform........................................4 B2

**SIGHTS & ACTIVITIES**
Festetics Kastély (Festetics Palace)......5 B1
Georgikon Major Múzeum
  (Georgikon Farm Museum)............6 A2
Helikon Könyvtár (Helikon Library)..(see 5)
Városi Strand (City Beach)................7 C4

**SLEEPING**
Bacchus.............................................8 C2
János Vajda College............................9 A3
Párizsi Udvar....................................10 B1
Phoenix Hotel..................................11 D3

**EATING**
Bacchus........................................(see 8)
Food Stands....................................12 C3
Margaréta Étterem...........................13 A2
Oázis...............................................14 C1

**ENTERTAINMENT**
Easy Rider.......................................15 B3
Jancsi Kocsmája..............................16 B2

**HUNGARY**

**Keszthely Tourist** ( ☎ 312 031; Kossuth Lajos utca 25; ⊙ 9am-5pm Mon-Fri) represents several private lodgings and apartment houses.

**Zalatour Camping** ( ☎ 312 782; kesztcamo@zalaszam.hu; Ernszt Géza sétány; camp & caravan sites 1450-2400Ft; bungalows 3000-4200Ft, apartments 7900-9300Ft; ⊙ mid-Apr–mid-Oct; P ☒ ) About 1km south of town, this waterfront camp has access to a rocky shore and a somewhat reedy beach. The apartments are a bit nicer than the bungalows (both sleep up to four). Don't come here for quiet; facilities include a restaurant, late-night bar, gift shop, sauna and sun beds, and a dog kennel in addition to sports stuff.

**János Vajda College** ( ☎ 311 361; Gagarin utca 4; dm 1600-3000Ft) This student dorm is open to all from July to August.

**Phoenix Hotel** ( ☎ 312 631; Balatonpart 4; s 5500-7300Ft, d 7000-8800Ft; P ) This is as close as you can get to the water for as little money as you can spend if you're not camping. The low-lying wood building is in a shady grove of trees at the edge of the lakefront park. Bike rental is only 300Ft for an hour and 900Ft for the day.

**Bacchus** ( ☎ 510 450; www.bacchushotel.hu; Erzsébet királyné utca 18; s €33-47, d €40-58; P ) Bacchus is positively Keszthely's best hotel. It has crisp rooms that open up to a little garden on the ground floor and balconies on the top, the staff is super-friendly and the cellar is a **wine museum** (admission free; ⊙ 10am-11pm) where wine tastings are available (six/10 types 1500/2400Ft). Not to mention the fabulous restaurant (p390).

**Párizsi Udvar** ( ☎ 311 202; www.hotels.hu/parizsi
_udvar; Kastély utca 5; d 7900-9900Ft, tr 9600-12,600Ft, 4-
bed r 13,000-15,000Ft, 5-bed r 13,500-15,600Ft) Large basic
rooms share kitchen facilities in what was once
part of the Festetics Kastély complex. The central courtyard adds to the quiet of the place.

## Eating

Open-air, self-service restaurant-stands and
bars line the trail between Kazinczy utca and
the waterfront, west of the ferry pier. In summer, places open between 8am and 10am and
close at 10pm or later. Off-season hours vary
but there's generally something open from
10am to 8pm. In town, Kossuth Lajos utca has
a number of pavement cafés in the pedestrian
area. There are a number of small grocery
shops just south on the same street.

**Oázis** ( ☎ 311 023; Rákóczi tér 3; lunches 430-520Ft;
🕒 11am-4pm Mon-Fri; ✗ ) A rare vegetarian eatery;
the small menu changes daily. It's not gourmet,
but it's tasty enough.

**Margaréta Étterem** ( ☎ 314 882; Bercsényi Miklós
utca 60; mains 600-1240Ft; 🕒 11am-10pm; ✗ ) Locals come for the good Hungarian food and
the casual, convivial vibe. Everyone here is
friendly. The patio with red-chequered tablecloths is cheery too.

## Entertainment

Numerous cultural performances take place
during the Balatonfest in May and the Dance
Festival in September. Tourinform has info
on events throughout the year.

Away from the waterfront, Kossuth Lajos
utca is where to look for pubs: **Jancsi Kocsmája**
(Kossuth Lajos utca 46; 🕒 noon-midnight Mon-Fri, 6pm-
midnight Sat & Sun), with tin advertising signs
hanging on the walls, is the most fun and is

mainly filled with young people. **Easy Rider**
( ☎ 319 842; Kossuth Lajos utca 79; 🕒 10am-10pm Sun-
Thu, 10am-4am Fri & Sat) turns into a disco at about
10pm on weekends.

## Getting There & Away

Buses to Hévíz (133Ft, 15 minutes) leave at least
every 30 minutes during the day. Other towns
served by buses include Badacsony (363Ft,
30 minutes, six daily), Balatonfüred (810Ft,
1½ hours, seven daily), Veszprém (1040Ft, two
hours, 12 daily) and Budapest (2780Ft, three
hours, six daily).

Keszthely is on a branch rail line linking
the lake's southeastern shore with Budapest
(2324Ft, three hours, eight daily). To reach
towns along Lake Balaton's northern shore by
train, you have to change at Tapolca.

From April to September, Mahart ferries
link Keszthely with Badacsonytomaj (1200Ft,
two hours, one to three daily) and other,
smaller lake towns.

---

**WORTH THE TRIP**

Just 6km northwest of Keszthely is the spa town (pop 4200) of **Hévíz** (www.heviz.hu). People have
utilised the warm mineral water here for centuries, first for tanning in the Middle Ages and
later for curative purposes (it was developed as a private resort in 1795). One of Europe's largest thermal lakes, the five-hectare **Gyógytó** (Parkerdő; admission 3 hr/day 900/1600Ft; 🕒 8.30am-5pm
May-Sep, 9am-4pm Oct-Apr) gurgles up in the middle of town. The hot spring is a crater some 40m
deep that disgorges up to 80 million litres of warm water a day. The surface temperature here
averages 33°C and never drops below 26°C, allowing bathing year-round. You can rent towels,
inner tubes and even swimsuits. Both the water and the bottom mud are slightly radioactive;
the minerals are said to alleviate various medical conditions.

To get here, take the bus from Keszthely station (127Ft, 15 minutes, every 15 to 30 minutes).
The lake park is across Deák tér from the Hévíz bus station. Walk right around the park to get
to the closest year-round entrance in the east.

# SOUTH CENTRAL HUNGARY

If you've had enough of the strait-laced Habsburg influence and want something a bit more Mediterranean, head to Southern Hungary. Historically, the area bordering Croatia and Serbia and Montenegro has often been 'shared' between Hungary and these countries, and it's here that the remnants of the 150-year Turkish occupation can be most strongly felt. In the Danube village of Mohács, the Hungarian army under King Lajos II was routed by a vastly superior Ottoman force in 1526.

The region is bounded by the Danube River to the east, the Dráva River to the south and west, and Lake Balaton to the north. Generally flat, the Mecsek and Villány Hills rise up in isolation from the plain. The weather always seems to be a few degrees warmer here than in other parts of the country; the sunny clime is great for grape growing, and oak-aged Villány reds are well regarded, if highly tannic.

## PÉCS

☎ 72 / pop 158,900

Pécs' (pronounced *paich*) sunny Jókai tér, paved in white marble, makes you think that the sea is close by. This lovely little town, near the southern border of Hungary, is going to be crowned European Culture Capital in 2010. This is where the Turks left their greatest monuments from 150 years of occupation; alongside are imposing churches, a lovely synagogue and more than a dozen galleries and museums, one dedicated entirely to Hungary's answer to Van Gogh, Tivadar Kosztka Csontváry. Green parks and great hiking in the Mecsek Hills only add to the appeal. Harkány is a nearby spa town that is an easy day trip.

History has far from ignored Pécs. The Roman settlement of Sopianae on this site was the capital of the province of Lower Pannonia for 400 years. Christianity flourished here in the 4th century and by the 9th century the town was known as Quinque Ecclesiae for its five churches. In 1009 Stephen I made Pécs a bishopric. The first Hungarian university was founded here in the mid-14th century. City walls were erected after the Mongol invasion of 1241, but 1543 marked the start of almost a century and a half of Turkish domination. In the 19th century the manufacture of Zsolnay porcelain and other goods, such as Pannonia sparkling wine, helped put Pécs back on the map.

### Orientation & Information

The train station is a little over 1km south of the old town centre. Take bus 30 for two long stops from the station to Kossuth tér to reach the centre, or you can walk up Jókai Mór utca. The bus station is a few blocks closer, next to the market. Follow Bajcsy-Zsilinszky utca north to get to the centre.

**Tourinform** ( ☎ 213 315; www.pecs.hu; Széchenyi tér 9; ☻ 8am-5.30pm Mon-Fri, 9am-4pm Sat May-Sep, 8am-4pm Mon-Fri Oct-Mar) has internet access (per hour 100Ft) and tons of local info, including a list of museums. The **main post office** (Jókai Mór utca 10) is in a beautiful Art Nouveau building (1904) with a colourful Zsolnay porcelain roof. There are plenty of banks and ATMs scattered around town. **Ibusz** ( ☎ 212 157; Apáca utca 1; ☻ 8am-5pm Mon-Fri, to 2pm Sat) travel agency has a currency exchange booth, rents private rooms and books transport tickets.

### Sights & Activities

The bizarrely named 'Mosque Church', which dominates the city's central square, is really quite striking. The **Mecset Templom** (Mosque Church; ☎ 321 976; Széchenyi tér; admission free; ☻ 10am-4pm Mon-Sat, 11.30am-4pm Sun mid-Apr–mid-Oct, 10am-noon Mon-Sat, 11.30am-2pm Sun mid-Oct–mid-Apr) has no minaret and has been a Christian place of worship for a long time, but the Islamic elements inside, such as the *mihrab* (prayer niche) on the southeastern wall, reveal its original purpose. Constructed in the mid-16th century from the stones of an earlier church, the mosque underwent several changes of appearance over the years – including the addition of a steeple and siding. In the late 1930s the building was restored to its medieval form.

West along Ferencesek utca at No 35, you'll pass the ruins of the 16th-century Turkish **Memi Pasa Fürdője** (Pasa Memi Bath) before you turn south on Rákóczi útca to get to the c 1540 **Hassan Jakovali Mecset** (Hassan Jakovali Mosque; ☎ 313 853; Rákóczi útca 2; adult/student 240/100Ft; ☻ 10am-1.30pm & 2-6pm Thu-Tue Apr-Sep). Though wedged between two modern buildings, this smaller mosque is more intact than its larger cousin and comes complete with a minaret. There's a small museum of Ottoman history inside.

North of Széchenyi tér, the minor **Régészeti Múzeum** (Archaeology Museum; ☎ 312 719; Széchenyi tér

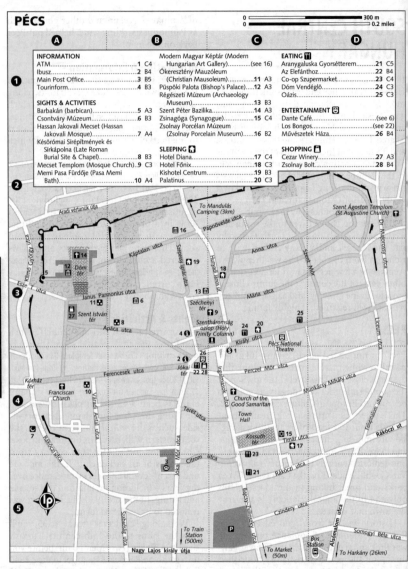

# PÉCS

0   300 m
0   0.2 miles

12; adult/student 300/150Ft; 🕙 10am-4pm Tue-Sun Apr-Oct) contains Roman artefacts found in the area. From here, climb Szepessy Ignéc utca and turn left (west) on Káptalan utca, which is a street lined with museums and galleries. **Zsolnay Porcélan Múzeum** (Zsolnay Porcelain Museum; 🕿 324 822; Káptalan utca 2; adult/student 700/350Ft; 🕙 10am-4pm Tue-Sun Apr-Oct) is on the eastern end of this strip.

English translations provide a good history of the artistic and functional ceramics produced from this local factory's illustrious early days in the mid-19th century to the present. The excellent **Modern Magyar Képtár** (Modern Hungarian Art Gallery; 🕿 324 822; Káptalan utca 4; adult/child 400/200Ft; 🕙 10am-6pm Tue-Sun Apr-Oct, to 4pm Tue-Sun Nov-Mar) is next door, and here you can get a comprehensive overview of Hungarian art from 1850 till today.

Continue west to Dóm tér and the walled bishopric complex containing the four-towered **Szent Péter Bazilika** ( ☎ 513 030; Dóm tér; complex ticket adult/student 1000/500Ft; ⏰ 9am-5pm Mon-Sat, 1-5pm Sun). The oldest part of the building is the 11th-century crypt. The 1770 **Püspöki Palota** (Bishop's Palace; admission free; ⏰ 2-5pm late-Jun–Aug) stands in front of the cathedral, and a 15th-century **barbakán** (barbican) is the only stone bastion to survive from the old city walls.

The early Christian cemeteries from the Roman town of Sopianae became part of the Unesco World Heritage list in 2000. Two interesting places are the 4th-century **Ókeresztény Mauzóleum** (Christian Mausoleum; ☎ 312 7190; Szent István tér 12; adult/student 350/200Ft; ⏰ 10am-4pm Tue-Sun Apr-Oct) and the **Késörómai Sírépítények és Sírkápolna** (Late Roman Burial Site & Chapel; Apáca utca 8 & 14; adult/student 350/200Ft; ⏰ 10am-4pm Tue-Sun Apr-Oct), which are both richly decorated.

East of the Christian Mausoleum is the **Csontváry Múzeum** ( ☎ 310 544; Janus Pannonius utca 11; adult/student 600/300Ft; ⏰ 10am-4pm Tue-Sun Apr-Oct), displaying the dreamy work of the wonderful Tivadar Kosztka Csontváry (1853–1919), whose use of vivid colour and texture in landscape painting, as well as his tragic life, has been compared to that of Van Gogh.

Pécs' beautifully preserved 1869 **zsinagóga** (synagogue; ☎ 315 881; Kossuth tér; adult/child 300/200Ft; ⏰ 10am-5pm Sun-Fri May-Oct) is south of Széchenyi tér.

## Sleeping

**Ibusz** ( ☎ 212 157; Apáca utca 1; ⏰ 8am-5pm Mon-Fri, to 2pm Sat) arranges private rooms for 2540Ft per person.

**Mandulás Camping** ( ☎ 515 655; Ángyán János utca 2; camp sites per person 1200Ft, motel/hotel r 3200/5800Ft; ⏰ May-Oct) From the centre, take bus 33 or 34 3km up into the Mecsek Hills.

**Kishotel Centrum** ( ☎ 311 707; www.hotels.hu/cen trum_kishotel; Szepessy Ignác utca 4; s/d/tr 4500/5800/8750Ft) Paintings cover just about every inch of wall space, bric-a-brac decorates shelves and the furniture is mix-and-match: it's just like staying at a Hungarian *nagymama* (grandma's) house. The central hall on the ground floor has a small fridge and a hot plate you can use, but there aren't many other facilities.

**Hotel Főnix** ( ☎ 311 680; www.fonixhotel.hu; Hunyadi János út 2; s 5290Ft, d 7990-9490Ft) Odd angles and sloping eaves characterise the asymmetrical Hotel Főnix. Rooms are plain and those on the top floor have skylights. This hotel is second choice to the Diana.

**Hotel Diana** ( ☎ 328 594; www.dianahotel.hu, Hungarian only; Tímár utca 4A; s/d 7700/11,000Ft; ✖ ) This small, immaculate hotel right next to the synagogue has rustic accents, such as split-wood chair rails in the guest and breakfast rooms. The rooms on the second floor are better than those on the first. Double room No 5 has a great skylight that opens.

**Palatinus** ( ☎ 889 400; palatinus.reservation@danubius group.hu; Király utca 5; s €58-86, d €66-94; **P** ) For some Art Nouveau glamour, Palatinus is *the* place in Pécs. An amazing, marble reception has a soaring Moorish-detailed ceiling, and the 'ballroom' makes you want to get your most expensive frock/tux on and waltz. It's a shame that the rooms are not as luxurious, but still, in Pécs, it's as good as it gets.

## Eating

Pubs, cafés and fast-food eateries line pedestrian Király utca.

**Aranygaluska Gyorsétterem** ( ☎ 310 210; Irgalmasok utca 4; mains 430-640Ft; ⏰ 7.30am-8pm Mon-Fri, to 5pm Sat & Sun; ✖ ) Working-class heroes gather here for the generously portioned, cafeteria meals – some say the best food in town. Office workers know it too: the place is packed at lunch. The *töltöt paprika* (stuffed peppers) alone fill you up.

**Oázis** ( ☎ 215 367; Király utca 17; mains 500-1000Ft; ⏰ 10am-11pm) Unlike most of the kebab shops across Hungary, the owner at this take-away actually hails from the Middle East. You can taste the difference.

**Az Elefánthoz** ( ☎ 216 055; Jókai tér 6; mains 1100-2000Ft; ⏰ 11am-11pm; ✖ ) An unatmospheric Italian restaurant that serves really good soups, pastas and pizzas. Salads, like the tuna and onions on lettuce, are meal-sized. The nonsmoking section is only three booths.

**Dóm Vendéglö** ( ☎ 210 088; Király utca 3; mains 1300-2500Ft; ⏰ noon-11pm; ✖ ✖ ) If you like meat and Art Nouveau décor, Dóm Vendéglö is for you. Beef, venison, pork, turkey and duck, surrounded by turn-of-the-century paintings. Enter at the rear of the courtyard under the Aranyhajó Fogadó hotel.

Get self-catering supplies at **Co-op Szupermarket** (cnr Irgalmasok & Tímár utcas).

HUNGARY

## Entertainment

Pécs has well-established opera and ballet companies as well as a symphony orchestra. **Tourinform** ( ☎ 213 315; www.pecs.hu; Széchenyi tér 9; 🕑 8am-5.30pm Mon-Fri, 9am-4pm Sat May-Sep, 8am-4pm Mon-Fri Oct-Mar) has schedule information. The free biweekly *Pécsi Est* lists what's on at nightclubs and the cinema.

**Művészetek Háza** ( ☎ 315 388; Széchenyi tér 7-8) The Artists' House is a cultural venue that hosts classical musical performances. A schedule is posted outside.

**Los Bongos** ( ☎ 06 20 468 9491; Jókai tér 6; admission 390-550Ft; 🕑 6pm-2am Mon-Sat) Fridays are a Latin fiesta, but every night sizzles. This nightclub is on the floor above Az Elefánthoz restaurant.

**Dante Café** ( ☎ 210 361; Janus Pannonius utca 11; 🕑 10am-1am) An intellectual and student crowd gathers on the ground floor below the Csontváry Múzeum. There's live jazz and other music from Thursday through Saturday.

## Shopping

**Cezar Winery** ( ☎ 214 490; Szent István tér 12; 🕑 9am-5.30pm Mon-Fri) This building is where the family of Janos Pannonius made sparkling wine from 1859 to 1995. You can still buy Pannonia *pezsgő* (champagne), under new owners, in the onsite shop and view the production facilities through glass walls.

**Zsolnay Bolt** ( ☎ 310 172; Jókai tér 2; 🕑 10am-4pm Tue-Sun) You can buy a set of kooky porcelain here.

## Getting There & Away

Buses for Harkány (484Ft, one hour) leave every 15 minutes throughout the day. At least four buses a day connect Pécs with Budapest (2660Ft, 4½ hours), two with Keszthely (1740Ft, three hours) and eight with Szeged (2310Ft, four hours).

Pécs is on a main rail line with Budapest's Déli train station (2610Ft, 2½ hours, eight daily). One daily train runs from Pécs (8.40pm) to Osijek (1880Ft, two hours) in Horvátország (Croatia).

## AROUND PÉCS
### Harkány

The hot springs at **Harkány** (www.harkany.hu, no English), 26km south of Pécs, have medicinal waters with the richest sulphuric content in Hungary. The indoor and outdoor baths and pools of **Gyógyfürdő** ( ☎ 480 251; www.harkanyfurdo.hu; Kossuth Lajos utca 7; adult/student 1790/1090Ft; 🕑 9am-10pm mid-Jun–Aug, to 8pm Sun-Thu & to 10pm Fri & Sat Sep–mid-

Jun) range in temperature from 26°C to 33°C in summer and from 33°C to 35°C in winter. You might consider booking a spa service, mud bath or massage. The town is basically the thermal bath complex in a 12-hectare park surrounded by holiday hotels and restaurants. Buses between Harkány and Pécs (484Ft, one hour) depart frequently, about every 15 minutes. The Harkány bus station is at the southeast corner of the park.

# SOUTHEASTERN HUNGARY

The mysterious Nagyalföld (Great Plain) is an area that has been central to Hungarian myth and legend for centuries. The Plain, and its horsemen and shepherds, have represented the Hungarian ethos in poems, songs, paintings and stories. It starts at the point where Tisza River drainage basin meets the wide expanse of level *puszta* (prairie or steppe). Much of the *alföld* has been turned into farmland for growing apricots and raising geese, but other parts are little more than grassy, saline deserts sprouting juniper trees. Kiskunsági Nemzeti Park, including the Bugac Puszta, protects this unique environment.

## KECSKEMÉT
☎ 76 / pop 108,180
Located about halfway between Budapest and Szeged, Kecskemét (*kech*-kah-mate) is a green, pedestrian-friendly city with interesting Art Nouveau architecture. Claims to fame include the locally produced *barack* (apricot) jam and *pálinka* (potent brandy), *libamaj* (goose liver) dishes, and the nearby Kiskunsági Nemzeti Park and horse farms.

## Orientation & Information

Central Kecskemét is made up of squares that run into one another, and consequently it's hard to tell them apart. The main bus and train stations are opposite each other in József Katona Park. A 10-minute walk southwest along Nagykőrösi utca brings you to the first of the squares, Szabadság tér.

**Tourinform** ( ☎ 481 065; www.kecskemet.hu; Kossuth tér 1; 🕑 8am-5pm Mon-Fri, 9am-1pm Sat Jul-Aug) is in the northeastern corner of the large Town Hall. Staff here can help you with information about Kiskunsági Nemzeti Park. The **OTP**

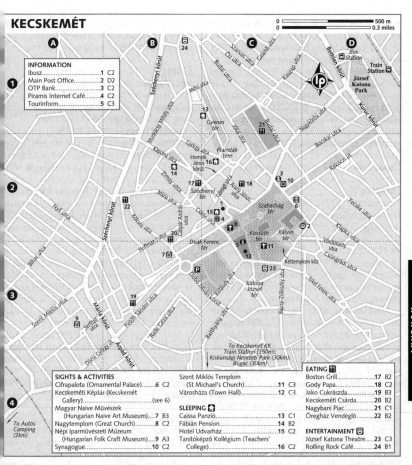

## KECSKEMÉT

HUNGARY

**Bank** (Szabadság tér 1/A) is central, does foreign exchange and has an ATM. The **main post office** (Kálvin tér 10) is to the southeast. Surf the Web at **Piramis Internet Café** ( ☎ 418 134; Csányi utca 1-3; per hr 540Ft; ☼ 10am-8pm Mon-Fri, 1-8pm Sat & Sun), upstairs in the courtyard of a small shopping mall.

## Sights

Walk around the park-like squares, starting at Szabadság tér, and admire the eclectic building styles, including the technicolour Art Nouveau of the 1902 **Cifrapalota** (Ornamental Palace; Rákóczi út 1), recently refurbished and covered in multicoloured majolica tiles. Check out the wonderful interiors of the **Kecskeméti Képtár** (Kecskemét Gallery; ☎ 480 776; Rákóczi út 1; adult/child 260/130Ft; ☼ 10am-5pm Tue-Sun). Across the street,

the Moorish building is the former **synagogue** (Rákóczi út 2), now an office building and exhibition hall called the House of Technology.

Kossuth tér is dominated by the massive 1897 Art Nouveau **Városháza** (Town Hall; admission free; ☼ 9am-5pm Mon-Fri), which is flanked by the baroque **Nagytemplom** (Great Church, 1806) and the earlier **Szent Miklós Templom** (St Michael's Church), dating from the 13th century. Nearby is the magnificent 1896 **József Katona Theatre** ( ☎ 483 283; Katona József tér 5; ☼ performance times only), a neobaroque theatre with a statue of the Trinity (1742) in front of it. All of these churches are open to the public during and around mass times and are free.

The town's museums are scattered around the main squares' periphery. Go first to the

**Magyar Naive Müvészek** (Hungarian Naive Art Museum; ☎ 324 767; Gáspár András utca 11; adult/student 150/50Ft; 🕓 10am-5pm Tue-Sun), in the Stork House (1730) northwest off Petőfi Sándor utca. It has an impressive small collection; the folk themes are especially noteworthy. Further to the southwest, the **Népi Iparmüvészeti Múzeum** (Hungarian Folk Craft Museum; ☎ 327 203; Serfőző utca 19a; adult/student 200/100Ft; 🕓 10am-5pm Tue-Sun) has a definitive collection of regional embroidery, weaving and textiles, as well as some furniture, woodcarving and agricultural tools. A few handicrafts are for sale at the entrance.

## Sleeping

Tourinform (p394) can help you locate the numerous colleges that offer dormitory accommodation in July and August; one good choice is the central **Tanítóképző Kollégium** (Teachers' College; ☎ 486 977; Piaristák tere 4; s/d 2000/4000Ft; 🕓 mid-Jun–Aug; Ⓟ ). **Ibusz** ( ☎ 486 955; Kossuth tér 3; 🕓 8am-5pm Mon-Fri Sep-Jun, 8am-5pm Mon-Fri, 9am-1pm Sat Jul-Aug) travel agency brokers private rooms from 2000Ft per person, with a four-night minimum.

**Autós Camping** ( ☎ 329 398; Csabai Géza körút 5; camp sites 1/2 people 1350/2100Ft, caravan sites 2200Ft, bungalows 5400Ft; 🕓 Apr-Oct) As the name implies, this place is more vehicle- than tent-camping oriented, with big treeless plots. Don't be surprised if it's jammed with caravans and Germanic speakers. Take bus 1 to get southwest of town.

**Caissa Panzió** ( ☎ 481 685; www.caissachessbooks.com; Gyenes tér 18, 4th fl; s/d/tr/q 6900/8900/10,300/11,700Ft) If you are a chess lover, stay here, at the Chess Panzió, where the manager has tournaments in the big lounge on the ground floor. The rooms are on several floors in an apartment block, and provide a slightly cheaper, shabby-chic alternative – some with shared bathrooms. There's no breakfast, but you can ask for a key and share the kitchen facilities.

**Fábián Pension** ( ☎ 477 677; www.hotels.hu/fabian; Kápolna utca 14; r 7500-9500Ft; ☒ 🐾 ) Definitely the town's best place to stay. Fábián is a family-run place, with picture windows, clean rooms and a spacious, flowery garden. Homemade jam and sweets are served along with your cold cuts and bread at breakfast, and mum and daughter will help you plan an independent trip to the national park or to a horse farm. You can also rent bicycles here for 1500Ft per day.

**Hotel Udvarház** ( ☎ 413 912; Csányi utca 1-3; s/d/tr 11,900/14,500/17,500Ft; Ⓟ ☒ ) Curvilinear blond and turquoise wood furnishings define the contemporary style of this hotel on the 1st floor above a shopping arcade (across from Piramis Internet Café). A few rooms have air-con; ask first, if this is important to you.

## Eating

**Jako Cukrászda** ( ☎ 505 949; Petőfi Sándor utca 7; cakes 110-265Ft; 🕓 7am-7pm Mon-Fri, 9am-7pm Sat & Sun) Cakes, puddings and strudels tempt from behind a long, modern glass-and-chrome case.

**Öregház Vendéglö** ( ☎ 496 973; Kölcsey utca 3; mains 600-1000Ft; 🕓 11am-10pm; ☒ ) Get yourself some proper Hungarian roast: the *cigany pecsenye* (literally 'Gypsy's roast') is a mixed grill with tender cutlets of pork and chicken, a piece of bacon and a sausage. Join the friends and families who gather here for Sunday lunches. Blue-and-white *kékfestö* (indigo-dyed) tablecloths and curtains make the place homy and it's completely nonsmoking – a real rarity.

**Kecskeméti Csárda** ( ☎ 488 686; Kölcsey utca 7; mains 1290-1990Ft; 🕓 11am-11pm; ☒ ) This is what a stereotypical Hungarian country inn (*csárda*) restaurant looks like – with a Romani musician and all. It may seem a bit touristy, but it's where residents go to celebrate special occasions. There's courtyard dining.

You can get some decent and cheap quick eats and a beer at **Boston Grill** ( ☎ 484 444; Kápolna utca 2; burgers 320-550Ft; 🕓 11am-10pm) or **Gody Papa** ( ☎ 415 515; Arany János utca 3; pizzas 330-550Ft; 🕓 11am-11pm). There is an open-air market, **Nagybani Piac** (Budai utca; 🕓 7am-1pm Mon-Sat) for self-catering.

## Entertainment

Tourinform (p394) has a list of what concerts and performances are on, or check out the free *Kecskeméti Est* (www.est.hu, Hungarian only) available at restaurants around town. Nightlife can be a little dull on weekdays outside the summer months, but you can always enjoy a coffee or a glass of wine from one of the cafés on Kossuth tér and watch the people go by.

**József Katona Theatre** ( ☎ 483 283; Katona József tér) See operettas and symphony performances in the 19th-century building.

**Rolling Rock Café** ( ☎ 506 190; Jókai utca 44; 🕓 noon-5am Thu-Sat, noon-midnight Tue-Wed) The coolest place in town for live music and a beverage.

## Getting There & Away

Frequent buses depart for Budapest (1040Ft, two hours, every 40 minutes) and for Szeged (1090Ft, two hours, hourly). A direct rail line links Budapest's Nyugati train station with Kecskemét (1212Ft, 1½ hours, 12 daily) and

Kecskemét with Szeged (1844Ft, 1¼ hours, hourly except at lunch time).

## KISKUNSÁG NATIONAL PARK

Totalling 76,000 hectares, **Kiskunsági Nemzeti Park** (Kiskunság National Park; www.knp.hu) consists of half a dozen 'islands' of protected land. Much of the park's alkaline ponds, dunes and grassy 'deserts' with juniper trees are off-limits. **Bugac** (*Boo*-gats) village, about 30km southwest of Kecskemét, is the most accessible part of the park. Here you can see the famous Hungarian cowboys ride at a daily horse show from May to October. The rest of the year, ask at the Kecskemét Tourinform (p394) to see if they know of a tour group you could join.

The company that owns the restaurant **Bugaci Karikás Csárda** ( ☎ 575 121; Nagybugac 135; mains 1200-2500Ft; ❤ 11am-11pm) runs the **horse show** (adult/student 1000/500Ft; ❤ 1.15pm May-Oct), which is the main attraction in the village. You can take a **wagon ride** (1000Ft; ❤ 12.15pm May-Oct) to go the few kilometres to the **Pásztor Múzeum** (Shepherd Museum; admission free; ❤ 10am-5pm May-Oct) first or just walk down the sand road to the staging ring. Once the show starts, the horse herders crack their whips, race one another bareback and ride 'five-in-hand', a breathtaking performance in which one *csikós* (cowboy) gallops five horses at full speed while standing on the backs of the rear two. And of course you can always stop for some wine and Romani music in the *csárda* afterwards.

The best way to get to Bugac is by bus from Kecskemét (423Ft). The 11am bus from the main terminal gets you to the park entrance around noon. Another option is to take the narrow-gauge train (326Ft) from the Kecskemét KK train station (south of the town centre) to the Móricgát stop (two after the Bugac stop) and walk across the field towards the conical-shaped roof of the Pásztor Múzeum. Departures are at 8am, 2.10pm and 7.50pm daily. After the show, the first bus back to Kecskemét passes by the park entrance at 5.15pm weekdays and 6.35pm weekends (a change at Jakabszállás is required for the last bus). The return train departs from Móricgát at 6.04pm and 11.54pm.

## SZEGED

☎ 62 / pop 175,500

Szeged (*seh*-ged) is one of Hungary's best off-the-beaten-track destinations, a place that draws far fewer visitors than it should. A couple of days in this lively college town on the southern Great Plain, right on the Tisza River just before Serbia, will get you acquainted with the many ornate and colourful one-time palaces that now contain businesses or house several families. The Maros River from Romania enters the Tisza just east of the centre, and flooding is not uncommon. Much of the old town is architecturally homogeneous, as it was rebuilt after the disastrous 1879 flood destroyed large parts of the city.

### Orientation & Information

The train station is south of the city centre on Indóház tér; tram 1 rides from it along Boldogasszony sugárút into the centre of town (five stops to Széchenyi tér). The bus station, on Mars tér, is to the west of the centre and is within easy walking distance via pedestrian Mikszáth Kálmán utca.

The **Tourinform** ( ☎ 488 699; Dugonics tér 2; ❤ 9am-5pm Mon-Fri) office is hidden in a courtyard. **Matrix Café** ( ☎ 423 830; Kárász utca 5; per hr 500Ft; ❤ 24hr) has dozens of internet terminals and just as many for game-addict use only.

**Main post office** (Széchenyi tér 1)

**OTP Bank** (Klauzál tér 4)

### Sights & Activities

East of Széchenyi tér, the huge, neoclassical **Móra Ferenc Múzeum** ( ☎ 549 040; Várkert; adult/student 400/250Ft; ❤ 10am-5pm Tue-Sun) peers down on the Tisza River. There are interesting exhibits on the Avar people (5th to 8th centuries) who lived in the area, on the area's folk life and art, as well as a room dedicated to the 1879 flood. North of the museum is a long, waterview park with walking paths and playground equipment.

To the west, the **Új Zsinagóga** (New Synagogue; ☎ 423 849; Gutenberg utca 13; adult/student 250/100Ft; ❤ 10am-noon & 1-5pm Sun-Fri Apr-Sep, 10am-2pm Sun-Fri Oct-Mar) is the most beautiful Jewish house of worship in Hungary and is still in use. An ornate, blue- and gold-painted interior graces the 1903 Art Nouveau building. Free organ concerts here are common on summer evenings. The nearby **Ó Zsinagóga** (Old Synagogue; Hajnóczy utca 12; admission free; ❤ service times) was built in 1843.

The **Szeged Open-Air Festival** is held in Dom tér from mid-July to late August. Running along three sides of the square is the **Nemzeti Emlékcsarnok** (National Pantheon), with statues and reliefs of 80 Hungarian notables. One block northeast, inside the **Szerb Ortodox Templom** (Serbian Orthodox Church; cnr Béla & Somogyi utca; adult/student 150/100Ft; ❤ 8am-8pm), have a look at

HUNGARY

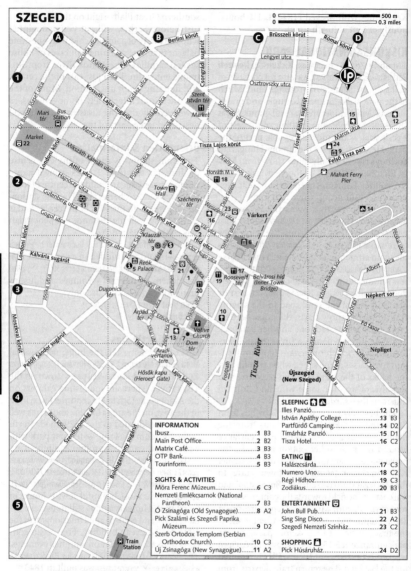

**SZEGED**

0 ___ 500 m
0 ___ 0.3 miles

the fantastic iconostasis – a central gold 'tree' with 60 icons hanging off its 'branches'.

Just north of the Old Town ring road is the **Pick Szalámi és Szegedi Paprika Múzeum** ( ☎ 421 814; Felső Tisza part 10; adult/student 320/240Ft; ☻ 3-6pm Tue-Fri & 1-4pm Sat). Two floors of exhibits and old photos show traditional methods of salami production. There's a small gift stand in

the museum and a butcher shop around the corner in this factory building.

## Sleeping

Plenty of student accommodation is open to travellers in July and August, including the central **István Apáthy College** ( ☎ 545 896; Eötvös utca 4; r 5000Ft; ✗ ). Ask Tourinform (p397) for more information. **Ibusz** ( ☎ 471 177; www.ibusz.hu; Oroszlán utca 3; per person 4000-5000Ft; 9am-5pm Mon-Fri, to 1pm Sat) travel agency can help with private rooms.

**Partfürdő Camping** ( ☎ 430 843; Közép-kikötő sor; camp sites per person 1200Ft, bungalows 12,000Ft; mid-May–Sep; P ) This green, grassy camp site is across the river in New Szeged. Bungalows sleep up to four people.

**Illes Panzió** ( ☎ 315 640; www.illespanzio.fw.hu; Maros utca 37; r 5900-7900Ft; P ) This newly refurbished old mansion north of the centre has fresh, clean rooms with wood panels, cool tile floors, TVs and polished woodwork.

**Tímárház Panzió** ( ☎ 425 486; Maros utca 26; s/d/tr 8200/10,000/17,600Ft; P ) Boxy rooms are sparsely furnished with low-lying modern beds and flat-faced armoires.

**Tisza Hotel** ( ☎ 478 278; www.tiszahotel.hu; Wesselényi utca 1; s/d €57/67; P ) The classy old mamma of Szeged, this 1885 hotel has imposing marble pillars, gilded décor and vast halls with low-hanging chandeliers. You can upgrade to a 'superior' room with colonial furniture for under €20 extra. The cheapest deals are rooms with a shower, but the toilet is in a shared restroom down the hall.

## Eating

**Numero Uno** ( ☎ 424 745; Széchenyi tér 5; mains 360-730Ft; 11am-11pm Mon-Sat, noon-11pm Sun; ) Good pizzas and calzones on the main square. There's a garden out back.

**Régi Hídhoz** ( ☎ 420 910; Oskola utca 4; mains 780-1200Ft; noon-11pm Sun-Thu, 11am-midnight Fri & Sat; ) This is the cheaper version of Halászcsárda (below), where many come to try Szeged's *halászlé* (fish soup). The rustic dining room has faux-treated yellow plaster walls and ceramics hanging as decorations.

**Zodiákus** ( ☎ 420 914; Oskola utca 13; mains 890-2100Ft; 11am-midnight Mon-Thu, 11am-1am Sat, 1-4pm Sun; ) Low lighting, barrel ceilings, amber walls and stylised zodiac-sign art make for a sultry, upscale environment. Imaginative entrées include options such as beef tenderloin topped with red currants and cheddar cheese.

**Halászcsárda** ( ☎ 555 980; Roosevelt tér 14; mains 1500-2000Ft) While in town you have to try Szegedi *halászlé*, the fish soup the area is known for. This is the place that wins all prizes for the local delicacy.

## Entertainment

This being a college town means that there is a vast array of bars, clubs and other nightspots, especially around Dugonics tér. Nightclub programmes are listed in the free *Szegedi Est* magazine.

**Szegedi Nemzeti Színház** ( ☎ 479 279; Deák Ferenc utca 12-14) Since 1886, the Szeged National Theatre has been the centre of cultural life in the city. Opera, ballet and drama performances take the stage.

**John Bull Pub** ( ☎ 484 217; Oroszlán utca 6; 10am-midnight Mon-Fri, to 1am Sat & Sun) Join the 20-somethings drinking on the small patio or in the cosy pub – if you can find a free table.

**Sing Sing Disco** (cnr Mars tér & Dr Baross József utca; 10pm-4am Wed-Sat) A place where the youngsters let loose on weekends, with guest DJs, rave parties and occasional theme nights (let's hope none of them include prison outfits). Admission starts at 500Ft, depending on the DJ.

## Shopping

**Pick Húsáruház** ( ☎ 421 879; Maros utca 21; 3-6pm Mon, 7am-6pm Tue-Fri, 6am-noon Sat) You can buy a stick of Pick salami, Szeged's brand product, as well as other meats, right from the factory store.

## Getting There & Away

Buses run to Budapest (2430Ft, three hours, six daily), Kecskemét (1090Ft, two hours, hourly) and Pécs (2310Ft, four hours, eight daily), among other destinations. If you're heading to Serbia, buses make the 1½ hour run to Subotica daily at 10am (800Ft).

Szeged is on the main rail line to Budapest's Nyugati train station (2324Ft, 2½ hours, 11 daily), stopping halfway along in Kecskemét (1844Ft, 1¼ hours, 11 daily). You have to change in Békéscsaba to get to Arad (2946Ft, 3½ hours, three daily) in Romania. Two daily trains (6.35am and 4.25pm) go direct from Szeged to Subotica (1434Ft, two hours) in Serbia.

# NORTHEASTERN HUNGARY

The level plains and grasslands give way to a chain of wooded hills as you head north and east. These are the foothills of the Carpathian Mountains (in modern-day Ukraine and Romania), which stretch along the Hungarian border with Slovakia. Though you'll definitely notice the rise in elevation, Hungary's highest peak of Kékes-tető is still only a proverbial bump in the road at 1014m. The microclimates in several of the hill groupings are quite conducive to wine production. Eger and Tokaj are known worldwide for their red and sweet dessert wines, respectively. Not far north of Eger is Szilvásvárad – the Hungarian home of the snow-white Lipizzaner horse makes a good day trip.

## EGER

**☎ 36 / pop 57,000**

After Budapest, Eger (egg-air) is probably next on any visitor's list, and the gallons of wine that are at your disposal here definitely have something to do with it. But that's not to say there's nothing else to draw travellers here – on the contrary. This attractive baroque city has a great hilltop castle and a walkable, quaint town centre. And then, of course, there's the wine.

It was here in 1552 that Hungarian defenders temporarily stopped the Turkish advance into Western Europe and helped preserve Hungary's identity. Legend has it that István Dobó fortified his badly outnumbered soldiers with red wine while they successfully defended Eger against the siege. When the Ottomans saw the red-stained beards, rumours circulated that the Hungarians were drinking bull's blood to attain their strength. Thus the name of the region's most famous red wine came to be Egri Bikavér (Eger Bull's Blood). The Ottomans returned in 1596 and captured Eger Castle. They were evicted in 1687.

In the 18th century, Eger played a central role in Ferenc Rákóczi II's attempt to overthrow the Habsburgs, and it was then that a large part of the castle was razed by the Austrians. Credit goes to the bishops of Eger for erecting most of the town you see today. Eger has some of Hungary's finest architecture, especially examples of Copf (Zopf in Hungarian), a transitional style between late baroque and neoclassicism found only in Central Europe. Just a 20-minute walk southwest of the centre, dozens of small wine cellars are to be found carved into the sides of Szépasszony völgy (Valley of the Beautiful Women).

### Orientation & Information

The main train station is a 15-minute walk south of town, on Vasút utca, just east of Deák Ferenc utca. Egervár train station, which serves Szilvásvárad and other points north, is a five-minute walk north of the castle along Vécseyvölgy utca. The bus station is west of Széchenyi István utca, Eger's main drag.

**Egri Est Café** ( ☎ 411 105; Széchenyi István utca 16; ☽ 11am-midnight Sun-Thu, to 4am Fri & Sat) internet access for 500Ft per hour.

**OTP Bank** (Széchenyi István utca 2)

**Post office** (Széchenyi István utca 22)

**Tourinform** ( ☎ 517 715; www.eger.hu; Bajcsy-Zsilinszky utca 9; ☽ 9am-5pm Mon-Fri, to 1pm Sat, to 6pm Mon-Fri Jul-Aug) The helpful staff here has lots of regional information on hand, including an accommodation guide.

### Sights & Activities

The most striking attraction and the best views of town are from **Egri Vár** (Eger Castle; ☎ 312 744; Vár 1; adult/student combined ticket 900/450Ft; ☽ 8am-8pm Tue-Sun Apr-Aug, to 7pm Sep, 8am-6pm Oct & Mar, to 5pm Nov-Feb), a huge walled complex at the top of the hill off Dózsa tér. First fortified after an early Mongol invasion in the 13th century, the earliest ruins onsite are the foundations of St John's Cathedral, built in the 12th century and destroyed by the Turks. The excellent **István Dobó Múzeum** (admission included with castle), inside the Bishop's Palace (1470), explores the history and development of the castle and the town. Other exhibits such as the **Panoptikum** (Waxworks; adult/student 350/250Ft) and the **Éremverde** (Minting Exhibit; adult/student 240/120Ft) cost extra. Even on days when the museums are closed, you can walk around the grounds and battlements and enjoy the views if you buy a *sétaljegy* (strolling ticket, adult/child 400/200Ft).

A surprise awaits you west of the castle hill: a 40m-high **minaret** (Knézich Károly utca; admission 200Ft; ☽ 10am-6pm Mar-Oct), minus the mosque, is allegedly Europe's northernmost remains of the Ottoman invasion in the 16th century. The **Minorita Templom** (Minorite Church; Dobó István tér; admission free; ☽ mass times), built in 1771, is a glorious baroque building. In the square in front are statues of national hero István Dobó and his comrades-in-arms routing the Turks in 1552.

The first thing you see as you come into town from the bus or train station is the neoclassical **Egri Bazilika** (Eger Cathedral; Pyrker János tér 1), built in 1836. Directly opposite is the Copf-style **Líceum** (Lyceum; ☎ 520 400; Esterházy tér 1; admission free; ☽ 9.30am-3.30pm Tue-Sun Apr-Sep, to 1pm Sat & Sun Oct-Mar), dating from 1765, with a 20,000-volume frescoed **könyvtár** (library; adult/student 500/350Ft) on the 1st floor and an 18th-century observatory in the **Csillagászati Múzeum** (Astronomy Museum; adult/student 500/350Ft) on the 6th floor. Climb three more floors up to

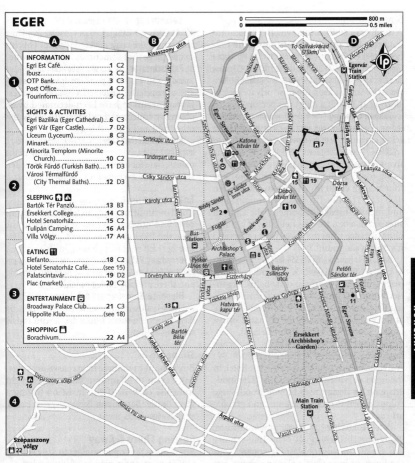

## EGER

0 — 800 m
0 — 0.5 miles

**INFORMATION**
Egri Est Café..........................1 C2
Ibusz.....................................2 C2
OTP Bank...............................3 C3
Post Office.............................4 C2
Tourinform............................5 C2

**SIGHTS & ACTIVITIES**
Egri Bazilika (Eger Cathedral)...6 C3
Egri Vár (Eger Castle)..............7 D2
Líceum (Lyceum).....................8 C3
Minaret..................................9 C2
Minorita Templom (Minorite
    Church).............................10 C2
Török Fürdő (Turkish Bath)....11 D3
Városi Térmalfürdő
    (City Thermal Baths).........12 D3

**SLEEPING**
Bartók Tér Panzió..................13 B3
Érsekkert College..................14 C3
Hotel Senatorház..................15 C2
Tulipán Camping...................16 A4
Villa Völgy............................17 A4

**EATING**
Elefanto................................18 C2
Hotel Senatorház Café........(see 15)
Palatscintavár......................19 D2
Piac (market)........................20 C2

**ENTERTAINMENT**
Broadway Palace Club...........21 C3
Hippolite Klub...................(see 18)

**SHOPPING**
Borachivum..........................22 A4

HUNGARY

---

the observation deck for a great view of the city and to try out the camera obscura, the 'eye of Eger', designed in 1776 to entertain the locals.

The Archbishop's Garden was once the private reserve of papal princes, but today the park is open to the public. Inside the park, the **Városi Térmalfürdő** (City Thermal Baths; ☎ 411 699; adult/child 500/350Ft; ☺ 6am-7.30pm Mon-Fri, 9am-7pm Sat & Sun May-Sep, 9am-6pm daily Oct-Apr) has open-air, as well as covered, pools with different temperatures (40°C being the hottest) and mineral contents. The **Török Fürdő** (Turkish Bath; Fürdő utca 3), built between 1610 and 1617, is open only to those with a doctor's order.

The prize for the most deceitful name of any attraction in the world could almost

definitely go to **Szépasszony völgy** (Valley of the Beautiful Women; off Király utca; ☺ 10am-5pm), home to dozens of small wine cellars that truck in, store and sell Bull's Blood and other regional red and white wines. Walk the horseshoe-shaped street through the valley and stop in front of one that strikes your fancy and ask ('*megkosztólhatok?*') to taste their wares (50Ft per decilitre). If you want wine to go, you can bring an empty plastic bottle and have it filled for about (600Ft per 1½ litres); they'll also sell you a kitschy little plastic barrel full. It's easy to drink a lot here, but remember that there is a zero-tolerance policy for driving in Hungary with any alcohol in your system, so walk the 20 minutes back to the centre or get a taxi (1000Ft).

## Sleeping

A number of colleges in town offer accommodation in July and August, including the 132-bed **Érsekkert College** ( ☎ 413 661; fax 520 440; Klapka György utca 12; dm 1400-2000Ft). **Ibusz** ( ☎ 311 451; www.ibusz.hu; Széchenyi István utca 9; ✆ 8am-4pm Mon-Fri, 9am-1pm Sat Jun-Sep) can help organise private rooms, starting at 3000Ft a night per person.

**Tulipán Camping** ( ☎ 410 580; www.home.zonnet.nl/tulipan/; Szépasszony völgy utca 71; camp sites per person 1450Ft, caravan sites with electricity per person 1950Ft, hotel r 7680Ft, 4-/5-person bungalows 5500/9900Ft; P ⚿ ) The five-person bungalow has one bedroom, a living room, a kitchen and a bathroom. The four-person cabin is just a room (no kitchen or bath). The hotel rooms have minifridges and include breakfast. Some of the caravan sites are in a big, treeless field. It's at a stumbling distance from the valley wine cellars and it's open year-round.

**Bartók Tér Panzió** ( ☎ 515 556; fax 515 572; Bartók Béla tér 8; s/d/tr 7000/9000/11,000Ft; ✗ ) A light, colourful place with basic rooms and skylights, organised around a courtyard in an old town building. The same people operate St Kristof Panzió, at the end of the square, for the same prices (contact Bartók Tér Panzió for details).

**Villa Völgy** ( ☎ 321 664; www.hotels.hu/villavolgy; Szépasszony völgy, Tulipánkert utca 5; s/d 8200/13,600Ft; P ✗ ) A stylish, country manor house–type hotel, in the heart of wine-tasting country. The modern interior design uses blonde wood, large colourful prints on the curtains, and graphic art rugs.

**Hotel Senatorház** ( ☎ 320 466; www.senatorhaz.hu; Dobó István tér 11; r €56-70; P ⚿ ) This 18th-century inn sitting on the cobblestone square, with the lights of Eger Castle glowing above, has the best location in town. The reception is cluttered with tasteful antiques, leather sofas and old photographs, and traditional wood furnishings decorate the well-equipped 11 guest rooms.

## Eating

At the base of Szépasszony völgy utca there are numerous small terrace *büfé* (snack bars) that resemble food stands, but employ a waiter to serve you at your picnic table. There are also numerous restaurants and cafés along pedestrian Széchenyi István utca in town. The area is known for its *pistrang* (trout) dishes.

**Piac** (market; Katona István tér; ✆ 6am-6pm Mon-Fri, to 1pm Sat, to 10am Sun) Come to the covered market to get fruit, vegetables, meat and bread.

**Elefanto** ( ☎ 411 031; Katona István tér 2; mains 1350-2500Ft, pizzas 490-900Ft; ✆ 11am-midnight; ✗ ) Dine alfresco on the large covered terrace. This is a casual place that sometimes has light music.

**Palatscintavár** ( ☎ 413 986; Dobó István utca 9; mains around 1200Ft) This is a pancake-lover's heaven, and a wonderful vegetarian option. The restaurant seems to have been decorated by an obsessive collector of old cigarette packs and other odd and lovely things.

**Hotel Senatorház Café** ( ☎ 320 466; Dobó István tér 11; mains 1400-3000Ft; ✆ 11am-midnight; ✗ ) Sitting in the main square for a meal is delightful. Even better, stop by in the evening for a candlelit dessert.

## Entertainment

The Tourinform office can tell you what concerts and musicals are on at theatres in the area, the Líceum and at Eger Cathedral. The free *Egri Est* magazine has nightlife listings.

**Broadway Palace Club** (Pyker János tér 3; ✆ 10am-6am Wed, Fri & Sat) A good atmosphere for dancing and there are café tables outside.

**Hippolite Klub** ( ☎ 411 031; Katona István tér 2; ✆ 10am-4am) A mild-mannered restaurant by day, Hippolite turns funky disco with music starting at 9pm.

## Shopping

Buy wine at the source in Szépasszony völgy. Ask a cellar to fill up your plastic jug straight from the cask, or if you insist on having a glass bottle, **Borachivum** (Szépasszony völgy utca 33; ✆ 10am-6pm) sells them.

## Getting There & Away

Buses make the trip from Eger to Szilvásvárad (405Ft, 45 minutes, nine daily). Other destinations include Budapest (1500Ft, two hours, 15 daily), Kecskemét (2080Ft, 4½ hours, three daily) and also Szeged (2660Ft, 5½ hours, three daily). To get to Tokaj by bus, you have to go past it to Nyíregyháza and switch.

Eight trains a day connect Egervár station with Szilvásvárad (312Ft, one hour). Departing from the main train station, change at Füzesabony to get to Tokaj (1762Ft, two hours, seven daily). Direct trains run from Eger to Budapest's Keleti station (1968Ft, two hours) four times a day.

## SZILVÁSVÁRAD

☎ 36 / pop 1850

Horse-lover? Then come this way. The quiet village of Szilvásvárad, 28km north of Eger, hides in the Bükk Hills, most of which fall within the 43,000-hectare **Bükk Nemzeti Park**. This is where you can see, ride and be pulled (in a carriage) by the precious white stallions, the Lipizzaner horses. Either make a day trip to the hills or base yourself at the park. Some 250 prize horses are kept in local stables. If you love hiking, you can base yourself at the Lipizzaner centre too, and although there's no tourist office here, the Tourinform in Eger (p400) has information and sells hiking maps.

The bus from Eger will drop you off in the centre on Egri út. Park utca is off Egri, north of the bus stop, Szalajka Völgy is to the south. You get off the train at Szilvásvárad-Szalajkavölgy, the first of the town's two stations. Follow Egri út east and then north (left) for about 10 minutes into town. At the turn, if you go right instead you'll get to the valley.

Learn more about Lipizzaner horses at the **Lipcsai Múzeum** ( ☎ 355 135; Park utca 8; adult/student 350/250Ft; ☼ 9am-noon & 1-4pm), which has historical exhibits and a few live animals in an 18th-century stable. Call a day ahead to arrange a carriage (from 4300/7400Ft for a two-/four-horse coach seating three people) or a horseback ride at the **Lipizzaner State Stud Farm** (Lipicai Állami Ménesgazdaság; ☎ 564 400; Fenyves utca; admission adult/child 300/200Ft; ☼ 10am-noon & 2-4pm Thu-Sun; rides 1800/2200Ft per hr in paddock/further afield).

At the beginning of Szalajka Völgy there are restaurants, souvenir shops and tracks where Lipizzaner coaches race some summer weekends. You can park here for 100Ft per hour. Hike from here further into the valley, or take a ride on a **keskeny nyomtávú vasút** (narrow-gauge railway; ☎ 355 197; Szalajka völgy utca 6; one way adult/student 300/150Ft; ☼ May-Sep).

Nine daily buses connect Szilvásvárad and Eger (405Ft, 45 minutes). Trains to Egervár train station take about an hour (312Ft, eight daily).

# TOKAJ
☎ 47 / pop 4650

The region has been on the Unesco World Heritage list since 2002, although grapevines have been grown in the hills surrounding Tokaj village for at least 1000 years. The volcanic soil and unique microclimate promote the growth of *Botrytis cinerea* (noble rot) on the grapes. It's these ugly, shrivelled-up grapes covered with fungus that produce Tokaji Aszú,

a world-class dessert wine. The sweetness is rated from 3 (least) to 6 (the most). Tokaj also produces less sweet wines: Szamorodni (like dry sherry), Furmint and Háslevelú (the driest of all). The village itself spreads out in a valley at the confluence of the Tisza and the Bodrog Rivers. Look for the nesting storks on telephone poles and chimneys from March through September.

## Orientation & Information

Trains arrive 1200m south of the town centre; walk north on Baross Gábor utca, turn left on Bajcsy-Zsilinszky út and it turns into Rákóczi út, the main thoroughfare. The bus station is much more convenient, in town, on Seráz utca.
**Tourinform** ( ☎ 552 070; www.tokaj.hu; Serház utca 1; ☼ 9am-4pm Mon-Fri) is just off Rákóczi út.

## Sights & Activities

Start at the **Tokaji Múzeum** ( ☎ 352 636; Bethlen Gábor utca 13; adult/student 400/200Ft; ☼ 10am-4pm Tue-Sun May-Nov), which leaves nothing unsaid about the history of Tokaj, the region and its wines. After you're thoroughly knowledgeable, head to the 600-year-old cellar **Rákóczi Pince** ( ☎ 352 408; Kossuth tér 15; ☼ 10am-6pm) for a tasting and a tour. Bottles of wine mature underground in the long cave-like corridors (one measures 28m by 10m). A flight of six Tokaj wines costs 2100Ft. The correct order of sampling Tokaj wines is: Furmint, dry Szamorodni, sweet Szamorodni and then the Aszú wines – from three to six *puttony* (the sweetest). If you only want to taste the Aszú, a three-decilitre glass costs 216Ft to 636Ft, with a minimum of four glasses to taste.

There are less formal wine cellars (*pincek*) that offer tastings. They are scattered along the roads leading into town (Tarcali) and out of (Bodorgkeresztúrí) town. Look for signs on Rákóczi út, on Bem út and on Hegyalja utca (southeast of town off Bajcsy-Zsilinszky út). Other town attractions include the **Tokaji Galéria** ( ☎ 352 003; Bethlen Gábor utca 17; admission free; ☼ 10am-4pm May-Oct), in an 18th-century Greek Orthodox church, with works by local artists. The **Nagy Zsinagóga** (Great Synagogue; Serház utca 55), has been restored from its crumbling state.

## Sleeping & Eating

**Tourinform** (www.tokaj.hu) lists searchable private accommodation on its website. The newest, nicest pensions are southeast of town and require at least a 20-minute walk to get to the centre.

**HUNGARY**

**Lux** ( ☎ 352 145; Serház utca 14; d/tr 5400/7500Ft) This friendly six-room pension has obviously been well loved, and well used, but it is *central*. No breakfast.

**Tisza Panzió** ( ☎ 552 008; fax 552 009; Tarcali út 52; s/d 4000/6000Ft; P ✗ ) This *panzió* has simple and modern rooms, with TV and telephone. Tarcali út is about 25 minutes south of town along Bajcsy-Zsilinszky út (southwest of the train station).

**Millennium Hotel** ( ☎ 352 242; www.tokajmillennium .hu; Bajcsy-Zsilinszky út 34; s/d 8800/10,200Ft; P ✗ ) Sleek décor and up-to-date amenities, such as unlimited wireless internet connection in the guest rooms, live up to the new century name. Use of the wellbeing centre is included, but breakfast is 1100Ft extra. The hotel sits near the confluence of the Bodrog and Tisza Rivers.

**Róna** ( ☎ 352 116; Bethlen Gábor utca 19; mains 1300-1900Ft; ☽ 11am-10pm, to 9pm Nov-Feb) The speciality of the house is fish, caught in nearby rivers, but there are other Hungarian options on the menu here as well, although they are nothing fancy.

**Degenfeld** ( ☎ 553 050; Kossuth tér 1; mains 1800-2600Ft; ☽ 11.30am-10pm; ✗ ☒ ) Delight your tastebuds with lemon-tarragon venison or orange-ginger duck breast. The Degenfeld palace was built in 1870 and has lovely white tablecloths, fresh flowers and upholstered French imperial chairs in the dining room. A few rooms upstairs are for rent.

## Shopping

You can buy wine at any of the places mentioned for tasting or stop at the **Furmint Vinotéka** ( ☎ 353 340; Bethlen Gábor utca 12; ☽ 9am-5pm) wineshop for a large local selection.

## Getting There & Away

No direct buses connect Tokaj with Budapest or Eger. Two buses a day go to Nyíregyháza (463Ft, 40 minutes), where you can connect to either.

Four express trains a day travel to and from Budapest's Keleti station (2610Ft, two hours 45 minutes) and one local to Budapest's Nyugati (2762Ft, 4½ hours). Change at Füzesabony to get to Eger (1762Ft, two hours, five daily). Up to 18 trains a day connect Tokaj with Nyíregyháza (442Ft, 40 minutes), from where you can take a train to the Hungarian border town of Záhony and into Csop, in the Ukraine.

# HUNGARY DIRECTORY

## ACCOMMODATION

Budapest has the widest variety of lodging prices, but even in provincial towns you can find camping grounds, hostels and private rooms in the budget range; *panziók* (pensions), guesthouses and small hotels in the midrange; and multiamenity hotels at the top end. Reviews in this chapter are ordered according to price. Hungary's more than 400 camping grounds are listed in Tourinform's *Camping Hungary* map/brochure (www.camping.hu). Facilities are generally open May to October and difficult to reach without a car.

The **Hungarian Youth Hostel Association** (Map pp358-9; Mellow Mood Ltd; ☎ 1-413 2065; www.youthhostels.hu; VII Baross tér 15, 3rd fl, Budapest) keeps a list of year-round hostels throughout Hungary. In general, year-round hostels have a communal kitchen, laundry and internet service, sometimes a lounge, and a basic bread-and-jam breakfast may be included. Having a HI card is not required, but it may get you a 10% discount. From July to August, students vacate college and university dorms and administration opens them to travellers. Local Tourinform offices can help you locate such places.

Renting a private room in a Hungarian home is a good budget option and can be a great opportunity to get up close and personal with the culture: you generally share a bathroom with the family. Prices outside Budapest run from 2200Ft to 5500Ft per person per night.

Midrange accommodation may or may not have a private bathroom, satellite TV and in-room phone, but all top-end places do. A cold breakfast buffet is usually included in the price at pensions, and there are hot breakfasts included at hotels. A reasonable place might bill itself as a *kishotel* (small hotel) because it has satellite TV and a minibar. Air-conditioning is scarce nationwide, but you're more likely to find it at higher-priced establishments.

An engaging alternative is to stay in a rural village or farm house, but only if you have wheels – most places are truly remote. Contact Tourinform, the **National Association of Village Tourism** (Map p362; FAOS; ☎ 1-268 0592; VII Király utca 93) or the **Centre for Rural Tourism** (Map pp358-9; FTC; ☎ 1-321 4396; www.ftur.hu; VII Dohány utca 86) in Budapest.

# ACTIVITIES

Hungary has more than 100 thermal baths open to the public and many are attached to hotels with wellbeing packages. Two thermal baths in Budapest, one at Harkány (p394) and the large thermal lake at Hévíz (p390) are covered in this chapter. Request the Hungarian National Tourist Office (HNTO) brochure *Water Tours in Hungary* from Tourinform; it's a gold mine of information for planning spa itineraries.

There's also a helpful HNTO *Riding in Hungary* booklet on equestrian tourism, or you could contact the **Hungarian Equestrian Tourism Association** (Map p362; MLTSZ; ☎ 1-456 0444; www.equi.hu; IX Ráday utca 8, Budapest). **Pegazus Tours** (Map p362; ☎ 1-317 1644; www.pegazus.hu; V Ferenciek tere 5, Budapest) organises horse-riding tours, and occasionally bicycle tours as well.

Hiking enthusiasts may enjoy the trails around Tihany at Lake Balaton, the Bükk Hills north of Eger or the plains at Bugac Puszta south of Kecskemét. Hiking maps usually have yellow borders. Bird-watchers could explore these same paths or take a tour with **Birding Hungary** ( ☎ 70-214 0261; www.birdinghungary.com; PF 4, Budapest 1511).

All admission prices in this chapter are listed as they are quoted on signs in Hungary (adult/student). Usually, children and pensioners can get into places for the same discounted price.

# BOOKS

Not to be modest, an excellent overall guidebook is Lonely Planet's *Hungary*, while the *Budapest* guide takes an in-depth look at the capital. For an easy introduction to the nation's past, check out *An Illustrated History of Hungary* by István Lázár. Read László Kontler's *A History of Hungary* for a more in-depth, but easy-to-read, study.

# BUSINESS HOURS

With some rare exceptions, opening hours *(nyitvatartás)* are posted on the front door of establishments; *nyitva* means 'open' and *zárva* is 'closed'. Large, chain grocery stores are usually open from 7am to 6pm Monday through Friday, and to 1pm on Saturday. Smaller ones, especially in Budapest, may be open on Sunday or holidays as well. Most towns have a 'nonstop' convenience store, and many have hypermarkets, such as Tesco, that are open 24 hours. Main post offices are open 8am to 6pm weekdays, and to noon or 1pm Saturday.

Bank hours are from 8am to 4pm Monday to Thursday and 8am to 1pm on Friday. Hospitality opening hours vary between bigger and smaller towns, but generally restaurants open from 11am to 11pm, and bars and cafés open from 8am to midnight.

# COURSES

The granddaddy of all Hungarian language schools, **Debreceni Nyári Egyetem** (Debrecen Summer University; ☎ 52-489 117; www.nyariegyetem.hu; Egyetem tér 1, PO Box 35, Debrecen 4010), in eastern Hungary, is the most well known and the most well respected. It organises intensive two- and four-week courses during July and August and 80-hour, two-week advanced courses during winter. The **Debrecen Summer University Branch** (Map p362; ☎ 1-320 5751; XIII Jászai Mari tér 6) in Budapest puts on regular and intensive courses.

# CUSTOMS

You can bring and take out the usual personal effects, 200 cigarettes, 1L of wine or champagne and 1L of spirits. You are not supposed to export valuable antiques without a special permit; this should be available from the place of purchase. You must declare the import/export of any amount of cash exceeding 1,000,000Ft.

# DISABLED TRAVELLERS

Most of Hungary has a long way to go before it becomes accessible to the disabled, although audible traffic signals are becoming more common and there are Braille markings on the higher-denominated forint notes. For more information, contact the **Hungarian Disabled Association** (Map pp358-9; MEOSZ; ☎ 1-388 5529; meosz@matavnet.hu; III San Marco utca 76, Budapest).

# DISCOUNT CARDS

Those planning extensive travel in Hungary might consider the **Hungary Card** ( ☎ 1-266 3741; www.hungarycard.hu), which gives 50% discounts on seven return train fares; three 33%-off one-way train trips; 50% off some bus and boat travel; free entry to some museums and attractions outside Budapest; up to 25% off selected accommodation; and 20% off the price of the Budapest Card (p360). Available at Tourinform and Volánbusz offices, larger train stations, some newsagents and petrol stations throughout Hungary, the card costs 7935Ft and is valid for one year.

## EMBASSIES & CONSULATES

To find out more about Hungarian embassies around the world, or foreign representation in Hungary, contact the **Ministry of Foreign Affairs** (☎ 1-458 1000; www.kum.hu).

### Hungarian Embassies & Consulates

Hungarian embassies around the world include the following.

**Australia** ( ☎ 02-6282 2555; 17 Beale Cres, Deakin, ACT 2600)
**Canada** ( ☎ 613-230 9614; 299 Waverley St, Ottawa, Ontario K2P 0V9)
**France** ( ☎ 01 5636 0754; 7-9 Sq Vergennes, 75015 Paris)
**Germany** ( ☎ 030-203 100; Unter den Linden 76, 10117 Berlin)
**Ireland** ( ☎ 01-661 2902; 2 Fitzwilliam Pl, Dublin 2)
**Netherlands** ( ☎ 70-350 0404; Hogeweg 14, 2585 JD Den Haag)
**UK** ( ☎ 020-7235 5218; 35 Eaton Pl, London SW1X 8BY)
**USA** ( ☎ 202-362 6730; 3910 Shoemaker St NW, Washington, DC)

### Embassies & Consulates in Hungary

Embassies in Budapest (phone code ☎ 1) include the following.

**Australia** (Map pp358-9; ☎ 457 9777; XII Királyhágó tér 8-9; ☻ 9am-5pm Mon-Thu, to 2pm Fri)
**Austria** (Map p362; ☎ 479 7010; VI Benczúr utca 16; ☻ 8am-10am Mon-Fri)
**Canada** (Map pp358-9; ☎ 392 3360; XII Zugligeti út 51-53; ☻ 8am-4pm Mon-Fri)
**Croatia** (Map p362; ☎ 269 5854; VI Munkácsy Mihály utca 15; ☻ 9am-5pm Mon-Fri)
**France** (Map pp358-9; ☎ 374 1100; VI Lendvay utca 27; ☻ 9am-noon Mon-Fri)
**Germany** (Map p362; ☎ 488 3500; I Úri utca 64-66; ☻ 9am-noon Mon-Fri)
**Ireland** (Map p362; ☎ 302 9600; V Szabadság tér 7-9; ☻ 9.30am-1pm & 2-4pm Mon-Fri)
**Netherlands** (Map pp358-9; ☎ 336 6300; II Füge utca 5-7; ☻ 10am-noon Mon-Fri)
**Romania** (Map pp358-9; ☎ 348 0271; XIV Thököly út 72; ☻ 9.30am-noon, closed Wed)
**Serbia** (Map pp358-9; ☎ 322 9838; VI Dózsa György út 92/b; ☻ 10am-1pm Mon-Fri)
**Slovakia** (Map pp358-9; ☎ 460 9011; IV Stefánia út 22-24; ☻ 9.30am-noon Mon-Fri)
**Slovenia** (Map pp358-9; ☎ 438 5600; II Cseppkő utca 68; ☻ 9am-noon Mon-Fri)
**South Africa** (Map pp358-9; ☎ 392 0999; II Gárdonyi Géza út 17; ☻ 9am-12.30pm Mon-Fri)
**UK** (Map p362; ☎ 266 2888; V Harmincad utca 6; ☻ 10.30am-1.30pm & 2.30-5.30pm Mon-Fri)
**Ukraine** (Map pp358-9; ☎ 422 4120; XIV Stefánia út 77; ☻ 9am-noon Mon-Wed & Fri by appointment only)

**USA** (Map p362; ☎ 475 4400; V Szabadság tér 12; ☻ 8.15am-5pm Mon-Fri)

## FESTIVALS & EVENTS

The best annual events include the following.
**Budapest Spring Festival** (Mar)
**Balaton Festival** (May) Based in Keszthely.
**Hungarian Dance Festival** (late Jun) In Győr.
**Sopron Festival Weeks** (late Jun–mid-Jul)
**Győr Summer Cultural Festival** (late June-late Jul)
**Hortobágy International Equestrian Days** (Jul)
**Szeged Open-Air Festival** (Jul-Aug)
**Kőszeg Castle Theatre Festival** (mid-late Jul)
**Pepsi Sziget Music Festival** (late Jul-early Aug) On Óbudai hajógyári-sziget (Óbuda Shipbuilding Island) in Budapest.
**Hungaroring Formula One Grand Prix** (mid-Aug) At Mogyoród, 24km northeast of Budapest
**Budapest Autumn Festival** (mid-Oct-early Nov)

## GAY & LESBIAN TRAVELLERS

There is no openly antigay sentiment in Hungary, but neither is there a large openly gay population. The organisations and nightclubs that do exist are generally in Budapest. For up-to-date information on venues, events, groups etc, contact **GayGuide.Net** ( ☎ 06 30 932 3334; http://budapest.gayguide.net).

## HOLIDAYS

Hungary's 10 public holidays:
**New Year's Day** 1 January
**1848 Revolution Day** 15 March
**Easter Monday** March/April
**International Labour Day** 1 May
**Whit Monday** May/June
**St Stephen's Day** 20 August
**1956 Remembrance Day** 23 October
**All Saints' Day** 1 November
**Christmas Day** 25 December
**Boxing Day** 26 December

## LANGUAGE

Hungarians speak Magyar (Hungarian), and unlike the vast majority of tongues you'll hear in Europe, it is not an Indo-European language. It is traditionally categorised as Finno-Ugric, distantly related only to Finnish and Estonian. Many older Hungarians, particularly in the western part of the country, can understand German and many young people, particularly in Budapest, speak some English. Any travel-related business will have at least one staff member who can speak English.

Hungarians always put surnames before given names, in writing and in speech. But don't worry, no one expects foreigners to reverse their names upon introduction.

## MEDIA

Budapest has two English-language weeklies: the expat-oriented *Budapest Sun,* with a useful 'Style' arts and entertainment supplement, and the *Budapest Business Journal* (550Ft). Some Western English-language newspapers, including the *International Herald Tribune,* are available on the day of publication in Budapest and in other large western Hungary cities. Many more newspapers, mainly British, French and German, are sold a day late. International news magazines are also widely available.

## MONEY

The unit of currency is the Hungarian forint (Ft). Coins come in denominations of one, two, five, 10, 20, 50 and 100Ft, and notes are denominated 200, 500, 1000, 2000, 5000, 10,000 and 20,000Ft. ATMs are quite common throughout the country, including train stations, and they accept most credit and cash cards. Banks usually offer exchange services as well as ATMs. Branches can be found around the main square in an Old Town centre, or on the main thoroughfare leading to it. Bank hours are from 8am to 4pm Monday to Thursday and 8am to 1pm on Friday. Visa and MasterCard are the most widely accepted credit cards, but some smaller lodgings still only accept cash. Some businesses quote prices in euros; prices in this chapter conform to quotes of individual businesses.

## POST

A postcard costs 50Ft within Hungary, 110Ft within Europe, and 150Ft to the rest of the world. A *légiposta* (airmail) letter costs 190Ft within Europe, 380Ft to the rest of the world for up to 20g. Although you can buy stamps at some youth hostels and hotels, go to a post office to actually send your letter or card. If you put it in a post box on the street, it may languish for weeks. Otherwise, service is pretty speedy – a few days to Europe and about a week to the US.

Mail addressed to poste restante in any town or city will go to the main post office (*főposta*). When collecting poste-restante mail, look for the sign '*postán maradó küldemények*'. If you hold an Amex credit card or are carrying their travellers cheques, you can have your mail sent to **American Express** (Map p362; V Deák Ferenc utca 10, Budapest), where it will be held for one month.

## TELEPHONE & FAX

Hungary's country code is ☎ 36. To make an outgoing international call, dial ☎ 00 first. To dial city-to-city (and all mobile phones) within the country, first dial ☎ 06 (dialling in from out of the country, leave off the 06), wait for the second dial tone and then dial the city code and phone number. All localities in Hungary have a two-digit city code, except for Budapest, whose code is ☎ 1. Mobile phone numbers all start with the prefix ☎ 06 but are countrywide numbers (ie they have no city code). Budapest numbers have seven digits, most others six digits.

The best place to make international telephone calls is from a phone box with a phone card, which you can buy at newsstands in 2000Ft and 5000Ft denominations. Some cards, such as Neophone, get you an international call for as little as 19Ft per minute. Buy a Matáv *telefonkártya* at newsstands (800Ft) to make domestic calls at card-operated machines. Some pay phones still take coins. Telephone boxes with a black-and-white arrow and red target on the door and the word '*Visszahívható*' display a telephone number, so you can be phoned back.

## TOURIST INFORMATION

The HNTO has a chain of 120 **Tourinform** (☎ hotline 30 30 30 600; www.tourinform.hu, www.hungary.com) information offices across the country and is represented in 19 countries abroad. These are the best places to ask general questions and pick up brochures. The HNTO also operates a Tourinform hotline in Hungarian, English and German.

---

**EMERGENCY NUMBERS**

- General emergency ☎ 112 (English spoken)
- Police ☎ 107
- Fire ☎ 105
- Ambulance ☎ 104
- English-language crime hotline ☎ 1-438 8000
- Car assistance (24 hours) ☎ 188

HUNGARY

If your query is about private rooms, flights or international train travel, you may have to ask a commercial travel agency; most towns have at least a couple. The oldest, Ibusz, is arguably the best for private accommodation.

## VISAS

To enter Hungary, everyone needs a valid passport, or for citizens of the European Union, a national identification card. Citizens of virtually all European countries, the USA, Canada, Israel, Japan, New Zealand and Australia do not require visas to visit Hungary for stays of up to 90 days within a six-month period. UK citizens do not need a visa for a stay of up to six months. South Africans, however, do require a visa. Check with the **Ministry of Foreign Affairs** ( ☎ 1-458 1000; www.kum .hu) for an up-to-date list of which country nationals require visas.

Visas are issued at Hungarian consulates or missions, most international highway border crossings, Ferihegy airport and the International Ferry Pier in Budapest. However, visas are never issued on trains and rarely on buses.

## WOMEN TRAVELLERS

Some Hungarian men can be very sexist in their thinking, but they are also big on being polite, so women do not suffer any particular form of harassment.

For assistance and/or information ring the **Women's Line** (Nővonal; ☎ 06 80 505 101) or **Women for Women against Violence** (NANE; ☎ 1-267 4900), which operates from 6pm to 10pm daily.

## WORK

Working legally in Hungary always involved a Byzantine paper chase and it looks like it will get harder given EU membership requirements. The government has announced it will crack down on illegal workers. No-one thinks they're going to target English teachers, but the work situation for foreigners *is* in a state of flux.

# TRANSPORT IN HUNGARY

## GETTING THERE & AWAY
### Air

From Budapest's Ferihegy 2 airport you can reach destinations in Eastern and Western Europe, the UK, Russia and connect to places beyond. Malév is the Hungarian national airline. Low-cost airlines fly from Ferihegy 1 to off-market airports in Western Europe, such as London Stansted.

Vienna's Schwechart airport is only about three hours from Budapest by bus, less to western Hungary, and often has less expensive international airfares since it handles more traffic.

**Aeroflot** (code SU; ☎ 318 5955; www.aeroflot.com) Flights to Russia.

**Austrian Airlines** (code OS; ☎ 327 9080; www.aua.com) Less than an hour's flight to Vienna.

**ČSA** (code OK; ☎ 318 3175; www.czech-airlines.com) At least three flights daily to/from Prague.

**Lot Polish Airlines** (code LO; ☎ 266 4772; www.lot.com) Budapest direct to Warsaw and connecting to other Polish and Russian cities.

**Malév Hungarian Airlines** (code MA; ☎ 235 3888; www.malev.hu) Flights to Vienna, Kyiv and Odesa in Ukraine, Timişoara in Romania, Split and Dubrovnik in Croatia, Varna and Sofia in Bulgaria, Prague in the Czech Republic, Kraków and Warsaw in Poland, and Moscow in Russia.

**Sky Europe** (code NE; ☎ 777 7000) A low-cost airline that flies daily to Warsaw and three days a week to Split and Dubrovnik.

**Tarom Romanian Air Transport** (code RO; ☎ 235 0809; www.tarom.ro) Direct flights to and from Bucharest.

### Land

Hungary has excellent land transport connections with its neighbours. Most of the departures listed are from Budapest, though other cities and towns closer to the various borders can also be used as springboards.

#### BICYCLE & WALKING

Cyclists may have a problem crossing at Hungarian border stations since bicycles are banned on motorways and national highways with single-digit route numbers.

If you're heading north, there are three crossings to and from Slovakia where you should not have any problems. Bridges link Esztergom with Štúrovo and Komárom with Komárno. At Sátoraljaújhely, northeast of Miskolc, there's a highway border crossing over the Ronyva River that links the centre of town with Slovenské Nové Mesto.

#### BUS

Most international buses arrive at the Népliget bus station (p373) in Budapest. **Eurolines** ( ☎ 1-219 8080; www.eurolines.com), in conjunction with its Hungarian affiliate, **Volánbusz** ( ☎ 1-219 8080; www.volanbusz.hu), is the international bus company of Hungary. There's a 10% youth discount for those under 26. Useful international buses include those from Budapest to Vienna city centre (5490Ft, 3½ hours, four daily), Bratislava, Slovakia (Pozsony; 4400Ft, four hours, one daily), Subotica in Serbia (Szabatka; 3300Ft, four hours, daily), Rijeka in Croatia (7900Ft, 10 hours, one weekly), Prague in the Czech Republic (9500Ft, eight hours, five weekly), and Sofia in Bulgaria (12,500Ft, 15 hours, four weekly).

Four buses a day (7.30am, 11.15am, 5.15pm and 7.15pm) run from Vienna International Airport in Austria to the Népliget bus station in Budapest (€28). **Mitch's Tours** ( ☎ 06 70 588 306; www.mitchstours.com; adult/student €32/29) runs a shuttle-bus service between Deák tér or several hostels in the Budapest area and the airport or hostels in Vienna (departs Vienna 8.30am, departs Budapest 1.30pm).

### CAR & MOTORCYCLE
Border controls between Hungary and her EU neighbours (as of 1 May, 2004), Slovakia and Austria, were not scheduled to be removed at the time of research, but there will be no more customs checks at these points. Third-party insurance is compulsory for driving in Hungary. If your car is registered in the EU, it's assumed you have it. Other motorists must show a Green Card or buy insurance at the border.

### HITCHING
In Hungary, hitchhiking is legal except on motorways. Hitchhiking is never an entirely safe way to travel and we don't recommend it, but if you're willing, **Kenguru** (Map p362; ☎ 1-266 5837; www.kenguru.hu; VIII Kőfaragó utca 15, Budapest; ☀ 8am-6pm Mon-Fri, 10am-4pm Sat) is an agency that matches riders with drivers. Hitch a ride to Amsterdam (11,000Ft), Munich (5500Ft) or Paris (11,700Ft), among other destinations.

### TRAIN
The Hungarian State Railways, **MÁV** ( ☎ international information 1-461 5500; www.elvira.hu Hungarian only, www.mav.hu) links up with international rail networks in all directions and its schedule is available online. MÁV sells Inter-Rail passes to European nationals (or residents of at least six months). Hungary is in Zone D along with the Czech Republic, Slovakia, Poland and Croatia. The price for any one zone is €226/158/113 for adult/youth (12-26)/child (four-12). There are big discounts on return fares only between Hungary and former communist countries: up to 65% to Slovakia, Slovenia and Croatia; 70%

to Romania; 40% to Serbia; 40% to the Czech Republic and Poland; and 50% to Ukraine, Bulgaria, Belarus and Russia. For tickets to Western Europe you'll pay the same as everywhere else unless you're aged under 26 and qualify for the 30% to 50% BIJ discount. For tickets or more information about passes and discounts, ask at the MÁV Ticket Office (p373) in Budapest.

Eurail passes are valid, but not sold, in Hungary. EuroCity (EC) and Intercity (IC) trains require a seat reservation and payment of a supplement. Most larger train stations in Hungary have left-luggage rooms open at least 9am to 5pm. There are three main train stations in Budapest, so always note the station when checking a schedule online; for more information see p373.

Some direct connections from Budapest to neighbouring countries include Vienna (6600Ft, 3½ hours, five daily); Bratislava, Slovakia (Pozsony; 5600Ft, 2½ hours, eight daily); Arad (7400Ft, 4½ hours, six daily) and Bucharest, Romania (18,600Ft, 13 to 15 hours, five daily); Csop (7600Ft, 4½ hours, two daily) and Kyiv, Ukraine (18,400Ft, 24 hours, one daily), continuing to Moscow (25,400Ft, 37 hours, one daily); Zagreb, Croatia (9000Ft, 5½ to 7½ hours, three daily); Belgrade, Serbia (9400Ft, seven hours, two daily); Ljubljana, Slovenia (13,700Ft, 8½ hours, three daily).

Other direct train destinations in Eastern Europe include Prague, Czech Republic (14,850Ft, nine hours, two daily); Kraków, Poland (13,500Ft, 10½ hours, one daily); Sofia, Bulgaria (18,200Ft, 18 to 26 hours, two daily). Fares listed are for second-class tickets without seat reservation; first-class tickets are usually 50% more. For information on international destinations outside Eastern Europe, see the main Transport chapter of this book (p924).

## River
There's an international Mahart PassNave hydrofoil service on the Danube daily from April to early November between Budapest and Vienna (5½ hours), stopping in Bratislava (four hours). Adult one-way/return fares for Vienna are €75/99, for Bratislava €69/93. Students with ISIC cards pay €59/84. Boats leave from the Nemzetközi hajóállomás (International Ferry Pier), next to the **Mahart PassNave Ticket Office** (Map p362; ☎ 484 4013; www .mahartpassnave.hu; Belgrád rakpart). The ticket office in Vienna is **Mahart PassNave Wien** ( ☎ 01-72 92 161; Handelskai 265).

# GETTING AROUND

## Air

Hungary does not have any scheduled internal flights.

## Bicycle

Hungary now counts 2500km of dedicated bicycle lanes around the country, with more on the way. For information and advice, contact the helpful **Hungarian Bicycle Touring Association** (MKTSZ; Map p362; ☎ 1-311 2467; mktsz@enternet.hu; VI Bajcsy-Zsilinszky út 31) in Budapest.

## Boat

In summer there are regular passenger ferries on Lake Balaton and on the Danube from Budapest to Szentendre, Visegrád and Esztergom. Details of the schedules are given in the relevant destination sections.

## Bus

Domestic buses, run by **Volánbusz** ( ☎ 1 219 8080; www.volanbusz.hu) cover an extensive nationwide network. The buses are generally relatively new, and everybody and their grandmother takes them, so they are safe. Bus fares average 1270Ft per 100km.

Timetables are posted at stations and stops. Some footnotes you could come across include *naponta* (daily), *hétköznap* (weekdays), *munkanapokon* (on work days), *munkaszüneti napok kivételével naponta* (daily except holidays), and *szabad és munkaszüneti napokon* (on Saturday and holidays). A few large bus stations have luggage rooms, or a bathroom attendant who you pay to watch your bags, but these generally close by 6pm.

## Car & Motorcycle

Limited access Motorways (M1, M3, M7) require toll passes (10-day, 2000Ft) that can be purchased at petrol stations and at some motorway entrances. Check with your rental company; the car may already have an annual pass.

Many cities and towns require that you 'pay and display' when parking. The cost averages about 100Ft an hour in the countryside, and up to 180Ft on central Budapest streets.

### AUTOMOBILE ASSOCIATIONS

The so-called 'Yellow Angels' of the Hungarian Automobile Club do basic breakdown repairs for free if you belong to an affiliated organisation such as AAA in the USA or AA

in the UK. You can telephone 24 hours a day on ☎ 188 nationwide.

### DRIVING LICENCE

Your normal, home country driving licence is sufficient for driving in Hungary.

### FUEL & SPARE PARTS

Unleaded (*ólommentes*) petrol (*benzin*) in 95 and 98 octane is available all over the country and costs from 285 per litre, respectively. Most stations also have diesel fuel (*gázolaj*) costing around 240Ft per litre. You can pay by credit card. The Hungarian Automobile Club can assist with repairs.

### HIRE

In general, you must be at least 21 years old and have had your licence for at least a year to rent a car. Drivers under 25 often have to pay a surcharge.

### INSURANCE

Third-party insurance is compulsory. If your car is registered in the EU, it's assumed you have it. Other motorists must show a Green Card or buy insurance at the border. Rental cars come with Green Cards.

### ROAD RULES

The most important rule to remember is that there's a 100% ban on alcohol when you are driving, and this rule is *very* strictly enforced. (Police even stalk the parking lots of expensive, outlying restaurants.) Do not think you will get away with one glass of wine at lunch; if caught with 0.001% alcohol in your blood, you will be fined up to 30,000Ft. If your blood alcohol level is high, you will be arrested and your licence taken away.

Using a mobile phone while driving is prohibited in Hungary. *All* vehicles must have their headlights switched on throughout the day outside built-up areas. Motorcyclists must have their headlights on at all times.

## Local Transport

Public transport is efficient and extensive, with city bus and, in many towns, trolleybus services. Budapest and Szeged also have trams, and there's an extensive metro (underground or subway) and a suburban commuter railway in Budapest. Purchase tickets at newsstands before travelling and validate them once aboard. Inspectors do check tickets, especially on the metros in Budapest.

## Train

**MÁV** ( ☎ domestic information 1-461 5400; www.elvira.hu Hungarian only, www.mav.hu) operates reliable train services on its 8000km of tracks. Schedules are available online and computer information kiosks are popping up at rail stations around the country. Second-class domestic train fares are 824Ft per 100km, 1st-class fares are usually 50% more. IC trains are express trains, the most comfortable and the newest. *Gyorsvonat* (fast trains) take longer and use older cars; s*zemélyvonat* (passenger trains) stop at every village along the way. Seat reservations *(helyjegy)* cost extra and are required on IC and some fast trains; these are indicated on the timetable by an 'R' in a box or a circle. (A plain 'R' means seat reservations are available.)

In all stations a yellow board indicates departures *(indul)* and a white board arrivals *(érkezik)*. Express and fast trains are indicated in red, local trains in black. In some stations, large black-and-white schedules are plastered all over the walls. To locate the timetable you need, first find the posted railway map of the country, which indexes the route numbers at the top of the schedules.

Most train stations have left-luggage offices that are open at least from 9am to 5pm.

You might consider purchasing a Hungarian Rail Pass before entering the country. The cost is US$76 for five days of 1st-class travel within 15 days and US$95 for 10 days within a month. You would, however, need to use it a lot to get your money's worth.

# Latvia

These are heady days for little Latvia. Not only is it finally part of the EU, but its economy is humming along at the fastest clip in Europe. Traffic seems to double annually at its flashy new airport. Its capital, Rīga, is maturing like a fine wine, sprouting a lively cultural scene to match the exuberance of its world-class architecture.

Count Latvia as one country that's ready for prime time. Ancient Rīga, stunningly diverse architecturally and fun, fun, fun, is a jewel of a city, despite the long winters. Outside of Rīga lies an outdoors-lover's paradise, with hectares of forested national parkland beckoning bikers, hikers and bird-watchers. There are quaint castle towns, happening beach towns and, just as importantly, good domestic beer to enjoy in either.

You won't be the first one you know to come here any more, but you'll still be plenty charmed. Sure, Latvia retains some of its gruff old Sovietness, but that will soon be just another feather in its tourist-magnet cap. After all, you're not supposed to be able to witness old Soviet buildings in places that are so damn, well, nice.

## FAST FACTS

- **Area** 64, 600 sq km
- **Capital** Rīga
- **Currency** Lats (Ls); €1=0.70Ls; US$1=0.55Ls; UK£1=1.03Ls; A$1=0.41Ls; ¥100=0.47Ls; NZ$1=0.35Ls
- **Famous for** Rīga's black balsam, ice hockey, Eurovision eureka in 2002
- **Official Language** Latvian
- **Phrases** *labdien/sveiki* (hello); *cik?* (how much?); *paldies* (thank you); *lūdzu* (please/ you're welcome)
- **Population** 2.3 million
- **Telephone Codes** country code ☎ 371; international access code ☎ 00
- **Visas** none required for stays of up to 90 days for Australian, Canadian, EU, New Zealand or US citizens

LATVIA

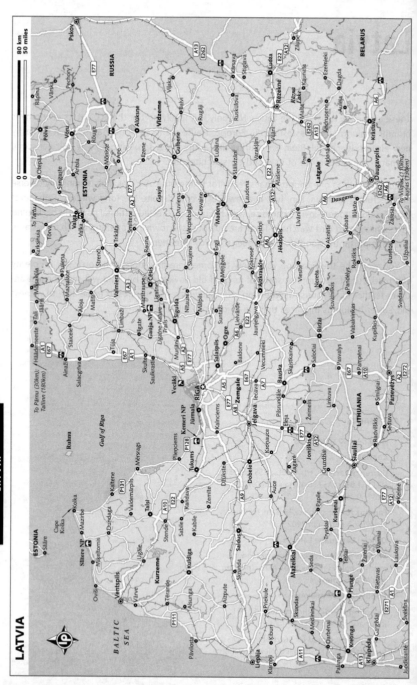

# HIGHLIGHTS

- Delight in vivacious **Rīga** (p417), with cobbled Old Town streets, delectable Art Nouveau and seething nightlife.
- Take a bobsled ride at 100km/h, bungee jump or just stroll among woods and castles in magnificent **Sigulda** (p428).
- Go to the beach in **Jūrmala**, but also take in the distinctive wooden architecture (p427).
- Get down in Latvia's hippest city, **Liepāja** (p433), a haven for cool clubs, raucous festivals and funky design.
- Witness the raw power of nature and explore Liv culture at desolate, solitary **Cape Kolka** (p431).

## HOW MUCH?

- **Public transport ticket** 0.2Ls
- **Loaf of bread** 0.3Ls
- **Hostel bed in Rīga** 8Ls
- **Bottle of vodka** 4Ls
- **Take-away hamburger** 1.04Ls

## LONELY PLANET INDEX

- **Litre of petrol** 0.62Ls
- **Litre of water** 0.2Ls
- **Bottled beer** 0.3/1Ls in store/bar
- **Souvenir T-shirt** 7Ls
- **Street snack (hotdog)** 0.5Ls

# ITINERARIES

- **Three days** Spend one day exploring Rīga's Old Town, then a morning in the Art Nouveau district before taking a half-day trip to Rundāle Palace and/or Salaspils. On the third day visit Sigulda or Jūrmala.
- **One week** Spend three days in Rīga, with a day trip thrown in. Spend two days castle-crawling and/or engaging in outdoor activities in Sigulda and Cēsis. Lastly, drive to Liepāja via Cape Kolka and Ventspils before heading back to Rīga for one last big night out on the town.

# CLIMATE & WHEN TO GO

Latvia's climate is wet, with relatively harsh, long winters and warm, short summers. The winter is a great time to visit Rīga, as the crowds thin, but bring your thermals. Beer gardens, sunbathing, and super-long days are compelling reasons to visit in the summer. Autumn and spring are hit or miss. The average summer temperature is 15.8°C and in winter a brisk minus 4.5°C.

# HISTORY

Latvia's history is a troubled whirlwind of fierce struggle and long periods of occupation. Latvians descended from tribes that migrated north from around Belarus and settled on the territory of modern Latvia around 2000 BC. These tribes settled in coastal areas to fish and take advantage of rich deposits of amber, which was more precious than gold in many places until the Middle Ages.

Eventually, four main Baltic tribes evolved: the Selonians, the Letts (or Latgals), the Semigallians and the Cours. From the latter three derived the names of three of Latvia's four principal regions: Latgale, Zemgale and Kurzeme. The fourth region, Vidzeme (Livland), derived its name from the Livs, a Finno-Ugric peoples unrelated to the Balts (p431).

During succeeding centuries of foreign rule these tribes merged into one Latvian identity. They were pagan until the first Christian missionaries arrived and began converting them in the late 12th century.

In 1201, at the bequest of the pope, German crusaders, led by Bishop von Buxhoevden of Bremen, conquered Latvia and founded Rīga, which became the major city in the German Baltic. He also founded the Knights of the Sword, who made Rīga their base for subjugating Livonia.

Latvia was conquered by Poland in 1561 and Catholicism was firmly entrenched. Sweden then colonised Latvia (seen by many as a golden age for Latvia) in 1629 until the Great Northern War (1700–21), after which the country was under Russian rule.

Out of WWI rose an independent Latvian state, declared on 18 November 1918. The Soviets were the first to recognise Latvia's independence, but the honeymoon didn't last long. Soviet occupation began in 1939 with the Molotov-Ribbentrop Pact. Nationalisation, killings and mass deportations to Siberia followed. Latvia was occupied partly or wholly by Nazi Germany from 1941 to 1945, when an estimated 175,000 Latvians, mostly Jews, were killed or deported.

LATVIA

---

**BLUE MOOER**

It sounds like your classic old wives' tale: blue cows delivered from the sea by mermaids. Yet at least part of this Liv legend is true – Latvia does indeed have blue cows. About 100 of them, to be exact, making it the world's rarest breed of cow.

These curious ruminants originated in Latvia's Kurzeme region. The first ones appeared in the early 1900s. No-one is sure why or how they appeared, which is why the bit about mermaids can't be completely ruled out, but their star quickly waxed as they proved remarkably resistant to cold, rain and wind – three things that Latvia has in great supply.

The blue cow population dwindled to less than 50 in Soviet times, but began to rebound in the 1990s as geneticists realised the value in cross-breeding with these hearty beasts. Your best bet for seeing one is to ask at the Information Centre of Ķemeri National Park (p428), where several of them roam.

---

The first major public protest of the *glasnost* (openness) era was on 14 June 1987 when 5000 people rallied at Rīga's Freedom Monument to commemorate the 1941 Siberia deportations. On 23 August 1989 about two million Latvians, Lithuanians and Estonians formed a 650km human chain from Vilnius, through Rīga, to Tallinn, to mark the 50th anniversary of the Molotov-Ribbentrop Pact.

The Latvian Popular Front was formed to fight for independence. After its supporters won a big majority in the March 1990 elections, Russia barged back in on 20 January 1991. Soviet troops stormed the Interior Ministry building in Rīga, killing four people.

The August 1991 coup attempt in Moscow turned the tables and Latvia declared full independence on 21 August. On 6 September, the USSR recognised Latvia's independence. The country held its first democratic elections in June 1993.

On 1 May 2004 the EU opened its doors to 10 new members, including Latvia, and the economy took off almost immediately. Long the Baltic laggard, Latvia registered the highest economic growth in the EU in 2004–05, even as thousands of Latvians left for jobs in Ireland and elsewhere. In long-time President Vaira Vike-Freiberga – known as the 'Baltic Iron Lady' – Latvia has an internationally respected leader who at press time was being mentioned as a strong contender to succeed Kofi Annan as UN secretary-general.

## PEOPLE

Latvia's 2.3 million inhabitants are made up of Latvians (59%) and Russians (29%), with Belarusians (4%), Poles (2.6%) and Ukrainians (2.5%) leading the rest of the pack.

Latvians are known for their steely demeanour and they often have to be coaxed into friendship – hardly surprising considering their history of oppression and the fact that Latvians are still a minority group in Rīga and most other urban areas. But they also know how to unwind, as a Friday night out in Rīga will attest.

## RELIGION

The Roman Catholic Church has the largest following with roughly 500,000 adherents, followed by Lutheran (300,000) and Russian Orthodox (100,000).

## ARTS

The traditional importance of song as Latvia's greatest art form is shown in the 1.4 million *dainas* (folk songs), identified and collected by Krišjānis Barons (1835–1923). Latvia has held a national song festival in Rīga every five years for the last 125 years (p434). In 2003 the festival was inscribed on Unesco's list of 'Oral and Intangible Heritage of Humanity' masterpieces.

Prāta Vētra (Brainstorm) is the country's biggest rock band. The group finished third place in the Eurovision Song Contest in 2000, two years before another Latvian, Marija Naumova, won the contest and became a national hero.

You can both learn about folk music and buy Brainstorm and other Latvian pop and folk albums at Upe (p426) in Rīga.

The most celebrated figure in Latvian literature is Jānis Rainis (1865–1929), yet his criticism of political oppression meant he was exiled to Siberia and Switzerland. There's a monument to him in the Esplanāde park near the State Museum of Art in Rīga.

## ENVIRONMENT

Latvia is 64,589 sq km in area – slightly smaller than Ireland. Forest covers almost half of it, providing a home to creatures such as wild boar, wolves and deer – though you're not likely to bump into any of these creatures in the wild without some guidance. Latvia protects more than a million hectares as national parkland.

### Environmental Issues

Soviet factories and chemical plants left quite a few stains on Latvia's environment, but the government and various national organisations have made cleaning up the environment a top priority and Latvia's pollution problems are now being addressed.

## FOOD & DRINK

Half-Russian, half-Germanic, Latvian cuisine is hearty food designed to keep the cold out. Pork is especially popular – try the pork knuckle in any Lido restaurant (p424) – as are potato-based dishes, *zupa* (soups), *siļe* (herring) and *lasis* (salmon). *Pīrāgi* (small pies or pasties) are another favourite and come stuffed with just about anything. Vegetarian options are few outside of Rīga.

Eating is not a drawn-out affair; it's traditionally done to refuel before resuming work, but Rīga has many top-class restaurants for those who prefer sumptuous, relaxed dining. If you're lucky enough to be invited for a meal with a local, make sure you bring flowers (an odd number only, for superstitious reasons) and don't even think about being vegetarian. Grin and eat until your combats won't fit anymore then waddle home content.

One thing that will warm your cockles is the infamous Rīga Black Balsam, a treacly alcoholic beverage with potent medicinal qualities – apparently. It tastes fairly vile straight up, but it's tasty mixed with coffee or blackcurrant juice in a heavenly concoction called Hot Balzams. Latvia's also a huge beer-drinking country. Less-popular brands Užavas and Tērvetes are the best of the lot.

# RĪGA

**pop 790,000**

The Baltics' thumping heart lies in Rīga, a glorious marriage of gracious old-world charmer and relentless, unabashedly liberated temptress. The charmer is Old Rīga (known as Old Town), a maze of narrow medieval streets lorded over by brooding Gothic spires and stone façades reflecting a dizzying array of centuries-old architectural styles. The temptress is New Town, bursting at the seams with bold Art Nouveau and seething nightlife.

Rīga was founded in 1201 when the Germans established it as their primary bastion of power on the Baltic Coast. Since then it has grown into one of the few things in the Baltics you might call 'big' (aside from Soviet-era sanatoriums). But unlike most former Soviet cities, Rīga can hold your attention even outside of its Unesco-honoured centre. In the sprawling suburbs you'll find old wooden houses, brick factories, hidden churches and parkland galore.

Thanks in part to budget airlines, Rīga is no longer a secret. The maddening summer crowds can make getting a room, or even getting a seat in a beer garden, difficult. Weekend stag parties will continue to make their presence felt until somebody figures out a way to herd them out of Old Town. You can avoid the crowds, yet still absorb every morsel of what Rīga has to offer, by visiting in the low season. Or just take the crowds in your stride and make friends with fellow travellers similarly inebriated by Rīga's bounty.

## ORIENTATION

Rīga straddles the Daugava River, with Old Town resting on its eastern flank. Old Town's skyline is dominated by three steeples: St Peter's, Dome Cathedral and St Jacob's. To the north and west of Old Town

---

**RĪGA IN TWO DAYS**

Head out to the **Latvian Ethnographic Open Air Museum** (p422) for a glimpse of what Latvia once was. You'll better appreciate what it has become when you return to Rīga for lunch on Hotel Gūtenberg's **rooftop terrace** (p423). Spend the rest of the day just taking in the many architectural flavours of Old Town.

The next day you're back in Old Town for a morning trip up the steeple of **St Peter's** (p420) and a trip to the **Museum of the Occupation of Latvia** (p421). Spend the afternoon walking around the **Art Nouveau district** (p422) in New Town before ending the day with a well-deserved cocktail at **Skyline Bar** (p425).

LATVIA

# CENTRAL RĪGA

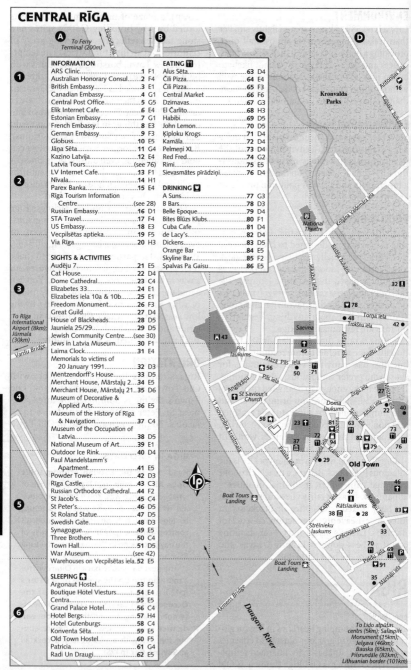

**INFORMATION**
ARS Clinic....................................1 F1
Australian Honorary Consul......2 F4
British Embassy...........................3 E1
Canadian Embassy......................4 G1
Central Post Office......................5 G5
Elik Internet Cafe........................6 E4
Estonian Embassy........................7 G1
French Embassy...........................8 E3
German Embassy..........................9 F3
Globuss.....................................10 E5
Jāṇa Sēta...................................11 G4
Kazino Latvija.............................12 E4
Latvia Tours...........................(see 76)
LV Internet Cafe........................13 F1
Nīvala.......................................14 H1
Parex Banka..............................15 E4
Rīga Tourism Information
    Centre..............................(see 28)
Russian Embassy........................16 D1
STA Travel.................................17 F4
US Embassy...............................18 E3
Vecpilsētas aptieka....................19 F5
Via Rīga....................................20 H3

**SIGHTS & ACTIVITIES**
Audēju 7...................................21 E5
Cat House.................................22 D4
Dome Cathedral........................23 C4
Elizabetes 33............................24 E1
Elizabetes iela 10a & 10b..........25 E1
Freedom Monument...................26 F3
Great Guild...............................27 D4
House of Blackheads.................28 D5
Jauniela 25/29..........................29 D5
Jewish Community Centre.....(see 30)
Jews in Latvia Museum..............30 F1
Laima Clock..............................31 E4
Memorials to victims of
    20 January 1991...................32 D3
Mentzendorff's House................33 D5
Merchant House, Mārstaļu 2......34 E5
Merchant House, Mārstaļu 21.....35 D6
Museum of Decorative &
    Applied Arts.........................36 E5
Museum of the History of Rīga
    & Navigation........................37 C4
Museum of the Occupation of
    Latvia..................................38 D5
National Museum of Art............39 E1
Outdoor Ice Rink......................40 D4
Paul Mandelstamm's
    Apartment...........................41 E5
Powder Tower...........................42 D3
Rīga Castle...............................43 C3
Russian Orthodox Cathedral......44 F2
St Jacob's.................................45 C4
St Peter's.................................46 D5
St Roland Statue.......................47 D5
Swedish Gate............................48 D3
Synagogue................................49 E5
Three Brothers..........................50 C4
Town Hall.................................51 D5
War Museum........................(see 42)
Warehouses on Vecpilsētas iela..52 E5

**SLEEPING**
Argonaut Hostel........................53 E5
Boutique Hotel Viesturs.............54 E4
Centra......................................55 E5
Grand Palace Hotel...................56 C4
Hotel Bergs..............................57 H4
Hotel Gutenbergs......................58 C4
Konventa Sēta..........................59 E5
Old Town Hostel.......................60 F5
Patricia....................................61 G4
Radi Un Draugi.........................62 E5

**EATING** 🍴
Alus Sēta..................................63 D4
Čili Pizza..................................64 E4
Čili Pizza..................................65 F3
Central Market..........................66 F6
Dzirnavas.................................67 G3
El Čarlito..................................68 H3
Habibi......................................69 D5
John Lemon..............................70 D5
Ķiploku Krogs...........................71 D4
Kamāla.....................................72 D4
Pelmeņi XL...............................73 D4
Red Fred..................................74 G2
Rimi.........................................75 E5
Sievasmātes pīrādziņi................76 D4

**DRINKING** 🍷
A Suns......................................77 G3
B Bars......................................78 D3
Belle Epoque............................79 D4
Bites Blūzs Klubs.......................80 F1
Cuba Cafe.................................81 D4
de Lacy's..................................82 D4
Dickens....................................83 D5
Orange Bar...............................84 E5
Skyline Bar ..............................85 F2
Spalvas Pa Gaisu......................86 E5

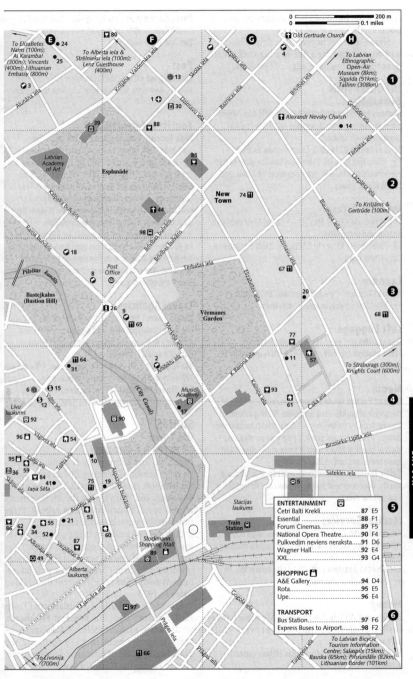

runs a wide band of 19th-century parks and boulevards.

New Town lies beyond that strip. The train and bus stations are a five-minute walk apart, near the southeastern edge of Old Rīga.

# INFORMATION
## Bookshops

**Globuss** ( ☎ 2722 6957; Vaļņu iela 26; ☼ 8am-10pm) International mag titles downstairs and a few English-language novels upstairs.

**Jāņa sēta** ( ☎ 2724 0892; Elizabetes iela 83/85; ☼ 10am-7pm Mon-Fri, 11am-5pm Sat) The place to find every map under the sun, reference books on Latvia, and Lonely Planet guides.

## Internet Access

**Elik** (Vaļņu iela 41; per 3hrs 1Ls; ☼ 24hr) Great Old Town location and cheap rates.

**LV** (Dzirnavu iela 53; per hr 0.50Ls; ☼ 24hr) Best internet café in New Town.

## Laundry

**Nīvala** (Akas iela 4; wash/dry per load 2.40/0.80Ls; ☼ 24hr) Self-service, or leave it with them.

## Left Luggage

**Bus station** (per piece 1Ls; ☼ 5.30am-11pm)
**Train station** (per piece 1Ls; ☼ 4.30am-midnight) In the basement.

## Media

**In Your Pocket** (www.inyourpocket.com/latvia/en) Of the gaggle of pocket-sized city guides floating around, *In Your Pocket* is by far the most credible. It features sardonic listings, a good city and public transportation map, and loads of practical information. It's free at the airport and many hotels and costs 1.20Ls elsewhere.

**Baltic Times** (www.baltictimes.com) English-language weekly. Good source of pan-Baltic news and listings for Rīga cultural events.

## Medical Services

**ARS Clinic** ( ☎ 2720 1001/3, emergency home service ☎ 2720 1003; Skolas iela 5; ☼ 24hr) English-speaking service.

**Vecpilsētas aptieka** ( ☎ 2721 3340; Audēju iela 20; ☼ 24hr) Excellent pharmacy.

## Money

Banks and ATMs dot the city. Most big banks cash travellers cheques and provide cash advances.

**Kazino Latvija** (Kaļķu iela 24) Has 24-hour currency exchange.

**Parex Banka** (Kaļķu iela 28; ☼ 9am-8pm Mon-Sat) Great location and hours; has currency exchange between 8am and 10pm daily.

## Post

**Central post office** (Stacijas laukums 1; ☼ 8am-8pm Mon-Fri, 8am-6pm Sat, 8am-4pm Sun) Next to the train station.

## Tourist Information

**Rīga Tourism Information Centre** main office ( ☎ 2703 7900; www.rigatourism.com; Rātslaukums 6; ☼ 10am-7pm); bus station ( ☎ 2722 0555; ☼ 9am-7pm); train station ( ☎ 2723 3815; ☼ 10am-6.30pm) Gives out free maps and has loads of information. They can arrange accommodation and book walking, bus or boat tours from a variety of tour operators. Website has great Old Town walking tour suggestions. They sell the Rīga Card, a discount card costing 8Ls for 24 hours, 12Ls for 48 hours or 16Ls for 72 hours (half-price for under 16s). You get a free walking tour, free rides on trolleybuses and trams, free entry to some museums, a copy of *In Your Pocket* and other discounts.

## Travel Agencies

**Latvia Tours** ( ☎ 2708 5001; www.latviatours.lv; Kaļķu iela 8; ☼ 9am-7pm Mon-Fri) Large agency offers visa assistance to Russia and Belarus and replaces American Express travellers cheques.

**Via Rīga** ( ☎ 2781 2624; www.viariga.com; K Barona iela 7/9) Ferry and plane tickets and a range of tours.

**STA Travel** ( ☎ 2700 7777; www.statravel.lv; Raiņa bulvaris 23; ☼ 9am-5pm Mon-Fri) Handles ISIC cards.

# SIGHTS
## Old Town
### ST PETER'S & AROUND

Rīga's skyline centrepiece is gothic **St Peter's** (Sv Pētera baznīca; lift admission 2/0.70Ls adult/student; ☼ 10am-5pm, closed Mon), thought to be about 800 years old. Don't miss the view from its famed spire, which has been rebuilt three times in the same baroque form. Legend has it that in 1667 builders threw glass from the top – the number of pieces it broke into was the number of years it would stand. It landed on straw and didn't break, and a year later it burned down. The spire's current incarnation dates to 1973.

St. Peter's overlooks the **Rātslaukums** (Town Hall Square) and the **House of Blackheads**, (Rātslaukums 6; admission 1.50Ls; ☼ 10am-5pm, closed Mon), originally built in 1344 to house the Blackheads' guild of unmarried foreign merchants. Facing the House of Blackheads across the square is the **Town Hall**. Both buildings were destroyed in WWII and rebuilt from scratch in recent years. A statue of Rīga's patron saint, **St Roland** (Rātslaukums), stands between the two buildings. It's a replica of the original, erected in 1897, which now sits in St Peter's.

The entire area south of St Peter's square is a fine place to wander. There are 16th- and 17th-century **warehouses** (Vecpilsētas iela), the only Old Town **synagogue** (Pietavas iela 6-8) to survive the war, and even some Art Nouveau – check out **Paul Mandelstamm's apartment** (Kalēju iela 23) and, a little north of Town Hall Square, **Jauniela 25/29**. You can see how wealthy Rīgans once lived at 17th-century **Mentzendorff's House** ( ☎ 2721 2951; Grēcinieku iela 18; adult/child 1.20/0.40Ls; ☻ 10am-5pm Wed-Sun). More old baroque **merchant houses** are at Mārstaļu iela 21 and 2.

### DOME CATHEDRAL
The Baltic's largest **cathedral** (Doma baznīca; Doma laukums; admission 0.50Ls; ☻ 11am-6pm Tue-Fri, 10am-2pm Sat) also boasts a marvellous 6768-pipe organ, which was the world's largest when it was completed in 1884. The cathedral's foundations were laid in 1211 and the stone tombs it contains were blamed for a cholera epidemic that broke out after a flood in 1709 and killed one-third of the city's residents. Mass is held at 8am Monday to Saturday, and at noon Sunday in its cavernous belly, which lost much of its décor in the Soviet era.

### NORTH OF DOME CATHEDRAL
Heading north from busy Doma laukums (Dome Square), you'll spot **St Jacob's Cathedral** (Sv Jēkaba katedrāle; Mazā Pils iela), with an interior dating back to 1225. Nearby are the **Three Brothers** (Mazā Pils iela 17, 19 & 21), Rīga's oldest stone houses. In Old Town's northeast corner, medieval **Rīga Castle** (Pils laukums 3) now houses the president and a couple of museums.

Meandering back toward the centre of Old Town, look for **Trokšņu iela**, Old Rīga's narrowest street. It leads to the **Swedish Gate** (cnr Trokšņu & Aldaru ielas), which was built into the city walls in 1698 to celebrate Swedish occupation. East of that is the round 14th-century **Powder Tower**, the only survivor of the 18 towers in the old city wall and home to the War Museum (right).

### LĪVU LAUKUMS
This square, near the busiest entrance to Old Town along Kaļķu iela, features beer gardens

by summer and an **outdoor ice rink** (admission free; skate rental per hr 0.50Ls; ☻ 10am-1am Nov-Mar, depends on temperature) by winter. The square is overlooked by the **Great Guild** (see p426), which faces the yellow-painted **Cat House** (Meistaru iela 19) that adorns many a postcard.

Venturing north towards Brīvības bulvāris, you'll encounter **Laima Clock**, favoured meeting spot for lovers and just about everybody else. From here, the city's old defensive moat – now a canal – snakes through parks between wide 19th-century boulevards.

Just over the canal, the **Freedom Monument** (Brīvības bulv). During the Soviet years the Freedom Monument was off-limits, and placing flowers at its base was a crime for which people were deported to Siberia.

Beneath **Bastejkalns** (Bastion Hill), west of the monument, five red stone slabs lie as **memorials** to the victims of 20 January 1991, who were killed here when Soviet troops stormed the nearby Interior Ministry. No-one who has seen filmmaker Jūris Podnieks' documentary, *Homeland – Postscript*, will forget the last footage shot by Andris Slapins or his gasped words 'keep filming…' as he lay dying.

### MUSEUMS
Both the Soviet and Nazi occupations of Latvia during the last 65 years are chronicled in the chilling yet spirited **Museum of the Occupation of Latvia** (Strēlnieku laukums 1; www.occupationmuseum .lv; admission free; ☻ 11am-5pm May-Sep, closed Mon Oct-Apr, closed major holidays). A gaggle of young tour guides gives free tours in English, and there's also a worthwhile one-hour audio guide available (3Ls). Here you can also buy historical books on the occupation and dissident memoirs translated into English.

The absorbing **Museum of Decorative & Applied Arts** (www.dlmm.lv; Skārņu iela 10; student/child 1.50/0.50Ls; ☻ 11am-5pm, closed Mon), in a restored 13th-century church, presents an eccentric melee of Latvian textiles, china and tapestry.

The **Museum of the History of Riga & Navigation** (www.vip.latnet.lv/museums/Riga; Palasta iela 4; adult/student 1.50/0.50Ls; ☻ 11am-5pm Wed-Sun) is in a cloister next to Dome Cathedral. The gruesome mummified hand of a criminal and the 16th-century executioner's sword are highlights.

The violent history of this tiny nation is depicted in photos and war relics at the **War Museum** (Powder Tower, Smilšu iela 20; www.karamuzejs.lv; adult/child 0.5/0.25Ls; ☻ 10am-5pm Wed-Sun).

**LATVIA**

## New Town & Beyond

Extending north and east of the Freedom Monument, Rīga's 'New Town' isn't particularly new. A vast area of wide boulevards lined with modern shops, stately embassies and regal townhouses, it began to take shape in the 18th century and rose to prominence as the centre of Rīga's Art Nouveau movement (see below) in the early 20th century.

Just north of the Freedom Monument is Esplanāde park and the fabulous 19th-century **Russian Orthodox Cathedral** (Brīvības bulv 23). Across the park is the **National Museum of Art** ( ☎ 2732 4461; www.vmm.lv; K Valdemāra iela 10a; permanent/rotating exhibits 1.50/1Ls; ☺ 11am-5pm Wed-Mon), where pre-WWII Russian and Latvian art is on display among the Soviet grandeur of ruched net curtains, marble columns and red carpets.

The **Jewish community centre** ( ☎ 2728 3484; Skolas iela 6) shares a building with the **Jews in Latvia Museum** (admission by donation; ☺ noon-5pm Sun-Thu), which recounts Latvian Jewish history from the 16th century to 1945.

Located way out on the outskirts of the city, the **Latvian Ethnographic Open-Air Museum** ( ☎ 2799 4515; Brīvības gatve 440; www.ltg.lv/english /brivdabas.muzejs; adult/child 1/0.50Ls; ☺ 10am-5pm) is a Rīga essential. The dozens of farmhouses, churches and windmills on the grounds provide a record of bygone country life. The National Fair of Applied Arts (held early June) and several festivals take place here. Take bus 1 from the corner of Merķeļa iela and Tērbatas iela to the Brīvdabas muzejs stop.

## FESTIVALS & EVENTS

For more on festivals see p434. For a complete list see www.km.gov.lv.

**International Baltic Ballet Festival** (www.ballet -festival.lv) Performances by Latvian and international companies, in March.

**Rīga Opera Festival** (www.music.lv/opera) Takes place in June over 10 days.

**Arsenāls Film Forum** (www.arsenals.lv) International film festival held in even years in September.

## SLEEPING
### Budget

**Old Town Hostel** ( ☎ 2722 3406; www.rigaoldtownhostel .lv; Vaļņu iela 43; dm from 7Ls, d 20Ls; ✖ ▢ ) Not only is this a top-three hostel, but it also owns a pair of funky doubles that, if you can somehow reserve them, are the best value in Old Town. The always-lively pub downstairs is a great place to meet people.

**Argonaut Hostel** ( ☎ 2614 7214; www.argonauthostel .com; Kalēju iela 50; dm from 9Ls, d with shared bathroom 34Ls; ▢ ) Adventure lovers need look no further than this popular hostel, which boasts its own bobsled, and doubles as an adventure-tour agency. The kitchen could use a sink, but camaraderie runs rife among the wannabe Xgamer clientele.

**Knight's Court** ( ☎ 2736 4950; www.knightscourt.lv; Bruņinieku iela 75b; dm/d from 8/32Ls; P ▢ ) A hostel-hotel hybrid with clean, well-above-average dorm rooms in the main building, and an annex out back with 10 great-value private rooms. No hostel in Rīga is guaranteed quiet, but its location well out of Old Town gives it a chance. Free basic breakfast for all.

---

### NEW TOWN'S ART NOUVEAU

The flamboyant Art Nouveau district is New Town's delicious answer to the refined elegance of Old Town. A walk around here reveals a dizzying display of façades festooned with nude nymphs, lordly lions, ghastly goblins, and all manner of menacing mug – typical features of the 19th-century German Art Nouveau school, known as Jugendstil.

Based on the idea that design should embrace the decadent and expressive, the Art Nouveau movement started in Paris, Munich and Vienna, but it was Rīga that arguably took it the furthest. Today Rīga's Art Nouveau collection – which unlike that of many German cities, survived the war – is credited by Unesco as being the finest in Europe.

The Art Nouveau district is centred around Alberta iela, but you'll find fine examples of Jugendstil scattered throughout the New Town and it even crops its head up – quite literally – in Old Town (Rīga's first Art Nouveau building is in Old Town at **Audēju 7**). Don't miss the renovated façades of **Strēlnieku 4a** and **Elizabetes 10a, 10b and 33**. Those and most of the buildings on Alberta were designed by the Jugendstil movement's foremost practitioner in Rīga, Mikhail Eisenstein. Examples of the Latvian Art Nouveau style, known as National Romanticism, are on Antonijas iela.

**Livonija** ( ☎ 2720 4180; livonija@nite.lv; Maskavas iela 32; s/d from 20/24Ls) Quite simply the cheapest true hotel in Rīga. Its location in the gritty Russian Maskavas district turns some people off, but in reality it's a fine location. You're just three short stops on tram 7 from the bus station, and four stops from Old Town.

**Lenz Guesthouse** ( ☎ 2733 3343; www.lenz.lv; Lenču iela 2; s/d 32/35, with shared bathroom 27/32Ls; (P) (🖳) ) This quiet guesthouse on the fringes of the Art Nouveau district occupies that grey area between hostel and hotel. It's that rare budget hotel that pays attention to the details, including a big breakfast laid out in one of Rīga's nicest communal kitchens.

Also recommended:

**Patricia** ( ☎ 2728 4868; www.patriciahotel.com; Elizabetes iela; apt from 27Ls, min 2-nights) Rents out private flats in the centre.

**Riga Hostel** ( ☎ 2722 4520; www.riga-hostel.com; Mārstaļu iela 12; dm/d with shared bathroom from 9/40Ls; (🖳) ) Spanish run hostel with nice chill-out room.

## Midrange

**Radi un Draugi** ( ☎ 2782 0200; www.draugi.lv; Mārstaļu iela 1; s/d from 37/46Ls; (🖳) ) Great Old Town location? Check. Harmonious design? Check. Elegant bar and restaurant? Check. Kettles in all rooms? Check. Major weaknesses? Negative. All this for well under 50L? Affirmative! Several hotels in Rīga charge twice as much and deliver half the quality. The junior suites, only 6L more than doubles, are the hotel's triumphant signature.

**Krišjānis & Gertrūde** ( ☎ 2750 6603; www.kg.lv; s/d from 35/50Ls; (🗙) (🖳) ) It would be hard to find better value than this friendly, family-run B&B in the heart of New Town. You can save even more money by self-catering in the kitchen. There are only five rooms, so book well ahead.

**Konventa Sēta** ( ☎ 2708 7501; www.konventa.lv; Kalēju iela 9/11; s/d from €90/95; (P) ) Beyond its location in a 15th-century Old Town convent, there's nothing particularly special about this 140-room spread out among seven buildings. Turn your expectations down a notch and Konventa Sēta offers pretty good bang-for-the-buck, however.

**Centra** ( ☎ 2722 6441; www.centra.lv; Audēju iela 1; s/d €110/120; (🗙) (🔀) (🖳) ) Smoke-free hotels in Rīga are about as common as flying moose. Not only is Centra smoke free, but it also has some of the most tastefully designed, comfortable, and downright humungous rooms in Old

Town. The gigantic junior suites cost only €20 more than the doubles. The upper-floor rooms are quieter and have views.

**ElizaBetes Nams** ( ☎ 2750 9292; www.elizabetesnams.lv; Elizabetes iela 27; s/d from 40/60Ls; (P) (🗙) ) This romantic boutique hardly fits the profile of a business hotel, yet it plays home-away-from-home for a loyal cadre of business travellers looking for an after-work sanctuary. No rooms are the same, but all ooze character and are outstanding values.

**Hotel Gutenbergs** ( ☎ 2781 4090; www.gutenbergs.lv; Doma laukums 1; s/d from 60/80Ls; (P) (🗙) (🖳) ) Its rooftop restaurant has the best view in Rīga. You don't look down on the spires of Old Town, you sit among them. The restaurant's a tough act to follow, but the cosy rooms, some with sloping ceilings, are up to the task. The newer wing lacks the character of the older wing, however.

## Top End

**Boutique Hotel Viesturs** ( ☎ 2735 6060; www.hotelviesturs.lv; 5 Mucinieku iela; s/d/ste 59/89/159L; (🔀) ) Rooms in this quaint 17th-century boutique are small but positively exquisite – especially the bathrooms. The loft suite, with balcony views of St Peter *and* Dome Cathedral, might just be the best room in Rīga. The entire place is littered with amazing antiques.

**Grand Palace Hotel** ( ☎ 2704 4000; www.schlossle-hotels.com/grandpalace; Pils iela 12; s/d from €215/260; (P) (🗙) (🔀) (🖳) ) If you don't mind smallish rooms, you'll find no better place to be pampered than the lavish Grand Palace. Hotel staff wax nostalgic about the various luminaries

LATVIA

who have stayed here, such as Catherine Deneuve and REM, but it's actually more fit for royalty than rock stars.

## EATING

The days when there was little to choose from in Rīga outside smoky cafés and a handful of overplayed expat joints are long gone. Today you'll find a veritable cornucopia of ethnic restaurants and most of them are smoke-free thanks to a strict new antismoking law.

In Old Town you can't toss one of Rīga's trademark fluffy alley cats without it landing (on its feet) in a restaurant. Smart money follows the locals to New Town to escape the crowds.

### Restaurants

#### OLD TOWN

**John Lemon** (Peldu iela 21; mains 1.50-4Ls) This small diner with orange walls and a pink bar is open until 5am on Friday and Saturday nights, but is a great spot for noshing any time. The calzone-like *lavash* are a bargain.

**Kamāla** (Jauniela 14; mains 2-4Ls) Trancey Indian music, ornately carved furniture and apsaras set the dreamy vibe at this intimate vegetarian restaurant. The exceptional Indian soup is among 25 on the menu, and many dishes are Ayurvedic.

**Ķiploku krogs** (Jēkaba iela 3/5; mains 2.50-5Ls) The 'garlic pub' dices up garlic and sticks it into hearty dishes of all shapes, sizes and guises. The pasta dishes are especially good, and cheap to boot. Not a place for calorie counters.

**Habibi** ( ☎ 2722 8551; Peldu iela 24; mains 5-7Ls) This totally cool Egyptian-run hookah joint serves up Middle Eastern and Central Asian food in a rich, cushiony interior.

#### NEW TOWN

**Ai Karamba!** (Pulkveža Brieža 2; mains 3-4Ls) American country kitchen meets greasy spoon at this colourful Canadian-owned diner. There's a chill-out room upstairs and surprises like stuffed schnitzel on the menu.

**el Čarlito** ( ☎ 2777 0586; Blaumaņa iela 38/40; mains 3-5Ls) This bustling Mexican eatery features margaritas and decent fajitas and quesadillas (3Ls).

**Red Fred** (Dzirnavu iela 62; mains 3-6Ls) It's unlikely that the urban hipsters bathing in the sublime red glow of this eatery have too much experience using the pick-axes and hard hats that line the walls. But you can't blame them for liking the eclectic food.

**Vincents** ( ☎ 2733 2634; Elizabetes iela 19; mains 8-12Ls) Inspired by Van Gogh, this fancy local institution boasts Rīga's finest European cuisine cooked up by Latvia's most famous chef, Mārtiņš Rītiņš.

### Cheap Eats

In addition to the following places, the train station has a wealth of cheap and quick eating options.

**Sievasmātes pīrādziņi** (Kaļķu iela 10; ✆ 9am-9pm) This is the most centrally located of Rīga's beloved *pīrāgi* shops; you can go local and fill up on a few of these for under 2Ls.

**Pelmeņi XL** (Kaļķu iela 7; meals 1-2Ls; ✆ 9am-4am) Hungry mobs flock to this dirt-cheap cafeteria on Old Town's main drag for huge bowls of *pelmeni* (Russian dumplings) and *varenyky* (Ukrainian dumplings).

**Čili Pizza** (meals 2-3Ls; Old Town (Brīvbas bulv 26); New Town (Raina bulv 15) With five locations in Riga and counting, this reliable Lithuanian chain is fast becoming ubiquitous.

---

#### LATVIA'S LIDO LOVE AFFAIR

If you want to sample Latvian food look no further than the wildly popular buffet-style Lido restaurants. The chain's flagship enterprise is the gargantuan, amusement park–like **Lido atpūtas centrs** (Krasta iela 76; ✆ 10am-11pm), where you can easily get lost amid endless buffet rows of pork knuckle, potato pancakes, fried cabbage and, oh, about a thousand other dishes. With an ice-skating rink and its own outdoor ethnographic park, it's a huge draw for Latvian families. From the bus station it's an easy 15-minute ride out to the 'Lido' stop on tram 7.

The other Lido restaurants are basically miniature versions of the original without all the bells and whistles. The only one in Old Town is **Alus sēta** (Tirgoņu iela 6; ✆ 10am-1am). In New Town the best options are **Staburags** (A Čaka iela 55; ✆ noon-midnight) and **Dzirnavas** (Dzirnavu iela 76; ✆ 8am-11pm).

A decidedly heavy meal with a pint of *alus* (beer) at any of these places shouldn't set you back more than 5Ls.

## Self-Catering

**Central market** (Centrālirgus iela; ☉ 8am-6pm) Located in five huge hangars behind the bus station, this colourful, Soviet-style market is one of the largest in Europe and has Rīga's cheapest produce.

**Rimi** (Universālveikals Centrs, cnr Audēju & Vaļņu ielas; ☉ 9am-10pm) The biggest and best-located supermarket in Old Town.

# DRINKING

Rīga thoroughly deserves its reputation as a party mecca. Don't be surprised to find yourself still out dancing at 7am on a weekday morning. Many harmless-seeming daytime cafés turn into raucous bars by night.

## Old Town

In the summer, the numerous outdoor beer gardens on Old Town's two main squares, Līvu laukums and Doma laukums, make fine places for pints.

**Orange Bar** (Jāņa sēta 5) Check your inhibitions at the door of this grungy alternative venue, where peeps are not afraid to dance on the bar. Can get ugly late at night – in a good way.

**Spalvas Pa Gaisu** (Grēcinieku 8) A classy outfit with a mean streak, it showcases thirty-somethings going bananas to a mix of Latino and Latvian music.

**Cuba Café** (Jauniela 15; light meals 3-6Ls) This lively spot pulls no punches with its mojitos and draws a hip, energetic crowd that clearly appreciates that.

**Belle Epoque** (Mazā monētu iela 6) Students flock to this basement bar to power down its trademark 'apple pie' shots. Also called French Bar, it's relatively immune to stag parties.

**B Bars** (Toŗņa iela 4) Do not – repeat *do not* – leave Rīga without stopping by here for a mug of their heavenly Hot Balzams. It puts mulled wine to shame. Happy hour is two-for-one.

**Dickens** (Grēcinieku iela 9/1) Old Town has an inordinate number of Irish bars that show sports on TV and get taken over by stag parties on weekends. This is probably the rowdiest of the bunch.

**de Lacy's** (Šķūņu iela 4) You'll have a slightly better chance of enjoying a pint of Guinness and a good Irish meal in peace at this expat hang-out.

## New Town

**Skyline Bar** (Elizabetes iela 55) The glam crowd and the stunning view make this newly redesigned window palace on the 26th floor of the Reval Hotel Latvija decidedly *de rigueur*.

**A Suns** (Elizabetes iela 83/85) If you happen to visit this popular expat hang-out in Berga bazārs, make a point of visiting the men's room for a truly warped example of artistic creation.

**Bites Blūzs Klubs** ( ☎ 2733 3125; Dzimavu 34a; cover 3Ls Fri & Sat) It has great live blues and a proper bar – the kind where the bartender can slide a beer from one end and it will take several seconds to reach a customer at the other end.

# ENTERTAINMENT

*In Your Pocket* has a full listing of movie venues as well as listings for opera, ballet and classical music. Ballet, opera and theatre break for summer holidays, from around June to September. Check www.livas.lv for movie listings.

## Nightclubs

**Pulkvedim neviens neraksta** (No-one Writes to the Colonel; ☎ 2721 3886; Peldu iela 26-28; cover 1-3Ls Thu-Sat) There's no such thing as dull night at 'Pulkvedis,' which serves up 1980s and '90s hits on the ground floor and trancier beats downstairs.

**Essential** ( ☎ 2724 2289; www.essential.lv; Skolas iela 2; cover 5-7Ls; ☉ Thu-Sun) Rīga's hottest club is a spectacle of beautiful bodies boogieing to some of Europe's top DJ talent in three dance chambers. Overzealous security aside, there's no safer bet if partying till dawn is your mission. Sorry, no local beer – just 4Ls Coronas. Drink cocktails.

**Četri Balti Krekli** (Four White Shirts; ☎ 2721 3885; www.krekli.lv; Vecpilsētas iela 12; cover 1-5Ls) This is the place to see live Latvian rock bands any night of the week.

**XXL** ( ☎ 2728 2276; Kalniņa iela 4; cover 1-10Ls) Rīga's best gay club features a thriving disco on Friday and Saturday nights, go-go dancers and plenty of dark rooms to get cosy.

## Ballet & Opera

The awesome **National Opera Theatre** ( ☎ 2707 3777; www.opera.lv; Aspazijas bulv 3; box office ☉ 10am-7pm) is home to the Rīga Ballet, where Mikhail Baryshnikov made his name, and the Latvian National Opera.

## Cinemas

Films are generally shown in their original language with Latvian or Russian subtitles. The Leviathan **Forum Cinemas** (13 Janvāra 8; www.forumcinemas.lv) is the second-largest movie

**LATVIA**

theatre in Northern Europe. Tickets average 2Ls at most theatres.

## Classical Music

**Great Guild** (Lielā ģilde; ☎ 2721 3643; www.music.lv /orchestra; Amatu iela 6; tickets 2-7Ls; box office ☺ noon-6pm) This lovely 14th-century building is the concert hall of the renowned Latvian National Symphony Orchestra.

Music performances are also held at the following places.

**Dome Cathedral** ( ☎ 2721 3213; Doma laukums 1; tickets 1-3Ls; box office ☺ 10am-5pm Mon-Sat & 30min before concerts) Organ concerts at least weekly at 7pm.

**St Peter's Church** ( ☎ 2722 9426) Free concerts every Tuesday at 6pm.

**Wagner Hall** ( ☎ 2721 0814; Vāgnera iela 4; box office ☺ noon-3pm & 4-7pm) Chamber and solo concerts.

## SHOPPING

**A&E Gallery** (Jauniela iela 17) The place to shop for amber and art, it's a favourite with visiting dignitaries and celebs.

**Rota** (Kalēju iela 9/11; ☺ 10am-11pm) Good selection of amber jewellery set in silver.

**Upe** (Vāgnera iela 5) The place to learn about and/or buy traditional Latvian folk instruments and albums. Also has a small selection of carefully selected, cheese-free Latvian rock.

## GETTING THERE & AWAY

For information on airline offices in Rīga and international flights, bus, train and ferry services see p436.

### Land

The Rīga **bus station** ( ☎ 2900 0009; Prāgas iela 1) is a three-minute walk south of Old Town across 13 Janvāra iela.

The **train station** ( ☎ 2723 3113; Stacijas laukums) is about a five-minute walk beyond that. For information on domestic buses and trains going to/from Rīga, see p436.

## GETTING AROUND
### To/from the Airport

**Rīga international airport** (RIX; Lidosta Rīga; ☎ 2720 7009; www.riga-airport.com) is about 8km west of the city centre. Bus 22 runs at least every 30 minutes from 5.45am to 11.40pm between the airport and the stop on 13 Janvāra iela opposite the bus station in Rīga (0.20Ls, 30 minutes). Express bus 22A (0.25Ls) drops you off at the Orthodox Cathedral on Brīvības

bulvāris and is 10 minutes quicker, but it only runs about every hour.

A taxi from the Old Town to the airport costs 10Ls; agree on a price beforehand and insist the driver takes the short route over the Vanšu Bridge (Vanšu tilts) or they *will* try to rip you off.

### Car & Motorcycle

For information on car rentals, see p437. Motorists must pay 5Ls per hour to enter the Old Town.

### Public Transport

Rīga's user-friendly Soviet-era public transport system is worth mastering if you plan to venture out of Old Town. All bus, trolleybus and tram routes are clearly marked on any decent city map. Tickets (0.20Ls) are sold on board by conductors and there is no need to punch your ticket. Five-day passes (3.80Ls) for all three are sold at news kiosks. Most city transport runs from 5.30am to 12.30am daily, but some trams run sporadically all night. For Rīga public transport routes and schedules visit www.rigassatiksme.lv.

### Taxi

Taxis officially charge 0.3Ls per km by day and 0.4Ls per km by night, but drivers employ every unofficial trick in the book to rip off foreigners. Insisting the meter is switched on is always a good idea, but some – not all – cab companies quadruple their rates late at night. If the meter is counting off santīmi faster than your watch is counting off seconds, stop the cab and get out! You can hail cabs on the street, find them in rank at several points throughout the city, or call **Rīgas Taksometru Parks** ( ☎ 2800 1313) or **Rīga Taxi** ( ☎ 2800 1010).

## AROUND RĪGA
### Salaspils

'Behind this gate the earth groans', reads the inscription on the large concrete bunker that marks the entrance to the **Salaspils Concentration Camp**.

Between 1941 and 1944 an estimated 45,000 Jews from Rīga and approximately 55,000 other people, including Jews from other Nazi-occupied countries and prisoners of war, were murdered here, 15km southeast of Rīga. Today the site is a place of peaceful solitude amid whispering pine trees. A metronome encased inside a black marble wall beats out never-ending time. Several giant, gaunt sculptures stand near the middle of the 40-hectare site. It is a haunting memorial.

The concrete sculpture on the left upon entering reads: 'On this way went crying children, mothers, fathers and grandfathers – all went to die. Who will count those unsaid words? Who will count the lost years which Nazi bullets killed…?' Inside the bunker a small exhibition recounts the horrors of the camp.

To get there from Rīga, take a suburban train on the Ogre–Krustpils line to Dārziņi (not Salaspils) station. A hidden path leads from the station to the *piemineklis* (memorial), a 15-minute walk away. If you're driving from Rīga on the A6 highway, the hard-to-spot turnoff is on the left 300m before the A5/E77 highway.

## Rundāle Palace

If you only have time for one day trip out of Rīga, make it **Rundāle Palace** ( ☎ 2396 2197; www rundale.net; adult/student 2.50/1.50Ls; ☺ 10am-7pm Jun-Aug, to 6pm Sep-Oct & May, to 5pm Nov-Apr), 75km south of the capital in the tiny town of Pilsrundāle. A monument to aristocratic ostentatiousness, it was gifted by Empress of Russia Anna Ioannovna to her favourite advisor (and lover), Baron Ernst von Bühren, whom she later appointed Duke of Courland.

The architect of this sprawling complex was the Italian baroque genius Bartolomeo Rastrelli, best known for designing the Winter Palace in St Petersburg. Rastrelli wasn't able to complete Rundāle before Empress Anna died in 1740, and Von Bühren was forced into exile. But when Catherine the Great took the Russian throne in the 1760s Von Bühren returned with Rastrelli to finish the mothballed palace. It was completed, with rococo elements, in 1768, and served as the Duke's summer home until his death in 1772.

Today about 40 of the palace's 138 rooms are open to visitors, as are the extensive, wonderfully landscaped gardens. Although the furnishings in the rooms are not original – they were donated or bought when the palace was restored in the 1970s – they are positively exquisite. Outside the palace ballroom, a real stork's nest is visible in a chimney, bizarrely mirroring a stork's nest engraving in the ceiling of the ballroom, which was painted white

to better highlight the bright plumage worn by ball guests.

To get here take a bus from Rīga to Bauska (1.60Ls, 1¼ hours, hourly), 12km west of Pilsrundāle. Buses run sporadically from Bauska to Pilsrundāle – the tourist office in Rīga has details.

You may also wish to check out Rastrelli's **Jelgava Palace** in Jelgava, 30km east of Pilsrundāle, which today houses a university. There's also an interesting **castle** in Bauska.

## Jūrmala
### pop 56,000
They call it the Baltic Riviera, and while the weather's a bit too fickle to justify the moniker, this endless stretch of sandy beach, backed by an odd mix of quaint wooden Art Nouveau houses and shocking Soviet-era sanatoriums, makes a delightful respite from the hustle and bustle of Rīga.

Jūrmala actually consists of 14 townships spread out over 32km due west of Rīga. Unless you have a car or bicycle (in which case you can explore several townships), you'll want to head straight to the two main townships of Majori and Dzintari, linked by Jumas iela, a 1km pedestrian street that constitutes Jūrmala's main drag.

**Jūrmala Tourism Information Centre** ( ☎ 2714 7900; www.jurmala.lv; Lienes iela 5, Majori; ☺ 9am-7pm Mon-Fri, 10am-5pm Sat, 10am-3pm Sun) disseminates free maps and a useful brochure outlining walks, bike rides and tourist attractions in the area. It can arrange accommodation in private homes for as little as 5Ls.

### SIGHTS & ACTIVITIES
Besides its 'Blue Flag' beach, Jūrmala's main attraction is its colourful Art Nouveau **wooden houses**, distinguishable by frilly awnings, detailed façades and elaborate towers. These houses are found all over Jūrmala, but you can get your fill by taking a leisurely stroll along Jūras iela, which parallels Jomas iela in Majori and Dzintari. The houses are in various states of repair; some are dilapidated and abandoned, others are beautifully renovated, and still others are brand new constructions.

Way at the other end of the architectural spectrum are several particularly gaudy beachfront Soviet-era sanatoriums. No specimen glorifies the genre quite like the **Vaivari sanatorium** (Asaru prospekts 61), on the main road

5km west of Majori. It resembles a giant, beached cruise ship that's been mothballed since the Brezhnev era. Surprisingly it still functions, catering to an elderly clientele who have been visiting regularly since, well, the Brezhnev era.

You can rent **bicycles** at several places around town, including most hotels, for 5Ls per day. Check www.jask.lv for **kiteboarding** information.

### Ķemeri National Park

Jūrmala is the jumping-off point for this 42,790-hectare **national park** (www.kemeri.gov.lv). Ancient bogs, swamps, lakes and forests are all found here, along with a wealth of flora and fauna. You can get information on hikes and canoe trips in the park from the **Information Centre** ( ☎ 2773 0078; Meža māja; ☻ 9am-6pm May-Sep) in Ķemeri, the westernmost township of Jūrmala.

#### SLEEPING & EATING

There's a dizzying array of lodging options here, few of them good values. Many offer a full range of spa services. Prices go way down outside the peak months of July and August.

**Kempings Nemo** ( ☎ 2773 2349; nemo@nemo.lv; Atbalss iela 1, Vaivari; cottages 5-24Ls, per camp site/person 1/1Ls; P ☻ ) It's right next to Nemo Water Park and the beach, but it's a long way from most of the action.

**Elina** ( ☎ 2776 1665; www.elinahotel.lv; Lienes iela 43; d from 25Ls; P ) There's nothing particularly special about this place except for the price. Rooms are basic but have what you need – namely a bed, closet and TV.

**Baltic Beach Hotel** ( ☎ 2777 1400; www.balticbeach.lv; Jūras iela 23-25, Majori; s 50-100Ls, d 55-120Ls; P ☒ ☒ ☻ ☻ ) The hulking Soviet exterior here belies a crisp lobby and impeccably renovated rooms, many with balconies overlooking the beach. It has a top-notch spa, good restaurant and a primo location.

**Slavu** (Jomas iela 57; meals 4-9Ls) A rare year-round eatery in Jūrmala, it serves a ferociously good chicken shashlyk among other dishes. There's a weekend nightclub here in the summer.

#### GETTING THERE & AWAY

Suburban trains go every 20 minutes or so to/from Rīga (0.51Ls, 40 minutes). All stop in Dubulti and most stop in Dzintari, Majori and the other townships.

# EASTERN LATVIA

Heading east out of Rīga, cobblestones quickly yield to conifers as you enter the wild and woolly Vidzeme region. The region's highlight is the Gauja National Park, an outdoor lovers' paradise with hiking, canoeing, mountain biking, berry picking, fishing and even skiing (albeit on modest slopes) on offer. The region is also dripping with history, as a slew of medieval castles attests.

Much of Sigulda and all of Cēsis – the only two towns covered here – lie within the 49,000-hectare national park.

## GAUJA NATIONAL PARK

Much of Vidzeme's prime forest-clad real estate falls within this highly accessible **national park** (www.gnp.gov.lv). Some 150 bird species and almost 50 different mammals can be found frolicking amid its rivers, cliffs and pine forests. The park's extensive network of camping grounds makes it a fine place for human frolicking as well. The best camping grounds line the Gauja River between the Cēsis and Sigulda.

## SIGULDA

### pop 10,855

It's hard to believe that this tranquil paradise, spread out over a ridge above the Gauja River and cloaked in a blanket of pine forest, is only a half-hour (50km) drive from Rīga. Like all of Latvia, Sigulda lacks high mountains, but that hasn't stopped it from becoming Latvia's outdoor activities capital. As its medieval castles attest, it's also pretty darn old – 800 years old, to be exact, as of 2007.

### Information

The helpful **Gauja National Park Visitor Centre** ( ☎ 2780 0388; www.gnp.gov.lv; Baznīcas iela 3, Sigulda; ☻ 9.30am-7pm Apr-Oct, 10am-4pm Nov-Mar) can arrange guided tours of Sigulda and the national park. **Sigulda Tourism Information Centre** ( ☎ 2797 1335; www.sigulda.lv; Ausekla iela 6; ☻ 10am-7pm May-Oct, to 5pm Nov-Apr) has maps and loads of other information. There's also an **internet café** (Pils iela 3; per hr 0.70Ls; ☻ 10am-10pm).

### Sights

Stunning **Turaida Castle** occupies an enviable knoll overlooking the Gauja River inside the **Turaida Museum Reserve** ( ☎ 2797 1402; www.turaida-muzejs.lv; admission 1.50Ls; castle & museum ☻ 9am-7pm

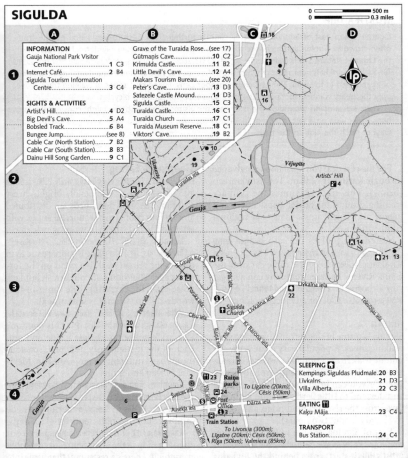

## SIGULDA

**INFORMATION**
Gauja National Park Visitor
  Centre.............................**1** C3
Internet Café...........................**2** B4
Sigulda Tourism Information
  Centre.............................**3** C4

**SIGHTS & ACTIVITIES**
Artist's Hill............................**4** D2
Big Devil's Cave......................**5** A4
Bobsled Track.........................**6** B4
Bungee Jump......................(see 8)
Cable Car (North Station).......**7** B2
Cable Car (South Station).......**8** B3
Dainu Hill Song Garden..........**9** C1

Grave of the Turaida Rose....(see 17)
Gūtmaņis Cave......................**10** C2
Krimulda Castle.....................**11** B2
Little Devil's Cave..................**12** A4
Makars Tourism Bureau......(see 20)
Peter's Cave..........................**13** D3
Satezele Castle Mound..........**14** D3
Sigulda Castle.......................**15** C3
Turaida Castle.......................**16** C1
Turaida Church......................**17** C1
Turaida Museum Reserve.......**18** C1
Viktors' Cave........................**19** B2

**SLEEPING**
Kempings Siguldas Pludmale.**20** B3
Līvkalns.................................**21** D3
Villa Alberta..........................**22** C3

**EATING**
Kaķu Māja.............................**23** C4

**TRANSPORT**
Bus Station............................**24** C4

---

May-Oct, 10am-6pm Oct-Apr, grounds till 9pm Jun-Aug). Turaida means 'garden of god' in ancient Liv, and its an apt enough moniker for this serene sanctuary – even if the Liv gods might frown on the big summer crowds. The sprawling grounds include the sculpture-festooned **Dainu Hill Song Garden**, the quaint wooden-spired **Turaida Church** and a local-history **museum** in a 15th-century granary. In the churchyard two lime trees shade the **grave** of the legendary Turaida Rose; read her heartbreaking story in the museum.

The 18th-century Great Northern War left **Sigulda Castle** in ruins, but it's enchanting to scramble around this once-formidable knight's stronghold and enjoy the views of Turaida Castle across river. There are outdoor concerts here in the summer. Across the street is a scenic **cable car** (return tickets weekdays/weekend 1/1.50Ls; departs half-hourly 10am-7.30pm May-Sep, departs hourly 10am-4pm Oct-Apr) that runs across the valley to the ruins of **Krimulda Castle**.

## Activities

One experience you'll never forget is the hair-raising ride down Sigulda's **bobsled track** (Šveices iela 13; tourist/authentic bobsled 4/35Ls; all evenings & 11am-5pm weekends Nov-Mar, 11am-5pm weekends May-Sep) with a professional driver at 100km/h. Think of the scariest rollercoaster you've ever been on and multiply the fear factor by three. Less intrepid souls can negotiate the track in a five-man 'tourist bob' resembling an oversized raft, and there's a wheeled bob for summer sliding.

LATVIA

**WORTH A TRIP**

Līgatne, 20km east of Sigulda and only slightly further from Cēsis, offers a fine escape from often-crowded Sigulda and a chance to see animals roaming in relatively natural confines near the **Līgatne Nature Trails** (visitor centre ☎ 2415 3313; adult/child 1/0.50Ls; ⌚ 9.30am-5pm Mon, to 6.30pm Tue-Sun). The animals here, most of which are indigenous to Latvia, were rescued after being injured or abandoned in the wild. Their spacious outdoor pens, linked by a series of walking trails, leave only the bears wanting for space. There's also a loop for cars and bicycles.

There's a camping ground on the river near the visitor centre, and you might consider floating back to Sigulda on a raft, canoe or innertube (below). To get here, take a train to Līgatne and walk or hitch the 4km to the trails.

For the real deal you *must* book in advance through Karīna at Makars Tourism Bureau (below). This track was once the primary training ground for Soviet bobsledders and lugers, and it still hosts many big regional competitions.

Adrenaline junkies can also **bungee jump** (☎ 2921 2731; www.lgk.lv; jumps from 17Ls; ⌚ Fri-Sun May-Oct from 6.30pm) from the cable car over the Gauja River. The same company can also get you airborne in a **vertical wind tunnel** (⌚ 2838 4400; per min 5Ls). Call for advance booking.

### HIKING

Sigulda is prime hiking territory so bring your walking shoes. A popular easy route is the 40-minute walk from Krimulda Castle to Turaida Museum Reserve via **Gūtmaņis Cave** and **Viktors' Cave**. Or you can head south from Krimulda and descend to **Little Devil's Cave** and **Big Devil's Cave**, cross the river via footbridge, and return to Sigulda (about two hours).

East of Sigulda, try the well-marked loop that joins **Peter's Cave**, **Satezele Castle Mound** and **Artist's Hill**; it starts from behind the Līvkalns hotel and takes about 1½ hours. The view of Turaida Castle and the Gauja River valley from Artists' Hill is spectacular.

The Gauja National Park Visitor Centre (p428) has details on longer walks.

### FLOATING

Floating down the peaceful Gauja River is a great way to observe this pristine area and have a few wildlife encounters if you're lucky. There are camping grounds all along the stretch of river from Cēsis to Sigulda. **Makars Tourism Bureau** (☎ 2924 4948; www.makars .lv; Peldu iela 2; tours per boat 10-40Ls) is one of several organisers of boat trips along the Gauja, or you can just head upstream, stick your arse in an innertube, and float back to town.

## Sleeping & Eating

**Livonija** (☎ 2797 3066; www.livonija.viss.lv, Pulkveža Brieža iela 55; dm/s/d 8/15/22Ls; P ) Friendly, bright, cheery and fun. The nine dorm beds are distributed among four rooms in a wonderful annex with satellite TV and a free (!!) washing machine.

**Līvkalns** (☎ 2797 0916; www.livkalns.lv; Pēteralas iela; s/d from 24/28Ls; P ) No place is more rustic than this idyllic retreat next to a pond on the forest's edge. The rooms are pine-fresh but lack noise-reducing carpeting. The cabin-in-the-woods-style restaurant is sensational.

**Villa Alberta** (☎ 2797 1060; www.villaalberta.lv; Līvkalna iela 10a; s/d from 35/40Ls; P ) This boutique in a brick house oozes class inside and out. Each of the meticulously designed, spacious rooms has a different theme – Alaskan, Mexican, Mayan and more.

**Kempings Siguldas Pludmale** (☎ 2924 4948; www .makars.lv; Peldu iela 2; camp sites per person/tent/car/caravan 1/1/1/2Ls; ⌚ 15 May–15 Sep) Wonderful riverside camping spot that rents tents for 4Ls a day.

**Kaķu Māja** (☎ 2700 272; Pils iela 8; mains 3-5Ls) Your one-stop shop in the town centre for just about everything. There's a restaurant that turns into a club on weekends, a basement sports bar and a cheap caféteria-style canteen next door.

## Getting There & Around

For information on buses and trains to/from Rīga, see p436.

There's at least one public bus per hour between Sigulda train station and Turaida until about 8pm (0.25Ls). Hitching is popular around here, but take the usual precautions.

## CĒSIS

pop 17,588

Stinking of history, ecologically well-endowed and quaint to the core, Cēsis can trap you for days. Latvians say that this town is quintessentially Latvian and pay it due homage by drinking lots of Cēsu *alus*, which recently became the country's most popular beer.

Pick up a map at the **Cēsis Tourist Information Centre** ( ☎ 2412 1815; www.cesis.lv; Pils laukums 2; ☺ 9am-6pm Mon-Sat, 10am-5pm Sun May-Sep, 10am-5pm Oct-Apr) near the castle. **Capital Datorsalons** ( ☎ 2410 7111; Rīgas iela 7; per hr 0.50Ls; ☺ 9am-6pm Mon-Fri, 10am-4pm Sat) has internet access.

## Sights

Endearing **Cēsis Castle** (Pils laukums 11; adult/student incl park & museum 1.50/0.70Ls; ☺ 10am-5pm Tue-Sun Oct-Apr, to 6pm Tue-Sun May-Sep), with its magnificent twin towers, is Latvia's best-preserved castle. The Master of the Livonian Order chose it as his residence in 1237 when Cēsis was the capital of Livonia. The castle's western tower has a viewpoint overlooking **Castle Park**, and the adjoining 18th-century New Castle contains a museum of history and art. The city's old **Lenin Statue** lies in an open coffin on the castle grounds.

There are plenty of outdoor activities going on here, including boat trips down the Gauja (opposite).

## Sleeping & Eating

**Hostel Putiņkrogs** ( ☎ 2412 0290; cdzp@apollo.lv; Saules iela 23; d with shared bathroom per person 6Ls; Ⓟ ) Inside this grimy Soviet-style building, 1km west of the train station, lurk perfectly fine rooms for peanuts. You can buy food at the store downstairs and self-cater in the nice kitchen.

**Katrina** ( ☎ 2410 7700; www.hotelkatrina.lv; Mazā Katrīnas iela 8; s/d 28/36Ls; Ⓟ ) This pinkish building near the centre of the action is the best midrange option in town. Rooms are bright with light-wood furniture and have free internet access.

**Hotel Cēsis** ( ☎ 2412 0122; www.hotel.kolonna.com; Vienības laukums 1; s/d 30/42Ls; Ⓟ ⊠ 🖥 ) This rather stately place is Cēsis's best hotel. Rooms are spacious and comfortable and the English-speaking staff are superhelpful. The inhouse restaurant serves Latvian and European cuisine in a formal setting and is excellent, as well as having a lovely garden where you can dine outside.

**DivasPuses** (Rīgas iela 4) This well-situated bar has decent pizzas and stays open late on Saturday nights, catering to a diverse crowd.

## Getting There & Away

For information on buses and trains to/from Rīga, see p436.

# WESTERN LATVIA

Sandy beaches meet rocky seaside points, rolling farmland yields to thick forests, and cobbled medieval towns bump heads with thriving urban centres in Latvia's enchanting western Kurzeme region. Known as the Courland in English, it's named after the Baltic Cours who lived here before the 13th-century German invasion. The country's most diverse region, it presents off-the-beaten-track exploring around Cape Kolka and more accessible delights in Kuldīga, Ventspils and Liepāja.

## KOLKA & CAPE KOLKA

The Gulf of Rīga meets the Baltic sea in dramatic fashion at **Cape Kolka**, a desolate moonscape of wind-swept sand bars and angry currents. The raw, powerful effect of this desolate point was amplified by a biblical winter storm in 2005, which uprooted dozens of trees and tossed them like matchsticks onto the sandy beach, where they remain hideously entombed, roots in the air.

The monument near the entrance to the beach was put up in 2002 after three Swedes

---

**THE LAST OF THE LIVS**

Kurzeme is home to some of the last remaining Livs, a Finno-Ugric peoples who first migrated to northern Latvia 5000 years ago. Although many Latvians descended from this fishing tribe, less than 200 Livs remain in Latvia today, clustered in 14 fishing villages along the coast south of Cape Kolka. Hungary, Finland and Estonia also have small Liv populations, but they consider this area their homeland and return every August for the **Liv Festival** in Mazirbe, 18km southwest of Kolka.

While the Liv language is still taught in local elementary schools and at Tartu University in Estonia, there are fewer than 10 native speakers remaining in the world. You can learn about the Livonians at the small **Livonian Centre** ( ☎ 2327 7267; ☺ 9am-6pm Mon-Fri) behind the library on the main street in Kolka, and in a few other Kurzeme towns.

LATVIA

drowned in the cape's shallow but treacherous, quicksand-bottomed waters. One side reads, 'For people, ships and Livian earth'; the other, 'For those the sea took away.' Locals claim the cape's waters are littered with more shipwrecks than anywhere else in the Baltics. Cape Kolka's beauty is best admired from the beach.

Kolka's only hotel is the basic **Zitari** ( ☎ 2324 7145; d 15Ls) on the main street.

## Getting There & Away

Cape Kolka is less than two hours from Rīga by car, making an easy day trip. Two daily buses make the trip but can take up to five hours.

For more active sorts, an excellent way to get up here is by bicycle from Jūrmala. It starts off bumpy but the road soon turns into the beautifully paved, incredibly scenic, two-lane Hwy P131. It's about 130km from Jūrmala to Cape Kolka, and there are many campsites and guesthouses along the along the way, particularly in Purciems, 22km south of Kolka.

## VENTSPILS

**pop 44,000**

Latvia's main port sure doesn't feel like the gritty, industrial hub it's supposed to be. It's relatively quiet, with lots of parks, a clean beach, some rustic old wooden houses and a lovely promenade along the canal port. Each year the city plays host to the country's Eurovision contest finals – quite a distinction in Latvia.

## Information

**Ventspils Tourism information centre** ( ☎ 2362 2263; www.tourism.ventspils.lv; Tirgus iela 7; ☼ 8am-7pm Mon-Fri, 10am-5pm Sat, 10am-3pm Sun May-Sep, 8am-5pm Mon-Fri, 10am-3pm Sat & Sun Nov-Apr) can arrange cheap hostel accommodation in summer. **Ventspils Library** (Akmeņu iela 2; per hr 0.50Ls; ☼ 10am-7pm Mon-Fri, 10am-4pm Sat) is a superb new facility with internet access.

## Sights

Ventspils' 13th-century **Livonian Order Castle** (Jāņa iela 17) hosts a cutting-edge **museum** ( ☎ 2362 2031; adult/child 1/0.50 Ls; ☼ 9am-6pm May-Oct, 10am-5pm Nov-Apr) with an interactive display on castle history and two panoramic telescopes for visitors to enjoy an eagle-eye view of the port and city.

## Sleeping & Eating

**Piejūras Kempings** ( ☎ 2362 7925; www.camping .ventspils.lv; Vasarnicu iela 56; camp sites per person 1.50Ls; basic/equipped 4-person cottages from 12/24Ls; P ) This superb camping ground is just a five-minute walk from the beach, and rents gorgeous wooden cottages year-round.

**Olimpiskā Centra Ventspils** ( ☎ 2362 8032; www .ocventspils.lv; Lielais prospekts 33; r 13Ls; P ☒ ) This hotel is effectively the institutional arm of Ventspils' state-of-the-art Olympic Centre is easily the best hotel deal in all of Latvia.

**Melanis Sivēns** (Jāna iela 17; mains 2-4Ls) Ventspils' nicest restaurant is in the Livonian Order Castle dungeon.

**Kosmos** (Ganību 22/24; mains 2-4Ls) While best known as a club, this warehouse-style space is also a tasty option for lunch or dinner.

## Getting There & Away

Buses run to/from Kuldīga (1.35Ls, one hour, seven daily), Liepāja (3.40Ls, two hours, seven daily) and Rīga (2.30Ls, 3¼ hours, at least hourly).

For international ferry schedules see p436.

## KULDĪGA

**pop 14,000**

Picturesque Kuldīga is a mellow medieval masterpiece. The antithesis of nearby Liepāja, it doesn't have a whole lot to do besides stroll its narrow streets, chill out down by the river and soak up the old-world charm.

The **Tourist Information Centre** ( ☎ 2332 2259; www.kuldiga.lv; Baznīcas iela 5; ☼ 9am-5pm Mon-Fri, 10am-4pm Sat, 10am-2pm Sun May-Oct, 9am-5pm Mon-Fri Nov-Apr) in the old Town Hall has a great brochure explaining the fascinating history of the town, which dates to 1242 when the German Order of Knights built a castle on the Venta River.

All that remains of the castle today are a few mounds and ditches scattered around pleasant, sculpture-laden **Pils parks**, a short walk east of the tourist centre. From here you get a good vantage point of gentle **Kuldīga waterfall**. At 275m, it's said to be Europe's widest – just don't expect Niagara Falls!

Kuldīga's main drag, pedestrian **Liepājas iela**, is a fine place to plop down in a streetside café and watch the world go by. **Jāņa Nams** ( ☎ 2332 3456; Liepājas iela 36; s/d 20/22Ls; P ) is a clean middle-of-the-road sleeping option; inquire at the tourist centre if you prefer something more up- or downmarket.

Buses run to/from Ventspils (1.35Ls, one hour, seven daily), Liepāja (2.20Ls, 1¼ hours, eight daily) and Rīga (2.30Ls, 3¼ hours, hourly). Use the bus stop near Rimi supermarket on Sūru iela to avoid a long hike to/from the bus station.

## LIEPĀJA

**pop 90,000**

Liepāja's irrepressible party spirit and exuberant embrace of design make it one of Latvia's hippest cities. Known as 'the cradle of Latvian rock', the city doesn't turn out bands like it used to, but it has two of the world's funkiest clubs and a great beach where the Baltics' craziest summer beach party is held.

**Liepāja Tourist Information Office** ( ☎ 2348 0808; www.liepaja.lv/turisms; Rožu laukums iela 11; ☻ 9am-7pm Mon-Fri, 9am-4pm Sat, 10am-3pm Sun May-Sep, 9am-5pm Mon-Fri Oct-Apr) can help with accommodation and has details on getting to Liepāja's one must-see attraction, **Karosta Prison**, in the crumbling Karosta district south of the centre. Among the tours here is the quirky and unique 'prison experience' tour that involves donning prisoner garb and spending the night. Whilst in Karosta check out the crumbling old Tsarist forts slipping into the sea and the ubiquitous red-brick turn-of-the-century architecture.

### Sleeping & Eating

**Hotel Fontaine** ( ☎ 2342 0956; www.fontaine.lv; Jūras iela 24; r from 15Ls; ⓟ 🖳 ) Liepāja's reputation as a boutique haven rests largely on the doorstep of this kitschy hotel. The themed rooms here are brimming over with curiosities such as old Soviet army footlockers, B-movie posters, and quilted bedspreads. Reception doubles as a curiosity shop, crammed with dusty Soviet-era gas masks and an array of secondhand clothing.

More fastidious types might prefer the more minimalist boutique **Porins** ( ☎ 2915 0596; www.porins.lv; Palmu iela 5; s/d 18/25Ls; ⓟ ) or the **Beach Hotel Liepāja** ( ☎ 2342 2095; www.liepajahotel.lv; Kr. Barona 14; s/d 15/30Ls; ⓟ ).

Porins and Pablo (see Entertainment) have good restaurants, or for something a little fancier try **Vecais Kapteinis** ( ☎ 342 5522; Dubelsteina iela 14; mains 3-7Ls), a marvellous seafood restaurant that also serves meat and pasta dishes.

### Entertainment

**Fontaine Palace** ( ☎ 2348 8510; www.fontainepalace.lv; Dzirnavu iela 4) If you like Hotel Fontaine, you'll love this inimitable nightclub–concert venue

housed in a gorgeous 18th-century warehouse. Note the giant phallus standing at attention over the main dance floor.

**Pablo** ( ☎ 2348 1555; www.pablo.lv; Zivju iela 4/6) Liepāja's other stroke of genius is this four-storey party palace, also known as 'Latvia's 1st Rock Café'. It's essentially a shrine to Latvian rock'n'roll, complete with a live-music stage, restaurant and rollicking nightclub.

Every July Pablo helps throw the **Baltic Beach Party** (www.balticbeachparty.lv), fast becoming a must-stop on the Eastern Europe party circuit. In August it helps put on the **Amber of Liepāja** (www.liepajasdzintars.lv) rock festival.

### Getting There & Away

Buses run to/from Kuldīga (2.20Ls, 1¼ hours, eight daily) and Ventspils (3.40Ls, two hours, seven daily), and there are several buses (4.30Ls, 3¼ hours) and one early morning train (3.40Ls, 3¼ hours) to/from Rīga.

# LATVIA DIRECTORY

## ACCOMMODATION

Rīga was already becoming popular before Ryanair entered the scene in 2005, resulting in a huge spike in both stag parties and more civilised forms of tourism, and making it hard to get a room in the peak season (June to August). Several Rīga hotels opened and/or expanded in advance of the May 2005 World Ice Hockey Championships, which has alleviated the room crunch somewhat, but you should still book well in advance.

A recent spate of hostel openings in Rīga means a cheap bed is no longer so hard to come by – but again, book ahead. You can find listings for hostels across Latvia and book beds at the website of the **Latvian Youth Hostel Association** (www.hostellinglatvia.com). Prices range from 5Ls to 15Ls per night. There are plenty of good camping grounds across the country, both with and without facilities.

For a double room in the high season expect to pay 25Ls to 40Ls for budget lodging in Rīga, and up to 150Ls at the top end. You'll pay much less in the regions, where good budget rooms start at about 12Ls. Rates are typically at least 20% cheaper during the low season (generally around October to April).

LATVIA

## ACTIVITIES

With hectare after hectare of unspoilt forest and national parkland, Latvia is ideal for camping, hiking, bird-watching, berry-picking, mushrooming or picnicking in the woods.

Sigulda (p428), on the border of the Gauja National Park, is a haven for adventure enthusiasts looking to float the Gauja River, bungee jump, bobsled, or ski down one of Latvia's modest slopes. Argonaut Hostel (p422) runs a series of unique adventure tours, many of them around Sigulda.

The country's extensive coastline lends itself to kiteboarding and windsurfing – notoriously windy Liepāja (p433) is a hotbed. Locals simply love to while away the winter hours ice fishing on the country's many lakes and estuaries.

## BUSINESS HOURS

Most shops open between 10am and 6pm in the larger towns and cities on weekdays and Saturdays. Banks generally open from 9am to 5pm weekdays. Most bars and restaurants open between 10am and noon and close around 11pm. Bars and some restaurants stay open much later on weekends – until 2am or till the last customer leaves.

## DISABLED TRAVELLERS

The cobbled streets of Rīga's Old Town make life difficult for wheelchair users, but the city is slowly coming around, and about half the city's buses (but none of the trams or trolleybuses) are now equipped for disabled travellers. Most of the newer hotels have at least a couple of rooms kitted out for disabled travellers.

## EMBASSIES & CONSULATES

Check www.mfa.gov.lv/en/ministry/mission for a full listing of Latvian missions abroad and foreign missions in Latvia.

### Latvian Embassies & Consulates Abroad

**Australia** ( ☎ 02-9744 5981; dalins@optusnet.com.au; 32 Parnell St, Strathfield NSW 2135)
**Canada** ( ☎ 613-238 6014; www.ottawa.am.gov.lv; 350 Sparks Street, Suite 1200, Ottawa, Ontario, K1R 7S8)
**Estonia** ( ☎ 2-627 7850; embassy.estonia@mfa.gov.lv; Tõnismägi 10, EE10119 Tallinn)
**France** ( ☎ 01 53 64 58 10; www.paris.am.gov.lv; 6 Villa Said, 75116 Paris)
**Germany** ( ☎ 030-8260 02 22; www.am.gov.lv/berlin; Reinerzstrasse 40-41, D-14193 Berlin)

**Ireland** ( ☎ 01 662 1610; embassy.ireland@mfa.gov.lv; 14 Lower Leeson St, Dublin 2)
**Lithuania** ( ☎ 52-131 220; embassy.lithuania@mfa.gov.lv; Čiurlionio gatvė 76, LT-03100 Vilnius)
**Russia** ( ☎ 495-232 9760; www.am.gov.lv/lv/moscow; ul Chapligina 3, Moscow)
**UK** ( ☎ 020-7312 0040; www.london.am.gov.lv; 45 Nottingham Place, London W1U 5LY)
**USA** ( ☎ 202-328-2840; www.latvia-usa.org; 2306 Massachusetts Avenue NW, Washington, DC 20008)

### Embassies & Consulates in Latvia

The following diplomatic offices are in Rīga.
**Australia** ( ☎ 2722 4251; australia@apollo.lv; Arhitektu iela 1-305)
**Canada** ( ☎ 2781 3945; www.dfait-maeci.gc.ca/canada-europa/baltics; Baznīcas iela 20/22)
**Estonia** ( ☎ 2781 2020; www.estemb.lv; Skolas iela 13)
**France** ( ☎ 2703 6600; www.ambafrance-lv.org; Raiņa bulv 9)
**Germany** ( ☎ 2708 5100; www.deutschebotschaft-riga.lv; Raiņa bulv 13)
**Lithuania** ( ☎ 2732 1519; http://lv.urm.lt; Rūpniecības iela 24)
**Russia** ( ☎ 2733 2151; www.latvia.mid.ru; Antonijas iela 2)
**UK** ( ☎ 2777 4700; www.britain.lv; Alunāna iela 5)
**USA** ( ☎ 2703 6200; www.usembassy.lv; Raiņa bulv 7)

## FESTIVALS & EVENTS

During the midsummer **Līgo** celebration on the night of 23 June (St John's Eve), the entire country retreats to feast on country food, jump over fires and reenact other pagan rituals. It's not always the best time to visit, however: Latvians joke (somewhat justifiably) that 'it always rains on Līgo'.

Undoubtedly Latvia's biggest festival, held every five years, is its **national song festival** (www.dziesmusvetki2008.lv). The 24th edition of the festival is scheduled for 2008.

Latvia hosts the pan-Baltic **Baltica International Folklore Festival** every three years; the next one is scheduled for 2009.

## GAY & LESBIAN TRAVELLERS

The Baltics first gay pride event – a march in Rīga in July 2005 – was a milestone for gay-rights activists. Rīga's gay scene revolves around established club XXL (p425). Compared to gay scenes across the rest of Europe, Latvia's is a fledgling operation but no less fun. There are links to gay and lesbian clubs, groups and information at www.gay.lv (in Latvian).

# HOLIDAYS

Latvia's official public holidays:

**New Year's Day** 1 January
**Good Friday** March/April
**Easter Sunday** March/April
**Day after Easter** March/April
**Convocation of the Constitutional Assembly of Latvia** 1 May
**Declaration of Independence from USSR** 4 May
**Mother's Day** 2nd Sunday in May
**Ligo** 23 June, Midsummer Night (St John's Eve)
**Jani** 24 June, Midsummer Day (St John's Day)
**National Day** Anniversary of proclamation of Latvian Republic, 1918, on 18 November
**Christmas Eve & Day** 24 and 25 December
**Boxing Day** 26 December
**New Year's Eve** 31 December

# INTERNET ACCESS

Rīga has myriad 24-hour internet cafés and most reasonably sized provincial towns have a few places to log on. If you are paying much more than 0.50Ls per hour you are getting ripped off.

Rīga airport, some provincial hotels and many cafés, restaurants and hotels in Rīga provide paid wi-fi access through the monopolistic national telecoms company **Lattelkom** (per hour/day 0.95/9.95Ls). A few hotels in Rīga offer wi-fi free of charge to guests, but free wi-fi is not nearly as ubiquitous in Latvia as it is in neighbouring Lithuania and Estonia.

# LANGUAGE

Latvian is one of only two surviving Baltic branches of the Indo-European language group (the other is Lithuanian). It is distantly related to the Germanic and Slavic language families.

Russian is the first language of 37.5% of Latvians, and is widely understood by anybody over the age of 25. You should have no trouble getting by with English in Rīga. Knowledge of English is growing in the provinces, but learning a few Latvian phrases is a good idea.

# MONEY

The national currency is the Lat (Ls). One Lat equals 100 santīmi and is roughly equivalent in value to a British pound. Latvia was originally planning to adopt the euro by 2008, but because of high inflation this does not look likely to happen before 2010.

You should be able to find an ATM machine in any town where humans outnumber barnyard animals. Most big banks cash travellers cheques and most major currencies. Credit cards are widely accepted.

National bank **Latvijas Bankas** (www.bank.lv) posts exchange rates on its website.

# POST

Latvia's postal system is almost completely reliable. It costs 0.36/0.45Ls to send a postcard/letter to Europe and 0.40/0.55 to other countries. Mail to North America takes about 10 days, and to Europe about a week. Stamps are sold at a post office (*pasts*).

# TELEPHONE

Both mobile and fixed Latvian telephone numbers have seven digits. As of 2007 you have to dial a 2 before *any* number (both mobile and fixed), but there are no city codes. To make a call, simply dial 2 followed by the seven-digit number (of course you must also dial the country code ☎ 371, if you're calling from outside the country).

Calls can be made from cardphones using a telekarte, worth 2Ls, 3Ls or 5Ls and sold at kiosks and post offices, or with a major credit card; instructions in English are included in every booth. International cards are done by **Telenets** (www.telenets.lv) and **lattelekom** (www.lattelekom.lv). To make an international call, dial the international access code ☎ 00, followed by the country code, city code and number.

If you're going to be around for awhile, pick up a local SIM card (basically free with the purchase of credits) from any kiosk or supermarket and stick it in your mobile phone. The options are **Latvijas Mobilais Telfons' Okarte** (www.lmt.lv) and **Tele2** (www.tele2.lv). Local calls cost around 0.20Ls per minute, and you can send texts abroad for a nominal fee (international calls, on the other hand, will sap your credits in a hurry!). Mobile telephones likewise have seven digits and need no area code.

---

**EMERGENCY NUMBERS**

- Emergency ☎ 112
- Police ☎ 02
- Fire ☎ 01
- Ambulance ☎ 03

## VISAS

Holders of EU passports don't need a visa to enter Latvia; nor do Australian, Canadian, Israeli, New Zealand, Swiss and US citizens, if staying for less than 90 days. South Africans are among some nationalities that do require visas. For information on obtaining visas and seeing if you need one, please visit www.mfa .gov.lv/en/service/visas.

# TRANSPORT IN LATVIA

## GETTING THERE & AWAY

### Air

All flights to Latvia land at **Riga international airport** (RIX; ☎ 2720 7009; www.riga-airport.com), which has flight schedules and a full list of airlines flying to Rīga on its website. There is no departure tax.

Latvia's flagship carrier is **Air Baltic** (www .airbaltic.lv; ☎ 2720 7777), with direct flights to about 30 cities in Europe.

Other major carriers with direct flights to Rīga include the following:

**Aeroflot** ( ☎ 2724 0228; www.aeroflot.ru)
**AeroSvit** ( ☎ 2720 7502; www.aerosvit.ua)
**Air Lingus** ( ☎ 2735 7736; www.aerlingus.com)
**Austrian Airlines** ( ☎ 2750 7700; www.aua.com)
**British Airways** ( ☎ 2720 7097; www.britishairways.com)
**Czech Airlines** ( ☎ 2720 7636; www.czech-airlines.com)
**KLM** ( ☎ 2766 8600; www.klm.com)
**LOT** ( ☎ 2722 7234; www.lot.com)
**Lufthansa** ( ☎ 2750 7711; www.lufthansa.com)

### Land

#### BORDER CROSSINGS

Lines are small at the Lithuania and Estonia borders and shouldn't hold you up more than 10 minutes. Have your passport, insurance and registration documents ready to expedite the process. See opposite for information on road rules and car hire.

If you're planning on crossing into Russia or Belarus in a rental car, check your rental conditions very carefully, most rental companies forbid this. For all road crossings into Russia or Belarus, see the boxed text on p929.

#### BUS

International bus companies **Eurolines** ( ☎ 2721 4080; www.eurolines.lv) and **Ecolines** ( ☎ 2721 4512; www .ecolines.lv) are based at the Rīga bus station.

Eurolines and a few smaller carriers have buses from Rīga to Vilnius (7.50Ls, five hours, at least four daily), Moscow (15Ls, 17 hours, two daily), Tallinn (7Ls, 4½ hours, 10 to 15 daily), St Petersburg (12Ls, 13 hours, two daily) and Kaliningrad (8.50Ls, nine hours, two daily).

Ecolines and Eurolines serve various cities in Poland, Germany and other Western European countries, including Warsaw (22Ls, 10 hours, daily), Berlin (30Ls, 20 hours, daily) and London (81Ls, 36 hours, four weekly). See their websites for full schedules.

#### TRAIN

Rīga is linked by direct train to the following international destinations: Moscow (from 25Ls, 18 hours, twice daily), St Petersburg (from 10Ls, 13 hours, daily), Kyiv (from 25Ls, 20½ hours, even days October to May, daily June to September), Lviv (from 18Ls, 26 hours, even days), and Vilnius (from 10Ls, five hours, even days). Visit www.ldz.lv for updated international train schedules.

### Sea

Tickets for all ferries can be purchased through the carriers or through travel agents. Schedules change often and vary according to season.

#### RĪGA

**DFDS Tor Line** ( ☎ 2735 3523; www.dfdstorline.lv; Zivju iela 1) goes to/from Lübeck, Germany (from 45Ls, 34 hours, two weekly). Estonia's **Tallink** ( ☎ 2709 9700; www.tallink.lv; Eksporta iela 3a) goes to/ from Stockholm (from 25Ls, 16 hours, every other day).

#### VENTSPILS

Tickets for most ferries originating in Ventspils must be bought at the **ferry information office** ( ☎ 2360 7358; 7 Plosta iela). **Scandlines** (www .scandlines.lt) goes to/from Rostock, Germany (from €40, 27 hours, four weekly); Karlshamn, Sweden (info@becoship.se; from 55Ls, 17 hours, three weekly); and Nynäshamn, Sweden (jacob.norling@bourgergroup.se; from 50Ls, 11 hours, five weekly). **SSC** ( ☎ 2371 3607; ventspils@slkferries.ee; 5 Plosta iela) goes to/from Mõntu, Estonia (from 15Ls, four hours, four weekly).

## GETTING AROUND

### Air

There are no commercial domestic flights (Latvia's too tiny!).

## Bicycle

Cycling is a great way to get around, as Latvia is as flat as a *blini* and its once-dismal roads are increasingly well-kept. The 160km ride from Rīga up to Cape Kolka (p431) is an excellent two- to three-day ride. The **Latvian Bicycle Tourism Information Centre** (www.velokurjers.lv; Jēkabpils iela 19a) in Rīga has cycling advice.

## Bus

Buses are quicker, cheaper and more frequent than trains. Timetables are to the right inside Rīga's bus station. Carefully check schedules so as not to get stranded at your destination; along some of these routes the last bus of the day departs as early as 6pm.

| Destination | Cost | Duration | Frequency |
| --- | --- | --- | --- |
| Bauska | 1.60Ls | 1½hr | at least hourly |
| Cēsis | 2Ls | 2hr | at least 2 hourly |
| Kolka | 3.40Ls | 5hr | 2 daily |
| Kuldīga | 3.30Ls | 3¼hr | at least hourly |
| Liepāja | 4.30Ls | 3¼hr | at least hourly |
| Sigulda | 1Ls | 1hr | at least 3 hourly |
| Ventspils | 4.30Ls | 3¼hr | hourly |

## Car & Motorcycle

Driving is the best way to get around the Latvian countryside. The road network is extensive and the roads in pretty good shape, even if most 'highways' are simple two-lane jobs. To drive from one end of the country to the other shouldn't take much more than four hours.

Driving is on the right-hand side. There's zero tolerance of drinking and driving (and a hefty fine of 500Ls plus a possible 15-day jail sentence if caught). Speed limits are generally 50km/h within towns and between 70km/h and 110km/h on highways), and are vigorously enforced. Headlights must be on at all times while driving.

Of all the airport's car-rental agencies, **Budget** ( ☎ 2720 7327) seems to have the cheapest economy cars. Others airport agencies include **National** ( ☎ 720 7710) and **Europcar** ( ☎ 2720 7825), which has discounts for Rīga Card holders. You can generally save money by renting an older car from a local agency, such as **Auto** ( ☎ 2958 0448), which can also supply you with a driver. Car-rental companies usually allow you to drive in all three Baltic countries, but not beyond.

To drive in Latvia you're technically required to have an International Driving Permit, but most rental car agencies won't hold you to it, nor will the cops.

## Hitching

Hitching is never totally safe, and Lonely Planet doesn't recommend it. That said, hitching is popular in certain areas of the country, especially around Sigulda and Cēsis, and will often save you a lengthy bus wait.

## Local Transport

Most reasonably sized cities have excellent public transport networks featuring a mix of trams, buses and trolleybuses (buses attached to overhead electric wires). Tickets generally cost 0.20Ls and can be bought on board. In smaller towns, such as Sigulda, taking a taxi may save you a long wait. For tips on public transport in Rīga see p426.

## Train

Train travel in Latvia is deliberate, to say the least, but the country is so small that it hardly matters. Suburban trains are the best way to get from Rīga to Jūrmala (0.51Ls, 40 minutes, at least two hourly) and are a reasonable way to get from Rīga to Sigulda (0.71Ls, one hour, 12 daily), Cēsis (1.10Ls, 1½ hours, five daily) and Liepāja (3.40Ls, three hours, daily). For complete domestic train timetables see www.ldz.lv.

**LATVIA**

# Lithuania

The image of the reticent Balt fades away when you enter iconoclastic Lithuania, a country dripping with history and boasting enough star attractions to make Unesco drool four times over.

It's so small you could miss it on a map, but it has done some big things over the years, most notably becoming the first country to formally declare its independence from the Soviet Union. It almost slew another superpower in 2000 when its basketball team came within a basket of beating the US 'Dream Team' at the Athens Olympics. The team settled for its third straight bronze – one of the greatest overachievements in sporting history.

Such large deeds bring to mind the large place Lithuania once was. In the 1400s the country extended all the way to the Black Sea. The good times wouldn't last, but even today Lithuanians brim with pride and confidence befitting their mighty heritage.

They certainly have a lot to be proud of. For starters there's effortlessly charming Vilnius and its skyline of baroque spires. The eerie Hill of Crosses near Šiaulia is a truly unique experience. In the west thousands of migratory birds make the Curonian Spit their primary port of call. With the arrival of budget airlines, more tourists are likewise making Lithuania a port of call, but don't let that scare you away. There are plenty of delights to go around in this Baltic beauty.

## FAST FACTS

- **Area** 65,300 sq km
- **Capital** Vilnius
- **Currency** litas (Lt); A$1 = 2.03 Lt; €1 = 3.45 Lt; ¥100 = 2.37 Lt; NZ$1 = 2.03 Lt; UK£1 = 4.99 Lt; US$1 = 2.70 Lt
- **Famous for** basketball, baroque churches, *cepelinai* (dough shaped like zeppelins, stuffed with meat and potato)
- **Official Language** Lithuanian
- **Phrases** *labas* (hello), *ačiū* (thanks), *prašau* (please/you're welcome), *taip* (yes), *ne* (no), *viso gero* (goodbye)
- **Population** 3.45 million
- **Telephone Codes** country code ☎ 370; international access code ☎ 00
- **Visa** none required for stays of up to 90 days for Australian, Canadian, EU, New Zealand or US citizens

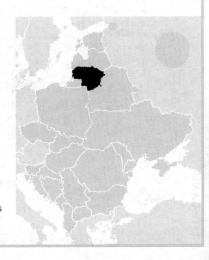

LITHUANIA

80 km
50 miles

To Minsk

BELARUS

Maltra
E262
A13
Agona
Preili
Kräslava
Atašiene
Ivári
Daugavpils
A6
E262
Ilükste
LATVIA
E22
Daugava
Zarasai
Vesplinas
Subate
Akniste
Dūkštos
Uzpaliai
Daugailiai
Utena
Aukštaitija NP
Paluše
Ignalina
Jēkabpils
Viešite
Nereta
Suviniškis
Pandelys
Rokiškis
Švedasai
Anykščiai
A6
Molėtai
Sveizionys
Giedraičiai
Pabradé
Nemenčine
Vilnius
A3
Juozapine (294m)
E85
Dieveniškes
Biržai
Saločiai
Pasvalys
Pampėnai
Kupiškis
Ragava
E272
Ukmergė
E262
A2
Neris
Maišiagala
Trakai
Kernavė
E85
Švenčionys
Dievenškes
Bauska
A7
Pilsundale
Žeimelis
Linkuva
A10
Smilgiai
Panevėžys
A8
E67
Šeta
A6
Jonava
E262
Kaišiadorys
A1
Vievis
Lentvaris
Trakai Istorinė NP
A16
E28
Rūdiškes
Satekškos
E85
Eišiškes
Bielai
E77
Žagarė
Joniškis
Gruzdžiai
A12
E272
Šiauliai
A9
Radviliškis
Grinkiškis
Raseiniai
Kėdainiai
A1
E85
Kaunas
E67
Darsūniškis
Prienai
A16
E28
Marijampolė
A4
Varėna
Marcinkonys
Auce
Papile
Kuršėnai
A12
E77
Kelmė
Šiluvė
Erzvilkas
Jurbarkas
Nemunas
Simkaičiai
Sakiai
Kutuzovo
Vilkaviškis
E28
A7
Kalvarija
E67
Suwałki
Lazdijai
Merkinė
Druskininkai
Dzūkija NP
Alytus
A3
Seštokai
Kybartai
To Warsaw (220km)
Mažeikiai
Seda
Tryškiai
Varniai
Žarėnai
Laukuva
A1
E85
A12
E77
Tauragė
Šilalė
Skaudvilė
Viešvilė
Nēšvkove
POLAND
Elk
Kibūri
Krumini
Medininkai
Skuodas
Barėnai
E272
A11
Plungė
Žemaitija NP
Rietavas
Žemaičiu Naumiestis
Silutė
Švekšna
Gargždai
Priekulė
Sovetsk
Chernyakhovsk
E28
RUSSIA
To Liepāja
Klaipėda
Palanga
Smiltynė
Kretinga
A13
Juodkrantė
Neringa
Nida
Curonian Spit NP
Curonian Spit
Nemunas Delta Regional Park
Žemaičiu Naumiestis
Svetlogorsk
Zelenogradsk
Kaliningrad
E28
A1
Svetlogorsk
BALTIC SEA
Curonian Lagoon
Baltiysk
E77
Olsztyn

## HIGHLIGHTS

- Exploring beautiful baroque **Vilnius** (p443), with its cobbled streets and skyline of church spires.
- Hearing the wind breathe between the thousands of crosses at the eerie Hill of Crosses in **Šiauliai** (p459).
- Breathing the pure air within the fragrant pine forests and high sand dunes of the enchanting **Curonian Spit** (p463).
- Checking out the stunning island castle in **Trakai** (p454), home of the rare Karaite people.
- Leaving people behind and chasing critters at **Aukštaitija National Park** (p455).

## ITINERARIES

- **Three days** Explore Vilnius for two days (p446), then day-trip to Trakai to explore its spectacular island castle and the homesteads of the Karaite people, stopping off at Paneriai on the way.
- **One week** Spend four nights in Vilnius with day trips to both Trakai and the Soviet Sculpture Park near Druskininkai. Go to Šiauliai to see the Hill of Crosses, then spend two or three days exploring some serious nature on the Curonian Spit. Head back east via Klaipėda and Kaunas.

## CLIMATE & WHEN TO GO

Lithuania tends to have a beautiful but short summer, a crisp autumn, a long winter and a dreary spring. Summer is the ideal time for

---

### HOW MUCH?

- **Public transport ticket** 1.10 Lt
- **Loaf of bread** 1 Lt
- **Two-scoop ice cream** 2 Lt
- **Bottle of vodka** 10 Lt
- **Short taxi ride** 10 Lt

### LONELY PLANET INDEX

- **Litre of petrol** 2.5 Lt
- **Litre of water** 2 Lt
- **Bottled beer in store/bar** 2/5 Lt
- **Souvenir T-shirt** 20 Lt
- **Street snack (hot dog)** 3 Lt

---

forays to coastal areas and inland national parks. Vilnius is enchanting any time of the year, but is much less crowded in the winter.

## HISTORY

Lithuania's history is a story of riches to rags and then back to riches again. It all started when ancient tribes fanned out across the Baltics to take advantage of the region's plentiful amber deposits. In 1009 those tribes were sufficiently assimilated for Lithuania to be mentioned for the first time in writing. Vilnius will open its reconstructed Royal Palace on the 1000-year anniversary of this event in 2009 (p447).

By the 12th century Lithuania's peoples had split into two tribal groups: the Samogitians (lowlanders) in the west and the Aukštaitiai (highlanders) in the east and southeast. In the mid-13th century Aukštaitiai leader Mindaugas unified Lithuanian tribes to create the Grand Duchy of Lithuania, of which he was crowned king in 1253 at Kernavė (p454).

It was the mighty Lithuanian leader Gediminas who pushed Lithuania's borders south and east between 1316 and 1341. In 1386 marriage forged an alliance with Poland against the Teutonic Order – Germanic crusaders who were busy conquering much of the region – that lasted 400 years. The alliance defeated the German knights in 1410 at the battle of Grünwald in Poland, ushering in a golden period during which Vilnius was born and Lithuania became one of Europe's largest empires.

But Lithuania was destined to disappear off the maps of Europe. In the 18th century, the Polish–Lithuanian state was so weakened by division that it was carved up by Russia, Austria and Prussia (successor to the Teutonic Order) in the partitions of Poland (1772, 1793 and 1795–96).

Vilnius was a bastion of Polish culture in the 19th century and a focus of uprisings against Russia. It also became an important Jewish centre; Jews made up almost half of its 160,000-strong population by the early 20th century (p448).

Lithuanian nationalists declared independence on 16 February 1918 with Kaunas as the capital, as Polish troops had annexed Vilnius from the Red Army in 1920. Lithuania's first president, Antanas Smetona, ruled the country with an iron fist during this time.

In 1940, after the Molotov–Ribbentrop Pact, Lithuania was forced into the USSR. Within a year 40,000 Lithuanians were killed

LITHUANIA

or deported. Up to 300,000 more people, mostly Jews, died in concentration camps and ghettos during the 1941–44 Nazi occupation, many of them at Paneriai (p453).

The USSR ruled again between 1945 and 1991. An estimated 250,000 people were murdered or deported to Siberia while armed partisans resisted Soviet rule from the forests. The bloody period of resistance, which petered out in 1953, is chronicled in a brand-new wing of Vilnius' Museum of Genocide Victims (p449).

In the late 1980s Lithuania led the Baltic push for independence. The popular front, Sajūdis, won 30 seats in the March 1989 elections for the USSR Congress of People's Deputies. Lithuania was the first Soviet state to legalise noncommunist parties. In February 1990 Sajūdis was elected to form a majority in Lithuania's new Supreme Soviet (now the parliament), which on 11 March declared Lithuania independent.

Moscow marched troops into Vilnius and cut off Lithuania's fuel supplies. On 13 January 1991, Soviet troops stormed key buildings in Vilnius. Fourteen people were killed at Vilnius' TV tower and Lithuanians barricaded the Seimas (their parliament). In the wake of heavy condemnation from the West, the Soviets recognised Lithuanian independence on 6 September, bringing about the first of the Baltic republics.

The last Soviet troops left the country on 31 August 1993. Lithuania replaced the rouble with the litas, joined NATO in April 2004, and entered the EU a month later. True to form, bold Lithuania forthrightly ratified the EU constitution in November 2004, becoming the first of the 25 EU member countries to do so.

Lithuania's eager embrace of all things European hit a speed bump in May 2006 when the EU rejected Lithuania's bid to adopt the euro, citing inflation concerns. The country now hopes to adopt the common currency in 2009 at the earliest. But despite that, and despite an animated political climate that saw a president impeached over corruption allegations in 2004, proud Lithuania remains unabashedly optimistic about its future.

## PEOPLE

Easily the most ethnically homogeneous population of the three Baltic countries, Lithuanians count for 83% of the total population. Poles form 6.7% and Russians 6.3%.

Lithuanians are an outgoing, cheeky bunch, especially compared with their reticent neighbours in Latvia and Estonia. That has led some to call them the 'Spanish of the Baltics'. Others call them the 'Italians of the Baltics', citing their fierce pride – a result of the many brutal attempts to eradicate their culture and the memories of their long-lost empire.

## ARTS

Lithuania's best-known national artist will always be Mikalojus Konstantinas Čiurlionis (1875–1911), a depressive painter who also composed symphonic poems and piano pieces. The best collection of his paintings are in the National Čiurlionis Art Museum in Kaunas (p457).

Lithuania has a thriving contemporary art scene. Vilnius artists created the tongue-in-cheek Republic of Užupis (p449), which hosts alternative art festivals, fashion shows and exhibitions in its breakaway state. Other home-grown artists can be seen at **Europas Parkas Sculpture Park** (www.europosparkas.lt) at the geographical centre of Europe (19km from Vilnius; ask a tourist office for details).

Music is at the heart of the Lithuanian spirit, and Lithuania is the jazz giant of the Baltics, with its highlight the Kaunas Jazz Festival.

Lithuanian fiction began with the late-18th-century poem 'Metai' (The Seasons) by Kristijonas Donelaitis. Antanas Baranauskas' 1860 poem 'Anykščiai Pine Forest' uses the forest as a symbol of Lithuania. Literature suffered persecution from the tsarist authorities, who banned the use of the Latin alphabet.

Several major Polish writers grew up in Lithuania and regarded themselves as partly Lithuanian, most notably Adam Mickiewicz (1798–1855), the inspiration of 19th-century nationalists, whose great poem 'Pan Tadeusz' begins 'Lithuania, my fatherland…'

## ENVIRONMENT
### The Land

Lush forests and more than 4000 lakes mark the landscape of Lithuania, a country that is largely flat with a 100km-wide lowland centre. Forest covers a third of the country and contain creatures such as wild boar, wolves, deer and elk. Aukštaitija National Park (p455) is one place where these beasts roam, although you are unlikely to encounter them without a guide. You're more likely to spot a stork –

Lithuania has Europe's highest concentration of storks, and their nests crop up in the unlikeliest places.

### Environmental Issues

A huge amount of EU money is being sunk into cleaning up Lithuania's environment, which continues to suffer from years of Soviet mismanagement and indifference.

For years the hot potato has been the Ignalina Nuclear Power Plant, 120km north of Vilnius. One of two reactors similar in design to Chornobyl was closed in December 2004, and the final shutdown of the plant is scheduled for 2009 at a massive cost of €3.2 billion.

Other problems Lithuania faces include the threat of large-scale pollution from a recently discovered arsenal of decomposing chemical weapons. About 40,000 bombs and mines lie on the seabed 70 nautical miles off Klaipėda, where Soviet forces sank German ships, and the cargo from these ships could threaten the fragile coastline of the Curonian Spit. The spit is also threatened by oil rigs being built offshore by Lukoil (p733).

The Būtingė oil terminal, off the northwestern coast near Latvia, continues to enrage environmentalists; it was the site of a 60-ton oil spill in November 2001.

To do your part for the environment, camp only in designated areas and, when required, keep to the marked trails on the sand dunes of the Curonian Spit and in other national parks.

### FOOD & DRINK

Unbuckle your belts for the gastronomic delights of good, hearty Lithuanian cooking. The food was tailor-made for those peasants out working the fields so it's seriously stodgy comfort eating rather than delicate morsels. Based on potatoes, meat and dairy goods, it's not ideal for vegetarians so we've highlighted options for those who shun the pleasures of pigs trotters and pork knuckles.

The national dish is the hearty, jiggle-when-they-wiggle *cepelinai* (zeppelins): airship-shaped parcels of thick potato dough stuffed with cheese, *mesa* (meat) or *grybai* (mushrooms). It comes topped with a rich sauce made from onions, butter, sour cream and bacon bits. Another artery-hardening favourite is sour cream–topped *kugelis*: a dish that bakes grated potatoes and carrots in the oven. *Koldūnai* are hearty ravioli stuffed with meat or mushrooms, and *virtiniai* are stodgy dumplings.

Lithuanians drink their share of *alus* (beer) and it's all pretty good. The most popular brand is vyturys, but try Utenos, Kalnapilis and Gubernija as well. No beer is complete without the world's most fattening bar snack, *kepta duona* (deep-fried black bread with garlic).

*Midus* (mead) originated in the Middle Ages but is making a comeback these days. It's made of honey boiled with water, berries and spices, then fermented with hops.

### RELIGION

Lithuania was the last pagan country in Europe, explaining why so much of its religious art, national culture and traditions have raw pagan roots. Today the country is 70% to 80% Roman Catholic by most estimates, with strong Lutheran and Russian Orthodox minorities.

# VILNIUS

☎ 5 / pop 600,000

Picture the quintessentially quaint Old World European capital, and chances are you'll come up with something pretty close to Vilnius. A spider web of cobbled streets snaking amid some of the world's most fantastic baroque churches, its appeal is blatant, its charm intoxicating.

It is essential to avoid tunnel vision as you walk around Vilnius. Its churches, too numerous to count, are pleasantly prone to present themselves perfectly framed by narrow streets. Look down, too: Vilnius was built on a swamp, and many buildings, especially along Pilies gatvė and Aušros Vartų gatvė, have sunk up to a metre below street level. Perhaps that explains the city's quirky streak, epitomised by a number of strange monuments (see p447) and by a decidedly animated political scene.

Vilnius feels tiny, but that's a bit deceptive because the sprawling suburban jacket that surrounds the Unesco-listed Old Town is a fairly typical Soviet-style mess of snarled traffic, car shops and concrete. Unlike, say, Rīga, there's not much reason to stray far from the Old Town, although the suburbs do support some mighty fine parks.

LITHUANIA

# VILNIUS

0 — 200 m
0 — 0.1 miles

To Russian Embassy (2km)

Ukmergės gatvė

To Kalvarijų Market (700m); Europas Parkas (19km)

Šeimyniškių gatvė

Upės gatvė

Kalvarijų gatvė

Juozapavičiaus gatvė

Žalgirio Stadium

To Kernavė (35km)

Neris

Goštauto gatvė

Žaliasis Tiltas

Žygimantų gatvė

Tumo-Vaižganto gatvė

Vasario 16-osios gatvė

Jaušo gatvė

Vienuolio gatvė

Vilniaus gatvė

Tilto gatvė

Lukiškių aikštė

To Seimas (400m); Pacha (400m); Estonian Embassy (1km); Orthodox Church of the Apparition (1km); Russian Embassy (2.4km)

To St Peter & Paul Church (600m)

To British Embassy (500m); Baltic-American Medical & Surgical Clinic (1km); Polish Embassy (2.5km)

Mindaugo Tiltas

Žvejų gatvė

Arsenalo gatvė

Kalnų Park

Savivaldybės aikštė

Gedimino prospektas

Pamėnkalnio gatvė

Jogailos gatvė

Taurakalnis

Gediminas Hill

Three Crosses Hill

Katedros aikštė

Totorių gatvė

Vrublevskio gatvė

Pylimo gatvė

To German Embassy (300m); Latvian Embassy (750m); Vingis Park (1.2km)

Kalinausko gatvė

Akmenų gatvė

Tauro gatvė

Liejyklos gatvė

Sereikiškių gatvė
Youth Park (Sereikiškių Parkas)

To Tores (250m); Filaretai Hostel (500m)

Stiklių gatvė

Dominikonų gatvė

Šventaragio gatvė

Barboros Radvilaitės gatvė

Universiteto gatvė

Daukanto aikštė

President's Palace

Vilnius University

Bernardinų gatvė

Sv Mykolo gatvė

Literatų gatvė

Maironio gatvė

Užupis

Vilnia

Krivų gatvė

Palangos gatvė

Klaipėdos gatvė

Trakų gatvė

Vilniaus gatvė

Sv Jono gatvė

Švarco gatvė

To Youth Tourist Centre (400m)

Užupio gatvė

Paupio gatvė

Basanavičiaus gatvė

To Lithuanian Student & Youth Travel Bureau (750m); Teacher's University Hostel (800m); Coca-Cola Plaza (800m); TV Tower (1.5km); Paneriai (10km); Trakai (28km); Kaunas (100km); Druskininkai (112km); Klaipėda (310km)

Pylimo gatvė

Volkočio gatvė

Žydų gatvė

Arklių gatvė

Karmelitų gatvė

Mikalojaus gatvė

Šv Stepono gatvė

Old Town

Savičiaus gatvė

Rokšto gatvė

Aukštaičių gatvė

To Paupio Namai (50m)

Rotušės aikštė

Lydos gatvė

Žemaitijos gatvė

Naugarduko gatvė

Ligoninės gatvė

Rūdninkų gatvė

Mėsinių gatvė

Šv kazimiero gatvė

Subačiaus gatvė

Aušros Vartų gatvė

Bazilijonų gatvė

To E-Guest House (400m); Mens Factory (400m)

Algirdo gatvė

Aguonų gatvė

Mindaugo gatvė

Sopeno gatvė

Sodų gatvė

Seinų gatvė

Daukšos gatvė

Rasų gatvė

Kauno gatvė

Šv Stepono gatvė

Geležinkelio gatvė

Pelesps gatvė

Pelesos gatvė

Liepkalnio gatvė

To Vilnius International Airport (4km)

Train Station

LITHUANIA

## ORIENTATION

Most of the action in Vilnius takes place in Old Town. Vokiečių gatvė is the most commercial street in Old Town; Pilies gatvė the most touristy. Old Town's northern border merges with New Town at Gedimino prospektas, a wide, part-time pedestrianised avenue that runs west-to-east from parliament to Katedros aikštė (Cathedral Square), the spiritual, if not the geographical, heart of Vilnius.

## INFORMATION
### Bookshops

**Akademinė Knyga** (Universiteto gatvė 4) Some translated Lithuanian works, and Lonely Planet travel guides.
**Littera** (Šv Jono gatvė 12) Inside Vilnius University courtyard; enter on Universiteto gatvė 3.

### Cultural Centres

**American Center** ( ☎ 266 5682; www.usembassy.lt/irc .asp; Pranciškonų gatvė 3-6; ⏰ 10am-5.30pm Mon-Fri) American media in a 14th-century monastery.
**British Council** ( ☎ 264 4890; www.britishcouncil .lt; Jogailos gatvė 4; ⏰ 11am-6pm Tue-Sat, closed 15 Jul-19 Aug)
**Centre Culturel Français** ( ☎ 231 2984; www.centre francais.lt; Didžioji gatvė 1; ⏰ 1.30-6.30pm Mon-Fri, 10am-3pm Sat)

### Internet Access & Telephone

Portions of Vokiečių gatvė, Pilies gatvė and Gedimino prospektas are free wi-fi zones.
**Alderada** (Pylimo gatvė 21; per hr 5 Lt; long-distance VOIP calls per min 0.12 Lt) Phone and internet.
**Collegium** (Pilies gatvė 22; per hr 8 Lt; ⏰ 8am-11pm) Good location; terrible prices.

**Omnitel** (Gedimino prospektas 12; per hr 2 Lt; ☾ 9am-6pm Mon-Sat) internet access.
**Renta Rentoma** (Stiklių gatvė 16; per hr 2 Lt; ☾ 10am-7pm) internet access.

## Left Luggage
Ask for the *bagažinė*.
**Bus station** (per bag per 24hr 3 Lt; ☾ 5.30am-9pm Mon-Sat, 7am-9pm Sun)
**Train station** (per bag per 24hr 3 Lt; ☾ 5.30am-9pm Mon-Fri, 7am-9pm Sat)

## Media
**Vilnius in Your Pocket** (www.inyourpocket.com/lithuania/en) Quality city guide published every two months, available as PDF download or in bookshops, tourist offices and newspaper kiosks (5 Lt).
**Baltic Times** (www.baltictimes.com) English-language weekly with pan-Baltic news and listings of cultural events in Vilnius.

## Medical Services
**24-hour pharmacy** (Gedimino Vaistinė; ☎ 261 0135; Gedimino prospektas 27)
**Baltic-American Medical & Surgical Clinic** ( ☎ 234 2020; www.bak.lt; Antakalnio gatvė 124; ☾ 24hr) English-speaking health care inside Vilnius University Antakalnis hospital, approximately 1km north of town.

## Money
Vilnius is littered with ATMs and banks, and most offer the usual exchange, money transfer, travellers cheques and cash-advance services. Many are concentrated on Vokiečių gatvė.
**American Express** ( ☎ 212 5805, 24hr emergency 8-616 81255; www.amextravel.lt; Vokiečių gatvė 13) Travel agency that replaces lost Amex travellers cheques.
**Parex Bankas Currency Exchange** (Geležinkelio gatvė 6; ☾ 24hr) Currency exchange with ATM; exit the train station and head left.

## Post
**Branch post office** (Vokiečių gatvė 7)
**Central post office** (Gedimino prospektas 7)

## Tourist Information
**Vilnius Tourist Information Centres** (www.vilnius-tourism.lt; ☾ 9am-6pm Mon-Fri, 10am-4pm Sat & Sun); Town Hall ( ☎ 262 0762; Didžioji gatvė 31); Vilniaus gatvė ( ☎ 262 9660; Vilniaus gatvė 22); train station ( ☎ 269 2091) These friendly centres have a wealth of glossy brochures and general information. They also arrange tour guides, book accommodation (hotel reservation fee of 6 Lt applies), and rent bicycles for use in Old Town only.

## Travel Agencies
**Kelvita** ( ☎ 210 6130; www.kelvita.lt; train station international hall, kiosk 30; ☾ 8am-6pm Mon-Fri) No-frills agency with the cheapest Russian and Belarusian visas.
**Lithuanian Student & Youth Travel Bureau** ( ☎ 239 7397; www.jaunimas.lt, in Lithuanian; Basanavičiaus gatvė 30/13) Cheap fares for ISIC holders.
**Vilnius City Tour** ( ☎ 261 5558; www.vilniuscitytour.com; Aušros Vartų gatvė 7) Runs thrice-daily city tours and organises excursions outside Vilnius.

# SIGHTS
Baroque churches are what Vilnius is most famous for, but don't get caught up in rushing from church to church. Savour the walk around Old Town instead. Pop your head into a courtyard behind a centuries-old façade for a glimpse of everyday life in Vilnius: an old lady hanging laundry; men hovering over an open car-bonnet; rogue teens sneaking a smoke. A walk around Old Town at night, with the steeples illuminated by soft flood lights, is truly magical.

## Gediminas Hill & Cathedral Square
Vilnius was founded on 48m-high Gediminas Hill, topped since the 13th century by the oft-rebuilt tower of ruined **Gediminas Castle**. There are spectacular views of Old Town from the top of the tower, which houses the **Upper Castle Museum** ( ☎ 261 7453; adult/child 4/2 Lt; ☾ 10am-7pm May-Oct, 11am-5pm Tue-Sun Nov-Apr). From here you'll also see the white **Three Crosses** on a hill to the east, erected in memory of three crucified monks.

At the base of Gediminas Hill sprawls Cathedral Square (Katedros aikštė), dominated

---

**VILNIUS IN TWO DAYS**

Spend your first day taking in the magic of **Old Town** (opposite). Start off – naturally – at the **Gates of Dawn** (p448), then spend a few hours snaking your way toward **Cathedral Square** (above). Climb **Gediminas Hill** (above) for sunset, and crown the day with a home brew at **Avilys** (p452).

On day two, devote some time to the **Museum of Genocide Victims** (p449) and take in another museum or two near Cathedral Square. Then either explore the old **Jewish Quarter** (p448) or cross the Vilnia River into bohemian **Užupis** (p449), where another fine sunset panorama beckons at **Tores** (p451).

**TOP FIVE QUIRKY ATTRACTIONS**

Vilnius has an undeniable mischievous streak, as the following attest:

■ **Frank Zappa memorial** (Kalinausko gatvė 1) The world's first Zappa statue is oddly situated in a grim, graffiti-splashed courtyard west of Old Town. It was erected in 1995 by the local Zappa fan club.

■ **Angel of Užupis statue** (Užupio & Malūnro gatvė) This statue of an angel blowing a trumpet and standing on an egg is the oddball symbol of Vilnius' strangest district.

■ **Egg statue** (cnr Šv Stepono & Raugyklos gatvė) This oversized egg on a nest of real twigs resided on U upis' main square until it 'hatched' the Angel of U upis in 2002 and moved to a grim square west of Old Town.

■ **Žaliasis Tiltas (Green Bridge)** The sculptures on this bridge are a blatant reminder of Lithuania's communist past – and yet weren't torn down like the rest of the Lenins and comrades because the locals adore them!

■ **The ¿ building** (Kauno gatvė 5) This dilapidated building with an upside-down question mark dangling from its façade undoubtedly hides secrets behind its boarded-up windows.

by **Vilnius Cathedral** (☺ 7am-7.30pm, Sunday mass at 9am, 10am, 11.15am & 7pm) and its 57m-tall **belfry**, a Vilnius landmark. The square buzzes with local life, especially during Sunday morning mass. Amuse yourself by hunting for the secret *stebuklas* (miracle) tile, which if found can grant a wish if you stand on it and turn around clockwise. It marks the spot where the Tallinn–Vilnius human chain ended in 1989.

The first wooden cathedral, built here in 1387–88, was in Gothic style but has been rebuilt many times since then. The most important restoration was completed from 1783 to 1801, when the outside was redone in today's classical style. The interior retains more of its original aspect. Its showpiece is the baroque **St Casimir's Chapel**, with white stucco sculptures and frescoes depicting the life of St Casimir (Lithuania's patron saint), whose silver coffin lies within.

At the square's eastern end is an **equestrian statue of Gediminas**, built on an ancient pagan site. The massive construction project going on behind the statue, at the base of Gediminas Hill, is the rebuilding of the **Royal Palace** (Valdovů rumai). The palace buzzed with masked balls, gay banquets and tournaments in the 16th century. But in 1795 the Russians occupied Lithuania and demolished the palace along with the Lower Castle and city defence wall.

The palace is currently being rebuilt, red brick by red brick, and will rise from the ashes on 6 July 2009 to mark the millennium anniversary of the first known mention of Lithuania in writing. Archaeologists are digging up all kinds of ancient coins and other treasures as the project proceeds.

Exhibitions on the ambitious reconstruction project fill the must-see **Museum of Applied Arts** (☎ 262 8080; Arsenalo gatvė 3a; admission 8 Lt; ☺ 11am-6pm Tue-Sat, 11am-4pm Sun), in the old arsenal at the foot of Gediminas Hill. The museum also has many items from the original palace on display.

A little north of Cathedral Square, the **National Museum** (☎ 262 9426; Arsenalo gatvė 1; adult/child 4/2 Lt; ☺ 10am-5pm Tue-Sat, 10am-3pm Sun May-Sep, 10am-5pm Wed-Sun Oct-Apr) has ethnographic exhibits, art and other displays looking at Lithuanian life up to WWII. Exhibits are in Lithuanian and Russian.

East of Cathedral Square, magnificent **St Peter & Paul Church** is one of Vilnius' finest baroque churches. It's a treasure trove of sparkling white stucco sculptures of real and mythical people, animals and plants, with touches of gilt, paintings and statues. The decoration was done by Italian sculptors between 1675 and 1704.

## Old Town

Eastern Europe's largest old town deserves its Unesco status. The area stretches 1.5km south from Cathedral Square and the eastern end of Gedimino prospektas.

### VILNIUS UNIVERSITY & ST JOHN'S CHURCH

The students of **Vilnius University** (☎ 268 7298; Universiteto gatvė 3; adult/child 5/2.50 Lt; ☺ 9am-6pm Mon-Sat Mar-Oct, 9am-5pm Mon-Sat Nov-Feb) attend school

---

**JEWISH VILNIUS**

Dubbed by Napoleon as the 'Jerusalem of the north', Vilnius had one of Europe's most prominent Jewish communities until Nazi brutality virtually wiped it out (with assistance from the Soviets).

The old Jewish quarter lay in the streets west of Didžioji gatvė, including present-day Žydų gatvė (Jews St) and Gaono gatvė, named after Vilnius' most famous Jewish resident, Gaon Elijahu ben Shlomo Zalman (1720–97), a sage who recited the entire Talmud by heart at the age of six.

Jewish Vilnius is far too rich a topic to adequately cover here, but there are several excellent resources available if you want to dig deeper into Lithuania's Jewish past.

A good place to start your tour is at any of the three branches of the **Vilna Gaon Jewish State Museum of Lithuania** (www.jmuseum.lt): **The Green House** ( ☎ 262 0730; Pamėnkalnio gatvė 12; admission by donation; ☷ 9am-5pm Mon-Thu, 9am-4pm Fri, 10am-4pm Sun), dedicated to the holocaust in Lithuania; the **Tolerance Centre** ( ☎ 231 2356; Naugarduko gatvė 10; ☷ 9am-5pm Mon-Thu, 9am-4pm Fri, 10am-4pm Sun), which stages community events and exhibits the works of prominent Lithuanian Jewish artists; and another **branch** ( ☎ 212 7912; Pylimo gatvė 4; ☷ 9am-1pm Mon-Fri) that shares a building with the Jewish Community Centre. The city's Jewish population today numbers about 4000. The main **synagogue** (Pylimo gatvė 39) is near the Tolerance Centre.

All three museums sell the handy self-guide *Memorable Sites of Jewish History and Culture* (12 Lt). For a more casual glimpse of Jewish life, walk down Žydų gatvė to the memorial **bust of Gaon Elijahu** (Žydų gatvė 3), imagining how life once was. There's a **map** of the two main Jewish ghettos during WWII at Rūdninkų gatvė 18, which used to be the single gate to the largest ghetto.

---

on a spectacular campus featuring 13 courtyards framed by 15th-century buildings and splashed with 300-year-old frescoes.

Founded in 1579 during the Counter-Reformation, Eastern Europe's oldest university was run by Jesuits for two centuries and became one of the greatest centres of Polish learning before being closed by the Russians in 1832. It reopened in 1919.

The library here, with five million books, is Lithuania's oldest. The university also houses the world's first **Centre for Stateless Cultures** ( ☎ 268 7293; www.statelesscultures.lt), established for those cultures that lack statehood, such as Jewish, Roma and Karaimic (Karaite) cultures, in its history faculty.

You need to go through the university entrance on Universiteto to access both Littera bookshop (p445) and **St John's Church** ( ☷ 10am-5pm Mon-Sat), a baroque gem. Founded in 1387 – well before the university arrived – its 17th-century bell tower is the highest structure in Old Town.

You can exit (but not enter) St John's on Pilies gatvė, the hub of tourist action and the main entrance to the Old Town from Cathedral Square.

### THE GATES OF DAWN

Located at the southern border of Old Town, the 16th-century **Gates of Dawn** (Aušros Vartai)

is the only one of the town wall's original nine gates still intact. The gate houses the **Chapel of the Blessed Virgin Mary** ( ☷ 6am-7pm) and the black-and-gold 'miracle-working' **Virgin Mary icon**. A gift from the Crimea by Grand Duke Algirdas in 1363, it is one of the holiest icons in Polish Catholicism, and the faithful arrive in droves to offer it whispered prayer.

When the Russians destroyed the old city walls in the 18th century, they spared Aušros Vartai, fearing bad luck if they tampered with the resting place of the Virgin icon. The Soviets likewise refused to touch it. Look up as you're exiting Old Town and you can spot the icon through the window of the chapel.

There are four stunning churches in the immediately vicinity of the Gates of Dawn. Catholic **St Teresa's Church** is early baroque (1635–50) outside and more elaborate late baroque inside. Roughly behind it is the big, pink, domed 17th-century **Orthodox Church of the Holy Spirit**, Lithuania's chief Russian Orthodox church and another fine baroque specimen. Directly across the street, through a late baroque archway known as the **Basilian Gates** (Aušros Vartų gatvė 7), is the dilapidated **Holy Trinity Church**. And further up Aušros Vartų gatvė on the eastern side is ravishing **St Casimir's Church**, the oldest of Vilnius' baroque masterpieces. It was built by Jesuits (1604–15) and under Soviet rule was a museum of atheism.

## VOKIEČIŲ GATVĖ & AROUND

Vokiečių gatvė, Old Town's main commercial street, makes a good jumping-off point for explorations of the old Jewish quarter (opposite) and offers fine views of several churches. Peering north from Vokiečių you'll spot **St Catherine's Church** (Vilniaus gatvė 30) displaying Vilnius' trademark peach baroque style; to the south lies the unsung and similarly peach-hued **Church of All Saints** (Rūdninkų 20/1).

The **Holy Spirit Church** (Dominikonų gatvė 8) is Vilnius' primary Polish church (1679) and has one of the most elaborate baroque interiors you'll find anywhere. The recently reconsecrated **Church of the Assumption** (Trakų gatvė 9/1) is symbolic of the incredible renovation sweeping through the Old Town.

## New Town

Vilnius' 19th-century New Town boasts a true European boulevard after its premier street, Gedimino prospektas, was given a face-lift between 2002 and 2003. It's a grand road with Vilnius Cathedral at one end and the silver-domed **Orthodox Church of the Apparition** (Mickevičiaus 1) at the other. Much of Gedimino becomes a pedestrian street outside working hours, when fashionable types flock here to see, be seen and peruse the sundry Western brands on display in the shop fronts.

Lenin once stood on Lukiškių Aikštė, a square that used to bear the name of the levelled statue, which is now displayed in Druskininkai's Soviet sculpture park, Gruto Parkas (p455).

The building facing the square was the notorious KGB headquarters and prison, but is now the **Museum of Genocide Victims** ( ☎ 249 6264; muziejus@genocid.lt; Aukų gatvė 2a; admission 4 Lt; ☒ 10am-5pm Tue-Sat, 10am-3pm Sun). Called the 'KGB Museum' by locals, it is Vilnius' most important and most popular museum. It is best taken in with an English-speaking guide (30 Lt, reserve in advance) or headphone audio tour (8 Lt).

Names of those who were murdered in the former KGB prison are carved into the stone walls outside – note how young many victims were. Inside, inmate cells and the execution cell where prisoners were shot or stabbed in the skull between 1944 and the 1960s can be visited. Two new permanent exhibits recently opened: one documenting the post-WWII Lithuanian resistance movement, the other on the gulags.

At the west end of Gedimino prospektas is the **Seimas** (parliament) building. Further along lies pleasant **Vingis Park**, and beyond that the 326m-tall **TV Tower**, where wooden crosses remember the victims of 13 January 1991 (p442).

## Užupis

The cheeky streak of rebellion pervading Lithuania flourishes in this district just east of Old Town. In 1998 the resident artists, dreamers, squatters and drunks officially unofficially declared this a breakaway state known as the **Užupis Republic**. The state has its own tongue-in-cheek president, anthem, flags and a 41-point constitution that, among other things, gives inhabitants the right to cry, the right to be misunderstood and the right to be a dog. Read the entire thing in English, French or Lithuanian on a wall on Paupio gatvė.

The best time to visit Užupis is April Fool's Day. Mock border guards set up at the main bridge into town and stamp visitors' passports and a huge party rages all day and all night. However, it's worth visiting any time of year for its galleries, craft workshops and bohemian vibe.

Just over the Užupis' northern bridge you'll find baroque **Bernardine Church** and pint-sized Gothic **St Anne's Church** essentially fused together like mismatched Siamese twins.

## FESTIVALS & EVENTS

See p465 for more festivals, and a comprehensive list is at www.vilniusfestivals.lt.

**Vilnius Festival** A month-long summer festival (May to June) of classical music organised by the Lithuanian National Philharmonic Society.

**Vilnius Days** Five-day celebration of carnivals, street theatre, dancing, masked parades and craft fairs in the streets, in September.

## SLEEPING

For tips on booking accommodation in Vilnius, see p464.

### Budget

**Filaretai Hostel** ( ☎ 215 4627; www.filaretaihostel.lt; Filaretų gatvė 17; dm from 31 Lt; s/d with shared bathroom 68/86 Lt; ☐ ) A recent renovation has added rooms and polish to this chilled-out hostel in arty Užupis. If you want more privacy, the doubles are a great value. Take bus 34 to the Filaretų stop.

LITHUANIA

**Old Town Hostel** ( ☎ 262 5357; www.lithuanianhostels .org; Aušros Vartų gatvė 20/10; dm 32 Lt, d per person 100 Lt; 🖳 ) It's nothing special by world standards, but it sticks out in Vilnius because of its perfect location, two minutes from both Old Town and the train station. You'll have few problems finding a drinking buddy here.

**Paupio Namai** ( ☎ 264 3113; www.hotel.paupio.lt; Paupio gatvė 31a; dm/s/d with shared bathroom from 45/80/100 Lt; 🅿 🖳 ) Vilnius' best 'hostel' is actually more of a pension or a guesthouse. The small singles are a phenomenal option for solo travellers wary of communal living but keen on a cheap bed. There's a small kitchen.

**Litinterp** ( ☎ 212 3850; www.litinterp.lt; Bernardinų gatvė 7-2; s/d 100/160 Lt, with shared bathroom 80/140 Lt; 🅿 ) In year two of Lithuanian independence, the hotel gods looked upon the country's feeble accommodation selection and said, 'Let there be an unobtrusive guesthouse with bright pinewood floors that will forever remain the best deal in Vilnius,' and thus was born Litinterp. And it was good.

**Domus Maria** ( ☎ 264 4880; http://domusmaria.vil nensis.lt; Aušros Vartų gatvė 12; dm/s/d 75/179/249 Lt; 🅿 ✕ 🖳 ) Positively unique and immensely popular, this guesthouse-within-a-monastery captures the soul of Vilnius without capturing too much of your hard-earned cash. It stays true to its monastic origins with wide arched corridors and spartan white rooms. Laptop hire available for 50 Lt per day.

Other recommended hostels:

**Teacher's University Hostel** ( ☎ 213 0704; Vivulskio gatvė 36; d & tr per person with shared bathroom 24 Lt; deluxe d 120 Lt) Soviet through and through, but ultracheap. No self-catering.

**Youth Tourist Centre** ( ☎ 261 1547; vjtc@delfi.lt; Polocko gatvė 7; dm 26 Lt) Cheap, clean and basic alternative in Užupis if Filaretai is full.

## Midrange

**Ecotel** ( ☎ 210 2700; www.ecotel.lt; Slucko gatvė 8; s/d from 159/169 Lt; 🅿 ✕ ) Economy business-class rooms tend to be pretty abominable in Vilnius, but this 168-room property on the north bank of the Neris bucks the trend by offering squeaky-clean rooms with smart, simple furnishings.

**E-Guest House** ( ☎ 266 0730; www.e-guesthouse .lt; Ševčenkos gatvė 16; d/apt 180/260 Lt; 🅿 ⯁ 🖳 ) If you're willing to roost slightly outside the centre, you'll have trouble beating the value of this quirky, tech-inclined nugget, where laptop rental costs 20 Lt and internet-ready

computers line the corridors. The rooms are airy, modern and crisp.

**City Gate** ( ☎ 210 7306; www.citygate.lt; Bazilijonų gatvė 3; s/d from 200/300 Lt; 🅿 ✕ ) Friendly, warm reception area (think brick walls, cosy sitting room and big smile on the receptionist) gives a hint of the treats you are in for at this low-risk, high-return outfit between Old Town and the train station.

**Ramada** ( ☎ 255 3555; www.ramadavilnius.lt; Subačiaus gatvė 2; s/d from €81/100; ✕ 🖳 ) Of all the fancy chain hotels in Vilnius, the Ramada delivers the best value. Discounting the strange art (Sailboats? Beaches?) in the somewhat small rooms, the hotel affects a 19th-century vibe, with cream colours and elegant curtains. Its location near Gates of Dawn is ideal.

**AAA Guest House Mano Liza** ( ☎ 212 2225; www .hotelinvilnius.lt; Ligoninės gatvė 5; d from 220 Lt) This quirky little guesthouse is a poor man's version of sumptuous Grotthuss next door, which is hardly an insult. The eight rooms have cheerful colours and flowery designs. It's a super deal in the low season.

**Scandic Neringa** ( ☎ 261 0516; www.scandic-hotels .com; Gedimino prospektas 23; s/d from 270/339 Lt; 🅿 ✕ 🖳 ) Delivers some of the finest service in town in a Soviet-cum-Scandinavian atmosphere. Dirt and dust – enemies No 1 and 2 – face instant eradication. Breakfast on the street terrace provides varsity people-watching. Steep weekend discounts make it ideal for weekend escapes.

## Top End

**Reval Hotel Lietuva** ( ☎ 272 6272; www.revalhotels .com; Konstitucijos prospektas 20; s/d from €120/140; 🅿 ✕ ⯁ 🖳 ⯁ ) The burly, bustling Reval is the antidote to Vilnius' plethora of quaint boutique hotels, with well-appointed business-class rooms, the best casino in Vilnius and a rare fitness centre that's worthy of the name. The top-floor Sky Bar has the city's best views.

**Grotthuss** ( ☎ 266 0322; www.grotthusshotel.com; d from €128; 🅿 ✕ ⯁ 🖳 ) There's nary a hair out of place in this classy and opulent gem, which the German-baroness owner has managed to make fit for a baroness without being too aristocratic and stuffy. The scents wafting up from the kitchen of Le Pergola restaurant – arguably Vilnius' finest – are to die for.

**Shakespeare Boutique Hotel** ( ☎ 266 5885; www .shakespeare.lt; Bernardinų gatvė 8/8; s/d from 360/600 Lt;

P ⊠ ⊠ 🖥 ) This jewel of a boutique exudes old-world elegance and culture from every pore. Each room pays homage to a different writer, and a beautiful rug, huge impressionist-style painting or gorgeous antique comes into view at every turn.

# EATING

Whether it's curry, *cepelinai* (gut-busting meat and potato zeppelins) or *kepta duona* (fried bread sticks oozing garlic) you want, Vilnius has a mouth-watering selection of local and international cuisine.

**Amatininkų Užiega** (Didžioji gatvė 19/2; mains 15-20 Lt; ☾ 11am-5am) This perfectly located spot is a great place to sample country Lithuanian fare or grab a steak in the wee hours of the morning, and meet a random character or two at the bar.

**Žemaičiai** (Vokiečių gatvė 24; mains 15-35 Lt) Of the many brick-walled, old-style Lithuanian theme restaurants in Vilnius, this institution, famous for its pigs trotters (14 Lt), offers the most authentic Lithuanian experience.

**Saint Germain** (Literatų gatvė 9; mains 20 Lt) Paris is the inspiration behind this shabby-chic wine-bar-cum-restaurant with modern art splashed on the wall, groovy French lounge music and funky handwritten menus. Advance reservations for its street terrace are essential.

**Aukštaičiai** (Antokolskio gatvė 13; mains 20-50 Lt; ☾ 8am-4am) Occupying half a length of a quaint old Jewish quarter street in the warm months, it's a bit pricier than most Lithuanian-food establishments, but then again the food's better. It serves a mean breakfast.

**Medininkai** ( ☎ 266 0771; Aušros Vartų gatvė 8; mains 30-50 Lt) Dine amid vaulted ceilings and ancient frescoes in this gorgeous space in the prettiest part of town. The delicious European cuisine only enhances the ambience.

Fans of Italian food have two good options near each other on Vilniaus gatvė. The

cheaper restaurant, **Pomodoro** (Vilniaus gatvė 15; pizzas/mains from 8/15 Lt), may be a chain but it's pretty good with a great atrium seating area within the Centro Pazažas mall. The more upmarket **Da Antonio** ( ☎ 262 0109; Vilniaus gatvė 23; mains 25 Lt) has the best homemade pasta in town, served up in a cosy classical space.

## Quick Eats

**Delano** (Gedimino prospektas 24; meals from 10 Lt) This big basement cafeteria-style eatery is a great place for budget travellers to fill up on greasy Lithuanian food. It's reminiscent of Lido in Latvia (see p424), only cheaper and not as good.

**Ephesus** (Trakų gatvė 15; kebab 5 Lt; ☾ 11-6am Tue-Sat, 11-1am Sun & Mon) Ravenous night owls can munch on kebabs into the really wee hours at this small Turkish joint.

## Self-Catering

Fresh fruit, honey, smoked eels and cheap staples can all be found at **Kalvarijų market** ( ☾ 7am-noon Tue-Sun), located north of the Neris River. There are two branches of the small supermarket **Ikiukas** (Pylimo gatvė 21); Old Town (Jogailos gatvė 12).

---

### EATING IN UŽUPIS

There are few eateries in bohemian Užupis, but most of them are noteworthy. Mountain lodge-style **Tores** ( ☎ 262 9309; Užupio gatvė 40; meals 30-50 Lt) has good food and atmosphere, but the main reason to come is for the stunning panorama of Gediminas Castle and the Cathedral across Vilnia River valley. Take it all in from the outdoor patio while sipping Švyturys pints (5 Lt).

**Užupio kavinė** (Užupio gatvė 2; mains 10-20 Lt), right on the river as you enter Užupis, is a legendary spot known for its arty clientele and good cheap breakfasts. Ask the bartender for a copy of the Užupis constitution in English. Lastly, **Prie Angelo Kavinė** (Užupio gatvė 9; pizzas 15 Lt; ⊠ ), on the main square, fires up what may be Vilnius' best pizzas.

LITHUANIA

---

**PUFFERS SNUFFED OUT**

From 1 January 2007, smoking in all restaurants and bars was banned in the whole of Lithuania. Lithuania is among the first of the EU countries to introduce this ban, but they sure won't be the last.

---

# DRINKING

Vilnius' riotous party culture centres on clubs in the cold months and outdoor cafés in the summer.

On the weekends, many cafés turn into clubs and many restaurants turn into raucous bars.

**Cozy** (Dominikonų gatvė 10; sandwiches/mains 8/15 Lt) Cozy has excellent lunch specials (15 Lt) by day and draws an alternative student crowd from nearby Vilnius University by night. The basement DJ club has all-night soirees on Friday and Saturday, and smaller parties on Monday and Thursday.

**Sole Luna** (Universiteto gatvė 4; mains from 8 Lt; ☾ Mon-Sat) Students love the cheap food at this Italian-owned café near Vilnius University, but the main draw is the outdoor dining and weekend dancing in a 16th-century courtyard.

**Skonis ir Kvapas** (Trakų gatvė 8; mains 15-20 Lt) Now this is how a café should look: original frescoes on the ceiling and walls, working fireplace and a worn wooden floor. Vilnius' best tea list comes presented on an mock hand fan.

**Avilys** (Gedimino prospektas 5; pints of beer 7-8 Lt) 'Beehive' draws a refined crowd to sample its excellent home brew – the dark and honey beers especially – and a variety of dishes cooked in beer.

---

**AUTHOR'S CHOICE**

**Manu Kavinė** (Bokšto gatvė 7; mains 10-20 Lt; ☾ 11-2am) This bar has something for everybody: an extensive tea list; a wide selection of beer on tap, including Guinness; and an exceptionally priced menu with delights such as German sausages (12 Lt), and salmon wrapped in tin foil (16.50 Lt). It would be enough to stop there, but the amiable owner throws in complimentary internet access on two computers and – get this, sports fans – free darts and foosball in the backroom sports bar.

---

# ENTERTAINMENT

*In Your Pocket* publishes a list of movie theatres as well as listings for opera, theatre, classical music and other big events. Most such venues break for the summer. The tourist offices also post events listings. Check www.cinema.lt (in Lithuanian) for movie listings.

## Cinemas

Films are screened in English at the 12-screen **Coca-Cola Plaza** ( ☎ 265 6565; www.forumcinemas.lt; Savanorių 7) and are usually dubbed in Lithuanian elsewhere.

## Classical Music

**Lithuanian Opera & Ballet Theatre** ( ☎ 262 0636; www.opera.lt; Vienuolio gatvė 1) Classical productions in a grand, gaudy building near the river.

**National Philharmonic** ( ☎ 266 5233; www.filharmonija.lt; Aušros Vartų gatvė 5; ☾ box office 10am-7pm Tue-Sat, 10am-noon Sun) The country's most renowned orchestras perform here.

## Theatre

**National Drama Theatre** ( ☎ 262 9771; www.teatras.lt; Gedimino Prospektas 4; ☾ 10am-6pm Mon-Fri, 11am-6pm Sat & Sun) stages national and international productions in Lithuanian.

## Nightclubs

With cover charges increasing by the month, crowds at most Vilnius clubs are increasingly bling-bling and the velvet-rope policies increasingly obnoxious.

**Brodvėjus** ( ☎ 210 7208; Mėsinių 4; cover 10-15 Lt) Every big city in Eastern Europe has one – a place where hordes of expats and pretty young things flock night after night to dance to 'I Will Survive', 'Mambo No 5' and the same tired-but-innocuous soundtrack until way past bedtime. Brodvėjus is a classic example of the genre.

**Pabo Latino** ( ☎ 262 1045; Trakų gatvė 3; cover 30 Lt; ☾ Thu-Sat) This was the best club in Vilnius until its growling bouncers were charged with stepping up face control. Still, there's always hope that it will return to its vibrant salsa-infused glory.

**Pacha** (www.pacha.com) The legendary chain of Ibiza fame promises to reinvigorate the Vilnius club scene when it opens its doors in 2007.

**Men's Factory** ( ☎ 8-699 85009; Švencenkos gatvė 16/10; cover 5-40 Lt; ☾ Wed-Sat) This wildly popular gay club west of Old Town draws plenty of straight club-goers, too.

## SHOPPING

**Amber Museum-Gallery** ( ☎ 212 0499; Šv Mykolo gatvė 8; ☻ 10am-7pm) Exquisite pieces for sale plus displays on the history and chemistry of amber.

**Craft market** (meeting point of Didžioji & Pilies gatvė) Traditional crafts and amber in abundance at this daily market.

**Devyni du penki** (Stiklių gatvė 12) Sells gorgeous chunky silver jewellery, some embedded with amber.

**Jonas Bugailiškis** ( ☎ 261 7667; Aušros Vartų gatvė 17-10) The place to buy authentic Lithuanian-style wooden crosses, toys and traditional folk instruments.

## GETTING THERE & AWAY

For information on international and domestic flights, bus, train and ferry services to Vilnius, see p466.

The **train station** ( ☎ 233 0087/6; Geležinkelio gatvė 16) is a five-minute walk south of Old Town. The **bus station** ( ☎ 216 2977; Sodų gatvė 22) is across the street from the train station.

## GETTING AROUND
### To/From the Airport

**Vilnius International Airport** ( ☎ 230 6666; www.vilnius-airport.lt; Rodūnios gatvė 2) sits 5km south of the city.

Getting from the airport to the centre of Vilnius is a doddle: just hop on bus 1, which runs every hour to the train station (1 Lt, 20 minutes).

Alternatively you can take the more frequent bus 2 towards Lukiškių Aikštė. on Gedimino prospektas in New Town. Minibus 15 (2 Lt) also plies this route.

A taxi from the airport to the city centre should cost no more than 20 Lt.

### Car

For tips on car rental see p468. There's a huge **free parking lot** (Maironio gatvė) on the western edge of Old Town, and numerous guarded paid car parks around town.

### Public Transport

Unless you're heading well out of Old Town, you won't have much need for public transport in Vilnius, although the route from the train station to New Town via Pylimo gatvė is handy. It is serviced by trolleybuses 2 and 5, and by buses 26, 26a and 53.

Tickets cost 1.40 Lt at news kiosks and 1.10 Lt direct from the driver; punch tickets

on board in a ticket machine or risk a 20 Lt on-the-spot fine.

### Taxi

Taxis officially charge 2 Lt per kilometre (more at night) and must have a meter. Drivers often try to rip tourists off, especially if flagged down on the street. You can phone a **taxi** ( ☎ 1409, 1423, 1445, 1422, 1800), or queue up at one of numerous taxi ranks. Popular spots are outside the train station and at the southern end of Vokiečių gatvė.

## AROUND VILNIUS
### Paneriai

During WWII the Nazis, aided by Lithuanian accomplices, exterminated three-quarters of Vilnius' 100,000-strong Jewish population at this site, 10km southwest of central Vilnius.

From the entrance a path leads to the small **Paneriai Museum** ( ☎ 5-260-2001; Agrastų gatvė 15; ☻ 11am-6pm Mon, Wed, Fri & Sun Mar-Dec), near which there are two monuments – one Jewish (marked with the Star of David), the other one Soviet (an obelisk topped with a Soviet star).

Paths lead from here to grassed-over pits where the Nazis burnt the exhumed bodies of their victims to hide the evidence of their crimes.

There are about 20 suburban trains daily from Vilnius to Paneriai station (1.20 Lt, 20 minutes). From the station, it is a 1km walk southwest along Agrastų gatvė to the site.

### Trakai
☎ 528 / pop 6,110

Talk about your perfect day trip: Lithuania's ancient capital, just 28km west of Vilnius, has a little bit of everything, including bucolic lakes, two castles – with one that will truly make your jaw drop – and a rare Middle Eastern religious sect.

That sect is the Karaites, named after the term *Kara*, which means 'to study the scriptures' in both Hebrew and Arabic. The sect originated in Baghdad and practises strict adherence to the Torah (rejecting the rabbinic Talmud). Grand Duke of Lithuania Vytautas brought about 380 Karaite families to Trakai from Crimea, in around 1400, to serve as bodyguards. Only 63 remain in Trakai today and their numbers – about 280 in Lithuania – are dwindling rapidly.

This area has protected status as the **Trakai Historical National Park** (www.seniejitrakai.lt). The

LITHUANIA

**tourist information centre** ( ☎ 51934; www.trakai .lt; Vytauto gatvė 69; ⏰ 8am-5pm Mon-Thu, 8am-3.45pm Fri Sep-Apr; 8.30am-4.15pm Mon, 8.30am-5.30pm Tue-Fri, 9am-3pm Sat May-Aug) sells maps, books accommodation, rents bikes (24 Lt per day) and has information on fishing, sailing, scuba diving, horse riding and a range of other activities.

### SIGHTS

Trakai's trophy piece is the fairytale **Island Castle** ( ☎ 53946; adult/student 10/5 Lt; ⏰ 10am-7pm May-Sep, 10am-5pm Tue-Sun Oct-Apr), occupying a small island in Lake Galvė. The painstakingly restored, red-brick Gothic castle dates from the late-14th century when Prince Kęstutis, father of Vytautas, once ruled the area. Vytautas completed what his father started in the early 1400s and died in the castle in 1430.

A footbridge links the Island Castle to the shore. Inside the castle is a branch of the **Trakai History Museum** ( ☎ 53946; www.trakaimuziejus.lt) in which the history of the castle is charted. In summer the castle courtyard is a magical stage for concerts and plays.

The museum has two other branches in town: an **Exhibition of Religious Art** ( ☎ 53941; Kestučio gatvė 4; adult/student 4/2 Lt; ⏰ 10am-6pm Wed-Sun) and the **Karaite Ethnographic Exhibition** ( ☎ 55286; Karaimų gatvė 22; adult/student 4/2 Lt; ⏰ 10am-6pm Wed-Sun). The latter provides a good introduction to the fascinating Karaite culture. Karaimų gatvė No 30 is a beautifully restored early-19th-century **Kenessa** (prayer house) of the Karaites.

The ruins of Trakai's **Peninsula Castle**, built from 1362 to 1382 by Kęstutis and destroyed in the 17th century, are at the northern end of town.

### SLEEPING & EATING

**Kempingas Slėnyje** ( ☎ 53880; www.camptrakai.lt; Slėnio 1; camping per person/car/tent 16/5/6 Lt, cottage 250 Lt, r in summer house/guesthouse from 70/120 Lt; Ⓟ ) This sublime complex is 5km out of Trakai on the northern side of Lake Galvė. You can pitch your tent by the lake or stay in wooden cabins or the spectacular guesthouse with lakeside balconies. Activities include horse riding, canoeing and hot-air balloon rides.

**Sport Centre** ( ☎ 53200; www.sc.trakai.com; Karaimų gatvė 73; s/d 144/156 Lt; Ⓟ ) Rooms here are basic but big and clean, and half have wonderful lakeside views. As the name implies, it doubles as a mighty fine activity centre.

**Apvalaus Stalo Klubas** (Round Table Club; ☎ 55595; Karaimų gatvė 53; pizzas 15 Lt, mains 35 Lt; ✖ ) A lovely waterside French restaurant with separate pizzeria and stunning sunset views.

There are two good options for trying out Karaite food – especially *kibinai*, meat-stuffed pastries that are similar to empanadas. Prices at both will seem refreshing after Vilnius. **Kibininė** (Karaimų gatvė 65; kibinai 2.50-5 Lt) has a dreamy location right on the lake, while **Kybynlar** (Karaimų gatvė 29; meals 15 Lt; ✖ ) has a more Turkic feel. The writing on the wall is in the endangered Karaim language.

### GETTING THERE & AWAY

There are at least two buses hourly to/from Vilnius (4 Lt, 45 minutes), plus seven daily trains (4 Lt, 45 minutes).

## Kernavė

Deemed an 'exceptional testimony to some 10 millennia of human settlements in this region' by Unesco, which made it a World Heritage site in 2004, Kernavė is the 'Pompeii of Lithuania' and a must-see. Thought to have been the spot where Mindaugas (responsible for uniting Lithuania for the first time) celebrated his coronation in 1253, the rural cultural reserve comprises four old castle mounds and the archaeological remains of a medieval town.

Unfortunately, the **Archaeological & Historical Museum** ( ☎ 382-47385; www.kernave.org; Kerniaus gatvė 4a) is undergoing renovation and won't reopen until the spring of 2008. However, you can still explore the grounds and observe ongoing excavations in the pleasant, 194.4 hectare **Kernavė Cultural Reserve** (www.kernave.org).

To reach Kernavė, 35km northwest of Vilnius in the Neris Valley, follow the road through Dūksvos from Maisiagala on the main road north to Ukmergė.

# EASTERN & SOUTHERN LITHUANIA

The mythical forests and famous spas of eastern and southern Lithuania make easy day trips from Vilnius – although outdoor enthusiasts should not hesitate to spend more time here camping, cross country skiing, canoeing, hiking, bird-watching or berry-picking.

## AUKŠTAITIJA NATIONAL PARK

☎ 386

Lithuania's first national park (founded in 1974) is a 400-sq-km wonderland of rivers, lakes, centuries-old forests and tiny villages still steeped in rural tradition. Around 70% of the park comprises pine, spruce and deciduous forests, inhabited by elk, deer, wild boar, storks, and white-tailed and golden eagles. Its highlight is a labyrinth of 126 lakes, the deepest being Lake Tauragnas (60.5m deep).

The park is mainly for outdoor lovers, but there are also some cultural attractions, including several settlements that are protected ethnographic centres. For those interested in getting deeper under the skin of this enchanting area, the **Aukštaitija National Park Office** ( ☎ 47430; www.tourism.lt/nature/parks/aukstaitija.html; ☿ 9am-6pm Mon-Fri, 10am-6pm Sat) in Palūšė has everything you need to know. Another good resource is the **Tourism Centre Palūšė** ( ☎ 47430; www.paluse.lt), which also runs a camping ground.

To get here jump on a train from Vilnius to Ignalina (10 Lt, two hours, seven daily), from where you have to walk, hitch or take a taxi to Palūšė.

## DRUSKININKAI

☎ 313 / pop 20,000

Druskininkai, 130km south of Vilnius, is Lithuania's most famous health resort. In recent years it has gained notoriety as the home to the somewhat controversial Soviet sculpture museum known as Grūto Parkas.

People have been taking in the incredibly salty waters in this leafy riverside town since the 18th century. Today there's a mix of both Soviet-style and more modern treatments to be had if you're in the mood for pampering. At **Druskininkų Gydykla** (Vilniaus gatvė 11; per cup 0.30 Lt) you can sample several types of genuine Druskininkai mineral water, which tastes downright foul but promises eternal beauty.

The **Tourist Information Centres** (www.druskininkai .lt; town centre ☎ 51777; www.druskininkiai.lt; Čiurlionio gatvė 65; ☿ 10am-6.45pm Mon-Sat, 10am-5pm Sun; old train station ☎ 60800; Gardino gatvė 3; ☿ 8.30am-5.15pm Mon-Fri) can help you out with accommodation and information on the town's dozens of spas. The branch at the old train station also runs an excellent camping ground with a few no-frills mobile homes for rent (from 70 Lt).

But chances are you are here to see **Grūto Parkas** ( ☎ 55511; www.grutoparkas.lt; adult/child 10/3 Lt; ☿ 9am-sunset), 8km west of town in the village

of Grūtas. The park has been an enormous hit since it opened to much fanfare in 2001. The sprawling grounds contain dozens of statues of Soviet heroes, exhibits on Soviet history and loudspeakers bellowing Soviet anthems. The statues once stood confidently in parks or squares across Lithuania.

There are nine daily buses between Druskininkai and Vilnius, and 10 daily buses to/from Kaunas (both 20 Lt, two hours). If you're going straight to Grūto Parkas, ask to be let off at the park turnoff, then walk the final 1km walk to the park.

# CENTRAL LITHUANIA

Most view Lithuania's nondescript interior as little more than something you must cross to get to the west coast or Latvia, but it does offer a few worthwhile diversions, including the country's signature tourist attraction, the Hill of Crosses in Šiaulia.

## KAUNAS

☎ 37 / pop 378,900

Lithuania's second city remains stubbornly provincial, but holds some appeal for those willing to scratch beneath its hard-edged surface. That appeal lies mainly in its attractive Old Town, a seemingly endless central pedestrian street, its wide range of museums and its red-hot basketball team, Žalgiris.

The capital of Lithuania in the dark days between the two world wars, Kaunas is enjoying a renaissance of sorts as several budget airlines have made it their Lithuanian hub. But its hotels and restaurants need to improve if it is to lure more than a fraction of those who use its airport, most of whom head straight to Vilnius.

For now, Kaunas is a convenient overnight stopover and, in the warmer months, a decent place to experience the real Lithuania away from the crowds of Vilnius. A great time to visit is in April when the city comes alive during the four-day **Kaunas Jazz Festival** (www .kaunasjazz.lt).

### Information

Casinos have 24-hour currency exchanges. All major banks cash travellers cheques and have ATMs.

**Hansa Bankas** Old Town (Vilniaus gatvė 13); New Town (Laisvės alėja 79) Both branches have an ATM.

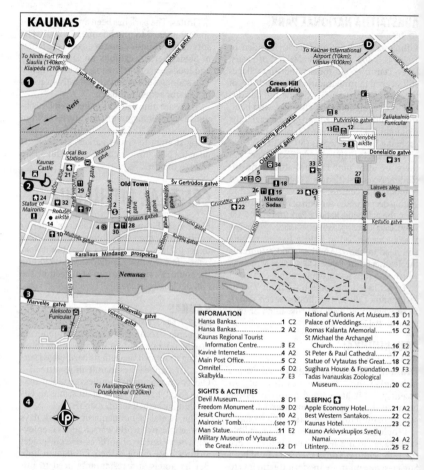

# KAUNAS

**INFORMATION**
Hansa Bankas.................................1 C2
Hansa Bankas.................................2 A2
Kaunas Regional Tourist
   Information Centre......................3 E2
Kavinė Internetas..........................4 A2
Main Post Office............................5 C2
Omnitel.........................................6 D2
Skalbykla.......................................7 E3

**SIGHTS & ACTIVITIES**
Devil Museum................................8 D1
Freedom Monument .....................9 D2
Jesuit Church................................10 A2
Maironis' Tomb.....................(see 17)
Man Statue...................................11 E2
Military Museum of Vytautas
   the Great..................................12 D1

National Čiurlionis Art Museum.13 D1
Palace of Weddings.....................14 A2
Romas Kalanta Memorial............15 C2
St Michael the Archangel
   Church.....................................16 E2
St Peter & Paul Cathedral............17 A2
Statue of Vytautas the Great....18 C2
Sugihara House & Foundation..19 F3
Tadas Ivanauskas Zoological
   Museum...................................20 C2

**SLEEPING**
Apple Economy Hotel..................21 A2
Best Western Santakos................22 C2
Kaunas Hotel...............................23 C2
Kauno Arkivyskupijos Svečių
   Namai......................................24 A2
Litinterp......................................25 E2

---

**Kaunas in Your Pocket** (www.inyourpocket.com)
Annual city guide sold in hotels, art galleries and news
kiosks for 5 Lt.

**Kaunas Regional Tourist Information Centre**
( ☎ 323 436; http://visit.kaunas.lt; Laisvės alėja 36;
⏰ 9am-6pm Mon-Fri, 9am-1pm Sat, 2-4pm Sun Jun-Aug;
9am-6pm Mon-Fri, 9am-3pm Sat May & Sep; 9am-6pm
Mon-Thu, 9am-5pm Fri Oct-Apr) Books accommodation,
sells maps and arranges bicycle rental. There's a travel
agency in the same office that sells bus, plane and ferry
tickets and can obtain visas.

**Kavinė Internetas** (Vilniaus gatvė 24; per hr 4 Lt;
⏰ 8.30am-11pm) Good internet café that serves drinks.

**Main post office** (Laisvės alėja 102; ⏰ 7am-7pm Mon-
Fri, 7am-5pm Sat)

**Omnitel** (43 Laisvės alėja; per hr 3 Lt; ⏰ 8am-6pm
Mon-Fri, 10am-4pm Sat) internet access.

**Skalbykla** (laundromat; Gedimino gatvė 11; per kg 4 Lt;
⏰ 8.30am-5pm Mon-Sat) Same-day service available.

## Sights

### OLD TOWN

Start any trip to Kaunas wandering through its
lovely little Old Town, where most streets lead
to Rotušės aikštė (Central Square). Surrounding the square are 15th- and 16th-century
German merchants' houses. The 18th-
century, white, baroque former city hall is
now the **Palace of Weddings**. The southern side
of the square is dominated by an 18th-century
twin-towered **Jesuit church**.

   **St Peter & Paul Cathedral** (Vilniaus gatvė 1) on the
northeastern corner of the square, owes much
to baroque reconstruction, but its early-15th-

century Gothic-shaped windows remain. **Maironis' tomb** is outside the cathedral's south wall.

## NEW TOWN

Kaunas expanded east from the Old Town in the 19th century, giving birth to the modern centre and its striking 1.7km-long pedestrian street, Laisvės alėja, which today is lined with bars, shops and restaurants.

Near the western end you'll find Miestos Sodas (City Garden), where a **memorial to Romas Kalanta** – a Kaunas student who set himself on fire on 14 May 1972 in protest at tyrannical communist rule – takes the form of several stone slabs.

The **Tadas Ivanauskas Zoological Museum** (☎ 229 675; Laisvės alėja 106; adult/child 5/3 Lt; 11am-7pm

Tue-Sun) contains 13,000 stuffed animals to amuse and educate children of all ages. Nearby stands a **statue** of Vytautas the Great.

The blue, neo-Byzantine **St Michael the Archangel Church** (1893) dominates the eastern end of Laisvės alėja from its position on the adjacent Nepriklausomybės aikštė (Independence Square). On the same square, the **statue of man**, modelled on Nike the Greek god of victory, caused a storm of controversy when his glorious pose exposing his manhood was unveiled.

East of here is the **Sugihara House & Foundation** (☎ 332 881; Vaižganto gatvė 30; admission free; 10am-5pm Mon-Fri, 11am-4pm Sat & Sun May-Oct; 11am-3pm Mon-Fri Nov-Apr) tells the story of Chiune Sugihara, the Japanese consul to Lithuania (1939–40), known as 'Japan's Schindler'. He saved 12,000 lives by issuing visas (against orders) to Polish Jews who faced being forced into Soviet citizenship.

North of Laisvės alėja, Vienybės aikštė (Unity Square) contains the **Freedom Monument**, which honours 16 February 1918 – the day Lithuania declared independence. It was erected in 1928. It was hidden during the Stalin era, and put back in place on 16 February 1989.

Two museums share the large building on the north side of the square. The **Military Museum of Vytautas the Great** (☎ 320 939; Donelaičio gatvė 64; adult/child 2/1 Lt; 11am-6pm Wed-Sun) recounts Lithuania's history from prehistoric times to the present day. The **National Čiurlionis Art Museum** (☎ 221 417; Putvinskio gatvė 55; 11am-5pm Tue-Sat) has an extensive collection of the romantic symbolic paintings of Mikalojus Konstantinas Čiurlionis (1875–1911), Lithuania's beloved artist and composer.

Nearby is the bizarre **Devil Museum** (☎ 221 587; Putvinskio gatvė 64; 11am-5pm, closed Mon), which contains more than 2000 devil statuettes. Note the satanic figures of Hitler and Stalin, formed from tree roots, and performing a deadly dance over Lithuania.

Leaving town, the 19th-century **Ninth Fort** (☎ 377 715; Žemaičių plentas 73; adult/child 5/3 Lt; 10am-6pm Wed-Mon Mar-Nov, 10am-4pm Wed-Sun Dec-Feb), 7km from Kaunas, was used by the Russians in WWI to defend their western frontier against Germany. During WWII the Nazis murdered an estimated 80,000 people, mostly Kaunas Jews, here. Take bus 35 or 23 to the IX Fortas bus stop, then walk for 1km.

## Sleeping

**Litinterp** ( ☎ 228 718; www.litinterp.lt; Gedimino gatvė 28-7; s/d 100/160 Lt, with shared bathroom 80/140 Lt) Much like the Soviets once did, the Litinterp folks manage to make all their properties look identical down to the last light switch. Unlike the Soviets – and unlike many budget hotels – their identical stuff always works. Budget paradise.

**Kaunas Hotel** ( ☎ 750 861; www.kaunashotel.lt; Laisvės alėja 79; d from 320 Lt;  P ☒ ☒ ⬚ ) This centrally located hotel is as dependable as they come in Kaunas, with airy if nondescript rooms and a host of business-traveller treats like free wi-fi and one of the best hotel fitness centres in Lithuania.

**Apple Economy Hotel** ( ☎ 321 404; www.applehotel.lt; Valančiaus gatvė 19; s/d from 135/190 Lt;  P ☒ ☒ ) Fans of minimalism will crave a stay at the quirky Apple. Spot the green-apple motif on your pillows and on the silk wall hangings that add a splash of colour to the otherwise white rooms.

**Best Western Santakos** ( ☎ 302 702; www.santaka.lt; Gruodžio gatvė 21; s/d from 360/480 Lt;  P ☒ ☒ ⬚ ) Kaunas' swankiest hotel by a long shot feels nothing like a chain. The enormous rooms in the old wing boast opulent bathrooms with swinging double doors and a generously fur-nished sitting area fit for a small party.

## Eating

It's no Vilnius but Kaunas' restaurant scene is gradually improving, and food tends to be cheaper than in the capital.

**Pizza Jazz** (Laisvės alėja 68; mains 10-20 Lt) Sure it's a chain, but it's still one of the best cheap-eating options in Kaunas. Has a lively bar on one side and a surprisingly posh-feeling restaurant on the other.

**Miesto Sodas** (Laisvės alėja 93; mains 15-20 Lt;  ⏱ 11am-midnight) Kaunas' trendiest eatery has more than passable steaks, rarity of all rarities, a salad bar. Service can be snail-slow. Siena nightclub in the basement is a great place to watch Žalgiris basketball games.

**Yakata** (Valančiaus gatvė 14; sushi boats 32 Lt, mains 20 Lt) A cosy, tastefully done little Japanese place with superb chicken teriyaki, OK sushi and well-priced beer (5 Lt).

**Senieji Rūsiai** (Vilniaus gatvė 34; mains 25-35 Lt) Easily the tastiest restaurant in Kaunas, this candle-lit 17th-century cellar offers European special-ties such as ostrich and beefsteak flambéed at your table.

## Drinking

**Skliautai** (Rotušės aikštė 26) A cool basement café that creates instant fans with its Old Town courtyard patio and arty crowd.

**Avilys** (Vilniaus gatvė 34; mains 15-25 Lt) Expect the same fine food and award-winning home brew produced by this brew-pub's Vilnius branch (p452).

## Entertainment

**Fortas** (Donelaičio gatvė 65; mains 10-25 Lt) The best bar in town has an Irish feel and draws rowdy college kids to hear DJs or live music upstairs most nights of the week.

**Ex-It** ( ☎ 202 813; Maironio 19; cover 20-100 Lt;  ⏱ Fri & Sat) Many vote this pulsating, multichambered dance cathedral the best club in Lithuania.

**Kaunas Philharmonic** ( ☎ 200 478; www.kaunofilhar monija.lt; Sapiegos gatvė 5) This is the main concert hall for classical music.

**Kaunas Musical Theatre** ( ☎ 200 933; www.muzikini steatras.lt; Laisvės alėja 91) This 1892 building hosts operettas from September to June.

## Getting There & Away

### AIR

For information on international flights, see p466).

### BUS

International routes to/from the **long-distance bus station** ( ☎ 409 060; Vytauto prospektas 24) include St Petersburg, Kaliningrad, Rīga (45 Lt, 3½ hours, one daily) and Tallinn (110 Lt, 12 hours, one daily).

Domestic routes include Vilnius (19 Lt, 1½ hours, three hourly), Druskininkai (24 Lt, two to three hours, six buses via Alytus), Klaipėda (38 Lt, three hours, 10 daily), Palanga (40 Lt,

3½ hours, 10 to 15 daily) and Šiauliai (23 Lt, three hours, 15 daily).

### TRAIN
From the **train station** ( ☎ 221 093; Čiurlionio gatvė 16) there are 13 trains daily to/from Vilnius (11 Lt, 1¼ hours) and an incredibly slow overnight train to/from Klaipėda (25 Lt, six hours).

## Getting Around
### TO/FROM THE AIRPORT
**Kaunas International Airport** ( ☎ 399 307; Savanorių prospektas) is 10km north of the Old Town in the suburb of Karmėlava. To get there take minibus 120 from the big stop at Šv Gertrūdos gatvė (1 Lt).

## ŠIAULIAI
☎ 41 / pop 147,000
Lithuania's fourth-largest city is usually just a stopover for peeps making the pilgrimage to the legendary Hill of Crosses, 12km to the north. But a recent facelift on its main pedestrian walkway signals that it's preparing for bigger things.

Once home to the USSR's largest military base outside Russia, Šiauliai today is a symbol of Lithuania's determined westward push, as it provides a base for the NATO forces policing Baltic skies.

You can get your bearings at the **tourism information centre** ( ☎ 523 110; www.siauliai.lt/tic; Vilniaus gatvė 213; ☼ 9am-6pm Mon-Fri, 10am-5pm Sat, 10am-4pm Sun).

## Sights & Activities
Recently renovated **Vilniaus gatvė** is the city's main drag and is a great place to stroll or plop down in a street-side café and watch the world go by. It's also a free wi-fi zone.

The city's quirky symbol is a bizarre golden **sundial** (cnr Salkausko gatvė & Ežero gatvė), topped by a gleaming statue of an archer. It stands on the shore of Lake Tal os, about five minutes' walk north from the centre.

**Zoknia Military Airfield**, with runways large enough to land a space shuttle on, can be visited by guided tours arranged at least one week in advance through the tourism information centre. Many of the 50 or so Soviet aircraft hangars (which once housed MiG-29 fighters) remain, as does the subterranean command post sturdy enough to survive a nuclear attack. About 120 NATO personnel and four F-16 jet fighters are currently stationed at Zokniai.

### HILL OF CROSSES
Lithuania's most incredible, awe-inspiring sight is the legendary **Hill of Crosses** (Kryžių kalnas). It is a two-hump hillock blanketed by thousands of crosses. The sound of the evening breeze tinkling through the crosses that appear to grow on the hillock is indescribable and unmissable. Each and every cross represents the amazing spirit, soulfulness and quietly rebellious nature of these people.

Legend says the tradition of planting crosses began in the 14th century. The crosses were bulldozed by the Soviets, but each night people crept past soldiers and barbed wire to plant yet more, risking their lives or freedom to express their national and spiritual fervour. Today Kryžių kalnas is a place of national pilgrimage.

Some of the crosses are devotional, others are memorials (many for people deported to Siberia) and some are finely carved folk-art masterpieces.

This strange place lies 12km north of Šiauliai – 10km north up highway A12, then 2km east from a well-marked turnoff (the sign says 'Kryžių kalnas 2'). You can rent a bike from the tourist information centre (first hour 3.50 Lt, per additional hour 2.50 Lt) and pedal out here, or take one of eight buses. The bus schedule is in the tourist centre. A round-trip taxi with a half hour to see the crosses should cost 30 Lt.

## Sleeping & Drinking
**Šiaulių Kolegijos Youth Hostel** ( ☎ 523 764; administraija@siauliaikolegija.lt; Tilžės gatvė 159; s/d/tr/q with shared bathroom 50/60/75/100 Lt; P ✗ ) has spick-and-span rooms at incredibly low prices – and even throws free wireless internet into the mix.

**Šaulys** ( ☎ 520 812; www.saulys.lt; Vasario 16-osios gatvė 40; s/d from 180/250 Lt; P ✗ ✗ ☐ ☐ ) Šiauliai's swankiest choice has all the mod cons and a decent fitness centre. If that's not enough activity for you, they organise paragliding and parachuting expeditions.

**Arkos** (Vilniaus gatvė 213; mains 15-20 Lt) Good bar with passable munchies in a brick cellar.

## Getting There & Away
Šiauliai is roughly 140km from both Kaunas and Rīga. With your own wheels you could feasibly visit the Hill of Crosses as a day trip from either.

LITHUANIA

Services from the **bus station** ( ☎ 525 058; Tilzes gatvė 109) include Vilnius (32 Lt, three hours, nine daily), Kaunas (23 Lt, three hours, 15 daily), Klaipėda (23 Lt, 2½ hours, six daily) and Rīga (20 Lt, 2½ hours, 10 daily).

From the **train station** ( ☎ 430 652; Dubijos gatvė 44) there are trains to Vilnius (26 Lt, four hours, five to eight daily) and Rīga (16 Lt, 2½ hours, at least one daily).

# WESTERN LITHUANIA

Lithuania's lively left coastline is only 99km long but it packs plenty of fire power, with a thriving port city, a thumping party town and its crown jewel, the starkly beautiful, sand dune–infested Curonian Spit – a Unesco World Heritage site. Toss in a few fine festivals, add a dollop of German history and there will be plenty to keep you occupied in this wonderful part of the world.

## PALANGA
☎ 460 / pop 19,550

Downright dull by winter, beachside Palanga, just 25km north of Klaiepėda, explodes into Lithuania's undisputed party capital in the summer months.

The **tourist information centre** ( ☎ 48811; www .palangatic.lt; Kretingos gatvė 1; ☼ 9am-6pm Mon-Fri, 9am-3.30pm Sat & Sun May-Aug; 9am-5pm Mon-Fri Sep-Apr) adjoins the tiny bus station, east of Palanga's lengthy main artery, pedestrian Basanavičiaus gatvė.

For a peaceful escape from the crowds of Basanavičiaus gatvė, walk or cycle south along Meilės alėja, the main beachfront path, to Palanga's **Botanical Park**, where you'll discover lush greenery and swans gliding on still lakes The park's highlight is the **Amber Museum** ( ☎ 51319; Vytauto gatvė 17; adult/child 5/2.50 Lt; ☼ 10am-8pm Tue-Sat, 10am-7pm Sun), inside the sweeping former palace of the noble Polish Tyszkiewicz family.

### Sleeping & Eating

Room rates change by the week in the summer. Litinterp in Klaipėda (p462) can arrange B&Bs in Palanga. For cheap digs try haggling with one of the dozens of locals who stand at the eastern end of Kretingos gatvė touting *nuomojami kambariai* (rooms for rent). Expect to pay 25 to 100 Lt per head.

Two fabulously designed hotels located across from each other and sharing an owner

are the **Palanga Hotel** ( ☎ 41414; www.palanga hotel.lt; Birutės gatvė 60; r from 500 Lt; P ☒ ☒ ☐ ☒ ) and the **Vandenis** ( ☼ 52987; www.vandenis.lt; Birutės gatvė 47; d/ste from 250/300 Lt; P ☒ ☒ ☐ ). The refreshingly unique Palanga is the snazziest hotel in town, while the up-and-coming Vandenis has live tunes nightly in its large, flashy music bar.

There are scores of eating options along Basanavičiaus gatvė. One that stands out is rustic **1925 Baras** (Basanavičiaus gatvė 4; mains 15-20 Lt), which has a less carnival atmosphere than many Palanga restaurants.

### Getting There & Away

For details on summer Palanga–Vilnius flights see p467. There are regular daily buses to Vilnius (52 Lt, four hours, six daily), Kaunas (40 Lt, 3½ hours, five daily), Klaipėda (bus/minibus 1.50/3 Lt, 45 minutes, every 20 minutes) and Rīga (40 Lt, five hours, two daily).

## KLAIPĖDA
☎ 46 / pop 194,000

Gritty Klaipėda is Lithuania's main port city and gateway to the lush natural beauty of the Curonian Spit. It boasts a fascinating history as the East Prussian city of Memel, and many Germans enjoy visiting to dig into Klaipėda's Prussian past and waltz among the few buildings still standing from that era.

**Krantas Travel** ( ☎ 395 111; Teatro gatvė 5) sells ferry tickets to Kiel. **Omnitel** ( ☎ 412 360; Manto gatvė 18; per hr 3 Lt; ☼ 9am-6pm Mon-Fri, 10am-4pm Sat) has internet access.

The **tourist information centre** ( ☎ 412 186; www .klaipedainfo.lt; Turgaus gatvė 7; per hr 2 Lt; ☼ 9am-7pm Mon-Fri, 10am-4pm Sat & Sun May-Aug; 9am-6pm Mon-Fri Sep-Apr) arranges accommodation and tours and has two computers for internet surfing.

### Sights

What little remains of Klaipėda's **Old Town** (most of it was destroyed in WWII) is wedged between the Danės River and recently renovated Turgaus gatvė. There are several well-preserved old German half-timbered buildings in the vicinity of Teatro aikštė (Theatre Square), which is Klaipėda's spiritual heart.

The square's dominant building is the **Drama Theatre** (Teatro aikštė 2), where in 1939 Hitler stood on the balcony and announced the incorporation of Memel into Germany. Occupying the middle of the square is the much-loved **statue of Ännchen von Tharau** – a

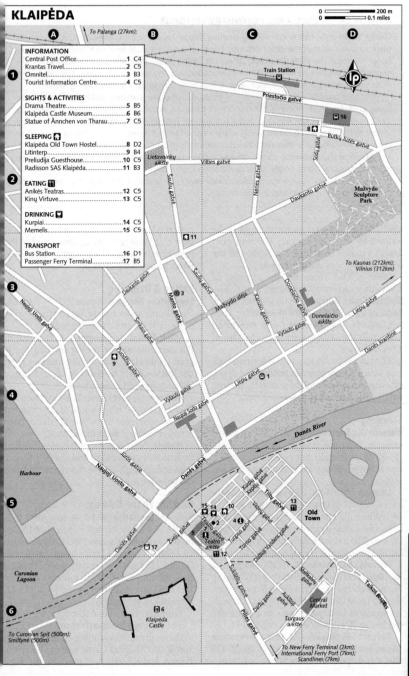

# KLAIPĖDA

| 0 | 200 m |
| 0 | 0.1 miles |

**INFORMATION**
Central Post Office.................................**1** C4
Krantas Travel......................................**2** C5
Omnitel..................................................**3** B3
Tourist Information Centre..................**4** C5

**SIGHTS & ACTIVITIES**
Drama Theatre......................................**5** B5
Klaipėda Castle Museum.....................**6** B6
Statue of Ännchen von Tharau...........**7** C5

**SLEEPING**
Klaipėda Old Town Hostel...................**8** D2
Litinterp................................................**9** B4
Preliudija Guesthouse..........................**10** C5
Radisson SAS Klaipėda.........................**11** B3

**EATING**
Anikės Teatras.......................................**12** C5
Kinų Virtuve...........................................**13** C5

**DRINKING**
Kurpiai...................................................**14** C5
Memelis..................................................**15** C5

**TRANSPORT**
Bus Station............................................**16** D1
Passenger Ferry Terminal.....................**17** B5

To Palanga (27km);

Train Station

Priestočio gatvė

Butkų Juzės gatvė

Lietuvninkų aikštė

Vilties gatvė

Mažvydo Sculpture Park

To Kaunas (212km);
Vilnius (312km)

Donelaičio aikštė

Danės krantinė

Danės River

Harbour

Danės gatvė

Old Town

Curonian Lagoon

Teatro aikštė

Central Market

Turgaus aikštė

Klaipėda Castle

To Curonian Spit (500m);
Smiltynė (500m)

To New Ferry Terminal (2km);
International Ferry Port (7km);
Scandlines (7km)

LITHUANIA

**AUTHOR EXPERIENCE – THE LEGENDARY VIKTORIJA**

Creaky Soviet-style hotels manned by snarling babushkas are a dying breed in the Baltics, yet there's a true classic of the genre defiantly hogging real estate in downtown Klaipėda. Sentimentalists might call the **Viktorija Hotel** ( ☎ 412 190; Šmikaus gatvė 2; s/d/tr with shared bathroom 45/68/90) a masterpiece. Modernists would call it an abomination. As many travellers do, I ended up calling one of its single rooms home for a night after failing to find a remotely better deal in Klaipėda.

'Positively ghastly' is how one local city guide describes the Viktorija, and quite frankly that's being kind. My room featured hideous Soviet furniture, pockmarked walls covered (barely) by 1970s wallpaper, broken windows and a solitary sink spitting rusty cold water. The bed sagged almost to the floor and groaned loudly at the slightest hint of movement. Deafening street noise streamed through the broken windows. But what truly made the room stand out was the stench, a surly mix of stale cigarette smoke, mildew and human sweat that uncannily grew worse as the night progressed. Quite simply, it rendered sleep impossible.

Surely the Baltics' most authentic Soviet experience, the Viktorija really has to be experienced to be believed. But experience it with caution.

character from a love poem thought to be written by the 17th-century German poet Simon Dach. The statue is a replica of the original destroyed during the war.

West of Old Town are the remains of Klaipėda's old moat-protected castle. The **Klaipėda Castle Museum** ( ☎ 410 524; Pilies gatvė 4; adult/child 4/2 Lt; ☼ 10am-6pm Wed-Sun Jun-Aug, 10am-6pm Tue-Sat Sep-May) inside the one remaining tower tells the castle's story from the 13th to 17th centuries.

The city celebrates its nautical heritage each July with a flamboyant **Sea Festival** that draws crowds for a weekend of concerts, parties, exhibitions and nautical manoeuvres.

## Sleeping

**Klaipėda Old Town Hostel** ( ☎ 211 879; guest lace@ yahoo.com; Butkų Juzės gatvė 7/4; dm 32 Lt, linen 2 Lt; P ✗ ▣ ) A friendly but generally unexceptional hostel, poorly located next to the bus station.

**Litinterp** ( ☎ 310 296; klaipeda@litinterp.lt; Puodžių gatvė 17; s/d 100/160 Lt, with shared bathroom 80/140 Lt; P ) While it's not for everyone, those who subscribe to the pinewood-heavy, breakfast-on-a-nightstand formula here wish there were Litinterps scattered throughout the world.

**Preliudija Guesthouse** ( ☎ 310 077; www.preliudija .com; Kepėjų gatvė 7; s/d from 160/180 Lt; P ) While the big boys charge big bucks for half the quality, this six-room Old Town offering has minimalist, spacious L-shaped rooms in a charming old house. Breakfast costs an extra 17 Lt.

**Radisson SAS Klaipėda** ( ☎ 490 800; www.radisson sas.com; Šaulių gatvė 28; s/d €125/135; P ✗ ⚇ ▣ ) The shipshape rooms here have candy cane–

patterned bedspreads and a tasteful nautical theme. It finishes many lengths ahead of the pack in the regatta to be Klaipėda's best hotel. Rates go down big-time on weekends.

## Eating & Drinking

**Kinų Virtuve** (Tiltų gatvė 15; mains 10 Lt; ☼ 11am-2am) Hole-in-the-wall Chinese resto provides some of the only cheap eats in Klaipėda.

**Anikės Teatras** (Sukilėlių gatvė 8-10; mains 20-35 Lt) For more upmarket dining try this European food palace with a plump terrace right on Teatro aikštė. Its sister restaurants serve Lithuanian and Chinese food.

**Kurpiai** (Kurpių gatvė 1a; mains 15-20 Lt; ☼ noon-3am) Eat fresh seafood to the sound of saxophone at this legendary jazz bar where the dance floor is jumping every night of the week.

**Memelis** (Žvejų Žėjų gatvė 4; mains 15-20 Lt) The first floor is a microbrewery and the 3rd floor a salsa-infused nightclub in this character-laden old storehouse.

## Getting There & Away

Klaipėda **bus station** ( ☎ 411 547; Butkų Juzės 9) welcomes daily buses from Vilnius (49 Lt, 3¼ hours, 14 daily), Kaunas (38 Lt, three hours, 10 daily), Liepaja (14 Lt, 2½ hours, two daily), Šiauliai (23 Lt, 2½ hours, six daily), Palanga (bus/minibus 1.50/3 Lt, 45 minutes, every 20 minutes) and Kaliningrad via Nida (25 Lt, three hours, three daily).

For international bus schedules see p467.

The **passenger terminal** (Žvejų gatvė 8) for ferries to the Smiltynė ferry landing on the Curonian Spit is near Klaipėda Castle west of Old Town. Ferries leave every half-hour in the high season and cost 1.50 Lt return (10 minutes). Vehicles must use the **New Ferry Terminal** (Nemuno gatvė 8; per car 32 Lt), 2.5km south of the passenger terminal. Services depart at least hourly.

The **International Ferry Port** ( ☎ 395 050; www .spk.lt; Perkėlos gatvė 10) is another 5km south of the New Ferry Terminal. Take bus 1 or 1a (1 Lt) to both the New Ferry Terminal (10 minutes) and the International Ferry Port (30 minutes).

# CURONIAN SPIT

This magical pigtail of land, dangling off the western rump of Lithuania, hosts some of the world's most precious sand dunes and a menagerie of elk, deer and avian wildlife. Just 3.8km at its widest point, the spit looks positively brittle on a map, but in person it seems much sturdier, thanks to the pine forests that cover 70% of its surface. A few dunes rise high above those forests, creating a surreal effect.

The fragile spit, which Unesco recognised as a World Heritage site in 2000, has faced a number of environmental threats over the years, beginning with the clear felling of its forests in the 16th century. Lately the dunes have been eroding rapidly and tourism is exacerbating the problem. When observing the dunes, stick to the marked paths.

The entire Curonian Spit was Prussian territory until WWI. These days the spit is divided roughly evenly between Lithuania and Russia's Kaliningrad region in the south. Lithuania's share of the spit is protected as the **Curonian Spit National Park** (www.nerija.lt), which has two **visitors centres** Smiltynė ( ☎ 46-402 257; Smiltynės plentas 11; ☘ 8am-5pm Mon-Fri, 9am-4pm Sat, 9am-2pm Sun Jun-Aug, closed Sat & Sun Sep-May); Nida ( ☎ 51256; Naglių gatvė 8; ☘ 9am-5pm Mon-Sat, 9am-2pm Sun May-Sep) with abundant information on walking, cycling, boating and lazing activities.

Administratively, the Lithuania side is divided into two regions: the township of Smiltynė, which is part of Klaipėda; and the Neringa municipality, which contains the townships Alksnynė, Juodkrantė, Pervalka, Preila and touristy Nida.

## GETTING THERE & AWAY

To get to the spit you need to take a ferry or bus from Klaipėda or take the Kaliningrad–Klaipėda bus (see opposite).

From Smiltynė, buses and microbuses (7 Lt, 1¼ hr) run regularly to/from the **Nida bus station** ( ☎ 54859; Naglių gatvė 20) via Juodkrantė.

## Smiltynė
☎ 46

Smiltynė is where the ferries from Klaipėda dock. The visitor centre here is a good place to plot strategies for forays south and has a small nature museum.

On summer weekends Klaipėda residents cram Smiltynė, flocking to its beaches and to the **Lithuanian Sea Museum** ( ☎ 490 740; adult/student 9/5 Lt, dolphin/sea lion show 13/3 Lt; ☘ 10.30am-6.30pm Tue-Sun Jun-Aug; 10.30am-5.30pm Wed-Sun May & Sep; 10.30am-4.30pm Sat & Sun Oct-Apr), which contains an aquarium with seal and sea-lion shows.

## Neringa
☎ 469 / pop 2600

South of Smiltynė the crowds begin to thin and you enter Neringa, which slinks majestically southward all the way to the Russian border. The fresh air and scent of pine grow headier as you get further and further away from civilisation.

### JUODKRANTĖ

Juodkrantė has a few rather strange attractions and is a popular place to engage in one of Neringa's trademark activities: buying and tasting freshly caught and smoked fish, which is sold from several wooden houses along the main road, Rėzos gatvė.

Top of the strange sights list is the **Raganų Kalnas** (Witches' Hill), a spooky sculpture trail through gorgeous forest with large, fairytale Lithuanian wooden carvings.

Less than 1km south of Juodkrantė is one of Neringa's must-see attractions: a massive **colony of grey herons and cormorants**. Wooden steps lead from the road to a viewing platform where the panorama of thousands of nests amid pine trees – cormorants to the north, herons to the south – is breathtaking. In March and April the air is thick with birds carrying huge sticks to build their nests; in May the cacophony rises to a deafening crescendo as the chicks are born.

In Juodkrantė stay at the marvellously rustic **Vila Flora** ( ☎ 53024; www.vilaflora.lt; Kalno gatvė 7a; s/d/tr 220/250/300 Lt; meals 30 Lt; P 🖳 ), which also serves up some of the best food on the spit.

### NIDA

Neringa's southernmost settlement is Nida, a charming resort town that slumbers much of the year but in the summer becomes Neringa's tourist nerve centre. It truly is a special place that somehow manages to maintain its charm and laid-back feel even when the crowds pick up.

**Hansabank** (Taikos gatvė 5) has an ATM. The **tourist information centre** ( ☎ 52345; Taikos gatvė 4; www.visitneringa.lt; 9am-8pm Mon-Sat, 9am-3pm Sun Jun-Aug, 10am-6pm Mon-Fri Sep-May) books accommodation and stocks loads of useful information on walks, bike rides, fishing boat trips etc.

### Sights & Activities

An excellent way to see the spit is on a **bicycle**. A flat cycling trail runs all the way from Nida to Smiltynė, and you stand a good chance of seeing elk or other wildlife at any point along that path. There are bicycles for hire on almost every street corner in Nida; some allow you to leave your bike in Smiltynė and bus it back to Nida.

The Curonian Spit's awe-inspiring sand dunes are on full display from the smashed granite sundial atop the 52m-high **Parnidis Dune**. The panorama of coastline, forests and the spit's most stunning dune extending into Kaliningrad to the south is unforgettable. You can walk up here from town on a nature trail (ask at the tourist information centre for a map) or drive via Taikos gatvė.

Back in Nida, check out the **Ethnographic Museum** ( ☎ 52372; Naglių gatvė 4; admission 2 Lt) and the **Thomas Mann Memorial Museum** ( ☎ 52260; Skruzdynės gatvė 17; adult/child 2/0.50 Lt; 10am-6pm Tue-Sun) in the Nobel Prize–winning German writer's former summer house.

Another of Nida's many highlights is its **architecture**, a mix of classic German half-timbered construction and quaint wooden houses with frilly eaves and intricate façades.

### Sleeping & Eating

The tourist information centre or Litinterp (p462) in Klaipėda can help arrange accommodation in private houses, but contact them weeks in advance in the summer. In the winter expect steep discounts on listed prices here.

**Medikas** ( ☎ 52985; Kuverto gatvė 14; dm/r from 30/130 Lt; **P** ) They're nothing fancy, but the cheap bare-bones rooms at this Soviet place will satisfy bargain hunters.

**Vandeja** ( ☎ 52742; www.forelle.lt; Naglių gatvė 17; d/apt from 120/350 Lt; **P** ) Just one of many exceptional little guesthouses in Nida, with huge, extraordinarily comfortable rooms and all the mod cons you could want. Has an enviable location down by the water.

**Miško namas** ( ☎ 52290; www.miskonamas.com, Pamario gatvė 11-2; d/ste 110/250 Lt; **P** **□** ) Another charmer – every room here has its own fridge, sink and kettle and a couple have balconies. Self-cater in the cosy communal kitchen. Take note of the 180-year-old twisting wooden staircase.

# LITHUANIA DIRECTORY

## ACCOMMODATION

Vilnius has a serious room crunch so book ahead in the high season. The tourist information offices can help in a pinch, but they tend to utilise unexceptional midrange hotels. Coastal locations such as Palanga and the Curonian Spit are popular with Lithuanians as well as foreigners, and rooms fill up months ahead in the summer.

Vilnius has no shortage of excellent top-end lodgings. Many fine business hotels reduce their rates at weekends. Good budget accommodation is scarce in Vilnius and most other cities; the few deals that exist are highlighted prominently in this book. Vilnius has a few hostels; none are state-of-the-art, but expect that to change in the near future. Outside of Vilnius most hostels are grim Soviet affairs, but in rural areas you can find perfectly fine hotel rooms at hostel prices. Most camping grounds are cheap and basic (10 Lt to 25 Lt for a camp site), but they are gradually improving.

For a double room in Vilnius in the May to September high season you'll pay about 150 Lt for budget lodging and up to 600 Lt at the top end. You'll pay much less in the regions, where good budget rooms start as low as 50 Lt.

If you can't find a room somewhere, check with the local tourist information office for help. **In Your Pocket** (www.inyourpocket.com) has complete hotel listings for Vilnius, Kaunas, Šiauliai and Klaipėda.

## ACTIVITIES

Lithuania is conducive to any activity revolving around its gazillion forests: hiking, mushrooming, berry-picking, picnicking and bird-watching are at the top of the list. Lakes are also abundant, especially in the wilderness of Aukštaitija National Park (p455), where both hiking and boating activities abound.

Cycling is becoming more popular in flat Lithuania. Most towns and cities have several outlets that rent out bikes. Good places for long day-rides include the Curonian Spit (p463), and Druskininkai (p455).

In hoops-mad Lithuania it's not hard to find a pick-up basketball game at any time, anywhere. Palanga (p460) is popular for kite surfing.

## BUSINESS HOURS

Most shops open at 9am or 10am and close around 6pm on weekdays and Saturday. Banks are generally open between 8am and 5pm on weekdays. Restaurants tend to open around 10am and close around 11pm, but many stay open much later on weekends, especially in cities.

## DISABLED TRAVELLERS

Lithuania is not the most friendly country for disabled travellers; the cobbled streets of Vilnius' Old Town make it difficult for wheelchair users and the visually impaired. However, public transport in Vilnius has disabled access and most of the nicer hotels in Vilnius and other cities do have a room or two kitted out for mobility-impaired guests.

## EMBASSIES & CONSULATES
### Lithuanian Embassies & Consulates

Check www.urm.lt for a full listing of Lithuanian missions abroad and foreign missions in Lithuania.

**Australia** ( ☎ 02-9498 2571; 40B Fiddens Wharf Rd, Killara, Sydney, NSW 2071)

**Canada** ( ☎ 613-567 5458; 130 Albert St, Ste 204, Ottawa, Ontario K1P 5G4)

**Estonia** ( ☎ 2-631 4030; Uus tänay 15, Tallinn)

**France** ( ☎ 01 40 54 50 50; 22 Blvd de Courcelles, 75017 Paris)

**Germany** ( ☎ 030-890 68 10; Charitestrasse 9, 10711 Berlin)

**Ireland** ( ☎ 01 6688292; Merrion Rd, Ballsbridge, Dublin 4)

**Latvia** ( ☎ 2732 1519; Rūpniecibas iela 24, 1010 Rīga)

**New Zealand** ( ☎ 09-336 7711; 28 Heather St, Parnell, Auckland)

**Russia** Moscow ( ☎ 495-785 8605, Borisoglebsky per 10, Moscow 121069); Kaliningrad ( ☎ 401-2-957 688; ul Proletarskaya 133, Kaliningrad)

**UK** ( ☎ 020-7486 6401; 84 Gloucester Pl, London W1H 3HN)

**USA** ( ☎ 202-234-5860; 2622 16th St NW, Washington, DC 20009)

### Embassies & Consulates in Lithuania

The following embassies and consulates are in Vilnius:

**Australia** ( ☎ 5-212 3369, emergency 8-687 11117; australia@consulate.lt; Vilniaus gatvė 23)

**Belarus** ( ☎ 5-266 2200; www.belarus.lt; Mindaugo gatvė 13)

**Canada** ( ☎ 5-249 0950; www.canada.lt; Jogailos gatvė 4)

**Estonia** ( ☎ 5-278 0200; www.estemb.lt; Mickevičiaus gatvė 4a)

**France** ( ☎ 5-212 29 79; www.ambafrance-lt.org; Švarco gatvė 1)

**Germany** ( ☎ 5-210 6400; www.deutschebotschaft -wilna.lt; Sierakausko gatvė 24/8)

**Latvia** ( ☎ 5-213 1260; embassy.lithuania@mfa.gov.lv; Čiurlionio gatvė 76)

**Poland** ( ☎ 5-270 9001; ambpol@tdd.lt; Smėlio gatvė 20a)

**Russia** ( ☎ 5-272 1763; www.rusemb.lt; Latvių gatvė 53/54)

**UK** ( ☎ 5-246 2900; www.britain.lt; Antakalnio gatvė 2)

**USA** ( ☎ 5-266 5500; www.usembassy.lt; Akmenų gatvė 6)

## FESTIVALS & EVENTS

There's no better time to observe Lithuanian culture than during its stupendous Unesco-honoured **national song festival** (www.lfcc.lt), held every four years in July in Vilnius. The next one is scheduled for 2007.

The pan-Baltic **Baltica International Folklore Festival** takes place all over Lithuania every three years. Lithuania is due to host the festival in 2008.

## HOLIDAYS

**New Year's Day/National Flag Day** 1 January

**Independence Day** 16 February (anniversary of 1918 independence declaration)

**Restoration of the Independent Lithuanian State** 11 March

**Easter** (Good Friday and Easter Monday) April

**International Labour Day** 1 May

**Feast of St John (Midsummer)** 24 June

**Statehood Day** 6 July; commemoration of Grand Duke Mindaugas' coronation in 13th century

**Feast of the Assumption** 15 August

**Vytautas the Great's Coronation** 8 September

**25 October** Constitution Day

**All Saints' Day** 1 November

**Christmas** 25 and 26 December

## INTERNET ACCESS

Vilnius has surprisingly few internet cafés – and none that are open 24 hours – but several main streets are free wi-fi zones, as are the airport and scores of cafés and hotels. Most

LITHUANIA

reasonably sized provincial towns have at least one place to log on. The entire country is growing increasingly wi-fi-friendly.

## LANGUAGE

Lithuanian is the older of the two surviving Baltic branches of the Indo-European language group.

English is widely spoken in Vilnius but is not well understood outside the capital. Most Lithuanians over the age of 25 speak fluent Russian, while German is a popular second language on the formerly Prussian west coast.

## MONEY

Lithuania's plan to adopt the euro in 2007 did not pan out as the country could not meet its required inflation targets. Thus, the litas (the plural is litai; Lt) will be the country's currency for at least a couple more years. The litas is divided into 100 centai. It is pegged to the euro at the rate of 3.45 Lt per euro.

All but the smallest Lithuanian towns usually have at least one bank with a functional ATM. Most big banks cash travellers cheques and exchange most major currencies. Credit cards are widely accepted.

## POST

Sending a postcard/letter abroad costs 1.20/1.70 Lt. Mail to North America takes about 10 days, and to Europe about a week.

## TELEPHONE

Lithuania's digitalised telephone network is run by **Lietuvos Telekomas** (www.telecom.lt).

To call other cities within Lithuania, dial ☎ 8 followed by the city code and phone number. To make an international call dial ☎ 00 before the country code.

To call Lithuania from abroad, dial ☎ 370 then the city code, followed by the phone number.

Picking up a local prepaid SIM card allows for pain-free and relatively cheap calling

---

**EMERGENCY NUMBERS**

■ Ambulance ☎ 03

■ Emergency ☎ 112 from mobile phone

■ Fire ☎ 01

■ Police ☎ 02

---

and texting. Mobile companies **Bitė** (www.bite .lt), **Omnitel** (www.omnitel.lt) and **Tele 2** (www.tele2 .lt) sell prepaid SIM cards; Tele2 is the only one to offer pan-Baltic roaming with prepaid cards.

To call a mobile phone within Lithuania, dial ☎ 8 followed by the eight-digit number; to call a mobile from abroad dial ☎ 370 instead of ☎ 8.

Public telephones, which are increasingly rare given the widespread use of mobiles, are blue and only accept phonecards, which are sold in denominations of 9 Lt, 13 Lt, 16 Lt and 30 Lt at newspaper kiosks.

## VISAS

Citizens from the EU, Australia, Canada, Israel, Japan, New Zealand, Switzerland and the US do not require visas for entry into Lithuania if staying for less than 90 days. South African nationals are required to obtain a visa. For information on other countries and obtaining a visa, visit www .migracija.lt.

# TRANSPORT IN LITHUANIA

## GETTING THERE & AWAY
### Air

The Europe-wide budget-airline explosion has hit Lithuania with a vengeance. Kaunas, not Vilnius, is the destination for budget flights, but most tourists landing in Kaunas immediately hop in a car or bus for the one-hour drive to Vilnius. Flights to Kaunas land at **Kaunas International Airport** ( ☎ 750 195; www.kaunasair.lt) about 12km north of the centre. Its website has updated timetables.

Most international traffic to Lithuania still goes through **Vilnius International Airport** ( ☎ 230 6666; www.vilnius-airport.lt; Rodūnios gatvė 2). See the airport website for updated timetables and a full list of airlines flying to/from Vilnius. Local budget provider **Lithuania Airlines** ( ☎ 252 5555; www.lal.lt) runs some seasonal flights in and out of **Palanga Airport** ( ☎ 460-52020; www.palanga-airport .lt). **SAS** ( ☎ 460-52300; Palanga airport) flies to Palanga from Copenhagen.

**Air Baltic** (www.airbaltic.com); Old Town ( ☎ 234 0618; Universiteto gatvė 10-7); airport ( ☎ 235 6000) runs direct flights between Vilnius and about a dozen Western European destinations.

Major international carriers with direct flights to Vilnius include the following:

**Aeroflot** (code SU; ☎ 212 4189; www.aeroflot.ru)

**Austrian Airlines** (code OS; ☎ 279 1416; www.aua .com)

**British Airways** (code BA; ☎ 720 7097; www.brit ishairways.com)

**ČSA** (Czech Airlines; code OK; ☎ 215 1503; www.czech -airlines.com)

**Estonian Air** (code OV; ☎ 273 9022; www.estonian-air .com)

**Finnair** (code AY; ☎ 261 9339; www.finnair.com)

**LOT** (code LO; ☎ 273 9020; www.lot.com)

**Lufthansa** (code LH; ☎ 232 9290; www.lufthansa.com)

**SAS Scandinavian Airlines** (code SK; ☎ 235 6000; www .sas.lt)

## Land
### BORDER CROSSINGS
Crossing into Latvia or Poland is painless: just present your passport for stamping and you'll most likely be on your way.

If you're planning on crossing into Russia (Kaliningrad) or Belarus in a rental car, check your rental conditions very carefully – most rental companies forbid this. For all road crossings into Russia (Kaliningrad) or Belarus, see the boxed text on p929.

### BUS
The main international bus companies operating in Lithuania are **Eurolines** (www.eurolines.lt; Vilnius bus station ☎ 5-215 1377; Kaunas bus station ☎ 37-202 020; Klaipėda ☎ 46-415 555) and **Ecolines** (www.ecolines .lt; Vilnius ☎ 5-262 0020; Vilniaus gatvė 45; Kaunas bus station ☎ 37-320 2020; Klaipėda ☎ 46-310 103; Šiaulia bus station ☎ 41-399 400).

Eurolines, Ecolines or one of a few smaller carriers have services between Vilnius and the following destinations in Eastern Europe: Riga (45 Lt, five hours, at least four daily), Kaliningrad (50 Lt, seven hours, two daily), Tallinn (95 Lt, 12 hours, two daily), Warsaw (97 Lt, nine hours, three daily), Moscow (99 Lt, 13 hours, daily), Minsk (30 Lt, four hours, at least five daily) and Gdansk (110 Lt, 10½ hours, nightly). A few of these bus services continue westward to Kaunas and/or Klaipėda; some northbound buses stop in Šiauliai.

There are a couple of weekly buses from Vilnius to Kyiv and a handful of Western European cities, including London and several German cities. There's a daily bus to Berlin (from 170 Lt, 16 hours).

### CAR & MOTORCYCLE
Coming from the south, you're looking at a 30-minute to one-hour wait at the two Polish border crossings (Ogrodniki and Budzisko). Lines at the Latvian border in the north are smaller. Have your passport, insurance and registration documents ready.

### TRAIN
Vilnius is linked by regular direct trains to Moscow (from 110 Lt, 15 hours, two to three daily), St Petersburg (from 94 Lt, 20 hours, daily), Kaliningrad (from 45 Lt, seven hours, at least twice daily), Warsaw (from 85 Lt, 12 hours, three weekly) and Minsk (40 Lt, 4½ hours, at least five daily). You'll need a Belarus visa for the Moscow train. There is also sporadic service to Lviv and Kyiv in Ukraine, but these also go through Belarus.

## Sea
Klaipėda is the port of call for all international ferries bound for Lithuania. The vast majority are cargo ferries, some with room for a few passengers.

**DFDS Lisco** ( ☎ 46-395 050; www.dfdslisco.com; bookings: pfei@dfdslisco.com) has a passenger ferry service between Klaipėda and Kiel (230 Lt, 21 hours, six weekly). Book through Krantas Travel (p460).

**Scandlines** ( ☎ 46-310561; www.scandlines.lt; reservations: ferry@scandlines.lt; Naujosis Sodo gatvė 1) has limited passenger space on its twice weekly cargo ferries between Klaipėda and Aabenraa (Denmark; adult/student €136/120, 32 hours) via Århus (Denmark; 17 hours).

## GETTING AROUND
### Air
**Lithuanian Airlines** ( ☎ 252 5555; www.lal.lt) has three to seven weekly flights from Vilnius to Palanga and return from May to September only.

### Bicycle
Get everything you need to know about bike touring in Lithuania from the website of the **Lithuanian Bicycle Information Centre** (www.bicycle .lt). Lithuania is flat and its once-disastrous roads are gradually improving. For more on bike riding see p465.

### Bus
Timetables for local buses are displayed prominently in most train stations. From Vilnius

you can get to/from the following destinations by bus:

| Destination | Cost | Duration | Frequency |
| --- | --- | --- | --- |
| Druskininkai | 19 Lt | 2hr | 11 daily |
| Kaunas | 19 Lt | 1½hr | 2-3 hourly |
| Klaipėda | 49 Lt | 3¼hr | 14 daily |
| Palanga | 52 Lt | 4hr | 7 daily |
| iauliai | 32 Lt | 3hr | 9 daily |
| Trakai | 4 Lt | 45min | 2-3 hourly |

To Kaunas there are also regular minibuses, which are quicker.

## Car & Motorcycle

You can drive from any one point in Lithuania to another in a couple of hours. Modern four-lane highways link Vilnius–Klaipėda (via Kaunas) and Vilnius–Panavėžys.

The big international car-rental agencies are well represented at Vilnius Airport. Try **Avis** ( ☎ 232 9316; www.avis.lt), **Budget** ( ☎ 230 6708; www .budget.lt) or **Sixt** ( ☎ 239 5636; www.sixt.lt). You'll save a ton of money by renting from a local opera-tor. Charismatic **Rimas** ( ☎ 277 6213, 8-698-21662; rimas.cars@is.lt) rents older cars at the lowest rates in town and just might invite you ice fishing.

The speed limit in Lithuania is 50km/h in cities and 90km/h to 110km/h outside the city and on highways. Headlights must be switched on at all times and winter tyres must be fitted between 1 November and 1 March.

## Local Transport

Lithuanian cities are generously covered by networks of buses, trolleybuses and minibuses. In most towns you must punch your bus ticket or you'll risk a fine.

## Train

You can lumber from Vilnius to a few domestic destinations on Lithuania's clunky suburban trains. Destinations include Kaunas (11 Lt, 1¼ hours, 13 daily), Klaipėda (40 Lt, five hours, two daily), Paneriai (1.20 Lt, 20 minutes, 23 daily), Šiauliai (24 Lt, four hours, five to eight daily), Ignalina (10 Lt, two hours, seven daily) and Trakai (2.50 Lt, 40 minutes, seven daily).

# Macedonia Македонија

Mountainous Macedonia still has an air of mystery to it. Simultaneously ancient and brand new, it's struggling to find its place in the postcommunist world. Black-clad Orthodox monks are just as much a part of this renewal as the hordes of teenagers, bedecked in the latest Italian fashions, sipping coffee in the stylish bars of the capital.

For outdoors types it's a paradise. Its extensive wilderness allows ample opportunities for hikers, mountain climbers and skiers.

Its ancient ruins will fascinate anyone with even a smidgen of interest in history and its wealth of art ranges from doe-eyed Byzantine icons to square-jawed socialist-realist statues.

In short, for a little place it's crammed with something for just about everyone.

Quite apart from Macedonia's spectacular peaks, lakes and rivers, it's the hospitality of the people of this most southern of Slavic nations that will make your visit truly memorable.

## FAST FACTS

- **Area** 25,713 sq km
- **Capital** Skopje
- **Currency** Macedonian Denar (MKD); €1 = 64.10MKD; US$1=50.50MKD; UK£1 = 94.70MKD; A$1 = 37.95MKD; ¥100 = 42.90MKD; NZ$1 = 32.50MKD
- **Famous for** Alexander the Great, Mother Teresa (born in Skopje), Lake Ohrid
- **Official Languages** Macedonian, Albanian
- **Phrases** *zdravo* (hello); *blagodaram/fala* (thanks); *molam* (please); *do gledanje* (goodbye)
- **Population** 2,050,554
- **Telephone Codes** country code ☎ 389; international access code ☎ 00
- **Visas** not needed for citizens of the EU, USA and New Zealand; most others do require one, see p490

MACEDONIA

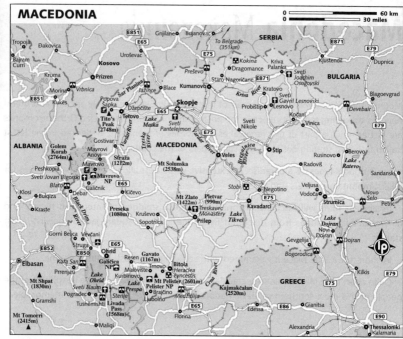

## MACEDONIA

0 ————— 60 km
0 ————— 30 miles

## HIGHLIGHTS

■ Combine history, culture, natural beauty and groovy bars by the lake at spectacular **Ohrid** (p481)

■ Get a whiff of Ottoman grandeur at stylish **Bitola** (p485), with a national park on its doorstep and the nicest urban space in Macedonia

■ Whet your appetite for this ancient land with Macedonia's capital **Skopje** (p474), which dishes up great cuisine, buzzy bars and historic sites

■ Follow in the footsteps of hermits, monks and revolutionaries via the mountainous paths around beautiful **Lake Matka** (p480)

## ITINERARIES

■ **Three days** Spend a day exploring the sights of Skopje. Then get a bus to Ohrid and spend two days poking about the churches and lazing around and in the glorious lake.

■ **One week** As above, but take an extra day in Skopje to visit Lake Matka. From Ohrid visit the Sveti Naum monastery for a day of ancient frescoes, posing peacocks and

boating on the lake. Head on to Bitola to stroll about the Heraclea Lyncestis ruins, before staking out a spot on the fashion runway that masquerades as the main street. If you're not ruined out, see the ancient city of Stobi on returning to Skopje.

### HOW MUCH?

■ **Cup of coffee** 70MKD

■ **Loaf of bread** 20MKD

■ **Souvenir icon** 186MKD

■ **Six pieces of kebapci (meat rolls)** 90MKD

■ **Short taxi ride** 50MKD

### LONELY PLANET INDEX

■ **Litre of petrol** 60MKD

■ **Litre of bottled water** 20MKD

■ **Skopsko beer** 80MKD

■ **Souvenir T-shirt** 450MKD

■ **Street snack (burger)** 60MKD

## CLIMATE & WHEN TO GO

Temperatures vary widely: summer temperatures can reach 40°C, while in winter it can drop as low as minus 30°C. The average annual temperatures are above 10°C almost everywhere. Summers are hot and dry, while in winter the snow falls in the mountains from November to April.

The best time to enjoy Macedonia is between May and September, and the peak tourist season is from mid-July to mid-August, when locals take their holidays.

## HISTORY
### Early History

Historical and geographical Macedonia is divided between the Republic of Macedonia, the Greek province of Macedonia and a corner of Bulgaria called Pirin Macedonia. The largest portion of the historic Macedonia region is now Greek territory, a point that Greeks are always quick to make when disputing Macedonia's use of the name, as they invariably do. In any case, the region was the homeland of Alexander the Great, who sallied forth to conquer the ancient world in the 4th century BC. Rarely independent, the territory of the Republic of Macedonia has often been a staging post for invaders. Roman rule was entrenched after the conquest of Macedonia in 168 BC, and over the next 500 years the ancestors of the Vlach people developed a Latin dialect. Today's Vlach community speak a language called Aromanian, which, as the names suggests, is related to Romanian and Latin. Many Vlach villages lie along the route of the Roman Via Egnatia, a vital military road and trade route that stretched from Durrës in Albania to Istanbul (Constantinople) in Turkey. When the Roman Empire was divided in the 4th century AD, this region came under the Eastern Roman Empire, ruled from Constantinople. Slavs started settling in the area in the 7th century AD, and not long after adopted the Christian faith of earlier residents.

In the 9th century the region was conquered by Car Simeon (r 893–927) and later, under Car Samoil (r 980–1014), Macedonia was the centre of a powerful Bulgarian state. Samoil's defeat by Byzantium in 1014 ushered in a long period when Macedonia passed back and forth between Byzantium, Bulgaria and Serbia. Around this time the first Roma (also known as Gypsy) people arrived in the area after a long migration from northern India.

After the crushing defeat of Serbia by the Ottomans in 1389, Macedonia became part of the Ottoman Empire.

The Ottomans divided civil life according to religious affiliation, in what was called the *millet* system. The Greek Orthodox Church was given much power over the Macedonian Christians, causing great resentment.

In 1878 Russia defeated Turkey, and Macedonia was ceded to Bulgaria by the Treaty of San Stefano. The Western powers, fearing the creation of a powerful Russian satellite in the heart of the Balkans, forced Bulgaria to return Macedonia to Ottoman rule.

### Nationalism

In 1893 Macedonian nationalists formed the Internal Macedonian Revolutionary Organization (VMRO) to fight for independence from Turkey, culminating in the Ilinden uprising of August 1903, which was brutally suppressed in October of the same year. Although the nationalist leader Goce Delčev died before the revolt, he has become the symbol of Macedonian nationalism.

The First Balkan War of 1912 saw Greece, Serbia, Bulgaria and Montenegro fighting together against Turkey. During the Second Balkan War in 1913, Greece and Serbia ousted the Bulgarians and carved up Macedonia. Frustrated by this, VMRO continued the struggle against the new rulers, and in response the interwar government in Belgrade banned the Macedonian language and the name Macedonia. Though some VMRO elements supported Bulgarian occupation during WWII, many more joined Josip Broz Tito's partisans, and in 1943 it was agreed that postwar Macedonia would have full republic status in a future Yugoslavia. Tito led the communist resistance to German occupation in WWII and later became prime minister, then president, of Yugoslavia.

The end of WWII brought Macedonians hope of unifying their peoples. This was encouraged by the Greek Communist Party and Bulgaria's recognition of its Macedonian minorities. However the Stalin-Tito split of 1948, and the end of the Greek civil war in 1949, put an end to such hopes. Nonetheless, the first Macedonian grammar was published in 1952 and an independent Macedonian Orthodox Church was reinstated.

Over the subsequent 40 years Yugoslavia prospered by comparison with other Eastern

European states, with citizens free to travel and worship as they wished. The country was also open as a tourist destination.

## Independence

On 8 September 1991 Macedonians held a referendum on independence. Seventy-four percent voted in favour and in January 1992 the country declared its full independence from the former Yugoslavia. Macedonian leader Kiro Gligorov artfully negotiated the only peaceful withdrawal of the Yugoslav army from any of the former republics.

Greece withheld diplomatic recognition of Macedonia and demanded that the country find another name, worried that it implied territorial claims over Aegean Macedonia, which they had obtained in the 1913 carve-up. At Greek insistence, Macedonia was forced to use the 'provisional' title Former Yugoslav Republic of Macedonia (FYROM) in order to be admitted to the UN in April 1993. When the USA (following six EU countries) recognised FYROM in February 1994, Greece declared an economic embargo against Macedonia and closed the Aegean Macedonian port of Thessaloniki to trade. The embargo was lifted in November 1995 after Macedonia changed its flag and agreed to discuss its name with Greece. To date, there's been no resolution of this thorny issue. Increasingly the name Macedonia is being used internationally, despite Greek intransigence.

Meanwhile, the country's ethnic Albanian minority was seeking better representation on the political and cultural fronts, and tried to set up an Albanian-speaking university in Tetovo in 1995. Since Macedonian was the only official language according to the country's constitution, the authorities declared the university illegal and tried to close it down. Soon after, President Gligorov lost an eye in an assassination attempt and tensions increased.

Over the following years, an Albanian rebel group called the National Liberation Army was formed and claimed responsibility for a number of bombings. This escalated in February 2001 into armed conflict in western Macedonia. Hostilities did not last long, however. With the signing of the Ohrid Framework Agreement in August 2001, the Macedonian government agreed to greater political participation for the Albanian minority, official recognition of the

Albanian language, as well as an increase in the number of ethnic Albanian police officers throughout the country.

Macedonia became an official candidate for EU membership in December 2005 and has been steadily progressing towards that goal. Stumbling blocks may be the name issue with Greece and increasing European concerns about enlargement. Macedonia also hopes to join NATO before the end of the decade.

At the time of writing Macedonia has found itself caught between European justice and a possible NATO partner, in a case where a German man was allegedly detained by Macedonian officials when entering the country before being handed over to America's CIA, kidnapped and flown to Afghanistan for interrogation. There is some concern that Macedonia's non-cooperation with European investigators may prove a stumbling block to EU membership.

## PEOPLE

There's a reason why the French call a mixed salad a *salade macédoine*. It's hard to imagine a place where ethnicity is such a confused topic. Bulgarians think that Macedonians are really Bulgarians, some Serbs think they're actually Serbs. Greeks think they're anything but Macedonian – a name they consider they own the rights to, even though it's well documented that the Ancient Greeks despised the ancient Macedonians.

As for the Macedonians themselves? One thing they're sure of is that they're Macedonian. Most will accept that they're of Slavic origin, although some will argue black and blue that they're Slavicised descendents of the ancient Macedonian people.

Like much of the Balkans, ethnicity rather than nationhood defines people's identities. Local Albanians and Turks are never referred to (or refer to themselves) as Macedonian, even if their families have lived in the area for several generations.

According to the 2002 census the total population of just over two million is made up of Macedonians of Slav ethnicity (64%), Albanians (25.2%), Turks (3.9%), Roma (2.7%), Serbs (1.8%), and others such as Vlachs, Bosniaks and Bulgarians (2.4%).

Relations between Albanians and Macedonians can be problematic. Other predominately Islamic ethnic groups tend to get lumped in with the Albanians – except the Roma who are so economically deprived and socially stigmatised as to be an underclass all on their own.

Despite all this, it is absolutely the case that all communities are generous and hospitable, and if the topic of community relations comes up, most people will say they get along just fine with everyone and it's the politicians who stir up trouble for their own benefit. Just be aware that it is a sensitive topic.

## RELIGION

Most Macedonians belong to the Macedonian Orthodox Church, and most Albanians, Turks and Roma to Islam. There is also a smallish Catholic community, nearly all ethnically Albanian, whose most famous daughter was Mother Teresa. The once-sizable Jewish community was deported en masse for the death camps at Treblinka and Auschwitz during WWII.

## ARTS
### Cinema

The most significant Macedonian film is *Before the Rain* (1995), directed by Milčo Mančevski. Visually stunning, with a great cast and a haunting soundtrack, the film is a manifold take on the tensions between Macedonians and ethnic Albanians. Filmed partly in London and partly in Macedonia, you will be able to spot the Sveti Jovan at Kaneo church and the Treskavec monastery. Mančevski also released *Dust* in 2001, starring Joseph Fiennes and David Wenham. It's a Western linking the American frontier and the badlands of wild Macedonia at the turn of the 20th century.

### Music

The oldest form of Macedonian folk music involves the *gajda* (bagpipes). This instrument is played solo or is accompanied by the *tapan* (two-sided drum), each side of which is played with a different stick to obtain a different tone. These are often augmented by *kaval* (flute) and/or *tambura* (small lute with two pairs of strings). Macedonia has also inherited (from a long period of Turkish influence) the *zurla* (double-reed horn), and the *Čalgija* music form. Bands playing folk music may be heard and enjoyed at festivals such as the Balkan Festival of Folk Dances & Songs in Ohrid in early July, or the Ilinden Festival in Bitola in early August.

Roma bands are another musical treat in Macedonia. One of the most popular Roma singers, the velvety-voiced Esma Redžepova, is from Skopje.

Young Macedonians generally prefer to listen to their own pop music over English-language artists, although hip-hop and metal have their fans. Macedonian pop tends to be of the Eurovision style – upbeat synth-heavy numbers with a vaguely gypsy feel.

### Dance

The most famous Macedonian folk dance is probably *teškoto oro* (difficult dance). Music for this beautiful male dance is provided by the *tapan* and *zurla*. Performed in traditional Macedonian costume, it is often included in festivals or concerts.

Other dances include *komitsko oro,* which symbolises the struggle of Macedonian freedom fighters against the Turks, and *Tresenica,* a women's dance from the Mavrovo region. The *oro* is similar to the *kolo,* a circle dance that is danced throughout the Balkans.

## ENVIRONMENT
### The Land

Most of Macedonia's 25,713 sq km consists of a plateau between 600m and 900m above sea level, hemmed in by high mountains on its western borders – 16 of which are higher than 2000m. Golem Korab (2864m), on the border with Albania, is the country's highest peak. The Vardar River crosses the middle of the country, passing Skopje on its way to the Aegean Sea near Thessaloniki. Lakes Ohrid and Prespa drain into the Adriatic via Albania.

### Wildlife

Macedonia belongs to the eastern Mediterranean and Euro-Siberian vegetation region and is home to a large number of plant species in a relatively small geographical area. The high mountains are dominated by pines, with beech and oak on the lower slopes.

Macedonia is a boundary area between two different zoological zones – the high mountain region and the low Mediterranean valley region. The fauna of the forests is abundant and includes bears, wild boar, wolves, foxes, squirrels, chamois and deer. The lynx is found, although very rarely, in the mountains of western Macedonia. Forest birds include the blackcap, grouse, black grouse, imperial eagle and forest owl.

The famous shepherd dog (*šarplaninec*), from the Šar Planina mountains, stands some 60cm tall and is a fierce fighter in defending flocks from bears or wolf packs. Don't mess with them.

Lakes Ohrid, Prespa and Dojran are separate fauna zones, a result of territorial and temporal isolation. Lake Ohrid's fauna is a relic of an earlier era – including the endangered letnica trout (also known as Lake Ohrid trout on English-language menus, and *koran* in Albania) and a genus of snail dating back 30 million years. It is also home to the mysterious European eel, which comes to Lake Ohrid from the distant Sargasso Sea to live for up to 10 years. It makes the trip back to the Sargasso Sea to breed, then dies and its offspring start the cycle anew.

## National Parks

Macedonia's three national parks protect 205,235 hectares of mountain wilderness – 8.07% of the country. They are Pelister (p485), Galičica (between Lakes Ohrid and Prespa) and Mavrovo (p480). Additionally, Lake Ohrid is on the World Heritage List. Pelister and Galičica are both part of a broader nature protection zone around Lake Prespa, shared with adjacent areas in Albania and Greece. Being mountainous, hiking is only possible during the warmer months. Mavrovo and Pelister both have ski runs. All three are accessible by road (though not really by public transport), and none require any permits from park officers. The onus is on visitors to keep the parks as pristine as possible.

## Environmental Issues

Lake Ohrid's unique trout, known locally as letnica has nearly been fished to extinction, and yet it is still served (illegally) at restaurants throughout the country. Other problems include illegal logging, hunting and dumping of waste. Nonbiodegradable litter is a major eyesore, particularly in the west of the country. Try to refuse unnecessary plastic carrier bags in shops.

## FOOD & DRINK

If one word sums up Macedonian cuisine, it's *skara* (barbecue). Pork, chicken or lamb – Macedonians are mad on meat. Vegetarians shouldn't get overly excited by all the stuffed vegetables and vine leaves on the menu – they're delicious, but they'll probably be stuffed with meat. Stuffed meat is also popular, in which case it'll be filled with cheese.

Don't order the Lake Ohrid trout – it's an endangered species, not to mention horribly expensive. Even the most expensive restaurants (ресторан) tend to have cheap options on the menu, especially salads or pasta. Balkan *burek* (cheese, spinach, potato or meat in filo pastry) or *kebapci* (kebabs) make for a cheap snack. Italian food is available just about everywhere, and should give vegetarians a welcome relief from salads.

The terms café and bar are interchangeable as they both tend to serve coffee and alcohol. Don't expect to find any food at a café. The national firewater is *rakija*, a strong distilled spirit popular throughout the Balkans. A particularly Macedonian variety is the ouzo-like *mastika*.

Macedonia produces excellent wine which is exported throughout the region. The two main varieties grown are Vranec, a rich fruity red, and Smederevka, a light white with citrus notes.

# SKOPJE СКОПЈЕ

☎ 02 / pop 507,000

Skopje fits many of the stereotypes of a contemporary Eastern European city. Communist-era housing blocks dominate the skyline, public buildings are chunky behemoths, and there's a certain greyness and griminess that pervades. However, scratch the surface and a different Skopje reveals itself. Delicate minarets rise above the cobbled lanes of the Čaršija (Turkish bazaar), where Orthodox churches sit alongside copper-domed bathhouses and historic Ottoman trading inns.

The Vardar is no sluggish stream. It rages between the old and new halves of the city – a fitting symbol of the Muslim and Orthodox divide – spanned by the elegant arches of the Kamen Most (Stone Bridge). On the south side, stylish bars and cafés buzz with a fashion-conscious young crowd, undisturbed by the English stag-partiers currently plaguing other European capitals. Foodies won't be disappointed by the traditional cuisine on offer in a number of atmospheric little eateries, nor the selection of excellent local

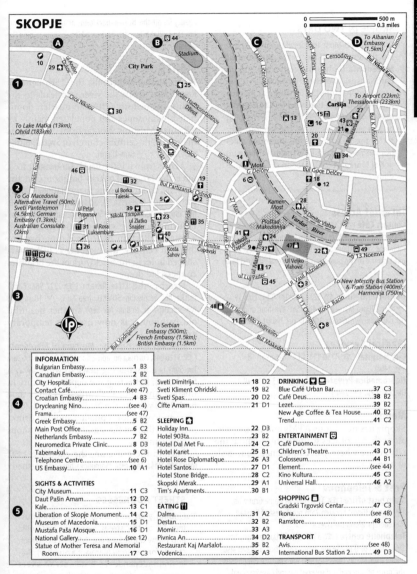

# SKOPJE

0 .................. 500 m
0 .................. 0.3 miles

wines. Likewise, history buffs and art-lovers will find their palates well served.

## ORIENTATION

Skopje is centred around the large square Ploštad Makedonija on the south bank of the Vardar River. The train and bus station is a 15-minute walk southeast. Mount Vodno,

with its giant illuminated cross, rises to the south.

## INFORMATION
### Bookshops

**Tabernakul** ( ☎ 3115 329; Dimitrie Čupovski 4) In the back right-hand corner you'll find a small collection of Macedonian books in English as well as other English-language titles.

**MACEDONIA**

---

## Internet Access

**Contact Café** ( ☎ 3298 023; 1st fl, Gradski Trgovski
Centar; per hr 120MKD; ☙ 9am-midnight Mon-Fri, 10am-
midnight Sat, 3-10pm Sun) This is the best, fastest and
most central of the numerous internet cafés around town.

## Laundry

**Drycleaning Nino** ( ☎ 3222 446; Ivo Ribar Lola 59;
☙ 8am-10pm Mon-Fri, to 4pm Sat) Washing and drying
per pair underwear/socks 10MKD, per T-shirt 50MKD.

## Medical Services

**City Hospital** ( ☎ 3130 111; Ul 11 Oktomvri 53;
☙ 24hr)
**Neuromedica Private Clinic** ( ☎ 3133 313; Ul 11
Oktomvri 25; ☙ 24hr)

## Money

Skopje has numerous ATMs and many private exchange offices scattered throughout the
city centre where you can change your cash
at a good rate.

## Post & Telephone

**Main post office** ( ☎ 3141 141; Ul Dame Gruev bb;
☙ 7am-5.30pm) Located 75m northwest of Ploštad
Makedonija, along the river.
**Telephone centre** ( ☎ 3141 141; Ul Dame Gruev bb;
☙ 7am-10pm) Inside the main post office. You can also
phone from kiosks (newsagents) with private telephones.
The price of your call is displayed digitally as you speak.

## Travel Agencies

**Frama** ( ☎ 3115 124; www.frama.com.mk; 1st fl Gradski
Trgovski Centar) Flight prices are listed in euro on a board
by the door of this large central agency with an English-
speaking staff.
**Go Macedonia Alternative Travel** ( ☎ 3071 265;
www.gomacedonia.com; Ul Ankarska 29a) The best

agency for off-the-beaten-track tours of any sort, including
eco- and village-tourism, hiking, biking, caving, wining
and dining.

## SIGHTS

From **Ploštad Makedonija** the 15th-century
**Kamen Most** spans the river and leads to the
**Čaršija**, the historic Ottoman quarter, dominated by mosques and populated mainly by
Albanian Muslims. Not far from the bridge is
the cute 19th-century church of **Sveti Dimitrija**
( ☎ 3232 919; ☙ 6am-10pm).

Across from it is the **Daut Pašin Amam** (1466),
once the largest Turkish bathhouse in the
Balkans, and now home to the **National Gallery**
( ☎ 3133 102; Kruševska 1A; adult/concession 50/20MKD;
free Sun; ☙ 10am-6pm Tue-Sun Oct-Mar, to 9pm Apr-Sep).
Housing some excellent modern art and
a small collection of icons dating back to
the 14th century, the building is lit by star-
shaped holes in the brickwork of the beautiful
copper-clad domes.

Nearby, the **Čifte Amam** ( ☎ 3227 986; Bitpazarska bb; admission 50MKD, free Sun; ☙ 10am-6pm
Tue-Sun Oct-Mar, to 9pm Apr-Sep) another beautiful
old bathhouse, is now used for temporary
exhibitions.

Just up the hill the **Museum of Macedonia**
( ☎ 3116 044; Čurčiska bb; admission 50MKD; ☙ 9am-3pm
Tue-Sun) is a fascinating place to while away a
few hours. Reflecting the depth of culture in
this ancient land, the earliest exhibits date
back 7500 years to the Neolithic period. Keep
your eyes open for a phallus-spouted drinking vessel that set the standard for joke shops
for millennia.

Beyond the museum, the exquisite 1492
**Mustafa Paša Mosque** (Samoilova bb) has a shady

---

garden with a fountain and an earthquake-cracked dome. The ruins of the **Kale**, across the street from the mosque, has panoramic views of Skopje from the 11th century Cyclopean wall.

The tiny monastery **Sveti Spas** (admission 100MKD; ✆ 9am-5pm Tue-Fri, to 3pm Sat & Sun) was built below ground level because during Ottoman times it was illegal for a church to be taller than a mosque. It boasts an iconostasis 10m wide and 6m high, beautifully carved in the early 19th century. Look for the carvers' miniature self-portrait in the left side of the carving. Across the cloister is a room with the **Tomb and Museum of Goce Delčev**, independence campaigner and national hero, killed by the Ottomans in 1903.

Back on the south side of the bridge, a hefty bronze commemorates the **liberation of Skopje** by the partisans, with chisel-jawed men, scary mommas in headscarves and heroic children, all sporting serious weaponry.

The crazy insect-like building across the boulevard is the city's **main post office** (opposite). It was designed during the Yugoslav era to be an abstract take on church architecture. Enter from the river side to check out the socialist murals in the large circular main hall.

The massive modern church of **Sveti Kliment Ohridski** ( ✆ 3237 218; Bul Sveti Kliment Ohridski bb) does a good impersonation of a mosque, with its large interlocking domes and freestanding bell tower.

South of the centre, the only interesting thing about the **City Museum** ( ✆ 3114 742; MH Jasmin Mito Hađivasilev bb; admission free; ✆ 9am-5pm Tue-Sat, 9am-1pm Sun) is its partly-ruined exterior. The clock is frozen at 5.17 on the morning of the tragic Skopje earthquake of 27 July 1963, which killed 1066 people and almost demolished the city. On the left is Tito's message of support to the shattered citizens. Go around to the back for a strange mix of decaying shops and bars amid abandoned railway carriages and artillery.

A 2.5m bronze **statue of Mother Teresa** stands sentinel at the entrance to a small square, not far from the now-demolished house where she was raised. Her simple **Memorial Room** ( ✆ 070-704 894; Ul Maršal Tito; admission free; ✆ 1-4pm) is in the base of an 18th-century feudal tower. A superb socialist relief fronts the Army House to the right of the tower.

For a great view of the city, take the 20-minute taxi ride up Mount Vodno to the

**Sveti Pantelejmon monastery** ( ✆ 3081 255; ✆ 9am-11pm) with its sweet little 12th-century church and excellent traditional restaurant (meals 400MKD).

## SLEEPING

Skopje's hotels are geared towards visitors from charge-account land – business travellers and those from organisations trying to resolve the mess in neighbouring Kosovo. Hence there's no shortage of pricey establishments, but cheaper options for tourists are more limited.

### Budget

**Hotel Santos** ( ✆ 3226 963; Ul Bitpazarska 69; s/d €20/25) With refurbished rooms complete with TV sets and clean bathrooms, this is the nicest of the cheap hotels among the evocative cobbled laneways of the Čaršija. It's set back from Bitpazarska in its own little laneway near the corner of Ulica Evlija Čelebi.

**Hotel 903ta** ( ✆ 3211 345; Ul Nikola Trimpare 9; s/d €30/50) This little family-owned hotel, right in the midst of a lively neighbourhood, offers two spacious apartments with leather couches, two rooms with their own bathroom and two that share. It's clean and comfortable and very newly renovated.

**Hotel Kanet** ( ✆ 3238 353; www.hotelkanet.com.mk; Ul Jordan Hadžikonstantinov Džinot 20; s/d €45/60; P 🛏 ) The varnished wood and park-side setting is more redolent of a mountain cabin than an inner-city hotel. The rooms are spotless and comfy, and the large covered terrace is a great spot to soak up the park vibe.

### Midrange

**Hotel Dal Met Fu** ( ✆ 3239 584; www.dalmetfu.com.mk; Ploštad Makedonija; s €59-69, d €69-79, apt s €85-145, apt d €100-170; P 🛏 ⬜ ) Positioned on the main square, this bright and cheerful minihotel (three rooms and three apartments) is above the overrated restaurant of the same name. It has nicely designed rooms with a fashionable edge, friendly staff and a location that is unbeatably central.

**Hotel Rose Diplomatique** ( ✆ 3135 469; rosediplomatique.tripod.com; Ul Roza Luksemburg 13; s €65-85, d €85-105) This boutique B&B has eight charming rooms, caring staff and a cute garden. The décor has a gentle feminine touch (lots of frills and ornaments) and breakfast includes delicious homemade jams on a well-laden buffet table.

MACEDONIA

**Tim's Apartments** ( ☎ 3237 650; www.tims.com.mk; Ul Orce Nikolov 120; s/d €69/89, ste €86-128; 🐾 ) This handsome apartment-hotel has a range of rooms, self-catering apartments and two-bedroom 'residences' on a quiet street in an inner suburb.

**Skopski Merak** ( ☎ 3090 755; Ul Andon Dukov 27; s/d €70/100; 🐾 🖳 ) Situated above a popular fish restaurant, this snug family-run hotel has 15 spotless rooms and a separate apartment nearby. In winter there's an open fire lit in the central atrium.

### Top End

**Hotel Stone Bridge** ( ☎ 3244 900; www.stonebridge -hotel.com; Kej Dimitar Vlahov 1; s €129-189, d €149-229, ste €299-549; P 🐾 🖳 🏃 ) From the beautiful white marble Turkish bath to the lavishly upholstered furniture, you can tell that these newcomers take luxury seriously. Visiting royalty or rappers would feel quite at home among all the gilt in the Apartment Sultan. Ordinary mortals will find the standard rooms luxurious and the location is perfect.

**Holiday Inn** ( ☎ 3292 929; www.holiday-inn.com/sko pje; Ul Vasil Adzilarski 2; s €224-251, d €238-285, ste €317-500; P 🗶 🐾 🏃 ) A conveniently located business-class establishment next to the Gradski Trgovski Centar on the south side of the Vardar, this is the only hotel in Skopje to have a specially designed wheelchair-accessible room.

### EATING

There are a surprising number of great eating options in Skopje. The Čaršija is littered with affordable *kebapci* places and bakeries, and you can find fresh produce at its large open market. Also check out the impressive new supermarket in the Ramstore (opposite).

**Destan** (Bunjakovec Centar, Bul Partizanski Odredi; 6 pieces of kebaps 90MKD) Situated at the back of the shopping centre on the ground floor, Destan serves *kebaps* (barbequed meat rolls) with delicious grilled Turkish bread, raw onion and hot peppers.

**Harmonija** ( ☎ 2460 985; Bul Jane Sandanski 37; mains 100-250MKD; 🕒 8am-12pm Sun-Fri, 8am-1am Sat) This hard-to-find restaurant provides a full menu of fantastic vegetarian food including a wonderful macrobiotic platter. It's located in the Skopjanka mall, a motley collection of run-down shops a block east of the station, on the left past the first street. The restaurant's yellow sign points down a set of stairs that juts out into the footpath next to a florist.

**Pivnica An** ( ☎ 3212 111; Kapan An, Čaršija; mains 170-400MKD) Marvellous Macedonian food and a great atmosphere, located in a historic Ottoman trading inn.

**Dalma** ( ☎ 070-260 410; Ul Petar Poparsov 22; mains 160-450MKD) Offers beautiful Mediterranean cuisine in the most stylish of surroundings.

**Momir** ( ☎ 3211 011; Bul Ivo Ribar Lola 79; mains 450MKD) This is a great fish restaurant where you can try specialities such as squid stuffed with yellow cheese and ham.

**Vodenica** ( ☎ 3232 877; Bul Ivo Ribar Lola 69; mains 300-650MKD) The food is excellent in this upmarket Italian eatery, which takes its name from the waterwheel in its romantic garden.

### DRINKING

Skopje has a lively enough bar-café scene to suit any taste. Explore around the Gradski Trgovski Centar and neighbouring riverside promenade, where there are dozens of establishments ranging from stylish cocktail bars to the ubiquitous Irish boozer.

**Lezet** ( ☎ 3225 003; Ul Nikola Trimpare bb) The soft lighting, chilled music and harem furnishings

---

**AUTHOR'S CHOICE**

**Restaurant Kaj Maršalot** (Bul Sveti Kliment Ohridski bb; mains 100-500MKD) A life-size cardboard cutout of Tito cheerily raises his glass as you enter this bizarre socialist-themed restaurant where, according to the advertising, 'proletarians as well as the capitalists feel the equality of the transition'. Among the communist posters and busts, our leading English-speaking revolutionaries Bob Marley and John Lennon smile down benignly, exhorting us simultaneously to 'Get Up Stand Up' and 'Let It Be'. Surely 'imagine no possessions' would be a more appropriate slogan for the latter, especially given that McCartney was responsible for the laid-back lyric they've chosen. There's no such confusion with the food, which is wonderfully authentic Macedonian fare. Order a bottle of excellent local wine along with a mixed platter of yummy breaded olives, vine leaves stuffed with mince and the supersharp local 'yellow' cheese.

seem to encourage couples to pair up in the cosy corners of this groovy bar.

**New Age Coffee & Tea House** ( ☎ 3117 559; Kosta Šahov 9) This bohemian hipster haunt is like a farmhouse, with dogs and roosters roaming around the yard out front. It's rumoured that aside from the generally alternative clientele, this is also a gay and lesbian hangout.

**Blue Café Urban Bar** ( ☎ 3123 355; Ul Veljko Vlahović 4 2/3; ✗ ) A truly stylish, modern bar with fab cocktails and a large selection of special coffees and teas.

**Café Deus** ( ☎ 3135 415; Ul Leninova 22) Cosy, smoky and atmospheric, Deus does a good impersonation of a Parisian café, with dark wood furnishings and little tables adorned with roses.

**Trend** ( ☎ 3132 425; Ul Nikola Vapcarov 2/4) The name says it all. This combination restaurant, café and cocktail bar with a nightclub downstairs is the current place to be seen.

## ENTERTAINMENT

For up-to-date info on clubs and special events, check out www.skopjeclubbing.com.mk.

**Universal Hall** ( ☎ 3224 158; Bul Partizanski Odredi bb; tickets 100-200MKD) The home to classical and other music performances, as well as Skopje's jazz festival in October every year.

**Children's Theatre** ( ☎ 3290 111; Ul Evliya Čelebi 4; tickets €1) This cute little theatre in the Čaršija puts on musicals and puppet shows for the little 'uns.

**Kino Kultura** ( ☎ 3236 578; Ul Luj Paster 2; tickets 60-120MKD) Screens recent English-language movies.

**Café Duomo** ( ☎ 3127 300; Bul Ivo Ribar Lola 67; ✹ 10pm-4am Sun-Thu, 10pm-5am Fri & Sat) Dance the night away in this upmarket late-night bar, which hosts live music and cabaret.

**Colosseum** (City Park; www.colosseumsummerclub.com; special events 250-400MKD) and **Element** (City Park; www.element.com.mk) in the city park are *the* places for summer outdoor clubbers and international DJs.

## SHOPPING

The Čaršija teems with little shops that sell souvenirs such as copper coffee pots and rugs. The two main shopping malls, **Gradski Trgovski Centar** (Ploštad Makedonija; ✹ 9am-7pm; Ⓟ ) and the flash new **Ramstore** (MH Jasmin Mito Hadivasilev bb; ✹ 10am-10pm; Ⓟ ), are full of fashion kids cruising the boutiques, bars and cafés. The former has a small souvenir kiosk just inside

the carpark end, but you'll find more interesting memorabilia at the stall selling socialist medals near the opposite entrance. Check out **Ikona** ( ☎ 3224 403) on the ground floor of Ramstore for beautiful hand-painted icons.

## GETTING THERE & AWAY
### Air

A host of airlines serve Skopje's **Petrovec airport** ( ☎ 3148 333; www.airports.com.mk), 21km east of the city.

It may be cheaper to fly into Thessaloniki in northern Greece; try to coordinate the flight times with the two to three daily trains that connect Thessaloniki with Skopje.

### Bus

Skopje's **New Intercity Bus Station** (Nova Avtobuska Stanica; ☎ 3236 254) is underneath the train station on bul Jane Sandanski. There is a comprehensive network to all Macedonian towns, with at least 13 buses daily to Prilep (320MKD, 2¼ hours, 139km), seven to Bitola (350MKD, 2½ hours, 185km), 21 to Tetovo (100MKD, 40 minutes, 42km), three to Mavrovi Anovi (270MKD, 1½ hours, 88km), 10 to Ohrid via Kičevo (380MKD, three hours, 167km) and four to Ohrid via Bitola (380MKD, four hours, 261km).

International buses either leave from here or from International Bus Station 2, along from the Holiday Inn on Kej 13 Noemvri, where there are offices for several private lines. To catch a direct bus to Tirana in Albania you will first need to head to Tetovo.

### Train

Skopje's ageing **train station** ( ☎ 3234 255; Bul Jane Sandanski) serves both domestic and international routes. For details on international trains, see p491. The most useful domestic route for tourists goes through Veles and on to Prilep and Bitola (four trains daily, some at ghastly hours). A little Cyrillic will be useful to make sense of the timetables, so come prepared with your phrasebook.

## GETTING AROUND
### To/From the Airport

There is no public transport from the airport. Airport taxi drivers can charge between 1290MKD and 2200MKD, though the fare shouldn't be more than 700MKD. It's best to arrange a taxi through your hotel before you arrive, although even then be aware that some hotels may try to bump up the price. Only use taxis that have the official 'taxi' sign.

## Bus

Skopje is easily explored on foot and taxis are cheap, so chances are you won't need to brave the bus system. Inner-suburban city buses in Skopje cost between 15MKD and 30MKD per trip.

## Car

Skopje is awash with car-rental agencies, from the large ones to small local companies. Rental prices generally start at around €35 per day. Try **Avis** ( ☎ 3222 046; lower ground, Ramstore; 🕑 9am-5pm). Parking is a cultural experience of its own – people park anywhere, including the strip in the middle of the road.

## Taxi

Skopje's taxis are cheap and excellent, once you get past the shysters at the airport. All official taxis have meters, which are turned on without prompting. The first few kilometres are a flat 50MKD, and then it's 15MKD per kilometre. Watch out for the unofficial drivers who hang around the train-bus station. They'll try to load your bags into their boot before you notice they don't have a taxi sign, and then overcharge you for an unmetered trip.

## AROUND SKOPJE
### Lake Matka ЕЗЕРО МАТКА

Only half an hour's drive from Skopje, Matka is a place of calm cool nature, where the steep canyon reflects in the lake's green mirrored surface. For centuries the area has been a retreat from society, attracting hermits, monks and early Macedonian revolutionaries. Now the lake, created by the damming of the Treška River, is a magnet for day-trippers and action-seekers, with opportunities for kayaking, hiking, rock climbing and caving.

The lakeside path starts at the end of the road. Follow it to see the 14th-century **Sveti Andrea monastery**, with its impressive frescoes. Next door is the very basic **Matka Mountain Hut** ( ☎ 3052 655; beds €7), where in summer you can spend the night or hire guides. The staff operate a small boat across the lake where it is a 15-minute climb to Matka's most beautiful church, **Sveti Šiševo**. You will need to bang on the metal to get the boat to collect you, but let them know your return time in advance.

If you are stranded, it's a long and difficult three-hour hike from here to Skopje, via Mt Vodno.

Back along the road is the peaceful **Monastery of Sveta Bogorodica** ( 🕑 10am-noon & 5-7pm Tue & Thu, all day Sat & Sun). From here the hardy can follow a steep path for 90 minutes to the little churches of **Sv Spas, Trojica** and **Nedala**. Just below the monastery, **Manastirski Peštera** ( ☎ 3352 512; mains 170-700MKD) is an atmospheric restaurant serving all manner of game, built into the hillside in a dimly lit cave.

A taxi to Lake Matka shouldn't cost more than 350MKD, or you can take your chances on bus 60 (50MKD, 40 minutes), which leaves somewhat erratically from Bulevar Partizanski Odredi.

# WESTERN MACEDONIA

## MAVROVO NATIONAL PARK
### МАВРОВО НАЦИОНАЛНИ ПАРК
☎ 042

Along with the country's best skiing facilities, Mavrovo National Park offers 73,088 hectares of birch and pine forest, lake, karst fields, waterfalls and alpine plain to be explored. It contains cultural treasures and quite a few mountain villages, including Galičnik with its famous July wedding festival. Accommodation is mostly in the ski village of Mavrovo on the southern side of the lake and public transport is limited, but in all but the depths of winter it's a cinch to get around with your own wheels.

## Sights & Activities

The **Zare Lazarevski ski centre** ( ☎ 042-489 002; www .zarelaz.com; Mavrovo village; ski pass per day 850MKD, ski hire 600MKD) is Macedonia's biggest and most modern ski resort, and by all accounts the skiing is very good, lasting from 15 November until as late as the middle of April. Compared with other European resorts it's dirt cheap, but it doesn't offer a huge amount of après-ski activity. The ski lifts operate all year (200MKD for nonskiers) and in summer you can hire mountain bikes for €10. The whole operation is run from the Hotel Bistra (see below).

**Sveti Jovan Bigorski** ( ☎ 042-478 675; bigorski@mt .net.mk; admission free) is a fully working monastery and one of the most popular with visitors in Macedonia. It was first established in 1020 on the spot where the icon of Sveti Jovan Bigorski (St John the Forerunner, eg St John the Baptist) appeared, and has been rebuilt many times over the centuries. The miraculous icon kept reappearing and the monastery kept being 'resurrected'. The present day structures date from the 18th and 19th centuries, and houses one of the three icon-ostases carved by Makarije Frčkovski and the Filipovski brothers, who also carved the one in Sveti Spas in Skopje. The monastery has dormitories (€5 to €15) with self-catering facilities where you can stay overnight, as well as a little shop selling painted icons and Mastika, the aniseed-flavoured *rakija* made by the monks.

The old Vlach village of **Galičnik** lies deep within the park, about 17km from Mavrovo. The road to Galičnik from Mavrovo is often snowed-in as late as May and closes as early as November. The village hosts a very popular wedding festival in the middle of July. The bridal costumes weigh up to 30kg! The festival is rich in traditions, with lots of dances, folk music…and a few tears.

## Sleeping & Eating

**Hotel Srna** ( ☎ 042-388 083; www.hotelsrna.cjb.net; Mavrovo village; s/d/tr €42/60/75; **P** ) A friendly little hotel, 400m from the chairlifts, Srna has spotless airy rooms (some with balconies), a cheerful bar and a restaurant with lots of antlers and pelts. Half-board costs an extra €5 per person.

**Hotel Bistra** ( ☎ 042-489 027; www.bistra.com; Mavrovo village; 15 Apr-15 Nov s €45-65, d €75-100, 16 Nov–14 Apr s €90-115, d €120-160; **P** **⃟** ) This sprawling resort hotel has comfortable rooms with satellite TV, a large restaurant with an open fire, a bar (of course), plus a swimming pool, fitness centre and sauna. The more expensive rooms have Jacuzzis. The Bistra also runs the nearby Hotel Ski Škola and Hotel Mavrovski, which offer simpler rooms at a cheaper price, while still having access to the main hotel's facilities.

## Getting There & Away

Buses don't go directly to Mavrovo village but pass through the town of Mavrovo Anovi on the other side of the lake. There are seven buses a day to Debar (120MKD, 46km), five to Tetovo (140MKD, 45km), and three to Skopje (270MKD, 1½ to 2½ hours depending on conditions, 88km). For Sveti Jovan Bigorski take the bus to Debar and ask to be let off at the turnoff to the monastery. From here it is a steep 500m climb to the complex.

# SOUTHERN MACEDONIA

## OHRID ОХРИД

☎ 046 / pop 55,700

The highlight of any trip to Macedonia, Ohrid is a place of dramatic beauty, steeped in history and culture. The crystalline waters of the lake and plentiful budget accommodation make it a magnet for summer holidaymakers, turning this sleepy little place, with its evocative cobbled laneways peppered with picturesque churches, into a vibrant party town.

For Orthodox Macedonians it is the spiritual heart of their country and a focus of nationalistic pride. It was here that Sts Clement and Naum in the 9th century founded the first Slavic university. Later Ohrid was the capital of the 10th-century kingdom of Tsar Samoil, with its bishop an independent Patriarch. The revival of the archbishopric of Ohrid in 1958, and its independence from the Serbian Orthodox Church in 1967, were important steps on the road to modern nationhood.

However its history goes back much further than that. The tectonic lake itself is one of the oldest in the world and at 294m is the deepest in the Balkans. The area has been settled for 8000 years, while the town was first mentioned under the Greek name Lychnidos, before being conquered by the Ancient Macedonians in the 4th century BC. Under the Romans it became a stopping point on the Via Egnatia, which ran

MACEDONIA

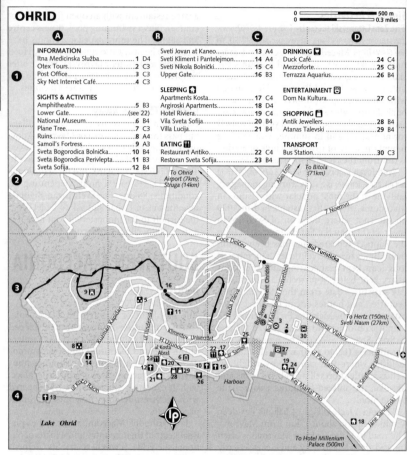

# OHRID

0 _____ 500 m
0 _____ 0.3 miles

| INFORMATION | | |
| --- | --- | --- |
| Itna Medicinska Služba | 1 | D4 |
| Otex Tours | 2 | C3 |
| Post Office | 3 | C3 |
| Sky Net Internet Café | 4 | C3 |

| SIGHTS & ACTIVITIES | | |
| --- | --- | --- |
| Amphitheatre | 5 | B3 |
| Lower Gate | (see 22) | |
| National Museum | 6 | B4 |
| Plane Tree | 7 | C3 |
| Ruins | 8 | A4 |
| Samoil's Fortress | 9 | A3 |
| Sveta Bogorodica Bolnička | 10 | B4 |
| Sveta Bogorodica Perivlepta | 11 | B3 |
| Sveta Sofija | 12 | B4 |

| | | |
| --- | --- | --- |
| Sveti Jovan at Kaneo | 13 | A4 |
| Sveti Kliment i Pantelejmon | 14 | A4 |
| Sveti Nikola Bolnicki | 15 | C4 |
| Upper Gate | 16 | B3 |

| SLEEPING | | |
| --- | --- | --- |
| Apartments Kosta | 17 | C4 |
| Argiroski Apartments | 18 | D4 |
| Hotel Riviera | 19 | C4 |
| Vila Sveta Sofija | 20 | B4 |
| Villa Lucija | 21 | B4 |

| EATING | | |
| --- | --- | --- |
| Restaurant Antiko | 22 | B4 |
| Restoran Sveta Sofija | 23 | B4 |

| DRINKING | | |
| --- | --- | --- |
| Duck Café | 24 | C4 |
| Mezzoforte | 25 | C3 |
| Terrazza Aquarius | 26 | B4 |

| ENTERTAINMENT | | |
| --- | --- | --- |
| Dom Na Kultura | 27 | C4 |

| SHOPPING | | |
| --- | --- | --- |
| Antik Jewellers | 28 | B4 |
| Atanas Talevski | 29 | B4 |

| TRANSPORT | | |
| --- | --- | --- |
| Bus Station | 30 | C3 |

from present-day Albania's port of Durrës to Istanbul in Turkey.

The lake's mountainous fringes include the Galičica National Park, on the way to the marvellous monastery of Sveti Naum, 29km south towards the Albanian border.

## Orientation

The Old Town of Ohrid is easy to get around on foot. The lake is to the south, and the picturesque Old Town descends from Samoil's Fortress on the hill to the west.

## Information

### INTERNET ACCESS

**Sky Net Internet Café** ( ☎ 258 381; skynet@mt.net .mk; 1st fl, TC Amam, Ul Sveti Kliment Ohridski; per hr

60MKD; 🕑 9am-2am) Offers the best and fastest internet access as well as super cheap international phone calls.

### MEDICAL SERVICES

**Itna Medicinska Služba** ( ☎ 266 217; Dimitar Vlahov bb; 🕑 24hr) Accident and Emergency clinic, at the back left side of the Ambulanta Malariena building.

### MONEY

There are several ATMs and banks around Bulevar Makedonski Prosvetiteli and Ulica Sveti Kliment Ohridski.

### POST & TELEPHONE

**Post office** (Bul Makedonski Prosvetiteli). You can also change money here. There is a wall of payphones right outside.

## TOURIST INFORMATION & TRAVEL AGENCIES

There's no official tourist office, but there are many travel agencies around the bus station that can provide information and arrange private accommodation and tours.

**Otex Tours** ( ☎ 261 244; biteli@yahoo.com; Ul Partizanska bb)

## Sights

Most of Ohrid's churches charge an entry fee of 100MKD. If not, it is customary to leave some money at the icons; this contributes towards preserving these historical sites. Winter opening hours seem to depend on how cold it is.

A gnarled 900-year-old **plane tree** (Ul Sveti Kliment Ohridski) lies in the heart of Ottoman Ohrid. It has apparently housed a café and a barber shop at different points in its long life.

Enter the old town through the remains of the **Lower Gate** (Ul Car Samoil). Ohrid's fortifications date back to the Roman period, although they were reconstructed in the Middle Ages. They completely enclosed the town until the Ottoman invasion of 1395, when the centre of civic life moved to the bazaar that sprung up on the flat land outside the ramparts.

The small 14th-century churches of **Sveta Bogorodica Bolnička** and **Sveti Nikola Bolnički** ( 🕙 9am-2pm 5-7pm) were originally hospital churches, where people were quarantined during times of plague before being allowed to enter the town.

On Ulica Car Samoil, the **National Museum** ( ☎ 267 173; Ul Car Samoil 62; adult/student 100/50MKD; 🕙 9am-2pm Tue-Sun) is an Ottoman-era house with exquisite carved ceilings and amazing views over the lake. It is the star exhibit in its own collection of Ohrid's archaeological and ethnographic relics.

The grandiose 11th-century **Sveta Sofija** (admission 100MKD; 🕙 10am-noon & 5-8pm Tue-Sun, 9am-3pm winter) was originally built as a cathedral. The frescoes are extremely well preserved thanks to having been whitewashed during the church's days as a mosque.

**Sveti Jovan at Kaneo** (Ul Koćo Racin) is a breathtakingly beautiful little 13th-century church perched on the cliffs, and provides the perfect foreground to the most iconic view of the lake.

Ohrid's main church, **Sveti Kliment i Pantelejmon** (Ul Kuzman Kapidan), is newly built on the frescoed foundations of an earlier church. It houses the remains of St Clement. Nearby, the **ruins** of a 5th-century basilica and 4th-century church have their intricate mosaics uncovered in the summer months from the layer of sand that preserves them. One of the mosaics shows a swastika – an old Indo-Aryan sun symbol long before the Nazis appropriated it.

The emphatically restored 10th-century **Samoil's Fortress** (admission 30MKD; 🕙 9am-4pm), on the town's heights, is most interesting from a distance, but there are splendid views from the crenulated walls and towers.

Down the hill, Ohrid's **Amphitheatre** was built around the time of the birth of Christ, and wasn't fully uncovered until 1984. It was originally used for plays and oratory, but in the late Roman era the first 10 rows were pulled out and replaced with a wall to convert it into an arena for bloodsports.

Continue towards the **Upper Gate** (Gorna Porta) to the gorgeous 13th-century **Sveta Bogorodica Perivlepta** (Sveti Kliment; admission 100MKD; 🕙 10am-3pm), adorned inside with vivid frescoes.

## Festivals & Events

The five-day Balkan Festival of Folk Dances & Songs, held at Ohrid in early July, draws folkloric groups from around the Balkans. The **Ohrid Summer Festival** (www.ohridsummer.com.mk), held from mid-July to mid-August, features classical concerts in the Sveta Sofija church, open-air theatre and many other events. An international poetry festival, replete with food and drink in the streets, is held annually in nearby Struga in the second half of August.

Ohrid hosts a **swimming marathon** (www.pfm .org.mk) each summer, when swimmers race the 30km across Lake Ohrid from Sveti Naum. A briefer but no less gruelling endurance event is held on the feast of the Epiphany (January 19), when young men compete for the honour of retrieving a golden cross thrown into the icy lake by the archbishop.

## Sleeping

### BUDGET

Everyone in Ohrid seems to have a room to rent (€5 to €15 per person), and if you're arriving in season you'll probably be approached by someone at the bus station. Otherwise they can be organised in advance through local agencies such as Otex Tours (see left).

**Villa Lucija** ( ☎ 265 608; lucjia@mt.net.mk; Ul Kosta Abraš 29; s/d/tr/q €15/25/30/35) The best of the private

MACEDONIA

accommodation on offer, right in the centre of the Old Town, Villa Lucija's rooms are clean and spacious, balconies overlook the lake, and the patio is right on the water for a swim.

**Apartments Kosta** ( ☎ 267 243; vilakosta@gmail.com; Ul Car Samoil 26; s/d/tr/q €15/25/30/45) The Kostas have gone all out to provide little extra comforts for their budget guests, including slippers, hairdryers, good quality linen, free tea- and coffee-making facilities and use of the family's laundry facilities and BBQ.

**Argiroski Apartments** ( ☎ 262 844; Kej Maršal Tito bb; apt €20-25) This modern block is set back from the main lakeside road, down a drive where it seems that all the neighbours have rooms to rent. Sleeping three to four people at a squeeze, the apartments are sparkling and new with self-catering facilities.

### MIDRANGE & TOP END
**Hotel Riviera** ( ☎ 268 735; hotelriviera@mt.com.mk; Kej Maršal Tito 4; s/d €31/48, ste €60-79; 🟦) Step back into 1970s Yugoslavia. The dated décor and crazy antique collection in the lobby are part of this place's love-it-or-hate-it charm. The three lakeside suites are wonderful for the price, sleeping up to four people.

**Vila Sveta Sofija** ( ☎ 254 368; www.vilasofija.com; Ul Kosta Abraš 64; s/d €35/60, ste €80-120; 🟦) Tucked into the lower part of the old town, this converted Ottoman house combines opulent traditional furnishings and old-world charm with space-age bathroom design. The luxury suite is impossibly romantic and the food is wonderful. This is the best boutique hotel in Macedonia.

**Hotel Millenium Palace** ( ☎ 263 361; www.milleni umpalace.com.mk; Kej Maršal Tito bb; s/d €49/66, ste €99-124; 🅿 🟦 🖳 🟦) It's amazing to think that this uber-'80s monstrosity was built this millennium. Once you get past the aesthetics, the facilities within are very good – comfy beds, all mod cons, a small gym, sauna and an indoor swimming pool with a cocktail bar. The suites have terraces overlooking the lake.

## Eating & Drinking
Ohrid has a great selection of cafés and bars, many of which host live music. The quality of its restaurants is rather less impressive.

**Restoran Sveta Sofija** ( ☎ 267 403; Ul Car Samoil 88; mains 160-690MKD) This classy bistro serves a wide range of Macedonian dishes. The view from the terrace onto the ancient church is the very soul of Ohrid, made all the more evocative on the weekend when the folk band plays.

**Restaurant Antiko** ( ☎ 265 523; Ul Car Samoil 30; mains from 350MKD) Built into the ancient city gate, this is the best place for traditional Macedonian food. Beware – it is rather pricey and local specialities need to be ordered up to three hours in advance.

**Terrazza Aquarius** ( ☎ 252 625; Ul Kosta Abraš 30) In winter it's a cosy bar, but in summer this large lakeside terrace becomes party central, with its weekend hours extending until 3am. Expect a big sound system, guest DJs and lots of cocktails.

**Mezzoforte** (Ul Car Samoil 8) A groovy young crowd populates this stylish Old Town bar, with vaulted brick ceilings, comfy sofas and chilled music.

**Duck Café** ( ☎ 256 818; Kej Maršal Tito 12) This large booze barn hosts some great live bands from Thursday to Saturday, playing everything from jazz to rock and blues.

## Entertainment
Ohrid's movie theatre and concert hall, **Dom Na Kultura** (Ul Grigor Prličev; admission 50-100MKD), faces the lakeside park.

## Shopping
**Antik Jewellers** ( ☎ 250 999; Ul Kosta Abraš 13) Ohrid Pearls have been crafted by local families since the secret of fashioning pearl-like jewellery from fish bones was brought to Ohrid by Russian artisans fleeing the revolution. Unlike the cheaper versions to be found in every second shop on Ul Car Samoil, these are the real deal.

**Atanas Talevski** ( ☎ 254 059; Ul Kosta Abraš 19) A wonderful photographer, whose intimate studies of elderly villagers are astoundingly good. With small prints only costing 200MKD, they make brilliant gifts for art-minded friends.

## Getting There & Away
### AIR
**Ohrid airport** (OHD; ☎ 252 820; www.airports.com.mk) is served from only a handful of European cities – Skopje (Macedonian), Belgrade (JAT), Ljubljana (Adria), Zurich (Helvetic and Macedonian) and Vienna (Macedonian). A taxi to the airport, 7km north of Ohrid, costs 250MKD.

### BUS
Buses to Struga (14km) leave roughly every 15 minutes (5am to 9pm) from stand 1 at

the **bus station** ( ☎ 262 490; Ul Dimitar Vlahov). Enter through the back doors and pay the conductor (30MKD).

About 10 buses a day run between Ohrid and Skopje via Kičevo (380MKD, three hours, 167km). Another four go via Bitola (380MKD, four hours, 261km). The first route is shorter, faster and more scenic, so try to take it. There are at least six buses a day travelling to Bitola (170MKD, 1½ hours, 71km). Three of these continue on to Belgrade (1500MKD, about 12 hours, 692km).

For Albania, catch a Sveti Naum bus to the border crossing (80MKD, 50 minutes, 29km, four daily). From Albanian customs it's 6km to Pogradec; taxis are waiting and should charge only €5 for the ride.

### CAR
There's a branch of **Hertz** ( ☎ 261 237; Bul Turistička bb; ☙ 8am-10pm Mon-Fri, 8am-2pm Sat) in Ohrid.

## AROUND OHRID
### Sveti Naum Свети Наум
The magnificent grounds of the Sveti Naum monastery, near the Albanian border 29km south of Ohrid, are a real treat. The grounds are patrolled by peacocks and contain the source of Lake Ohrid's water. The beautiful 17th-century **Church of Sveti Naum** (admission 100MKD) rises on a hill above the lake, surrounded by the buildings of the Hotel Sveti Naum, which has taken over the historic monastery complex.

The original church of the Holy Archangels was built in 900 by St Naum, and the saint himself is buried here. They say that you can still hear his heartbeat if you put your ear on his tomb inside the chapel. The monastery grounds also offer a view of the Albanian town of Pogradec across the lake. In the summer months you can take a half-hour boat trip from the monastery to the bubbling springs that feed Lake Ohrid (€1 to €5 per person depending on party size).

### SLEEPING & EATING
**Hotel Sveti Naum** ( ☎ 046-283 080; www.hotel-stnaum .com.mk; s €44-50, d €70-80, apt €100-120; ▣ ) Standing at the heart of the monastery, this lovely hotel has magical views, excellent rooms with satellite TV, phone, central heating and traditional stylings. The hotel restaurant serves traditional Macedonian food (120MKD to 600MKD).

### GETTING THERE & AWAY
Four buses a day run from Ohrid to Sveti Naum (80MKD, 50 minutes, 29km, four daily). The bus continues on to the Albanian border before heading back. A taxi will get you there in 35 minutes and set you back €10.

In summer you can also come by boat but it only leaves when a group of about five to eight people is present; ask about times at the wharf or at the travel agencies in town. The fare is about 150/200MKD one way/return.

## BITOLA & PELISTER NATIONAL PARK
### БИТОЛА И ПЕЛИСТЕР НАЦИОНАЛНИ ПАРК
☎ 047
Easily the most handsome and quite possibly the friendliest city in Macedonia, chilly Bitola sits on a 660m-high plateau at the foot of Mt Pelister, just north of the Greek border. Named Manastir under Ottoman rule, it surpassed even Skopje as the most important city in the region, with its prestigious military academy attracting the likes of a young Kemal Ataturk, the father of modern Turkey. Its past prosperity has graced it with a fine central promenade, Ulica Maršal Tito, which is lined with 19th-century buildings including the three remaining consulates – Turkish, British and French. In winter the temperatures can reach minus 30°C, but this doesn't stop the locals strutting their stuff up and the down this street or hanging out in its stylish bars and cafés.

### Information
The local info source is the newly opened **Tourist Info Center** ( ☎ 241 641; Sterjo Georgiev 1; ☙ Mon-Fri 9am-4pm). For internet access we recommend **Internet Caffe Mouse** ( ☎ 047-241 194; Ul Maršal Tito; per hr 30MKD).

### Sights & Activities
Clustered around the Dragor River, the magnificent minarets of three **16th-century mosques** pierce the sky. North of the river the city's colourful **old bazaar** has about 6000 shops to explore. On the south side **Sveti Dimitri** (Ul 11 Oktomvri) boasts a large lavish interior with exquisite frescoes, ornate lamps, a huge iconostasis and storm clouds covering the ceiling.

As you wander down Ulica Maršal Tito and into the park you'll notice the number of well-tended socialist-realist **statues** of square-jawed partisans. Tito's bust is rarely without fresh flowers, but more surprising is the bronze Partisan memorial erected in Goce Delčev square as recently as 2004.

Follow the signs in the park to the fascinating ruins of **Heraclea Lyncestis** (admission 100MKD, photos 500MKD; ☺ 9am-3pm Nov-Apr, 9am-5pm May-Oct). Founded in the 4th century BC by Philip II of Macedon, Heraclea was conquered by the Romans two centuries later and became an important stage on the Via Egnatia, the Roman road that connected ports on the Adriatic with Byzantium. Excavations only started in 1936 and are continuing as money allows, but the well-preserved theatre, baths, portico, two early Christian basilicas and the episcopal palace are now visible. The site's 1300 sq metres of mosaics are protected by sand (and often buried by snow) in the winter, but they are uncovered from 1 May to 15 October every year.

**Pelister National Park**, only 10km from Bitola, covers 12,500 hectares of pine forest and the great granite dome of **Mt Pelister** (2601m). The park protects some 88 species of trees, included the rare five-leafed Macedonian pine (*Pinus peuce*). There is a small **ski slope** (day pass 300MKD), which usually operates from the beginning of December until early March. In summer you can hike to the crystal-clear lakes on top of the mountain, enjoying the views over Lake Prespa to the west.

On the edge of the park is the rugged old Vlach village of **Malovište**. The village has been slowly losing its population for decades, but its collection of two-storey stone houses is one of the finest ensembles of traditional architecture in Macedonia. A little river burbles through the village, crossed by many quaint little bridges. The lanes are made of rough cobblestones – sturdy footwear will help save your ankles. The massive church of **Sveti Petka** (built in 1856) shows how wealthy the community had grown through cattle breeding. The interior is full of frescoes and over 100 icons. About 2km from the village, in the middle of a dense beech forest, is the little church of **Sveta Ana**. It takes about 30 minutes to hike there – it's 400m higher in altitude. Tradition has it that an acorn taken from the tree here will bring you luck in love. Hotels in Bitola can arrange transport to/from Malovište, with one hour at the village, for about 500MKD. Malovište is 4km off Hwy E65 between Bitola and Resen – turn off at Kazani, take the first left and then another left through a tunnel under the highway.

The **Ilinden Festival**, the most important event of the year, takes place on 2 August, and celebrates the uprising against the Ottomans with traditional food, music and general joy.

## Sleeping & Eating

Accommodation in the centre of Bitola is limited and overpriced. Better deals can be found in the villages on the road through Pelister National Park, even allowing for the cost of taxis to the centre.

**Hotel Šumski Feneri** ( ☎ 047-293 030; sfeneri@mt .net.mk; Trnovo village; s/d/tr €25/40/50, apt €60; P ) This charming family-owned hotel lies on the lower slopes of Mt Pelister in the village of Trnovo, 9km from the centre of Bitola (200MKD by taxi) and 6km to the ski-field chairlifts. It has four apartments, which can fit four people, an extraordinary number of potted plants and a large restaurant filled with unintentionally hilarious art. Naomi Campbell and Joseph Fiennes have both stayed here. To get there take the Pelister National Park road up the mountain towards Molika.

**Hotel Molika** ( ☎ 047-229 406; www.hotelmolika.com .mk; Molika, Pelister National Park; s/d €32/46; P ✕ ◻ ) Located at the foot of the chairlifts 1420m up Mt Pelister but only 15km from Bitola, this 56-room mountain lodge also offers full or half-board to weary skiers and hikers. The furnishings are faded but the rooms are fine, with great views from the balconies at the front.

**Hotel De Niro** ( ☎ 047-229 656; www.hotel-deniro .com; Ul Kiril i Metodij 5; s/d €35/50, ste €80; ✕ ◻ ) The location is perfect for this new little hotel, around the corner from the consulates on Maršal Tito and above a popular Italian restaurant of the same name. The rooms are very clean but small, especially the single – where your shower looks out at the factory next door via an upper-torso-revealing piece of unfrosted glass.

**Hotel Epinal** ( ☎ 047-224 777; www.hotelepinal.com; Ul Maršal Tito bb; s €75-84, d €120-140; ✕ ▣ ) The only large hotel in the centre of Bitola, Epinal has some great facilities – such as an excellent swimming pool and gym – but the rooms are overpriced. Use of the air-conditioning will set you back an extra €10 per person. The open-air café under a wrought-iron roof at the front of the hotel, on the other hand, is an excellent spot for traditional Macedonian fare, especially fish (mains 300MKD to 900MKD).

> ### WORTH A TRIP
>
> The remote and magnificent **Treskavec Monastery**, 10km to the north of Prilep on the top of rocky Mt Zlato, can only be reached by a two-hour climb or by 4WD up a muddy mountain track, weather permitting. Take a taxi to Dabnica village and ask the driver to point you at the cobbled track leading up the mountain. Go up the road, and after you reach the water fountain, continue on the straight path. The monastery itself was rebuilt in the early 1990s after it was destroyed by a fire, and forms a sort of pentagon with a courtyard and 14-century church at its centre, decorated with fine frescoes. Built on what was an ancient town, the site once housed a temple to Apollo and Artemis. The monastery's guardians will welcome you, cook you dinner and let you sleep in the rooms for free. Beds and blankets are provided. Leave some money at the icons; how much is up to you, but we recommend at least 200MKD per person.

## Getting There & Away

The **bus station** ( ☎ 047-391 391; Ul Nikola Tesla) and **train station** ( ☎ 047-392 904; Ul Nikola Tesla) are adjacent to each other, about 1km south of the town centre. There are seven buses daily to Skopje between 5am and 4.30pm (350MKD, 2½ hours, 185km), which also stop in Prilep (110MKD, 30 minutes, 46km). The train follows a similar route but takes four hours to reach its destination (four daily). There are at least six buses to Ohrid, with more services in summer (170MKD, 1½ hours, 71km).

To get to the Greek border, take a taxi from the bus station (€6, 15 minutes, 15km) and then order a taxi on the Greek side to the nearest town, Florina (€12, 15 minutes, 17km). From here it will take about three hours by bus and a little longer by train to reach Thessaloniki.

There's a branch of **Hertz** ( ☎ 047-237 087; Ul Kliment Ohridski 2; per day from €40) in town.

# MACEDONIA DIRECTORY

## ACCOMMODATION

City hotels are expensive, as they tend to cater to business and government travellers. In areas where locals take their holidays, accommodation is generally good and affordable, with plenty of private options. In Skopje you'll be lucky to find a midrange single for less than €60 per night, whereas in Ohrid there are plenty under €40. Booking early is recommended for visits during the summer season, Orthodox Christmas (7 January) and Orthodox Easter.

## ACTIVITIES

There is great skiing at Mavrovo (p481), along with less-developed facilities at Pelister (opposite) and Popova Šapka (1845m), 18km west of Tetovo near the border with Kosovo. Hiking is spectacular in any of the three national parks (Galičica, Pelister and Mavrovo) and at Lake Matka (p480) near Skopje. Unsurprisingly, Macedonia has a great tradition of mountaineering. The **Macedonian Mountaineering Sports Federation** ( ☎ 02-3165 540; spsm@mt.net.mk) can put you in touch with guides throughout the county for alpine hikes, rock- or ice-climbing, as well as hiring tents, cooking equipment and providing maps and details of mountain huts.

## BOOKS

Lonely Planet's *Eastern Europe Phrasebook* will help you with the language. A decent background book is *Who Are the Macedonians?* by Hugh Poulton, a very readable political and cultural history. Also addressing the issue of Macedonian identity is Will Myer's *People Of The Storm God: Travels In Macedonia*. A *Hitchhiker's Guide to Macedonia...and my soul*, by Carol Maria Cho, is a laugh-out-loud funny journal, if a little self-indulgent in parts.

## BUSINESS HOURS

Businesses tend to stay open late in Macedonia. Travellers will generally find them open from 8am to 8pm weekdays and 8am to 2pm on Saturday. In smaller centres they may close for lunch from around 1pm, and reopen at 4pm. Post offices open from 7am to 5.30pm and banks from 7am to 5pm, Monday to Friday. Restaurants, bars and cafés tend to open at 9am and close at midnight, extending to 1am on Friday and Saturday.

## DANGERS & ANNOYANCES

In general, Macedonia is a safe and easygoing country. Watch out for pickpockets in crowded areas, and taxi drivers charging exorbitant fares from the airport. A more specific annoyance can be the persistence of young beggars, particularly around the riverfront and square in Skopje, and at traffic lights. While they are unlikely to hurt you, it can be quite intimidating to have half a dozen rug rats hanging off every pocket for 15 minutes at a time, getting progressively more aggressive. Keep your hands firmly on your valuables and walk quickly into the nearest café or store if you're unable to shake them.

## DISABLED TRAVELLERS

Wheelchair accessibility in Macedonia is almost nonexistent. Few public buildings or hotels have ramps and only the very expensive Holiday Inn in Skopje has a specifically designed wheelchair-accessible room. There is no disabled access on public transport.

## EMBASSIES & CONSULATES
### Macedonian Embassies & Consulates

A full list of Macedonian embassies abroad and embassies and consulates in Macedonia can be found at www.mfa.gov.mk.

**Albania** ( ☎ 04-233 036; makambas@albnet.net; cnr Rr Skënderbej & Rr e Kavajës, Tirana)

**Australia** ( ☎ 0612-6249 8000; info@macedonianemb.org .au; Perpetual Bldg, Ste 2:05, 10 Rudd St, Canberra ACT 2601)

**Bulgaria** ( ☎ 02-870 1560; todmak@bgnet.bg; Ul Frederic Joliot-Curie 17, Block 2, fl 1, Ste 1, Sofia 1113)

**Canada** ( ☎ 613-234 3882; www3.sympatico.ca/emb.mace donia.ottawa/; 130 Albert St, Ste 1006, Ottawa ON, K1P 5G4)

**France** ( ☎ 01 45 77 10 50; ambassade@fr.oleane.com; 5 Rue de la Faisanderie, 75116 Paris)

**Germany** ( ☎ 030-890 69 50; makedonische.bot schaft@t-online.de; Koenigsallee 2, 14193 Berlin)

**Greece** Athens ( ☎ 210 674 9585; lormak@teledomenet .gr; Marathonoudromou 13, P Psychico, 154 52); Thessaloniki ( ☎ 2310 277 347; dkpsolun@mfa.com.mk; Tsimiski 43)

**Kosovo** ( ☎ 038-247 462; fax 247 463; Ul 24 Maj 121, Prishtina)

**Netherlands** ( ☎ 0704-27 22 64; repmak@wanadoo.nl; Laan can Meerdevoort 50-C, 2517Am Den Haag)

**Serbia & Montenegro** Belgrade ( ☎ 011-328 4924; macemb@eunet.yu; Gospodar Jevremova 34, 11000); Podgorica ( ☎ 081-667 415; mkgkpodgorica@cg.yu; Hercegovacka 49/3, 81000)

**UK** ( ☎ 020 7976 0535; www.macedonianembassy.org .uk; Suites 2.1 & 2.2, Buckingham Court, 75-83 Buckingham Gate, London SW1E 6PE)

**USA** ( ☎ 202-667-0501; www.macedonianembassy.org; 2129 Wyoming Ave, Washington DC, 20008)

### Embassies & Consulates in Macedonia

All of the following are located in Skopje unless indicated otherwise:

**Albania** ( ☎ 02-2614 636; ambshqip@mt.net.mk; Ul HT Karpoš 94a)

**Australia** ( ☎ 02-3061 114; austcon@mt.net.mk; Ul Londonska 11b)

**Bulgaria** ( ☎ 02-3229 444; bgemb@mol.com.mk; Ul Ivo Ribar Lola 40)

**Canada** ( ☎ 02-3225 630; honcon@unet.com.mk; Bul Partizanska Odredi 17a)

**Croatia** ( ☎ 02-3127 350; velhrskp@mpt.com.mk; Ul Ivo Ribar Lola 44)

**France** ( ☎ 02-3244 300; www.ambafrance-mk.org; Ul Salvador Aljende 73); Bitola ( ☎ 047-223 192; fax 047-223 594; Ul Maršal Tito 42)

**Germany** ( ☎ 02-3093 900; dt.boskop@mol.com.mk; Ul Lerinska 59)

**Greece** ( ☎ 02-3219 260; grfyrom@unet.com.mk; Ul Borka Taleski 6); Bitola ( ☎ 047-238 310; fax 047-220 310; Ul Tomaki Dimitrovski 43)

**Netherlands** ( ☎ 02-3129 319; www.nlembassy.org.mk; Ul Leninova 69-71)

**Serbia** ( ☎ 02-3129 298; yuamb@unet.com.mk; Ul Pitu Guli 8)

**UK** ( ☎ 02-3299 299; beskopje@mt.net.mk; Ul Salvador Aljende 73); Bitola ( ☎ /fax 047-228 765; Ul Maršal Tito 42)

**USA** ( ☎ 02-3116 180; skopje.usembassy.gov; Bul Ilinden bb)

## FESTIVALS & EVENTS

There are a good few festivals in Macedonia, especially in the summertime. July brings open-air evening concerts, opera and theatre to both Ohrid and Skopje. There is also a fun folklore festival in Ohrid in early July (see p483). Summer sees the International Swimming Marathon on Lake Ohrid.

One festival that all Macedonians rave about is the Galičnik wedding festival (see p481), held on the second weekend in July. Skopje's autumn days are brightened up with the flickering screens of the international film festival and the warm sounds of the **Skopje Jazz Festival** (www.skopjejazzfest.com.mk) in October.

## GAY & LESBIAN TRAVELLERS

For a country that is quick to lay claim to the legacy of Alexander the Great (whose great love was fellow soldier-boy Hephaistion), acceptance of gays and lesbians is shamefully lacking. Homosexuality was decriminalised in Macedonia in 1996, but there is little social acceptance. Any scene that may exist is so underground it's completely inaccessible to tourists, not to mention many locals.

MACEDONIA

## HOLIDAYS
**New Year** 1 & 2 January
**Orthodox Christmas** 7 January
**International Women's Day** 8 March
**Orthodox Easter Week** March/April
**Labour Day** 1 May
**Sts Cyril & Methodius Day** 24 May
**Ilinden or Day of the 1903 Rebellion** 2 August
**Republic Day** 8 September
**Partisan Day** 11 October

## INTERNET ACCESS
Bring your laptop – Macedonia's on its way to being the world's first completely wireless country.

## INTERNET RESOURCES
**Culture – Republic of Macedonia** (www.culture.in.mk)
**Exploring Macedonia** (www.exploringmacedonia.com)
**Macedonia FAQ** (faq.macedonia.org)
**Skopje Online** (www.skopjeonline.com.mk)

## LANGUAGE
Macedonia's two official languages are Macedonian and Albanian. Macedonian, a South Slavic language, is spoken by most of the population. There are some grammatical similarities between Macedonian and Bulgarian, such as the omittance of case. Speakers of Bulgarian, Serbian, Croatian and, to a lesser extent, Russian should get by without too much difficulty. For others, we recommend a good phrasebook, such as Lonely Planet's *Eastern Europe Phrasebook*.

Macedonian uses the Cyrillic alphabet, based on the Glagolitic script, which originated in Macedonia and spread across the eastern Slavic world. Though Latin script appears on road signs and some shop names, the Cyrillic alphabet is predominant and street names are printed in Cyrillic only, so it's a good idea to learn the alphabet before travelling to the country. For a quick introduction to useful Macedonian and Albanian words and phrases, see the Language chapter, p944.

## MONEY
Macedonian denar (MKD) notes come in denominations of 10, 50, 100, 500, 1000 and 5000, and there are coins of one, two and five denar. The denar isn't convertible outside Macedonia. Restaurants, hotels and some shops will accept payment in euro (usually) and US dollars (sometimes). In this book we've used whatever currency the prices were listed in, which is usually euro for hotels and denar for other transactions.

Small private exchange offices throughout central Skopje and Ohrid exchange cash for a rate that is only slightly better than at banks. ATMs can be found in all of the major towns and tourist centres but not in out-of-the-way places. Travellers cheques are a real hassle to change and we advise against relying on them, except as a form of emergency back-up money. Credit cards are widely accepted, but don't take it for granted, even at a hotel or restaurant. Diners Club is surprisingly popular.

## POST
Mail services to/from Macedonia are efficient and reasonably fast, although sending money or valuables through normal post is not recommended as they may mysteriously disappear. Letters to the USA cost 38MKD, to Australia 40MKD and to Europe 35MKD. There are poste-restante services at major post offices.

## RESPONSIBLE TRAVEL
Lake Ohrid trout is almost extinct, and in 2004 the government issued a seven-year ban on catching it. Despite this, many restaurants still offer it, thereby encouraging illegal trout fishing. Don't order it.

Although in the majority of larger towns and cities dress is tight, colourful and revealing among women and men, do dress modestly when visiting a church, monastery or mosque.

## TELEPHONE & FAX
A long-distance call costs less at main post offices than in hotels. Drop the initial zero in the city codes when calling Macedonia from abroad. Buy phonecards in units of 100 (200MKD), 200 (300MKD), 500 (650MKD) or 1000 (1250MKD) from post offices. Some larger kiosks also sell the 100-unit cards. You can often make cheap international calls at internet cafés for around 15MKD per minute.

Macedonia has a digital mobile phone network (MobiMak); mobile numbers are preceded by ☎ 070. Some providers may have

---

**EMERGENCY NUMBERS**

- Ambulance ☎ 194
- Police ☎ 192
- Highway & Roadside Assistance ☎ 15555

global-roaming agreements with Macedonia's domestic network, so check before departing.

Fax services are available at the main post offices in Skopje and Ohrid.

## VISAS

Citizens of EU countries, Argentina, Barbados, Bosnia, Botswana, Croatia, Cuba, Iceland, Israel, Japan, New Zealand, Maldives, Norway, Switzerland and the USA don't need visas for Macedonia and are allowed to stay for up to three months. Visas are required for most others and cost €20 to €50 depending on where you apply for it and whether it is single- or multiple-entry. Even though some visas can be obtained at the airport for some nationalities, it is much safer to apply in advance. The regulations change quite frequently – check www.mfa.gov.mk for the latest information.

## WOMEN TRAVELLERS

Women travellers should feel no particular concern about travel in Macedonia. Other than possible cursory interest from men, travel is hassle-free and easy.

# TRANSPORT IN MACEDONIA

## GETTING THERE & AWAY
### Air

Macedonia has two international airports, Skopje's **Petrovec airport** (SKP; ☎ 02-3148 333; www.airports.com.mk) and the much smaller **Ohrid airport** (OHD; ☎ 046-252 820; www.airports.com.mk). There is no departure tax.

### AIRLINES

**Adria Airways** (code JP; ☎ 02-3117 009; www.adria.si; Ljubljana)

**Air France** (code AF; no local office; www.airfrance.com; Prague)

**Croatia Airlines** (code OU; ☎ 02-3115 858; www.croatiaairlines.hr; Zagreb)

**Czech Airlines** (code OK; ☎ 02-3290 572; www.czechairlines.com; Prague)

**JAT Airways** (code JU; ☎ 02-3118 306; www.jat.com; Belgrade)

**Lufthansa** (code LH; ☎ 02-3216 120; www.lufthansa.com; Ljubljana)

**Malév Hungarian Airlines** (code MA; ☎ 02-3111 214; www.malev.hu; Budapest)

## Land

Macedonia shares land borders with Greece, Albania, Bulgaria, Serbia and the UN-monitored territory of Kosovo. Access to/from all neighbouring states is generally trouble-free and unrestricted.

### BORDER CROSSINGS
#### Albania

There are four border crossings with Albania – the two main ones are on either side of Lake Ohrid (Kafa San/Qafa e Thanës, 12km southwest of Struga, and Sveti Naum/Tushëmishti, 29km south of Ohrid). There are two smaller ones at Blato, 5km northwest of Debar, and at Stenje on the western shore of Lake Prespa.

#### Bulgaria

The main crossings are just east of Kriva Palanka (between Sofia and Skopje), east of Delčevo (26km west of Blagoevgrad) and at Novo Selo (between Petrič and Strumica).

#### Greece

There are crossings at Gevgelija (between Skopje and Thessaloniki), Dojran (just east of Gevgelija) and Medžitlija. To get to this crossing, take a taxi from the Bitola bus station (€6, 15 minutes, 15km) and then order a taxi on the Greek side to the nearest town, Florina (€12, 15 minutes, 17km).

#### Kosovo

The main border crossing at Blace is just a 20-minute trip north from Skopje. There is another crossing point close by at Jazince, used by vehicles coming from Tetovo.

#### Serbia

The main crossing point into Serbia is Tabanovce, either on the motorway or by train. There's a much smaller crossing point at Pelince about 25km northeast of Tabanovce.

### BUS

From Skopje buses travel to Belgrade (1350MKD, six hours, 431km, 16 daily), Prishtina (300MKD, 1¾ hours, 87km, six daily), Sofia (640MKD, six hours, 222km, six daily) and further-flung Eastern European centres such as Sarajevo, Zagreb and Ljubljana. Many of these routes pass through smaller centres, including Ohrid and Bitola.

To/from Albania you can travel from Tetovo via Struga to Tirana by bus (900MKD, six to seven hours, two daily on Monday, Wednesday and Friday). From Ohrid you can catch a Sveti Naum bus to the border (80MKD, 50 minutes, 29km, four daily) and cross on foot.

## CAR & MOTORCYCLE
None of the border crossings should pose any particular problems. You will need a Green Card endorsed for Macedonia to bring a car into the country. For further information on driving around Macedonia see below.

## TRAIN
Trains from Skopje head to Belgrade via Niš (1209MKD, nine hours, two daily), Prishtina (€4, 2½ hours, two daily), Podgorica via Niš (2000MKD, 17½ hours, daily), Zagreb (2050MKD, 18 hours, daily) and Ljubljana (2690MKD, 20½ hours, daily). Sleepers are available. You can find timetables for international routes on the website of **Macedonian Railways** (www.mz.com.mk/patnichki/timetable.htm).

# GETTING AROUND
## Air
It is possible to fly between Skopje and Ohrid on MAT (see p484) but buses are definitely the best and cheapest option.

## Bicycle
Cycling around Macedonia is becoming more popular. The country offers generally good road conditions and relatively light traffic – though beginners should be warned it is a mountainous country.

## Bus
The bus network is well developed in Macedonia, with frequent services from Skopje to all major centres in safe and fairly comfortable coaches. It's a good idea to buy a ticket from the station a day or two in advance when travelling to Ohrid in the busy summer season. For further information see the Getting There & Away section of each destination chapter.

## Car & Motorcycle
### DRIVING LICENCE
Usually your country's driving licence will suffice, but it is a good idea to have an International Driving Permit as well.

### HIRE
Skopje is full of rental-car agencies, from the large ones (Hertz, Avis, Sixt) to dozens of local companies. The choices in Ohrid and Bitola are more limited. Tourist brochures give comprehensive lists. A smallish sedan like a Ford Focus costs about €40 a day, including insurance. You need to present your passport, driving licence and a credit card. You normally need to have held a full driving licence for one year.

### INSURANCE
Rental agencies provide insurance for around €15 to €25 a day, depending on the type of car, with a nonwaivable excess of €1000 to €2500. Green Card insurance is accepted, and third-party insurance is compulsory.

### ROAD RULES
Driving is on the right-hand side of the road. Speed limits for cars and motorcycles are 120km/h on motorways, 80km/h on the open road and 50km/h to 60km/h in towns. Speeding fines start from around 1500MKD. It is compulsory to wear a seat belt and to have the headlights on (dipped) at all times for both cars and motorcycles. It is also compulsory to carry a replacement set of bulbs, two warning triangles, a first-aid kit, and between 15 November and 15 March cars must carry snow chains. Motorcyclists and their passengers must wear helmets. Macedonia has a relatively high death toll from accidents and the busy traffic police are vigilant on speeding, drink driving and headlights in particular. Fines are issued on-the-spot. The legal blood-alcohol limit is 0.05%.

## Taxi
Taxis are a snappy way of getting to out-of-the-way monasteries and other sights if buses aren't convenient. Macedonian taxis are very cheap by European standards – Skopje has some of the cheapest capital-city taxis. A half-hour trip, from Skopje to Lake Matka for example, should cost around 350MKD.

## Train
Macedonia has a limited network of domestic destinations reachable by train. Possibly the only one of any real interest is the four-hour, three-times-daily service to Bitola via Prilep from Skopje. The most you'll pay for a domestic ticket is 370MKD for a return to Bitola. Timetables are available on the website of **Macedonian Railways** (www.mz.com.mk/patnichki/timetable.htm).

Downtown Minsk (p80), Belarus

BRUCE YUAN-YUE BI

The colourful façades of Tirana's (p51) apartment blocks, Albania

DOUG MCKINLAY

White Ottoman houses cling to the rugged mountain slopes of Berat (p62), Albania

PAUL DAVID HELLANDER

PAUL GREENWAY

The Yantra River wends its way past the town of Veliko Târnovo (p162), Bulgaria

PATRICK HORTON

Pilgrims at the site of the alleged apparition of the Virgin Mary, Međugorje (p121), Bosnia and Hercegovina

The healing waters of Gellért thermal baths (p364) in Budapest, Hungary

MARTIN MOOS

WITOLD SKRYPCZAK

The picturesque town of České Budějovice (p289), Czech Republic

JONATHAN SMITH

Kuressaare's fairytale Bishop's castle, Saaremaa (p343), Estonia

Al fresco dining on Placa, Dubrovnik (p233), Croatia

RICHARD I'ANSON

MARTIN MOOS

The wining and dining hub of Király utca, Pécs (p391), Hungary

JANE SWEENEY

The legendary Hill of Crosses (p459), Šiauliai, Lithuania

Picturesque Kotor (p533) overlooks the majestic Kotor fjord, Montenegro

PATRICK

The tiny 13th-century church, Sveti Jovan at Kaneo (p483), overlooking Lake Ohrid, Macedonia

The peaks of Međed rise behind Crno jezero (Black Lake) in the stunning Durmitor National Park (p536), Montenegro

The famed spire of the Gothic St Peter's Church, Rīga (p420), Latvia

A sunny afternoon in Ştefan cel Mare Park, Chişinău (p506), Moldova

One of Belgrade's enticing hidden-away bars (p759), Serbia

*Last Judgement* fresco of Voroneț Monastery (p674), Romania

The historic thoroughfare of Długi Targ (Long Market), Gdańsk (p597), Poland

MARTIN MOOS

Cathedral of the Assumption, Sergiev
Posad (p717), Russia

RICHARD NEBESKY

Historic buildings fringe the bustling
Hviezdoslavovo square, Bratislava (p786), Slovakia

Moscow's impressive Red Square (p705), home to Lenin's Mausoleum, Russia

JONATHAN SMITH

JONATHAN SMITH

Ljubljana (p827), Slovenia – home to an eclectic array of inviting restaurants and bars

PETER WILLIAM T

The golden domes of St Michael's Monastery (p869), Kyiv, Ukraine

Cobblestone streets and historic buildings of Lviv (p874), Ukraine

JONATH.

# Moldova

For a country that's only vaguely known in Europe and all but anonymous to the rest of the world, Moldova has a cultural, political and economic, erm, 'liveliness' equalled by few. News briefs that emerge from the region are punctuated by tales of civil war, breakaway republics, organised crime, arms dealing, human trafficking and a curious return to communism.

Rarely mentioned is the country's first-rate, and bargain-priced, wine industry. The beguiling attractions between the vineyards get no press at all; remote monasteries cut into limestone cliffs, sunflower fields, enormous watermelons, bucolic pastoral lands, amazingly friendly people and one of Europe's most party-bent capitals. The tiny breakaway regions of Transdniestr and Gagauzia are exquisite idiosyncratic wonders, with the former arguably ranking as one of Europe's top curiosities. Chişinău's grossly inflated accommodation prices notwithstanding, this is one of Europe's best travel bargains and far and away the best wine (ad)venture on the planet.

**MOLDOVA**

## FAST FACTS

- **Area** 33,700 sq km
- **Capital** Chişinău
- **Currency** leu; €1 = 15.48 lei; US$1 = 12.37 lei; UK£1 = 22.30 lei; A$1 = 9.01 lei; ¥100 = 11.41 lei; NZ$1 = 8.48 lei
- **Famous for** wine, folk art
- **Official Languages** Moldovan, Russian
- **Phrases** *bună* (hello); *merci* (thank you); *cum vă numiţi?* (what's your name?)
- **Population** 4.43 million
- **Telephone Codes** country code ☎ 373; international access code ☎ 22
- **Visas** required for Australian and New Zealand passport holders; see p523 for details

## HIGHLIGHTS

- Stroll **Chişinău's** (p506) tree-studded avenues and experience its kick-ass nightlife
- Visit the fantastic cave monastery of 13th-century monks at **Orheiul Vechi** (p514)
- Take an organised or improvised wine tour at the country's world-famous cellars in **Cricova** (p513) and sip from the fruit of the gods
- Visit the self-styled republic, **Transdniestr** (p515), a surreal, living museum of the Soviet Union, for an off-the-beaten-track experience

## ITINERARIES

- **One week** Arrive in Chişinău – buy and uncork several bottles of wine to fuel a couple of days' partying. Use Chişinău as your base, making a trip out to the cave monasteries at Orheiul Vechi. Tour a big-name vineyard.
- **Two weeks** Follow the one-week itinerary, plus add on a few days travelling back in time in Transdniestr, the country that doesn't officially exist, then tack on a few smaller vineyard tours around Chişinău, purchasing your customs limit, before returning home.

## CLIMATE & WHEN TO GO

Moldova has moderate winters and warm summers. Hikers and wine enthusiasts would do well to travel between May and September, when you have more guarantees that camping grounds and attractions will be open. As there is little tourism in Moldova, there's no real low or high season.

## HISTORY

Moldova today straddles two historic regions divided by the Nistru (Dniestr) River. Historic Romanian Bessarabia incorporated the region west of the Nistru, while tsarist Russia governed the territory east of the river (Transdniestr).

Bessarabia, part of the Romanian principality of Moldavia, was annexed in 1812 by the Russian empire. In 1918, after the October Revolution, Bessarabia declared its independence. Two months later the newly formed Democratic Moldavian Republic united with Romania. Russia never recognised this union.

Then in 1924 the Soviet Union created the Moldavian Autonomous Oblast on the eastern banks of the Nistru River, and incorporated

### HOW MUCH?

- **Bottle of Cricova table wine** $1 to $3
- **Museum admission (adult)** $0.20 to $1
- **Short taxi ride** $2
- **Local bus ticket** $0.15
- **Internet access** $0.25 per hr

### LONELY PLANET INDEX

- **Litre of petrol** $0.50
- **Litre of water** $0.35
- **Beer (Chişinău in a bar)** $0.45 to $1
- **Souvenir T-shirt** $3 to $5
- **Pizza slice from street kiosk** $0.50

Transdniestr into the Ukrainian Soviet Socialist Republic (SSR). A few months later the Soviet government renamed the oblast the Moldavian Autonomous Soviet Socialist Republic (Moldavian ASSR). During 1929 the capital was moved to Tiraspol from Balta (in present-day Ukraine).

In June 1940 the Soviet army, in accordance with the terms of the secret protocol associated with the Molotov-Ribbentrop Pact, occupied Romanian Bessarabia. The Soviet government immediately joined Bessarabia with the southern part of the Moldavian ASSR – specifically, Transdniestr – naming it the Moldavian Soviet Socialist Republic (Moldavian SSR). The remaining northern part of the Moldavian ASSR was returned to the Ukrainian SSR (present-day Ukraine). Bessarabia suffered terrifying Sovietisation, marked by the deportation of 300,000 Romanians.

During 1941 allied Romanian and German troops attacked the Soviet Union, and Bessarabia and Transdniestr fell into Romanian hands. Consequently, thousands of Bessarabian Jews were sent to labour camps and then deported to Auschwitz. In August 1944 the Soviet army reoccupied Transdniestr and Bessarabia. Under the terms of the Paris Peace Treaty of 1947, Romania had to relinquish the region and Soviet power was restored in the Moldavian SSR.

Once in control again the Soviets immediately enforced a Sovietisation programme on the Moldavian SSR. The Cyrillic alphabet was imposed on the Moldovan language (a dialect of Romanian) and Russian became

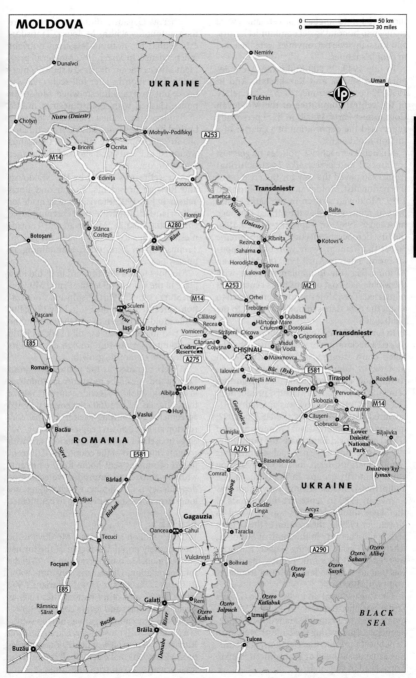

# MOLDOVA

the official state language. Street names were changed to honour Soviet communist heroes, and Russian-style patronymics were included in people's names.

In July 1949, 25,000 Moldovans were deported to Siberia and Kazakhstan. And in 1950–52 Leonid Brezhnev, then first secretary of the central committee of the Moldovan Communist Party, is said to have personally supervised the deportation of a quarter of a million Moldovans.

Mikhail Gorbachev's policies of *glasnost* (openness) and *perestroika* (restructuring) from 1986 paved the way for the creation of the nationalist Moldovan Popular Front in 1989. Moldovan written in the Latin alphabet was reintroduced as the official language in August 1989. In February–March 1990 the first democratic elections to the Supreme Soviet (parliament) were won by the Popular Front. Then in April 1990 the Moldovan national flag (the Romanian tricolour with the Moldavian coat of arms in its centre) was reinstated. Transdniestr, however, refused to adopt the new state symbols and stuck to the red banner.

In June 1990 the Moldovan Supreme Soviet passed a declaration of sovereignty. After the failed coup attempt against Gorbachev in Moscow in August 1991, Moldova declared its full independence and Mircea Snegur became the democratically elected president in December 1991. Moldova was granted 'most-favoured nation' status by the USA in 1992, qualifying for International Monetary Fund (IMF) and World Bank loans the same year.

Counteracting these nationalist sentiments was an emerging desire for autonomy among ethnic minority groups. In Transdniestr, the Yedinstivo-Unitatea (Unity) movement was formed in 1988 to represent the interests of the Slavic minorities. This was followed in November 1989 by the creation of the Gagauz Halki political party in the south of Moldova, where the Turkic-speaking Gagauz minority was centred. Both ethnic groups' major fear was that an independent Moldova would reunite with Romania.

The Gagauz went on to declare the Gagauz Soviet Socialist Republic in August 1990. A month later the Transdniestrans declared independence, establishing the Dniestr Moldovan Republic. In presidential elections, Igor Smirnov came out as head of Transdniestr, Stepan Topal head of Gagauzia.

Whereas Gagauzia didn't press for more than autonomy within Moldova, Transdniestr settled for nothing less than outright independence. In March 1992 Moldovan president Mircea Snegur declared a state of emergency. Two months later full-scale civil war broke out in Transdniestr when Moldovan police clashed with Transdniestran militia in Bendery (then called Tighina), who were backed by troops from Russia. An estimated 500 to 700 people were killed and thousands wounded in events that shocked the former Soviet Union.

A ceasefire was signed by the Moldovan and Russian presidents, Snegur and Boris Yeltsin, in July 1992. Provisions were made for a Russian-led, tripartite peacekeeping force comprising Russian, Moldovan and Transdniestran troops to be stationed in the region. Troops remain here today, maintaining an uneasy peace.

Moldova took a step forward in its bid for a place in the EU when Deputy Prime Minister Ion Sturza signed a Partnership and Cooperation Agreement with the EU in May 1999. But while Moldova is keen to join the ranks of the EU, two major obstacles still block its path: the country's mounting foreign debt and its inadequate economic growth.

Widely regarded as the poorest nation in Europe and one of the most corrupt countries in the world, Moldova is endeavouring to shake these stigmas. In late 2005 the country signed agreements committing itself to combat corruption and lock down people-trafficking. Average household income remains low, and with roughly one-third of the country's GDP comprised of monies sent home from emigrants working abroad, an unproductive economic dependency is developing, which will require long-term domestic cultivation to counteract.

## PEOPLE

With 4.5 million inhabitants, Moldova is the most densely populated region of the former Soviet Union. Moldovans make up 78.2% of the total population, Ukrainians constitute 8.4%, Russians 5.8%, Gagauz 4.4%, Bulgarians 1.9%, 'other' 1.5%, and other nationalities such as Belarusians, Poles and Roma compose 1.3%.

Most Gagauz and Bulgarians inhabit southern Moldova. In Transdniestr, Ukrainians and Russians make up 58% of the region's population; Moldovans make up 34%. It is one of the least urbanised countries in Europe.

---

**NOT EXACTLY A NATIONAL SPORT**

Did you know that Moldova is world famous for its underwater hockey teams? Well, OK, *infamous* then.

You wouldn't normally associate such a sport as underwater hockey with Moldova (come to think of it, there aren't any countries you'd associate it with, but that's another story…). However, in the 2000 Underwater Hockey Championships held in the world-renowned underwater-hockey metropolis of Hobart, in Tasmania, Australia, the Moldovan men's team puzzled referees and judges by not even knowing how to put their fins and flippers on properly. After being trounced by such stalwarts as Columbia 30-0 and Argentina 23-0, it was revealed that the entire team had filed for (and eventually received) refugee status with the Australian government.

It's a good thing for Moldovans that Canadians aren't known for their good memories or efficient bureaucracy. Two years later, after much hounding from a so-called Moldovan Underwater Hockey Federation based in Tiraspol (in probably the only time Transdniestran officials called themselves 'Moldovan'), the Canadian embassy in Bucharest granted the women's team visas to participate in the world championships in Calgary.

There was much head scratching as the Moldovan national anthem was played – and no team came out to play. But how could they? They were in Toronto, filing for refugee status. In this elaborate visa scam, each woman on the team (who no doubt wouldn't know what to do with an underwater puck even if it bit her) had paid organisers some $1200 – not bad for refugee status in Canada.

While this incident sadly spells out an uncertain future for the world of underwater hockey in Moldova, it does speak volumes about the creativity and persistence of Moldovans!

---

# RELIGION

Moldova stays on course with the region's religious leanings; the vast majority being Eastern Orthodox (98%), with the recovering Jewish community (1.5%) at a distant second. Baptists and 'other' make up the remaining 0.5%.

# ARTS

There is a wealth of traditional folk art in Moldova, with carpet making, pottery, weaving and carving predominating.

Traditional dancing in Moldova is similar to the traditional dances of other Eastern European countries. Couples dance in a circle, a semicircle or a line to the sounds of bagpipes, flutes, panpipes and violins.

Two of Moldova's most prolific modern composers are Arkady Luxemburg and Evgeny Doga, who have both scored films and multimedia projects, as well as written songs, concertos, suites and symphonies. Dimitrie Gagauz has for over three decades been the foremost composer of songs reflecting the folklore of the Turkic-influenced Gagauz population of southern Moldova.

The biggest name in Moldovan painting is Mihai Grecu (1916–98), who cofounded the National School of Painting and was also a poet and free love advocate. In sculpture, Anatol Coseac today produces some highly original woodworks.

# ENVIRONMENT
## Land

Moldova is tiny and landlocked. It's a country of gently rolling steppes, with a gradual sloping towards the Black Sea. With one of the highest percentages of arable land in the world, Moldova is blessed with rich soil. Fields of grains, fruits and sunflowers are characteristic of the countryside. Moldova counts some 16,500 species of animals (460 of which are vertebrates) as its citizens.

## National Parks

There are five scientific reserves (totalling 19,378 hectares) and 30 protected natural sites (covering 22,278 hectares). The reserves protect areas of bird migration, old beech and oak forests, and important waterways. The Codru reserve, Moldova's oldest, boasts 924 plant species, 138 kinds of birds and 45 mammals; this is the most frequently visited reserve.

## Environmental Issues

A great effort has been made by environmental groups to protect Moldova's wetland regions along the lower Prut and Nistru Rivers.

Never heavily industrial, Moldova faces more issues of protection and conservation than pollution. The majority of its 3600 rivers and rivulets were drained, diverted or dammed, threatening ecosystems.

MOLDOVA

## FOOD & DRINK

Hearty meals fit for an explorer are the name of the game here. No point in fussing about calories and arteries – food, as with life itself, is meant to be enjoyed to the full. It's easier to give in and enjoy.

In Moldova, some Russian influences have seen that pickled fruits and vegetables are popular, as are Russian meals like *pelmeni* (similar to ravioli). A Turkic influence has arguably been strong here; in the south you may find the delicious Gagauz *sorpa*, a spicy ram soup.

There's no beating about the bush – vegetarians will find their meals limited. Locally grown fresh fruit and veg is always a bonus, but expect to find few vegetarian choices. We've pointed them out when we've found them.

In Moldova, outside of Chişinău, where the choice of eateries is astounding, you'll be lucky to find a decent restaurant and will be stuck with hotel dining rooms, bars or cafeterias.

Moldova produces excellent wines and brandies. Red wines are called *negru* and *roşu*, white wine is *vin alb*, while *sec* means dry, *dulce* is sweet and *spumos* translates as sparkling.

# CHIŞINĂU

☎ 22 / pop 664,325

In Chişinău (kish-i-now in Moldovan, kish-i-nyov in Russian) fleets of BMWs and Mercedes dominate traffic, while fashionably dressed youth strut down boutique-lined avenues and dine in fancy restaurants. How did this excessive wealth find its way to the capital of one of Europe's poorest countries? Answer: you don't wanna know and we ain't asking. The stunning contrast between rich and poor is only overshadowed by certain individuals who are clearly above the law and shamelessly conduct themselves as such. While this dodginess may be inordinately distracting for visitors, citizens of this vibrant, good-natured city have long since dismissed these oddities in favour of what really counts: having a good time.

First chronicled in 1420, Chişinău became a hotbed of anti-Semitism in the early 20th century; in 1903 the murder of 49 Jews sparked protests from Jewish communities worldwide. In 1941 a Nazi-driven deportation scheme and massacre was launched in Chişinău by the same group that had instigated the Iasi pogrom.

---

### CHIŞINĂU IN TWO DAYS

Sightseeing options are engaging but thin and easily covered in a half-day amble. Spend both nights ensconced in Chişinău's legendary nightlife. On your first day eat at the **Beer House** (p510), then sample its home-brew before moving on to cocktails at **Déja Vu** (p511). Dance the night away at **People** (p512).

On your second day get a hearty breakfast at **Cactus Café** (p510). Wander through the **National Archaeology and History Museum** (p509) and **National Museum of Fine Arts** (p509) until recovered. Then do it all again until 6am at **City Club** (p512).

---

Chişinău was the headquarters of the USSR's southwestern military operations during Soviet rule. Between 1944 and 1990 the city was called Kishinev, its Russian name, which is still used by some of the few travel agencies abroad who actually know where it is.

## ORIENTATION

Chişinău's street layout is a typically Soviet grid system of straight streets.

The train station is a five-minute walk from the city centre on Aleea Gării. Exit the train station, turn right along Aleea Gării to Piaţa Negruzzi, then walk up the hill to Piaţa Libertăţii. From here the main street, B-dul Ştefan cel Mare, crosses the city from southeast to northwest. The city's main sights and parks radiate off this street.

## INFORMATION
### Bookshops
**Cartea Academica** (B-dul Ştefan cel Mare 148; ◷ 9am-6pm Mon-Sat) Your best bet for English-language titles.
**Librărie Eminescu** (B-dul Ştefan cel Mare 180; ◷ 9am-6pm Mon-Fri, 9am-5pm Sat) Much larger, but devoid of English.

### Cultural Centres
**Alliance Française** ( ☎ 234 510; Str Sfatul Ţării 18; ◷ 9am-6.30pm Tue-Sat) Has a well-equipped *media-thèque* (media centre) and hosts regular cultural events.

### Internet Access
**Central Telephone Office** (B-dul Ştefan cel Mare 65; per hr $0.60; ◷ 24hr)
**Internet** ( ☎ 540 305; Hotel National, B-dul Ştefan cel Mare 4; per hr $0.50; ◷ 24hr)

## Left Luggage

The **train station** ( ☎ 252 737; Aleea Gării; ✆ 24hr) has a 24-hour left-luggage service, 100m north of the main entrance alongside the platform.

## Medical Services

Contact the US embassy (p522) for a list of English-speaking doctors.

**Felicia** ( ☎ 223 725; B-dul Ştefan cel Mare 62; ✆ 24hr) Well-stocked pharmacy.

**Hotel National** ( ☎ 540 305; 4th f l, B-dul Ştefan cel Mare 4) Has a medical-care room.

**Municipal Clinical Emergency Hospital** ( ☎ 248 435; www.ournet.md/~scmu; Str Toma Ciorba 1; ✆ 24hr) Provides a variety of emergency services, and a good likelihood of finding English-speaking staff.

## Money

There are ATMs all over the city centre, in all the hotels and in shopping centres. Currency exchanges are concentrated around the bus and train stations, and also along B-dul Ştefan cel Mare.

**Eximbank** ( ☎ 272 583; B-dul Ştefan cel Mare 6; ✆ 9am-5pm Mon-Fri) Can give you cash advances in foreign currency.

**Victoriabank** ( ☎ 233 065; Str 31 August 1989, 141; ✆ 9am-4pm Mon-Fri) Amex's representative in Moldova.

## Post

**Central post office** ( ☎ 227 737; B-dul Ştefan cel Mare 134; ✆ 8am-7pm Mon-Sat, to 6pm Sun) There is also a post office on Aleea Gării (open to 8pm).

## Telephone

**Central telephone office** (B-dul Ştefan cel Mare 65; ✆ 24hr) Book international calls inside the hall marked 'Convorbiri Telefonice Internaţionale'. Faxes and telegrams can also be sent from here. Receive faxes at ☎ 549 155.

## Travel Agencies

There's no tourist information centre in Moldova, but there are plenty of agencies where you can get information. Most offer discounted rates in some hotels.

**Moldovar Tur** ( ☎ 270 488; moldovatur@travels.md; B-dul Ştefan cel Mare 4; ✆ 9am-5pm Mon-Fri) The official state tourist agency can arrange Cricova and other vineyard tours. It can also find you chauffeured cars.

**Soleil Tours** ( ☎ 271 314; B-dul Negruzzi 5; ✆ 8am-6pm Mon-Sat, 9am-5pm Sun) A very efficient organisation, it can book accommodation and transport tickets, but is known for its multiday excursions into remote Moldova, taking in monasteries, places of interests and incorporating rural homestays.

Sometimes travel agencies take a while to reply to emails (if ever). A better bet for pre-trip contact would be **Marina Vozian** ( ☎ 488 258, 0691-557 53; www.marisha.net), an independent guide and authority on all things Moldovan, or **Radu Sargu** ( ☎ in Moldova 0691-389 53, in US 432-224 7377; www.moldova-travel.com), who arranges apartment rentals and provides local information and assistance.

## DANGERS & ANNOYANCES

Bucharest-style restaurant pricing scams are emerging, particularly in tourist-friendly basement joints. Never order anything, particularly wine, without confirming the price *in writing* (eg menu) to avoid surprises on the bill. If you've been victimised, keep all receipts and report it to the police.

Travellers are required to have their passports with them *at all times*. Cheeky police are prone to random checks.

## SIGHTS

No one can accuse Chişinău of being overburdened with tourist sights. Lacking in 'must-sees', it's more a pleasant city to wander about in and discover as you go. As it was heavily bombed during WWII, little remains of its historic heart. Still, there are some great museums and parks, and it's fun to see how communist iconography merges with symbols of Moldovan nationalism.

A good place to begin is smack in the city centre, where Chişinău's best-known parks diagonally oppose each other, forming two diamonds at the city's core. The highlights here are the Holy Gates (1841), more commonly known as Chişinău's own **Arc de Triomphe**. To its east sprawls **Parcul Catedralei** (Cathedral Park), dominated by the city's main **Orthodox Cathedral**, with its lovely bell tower (1836). On the northwestern side of the park is a colourful 24-hour **flower market**.

**Government House**, where cabinet meets, is the gargantuan building opposite the Holy Gates. The parliament convenes in **Parliament House** (B-dul Ştefan cel Mare 123) further north. Opposite this is the **Presidential Palace**.

**Grădina Publică Ştefan cel Mare şi Sfînt** (Ştefan cel Mare Park) is the city's main strolling, cruising area. The park entrance is guarded by a **statue** (1928) of Ştefan himself; this medieval prince of Moldavia is the greatest symbol of Moldova's strong, brave past.

**MOLDOVA**

# CENTRAL CHIŞINĂU

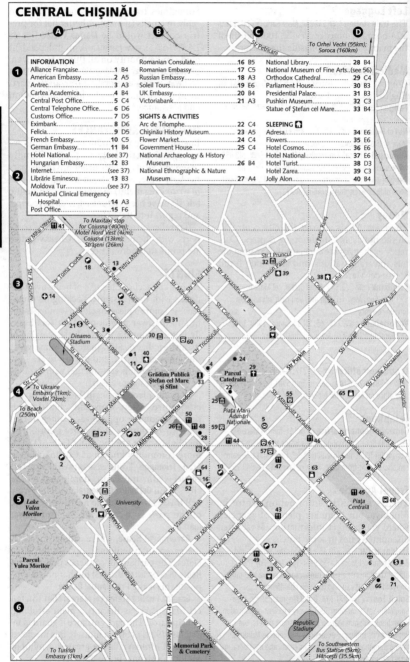

**INFORMATION**
Alliance Française.......................1 B4
American Embassy.....................2 A5
Antrec.........................................3 A3
Cartea Academica.....................4 B4
Central Post Office....................5 C4
Central Telephone Office.........6 D6
Customs Office..........................7 D5
Eximbank...................................8 D6
Felicia.........................................9 D5
French Embassy.......................10 C5
German Embassy.....................11 B4
Hotel National...................(see 37)
Hungarian Embassy................12 B3
Internet...............................(see 37)
Librărie Eminescu....................13 B3
Moldova Tur......................(see 37)
Municipal Clinical Emergency
    Hospital................................14 A3
Post Office...............................15 F6

Romanian Consulate...............16 B5
Romanian Embassy..................17 C5
Russian Embassy......................18 A3
Soleil Tours..............................19 E6
UK Embassy..............................20 B4
Victoriabank............................21 A3

**SIGHTS & ACTIVITIES**
Arc de Triomphe......................22 C4
Chişinău History Museum........23 A5
Flower Market..........................24 C4
Government House...................25 C4
National Archaeology & History
    Museum................................26 B4
National Ethnographic & Nature
    Museum................................27 A4

National Library.......................28 B4
National Museum of Fine Arts..(see 56)
Orthodox Cathedral................29 C4
Parliament House.....................30 B3
Presidential Palace...................31 B3
Pushkin Museum......................32 C3
Statue of Ştefan cel Mare........33 B4

**SLEEPING**
Adresa.......................................34 E6
Flowers......................................35 E6
Hotel Cosmos...........................36 E6
Hotel National..........................37 E6
Hotel Turist...............................38 D3
Hotel Zarea..............................39 C3
Jolly Alon..................................40 B4

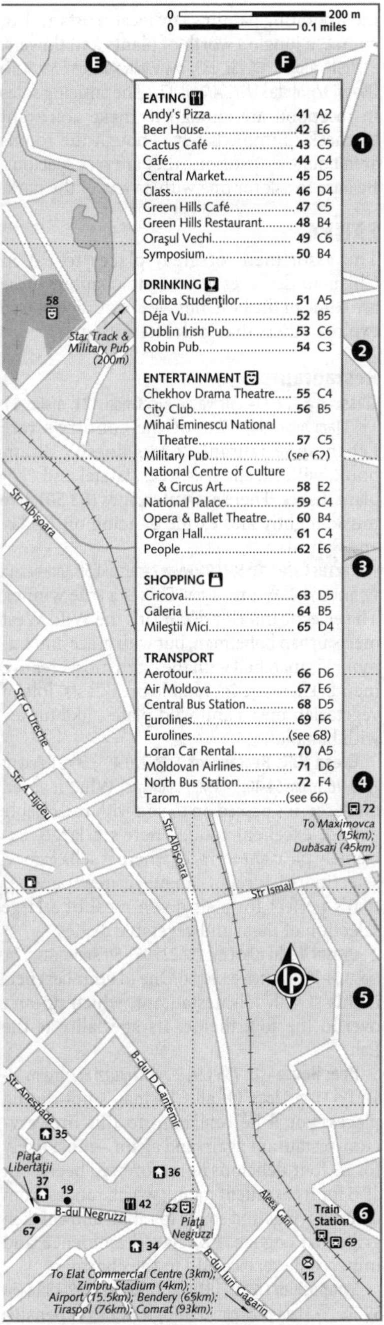


### Museums

The very worthwhile **National Archaeology & History Museum** (☎ 242 194; muzeum@mac.md; Str 31 August 1989, 121A; admission/photo $1.15/0.75; 9am-6pm Tue-Sat) is the granddaddy of Chişinău's museums. There are archaeological artefacts from Orheiul Vechi, including Golden Horde coins, Soviet-era weaponry and a huge WWII diorama on the 1st floor, where you can speak to a man who spent 12 years as a political prisoner at a worker's camp in desolate Vorkuta. A **statue** of Lupoaica Romei (the wolf of Rome) and the abandoned children Romulus and Remus stands in front of the museum. To Moldovans, this is a symbol of their Latin ancestry.

Opposite the **National Library** is the **National Museum of Fine Arts** (Muzeul de Arte Plastice; ☎ 241 730; Str 31 August 1989, 115; admission $0.75; 10am-6pm Tue-Sun), which has an interesting collection of contemporary European (mostly Romanian and Moldovan) art, folk art, icons and medieval knick-knacks.

The highlight of the **National Ethnographic & Nature Museum** (☎ 244 002; Str M Kogălniceanu 82; adult/child $1/0.50; 10am-6pm Tue-Sun) is a life-size reconstruction of a mammal skeleton, which was discovered in the Rezine region in 1966. The museum has some pop art, lots of stuffed animals, and exhibits covering the sciences of geology, botany and zoology. An English-language tour costs $5.

The **Chişinău History Museum** (☎ 241 584; Str Mateevici 60A; admission $0.40; 10am-6pm Tue-Sun) surveys the city's history from its founding onwards, with archaeological exhibits and photographs; it's a treat mainly to visit the old water tower (1892) it's housed in. The museum was mysteriously closed at the time of writing.

Several blocks northeast of the central parks is the **Pushkin Museum** (☎ 292 685; Str Anton Pann 19; admission $1.15; 10am-4pm Tue-Sun), housed in a cottage where Russian poet Alexander Pushkin (1799–1837) spent an exiled three years between 1820 and 1823. It was here that he wrote *The Prisoner of the Caucasus* and other classics. An English-language tour costs $7.

## SLEEPING

### Budget

Check out **Marisha** (www.marisha.net) for cheap homestays in Chişinău

**Hotel Turist** (☎ 220 637; B-dul Renaşterii 13; s $26-50, d $25) For a kitsch blast of the Soviet past, try this friendly place: it overlooks a giant Soviet memorial to communist youth and sports a

MOLDOVA

**AUTHOR'S CHOICE**

**Adresa** ( ☎ 544 392; www.adresa.md; B-dul Negruzzi 1; apt from $20; ☒ 24hr) For short- or long-term stays, this reliable agency offers great alternatives to hotels, renting out one- to three-room apartments throughout the city. Although often in large concrete buildings, they are completely private, comfortable and have kitchens. It's also a great way to live as the locals do, using rusty lifts (elevators) or climbing staircases somewhat less than sparkling. Still, they're all safe and clean. Check out the photo album of its options before you agree on one; most aren't right in the city centre but are a short taxi ride away.

snazzy socialist mural on its façade. The low-end singles are in tatty condition.

**Hotel Zarea** ( ☎ 227 625; Str Anton Pann 4; d 'deluxe' $30, s/d with shared bathroom $10/20) This drab high-rise has dour, smoky rooms that are appropriately priced. There's a bar and billiard club. Breakfast isn't included.

## Midrange

**Motel Nord Vest** ( ☎ 759 828; Calea Eşilor 30; s/d $38/51) This pleasant 100-bed motel is 4km northwest of the city centre on the main Chişinău–Cojuşna highway. The motel has a tennis court, sauna, restaurant and bar. Maxitaxis 135 and 136, as well as all buses to Cojuşna, stop right at the front.

**Hotel National** ( ☎ 540 305; www.moldovatur.travels.md; B-dul Ştefan cel Mare 4; s/d $47/60; ☒ ☐ ) This 17-floor giant, with 319 ho-hum, mildly overpriced rooms, is run by Moldova Tur. It has good services, like a small post office, a medical-care room, shops, bar, restaurant and internet café.

**Hotel Cosmos** ( ☎ 542 757; cosmos@moldova.net; Piaţa Negruzzi 2; s/d from $63/74; ☒ ) There's no good reason to stay in this concrete tower with dull, plasticised, overpriced rooms, save for access to the shopping centre downstairs, its full-service desk and central location.

## Top End

**Flowers** ( ☎ 277 262; hotelflowers@hotbox.ru; Str Anestiade 7; s/d/ste $120/140/160; ☒ ☒ ☐ ) If your credit limit's in good standing, this is the place for a splurge. Enormous rooms with high ceilings are exquisitely decorated with tasteful restraint,

incorporating paintings by local artists and, of course, a jungle's worth of plants and flowers.

**Jolly Alon** ( ☎ 232 233; www.jollyalon.com; Str Maria Cibotari 37; s/d/ste $172/204/249; ☐ ) The enticing sofas in reception are enough to make you want to check-in immediately. Though the rooms aren't quite as luxurious, they are very spacious. Be sure to ask for one with a view of the park.

# EATING

The assortment of great places to eat in Chişinău deserves a separate chapter; these are some of the best, but we encourage you to explore others that look interesting.

## Restaurants

**Class** ( ☎ 227 774; Str Vasile Alecsandri 121; mains $4; ☒ 11am-midnight) One of the country's rare Lebanese restaurants, Class doesn't disappoint, with excellent entrées, falafel and eggplant dishes. There are waterpipes ($2.50), live music nightly and exotic dancing on Friday and Saturday.

**Cactus Café** ( ☎ 504 094; www.cactus.md; Str Armenească 41; mains $4-8; ☒ 9am-10pm) This is a true winner. The eclectic interior décor (it's the Wild West meets urban bohemian, but with grace and humour) is matched with the city's most creative menu. There are incredible breakfasts, lots of vegetarian meals and wild plates, like turkey with bananas.

**Green Hills Restaurant** ( ☎ 220 451; Str 31 August 1989, 76; mains $4-10; ☒ 9am-midnight) What it saved on décor, it's passed on to you with reasonably priced, excellent food. There's a large, extremely pleasant terrace (where it sells a good selection of foreign-language newspapers!) that's perfect for a sit-down meal of a large selection of meat and vegetable dishes.

**Oraşul Vechi** (Old City; ☎ 225 063; Str Armenească 24; mains $4-10; ☒ noon-midnight) One of your best bets is this stylish folk restaurant, which doesn't overdo the folk theme. Its speciality is the fish.

**Beer House** ( ☎ 756 127; B-dul Negruzzi 6/2; mains $4-14; ☒ 11am-11pm) Of all Chişinău's hot dining places, you'll be returning to this brewery-cum-restaurant again and again – most likely for its four delicious home-brewed beers, but also for its excellent menu, which ranges from chicken wings and soups to rabbit and chicken grilled in cognac. Its relaxed ambience and impeccable service add to the charm.

**Symposium** ( ☎ 211 318; Str 31 August 1989, 78; mains $5-10; ☒ 11am-midnight) Though not as expensive as some top-class restaurants in Chişinău, this is regarded as one of the city's top dining experiences in terms of elegance and refinery. The French-style cuisine is succulent, with lamb dishes its speciality.

## Cafés

When the sun shines, outdoor cafés sprout like mushrooms. There is a popular terrace outside the Opera & Ballet Theatre (p512). There are also some good outside cafés opposite the main entrance to the university on Str A Mateevici and in the courtyard leading to Parcul Valea Morilor.

**Café** (Str Puşkin 22; mains $1-2; ⏰ 11am-11pm) This no-name cafeteria serves surprisingly succulent food priced for the university crowd.

**Green Hills Café** ( ☎ 220 451; B-dul Ştefan cel Mare 77; mains $4-10; ⏰ 8.30am-10pm Mon-Sat, 10am-10pm Sun) Though the meals are delicious here, most come for a quick fix – great coffee, cocktails or beer, and, of course, to people-watch while sitting on the city's main drag. This is run by the same bunch that operates the Green Hills Restaurant (opposite), featuring the same menu.

## Quick Eats

For the cheapest of cheap eats, there are some kiosks and small 'cafés' around the bus station and central market, where a dish of mystery meat or meat-filled pastries cost less than $1. Most go there for beer and vodka shots.

**Andy's Pizza** ( ☎ 210 210; B-dul Ştefan cel Mare 169; mains $2-4; ⏰ 7.30am-11pm) This popular chain has locations all around Chişinău, but this branch is a slick, almost techno-looking pizzeria, and is packed constantly. The thick and gooey pizzas, spaghetti and chicken wings keep clients happily purring.

## Self-Catering

**Central market** (Piaţa Centrală; ⏰ 7am-5pm) Since 1825 this market has been the place where Moldovans haggle over prices for fresh produce. It's well worth a visit for its choice of fresh food and lively ambience. It sprawls out around the central bus station on Str Tighina and Str Armeneasca.

## DRINKING

**Coliba Studenţilor** (Str A Mateevici; ⏰ 8am-11pm) This student hangout is opposite the university, just above the park. The terrace is a good place to bump into eager English speakers.

**Déja Vu** ( ☎ 227 693; Str Bucureşti 67; ⏰ 11am-2am) This is a true cocktail bar, where the drinks menu is tantalising and bartenders twirl glasses with aplomb. There's also a small dining hall serving meals, but most come here to lounge about being fabulous with multicoloured cocktails perched in their hands.

**Robin Pub** (Str Alexandru cel Bun 83; mains $5-11; ⏰ 11am-1am) A friendly local-pub feel reigns supreme in this relaxed, tastefully decorated hang-out with an extravagant menu. An ideal place to forget about the world for hours in a down-to-earth, unpretentious atmosphere.

**Dublin Irish Pub** ( ☎ 245 855; Str Bulgară 27; mains $2.50-12; ⏰ noon-11pm) The atmosphere is always lively at this relatively expensive but popular Celtic-cum-Moldovan Irish pub. While the bar is the highlight, the pricey restaurant is a temptation as well. A pint of the good stuff runs to about $5.50.

---

**MAKE NEW FRIENDS**

What with their friendly, outgoing disposition, you shouldn't have any trouble winning acquaintances in Moldova. However, if you want to be instantly embraced, and possibly kissed, steer the conversation towards music, then casually drop these names: 'Zdob şi Zdub' and 'Gândul Mâţei'.

Zdob şi Zdub (zdob-shee-zdoob; www.zdob-si-zdub.com) have been together since 1995, working Moldovan audiences into a lather with their Romanian-folk-meets-the-Red-Hot-Chili-Peppers sound fusion. In 2005 the group achieved a stunning sixth place finish in the Eurovision Song Contest. They are now touring so ferociously that poor Moldova hardly hears from them. Your best chance is to catch a show in Romania.

Gândul Mâţei (gun-dool muts-ehee; www.gm.md) nimbly run the gamut from lounge music to Coldplay-esque ballads to rocking *hard*. They're starting to break out of the Moldovan market, but still gig regularly in Chişinău.

Both bands have a very strong following in Moldova, and locals between the ages of 15 and 35 are guaranteed to become unwound with breathless reverence at the mere mention of their names. Moreover, their shows are nothing short of fabulous and are a highly recommended experience.

MOLDOVA

# ENTERTAINMENT

Posters listing 'what's on' are displayed on boards outside the city's various theatres.

## Nightclubs

Chişinău rocks in all directions throughout the night, but in some of the larger clubs be prepared to walk through metal detectors and deal with tough-guy posturing from goonish doormen.

**City Club** (Str 31 August 1989, 121; ☺ 10pm-6am) In the alley next to the Licurici Puppet Theatre, this 2nd-floor club is vying for the title of 'Hippest Place in Town'. You be the judge.

**People** ( ☎ 275 800; B-dul Negruzzi 2/4; ☺ 10pm-4am Thu-Sat) The best disco in town has lots of theme nights and special DJs. The doormen might try to lead male customers into their next-door strip club.

**Star Track** ( ☎ 496 207; Str Kiev 7; ☺ 10pm-4am Tue-Sun) The centrepiece of the Rîşcani district nightlife, the dark interior sports comfortable sofas and intimate booths where love-struck couples can smooch while keeping one eye open to catch the lacy dance performances in which scantily clad men and women prance around to techno tunes. Under Star Track is the less titillating but equally popular Military Pub.

## Theatre, Opera & Ballet

**Opera & Ballet Theatre** ( ☎ 244 163; B-dul Ştefan cel Mare 152; ☺ box office 10am-2pm & 5-7pm) This venue is home to the esteemed national opera and ballet company.

**Mihai Eminescu National Theatre** ( ☎ 221 177; B-dul Ştefan cel Mare 79; ☺ box office 11am-6.30pm) Contemporary Romanian productions can be seen at this theatre, founded in 1933.

**Chekhov Drama Theatre** (Teatrul Dramatic A Cehov; ☎ 223 362; Str Pârcălab 75) Plays in Russian are performed at the Chekhov Drama Theatre, situated where Chişinău's choral synagogue was located until WWII.

**National Palace** (Palatul Naţional; ☎ 213 544; Str Puşkin 21; ☺ box office 11am-5pm) Various cabarets, musicals and local theatre group productions are performed here.

## Circus

**National Centre of Culture and Circus Art** ( ☎ 496 803; B-dul Renaşterii 33; ☺ box office 9am-6pm) Itching for the man on the flying trapeze? Head to this loftily titled circus across the river. Performances are held at 6.30pm Friday, and noon,

3pm and 6.30pm Saturday and Sunday. Bus 27 from B-dul Ştefan cel Mare travels here. Renovations were under way at the time of writing and were expected to be completed by December 2007.

## Sport

Moldovans are big football fans and Chişinau has three stadiums to prove it. The new **Zimbru Stadium** is the city's first European regulation football stadium, located in Botanica. The **Republic Stadium** (Stadionul Republican), south of the city centre, has floodlighting. **Dinamo Stadium** (Stadionul Dinamo) is north of the city centre on Str Bucureşti. Moldovans like football so much, in fact, there's an American football team called the Chişinău Barbarians, who hold occasional matches, in full gear.

## Live Music

**Organ Hall** (Sala cu Orgă; ☎ 225 404; B-dul Ştefan cel Mare 79) Classical concerts and organ recitals are held at this hall, next to the Mihai Eminescu National Theatre. Performances start at 6pm; tickets are sold at the door.

**Philharmonic Concert Hall** ( ☎ 224 505; Str Mitropolit Varlaam 78) Moldova's National Philharmonic is based here.

# SHOPPING

**Cricova** ( ☎ 222 775; B-dul Ştefan cel Mare 126; ☺ 10am-7pm Mon-Fri, to 6pm Sat, to 4pm Sun) The commercial outlet of the Cricova wine factory. It stocks many types of affordable wines and champagnes (only $2 to $5 each), plus the crystal glasses to drink them in.

**Mileştii Mici** ( ☎ 211 229; www.milestii-mici.md; Str Vasile Alecsandri 137; ☺ 9am-4pm Mon-Sat) This is the outlet store for the Mileştii Mici wine cellars. They also have outlets on the 1st floor of the Elat Commercial Centre (4km southeast of the city centre) and the airport.

**Galeria L** ( ☎ 221 975; Str Bucureşti 64; ☺ 10am-7pm Mon-Fri, to 5pm Sat) Holds temporary art exhibitions, and sells small works of art and souvenirs crafted by local artists.

# GETTING THERE & AWAY
## Air

Moldova's only airport of significance is in Chişinău, **Chişinău international airport** (KIV; ☎ 526 060), 14.5km southeast of the city centre. Obviously, it has only international flights. For more information on airlines servicing Chişinău, see p523.

## Bus

Chişinău now has three bus stations. The **North Bus Station** (Autogară Nord; ☎ 439 489) is where nearly all domestic and international lines depart, except Transdniestr-bound lines (which depart from the Central Bus Station). Services include 12 daily buses to Străşeni, and regular buses to Bălţi, Recea, Ediniţa and Briceni. There are buses half-hourly between 9.15am and 10pm to Orhei.

There are daily buses to Bucharest ($14, 12 hours), Odesa ($7, four to five hours), Moscow ($35, 30 hours), St Petersburg ($33, 33 to 36 hours), Kiev ($14, 11 hours) and Minsk ($24, 26 hours). You can buy advance tickets here or from a tiny office at the train station. The information booth charges 1 leu ($0.07) per question.

Domestic and international maxitaxis operate from the **Central Bus Station** (Autogară Centrală; ☎ 542 185; Str Mitropolit Varlaam), behind the central market. Maxitaxis go to Tiraspol and Bendery ($2, 1½ hours, every 20 to 35 minutes) from 6.30am to 6.30pm, with reduced services until 10pm.

Bus services to/from Comrat, Hânceşti and other southern destinations use the less crowded **Southwestern Bus Station** (Autogară Sud-vest; ☎ 723 983; cnr Şoseaua Hânceşti & Str Spicului), located approximately 2km from the city centre. Daily local services include five buses to Comrat ($2.95) in Gagauzia and six to Hânceşti. A fleet of private maxitaxis to Iaşi, Romania ($10, four hours) also departs from here.

**Eurolines** ( ☎ 549 813, 271 476; www.eurolines.md), with an office at the train station, has regular routes to Italy, Spain and Germany (usually around $140 return).

## Train

International routes departing from Chişinau's sparkling new **train station** ( ☎ 252 737; Aleea Gării) include three daily trains to Moscow ($46, 28 to 33 hours), three daily trains to Kiev ($20, 12 hours), one each to St Petersburg ($45, 40 hours), Bucharest ($29.50, 14 hours), and Lviv ($15.50, eight hours), and two weekly services to Minsk ($35, 25 hours). To get to Budapest, you must change in Bucharest.

Due to the train service interruption through Transdniestr, there were no trains to Bendery, Tiraspol or Odesa at the time of writing.

There are five daily trains to Comrat ($4, three hours) and four to Ungheni ($4, three hours).

## GETTING AROUND
### To/From the Airport

Bus 65 departs half-hourly between 5am and 10pm from the Central Bus Station to the airport ($0.15).

Maxitaxi 65 departs every 20 minutes from Str Ismail, near the corner of B-dul Ştefan cel Mare, for the airport and return ($0.25).

### Bus & Trolleybus

Bus 45 and maxitaxi 45a run from the Central Bus Station to the Southwestern Bus Station. Bus 1 goes from the train station to B-dul Ştefan cel Mare.

Trolleybuses 1, 4, 5, 8, 18 and 22 go to the train station from the city centre. Buses 2, 10 and 16 go to the Southwestern Bus Station. Maxitaxis 176 and 191 go to the North Bus Station from the city centre. Tickets costing $0.15 for buses and $0.10 for trolleybuses are sold at kiosks or direct from the driver.

Most bus routes in town and to many outlying villages are served by nippy maxitaxis ($0.25 per trip, pay the driver). Route numbers, displayed on the front and side windows, are followed by the letter 'a' or 't'. Those with the letter 'a' follow the same route as the bus of the same number. Those with a letter 't' follow the trolleybus routes. Maxitaxis run regularly between 6am and midnight.

### Car & Motorcycle

Hire cars are available from **Loran Car Rental** ( ☎ 243 710; www.turism.md/loran; Str A Mateevici 79) from €34 per day (Dacia Logan), including insurance. All payments must be made in cash (euros) and a deposit is required.

### Taxi

Taxi-stand drivers often try to rip you off. A **taxi** ( ☎ 746 565/705/706/707) is cheaper; the official per-kilometre rate is $0.25.

## AROUND CHIŞINĂU
### Cricova

The grand duke of Moldovan wineries is **Cricova** ( ☎ 22-277 378; www.cricova.md; Str Ungureanu 1; ⏰ 8am-4pm) – and it knows it.

Its underground wine kingdom, 15km north of Chişinău in the village of Cricova, is one of Europe's biggest. It boasts 120km of

MOLDOVA

labyrinthine roadways, 60 of which are used for wine storage. These avenues are lined wall-to-wall with bottles. Up to 100m underground, the 'cellars' are kept at a temperature of between 12°C and 14°C, with humidity at 96% to 98%, to best protect the 1.25 million bottles of rare and collectable wine, plus the 30 million litres of wine the factory produces annually (during Soviet times, the output was two to three times this amount!). Tunnels have existed here since the 15th century, when limestone was dug out to help build Chişinău. They were converted into an underground wine emporium in the 1950s.

You must have private transport and advance reservations to get into Cricova. It's most easily done through travel agencies in Chişinău but you can call yourself and book a time. Your two-hour tour ($62 per person) includes trips down streets with names like Str Cabernet, Str Pinot etc, wine tasting, a light meal and a few 'complimentary' bottles. Though the tour is admittedly worthwhile, Cricova's starch formality and astonishing aversion to customer contact puts off many visitors.

Once you've finished at Cricova, head to the much-awarded **Acorex vineyard** (www.acorex .net; ☺ 9am-6pm), just down the hill. There's no tour, but its shop sells limited lines not available in most stores or outside Moldova.

## Cojuşna

Cricova's spunky, down-to-earth competitors operate 12km northwest of Chişinău in the village of Cojuşna. This is a moribund place in comparison with Cricova, but the tours are first rate and very friendly.

**Cojuşna** ( ☎ 22-744 820, 715 329; Str Lomtadze 4; ☺ 8am-6pm Mon-Fri), founded in 1908, is geared for tourists and is therefore very flexible – staff will open the wine cellars and wine-tasting rooms for you at any hour of any day. The cellars comprise six 'alleys', each 100m long. The wine tasting comes with a full meal, served in an impressive and seductively cosy hall decorated with wooden furniture carved by a young local and his father.

It is easy to organise your own tour of Cojuşna – you needn't pay exorbitant fees at Chişinău travel agencies – although Cojuşna will need advance warning if you require a tour in English (two- to three-hour tour per person $17). You can buy wines ($2 to $12 per bottle) from the Cojuşna shop in the complex.

Bus 2 runs every 15 minutes from Str Vasile Alecsandri in Chişinău towards Cricova. Catch one of the frequent maxitaxis leaving from Calea Eşilor (take trolleybus 1, 5 or 11 up Ştefan cel Mare to the Ion Creangă university stop), get off at the Cojuşna stop. Ignore the turning on the left marked 'Cojuşna' and walk or hitch the remaining 2km along the main road to the vineyard entrance, marked by a tall, totem pole–style pillar.

## Orheiul Vechi

Ten kilometres southeast of Orhei lies Orheiul Vechi ('Old Orhei', marked on maps as the village of Trebujeni), arguably Moldova's most fantastic sight. It's certainly among its most haunting places.

The **Orheiul Vechi Monastery Complex** (Complexul Muzeistic Orheiul Vechi; ☎ 235-34 242; admission $1.15; ☺ 9am-5pm Tue-Sun), carved into a massive limestone cliff in this wild, rocky, remote spot, draws visitors from around the globe.

The **Cave Monastery** (Mănăstire în Peştera), inside a cliff overlooking the gently meandering Răut River, was dug by Orthodox monks in the 13th century. It remained inhabited until the 18th century, and in 1996 a handful of monks returned to this secluded place of worship and are slowly restoring it. You can enter the cave via an entrance on the cliff's plateau.

Ştefan cel Mare built a fortress here in the 14th century, but it was later destroyed by Tartars. In the 18th century the cave-church was taken over by villagers from neighbouring Butuceni. In 1905 they built a church above ground dedicated to the Ascension of St Mary. The church was shut down by the Soviets in 1944 and remained abandoned throughout the communist regime. Services resumed in 1996, though it still looks abandoned. Archaeologists have uncovered remnants of a defence wall surrounding the monastery complex from the 15th century.

On the main road to the complex you'll find the headquarters where you purchase your entrance tickets, and where you can also arrange guides and get general information. It's forbidden to wear shorts and women must cover their heads while inside the monastery.

### SLEEPING

**Orheiul Vechi Monastery Headquarters** ( ☎ 235-56 912; d $23) has five pleasant rooms and a small restaurant. The rooms facing the monastery have spine-tingling views. Spending the night here is highly recommended.

### GETTING THERE & AWAY
From Chişinău daily buses depart every half-hour for Orhei ($1.50). Unfortunately, there's only a single daily bus from Orhei to Trebujeni at 6am (ask to be dropped off by the signposted entrance to the complex). Better yet, alight from the Orhei-bound bus at the Ivancea turn-off and hire to a taxi to Orheiul Vechi, striking a deal for return service, including a two-hour wait, for around $12, or one-way for about $6. There is a daily afternoon bus (3pm) to Orhei from Orheiul Vechi.

## Soroca
pop 38,492

Soroca is the Roma 'capital' of Moldova, but people come here to see the outstanding **Soroca fortress** ( ☎ 230-24 873; http://soroca-fortress.nflame.net; admission free; ☺ 9am-6pm Wed-Sun May-Oct, low season by appointment). Part of a medieval chain of military fortresses built by Moldavian princes between the 14th and 16th centuries to defend Moldavia's boundaries, the fortress was founded by Ştefan cel Mare and rebuilt by his son, Petru Rareş, in 1543–45.

The fortress is administered by the **Soroca Museum of History and Ethnography** ( ☎ 230-22 264; Str Independentei 68; admission $0.10; ☺ 10am-6pm Tue-Sun, low season by appointment). This well-designed museum is a real treat; its 25,000 exhibits cover archaeological finds, weapons and ethnographic displays.

The simple, but clean and bright rooms at the **Nistru Hotel** ( ☎ 230-23 783; Str Mihiel Malmut 20; d $19.50) are your best bet in Soroca. The hotel

---

**WORTH A TRIP**

**Satul Moldovenesc** ( ☎ 248-36 136; http://moldovacc.md/satmoldovenesc; Hârtopul Mare; 1-room house $15-45, 2-room house $52) Only 30km northeast of Chişinau (head towards Dubăsari then north to Hârtopul Mare and follow the signs), this full-service complex in the middle of nature offers a very active programme of rest and relaxation! You can rent an island for $12 and enjoy a picnic there, have a sauna, go horse riding (children can be 'accompanied on their ride of the donkey'), and go swimming or fishing in one of the three lakes nearby.

---

is hidden down an improbable side street one block east of the red-roofed Soroca city council building, which faces the park.

There are 12 daily buses to Soroca from Chişinău's North Bus Station.

# TRANSDNIESTR

pop 555,500

The self-declared republic of Transdniestr (Pridnestrovskaya Moldavskaya Respublika, or PMR in Russian) is one of the world's last surviving bastions of communism. At least that's what most people say.

Transdniestr incorporates a narrow strip of land covering only 3567 sq km on the eastern bank of the Nistru River. It was the scene of a bloody civil war in the early 1990s when the area declared independence from Moldova. Travellers will be stunned by a region that is very much an independent state in all but name. It has its own currency, police force, army and borders, which are controlled by Transdniestran border guards. Western travellers are grudgingly allowed to travel in the region. Russian is the predominant language. Transdniestrans boycott the Moldovan independence day and celebrate their own independence day on 2 September.

See **Images of Transdniestr** (http://geo.ya.com/travel images/transdniestr.html) for some excellent photos of the region, and www.president-pmr.org for the 'official' account of Transdniestr.

## History
Igor Smirnov was elected president of Transdniestr in 1991 following the region's declaration of independence four months prior. Transdniestr insists it's an independent country and a sovereign state within Moldova. Most of the time it pushes for the creation of a Moldovan federation, with proportionate representation between Moldova, Transdniestr and Gagauzia.

Neither Smirnov's presidency nor the Transdniestran parliament is recognised by the Moldovan – or any other – government. The Russian 14th army, headquartered in Tiraspol since 1956, covertly supplied Transdniestran rebels with weapons during the civil war. The continued presence of the 5000-strong Russian 'operational group' in Transdniestr today is seen by local Russian speakers as a guarantee of their security.

MOLDOVA

MOLDOVA

---

**TREAD LIGHTLY IN TRANSDNIESTR**

At the time of writing rising political and economic turmoil was making a day trip to Transdniestr more hair-raising than it's been in years. The happy-go-lucky days of benign Kafka-esque moments at the border and a time-travel stroll through Tiraspol have been replaced by social ostracism of foreigners and the creepy feeling of being watched at all times, as renewed paranoia deepens. There have been accounts of people being reported and then detained by police for simply speaking English or giving blankets to the poor in Tiraspol. Picture taking, no matter how innocent, is becoming decidedly uncool – I was barred entrance to a café I needed to review for this book after the owner spied me taking a quick photo down the street. Frosty merchants rush through transactions without a word.

The source of the trouble is a very complex political predicament, the latest chapter in a four-way theatre of one-upmanship between the Ukraine, Russia, Moldova and Transdniestr. Barring a sudden flash of diplomatic magic, the situation is expected to get far worse before it gets better. All train service in and out of Transdniestr had been suspended at the time of writing.

The upshot is that the border can still be amusingly memorable; bobbing and weaving around invented infractions and creative interpretations of the law. Shaky political climate notwithstanding, border guards still have a vested financial interest (bribes) in letting you through – budget around US$20 to $30 for this excitement, coming and going, depending on how dodgy you look or how big your camera bag is.

Entry permits are still (officially) $1 to $5 depending on your nationality, available *at the border* no matter what the guys on duty playfully tell you. If you stay under 24 hours, you needn't register with the authorities, and if you enter with a Moldovan national, you can be listed on their entry permit (as several names can be inscribed on one) for a few pennies.

If you're staying for over 24 hours, you'll need to register with the **OVIR** ( ☎ 533-79 083; ul Kotovskogo No 2A; ☺ 9am-5pm Mon-Fri). Enter through the rusting, prison-like gate and inquire at the hidden white building with the red roof. Outside of the OVIR business hours you must go to the **Tiraspol Militia Office** (formerly the Tiraspol Militia Passport Office; ☎ 533-34 169; Roza Luxemburg 66; ☺ 24hr) where registration is possible, but you'll probably be asked to check in at the OVIR office the following working day anyway. The registration fee is about $0.60. Some hotels won't even talk room availability with you until you've registered, no matter how long you're staying. Some top-end hotels will register you automatically.

As always, check the current political situation before heading into erratic territory.

---

The Ministry of State Security (MGB), a modern-day KGB, has sweeping powers, and has sponsored the creation of a youth wing, called the Young Guard, for 16- to 23-year-olds.

Alongside a number of agreements between Moldova and Transdniestr since 1991, there have been countless moves by both sides designed to antagonise or punish the other. In 2003 alone Smirnov, reacting to one of his demands being refused by Moldova, slapped exorbitant tariffs on all Moldovan imports, instantly halting trade over the 'border' and making life more difficult for ordinary people on both sides. In September 2003 Smirnov even severed phone connections between the two for a few weeks, so that calls could not be made between the regions.

While Smirnov is becoming increasingly mistrusted by his 'electorate', a large sub-

section of locals still refuse to criticise their government. Political and economic attitudes aside, popular opinion still strongly supports independence from Moldova.

See the boxed text (above) for current information on Transdniestr's political and economic climate. On 6 July 2006, a bomb blast on a local bus in Tiraspol killed eight people. Transdniestran politicians were quick to blame 'Moldovan provocateurs'. Popular opinion in Moldova is that a would-be arms dealer probably lost control of his merchandise.

## Language

The official state languages in Transdniestr are Russian, Moldovan and Ukrainian. Students in schools and universities are taught in Russian, and the local government and most official institutions operate almost solely in

Russian. All street signs are written in Russian, Moldovan and sometimes Ukrainian.

## Money

The only legal tender is the Transdniestran rouble (TR). Officially introduced in 1994, it quickly dissolved into an oblivion of zeros. To keep up with inflation, monetary reforms introduced in January 2001 slashed six zeros from the currency, with a new TR1 banknote worth one million roubles in old money. Some taxi drivers, shopkeepers and market traders will accept payment in US dollars – or even Moldovan lei or Ukrainian hryvnia, but generally you'll need to get your hands on some roubles (US$1 = TR8.30).

Spend all your roubles before you leave, as no one honours or exchanges this currency outside Transdniestr, though you can probably find takers at the bus station in Chişinău if you somehow get stuck with a large amount.

## Post

Transdniestran stamps featuring local hero General Suvorov can only be used for letters sent within the Transdniestran republic and are not recognised anywhere else. For letters to Moldova, Romania and the West, you have to use Moldovan stamps (available here, but less conveniently than in Moldova).

## Media

The predominantly Russian Transdniestran TV is broadcast in the republic between 6am and midnight. Transdniestran Radio is on air during the same hours. Bendery has a local TV channel that airs 24 hours.

The two local newspapers are in Russian. The *Transdniestra* is a purely nationalist affair advocating the virtues of an independent state; *N Pravda* is marginally more liberal.

## TIRASPOL

☎ 533 / pop 183,678

Tiraspol (from the Greek, meaning 'town on the Nistru'), 70km east of Chişinău, is the second-largest city in Moldova, sorry, make that the largest city and capital of Transdniestr! As Soviet-licious as they come and still a candidate for World's Largest Open-Air Museum; nevertheless MTV and Red Bull are making their presence felt. With

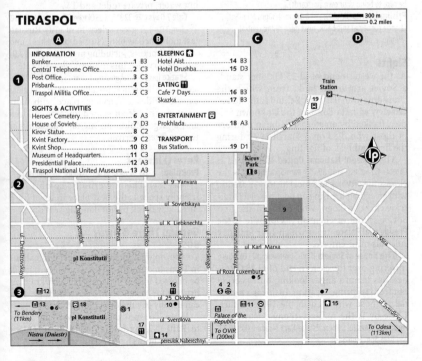

**TIRASPOL**

| | |
|---|---|
| **INFORMATION** | |
| Bunker...................................**1** B3 | |
| Central Telephone Office..........**2** C3 | |
| Post Office.............................**3** C3 | |
| Prisbank...............................**4** C3 | |
| Tiraspol Militia Office...............**5** C3 | |
| **SIGHTS & ACTIVITIES** | |
| Heroes' Cemetery....................**6** A3 | |
| House of Soviets......................**7** D3 | |
| Kirov Statue...........................**8** C2 | |
| Kvint Factory..........................**9** C2 | |
| Kvint Shop............................**10** B3 | |
| Museum of Headquarters..........**11** C3 | |
| Presidential Palace...................**12** A3 | |
| Tiraspol National United Museum....**13** A3 | |
| **SLEEPING** | |
| Hotel Aist............................**14** B3 | |
| Hotel Drushba.......................**15** D3 | |
| **EATING** | |
| Cafe 7 Days..........................**16** B3 | |
| Skazka.................................**17** B3 | |
| **ENTERTAINMENT** | |
| Prokhlada.............................**18** A3 | |
| **TRANSPORT** | |
| Bus Station............................**19** D1 | |

0 — 300 m
0 — 0.2 miles

Train Station

ul Lenina

Kirov Park

ul 9 Yanvara

ul Sovietskaya

ul K Liebknechta

ul Karl Marxa

ul Mira

pl Konstitutii

ul Roza Luxemburg

ul 25 Oktober

ul Sverdlova

Palace of the Republic

To OVIR (200m)

To Bendery (11km)

pl Konstitutii

Nistru (Dniestr)

pereulok Naberezhnyi

To Odesa (113km)

ul Sverdlova

**MOLDOVA**

questionable business dealings from the tiny elite rife, the have/have-not divide is glaring. The city was founded in 1792 following Russian domination of the region. Its inhabitants are predominantly Russian (41%), with ethnic Ukrainians comprising 32% and a much harassed ethnic Moldovan minority filling 17%.

## Orientation & Information

The train and bus stations are next to each other at the end of ul Lenina. Exit the train station and walk down ul Lenina, past Kirov Park, to ul 25 Oktober (the main street). Ul 25 Oktober, Tiraspol's backbone, is also its commercial strip, with most of the shops and restaurants.

**Bunker** (pereulok Naberezhnyi 1; per hr $0.40; ☺ 9am-11pm) A modern internet club.

**Central telephone office** (cnr ul 25 Oktober & ul Kommunisticheskaya; ☺ 7am-8.45pm) You can buy phonecards ($2.40 or $8) to use in the modern pay telephones.

**Post office** (ul Lenina 17; ☺ 7.30am-7pm Mon-Fri) Won't be of much use to you unless you want to send postcards to all your friends in Transdniestr (but if you do, be sure to bring your own postcards).

**Prisbank** (ul 25 Oktober; ☺ 8.30am-4.30pm Mon-Sat) Change money at this bank, next door to the central telephone office.

## Sights

At the western end of ul 25 Oktober stands a Soviet armoured tank, from which the Transdniestran flag flies. Behind is the **Heroes' Cemetery** with its Tomb of the Unknown Soldier, flanked by an eternal flame in memory of those who died on 3 March 1992 during the first outbreak of fighting.

The **Tiraspol National United Museum** (ul 25 Oktober 42; admission $0.30; ☎ 9am-5pm Sun-Fri) is the closest the city has to a local history museum, with an exhibit focusing on poet Nikolai Dimitriovich Zelinskogo, who founded the first Soviet school of chemistry. Opposite is the **Presidential Palace**, from which Igor Smirnov rules his mini-empire.

The **House of Soviets** (Dom Sovetovul; ul 25 Oktober), towering over the eastern end of ul 25 Oktober, has Lenin's angry-looking bust peering out from its prime location. Inside is a **memorial** to those who died in the 1992 conflict. Close by is the military-themed **Museum of Headquarters** (ul Kommunisticheskaya 34; admission $0.30; ☺ 9am-5pm Mon-Sat).

The **Kvint factory** (☎ 37 333; http://kvint.biz; ul Lenina 38) is one of Transdniestr's pride and joys – since 1897 it's been making some of Moldova's finest brandies. Buy some of its products either near the front entrance of the plant or at its **town centre store** (ul 25 Oktober 84; ☺ 24hr).

Further north along ul Lenina, towards the bus and train stations, is **Kirov park**, with a **statue** of the Leningrad boss who was assassinated in 1934, conveniently sparking mass repressions throughout the USSR.

## Sleeping & Eating

You must register at the **OVIR** (ul Kotovskogo No 2A; ☺ Mon-Fri) if staying more than 24 hours (see the boxed text, p516).

**Hotel Drushba** (☎ 34 266; ul 25 Oktober 116; r $20-40) There are several dozen categories of rooms on offer at this massive place that has hopefully seen better days. Some have hot water, TV, fridge, larger beds, private bathroom or shower.

**Hotel Aist** (☎ 37 174; pereulok Naberezhnyi 3; d $25-40) The grass in the cement cracks outside gives it a derelict feel, but this is a decent hotel. The more expensive rooms have luxuries, such as hot water, private toilet and TV.

**Cafe 7 Days** (☎ 32 311; ul 25 Oktober 77; mains $0.35-1.50; ☺ 9am-11pm) A great selection of tasty Russian fast food, such as blini (stuffed pancakes), and Western imports, including pizza, as well as salads, are served at this modern, pleasant café.

**Skazka** (pereulok Naberezhnyi 1; mains $2-3.50; ☺ 10am-8pm) The office building-calibre green and glass exterior hides a 'fairytale' place with half-hearted castle décor geared towards children and a large Moldovan menu. The summer terrace faces the river.

## Entertainment

**Prokhlada** (☎ 34 642; ul 25 Oktober 50; mains $2-4; ☺ 4pm-6am) This cavernous, sombre but friendly space is the best place in town for a meal, lazy drink or hot dancing session.

## Getting There & Away

### BUS

You can only pay for tickets to other destinations in Transdniestr with the local currency, but will be allowed to pay in Moldovan lei/Ukrainian hryvnia for tickets to Moldova/Ukraine. You can usually pay the driver directly.

From Tiraspol there are five daily buses to Bălţi ($7, six hours), 13 daily to Odesa ($5, three hours), once daily to Kyiv ($10, 14 hours) and once weekly to Berlin. Buses go to Chişinău nearly every half-hour from 5.50am to 8.50am, and maxitaxis run regularly from 6.30am to 6.10pm.

Trolleybus 19 ($0.10) and quicker maxitaxis 19 and 20 ($0.15) cross the bridge over the Dniestr to Bendery.

### TRAIN

All train service in and out of Transdniestr had been suspended at the time of writing. However, when in operation, tickets for same-day departures are sold in the main train station ticket hall. Advance tickets (24 hours or more before departure) are sold in the ticket office on the 2nd floor.

Most eastbound trains from Chişinău to Ukraine and Russia stop in Tiraspol. Seven daily trains go to Chişinău ($0.90), three daily to Odesa ($2), two daily to Moscow and Minsk, and once daily to St Petersburg.

## BENDERY

☎ 552 / pop 123,038

Bendery (sometimes called Bender, and previously known as Tighina), on the western banks of the Dniestr River, has made something of a miraculous recovery in recent years. Scars from the bloodshed in the early 1990s have noticeably healed. The city centre in particular is a breezy place, vastly more inviting than Tiraspol.

During the 16th century Moldavian prince Ştefan cel Mare built a large defensive fortress here on the ruins of a fortified Roman camp. In 1538 the Ottoman sultan, Suleiman the Magnificent, conquered the fortress and transformed it into a Turkish *raia* (colony), renaming the city Bendery, meaning 'belonging to the Turks'. During the 18th century Bendery was seized from the Turks by Russian troops who then massacred Turkish Muslims in the city. In 1812 Bendery fell permanently into Russian hands. Russian peacekeeping forces remain here to this day.

Bendery was hardest hit by the 1992 military conflict with Moldova, both in terms of destruction and loss of life. Though extensive repairs have been made, finding bullet-pocked buildings isn't uncommon.

### Information

**Central department store** (cnr ul Lenina & ul Kalinina; per hr $0.50) Has two internet clubs on the top floor.

**Currency exchange** (ul Sovetskaya) Change money here; located next to the Central Market.

**Pharmacy** (cnr ul Suvorova & ul S Liazo; ☺ 8am-8pm Mon-Sat, to 4pm Sun)

**Telephone office** (cnr ul S Liazo & ul Suvorova; ☺ 8am-6pm Mon-Fri, to 4pm Sat) International telephone calls can be booked from here.

### Sights

Bendery's main sight is, paradoxically, impossible to see. The great Turkish **Tighina fortress**, built in the 1530s to replace a 12th-century fortress built by the Genovese, is now being used by the Transdniestran military as a training ground and is strictly off-limits. The best view of it is from the bridge

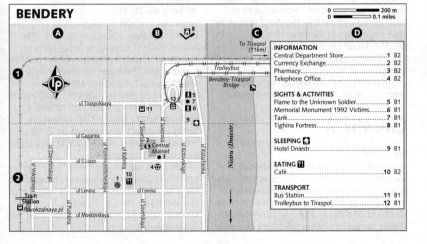

**BENDERY**

| | 0 | 200 m |
| 0 | | 0.1 miles |

**INFORMATION**
Central Department Store.....................1 B2
Currency Exchange...............................2 B2
Pharmacy.............................................3 B2
Telephone Office..................................4 B2

**SIGHTS & ACTIVITIES**
Flame to the Unknown Soldier...............5 B1
Memorial Monument 1992 Victims.........6 B1
Tank.....................................................7 B1
Tighina Fortress...................................8 B1

**SLEEPING**
Hotel Dniestr........................................9 B1

**EATING**
Café.....................................................10 B2

**TRANSPORT**
Bus Station...........................................11 B1
Trolleybus to Tiraspol...........................12 B1

To Tiraspol (11km)
Trolleybus
Bendery-Tiraspol Bridge
ul Tiraspolskaya
ul Gagarina
ul S Liazo
ul Dzerzhinskogo
ul Volozanaya
ul Lenina
Train Station
Privokzalnaya pl
ul Pushkina
ul Moskovskaya
ul Sovetskaya
Central Market
ul Suvorova
ul Kalinina
ul Kommunisticheskaya
ul Kotovskogo
ul Kalacheka
Nistru (Dniestr)

MOLDOVA

going towards Tiraspol. At the entrance to the city, close to the famous **Bendery–Tiraspol bridge**, is a **memorial park** dedicated to local 1992 war victims. An eternal flame burns in front of an armoured **tank**, from which flies the Transdniestran flag. Haunting **memorials** to those shot dead during the civil war are evident throughout many of the main streets in the city centre.

### Sleeping & Eating

A three-tier pricing system is intact here, with prices for locals; Moldovans, Ukrainians and Belarusians; and all other foreigners.

**Hotel Dniestr** ( ☎ 29 478; ul Katachenka 10; r $20) Pricier doubles have hot water, TV and fridge. There's an adjacent restaurant and terrace café.

**Café** (cnr ul Kalinina & ul Lenina; mains $1-2; ☺ 9am-11pm) Located in the park across from the department store, this small restaurant has a popular, pleasant terrace, where grilled-meat dishes are the favourite. It also doubles as a hang-out and bar.

### Getting There & Around

All train service in and out of Transdniestr had been suspended at the time of writing. However, when in operation, there are at least 15 daily trains to Chişinău, including ones coming from Moscow and Odesa. The train station is located at Privokzalnaya pl.

There are buses and maxitaxis every half-hour or so to Chişinău ($2, 1″ hours), and two daily to Comrat.

Trolleybus 19 for Tiraspol ($0.10) departs from the bus stop next to the main roundabout at the entrance to Bendery; maxitaxis also regularly make the 20-minute trip ($0.15). There are two daily buses to Odesa ($5, three hours) and one to Kiev ($10, 14 hours).

Local maxitaxis (70 kopeks) leave from the currency exchange near the central market.

# GAGAUZIA

**pop 171,500**

Subordinate to Moldova constitutionally and for foreign relations and defence, Gagauzia (Gagauz Yeri) is an autonomous region covering 1832 sq km of noncontiguous land in southern Moldova. The region eventually found its niche within Moldova through judicious mediation, but there's still simmering unrest between the two entities over language and economic issues.

Gagauzia is comprised of three towns and 27 villages dotted throughout three broken-up districts.

The Gagauz are a Turkic-speaking, Christian ethnic minority whose Muslim antecedents fled the Russo-Turkish wars in the 18th century. They were allowed to settle in the region in exchange for their conversion to Christianity. Their language is a Turkish dialect, with its vocabulary influenced by Russian Orthodoxy as opposed to the Islamic influences inherent in Turkish. Gagauz look to Turkey for cultural inspiration and heritage.

The republic has its own flag (blue, white and red stripes with three white stars in the upper left corner), its own police force, its own newspapers *(Sabaa Ildyzy, Gagauz Vesti* and *Guneshhik)*, and its own university. The official languages here are Gagauzi, Moldovan and Russian, though Russian is used almost everywhere, including the university. Gagauz autonomy was officially recognised by the Moldovan government on 23 December 1994; that day is now celebrated annually as Independence Day. Unlike the more militant separatists in Transdniestr, the Gagauz forfeited independence for large-scale autonomy. Theirs is a predominantly agricultural region with little industry to sustain an independent economy.

## COMRAT

☎ 298 / pop 25,197

Gagauzia's capital, 92km south of Chişinău, is no more than a dusty town with little of tourist interest outside of being an intriguing cultural and provincial oddity. In 1990 Comrat was the scene of clashes between Gagauz nationalists and Moldovan armed forces, pre-empted by calls from local leaders for the Moldovan government to hold a referendum on the issue of Gagauz sovereignty. Local protesters were joined by Transdniestran militia forces, who are always game for a bit of clashing.

Comrat is home to the world's only Gagauz university (taught in Russian). Most street signs are in Russian; some older ones are in Gagauzi but in the Cyrillic script. Since 1989, Gagauzi, alongside Moldovan, has used the Latin alphabet.

From the bus station, walk south along the main street, Str Pobedy, past the market to pl Pobedy (Victory Sq). St John's Church stands on the western side of the square, behind which lies the central park. Pr Lenina runs parallel to Str Pobedy, west of the park.

Change money at the **Moldovan Agrobank** (Str Pobedy 52; 8am-2pm Mon-Fri). A small currency exchange is inside the entrance to the market. You can make international calls at the **post office** (Str Pobedy 55; 8am-6pm Mon-Fri, to 5pm Sat). Surf the web at **IATP** (☎ 25 875; Str Lenina 160; per hr $0.40; 9am-6pm Mon-Fri).

The regional **başkani** (assembly) is on pr Lenina. The Gagauzi and Moldovan flags fly from the roof.

Next to the assembly is the **Gagauz Culture House**, in front of which stands a statue of Lenin. West of pr Lenina at Str Galatsăna 17 is the **Gagauz University** (Komrat Devlet Üniversitesi), founded in 1990. Four faculties (national culture, agronomy, economics and law) serve 1500 students, who learn in Russian and Gagauz. The main foreign languages taught are Romanian, English and Turkish.

### Getting There & Away

There are five daily return buses from Chişinău to Comrat ($3.90). From Comrat there are two buses daily via Bendery to Tiraspol, and one only as far as Bendery.

# MOLDOVA DIRECTORY

## ACCOMMODATION

Chişinău has a good range of hotels. Most towns have small hotels that have survived from communist days. Basic singles or doubles with a shared bathroom cost $30 to $50 per room in Chişinău, but outside the capitals singles will usually be $20 to $30 and doubles $25 to $40. Unless noted otherwise, all accommodation options include breakfast in the price.

You will be asked to briefly present your passport upon registration; they may keep it for several hours in order to register it.

Camping grounds *(popas turistic)* are practically nonexistent in Moldova. The good news is that wild camping is allowed anywhere unless otherwise prohibited.

The idea of homestays in Moldova is in its infancy. Check **Marisha** (www.marisha.net) for a growing list of options. There are no hostels in Moldova.

## BUSINESS HOURS

Banks can be expected to open from 9am to 3pm, with many closing for an hour around noon. Most shops are open from 9am or 10am to 6pm or 7pm, some closing on Sunday. Post offices are open from 8am to 7pm Monday to Friday, until 4pm Saturday and closed Sunday. Museums are usually open from 11am to 5pm, with most closing on Monday. Restaurants can be expected to stay open until at least 11pm nightly. Theatrical performances and concerts usually begin at 7pm.

## CUSTOMS

Moldova's customs procedures have loosened significantly and generally there should be little problem bringing whatever you like in and out of the country. See **Welcome to Moldova!** (www.turism.md) for the latest information on customs regulations.

There is no limit to the amount of foreign currency you can bring in or out of the country, but the amount must be declared upon entering on a customs declaration form you'll be given, and then again upon exiting the country; purportedly, this is to ensure you do not leave with more money than you arrived with. You might be asked to prove that you have at least $30 for each day of your stay.

You're allowed to cross the border either way with 1L of alcohol, 2L of beer and up to 200 cigarettes, though these rules are not strictly enforced. Visit the **customs office** (☎ 22-569 460; Str Columna 65) in Chişinău for official permission to take antiques or large art pieces out of the country.

## EMBASSIES & CONSULATES

### Moldovan Embassies & Consulates

Moldova has embassies and consulates worldwide.

**France** (☎ 01 40 67 11 20; www.ambassade-moldavie.com; 1 rue Sfax, 75116 Paris)

**Germany** (☎ 069-52 78 08; www.konsulat-moldova.de; Adelheidstrasse 8, 60433 Frankfurt)

**Romania** Embassy (☎ 01-230 0474; ambasadamoldova@zappmobile.ro; Aleea Alexandru 40, 011834 Bucharest) Consulate (☎ 01-410 9827; Str C Constantinescu 47, sec 1, 71326 Bucharest)

**Russia** (☎ 495-924 5353; www.moldembassy.ru; 18 Kuznetsky most, 103031 Moscow)

**Turkey** (☎ 312-446 5527; ambmold@superonline.com; Kaptanpasa Sok 49, 06700 Ankara)

MOLDOVA

**Ukraine** ( ☎ 044-280 7722; kiev@mfa.md; vul Sichnevogo Povstannya 6, 01010 Kyiv)
**USA** ( ☎ 202-667 1130; embassyofmoldova@mcihispeed .net; 2101 S St NW, Washington, DC 20008)

### Embassies & Consulates in Moldova

Following is a list of countries with embassies or consulates in Chişinău:
**France** ( ☎ 22-228 204; www.ambafrance.md; Str 31 August 1989, 101A)
**Germany** ( ☎ 22-234 607; ambasada-germana@riscom .md; Str Maria Cibotari 35)
**Romania** Embassy ( ☎ 22-228 126; ambrom@moldnet .md; Str Bucureşti 66/1) Consulate ( ☎ 22-237 622; Str Vlaicu Pircalab 39)
**Russia** ( ☎ 22-234 941; www.moldova.mid.ru; B-dul Ştefan cel Mare 153)
**Turkey** ( ☎ 22-509 100; turkembassy@arax.md; Str V Cupcea 60)
**UK** ( ☎ 22-225 902; www.britishembassy.md; Str Nicolae Iorga 18)
**Ukraine** ( ☎ 22-582 124; www.mfa.gov.ua, in Ukrainian; Str V Lupu 17)
**USA** ( ☎ 22-233 772; http://moldova.usembassy.gov; Str A Mateevici 103A)

### FESTIVALS & EVENTS

Moldova is not a festival-heavy country, perhaps as its citizens find any excuse to party anytime throughout the year. Their major festival is the **Wine Festival** on the second Sunday in October (and for several wine-drenched days preceding and following it). The government has even instituted a visa-free regime for this period. Chişinău's **City Day** is 14 October.

### GAY & LESBIAN TRAVELLERS

Before Moldova repealed its Soviet antigay law in 1995, it was one of only four European countries to still criminalise homosexuality. Now Moldova has among the most progressively liberal laws on the continent: homosexual activity is legal for both sexes at 14, the same age as for heterosexual sex. In 2003 the government adopted a National Human Rights Plan which would see the prohibition of discrimination against homosexuals enshrined in law. Gay Pride parades happen in Chişinău yearly in late April/early May.

However, homosexuality is still a hushed topic, and politicians still get away with antigay rhetoric. While most people take a laissez-faire attitude towards the notion of homosexuality, being visibly out is likely to attract unwanted attention. For more information, visit www.gay.md.

### HOLIDAYS

The following national holidays are celebrated in Moldova.
**New Year's Day** 1 January
**Orthodox Christmas** 7 January
**International Women's Day** 8 March
**Orthodox Easter** March/April/May
**Victory (1945) Day** 9 May
**Independence Day** 27 August
**National Language Day** 31 August

Transdniestrans boycott the Moldovan Independence Day; they celebrate their own Independence Day on 2 September.

### INTERNET RESOURCES

Get your everyday Moldova news and information at **Moldova Azi** (www.azi.md).

### MONEY

Moldovan lei come in denominations of 1, 5, 10, 20, 50, 100, 200 and 500 lei. There are coins for 1, 5, 10, 25 and 50 bani (there are 100 bani in a leu).

Note that the breakaway Transdniestran republic has its own currency, which is useless anywhere else in the world (see p517).

It's easy to find ATMs in Chişinău, but not in other towns in Moldova. Eximbank will cash travellers cheques and give cash advances on major credit cards. It's almost impossible to use travellers cheques in shops or restaurants. While credit cards won't get you anywhere in rural areas, they are widely accepted in larger department stores, hotels and most restaurants in cities and towns. In Moldova, prices are often quoted in US dollars, and so that's what we've quoted for costs in this chapter.

### POST

From Moldova, it costs $0.35 to send a postcard or letter under 20g to Western Europe, Australia and the USA.

**DHL** (www.dhl.com) is the most popular international courier service in the region. It has offices in Chişinău and Tiraspol. See its website for details.

### TELEPHONE

Moldtelecom, the wonderfully named, state-run telephone company, sells pay cards ($2.25 or $3) that can be used to dial any number

---

**EMERGENCY SERVICES**

- Ambulance ☎ 903
- Fire ☎ 901
- Police ☎ 902

---

within Moldova only. These are sold at any telephone centre in the country. To make an international call using a prepaid card, you need to use a private company like Treitelecom. Its cards cost $3.75 to $35 and are available at any Moldpressa newspaper stand (and can be used to make local calls, too).

Mobile phone service in Moldova is provided by Chişinău-based Moldcell (run by Moldtelecom) and **Voxtel** ( ☎ 22-575 757; www .voxtel.md; Str Alba Iulia 75, Chişinău).

## VISAS

From 1 January 2007 citizens of EU member states, USA, Canada and Japan will no longer need visas! Everyone else is still on the hook for visas. Additionally, Australians, New Zealanders and South Africans all require an invitation from a company, organisation or individual. When acquiring a visa in advance, payments to the consulates are usually in the form of a bank deposit at a specified bank.

Visas can be easily acquired on arrival at Chişinău airport (single/double entry $60/75) or, if arriving by bus or car from Romania, at three border points: Sculeni (north of Iaşi); Leuşeni (main Bucharest–Chişinău border); and Cahul. Visas are not issued at any other border crossings, nor when entering by train. Citizens of countries requiring an invitation must present the original document (copies/faxes not accepted) at the border if buying a visa there.

In 2002 Moldova generously started instituting a visa-free regime for all foreigners wishing to partake in its Wine Festival (second Sunday in October). These visa-free visits cannot exceed 10 days.

An HIV/AIDS test is required for foreigners intending to stay in Moldova longer than three months. Certificates proving HIV-negative status have to be in Russian and English.

See **Welcome to Moldova!** (www.turism.md) and follow the links to check for the latest changes in the visa regime.

### Costs & Registration

The price of a single-/double-entry tourist visa valid for one month is $60/75. Single-/double-entry transit visas valid for 72 hours are $30/60. Special rates apply for tourist groups of more than 10 persons, and for children, the handicapped and the elderly.

Visas can be processed within a day at the **Moldovan consulate** ( ☎ 40-21-410 9827; B-dul Eroilor 8, Bucharest) in Romania. Applications must be made between 8.30am and 12.30pm Monday to Friday. After paying for the visa at a specified bank in the city centre, you then collect your visa between 3pm and 4pm the same day.

# TRANSPORT

## GETTING THERE & AWAY

As a result of the Soviet legacy, travellers may experience some questioning or minor hassle on entering Moldova, but, thanks to the same legacy, any potential complication is easy to resolve on the spot – most often by offering a few dollars. Moldovan border guards are generally friendly and down-to-earth, although they may be curious about you, as they see few foreign tourists.

### Air

Moldova's only airport of significance is **Chişinău International** (KIV; ☎ 22-526 060), 14.5km south of the city centre. **Voiaj Travel** (www.voiaj .md) in Chişinău publishes the latest airport schedules. For information on flights to/from Western Europe and beyond, see p927.

There are two national airlines. **Moldavian Airlines** (code 2M; ☎ 22-549 339; www.mdv.md; B-dul Ştefan cel Mare 3, Chişinău), located in the **Air Service** (www.airservice.md) travel centre, offers 12 weekly flights to Timişoara and two daily flights to Budapest, from where it has connections to other European destinations. **Air Moldova** (code 9U; ☎ 22-546 464; www.airmoldova.md; B-dul Negruzzi 8, Chişinău) has daily flights between Chişinău and Bucharest, and to Timişoara.

Also in the Air Service travel centre is **Carpatair** (code V3; ☎ 22-549 339; www.carpatair.com), which flies to Timişoara and beyond six times weekly. **Aerotour** (code UN; ☎ 22-542 454; www .transaero.md; B-dul Ştefan cel Mare 4, Chişinău) has two flights daily to Budapest, one or two flights daily to Bucharest and two flights weekly to Prague.

**MOLDOVA**

MOLDOVA

**Tarom Romanian Air Transport** (code RO; ☎ 22-541 254; www.tarom.ro; B-dul Ştefan cel Mare, 3, Chişinău; ☯ 9am-5pm) flies to Bucharest eight times weekly.

The following airlines also fly to and from Moldova:

**Austrian Airlines** (code OS; ☎ 22-244 083; www .austrianair.com)

**Transaero** (code UN; ☎ 542 454; www.transaero.md) Flies between Chişinău and Bucharest.

**Turkish Airlines** (code TK; ☎ 22-527 078; www .turkishairlines.com)

## Land
### BUS
Moldova is well linked by bus lines to central and Western Europe. While not as comfortable as the train, buses tend to be faster, though not always cheaper.

**Eurolines** (www.eurolines.md) has a flurry of buses linking Moldova with Western Europe.

Buses between Chişinău and Kiev or Odesa run through Transdniestr and Tiraspol; even with a Moldovan visa, local authorities are likely to make you pay for an additional transit permit.

### CAR & MOTORCYCLE
The Green Card (a routine extension of domestic motor insurance to cover most European countries) is valid in Moldova. Extra insurances can be bought at the borders.

### TRAIN
From Chişinău, there is one daily train to Lviv and three to Moscow. Westbound, there are nightly trains to Romania and beyond.

There's an overnight service between Bucharest and Chişinău; at 12 hours, the journey is longer than taking a bus or maxitaxi (the train heads north to Iaşi, then south again), but is more comfortable if you want to sleep.

## GETTING AROUND
### Bicycle
Moldova is mostly flat, making cycling an excellent way of getting around. That is, it would

be if it weren't for the bad condition of most of the roads, and for the lack of infrastructure – outside of Chişinău, you'll have to rely on your own resources or sense of adventure (and trying to enlist help from friendly locals) if you run into mechanical trouble.

### Bus & Maxitaxi
Moldova has a good network of buses running to most towns and villages. Maxitaxis, which follow the same routes as the buses, are quicker and more reliable.

### Car & Motorcycle
It is now possible for foreigners to hire and drive a car in Moldova. In Chişinău, travel agencies can arrange car hire (see p513).

Be wary, however, as the roads are in poor condition. EU driving licences are accepted here; otherwise, bring both your home country's driving licence and your International Driving Permit, which is recognised in Moldova.

The intercity speed limit is 90km/h and in built-up areas 60km/h; the legal blood alcohol limit is 0.03%. For road rescue, dial ☎ 901. The **Automobile Club Moldova** (ACM; ☎ 22-292 703; www.acm.md) can inform you of all regulations and offer emergency assistance (this is a members-only service).

### Local Transport
In Moldova, buses cost about $0.15, trolley-buses $0.10 and city maxitaxis $0.25.

### Taxi
In Moldova, there are official (and unofficial) metered taxis, both of which may try to rip you off. It's best to call a taxi (p513). A taxi ride to anywhere inside Chişinău is unlikely to cost more than $3. The going rate is about $0.25 per km. The handy Russian-style practice of waving a private car down for a 'ride' with someone who just happens to be going your way (for a fee!) is the more common way of getting lifts. You'll often need to agree upon a price before driving off.

# Montenegro Црна Гора

Expect newly independent Montenegro to come out from its Yugoslav shadow and be seen for the beauty it is. No longer should visitors think they'd fall off the edge of the world if they journey east beyond Dubrovnik.

Croatia's sapphire blue Adriatic Sea does continue. However here it's backed by a craggy, grey mountain range leaving just enough room for a ribbon of coastal towns on a sweep of sandy beaches and small coves running down to the Albanian border.

Historic walled towns like Stari Bar, Budva, Kotor and Herceg Novi are perfect for exploring, and anywhere along the coast you can find private rooms in a laze-away seaside town.

The interior is a setting of dramatic mountains tufted with pine forests, dotted with lakes and scored by giddy-deep canyons. The highest region, the Durmitor National Park, is a favourite for winter skiing and summer hiking in a pristine mountainscape while below in Tara's deep canyon, intrepid rafters challenge its tumbling rapids. So much for a small country – the world's newest nation.

MONTENEGRO

## FAST FACTS

- **Area** 13,812 sq km
- **Capital** Podgorica
- **Currency** euro (€); US$1 = €0.77; UK£1 = €1.47; A$1 = €0.60; ¥100 = €0.70; NZ$1 = €0.49 €1 = 88din (Serbia)
- **Famous for** being the newest country in the world
- **Official Language** Serbian
- **Phrases** zdravo (hello); hvala (thanks); da (yes); ne (no); govorite li engleski? (do you speak English?)
- **Population** 716,000 (2005 est)
- **Telephone codes** ☎ 381, international access code ☎ 99
- **Visas** Not required by British, Australian, New Zealand, USA, and most EU or Canadian citizens

**MONTENEGRO GOES IT ALONE**

There comes a time in any unhappy marriage when one partner decides to leave home. Especially in a union called Serbia and Montenegro – essentially a shotgun marriage arranged by a potential parent-in-law, the EU. Montenegro has narrowly voted for independence and packed its bags, but it'll be a gradual separation as common assets are divvied up. There'll be embassies to establish and talks to have with the EU over membership. The brake on Serbian entry, and the handing over of war criminals, won't apply to Montenegro, which suddenly loses any taint by being associated with Serbia.

The results of the referendum came at about the same time as we were putting the finishing flourishes to a chapter titled Serbia & Montenegro. We've split and revised the information wherever possible but these are still early stages in nation-building and a number of joint organisations are still in, well, joint hands. For that reason we point you to various sections in the Serbia chapter.

## HIGHLIGHTS

- Gaze down on the broody Wagnerian fjord from the castle ruins above **Kotor's old town** (p533)
- Ski, hike, climb or raft the rapids in **Durmitor National Park** (p536)
- Laze, slurp on ice creams, and build sandcastles on just about any beach. Give **Budva** (p532) a go
- Wander the former capital, **Cetinje**, (p535) and discover the old embassies that might be needed again

## ITINERARIES

- **One week** Bum your way through the coastal towns. Definitely idle away some days in Kotor, soak up Budva's sun and build a sandcastle on one of Ulcinj's beaches.
- **Two to three weeks** Add in the interior with hiking and rafting in Durmitor, roaming around Cetinje and exploring Lake Skadar.

## CLIMATE & WHEN TO GO

The coast has a Mediterranean climate with short cool winters and long dry summers. Inland, the winters are longer and colder, and the summers shorter and hotter, while the mountain regions have cold snowy winters and warm summers.

The Montenegrin coast is at its best in May, June and September, but avoid July and August, when accommodation becomes quite scarce and expensive. The ski season is from December to March. And just to let you know – the summer sea temperature is 25°C to 28°C.

## HISTORY

Montenegro's history is one of dogged independence battled for against greater forces, which have crashed in failure against its rocky fortress interior. For 500 years Montenegro was the only country to defeat the Turkish forces that overran southeast Europe, and remain independent. While the size of its territory waxed and waned it was always centred on the central mountain fastness of Cetinje.

Only twice has the country not been master of its own affairs: first from 1166 for about 200 years when it was taken over by the Serbian kingdom of Raska, and second in 1916 during WWI when the Austrians invaded. On the back of that event Montenegro's ally Serbia took the opportunity to occupy Montenegro and then annex it in 1922.

Montenegro's development from tribal society to a modern state started with the *vladike*, the prince-bishops who ruled from the end of the 17th century; these *vladike* were

**HOW MUCH?**

- **Short taxi ride** €2
- **Internet access per hour** €1
- **Coffee** €1
- **Bottle of plum brandy** €8

**LONELY PLANET INDEX**

- **Litre of petrol** €1.05
- **Litre of bottled water** €1
- **Beer** €1
- **Souvenir T-shirt** €10
- **Street snack (slice of pizza)** €0.60

supposedly celibate so the line of succession went from uncle to nephew.

During Vladika Petar 1's rule and that of his successor, Petar II Petrovic Njegos, Montenegro was moulded into a state with the establishment of a central government supported by a taxation system.

Under Petar II's successors, Montenegro finally secured its territories with the defeat of the Turks in the Russo-Turkish war and recognition at the subsequent Congress of Berlin in 1878.

By the turn of the 19th century, Montenegro was developing into a modern state with a legal framework, education system, a telegraph and postal service and the development of roads and railways. Cetinje was also becoming a

social capital of southeastern Europe. Nikola I Petrovic, Montenegro's ruler, married six of his daughters into European royal and aristocratic families, and several embassies and diplomatic missions were established in Cetinje. Their fine buildings can still be seen today.

In 1910, Montenegro became a constitutional monarchy with Nikola as king, but within four years the country was at war and eight years later a Serbian satrapy. A popular revolt, the Christmas Uprising, erupted in 1919 and rumbled on until the exiled King Nikola withdrew his support. This period is marked by a large Montenegrin diaspora, mainly to the USA.

As a reward for its stalwart support of the partisans during WWII, Tito gave Montenegro republic status in the postwar Yugoslav

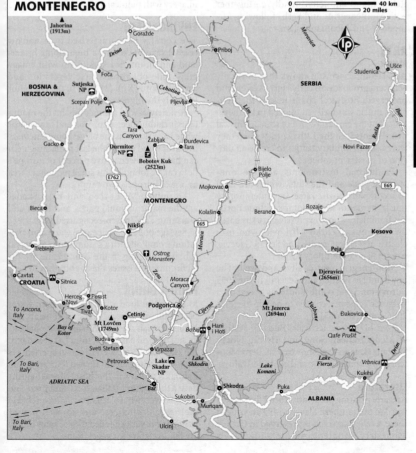

MONTENEGRO

federation. From then on Montenegro was a loyal member of all of Yugoslavia's incarnations culminating in the loose union of Serbia and Montenegro that came to an end with the pro-independence vote in May 2006.

Montenegro is now fully independent for the first time since 1916, and became the 192nd member of the UN on 28 June 2006.

## PEOPLE

Montenegro's 2003 census revealed a population of 673,000. The ethnic split is made up of 43% Montenegrins, 32% Serbs, 8% Bosnians, 5% Albanians and 12% other groups. There are large Slavic Muslim and Albanian minorities.

## RELIGION

Religion and ethnicity broadly go together with Montenegrins and Serbs following Orthodoxy and Albanians Islam.

## ARTS
### Music

A Palaeolithic whistle shows that musically Montenegro made an early start. A later, and preserved, liturgical chant reveals that religious music was well established in medieval times but the earliest record of secular musical instruments is in the 12th century when they were used in military tactics to create an illusion of greater numbers.

Traditional instruments are the one-stringed *gusle* and the flute, which are used to accompany poetic verse. In contemporary music, names to watch out for include Borislav Taminjzic, whose expressive work is based on folk music, Zarko Mirkovic, who uses electro-acoustical media, and Senad Gacevic, who makes contempory fusion.

Montenegrin pop is alive and well. The boy band No Name came seventh in the 2005 Eurovision Song contest but was booed off a Belgrade stage in a contest to decide the joint 2006 entry (see p751).

Two big music festivals, Budva's Festival of Mediterranean Song and Herceg Novi's Sunčane skale festival, showcase modern Montenegrin popular music and all its derivatives.

### Literature

An early printing press introduced the printed word to the southern Slavs in 1493 and one of these, a religious tract, is preserved in Cetinje Monastery. Montenegrin literature has its roots in folk poetry sung to the accompaniment of the *gusle*. The country's most famous poet was its Prince-Pishop Peter II, whose epic poem *Mountain Wreath* is a synthesis of Montenegrin and Serbian philosophy.

## Art

Montenegro's monasteries are the repositories of early art with some frescoes going back to the 10th century. Most of these and icons were executed in the traditional Byzantine style.

In subsequent centuries, Montenegrin artists were influenced by the Italian renaissance and the baroque, and by the 20th-century artists were adopting European styles, notably postimpressionism and expressionism. In the late 20th century a new generation of artists extended international styles by blending in Montenegrin imagery with political and social concerns.

## ENVIRONMENT

The country is characterised by a narrow coastal strip backed by a high alpine hinterland and an interior karst plain with craggy grey-white outcrops, sparse vegetation and caves. Bobotov Kuk (2523m) in the Durmitor Range is the highest mountain.

A variety of wild animals inhabit the mountains including deer, lynx, wolf and brown bear while Lake Skadar is the biggest bird sanctuary in Europe and one of the last remaining pelican habitats. Twenty-five percent of Europe's flora can be found in this small republic as well as one of Europe's two rainforests.

Durmitor, Mt Lovcen and Lake Skadar are the major national parks, and Kotor and Durmitor are Unesco-recognised sites.

Sewage pollution of coastal waters, air pollution from Podgorica's aluminium plant and rubbish dumping in the countryside are the environmental issues the country has to face.

## FOOD & DRINK

Montenegrin food is a mix of Eastern European with an emphasis on grilled meats and Mediterranean cuisine, with its traditional garlic and olive oil base. Fish, from Lake Skadar or the sea is plentiful. A continental speciality is *kajmak* (a salted cream turned to cheese) and Žabljak's variety is the best. Montenegrins have a thing about Italian food, and pizza and pasta is everywhere. Salads, *gibanica* (cheese pie), *zeljanica* (cheese and spinach pie) or *pasulj prebranac* (a cooked dish of spicy beans) are fall-back fare for vegetarians.

Nikšićko *pivo* (try saying that after a few) is the local beer and is a good thirst quencher. Many people distil their own *rakija* (brandy) out of plums and other fruit. Montenegrin red wine, *venac* especially, is a rich drop.

Coffee is usually served Turkish-style, 'black as hell, strong as death and sweet as love'. If you want anything other than herbal teas you should ask for Indian tea.

# PODGORICA
# ПОДГОРИЦА

☎ 081 / pop 179,500

The nation's capital has little to offer visitors, who usually pass through on their way to the mountains or the coast. Accommodation here is expensive compared to the coast, where a €40 room will fetch €250 in Podgorica.

## ORIENTATION

The train station and bus station are in the eastern part of the town. The commercial hub centres on Slobode and intersecting with it is Hercegovačka, the shopping-café heart of the town.

## INFORMATION

**Atlas Bank** ( ☎ 407 211; Stanka Dragojevića 4; ⏱ 8am-6pm Mon-Fri, to 12.30pm Sat) Cashes travellers cheques.

**Internet cg** ( ☎ 403 444; Vučedolska 13; per hr €1.50; ⏱ 8am-8pm Mon-Fri, 9am-2pm Sat)

**Left luggage** (bus station; per piece €1; ⏱ 6am-10pm)

## SLEEPING & EATING

There are some cheap eating places around the bus station and pleasant cafés in Hercegovačka.

In a city of overpriced hotels, modern and well-equipped **Europa** ( ☎ 623 444; Orahovačka 16; s/d €45/70; ⓟ ⓧ ⓛ ), near the train station, is a weary traveller's best friend, if a night in Podgorica is a necessity. There's free internet in each room, a fitness centre to tone you up and a sauna to sweat you out.

Found in most big town bus stations in Montenegro, canteen-style restaurants like **Express Restoran** (bus station; meals €2-4) dish up good cheap meals. It's all on display, so you point and pay without stretching your knowledge of the language.

**Buda Bar** ( ☎ 344 944; Stanka Dragojeviča 26; sandwiches €2.50) is a slinky ultramodern café-bar so laid-back the meditative golden Buddha statue seems completely out of it. Equally reflective customers read their newspapers or stare into their espressos searching for the eternal truth. Come evening and the mood changes to a bustling chatty meeting place.

## GETTING THERE & AWAY
### Air

**Montenegro Airlines** ( ☎ 664 411; www.montenegro -airlines.cg.yu; Slobode 21; ⏱ 8am-8pm Mon-Fri, to 2pm Sat) flies to European destinations from Podgorica and to Belgrade from Tivat. The airport tax is €8/15 for domestic/international flights.

**JAT** ( ☎ 664 740; www.jat.com; Ivana Milutinovica 20; ⏱ 9am-5pm Mon-Fri, 9am-1pm Sat) flies several times a day from Podgorica and Tivat to Belgrade. Flights to Belgrade are €73.

### Bus

Buses go from the **bus station** ( ☎ 620 430) to Belgrade (€20, nine hours, 11 buses), Žabljak (€8, four hours, at 1.10pm, 1.50pm and 3.30pm), Sarajevo (€14, nine hours, at 7.40am, 9.30am, 1.35pm and 11pm) and many to Rožaje, for Peja in Kosovo (€8, four hours).

### Train

Services from the **train station** ( ☎ 633 663) travel the scenic train route to Belgrade (€15 plus €10/5 for a three-/six-berth sleeper on overnight trains, eight hours). There are frequent trains to Bar and Sutomore on the coast.

## GETTING AROUND

Call **Bum** ( ☎ 9703) for a taxi to the airport (about €7). **Meridian** ( ☎ 234 944, 069 316 666; Cetinjski put; ⏱ 8am-2pm & 6-8pm Mon-Fri, 8am-2pm Sat) rents cars from €30 a day.

## AROUND PODGORICA
### Virpazar & Lake Skadar
ВИРПАЗАР & СКАДАРСКО ЈЕЗЕРО

A causeway carries both road and rail traffic from Podgorica to Bar, passing over the western edge of the 44km-long Lake Skadar. This beautiful lake, fringed by mountains, is the biggest lake in the Balkans, and is one of the largest bird sanctuaries and remaining pelican habitats in Europe. Jutting westward from the causeway is the 400-year-old Turkish castle of Lesendro. Ask around Virpazar for boat trips.

MONTENEGRO

The **Pelikan** ( ☎ 081-711 011; Virpazar; dishes €6-8) restaurant is renown for its cuisine and décor. The dining room is exotically decorated with dried plants, old photographs, nautical ephemera and a series of well-battered hats. Try any of the fish dishes, all made with fish fresh from the lake. The service is top-notch and dessert is on the house. On weekend evenings, May to September, there's live music. The Pelikan also has accommodation (d with shared bathroom €20).

# COASTAL MONTENEGRO

## BAR БАР
☎ 085 / pop 45000

Backed by a precipitous coastal range, the modern city of Bar is Montenegro's major port and a transport hub for the coast. Far more interesting, however, is the 1000-year-old Stari Bar (Old Bar). Whether arriving from the north or by ferry from Italy, Bar will be most people's first stop in coastal Montenegro.

## Orientation & Information
The ferry terminal in Bar is 300m from the town centre; the bus station and adjacent train station are about 2km southeast of the centre.

**Crnogorska Komercijalna Bank** (Obala Kralja Nikole bb) ATM; opposite ferry terminal.

**Komercijalna Bank** ( ☎ 311 827; Obala Kralja Nikole bb) Cashes travellers cheques.

**Tourist Information Centar** ( ☎ 311 633; tobar@cg .yu; Obala 13 Jula bb; ⏱ 8am-4pm Sep-Jun, 8am-8pm Jul & Aug) Helpful office with good information.

## Sights
The impressive **Stari Bar** (admission €1; ⏱ 9am-5pm Apr-Oct) stands on a bluff 4km northeast, off the Ulcinj road. A steep cobbled hill takes you up to a fortified entrance, from where a short dark passage pops you out into a huge garden of vine-clad walls, abandoned streets and ruins overgrown with grass and wild flowers.

The northern corner has an 11th-century fortress with views showing Stari Bar's isolated and beautiful setting amid mountains and olive groves. Also in the northern corner are the foundations of the church of St George, the patron saint of Bar. Originally a Romanesque church, the Turks rebuilt it into a mosque in the 17th century, but the unlucky spot was yet again

in ruins after an accidental explosion of gunpowder. Nearby are two preserved churches, **St Veneranda** and **St Catherine**, both from the 14th century. Around the corner is a Turkish bath from the 17th or 18th century – a solid, charming building. In the western part of the town are the remains of the **Church of St Nicolas**, with glimpses of Serbo-Byzantine frescoes.

Stand still and imagine the murmur of people and the scurrying of everyday life in this once-sophisticated city.

Nearby is the **Stara Maslina** (Old Olive Tree), which is reputedly 2000 years old. Ask for directions as there are many other gnarled and ancient trees around here.

## Sleeping & Eating
**Putnik Gold** ( ☎ 311 605; putnikgold@cg.yu; Obala 13 Jula bb; s/d from €10/20, breakfast/full board €3/10, apt without meals from €40; ⏱ 9am-5pm Mon-Sat Oct-May, 8am-8pm Mon-Sat Jun-Sep) Books accommodation along the coast.

**Pulena Pizza Pub** ( ☎ 312 816; Vladimira Rolovića bb; dishes €2.50-6) A busy eating and drinking place under the outer of the three spaceships that some architect thought was a good design for a market. Pizzas and pastas are on offer to be washed down with a beer or soft drink; otherwise the coffees are good. Beware, small pizzas are large.

**GMG Supermarket** ( ☎ 312 619; Vladimira Rolovića bb; ⏱ 6am-11pm) Sells all you need for a feed-yourself holiday.

## Getting There & Away
**Barska Plovidba** ( ☎ 312 336; mlinesagency@cg.yu; ferry terminal; ⏱ 8am-10pm sailing days, 8am-8pm other days) books Montenegro Lines, which sails to Bari (at 10pm Tuesday, Thursday & Sunday) and Ancona (at 4pm Wednesday and Friday, July to mid-September) in Italy. For schedule and prices check www.montenegrolines.net.

**Mecur** ( ☎ 313 617; merco@cg.yu; Obala 13 Jula bb; ⏱ 9am-3pm Mon-Sat Oct-May, to 8pm Mon-Sat Jun-Sep) books Azzurra Lines, which runs from Kotor to Bari on Mondays, June to September. For schedule and prices check www.azzurraline .com.

The **bus station** ( ☎ 346 141) has almost hourly services to the coastal towns and inland to Podgorica. Fares are between €1 and €3.

The **train station** ( ☎ 312 210) is on the Sutomore to Belgrade line with two daily services to Belgrade and frequent services to Podgorica or Sutomore.

# ULCINJ УЛЦИЊ

☎ 085 / 26,500

The town of Ulcinj heads a series of fine beaches from Mala Plaža (Small Beach) below the old town to Velika Plaža (Great Beach), a famous 12km beach stretching eastwards towards Albania. The Stari Grad (Old Town) is a maze of private houses intermingled with expensive restaurants exploiting the view.

The Turks ruled here for over 300 years and Ulcinj gained notoriety as a North African pirate base and slave market between 1571 and 1878. Today there is a significant Muslim population and the town is popular with Kosovars. An invasion happens every July and August when tens of thousands of holidaymakers flock to enjoy its beaches and Mediterranean climate. Ulcinj is also a transit point for travellers wanting to go on to Albania.

## Orientation & Information

The bus station is on the edge of town, off the Bar–Ada road. Travel into town by turning right onto 26 Novembar (Hafiz ali Ulquinaku) at the first major junction. Mala Plaža and Stari Grad are 3km below at the end of 26 Novembar. Velika Plaža begins about 5km southeast of the town.

**Komercijalna Bank** ( ☎ 421 995; 26 Novembar bb) Cashes travellers cheques; Visa ATM.

**SHPK Art Tours** ( ☎ 401 437; 0609 031 525; 26 Novembar bb; per hr €0.50; ☾ 9am-midnight) Internet and travel agency.

## Sights & Activities

Rising up from the sea's edge, the ramparts of Stari Grad (Old Ulcinj) overlook both town and Mala Plaža, and while earthquakes shattered many buildings in 1979 they have been faithfully reconstructed. Climbing up from the beach and wandering through to the upper gate brings you to a small **museum** ( ☎ 421 419; Stari Grad; admission €1; ☾ 8am-2pm Mon-Fri) with Montenegrin and Turkish artefacts.

Divers wanting a chance to swim around various wrecks and the remains of a submerged town should contact the **D'olcinium Diving Club** ( ☎ 421 612; www.uldiving.com) for information.

## Sleeping

**Real Estate Tourist Agency** ( ☎ 421 609; www.real estate-travel.com; 26 Novembar bb; r from €7-20, B&B from €19, 2-/3-/4-bed per apt €20/30/40; ☾ 8am-9pm) This agency (200m above Mala Plaža) arranges accommodation in private rooms and apartments that usually come with cooking facilities. It also runs local tours.

**Bella Vista Travel Agency** ( ☎ 402 088; bellavista@cg .yu; 26 Novembar bb; s/apt B&B from €12/25) The family restaurant opposite Real Estate has several rooms and apartments available. It also sells air and ferry tickets, and runs day excursions.

**Dvori Balšića** and the adjacent **Palata Venecija** ( ☎ /fax 421 457; leart@cg.yu; Stari Grad; 2-/4-/6-person apt from €47/87/127 Sep-Jun, €66/127/181 Jul & Aug) are the steal of the Adriatic! Spacious apartments with kitchenette and views out over the Old City walls to the lapping sea. The stone terrace outside has waiter service for those sundowner drinks as you laze back and consider yourself 'king of the castle', as indeed the previous owners were.

There are two camping grounds, **Tomi** (Ada road; ☾ May-Sep) and **Neptun** ( ☎ 412 888; Ada road; ☾ May-Sep), and a holiday camp **HTP Velika Plaža** ( ☎ 413 131; www.velikaplaza.cg.yu; Ada road; r/apt half-board from €19/25; ☾ May-Sep) about 1km east of Milena and adjacent to Velika Plaža.

## Eating & Drinking

**Bella Vista** ( ☎ 402 088; 26 Novembar bb; dishes €4-8) Suitable for an early breakfast or late-night drink and snack, if you're in private, bed-only accommodation.

**Manhattan** ( ☎ 069 032 400; 26 Novembar bb; dishes €4.50-8) Tables crowded with shiny glasses, peaked napkins and a bottle ready to open says that this is an establishment with standards to fulfil. 'Do you like fish?' the waiter asks. 'Let me show you.' And he returns with a platter of sparkling-eyed fish that can be grilled or seasoned with oil, garlic and lemon. Pizza and pasta are also on the menu.

**Kafana Bazar** ( ☎ 421 639; 26 Novembar bb; dishes €5-8) An upstairs restaurant that's an ideal idling place when the streets below are heaving with tourists. Gloat in comfort as you enjoy a plate of fried *lignje na žaru* (calamari) or a sublime lunchtime fish soup.

**Marinero** ( ☎ 423 009; Mala Plaža; dishes €5-9) The owner was once a ship's cook, and ship's cooks don't last long unless they're good. Often seafaring mates gather here, speaking three or four languages, so for a coffee or *rakija* you'll get the history of the town and tales of the sea. You'll also enjoy a slap-up seafood meal.

## Getting There & Away

**Minibuses** ( ☎ 462 690) to Shkodër, Albania (€4, one hour, at 6am and 1pm) departs from

MONTENEGRO

outside the post office on 26 Novembar. A service on Monday, Wednesday and Saturday links Montenegro with Dubrovnik and Split (€28) in Croatia. Services depart from Ulcinj (at 5am), Budva (at 6.20am), Kotor (at 7.10am), Herceg Novi (at 8.10am), Dubrovnik (at 9.20am), arriving at Split at 1.50pm. The return leaves at 4pm.

The **bus station** ( ☎ 413 225) has services along the coast to the Montenegro–Croatia border at Igo (€7.50, three hours, at 5.20am, 7am and 12.45pm), Podgorica (€5, two hours, at 5.45am, noon and 2.50pm) and Prishtina, Kosovo (€27, nine hours, at 7.30pm).

Many minibuses ply the road to Ada (and Velika Plaža) from the market place (€1.50) in July and August.

## BUDVA БУДВА
☎ 086 / pop 16,000

Budva is the hub of the Montenegrin holiday coast with fine beaches punctuating the coastline all the way from Budva to Sveti Stefan. Backing them is a large strip of hotels, cafés and shops.

In June the town hosts a pop-orientated music festival plus a summer festival with music, theatre and visual arts in July and August.

### Orientation & Information

The bus station is about 1km from the Stari Grad (Old Town). The road called Mediteranska leads into Budva, ending at the harbour and Stari Grad. **Crnogorska Komercijalna Bank** ( ☎ 451 075; Mediteranska 7; ◷ 8am-8pm Mon-Sat) has an ATM, and cashes travellers cheques. There's also a **Tourist information office** ( ☎ 402 814; Stari Grad; ◷ 11.30am-6.30pm Mon-Fri, 1.30pm-6.30pm Sat Oct-Apr, 9am-9pm May-Sep).

### Sights & Activities

Budva's big tourist-puller is its its old **walled town**. Levelled by two earthquakes in 1979, it has since been completely rebuilt and become a tourist attraction with small boutique shops, restaurants, cafés and bars. It's so picturesque it seems almost contrived.

The **Budva Museum** ( ☎ 453 308; Petra I Petrovića 11, Stari Grad; adult/child €1.50/0.50; ◷ 8am-8pm Tue-Fri, 10am-4pm Sat & Sun) proudly shows off its three floors of well-laid-out exhibits covering the everyday from pre-Roman to the late 1700s. On the top floor is the best piece, a bronze 5th-century helmet with holes in the back that

maybe tell of the wearer's final day. Down on the ground floor, the floor is dug out to reveal the original street below.

The Stari Grad beach is pebbly and average. **Mogren Beach**, 500m to the right of the Grand Hotel Avala, is better but still pebbly, while for sandcastle building you need the 5km-string of **sandy beaches** arching towards Sveti Stefan. The beaches and swimming are the main attractions for the hordes of summer-break visitors, and in summer there are plenty of boat trips on offer at the harbour.

The former island fishing village of **Sveti Stefan**, now linked to the mainland, is an exclusive hotel complex with a €5 entrance fee for nonguests.

The tourist information office has an outline map of shortish walks and points of interest, around the Budva area.

### Sleeping

**Hippo Hostel** ( ☎ 452 206; www.hippo.com; Proleterska IV 37; dm/r €14/32; ⌨ ) A potentially good and well-needed hostel that has opened in Budva and seems to be doing well. Let us know what you think.

**JAMB Travel** ( ☎ 452 992; www.jamb-travel.com; Mediteranska 23; r €4.50-15, 2-/5-person apt €19/80; ◷ 8am-3pm Mon-Fri Nov-May, to 8pm Jun-Oct) Books accommodation and organises day tours around Montenegro.

**Hotel Mogren** ( ☎ 451 780; fax 452 041; Mediteranska 1; s/d €55/86) A bit like an elderly aunt you've become fond of, the Mogren has become a favourite of ours. Sure it's seen better days but the location (jostling the old city) and price are mighty tempters. Ask for a room with a view of the old city and the sea.

**Hotel Fontana** ( ☎ 452 153; fontana.lekic@cg.yu; Slovenska obala 23; s/d from €45/70) Sitting pretty in a garden area by the harbour. With a small terrace and café-bar to chat with fellow guests, the Fontana has the feel of a holiday home. Rooms are smallish but good, and most on the upper floors have sea views.

There are camping options at **Autocamp Avala** ( ☎ 451 205; Boreti; ◷ Jun-Sep) and **Budva Autocamp** (Jadranski put bb); contact JAMB Travel for details.

### Eating & Drinking

**Restaurant Jadran** ( ☎ 451 028; Slovenska Obala 10; dishes €5-10) When you want to feel special, dine at the Jadran, which is considered Budva's best restaurant. You can eat a lobster for €60 per kilogram, or a substantial soup or *ćevapčići* for €2 – the choice is your wallet's. Mussels Jadran is a justifiable excuse to enjoy a tangy jus of oil, lemon and garlic mopped up with wads of bread and washed down with a chilled Montenegrin white wine.

**Lazo i Milan** ( ☎ 451 468; 13 Jul bb; dishes €6-9) A simple restaurant hidden from most, except the discerning locals. Pasta dishes just like Mama makes them except this mama is a burly Montenegrin chef who can cook up a storm of gastronomic delight with his sauces.

**Old Fisherman's Pub** ( ☎ 069 553 347; Slovenska Obala bb; dishes €3-6) A large drinking place with a patio, on the edge of the harbour. Snacks and an English breakfast are available.

**Chest O'Sheas** ( ☎ 069 579 468; Stari Grad; ⏰ 6pm-late) Near the tourist office, this shoebox of a bar, with Guinness on tap to attract those who haven't made the jump to Montenegrin beer.

**Bus station café** (Ivana Milutinovića; dishes €2-3). The best cheapie in town in a choose-and-point caféteria.

## Getting There & Away

The **bus station** ( ☎ 456 000; Ivana Milutinovića) has frequent, almost hourly, services to the coastal towns and inland to Podgorica. fares are between €1 and €3.

# KOTOR KOTOP

☎ 082 / pop 23,500

Picturesque Kotor with its walled town nestling at the head of southern Europe's deepest fjord has Montenegro's most dramatic setting. In broody weather the atmosphere becomes all Wagnerian, dark shadows cut with fingers of sunlight while on a sunny day the wind-ripples on the purple water sparkle. Stari Grad (Old Town), lying under the lee of a mountain, is a labyrinth of cobbled laneways linking small squares containing ancient churches and former aristocratic mansions.

## Orientation

The western flank of the funnel-shaped Stari Grad lies against Kotor Bay. An 18th-century gateway off Jadranski Put, which runs along the waterside, leads into the old town. The bus station is 1km away on the Budva road.

## Information

**Forza** ( ☎ 304 352; Stari Grad; per hr €2) Two computer terminals in a library-styled bar.

**Information booth** ( ☎ 325 950; western gateway;

⏰ 9am-3pm Mon-Sat Oct-Apr, to 9pm Mon-Sat May-Sep) Tourist and private accommodation information; maps and brochures.

**Montenegrobanka** ( ☎ 323 946; Trg Octobarske Revolucije) ATM; cashes travellers cheques.

## Sights

The fun is simply in wandering around this atmospheric town popping into old churches, dawdling for coffee at the pavement cafés, and people-watching. The energetic can slog up to the old fortifications on the mountainside above Kotor to scan the huge fjord in which Kotor hides. Similar views can be seen from the string of hairpin bends that lead over the mountains to Cetinje.

As a former Mediterranean naval power, Kotor has a proud history and the **Maritime Museum** ( ☎ 304 720; Stari Grad; admission €1.50; ⏰ 8am-2pm Mon-Fri, 9am-noon Sat & Sun) covers much of it in its three storeys of displays. A leaflet in English helps explain its magnificent collection of photographs, uniforms, weapons, painting and models of ships.

**St Tryphon Cathedral** was originally built in the 11th century but earthquakes have meant subsequent reconstructions. The interior is a masterpiece of Romanesque-Gothic architecture with slender columns thrusting upwards to support a series of vaulted roofs. A reliquary chapel holds some of the remains of St Tryphon, the patron saint of Kotor, plus a portion of the Holy Cross.

Breathe in the smell of incense and beeswax in the plain and unadorned 1909 Orthodox **St Nicholas Church**. The silence, the iconostasis with its silver panels in bas relief, the dark wood against bare grey walls and the filtered rays of light through the upper dome create an eerie atmosphere.

## Sleeping

The best deals are private rooms starting from €10 per person. Ask around, at the information booth or a travel agency. In summer you're likely to be approached at the bus station.

**Meridian Travel Agency** ( ☎ 323 448; travel@cg.yu; Stari Grad; r €10-20, apt €30-40; ⏰ 9am-2pm & 6-7pm Mon-Fri, 9am-2pm Sat) This ever-helpful agency in a small lane behind the clock tower books private and hotel accommodation in and around the city.

**Hotel Vardar** ( ☎ 325 084; vardar@cg.yu; Trg Octobarske Revolucije; s/d from €32/48) Decorated in dark brown, cream and white that's sooo old-Yugoslavia.

MONTENEGRO

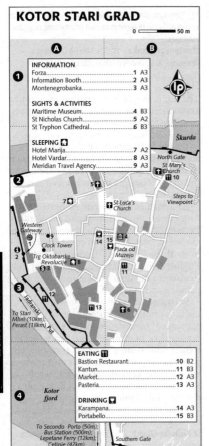

**KOTOR STARI GRAD**

0 ——— 50 m

**INFORMATION**
Forza...............................................1  A3
Information Booth.............................2  A3
Montenegrobanka.............................3  A3

**SIGHTS & ACTIVITIES**
Maritime Museum.............................4  B3
St Nicholas Church............................5  A2
St Tryphon Cathedral........................6  B3

**SLEEPING**
Hotel Marija......................................7  A2
Hotel Vardar.....................................8  A3
Meridian Travel Agency.....................9  A3

**EATING**
Bastion Restaurant..........................10  B2
Kantun............................................11  B3
Market.............................................12  A3
Pasteria...........................................13  A3

**DRINKING**
Karampana......................................14  A3
Portobello........................................15  B3

break, cherry strudel – a juicy speciality of the region.

**Kantun** ( ☎ 325 757; Pjaća od muzejo; dishes €3-8) Without the techno music, this wood-beam restaurant with a bare stone interior, could be a rural *kafana* (small basic café) serving up traditional Montenegrin fare to rough-handed farmers, rather than occupying Kotor prime real estate. Make sure you sample the Njegoša cheeses and the *roštiljska kobasica* (homemade sausages).

**Pasteria** ( ☎ 322 269; Pjaca Sveti Tripuna, Stari Grad; dishes €3-10) Choose pizza, pasta or snacks from the multilingual menu. Sited opposite the twin towers of St Tryphon Cathedral, this elegant eatery has one of the best reputations in the old city. Late risers can breakfast here until 2pm. While waiting for your order, study the large photographs of 19th century Kotor on the wall.

**Stari Mlini** ( ☎ 333 555; Ljuta bb; dishes €5-30) On the road 10km towards Perast, this is an old converted mill on the edge of a river that races through the restaurant's terrace area. Inside is all stonework, heavy wooden beams and tables set with glistening glasses, silver cutlery and white linen – all illuminated by warm candlelight. Large 200-year-old stone jars contain cheese stored in oil, a house speciality on a traditional Montenegrin menu enlivened by a variety of fish dishes. Come for a lazy afternoon meal on the terrace or an intimate dinner inside.

**Bastion Restaurant** ( ☎ 322 116; dishes €6-30) By St Mary's church, Bastion Restaurant is a busy lunchtime venue so it's best to get there early. Any slight indecision in ordering and the waiter will wheel in a platter of fish to tempt you, and if those don't say 'eat me', there's a varied menu with veggie options to choose from. The seafood salad starter is recommended.

**Market** (Jadranski put; ☑ 7am-2pm) Kotor's produce market is just outside the city walls. Big juicy hamburgers can be bought for €1 plus a variety of fruit, bread and cheeses.

**Secondo Porto** ( ☎ 334 342; cnr Budva Rd & Njegoša; admission €2-10; ☑ 11pm-late) Indeed the 'second port' for Kotor's revellers who mass onto the disco's three floors after the old town's bars close. Local and 'imported' star DJs spin the music.

Kotor's cafés and bars, which are quiet places by day, turn werewolf on weekend nights when they throb to techno and other rhythms. Try the **Portobello** ( ☎ 068 407 200; Pjaća od muzejo; ☑ 8am-11am Oct-Apr, 8am-1am May-Sep) and around the corner, the **Karampana** ( ☎ 051 451).

However it's an affordable place commanding the square just inside the city walls where the big plus is not having to lug your bags far into this pedestrian-only city.

**Hotel Marija** ( ☎ 325 062; hotel.marija.kotor@cg.yu; Stari Grad; s/d/tr/q from €44/63/84/112; ☒ ☐ ) Converted from a historic mansion, this boutique hotel is tucked away in the cobbled laneways of the old city. The oak panelling throughout adds a charm, distinction and warmth. A small lobby bar provides conspiratorial planning space for the day's sightseeing, and comfort for tired feet on your return.

## Eating & Drinking

The lanes house several bakeries. Munch on *burek,* pizza slices and, for an afternoon

## Getting There & Away

If you are driving, the shortest way to Herceg Novi is via the ferry at Lepetane (€3.50 per car, every half-hour). The bus station has frequent services along the coast.

The **bus station** ( ☎ 325 809) has frequent, almost hourly, services to the coastal towns and inland to Podgorica. fares are between €1 and €3.

## AROUND KOTOR

**Perast** is a small waterside village about 18km from Kotor and out in the bay is the remarkable, artificial island called **Lady of the Rock**. Every 22 July over the last 550 years, local people have sailed here to drop stones overboard. Their efforts at island creation have been made that bit easier by using a large underwater rock as a foundation, and by the later sinking of 87 captured ships loaded with rocks.

In the village, St Nicholas is an unfinished church housing a small **museum** (admission €0.50; ☺ 9am-5pm) with a collection of vestments, icons and copies of Italian religious art.

Between mid-May and mid-October boats regularly ply between the island and Perast (€1 return); just ask on the waterfront. An hourly minibus service connects with Kotor (€1).

## CETINJE ЦЕТИЊЕ

☎ 086 / pop 19,000

Nestled in a green vale surrounded by rough, grey mountains, Cetinje is an odd mix of former capital and overgrown village where single-storey cottages and stately mansions share the same street.

Several of those mansions, dating from royal times when European ambassadors fêted the social scene, have become museums or schools for art and music. Cetinje Monastery, also with a significant museum, is the town's spiritual home.

Further afield lies some astounding scenery, the panoramic view of Lake Skadar from Pavlova Strana, the old bridge at Rijeka Crnojevića, and the plummeting road down to Kotor.

When that seaside heat has burnt just a little too much, Cetinje is a pleasantly cool and enjoyable day trip up from the coast.

## Orientation & Information

A short walk from the bus stand leads to Balšica Pazar, the main square, with a big wall map to help you get oriented. There are no banks or ATMs here.

## Sights

### MUSEUMS

The former parliament, and Cetinje's most imposing building, is now the **National Museum of Montenegro** ( ☎ 230 555; Novice Cerovića; admission €5; ☺ 9am-5pm Mon-Fri Dec-Apr, to 5pm May-Nov), which comprises a history section and an art gallery. The entrance ticket also covers Cetinje's other museums.

The Art Gallery celebrates Montenegrin and regional art but the prime exhibit is the precious 5th-century Icon of Phillarmos, Madonna and Child. The History exhibits showcase Montenegro from 60,000 BC to the present day. On display are many old books, copies of frescoes, 44 captured Turkish flags and the coat (three bullet holes in the back) of Duke Danilo. He was the last *vladika* of Montenegro and was assassinated in Kotor in 1860 by an aggrieved tribal leader.

The **Biljarda Hall** (Billiard Hall; ☎ 231 050; ☺ 9am-5pm Apr-Oct, to 3pm Mon-Fri Nov-Mar) opposite the National Museum, was the 1832 residence of *vladika* Petar II Petrovic Njegos, and is now a museum dedicated to him. The hall housed the nation's first billiard table, hence the name, and now shelters a fascinating scale relief map of Montenegro created by the Austrians in 1917.

The 1871 **State Museum** ( ☎ 230 555; King Nikola Sq; ☺ 9am-5pm Apr-Oct, to 5pm Mon-Fri Nov-Mar) was the former residence of Nikola Petrović I, last king of Montenegro. Although looted during WWII, sufficient furnishings, many stern portraits and period weapons remain to give a picture of the times. The souvenir shop sells an illustrated map showing the 12 former 18th- and 19th-century embassies in Cetinje. Some were just plain townhouses (Belgium), while others were ornate three-storey mansions with baroque flourishes (Russia).

The new **Ethnographic Museum** (King Nikola Sq; ☺ 9am-3pm Nov-Apr, to 5pm May-Oct) has displays of traditional Montenegrin clothing. If there have ever been reports of yeti in the mountains of Montenegro then it might be down to the black, hooded, long-haired, full-length cape that shepherds wear, and there's an example here.

### CETINJE MONASTERY

Founded in 1484, and rebuilt in 1785, **Cetinje Monastery** ( ☎ 231 021; ☺ 8am-7pm May-Oct) has for the curious, or devout, a portion of the true Cross. But their proudest possession is the mummified right hand of St John the Baptist, set in a bejewelled casket with a little glass

MONTENEGRO

window. You will have to be really persuasive to see it, as it's not normally shown to visitors.

The monastery **museum** contains a copy of the 1494 *Oktoih* (Book of the Eight Voices), one of the oldest collections of liturgical songs in a Slavic language. There's also a collection of portraits, vestments, ancient handwritten texts and gifts from Russian churches. Again, you will have to be persuasive.

There are frequent, almost hourly, services to Budva and Kotor, and inland to Podgorica. Fares are between €1 and €3.

## AROUND CETINJE

At **Rijeka Crnojevića**, 14km from Cetinje, is an old and pretty four-arch pedestrian bridge that spans the tail end of Lake Skadar. The bridge is best seen in the golden glow of the setting sun when the light paints a mirror image in the still waters.

Then 5km further on, **Pavlova Strana** provides a bird's-eye view of a sweeping double-back bend as the lake turns around a mountain spur shaped like a turtle-shell. In the distance, under a two-humped mountain, you should see the town of Virpazar glistening white above the lake.

Twenty kilometres from Cetinje is **Mt Lovćen** (1749m), the 'Black Mountain' that gave Montenegro its Italian name (*monte* means 'mountain', *negro* means 'black'). From the end of the road 461 steps take you to the summit and the mausoleum of Petar II Petrovic Njegoš, revered poet and ruler. From the top are sweeping views of the Bay of Kotor, mountains, coast and reputedly, on a clear morning, Italy.

## HERCEG NOVI ХЕРЦЕГ НОВИ
☎ 088 / pop 34,000

Herceg Novi, another attractive walled town, a day trip from Kotor or Dubrovnik is the nearest town to the Croatian border. The bus station is on the main highway. There's a three-day music festival **Sunčane skale** (Sunny Steps) in the second week of July.

The travel agency **Gorbis** ( ☎ 322 085; Njegoševa 64; s/d/apt from €10/14/20; ☺ 8am-7pm) books accommodation, flight and ferry tickets. **Crnogorska Komercijalna Bank** ( ☎ 322 666; Trg Nikole Đurkovića; ☺ 7am-8pm Mon-Sat) cashes travellers cheques and has an ATM.

### Sleeping & Eating

Private rooms are a good option. If you're here to catch a bus, contact the **Poznanović family**

( ☎ 323 708; s/d €15/20) in the house behind the bus station or contact Gorbis.

While other cafés dot this square **Lokanda** ( ☎ 321 699 10; Đurokevice Trg bb; pizzas €3.50-5 pasta €4 ice cream sundaes €2-2.50) seems to have the public's affection; people come here to meet, take coffee or read the paper. Enjoy a refreshing lemonade prepared from real lemons, or squander your appetite on a pizza or creamy sundae.

There are plenty of very tasty cheap fill-up meals at **Konoba Hercegovina** ( ☎ 332 800; 18 Đurokevice Trg; €2-3), an unpretentious national-cuisine restaurant.

### Getting There & Away

The **bus station** ( ☎ 21 225) has frequent, almost hourly, services along the coast and inland to Podgorica. Fares are between €1 and €3.

A comfortable Centrotrans coach travels daily to Mostar (€9, 4½ hours, at 8am) and onto Sarajevo (€17, seven hours); other services leave at 6.45am, 7.30pm, 9pm and 10pm. Buses also go to Dubrovnik (€9, two hours, at 9.30am and 3.30pm).

# NORTHERN MONTENEGRO

## OSTROG MONASTERY
ОСТРОГ МАНАСТИР

Some 20km south of Nikšić is the **monastery of Ostrog**, precipitously resting on a cliff face, 900m above the Zeta valley. A long windy road off the Podgorica–Nikšić road eventually makes it to a lower car park, from where penitent pilgrims then plod another 3km uphill to the monastery. Nonpilgrims and the pure of heart may drive to the upper carpark.

The monastery was built out of two caves in 1665 to hide Archbishop Vasilije Jovanovic, when he was fleeing from the Turks. Vasilije never left, and praying over his bones is credited with curing the most serious of illnesses, which accounts for the pilgrims. It's also alleged that the Bosnian Serb war criminals Radovan Karadžić and Ratko Mladić have hidden here too.

## DURMITOR NATIONAL PARK
ДУРМИТОР

Magnificent scenery ratchets up to the stupendous in this national park, where ice has carved out a dramatic mountain landscape. Some 18 lakes dot the Durmitor Range with the largest, **Crno jezero** (Black Lake), a pleasant 3km walk from Žabljak. Dominating all is the rounded mass of **Međed** (2287m) rearing up behind the lake and flanked by other peaks, including **Bobotov Kuk** (2523m). Slitting the earth's crust for 80km, the 1.3km-deep **Tara Canyon** is best seen from a rock promontory at Curevac, a €10 taxi ride away from Žabljak.

From December to March, Durmitor is Montenegro's major ski resort while in summer it's a popular place for hiking, rafting and many other activities. The weather is very changeable so be prepared, even in summer.

## Orientation & Information

The centre of Žabljak is where the Nikšić road meets the Đurđevica Tara bridge road. Here there's a **tourist information centre** (☎ 089-361 569; ⏱ 8am-8pm Dec-Mar, to 3pm Apr-Nov), with maps and fine picture books, a taxi stand and a bus stop. The bus station, on the Nikšić road, is at the southern end of town.

Visa cardholders can withdraw cash at the Hotel Jezera where there's also **internet access** (per 30min €1). **Durmitor National Park** (www.durmitorcg .com) has a useful website.

## Sleeping & Eating

All the hotel restaurants are open to non-residents.

**Sveti Đorđije** (☎ /fax 089-361 367; tasaint@cg.yu; Njegoševa bb; s/d from €11/16, 2-/3-/4-person apt from €22/33/44, B&B/half-board from €4/9; ⏱ 9am-9pm) This agency has its finger on Žabljak's private-accommodation pulse.

**Hotel Jezera** (☎ 089-360 206; hmdurmitor@hotmail .com; Njegoševa bb; s with half-board €30-35, d €50-60, tr €60-75; **P**) OK if you're happy in crowds, as this large hotel takes big groups of skiers and summer holidaymakers. The rooms are spacious, there's a pleasant restaurant and an aperitif bar, and a summer swimming pool (nonguests €5).

**Planinka** (☎ 089-361 344; Narodni Heroja 5; s/d/tr B&B €23/40/48; **P**) Much the same as the Jezera but with no swimming pool.

**Restaurant Durmitor** (☎ 060 657 316; Božidara Žugića bb; dishes €4-8) 'Don't hesitate to tell us if you have a complaint', says the menu, which shows a (justifiable) confidence in its food – special home-cooking in what is just a small

wooden hut seating 20 bodies. Should be warm in winter.

**National Restaurant** (☎ 089-261337; Božidara Žugića 8; dishes €4.50-8) A pearl of a place that's small, but not crowded, and offers the best food around. There are broths and hot appetisers with slugs of domestic brandy to defeat the winter chill, or grilled trout and salad in summer. They also have pleasant rooms (singles/doubles €24/48) upstairs if you want some quiet accommodation.

Autocamp Ivan-do and Autocamp Mlinski Potok are camping grounds, without facilities, uphill from the national park office.

## Activities

In winter there's skiing, snowboarding or scooting around behind a dog-drawn team. In summer rafting trips charge through the steeply forested Tara Gorge and spill over countless foaming rapids. The park also offers horse riding, cycling, mountaineering and hiking on various marked trails around the mountain slopes.

**Ski Centar Durmitor** (☎ 089-361 579; www.durmit orcg.com/ski_centar.php; ⏱ 8am-6pm Mon-Sat), opposite Hotel Žabljak, arranges ski passes (€12/70 per day/week), ski lessons (€5 to €10 per lessons) and equipment rental (€5 to €10 per day).

While rafting is a group activity individuals can join in, if there's space available. Contact **Sveti Đorđije** (☎ /fax 089-31 367; tasaint@cg .yu; ⏱ 8am-8pm), which is a fount of information (in English), and offers all-inclusive half-/one-/two-day trips costing €60/120/250.

Sveti Đorđije also organises summer day tours typically for six to eight people (individuals may join) at €30 each to the **Piva Monastery**, which is near the Bosnian border, and has remarkable frescoes.

The **Durmitor National Park office** (☎ 089-360 228; ⏱ 7am-2pm Mon-Fri), next to Hotel Durmitor, has park maps and runs rafting trips (€150 for a group of 10), horse-riding tours (half/whole day €25/50) led by an English-speaking guide, and walking tours.

## Getting There & Away

There are buses to Belgrade (€18, 10 hours, at 9.30am, 11am and 4.30pm) and Podgorica (€6, 3½ hours, at 8am, 8.30am and 12.45pm). However check with the **bus station** (☎ 089-61 318) as schedules change regularly.

# MONTENEGRO DIRECTORY

## ACCOMMODATION

Most Montenegrin hotels, when compared to accomodation on the coast and Žabljak, are quite expensive, so look out for signs saying 'rooms', 'sobe' or 'zimmer'. These can often be of a hotel standard but rather more personable; they range from just a room sharing a bathroom to an apartment with several rooms including a kitchen and private bathroom. The coast has some summer camping grounds as do the national parks.

Where there are seasonal differences we quote the high-season price and, unless otherwise mentioned, the tariff includes breakfast, except in private accommodation, and rooms have private bathrooms. Don't forget to bargain for a discount for several days' stay.

## ACTIVITIES

Durmitor (p536) is Montenegro's main activity centre. In winter it's the country's main resort for skiing, snowboarding and snow sledging by dog or motor. In the summer hikers and climbers flock to the same mountains while the brave and nervous shoot the rapids down below in the Tara canyon.

## BOOKS

Tim Judah has a good eye on the regional scene so try *The Serbs: History, Myth and the Destruction of Yugoslavia*. Sabrina Ramet's *Balkan Babel* is an engaging look at Yugoslavia from Tito to Milošević, while *Montenegro: The Divided Land*, by Thomas Fleming, is an in-depth history of the country.

*Wild Europe*, by Bozidar Jezenik, is a great read and full of quirky nuggets of information, see the boxed text on right for more information.

The fictional work *Montenegro*, by Starling Lawrence, is a turn-of-the-20th-century political potboiler about a British spy lurking around Montenegro, seeking to advantage his country's interests as the Ottoman empire collapses.

## BUSINESS HOURS

Banks keep long hours, often 8am to 7pm weekdays and 8am to noon Saturday. Shops open at 8am and close at 8pm on weekdays

---

**HEAD COUNT**

According to Bozidar Jezenik's *Wild Europe*, the Montenegrins decapitated their dead or wounded enemies, and kept the heads as a sign of their valour. In a society that did not have hereditary rank it was a means of establishing one's social prestige, so the more heads the better. The custom persisted into the mid-19th century and old men well into the 20th century would boast of the heads they had taken in their youth. Visitors may rest assured that now they'll always keep their heads in Montenegro.

---

and 4pm on Saturdays; during summer, shops in holiday resorts will stay open longer and also open on Sundays. Cafés, restaurants and bars usually open around 8am and close at midnight. Most government offices close on Saturday and Sunday.

## DANGERS & ANNOYANCES

Despite new laws, which most seem to ignore, the major annoyance is the incessant smoking in public places.

It's fine to discuss politics but be prepared to listen and ask people's opinions rather than foisting your own upon them.

Check with the police before photographing any official building they're guarding.

## EMBASSIES & CONSULATES

At the time of writing Montenegro still had to establish embassies or consulates in other countries. Your own government's department of foreign affairs or the Serbian Embassy in your country (p777) may be able to help.

### Embassies & Consulates in Montenegro

For countries not on this list, contact their offices in Belgrade, which may still handle representation for Montenegro. See p777 for addresses. The following (except Croatia) are represented in Podgorica.

**Bulgaria** ( ☎ 655 009; 10 Vukitze Mitrovitch)
**Croatia** ( ☎ 082-323 127; Šuranj 248, Kotor)
**France** ( ☎ 665 148; Hercegovacka 10)
**Germany** ( ☎ 201 070; Hercegovacka 10)
**Hungary** ( ☎ 602880; Kralje Nikole 104)
**Romania** ( ☎ 618 040; 40 Vukice Mitrovic)
**UK** ( ☎ 205 461; Trg Vektra, zgrada Cijevna Komerc 11/3)
**USA** ( ☎ 225 417; Kruševac bb)

## HOLIDAYS

Orthodox churches celebrate Easter one to five weeks later than other churches. Public holidays in Montenegro include the following:

**New Year** 1 and 2 January
**Orthodox Christmas** 7 January
**International Labour Days** 1 and 2 May
**Statehood Day** 13 July

## INTERNET RESOURCES

**Montenegro Tourist Organisation** (www.visit -montenegro.cg.yu)
**Montenegro Beauty** (www.montenegrobeauty.com) Tourist information.
**Montenegrin Association of America** (www.monte -negro.org) Has a few worthwhile pages, some out of date.
**Government of the Republic of Montenegro** (www.gom.cg.yu)

## MONEY

Montenegro uses the euro. ATMs accepting Visa, MasterCard and their variants are widespread in major towns. MasterCard, Visa and Diners Club are widely accepted by businesses too. **Western Union** (www.westernunion.com) transfers can be made at most banks and major post offices. Most banks cash hard-currency travellers cheques and again the euro is preferable.

## POST

Parcels should be taken unsealed to the main post office for inspection. Allow time to check the post office's repackaging and complete the transaction. You can receive mail, addressed poste restante, in all towns for a small charge.

## TELEPHONE

Press the i button on public phones for dialling commands in English. The international operator is ☎ 901.

### Mobile Phones

Numbers starting with ☎ 069 reputedly gives the best service and a starter pack containing

---

**EMERGENCY NUMBERS**

- Police ☎ 92
- Ambulance ☎ 94
- Fire brigade ☎ 93
- Motoring Assistance ☎ 987
- Road Conditions ☎ 9807

---

a SIM card costs €10, including €5 worth of calls. We had occasional problems with text messages to and from abroad.

### Phonecards

Phone cards worth €2 and €5 don't give enough time for a decent international call, so use telephone centres at post offices.

## VISAS

Tourist visas are not required for citizens of most European countries, Australia, Canada, Israel, Japan, New Zealand, and the USA. South Africans and everyone else need to apply for visas. The website of the Montenegrin government (www.gom.cg.yu) has details.

## WOMEN TRAVELLERS

Other than a cursory interest shown in them by men, solo women should find travelling is hassle-free and easy in Montenegro.

# TRANSPORT IN MONTENEGRO

## GETTING THERE & AWAY
### Air

Apart from holiday charter flights, Montenegro is not well served by international airlines; this may change with independence. Currently Adria and Austrian Airlines are the only regional airlines serving international hubs like London and Vienna. European discount airlines have yet to fly to Montenegro and currently Dubrovnik and Split (Croatia) are the nearest airports.

Montenegro is served by **Podgorica airport** (TGD; ☎ 081-243 726) and **Tivat airport** (TIV; ☎ 082-673 551); only JAT and Montenegro Airlines fly from Tivat.

**Adria Airlines** (code JP; ☎ 081-241 154; www.adria -airways.com)
**Austrian Airlines** (code OS; ☎ 081-606 170; www .aua.com)
**JAT** (code JU; ☎ 081-664 740; www.jat.com)
**Montenegro Airlines** (code YM; ☎ 081-664 411; www.montenegro-airlines.cg.yu)

### Land
#### BORDER CROSSINGS

You can easily enter Montenegro by land from any of its neighbours and no bus changes are required. Entering Albania involves a €10 fee.

### BICYCLE

You will have no problems bringing a bicycle into Montenegro but remember it's a hilly country. There are few cyclists so road-users are not cycle savvy.

### BUS

There's a well-developed bus service along the coast to Dubrovnik and Split (see p531) plus a service from Herceg Novi to Mostar and Sarajevo in Bosnia and Hercegovina (p536). Twice daily minibuses ply from Ulcinj to Shkodër, Albania (see p531). Every bus station will have services to Belgrade in Serbia; on average the journey time is nine hours and the fare €20.

### CAR & MOTORCYCLE

Drivers need an International Driving Permit, and vehicles need Green Card (international third-party) insurance, or insurance (from €80 a month) must be bought at the border.

### TRAIN

Montenegro's only international rail connection is to Belgrade, Serbia, from Bar on the coast via Sutomore and Podgorica. For onward connections see p779.

## Sea

Ferries sail between Bar, Kotor and Italy, see p530.

---

**DRIVING OFFENCES**  *Patrick Horton*

Within 10 minutes of driving away from the Podgorica hire car office I copped a €15 fine from a traffic policeman for not obeying a turn right arrow. That was in 2004; in 2006 I managed 30 minutes before being pulled over. I was told that I had committed two offences; my fog lights were on as well as the parking lights that the car hire firm told me were now mandatory for daylight driving. I handed over my documents, which the policeman clutched as tightly as a wad of euro in a high wind. He read them and announced that I would have to go back to the post office in Podgorica, pay the fine and return to him with the receipt before I could have the documents. No way, I thought, so I put on my best dumb foreigner act and he relented. Later I found out that he had no right to retain my documents but I never found out what the second offence was.

---

## GETTING AROUND

### Bicycle

Cyclists are a rare species even in the cities. There are no special provisions for them and don't expect drivers to be careful around cyclists.

### Bus

The bus service is extensive and reliable and covers all of Montenegro. The usual fare between towns is about €2; luggage carried below is charged at €0.50 per piece.

### Car & Motorcycle

Independent travel is an ideal way to gad about and discover the country. Beware of traffic police with speed radar guns; they also do spot checks of your documents and the car.

#### AUTOMOBILE ASSOCIATIONS

The **Auto-Moto Savez Serbia and Montenegro** (Serbia & Montenegro Automotive Association; ☎ 9800; www.amsj .co.yu) web page has details on Montenegrin road conditions.

#### HIRE

The major European car-hire companies have a presence in Podgorica but **Meridian Rent a Car** ( ☎ 081-234 944, 069 316 66), which has offies in Podgorica, Budva and Bar, is a good, cheap option.

Make sure the tyres are good and all lights and indicators work. Cars are required to carry a first-aid kit, an emergency stop warning triangle, spare tyre and spare bulbs; the police can fine you for not having these.

#### ROAD RULES

In Montenegro, driving is on the right, seat belts must be worn and the drink-driving limit is 0.05%. Speed limits are 80km/h on main roads and 40km/h in urban areas. A recently introduced law requires you to drive with your parking lights on during the day.

### Train

At the time of research **Jugoslovenske Železnice** (JŽ, Yugoslav Railways; www.yurail.co.yu, in Serbian) were operating the trains from Belgrade that run along the highly scenic line down through Podgorica to Bar and terminating at Sutomore; their website gives timetable details. Other railway lines in Montenegro were not operational but may one day form a network for a Montenegrin Railways organisation.

# Poland

A flat, fertile nation in the centre of Europe, often surrounded by conquest-happy empires, can expect life to be turbulent at times. And that's been the experience of Poland, as it's grappled with centuries of war, invasion and foreign occupation. Nothing, however, has succeeded in suppressing the Poles' strong sense of nationhood and cultural identity, as exemplified by the ancient royal capital of Kraków, with its breathtaking castle, and bustling Warsaw, with its painstaking postwar reconstruction of its devastated Old Town.

Although early euphoria at joining the EU has subsided into a more realistic expectation of membership, there's a distinct sense of confidence and optimism in the big cities, and among young people in particular. As a result, regional centres such as urbane Gdańsk, cultured Wrocław and lively Poznań exude a cosmopolitan energy that's a heady mix of old and new.

Away from the cities, Poland is a diverse land, from its northern sandy beaches and magnificent southern mountains to the lost-in-time forests of the east. And everywhere there are seldom-visited towns to discover, with their own ruined castles, picturesque squares and historic churches.

Poland is still good value for travellers and has a transport system that makes it easy to get around. As Poland continues to reconcile its rediscovered European identity with its hard-won political and cultural freedoms, it's a fascinating time to visit this beautiful country.

## FAST FACTS

- **Area** 312, 685 sq km
- **Capital** Warsaw
- **Currency** złoty; €1=3.98zł; US$1=3.13zł; UK£1=5.92zł; A$1=2.35zł; C$1 = 2.81zł; Ą100=2.68zł; NZ$1=2.06zł
- **Famous for** Chopin, Copernicus, Marie Curie, Solidarity, vodka
- **Official Language** Polish
- **Phrases** *dzień dobry* (good morning/afternoon), *dziękuję* (thank you), *proszę* (please), *Gdzie jest dworzec autobusowy/kolejowy?* (Where's the bus/train station?)
- **Population** 38 million
- **Telephone Codes** country code ☎ 48; international access code ☎ 00
- **Visas** not required for EU citizens; US, Canadian, New Zealand and Australian citizens do not need visas for stays of less than 90 days

POLAND

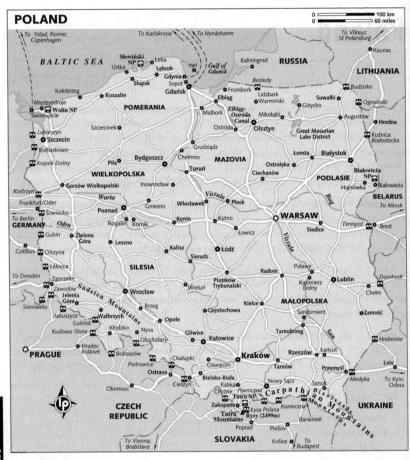

POLAND

## HIGHLIGHTS

- Experience the beauty and history of Kraków's **Wawel Castle** (p561)
- Meet European bison and other magnificent fauna at **Białowieża National Park** (p559)
- Soak up the cosmopolitan vibe of **Gdańsk** (p597) and take a dip in the Baltic at nearby **Sopot** (p602)
- Enjoy the skiing or hiking life of the **Tatra Mountains** (p574)
- Discover Warsaw's tragic wartime history at the **Warsaw Rising Museum** (p553)

## ITINERARIES

- **One Week** Spend a day exploring Warsaw with a stroll round the Old Town and a

stop at the Warsaw Rising Museum. The next day, head to Kraków for three days, visiting the Old Town, Wawel Castle, the former Jewish district of Kazimierz, and Wieliczka. Take a day trip to Oświęcim, then head on to Zakopane for two days.

- **Two Weeks** Follow the above itinerary, then on the eighth day travel to Wrocław for two days. Progress north to Toruń for a day, then onward to Gdańsk for two days, exploring the Old Town and visiting Westerplatte. Wind down with a couple of days at the seaside in Sopot.

## CLIMATE & WHEN TO GO

Poland's weather can be unpredictable. Summer is usually warm and sunny, with July the hottest month, but it's also the season with the highest rainfall. Spring and autumn are pleasantly warm but can also be wet. Snow can fall anywhere in Poland between December and March, lingering until April or even May in the mountains.

The tourist season runs roughly from May to September, peaking in July and August. Many Polish families go on holidays during these two months, so transport is crowded and accommodation limited. Most theatres and concert halls are also closed at this time. From midautumn to midspring, outdoor activities are less prominent and many camping grounds and youth hostels are closed. See the climate charts on p911, for more information.

## HISTORY

Poland's history started with the Polanians (People of the Plains). During the early Middle Ages, these Western Slavs moved into the flatlands between the Vistula and Odra Rivers. Mieszko I, Duke of the Polanians, adopted Christianity in 966 and embarked on a campaign of conquest. A papal edict in 1025 led to Mieszko's son Bolesław Chrobry (Boleslaus the Brave) being crowned Poland's first king.

Poland's early success proved fragile, and encroachment from Germanic peoples led to the relocation of the royal capital from Poznań

---

**HOW MUCH?**

- **Night in a hostel** 45zł

- **Night in a midrange double room** 200zł

- **Three-course restaurant meal for two** 120zł

- **Postcard** 1zł

- **Postage stamp** 3zł

**LONELY PLANET INDEX**

- **Litre of petrol** 3.75zł

- **Litre of water** 2zł

- **Beer** 5-7zł

- **Souvenir T-shirt** 35zł

- **Street snack** (*zapiekanka*, a toasted roll with cheese, mushrooms and tomato sauce) 2-5zł

---

to Kraków in 1038. More trouble loomed in 1226 when the Prince of Mazovia invited the Teutonic Knights to help convert the pagan tribes of the north. These Germanic crusaders used the opportunity to create their own state along the Baltic coast. The south had its own invaders to contend with, and Kraków was attacked by Tatars twice in the mid-13th century.

The kingdom prospered under Kazimierz III 'the Great' (1333–1370). During this period of rebirth, many new towns sprang up, while Kraków blossomed into one of Europe's leading cultural centres.

When the daughter of Kazimierz's nephew married the Grand Duke of Lithuania, Jagiełło, Poland and Lithuania were united as the largest state in Europe, stretching from the Baltic to the Black Sea.

The Renaissance was introduced to Poland by the enlightened King Zygmunt during the 16th century, as he lavishly patronised the arts and sciences. By asserting that the Earth travelled around the sun, Nicolaus Copernicus revolutionised the field of astronomy in 1543.

The 18th century was a period of disaster and decline for Poland. First it was subject to Swedish and Russian invasions, and at century's end it faced partition by surrounding empires. In 1773 Russia, Prussia and Austria seized Polish territory in the First Partition; by the time the Third Partition was completed in 1795, Poland had vanished from the map of Europe.

Although the country remained divided through the entire 19th century, Poles steadfastly maintained their culture. Finally, upon the end of WWI the old imperial powers dissolved, and a sovereign Polish state was restored. Very soon, however, Poland was again at war. Under the command of Marshal Jozef Piłsudski, Poland defended its eastern territories from long-time enemy Russia, now transformed into the Soviet Union and determined to spread its revolution westward. After two years of impressive fighting by the outnumbered Poles, an armistice was signed, retaining Vilnius and Lviv within Poland.

Though Polish institutions and national identity flourished during the interwar period, disaster soon struck again. On 1 September 1939, a Nazi blitzkrieg rained down from the west; soon after, the Soviets invaded

POLAND

---

**TOP FIVE REMNANTS OF COMMUNISM**

It's been less than two decades since the end of communist rule in Poland, but evidence of the era is fading fast. If you want to delve into the days of the Eastern Bloc, check out these remains.

- Nowa Huta – Everyone visits Kraków for its medieval splendour, but there's another side to the former royal capital that few tourists see. Catch a tram to the eastern suburb of Nowa Huta for a glimpse of the planned 'workers' paradise' district, built in the 1950s to counter the influence of the city's religious and intellectual elite.

- Stadion Dziesięciolecia – Just over the river from central Warsaw is the 10th Anniversary Stadium, constructed in the 1950s from the rubble of buildings destroyed in WWII. Initially the jewel in communist Poland's sporting crown, it was abandoned as a sporting venue in the 1980s, and now houses a huge open-air market.

- Warszawa Centralna – Opened by communist bigwigs in 1975, Warsaw's massive main train station was seen as a triumph of modern socialism over the inefficient structures of the past. However, current opinion is mixed. Many travellers have experienced the disorientating sensation of traversing its labyrinthine corridors, and Poles have pondered whether it should be torn down.

- Gdańsk Shipyards – Constructed after WWII, this sprawling industrial site north of Gdańsk's Old Town was originally known as the Lenin Shipyards. It hit the international headlines as the birthplace of the Solidarity trade union in 1980, and became the hub of the decade-long struggle to overthrow the communist system.

- Milk bars – The *bar mleczny* is a humble institution which survived the regime that founded it. Milk bars were conceived by the communist government as low-cost cafeterias for workers, serving basic vegetarian dishes. Nowadays they're a living reminder of the era, and a great place to find straightforward, unfussy Polish food.

---

Poland from the east, dividing the country with Germany. This agreement didn't last long, as Hitler soon transformed Poland into a staging ground for the Nazi invasion of the Soviet Union. Six million Polish inhabitants died during WWII (including the country's three million Jews), brutally annihilated in death camps. At the war's end, Poland's borders were redrawn yet again. The Soviet Union kept the eastern territories and extended the country's western boundary at the expense of Germany. These border changes were accompanied by the forced resettlement of more than a million Poles, Germans and Ukrainians.

Peacetime brought more repression. After WWII, Poland endured four decades of Soviet-dominated communist rule, punctuated by waves of protests, most notably the paralysing strikes of 1980–81, led by the Solidarity trade union. Finally, in the open elections of 1989, the communists fell from power and in 1990 Solidarity leader Lech Wałęsa became Poland's first democratically elected president.

The postcommunist transition brought radical changes, which induced new social hardships and political crises. But within a decade Poland had built the foundations for a market economy, and reoriented its foreign relations towards the West. In March 1999, Poland was granted full NATO membership, and it joined the EU in May 2004.

Despite a strong economy, the nation swung to centre-right parties in the 2005 parliamentary elections, partly in reaction to continuing high unemployment, government spending cuts and corruption scandals. The new political tone was underlined a few weeks later by the presidential election victory of Lech Kaczyński, well known for his social conservatism.

## PEOPLE

For centuries Poland was a multicultural country, home to large Jewish, German and Ukrainian communities. Its Jewish population was particularly large, and once numbered more than three million. However, after Nazi genocide and the forced resettlements that followed WWII, the Jewish population declined to 10,000 and Poland became an ethnically homogeneous country, with some 98% of the population being ethnic Poles.

More than 60% of the citizens live in towns and cities. Warsaw is by far the largest urban settlement, followed by Łódź, Kraków, Wrocław, Poznań and Gdańsk. Upper Silesia (around Katowice) is the most densely inhabited area, while the northeastern border regions remain the least populated.

Between five and 10 million Poles live outside Poland. This émigré community, known as 'Polonia', is located mainly in the USA (particularly Chicago).

Poles are friendly and polite, but not overly formal. The way of life in large urban centres increasingly resembles Western styles and manners. In the countryside, however, a more conservative culture dominates, evidenced by traditional gender roles and strong family ties. In both urban and rural settings, many Poles are devoutly religious.

The Poles' sense of personal space may be a bit cosier than you are accustomed to – you may notice this trait when queuing for tickets or manoeuvring along city streets. When greeting each other, Polish men are passionate about shaking hands. Polish women often shake hands with men, but the man should always wait for the woman to extend her hand first.

## RELIGION

Roman Catholicism is the dominant Christian denomination, adhered to by more than 80% of Poles. The Orthodox church's followers constitute about 1% of the population, mostly living along a narrow strip on the eastern frontier.

The election of Karol Wojtyła, the archbishop of Kraków, as Pope John Paul II in 1978, and his triumphal visit to his homeland a year later, significantly enhanced the status of the church in Poland. The country was proud of the late Pope: even now his image can be seen in public places and private homes throughout the country.

The overthrow of communism was as much a victory for the Church as it was for democracy. The fine line between the Church and the state is often blurred in Poland, and the Church is a powerful lobby on social issues. Some Poles have grown wary of the Church's increasing influence in society and politics, but Poland remains one of Europe's most religious countries, and packed-out churches are not uncommon.

## ARTS
### Literature

Poland has inherited a rich literary tradition dating from the 15th century, though its modern voice was shaped in the 19th century, during the long period of foreign occupation. It was a time for nationalist writers such as the poet Adam Mickiewicz (1798–1855), and Henryk Sienkiewicz (1846–1916), who won a Nobel prize in 1905 for *Quo Vadis?* This nationalist tradition was revived in the communist era when Czesław Miłosz was awarded a Nobel prize in 1980 for *The Captive Mind*.

At the turn of the 20th century, the avant-garde 'Young Poland' movement in art and literature developed in Kraków. The most notable representatives of this movement were the writer Stanisław Wyspiański (1869–1907), also famous for his stained-glass work; the playwright Stanisław Ignacy Witkiewicz (1885–1939), commonly known as Witkacy; and the Nobel laureate Władysław Reymont (1867–1925). In 1996, Wisława Szymborska (b 1923) also received a Nobel prize for her ironic poetry.

### Music

The most famous Polish musician was undoubtedly Frédéric Chopin (1810–49), whose music displays the melancholy and nostalgia that became hallmarks of the national style. Stanisław Moniuszko (1819–72) injected a Polish flavour into 19th-century Italian opera music by introducing folk songs and dances to the stage. His *Halka* (1858), about a peasant girl abandoned by a young noble, is a staple of the national opera houses.

### Visual Arts

Poland's most renowned painter was Jan Matejko (1838–93), whose monumental historical paintings hang in galleries throughout the country. Wojciech Kossak (1857–1942) is another artist who documented Polish history; he is best remembered for the colossal painting *Panorama of Racławicka,* on display in Wrocław (p584).

A long-standing Polish craft is the fashioning of jewellery from amber. Amber is a fossil resin of vegetable origin that comes primarily from the Baltic region, and appears in a variety of colours from pale yellow to reddish brown. The best places to buy it are Gdańsk, Kraków and Warsaw.

POLAND

Polish poster art has received international recognition; the best selection of poster galleries is in Warsaw and Kraków.

## Cinema

Poland has produced several world-famous film directors. The most notable is Andrzej Wajda, who received an Honorary Award at the 1999 Academy Awards. Western audiences are probably more familiar with the work of Roman Polański, who directed critically acclaimed films such as *Rosemary's Baby* and *Chinatown*. In 2002 Polański released the incredibly moving film *The Pianist*, which was filmed in Poland and set in the Warsaw Ghetto of WWII. The film went on to win three Oscars and the Cannes Palme d'Or. The late Krzysztof Kieślowski is best known for the trilogy *Three Colours Trilogy*.

## ENVIRONMENT
### The Land

Poland covers an area of 312,677 sq km, approximately as large as the UK and Ireland put together, and is bordered by seven states and one sea.

The northern edge of Poland meets the Baltic Sea. This broad, 524km-long coastline is spotted with sand dunes and seaside lakes. Also concentrated in the northeast are many postglacial lakes – more than any country in Europe except Finland.

The southern border is defined by the mountain ranges of the Sudetes and Carpathians. Poland's highest mountains are the rocky Tatras, a section of the Carpathian Range it shares with Slovakia. The highest peak of the Polish Tatras is Mt Rysy (2499m).

The area in between is a vast plain, sectioned by wide north-flowing rivers. Poland's longest river is the Vistula (Wisła), which winds 1047km from the Tatras to the Baltic.

## Wildlife & National Parks

About 28% of Poland is covered by forest and, admirably, up to 130 sq km of new forest is planted each year. Some 60% of the forests are pine trees, but the share of deciduous species, such as oak, beech and birch, is increasing.

Poland's fauna includes hare, red deer, wild boar and, less abundantly, elk, brown bear and wildcat. European bison, which once inhabited Europe in large numbers, were brought to the brink of extinction early in the 20th century and a few hundred now live in Białowieża

National Park. The Great Masurian Lakes district attracts a vast array of bird life, such as storks and cormorants. The eagle, though rarely seen today, is Poland's national bird and appears on the Polish emblem.

Poland has 23 national parks, but they cover less than 1% of the country. No permit is necessary to visit these parks, but most have small admission fees. Camping in the parks is sometimes allowed, but only at specified sites. Poland also has a network of less strictly preserved areas called 'landscape parks'. About 105 of these parks, covering 6% of Poland, are scattered throughout the country.

## FOOD & DRINK

The cheapest place to eat Polish food is a *bar mleczny* (milk bar), a no-frills, self-service cafeteria, popular with budget-conscious locals and backpackers alike. Up the scale, the number and variety of *restauracja* (restaurants) has ballooned in recent years, especially in the big cities. Pizzerias have also become phenomenally popular with Poles. And though Polish cuisine features plenty of meat, there are vegetarian restaurants to be found in most cities.

Menus usually have several sections: *zupy* (soups), *dania drugie* (main courses) and *dodatki* (accompaniments). The price of the main course may not include a side dish – such as potatoes, fries and salads – which you choose separately (and pay extra for) from the *dodatki* section. Also note that the price for some dishes (particularly fish and poultry) is often listed per 100g, so the price will depend on the total weight of the fish or meat.

Poles start their day with *śniadanie* (breakfast); and the most important and substantial meal of the day, *obiad*, is normally eaten between 2pm and 5pm. The third meal is *kolacja* (supper). Most restaurants open from midmorning until midnight, though milk bars and snack bars are open from early morning.

## Staples & Specialities

Various cultures have influenced Polish cuisine, including Jewish, Ukrainian, Russian, Hungarian and German. Polish food is hearty and filling, abundant in potatoes and dumplings, and rich in meat.

Poland's most famous dishes are *bigos* (sauerkraut with a variety of meats), *pierogi* (ravioli-like dumplings stuffed with cottage cheese, minced meat, or cabbage and wild mushrooms) and *barszcz* (red beetroot soup, better known by the Russian word *borscht*).

Hearty soups such as *żurek* (sour soup with sausage and hard-boiled eggs) are a highlight of Polish cuisine. Main dishes are made with pork, including *golonka* (boiled pig's knuckle served with horseradish) and *schab pieczony* (roast loin of pork seasoned with prunes and herbs). *Gołąbki* (cabbage leaves stuffed with mince and rice) is a tasty alternative.

*Placki ziemniaczane* (potato pancakes) and *naleśniki* (crepes) are also popular dishes.

### Drinks

Poles claim the national drink, *wódka* (vodka), was invented in their country. It's usually drunk neat and comes in a number of flavours, including *myśliwska* (flavoured with juniper berries), *wiśniówka* (with cherries) and *jarzębiak* (with rowanberries). The most famous variety is *żubrówka* (bison vodka), flavoured with grass from the Białowieża Forest. Other notable spirits include *krupnik* (honey liqueur), *śliwowica* (plum brandy) and *goldwasser* (sweet liqueur containing flakes of gold leaf).

Poles also appreciate the taste of *zimne piwo* (cold beer); the top brands, found everywhere, include Żywiec and Okocim, while regional brands are available in every city.

# WARSAW

☎ 022 / pop 1.69 million

Poles and visitors alike agree: Warsaw (Warszawa in Polish, vah-*shah*-vah) is different. The business centre of Poland, its postcommunist commercial character is symbolised by capitalist towers rivalling the Stalinist-era Palace of Culture for prominence on the skyline. A spin-off from all this international trade is the city's excellent array of dining, entertainment and nightlife options.

The city's tumultuous past is reflected in its present-day appearance. The beautiful Old Town district was devastated in WWII but reconstructed with unerring accuracy, and is the most attractive part of the city. The nearby Royal Way, and the former Royal Parks, are also pleasant places to linger. Other districts feature communist-era concrete blocks and are less agreeable.

With its many museums, galleries and entertainment options, Warsaw can keep visitors

occupied for several days. As it's also Poland's central transport hub, the capital makes a good base for short trips into the surrounding countryside.

## HISTORY

The Mazovian dukes were the first rulers of Warsaw, establishing it as their stronghold in the 14th century. The city's strategic central location led to the capital being transferred from Kraków to Warsaw when Poland and Lithuania were unified in 1569.

Although the 18th century was a period of catastrophic decline for the Polish state, Warsaw underwent a period of prosperity during this period. Many magnificent churches, palaces and parks were built, and cultural and artistic life blossomed. The first (shortlived) constitution in Europe was instituted in Warsaw in 1791.

In the 19th century Warsaw declined in status to became a mere provincial city of the Russian empire. Following WWI, the city was reinstated as the capital of a newly independent Poland and once more began to thrive. Following the Warsaw Rising of 1944 the city centre was devastated, and the entire surviving population forcibly evacuated. Upon war's end, the people of Warsaw returned to the capital, and set about rebuilding its historic heart.

## ORIENTATION

The Vistula River divides Warsaw into two very different areas. The western left-bank sector features the city centre, including the Old Town, the historic nucleus of Warsaw. Almost all tourist attractions, as well as most tourist facilities, are on this side of the river. The eastern part of Warsaw, the suburb of Praga, has no major sights and sees few tourists.

If arriving by train, Warszawa Centralna station is, as the name suggests, within walking distance of the city centre and major attractions. If you arrive by bus at Dworzec Centralny PKS station, hop on a train from the adjoining Warszawa Zachodnia station into the centre. From the Dworzec PKS Stadion, you can catch a train to Warszawa Centralna from the Stadion train station.

## INFORMATION
### Bookshops

**American Bookstore** (Map p550; ☎ 827 48 52; ul Nowy Świat 61) Offers a wide selection of Lonely Planet titles, English publications and maps.

POLAND

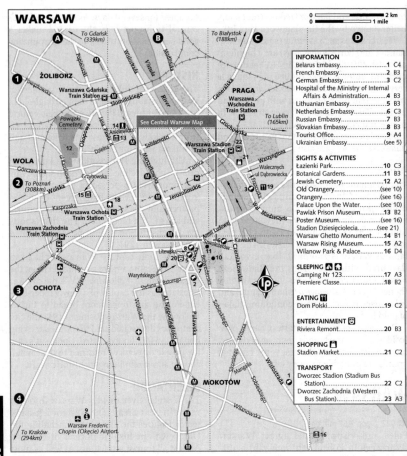

## WARSAW

| INFORMATION | |
| --- | --- |
| Belarus Embassy | **1** C4 |
| French Embassy | **2** B3 |
| German Embassy | **3** C2 |
| Hospital of the Ministry of Internal | |
| Affairs & Administration | **4** B3 |
| Lithuanian Embassy | **5** B3 |
| Netherlands Embassy | **6** C3 |
| Russian Embassy | **7** B3 |
| Slovakian Embassy | **8** B3 |
| Tourist Office | **9** A4 |
| Ukrainian Embassy | (see 5) |

| SIGHTS & ACTIVITIES | |
| --- | --- |
| Łazienki Park | **10** C3 |
| Botanical Gardens | **11** B3 |
| Jewish Cemetery | **12** A2 |
| Old Orangery | (see 10) |
| Orangery | (see 16) |
| Palace Upon the Water | (see 10) |
| Pawiak Prison Museum | **13** B2 |
| Poster Museum | (see 16) |
| Stadion Dziesięciolecia | (see 21) |
| Warsaw Ghetto Monument | **14** B1 |
| Warsaw Rising Museum | **15** A2 |
| Wilanow Park & Palace | **16** D4 |

| SLEEPING | |
| --- | --- |
| Camping Nr 123 | **17** A3 |
| Premiere Classe | **18** B2 |

| EATING | |
| --- | --- |
| Dom Polski | **19** C2 |

| ENTERTAINMENT | |
| --- | --- |
| Riviera Remont | **20** B3 |

| SHOPPING | |
| --- | --- |
| Stadion Market | **21** C2 |

| TRANSPORT | |
| --- | --- |
| Dworzec Stadion (Stadium Bus | |
| Station) | **22** C2 |
| Dworzec Zachodnia (Western | |
| Bus Station) | **23** A3 |

**EMPiK Megastore** Galeria Centrum (Map p550; ☎ 551 44 86; ul Marszałkowska 116/122); ul Nowy Œwiat (Map p550; ul Nowy Świat 15/17) For a large array of foreign newspapers and magazines, with several other branches around town.

## Emergency

**Ambulance** ☎ 999
**Fire** ☎ 998
**Police** ☎ 997, from mobiles ☎ 112

## Internet Access

Expect to pay around 9zł to 10zł per hour for internet access in Warsaw. Several convenient but dingy internet cafés are also located within Warszawa Centralna train station.

**Casablanca** (Map p550; ☎ 828 14 47; ul Krakowskie Przedmieście 4/6; ☼ 9am-1am Mon-Fri, 10am-2am

Sat, 10am-midnight Sun) Enter around the corner off ul Oboźna.

**Internet Café** (Map p550; ☎ 826 60 62; ul Nowy Świat 18/20; ☼ 9am-11pm Mon-Fri, 10am-10pm Sat & Sun)

**Verso Internet** (Map p550; ☎ 831 28 54; ul Freta 17; ☼ 8am-8pm Mon-Fri, 9am-5pm Sat, 10am-4pm Sun) Enter from the back of the building, off ul Świętojerska.

## Medical Services

**Apteka Grabowskiego** (Map p550; ☎ 825 69 86; Warszawa Centralna train station) An all-night pharmacy.

**CM Medical Center** (Map p550; ☎ 458 70 00; 3rd fl, Marriott Hotel, al Jerozolimskie 65/79) Offers specialist doctors, carries out laboratory tests and makes house calls.

**Dental-Med** (Map p550; ☎ 629 59 38; ul Hoża 27) A central dental practice.

POLAND

**Hospital of the Ministry of Internal Affairs & Administration** (Map p548; ☎ 602 15 78; ul Wołoska 137) A hospital preferred by government officials and diplomats.

## Money

Foreign-exchange offices *(kantors)* and ATMs are easy to find around the city centre. *Kantors* open 24 hours can be found at the Warszawa Centralna train station, and either side of the immigration counters at the airport, but exchange rates at these places are about 10% lower than in the city centre. Avoid changing money in the Old Town, where the rates are even lower. The following places change major-brand travellers cheques, offer cash advances on Visa and MasterCard, and have ATMs that take just about every known credit card.

**American Express** (Map p550; Marriott Hotel, al Jerozolimskie 65/79)

**Bank Pekao** (Map p550; Krakowskie Przedmieście 1) Bank Pekao has a dozen branches in the city, including one next to the Church of the Holy Cross.

**PBK Bank** (Map p550; ground fl, Palace of Culture & Science Bldg)

**PKO Bank** (Map p550; plac Bankowy 2).

## Post

**Main post office** (Map p550; ul Świętokrzyska 31/33; ☺ 24hr)

## Tourist Information

Each tourist office provides free city maps and free booklets, such as the handy *Warsaw in Short* and the *Visitor*, sells maps of other Polish cities, and helps book hotel rooms. They also sell the Warsaw Tourist Card (one/three days 35/65zł), which gives free or discounted access to museums, and includes public transport and discounts at some theatres, sports centres and restaurants.

Free monthly tourist magazines worth seeking out include *Poland: What, Where,*

*When, What's Up in Warsaw* and *Welcome to Warsaw*. The comprehensive monthly *Warsaw Insider* (8zł) and *Warsaw in Your Pocket* (5zł) are also useful.

**Official tourist organisation** ( ☎ 9431; www.warsawtour.pl) Has several branches, including: Royal Way (Map p550; ul Krakowskie Przedmieście 39; ☺ 9am-8pm May-Sep, 9am-6pm Oct-Apr) **Central office;** Okęcie and Etiuda airport arrivals halls (Map p548; ☺ 8am-8pm May-Sep, 8am-6pm Oct-Apr); main hall of Warszawa Centralna train station (Map p550; ☺ 8am-8pm May-Sep, 8am-6pm Oct-Apr).

**Warsaw Tourist Information Centre** (Map p550; ☎ 635 18 81; www.wcit.waw.pl; pl Zamkowy 1/13; ☺ 9am-6pm Mon-Fri, 10am-6pm Sat, 11am-6pm Sun May-Sep; 9am-6pm Mon-Thu, 9am-8pm Fri, 10am-8pm Sat, 11am-8pm Sun Oct-Apr) Helpful privately-run tourist office in the Old Town.

## Travel Agencies

**Almatur** (Map p550; ☎ 826 35 12; www.almatur.pl; ul Kopernika 23)

**Orbis Travel** (Map p550; ☎ 827 72 65; ul Bracka 16) Has branches all over Warsaw, as well as at the airport.

**Our Roots** (Map p550; ☎ 0501 23 61 17; ul Twarda 6) Warsaw's primary agency for anyone interested in tours about local Jewish heritage.

**Trakt** (Map p550; ☎ 827 80 68; www.trakt.com.pl; ul Kredytowa 6) Guided tours of Warsaw and beyond, in English and several other languages.

## SIGHTS
### Old Town

The main gateway to the Old Town is **Plac Zamkowy** (Castle Square). All the buildings here were superbly rebuilt from their foundations after WWII, earning the Old Town a place on Unesco's World Heritage List. Within the square stands the **Monument to Sigismund III Vasa**, who moved the capital from Kraków to Warsaw.

The dominant feature of the square is the massive 13th-century **Royal Castle** (Map p550;

**POLAND**

---

### WARSAW IN TWO DAYS

Wander through the **Old Town** (above), and tour the **Royal Castle** (above), having lunch afterwards at **Karczma Gessler** (p547). Walk along the **Royal Way** (p551), dropping into the **Chopin Museum** (p552) en route. Take the lift to the top of the **Palace of Culture & Science** (p552) for views of the city, before promenading through the nearby **Saxon Gardens** (p552).

The next day, visit the **Warsaw Rising Museum** (p553) in the morning, followed by lunch at one of the many restaurants along ul Nowy Świat. Spend the afternoon exploring **Łazienki Park** (p552), before sipping a cocktail at **Sense** (p556). Finish off the day with a visit to the nightclub district around ul Mazowiecka, or enjoy a performance at **Teatr Wielki** (p557).

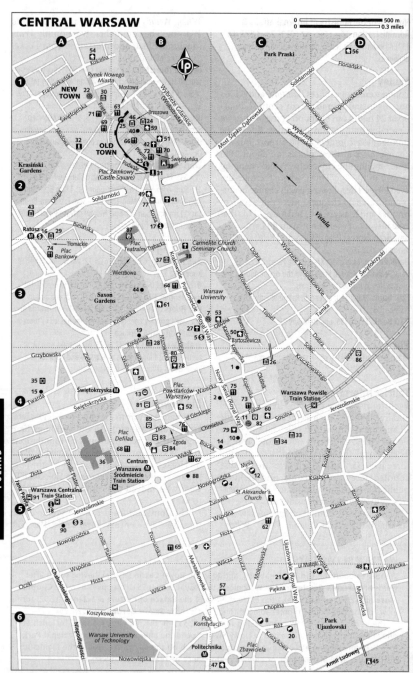

# CENTRAL WARSAW

POLAND

☎ 657 21 70; plac Zamkowy 4; adult/child 18/12zł, free Sun; 🕑 10am-4pm Mon-Sat, 11am-4pm Sun, closed Mon Oct-Apr), also reconstructed after the war. The highlight of the sumptuously decorated rooms is the Senators' Antechamber, where landscapes of 18th-century Warsaw by Bernardo Bellotto (Canaletto's nephew) are on show.

From the castle, walk down ul Świętojańska to Warsaw's oldest church, the 15th-century Gothic **St John's Cathedral** (Map p550; ul Świętojańska 8; admission crypt 1zł; 🕑 10am-1pm & 3-5.30pm Mon-Sat). This street continues to the magnificent **Rynek Starego Miasta** (Old Town Market Square).

Off the square is the **Warsaw Historical Museum** (Map p550; ☎ 635 16 25; Rynek Starego Miasta 42; adult/child 6/3zł, free Sun; 🕑 11am-6pm Tue & Thu, 10am-3.30pm Wed & Fri, 10.30am-4.30pm Sat & Sun). At noon it shows an English-language film depicting the wartime destruction of the city.

Nearby is the **Adam Mickiewicz Museum of Literature** (Map p550; ☎ 831 76 91; Rynek Starego Miasta 20; adult/child 5/4zł, free Sun; 🕑 10am-3pm Mon, Tue & Fri, 11am-6pm Wed & Thu, 11am-5pm Sun), featuring exhibits on Poland's most revered literary figure and other leading writers.

Walk west for one block to the **Barbican**, part of the medieval city walls. North along ul Freta is the **Marie Skłodowska-Curie Museum** (Map p550; ☎ 831 80 92; ul Freta 16; adult/child 6/3zł; 🕑 10am-4pm Tue-Sat, 10am-2pm Sun), which features modest displays about the great lady, who, along with husband Pierre, discovered radium and polonium, and laid the foundations for radiography, nuclear physics and cancer therapy.

Heading southwest, you'll reach the **Monument to the Warsaw Rising** (Map p550; cnr ul Długa & ul Miodowa). This striking set of statuary honours the heroic Polish revolt against German rule in 1944.

Not far away, the **State Archaeological Museum** (Map p550; ☎ 831 15 37; ul Długa 52; adult/child 8/4zł, free Sun except 3rd Sun of month; 🕑 9am-4pm Mon-Thu, 11am-6pm Fri, 10am-6pm Sun) is located in a 17th-century former arsenal.

## Royal Way (Szlak Królewski)

This 4km route links the Royal Castle with Łazienki Park (see p552) via ul Krakowskie Przedmieście, ul Nowy Świat and al Ujazdowskie. Bus 180 stops at most places along this route and continues to Wilanów Park (Map p548). Bus No 100 also runs on Saturday and Sunday from May to September, between plac Zamkowy and Łazienki Park.

Just south of the Royal Castle is the ornate 15th-century **St Anne's Church** (Map p550; ul Krakowskie Przedmieście 68; 🕑 daylight hr), with impressive views from its **tower** (adult/child 3/2zł;

**POLAND**

⊙ 10am-6pm Tue-Sun). About 300m further south is **Radziwiłł Palace** (Map p550; not open to the public), the residence of the Polish president. Opposite, **Potocki Palace** (Map p550; ☎ 421 01 25; ul Krakowskie Przedmieście 15/17; admission free; ⊙ 10am-8pm) houses a contemporary art gallery.

To the west are the **Saxon Gardens** (admission free; ⊙ 24hr). At the entrance is the small but poignant **Tomb of the Unknown Soldier** (Map p550), though it's not open to the public. The ceremonial changing of the guard takes place here at noon on Sunday.

South of the tomb is the **Ethnographic Museum** (Map p550; ☎ 827 76 41; ul Kredytowa 1; adult/child 8/4zł, Wed free; ⊙ 9am-4pm Tue, Thu & Fri, 11am-6pm Wed, 10am-5pm Sat & Sun). It displays Polish folk costumes, and regional arts and crafts.

Back along the Royal Way is the 17th-century **Church of the Holy Cross** (Map p550; ul Krakowskie Przedmieście 3; ⊙ erratic). Chopin's heart is preserved in the second pillar on the left-hand side of the main nave. It was brought from Paris, where he died of tuberculosis aged only 39. If you want to know more, head along ul Tamka to the small **Chopin Museum** (Map p550; ☎ 827 54 71; ul Okólnik 1; adult/child 10/5zł, free Wed; ⊙ 10am-5pm Mon, Wed & Fri, 12-6pm Thu, 10am-2pm Sat & Sun May-Sep; 10am-2pm Mon-Wed, Fri & Sat, noon-6pm Thu Oct-Apr). On show are letters, handwritten musical scores and the great man's last piano.

East of the junction of ul Nowy Świat and al Jerozolimskie is the **National Museum** (Map p550; ☎ 621 10 31; al Jerozolimskie 3; adult/child 12/7zł, incl temporary exhibitions 19/12zł, museum free Sat; ⊙ 10am-4pm Tue, Wed & Fri-Sun, 10am-6pm Thu) with an impressive collection of Greek and Egyptian antiquities, Coptic frescoes, medieval woodcarvings and Polish paintings; look out for the surrealistic fantasies of Jacek Malczewski. Next door is the **Museum of the Polish Army** (Map p550; ☎ 629 52 71; al Jerozolimskie 3; museum adult/child 6/3zł, grounds free; ⊙ 10am-5pm Wed-Sun May-Sep, 10am-4pm Wed-Sun Oct-Apr), with army vehicles outside and miscellaneous militaria within.

Go south along al Ujazdowskie and cross busy ul Armii Ludowej. Over the road is the cutting-edge **Centre for Contemporary Art** (Map p550; ☎ 628 12 72; al Ujazdowskie 6; adult/child 12/6zł, free Thu; ⊙ 11am-5pm Tue-Thu, Sat & Sun, 11am-9pm Fri). It's housed in the reconstructed **Ujazdów Castle** (Map p550), originally built during the 1620s. Further down (towards the south) are the small **Botanical Gardens** (Map p548; ☎ 553 05 23; adult/child 4.50/2.50zł; ⊙ 10am-8pm).

## Łazienki Park

This large, shady and popular **park** (admission free; ⊙ daylight hr) is best known for the 18th-century **Palace upon the Water** (Map p548; ☎ 621 62 41; adult/child 12/9zł; ⊙ 9am-4pm Tue-Sun). It was the summer residence of Stanisław August Poniatowski, the last king of Poland, who was deposed by the Russian army and confederation of Polish magnates in 1792. The park was once a royal hunting ground attached to Ujazdów Castle.

The **Old Orangery** (Map p548; ☎ 621 62 41; by reservation only adult/child 6/4zł) contains a sculpture gallery and an 18th-century theatre. Between noon and 4pm every Sunday from May to September, piano recitals are held among the rose gardens.

## Wilanów Park

Another magnificent **park** (Map p548; ul Wisłostrada; admission free; ⊙ 9.30am-dusk) lies 6km southeast of Łazienki Park. Its centrepiece is the splendid **Wilanów Palace** (Map p548; ☎ 842 07 95; adult/child 20/10zł, free Thu; ⊙ 9am-4pm Mon & Thu-Sat, 9am-6pm Wed, 9am-7pm Sun May-Sep, 9am-4pm Wed-Mon Oct-May), the summer residence of King Jan III Sobieski, who ended the Turkish threat to Central Europe by defeating the Turks at Vienna in 1683. In summer, be prepared to wait. The last tickets are sold two hours before closing time.

In the well-kept park behind the palace is the **Orangery** (Map p548; admission fee varies with exhibitions; ⊙ 9.30am-3.30pm Wed-Mon), which houses an art gallery. The **Poster Museum** (Map p548; ☎ 842 26 06; adult/child 8/5zł, free Wed; ⊙ noon-3.30pm Mon, 10am-3.30pm Tue-Sun) in the former royal stables is a repository of Poland's world-renowned poster art.

To reach Wilanów, take bus 180 from anywhere along the Royal Way.

## Palace of Culture & Science

Massive, brooding and inescapable, this **towering structure** (Map p550; ☎ 656 76 00; plac Defilad; ⊙ 9am-8pm Mon-Thu, 9am-midnight Fri-Sun Jun-Aug, 9am-6pm Sep-May) has become an emblem of the city, as it's slowly rehabilitated from its Stalinist past. It has a particularly sinister aspect at dusk, though it's also a handy landmark. The Palace was built in the early 1950s as a 'gift of friendship' from the Soviet Union, and is still one of Europe's tallest buildings (234m).

The **observation terrace** (adult/child 20/15zł; ⊙ 9am-6pm) on the 30th floor provides a panoramic view, though it can be very cold and windy up there.

## Warsaw Rising Museum

This impressive **museum** (Map p548; ☎ 626 95 06; ul Grzybowska 79; adult/child 4/2zł, free Sun; ⏰ 10am-6pm Wed, Fri-Sun, 10am-8pm Thu) commemorates Warsaw's insurrection against its Nazi occupiers in 1944, which was destined to end in defeat and the destruction of much of the city and its population. The Rising was viciously suppressed by the Germans (while the Red Army stood by on the opposite bank of the Vistula), with more than 200,000 Poles dying by its conclusion.

The moving story of the Rising is retold here via photographs, exhibits and audiovisual displays. The centrepiece is a massive memorial wall emitting a heartbeat and selected audio recordings. At the end of the journey there's a replica 1944 café, underlining the fact that life went on, even in the worst days of the struggle. Captions are in Polish and English. Catch trams 8, 12, 22 or 24 from al Jerozolimskie, heading west.

## Jewish Heritage

The suburbs northwest of the Palace of Culture & Science were once predominantly inhabited by Jewish Poles. During WWII the Nazis established a Jewish ghetto in the area, but razed it to the ground after crushing the Warsaw Ghetto Uprising in April 1943.

The **Warsaw Ghetto Monument** (Map p548; cnr ul Anielewicza & ul Zamenhofa) remembers the Nazis' victims via pictorial plaques. The nearby **Pawiak Prison Museum** (Map p548; ☎ 831 13 17; ul Dzielna 24/26; admission free; ⏰ 9am-5pm Wed, 9am-4pm Thu & Sat, 10am-5pm Fri, 10am-4pm Sun) was a Gestapo prison during the Nazi occupation. Moving exhibits include letters and other personal items.

The most poignant remainder is Europe's largest **Jewish Cemetery** (Map p548; ul Okopowa 49/51; admission 4zł; ⏰ 10am-5pm Mon-Thu, 9am-1pm Fri, 9am-4pm Sun). Founded in 1806, it has more than 100,000 gravestones. Visitors must wear a head-covering to enter, and it's accessible from the Old Town on bus 180.

The **Jewish Historical Institute** (Map p550; ☎ 827 92 21; ul Tłomackie 3/5; adult/child 10/5zł; ⏰ 9am-4pm Mon-Wed & Fri, 11am-6pm Thu) has permanent exhibits about the Warsaw Ghetto, as well as local Jewish artworks. Further south is the neo-Romanesque **Nożyk Synagogue** (Map p550; ☎ 620 43 24; ul Twarda 6; admission 3.50zł; ⏰ 10am-8pm Sun-Thu, 10am-4pm Fri), Warsaw's only synagogue to survive WWII.

A walking tour of Jewish sites is detailed (in English and with a map) in the free pamphlet, *Jewish Warsaw*, available from tourist offices.

## SLEEPING

Not surprisingly, Warsaw is the most expensive Polish city for accommodation, though there's a number of reasonably priced hostels around town. The tourist offices can help find a room.

## Budget

**Smolna Youth Hostel No 2** (Map p550; ☎ /fax 827 89 52; ul Smolna 30; dm 36zł, s/d 65/120zł) Very central and very popular, though there's a midnight curfew. However, the light tidy dorms have a reasonable amount of space, the tiled bathrooms are clean, and there's a lounge and kitchen area. Note that guests are separated into dorms according to gender, and reception is up four flights of stairs.

**Oki Doki** (Map p550; ☎ 826 51 12; www.okidoki.pl; plac Dąbrowskiego 3; dm 45zł, s/d 110/145zł) There are no drab dorms here. Each is decorated thematically using the brightest paints available; try the Communist (red with a big image of Lenin). Lower bunks have good headroom, and the shared bathrooms are clean and bright. The hostel also has a bar, free washing machine and kitchen, and hires out bikes.

**Hostel Helvetia** (Map p550; ☎ 826 71 08; www.hostel-helvetia.pl; ul Kopernika 36/40; dm 45zł, s/d 110/150zł; 🖳 ) Bright hostel with an attractive combined lounge and kitchen. Dorms have lockers available, and some rooms feature bicycle-related images in deference to the cycling-enthusiast owner. Unsurprisingly, the hostel hires out bikes. Enter from the street behind, ul Sewerynów.

**Nathan's Villa Hostel** (Map p550; ☎ 622 29 46; www.nathansvilla.com; ul Piękna 24/26; dm 45zł, s/d 130/160zł; 🖳 ) Nathan's is the standard by which all Warsaw hostels should be judged. A sunlit courtyard leads to well-organised dorms, while private rooms are comfortable and decorated with monochrome photographs of Polish attractions. The kitchen is well set up, and there's a free laundry, a book exchange, and games to while away rainy days.

**Hostel Kanonia** (Map p550; ☎ 635 06 76; www.kanonia.pl; ul Jezuicka 2; dm 55zł, s/d 140/180zł; 🖳 ) Housed in a historic building in the heart of the Old

Town, accommodation is mostly in dorms, with only one dedicated double room. Some rooms have picturesque views onto the cobble stone streets, and there's a pleasant dining room with basic kitchen facilities.

**Dom Gościnny** (Map p550; ☎ 628 42 61; www.sezam.pw.edu.pl; ul Górnośląska 14; s/d 90/140zł, ste from 180zł; P 🖳) If you want to enjoy the pleasures of the city centre without sleeping there, this accommodation in the peaceful nearby embassy area is a good choice. Rooms have simple furnishings and plain carpets, but there's plenty of cupboard space and a kitchen.

**Camping Nr 123** (Map p548; ☎ 823 37 48; ul Warszawskiej 1920r 15/17; tents 12zł, plus per person 12zł; P 🖳) Set in extensive grounds near the Dworzec Zachodnia bus station, cabins (40zł per person) are also available and there's a tennis court nearby.

## Midrange

**Hotel Praski** (Map p550; ☎ 818 49 89; www.praski.pl; al Solidarności 61; s 147-210, d 160-230zł; P) The rooms of this inexpensive hotel vary in size, but have attractive high ceilings and comfortable beds. Bathrooms are clean, red carpets add old-fashioned charm, and some rooms have views of Praski Park. It's an easy walk across the river to the Old Town.

**Premiere Classe** (Map p548; ☎ 624 08 00; ul Towarowa 2; d from 179zł; P ✕ 🖳) If you're not bothered too much by room size, this modern hotel makes a good base. Rooms are small but bright, and neatly set up with modern furnishings. Friendly staff are a plus. Guests can use the restaurant, bar and fitness centre in the neighbouring sister hotels.

**Hotel Powiśle** (Map p550; ☎ 621 03 41; www.hotel powisle.oit.pl; ul Szara 10a; s/d 160/180zł; P) If Agatha Christie had set one of her mysteries in Poland, she would have chosen somewhere like this accommodation, pleasantly reminiscent of an old-fashioned country hotel. Although it's slightly scuffed, the generous use of wood panelling and the out-of-date carpets make for a comforting old-world feel. There's a bar and restaurant on site.

**City Apartments** (Map p550; ☎ 825 39 12; www.hotel inwarsaw.pl; ul Nowowiejska 1/3; apt from €60-120) A range of apartments are on offer here, from the Old Town to the city centre. They provide privacy and space, and allow for some cost-cutting via the fully equipped kitchen facilities. Although, as always happens with these places, you won't find every utensil you need.

**Sofitel Victoria** (Map p550; ☎ 657 80 11; www.sofi tel.com; ul Królewska 11; d/ste from €70/200; P ✕ 🖳 🖳 🖳) The very model of a modern business hotel, with a spacious marble foyer, and a lounge area housing a small library of books on Polish culture and history. The rooms are conservatively decorated, with gleaming bathrooms. The cheaper doubles are great value.

**Old Town Apartments** (Map p550; ☎ 887 98 01; www.warsawshotel.com; Rynek Starego Miasta 12/14; apt from €80) These modern renovated apartments lend you the pleasant illusion of being a local. Décor is bright and contemporary, most apartments have washing machines, and all have fully operational kitchens. Some can house up to six people.

**Hotel Harenda** (Map p550; ☎ 826 00 71; www.hotel harenda.com.pl; ul Krakowskie Przedmieście 4/6; s/d/ste from 250/270/460zł; P 🖳) Boasts a great location just off the Royal Way, although the green-and-brown colour scheme may deter some; the Harenda's rooms are neat and clean, with solid timber furniture. There's an old-fashioned feel to the hotel's interiors, and an expensive antique shop just off the foyer if retail therapy is required.

## Top End

**Dom Literatury** (Map p550; ☎ 828 39 20; www.fundac jadl.com; ul Krakowskie Przedmieście 87/89; s/d 220/370zł) Within a grand historic building, this accommodation features rambling halls and staircases bedecked with pot plants and sizeable paintings. There are a maze of comfortable rooms, many of which have excellent views of the Old Town and the Vistula. Don't, however, expect too much English from the friendly staff.

**Hotel Gromada Centrum** (Map p550; ☎ 582 99 00; www.gromada.pl; plac Powstańców Warszawy 2; s/d from 320/350zł; P ✕ 🖳) Centrally located, the Gromada is a great launching pad for exploring the central city. Upstairs from the funky green foyer, however, the featureless brown-carpeted corridors stretch out into the distance like an optical illusion. The rooms are plain, but clean and spacious.

**Hotel Le Regina** (Map p550; ☎ 531 60 00; www.leregina.com; ul Kościelna 12; d/ste from €250/600; P ✕ 🖳 🖳 🖳) It's not cheap, but the Le Regina is a jaw-dropping combination of traditional architecture and contemporary design. The enormous rooms feature king-size beds with headboards of dark, polished wood. Deluxe rooms also have timber floors, and terraces with courtyard views. All rooms sport spectacular bathrooms with marble benchtops.

# EATING

The most recent revolution to conquer the Polish capital has been a gastronomic one. A good selection of restaurants can be found in the Old Town and around ul Nowy Świat.

## Polish

**Bar Pod Barbakanem** (Map p550; ☎ 831 47 37; ul Mostowa 27/29; mains 8-12zł; ☾ 8am-5pm) Opposite the Barbican, this popular former milk bar survived the fall of the Iron Curtain and continues to serve cheap, unpretentious food in an interior marked by tiles: on the floor, walls and tabletops. Fill up while peering out through the lace curtains at the passing tourist hordes.

**Zgoda Grill Bar** (Map p550; ☎ 827 99 34; ul Zgoda 4; mains 18-35zł; ☾ 10am-11pm) A bright, informal place serving up cheap and tasty Polish standards. If you're not in the mood for Polish, there are Turkish, Italian and Mexican places just along the street.

**Dom Polski** (Map p548; ☎ 616 24 32; ul Francuska 11; mains 26-64zł; ☾ noon-midnight) This classy restaurant, in its yellow stucco building set back from the street, is perennially popular with tour groups and out-of-towners looking for tasty food and reasonable prices. It's worth the walk over the bridge.

**Restauracja Przy Zamku** (Map p550; ☎ 831 02 59; plac Zamkowy 15; mains from 32-80zł; ☾ 11am-midnight) An attractive, old-world kind of place with hunting trophies on the walls and attentive, white-aproned waiters. The top-notch Polish menu includes fish and game and a bewildering array of entrées – try the excellent hare pâté served with pickles and cranberry sauce.

**Karczma Gessler** (Map p550; ☎ 831 44 27; Rynek Starego Miasta 21/21a; mains 50-120zł; ☾ 11am-midnight) The décor of this romantic cellar is spectacular, with exposed timber beams and lots of rustic items such as cart wheels about the place. The food is pricey but impressive. Some dishes (such as the whole goose) can be shared by three.

**Café Design** (Map p550; ☎ 828 57 03; ul Krakowie Przedmieście 11; mains 69-79zł; ☾ 10am-11.30pm) Classy eatery serving tradition-inspired Polish cuisine in an ultramodern venue on the Royal Way, with circular platforms supporting tables below sleek wooden panelling. English-language newspapers and magazines are at hand, and mains include dishes involving rabbit, duck, lamb and deer.

## International

**Dziki Ryż** (Map p550; ☎ 621 50 15; ul Hoża 54; mains 18-25zł; ☾ 11am-7pm Mon-Fri, 1-5pm Sat & Sun) This hidden gem serves a range of Asian dishes, covering Chinese, Japanese, Korean and Thai cuisine. Though small (just six tables), it has loads of personality, with dark timber surfaces, bamboo place mats and Japanese newspapers plastering the walls. Red and green curries lead the way on the menu, including tofu versions, though they've been toned down for Polish palates.

**Restauracja Pod Samsonem** (Map p550; ☎ 831 17 88; ul Freta 3/5; mains 18-30zł; ☾ 10am-11pm) Situated in the New Town, and frequented by locals looking for inexpensive and tasty meals with a Jewish flavour. Interesting appetisers include Russian pancakes with salmon, and 'Jewish caviar'. Spot the bas relief of Samson and the lion above the next door along from the entrance.

**Tam Tam** (Map p550; ☎ 828 26 22; ul Foksal 18; mains from 20zł; ☾ noon-midnight) Housed in a subterranean 'African-style' place with a street-level bar. The varied menu includes pasta, goulash and kebabs, and a big list of teas and coffees. There's occasional live music in the evenings.

**Podwale Piwna Kompania** (Map p550; ☎ 635 63 14; ul Podwale 25; mains 21-55zł; ☾ 11am-1am) The restaurant's name (The Company of Beer) gives you an idea of the lively atmosphere in this eatery just outside the Old Town's moat. The menu features lots of grilled items and dishes such as roast duck, Wiener schnitzel, pork ribs and roasted pork knuckle. There's a courtyard for outdoor dining.

**London Steakhouse** (Map p550; ☎ 827 00 20; al Jerozolimskie 42; mains 32-66zł; ☾ 11am-midnight) You'll find it hard to convince yourself you're in London, but it's fun to spot the UK memorabilia among the cluttered décor, while being served by waitresses wearing Union Jack neckties and miniskirts. Steaks dominate the menu, which also includes fish and chips. There's roast beef and Yorkshire pudding on weekends.

**Adler Bar & Restaurant** (Map p550; ☎ 628 73 84; ul Mokotowska 69; mains 35-50zł; ☾ 8am-midnight Mon-Fri, 1pm-midnight Sat & Sun) A tiny oasis in the concrete jungle, housed within a curious circular building. Service is impeccable and a good variety of Polish and Bavarian *nouvelle cuisine* is on offer. Try the ice-meringue with strawberry mousse.

**Puszkin** (Map p550; ☎ 635 35 35; ul Świętojańska 2; mains 48–87zł; ☻ noon–midnight) An upmarket Russian restaurant where waiters in Cossack outfits serve up traditional dishes such as caviar, sturgeon and wild boar in opulent surrounds.

## Vegetarian

**Vega** (Map p550; ☎ 828 64 28; ul Nowy Świat 52; soups 5zł, mains 5–20zł; ☻ 11am–8pm) Cheap and delicious vegetarian food from a place tucked away in a courtyard. Try the *naleśniki* (crepes wrapped around a variety of fillings). There's also a good number of vegan items on the menu.

**Tukan Salad Bar** (Map p550; ☎ 531 25 20; plac Bankowy 2; mains from 5zł; ☻ 8am–8pm Mon–Fri, 10am–6pm Sat & Sun) This place has several outlets around the capital offering possibly the widest choice of salads in Poland. As the name suggests, look for the toucan on the door. This branch is hidden from the street in the arcade running parallel.

## Self-Catering

The most convenient places for groceries are the **MarcPol Supermarket** (Map p550; plac Defilad) in front of the Palace of Culture & Science building, and the **Albert Supermarket** (Map p550; Galeria Centrum, ul Marszałkowska) close by.

## DRINKING

**Sense** (Map p550; ☎ 826 65 70; ul Nowy Świat 19; ☻ noon–1am Mon–Thu, noon–3am Fri & Sat, noon–10pm Sun) A very modern venue with a mellow atmosphere. Comfortable banquettes sit beneath strings of cube-shaped lights, and there's an extensive wine and cocktail list, with some drinks measured in a 'Palace of Culture' (a tall scientific beaker). Try the house speciality, ginger rose vodka. There's also a food menu if you're hungry.

**Paparazzi** (Map p550; ☎ 828 42 19; ul Mazowiecka 12; ☻ noon–1am) This is one of Warsaw's flashest venues, where you can sip a bewildering array of cocktails under blown-up photos of Hollywood stars. It's big and roomy, with comfortable seating around the central bar, and does a good line in bar food, including some tasty salads.

**Pub Harenda** (Map p550; ☎ 826 29 00; ul Krakowskie Przedmieście 4/6; ☻ 9am–3am) Located at the back of Hotel Harenda, this pub is often crowded. However, it's a friendly, atmospheric place – the front section feels like a wood cabin out in the forest. There's dance music on weekends.

**Demmers Teahouse** (Map p550; ☎ 828 21 06; ul Krakowskie Przedmieście 61/63; ☻ 11am–7pm Mon–Fri, 11am–6pm Sat & Sun) On the Royal Way, Demmers has a staggering array of teas to try.

## ENTERTAINMENT
### Nightclubs

There's no shortage of good clubs in Warsaw. Explore ul Mazowiecka, ul Sienkiewicza and the area around ul Nowy Świat for more nightclub action.

**Enklawa** (Map p550; ☎ 827 31 51; ul Mazowiecka 12; ☻ 9pm–3am Wed–Sat) Funky red-and-orange space with comfy plush seating, mirrored ceilings, two bars and plenty of room to dance. Check out the long drinks list, hit the dance floor or observe the action from a stool on the upper balcony. Wednesday night is 'old school' night, with music from the '70s to '90s.

**Foksal 19** (Map p550; ☎ 829 29 55; ul Foksal 19; ☻ bar 5pm–1am Mon–Thu, 5pm–3am Fri & Sat, nightclub 11pm–5am Fri & Sat) Ultramodern playpen for Warsaw's bright young things. Downstairs is a cool drinking zone with a backlit bar, subdued golden lighting and comfy couches. Upstairs is the nightclub – a blue-lit contemporary space with DJs playing a variety of sounds.

**Hybrydy** (Map p550; ☎ 822 30 03; ul Złota 7/9; ☻ 9pm–3am) This joint has been going for decades, and features all sorts of live music most nights.

**Riviera Remont** (Map p548; ☎ 660 91 11; ul Waryńskiego 12; ☻ Jun–Sep) A popular, cheap student club offering regular live music.

In Łazienki Park (p552), piano recitals are held every Sunday from May to September, and chamber concerts are staged in summer at its Old Orangery.

Free jazz concerts also take place in the Old Town Market Square on Saturday at 7pm in July and August.

### Theatre

Advance tickets for most theatrical events can be bought at **ZASP Kasy Teatralne** (Map p550; ☎ 621 93 83; al Jerozolimskie 25; ☻ 11am–6.30pm Mon–Fri) or the **EMPiK Megastore** (Map p550; ☎ 551 44 43; ul Marszałkowska 104/122).

**Teatr Ateneum** (Map p550; ☎ 625 73 30; ul Jaracza 2) This place leans towards contemporary Polish-language productions.

**Teatr Wielki** (Map p550; ☎ 692 02 00; www.teatrwielki .pl; plac Teatralny 1) Wielki hosts opera and ballet in its grand premises.

**Filharmonia Narodowa** (Map p550; ☎ 551 71 11; ul Jasna 5) Classical-music concerts are held here.

## Cinemas

To avoid watching Polish TV in your hotel room, catch a film at the central **Kino Atlantic** (Map p550; ☎ 827 08 94; ul Chmielna 33) or **Kino Relax** (Map p550; ☎ 828 38 88; ul Złota 8). Tickets cost around 18zł.

## SHOPPING

**Stadion Market** (Map p548; al Jerozolimskie; ☯ dawn-around noon) This huge bazaar is situated within a former stadium in the suburb of Praga. It's busiest on weekends – beware of pickpockets.

**Galeria Centrum** (Map p550; ul Marszałowska 104/122) A sprawling modern shopping mall in the city centre.

There are also plentiful antique, arts and crafts shops around Rynek Starego Miasta in the Old Town, so brandish your credit card and explore.

## GETTING THERE & AWAY
### Air

The **Warsaw Frédéric Chopin airport** (Map p548; www.lotnisko-chopina.pl) is more commonly called Okęcie airport. Domestic arrivals and departures occupy a separate part of the same complex. The separate Etiuda terminal mostly handles discount airlines.

The useful tourist office is on the arrivals level of the international section. There's also a tourist office at the Etiuda terminal.

At the arrivals level there are ATMs and several *kantors*. There are also car-rental companies, a left-luggage room and a newsagent where you can buy public transport tickets.

Domestic and international flights can be booked at the **LOT office** (Map p550; ☎ 9572; ul Jerozolimskie 65/79), or at any travel agency. Other airline offices are listed in the *Welcome to Warsaw* magazine, and on p616.

### Bus

Warsaw has two major bus terminals for PKS buses. **Dworzec Zachodnia** (Western Bus Station; Map p548; al Jerozolimskie 144) handles domestic buses heading south, north and west of the capital, including six daily to Częstochowa (30zł), seven to Gdańsk (50zł), four to Kraków (39zł), seven to Olsztyn (32zł), eight to Toruń (35zł), three to Wrocław (46zł), and three to Zakopane (54zł). This complex is southwest of the city centre and adjoins the Warszawa Zachodnia train station. Take the commuter train that leaves from Warszawa Śródmieście station.

**Dworzec Stadion** (Stadium Bus Station; Map p548; ul Sokola 1) adjoins the Warszawa Stadion train station. It is also easily accessible by commuter train from Warszawa Śródmieście. Dworzec Stadion handles some domestic buses to the east and southeast, including 20 daily to Lublin (25zł), five to Białystok (23zł to 29zł), 12 to Zamość (37zł), and seven to Kazimierz Dolny (22zł).

**Polski Express** (Map p550; ☎ 844 55 55; www.polskiexpress.pl) operates coaches from the airport, but passengers can get on or off and buy tickets at the kiosk along al Jana Pawła II, next to the Warszawa Centralna train station. Polski Express buses travel to Białystok (34zł, one daily), Częstochowa (50zł, two daily), Gdynia, via Gdańsk (72zł, two daily), Kraków (67zł, one daily), Lublin (34zł, seven daily), Szczecin (80zł, two daily) and Toruń (48zł, 12 daily).

International buses depart from and arrive at Dworzec Zachodnia or, occasionally, outside Warszawa Centralna. Tickets are available from the bus offices at Dworzec Zachodnia, from agencies at Warszawa Centralna or from any of the major travel agencies in the city, including Almatur.

### Train

Warsaw has several train stations, but the one that most travellers will use is **Warszawa Centralna** (Map p550; Warsaw Central; al Jerozolimskie 54). Refer to the relevant destination sections in this chapter for information about services to/from Warsaw.

Warszawa Centralna is not always where trains start or finish, so make sure you get on or off promptly; and guard your belongings against pickpocketing and theft at all times.

The station's main hall houses ticket counters, ATMs and snack bars, as well as a post office, newsagents and a tourist office. Along the underground mezzanine level leading to the platforms are a dozen *kantors* (one of which is open 24 hours), a **left-luggage office** ( ☯ 7am-9pm), lockers, eateries, outlets for local public transport tickets, internet cafés and bookshops.

POLAND

Tickets for domestic and international trains are available from counters at the station (but allow at least an hour for possible queuing) or, in advance, from any major Orbis Travel office (p549). Tickets for immediate departures on domestic and international trains are also available from numerous, well-signed booths in the underpasses leading to Warszawa Centralna.

Some domestic trains also stop at Warszawa Śródmieście station, 300m east of Warszawa Centralna, and Warszawa Zachodnia, next to Dworzec Zachodnia bus station.

## GETTING AROUND

### To/From the Airport

The cheapest way of getting from the airport to the city centre is bus 175, which leaves every 10 to 15 minutes for the Old Town, via ul Nowy Świat and the Warszawa Centralna train station. If you arrive in the wee hours, night bus 611 links the airport with Warszawa Centralna every 30 minutes.

The taxi fare between the airport and the city centre is from 30zł to 35zł. Official taxis displaying a name, telephone number and fares can be arranged at the official taxi counters at the international arrivals level. Unauthorised 'Mafia' cabs still operate and charge astronomical rates.

### Car

Warsaw traffic isn't fun, but there are good reasons to hire a car for jaunts into the countryside. Major car-rental companies are listed in the local English-language publications, and include **Avis** (☎ 650 48 72; www.avis.pl), **Hertz** (☎ 650 28 96; www.hertz.com.pl) and **Sixt** (☎ 650 20 31; www.sixt.pl). For more details about car hire see p617.

### Public Transport

Warsaw's public transport operates from 5am to 11pm daily. The fare (2.40zł) is valid for one ride only on a bus, tram, trolleybus or metro train travelling anywhere in the city.

Warsaw is the only place in Poland where ISIC cards get a public-transport discount (of 48%).

Tickets are available for 60/90 minutes (3.60/4.50zł), one day (7.20zł), three days (12zł), one week (24zł) and one month (66zł). Buy tickets from kiosks (including those marked 'RUCH') before boarding, and validate them on board.

A metro line operates from the Ursynów suburb (Kabaty station) at the southern city limits to Plac Wilsona, via the city centre (Centrum), but is of limited use to visitors. Local commuter trains head out to the suburbs from the Warszawa Śródmieście station.

### Taxi

Taxis are a quick and easy way to get around – as long as you use official taxis and drivers use their meters. Beware of unauthorised 'Mafia' taxis parked in front of top-end hotels, at the airport, outside Warszawa Centralna train station and in the vicinity of most tourist sights.

# MAZOVIA & PODLASIE

After being ruled as an independent state by a succession of dukes, Mazovia shot to prominence during the 16th century, when Warsaw became the national capital. The region has long been a base for industry, the traditional mainstay of Poland's second largest city, Łódź. To the east of Mazovia, toward the Belarus border, lies Podlasie, which means 'land close to the forest'. The main attraction of this region is the impressive Białowieża National Park.

## ŁÓDŹ

**☎ 042 / pop 785,000**

Łódź (pronounced woodge) became a major industrial centre in the 19th century, attracting immigrants from across Europe. Little damaged in WWII, it's a lively, likeable city with attractive Art Nouveau architecture, and the added bonus of being well off the usual tourist track. It's an easy day trip from Warsaw.

Many of the attractions – and most of the banks, *kantors* and ATMs – are along ul Piotrkowska, the main thoroughfare. You can't miss the bronze statues of local celebrities along this street, including pianist Arthur Rubenstein, seated at a baby grand. The helpful **tourist office** (☎ 638 59 55; www.cityoflodz.pl; ul Piotrkowska 87; 8.30am-4.30pm Mon-Fri, 9am-1pm Sat) hands out free tourist brochures, including the useful *1-2-3 Days in Łódź*.

The **Historical Museum of Łódź** (☎ 654 03 23; ul Ogrodowa 15; adult/child 7/4zł, free Sun; 10am-4pm Tue & Thu, 2-6pm Wed, 10am-2pm Fri-Sun) is 200m northwest of plac Wolności, at the northern end of the main drag. Also worthwhile is the **Museum of Ethnography & Archaeology** ( ☎ 632 84 40; plac Wolności 14; adult/child 6/4zł, free Tue; 10am-5pm Tue, 11am-6pm Thu, 9am-4pm Wed, Fri-Sun).

**Herbst Palace** ( ☎ 674 96 98; ul Przędalniana 72; adult/ child 7/4.50zł; 10am-5pm Tue, noon-5pm Wed & Fri, noon-7pm Thu, 11am-4pm Sat & Sun) has been converted into an appealing museum. It's accessible by bus 55 heading east from the cathedral at the southern end of ul Piotrkowska. The **Jewish Cemetery** (www.jewishlodzcemetery.org; ul Bracka 40; admission 4zł, free first Sun of month; 9am-5pm Sun-Thu, 9am-3pm Fri Apr-Oct, 9am-3pm Sun-Fri Nov-Mar) is one of the largest in Europe. It's 3km northeast of the city centre and accessible by tram 1 or 6 from near plac Wolności. Enter from ul Zmienna.

The tourist office can provide information about all kinds of accommodation. The **youth hostel** ( ☎ 630 66 80; www.youthhostel.lodz.wp.pl; ul Legionów 27; dm from 30zł, s/d from 45/70zł; ) is excellent, so book ahead. It features nicely decorated rooms in a spacious old building, with free laundry and a kitchen. It's 250m west of plac Wolności.

The **Hotel Savoy** ( ☎ 632 93 60; www.hotelsavoy.pl; ul Traugutta 6; s/d from 87/200zł) is well positioned just off central ul Piotrkowska. Don't be put off by the scuffed corridors and stencilled door numbers: they conceal spacious, light-filled rooms with gleaming bathrooms.

Around the corner, the **Grand Hotel** ( ☎ 633 99 20; www.orbis.pl; ul Piotrkowska 72; s/d from 280/357zł) offers a touch of faded, if overpriced, *fin-de-siècle* grandeur.

Opposite the Grand, **Puenta** ( ☎ 630 80 87; ul Piotrkowska 65; mains 14-32zł; noon-10pm) is a brightly decorated restaurant, full of locals and visitors having a good time. The menu includes pasta, salads and a good selection of chicken and fish dishes. **Esplanada** ( ☎ 630 59 89; ul Piotrkowska 100; mains 35-60zł) is an excellent *belle époque*–style eatery serving quality Polish cuisine, sometimes accompanied by live folk music.

**LOT** ( ☎ 630 15 40; ul Piotrkowska 122) flies the 20-minute hop to Warsaw nine times a week. From the Łódź Kaliska train station, 1.2km southwest of central Łódź, trains go regularly to Wrocław (110 zł), Poznań (79 zł), Toruń (31 zł) and Gdańsk (46 zł). For Warsaw (29zł) and Częstochowa (23 zł), use the Łódź Fabryczna station, 400m east of the city centre. Buses go in all directions from the bus terminal, next to the Fabryczna train station.

## BIAŁOWIEŻA NATIONAL PARK
☎ 085

Once a centre for hunting and timber-felling, Białowieża (Byah-wo-*vyeh*-zhah) is now Poland's oldest national park. Its significance is underlined by Unesco's unusual recognition of the reserve as both a Biosphere Reserve *and* a World Heritage Site. The forest contains 120 species of birds, along with elk, wild boars and wolves. Its major drawcard is the magnificent European bison, which was once extinct outside zoos, but has been successfully reintroduced to its ancient home.

The logical visitor base is the charming village of Białowieża. The main road to Białowieża from Hajnówka leads to the southern end of Palace Park (the former location of the Russian tsar's hunting lodge), then skirts around the park to become the village's main street, ul Waszkiewicza. At the western end of this street is the **post office** ( 7am-7pm Mon-Fri, 7am-2pm Sat).

Money can be changed at the Hotel Żubrówka, but not travellers cheques or anything as exotic as Australian dollars. The hotel also has an ATM by the entrance, and public internet access for the scary rate of 10zł per half-hour.

You'll find the **PTTK (Polskie Towarzystwo Turystyczno-Krajoznawcze) office** (Polish Tourist Country Lovers Society; ☎ 681 22 95; www.pttk.bialowieza.pl; ul Kolejowa 17; 8am-4pm) at the southern end of Palace Park. Serious hikers should contact the **National Park Office** ( ☎ 682 97 02; www.bpn .com.pl; 9am-4pm) inside Palace Park. Most maps of the national park (especially the one published by PTOP – Północnopodlaskie Towarzystwo Ochrony Ptaków, North Podlasian Bird Protection Society) detail several enticing hiking trails.

### Sights & Activities
A combined ticket (12zł) allows you entry to the museum, the bison reserve and the nature reserve. Alternatively, you can pay for each attraction separately.

The elegant **Palace Park** (admission free; daylight hr) is only accessible on foot, bicycle or horse-drawn cart across the bridge from the PTTK office. Over the river is the excellent **Natural & Forestry Museum** (adult/child 10/5zł; 9am-4.30pm Apr-Sep, 9am-4pm Tue-Sun Oct-Mar), with displays on local flora and fauna, and beekeeping.

The **European Bison Reserve** (Rezerwat Żubrów; ☎ 681 23 98; adult/child 6/3zł; 9am-4pm) is an open-plan zoo containing many of these

POLAND

mighty beasts, as well as wolves, strange horselike tarpans and mammoth żubroń (hybrids of bisons and cows). Entrance to the reserve is just north of the Hajnówka-Białowicża road, about 4.5km west of the PTTK office – look for the signs along the żebra żubra (bison's rib) trail, or follow the green or yellow marked trails. Alternatively, catch a local bus to the stop at the main road turn-off (2.50zł) and walk a kilometre to the entrance, but ask the driver first if the bus is taking a route past the reserve.

The main attraction is the **Strict Nature Reserve** (adult/child 6/3zł; ☉ 9am-5pm), which starts about 1km north of Palace Park. It can only be visited on a three-hour tour with a licensed guide along an 8km trail (195zł for an English- or German-speaking guide). Licensed guides (in many languages) can be arranged at the PTTK office or any travel agency in the village. Note that the reserve does close sometimes, due to inclement weather.

A more comfortable way to visit the nature reserve is by horse-drawn cart, which costs 162zł in addition to guide and entry fees (three hours) and holds four people. Otherwise, it may be possible (with permission from the PTTK office) to visit the reserve by bicycle (with a guide).

The Dom Turysty PTTK hires out bikes (25zł per day), as do several other hotels and *pensions*.

### Sleeping & Eating

There are plenty of homes along the road from Hajnówka offering private rooms for about 40/70zł for singles/doubles.

**Paprotka Youth Hostel** ( ☎ 681 25 60; www.paprotka.com.pl; ul Waszkiewicza 6; dm from 16zł, d 50zł; Ⓟ ☒ 🖵 ) One of the best in the region: the rooms are light and spruce, with high ceilings and potted plants; the newly renovated bathrooms are clean; and the kitchen is excellent. There's a washing machine as well.

**Dom Turysty PTTK** ( ☎ 681 25 05; dm from 24zł, d/tr from 66/111zł; Ⓟ ) Inexpensive accommodation inside Palace Park. It has seen better days, but the position and rates are hard to beat. It has a pleasant restaurant with a bison-head motif.

**Pension Gawra** ( ☎ 681 28 04; fax 681 24 84; ul Poludnlowa 2; d 60-120zł; Ⓟ ) A quiet, homely place with large rooms lined with timber in a hunting lodge style, overlooking a pretty garden just behind the Hotel Żubrówka. The doubles

with bathrooms are much more spacious than those without.

**Pensjonacik Unikat** ( ☎ 681 27 74; ul Waszkiewicza 39; s/d/tr from 80/100/160zł; Ⓟ ⓰ ) A bit too fond of dead creatures' hides as décor, but good value with its tidy wood-panelled rooms, one of which is designed for disabled access. The restaurant offers specialities such as Belarus-style potato pancakes, and has a menu in both German and English.

**Hotel Żubrówka** ( ☎ 681 23 03; ul Olgi Gabiec 6; s/d/ste from 280/320/450zł; Ⓟ ☒ 🖵 ) Just across the way from the PTTK office, this is the town's best hotel. It's eccentrically decorated with animal hides, a working miniature water wheel, and pseudo cave drawings along the corridors. Rooms are predictably clean and comfortable, and there's a café, restaurant and nightclub on the premises.

### Getting There & Away

From Warsaw, take the express train from Warszawa Centralna to Siedlce (1½ hours), wait for a connection on the slow train to Hajnówka (two hours), and then catch one of the nine daily PKS bus services to Białowieża (5zł, one hour). Two private companies, Oktobus and Lob-Trans, also run fairly squeezy minibuses between Hajnówka and Białowieża (5zł, one hour, five to seven daily). For the latest timetable information, check out www.turystyka.hajnowka.pl/ctrpb/english/

Five buses a day travel from the Dworzec Stadion station in Warsaw to Białystok (23zł to 29zł, four hours), from where two buses travel to Białowieża (15zł, three hours). You may need to stay overnight in Białystok to catch the connecting services. Polski Express also runs one daily bus between Białystok and Warsaw (34zł, 3½ hours).

# MAŁOPOLSKA

Małopolska (literally 'lesser Poland') is a historic region covering all of southeastern Poland, from the Carpathian Mountains along the nation's southern borders, to the Lublin Uplands further north. It's a beautiful area, within which the visitor can spot remnants of traditional agricultural life. The biggest attraction, however, is the former royal capital, Kraków, and the majestic Tatra Mountains to the city's south.

# KRAKÓW

☎ 012 / pop 758,000

A city founded upon the defeat of a dragon is off to a promising start when it comes to attracting visitors, and Kraków doesn't disappoint. As it was the royal capital of Poland until 1596, Kraków is packed with beautiful buildings and streets dating back to medieval times. The city's centrepiece, Wawel Castle and Cathedral, is a stunning reminder of the city's luck in avoiding major damage in WWII.

Just outside the Old Town lies Kazimierz, the former Jewish quarter, its silent synagogues reflecting the tragedy of the recent past. The district's tiny streets and low-rise architecture make it an interesting place to explore.

As the nation's biggest tourist drawcard, Kraków is also replete with diversions of a more modern variety, with hundreds of restaurants, bars and other venues tucked away in its laneways and cellars. Though hotel prices are above the national average, and visitor numbers high in summer, this vibrant, cosmopolitan city is an essential part of any tour of Poland.

## Information

### BOOKSHOPS

**EMPiK Megastore** (Map p562; ☎ 429 42 34; Rynek Główny 5; ⏲ 9am-10pm) Sells foreign newspapers, magazines, novels and maps.

**Księgarnia Hetmańska** (Map p562; ☎ 430 24 53; Rynek Główny 17) An impressive selection of English-language books, including non-fiction on Polish history and culture.

**Jarden Jewish Bookshop** (Map p564; ☎ 429 13 74; ul Szeroka 2) Located in Kazimierz.

**Sklep Podróżnika** (Map p562; ☎ 429 14 85; ul Jagiellońska 6; ⏲ 11am-7pm Mon-Fri, 10am-3pm Sat) Sells a wide selection of regional and city maps, as well as Lonely Planet titles.

### INTERNET ACCESS

**Internet Café U Luisa** (Map p562; ☎ 617 02 22; Rynek Główny 13; per hr 4zł; ⏲ 10am-10pm)

**Klub Garinet** (Map p562; ☎ 423 22 33; ul Floriańska 18; per hr 4zł; ⏲ 9am-midnight)

### MONEY

*Kantors* and ATMs can be found all over the city centre. It's worth noting, however, that many *kantors* close on Sunday, and areas near the Rynek Główny and the main train station offer terrible exchange rates. There are also exchange facilities at the airport.

**Bank Pekao** (Map p562; Rynek Główny 32) Cashes travellers cheques and provides cash advances on MasterCard and Visa.

### POST

**Main post office** (Map p562; ul Westerplatte 20; ⏲ 8am-8pm Mon-Fri, 8am-2pm Sat, 9-11am Sun)

### TOURIST INFORMATION

The Kraków Card (www.krakowcard.com), available from tourist offices, includes travel on public transport and entry to many museums for 45/65zł for two/three days .

Two free magazines, *Welcome to Cracow & Małopolska* and *Visitor: Kraków & Zakopane* are available at tourist offices and some travel agencies and upmarket hotels. The *Kraków in Your Pocket* booklet is also very useful.

**Tourist Information Centre** (Map p562; ☎ 421 77 87; www.karnet.krakow.pl; ul Św. Jana 2; ⏲ 10am-6pm Mon-Sat) Central city-run agency giving assistance to visitors.

**Małopolska Tourism Information Centre** (Map p562; ☎ 421 77 06; www.mcit.pl; Rynek Główny 1/3; ⏲ 9am-7pm Mon-Fri, 9am-4pm Sat & Sun Apr-Sep, 10am-5pm Mon-Fri, 10am-4pm Sat Oct-Mar) Helpful privately run tourist office centrally located in the Cloth Hall.

**Tourist office** (Map p562; ☎ 433 73 10; Rynek Główny 1; ⏲ 9am-7pm Apr-Sep, 9am-5pm Oct-Mar) In the Town Hall Tower.

**Tourist office** (Map p562; ☎ 432 01 10; ul Szpitalna 25; ⏲ 8am-8pm Mon-Fri, 9am-5pm Sat & Sun) Near the main train station, this place is smaller and less harried.

**Tourist office** (Map p564; ☎ 422 04 71; ul Józefa 7; ⏲ 10am-4pm Mon-Fri) In Kazimierz, providing information about Jewish heritage and local attractions.

## Sights & Activities

### WAWEL HILL

Kraków's main draw for tourists is **Wawel Hill** (Map p562; grounds admission free; ⏲ 6am-8pm May-Sep, 6am-5pm Oct-Apr). South of the Old Town, the hill is crowned with a castle and cathedral, both of which are enduring symbols of Poland.

You can choose from several attractions within the castle, each requiring a separate ticket, valid for a specific time. There's a limited daily quota of tickets for some parts, so arrive early if you want to see everything.

Within the magnificent **Wawel Castle** (Map p562; ☎ 422 51 55; www.wawel.krakow.pl) are the **State Rooms** (adult/child 14/8zł, free Mon; ⏲ 9.30am-noon Mon, 9.30am-4pm Tue & Fri, 9.30am-3pm Wed, Thu & Sat,

**POLAND**

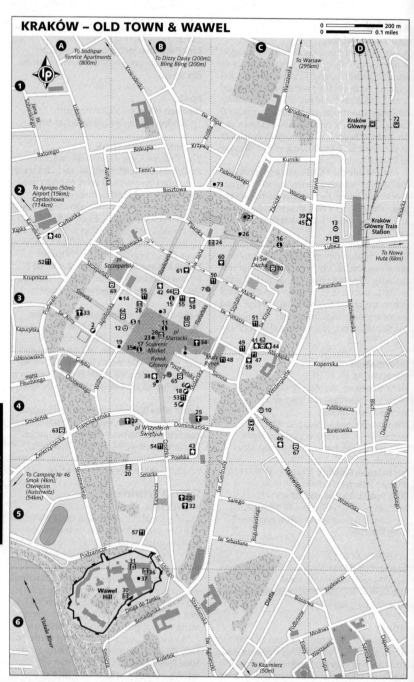

# KRAKÓW – OLD TOWN & WAWEL

POLAND

**INFORMATION**
Bank Pekao....................................1 B3
British Consulate............................2 A3
Cracow Tours................................3 A3
EMPiK Megastore...........................4 B3
French Consulate...........................5 B4
German Consulate..........................6 B4
Internet Café U Luisa.....................7 B4
Klub Garinet..................................8 B3
Księgarnia Hetmańska...................9 B3
Main Post Office..........................10 C4
Maloposka Tourism
    Information Centre...................11 B3
Police Station...............................12 B3
Post Office...................................13 D2
Sklep Podróżnika.........................14 B3
Tourist Information Centre............15 B3
Tourist Office...............................16 C2
Tourist Office...............................17 B3
US Consulate...............................18 B4

**SIGHTS & ACTIVITIES**
Almatur........................................19 B3
Archaeological Museum................20 B5
Barbican......................................21 C2
Church of SS Peter &
    Paul...........................................22 B5
Cloth Hall....................................23 B3
Czartoryski Museum.....................24 C2
Dominican Church........................25 B4
Florian Gate.................................26 C2
Franciscan Church........................27 B4

Gallery of 19th-Century Polish
    Painting....................................28 B3
Historical Museum of Kraków......29 B3
Lost Wawel..................................30 B6
Museum of Oriental Art...............31 B5
St Andrew's Church......................32 B5
St Anne's Church..........................33 A3
St Mary's Church..........................34 B3
Town Hall Tower..........................35 B3
Treasury & Armoury.....................36 B6
Wawel Castle...............................37 B6

**SLEEPING**
Cracow Hostel.............................38 B4
Greg & Tom Hostel......................39 C2
Hotel Alexander...........................40 A2
Hotel Amadeus............................41 C3
Hotel Saski..................................42 B3
Hotel Wawel................................43 B4
Hotel Wit Stwosz.........................44 C3
Jordan Tourist Information &
    Accomodation..........................45 C2
Wielopole Guest Rooms...............46 C4

**EATING**
Bombaj Tandoori..........................47 C4
Casa della Pizza...........................48 C4
Green Way Bar Wegetariański.....49 C3
Gruzińskie Chaczapuri..................50 C3
Ipanema......................................51 C3
Metropolitan Restaurant..........(see 42)
Nostalgia.....................................52 A3

Orient Ekspres............................**53** B4
Pod Aniolami..............................**54** B4
Reatauracja Chłopskie
    Jadło.......................................**55** B3
Restauracja Pod Gruszką........**56** B3
Smak Ukraiński...........................**57** B5

**DRINKING**
Café Camelot..............................**58** B3
Paparazzi....................................**59** C4
Piwnica Pod Złotą Pipą..............**60** C3
Pod Papugami............................**61** B3

**ENTERTAINMENT**
Black Gallery...............................**62** C3
Filharmonica Krakówska............**63** A4
Frantic........................................**64** B3
Kino Pasaż..................................**65** B4
Kino Sztuka................................**66** B3
Łubu-Dubu.................................**67** C4
Piano Rouge...............................**68** B3
Stary Teatr..................................**69** B3
Teatr im Słowackiego.............**70** C3

**TRANSPORT**
Biuro Turystyki i Zakwaterowania
    Waweltur.............................(see 45)
Bus 192 to Airport.....................**71** D2
Bus Terminal...............................**72** D1
LOT Office..................................**73** C2
Minibuses to Wieliczka...............**74** C4
Pol-Tur......................................(see 39)

---

10am-3pm Sun) and the **Royal Private Apartments** (adult/child 18/13zł; 9.30am-4pm Tue & Fri, 9.30am-3pm Wed, Thu & Sat, 10am-3pm Sun). Entry to the latter is only allowed on a guided tour; you may have to accompany a Polish language tour if it's the only one remaining for the day. If you want to hire a guide who speaks English, French or German, contact the onsite **guides office** ( 429 33 36).

The 14th-century **Wawel Cathedral** (Map p562; adult/child 10/5zł; 9am-3.45pm Mon-Sat, 12.15-3.45pm Sun) was the coronation and burial place of Polish royalty for four centuries, and houses **Royal Tombs**, including that of King Kazimierz Wielki. The **bell tower** of the golden-domed **Sigismund Chapel** (1539) contains the country's largest bell (11 tonnes).

Ecclesiastical artefacts are displayed in the small **Cathedral Museum** (Map p562; adult/child 5/2zł; 10am-3pm Tue-Sun).

Other attractions include the **Museum of Oriental Art** (adult/child 6/4zł, free Mon; 9.30am-noon Mon, 9.30am-4pm Tue & Fri, 9.30am-3pm Wed, Thu & Sat, 10am-3pm Sun); the **Treasury & Armoury** (adult/child 14/8zł, free Mon; 9.30am-noon Mon, 9.30am-4pm Tue & Fri, 9.30am-3pm Wed, Thu & Sat, 10am-3pm Sun); the **Lost Wawel** (adult/child 6/4zł, free Mon; 9.30am-noon Mon, 9.30am-4pm Tue & Fri, 9.30am-3pm Wed, Thu & Sat,

10am-3pm Sun), a well-displayed set of intriguing archaeological exhibits; and the atmospheric **Dragon's Cave** (Map p562; admission 3zł; 10am-5pm May-Oct). Go here last, as the exit leads out onto the riverbank.

**OLD TOWN**
The focus of the Old Town is **Rynek Główny** (Main Market Square), Europe's largest medieval town square (200m by 200m). At its centre is the 16th-century Renaissance **Cloth Hall** (Sukiennice; Map p562). Downstairs is a large **souvenir market** and upstairs is the **Gallery of 19th-Century Polish Painting** (Map p562; 422 11 66; adult/child 8/5zł, free Sun; 10am-3.30pm Tue, Thu, Sat & Sun, 10am-6pm Wed & Fri), with famous works by Jan Matejko.

The 14th-century **St Mary's Church** (Map p562; Rynek Główny 4; adult/child 4/2zł; 11.30am-6pm Mon-Sat, 2-6pm Sun) fills the northeastern corner of the square. The huge main altarpiece by Wit Stwosz (Veit Stoss in German) of Nuremberg is the finest Gothic sculpture in Poland, and is opened ceremoniously each day at noon. Every hour a *hejnał* (bugle call) is played from the highest tower of the church. The melody, played in medieval times as a warning call, breaks off abruptly to symbolise the

**POLAND**

moment when, according to legend, the throat of a 13th-century trumpeter was pierced by a Tatar arrow.

West of the Cloth Hall is the 15th-century **Town Hall Tower** (Map p562; ☎ 422 99 22, ext 218; admission 4zł; ⏱ 10.30am-6pm May-Oct), which you can climb. The **Historical Museum of Kraków** (Map p562; ☎ 422 15 04; Rynek Główny 35; adult/child 5/3.50zł; free Sat; ⏱ 9am-4pm Wed & Fri-Sun, 10am-5pm Thu) has paintings, documents and oddments relating to the city.

From St Mary's Church, walk up (northeast) ul Floriańska to the 14th-century **Florian Gate**. Beyond it is the **Barbican** (Map p562; adult/child 5/3zł; ⏱ 10.30am-6pm Apr-Oct), a defensive bastion built in 1498. Nearby, the **Czartoryski Museum** (Map p562; ☎ 422 55 66; ul Św Jana 19; adult/child 9/6zł, free Thu; ⏱ 10am-6pm Tue & Thu, 10am-7pm Wed, Fri & Sat, 10am-3pm Sun) features an impressive collection of European art, including Leonardo da Vinci's *Lady with an Ermine*. Also on display are Turkish weapons and artefacts, including a campaign tent from the 1683 Battle of Vienna.

South of Rynek Główny, plac Wszystkich Świętych is dominated by two 13th-century monastic churches: the **Dominican Church** (Map p562; ul Stolarska 12; admission free; ⏱ 9am-6pm) to the east and the **Franciscan Church** (Map p562; plac Wszystkich Świętych 5; admission free; ⏱ 9am-5pm) to the west. The latter is noted for its stained-glass windows.

To the south, you'll find the **Archaeological Museum** (Map p562; ☎ 422 75 60; ul Poselska 3; adult/child 7/5zł; ⏱ 9am-2pm Mon-Wed, 2-6pm Thu, 10am-2pm Fri & Sun), with displays on local prehistory and ancient Egyptian artefacts, including animal mummies.

Continuing south along ul Grodzka is the early 17th-century Jesuit **Church of SS Peter & Paul** (Map p562; ul Grodzka 64; ⏱ dawn-dusk), Poland's first baroque church. The Romanesque 11th-century **St Andrew's Church** (Map p562; ul Grodzka 56; ⏱ 9am-6pm Mon-Fri) was the only building in Kraków to withstand the Tatars' attack of 1241.

### KAZIMIERZ

Founded by King Kazimierz the Great in 1335, Kazimierz was originally an independent town. In the 15th century, Jews were expelled from Kraków and forced to resettle in a small pre-

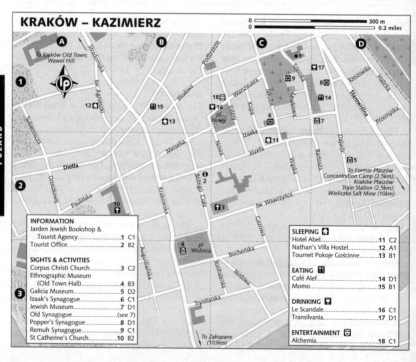

**KRAKÓW – KAZIMIERZ**

0 ────── 300 m
0 ────── 0.2 miles

| INFORMATION | |
| --- | --- |
| Jarden Jewish Bookshop & Tourist Agency | 1 C1 |
| Tourist Office | 2 B2 |

| SIGHTS & ACTIVITIES | |
| --- | --- |
| Corpus Christi Church | 3 C2 |
| Ethnographic Museum (Old Town Hall) | 4 B3 |
| Galicia Museum | 5 D2 |
| Izaak's Synagogue | 6 C1 |
| Jewish Museum | 7 D1 |
| Old Synagogue | (see 7) |
| Popper's Synagogue | 8 D1 |
| Remuh Synagogue | 9 C1 |
| St Catherine's Church | 10 B2 |

| SLEEPING | |
| --- | --- |
| Hotel Abel | 11 C2 |
| Nathan's Villa Hostel | 12 A1 |
| Tournet Pokoje Gościnne | 13 B1 |

| EATING | |
| --- | --- |
| Café Alef | 14 D1 |
| Momo | 15 B1 |

| DRINKING | |
| --- | --- |
| Le Scandale | 16 C1 |
| Transilvania | 17 D1 |

| ENTERTAINMENT | |
| --- | --- |
| Alchemia | 18 C1 |

scribed area in Kazimierz, separated by a wall. The Jewish quarter later became home to Jews fleeing persecution from throughout Europe.

By the outbreak of WWII there were 65,000 Jewish Poles in Kraków (around 30% of the city's population), and most lived in Kazimierz. During the war the Nazis relocated Jews to a walled ghetto in Podgórze, just south of the Vistula River. They were exterminated in the nearby **Płaszów Concentration Camp**, as portrayed in Steven Spielberg's haunting film *Schindler's List*.

Kazimierz's western Catholic quarter includes the 14th-century Gothic **St Catherine's Church** (Map p564; ul Augustian 7; admission free; 🕑 only during services), with an imposing 17th-century gilded high altar, while the 14th-century **Corpus Christi Church** (Map p564; ul Bożego Ciała 26; admission free; 🕑 9am-5pm Mon-Sat) is crammed with baroque fittings. The **Ethnographic Museum** (Map p564; ☎ 430 55 63; plac Wolnica 1; adult/child 6.50/4zł, free Sun; 🕑 10am-6pm Mon, 10am-3pm Wed-Fri, 10am-2pm Sat & Sun) in the Old Town Hall has a collection of regional crafts and costumes.

The eastern Jewish quarter is dotted with synagogues. The 15th-century **Old Synagogue** is the oldest Jewish religious building in Poland. It now houses the **Jewish Museum** (Map p564; ☎ 422 09 62; ul Szeroka 24; admission 6zł; 🕑 10am-2pm Mon, 9am-4pm Wed & Thu, Sat & Sun, 9am-5pm Fri), with exhibitions on Jewish traditions.

Not far away, the **Galicia Museum** (Map p564; ☎ 421 68 42; www.galiciajewishmuseum.org; ul Dajwór 18; adult/child 7/5zł; 🕑 9am-8pm) features an impressive photographic exhibition, depicting modern-day traces of southeastern Poland's once thriving Jewish community.

A short walk north is the small 16th-century **Remuh Synagogue** (Map p564; ☎ 422 12 74;

ul Szeroka 40; adult/child 5/2zł; 🕑 9am-4pm Mon-Fri), still used for religious services. Behind it, the **Remuh Cemetery** (admission free; 🕑 9am-4pm Mon-Fri) boasts some extraordinary Renaissance gravestones. Nearby, the restored **Izaak's Synagogue** (Map p564; ☎ 430 55 77; ul Jakuba 25; admission 7zł; 🕑 9am-7pm Sun-Fri) shows documentary films about life in the Jewish ghetto.

It's easy to take a self-guided walking tour around Kazimierz with the booklet *Jewish Kazimierz Short Guide*, available from the Jarden Jewish Bookshop (see p561).

### WIELICZKA SALT MINE

Wieliczka (vyeh-*leech*-kah), 15km southeast of the city centre, is famous for the **Wieliczka Salt Mine** ( ☎ 278 73 02; www.kopalnia.pl; ul Daniłowicza 10; adult/child 65/55zł, 20% discount after 6pm & Nov-Feb; 🕑 7.30am-7.30pm Apr-Oct, 8am-5pm Nov-Mar). It's an eerie world of pits and chambers, and every single element from chandeliers to altarpieces was hewn by hand from solid salt. The mine is included on Unesco's World Heritage List.

The highlight of a visit is the richly ornamented **Chapel of the Blessed Kinga**, a church measuring 54m by 17m, and 12m high. Construction of this underground temple took more than 30 years (1895–1927), resulting in the removal of 20,000 tonnes of rock salt.

The obligatory guided tour through the mine takes about two hours (a 2km walk). Tours in English (July to August) operate half-hourly from 8.30am to 6pm; from September to June they're approximately hourly from 9am to 5pm. There are at least two tours a day in German, and more frequently in July and August. If you're visiting independently, you must wait for a tour to start. Last admission to the mine is shortly before closing time.

---

### THE LAJKONIK OF KRAKÓW

As you're walking through Kraków's mighty market square, you may see a street performer dressed as a man riding a richly decorated horse, with a pointed hat on his head. This is an everyday version of the Lajkonik, the central figure of an annual parade through the city.

Exact details of the Lajkonik's origin are hard to pin down, but one story involves a Tatar assault on Kraków in 1287. A group of raftsmen discovered the tent of the commanding khan on a foray outside the city walls, and dispatched the unsuspecting Tatar leader and his generals in a lightning raid. The raftsmen's leader then wore the khan's richly decorated outfit back to the city.

To commemorate the victory, each year on the first Thursday following Corpus Christi (May or June), a colourful parade takes place. Starting from the Premonstratensian monastery in Zwierzyniec, the elaborately costumed Lajkonik marches through Kraków's streets to the Main Market Square (Rynek Główny), accompanied by folk musicians. In the square, the Lajkonik prances in a lively fashion, recreating the Cracovian citizens' joy when the siege was lifted.

Minibuses to Wieliczka town depart every 10 minutes between 6am and 8pm from a location on ul Starowiślna, near the main post office in Kraków, and drop passengers outside the salt mine (2.50zł). Trains between Kraków and Wieliczka (3.80zł) leave every 45 minutes throughout the day, but the train station in Wieliczka is a fair walk from the mine.

## Tours

The following companies operate tours of Kraków and surrounding areas:

**Almatur** (Map p562; ☎ 422 46 68; Rynek Główny 27) Arranges various outdoor activities during summer.

**Cracow Tours** (Map p562; ☎ 422 40 35; www.cracow tours.pl; Rynek Główny 41) Inside Orbis Travel, offering city tours, and tours of Auschwitz and the salt mines.

**Crazy Guides** (☎ 0888 68 68 71; www.crazyguides .com) Offers entertaining tours of the city's communist-era suburbs, in restored East German cars.

**Jarden Jewish Bookshop & Tourist Agency** (Map p564; ☎ 421 71 66; www.jarden.pl; ul Szeroka 2) The best agency for tours of Polish Jewish heritage. Its showpiece, 'Retracing Schindler's List' (two hours by car), costs 65zł per person. All tours require a minimum of three and must be arranged in advance. Tours are in English, but French- and German-speaking guides can be arranged.

## Sleeping

Kraków is unquestionably Poland's major tourist destination, with prices to match. Booking ahead in the busy summer months is recommended.

### BUDGET

**Bling Bling** (☎ 634 05 32; www.blingbling.pl; ul Pędzichów 7; dm 45zł, d/tr 120/180zł; 🖳) Comfortable hostel north of the Old Town, offering inexpensive, good quality accommodation. High ceilings make the dorms feel spacious, though the lounge is a little dark. Laundry available.

**Cracow Hostel** (Map p562; ☎ 429 11 06; www.cracow hostel.com; Rynek Główny 19; dm 45-60zł; 🖳) Budget accommodation is hard to find in the centre of the Old Town, but this place is perched high above the market square, with an amazing view of St Mary's Church from the roomy but comfortable lounge. There's also a kitchen and washing machine.

**Greg & Tom Hostel** (Map p562; ☎ 422 41 00; www .gregtomhostel.com; ul Pawia 12; dm 50zł, d/tr 120/150; 🖳) This well-run hostel is spread over two locations; the private rooms are a 10-minute walk away on ul Warszawska. The staff are friendly, the rooms are clean, and laundry facilities are included. Note that reception is up four flights of stairs, and the private rooms are above a (seemingly peaceful) massage parlour.

**Nathan's Villa Hostel** (☎ 422 35 45; www.nathansvilla .com; ul Św. Agnieszki 1; dm/d from 50/160zł; 🗶 🖳) The best hostel in town is conveniently located between the Old Town and Kazimierz. Comfy rooms, sparkling bathrooms, free laundry and a friendly atmosphere make this place a big hit with backpackers. The addition of a cellar bar, mini-cinema and pool table have kept Nathan's ahead of the pack.

**Dizzy Daisy** (☎ 292 01 71; www.hostel.pl; ul Pędzichów 9; dm/d/tr 60/160/210zł; 🖳) A modern chain-hostel with great facilities and light, clean rooms, frequented by an international crowd of party people. Laundry and kitchen are available.

**Camping Nr 46 Smok** (☎ 429 83 00; ul Kamedulska 18; per person/tent 15/19zł; 🅿) It's small, quiet and pleasantly located 4km west of the Old Town. To get here from outside the Kraków Główny train station building, take tram 2 to the end of the line in Zwierzyniec and change for any westbound bus (except No 100).

### MIDRANGE

An agency offering decent rooms around town is **Jordan Tourist Information & Accommodation Centre** (Map p562; ☎ 422 60 91; www.jordan.krakow .pl; ul Pawia 8; ⏲ 8am-6pm Mon-Fri, 9am-2pm Sat & Sun; s/d around 110/130zł).

**Sodispar Service Apartments** (☎ 0602 247 438; www.sodispar.com.pl; ul Lubelska 12; apt €30-140) Several comfortable, modern apartments sleeping up to four people, north of the Old Town. Cheaper rates are available for longer stays.

**Apropo** (☎ 0506 102 924; www.apropo.info; ul Karmelicka 36; d/tr 150/225zł) Set of comfortable rooms within a fully renovated old apartment, with access to shared bathrooms, a light-filled kitchen and laundry facilities. It's in a convenient location not far from the Old Town.

**Tournet Pokoje Gościnne** (Map p564; ☎ 292 00 88; www.accommodation.krakow.pl; ul Miodowa 7; s/d/tr from 140/180/220zł) This is a neat *pension* in Kazimierz, offering simple but comfortable and quiet rooms. The bathrooms, however, are tiny.

**Hotel Royal** (Map p562; ☎ 421 35 00; www.royal .com.pl; ul Św. Gertrudy 26-29; s 140-210zł, d 220-300zł, tr 300-330zł, ste 300-360zł; 🅿) Impressive Art Nouveau edifice with loads of old-world charm, just below Wawel Castle. It's split into two sections: the higher-priced two-star rooms are cosy, and far preferable to the fairly basic one-star rooms at the back.

**Hotel Abel** (Map p564; ☎ 411 87 36; www.hotelabel .pl; ul Józefa 30; s/d/tr 170/230/260) Reflecting the character of Kazimierz, this hotel has a distinctive personality, evident in its polished wooden staircase, arched brickwork and age-worn tiles. The comfortable rooms make a good base for exploring the historic Jewish neighbourhood.

**Wielopole Guest Rooms** (Map p562; ☎ 422 14 75; www.wielopole.pl; ul Wielopole 3; s/d from 190/280zł; P ⊠ &) Smart and simple modern rooms in a renovated block on the eastern edge of the Old Town, with narrow beds but spotless bathrooms. One room is designed for disabled access, and breakfast is only included for stays of two nights or more.

**Hotel Wit Stwosz** (Map p562; ☎ 429 60 26; www.wit -stwosz.com.pl; ul Mikołajska 28; s/d/tr €75/86/99, ste €130) In a historic town house belonging to St Mary's church, and decorated in a suitably religious theme. Rooms are compact and simply furnished, but tasteful and attractive.

### TOP END

**Hotel Saski** (Map p562; ☎ 421 42 22; www.hotelsaski.com .pl; ul Sławkowska 3; s/d/ste 295/360/450zł; ⊠) The Saski occupies a historic mansion, complete with a uniformed doorman, rattling old lift and ornate furnishings. The rooms themselves are comparatively plain, though some singles are surprisingly spacious.

**Hotel Wawel** (Map p562; ☎ 424 13 00; www.hotel wawel.pl; ul Poselska 22; s/d 260/380zł; ⊠) Ideally located just off busy ul Grodzka, this is a pleasant place offering tastefully decorated rooms with timber highlights. It's far enough back from the main drag to avoid most of the noise.

**Hotel Alexander** (Map p562; ☎ 422 96 60; www.alex hotel.pl; ul Garbarska 18; s/d 340/400zł; P ⊠ &) The Alexander is a bright and very modern place, offering standard three-star comfort. It's on a shabby but quiet street just west of the Old Town. One room is designed for disabled access.

**Hotel Amadeus** (Map p562; ☎ 429 60 70; www.hotel -amadeus.pl; ul Mikołajska 20; s/d €156/166, ste €240; ⊠ &) Everything about this hotel says 'class'. The rooms are tastefully furnished, though singles are rather small given the price. One room has disabled access, and there's a sauna, a fitness centre, and a well-regarded restaurant. While hanging around the Amadeus' foyer, you can check out photos of famous guests.

## Eating

Kraków is a food paradise, tightly packed with restaurants serving a wide range of international cuisines.

One local speciality is *obwarzanki* (ring-shaped pretzels powdered with poppy seeds, sesame seeds or salt) available from street vendors dozing next to their barrows.

### POLISH

**Restauracja Pod Gruszką** (Map p562; ☎ 422 88 96; ul Szczepańska 1; mains 12-55zł; ☾ noon-midnight) A favourite haunt of writers and artists, this upstairs establishment is the eatery that time forgot, with its elaborate old-fashioned décor featuring chandeliers, lace tablecloths, age-worn carpets and sepia portraits. The menu covers a range of Polish dishes, the most distinctive being the soups served within small bread loaves.

**Restauracja Chłopskie Jadło** (Map p562; ☎ 429 51 57; ul Św. Jana 3; mains 12-80zł; ☾ noon-midnight) Arranged as an old country inn with wooden benches and traditional music, and serving tasty Polish food. Try the *żurek* (sour soup) with sausage and egg, for a light but filling meal. There are some vegetarian options on the menu, but brace yourself for the meat products hanging off the walls.

**Nostalgia** (Map p562; ☎ 425 42 60; ul Karmelicka 10; mains 13-36zł; ☾ noon-11pm) A refined version of the traditional Polish eatery, Nostalgia features a fireplace, overhead timber beams, uncrowded tables and courteous service. Wrap yourself around Russian dumplings, pork loins in green pepper sauce, or veggie options such as potato pancakes. In warm weather there's an outdoor dining area.

**Pod Aniołami** (Map p562; ☎ 421 39 99; ul Grodzka 35; mains 25-60zł; ☾ 1pm-midnight) This eatery 'under the angels' offers high-quality Polish food in a pleasant cellar atmosphere, though it can get a little smoky. Specialities include the huntsman's smoked wild boar steak.

### INTERNATIONAL

**Gruzińskie Chaczapuri** (Map p562; ☎ 0509 542 800; cnr ul Floriańska & ul Św. Marka; mains 10-18zł; ☾ 10am-midnight) Cheap and cheerful place serving up tasty Georgian dishes. Grills, salads and steaks fill out the menu, and there's a separate vegetarian selection with items such as the traditional Georgian cheese pie with stewed vegetables.

**Bombaj Tandoori** (Map p562; ☎ 422 37 97; ul Mikołajska 11; mains 11-32zł; ☾ noon-11pm) The Bombaj

**POLAND**

Tandoori is the best curry house in Kraków, with friendly staff and a lengthy menu of Indian standards. The four-person set menu (85zł) is excellent value, and there's also a takeaway and local delivery service.

**Casa della Pizza** (Map p562; ☎ 421 64 98; Mały Rynek 2; mains 12-32zł; ☼ 11am-midnight) This unpretentious place is away from the bulk of the tourist traffic, with a menu of pizzas and pasta. The downstairs bar section is the Arabian-styled Shisha Club, serving Middle Eastern food.

**Orient Ekspres** (Map p562; ☎ 422 66 72; ul Stolarska 13; mains 15-48zł; ☼ 11am-11pm) Hercule Poirot might be surprised to find this elegant eatery here, well off the route of its railway namesake. The food is mainly Polish, with some international additions, accompanied by wine by the glass. Mellow music and candlelight make it a good place for a romantic rendezvous.

**Smak Ukraiński** (Map p562; ☎ 421 92 94; ul Kanonicza 15; mains 15-50zł; ☼ 11am-9pm) This Ukrainian restaurant presents authentic dishes in a cosy little cellar decorated with provincial flair. Expect lots of dumplings, *borscht* and waiters in waistcoats.

**Café Alef** (Map p564; ☎ 421 38 70; ul Szeroka 17; mains 16-45zł; ☼ noon-11pm) This is a quaint place in the heart of Kazimierz, with gilt-edged mirrors and lace tablecloths. It offers an array of Jewish-inspired dishes such as chicken *knedlach* (dumplings) and stuffed goose neck.

**Ipanema** (Map p562; ☎ 422 53 23; ul Św. Tomasza 28; mains from 16zł; ☼ noon-11pm) A banana palm as décor may seem out of place in Poland, but this bright place pulls it off. The Brazilian menu features steaks, grills and a range of interesting Afro-Brazilian dishes.

**Metropolitan Restaurant** (Map p562; ☎ 421 98 03; ul Sławkowska 3; mains 22-68zł; ☼ 7.30am-midnight Mon-Sat, 7.30am-10pm Sun) Attached to Hotel Saski, this place has nostalgic B&W photos of international locales plastering the walls, and is a great place for breakfast. It also serves pasta, grills and steaks, and luxurious items such as honey and orange roasted leg of duck.

### VEGETARIAN

**Momo** (Map p564; ☎ 0609 685 775; ul Dietla 49; mains 4-12zł; ☼ 11am-8pm) Vegans will cross the doorstep of this Kazimierz restaurant with relief – the majority of the menu is completely animal-free. The space is decorated with Indian craft pieces, and serves up subcontinental soups, stuffed pancakes and rice dishes, with a great range of cakes. The Tibetan dumplings are a treat worth ordering.

**Green Way Bar Wegetariański** (Map p562; ☎ 431 10 27; ul Mikołajska 14; mains 10-15zł; ☼ 10am-10pm Mon-Fri, 11am-9pm Sat & Sun) The Green Way offers good value vegetarian fare such as veggie kofta, enchiladas and salads.

## Drinking

There are hundreds of pubs and bars in Kraków's Old Town, many housed in ancient vaulted cellars, which get very smoky. Kazimierz also has a lively bar scene, centred on plac Nowy and its surrounding streets.

**Paparazzi** (Map p562; ☎ 429 45 97; ul Mikołajska 9; ☼ 11am-1am Mon-Fri, 4pm-4am Sat & Sun) If you haven't brought any reading material with you to this bar, look up – the ceiling is plastered with pages from racy tabloid newspapers. It's a bright, modern place, with black-and-white press photos covering the walls. The drinks menu includes cocktails such as the Polish Express, built around vanilla vodka. There's also inexpensive bar food.

**Le Scandale** (Map p564; ☎ 430 68 55; plac Nowy 9; ☼ 8am-3am) Smooth Kazimierz drinking hole with low black leather couches, ambient lighting and a gleaming well-stocked bar. Full of mellow drinkers sampling the extensive cocktail list.

**Transilvania** (Map p564; ☎ 0692 335 867; ul Szeroka 9; ☼ 10am-3am) The Transilvania is another convivial place in Kazimierz, with a vampire theme going on. Check out the portrait of Vlad the Impaler over the bar.

**Pod Papugami** (Map p562; ☎ 422 82 99; ul Św. Jana 18; ☼ 1pm-2am Mon-Sat, 3pm-2am Sun) This is a vaguely 'Irish' cellar pub decorated with old motorcycles and other assorted odds and ends. A good place to hide from inclement weather, with its pool table and tunnel-like maze of rooms.

**Piwnica Pod Złotą Pipą** (Map p562; ☎ 421 94 66; ul Floriańska 30; ☼ noon-midnight) Less claustrophobic than other cellar bars, with lots of tables for eating or drinking. Decent bar food and international beers on tap.

**Café Camelot** (Map p562; ☎ 421 01 23; ul Św. Tomasza 17; ☼ 9am-midnight) For coffee and cake, try this genteel haven hidden around an obscure street corner in the Old Town. Its cosy rooms are cluttered with lace-covered candlelit tables, and a quirky collection of wooden figurines featuring spiritual or folkloric scenes.

## Entertainment

The comprehensive Polish-English booklet *Karnet* (3zł), published by the Tourist Information Centre (see p561), lists almost every event in the city.

### NIGHTCLUBS

**Piano Rouge** (Map p562; ☎ 431 03 33; Rynek Główny 46; ☻ noon-3am) A sumptuous cellar venue decked out with classic sofas, ornate lampshades and billowing lengths of colourful silk. There's live jazz every night from Wednesday to Sunday.

**Łubu-Dubu** (Map p562; ☎ 423 05 21; ul Wielopole 15; ☻ 4pm-2am Sun-Thu, 5pm-4am Fri & Sat) The name of this place (*woo*boo-*doo*boo) is as funky as its décor. This grungy upstairs joint is an echo of the past, from the garish colours to the collection of objects from 1970s Poland. A series of rooms creates spaces for talking or dancing as the mood strikes.

**Alchemia** (Map p564; ☎ 421 22 00; ul Estery 5; ☻ 9am-3am) This Kazimierz venue exudes a shabby-is-the-new-cool look with rough-hewn wooden benches, candlelit tables and a companionable gloom. It hosts regular live music gigs and theatrical events through the week.

**Black Gallery** (Map p562; ul Mikołajska 24; ☻ noon-6am) Underground pub-cum-nightclub with a modern aspect: split levels, exposed steel frame lighting and a metallic bar. It really gets going after midnight. It also has a more civilised courtyard.

**Frantic** (Map p562; ☎ 423 04 83; ul Szewska 5; ☻ 6pm-4am) Occupying vast brick cellars, Frantic is trendy, attractive and popular with foreigners.

### THEATRE

**Stary Teatr** (Map p562; ☎ 422 40 40; www.stary-teatr.pl; ul Jagiellońska 5) The best-known venue, Stary offers quality theatre.

**Teatr im Słowackiego** (Map p562; ☎ 422 40 22; plac Św. Ducha 1) This grand place, built in 1893, focuses on Polish classics and large productions.

**Filharmonia Krakówska** (Map p562; ☎ 422 94 77; ul Zwierzyniecka 1) Hosts one of the best orchestras in the country; concerts are usually held on Friday and Saturday.

### CINEMAS

Two convenient cinemas are **Kino Sztuka** (Map p562; ☎ 421 41 99; cnr Św. Tomasza & Św. Jana), and the tiny **Kino Pasaż** (Map p562; ☎ 422 77 13; Rynek Główny 9). Tickets cost from 11zł.

## Getting There & Away

For information on travelling from Kraków to Zakopane, Częstochowa or Oświęcim (for Auschwitz), refer to the relevant destination sections later.

### AIR

The **John Paul II International airport** (www.lotnisko-balice.pl) is more often called the Balice airport, after the suburb in which it's located, about 15km west of the Old Town. The airport terminal hosts several car-hire desks, along with currency exchanges. You can buy tickets for bus 192 to the city centre from the newsagency upstairs.

LOT flies between Kraków and Warsaw several times a day, and offers direct flights from Kraków to Frankfurt and Munich. Bookings for all flights can be made at the **LOT office** (Map p562; ☎ 422 42 15; ul Basztowa 15).

A range of other airlines, including budget operators, connect Kraków to cities in Europe. There are direct flights to and from London via British Airways, Centralwings (April to October), Easyjet, Sky Europe and Ryanair. Dublin is serviced by Ryanair (May to October), Sky Europe and Aer Lingus.

### BUS

If you've been travelling by bus elsewhere in Poland, Kraków's modern main **bus terminal** (Map p562; ul Bosacka 18) will seem like a palace compared to the usual facility. It's located on the other side of the main train station from the Old Town. However, bus services are limited to regional centres of minimal interest to travellers, as well as Lublin (40zł, four daily), Zamość (42zł, five daily), Warsaw (39zł, four daily), Wrocław (42zł, four daily) and Cieszyn (18zł, 10 daily) on the Czech border.

A daily Polski Express bus to Warsaw also departs from the bus terminal (67zł), but takes eight hours to reach the capital.

### TRAIN

The lovely old **Kraków Główny train station** (Map p562; plac Dworcowy), on the northeastern outskirts of the Old Town, handles all international trains and most domestic rail services. The railway platforms are about 150m north of the station building.

Each day from Kraków, 10 fast trains head to Warsaw (43zł, 2¾ hours). There are also 10 fast trains daily to Wrocław (41zł, 3¾ hours), six to Poznań (48zł, six hours), two to Lublin

**POLAND**

(44zł, five hours), and eight to Gdynia, via Gdańsk (101zł, 7¼ hours).

Advance tickets for international and domestic trains can be booked directly at the station or from Cracow Tours (p566).

## OŚWIĘCIM

☎ 033 / pop 48,000

Few place names have more impact than Auschwitz, which is seared into public consciousness as the location of history's most extensive experiment in genocide. Every year hundreds of thousands visit Oświęcim (osh-*fyen*-cheem) to learn about the infamous Nazi death camp's history, and to pay respect to the dead.

Established within disused army barracks in 1940, Auschwitz was initially designed to hold Polish prisoners, but was expanded into the largest centre for the extermination of European Jews. Two more camps were subsequently established: Birkenau (Brzezinka, also known as Auschwitz II), 3km west of Auschwitz; and Monowitz (Monowice), several kilometres west of Oświęcim. In the course of their operation, between one and 1.5 million people were murdered in these death factories – about 90% of these were Jews.

### Auschwitz

Auschwitz was only partially destroyed by the fleeing Nazis, so many of the original buildings remain as a bleak document of the camp's history. A dozen of the 30 surviving prison blocks house sections of the **State Museum Auschwitz-Birkenau** ( ☎ 844 81 00; www .auschwitz.org.pl; admission free; 8am-7pm Jun-Aug, 8am-6pm May & Sep, 8am-5pm Apr & Oct, 8am-4pm Mar & Nov, 8am-3pm Dec-Feb).

About every half-hour, the cinema in the **visitors centre** at the entrance shows a 15-minute documentary film (admission 3.50zł) about the liberation of the camp by Soviet troops on 27 January 1945. It's shown in several languages throughout the day; check the schedule at the information desk as soon as you arrive. The film is not recommended for children under 14 years old. The visitors centre also has a cafeteria, bookshops, a *kantor* and a left-luggage room.

Some basic explanations in Polish, English and Hebrew are provided on site, but you'll understand more if you buy the small *Auschwitz Birkenau Guide Book* (translated into about 15 languages) from the visitors centre.

An English-language tour (26zł per person, 3½ hours) of Auschwitz and Birkenau leaves at 11am daily, with others starting at 10am, 1pm and 3pm if there's enough demand. Tours in German or Polish commence when a group of seven or eight can be formed; otherwise, tours in a range of languages can be arranged in advance. But make sure you receive your allotted time; some guides tell you to wander around Birkenau by yourself and to make your own way back to Auschwitz.

### Birkenau

**Birkenau** (admission free; 8am-7pm Jun-Aug, 8am-6pm May & Sep, 8am-5pm Apr & Oct, 8am-4pm Mar & Nov, 8am-3pm Dec-Feb) was actually where the murder of huge numbers of Jews took place. This vast (175 hectares), purpose-built and grimly efficient camp had more than 300 prison barracks and four huge gas chambers complete with crematoria. Each gas chamber held 2000 people and electric lifts raised the bodies to the ovens. The camp could hold 200,000 inmates at one time.

Although much of the camp was destroyed by retreating Nazis, the size of the place, fenced off with barbed wire stretching almost as far as the eye can see, provides some idea of the scale of this heinous crime. The viewing platform above the entrance provides further perspective. In some ways, Birkenau is even more shocking than Auschwitz and there are far fewer tourists.

### Sleeping & Eating

For most visitors, Auschwitz and Birkenau are an easy day trip from Kraków. The cafeteria in the visitors centre is sufficient for a quick lunch.

**Centrum Dialogu i Modlitwy** ( ☎ 843 10 00; www .centrum-dialogu.oswiecim.pl; ul Kolbego 1; camp sites from 22zł, r per person with shared bathroom from 88zł; ) This place is 700m southwest of Auschwitz. It's comfortable and quiet, and the price includes breakfast. Rooms with private bathroom cost slightly more, and full board is also offered.

### Getting There & Away

From Kraków Główny station, 12 mostly slow trains go to Oświęcim (10zł, 1½ hours) each day, though more depart from Kraków Płaszów station.

Far more convenient are the 16 buses per day to Oświęcim (8zł, 1½ hours), which depart from the bus station in Kraków, four of which terminate at the museum. For the others, get off at the final stop, 200m from the entrance to Auschwitz. The return bus timetable to Kraków is displayed at the Birkenau visitors centre.

Every half-hour from 11.30am to 4.30pm between 15 April and 31 October, buses shuttle passengers between the visitor centres at Auschwitz and Birkenau (buses run later to 5.30pm in May and September, and until 6.30pm from June to August). Otherwise, follow the signs for an easy walk (3km) or take a taxi. Auschwitz is also linked to the town's train station by buses 24, 25, 28 and 29 every 30 to 40 minutes.

Most travel agencies in Kraków offer organised tours of Auschwitz (including Birkenau), from 100zł to 150zł per person. Check with the operator for exactly how much time the tour allows you at Auschwitz, as some run to a very tight schedule.

## CZĘSTOCHOWA
☎ 034 / pop 251,000

Częstochowa (chen-sto-*ho*-vah), 114km northwest of Kraków, is an attractive pilgrimage town, dominated by the graceful Jasna Góra monastery atop a hill at its centre. The monastery, founded by the Paulites of Hungary in 1382, is the home of the Black Madonna, and owes its fame to a miracle. In 1430 a group of Hussites stole the holy icon, slashed it and broke it into three pieces. Legend has it that the picture bled, and the monks cleaned the retrieved panel with the aid of a spring, which rose miraculously from the ground. Though the picture was restored, the scars on the Virgin's face were retained in memory of the miracle.

The Madonna was also credited with the fortified monastery's resistance to the Swedish sieges of the 1650s. In 1717 the Black Madonna was crowned Queen of Poland.

From the train station, and adjacent bus terminal, turn right (north) up al Wolności – along which are several internet cafés – to the main thoroughfare, al Najświętszej Marii Panny (simplified to al NMP). At the western end of this avenue is the monastery and at the eastern end is plac Daszyńskiego. In-between is the **tourist office** ( ☎ 368 22 60; al NMP 65; ☽ 9am-5pm Mon-Sat) and several banks and *kantors*.

## Sights
The **Paulite Monastery on Jasna Góra** ( ☎ 365 38 88; www.jasnagora.pl; admission free; ☽ dawn-dusk) retains the appearance of a hilltop fortress. Inside the grounds are three **museums** (donations welcome; ☽ 9am-5pm): the **Arsenal**, with a variety of old weapons; the **600th-Anniversary Museum** (Muzeum Sześćsetlecia), which contains Lech Wałęsa's 1983 Nobel Peace Prize; and the **Treasury** (Skarbiec), featuring offerings presented by the faithful.

The **tower** ( ☽ 8am-4pm Apr-Nov) is the tallest (106m) historic church tower in Poland. The baroque church beneath is beautifully decorated. The image of the Black Madonna is on the high altar of the adjacent chapel, entered from the left of the church aisle. It's hard to see, so a copy is on display in the **Knights' Hall** (Sala Rycerska) in the monastery. Note that the Madonna is sometimes concealed by a silver cover; if so, check with the on-site information office for the next scheduled uncovering. It's quite an event, as priests file in, music plays and the image slowly emerges.

On weekends and holidays expect long queues for all three museums. The crowds in the chapel may be so thick that you're almost unable to enter, much less get near the icon.

In the Town Hall the **Częstochowa Museum** ( ☎ 360 56 31; al NMP 45; adult/child 4/3zł; ☽ 9am-3.30pm Tue, Thu & Fri, 11am-5.30pm Wed, 10am-4pm Sat & Sun) features an ethnographic collection and modern Polish paintings.

## Festivals & Events
The major Marian feasts at Jasna Góra are 3 May, 16 July, 15 August (especially), 26 August, 8 September, 12 September and 8 December. On these days the monastery is packed with pilgrims.

## Sleeping & Eating
**Youth Hostel** ( ☎ 324 31 21; ul Jasnogórska 84/90; dm 20-36zł; ☽ Jul-Aug) This hostel, two blocks north of the tourist office, has modest facilities. Look for the triangular green sign on the building's wall.

**Dom Pielgrzyma** ( ☎ 377 75 64; ul Wyszyńskiego 1/31; dm 23zł, s/d from 70/100zł) A huge place behind the monastery, it offers numerous quiet and comfortable rooms, and is remarkably good value.

Plenty of **eateries** can be found near the Dom Pielgrzyma. Better restaurants are dotted along al NMP.

**Restaurant Cleopatra** ( ☎ 368 01 01; al NMP 71; mains 10-18zł; ☽ 11am-11pm) The cheerfully out-of-place Cleopatra, near the tourist office, serves pizzas, kebabs and sandwiches among pillars painted with ancient Egyptian designs.

POLAND

**Bar Viking** ( ☎ 324 57 68; ul Nowowiejskiego 10; mains 6-40zł; ☒ 10am-10pm) About 200m south of the Częstochowa Museum is a friendly place with a good range of dishes, including vegetarian choices.

## Getting There & Away

Every day from the **bus terminal** (al Wolności 45) nine buses go to Kraków (14zł to 34zł), five travel to Wrocław (21zł to 29zł), eight head for Zakopane (30zł to 41zł) and seven depart for Warsaw (30zł to 46zł).

From the impressive **train station** (al Wolności 21) five trains a day go to Warsaw (38zł, 3½ hours). There are also three daily trains to Gdynia via Gdańsk (55zł, nine hours), four to Łódź (30zł, two hours), one to Olsztyn (52zł,

7½ hours), one to Zakopane (26zł, six hours), four to Kraków (29zł, two hours) and two to Wrocław (32zł, three hours).

## ZAKOPANE

☎ 018 / pop 30,000

Nestled at the foot of the Tatra Mountains, Zakopane is Poland's major winter sports centre, though it's a popular destination year-round. It may resemble a tourist trap, with its overcommercialised, overpriced exterior, but it also has a relaxed, laid-back vibe that makes it a great place to chill out for a few days, even if you're not intending to ski or hike.

Zakopane also played an important role in keeping Polish culture alive during the long years of foreign rule in the 19th century. Many

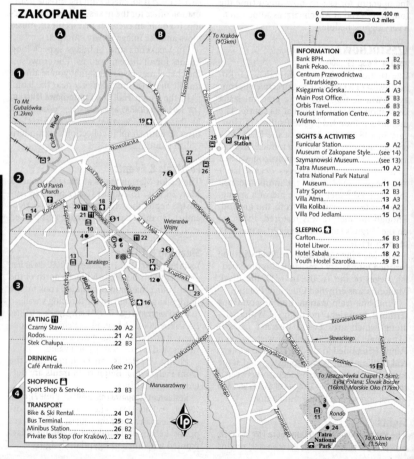

ZAKOPANE

**INFORMATION**
Bank BPH...........................................1 B2
Bank Pekao.........................................2 B3
Centrum Przewodnictwa
  Tatrańskiego.....................................3 D4
Księgarnia Górska................................4 A3
Main Post Office..................................5 B3
Orbis Travel........................................6 B3
Tourist Information Centre...................7 B2
Widmo................................................8 B3

**SIGHTS & ACTIVITIES**
Funicular Station..................................9 A2
Museum of Zakopane Style.....(see 14)
Szymanowski Museum............(see 13)
Tatra Museum....................................10 A2
Tatra National Park Natural
  Museum...........................................11 D4
Tatra Sport........................................12 B3
Villa Atma..........................................13 A3
Villa Koliba........................................14 A2
Villa Pod Jedlami...............................15 D4

**SLEEPING**
Carlton..............................................16 B3
Hotel Litwor......................................17 B3
Hotel Sabała......................................18 A2
Youth Hostel Szarotka........................19 B1

**EATING**
Czarny Staw.......................................20 A2
Rodos................................................21 A2
Stek Chałupa......................................22 B3

**DRINKING**
Café Antrakt...................................(see 21)

**SHOPPING**
Sport Shop & Service..........................23 B3

**TRANSPORT**
Bike & Ski Rental................................24 D4
Bus Terminal......................................25 C2
Minibus Station..................................26 B2
Private Bus Stop (for Kraków)...........27 B2

artistic types settled in the town, including composer Karol Szymanowski and the writer and painter, Witkacy. Witkacy's father, Stanisław Witkiewicz, was inspired by traditional local architecture to create the famous Zakopane style. Some of his buildings still stand.

## Information

### INTERNET ACCESS

**Widmo** ( ☎ 206 43 77; ul Galicy 6; per hr 4.50zł; ☻ 7.30am-midnight Mon-Fri, 9am-midnight Sat & Sun)

### MONEY

Dozens of *kantors* can be found along the main streets. There are several banks along the pedestrian mall.

**Bank Pekao** ( ☎ 201 40 84; al 3 Maja 5)

**Bank BPH** ( ☎ 201 49 09; ul Krupówki 19)

### POST

**Main post office** (ul Krupówki)

### TOURIST INFORMATION

**Tourist Information Centre** ( ☎ 201 22 11; ul Kościuszki 17; ☻ 8am-8pm Jun-Sep, 9am-6pm Oct-May) Helpful English-speaking staff provide advice, and sell hiking and city maps. The centre can also arrange rafting trips down the Dunajec River (see p576).

### TRAVEL AGENCIES

**Centrum Przewodnictwa Tatrzańskiego** (Tatra Guide Centre; ☎ 206 37 99; ul Chałubińskiego 42/44; ☻ 9am-3pm) Able to arrange English- and German-speaking mountain guides.

**Księgarnia Górska** (ul Zaruskiego 5) In the reception area of the Dom Turysty PTTK, this is the best place for regional hiking maps.

**Orbis Travel** ( ☎ 201 50 51; ul Krupówki 22) Offers the usual services, as well as accommodation in hotels and *pensions*. Also has an in-house *kantor*.

## Sights & Activities

Check out exhibits about regional history, ethnography and geology at the **Tatra Museum** ( ☎ 201 52 05; ul Krupówki 10; adult/child 5/4zł, free Sun; ☻ 9am-4pm Tue-Sat, 9am-3pm Sun May-Oct, 9am-4pm Wed-Sat, 9am-3pm Sun Nov-Apr), along with displays on local flora and fauna. Head southwest to **Villa Koliba** (ul Kościeliska 18), the first design (1892) by Witkiewicz in the Zakopane style. Fittingly, it now houses the **Museum of Zakopane Style** ( ☎ 201 36 02; adult/child 5/4zł; ☻ 9am-5pm Tue-Sat, 9am-3pm Sun).

About 350m southeast is **Villa Atma** (ul Kasprusie 19) with its **Szymanowksi Museum** ( ☎ 201 34 93; adult/child 5/3zł, free Sun; ☻ 10am-3.30pm Wed, Thu, Sat &

Sun, 10am-6pm Fri), dedicated to the great musician who once lived there. There are piano recitals here in summer.

The **Tatra National Park Natural Museum** ( ☎ 206 32 03; ul Chałubińskiego 42a; admission free; ☻ 8am-3pm Mon-Sat), near the Rondo en route to the national park, has some mildly interesting exhibits about the park's natural history.

A short walk northeast up the hill leads to **Villa Pod Jedlami** (ul Koziniec 1), another splendid house built in the Zakopane style (the interior cannot be visited). Perhaps Witkiewicz's greatest achievement is the **Jaszczurówka Chapel**, about 1.5km further east along the road to Morskie Oko.

**Mt Gubałówka** (1120m) offers excellent views over the Tatras and is a popular destination for tourists who don't feel overly energetic. The **funicular** (tickets adult/child 8/6zł, return 14/10zł; ☻ 9am-9pm May-Sep, 8am-7pm Oct-Apr) covers the 1388m-long route in less than five minutes, climbing 300m from the funicular station just north of ul Krupówki.

## Sleeping

Given the abundance of private rooms and decent hostels, few travellers actually stay in hotels. The tourist office usually knows of great bargains in guesthouses.

Some travel agencies in Zakopane can arrange private rooms, but in the peak season they may not want to offer anything for less than three nights. Expect a double room (singles are rarely offered) to cost about 70zł in the peak season in the town centre, and about 50zł for somewhere further out.

Locals offering private rooms may approach you at the bus or train stations; alternatively, just look out for signs posted in the front of private homes – *noclegi* and *pokoje* both mean 'rooms available'.

Like all seasonal resorts, accommodation prices fluctuate considerably between low season and high season (December to February and July to August). Always book accommodation in advance at these peak times, especially on weekends. The following rates are for high season.

**Youth Hostel Szarotka** ( ☎ 201 36 18; www.szarotka ptsm.republika.pl; ul Nowotarska 45; dm/d 35/90zł; Ⓟ ✗ ) This friendly, homely place gets packed in the high season. There's a kitchen and washing machine on site, and bed linen costs 5zł extra. It's on a noisy road about a 10-minute walk from the town centre.

**Carlton** ( ☎ 201 44 15; www.carlton.pl; ul Grunwaldzka 11; s/d/tr 90/180/270zł; P 💻 ) Good value *pension* in a grand old house away from the main drag, featuring light-filled rooms with modern furniture. There's an impressive shared balcony overlooking the road, and a big comfy lounge lined with potted plants.

**Hotel Sabała** ( ☎ 201 50 92; www.sabala.zakopane.pl; ul Krupówki 11; s/d/ste from 275/370/480zł; P ✕ 💻 ) Built in 1894 but thoroughly up-to-date, this striking timber building has a superb location overlooking the picturesque pedestrian thoroughfare. It offers cosy, attic-style rooms, and there's a sauna and solarium on the premises. A candlelit **restaurant** (mains 12-42zł) has views of street life.

**Hotel Litwor** ( ☎ 202 42 00; www.litwor.pl; ul Krupówki 40; s/d 425/575zł, ste from 600zł; P ✕ 💻 🍴 ) This sumptuous four-star place, with large, restful rooms, has all the usual top-end facilities, including a gym and sauna. A discount applies to advance bookings. It also has an excellent restaurant serving classy versions of traditional dishes.

## Eating & Drinking

The main street, ul Krupówki, is lined with all sorts of eateries.

**Czarny Staw** ( ☎ 201 38 56; ul Krupówki 2; mains 11-35zł; 🕙 10am-1am) Offers a tasty range of Polish dishes, including fish, much of it cooked before your very eyes on the central grill. There's a good salad bar, and live music most nights.

**Rodos** (ul Krupówki 6; mains 13-29zł; 🕙 9am-10pm) If you need a break from Polish food served by waiters in Tatran costume, this Greek eatery provides a good range of kebabs, gyros and pasta dishes, in a space decorated with Mediterranean scenes and the odd off-theme prop from the Middle East.

**Stek Chałupa** ( ☎ 201 59 18; ul Krupówki 33; mains 16-36zł; 🕙 11am-11pm) Big friendly barn of a place, with homely décor and waitresses in traditional garb. The menu features meat dishes, particularly steaks, though there are vegetarian choices among the salads and *pierogi*.

**Café Antrakt** ( ☎ 201 73 02; ul Krupówki 6; 🕙 11am-midnight) A mellow venue for an alcoholic or caffeine-laden drink, hidden away above Rodos with an ambient old-meets-new décor. It occasionally hosts live jazz.

## Getting There & Away

From the **bus terminal** (ul Chramcówki), fast PKS buses run to Kraków every 45 to 60 minutes

(13zł, 2½ hours). Two private companies, Trans Frej (www.trans-frej.com.pl, in Polish) and Szwagropol (www.szwagropol.pl, in Polish), also run comfortable buses (15zł) at the same frequency. These private buses leave from a stop along ul Kościuszki in Zakopane, and from the bus terminal in Kraków. At peak times (especially weekends), buy your tickets for the private buses in advance from counters outside the departure points in Zakopane. Tickets are also available in Kraków for Trans Frej buses from **Biuro Turystyki i Zakwaterowania Waweltur** (Map p562; ul Pawia 8) and for Szwagropol buses from **Pol-Tur** (Map p562; ul Pawia 12). The minibus station opposite the bus terminal is most useful for journeys to towns within the Tatra Mountains.

From Zakopane, PKS buses also go once daily to Lublin (57zł, six hours), Sanok (35zł, 6½ hours), Oświęcim (23zł) and Przemyśl; and four times daily to Warsaw (54zł, eight hours). At least one bus daily heads to Poprad in Slovakia (19zł). PKS buses – and minibuses from opposite the bus terminal – regularly travel to Lake Morskie Oko and on to Polana Palenica. To cross into Slovakia, get off this bus/minibus at Łysa Polana, cross the border on foot and take another bus to Tatranská Lomnica in Slovakia.

From the **train station** (ul Chramcówki), trains for Kraków (19zł, 3½ hours) leave every two hours or so, but avoid the slow train, which takes up to five hours. Between one and three trains a day go to Częstochowa, Gdynia via Gdańsk, Lublin, Łódź and Poznań, and five head to Warsaw.

# TATRA MOUNTAINS
☎ 018

The Tatras, 100km south of Kraków, are the highest range of the Carpathian Mountains. Roughly 60km long and 15km wide, this mountain range stretches across the Polish–Slovak border. A quarter is in Poland and is mostly part of the Tatra National Park (about 212 sq km). The Polish Tatras contain more than 20 peaks over 2000m, the highest of which is Mt Rysy (2499m).

## Cable Car to Mt Kasprowy Wierch

The **cable car** (return adult/child 30/20zł; 🕙 7am-9pm Jul-Aug, 7.30-5pm Mar-Jun & Sep-Oct, 8am-4pm Nov-Feb) from Kuźnice (3km south of Zakopane) to the summit of Mt Kasprowy Wierch (1985m) is a classic tourist experience enjoyed by Poles and foreigners alike. At the end of the trip, you can get off and stand with one foot in Poland and the other in Slovakia. The one-way journey takes 20 minutes and climbs 936m. The cable car normally shuts down for two weeks in May and November, and won't operate if the snow and, particularly, the winds are dangerous.

The view from the top is spectacular (clouds permitting). Two chairlifts transport skiers to and from various slopes between December and April. A small cafeteria serves skiers and hikers alike. In summer, many people return to Zakopane on foot down the Gąsienicowa Valley, and the most intrepid walk the ridges all the way across to Lake Morskie Oko via Pięciu Stawów, a strenuous hike taking a full day in good weather.

If you buy a return ticket, your trip back is automatically reserved for two hours after your departure, so buy a one-way ticket to the top (19zł) and another one down (14zł), if you want to stay longer. Mt Kasprowy Wierch is popular; so in summer, arrive early and expect to wait. PKS buses and minibuses to Kuźnice frequently leave from Zakopane.

## Lake Morskie Oko

The emerald-green Lake Morskie Oko (Eye of the Sea) is a popular destination and among the loveliest lakes in the Tatras. PKS buses and minibuses regularly depart from Zakopane for Polana Palenica (30 minutes), from where a road (9km) continues uphill to the lake. Cars, bikes and buses are not allowed up this road, so you'll have to walk, but it's not steep (allow about two hours one way). Alternatively, take a horse-drawn carriage (32/25zł uphill/downhill, but very negotiable) to within 2km of the lake. In winter, transport is by horse-drawn four-seater sledge, which is more expensive. The last minibus to Zakopane returns between 5pm and 6pm.

## Hiking

If you're doing any hiking in the Tatras get a copy of the *Tatrzański Park Narodowy* map (1:25,000), which shows all hiking trails in the area. Better still, buy one or more of the 14 sheets of *Tatry Polskie*, available at Księgarnia Górska in Zakopane (p573). In July and August these trails can be overrun by tourists, so late spring and early autumn are the best times. Theoretically you can expect better weather in autumn, when rainfall is lower.

Like all alpine regions, the Tatras can be dangerous, particularly during the snow season (November to May). Remember the weather can be unpredictable. Bring proper hiking boots, warm clothing and waterproof rain gear – and be prepared to use occasional ropes and chains (provided along the trails) to get up and down some rocky slopes. Guides are not necessary because many of the trails are marked, but can be arranged in Zakopane (see p573 for details) for about 230z³ per day.

There are several picturesque valleys south of Zakopane, including the **Dolina Strążyska**. You can continue from the Strążyska by the red trail up to **Mt Giewont** (1909m), 3½ hours from Zakopane, and then walk down the blue trail to Kuźnice in two hours.

Two long and beautiful forested valleys, the **Dolina Chochołowska** and the **Dolina Kościeliska**, are in the western part of the park, known as the Tatry Zachodnie (West Tatras). These valleys are ideal for cycling. Both are accessible by PKS buses and minibuses from Zakopane.

The Tatry Wysokie (High Tatras) to the east offer quite different scenery: bare granite peaks and glacial lakes. One way to get there is via cable car to **Mt Kasprowy Wierch**, then hike eastward along the red trail to Mt Świnica (2301m) and on to the Zawrat pass (2159m) – a tough three to four hours from Mt Kasprowy. From Zawrat, descend northwards to the Dolina Gąsienicowa along the blue trail and then back to Zakopane.

Alternatively, head south (also along the blue trail) to the wonderful **Dolina Pięciu Stawów** (Five Lakes Valley), where there is a mountain refuge 1L hours from Zawrat. The blue trail heading west from the refuge passes **Lake Morskie Oko**, 1½ hours from the refuge.

## Skiing

Zakopane boasts four major ski areas (and several smaller ones) with more than 50 ski lifts. **Mt Kasprowy Wierch** and **Mt Gubałówka** offer the best conditions and most challenging slopes in the area, with the ski season extending until early May. Lift tickets cost 10zł for one ride at Mt Kasprowy Wierch, and 2zł on the much smaller lift at Mt Gubałówka. Alternatively, you can buy a 10-ride card (70zł Mt Kasprowy Wierch, 18zł Mt Gubałówka) which allows you to skip the queues. Purchase your lift tickets on the relevant mountain.

**POLAND**

Ski equipment rental is available at all facilities except Mt Kasprowy Wierch. Otherwise, stop off on your way to Kuźnice at the **ski rental** place near the Rondo in Zakopane. Other places in Zakopane, such as **Tatry Sport** (ul Piłsudskiego 4) and **Sport Shop & Service** (ul Krupówki 52a), also rent ski gear.

## Sleeping

Tourists are not allowed to take their own cars into the park; you must walk in, take the cable car or use an official vehicle owned by the park or a hotel or hostel.

Camping is also not allowed in the park, but eight PTTK mountain refuges/hostels provide simple accommodation. Most refuges are small and fill up fast; in midsummer and midwinter they're invariably packed beyond capacity. No one is ever turned away, however, though you may have to crash on the floor if all the beds are taken. Do not arrive too late in the day, and bring along your own bed mat and sleeping bag. All refuges serve simple hot meals, but the kitchens and dining rooms close early (sometimes at 7pm).

The refuges listed here are open all year, but some may be temporarily closed for renovations or because of inclement weather. Check the current situation at the Dom Turysty PTTK in Zakopane or the regional **PTTK headquarters** ( ☎ 018-443 74 57) in Nowy Sącz.

The easiest refuge to reach from Zakopane is the large and decent **Kalatówki Hotel** ( ☎ 206 36 44; s/d/tr from 46/90/111zł), a 40-minute walk from the Kuźnice cable-car station. About 30 minutes beyond Kalatówki on the trail to Giewont is **Hala Kondratowa Hostel** ( ☎ 201 91 14; dm 20-22zł). It's in a great location and has a great atmosphere, but it is small.

Hikers wishing to traverse the park might begin at the **Roztoka Hostel** ( ☎ 207 74 42; dm 22-30zł), accessible by the bus or minibus to Morskie Oko. An early start from Zakopane, however, would allow you to visit Morskie Oko in the morning and stay at the **Morskie Oko Hostel** ( ☎ 207 76 09; dm from 40zł), or continue through to the **Dolina Pięciu Stawów Hostel** ( ☎ 207 76 07; dm from 25zł). This is the highest (1700m) and most scenically located refuge in the Polish Tatras.

## DUNAJEC GORGE

An entertaining and leisurely way to explore the Pieniny Mountains is to go **rafting** on the Dunajec River, which winds along the Polish–Slovak border through a spectacular and deep gorge.

The trip starts at the wharf (Przystan Flisacka) in Kąty, 46km northeast of Zakopane, and finishes at the spa town of Szczawnica. The 17km (2″ hours) raft trip operates between May and October, but only starts when there's a minimum of 10 passengers.

The gorge is an easy day trip from Zakopane. In summer, 10 PKS buses to Kąty leave from the bus station. Alternatively, catch a regular bus to Nowy Targ (30 minutes) from Zakopane and one of six daily buses (one hour) to Kąty. From Szczawnica, take the bus back to Zakopane or change at Nowy Targ. Each day, five buses also travel between Szczawnica and Kraków.

To avoid waiting around in Kąty for a raft to fill up, organise a trip at any travel agency in Zakopane or at the tourist office. The cost is around 60zł to 70zł per person, and includes transport, equipment and guides.

## SANOK

☎ 013 / pop 40,000

Nestled in a picturesque valley in the foothills of the Bieszczady Mountains, Sanok has been subject to Ruthenian, Hungarian, Austrian, Russian, German and Polish rule in its eventful history. Although it contains an important industrial zone, it's also a popular base for exploring the mountains.

The helpful **PTTK office** ( ☎ 463 21 71; www.pttk .sanok.com.pl; ul 3 Maja 2; ☯ 8am-5pm Mon-Fri), near the market square, is the best place to find brochures on Sanok's attractions. There's also a tourist information desk inside **Orbis Travel** ( ☎ 463 28 59; ul Grzegorza 4; ☯ 9am-5pm Mon-Fri, 9am-1pm Sat). There's a **Bank Pekao** (cnr ul Grzegorza & ul Kościuszki) nearby, and you can check email at **Prox** ( ☎ 464 22 50; ul Kazimierz Wielkiego 6; per hr 3.50zł) further west.

Sanok is noted for its unique **Museum of Folk Architecture** ( ☎ 463 16 72; ul Rybickiego 3; adult/child 9/6zł; ☯ 8am-6pm May-Oct, 8am-2pm Nov-Apr), which features architecture from regional ethnic groups. Walk north from the town centre for 2km along ul Mickiewicza and ul Białogórska, then cross the bridge and turn right. The **Historical Museum** ( ☎ 464 13 66; ul Zamkowa 2; adult/child 10/7zł; ☯ 9am-5pm Tue & Wed, 8am-3pm Thu & Fri, 9am-3pm Sat & Sun Apr-Oct; 8am-3pm Mon, Thu & Fri, 9am-5pm Tue & Wed, 9am-3pm Sat & Sun Nov-Mar) is housed in a 16th-century castle and contains an impressive collection of Ruthenian icons.

Sanok's surrounding villages are attractions in their own right, as many have lovely old churches. The marked **Icon Trail** takes hikers or cyclists along a 70km loop, passing by 10 village churches, as well as attractive mountain countryside. Trail leaflets and maps (in English, German and French) are available from the PTTK and Orbis offices.

Convenient budget accommodation is available at **Hotel Pod Trzema Różami** ( ☎ 463 09 22; trzyroze@ooh.pl; ul Jagiellońska 13; s/d/tr 80/100/120zł; **P** **里** ), about 300m south of the main square. Further south (another 600m) and up the scale is **Hotel Jagielloński** ( ☎ /fax 463 12 08; ul Jagiellońska 49; s/d/tr/ste from 90/110/130/140zł; **P** ), with distinctive wooden furniture, parquetry floors and a very good **restaurant** (mains 14-35zł). Another comfortable option is **Hotel Sanvit** ( ☎ 465 50 88; www.sanvit.sanok.pl; ul Łazienna 1; s/d/tr 115/135/165zł, ste from 155zł; **P** **里** **里** ), just west of the square, with bright, modern rooms, shining bathrooms and a restaurant.

**Karczma Jadło Karpackie** ( ☎ 464 67 00; Rynek 12; mains 8-20zł; ⏱ 9am-10pm) is an amenable, down-to-earth bar and restaurant on the main square. A good place to have a drink, alcoholic or otherwise, is **Weranda Caffe** ( ☎ 0609 741 936; ul 3 Maja 14; ⏱ 10am-10pm), a cosy café-bar with a fireplace, and outdoor seating in summer.

The bus terminal and adjacent train station are about 1km southeast of the main square. Four buses go daily to Przemyśl (11zł, two hours), and one to Zakopane (35zł, 6½ hours). Buses also head regularly to Kraków and Warsaw. Train journeys to these destinations, however, may require multiple changes.

## PRZEMYŚL

☎ 016 / pop 68,000

Everything about Przemyśl (*psheh*-mishl) feels big: its sprawling market square, the massive churches surrounding it, and the broad San River flowing through the city.

Luckily the area of most interest to visitors – its sloping and well-preserved **Rynek** (Market Square) – is compact and easily explored. The **tourist office** ( ☎ 675 16 64; www.parr.pl; Rynek 26; ⏱ 8am-4pm Mon-Fri, 9am-3pm Sat) is on the northwest corner of the square as it stretches down toward the river. Check your emails at **Blue Net** ( ☎ 678 55 62; ul Słowackiego 14; per hr 3zł), along the main road on the eastern edge of the Old Town.

About 350m southwest of the Rynek are the ruins of a 14th-century **castle** (ul Zamkowa), built by Kazimierz Wielki. The **Regional Museum** ( ☎ 678 33 25; plac Czackiego 3; adult/child 5/3zł;

⏱ 10.30am-5pm Tue & Fri, 10am-2pm Wed, Thu, Sat & Sun) houses a splendid collection of Ruthenian icons and Austro-Hungarian militaria, and a dry display of local archaeological finds. It's about 150m southeast of the Rynek.

For variety, visit the curious **Museum of Bells and Pipes** ( ☎ 678 96 66; ul Władycze 3; adult/child 5/3zł; ⏱ 10.30am-5.30pm Tue & Fri, 10am-2.30pm Wed, Thu & Sat, 12.15-3.45pm Sun Apr-Oct) in the old Clock Tower, where you can inspect several floors worth of vintage bells, elaborately carved pipes and cigar cutters (the city has long been famous across Poland for manufacturing these items). From the top of the tower, there's a great view of town.

Back in the Rynek, the **Museum of the City of Przemyśl** ( ☎ 678 65 01; Rynek 9; adult/child 5/3zł; ⏱ 10.30am-5pm Tue & Fri, 10am-2pm Wed, Thu, Sat & Sun) showcases furniture, photographs and other items from the 19th and 20th centuries.

Przemyśl has a wide selection of inexpensive accommodation, including the central **Dom Wycieczkowy Podzamcze** ( ☎ 678 53 74; ul Waygarta 3; dm 20-24zł, d/tr 58/72zł), on the western edge of the Old Town. Its rooms have seen some wear, but have recently been repainted, and the largest dorm is decked out with potted plants and a TV. **Hotelik Pod Basztą** ( ☎ 670 82 68; ul Królowej Jadwigi 4; s/d/tr from 49/59/79zł) is just below the castle. Rooms are a little old-fashioned, with shared bathrooms, but many have castle or city views. The one 'superior' room boasts a spectacular balcony overlooking the Old Town.

More comfort is available at **Hotel Europejski** ( ☎ 675 71 00; ul Sowińskiego 4; s/d/tr 90/120/140zł) in a renovated old building facing the attractive façade of the train station. An impressive staircase leads to simple, light rooms with high ceilings and modern bathrooms.

**Restauracja Karpacka** ( ☎ 678 90 57; ul Kościuszki 5; mains 8-18zł; ⏱ 10am-10pm), just west of the tourist office, is an old-fashioned eatery featuring bow-tied waiters, a timber ceiling and yellow stucco walls. It serves a good range of Polish standards, and Ukrainian *borscht* in a nod to the neighbours just down the road.

Another worthy place to eat is **Restauracja Piwnica Mieszczańska** ( ☎ 675 04 59; Rynek 9; mains 8-25zł; ⏱ 11am-11pm), in the same building as the city museum. Its cellar setting is decorated with mini-chandeliers and lace tablecloths. The bourgeoisie platter (three kinds of meat) will interest ardent carnivores, and there's a reasonable selection of soups and fish dishes.

From Przemyśl, buses run to Lviv (95km) in Ukraine six times a day and regularly to all towns in southeastern Poland, including Sanok (11zl, two hours, four daily). Trains run regularly from Przemyśl to Lublin, Kraków and Warsaw, and stop here on the way to/ from Lviv. The bus terminal and adjacent train station in Przemyśl are about 1km northeast of the Rynek.

## LUBLIN

☎ 081 / pop 358,000

Lublin is a city resonant with important moments in Polish history. In 1569 the Lublin Union was signed here, uniting Poland and Lithuania; and at the end of WWII, the Soviet Union set up a communist government in Lublin, prior to the liberation of Warsaw. Throughout history the city has faced numerous invasions by warlike neighbours, though today its beautifully preserved Old Town is a peaceful blend of Gothic, Renaissance and baroque architecture.

### Information

Plenty of ATMs can be found on ul Krakowskie Przedmieście, and at several *kantors* along ul Peowiaków.

**Bank Pekao** (ul Królewska 1) Changes travellers cheques and gives cash advances on Visa and MasterCard. There's a branch at ul Krakowskie Przedmieście 64.

**EMPiK Megastore** (Galeria Centrum, 3rd fl, ul Krakowskie Przedmieście 16) Maps, books and international newspapers are available here.

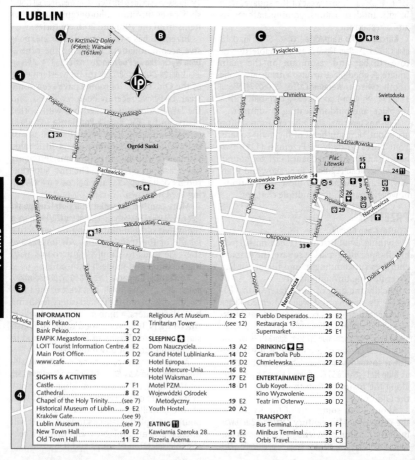

**LOIT Tourist Information Centre** ( ☎ 532 44 12; www.lublin.pl; ul Jezuicka 1/3; ⊙ 10am-6pm Mon-Fri, 10am-4pm Sat, 10am-3pm Sun May-Sep, 9am-5pm Mon-Fri, 10am-3pm Sat Oct-Apr) Has helpful English-speaking staff, and lots of free brochures, including the city walking-route guide *Tourist Routes of Lublin*. It also sells maps of various Polish and Ukrainian cities.

**Main post office** (ul Krakowskie Przedmieście 50)

**www.café** ( ☎ 442 35 80; 3rd fl, Rynek 8; per hr 3zł; ⊙ 10am-10pm)

## Sights

### CASTLE

The substantial castle, standing on a hill northeast of the Old Town, has a dark history. It was built in the 14th century, then was rebuilt as a prison in the 1820s. During the

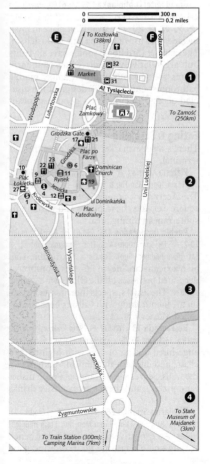

Nazi occupation, more than 100,000 people passed its doors before being deported to the death camps. Its major occupant is now the **Lublin Museum** ( ☎ 532 50 01; www.zamek-lublin.pl; ul Zamkowa 9; adult/child 6.50/4.50zł; ⊙ 9am-4pm Wed-Sat, 9am-5pm Sun). On display are paintings, silverware, porcelain, wood-carvings and weaponry, mostly labelled only in Polish. Check out the alleged 'devil's paw-print' on the 17th-century table in the foyer, linked to an intriguing local legend.

At the eastern end of the castle is the gorgeous 14th-century **Chapel of the Holy Trinity** (adult/child 6.50/4.50zł, incl museum 10/6zł; ⊙ 9am-3.45pm Mon-Sat, 9am-4.45pm Sun), accessible via the museum. Its interior is covered with polychrome Russo-Byzantine frescoes painted in 1418 – possibly the finest medieval wall paintings in Poland.

### OLD TOWN

The compact historic quarter is centred on the **Rynek**, the main square surrounding the neoclassical **Old Town Hall** (1781). The **Historical Museum of Lublin** ( ☎ 532 60 01; plac Łokietka 3; adult/child 3.50/2.50zł; ⊙ 9am-4pm Wed-Sat, 9am-5pm Sun), displaying documents and photos, is inside the 14th-century **Kraków Gate**, a remnant of medieval fortifications. Daily at noon, a bugler plays a special tune atop the **New Town Hall** opposite the gate. (If you're a bugling addict, don't miss the annual **National Bugle Contest** on 15 August.)

For an expansive view of the Old Town, climb to the top of the **Trinitarian Tower** (1819), which houses the **Religious Art Museum** ( ☎ 743 64 33; plac Katedralny; adult/child 5/3zł; ⊙ 10am-5pm Apr-Oct, 10am-3pm Sat & Sun Nov-Mar). Nearby is the 16th-century **cathedral** (plac Katedralny; ⊙ dawn-dusk) and its impressive baroque frescoes. The painting of the Virgin Mary is said to have shed tears in 1949, so it's a source of pride and reverence for local believers.

### MAJDANEK

About 4km southeast is the **State Museum of Majdanek** ( ☎ 744 26 40; admission free; ⊙ 8am-6pm May-Sep, 8am-3pm Oct-Apr). It commemorates one of the largest Nazi death camps, where some 235,000 people, including more than 100,000 Jews, were massacred. Barracks, guard towers and barbedwire fences remain in place; even more chilling are the crematorium and gas chambers.

A short explanatory film (admission 2zł) can be seen in the visitors centre, from which

POLAND

a marked 'visiting route' (5km) passes the massive stone **Monument of Fight & Martyrdom** and finishes at the domed **mausoleum** holding the ashes of many victims.

Trolleybus 156 from near the Bank Pekao along ul Królewska goes to the entrance of Majdanek.

Pick up the free *Tourist Routes of Lublin* guide, which includes a *Heritage Trail of the Lublin Jews* chapter, from the tourist office, if you want to walk along the marked **Jewish Heritage Trail** around Lublin.

## Sleeping

### BUDGET

**Youth Hostel** ( ☎ & fax 533 06 28; ul Długosza 6; dm/d/tr 19/50/75zł) Modest but well run. Simple rooms are decorated with potted plants, and there's a kitchen and a pleasant courtyard area with seating. Bed linen costs 6zł extra and it's 100m up a lane off ul Długosza.

**Wojewódzki Ośrodek Metodyczny** ( ☎ 532 92 41; www.wodn.lublin.pl; ul Dominikańska 5; dm 45zł) This place in an atmospheric Old Town building has rooms with between two and five beds. It's good value and often busy, so book ahead. Look for the sign 'Wojewódzki Ośrodek Doskonalenia Nauczycieli' outside.

**Dom Nauczyciela** ( ☎ 533 82 85; www.oupislublin .republika.pl; ul Akademicka 4; s/d/tr from 90/106/189zł) Value-packed accommodation in the heart of the university quarter, west of the Old Town. Rooms have old-fashioned décor but are clean, with good bathrooms. Some rooms have views over the city, and there are bars and eateries nearby.

**Camping Marina** ( ☎ 745 69 10; fax 744 10 70; ul Krężnicka 6; per tent 8zł, cabins from 55zł; ☯ May-Sep) Lublin's only camping ground is serenely located on a lake about 8km south of the Old Town. To get there take bus 17, 20 or 21 from the train station to Stadion Sygnał and then catch bus 25.

### MIDRANGE & TOP END

**Motel PZM** ( ☎ 533 42 32; ul Prusa 8; s/d from 120/160zł; P ☒ ) This car-friendly accommodation is housed in an uninspiring concrete pile, but it's handy for the bus station. The rooms have recently been renovated, with new furniture and freshly tiled bathrooms.

**Hotel Waksman** ( ☎ 532 54 54; www.waksman.pl; ul Grodzka 19; s/d 180/200zł, ste from 240zł; P ☒ 🖳 ) This small gem is excellent value for its quality and location. Just within the Grodzka Gate in the

Old Town, it offers elegantly appointed rooms with different colour schemes, and an attractive lounge with tapestries on the walls. One room has a waterbed.

**Hotel Europa** ( ☎ 535 03 03; www.hoteleuropa.pl; ul Krakowskie Przedmieście 29; s/d 290/380zł; P ☒ ☒ 🖳 ⓖ ) Central hotel offering smart, thoroughly modernised rooms with high ceilings and elegant furniture, in a restored 19th-century building. Two rooms are designed for disabled access, and there's a nightclub downstairs.

**Hotel Mercure-Unia** ( ☎ 533 72 12; www.orbis.pl; al Racławickie 12; d from 245zł; P ☒ ☒ 🖳 ) This business hotel is big, central and convenient, and offers all modern conveniences, though it's lacking in atmosphere. There's a gym, bar and restaurant on the premises.

**Grand Hotel Lublinianka** ( ☎ 446 61 00; www.lublin ianka.com; ul Krakowskie Przedmieście 56; s/d from 300/340zł; P ☒ ☒ 🖳 ⓖ ) The swankiest place in town includes free use of a sauna and Turkish bath. The cheaper (3rd floor) rooms have skylights but are relatively small, while 'standard' rooms are spacious and have glitzy marble bathrooms. One room is designed for disabled access, and there's a good restaurant downstairs.

## Eating & Drinking

There's a supermarket located near the bus terminal.

**Pizzeria Acerna** ( ☎ 532 45 31; Rynek 2; mains 10-24zł; ☯ 11am-10pm Mon-Thu & Sun, 11am-midnight Fri & Sat) The Acerna is a popular eatery on the main square, serving cheap pizzas and pasta in its subterranean dining area.

**Pueblo Desperados** ( ☎ 534 61 79; Rynek 5; mains 10-27zł; ☯ 9am-10pm Mon-Thu, 9am-midnight Fri & Sat, 10am-midnight Sun) Takes a reasonable stab at Mexican cuisine in its tiny sombrero-decorated premises off the Old Town's central square. The usual suspects (burritos, tacos) are on the menu, along with Corona beer and so-called Mexican pizzas.

**Restauracja 13** ( ☎ 532 29 19; ul Krakowskie Przedmieście 13; mains 10-26zł; ☯ 9am-midnight) Cosy orange-hued dining option with high-backed chairs and curious 'thumbprint' patterns on the walls. Serves a good range of Polish dishes (and pizzas), and there's an extensive drinks list.

**Kawiarnia Szeroka 28** ( ☎ 534 61 09; ul Grodzka 21; mains 15-40zł; ☯ 11am-11pm Mon-Thu, 11am-midnight Fri-Sun) An evocative place with timber bench seating and a flagstone floor, offering good

Jewish and Polish cuisine. There's a terrace at the back and regular live *klezmer* bands in the evenings playing traditional Jewish music (15zł extra).

**Chmielewska** ( ☎ 743 72 96; ul Krakowskie Przedmieście 8; ⏰ 10am-10pm) Charming old-fashioned café that looks like it dropped in from a bygone century. The menu is full of classic Polish cakes such as *sernik* (cheesecake) and *szarlotka* (apple pie), with a wide selection of coffee, tea and alcoholic drinks.

**Caram'bola Pub** ( ☎ 534 63 80; ul Kościuszki 8; ⏰ 11am-midnight Mon-Thu, 11am-2am Fri & Sat, noon-midnight Sun) This pub is a pleasant place for a beer or two. It also serves inexpensive bar food, including the ubiquitous pizzas.

## Entertainment

**Club Koyot** ( ☎ 743 67 35; ul Krakowskie Przedmieście 26; ⏰ 5pm-late Sat-Thu, noon-late Fri) This club is concealed in a courtyard and features live music or DJs most nights.

**Kino Wyzwolenie** ( ☎ 532 24 16; ul Peowiaków 6; adult/child 15/13zł) If you'd prefer a movie to music, this is a classic 1920s cinema in a convenient location.

**Teatr im Osterwy** ( ☎ 532 42 44; ul Narutowicza 17) Lublin's main theatrical venue which features mostly classical plays.

## Getting There & Away

From the **bus terminal** (al Tysiąclecia), opposite the castle, buses head to Białystok (24zł, three daily), Kraków (38zł to 46zł, two daily), Łódź (33zł, three daily), Olsztyn (65zł, one daily), Toruń (63zł, one daily) and Zakopane (43zł, five daily). Six buses also go daily to Przemyśl (14zł), 12 head to Zamość (13zł) and more than two dozen travel to various destinations within Warsaw (30zł, three hours). From the same terminal, Polski Express offers seven daily buses to Warsaw (34zł, three hours). Private minibuses head to various destinations, including Warsaw (30zł, 2½ hours, every half-hour), from bus stops north and west of the bus terminal.

The **Lublin Główny train station** (plac Dworcowy) is 1.2km south of the Old Town and accessible by bus 1 or 13. When leaving the station, look for the bus stop on ul Gazowa, to the left of the station entrance as you walk down the steps (not the trolleybus stop). Alternatively, trolleybus 150 from the station is handy for the university area and the youth hostel. At least a dozen fast trains go daily to Warsaw

(32zł, 2½ hours) and two fast trains travel to Kraków (46zł, five hours). Buy tickets from the station or **Orbis Travel** ( ☎ 532 22 56; www .orbistravel.com.pl; ul Narutowicza 33a).

## Around Lublin
### KOZŁÓWKA

The hamlet of Kozłówka (koz-*woof*-kah), 38km north of Lublin, is famous for its sumptuous late-baroque **palace**, which houses the **Museum of the Zamoyski Family** ( ☎ 852 83 00; www .muzeumzamoyskich.lublin.pl; adult/child 24/12zł; ⏰ 10am-4pm Mon-Fri, 10am-5pm Sat & Sun Mar-Oct, 10am-3pm Nov-Dec). It features original furnishings, ceramic stoves and a large collection of paintings.

Even more interesting is its incongruous **Socialist-Realist Art Gallery** (adult/child 5/3zł; ⏰ 10am-4pm Mon-Fri, 10am-5pm Sat & Sun Mar-Oct, 10am-3pm Nov-Dec), decked out with numerous portraits and statues of communist-era leaders. It also features many idealised scenes of farmers and factory workers striving for socialism.

You can stay in the **palace rooms** and on an 'agrotourist' **farm** ( ☎ 852 83 00). Contact staff in advance about availability and current costs.

From Lublin, two buses head to Kozłówka each morning, usually on the way to Michów. Only a few buses return directly to Lublin in the afternoon, so check the timetable before visiting the museum. Alternatively, you can catch one of the frequent buses to/from Lubartów, which is regularly connected by bus and minibus to Lublin.

## ZAMOŚĆ
☎ 084 / pop 67,000

While most Polish cities' attractions centre on their medieval heart, Zamość (*zah*-moshch) is pure Renaissance. It was founded in 1580 by Jan Zamoyski, the nation's chancellor and commander-in-chief. Designed by an Italian architect, the city was intended as a prosperous trading settlement between Western Europe and the region stretching east to the Black Sea.

In WWII, the Nazis earmarked the city for German resettlement, sending the Polish population into slave labour or concentration camps. Most of the Jewish population of the renamed 'Himmlerstadt' was exterminated.

The splendid architecture of Zamość's Old Town escaped destruction in the war's latter stages, and was added to Unesco's World Heritage List in 1992.

**POLAND**

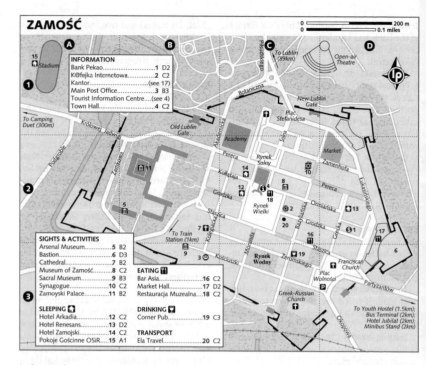

**ZAMOŚĆ**

**INFORMATION**
| | |
|---|---|
| Bank Pekao | 1 D2 |
| K@fejka Internetowa | 2 C2 |
| Kantor | (see 17) |
| Main Post Office | 3 B3 |
| Tourist Information Centre | (see 4) |
| Town Hall | 4 C2 |

**SIGHTS & ACTIVITIES**
| | |
|---|---|
| Arsenal Museum | 5 B2 |
| Bastion | 6 D3 |
| Cathedral | 7 B2 |
| Museum of Zamość | 8 C2 |
| Sacral Museum | 9 B3 |
| Synagogue | 10 C2 |
| Zamoyski Palace | 11 B2 |

**EATING**
| | |
|---|---|
| Bar Asia | 16 C2 |
| Market Hall | 17 D2 |
| Restauracja Muzealna | 18 C2 |

**SLEEPING**
| | |
|---|---|
| Hotel Arkadia | 12 C2 |
| Hotel Renesans | 13 D2 |
| Hotel Zamojski | 14 C2 |
| Pokoje Gościnne OSiR | 15 A1 |

**DRINKING**
| | |
|---|---|
| Corner Pub | 19 C3 |

**TRANSPORT**
| | |
|---|---|
| Ela Travel | 20 C2 |

## Information

There's a *kantor* in the Market Hall.

**Bank Pekao** (ul Grodzka 2) Has an ATM, cashes travellers cheques and gives advances on Visa and MasterCard.

**K@fejka Internetowa** ( ☎ 639 29 32; Rynek Wielki10; per hr 3zł) internet access.

**Main post office** (ul Kościuszki) Near the cathedral.

**Tourist Information Centre** ( ☎ 639 22 92; Rynek Wielki 13; ☺ 8am-6pm Mon-Fri, 10am-6pm Sat & Sun May-Sep, 8am-5pm Mon-Fri, 9am-2pm Sat Oct-Apr) This helpful office in the town hall sells *Along the Streets of Zamość* (2zł; in English, German and Italian) and the glossy *Zamość – A Short Guidebook* (8zł), along with a good stock of maps.

## Sights

**Rynek Wielki** is the heart of Zamość attractive Old Town. The impressive Italianate Renaissance square (exactly 100m by 100m) is dominated by the lofty, pink **Town Hall** and surrounded by colourful arcaded burghers' houses, many adorned with elegant designs. The **Museum of Zamość** ( ☎ 638 64 94; ul Ormiańska 30; adult/child 5/2.50zł; ☺ 9am-5pm Tue-Sun) is based in two of the loveliest buildings on the Rynek and houses interesting exhibits, including

paintings, folk costumes, archaeological finds and a scale model of the 16th-century town.

Southwest of the square is the mighty 16th-century **cathedral** (ul Kolegiacka; ☺ dawn-dusk), which hosts the tomb of Jan Zamoyski in the chapel to the right of the high altar. The **belfry** (1zł; ☺ May-Sep) can be climbed for good views of the historic cathedral bells and the Old Town. In the grounds, the **Sacral Museum** (admission 1zł; ☺ 10am-4pm Mon-Fri, 10am-1pm Sat & Sun May-Sep, 10am-1pm Sun Oct-Apr) features various robes, paintings and sculptures.

**Zamoyski Palace** (closed to the public) lost much of its character when it was converted into a military hospital in the 1830s. Today it's used for government offices. Nearby, the **Arsenal Museum** ( ☎ 638 40 76; ul Zamkowa 2; adult/child 5/2.50zł; ☺ 9am-5pm Mon-Fri) holds an unremarkable collection of cannon, swords and firearms. To the north of the palace stretches a beautifully landscaped **park**.

Before WWII, Jewish citizens accounted for 45% of the town's population (of 12,000) and most lived in the area north and east of the palace. The most significant Jewish architectural relic is the Renaissance **synagogue** (☎ 0608 409 055; ul Pereca 14; admission 2zł; ☺ 10am-3pm Mon-Fri, 10am-5pm Sat & Sun May-Sep, by appointment Oct-Apr), built in the early 17th century. Until recently it was used as a public library, but is now empty and awaiting transformation into a museum. In the meantime you can visit and see its original wall and ceiling decoration.

On the eastern edge of the Old Town is the antiquated but bustling **Market Hall** (Hala Targowa). Behind it is the best surviving **bastion** from the original city walls.

## Sleeping

### BUDGET

**Youth Hostel** (☎ 627 91 25; ul Zamoyskiego 4; dm 12-16zł; ☺ Jul & Aug) You can find this hostel in a school building 1.5km east of the Old Town, not far from the bus terminal. It's basic but functional and very cheap.

**Pokoje Gościnne OSiR** (☎ 638 60 11; ul Królowej Jadwigi 8; dm 23.50zł, s/d/tr 90/125/150zł; ⓟ ⊠) Located in a sprawling sporting complex a 15-minute walk west of the Old Town, and packed with old trophies and students playing table tennis. Rooms are plainly furnished, clean and comfortable, although the bathrooms fall short of the ideal.

**Camping Duet** (☎ 639 24 99; ul Królowej Jadwigi 14; s/d/tr 70/85/110zł; ⓟ ⛎) About 1.5km west of the Old Town, Camping Duet has neat bungalows, tennis courts, a restaurant, sauna and Jacuzzi. Larger bungalows sleep up to six.

### MIDRANGE & TOP END

**Hotel Arkadia** (☎ 638 65 07; www.arkadia.zamosc.pl; Rynek Wielki 9; s/d/tr 100/150/180zł; ⓟ) With just seven rooms, this compact place offers a pool table and restaurant in addition to lodgings. It's charming but shabby, though its location right on the market square is hard to beat.

**Hotel Jubilat** (☎ 638 64 01; hoteljubilat@hoga.pl; ul Kardynała Wyszyńskiego 52; s/d 134/173zł; ⓟ ⊡) An acceptable, if slightly drab, place to spend the night, right beside the bus station. It couldn't be handier for late arrivals or early departures, but it's a long way from anywhere else. It has a restaurant and fitness club.

**Hotel Renesans** (☎ 639 20 01; hotelrenesans@hoga .pl; ul Grecka 6; s/d 139/198zł; ⓟ ⊡) It's ironic that a hotel named after the Renaissance is housed in the Old Town's ugliest building. However, it's central and the rooms are comfortable enough, if you can ignore the brown-patterned carpets.

**Hotel Zamojski** (☎ 639 25 16; www.orbis.pl; ul Kołłątaja 2/4/6; s/d/ste 192/285/415zł; ⓟ ⊠) The best joint in town is situated within three connected old houses, just off the square. The rooms are modern and tastefully furnished, and there's a good on-site restaurant and cocktail bar, along with a fitness centre.

## Eating & Drinking

There are a few cheap fast-food outlets in the Market Hall.

**Bar Asia** (☎ 639 23 04; ul Staszica 10; mains 5-8zł; ☺ 8am-5pm Mon-Fri, 8am-4pm Sat) For hungry but broke travellers, this popular-style place is ideal. It serves cheap and tasty Polish food including several variants of *pierogi*, in a plain space with lace tablecloths and potted plants.

**Restauracja Muzealna** (☎ 638 73 00; ul Ormiańska Ormianska 30; mains 8-18zł; ☺ 11am-10pm Mon-Sat, 11am-9pm Sun) Subterranean restaurant in an atmospheric cellar below the main square, bedecked with ornate timber furniture and portraits of nobles. It serves a better class of Polish cuisine at reasonable prices, and has a well-stocked bar.

**Corner Pub** (☎ 627 06 94; ul Żeromskiego 6; ☺ 11am-11pm) This cosy Irish-style pub is a good place to have a drink. It has comfy booths and the walls are ornamented with bric-a-brac such as antique clocks, swords and model cars.

## Getting There & Away

Buses are usually more convenient and quicker than trains. The **bus terminal** (ul Hrubieszowska) is 2km east of the Old Town and linked by frequent city buses, primarily route Nos 0 and 3. Daily, one or two fast buses go to Kraków (40zł, four hours), four to Warsaw (37zł, five hours) and nine to Lublin (13zł, two hours).

Quicker and cheaper are the minibuses that travel every 30 minutes between Lublin and Zamość (10zł, 1½ hours). They leave from the minibus stand opposite the bus terminal in Zamość and from a disorganised corner northwest of the bus terminal in Lublin. Check the changeable timetable for departures to other destinations, including Warsaw and Kraków.

From the train station, about 1km southwest of the Old Town, several slow trains head to Lublin (about four hours) every day and one plods along to Warsaw (six hours). **Ela Travel** (☎ 638 57 75; ul Grodzka 18) sells international bus and air tickets.

**POLAND**

# SILESIA

Silesia (Śląsk) has a history of ethnic and political flux, having been governed by Polish, Bohemian, Austrian and German rulers. After the devastating Mongol invasion of Europe in the 13th century, Silesia's rulers welcomed German immigration to rebuild population numbers, unwittingly foreshadowing future tensions between Poles and ethnic Germans. After two centuries as part of Prussia and Germany, the territory was largely included within Poland's new borders after WWII.

Nowadays Upper Silesia is the nation's industrial heart, while Lower Silesia is a fertile farming region centred on Wrocław. Along the region's southwestern edge run the Sudeten Mountains, forming the border with the Czech republic.

The industrial zone around Katowice has limited attraction for visitors. However, Wrocław is a beautiful historic city with lively nightlife, and the Sudeten Mountains draw hikers and other nature lovers.

## WROCŁAW

☎ 071 / pop 639,000

When citizens of beautiful Kraków enthusiastically encourage you to visit Wrocław (*vrots-wahf*), you know you're onto something good. The city's beautiful Old Town is a gracious mix of Gothic and baroque styles, and its large student population ensures a healthy number of restaurants, bars and nightclubs.

Wrocław has been traded back and forth between various rulers over the centuries, but began life in the year 1000 under the Polish Piast dynasty and developed into a prosperous trading and cultural centre. In the 1740s it passed to Prussia, under the German name of Breslau. Under Prussian rule, the city became a major textile manufacturing centre, greatly increasing its population.

Upon its return to Poland in 1945, Wrocław was a shell of its former self, having sustained massive damage in WWII. Though 70% of the city was destroyed, sensitive restoration has returned the historic centre to its former beauty.

## Information

### BOOKSHOPS

**EMPiK Megastore** ( ☎ 343 39 72; Rynek 50) For the widest choice of foreign-language newspapers and magazines.

**Księgarnia Podróżnika** ( ☎ 792 30 65; ul Wita Stwosza 19/20) The best place for maps and guidebooks.

### INTERNET ACCESS

**Dr Joystick** ( ☎ 322 14 88; ul Staromłyńska 2a; per hr 3zł; ⏲ 10.30am-10.30pm)

**W Sercu Miasta** ( ☎ 342 46 75; ul Przejście Żelaźnicie; per hr 5zł; ⏲ 24hrs) Down a laneway in the middle of the Rynek.

### MONEY

There are *kantors* through the city centre and a number in the bus and train stations.

**Bank Pekao** (ul Oławska 2) Offers the usual financial services.

### POST

**Main post office** (Rynek 28; ⏲ 6.30am-8.30pm)

### TOURIST INFORMATION

**Tourist office** ( ☎ 344 31 11; www.wroclaw.pl; Rynek 14; ⏲ 9am-9pm May-Sep, 9am-8pm Oct-Apr) Provides a variety of free brochures and maps and sells souvenirs.

## Sights

Wrocław's pride and joy is the giant **Panorama of Racławicka** ( ☎ 344 23 44; ul Purkyniego 11; adult/child 20/15zł; ⏲ 9am-5pm Tue-Sun May-Oct, 9am-4pm Tue-Sun Nov-Apr), a 360-degree painting of the 1794 Battle of Racławice, in which the Polish peasant army, led by Tadeusz Kościuszko, defeated Russian forces intent on partitioning Poland. Created by Jan Styka and Wojciech Kossak for the centenary of the battle in 1894, the painting is an immense 114m long and 15m high, and was brought here by Polish immigrants displaced from Lviv after WWII. Due to the communist government's uneasiness about glorifying a famous Russian defeat, however, the panorama wasn't re-erected until 1985, in a circular building east of the Old Town. Obligatory tours (with audio in English, French, German, Spanish, Russian and other languages) run every 30 minutes from 9am to 4.30pm April to November, and 10am to 3pm from December to March. The ticket also allows entry to the National Museum on the same day.

Located nearby, the **National Museum** ( ☎ 343 88 39; plac Powstańców Warszawy 5; adult/child 15/10zł, free Sat; ⏲ 9am-4pm Wed-Fri & Sun, 10am-6pm Sat) exhibits Silesian medieval art, and a fine collection of modern Polish painting. Entry is included with a ticket to the Panorama.

In the centre of the Old Town is the **Rynek**, Poland's second-largest old market square

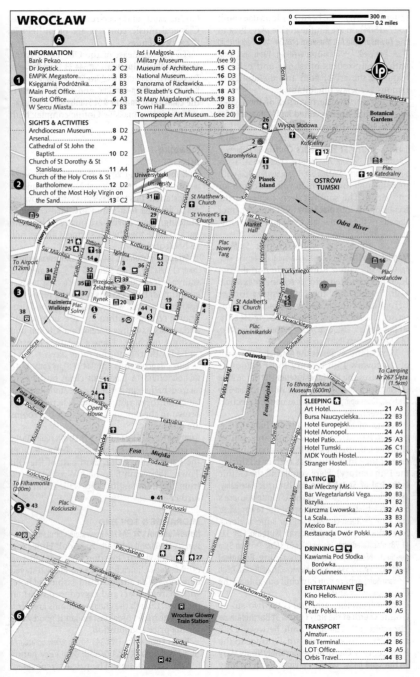

# WROCŁAW

**INFORMATION**
Bank Pekao.....................................1 B3
Dr Joystick.....................................2 C2
EMPiK Megastore...........................3 B3
Księgarnia Podróżnika.....................4 B3
Main Post Office.............................5 B3
Tourist Office.................................6 A3
W Sercu Miasta..............................7 B3

**SIGHTS & ACTIVITIES**
Archdiocesan Museum.....................8 D2
Arsenal..........................................9 A2
Cathedral of St John the
    Baptist.....................................10 D2
Church of St Dorothy & St
    Stanislaus.................................11 A4
Church of the Holy Cross & St
    Bartholomew.............................12 D2
Church of the Most Holy Virgin on
    the Sand..................................13 C2

Jaś i Małgosia...............................14 A3
Military Museum.......................(see 9)
Museum of Architecture................15 C3
National Museum..........................16 D3
Panorama of Racławicka................17 D3
St Elizabeth's Church....................18 A3
St Mary Magdalene's Church.........19 B3
Town Hall.....................................20 B3
Townspeople Art Museum...(see 20)

**SLEEPING**
Art Hotel......................................21 A3
Bursa Nauczycielska.....................22 B3
Hotel Europejski............................23 B5
Hotel Monopol..............................24 A4
Hotel Patio...................................25 A3
Hotel Tumski................................26 C1
MDK Youth Hostel........................27 B5
Stranger Hostel.............................28 B5

**EATING**
Bar Mleczny Miś...........................29 B2
Bar Wegetariański Vega.................30 B3
Bazylia.........................................31 B2
Karczma Lwowska.........................32 A3
La Scala.......................................33 B3
Mexico Bar...................................34 A3
Restauracja Dwór Polski................35 A3

**DRINKING**
Kawiarnia Pod Słodka
    Borówka...................................36 B3
Pub Guinness................................37 A3

**ENTERTAINMENT**
Kino Helios...................................38 A3
PRL.............................................39 B3
Teatr Polski..................................40 A5

**TRANSPORT**
Almatur.......................................41 B5
Bus Terminal................................42 B6
LOT Office...................................43 A5
Orbis Travel.................................44 B3

POLAND

(after Kraków). The beautiful **Town Hall** (built 1327–1504) on the southern side plays host to the **Townspeople Art Museum** ( ☎ 347 16 90; adult/child 7/5zł, free Wed; 11am-5pm Wed-Sat, 10am-6pm Sun), with stately rooms on show, and exhibits featuring the art of gold and the stories of famous Wrocław inhabitants.

In the northwestern corner of the Rynek are two small houses called **Jaś i Małgosia** (ul Św. Mikołaja) linked by a baroque gate (closed to the public). Behind them is the monumental 14th-century **St Elizabeth's Church** (ul Elżbiety 1; admission 5zł; 9am-7pm Mon-Fri, 11am-5pm Sat, 1-5pm Sun May-Oct, 10am-5pm Mon-Sat, 1-7pm Sun Nov-Apr) with its 83m-high tower, which you can climb for city views. The southwestern corner of the Rynek opens into **plac Solny** (Salt Square), once the site of the town's salt trade and now home to a 24-hour flower market.

One block east is the Gothic **St Mary Magdalene's Church** (ul Łaciarska; admission free; 9am-4pm Mon-Sat) with a Romanesque portal from 1280 incorporated into its southern external wall. Further east, the 15th-century former Bernardine church and monastery encompasses the **Museum of Architecture** ( ☎ 344 82 78; ul Bernardyńska 5; adult/child 7/5zł; 10am-4pm Tue, Wed, Fri & Sat, noon-6pm Thu, 11am-5pm Sun).

West of the Rynek is the **Arsenal**, a remnant of the town's 15th-century fortifications. It now houses the **Military Museum** ( ☎ 347 16 96; ul Cieszyńskiego 9; adult/child 7/5zł, free Wed; 11am-5pm Wed-Sat, 10am-6pm Sun), with the usual collection of old weapons.

North of the river is **Ostrów Tumski** (Cathedral Island), a picturesque area full of churches, though it's no longer an island (an arm of the Odra River was reclaimed during the 19th century). Here you'll find the Gothic **Cathedral of St John the Baptist** (plac Katedralny; 10am-8pm except during services). Uniquely, there's a lift to whisk you to the top of the **tower** (adult/child 4/3zł; 10am-6pm Mon-Sat) for superb views. Next door is the **Archdiocesan Museum** ( ☎ 327 11 78; plac Katedralny 16; adult/child 3/2zł; 9am-3pm Tue-Sun). Nearby are the charming **Botanical Gardens** ( ☎ 322 59 57; ul Sienkiewicza 23; adult/child 7/5zł; 8am-6pm), where you can chill out among the chestnut trees and tulips.

West from the cathedral is the two-storey Gothic **Church of the Holy Cross & St Bartholomew** (plac Kościelny; 9am-6pm), built between 1288 and 1350. Cross over the small bridge to the 14th-century **Church of the Most Holy Virgin Mary on the Sand** (ul Św. Jadwigi; erratic) with its lofty Gothic vaults and year-round nativity scene. Classical music concerts are often held in these two venues.

To the southeast of the Old Town is the **Ethnographical Museum** ( ☎ 344 33 13; ul Romualda Traugutta 111; adult/child 5/4zł, free Sat; 10am-4pm Tue, Wed & Fri-Sun, 11am-4pm Thu) and to the south is the **Church of St Dorothy & St Stanislaus** (ul Świdnicka; dawn-dusk), a massive Gothic complex built in 1351.

## Sleeping
### BUDGET
**MDK Youth Hostel** ( ☎ 343 88 56; mdkkopernik.wp.pl; ul Kołłątaja 20; dm/d from 22/29zł) Not far from the train station, this is a basic, recently renovated place, located in a grand mustard-coloured building. Some dorms are huge and beds are packed close together. It's almost always full, so book ahead.

**Stranger Hostel** ( ☎ 344 12 06; www.thestrangerhostel .com; ul Kołłątaja 16; dm 50zł; ) A tatty old staircase leads up to Wrocław's best budget accommodation. Dorms are set in renovated apartment rooms with ornate lamps and decorative ceilings. Bathrooms are shiny clean, and guests have free access to a kitchen and washing machine. There's a games console and a DVD projector for rainy days.

**Bursa Nauczycielska** ( ☎ 344 37 81; ul Kotlarska 42; s/d/q 50/90/104zł) A basic but clean hostel with shared bathrooms, ideally located just one block northeast of the Rynek. There's a lot of brown in the colour scheme, but the rooms are quite cosy.

**Camping Nr 267 Ślęza** ( ☎ 372 55 11; ul Na Grobli 16/18; per person/tent 14/3zł, d/tr bungalows 60/90zł; P ) On the bank of the Odra, 2km east of the Old Town. Take tram 5 to plac Wróblewskiego from the train station and walk about 1km further east.

### MIDRANGE & TOP END
**Hotel Monopol** ( ☎ 343 70 41; www.orbis.pl; ul Modrzejewskiej 2; s 122-182zł, d 164-264zł; ) Adolf Hitler was a frequent visitor, but don't let that put you off: Marlene Dietrich and Pablo Picasso stayed here too. It's an attractive old-fashioned hotel with marble pillars and carved woodwork in the foyer, though the cheapest rooms are fairly basic. The buffet breakfast makes it good value for the price and location.

**Hotel Europejski** ( ☎ 343 10 71; www.odratourist .pl; ul Piłsudskiego 88; s/d 195/205zł; ) Very handy for the train station. The pricier 'renovated'

POLAND

rooms are large and comfortable, though the décor's a bit dated.

**Old Town Apartments** (Map p550; ☎ 022-887 98 00; www.warsawshotel.com; Rynek Starego Miasta 12/14, Warsaw; apt 250-420zł) Warsaw-based agency with modern, fully furnished one-bedroom apartments around Wrocław's main square. Weekly rates are available.

**Hotel Tumski** (☎ 322 60 99; www.hotel-tumski.com .pl; Wyspa Słodowa 10; s/d/ste 230/320zł/480zł; ☒ ) This is a neat hotel in a peaceful setting overlooking the river, offering reasonable value for money. It's ideal for exploring the lovely ecclesiastical quarter, and there's a good restaurant attached.

**Hotel Patio** (☎ 375 04 00; www.hotelpatio.pl; ul Kiełbaśnicza 24; s/d/ste from 280/310/395zł; P ☒ ☐ ) Pleasant lodgings a short hop from the main square, and actually within two buildings linked by a covered sunlit courtyard. Rooms are clean and light, sometimes small but with reasonably high ceilings. There's a restaurant, bar and hairdresser on site.

**Art Hotel** (☎ 787 71 00; www.arthotel.pl; ul Kiełbaśnicza 20; s/d/ste from 320/360/430zł; P ☒ ☒ ☐ ) Superelegant accommodation in a renovated apartment building. Rooms feature tastefully restrained décor, quality fittings and gleaming bathrooms. Within the arched brick cellar is a top-notch restaurant, and there's a fitness room to work off the resultant calories.

## Eating & Drinking

**Bar Mleczny Miś** (☎ 343 49 63; ul Kuźnicza 45-47; mains 3-12zł; ⌚ 7am-6pm Mon-Fri, 8am-5pm Sat) In the university area, this classic cheap-eats cafeteria is basic but popular with frugal university students. Look for the bear above the sign.

**Bazylia** (plac Uniwersytecki; mains 4-9zł; ⌚ 8am-8pm Mon-Fri, 7.30am-8pm Sat) Inexpensive and bustling modern take on the classic *bar mleczny*, in a curved space with huge plate-glass windows overlooking the venerable university buildings. The menu has a lot of Polish standards such as *bigos* and *gołąbki*, and a decent range of salads and other vegetable dishes.

**Bar Wegetariański Vega** (☎ 344 39 34; Rynek 1/2; mains 5-12zł; ⌚ 8am-7pm Mon-Fri, 9am-5pm Sat) This is a cheap cafeteria in the centre of the Rynek, offering veggie dishes in a light green space. Good choice of soups and crepes.

**Mexico Bar** (☎ 346 02 92; ul Rzeźnicza 34; mains 11-39zł; ⌚ noon-midnight) Compact, warmly lit restaurant featuring sombreros, backlit masks and a chandelier made of beer bottles. There's

a small bar to lean on while waiting for a table. All the Tex-Mex standards are on the menu, but book at least two days ahead for a table on weekends.

**Karczma Lwowska** (☎ 343 98 87; Rynek 4; mains 20-37zł; ⌚ noon-midnight) Has a great spot on the main square, with outdoor seating in summer, and offers the usual meaty Polish standards in a space with a rustic rural look. It's worth stopping by to try the beer, served in ceramic mugs.

**La Scala** (☎ 372 53 94; Rynek 38; mains 23-75zł; ⌚ 10am-midnight) Offers authentic Italian food and particularly good desserts. Prices are high, but you're paying for the location. There's a cheaper trattoria at ground level.

**Restauracja Dwór Polski** (☎ 372 48 96; Rynek 5; mains 35-45zł; ⌚ noon-midnight) This eatery is a classy place to sample good-quality Polish cuisine on the main square, in a rather grand room with silver candelabra and white table-cloths.

**Pub Guinness** (☎ 344 60 15; plac Solny 5; ⌚ noon-2am) No prizes for guessing what this pub serves here. A lively, fairly authentic Irish pub, spread over three levels on a busy corner. The ground-floor bar buzzes with student and traveller groups getting together, and there's a restaurant and beer cellar as well. A good place to wind down after a hard day's sightseeing.

**Kawiarnia Pod Słodka Borówka** (☎ 343 68 56; Rynek 45; ⌚ 9am-10pm) If you're after a heart-starter, try the *kawa* (coffee) and cakes here. Nice cherry pie, and an odd collection of old hats along the wall.

## Entertainment

Check out the bimonthly *Visitor* (free and in English) for details of what's on in this important cultural centre. It's available from the tourist office and upmarket hotels.

**PRL** (☎ 342 55 26; Rynek Ratusz 10; ⌚ noon-3am) The dictatorship of the proletariat is alive and well in this tongue-in-cheek venue inspired by communist nostalgia. Disco lights play over a bust of Lenin, propaganda posters line the walls, and red menace memorabilia is scattered through the maze of rooms. Descend to the basement – beneath the portraits of Stalin and Mao – if you'd like to hit the dance floor.

**Teatr Polski** (☎ 316 07 77; ul Zapolskiej 3) Wrocław's main theatrical venue stages classic Polish and foreign drama.

POLAND

**Filharmonia** ( ☎ 342 20 01; www.filharmonia.wroclaw.pl; ul Piłsudskiego 19) This place hosts concerts of classical music, mostly on Friday and Saturday nights.

**Kino Helios** ( ☎ 781 55 70; www.heliosnet.pl; ul Kazimierza Wielkiego 19a) If you're after a movie head to this modern multiplex screening English-language films.

## Getting There & Away

**Orbis Travel** ( ☎ 343 26 65; Rynek 29) and **Almatur** ( ☎ 343 41 35; ul Kościuszki 34) offer the usual services. If you're travelling to/from Wrocław at the weekend, you'll be in competition with thousands of itinerant university students, so book your ticket as soon as possible.

### AIR

Every day, LOT flies four to seven times between Wrocław and Warsaw, once between Wrocław and Frankfurt-am-Main, and once to Munich. Tickets can be bought at the **LOT office** ( ☎ 342 51 51; ul Piłsudskiego 36). There's also a Direct Fly flight to Gdańsk on weekdays.

The airport is in Strachowice, about 12km west of the Old Town. Bus 406 links the airport with Wrocław Główny train station and bus terminal, via the Rynek.

### BUS

The **bus terminal** (ul Sucha 11) is south of the main train station. Several PKS buses go daily to Warsaw (37zł, five hours), Poznań (22zł to 35zł, 2½ hours), Częstochowa (22zł, three hours) and Białystok (66zł, seven hours). For most travel, however, the train is more convenient.

### TRAIN

The **Wrocław Główny station** (ul Piłsudskiego 105) was built in 1856 and is a historical monument in itself. Every day, fast trains to Kraków (42zł, 3¾ hours) depart every one or two hours, and several InterCity and express trains go to Warsaw (88zł, six hours), usually via Łódź. Wrocław is also regularly linked by train to Poznań (32zł, 3½ hours), Częstochowa (32zł, 3½ hours, four daily), Szczecin (47zł, five hours, 10 daily), and Lublin (52zł, 9½ hours, two daily).

## SUDETEN MOUNTAINS

The Sudeten Mountains (Sudety) run for over 250km along the Czech–Polish border. The Sudetes feature dense forests, amazing rock formations and deposits of semiprecious stones, and can be explored along the extensive network of trails for **hiking** or **mountain biking**. The highest part of this old eroded chain is Mt Śnieżka (1602m).

**Szklarska Poręba**, at the northwestern end of the Sudetes, offers superior facilities for **hiking** and **skiing**. It's at the base of Mt Szrenica (1362m), and the town centre is at the upper end of ul Jedności Narodowej. The small **tourist office** ( ☎ 075-754 77 40; www.szklarskaporeba.pl; ul Pstrowskiego 1) has accommodation information and maps. Nearby, several trails begin at the intersection of ul Jedności Narodowej and ul Wielki Sikorskiego. The red trail goes to Mt Szrenica (two hours) and offers a peek at Wodospad Kamieńczyka, a spectacular waterfall.

**Karpacz** to the southeast has more nightlife on offer, though it attracts fewer serious mountaineers. It's loosely clustered along a 3km road winding through Łomnica Valley at the base of Mt Śnieżka. The **tourist office** ( ☎ 075-761 86 05; www.karpacz.com.pl; ul Konstytucji 3 Maja 25a) should be your first port of call. To reach the peak of Mt Śnieżka on foot, take one of the trails (three to four hours) from Hotel Biały Jar. Some of the trails pass by one of two splendid postglacial lakes; Mały Staw and Wielki Staw.

The bus is the fastest way of getting around the region. Every day from Szklarska Poręba, about five buses head to Wrocław and one train plods along to Warsaw (55zł, 12 hours). From Karpacz, get a bus to Jelenia Góra, where buses and trains go in all directions.

For the Czech Republic, take a bus from Szklarska Poręba to Jakuszyce, cross the border on foot to Harrachov (on the Czech side) and take another bus from there.

# WIELKOPOLSKA

Wielkopolska (Greater Poland) is the region where Poland came to life in the Middle Ages, and is referred to as the Cradle of the Polish State. As a result of this prominent role, its cities and towns are full of historic and cultural attractions.

The royal capital moved from Poznań to Kraków in 1038, though Wielkopolska remained an important province. Its historic significance didn't save it from international conflict, however, and the region became part of Prussia in 1793. Despite intensive Germanisation, Wielkopolska rose against German rule at the end of WWI and became part of the reborn Poland. The battles of WWII later caused widespread destruction in the area.

Poznań, the region's major city, is well known for its regular trade fairs dotted throughout the calendar. It's also home to attractive architecture and museums, and the surrounding countryside is good for cycling and hiking.

## POZNAŃ

☎ 061 / pop 577,000

No-one could accuse Poznań of being too sleepy. Between its regular trade fairs, student population and visiting travellers, it's a vibrant city with a wide choice of attractions.

It grew from humble beginnings, when 9th-century Polanian tribes built a wooden fort on the island of Ostrów Tumski. From 968 to 1038 Poznań was the de facto capital of Poland. Its position between Berlin and Warsaw has always underlined its importance as a trading town, and in 1925 a modern version of its famous medieval trade fairs was instituted. The fairs, filling up the city's hotels for several days at a time, are the lynchpin of the city's economy.

Poznań has a beautiful Old Town at its centre, with a number of interesting museums, and a range of lively bars, clubs and restaurants. It's both a cosmopolitan place with an active cultural scene, and a good transport hub from which to explore the region.

## Information
### BOOKSHOPS
**EMPiK Megastore** ( ☎ 852 66 90; plac Wolności) Offers the largest choice of foreign magazines and newspapers.
**Globtroter Turystyczna** (ul Żydowska) Excellent for maps and Lonely Planet guidebooks.

### INTERNET ACCESS
**Internet Café Bajt** ( ☎ 853 18 08; ul Zamkowa 5; per hr 3zł; ☼ 24hr)

### MONEY
A few of the *kantors* in the city centre are shown on the map; there's also one in the bus terminal and another (open 24 hours) in the train station.
**Bank Pekao** (ul Św. Marcin 52/56) Probably the best place for travellers cheques and credit cards. There's another branch at ul 23 Lutego.

### POST
**Main post office** (ul Kościuszki 77; ☼ 7am-9pm Mon-Fri, 9am-5pm Sat, 10am-4pm Sun)

### TOURIST INFORMATION
**City Information Centre** ( ☎ 851 96 45; ul Ratajczaka 44; ☼ 10am-7pm Mon-Fri, 10am-5pm Sat) Handles bookings for cultural events.
**Tourist Information Centre** ( ☎ 852 61 56; Stary Rynek 59; ☼ 9am-6pm Mon-Fri, 10am-4pm Sat May-Sep, 9am-5pm Mon-Fri Oct-Apr) Helpful.

## Sights
### OLD TOWN
If you're in the attractive **Stary Rynek** (Old Market Square) at noon, keep an eye out for the goats in the Renaissance **Town Hall** (built 1550–60). Every midday two metal goats above its clock butt their horns together 12 times, echoing an improbable centuries-old legend of two animals escaping a cook and fighting each other in the town hall tower. Inside the building, the **Poznań Historical Museum** ( ☎ 852 56 13; adult/child 5.50/3.50zł; ☼ 9am-4pm Mon & Tue, 11am-6pm Wed, 9am-6pm Fri, 10am-3pm Sun) displays splendid period interiors.

Also within the square are the **Wielkopolska Military Museum** ( ☎ 852 67 39; Stary Rynek 9; adult/child 3.50/2.20zł; ☼ 9am-4pm Tue-Sat, 10am-3pm Sun) and the **Museum of Musical Instruments** ( ☎ 852 08 57; Stary Rynek 45/47; adult/child 5.50/3.50zł, free Sat; ☼ 11am-5pm Tue-Sat, 10am-3pm Sun), along with the **Museum of the Wielkopolska Uprising** ( ☎ 853 19 93; Stary Rynek 3; adult/child 4/2zł, free Sat; ☼ 10am-5pm Tue, Thu & Fri, 10am-6pm Wed, 10am-3pm Sat & Sun), which details the conflict in the region between German and Polish fighters after WWI.

The **Archaeological Museum** ( ☎ 852 82 51; ul Wodna 27; adult/child 6/3zł, free Sat; ☼ 10am-4pm Tue-Fri, 10am-6pm Sat, 10am-3pm Sun) contains Egyptian mummies and displays on the prehistory of western Poland.

The 17th-century **Franciscan Church** (ul Franciszkańska 2; ☼ 8am-8pm), one block west of the Rynek, has an ornate baroque interior, complete with wall paintings and rich stucco work. Above the church, on a hill, is the **Museum of Applied Arts** ( ☎ 852 20 35; adult/child 5.50/3.50zł, free Sat; ☼ 10am-4pm Tue, Wed, Fri & Sat, 10am-3pm Sun), featuring glassware, ceramics, silverware and clocks.

The nearby **National Museum: Paintings & Sculpture Gallery** ( ☎ 856 80 00; al Marcinkowskiego 9; adult/child 10/6zł, free Sat; ☼ 10am-6pm Tue, 9am-5pm Wed, 10am-4pm Thu, 10am-5pm Fri & Sat, 10am-3pm Sun) displays mainly 19th- and 20th-century Polish paintings.

**POLAND**

# POZNAŃ

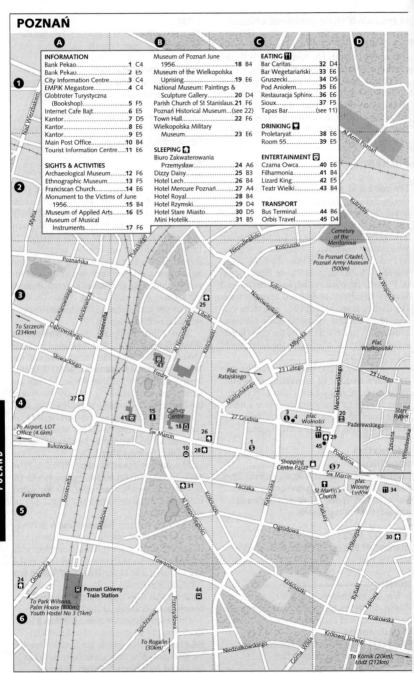

## INFORMATION
| | |
|---|---|
| Bank Pekao | 1 C4 |
| Bank Pekao | 2 E5 |
| City Information Centre | 3 C4 |
| EMPiK Megastore | 4 C4 |
| Globtroter Turystyczna (Bookshop) | 5 F5 |
| Internet Cafe Bajt | 6 E5 |
| Kantor | 7 D5 |
| Kantor | 8 E6 |
| Kantor | 9 E5 |
| Main Post Office | 10 B4 |
| Tourist Information Centre | 11 E6 |

## SIGHTS & ACTIVITIES
| | |
|---|---|
| Archaeological Museum | 12 F6 |
| Ethnographic Museum | 13 F5 |
| Franciscan Church | 14 E6 |
| Monument to the Victims of June 1956 | 15 B4 |
| Museum of Applied Arts | 16 E5 |
| Museum of Musical Instruments | 17 F6 |
| Museum of Poznań June 1956 | 18 B4 |
| Museum of the Wielkopolska Uprising | 19 E6 |
| National Museum: Paintings & Sculpture Gallery | 20 D4 |
| Parish Church of St Stanislaus | 21 F6 |
| Poznań Historical Museum | (see 22) |
| Town Hall | 22 F6 |
| Wielkopolska Military Museum | 23 E6 |

## SLEEPING
| | |
|---|---|
| Biuro Zakwaterowania Przemysław | 24 A6 |
| Dizzy Daisy | 25 B3 |
| Hotel Lech | 26 B4 |
| Hotel Mercure Poznań | 27 A4 |
| Hotel Royal | 28 B4 |
| Hotel Rzymski | 29 D4 |
| Hotel Stare Miasto | 30 D5 |
| Mini Hotelik | 31 B5 |

## EATING
| | |
|---|---|
| Bar Caritas | 32 D4 |
| Bar Wegetariański | 33 E6 |
| Gruszecki | 34 D5 |
| Pod Aniołem | 35 E6 |
| Restauracja Sphinx | 36 E6 |
| Sioux | 37 F5 |
| Tapas Bar | (see 11) |

## DRINKING
| | |
|---|---|
| Proletaryat | 38 E6 |
| Room 55 | 39 E5 |

## ENTERTAINMENT
| | |
|---|---|
| Czarna Owca | 40 E6 |
| Filharmonia | 41 B4 |
| Lizard King | 42 E5 |
| Teatr Wielki | 43 B4 |

## TRANSPORT
| | |
|---|---|
| Bus Terminal | 44 B6 |
| Orbis Travel | 45 D4 |

POLAND

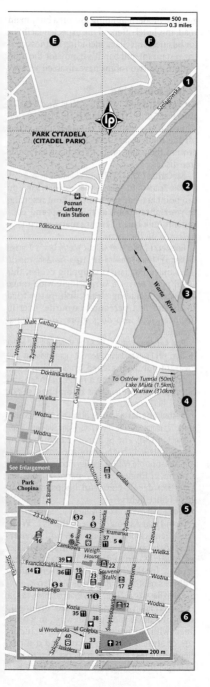

Two blocks south of Stary Rynek is the large, pink, baroque **Parish Church of St Stanislaus** (ul Gołębia 1; ☺ erratic) with monumental altars built in the mid-17th century. A short stroll southeast is the **Ethnographic Museum** ( ☎ 852 30 06; ul Grobla 25; adult/child 5.50/3.50zł; free Sat; ☺ 10am-4pm Tue, Wed, Fri & Sat, 10am-3pm Sun), presenting a collection of woodcarving and traditional costumes.

The 19th-century Prussian **Poznań Citadel**, where 20,000 German troops held out for a month in February 1945, lies about 1.5km north of the Old Town. The fortress was destroyed by artillery fire but a park was laid out on the site, which incorporates the **Poznań Army Museum** ( ☎ 820 45 03; al Armii Poznań; adult/child 4/2zł, free Fri; ☺ 9am-4pm Tue-Sat, 10am-4pm Sun).

In a park in the new city centre, the moving **Monument to the Victims of June 1956** commemorates the dead and injured of the massive 1956 strike by the city's industrial workers, which was crushed by tanks. Next door in the Cultural Centre; there's more detail in the **Museum of Poznań June 1956** ( ☎ 852 94 64; ul Św. Marcin 80/82; adult/child 2/1zł; ☺ 10am-6pm Wed or by arrangement).

In **Park Wilsona**, 1km southwest of the train station, is the **Palm House** ( ☎ 865 89 07; ul Matejki 18; adult/child 5.50/4zł; ☺ 9am-4pm Thu-Sat, 9am-5pm Sun). This huge greenhouse (built in 1910) contains 17,000 species of tropical and subtropical plants.

**Ostrów Tumski** is 1km east of the Old Town (take any eastbound tram from plac Wielkopolski). This river island is dominated by the monumental, double-towered **Poznań Cathedral** (ul Ostrów Tumski), originally built in 968. The Byzantine-style **Golden Chapel** (1841) and the **mausoleums** of Mieszko I and Boleslaus the Brave are behind the high altar. Opposite the cathedral is the 15th-century Gothic **Church of the Virgin Mary** (ul Panny Marii 1/3).

Some 2.5km east of the Old Town is **Lake Malta**, a favourite weekend destination for Poles. It holds sailing regattas, outdoor concerts and other events in summer, and in winter there's a ski slope in operation. To get to the lake, take tram 1, 4 or 8 from plac Wielkopolski.

## Sleeping

During trade fairs, the rates of Poznań's accommodation dramatically increases. A room may also be difficult to find, so it pays to book ahead. Prices given here are for outside trade-fair periods.

**POLAND**

## BUDGET

Check out **Biuro Zakwaterowania Przemysław** ( ☎ 866 35 60; www.przemyslaw.com.pl; ul Głogowska 16; ⊗ 8am-6pm Mon-Fri, 10am-2pm Sat; s/d from 43/65zł, apt from 150zł), an accommodation agency not far from the train station. Rates for weekends and stays of more than three nights are cheaper than the prices quoted here.

**Youth Hostel No 3** ( ☎ 866 40 40; ul Berwińskiego 2/3; dm 25zł) Cheap lodgings about a 15-minute walk southwest of the train station along ul Głogowska, adjacent to Park Wilsona. It's a basic 'no frills' option, but fills up fast with students and school groups. There's a 10pm curfew.

**Dizzy Daisy** ( ☎ 829 39 02; www.hostel.pl; al Niepodległości 26; dm/s/d 30/50/100zł; 🖳 ) This is one of the most comfortable hostels in town, with free laundry and no curfew. Outside July to August, however, it has limited places for travellers, as it's also used as student quarters.

**Mini Hotelik** ( ☎ 863 14 16; al Niepodległości 8a; s/d from 54/107zł) Like it says on the label, this is a small place in an old building between the train station and the Old Town. It's basic but clean, with colourfully painted chambers. Some rooms share a bathroom. Enter from ul Taylora.

## MIDRANGE & TOP END

**Hotel Lech** ( ☎ 853 01 51; www.hotel-lech.poznan.pl; ul Św. Marcin 74; s/d 162/244zł) Hotel Lech has standard three-star décor, but rooms are relatively spacious and the bathrooms are modern. Flash your ISIC card for a discount.

**Hotel Stare Miasto** ( ☎ 663 62 42; www.hotelstare miasto.pl; ul Rybaki 36; s/d 195/295zł; 🅿 ⊠ 🖳 ) Elegant value-for-money hotel with a tasteful chandeliered foyer and spacious breakfast room. Rooms can be small, but are clean and bright with lovely starched white sheets. Some upper rooms have skylights in place of windows.

**Hotel Rzymski** ( ☎ 852 81 21; www.rzymskihotel .com.pl; al Marcinkowskiego 22; s/d 210/270zł) Offers the regular amenities of three-star comfort, and overlooks plac Wolności. The décor has a lot of brown, and rooms aren't quite as grand as the elegant façade suggests, but they're a decent size.

**Hotel Royal** ( ☎ 858 23 00; www.hotel-royal.com.pl; ul Św. Marcin 71; s/d 320/420zł; 🅿 ) This is a gorgeous place set back from the main road. Rooms have huge beds and sparkling bathrooms.

**Hotel Mercure Poznań** ( ☎ 855 80 00; www.orbis.pl; ul Roosevelta 20; s/d from €122/142; 🅿 ⊠ 🅧 🖳 ⓖ ) In a gigantic modern building just off a busy main road, this hotel offers all the expected facilities for business travellers, including a fitness centre, restaurant and bar. It's handy for the train station, and two rooms have disabled access.

## Eating & Drinking

**Bar Wegetariański** ( ☎ 821 12 55; ul Wrocławska 21; mains from 5zł; ⊗ 11am-6pm Mon-Fri, 11am-3pm Sat) This cheap vegetarian eatery is in a cellar off the main road, bedecked with plant life around the walls, and offers the usual meat-free dishes.

**Bar Caritas** ( ☎ 852 51 30; plac Wolności 1; mains 8-15zł; ⊗ 8am-7pm Mon-Fri, 10am-5pm Sat, noon-5pm Sun) You can point at what you want without resorting to your phrasebook at this cheap and convenient milk bar. There are many variants of *naleśniki* on the menu.

**Gruszecki** ( ☎ 850 89 42; plac Wiosny Ludów 2; mains 15-38zł; ⊗ 10am-9pm Mon-Sat, 11am-7pm Sun) Inside the Kupiec Poznański shopping centre, this small place serves a surprisingly wide range of dishes, including steaks, fish, pasta, fried snails and that perennial favourite, liver in raspberries. It also does more conventional breakfasts.

**Pod Aniołem** ( ☎ 852 98 54; ul Wrocławska 4; mains 16-28zł; ⊗ 11am-midnight Mon-Sat, 1pm-midnight Sun) Pleasant pub with arched brick ceilings and candlelit tables, serving a range of cheap and filling Polish fare such as dumplings, salads and grilled meats.

**Restauracja Restaurant Sphinx** ( ☎ 852 80 25; Stary Rynek 77; mains 16-50zł; ⊗ 11am-11pm Sun-Thu, 11am-midnight Fri & Sat) The Sphinx is a branch of the ubiquitous kebab-and-cabbage chain, offering reasonable-value grills and salads, and a menu in English. Be prepared for ancient Egyptian décor, colourful lampshades and lots of fairy lights.

**Sioux** ( ☎ 851 62 86; Stary Rynek 93; mains 22-58zł; ⊗ noon-11pm) As you'd expect, this is a 'Western'-themed place, complete with waiters dressed as cowboys. Bizarrely named dishes such as 'Marinated Fist of Dancer with Wolves' (pork steak) are on the menu, along with lots of steaks, ribs, grills and tacos.

**Tapas Bar** ( ☎ 852 85 32; Stary Rynek 60; mains 28-45zł; ⊗ noon-midnight) Atmospheric place dishing up authentic tapas and Spanish wine, in a room lined with intriguing bric-a-brac including jars of stuffed olives, a cactus and a model elephant. Most tapas dishes cost 16zł to 18zł, so forget the mains and share with friends.

**Proletaryat** ( ☎ 851 32 15; ul Wrocławska 9; ◷ 1pm-2am Mon-Sat, 3pm-2am Sun) Small red communist nostalgia bar with an array of socialist-era gear on the walls, including the obligatory bust of Lenin in the window, and various portraits of the great man and his comrades. Play 'spot the communist leader' while sipping a boutique beer from the Czarnków Brewery.

**Room 55** ( ☎ 855 32 24; Stary Rynek 80/82; ◷ 9am-midnight Mon-Sat, noon-midnight Sun) One of several trendy places on the main square to enjoy a drink and something to eat. Features mellow red chairs and banquettes, with a mezzanine area for observing the beautiful people below.

## Entertainment

**Lizard King** ( ☎ 855 04 72; Stary Rynek 86; ◷ noon-2am) Simultaneously happening and laid-back, this venue is easily spotted by the big guitar on its outside wall. Friendly crowds sit drinking and eating in the split-level space, casting the occasional glance at the lizard over the bar. There's live music later in the week, usually from 9pm.

**Czarna Owca** ( ☎ 853 07 92; ul Jaskółcza 13; ◷ noon-2am Mon-Fri, 5pm-2am Sat) Literally 'Black Sheep', this is a popular club with nightly DJs playing a mix of genres including R&B, house, pop and rock. There's a dance mix on weekends and a retro night on Thursday.

**Teatr Wielki** ( ☎ 852 82 91; ul Fredry 9) is the main venue for opera and ballet, while not far away, the **Filharmonia** ( ☎ 852 47 08; ul Św. Marcin 81) offers classical concerts at least every Friday night.

## Getting There & Away

LOT flies five times a day between Warsaw and Poznań. There are flights from Poznań to Frankfurt and Munich most days; and LOT and SAS fly daily to Copenhagen. Tickets are available from the **LOT office** ( ☎ 849 22 61; airport) or from **Orbis Travel** ( ☎ 851 20 00; al Marcinkowskiego 21). The airport is in the western suburb of Ławica, 7km from the Old Town and accessible by bus 59 or 78.

The **bus terminal** (ul Towarowa 17) is a 10-minute walk east of the train station. Bus services are relatively poor, but buses do travel from Poznań five times a day to Łódź, twice a day to Toruń and twice a day to Wrocław.

The busy **Poznań Główny train station** (ul Dworcowa 1) offers services to Kraków (48zł, 6½ hours, 11 daily), Szczecin, some of which continue to Świnoujście (34zł, two hours,

18 daily), to Gdańsk and Gdynia (43zł, five hours, seven daily), Toruń (30zł, 3½ hours, three daily) and Wrocław (32zł, 3½ hours, 15 daily). More than 20 trains a day also head to Warsaw, including nine express (78zł, five hours) and eight InterCity services (86zł, three hours).

# POMERANIA

Pomerania (Pomorze) had spent a millennium being fought over by Germanic and Slavic peoples, before being returned to Poland after WWII. The region covers a large swathe of territory along the Baltic coast, from the German border in the west, to the lower Vistula Valley in the east. The major urban centres are western Szczecin, and Gdańsk on Poland's northern coast. A sandy coastline stretches between them, a popular destination for holidaymakers in summer. The attractive Gothic city of Toruń lies inland, within a belt of forests and lakes.

## TORUŃ

☎ 056 / pop 211,000

The first thing to strike you about Toruń is its massive red-brick churches, looking more like fortresses than places of worship. The city is defined by its striking Gothic architecture, which gives its Old Town a distinctive appearance.

Toruń is also famous as the birthplace of Nicolaus Copernicus, a figure you cannot escape as you walk the streets of his home town – you can even buy gingerbread men in his likeness. The renowned astronomer spent his youth here, and the local university is named after him.

Historically, Toruń is intertwined with the Teutonic Knights, who established an outpost here in 1233. Following the Thirteen Years' War (1454–66), the Teutonic Order and Poland signed a peace treaty here, which returned to Poland a large area of land stretching from Toruń to Gdańsk. In the following centuries, Toruń suffered a fate similar to that of the surrounding region: Swedish invasions and German domination until the early 20th century.

Toruń was fortunate to escape major damage in WWII, and as a result is the best-preserved Gothic town in Poland. The Old Town was added to Unesco's World Heritage List in 1997.

POLAND

# TORUŃ

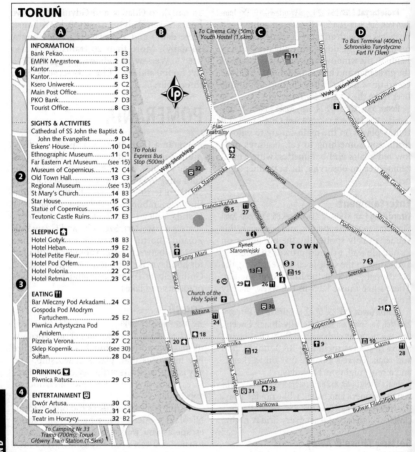

**INFORMATION**
| | | |
|---|---|---|
| Bank Pekao | 1 | E3 |
| EMPiK Megastore | 2 | C3 |
| Kantor | 3 | C3 |
| Kantor | 4 | E3 |
| Ksero Uniwerek | 5 | C2 |
| Main Post Office | 6 | C3 |
| PKO Bank | 7 | D3 |
| Tourist Office | 8 | C3 |

**SIGHTS & ACTIVITIES**
| | | |
|---|---|---|
| Cathedral of SS John the Baptist & John the Evangelist | 9 | D4 |
| Eskens' House | 10 | D4 |
| Ethnographic Museum | 11 | C1 |
| Far Eastern Art Museum | (see 15) | |
| Museum of Copernicus | 12 | C4 |
| Old Town Hall | 13 | C3 |
| Regional Museum | (see 13) | |
| St Mary's Church | 14 | B3 |
| Star House | 15 | C3 |
| Statue of Copernicus | 16 | C3 |
| Teutonic Castle Ruins | 17 | E3 |

**SLEEPING**
| | | |
|---|---|---|
| Hotel Gotyk | 18 | B3 |
| Hotel Heban | 19 | E2 |
| Hotel Petite Fleur | 20 | B4 |
| Hotel Pod Orłem | 21 | D3 |
| Hotel Polonia | 22 | C2 |
| Hotel Retman | 23 | C4 |

**EATING**
| | | |
|---|---|---|
| Bar Mleczny Pod Arkadami | 24 | C3 |
| Gospoda Pod Modrym Fartuchem | 25 | E2 |
| Piwnica Artystyczna Pod Aniołem | 26 | C3 |
| Pizzeria Verona | 27 | C2 |
| Sklep Kopernik | (see 30) | |
| Sułtan | 28 | D4 |

**DRINKING**
| | | |
|---|---|---|
| Piwnica Ratusz | 29 | C3 |

**ENTERTAINMENT**
| | | |
|---|---|---|
| Dwór Artusa | 30 | C3 |
| Jazz God | 31 | C4 |
| Teatr im Horzycy | 32 | B2 |

## Information

### BOOKSHOPS
**EMPiK Megastore** ( ☎ 622 48 95; ul Wielkie Garbary 18)

### INTERNET ACCESS
**Ksero Uniwerek** ( ☎ 621 92 79; ul Franciszkańska 5; per hr 3zł; ⏱ 8am-7pm Mon-Fri, 9am-4pm Sat)

### MONEY
ATMs can be found along ul Różana and ul Szeroka. A couple of handy *kantors* are shown on the map.
**Bank Pekao** (ul Wielkie Garbary 11)
**PKO Bank** (ul Szeroka)

### POST
**Main post office** (Rynek Staromiejski; ⏱ 7am-9pm)

### TOURIST INFORMATION
The free, glossy *Toruń Tourist & Business Guide*, available from most decent hotels, advertises local eateries and nightclubs.
**Tourist office** ( ☎ 621 09 31; www.it.torun.pl; Rynek Staromiejski 25; ⏱ 9am-4pm Mon & Sat, 9am-6pm Tue-Fri, 9am-1pm Sun May-Aug, 9am-4pm Mon & Sat, 9am-6pm Tue-Fri Sep-Apr) Very helpful.

## Sights
The starting point for any exploration of Toruń is the **Rynek Staromiejski** (Old Town Market Square), the focal point of the Old Town. The **Regional Museum** ( ☎ 622 70 38; www.muzeum.torun.pl; Rynek Staromiejski 1; adult/child 10/6zł; ⏱ 10am-6pm Tue-Sun May-Aug, 10am-4pm Tue-Sun Sep-Apr) sits within the massive 14th-century **Old Town Hall**, featuring a

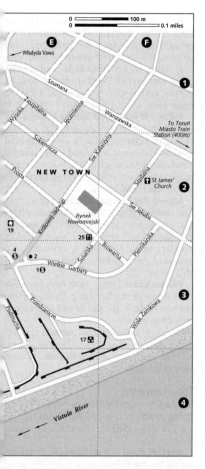

fine collection of 19th- and 20th-century Polish art. Other displays recall the town's guilds, and there's an exhibition of medieval stained glass and religious paintings. Climb the 40m-high **tower** (adult/child 10/6zł; 10am-4pm Tue-Sun Apr, 10am-7pm Tue-Sun May-Sep) for great views.

In front of the Town Hall is an elegant **statue** of Copernicus. Look for other interesting items of statuary around the square, including a dog and umbrella from a famous Polish comic strip, and a fabled violinist who saved Toruń from a plague of frogs.

The richly decorated, 15th-century **Star House**, with its baroque façade and spiral wooden staircase, contains the **Far Eastern Art Museum** ( 622 70 38; Rynek Staromiejski 35; adult/child 7/4zł; 10am-4pm Tue-Sun).

Just off the northwestern corner of the square is the late-13th-century **St Mary's Church** (ul Panny Marii; dawn-dusk), a Gothic building with magnificent 15th-century stalls.

In 1473, Copernicus was born in the brick Gothic house that now contains the dry **Museum of Copernicus** ( 622 70 38; ul Kopernika 15/17; adult/child 10/7zł; 10am-6pm Tue-Sun May-Aug, 10am-4pm Tue-Sun Sep-Apr), with replicas of the great astronomer's instruments.

One block east is the **Cathedral of SS John the Baptist & John the Evangelist** (ul Żeglarska; adult/child 2/1zł; 9am-5.30pm Mon-Sat, 2-5.30pm Sun Apr-Oct), founded in 1233 and completed more than 200 years later, with its massive **tower** (adult/child 6/4zł) and bell.

Behind the church, the **Eskens' House** ( 622 70 38; ul Łazienna 16; adult/child 7/4zł; 10am-4pm Tue-Sun) is a disappointing affair displaying old photographs, a few swords and archaeological finds, labelled in Polish. Further east are the ruins of the **Teutonic Castle** ( 622 70 39; ul Przedzamcze; adult/child 2/1zł; 9am-8pm), destroyed in 1454 by angry townsfolk protesting against the knights' oppressive regime.

In a park just north of the Old Town is the **Ethnographic Museum** ( 622 80 91; ul Wały Sikorskiego 19; adult/child 8/5zł; 9am-4pm Mon, Wed & Fri, 10am-6pm Tue, Thu, Sat & Sun Apr-Sep, 9am-4pm Tue-Sun Oct-Mar), showcasing traditional customs, costumes and weapons.

## Sleeping

Budget lodgings are a distance from the Old Town, but in summer extra student accommodation opens its doors to travellers. Check with the tourist office for updated details.

### BUDGET

**Camping Nr 33 Tramp** ( 654 71 87; www.tramp.mosir.torun.pl; ul Kujawska 14; camping per person 8zł, tents 5-10zł, d/tr/q 60/75/75zł; May-Sep) The cabins here are basic and it's alarmingly close to the train line. It's a five-minute walk west of the main train station.

**Schronisko Turystyczne Fort IV** ( 655 82 36; www.fort.torun.pl; ul Chrobrego 86; dm 17-23zł) Atmospherically located in an old Prussian fort, with long, solid brick corridors built to withstand sieges, and leading to plain, barrack-like dorms. Although inconvenient for town, it's an easy ride on bus 14 from the bus terminal or main train station.

**Youth Hostel** ( 659 61 84; ul Św. Józefa 22/24; dm 20zł) Offers plain but bright facilities

POLAND

overlooking parkland, 1.6km northwest of the centre. Catch bus 11 from the main train station or Old Town, to the first stop on ul Św. Jozefa. Reception closes between 10am and 5pm daily, and there's a 10pm curfew.

### MIDRANGE & TOP END

**Hotel Pod Orłem** ( ☎ 622 50 24; www.hotel.torun.pl; ul Mostowa 17; s/d 110/140zł, apt 200zł; P ✕ 🖳 ) This hotel is great value, and although the rooms are smallish, have squeaky wooden floors, and some contain poky bathrooms, the service is good and it's central. The foyer and corridors are fun with their jumble of framed pop-art images and old photos.

**Hotel Polonia** ( ☎ 657 18 00; www.polonia.torun.pl; plac Teatralny 5; s/d 150/180zł) The Polonia has smart, attractively furnished rooms with soothing green tones, high ceilings and good bathrooms, in a restored 19th-century building a short walk from the main square. The hotel also has its own *kantor*.

**Hotel Gotyk** ( ☎ 658 40 00; www.hotel-gotyk.com .pl; ul Piekary 20; s/d from 150/250zł) Housed in a fully modernised 14th-century building just off the main square, rooms are very neat, with ornate furniture and high ceilings, and all come with sparkling bathrooms.

**Hotel Retman** ( ☎ 657 44 60; www.hotelretman.pl; ul Rabiańska 15; s/d 160/210zł) Relatively new accommodation offering spacious, atmospheric rooms with red carpet and solid timber furniture. Downstairs is a good pub and restaurant.

**Hotel Petite Fleur** ( ☎ 663 44 00; www.petitefleur .pl; ul Piekary 25; s/d from 190/250zł; 🖳 ) Just opposite the Gotyk, the Petite Fleur offers fresh, airy rooms in a renovated old town house, some with exposed original brickwork and rafters. It also has a French cellar restaurant.

**Hotel Heban** ( ☎ 652 15 55; www.hotel-heban.com.pl; ul Małe Garbary 7; s/d/ste from 190/300/350zł; P ✕ 🖳 ) This is a stylish, upmarket hotel occupying an historic 17th-century building in a quiet street. It also has a good restaurant, situated off a lavish foyer with painted wooden ceilings and a 24-hour bar.

## Eating & Drinking

**Bar Mleczny Pod Arkadami** ( ☎ 622 24 28; ul Różana 1; mains 3-8zł; ⏲ 9am-7pm Mon-Fri, 9am-4pm Sat) This classic milk bar is just off the Old Town Square, with a range of low-cost dishes. It also has a takeaway window serving a range of *zapiekanki* (toasted rolls with cheese, mushrooms and ketchup) and sweet waffles.

**Pizzeria Verona** ( ☎ 622 04 80; ul Chełmińska 11; mains 7-26zł; ⏲ 11am-midnight) The Verona offers a big menu of pizzas, plus a few pasta and salad options. It's in a great cellar location with fairy lights, wicker lampshades and candles in old wine bottles. Don't attempt to descend the precipitous stairs if you've had a few too many beers.

**Sułtan** ( ☎ 621 06 07; ul Mostowa 7; mains 8-12zł; ⏲ 11am-midnight Sun-Thu, 11am-1am Fri & Sat) A splash of Middle Eastern cuisine in western Poland in a cheerful venue decorated with colourful lanterns and Arabic script. The menu contains pides, kebabs, shwarma and gyros, along with soups, salads and pizzas.

**Gospoda Pod Modrym Fartuchem** ( ☎ 622 26 26; Rynek Nowomiejski 8; mains 16-29zł; ⏲ 10am-10pm) This is a very pleasant, unpretentious 15th-century pub on the New Town Square, once visited by Polish kings and Napoleon. It serves the usual meat-and-cabbage Polish dishes at reasonable prices.

**Piwnica Ratusz** ( ☎ 621 02 92; Rynek Staromiejski 1) This is a great place for a drink, offering outdoor tables in the square and a cavernous area downstairs.

Toruń is famous for its *pierniki* (gingerbread), which come in a variety of shapes, and can be bought at **Sklep Kopernik** ( ☎ 622 88 32; Rynek Staromiejski 6).

## Entertainment

**Piwnica Artystyczna Pod Aniołem** ( ☎ 622 70 39; Rynek Staromiejski 1) Set in a splendid spacious cellar in the Old Town Hall, this bar offers live music some nights.

**Jazz God** ( ☎ 652 13 08; ul Rabiańska 17; ⏲ 5pm-2am Sun-Thu, 5pm-4am Fri & Sat) This is a lively cellar bar with rock DJs every night from 9pm. On Sunday there's live jazz around 8pm.

**Teatr im Horzycy** ( ☎ 622 52 22; plac Teatralny 1) The main stage for theatre performances.

**Dwór Artusa** ( ☎ 655 49 29; Artus Court, Rynek Staromiejski 6) This place often presents classical music.

**Cinema City** ( ☎ 664 64 64; ul Czerwona Droga 1; tickets 15zł) A moviehouse showing current film releases in a 12-screen multiplex.

## Getting There & Away

The **bus terminal** (ul Dąbrowskiego) is a 10-minute walk north of the Old Town, though it offers surprisingly few long-distance buses. **Polski Express** (ul Mickiewicza) has 12 buses a day to Warsaw (48zł, four hours) and two a day to Szczecin.

The **Toruń Główny train station** (al Podgórska) is on the opposite side of the Vistula River and linked to the Old Town by bus 22 or 27 (get off at the first stop over the bridge). Some trains stop and finish at the more convenient Toruń Miasto train station, about 500m east of the New Town.

From the Toruń Główny station, there are fast train services to Poznań (30zł, 3½ hours, six daily), Gdańsk and Gdynia (36zł, five hours, nine daily), Kraków (50zł, 6½ hours, six daily), Łódź (32zł, eight daily), Olsztyn (32zł, eight daily), Szczecin (45zł, five hours, direct twice a week), Wrocław (43zł, 4½ hours, two daily) and Warsaw (40zł, four hours, seven daily). Trains travelling between Toruń and Gdańsk often change at Bydgoszcz, and between Toruń and Kraków you may need to get another connection at Inowrocław.

# GDAŃSK
☎ 058 / pop 462,000

Few Polish cities occupy such a pivotal position in history as Gdańsk. Founded more than a millennium ago, it became the focus of territorial tensions when the Teutonic Knights seized it from Poland in 1308. The city joined the Hanseatic League in 1361, and became one of the richest ports in the Baltic through its membership of the trading organisation. Finally, the Thirteen Years' War ended in 1466 with the Knights' defeat and Gdańsk's return to Polish rule.

This to-and-fro between Germanic and Polish control wasn't over – in 1793 Gdańsk was incorporated into Prussia, and after WWI became the autonomous Free City of Danzig. The city's environs are where WWII began, when the Nazis bombarded Polish troops stationed at Westerplatte. Gdańsk suffered immense damage in the war, but upon its return to Poland in 1945, its historic centre was faithfully reconstructed.

In the 1980s, Gdańsk achieved international fame as the home of the Solidarity trade union, whose rise paralleled the fall of communism in Europe. Today it's a lively, attractive city that makes a great base for exploring the Baltic coast.

## Information
### BOOKSHOPS
**EMPiK Megastore** ( ☎ 301 72 44; ul Podwale Grodzkie 8) Opposite the main train station.

### INTERNET ACCESS
**Jazz 'n' Java** ( ☎ 305 36 16; ul Tkacka 17/18; per hr 5zł; ◷ 10am-10pm)
**Rudy Kot** (ul Garncarska 18/20; per hr 4zł; ◷ 10am-10pm)

### MONEY
The *kantor* at the main train station is open 24 hours.
**Bank Millennium** Old Town (ul Wały Jagiellońskie 14/16); Main Town (ul Długi Targ 14/16) Has more branches at central locations.
**Bank Pekao** (ul Garncarska 23) Will provide cash advances on Visa and MasterCard.

### POST
**Main post office** (ul Długa 22; ◷ 8am-8pm Mon-Fri, 9am-3pm Sat)

### TOURIST INFORMATION
**PTTK office** ( ☎ 301 13 43; www.pttk-gdansk.pl; ul Długa 45; ◷ 9am-5pm)

### TRAVEL AGENCIES
**Almatur** ( ☎ 301 24 24; Długi Targ 11)
**Orbis Travel** ( ☎ 301 45 44; ul Podwale Staromiejskie 96/97)

## Sights
### MAIN TOWN
Ul Długa (Long Street) and Długi Targ (Long Market) form the city's main historic thoroughfare, and are known collectively as the **Royal Way**. Polish kings traditionally paraded through the **Upland Gate** (built in the 1770s on a 15th-century gate), onward through the **Golden Gate** (1614), and proceeded east to the Renaissance **Green Gate** (1568).

**Gdańsk History Museum** ( ☎ 767 91 00; ul Długa 47; adult/child 8/4zł, adult/child incl Artus Court Museum & Dom Uphagena 12/6zł; ◷ noon-6pm Tue-Fri, noon-4pm Sat & Sun) is inside the towering Gothic **Main Town Hall**. On show are photos of old Gdańsk, and the damage caused during WWII.

**Artus Court Museum** ( ☎ 767 91 00; ul Długi Targ 43/44; adult/child 8/4zł, free Wed; ◷ noon-6pm Tue-Fri, noon-4pm Sat & Sun), where merchants used to congregate, stands behind **Neptune's Fountain** (1633). The adjacent **Golden House** (1618) has a strikingly rich façade. Further west, the 18th-century **Dom Uphagena** ( ☎ 301 13 63; ul Długa; adult/child 8/4zł, free Sun; ◷ noon-6pm Tue-Fri, 10am-4pm Sat, 11am-4pm Sun) features ornate furniture.

North of the Green Gate is the 14th-century **St Mary's Gate**, which houses the **State Archaeological Museum** ( ☎ 301 50 31; ul Mariacka 25/26;

**POLAND**

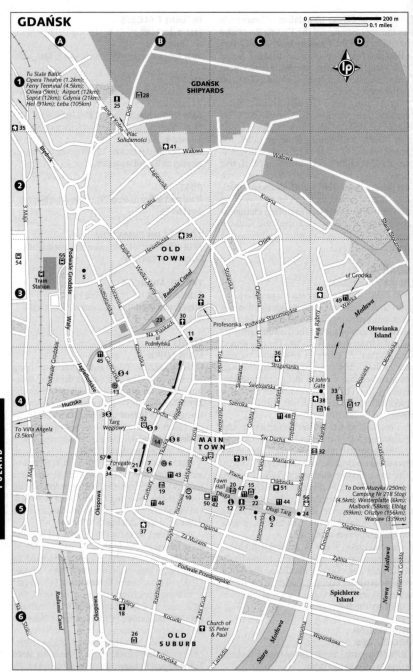

# GDAŃSK

POLAND

0 — 200 m
0 — 0.1 miles

**GDAŃSK SHIPYARDS**

To Stałe Bałtic
Opera Theatre (1.2km);
Ferry Terminal (4.5km);
Oliwa (5km); Airport (12km);
Sopot (12km); Gdynia (21km);
Hel (91km); Łeba (105km)

Plac Solidarności

**OLD TOWN**

Radunia Canal

Train Station

**MAIN TOWN**

Ołowianka Island

St John's Gate

To Villa Angela (3.5km)

Town Hall

Długi Targ

To Dom Muzyka (250m);
Camping Nr 218 Stogi
(4.5km); Westerplatte (6km);
Malbork (58km); Elbląg
(59km); Olsztyn (156km);
Warsaw (339km)

Spichlerze Island

**OLD SUBURB**

Church of SS Peter & Paul

adult/child 5/4zł; 9am-4pm Tue, Thu & Fri, 10am-5pm Wed, Sat & Sun). It features an overly generous number of formerly diseased ancient human skulls, displays of amber, and river views from the adjacent **tower** (admission 2zł). Through this gate, picturesque **ul Mariacka** (St Mary's St) is lined with 17th-century burgher houses and amber shops.

At the end of ul Mariacka is the gigantic 14th-century **St Mary's Church** (adult/child 2/1zł; 8am-8pm, except during services). Watch little figures troop out at noon from its 14m-high astronomical clock, adorned with zodiacal signs. Climb the 405 steps of the **tower** (adult/child 3/1.50zł) for a giddy view over the town. West along ul Piwna (Beer St) is the Dutch Renaissance **Arsenal** (1609), now occupied by a market.

Further north along the waterfront is the 15th-century **Gdańsk Crane**, the largest of its kind in medieval Europe and capable of hoisting loads of up to 2000kg. It's now part of the **Central Maritime Museum** ( 301 86 11; ul Ołowianka 9-13; one section 6zł, all four sections 14zł; 10am-5pm Tue-Sun). The museum offers a fascinating insight into Gdańsk's seafaring past, including the **Sołdek Museum Ship**, built here just after WWII.

### OLD TOWN
Almost totally destroyed in 1945, the Old Town has never been completely rebuilt. However, among its gems are **St Catherine's Church** (ul Wielke Młyny; 8am-6pm Mon-Sat), Gdańsk's oldest church (begun in the 1220s). Opposite, the **Great Mill** (ul Wielke Młyny) was built by the Teutonic Knights in around 1350. It

used to produce 200 tonnes of flour per day and continued to operate until 1945.

Right behind St Catherine's is **St Bridget's Church** (ul Profesorska 17; 10am-6pm Mon-Sat). Formerly Lech Wałęsa's place of worship, the church was a strong supporter of the shipyard activists in the 1980s.

The soaring **Monument to the Shipyard Workers** (plac Solidarności) stands at the entrance to the Gdańsk Shipyards to the north. It was erected in late 1980 in memory of 44 workers killed during the riots of December 1970. Down the street is the evocative **Roads to Freedom Exhibition** (Solidarity Museum; 769 29 20; ul Doki 1; adult/child 6/4zł, free Wed; 10am-4pm Tue-Sun). Look out for the section of the Berlin Wall outside.

### OLD SUBURB
The **National Museum** ( 301 70 61; ul Toruńska 1; adult/child 9/5zł; 9am-4pm Tue-Fri, 10am-4pm Sat & Sun) is famous for its Dutch and Flemish paintings, especially Hans Memling's 15th-century *Last Judgment*.

Adjoining the museum is the former Franciscan **Church of the Holy Trinity** (ul Św. Trójcy; 10am-8pm Mon-Sat), built at the end of the 15th century.

### OLIWA
Some 9km northwest is the lovely **Park Oliwski** (ul Cysterśów), surrounding the towering **Oliwa Cathedral** ( 8am-8pm), built in the 13th century with a Gothic façade and a long, narrow central nave. The famous baroque organ is used for recitals each hour between 10am and 3pm Monday to Saturday in June, July and August. Nearby is the **Ethnographic Museum** ( 552 12 71;

**POLAND**

ul Cystersów 19; adult/child 8/5zł; ☻ 9am-4pm Tue-Fri, 10am-4pm Sat & Sun) in the Old Granary, and the **Modern Art Gallery** ( ☎ 552 12 71; adult/child 6/3zł; ☻ 9am-4pm Tue-Sun) in the former Abbots' Palace.

To reach the park, take the commuter train to the Gdańsk Oliwa station (2.80zł). From there, it's a 10-minute walk; head (west) up ul Poczty Gdańsk, turn right (north) along the highway and look for the signs (in English) to 'Ethnographic Museum' and 'Cathedral'.

### WESTERPLATTE

WWII began at 4.45am on 1 September 1939, when the German battleship *Schleswig-Holstein* began shelling the Polish naval post at Westerplatte, 7km north of Gdańsk's Main Town. The 182-man Polish garrison held out against ferocious attacks for a week before surrendering.

The enormity of this event is marked by a hilltop **memorial** (free; ☻ 24hr), a small **museum** ( ☎ 343 69 72; ul Sucharskiego 1; admission 2zł; ☻ 8am-7pm) and **ruins** remaining from the Nazi bombardment.

Bus 106 (25 minutes) goes to the park every 15 minutes from a stop outside the main train station in Gdańsk. Alternatively, excursion boats (23/39zł one way/return) to and around Westerplatte leave from a dock near the Green Gate in Gdańsk between 1 April and 30 October.

## Sleeping

If you're having trouble finding accommodation, check with the PTTK office. Also consider staying in nearby Sopot or Gdynia.

### BUDGET

**Youth Hostel** ( ☎ /fax 301 23 13; ul Wałowa 21; dm/s/d from 12/25/50zł; Ⓟ ✗ ) Old-style hostel in a quiet, old building on the doorstep of the Gdańsk Shipyards, Lech Wałęsa's old stamping grounds. Rooms are brown and basic, but clean. Book ahead, particularly in summer. Smoking and drinking are strictly forbidden and there's a midnight curfew.

**Dom Harcerza** ( ☎ 301 36 21; www.domharcerza.prv.pl; ul Za Murami 2/10; dm 25zł, s/d/tr from 50/100/120zł) The rooms are small but cosy, and the bathrooms are clean at this place, which offers the best value and location for any budget-priced hotel. It's popular (so book ahead), and can get noisy when large groups are staying here. There's a charming old-fashioned restaurant on the ground floor.

**Baltic Hostel** ( ☎ 721 96 57; www.baltichostel.com; ul 3 Maja 25; dm 35zł, s/d 50/100zł; Ⓟ ✗ 💻 ) Aimed at the international budget traveller, this hostel near the train and bus stations has basic, newly-furnished rooms with high ceilings. Bathrooms are clean, and there's a homely light-filled lounge area with ceramic fish on the wall. The entrance is right at the end of the long brown apartment block, around to the right.

**Targ Rybny** ( ☎ 301 56 27; www.gdanskhostel.com; ul Grodzka 21; dm from 40zł, s/d/tr from 90/140/180zł; Ⓟ ✗ 💻 ) A popular modern hostel in a great central location overlooking the quay. It's a little cramped, but clean and sociable, with a comfy lounge area. It also offers bike rental.

**Camping Nr 218 Stogi** ( ☎ 307 39 15; www.camping-gdansk.pl; ul Wydmy 9; per person/tent 10/10zł, cabins 40-100zł; ☻ Apr-Oct; Ⓟ ) This camping ground is only 200m from the beach in the seaside holiday centre of Stogi, about 5.5km northeast of the Main Town. Tidy cabins sleep between two and five people, and facilities include a volleyball court and children's playground. Take tram 8 or 13 from the main train station in Gdańsk.

### MIDRANGE & TOP END

**Apartments Poland** ( ☎ 346 98 64; www.apartmentpoland.com; apt from €50) is an agency with renovated properties scattered through the Tri-City Area (Gdańsk/Sopot/Gdynia), including a number in central Gdańsk. Some are big enough for families or other groups. Be aware of the additional electricity charge when checking out, based on a meter reading.

**Villa Angela** ( ☎ 302 23 15; www.villaangela.pl; ul Beethowena 12; s/d/tr 175/210/285zł; Ⓟ ✗ 💻 ) Comfortable lodgings west of the centre, with spacious recently renovated rooms (some with balconies), good furniture and gleaming bathrooms. It's accessible by buses 130, 184 or 384, or night bus N6, from the main train station.

**Dom Muzyka** ( ☎ 300 92 60; www.dom-muzyka.pl; ul Łąkowa 1/2; s/d from 180/255zł; Ⓟ ✗ 🎾 💻 ) Gorgeous white rooms with arched ceilings and quality furniture, inside the Music Academy some 300m east of the city centre. From July to August, a second wing of the building offers cheaper student-style accommodation. It's hard to spot from the street; head for the door on the city end of the courtyard within the big yellow-brick building.

**Dom Aktora** ( ☎ 301 59 01; www.domaktora.pl; ul Straganiarska 55/56; s/d/ste from 200/300/360zł) The Dom

Aktora is an historic and convenient place which is always popular, but it's a little old-fashioned in appearance.

**Mercure Hevelius Gdańsk** ( ☎ 321 00 00; www.orbis .pl; ul Heweliusza 22; s/d from 360/430zł; P ✕ ⌷ ⏦ ) Though the foyer still hints at its origins in the late Cold War days, this business-friendly hotel offers good quality rooms and facilities including a restaurant, bar and·sauna. Two rooms are designed for disabled access, and some upper rooms have great views of the Old Town.

**Hotel Hanza** ( ☎ 305 34 27; www.hanza-hotel.com.pl; ul Tokarska 6; s/d 665/695zł; P ✕ ✕ ⌷ ) The Hanza is attractively perched along the waterfront near the Gdańsk Crane, and offers elegant, tasteful rooms in a modern building. Some rooms have enviable views over the river.

## Eating & Drinking

For self-catering, visit the supermarket inside the former Arsenal facing Targ Węglowy.

**Bar Mleczny Neptun** ( ☎ 301 49 88; ul Długa 33/34; mains 2-10zł; ✆ 7.30am-6pm Mon-Fri, 10am-5pm Sat, 11am-5pm Sun) This joint is a cut above your run-of-the-mill milk bar, with potted plants, lace curtains, decorative tiling and old lamps for décor.

**Green Way** ( ☎ 301 41 21; ul Garncarska 4/6; mains 7-10zł; ✆ 10am-7pm Mon-Fri, noon-7pm Sat & Sun) Popular with local vegetarians, this eatery serves everything from soy cutlets to Mexican goulash in an unfussy blue-and-yellow space.

**Grand Café Rotterdam** ( ☎ 305 45 80; Długi Targ 33/34; mains 12-27zł; ✆ 10am-2am) On the ground floor of the Dutch consulate, this café serves especially good savoury pancakes. It also has a good range of seafood dishes, including

stir-fried mussels. It's a pleasant spot for an alfresco beer, and has a well-stocked cellar wine bar.

**Kansai** ( ☎ 324 08 88; ul Ogarna 124/125; mains 22-36zł; ✆ noon-10pm Tue-Sun) You'd expect fish to be served in a seaport, but Kansai adds an exotic twist by serving sushi in full-on Japanese ambience. Waiters are dressed in traditional robes, there's a samurai sword on the counter, and the menu has dishes made from tuna, salmon and butterfish, along with classic California rolls.

**Restauracja Kubicki** ( ☎ 301 00 50; ul Wartka 5; mains 25-43zł; ✆ 11.30am-11.30pm) The Kubicki is a decent midpriced place to try Polish food, especially seafood. It's one of the oldest eateries in Gdańsk, established in the Danzig days of 1918, and offers appropriately old-fashioned décor and service off a scenic laneway next to the river.

**Pod Łososiem** ( ☎ 301 76 52; ul Szeroka 52/54; mains 45-95zł; ✆ noon-10pm) This is one of Gdańsk's oldest and most highly regarded restaurants, and is particularly famous for its salmon dishes. Red leather seats, brass chandeliers and a gathering of gas lamps fill out the sombre interior.

**Piwinica Rajców** ( ☎ 300 02 80; ul Długi Targ 44; mains 20-110zł; ✆ 10am-midnight) An excellent cellar-restaurant below a striking entrance that's topped by a statue of the god Mercury. The menu features some of the finest Polish cuisine to be had in Gdańsk, particularly wild boar, and extends to more exotic dishes such as springbok fillet.

**U Szkota** ( ☎ 301 49 11; ul Chlebnicka 9/12; ✆ noon-midnight) If you're in the mood to be served by buzz-cut Polish waiters dressed in kilts, this Scottish-themed venue is the place to go. The bar is small but cosy, with good-natured staff, and there's a decent selection of whiskies on the drinks list. The attached restaurant serves a largely Polish menu.

**Maraska** ( ☎ 301 42 89; ul Długa 31/32; ✆ 9am-9pm) The Maraska is a cosy teahouse with vintage wallpaper, framed pictures of yachts, and tea paraphernalia for sale. There's a good choice of desserts, and a counter selling chocolates and other sweets.

## Entertainment

**Yesterday** ( ☎ 301 39 24; ul Piwna 50/51; ✆ 6pm-2am) Groovy cellar venue decked out in a 1960s theme, with colourful flower-power décor including cartoon characters and a fluorescent

POLAND

portrait of Chairman Mao. DJs play a variety of sounds from 9pm every night, and there's the occasional live gig. Tuesday night is British music night.

**State Baltic Opera Theatre** ( ☎ 763 49 12; www .operabaltycka.pl; al Zwycięstwa 15) This place is in the suburb of Wrzeszcz, not far from the train station at Gdańsk Politechnika.

**Teatr Wybrzeże** ( ☎ 301 70 21; ul Św. Ducha 2) Next to the Arsenal is the main city theatre. Both Polish and foreign classics (all in Polish) are part of the repertoire.

## Getting There & Away

For information about international ferry services to/from Gdańsk and Gdynia, see p617.

### AIR

From Gdańsk, LOT has six to seven daily flights to Warsaw, two a day to Frankfurt, and one to Hamburg and Munich. Tickets can be bought at the **LOT office** ( ☎ 0801 703 703; ul Wały Jagiellońskie 2/4).

### BOAT

Polferries uses the **ferry terminal** (ul Przemysłowa) in Nowy Port, about 5km north of the Main Town and a short walk from the local commuter train station at Gdańsk Brzeżno. Orbis Travel and the PTTK Office in Gdańsk provide information and sell tickets.

Between 1 May and 30 September, excursion boats leave regularly from the dock near the Green Gate in Gdańsk for Sopot (35/51zł one way/return) and Gdynia (41/61zł) – and you can even go to Hel (61/92zł)! From the same dock, boats also head out to Westerplatte (23/39zł) between 1 April and 30 October.

### BUS

The **bus terminal** (ul 3 Maja 12) is behind the main train station and connected to ul Podwale Grodzkie by an underground passageway. Every day there are buses to Olsztyn (26zł, seven daily), Toruń (27zł, two daily), and Warsaw (50zł, six hours, five daily), and one or two to Białystok and Świnoujście. Polski Express also offers buses to Warsaw (72zł, two daily).

### TRAIN

The city's main train station, **Gdańsk Główny** (ul Podwale Grodzkie 1), is conveniently located on the western outskirts of the Old Town. Most long-distance trains actually start or finish at

Gdynia, so make sure you get on/off quickly here.

Each day more than 20 trains head to Warsaw, including eight express trains (82zł, 5½ hours) and five InterCity services (90zł, 3½ hours). There are fast trains to Olsztyn (32zł, three hours, nine daily), Kraków (115zł, eight hours, 13 daily), Poznań (45zł, five hours, seven daily), Toruń (37zł, three hours, eight daily) and Szczecin (47zł, 4½ hours, four daily). Trains also head to Białystok and Lublin three times a day.

## Getting Around

The airport is in Rębiechowo, about 12km northwest of Gdańsk. It's accessible by bus 110 from the Gdańsk Wrzeszcz local commuter train station, or less frequently by bus B from outside the Gdańsk Główny train station. Taxis cost 40zł to 50zł one way.

The local commuter train, the SKM, runs every 15 minutes between 6am and 7.30pm, and less frequently thereafter, between Gdańsk Główny and Gdynia Główna stations, via Sopot and Gdańsk Oliwa stations. (Note: the line to Gdańsk Nowy Port, via Gdańsk Brzeżno, is a separate line that leaves less regularly from Gdańsk Główny.) Buy tickets at any station and validate them in the machines at the platform entrance.

## AROUND GDAŃSK

Gdańsk is part of the so-called Tri-City Area including Gdynia and Sopot, which are easy day trips from Gdańsk.

### Sopot

☎ 058 / pop 43,000

Sopot, 12km north of Gdańsk, has been one of the Baltic coast's most fashionable seaside resorts since the 19th century. It has an easy-going atmosphere and long stretches of sandy **beach**.

The **tourist office** ( ☎ 550 37 83; www.sopot.pl; ul Dworcowa 4; ☼ 9am-8pm Jun-Aug, 10am-6pm Sep-May) is about 50m from the main train station. A short walk to the east of the station is **Gamer** ( ☎ 555 01 83; ul Chopina 1; per hr 4zł; ☼ 9am-10pm), an internet café.

From the tourist office, head down ul Bohaterów Monte Cassino, one of Poland's most attractive pedestrian streets, and past the church to Poland's longest **pier** (515m).

Opposite Pension Wanda, **Museum Sopotu** ( ☎ 551 22 66; ul Poniatowskiego 8; adult/child 5/3zł;

(☑) 10am-4pm Tue-Fri, 11am-5pm Sat & Sun) has displays recalling the town's 19th-century incarnation as the German resort of Zoppot.

### SLEEPING & EATING

There are no real budget options in Sopot, and prices increase during the busy summer season. Bistros and cafés serving a wide range of cuisines sprout up in summer along the promenades.

**Hotel Eden** (☎ 551 15 03; www.hotel-eden.com.pl; ul Kordeckiego 4/6; s 100-180zł, d 170-260zł, tr 320zł, q 340zł, ste 410zł; **P** **☐**) One of the less expensive places in town. It's a quiet, old-fashioned *pension* with high ceilings and old-fashioned furniture, overlooking the town park one street from the beach. The cheaper rooms don't have private bathrooms.

**Willa Karat II** (☎ 550 07 42; ul 3 Maja 31; s/d/tr 150/250/270zł) Cosy budget lodgings a few blocks from the beach, with light, spacious rooms and clean bathrooms, and plants decorating the corridors. There's a kitchen and dining area for guest use. From the train station, walk right along ul Kościuszki, then left along ul 3 Maja toward the coast.

**Pension Wanda** (☎ 550 30 38; fax 551 57 25; ul Poniatowskiego 7; s/d/tr from 200/300/410zł, ste from 360zł; **P** **☒**) The Wanda is a homely place with light, airy rooms, in a handy location about 500m south of the pier. Some rooms have sea views.

**Zhong Hua Hotel** (☎ 550 20 20; www.hotelchinski.pl; al Wojska Polskiego 1; s/d/ste 430/455/565zł; **☒** **☐**) Attractive accommodation in a striking wooden pavilion on the seafront. The foyer is decked out in Chinese design, with hanging lanterns and beautiful timber furniture. The theme extends to the small but pleasant rooms, with views of the water.

The classy **Café del Arte** (☎ 555 51 60; ul Bohaterów Monte Cassino 53; (☑) 10am-10pm) is a great place to enjoy coffee, cake and ice cream surrounded by artistic objects in the combined café-gallery. At the same address is **Caipirinha** (☎ 555 53 80; ul Bohaterów Monte Cassino 53; mains 12-20zł; (☑) 10am-midnight), a bar and eatery serving light meals and plenty of cocktails. Its surrealistic 'melting' architecture is what sets this building apart; you really can't miss it.

### GETTING THERE & AWAY

From the **Sopot train station** (ul Dworcowa 7), local commuter trains run every 15 minutes to Gdańsk Główny (2.80zł, 15 minutes) and

Gdynia Główna (1.20zł, 10 minutes) stations. Excursion boats leave several times a day (May to September) from the Sopot pier to Gdańsk, Gdynia and Hel.

## Gdynia
☎ 058 / pop 254,000

Gdynia, 9km north of Sopot, was greatly expanded as a seaport after this coastal area (but not Gdańsk) became part of Poland following WWI. Less atmospheric than Gdańsk or Sopot, it's a young city with a busy port atmosphere.

From the main Gdynia Główna train station on plac Konstytucji, where there is a **tourist office** (☎ 721 24 66; www.gdynia.pl; (☑) 8am-6pm May-Sep, 10am-5pm Oct-Apr), follow ul 10 Lutego east for about 1.5km to the pier. At the end of the pier is the **Oceanographic Museum & Aquarium** (☎ 621 70 21; adult/child 11/7zł; (☑) 10am-5pm Tue-Sun), which houses a vast array of sea creatures, both alive and embalmed.

A 20-minute walk uphill (follow the signs) from Teatr Muzyczny on plac Grunwaldzki (about 300m southwest of the start of the pier) leads to **Kamienna Góra**, a hill offering wonderful views.

### SLEEPING & EATING

Gdynia is probably best visited as a day trip, but it does have a vibrant restaurant scene. There are several milk bars in the city centre, and upmarket fish restaurants along the pier.

**China Town Hotel** (☎ 620 92 21; www.chinahotel.pl; ul Dworca 11a; s/d 100/130zł) Inexpensive lodgings can be found here, opposite the train station. The rooms are plain but serviceable for a night, though singles are very small. There's a sushi restaurant in the same building.

**Hotel Antracyt** (☎ 620 12 39; ul Korzeniowskiego 19; www.hotel-antracyt.pl; s/d from 170/240zł; **P** **☒** **☐**) This place is further south, on a hill in an exclusive residential area, with fine views over the water.

**Willa Lubicz** (☎ 668 47 40; www.willalubicz.pl; ul Orłowska 43; s/d 380/410zł; **☒**) If you're looking for style you could try this quiet, upmarket place with a chic 1930s ambience at the southern end of town; Gdynia Orłowo is the nearest train station. Third-floor rooms have views of the sea.

**Bistro Kwadrans** (☎ 620 15 92; Skwer Kościuszki 20; mains 9-13zł; (☑) 9am-10pm Mon-Fri, 10am-10pm Sat, noon-10pm Sun) One block north of the median

POLAND

strip along ul 10 Lutego, this is a great place for tasty Polish food. It also serves up pizzas, including an improbable variant involving banana and curry.

### GETTING THERE & AWAY

Local commuter trains link **Gdynia Główna** station with Sopot and Gdańsk every 15 minutes (4zł, 25 minutes). From the same station, regular trains run to Hel (12zł) and Lębork (for Łeba). From the small **bus terminal** outside, minibuses also go to Hel (11zł) and Łeba, and two buses run daily to Świnoujście.

Stena Line uses the **Terminal Promowy** (ul Kwiatkowskiego 60), about 5km northwest of Gdynia. Take bus 150 from outside the main train station.

Between May and September, excursion boats leave regularly throughout the day to Gdańsk, Sopot and Hel from the Gdynia pier.

## Hel

Never was a town more entertainingly named – English speakers can spend hours creating amusing twists on 'to Hel and back', or 'a cold day in Hel'. In fact, this old fishing village at the tip of the Hel Peninsula north of Gdańsk is an attractive place to visit, and a popular beach resort. The pristine, windswept **beach** on the Baltic side stretches the length of the peninsula. On the southern side the sea is popular for **windsurfing**; equipment can be rented in the villages of Władysławowo and Jastarnia.

The **Fokarium** ( ☎ 675 08 36; ul Morska 2; admission 1zł; ☯ 8.30am-8pm), off the main road along the seafront, is home to endangered Baltic grey seals. It also has a good souvenir shop for those 'I'm in Hel' postcards to friends back home. The 15th-century **Gothic church** (ul Nadmorksi 2), further along the esplanade, houses the **Museum of Fishery** ( ☎ 675 05 52; adult/child 5/3zł; ☯ 10am-4pm Tue-Sun).

Visitors often stay in **private rooms** offered within local houses (mostly from May to September), at about 90zł per double. **Captain Morgan** ( ☎ 675 00 91; www.captainmorgan.hel.org.pl; ul Wiejska 21; d/tr 100/140zł) also offers plain, clean rooms, and good seafood in a quirky pub stuffed with maritime memorabilia.

To Hel, minibuses leave every hour or so from the main train station in Gdynia (11zł). Several slow trains depart from Gdynia daily (12zł), and from May to September from Gdańsk. Hel is also accessible by excursion boat from Gdańsk, Sopot and Gdynia.

## Łeba

☎ 059 / pop 4100

Łeba (weh-bah) transforms from quiet fishing village to popular seaside resort between May and September. The wide sandy **beach** and clean water is ideal if you're looking for a beach break.

From the train station, or adjacent bus stop, head east along ul 11 Listopada as far as the main street, ul Kościuszko. Then turn left (north) and walk about 1.5km to the better eastern beach via the esplanade (ul Nadmorska); if in doubt, follow the signs to the beachside Hotel Neptune.

The **tourist office** ( ☎ 866 25 65; ☯ 8am-4pm Mon-Fri May-Sep) is inside the train station. There are several kantors along ul 11 Listopada.

### SŁOWIŃSKI NATIONAL PARK

Beginning just wwest of Łeba, this park stretches along the coast for 33km. It contains a diversity of habitats, including forests, lakes, bogs and beaches, but the main attraction is the huge number of massive (and shifting) **sand dunes** that create a desert landscape. The wildlife and birdlife is also remarkably rich.

From Łeba to the sand dunes, follow the signs from near the train station northwest along ul Turystyczna and take the road west to the park entrance in the hamlet of Rąbka. Minibuses ply this road in summer from Łeba; alternatively, it's a pleasant walk or bike ride (8km). No cars or buses are allowed beyond the park entrance.

### SLEEPING & EATING

Many houses offer private rooms all year round, but finding a vacant room during summer can be tricky. There are plenty of decent eateries in the town centre and along ul Nadmorska.

**Hotel Wodnik** ( ☎ 866 13 66; www.wodnik.leba.pl; ul Nadmorska 10; s/d from 232/363zł; P ♨ ) One of several pensions along the esplanade on the eastern side of the beach.

**Camping Nr 41Amber** ( ☎ 866 24 72; www.ambre .leba.pl; ul Nadmorska 9a; per person/tent from 11/6zł; P ) This is a decent camping ground, but bring mosquito repellent if you don't want to be eaten alive.

### GETTING THERE & AWAY

The usual transit point is Lębork, 29km south of Łeba. In summer there are several daily trains between the two destinations (7zł). To

Lębork, slow trains run every hour or two from Gdańsk, via Gdynia, and there are buses every hour from Gdynia. In summer (June to August), two buses and two trains run directly between Gdynia and Łeba, and one train a day travels to/from Wrocław (55zł, 10 hours).

## Malbork

☎ 055 / pop 42,000

**Malbork Castle** ( ☎ 647 08 00; www.zamek.malbork.pl; adult/child 25/15zł; �9am-7pm Tue-Sun May-Aug, 10am-5pm Tue-Sun Apr & Sep, 10am-3pm Tue-Sun Oct-Mar) is the centrepiece of this town, 58km southeast of Gdańsk. It's the largest Gothic castle in Europe, and was once known as Marienburg, headquarters to the Teutonic Knights. It was constructed by the Order in 1276 and became the seat of their Grand Master in 1309. Damage sustained in WWII has been repaired since the conflict's end, and it was placed on the Unesco World Heritage List in 1997.

The **Youth Hostel** ( ☎ 272 24 08; gimnazjum@malbork .com; ul Żeromskiego 45; dm/d 20/46zł) is a reasonable budget option in a local school about 500m south of the castle. Bed linen costs an extra 5zł per person.

**Hotel & Restaurant Zbyszko** ( ☎ 272 26 40; www .hotel.malbork.pl; ul Kościuszki 43; s/d from 140/210zł; P ) is a fairly drab but conveniently located place along the road to the castle. The unremarkable rooms are serviceable for a night.

**Hotel & Restaurant Zamek** ( ☎ 272 33 67; biuro@ hotelzamek.pl; ul Starościńska 14; s/d/ste 230/300/660zł; P ⊠ ⚄ ) is inside a restored medieval building in the Lower Castle. The rooms are a bit old-fashioned, but the bathrooms are up-to-date and the restaurant has character.

The castle is 1km west of the train and bus stations. Leave the train station, turn right, cut across the highway, head down ul Kościuszki and follow the signs. Malbork is an easy day trip by train from Gdańsk (10zł, 45 minutes). There are buses every hour to Malbork from Gdynia and five daily from Gdańsk. From Malbork, trains also regularly go to Toruń and Olsztyn.

## SZCZECIN

☎ 091 / pop 415,000

Szczecin (*shcheh*-cheen) is the major city and port of northwestern Poland. Massive damage in WWII accounts for the unaesthetic mishmash of new and old buildings in the city centre, but enough remains to give a sense of the pre-war days. The broad streets and massive historic buildings bear a strong resemblance to Berlin, for which Szczecin was once the main port as the German city of Stettin. Szczecin may not have the seamless charm of Toruń or Poznań, but it's worth a visit if you're travelling to/from Germany.

The **tourist information office** ( ☎ 434 04 40; al Niepodległości 1; �9am-5pm Mon-Fri, 10am-2pm Sat Jun-Aug, 9am-5pm Mon-Fri Sep-May) is helpful, as is the **cultural & tourist information office** ( ☎ 489 16 30; �10am-6pm) in the castle. The **post office** and most *kantors* are along al Niepodległości, the main street. There's a handy internet café, **Portal** ( ☎ 488 40 66; ul Kaszubska 53; per hr 4zł; �24hr), in the side street opposite the tourist office.

The huge and austere **Castle of the Pomeranian Dukes** (ul Korsazy 34; admission free; �dawn-dusk) lies 500m northeast of the tourist office. Originally built in the mid-14th century, it was enlarged in 1577 and rebuilt after WWII. Its **Castle Museum** ( ☎ 434 73 91; adult/child 4/3zł; �10am-6pm Tue-Sun) explains the building's convoluted history, with special exhibitions mounted from time to time.

A short walk down (south) from the castle is the 15th-century **Old Town Hall** (ul Mściwoja 8), which contains the **Museum of the City of Szczecin** ( ☎ 431 52 53; adult/child 6/3zł; �11am-6pm Tue, 10am-4pm Wed-Sun). Nearby is the charmingly rebuilt **Old Town** with its cafés, bars and clubs. Three blocks northwest of the castle is the **National Museum** ( ☎ 431 52 36; ul Staromłyńska 27; adult/child 6/3zł; �10am-6pm Tue, Wed & Fri, 10am-4pm Thu, Sat & Sun).

## Sleeping & Eating

**Youth Hostel PTSM** ( ☎ 422 47 61; www.ptsm.home.pl; ul Monte Cassino 19a; dm 16-18zł, d 44zł; P 🖳 ) This hostel has clean, spacious rooms and is located 2km northwest of the tourist office. Catch tram 1 north to the stop marked 'Piotr Skargi', then walk right one block. Bed linen costs 6zł extra.

**Hotelik Elka-Sen** ( ☎ 433 56 04; www.elkasen.szc zecin.pl; al 3 Maja 1a; s/d 120/140zł; 🖳 ) Simple, clean rooms in a basement location in the centre of town. Just south of the tourist office, enter from the side street.

**Hotel Podzamcze** ( ☎ 812 14 04; www.podzamcze .szczecin.pl; ul Sienna 1/3; s/d 185/235zł; P ) This hotel is in a charming location near the Old Town Hall, with neat, well-maintained rooms and a small restaurant.

**Haga** ( ☎ 812 17 59; ul Sienna 10; mains 10-20zł; �11am-11pm) This informal place in the Old

Town produces Dutch-style filled pancakes from a menu listing more than 400 combinations.

**Restauracja Stary Szczecin** ( ☎ 433 62 30; plac Batorego 2; mains 18-85zł; ☻ noon-midnight) A more upmarket option serving a range of traditional Polish dishes in elegant surrounds.

**Camping PTTK Marina** ( ☎ /fax 460 11 65; ul Przestrzenna 23; per person/tent 10/7.50zł, s/d/tr/q cabins 42/70/100/160zł; ☻ May-Sep; **P** ) On the shore of Lake Dąbie – get off at the Szczecin Dąbie train station and ask for directions (2km).

### Getting There & Away

LOT flies between Szczecin and Warsaw four times a day. Book at the **LOT office** ( ☎ 488 35 58; ul Wyzwolenia 17), about 200m from the northern end of al Niepodegłości.

The **bus terminal** (plac Grodnicki) and the nearby **Szczecin Główny train station** (ul Kolumba) are located 600m southeast of the tourist office. Three bus services a day head for Warsaw (61zł, six hours), two via Poznań. Fast trains travel regularly to Poznań (37zł, four hours) and Gdańsk (47zł, 3½ hours) and expresses run to Warsaw (88zł, seven hours). Slow trains plod along every two hours to Świnoujście (16zł).

Advance tickets for trains and ferries are available from **Orbis Travel** ( ☎ 434 26 18; plac Zwycięstwa 1), about 200m west of the main post office.

# WARMIA & MASURIA

Like much of northern Poland, Warmia and Masuria have changed hands between Germanic and Polish rulers over the centuries. The countryside is a beautiful postglacial landscape dominated by 3000 lakes, linked to rivers and canals, which host aquatic activities like yachting and canoeing. This picturesque lake district has little industry, and as a result remains unpolluted and attractive, especially in summer.

## OLSZTYN

☎ 089 / pop 173,000

Olsztyn (ol-shtin) is another city on the Copernicus trail, as the great astronomer once served as administrator of Warmia, commanding Olsztyn Castle from 1516 to 1520. From 1466 to 1772 the town belonged to the kingdom of Poland. With the first partition

of the nation, Olsztyn became Prussian Allenstein, until it returned to Polish hands in 1945.

Nowadays it's a pleasant city whose rebuilt Old Town is home to cobblestone streets, art galleries, cafés, bars and restaurants. As a busy transport hub, it's also the logical base from which to explore the region, including the Great Masurian Lakes district (p608).

The **tourist office** ( ☎ 535 35 65; www.warmia.mazury.pl; ul Staromiejska 1; ☻ 8am-4pm Mon-Fri) is helpful. For money matters, try the **PKO Bank** (ul Pieniężnego).

For snail mail, go to the **main post office** (ul Pieniężnego); for cybermail, try **Klub Internetowy** (ul Kościuszki 26; per hr 3.50zł; ☻ 10am-9pm Mon-Sat, 11am-8pm Sun) near the train station. Books and maps are sold at **EMPiK** (ul Piłsudskiego 16) inside the Alfa Centrum shopping mall.

### Sights

The **High Gate** (Upper Gate) is the remaining section of the 14th-century city walls. Further west, the 14th-century **Castle of the Chapter of Warmia** (ul Zamkowa 2) contains the **Museum of Warmia & Mazury** ( ☎ 527 95 96; adult/child 6/4zł; ☻ 9am-5pm Tue-Sun May-Sep, 10am-4pm Tue-Sun Oct-Apr). Its exhibits star Copernicus, who made some astronomical observations here in the early 16th century, along with coins and art.

The **Rynek** (Market Square) was rebuilt after WWII destruction. To the east, the red-brick Gothic **Cathedral of Św. Jakuba Większego** (ul Długosza) dates from the 14th century. Its 60m tower was added in 1596.

### Sleeping

**Hotel Wysoka Brama** ( ☎ 527 36 75; www.hotel wysokabrama.olsztyn.pl; ul Staromiejska 1; s/d/ste 45/60/160zł) Offers cheap but basic rooms that are in a very central location next to the High Gate.

**Hotel Pod Zamkiem** ( ☎ 535 12 87; www.hotel-olsztyn.com.pl; ul Nowowiejskiego 10; s/d 150/190zł; **P** **☐** ) Cosy *pension*, with charmingly old-fashioned rooms, reached via an extravagant stairwell constructed of dark timber carved with German text. It's located in a convenient spot near the castle.

**Polsko-Niemieckie Centrum Młodzieży** ( ☎ 534 07 80; www.pncm.olsztyn.pl; ul Okopowa 25; s/d 190/240zł; **P** **☐** ) This place is also situated next to the castle. The rooms (some with views of the castle) are plain, but have gleaming

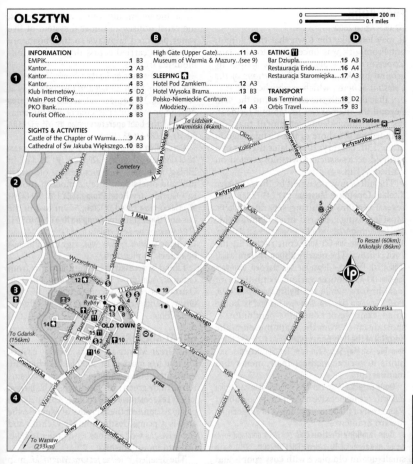

## OLSZTYN

| INFORMATION | | High Gate (Upper Gate)............**11** A3 | EATING |
|---|---|---|---|
| EMPiK..............................**1** B3 | | Museum of Warmia & Mazury...(see 9) | Bar Dziupla.........................**15** A3 |
| Kantor.............................**2** A3 | | | Restauracja Eridu................**16** A4 |
| Kantor.............................**3** B3 | | SLEEPING | Restauracja Staromiejska....**17** A3 |
| Kantor.............................**4** B3 | | Hotel Pod Zamkiem...............**12** A3 | |
| Klub Internetowy.............**5** D2 | | Hotel Wysoka Brama............**13** B3 | TRANSPORT |
| Main Post Office................**6** B3 | | Polsko-Niemieckie Centrum | Bus Terminal......................**18** D2 |
| PKO Bank..........................**7** B3 | |   Młodzieży........................**14** A3 | Orbis Travel.......................**19** B3 |
| Tourist Office....................**8** B3 | | | |
| | | | |
| SIGHTS & ACTIVITIES | | | |
| Castle of the Chapter of Warmia........**9** A3 | | | |
| Cathedral of Św Jakuba Większego..**10** B3 | | | |

---

bathrooms. There's a sunlit restaurant off the foyer.

## Eating

**Bar Dziupla** ( ☎ 527 50 83; Rynek 9/10; mains 11-15zł; ⏲ 8.30am-8pm Mon-Fri, 9am-8pm Sat, 9am-7.30pm Sun) This small place is renowned among locals for its tasty Polish food, such as *pierogi*. It also does a good line in soups, including Ukrainian *borscht*.

**Restauracja Eridu** ( ☎ 534 94 67; ul Prosta 3/4; mains 13-18zł; ⏲ 11am-8pm) The Eridu offers some inexpensive Middle Eastern choices in a vaguely Arabian setting. Also serves takeaway kebabs from a street window.

**Restauracja Staromiejska** ( ☎ 527 58 83; ul Stare Miasto 4/6; mains 16-36zł; ⏲ 11am-10pm) In classy premises on the Rynek, this restaurant serves quality Polish standards at reasonable prices. There's a range of *pierogi* and *naleśniki* on the menu.

## Getting There & Away

From the **bus terminal** (ul Partyzantów), buses travel to Białystok (40zł, five daily), Gdańsk (30zł, three hours, six daily) and Warsaw (32zł, five hours, 10 daily).

Trains depart from the **Olsztyn Główny train station** (ul Partyzantów) to Białystok (42zł, two daily), Warsaw (38zł, three daily), Gdańsk (35zł, six daily), Poznań (44zł, three daily), Wrocław (50zł, two daily) and Toruń (32zł, seven daily). **Orbis Travel** ( ☎ 522 06 13; al Piłsudskiego) sells advance train tickets.

POLAND

## FROMBORK

☎ 055 / pop 2600

It may look like the town that time forgot, but Frombork was once home to Nicolaus Copernicus. It's also where he wrote his ground-breaking *On the Revolutions of the Celestial Spheres,* which established the theory that the earth travelled around the sun. Beyond the memory of its famous resident, it's a charming sleepy settlement that was founded on the shore of the Vistula Lagoon in the 13th century. It was later the site of a fortified ecclesiastical township, erected on Cathedral Hill.

The hill is now occupied by the extensive **Nicolaus Copernicus Museum** (☎ 243 72 18), with several sections requiring separate tickets. Most imposing is the red-brick Gothic **cathedral** (adult/child 4/2zł; ⏱ 9.30am-5pm Mon-Sat May-Sep, 9am-3.30pm Tue-Sun Oct-Apr), constructed in the 14th century. The nearby **Bishop's Palace** (adult/child 4/2zł; ⏱ 9am-4.30pm Tue-Sun May-Sep, 9am-4pm Tue-Sun Oct-Apr) houses various exhibitions on local history, while the **Belfry** (adult/child 4/2zł; ⏱ 9.30am-5pm May-Sep, 9am-4pm Oct-Apr) is home to an example of Foucault's pendulum. A short distance from the main museum, the **Hospital of the Holy Ghost** (adult/child 4/2zł; ⏱ 10am-6pm Tue-Sat May-Sep, 9am-4pm Tue-Sat Oct-Apr) exhibits historical medical instruments and manuscripts.

**Dom Dziecka** (☎ 243 72 15; ul Braniewska 11; dm 20zł) offers inexpensive accommodation about 500m east of the museum, along ul Kopernika toward Braniewo.

**Dom Familijny Rheticus** (☎ 243 78 00; domfamilijny@ wp.pl; ul Kopernika 10; s/d/ste 88/120/240zł; P) is a small, quaint old place with cosy rooms and good facilities, a short walk to the east of the bus stop.

The bus and train stations are along the riverfront about 300m northwest of the museum, but trains are slow and infrequent. Frombork can be directly reached by bus from Elbląg (6zł, hourly) and Gdańsk (16zł, five daily). The best place to get on and off is the bus stop directly below the museum on ul Kopernika.

## ELBLĄG-OSTRÓDA CANAL

The longest navigable canal still used in Poland stretches 82km between Elbląg and Ostróda. Constructed between 1848 and 1876, this waterway was used to transport timber from inland forests to the Baltic. To over-come the 99.5m difference in water levels, the canal utilises an unusual system of five water-powered slipways so that boats are sometimes carried across dry land on rail-mounted trolleys.

Usually, **excursion boats** (⏱ mid May-late Sep) depart from both Elbląg and Ostróda daily at 8am (85zł, 11 hours), but actual departures depend on available passengers. For information, call the **boat operators** (Elbląg ☎ 055-232 43 07, Ostróda ☎ 089-646 38 71; www.zegluga.com.pl).

**Hotel Młyn** (☎ 055-235 04 70; www.hotelmlyn.com .pl; ul Kościuszki 132; s/d from 220/310zł; P ⌧ ⌘), in Elbląg, is located in a picturesque old water mill and offers comfortable modern rooms. In Ostróda, try **Hotel Promenada** (☎ 089-642 81 00; ul Mickiewicza 3; s/d 120/180zł), 500m east of the bus and train stations. **Camping Nr 61** (☎ 055-232 43 07; www.camping-elblag.alpha.pl; ul Panieńska 14; tents 12zł, cabins 60-80zł; ⏱ May-Sep), right at Elbląg's boat dock, is pleasant.

Elbląg is accessible by train and bus from Gdańsk, Malbork, Frombork and Olsztyn. Ostróda is regularly connected by train to Olsztyn and Toruń, and by bus to Olsztyn and Elbląg.

## GREAT MASURIAN LAKES

The Great Masurian Lakes district east of Olsztyn has more than 2000 lakes, which are remnants of long-vanished glaciers, and surrounded by green hilly landscape. The largest lake is **Lake Śniardwy** (110 sq km). About 200km of canals connect these bodies of water, so the area is a prime destination for yachties and canoeists, as well as those who prefer to hike, fish and mountain-bike.

The detailed *Wielkie Jeziora Mazurskie* map (1:100,000) is essential for anyone exploring the region by water or hiking trail. The *Warmia i Mazury* map (1:300,000), available at regional tourist offices, is perfect for more general use.

### Activities

The larger lakes can be sailed from Węgorzewo to Ruciane-Nida, while canoeists might prefer the more intimate surroundings of rivers and smaller lakes. The most popular kayak route takes 10 days (106km) and follows rivers, canals and lakes from Sorkwity to Ruciane-Nida. Brochures explaining this route are available at regional tourist offices. There's also an extensive network of **hiking** and **mountain-biking** trails around the lakes.

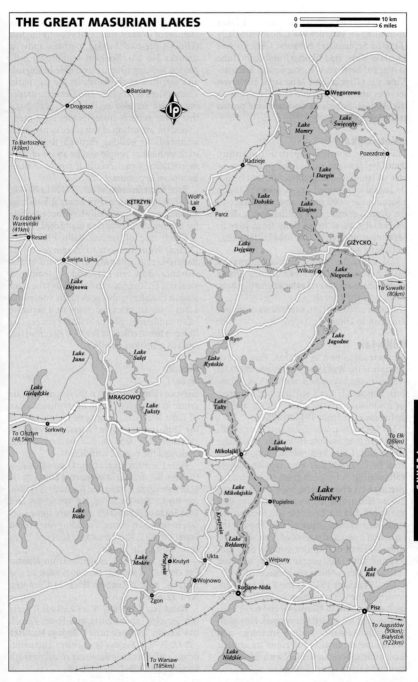

# THE GREAT MASURIAN LAKES

| 0 | 10 km |
| 0 | 6 miles |

Barciany

Drogosze

Węgorzewo

To Bartoszyce
(43km)

Lake
Mamry

Lake
Święcajty

Pozezdrze

Radzieje

Lake
Dargin

KĘTRZYN

Wolf's
Lair

Parcz

Lake
Dobskie

Lake
Kisajno

To Lidzbark
Warmiński
(41km)

Reszel

GIŻYCKO

Lake
Dejguny

Święta Lipka

Wilkasy

Lake
Niegocin

To Suwałki
(80km)

Lake
Dejnowa

Ryn

Lake
Jagodne

Lake
Juno

Lake
Sałęt

Lake
Ryńskie

Lake
Giełądzkie

MRĄGOWO

Lake
Juksty

Lake
Tałty

To Olsztyn
(48.5km)

Sorkwity

Mikołajki

Lake
Łuknajno

To Ełk
(28km)

**POLAND**

Lake
Białe

Lake
Mikołajskie

Popielno

Lake
Śniardwy

Krutynia

Lake
Mokre

Krutyń

Ukta

Lake
Bełdany

Wejsuny

Lake
Roś

Wojnowo

Ruciane-Nida

Zgon

Pisz

To Augustów
(90km);
Białystok
(122km)

To Warsaw
(185km)

Lake
Nidzkie

Most travellers prefer to enjoy the lakes in comfort on **excursion boats**. Boats run daily (May to September) between Giżycko and Ruciane-Nida, via Mikołajki; and daily (June to August) between Węgorzewo and Ruciane-Nida, via Giżycko and Mikołajki. However, services are more reliable from late June to late August. Schedules and fares are posted at the lake ports.

## Święta Lipka

This village boasts a superb 17th-century **church** (☼7am-7pm), one of the purest examples of late-baroque architecture in Poland. Its lavishly decorated organ features angels adorning the 5000 pipes, and they dance to the organ's music. This mechanism is demonstrated several times daily from May to September, and recitals are held Friday nights from June to August.

Ask any of the regional tourist offices for a list of homes in Święta Lipka offering **private rooms**. There are several **eateries** and places to drink near the church.

Buses run to Kętrzyn every hour or so, but less often to Olsztyn.

## Wolf's Lair

An eerie attraction at Gierłoż, 8km east of Kętrzyn, is the **Wolf's Lair** (Wilczy Szaniec; ☎ 089-752 44 29; www.wolfsschanze.home.pl; adult/child 8/5zł; ☼8am-dusk). This was Hitler's wartime headquarters for his invasion of the Soviet Union, and his main residence from 1941 to 1944.

In 1944 a group of high-ranking German officers tried to assassinate Hitler here. The leader of the plot, Claus von Stauffenberg, arrived from Berlin on 20 July for a regular military staff meeting. A frequent guest, he entered the meeting with a bomb in his briefcase. He placed it near Hitler and left to take a prearranged phone call, but the briefcase was then unwittingly moved by another officer. Though the explosion killed and wounded several people, Hitler suffered only minor injuries. Stauffenberg and some 5000 people allegedly involved in the plot were subsequently executed.

On 24 January 1945, as the Red Army approached, the Germans blew up Wolfsschanze (as it was known in German), and most bunkers were at least partly destroyed. However, huge concrete slabs – some 8.5m thick – and twisted metal remain. The ruins are at their most atmospheric in winter, with fewer visitors and a thick layer of snow.

A large map is posted at the entrance, with features of interest clearly labelled in English (Hitler's personal bunker, perhaps aptly, is unlucky No 13). Booklets outlining a self-guided walking tour are available in English and German at the kiosk in the car park. The services of English- and German-speaking guides are also available for 50zł. Note that some reports from visitors have mentioned the attraction of this place to neo-Nazi skinheads. If walking through the woods, stick with other people and be aware of your surroundings, particularly if you're of non-European appearance.

**Hotel Wilcze Gniazdo** ( ☎ 089-752 44 29; fax 752 44 92; s/d/tr 70/80/130zł), situated in original buildings within the complex, is fairly basic but adequate for one night. A restaurant is attached.

Catch one of several daily PKS buses (3.20zł) from Kętrzyn to Węgorzewo (via Radzieje, not Srokowo) and get off at the entrance. Between May and September, a local bus (2.50zł, 9am to 6pm) from the train station in Kętrzyn also goes to the site, either a bus 1 on an extended route or a separate bus bound especially for Wilczy Szaniec. The Kętrzyn **tourist office** ( ☎ 089-751 47 65) can advise current transport details.

## Giżycko

☎ 087

Giżycko (ghee-*zhits*-ko) is the largest lakeside centre in the region, set on the northern shore of Lake Niegocin. A notable historic site is the 19th-century **Boyen Fortress** (ul Turystyczna 1; adult/child 6/3zł; ☼8am-7pm), built by the Prussians to defend the border with Russia.

Near the main square (plac Grunwaldzki) is the very helpful **tourist information office** ( ☎ 428 52 65; www.gizycko.turystyka.pl; ul Warszawska 7; ☼8am-5pm May-Jun, 8am-7pm Jul-Sep, 8am-4pm Oct-Apr) and **Bank Pekao** (ul Olsztyńska 17). There are some *kantors* in the town centre, including one at **Orbis Travel** ( ☎ 428 35 98; ul Dąbrowskiego 3), about 250m east of the main square.

Sailing boats are available from **Almatur** ( ☎ 428 59 71; ul Moniuszki 24), 700m west of the fortress, and at **Centrum Mazur** at Camping Nr 1 Zamek.

**Wama Tour** ( ☎ 429 30 79; ul Konarskiego 1) rents out bicycles (about 20zł), and Hotel Zamek has kayaks (8zł per hour). **Żegluga Mazurska** ( ☎ 428 25 78; ul Kolejowa 8) operates excursion boats, and you can arrange car rental through **Łuczany** ( ☎ 428 26 62; ul Suwalska 19b).

## SLEEPING & EATING

**Boyen Fortress Youth Hostel** ( ☎ 428 29 59; tmtb@wp .pl; dm 15-20zł) Has a character-packed location within the battlements, and offers the usual basic but clean facilities.

**Hotel Zamek** ( ☎ 428 24 19; d 144zł; ⊗ May-Sep; P ) This place provides a decent standard of accommodation for the price.

**Hotel Wodnik** ( ☎ 428 38 71; www.cmazur.pl; ul 3 Maja 2; s/d from 180/250zł; P ✗ ▣ ) A big barn of a place just off the main square, with plain but tidy rooms and modern bathrooms. There's a restaurant, bar and billiards room on the premises.

**Camping Nr 1 Zamek** ( ☎ 428 34 10; ul Moniuszki 1; per person/tent 15/10zł; ⊗ May-end Sep; P ) Just west of the canal, this camping ground is simple but central.

**Kuchnie Świata** ( ☎ 429 22 55; plac Grunwaldzki 1; mains 15-40zł; ⊗ 11am-11pm) A good dining choice is this cheery red-and-orange space serving up an eclectic range of dishes including pizza and pasta, along with *placki ziemniaczane* and other Polish favourites.

## GETTING THERE & AWAY

From the train station, on the southern edge of town near the lake, around seven trains run daily to Kętrzyn and Olsztyn, and two head to Gdańsk.

From the adjacent bus terminal, buses travel regularly to Mikołajki (9zł, one hour), Kętrzyn (8zł, 45 minutes) and Olsztyn. Five buses daily head to Warsaw.

## Mikołajki
☎ 087

Mikołajki (Mee-ko-*wahy*-kee), 86km east of Olsztyn, is a great base for exploring the lakes, and it's a picturesque little village in its own right. The **tourist office** ( ☎ 421 68 50; www.mikolajki .pl; plac Wolności 3; ⊗ 9am-8pm May-Sep) is in the town centre, though in the low season tourist advice is available at the **local government offices** (ul Kolejowy 7; ⊗ 10am-3pm Oct-Apr). There are *kantors* and ATMs near the tourist office, but nowhere to change travellers cheques or get cash advances.

Sailing boats and kayaks can be hired from **Cicha Zatoka** ( ☎ 421 50 11; al Spacerowa 1) at the waterfront on the other side of the bridge from the town centre, and also from the appropriately named **Fun** ( ☎ 421 62 77; ul Kajki 82).

Lake Śniardwy and Lake Łuknajno are ideal for **cycling**. The tourist office can provide details and maps, and bikes can be rented from Pensionjat Mikołajki.

## SLEEPING & EATING

*Pensions* and homes offering private rooms are dotted along ul Kajki, the main street leading around Lake Mikołajskie; more *pensions* can be found along the roads to Ruciane-Nida and Ełk. There are plenty of eateries along the waterfront and around the town square to cater for peak-season visitors.

**Pensjonat Mikołajki** ( ☎ 421 64 37; www.pensjonat mikolajki.prv.pl; ul Kajki 18; s/d 100/200zł) An attractive place to stay, with timber panelling and a prime lake-front location. Some rooms have balconies overlooking the water.

**Camping Nr 2 Wagabunda** ( ☎ 421 60 18; ul Leśna 2; per person/tent 15/12zł, cabins 80zł; ⊗ May-Oct) Across the bridge, this camping ground is 1km southwest of the town centre.

**Pizzeria Królewska** ( ☎ 421 63 23; ul Kajki 5; mains 8-22zł; ⊗ noon-10pm) A reasonable pizza restaurant open year-round, in cosy cellar premises.

## GETTING THERE & AWAY

From the bus terminal, next to the bridge at plac Kościelny, six buses go to Olsztyn (13zł, two hours) each day. Otherwise, get a bus (hourly) to Mrągowo and change there for Olsztyn. Several buses also go daily to Giżycko (9zł, one hour) and three depart in summer for Warsaw. A private company, **Agawa** ( ☎ 0698 256 928) runs an express service daily to Warsaw year-round, departing from the bus terminal.

From the dozy train station, two slow trains shuttle along daily to Olsztyn (14zł), and two to Ełk (11zł), and one fast train heads to Poznań via Olsztyn in summer. In quiet times, the ticket office only opens 30 minutes (or less) before departures.

# POLAND DIRECTORY

## ACCOMMODATION
### Camping

Poland has hundreds of camping grounds, and many offer good-value cabins and bungalows. Most open May to September, but some only open their gates between June and August.

### Hostels

*Schroniska młodzieżowe* (youth hostels) in Poland are operated by Polskie Towarzystwo

Schronisk Młodzieżowych (PTSM), a member of Hostelling International. Most only open in July and August, and are often very busy with Polish students; the year-round hostels have more facilities. Youth hostels are open to all, with no age limit. Curfews are common, and many hostels close between 10am and 5pm.

A number of privately-operated hostels operate in the main cities, and are geared towards international backpackers. They are usually open 24 hours and offer more modern facilities than the old youth hostels, though prices are higher. These hostels usually offer free use of washing machines, in response to the absence of laundromats in Poland.

A dorm bed can cost anything from 15zł to 50zł per person per night. Single/double rooms, if available, cost from about 80/100zł.

### Hotels

Hotel prices often vary according to season, and are posted at hotel reception desks. Top-end hotels sometimes quote prices in euros, and discounted weekend rates are often available. Rooms with a private bathroom can be considerably more expensive than those with shared facilities. Most hotels offer 24-hour reception.

If possible, check the room before accepting. Don't be fooled by hotel reception areas, which may look great in contrast to the rest of the establishment. On the other hand, dreary scuffed corridors can sometimes open into clean, pleasant rooms.

Two reliable companies can arrange accommodation (sometimes with substantial discounts) over the internet through www .poland4u.com and www.hotelspoland.com.

### Mountain Refuges

PTTK runs a chain of *schroniska górskie* (mountain refuges) for trekkers. They're usually simple, with a welcoming atmosphere, and serve cheap, hot meals. The more isolated refuges are obliged to accept everyone, so can be crowded in the high season. Refuges are normally open all year, but confirm with the nearest PTTK office before setting off.

### Private Rooms & Apartments

Some destinations have agencies (usually called *biuro zakwaterowania* or *biuro kwater prywatnych*), which arrange accommodation in private homes. Rooms cost about 70/100zł per single/double. The most important factor

to consider is location; if the home is in the suburbs, find out how far it is from reliable public transport.

During the high season, home owners also directly approach tourists. Prices are open to bargaining, but you're more likely to be offered somewhere out in the sticks. Also, private homes in smaller resorts and villages often have signs outside their gates or doors offering a *pokoje* (room) or *noclegi* (lodging).

In Warsaw, Kraków, Wrocław and Gdańsk, some agencies offer self-contained apartments, which are often an affordable alternative to hotels.

## ACTIVITIES

Hikers and long-distance trekkers can enjoy marked trails across the Tatra (p575) and Sudeten Mountains (p588), around Białowieża National Park (p559) and the Great Masurian Lakes district (p608), and at places near Poznań (p589) and Œwinoujœcie. Trails are easy to follow and detailed maps are available at most larger bookshops.

As Poland is fairly flat, it's ideal for cyclists. Bicycle routes along the banks of the Vistula River are popular in Warsaw (p547), Toruń (p593) and Kraków (p561). Many of the national parks – including Tatra (near Zakopane), Wolin (near Świnoujście) and Słowinski (near Łeba) – offer bicycle trails, as does the Great Masurian Lakes district. Bikes can be rented at most resort towns and larger cities (see also p617).

Zakopane (p572) will delight skiers from December to March. Facilities are cheaper than – though not as developed as – the ski resorts of Western Europe.

Throngs of yachties, canoeists and kayakers enjoy the network of waterways in the Great Masurian Lakes district every summer; boats are available for rent from all lakeside towns. Windsurfers can head to the beaches of the Hel Peninsula (p604).

## BOOKS

*God's Playground: A History of Poland,* by Norman Davies, offers an in-depth analysis of Polish history. The condensed version, *The Heart of Europe: A Short History of Poland,* also by Davies, has greater emphasis on the 20th century. *The Polish Way: A Thousand-Year History of the Poles and their Culture,* by Adam Zamoyski, is a superb cultural overview. The wartime Warsaw Rising is vividly brought to life in Norman Davies' *Rising '44*, and *The Polish Revolution: Solidarity 1980–82*, by Timothy Garton Ash, is entertaining and thorough. *Jews in Poland* by Iwo Cyprian Pogonowski, provides a comprehensive record of half a millennium of Jewish life.

## BUSINESS HOURS

Most shops are open from 9am to 6pm Monday to Friday, and until 2pm on Saturday. Supermarkets and larger stores often have longer opening hours. Banks in larger cities are open from about 8am to 5pm weekdays (sometimes until 2pm on Saturday), but have shorter hours in smaller towns. *Kantors* generally follow shop hours.

## DANGERS & ANNOYANCES

Poland is a relatively safe country, but be alert for thieves and pickpockets around major train stations, such as Warszawa Centralna. Robberies have become a problem on night trains, especially on international routes. Try to share a compartment with other people if possible. Watch out too for bogus ticket-inspectors on public transport – ask to see ID if they try to fine you.

Theft from cars is a widespread problem, so keep your vehicle in a guarded car park whenever possible. Heavy drinking is common and drunks can be disturbing, though rarely dangerous. Smoking is common in public places, especially in bars and restaurants. However, it's becoming more common for hotels and restaurants to offer nonsmoking options.

As Poland is an ethnically homogeneous nation, travellers who look racially different may attract curious stares from locals in outlying regions. Football (soccer) hooligans are not uncommon, so avoid travelling on public transport with them (especially if their team has lost!).

## DISABLED TRAVELLERS

Poland is not well set-up for people with disabilities, although there have been significant improvements over recent years. Wheelchair ramps are only available at some upmarket hotels, and public transport will be a real challenge for anyone with mobility problems. However, many top-end hotels now have at least one room specially designed for disabled access – book ahead for these. There are also some low-floor trams now running on the Warsaw public transport network. Informa-

tion on disability issues is available from **Integracja** ( ☎ 022-635 13 30; www.integracja.org).

## EMBASSIES & CONSULATES
### Polish Embassies & Consulates

**Australia** ( ☎ 02-6273 1208; 7 Turrana St, Yarralumla, ACT 2600); Sydney ( ☎ 02-9363 9816; 10 Trelawny St, Woollhara, NSW 2025)
**Canada** ( ☎ 613-789 0468; 443 Daly Ave, Ottawa 2, Ontario K1N 6H3); Toronto ( ☎ 416-252 5471; 2603 Lakeshore Blvd West); Vancouver ( ☎ 604-688 3530; 1177 West Hastings St, Suite 1600)
**France** ( ☎ 01 43 17 34 00; 1 Rue de Talleyrand, 75007 Paris)
**Germany** ( ☎ 030-22 31 30; Lassenstrasse 19-21, 14193 Berlin); Hamburg ( ☎ 040-611870; Gründgensstrasse 20)
**Netherlands** ( ☎ 070-799 01 00; Alexanderstraat 25, 2514 JM The Hague)
**UK** ( ☎ 0870-774 27 00; 47 Portland Pl, London W1B 1JH); Edinburgh ( ☎ 0131-552 0301; 2 Kinnear Rd, EH3 5PE); Sheffield ( ☎ 0114- 276 6513; 4 Palmerston Rd, S10 2 TE)
**USA** ( ☎ 202-234 3800; 2640 16th St NW, Washington, DC 20009); New York ( ☎ 212-686 1541; 233 Madison Ave); Chicago ( ☎ 312-337 8166; 1530 North Lake Shore Dr); Los Angeles ( ☎ 310-442 8500; 12400 Wilshire Blvd)

### Embassies & Consulates in Poland

All diplomatic missions listed are in Warsaw unless stated otherwise.
**Australia** (Map p550; ☎ 022-521 34 44; www.australia .pl; ul Nowogrodzka 11)
**Belarus** (Map p548; ☎ 022-742 09 90; ul Wiertnicza 58)
**Canada** (Map p550; ☎ 022-584 31 31; www.canada.pl; ul Matejki 1/5)
**Czech Republic** (Map p550; ☎ 022-628 72 21; warsaw@embassy.mzv.cz; ul Koszykowa 18)
**France** (Map p548; ☎ 022-529 30 00; ul Puławska 17); Kraków (Map p562; ☎ 012-424 53 00; ul Stolarska 15)
**Germany** (Map p548; ☎ 022-584 17 00; www.amba sadaniemiec.pl; ul Dąbrowiecka 30); Kraków (Map p562; ☎ 012-424 30 00; ul Stolarska 7)
**Ireland** (Map p550; ☎ 022-849 66 33; www.irlandia .pl; ul Mysia 5)
**Lithuania** (Map p548; ☎ 022-625 33 68; litwa.amb@ waw.pdi.net; al Szucha 5)
**Netherlands** (Map p548; ☎ 022-559 12 00; www.nl embassy.pl; ul Kawalerii 10)
**Russia** (Map p548; ☎ 022-621 34 53; ul Belwederska 49)
**Slovakia** (Map p548; ☎ 022-528 81 10; ul Litewska 6)
**Ukraine** (Map p548; ☎ 022-629 34 46; al Szucha 7)
**UK** (Map p550; ☎ 022-311 00 00; www.britishembassy .pl; al Róż 1); Kraków (Map p562; ☎ 012-421 70 30; ul Św. Anny 9)
**USA** (Map p550; ☎ 022-504 20 00; www.usinfo.pl; al Ujazdowskie 29/31); Kraków (Map p562; ☎ 012-424 51 00; ul Stolarska 9)

## FESTIVALS & EVENTS

### Warsaw

**International Book Fair** (www.bookfair.pl) Held in May.

**Warsaw Summer Jazz Days** (www.adamiakjazz.pl) Held in July.

**Mozart Festival** Held in June/July.

**International Street Art Festival** (www.sztukaulicy .pl) Held in July.

**Warsaw Autumn Festival of Contemporary Music** (www.warsaw-autumn.art.pl) Held in September.

### Kraków

**Organ Music Festival** Held in March.

**Jewish Culture Festival** (www.jewishfestival.pl) Held in June/July.

**International Festival of Street Theatre** (www .teatrkto.pl, under 'Festiwale' link) Held in July.

**Summer Jazz Festival** (www.cracjazz.com) Held in July.

### Czêstochowa

The major Marian feasts at Jasna Góra are 3 May, 16 July, 15 August (especially), 26 August, 8 September, 12 September and 8 December.

### Wrocław

**Musica Polonica Nova Festival** (www.musicapoloni canova.pl, in Polish only) Held in February.

**Jazz on the Odra International Festival** (www .jnofestival.pl) Held in April.

**Wrocław Marathon** (www.wroclawmaraton.pl) Held in April.

**Wrocław Non Stop** (www.wroclawnonstop.pl) Held in June/July.

**Wratislavia Cantans** (www.wratislavia.art.pl) Held in September.

### Poznań

The largest trade fairs take place in January, June, September and October.

**St John's Fair** Cultural event in June.

**Malta International Theatre Festival** (www.malta -festival.pl) Held in late June.

### Gdańsk

**International Organ Music Festival** (www.gdanskie -organy.com, under concerts) Organ recitals are held at the Oliwa Cathedral twice a week (mid-June to late August).

**International Street & Open-Air Theatre Festival** (www.feta.pl) Popular event held in July.

**International Organ, Choir & Chamber Music Festival** (www.gdanskie-organy.com, under concerts) Every Fri in July and August, at St Mary's Church.

**St Dominic's Fair** (www.mtgsa.pl, under Jarmark Św. Dominika) An annual shopping fair held in August.

## GAY & LESBIAN TRAVELLERS

With the Church remaining influential in social matters, and with senior government figures accused of homophobia, gay acceptance in Poland is still in development. As a result, the Polish gay and lesbian scene remains fairly discreet. Warsaw and Kraków are the best places to find gay-friendly bars, clubs and accommodation. The free tourist brochure, the *Visitor*, lists a few gay nightspots.

The best source of information on Warsaw and Kraków is online at www.gayguide.net. **Innastrona** (www.innastrona.pl) is also useful. **Lambda** ( ☎ 022-628 52 22; www.lambda.org.pl) is a national gay rights and information service. Newsstands and gay bars in Warsaw may also stock copies of *Nowy Men*, a gay listings magazine.

## HOLIDAYS

Poland's official public holidays:

**New Year's Day** 1 January
**Easter Monday** March or April
**Labour Day** 1 May
**Constitution Day** 3 May
**Corpus Christi** A Thursday in May or June
**Assumption Day** 15 August
**All Saints' Day** 1 November
**Independence Day** 11 November
**Christmas** 25 and 26 December

## INTERNET RESOURCES

**InsidePoland** (www.insidepoland.com) Current affairs and reasonable links.

**Poland What Where When** (www.what-where-when .pl) Online version of the handy tourist magazine.

**Poland.pl** (www.poland.pl) Excellent place to start surfing.

**POLISHWORLD** (www.polishworld.com) Directories and travel bookings.

**VirtualTourist.com** (www.virtualtourist.com) Poland section features postings and discussion by travellers.

**VISIT.PL** (www.visit.pl) Online accommodation booking service.

## MEDIA

The glossy, English-language *Poland Monthly* and the *Warsaw Business Journal* are aimed at the business community, while *Warsaw Insider* has more general-interest features, listings and reviews.

The free *Welcome to...* series of magazines covers Poznań, Kraków and Warsaw monthly, with special editions released irregularly on other cities including Gdańsk and Wrocław. The free magazine *Poland: What, Where, When* covers Warsaw, Kraków and Gdańsk.

Recent newspapers and magazines from Western Europe and the USA are readily available at EMPiK bookshops, which are *everywhere,* and at newsstands in the lobbies of upmarket hotels.

The state-run Polish Radio (Polskie Radio) is the main broadcaster, while Warsaw-based Radio Zet and Kraków-based RFM are two nationwide private broadcasters.

Poland has several private TV channels, including PolSat, and two state-owned countrywide channels. Foreign-language programmes are painfully dubbed with one male voice covering all actors (that's men, women and children) and no lip-sync, so you can still hear the original language underneath. Most major hotels have access to European and US channels.

Cinemas are present in all city centres, including modern multiplexes. English-language films are usually subtitled rather than dubbed into Polish.

## MONEY

The Polish currency is the złoty (*zwo*-ti), abbreviated to zł. (The currency is also sometimes referred to by its international currency code, PLN.) It's divided into 100 groszy (gr). Denominations of notes are 10, 20, 50, 100 and 200 złoty (rare), and coins come in one, two five, 10, 20 and 50 groszy, and one, two and five złoty.

### ATMs

*Bankomats* (ATMs) accept most international credit cards and are easily found in the centre of all cities and most towns. Banks without an ATM may provide cash advances over the counter on credit cards.

### Moneychangers

Private *kantors* (foreign-exchange offices) are *everywhere*. *Kantors* require no paperwork and charge no commission. Rates at *kantors* in the midst of major tourist attractions, in top-end hotels and at airports are generally poor.

The most widely accepted currencies are the euro, the US dollar and the pound sterling (in that order), though most *kantors* will change a range of other currencies. Foreign banknotes should be in perfect condition or *kantors* may refuse to accept them.

Travellers cheques are more secure than cash, but *kantors* rarely change them. Not all banks do either, and most charge 2% to 3% commission. The best place to change travellers cheques are branches of Bank Pekao or PKO Bank. In remote regions, finding an open bank that cashes travellers cheques may be tricky, especially on weekends.

## POST

Postal services are operated by Poczta Polska. Most cities have a dozen or more post offices, of which the Poczta Główna (main post office) has the widest range of services.

Letters and postcards sent by air from Poland take a few days to reach a European destination and a week or so to anywhere else. The cost of sending a normal-sized letter (up to 20g) or a postcard to other European countries is 3zł, rising to 3.20zł for North America and 4.50zł for Australia.

## TELEPHONE

All land-line numbers throughout Poland have seven digits. Note that it's necessary to dial both the area code and the local number, even for calls within the local area.

To call Poland from abroad, dial the country code ☎ 48, then the two-digit area code (drop the initial '0'), and then the seven-digit local number. The international access code for overseas calls from Poland is ☎ 00. If you need help, try the operators for local numbers ( ☎ 913), national numbers and codes ( ☎ 912) and international codes ( ☎ 908), but don't expect anyone to speak English.

### Mobile Phones

The three mobile telephone providers are Orange, Era and Plus GSM. Reception is generally good and covers the whole country. Mobile numbers are often quoted as nine digits, but require an initial zero to be dialled from land-line phones.

The website www.roaming.pl has plenty of information about using a mobile in Poland.

---

**EMERGENCY NUMBERS**

- Police ☎ 997, from mobiles ☎ 112
- Ambulance ☎ 999
- Fire brigade ☎ 93
- Roadside Assistance ☎ 981

**POLAND**

## Phonecards

Most public telephones use magnetic phonecards, available at post offices and kiosks in units of 15 (9zł), 30 (15zł) and 60 (24zł) – one unit represents one three-minute local call. The cards can be used for domestic and international calls.

## VISAS

EU citizens do not need visas to visit Poland and can stay indefinitely. Citizens of Australia, Canada, Israel, New Zealand, Switzerland and USA, can stay in Poland up to 90 days without a visa. South African citizens do require a visa.

Other nationals should check with Polish embassies or consulates in their countries for current visa requirements. Updates can be found at the website of the Ministry of Foreign Affairs: www.msz.gov.pl.

# TRANSPORT IN POLAND

## GETTING THERE & AWAY
### Air

The vast majority of international flights to Poland arrive at Warsaw's Okęcie airport (some at the Etiuda terminal), while other important airports include Kraków Balice, Gdańsk and Wrocław. The national carrier **LOT** (LO; www.lot.com; ☎ 0801 703 703) flies to all major European cities.

Other major airlines flying to Poland include the following:

**Aeroflot** (code SU; ☎ 022-628 25 57; www.aeroflot.com)
**Air France** (code AF; ☎ 022-556 64 00; www.airfrance.com)
**Alitalia** (code AZ; ☎ 022-692 82 85; www.alitalia.it)
**British Airways** (code BA; ☎ 022-529 90 00; www.ba.com)
**Centralwings** (code C0; ☎ 022-558 00 45; www.centralwings.com)
**EasyJet** (code U2; ☎ 0044 870 6 000 000; www.easyjet.com)
**KLM** (code KL; ☎ 022-556 64 44; www.klm.pl)
**Lufthansa** (code LH; ☎ 022-338 13 00; www.lufthansa.pl)
**Malév** (code MA; ☎ 022-697 74 72; www.malev.hu)
**Ryanair** (code FR; ☎ 0353-1-249 7791; www.ryanair.com)
**SAS Scandinavian Airlines** (code SK; ☎ 022-850 05 00; www.scandanavian.net)
**SkyEurope** (code NE; ☎ 022-433 07 33; www.skyeurope.com)
**Wizz Air** (code W6; ☎ 022-351 94 99; www.wizzair.com)

## Land
### BORDER CROSSINGS

Below is a list of major road border-crossings that accept foreigners and are open 24 hours.
**Belarus** South to north Terespol and Kuźnica Białostocka.
**Czech Republic** West to east Porajów, Zawidów, Jakuszyce, Lubawka, Kudowa-Słone, Boboszów, Głuchołazy, Pietrowice, Chałupki and Cieszyn.
**Germany** North to south Lubieszyn, Kołbaskowo, Krajnik Dolny, Osinów Dolny, Kostrzyn, Słubice, Ścwiecko, Gubin, Olszyna, Łęknica, Zgorzelec and Sieniawka.
**Lithuania** East to west Ogrodniki and Budzisko.
**Russia (Kaliningrad)** West to east Gronowo and Bezledy.
**Slovakia** West to east Chyżne, Chochołów, Łysa Polana, Niedzica, Piwniczna, Konieczna and Barwinek.
**Ukraine** South to north Medyka, Hrebenne, Dorohusk and Zosin.

If you're heading to Russia or Lithuania and your train/bus passes through Belarus, be aware that you need a Belarusian transit visa and you must obtain it in advance; see p95 for details.

### BUS

International bus services are offered by dozens of Polish and international companies. They're cheaper than trains, but not as comfortable or fast.

One of the major operators is **Eurolines** ( ☎ 032-351 20 20; www.eurolinespolska.pl), which operates to a range of European destinations, including eastern cities such as Minsk, Brest, Vilnius, Tallinn and Riga. For more details of international bus travel into Poland, see p930.

### CAR & MOTORCYCLE

To drive a car into Poland, EU citizens need their driving licence from home, while other nationalities must obtain an International Drivers Licence in their home country. Also required are vehicle registration papers and liability insurance (Green Card). If your insurance is not valid for Poland you must buy an additional policy at the border.

### TRAIN

Trains link Poland with every neighbouring country and beyond, but international train travel is not cheap. To save money on fares, investigate special train tickets and rail passes (see p939). Domestic trains in Poland are significantly cheaper, so you'll save money if you buy a ticket to a Polish border destination, then take a local train.

Do note that some international trains to/from Poland have become notorious for theft. Keep a grip on your bags, particularly on the Berlin-Warsaw, Prague-Warsaw and Prague-Kraków overnight trains, and on *any* train travelling to/from Gdańsk. Some readers have reported being gassed while in their compartments and have had everything stolen while they 'slept'. Always reinforce your carriage and, if possible, sleep in a compartment with others. First-class carriages, in theory, should be safer.

## Sea

Three companies operate passenger and car ferries all year:

**Polferries** (www.polferries.pl) Offers services between Gdańsk and Nynäshamn (18 hours) in Sweden every other day in summer (less frequently in the off season). It also has daily services from Świnoujście to Ystad (9½ hours) in Sweden, every Saturday to Rønne (six hours) in Denmark, and five days a week to Copenhagen (10½ to 11 hours).

**Stena Line** (www.stenaline.com) Operates between Gdynia and Karlskrona (11 hours) in Sweden.

**Unity Line** (www.unityline.pl) Runs ferries between Świnoujście and Ystad (eight hours).

Any travel agency in Scandinavia will sell tickets for these services. In Poland, ask at any Orbis Travel office. In summer, passenger boats ply the Baltic coast from Świnoujście to Ahlbeck, Heringsdorf, Bansin and Sassnitz in Germany.

## GETTING AROUND

### Air

The only domestic carrier, LOT (www.lot.com), runs flights several times a day from Warsaw to Gdańsk, Kraków, Łódź, Poznań, Szczecin and Wrocław. So, flying between, for example, Kraków and Gdańsk means a connection in Warsaw, which is not necessarily convenient.

### Bicycle

Cycling is not great for getting around cities, but is often a good way to travel between villages. Major roads are busy but generally flat, while minor roads can be bumpy. If you get tired, it's easy to place your bike in the special luggage compartment of a train. These compartments are at the front or rear of slow passenger trains, but rarely found on fast or express trains, and never on InterCity or EuroCity services. You'll need a special ticket for your bike from the railway luggage office.

## Bus

Buses can be useful on short routes and through the mountains in southern Poland; but usually trains are quicker and more comfortable, and private minibuses are quicker and more direct.

Most buses are operated by the state bus company, PKS. It provides two kinds of service from its bus terminals *(dworzec autobusowy PKS)*: ordinary buses (marked in black on timetables), and fast buses (marked in red), which ignore minor stops.

Timetables are posted on boards inside or outside PKS bus terminals. Additional symbols next to departure times may indicate the bus runs only on certain days or in certain seasons. Terminals usually have an information desk, but it's rarely staffed with English speakers. Tickets for PKS buses are usually bought at the terminal, but sometimes from drivers.

The largest private bus operator is **Polski Express** (www.polskiexpress.pl), which operates long-distance routes to/from Warsaw (p557). Polski Express buses normally arrive and depart from PKS bus terminals – exceptions are mentioned in the relevant destination sections.

### COSTS

The price of bus tickets is determined by the length, in kilometres, of the trip. Prices start at roughly 2zł for a journey of up to 5km. Minibuses charge set prices for journeys, and these are normally posted in their windows or at the bus stop.

## Car & Motorcycle

### FUEL & SPARE PARTS

Petrol stations sell several kinds of petrol, including 94-octane leaded, 95-octane unleaded, 98-octane unleaded and diesel. Most petrol stations are open from 6am to 10pm (from 7am to 3pm Sunday), though some operate around the clock. Garages are plentiful. Poland's roadside assistance number is ☎ 981.

### HIRE

Major international car-rental companies, such as **Avis** (www.avis.pl), **Hertz** (www.hertz.pl) and **Europcar** (www.europcar.com.pl), are represented in larger cities and have smaller offices at airports. Rates are comparable to full-price rental in Western Europe.

Some companies offer one-way rentals, but no agency will allow you to drive their precious vehicle into Russia, Ukraine or Belarus.

Rental agencies will need to see your passport, your local driving licence (which must be held for at least one year) and a credit card (for the deposit). You need to be at least 21 or 23 years of age to rent a car; sometimes 25 for a more expensive car.

It's usually cheaper to prebook a car in Poland from abroad, rather than to front up at an agency inside the country. It would be even cheaper to rent a car in Western Europe (eg Berlin or Geneva), and drive it into Poland, but few rental companies will allow this. If they do, special insurance is required.

### ROAD RULES

The speed limit is 130km/h on motorways, 100km/h or 110km/h on two- or four-lane highways, 90km/h on other open roads and 60km/h in built-up areas (50km/h in Warsaw). If the background of the sign bearing the town's name is white you must reduce speed to 60km/h; if the background is green there's no need to reduce speed (unless road signs indicate otherwise). Radar-equipped police are very active, especially in villages with white signs.

Unless signs state otherwise, cars may park on pavements as long as a minimum 1.5m-wide walkway is left for pedestrians. Parking in the opposite direction to traffic flow is allowed. The permitted blood alcohol level is a low 0.02%, so it's best not to drink if you're driving. Seat belts are compulsory for front seats. Motorbike helmets are also compulsory. Between 1 October and the end of February, all drivers must use headlights during the day (and night!).

## Train

Trains will be your main means of transport. They're cheap, reliable and rarely overcrowded (except for July and August peak times). The **Polish State Railways** (PKP; www.pkp.pl) operates trains to almost every place listed in this chapter.

InterCity trains operate on major routes out of Warsaw, including Gdańsk, Kraków, Poznań, Wrocław and Szczecin. They only stop at major cities and are the fastest way to travel by rail. These trains require seat reservations.

Down the pecking order but still quick are *pociąg ekspresowy* (express trains) and the similar but cheaper *pociąg TLK* (TLK trains). *Pociąg pospieszny* (fast trains) are a bit slower and more crowded. *Pociąg osobowy* (slow passenger trains) stop at every tree at the side of the track and should be used only for short trips. Express and fast trains do not normally require seat reservations except at peak times; seats on slow trains cannot be reserved.

Almost all trains carry two classes: *druga klasa* (2nd class) and *pierwsza klasa* (1st class), which is 50% more expensive. The carriages on long-distance trains are usually divided into compartments: 1st-class compartments have six seats; 2nd-class ones contain eight seats.

In a couchette on an overnight train, compartments have four/six beds in 1st/2nd class. Sleepers have two/three people (1st/2nd class) in a compartment fitted with a washbasin, sheets and blankets. Most 2nd-class and all 1st-class carriages have nonsmoking compartments.

Train *odjazdy* (departures) are listed on a yellow board and *przyjazdy* (arrivals) on a white board. Ordinary trains are marked in black print, fast trains in red. An additional 'Ex' indicates an express train, and InterCity trains are identified by the letters 'IC'. The letter 'R' in a square indicates the train has compulsory seat reservation. The timetables also show which *peron* (platform) it's using. Be aware that the number applies to *both* sides of the platform. If in doubt, check the platform departure board or route cards on the side of carriages, or ask a fellow passenger.

Timetable and fare information in English is on the PKP website. *Miejsca sypialne* (sleepers) and *kuszetki* (couchettes) can be booked at special counters in larger train stations or from Orbis; pre-booking is recommended.

If a seat reservation is compulsory on your train, you will automatically be sold a *miejscówka* (reserved) seat ticket. If you do not make a seat reservation, you can travel on *any* train (of the type requested, ie slow, fast or express) to the destination indicated on your ticket on the date specified.

Your ticket will list the *klasa* (class); the *poc* (type) of train; where the train is travelling *od* (from) and *do* (to); the major town or junction the train is travelling *prez* (through); and the total *cena* (price). If more than one place is listed under the heading *prez* (via), find out from the conductor *early* if you have to change trains at the junction listed or be in a specific carriage (the train may separate later).

If you get on a train without a ticket, you can buy one directly from the conductor for a small supplement – but do it right away. If the conductor finds you first, you'll be fined for travelling without a ticket. You can always upgrade from 2nd to 1st class for a small extra fee (about 5zł), plus the additional fare.

# Romania

A world where video speed–traps monitor zooming Audis and horse carts ca_____ ___ake and real Dracula sites dot the landscape where shepherds tend to flocks and n__ __armers plough by hand – Romania may well be Europe's most interesting country. It's certainly beautiful. The mountains that spread and curl across Transylvania create a world of hiking, biking and skiing options. Gothic towns like Braşov still have walls guarding cobbled cores with buildings from the Austro-Hungarian Empire standing still with chipped paint-jobs.

Sometimes con-artist taxi drivers unfortunately give Romanians a tainted name across the region, but it's far from the truth – here, couples of all ages show more sickening PDA (public displays of affection) than any country in Eastern Europe, and volunteer to help you get unlost. After joining the EU in 2007, some locals worry that the West will touch areas that communism missed, like bucolic Maramureş, with its 'merry cemetery' and lush rural life evoking (way) past eras. Those who limit their trip to chasing Dracula – and the real Vlad Ţepeş (that moustached impaler from the 14th century) is revered here – will miss out on a lot.

## FAST FACTS

- **Area** 237, 500 sq km
- **Capital** Bucharest
- **Currency** nou leu: €1 = 3.51 lei; US$1 = 2.72 lei; UK£1 = 5.09 lei; A$1 = 2.04 lei; ¥100 = 24.25 lei; NZ$1 = 1.72 lei; see p687 for details on the changed currency as of 2007
- **Famous for** Dracula, Transylvania, Nadia Comaneci's 10.0 in the '76 Olympics
- **Official Language** Romanian
- **Phrases** bună (hello); da (yes); nu (no); mulţumesc (thank you)
- **Population** 22.3 million
- **Telephone Codes** country code ☎ 40, international access code ☎ 00
- **Visas** Citizens of the EU, USA, Canada, Japan, Australia and New Zealand visa-free for up to 90 days. Many others require a visa; see p688

ROMANIA

ROMANIA

...UCH?

- **Bottle of Mufatlar table wine** €2.50
- **Museum admission (adult)** €0.60 to €2 (usually)
- **Local bus trip** €0.30
- **Short taxi ride** €3
- **Phonecard** €2.85

### LONELY PLANET INDEX

- **Litre of petrol** €1
- **Litre of water** €0.60
- **Beer (in a Bucharest bar)** €0.60 to €1.50
- **Souvenir item** €3 to €6
- **Street snack (kebab)** €1.50-3

## HIGHLIGHTS

- Castle-hop or hike the Carpathian Mountains by basing yourself in the lively medieval paradise of **Braşov** (p640).
- Hike or bike between painted monasteries in **Southern Bucovina** (p670), collectively grouped as a Unesco World Heritage site
- Go back in time, drink the local homebrew, dance by a camp fire in the heart of rural Romania, **Maramureş** (p663).
- Follow the heroic trail of the 1989 revolution in tenacious **Timişoara** (p659).
- Rent a rowboat and venture out onto tributaries at the fragile, rich-with-birdlife **Danube Delta** (p682).

## ITINERARIES

- **10 days** See Ceauşescu's grandiose buildings in Bucharest, then train to Sinaia, to see Peleş Castle and hike or bike atop the Bucegi Mountains. Continue north to Braşov, for castles by day and beer-slurps by night. Head north to Sighişoara for a look at its medieval citadel, then train back to Bucharest or on to Budapest.
- **One month** It's hard to do some backtracking. Start with three days in Bucharest, then head through Transylvania, stopping off for a day or two each at Sinaia, Braşov, Sighişoara and Sibiu, then west to Timişoara. Cross back into Transylvania to the student town Cluj-Napoca, then up to Maramureş for a four or five days

of chilling out. Continue the rural experience to the east in Southern Bucovina's painted monasteries, finishing in Iaşi.

## CLIMATE & WHEN TO GO

Romania is a year-round destination, with much variation in its climate: the average annual temperature in the south is 11°C, 7°C in the north and only 2°C in the mountains. In the summer months, temperatures have risen to above 40°C in recent years in Bucharest and along the Black Sea Coast, while winter chills of below -35°C are not unknown in the Braşov depression. See Climate Charts p911.

## HISTORY

### Ancient Romania & Dracula

Ancient Romania was inhabited by Thracian tribes, more commonly known as Dacians. The Greeks established trading colonies along the Black Sea from the 7th century BC and the Romans conquered in AD 105–06. The slave-owning Romans brought with them their superior civilisation and the Latin language.

From the 10th century the Magyars (Hungarians) expanded into Transylvania and by the 13th century all of Transylvania was under the Hungarian crown.

The Romanian-speaking principalities of Wallachia and Moldavia offered strong resistance to the Ottomans' northern expansion in the 14th and 15th centuries. Mircea the Old, Vlad Ţepeş and Ştefan cel Mare (Steven the Great) were legendary figures in this struggle.

Vlad Ţepeş, ruling prince of Wallachia from 1456 till 1462 and 1476 till 1477, gained the name Ţepeş (Impaler) after his primary form of punishing his enemies – impaling. A wooden stake was carefully driven through the victim's backbone without touching any vital nerve, ensuring at least 48 hours of conscious suffering before death. He is perhaps more legendary as the inspiration for 19th-century novelist Bram Stoker's Count Dracula. (Vlad was called Dracula, meaning 'son of the dragon', after his father, Vlad Dracul, a knight of the Order of the Dragon.)

When the Turks conquered Hungary in the 16th century, Transylvania became a vassal of the Ottoman Empire. In 1600 the three Romanian states – Transylvania, Wallachia and Moldavia – were briefly united under Mihai Viteazul (Michael the Brave). In 1687 Transylvania fell under Habsburg rule.

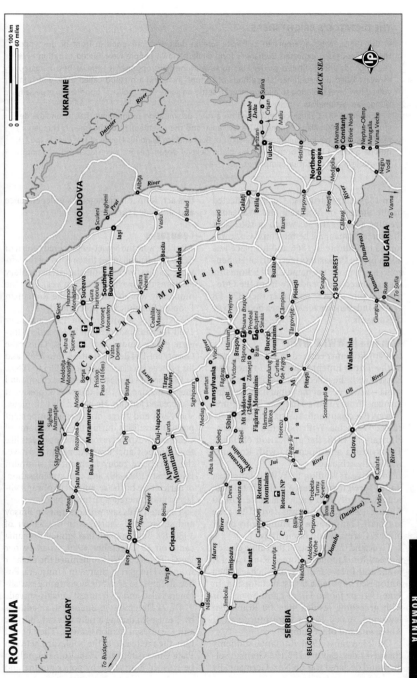

---

**THE DICTATOR'S BRIGHT IDEAS**

In the 1980s, in his attempts to eliminate foreign debt and look good in front of the world, Nicolae Ceauşescu exported Romania's food while his own people were forced to ration even staple goods and instituted power cuts to save money. His opponents were at best harassed, at worst killed by experimental methods of torture, including a method called *radu*, which involved low-level radiation to allow cancer to settle on some of his political opponents, especially Hungarian nationalists.

In March 1987 Ceauşescu embarked on a rural urbanisation programme that meant the destruction of 8000 villages (many in Transylvania) and the resettlement of the (mainly Hungarian) residents. After having bulldozed one-sixth of Bucharest to build his House of the People (p627), no-one doubted he'd proceed with his plans. Several dozen villages were razed, but thankfully the whole project went uncompleted.

---

In 1859 Alexandru Ioan Cuza was elected to the thrones of Moldavia and Wallachia, creating a national state, which in 1862 took the name Romania. The reformist Cuza was forced to abdicate in 1866 and his place was taken by the Prussian prince Karl of Hohenzollern, who took the name Carol I. Romania then declared independence from the Ottoman Empire in 1877 and, after the 1877–78 War of Independence, Dobrogea became part of Romania.

## Romania in WWI & WWII

In 1916 Romania entered WWI on the side of the Triple Entente (Britain, France and Russia) with the objective of taking Transylvania – where 60% of the population was Romanian – from Austria-Hungary. The Central Powers (Germany and Austria-Hungary) occupied Wallachia. With the defeat of Austria-Hungary in 1918, the unification of Banat, Transylvania and Bucovina with Romania was finally achieved.

In the years leading to WWII, Romania, under foreign minister Nicolae Titulescu, sought security in a French alliance. On 30 August 1940 Romania was forced to cede northern Transylvania to Hungary by order of Nazi Germany and fascist Italy.

To defend the interests of the ruling classes, General Ion Antonescu forced King Carol II to abdicate in favour of his son Michael. Then Antonescu imposed a fascist dictatorship. In June 1941 he joined Hitler's anti-Soviet war with gruesome results: 400,000 Romanian Jews and 36,000 Roma were murdered at Auschwitz and other camps.

On 23 August 1944 Romania suddenly changed sides, captured 53,159 German soldiers and declared war on Nazi Germany. By this act, Romania salvaged its independence and shortened the war.

## Ceauşescu

After the war, the Soviet-engineered return of Transylvania enhanced the prestige of the left-wing parties, which won the parliamentary elections of November 1946. A year later the monarchy was abolished and the Romanian People's Republic was proclaimed.

Soviet troops withdrew in 1958 and after 1960 Romania adopted an independent foreign policy under two leaders, Gheorghe Gheorghiu-Dej (leader from 1952 to 1965) and his protégé Nicolae Ceauşescu (1965 to 1989).

Ceauşescu's domestic policy was chaotic and megalomaniac. In 1974 the post of president was created for him. He placed his wife Elena, son Nicu and three brothers in important political positions during the 1980s. Some of Ceauşescu's expensive follies were projects like the Danube Canal from Agigea to Cernavo, the disruptive redevelopment of southern Bucharest (1983–89) and the 'systemisation' of agriculture by the resettlement of rural villagers into concrete apartment blocks.

The late 1980s saw workers' riots in Braşov and severe food shortages in the winter of 1988–89. But the spark that ignited Romania came on 15 December 1989, when Father László Tökés publicly condemned the dictator from his Hungarian church in Timişoara. Police attempts to arrest demonstrating parishioners failed and civil unrest quickly spread.

On 21 December in Bucharest, an address by Ceauşescu during a rally was cut short by anti-Ceauşescu demonstrators. They booed him, then retreated to the boulevard between Piaţa Universităţii and Piaţa Romană, only to be crushed hours later by police gunfire and armoured cars. The next morning thousands more demonstrators took to the streets. At midday Ceauşescu reappeared with his wife on the balcony of the Central Committee building to speak, only to be forced to flee by helicopter. The couple were arrested in Târgovişte, taken to a military base and, on 25 December, executed by a firing squad.

The National Salvation Front (FSN) swiftly took control. In May 1990 it won the country's first 'democratic' elections, placing Ion Iliescu at the helm as president and Petre Roman as prime minister. In Bucharest, student protests against this former communist ruler were ruthlessly squashed by 20,000 coal miners shipped in courtesy of Iliescu. Ironically, when the miners returned in September 1991, it was to force the resignation of Petre Roman, who was blamed for worsening living conditions.

### Modern Romania

Romania's birth as a modern nation has been a difficult one. In December 1999 President Constantinescu dismissed Radul Vasile and replaced him with former National Bank of Romania governor, Mugur Isărescu. But by mid-2000 Isărescu was fighting for his political life after the opposition accused him of mismanagement of the State Property Fund. This was followed in May 2000 by the collapse of the National Fund for Investment (NFI), which saw thousands of investors lose their savings.

Romania joined the Council of Europe in 1993. The EU started accession talks with Romania in March 2000 and joined NATO in 2002. All this came as Romania chummed up with the USA, allowing Iraq-bound military to set up bases and granting lucrative constructive projects to American companies – something some EU members weren't happy with. At the last minute in 2006, the EU granted Romania membership in 2007 – though Brussels warned it will continue to monitor progress in fighting corruption and organised crime.

## PEOPLE

Romanians make up 89% of the population; Hungarians are the next largest ethnic group (7%), followed by Roma (2%), and smaller populations of Ukrainians, Germans, Russians and Turks. Germans and Hungarians live almost exclusively in Transylvania, while Ukrainians and Russians live mainly near the Danube Delta, and Turks along the Black Sea Coast.

The government estimates that only 400,000 Roma people live in Romania, although other sources estimate between 1.5 and 2.5 million. A good site to learn more about the Roma is the Budapest-based **European Roma Rights Centre** (http://errc.org).

## RELIGION

The majority of Romania's population (87%) is Eastern Orthodox Christian. The rest is split between Protestant (6.8%), Catholic (5.6%), Muslim (0.4%), plus there are some 39,000 Jehovah's Witnesses and 10,000 Jews.

## ARTS

Painting on glass and wood remains a popular folk art. Considered to be of Byzantine origin, this traditional peasant art was widespread in Romania from the 17th century onwards. Superstition and strong religious beliefs surrounded these icons, which were painted to protect a household from evil spirits.

The paintings of Nicolae Grigorescu (1838–1907) absorbed French impressionism and created canvasses alive with the colour of the Romanian peasantry.

Romania's most famous sculptor is Constantin Brancusi (1876–1957), whose polished bronze and wood works are held at museums in Paris, New York, Canberra and in Romania at the Museum of Art in Craiova and Bucharest's National Art Museum (p629).

Modern literature emerged in the mid-19th century in the shape of romantic poet Mihai Eminescu (1850–89), who captured the spirituality of the Romanian people in his work.

The Romanian classical-music world is nearly synonymous with George Enescu (1881–1955), whose Romanian Rhapsodies

Nos 1 and 2 and opera *Odeipe* are generally considered classics.

Most Romanians and world residents are less charitable of the Cheeky Girls, Cluj-Napoca-born twins who made the big time (or at least a hit single) after leaving for the UK.

In the cinema world, Romania has scored a couple of recent international hits, with Nae Caranfil's comedy *Filantropica* (2002) and Cristi Puiu's *The Death of Mr Lăzărescu* (2005).

## ENVIRONMENT
### The Land

Covering 237,500 sq km, Romania – shaped a bit like a pufferfish – is made up of three main geographical regions, each with its particular features. The mighty Carpathian Mountains form the shape of a scythe swooping down into the country's centre from the Ukraine and curling up northwards.

West of this are large plateaus where villages and towns lie among the hills and valleys. East of the mountains are the low-lying plains (where most of the country's agricultural output comes from), which end at the Black Sea and Europe's second- largest delta region where the Danube spills into the sea.

### Wildlife

Rural Romania has thriving animal populations, which include chamois, lynx, fox, deer, wolf, bear and badger. There are 33,792 species of animals here (707 of which are vertebrates; 55 of these are endangered) as well as 3700 species of plants (39 of which are endangered).

Birdlife in the Danube Delta (p682) is unmatched. It is a major migration hub for numerous bird species and home to 60% of the world's small pygmy cormorant population.

### National Parks

Romania has nearly 600 protected areas, including 13 national parks, three biosphere reserves and one Natural World Heritage site (the Danube Delta), totalling over 12,000 sq km protected.

### Environmental Issues

Romania may very well have more rubbish bins than any country on earth (look around, it's stunning) – the problem is getting people to use them. NGOs such as **Pro Natura** (www.pronatura.ro) and the

**Transylvania Ecological Club** (www.greenagenda .org) work to spread word about how to diminish the impact of tourism on the country's environment.

Romania has the ongoing problem of cleaning up the pollution left by communist-era chemical plants. If you're on the train between Sighişoara and Cluj-Napoca, look out for the dilapidated, blackened plants in Copşa Mică, which were so dangerous to the local community until the early 1990s that some two-thirds of the children showed signs of mental illness.

## FOOD & DRINK

Let's leave the debate as to whether or not something called Romanian cuisine actually exists and plunge, mouth open wide, into a world of tasty, hearty, simple food: Romanian cooking. Relying heavily upon pork and staples such as potatoes and cabbage, with liberal borrowings from the cultures that have traversed and occupied its land, Romanian cooking is not for those seeking to diet.

*Mămăligă* is a cornmeal mush that's boiled or fried and served at every meal. *Ciorbă* (soup) is the other mainstay of the Romanian diet. Favourites include *ciorbă de burta* (tripe soup served with dollop of sour cream) and *ciorbă de legume* (vegetable soup cooked with meat stock).

Other common dishes are *muşchi de vacă/ porc/miel* (cutlet of beef/pork/lamb), *ficat* (liver), *piept de pui* (chicken breast) and *cabanos prajit* (fried sausages). Typical desserts include *plăcintă* (turnovers), *clătite* (crepes) and *cozonac* (a brioche).

Thanks to the Orthodox diet, you can always find some vegetarian dishes, unexciting and repetitious as they will come to be. If a plate of *mămăligă* does not turn you on, try *caşcaval pâine* (cheese covered in breadcrumbs and fried), *salată roşii* (tomato salad), *salată castraveţi* (cucumber salad) and *salată asortată* (mixed salad, usually just a mix of – guess what? – tomatoes and cucumbers). When you're really lucky, you'll find vegetable soup or stew, or a dish made from aubergine.

Among the best Romanian wines are Cotnari, Murfatlar, Odobeşti, Târnave and Valea Călugărească.

*Ţuica* is a once-filtered clear brandy made from fermented fruit (the tastiest and most popular is plum *ţuica*), usually 30-proof.

# BUCHAREST

☎ 021 / pop 2.1 million

Much of Romania slags it, some travellers have had enough of it after a couple of days, but Bucharest is a fascinating working experiment of mixed eras, not to mention lots of (uncute) stray dogs. Wide boulevards with century-old villas, fashioned in the best Paris style, mingle with (scattered and hidden) 18th-century monasteries, communist-built housing blocks and statement-making government headquarters (some tagged with bullet holes from the 1989 revolution). Less than two decades since the city violently ended Nicolae Ceauşescu's stranglehold on the country, life does boom here in Romania's capital – museums are super, and people are a lot nicer than some give them credit for. It's a city that's changing, and that makes it a worthy stop for those willing to poke around and find its elusive soul.

## ORIENTATION

Bucharest's main train station, Gară de Nord, is a few kilometres northwest of Bucharest's centre. The station is connected by the metro to Piaţa Victoriei on the northern side of the centre or to Piaţa Unirii on the southern side. Bus 133 will take you just north of the centre to Piaţa Romană; bus 85 goes to Piaţa Universităţii.

Bucharest's most historic areas spread to either side of the main boulevard B-dul Bălcescu, which changes its name to B-dul General Mageru to the north, and B-dul IC Brătianu south of Piaţa Universităţii.

## Maps

By far the best Bucharest map, available at bus ticket stands, is the *100% Planul Oraşului Bucareşti Map* (1:200,000; 11 lei), with all transport routes.

## INFORMATION
### Bookshops

**Librărie Noi** (Map p628; ☎ 311 0700; Blvd Nicolae Bălcescu 18; ☺ 9.30am-8.30pm Mon-Sat, 11am-7pm Sun) Best bookshop, with English-language novels, LP guides, lots of maps and a fab antiques section.

## Cultural Centres

**British Council Library** (Map p626; ☎ 307 9600; www.britishcouncil.ro; Calea Dorobanţilor 14; ☺ 9am-7pm Mon-Fri, to 1pm Sat) Library, internet access and café.

**French Institute** (Map p626; ☎ 316 0224; www.culture-france.ro; B-dul Dacia 77; ☺ 9am-6.30pm Mon-Thu, 9am-4.30pm Fri, 10am-2.30pm Sat) Film screenings, internet and bistro.

## Emergency
**Ambulance** ☎ 973
**Emergency** ☎ 112
**Police** ( ☎ 955, central station ☎ 311 2021)

## Internet Access

Many hotels and hostels have internet access. Look for red-and-white 'Zapp Hotspot' signs advertising wi-fi access around town.

**Access Internet** (Map p626; ☎ 650 7879; Blvd Lascar Catargiu 6; per hr €0.75-0.90; ☺ 24hr) International calls are US$0.04 per minute.

**Access Internet** (Map p628; B-dul Nicolae Balcescu 24; per 20min €0.30; ☺ 7am-2am)

**Internet & Games** (Map p628; ☎ 0721-877-866; B-dul Regina Elisabeta 25; per hr €0.90; ☺ 24hr)

## Left Luggage

There's **left luggage** (Map p626; Piaţa Gară de nord 1; per day small/big bag €0.90/1.80; ☺ 24hr) at the train station, right in the hallway leading to front exit.

## Medical Services

**Emergency Clinic Hospital** (Map p626; ☎ 230 0106; Calea Floreasca 8; ☺ 24hr) Bucharest's best state hospital.

**Pro-Dental Care** (Map p628; ☎ 313 4781; Str Hristo Botev 7; ☺ 10am-8pm Mon-Fri, to 4pm Sat)

**Sensi-Blu** (Map p628; ☎ 305 7314; B-dul Nicolae Bălcescu 7; ☺ 24hr) Reliable pharmacy chain with 18 Bucharest locations.

## Money

Currency exchanges and ATMs are everywhere – including several along B-dul Nicolae Bălcescu in the centre. Avoid the currency-exchange counters at the airport; there are ATM machines in the arrivals hall.

**Banca Comercială Română** (Map p628; B-dul Regina Elisabeta 5; ☺ 8.30am-5.30pm Mon-Fri, to 12.30pm Sat)

## Post

**Central post office** (Map p628; ☎ 315 9030; Str Matei Millo 10; ☺ 7.30am- 8pm Mon-Fri, 8am-2pm Sat) Collect post-restante mail from the central post office on Str Matei Millo.

## Telephone

RomTelecomm cards (from 10 lei) are available at newsstands. Most phone booths are neglected, but still work. You'll have no problem

ROMANIA

# GREATER BUCHAREST

| | |
|---|---|
| 0 | 500 m |
| 0 | 0.3 miles |

**AVIATIEI**

To Bus No 452 to Căldăruşani Monastery (400m); Gară Băneasa (750m); Băneasa Airport (8km); Casa Albă (8km); Henri Coandă (Otopeni) Airport (17km); Căldăruşani Monastery (41km); Braşov (168km)

### INFORMATION
| | |
|---|---|
| Access Internet | 1 B4 |
| Australian Consulate | 2 D6 |
| Banca Comercială Română | 3 B4 |
| Branch Post Office | 4 A4 |
| Branch Post Office | 5 B4 |
| British Council Library | 6 B4 |
| Canadian Embassy | 7 B4 |
| Emergency Clinic Hospital | 8 C3 |
| French Embassy | 9 B4 |
| French Institute | 10 C4 |
| German Embassy | 11 B3 |
| IDM Exchange | 12 A4 |
| Irish Embassy | 13 C4 |
| Left Luggage | 14 A4 |
| Moldovan Consulate | 15 A5 |
| Moldovan Embassy | 16 B3 |
| UK Embassy | 17 C4 |
| Wasteels | (see 14) |

### SIGHTS & ACTIVITIES
| | |
|---|---|
| Antim Monastery | 18 B6 |
| Ferry and Row Boats | 19 A1 |
| Jewish History Museum | 20 C6 |
| Mănăstirea Radu Vodă | 21 C6 |
| Museum of the Romanain Peasant | 22 A3 |
| National Institue for Science and Technology | 23 B6 |
| National Military Museum | 24 A5 |
| National Museum of Contemporary Art (Entry) | 25 A6 |
| National Village Museum | 26 A2 |
| Palace of Parliament | 27 B6 |
| Palace of Parliment Entry | 28 B6 |
| Patriarchal Cathedral | 29 B6 |
| Press House | 30 A1 |
| Triumphal Arch | 31 A2 |

### SLEEPING
| | |
|---|---|
| Butterfly Villa Hostel | 32 A2 |
| Funky Chicken | 33 A5 |
| Golden Tulip | 34 B4 |
| Hotel Astoria | 35 A4 |
| Hotel Duke | 36 B4 |
| Hotel Elizeu | 37 A4 |
| Hotel Helios | 38 A4 |
| Villa 11 | 39 A4 |
| Youth Hostel Villa Helga | 40 C4 |

### EATING
| | |
|---|---|
| Smart's | 41 C4 |

### DRINKING
| | |
|---|---|
| Dubliner | 42 A3 |

### ENTERTAINMENT
| | |
|---|---|
| Hollywood Multiplex | (see 45) |
| Opera House | 43 A5 |
| Queen's | 44 C6 |

### SHOPPING
| | |
|---|---|
| Bucureşti Mall | 45 D6 |
| Gift Shop | (see 22) |

### TRANSPORT
| | |
|---|---|
| Bus Stop to Ghencea Cemetery | 46 A6 |
| Central Bus Station | 47 A4 |
| Eurolines | 48 A4 |
| Toros | 49 A4 |

Piaţa Presei Libere

Herăstrău Lake

Parcul Herăstrău

Str Dumitru Zosima

B-dul C Prezan

B-dul Prim Verii

Piaţa de Charles de Gaulle

**FLOREASCA**

Str Muzeul Zambaccian

Piaţa Dorobanţilor

Str A.I. Mincu

Calea Dorobanţilor

Parcul Circului

Colentina Hospital

**Piaţa Victoriei**

B-dul Iancu de Hunedoara

Str Grigore Alexandrescu

Şos Ştefan cel Mare

Obor Market

Str Occidentului

Str Nicolae Iorga

Piaţa Romana

Piaţa Lahovari

Str Mihai

Piaţa Gemeni

To Gară Obor Station (1.3km); C&I Bus Station (1.5km)

**Gară de Nord**

Piaţa Gară de Nord

Piaţa Dacia

B-dul Dacia

Str Dumbrava Roşie

Piaţa Cantacuzino

Str Gen Berthelot

Str Ştirbei Vodă

Piaţa Revoluţiei

To Piranha Club (1.25km)

Cişmigiu Lake

Piaţa Victor Babeş

B-dul Regina Elisabeta

Piaţa Universităţii

Str Lipscani

**Historic Quarter**

See Central Bucharest Map

Biserica Sfinţii Apostoli

Piaţa Uniri

B-dul Unirii

Str Antim

Str Bibescu Voda

Unirea Shopping Centre

Biserica Bucur Ciobanul

Calea 13 Septembrie

Piaţa G Coşbuc

To Ghencea Civil Cemetery (1.5km)

B-dul Regina Maria

B-dul Dimitrie Cantemir

B-dul Mărăşeşti

B-dul Unirii

B-dul Mircea Vodă

B-dul O Goga

Calea Dudeşti

**ROMANIA**

finding a shop selling Orange or Vodaphone SIM cards for your mobile phone – try a central street like B-dul Magheru.

Access Internet (p625) can help with international calls too.

## Tourist Information

Sometimes you have to wonder if the Bucharest government just doesn't care about the city, as the nation's capital is woefully unrepresented in the world of information. The many travel agencies are focussed on getting you out of the country. Hostels tend to be excellent sources of info, helping with rental cars or day trips to Snagov or even Bran Castle.

**ONT Carpați** (Map p628; ☎ 314 1922; www.ont.ro; B-dul General Magheru 7; ⏰ 9am-6.30pm Mon-Fri, to 2pm Sat) Lots of outbound business, but staff are happy to talk through a Romania trip, arrange daily guides (€30) and offer city tours (from €40 with driver).

**Wasteels** (Map p626; ☎ 317 0370; www.wasteelstravel .ro; Gară de Nord; ⏰ 8am-7pm Mon-Fri, to 2pm Sat) Conveniently located on the left side of the exit hallway of the train station, Wasteels can rent cars for you, help with train reservations, and may be able to call you a reliable taxi.

## DANGERS & ANNOYANCES

It's said that Bucharest's stray dogs (politically correct term of late: 'community dogs') number from 100,000 to 200,000. Though it's rarely a problem, travellers are occasionally bitten, and in 2006 a Japanese businessmen bled to death following a freak bite that severed an artery. If bitten, go to a hospital within 36 hours for antirabic injections. Avoid any packs of dogs, who occasionally occupy empty lots behind buildings.

Another 'danger' are the taxi drivers who charge extortionately high prices. Worst are those outside Gară de Nord. Avoid using these (we've heard of travellers paying US$150 for a US$5 ride!). Wasteels (above) can usually call for a taxi from the train station, if you don't have a phone to call the reliable companies listed on p635.

## SIGHTS

Bucharest teems with museums and attractions, all relatively dirt cheap and many among the nation's best. The historic thoroughfare Calea Victoriei makes a nice walk, as it connects the two main squares of the city: Piața Victoriei in the north, and Piața Revoluției in the centre. Follow the river east to where it does under the sprawling Piața Unirii.

## Ceaușescu's Bucharest

Inspired by a trip to Pyongyang and Beijing, Nicolae Ceaușescu unleashed a feverish reconstruction campaign on Bucharest (and Romania) in the 1980s, and this is most evident along **B-dul Unirii** in southern Bucharest. Intended to be Romania's 'Champs Elysées', the busy, fountain-lined 3.2km boulevard – famously 6m longer than the Paris prototype – meant destroying an entire suburb of historic buildings. (To get a sense of what it replaced, stroll just north into the historic centre; see p629).

From central **Piața Unirii** (under which the city's crippled Dâmbovița River is submerged), look southwest, where the **Patriarchal Cathedral** (Catedrala Patriahală; Map p626; Str Dealul Mitropoliei) – the centre of Romanian Orthodox faith, and built between 1656 and 1658 – peeks out from once-grand housing blocks – a rare religious site that gets views of the centre. B-dul Unirii's housing blocks were designed to 'hide' churches across the city, such as the **Antim Monastery** (Mănăstirea Antim; Map p626; Str Antim), which is south just one block before the boulevard ends, and dates from 1715.

Facing the boulevard is the impossible-to-miss **Palace of Parliament** (Palatul Parlamentului; Map p626; ☎ 311 3611; B-dul Națiunile Unite; adult/student €6/3; ⏰ 10am-4pm), the world's second-largest building (after the US Pentagon). Built in 1984 (and still 10% unfinished), the building's 12 storeys and 3100 rooms covers 330,000 sq metres, and cost an estimated €3.3 billion. Rushed, but interesting, 45-minute tours go every half-hour or so and lead into a handful of marble rooms – still rented out for conferences – finishing at the balcony Nicolae didn't live long enough to speak from. Facing the Palace of Parliament

## CENTRAL BUCHAREST

0 _____ 300 m
0 _____ 0.2 miles

**INFORMATION**
Access Internet...................1 C3
Banca Commercială
  Română...........................2 C4
Central Post Office...............3 B4
Internet & Games...............4 B4
Librărie Noi.......................5 C3
Main Police Station............6 B4
ONT Carpaţi.......................7 B2
Pro-Dental Care.................8 D4
Sensi-Blu...........................9 C3
US Consulate....................10 C3
US Embassy......................11 C3

**SIGHTS & ACTIVITIES**
Athénéé Palace................12 B2
Black Cross.....................(see 5)
Building Shell................(see 28)
Central Committee of the
  Communist Party
  Building.......................13 B3

Cişmigiu Garden.........14 A3
Economic Consortium
  Palace........................15 B5
National Art Museum..16 B3
Natural History
  Museum......................17 B3
Old Princely Court......18 C5
Stavropoleos Church..19 B5

**SLEEPING**
Hanul lui Manuc......20 C5
Hotel Carpaţi.............21 B4
Hotel Muntenia........22 B3
Hotel Opera..............23 B3
Rembrandt Hotel.......24 C5

**EATING**
Bistro Vilacrosse...............25 B4
Casa Veche.....................26 B2
Count Dracula Club.........27 B5
IO Coffee Bar.................28 B3
La Mama.........................29 B2
Mediterraneo..................30 D2
Paradis...........................31 D4
Red Lion.........................32 B4
Snack Attack!..................33 C3

**DRINKING**
Amsterdam Grand Café.....34 C5
Fire Club.........................35 C5
La Butoaie......................36 C3

**ENTERTAINMENT**
Cinema Pro.....................37 C4
Club A............................38 C5
Twice..............................39 D5

**SHOPPING**
Librărie Noi....................(see 5)

**TRANSPORT**
Agenţie de Voiaj CFR
  office...........................40 B4
Autogara Diego...............41 B5
Tarom.............................42 B5

from B-dul Unirii, the entrance is around to the right (a 12-minute walk).

Back on the building's west side, walk back past B-dul Unirii to the building's south side, noting the half-finished **National Institute for Science & Technology** (Map p626; cnr B-dul Libertăţii & Calea 13 Septembrie); half-done or abandoned buildings like this litter Bucharest. At the

back of the Palace of Parliament is the superb **National Museum of Contemporary Art** (Muzeul Naţionalde Arta Contemporana; Map p626; ☎ 318 9137; www.mnac.ro; Calea 13 Septembrie; adult/student €1.50/free; ✆ 10am-6pm Wed-Sun), which opened in 2004. A fully changing four-floor exhibition space features eclectic European artists – including installation and video art – and is easily one of Eastern Europe's most provocative spaces. There's a top-floor open-air café.

A 45-minute rather-dreary walk west (or accessed via bus 385 from outside the Parliament ticket office on B-dul Naţiunile Unite) is **Ghencea Civil Cemetery** (Cimitriul Civil Ghencea; Map p626; ☎ 413 8590; Calea 13 Septembrie; ☻ 8am-8pm), where you can see the resting spots of Nicolae Ceauşescu (row I-35, marked with a red cross, to the left of the entry path) and his wife Elena (H25, across to the right of the entry path), both executed on Christmas in 1989.

## Historic Centre

Some of the fiercest fighting during the 1989 revolution took place at **Piaţa Universităţii** (Map p628; Ⓜ Piaţa Universităţii), which straddles Bucharest's most evocative, historic streets. Journalists watched tanks roll over Romanian freedom-fighters and soldiers shoot into crowds of protestors from their viewpoint inside Hotel Inter-Continental. Scour the area and you'll find bullet marks in some buildings and 10 stone crosses commemorating those killed. A **black cross** and plaque on the wall at B-dul Nicolae Bălcescu 18 marks the spot where the first protestor, Mihai Gătlan, died at 5.30pm on 21 December 1989.

Much of the historic centre looms in the blocks to the southwest. A good access way is along historic **Calea Victoriei**, built in 1692 under Brâncoveanu's orders to link the centre with his summer palace in Mogoşoaia, 14km northwest. Three blocks south is **Str Lipscani**; its blocks to the east of Calea Victoriei become a centre of bohemian ballyhoo at night, especially in summer.

Another block south is the ritzy **Economic Consortium Palace** (Casa de Economii şi Consemnaţiuni), designed by French architect Paul Gottereau between 1894 and 1900. Across the street is the **National History Museum** (Map p628; ☎ 311 3356; Calea Victoriei 12; adult/student €0.90/0.45; ☻ 9am-5pm), housed in the neoclassical former Post Office Palace (1894). The museum is mostly under a long-winded renovation, but it's worth seeing for the dismantled replica of the 2nd-century 40m Trajan's Column; its 2500 characters retell the Dacian Wars against Rome. (Go to panel 18 to see decapitated heads.) There's also a gold-crammed treasury.

A block east of the museum, the **Stavropoleos Church** (Map p628; Str Stavropoleos), on a street meaning 'town of the cross', dates from 1724 and is one of Bucharest's most atmospheric

churches, with a courtyard filled with old tombstones and an ornate wood interior.

The centre of the old historic centre is around the **Old Princely Court** (Palatul Voievodal; Map p628; Curtea Veche; ☎ 314 0375; Str Franceza 21-23; admission €0.60; ☻ 10am-5pm), a busted-up court from the 15th century with a Vlad Tepeş statue out front.

Just southeast, **Hanul lui Manuc**, an active hotel with a courtyard restaurant-bar (p631), was built to shelter travelling merchants, and is one of the few remaining buildings of the era.

To the southeast, just beyond Piaţa Unirii, the interesting **Jewish History Museum** (Muzeul de Istorie al Comunitaţilor Evreieşti din România; Map p626 ☎ 311 0870; admission by donation; ☻ 9am-1pm Sun-Fri) is housed in a colourful synagogue that dates from 1836 (but was rebuilt in 1910). Exhibits (in English and Romanian) outline Jewish contributions in Romanian history, which is not something all Romanians know about. In 1941, 800,000 Jews lived in Romania; today only 10,000 remain. You need your passport to enter.

## Piaţa Revoluţiei

The scene of Ceauşescu's infamous last speech of 21 December 1989 was on the balcony of the former **Central Committee of the Communist Party building** (Map p628), a few blocks northwest of Piaţa Universităţii. Amid cries of 'Down with Ceauşescu' he briefly escaped in a helicopter from the roof. Meanwhile, the crowds were riddled with bullets, and many died.

The **building shell** (Map p628; cnr Str DI Dobrescu & Str Boteanu) once housed the hated Securitate and was destroyed by protestors in 1989. Now a modern glass structure stands inside it; you can get hipster coffee in the basement IO Coffee House (p632).

Housed in the early 19th-century Royal Palace, the **National Art Museum** (Muzeul Naţional de Artă; Map p628; ☎ 313 3030; http://art.museum.ro; Calea Victoriei 49-53; combo ticket adult/student €3.60/1.80, Romanian & European collections €2.40/1.20, first Wed of month free; ☻ 10am-6pm Wed-Sun) is a super three-part museum. The north door leads to the **Gallery of Romanian Art** (adult/student €2.10/0.90), with hundreds of icons saved from communist-destroyed churches and many paintings, including arresting portraits of Nicolae Grigorescu. Also in the building is the small **Treasures of Roman Art** (adult/student €1.50/0.60). The south door leads to the absorbing **Gallery of European Art** (Map p628; adult/student €1.20/0.60), a 12,000-piece collection, which was largely assembled from Tsar Carol I's collection,

ROMANIA

which covers all things from Rembrandt and Bartolomeo to Rodin and Monet.

Just to the north is the **Athénée Palace** (Str Episcopiei 1-3), so evocatively captured in its post-revolutionary, prostitute-teeming state by Robert Kaplan in *Balkan Ghosts*. Designed to out-do Paris in 1918, the hotel later served as a hotbed for Romania's 'KGB', the Securitatae. Now Hilton has cleaned it up – and priced rooms beyond their worth.

Just east is the grand domed **Ateneul Român** (Romanian Athenaeum; Map p628; ☎ 315 6875), which hosts prestigious concerts. Built in 1888, this is where George Enescu made his debut in 1898. Today it's home to the George Enescu Philharmonic Orchestra.

Just west is the local-loved **Cişmigiu Garden**, with shady walks, cafés and a ridiculous number of benches on which to sit and stare at Bucharestians going by.

## Northern Bucharest

Bucharest's most luxurious villas and parks hug the grand avenue **Şoseaua Kiseleff**, which begins at **Piaţa Victoriei** (Map p626; Ⓜ Piaţa Victoriei). A leafy walk north are two museums that pay tribute to Romania's rural heart.

About 200m north, the **Museum of the Romanian Peasant** (Muzeul Ţăranului Român; Map p626; ☎ 212 9661; Şos Kiseleff 3; adult/student €1.80/0.60; ☉ 10am-6pm Tue-Sun) is so good you may want to hug it. Chosen as Europe's best museum in 1996, it makes the best of little money. Hand-made cards (in English) personalise exhibits, such as a full 19th-century home located upstairs, a heartbreakingly sweet room devoted to grandmas, and 'hidden' rooms that hand-scrawled directions usher you to. Don't miss the (rare) communism exhibit downstairs, with Lenin busts and portraits of Romanian leader Gheorghiu-Dej. An 18th-century Transylvanian church is in the back lot, as is the museum's **gift shop**.

About a kilometre north is the **Triumphal Arch** (Arcul de Triumf; Map p626), based on the Paris monument, and devoted to WWI and the reunification of Romania in 1918 (built 1935–36). Traffic roars by, so it's tricky to reach; its viewing platform at the top was closed at the time of writing.

Pathways just east lead to the lovely **Herăstrău Park** (Parcul Herăstrău), which hugs the chain of lakes that stripe northern Bucharest. There are plenty of cafés around. On the east side, about 500m north, a **ferry** crosses the lake regularly (3 lei one-way), and there are **rowboats**

(per hr 5 lei) to rent. Adjoining the park, but best accessed from Şos Kiseleff, is the **National Village Museum** (Muzeul Naţional al Satului; Map p626; ☎ 317 9110; Şos Kiseleff 28-30; adult/student €1.50/0.60; ☉ 9am-7pm Tue-Sun, to 4pm Mon May-Sep, to 5pm Tue-Fri, to 4pm Mon Oct-Apr), a terrific open-air collection of several dozen homesteads, churches, mills and windmills that have been relocated from rural Romania. At times in July and August artisans in traditional garb show off various rural trades.

At the north end of Şos Kiseleff is the Stalinesque **Press House** (Casa Presei Libre), built in 1956. Note the imprint of the former hammer and sickle midway up the tower.

## Western Bucharest

Not far from the train station, the pinky-peach **National Military Museum** (Muzeul Militar Naţional; Map p626; ☎ 319 6015; Str Mircea Vulcănescu 125-127; adult/student €1.50/0.75; ☉ 9am-5pm Tue-Sun) doubles nicely as a Romanian history museum. Note the 1988 communist mural in the entry; in back is a superb hangar with Aurel Vlaicu's famed 1911 plane, which Romanians attest made the first 'real' flight.

## SLEEPING

If you only have a couple of days, it may be worth trying to stay near the centre. The area around the grotty Gară de Nord has some cheaper options. Breakfast is included unless otherwise noted.

### Budget

#### CENTRAL BUCHAREST

**Hotel Muntenia** (Map p628; ☎ 314 6010; Str Academiei 19-21; s/d with shared bath €15/21, d with private bath €51) Walls are yellowing and the façade's chipping, but the rooms are clean. Skip the private-bath option; it's hardly worth the extra euros. No breakfast.

#### NEAR THE TRAIN STATION

**Vila 11** (Map p626; ☎ 0722 495 900; vila11bb@hotmail .com; Str Institutul Medico Militar 11; dm/s/d €10/18/28) Run by a Canadian family, this homy *pension* is on a back street. Call ahead; sometimes no one's around.

#### OUTSIDE THE CENTRE

**Casa Albă** (Map p626; ☎ 230 4525; Alea Privighetorilor 1-3; camp sites per tent €6, bungalows €22) This camping ground is in way-north Bucharest. Take bus 301 north from Piaţa Romană; get off a stop after the Băneasa airport and walk 500m east.

**Funky Chicken** (Map p626; ☎ 312 1425; funkychicken hostel@hotmail.com; Str Gen Berthelot 63; dm €8) Just a couple of blocks from Cişmigiu Gardens, this hostel occupies an historic home on a shady street, with three dorm rooms that sleep 18. No breakfast, but there's a kitchen and free cigarettes.

**Butterfly Villa Hostel** (Map p626; ☎ 0747 032 644; www.villa-butterfly.com; Str Dumitru Zosima 82; dm/s/d €9/14/26; ⚡ ▯ ) By far Bucharest's best hostel, run by a German-Romanian couple, Butterfly is not necessarily the best located. Free laundry, a roof terrace, all-day breakfasts and courtyard are bonuses. Bus 282 leaves from the train station, and bus 300 from Piaţa Romana.

**Youth Hostel Villa Helga** (Map p626; ☎ 610 2214; www.rotravel.com/hotels/helga; Str Salcâmilor 2; dm/s/d €12/16/28; ⚡ ▯ ) A converted old villa east of the centre has nice, clean rooms, with a new kitchen to use, two private rooms, and patio seats under the vine shade. Prices drop after summer.

## Midrange
### CENTRAL BUCHAREST
**Hanul lui Manuc** (Manuc's Inn; Map p628; ☎ 313 1415; hmanuc@rnc.ro; Str Franceză 62-64; s/d €36/60) Originally a 19th-century merchants' inn (caravanserai), this hotel is one of the city's oldest buildings and has an equally colourful guest list from its past including prostitutes, criminals and Lonely Planet authors. Sculpted wooden balconies line the terrace overlooking the courtyard. It's a bit dated, but the location and price make it a steal.

**Rembrandt Hotel** (Map p628; ☎ 313 9315; www.rembrandt.ro; Str Smârdan 11; s €63, d Mon-Fri €91-113, d Sat & Sun €81-93; ⚡ ▯ ) This wonderful, relatively new 15-room, Dutch-owned hotel faces the landmark National Bank in the historic centre. Rooms win serious points for polished wood floors, wall-size timber headboards and DVD players.

---

**AUTHOR'S CHOICE**

If you're looking to save and be central, it's hard to beat **Hotel Carpaţi** (Map p628; ☎ 315 0140; carpati@compace.ro; Str Matei Millo 16; s/d with shared bath €26/42, d with private bath d €55-68), which has 40 recently renovated rooms – some are tiny, with little light – and a fun, rather scary, two-door lift. Breakfast comes with a little pomp in the Paris-style lobby lounge. All rooms have a TV and a sink.

---

### NEAR THE TRAIN STATION
**Hotel Astoria** (Map p626; ☎ 318 9989; B-dul Dinica Golescu 27; s/d €30/45) Facing the station, the nine-floor Astoria, beside the railway tracks, carries some yesteryear grace.

**Hotel Elizeu** (Map p626; ☎ 319 1734; rezervari@hotelelizeu.ro; Str Elizeu 11-13; s/d €46/57; ⚡ ) A notch up from the rest, this 54-room hotel is comfortable and modern, if a bit standard. It's in a quiet residential area a few blocks north of the station.

### OUTSIDE THE CENTRE
**Hotel Helios** (Map p626; ☎ 310 7083; Str Iulia Haşden 16; s/d €66/77; ⚡ ▯ ) This 15-room hotel is only a few blocks from the train station, but feels far away – it faces a quaint Orthodox church. Stylish rooms have floor-to-ceiling wardrobes. Prices drop 20% Saturday and Sunday.

## Top End
### CENTRAL BUCHAREST
**Hotel Opera** (Map p628; ☎ 312 4857; www.hoteloprea.ro; Str Ion Brezoianu 37; s/d €120/140; ⚡ ▯ ) Set on a back-street corner, this 33-room, faintly Art Deco hotel goes all-out music theme inside. The rooms are small, but nicely arranged. Rates don't include 9% VAT.

### OUTSIDE THE CENTRE
**Hotel Duke** (Map p626; ☎ 317 4186; www.hotelduke.ro; B-dur Dacia 33; s/d €130/150; ⚡ ▯ ) At Piaţa Romana, the 38-room Duke is a pleasant business-style hotel with mint-and-caramel rooms, and attentive staff. There's internet in the lobby, and a casual bar where suits chat, and it's located near central attractions and restaurants.

**Golden Tulip** (Map p626; ☎ 212 5558; www.goldentulip bucharest.com; Calea Victoriei 166; r €160 & €180; ⚡ ▯ ) This very stylish 82-room hotel opened close to the centre in 2005, giving Bucharest a needed modern push. Plush red chairs are set before full-wall glass windows in the stark rooms. Rates drop 20% Friday to Sunday.

# EATING
## International
**Paradis** (Map p628; ☎ 315 2601; Str Hristo Botev 10; dishes €1.80; ⌚ 8am-10.30pm) Try the brilliant-value buffet lunch at this Lebanese joint: spicy aubergine stew or spinach over rice spinach stews, meatballs in tomato sauce, and mounds of flat bread.

**Mediterraneo** (Map p628; ☎ 211 5308; Str Icoanei 20; mains €3.60-6; ⌚ 10am-midnight or later) This great little corner restaurant on a cobbled back lane

ROMANIA

draws expats and locals for Turkified Medi-terranean fare (fish, kebabs, pastas). Sunday brunch (35 lei) is a big deal.

**Smart's** (Map p626; ☎ 211 9035; Str Alex Donici 14; mains €4.50-9; ☺ 11am-late) On a shady lane, this great, popular pub serves (rather Romanian) pub fare, with a selection of salads (11 to 14 lei) and pastas (15 to 20 lei). It's popular, and a fine spot to sit over a bottle of Leffe.

**Red Lion** (Map p628; ☎ 315 1526; Str Academiei 1a; pizza €2.70-5.10; ☺ 9am-midnight Mon-Fri, 3pm-midnight Sat & Sun) This popular pizza-pasta place near the university fills two rooms, with locals look-ing for beer on draft (2 lei), pizzas (go for the large) and pastas (6 to 13 lei).

**Casa Veche** (Map p628; ☎ 0724 232 631; Str Enescu 15; pizza €4.20-6.60; ☺ noon-midnight) With courtyard seats under vines, and traditional upstairs seating, this place wins Bucharest hearts for its great-quality crispy pizzas and a winner setting near the centre.

## Romanian

**Count Dracula Club** (Map p628; ☎ 312 1353; www.count -dracula.ro; Splaiul Independenței 8a; meals €20; ☺ lunch & dinner) Sometimes you have to succumb to things, like this: a spooky home with blood-dripping walls and cosy rooms themed as hunting, medieval and Transylvanian, and a chapel-coffin room with impaled heads, hands reaching through walls, and blood-red lights. Plus, Drac himself shows up 'for a show' at 9.30pm on Tuesday and Friday.

**La Mama** (Map p628; ☎ 312 9797; Str Epislopiei 9; mains €3-5; ☺ 10am-2am Sun-Thu, to 4am Fri & Sat) This converted villa, with its sprawling covered deck that's filled all hours, dates from the late 19th century. Its menu is stuffed with very tasty, meat-heavy options. The roasted pork neck (13 lei), with country-style potatoes, is unbeatable.

## Cafes & Quick Eats

**10 Coffee Bar** (Map p628; ☎ 315 6098; Str Demetrie Dobrescu 5) In a chic spot looking out from a blown-out ruin of the 1989 clash at nearby Piața Revoluți, this two-floor café has back-lit wall-length B&W prints of the 1989 scene and candles on the table.

**Snack Attack!** (Map p628; ☎ 312 7664; Str Ion Câmpineanu 10; sandwiches €1.50; ☺ 8am-8pm Mon-Fri, to 2pm Sat) Fresh and cheap take-out panini, salads (including hummus and tabbouleh with tortillas).

# DRINKING

Bucharest's budding bar scene is liveliest in the Str Lipscani area. Piața Universității is alive with revellers at the weekend, and hosts free outdoor pop concerts in summer.

**Amsterdam Grand Café** (Map p628; ☎ 313 7580; Str Covaci 6; ☺ 10am-2am) This rustic, wood-floor café has high ceilings and nooks to sit in, drink, and catch some live jazz some afternoons. There's food, but it's better for drinks.

**Dubliner** (Map p626; Șos Nicolae Titulescu 18; ☺ 9-2am) A long-time expat hang-out for Guinness on draft and football games, attracting a grab bag of fans; the steak sandwich (pricey at €6.60) is super.

**Fire Club** (Map p628; ☎ 0722-390 946; Str Gabroveni 12) This big red-brick room usually has groups of students crouching on stools around small tables with bottles of Tuborg in hand. Rock and punk shows are staged in the basement.

**La Butoaie** (Map p628; B-dul Nicolae Bălcescu 2) Huge with uni students, this lively open-deck bar on the 5th floor of the Ion Luca Caragiale National Theatre fits hundreds, with benches and big pillows in seating areas. It fills early on warm days.

# ENTERTAINMENT

**Şapte Seri** (Seven Evenings; www.sapteseri.ro) and *24 Fun* are free, weekly entertainment listings magazines (in Romanian).

## Cinemas

Bucharest is fond of the movies, and plays foreign-language films in their original language. A few options include:

**Cinema Pro** (Map p628; ☎ 824 1360; Str IC Brătianu 6; tickets €2.40-3)

**Hollywood Multiplex** (Map p626; ☎ 327 7020; Bucureşti Mall, Calea Vitan 55-59; tickets €2.50-4.50) Multi-screen jobbie.

## Clubs

**Club A** (Map p628; ☎ 315 6853; Str Blănari 14) Run by students, this club is a classic and is beloved by all who go there. Indie pop-rock tunes rock the house until 5am Friday and Saturday nights.

**Twice** (Map p628; ☎ 313 5593; Str Sfânta Vineri 4, Sect 3; ☒ 9pm-5am) DJs and amateur stripping are part of the hip-to-hip youth dancing to two beats across two rooms. Come along and be prepared to sweat.

## Gay & Lesbian Venues

The main gay venue in town is **Queen's** (Map p626; ☎ 0722 988 541; Str Juliu Barach 13; ☒ noon-3am).

For more information on Romania's gay and lesbian community, see p687.

## Opera & Classical Music

For information on seeing the philharmonic at the Ateneul Român (Romanian Athenaeum) see p630.

At the **Opera House** (Opera Română; Map p626; ☎ 313 1857; B-dul Mihail Kogălniceanu 70) you can enjoy a full-scale opera in a lovely building for between €1 and €4.

# SHOPPING

For beautifully made woven rugs, table runners, national Romanian costumes, ceramics and other local crafts, don't miss the excellent folk-art shop inside the Museum of the Romanian Peasant (p630).

Librăria Noi (p625) has a great collection of antique books and maps.

# GETTING THERE & AWAY
## Air

International flights use the **Henri Coanda Airport** (formerly Otopeni; ☎ 201 4788; www.otp-airport.ro; Şos

Bucureşti-Ploieşti), 16km north of Bucharest on the road to Braşov.

Arrivals and departures use marked side-by-side terminals (arrivals are to the north). There are **information desks** ( ☎ 204 1220; ☒ 24hr) in both terminals.

Romania's national airline is **Tarom** (Transporturile Aeriene Române; www.tarom.ro; Airport ☎ 201 400; Centre ☎ 337 0400; Spl Independenţei 17; ☒ 8.30am-7.30pm Mon-Fri, 9am-2pm Sat).

**Air Moldova** ( ☎ 312 1258; www.airmoldova.md) also serves Henri Coanda.

**Băneasa Airport** ( ☎ 232 0020; Şos Bucureşti-Ploieşti 40), 8km north of the centre, is used for some internal and charter flights.

## Bus
### DOMESTIC DESTINATIONS

Bucharest's bus system is frankly a mess, scarred by ever-changing departure locations, companies and schedules. Try checking websites such as www.cdy.ro and www.autogara.ro, or asking your hotel to help with the latest. Or stick with the train.

The most popular routes are the maxitaxis to Braşov (€5.10, 2½ hours), which stop in Sinaia, Buşteni and Predeal on the way; **C&I** ( ☎ 256 8039; Str Ritmului 35) runs these from its 'station' 3.25km east of Piaţa Romana – it's four blocks north of metro station Piaţa Iancului. Buses 69 and 85 go there from Gară de Nord. Some continue on to Sighişoara (€8.10, five hours).

Every 45 minutes or so, maxitaxis head for Costanţa (€9) from the so-called **Central Bus Station** (Autogara Gară de Nord; Map p626), which is located about 350m southeast of the train station.

See p635 for details on getting to Snagov.

### INTERNATIONAL BUSES
#### Bulgaria

Maxitaxi service departs three times daily from the roadside '**Autogara Diego**' (Map p628; ☎ 311 1283; Splaiul Independenţei 2K) and heads to Ruse, Bulgaria (€12 one way, three to four hours).

#### Turkey

Those who are Turkey-bound have several options leaving from around Gară de Nord, including **Ortadoğu Tur** ( ☎ 318 7538; Str Gară de Nord 6-8) and **Toros** (Map p626; ☎ 233 1898; Calea Griviţei 134-136). The 12-hour trip costs about €36 one-way.

ROMANIA

## Western Europe

The biggest name in international buses is **Eurolines** ( ☎ 316 3661; www.eurolines.ro; Str Buzeşti 44; ☒ 24hr), which links many Western European destinations with Bucharest, including two weekly buses to Athens (€80, 22 hours) and Berlin (€115), daily service to Rome (€115) and Vienna (€64), and three weekly to Paris (€125). Working with Eurolines, Atlassib (www.atlassib.ro) handles Italian destinations.

## Car & Motorcycle

Bucharest offers some of the country's cheapest car-rental rates. Major car-rental agencies can be found at the Henri Coanda Airport arrivals hall. Cheaper is **C&V** ( ☎ 201 4611, 0788-998 877; www.dvtouring.ro), which offers Dacia Solenzas for €42 per day (including unlimited mileage and insurance); it falls to €27 per day if you rent over a week.

Parking a car in the centre, particularly off Piaţa Victoriei and Piaţa Universităţii, costs €0.30; look for the wardens in yellow-and-blue uniforms. In many places you can just pull onto the sidewalk.

## Train

**Gară de Nord** (Map p626; ☎ 223 2060; Piaţa Gară de Nord 1) is the central station for national and international trains. Call ☎ 9521 or ☎ 9522 for telephone reservations. It has two halls, where same-day tickets can be purchased. Facing the station, the one to the right sells 1st- and 2nd-class domestic tickets; the one to the left sells international (marked 'casa internaţionale') and 1st-class domestic tickets. If you don't have a ticket, you have to pay €0.15 to get on the platform.

For all advance tickets (over 24 hours before departure), go to **Agenţie de Voiaj CFR office** (Map p628; ☎ 313 2643; www.cfr.ro; Str Domnita Anastasia 10-14; ☒ 7.30am-7.30pm Mon-Fri, 9am-1.30pm Sat). A seat reservation is compulsory if you are travelling with an Inter Rail or Eurail pass. Wasteels agency on the platform (see p627) can help out too. International tickets must be bought in advance.

Some local trains to/from Constanţa use Gară Obor station, east of the centre. Bus 85 goes between the two stations.

Check the latest train schedules on either www.cfr.ro or the reliable German site www.bahn.de.

Sample direct daily service includes:

| Destination | Price | Duration | Daily Departures |
| --- | --- | --- | --- |
| Braşov | €7.60 | 2½hr | hourly |
| Cluj-Napoca | €11-16 | 7½hr | six |
| Costanţa | €8.75 | 2˝-4hr | almost hourly |
| Iaşi | €14.50 | 7hr | five |
| Sibiu | €14 | 5hr | three |
| Sighişoara | €8-12 | 4½hr | nine |
| Suceava | €15.50 | 8hr | one |
| Timişoara | €22.50 | 8hr | eight |
| Tulcea | €9.80 | 6hr | one |

Daily international services include six trains to Budapest (13 to 15 hours); two trains to Sofia (11 hours) and Gorna Oryakhovitsa (near Veliko Târnovo, Bulgaria; 6½ hours); and one train to Belgrade (12 hours), Chişinău (13 hours), Istanbul (19 hours) and Kiev (27 hours), Moscow (39 hours).

# GETTING AROUND
## To/From the Airport
### BUS

To get to Henri Coanda (Otopeni) or Băneasa airport take bus 783 from the city centre, which departs every 15 minutes between 5.37am and 11.23pm (every half-hour at weekends) from Piaţa Unirii and goes via Piaţa Victoriei.

Buy a ticket, valid for two trips, for €1 at any RATB (Régie Autonome de Transport de Bucureşti) bus-ticket booth near a bus stop. Once inside the bus remember to feed the ticket into the machine.

Băneasa is 20 minutes from the centre; get off at the 'aeroportul Băneasa' stop.

Henri Coanda is about 40 minutes from the city centre. The bus stops outside the departures hall then continues to arrivals.

To get to the centre from Otopeni, catch bus 783 from the downstairs ramp outside the arrivals hall; you'll need to buy a ticket from the stand at the north end of the waiting platform (to the right as you exit).

### TAXI

Taking a reputable taxi from the centre to Otopeni should cost no more than €6 or €7.

Fly Taxi monopolises airport transfers and charges about €15 to the centre – go for a flat rate, and don't rely on the meter.

## Public Transport

For buses, trams and trolleybuses buy tickets (€0.35) at any **RATB** (www.ratb.ro) street kiosk, marked 'casa de bilete' or simply 'bilete'.

Punch your ticket on board or risk a €10 on-the-spot fine.

Public transport runs from 5am to about 11pm (reduced service on Sunday). There's some info online. See p625 for a good map with routes.

Bucharest's metro dates from 1979 and has four lines and 46 stations. Trains run every five to seven minutes during peak periods and about every 20 minutes off-peak between 5.30am and 11.30pm.

To use the metro, buy a magnetic-strip ticket at the subterranean kiosks inside the main entrance to the metro station. Tickets valid for either two/10 journeys cost €0.60/1.90. A one-month unlimited travel ticket costs €5.75.

## Taxi

Opt for a cab with a meter, and avoid the guys outside Gară de Nord. It's best to call one, or have a restaurant or hotel call for you. Reputable companies include **Cobalcescu** ( ☎ 9451), **CrisTaxi** ( ☎ 9461) and **Taxi Sprint** ( ☎ 9495). Check the meter is on; rates are posted on the door.

## AROUND BUCHAREST

The tomb of infamous tyrant Vlad Ţepeş lures visitors to **Snagov** (about 35km north of Bucharest) – as much as the large lake and leisure complex. Devour the legend of Dracula by visiting the grave where his headless torso is said to lie, buried in the famous 16th-century **church and monastery,** on an island in Snagov Lake.

Most visitors go by organised day trip – and hostels like Butterfly Villa (p631) in Bucharest arrange these, usually dropping by **Căldăruşani Monastery** 6km southeast.

It's possible to go by maxitaxi, which leave hourly from Piaţa Universităţii via Piaţa Romana, and the Press House in Bucharest (€1 each way). Once there, a good destination is **Complex Astoria** ( ☎ 316 7550; r€30-45), which has a pool, tennis courts and boats to rent to take to the church. It's on the south side of the lake a few kilometres east of the town centre.

# WALLACHIA

With competition like the rural idyll of Maramureş, the elegant Hapsburgs cities of Crişana and Banat and the tempting offerings just north in Transylvania, Wallachia (Ţara Românească) is ignored by most travellers. All the better for you.

Occupying Romania[...] swipe are some of the cou[...] and peaceful monasterie[...] tour buses. The heart of t[...] can be found here, teari[...] on horse-drawn carts a[...] houses. In the summer months, fearless drivers will want to navigate the heart-stopping Transfăgărăşan road – said to be one of the highest roads in Europe – cutting dramatically across the Făgăraş Mountains from its start point at Curtea de Argeş.

## CURTEA DE ARGEŞ

☎ 0248 / pop 33,365

Curtea de Argeş was a princely seat in the 14th century and its church is considered to be the oldest monument preserved in its original form in Wallachia. The exquisite monastery (or Episcopal cathedral), sculpted from white stone, is unique for its chocolate-box architecture and the royal tombs it hides.

The historic town is a gateway to the Făgăraş Mountains.

### Orientation

The train station, a 19th-century architectural monument, is 100m north of the bus station on Str Albeşti. The centre is a 10-minute walk along Str Albeşti then up the cobbled Str Castanilor and along Str Negru Vodă. Continue on until you reach a statue of Basarab I, from where all the major sights, a camping ground and hotels (signposted) are a short walk.

### Information

There is a **tourist office** ( ☎ 721 451; B-dul Basarabilor 27-29; ⏲ 9am-5pm Mon-Fri) within Hotel Posada. **Raiffeisen Bank** (B-dul Basarabilor; ⏲ 8.30am-6.30pm Mon-Fri) is next to Hotel Posada.

The **post office** (B-dul Basarabilor 17-19; ⏲ 7am-8pm Mon-Fri) and the telephone office are in the same building.

### Sights
#### PRINCELY COURT

The ruins of the **Princely Court** (Curtea Domnească; ⏲ 9am-6pm; admission €0.60), which originally comprised a church and palace, are in the city centre. The church was built in the 14th century by Basarab I, whose statue stands in the square outside the entrance to the court.

Basarab died in 1352. His burial place near the altar in the princely church at Curtea de Argeş was discovered in 1939. The princely was rebuilt by Basarab's son, Nicolae xandru Basarab (r 1352–68), and completed by Vlaicu Vodă (r 1361–77). While little remains of the palace today, the 14th-century church (built on the ruins of a 13th-century church) is almost perfectly intact.

### HISTORIC CENTRE

The **County Museum** (Muzeul Orăşenesc; ☎ 711 446; Str Negru Vodă 2; ☉ 9am-4pm Tue-Sun) charts the history of the region. Rising on a hill are the ruins of the 14th-century **Biserica Sân Nicoară** (Sân Nicoară Church).

### CURTEA DE ARGEŞ MONASTERY

This fantastical **Episcopal cathedral** (Mănăstirea Curtea de Argeş; admission €0.60; ☉ 8am-7pm) was built between 1514 and 1526 by Neagoe Basarab (r 1512–21) with marble and mosaic tiles from Constantinople. Legend has it that the wife of the master stonemason, Manole, was embedded in the church's walls, in accordance with a local custom obliging the mason to bury a loved one alive within the church to ensure the success of his work. Manole told his workers that the first wife to bring their food the next day would be entombed. The workers duly went home and warned their women – and so Manole's wife arrived first.

The current edifice dates from 1875 when French architect André Lecomte du Nouy was brought in to save the monastery, which was in near ruins.

The white marble tombstones of Carol I (1839–1914) and his poet wife Elizabeth (1853–1916) lie on the right in the monastery's *pronaos* (entrance hall). On the left of the entrance are the tombstones of King Ferdinand I (1865–1927) and British-born Queen Marie (1875–1938) whose heart, upon her request, was put in a gold casket and buried in her favourite palace in Balcic in southern Dobrogea. Following the ceding of southern Dobrogea to Bulgaria in 1940, however, her heart was moved to a marble tomb in Bran. Neagoe Basarab and his wife are also buried in the *pronaos*.

In the park opposite lies the legendary **Manole's Well**. Legend has it that Manole tried – and failed – to fly from the monastery roof when his master, Neagoe, removed the scaffolding to prevent him building a more beautiful structure for anyone else. The natural spring marks the hapless stonemason's supposed landing pad.

## Sleeping

**Pensiunea Ruxi** ( ☎ 0727-827 675; Str Negru Voda 104; www .pensiunea-ruxi.ro; r €19) Directly across from Hotel Confarg. While the rooms are new and comfortable, the real treat is the homy atmosphere; the family will go to heart-breaking lengths to make sure you're taken care of. Breakfast costs €2.

**Hotel Posada** ( ☎ 721 451; www.posada.ro; B-dul Basarabilor 27-29; 1-star s €19, 2-star s/d €23/30, 3-star €30/40; ▣ ) Try to get a front room here to watch the sunset over the mountains. It offers both renovated and unrenovated rooms.

**Hotel Confarg** ( ☎ 728 020; Str Negru Vodă 5; s/d/ste €26/34/46) Possibly the best value hotel in Romania! Rooms are large, clean and modern. Doubles have huge tubs and the suites are admirably swanky for the price.

## Eating & Drinking

**Montana Pizzerie** (B-dul Basarabilor; pizza €2) This place serves up fresh pizzas and beer. Most nights there is live music.

**Restaurant Capra Neagră** ( ☎ 721 619; Str Alexandru Lahovary; mains €2) Sit on the terrace here and enjoy Romanian dishes.

**Be Happy Cafe** (B-dul Basarabilor; admission €0.75; ☉ to 5am) A café during the week, this place transforms into a thumping club on the weekends.

## Getting There & Away

There are six daily trains running to/from Piteşti; change at Piteşti for all train routes.

State buses run from the bus station to/ from Arefu, Câmpulung Muscel, Braşov and Bucharest (two daily). Some buses travel only on weekdays, others only on weekends.

A daily maxitaxi to Bucharest via Piteşti leaves at 8am from outside Hotel Posada. Other maxitaxis go to/from Arefu and Piteşti from an unofficial **maxitaxi stop** (cnr Str Mai 1 & Str Lascăr Catargiu).

# TRANSYLVANIA

Probably no place in Eastern Europe gets more imaginative awe than Transylvania, where you find Gothic castles that look as if fanged goons would climb down their walls and wing-flap over moats to villages where they would pick and choose their daily meal of human flesh. Beyond the myths, Transylvania is flat-out gorgeous. Separated from Wallachia to the south by a curling stripe of the giant Carpathian Mountains – the so-called Transylvania

Alps – here's what travel's about: mountain hikes and skiing, valleys of Saxon towns with fortified churches from the Middle Ages, and (yes) a Dracula site or two. The two main entry points are Braşov (a few hours north of Bucharest), with castles nearby and cobbled glory in town; to the northwest, en route to Budapest, is Cluj-Napoca, a booming student town.

Picking an itinerary around plump Transylvania is up for grabs. The 'main-three' for most visitors – and easily visited in tandem – are Braşov, the must-see citadel town of Sighişoara; and Sibiu, an EU 'Cultural Capital' in 2007. Some say, and with reason, that Romania begins only when you get to the villages. If you can, get some wheels and venture out on your own into Saxon villages between the two, or further afield, where horse carts and feet are the primary ways of getting about.

## SINAIA
**☎ 0244 / pop 14,240**

A Carpathian resort that attracted kings and queens, and now – being on the Bucharest–Braşov highway – hordes of vacationing Romanian families, Sinaia is set on the fir-clad towering Bucegi Mountains with ski runs and hiking trails for year-round fun. Sinaia can be quiet despite all the hubbub, but King Carol I's Peleş Castle reckons to out-majestify Bran's for day-trippers looking for jaw-dropping excess. There's plenty of century-old buildings, made to impress the passing royalty (some now fashioned into hotels) to gawk at too.

The resort is alleged to have gained its name from Romanian nobleman Mihai Cantacuzino, who, following a pilgrimage to Mt Sinai in Israel in 1695, founded the Sinaia Monastery. Sinaia developed into a major resort after King Carol I selected the area for his summer residence in 1870.

### Orientation & Information

The train station is directly below the centre of town. From the station climb up the stairway across the street to busy B-dul Carol I. The centre and cable car are to the left; the palace is uphill to the right.

Amco's fold-out *Ploieşti* map includes a so-so city map. Better is the SunCart *Sinaia* map (8.70 lei), which also includes Buşteni.

### BOOKSHOPS

**Flower Power** (B-dul Carol I; ☺ 8am-6pm Mon-Fri) Carries area maps, man.

### EMERGENCY

**Salvamont** ( ☎ 313 131; Primărie, B-dul Carol I) Also at Cota 2000 at top of chairlift; 24-hour mountain-rescue service.

### INTERNET ACCESS

**Internet Cafe** (Str Aosta 3; per hr €0.90; ☺ 9am-11pm) Sign points to side of building.

### LAUNDRY

**Eco Laundry** ( ☎ 0788 660 788; per load €2.40; B-dul Carol I 31; ☺ 7am-11pm) Drop-off laundry behind the big grey building.

### MONEY

**Banca Transilvania** (B-dul Carol I 14; ☺ 9am-5pm Mon-Fri, 9.30am-12.30pm Sat) Has a 24-hour ATM; foreign-exchange service is next door.

### POST & TELEPHONE

**Central post office** ( ☎ 311 591; B-dul Carol I 3; ☺ 7am-8pm Mon-Fri, 8am-noon Sat)
**Telephone office** ( ☺ 10am-6pm Mon-Fri, to 2pm Sat) In the same building as the central post office.

### TOURIST INFORMATION & TRAVEL AGENCIES

**Sinaia Tourism Information Centre** ( ☎ 315 656; CIPT_Sinaia@yahoo.com; B-dul Carol I 47; ☺ 9am-4.30pm Mon-Fri, 'optional' Sat) Snappy attendants soften with patience. Lots and lots of information and brochures and maps, but can't book rooms.
**Dracula's Land** ( ☎ 311 441; B-dul Carol I, 14; ☺ 9am-5pm or 6pm) It hides its tacky name for the street (sign merely says 'Tourist Office'), but some chummy blokes inside can help find a villa or hotel room for you, arrange hiking guides, or change money.

### Sights

Full of pomp and brimming with confidence of the then new Romanian monarchy, King Carol I's magnificent **Peleş Castle** ( ☎ 310 205; compulsory tours adult/child €3.60/1.50; ☺ 11am-5pm Wed, 9am-5pm Thu-Sun), a 20-minute walk up from the centre, is really a palace, with its fairy-tale turrets rising above acres of green meadows and grand reception halls fashioned in Moorish, Florentine and French styles. Endless heavy wood-carved ceilings and gilded pieces practically overwhelm our wee mortal minds. Worthwhile tours take in the first floor only – note the central vacuuming system.

About 100m up the hill from the castle, the German-medieval **Pelişor Palace** ( ☎ 310 918; compulsory tours adult/child €2/0.65; ☺ 11am-5pm Wed, 9am-

ROMANIA

# TRANSYLVANIA

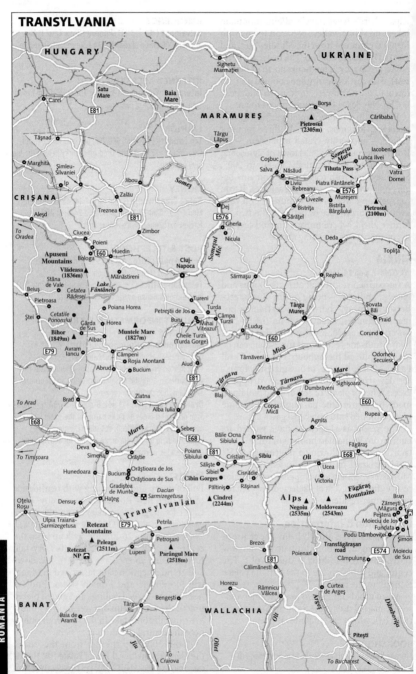

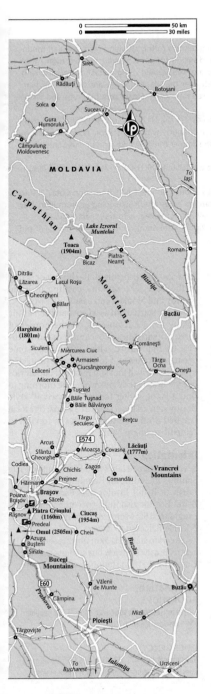

5pm Thu-Sun) has a hard time competing with its neighbour. Built by King Carol to house his nephew (and future king) Ferdinand (1865–1927) and wife Marie (who didn't get on well with King C and loathed Peleş). Its Art Nouveau style is certainly less showy. The popular Marie died in the arched gold room upstairs.

## Activities

Near the cable car, **Snow** ( ☎ 311 198; Str Cuza Voda 2a; ☺ 9am-6pm) rents out skis and snowboards for €10.50 per day, and bikes for €12.

Skis can also be rented at Cota 1400; mountain bikes can be rented at the **bike outlet** ( ☎ 314 906; Str Octavia Goga 1; per hr/day €2.40/12; ☺ 8am-7pm or 8pm).

## Sleeping

Travel agencies around town can find you a room in one of the countless pensions starting from €22. In the Bucegi mountains there are several cabanas that, purportedly, always have a space for a hiker in need of winks. Some have no electricity.

**Hotel Furnica** ( ☎ 311 151; Str Furnica 50; s €19, d €30-38) Built by the Peleş architects, the century-old, faux-Jacobian 26-room Furnica (250m west of Peleş) gives you a sense of royalty for cheap. Rooms are clean but dated, with varied layouts, and some overlooking the interior courtyard with restaurant.

**Hotel Caraiman** ( ☎ 313 551; B-dul Carol I, 4; palace@rdslink.ro; s/d/apt €33/44/61) Of the faded-glory century-old hotels – and Sinaia teems with the guys – we like the 1881 red-and-white Caraiman most, for being less royal ball and more rustic and laid-back.

**Marami Hotel** ( ☎ 315 560; www.marami.ro; Str Furnica 52; s/d/ste €50/55/60; ☒ ☐ ) The chalet-style frame looks a little cheap, but inside the Marami's 17 rooms are probably Sinaia's best midrange option. The vibe is slightly Art Deco, with pink-sand bedspreads and rust carpets.

## Eating

There are a few fast-food stands and pizza places along B-dul Carol I.

**Irish House** ( ☎ 310 060; www.irishhouse.ro; B-dul Carol I, 80; mains €2-6; ☺ 10am-midnight) Guinness is on tap (€1.65), ceilings are green, and a few token Irish dishes are on the menu, but the House's two-room rustic spot fills for its good Romanian food.

**Snow** ( ☎ 311 198; Str Cuza Voda; mains €3-6; ☺ 8am-midnight) Snow gets busiest with ski and bike

### BUCEGI MOUNTAINS

Sinaia and Buşteni, 5km north, are the principal gateways to this stunning (and popular) mountain range of dizzying skiing, mountain bike and hiking fun on a plateau situated high up on the border of Transylvania and Wallachia. Hikes are well-marked – some make for great biking. Things get harsh when winds and weather rush over the plateau. There are cabanas up here, but most visitors go as a day trip. Talk to Snow (see this box) in Sinaia about ski runs and biking trails or to get equipment.

From Sinaia, the 30-person **cable-car station** ( ☎ 311 764, 311 872; to Cota 1400/2000 €3/5.70, return €5.40/10.80; ☒ 8.30am-4pm or 5pm Tue-Sun) leaves half-hourly with two station points marked by elevation, but lines stack for a couple of hours in summer (roughly mid-June to mid-September); get there by 7am.

**Buşteni's cable-car station** ( ☎ 320 306; one-way/return €5.70/11.40; ☒ 8am-3.45pm Wed-Mon) is another access point.

It's possible to hike from the top to Bran – it's about five hours' hike from atop Cota 1200 to Cabana Omul, and another five downhill into Bran. It's a *very* rough hike going up from Bran. Day or overnight trips require the 1:70,000 Dimap trail map of Bucegi with trail marker details.

In town **Snow** ( ☎ 311 198; Str Cuza Voda 2a; ☒ 9am-6pm) rents skis (€10 per day) and bikes in summer.

---

rentals, but it's outdoor-indoor Romanian restaurant is about as good as the centre gets.

**La Brace** ( ☎ 310 348; Str Coştilei 27; mains €3-9; ☒ 10am-midnight Sun-Fri, 10-1am Fri) Amid trees, and near where the cable car passes, this fun multifloor place gets busy for pizza mostly – and the oven-baked pies are well done. It's a 15-minute walk from the centre; follow the many signs.

### Getting There & Away

Sinaia is on the Bucharest–Braşov rail line – 126km from the former and 45km from the latter – so jumping on a train to Bucharest (1½ hours) or Braşov (€4, one hour) is a cinch.

Buses and maxitaxis run every 45 minutes between roughly 7am and 10pm from the central bus stop on B-dul Carol I to Azuga and Buşteni, some all the way to Bucharest or Braşov. Rates are less than the train, and they go quicker too; pay the driver when you board. There's little room for luggage usually.

## BRAŞOV

☎ 0268 / pop 284,600

Transylvania's number-one hub is also the first Saxon town north of Bucharest, and its setting, ringed by mountains and verdant hills, ensures Braşov (Brassó in Hungarian) fills with tourists. But locals don't have the cynical jadedness some touristy towns get. Baroque façades and bohemian outdoor cafés spill onto brick sidewalks around the centre, particularly around lovely Piaţa Sfatului, one of Romania's finest squares. City strolls, good

food and day-trip potential – hiking or skiing in the Bucegi Mountains, castling in Bran, Râşnov and Sinaia – can easily fill a week.

Braşov started out as a German mercantile colony named Kronstadt. At the border of three principalities, it became a major medieval trading centre. The Saxons built some ornate churches and town houses, protected by a massive wall that still remains. Earlier this decade Braşov residents woke one morning to find a giant, rather tacky, 'Hollywood'-style Braşov sign on the facing Mt Tâmpa; one local laughed it off, 'Do they think I'm too old to remember where I am?'

### Orientation

Several brick ped lanes lead from central Piaţa Sfatului, including Str Republicii, which leads north to B-dul Eroilor and Parcul Central. B-dul Eroilor also links two other main thoroughfares, Str Mureşenilor to its west and Str Nicolae Bălcescu to its east.

The train station is 3km northeast of the city centre. Braşov has a few bus stations – Autogară 1, next to the train station, is the most active.

### Information
#### BOOKSHOPS

**Librărie George Coşbuc** ( ☎ 444 395; Str Republicii 29; ☒ 9am-7pm Mon-Fri, 10am-4pm Sat)

#### EMERGENCY

**Salvamont** ( ☎ 471 517, 0725-826 668; Str Varga 23) Does 24-hour emergency rescue for the mountains.

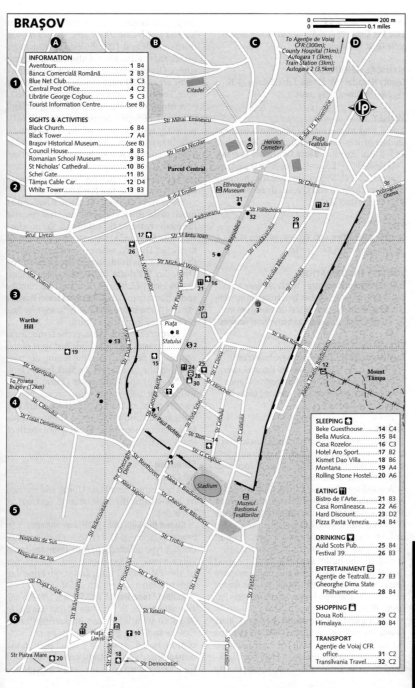

# BRAŞOV

| | |
|---|---|
| 0 | 200 m |
| 0 | 0.1 miles |

**INFORMATION**
| | |
|---|---|
| Aventours.............................. | **1** B4 |
| Banca Comercială Română.......... | **2** B3 |
| Blue Net Club.......................... | **3** C3 |
| Central Post Office.................... | **4** C2 |
| Librărie George Coşbuc.............. | **5** C3 |
| Tourist Information Centre.......... | (see 8) |

**SIGHTS & ACTIVITIES**
| | |
|---|---|
| Black Church........................... | **6** B4 |
| Black Tower............................ | **7** A4 |
| Braşov Historical Museum......... | (see 8) |
| Council House.......................... | **8** B3 |
| Romanian School Museum.......... | **9** B6 |
| St Nicholas' Cathedral.............. | **10** B6 |
| Schei Gate............................. | **11** B5 |
| Tâmpa Cable Car..................... | **12** D4 |
| White Tower........................... | **13** B3 |

To Agenţie de Voiaj
CFR (300m);
County Hospital (1km);
Autogara 1 (3km);
Train Station (3km);
Autogara 2 (3.5km)

Citadel

Str Mihai Eminescu

Str Iorga Nicolae

Heroes'
Cemetery

Piaţa
Teatrului

Parcul Central

B-dul Erollor

Ethnographic
Museum

Str Cherea

Str Sadoveanu

Str Dobrogeanu
Gherea

Şirul Livezii

Str Sfântu Ioan

Calea Poienii

Str Michael Weiss

Str Postăvarului

Str Nicolae Bălcescu

Str Castelului

Warthe
Hill

Str Piaţa Enescu

Str Julius Roper

Piaţa
Sfatului

Aleea Tiberiu Brediceanu

Mount
Tâmpa

To Poiana
Braşov (12km)

Str Stejeriş̧ului

Str George Barlţu

Str Cibinului

Str Hirscher

Str Traian Demetrescu

Str Poria Schei

Str Cerbului

Str Castelului

Str Paul Richter

Str Stonii

Str G Coşbuc

Str Gheorghe
Dima

Aleea T Brediceanu

Stadium

Muzeul
Bastionul
Ţesătorilor

Str Gheorghe
Beethoven

Aleea Saguna

Str Gheorghe Băiulescu

Str Brâncoveanu

Str Trotuş

Nisipulni de Sus

Nisipului de Jos

Str După Iniste

Str Prundului

Str L Arbore

Str Lacea

Str Retezat

Str Petofi

Str Curcanilor

Piaţa
Unirii

Str Vasile Saftu

Str Democraţiei

Str Piatra Mare

**SLEEPING**
| | |
|---|---|
| Beke Guesthouse......... | **14** C4 |
| Bella Musica............... | **15** B4 |
| Casa Rozelor.............. | **16** C3 |
| Hotel Aro Sport.......... | **17** B2 |
| Kismet Dao Villa......... | **18** B6 |
| Montana.................... | **19** A4 |
| Rolling Stone Hostel.... | **20** A6 |

**EATING**
| | |
|---|---|
| Bistro de l'Arte........... | **21** B3 |
| Casa Româneasca....... | **22** A6 |
| Hard Discount............ | **23** D2 |
| Pizza Pasta Venezia.... | **24** B4 |

**DRINKING**
| | |
|---|---|
| Auld Scots Pub........... | **25** B4 |
| Festival 39................. | **26** B3 |

**ENTERTAINMENT**
| | |
|---|---|
| Agenţie de Teatrală.... | **27** B3 |
| Gheorghe Dima State | |
| Philharmonic.......... | **28** B4 |

**SHOPPING**
| | |
|---|---|
| Doua Roti.................. | **29** C2 |
| Himalaya................... | **30** B4 |

**TRANSPORT**
| | |
|---|---|
| Agenţie de Voiaj CFR | |
| office..................... | **31** C2 |
| Transilvania Travel...... | **32** C2 |

ROMANIA

## INTERNET ACCESS
**Blue Net Club** ( ☎ 0740-839 449; Str Michael Weiss 26; per hr €0.50; ☯ 24hr)

## MEDICAL SERVICES
**County Hospital** ( ☎ 333 666; Calea Bucureşti 25-27; ☯ 24hr) Northwest of the centre.

## MONEY
You'll find numerous ATMs, banks and exchange offices on and around Str Republicii and B-dul Eroilor. **Banca Comercială Română**, (Piaţa Sfatului 14; ☯ 8.30am-5pm Mon-Fri, to 12.30pm Sat), charges 1.5% (US$5 minimum) for changing travellers cheques and gives cash advances on Visa or MasterCard.

## POST
**Central post office** ( ☎ 411 609; Str Iorga Nicolae 1; ☯ 7am-8pm Mon-Fri, 8am-1pm Sat)

## TOURIST INFORMATION
**Tourist information centre** ( ☎ 419 078; www.brasov city.ro; Piaţa Sfatului 30; ☯ 9am-5pm) In the gold city council building, the English-speaking staff can point you to tour services, offer free brochures and track down hotel vacancies.

## TRAVEL AGENCIES
**Aventours** ( ☎ 472 718; www.discoveromania.ro; Str Paul Richter 1; ☯ 10am-3pm Mon-Fri) This small agency, led by English-speaking guides, offers great tailor-made tours (particularly mountain-based ones) and oodles of information on the area.

## Sights
Though many of the attractions (including a handful not mentioned here) hardly compete with Bucharest's, Braşov's sense of medieval glory still stands strong.

A good starting point for a walk is central **Piaţa Stafalui**, where witches were once burned and prisoners tortured in the gold **Council House** (Casa Sfatului), which dates from 1420; listen closely when passing (we hear a caretaker quit after hearing 'ghostly screams' from the tower at night). The building also houses the good tourist information centre and unmemorable **Braşov Historical Museum** ( ☎ 472 350; adult/student €0.85/0.57; ☯ 10am-6pm Tue-Sun Jun-Sep, 9am-5pm Tue-Sun Oct-May).

Peeking up from the south, the Gothic **Black Church** (Biserica Neagră; adult/child €1/0.50; ☯ 10am-5pm Mon-Sat, mass at 10am Sun), built between 1384 and 1477, gained its name after a 1689 fire blackened its walls. Inside the church (supposedly

the largest Gothic place of worship between Vienna and Istanbul) see apse statues moved from outside and 120 fabulous Turkish rugs, merchants' gifts after Ottoman shopping sprees. Organ recitals on the 4000-pipe instrument are usually held in July and August, at 6pm Tuesday, Thursday and Saturday (4 lei).

A couple of blocks east, cobblestone **Str Sforii** is one of Europe's narrowest 'streets', with perfectly framed views of the 'Hollywood'-style Braşov sign that looks over town from Mt Tâmpa. To reach it, take the **Tâmpa cable car** (Telecabina; ☎ 478 657; one-way/return €0.90/1.80; ☯ 9.30am-5pm Tue-Sun), well worth it for the stunning views of town and access to a few hiking trails.

From the cable-car station, you'll notice that much of the town's original walls still encircle the town centre. At the south end, the neoclassical **Schei Gate** (1828) separated the centre with the Schei District, where – in Saxon days – the Romanians lived. Stop by the black-spired Orthodox **St Nicholas' Cathedral** (St Nicolae din Scheii; ☯ 6am-9pm), which dates from the 14th century and is home to the small **Romanian School Museum** ( ☎ 511 411; adult/student €0.90/0.60; ☯ 9am-5pm Tue-Sun). It's accessed from Piaţa Unirii.

Leave time to look out over the centre from the two towers on the hillside just west of the centre – it's popular when the setting sun puts a golden hue on Braşov; the **Black Tower** (Turnul Neagru) and **White Tower** (Turnul Alba), which are actually rather white, are reached on a lovely promenade alongside the western city walls and a rushing stream. A sideroad leads to the promenade from about 200m south of the Black Church.

## Sleeping
### HOSTELS
Both hostels are near Piaţa Unirii, and reached by bus 4 from the train station (get out at last stop).

**Kismet Dao Villa** ( ☎ 514 296; www.kismetdao.ro; Str Democratiei 2B; dm €10-11, d €24) Set up in a rather dorm-y type building, the four-floor, six-room villa is a good budget choice with video games on the TV, playful staff, and good-value day trips to Bran and area attractions.

**Rolling Stone Hostel** ( ☎ 513 965, 0744-876 970; www.rollingstone.ro; Str Piatra Mare 2A; dm/r from €10/28; ☒ ) Run by a long-time Braşov institution (Maria and Grig Bolea), the Stone is a welcoming hostel spot, with a small pool in the outside courtyard. Some guests have a hard time keeping up with the staff's energy. It's homy and scenic, but skip the overpriced tours.

### GUESTHOUSES & HOTELS

**Hotel Aro Sport** ( ☎ 478 800; Str Sfântu Ioan 3; s/d €11/16) Here's what Eastern Europe travel used to be about – old boxy rooms, a sink in the corner, a shower down the hall. It's quite clean though and the price is right. There's no breakfast.

**Beke Guesthouse** ( ☎ 511 997; Str Cerbului 32; r €11-14) Ever homy, this lovely Hungarian-speaking couple runs a handful of simple rooms (with shared bath) that look over a vine-covered courtyard. Often they'll bring by a jug of homemade wine. No breakfast, no sign, no English.

**Montana** ( ☎ 0723 614 534; Calea Poienii; s €42-44, d €52-54) This super Brady Bunch–style Kermit-green six-room hillside guesthouse is up the hill from the White Tower. It has slanted cedar roofs and seriously pastel room themes. Pay €2 more for rooms with fridge and balcony.

**Bella Musica** ( ☎ 477 956; www.bellamusica.ro; Piaţa Sfatului 19; s/d €63/77; ☒ ▢ ) Opened in 2005, the terrific 22-room Musica has very stylish rooms with soft lighting, textured orange walls and old-style wood desks to write poems on.

**Casa Rozelor** ( ☎ 475 212; www.casarozelor.ro; Str Michael Weiss 20; r €88; ▢ ) In a central back alley, this lovely German-run three-room guest-house mixes up themes (eg a loft with a red-leather sofa facing a 15th-century brick wall). There are no TVs.

### Eating

**Hard Discount** (Str Nicolae Bălcescu; ☒ 24hr) Fully stocked supermarket next to the indoor-outdoor fruit and vegetable market.

**Pizza Pasta Venezia** ( ☎ 470 511; Str Hirscher 2; pastas & pizzas from €2.50; ☒ 11am-midnight or 1am) Wall-sized Venetian paintings and soft lighting – and cheaper prices – helps this cosy Italian restaurant fill before its similar-themed neighbours.

**Bistro de l'Arte** ( ☎ 0722 219 980; Piaţa Enescu 11; mains €2.50-4.50; ☒ 9am-1am Mon-Sat, noon-midnight Sun) In the bottom of a cosy 15th-century building, the Bistro serves great meals – sandwiches, fish *filets*, breakfasts. There's excellent loose teas and wi-fi access.

**Casa Româneasca** (Piaţa Unirii; mains €3-6; ☒ noon-midnight) Deep in the Schei district, away from trolling tourists, this *casa* serves tasty *sarma-lute cu mamaliguta* (boiled beef rolled with vegetables and cabbage).

### Drinking

**Auld Scots Pub** ( ☎ 470 183; Str Hirscher 10; ☒ 11am-2am) Capturing local imagination, the kilts and Connery on the walls of this inviting bar can be forgiven because of its tasteful sitting areas, three-board dart room and far better-than-average pub fare.

**Festival 39** ( ☎ 478 664; Str Mureşenilor 23; ☒ 10-1am) Cosy dark-lit room with happy locals filling the tables and bars when other bars are empty.

### Entertainment

The **Gheorghe Dima State Philharmonic** ( ☎ 473 058; www.sfbv.home.ro; Str Hirscher 10) performs mainly between September and May. Tickets can be purchased at the **Agenţie de Teatrală** ( ☎ 471 889; Str Republicii 4; ☒ 10am-5pm Tue-Fri, to 2pm Sat).

### Shopping

**Himalaya** ( ☎ 477 855; www.himalaya.ro; Piaţa Sfatului 17; ☒ 10am-7pm Mon-Fri, to 2pm Sat) A great sports store with ski and hiking boots, sleeping bags, rock-climbing gear. Staff double as guides.

**Doua Roti** ( ☎ 0740 125 984; Str Nicolae Bălcescu 55; ☒ 8.30am-5pm Mon-Fri, 9am-1pm Sat) Bike shop with used bikes.

### Getting There & Around
#### BUS

Maxitaxis and microbuses are the best way to reach places near Braşov, including Bran, Râşnov and Sinaia. Otherwise it's generally better to go by train.

The most accessible station is **Autogară 1** ( ☎ 427 267), next to the train station (reached by bus 4 from the centre), a ramshackle lot with a booming maxitaxi business (hourly jobs go to-and-fro on the Târgu Mureş–Sighişoara–Braşov–Buşteni–Bucharest route) and some long-distance buses. From 6am to 7.30pm maxitaxis leave every half-hour for Bucharest (€5.25, 2½ hours), stopping in Buşteni and Sinaia. About four or five maxitaxis leave for Sibiu (€3.90, 2½ hours), stopping in Făgăraş town, and Iaşi (€10). Bus 4 reaches the centre from the train station (pre-buy ticket). From the centre, hail a bus at the corner of Str Nicolae Bălcescu and Str Gherea.

**Autogară 2** (Bartolomeu; ☎ 426 332; Str Avram Iancu 114), a kilometre west of the train station, sends half-hourly buses to Râşnov (€0.45, 25 minutes) and Bran (€0.75, 40 minutes) from roughly 6.30am to 11.30pm. A dozen daily buses go to Zărneşti (€0.75, one hour), less

ROMANIA

on weekends. Take bus 12 to/from the centre (it stops at the roundabout just north of the station).

### CAR & MOTORCYCLE

Car-rental rates are more expensive than in Bucharest, Sibiu or Cluj. **Transilvania Travel** ( ☎ 477 623; www.transilvaniatravel.com; Str Republicii 62; ⏱ 9am-5pm Mon-Fri, to 1pm Sat) rents cars from €45 daily; prices will drop by €10 daily if you rent for a week or more.

### TAXI

Taxi drivers seem pretty honest in Braşov. A couple of good agencies include **Martax** ( ☎ 313 040) and **Tod** ( ☎ 321 111). Taking a taxi to the 'three castles' in Bran, Râşnov and Sinaia costs about €70.

### TRAIN

Advance tickets are sold at the **Agenţie de Voiaj CFR office** ( ☎ 477 015; Str 15 de Noiembre 43; ⏱ 8am-7.30pm Mon-Fri).

Daily domestic train service includes the following (prices are for second-class seats on rapid trains): at least hourly to Bucharest (€7.50, 2½ hours), a dozen to Sighişoara (€6.50, 2½ hours), nine to Sibiu (€7, 2¾ hours), five to Cluj-Napoca (€11.70, six hours), one to Iaşi (€10.50, 8½ hours).

International links include three daily trains to Budapest (€40/70 seat/sleeper, 14 hours), two to Vienna (€75/100, 18 hours) and also one daily train to Prague (21 hours) and Istanbul (19 hours).

The **left-luggage office** (per day small/big bag €0.60/1.80; ⏱ 24hr) is located in the underpass that leads out from the tracks.

## AROUND BRAŞOV
### Bran & Râsnov
☎ 0268

No Dracula or vampires await, and in fact Vlad Ţepeş supposedly only dropped by once in the 15th century, but it's hard to skip so-called 'Dracula's castle', 30km south of Braşov. The (surprisingly) famous **Bran Castle** ( ☎ 238 332; www.brancastlemuseum.ro; adult/students & child €3/1.50; ⏱ 9am-6pm Tue-Sun, noon-6pm Mon May-Sep, 9am-4pm Tue-Sun) dates from 1378. At first look, the 60m castle, set on a rocky outcrop between facing hills, certainly seems vampirific, but inside – elbowing past tour groups – it's a little bit of an anticlimax. Queen Marie made many summer retreats here in the 1920s, highlighted with exhibits inside.

Râsnov, 12km toward Braşov, doubles the castle intake with its own appealing offer. The ruins of the 13th-century **Râsnov fortress** (Cetatea Râsnov; ☎ 230 255; adult/child €2.70/1.50; ⏱ 9am-8pm May-Oct, to 6pm Nov-Apr). From the central square, steps lead up the hill where inclined alleys and a museum await.

### SLEEPING

Generally Bran is a less appealing base than Braşov or other villages in the area. **Antrec** ( ☎ 236 340, 0788-411 450; www.antrec.ro; Str Principală 509; ⏱ 9am-5pm Mon-Fri, to 1pm Sat) arranges private accommodation in the area. Cabana Bran

---

**DRACULA VS VLAD!**

We'll never know who'd win in a fight, but at least here's a comparison between the very-real Vlad Ţepeş (1431–76) and the very-fake wing-capable Dracula.

**Lived in Transylvania?**
Drac: Yes, Bram Stoker puts his home near Bistriţa, northeast of Cluj-Napoca.
Vlad: No, his real home is south of the Carpathians in Poienari, Wallachia.

**Fearful feasts?**
Drac: Yes, he ate people.
Vlad: Yes, he ate steaks while Turks wriggled on skin-piercing rectum-to-underarm stakes.

**Bi-curious?**
Drac: Yes! The giveaway is when the fanged fluid-changer stops female demons from devouring Jonathan Harker and cries out 'this man belongs to me!' – indeed.
Vlad: Probably (note his handle-bar moustache).

**How did he die?**
Drac: Wooden stake through the heart, followed by decapitation.
Vlad: No-one's sure, may have died in battle or assassinated by rival nobles; eventually Turks decapitated his body though!

Castel, just 600m from the castle, was closed for renovation at research time.

**Vila Bran** ( ☎ 236 866; www.vilabran.ro; Str Principală 238; r €28-40) This 58-room five-building complex is a bit touristy – there are three restaurants, a zip line (flying fox) over a creek, an indoor BB court – but the view of the hills is worth it.

**Casa Contelui** ( ☎ 0723-005 378; www.casacontelui.ro; Str Bălcescu 16; r with shared/private bathroom €23/28) Green signs from Râsnov centre point to this lovely fenced-off six-room farmhouse-guesthouse with an English-speaking owner.

### GETTING THERE & AWAY

Buses marked 'Bran-Moeciu' (€0.70, one hour) depart every half-hour from Braşov's Autogară 2. Return buses to Braşov leave Bran every half-hour from roughly 7am to 6pm in winter, 7am to 10pm in summer. All buses to Braşov stop each way at Râsnov.

From Bran there are about a dozen buses daily to Zărneşti (€0.70, 40 minutes).

## Poiana Braşov

Braşov's skiers prefer this **mountain** (www.poiana -brasov.ro), 14km from Braşov, over Sinaia's, reached by an easy bus trip. Skis can be rented for €12, an all-day pass is about €17. There are good intermediate runs, and a couple of advanced slopes, plus hiking trails in summer.

**Cabana Cristianul Mare** ( ☎ 0741 110 092; r with shared bathroom per person €10, d with private bathroom €34), just down from the top of the lift, is a super place to kick back over berry tea or beer; rooms are available.

Bus 20 leaves from B-dul Eroilor in front of the County Library in Braşov every half-hour for Poiana Braşov (€0.75), where it's a 20-minute walk to the slopes.

## Zărneşti

☎ 0268

This windswept and rather down-and-out town at the edge of the lovely, rugged Piatra Craiului National Park gives off a bit of a *Twilight Zone* vibe. If only Nicole Kidman had hung around a little – or at all – when she was a couple of kilometres away filming *Cold Mountain*. Locals are particularly nice, and Zărneşti provides an excellent springboard to nearby hikes.

### ORIENTATION & INFORMATION

Buses stop at a roundabout, near the post office and about 100m past the city hall along

Str Metropolit... is about 1km ...

The helpful... ( ☎ 223 165; ww... 6pm Mon-Fri), abo... (west) from th... guides (from €...

### HIKING

The 14,800-he.... Piatra Craiului and its twin-peaked Piatra Mică (Stone of the Prince; no jokes) rise southwest of town. Day-hike loops are an option. Follow the blue vertical-stripe signs along the road south of town, then the yellow vertical-stripe signs back, for a four- or five-hour trip that goes through the gorge where Jude Law got shot in *Cold Mountain*. More difficult hikes scale the peaks from the back (north) side; ask at the park office.

### SLEEPING

**Cabana Gura Raului** ( ☎ 0722-592 375; s/d €8.50/17) A bit wobbly, but set at the outset of Zărneşti Canyon at the end of town (follow Str Raului 500m past the national park office), this fading cabana offers 17 boxy rooms and food.

**Pensuine Fabius** ( ☎ 0722-523 199; Str Dr Senchea 7; r €19) Run by a lovely family (which includes *two* priests), the five-room Fab, which is in town, offers semirustic rooms with TV and private bath. It's about 75m south from the bus stop.

### GETTING THERE & AWAY

There are 14 buses leaving weekdays to Autogară 2 in Braşov (€0.70, one hour), and about half that at weekends. About five or six daily buses head to Bran (€0.70, 40 minutes).

By rail, five daily trains link Braşov with Zărneşti (€0.80, 50 minutes), stopping at Râsnov on the way.

## SIGHIŞOARA

☎ 0265 / pop 32,300

He was born here. And for many visitors to this dreamy, medieval citadel town – with half-a-millennium-old townhouses of bright colours overlooking hilly cobbled streets and church bells that clang in the early hours – seeing where Dracula made his first steps is enough to justify a quick drop-by. But it's hardly the end of Sighişoara (Schässburg in German, Segesvár in Hungarian). Cute little museums uncover some colourful local history. The low hills that flank the town lead to pastures and forests that are home to traditional Saxon villages. Yes, bus

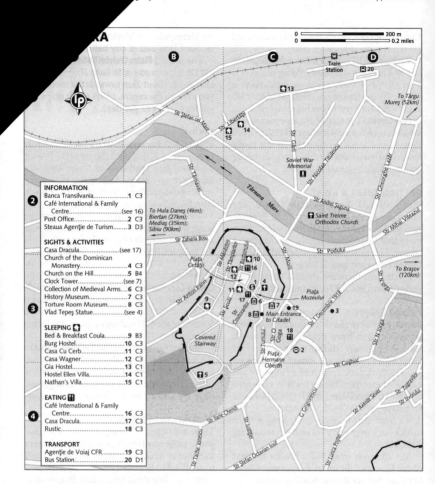

tours come in'n'out in summer, and even some backpackers feel one day's enough – but some days are better than others.

Good day-trips from here include Saxon Land towns (p648) or a day (or two) in the half-Hungarian town of Târgu Mureş (p652).

## Information
### INTERNET ACCESS
**Café International & Family Centre** (Piaţa Cetăţii 8; per hr €0.60;  8am-8pm Mon-Sat Jun-Sep, 1-7pm Mon-Sat Oct-May) Christian pop accompanies your web-surf board.

### MONEY
There are numerous exchange offices lining the city's main street, Str 1 Decembrie 1918.

Banca Transilvania has a 24-hour ATM in the citadel; between Piaţa Cetăţii and Muzeulul.

### POST
**Post office** (Str 1 Decembrie 1918, 17;  7am-8pm Mon-Fri) In a funny yellow-panel building.

### TRAVEL AGENCIES
Sighişoara was hoping to finally open a tourist information centre at research time.
**Steaua Agenţie de Turism** ( 772 499; Str 1 Decembrie 1918, 10;  9.30am-4pm Mon-Fri) Can find private accommodation (€10 per person per night) in the residential area northwest of the citadel.
**Café International & Family Centre** ( 777 844; Piaţa Cetăţii 8;  8am-8pm Mon-Sat Jun-Sep) Volunteer staff of this nonprofit agency double as a tourist office in

**COMBO TICKET**

It's not made clear, but you can visit the History Museum, the medieval arms collection, and the Torture Room Museum for a combo ticket price of €2.15 (about the same price as the student discounts for all three).

summer (only); they arrange walking tours, rent bikes, and can point you to area hikes.

## Sights

Most of Sighişoara's sights are clustered in the compact old town – the delightful medieval **citadel** – perched on a hillock and fortified with a 14th-century wall, to which 14 towers and five artillery bastions were later added. Today the citadel, which is on the Unesco World Heritage list, retains just nine of its original towers (named for the guilds in charge of keeping them up) and two of its bastions.

Entering the citadel, you pass under the massive **clock tower** (Turnul cu Ceas), which dates from 1280. Inside is the great little **History Museum** (☎ 771 108; Piaţa Muzeului 1; adult/child €1.50/1.10; ⏰ 10am-6pm Mon, 9am-6.30pm Tue-Fri, 9am-4.30pm Sat & Sun mid-May–mid-Sep, 9am-3.30pm Tue-Fri, 10am-3.30pm Sat & Sun mid-Sep–mid-May), with small rooms that tell Sigh's tale and are off the steps that wind up to the 7th-floor look-out above the clock for superb panoramic views.

Under the clock tower on the right (if heading out of the old town) is the small, dark **Torture Room Museum** (admission €0.60; ⏰ same as History Museum), which shows how fingers were smashed and prisoners burned with coals. If it's closed, ask at the medieval arms collection for entry.

Towards Piaţa Cetăţii on the left, the small **Collection of Medieval Arms** (adult/student €0.90/0.60; ⏰ same as History Museum) has four rooms devoted to medieval helmets, shields, crossbows and maces.

Hidden away behind the 15th-century **Church of the Dominican Monastery** (Biserica Mănăstirii), across from the museum, is a **Vlad Ţepeş statue**, showing the legend with his trademark circa-1981 porno moustache.

Speaking of, continuing west towards Piaţa Cetăţii, you come to the renovated **Casa Dracula** (now a restaurant; see p648), in which Vlad Ţepeş reputedly lived until the age of four.

The quiet, miniscule **Piaţa Cetăţii** is the heart of old Sighişoara. It was here that markets and public executions were held.

From the square, turn left up Str Şcolii to the 172 steps of the **covered stairway** (scara acoperit), to the 1345 Gothic **Church on the Hill** (Biserica din Deal; Bergkirche; ⏰ mid-Apr–Oct), a 429m Lutheran church with an atmospheric German cemetery just behind.

## Sleeping

### BUDGET

**Burg Hostel** (☎ 778 489; www.ibz.ro; Str Bastionului 4-6; dm/s/d €7.25/11.50/17.25) Perhaps more focused on its basement lounge (rock music, internet) and restaurant, this very clean, slightly sterile hostel has functional rooms of various bed counts – all with their own private bathroom. Breakfast is €2.80.

**Gia Hostel** (☎ 772 486; giahouse@myx.net; Str Libertăţii 41; dm from €7, r €18-23; 💻) It backs onto the railway line in a slightly dodgy area (about a 15-minute walk to the citadel) and the rooms are a bit of a rush job, but the nine-room hostel has lots of good services (bike rental, car rental for €35 per day, and an hour's free internet).

**Nathan's Villa** (☎ 772 546; www.nathansvilla.com; Str Libertăţii 8; dm/d €8/20) This traditionally popular choice (with free laundry and a bar) stays open from April to November only. It's 200m west of the train station.

**Hostel Ellen Villa** (☎ 776 402; www.elenvillahostel.com; Str Libertăţii 10; dm/r €10/20) This homy place, next to Nathan's, feels more guesthouse-y.

### MIDRANGE

**Casa Cu Cerb** (Stag House; ☎ 777 349; Str Şcolii 1; s €35, d €40-50; ⊠) First thing you see walking into this all-restored 1693 building is Prince Charles' mug – he stayed here a few days in 2002. It's a good choice, with cast-iron bed frames and rattan rugs by the TV sitting area. No breakfast.

**Casa Wagner** (☎ 506 014; www.casa-wagner.com; Piaţa Cetăţii 7; s €40, d €45-50, ste €70) This 22-room beauty on the main square has a mix of rooms; singles

**AUTHOR'S CHOICE**

**Bed & Breakfast Coula** (☎ 777 907; Str Tâmplarilor 40; r €15) Those looking for a homy budget base in the citadel will enjoy this unsigned 400-year-old home, run by an English-speaking family who can help arrange Saxon church trips and rent you bikes. There are six rooms (only one's in use in winter).

are a bit cramped, but some of the others sprawl. The ground-floor restaurant is quite good.

## Eating

**Café International & Family Centre** ( ☎ 777 844; Piaţa Cetăţii 8; mains €2-3.50; 🕒 8am-8pm Mon-Sat Jun-Sep, 10am-6pm Mon-Sat Oct-May) This two-room café, with chairs in the square, is the perfect lunch spot, with daily-made mostly vegetarian fare, including quiches or lasagne, plus desserts.

**Rustic** (Str Decembrie 1, 7; mains €3-10; 🕒 8am-midnight) A wood-and-brick 'man's man' bar-restaurant down from the citadel; eggs served all day, plus the usual grilled meats.

**Casa Dracula** ( ☎ 771 596; Str Cositorarilor 5; mains €4.50-8.50; 🕒 10am-midnight) The food can't compete with Casa Wagner's restaurant (p647), but this three-room candle-lit restaurant is too tempting to pass by – juicy meats in Dracula's first home. It's OK to come for a red wine only.

## Getting There & Away

About a dozen trains connect Sighişoara with Braşov (€3 to €8, two hours), nine of which go on to Bucharest (€8 to €12, 4½ hours). Five daily trains go to Cluj-Napoca (€7.40 to €10, 3½ hours). You'll need to change trains in Mediaş to reach Sibiu (€2.75, 2½ hours), but these are timed for easy transfers. Three daily trains go to Budapest (€38, nine hours); the night one has a sleeper (from €49). Buy tickets at the **train station** ( ☎ 771 886), or at the central **Agenţie de Voiaj CFR** ( ☎ 771 820; Str O Goga 6A; 🕒 8am-3pm Mon-Fri).

Next to the train station on Str Libertăţii, the **bus station** ( ☎ 771 260) sends buses of various size and colour to Budapest (€20, eight hours, two weekly), Făgăraş (€3.50, three hours, one daily), Sibiu (€3.50, 2½ hours, five daily). Maxitaxis pass by every couple of hours for Braşov.

## SAXON LAND

Sighişoara, Sibiu and Braşov envelop the rolling hills that make up the heart of dozens of Saxon villages. These yester-century villages are generally dotted with impressive fortified churches dating from the 12th century. Some can be accessed by rather rough dirt roads. Even just a kilometre or two off the main highway towards Braşov or Sibiu opens up a world where horse carriages and walking is generally the only way anyone gets around, and a car – any car – gets wide stares.

Popular destinations include **Biertan** (28km southwest of Sighişoara) and **Viscri** (about 40km east). The latter misses some of the

tour buses, as the road south of Buneşti is quite rough. Call **Carolina Fernolend** ( ☎ 0740 145 397) to arrange private accommodation in Viscri (about €18 to €20 per person including meals) and a look at the church.

Bus service is infrequent and unreliable. Renting a car is cheapest from Sibiu (p651) but Gia Hostel rents a car from Sighişoara, or you can arrange a taxi.

## SIBIU

☎ 0269 / pop 154,890

Of the Transylvanian Saxon towns, Sibiu has always been the most important – the capital, the culturally most active – but has trailed Sighişoara, Braşov and Cluj in terms of travel appeal. Things look to change, as 2007 marks Sibiu as an EU-designated 'Capital of Culture' (along with Luxembourg), and year-long events will be putting Sibiu on the map for more visitors. The town is certainly enchanting enough on its own – with a just-scrubbed centre, newly cobblestoned squares and pedestrian malls – and the unique 'eye-lid' rooftop windows looking over buildings painted in pastels.

Founded in the 12th century on the site of the former Roman village of Cibinium, Sibiu (Hermannstadt to the German Saxons, Nagyszében to Hungarians) served as the seat of the Austrian governors of Transylvania under the Habsburgs from 1703 to 1791, and again from 1849 to 1867.

## Orientation

The adjacent bus and train stations are near the centre of town. Exit the station and stroll up Str General Magheru four blocks to Piaţa Mare, the historic centre.

## Information

### BOOKSHOPS

**Librăria Humanitas** ( ☎ 211 434; Str Nicolae Bălcescu 16; 🕒 10am-7pm Mon-Fri, 11am-5pm Sat) Good map selection.

### EMERGENCY

**Salvamont** ( ☎ 216 477, 0745-140 144; Str Nicolae Bălcescu 9; 🕒 8am-4pm Mon-Fri) Provides 24-hour mountain-rescue service.

### INTERNET ACCESS

**Click** (Str Ocnei 11; per hr €0.45; 🕒 9-2am Mon-Fri, 10-2am Sat, 2pm-2am Sun)

**Schuponet** (Str Dr I Lupas 21; per hr €0.45; 🕒 24hr)

## LEFT LUGGAGE
**Train Station** (Piaţa 1 Decembrie 1918; per day €0.90; ⏲ 24 hr)

## MONEY
ATMs are located all over the centre as well as in most hotels.

**Banca Comercială Română** (Str Nicolae Bălcescu 11; ⏲ 8.30am-5.30pm Mon-Fri, to 12.30pm Sat) Changes travellers cheques and gives cash advances.

## POST
**Central post office** (Str Mitropoliei 14; ⏲ 7am-8pm Mon-Fri, 8am-1pm Sat)

## TOURIST INFORMATION & TRAVEL AGENCIES
**Casa Luxemburg** ( ☎ 216 854; www.kultours.ro; Piaţa Mică 16; ⏲ 9am-9pm) Travel agent offering loads of city tours (€6 to €15) and day trips (€25 to €50); also has a useful free Sibiu map.

**Tourist Information Centre** ( ☎ 208 913; www.sibiu .ro; Piaţa Mare 2; ⏲ 9am-5pm Mon-Sat, 10am-1pm Sun) A pioneer in self-organisation, this superb can-do office is slated to take over a primo spot on the ground floor of the new city hall for 2007. Staff help with bus schedules, and book accommodation.

## Sights
### CENTRE
The expansive Piaţa Mare was the very centre of the old walled city. A good start for exploring the city is to climb to the top of the former **Turnul Sfatului** (Council Tower; 1588; admission €0.30; ⏲ 10am-6pm), which links Piaţa Mare with its smaller sister square, Piaţa Mică.

The **Brukenthal Museum** ( ☎ 217 691; Piaţa Mare 4-5; adult/child €1.80/0.90; ⏲ 10am-5pm Tue-Sun) is the oldest and likely finest art gallery in Romania. Founded in 1817, the museum is in the baroque palace (1785) of Baron Samuel Brukenthal (1721–1803), former Austrian governor. There are excellent collections of 16th- and 17th-century Flemish, Italian, Dutch and Austrian paintings, including a giant painting of Sibiu from 1808.

The square's most impressive building, however, is the **Banca Agricola** (Piaţa Mare 2), which now houses the town hall. Just west of here is the lovely Primăria Municipiului (1470), now the **City History Museum** (Str Mitropoliei 2), which was closed at research time but should re-open by mid-2007.

Nearby, on Piaţa Huet, is the Gothic **Biserica Evanghelică** (Evangelical Church; ⏲ 9am-3pm Mon-Fri, 10am-4pm Sat, 11am-4pm Sun), which was built from 1300 to 1520, and has a great five-pointed tower that's visible from afar. Don't miss the four magnificent baroque funerary monuments on the upper nave on the north wall, and the 1772 organ with 6002 pipes (it's Romania's largest). The tomb of Mihnea Vodă cel Rău (Prince Mihnea the Bad), son of Vlad Ţepeş, is in the closed-off section behind the organ (ask for entry). This prince was murdered in front of the church in 1510. You can climb the **church tower** (admission €0.90); ask for entry at Casa Luxemburg (left).

North of the centre is the interesting lower town, reached from under the photogenic **Iron Bridge** (1859) facing Piaţa Mică.

Also on Piaţa Mică, the **Pharmaceutical Museum** ( ☎ 218 191; adult/child €1.20/0.60; ⏲ 10am-6pm Tue-Sun) is a three-room collection packed with pills and powders and scary medical instruments.

It's worth walking along the 16th-century **city walls** and watchtowers, accessible a few blocks southeast of Piaţa Mare, along Str Cetăţii.

### OUTSIDE THE CENTRE
Sibiu's top highlight is some 5km from the centre. The large **Museum of Traditional Folk Civilization** (Muzeul Civilizaţiei Populare Tradiţionale Astra; ☎ 242 599; Calea Răşinarilor 14; adult/child €3.60/1.80; ⏲ 10am-6pm Tue-Sun, to 8pm depending on the weather), is a sprawling open-air museum with 120 traditional dwellings, mills and churches brought from around the country. There's a **restaurant** with creek-side bench seats. Trolleybus 1 from the train station goes there (get off at the last stop and keep walking under 1km, or take the hourly Răşinari tram). A taxi is about €3 one way.

## Sleeping
### BUDGET
**Old Town Hostel** ( ☎ 216 445; www.hostelsibiu.ro; Piţa Mică 26; dm/d €12/27) In a 450-year-old building

---

**AUTHOR'S CHOICE**

**Pensiunea Ela** ( ☎ 215 197; www.hotel-ela .as.ro; Str Nová 43; s/d €29/38) One of Sibiu's best bets, this Lower Town guesthouse has just nine rooms, all clean and comfy, if a little small. The owners care for every detail (and you're asked to remove your shoes in the room). The €4.50 breakfast is a bit disappointing. Laundry service is available.

**ROMANIA**

with spacious dorms looking over a main square, this simple hostel actually boasts the most atmospheric location in Sibiu. Dorms have more light than the private room. There's no breakfast, but there is a kitchen. Laundry service costs €2.

**Hotel Halemadero** ( ☎ 212 509, Str Măsarilor 10; d/tr €24/32) Friendly, family-run four-room deal

in a slightly scrappy patch of Lower Town. Rooms are old-school, with TV, shared bathroom and three or four beds. The family runs a beery patio café. There's no breakfast.

**Hotel Podul Minciunilor** ( ☎ 217 259; www.hotel-ela .as.ro; Str Azilului 1; d/tr €27/36) Located half a block from Liar's Bridge in Lower Town, this six-room guest house is a bit cuter from outside

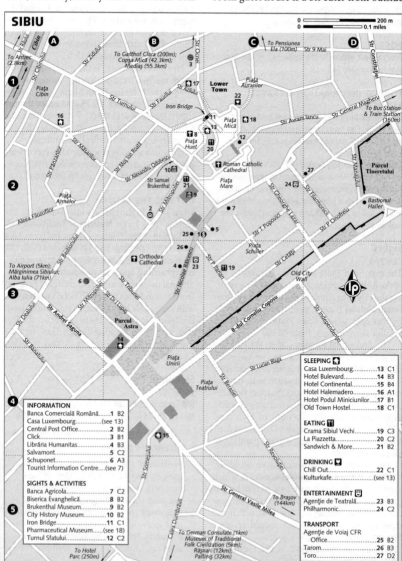

**SIBIU**

0 ————— 200 m
0 ————— 0.1 miles

than in, but has basic clean rooms with TVs. No breakfast.

**Casa Luxemburg** ( ☎ 216 854; www.kultours.ro; Piaţa Mică 16; s/d/tr €33/57/77) It's a little dormy, but this six-room job overlooks the Evangelical Church and Piaţa Mică.

### MIDRANGE

Unfortunately much of the hotel boom is on the highway outside town. A few other hotels in the centre were in the works, or under renovation, at research time.

**Gasthof Clara** ( ☎ 222 914; www.gastofclara.rom; s/d €45/56) It's on unappealing, dusty street, but that evaporates once inside this cheerful six-room guesthouse with a terrace restaurant.

**Hotel Parc** ( ☎ 424 455; www.hotelparcsibiu.ro; Str Şcoala de Înot 1-3; s/d €58/73; 🗱 🖳 ) This former grey blob 1km southwest of the centre went and did itself up. It has a fresh gold exterior, with 59 fully modern, if slightly unexciting, interiors.

**Hotel Continental** ( ☎ 218 100; www.continentalhotels .ro; Calea Dumbrăvii 2-4; s/d €56/77; 🗱 🗱 ) Grey grey grey on the outside, this 13-floor, 182-room hotel is plain but quite well kept inside.

## Eating

**Sandwich & More** (Str Samuel Brukenthal; sandwiches €1; 🕑 8am-8pm Mon-Sat) This window spot serves veggie sandwiches, and Asian-style pastas – by far Sibiu's best fast-food option.

**Crama Sibiul Vechi** (Str Ilarian; mains €2.50-6; 🕑 noon-midnight) This popular, evocative brick-cellar spot off the main crawl reels in locals for its tasty Transylvanian armoury of muttons, sausages, beefs and fish. There's live music most nights.

**La Piazzetta** ( ☎ 230 879; Piaţa Mică 15; pizza & pasta €3-6) This square pizza shop is livelier than most, with smoking couples and babies eating pizza at red-chequered tables.

## Drinking

Piaţa Mică is the drinking headquarters.

**Kulturkafe** (Piaţa Mică 16; 🕑 10am-3am Mon-Fri, 1pm-3am Sat, 3am-3pm Sun) Good table spots on the square, slightly more adult-like inside.

**Chill Out** (Piaţa Mică 23; 🕑 10am-2am) Local students hightail it to this fun, loud, enigmatic spot with a well-lit room and a dark one, where themed nights and DJs rule the night.

## Entertainment

Sibiu's International Astra Film Festival is held in May.

**Agenţie de Teatrală** ( ☎ 217 575; Str Nicolae Bălcescu 17; 🕑 10am-5pm Mon-Fr, 11am-3pm Sat) Tickets for major events are sold here.

**Philharmonic** ( ☎ 210 264; Str Filarmonicii 2) A big cultural player since 1949.

## Getting There & Around

### AIR

**Sibiu airport** ( ☎ 229 161; Sos Alba Iulia 73) is 5km west of the centre. **Tarom** ( ☎ 211 157; Str Nicolae Bălcescu 10; 🕑 9am-12.30pm, 1.30-5pm Mon-Fri) has three weekly flights to Bucharest (€60 to €100 one-way), daily service to Munich (€250) and five weekly to Vienna (€300). Trolleybus 8 runs between the airport and the train station.

**Carpatair** ( ☎ 229 161; www.carpatair.com), which has an office at the airport, flies to Germany and Italy via Timişoara.

### BUS

The **bus station** ( ☎ 217 757; Piaţa 1 Decembrie 1918) is located opposite the train station. Daily bus and maxitaxi service includes 13 to Braşov (€4.50, 2½ hours), four or five services to Bucharest (€8.50, 5½ hours), nine to Cluj-Napoca (€6, 3½ hours), four to Sighişoara (€3.50 lei, two hours), as well as two to Timişoara (€9, six hours).

### CAR & MOTORCYCLE

For a cheap rental option try **Toro** ( ☎ 232 237, 0745-425 441; Str Filarmonicii 5; 🕑 8am-4pm Mon-Fri, to 1pm Sat), which has Dacias to rent from €30 to €38 per day.

### TAXI

To call a taxi dial ☎ 953.

---

**WORTH THE TRIP**

About 20km west of Sibiu, and a serious world away, **Mioritica** ( ☎ 0740-175 287; Sibiel village; r from €15; 🖳 ) is 'paradise' to Sorian, the English- and German-speaking owner of this remarkable streamside four-room guesthouse. Three bridges go over the roaring stream, and a garden includes exhibits of found objects that Sorian, a local history teacher, rescues from the ages. Meals are provided, and they can point you to hiking trails, nearby villages, and an icon museum in town. It's hard to leave. Follow the stream towards the hills, west of the centre.

**TRAIN**

Sibiu lies at an awkward rail junction; sometimes you'll need to change trains. But there are three daily direct trains to Braşov (€6.75, 2½ hours), three to Bucharest (€14, five hours), Timişoara (€14, five hours). Buy tickets at the **Agenţie de Voiaj CFR office** ( ☎ 216 441; Str Nicolae Bălcescu 6; ☻ 7.30am-7.30pm Mon-Fri).

Trolleybus 1 connects the train station with the centre, but it's only a 450m walk along Str General Magheru.

## FĂGĂRAŞ MOUNTAINS
☎ 0268

The dramatic peaks of the Făgăraş Mountains cut a serrated line south of the main Braşov–Sibiu road and shelter dozens of glacial lakes. The famed **Transfăgăraşan road** (generally open only from June to August due to snow) cuts through the range from north to south. No buses ply the route.

Despite its name, Făgăraş town (pop 43,900) is not the prime access point to the Făgăraş Massif. Most hikers head south to the mountains from the commie-ho town Victoria.

## TÂRGU MUREŞ (MAROSVÁSÁRHELY)
☎ 265 / pop 166,100

The clear boom town of Transylvania's Székely Land (home to the ethnic Hungarian population – sometimes a *buna ziua* gets a shrug), Târgu Mureş' Habsburg-styled architecture, pleasant centre and Hungarian accent gives it a distinctive feel from surrounding Transylvanian towns like Sighişoara 55km south. In 2006 Wizz Air began service from Budapest, making it a potentially cheaper hub to reach Romania from Western Europe.

### Orientation & Information

Central Piaţa Trandafirilor runs several blocks in the busy commercial heart, where you can find ATMs, bars and food. At its northeastern end stands the landmark Orthodox Church. Str Bernady György leads east from there past the 14th-century citadel. The train station is 1km south and the bus station 1.5km south.

Two blocks west of the Orthodox Church, **Complex Charis** (cnr Str Arany Ianoş & Str Aurel Filmon; per hr €0.60; ☻ 9am-9pm Mon-Fri, 3-9pm Sat, 6-9pm Sun) is a Christian organisation with a slick reading room that has computers on which you can check email.

**Tourism Information Centre** ( ☎ 365 404 934; www.cjmures.ro/turism; cnr Piaţa Trandafirilor & Str Enescu; ☻ 8am-8pm Tue-Thu, to 4pm Mon & Sat), in the Culture Palace, is a superbly run centre offering free maps and information on the region.

### Sights

At the southwestern end of Piaţa Trandafirlor, the **Culture Palace** (Palatul Culturii; cnr Piaţa Trandafirilor & Str Enescu; adult/student €0.75/1.50; ☻ 9am-6pm Tue-Sun) is Târgu Mureş' beloved landmark and top attraction. Inside its glittering, tiled, steepled roof is an often-used concert hall and several worthwhile museums (all included in the entry price). The best is the **Hall of Mirrors** (Sala Oglinzi), with 12 stained-glass windows lining a 45m hallway – a tape in various languages explains the folktales each portrays. The **Art Museum** (2nd floor) houses many large late-19th and early 20th-century paintings; the **Archaelogical Museum** (1st floor) explains Dacian pieces found in the region in English.

### Sleeping

**Hotel Sport** ( ☎ 231 913; Str Liviu Rebreanu 29A; r with shared/private bathroom €10/22) Crusty and a bit musty, this OK 44-room cheapie (five minutes north of the train station on foot) is for shoestringers only. No breakfast.

**Pensiune Ana Maria** ( ☎ 264 401; Str AL Papui Ilarian 17; s/d/apt €26/29/37) Something like a home for Elvis Habsburg, this playful eight-room guesthouse mixes a bit of green Vegas garishness

---

**HIKING FROM VICTORIA**

One of the best stations to get off is Ucea (59km from Sibiu), from where you can catch a bus (or walk the 7km) to **Victoria**. From here you can hike to **Cabana Turnuri** (1520m; 20 beds) in about six hours. The scenery is stunning once you start the ascent. The next morning head for **Cabana Podragu** (2136m; 68 beds), four hours south.

Cabana Podragu makes a good base if you want to climb **Mt Moldoveanu** (2544m), Romania's highest peak. It's a tough uphill climb, but the views from the summit are unbeatable. Otherwise, hike eight hours east, passing by Mt Moldoveanu, to Cabana Valea Sambetei (1407m). From Cabana Valea Sambetei you can descend to the railway in Ucea, via Victoria, in a day.

and Austrian tradition – breakfasts are huge and superb. Go past the citadel and turn right at Str AL Papui Ilarian.

**Hotel Concordia** ( ☎ 260 602; Piaţa Trandafirilor 45; s/d €96/112; ❄ ▣ ) One of Romania's most chic boutique hotels; splurgers go for the stark and giant rooms (with zebra-print chairs and fashion prints on the walls).

## Eating

**Leo** (Piaţa Trandafirilor 36-38; mains €2.75-4; ❧ 24hr) On the eastern side of the square, this outdoor-indoor spot gets busy with pizzas and quite tasty Romanian food.

**Kebab** (Str Bolyai 10; kebabs €1.50; ❧ 6.30am-10pm) A block north of the square, this budget spot has comfy indoor-outdoor seats plus pick-and-point eats, including kebab lunch specials.

## Getting There & Away

Daily bus and maxitaxi service from the **bus station** ( ☎ 221 451; Str Gheorghe Doja) includes 18 or so to Sighişoara (€2, 1½ hours), continuing on to Braşov (€5.50; 3½ hours); plus five daily to Cluj-Napoca (€3.50 to €4, 2½ hours) and two to Sibiu (€3.50, three hours). Bus 18 connects the centre with the station.

The **Agenţie de Voiaj CFR** ( ☎ 266 203; Piaţa Te-atrului 1; ❧ 7.30am-7.30pm Mon-Fri), facing Piaţa Trandafirilor near its northwestern corner, sells tickets for daily trains including two daily to Bucharest (€16, 8½ hours) and Sibiu (€4, 5½ hours), plus one to Cluj-Napoca (€6.75, 2½ hours), Timişoara (€9.25, 6½ hours) and Budapest (€37, 7½ hours). Bus 5 connects the station with the centre.

# CLUJ-NAPOCA

☎ 0264 / pop 317,950

Just one letter away from 'club', Cluj-Napoca isn't as pretty or mountainous as the Saxon towns to the south, but it earns much of its nationwide fame and rep for its dozens of cavernous, unsnooty discos. Outside the clubs, though, Cluj (everyone calls it just 'Cluj') is one of Romania's most welcoming and energised cities – a 'real' city where there's everything going on (football, opera, espresso, heated politics, trams), regardless of who visits or not. Its attractions don't hit you over the head like Dracula's 'homes' do, but if you look closer, Cluj's are some of Transylvania's most arresting. It's also a great base for renting a car – it's far cheaper here than in Braşov – and

serves as a common shooting-off point for Maramureş (p663).

## History

In AD 124, Roman Emperor Marcus Aurelius elevated the Dacian town of Napoca to a colony. From 1791 to 1848 and again after the union with Hungary in 1867, Cluj-Napoca served as the capital of Transylvania.

In the mid-1970s the old Roman name of Napoca was added to the city's official title to emphasise its Daco-Roman origin In the 1990s, ex-mayor George Funar furthered that Romanian nationalist swipe (painting trash bins in Romanian colours) that embarrassed many locals.

## Orientation

The *gară* (train station) is 1.5km north of the city centre. Walk left out of the station and cross the street to catch tram 101 or a trolley-bus south down Str Horea. Most buses arrive and depart from Autogară 2, north of town.

### MAPS

The best map for the city is Cartographia's 1:12,000 *Cluj-Napoca* (€3).

## Information
### BOOKSHOPS

**Gaudeamus** ( ☎ 439 281; Str Iuliu Mariu 3; ❧ 10am-7pm, 11am-2pm Sat) Has some maps and many Hungarian titles.

**Librăria Humanitas** (Str Napoca 7; ❧ 10am-7pm Mon-Fri, to 6pm Sat)

### INTERNET ACCESS

**Blade Net** (Str Iuliu Maniu 17; per hr €0.60; ❧ 7am-midnight)

**Net Zone** (Piaţa Muzeului 5; per hr €0.40; ❧ 24hr 'approximately')

### LANGUAGE COURSES

**Access** ( ☎ 420 476; www.access.ro; Str Tebei 21, 3rd fl; ❧ 10am-6pm Mon & Thu, 2-8pm Tue-Wed, 2-6pm Fri) Offers Romanian-language courses.

### LAUNDRY

**Perado Laundry** (Str Calera Turzeii 13; per load €4.50; ❧ 10am-7pm Mon-Sat) The ever-valuable wash-fold-and-dry service.

### LEFT LUGGAGE

Plan ahead: the train station has no left luggage.

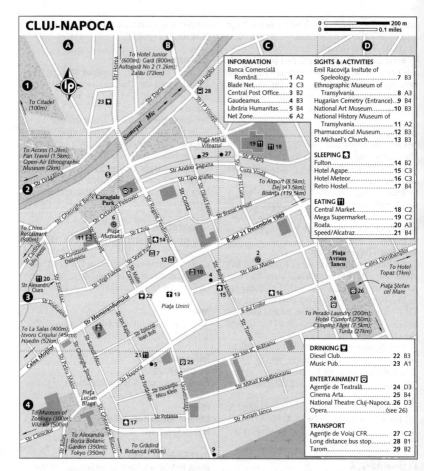

## CLUJ-NAPOCA

| 0 | 200 m |
| 0 | 0.1 miles |

**INFORMATION**
Banca Comercială
  Română...................1 A2
Blade Net...................2 C3
Central Post Office......3 B2
Gaudeamus................4 B3
Librăria Humanitas.....5 B4
Net Zone...................6 A2

**SIGHTS & ACTIVITIES**
Emil Racoviţa Insitute of
  Speleology..............7 B3
Ethnographic Museum of
  Transylvania............8 A3
Hugarian Cemetry (Entrance)..9 B4
National Art Museum...........10 B3
National History Museum of
  Transylvania............11 A2
Pharmaceutical Museum........12 B3
St Michael's Church............13 B3

**SLEEPING**
Fulton..........................14 B2
Hotel Agape....................15 C3
Hotel Meteor...................16 C3
Retro Hostel....................17 B4

**EATING**
Central Market.................18 C2
Mega Supermarket.............19 C2
Roata..........................20 A3
Speed/Alcatraz................21 B4

**DRINKING**
Diesel Club.......................22 B3
Music Pub.........................23 A1

**ENTERTAINMENT**
Agenţie de Teatrală............24 D3
Cinema Arta.....................25 B4
National Theatre Cluj-Napoca..26 D3
Opera...............................(see 26)

**TRANSPORT**
Agenţie de Voiaj CFR..........27 C2
Long distance bus stop........28 B1
Tarom...............................29 B2

---

### MONEY

**Banca Comercială Română** (Str Gheorghe Bariţiu 10-12; 8.30am-6pm Mon-Fri, 8.30am-12.30pm Sat) Gives cash advances and changes travellers cheques.

### POST

**Central post office** (Str Regele Ferdinand 33; 7am-8pm Mon-Fri, 8am-1pm Sat)

### TOURIST INFORMATION & TRAVEL AGENCIES

Cluj still has no tourist information centre. See www.cjnet.ro for general information on the city, or try the following.

**Green Mountain Holidays** ( 0744-637 227; www.greenmountainholidays.ro) Terrific ecotourism agency providing activity-filled trips in the Apuseni Mountains.

**Pan Travel** ( 420 516; www.pantravel.ro; Str Grozavescu 13; 9am-5pm Mon-Fri) This top-notch outfit can book accommodation, car rental (from €30 per day), provide guides and arrange Maramureş trips. It's best to contact ahead of time.

**Transylvania Ecological Club** (Clubul Ecologic Transilvania; 431 626; www.greenagenda.org, www.cdtcluj.ro) Grass-roots environmental group focuses on eco-travel in the region. At research time it was looking for a new location.

## Sights

### CENTRAL CLUJ-NAPOCA

The vast 14th-century **St Michael's Church** dom-inates Piaţa Unirii. The neo-Gothic tower (1859) topping the Gothic hall church creates a great landmark. Outside is a huge equestrian statue (1902) of the famous Hungarian king Matthias Corvinus (r 1458–90), who was born in town. (At night compare the half-hearted lighting on this compared with the elaborate lighting of the namesake Romanian hero on **Piaţa Avram Iancu**, three blocks east.)

Facing Piaţa Unirii is the interesting **National Art Museum** ( ☎ 496 952; Piaţa Unirii 30; adult/child €1.50/0.75; ☉ noon-7pm Wed-Sun Jun-Oct, 11am-6pm Wed-Sun Nov-May), housed inside the baroque Banffy Palace (1791).

The small three-room **Pharmaceutical Museum** ( ☎ 597 567; Str Regele Ferdinand 1; adult/child €0.60/0.30; ☉ 10am-4pm Mon-Sat) is housed in Cluj's first apothecary (1573). Old glass cases housing grounded mummy dust, 18th-century aphrodisiacs and medieval alchemy symbols are brought to life by the hilarious guide, who ushers you around as if showing off game-show prizes.

A block north, the museum for the **Emil Racoviţa Institute of Speleology** (Str Sextil Puşcariu 10) should be open in its new location by the time you arrive. The much-travelled scientist Racoviţa opened the world's first cave institute in Cluj in 1920.

Just off lovely Piaţa Muzeului is the **National History Museum of Transylvania** ( ☎ 495 677; Str Constantin Daicoviciu 1; adult/child €0.60/0.30; ☉ 10am-4pm Tue-Sun), filled with ghoulish remains of ancient tombs and many Roman pieces – the modern sections were under renovation at research time.

Closed for renovation at research time, the **Ethnographic Museum of Transylvania** (Muzeul Etnografic al Transilvaniei; ☎ 592 344; Str Memorandumului 21) runs an open-air museum (adult/student €1.20/0.6; ☉ 10am-6pm May-Sep, 8am-4pm Oct-Mar, closed Apr), with 14 traditional buildings; take bus 27 to Hoia forest from the train station.

### OUTSIDE THE CENTRE

In the 'student ghetto' west of the centre, inside the wooded **Biology and Geology Faculty**, you'll find the surprisingly rewarding **Museum of Zoology** ( ☎ 595 739; Str Clinicolor 5-7; adult/student €0.45/0.23; ☉ 9am-3pm Mon-Fri, 10am-2pm Sat & Sun), an L-shaped lab that looks like it hasn't changed in five decades. From Str Clinicilor, veer left through the brick gate.

Just south, head past fast-food joints up Str Bogdan P Haşdeu to Str Pasteur to reach the fragrant 1930 **Alexandru Borza Botanic Gardens** ( ☎ 592 152; Str Republicii 42; adult/student €1.20/0.60;

☉ 9am-6pm), with shaded green lawns and a super Japanese garden.

Just east of here, most easily reached from Str Avram Iancu down the hill, is an immense, highly memorable **Hungarian cemetery** (Házsongárdi temető).

For an overall view of Cluj-Napoca, climb up the **citadel** (cetatea; 1715), northwest of the centre.

## Sleeping

### BUDGET

**Retro Hostel** ( ☎ 450 452; www.retro.ro; Str Potaissa 13; dm from €10, r €15 per person; 🖳 ) On a quiet lane amid 16th-century citadel wall fragments, the superbly run Retro is one of Romania's best hostels. It's a little tight – only a couple of bathrooms, and one private room is only accessible through the other private room. Staff offer good-value day trips. Breakfast is €2.50.

**Camping Făget** ( ☎ 596 234; tent sites €2.25, 2-person huts €15) This hill-top collection of OK cabanas and tent spots is 7km south of the centre. Take bus 35 to the end of the line, from where it's a 2km marked hike.

**Hotel Junior** ( ☎ 432 028; www.pensiune-junior.ro; Str Câri Ferate 12; s/d €23/27) Hot-pink building and simple rooms, on a dusty, unappealing street just down from the trains. No breakfast.

**Vila 69** ( ☎ 591 592; vila69@email.ro; Str Haşden 69; s/d €28.50/37; 🖳 ) Seventeen rather plain, modern rooms in a happy little place. Take Str Clinicolor, turn right on Str Piezişă – it's 200m up the street.

### MIDRANGE

**Hotel Meteor** (591 060; www.hotelmetro.ro; B-dul Eroilor 29; s €35, d €40 & €44) Slightly faded modern hotel – some rooms are quite small, but staff are nice and there's laundry service. The restaurant's alley tables mean night-time noise in good weather.

**Fulton** ( ☎ 597 898; www.fulton.ro; Str Sextil Puşcariu 10; s €40-60, d €45-65; 🖳 ) The closest to boutique style, this back-street central inn has earth-toned striped walls, wrought-iron bed frames, and a laid-back covered patio bar. Plug-in internet's free.

### TOP END

**Hotel Agape** ( ☎ 406 523; www.hotelagape.ro; Str Iuliu Maniu 6; s/d €59/71; ✕ 🖳 ) Run by Hungarian locals, this 40-room hotel has *six* restaurants and giant rooms.

## Eating

**Tokyo** ( ☎ 598 662; Str Marinescu 5; sushi & rolls from €3; ⊗ 11am-midnight) Japanese pop on the stereo and the Shinto gate out front are certainly a break from all the traditional Romanian restaurants around town. Go south on Str Babeş from the centre, turn right on Str Marinescu.

**Roata** ( ☎ 592 022; Str Alexandru Ciura 6A; mains €4.50-8.50; ⊗ noon-midnight Tue-Sat, 1pm-midnight Sun-Mon) Housed in a back alley house, and with tasty traditional Romanian dishes served in clay plates. Best is sitting on the small terrace vying for space amid potted plants and moss-covered stones.

### QUICK EATS

There are heaps of good pizza, hamburger and kebab options on Str Piezişă in the 'student ghetto' and more centrally on Piaţa Lucian Blaga and Str Napoca.

**Speed/Alcatraz** (Str Napoca 4-6; pizzas 11 lei, sandwiches €1.25-2; ⊗ 24hr) Busy fast-food option with good seating options, including some in the 'Al Capone' jail cages.

### SELF-CATERING

For fresh produce, stroll through the quite colourful **central market**, behind the Complex Commercial Mihai Viteazul shopping centre on Piaţa Mihai Viteazul, which also houses **Mega Supermarket** ( ⊗ 7am-9pm Mon-Fri, 8am-8pm Sat, 8am-7pm Sun).

## Drinking

Piaţa Unirii is the site of many subterranean watering holes, but clubs and bars are spread out throughout the centre. It pays to explore.

**Diesel Bar** ( ☎ 493 043; Piaţa Unirii 17) Walk past the hipsters in the all-glass entry and go downstairs into a towering cavernous room, with red-spotlit tables, and giant rooms for 15-lei gin and tonics.

**Music Pub** ( ☎ 432 517; Str Horea 5; ⊗ 9-3am Mon-Fri, 11am-3pm Sat, 5pm-3am Sun) A little wild west up front, the sprawling pub is a great, more casual, place for buddy blokes and indie-pop flirters.

The 'student ghetto', found southwest of Cluj-Napoca's centre (on and off Str Piezişă, reached by Str Clinicilor about 300m from Piaţa Lucian Blaga), teams with lively open-air bars, including **La Salas** (Str Piezişă; ⊗ 10-2am or 3am).

## Entertainment

**Şapte Seri** (www.sapteseri.ro) and *24-Fun* are free biweekly booklets listing all the latest goings-on (in Romanian).

### CINEMAS

**Cinema Arta** ( ☎ 596 616; Str Universitaţii 3) screens Hollywood films in English. Tickets cost about €1.75.

### THEATRE & CLASSICAL MUSIC

The **Agenţie de Teatrală** ( ☎ 595 363; Piaţa Ştefan cel Mare 14; ⊗ 11am-5pm Tue-Fri) sells tickets for theatre, opera and the philharmonic, which hit the stage at the **National Theatre Cluj-Napoca** ( ☎ 590 272; Piaţa Ştefan cel Mare 2-4).

## Getting There & Around

### AIR

Air Tarom has at least two daily direct flights to Bucharest (one-way/return from €103/153). Tickets can be bought at the airport (8km east of town, reached by bus 8) or at the **Tarom city office** ( ☎ 432 669; Piaţa Mihai Viteazul 11; ⊗ 8am-6pm Mon-Fri, 9am-1pm Sat).

### BUS

At research time, daily bus service from **Autogară 2** (Autogară Beta; ☎ 455 249), 350m northwest of the train station (take the overpass), included the following: two daily buses to Braşov (€8), four to Bucharest (€9.25), five to Budapest (€17), one to Chişinău (€20), one to Iaşi (€12 to €15) and three to Sibiu (€6, three hours). Note that there is no Autogară 1. Budapest-bound maxitaxis stop at the international bus station there and finish at the Budapest airport.

### CAR

Cluj has some of the best car-rental rates in the country. Pan Travel (p654) rents Dacias for €30 per day. **Rodna** ( ☎ 416 773; www.rodna-trans .ro; Str Traian Vuia 62), towards the airport, rents newish Dacia Logans from €30 per day, and foreign cars for a bit more.

### TAXI

**Diesel Taxi** ( ☎ 953, 946) is a well-regarded, meter-using local company.

### TRAIN

The **Agenţie de Voiaj CFR** ( ☎ 432 001; Piaţa Mihai Viteazul 20; ⊗ 7am-7pm Mon-Fri) sells domestic and international train tickets in advance. Sample fares for *accelerat* trains include:

| Destination | Price (€) | Duration | No of daily trains |
|---|---|---|---|
| Braşov | 8.60 | 4 | 6 |
| Bucharest | 11 | 7½ | 6 |
| Budapest | 34.50 | 5 | 2 |
| Iaşi | 10.50 | 9hr | 4 |
| Oradea | 5.75 | 2¼-4 | 12 |
| Sibiu | 9 | 4 | 1 |
| Sighişoara | 7.30 | 3½ | 6 |
| Suceava | 8.60 | 7 | 4 |
| Timişoara | 8.60 | 7 | 6 |

## AROUND CLUJ-NAPOCA
### Turda

Amidst the rolling plains 27km south of Cluj, the unfortunately named Turda is a town of two massive drops – one natural, the other in a mine – which justify a nice day trip.

The **Cheile Turzii** (Turda Gorge) is 9km south-west, walked in a few hours in gently rising fields filled with sheep; the red-cross trail leads through the gorge, and a red-dot one up and over the peak. Ask for trail info at the **tourist information centre** ( ☎ 314 611; Piaţ,\a 1 Deciembrie 1918; ☽ 9am-6pm Mon-Sat), about 250m south of Piaţa Republicii, where buses to/from Cluj stop.

In town, about 1km north of Piaţa Republicii, is Turda's massive **salt mine** ( ☎ 311 690; Str Salinelor 54; adult/child €2.40/1.20; ☽ 9am-3.30pm summer, to 1.30pm Mon-Fri, to 3.30pm Sat & Sun winter), reached along a seemingly endless (500m) tunnel. One mine descends 13 stories down, where can peer farther down into a 'lake' far below.

**Hotel Potaissa** ( ☎ 312 691; Str Republicii 6; s/d €27/36, with shared bath €12/24) Clean and central hotel from 1947 with loud carpets.

**Hunter Prince Castle** (aka 'Dracula Hotel'; ☎ 316 850; www.huntercastle.ro; Str Sulutiu 4-6; r €51 & 65; ☒ ) Just off the main strip, this kitschy, fun 'castle' hotel plugs Dracula and hunting, with a good restaurant.

Maxitaxis leave frequently from the centre to Cluj-Napoca's Piaţa Mihai Viteazul (€1.20, 40 minutes) until 8.30pm or so. A taxi back is about €15.

# CRIŞANA & BANAT

While flaunting three of Romania's most 'European' cities (Oradea, Arad and Timişoara), in both essence and crumbling Hapsburg architecture, the areas of Crişana (north of the Mureş River) and Banat (to the south) are also sprinkled with tempting offerings like the soaring Apuşeni Mountains, ski runs, deep caves, gorges, waterfalls and curative thermal waters. Zigzag from giddying excitement to recuperative leisure all within a few hours drive.

It was in Timişoara that the seeds of the 1989 revolution were sewn, a fact that has left these charming and proud people with a scarcely concealed perma-grin.

Crişana and Banat once merged imperceptibly into Vojvodina (Serbia) and Hungary's Great Plain. Until 1918 all three regions were governed jointly.

## ORADEA

☎ 0259 / pop 209,571

Elegant Oradea lies a few kilometres east of the Hungarian border, in the centre of the Crişana region, at the edge of the Carpathian Mountains.

Of all the cities of the Austro-Hungarian Empire, Oradea best retains its 19th-century romantic style. It was ceded to Romania in 1920 and has since taken on an air of faded grandeur, but it is a lovely place to stop.

### Orientation

The train station is a couple of kilometres north of the centre; trams 1 and 4 run south from Piaţa Bucureşti (outside the train station) to Piaţa Unirii, Oradea's main square. Tram 4 also stops at the northern end of Calea Republicii, a five-minute walk south to the centre.

The main square north of the river is Piaţa Republicii (also called Piaţa Regele Ferdinand I).

### Information

**24-hour pharmacy** ( ☎ 418 242; cnr Str Libertăţii & Piaţa Ferdinand)

**Game Star Internet Café** (Str Mihai Eminescu 4; per hr €0.40; ☽ 24hr)

**HVB Bank** ( ☎ 406 700; Piaţa Unirii 24; ☽ 9am-4pm Mon-Fri) Has all services.

**Panda Tours** ( ☎ 477 222; Str Iosif Vulcan 6; ☽ 9am-7pm Mon-Fri, to 1pm Sat) There's no official tourist information.

**Post office** ( ☎ 136 420; Str Roman Ciorogariu 12; ☽ 7am-7.30pm Mon-Fri)

**Telephone office** (Calea Republicii 5; ☽ 8am-8pm)

### Sights

Oradea's most imposing sights are on its two central squares, Piaţa Unirii and Piaţa Republicii.

ROMANIA

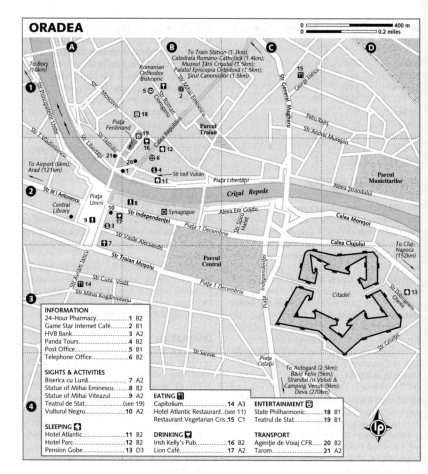

### ORADEA

| INFORMATION | |
|---|---|
| 24-Hour Pharmacy | 1 B2 |
| Game Star Internet Café | 2 B1 |
| HVB Bank | 3 A2 |
| Panda Tours | 4 B2 |
| Post Office | 5 B1 |
| Telephone Office | 6 B2 |

| SIGHTS & ACTIVITIES | |
|---|---|
| Biserica cu Lună | 7 A2 |
| Statue of Mihai Eminescu | 8 B2 |
| Statue of Mihai Viteazul | 9 A2 |
| Teatrul de Stat | (see 19) |
| Vulturul Negru | 10 A2 |

| SLEEPING | |
|---|---|
| Hotel Atlantic | 11 B2 |
| Hotel Parc | 12 B2 |
| Pension Gobe | 13 D3 |

| EATING | |
|---|---|
| Capitolium | 14 A3 |
| Hotel Atlantic Restaurant | (see 11) |
| Restaurant Vegetarian Cris | 15 C1 |

| DRINKING | |
|---|---|
| Irish Kelly's Pub | 16 B2 |
| Lion Café | 17 A2 |

| ENTERTAINMENT | |
|---|---|
| State Philharmonic | 18 B1 |
| Teatrul de Stat | 19 B1 |

| TRANSPORT | |
|---|---|
| Agenţie de Voiaj CFR | 20 B2 |
| Tarom | 21 A2 |

## PIAŢA UNIRII

The 1784 Orthodox **Biserica cu Lună** (Moon Church; Piaţa Unirii) has an unusual lunar mechanism on its tower that adjusts position in accordance with the moon's movement.

In the centre of Piaţa Unirii stands an equestrian **statue of Mihai Viteazul**, the prince of Wallachia (r 1593–1601), who is said to have rested in Oradea in 1600. East of this statue, overlooking the Crişul Repede River, you'll find the magnificent **Vulturul Negru** (Black Vulture; 1908) hotel and covered arcade, which links Piaţa Unirii with Str Independenţei and Str Vasile Alecsandri. A **statue of Mihai Eminescu**, the 19th-century Romantic poet, overlooks the river's southern bank.

Further east of Piaţa Unirii is **Parcul Central**, with a large monument, and a citadel, which was built in the 13th century, and now serves as government offices.

## PIAŢA REPUBLICII & NORTH

Across the bridge the magnificent neoclassical **Teatrul de Stat** (State Theatre), designed by Viennese architects Fellner and Hellmer in 1900, dominates Piaţa Republicii. To its right begins the long, pedestrianised Calea Republicii, lined with bookshops and cafés.

A block southwest of the train station is **Şirul Canonicilor** (Canon's Corridor), a series of archways that date back to the 18th century.

The **Catedrala Romano-Catolică** (Roman Catholic Cathedral; 1780) is the largest in Romania.

The adjacent **Palatul Episcopia Ortodoxă** (Episcopal Palace; 1770), with 100 fresco-adorned rooms and 365 windows, was modelled after Belvedere Palace in Vienna. It houses the **Muzeul Țării Crişului** (Museum of the Land of the Criş Rivers; ☎ 412 725; B-dul Dacia 1-3; admission €0.60; ☺ 10am-5pm Tue-Sun), with history and art exhibits relevant to the region.

## Sleeping

**Strandul cu Voluti** (cabins/camp sites per person €14.50/3; ☺ May–mid-Sep) Camping in Băile 1 Mai, 9km southeast of Oradea. Take a southbound tram 4 (black number) from the train station, or an eastbound tram 4 (red number) from Piața Unirii to the end of the line, then bus 15 to the last stop.

**Camping Venus** (☎ 318 266; tents & 2-/3-bed bungalows per person €10) This camping ground is 500m from Strandul cu Voluti.

**Hotel Parc** (☎ 411 699; Calea Republicii 5-7; s with shared toilet €14, €d 23) Oradea's only budget option. Ignore the crumbling façade – these large rooms are worn, but reasonably clean.

**Pension Gobe** (☎ 414 845; Str Dobrogeanu Gherea 26; s/d €30/40) This family-owned *pension* has several charming rooms, a small restaurant, and a bar.

**Hotel Atlantic** (☎ 426 911; www.hotelatlantic.ro; Str Iosif Vulcan 9; s/d/ste €45/50/60) These spacious, contemporary rooms sport *huge* marble bathrooms, some with spas, and your own private bar! The Blue Suite has a bed the size of a trampoline.

## Eating & Drinking

Calea Republicii is lined with cheap and cheerful eateries and cafés.

**Restaurant Vegetarian Cris** (☎ 441 593; George Enescu 30; mains €1.5; ☺ 9am-9pm Sun-Thu, to 4pm Fri) This place is the only vegetarian restaurant in Romania! Choose from a tantalisingly cheap menu featuring soups, stuffed peppers, minced-pumpkin balls, lentils, macaroni and cabbage, celery schnitzel, mushroom haggis, and soy, soy, soy!

**Capitolium** (☎ 420 551; Str. Avram Iancu 8; mains €5; ☺ 8am-12am) Bask in doting service and huge portions at this Romanian restaurant.

**Hotel Atlantic Restaurant** (☎ 414 953; Str Iosif Vulcan 9; mains €5) With an elegant interior, it has the best menu in town: hearty goulash, Mexican chicken and speciality steak dishes.

Most of Oradea's terrace cafés and restaurants double as bars in the evening.

**Irish Kelly's Pub** (☎ 413 419; Calea Republicii 2) Caters for a rowdy crowd on its outside terrace.

**Lion Café** (Str Independenței 1; ☺ 7am-1am) Trendy by day, packed by night.

## Entertainment

Tickets for performances at the **State Philharmonic** (Filarmonica de Stat; ☎ 430 853; Str Moscovei 5; tickets €2) can be purchased from its **ticket office** (☺ 10am-6pm Mon-Fri), inside the **Teatrul de Stat** (State Theatre; ☎ 130 885; Piața Ferdinand 4-6; tickets €3-12; ☺ 10-11am, 5-7pm).

## Getting There & Away

### AIR

**Tarom** (☎ 131 918; Piața Ferdinand 2; ☺ 8am-6pm Mon-Fri, 10am-1pm Sat) has three weekly flights to Baia Mare, daily flights to Bucharest and two weekly flights to Satu Mare from **Oradea airport** (☎ 416 082; www.oradea-online.ro/oradea/3/oradea_airport.htm; Calea Aradului km6). Note that Tarom accepts US dollars but not euros.

### BUS

From Oradea **Autogară** (☎ 418 998; Str Râzboieni 81), south of the centre, there are daily services to Beiuş, Deva and Satu Mare. More than 20 maxitaxis run daily to and from Băile Felix.

A daily state bus runs to Budapest (€17, 10 hours) leaving from outside the train station. Purchase tickets from the driver.

Maxitaxis run daily to Budapest from outside the train station (€20).

### CAR & MOTORCYCLE

The border crossing into Hungary for motorists is at Borş, 16km west of Oradea, and is open 24 hours.

### TRAIN

The **Agenție de Voiaj CFR** (☎ 130 578; Calea Republicii 2; ☺ 7am-7pm Mon-Fri) sells advance tickets.

Daily fast trains from Oradea include three to Budapest (€28), two to Bucharest (€22), five to Băile Felix, three to Cluj-Napoca (€11), one to Braşov and three to Timişoara (€7).

## TIMIȘOARA

☎ 0256 / pop 321,930

In the Banat region, tenacious Timişoara stunned the world as the birthplace of the 1989 revolution. Romania's fourth-largest city is known by residents as Primul Oraş Liber (First Free Town). It's a city that's loved by residents and tourists alike, with a charming Mediterranean air, regal Habsburg buildings and thriving culture and sport. Timişoara

ROMANIA

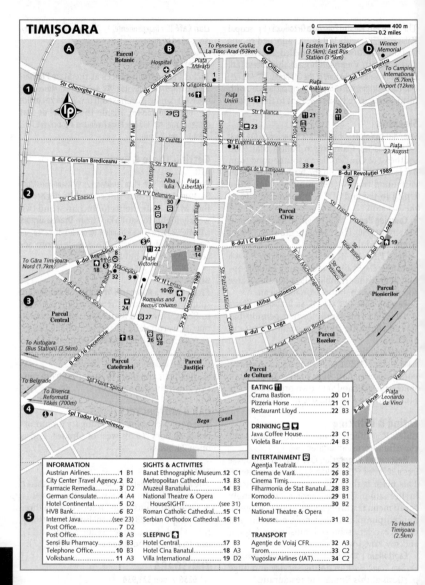

# TIMIȘOARA

is the hub of Carpatair, Romania's thriving semibudget airline, and as such is an excellent entry point for international visitors.

## Orientation

The Old Town has retained its circular orientation, with major streets and boulevards jutting out, pinwheel-like. Confusingly, Timișoara-Nord (the northern train station) is west of the city centre. Walk east along B-dul Republicii to the Opera House and Piața Victoriei. To the north is Piața Libertății; Piața Unirii, the old town square, bookended by the Roman Catholic Cathedral and the Serbian Orthodox Church, two blocks further north. Timișoara's bus station is beside the Idsefin Market, three blocks from the train station. Take B-dul General Drăgălina south to the canal, cross the bridge and head west to the next bridge. Boulevard C D Loga, south of the centre, swoops past a series of lovely parks, as well as the Metropolitan Cathedral. To get to the Eastern Train Station and international bus terminal, follow Aleea Demetriade northeast of the Old Town.

## Information

### INTERNET ACCESS

**Internet Java** ( ☎ 432 495; Str Pacha 6; per hr €1; ☻ 24hr) Inside the Java Coffee House.

### MEDICAL SERVICES

**Farmacie Remedia** (B-dul Revoluţiei 1989; ☻ 7am-8pm Mon-Fri, 7am-8pm Sat)
**Sensi Blu Pharmacy** ( ☎ 406 153; Piaţa Victoriei 7; ☻ 8am-8pm Mon-Fri, 9am-8pm Sat & Sun)

### MONEY

**City Centre Travel Agency** (B-dul Republicii 4; ☻ 9am-6pm Mon-Fri) Has an ATM and currency exchange.
**Hotel Continental** (B-dul Revoluţiei 3; ☻ 8am-6pm Mon-Fri, to 1pm Sat) Has a currency exchange.
**HVB Bank** ( ☎ 306 800; Piaţa Victoriei 2; ☻ 9am-4pm Mon-Fri)
**Volksbank** ( ☎ 406 101; Str Piatra Craiului 2)

### POST

**Post office** B-dul Revoluţiei ( ☎ 491 999; B-dul Revoluţiei 2; ☻ 8am-7pm Mon-Fri, to noon Sat); Str Macieşilor (Str Macieşilor; ☻ 8am-7pm Mon-Fri) The central post office on B-dul Revoluţiei can get busy; if so, try the branch on Str Macieşilor.

### TELEPHONE

**Telephone office** (Str N Lenau; ☻ 7am-9pm) Has fax facilities.

### TOURIST INFORMATION

**City Centre Travel Agency** (tourism ☎ 292 960, plane tickets 292 961; www.aerotravel.ro; B-dul Republicii 4; ☻ 9am-6pm Mon-Fri) A dynamic agency with people dedicated to all varieties of domestic tourism, car rental and flight bookings.

## Sights

The centre of town is Piaţa Victoriei, a beautifully landscaped pedestrian mall lined with shops, cinemas and cafés, with the **National Theatre & Opera House** (p662) at its head. Note the column topped with the classic scene of **Romulus and Remus** feeding from the mother wolf – a gift from the city of Rome. It was here

that thousands of demonstrators gathered on 16 December 1989 (see p622), following the siege on László Tökés' house. A memorial plaque on the front of the Opera House today reads: 'So you, who pass by this building, will dedicate a thought for free Romania.'

Just east of the *piaţa* is the 15th-century Huniades Palace, housing the **Muzeul Banatului** (Banat History Museum; ☎ 491 339; Piaţa Huniade 1; admission €0.60; ☻ 10am-4.30pm), which is worth visiting for its displays on natural history, geology, armour, weapons, archaeology, ceramics, tools and scale-model countryside shelters.

Towering over the mall's southwestern end is the 1946 Romanian Orthodox **Metropolitan Cathedral** with unique electrical bells. Next to the cathedral is Parcul Central, and just south of it the Bega Canal.

The 1989 revolution began on 15 December 1989 at the **Biserica Reformată Tökés** (Tökés Reformed Church; ☎ 492 992; Str Timotei Cipariu 1), off B-dul 16 Decembrie just southwest of the centre, where Father László Tökés spoke out against the dictator.

Piaţa Libertăţii and the Primăria Veche (Old Town Hall; 1734) lie north. Piaţa Unirii is Timişoara's most picturesque square featuring a baroque 1754 **Roman Catholic Cathedral**, and the 1754 **Serbian Orthodox Cathedral**. Housed in the oldest fortress in Timişoara, **Banat Ethnographic Museum** ( ☎ 434 967; Str Popa Şapcă 4; admission €0.50; ☻ 10am-4pm Tue-Sun) is within the city's remaining 18th-century bastion.

## Sleeping

**Camping International** ( ☎ 208925; campinginternational@yahoo.com; Aleea Pădurea Verde 6; camp sites per tent €2.50, chalets with central heating s/d/q €34/46/63) Nestled in the Green Wood forest on the opposite side of town from Timişoara-Nord train station. The main entrance of this excellent camping ground is on Calea Dorobanţilor. From the station catch trolleybus 11 to the end of the line. The bus stops less than 50m from the camping ground. The site has a restaurant.

**Hostel Timişoara** ( ☎ 293 960; Str Arieş 19, 'Baron' Bldg; dm €9) Two kilometres from the city centre, take tram 8 from the northern train station to this four-room, bare-bones hostel located on the top floor of a university building.

**Pensiune Giulia** ( ☎ 283 102; www.pensiuneagiulia.go.ro; Str Etolia 3; s/d €29/34.50) A gorgeous *pension* with contemporary art on the walls and all mod-cons near the city limits. No public transport access.

ROMANIA

**Hotel Cina Banatul** ( ☎ 491 903; B-dul Republicii 3-5; s/d €29/40) The best-value pad with clean, ultra-modern rooms and a good restaurant.

**Hotel Central** ( ☎ 490 091; www.hotel-central.ro; Str N Lenau 6; s/d €40/46) Recent renovations have left this place glistening, modern and comfortable.

**Villa International** ( ☎ 499 339; B-dul CD Loga 48; s/d €50/60) Part villa, part curiosity. The Ceauşescus only slept here for two nights, but their apartments still contain 'personal effects', free for guest use. The villa has an unusual faded glory. Rooms are achingly outmoded and bare, but clean. A sneak-peak at the dated lobby is highly recommended.

## Eating & Drinking

There are plenty of lovely terrace cafés lining Piaţ Unirii and Piaţa Victoriei, where you can while away the time or plot the next revolution. Hang out with sociable locals at night in the terrace café-bars on Piaţa Victoriei, downing bottles of the local Timişoreana Pils beer for around €1 a bottle.

**Pizzeria Horse** ( ☎ 229 666; Str Popa Şapcă 4; mains €5) Slabs of mouth-watering pizza starting at €1!

**La Tino** ( ☎ 226 455; Calea Aradului 14; mains €4) There's classy Italian food and scrummy pizzas at this place north of the city centre.

**Crama Bastion** ( ☎ 221 199; Str Hector 1; mains €6) Classic Romanian dishes vie with the wine list for attention in this traditional restaurant in 18th-century fortifications.

**Restaurant Lloyd** ( ☎ 294 949; Piaţa Victoriei 2; meals €8-12) Exquisite international-Romanian menu of shark, smoked salmon and a spit-roast joint.

**Violeta Bar** (Piaţa Victoriei) At the southern end of the square, this bar is particularly popular.

**Java Coffee House** ( ☎ 432 495; Str Pacha 6; ☼ 24hr) Gulp caffeine with one hand, check email with the other.

## Entertainment

### CINEMAS

**Cinema Timiş** ( ☎ 491 290; Piaţa Victoriei 7; tickets €2-3) Movies are screened in their original language.

**Cinema de Vară** (B-dul CD Loga 2) Tickets at this brilliant outdoor cinema cost the same but it's far more fun!

### NIGHTCLUBS

Be seen in these funky haunts.

**Lemon** (Str Alba Iulia 2; from ☼ 10pm) This club in the cellar of a piano bar has hip-hop and house DJs.

**Komodo** (Str Ungureanu 9) So trendy it hurts, this large, colourfully lit eclectic bar has techno-house DJs on weekends.

### THEATRE & CLASSICAL MUSIC

Buy tickets (starting at €1) from **Agenţia Teatrală** ( ☎ 499 908; Str Mărăşeşti 2; ☼ 10am-1pm, 5-7pm Tue-Sun) for performances at the following venues.

Classical concerts are held most evenings at the **Filharmonia de Stat Banatul** (State Philharmonic Theatre; ☎ 492 521; B-dul CD Loga 2). Tickets can also be bought at the box office inside.

The **National Theatre & Opera House** (Teatrul Naţional şi Opera Română; ☎ 201 284; Str Mărăşeşti 2) is highly regarded.

## Getting There & Away

### AIR

The airport is 12km east of the centre. **Tarom** ( ☎ 200 003; B-dul Revoluţiei 1989 3-5; ☼ 8am-8pm Mon-Fri, 7am-1pm Sat) has four daily flights to Bucharest (US$75 plus tax US$5; note Tarom does not accept euros) and several weekly international flights.

Timişoara is the hub of **Carpatair** (www.carpatair.ro), Romania's thriving semibudget airline, with service to nine key cities as well as a growing list of international destinations. Strangely Carpatair doesn't have an office in its hub city, only out at the airport.

**Yugoslav Airlines** (JAT; ☎ 495 747; Str Eugeniu de Savoya 7) runs daily international flights to Europe.

**Austrian Airlines** ( ☎ 490 320; all-tsr-to@aua.com; Piaţa Unirii 6) has daily flights to Vienna costing about €200.

### BUS

The small, shabby **Autogară** ( ☎ 493 471; B-dul Maniu Iuliu 54; ☼ 6am-8pm Mon-Fri) has six platforms from where slow state buses run daily to Campeni, Arad, Sibiu and Rimincu Valcea. Maxitaxis run daily to Oradea, Arad, Deva and Campeni.

International buses leave from the **East Bus Station** (Autogară Est), which is merely a few kiosks cluttered outside the east train station. **Atlasib** ( ☎ 226 486) goes to Italy, Spain and even Sweden. **Eurolines** ( ☎ 288 132; timisoara.ag@eurolines.ro) goes to Budapest, Greece, Switzerland and Portugal, among others. **Murat** ( ☎ 0744-144 326, in Romanian) goes to Istanbul (€100).

### TRAIN

All major train services depart from **Gară Timişoara-Nord** (Northern Train Station; ☎ 491 696; Str Gării 2). Purchase tickets in advance from the

**Agenţie de Voiaj CFR** ( ☎ 491 889; cnr Strs Măcieşilor & V Babeş; ☺ 8am-8pm Mon-Fri, international tickets 9am-7pm Mon-Fri). Daily trains include eight to Bucharest (€22.50), one to Cluj-Napoca (€11.50), five to Băile Herculane (€8.40), one to Baia Mare via Arad (€12.60) and three sadistically slow runs to Iaşi (16 hours). Additionally, three go to Budapest (€38) and one to Belgrade (€14).

# MARAMUREŞ

Dismount from the horse-drawn cart and tip your chauffer in cigarettes. You've found one of the last places where rural European medieval life remains intact. Where peasants live off the land as countless generations did before them. Even Romanians joke that nothing has changed here for 100 years – welcome to Maramureş.

The last peasant culture in Europe is thriving here, with hand-built wooden churches, traditional music, colourful costumes and ancient festivals. Villagers' homes are still fronted with traditional, giant, ornately carved wooden gates. Ear-smoking, 100-proof plum-brandy (*ţuica*) stills percolate in the garden, usually tended by a rosy-cheeked patriarch. Discovering this part of the world is a time-travel adventure, verily stunning Western visitors.

The region was effectively cut off from Transylvania by a fortress of mountains and has remained untouched by the 20th-century (and the 19th century, and the 18th century…). It escaped the collectivisation of the 1940s, systemisation of the '80s and the Westernisation of the '90s and as such is living history.

## SIGHETU MARMAŢIEI
☎ 0262 / pop 41,425
Sighetu Marmaţiei is the northernmost town in Romania, almost touching the Ukrainian border. Its name is derived from the Thracian and Dacian word *seget* (fortress).

Sighet (as it's known locally) is famed for its vibrant **Winter Festival**. Its former maximum-security prison is now open as a museum and is a sobering and informative highlight of any visit to northern Romania.

### Information
**ATM** (Piaţa Libertăţii 8) Outside Hotel Tisa.
**Banca Română** (Calea Ioan Mihaly de Apşa 24; ☺ 9am-5pm Mon-Fri) ATM, and cash transfer and exchange facilities.
**Fundaţia OVR Agro-Tur-Art** ( ☎ 330 171; www .vaduizei.ovr.ro) In Vadu Izei (6km south) is the region's best source of beds, books and information.
**Millennium** (Str Corneliu Coposu; per hr €1.40; ☺ 9am-10pm Tue-Sat, noon-10pm Sun) Internet access.
**MM Pangaea Proiect Turism** ( ☎ 312 228; www .pangaeaturism.ro; Piaţa Libertăţii 15; ☺ 9am-4pm Mon-Fri) Offers simple maps and group tours.
**Post & telephone office** (Str Ioan Mihaly de Apşa 39) Opposite the Maramureş Museum.

### Sights
On Piaţa Libertăţii, the **Hungarian Reformed Church** was built during the 15th century. Close by is the 16th-century **Roman Catholic Church**.

Nearby, the **Maramureş Museum** (Piaţa Libertăţii 15; admission €0.50; ☺ 10am-6pm Tue-Sun) displays colourful folk costumes, rugs and carnival masks.

Just off the square is Sighet's only remaining **synagogue** (Str Bessarabia 10). Before WWII there were eight synagogues serving a large

---

### SIGHET PRISON

In May 1947 the Communist regime embarked on a reign of terror, slaughtering, imprisoning and torturing thousands of Romanians. While many leading prewar figures were sent to hard-labour camps, the regime's most feared intellectual opponents were interned in Sighet's maximum-security prison. Between 1948 and 1952, about 180 members of Romania's academic and government elite were imprisoned here.

Today four white marble plaques covering the barred windows of the prison list the 51 prisoners who died in the Sighet cells, notably the academic and head of the National Liberal Party (PNL), Constantin Brătianu; historian and leading member of the PNL, Gheorghe Brătianu; governor of the National Bank, Constantin Tătăranu; and Iuliu Maniu, president of the National Peasants' Party (PNŢ).

The prison, housed in the old courthouse, was closed in 1974. In 1989 it re-opened as the **Muzeu al Gândirii Arestate** (Museum of Arrested Thought; ☎ 314 224, 316 848; Str Corneliu Coposu 4; admission free; ☺ 9.30am-6.30pm, to 4.30pm 15 Oct-15 May). Photographs are displayed in the torture chambers and cells.

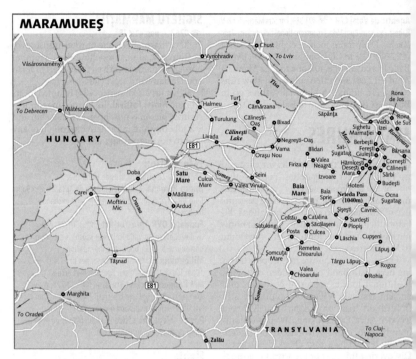

MARAMUREŞ

Jewish community, which comprised 40% of the town's population.

The Jewish writer and 1986 Nobel Peace Prize winner, Elie Wiesel, who coined the term 'Holocaust', was born in (and later deported from) Sighet. His **house** is on the corner of Str Dragoş Vodă and Str Tudor Vladimirescu. Along Str Gheorghe Doja, there is a **monument** (Str Mureşan) to the victims of the Holocaust.

Visit traditional peasant houses from the Maramureş region at the open-air **Muzeul Satului** (Village Museum; ☎ 314 229; Str Dobăieş 40; adult/child €0.90/0.50; ☺ 9am-4pm), southeast of Sighet's centre. Allow at least half a day to wander through the incredible constructions. Children love the wood dwellings, cobbled pathways and 'mini' villages. You can even stay overnight in tiny wooden cabins (€5.50).

## Sleeping & Eating

For homestays in the area check out www.ruraltourism.ro and www.pensiuni.info.ro.

**Hotel Tisa** ( ☎ 312 645; Piaţa Libertăţii 8; d/tr €24/29) Smack-bang in the centre of Sighet, the ailing rooms here were enjoying renovation at the time of writing.

**Motel Buţi** ( ☎ 311 035; Str Ştefan cel Mare 6; s/d/tr €21/28/41) This charming villa has spotlessly clean but small rooms, as well as a bar and pool table downstairs.

**David's** (Str Ioan Mihaly de Apşa 1; ☺ 7am-10pm; mains €3) is the lively bar-of-the-moment, with a menu long on drinks and short on food.

## Getting There & Away

### BUS

The **bus station** (Str Gării) is opposite the train station. There are several local buses daily to Baia Mare (€2, 65km), Satu Mare (€2.50, 122km), Borşa (€1), Budeşti (€1), Călineşti (€1), Vişeu de Sus (€1.50), and one bus daily to Bârsana, Botiza, Ieud and Mara.

### TRAIN

Tickets are sold in advance at the **Agenţie de Voiaj CFR** ( ☎ 312 666; Piaţa Libertăţii 25; ☺ 7am-2pm Mon-Fri). There's one daily fast train that runs to Timişoara (€20), Bucharest (€20, 12 hours), Cluj-Napoca (€12.50, six hours) and Arad (€18).

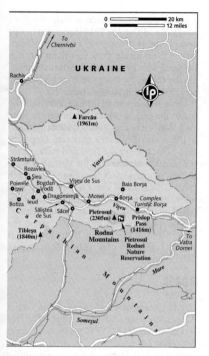

## SĂPÂNŢA
☎ 0262

Săpânţa village has a unique place in the hearts of Romanians. It boasts the **Merry Cemetery**, which is famous for the colourfully painted wooden crosses that adorn its tombstones. Shown in art exhibitions across Europe, the crosses attract coachloads of visitors who marvel at the gentle humour and human warmth that created them.

Five hundred metres off the main road, a new wooden church claiming to be the **tallest wooden structure in Europe** (75m) is being built with a controversial stone base.

The village itself lies 12km northwest of Sighetu Marmaţiei, just 4km south of Ukraine. Find rooms at **Pensiunea Stan** ( ☎ 372 337; d €20), opposite the cemetery entrance, and **Pensiunea Ileana** ( ☎ 372 137; d €14), a green-tiled house to the right of Pensiunea Stan.

**Camping Poieni** ( ☎ 372 228; camp sites €1.50, cabins per person €3; ☼ 1 Jun-31 Aug), 3km south of Săpânţa, and has an excellent trout restaurant.

A bus leaves for Săpânţa from Sighetu Marmaţiei every hour (8am to 2pm), returning at 4pm and 5pm.

## VALEA IZEI
☎ 0262 / pop 3000

The Valea Izei (Izei Valley) follows the Iza River eastward from Sighetu Marmaţiei to Moisei. The valley is lined with small peasant villages that are renowned for their elaborately carved wooden gates and tall wooden churches.

Tourism is gradually developing in this region, providing visitors with the opportunity to sample traditional cuisine or try their hand at woodcarving, wool weaving and glass painting.

In mid-July, Vadu Izei, together with the neighbouring villages of Botiza and Ieud, hosts the **Maramuzical Festival**, a lively four-day international folk-music festival.

### Vadu Izei

Vadu Izei is at the confluence of the Iza and Mara Rivers, 6km south of Sighetu Marmaţiei.

**Fundaţia OVR Agro-Tur-Art** ( ☎ 330 171; www.va duizei.ovr.ro; house No 161) is an unrivalled source of local information and has rooms for rent in private homes (€15 to €20). **Nicolae Prisăcaru** ( ☎ 0721-046 730; prisnic@conseco.ro) and the lovely **Ramona Ardelean** ( ☎ 0744-827 829; aramona@gmx .de) arrange excellent guided tours in French or English (€13/25 per half-/full day plus €0.25 per kilometre), as well as picnics, woodcarving or icon-painting workshops, and homestays.

### Bârsana

From Vadu Izei continue southeast for 12km to Bârsana. Dating from 1326, the village acquired its first church in 1720 (its interior paintings were done by local artists). The Orthodox **Bârsana Monastery** is a popular pilgrimage spot in Maramureş. It was the last Orthodox monastery to be built in the region before Serafim Petrovai, head of the Orthodox church in Maramureş, converted to Greco-Catholicism in 1711.

**Maria Paşca** ( ☎ 331 165; house No 377; bed €20, with full-board €30) has rooms to rent at her home.

### Rozavlea

Continue south though Strâmtura to Rozavlea, first documented under the name of Gorzohaza in 1374. Its fine **church**, dedicated to the archangels Michael and Gabriel, was built between 1717 and 1720 in another village, then erected in Rozavlea on the site of an ancient church destroyed by the Tatars.

ROMANIA

## Botiza

From Rozavlea continue south for 3km to Şieu, then turn off for Botiza. Botiza's **old church**, built in 1694, is overshadowed by the large **new church** constructed in 1974 to serve the 500 or so devout Orthodox families.

Opération Villages Roumains (OVR) runs an efficient agrotourism scheme in Botiza. Bookings can be made with local representative **George Iurca** ( ☎ 334 110, 0722-942 140; botizavr@sintec.ro; house No 742; ☯ 8am-10pm), whose house is signposted. George also runs German-, French- and English-speaking tours of Maramureş (€10 to €15 per day) and Transylvania, rents out mountain bikes (€5 per day) and organises fishing trips.

## Ieud

The oldest wooden church in Maramureş, dating from 1364, is in Ieud, 6km south of the main road from Şieu. Ieud was first documented in 1365. Its fabulous Orthodox **Church on the Hill** was built from fir wood and used to house the first document known to be written in Romanian (1391–92), in which the catechism and church laws pertaining to Ieud were coded. The church was restored in 1958 and in 1997.

Ieud's second **church** is Greco-Catholic, and was built in 1717. It is unique to the region as it has no porch. At the southern end of the village it houses one of the largest collections of icons on glass found in Maramureş.

OVR runs a small agrotourism scheme in Ieud. You can make advance bookings through the office in Vadu Izei (p665) or go straight to local representatives **Vasile Chindris** ( ☎ 336 197; house No 201; bed €12, with full-board €25), **Liviu Ilea** ( ☎ 336 039; house No 333; bed €12, with full-board €18) or **Vasile Rişco** ( ☎ 336 019; house No 705; r with half-/full-board €12/18).

## Moisei

Moisei lies 7km northeast of Săcel, at the junction of route 17C and route 18. A small town at the foot of the Rodna Massif, Moisei is known for its traditional crafts and customs. It gained fame in 1944 when retreating Hungarian (Horthyst) troops gunned down 31 people before setting fire to the village.

In 1944, following the news that the front was approaching Moisei, villagers started to flee, including those forced-labour detachments stationed in the village. Occupying Hungarian forces organised a manhunt to track down the deserters. Thirty-one were captured and detained in a small camp in nearby Vişeu de Sus without food or water for three weeks. On 14 October 1944 Hungarian troops brought the 31 prisoners to a house in Moisei, locked them inside, then shot them through the windows – 29 were killed. Before abandoning the village, the troops set it on fire, leaving all 125 remaining families homeless.

Only one house in Moisei survived the blaze: the one in which the prisoners were shot. Today it houses a small **museum** in tribute to those who died in the massacre. Opposite, on a hillock above the road and railway line, is a circular **monument** to the victims. The 12 upright columns symbolise sun and light. Each column is decorated with a traditional carnival mask, except for two that bear human faces based on the features of the two survivors.

The museum and monument are at the eastern end of the village. If the museum is locked, knock at the house next door and ask for the key.

## BORŞA

☎ 0262

Ore has been mined at Borşa, 12km east of Moisei, since the mid-14th century. The area was colonised in 1777 by German miners from Slovakia; later, Bavarian-Austrian miners moved to Baia Borşa, 2km northeast of the town, to mine copper, lead and silver.

The **Complex Turistic Borşa**, a small ski resort and tourist complex 10km east of Borşa town, is a main entry point to the **Rodna Mountains**, part of which form the Pietrosul Rodnei Nature Reservation (5900 hectares). For useful information on the hiking trails leading into the massif talk to staff at the two-star **Hotel Cerbal** ( ☎ 344 199; Str Fântâna; s/d/tr incl breakfast €31/37/47).

In winter, you can ski down the 2030m-long ski run at the complex (beginner to intermediate). There's a **ski lift** (Str Brădet 10; ☯ 7am-6pm), but ski hire is not available.

## PRISLOP PASS

Famed for its remoteness, the Prislop Pass is the main route from Maramureş into Moldavia. Hikers can trek east from Borşa across the pass.

From Moldavia you can head northeast to Câmpulung Moldovenesc and on to the monasteries of southern Bucovina; or south to the natural mineral waters of Vatra Dornei and through to the fantastic Bicaz Lake.

At 1416m a roadside monument marks the site of the last Tartar invasion prior to their final flight from the region in 1717. Nearby is the Hanul Prislop, site of the Hora de la Prislop, the major Maramureş festival, held yearly on the second Sunday in August.

# MOLDAVIA

With thickly forested hills and tranquil valleys undulating off into the horizon, Moldavia mixes the rich folklore, natural beauty and turbulent history of Transylvania and the quietly appealing, bucolic paradise of Maramureş into its own lovely hybrid of the best of Romania. Cavort through the countryside, then urbanise in Iaşi and Suceava, where the first generation to have no vivid memories of Ceauşescu is rapidly developing a taste for food, shopping and late-night debauchery.

## IAŞI

☎ 0232 / pop 326,502

Iaşi (pronounced 'yash') has an energy and depth of character that would be instantly giddying if one had the power to see through concrete. Those without this endowment will need a few days to pinpoint the numerous joys of Romania's second-largest city.

Iaşi's past as Moldavia's capital since 1565 has resulted in a city scattered with fabulous buildings, important monasteries, parks and unpretentious cultural treasures. Moreover, it's the perfect staging area for travellers heading to the Moldovan border, 20km away.

Modern Iaşi is among Romania's most vibrant cities, teeming with beautiful people, restaurants, bars and hot night spots. **Iaşi Days** (second week in October) is an unhinged street party, fuelled by a river of *must* (a sweet, fermented not-quite-wine brew).

## Orientation

Iaşi's street design was seemingly laid out by a crayon-wielding two-year-old. To reach Iaşi's bus station (Autogara Iaşi Vest) from Gară Centrală train station, walk northwest along Str Străpungerea Silvestru for about 1km. To reach Piaţa Unirii from Gară Centrală train station, walk northeast along Str Gării for two blocks, then turn right onto Şos Arcu. From Piaţa Unirii, B-dul Ştefan cel Mare şi Sfânt runs southeast past the Mitropolia Moldovei (Moldavian Metropolitan Cathedral) and the Church of the Three Hierarchs, ending at the Palatul Culturii (Palace of Culture). B-dul Carol I starts at Piaţa Mihai Eminescu and runs northwest, past the university, Parcul Copou and the Botanical Gardens.

## Information

### INTERNET ACCESS

**Bar-Cafe Internet** (B-dul Ştefan cel Mare şi Sfânt 8, per hr €1.50; ☽ 24hr) Inside the mall.

**Take Net** (Şos Arcu 1; per hr €0.60; ☽ 24hr)

### EMERGENCY

For any emergency within the city, dial ☎ 112.

### MEDICAL SERVICES

**Sfântu Spiridon University Hospital** ( ☎ 210 690; B-dul Independenţei 1) The city's largest, most central hospital.

### MONEY

**Raiffeisen Bank** (B-dul Ştefan cel Mare şi Sfânt 2; ☽ 8.30-6.30pm Mon-Fri, 9am-2pm Sat)

### POST

**Post office** ( ☎ 212 222; Str Cuza Vodă 10; ☽ 8am-7pm Mon-Fri, to 1pm Sat)

### TELEPHONE

**Telephone centre** (Str Alexandru Lăpuşneanu; ☽ 8am-8pm Mon-Fri, to 3pm Sat)

### TOURIST INFORMATION

Iaşi has no official tourist office.

**Cliven Turism** ( ☎ 258 326; www.reservation.ro; B-dul Ştefan cel Mare şi Sfânt 8-12; ☽ 9am-6pm Mon-Fri, to 2pm Sat) As agents for Antrec, these adept English-speakers can arrange rural accommodation, city tours and car rental.

## Sights

### B-DUL ŞTEFAN CEL MARE ŞI SFÂNT & AROUND

Start your city tour on Piaţa Unirii, the main square, with a trip to the 13th floor restaurant of **Hotel Unirea** for a bird's-eye view of Iaşi.

Eastwards the tree-lined B-dul Ştefan cel Mare şi Sfânt leads to the **Moldavian Metropolitan Cathedral** (Mitropolia Moldovei; 1833–39) with its cavernous interior painted by Gheorghe Tattarescu. In mid-October thousands of pilgrims flock here to celebrate the day of St Paraschiva, the patron saint of the cathedral and of Moldavia.

Opposite is a park and at the northeastern end is the **Vasile Alecsandri National Theatre**

(1894–96). In front of it is a statue of its founder Vasile Alecsandri (1821–90), a poet who single-handedly created the theatre's first repertoire with his Romanian adaptation of a French farce.

The boulevard's shining pearl is the fabulous **Biserica Sfinţilor Trei Ierarhi** (Church of the Three Hierarchs; 1637–39), unique for its rich exterior, which is embroidered in a wealth of intricate patterns in stone. Built by Prince Vasile Lupu, the church was badly damaged by Tatar attacks in 1650 but later restored. Inside are the marble tombs of Prince Vasile Lupu and his family, as well as Prince Alexandru Ioan Cuza and Moldavian prince Dimitrie Cantemir.

At the southern end of B-dul Ştefan cel Mare şi Sfânt stands the giant neo-Gothic

**Palatul Culturii** (Palace of Culture; ☎ 218 383; adult/child each museum €0.70/0.50, all 4 museums €2.25/1.50; ☀ 10am-4.30pm Tue-Sun), built between 1906 and 1925 on the ruins of the **old princely court**, founded by Prince Alexandru cel Bun (r 1400–32) in the early 15th century.

The main attraction of the 365-room building today is the four first-class museums it houses: the **Ethnographic Museum**, which has exhibits ranging from agriculture, fishing and hunting to wine-making, as well as traditional costumes and rugs; the **Art Museum** containing works by Romanian artists including Nicolae Grigorescu and Moldavian-born Petre Achiţemie; the **Muzeul de Istorie** (History Museum), where the exhibits include portraits of all of Romania's rulers from AD 81; and

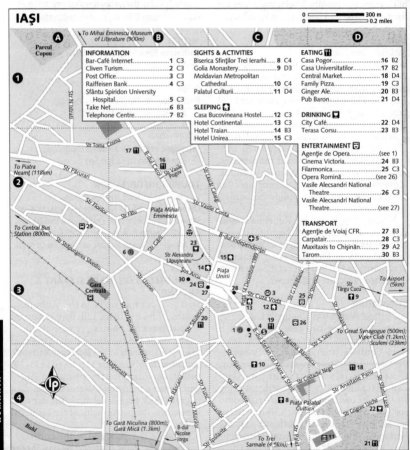

**IAŞI**

0 _____ 300 m
0 _____ 0.2 miles

**INFORMATION**
Bar-Café Internet.....................1 C3
Cliven Turism...........................2 C3
Post Office...............................3 C3
Raiffeisen Bank........................4 C3
Sfântu Spiridon University
  Hospital................................5 C3
Take Net..................................6 B3
Telephone Centre.....................7 B2

**SIGHTS & ACTIVITIES**
Biserica Sfinţilor Trei Ierarhi.....8 C4
Golia Monastery.......................9 D3
Moldavian Metropolitan
  Cathedral............................10 C4
Palatul Culturii........................11 D4

**SLEEPING**
Casa Bucovineana Hostel.......12 C3
Hotel Continental...................13 C3
Hotel Traian..........................14 B3
Hotel Unirea..........................15 C3

**EATING**
Casa Pogor.............................16 B2
Casa Universitatilor.................17 B2
Central Market.........................18 D4
Family Pizza............................19 D4
Ginger Ale...............................20 B3
Pub Baron...............................21 D4

**DRINKING**
City Café.................................22 D4
Terasa Corsu...........................23 B3

**ENTERTAINMENT**
Agenţie de Opera................(see 1)
Cinema Victoria.......................24 B3
Filarmonica.............................25 C3
Opera Rominä......................(see 26)
Vasile Alecsandri National
  Theatre................................26 C3
Vasile Alecsandri National
  Theatre............................(see 27)

**TRANSPORT**
Agenţie de Voiaj CFR.............27 B3
Carpatair.................................28 C3
Maxitaxis to Chişinän.............29 A2
Tarom....................................30 B3

the **Science & Technical Museum** which displays various mechanical creations and musical instruments.

A few blocks north, past the central market, is the fortified **Golia Monastery** (admission free; Str Cuza Vodă), which was constructed in a late-Renaissance style. The monastery's walls and the 30m Golia tower at the entrance shelter a 17th-century church, noted for its vibrant Byzantine frescoes and intricately carved doorways.

### PARCUL COPOU

To get to **Parcul Copou** (Copou Park; laid out between 1834 and 1848) catch tram 1 or 13 north from Piaţa Unirii. The park, which was established during the princely reign of Mihail Sturza, is famed as being a favourite haunt of the legendary poet Mihai Eminescu (1850–89). He allegedly penned some of his best works beneath his favourite linden tree in this park.

The tree is still standing, behind a 13m-tall **monument of lions**, and opposite the main entrance to the park. A bronze bust of Eminescu stands in front of it. Here is the **Mihai Eminescu Museum of Literature** ( ☎ 0747-499 405; admission €0.30; ☺ 10am-5pm Tue-Sun), which recalls the life and loves of Eminescu, Romania's most cherished writer and poet.

## Sleeping

**Casa Bucovineana Hostel** ( ☎ 222 913; Str Cuza Voda 30; s/d/ste with shared bathroom €19.60/30/56) Recent renovations have made the rooms here much more palatable. Some doubles have in-room showers. All rooms have TVs and phones. Breakfast not included.

**Hotel Continental** ( ☎ 211 846; Piaţa 14 Decembrie 1989; s/d €30/40.50, with shared bathroom €25.50/30) The rooms here have been freshened, but so have the prices. The shared bathrooms are clean and private bathrooms are new and immaculate – very much worth the upgrade. Try to get a room away from the noisy street.

**Hotel Traian** ( ☎ 266 666; Piaţa Unirii 1; s/d/ste €63/79/97) The multilingual staff here will make you feel at home in this elegant hotel, designed by Gustave Eiffel. The high-ceiling rooms are awash in old-world comfort, with large, modern bathrooms.

**Casa Universitatilor** ( ☎ 340 029 B-dul Carol I, 9; mains €1-3) Meals are geared for destitute students, but the lime tree-festooned terrace is great for a lazy beer.

## Eating & Drinking

**Family Pizza** ( ☎ 262 400; Str Gl Brătianu; mains €2-4; ☺ 24hr) This lively, brightly lit parlour has 25 types of pizza, plus pasta and a week's worth of pastries to choose from. They also deliver.

**Pub Baron** ( ☎ 206 076; Str Sfântu Lazăr 52; mains €2-4; ☺ 24hr) Cosy wooden interiors and a great eating option. They're heavy on fresh grills, cooked in brick ovens in the dining room, but there are many salads and fish dishes too.

**Casa Pogor** ( ☎ 243 006; Str Vasile Pogov 4; mains €2-4; ☺ 11am-midnight) Where to sit? In the insanely cosy basement that used to house the famed Junimea wine cellar, the main dining hall furnished with antiques or on the multitiered terrace looking out onto a quiet square? Iaşi's most pleasant restaurant (with the patchiest wait-staff) also has vegetarian choices.

**Ginger Ale** ( ☎ 276 017; Str Săulescu 23; mains €2-5; ☺ 11-1am) This place feels like an oversized, old-fashioned café with its antique furniture and cosy dining room. A great place for drinks or a full meal, they also offer 20% to 50% discounts daily from noon to 4pm.

**Trei Sarmale** ( ☎ 237 255; Str Bucium 52; mains €2-5; ☺ 9-2am) This traditional Romanian restaurant teeters on the edge of kitsch with it's folkier-than-thou décor, but the food is mouthwatering. Check before you head out there as it is often booked by tour groups. Take a €3 taxi or bus 30 or 46 from Piaţa Mihai Eminescu; ask the driver for 'Tre Sarmale'.

**City Café** (Str Sfântu Lazăr 34; ☺ 11-1am) This is where Iaşi's beautiful, moneyed people come for relaxed posing sessions. A high-tech, blue-lit, ultracool bar, it's known for its many cocktails.

**Terasa Corso** ( ☎ 276 143; www.corsoterasa.ro; Str Alexandru Lăpuşneanu 11; ☺ 11am-midnight Mon, 9-1am Tue-Sun) The concept of a 'bar' is stretched in this huge, amphitheatre-shaped pub with a well-tended garden in the middle.

**Central market** ( ☺ 8am-4pm) Get fresh fruit and vegetables at this indoor market, with entrances on Str Costache Negri and Str Anastasie Panu.

## Entertainment

**Viper Club** (Iulius Mall; ☺ 24hr, disco 11pm-4am) This rainy-day, entertainment emporium about a kilometre out of the centre, features bowling alleys, billiards and video games, and transforms itself into a House-music haven come night-time.

**Cinema Victoria** ( ☎ 312 502; Piaţa Unirii 5) See your favourite Hollywood schlockbuster with Romanian subtitles here!

**Filarmonica** (Philharmonic; ☎ 212 509; www.filarmonicais.ro; Str Cuza Vodă 29; box office ☷ 10am-1pm & 5-7pm Mon-Fri) When the much-revered Iaşi State Philharmonic Orchestra is in town, its concerts are massively popular. Tickets cost from €2 with 50% student discounts.

**Vasile Alecsandri National Theatre** ( ☎ 316 778; Str Agatha Bârsescu 18) and the **Opera Română** ( ☎ 211 144) are located in the same impressive neo-baroque building. For advance bookings go to the **Agenţia de Opera** ( ☎ 255 999; B-dul Ştefan cel Mare şi Sfânt 8; ☷ 10am-5pm Mon-Sat). Tickets cost from €1.50, with 50% student discounts.

## Getting There & Away

### AIR
**Tarom** ( ☎ 267 768; Şos Arcu 3-5; ☷ 9am-5pm Mon-Fri) has daily flights to Bucharest (about US$75 plus tax US$5; note Tarom does not accept euros).

**Carpatair** ( ☎ 215 295; www.carpatair.com; Str Cuza Voda 2; ☷ 9am-6pm Mon-Fri) has flights to Timişoara Monday to Saturday, from where you can catch connecting flights to Italy, Germany and Paris.

### BUS
The **central bus station** (Autogara Iaşi Vest; ☎ 214 720), behind the large building labelled 'Auto Center', has four daily maxitaxis each to Târgu Neamţ (€2.85) and Suceava (€5.15), eight to Bucharest (€11.40), 18 to Bacau and almost 20 to Piatra Neamţ (€4.30). Slower buses run to Vatra Dornei, Tulcea and Braşov.

Maxitaxis to Chişinău leave from outside the Billa supermarket three to four times daily while up to six daily (slower) buses to Chişinău depart from the bus station.

### TRAIN
Nearly all trains arrive and depart from the Gară Centrală (also called Gară Mare and Gară du Nord) on Str Garii. Trains to Chişinău depart from the Gară Niculina (also called Gară International) on B-dul Nicolae Iorga about 800m south of the centre, and tickets for the trip must be bought from Gară Mică (the one with the sign saying 'Niculina' on it!), 500m south on Aleea Nicolina. The **Agenţie de Voiaj CFR** ( ☎ 242 620; Piaţa Unirii 10; ☷ 7.30am-8.30pm Mon-Fri) sells advance tickets.

There are five daily trains to Bucharest (€14.50, seven hours), one service daily to each of Oradea, Galaţi, Mangalia and three

to Timişoara (via Oradea, affectionately called the 'horror train' by locals).

# SOUTHERN BUCOVINA

Southern Bucovina is a rural paradise as magical and deeply revered as Maramureş. Its painted churches are among the greatest artistic monuments of Europe – in 1993 they were collectively designated World Heritage sites by Unesco. Apart from religious art and fantastic churches, southern Bucovina is well worth visiting for its folklore, picturesque villages, bucolic scenery and colourful inhabitants, all as memorable as you'll find elsewhere in Romania.

Southern Bucovina embraces the northwestern region of present-day Moldavia; northern Bucovina is in Ukraine.

## SUCEAVA
☎ 0230 / pop 111,200
Suceava, the capital of Moldavia from 1388 to 1565, was a thriving commercial centre on the Lviv–Istanbul trading route. Today it's the seat of Suceava County and gateway to the painted churches of Bucovina.

### Orientation
Piaţa 22 Decembrie is the centre of town, with most sites of note being within a 400m radius. Suceava has two train stations, Suceava and Suceava Nord, both north of the city centre and easily reached by trolleybus or maxitaxi. From Suceava station, cross the street, buy a ticket at a kiosk and take trolleybus 2 or 3 to the centre of town. From Suceava Nord take trolleybus 5 or maxitaxi 1 (pay the driver). From Piaţa 22 Decembrie, walk south along Str Ştefan cel Mare past Central Park and Bucovina Mall to the Bucovina History Museum. Or head north for St Dimitru's Church and the Central Market. The City of Residence citadel is east of the centre, down Str Cetăţii, over the creek and through Parcul Şipote.

### Information
#### INTERNET ACCESS
**Assist** ( ☎ 523 044; Piaţa 22 Decembrie; per hr €0.50; ☷ 9am-11pm)

#### MONEY
There are several ATMs on Piaţa 22 Decembrie and along Str Ştefan cel Mare.

ROMANIA

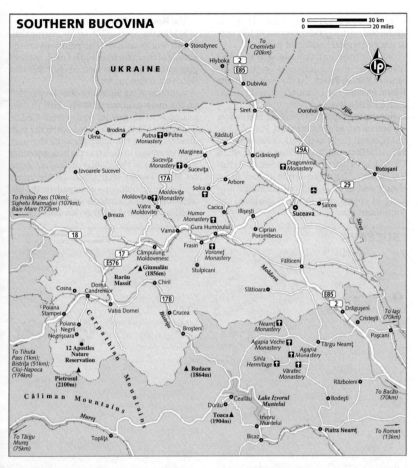

**Raiffeisen Bank** (Str Nicolai Bălcescu 2; ⏱ 8.30am-6.30pm Mon-Fri, 9am-3pm Sat)

### POST

**Post office** ( ☎ 512 222; Str Dimitrie Onciul; ⏱ 7am-7pm Mon-Fri, 8am-4pm Sat)

### TELEPHONE

**Telephone centre** (cnr Str Nicolae Bălcescu & Str Dimitrie Onciu; ⏱ 7am-9pm Mon-Fri, 8am-4pm Sat)

### TOURIST INFORMATION

Not surprisingly, Suceava is bursting with tourist resources. Start while you're still at home by visiting www.lasuceava.ro.
**Unita Tour Suceava** ( ☎ 523 024; unitatour.sv@unita-turism.ro; Str Nicolae Bălcescu 2; ⏱ 8am-8pm Mon-Fri,

to 5pm Sat) Inside Hotel Suceava, this small office can arrange monastery tours with multilingual guides for between €80 and €90 (€20 to €25 extra for guide) per group.
**Ciprian Slemcho** ( ☎ 0744-292 588; www.mtour.go.ro) This highly recommended private tour guide is a specialist in both religion and history. He's also a can-do kind of guy and arranges tours to suit your schedule.
**Infoturism** ( ☎ 551 241, 0722-331 502; infoturism@suceava.rdsnet.ro; Str Mihai Eminescu 8; ⏱ 8am-8pm) This is the official tourism office of Suceava county.

## Sights

The bulky **Casa de Cultură** (House of Culture) is at the western end of Piaţa 22 Decembrie, the city's main square. West of Piaţa 22 Decembrie is Hanul Domnesc, a 16th-century guesthouse that now houses an **Ethnographic Museum** ( ☎ 214

081; Str Ciprian Porumbescu 5; adult/child €0.60/0.30; ⏰ 9am-5pm Tue-Sun), with a good collection of folk costumes and typical household items.

North of the bus stop along B-dul Ana Ipătescu lie the foundations of the 15th-century **Princely Palace**. To the west is **Biserica Sfântul Dumitru** (St Dimitru's church; 1535) built by Petru Rareş.

Return to Piaţa 22 Decembrie and follow Str Ştefan cel Mare south past Parcul Central (Central Park) to the informative **Muzeul Naţional al Bucovinei** (Bucovina History Museum; ☎ 216 439; Str Ştefan cel Mare 33; adult/child €0.90/0.30; ⏰ 9am-5pm Tue-Sun). The presentation comes to an abrupt end at 1945 and old paintings now hang in rooms that formerly glorified the communist era.

The **Mănăstirea Sfântu Ioan cel Nou** (Monastery of St John the New; 1522), off Str Mitropoliei, is well worth visiting. The paintings on the outside of the church are badly faded, but they give you an idea of the painted churches that Bucovina is famous for.

Continue along Str Mitropoliei, keeping left on the main road out of town, until you see a large wooden gate marked 'Parcul Cetăţii' on the left. Go through it and, when the path divides, follow the footpath with the park benches around to the left to the huge **equestrian statue** (1966) of the Moldavian leader, Ştefan cel Mare. Twenty metres back on the access road to the monument is a footpath on the left, which descends towards the **Cetatea de Scaun** (City of Residence; adult/child €0.45/0.30; ⏰ 9am-6pm), a citadel

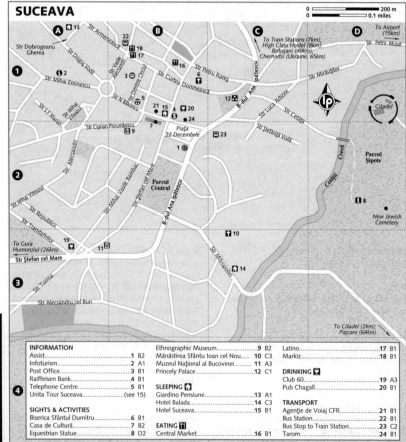

## SUCEAVA

fortress that held off Mehmed II, conqueror of Constantinople (Istanbul) in 1476.

## Sleeping

**High Class Hostel** ( ☎ 525 213, 0723-782 328; www.class hostel.ro; Str Aurel Vlaicu 195; per person €14.50; 🖳 ) This hostel is on the edge of the city, but you'll feel as if you're in the country in this peaceful, spacious and ultra-modern two-floor house. Monica, your interminably good-natured host, can arrange monastery tours if you like, or show you around the city too. It's a super-friendly hostel, and one of the country's best, 1km west of Gară de Nord.

**Giardino Pensiune** ( ☎ 531 778, www.giardino.ro; Str Dobrogeanu Gherea 2; s/d €28/35; 🖳 ) Opened in 2005 this three-star *pension* still reeks of brand new everything. The breakfast (included), is overwhelming. Just 200m from the bus station. Psst! 'Prices are negotiable for backpackers'!

**Hotel Suceava** ( ☎ 521 079; www.unita-turism.ro; Str Nicolae Bălcescu 2; unrenovated s/d €25/34, renovated s/d/tr €32/43/52) Smack in the city centre and featuring old-fashioned but perfectly comfortable rooms, with new bathrooms, this is a very pleasant place. Refrigerators are available upon request.

**Hotel Balada** ( ☎ 520 408; www.balada.ro; Str Mitropoliei 3; s/d/ste €59/70/111.50; 😆 🖳 ) One of the top hotels in the region, this three-storey hotel offers elegance and comfort over pure luxury; rooms have everything you need but are simply furnished. It's on a lovely, quiet street.

## Eating & Drinking

**Latino** ( ☎ 523 627; Str Curtea Domnească 9; mains €2-8; ⏰ 11am-midnight) The classy, subdued décor is accentuated by impeccable service and a dazzlingly varied menu that runs the gamut from over 25 kinds of pizza (with real mozzarella!; €5), to a dozen first-rate pasta dishes (€4) and steaming, fresh fish dishes (€5 to €8).

**Markiz** ( ☎ 520 219; Str Vasile Alecsandri 10; mains €2-4; ⏰ 8am-11pm) Its once grand reputation diminished, this budget-friendly Middle Eastern restaurant may nevertheless be your best chance at culinary diversity until you get back to Bucharest. The terrace remains a pleasant and favoured place to have a few drinks.

The **central market** (cnr Strs Petru Rareş & Ştefan cel Mare) is close to the bus station.

**Pub Chagall** ( ☎ 0723 961 127; Str Ştefan cel Mare; mains €3-7; ⏰ 11am-1am) Cosy cellar pub and diner.

Though it has a full menu of tasty meals (€1 to €3), it's mostly used as a drinking hole.

**Club 60** ( ☎ 209 440; Str Ştefan cel Mare; ⏰ 1pm-1am) Enter here at your own risk: you may never want to leave! Emanating some of the smoothest vibes of any club in the country is this vast, loft-style lounge-bar with wooden floors, antique furnishings, comfy sofas and billiard tables. Enter from the back of the Universal Department Store and climb the stairs to the 2nd floor.

## Getting There & Away

### AIR

Suceava's **Ştefan cel Mare airport** (www.aeroportsuceava .ro) is about 15km northeast of the centre.

**Tarom** ( ☎ 214 686; www.tarom.ro; Str Nicolae Bălcescu 2; ⏰ 9am-7pm Mon-Fri, to 2pm Sat) has four weekly flights to Bucharest (US$104 plus tax US$5; Tarom does not accept euros).

**Carpatair** ( ☎ 529 559; www.carpatair.com) doesn't have an office in Suceava, but it does fly to Timişoara and points beyond there, three times a week.

### BUS

The **bus station** ( ☎ 216 089) is in the centre of town at Str Armenească.

Bus and maxitaxi services include 13 daily to Gura Humorului (€1.40), eight to Botoşani (€1.40), six to Rădăuţi (€1.40), five to Iaşi (€4.50) and Vatra Dornei (€3), four to Bucharest (€9.20) and three to Târgu Neamţ (€2.30). Five daily buses go to Chernivtsi (Cernăuţi) in Ukraine (€5.70) and three a week to Chişinău in Moldova (€8.60).

### TRAIN

The bus stop to the train station is east of Piaţa 22 Decembrie, across B-dul Ana Ipătescu, next to McDonald's. The **Agenţie de Voiaj CFR** ( ☎ 214 335; Str Nicolae Bălcescu 8; ⏰ 7am-8pm Mon-Fri) sells advance tickets. Trains that originate or terminate in Suceava arrive and depart at Suceava Nord. Most trains arrive and depart from the newly spruced Gară Burdujeni (also known as Gară Sud or Gară Principala), which is a half-scale replica of Milan's stunning Central Station.

Train service includes nine to Gură Humorului (€2.10, 70 minutes), seven to Vatra Dornei (€7, 3¼ hours), three to Iaşi (€4.40, 2½ hours) and Timişoara (€18, 13½ hours) and one daily to Bucharest (€15.50, seven hours). To get to Moldoviţa, change at Vama.

ROMANIA

# BUCOVINA MONASTERIES

☎ 0230

## Voroneţ

The *Last Judgment* fresco, which fills the entire western wall of the **Voroneţ Monastery** (adult/child €1.20/0.60; ☼ 8am-8pm), is perhaps the most marvellous Bucovine fresco. At the top, angels roll up the signs of the zodiac to indicate the end of time. The middle fresco shows humanity being brought to judgment. On the left, St Paul escorts the believers, while on the right Moses brings forward the nonbelievers. Below is the *Resurrection*.

On the northern wall is *Genesis*, from Adam and Eve to Cain and Abel. The southern wall features a tree of Jesse (see opposite for details of the Suceviţa Jesse tree) with the genealogy of biblical personalities. In the vertical fresco to the left is the story of the martyrdom of St John of Suceava (who is buried in the Monastery of Sfântu Ioan cel Nou in Suceava). The vibrant, almost satiny blue pigment used throughout the frescoes is known worldwide as 'Voroneţ blue'.

In the narthex lies the tomb of Daniel the Hermit, the first abbot of Voroneţ Monastery. It was upon the worldly advice of Daniel, who told Ştefan cel Mare not to give up his battle against the Turks, that the Moldavian prince went on to win further victories against the Turks and then to build Voroneţ Monastery out of gratitude to God.

In 1785 the occupying Austrians forced Voroneţ's monks to abandon the monastery. Since 1991 the monastery has been inhabited by a small community of nuns.

### SLEEPING & EATING

The town of Gura Humorlui is a perfect base to visit Voroneţ. Every second house takes in tourists. The usual rate per person per night in a so-called 'vila' is about €15 to €20. There's wild camping possible on the south bank of the Moldova River, 500m south of the bus station; follow the only path and cross the river.

**Pensuinea Lions** ( ☎ 235 226; www.motel-lions.ro, in Romanian; Str Ştefan cel Mare 39; s/d €23/29) This three-star *pension*-restaurant minicomplex is warm, homy and clean. Beds are decent and all rooms have a balcony.

**Hotel Simeria** ( ☎ 230 227; Mihail Kogalniceanu 2; s €27, d per person €30) This is a modern, impeccably clean and pleasant three-storey hotel. Some rooms have balconies, all have refrigerator and TV.

**Casa Elena** ( ☎ 230 651; www.casaelena.ro; s/d €44/59) A quick 3.5km trip from Gura Humorului on the northern edge of Voroneţ Monastery, this four-star option has 31 rooms in five different villas, all in a large, luxurious complex. The hotel also has a billiard room, sauna and 24-hour restaurant.

### GETTING THERE & AWAY

See p673 for bus and train services from Suceava to Gura Humorului. There are buses on weekdays from Gura Humorului to Voroneţ, departing at 7am, 12.30pm and 2.45pm. A lovely option is to walk the 4km along a narrow village road to Voroneţ. The route is clearly marked and it's impossible to get lost.

## Humor

Of all the Bucovina monasteries, **Humor Monastery** (Mănăstirea Humorului; adult/child €1.20/0.60; ☼ 8am-8pm) has the most impressive interior frescoes.

On the church's southern exterior wall (AD 1530) the 1453 siege of Constantinople is depicted, with the parable of the return of the prodigal son beside it. On the porch is the *Last Judgment* and, in the first chamber inside the church, scenes of martyrdom.

Aside from hitching a ride the 6km from Gura Humorlui, there are regular maxitaxis that depart from next to the towering Best Western Hotel, at the start of the road towards the monastery.

## Moldoviţa

**Moldoviţa Monastery** (adult/child €1.20/0.60; ☼ 10am-6pm) is in the middle of a quaint village. It's a fortified enclosure with towers and brawny gates, and a magnificent painted church at its centre. The monastery has undergone careful restoration in recent years.

The fortifications here are actually more impressive than the frescoes. On the church's southern exterior wall is a depiction of the defence of Constantinople in AD 626 against Persians dressed as Turks, while on the porch is a representation of the *Last Judgment*, all on a background of blue. Inside the sanctuary, on a wall facing the original carved iconostasis, is a portrait of Prince Petru Rareş (Moldoviţa's founder) and his family offering the church to Christ. All these works date from 1537. In the monastery's small museum is Petru Rareş' original throne.

## SLEEPING & EATING

See www.ruraltourism.ro for some great homestays in Vama, a small village 14km south of Moldoviţa on the main Suceava–Vatra Dornei road.

**Mărul de Aur** ( ☎ 336 180; camping free, cabins €3.50) Located in Moldoviţa between the train station and the monastery, Mărul de Aur has pitiable rooms that are not recommended, however it operates a camping ground, 3km out of town on the road to Suceviţa.

**Letitia Orsvischi Pension** ( ☎ 745 869 529; orsiv schiletita@yahoo.fr; Str Gării 20; per person €25; 🖵 ) This large, two-house property in Vama has a massive painted-egg exhibit and a private ethnographic museum. Rooms are simple, but clean, with shared bathroom. Breakfast, dinner *and* internet included! Follow the signs with painted eggs. No English is spoken.

**Casa Alba** ( ☎ 340 404; www.casa-alba.suceava.ro; s/d/ste €46/54.50/77) You certainly won't feel a monastic asceticism in this lush, ultra-modern and very comfortable villa. Follow the one road heading south 5km west of Frasin about 3km east of Vama.

## GETTING THERE & AWAY

Moldoviţa Monastery is right above Vatra Moldoviţei's train station (be sure to get off at Vatra Moldoviţei, not Moldoviţa). From Suceava there are nine daily trains to Vama (1½ hours), and from Vama three trains leave daily for Vatra Moldoviţei (35 minutes).

## Suceviţa

**Suceviţa Monastery** (adult/child €1.20/0.60; ☼ 8am-8pm) is perhaps the largest and finest of the Bucovina monasteries.

The church inside the fortified quadrangular enclosure (built between 1582 and 1601) is almost completely covered in frescoes. As you enter you first see the *Virtuous Ladder* fresco covering most of the northern exterior wall, which depicts the 30 steps from hell to paradise. On the southern exterior wall is a tree symbolising the continuity of the Old and New Testaments. The tree grows from the reclining figure of Jesse, who is flanked by a row of ancient philosophers. To the left is the Virgin as a Byzantine princess, with angels holding a red veil over her head. Mysteriously, the western wall remains blank. Legend has it that the artist fell off his scaffolding and died, leaving artists of the time too scared to follow in his footsteps.

## SLEEPING & EATING

It's worth spending a night here and doing a little hiking in the surrounding hills. Wild camping is possible in the field across the stream from the monastery, as well as along the road from Moldoviţa. The road from Marginea to Suceviţa is littered with *cazare* (room for rent) signs.

**Pensiunea Emilia** ( ☎ 0740 117 277; Str Bercheza 173; s/d €14.50) Of the handful of *pensions* in the immediate area, this one is most appealing. It has only five rooms, but all feel like home. Walk 700m up the road opposite the monastery.

**Pensiunea Silva** ( ☎ 0230 417 019; www.pensiuneasilva .ro; Suceviţa 391; r per person incl full-board €24; 🖵 ) The hunting-lodge motif here is punctuated by a gaggle of taxidermied critters inside the front door. Located on the western edge of nearby Suceviţa village by the Info-Tur office, it's an easy 3km walk to the monastery.

## GETTING THERE & AWAY

Suceviţa is the most difficult monastery to reach on public transport. There are only two daily buses from Rădăuţi (six maxitaxis daily travel to Rădăuţi from Suceava; €1.40). Hitching or biking are your best bets.

# NORTHERN DOBROGEA

Northern Dobrogea is undeniably a kingdom unto itself within Romania. Although it lacks prevailing Romanian icons (breathtaking mountains, ancient churches, the undead), both the Danube River (Râul Dunărea) and the Black Sea coast (Marea Neagră) contain offerings ranging from all nature to *au natural*.

Though widely considered to be the least 'Romanian' part of the country, this is ironically where the strongest evidence of Romania's conspicuously proud connection to ancient Rome can be found in the form of statues, busts, sarcophagi and other archaeological finds.

In Mamaia humans converge in beach resort towns to sooth their bodies with sunshine and curative mud. Alternatively, the calming and less opulent Danube Delta draws bird-lovers and seekers of solitude into a tangled web of ever-eroding canals, riverbeds and wetlands.

## CONSTANŢA

☎ 0241 & 0341 / pop 314,490

Constanţa is the gateway to Romania's seaside activities. Sadly, sharp annual price hikes have

ROMANIA

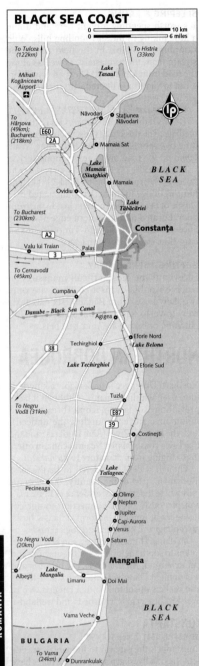

**BLACK SEA COAST**

0 ——————— 10 km
0 ——————— 6 miles

To Tulcea
(122km)

To Histria
(33km)

Lake
Tasaul

Mihail
Kogălniceanu
Airport

To
Hârşova
(49km);
Bucharest
(218km)

E60
2A

Năvodari  Staţiunea
Năvodari

Mamaia Sat

Lake
Mamaia
(Siutghiol)

Mamaia

B L A C K
S E A

Ovidiu

Lake
Tăbăcăriei

To Bucharest
(230km)

**Constanţa**

A2

Valu lui Traian  Palas
3

To Cernavodă
(45km)

Cumpăna

Danube – Black Sea Canal

Agigea

38

Techirghiol

Eforie Nord
Lake Belona

Lake Techirghiol

Eforie Sud

Tuzla

To Negru
Vodă (31km)

E87

39

Costineşti

Lake
Tallageac

Pecineaga

Olimp
Neptun
Jupiter
Cap-Aurora
Venus
Saturn

To Negru Vodă
(20km)

**Mangalia**

Lake
Mangalia

Albeşti  Limanu  Doi Mai

B L A C K
S E A

Vama Veche

B U L G A R I A

To Varna
(24km)  Dunrankulak

ROMANIA

made a trip here fairly expensive, even by
Western European standards, though staying
in private homes, camping or hotel-room
stuffing can ease expenses (see opposite).

Old Constanţa evokes romantic notions
of ancient seafarers, the Roman poet Ovid
and even the classic legend of Jason and the
Argonauts (they fled here from King Aietes).
Constanţa's original name Tomis means 'cut to
pieces', in reference to Jason's beloved Medea,
who cut up her brother Apsyrtus and threw the
pieces into the sea near the present-day city.

After Constanţa was taken by Romania in
1877 a railway line was built to Bucharest. By
the early 1900s it was a fashionable seaside
resort frequented by European royalty.

The city offers a bit of everything: beaches,
a picturesque Old Town, archaeological treasures and a few excellent museums.

## Orientation

Constanţa sprawls up the Black Sea coast
from the port in the south to Mamaia in the
north. The train station is about 2km west
of the centre. To reach Constanţa's centre,
exit the station, buy a ticket from the kiosk
to the right and take trolleybus 40, 41 or 43
down B-dul Ferdinand to Parcul Arheologic
(Archaeological Park) four stops from the
station; or just walk along B-dul Ferdinand.
North of B-dul Ferdinand is Constanţa's business district and many of its best restaurants.
The area around Str Ştefan cel Mare is lined
with shops, restaurants and theatres. South
of B-dul Ferdinand are the tiny streets of the
Old Town, sporting the city's best museums,
churches and neglected buildings.

## Information

Most hotels and travel agencies have exchange
outlets, and there are numerous exchange
offices, several of which are open around the
clock and line B-dul Tomis south of B-dul
Ferdinand.

**Banca Comercială Română** ( ☎ 638 200; Str Traian 1;
⏱ 8.30am-5.30pm Mon-Fri, to 12.30pm Sat) Changes
travellers cheques, gives unlimited cash advances on Visa
and MasterCard and has an ATM.

**Central post office** ( ☎ 552 222; B-dul Tomis 79-81;
8.30am-8pm Mon-Fri, to 1pm Sat)

**County Hospital** (Spitalul Judetean; ☎ 662 222; B-dul
Tomis 145) North of the centre.

**Latina Tourism** ( ☎ 639 713; latina@latina.ro; B-dul
Ferdinand 70; ⏱ 9am-5pm Mon-Fri) A recommended
travel agency with all the normal services.

**Planet Games** ( ☎ 552 377; cnr Str Ștefan cel Mare & Str Răscoala din 1907; per hr €0.65; ☒ 24hr)
**Telephone office** (B-dul Tomis 79-81; ☒ 8.30am-10pm) Shares the same building as the central post office.

## Sights

Constanța's most renowned attraction is the **History & Archaeological Museum** ( ☎ 618 763; Piața Ovidiu 12; adult/child €3/1.50; ☒ 9am-8pm Jun-Sep, 10am-6pm Tue-Sun Oct-May). There's something here for everyone. Kids will be impressed by the bones of a 2nd-century woman and the mammoth tusks.

The archaeological fragments of Roman Tomis spill over onto the surrounding square. Facing these is a glass museum, which shelters a gigantic 3rd-century **Roman mosaic** discovered in 1959. The **statue of Ovid**, erected on Piața Ovidiu in 1887, commemorates the Latin poet who was exiled to Constanța in AD 8; rumour has it that he hated the place.

A block south is **Moscheia Mahmudiye** (Mahmudiye Mosque; Str Arhiepiscopiei), dating from 1910, and with a 140-step minaret you can climb when the gate is unlocked. Two blocks further down the same street is an Orthodox **Catedrala** (1885). Along the promenade is the **Genoese lighthouse** (1860) and pier, with a fine view of old Constanța.

Another museum in town worth checking out is the **Muzeul de Artă Populară** (Folk Art Museum; ☎ 616 133; B-dul Tomis 32; adult/child €1.25/0.50; ☒ 9am-8pm Jul & Aug, 10am-6pm Tue-Sun Sep-Jun), which has handicrafts and costumes. Further north along the boulevard is the **Art Museum & Gallery** ( ☎ 617 012; B-dul Tomis 84; adult/child €1.75/1; ☒ 10am-6pm Tue-Sun), with mostly still-life and landscape paintings and sculptures. Contemporary exhibits are held in an adjoining art gallery. The **Muzeul Marinei Române** (Naval History Museum; ☎ 619 035; Str Traian 53; adult/child €1.50/0.50; ☒ 10am-6pm Tue-Sun Jun-Sep, 9am-5pm Tue-Sun Oct-May) is housed in the old Navy high school. The captions are in Romanian.

Near the city's main intersection, B-dul Ferdinand and B-dul Tomis, is Parcul Victoriei, which has remains of the 3rd-century **Roman city wall** and the 6th-century Butchers' tower, loads of Roman sculptures and the modern **Victory monument** (1968).

Heading north towards Mamaia, you pass Constanța's **Planetarium** ( ☎ 831 553; B-dul Mamaia; adult/child €2/1; ☒ 8am-9pm Jun–mid-Sep, to 4pm mid-Sep-May), on the southeastern shores of Lake Tăbăcăriei.

## Activities

You can sail on the **Condor** ( ☎ 0744-689 228; tours per person per hr for groups of 14 €5; ☒ at around 9am May-Sep), moored at the Tomis Turist Port, at the east end of Str Remus Opreanu.

**Delphi** ( ☎ 0722-336 686) provides a flexible range of scuba-diving opportunities.

## Sleeping

A small legion of people with spare rooms meet every arriving train offering very cheap accommodation. Prices range from 20 to 40 lei (€5.75 to €11.50). The rooms are always plain, with shared bath, but acceptable, though privacy is non-existent.

The nearest camping ground is north of Mamaia (see p680).

**Hotel Tineretului** ( ☎ 613 590; fax 611 290; B-dul Tomis 24; s/d €24/26.50) Cheap for good reason; the rooms are worn, the bedding half-heartedly laundered, the bathrooms woeful and the reception indifferent.

**Hotel Maria** ( ☎ /fax 616 852; B-dul 1 Decembrie 1918; s/d €40/51.50; ☒ ) This more modern option, across from the park that faces the train station, has lots of glass, chrome and deep blue to soothe your sun-withered nerves. There's only 12 rooms, so it's cosy and quiet.

**Hotel Class** ( ☎ 660 766; www.hotelclass.ro; Str Răscoala din 1907 1; s/d/ste €57.50/68.50/86; ☒ 🖳 ) Opened in January 2006, everything here is new or new-looking enough to make it worth the price.

**Hotel Guci** ( ☎ /fax 695 500; www.blackseahotels.ro; Str Răscoala din 1907, 23; s/d/ste €60/67/85; ☒ ☒ ) Modern, moderately luxurious three-star hotel offering a Jacuzzi, laundry, massage and a gym.

## Eating

**Café D'Art** ( ☎ 612 133; B-dul Tomis 97; mains €1-3; ☒ 9-1am) This is an intimate place snuggled up to the Drama Theatre. Especially popular as an evening drinking hole (cocktails €2), it's also packed during the day with those seeking a good place to people-watch while enjoying a light meal.

**Pizzico** ( ☎ 615 555; Piața Ovidiu 7; mains €3-5; ☒ 24hr) While the wood-fire pizza and summer terrace are its main draw, Pizzico has a menu that offers truffles, pasta, buffalo wings, fish (summer only), salads and a large, inexpensive wine list.

**Beta** ( ☎ 673 663; www.la-beta.ro; Str Ștefan cel Mare 6A; mains €3-6; ☒ 7-1am) This modern food emporium and bar with a sprawling terrace is sure to satisfy all. Menu items include full

ROMANIA

breakfast, vegetarian dishes, pizza, salad and children's meals.

**Marco Polo** ( ☎ 617 537; Str Mircea cel Bătrân 103; mains €2-5; ☷ 11am-midnight) A splendid Italian restaurant where tables are separated from each other by plants, making you feel like you're in a private garden, only one with doting waiters! Portions are generous, and the service kind and attentive. The pizza, pasta, meat, fish and veg dishes are delicious.

**Casa Tărănească** ( ☎ 665 606; Str Negru Voda 9; mains €3.50-7; ☷ 24hr) This traditional restaurant stays open day and night, offering detoxing clubbers Romanian comfort food such as *sarmale* (ground beef, vegetables, rice and spices wrapped up like a burrito in cabbage or vine leaves), *ciorbă* and *mămăligă*,

knuckle of pork and, um, 'bear with wild sauce' (dare you).

## Entertainment

New foreign films are presented at **Cinema Studio** ( ☎ 611 358; cnr B-bul Tomis & Str Negru Voda). In summer, films are also screened at **Cinema Grădină Tomis** (B-dul Ferdinand), an outside cinema in Archaeological Park.

Tickets for the **Metamorfoze State Drama Theatre & Opera** ( ☎ 615 268; Str Mircea cel Bătrân 97) are sold at the **ticket office** (B-dul Tomis 97; ☷ 9am-6pm Mon-Fri, 9am-noon Sat, 5-6.50pm Sun) or the **Agenţie de Bilete** ( ☎ 664 076; Str Ştefan cel Mare 34; ☷ 10am-5pm). The theatre is also home to the Filarmonica Marea Neagră (Black Sea Philharmonic) and the **Oleg Danovski Ballet Theatre** ( ☎ 488 202).

CONSTANŢA

0 —————— 200 m
0 —————— 0.1 miles

BLACK SEA

To County Hospital (700m); Mihail Kogălniceanu Airport (24km)

To Autogară Nord (2.9km)

To Lake Tabacariei (3.4km); Planetarium (3.4km); Mamaia (6.4km)

Modern Beach (Plaja Modern)

Tomis Department Store

Archaeological Park — Prefectura

To Hotel Maria (900m); Autogară Sud (1.5km); Train Station (1.5km)

Marina (Tomis Turist Port)

Constanţa Port (Portul Constanţa)

Marina

**SLEEPING** 🏠
Hotel Class.....................17 B2
Hotel Guci.......................18 B2
Hotel Tineretului.............19 C3

**EATING** 🍴
Beta..............................20 B1
Café D'Art......................21 B1
Casa Tărănească............ 22 B2
Marco Polo.....................23 B1
Pizzaco..........................24 C3

**ENTERTAINMENT** 🎭
Agenţie de Bilete......... 25 A2
Cinema Grădină Tomis... 26 B2
Cinema Studio...............27 B2
Metamorfoze State Drama Theatre & Opera.........28 B1
Oleg Danovski Ballet Theatre..................(see 28)
Ticket Office for Metamorfoze State Drama Theatre & Opera.........................29 B1

**TRANSPORT**
Agenţie de Voiaj CFR....... 30 C3
Tarom.............................31 B1

**INFORMATION**
Banca Comercială Română..... 1 C3
Central Post Office.................2 B1
Latina Tourism........................3 A2
Planet Games..........................4 B2
Raiffeisen Bank.......................5 A3
Telephone Office.................(see 2)

**SIGHTS & ACTIVITIES**
Art Museum & Gallery............6 B2
Catedrala.................................7 C4
Genoese Lighthouse............. 8 D4
History & Archaeological Museum...............................9 C3
Moscheia Mahmudiye..........10 C3
Muzeul de Artă Populară......11 C3
Muzeul Marinei Române.......12 A3
Roman City Wall....................13 B2
Roman Mosaic.......................14 C4
Statue of Ovid.......................15 C3
Victory Monument................16 B2

ROMANIA

## Getting There & Away

### AIR

In summer there are international flights from Athens and sometimes Istanbul to/from Constanţa's **Mihail Kogalniceanu Airport** ( ☎ 255 100; aeroport@aic.ro), 25km from the centre.

**Tarom** ( ☎ 662 632; Str Ştefan cel Mare 15; ☽ 8am-6pm Mon-Fri, 8.30am-12.30pm Sat) has a once-weekly flight to Bucharest (US$75 plus tax US$5; Tarom does not accept euros). **Carpatair** ( ☎ 255 422; constanta@carpatair.com) flies to Timişoara six days a week with connections to numerous cities beyond. Their office is at Constanţa's airport.

### BUS

Constanţa has two bus stations. From the **Autogară Sud** (Southern Bus Station; ☎ 665 289; B-dul Ferdinand), next to the train station, buses to Istanbul (17½ hours) depart daily. Tickets are sold in advance from **Özlem Tur** ( ☎ 514 053) just outside the bus station. There are three maxitaxis daily to Braila (€5.60) and 10 daily to Galaţi (€6.70), each of which stop at the **Autogară Nord** (Northern Bus Station; ☎ 641 379; Str Soveja 35) on the way. Maxitaxi 23 to Mamaia also departs from here.

From Constanţa's northern bus station services include at least one daily maxitaxi to Chişinău (€13, nine hours) and Iaşi (€11.20, seven hours), and four to Histria (€1.75). Maxitaxis leave for Tulcea (€3.70, 2½ hours) every 30 minutes from 6am to 7.30pm.

If you're travelling south along the Black Sea Coast, buses are infinitely more convenient than trains. Exit Constanţa's train station, turn right and walk 50m to the long queue of maxitaxis, buses and private cars destined for Mangalia, stopping at Eforie Nord, Eforie Sud, Neptun-Olimp, Venus and Saturn.

### TRAIN

Constanţa's train station is near the southern bus station at the west end of B-dul Ferdinand.

The **Agenţie de Voiaj CFR** ( ☎ 617 930; Aleea Vasile Canarache 4; ☽ 7.30am-8.30pm Mon-Fri, 8am-1pm Sat) sells long-distance tickets only; for the local train service (down the coast) buy tickets at the train station.

There are 11 to 15 daily trains to Bucharest (€8.75, 2½ to 4½ hours). There are daily services to Suceava, Cluj-Napoca, Satu Mare, Galaţi, Timişoara and other destinations. As many as 19 trains a day head from Constanţa to Mangalia (€1.30, one to 1¼ hours). There are one to two daily trains to Chişinău in

Moldova (€20, 12 hours). The Ovidius train to Budapest also runs overnight (17 hours) via Bucharest and Arad.

## MAMAIA
☎ 0241

Mamaia is where the real action is, if by 'action' you mean pretty beaches, pretty people and pretty dreadful hangovers. It's a mere 8km strip of beach between the freshwater Lake Mamaia (also known as Lake Siutghiol) and the Black Sea, but it's Romania's most popular resort. It gloats over golden sands, an aqua park, restaurants, nightclubs and a raucous atmosphere.

## Information

**Info Litoral Tourist Information Centre** ( ☎ 555 000; www.infolitoral.ro; 185 Al Lăpuşneanu Blvd, Constanţa Chamber of Commerce Bldg; ☽ 9am-5pm Mon-Fri) is a highly recommended first stop. The friendly, well-informed staff will help answer any kind of questions. They also sells maps and booklets.

Every hotel has a currency exchange, and ATMs are easy to find, but to change travellers cheques you have to go to Constanţa.

The **post office & telephone** ( ☽ 8am-8pm Mon-Fri) is 200m south of the Cazino complex on the promenade.

## Sights & Activities

Mamaia's number-one attraction is its wide, golden **beach**, which stretches the length of the resort. The further north you go, the less crowded it becomes.

In summer, **boats** ( ☎ 252 494; return €3; ☽ departing every 30min 9am-midnight) ferry tourists across Lake Mamaia to **Insula Ovidiu** (Ovidiu Island, where the poet's tomb is located) from the Tic-Tac wharf opposite the Statia Cazino bus stop.

There's a huge **Aqua Park** (adult/child under 12/child under 3 €10/6/free; ☽ 8am-10pm mid-May–mid-Sep) opposite Hotel Perla at Mamaia's main entrance.

Some 50m north of Hotel Bucureşti, by the banks of Lake Mamaia, is a **water-sports school** ( ☎ 588 888), offering waterskiing, yachting, windsurfing and rowing.

## Sleeping

For information about rooms in private homes, see p677). Most private homes will be a 15- to 20-minute maxitaxi ride from the beach. Camping is no longer allowed on the beach in Mamaia proper. **Centrul de Cazare Cazino** ( ☎ 831 200, 555 555; ☽ 10am-9pm mid-Jun–mid-Sep) has lists of available accommodation. Booking hotel

ROMANIA

rooms through travel agencies (see p679) can save you as much as 15% on the rack rate.

**Popas Hanul Piraţilor** ( ☎ 831 454; tent sites €3, 2-room huts €8) A camping ground 3km north of Mamaia's northern limit, this has shabby huts, but an on-site café and stretches of fine sand nearby. Bus 23 and maxitaxi 23E stop in front of it.

**Hotel Turist** ( ☎ 831 006; B-dul Mamaia 288; s/d €32/41) Comfortable and clean rooms for those wanting the beach scene without the beach nightlife blaring through the walls. It's slightly off the main drag, about a 15-minute walk from the beach. Take bus 40 from the train station.

**Hotel Perla** ( ☎ 831 995; s/d/ste €43/48/75; ⚇ 🖳 ♿ ) Lording over the resort's main entrance, this huge hotel is both a landmark and reliable service centre. It's a busy, efficiently run place.

**Hotel Bulevard** ( ☎ 831 533; www.complexbulevard.ro; B-dul Mamaia 294; s/d €49/58; ⚇ 🖳 ♨ ) Modern and offering full services. Next to Hotel Turist.

**Flora Hotel** ( ☎ 831 059; d with/without breakfast €26/22.50) and neighbouring **Victoria Hotel** ( ☎ 831 028; www.hotelvictoria.ro; s/d €31.50/36) are virtually identical. The rooms here are very basic, but clean. Ever-frugal university students often book a double room and cram in eight people for an extreme budget weekend at the beach. Hint, hint.

## Eating

Almost every hotel has an adjoining restaurant and there are numerous fast-food stands and restaurants lining the boardwalk. **Orange Plazza** ( ☎ 0722-500 577; mains €2-5; ⏱ 10-6am) is located in the northern part of the resort and a good bet. The eclectic international menu changes every three months. There's also an on-site pub and disco.

## Getting There & Around

Tickets for trains to Mamaia departing from Constanţa (see opposite) can be bought in advance at the **Agenţie de Voiaj CFR** ( ☎ 617 930), adjoining the post and telephone office on the promenade.

The quickest way to travel between Constanţa and Mamaia is by maxitaxi. Maxitaxis 23, 23E and 301 depart regularly from Constanţa's train station, stopping at major hotels. Buses 41 and 47 also take you from Constanţa to the northern end of Mamaia.

In summer a shuttle runs up and down Mamaia's 5km boardwalk.

Currently, vehicles not registered in Constanţa must pay a €0.50 road tax at the entrance to Mamaia, though this may be discontinued in 2007.

# EFORIE NORD
☎ 0241
Eforie Nord, 14km south of Constanţa, is the first large resort south of the city. Beaches are below 10m-to-20m cliffs and are as crowded as in Mamaia.

## Orientation
The train station is only a few minutes' walk from the post office and main street, B-dul Republicii. Exit the station and turn left; turn left again after Hotel Belvedere and then right onto B-dul Republicii.

Most hotels and restaurants are on Str Tudor Vladimirescu, which runs parallel to B-dul Republicii along the beach.

## Information
There is a currency exchange in practically every hotel. The **telephone office** ( ☎ 7am-9pm Mon-Fri, 11am-7pm Sat & Sun) is inside the **central post office** (B-dul Republicii 11; ⏱ 8am-8pm Mon-Fri, to 6pm Sat).

## Sights & Activities
Tiny **Lake Belona**, just behind the southern end of the beach, is a popular bathing spot, as its water is warmer than the Black Sea.

Southwest of Eforie Nord is **Lake Techirghiol**, a former river mouth famous for its black sapropel mud, which is effective against rheumatism. The lake is 2m below sea level, and its waters are four times saltier than the sea.

## Sleeping & Eating
**Camping Meduza** ( ☎ 742 385; tent sites €3, d €10, 2-bed huts €12) This cramped space is behind the Prahova Hotel at the northern end of town. Doubles are in a drab concrete building. The place is always noisy but it's close to the action and offers laundry service.

**Villa Horiana** ( ☎ 741 388; Str Alexandru Cuza 13; s/d €40/60; ⚇ ) No doubt the best place to lay your party-weary head in Eforie Nord is here, in this converted bungalow. Some rooms have their own balcony and the home cooking by the super-friendly owners is reason enough to stay here.

**Pensiunea Colonial** ( ☎ 741 561; B-dul Republicii 17; per person €35; ⚇ 🖳 ) This three-star property, has simple, clean rooms, a street-front terrace and a cosy common area. Breakfast is not included.

**Cofetăria Pescăruş** (B-dul Republicii; mains €1-3; ☒ 11-1am) Opposite the post office, this cafeteria-style joint is handy because you can point to the type of grease you want. It's good for a cheap fill-up and has live music from 9pm.

**Nunta Zamfirei** ( ☎ 741 651; Str Republicii; mains €2-6; ☒ 6pm-1am) This Romanian restaurant is famed for its folk song-and-dance shows. Walk north along B-dul Republicii and turn left onto the small track opposite the public thermal baths.

## Getting There & Away

The **Agenţie de Voiaj CFR** ( ☎ 617 930; B-dul Republicii 11) is inside the post office building.

All trains between Constanţa and Mangalia stop at Eforie Nord, but you're better off in a maxitaxi (€0.50).

## NEPTUN-OLIMP

☎ 0241

Before the 1989 revolution, Neptun-Olimp was the exclusive tourist complex of Romania's Communist Party. Neptun-Olimp is in fact two resorts in one. Olimp, a huge complex of hotels facing the beach, is the party place. Neptun, 1km south, is separated from the Black Sea by two small lakes amid some lush greenery. Together they form a vast expanse of hotels and discos.

Neptun-Olimp is perhaps the nicest and most chic of the Romanian Black Sea resorts. The Info Litoral Tourist Information Centre (p679) in Mamaia can provide you with detailed information about these resorts, and they or any travel agency in Constanţa can help with hotel bookings.

The resort complex offers a reasonable range of **activities**: tennis, windsurfing, jet-skiing, sailing, minigolf, bowling and discos.

**Hotel Albert** ( ☎ 731 514; hotelalbert@idilis.ro elena borcha@yahoo.com; d/ste from €51.50/72) is one of the best bets along the coast, located smack in between Neptun and Olimp. It's slightly secluded from the bustle and tastefully mixes modernity with rustic décor.

Halta Neptun train station is within walking distance of the Neptun-Olimp hotels, midway between the two resorts. All trains travelling from Bucharest or Constanţa to Mangalia stop at Halta Neptun.

The **CFR office** (Str Plopilor) is inside Neptun's Hotel Apollo, northwest of Lake Neptun II.

Private maxitaxis run between the resort towns and Mangalia.

## MANGALIA

☎ 0241 / pop 44,300

Formerly ancient Greek Callatis, Mangalia, founded in the 6th century BC, contains several minor archaeological sites. It is a quiet town, not a place for partying, and attracts many elderly European tour groups.

## Orientation & Information

Mangalia spreads beach town-like along the coast, with nothing of note being further than a few blocks inland. The train station is 1km north of the centre. Turn right as you exit and follow Şos Constanţei (the main and only road you're ever likely to use, aside from the beachfront road) south. At the roundabout, turn left for Hotel Mangalia, the Izvor Hercules fountain and the beach or go straight ahead for the pedestrianised section of Şos Constanţei and most facilities, including the Callatis Archaeological Museum and the Casă de Cultură. Private and city buses stop in front of the train station.

There is a small tourist **information kiosk** ( ☒ 8.30am-4pm) outside the train station that gives out leaflets and can help with booking accommodation.

Most hotels have currency exchanges. One of the numerous **currency exchange offices** (Str Stefan cel Mare 16; ☒ 7.30am-10pm) is opposite the post office. Cash travellers cheques or get cash advances on Visa and MasterCard at the **Banca Comercială Română** (Şos Constanţei 25; ☒ 8am-4pm Mon-Fri).

The **telephone office** (Str Ştefan cel Mare 14-15; ☒ 7am-10pm) and **post office** ( ☒ 7am-9pm Mon-Fri, 8am-4pm Sat, 11am-7pm Sun) are in the same building.

**La Maxim** (per hr €0.65; ☒ 24hr) is an internet shack right on the beach, in front of Hotel Zenit.

## Sights

The **Callatis Archaeological Museum** ( ☎ 753 580; Str Şoseaua Constanţei 26; ☒ 8am-8pm) has a good collection of Roman sculptures. Just past the high-rise building next to the museum are some remnants of a 4th-century **Roman-Byzantine necropolis**.

At the south side of Hotel Mangalia, along Str Izvor, are the ruins of a 6th-century **Palaeo-Christian basilica** and a **fountain** (Izvorul Hercules) dispensing sulphurous mineral water that, despite the smell, some people drink.

Cultural events take place in the **Casă de Cultură**, which has a large socialist mural on its façade. One block east of the post office is the Turkish **Moscheea Esmahan Sultan** (Sultan Esmahan

ROMANIA

Mosque; Str Oituz; admission €0.65; 🕑 9am-8pm). Built in 1525, it's surrounded by a lovely garden and well-kept cemetery.

From here, head east down Str Oituz to the beachfront, where, in the basement of Hotel President, remains of the walls of the Callatis citadel dating from the 1st to the 7th centuries are open in the **Muzeul Poarta Callatiana** (Callatiana Archaeological Reservation; 🕑 24hr).

## Sleeping & Eating

**Antrec** ( ☎ 759 473; Str George Murnu 13, Block D, Apt 21; 🕑 24hr, calls only) They arrange rooms in private homes in Mangalia and other costal resorts from €13 a night.

**Hotel Zenit** ( ☎ 751 645; Str Teilor 7), **Hotel Astra** ( ☎ 751 673; Str Teilor 9) and **Hotel Orion** ( ☎ 751 156; Str Teilor 11) are surprisingly pleasant three-star options on the promenade. All have singles/doubles with private bathroom for €32/43.

**Hotel Paradiso** ( ☎ 752 052; Str Rozelor 35; s/d €42.50/60; 🔥 ) A 1960s holdout, this is a popular choice. It's one of the few hotels on the coast with full wheelchair access; there are ramps onto the beach.

**Hotel President** ( ☎ 755 861; www.hpresident.com; Str Treilor 6; s/d/ste from €53/91/147) This is the top place to stay south of Constanţa, a four-star luxury hotel with a fully-fledged business centre.

**Cafe del Mar** ( ☎ 0723 356 610; Str Treilor 4; mains €2-4; 🕑 24hr) You can't go wrong here. There's a great double-decker terrace, stylish interiors and one of the most varied, fanciful menus around – it's the only place on the coast to get US-style buffalo wings (€2.60) and potato skins (€4)! It's next to Hotel President.

## Getting There & Away

### BUS

Maxitaxis from Constanţa stop at Mangalia's train station and in front of the post office, where all maxitaxis running up the coast to Olimp (every 20 minutes) and down to Vama Veche stop. Maxitaxis to Constanţa (€1) run regularly from 5am to 11pm.

### TRAIN

The **Agenţie de Voiaj CFR** ( ☎ 752 818; Str Stefan cel Mare 14-15; 🕑 7.30am-8.30pm Mon-Sat, 8.30am-1.30pm Sun) adjoins the central post office.

Mangalia is at the end of the line from Constanţa. From Constanţa there are 19 trains daily in summer to Mangalia (one to 1¼ hours), five of which are direct to/from Bucharest's Gară Obor (€10, 4½ hours). In summer there are also express trains to/from Iaşi, Sibiu, Suceava, Cluj-Napoca and Timişoara.

# DANUBE DELTA

The mighty Danube River empties into the Black Sea just south of the Ukrainian border. At this point the Danube splits into three separate channels: the Chilia, Sulina and Sfântu Gheorghe arms, creating a 4187 sq km wetland of marshes, floating reed islets and sandbars, providing sanctuary for 300 species of birds and 160 species of fish. Reed marshes cover 156,300 hectares, constituting one of the largest single expanses of reed beds existing in the world.

The Danube Delta (Delta Dunarii) is under the protection of the Administration of the Danube Delta Biosphere Reserve Authority (DDBRA), set up in response to the ecological disaster that befell the delta region during Ceauşescu's attempt to transform it into an agricultural region. Now there are 18 protected reserves (50,000 hectares) that are off-limits to tourists or anglers, including the 500-year-old Leţea Forest and Europe's largest pelican colony. The Delta is also included in Unesco's World Heritage list.

The part of the delta most accessible to foreigners is the middle arm (Sulina), which cuts directly across from Tulcea to Crişan and Sulina (71km). Most river traffic uses the Sulina arm, including the ferries and touring boats from Tulcea.

It's also a bird-watcher's paradise with protected species such as the roller, white-tailed eagle, great white egret, mute and whooper swans, falcon and bee-eater.

## Getting Around

Ibis Tours (p684) in Tulcea arranges bird-watching trips.

In the delta proper it's easy to hire rowing boats from fishermen. This is the only way to penetrate the delta's exotic backwaters.

### FERRY

**Navrom** ( ☎ 0240-511 553; www.navrom.x3m.ro, Romanian only) operates passenger ferries year-round to towns and villages in the delta. It also runs its own tours on weekends. On Saturday, tours head to Sulina, leaving at 8am and returning at 8pm (€4.80); on Sunday at the same hours tours sail to Sfântu Gheorghe (€4.80). You get

ROMANIA

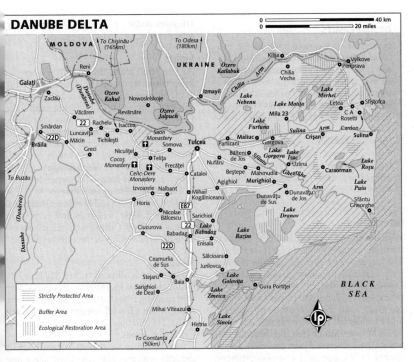

## DANUBE DELTA

0 ——— 40 km
0 ——— 20 miles

Strictly Protected Area

Buffer Area

Ecological Restoration Area

to see the landscape but there is little time for true exploring.

There are fast and slow ferries to Sulina from Tulcea; the slow ferry departs Tulcea at 1pm (€5.20, four hours, Monday to Friday), returning at 7.30am (Tuesday, Friday and Sunday) and the fast ferry leaves Tulcea at 2pm (€10, 1½ hours, daily) returning at 7.30am (daily). Buy a round-trip ticket on the fast ferry to guarantee a return seat.

The slow ferry to Sfântu Gheorghe departs from Tulcea at 1.30pm (€5.75, 5½ hours, on Monday, Wednesday and Friday), returning at 7am (Tuesday, Thursday and Saturday). The fast ferry departs Tulcea at 3pm (€10.50, two hours, on Tuesday and Saturday), returning at 7am (Wednesday and Sunday).

Ferries to Periprava from Tulcea depart at 1.30pm (€5, four hours, on Monday, Wednesday, Thursday and Friday), stopping at Chilia Veche. Return ferries leave Periprava at 6am (Tuesday, Thursday, Friday and Sunday).

Ferry tickets can be purchased at Tulcea's Navrom terminal from 11.30am to 1.30pm. There are also ticket counters on the ferries themselves.

### HYDROFOIL

Hydrofoils to Sulina (1½ hours, €5.25) depart from Tulcea's AFDJ Galaţia terminal, next to the floating ambulance, every day at 2pm. They stop in Maliuc (€1.80) and Crişan (€2.65) on the way. The return trip is at 7pm. Purchase tickets on board.

## TULCEA

☎ 0240 / pop 96,158

Tulcea (tool-*cha*) is an important port and gateway to the Danube Delta paradise. It is usually passed through quickly en route to the delta, so most tourists miss its unassuming appeal. Despite visual reminders that Tulcea is mainly an industrial town, it has a lively energy and an allure of its own, with nightclubs and a sizable Turkish population, which lends it a multiethnic flavour.

It was settled by Dacians and Romans from the 7th to 1st centuries BC.

Tulcea hosts the annual International Folk Festival of Danubian Countries in August, when local songs, games and traditional activities are played out to a Danubian backdrop.

ROMANIA

---

**DELTA PERMITS**

In principle, visitors need travel permits to travel in the delta. If on a group excursion of any kind, these are automatically handled by the operator. If you hire a local fisherman, ask to see his valid permit. The only time you'll need to buy one (€1) is if you go boating or foraging independently. The Information & Ecological Education Centre (below) in Tulcea can issue these for you. If inspectors (and there are many of them) find you without one, you can be liable for a fine of up to €200. You need separate permits to fish or hunt.

---

## Orientation

With the hills to the south and the Danube to the north, getting oriented in Tulcea is a breeze. The bus and train stations, and the Navrom ferry terminal, are adjacent, overlooking the Danube at the western end of the riverfront promenade, which stretches for about a kilometre east along the river past Hotel Delta and into a residential area with museums and the Azizie Mosque. Most hotels and shopping start a block back from the river and continue up the hill. Lake Ciuperca is west of the stations. Inland two blocks, between Str Păcii and Str Babadag, is Piața Unirii, the centre of Tulcea.

## Information

All the hotels have currency exchanges.

**Anason Pharmacy** (☎ 513 352; Str Babadag 8) Has an all-night dispenser.

**Floating ambulance station** (stația de ambulanță; ☉ 24hr) Moored in front of the Culture House on the riverfront. Some of its crew speak English.

**Ibis Tours** (☎ /fax 512 787; www.ibis-tours.ro; Str Babadag 6, Apt 14) Arranges wildlife and bird-watching tours in the delta and Dobrogea, led by professional ornithologists, from €30 a day.

**Information & Ecological Education Centre** (☎ 519 214; www.deltaturism.ro; Str Portului 34A; ☉ 8am-6pm) A representative of Antrec and run by the Danube Delta Biosphere Reserve (DDBR). In a glass booth inside the building opposite the AFDJ hydrofoil terminal, it can book accommodation in homes, hotels and *pensions* and assist in making tours. It can also help you get fishing, hunting and travel permits.

**Post office** (☎ 512 869; Str Babadag 5; ☉ 7am-8pm Mon-Fri, 8am-noon Sat)

**Raiffeisen Bank** (☉ 8am-5pm Mon-Fri) Directly across from Hotel Delta.

**Telephone centre** (☉ 7am-8pm) In the same building as the post office.

## Sights

As you stroll along the river you'll see the **Independence Monument** (1904) on Citadel Hill, at the far eastern end of town. You can reach this by following Str Gloriei from behind the Egreta Hotel to its end; the views are superb.

The **Natural History Museum & Aquarium** (☎ 515 866; Str Progresului 32) highlights the delta's fauna with lots of stuffed birds and a basement aquarium. The minaret of **Moscheia Azizie** (Azizie Mosque; 1863) is down Str Independenței.

The **Folk Art & Ethnographic Museum** (☎ 516 204; Str 9 Mai, 4) has Turkish and Romanian traditional costumes, fishing nets, rugs and carpets. In front of the Greek Orthodox church is a **memorial** to the local victims of the 1989 revolution.

## Sleeping

No camping is allowed within Tulcea's city limits. However, there are many areas where wild camping is permitted on the banks of the canal within a few kilometres of the city; ask at the Information & Ecological Education Centre for details.

The formerly stout boat hotel ('boatel') industry, with multiday delta tours, was going through a lull at the time of writing. Keep an eye out for new companies opening to fill the void.

**Hotel Europolis** (☎ 512 443; www.europolis.ro; Str Păcii 20; s/d €24.50/34.50; ☒ ) Rejoice over the spacious rooms with huge bathrooms. For the same prices, you can stay at its Complexul Touristic Europolis, a resort-like hotel by Lake Câsla, 2km outside of Tulcea's city limits. Though favoured by groups, the site is lovely, in the thick of nature. Water-bikes and small boats can be rented and there are walking trails.

**Insula Complex** (☎ 530 908; Lake Ciuperca; s/d €26/35) Seconds from the train station on Lake Ciuperca, this two-star option has an on-site restaurant and pleasant rooms. Turn right out of the train station and cross the bridge to the island.

**Hotel Delta** (☎ 514 720; www.deltahotelro.com; Str Isaccei 2; s/d €48/60; ☒ ☐ ☒ ☒ ) A city landmark, it boasts the most luxurious rooms around, some affording a unimpeded views of the river. There's a restaurant and bar.

**Casa Albastra Hotel** (☎ 535 662; s/d without breakfast €16/20) Near Insula Complex is this typical Romanian sport hotel.

## Eating & Drinking

There's a string of cafés, and kebab and fast-food joints along Str Unirii.

**Restaurant Select** ( ☎ 510 301; Str Păcii 6; mains €3-9; ☺ 9am-midnight) Treat yourself to a top-notch meal here. From its varied menu, choose from fish, frog legs, pizza and the local speciality, *tochitura Dobrogeana* (pan-fried meat with spicy sauce).

**Fast Food Trident** (Str Babadag; mains €2-4; ☺ 8am-11pm) This is an excellent spot for cheesy pizzas and pasta. It's opposite the Winmarket Department Store.

**Carul cu Bere** (Str Păcii 6; mains €1-3; ☺ 9am-midnight) Adjoins Restaurant Select and has a terrace; enjoy a beer and people-watch. Meals are courtesy of Restaurant Select.

## Getting There & Away

The **Agenţie de Voiaj CFR** ( ☎ 511 360; Str Unirii 4; ☺ 9am-4pm Mon-Fri) is on the corner of Str Babadag. From the **train station** ( ☎ 513 706; Str Portului) there are only two, slow trains a day to Constanţa (€5.10, five hours). There's one daily train to Bucharest (€9.80, six hours).

The **bus station** ( ☎ 513 304) adjoins the **Navrom ferry terminal** (Str Portului). As many as 15 buses and maxitaxis head to Bucharest (€9.80), at least nine to Galaţi (€3.15) and one a day each to Iaşi (€12.60) and Piatra Neamţ (€13.70). Maxitaxis to Constanţa (€4) leave every half-hour from 5.30am to 8pm. One bus a day heads to Istanbul (€40).

## TULCEA TO SULINA
☎ 0240

The Sulina arm, the shortest channel of the Danube, stretches 63.7km from Tulcea to Sulina. The Navrom ferry's first stop is at **Partizani**, from where you can find a fisherman to row you to the three lakes to the north, Tataru, Lung and Mester. Next stop is **Maliuc**, where there is a hotel and camping ground for 80 people. North of Maliuc is **Lake Furtuna**, a snare for bird-watchers.

The next stop for the ferry is the junction with Old Danube, 1km upstream from **Crişan**. There are several *pensions* in the village, all charging about €10 per person. Try **Pensiune Gheorghe Silviu** ( ☎ 511 279) or **Pensiune Pocora** ( ☎ 511 279). There is also the DDBR's **Crişan Centre for Ecological Information & Education** ( ☎ 519 214; office@deltaturism.ro; ☺ 8am-4pm Tue-Sun), which features wildlife displays, a library and a video room. At the main Crişana

ferry dock, ask about side trips to **Mila 23** or **Caraorman**.

There is a camping area on the road to the beach.

A few hundred metres west along the river-front from the Sulina Cinema is a small sign pointing to **Pensiune Astir** ( ☎ 543 379; s/d €10/20). The **Pensiune Delta Sulina** ( ☎ 0722-275 554; r with/without breakfast & dinner €40/30) is a comfortable, three-star option.

For information on ferries and hydrofoils see p682 at the start of this Danube Delta section.

# ROMANIA DIRECTORY

## ACCOMMODATION

Prices for Romanian accommodation have risen in recent years. There are five basic options: hostels, private homestays (promoted by the 'bum-rush the traveller' at the train station technique), family-style guesthouse *pensions (pensiunes)*, hotels (a grab-bag of communist leftovers and comfy, if standard, business hotels), and camping grounds that usually include simple *căsuţe* (wooden huts).

Budget travellers should look out for *pensions,* which are often lovingly run, offer insight into how Romanians live, and cost about €15 to €20 per person (an extra €5 or more for full board), and a little more in cities. The best online resource is www.ruraltourism.ro; otherwise contact **Antrec** (National Association of Rural, Ecological & Cultural Tourism; www.antrec.iiruc.ro), whose headquarters is in Bran (p644).

Hostels usually cost around €10 for a dorm bed; sometimes private rooms (with shared bath) are available for between €20 and €30. Hostels vary in quality, with Bucharest's topping in terms of travel-savvy hang-outs. **Youth Hostels Romania** (www.hihostels-romania.ro) has information on HI hostels.

Hotel prices have risen in recent years, but these tend to offer the most privacy and comfort. Some old stalwarts have been scrubbed up. The polished B&B world hasn't made much of a dent in Romania. Midrange hotels tend to cost from €30 to €60, more so in Bucharest.

In-town camping is often in less-than-ideal locations, and conditions are sometimes quite shoddy. In most mountain areas there's a network of cabanas (cabins or chalets) with

ROMANIA

restaurants and dormitories. Prices are much lower than those of hotels and no reservations are required, but arrive early if the cabana is in a popular location.

*Apă caldă* (hot water) is common at most accommodation, but air-conditioning is a luxury. Many hotels advertise 'internet connections', meaning just plug-in capability if you have a local ISP.

All reviews in this chapter include breakfast unless otherwise noted. Listings are ordered by price.

## ACTIVITIES

Most outdoor fun sticks with Romania's Carpathians, which stripe the country impressively. Emergency rescue is provided by **Salvamont** (www.salvamont.org, in Romanian), a voluntary mountain-rescue organisation with 21 stations countrywide.

### Biking

Mountain-biking has taken off in recent years. Some roads can be hair-rising to ride along as traffic zooms by. A great place to go is Sinaia (p637), where you can rent a bike and take it to the plateau atop the Bucegi Mountains by lift. **Clubul de Cicloturism Napoca** (office@ccn.ro; Cluj-Napoca) was looking for a new office at research time, but can offer bike-rental advice. **Transylvania Adventure** (www.adventuretransylvania.com) offers eight-day trips (including bike and accommodation) from mid-May to mid-October for about €700.

### Bird-Watching

Europe's greatest wetlands, the Danube Delta (p682), is home to the continent's largest pelican colony, plus most of the world's population of red-breasted geese (up to 70,000) winter here.

### Hiking

Hiking is the number-one activity, which is not surprising considering the intensity of the Carpathians cutting across the country. The most popular places are in the Bucegi (p640), and Făgăraş (p652) and the Piatra Craiului (p645).

Trails are generally well marked, and a system of cabanas, huts and hotels along the trails on the mountain tops and plateaus make even a several-day trek more than comfortable. A good source of guides can be found at www.alpineguide.ro.

### Skiing

Ski and snowboard centres are popular, but ski runs tend to be fewer (and costlier) than many Bulgarian slopes. Sinaia (p637) and Poiana Braşov (p645) are the most popular ski slopes. The ski season runs from December through March. Resorts rent skis and snowboards (about €10 to €12 per day); lift tickets are sometimes bundled by number of trips (10 trips can run €20).

## BUSINESS HOURS

Banks can be expected to open from 9am to 5pm Monday to Friday and 9am to noon on Saturday. Most museums open from 9am or 10am to 5pm or 6pm Tuesday to Sunday. Opening hours for many institutions change slightly following daylight-savings. Restaurants can be expected to stay open roughly from 10am to midnight.

## CUSTOMS

Officially, you're allowed to import hard currency up to a maximum of US$10,000. Valuable goods and foreign currency over US$1000 should be declared upon arrival. For foreigners, duty-free allowances are 4L of wine, 2L of spirits and 200 cigarettes. For more information check www.customs.ro.

## DANGERS & ANNOYANCES

Romania's sometimes gets a rip-off reputation that's hardly justified. Taxi drivers at train stations are likely to overcharge, a few Bucharest restaurants add extra charges to some bills, and pick-pockets target wallets and mobile phones (cellphones) in busy areas such as buses. Another problem are the many stray dogs seen nationwide, but particularly in Bucharest. Take the necessary precautions and you're likely to have a trouble-free visit.

The biggest annoyances are trying to get someone to change a 50 lei note, museums that charge upwards of €15 to take photographs, and the lack of laundry facilities.

Also be sure to take some food and water and lots of mosquito repellent on any expedition into the Danube delta. Warning: do not drink Danube water!

## EMBASSIES & CONSULATES
### Romanian Embassies & Consulates
Romanian embassies and consulates abroad:
**Australia** ( ☎ 02-6286 2343; http://canberra.mae.ro; 4 Dalman Crescent, O'Malley, ACT, Canberra)

**Canada** ( ☎ 613-789 5345; www.cyberus.ca/~romania; 655 Rideau St, Ottawa, Ontario)

**France** ( ☎ 01 47 05 10 46; www.amb-roumanie.fr, in French; 5 rue de l'Exposition, Paris)

**Germany** ( ☎ 030-212 39 202; www.rumainische-bot schaft.de; Dorotheenstr 62-66, Berlin)

**Ireland** ( ☎ 031-668 1275; ambrom@eircom.net; 26 Waterloo Rd, Dublin)

**Moldova** ( ☎ 22-228 126; http://chisinau.mae.ro; Str Bucureşti 66/1, Chişinău)

**UK** ( ☎ 020-7937 9666; www.roemb.co.uk; 4 Palace Green, Kensington Gardens, London)

**USA** ( ☎ 202-232 3694; www.roembus.org; 1607 23rd St NW, Washington DC)

## Embassies & Consulates in Romania

Unless stated otherwise, the following embassies are in Bucharest.

**Australia** (Map p626; ☎ 021-316 7558; don.cairns@ austrade.gov.au; B-dul Unirii 74)

**Canada** (Map p626; ☎ 021-307 5000; bucst@dfait -maeci.gc.ca; Str Nicolae Iorga 36)

**France** (Map p626; ☎ 021-303 1000; www.ambafrance -ro.org; Str Biserica Amzei 13-15)

**Germany** Bucharest (Map p626; ☎ 021-202 9830; www .bukarest.diplo.de; Str Gheorghe Demetriade 6-8); Sibiu ( ☎ 0269-211 133; www.hermannstadt.ro; Str Lucian Blaga 15-17); Timişoara ( ☎ 0256-309 800; www.german consultimisoara.ro; Spl Vladimirescu 10, Timişoara)

**Ireland** ( ☎ 021-212 2088; embassybucharest@yahoo.ie; Str Vasile Lascăr 42-44)

**Moldova** Bucharest (Map p626; ☎ 021-230 0474; ambasadamoldova@zappmobile.ro; Aleea Alexandru 40); Bucharest (Map p626; ☎ 021-410 9827; B-dul Eroilor 8)

**UK** (Map p626; ☎ 021-201 7200; www.britishembassy .gov.uk/romania; Str Jules Michelet 24)

**USA** Bucharest (Map p628; ☎ 021-210 4042; www.us embassy.ro; Str Tudor Arghezi 7-9); Bucharest (Map p628; ☎ 021-316 4052; Str Nicolae Filipescu 26)

## GAY & LESBIAN TRAVELLERS

Romania became one of Europe's last countries to decriminalise homosexual activity in 2001. Bucharest has the most active gay and lesbian scene, including the emergence of GayFest in late May that features events, films and disco nights. **Accept** (www.accept-romania.ro) is a gay-, lesbian- and transgender-rights group.

## FESTIVALS & EVENTS

A few favourite festivals include the following (but watch out for horse trades and shepherd cheese measurement celebrations):

**Juni Pageant** (April) Braşov

**Bucharest Carnival** (late May to early June) Bucharest

**Medieval Festival of the Arts** (July) Sighişoara

**International Folk Music & Dance Festival of Ethnic Minorities in Europe** (August) Cluj-Napoca

**Sâmbra Oilor** (September) Bran

**Iaşi Days** (mid-October) Iaşi

**De la Colind la Stea** (December) Braşov

## HOLIDAYS

Public holidays in Romania:

**New Year** 1 and 2 January

**Catholic & Orthodox Easter Mondays** In March/April

**Labour Day** 1 May

**Romanian National Day** 1 December

**Christmas** 25 and 26 December

## LEGAL MATTERS

If you are arrested, you can insist on seeing an embassy or consular officer straight away. It is not advisable to present your passport to people on the street unless you know for certain that they are authentic officials – cases of theft have been reported.

Romanians can legally drink, drive and vote (though not simultaneously!) at 18. The age of consent in Romania is 15.

## MONEY

In Romania the only legal tender is the leu (plural: lei). From January 2007, the old lei was taken out of circulation, and the new lei (abbreviated 'RON') – with four less zeroes – took over. If someone offers an old note (say a 500,000-lei note instead of a 50 RON note), don't take it. The new lei comes in denominations of 2000, 10,000, 50,000, 100,000 and 500,000. There are (heavy) coins for one, five, 10, 20, 50, 100, 500 and 1000 lei.

Prices are frequently quoted in euros – especially at hotels – and prices in this chapter are quoted in euro. If Romania joins the EU, it's possible prices may rise.

ATMs are everywhere and give 24-hour withdrawals in lei on your Cirrus, Plus, Visa, MasterCard and Eurocard. Some banks, such as Banca Comercială Română, give cash advances on credit cards in your home currency.

Moneychangers are just as ubiquitous. Dollars and euros are easiest to exchange, though British pounds are widely accepted. You often must show a passport to change money. Be wary of changers with bodyguard goons out front. Some changers advertise juicy rates, but subtly disguise a '9' as a '0' etc. Count your money carefully.

ROMANIA

All branches of the Banca Comercială Română, among others, will cash travellers cheques. Credit cards won't get you anywhere in rural areas, but they are widely accepted in larger department stores, hotels and most restaurants in cities and towns.

## POST

A postcard or letter under 20g to Europe from Romania costs €0.85 and takes seven to 10 days. The postal system is reliable, if slow.

Poste restante is held for one month (addressed c/o Poste Restante, Poştă Romană Oficiul Bucureşti 1, Str Matei Millo 10, RO-70700 Bucureşti, Romania) at Bucharest's central post office (p625).

## TELEPHONE

Romania's telephone centres and phone booths are a sad sight, almost completely ignored amid mobile-phone revolutionaries. Cellphones are preferable to land lines for many Romanians. Cellphone numbers are 10 digits, beginning with 07. Phonecards (€3) can be bought at newsstands and used in phone booths for domestic or international calls.

European cellphones with roaming work in Romania; otherwise you can get a Romania number from Orange or Vodaphone, which have shops everywhere. The SIM card costs about US$5 including credit; calls are about US$0.10 to US$0.30 per minute.

Romania's international operator can be reached by dialling ☎ 971.

## TOURIST INFORMATION

Information is a problem, as very few towns keep open tourism information centres (Sibiu's is the darling of info); there's no national tourist-office network and even Bucharest lacks even the dinkiest info centre. Most travel agents are geared to get you out of Romania, but some can help, or will try to. The best information often comes from travel-oriented accommodation such as hostels or *pensions* that offer day trips.

The so-called **Romanian National Tourist Office** (www.romaniantourism.ro) amazingly has no offices in Romania, but keeps an active **London office**

---

**EMERGENCY NUMBER**

Call ☎ 112 for an ambulance or other emergency services.

---

( ☎ 020-7224 3692; infoUK@RomaniaTourism.com; 22 New Cavendish St) and **New York City office** ( ☎ 212-545-8484; infoUS@RomaniaTourism.com; 355 Lexington Ave, 19th fl).

## VISAS

Your passport's validity must extend to at least six months beyond the date you enter the country in order to obtain a visa.

Citizens of all EU countries, USA, Canada, Japan and many other countries may travel visa-free for 90 days in Romania. Australians and New Zealanders no longer need to arrange visas prior to arriving in Romania. As visa requirements change frequently, check with the **Ministry of Foreign Affairs** (www.mae.ro) before departure.

Romania issues two types of visas to tourists: transit and single-entry. Transit visas (for those from countries other than the ones mentioned earlier) are for stays of no longer than three days, and cannot be bought at the border.

To apply for a visa you need a passport, one recent passport photograph and the completed visa application form accompanied by the appropriate fee. Citizens of some countries (mainly African) need a formal invitation from a person or company in order to apply for a visa; see the Ministry of Foreign Affairs' website for details.

Regular single-entry visas (US$25) are valid for 90 days from the day you arrive. Single-entry visas are usually issued within a week (depending on the consulate), but for an extra US$6 can be issued within 48 hours.

Transit visas can be either single-entry (US$15) – valid for three days and allowing you to enter Romania once – or double-entry (US$25), allowing you to enter the country twice and stay for three days each time.

Check your visa requirements for Serbia and Montenegro, Hungary, Bulgaria and Ukraine, if you plan on crossing those borders. If you are taking the Bucharest–St Petersburg train, you need Ukrainian and Belarusian transit visas on top of the Russian visa.

# TRANSPORT IN ROMANIA

## GETTING THERE & AWAY

### Air

**Tarom** (Transporturile Aeriene Române; code RO; www.tarom .ro) is Romania's state airline. Nearly all international flights to Romania arrive at Bucharest's **Henri Coanda International Airport** (formerly

Otopeni; OTP; ☎ 201 4788; www.otp-airport.ro; Şos Bucureşti-Ploieşti, Bucharest).

Major airlines flying into the country:

**Air France** (code AF; ☎ 021-319 2705; www.airfrance.com)

**Air Moldova** (code 9U; ☎ 021-312 1258; www.airmoldova.md)

**Austrian Airlines** (code OS; ☎ 021-204 2208; www.austrianair.com)

**British Airways** (code BA; ☎ 021-303 2222; www.british-airways.com)

**ČSA** (Czech Airlines; code OK; ☎ 021-315 3205; www.csa.cz)

**KLM** (code KL; ☎ 021-312 0149; www.klm.com)

**LOT Polish Airlines** (code LO; ☎ 021-314 1096; www.lot.com)

**Lufthansa** (code LH; ☎ 021-204 8410; www.lufthansa.com)

**Swiss Airlines** (code LX; ☎ 021-312 0238; www.swiss.com)

**Turkish Airlines** (code TK; ☎ 021-311 2410; www.turkishairlines.com)

**Carpatair** ( ☎ 256 300 900; www.carpatair.com) connects Timişoara with Italy, France and Germany; it also runs a flight from Budapest to Cluj-Napoca. Air Moldova and Tarom together operate daily flights between Chişinău and Bucharest; **Wizz Air** (www.wizzair.com) started flying between Budapest and Târgu Mureş in 2006. and **Transaero** (www.transaero.md) also has flights on that route.

Maxitaxis connect Cluj-Napoca with the Budapest airport, making that cheaper hub an attractive alternative to Bucharest for those heading to Transylvania.

## Land
### BORDER CROSSINGS
Expect long queues at checkpoints, particularly on weekends. Carry food and water for the wait. Don't try bribing a Romanian official and beware of unauthorised people charging dubious 'ecology', 'disinfectant' or other dodgy taxes at the border.

### BUS
Romania is well linked by bus lines to central and Western Europe as well as Turkey. While not as comfortable as the train, buses usually tend to be faster, though not always cheaper.

**Eurolines** (www.eurolines.ro) has a flurry of buses linking numerous cities in Romania with Western Europe. Buses to Germany cost from €75 to €125 one-way, while buses to Paris and Rome cost about €125.

Eurolines and other private companies have many daily buses to Budapest from cities throughout Romania, including Bucharest, Arad, Braşov and Cluj-Napoca, with stops along the way.

Various companies connect Bucharest and Istanbul (p633); buses also leave from Constanţa.

### CAR & MOTORCYCLE
The best advice here is to ensure your documents (personal ID, insurance, registration and visas, if required) are in order before crossing into Romania. The Green Card (a routine extension of domestic motor insurance to cover most European countries) is valid in Romania. Extra insurance can be bought at the borders.

### TRAIN
International train tickets are rarely sold at train stations, but rather at CFR (Romanian State Railways) offices in town (look for the Agenţie de Voiaj CFR signs) or Wasteels offices. Tickets must be bought at least two hours prior to departure.

Those travelling on an Inter Rail or Eurail pass still need to make seat reservations (€4, or €15 if using a couchette) on express trains within Romania. Even if you're not travelling with a rail pass, practically all international trains require a reservation (automatically included in tickets purchased in Romania). If you already have a ticket, you may be able to make reservations at the station an hour before departure, though it's preferable to do so at a CFR office at least one day in advance.

There are five Budapest–Bucharest trips daily; the 873km trip takes 13 to 16 hours, by way of Arad and the Hungarian border town of Lököshaza. It's also possible to pick up the Budapest-bound train from other Romanian cities including Constanţa, Braşov and Cluj-Napoca.

The train service between Bucharest and Bulgaria is slow and crowded but cheap. Between Sofia and Bucharest (€18, 11 hours) there are two daily trains, both of which stop in Ruse.

Other train service from Bucharest includes three to Chişinău (13″ hours) and Istanbul (19 hours); one daily to Moscow (39 hours) – via Kyiv – and Vienna (17″ hours).

ROMANIA

## GETTING AROUND

### Air

State-owned carrier **Tarom** (www.tarom.ro) is Romania's main carrier. **Carpatair** (www.carpatair.com) runs domestic routes – and ones to Western Europe – from its hub in Timişoara, making this western city a great back-up hub for getting in/out of Romania.

### Bicycle

Cyclists have become a more frequent sight in Romania, particularly in Transylvania, Maramureş and Moldavia, but rental is not that widespread. There are generally bike and bike-repair shops in most major towns. A good place to rent one is Sinaia (p637).

### Boat

Boat is the only way of getting around much of the Danube Delta; see p682.

### Bus

A mix of clunky buses, microbuses and maxi-taxis combine to form the seriously disorganised Romanian bus system spread across a changing array of bus companies. Finding updated information can be tough without local help. Sometimes stations themselves move around, particularly the migratory lots where maxitaxis leave from. Some routes – such as Braşov–Sinaia, or Sibiu–Cluj-Napoca – are more useful than others. Generally it's easier to plan on the train.

Fares are cheap though and calculated per kilometre – it's about 1 lei (€0.29) per 10km; the 116km trip from Braşov to Sighişoara is about (€3.50).

This chapter reflects the situation at research time; the routes should remain roughly the same.

### Car & Motorcycle

Even if you're on a budget, it's well worth splitting the costs of a car – sometimes as low as €25 per day – and getting out into rural areas like Maramureş (p663) and Saxon Land (p648). It's amazing how much things can change only 2km from a 'main' paved highway. More than a couple of roads are best suited for 4WD, though everything in this chapter can be reached by a Dacia Solenza (the cheapest rental car, and a fine one), if you take extra precautions.

Braşov has some of the country's higher rental rates, whereas Bucharest, Sibiu and Cluj-Napoca have lower rates. Drop-off serv-ice is allowed by many companies, with an extra fee of not less than €50. See destination sections for car-rental recommendations.

#### TIPS

- Plan on time – Things go slower; flocks of sheep, horse carts, full-lane tractors, construction and giant potholes halt traffic.
- Get a map – A map is mandatory if you're planning to go back roads. Maps can be found in bookshops, but highway petrol stops don't tend to carry them. A good one is Cartographia's 1:800,000 *Romania* (about €3.50).
- Hitchhiking – It's a part of life, and you'll see old women, even children, hailing rides. Generally there are no problems doing so, though we 'enjoyed' the company of an extremely drunk man looking to go 500m.
- Parking – In most places, a sidewalk is fair game to park your car. In some, however, note the 'P cu plata' sign meaning payment is required. Usually a bloke trolls the area and charges €0.30 or €0.50 to park a few hours. A local in one town explained what happens if they get a ticket: 'It's their job to ticket us, and ours to throw it away.'

#### RULES

Your country's driving licence will be recognised here. There is a 0% blood-alcohol tolerance limit. Seat belts are compulsory in the front and back; children under 12 are forbidden to sit in the front.

Speed limits are 90km/h on major roads and 70km/h inside highway villages and towns unless otherwise noted. A few motorways allow faster driving. Speed traps – such as the video ones between Braşov and Bucharest – are common; drivers warn each other with a flash of the headlights.

### Local Transport

Buses, trams and trolleybuses provide transport within most towns and cities in Romania, although many are crowded. They usually run from about 5am to midnight, although services can get thin on the ground after 7pm in more remote areas. Purchase tickets at street kiosks marked *bilete* or *casă de bilete* before boarding, and validate them once aboard.

In many rural parts, the only vehicles around are horse-powered. Horse and cart is the most popular form of transport in Romania. Many carts will stop and give you a ride, the driver expecting no more than a cigarette in return.

Bucharest is the only city in Romania to boast a metro system.

## Train

Rail has long been the most popular way of travelling around Romania. **Căile Ferate Române** (CFR; Romanian State Railways; www.cfr.ro) runs trains over 11,000km of track, providing service to most cities, towns and larger villages in the country. The *mersul trenurilor* (national train timetable) is published annually and sold for €2 from CFR offices. It's also available at www .mercultrenurilorcfr.ro, but it's complicated picking the right array of destinations; better (for times, but no prices) is the German site www.bahn.de.

*Sosire* means 'arrivals' and *plecare* is 'departures'. On posted timetables, the number of the platform from which each train departs is listed under *linia*.

### CLASSES & TYPES OF TRAINS

In Romania there are five different types of train, all of which travel at different speeds, offer varying levels of comfort and charge different fares for the same destination.

The cheapest trains are local personal trains. These trains are achingly slow. *Accelerat* trains are faster, hence a tad more expensive and less crowded. Seat reservations are obligatory and automatic when you buy your ticket. There's little difference between *rapid* and *expres* trains. Both travel at a fair speed and often have dining cars. Pricier Inter-City trains are the most comfortable but aren't faster than *expres* trains.

*Vagon de dormit* (sleepers) are available between Bucharest and Cluj-Napoca, Oradea, Timişoara, Tulcea and other points. First-class sleeping compartments generally have two berths, 2nd-class sleepers generally have four berths and 2nd-class couchettes have six berths. Book these in advance.

Fares listed in this chapter generally indicate one-way, 2nd-class seats on *rapid* or *accelerat* trains.

### BUYING TICKETS

Tickets are sold in advance for all trains except local personal ones. Advance tickets are sold at an Agenţie de Voiaj CFR, a train-ticket office found in every city centre. When the ticket office is closed you have to buy your ticket immediately before departure at the station.

Theoretically you can buy tickets at CFR offices up to two hours before departure. Sometimes they don't sell tickets for same-day trips, so try to plan a day ahead.

You can only buy tickets at train stations two hours – and in some cases just one hour – before departure. Queues can be horrendous. At major stations there are separate ticket lines for 1st and 2nd classes; you may opt for 1st class when you see how much shorter that line is. Your reservation ticket lists the code number of your train along with your assigned *vagon* (carriage) and *locul* (seat).

If you have an international ticket right through Romania, you're allowed to make stops along the route but you must purchase a reservation ticket each time you reboard an *accelerat* or *rapid* train. If the international ticket was issued in Romania, you must also pay the *expres* train supplement each time.

In a pinch you can board a train and pay the ticket-taker for the ride; ask how much. As one local told us: 'This is Romania – you can do anything if you pay for it.'

### COMPARING TRAIN COSTS

This chart is here to help gauge how train fares ebb based on speed and condition. In our experience, the 1st-class price wasn't worth the hike; personal trains went nearly as quickly on some routes, but were scrappier and fuller.

| Trip | Personal | Accelerat | Rapid | Inter-City |
|---|---|---|---|---|
| 100km (1st Class) | €3.50 | €6.40 | €8.10 | €9 |
| 100km (2nd Class) | €2.20 | €4.40 | €5.80 | €6.65 |
| Bucharest-Braşov (1st) | €5.70 | €10 | €11.20 | €12.10 |
| Bucharest-Braşov (2nd) | €3.50 | €6.50 | €7.90 | €8.70 |

ROMANIA

# Russia Россия

Looming over the rest of Europe with its immense, inhuman size and dark, brutal history, Russia is an essential and fascinating destination, the flip side of modern Europe and still an unknown quantity to most travellers. Somehow Russia manages to pull off the truly impressive feat of being both a really exciting place to travel while never relenting on its tediously bureaucratic approach to life. Stay in the EU if you want things easy and hassle-free, but venture east for one of the last truly adventurous and unpredictable destinations on the continent.

Brash, vulgar but totally fascinating, Moscow is the biggest city in Europe, home to more billionaires than anywhere else in the world and the economic motor driving Russia's resurgence as a great power. Its rich history, vast highways, startling architecture and frenzied pace of development makes it a must on any trip to Eastern Europe. The flip side of the coin is St Petersburg, the former imperial capital of Russia and still its most beautiful and alluring city. With its colourful and often crumbling Italianate mansions, wending canals and enormous Neva River, this is one of the incontestable highlights of the continent.

If you want to really be outré, drop into ignored little Kaliningrad, the former German city of Königsburg, and an enclave of Russia wedged between Poland and Lithuania on the Baltic Sea, and probably the least visited area in this entire book.

---

## FAST FACTS

- **Area** 16,995,800 sq km
- **Capital** Moscow
- **Currency** rouble (R); €1 = R34; US$1 = R27; UK£1 = R51; A$1 = R20; ¥100 = R23; NZ$1 = R18
- **Famous for** vodka, communism, oil, gangsters
- **Official Language** Russian
- **Phrases** *privyet* (hi), *do svidaniya* (goodbye), *spasiba* (thanks), *izvinitye* (excuse me), *mozhno yesho stakanchik?* (may I have another little glassful?)
- **Population** 147 million
- **Telephone Codes** country code ☎ 7; international access code 8 (wait for second tone) 10, or just + from a mobile phone
- **Visas** required by all and can be a real headache – begin preparing well in advance of your trip! For more details, see p744

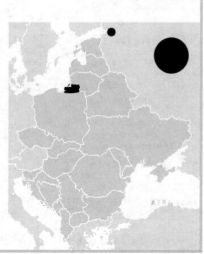

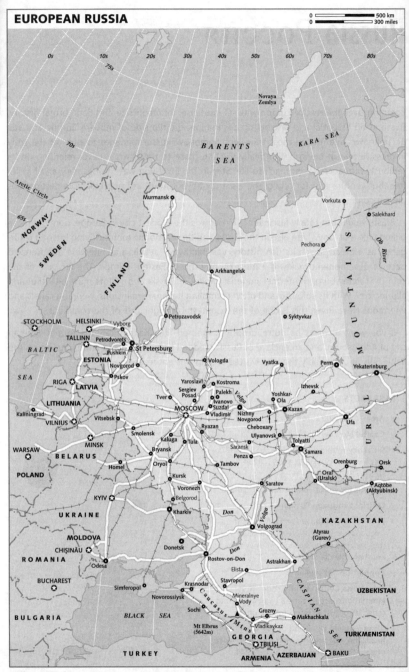

# EUROPEAN RUSSIA

0 ———— 500 km
0 ———— 300 miles

Novaya Zemlya

BARENTS SEA

KARA SEA

Arctic Circle

NORWAY

SWEDEN

FINLAND

Murmansk

Vorkuta

Salekhard

Pechora

Ob River

Arkhangelsk

URAL MOUNTAINS

STOCKHOLM

HELSINKI

TALLINN

Petrodvorets

Vyborg

Petrozavodsk

Syktyvkar

Pushkin

St Petersburg

ESTONIA

Novgorod

Vologda

Vyatka

Perm

Yekaterinburg

BALTIC

RIGA

LATVIA

Pskov

Yaroslavl

Kostroma

Izhevsk

SEA

LITHUANIA

Tver

Sergiev Posad

Palekh

Ivanovo

Yoshkar-Ola

Kaliningrad

VILNIUS

Vitsebsk

MOSCOW

Suzdal

Vladimir

Nizhny Novgorod

Kazan

Ufa

WARSAW

Smolensk

Ryazan

Cheboxary

Ulyanovsk

Tolyatti

BELARUS

Kaluga

Tula

Saransk

Samara

POLAND

Homel

Bryansk

Oryol

Penza

Orenburg

Orsk

Tambov

Saratov

Oral (Uralsk)

KYIV

Kursk

Aqtöbe (Aktyubinsk)

Voronezh

Belgorod

UKRAINE

Kharkiv

Don

Volga

KAZAKHSTAN

MOLDOVA

CHIŞINĂU

Donetsk

Volgograd

Atyrau (Gurev)

ROMANIA

Odesa

Rostov-on-Don

Don

Astrakhan

BUCHAREST

Elista

Simferopol

Krasnodar

Stavropol

CASPIAN

UZBEKISTAN

Novorossiysk

Mineralnye Vody

SEA

BULGARIA

BLACK SEA

Sochi

Caucasus Mts

Grozny

Makhachkala

Mt Elbrus (5642m)

Vladikavkaz

TURKMENISTAN

GEORGIA

TBILISI

TURKEY

ARMENIA

AZERBAIJAN

BAKU

## HIGHLIGHTS

- Smell the power in the air at the **Kremlin** (p707), the nerve centre of the world's largest country, and see Lenin on daily display at fabulous **Red Square** (p705).
- Take in a visual feast on St Petersburg's **Palace Sq** (p723), home to the **Winter Palace** (p723), and enjoy the art collection of the world-famous **Hermitage** (p723).
- Experience a city that truly never sleeps during the **St Petersburg white nights** (p726) in late June.
- See the real Russia in the 'Golden Ring' – the historic towns of **Suzdal** (p716), **Vladimir** (p716) and **Sergiev Posad** (p717) – famed for their beautiful monasteries and churches and just a short trip from Moscow.
- Ride in style on the **Moscow metro** (p715), one of the most efficient and beautiful mass-transit systems in the world.

## ITINERARIES

- **Three days in Moscow** Red Sq and the Kremlin have to be your first stop, followed by the Pushkin Museum and Church of Christ the Saviour on the Moscow River. On day two go south of the river to the sublime Novodevichy Convent, then take the stunning metro to the State Tretyakov Gallery. Check out Moscow's legendary nightlife in the evening. On day three strike out and see one of the delightful Golden Ring towns.
- **Three days in St Petersburg** Wander up Nevsky Prospekt, see Palace Sq, the mighty Neva River and the unforgettable Hermitage, where you can lose yourself for hours in the magnificent collection. Day two allows time for the historic St Peter & Paul Fortress, the Church on Spilled Blood and the Lavra Alexandra Nevskogo (Alexander Nevsky Monastery). On day three take an excursion out of the city and visit either Pushkin or Petrodvorets for a taste of how the tsars lived.

## CLIMATE & WHEN TO GO

If Russia can be called a land of extremes, then its weather is no exception. The winters are extremely cold – temperatures are regularly as low as -10°C or even -20°C in both Moscow and St Petersburg – while summers are hot and humid. Spring and autumn are both notional concepts, each lasting about a month.

---

**HOW MUCH?**

- **Second-class overnight train between Moscow and St Petersburg** R500 to R1300
- **Standard taxi fare within a city centre** R100
- **Metro journey in Moscow** R15
- **Bootleg DVD** R100
- **George W Bush novelty nesting doll** R800

**LONELY PLANET INDEX**

- **Litre of petrol** R16
- **Litre of water** R30
- **Bottle of Baltika beer** R30
- **Souvenir T-shirt** R300 to R500
- **Street snack (blin)** R40 to R50

---

Despite its extremes of temperature, most times of year can be good for visiting Russia. The snow and ice make St Petersburg look quite magical, and Moscow surprisingly clean. If possible, avoid March and early April – the 'thaw' is the least pleasant time. The snow and ice melt, creating a ubiquitous brown sludge and general muddiness that makes walking about unpleasant. The best months to visit are May, June and September. See p911 for more information on Russia's climate.

## HISTORY

Russia has its origins in countries it nowadays likes to think of as its satellites, effectively springing forth from Ukraine and Belarus in the Dark Ages, while taking its alphabet from Bulgaria, from where Christianity spread. The birth of the Russian state is usually identified with the founding of Novgorod in 862 AD, although until 1480 Russia was effectively a colony of the Mongols.

The medieval period in Russia was a dark and brutal time, never more so than during the reign of Ivan the Terrible (r 1547–84), whose sobriquet was well earned through his fantastically cruel punishments, such as boiling his enemies alive and, most famously, putting out the eyes of the architects who created his magnificent St Basil's Cathedral (p705) on Red Sq.

Despite Ivan the Terrible's conquest of the Volga basin and obsession with reaching the Baltic (at that time controlled by the Lithuanians and Swedes), it was not until the Romanov dynasty (1613–1917) that Russia began absorbing sparsely populated neighbouring regions and filling them with Russians. Territorial expansion between the 17th and 19th centuries saw the country increase in size exponentially to include Siberia, the Arctic, the Far East, Central Asia and the Caucasus, a massive land grab that created the huge country Russia is today.

Peter the Great (r 1689–1725) can in many ways be seen as the father of modern Russia. It was he who dragged the country kicking and screaming out of the dark ages, setting up a Russian navy, educational centres and beginning the construction of a new capital – St Petersburg – in 1703. Russia's capital moved north from Peter's hated Moscow in 1712, and was to remain the capital until the Bolsheviks moved it back to Moscow more than two centuries later.

Catherine the Great (r 1762–96), a provincial German princess with no legitimate claim to the throne, assumed power, having plotted to have her histrionic, pointless husband Peter III dispatched by palace guards. Catherine continued Peter the Great's progressive yet authoritarian policies to create a world power by the mid-18th century. Her 'enlightened despotism' saw the founding of the art collection that was to become the Hermitage, a huge expansion in the sciences and arts, a correspondence with Voltaire, and the strengthening of the nation. However, it also saw her brutal suppression of a Cossack rebellion and intolerance for any institution that would threaten her authority.

The 19th century saw feverish capitalist development undermined by successively autocratic and backwards tsars. Alexander I (r 1801–25) was too preoccupied with Napoleon (who invaded Russia and torched Moscow in 1812, but was eventually beaten by the Russian winter), and despite Alexander II's (r 1855–81) brave freeing of the serfs in 1861, which paved the way to a modern capitalist economy, political reform was nowhere on the cards.

The revolutionary movement grew in the late 19th century, mainly in Switzerland, where many exiled radicals had based themselves. Nicholas II, the last tsar of Russia, ascended the throne in 1894, and was even weaker and more scared of change than his predecessors. It was his refusal to countenance serious reform that precipitated the 1917 revolution. What began as a liberal revolution was hijacked later the same year in a coup led by the Bolsheviks under Lenin, which resulted in the establishment of the world's first communist state.

Between 1917 and 1920 the Bolsheviks fought a bloody Civil War against the 'whites', who supported the monarchy. The tsar and his family were murdered in 1918 to deprive the whites of any figurehead, and eventually resistance to the communists trickled out.

By the time Lenin died in 1924 – since when he has lain in state at his purpose-built mausoleum (p705) on Red Sq – Russia had become the principal member of the Union of Soviet Socialist Republics, a communist superpower absorbing some 14 neighbouring states between 1922 and 1945. It was Stalin who, with incredibly single-minded brutality, dragged Russia into the 20th century. His forced industrialisation of the country involved the deaths of millions, but he got his results, making him an oddly ambivalent figure in Russia today. He saw Russia through the devastation of WWII, during which some 20 million Soviets died, and by the time he himself died in 1953, the USSR had a full nuclear arsenal and half of Europe as satellite states.

After Stalin, Khrushchev (r 1957–64) began a cautious reform programme and denounced Stalin before being removed and replaced by Leonid Brezhnev, whose rule (1964–82) was marked by economic stagnation and growing internal dissent. Finally, Mikhail Gorbachev's period of reform, known as *perestroika,* began in 1985. Within six years the USSR had collapsed alongside communism, and reformer Boris Yeltsin was elected the first ever president of Russia in 1991.

Yeltsin led Russia into a new world of cutthroat capitalism, which saw the creation of a new superclass of oligarchs – businessmen who made billions from buying once stateowned commodities and running them as private companies – while prices soared and incomes dropped in real terms for the vast majority of the population.

Since 2000 Russia has been led by Vladimir Putin, an ex-KGB officer who has steered a careful course between reform and centralisation, alarming the West with his control of the media and brutal clampdown on the independence movement in Chechnya. The Beslan school siege in September 2004 was the latest large-scale terrorist assault on Russia from Chechen separatists, whose activities have bedevilled Putin's presidency. Despite this, Putin remains an extremely popular president and Russia is in the grip of very healthy economic growth, even though there's clearly still a long way to go. Russia looks set to regain its position as a superpower through its vast gas and oil reserves rather than its nuclear arsenal, something most people would have laughed at just a few years ago. With WTO membership on the cards and Putin's hosting of the G8 summit in 2006, economically at least things are looking up, although any real reform of the lumbering bureaucracy remains a distant dream.

## PEOPLE

There's some truth to the local saying 'scratch a Russian and you'll find a Tatar'. Russia has absorbed people from a huge number of nationalities: from the Mongols, the Tatars, Siberian peoples, Ukrainians, Jews, Caucasians and other national minorities who have all been part of Russia for centuries. This means that while the vast majority of people you meet will describe themselves as Russian, ethnic homogeneity is not always that simple.

On a personal level, Russians have a reputation for being dour, depressed and unfriendly. In fact, most Russians are anything but, yet find constant smiling indicative of idiocy and ridicule pointless displays of happiness commonly seen in Western culture. Even though Russians can be unfriendly and even downright rude when you first meet them (especially those working behind glass windows of any kind), their warmth as soon as the ice is broken is quite astounding. Just keep working at it.

## SPORT

Russia remains a formidable sporting presence in the world arena: at the 2000 Sydney Olympics Russia came away with 32 gold medals, second only to the USA, although at Athens in 2004 Russia found itself squeezed into third place by China, winning a still hugely impressive 28 gold medals. It excels at producing top-notch tennis stars, ice-hockey players and gymnasts.

On the ground, football is the game that interests Russians most, although many people care more passionately about the English premier league than their own teams, especially since Russian billionaire Roman Abramovich bought London club Chelsea for himself in 2003.

## RELIGION

The vast majority of Russians identify themselves as Orthodox Christians, although the proportion of those who actually practise their faith is small. The Russian Orthodox Church is led by Patriarch Alexei II. The church has become ever-more political in recent years, virulently condemning homosexuality, contraception and abortion.

Religious freedom exists in Russia – St Petersburg boasts the world's most northerly Mosque and Buddhist Temple. There can be unbelievable residual prejudice against Jews, although this is very rarely exhibited in anything other than the odd negative comment and some deeply entrenched stereotypes. There is certainly no reason for Jewish travellers to worry about coming to Russia.

## ARTS

Blame it on the long winter nights, the constant struggle against authoritarianism or the long-debated qualities of the mysterious 'Russian soul', but Russia's artistic contribution to the world is nothing short of gobsmacking.

### Literature

Russia's formal literary tradition began relatively late. It was set in motion in the early 19th century by playwright Griboyedov before reaching its zenith with the poetic genius of Alexander Pushkin (1799–1837), whose epic poem *Yevgeny Onegin* stands out as one of Russian literature's greatest achievements, an enormous, playful, philosophical poem from which any Russian can quote at least a few lines.

Pushkin's life was tragically cut short by a duel, and though his literary heir Mikhail Lermontov had the potential to equal or even surpass Pushkin's contribution – his novel *A Hero of Our Time* and his poetry spoke of incredible gifts – only a few years later Lermontov, too, was senselessly murdered in a duel in Southern Russia.

By the late 19th century Russia was producing some of the world's great classics – Leo

Tolstoy and Fyodor Dostoyevsky were the outstanding talents, two deeply different writers of unquestionable genius. Tolstoy brought the world enormous tapestries of Russian life, such as *War and Peace* and *Anna Karenina*, while Dostoyevsky wrote dark and troubled philosophical novels, such as *Crime and Punishment* and *The Brothers Karamazov*.

The early 20th century saw a continued literary flowering during what was widely known as the Silver Age, an enormously productive era of poetic creation, seeing movements as disparate as the acmeists, mystics and symbolists combine in unpredictable and often brilliant ways. This incredible literary ferment, which brought Blok, Akhmatova and Mandelstam worldwide fame, was dramatically curtailed by the revolution. Seismic changes in literature occurred in Russia post-1917. Despite an initial burst of creative energy – some of Russia's best writing, virtually unknown to audiences in the West, was written during the period between 1917 and 1925 – by the late 1920s, with Stalin's grip on power complete, all writers not spouting the party line were anathematised. Dissenting writers were either shot, took their own lives, fled or were silenced as Stalin revealed his socialist realist model of writing, which brought novels with titles such as *Cement* and *How the Steel Was Tempered* to the toiling masses. Despite this, many writers kept on writing in secret, and novels such as Mikhail Bulgakov's *The Master and Margarita* and poems such as Anna Akhmatova's *Requiem* survived Stalinism to become classics known the world over.

Despite Khrushchev allowing some literary debate to begin again (he allowed Solzhenitsyn's *A Day in the Life of Ivan Denisovich* to be published, a novella depicting life in one of Stalin's gulags), censorship continued until the mid-1980s when, thanks to Mikhail Gorbachev's policy of *glasnost* (openness), writers who had only been published through the illegal network of *samizdat* (the home printing presses), and were thus read only by the intelligentsia, suddenly had millions of readers.

Since the end of the Soviet Union Russian literature has developed quickly and embraced the postmodernism that was creatively proscribed by the Soviet authorities. Current literary big-hitters include Boris Akunin and Viktor Pelevin, both of whose works are widely available in English.

## Cinema & TV

Russia has produced some of the world's most famous film images – largely thanks to the father of the cinematic montage, Sergei Eisenstein, whose *Battleship Potemkin* (1925) and *Ivan the Terrible* (1944–46) are masterpieces and reference points for anyone serious about the history of film. Despite constant headaches with authority, Andrei Tarkovsky produced complex and iconoclastic films in the 1960s and 1970s; *The Mirror* and *Andrei Rublev* are generally considered to be his two greatest works.

In recent times Nikita Mikhailkov and Alexander Sokurov have established themselves as internationally renowned Russian directors. Mikhailkov was awarded the best foreign film Oscar in 1994 for his *Burnt by the Sun*, and seemed to find a more sentimental and Hollywood-friendly style for his underwhelming *The Barber of Siberia* (1999), the biggest-budget Russian film ever made. Alexander Sokurov has made his name producing art-house historical dramas, including *Taurus*, *Molokh* and 2002's astonishing *Russian Ark* – the only full-length film ever made using one long tracking shot. Andrei Zvyagintsev's stunning debut feature, *The Return* (2003), which scooped the Golden Lion at Venice is a sublime visual treat. *Night Watch* (2004), one of the few Russian thrillers to have been a hit internationally, is a blockbuster-style movie about Moscow's gangland.

Russian TV is not nearly as rich a feast, although the recent big-budget adaptation of *Master and Margarita* by national channel Rossiya was hailed as a great success. There are several channels available, although this varies across the country. The past few years have been characterised by a barely disguised attempt on the part of Putin's government to claw back the media control that the Kremlin had lost since *perestroika*. The takeover of once-trailblazing NTV, Russia's first professionally run TV station (and crucially, one critical of the Kremlin), has had a long-term effect on the vibrancy of the Russian media as a whole. In 2001 the Putin government effectively staged a takeover of the station on spurious legal grounds, leading to the mass resignation of NTV's journalists and editors. Since then NTV has been unable to re-establish the high standard of political journalism that was its trademark. There are currently no national TV channels independent of the Kremlin operating in Russia. Most channels run a dismal array of chat shows, old Soviet movies, chronic pop concerts and American straight-to-video movies clumsily dubbed into Russian with one voice.

## Music

Russia is, of course, famous for composers such as Tchaikovsky, Rimsky-Korsakov, Prokofiev and Shostakovich, and despite the enormous and almost universally horrific Russian pop-music industry, music is taken extremely seriously in modern Russia. Indeed, on any night of the week in Moscow or St Petersburg there's likely to be a good choice of concerts, gigs, ballet and opera to choose from.

Girl duo TATu remains one of the few Russian groups to be known beyond the former Soviet Union, although ginger matriarch Alla Pugacheva (a kind of Russian female version of Elton John complete with wardrobe) enjoys a cult following in some quarters.

## Painting

Russian painting is fairly unknown in the West, the most celebrated artists being the avant-garde painters of the early 20th century, such as Vasily Kandinsky and Kazimir Malevich. Most Russians will be surprised if you have heard of them and not the 'greats' of the 19th century, such as Ilya Repin and the *peredvizhniki* (wanderers) – the generation of painters who rejected the strict formalism of the St Petersburg Academy and painted realistic rural scenes with deep social messages.

Anyone visiting Russia will want to see the collection of foreign art held at the Hermitage (p723). The best galleries for Russian art are the Russian Museum (p725) in St Petersburg and the State Tretyakov Gallery (p709) in Moscow.

## Theatre & Dance

Theatre is one of the more vibrant art forms in Russia today. Since Chekhov revolutionised Russian drama in the late 19th century, Russia has seen countless innovations, from Stanislavsky, who created method acting, to Meyerhold, the theatrical pioneer whom Stalin had arrested and murdered.

Among the most celebrated contemporary theatre directors today are St Petersburg–based Lev Dodin and Moscow-based Roman Vityuk. The world-famous Bolshoi (p708) and Mariinsky (Kirov; p729) theatres have worked hard to reinvent themselves since the end of the Soviet Union, and their performances are regularly seen around the world on lucrative tours.

## ENVIRONMENT

While Russia as a country encompasses almost every conceivable type of landscape, European Russia around Moscow and St Petersburg is characterised by flatness. You can take the train from one city to the other and barely pass a hill or a valley.

Kaliningrad is strikingly different, with its half of the Kurshkaya Kosa (Curonian Spit), the Curonian Lagoon and the world's largest supply of amber.

The disastrous environmental legacy of communism is enormous. As well as both Moscow and St Petersburg being polluted from traffic and heavy industry, the countryside is frequently blighted by factories and other industrial plants. Environmental consciousness remains relatively low, although things are slowly changing with the emergence of a small but vocal Russian environmental movement.

## FOOD & DRINK

There's no denying it, Russian food is quite bland by most people's standards: spices are not widely used and dill is overwhelmingly the herb of choice, sprinkled onto almost everything. That said, you can eat extremely well in Russia – Caucasian food is popular throughout the country and is delicious. Moscow and St Petersburg both overflow with restaurants serving cuisine from all over the world. While the variety is hardly as great in Kaliningrad, world cuisine has also caught on and you can eat well there, too.

## Staples & Specialities

Russian soups are very good. Delicious *borsch* (beetroot soup), *solyanka* (a soup made from pickled vegetables) and *ukha* (fish soup) are always reliable. *Pelmeni* are Russian ravioli – beef parcels wrapped in dough and served with *smetana* (sour cream) – and are the lowest common denominator in Russian cooking. Other more interesting possibilities are *zharkoye* (literally 'hot' – meat stew in a pot), blini, caviar, beef Stroganov, *goluptsy* (mincemeat wrapped in cabbage leaves) and fish specialities, such as sturgeon, salmon and pikeperch.

## Where to Eat & Drink

Traditional cheap Soviet eateries have been almost entirely edged out by slick fast-food chains and upscale restaurants serving the latest fashionable cuisine. You can still find the odd *stolovoya* (canteen) or *cheburechnaya* (specialising in Caucasian lamb dumplings, or *chebureki*) in most places for an ultra-cheap eat or a flash back to 1982.

Russian restaurants themselves tend to be quite formal, although there's an increasing number of relaxed diner-style eateries in evidence in Moscow and St Petersburg. Cafés, a Western import, have become extremely popular, although bars and beer halls are where most Russians prefer to drink. These relaxed, generally cheap places usually combine beer and hearty Russian fare with live music of some description.

## Vegetarians & Vegans

Russia can be tough for vegetarians, and near impossible for vegans. Vegetarians will find themselves eating blini with sour cream, mushrooms, cheese or savoury *tvorog* (whey); mushroom julienne (mushrooms fried in garlic, cheese and cream); and visiting Georgian restaurants often. Vegans might be wishing they could go home.

## Habits & Customs

Food etiquette is fairly straightforward. Symbolic of its importance in Russian culture, it's drinking that is full of unspoken rules. First of all, never drink vodka without *zakuski* (snacks) – you'll get drunk otherwise, whereas (according to any Russian) that will *never* happen if you consume pickled herring or gherkins with your vodka. Once a bottle (vodka or otherwise) has been finished, it's considered rude to put it back on the table – always put it on the floor instead. Don't talk during toasts, and always appear to drink to the toast (even if you dribble it down your chin or drink nothing at all). Men should always down a vodka shot in one. Women are let off this requirement, although being able to down a large shot will garner respect from all quarters.

# MOSCOW МОСКВА

☎ 495 / pop 10 million

Moscow's sheer size is something most people aren't prepared for – while many come knowing this is the biggest city in Europe by far, this fact alone does not prepare most for the inhuman scale of the Russian capital. Brazen, ugly, intimidating, exciting and unforgettable, Moscow is many things to many people, and most visitors find their memories are a combination of positive and negative. History, power and wild capitalism hang in the air, beautiful buildings are demolished to build casinos, people continue to go about their never-easy lives as they have done here since time immemorial, and the city continues its maddening whirl.

That said, Moscow is a fascinating city full of museums, cathedrals, monumental architecture and exciting nightlife, and it's quite possible to find a quiet neighbourhood and create your own refuge from the chaos, or alternatively embrace the city and its infectious energy; few cities in the world have so much to spare.

## HISTORY

While Moscow has been inhabited for more than five millennia, it was mentioned for the first time only in 1147 by Prince Yury Dolgoruky, who to this day is acknowledged as the founder of the city by a huge equestrian statue of him on Tverskaya ul (p708). It was Yury who built wooden walls around the city and oversaw its rise as an economic centre. During the reign of the Mongol Horde in the 13th to 15th centuries Moscow outstripped rivals Vladimir and Suzdal as the principal town of the Muscovy principality. Under Ivan the Great and Ivan the Terrible in the 16th century the city expanded enormously, as Russia became a vast state absorbing Slav lands to the west, the Baltic, the Urals and the north. The Crimean Tatars sacked the city in 1571, burning much of it, which prompted the construction of stone walls around Kitay Gorod (p708) that can still be seen today. By the early 17th century Moscow was the biggest city in the world.

The 18th century saw a huge decline for Moscow – Peter the Great moved the capital to his new northern city of St Petersburg in 1712, and fire, economic downturn and bubonic plague took their toll. Napoleon's onslaught on

Moscow a century later was even more catastrophic – Muscovites burned most of the city
rather than surrender to the French, although
thankfully the Kremlin survived. Following
Napoleon's retreat and eventual rout, Moscow
regained its confidence and developed as Russia's economic powerhouse – becoming an
industrial city full of factories, slums and revolutionaries by the end of the 19th century.

It was the Russian revolution that restored
Moscow's prestige – the resulting Civil War
forced Lenin, fearing St Petersburg's proximity to hostile foreign governments, to move
the capital back to Moscow in 1918. As capital
of the USSR, Moscow became the nerve centre
of a superpower. Under Stalin the Nazis were
resisted (they came within 30km of the Kremlin, but never managed to take the city), the
vast and beautiful Moscow metro was built,
countless churches including the now reconstructed Church of Christ the Saviour (p709)
were demolished and huge, neo-Gothic buildings such as the Seven Sisters skyscrapers that
still define the city skyline became the order
of the day. Soviet Moscow's proudest moment
came when it hosted the 1980 Olympics – a
last big fling for a declining nation that was
soon to reform itself out of existence.

Moscow has seen no end of tumult since
*perestroika* – the 1991 coup against Gorbachev,
Yeltsin's attack on the parliament building in
1993, the terrible Ostankino TV Tower fire
in August 2000 (becoming a metaphor for
many despairing Muscovites of Russia's disintegrating infrastructure) and several large-scale
terrorist attacks. The most famous and horrific
terrorist assault was the Dubrovka Theatre
Siege of October 2002 when Chechen terror-
ists took an entire theatre audience hostage,
eventually culminating in a botched rescue
attempt during which some 129 people were

killed. Despite this, Moscow has reinforced
its position as Russia's economic powerhouse
and today it's a city looking far ahead into
the future.

## ORIENTATION

The medieval centre of the city, the Kremlin,
is a triangle on the northern bank of the Moscow River. The modern city centre radiates
around it, the main streets being Tverskaya
ul and ul Novy Arbat. The very centre of
the city is defined by the 'garden ring' – a
vast eight-lane highway that rings Moscow's
central district.

## INFORMATION
### Bookshops

**Anglia British Bookshop** (Map pp702-3; ☎ 299 7766;
www.anglophile.ru; Vorotnikovsky per 6; ☿ 10am-7pm
Mon-Fri, 10am-6pm Sat, 11am-5pm Sun; Ⓜ Mayakovskaya) Has an excellent selection of books in English,
including some antique Lonely Planet guides.

**Moskovsky Dom Knigi** (Map pp702-3; ☎ 290 4507;
www.mdk-arbat.ru, in Russian; ul Novy Arbat 8; ☿ 10am-
9pm Mon-Sat, 10am-8pm Sun; Ⓜ Arbatskaya) Moscow's
main bookshop, excellent but crowded, stocks books on
pretty much anything, including a very decent selection of
English-language novels.

### Internet Access

**Café Max** (Map pp702-3; ☎ 741 7571; www.cafémax.ru,
in Russian; ul Novoslobodskaya 3; per hr R50-100; ☿ 24hr;
Ⓜ Novoslobodskaya) This chain is in several locations
throughout the city, but its most central branch is here on the
3rd floor of the shopping centre opposite the metro station.

**Jagganath** (Map pp702-3; ☎ 928 3580; ul Kuznetsky
Most 11; ☿ 8am-11pm; Ⓜ Kuznetsky Most) A pleasant
alternative to loud, busy internet cafés – this veg café and
health-food shop (p712) is a relaxing place to surf. Wi-fi is
free to diners with laptops.

**NetCity** (Map pp702-3; ☎ 962 0111; www.netcitycafé
.ru, in Russian; Kamergersky per 6; per hr R60; ☿ 24hr;
Ⓜ Okhotny Ryad) An excellent spot right in the city centre.

### Left Luggage

The many metro stations around Moscow all
have left-luggage services, known as *kamera
khraneniya*. They charge minimal rates of R30
to R60 per 24 hours, although always check
their opening times as even 24-hour ones can
have 'technical breaks' of several hours.

### Media

Moscow's huge expat population has created a large market for English-language

# CENTRAL MOSCOW

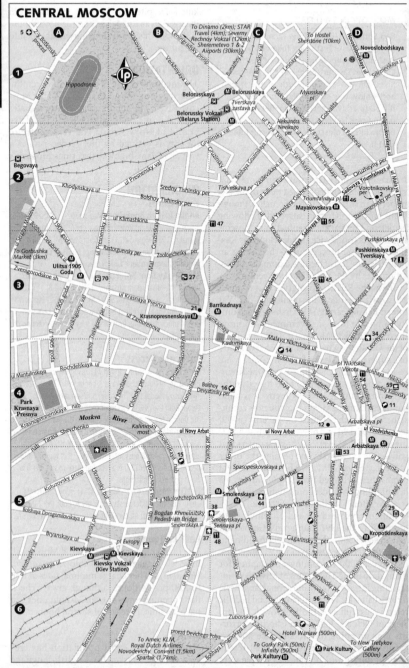

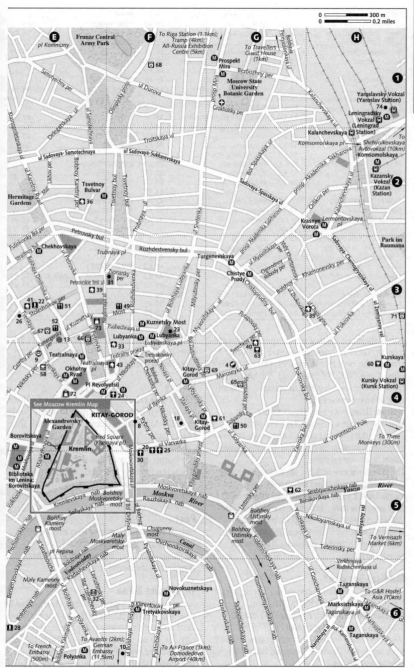

publications. All three newspapers below are free in various bars, cafés and restaurants around the city. For those who can read Russian, *Time Out*, *Ne Spat!* and *Afisha* are the three best-known listings magazines, all available at any newsstand.

**Moscow Times** (www.themoscowtimes.com) Most reliable is this daily, a professional and well-produced newspaper that is free and available everywhere. Its weekend edition is excellent for visitors and has comprehensive listings for all leisure activities.

**The Exile** (www.exile.ru) A free, satirical fortnightly paper that has consistently outraged and offended since it began in the late 1990s. It's a great read if you want to know what's really going on in town – its brutally honest bar and restaurant section, Bardak, is legendary and scripture to many.

**Element** (www.elementmoscow.ru) This weekly entertainment paper is another good source of information, reviews and listings.

## Medical Services

There are several expensive, foreign-run health services available in Moscow.

**American Medical Centre** (Map pp702-3; ☎ 933 7700; www.amcenter.ru/en; Grokholsky per 1; ⏰ 24hr; Ⓜ Prospekt Mira) Features an English-speaking pharmacy (open 8am to 8pm Monday to Friday, and 9am to 5pm Saturday and Sunday).

**Botkin Hospital** (Map pp702-3; ☎ 945 0045; 2-y Botkinsky proezd 5; ⏰ 24hr; Ⓜ Dinamo) A Russian facility where English is spoken.

## Money

ATMs and reliable moneychanging facilities are located on every corner. Russian banks include Alfa Bank, Bank Moskvy and Sberbank; banks work full days (usually 8am to 7pm Monday to Friday). Out of hours, most big hotels have a 24-hour bank or moneychanging facility. **Amex** ( ☎ 933 6636; fax 933 6635; ul Usacheva 33; Ⓜ Sportivnaya) cashes Amex travellers cheques.

## Post

**Central Telegraph** (Tsentralny Telegraf; Map pp702-3; Tverskaya ul 7; ⏰ postal counters 8am-10pm; Ⓜ Okhotny Ryad) This convenient office offers post, telephone, fax and internet services.

## Telephone & Fax

Nearly all hotels have IDD from their rooms at exorbitant rates. It's far better to buy a phonecard and call from any pay phone around the city, or go to the Central Telegraph (above) and use the booths there. You can also send faxes from there. The Moscow mobile-phone

---

**MOSCOW TELEPHONES CHANGE**

At the time of writing some Moscow telephone numbers changed – those beginning with the number 9 changed to number 6. Therefore if you have a telephone number and it doesn't work, try changing the first digit to a 6. Note also that Moscow's city code has changed from 095 to 495.

---

market is huge, and most international phones with roaming will automatically switch over to a local network. It's perfectly feasible to buy a local SIM card if you're staying in town for any amount of time – just go to any of the hundreds of mobile-phone shops around the city.

### Toilets

As a rule, the more you pay for a toilet, the worse it will be. Free toilets are normally available in museums, and there are nasty temporary toilets, which you pay around R10 for the honour of using, around metro stations. Free toilets in smart hotels, cafés and restaurants remain the best choice.

### Travel Agencies

**Avantix.ru** ( ☎ 787 7272; www.avantix.ru; ul Shchipok 11; Ⓜ Serpukhovskaya) One of the leading online ticket agencies, Avantix's office in Moscow sells air and train tickets and can deliver them free of charge to you anywhere in Moscow.

**Infinity** ( ☎ 234 6555; www.infinity.ru; Komsomolsky pr 13; Ⓜ Frunzenskaya) With an office in both south Moscow and St Petersburg, Infinity is well used to dealing with the needs of foreigners. The helpful English-speaking staff can make most travel arrangements.

**STAR Travel** ( ☎ 797 9555; www.startravel.ru; 3rd fl, ul Baltiiskaya 9; Ⓜ Sokol) The representative of STA Travel in Moscow, STAR can book student and young person's air and train tickets from its north Moscow office. Check its website for more offices in the city.

## DANGERS & ANNOYANCES

Red Sq and the area immediately around it repeatedly feature in travellers' tales of harassment by police. This can often involve document checks where the officers in question find something wrong with your (perfectly above board) visa or registration. See p741 for tips on how to deal with this. Other scams in the area have involved hackneyed tricks, such as someone dropping a wallet and their accomplice pointing this out to you. You pick up

and return the wallet to the man who dropped it, whereupon he miraculously finds lots of cash is missing and demands you pay him the cash back. Just don't get involved if you see someone drop his or her wallet.

## SIGHTS
### Red Square

Palpably the centre of Moscow and even Russia as a whole, **Red Sq** (Map p706; Ⓜ Pl Revolyutsii) is a massively impressive sight that brings back the full force of the Cold War, despite the two decades that have passed since *perestroika*. Something of a misnomer for this grey and rectangular strip to the east side of the Kremlin, Red Sq is surrounded by Lenin's Mausoleum to the west, the State History Museum to the north, GUM shopping centre to the east and fabulous St Basil's Cathedral to the south. Begin your visit to Moscow by coming here – there's nothing else like it.

Entering Red Sq through the **Voskressensky Gates** (Map p706), you'll emerge with a superb view of the magnificently flamboyant **St Basil's Cathedral** (Sobor Vasilia Blazhennogo; Map p706; ☎ 298 3304; admission R100; ⏰ 11am-5pm Wed-Mon; Ⓜ Pl Revolyutsii) on the far side. Ivan the Terrible was so keen to immortalise his victory over the Tatars at Kazan that he took the measure of blinding the architects after they completed the cathedral's dazzlingly bright onion domes in 1561 to ensure that nothing of comparable beauty could ever be built. Its design is the culmination of a wholly Russian style that had been developed through the building of wooden churches. The cathedral owes its name to the barefoot holy fool Vasily (Basil) the Blessed, who predicted Ivan's damnation (as yet unconfirmed) and added (correctly) that Ivan would murder his son. It's definitely worth going inside to see the stark medieval wall paintings. Look out for the **Lobnoye Mesto** (Map p706) just in front of the cathedral, a 13m-long circular stone platform from where Ivan the Terrible addressed the Muscovites in 1547 and where historically the tsar's orders, as well as notices of execution, were announced to the townsfolk. Now it's considered good luck to throw a coin into the raised centre of the platform.

**Lenin's Mausoleum** (Mavzoley V I Lenina; Map p706; ☎ 923 5527; admission free; ⏰ 10am-1pm Tue-Thu, Sat & Sun; Ⓜ Pl Revolyutsii) is global ground zero for nostalgic communists. Before joining the queue at the northwestern corner of Red Sq,

RUSSIA

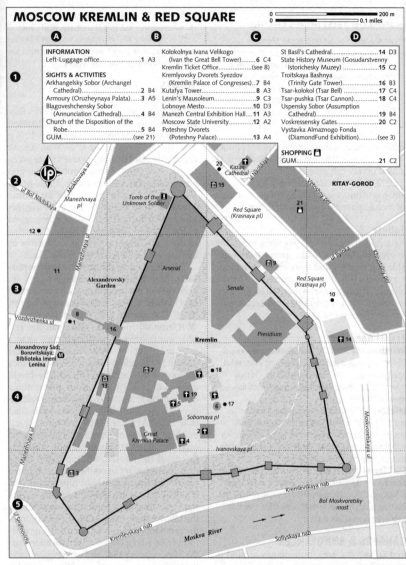

# MOSCOW KREMLIN & RED SQUARE

0 _____ 200 m
0 _____ 0.1 miles

| INFORMATION | | |
| --- | --- | --- |
| Left-Luggage office | 1 | A3 |

| SIGHTS & ACTIVITIES | | |
| --- | --- | --- |
| Arkhangelsky Sobor (Archangel | | |
| Cathedral) | 2 | B4 |
| Armoury (Oruzheynaya Palata) | 3 | A5 |
| Blagoveshchensky Sobor | | |
| (Annunciation Cathedral) | 4 | B4 |
| Church of the Disposition of the | | |
| Robe | 5 | B4 |
| GUM | (see 21) | |

| Kolokolnya Ivana Velikogo | | |
| --- | --- | --- |
| (Ivan the Great Bell Tower) | 6 | C4 |
| Kremlin Ticket Office | (see 8) | |
| Kremlyovsky Dvorets Syezdov | | |
| (Kremlin Palace of Congresses) | 7 | B4 |
| Kutafya Tower | 8 | A3 |
| Lenin's Mausoleum | 9 | C3 |
| Lobnoye Mesto | 10 | D3 |
| Manezh Central Exhibition Hall | 11 | A3 |
| Moscow State University | 12 | A2 |
| Poteshny Dvorets | | |
| (Poteshny Palace) | 13 | A4 |

| St Basil's Cathedral | 14 | D3 |
| --- | --- | --- |
| State History Museum (Gosudarstvenny | | |
| Istorichesky Muzey) | 15 | C2 |
| Troitskaya Bashnya | | |
| (Trinity Gate Tower) | 16 | B3 |
| Tsar-kolokol (Tsar Bell) | 17 | C4 |
| Tsar-pushka (Tsar Cannon) | 18 | C4 |
| Uspensky Sobor (Assumption | | |
| Cathedral) | 19 | B4 |
| Voskressensky Gates | 20 | C2 |
| Vystavka Almaznogo Fonda | | |
| (DiamondFund Exhibition) | (see 3) | |

| SHOPPING | | |
| --- | --- | --- |
| GUM | 21 | C2 |

drop your camera either at the left-luggage office inside the State History Museum (opposite) or at the **left-luggage office** (Map p706; per bag R60; 9am-6.30pm; Pl Revolyutsii) beneath Kutafya Tower, as you will not be allowed to take it with you. The hilariously sombre visit takes you into the very dark crypt under Red Sq where Lenin lies swathed in red velvet. Any

talking will provoke angry shushing from the soldiers who line the route. Bear in mind that Stalin had Lenin's brain removed in a rather fanciful attempt to study the 'pure communist' brain, leaving Vladimir Ilych looking decidedly green around the (probably wax) gills. Following the trip underground, you'll emerge beside the route along the Kremlin wall, where other greats, such as Stalin, Gagarin and Brezhnev, are buried. Yeltsin-era plans to rebury Lenin in St Petersburg (where he apparently wished to be buried next to his mother) have been abandoned, and it appears that he isn't going anywhere in a hurry.

The **State History Museum** (Gosudarstvenny Istoricheskny Muzey; Map p706; ☎ 292 4019; www.shm.ru, in Russian; adult/student R150/75; ⏰ 10am-6pm Mon, Wed-Sat, 11am-7pm Sun; Ⓜ Pl Revolyutsii) is the stunningly ornate red building at the northern end of the square. It has an enormous collection covering the whole of Russian history from the Stone Age on, and has been continually refurbishing its galleries since the 1990s. A joint ticket for the museum and St Basil's Cathedral saves a few roubles at R230.

Finally, drop into **GUM** (Map p706; ⏰ 10am-10pm; Ⓜ Pl Revolyutsii) to see the showpiece Soviet shopping centre turned designer mall for the new rich, with its stunning glass roof and centrepiece fountains.

## The Kremlin

The nerve centre of Russian politics, the ultimate goal of Cold War espionage, a symbol of power and intrigue recognised the world over – for most first-time visitors what's most unexpected about the Kremlin are the several huge cathedrals at its heart.

Kremlin simply means 'citadel' in Russian and any medieval Russian town had one. Moscow's is huge – in effect a walled city, the best views of which can be got from across the Moscow River; try standing on either the Bolshoy Moskvoretsky or the Bolshoy Kameny Bridges for a superb view of the complex. The Kremlin (first built in the 1150s) grew with the importance of Moscow's princes and in the 1320s it became the headquarters of the Russian Orthodox Church, which shifted here from Vladimir. Between 1475 and 1516 Ivan the Great brought master builders from Pskov and Italy to supervise the construction of new walls and towers, three great cathedrals and more.

Before entering the **Kremlin** (Map p706; ☎ 203 0349; www.kreml.ru; adult/student R300/150, photography R50; ⏰ 10am-5pm Fri-Wed; Ⓜ Aleksandrovsky Sad) deposit your bags at the **left-luggage office** (per bag R60; ⏰ 9am-6.30pm; Ⓜ Aleksandrovsky Sad), beneath the Kutafya Tower, just north of the main ticket office. The Kremlin ticket office, in the Aleksandrovsky Garden, closes at 4.30pm. The ticket covers admission to all buildings,

except the Armoury and Diamond Fund Exhibition (below).

### SOUTHWEST BUILDINGS

From the Kutafya Tower, which forms the main visitors' entrance, walk up the ramp and pass through the Kremlin walls beneath the **Troitskaya Bashnya** (Trinity Gate Tower; Map p706). The lane to the right (south) passes the 17th-century **Poteshny Dvorets** (Poteshny Palace; Map p706), where Stalin lived. The horribly out of place glass and concrete **Kremlyovksy Dvorets Syezdov** (Kremlin Palace of Congresses; Map p706) houses a concert and ballet auditorium, where incongruously enough lots of Western pop stars play when they are in Moscow.

### ARMOURY & DIAMOND FUND

In the southwestern corner of the Kremlin, the **Armoury** (Map p706; Oruzheynaya Palata; adult/student R350/175; Ⓜ Aleksandrovsky Sad) is a numbingly opulent collection of treasures accumulated over centuries by the Russian State and Church. Your ticket will specify a time of entry. Highlights include the Fabergé eggs in room two, and the reams of royal regalia in rooms six and nine.

If the Armoury hasn't sated your diamond lust, there are more in the separate **Vystavka Almaznogo Fonda** (Map p706; Diamond Fund Exhibition; adult/student R350/175; ⏰ closed for lunch 1-2pm; Ⓜ Aleksandrovsky Sad) in the same building.

### SOBORNAYA PLOSHCHAD

On the northern side of Sobornaya pl is the 15th-century **Uspensky Sobor** (Assumption Cathedral; Map p706), focal church of prerevolutionary Russia and the most impressive of the Kremlin ensemble. It's the burial place of the heads of the Russian Orthodox Church from the 1320s to 1700. The tombs are against the north, west and south walls.

The iconostasis dates from 1652, but its lowest level contains some older icons, including the *Virgin of Vladimir* (Vladimirskaya Bogomater), an early 15th-century Rublev School copy of Russia's most revered image. The 12th-century original, now in the State Tretyakov Gallery (p709), stood in the Assumption Cathedral from the 1480s to 1930. The oldest icon on display is the magnificent 12th-century red-clothed *St George,* brought here from Novgorod; it is positioned behind glass by the north wall.

The **Tserkov Rizopolozheniya** (Church of the Disposition of the Robe; Map p706), opposite the Assumption Cathedral, was built between 1484 and 1485 and includes a delightful wooden sculpture exhibition and some lovely frescoes. The domes and facades of the cathedrals are being progressively restored.

With its two golden domes rising above the eastern side of Sobornaya pl, the 16th-century **Kolokolnya Ivana Velikogo** (Ivan the Great Bell Tower; Map p706) is the Kremlin's tallest structure. Beside the bell tower stands the world's biggest bell, the **Tsar-kolokol** (Tsar Bell; Map p706), a 202-tonne monster that cracked before it ever rang. North of the bell tower is the mammoth **Tsar-pushka** (Tsar Cannon; Map p706), cast in 1586, but never shot.

Back on Sobornaya pl, the 1508 **Arkhangelsky Sobor** (Archangel Cathedral; Map p706), at the square's southeastern corner, was for centuries the coronation, wedding and burial church of tsars. The tombs of all of Russia's rulers from the 1320s to the 1690s are here bar one (Boris Godunov, who was buried at Sergiev Posad).

Dating from 1489, the **Blagoveshchensky Sobor** (Annunciation Cathedral; Map p706) at the southwest corner of Sobornaya pl contains the celebrated icons of master-painter Theophanes the Greek. He probably painted the six icons at the right-hand end of the diesis row, the biggest of the six tiers of the iconostasis. *Archangel Michael* (the third icon from the left on the diesis row) and the adjacent *St Peter* are ascribed to Russian master Andrei Rublev.

## Around Red Square

Manezhnaya pl, at the northwestern end of Red Sq, has transformed into the vast underground **Okhotny Ryad Shopping Mall** (Map pp702–3), worth a look just to shatter images of Russians queuing in the snow for bread. The former **Manezh Central Exhibition Hall** (Map p706), the long, low building on the southern side of the square, was home to some of Moscow's most popular art exhibitions until it was burnt to a shell in a mysterious fire in 2003. On the southwestern side of the square is the fine edifice of **Moscow State University** (Map p706), built in 1793. The classic Stalinist Hotel Moskva, once fronting the northeastern side of the square, was demolished in 2004 to make way for a huge underground car park. A replica of the original hotel (famous internationally for

being on Stolichnaya Vodka labels) is to be built after the car park is complete.

Teatralnaya pl opens out on both sides of Okhotny Ryad, 200m north of Manezhnaya pl. The northern half of the square is dominated by the **Bolshoi Theatre** (Map pp702–3), which was being renovated at the time of writing and is where Tchaikovsky's *Swan Lake* was premiered (to bad reviews) in 1877. Look out for the stunning Art Nouveau **Metropole Hotel** (Map pp702–3), one of Moscow's most historic, on Teatralny proezd facing the Bolshoi at an angle across the road.

Moscow's main avenue, elegant **Tverskaya ul** (Map pp702–3), replete with fashionable shops and costly cafés and restaurants, meanders uphill from Red Sq and continues pretty much in a straight line all the way to St Petersburg. There are also the lovely pedestrianised side streets of **Kamergersky per** (Map pp702–3) and **Stoleshnikov per** (Map pp702–3) to walk down. Further up on Tverskaya ul there's the **equestrian statue of Yury Dolgoruky** (Map pp702–3), the founder of the city, which now faces the **Moscow Mayor's Office** (Map pp702–3), where the Luzhkov administration concocts many of its hare-brained ideas.

Further up, on Pushkinskaya pl, there's the huge **Alexander Pushkin Statue** (Map pp702–3), a monument to Russia's national poet, behind which is the gaudy Rossiya cinema and casino complex. Another item of note on the square is Russia's first McDonald's, which saw lines stretching around the square when it opened in 1990. To this day it has the dubious honour of being the biggest McDonald's branch in the world, seating 700 burger munchers at any one time.

## Kitay Gorod

This 13th-century neighbourhood was the first in Moscow to grow up outside the Kremlin walls. While its name means China Town in modern Russian, do not expect anything Chinese – the name derives from an old Russian word meaning 'wattle', for the supports used for the walls that protected the suburb. This is the heart of medieval Moscow and parts of the suburb's walls are visible. The main places of interest are the collection of churches in the neighbourhood. Look out for the charming, brightly painted **Monastery of the Epiphany** (Map pp702–3) opposite Ploshchad Revolyutsii Metro station and the small churches along ul Varvarka, incongruously surrounded by general concrete sprawl. These is the 17th-century **Monastery of the Sign** (Map pp702–3), the **Church of St Maxim the Blessed** (1698; Map pp702–3) and **St Barbara's Church** (1795–1804; Map pp702–3). While the horrendous Hotel Rossiya has been demolished now, Sir Norman Foster is slated to build Europe's tallest skyscraper on the site, to be completed in 2011.

Communist history can be seen on Staraya pl, where the western side of the square is taken up with the **Central Committee Building** (Map pp702–3), once the most important decision-making organ of the communist party and thus the whole of the Soviet Union. Further up the hill, past Novaya pl, you'll see the huge and sinister **Lubyanka Building** (Map pp702–3) crowning Lubyanka Hill. This was the headquarters of the dreaded KGB and remains today the nerve centre of its successor organisation, the Federal Security Bureau.

## Pushkin Museum & Around

Moscow's premier foreign art museum is a short distance from the southwestern corner of the Kremlin. The **Pushkin Fine Arts Museum** (Map pp702–3; ☎ 203 7958; ul Volkhonka 12; adult/student R300/100, audio guide R200; ☼ 10am-6pm Tue-Sun; Ⓜ Kropotkinskaya) is famous for its impressionist and postimpressionist paintings, but also has a broad selection of European works from the Renaissance onward, mostly appropriated from private collections after the revolution. There are also interesting temporary exhibits on regular display.

Nearby is the gigantic **Church of Christ the Saviour** (Khram Khrista Spasatelya; Map pp702–3; ☎ 201 3847; Prechistenskaya nab; ☼ 10am-5pm; Ⓜ Kropotkinskaya), rebuilt at an estimated cost of US$360

million by Mayor Luzhkov on the site of the original cathedral, which was destroyed by Stalin, and replacing what was once the world's largest swimming pool. It's massively impressive with its vast golden dome, although the Tsereteli-designed interiors wouldn't look out of place in the equally gaudy Okhotny Ryad Shopping Mall (also Tsereteli designed).

## State Tretyakov Gallery

The world's best collection of Russian icons is found in the **State Tretyakov Gallery** (Gosudarstvennaya Tretyakovskaya Galereya; Map pp702–3; ☎ 951 1362; www.tretyakov.ru; Lavrushinsky per 10; adult/student R240/140, audio guide R140; ☼ 10am-6.30pm Tue-Sun; Ⓜ Tretyakovskaya), along with an outstanding collection of other prerevolutionary Russian art, particularly the 19th-century *peredvizhniki* (wanderers) and some incredible landscapes. A second building of the museum is the **New Tretyakov Gallery** (Map pp702–3; ☎ 230 7788; Krymsky Val 10; adult/student R240/140, audio guide R140; ☼ 10am-6.30pm Tue-Sun; Ⓜ Park Kultury), which houses a similarly brilliant collection of 20th-century art encompassing both socialist realism and the myriad of early 20th-century painting styles, as well as temporary exhibits.

## Novodevichy Convent

A cluster of sparkling domes behind turreted walls southeast of the city centre on the Moscow River, **Novodevichy Convent** (Novodevichy Monastyr; ☎ 246 8526; adult/student R150/75; ☼ 10am-5pm Wed-Mon; Ⓜ Sportivnaya) is resplendent with history and treasures. Founded in 1524 to celebrate the retaking of Smolensk from Lithuania, it gained notoriety as the place where Peter the Great imprisoned his half-sister Sofia for her part in the Streltsy Rebellion.

---

**TOP FIVE MOST AWFUL**

Mayor Luzhkov and his artist of choice, Zurab Tsereteli, are no strangers to controversy. Their taste for new, shiny, tasteless buildings beggars belief, but sadly for Moscow one has the power and the other has the 'vision' to see through these awful projects. Not all of these are creations of Tsereteli, but they are all classic examples of the horrendous taste that characterises the Russian capital.

- Peter the Great Monument (Map pp702–3; Bersenevskaya nab; Ⓜ Polyanka)
- Bogdan Khmelnitsky Pedestrian Bridge (Map pp702–3; Rostovskaya nab; Ⓜ Kievskaya)
- Interiors of the Church of Christ the Saviour (Map pp702–3; Soymonovsky pr; Ⓜ Kropotkinskaya)
- The water park outside the Kievskaya Station (Map pp702–3; pl Evropy; Ⓜ Kievskaya)
- Okhotny Ryad Shopping Centre (Map pp702–3; Manezhnaya pl; Ⓜ Okhotny Ryad)

You enter the convent under the red-and-white Moscow-baroque **Transfiguration Gate-Church**. The oldest and dominant building in the grounds is the white **Smolensk Cathedral** (1524–25). **Sofia's tomb** lies among others in the south nave. The **bell tower** against the convent's east wall, completed in 1690, is generally regarded as Moscow's finest. The adjacent **Novodevichy Cemetery** (adult/student R150/75; ☻ 9am-8pm) contains the tombs of Khrushchev, Chekhov, Gogol, Mayakovsky, Stanislavsky, Prokofiev, Eisenstein, Raisa Gorbachev, and other Russian and Soviet notables.

## ACTIVITIES

Moscow has some of the swankiest *banyas* (traditional Russian steam baths) in the country, and it would be a shame to leave without trying one out. The most famous is the excellent **Sandunovskiye Bani** (Map pp702-3; ☎ 925 4631/33; Neglinnaya ul 14; ☻ 8am-10pm; Ⓜ Tsvetnoy Bul), where you can enjoy a range of treats, from a communal bathing session, for R500 to R700, to a private and extremely luxurious bathing chamber from R1200. There are *banyas* everywhere throughout the city – ask at your hotel if you need a local recommendation.

## TOURS

**Capital Tours** (Map pp702-3; ☎ 232 2442; www.capitaltours.ru; ul Ilyinka 4; Ⓜ Pl Revolyutsii) offers both a city tour (US$25, 11am and 2.30pm daily) and a Kremlin Cathedrals and Armoury tour (US$46, 10.30am and 3pm Friday to Wednes-day) departing from its office off Red Sq. Both options are highly recommended.

## SLEEPING

Moscow is pricey, and nothing more so than its hotels. Bent on modernisation, the city has demolished the nasty but budget-friendly Intourist, Moskva, Minsk and Rossiya Hotels, and unfortunately, there are few budget places opening to bridge the gap. The good news is that Moscow has its first genuine hostels with both Godzilla and Sweet opening up in 2005. The bad news is that it's not always plain sailing for hostels, so double-check that they are operating before counting on them.

### Budget

**Galina's Flat** (Map pp702-3; ☎ 621 6038; galinas.flat@mtu-net.ru; Flat 35, ul Chaplygina 8; dm/s/d R350/800/1000; Ⓠ; Ⓜ Chistiye Prudy) Still the cheapest bed in the city despite a recent price hike, Galina's central apartment functions as a homestay and is a wonderful way to see 'real' Russian life. Galina herself is friendly and speaks passable English. There's internet access and a kitchen that guests can use, as well as breakfast for an extra R50. Transfers to/from any Moscow airport are available for R1000.

**Sweet Moscow** (Map pp702-3; ☎ 241 1446; www.sweetmoscow.com; 8th fl, Flat 31, ul Arbat 51; dm R900; Ⓜ Smolenskaya) One of Moscow's new breed of small, central hostels located in residential buildings, Sweet was forced to move to new premises on the old Arbat – a superb location

---

**BANYA RITUAL**

No experience is more Russian than the *banya*. Many Russians believe that it's the only true way to get clean, and for some it's the only place they ever wash. You can pay for a private (*lyuks*) *banya* if you are a mixed-sex group wanting to bathe together. For a more authentic experience, go to a communal *banya* – far cheaper and usually segregated.

You'll get *tapki* (sandals), and some *prostinya* (sheets) to cover yourself with. Before entering you should buy some snacks and drinks for your (equally important) breaks from the bathing ritual, and a bunch of birch *veniki* (twigs) .

Once inside, you strip down, put your sheet around you and head for the dry sauna, where you get nice and hot before plunging into the *parilka* (steam bath). Here you get seriously sweaty and beat the toxins out of your skin with the birch twigs. Normally, people do their own legs and arms, and then lie down and allow their friends to whip their backs and stomachs. It's actually not that painful, unless your friend displays sadistic tendencies. Once you're sweating more than you thought possible and are covered in bits of twig and leaf, run out of the *parilka* and jump into the freezing plunge pool (alternatively, if you are in the countryside run out naked into the snow and roll around in it). After a break to drink beer or tea and snack while discussing the world's problems, repeat – several times over. Don't miss Moscow's superb Sandunovskiye Bani (above) or St Petersburg's Krugliye Bani (p726), with its brilliant heated outdoor pool.

where it offers only dorms (six beds in three rooms). There's a basic kitchen and laundry facilities, but it's friendly and well run, with clean, smart little rooms.

**Godzilla's** (Map pp702-3; ☎ 629 8957; fax 692 1221; Bolshoy Karetny per 6; dm/s/d R900/2000/2000; Ⓜ Tsvetnoy Bulvar) At last Moscow has a real hostel! Centrally located, run by a friendly Englishman and with a suitably eccentric name, this is the answer to many people's prayers. There are 49 beds, also laundry facilities, a common room and kitchens, although the shower provision is tight and will hopefully soon be expanded. Grand plans to take over the whole building are afoot, which will be the best news for backpackers since the end of Intourist. Until then book way in advance as it's always fully booked in summer.

**Travellers Guest House** ( ☎ 631 4059; www.tgh.ru; 10th fl, Bolshaya Pereyaslavskaya ul 50; dm/r R950/2100; Ⓜ Prospekt Mira) Once a real boon for budget travellers, the TGH is no longer such a great deal. Resting on its laurels for more than a decade now, the rooms, never great, are fairly crappy and slowly disintegrating. It's in a depressing block a fair way from the metro, and frankly until it refurbishes it's hard to recommend.

**Hotel Tsentralnaya** (Map pp702-3; ☎ 629 8957; fax 692 1221; Tverskaya ul 10; s/d R1400/2100; Ⓜ Chekhovskaya) One of the city's best bargains – the Tsentralnaya is on Moscow's main street and offers great value, even if it's rooms are far more simple than the grand entrance suggests. While accommodation is basic and all facilities shared, this is a clean, safe option and highly recommended.

## Midrange

**Hotel Sverchkov** (Map pp702-3; ☎ 625 4978; Sverchkov per 8; s/d R2300/2600; Ⓜ Chistiye Prudy) This small hotel is really good value for money; set in an 18th-century Moscow residential building in the city centre. Rooms are fairly plain, but are comfortable and secure.

**Hotel Warsaw** ( ☎ 238 7701; warsaw@sovintel.ru; Leninsky pr 2; s/d R3200/3950; Ⓜ Oktyabrskaya) Despite sounding like the worst Intourist horror hotel imaginable, the Warsaw is in fact brand new. It's in a fairly ghastly building just off Oktyabrskaya Sq, but it's actually modern, clean and well run inside, and good value at these prices.

**Hotel Belgrade** (Map pp702-3; ☎ 248 2692; Smolenskaya ul 8; s/d R3200/4160; Ⓜ Smolenskaya) Once a notorious fleapit, the Belgrade has made a concerted effort to clean itself up. Rooms aren't great – and indeed, many have barely been touched since the 1980s – but this is a very well-located midrange option and its exterior neon lights at night have to be seen to be believed!

**Hotel Budapest** (Map pp702-3; ☎ 623 2356; www .hotel-budapest.ru; Petrovskie linii ul 2/18; s/d €110/155; Ⓜ Teatralnaya) An unassuming hotel in a small central side street, its rooms are stylishly decked out and the whole place has a rather elegant old-world feel. A new addition opened at the time of writing, the Pyotr Pervy Hotel (Peter the First Hotel), is smarter and gives itself four stars.

**Hotel Ukraina** (Map pp702-3; ☎ 243 3030; fax 956 2078; Kutuzovsky pr 2/1; s/d R4200/4650; Ⓜ Kievskaya) The magnificent Gothic-Stalinist façade of the Hotel Ukraina leaves you in no doubt that this was once one of the best hotels in the USSR. There are some stunning views over the river and the rooms are suitably grand. The whole place is set for total refurbishment, so prices will soon rise.

**East-West Hotel** (Map pp702-3; ☎ 290 0404; www.east westhotel.ru; Tverskoy bul 4; s/d R10,500/11,500; Ⓜ Pushkinskaya Tverskaya) Quite unlike any other Moscow hotel, this old mansion has been done up in very Russian (read garish) décor, and is gated from the street and thus very secure. The rooms are comfortable, although similarly located in interior-design purgatory.

## Top End

**Ararat Park Hyatt Moscow** (Map pp702-3; ☎ 783 1234; www.moscow.park.hyatt.com; Neglinnaya ul 4; r 12,000, ste R16,500/47,600; Ⓟ ⊠ ⌨ ⊠; Ⓜ Teatralnaya) Probably the best hotel in the city, as reflected in its prohibitive prices. The stunning lobby sets the tone, and the 219 extraordinarily luxurious rooms do not disappoint. There are three restaurants and a superb health club, too.

**Golden Ring Hotel** (Map pp702-3; ☎ 725 0100; www .hotel-goldenring.ru; Smolenskaya ul 5; s/d R12,880/14,500, ste R17,000/61,200; Ⓟ ⊠ ⌨; Ⓜ Smolenskaya) An excellent Swiss-run business hotel. What it lacks in atmosphere it makes up for in views, service and location. The corner suites overlooking the Ministry of Foreign Affairs are excellent.

## EATING

Moscow food has undergone a massive process of evolution (and a degree of revolution), which is still ongoing. You'll eat well here if

**RUSSIA**

you have money, less so on a budget, but it can be done. Check out ultracool Kamergersky per for a huge range of cafés and restaurants. For snacks on the run, there are plenty of street stands selling hot dogs, *chebureki* (Caucasian meat pasties) and blini around metro stations and on many central avenues.

**Lyudi kak Lyudi** (Map pp702-3; ☎ 921 1201; Solyansky tup 1/4; mains R150; ⏱ 8am-11pm Mon-Fri, 8am-6am Sat & Sun; Ⓜ Kitay Gorod) 'Everyday people' is a tiny but great little refuge popular with after-hours clubbers as well as young workers who swear by the excellent R120 business lunch.

**Il Patio** (Map pp702-3; ☎ 290 5070; Smolenskaya ul 3; mains R200; ⏱ 11am-11pm; Ⓜ Smolenskaya) With more than 15 outlets, this reliable Moscow chain changed its name from Patio Pizza to Il Patio recently. The pizza is the same, though – a big choice at reasonable prices.

**City Grill** (Map pp702-3; ☎ 299 0953; www.citygrill.ru, in Russian; Sadovaya Triumfalnaya ul 2/30; mains R350; ⏱ noon-midnight; Ⓜ Mayakovskaya) This once-pioneering Moscow institution is now nothing special in a city of such high culinary norms, but it's still a reliable and well-located place to grab a decent modern European meal of above average standard. The music can be quite loud.

**Sindibad's** (Map pp702-3; ☎ 291 7115; www.sindi bad.ru; Nikitsky bul 14; mains R350; ⏱ noon-11pm; Ⓜ Arbatskaya) The previous entirely Lebanese and Arabic menu here has been adapted to Muscovite taste and now includes sturgeon and pikeperch. However, you can still enjoy the excellent hummus, baba ganoush and pitta, among other Levantine specialities, in a cosy, convivial setting. Bookings advised on weekends.

**Correa's** (Map pp702-3; ☎ 933 4684; www.correas.ru; Bolshaya Gruzinskaya ul 32; mains R350-600; ⏱ 8am-midnight; Ⓜ Barrikadnaya) This New York–style deli has become a Moscow institution in just a few years of existence, often known among the expat community as Isaac's, the name of its American chef. The sandwiches are wonderful, and the fresh supplies unrivalled. There's also a great and extremely popular breakfast menu (book on weekends) and a delivery service available.

**Correa's** ( ☎ 725 6035; ul Bolshaya Ordynka 40/2; mains R350-600; ⏱ 8am-midnight) This branch, south of the river, is just as good as the original but roomier.

**Starlite Diner** (Map pp702-3; ☎ 290 9638; www.starli tediner.com; Bolshaya Sadovaya ul 16; mains R400; ⏱ 24hr; Ⓜ Mayakovskaya) A well-deserved favourite –

expats come to this surreal American diner for a taste of home. Food and service are great, and the breakfasts are authentic and wonderfully caloric. There's now a second branch to the south by the Oktyabrskaya metro station, although it's not nearly as nice – stuck on a traffic island without the outdoor seating of the original.

**Moskva-Roma** (Map pp702-3; ☎ 229 5702; www.mos cow-roma.ru, in Russian; Stoleshnikov per 12; mains R450; ⏱ 24hr; Ⓜ Teatralnaya) Funky and fun, Moskva-Roma combines a very high standard of modern Italian cooking with a happening atmosphere, with DJs most nights and some of the best staff in the city.

**Café Margarita** (Map pp702-3; ☎ 299 6534; www.cafe -margarita.ru; Malaya Bronnaya ul 28; mains R500; ⏱ noon-1am; Ⓜ Mayakovskaya) On Patriarch's Ponds, the gorgeous square immortalised by the opening chapter of Bulgakov's *Master and Margarita*, is this great place. Its prices are rather high, but there's nowhere else like it in the city, with its well-read crowd and literary connections, books lining the walls and live music nightly from 8pm (R100 charge per person). The set lunch (R200) is good value, too, and comes with a glass of red wine.

**Tiflis** (Map pp702-3; ☎ 290 2897; www.tiflis.ru, in Russian; ul Ostozhenka 32; mains R500-800; ⏱ noon-midnight; Ⓜ Park Kultury) A real treat, Moscow's best Georgian restaurant is a fantastic affair, with lots of outdoor seating in a traditional-style, rambling Georgian complex that looks like it's been lifted from Tbilisi. It's not cheap, but its wonderful *lobio* (traditional spicy bean paste), *khachapuri* (cheese pie cooked with runny egg and butter in the middle), *satsivi* (spicy chicken or turkey served cold in a herb sauce) and other classic Georgian dishes make it well worth a splurge.

## Cheap Eats

**Zhiguli** (Map pp702-3; ☎ 291 4144; ul Novy Arbat 11; mains from R50; ⏱ noon-2am; Ⓜ Arbatskaya) Smart self-service canteen with a Brezhnevian theme. Good Russian food and low, low prices just off the Arbat.

**Jagannath** (Map pp702-3; ☎ 928 3580; ul Kuznetsky Most 11; mains R50-250; ⏱ 8am-11pm; Ⓜ Kuznetsky Most) A life saver for vegetarians, this excellent health-food place with a strong Indian theme has both a self-service buffet and a sit-down restaurant. Food is superb, although if you want the really good stuff ordered à la carte you have to sit in the gloomy restaurant rather than the charming café area. There's free wi-fi and an internet café, too.

**Pyat Zvyozd** (Map pp702-3; ☎ 737 5545; Kamergersky per 6; sandwiches R75-95; ☑ 8.30am-11pm) Globalisation is complete! In a city where it was once said you could buy Prada or a Picasso but couldn't get a decent sandwich to go, here's the Russian franchise version of the UK sandwich chain Pret a Manger. Here you'll find a frighteningly similar setup, with a range of sandwiches, wraps and sushi perfect for eating on the run between sights.

**Prime** (Map pp702-3; ☎ 737 5545; sandwiches R75-95; ☑ 8.30am-11pm) Arbat (ul Arbat 9; Ⓜ Arbatskaya); Kamergersky per (Kamergersky per 5/7; Ⓜ Teatralnaya) The original Moscow sandwich shop, also a none-too-subtle rip off of Pret a Manger, has two main locations both near major tourist sights, making them perfect for a takeaway sandwich.

## DRINKING

Gravitate toward the **Hermitage Gardens** (Map pp702-3; Ⓜ Pushkinskaya Tverskaya) or the **Aleksandrovsky Garden** (Map pp702-3; Ⓜ Okhotny Ryad) during the summer months for relaxed beer drinking amid the greenery. Read the bar guide **The Exile** (www.exile.ru) for the latest cool places. Following are our long-time favourites:

**Doug & Marty's Boar House** (Map pp702-3; ☎ 917 9986; ul Zemlyanoy val 26; admission R60-100; ☑ noon-6am; Ⓜ Kurskaya) Run by Doug, the creator of the legendary Hungry Duck (once the wildest bar in Europe due to its famously hedonistic ladies night), the Boar House is busy throughout the week and attracts an expat and local crowd devoted to serious debauchery. Monday and Thursday are particularly busy (on Thursday women drink for free).

**Kitaysky Lyotchik** (Map pp702-3; ☎ 924 5611; Lyublyansky proezd; admission R150; ☑ 10am-8am; Ⓜ Kitay Gorod) The 'Chinese Pilot' is a long-standing favourite with the boho crowd, who come here for the live music and lack of aggressive door policy.

**Kult** (Map pp702-3; ☎ 917 5709; Yauzskaya ul 5; Ⓜ Kitay Gorod) A pretty laid-back club/bar with good DJs playing a big range of music for a young, up-for-it crowd.

**Proekt OGI** (Map pp702-3; ☎ 627 5366; www.proektogi .ru, in Russian; Potapovsky per 8/12; Ⓜ Chistiye Prudy) OGI is the acronym of a publishing house that diversified into bars and cafés and has become a phenomenon – the OGI bar/cafés (all with their own in-house bookshop) can be found all over central Moscow.

## Cafés

While it took off first in St Petersburg, the coffee culture in Moscow has grown into a huge industry. Our highest recommendation goes to **Coffee Mania** (Map pp702-3; ☎ 229 3901; www .coffeemania.ru; Bolshaya Nikitskaya ul 13; Ⓜ Arbatskaya), with its delicious food and cakes. Both chic **Shokoladnitsa** (Map pp702-3; ☎ 241 0620; www.shoko.ru, in Russian; ul Arbat 29; Ⓜ Arbatskaya) and **Coffee House** (Map pp702-3; www.coffeehouse.ru, in Russian; Tverskaya ul 6; Ⓜ Okhotny Ryad) serve decent coffee. All three have branches scattered throughout the city, and they're often the only breakfast venues in town.

## ENTERTAINMENT
### Nightclubs

Negotiating Moscow's legendarily lavish and hedonistic clubland is a challenge. 'Face control' (the Russian term for an unreasonable door policy administered by thugs) rules. **The Exile** (www.exile.ru) has an up-to-date, un-PC club guide.

While many clubs disappear overnight, some enduringly popular venues include the following:

**Propaganda** (Map pp702-3; ☎ 924 5732; Bol Zlatoustinksy per 7; admission R50-200; ☑ noon-7am; Ⓜ Kitay Gorod) Known to one and all as 'propka', this long-time fixture on the Moscow club scene is an oasis of good management and friendly security guards seen in very few other establishments here. Commercial techno and house dominate, with great local and international DJs.

**Art Garbage** (Map pp702-3; ☎ 928-8745; www.art -garbage.ru, in Russian; Starosadsky per 5; admission free-R250; ☑ 9pm-6am; Ⓜ Kitay Gorod). Extremely friendly, alternative night spot popular for gigs and late night parties and hugely popular with students and arty types.

## Cinemas

There are a few cinemas in Moscow that show films in the original language (usually English). Check the **Moscow Times** (www.themoscowtimes.com), which has a useful English-Language Movies section in its daily entertainment pages. One regular favourite is the **Dome Cinema** (Map pp702-3; ☎ 931 9873; www.domecinema.ru; The Renaissance Moscow Hotel, Olimpiisky Pr 18/1; Ⓜ Prospekt Mira).

## Gay & Lesbian Venues

Moscow is the centre of Russian gay life, and even if the gay population is barely visible, it's certainly a lot more socially acceptable than ever before in Russia to be queer. The first gay pride march in Russian history took place in 2006, despite openly homophobic comments from the city's mayor. The best resource for checking the ever-changing club scene is www.gay.ru/english.

**Three Monkeys** ( ☎ 916 3555; Nastavnichesky per 11; admission free-R300; Ⓨ 7pm-7am; Ⓜ Chkalovskaya) The most fun and accessible gay venue, Three Monkeys is the latest incarnation of the long-standing Moscow gay club, spread over several floors and busy on weekends.

## Theatre

Moscow has a long and proud theatrical tradition. A trip to the Bolshoi may be expensive, but it will usually be unforgettable, too. Otherwise, without speaking Russian you won't be able to enjoy the offerings of most theatres. Check the **Moscow Times** (www.themoscowtimes.com) or its weekend edition (out on Fridays) for regular listings and reviews.

**Chekhov Art Theatre** (Map pp702-3; ☎ 229 8760; www.mxat.ru, in Russian; Kamergersky per 3; tickets R100-500; Ⓜ Okhotny Ryad) The city's most famous dramatic venue is still known to most Muscovites as MKhAT, where, under Stanislavsky, method acting was born at the turn of the last century. It sometimes has performances in English.

**Bolshoi Theatre** (Map pp702-3; ☎ 250 7317; www .bolshoi.ru; Teatralnaya pl 1; tickets R200-1500; Ⓜ Teatralnaya) Sadly the main Bolshoi Theatre is closed for renovation until the end of 2008. In the meantime performances are held in the building next door. Unless you specifically want to see the Bolshoi troupe, consider going to the ballet in St Petersburg instead. Tickets are available online and through travel agencies at a premium, although the kiosks around the city (teatralnaya kassa) often offer some good bargains.

## Live Music

Moscow offers a great variety of gigs and concerts, and is an increasingly popular stop-off on European tours for big international acts. The **Moscow Times** (www.themoscowtimes.com) weekend edition (or website) is a useful source of information. The main big gig venues are the Olimpiisky Sports Complex ( Ⓜ Tsvetnoy Bulvar) and the Kremlin Palace (p707).

Following are more intimate smaller venues, where you can often see good Russian and foreign bands:

**Sixteen Tons** (Map pp702-3; ☎ 253 5300; www.16tons .ru; ul Presnensky val 1; admission for gigs only R200-800; Ⓨ 6pm-late; Ⓜ Ulitsa 1905 Goda) Atmospheric English-style pub with microbrewery downstairs and great gig and club venue upstairs featuring some of the best small gigs in the city.

**Tabula Rasa** (Map pp702-3; ☎ 508 4019; ul Kazakova 8A; admission for gigs only R100-400; Ⓨ 9pm-6am; Ⓜ Kurskaya) A great venue for international bands (indie and rock mainly) with a cosy interior complete with pool table and fireplace.

**Kitaysky Lyotchik** (Map pp702-3; ☎ 924 5611; Lyublyansky proezd; admission R150; Ⓨ 10am-8am; Ⓜ Kitay Gorod) The 'Chinese Pilot' is relaxed and unpretentious, has nightly concerts and is generally held to be the city's most reliable after hours hang out.

## Sport

Football is definitely Moscow's main spectator sport. There are several teams in the city – the best known internationally are **Spartak** ( ☎ 201 1164; Luzhniki Stadium, Luzhnetskaya nab 24; Ⓜ Sportivnaya) and **Dinamo** ( ☎ 612 7172; Dinamo Stadium, Leningradsky pr 36; Ⓜ Dinamo). You can usually buy tickets on match days without much problem, either at the gate or from the theatre-ticket kiosks in most metro stations; prices start at R100.

## SHOPPING

The new wealth of Russia has created a class of Russians for whom nothing is too expensive or extravagant. If you have the cash, check out the designer boutiques of Tretyakovsky proezd, where Prada, Gucci and Armani jostle for your attention. Nearby Stoleshnikov per is also full of designer labels. **GUM** (Map p706; Ⓨ 10am-10pm) and **TsUM** (Map pp702-3; ☎ 292 1157; www.tsum.ru; ul Petrovka 2; Ⓨ 9am-10pm Mon-Sat, 9am-9pm Sun; Ⓜ Teatralnaya) are also great for big brand names.

**Old Arbat** (Map pp702-3; ul Stary Arbat; Ⓜ Arbatskaya) The Old Arbat is the historic, pedestrian street famous in Moscow for its proliferation of souvenir sellers. It's extremely naff and usually overpriced, but if you want souvenirs – from nesting dolls to Soviet flags and engraved hip flasks – this is the place.

**Vernisazh Market** (Izmailovsky Park; Ⓨ 7am-6pm Sat & Sun; Ⓜ Izmailovsky Park) Far better value, but rather far-flung, this market has a huge collection of handicrafts, knick-knacks, souvenirs, clothing and art.

Although illegal in the West, pirated DVDs are available everywhere in Russia. In Moscow you'll see them on sale all over the place, usually in underpasses by metro stations and kiosks around the city.

**Gorbushka Market** ( ☎ 730 0006; Barklaya ul 8; ⊙ 10am-9pm; Ⓜ Bagrationovskaya) This famous electrical goods and pirate DVD market may be worth a visit if DVDs are your thing. It's a former TV factory that now houses an immense number of shops selling every conceivable type of technology at knock-down prices.

# GETTING THERE & AWAY
## Air
Moscow is served by three main international airports; Domodedovo, Sheremetyevo and Vnukovo, which connect Moscow to every major European city and to major hubs worldwide. For a list of carriers that serve the city and airport information see p745.

## Boat
The Moscow terminus for cruises to St Petersburg is 10km northeast of the city centre at the **Severny Rechnoy Vokzal** (Northern River Station; ☎ 105 3560; Leningradskoe shosse 51; Ⓜ Rechnoy Vokzal). Take the metro to Rechnoy Vokzal stop, then walk 15 minutes due west, passing under Leningradskoe shosse and through a nice park.

## Bus
Buses run to a number of towns and cities within about 700km of Moscow, but they tend to be crowded. However, they are usually faster than the *prigorodny* (suburban) trains, and are convenient to some Golden Ring destinations (p716). To book a seat you have to go 15km east of the city to the long-distance bus station, **Shchyolkovskaya Avtovokzal** (Shchyolkovskaya Bus Station; ☎ 468 0400; Shchyolkovskoye shosse 2; Ⓜ Shchyolkovskaya), beside Shchyolkovskaya metro.

## Train
Moscow is the heart of the Russian railway network, and internationally you can catch trains for destinations as far apart as Berlin and Beijing.

Of the nine stations in Moscow, use **Leningradsky Vokzal** (Leningrad Station; Map pp702-3; Ⓜ Komsomolskaya) for trains to St Petersburg, Novgorod, Estonia and Finland; **Rizhsky Vokzal** (Riga Station; Ⓜ Rizhskaya) for Latvia; **Belorussky Vokzal** (Belarus Station; Map pp702-3; Ⓜ Belorusskaya) for Belarus, Lithuania, Kaliningrad, Poland, Germany and the Czech Republic; and **Yaroslavsky Vokzal** (Yaroslavl Station; Map pp702-3; Ⓜ Komsomolskaya) for Siberia, Mongolia and China.

Besides the train stations proper, tickets are sold throughout the city at railway ticket offices, the main one being the **Moscow Central Train Booking Office** (Tsentralnoe Zheleznodorozhnoe Agentstvo; Map pp702-3; ☎ 266 8333; Komsomolskaya pl 5; ⊙ 9am-8pm Mon-Fri, 9am-5pm Sat & Sun; Ⓜ Komsomolskaya). Alternatively, travel agencies and other *kassa zheleznoy dorogi* (ticket offices) also sell tickets, sometimes for a small commission, but frankly it's worth it – it's much easier.

# GETTING AROUND
## To/From the Airports
Moscow's main international airport today is **Domodedovo** (www.domodedovo.ru), an easy train ride from central Moscow. An express (R120, 40 minutes, half-hourly) runs to/from Paveletsky Station, where you can transfer to the metro.

The other big international airport is ailing **Sheremtyevo 2** (www.sheremetyevo-airport.ru). From here minibuses 48 and 49 and bus 851 go to the nearest metro station, Rechnoy Vokzal, from where you can travel into central Moscow. A taxi can be ordered from the official taxi office in the arrivals area and should cost R700 to R900.

## Metro
The magnificent **Moscow metro** (www.mosmetro.ru) is probably the best in the world, and is currently introducing new trains to bring the Stalin-era system up to modern standards. More than 150 metro stations in all parts of the city and a train departure every two minutes make it the best way to get around. The flat fare is R15, although buying in bulk saves a lot of money (eg 10 rides cost R125).

## Trolleybus, Tram & Bus
Short-term visitors are unlikely to use public transport beyond the metro. However, a comprehensive and dirt-cheap, although painfully slow, network of buses, trams and trolleybuses exists all over Moscow. In far-flung places it can be necessary to take one of these to get to the nearest metro station. If so, buy tickets on board (around R10 per trip).

## Taxi
See p746 for information on hailing unofficial taxis in Russia. The standard rate for short

trips in unofficial taxis is R100, while longer ones cost R150 to R200. Official taxis cost more. You can book through the central **Taxi Reservation Office** ( ☎ 627 0000; ☻ 24 hr).

## AROUND MOSCOW

Do yourself a favour when in Russia and make an effort to see more than just its two most famous cities. Escaping Moscow is vital if you want to get some sense of how ordinary Russians live. The historic towns surrounding Moscow to the northeast (known as the Golden Ring due to their magnificent churches and medieval monasteries) are a great place to start. The most interesting and accessible towns, each of which preceded the present capital as the political and cultural heart of Russia, are Suzdal, Vladimir and Sergiev Posad. The towns' churches, monasteries, kremlins (citadels) and museums make a picturesque portfolio of early Russian art, architecture and history.

### Suzdal Суздаль
☎ 49,231 / pop 12,000

If you have the chance to visit only one of the Golden Ring towns, make it lovely Suzdal. Coming here from Moscow is a wonderful experience, as you'll see a traditional Russian town overflowing with old monasteries, convents, churches and intricately decorated *izbas* (wooden cottages) dotted in green fields around the meandering Kamenka River. Green fields reach right into Suzdal's centre, and the whole town is architecturally protected. A greater contrast from Moscow is hard to imagine.

#### SIGHTS

At the eastern end of ul Kremlyovskaya the 1.4km-long rampart of Suzdal's kremlin encloses the 13th-century **Rozhdestvensky Sobor** (Nativity of the Virgin Cathedral), the 1635 **bell tower** and the **Arkhiyereyskie Palati** (Archbishop's Chambers). The latter houses the **Suzdal History Exhibition** ( ☎ 21624; admission R30; ☻ 10am-5pm Wed-Mon), which includes the original 13th-century door from the cathedral, photos of its interior and a visit to the 18th-century **Krestovaya Palata** (Cross Hall).

Founded in the 14th century to protect the town's northern entrance, the **Spaso-Yevfimievsky Monastyr** (Saviour Monastery of St Euthymius; ☎ 20746; all-inclusive ticket R280, photos R100; ☻ 10am-6pm Tue-Sun) is at the northern end of ul Lenina.

Inside, standing before the seven-domed, 12th-and 13th-century **Cathedral of the Transfiguration of the Saviour**, a tall **bell tower** chimes a lovely 10-minute concert hourly. The old monastery **prison**, set up in 1764 for religious dissidents, now houses a fascinating exhibit on the monastery's prison life and military history, including displays on some of the better-known prisoners who stayed here.

#### SLEEPING & EATING

**Hotel Rizopolozhenskaya** ( ☎ 24314; ul Lenina; s/d from R680/1100) Although housed in the decrepit 19th-century Monastery of the Deposition, some of the rooms have been renovated, but not all. It's a good bargain, though, and an atmospheric location.

**Pokrovskaya Hotel** ( ☎ 20908; www.suzdaltour.ru; ul Pokrovskaya; s/d R1820/2400) This pleasant hotel is located within the walls of the Intercession Convent. The rooms are clean and have some charm, despite being modern.

**Kremlin Refectory** ( ☎ 21763; Kremlin; mains R100; ☻ 11am-11pm) Located in the Archbishop's Chambers in the kremlin, the food served is traditional and the atmosphere lively. Be sure to sample the local *medovukha*, a lightly alcoholic, honey-flavoured mead drink that is simply heavenly.

#### GETTING THERE & AWAY

Only buses serve Suzdal. There is one direct connection daily with Moscow's Shchyolkovskaya Avtovokzal, two buses daily to Kostroma, five to Ivanovo and regular services throughout the day to Vladimir. From Moscow it's often easier to take the train to Vladimir and then a bus to Suzdal.

### Vladimir Владимир
☎ 4922 / pop 360,000

Little remains in Vladimir, 178km northeast of Moscow, from its medieval heyday as Russia's capital. However, what does remain – several examples of Russia's most ancient and formative architecture – is worth pausing to see en route to or from the more charming town of Suzdal.

Begun in 1158, **Uspensky Sobor** (Assumption Cathedral; ☎ 325201; admission R100; ☻ 1.30-5pm) is a white-stone version of Kyiv's brick Byzantine churches, and contains magnificent frescoes by Andrei Rublev and others. Nearby the **Dmitrievsky Sobor** (Cathedral of St Dmitry), built from 1193 to 1197, is where the art of

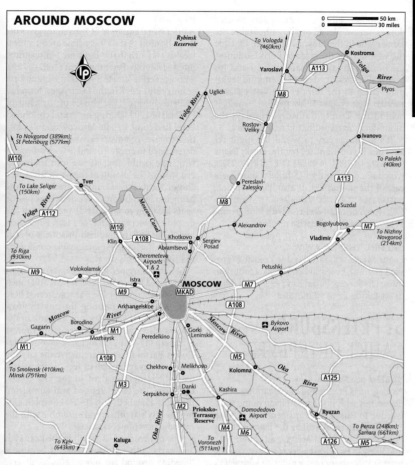

**AROUND MOSCOW**

Vladimir-Suzdal stone carving reached its pinnacle.

From Moscow's Kursky Vokzal (Kursk Station), there are numerous suburban trains and buses to Vladimir. There are also bus services to/from Moscow, Nizhny Novgorod, Kostroma, Ivanovo, Suzdal and Kazan.

## Sergiev Posad Сергиев Посад

☎ from Moscow 254, from elsewhere 49654 / pop 100,000

Charming Sergiev Posad was known as Zagorsk throughout the Soviet era, and many people still refer to it as that today. It's a sleepy town of unexpectedly huge cultural significance, due to the 15th-century Troitse-Sergieva Lavra (Trinity Monastery of St Sergius) –

the reason why it receives a steady stream of visitors year-round. At just 60km from central Moscow, it's a pleasant and easy day trip by train. For its concentrated artistry and its unique role in the interrelated histories of the Russian Church and State, it is well worth the trip.

**Troitse-Sergieva Lavra** (Trinity Monastery of St Sergius; ☎ 45356; admission free, photos R150; ⏱ 10am-6pm) was built in the 1420s; the dark yet beautiful **Troitsky Sobor** (Trinity Cathedral) is the heart of the Trinity Monastery. A memorial service for St Sergius (whose tomb stands in the southeastern corner) goes on all day, every day. The icon-festooned interior is largely the work of the great medieval painter Andrei Rublev and his students. **Uspensky Sobor**

(Assumption Cathedral), with its star-spangled domes, was modelled on the cathedral of the same name in the Moscow Kremlin. Outside the west door is the **grave** of Boris Godunov, the brother-in-law of Tsar Fyodor I and his eventual successor, despite having no legitimate claim to the throne. The **Vestry** (Riznitsa; admission R160; 🕙 10am-5.30pm Wed-Sun), which is behind the Trinity Cathedral, displays the monastery's extraordinarily rich treasury.

It's not necessary to spend the night really, but if you want to, try the **Russky Dvorik** ( ☎ 75392; fax 75391; ul Mitkina 14/2; s/d R1700/2100), which is a delightful small hotel a short walk east of the monastery. It also has a separate **restaurant** ( ☎ 45114; ul Krasnoy Armii 134; mains R300-500), which does get overrun with tour groups at lunch, but it's otherwise pleasant.

### GETTING THERE & AWAY
From Moscow's Yaroslavsky Vokzal (Yaroslavl Station), buses and *elektrichki* (suburban trains) to Sergiev Posad leave every half-hour or so, taking 75 to 90 minutes.

# ST PETERSBURG
# САНКТ ПЕТЕРБУРГ

☎ 812 / pop 5 million
As elegant as Prague and as enchanting as Budapest but with just a smattering of the tourists due to Russia's intransigent visa regime, St Petersburg really will be the next big thing once visa-free travel arrives, although with that likely to be at least a decade away, you still have St Petersburg pretty much to yourself by the standards of other tourist-filled cities in the Baltics and central Europe.

In fact, comparing this giant warehouse of Russian culture to any other city is unfair. Long before Eastern Europe became known for its incredible cities, St Petersburg was the most important city in the entire region, capital of one of the world's most powerful empires and centre of countless movements in all fields of art. Since being founded by Peter the Great in 1703, St Petersburg has grown to be Europe's fourth-largest city and easily one of its most culturally significant. A 'window on Europe', the city of Dostoyevsky and Shostakovich, cradle of the Russian Revolution, St Petersburg has more to offer the traveller than perhaps anywhere else in Russia.

## HISTORY
A brief visual survey of St Petersburg gives little indication that its incredible architectural wealth was originally built on a mosquito-infested swamp. Peter the Great (1682–1725), who wanted to create a modern capital for a country still stuck in the Dark Ages, founded St Petersburg on the shores of the Gulf of Finland in 1703. During his brutal childhood Peter had come to hate Moscow and its plotting coteries of *boyars* (aristocrats), and was determined to create a brand new city through which he could drag Russia into the modern world. The mouth of the Neva River was chosen for its accessibility for trade (Moscow being unnavigable from Western Europe due to its location so far inland) and with all the despotic powers at hand for a tsar, Peter soon had thousands of Swedish prisoners of war toiling in the toughest imaginable conditions to bring about his dream.

St Petersburg became the capital of Russia in 1713 and the court, government and much of Russian economic life was transferred here from Moscow, prompting the city to grow with extreme speed. Much of the look of the city was determined by the reign of Empress Elizabeth (1741–62), which saw favourite architect Bartolomeo Rastrelli give the city the warm, extravagant Italian feel, which is still overwhelmingly evident in the city today. Catherine the Great refined and completed many of Elizabeth's projects, complementing the city's architectural ensemble with the introduction of neoclassicism.

The city reached its zenith in the later 19th and early 20th centuries when it became a breeding ground for movements as diverse as style modern, the avant-garde, symbolist poetry and modern dance. Petrograd (as the city became in 1914, 'St Petersburg' being too Germanic when war broke out) was the setting for the 1917 revolution that saw Nicholas II abdicate, and then the communist coup later the same year, after which Lenin led the socialist government from the Smolny Institute. In 1918, in a significant blow to the city's future, Lenin moved the capital back to more easily defensible Moscow, where it remains today. In 1924, following Lenin's death, the city changed its name yet again to Leningrad.

Leningrad – already the focus of Stalin's brutal purges in the 1930s – experienced its darkest hour during WWII, when the German advance on the city led to a siege lasting almost 900 days. During that time more than one million people starved to death, a tragedy still fresh in the psyche of St Petersburgers today. Hitler's failure to take the city was, however, a huge dent to German morale and despite being badly damaged, Leningrad emerged as great a city as ever from the war.

After a 70-year experiment with communism, the city began a new era when it voted finally to change its name from Leningrad back to St Petersburg. With locally born-and-bred Vladimir Putin now running the country, the city has profited from central funding to restore many of its crumbling palaces. The city's 300th anniversary in 2003 set the tone for a new century of optimism and progress for Russia's graceful former capital.

## ORIENTATION
St Petersburg is spread out across many different islands, some real and some created through the construction of canals. The central street is Nevsky Prospekt, which extends for some 4km from the Lavra Alexandra Nevskogo (Alexander Nevsky Monastery) to the Hermitage. The vast Neva River empties into the Gulf of Finland, filtered through a number of islands. The most significant of these are Vasilevsky and Petrogradsky Islands.

## INFORMATION
### Bookshops
**Anglia Bookshop** (Map p724; ☎ 579 8284; www .anglophile.ru; nab reki Fontanki 38; ⊙ 10am-7pm; Ⓜ Gostiny Dvor) Has a decent selection of contemporary literature, history and travel writing.
**Dom Knigi** (Map p724; ☎ 570 6402; Nevsky pr 62; ⊙ 9am-9pm; Ⓜ Gostiny Dvor) The best place to buy Russian books. It may move back to its historic premises at Nevsky pr 28 soon.
**John Parsons Bookshop** (Map p724; ☎ 331 8828; nab reki Fontanki 38; ⊙ 10am-7pm; Ⓜ Gostiny Dvor) The best English-language bookshop in the city, John Parsons wins out simply with the space and thus selection of books it has. It's conveniently located in the same building as Anglia Bookshop.

### Internet Access
Nevsky pr boasts two internet cafés:
**Café Max** (Map p724; ☎ 273 6655; Nevsky pr 90/92; per hr R60; ⊙ 24hr; Ⓜ Mayakovskaya)
**Quo Vadis** (Map p724; ☎ 333 0708; Nevsky pr 76; per hr R60; ⊙ 9am-11pm; Ⓜ Mayakovskaya) Enter from Liteiny pr.

### Laundry
There's a centrally located **laundry service** (Map pp720-1; ☎ 273 5806; ul Pestelya 17/25; per kg R22; ⊙ 9am-8pm Mon-Sat, 9am-6pm Sun; Ⓜ Chernyshevskaya); look for the sign 'khimchistka i prachechnaya'. Otherwise, many minihotels and hostels offer a laundry service at perfectly reasonable rates.

### Left Luggage
You can leave your luggage at any kamera khraneniya (luggage office) of the big metro stations for R30 to R50 per day.

### Media
There is lots of St Petersburg–specific media. In English there's the St Petersburg Times, Pulse and the bottom-rate Neva News. Super useful for visitors is **In Your Pocket St Petersburg** (www.inyourpocket.com), available for free from hotels and hostels.

### Medical Services
**International Clinic** (Map p724; ☎ 336 3333; www .icspb.com; 6 ul Marata; ⊙ 24hr; Ⓜ Mayakovskaya) Pricey treatment is available at this clinic, which offers 24-hour emergency care and direct billing to insurance companies.
**Poliklinika No 2** (Map pp720-1; ☎ 316 6272; Moskovsky pr 22; ⊙ 24hr; Ⓜ Technologichesky Institut) This service is also recommended – and much cheaper.

Following are two 24-hour pharmacies:
**Apteka** (Map p724; ☎ 277 5962; Nevsky pr 83; ⊙ 24hr; Ⓜ Pl Vosstaniya)
**Apteka Petrofarm** (Map p724; ☎ 314 5401; Nevsky pr 22; ⊙ 24hr; Ⓜ Nevsky Pr)

### Money
Currency-exchange offices are located through the city. ATMs are inside every metro station, in hotels and department stores, in main post offices and along major streets. Travellers cheques can be exchanged at most Russian banks (with commission, of course).

### Post
**Central post office** (Glavpochtamt; Map pp720-1; ☎ 312 8302; Pochtamtskaya ul 9; ⊙ 9am-7.45pm Mon-Sat, 10am-5.45pm Sun; Ⓜ Sadovaya) Come here to send large parcels abroad (small post offices will usually refuse to take them).

### Telephone & Fax
You can make international calls from most modern call boxes. Telefonaya karta (phonecards) can be bought in kiosks around town, as well as at metro station ticket offices. Call

# CENTRAL ST PETERSBURG

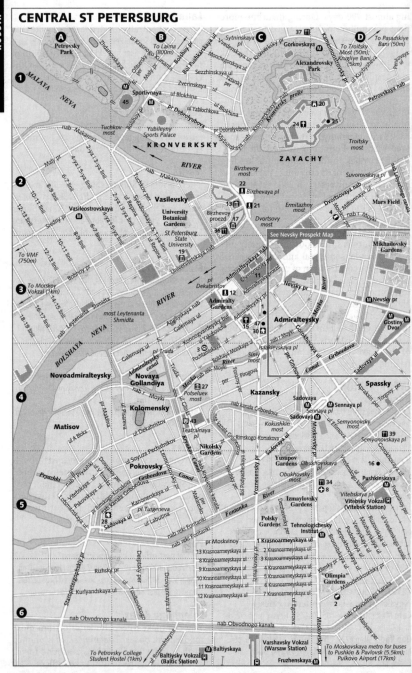

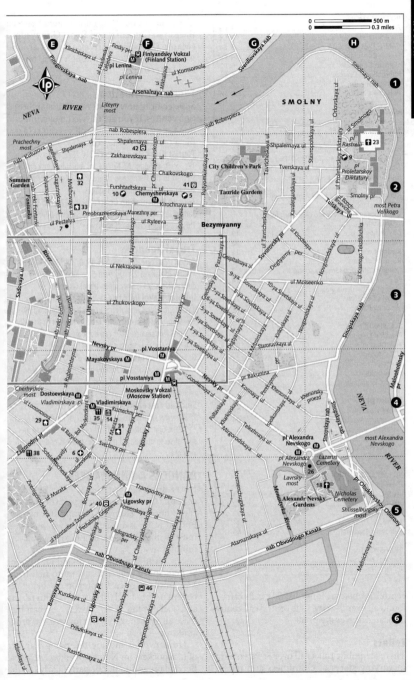

**RUSSIA**

centres for placing long-distance calls can be found all over the city. One central call centre is located at Nevsky pr 88.

## Toilets

There are public toilets all over St Petersburg in varying states of cleanliness and repair.

Convenient ones (R15) are located between the Kazan Cathedral and Kanal Griboyedova (Map p724). There are also toilets around most metro stations, although these tend to be a last resort.

## Tourist Information

St Petersburg now boasts two tourist information centres. If you are the victim of crime and don't speak Russian, these offices can help you file a report with the police.

**Tourist Kiosk** (Map p724; ☎ 310 2822; Dvortsovaya pl 12; ⏰ 9am-6pm; Ⓜ Nevsky pr) A helpful kiosk on Palace Sq next to the Hermitage where you can get information and buy guides in many languages.

**Tourist Information Centre** (Map p724; ☎ 310 8262; Sadovaya ul 14; ⏰ 9am-6pm; Ⓜ Sadovaya/Nevsky pr) This is a bigger centre off Nevsky pr.

## Travel Agencies

**Amex** (Map pp720-1; ☎ 326 4500; fax 326 4501; ul Malaya Morskaya 23; ⏰ 9am-5pm Mon-Fri; Ⓜ Sadovaya/Nevsky Pr) Only offers travel services.

**Infinity Travel** (Map pp720-1; ☎ 313 5085; www .infinity.ru; Hotel Angleterre, ul Bolshaya Morskaya 29; ⏰ 9am-6pm Mon-Sat; Ⓜ Nevsky Prospekt) A friendly and efficient service. Staff can book air and train tickets, and organise visa support and hotel bookings.

**Ost-West Kontaktservice** (Map p724; ☎ 327 3023; www.ostwest.com; 105 Nevsky pr; ⏰ 9am-6pm Mon-Sat; Ⓜ Pl Vosstaniya) A reliable outfit, Ost-West can organise registration for all visas, as well as offer visa support.

**Sindbad Travel International** (Map p724; ☎ 332 2020; www.sindbad.ru, in Russian; 2-ya Sovetskaya ul 12; ⏰ 9am-6pm Mon-Sat; Ⓜ Pl Vosstaniya) Sindbad are specialists in discounted travel for students and under 26 year olds.

## DANGERS & ANNOYANCES

Never drink tap water in St Petersburg as it contains *Giardia lamblia*, a parasite that can cause horrific stomach cramps and nausea. Bottled water is available everywhere. If you must drink tap water, boil it for a good few minutes first.

The humidity and marshland location of St Petersburg makes it mosquito hell from May until October. Be prepared – bring repellent or the standard anti-mosquito tablets and socket plug. Alternatively you can buy these all over the city – ask for *sredstva protif kamarov*.

Human pests include the rising number of pickpockets on Nevsky pr in recent years. Be vigilant and look out particularly for the infamous gangs of children who work the street.

Sadly racist attacks are a reality in the city. Skinhead gangs have killed an unprecedented number of mainly Caucasian and Central Asians in the past few years, and there's a climate of fear among ethnic minorities. Perhaps worst of all, the city Governor, Valentina Matvienko, had not at the time of writing ever publicly decried these attacks. We still encourage nonwhite travellers to visit, but suggest exercising far more caution here than anywhere else in the region. Avoid the suburbs whenever possible and try not to go out after dark alone.

## SIGHTS
### The Historic Heart
Unquestionably your first stop should be the **Palace Sq** (Dvortsovaya ploshchad; Map p724), where the baroque/rococo **Winter Palace** (Zimny dvorets; Map p724) appears like a mirage under the archway at the start of Bolshaya Morskaya ul. Empress Elizabeth commissioned the palace from Bartolomeo Rastrelli in 1754. Along with a number of neighbouring buildings, some of the Winter Palace's 1057 rooms now house part of the astonishing **Hermitage** (Map p724; ☎ 571 3465; www .hermitage.ru; adult R350, students & children free, free for all individuals on the 1st Thu of every month, no flash photo/ video ticket R100/350, audio guides R250; ☷ 10.30am-6pm Tue-Sat, 10.30am-5pm Sun; Ⓜ Nevsky Pr), which is one of the world's great art museums. Enter through the courtyard from Palace Sq. To avoid queues in the summer months, you can book tickets online very easily. The collection is vast and can be overwhelming for a first-time visitor. Get an English map at the information desk in the ticket hall.

If your time for visiting is limited, you should look out for the following highlights: the Jordan Staircase (positioned directly ahead of you when you enter); room 100 (Ancient Egypt); rooms 178–97 (the State rooms for the apartments of the last imperial family); room 204 (the Pavilion Hall); rooms 228–38 (Italian Art, 16th to 18th centuries); room 271 (the imperial family's cathedral); and concentrate most of your time on the fabulous 3rd floor, particularly rooms 333–50 for late-19th-century and early-20th-century European art, including a huge array of Matisse, Picasso, Monet, Van Gogh, Cézanne, Gaugin, Pissaro, Rodin and Kandinsky. There

are several cafés, internet access and shops within the museum, so you can easily spend a whole day here. Disabled access is now very good – call ☎ 110 9079 if you require any assistance.

Across the square from the winter palace is the fabulous **General Staff Building** (Map p724; adult/student R200/free; ☷ 10.30am-6pm Tue-Sun; Ⓜ Nevsky Pr), which also houses a museum and temporary exhibits, including French art of the 20th century and the former apartments of Prime Minister Count Nesselrohde, and in the middle of the square, the 47.5m **Alexander Column** (Map p724) commemorates the 1812 victory over Napoleon.

To the west across the road is the gilded spire of the **Admiralty** (Map pp720–1), which used to be the headquarters of the Russian navy. West of the Admiralty is **ploshchad Dekabristov** (Decembrists' Sq; Map pp720–1), named after the Decembrists' Uprising of 14 December 1825.

Falconet's famous statue of Peter the Great, the **Bronze Horseman** (Map pp720–1), stands at the end of the square towards the river. Behind looms the splendid golden dome of **Isaakievsky Sobor** (St Isaac's Cathedral; Map pp720-1; ☎ 315 9732; Isaakievskaya pl; admission to cathedral adult/ student R300/170, to colonnade R150/100; ☷ 10am-7pm Thu-Tue; Ⓜ Sadovaya/Nevsky Pr), built between 1818 and 1858. At this price think twice before going into the cathedral unless you like the ornate baroque style. The colonnade is far better value for money, however, giving superb views over the city.

### Nevsky Prospekt
The inner part of vast Nevsky pr runs from the Admiralty to Moskovsky Vokzal (Moscow Station) and is St Petersburg's main shopping thoroughfare. The most impressive sight along it is the great colonnaded arms of the **Kazansky Sobor** (Kazan Cathedral; Map p724; Kazanskaya pl 2; admission free; ☷ 9am-6pm; Ⓜ Nevksy Pr), built between 1801 and 1811.

At the end of Nevsky pr is the working **Lavra Alexandra Nevskogo** (Alexander Nevsky Monastery; Map pp720-1; ☎ 274 0409; adult/student R60/40; ☷ dawn-8pm in summer, dawn-dusk rest of year; Ⓜ pl Alexandra Nevskogo), where you'll find the **Tikhvin Cemetery** (Map pp720-1; admission R60/40; ☷ 11am-dusk Fri-Wed; Ⓜ pl Alexandra Nevskogo), the last resting place of some of Russia's most famous artistic figures, including Tchaikovsky and Dostoyevsky.

# NEVSKY PROSPEKT

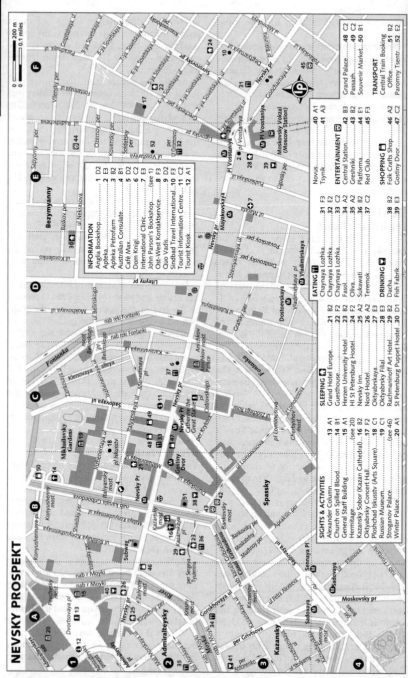

**INFORMATION**
| | |
|---|---|
| Anglia Bookshop | **1** D2 |
| Apteka | **2** E3 |
| Apteka Petrofarm | **3** B2 |
| Australian Consulate | **4** B1 |
| Café Max | **5** D2 |
| Dom Knigi | **6** C2 |
| International Clinic | (see 1) |
| John Parson's Bookshop | **8** F3 |
| Ost-West Kontaktservice | **9** D2 |
| Quo Vadis | **10** F3 |
| Sinbad Travel International | **11** C2 |
| Tourist Information Centre | **11** C2 |
| Tourist Kiosk | **12** A1 |

**SIGHTS & ACTIVITIES**
| | |
|---|---|
| Alexander Column | **13** A1 |
| Church on Spilled Blood | **14** B1 |
| General Staff Building | **15** A1 |
| Hermitage | (see 20) |
| Kazansky Sobor (Kazan Cathedral) | **16** B2 |
| Oktyabrsky Concert Hall | **17** F2 |
| Ploshchad Iskusstv (Arts Square) | **18** C1 |
| Russian Museum | **19** C1 |
| Stroganov Palace | (see 46) |
| Winter Palace | **20** A1 |

**SLEEPING**
| | |
|---|---|
| Grand Hotel Europe | **21** B2 |
| Guesthouse | **22** F2 |
| Herzen University Hostel | **23** B2 |
| HI St Petersburg Hostel | **24** F2 |
| Nevsky Inn | **25** A2 |
| Nord Hostel | **26** A2 |
| Oktyabrskaya | **27** E3 |
| Oktyabrsky Filial | **28** E3 |
| Rachmaninoff Art Hotel | **29** B2 |
| St Petersburg Puppet Hostel | **30** D1 |

**EATING**
| | |
|---|---|
| Chaynaya Lozhka | **31** F3 |
| Chaynaya Lozhka | **32** E2 |
| Chaynaya Lozhka | **33** C2 |
| Fasol | **34** A2 |
| Oliva | **35** A2 |
| Sukawati | **36** B2 |
| Teremok | **37** C2 |
| Novus | **40** A1 |
| Tsynik | **41** A3 |

**DRINKING**
| | |
|---|---|
| Dacha | **38** B2 |
| Fish Fabrik | **39** E3 |

**ENTERTAINMENT**
| | |
|---|---|
| Central Station | **42** B3 |
| Greshniki | **43** B2 |
| Platforma | **44** E1 |
| Red Club | **45** F3 |

**SHOPPING**
| | |
|---|---|
| Folk Crafts Shop | **51** B2 |
| Gostiny Dvor | **47** C2 |
| Grand Palace | **48** C2 |
| Passazh | **49** C2 |
| Souvenir Market | **50** B1 |

**TRANSPORT**
| | |
|---|---|
| Central Train Booking Office | **46** A2 |
| Parommy Tsent | **52** E2 |

## Between Nevsky & the Neva

A block north of Nevsky Pr metro station is lovely **ploshchad Iskusstv** (Arts Sq; Map p724), with a statue to national bard Alexander Pushkin at its centre.

The yellow Mikhailovsky Palace, now the **Russian Museum** (Gosudarstvenny Russky muzey; Map p724; ☎ 311 1465; www.rusmuseum.ru; adult/student R300/150; ☼ 10am-6pm Wed-Mon; Ⓜ Nevsky Pr), housing one of the country's finest collections of Russian art, makes up the far side of the square. This makes the perfect complement to the Hermitage, presenting a wonderful and easily navigable collection of Russian art throughout the ages in the palace's lovely halls. Behind it are the pleasant **Mikhailovsky Gardens** (Map p724), which are popular year-round for walking and relaxing.

The polychromatic domes of the **Church on Spilled Blood** (Map pp720-1; ☎ 315 1636; Konyushennaya pl; adult/student R300/170; ☼ 10am-8pm Thu-Tue; Ⓜ Gostiny Dvor) are close by and have become a symbol of the city despite being a total stylistic anomaly for St Petersburg with its giddy baroque overstatement. Also known as the Church of the Resurrection of Christ, it was built from 1887 to 1907 on the spot where Alexander II had been assassinated in 1881. The interior is incredible and somewhat overwhelming – having been restored from Soviet times, when the church was used as a potato warehouse – and it's well worth visiting.

The lovely **Summer Garden** (Letny Sad; Map pp720-1; ☼ 9am-10pm May-Oct, 10am-6pm Oct–mid-Apr, closed mid-Apr–late-Apr) is between the open space of Mars Field (Marsovo Pole) and the Fontanka River. Laid out for Peter the Great, with fountains and pavilions along a geometrical plan, it's a lovely place in which to relax.

The greatest thing about the unmistakable Rastrelli-designed **Smolny Cathedral** (Smolny Sobor; Map pp720-1; ☎ 278 5596; pl Rastrelli; admission R150; ☼ 11am-5pm Fri-Wed), 3km east of the Summer Garden, is the sweeping view from atop one of its 63m-high belfries.

## South & West of Nevsky Prospekt

A short walk down the Moyka River from Isaakievskaya pl (St Issac's Sq) is the fascinating **Yusupov Palace** (Map pp720-1; ☎ 314 9883; nab reki Moyki 94; adult/student R300/250; ☼ 11am-5pm; Ⓜ Sadovaya). Notorious as the scene of Rasputin's grisly murder in 1916, the palace has some of the most magnificent interiors in

the city. The entry price gets you a walkman, which guides you through the palace in English giving a very interesting tour of its rooms, including the wonderful private theatre. You can also join a special half-hour Rasputin tour (adult/under 16 years/student R300/150/250) that takes you to parts of the palace not visited on the audio tour and traces the last hours of Rasputin's life. It begins daily at 1.15 and 5.15pm.

Across the meandering Kanal Griboyedov is **Sennaya pl** (Map pp720–1), the heart of Dostoyevskyville. The author lived in several flats around here, and many of the locations turn up in *Crime and Punishment*. To find out more, head to the **Dostoyevsky Museum** (Map pp720-1; ☎ 571 4031; www.md.spb.ru; Kuznechny per 5/2; adult/student R100/50, audio tour in English R100; ☼ 11am-6pm Tue-Sun; Ⓜ Vladimirskaya), located in the house in which the writer died in 1881. It includes many original pieces of furniture and objects owned by the great man, as well as an interesting exhibit about his life.

## The Petrograd Side

The Petrograd Side refers to the cluster of delta islands between the Malaya Neva and the Bolshaya Nevka channels, including the large Petrogradsky Island and little Zaychy Island, home of the Peter & Paul Fortress.

The principal attraction here is the **Peter & Paul Fortress** (Petropavlovskaya Krepost; Map pp720-1 ☎ 230 0340; admission to grounds free, to all buildings adult/student R120/60; ☼ 10am-5pm Thu-Mon, 10am-4pm Tue; Ⓜ Gorkovskaya). Founded in 1703 as the original military fortress for the new city, it was mainly used as a political prison up to 1917: famous residents include Peter's own son Alexei, as well as Dostoyevsky, Gorky and Trotsky. At noon every day a cannon is fired from the **Naryshkin Bastion** (Map pp720–1), scaring the daylights out of tourists. It's fun to walk along the **battlements** (Map pp720–1). Most spectacular of all is the **St Peter & Paul Cathedral** (Map pp720–1), with its landmark needle-thin spire and magnificent baroque interior. All Russia's tsars since Peter the Great have been buried here. The latest addition was Nicholas II and his family, finally buried here by Yeltsin in 1998 – you'll find them in an anteroom to your right as you enter. Also look out for the famously ugly pinhead **statue** of Peter the Great in the centre of the fortress. The statue was created by Mikhail Shemyakin in 1990.

RUSSIA

## Vasilevsky Island

Peter the Great intended for Vasilevsky Island to become the centre of his new city and the buildings at the eastern end of the island are some of the oldest in St Petersburg. However, despite being the academic centre of the city, the lack of a bridge until the mid-19th century meant that development naturally focused on the other side of the Neva. There's plenty to be seen here, though – the Strelka (Tongue of Land), beside the unusual red **Rostral Columns** (Map pp720–1; elaborate oil-fired navigation beacons, now only lit on special occasions), gives a magnificent view across the Neva and is a social hub during the summer months. The old Stock Exchange is now the grand **Central Naval Museum** (Map pp720-1; ☎ 328 2502; Birzhevaya pl 4; adult/student R320/110; ☽ 11am-5pm Wed-Sun; Ⓜ Sportivnaya/Vasileostrovskaya), a tribute to Russia's naval muscle.

On the University Embankment, the pale blue and white building with the steeple is the **Kunstkamera** (Museum of Anthropology & Ethnography; Map pp720-1; ☎ 328 1412; www.kunstkamera.ru; Universitetskaya nab 3; adult/student R200/100; ☽ 11am-6pm Tue-Sun; Ⓜ Sportivnaya/Vasileostrovskaya); the entrance is around the corner on Tamozhyonny per. Founded by Peter himself in 1714, it contains his personal collection of 'curiosities' that were originally displayed to educate the populace. You'll see a ghoulish collection of babies in jars with a variety of physical defects.

The single most interesting place to visit on Vasilevsky Island is the **Menshikov Palace** (Map pp720-1; ☎ 323 1112; Universitetskaya nab 15; adult/student R200/100; ☽ 10.30am-4.30pm Tue-Sun; Ⓜ Sportivnaya/Vasileostrovskaya). Now part of the Hermitage Museum, this 1712 palace was built for Peter the Great's close friend (and some say lover) Alexander Menshikov, the first governor of St Petersburg. The interiors are not much on the far later Yusupov Palace interiors, but are very revealing for anyone interested in the Petrine era. The very heavy, Dutch-influenced décor and furnishings were totally outmoded by the 19th century, but are very representative of the style of the times.

## ACTIVITIES

There is plenty of opportunity to try out a Russian *banya* in St Petersburg. One of the most popular in town is **Krugliye Bani** ( ☎ 247 6409; ul Karbysheva 29A; ☽ 8am-9pm Fri-Tue; Ⓜ Pl Muzhestva), which also has a fantastic open-air heated pool that is great in the winter evenings. It's popu-

lar with expats on Wednesday. A more central option is **Kazachiye Bani** (Map pp720-1; ☎ 764 7812; Bolshoy Kazachy per 11; ☽ 9am-9pm; Ⓜ Pushkinskaya).

Swimming is also possible year-round, both inside and out. There are lots of pools in the city – try the **VMF** ( ☎ 322 4505; Sredny pr 87; ☽ 7am-9pm; Ⓜ Vasileostrovskaya) – a huge pool on Vasilevsky Island. However, for the quintessential Russian experience (or just to watch something quite spectacular during winter) head down to Zaychy Island (where the Peter & Paul Fortress is located) and watch the famous ice swimmers, or 'walruses', who start the day with a bracing dip in the water, through a hole carved into the ice.

## TOURS

It is quite hard to imagine a better deal than **Peter's Walking Tours** (www.peterswalk.com), run by Peter Kozyrev and his fantastic team of English-speaking guides. The tours leave from the HI St Petersburg Hostel (opposite) or Quo Vadis (p719). Prices cost R400 to R600 per person for the various tours, which include a six-hour epic Siege of Leningrad Tour. Other walks include the Dostoyevsky and Communist Legacy Walks, as well as more standard city tours.

## FESTIVALS & EVENTS

St Petersburg celebrates **City Day** on 27 May, which marks the founding of the city with mass festivities. The **white nights** (around the summer solstice in late June) are truly unique. The city comes alive and parties all night as the sun only barely sinks below the horizon, leaving the sky a magical grey-white throughout the night.

## SLEEPING

As St Petersburg has a very definite 'season', room prices are at a premium between May and September. Outside this period, room prices decrease by between 10% and 30% on those quoted here.

### Budget

**Hotel California** (Map pp720-1; ☎ 901 301 6061; www.hotelcalifornia.ru; Apt 36, ul Marata 67/17; dm R600; Ⓜ Vladimirskaya) The cheapest bed in the city, not to mention the place you're most likely to meet cool Russian musicians as well as foreign backpackers. Run by local rock legends Dva Samaliota, this hostel is great, although it can be quite lively at night. Dorm rooms sleep eight people.

**St Petersburg Puppet Hostel** (Map p724; ☎ 272 5401; www.hostelling-russia.ru; ul Nekrasova 12; dm/d R672/1664; ▢; Ⓜ Mayakovskaya) A popular and reliable place in central St Petersburg, next to the city's puppet theatre. The rooms are very simple but perfectly clean. Visa support is offered, and all visas are registered for free.

**HI St Petersburg Hostel** (Map p724; ☎ 329 8018; www.ryh.ru; 3-ya Sovetskaya ul 28; dm/d R690/1680; ▢; Ⓜ Pl Vosstaniya) A 300m walk from Moscow Station, this hostel is popular. Spotless dorms have three to six beds and there's one double; all are slightly cheaper in winter and for holders of ISIC and HI cards.

**Sleep Cheap** (Map pp720-1; ☎ 715 1304; www.sleepcheap.spb.ru; Mokhovaya ul 18/32; dm R700; ▢; Ⓜ Chernyshevskaya) A rather crowded place, Sleep Cheap is still waiting to expand, and hopefully once it does the dorms won't be so full. Despite this, everything is modern and clean, with washing facilities and a good location. The hostel is unmarked from the street – go through into the courtyard of No 18 and the hostel is on the left.

**Nord Hostel** (Map p724; ☎ 517 0342; www.nordhostel.com; Bolshaya Morskaya ul 10; dm/d 825/2250; ▢; Ⓜ Nevsky Pr) Run by friendly Russian staff along the lines of a traditional travellers hostel, the Nord is a real winner, with by far the best location of any of the city's hostels, next to the Hermitage, and huge, beautiful dorm rooms (one has its own piano) and a few doubles as well. Book ahead – this is our hostel of choice.

## Midrange

**Hotel Neva** (Map pp720-1; ☎ 578 0500; fax 273 2593; ul Chaikovskogo 17; s/d unmodernised R1700/2200, modernised R2500/3500; ▢; Ⓜ Chernyshevskaya) One of the city's oldest functioning hotels, the Neva opened its doors in 1913 and has a spectacular staircase to show for it. Unfortunately the rooms are not quite as grand, but they're still comfortable and clean. The location is good, a short walk from the Fontanka and the Neva Rivers.

**Domik v Kolomne** (Map pp720-1; ☎ 710 8351; www.domkolomna.nm.ru; nab Kanala Griboedova 74a; s/d R1800/2100; Ⓜ Sadovaya) Pushkin's family once rented rooms in this house, and the atmosphere of a large flat remains. Rooms have a homey Russian feel, there are private bathrooms and guests will be well looked after. Some rooms have lovely views over the canal.

**Herzen University Hotel** (Map p724; ☎ 314 7472; fax 315 5716; Kazanskaya ul 6; s/d/t R1950/2600/2800; Ⓜ Nevsky Pr) A well-run Russian hostel with a brilliant location, this place is used to foreigners, although it's very much a university hall of residence, so don't expect your usual hostel vibe. It's mainly popular with groups, but its clean and simple rooms (nearly all with en suite facilities) are a great deal.

**Nevsky Inn** (Map p724; ☎ 924 9805; www.nevskyinn.ru; Flat 19, Kirpichny per 2; s/d R2250/2750; Ⓜ Nevksy Pr) Run by a joint British-Russian management, the Nevsky is one of the best places to stay in the city. Rooms are clean and comfortable, and there's a modern kitchen that guests can use, perfectly combining comfort and economy. Highly recommended.

**Guesthouse** (Map p724; ☎ 271 3089; www.ghspb.ru; Grechesky per 13; s/d R2720/3400; Ⓜ Pl Vosstaniya) A great little place, despite its rather unimaginative name. Set behind the enormous Oktyabrsky Concert Hall, it's just a few minutes from Nevsky pr. Rooms are cosy and clean.

**Hotel Oktyabrskaya** (Map p724; ☎ 578 1515; www.oktober-hotel.spb.ru; Ligovsky pr 10; s/d R3000/4300; Ⓜ Pl Vosstaniya) This enormous hotel around Pl Vosstaniya has two buildings – the main one spans one side of the square and the smaller annexe, Oktyabrsky Filial, is to one side of Moscow Station. While it's enormous and impersonal, it's also well located and the rooms have all been renovated to a decent standard.

**Rachmaninoff Art Hotel** (Map p724; ☎ 327 7466; www.kazansky5.com; 3rd fl, Kazanskaya ul 5; s/d R4000/4850; ▨ ▢; Ⓜ Nevsky Pr) Perfectly located and beautifully designed, the Rachmaninoff attracts in-the-know arty types staying in the city. Stuffed full of antiques, the understated rooms nonetheless enjoy a thoroughly modern, boutique feel. And there's free wi-fi – luxury hotels take note!

**Five Corners Hotel** (Map pp720-1; ☎ 380 8181; www.5ugol.ru; Zagorodny pr 13; s/d/ste R4900/5600/6650; ▨ ▢; Ⓜ Dostoyevskaya) This place is very stylish indeed. Its suites are some of the coolest in the city and overlook a trendy hub of streets just a short walk from Nevsky pr. Staff are polite and efficient, and recent expansion to 35 rooms suggests it's deservedly popular. There's free wi-fi throughout.

## Top End

**Hotel Astoria** (Map pp720-1; ☎ 313 5757; www.astoria.spb.ru; 39 Bolshaya Morskaya ul; s/d R13,500/15,500; ℗ ▨ ▢; Ⓜ Sadovaya/Nevsky Pr) Given a new lease of life by the Rocco Forte group, which purchased this classic St Petersburg hotel in 1997, the Astoria is the only real rival to the Grand Hotel Europe as the city's best hotel. Guests have included polar opposites, such as Lenin and George W Bush, and while rates are very steep, there's no doubting that this is a gorgeously designed five-star place.

**Grand Hotel Europe** (Map p724; ☎ 329 6000; www .grandhoteleurope.com; Mikhailovskaya ul 1/7; r from R16,000; ⓟ ⚄ 🖳 ; Ⓜ Nevsky Pr) Pricey, but spectacular, the Grand Hotel Europe remains the best hotel in St Petersburg. The new management is renovating the hotel in a classical Russian style, bringing the tsarist opulence of the nearby Russian Museum into every room. Its faultless location, gorgeous rooms and superb service makes this the choice of everyone from royalty to rock stars, and its famous brunch ($80) on Sunday is the best in the city.

## EATING

Like Moscow, St Petersburg is an ever-increasingly exciting place to eat, although mainly in the upper price brackets. Those on a budget should look out for blini kiosks throughout the city. Their delicious blini are superb value (R30 to R50) and a great place to snack. As in Moscow, street food is sold around metro stations.

**Fasol** (Map p724; ☎ 571 9695; Gorokhovaya ul 17; mains R150; Ⓜ Sennaya pl) Delightful respite from the norms of the Russian eating experience, Fasol combines friendly, efficient service with good food at low prices. It's a cool place to come any time of day, although it's particularly busy in the evening. There's an English menu.

**Oliva** (Map p724; ☎ 314 6563; Bolshaya Morskaya ul 31; mains R160-300; ⏰ 10am-midnight; Ⓜ Nevsky Pr) An authentic Greek addition to the St Petersburg dining scene, though there is nothing taverna-like about this cavernous place, subtly painted and decorated in an array of Greek styles. The menu is traditional, and food is both excellent value and extremely good.

**Sukawati** (Map p724; ☎ 312 0504; Kazanskaya ul 8; mains R250-350; Ⓜ Nevsky Pr) Sleek Indonesian/Japanese fusion place set back behind the Kazan Cathedral. The Nasi Goreng is delicious, and the whole menu far more imaginative than most Asian restaurants in town.

**Vostochny Ugolok** (Map pp720-1; ☎ 713 5747; Gorokhovaya ul 52; mains 250-500; ⏰ 24hr; Ⓜ Pushkin-skaya/Sennaya pl) A taste of the Caucasus in St Petersburg, the 'Eastern Nook' serves brilliant trans-Caucasian dishes from Georgian *pkhali*

(mixed vegetables crushed up and served in crushed walnut and garlic) to Azeri *shashlyk* (kebab), all in a warm atmosphere of southern hospitality.

**Dickens** (Map pp720-1; ☎ 380 7888; nab reki Fontanki 108; breakfast R290; ⏰ 8am-2am; Ⓜ Sennaya pl) OK, we're not in the habit of recommending English or Irish pubs anywhere, but Dickens is exempt from that rule as it's the only place you can get a good English breakfast in the city without spending a fortune at a five-star hotel. It's a little out of the way, but has a friendly atmosphere and is popular with locals.

**Salkhino** (Map pp720-1; ☎ 232 7891; Kronverksy pr 25; mains R300-500; Ⓜ Gorkovskaya) This place is our favourite Georgian in the city, serving unfussy, delicious Georgian fare and a great selection of wines. Try the Adjaran *khachapuri* and the aubergines in walnut paste.

**Restoran** (Map pp720-1; ☎ 327 8979; Tamozhenny per 2; mains R400-600; ⏰ noon-1am; Ⓜ Vasileostrovskaya) Beautifully designed and lit, Restoran harks back to the days of Romanov splendour, despite its modern-minimalist décor being the polar opposite of Romanov taste. The Russian cuisine is well realised and beautifully presented.

### Cheap Eats

**Teremok** (Map p724; Nevsky 60; mains R60; Ⓜ Nevsky Pr) Already firmly established as the city's premier fast-food blini kiosk, Teremok now has its own sit-down restaurant on Nevsky pr – great for a quick and filling lunch.

**Chaynaya Lozhka** (Map p724; Nevsky pr 44; mains R100; ⏰ 9am-10pm; Ⓜ Pl Vosstaniya) This excellent chain serves delicious blini and offers a wide range of salads. The orange-clad staff members are extremely helpful and the meals are very cheap. There are also branches at Nevsky prospekt 136 and ul Vosstaniya 13. It can get busy at lunchtime.

**Troitsky Most** Kamennoostrovsky Pr ( ☎ 232 6693; Kamennoostrovsky Pr 9/2; mains R100-200; Ⓜ Gorkovskaya); Zagorodny Pr (Map pp720-1; ☎ 115 1998; Zagorodny Pr 38; Ⓜ Vladimirskaya) Superb vegetarian chain operating in multiple locations across the city. Its mushroom lasagne is legendary, and its salads freshly made and delicious.

Out of the city's food markets, **Kuznechny Market** (Map pp720-1; Kuznechny per 3; ⏰ 9am-9pm; Ⓜ Vladimirskaya) should not be missed. The most colourful and pricey of the city's food halls, you can taste delicious fruit, honey and cheese here, although you'll inevitably be charmed into making some purchases.

# DRINKING

**Novus** (Map p724; ☎ 569 3818; Bolshaya Morskaya ul 8; ☺ 6pm-6am; Ⓜ Nevsky pr) The current favourite for young expats and travellers, Novus is named after a highly eccentric Latvian hybrid of backgammon and pool. Packed nightly, this is a great place to meet a young and beautiful international crowd. Enter through the takeaway section downstairs.

**Dacha** (Map p724; Dumskaya ul 9; ☺ 6pm-6am; Ⓜ Nevsky pr) The bar sensation of 2005, when everyone in the city suddenly flocked here, indie bar Dacha now looks like an old timer, but still features on many people's list for a good night out. The R100 admission charge includes two free beers.

**Tsynik** (Map p724; ☎ 312 9526; per Antonenko 4; ☺ 1pm-3am Mon-Fri, 1pm-7am Sat & Sun; Ⓜ Sennaya pl) Famous for its rowdy crowd and *grenki* (fried garlic black bread), this is the place to be seen misbehaving. Vodka is served in teapots and the toilets are scrawled with intellectual graffiti.

**Fish Fabrik** (Map p724; ☎ 164 4857; Ligovsky pr 53; ☺ 3pm-6am; Ⓜ Pl Vosstaniya) An institution everyone should visit, Fish Fabrik is a dive bar for drunken artists and student slackers. Come here for beer, foosball (table football), cult movies and decent bar food.

# ENTERTAINMENT
## Nightclubs

Some of the best clubs include the following:

**Griboedov** (Map pp720-1; ☎ 764 4355; www.griboedovclub.ru, in Russian; Voronezhskaya ul 2A; admission R100-200; Ⓜ Ligovsky Pr) An alternative venue (see right).

**Jet Set** (Map pp720-1; ☎ 275 9288; Furshtadskaya ul 58B; Ⓜ Chernyshevskaya) In-crowd heaven.

**Metro** (Map pp720-1; ☎ 766 0204; www.metroclub.ru; Ligovsky pr 174; Ⓜ Ligovsky pr) Student super-club.

## Cinemas

The main cinemas in town line Nevsky pr. With very few exceptions, foreign films (the majority of what is screened) are dubbed into Russian, and so aren't great for non Russian–speaking visitors. The *St Petersburg Times* usually lists films (if any) being shown in English.

## Gay & Lesbian Venues

St Petersburg has four gay clubs and Russia's first lesbian club: check out **Excess** (www.xs.gay.ru) for the latest city-specific information. The two biggest and busiest clubs are next to each other:

**Central Station** (Map p724; ☎ 312 3600; www.centralstation.ru; ul Lomonosova 1; Ⓜ Nevsky pr) Slick new venue.

**Greshniki** (Map p724; ☎ 318 4291; www.greshniki.ru; nab kanala Griboedova 28A; Ⓜ Nevsky pr) An old timer.

## Theatre

St Petersburg is arguably Russia's cultural capital and there's a huge range of theatre, ballet, opera and classical concerts. Check the Friday *St Petersburg Times* for listings.

**Mariinsky Theatre** (Map pp720-1; ☎ 326 4141; www.mariinsky.ru; Teatralnaya pl 1; Ⓜ Sennaya Pl) A visit here should not be missed, especially as the Bolshoi in Moscow is being renovated and its main hall is closed until 2008.

## Live Music

There's a lively rock scene in St Petersburg, home to classic Soviet rock groups, such as Aquarium and Kino, and more recently rock stars-cum-performance artists Leningrad. There's always plenty going on.

**Griboedov** (Map pp720-1; ☎ 764 4355; www.griboedovclub.ru, in Russian; Voronezhskaya ul 2A; admission R100-200; Ⓜ Ligovsky Pr) Run by local ska band Dva Samaritan and a favourite venue.

**Platforma** (Map p724; ☎ 314 1104; ul Nekrasova 40; ☺ 24hr; Ⓜ Pl Vosstaniya)

**Red Club** (Map p724; ☎ 717 0000; www.clubred.ru; Poltavskaya ul 7; ☺ 6pm-6am; Ⓜ Pl Vosstaniya)

There's also a lively jazz scene. Check out the *St Petersburg Times* for other jazz gigs.

**JFC Jazz Club** (Map pp720-1; ☎ 272 9850; www.jfc.sp.ru; 33 Shpalernaya ul; admission R50-200; Ⓜ Chernyshevskaya)

## Sport

The local soccer team Zenith provokes feverish passion in the hearts of young Petersburgers, and after a match there are always rowdy street scenes as mobs of blue-clad youth stream, drunk and excitable, from the stadium. You can usually buy tickets to see Zenith play all over the city (ask at any *teatralnaya kassa* in a metro station), and the season runs from October to April. Its home ground is the **Petrovsky Stadium** (Map pp720-1; ☎ 119 5700; Petrovsky ostrov 2; admission R180; Ⓜ Sportivnaya).

# SHOPPING

**Gostiny Dvor** (Map p724; ☎ 710 5408; Nevsky pr 35; ☺ 10am-10pm; Ⓜ Gostiny Dvor) The enormous Gostiny Dvor was one of the world's first shopping arcades, being built in the mid-18th century. You'll find almost everything here, and despite the first floor being increasingly devoted to designer outlets, the ground floor retains much of its Soviet-era feel.

**Souvenir Market** (Map p724; Konyushennaya pl; **M** Gostiny Dvor) The best places for souvenir hunting include this market, next to the Church on Spilled Blood, where you can find an endless array of *matryoshki* (Russian nesting dolls) and Soviet memorabilia. You should most definitely haggle.

**Folk Crafts Shop** (Map p724; Stroganov Palace; **M** Nevsky pr) Another good place for traditional Russian gifts.

Other smart shopping malls include the designer-heavy **Grand Palace** (Map p724; ☎ 449 9344; Nevsky pr 44; ⊗ 11am-9pm; **M** Gostiny Dvor) and the charming 19th-century **Passazh** (Map p724; ☎ 312 2210; Nevsky pr 48; ⊗ 11am-9pm; **M** Gostiny Dvor).

## GETTING THERE & AWAY
### Air
St Petersburg is served by Pulkovo airport (LED), to the south of the city. There are two terminals – Pulkovo-1 is for domestic flights and Pulkovo-2 is international. For international connections and the carriers that fly here, see p745.

### Boat
From April to September St Petersburg has regular boats to/from Tallinn (R850, 14 hours) and a weekly service to Kaliningrad; see **Baltfinn** (www.baltfinn.ru) for details. For boat services from outside Eastern Europe, see p745. Boats leave from the **Morskoy Vokzal** ( ☎ 322 6052; pl Morskoy Slavy; **M** Primorskaya), but it's a long way from the metro, so it's easiest to take bus 7 or trolleybus 10 from outside the Hermitage.

### Bus
Buses arrive and depart from **Avtovokzal No 2** ( ☎ 766 5777; nab Obvodnogo kanala; **M** Ligovsky Pr). They are the cheapest way to travel between Moscow and St Petersburg (R515, 10 to 12 hours, eight daily), as well as being the cheapest option to get to Tallinn (R580 to R670, 7½ hours, seven daily) and Rīga (R540, 11 hours, two daily).

### Train
St Petersburg is well connected to the Baltics, Eastern Europe and the rest of Russia by train. Trains to/from Moscow go from **Moskovsky Vokzal** (Moscow Station; Map p724; ☎ 768 4597; pl Vosstaniya; **M** pl Vosstaniya), while services to/from the Baltics, Ukraine, Belarus and Poland run from **Vitebsky Vokzal** (Vitebsk Station; Map pp720-1; ☎ 768 5807; Zagorodny pr 52; **M** Pushkinskaya). See **Your Train – CIS Railway Table** (www.poezda.net) for timings and prices. For details of trains to Finland, see p930.

## GETTING AROUND
### To/From the Airports
St Petersburg's Pulkovo airport is 17km south of the city centre and has two terminals: Pulkovo-1 handles domestic flights and Pulkovo-2 is the international terminal. To Moskovskaya metro station, from where you can travel into the city centre, bus 13 runs from Pulkovo-2 and bus 39 runs from Pulkovo-1. A taxi into the city centre will cost around R600. All hotels can organise transfers, which can be a better option than haggling with unscrupulous taxi drivers. *Marshrutkas* (minibuses) K3 and K39 run between the two airport terminals and Sennaya Pl and Pl Vosstaniya metro stations respectively.

### Marshrutkas
Around the city centre, *marshrutkas* (minibuses) are a quick alternative to the slow trolleybuses. Costs vary on each route, but the average fare is R18, and fares are displayed prominently inside each van. To stop a *marshrutka*, simply hold out your hand and it will stop. Jump in, sit down, pass the cash to the driver (a human chain operates if you are not seated nearby), and then call out '*ostanovityes pozhalsta!*' when you want to get out and the driver will pull over. *Marshrutkas* are a very good way of getting from one end of Nevsky pr to another.

### Metro
The metro (R12 flat fare) is best for covering large distances across the city. The four lines cross over in the city centre and go out to the suburbs. The most confusing aspect of the system is that all labelling is in Cyrillic. Listen out for the announcements of the station names, or ask locals who will usually go out of their way to help. A further confusion is that two stations sharing an exit will have different names. For example, Nevsky pr and Gostiny Dvor are in the same place, but as they are on different lines, they have different names.

## Taxi

Holding your arm out will cause unofficial taxis to stop very quickly. The standard rate for a short distance (1km to 2km) is R50, R100 for a journey roughly between 2km and 5km, and whatever you can negotiate for trips longer than about 5km. As a foreigner, expect to have the price raised – always agree on a price before getting into the taxi. To call an official taxi, dial ☎ 068. For more information about taxis in Russia, see p746.

# AROUND ST PETERSBURG
## Petrodvorets Петродворец
☎ 812

The most popular of the tsarist palaces that stud the countryside around St Petersburg, **Petrodvorets** ( ☎ 427 9527; www.peterhof.ru; admission to grounds adult/student R300/150, free after 5pm; ⏱ 9am-9pm) has an imposing position 29km west of St Petersburg overlooking the Gulf of Finland. Despite its stunningly grand appearance, the **Grand Palace** (adult/student R430/220; ⏱ 10am-6pm Tue-Sun) was in fact almost totally destroyed by the German advance into Russia during WWII – the restored interiors are still as opulent as those befitting any despotic emperor. In fact, the only room in the palace that survived the Nazi occupation was Peter's simple study.

In summer the most impressive sight is the centrepiece of the grounds, the magnificent (if thoroughly over-the-top) **Grand Cascade & Water Avenue**, a symphony of more than 64 fountains and 37 bronze statues. This work of undoubted engineering genius extends from the palace all the way to the Gulf of Finland, and looks magnificent in an idiosyncratically look-how-rich-and-powerful-I-am imperialist manner.

Walking around the grounds is a treat, although during summer bring some anti-mosquito spray or you may well be eaten alive in the woods.

Elsewhere in the large grounds are several other buildings of interest. Most significant is **Monplaisir**, Peter's two-floor villa, and the lovely **Marly Guesthouse**, which takes its name from Louis XIV's hunting lodge at Versailles, and was a comfortable retreat for royals and their guests. It overlooks a small lake and has some wonderful interiors.

### GETTING THERE & AWAY

In summer the pricey Meteor hydrofoils (R500, 30 minutes) leave from outside St Petersburg's Hermitage museum every 20 to 30 minutes from 9.30am to at least 7pm. The trip is great, although don't leave it too late when returning, as the crowds can be massive and you may have to wait for up to an hour to get on a boat.

Far cheaper is taking a suburban train (R22, 40 minutes, every 20 to 40 minutes); take any train terminating at Oranienbaum or Kalishe from the Baltic Station ( Ⓜ Baltiiskaya) and alight at Novy Petrodvorets station. The station is still quite a walk (about 2km) from the palace, but buses run frequently from here.

## Tsarskoye Selo & Pavlovsk
Царское Село & Павловск
☎ 812

Literally the 'tsar's village', Tsarskoye Selo is the captivating palace 25km south of St Petersburg, just outside the town of Pushkin. Nearby is Pavlovsk, the smaller but equally impressive palace 4km beyond. Both are connected to specific rulers of Russia, although arguably Tsarskoye Selo's association with Catherine the Great draws far more interest than Pavlovsk's associate with her son, the mentally disturbed Paul I. It's perfectly possible to visit both in one day, although if time allows do them separately as they're both great trips in themselves.

**Tsarskoe Selo** was created by Empresses Elizabeth and Catherine the Great between 1744 and 1796. The big drawcard here is the Rastrelli-designed, baroque **Catherine Palace** ( ☎ 465 5308; www.tzar.ru; adult/student R520/250; ⏱ 10am-5pm Wed-Mon, closed last Mon of the month), built between 1752 and 1756, but practically destroyed in WWII. The exterior and 20-odd rooms have been expertly restored; the gilt-adorned and mirrored Great Hall is particularly dazzling.

The most famous room in the Catherine Palace is the Amber Room – which was removed by the Nazis in 1941 and was believed to be the world's most valuable piece of missing art, valued at some $140m. The room was created by Rastrelli under Empress Elizabeth from priceless amber panels given to Peter the Great by Frederick I of Prussia in 1716. The panels sat alongside magnificent diamond mosaics and mirrors, creating a dazzling ensemble. The Amber Room took more than a decade to restore and was reopened in 2003. The original was recently discovered to have been destroyed in Kaliningrad during the war (p737).

Just wandering around **Catherine Park** (adult/student R140/70; 9am-5.30pm), which surrounds the palace, is a pleasure. In the outer section of the park is the **Great Pond**, fringed by an intriguing array of structures, including a Chinese Pavilion, a purposely Ruined Tower and a Pyramid where Catherine the Great buried her dogs.

To escape the masses, head 4km further south to **Pavlovsk** (www.pavlovskart.spb.ru; admission to grounds adult/student R80/40; 9am-6pm), the park and palace designed by Charles Cameron between 1781 and 1786, and one of the most exquisite in Russia. Pavlovsk's **Great Palace** ( 470 2155; adult/student R370/185; 11am-5pm Sat-Thu), also partly restored after a trashing in WWII, has some delightful rooms, but it's the sprawling, peaceful park that's the real attraction.

### GETTING THERE & AWAY

The most convenient way of getting to both Tsarskoye Selo and Pavlovsk is to hop on one of the frequent *marshrutkas* (R26, 30 minutes) that leave from outside Moskovskaya metro station – not to be confused with the Moskovsky Vokzal (Moscow Station) – 8km south of the city centre; the *marshrutkas* stop within walking distance of Tsarskoe Selo and outside Pavlovsk. You can also take a train from Vitebsky Vokzal's (Vitebsk Station) platform 1 to Detskoe Selo (Tsarskoe Selo's train station) and to Pavlovsk station for Pavlovsk (it's a 30-minute trip to either). Note that while there are several trains prior to 9am, there are far fewer later in the day.

# KALININGRAD REGION
# КАЛИНИНГРАДСКАЯ ОБЛАСТЬ

**pop 955,000**

One part German, two parts Russian and wedged inextricably between a Europe-thirsty Lithuanian rock and a proud Polish hard place, Kaliningrad is a region with an identity problem. Should it be resurrecting its German past, flaunting its undeniable Russianness, or forging ahead on a brave new path?

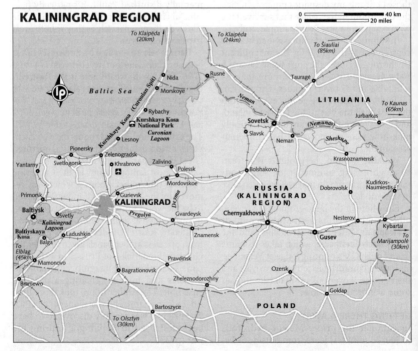

**KALININGRAD REGION**

Brashly, everybody's favourite Russian exclave does all three. The result is one of Eastern Europe's most exotic – and least travelled – locales. You'll definitely feel like you're in Russia, but it will seem a tad more liberal, a tad more open-minded and a tad more Western-oriented than the rest of the country.

If you, too, stay open-minded, you're in for a treat. In addition to a quirky capital – formerly the legendary German city of Königsberg – Kaliningrad has Prussian castle ruins, the world's largest amber-producing mine, long stretches of pristine beach and some of Europe's highest sand dunes.

Seeing all of this won't be easy. As an independent traveller here, you're about as common as a purple giraffe and people are likely to treat you accordingly. Tourism facilities are pretty much nonexistent. Do yourself a favour and bone up on the Cyrillic alphabet and some basic Russian phrases before you arrive.

## HISTORY

From the 13th century until 1945 the area was German, part of the core territory of the Teutonic Knights and their successors, the dukes and kings of Prussia. Its centrepiece was Königsberg, capital of East Prussia. Once one of Europe's most beautiful cities, Königsberg was a liberal and academically advanced Prussian outpost on the Baltic. Albertina University, founded in 1544 (whose most famous graduate was Immanuel Kant), helped ensure the city's position as a major educational, spiritual and cultural centre.

Königsberg lost its dignity forever in a four-day series of intense British air raids in August 1944 that destroyed most of the city. The three-month campaign by which the Red Army took it in 1945 was one of the fiercest of the war, with hundreds of thousands of casualties on both sides. After the war insult was added to injury and East Prussia was handed over to Stalin. The Soviets proceeded to ship out all the Germans, and out of the rubble of Königsberg rose Kaliningrad, which was meant to be the finest example of a Soviet planned city. The result was what you see today: a blinding expanse of concrete that is extreme even by Soviet standards.

Russia's Baltic Fleet is headquartered at Baltiysk (about 50km due west of Kalinigrad), and therefore the entire region was closed to Westerners until 1991. Despite a massive military downsizing since the 1990s, the ex-clave is still heavily militarised – a nod to its continued strategic importance to Russia as a buffer to the expanding EU.

Kaliningrad suffered through economically tragic times in the early 1990s. Things have much improved since then, and as the region becomes increasingly isolated from mainland Russia, many locals are pinning their hopes and futures more on Europe than Mother Russia.

Every year, into this strange brew waltz thousands of elderly German tourists returning to see the homeland of their ancestors or, in some cases, their own homeland.

## PEOPLE

Kaliningrad's remaining German population of about 200,000 was deported to Germany or Siberia after WWII – one of the most effective ethnic-cleansing campaigns in European history. The population's now made up of almost 80% Russians, 10% Belarusians, 6% Ukrainians, and the rest Lithuanians and others.

## ENVIRONMENT
### The Land

The Kaliningrad region is tiny – only 15,100 sq km, or less than a quarter the size of hardly immense Lithuania next door. Its coastline stretches 147km, 100km of which is sandy beaches and 50km of which is made up of the Kurshkaya Kosa (Curonian Spit), shared with Lithuania. The spit features Europe's second-highest sand dunes, measuring up to 60m in height. Much of the land is flat (some below sea level and protected by dykes), with elevations in the southeast rising to 231m.

### Environmental Issues

Unesco placed the Kurshkaya Kosa on its list of World Heritage sites in 2000, securing the unique ecosystem's importance and its protection under international law. About the same time Russian oil giant Lukoil announced plans to build D6 – a large series of oil rigs and an underwater pipeline – just 22km from the spit's shores. Drilling commenced in 2004.

In the event of a spill Lukoil can breathe easy: it will only have responsibility to clean oil from the sea, not from the shore, where it would inevitably wash up. Kaliningrad-based environmental NGO **Ecodefense** (www.ecodefence .ru) cites several incidents of oil pollution near Kaliningrad since the early 1990s, which were downplayed by the authorities.

# KALININGRAD КАЛИНИНГРАД

☎ within the region 2, from elsewhere 4012
pop 425,600

As with many provincial Russian cities, part of Kaliningrad's charm lies in its apparent lack of charm – its rows of Soviet-era apartment blocks, its neon-lit slot machine parlours, the stony faces of passers-by on the street. Yet hidden behind the brooding concrete facades lies a vibrant, fun-loving city with some more-traditional tourist appeal.

Much of that appeal lies in its Prussian past life. While allied bombing raids destroyed much of the city in WWII, some gems from old Prussia remain – a few attractive residential neighbourhoods with rows of old German houses, the remains of the old wall that once surrounded the city and its medieval castle, and a network of 19th-century red-brick gates that provided access through that wall.

While a hideous and heretofore unused Soviet monstrosity now occupies the plot where the castle once stood, the city has done a good job of rebuilding the main cathedral nearby, and contractors are hard at work installing a modern business and tourism Mecca – curiously named Fish Village – on the banks of the Pregolya River.

That's the future. In the present there is absolutely no tourist infrastructure. All maps, menus and street signs are in Russian only, there is no tourist information office to speak of and there's very little in the way of English-language guides – either written or breathing. The new tourism minister promises to make the city more user-friendly, but for now you're pretty much on your own.

## Orientation

Leninsky pr, a broad north–south avenue, is Kaliningrad's main artery, running more than 3km from the main train station, Yuzhny Vokzal (South Station), all the way to central ploshchad Pobedy (Victory Sq). Halfway it crosses the Pregolya River and passes Kaliningrad Cathedral, the city's major landmark.

## Information

### INTERNET ACCESS, POST & TELEPHONE

**Kaliningrad State Technical University information centre** (Room 155, KGTU Bldg, Sovetsky pr 1; per hr R36; ☺ 9am-9pm Mon-Fri, 9am-7pm Sat) Offers internet access.

**Post office** (ul Chernyakhovskogo 32; per hr R30; ☺ post office 10am-2pm & 3-7pm Mon-Fri, 10am-2pm & 3-6pm Sat, internet room 10am-2pm & 3-10pm Mon-Sat) Internet access and postal services.

**Post office** (ul Chernyakhovskogo 58; per hr R30; ☺ 9am-7pm Mon-Sat) Internet access and postal services.

**Telekom** (ul Teatralnaya 13; calls to US/UK per min R24/19.50, internet per hr R30; ☺ 8am-10pm) For long-distance calls, fax and internet access.

**Telekom** (Leninsky pr 2-4; calls to US/UK per min R24/19.50, internet per hr R30) For long-distance calls, fax and internet access.

### MEDICAL SERVICES

**Emergency Hospital** ( ☎ 466 989; ul Nevskogo 90; ☺ 24hr)

**Formula Zdorovya** ( ☎ 777 003; Leninsky pr 63-67; ☺ 24hr) Well-stocked pharmacy.

### MONEY

There are ATMs and/or 24-hour currency-exchange booths in most hotels, supermarkets, slot-machine parlours, and bus and train stations, as well as in various locations along Leninsky pr.

**Stroivestbank** ( ☎ 212 975; ul Gendelya 3a; ☺ 9am-5pm Mon-Fri) Gives credit-card cash advances.

---

### WHAT'S IN A NAME? NOT MUCH

Königsberg city was renamed in 1946 after Mikhail Kalinin, one of Lenin's henchmen, had conveniently died just as a new name for the city was needed. A former president of the Supreme Soviet, Kalinin had never even visited the region.

Not surprisingly, few residents have any association with Kalinin, and those who do know of him would rather forget him. Among other rotten deeds, Kalinin turned his back on the famine in Ukraine in 1932, when millions starved, and authorised the massacre of thousands of Polish officers in Katyn forest, which was later blamed on the Nazis.

A modest movement to rename the city has all but petered out. It appears the name 'Kaliningrad' will remain, for better or for worse, a symbol of the city's ambivalence about its place in history.

**RUSSIA**

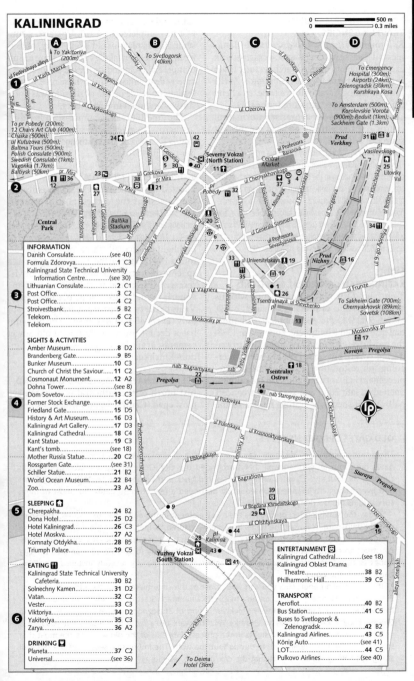

# KALININGRAD

0 _____ 500 m
0 _____ 0.3 miles

## TOURIST INFORMATION & TRAVEL AGENCIES

*Kaliningrad Historical and Cultural Monuments* (Памятники Истории и Культуры Калининград) is an excellent guide to the city's architecture. It's in Russian, but there are scores of photos. At the time of writing it was only available for a hefty price at the Amber Museum (opposite).

Kaliningrad lacks a tourist information centre, so private travel agencies are the best source of advice.

**Baltma Tours** ( ☎ 916 416; www.baltma.ru; pr Mira 94) This friendly, efficient, multilingual bunch is the best source of regional information in the city. Staff can arrange hotel accommodation, and provide tailored city tours and a surprising array of local excursions – including one to Yantarny, home of what was once the world's largest amber mine, and another to the military port city of Baltiysk (formerly Pillau), which requires a special permit to enter. Car hire with a driver is R620 per hour; guides cost R2800 per day.

## Sights

### KALININGRAD CATHEDRAL & AROUND

Tsentralny Ostrov (Central Island) with its striking Gothic **cathedral** (adult/student R70/30; 🕙 9am-5pm) was the geographical and spiritual heart of old Königsberg. Founded in 1333, the red-brick cathedral was almost destroyed during WWII, but since 1992 has been undergoing full restoration. The building's showpiece main hall, with fabulous vaulted ceilings, opened in late 2006 and serves as a concert hall. A painstakingly crafted replica of the

cathedral's 16th-century, 38,000-pipe organ will be completed by 2010. Upstairs, a museum has displays of old Königsberg, objects from archaeological digs and a shrine to Immanuel Kant – including the old philosopher's creepy death mask. Kant, whose rose-marble **tomb** lies outside on the north side, was born, studied and died in Königsberg.

The fine blue Renaissance-style building just across the river to the south of the cathedral is the former **Stock Exchange** (Leninsky pr 83), built in the 1870s.

### WORLD OCEAN MUSEUM

Located along the Petra Velikogo embankment west of the cathedral, this **museum** ( ☎ 340 244; www.vitiaz.ru; nab Petra Velikogo 1; all 3 sections adult/student R80/40; 🕙 11am-6pm Wed-Sun Apr-Oct, 10am-5pm Wed-Sun Nov-Mar) is a Kaliningrad highlight. It's actually three museums in one: tour a B-413 submarine; learn about sea and space exploration aboard two giant Soviet research ships; or visit its fairly uninspiring aquarium and learn about oceanography. Visits to the two ships are by free guided tour only (every 45 minutes or so). The museum has a decent souvenir shop with old Soviet cameras, army-issue gadgets and other random knickknacks.

### TSENTRALNAYA PLOSHCHAD & AROUND

Just north of the cathedral is Tsentralnaya ploshchad (Central Sq), on which sits one of

---

### OLD GATES SPROUT NEW LIFE

There was a time when the only way into the heart of Königsberg was through a network of gates built into an earthen wall that surrounded the city. Originally constructed in the 14th century, the wall and 13 gates were rebuilt of red brick in the middle of the 19th century. Wars and overzealous city planners subsequently destroyed a few of these gates, but most of them survived, as did portions of the wall.

Today the surviving red-brick gates are a key element in the city's plan to resurrect the spirit of old Königsberg. A few of the gates have been restored to their former glory and now house museums. The **Brandenberg Gate** (ul Zheleznodorozhnaya) is open to traffic. The city plans to reconstruct an entire section of the old wall near **Prud Verkhny** (Upper Pond) – an area the city hopes to transform into a buzzing hive of tourist activity. The city recently installed a walking path around the pond.

If you're feeling energetic, you can walk most of the circumference of the old wall, the outline of which is clearly visible on any map of Kaliningrad. Start at the southern boundary of the wall along pr Kalinina and walk clockwise along ul Zheleznodorozhnaya, Gvardeysky pr, ul Chernyakhovskogo and finally ul Litovsky Val. The walk takes most of the day, but you'll pass near many of Kaliningrad's best sights in the process. Remains of the old wall and the moat that surrounded the old city are visible throughout the walk. The impressive section of the old wall along ul Litovsky Val is the part that the city plans to rebuild.

the ugliest of Soviet creations, the H-shaped **Dom Sovetov** (House of Soviets). On this site stood a magnificent 1255 castle, damaged during WWII but dynamited out of existence by narrow-minded Soviet planners in 1967–68. In its place this eyesore was built (over 10 long years), but it has never been used after builders discovered that the ground beneath it is hollow, with a (now flooded) four-level underground passage connecting to the cathedral. Duh.

Heading northwest along Leninsky pr from Tsentralnaya ploshchad, follow the signs leading to the unique **Bunker Museum** (Muzey Blindazh; ☎ 536 593; ul Universitetskaya 2; admission R30; ☼ 10am-6pm), the underground German command where General Otto Lasch capitulated to the Soviets in 1945. There are some excellent dioramas here depicting the WWII bombing of Königsberg. Free guided tours are available in Russian and German.

Head towards the **Kant statue** and keep heading east, crossing the pretty Prud Nizhny (Lower Pond), to get to the highly worthwhile **History & Art Museum** ( ☎ 466 888; ul Klinicheskaya 21; adult/student R40/20; ☼ 10am-6pm Tue-Sun). Housed in a reconstructed 1912 concert hall, the museum displays a fairly open history of the city and has heart-wrenching photos of the dynamiting of the city's castle. Exhibits are in Russian only.

The **Kaliningrad Art Gallery** ( ☎ 467 166; Moskovsky pr 62; ☼ 11am-7pm Tue-Sun) features exhibitions by local artists.

### PLOSHCHAD POBEDY TO PROSPEKT MIRA

At the northern terminus of Leninsky pr lies the concrete expanse known as ploshchad Pobedy (Victory Sq), once dominated by Lenin but now lorded over by the newly built **Church of Christ the Saviour**.

Extending west of the square is pr Mira, a pleasant artery leading to some of the city's prettiest areas and lined with shops and cafés. Past the Schiller statue is the **zoo** (pr Mira 24; adult/student R40/20; ☼ 9am-8pm). Further west is the splendid **Cosmonaut Monument**, a gem of Soviet iconography honouring several cosmonauts from the region.

Just where pr Pobedy branches out from pr Mira is the entrance to bustling **Central Park**, favourite strolling ground for local families in the warm months. There's a small amusement park, a few outdoor eating options and plenty of greenery.

Walks through the linden-scented, tree-lined old **German neighbourhoods** are the best way to experience old Königsberg: the entire area previously known as Amalienau between prs Pobedy and Mira is enchanting (ul Kutuzova especially), as is the slightly rundown area north of pr Mira centred around ul Komsomolskaya.

### OTHER MUSEUMS

The fascinating **Amber Museum** ( ☎ 466 888; pl Vasilevskogo 1; admission R80; ☼ 10am-6pm Tue-Sun) has some 6000 amber art works (including some wild Soviet symbols), plus copies of sections of the famous Amber Room, which the Nazis stole wholesale from St Petersburg in 1941 and brought to Königsberg's castle. It was then destroyed by fire while under Red Army occupation. The museum is located within **Dohna Tower**, which served as a fortress to protect adjacent **Rossgarten Gate** (pl Vasilevskogo 3).

Impressively renovated **Korolevskie Vorota** (King's Gate; ☎ 581 272; ul Frunze 112; student/adult R80/40; ☼ 11am-6pm Wed-Sun) houses a museum with cool models of old Königsberg and exhibits on the personalities who shaped the region's history. A little south of here is the twin-towered **Sackheim Gate** (cnr pr Moscovsky & Litovsky Val).

Newly restored **Friedland Gate** (pr Kalinina 6; adult/child R20/10; ☼ 10am-5pm Tue-Sun) contains a small museum with a great map plotting the locations of the 13 original city gates. There's an intriguing arms display, and the original cobblestone road that ran through the gate is visible inside.

## Sleeping

Breakfast costs extra unless otherwise stated.

**Chaika** ( ☎ 210 729; www.hotel.kaliningrad.ru; ul Pugacheva 13; s/d from R1100/1300) This excellent-value hotel in an attractive residential area has an antique charm associated with being a converted townhouse as opposed to a converted Soviet monstrosity. The 24 rooms smell a bit musty, but have ample space and furniture.

**Hotel Kaliningrad** ( ☎ 536 021; www.hotel.kaliningrad.ru; Leninsky pr 81; budget s/d R1100/1600, business class s/d R2000/2800; P ☒ ☒ ☐ ) In the middle of the city, this concrete monster, with a certain surly Soviet charm, couldn't be louder, but its clean, no-frills budget rooms get the job done for a decent price. Wheelchair access is available.

RUSSIA

**Deima Hotel** ( ☎ 710 814; www.deima-tour.com; ul Tolstikova 15/2; business class s/d R1400/1800, economy d/tr with shared bathroom R600/990; P ) There's a dizzying variety of rooms to match the dizzying pace of activity in the lobby, bar and billiard room. The cramped dorm-style economy rooms are the city's best budget option. The location is poor, though – it's a 10-minute taxi ride (R50) south from the train station.

**Dona Hotel** ( ☎ 351 650; http://dona.kaliningrad.ru; pl Vasilevskogo 2; s/d from R2100/2700; P ⊠ 🖳 ) The Dona is an oasis of modernity, smiles and sleek design in a city where most hotels are still struggling to shake their Soviet shackles. It's Kaliningrad's best hotel, and its Dolce Vita eatery and jazz club is arguably the city's best restaurant.

**Cherepakha** ( ☎ 957 500; www.hotel.kaliningrad.ru; Zoologichesky tupik 10; s/d R2200/2900, ste R3900-4900; P ⊠ ) You can wake up to elephant calls in this intimate red-brick guesthouse tucked away in a residential neighbourhood behind the zoo. 'The Turtle' is known for its elegant furnishings, excellent a-la-carte breakfast and truly lavish deluxe rooms with huge flat-screen TVs.

Other recommendations:
**Komnaty Otdykha** ( ☎ 586 447; pl Kalinina; s/d/tr per person from R490/435/350) Surprisingly clean rooms above the train station, but watch your neighbour.
**Hotel Moskva** ( ☎ 352 333; www.hotel.kaliningrad.ru; pr Mira 19; s/d R2000/2800; P 🖳 ) Nicely renovated and perfectly located, if overpriced, 171-room behemoth.
**Triumph Palace** (Per Bolshevitsky 3) Newly opened top-end hotel.

## Eating

A recent restaurant explosion is one sure sign of progress in Kaliningrad, but possibly the best place to eat remains the summertime *shashlyk* stands in Central Park. A pork kebab washed down by a bottle of Baltika won't set you back much more than R100.

**Kaliningrad State Technical University caféteria** (KGTU Stolovaya; Basement, Sovietsky pr 1; mains R40-75; ��� 9am-6pm Mon-Sat) Every visitor to Russia should visit an authentic *stolovaya* (cafeteria) to fill up on cheap, hearty Russian food. This is a fine specimen in a great location.

**Vatan** (ul Chernyakhovskogo 12a-16a; mains R100-200; ☯ 11am-11pm; ✗ ) If you're not familiar with the wonders of central Asian cuisine, become so at this fun, affordable basement eatery with rare nonsmoking section. Its easy-to-navigate English menu features Uzbek mainstays such

as *plov* and *manty* (spicy dumplings) as well as more exotic offerings, and you can guzzle pints of Czech Primator beer for just R40.

**Zarya** (pr Mira 43; meals R100-250; ☯ 10am-3am) This highly fashionable spot in the lobby of a cinema has an old Europe flavour, with good fish dishes and a vegetarian menu.

**Yakitoriya** Leninsky (Leninsky pr 18; ☯ 24hr); Leonova (Leonova 59; mains R150-300; ☯ 11am-6am) Twenty four–hour Japanese food in once restaurant-starved Kaliningrad? You betcha. Not quite authentic, but not bad for the price. It has an English-picture menu.

**Solnechny Kamen** (pl Vasilevskogo 3; mains R150-500) Although the food is good (if a bit expensive), the main attraction is the atrium dining area overlooking Prud Verkhny. It's located inside Rossgarten Gate.

**12 Chairs Art Club** (pr Mira 67; mains R200-400; ☯ noon-1am) A masterpiece of cosy interior design, this dimly lit basement maze emanates class from every antique-filled nook. From the service to the scrumptious house specialities to the mouth-watering dessert menu highlighted by chocolate fondue, they get it all right here.

Self-caterers should visit the following supermarkets:
**Viktoriya** (ul 9-go Aprela 9; ☯ 9am-midnight) Large Western-style supermarket.
**Vester** (Leninsky pr 16; ☯ 10am-9pm)

## Drinking

**Reduit** ( ☎ 469 401; Litovsky Val 27; mains R200; ☯ noon-midnight) Freshly brewed beer fills pint glasses and flavours many of the food recipes at this brewpub in one of the old city defence bastions near Korolevskie Vorota. Unfiltered (R70) is the way forward. A guided beer tasting/fortress tour costs R170 – call ahead to reserve.

## Entertainment

**Kaliningrad Oblast Drama Theatre** ( ☎ 212 422; pr Mira 4; admission R100-180; ☯ box office 10am-7pm) Plays, classical concerts and other events are regularly staged here. Pick up the schedule at the box office.

**Kaliningrad Cathedral** ( ☎ 272 583; Tsentralny Ostrov) The Kaliningrad Chamber Choir holds concerts in a small room upstairs every Tuesday and Saturday at 4pm (admission R50). The newly restored main hall hosts concerts.

**Philharmonic Hall** ( ☎ 448 890; ul Bogdana Khmelnitskogo 61a; admission from R30) Boasting excellent acoustics, this beautifully restored neo-

Gothic church hosts organ concerts, chamber music recitals and the occasional symphony orchestra.

### NIGHTCLUBS

Kaliningrad's nightclubs often draw top DJs from Moscow and Western Europe. The big clubs loudly announce upcoming events on banners lining Leninsky pr and other major arteries. Most clubs besides Planeta tend to be either quiet or closed on weekdays.

**Universal** ( ☎ 952 996; www.club-universal.com; pr Mira 43; admission from R300) You gotta love a place where the bartenders wear (unedited) miniskirts with 'bar stuff' written across the bum. Nevertheless, it's Kaliningrad's classiest club and, unlike many places, won't leave you feeling way, way too old.

**Vagonka** ( ☎ 956 677; Stanochnaya ul 12; admission from R150) Located west of Kalinin Park, this one's not easy to find, but it's the best option for the under-21 crowd and drinks are cheap (R60 pints and R40 vodka shots).

**Planeta** ( ☎ 533 809; ul Chernyakhovskogo 26; admission Mon-Fri R150, Sat & Sun R400) Your one-stop shop for all things hedonistic goes off until the wee hours every night of the week. Upstairs is the glitzy nightclub proper, while downstairs an older crowd gets decidedly ugly dancing to Russian hits in the more intimate confines of the Diky Diuk restaurant.

**Amsterdam** (38/11 Litovsky Val; ☺ 8am-2am Sun-Thu, 8am-6am Fri & Sat) Kaliningrad's only gay club is hidden 200m down an unnamed sidestreet off Litovsky Val.

## Getting There & Away

### AIR

Kaliningrad's Khrabrovo **domestic** ( ☎ 355 083) and **international** ( ☎ 355 095) airports are 24km north of the city near Khrabovo village. For international connections, see p745. **Aeroflot** ( ☎ 916 455; pl Pobedy 4) has two to four daily flights to Moscow (from R2000 one way, 1¾ hours) and **Pulkovo Airlines** ( ☎ 716 663; pl Pobedy 4) has one to two daily flights to St Petersburg (from R2800 one way, 1½ hours). **Kaliningrad Airlines** ( ☎ 466 066; pl Kalinina 1) flies twice daily to Moscow and thrice weekly to St Petersburg.

### BUS

The **bus station** ( ☎ 443 635, international tickets ☎ 446 261; pl Kalinina) is next to the Yuzhny Vokzal (South Station). International destinations served: Klaipėda (R183, three hours, four

daily), Kaunas/Vilnius (R300/450, six/eight hours, twice daily), Rīga (R500, nine hours, twice daily), Tallinn (R800, 14 hours, daily), Olshtyn/Gdansk (R270/320, four/five hours, twice daily) and Warsaw (R450, nine hours, daily). **König Auto** ( ☎ 460 304) has several buses weekly to Berlin and other German cities.

The best way to Svetlogorsk and Zelenogradsk is via microbus or bus from the bus stop next to the Severny Vokzal (North Station) on Sovetsky pr. They run about every 15 minutes or so until about 8pm (microbus/bus to Zelenogradsk R25/30, 45/35 minutes; to Svetlogorsk R35/40, 60/45 minutes). All other domestic bus routes originate from the main bus station.

### CAR & MOTORCYCLE

There are three border crossings from Poland and four from Lithuania; the lines at the Lithuanian borders are not as monstrous.

### TRAIN

There are two stations in the city: **Severny Vokzal** (North Station; ☎ 601 838) and the larger **Yuzhny Vokzal** (South Station; ☎ 499 991). All long-distance and many local trains go from Yuzhny Vokzal, passing through but not always stopping at Severny Vokzal.

There are at least three daily trains to Vilnius (R550, six hours), at least one daily to Moscow (R950, 23 hours), one daily to Berlin (R2600, 15 hours), and one every second day to both Kyiv (R1200, 25 hours) and St Petersburg (R800, 26 hours).

Local trains include 12 daily to Svetlogorsk (R42, one hour), six daily to Zelenogradsk (R35, 45 minutes), and two daily to both Chernyakhovsk (R70, two hours) and Sovetsk (R100, three hours).

## Getting Around

### TO/FROM THE AIRPORT

To get to the domestic airport, take bus 128 from the bus station (R50, one hour, hourly). You have to take a taxi for the final 3km from the domestic airport to the international airport. Taxis ask at least R400 for the ride from the airport to the city centre, but it's cheaper going in the other direction (to the airport).

### PUBLIC TRANSPORT

Tickets for trams, trolleybuses, buses and microbuses are sold only by controllers on board (R6 to R7 within the city).

## SVETLOGORSK СВЕТЛОГОРСК

☎ within the region 53, from elsewhere 40153
pop 13,000

This sleepy beach town with some impressive Prussian-era half-timbered mansions makes an easy day trip from Kaliningrad. You can bag rays on the long, narrow beach or stroll along the promenade that separates the beach from the steep, sandy slopes that lead up to the town. Other favourite pastimes include amber shopping along the main drag, ul Lenina, and enjoying a lazy lunch with a view at one of several beachside eateries. Pick up a town map at any kiosk.

The town's main attraction are the gallant wooden houses in the tranquil residential neighbourhood east of the town centre. After WWII the Soviets confiscated these houses from their original owners and many became dachas for elite apparatchiks. From the water tower on ul Oktyabrskaya, walk east and you'll soon come to the quaint, half-timbered **Makar Organ Hall** ( ☎ 21761; ul Kurortnaya 3) in a converted stable. You can hear concerts of Bach, Handel and others throughout the week. Most begin at 5pm.

About 200m east of the main beach promenade is an impressive, colourful **sundial**, believed to be the largest in Europe. You can hire **bicycles** (per hr R40) on ul Leninska 100m east of ul Oktyabrskaya.

**Stary Doktor** ( ☎ 21362; www.alter-doctor.ru; ul Gagarina 12; s/d R1550/1850; ℗ ), in a beautiful German mansion, has tastefully austere rooms and a good restaurant. Beachfront **Hotel Grand Palace** ( ☎ 21655; www.grandhotel.ru; s/d from R5200/6900; ✖ 🖥 🕭 ) is the fanciest hotel in all of Kaliningrad, with lavish furnishings and a big plasma TV in every room; it also has wheelchair access.

If sitting outdoors at one of the many streetside eating spots on ul Leninska munching on *shashlyk* (chicken/pork R75/80), drinking *pivo* (R25) and listening to cheesy Russian pop doesn't make you happy, you're in the wrong country. Down by the beach, **Taverna Dom Rybaka** (Beregovaya 16; mains R200-300; ✖ ) has a great outdoor patio and serves tasty seafood.

### Getting There & Away

The best way to get to Svetlogorsk is via microbus or bus from the bus stop next to Kaliningrad's Severny Vokzal (North Station) on Sovetsky pr. They run every 15 minutes or so until about 8pm (bus/microbus R35/40, 60/45

minutes). Trains run approximately hourly from 8am to 9pm (to North Station R35, one hour; to South Station R40, 1¼ hours).

## KURSHKAYA KOSA NATIONAL PARK КУРШКАЯ КОСА

☎ within the region 50, from elsewhere 40150

The 98km-long Kurshkaya Kosa (Curonian Spit) is a remote and dramatic landscape with high sand dunes, pine forests, an exposed western coast and a calm lagoon that is shared by Russia and Lithuania. A Unesco World Heritage site, it's a paradise for elk, birds, and intrepid travellers who like to get way off the beaten track.

The Russian half of the Kurshkaya Kosa has far fewer services than the Lithuanian side, which is part of its appeal. You're not allowed to walk on the dunes, so access to the coast is mainly from the spit's three main towns – Lesnoy, Rybachy and, furthest north, Morskoye.

The best way for adventurers to experience the spit is on bike. You can hire bikes at the National Park's **Ecotourism Information Centre** ( ☎ 45275; Tsentralnaya ul 26) in Lesnoy, which also organises ecologically friendly excursions.

The **Kurshkaya Kosa National Park** ( ☎ 41346; www.kurshkayakosa.ru; Lesnaya ul 7; ☺ 8am-5pm Mon-Fri) is headquartered in Rybachy, but its **bird-ringing centre**, 7km north of Lesnoy, is the spit's main highlight. Massive bird-trapping nets (one is 15m high, 30m wide and 70m long) trap an average of 1000 birds a day for tagging.

To get to Kurshkaya Kosa, take a bus from Kaliningrad to Zelenogradsk (see p739), then hop on a northbound bus (about seven daily) or hire a taxi (R300/500/600 to Lesnoy/Rybachy/Morskoye).

# RUSSIA DIRECTORY

## ACCOMMODATION

Prices in this chapter are listed in budget order (from cheapest to most expensive). Budget accommodation is still hard to come by in Russia, and you are strongly recommended to book ahead during summer. During the white nights in St Petersburg in late June, booking early is essential. In this chapter, Budget is anything under R2000 per double per night, mid-range is R2000 to R12,000 per double per night, and Top End anything more than R12,000.

Both Moscow and St Petersburg have a number of well-established and reliable youth hostels, significantly more expensive than in most countries (budget beds cost €25 per night). Hotels start from about €35, although these are mainly fairly shabby Intourist relics. More independent and even boutique hotels are opening up and things are improving.

## BUSINESS HOURS

Russians work from early in the morning until the midafternoon. Shops usually open between 9am and 11am and often stay open until 8pm or 9pm. Banks have more traditional opening hours – usually 9am to 6pm Monday to Friday. Bars and restaurants will often work later than their stated hours if the establishment is full. In fact, many simply say that they work *do poslednnogo klienta* (until the last customer leaves).

## CHILDREN

While Russia isn't an obvious place to take children, there's more than you might expect for them to get out of a visit. In Moscow, **Gorky Park** (Krymsky Val; dawn-dusk; Park Kultury) is the obvious choice, where there's always plenty to do. You'll find fairground attractions, boats on the small lakes and plenty of other activities including a large ferris wheel.

The sprawling **Moscow Zoo** (Map pp702-3; 495-255 6034; www.zoo.ru; Bolshaya Gruzinskaya ul 1; adult/under 18yr R80/free; 9am-8pm Tue-Sun summer, 9am-5pm winter; Barrikadnaya) is also worth a visit. In St Petersburg the ghoulish freak show at the Kunstkamera (Museum of Anthropology & Ethnography; p726) is great fun for older kids, although younger ones may find its mutants rather upsetting. The **Alexandrovsky Park** (Map pp720-1; Kropnverksky Pr; 24hr; Petrogradskaya) behind the Peter & Paul Fortress has fairground rides, a small zoo and other activities that kids will enjoy.

## CUSTOMS

Customs controls in Russia are relatively relaxed these days and bag searches beyond the perfunctory are quite rare. Apart from the usual limits, bringing in and out large amounts of cash is restricted, although the amount at which you have to go through the red channel changes frequently. At the time of writing it was US$10,000.

On entering Russia you'll be given a *deklaratsiya* (customs declaration), which you should fill out with a list of any currency you're carrying plus any items of worth. You should list mobile phones, cameras and laptops to avoid any potential problems upon leaving Russia.

It's best if you can get your declaration stamped on entry and then simply show the same declaration when you exit Russia. However, sometimes customs points are totally unmanned, so it's not always possible. The system seems to be in total flux, with officials usually very happy for you to fill out exit declarations on leaving the country if necessary.

## DANGERS & ANNOYANCES

Despite the media fascination with gangland killings and the 'Russian mafia', travellers have nothing to fear on this score – the increasingly respectable gangster classes are not interested in such small fry. Travellers need to be very careful of pickpockets, though – most foreigners stand out a mile in Russia and, while this is no problem in itself, there's inevitably an increased chance you'll be targeted. Also be aware that there are some local gangs that can surround and rob travellers quite brazenly in broad daylight, although these are rare.

Bear in mind that, while things have improved slowly, many police officers and other uniformed officials are on the make – some are not much better than the people they are employed to protect the public from. Never allow them to go through your wallet or pockets, as you may find something is missing later on. If you feel you are being unfairly treated or the police try to make you go somewhere with them, pull out your mobile phone and threaten to call your embassy (*'ya pozvonyu svoyu posolstvu'*). This will usually be sufficient to make them leave you alone. However, if they still want you to go somewhere, it's best to call your embassy immediately.

There's a nasty skinhead tradition of attacking nonwhite people on Hitler's birthday (20 April). This should not cause undue concern to travellers, as targets are nearly always unfortunate people from the Caucasus, but nonwhite travellers should be aware of this disgusting behaviour, despite the very small chance of anything happening to them.

## DISABLED TRAVELLERS

Disabled travellers aren't well catered for in Russia. There's a lack of access ramps and lifts for wheelchairs. However, attitudes are enlightened, and things are slowly changing. Major museums, such as the Hermitage and the Russian Museum, offer very good disabled access.

# EMBASSIES & CONSULATES
## Russian Embassies & Consulates
Check the **Russian Federation Embassy & Consulate Locator** (www.russianembassy.net) for more listings of Russian embassies abroad. The following addresses are of consular sections where visas can be obtained.

**Australia** ( ☎ 02-9326 1188; www.australia.mid.ru; 7 Fullerton St, Woollahra, NSW 2025)

**Canada** ( ☎ 613-236 7220; www.rusembcanada.mid.ru; 52 Range Rd, Ottawa, Ontario, K1N 8J5)

**Finland** ( ☎ 09-661 877; www.helsinki.rusembassy.org; Tehtaankatu 1B, FIN-00140 Helsinki)

**Germany** ( ☎ 030/22-65-11-84; www.russische-botschaft.de; Behrenstr 66, 10117 Berlin)

**UK** ( ☎ 020-7229 8027, visa information message 0891-171 271; www.rusemblon.org; 5 Kensington Palace Gardens, London W8 4QS)

**USA** ( ☎ 202-939 8907; www.russianembassy.org; 2641 Tunlaw Rd NW, Washington, DC 20007)

## Embassies in Moscow
**Australia** (Map pp702-3; ☎ 495-956 6070; www.australianembassy.ru; Kropotkinsky per 2;  Ⓜ Kropotkinskaya)

**Belarus** (Map pp702-3; ☎ 495-924 7031; fax 095-928 6633; Maroseyka ul 17/6, 101000 Moscow;  Ⓜ Krasnye Vorota)

**Canada** (Map pp702-3; ☎ 495-105 6000; fax 105 6025; Starokonyushenny per 23;  Ⓜ Kropotkinskaya)

**France** ( ☎ 495-937 1500; www.ambafrance.ru; ul Bolshaya Yakimanka 45;  Ⓜ Oktyabrskaya)

**Germany** ( ☎ 495-937 9500; www.moskau.diplo.de; ul Mosfilmovskaya 56;  Ⓜ Park Pobedy)

**Netherlands** (Map pp702-3; ☎ 495-797 2900; www.netherlands-embassy.ru; Kalashny per 6;  Ⓜ Arbatskaya)

**New Zealand** (Map pp702-3; ☎ 495-956 3579; www.nzembassy.msk.ru; ul Povarskaya 44;  Ⓜ Barrikadnaya)

**UK** (Map pp702-3; ☎ 495-956 7200; fax 956 7201; Smolenskaya nab 10;  Ⓜ Smolenskaya)

**Ukraine** ( ☎ 495-229 1079; emb_ru@mfa.gov.ua; Leontevsky pereulok 18;  Ⓜ Pushkinskaya)

**USA** (Map pp702-3; ☎ 495-728 5000; www.moscow.usembassy.com; Bolshoy Devyatinsky per 8;  Ⓜ Barrikadnaya)

## Consulates in St Petersburg
**Australia** (Map p724; ☎ 812-325 7333; www.australianembassy.ru; Italyanskaya ul 1;  Ⓜ Nevsky Pr)

**Canada** (Map pp720-1; ☎ 812-325 8448; fax 325 8393; Malodetskoselsky pr 32B;  Ⓜ Tekhnologichesky Institut)

**France** (Map pp720-1; ☎ 812-332 2270; www.consulfrance-saint-petersbourg.org; nab reki Moyki 15;  Ⓜ Nevsky Pr)

**Germany** (Map pp720-1; ☎ 812-320 2400; www.sankt-petersburg.diplo.de; Furshtadtskaya ul 39;  Ⓜ Chernyshevskaya)

**UK** (Map pp720-1; ☎ 812-320 3200; www.britain.spb.ru; pl Proletarskoy Diktatury 5;  Ⓜ Chernyshevskaya)

**USA** (Map pp720-1; ☎ 812-331 2600; www.stpetersburg-usconsulate.ru; ul Furshtadtskaya 15;  Ⓜ Chernyshevskaya)

## Consulates in Kaliningrad
**Denmark** ( ☎ 401-2-716 868; 4th fl, pl Pobedy 4)

**Lithuania** ( ☎ 401-2-957 688; ul Proletarskaya 133)

**Poland** ( ☎ 401-2-950 419; Kashtanovaya alleya 51)

**Sweden** ( ☎ 401-2-959 400; ul Kutuzova 29)

# GAY & LESBIAN TRAVELLERS
Homosexuality was legalised in Russia in the early 1990s but remains a divisive issue throughout the country. Young people have a fairly relaxed attitude towards both gay and lesbian relationships, especially in Moscow and St Petersburg – by far the most cosmopolitan cities in the country. But attempts in the Duma as recently as 2002 to ban homosexuality altogether reflect the strong conservative traditionalism of many older Russians who see homosexuality as some kind of Western import. In 2006 ultra-right-wing groups backed by extremists from the Russian Orthodox Church attacked clubbers attempting to go to a gay night in Moscow, although luckily only a few people were hurt. In the same year Moscow Mayor Yuri Luzhkov illegally refused to even consider an application by gay groups to stage Russia's first ever gay pride march. There's still a long way to go, although on a practical level most same-sex couples will have no trouble booking a double room in a hotel.

# HOLIDAYS
Following are Russia's main public holidays:
**New Year's Day** 1 January
**Russian Orthodox Christmas Day** 7 January
**International Women's Day** 8 March
**International Labour Day/Spring Festival** 1 & 2 May
**Victory (1945) Day** 9 May
**Russian Independence Day** 12 Jun
**Day of Reconciliation and Accord (the rebranded Revolution Day)** 7 Nov

Other days that are widely celebrated are Defenders of the Motherland Day (23 February), Easter Monday and Constitution Day (12 December).

## INTERNET RESOURCES

There is a huge amount of travel information about Russia on the internet. The most up-to-date and accessible news sites are **Moscow Times** (www.themoscowtimes.com) and the **St Petersburg Times** (www.sptimesrussia.com), while **The Exile** (www.exile.ru) offers far more trenchant analysis of what's going on in the country's corrupt political landscape.

For specific and current tourist guides for St Petersburg and Kaliningrad (but oddly, not Moscow) see **In Your Pocket** (www.inyourpocket .com), which is updated monthly and includes the latest information on hotels, restaurants and nightlife. One of the best general sites for visitors is the excellent **Way To Russia.Net** (www .waytorussia.net), an online information portal with up-to-the-minute visa and travel information, listings for bars and clubs, travel tips, and background on Russia and its culture.

For those planning railway trips in Russia and the former Soviet Union, **Your Train** (www .poezda.net) is an invaluable resource, with a fully updated rail timetable uploaded to assist with planning any trip, as well as an online booking system to help you avoid the queues at train stations.

## LANGUAGE

Russian is spoken – not to mention written – everywhere. Young people usually speak some broken English, but generally knowledge of foreign languages is very low. After English, German is the most commonly understood language. It's pretty easy to pick up some basic Russian phrases, although what will really improve your enjoyment of Russia is making an effort to learn the (surprisingly easy) Cyrillic alphabet (see p960). Without it, you'll find everything extremely hard work.

## MEDIA

The Russian media has been the subject of an intense power struggle since the beginning of Putin's era in power. Seeking to claw back the control of the media lost since the end of communism, the Kremlin has been accused of illegally taking control of certain media groups that were critical of the government.

The most spectacular example of this was the takeover of national channel NTV by the Kremlin in 2001. Most Russian media outlets today are controlled by either the government or oligarchs with their own agenda.

## Magazines

There is a huge range of magazines on sale in Russia – many Western titles such as *Vogue* and *Elle* have their own Russian editions, and there is also plenty of homegrown talent. *Itogi* is the Russian equivalent to the *Economist* and has some very interesting news analysis pieces.

## Newspapers

The tabloid is king in the new Russia, as pioneered by the weekly *Argumenti I Fakti* and also *Moskovsky Komsomolets,* the trashy, huge-selling daily that has defined post-communist Russia's fascination with the grubby celebrity classes of the Russian showbiz world. Far better for news and analysis are *Izvestia, Kommersant* and *Vedomsti* (affiliated with the *Financial Times* and *Wall Street Journal*). The *Moscow Times,* a free English-language daily, has built its reputation on healthy scepticism of the Kremlin and pioneering investigative writing. It's twice-weekly sister paper, the *St Petersburg Times,* is the best source of local news from Russia's second city.

## Radio

The Moscow station *Ekho Moskvy* (Echo of Moscow) is the only independent station in the country and has a huge following. Other Russian stations have a huge amount of advertising and are of negligible quality.

## TV

The state-run ORT is the government mouthpiece and has been slowly raising broadcasting standards over the past decade to match NTV and RTR, its two main commercial rivals. A huge number of channels broadcast regionally as well. Other national channels include Kultura (the culture channel, showing highbrow documentaries, films and concerts) and the ultraglossy MTV Russia, which has been broadcasting in Russia since 1998, showing a mix of Russian and Western pop music.

## MONEY

The currency in Russia is the rouble, which is made up of 100 kopeks. Notes come in denominations of 5000, 1000, 500, 100, 50 and 10 roubles; coins come in five-, two- and one-rouble, and 50- and 10-kopek denominations. You can use all major credit and debit cards (including Cirrus and Maestro) in ATMs, and in good restaurants and hotels. It's possible to exchange travellers cheques, although at a price. Euro or US dollar cash is the best to bring, and in general should be in pristine condition – crumpled or old notes are often refused. Most major currencies can be exchanged at change booths all over any town in Russia. Look for the sign *obmen valyut*. You may be asked for your passport.

## POST

The Russian postal service gets an unfair rap. Postcards, letters and parcels sent abroad usually arrive within a couple of weeks, but there are occasional lapses. A postcard to anywhere in the world costs R17 and a letter R20.

## TELEPHONE

The international code for Russia is ☎ 7. The international access code from normal phones in Russia is ☎ 8, followed by 10 after the second tone, followed by the country code. From mobile phones, however, just dial +[country code] to place an international call.

## TRAVEL AGENCIES

Independent travellers may need to use travel agents to secure visa invitations (see right) and to book internal travel, as without Russian-language skills this can sometimes be tricky to organise yourself if you want to arrange more than a simple train or plane ticket. The following services are recommended:

**IntelService Center USA** ( ☎ 1-800 339 2118; www .intelservice.ru; 1227 Monterey St, Pittsburgh, PA 15212) With offices in both the US and Moscow, the IntelService Center has plenty of experience in organising travel in Russia. As well as visa invitations, it can arrange discounted hotel rates and tours.

**Travel Document Systems** ( ☎ 1-800 874 5100; www .traveldocs.com; 925 15th St NW, Ste 300, Washington, DC 20005) The Washington-based TDS deals exclusively in visa documentation and can fax visa invitations anywhere in the world.

**Way to Russia** (www.waytorussia.net) An entirely online travel agency, this Russian-based website is probably the ultimate resource for travellers. Some of the best visa support and most up-to-date information can be found here. Highly recommended.

---

**EMERGENCY NUMBERS**

- Fire ☎ 01
- Police ☎ 02
- Ambulance ☎ 03

---

## VISAS

Everyone needs a visa to visit Russia, and it will probably be your biggest single headache, so allow yourself at least a month before you travel to secure one. There are several types of visa, but most travellers will apply for a tourist visa, valid for 30 days from the date of entry. Your visa process has three stages – invitation, application and registration.

First of all you need an invitation. For a small fee (usually around €30) most hotels and hostels will issue an invitation (or 'visa support') to anyone staying with them. The invitation then allows you to apply for a visa at any Russian embassy. Costs can vary enormously, from $20 to $200 for same-day service, so try to plan as far ahead as possible. If you're not staying in a hotel or hostel, you'll need to buy an invitation. This can be done through almost any travel agent dealing with Russia.

On arrival you will need to fill out a *migratsionnaya karta* (migration card) – a long white form issued at passport control throughout the country. You surrender one half of the form immediately to the passport control and keep the other for the duration of your stay, giving it up only when you exit Russia. It is essential that you don't lose this, as leaving Russia without it will be an expensive nightmare. Some hotels will not accept travellers without one either.

Finally, once you arrive in Russia you are – officially at least – obliged to register your visa within three working days. This can nearly always be done by your hotel or hostel, but if you are not staying in one, you will need to pay a travel agency (usually $30) to register it for you. Not registering your visa is a gamble – some travellers report leaving Russia unhindered without registration, but officially you are liable to large fines. It's best not to take chances.

## WOMEN TRAVELLERS

The most common problem faced by foreign women in Russia is sexual harassment. It can be quite common to be propositioned in public, especially if you are walking alone at night. Unpleasant as it may be, this is rarely dangerous and a simple '*kak vam ne stydno*' ('you should be ashamed of yourself') delivered in a suitably stern manner should send anyone on their way.

That said, Russian men are generally extremely polite, and will open doors, give up their seats and wherever possible help any female out to a far greater degree than their Western counterparts. Women are also very independent, and you won't attract attention by travelling alone as a female.

# TRANSPORT IN RUSSIA

## GETTING THERE & AWAY
### Air

Moscow's three international airports are modern **Domodedovo Airport** (DME; ☎ 933 6666; www.domodedovo.ru), crappy Soviet-era relic **Sheremetyevo Airport** (SVO; ☎ 232 6565; www.sheremetyevo-airport.ru) and recently done up **Vnukovo Airport** (VKO; ☎ 436 2813; www.vnukovo.ru). Between them Moscow is connected to nearly all European capitals, New York, Washington, Los Angeles, Beijing, Tokyo, Hong Kong, Singapore and Delhi.

St Petersburg's recently renovated **Pulkovo-2 Airport** (LED; ☎ 704 3444; www.pulkovo.ru) is the city's international gateway. It's not as well connected as Moscow, but has regular connections throughout Europe, including Prague.

Kaliningrad's **Khrabrovo International Airport** (KGD; ☎ 4012-355 083) has daily flights to Warsaw on **LOT Airlines** (Leninsky pr 5).

The following list of carriers fly to/from Russia. Telephone numbers are included as applicable for Moscow (prefixed 495), St Petersburg (812) and Kaliningrad (401).
**Aeroflot** (code SU; ☎ 495-223 5555; 812-327 3872, 401-2-916 455; www.aeroflot.com)
**Air France** (code AF; ☎ 495-937 3839, 812-336 2900; www.airfrance.com)
**American Airlines** (code AA; ☎ 495-234 4074/5/6; www.aa.com)
**Austrian Airlines** (code OS; ☎ 495-995 0995, 812-331 2005; www.aua.com)
**British Airways** (code BA; ☎ 495-363 2525, 812-380 0626; www.ba.com)
**ČSA** (code OK; ☎ 495-737 6637, 812-315 5259; www .czechairlines.com)
**Delta Airlines** (code DL; ☎ 495-937 9090, 812-117 5820; www.delta.com)
**Finnair** (code AY; ☎ 495-933 0056, 812-303 9898; www.finnair.com)
**Germania Express** (code ST; www.gexx.de) Web-based sales only.
**Japan Airlines** (code JL; ☎ 495-730 3070; www.jal.com)
**Kaliningrad Airlines** (code K8; ☎ 401-2-355 095)
**KLM** (code KL; ☎ 495-258 3600, 812-346 6868; www.klm .com)

**LOT** (code LO; ☎ 495-775 7737, 812-273 5721, 401-2-342 707; www.lot.com)
**Lufthansa** (code LH; ☎ 495-737 6400, 812-320 1000; www.lufthansa.com)
**Pulkovo Airlines** (code FV; ☎ 495-299 1940, 812-303 9268, 401-2-716 663; www.pulkovo.ru)
**SAS Scandinavian Airlines** (code SK; ☎ 495-775 4747, 812-326 2600; www.scandinavian.net)
**Siberia Airlines** (code S7; ☎ 495-777 9999, 812-718 8676; www.s7.ru)
**Transaero Airlines** (code UN; ☎ 495-788 8080; www .transaero.ru)

### Land
#### BORDER CROSSINGS
The Russian Federation has a huge number of border crossings, adjoining as it does some 13 countries. From Eastern Europe you are most likely to enter from Finland at Vyborg, Estonia at Narva, Latvia at Rēzekne, Belarus at Krasnoye or Ezjaryshcha, and Ukraine at Chernihiv. You can enter Kaliningrad from Lithuania and Poland at any of six border posts. If you're going west to Europe through Belarus, note that you do need a transit visa and you must obtain it in advance; see p95 for details.

### Sea
St Petersburg has regular ferries from Helsinki, Tallinn and Rostok (in Germany). They are a slow and not particularly cheap method of transport. Tickets can be bought at the sea port (Morskoy Vokzal) and through the **Paromny Tsentr** (Map p724; ☎ 812-327 3377; www .paromy.ru, in Russian; ul Vosstaniya 19; Ⓜ Pl Vosstaniya), which sells tickets on all ferries. Prices for St Petersburg–Tallinn begin at R1500 for an armchair and at R2300 for a bed in a four-berth cabin.

## GETTING AROUND
### Air
In a country of Russia's size, travelling by air is often the only reasonable way to get around. Flights link nearly every city in Russia to Moscow, and most to St Petersburg.

When flying, reckon on paying two to three times the train fare for the same journey. Flights between Moscow and St Petersburg go every hour, and a seat costs from R1300/2400 (one way/return).

You can buy tickets at any *aviakassa* (air ticket office), at travel agents or directly from the airlines (see left).

## Bus

The cheapest way to get around Russia is by bus. The enormous size of the country makes it rather unappealing, but for short trips from major cities it can be faster than the train and there are more regular connections. Some sample costs are R515 (Moscow–St Petersburg) and R170 (St Petersburg–Novgorod).

### RESERVATIONS

There's almost no need to reserve a seat, and in most places it's impossible anyway. Just arrive a good 30 minutes to one hour before the departure is scheduled and buy a ticket.

The long-distance bus stations are at the following addresses:

**Avtovokzal No 2** (Map pp720-1; ☎ 812-166 5777; nab Obvodnogo Kanala 36, St Petersburg; Ⓜ Ligovsky Pr)

**Bus station** ( ☎ 4012-443 635, international tickets 446 261; pl Kalinina, Kaliningrad)

**Shchyolkovskaya Avtovokzal** (Shchyolkovskaya Bus Station; ☎ 495-468 0400; Shchyolkovskoye shosse 2, Moscow; Ⓜ Shchyolkovskaya)

## Car & Motorcycle

It's perfectly possible to bring your own vehicle into Russia, but expect delays, bureaucracy and the attention of the roundly hated GAI (traffic police), who take particular delight in stopping foreign cars for document checks.

To enter Russia with a vehicle you will need a valid International Driving Permit, your passport, and the insurance and ownership documents for your car. *Benzin* (petrol) is no problem to find, although unleaded is still rare outside Moscow and St Petersburg. Avoid 76 petrol, and pay more for 95 or 98.

Driving in Russia is on the right-hand side, and traffic coming from the right has the right of way. Any amount of alcohol in your blood is likely to lead to complications if you are breathalysed. However, you have the right to demand a hospital blood test.

### HIRE

Hiring a car is far preferable to bringing your own vehicle into Russia. As you don't really need a car to get around big cities, they are mainly of use when making trips out of town where public transport may not be so good. All the major agencies have offices in Moscow and St Petersburg. Check out **Hertz** (www.hertz .com) and **Avis** (www.avis.com).

## Hitching & Unofficial Taxis

Hitching for free is something of an alien concept in Russia, but paying a small amount to be given a lift is a daily reality for millions. The system's honour code is so ingrained that drivers will often go to extraordinary lengths to get you to your destination. In cities you'll see people flagging down cars all the time; long-distance hitching is less common, but it's still acceptable if the price is right. Simply state your destination and ask '*skolko?*' (how much?). Obviously, use common sense: don't get into a car with more than one passenger and be careful if travelling alone at night.

## Train

Russia is crisscrossed with an extensive train network. Suburban or short-distance trains are called *elektrichkas* and do not require advance booking – you can buy your ticket at the *prigorodny poezd kassa* (suburban train ticket offices) at train stations. Long-distance services need to be booked in advance to guarantee a seat. See p938 for details of classes on Russian trains. Train travel is pricier than bus travel, but it's still perfectly affordable and far more comfortable. Prices between Moscow and St Petersburg in 2nd class begin at R500, going up to R1500 for the fast day trains.

### RESERVATIONS

You're advised to reserve at least 24 hours in advance for any long-distance journey. It's quite a bureaucratic process, so bring your passport (or a photocopy), as without it you'll be unable to buy tickets. You can buy tickets for others if you bring their passports or photocopies. Queues can be very long and move with interminable slowness. If you're in a hurry, go to the service centres that exist in most big train stations. Here you pay a R100 surcharge; thus, there are no queues. Alternatively most travel agents will organise the reservation and delivery of train tickets for a generous mark-up.

You can buy train tickets in all mainline train stations, and at the central reservation offices in both Moscow and St Petersburg.

**Moscow Central Train Booking Office** (Map pp702-3; ☎ 495-266 8333; Komsomolskaya pl 5; ◷ 9am-8pm Mon-Fri, 9am-5pm Sat & Sun; Ⓜ Komsomolskaya)

**St Petersburg Central Train Booking Office** (Map p724; ☎ 812-162 3344; nab Kanala Griboeedova 24; ◷ 8am-8pm Mon-Sat, 8am-4pm Sun; Ⓜ Nevsky Pr)

# Serbia Србија

SERBIA

Serbia (Srbija) is yet to come within most tourists' comfort zone, but having got rid of Slobodan Milošević and become a democracy, the nation is now knocking on the doors of Europe, and in the meantime is a safe and welcoming place to visit. The most exciting spot is undoubtedly its capital, Belgrade, a gritty, energetic city. Cultural buffs can revel in its architecture and museums, foodies in its restaurants, while party animals will get no rest exploring its incessant nightlife.

Vojvodina's flat plains and the tranquil Fruška Gora monasteries provide an effective antidote to urban chaos, while Novi Sad is home to the world-famous Exit music festival. Serbia's proud and traditional south is a land of lush rolling hills and wooded valleys brushing up against rugged mountains. The medieval monasteries of Manasija, Sopoćani and Studenica remain the keepers of Serbian faith and Byzantine art, while the mountains of Zlatibor and Kopaonik provide snow fun in winter and glorious hiking in summer. Mosques mix with monasteries in Novi Pazar, where life in the Turkish quarter continues much as it did a century ago when the Turks were still in power.

A few kilometres south lies Kosovo, a disputed land riven by different interpretations of history. For Serbs it is the cradle of their nationhood, for Kosovo Albanians it is their future independence. The UN still recognises Kosovo as part of Serbia until current talks decide its future.

---

## FAST FACTS

- **Area** 102,350 sq km
- **Capital** Serbia – Belgrade; Kosovo – Prishtina
- **Currency** Serbia – dinar (din): €1 = 88din; US$1 = 63din; UK£1 = 117din; A$1 = 47din; ¥100 = 58din; NZ$1 = 43din; Kosovo – euro: US$1 = €0.79; UK£1 = €1.47; A$1 = €0.59; ¥100 = €0.67; NZ$1 = €0.50
- **Famous for** Basketball players, Slobodan Milošević
- **Official Language** Serbia – Serbian; Kosovo – Albanian
- **Phrases** Serbian – *zdravo* (hello), *hvala* (thanks), *da* (yes), *ne* (no), *govorite li engleski?* (do you speak English?); Albanian – *allo* (hello), *ju falem nderit* (thanks), *po* (yes), *jo* (no), *a flisni Anglisht?* (do you speak English?)
- **Population** 7.5 million, excluding Kosovo (estimate 1.9 million)
- **Telephone Codes** ☎ 381 international access code ☎ 99
- **Visas** not required by most visitors, see p778

**SERBIA**

## HIGHLIGHTS

- Tap into Belgrade's infectious **party scene** (p760).
- Explore old Serbian villages and sip plum brandy with the locals around **Zlatibor** (p769).
- Gawk at the wondrous and ancient frescoes in central Serbia's **medieval monasteries** (p770).
- Wander around Turkish-influenced **Prizren** (p775), which is dominated by an old castle, and take in a mosque, baths and riverside bars and cafés.

## ITINERARIES

- **One week** Revel in Belgrade's attractions and take some day trips to Novi Sad, Topola, Smederevo and Manasija Monastery.
- **Two to three weeks** Add in Subotica, catch the bus or train to Užice, and enjoy the mountains and old Serbian villages around Zlatibor. From Novi Pazar the curious can slip into Kosovo.

## CLIMATE & WHEN TO GO

The north has a continental climate with relatively cold winters and hot summers. The upland regions have hot, dry summers and cold winters, while the mountain areas have heavy snowfalls. The ski season is generally from December to March.

## HISTORY

A nation is often shaped by external events. Serbia's history has been punctuated by foreign invasions, from the time the Celts supplanted the Illyrians in the 4th century BC, through to the arrival of the Romans 100 years later, the Slavs in the 6th century AD, the Turks in the 14th century, the Austro-Hungarians in the late 19th and early 20th

---

**HOW MUCH?**

- **Short taxi ride** Serbia/Kosovo150din/€2
- **Internet access** 60-100din/€1 per hour
- **Coffee** 75din/€1
- **Bottle of plum brandy** 600din/€7

**LONELY PLANET INDEX**

- **Litre of petrol** Serbia/Kosovo 82.50din/€0.95
- **Litre of bottled water** 70din/€1
- **Beer** 60-80din/€ 1
- **Souvenir T-shirt** Serbia 1000din
- **Street snack (slice of pizza)** 50din/€0.60

---

centuries, and the Germans briefly in WWII. A pivotal nation-shaping event occurred in AD 395 when the Roman Emperor Theodosius I divided his empire giving Serbia to the Byzantines, thereby locking the country into Eastern Europe. This was further cemented in 879 when Sts Cyril and Methodius converted the Serbs to the Orthodox religion.

Serbian independence briefly flowered from 1217 with a golden age during Stefan Dušan's reign (1346–55). After his death Serbia declined and at the pivotal Battle of Kosovo in 1389 the Turks defeated Serbia, ushering in 500 years of Islamic rule. Early revolts were crushed but one in 1815 led to de facto Serbian independence that became complete in 1878.

On 28 June 1914 Austria-Hungary used the assassination of Archduke Franz Ferdinand by a Bosnian Serb to invade Serbia, sparking WWI. In 1918 Croatia, Slovenia, Bosnia and Hercegovina, Vojvodina, Serbia and its Ko-

---

**MONEY MATTERS**

During the 1990s, economic sanctions and gross mishandling of the economy led to the worst hyperinflation in European history. Bank notes became so worthless that it was cheaper to use them to paper walls rather than buy wallpaper and, in the end, smaller notes were only printed on one side to save ink. At the height of inflation (330,000%), a 500-billion-dinar banknote was issued to replace a 50-billion-dinar note that had only been in circulation one week.

Many state industries couldn't pay their employees so they were paid in kind or issued worthless shares. Later, when a multinational bought up the local brewery in the small town of Apatin, the locals found their shares to be worth a fortune. Apatin is now one of the richest municipalities, per capita, in Serbia.

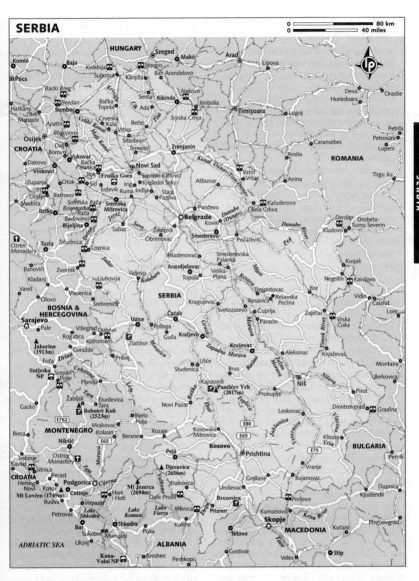

sovo province, Montenegro and Macedonia were joined together into the Kingdom of Serbs, Croats and Slovenes under the king of Serbia. This lengthy title remained until 1929 when the country became Yugoslavia (southern Slavs).

In March 1941 Yugoslavia joined the fascist Tripartite Alliance, which sparked a military coup and an abrupt withdrawal from the alliance; Germany's reaction was to bomb Belgrade. Rival resistance movements fought both each other and the Germans, with the communist partisans led by Josip Broz Tito gaining the upper hand. In 1945 they formed the government, abolished the monarchy and declared a federal republic, which included

## FOR SALE: ONE NAVY

Montenegro's vote for independence in May 2006 closes the book on Yugoslavia, a federation that lasted in various forms for 88 years. Montenegro's vote also means independence for Serbia, which less than a decade ago was led by a leader hell-bent on creating a greater Serbia. Now Serbia has shrunk to a shadow of its former self and will get smaller if Kosovo gains independence.

Serbia is now a landlocked country. What will it do with its navy, and will Montenegro give it port facilities at Bar? Probably some deal will be done, and regardless of the separation, Serbs will still flock to the Montenegrin coastline for holidays. Montenegrins would also like to continue their free access to medical and education services in Serbia.

Serbia and its autonomous provinces Kosovo and Vojvodina.

Tito broke with Stalin in 1948 and Yugoslavia became a nonaligned nation, albeit bolstered by Western aid. Within the nation, growing regional inequalities and burgeoning Serbian expansionism pushed demands by Slovenia, Croatia and Kosovo for more autonomy.

By 1986 Serbian nationalists were espousing a 'Greater Serbia' to encompass Serbs in the other republics. This doctrine was appropriated by Slobodan Milošević, Communist Party leader in Serbia, to attempt to dominate Yugoslavia. This horrified the other republics, which then had to fight bloody wars against the Serbian-controlled Yugoslav army to gain their independence.

In April 1992 the remaining republics, Serbia and Montenegro, formed a 'third' Yugoslav federation without any provision of autonomy for Kosovo. This was the latest event in a series of brutal repressions by Serbia of the majority Albanians in Kosovo and violence, largely provoked by the army and police, erupted in January 1998.

The West produced a storm of protest plus an arms embargo. In March 1999 peace talks in Paris failed when Serbia rejected a US-brokered peace plan. In response to organised resistance in Kosovo, Serbian forces moved to empty the country of its Albanian population. Hundreds of thousands fled into Macedonia and Albania, galvanising the US and NATO into a 78-day bombing campaign. On 12 June 1999 Serbian forces withdrew from Kosovo.

In the September 2000 presidential elections, the opposition parties, led by Vojislav Koštunica, declared victory but their claim was denounced by Milošević. Opposition supporters from all over the country swarmed to Belgrade, took over the streets and occupied parliament. When Russia then recognised Koštunica's win, it was all over for Milošević, who had to acknowledge defeat.

Koštunica restored ties with Europe, acknowledged Yugoslav atrocities in Kosovo and rejoined the UN. In April 2001 Milošević was arrested and extradited to the international war-crimes tribunal in The Hague.

In April 2002 a loose union of Serbia and Montenegro replaced Yugoslavia. The EU-brokered deal was intended to stabilise the region by accommodating Montenegrin demands for independence, but allowed for a referendum after three years. In May 2006 Montenegrins voted by 55.5% to leave the union.

In March 2003 Serbia's prime minister, Zoran Đinđić, was assassinated. He had been instrumental in extraditing Milošević and had been trying to get rid of criminal elements from politics and business. His alleged killers were crime bosses and Milošević-era paramilitary commanders.

Between 2003 and 2004 three attempts were made to elect a new president but they failed due to voter apathy. Parliamentary elections in December 2003 were inconclusive but saw a worrying resurgence of nationalism. Power-sharing deals installed Koštunica as head of a centre-right coalition relying on support from Milošević's Socialist Party. Finally, in June 2004, Serbia gained a new president in pro-European Boris Tadić.

On 11 March 2006 Milošević was found dead in his Hague cell, ending another chapter in the region's history. In the same month talks commenced on independence for Kosovo but these look headed for a stalemate. Serbia will give everything but independence and Kosovo Albanians want nothing but independence.

## PEOPLE

Serbia's 2002 census excluding Kosovo (estimate 1.9 million) revealed a population of 7.5 million. Ethnically Serbia (excluding Kosovo) is made up of 83% Serbs, 4% Hungarians, 2% Bosniaks, 1.5% Roma, 1% Albanians, 1%

**VOX POP**

*Who are you?* Nikola Vrzić, trained as an anthropologist but working part time as a video editor in Belgrade.

*What do you like best about Serbia?* Wait, I have to think about that.

*What would you like to change?* Mentality of the people, not to live in the past.

*Will you give up smoking?* In 10 years I suppose.

Montenegrins and 7.5% other groups. Vojvodina is more multicultural, with perhaps 28 ethnic groups and sizable populations of Hungarians, Slovaks and Romanians.

There are large Slavic Muslim and Albanian minorities in southern Serbia and about 10,000 Muslims live in Belgrade.

In Kosovo the minority Serbs (7%) live in ghettoes protected by Kosovo Force (KFOR).

## RELIGION

Religion and ethnicity broadly go together. About 65% of the population is Orthodox; Roman Catholics, who are Vojvodinan Hungarians, comprise 4%; Albanian Kosovars and Slavic Muslims make up 19%.

## ARTS
### Literature

Bosnian-born but a former Belgrade resident, Ivo Andrić was awarded the Nobel Prize for literature in 1961 for his *Bridge over the Drina.* Other books worthy of the traveller's perusal are *In the Hold,* by Vladimir Arsenijević; *Words Are Something Else,* by David Albahari; *Petrija's Wreath,* by Dragoslav Mihailović; and *Fear and its Servant,* by Mirjana Novaković.

### Cinema

The award-winning film *Underground,* by director Emir Kusturica, deals with Yugoslav history in a chaotic, colourful style. His latest film *Zivot Je Cudo* (Life Is a Miracle) is a dramatic story of a man who shuts his eyes to war and builds a scenic railway to attract tourists.

Bosnian director Danis Tanovic's *No Man's Land* deals superbly with an encounter between a Serbian soldier and a Bosnian soldier stuck in a trench on their own during the Bosnian war.

### Music

Serbia's vibrant dances are led by musicians playing bagpipes, flutes and fiddles. Kosovar music bears the deep imprint of five centuries of Turkish rule with high-whine flutes carrying the tune above the beat of a goatskin drum.

*Blehmuzika* (brass music influenced by Turkish and Austrian military music) has become the national music of Serbia, with an annual festival at Guča in August.

The modern music scene is fractured and covers everything from wild Roma music to house, techno, blues, jazz, drum'n'bass, or ethnic folk updated and crossed with techno, producing a variant that many call turbofolk.

**SINGING FOR EUROPE**

In 2004 Serbia and Montenegro entered the Eurovision Hall of Fame by coming second with a haunting love ballad by a Serbian group that blended Serbian and Turkish influences. That song, issuing forth from radios, cafés, bars and mobile phones, then proceeded to annoy everyone for the next three months.

The 2006 entry was to be decided through a televised contest in Belgrade, where a Serbian entry would compete against one from Montenegro. The Serbian audience took exception to the Montenegrin boy band – aptly titled 'No Name' – (as you would), and booed them off the stage after they were judged to be the winners. The Serbs accused the Montenegrin judges of tactical voting.

Several Montenegrin newspapers expressed their annoyance the next day by saying that the union between the two countries couldn't even work musically let alone politically. A former Serbian prime minister commented later that the event had caused more excitement than the death of Milošević on the same weekend.

In the end no agreement on who should represent the union could be reached and Serbia and Montenegro withdrew from the contest. Coincidently the Eurovision contest was held on the day before the Montenegrins decided that their future lay in independence.

## ENVIRONMENT

In the north of the country, Vojvodina is pancake-flat agricultural land. South of the Danube the landscape rises through rolling green hills that crest where the Dinaric Alps slice southeastwards across the country. Within these mountains is Kosovo, a lowland vale.

The highest mountain is Djeravica (2656m) in western Kosovo, and the mountain ranges of Zlatibor and Kopaonik are the country's major ski resorts.

Wild animals inhabiting the mountains include the lynx, wolf and brown bear but they avoid humans so visitors are unlikely to come across them.

The major national parks are Fruška Gora and Kopaonik, and Unesco-recognised sites are Sopoćani and Studenica monasteries.

Sewage pollution of river waters, air pollution around Belgrade and emissions from decaying industrial plants are the environmental issues the country has to face. The most likely remedy for these problems will come with eventual EU ascension, when strict new laws will come into force.

## FOOD & DRINK
### Staples & Specialities

A favourite cheap snack is *burek*, a greasy-pastry pie made with *sir* (cheese), *meso* (meat), *krompiruša* (potato) or occasionally *pecurke* (mushrooms); with yogurt it makes a good breakfast. *Čorba* (soup) or *ćevapčići* (grilled kebab) can make a filling midday meal.

Serbia is famous for its grilled meats, such as *ćevapčići*, *pljeskavica* (spicy hamburger), *ražnjići* (pork or veal kebabs) and *duveć* (grilled pork cutlets with spicy stewed peppers, courgettes and tomatoes on rice).

Regional cuisines range from spicy Hungarian goulash in Vojvodina, to Turkish kebab in Kosovo. In southern Serbia try *kajmak* (a salted cream turned to cheese).

*Pivo* (beer) is universally available. Many people distil their own *rakija* (brandy) out of plums and other fruit, and Montenegrin red wine, *venac* especially, is a rich drop.

Coffee is usually served Turkish-style, 'black as hell, strong as death and sweet as love'. Superb espresso and cappuccino is available at most cafés, restaurants and bars, and if you want regular tea, ask for Indian tea.

### Vegetarians & Vegans

Eating here is a trial for vegetarians and almost impossible for vegans. Try the following salads, which can be satisfying: *Srpska salata* (Serbian salad) containing raw peppers, onions and tomatoes, seasoned with oil and vinegar; and *šopska salata,* consisting of chopped tomatoes, cucumber and onion, topped with grated soft white cheese. Also ask for *gibanica* (cheese pie), *zeljanica* (cheese pie with spinach) or *pasulj prebranac* (a dish of cooked and spiced beans). If you eat fish there's plenty of seafood and trout. As always, there's the ubiquitous vegetarian pizza.

### Habits & Customs

Locals tend to skip breakfast and grab something on the way to work. Most people's work usually ends around 3.30pm, which becomes the time for lunch. This slides dinner back to 8pm, 9pm or 10pm if eating out.

# BELGRADE БЕОГРАД

☎ 011 / pop 1.58 million

Belgrade is not a beautiful city – even Belgraders agree on that – but it is an interesting city that's full of hedonism, passion and finesse. Architecturally, it's a mishmash of two centuries of grandiose buildings and ugly Soviet-style concrete blocks.

Regardless, the city holds some real gems. Perched between the Danube and Sava Rivers, the ancient Kalemegdan Citadel has always sought (not always successfully) to protect the city. Leading from it into the city heart is the princely Knez Mihailova, a street of restaurants, bookshops, galleries and shops full of pretty things. Belgraders love to shop and party, which probably developed as an antidote to the numbness of the Milošević years.

'Does anyone work here?' you wonder, as you roam streets full of people. Every day seems to be Saturday; and if every day is Saturday, then every night is Friday night, with plenty happening. Belgrade's ultimate appeal is its nightlife. There's always another place to go to: underground clubs, apartment bars, and floating bars and clubs on the rivers. Everyone is ready to party at any time, dance the night away and go straight to work the next day.

Cheap food and drink, plus a distinctive national cuisine, make for a host of decent

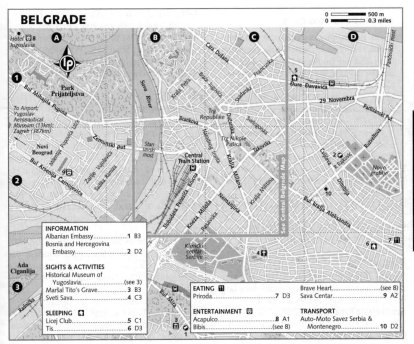

**BELGRADE**

0 ——— 500 m
0 ——— 0.3 miles

INFORMATION
Albanian Embassy....................1 B3
Bosnia and Hercegovina
   Embassy.............................2 D2

SIGHTS & ACTIVITIES
Historical Museum of
   Yugoslavia.......................(see 3)
Maršal Tito's Grave................3 B3
Sveti Sava.............................4 C3

SLEEPING 🏠
Licej Club............................5 C1
Tis.......................................6 D3

EATING 🍴
Priroda.................................7 D3

ENTERTAINMENT 🎭
Acapulco..............................8 A1
Bibis................................(see 8)

Brave Heart........................(see 8)
Sava Centar..........................9 A2

TRANSPORT
Auto-Moto Savez Serbia &
   Montenegro.....................10 D2

SERBIA

restaurants bursting with lively eaters. Just check out the bohemian quarter of Skadar-ska. When it all gets too much, there are places to escape to and relax. Ada Ciganlija swarms with swimmers during hot summer days, and the nearby park has forests to walk in.

## ORIENTATION
The central train station and two adjacent bus stations are on the southern side of the city centre. From a couple of blocks northeast, Terazije runs up to Trg Republike, the heart of Belgrade, from where Knez Mihailova, Belgrade's lively pedestrian boulevard, leads to the Kalemegdan Citadel.

## INFORMATION
### Bookshops
**Mamut** (Map p756; ☎ 639 060; cnr Knez Mihailova & Sremska; ☾ 9am-10pm Mon-Sat, noon-10pm Sun) Browsers heaven; books in English, CDs, DVDs, gifts and top-floor café.

**Plato Bookshop** (Map p756; ☎ 625 834; Knez Mihailova 48; ☾ 9-11am Mon-Sat, noon-11pm Sun) English literature, maps, books on Serbia and stationery.

### Internet Access
**SBB** (Map p756; ☎ 324 3177; per hr 80din; ☾ 9am-midnight Mon-Sat, 11am-midnight Sun) Located behind Makedonska 4.

**XPlato** (Map p756; ☎ 303 0633; Vase Čarapiča 19; per hr 100din; ☾ 9am-11.30pm)

### Internet Resources
**Belgrade City** (www.beograd.org.yu)
**Tourist Organisation of Belgrade** (www.belgrade tourism.org.yu)

### Laundry
**Wash Center** (Map p756; ☎ 306 5924; Admirala Geparta Br 3; ☾ 8am-8pm Mon-Sat) Washers and dryers; DIY laundry costs about 390din.

### Left Luggage
**Central train station** (Map p756; Savski Trg 2; per piece per day 90din)

### Medical Services
**Emergency Centre** (Map p756; ☎ 361 8444; Miloša Porcerca Pasterova 2; ☾ 24hr) Medical clinics.
**Prima 1** (Map p756; ☎ 361 0999; Nemanjina 2; ☾ 24hr) Pharmacy opposite train station.

---

**BELGRADE IN TWO DAYS**

Roam the mighty **Kalemegdan Citadel** (right), stroll through Knez Mihailova taking in a coffee on Trg Republike and checking out the sparks at the **Nikola Tesla Museum** (opposite). Explore the **Ethnographic Museum** (opposite), and take an aperitif at **Rezime** (p759) before dining out at **Šešir Moj** (p759) in Skadarska.

Have a peek at the mighty **Sveti Sava** (opposite) and **Sveti Marko** (opposite) in central Belgrade, then catch a bus to Zemun for a late lunch at **Reka** (p762). Rest up and then rev up with cocktails at **Ben Akiba** (p759) before clubbing at **Ana 4 Pistolja** (p760).

---

**Saski Venac Hospital** (Map p756; ☎ 361 9088; Pasterova 1; ⏲ 7am-7pm Mon-Fri)

## Money

More ATMs than your bank balance can manage. Exchange offices, recognisable by a large blue diamond sign, are widespread.

**Komercijalna Bank** (Map p756; ☎ 323 5087; Trg Nikole Pašića 2; ⏲ 8am-8pm Mon-Sat, 9am-3pm Sun) Busy bank with a useful Sunday opening; location is Terazije rather than Nikole Pašića, despite its address.

## Post

**Central post office** (Map p756; ☎ 363 3492; Zmaj Jovina 17; ⏲ 8am-7pm Mon-Sat)

## Telephone

**Telephone centre** (Map p756; ☎ 323 4484; Takovska 2; ⏲ 7am-midnight Mon-Fri, 7am-10pm Sat & Sun) In the post office by Sveti Marko church.

## Tourist Information

**Tourist Organisation of Belgrade** (Map p756; ☎ 324 8404; www.belgradetourism.org.yu; underpass; ⏲ 9am-8pm Mon-Fri, 9am-5pm Sat, 10am-4pm Sun) Friendly and knowledgeable outfit with useful brochures, city maps and a *Welcome to Belgrade* pamphlet.
**Yellow Cab** Events magazine (with some English) available at kiosks (90din).

## Travel Agencies

**Bas Turist** (Map p756; ☎ 263 6299, fax 784 859; BAS bus station) International buses.
**KSR Beograd Tours** (Map p756; ☎ 264 1258; fax 687 447; Milovana Milovanovića 5; ⏲ 8am-7pm Mon-Fri, 8am-3pm Sat) Train tickets and Eurail passes at station prices without the crowds.

**Lasta** (Map p756; ☎ 264 1251; www.lasta.co.yu; Milovana Milovanovića 1; ⏲ 7am-9pm) International buses.
**Wasteels** (Map p756; ☎ 265 8868; wasteels@eunet.yu; central train station, Savski Trg 2; ⏲ 9am-4pm Mon-Sat) Multilingual staff sell international train tickets, Eurail and Balkan flexipasses at station prices.

# SIGHTS
## Kalemegdan Citadel

Capture the hill protected by the junction of the Sava and Danube Rivers and you control the land to the south. This explains why there has been a fortified settlement here since Celtic times, but such prime real estate attracts enemies. Over the last 2300 years some 115 battles have been fought over this site, and parts of it and the outer city have been razed 44 times, as one conqueror removed another.

What remains today dates from the 18th century. The core of the fortifications is the Upper Citadel, accessed by several massive gates and bridges (now wooden) over deep moats.

The main entrance is the Stambol Gate, built by the Turks around 1750. This leads to the **Military Museum** (Map p756; ☎ 334 4408; admission 100din; ⏲ 10am-5pm Tue-Sun), which presents a complete military history of former Yugoslavia. Proudly displayed are captured Kosovo Liberation Army (KLA) weapons and bits of the American stealth fighter that was shot down in 1999. Outside are several bombs and missiles, which have been contributed from the air by NATO, plus a line-up of old guns and tanks, some quite rare. There's a guidebook in English (150din).

Most of the Upper Citadel is now parkland, and the massive walls are a favourite place for Belgraders to snatch an alfresco lunch on work days, or for young couples to find a bit of romantic solitude.

## Stari Grad

South of the citadel lies Stari Grad (Old Town), built mostly when the Habsburgs grabbed Belgrade from the declining Ottoman Empire.

The 3rd floor of the **National Museum** (Map p756; ☎ 330 6000; Trg Republike; admission 200din, free Sun; ⏲ 10am-5pm Tue, Wed & Fri, noon-8pm Thu & Sat, 10am-2pm Sun) is an art gallery displaying just part of a very large collection of national and European art, including works by Picasso and Monet. Nadežeta Petrović (1873–1915), one of

Serbia's first female artists, is well represented. The lower floors (prehistory) have been closed for several years.

Nearby is the outstanding **Ethnographical Museum** (Map p756; ☎ 328 1888; Studentski Trg 13; admission 100din; 10am-5pm Tue, 10am-10pm Thu, 9am-5pm Sat, 9am-1pm Sun) with a comprehensive collection of Serbian costumes, folk art and items of everyday existence. The costumes show a superb quality of weaving and embroidery using russet browns, wine reds and muted yellows. Some retro-designer just has to discover these patterns. Agrarian tools and equipment take up much of the top floor, with several displays of rooms furnished to reflect various periods of time and different communities. Explanations are in English and a small shop sells examples of the crafts.

You should visit the nearby **Gallery of Frescoes** (Map p756; ☎ 621 491; Cara Uroša 20; admission 50din; 10am-5pm Mon, Tue & Thu-Sat, 10am-2pm Sun) just to appreciate the artistic wealth cloistered in this country's monasteries. There are some originals but otherwise they're exact replicas, faithful to the last blotch and scratch. These you can photograph, whereas in most cases you can't photograph the originals in the monasteries.

The **Palace of Princess Ljubice** (Map p756; ☎ 638 264; Kneza Sime Markovića 8; admission 150din; 10am-5pm Tue-Fri, 10am-4pm Sat & Sun) is a Balkan-style palace built for the wife of Prince Miloš in 1831. Mostly, it's a collection of period furnishings, carpets and paintings but it desperately needs the addition of personal items to bring out how the princess led her life. To one side is a little *hammam* (Turkish bath), where the princess would have had steam baths and massages, and were she a woman of today, her yoga or Pilates class.

## Skadarska

Often hailed as Belgrade's Montmartre, Skadarska was the bohemian hang-out of poets and artists in the early 1900s. Today this cobbled street is famous for its Balkan taverns, strolling musicians, cafés and art galleries. In summer, the restaurants spill out onto the street, and music, theatre and cabaret performers entertain customers and passers-by.

The restaurants rejoice in unusual names, such as Tri Šešira (Three Hats – it was once a millinery), Ima Dana (There Are Days), Dva Jelena (Two Deer) and Dva Bela Goluba (Two White Doves).

## Central Belgrade

Behind the post office stands **Sveti Marko** (Map p756; Bulevar Kralja Aleksandra 17), a solid church supported by four massive internal pillars containing the grave of the Emperor Dušan (1308–55). Behind, and dwarfed, is a petite blue-domed **Russian Church** erected by refugees who fled the October Revolution.

Started in 1935 and interrupted by Hitler, communism and lack of cash, **Sveti Sava** (Map p753; Svetog Save) is billed as the biggest Orthodox church in the world. The church lies on the reputed site where the Turks burnt the relics of St Sava, the youngest son of a 12th-century ruler and founder of the independent Serbian Orthodox church.

The **Museum of Automobiles** (Map p756; ☎ 303 4265; Majke Jevrocime 30; admission 50din; 11am-7pm) is a private collection of cars and motorcycles in Belgrade's first garage. First choice for our garage would be the '57 Cadillac convertible, with only 25,000km and one careful owner – President Tito.

One of Belgrade's more interesting museums is the **Nikola Tesla Museum** (Map p756; ☎ 433 886; www.tesla-museum.org; Krunska 51; admission 50din; 10am-6pm Tue-Fri, 10am-1pm Sat & Sun), dedicated to one of Serbia's few heroes, the man who discovered alternating current. Apart from demonstrations of Tesla's fascinating inventions, the big thrill is when the curator turns on a high-frequency oscillator that lights up the (unconnected) fluorescent tube you're gingerly holding in your hand. Shades of *Star Wars*' light sabres!

## Outer Belgrade

Don't miss **Maršal Tito's grave** (Map p753; House of Flowers; ☎ 367 1485; Bulevar Mira; admission free; 9am-5pm Tue-Sun) with a curious museum of gifts (embroidery, dubious-purpose smoking pipes, saddles and weapons) given by toadying comrades and fellow travellers. Check the adjacent **Historical Museum of Yugoslavia** (Map p753; ☎ 367 1485; exhibitions 9am-2pm Tue-Sun) for an occasional exhibition. Trolleybus 40 or 41.

The UFO parked near the airport just happens to be a futuristic building housing the exceptional **Yugoslav Aeronautical Museum** ( ☎ 670 992; admission 300din; 9am-2pm Tue-Sun Nov-Apr, 9am-7pm Tue-Sun May-Oct), which is sure to engross any aircraft buff. On display are rare planes from WWII, bits of that infamous American stealth fighter and a parking lot of 'make me an offer' MiG21s.

# CENTRAL BELGRADE

0 ————————— 500 m
0 ————————— 0.3 miles

SERBIA

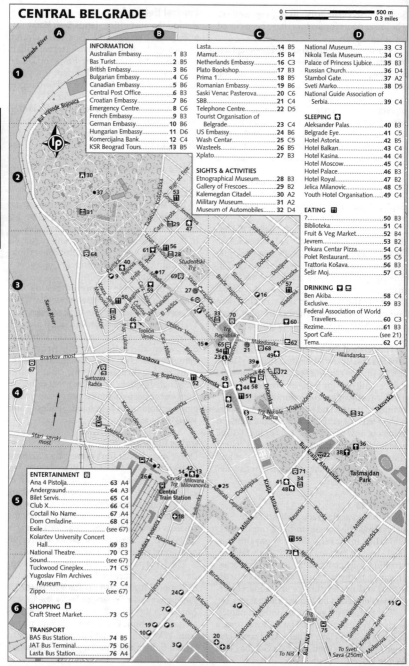

## INFORMATION
| | | |
|---|---|---|
| Australian Embassy | 1 | B3 |
| Bas Turist | 2 | B5 |
| British Embassy | 3 | B6 |
| Bulgarian Embassy | 4 | C6 |
| Canadian Embassy | 5 | B6 |
| Central Post Office | 6 | B3 |
| Croatian Embassy | 7 | B6 |
| Emergency Centre | 8 | C6 |
| French Embassy | 9 | B3 |
| German Embassy | 10 | B6 |
| Hungarian Embassy | 11 | D6 |
| Komercijalna Bank | 12 | C4 |
| KSR Beograd Tours | 13 | B5 |

| | | |
|---|---|---|
| Lasta | 14 | B5 |
| Mamut | 15 | B4 |
| Netherlands Embassy | 16 | C3 |
| Plato Bookshop | 17 | B3 |
| Prima 1 | 18 | B5 |
| Romanian Embassy | 19 | B6 |
| Saski Venac Pasterova | 20 | C6 |
| SBB | 21 | C4 |
| Telephone Centre | 22 | D5 |
| Tourist Organisation of Belgrade | 23 | C4 |
| US Embassy | 24 | B6 |
| Wash Centar | 25 | C5 |
| Wasteels | 26 | B5 |
| Xplato | 27 | B3 |

## SIGHTS & ACTIVITIES
| | | |
|---|---|---|
| Etnographical Museum | 28 | B3 |
| Gallery of Frescoes | 29 | B2 |
| Kalemegdan Citadel | 30 | A2 |
| Military Museum | 31 | A2 |
| Museum of Automobiles | 32 | D4 |

| | | |
|---|---|---|
| National Museum | 33 | C3 |
| Nikola Tesla Museum | 34 | C5 |
| Palace of Princess Ljubice | 35 | B3 |
| Russian Church | 36 | D4 |
| Stambol Gate | 37 | A2 |
| Sveti Marko | 38 | D5 |
| National Guide Association of Serbia | 39 | C4 |

## SLEEPING
| | | |
|---|---|---|
| Aleksander Palas | 40 | B3 |
| Belgrade Eye | 41 | C5 |
| Hotel Astoria | 42 | B5 |
| Hotel Balkan | 43 | C4 |
| Hotel Kasina | 44 | C4 |
| Hotel Moscow | 45 | C4 |
| Hotel Palace | 46 | B3 |
| Hotel Royal | 47 | B2 |
| Jelica Milanovic | 48 | C5 |
| Youth Hotel Organisation | 49 | C4 |

## EATING
| | | |
|---|---|---|
| ? | 50 | B3 |
| Biblioteka | 51 | C4 |
| Fruit & Veg Market | 52 | B4 |
| Jevrem | 53 | B2 |
| Pekara Centar Pizza | 54 | C4 |
| Polet Restaurant | 55 | C5 |
| Trattoria Košava | 56 | C3 |
| Šešir Moj | 57 | C3 |

## DRINKING
| | | |
|---|---|---|
| Ben Akiba | 58 | C4 |
| Exclusive | 59 | B3 |
| Federal Association of World Travellers | 60 | C3 |
| Rezime | 61 | B3 |
| Sport Café | (see 21) | |
| Tema | 62 | C4 |

## ENTERTAINMENT
| | | |
|---|---|---|
| Ana 4 Pistolja | 63 | A4 |
| Andergraund | 64 | A3 |
| Bilet Servis | 65 | C4 |
| Club X | 66 | C4 |
| Coctail No Name | 67 | A4 |
| Dom Omladine | 68 | C4 |
| Exile | (see 67) | |
| Kolarčev University Concert Hall | 69 | B3 |
| National Theatre | 70 | C3 |
| Sound | (see 67) | |
| Tuckwood Cineplex | 71 | C5 |
| Yugoslav Film Archives Museum | 72 | C4 |
| Zippo | (see 67) | |

## SHOPPING
| | | |
|---|---|---|
| Craft Street Market | 73 | C5 |

## TRANSPORT
| | | |
|---|---|---|
| BAS Bus Station | 74 | B5 |
| JAT Bus Terminal | 75 | D6 |
| Lasta Bus Station | 76 | A4 |

**Ada Ciganlija** (Map p753), a green and sandy island park in the Sava River, is Belgrade's summer retreat. Gentle choices are swimming in the lake (naturists 1km upstream, please), renting a bicycle or just strolling through the woodland. Adrenaline junkies might fancy the bungy jumping or the water-ski tow. Plenty of places overlooking the lake sell restorative cold beers.

## TOURS
**Romantika** ( ☯ Train trips May-Sep) Steam-hauled train to Sremski Karlovci. Contact KSR Beograd Tours (p754).
**Tourist Guides Association of Serbia** (Map p756; ☎ 323 5910; 5th fl, Dučanska 8; ☯ 9.30am-3pm Mon-Fri) Independent and licensed guides for city or country tours.
**Tourist Organisation of Belgrade** (p754) Runs bus, boat (May to October) and guided walking tours.

## FESTIVALS & EVENTS
**FEST film festival** (www.fest.org.yu) An international festival of film, held during February and March, with guest appearances from foreign directors and actors.
**Belgrade Beer Fest** (www.belgradebeerfest.com) A heady mix of rock music, a wide variety of domestic and foreign beers, and thousands of people who just like both. Held in August.
**Belgrade International Theatre Festival** (Bitef; www.bitef.co.yu) One of Europe's older and most important festivals of theatre. Its programme celebrates the avant-garde with theatre and street performances. Held in September.
**BEMUS** (www.bemus.co.yu) A classical music festival attracting some of the world's top orchestras, conductors and other music ensembles, and held in October.

## SLEEPING
Backpacker hostels are making an appearance in Belgrade, and some scruffy midrange hotels are getting a makeover in style, service and price. Some budget stalwarts are resisting the tide. At the top end of the range the Aleksander Palas has set the new standard for centrally located posh hotels.

## Budget
### HOSTELS
**Belgrade Eye** (Map p756; ☎ 334 6423; www.belgradeeye.com; Krunska 6b; dm/d/tr per person with shared bathroom €11.50/17.50/14; ☐ ) The Eye has doubles and dorms with luggage lockers. There's a kitchen for DIY catering and free tea and coffee are always on tap. The terrace is for good-weather lazing or for firing up the barbecue. For longer

stays, the helpful owners have apartments for rent.
**Tis** (Map p753; ☎ /fax 380 6050; terranova@sbb.co.yu; Koste Abraševića 17; bed per person from €15; ☐ ☐ ) Look for the striking yellow and green building two streets south of Bulevar Kralje Aleksandra, just east of its junction with Stanislava Sremčevića (take tram 2, 5 or 7). Recently opened, the fresh dorms and doubles are still untainted by backpacker socks, which if you have any can be done here for 400din a load. Some doubles have TVs and there's a common room with free internet access. You can buy sandwiches, coffee, tea and beer, and lounge in the secluded garden.
**Licej Club** (Map p753; ☎ 339 2466; www.licejkon.com; Venizelosova 31; s/d with shared bathroom €20.50/31; ☐ ) At the time of research this hostel had yet to open; let us know what you think.
The **Youth Hostel Organisation** (Map p756; Ferijalni Savez Beograd; ☎ 324 8550; www.hostels.org.yu; 2nd fl, Makedonska 22; ☯ 9am-4pm Mon-Fri) has a deal for discounted rooms with the **Hotel Astoria** (Map p756; ☎ 264 5422; Milovana Milovanovića 1a; s/d €22/29). It also books holiday student accommodation at the **Jelica Milanovic** (Map p756; ☎ 323 1268; Krunska 8; per person €11, with shared bathroom €9; ☯ Jul & Aug).

### HOTELS
**Hotel Royal** (Map p756; ☎ 263 4222; www.hotelroyal.co.yu; Kralja Petra 56; s/d from €25/33.50; ☐ ) Very central and cheap, the Royal's about the best budget value hotel and consequently it's often bursting. Sure, it's worn, and the breakfasts are iron rations, but it's kept tidy and the always-open bar means there's somewhere to slip away to if you can't sleep.

## Midrange
**Hotel Palace** (Map p756; ☎ 218 5585; www.palacehotel.co.yu; Topličin Venac 23; s/d/apt €65/92/110; ☐ ) From leather armchairs and a tinkling atrium waterfall to the pleasantly revived rooms, this hotel shows how a bit of TLC can resuscitate a state hotel. The rooms are large and have phones, TVs and bidets. We liked the look of rooms 514 and 511. Up on the top floor, the Panorama restaurant reveals a city view. Not that you would know it but the Palace was the Gestapo headquarters in WWII, and the French embassy afterwards.
**Hotel Balkan** (Map p756; ☎ 363 6000; www.balkanhotel.net; Prizrenska 2; s/d/tr €27/38/45; ☒ ) This is new Belgrade. Due to recent renovations by its new owner, an electronics company, the Balkan

now comes in seductive coffee browns and peachy cream with lots of bold artwork on the walls. It's been redesigned with thought. As befits a electronics company, it's plush with TVs and plasma screens around the place. The restaurant, the Orient Express, is named for the time when the hotel accommodated overnight passengers from the original *Orient Express*, which ran to Istanbul.

**Hotel Kasina** (Map p756; ☎ 323 5574; Terazije 25; s/d from €27/40; ✗ ▢ ) Opposite the Moscow, the Kasina is almost lost in a bank of similar buildings but stands out in Belgrade's history as its oldest hotel (1856). Inside is a good choice of rooms from cheap shoe-box singles to plush apartments. Breakfast is a buffet, there's a reasonable restaurant, and better still a rollicking beer hall.

**Hotel Moscow** (Map p756; Moskva; ☎ 268 6255; www .hotelmoskva.co.yu; Balkanska; s/d/tr from €57/122/152; ✗ ) A hotel with character, as the 1906 secessionist-period exterior suggests. Indira Gandhi and Orson Welles stayed here (unfortunately for the gossip mags, not in the same room and not at the same time). The downstairs café-bar has huge windows looking out onto Terazije; locals and visitors throng here to drink coffee, gorge on delicious cakes and watch their fellow citizens through the glass.

## Top End

**Aleksandar Palas** (Map p756; ☎ 330 5300; www.ale ksandarpalas.com; Kralja Petra 13-15; apt from €260 Mon-Fri, Sat & Sun €200; ✗ ▢ ) No simple rooms here, just beautiful apartments kitted out with the best furnishings and mod cons: home cinema with six speakers, and CD and DVD players. Bathrooms have space-age shower cabinets that spray and steam, while music plays in the background. Fortunately, the instructions are waterproof. Would you ever want to go outside?

# EATING

Belgraders enjoy eating out, and are well rewarded with many fine restaurants offering good affordable food. Many of these are packed around the streets of Knez Mihailova, 29 Novembra, Makedonska and the famous Skadarska.

## City Centre
### BUDGET

Kiosks and cafés offering *burek*, *ćevapčići*, pastries and some inventive pizza are scattered everywhere and you can fill up at these for under 100din. Many, like those around Trg Republike and the bus and train stations, are open 24 hours.

**Pekara Centar Pizza** (Map p756; Kolarčeva 10; pizza 60din; ✆ 24hr) With its ever-open doors, Pekara has a bright and cheery interior and trays of freshly made pizzas that beckon. There are stand-up tables if you want to stay and eat. You may need more than one slice.

Belgrade's main fruit and veg **market** (Map p756; cnr Brankova Prizrenska & Narodnog Fronta; ✆ 6am-1pm) is a fertile ground for self-catering. Belgrade has many supermarkets.

### MIDRANGE

**Biblioteka** (Map p756; Terazije 27; meals 240-300din) We've always felt that a library and a drinking den were a natural combination of pleasures. Biblioteka provides both. Books and magazines are racked up for reading, while waiters in cheeky red-banded bowlers, green checked shirts and large skirt aprons flit around to help with your drink and food requests. Many come here to meet friends, and the unobtrusive background music allows for quiet conversation or reading. Breakfasts are served until 1pm.

**Polet Restaurant** (Map p756; ☎ 323 2454; Kralja Milana 31; dishes 200-500din) Fat shiny brass ship-railings around the mezzanine floor, slatted shutters over portholes and a Mediterranean décor of blues and whites provide the ambience for this hideaway seafood restaurant. Enter from the street through the blue frontage; don't linger at the bar but descend 'below decks'. The menu ranges from the tasty fish soup (100din) to *scampi à la Parisienne* (1300din). The calamari is chargrilled to perfection, misted with lemon, and succulent (550din).

**Trattoria Košava** (Map p756; ☎ 627 344; Kralja Petra 6; dishes 400-600din; ✆ 9am-1am Mon-Fri, noon-1am Sat & Sun) This Mediterranean-style Italian restaurant is light and airy with a 'cheer you up on a bad day' pastel décor. Options include the downstairs café for a blow-in pizza snack, coffee and a give-me-more cherry strudel, or the restaurant upstairs for some serious eating.

**Jevrem** (Map p756; ☎ 328 4746; Gospodar Jevremova 36; meals 400-850din; ✆ 11am-1am Mon-Sat) Set in a restored old Dorćol house, Jevrem is furnished as if time stopped in the 1920s, confirmed by the old photographs of Belgrade on the sunflower yellow walls. The food is traditional and simple; for afters try the spiced hot brandy with baklava and Serbian coffee.

---

**AUTHOR'S CHOICE**

**?** (Map p756; ☎ 635 421; Kralja Petra 6; dishes 200-350din) The shortest restaurant name in town came about because of a dispute between a long-past owner and the abstemious clergy of the Orthodox cathedral opposite, who objected to its then name, Cathedral Tavern. The clergy threatened action so the landlord changed the signboard to a '?' signalling his perplexity as to what the fuss was about. Inside is an original Balkans tavern that could be a set for a noir film. Chiaroscuro light from panelled windows creeps in to pick up cigarette smoke and dust specks dancing through the sunbeams. Furniture and foot-polished floorboards glow with a patina of antiquity, diners sit at low wooden tables on equally low half-moon chairs while old men in window seats sip coffee and *rakija*, and put the day to rights. Caravaggio could have painted this scene. The cuisine is Serbian, with a robust selection of grilled meats.

---

**Šešir Moj** (My Hat; Map p756; ☎ 322 8750; Skadarska 21; dishes 480-800din) An intimate little restaurant that has alcoves decorated with an art gallery of oils and pastels. A place for romantics, especially when members of a Roma band swirl in, playing their hauntingly passionate music. Go for the *punjena belavešanica*, which is a pork fillet stuffed with *kajmak*. Finish with Serbian coffee and a piece of *orasnica* (walnut cake) if you've any room left.

## Outer Belgrade

**Priroda** (Map p753; ☎ 241 1890; Batutova 11; dishes 540-890din; ◷ 11am-8pm Nov-Apr, 8am-11pm May-Oct) Give this restaurant owner a medal for battling against adversity. Why? Priroda perseveres as a superb vegetarian restaurant in a land of carnivores. Discover the delicate flavours, oozing from vegetables and pulses, that are absent in traditional Serbian cuisine. Try the Vivaldi Plate for its smoked tofu, sea vegetables and cereals, and finish with the macrobiotic cake – a stunner.

## DRINKING
### Cafés

Belgrade has some top-class café-bars offering damn good coffee straight from the bean; many places also serve beer, wines and spirits. Nearly all are open daily from early morning to midnight, with a later start on Sunday. Most don't offer food. As the weather warms up and the trees start to bud, many pavement and pedestrian areas around Trg Republike blossom into café terraces.

**Rezime** (Map p756; ☎ 328 4276; Kralja Petra 41) When you're hangover-hobbled, slink up here and collapse in the leather armchairs. Try to wrangle your body back to some normality with the buck-you-up coffee or vast range of teas (cherry is our favourite), maybe the

supersmooth chilled chocolate mousse as well. But you don't have to abuse yourself to qualify for the Rezime treatment.

**Tema** (Map p756; ☎ 337 3859; Makedonska 11-13) A subtly lit modern bar that both young and old are welcome to linger in. Chilly days become more bearable after one of the coffees with a spirit kick.

**Sport Café** (Map p756; ☎ 324 3177; Makedonska 4) Punters come here for the 20-plus TV screens showing all manner of sports, rather than for the coffee.

### Bars

Many of Belgrade's clubs and bars are hidden away, below ground in basements or in seemingly innocent apartment blocks.

**Federal Association of World Travellers** (Map p756; ☎ 324 2303; 29 Novembra 7; ◷ 1pm-midnight Mon-Fri, 3pm-late Sat & Sun) A wonderfully eclectic basement bar in which you feel you've gate-crashed a surrealists' house party, and been welcomed in. It's decorated as though various members have returned from the four corners of the earth bearing one object as a contribution to

---

**AUTHOR'S CHOICE**

**Ben Akiba** (Map p756; ☎ 323 7775; Nušićeva 8; ◷ 9am-very late) We liked this place, its bubbly atmosphere and those cocktails – so smooth, so seductive and so moreish. You could easily leave here early in the morning brain- and wallet-drained. Another one of Belgrade's hidden bars, Ben Akiba started out as a secret drinking den for liberals opposed to Milošević. Slip round the back of the main building, go up to the 1st floor and knock. Then be prepared to heave yourself into the happy mass.

---

the furnishings. Just open the big black gate, follow the lights that come on, and listen for the music, which is live every night.

**Exclusive** (Map p756; ☎ 328 2288; Knez Mihailova 41-45; 🕑 9am-2am Mon-Sat, noon-1am Sun) A basement beer joint, Exclusive is Belgrade's answer to a Munich beer hall. There's plenty of knees-up music in this lads' bar, with big snacks – sausage, bread and chips (85din) – as a sound bedrock for serious drinking.

# ENTERTAINMENT
## Cinemas

**Yugoslav Film Archives Museum** (Map p756; ☎ 324 8250; www.kinoteka.org.yu; Kosovska 11; 🕑 11am-7pm Tue-Sun) This is the home of the Yugoslav film archives and screens classic Balkan and European films.

**Tuckwood Cineplex** (Map p756; ☎ 323 6517; Kneza Miloša 7; tickets 200-280din) This place shows the latest releases in English or with English subtitles.

## Live Music & Theatre

More big acts, such as Sting, Deep Purple, Lou Reed, Simple Minds and Boy George, are appearing in Belgrade. The ticketing agency **Bilet Servis** (Map p756; ☎ 628 342; www.biletservis.co.yu; Trg Republike 5; 🕑 9am-8pm) sells tickets for concerts and theatre.

The **Sava Centar** (Map p753; ☎ 213 9840; www .savacentar.com; Milentija Popovića 9, New Belgrade) and **Dom Omladine** (Map p756; ☎ 324 8202; Makedonska 22) host major concerts, film festivals and multimedia events.

The Belgrade Philharmonia often performs at **Kolarčev University Concert Hall** (Map p756; ☎ 630 550; Studentski Trg 5; box office 🕑 10am-noon & 6-8pm).

In winter there's opera staged at the elegant **National Theatre** (Map p756; ☎ 328 1333; Francuska 3; box office 🕑 10am-2pm Tue-Sun).

For some free Sunday entertainment wander along to the Kalemegdan, where folk come to dance hand in hand the traditional way to pipe, accordion and drum.

## Nightclubs

Clubs come and go out of fashion quickly – check *Yellow Cab* or ask a young Belgrader for the latest hot spot. Many clubs have regular bands at weekends or import the best DJs Europe has to offer. Summer party life also revolves around the many barges and boats moored on the Sava and Danube Rivers.

**Plastic** (Map p756; ☎ 328 5437; cnr Dalmatinska & Takovska; 🕑 10pm-5pm) The sizable dance floor

with a seamless mix of house, techno and drum'n'bass keeps Belgrade's clubbers up to all hours. Plastic is very popular; you may have to queue a while.

**Ana 4 Pistolja** (Map p756; ☎ 065 223 8474; Svetozara Radića 4; 🕑 10pm-4am Thu-Sun) Descend the spiralling path through the rock garden into the depths, where, in caverns beneath the streets, DJs spin everything from techno to trance for a heaving mixed-ages throng. Sometimes there's an entrance fee of 100din for males.

**Andergraund** (Map p756; ☎ 625 681; Pariska 1a; 🕑 noon-midnight Sun-Thu, noon-2am Fri & Sat; 🚻 ) Once an air-raid shelter and then a mushroom farm, (still smells a bit that way), Andergraund is a warren of caverns where the big-name DJs play. Live music is usually on Saturday, and whenever there's a big sports event the large TV on the outside terrace is fired up. This is about the only nightclub in Belgrade with wheelchair access.

**Club X** (Map p756; ☎ 064 434 5827; Nušićeva 27; 🕑 11pm-4am Wed-Sun) Another cruisy basement joint that's Belgrade's only gay and lesbian club. The place throbs to DJ beats, and Saturday is reputedly the best night.

### DANUBE RIVER BARGES

Adjacent to Hotel Jugoslavija in Novi Beograd (New Belgrade) is a kilometre-long strip of some 20 barges. Buses 15, 68, 603 and 701 from Trg Republike go to Hotel Jugoslavija.

**Brave Heart** (Map p753; Hrabo Scre; ☎ 851 1480; 🕑 10pm-4am) Heaves till late and appeals to Belgrade's young 'businessmen' and their trophy girls. It's a place to chill out with DJ music until midnight and then kick in when the live music starts up.

**Bibis** (Map p753; ☎ 319 2150; 🕑 10am-2am) A quiet place that's a useful starter to a night out; sit over a drink and decide where to rock on to next. It's popular in winter when other barges are closed.

**Acapulco** (Map p753; ☎ 784 760; 🕑 noon-3am) Where young businessmen come to flaunt their money and female attachments. Mockingly referred to as 'sponsorship girls', these women work on the basis of 'look after me (plenty of gifts), and I'll look gorgeous beside you'. Music is fast and furious turbofolk.

### SAVA RIVER BARGES

On the western bank of the Sava River is another 1.5km strip of floating bars, restaurants and discos that open in summer. Here you'll find Cocktail No Name (Map p756) playing pop and '80s music, Zippo (Map p756) for Serbian folk music, Exile (Map p756) pounding out techno and nearby Sound (Map p756) playing house and disco. Get there by walking over the Brankov Most or by catching trams 7, 9 or 11.

## SHOPPING

Belgrade's not a place for tacky souvenirs – yet. Instead there's a variety of homemade craftwork available, such as the lace and knitted woollens you'll find on sale in Kalemgdan Park. Knez Mihailova and the Terazije underpass are also good places to look for things to take home.

A **craft street market** (Map p756; cnr Kralja Milana & Njegoševa; ☺ 8am-5pm Mon-Sat) sells handcrafted jewellery items and original oil paintings.

Street sellers may offer you a set of 1990s currency from when unimaginable hyperinflation ruined Serbia; included should be a 500-billion-dinar note.

## GETTING THERE & AWAY
### Bus

Belgrade has two adjacent bus stations: **BAS** (Bus; Map p756; ☎ 636 299; Železnička 4) serves regional Serbia and some Montenegro destinations, while **Lasta** (Map p756; ☎ 625 740; Železnička bb) serves destinations around Belgrade.

There are services to Subotica (700din, three hours), Niš (800din, three hours), Podgorica (1500din, nine hours), Budva (1800din, 12 hours), Novi Pazar (800din, five hours) and Prishtina (1335din, seven hours).

International services are good with daily buses to destinations in Western Europe; see p779.

### Train

The **central train station** (Map p756; ☎ 629 400; Savski Trg 2) has a very helpful **information office** ( ☎ 361 8487; platform 1; ☺ 7am-7pm). There's also a **tourist office** ( ☎ 361 2732; ☺ 9am-8pm Mon-Fri, 9am-5pm Sat) for basic city information, an **exchange bureau** ( ☺ 6am-10pm) and **Wasteels** (Map p756; ☎ 265 8868; wasteels@eunet.yu; central train station, Savski Trg 2; ☺ 9am-4pm Mon-Sat) for rail passes and international tickets.

Overnight trains run from Belgrade to Bar (1280din plus 890/445din per three-/six-berth couchette, 11½ hours). Frequent trains go to Novi Sad (from 185din, 1½ hours) and Subotica (from 400din, three hours).

For international trains see p779.

## GETTING AROUND
### To/From the Airport

**Nikola Tesla airport** ( ☎ 601 555, 605 555; www.airport -belgrade.co.yu) is 18km west of Belgrade. The **JAT bus** ( ☎ 675 583; 160din; ☺ from airport hourly 5am-9pm, from town hourly 7am-10pm) connects the airport with Trg Slavija and the central train station. Ignore the taxi sharks prowling inside the airport; go outside and catch a cab to town for about 600din.

### Public Transport

Belgrade has trams, trolleybuses and buses. Tickets cost 25din from a street kiosk or 40din from the driver; make sure you validate the ticket in the machine on board.

Tram 2 is useful for connecting Kalemegdan citadel with Trg Slavija, bus stations and the central train station.

### Taxi

Belgrade's taxis are plentiful and most use meters; flag fall is 45din plus 38din per kilometre. Taxi sharks, usually in flash cars, prey around the airport, train and bus stations looking for a rich fare. At the stations move away from the entrance and pick up a cruising cab.

Have your hotel call you a taxi or phone **Maxis** ( ☎ 9804) or **Pink** ( ☎ 9803).

## AROUND BELGRADE
### Zemun Земун

On the southern bank of the Danube, some 8km northwest of central Belgrade, lies the small town of Zemun. Visitors come for lazy meals at the river-edge restaurants, boating or just ambling alongside the river.

Catch bus 83 from outside Belgrade's train station and get off in Zemun's main street, Glavna. From here the pedestrian-only Lenyinova street leads through a **market** down to the Danube. This older area of town has some once-resplendent 19th-century mansions proudly standing out from the post-WWII concrete.

From the market area, narrow cobbled streets lead uphill towards the **Gardoš**, a fortress with 9th-century origins. All that remains now are some 15th-century walls and the **Tower of Sibinjanin Janko**, built in 1896 to celebrate the millennial anniversary of the Hungarian state. Zemun was the most southerly point of the Austro-Hungarian empire and the tower was a useful vantage point to spy on the Turks, who were in control of Belgrade on the other side of the Sava.

SERBIA

Below the hill is the 1731 Orthodox **Nikola-jevska Church** (Njegoševa 43). Inside, gleaming out of the shadows, is an astoundingly beautiful iconostasis, carved from wood in the baroque style, gold-plated and bearing rows of saints painted onto golden backgrounds.

**Zemun Museum** ( ☎ 617 766; Glavna 9; admission 100din; ☯ 9am-4pm Tue-Fri, 9am-3pm Sat & Sun) has a huge collection demonstrating the development of Serbian applied arts. At the time of research it was closed for renovation.

There are a host of restaurants to choose from. In summer, patrons sit out on the terraces to drink the sunset down, listen to music and belt out old Serbian favourites once the *slivovitz* (plum brandy) has lubricated their throats.

**Reka** ( ☎ 611 625; dishes 500-800din; ☯ noon-3.30am, doors close 9pm) overlooks the Danube and has an abundance of character. To start, the menu has a list of the waiting staff and their foibles. Choose 'Grandma if you're not hungry and are very patient', 'Kacia will give you the stars from the sky if you ask' or 'Vesna, elegant, reserved and polite, she needs a special customer to inspire her dancing'. We suggest a table on the terrace, plenty of entrées, a fish platter and a bottle of wine or more. The restaurant has that special 'stay all day' atmosphere, but if you come here in the evening you'll have to book and arrive before 9pm. Most evenings there's live music.

## Smederevo Смедерево

The largest 'built on flat land' fortress in Europe dominates the Danube in the small town of Smederevo, some 46km southeast from Belgrade. A frequent bus service (245din, 1½ hours) from Belgrade's Lasta bus station makes this a pleasant day trip.

**Smederevo Fortress** ( ☎ 026-612 840; admission 20din; ☯ daylight hr) is a massive triangular fort with 25 towers built on early Roman fortifications; look for the odd bits of Roman-era sculpture used as masonry in the more modern walls. Built by despot Đurađ Brankovic, it served as his capital from 1428 to 1430 but was never really tested in battle. The greatest damage was caused by the detonation of a German ammunition train in the adjacent railway sidings in WWII.

**Smederevo Museum** ( ☎ 026-612 840; admission 20din; ☯ 10am-5pm Mon-Fri, 10am-3pm Sat & Sun) is a 'history of the town' museum with artefacts dating from Roman times, plus some interesting frescoes.

# VOJVODINA
# ВОJВОДИНА

This is big-sky country, where an extensive, almost featureless plain sweeps down from Hungary to the banks of the Danube. Incredibly fertile, it provides much of the food that fills the nation's larders. A hilly exception is the Fruška Gora National Park, an 80km-long upland island of rolling hills dotted with vineyards and some 14 monasteries.

## NOVI SAD НОВИ САД
☎ 021 / pop 299,000

For much of the year Novi Sad is 'Belgrade on Valium', having much of what the capital has to offer but at a far more sedate pace. A variety of interesting cafés, bars, museums, pedestrian streets and the mighty Petrovaradin Citadel merit a day jaunt from Belgrade, or a longer period to explore the monasteries and vineyards of Fruška Gora.

Come July the town explodes with a flood of festival-goers, who troop in for the annual Exit Festival (see opposite).

## Orientation

The adjacent train and intercity bus stations lie at the northern end of Bulevar Oslobođenja. It's a 2.5km walk to the city centre or a bus ride (No 4) to the city bus station. One block south is Zmaj Jovina leading into Trg Slobode, which is the heart of Novi Sad, and dominated by the Catholic cathedral and its chequered-tile roof. Leading off Zmaj Jovina is Dunavska. This small cobbled street is the entertainment hub of Novi Sad, with a mix of brand-name clothing shops, cafés, restaurants and antique shops. A road bridge leads over the Danube to the eastern bank and the old town, where stairs beside the large church lead up to Petrovaradin citadel.

## Information

**Delta Bank** ( ☎ 487 000; Mihajla Pupina 4) Cashes travellers cheques; ATM.

**KYM** ( ☎ 423 161; Mituruzic 4; per hr 60din) Internet access.

**Main post office & telephone centre** ( ☎ 614 708; Narodnih Heroja 2; ☯ 7am-7pm Mon-Sat, 8am-3pm Sun)

**Tourist Information Centre** ( ☎ 421 811; www .novisadtourism.com; Mihajla Pupina 9; ☯ 8.30am-8pm Mon-Fri, 9am-1.30pm Sat) On-the-button office with plenty of info including a walking-tour leaflet.

### EXIT FESTIVAL

If the Exit Festival (www.exitfest.org) is not Europe's biggest music event then at least it's the most talked about. Using the fortifications of the Petrovaradin Citadel as natural amphitheatres, organisers put up at least 19 stages to present the best in rock, blues, latino, roots, heavy metal, hip-hop and techno by world-class acts. Festival-goers say it's the atmosphere here that makes it special. There's not a huge crowd in one place, but the event is like several different festivals going on at the same time.

Performers in 2006 included Morrissey, Franz Ferdinand, The Cardigans and Pet Shop Boys, plus DJs Steve Lawler, Junkie XL, Jeff Mills and local Marko Nastic. The website has a ticket-booking service and reservations for the Danube-side camping ground.



## Sights

Built on a plug of volcanic rock and dominating the town and the Danube, the mighty **Petrovaradin Citadel** is a massive piece of work often referred to as the 'Gibraltar of the Danube'. It was built by slave labour between 1699 and 1780, and had been designed by the French architect Vauban to protect the town from Turkish invasions. It was mainly populated by Austro-Hungarian soldiers, and the village below grew up around the taverns that entertained them with 'ladies of the night' and the best Hungarian Roma musicians. Famous prisoners at Petrovaradin were Karageorge Petrović, leader of the Serbian uprising in 1804, and Tito.

The citadel contains a **City Museum** (☎ 433 155; admission 200din; 🕒 9am-5pm) and a **planetarium** (☎ 350 122; admission 40din; shows at 7pm Thu, 5pm Sat & Sun). The stables are now charming artist **studios** (🕒 9am-5pm Mon-Sat); visitors are welcome, and maybe over a coffee you'll find just the piece for that bare wall back home. Walking the walls gives a fine view of the Danube and Novi Sad on the opposite bank. Have a close look at the clock tower and you'll see that the hour hand is the longer one; this makes the clock more readable from the river.

Novi Sad's main museum is **Muzej Vojvodine** (☎ 420 566; Dunavska 35-37; admission 70din; 🕒 9am-7pm Tue-Fri, 9am-2pm Sat & Sun), housed in two buildings: No 35 covers the history of Vojvodina, from Palaeolithic times to the late 19th century; No 37 takes the story to 1945 with an emphasis on WWI and WWII. The collection is impressive in its thoroughness; the main explanatory panels are in English.

## Sleeping

**Bela Lađa** (☎ 661 6594; www.belaladja.com; Kisačka 21; s/d/tr per person with shared bathroom from €10; **P**) Several rooms above this intriguing old restaurant can provide homely comfort to 22 guests. Prices rise by 50% during the Exit Festival but this still makes it Novi Sad's cheapest option. Breakfast is available for €2.

**Brankovo Kolo** (☎/fax 528 263; www.hostelns.com; Episkopa Visariona 3; d/tr/q per person with shared bathroom €12/13/14; 🕒 1 Jul-25 Aug; **P** 💻) Novi Sad's cheapie is student accommodation only available in summer but fortunately that includes the Exit Festival.

**Boarding House Fontana** (☎ 662 1779, fax 621 779; Nikole Pašićeva 27; s/d/tr 2500/3000/3500din; **P**) There's a pleasant feel to these comfortable wood-panelled rooms, which are above the Restaurant Fontana in a quiet street near the local bus station. They're also a good find in a town stretched for cheap accommodation.

**Hotel Vojvodina** (☎ 662 2122 vojvodina@visitnovisad.com; Trg Slobode 2; s/d/tr/apt from 2500/3800/4800/4200din) An atmospheric old hotel (1854) caught in a time warp of dark wood, glass panelling, brass handrails and stained-glass windows. The rooms show their age.

**Zenit** (☎ 662 1444; www.hotelzenit.co.yu; Zmaj Jovina 8; s/d €45/55-65; **P** 💻) This boutique hotel features a big glass frontage. Zenit is popular with foreign visitors, who appreciate the luxurious, comfortable and homely feel of the place.

## Eating & Drinking

**Nešić** (Pašićeva 23; 🕒 8am-9pm Mon-Sat) Worth a visit as much to buy a squidgy cake and coffee as to appreciate this 1950s cake shop that's still authentic with its red leatherette bench seats.

**Gušan** (Zmaj Jovina 4; dishes 110-400din; 🕒 9am-11pm Mon-Thu, 9am-1am Fri & Sat, 5pm-midnight Sun) A basic eatery and beer bar downstairs from an alley off Zmaj Jovina. Monday to Friday there's a set meal, which you might want to avoid on Wednesday, when it's essentially pig guts. The stylised countryside murals on the wall add a rural touch.

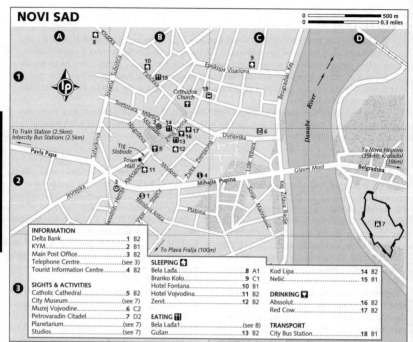

**NOVI SAD**

0 ──── 500 m
0 ──── 0.3 miles

| INFORMATION | | |
| --- | --- | --- |
| Delta Bank.......................1 B2 | | |
| KYM..............................2 B1 | | |
| Main Post Office.................3 B2 | | |
| Telephone Centre...............(see 3) | SLEEPING | Kod Lipa........................14 B2 |
| Tourist Information Centre......4 B2 | Bela Lađa......................8 A1 | Nešić...........................15 B1 |
| | Branko Kolo...................9 C1 | |
| SIGHTS & ACTIVITIES | Hotel Fontana.................10 B1 | DRINKING |
| Catholic Cathedral...............5 B2 | Hotel Vojvodina...............11 B2 | Abssolut.......................16 B2 |
| City Museum...................(see 7) | Zenit...........................12 B2 | Red Cow.......................17 B2 |
| Muzej Vojvodine.................6 C2 | | |
| Petrovaradin Citadel.............7 D2 | EATING | TRANSPORT |
| Planetarium....................(see 7) | Bela Lađa1....................(see 8) | City Bus Station...............18 B1 |
| Studios........................(see 7) | Gušan..........................13 B2 | |

**Bela Lađa** ( ☎ 661 6594; dishes 200-600din; Kisačka 21) Mileva and Albert might have dined here before they became Mr and Mrs Einstein – she once lived over the road. There's been a restaurant here since 1852 – time enough to start the collection of hundreds of bottles of wine that line the walls. Time also to perfect the 150 dishes on the traditional Vojvodinan menu.

**Plava Frajla** ( ☎ 661 3675; Sutjeska 2; dishes 300-400din) A popular knees-up restaurant just southwest of the centre. On Thursday and weekends traditional musicians play their hearts out, the clientele joins in with gusto and the party rips on until dawn. A good taster of local food is the *paprika u pavlaci* (an appetiser of yellow peppers fermented in cream cheese). We never understood why there were chairs fixed to the ceiling.

**Kod Lipa** ( ☎ 615 259; Svetozara Miletića 7; dishes 450-650din) This is an 1880s restaurant, where little has changed, as the old photographs on the wall testify. Age and atmosphere, plus traditional Vojvodinan food, come together to make this a must-visit restaurant. Downstairs in the converted cellars vast wine barrels on their sides form secluded alcoves with seating within. The appetising aroma of mellow wine still lingers.

**Absolut** ( ☎ 422 469; Zmaj Jovina 12; ☼ 9am-midnight Mon-Sat, 5pm-midnight Sun) The quasi-Palladian interior and cool Regency colours and furniture suggest a gentleman's club, where you feel you should be taking afternoon tea with Aunt Maud rather than guzzling the *slivovitz*.

**Red Cow** (cnr Dunavska & Zmaj Jovina) More Green Cow than Red, given the paint job, the Cow is an Irish-lookalike pub with a warm, woody and beery atmosphere. Halt here for a refreshing Guinness, draught Nikšić or an evening out.

## Getting There & Away

Frequent trains link the **train station** ( ☎ 443 200; Bulevar Jaše Tomića 4) with Belgrade (180din, two hours) and Subotica (240din, 1½ hours).

Frequent buses leave the **bus station** ( ☎ 444 021; Bulevar Jaše Tomića 6) for Belgrade (250din, 1½ hours).

## AROUND NOVI SAD

### FRUŠKA GORA ФРУШКА ГОРА

As a small island of rolling hills rising from the Vojvodina plain, Fruška Gora is known for its vineyards, orchards and monasteries. Thirty-five monasteries were built here between the 15th and 18th centuries to protect Serbian culture and religion from the Turks rampaging up from the south. Fifteen are preserved today and Krušedol and Novo Hopovo are the best known and most accessible.

**Krušedol Monastery** (near Krušedol Selo) was built by Serbian ruler Đorđe Brankovic in the early 1500s. Like many monasteries in this area, the church was severely damaged during a Turkish invasion and later rebuilt. Vivid frescoes, some original, leap out from the walls as a storyboard of biblical events.

**Novo Hopovo** (near Irig) is one of the oldest monasteries (1576) in the region and influenced the design of later churches, but suffered severe damage during WWII. Restoration of the frescoes has revealed earlier work painted under the influence of Cretan masters, who worked at Mt Athos Monastery in Greece. Many of the frescoes are incomplete but still present powerful images.

## SUBOTICA СУБОТИЦА

☎ 024 / pop 148,400

The attraction for visitors is the town's Hungarian-style Art Nouveau architecture (1908–12), which adds magic to the relaxed atmosphere. There's also the lakeside resort at Palić. At 10km from the border, the town is a useful transit point to/from Szeged (Hungary); it's worth a day trip from Belgrade.

## Orientation

Walk out of the train station and through the park to Đure Đrakovica. Left, (southeast), leads to the bus station and on to Palić. Staring at you on the right is the amazing Art Nouveau Modern Art Gallery. Also to the left is Korzo, a pedestrian street leading down to the old heart of Subotica, Trg Republike and the town hall.

## Information

**Exchange office** (train station; ⏰ 7am-7pm Mon-Sat, 7am-noon & 3-7pm Sun)

**Fiesta Internet Café** ( ☎ 559 490; Korzo 9; per hr 70din; ⏰ 10am-2pm & 4pm-midnight) Through an alley behind Korzo.

**Komercijalna Bank** ( ☎ 524 010; Korzo 10) ATM; cashes travellers cheques.

**Left-luggage** (train station; per item 90din; ⏰ 24hr)

**Tourist Information Office** ( ☎ 670 350; ticsu@yunord.net; Korzo 15; ⏰ 8am-8pm Mon-Sat,

8am-noon Sun) Very helpful folk with maps, pamphlets and advice.

## Sights

The imposing secessionist or Art Nouveau **town hall** (Trg Republike), built in 1910, contains an engaging **historical museum** ( ☎ 555 128; admission 50din; ⏰ 9am-4pm Tue, Wed & Fri, 11am-6pm Thu, 10am-2pm Sat) displaying regional life and the skull of a mammoth. You might also enjoy a look at the flogging trolley and the giant's broadsword. If you can visit the exquisitely decorated council chambers, the dark varnished wood, green baize cloth and high-back chairs give an air of petty municipal power.

An equally exquisite piece of Art Nouveau architecture is the sinuously decorated **Modern Art Gallery** ( ☎ 553 725; Trg Lenina 5; ⏰ 8am-2pm Mon, Wed & Fri, 8am-6pm Tue & Thu, 8am-noon Sat). One of the most beautiful buildings in Serbia, it's all swirling lines employing ceramic tiles, mosaics, stained-glass windows and finished off with a blue-tile roof.

Another wonderful piece of similar architecture is the disused **Synagogue** (cnr Trg Sinagoge) that's listed as an endangered monument by the **World Monuments Fund** (www.wmf.org). A casual passer-by might think it another Orthodox church but for the Star of David.

## Sleeping & Eating

Subotica isn't big on eating-places, apart from those below there's a slew of pizza joints around the Korzo.

**Dom Ucenika Srednjih Skola** ( ☎ 555 510; Harambašićeva 22; dm/s/d 540/1080/1728din; Ⓟ ) Student accommodation with rooms available throughout the year. While it's mostly for weekend and school holidays, weekday accommodation is possible, but it's best to phone and check; staff speak good English. Breakfast/lunch/dinner cost 1062/2242/2006din.

**PBG Hotel** ( ☎ /fax 556 542; Harambašićeva 21; s/d 3380/5060din; Ⓟ ) A pleasant hotel in backstreets that ensure a quiet night and good parking. While unexciting, the rooms are well furnished, the management pleasant and large get-you-started breakfasts are served.

**Lipa** (Đure Đrakovića 13; bureks 70din; ⏰ 24hr) A famous bakery and *burek* shop that's a brekkie or late-night snack stop. A cheese-and-mushroom *burek* and yogurt is a cure-all for hunger or hangover.

**Ravel** ( ☎ 554 670; Nušićeva 2; cakes 50-100din) Think Paris – the best in luscious cakes and superb

SERBIA

coffee, served with elegance in a beautifully decorated Art Nouveau interior with pastel green walls, stained-glass partitions and golden lamps.

**Népkör** (☎ 555 480; Žarka Zrenjanina 11; mains 400-1100din, set lunches 250din; ⏰ 10am-midnight Mon-Sat, 10am-5pm Sun) A chance to sample Hungarian cuisine; spoon into the steaming goulash or *gombásztál* (mushroom-and-cheese dish). The best feed is the three-course business lunch.

### Getting There & Away

From the **train station** (☎ 555 606) one international and two local trains go to Szeged in Hungary (155din, 1¾ hours). Trains travelling to Belgrade (480din, 3½ hours) also stop at Novi Sad.

For day trips there's a handy train leaving Belgrade at 8.20am, arriving at Novi Sad at 11.28am and leaving at 5.14pm to arrive back in Belgrade at 8.15pm.

The **bus station** (☎ 555 566; Marksov Put) has regular services to Szeged (210din, 1½ hours), hourly buses to Novi Sad (400din, two hours) and Belgrade (525din, 3½ hours).

## PALIĆ ПАЛИЋ

The park resort of Palić, 8km west of Subotica, edges onto a 5.5-sq-km lake that provides for boating, swimming, fishing and sailing. Outside the park on the Subotica road is a string of shops, pizza joints and a supermarket. In mid-July Palić hosts an international film festival (www.palicfilmfestival.com).

Bus 6 from outside the Hotel Patria in Subotica goes to Palić (35din, 20 minutes).

# SOUTHERN SERBIA

## DESPOTOVAC ДЕСПОТОВАЦ

☎ 035 / pop 25,500

The redoubtable Manasija Monastery and famous Resava Cave make Despotovac a worthwhile stopover on a casual wander south. The adventurous might also like to check out the coal-mining museum on the Cuprija–Despotovac road, and the Veliki Buk waterfalls in the area.

### Sleeping & Eating

**Kruna Motel** (☎ 611 659; Rudnička bb; s/d 1050/1900din; Ⓟ), on the western edge of town, is a welcome surprise. The bedroom slippers are a fine extra touch. The hotel will organise transport to the cave and monastery for 1500din.

**Grand Restaurant** (☎ 614 235; opposite bus station; dishes 280-400din; ⏰ 6am-midnight Mon-Sat, 3pm-midnight Sun) is a surprisingly good restaurant that at first glance seems no more than a bus station café; the grilled local trout is a good choice.

### Sights

**MANASIJA MONASTERY** МАНАСТИР МАНАСИЈА

This famous monastery defies the concept of a monastery as a haven of peace and spirituality, for confronting the visitor from the outside is a massive fortress sheltering a small church.

Dating from the early 1400s, the church was built to protect a community that had escaped the Turkish takeover of Kosovo. Despite seeming an impenetrable bulwark, the monastery was occupied several times by the Turks and consequently the remaining frescoes are only patchy. However, what's left is enough to startle the viewer with its vitality, colour and realism; it's as if the yet-to-come Italian Renaissance visited here first. Manasija is 2km north of the town.

### Resavska Pećina Ресавска Пећина

**Resava Cave** (☎ 611 110; respec@milnet.co.yu; 200din; ⏰ 9am-5pm Apr-Oct, arrange by phone Nov-Mar) is an exhibition or show cave up in the hills 20km beyond Despotovac. It was only discovered in 1962; some 4km have been explored although less than 1km is open to the public. Tours taking about 40 minutes lead through a series of winding passages to halls adorned with ancient stalactites and stalagmites. It's always cool down below so bring a jacket.

There's no public transport from Despotovac so take a taxi (1500din). Belgrade buses leave six times a day from Despotovac (380din, three hours).

## TOPOLA ТОПОЛА

☎ 034 / pop 25,000

Many Serbs regard this small rural town as sacred because it was from here that Karageorge Petrović pitched the Serbian insurrection against the Turks in 1804.

The **Tourist Organisation** (☎ 811 172; Kneginje Zorke 13; ⏰ 8am-4pm Mon-Fri, 10am-3pm Sat) has some pieces in English on Karageorge plus a town map. Alternatively, there's an information desk at the Hotel Oplenac.

There are no ATMs in town.

SERBIA

## Sights

The **museum** ( ☎ 811 781; Kralijice Marije; admission 150din; ☻ 9am-4pm) is a remnant of the fortified town built by Karageorge and his followers, and houses period artefacts and personal effects. Karageorge's personal canon, with one handle missing, dominates the entrance. This was removed by his grandson, King Petar I, and forged into his crown for when he succeeded to the Serbian throne in 1904.

The museum ticket also gives entry to the Church of St George and Petar House. Set in wooded parkland atop a hill, the **Church of St George** (Avenija Kralja Petra I; ☻ 8am-7pm Apr-Oct, 8am-4pm Nov-Mar) was erected between 1904 and 1912 by King Petar I as a memorial to his grandfather, Karageorge. The marble interior is decorated with copies of the best Serbian medieval frescoes and executed in millions of glistening mosaic pieces. Further mosaics depict the medieval kings of Serbia holding the monasteries they founded. The southern tomb here is Karageorge's while the other houses King Petar's remains.

Just downhill from the church is **Petar House** ( ☻ 8am-7pm Apr-Oct, 8am-4pm Nov-Mar), used by workmen who built the church and King Petar when he came to inspect the building progress. Today it houses temporary historical and art exhibitions.

## Sleeping

**Hotel Oplenac** ( ☎ 811 430; Avenija Kralja Petra I; s/d 1280/2160din; ℗ ) The only joint in town, it has comfortable but timeworn rooms.

## Getting There & Away

The bus station has frequent services to Belgrade (400din, three hours).

## NIŠ НИШ

☎ 018 / pop 250,000

Niš is mostly used as a stopover on the way to Sofia, Skopje or Thessaloniki. It hasn't much to lure the visitor, except for the infamous tourist attraction, the Ottoman skull-tower known as Ćele Kula.

Niš was first settled in pre-Roman times and flourished during the time of local boy made good, Emperor Constantine (AD 280–337). His extensive palace ruins lie 4km east of the town.

Turkish rule lasted from 1386 until 1877 despite several Serb revolts; the Ćele Kula is a grim pointer to their failure. The massive Tvrđava citadel is a reminder of the Ottoman supremacy.

## Orientation

The mighty Tvrđava Citadel dominates the north side of the Nišava River. Nearby is the market and the bus station, while the train station is to the west on Dimitrija Tucovića. The city centre is south of the river.

The citadel hosts a **blues, rock and pop festival** in July, and a **jazz festival** in October.

## Information

**KSR Beograd** ( ☎ 523 808, fax 523 840; Trg Oslobođenja 9; ☻ 8am-4pm Mon-Fri, 9am-2pm Sat) Sells train tickets and rail passes.
**Post Office** (Voždova Karađorđa 13a; internet access per hr 50din; ☻ 8am-8pm Mon-Sat)
**Tourist Office** ( ☎ 523 118; torg@bankerinter.net; Voždova Karađorđa 7; ☻ 7.30am-7pm Mon-Fri, 9am-1pm Sat) Basic tourist literature; books domestic buses.

## Sights

The Turks built the **Tvrđava** (Jadranska) on the site of a Roman fortress in 1396 to consolidate their hold on the region. The entrance through the redoubtable Stamboul Gate leads to a courtyard with souvenir shops and cafés.

The macabre **Ćele Kula** (Tower of Skulls; ☎ 222 228; Brače Tankosić bb; admission 100din; ☻ 9am-4pm Mon-Sat, 10am-2pm Sun Nov-Apr, 8am-8pm May-Oct; ℗ ) was erected by the Turks in 1809 as a ghoulish warning to would-be Serbian rebels. Commanded by the duke of Resava, the rebels were fighting to liberate Niš from a much larger force of Turks. The Serbs had suffered heavily and the duke desperately rushed the Turkish defences and fired his pistol into their powder magazine. The resulting explosion reportedly wiped out 4000 Serbs and 10,000 Turks, but not enough to deny the Turks victory. The dead Serbs were beheaded, scalped and their skulls embedded in this squat tower, but only 58 remain today. The admission ticket also includes a visit to Mediana.

**Mediana** ( ☎ 550 433; Bulevar Cara Konstantina bb; ☻ 9am-4pm Tue-Sat, 10am-2pm Sun) is the remains of a 4th-century Roman palace complex, possibly that of Constantine. Archaeological digging has revealed a palace, forum and an extensive grain-storage area with some sizable, almost intact, pottery vessels. The museum shelters some important mosaics and a collection of artefacts.

## Sleeping & Eating

Accommodation in Niš has been pathetic for some time. At the time of research there was only one city hotel open and the others were closed or on strike.

**Centrotourist Hotel** ( ☎ 527 267; 9 Brigada 10; s/d 1600/3200din; **P** ) The Centrotourist would not appear here but for being the only hotel in town. Indifferent reception staff, lack of maintenance and an unreasonable tariff count against it; on the plus side it's centrally located by the sports stadium and the rooms are clean.

**Mama Pizza** ( ☎ 245 044; Nade Tomić 10; dishes from 350din) A two-storey restaurant where the downstairs has a very much crisp-white-tablecloth, behave-yourself atmosphere while upstairs has more of a bistro feel. The pizzas, the best in town, are very large; consider sharing unless you haven't eaten for a week.

**Tramvaj** (Tramway; ☎ 547 909; Pobode 20) Take two trams and slice, build a servery out of one and surround it with seats from the other. A rattling good cup of coffee is just the ticket after a slog around town.

**Broz** ( ☎ 064 979 9909; Pobode 20; ☽ 10am-late) The basement is a cool retro homage to Josip Broz Tito and comes kitted out in shiny metal and red leatherette. A silver head of the big fella, hanging outside the 'girls', greets you as you slip down the stairs, and throughout the club are photos of Broz sucking on a big Havana with fellow socialist, Fidel Castro. Music is cool drum'n'bass and drinks include a fine range of malt whiskies.

## Getting There & Away

The **bus station** ( ☎ 255 117; Kneginje Ljubice) has services to Belgrade (640din, three hours, 10 buses), Brus for Kopaonik (380din, 1½ hours, at 10am and 3pm), Novi Pazar (700din, four hours, at 10am, 3.15pm and 7pm), Užice for Zlatibor (700din, five hours, at 7.25am, 12.05pm and 6.05pm) and Sarajevo (1380din, 10 hours, at 6.10am and 9pm).

Eight trains go to Belgrade (640din, 4½ hours) and two to Bar (seat/berth €17/26, 11½ hours).

Montenegro Airlines and JAT Airlines fly to Zurich from **Niš airport** ( ☎ 580 023; www.airportnis.co.yu).

## KOPAONIK КОПАОНИК

Kopaonik, Serbia's prime ski resort, is great for those looking for snow fun without the glamour. It has prices to match and a rather long season. It's based around Pančićev Vrh peak (2017m) overlooking Kosovo. Ski runs, served by 22 lifts, total 44km in length and range from nursery slopes to difficult; they're also linked to 20km of cross-country runs. The ski season runs from the end of November to the end of March, or even early April.

## Orientation & Information

Commercial and Delta banks cash travellers cheques and have ATMs around the resort. The website www.kopaonik.net has basic information and an area map.

There are several ski schools and equipment rental places, and daily and weekly lift passes are available.

## Activities

There are all the usual winter activities you'd expect: skiing, snowboarding and snowmobiles. In summer there's hiking, horse riding and mountain biking.

## Sleeping & Eating

There are several large-scale hotels with restaurants, gym facilities, pizzerias, discos and shops. Expect to pay €50 for a single and €84 per double (with half-board) in high season.

Possible accommodation options are the two-star **Hotel Jugobank** ( ☎ 036-71 040; Kopaonik) and **Hotel Junior** ( ☎ 037-825 051, fax 823 033; Brzeće), which is part of the Youth Hostel organisation. Inquiries can be made through the Youth Hostel organisation (see p757).

**Balkan Holidays** (www.balkanholidays.co.uk) is a British outfit that books ski holidays in Kopaonik. Its website has a topographical map showing the ski runs.

## Getting There & Away

From November to March and June to August there are three daily buses from Belgrade, and two from Niš.

## ZLATIBOR ЗЛАТИБОР

☎ 031 / pop 156,000

This large upland area in southwest Serbia is another ski resort but the season (January and February) is shorter than Kopaonik's due to its lower altitude. The summer season (June to August) draws more visitors for its mountain scenery and walking on marked routes.

## Orientation & Information

Zlatibor is a patchwork of small settlements centred on Tržni centar, a village of shops, eating and drinking places, a market and a bus stop.

**Anitours** ( ☎ /fax 841 855; www.anitours.co.yu; Tržni centar; ☽ 8am-7pm) Books tours and accommodation.

**Caffe Green** (Tržni centar; per hr 120din; ☽ 9am-2am) Internet access.

**Era Ski Service** (Tržni centar; ski lessons per hr 500din; equipment rental per day 500din)

**Komercijalna Bank** ( ☎ 845 182; Tržni centar) Cashes travellers cheques; ATM.

**Miros** ( ☎ 845 000; Tržni centar; ☽ 7am-9pm) Books accommodation and organises tours.

**Tourist organisation** ( ☎ 841 230; www.zlatibor.co.yu; ☽ 8am-8pm Jan-Feb, 8am-4pm Jun-Aug) By the bus stop; provides information, arranges private accommodation, organises day trips and sells bus tickets.

## Sights & Activities

Zlatibor skiing is easy stuff as there's a ski pull, although harder runs are in preparation. Ski schools and equipment-rental places can be found around Tržni centar.

Summer activities can include visits to the **museum village** at Sirogojno, the **Stopića cave** at Rožanstvo, **Uvac Monastery** at Stublo, and **old wooden churches** at Dobroselica, Jablanica and Kucani. **Mileševa Monastery**, with the famous white-angel fresco, is not too far away. More energetic pursuits include **rafting**, **walking**, **horse riding** and **mountain biking**; check with any travel agency.

The museum village of **Sirogojno** ( ☎ 802 291; www.sirogojno.org.yu; admission incl English-speaking guide 100din; ☽ 8.30am-7pm Apr-Oct, 8.30am-4pm Nov-Mar), 25km from Tržni centar, is set on a picturesque hillside. The museum is a collection of typical mountain-region buildings dating from the late 19th century, although the architectural styles belong to the 13th and 14th centuries. The buildings have been kitted out with furnishings and tools of trade to bring the place to life.

A day trip can also incorporate the **Šargan 8 narrow-gauge steam railway** (Kremna to Mokra Gora; 2½hr trip 400din; ☽ May-Sep), famous for its tortuous ascent over the mountains. This very scenic section is just one small part of the line that once connected Belgrade with Sarajevo via Užice and Višegrad. Work is going on to rebuild the line onto Višegrad in Bosnia and Hercegovina so when it's completed you'll need your passport for a ride.

This region of Serbia is famed for its wooden buildings. Some you'll have seen at Sirogojno but while you're in Mokra Gora have a look at the pretty wooden **Church of St Ilija**, down on the main road. Two kilometres outside on a bluff above the town is **Mećavnik** ( ☎ 800 686; admission 160din; ☽ 9am-9pm), a wooden town, built as a setting for Emir Kusturica's film *Zivot Je Cudo* (Life Is a Miracle).

## Sleeping & Eating

Accommodation prices quoted are for the January to February and June to August seasons; expect to pay 10% to 20% less out of season. Most visitors choose to stay in private rooms and apartments, which are modern, well furnished and usually have light cooking facilities. Typically, apartments cost €20 to €80 for two to six people, and €15 for singles; private rooms with shared bathrooms cost €8 to €12. The hotels reviewed are open all year.

**Olimp** ( ☎ 842 555; hotelolimp@ptt.yu; Naselje Sloboda bb; s/d B&B from 3740/6160din; P ☒ ☒ ) A modern hotel that's well decorated throughout, with some striking works of art; prices remain the same all year but reduce after three days' stay. The penthouse apartment is suitable for six with three double bedrooms and a large living area. A big outdoor pool keeps everyone cool in summer.

**Hotel Jugopetrol** ( ☎ 841 467; s/d/tr B&B from 3300/3600/4800din; s/d/tr half-board 2100/3600/5700din; P ☒ ) This big hotel sits on a hill about 300m southwest of Tržni centar, making our choice a top-floor room because of the view. All rooms are large with TV, phone and small balconies. The enormous lobby houses many services such as moneychanging, and there's a pool, table tennis, ski-equipment hire and shops. There's even figure-enhancing treatment, which will surely be needed after visiting the pastry shop in the conservatory.

**Zlatni Bor Restaurant** ( ☎ 841 077; dishes from 250din) A good place for a hunger-stopping breakfast. Try the *kajmak* and *lepinja* (traditional bread). It overlooks the lake, about 50m northeast of Tržni centar.

**Zlatiborska Koliba** ( ☎ 841 638; dishes 300-650din) Wooden ceilings, a big brick-arched bar, an open fireplace and good Serbian food chased by slugs of *rakija* make this a suitable place to recover from the exhaustion of skiing or hiking. In season there's live traditional music. The house speciality is *teleće grudi* – a stew of

**SERBIA**

veal, potatoes, *kajmak* and vegetables cooked in an earthenware pot over an open fire.

There are more pizza and *ćevapčići* joints, cafés and bars than you could visit in a month.

## Shopping

Apart from fruit and veg, the market sells all manner of interesting things. For the nippy weather there's a range of brightly coloured chunky pullovers and gloves; consider buying intricate lacework, a pair of *opanak* (traditional Serbian leather shoes) with curly toes or *čutura* (wooden bottles) for holding your *rakija* stash.

On the food and drink front there's plenty of domestic *rakija*, honey, pickles, several varieties of *kajmak, pršuta* (smoked meats) and dried herbs for tea.

## Getting There & Around

Buses leave the **bus stand** ( ☎ 841 587) for Belgrade (520din, four hours, six buses), Niš (500din, four hours, at 7am) and the nearest railhead at Užice (80din, 45 minutes, hourly).

Minibuses ply the villages in season.

## NOVI PAZAR НОВИ ПАЗАР

☎ 020 / pop 86,000

The Turks were not ousted until 1912 and Novi Pazar is perhaps the best visible example of their culture in Serbia, outside of Kosovo. It's also an Orthodox heartland with significant monasteries well worth visiting. This is also a gateway town for Kosovo.

## Orientation & Information

The piddly Raška River runs through the town, placing the old Turkish fortress, Turkish quarter and the mosque of Altun Alem on the southern side. Spanning the river is the strange Hotel Vrbak. Also crossing the river is 28 Novembar, which on the northern side has numerous cafés, bars and restaurants.

## Sights

Wandering around the old town, with its curious shops, can be an absorbing half-day. Here workshops with old crafts like cobbling and tinsmithing sit alongside small cafés, where old men sip strong coffee, play cards and talk. Spare a glance for the unusual apartment blocks and the circular spaceship, Hotel Vrbak – a freak show of Yugoslav central planning or an architect on acid?

### SOPOĆANI MONASTERY

King Uroš erected this **monastery**, 16km southwest of Novi Pazar, in line with the usual practice of medieval kings endowing monasteries to a saint, who would then intercede for them at the Day of Judgment – a sort of afterlife insurance. The 13th-century monastery is a remarkable story of survival, having been destroyed by the Turks at the end of the 17th century and abandoned until restored in the 1920s. The remaining frescoes show the definite influence of Romanesque art by giving the figures a rhythm, plasticity and vibrancy.

### PETROVA CRKVA

Surrounded by an ancient cemetery, the small **Church of St Peter** stands on a bluff above the Kraljevo road on the edge of town. It's Serbia's oldest church, with sections dating from the 8th century. Inside, the coarse masonry, the step-into baptismal well and the feet-polished flagstones provide a tangible sense of the ancient. The 13th-century frescoes are incomplete due to damage. If the church is locked, ask at the nearest house for the keeper of the huge iron key.

### ĐURĐEVI STUPOVI MONASTERY

Rising out of a copse, 3km uphill from Petrova Crkva, is the still-damaged monastery of **Đurđevi Stupovi** (Columns of St George), the oldest in Serbia and dating from 1170. The story goes that St Simeon, then Stefan Nemanja and ruler of much of what is now southern Serbia, was captured by the Turks in 1172. He promised God that if he regained his freedom he would endow a monastery to St George. Eventually he was released and abdicated later in life to become the monk Simeon, who endowed this monastery as promised. He was later buried here.

The church was extensively damaged by the Turks in the same bout of destruction that befell Sopoćani. Repairs were done in the 1900s but undone in WWII, when German troops removed stonework for their defences. Consequently only the western and northern sides of the church remain today.

## Sleeping & Eating

**Hotel Vrbak** ( ☎ 315 300; Maršala Tita bb; s/d from 1200/2200din; [P] ) This architectural spaceship, resting on cotton reel–shaped legs, and berthed in the main square, is the town's major hotel. The rooms have seen too many guests and the whole place needs a makeover, but you don't get many chances to stay in a strange place like this. As you check in, consider how they clean the huge translucent windows of the dome many metres above.

**Hotel Kan** (Cannes; ☎ /fax 315 300; Rifata Burdžovića 10; s/d 1740/2690din) This modern hotel, built in an Oriental style, has rather smallish rooms with half-carpeted walls compensated for by cable TV and minibar; it's clean and in reasonable condition.

**Kafana Centar** ( ☎ 27 799; 28 Novembar 21; dishes 150-170din) In contrast to this street's open-front eateries, this traditional café, a favourite hangout of the town's older folk, hides behind lace curtains. The smiling matron welcomes foreigners, excuses their poor Serbian, and dishes up a mighty helping of *ćevapčići* and salad.

**Hotel Tadz** ( ☎ 311 904; Rifata Burdževića 79; dishes 350-600din) Sometimes hotel kitchens surprise with the quality of their food, a fact the well-heeled clientele of the town have discovered with the Tadz. We enjoyed their *pièce de résistance*, the *pstrmka* (trout), served with a luscious garlic sauce.

## Getting There & Away

The **bus station** ( ☎ 318 354; Omladinska bb) has services to Belgrade (720din, five to six hours, half-hourly), Sarajevo (1131din, seven hours, at 7am, 10am, 11am and 10pm), Prishtina in Kosovo (450din, three hours, at 5.30am, 5.45am, 6am, 9am and 12.40pm) and Podgorica in Montenegro (650din, five hours, at 9.30am, 1pm, 1.30pm and 10.15pm).

# KOSOVO КОСОВО

The ebb and flow of Islam and Orthodox Christianity has left Kosovo a legacy of several artistically beautiful buildings, such as Gračanica Monastery near Prishtina, Decani Monastery near Peja, and the Sinan Pasha Mosque in Prizren. These all escaped the violence of 1999 and 2004.

The countryside is visually attractive – wide-open plains in some places and rolling hills patchworked with fields in others. Rearing up behind Peja in the southwest are tall mountains, often snow-clad, and including Djeravica (2656m), the tallest mountain in pre-1999 Serbia. Further east, nearer Macedonia, the mountains provide the ski slopes of Brezovica.

Serb influence in the province has ended, and been replaced by an Albanian one. In Prishtina new monuments celebrate Albanian heroes while the displays in the museums of Prishtina and Prizren are exploring the province's Illyrian and Albanian past.

## HISTORY

Following their defeat in 1389 by the Turks, the Serbs abandoned the region to the Albanians, descendants of the Illyrians who were the original inhabitants. Serbia regained control after the Turks departed in 1913 and in the ensuing years 500,000 Albanians emigrated, and Serbs were brought in to settle the vacated land. During WWII the territory was incorporated into Italian-controlled Albania and then liberated in October 1944 by Albanian partisans.

Three postwar decades of pernicious neglect followed until an autonomous province was created in 1974 and economic aid increased. Little changed and the standard of living in Kosovo stagnated at a quarter of the Yugoslav average. There was agitation for full republic status and in 1981 demonstrations were violently put down by the Serbian military. 300 people died and 700 were imprisoned.

Trouble reignited in November 1988 with demonstrations against the sacking of local officials and President Azem Vllasi. Further unrest and strikes in February 1989 produced a Serbian-declared state of emergency; in serious rioting, 24 Albanian Kosovars were shot dead. In July 1990 Kosovo's autonomy was

SERBIA

**SERBIA**

---

**VISITING KOSOVO FIRST?**

Legally Kosovo is still part of Serbia so there are no border posts or immigration controls between the two. So if you arrive in Kosovo first you can only enter Serbia via another country giving you a legitimate Serbian entry stamp.

---

cancelled, broadcasts in Albanian ceased, the only Albanian-language newspaper was banned, and 115,000 Albanians had their jobs taken by loyalist Serbs. A referendum held against Serbian opposition produced a 90% turnout with 98% voting for independence.

Frustrated attempts to negotiate autonomy encouraged the formation of the Kosovo Liberation Army (KLA) in 1996, and using guerrilla tactics they began to harass the Serbs.

In March 1999 a US-backed plan to return Kosovo's autonomy was rejected by Serbia. Stepping up attacks on the KLA, Serbia moved to empty the province of its non-Serbian population. Nearly 850,000 Kosovo Albanians fled to Albania and Macedonia; Serbia ignored demands to desist and NATO unleashed a bombing campaign on 24 March 1999. On 2 June Milošević acquiesced to a UN settlement, Serbian forces withdrew and the Kosovo Force (KFOR) took over. Since June 1999 Kosovo has been administered as a UN-NATO protectorate.

Kosovo slipped from the world's eye until March 2004, when two Albanian children, allegedly chased by Serbs, drowned in a river. Investigations disproved this allegation but at the time it sparked off a simmering discontent, mostly among youths. Nineteen Serbs were killed, 600 homes burnt and 29 Orthodox monasteries and churches, many medieval, were destroyed. KFOR, which could have controlled much of the outrage, was disastrously slow to act.

Independence negotiations commenced in February 2006. The Kosovo Albanians demand independence, whereas the Serbian

---

**MOBILE PHONING**

Kosovo doesn't have its own mobile-phone network so it's latched onto Monaco's. When dialling a mobile number from outside Kosovo just add a ☎ 0377 prefix.

---

stance hovers between rejection and accepting some form of Kosovar–Serb autonomy in an independent Kosovo.

## DANGERS & ANNOYANCES
The province is thought to have been cleared of landmines but there is still unexploded ordnance about. If you intend to go off the beaten track then check with KFOR or the police.

## PRISHTINA
☎ 038 / pop 165,000
Prishtina is a bustling capital inflated with the activity and personnel of foreign agencies, plus all the bars, restaurants and internet cafés to service them. There's a day's sightseeing within the city but a reliable bus service makes Prishtina a good base for forays into the countryside, Peja and Prizren.

### Orientation
Bulevardi Nëna Terezë (Mother Teresa), the main street, houses the UN Interim Administration Mission in Kosovo (Unmik) headquarters. West of this is the Sports Complex shopping mall with restaurants and a supermarket. Bulevardi Bil Klinton (yes, him) runs southwest from Bulevardi Nëna Terezë passing the bus station, the airport (17km) and onto Peja.

### Information
**Airprishtina** ( ☎ 243 557; Bulevardi Nëna Terezë 25a; ◷ 8am-6pm Mon-Sat, 8am-noon Sun) Flight bookings.
**Barnatorja Pharmacy** ( ☎ 224 245; Bulevardi Nëna Terezë; ◷ 7.30am-8pm)
**Dukagjini** ( ☎ 248 143; Bulevardi Nëna Terezë 20; ◷ 8am-8pm Mon-Sat) Novels and art books in English, and city maps.
**Internet** ( ☎ 044 608 549; per hr €1; ◷ 9am-midnight) Internet and cheap international calls; downtown opposite Unmik.
**Newsstand** (Luan Haradinaj; ◷ 9am-late) Foreign newspapers and magazines; latest papers arrive at 6pm; outside Monaco restaurant.
**Post Telephone Kosova** (PTK; ☎ 245 339; Bulevardi Nëna Terezë; ◷ 8am-10pm) Post and telephone.
**Pro Credit Bank** ( ☎ 240 248; UÇK; ◷ 9am-4pm Mon-Fri) Cashes travellers cheques; ATM.

### Sights
**Kosovo Museum** ( ☎ 249 964; Marte e Driele; admission €1.50; ◷ 10.30am-7pm Tue-Sun) has a thoughtful and well-captioned exhibition on premedieval Kosovo. As they point out, most of the collection was looted and taken to Belgrade.

---

**VOX POP**

*Who are you?* Naim Shala, photographer living in Prishtina.

*What do you like best about Kosovo?* I love my country. As a photographer, it still has unspoilt countryside and mountains. Yes, it's a beautiful country; people are friendly, especially to foreigners.

*What would you like to change?* We have to start thinking about this as our home, no longer as a communist property.

*Will you give up smoking?* When it will kill me. Ah, seriously, I am thinking of giving up.

---

Behind the museum is the **Jashar Pasha mosque** with notable floral designs, a huge chandelier and a finely decorated mihrab. Around the corner is a well-restored Balkan-style house, the home of the **Academy of Science and Arts**.

Nearby, a second mosque, the **Sultan Fatih Mehemit**, dates from the mid-15th century. Again there's exquisite decorative work and, interestingly, some carved marble stones from some earlier use can be found among the courtyard flagstones.

Much of the old Turkish quarter was destroyed by WWII bombing but odd bits remain. Almost opposite Jashar Pasha is a **ruined hammam** (Turkish bath; Vasil Andori), and if you walk down this street to Xhemajl Prishtina and the market, you'll come across several old houses.

## Sleeping

**Velania Guest House** (Pansion Profesor; ☎ 531 742, 044 167 455; Velania 4, 34; s/d €13/18, with shared bathroom €10/15) A noble professor has opened his house to budget travellers and provides 17 rooms on three floors, and a small kitchen on each floor. Tea and coffee ingredients are free, as is the laundry service. The professor intends to open another house with dormitory accommodation.

**Iliria** ( ☎ 224 275, fax 548 117; Bulevardi Nëna Terezë; s with shared toilet €30, d €40; **P** ) The old rambling Iliria is holding its own against private competition with reduced prices. Doubles bathrooms are large with hot waterfall-style showers. It's a central safe haven for the party animal, and comes with very helpful staff.

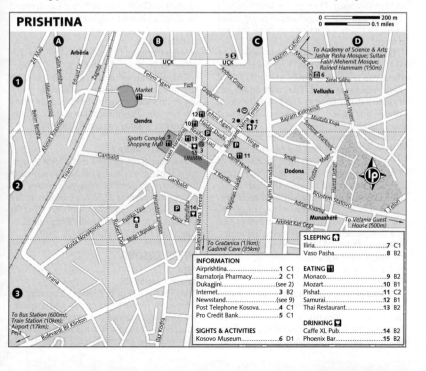

**Hotel Prishtina** ( ☎ 223 284; www.hotelprishtina.com; Vaso Pasha 20; s/d/apt €69/92/135; 🖭 ) One of Prishtina's new postwar hotels that's well equipped, but as it's spread over four floors you'd think there'd be a lift. The doubles are better value than the apartments. The hotel claims a high occupancy rate, so it's wise to book ahead. Breakfast is a very decent buffet.

## Eating & Drinking

There are plenty of small cafés selling *burek* and burgers.

**Monaco** ( ☎ 227 490; Luan Haradinaj; pizzas €3-6) Eat here or maybe buy your newspaper from the vendor outside and stretch your reading time inside with drinks and cakes. A big expat crowd always means there's something sporty on the box. The owner is the director of Prishtina's basketball team and that explains the slew of shiny cups on top of the TV, and the beer fridges.

**Pishat** ( ☎ 245 333; Qamil Hoxha 11; dishes €3-6) This place is decorated in strong earth, blue and yellow colours, giving a bright interior that's like a blast of sunshine on a dull day. A big stomach-filling breakfast costs €2. Feeling midday-snackish? Then go for *tavë e kuge*, a veggie hotpot with a large hunk of newly baked bread. To finish, a macchiato coffee – the best in town.

**Thai Restaurant** ( ☎ 044 163 598; dishes €7-11; ⏱ 11am-3pm & 6-11pm Mon-Sat) Just the place for when you're tired of grills and pizza, and fancy something spicy. Thai restaurants out of their natural habitat don't usually work, but this one's good. It's between Unmik and Luan Haradinaj.

**Samurai** ( ☎ 044 393 111; Fehmi Agani; €5-14; ⏱ 11.30am-2.30pm & 6-10pm Mon-Fri, 6-10.30pm Sat & Sun) Another refuge from local food with lots of snacky things – fried eggplant, yogurt garlic dips and marinated octopus that can be assembled into a meal. In addition there's tempura and sushi plus a special mussel soup. The bill comes in a woven palm box accompanied by a complimentary 'secret recipe' liqueur.

**Mozart** ( ☎ 044 425 555; Luan Haradinaj) A place for afters with ice-cream delights, waffles, fruit-and-cream concoctions and other deadly delights.

**Phoenix Bar** (snacks €2.50-4) A lads-away-from-home bar decorated with football team colours and scarves. Phoenix serves cholesterol-damaging breakfasts, coffee and snacks all day plus a traditional English roast on Sunday.

There's live music some weekends. It's opposite Unmik.

**Caffe XL Pub** (Bulevardi Nëna Terezë) One block south of the Grand Hotel, this British-style pub serves just drinks. Try the very palatable local beer, Birrë e Pejës.

## Getting There & Away

International and domestic services leave from the **bus station** ( ☎ 550 011; Mitrovicë-Prishtinë).

Kosovo's **airport** ( ☎ 038 5958; www.airportpristina .com) is 17km west of Prishtina on the Peja road. The only transport there is taxi. Try **Taxi Velana** ( ☎ 044 225 325); the fare should be about €20.

# AROUND PRISHTINA
## GRAČANICA

The superbly decorated Gračanica Monastery, built by the Serbian King Milutin in the early 14th century, is some 13km southeast of Prishtina. It's in the shape of a five-dome building on a cross-in-a-square plan, typical of the best Byzantine architecture of the period. Most of the frescoes date from then and cover all the walls.

Entry is no problem once you've identified yourself to KFOR at the entrance. Catch one of the frequent buses to Gjilan that pass outside.

### GADIMË CAVE

Worth a plunge underground, **Gadimë Cave** (Marble Cave; ☎ 044 285 941; adult/child €2.50/1; ⏱ 9am-6pm) is Kosovo's only exhibition or 'show' cave. It's famous for its helictites, thin stalactites growing at impossible angles. Several daily buses run here from Prishtina, 35km to the north; an alternative is a taxi (return €30 to €40).

### MEMORIAL PREKAZ

This **memorial** ( ⏱ 8am-8pm) to the 1998 slaughter of the Jeshari clan by the Serbs consists of the shelled remains of their two houses and the cemetery where all 53 are buried. Catch a bus to Skënderaj (€4, two hours), get off at the lurid green mosque and walk 500m uphill, or take a taxi from Prishtina (€50).

# OUTER KOSOVO
## Peja

☎ 039 / pop 69,000

Peja (Peč) is a mix of modern Yugoslav development in the town centre and Turkish-era buildings around the bazaar. The major attractions of the Patrijaršija Monastery, the Rugova Gorge and the Decani Monastery lie outside town. Rearing up behind the town, several 2000m-plus mountains form a picture-postcard backdrop.

## ORIENTATION & INFORMATION
The Prishtina road runs into the northern part of town to meet the main street, which then strikes south into the town centre. The bus station is at the intersection of these two routes. Many streets have yet to be labelled with their new names.

## SIGHTS
Peja's colourful **bazaar** is the place to acquire a carpet, a horse collar, bulk tobacco, daggy tracksuits, wedding outfits or a *plis* (white-felt domed Albanian hat).

**Patrijaršija Monastery**, seat of the Peč patriarchy, is 2km west of Peja, and visiting may take a little organising with the Italian KFOR troops at the gate. Inside the walls, in a garden of ruins and ancient trees, is the monastery, which consists of three ancient churches sharing a common narthex or entrance hall. The stone floors polished by centuries of shuffling monastic feet, the gloomy interiors and the smell of incense immediately stun you and draw you back centuries. The frescoes are incredible; no doubt about it, this is the Sistine Chapel of the Serbian Orthodox world.

The monastery is at the mouth of the **Rugova Gorge**, which slices into the mountains. It's worthwhile driving to one of the restaurants up the gorge. One day these mountains may achieve their potential for hiking and climbing.

**Decani Monastery** (1335) is 15km south and accessible by bus and a 2km walk. The monastery was the endowment of King Stefan (later a saint) whose body is buried within the church. According to the monks it is still uncorrupted (not yet decayed), which is the hallmark of a saint.

## GETTING THERE & AWAY
The **bus station** ( ☎ 32 527) has hourly services to Prishtina and Prizren. Fares are €2 to €3.

## Prizren
☎ 029 / pop 108,000
Although Prizren was the medieval capital of 'Old Serbia', the architectural influence is Turkish. Of all the towns mentioned in this chapter, Prizren has the largest remaining treasury of Turkish-era buildings, including the remarkable mosque and baths. Wander through the narrow streets and soak up the history and atmosphere from every cobble, over-hanging building and part-open wooden doorway, and then mull over it all at an outdoor café in the Shadrvan.

Unfortunately, Albanian Kosovar firing of Serb houses in 1999, and again in 2004, has left an ugly scar of burnt-out houses up the hillside. Moreover, the Orthodox churches have been gutted.

## ORIENTATION & INFORMATION
The town is built around the river and Shadrvan, a cobblestone plaza with a fountain in the middle. The bus station is on the Peja road about 2km northwest from the centre.

The Prishtina road arrives from the northeast and ends at the main bridge over the river. Crossing the river just west of here is a 'new' medieval bridge, built to replace the old one destroyed by floods in 1979.

An increasingly important documentary film and photographic exhibition, **Dokufest** (www.dokufest.com) happens in the first week of September.

## SIGHTS
A slow plod up from behind the Shadrvan brings you to the ruins of a castle that has passed through Roman, Turkish, Serbian and KFOR hands. The views are quite stupendous and if you're there when the imams call for prayers from their mosques, you'll hear a wave of chanting sweep across the town.

The 1561 **Sinan Pasha Mosque** on the riverside dominates the centre and can be visited for its fine, decorated high-domed ceiling.

Near the Theranda Hotel, the restored **Gazi Mehmed Pasha Baths** (1563) have become an occasional exhibition space. The internal upper floor was destroyed during WWII; maybe it couldn't cope with being an Italian bordello.

Opposite the post office is a solitary **minaret-like tower** with the Star of David; it's believed to be the remnants of a synagogue.

Some 200m upriver from the Theranda Hotel is a small **museum complex** ( ☎ 31 487; Seshi i Lidhjse bb; adult/child €1/0.20; ☉ 10am-10pm Sun-Tue) celebrating the Albanian League of Prizren. This was an independence movement in Turkish times and the museum celebrates the league and historical Prizren.

A 2km walk up by the river brings you into a ravine and the ruins of a 14th-century **castle**, the seat of the Serbian King Dušan. At present the interior is occupied by KFOR and isn't open to the public.

### GETTING THERE & AWAY
**The bus station** ( ☎ 631 152; Geromin de Rada) has hourly services to Prishtina and Peja. Fares are €2 to €3.

## Brezovica
This ski resort, 60km south of Prishtina, is seen as a bright spot in Kosovo's tourism future. The snow season is exceptionally long and runs from December up until May in some years.

Nine ski runs, served by seven chairlifts (day pass €10), lead down from 2500m; ski equipment and snowboards can be hired (€5 to €10 per day) and lessons (€15 per hour) are available. Even if you're not a skier, a trip up the ski lift is worth it to view the snowy mountains.

The **Molika Hotel** ( ☎ 290-70 452; per person B&B/half-board/full-board €35/35/40), with a restaurant, bars and cafés, is the only hotel on the slopes and is open only from 25 December to early May.

## GETTING THERE & AWAY
### Air
For airlines operating from **Prishtina airport** ( ☎ 548 430) see p779. Departure tax is €15 unless included in the ticket price.

### Bus
#### INTERNATIONAL
International buses serve much of Europe, including Skopje, Macedonia (€5, 1½ hours), Tirana, Albania (€35, 10 hours), Istanbul, Turkey (€40, 20 hours), and Sarajevo, Bosnia and Hercegovina (€30, 10 hours).

#### MONTENEGRO
From Peja there's an overnight bus to Podgorica (€15, seven hours). Alternatively minibuses (€5) and taxis (€25) go to Rožaje from outside the Peja bus station.

#### SERBIA
Buses connect Prishtina and Novi Pazar (€5.50, 3½ hours, at 10am, at 12.20pm, 5.30pm and 6.30pm) and Belgrade (€14, seven hours, at 10.30pm and 11pm).

### Train
There's now a service to Skopje (€10, 2½ hours, 6.24am and 1.04pm) from the **Fushë Kosovë station** ( ☎ 536 355) outside Prishtina.

## GETTING AROUND
A reliable bus service links all the main towns and villages with buses operating between Prishtina, Prizren and Peja (€3 to €4, two hours) on a half-hourly basis.

# SERBIA DIRECTORY

## ACCOMMODATION
Belgrade's new hostels are providing much-needed budget accommodation for travellers. While several state hotels have been privatised, tarted up and yanked up their prices, there are still a few reasonably priced midrange hotels. In Kosovo accommodation prices have stabilised as more hotels are built and expense-account customers (UN and nongovernmental organisations) go on to the next hot spot.

The cheapest option in the ski resorts is a private room. These can be as good as hotel rooms and certainly more personable; they range from a room sharing a bathroom up to an apartment with several rooms including kitchen and private bathroom. Look out for signs saying 'rooms', 'sobe' or 'zimmer'.

Where there are seasonal differences we quote the high-season price. Unless otherwise mentioned the tariff includes breakfast and the rooms have private bathrooms. Don't forget to bargain for a discount for several days' stay.

## ACTIVITIES
Serbia's main ski resorts are Zlatibor (p768) and Kopaonik (p768), while Kosovo's resort is at Brezovica (left). The ski season is from December to March; the resorts are also popular for summer activities.

## BOOKS
Tim Judah has a good eye for the regional scene, so try one of his books, *The Serbs: History, Myth and the Destruction of Yugoslavia* and *Kosovo: War and Revenge.* Also for Kosovo consider *Kosovo: A Short History,* by Noel Malcolm. Sabrina Ramet's *Balkan Babel* is an engaging look at Yugoslavia from Tito to Milošević.

Get your hands on *Guerrilla Radio* (alternative title – *Guerilla Radio: Rock'n'Roll Radio and Belgrade's Underground Resistance*), a riveting account by Matthew Collin of the role of the B92 radio station in undermining the Milošević regime. *With Their Backs to the World*, by Ĺsne Seierstad, is a compelling read of a cross section of Serbian lives during and after the Milošević years; she dispassionately lets the people tell their own stories.

## BUSINESS HOURS

Banks keep long hours, often 8am to 7pm weekdays and 7am to noon Saturday. On weekdays many shops open at 7am, close from noon to 4pm but reopen until 8pm. Department stores, some major shops and supermarkets are open all day. Cafés, restaurants and bars usually open around 8am and work to midnight. Most government offices close on Saturday but shops stay open until around 4pm.

## CUSTOMS

If you're bringing in more than €2000 in cash then you have to complete a currency declaration form on arrival and show it on departure. In practice it's ignored but if customs officials wanted to play by the rules, they could confiscate your money. Play safe and declare.

## DANGERS & ANNOYANCES

Travel nearly everywhere is safe but government travel advisories will warn against travel to Kosovo, see the boxed text on p771.

The major downer is the incessant smoking in public places. The majority of people are smokers, and the rest want to be when they are old enough. 'No smoking' signs are regularly ignored.

It's fine to discuss politics if you're also willing to listen.

Check with the police before photographing any official building they're guarding.

## EMBASSIES & CONSULATES
### Serbian Embassies & Consulates

**Albania** ( ☎ 042-23 042, 042-232 091; ambatira@icc-al.org; Skender Beg Bldg 8/3-II, Tirana)
**Australia** ( ☎ 02-6290 2630; scgembau@iprimus.com.au, O'Malley, ACT 2606)
**Bosnia and Hercegovina** ( ☎ 033-260 090; yugoamba@bih.net.ba; Obala Marka Dizdara 3a, Sarajevo 71000)
**Bulgaria** ( ☎ 02-946 1635, 946 1059; ambasada-scg-sofija@infotel.bg; Veliko Tmovo 3, Sofia 1504)
**Canada** ( ☎ 613-233 6289; www.embscg.ca/consular.html; 17 Blackburn Ave, Ottawa, Ontario, K1N8A2)
**Croatia** ( ☎ 01-457 9067ambasada@ambasada-srj.hr; Pantovcak 245, Zagreb)

**France** ( ☎ 01 40 72 24 24; ambasadapariz@wanadoo.fr; 5 rue Leonard da Vinci, 75016 Paris)
**Germany** ( ☎ 030-895 77 00; info@botschaft-smg.de; Taubert Strasse 18, Berlin D-14193)
**Hungary** ( ☎ 1-322 9838; ambjubp@mail.datanet.hu; Dozsa Gyorgy ut 92/b, Budapest H-1068)
**Netherlands** ( ☎ 0703 63 23 97; yuambanl@bart.nl; Groot Hertoginnelaan 30, The Hague 2517 EG)
**Romania** ( ☎ 021-211 98 71; ambiug@ines.ro; Calea Dorobantilor 34, Bucharest)
**UK** ( ☎ 0207-235 9049; www.yugoslavembassy.org.uk; 28 Belgrave Sq, London, SW1X 8QB)
**USA** ( ☎ 202-332 0333; www.yuembusa.org; 2134 Kalorama Rd NW, Washington, DC, 20008)

### Embassies & Consulates in Serbia
The following are represented in Belgrade:
**Albania** (Map p753; ☎ 011-306 6642; Bulevar Mira 25A)
**Australia** (Map p756; ☎ 011-330 3400; Čika Ljubina 13)
**Bosnia and Hercegovina** (Map p753; ☎ 011-329 1277; Milana Tankosića 8)
**Bulgaria** (Map p756; ☎ 011-361 3980; Birčaninova 26)
**Canada** (Map p756; ☎ 011-306 3000; Kneza Miloša 75)
**Croatia** (Map p756; ☎ 011-361 0535; Kneza Miloša 62)
**France** (Map p756; ☎ 011-302 3500; Pariska 11)
**Germany** (Map p756; ☎ 011-306 4300; Kneza Miloša 74-6)
**Hungary** (Map p756; ☎ 011-244 0472; Krunska 72)
**Netherlands** (Map p756; ☎ 011-361 8327; Simina 29)
**Romania** (Map p756; ☎ 011-361 8327; Kneza Miloša 70)
**UK** (Map p756; ☎ 011-264 5055; Resavska 46)
**USA** (Map p756; ☎ 011-361 9344; Kneza Miloša 50)

## FESTIVALS & EVENTS

See p757 for details on Belgrade's major festivals, and p763 for details on Novi Sad's Exit Festival.

On a different note there's the famous festival of brass band music at Guča near Čačak that takes place in the last week of August each year. For those who want to hear something different and tap into an exhibition of Serbian pride and culture, this is the festival to attend.

## GAY & LESBIAN TRAVELLERS

The general attitude in Serbia is very homophobic and hostile although less so in the more liberal Belgrade. Even so, gay and lesbian marches in Belgrade have been met by thuggish violence. Consequently gay and lesbian society keeps itself well hidden, although Belgrade now has one openly gay nightclub, Club X, p760.

## HOLIDAYS

Public holidays in Serbia:

**New Year** 1 and 2 January
**Orthodox Christmas** 7 January
**Constitution Day** 15 February
**International Labour Days** 1 and 2 May

Orthodox churches celebrate Easter between one and five weeks later than other churches.

In Kosovo, 28 November is Flag Day and Easter Monday is a public holiday.

## INTERNET RESOURCES

**B92** (www.b92.net) A good independent source of Serbian news.
**Fruška Gora National Park** (www.fruskagora-natl-park.co.yu)
**Serbia and Montenegro Government** (www.gov.yu)
**Serbian Government** (www.srbija.sr.gov.yu)
**Serbian Tourist Organisation** (www.serbia-tourism.org)

## LANGUAGE

Serbian is the common language in Serbia but Albanian is the required language for Kosovo. Many people know some English and German.

Hungarians in Vojvodina use the Latin alphabet; Serbs use both Latin and Cyrillic.

## MONEY

Kosovo uses the euro; Serbia retains the dinar but the inflation rate is about 10%. Many hotels will quote prices in euros, the favoured currency. ATMs accepting Visa, MasterCard and their variants are widespread in major towns and MasterCard, Visa and Diners Club are widely accepted by businesses. Many exchange offices in Serbia will change hard currencies into dinars and back again when you leave; look for their large blue diamond-shaped signs hanging outside. Some Belgrade banks and hotels have machines for changing foreign notes. A large number of banks cash hard-currency travellers cheques, and again the euro is preferable. **Western Union** (www.western union.com) transfers can be made at most banks and major post offices.

## POST

Parcels should be taken unsealed to the main post office for inspection. Allow time to check the post office's repacking and complete the transaction. You can receive mail,

---

**EMERGENCY NUMBERS**

- Police ☎ 92
- Ambulance ☎ 94
- Fire brigade ☎ 93
- Motoring Assistance ☎ 987
- Road Conditions ☎ 9800

---

addressed poste restante, in all towns for a small charge.

## TELEPHONE

Press the i button on public phones for dialling commands in English. The international operator's number is ☎ 901.

### Mobile Phones

In Serbia a 1000din card provides a local number and 500din of credit; the best coverage is gained with a number starting with ☎ 063, but ☎ 064 is cheaper.

### Phonecards

Phonecards don't give enough time for a decent international call so use telephone centres at post offices.

## TOURS

**Ace Cycling and Mountaineering Center** (www.ace-adventurecentre.com) Organises guided cycling and walking tours in Serbia.
**Balkan Holiday** (www.balkanholidays.co.uk)
**Regent Holidays** (www.regent-holidays.co.uk)

## VISAS

Tourist visas are not required for citizens of most European countries, Australia, Canada, Israel, New Zealand and the USA. The website of the **Ministry of Foreign Affairs** (www.mfa.gov.yu) has details. If you're not staying at a hotel or in a private home, then you have to register with the police within 24 hours of arrival and subsequently on changing address.

## WOMEN TRAVELLERS

Other than a cursory interest shown by men, solo women travellers should find travelling hassle-free and easy. In Muslim areas a few women wear headscarves but most young women adopt Western fashions. Dress more conservatively than usual in Muslim areas of Kosovo.

SERBIA

# TRANSPORT IN SERBIA

## GETTING THERE & AWAY

### Air

Hopefully it won't be long before the European discount airlines fly to Belgrade; currently Dubrovnik and Split (Croatia) are the nearest airports. For information on regional air links into Serbia, see p928.

Belgrade's **Nikola Tesla airport** ( ☎ 011-601 555, 605 555; www.airport-belgrade.co.yu) handles most international flights. Airline offices in Belgrade:

**Aeroflot** (code SU; ☎ 011-3235 814; www.aeroflot.com)
**Air France** (code AF; ☎ 011-638 378; www.airfrance .com)
**Alitalia** (code AZ; ☎ 011-3245 344; www.alitalia.com)
**Austrian Airlines** (code OS; ☎ 011-3248 077; www .aua.com)
**British Airways** (code BA; ☎ 011-3281 303; www .britishairways.com)
**ČSA** (code OK; ☎ 011-3614 592; www.csa.cz)
**Emirates** (code EK; ☎ 011-624 435; www.ekgroup.com)
**JAT** (code JU; ☎ 011-3024 077; www.jat.com)
**Lufthansa** (code LH; ☎ 011-3224 975; www.lufthansa .com)
**Malév** (code MA; ☎ 011-626 377; www.malev.hu)
**Montenegro Airlines** (code YM; ☎ 011-262 1122; www.Montenegro-airlines.com)
**Olympic Airways** (code OA; ☎ 011-3226 800; www .olympic-airways.gr)
**Swiss International Air Lines** (code LX; ☎ 011-3030 140; www.swiss.com)

### AIRLINES SERVING KOSOVO

Kosovo is served by **Prishtina airport** ( ☎ 038-548 430). Airline offices in Prishtina:

**Adria Airways** (code JP; ☎ 038-543 411; www.adria -airways.com)
**Albanian Airlines** (code LV; ☎ 038-242 056; www .albanianairlines.com.al)
**Austrian Airlines** (code OS; ☎ 038-242 424; www .aua.com)
**British Airways** (code BA; ☎ 038-548 661; www .britishairways.com)
**Malév** (code MA; ☎ 038-540 878; www.malev.hu)
**Turkish Airlines** (code TK; ☎ 038-502 052; www .turkishairlines.com)

### Land

#### BORDER CROSSINGS

You can easily enter Serbia by land from any of the neighbouring countries and no bus changes are required.

Kosovo can be entered from Serbia via Novi Pazar; see the boxed text on p772 for information on entry requirements.

### BUS

There's a well-developed bus service to Western Europe and Turkey from all major towns; contact any travel agency. Buses go from Belgrade to Malmo, in Sweden (€122, 34 hours, Friday), Munich (€82, 17 hours, daily), Paris (€88, 28 hours, Monday, Wednesday and Friday) and Zurich (€70, 23 hours, Wednesday and Saturday).

### CAR & MOTORCYCLE

Drivers need an International Driving Permit and vehicles need Green Card insurance, otherwise insurance (from €80 a month) must be bought at the border.

### TRAIN

All international rail connections out of Serbia originate in Belgrade with most calling at Novi Sad and Subotica heading north and west, and Niš going east. A good money-saver is to buy a Balkan flexipass (under/over 26 €50/80) that gives five days of travel in one month in Bulgaria, Greece, Macedonia, Serbia, Montenegro, Romania and Turkey.

Fares from Belgrade (all trains run daily):

| Destination | Duration | Fare (€) | Couchette (€) | Sleeper (€) |
| --- | --- | --- | --- | --- |
| Bucharest | 14hr | 30 | 10 | 17 |
| Budapest | 7hr | 16 | 16 | 22 |
| Istanbul | 26hr | 45 | 10 | 17 |
| Ljubljana | 10hr | 30 | * | 15 |
| Moscow | 50hr | 95 | * | 25 |
| Munich | 17hr | 110 | 15 | 30 |
| Sofia | 11hr | 12 | 8 | 12 |
| Thessaloniki | 16hr | 30 | 10 | 15 |
| Vienna | 11hr | 60 | 15 | 25 |
| Zagreb | 7hr | 20 | * | 15 |

* no couchette

## GETTING AROUND

### Bicycle

Cyclists are rare, even in the cities, and there are no special provisions. For cycling tours see opposite.

### Bus

The bus service is extensive and reliable and covers all of Serbia with a separate system

**SERBIA**

in Kosovo. Buses are rarely full and there's usually a row available for everyone; luggage carried below is charged at 70din/€0.50 (in Serbia/Kosovo) per piece.

### RESERVATIONS
Reservations are only worth considering for international buses, holiday times and long-distance journeys with infrequent services.

## Car & Motorcycle
Independent travel is an ideal way to gad about and discover the country. Beware of traffic police with speed radar guns; they also do spot checks of documents and the car.

### AUTOMOBILE ASSOCIATIONS
The **Auto-Moto Savez Serbia and Montenegro** (Serbia & Montenegro Automotive Association; Map p753; ☎ 9800; www.amsj.co.yu; Ruzveltova 18, Belgrade) web page has details on road conditions, tolls, insurance and petrol prices.

### DRIVING LICENCE
Generally your national driving licence will suffice but as a caution bring an International Driving Permit, available from your national motoring organisation.

### HIRE
Many hire companies such as **VIP** ( ☎ 011-369 1890), **Hertz** ( ☎ 011-334 6179) and **Budget** ( ☎ 011-313 3050) have offices at the airport and in Belgrade. **Master Rent a Car** ( ☎ 011-245 0842; www .mastercar.co.yu) rents out a basic Yugo car from €25 a day.

Make sure the tyres are in good condition, and all lights and indicators work. Cars are required to carry a first-aid kit, an emergency-stop warning triangle, spare tyre and spare bulbs; the police can fine you for not having these.

### ROAD RULES
Vehicles in Serbia drive on the right; seat belts must be worn and the drink-driving limit is .05.

Speed limits are 120km/h on motorways, 100km/h on dual carriageways, 80km/h on main roads and 60km/h in urban areas.

## Train
**Jugoslovenske Železnice** (JŽ; www.yurail.co.yu, in Serbian) provides trains from Belgrade to Novi Sad, Subotica and the highly scenic line down to Bar in Montenegro; the website gives timetable details. Trains are generally slower than buses due to lack of infrastructure investment.

Different types of train require different tickets, so when buying make sure you state the service you'll use.

The only train service in Kosovo is to Skopje.

# Slovakia

A 200-year-old log cabin with perfectly preserved white geometrics just waiting to be photographed. The smell of strong coffee enjoyed midday with pastries in an old town square café. Whimsical, foot-tapping folk music punctuated by a yee! ha! yip! The crunch of fresh snow under your boot at 2000m. Slovakia is not about overwhelming sights or superlatives, it's more about the experience of a place where nature and folkways still hold sway.

Bratislava bustles these days as post-EU membership investment pours in and new restaurants seem to open daily. The rabbit-warren old town is certainly worth a day or two's distraction. Get outside the city though and you can still find ancient castles, traditional villages, well-protected nature preserves and tourist walking trails connecting the country from end to end. Dense forests cover the low hills, and remnants of fortresses top the craggy cliffs. Medieval towns sit in sight of alpine peaks. You can hike past a waterfall in a gorge one day and search out nail-less wooden churches the next.

That's not to say that Slovakia's architecture wasn't affected by communism. Industrial blight and truly ugly concrete buildings are a part of the whole. But the country's come through it all with its folksy spirit intact. So pull up a plate of dumplings with *bryndza* (sheep's cheese) and dig in.

## FAST FACTS

- **Area** 49,035 sq km
- **Capital** Bratislava
- **Currency** koruna (Sk); €1 = 37Sk; US$1 = 29Sk; UK£1 = 55Sk; A$1 = 22Sk; ¥100 = 25Sk; NZ$1 = 19Sk
- **Famous for** ice hockey, beautiful women, mountain hiking, folk traditions
- **Official Language** Slovak
- **Phrases** *ahoj* (hello); *dovidenia* (goodbye); *d'akujem* (thank you); *este pivo prosím* (another beer please), *kde je WC* (veyt-say)? (where's the loo?)
- **Population** 5.4 million
- **Telephone Codes** country code ☎ + 421; international access code ☎ 00
- **Visas** citizens of the EU, USA, Canada, Australia, New Zealand and Japan can enter Slovakia for 90 days without a visa

**HOW MUCH?**

- **Night in hostel** 300-600Sk
- **Double room in pension** 1500Sk
- **Day's ski hire** 300Sk
- **Pair of hiking boots** 1800Sk
- **Postcard** 6Sk

**LONELY PLANET INDEX**

- **Litre of petrol** 44Sk
- **Litre of bottled water** 40Sk
- **Beer** 39Sk
- **Souvenir T-shirt** 250Sk
- **Street snack (hot dog)** 15Sk

## HIGHLIGHTS

- Ride one cable car then another to get to the precipitous summit of Lomnický štít in the **High Tatras** (p801).
- Turn your gaze east to the icon museum in **Bardejov** (p812), and at nearby Greek Catholic and Orthodox wooden churches.
- Delve into Slovakia's stony past at the country's largest extant fortress, now in ruins, **Spiš Castle** (p809).
- Climb the ladder- and chain-assist trails to get personal with the limestone gorges and rushing water of **Slovenský raj** (p811).

## ITINERARIES

- **Three days** Spend two days wandering the pedestrian streets and stopping in the sidewalk cafés of Bratislava's old town. Climb up castle hill (or take a ride up the New Bridge elevator) for a citywide view. On day three head for one of the castles within day-trip range: Devín and Trenčín are especially stunning.
- **One week** Add on a couple of days' hiking among the alps-esque peaks of the High Tatras. Further east, Bardejov beckons with a medieval town square, wooden churches, a nearby spa town and an excellent open-air village museum.

## CLIMATE & WHEN TO GO

The moderate climate averages -2°C in January and 25°C in August. Spring and autumn can be quite rainy and spring floods are not unheard of. Snow stays on the higher slopes of the High Tatras well into June, and standing snow is common in April even in the lower ranges.

The tourist season is from May to September. Lodging prices are lower outside those months (except for student dorms), but many sights in outlying areas aren't open. September is still quite warm, young wine is being harvested, and the mountains are snow-free (usually), making it one of the best times to visit. Rates skyrocket for the Easter and Christmas holidays nationwide.

## HISTORY

Slavic tribes wandered west into what would become Slovakia sometime round about the 5th century; by the 9th the territory was part of the short-lived Great Moravian Empire. It was about then that the Magyars (Hungarians) set up shop next door and subsequently lay claim to the whole territory. In the early 16th century, the Turks moved into Budapest pushing the Hungarian monarchs into Bratislava (then Pressburg, in German, or Pozsony, in Hungarian). Slovak intellectuals eventually cultivated ties with the Czechs, and after WWI, took their nation into the united Czechoslovakia.

The day before Hitler's troops invaded Czech territory in March 1939, leaders set up Slovakia as a fascist puppet and German ally. It was not, however, a populist move and in August 1944 Slovak partisans instigated the ill-fated Slovak National Uprising (Slovenské Národné Povstanie, or SNP), a source of ongoing national pride (and innumerable street names).

After the communist takeover in 1948, power was again centralised in Prague until 1989, when the Velvet Revolution brought down the curtains on the communists. Elections in 1992 saw the Movement for a Democratic Slovakia (HZDS) come to power and Vladimír Mečiar become prime minister. By that summer the Slovak parliament had voted to declare sovereignty, and the federation dissolved peacefully on 1 January 1993.

Mečiar's reign was characterised by antidemocratic laws and discrimination and the international community quickly turned on him. In part due to this pressure, the elections of 1998 ousted Mečiar and ushered in Mikuláš Dzurinda, leader of the right-leaning Slovak Democratic Coalition (SDK). Dzurinda

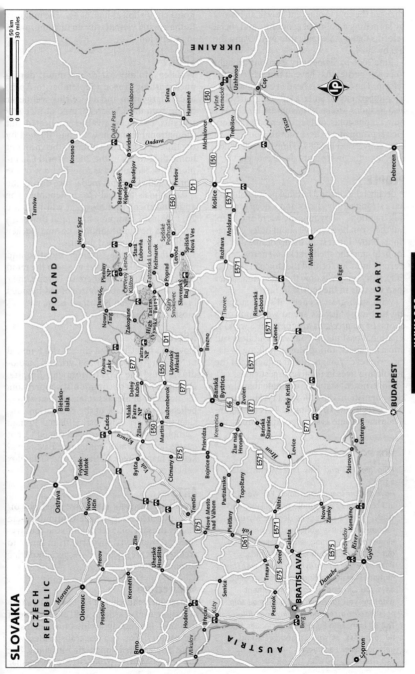

SLOVAKIA

changed the course of recent Slovakian history by launching a policy of economic and social reforms that got Slovakia into NATO and the EU by 2004.

June 2006 parliamentary elections brought to power parties that have at times been anti-reform. The coalition is headed by Prime Minister Robert Fico of Smer, a left-wing party, but also includes Mečiar's isolationist HZDS. For now, despite contradictory statements early on, Fico is promising to keep Slovakia on track to euro conversion in 2009. Time will tell which direction the government decides to go.

## PEOPLE

A deeply religious and familial people, Slovaks have strong family circles and a deep sense of folk traditions. The young are warm and open, but there can be a reserve about older generations. Show interest in their country, or ask for help, and the shell cracks. Generosity and warmth lurks just behind the stoicism. Thankfully, surly service is now the exception rather than the rule in the tourist industry.

With such great scenery, it's not surprising that most Slovaks spend weekends outdoors. Isť na prechadsku (going for a walk) is a national pastime so you will doubtless run into a backpack-toting Slovak walking in nature wherever you go. About a quarter of the population lives in the five largest cities.

Government statistics estimate that Slovakia's population is 86% Slovak, 11% Hungarian, 1.2% Czech and 1.7% Roma. This last figure is in some dispute as some groups estimate the

Roma population as high as 4%. The minority Roma are still viewed with an uncompromising suspicion.

## SPORT

Wander into any bar or restaurant during puck-pushing season (September to April) and 12 large men and an ice rink will never be far from the TV screen, even at nice restaurants. Local club rivalries are heated, but the national team showing had flagged by the time of research. Although they brought home the bronze in the 2003 World Championships, Slovakia was knocked out of the Torino 2006 Olympic medal race during the quarter finals by rival Czech Republic. The announcement that Slovakia will host the 2011 World Championships (and Bratislava will get a new multibillion–koruna hockey stadium) surely perked up fans.

Football fills the summer months, and while the Slovaks have yet to attain the rabid fanaticism found elsewhere in Europe, their club game is a reliable source of red-blooded bravado. SK Slovan Bratislava is the nation's most successful team.

## RELIGION

Slovakia's first Christian church was founded in Nitra in AD 833 after SS Cyril and Methodius visited the Great Moravian Empire. Despite 50 years of communist suppression, the majority of Slovaks retained their strong beliefs. Today, 84.1% of the population consider themselves religiously affiliated. Roman Catholics form the majority (about 60%), but evangelicals are also numerous; East Slovakia has many Greek Catholics and Orthodox believers.

## ARTS

Some city dwellers may have been put off by the clichéd image of the Communist-era 'happy peasant', but get out into the countryside and traditional folk arts, from music to architecture, are celebrated – especially during summer festivals

### Architecture

The wooden churches of East Slovakia, easily accessible from Bardejov (p812) are some of the most interesting architectural gems in the country. You can see transplanted versions at a skansen (open-air museum), like the one in Martin (p798), where vernacular

---

**VOX POP**

*Who are you and how old?* Martin Latal, age 29

*How do you spend your days?* I'm working at Accenture as a technology specialist, and studying for a manager's degree. My daily routine is of course work, but I go swimming almost every evening, and weekends I go out to a disco or pub with my friends.

*What's the best part of living in Bratislava?* The nightlife is really thrilling, and even on weekdays you can find good entertainment.

*What do you think about EU membership, possible euro ascension and Slovakia's future?* The EU is making Europe even smaller, better. Business, as well as goods trading, is getting easier each year.

village architecture is preserved. Levoča (p808) is known for its nearly complete medieval town walls and for the Gothic Church of St Jacob with a 18m-high altar carved by Master Pavol. Of course you can't miss the brutal socialist-realist architecture of the communist epoch, as evidenced by the New Bridge (Nový most, p792). Yes, it does resemble a UFO on a stick.

## Cinema

Slovak cinema first made its mark as part of the Czechoslovak New Wave of the 1960s, with classic films like *Smrt si rika Engelchen* (Death Calls Itself Engelchen, 1963) directed by Ján Kádar, and *Obchod na korze* (The Shop on the Main Street, 1965) by Elmar Klos. Martin Sulík was one of Slovakia's most promising new directors, winning an Oscar nomination for *Všetko, čo mám rád* (Everything I Like, 1992), and international acclaim for *Krajinka* (The Landscape, 2000). Unfortunately, lack of funding and the closing of the Koliba movie studios has meant little serious movie making since 2000.

## Music

Traditional Slovak folk instruments include the *fujara* (a 2m-long flute), the *gajdy* (bagpipes) and the *konkovka* (a strident shepherd's flute). Folk songs helped preserve the Slovak language during Hungarian rule, and in East Slovakia musical folk traditions are an integral part of village life.

In classical music, the 19th-century works of Ján L Bela and the symphonies of Alexander Moyzes receive world recognition. Slovakia's contemporary music scene is small, but vibrant. Modern musicians combine traditional lyrics or rhythms with a modern beat. Zuzana Mojžišová's music seems to have an almost Romany-like vibrancy, but stems from Slovak folk music. Marián Varga riffs on classical themes and the Peter Lipa band is granddaddy of the Bratislava Jazz Days festival.

# ENVIRONMENT
## The Land

Slovakia sits in the heart of Europe, straddling the northwestern end of the Carpathian Mountains. This hilly country forms a clear physical barrier between the plains of Poland and Hungary. Almost 80% of Slovakia is more than 750m above sea level, and forests, mainly beech and spruce, cover 40% of the country.

Southwestern Slovakia is a fertile lowland stretching from the foothills of the Carpathians down to the Danube River, which, from Bratislava to Štúrovo, forms the border with Hungary.

Central Slovakia is dominated by the High Tatras (Vysoké Tatry) mountains along the Polish border; Gerlachovský štít (2654m) being the highest peak. The forested ridges of the Low Tatras (Nízke Tatry) and the Malá Fatra are national park playgrounds. South are the gorges and waterfalls of Slovenský raj and the limestone caves of Slovenský kras. The longest river, the Váh, rises in the Tatras and flows 390km west and south to join the Danube at Komárno.

## Wildlife & National Parks

Slovakia's national parks contain bears, marmots, wolves, lynxes, chamois, mink and otters, though they're rarely seen. Deer, pheasants, partridges, ducks, wild geese, storks, grouse, eagles and other birds of prey can be seen across the country.

National parks and protected areas make up 20% of Slovakia. The parks in the High Tatras, Slovenský raj and Malá Fatra regions should not be missed.

## Environmental Issues

Slovakia is a mixed bag in environmental terms. No doubt due to most Slovaks' penchant for all things outdoorsy, large swathes of the countryside are protected parkland. On the other hand, the communist legacy left more than its fair share of grimy, industrial factories. Big centres such as Bratislava and Košice do suffer from air pollution.

The Gabčíkovo hydroelectric project, on the Danube west of Komárno, produces enough power to cover the needs of every home in Slovakia. But some believe it exacerbates the damage caused by annual floods. Events like Danube Day (www.danubeday.sk in Slovak) in June aim to raise awareness and money for river restoration.

## Responsible Travel

Tens of thousands of hikers pass through Slovakia's parks and protected areas every year – try to do your bit to keep them pristine. Wherever possible, carry out your rubbish, avoid using detergents or toothpaste in or near watercourses, stick to established trails (this helps prevent erosion), cook on a kerosene

SLOVAKIA

stove rather than an open fire and do not engage in or encourage – by purchasing goods made from endangered species – hunting.

After the famous Schöner Náci statue in Bratislava's old town was upturned one weekend, allegedly by a group of probably inebriated English-speaking men, police presence in the old town increased. Drink responsibly.

## FOOD & DRINK
### Staples & Specialities
Slovak cuisine is basic central European fare: various fried meat schnitzels with fries and hearty stews with potatoes. Soups like *cesnaková polievka* (garlic soup), either creamy or clear with croutons and cheese, and *kapustnica* (cabbage soup), with a paprika and pork base, start most meals. Slovakia's national dish is *bryndzové halušky*, gnocchilike dumplings topped with soft sheep's cheese and bits of bacon fat. Don't pass up an opportunity to eat in a *salaš* or a *koliba* (rustic wooden eateries) where these traditional specialities are the mainstay.

For dessert, try *palacinka* (crepes) stuffed with jam or chocolate. *Ovocné knedličky* (fruit dumplings) are round balls filled with fruit and coated with crushed poppy seeds or breadcrumbs, dribbled with melted butter and sometimes accompanied by fruit purée and ice cream – yum.

### Drinks
Slovak wine is…what do oenophiles say… highly drinkable (ie good and cheap). The Modra region squeezes dry reds, like Frankovka and Kláštorné. Slovak Tokaj, a white dessert wine from the southeast, is trying to give the Hungarian version a run for its money (though it falls short).

Slovak *pivo* (beer) is as good as the Czech stuff – try full-bodied Zlatý Bažant or dark, sweet Martiner. *Borovička* (a potent berry-based clear liquor) and *slivovice* (plum-based) are consumed as shots and are said to aid in digestion.

### Where to Eat & Drink
Self-service cafeterias (called *samoobsluha reštaurácie*, *jedáleň* or *bufet*) cater to office workers and are great places to eat during the day (they close early). Look for food stands near train and bus stations; you can buy fruits and vegetables at the local *tržnica* (market).

All manner of trendy world food has found a foothold in Bratislava, but most Slovak towns at least have a pizzeria or a Chinese takeaway. Cafés (spelled in English) are often as much bar or restaurant as coffee shop; *kaviareň* (cafés) may only serve beverages, but that includes alcohol, a *cukráreň* (pastry or sweet shop) has the best ice cream and cakes to go with coffee.

### Vegetarians & Vegans
It isn't easy being green in Slovakia. Some menus have a pasta or vegetable dish, but your only choice may be *vyprážaný syr* (fried cheese) and a *miešany šalat* (mixed salad). In this meat-lovers' haven even vegetable soups are made with chicken stock and *bezmäsa* (meatless) dishes aren't always meatless (those bacon crumbles on the dumplings apparently don't count). Things are looking up in Bratislava where a few vegetarian restaurants have sprung up. Other than that, pizzerias are always an option.

### Habits & Customs
Small tips (five to 10%) are customary, but your friends are likely to say you're spoiling the waiter. At least round up the bill to the next 20Sk (50Sk if the bill is over 500Sk).

# BRATISLAVA

☎ 02 / pop 421,155

Focus in on the compact historic centre and you see cobblestone roads, pedestrian plazas, pastel 18th-century rococo buildings, and sidewalk cafés galore. Expand your gaze and you can't miss the institutional housing blocks and bizarre communist constructions. An age-old castle shares the skyline with the 1970s, UFO-like New Bridge. That's Bratislava, a mixed but manageable city where both old and new merit a look.

Today the city hums as foreign investment helps upgrade roads, and beautiful people wearing black dine at the newest chichi pooh-pooh eatery. There's something a bit reckless about the development though. The old town zoning restrictions are taken lightly and weekend nights at least one gang of inebriated English-speaking blokes will likely pass by if you're out and about.

Who knows what the town will be in a few years, but for now the old centre is supremely

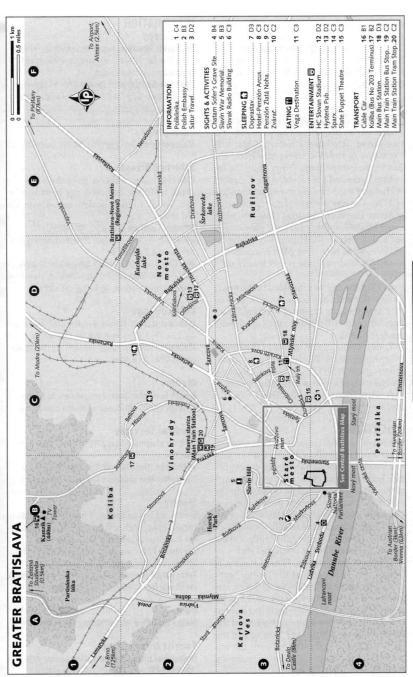

# GREATER BRATISLAVA

SLOVAKIA

strollable. Wander around the mazelike alleys, stopping for a coffee or two along the way. You may want to pop into a museum if it's raining, but otherwise the best thing to do is just take in the different views, even as it all changes before your eyes.

## HISTORY

Founded in AD 907, Bratislava was already a large city in the 12th century. In 1467 the Hungarian Renaissance monarch Matthias Corvinus founded a university here, the Academia Istropolitana. Then came the invading Turks and the capital of the Kingdom of Hungary was hurriedly moved to Bratislava in 1536. The city flourished during the reign of Maria Theresa of Austria (1740–80), when many of the imposing baroque palaces you see today were built. Hungarian monarchs were crowned here in St Martin's cathedral until 1830 and parliament met locally until 1848.

In 1918 the city was included in the newly formed Republic of Czechoslovakia, in 1969 it became the state capital of a federal Slovak Republic, and in 1993, the capital of an independent Slovakia.

Today, as the capital of one of the newest EU member states, Bratislava is a city under construction. With EU-inspired money and a proliferation of low-cost carrier flights, prices ain't what they used to be. Don't expect a bargain-basement visit.

## ORIENTATION

Bratislava's pedestrian centre starts south of Hodžovo nám. Follow Poštová down and you cross Obchodná (Shopping street) before getting to the Nám SNP and the heart of the old town bounded by the castle in the west and Tesco department store in the east. The large, plazalike Hviezdoslavovo nám is a convenient reference point, with the old town to the north, the Danube to the south, and the Slovak National Theatre on its east end.

The main train station, Hlavná stanica, is located just 1km north of the centre. Tram 13 runs from the station to Nám L Štúra, just south of Hviezdoslavovo nám, and bus 93 stops at Hodžovo nám. The main bus station, called Mlynské Nivy by locals because of the street it's on, is a little over 1km east of the old town. Bus 206 shuttles between the bus station and the main train station, stopping at Hodžovo nám in between.

## INFORMATION

### Bookshops

**Interpress Slovakia** (Map p790; Sedlárska 2; ☽ 9am-10pm Mon-Sat, 2-10pm Sun) Foreign newspapers and Bratislava periodicals in English.

**Next Apache** (Map p790; Panenská 28; ☽ 9am-10pm Mon-Fri, 10am-10pm Sat & Sun) Loads of used English books and a comfy café.

### Emergency

**Main police station** (Map p790; ☎ 159; Gunduličova 10)

### Internet Access

Getting online will cost from the price of a drink to 100Sk, but 60Sk per hour is average. Small internet outlets are all over the old town.

**Internet Centrum** (Map p790; ☎ 0903693577; Mikalská 2; ☽ 9am-4am) Four of the six computers have web cam and Skype access.

**Wifi Café** (Map p790; ground fl, Tatracentrum, Hodžovo nám; ☽ 8am-10pm Mon-Fri, 10am-10pm Sat, 11am-10pm Sun) Flat-screen terminals, smoke-free café with wi-fi.

### Left Luggage

**Main bus station** (Mlynské Nivy; Map p787; per bag per day 35Sk; ☽ 5.30am-10pm Mon-Fri, 6am-6pm Sat & Sun)

**Main train station** (Hlavná stanica; Map p787; per bag per day 45Sk; ☽ 6.30am-11pm)

### Media

**Slovak Spectator** (www.slovakspectator.sk) English-language weekly, with current affairs and event listings.

### Medical Services

**24-hour pharmacy** (Map p790; ☎ 5443 2952; Nám SNP 20)

**Poliklinika** (Map p787; ☎ 5296 2461; Bezručova 8) Twenty-four-hour emergency services, including dental.

### Money

Bratislava has an excess of banks and ATMs in the old town, with several convenient branches on Poštova and around Kamenné nám. There are also ATMs and exchange booths in the train and bus stations, and at the airport.

**Tatra Banka** (Map p790; Dunajská 4) Has staff that speak exceptional English and great English signage.

### Post

**Main Post Office** (Map p790; Nám SNP 34-35)

### Tourist Information

**Bratislava Culture & Information Centre** (BKIS; ☎ 5249 5906; www.bkis.sk) Centre (Map p790;

Klobučnícka 2; 8.30am-6pm Mon-Fri, 9am-3pm Sat); Main train station (Map p787; Hlavná stanica; 8am-7.30pm Mon-Fri & 8am-5pm Sat Jun-Sep, 8am-4.30pm Mon-Fri & 9am-2pm Sat Oct-May); Airport (MR Štefánik; 8am-7.30pm Mon-Fri, 10am-6pm Sat) The official central tourist point is a little sterile and the staff can seem uninterested, but keep pressing and they'll help.

**Bratislava Tourist Service** (BTS; Map p790; ☎ 5464 1271; www.bratislava-info.sk; Ventúrska 9; 10am-8pm) Tiny place, but it has a younger, more helpful staff and lots of maps and knick-knacks.

## Travel Agencies

**Satur** (Map p787; ☎ 5542 2828; www.satur.sk; Miletičova 1) Bratislava package trips and tours, transport tickets etc.

## SIGHTS & ACTIVITIES

**Bratislava Castle** (Bratislavský hrad; Map p790; grounds admission free; 9am-8pm Apr-Sep, to 6pm Oct-Mar) lords over the west side of the old town on a hill above the Danube. Winding ramparts and grounds provide a great vantage point for comparing ancient and communist Bratislava. The castle looks a bit like a four-poster bed, a shape that was well established by the 15th century. During the Turkish occupation of Budapest, this was the seat of Hungarian royalty. A fire devastated the fortress in 1811 and most of what you see today is a reconstruction from the 1950s (bland white interiors and all). The saving grace of the castle's ho-hum **Historical Museum** (Historické múzeum; Map p790; ☎ 5441 1441; www.snm.sk; adult/student 100/40Sk; 9am-6pm Tue-Sun) is that you can climb up the *korunná veža* (crown tower). At the time of writing

**MAN AT WORK**

The castle? The New Bridge? Nope, the most photo-opted sight in Bratislava ia a bronze statue called **The Watcher** (Čumil; Map p790). He peeps out of an imaginary manhole at the intersection of Panská and Sedlárska, below a 'men at work' sign. And he's not alone. There are other quirky statues scattered around the old town. See if you can find them: **The Frenchman** leans on a park bench, **The Photographer** stalks his subject paparazzi-style around a corner and the **Schöner Náci** tips his top hat on a square. Look up for other questionable characters, like a timepiece-toting monk and a rather naked imp, decorating building façades.

**BRATISLAVA IN TWO DAYS**

Start the morning by wandering up the ramparts of **Bratislava Castle** (left). Enter through the **Historical Museum** (left) to climb the *veža* (tower) for the highest views of the old town. On your way back down to town, stop at the **Museum of Jewish Culture** (below) before having lunch at **Prašná Bašta** (p793). Spend the afternoon strolling through the old town, stopping to drink at as many café terraces as you dare. If you schedule it right, you could catch an opera at the **Slovak National Theatre** (p794) or a band at the **Café Štúdio Club** (p793). The following day, trip out of town to explore **Devín Castle** (p795).

the tiny **treasury** (*klenotnica*) was closed for reconstruction. When it reopens, the highlight will still be the unbelievable 25,000-year-old fertility statue of a miniature headless naked woman carved from a mammoth tusk, the Venus of Moravany.

To see a more historically complete castle, take the bus beneath the bridge by Bratislava Castle to **Devín** (p795) 9km outside the city.

A series of old homes winds down the castle hill along Židovská in what was once the Jewish quarter. The **Museum of Clocks** (Múzeum hodín; Map p790; ☎ 5441 1940; Židovská 1; adult/student 40/20Sk; 10am-5pm Tue-Sun) is housed in the reputedly skinniest house in Slovakia. Further down, the **Museum of Jewish Culture** (Múzeum Židovskej kultúry; Map p790; ☎ 5441 8507; www.chatamsofer.com; Židovská 17; adult/student 200/20Sk; 11am-5pm Sun-Fri) displays moving exhibits about the community lost during WWII. Black-and-white photos show the old ghetto and synagogue ploughed under by the communists to make way for a highway and bridge. The staff can help arrange a visit to **Chatam Sofer's grave site** (Map p787; www.chatamsofer.com; Žižkova at tram tunnel; donations accepted; by appointment only), the resting place of the much revered 19th-century rabbi.

A relatively modest interior belies the elaborate history of **St Martin's Cathedral** (Dóm sv Martina; Map p790; admission €1.25; 9-11am & 1-5pm Mon-Sat, 1-5pm Sun). Eleven ruling monarchs (10 kings and one queen, Maria Theresa) were crowned in this 14th century church. The busy motorway almost touching St Martin's follows the moat of the former city walls and is shaking the building to its core.

**SLOVAKIA**

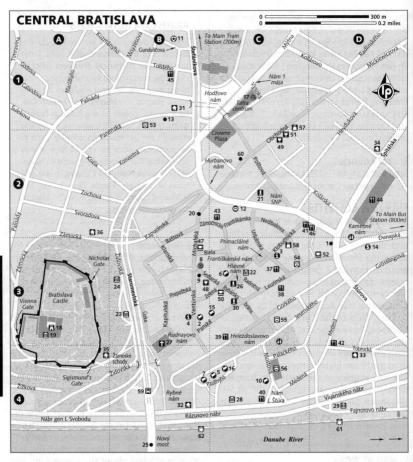

CENTRAL BRATISLAVA

Further east along the Danube, the 1st-floor exhibits of the **Slovak National Museum** (Slovenské Národné múzeum; Map p790; ☎ 5934 9122; www.snm.sk; Vajanského nábrežie 2; adult/student 60/20Sk; ⊙ 9am-5pm Tue-Sun) provide a super overview of the folk cultures and customs of Slovakia's regions. Skip the tired natural-history stuff upstairs.

An 18th-century palace and a Stalinist-modernist make interesting cohosts for the **Slovak National Gallery** (Slovenská Národná Galéria; Map p790; ☎ 5443 4587; www.sng.sk; Rázusovo nábrežie 2; adult/student 80/40Sk; ⊙ 10am-5pm Tue-Sun) and the nation's eclectic art collection – from Gothic to graphic design.

The old town's two opulent theatres are off Hviezdoslavovo nám, a broad, tree-lined plaza. The gilt neobaroque 1914 **Reduta Palace**

(see Slovak Philharmonic on p794) hosts the nation's symphony, and the ornate 1886 **Slovak National Theatre** (see p794) is the city's opera house. Neither is open for tours, but tickets are cheap if you want to see a show.

Bustling, narrow **Rybárska brána** runs through the pedestrian zone to Hlavné nám (Main Square), which is filled with café tables in summer, and a craft market at Easter and Christmas times. **Roland's Fountain** (Map p790) at the centre may have been built in 1572 as an old-fashioned fire hydrant. Flanking one side of the square is the 1421 **town hall** (radnica) containing the **Municipal Museum** (Mestské múzeum; Map p790; ☎ 5920 5130; Hlavné nám; adult/student 50/20Sk; ⊙ 10am-5pm Tue-Fri, 11am-6pm Sat & Sun). Buzz past the tedious archaeological cases and look for the stairs down to the cellar torture chambers, complete with illustrated murals.

The focal point of the Nám SNP is the **Monument to the Slovak National Uprising** and the heroes who fought fascism in WWII. On 31 December 2002, hundreds of thousands gathered here to ring in the new year – and a new nation – when separation from the Czech Republic became official.

## Hiking

To get out of the city and into the forest, take trolley bus 203 northeast from Hodžovo nám to the end of the line at Koliba, then walk up the road for about 20 minutes to the **TV tower** (Map p787) on Kamzík Hill (440m). Posted maps outline the many hiking possibilities in the forest surrounds and there are a couple of hotels with restaurants in the park. A **cable car** (lanovka; Map 000; ☎ 4425 9188; adult/student round-trip 90/60Sk; ☺ 10am-4pm Oct-May) makes the 15-minute journey downhill to the picnic areas and playgrounds of Železná studienka.

## FESTIVALS & EVENTS

Bratislava's best events are arts related. From June to September the **Cultural Summer Festival** (Kultúrne leto; ☎ 5441 3063) brings a smorgasbord of operas, plays and performances to the streets and venues around town. Classical music takes centre stage at the **Bratislava Music Festival** (Bratislavské hudobné slávnosti; ☎ 5443 4546;

www.bhsfestival.sk in Slovak), which runs from late September to mid-October. **Bratislava Jazz Days** (Bratislavských jazzových dní; ☎ 5293 1572; www.bjd.sk) swings for three days in September. Twenty-sixth of November is the usual start to the **Christmas market** on Hlavné nám.

## SLEEPING

Bratislava's no-longer-dirt-cheap lodging market is still cheaper than London, but don't expect comparable services. Bratislava Culture & Information Service (p788) can help with private rooms (from 1100Sk per person) and student dormitories (July and August, from 300Sk per person). To book an apartment, check out www.bratislavahotels.com.

## Budget

**Patio Hostel** (Map p790; ☎ 5292 5797; www.patio hostel.com; Špitalska 35; dm 450-550Sk, d per person 860-900Sk; ℗ ⊠ ▣ ) Clean and fresh and dorm-like (100 beds) – that is if you were allowed to paint the concrete block walls with bright colours and stylised graffiti at college. Each floor has a kitchenette and there's a courtyard patio in addition to the computer room and basement rec room (TV, fussball).

**Downtown Backpackers** (Map p790; ☎ 5464 1191; www.backpackers.sk; Panenská 31; dm 500-600Sk, d per person 1000Sk; ⊠ ▣ ) If you'd rather have lively conversation and laid-back Bohemian charm (exposed brick, red common-area walls) than

SLOVAKIA

---

**COMMUNIST BRATISLAVA**

Forty-five years of communist rule was bound to leave a mark. An obsession with modern functionalism led to many heinous buildings. The whole **Petržalka** (Map p787) concrete jungle housing estate is a key example. (We couldn't find any studies calculating how many people go to the wrong flat in an identical building down the road after a drink or two…) The adjacent **New Bridge** (Nový most; Map p790; ☎ 6252 0300; www.u-f-o.sk; Viedenská cesta; observation deck 100Sk; ☢ 10am-11pm), or the UFO (pronounced ew-fo) bridge, is a modernist marvel from 1972. After a three-year renovation it reopened in 2006 with an overhyped nightclub aloft, in addition to the prerequisite overpriced restaurant and viewing platform. And no, you're not seeing things, there is an upside down pyramid in the new town; that's the **Slovak Radio building** (Slovenský rozhlas; Map p787; cnr Mýtna & Štefanovičova).

On Slavín Hill, northwest of the old town, the **Slavín War Memorial** (Map p787) is one of the few remaining testaments to socialist realism as an art. It honours the Soviet soldiers who battled for Bratislava in 1945.

If you're nostalgic for the good old days, down a brewsky or two with Stalin, Lenin and the boys (or at least their statues) at the **KGB bar** (opposite).

---

a lock on your door, you've found your place. Some of the eight- and 10-bed dorm rooms act as a corridor to another. The gathering room has a bar. Take bus 93 two stops from the train station.

Other options:

**Doprastav** (Map p787; ☎ 5557 4313; www.dopra stav.sk/otherservices; Košická 52; dm 280-360Sk; s/d 625/952Sk) Hotel and dorm rooms near a shopping complex.

**Zvárač** (Map p787; ☎ 4924 6000; www.vuz.sk; Pionier-ska 17; s 700-900Sk, d 1100-1400Sk) Perfectly functional workers' hostel with attached bathrooms.

## Midrange

**Penzión Zlatá Noha** (Map p787; ☎ 5477 4922; www .zlata-noha.sk; Bellova 2, Koliba hill; s 1350Sk, d 1700-1900Sk; P X Q) Tranquillity and family-run attention make up for distance at this homy, modern guesthouse above town. If you want to use the wi-fi, ask for a room near the reception. Take bus 203 from Hodžovo nám and ring for the fifth stop, Jeséniova.

**Hotel-Penzión Arcus** (Map p787; ☎ 5557 2522; www .hotelarcus.sk; Moskovská 5; s 1400-1800Sk, d 2600Sk; P X) This friendly, popular hotel near the bus station is only 15 minutes' walk from the old town. Though updated in 2001, the varied rooms (some with balcony, some with courtyard views) still seem a little outmoded. But all the bathrooms are sparkly white.

**Pension Castle Club** (Map p790; ☎ 5464 1472; www .stayslovakia.com; Zámocké schody 4; s/d with shared bathroom €60/75, q €120; X) It's quite an uphill hike to this townhouse B&B near the castle. The few basic rooms book up fast. An attic quad (more

stairs!) has a bathroom, high-speed internet connection and two double beds.

**Penzión Chez David** (Map p790; ☎ 5441 3824; www .chezdavid.sk; Zámocká 13; s €64-74, d €78-88; P X) A cool blue colour scheme, great old photos of synagogues on the walls, and a primo location. You'll hardly even notice the building's boxy functionalism (though the rooms are small).

## Top End

**Hotel Marrol's** (Map p790; ☎ 5778 4600; www.hotelmarrols .sk; Tobrucká 4; s 7000Sk, d 7300-9600Sk; P X Q Q) Black-and-white movie stills, clubby leather chairs, sumptuous fabrics; Hotel Marrol's is straight off the silver screen – c 1940. Hard to imagine more retro refinement packed into one cultural landmark building.

**Hotel Danube** (Map p790; ☎ 5934 0000; www.hotel danube.com; Rybné nám 1; s €189-225, d €209-250; P X Q Q) A business behemoth, the Danube dominates the trade sector with serious services and a can-do staff. Oh, the riverfront location doesn't hurt either. Weekend rates and online packages bring the price way down.

## EATING

The old town certainly isn't lacking in dining options and tables pop up all along the pedestrian byways as soon as warm weather allows. Many of the restaurants are tourist- or expat-oriented, with correspondingly spiked prices (foreign language names are a giveaway). Student eateries line Obchodná, at the northern end of the pedestrian zone.

## Budget

Downtown **Tesco** (Map p790; ☎ 4446 4057; Kamenné nám; ☻ 8am-9pm Mon-Fri, 9am-7pm Sat & Sun) has a supermarket in the basement and a 2nd-floor cafeteria, tucked behind the garden department.

**Old Market** (Stara Tržnica; Map p790; Nám SNP 25; ☻ 7am-9pm Mon-Fri, 7am-6pm Sat, 1-6pm Sun) Fresh fruit-and-veggie vendors in the centre, hot food stands around the edge and a cafeteria upstairs.

**U Jakubu** (Map p790; ☎ 5441 7951; Nám SNP 24; mains 59-65Sk; ☻ 8am-6pm Mon-Fri) All the standard Slovak dishes lie before you; it's self-service at U Jakuba, where a soup-and-main costs as little as 90Sk.

**Divesta diétna jedáleň** (Map p790; Laurinská 8; mains 60-80Sk; ☻ 11am-3pm Mon-Fri) The big queues speak volumes about the veggie tucker at this central buffet.

## Midrange

**Prašná Bašta** (Map p790; ☎ 5443 4957; Zámočnicka 11; mains 105-215Sk) Good, reasonable Slovak food. The round, vaulted interior oozes old Bratislava charm.

**Archa** (Map p790; ☎ 5443 0865; Uršuľí Chicken sautéed with avocado? This is Slovak cuisine gone contemporary, with loads of vegetables. The interior is decorated to look like an ark.

Also recommended:

**Pizza Mizza** (Map p790; ☎ 5296 5034; Tobrucká 5; mains 99-160Sk) City's best slice.

**Vega Destination** (Map p787; ☎ 3352 6994; Malý trh 2; mains 120-180Sk; ✖ ) Space-age vegetarian.

## Top End

**Traja Mušketieri** (Map p790; ☎ 5443 0019; Sládkovičova 7; mains 350-600Sk) A stylised, upmarket version of a medieval tavern comes complete with a poetic menu. The waiters really know how to treat you well.

Of the many spiffy global food alternatives in the old town, **Kogo** (Map p790; ☎ 5464 5094; Hviezdoslavovo nám 21; mains 260-650Sk), for Italian seafood, is among the newest; and **Malecón** (Map p790; ☎ 0910274583; Nám L Štúra 4; mains 269-459Sk) has the most-praised Latin fare.

## DRINKING

From mid-April to October, just about any sidewalk café will do for a drink.

**Čokoládovňa** (Map p790; ☎ 5433 3945; Michalská 6; ☻ 9am-9pm) This tiny 'chocolate café' has cocktails, coffees and desserts made with the dark ambrosia.

**Roland Café** (Map p790; ☎ 5443 1372; Hlavné nám 5; ☻ 9am-1am) Was this Roland ever not on the main square? This institution has a full menu as well as cocktails and coffee and cakes.

**Kréma Gurmánov Bratislavy** (KGB; Map p790; ☎ 5273 1279; Obchodná 52; ☻ 10am-2am Mon-Fri, 4pm-3am Sat, 4pm-midnight Sun) Drink a dark and smoky toast to a statue of Stalin under a Soviet flag at KGB bar.

If you want to meet up and yarn with other English speakers, head to **Dubliner** (Map p790; ☎ 5441 0706; Sedlárska 6; ☻ 11am-3am Mon-Sat, to 1am Sun) or to **Slovak Pub** (Map p790; ☎ 5441 0706; Obchodná 62; ☻ 10am-midnight Mon-Thu, 10am-1am Fri & Sat, noon-midnight Sun). Otherwise, you may want to avoid them.

## ENTERTAINMENT
### Clubs

**Café Štúdio Club** (Map p790; ☎ 5443 1796; cnr Laurinská & Radničná; ☻ 10am-1am Mon-Wed; to 3am Thu & Fri, 4pm-3am Sat) Bop to the oldies, or chill out to jazz; most nights there's live music of some sort. A 1950s vibe prevails.

**Hysteria Pub** (Map p787; ☎ 0910447744; Odbojárov 9; ☻ 10am-1am Mon-Thu; to 5am Fri & Sat, 11am-midnight Sun) Comical murals depict inebriated

**AUTHOR'S CHOICE**

Thermal waters bubble under much of the country and Slovakia's premier spa site, **Piešťany** ( ☎ 33-775 7733; www.spa-piestany.sk; Kúpeľe ostrov), is only 87km north of Bratislava. Until recently most Slovak spas were medical facilities requiring a doctor's note. Not so today. OK, there's still a slightly antiseptic look about treatment rooms, but many of Piešťany's lovely 19th-century buildings sport a new coat of Maria Theresa yellow paint and others are under reconstruction. On Kúpelne ostrov (Spa Island) you can swim in thermal pools, breathe seaside-like air in a New Age salt cave and be wrapped naked in hot mud. Head to the *kasa* (cashier) at Napoleon 1 to book a service, or go online. There are several hotels on the island. Trains from Bratislava take 1¼ hours (130Sk, 12 daily) and you can continue on the same line to Trenčín (76Sk, 45 minutes).

cowboys downing tequila at this fun-loving restaurant-bar-disco. It's multigenerationally popular.

**Sparx** (Map p787; ☎ 0903403097; Cintorínska 32; ☺ 11am-midnight Mon-Wed, to 1am Thu, to 3am Fri & Sat) This cavernous bar (once a big beer hall) has live music Thursdays and becomes a disco at weekends.

### Gay & Lesbian Venues

**U Anjelov** (Map p790; ☎ 5443 2724; Laurinská 19; ☺ 9am-midnight Mon-Thu, until 1.30am Fri, 1pm-1.30am Sat, 1pm-midnight Sun) Bratislava's gay café serves creative mixed drinks, sometimes garnished with a candied marshmallow, while Frank Sinatra croons overhead.

**Apollon Club** (Map p790; ☎ 09-15-48 00 31; www.apollon-gay-club.sk; Panenská 24; ☺ 6pm-3am Mon-Thu & Sun, 6pm-5am Fri & Sat) The main gay dance club in town (not that there are many) with two bars and three stages. Boys only Thursdays.

### Sport

You can buy tickets online at www.ticketportal.sk.

**HC Slovan** (Map p787; ☎ 4445 6500; www.hcslovan.sk in Slovak; Odbojárov 3) Bratislava's hallowed ice-hockey team plays at a stadium northeast of the old town.

**SK Slovan** (☎ 4437 3083; Junácka 2) The home football team kicks it around nearby.

### Theatre & Concerts

**Slovak National Theatre** (Slovenské Národné Divadlo; Map p790; www.snd.sk; Hviezdoslavovo nám) Opera and ballet are performed at this ornate theatre. Get tickets ahead of time at the booking office (*pokladňa*; Map p790; ☎ 5443 3764) located behind the theatre, at the corner of Jesenského and Komenského. It's open from 8am to 5.30pm Monday to Friday, and from 9am to 1pm on Saturday.

**Slovak Philharmonic** (Slovenská Filharmónia; Map p790; ☎ 5920 8233; www.filharmonia.sk; cnr Nám L Štúra & Medená; ticket office ☺ 1-7pm Mon, Tue, Thu & Fri, 8am-2pm Wed) This state orchestra plays at a theatre in the Reduta Palace.

**State Puppet Theatre** (Štátne Bábkové Divadlo; Map p787; ☎ 5292 3668; www.babkovedivadlo.sk; Dunajská 36) Puts on puppet shows, usually at 10am and sometimes again at 2pm.

Folk dance and music ensembles, like **Sľuk** (☎ 6285 9125; www.sluk.sk) and **Lúčnica** (☎ 5292 0068; www.lucnica.sk), perform at various venues around town.

## SHOPPING

There are several crystal, craft and jewellery stores in and around Hlavné nám.

**Úľuv** (Map p790; ☎ 5273 1351; www.uluv.sk; Obchodná 64) For serious folk art shopping head to Úľuv, where there are two stores and a courtyard filled with artisans' studios. There's even a small restaurant serving folksy specials.

**Vinotéka Sv Urbana** (Map p790; ☎ 5433 2573; Klobučnícka 4) Has wines for sample and sale.

## GETTING THERE & AWAY
### Air

Bratislava's **MR Štefánika airport** (BTS; ☎ 3303 3353; www.airportbratislava.sk) is 7km northeast of the centre. **Sky Europe** (☎ 4850 4850; www.skyeurope.com) has two to three daily flights to Košice (50 minutes, three daily) for as little as 190Sk (plus 300Sk in taxes) if you book ahead. For more on flying within Eastern Europe, see this chapter's Transport section (p821). For more on getting to Slovakia from further afield, see the Transport chapter (p928).

**Vienna International airport** (VIE; www.viennaairport.com) is only 60km from Bratislava, and is connected by near-hourly buses.

### Boat

Floating down the Danube River is a cruisy way to get between Bratislava and Vienna (€21 one way, 1½ hours) or Budapest (€69 one way, four hours). From mid-April to September, **Slovenská plavba a prístavy** (☎ 5293 2226; www.lod.sk) runs at least one hydrofoil to Vienna and one to Budapest daily from the **hydrofoil terminal** (Map p790; Fajnorovo nábrežie 2). From June to October the **Twin City Liner** (☎ 09-03-61 07 16; www.twincityliner.com) operates three boats a day between the Bratislava **propeller terminal** (Map p790; Rázusovo nábrežie), in front of the Hotel Devin, and Vienna.

### Bus

The **main bus station** (autobusová stanica, AS; Map p787; reservations ☎ 5556 7349; www.eurolines.sk), is 1.5km east of the old town. Locals call it Mlynské Nivy, after the street it's on. Buses leave from here heading to towns across Slovakia, including Žilina (203Sk, three hours, seven daily), Poprad (345Sk, seven hours, four daily), Košice (441Sk, eight hours, nine daily) and Bardejov (491Sk, nine to 11 hours, three daily).

**Eurolines** (☎ 5556 7349; www.eurolines.sk) runs international buses from Bratislava to Prague (420Sk, four hours, three daily), Budapest (560Sk, four hours, one daily) and Kraków

For more on getting to Bratislava by bus from outside Eastern Europe, see (p930).

### Train

At least 12 daily trains leave the **main train station** (Hlavná stanica; www.zsr.sk), 1km north of the centre, to Košice (518Sk, 5½ to nine hours), most via Žilina (268Sk, 2¾ to four hours) and Poprad (420Sk, 4¾ to eight hours).

## GETTING AROUND
### To/From the Airport

Bus 61 links the airport with the main train station (18Sk; 20 minutes). To get to town by taxi shouldn't cost much more than 500Sk – make sure the meter is used.

### Bus & Tram

**Dopravný Podnik Bratislava** (DPB; ☎ 5950 5950; www.dpb .sk) runs an extensive tram, bus and trolleybus network. You can buy tickets (14/18/22Sk for 10/30/60 minutes) at the **DPB office** (Map p790; Obchodná 14; ☺ 9am-5.30pm Mon-Fri) and at news-stands. Validate on board. One-/two-/three-/ seven-day *turistické cestovné lístky* (tourist travel tickets) cost 90/170/270/310Sk and are sold at the DPB office and train and bus stations. Check routes and schedules at www.imhd.sk.

Bratislava Culture & Information Cen-tres (p788) sell the **Bratislava City Card** (1/2/3 days 200/300/370Sk), which covers city transport and provides discounted museum admissions among other benefits.

### Car

Numerous international rental agencies have offices at the airport; **Alimex** ( ☎ 5564 1641; www .alimex.sk) charges from 699Sk per day. **Avis** (Map p790; ☎ 5341 6111; www.avis.sk; Rybné nám 1) has a desk in the Hotel Danube, but prices are high (from 1200Sk per day).

### Taxi

Bratislava's taxis have meters, but they can be set to run at different rates. Cheating is becoming less common; within the old town a trip should cost no more than 300Sk. Call **Transtel Taxi** ( ☎ 16 301) or **Super Taxi** ( ☎ 16 616).

## AROUND BRATISLAVA

Hardcore castle aficionados should don their daypack and head to **Devín Castle** ( ☎ 6573 0105; Muranská; adult/student 80/30Sk; ☺ 10am-5pm Tue-Fri, to 6pm Sat & Sun mid-Apr-Oct), 9km west of Bratislava. Once the military plaything of 9th-century warlord

Prince Ratislav, the castle withstood the Turks but was blown up in 1809 by the French. Peer at the older bits that have been unearthed and tour a reconstructed palace museum. Bus 29 links Devín with Bratislava's New Bridge stop, under the bridge. Austria is just across the river.

# WEST SLOVAKIA

Snaking along the Small Carpathians on the main route northeast of Bratislava, watch for hilltop castle ruins high above the Váh River. Trenčín's magnificent, reconstructed castle is one of the most impressive along this once heavily fortified stretch.

## TRENČÍN
☎ 032 / pop 56,850

A mighty castle looms above the 18th- and 19th-century buildings in this lively university town. Roman legionnaires fancied the site, es-tablishing a military post, Laugaricio, in the 2nd century AD. A rock inscription recalls the 2nd legion's victory over the Germanic Kvad tribes. Trenčín Castle was first noted in a Viennese chronicle of 1069, but today's structure dates from around the 15th century. An excellent art museum rounds out the city's offerings.

### Orientation & Information

From the adjacent bus and train stations walk west through Park MR Štefánika and beneath the highway past the Hotel Tatra, where a street bears left uphill to Mierové nám, the main square. The whole centre is easily walkable.

#### EMERGENCY
**Police station** ( ☎ 159; Štúrovo nám 10)

#### INTERNET ACCESS
**Mike Studio** (Mierové nám 25; ☺ 9am-10pm Mon-Sat, 10am-10pm Sun; per min 1Sk) Just internet, no café.

#### MONEY
**VÚB Banka** (Mierové nám 37) ATM and exchange.

#### POST
**Main post office** (Mierové nám 21)

#### TOURIST INFORMATION
**Cultural Information Centre** ( ☎ 161 86; www.trencin .sk; City Office, Sládkovičova; ☺ 8am-6pm May-Sep, 8am-5pm Mon-Fri Oct-Apr) The helpful, well-informed staff can recommend one of the many local pensions.

SLOVAKIA

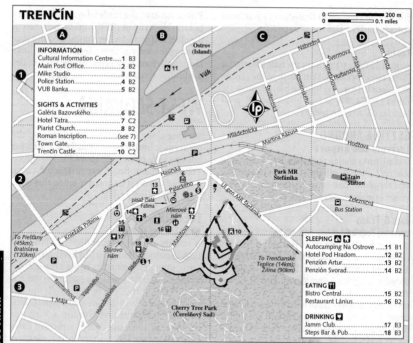

## TRENČÍN

0 _____ 200 m
0 _____ 0.1 miles

**INFORMATION**
Cultural Information Centre.....1 B3
Main Post Office.....................2 B2
Mike Studio...........................3 B2
Police Station........................4 B2
VUB Banka.............................5 B2

**SIGHTS & ACTIVITIES**
Galéria Bazovského.................6 B2
Hotel Tatra.............................7 C2
Piarist Church.........................8 B2
Roman Inscription...............(see 7)
Town Gate...............................9 B3
Trenčín Castle.......................10 C2

**SLEEPING** 🏠 🏡
Autocamping Na Ostrove ......11 B1
Hotel Pod Hradom.................12 B2
Penzión Artur........................13 B2
Penzión Svorad......................14 B2

**EATING** 🍴
Bistro Central........................15 B2
Restaurant Lánius..................16 B2

**DRINKING** 🍺
Jamm Club.............................17 B3
Steps Bar & Pub.....................18 B3

## Sights

Sitting astride a rocky crag above the town squares, **Trenčín Castle** (Trenčiansky hrad; ☎ 7435 657; adult/student 80/40Sk; ☉ 9am-5.30pm May-Oct, to 3.30pm Nov-Apr) would be hard to miss. At night, the castle is lit with green and purple lights. From up top you have sweeping views of the Váh River plain. Much of the castle you see is post-1950s reconstruction; a fire in the 1800s left the place in ruins. The Well of Love, purportedly dug by a man trying to win his lover back from servitude in the castle, is 70m deep. To go inside the palace, you have to join one of the frequent tours (in Slovak only, call two days ahead to arrange an English-speaking guide). The best time to visit is on summer evenings when two-hour **medieval night tours** (adult/student 100/50Sk) entertain you with sword fighting, minstrels, fun and staged frolics.

The famous **Roman inscription** of AD 179 is on the cliff behind the **Hotel Tatra** (☎ 6506 111; www.hotel-tatra.sk; Ulica gen MR Štefánika 2) and can only be seen through a viewing window on the hotel's staircase – ask at reception for permission to see it. The translation reads: 'To the victory of the emperor and the army

which, numbering 855 soldiers, resided at Laugaricio. By order of Maximianus, legate of the 2nd auxiliary legion.'

The **Galéria Bazovského** (☎ 7436 858; http://gmab.scot.sk in Slovak; Palackého 27; adult/student 40/10Sk; ☉ 9am-5pm Tue-Sun), in a restored 19th-century palace, houses a collection of works by local painter Miloš Bazovský (1899–1968). Temporary exhibits represent some of the best of 20th-century Slovak and Czech art.

At the western end of Mierové nám are the baroque **Piarist Church** (Piaristický kostol) and a 16th-century **town gate** (mestská brána).

## Sleeping

Trenčín has tonnes more pensions than we can list here, ask at the tourist office if the ones below are full.

**Autocamping na Ostrove** (☎ 7434 013; http://web .viapvt.sk/autocamping.tn; per car/tent 50/70Sk, per person in hut 200Sk; ☉ May–mid-Sep) On an island in the Váh River, walking distance from the city centre, this decent camping ground also has two five-bed chaty (huts).

**Penzión Svorad** (☎ 7430 322; www.svorad-trencin .sk; Palackého 4; s 450-800Sk, d 700-1200Sk; ✖) Frayed curtains, peeling linoleum – but oh, the castle views. It's clear this is in part of a grammar school; the staff is quite rule-oriented.

**Penzión Artur** ( ☎ 7481 029; www.arturtn.sk; Palackého 23; s/d/tr 1200/1500/2000Sk) Modular modern furniture in a colourful old town building. The wine restaurant and sidewalk café add to the appeal.

**Hotel Pod Hradom** ( ☎ 7442 507; www.podhradom .sk in Slovak; Matúšova 12; r 2300-2950Sk) On a winding wee street en route to the castle, this pretty little lodging has a prime location and patio. All rooms have minibars and broadband, many have sloped ceilings and skylights, some have a *mažeslka posteľ* (literally 'marriage bed', with one continuous queen-sized mattress).

### Eating & Drinking

**Bistro Central** (Štúrovo nám 10; mains 42-86Sk;  9am-7pm Mon-Thu, 9am-4am Fri, 7pm-4am Sat) You can nosh kebab meat in *langoš* (fried bread) from this food stand after the clubs let out.

**Restaurant Lánius** ( ☎ 7441 978; Mierové nám 20; mains 90-190Sk) Creaking beams, wood fires and wood floors; the rustic set up matches the hearty Slovak fare. Pass the dining room in the front; the one up the stairs at the rear of the courtyard is more fun.

**Steps Bar & Pub** ( ☎ 7446 252; Sládkovičova 4-6;  10.30am-1am Sun-Thu, to 4am Fri & Sat) The ground-floor pub has imports on tap. Upstairs the bar attracts a beautiful, college-age crowd.

**Jamm Club** (Štúrovo nám 5;  noon-1am Mon-Thu, to 3am Fri, 2pm-3am Sat, 2pm-1am Sun) Red and black painted walls make this cellar club seem extra dark. Live jazz and blues alternates with '70s and '80s disco nights.

### Getting There & Away

Trains are the quickest and most cost-efficient way to get here from Bratislava (180Sk, two hours, seven daily). Most continue on to Košice (420Sk, four hours). Twenty trains a day travel to Žilina (180Sk, 1½ hours) from here.

# CENTRAL SLOVAKIA

The rolling hills and forested mountain ranges of Central Slovakia are home to the shepherding tradition that defines Slovak culture. Watch roadside for farmers selling local sheep's cheese. The beautiful Malá Fatra mountain range is where this nation's Robin Hood, Juraj Jánošík, once roamed.

## ŽILINA
☎ 041 / pop 85,268

A Slavic tribe in the 6th century was the first to recognize Žilina's advantageous location on the Váh River at the intersection of several important trade routes. Today it makes a convenient base for exploring the Malá Fatra National Park, as well as the area's fortresses, towns and folk villages. There isn't much to see in town besides the old palace-castle on the outskirts.

### Orientation

The train station is on the northeastern side of the old town, near the Váh River. A 700m walk along Národná takes you past Nám A Hlinku up to Mariánské nám, the main square. From the south end of the bus station, follow Jána Milca northeast to Národná.

### Information

**CK Selinan** ( ☎ 5620 789; www.zilina.sk; Burianova medzierka 4;  8am-5pm Mon-Fri) Located in a lane off the western side of Mariánské nám, this travel agency is an official tourist office representative. It can also arrange accommodation in the Malá Fatras.

**Internet Caffe** ( ☎ 0903522226; Bottova 12; per min 1.5Sk;  10am-10pm Mon-Fri, 2-10pm Sat & Sun) Also has a full bar.

**Main post office** (Sládkovičova 1) Three blocks north of Mariánské nám.

**Tatra Banka** (cnr Mariánské nám & Farská) Has an ATM and change facility.

### Sights

North across the Váh River, the **Budatín Castle** (Budatínsky zámok; ☎ 5620 033; Topoľová 1; adult/student 50/30Sk;  9am-5.15pm Tue-Sun Jul & Aug, to 4pm Apr-Jun, Sep & Oct) is more mansion than stronghold. Inside, the **Považské Museum** contains exhibits of 18th- and 19th-century decorative arts as well as wire figures made by area tinkers. Other than that, you're left to a stroll through the pleasant old town.

### Sleeping

CK Selinan (above) can help with private rooms from 300Sk per person.

**Velký Diel** ( ☎ 5005 249; kadorova@dorm.utc.sk; Žilinská univerzita, Vysokoškolákov 20; dm 300-500Sk;  ) A student dorm open to travellers in July and August only, Velký Diel is worth contacting year-round just in case it has a vacancy. Take tram 1 from the bus or the train stations to get here.

**Penzión Majovey** ( ☎ 5624 152; fax 5625 239; Jána Milca 3; s/d 1000/1750Sk) The deep coral outside is more interesting than the stark white inside but bathrooms are huge and tile floors keep things cool throughout. Breakfast is an extra 100Sk.

**Hotel Grand** ( ☎ 5626 809; www.hotelgrand.sk; Sládkovičova 1; s/d 1590/2630Sk; [P] ) Floor-to-ceiling windows brighten up the bland rooms in this 90-year-old hotel off the main square. Go deluxe and ask for one with whirlpool tub and air-con (3180Sk).

## Eating & Drinking

**Voyage Voyage** ( ☎ 5640 230; Mariánske nám 191; mains 100-175Sk) With sleek neon and chrome, this is not your typical Slovak eatery. Dishes are as updated as the scene. Try one of the milk shakes.

**Pizzeria Carolina** ( ☎ 5003 030; Národná 5; pizzas 98-137Sk) Tables are filled weekdays to weekend; Carolina's is especially popular with college students. There's a mixed salad bar of sorts.

**Boston** ( ☎ 0905481214; Mariánské 24; ☺ 9am-midnight Sun-Thu, to 2am Fri & Sat) Live jazz Tuesday at 8pm; bar action nightly.

## Getting There & Away

Žilina is on the main railway line from Bratislava to Košice. Trains head to Trenčín (180Sk, one hour, 20 daily), Bratislava (268Sk, 2¾ hours, 12 daily) and Poprad (200Sk, two hours, 17 daily) and Košice (316Sk, three hours, 10 daily).

## AROUND ŽILINA

A few folk culture sights within an hour of Žilina are well worth exploring. The nearby town of **Martin** ( ☎ tourist information 4234 776; www .tikmartin.sk; Štefánika 9A) is industrial, but it also has the country's biggest *skansen* (open-air village museum), complete with working *krčma* (pub). Traditional plaster-and-log buildings from all over the region have been moved to the **Museum of the Slovak Village** (Múzeum Slovenské Dediny; ☎ 043-4239 491; adult/student 50/30Sk; ☺ 9am-6pm Mon-Sun). Take the bus to Martin (40Sk, 40 minutes, half-hourly), 35km south of Žilina. The village museum is 4km southeast of the city. Take bus 10 from the bus station to the last stop, Ľadovaň, and walk the remaining 1km up through the forest.

Dark log homes painted with contrasting patterns fill the traditional village of **Čičmany** (www.cicmany.viapvt.sk in Slovak), which is 50 minutes south of Žilina by bus (destination Čičmany, 47Sk, five daily). If you've seen a brochure or postcard of Slovakia, you've probably seen a photograph of a Čičmany house. Most are private residences, but **Radenov House** (No 42; adult/student 40/20Sk; ☺ 10am-4pm Tue-Sun) is a museum and **Penzión Katka** ( ☎ 041-5492 132; www.penzionkatka .sk; No 50; r per person 370-430Sk) rents rooms. Return bus times allow lots of hours to wander.

## MALÁ FATRA NATIONAL PARK
☎ 041

Sentinel-like formations stand watch at the rocky gorge entrance to the valley and precipitous peaks top the pine-clad slopes above. The Malá Fatra National Park (Národný park Malá Fatra) incorporates a chocolate box–pretty, 200-sq-km swathe of its namesake mountain range. The Vrátna Valley (Vrátna dolina), 25km east of Žilina, lies at the heart of the park. From here you can access the trailheads, ski lifts and a cable car to start your exploration. The long, one-street town of Terchová is at the lower end of the valley. Chata Vrátna is at the top. The village of Štefanová sits to the east, 1km uphill from Terchová.

---

**WORTH A TRIP**

**Bojnice Castle** (Bojnice zámok; ☎ 5430 633; www.bojnicecastle.sk; adult/child 200/70Sk; ☺ 9am-5pm Tue-Sun May, Jun & Sep, daily Jul & Aug, 10am-3pm Tue-Sun Oct-Apr) comes straight out of a fairy-tale dream. The original 12th-century fortification got an early 20th-century redo by the Pálffy family, who modelled it on French romantic castles. (Original Gothic and Renaissance parts do survive within.) The time to visit is during one of the many festivals and night-time tours. The biggest is the **International Festival of Ghosts and Ghouls** in May, which attracts thousands daily. Costumed guides re-enact legends and put on shows throughout the castle and grounds. The place also gets decked out for Christmas, Valentine's Day and medieval events, among others; check the website for schedules. A bus from Žilina to Prievidza takes 1½ hours (80Sk, eight daily), from Bratislava it's 3½ hours (198Sk, eight daily). Bojnice is 3km from Prievidza (via local bus 3). It's not on a main train line.

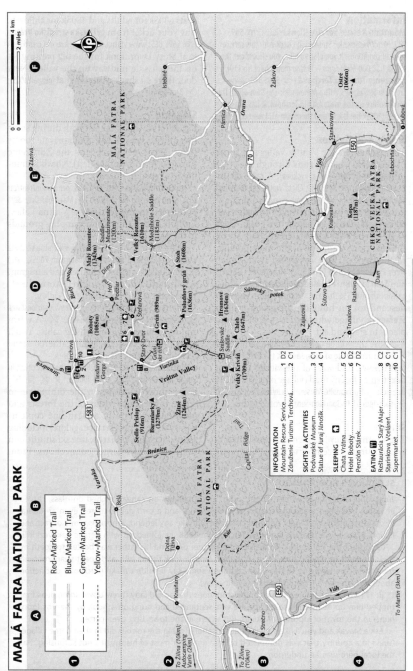

**MALÁ FATRA NATIONAL PARK**

Red-Marked Trail
Blue-Marked Trail
Green-Marked Trail
Yellow-Marked Trail

**SLOVAKIA**

| INFORMATION | |
|---|---|
| Mountain Rescue Service............................1 | D2 |
| Združenie Turizmu Terchová.....................2 | C1 |

| SIGHTS & ACTIVITIES | |
|---|---|
| Podvianské Museum..................................3 | C1 |
| Statue of Juraj Jánošík.............................4 | C1 |

| SLEEPING | |
|---|---|
| Chata Vrátna............................................5 | C2 |
| Hotel Boboty............................................6 | D2 |
| Penzión Stárek.........................................7 | D2 |

| EATING | |
|---|---|
| Reštaurácia Starý Majer...........................8 | C2 |
| Starinkova Vcelaren.................................9 | C1 |
| Supermarket............................................10 | C1 |

## Information

**Mountain Rescue Service** (Horská služba; ☎ 5695 232; http://his.hzs.sk/; Štefanová) Check with this service for trail conditions. If you plan to hike, you should get the VKÚ's 1:50,000 *Malá Fatra – Vrátna* map (sheet No 110).

**Združenie Turizmu Terchová** ( ☎ 5695 307; www .ztt.sk in Slovak; Sv Cyrila a Metoda 96; ☾ 9am-6pm) The tourist office on the main road in Terchová. It has internet access (100Sk per hour), and there's an ATM next door.

## Sights & Activities

The road enters the Vrátna Valley just south of Terchová, where it runs through the crags of **Tiesňavy Gorge** (Tiesňavy roklina). A **cable car** (kabínkova lanovka; ☎ 5993 049; Chata Vrátna; adult/student one way 250/170Sk; ☾ 8am-4pm) runs from above the hut at the top of the valley to **Snilov Saddle** (Snilovské sedlo; 1524m) below two peaks, **Chleb** (1647m) and **Velký Kriváň** (1709m). Both are on the red, ridge trail, one of the most popular in the park. A hike northeast from Chleb over **Poludňový grúň** (1636m), **Hromové** (1636m) and **Stoh** (1608m) to **Medziholie Saddle** (1185m) takes about 5½ hours. From there you can descend for an hour on the green trail to **Štefanová** village where there's a bus stop, places to stay and eat.

Above the village of Terchová is an immense aluminium **statue of Juraj Jánošík** (see the boxed text below), and west of the village bus stop next to the Obecný úrad (village office) is a little branch of **Podvanské Museum** (adult/student 20/10Sk; ☾ 9am-1pm & 1.30-3pm Mon-Sun) devoted to him.

### SKIING

The Vrátna Valley has plenty of tows and lifts are open from December to April. A day pass costs 680Sk for adults and 480Sk for children. Buy your ticket from **Lyžiarska stredisko Vrátna** ( ☎ 5695 055; www.vratna.sk). The *kasa* (cashier) is at Starý Dvor, look for the big parking lot on the left side midway up the valley. Next door there's a shack with **ski rental** (per pair 300Sk; ☾ 8am-4pm).

## Sleeping

Places to stay book up fast both during summer and ski season. Ask about private rooms (from 300Sk per person) at the Združenie Turizmu Terchová office (left). No wild camping is allowed in the park.

**Autocamp Varín** ( ☎ 5621 478; per person/tent/car 75Sk each, 4-person hut 1000Sk; ☾ May–mid-Oct; 🚲 ) Fifteen kilometres west of the Vrátna Valley, Varín is one of the closest camping grounds to the park.

**Chata Vrátna** ( ☎ 5695 739; www.vratna.sk/chata vratna/; dm 220Sk, d with shared bathroom 760Sk; P ) Muddy hikers, giggling children and a fragrant wood-smoke aroma fill this well-worn, chalet-style outfit at the top of Vrátna Valley.

**Penzión Stárek** ( ☎ 5695 359; www.penzionstarek .sk; Štefanová 124; d per person 400-540Sk; ✗ ) A warm and welcoming eight-room log cabin. You'll often find the owner's family gathered at the restaurant's outdoor picnic tables.

**Hotel Boboty** ( ☎ 5695 228; www.hotelboboty.sk in Slovak; Nový Dvor; s 800Sk, d 900-1900Sk; P ✗ 🖳 🚲 ) Skyscraping windows in the dining room create tremendous vistas of the forests and mountains beyond in a clean-line contemporary style. Expect services galore, including sauna, massage, billiards, free ski shuttle and some in-room internet connections. From

---

### SLOVAKIA'S ROBIN HOOD

Juraj Jánošík has been written about, sung about, painted on canvas, etched on glass, carved in wood; he's been made the subject of three movies and a card game, there's even an opera. It's hard to imagine a bigger national character. But like any legend, Jánošík is a mix of fact and fiction. Born into a peasant family in Terchová in 1688, he joined up with Ferenc Rákóvczi II in 1703 to fight the Habsburgs. While away his mother died and his father was beaten to death by their landlord for taking time off to bury her. Jánošík took to the hills and spent years robbing from the rich and giving to the poor (although some say he didn't make much of a distinction about who he stole from and didn't give it away).

In 1713 he was captured in a pub; the story goes that an old lady threw down some peas that tripped him up as he tried to escape. He was sentenced and hung on a hook by the ribs (gory huh?) in the town of Liptovský Mikuláš. But where in the town isn't even certain.

Ask a Slovak and you'll likely hear what sensational thing the robber did in their home village. Guess in a country that was dominated by foreigners for most of history, it's not surprising that the local hero was an underdog.

the bus stop at Nový Dvor, walk five minutes' uphill in the direction of Štefanová.

## Eating

The food situation in the park is pretty bleak; most Slovaks bring their own. There are takeaway stands at Starý Dvor and there's a **supermarket** *(potraviny)* at the valley turnoff in Terchová. Most hotels have restaurants. There's a pizzeria in Penzión Stárek (opposite).

**Starinkova Včeláreň** ( ☎ 5993 130; A Hlinku 246; snacks 20-50Sk) A friendly tearoom has scones and homemade honey to go with its brew.

**Reštaurácia Starý Majer** ( ☎ 5695 419; mains 1000-200Sk; ☼ 10am-9pm) Farm implements decorate the walls and hearty *halušky* top the menu.

## Getting There & Around

At least every two hours, more often on weekdays, buses link Žilina with Terchová (40Sk, 45 minutes) and Chata Vrátna (50Sk, one hour). Or you can change in Terchová for local buses that make multiple stops in the valley.

Ask at the Terchová information centre (opposite) about bicycle rental.

# EAST SLOVAKIA

Majestic? Ancient? Sublime? No one adjective well describes East Slovakia with its alpine peaks, old towns and even older castles. In one compact region you can hike the High Tatras, explore a medieval town square in Levoča, conquer the Špis Castle ruins, visit the Renaissance era in Bardejov and get back to city life in Košice. Though it's a distance from Bratislava, once you get here, the area is easy to traverse by bus. And Poland's just the other side of the mountains.

## HIGH TATRAS

☎ 052

When you first see the alpine, snow-strewn High Tatras (Vysoké Tatry) jutting out of the valley floor north of Poprad, you may do a double take. This isn't Switzerland after all. But Gerlachovský štít (2654m) is the highest in the Carpathian range, and the Tatras tower over most of Eastern Europe. The massif is only 25km wide, adding to the sense that some alien plopped these huge mountains here. The photo opportunities at higher elevations will get you fantasising about a career with *National Geographic* –

pristine snowfields, ultramarine mountain lakes, crashing waterfalls. Sadly, a massive windstorm in late 2004 uprooted the dense pine forest that surrounded the resort towns of Starý Smokovec and Tatranská Lomnica. Huge swathes will look barren and war ravaged for years to come. Trunks have been cleared leaving fields full of giant upturned stumps and dirt. This hasn't stopped the crowds from showing up.

Since 1949 most of the Slovak part of this jagged range has been included in the Tatra National Park (Tanap), complementing a similar park in Poland. A 600km network of hiking trails reaches all the alpine valleys and some peaks, with *chaty* (mountain huts) to stop at along the way. Routes are colour coded and easy to follow. Park regulations require you to keep to the marked trails and to refrain from picking flowers.

## Climate & When to Go

When planning your trip, keep in mind that the higher trails are closed from November to mid-June to protect the environment, and avalanches may close lower portions as well. There's snow by November that lingers at least until May. Always wear hiking boots and layer clothing. Know that the assistance of the Mountain Rescue Service is not free and beware of sudden thunderstorms on ridges and peaks where there's no protection. June and July are especially rainy. July and August are the warmest (and most crowded) months. Hotel prices and crowds are at their lowest from October to April.

For the latest weather and trail conditions stop by the **Mountain Rescue Service** (Horská Záchranná Služba; ☎ emergency 18 300; http://his.hzs.sk/; Starý Smokovec 23).

## Orientation

Starý Smokovec, a 20th-century resort town, is roughly central along the High Tatras chain, with Tatranská Lomnica, the smallest and quaintest resort, 5km to the east. Lakeside, development-crazy Štrbské Pleso, 11km to the west, was the only one of the big three resorts villages left with trees after the storm, and in some ways is the prettiest now. A narrow-gauge electric train connects Poprad with Štrbské Pleso via Starý Smokovec, where you have to change to get to Tatranská Lomnica. Roads lead downhill from the resorts to less expensive villages.

SLOVAKIA

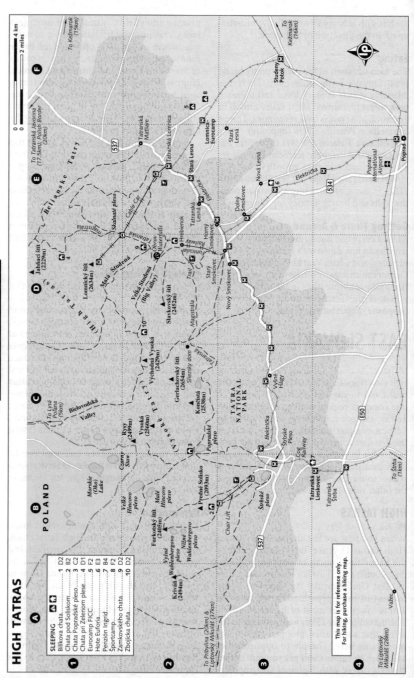

# HIGH TATRAS

This map is for reference only.
For hiking, purchase a hiking map.

## MAPS
Our High Tatras map is intended for orientation only, not as a hiking guide. Buy a proper VKÚ 1:25,000 (sheet No 2) or 1:50,000 *Vysoké Tatry* (sheet No 113) trail map when you arrive – both cost around 120Sk. They're usually available at hotels, shops and newsstands, as well as information offices. Green maps list summer *hiking turistka* (hiking trails) and the blue ones show winter ski routes.

## Information
### INTERNET ACCESS
**Hotel FIS** ( ☎ 4492 221; Areál FIS, Štrbské Pleso; per hr 100Sk; ☺ 24hr) Two lobby computers are available for general rental.
**Townson Travel** ( ☎ 4782 731; Tatranská Lomnica 94; per hr 80Sk; ☺ 9am-5pm Mon-Fri) This travel agency has one computer with access, but it closes sporadically.
**U Michalka Café** (Starý Smokovec 4; per hr 80Sk; ☺ 11am-10pm) One terminal in the corner.

### MONEY
All three main resorts have ATMs.
**Slovenská Sporiteľňa** (Cesta Slobody 24, Starý Smokovec) On the main road, has an ATM and exchange.

### POST
**Post Office** (off Cesta Slobody) Above Starý Smokovec train station.

### TOURIST INFORMATION
**Tatra Information Office** (TIK) Starý Smokovec ( ☎ 4423 440; www.tatry.sk; Dom služieb 24; ☺ 8am-8pm Mon-Fri, to 1pm Sat); Tatranská Lomnica ( ☎ 4468 118; Cesta Slobody; ☺ 10am-6pm Mon-Fri, 9am-1pm Sat) Oodles of info.
**Tatra National Park Info Centrum** ( ☎ 4492 391; www.tanap.sk; Štrbské Pleso; ☺ 9am-4pm) Next to Toliar department store; staff knows a lot about trails.

### TRAVEL AGENCIES
**T-Ski Travel** ( ☎ 4423 200; www.slovakiatravel.sk; Starý Smokovec 46; ☺ 9am-4pm Mon-Thu, to 5pm Fri-Sun) Books lodging, including some huts, and arranges ski and sport programmes. It's at the funicular station.

## Sights & Activities
### STARÝ SMOKOVEC
From Starý Smokovec a **funicular railway** (pozemná lanovka; ☎ 4467 618; www.tldtatry.sk; adult/student return 100/60Sk; ☺ 7.30am-7pm), or a 55-minute hike on the green trail, takes you up to **Hrebienok** (1280m). From here you have a great view of the Velká Studená Valley and a of couple

hiking options. The red trail, past the Bilíkova chata to **Obrov Waterfalls** (Obrovsky vodopad), takes about an hour. This is part of the **Tatranská Magistrála Trail** that follows the southern slopes of the High Tatras for 65km. Continuing on from the falls, it's a 35-minute hike to Zamkovského chata, and Skalnaté pleso (see below), with its cable car and trails down to Tatranská Lomnica.

### TATRANSKÁ LOMNICA
An extremely popular **cable car** (kabínková lanovka; www.tldtatry.sk; adult/student return 390/270Sk; ☺ 8.30am-7pm Jul-Aug, to 3.30pm Sep-Jun) links Tatranská Lomnica with the bustling lake and winter sports area of **Skalnaté pleso** (1751m). From there, another **cable car** (adult/student return 550/350Sk; ☺ 8.30am-7pm Jul-Aug, to 3.30pm Sep-Jun) goes on to the precipitous 2634m summit of **Lomnický štít** – bring a jacket. And queues are long during peak season, so get there early.

Alternatively, you can yomp it up to Skalnaté (2½ hours), where there is also an ordinary **chairlift** (adult/student 150/90Sk; ☺ 8.30am-5.30pm Jul-Aug, 8.30am-4.30pm Sep-Jun) running up to **Lomnické sedlo**, a 2190m saddle below the summit.

Is it a rollercoaster? Is it a summer bobsled? Both, it's **Tatrabob** ( ☎ 4467 951; Tatranská Lomnica 29; per ride 50Sk; ☺ 9am-10pm Jul & Aug, 9am-7pm Sep-Jun). Individual riders get hauled up on a track and then let go to control their own undulating descent.

### ŠTRBSKÉ PLESO
From the modern ski resort of Štrbské Pleso and its glacial lake (1346m), follow the red-marked Magistrála Trail (uphill from the train station) for about an hour up to **Popradské pleso**, an even more idyllic pond at 1494m. From Popradské pleso the Magistrála zigzags steeply up the mountainside then traverses east towards **Sliezsky dom** and **Hrebienok** (four hours).

There is also a year-round **chairlift** ( ☎ 4492 343; www.parksnow.sk; adult/student return 200/140Sk; ☺ 8am-3.30pm) to **Solisko**, from where it's a one-hour walk north along the red trail to the 2093m summit of **Predné Solisko**.

There's usually a guy hawking rides on a **snowmobile** (snižký skooter; 10 min 600Sk) in the field on the side of the road to the chairlift and Areál FIS.

### MOUNTAIN CLIMBING
You can reach the top of **Slavkovský štít** (2452m) via the blue trail from Starý Smokovec (seven

to eight hours return), but to scale the peaks without marked hiking trails (Gerlachovský štít included) you must hire a mountain guide (members of recognised climbing clubs excluded). Contact the **Mountain Guides Society Office** ( ☎ 4422 066; www.tatraguide.sk; Starý Smokovec 38; ✆ 10am-6pm Mon-Fri, noon-6pm Sat & Sun Jun-Sep, 10am-6pm Mon-Fri Oct-May), by the Hotel Smokovec. It runs classes too.

### SKIING, SNOWBOARDING & MOUNTAIN BIKING

Štrbské Pleso is probably the most poplar ski and snowboard area, but Starý Smokovec and Tatranská Lomnica both have lifts and runs. You can hire skis, snowboards, even mountain bikes, (all about 300Sk a day) from **Crystal Ski** ( ☎ 4492 834; www.crystalski.sk; Areál FIS; ✆ 8.30am-4.30pm) in Štrbské Pleso and from **Tatrasport** ( ☎ 4425 241; www.tatry.net/tatrasport; ✆ 8am-noon & 1-6pm) in Starý Smokovec, above the bus station parking lot.

## Sleeping

No wild camping is permitted within the national park, but there are a couple of camping grounds near Tatranská Lomnica. Lodging rates are high in the three main resorts; if you're looking for bargains you have to go downhill to towns like Nová Lesná, Stará Lesná and Tatranská Štrba. It's best to book private rooms ahead of time via the internet (www.tatry.sk and www.tanap.sk/homes.html) as tourist offices up here don't do bookings.

Up on the trails, a *chata* (mountain hut) can be anything from a shack to chalet. A bed goes for 300Sk to 500Sk; all may be full midsummer. Food is usually available, but you may want to bring some of your own supplies. A stay in a *chata* is one of the best mountain experiences the Tatras have to offer. Contact the *chata* directly to book ahead, essential in July and August. Someone usually speaks enough English to communicate.

### STARÝ SMOKOVEC & AROUND

**Pension Vesna** ( ☎ 4422 774; vesna@stonline.sk; Nový Smokovec 69; r per person 600Sk; **P** ) Both family-orientated and friendly. Most of the seven rooms at this guesthouse have three beds and a separate living area. Vesna's below Nový Smokovec train stop, behind the sanatorium.

**Hotel Euforia** ( ☎ 4783 061; www.hoteleuforia.sk; Nová Lesná 399; s/d 1150/1550Sk; **P** ) With blond wood and cobalt blue rugs, Euforia is fresher and

brighter (and newer) than most of what's up the hill. It's 3km south of Starý Smokovec, near the Nová Lesná train stop. A big terrace closes off with windows for winter.

**Grand Hotel** ( ☎ 4870 000; www.grandhotel.sk; Starý Smokovec 38; s/d 2300/3900Sk; **P** ⊠ ☎ ) More than 100 years of history are tied up in this full-service property front and centre in Starý Smokovec. It's a biggie.

Some mountain huts above:

**Bilíkova chata** (1220m; ☎ 4422 439; fax 4422 267) Hotel-like chalet with restaurant and one-, two- and three-bed rooms with shared bathrooms.

**Zbojnícka chata** (1960m; ☎ 0903638000; www.zbojnickachata.sk) Sixteen beds, dorm style, restaurant (breakfast included).

**Zamkovského chata** (1475m; ☎ 4422 636; www.zamka.sk) Twenty-four beds in four-bed rooms; board available.

### TATRANSKÁ LOMNICA & AROUND

**Eurocamp FICC** ( ☎ 4467 741; www.eurocamp-ficc.sk; per person/tent/car 110/80/80Sk, 2-/3-/4-bed bungalows 1200/1400/1600Sk; ✆ year-round; **P** ☎ ) Row upon row of caravans line up at this 1500-capacity ground. On site there are two restaurants, a bar, billiards, a supermarket, a swimming pool and sauna, and ball courts. It's five minutes' northeast of the Lomnica–Eurocamp train station on the line to Studený Potok.

**Športcamp** ( ☎ 4467 288; http://sportcamp.host.sk in Slovak; per person/tent/car 80/80/50Sk) Two kilometres south of Eurocamp FICC is a less hyper, 100-site camping ground with tennis and volleyball courts

**Penzión Encian** ( ☎ 4467 520; penzion.encian@sinet.sk; s/d 1000/1500Sk; **P** ) You couldn't ask for better hosts than Zdenka and Štefan Unák. They've warmed up the small restaurant with a fire in the hearth and old skiing memorabilia on display. Eave-top room 13 has a great view of Lomnický štít.

**Grandhotel Praha** ( ☎ 4467 941; www.grandhotel praha.sk; s/d 2900/3900Sk; **P** ⊠ ⧉ ☎ ) Remember when train travel was elegant? OK, so we're too young, but the 1899 Grandhotel isn't. Rooms are appropriately classic, if uninspired, and there's a new spa.

Take the cable car up from Tatranská Lomnica to Skalnaté pleso, and hike west to the huts above Starý Smokovec (above), or you can make the strenuous 2½-hour red-trail trek from Skalnaté pleso to **Chata pri Zelenom plese** (1540m; ☎ 4467 420; www.zelenepleso.sk). The lakeside hut has 50 beds.

## ŠTRBSKÉ PLESO & AROUND

**Penzión Pleso** ( ☎ 4492 160; Nové Štrbské Pleso 11; www
.penzionpleso.sk; r per person 650Sk, ste per person 800Sk; P ))
The inside of this refurbishment-in-progress
is well ahead of the outside. Go for contemporary suite 11 because of the views from corner,
full-length windows. Breakfast is 90Sk.

    **Penzión Ingrid** ( ☎ 0905108088; www.ingrid.sk; Tatranská Štrba 1121; apt per person 400-800Sk; P ✗ )) This
tidy new accommodation opened 500m from
the Tatranská Štrba zubačka (cog railway) in
late 2005. Apartments each have a two-burner
cooktop, a small fridge and an electric kettle.

    Mountain huts above Štrbské Pleso:

**Chata pod Soliskom** (1800m; ☎ 0905652036; www
.chatasolisko.sk) Nine beds, nice terrace and no hiking
required (it's next to the chairlift).

**Chata Popradské pleso** (1500m; ☎ 4492 177; www
.popradskepleso.sk) Sizeable chalet with restaurant and
132 beds in two eight-bed rooms. The attic floor sleeps 25
in sleeping bags.

## Eating & Drinking

The villages are close enough that it's easy to
eat in one and sleep in another. All of the hotels, and some of the *penzións* (homy hotels),
have restaurants; the grand ones have bars and
discos. Look for the local *potraviny* (supermarket) on the main road in each village.

    **Samoobslužná Reštaurácia** ( ☎ 4781 011; Hotel Toliar, Štrbské Pleso 21; mains 40-70Sk; ⏲ 7am-10pm) This
self-service cafeteria has one-dish meals (goulash, chicken stir-fry) and some vegetarian
options.

    **Reštaurácia Stará Mama** ( ☎ 4467 216; shopping centre Sintra, Tatranská Lomnica; mains 65-172Sk) Substantial
soups and homemade dumplings are the main
reason hikers frequent this rustic fave; but the
menu is actually quite extensive.

    **Pizzéria Albas** ( ☎ 4423 460; Albas, Starý Smokovec;
pizzas 100-170Sk) Everyone you talk to seems to
recommend this big, antiseptic pizzeria. It's
the pizza, not the place.

    **Zbojnícka Koliba** (Tatranská Lomnica; mains 150-350Sk)
Musicians play gypsy songs on the cimbalon
while your chicken roasts over the open fire.
Sit back, order some *bryndza* to spread on
bread, have some hot spiced wine and wait,
it'll take an hour to cook. The Koliba is on the
road up to the Grand Hotel Praha.

    **Tatry Pub** ( ☎ 4422 448; Starý Smokovec; ⏲ 1-11pm
Mon-Thu, 11am-midnight Fri-Sun) Refresh yourself at
the official watering hole of the Mountain
Guide Club. It's on the main road west and
up from the car park.

## Getting There & Away

To reach the Tatras from most destinations
you need to switch in Poprad (p806).

### BUS

Buses from Poprad travel to Starý Smokovec
(18Sk, 20 minutes, every half hour), Tatranská Lomnica (25Sk, 35 minutes, hourly) and
Štrbské Pleso (45Sk, 50 minutes, every 45
minutes). One daily, early-morning bus links
Bratislava with Starý Smokovec (346Sk, 6½
hours) directly.

    From Tatranská Lomnica buses leave for
Kežmarok (22Sk, 30 minutes) at least every
1½ hours.

### TRAIN

To reach the High Tatras by train you'll have
to change at Poprad (p806). There are frequent narrow-gauge electric trains between
Poprad and the High Tatras (see Getting
Around). All three main train stations have
left-luggage offices.

### WALKING INTO POLAND

There's a highway border crossing at Lysá
Poľana, 2.5km north of Tatranská Javorina,
which is accessible by bus from Tatranská
Lomnica (30Sk, 45 minutes, at least five daily).
From the Polish side there are regular public
buses and private minibuses to Zakopane
(26km).

## Getting Around

**Tatra electric train service** (Tatranská elekrická
železnica, TEZ) links most of the towns and
villages in the Tatras at least hourly. One line
runs from Poprad via Starý Smokovec (30
minutes) to Štrbské Pleso (one hour), with
frequent stops in between. Another line connects Starý Smokovec to Tatranská Lomnica
(15 minutes). A third route is from Tatranská
Lomnica through Studeny Potok (15 minutes) looping round to Poprad (25 minutes).
A 20Sk ticket covers a six to 14km ride. It's
easier to buy a one-/three-/seven-day pass for
100/200/360Sk. If there's not a ticket window
at your stop, buy one from the conductor.
Validate it on board.

    A cog railway connects Tatranská Štrba (on
the main Žilina–Poprad railway line) with
Štrbské Pleso (30Sk, 15 minutes, hourly).

    Local buses run between the resorts every
20 minutes and tend to be quicker than the
train – they have fewer stops though. Starý

Smokovec to Tatranská Lomnica (10Sk) takes 10 minutes, and to Štrbské Pleso (28Sk) takes 30 minutes.

The main road through the Tatras resorts is Rte 537, or Cesta Slobody (Freedom Way). You can connect to it from the E50 motorway through Tatranská Štrba, Poprad or Velká Lomnica.

Hire mountain bikes from Tatrasport in Starý Smokovec and Crystal Ski in Štrbské Pleso, which both also rent skis (see p804).

## POPRAD

☎ 052 / pop 55,400

Poprad is an important transportation transfer point for the High Tatras and Slovenský raj National Parks, and a possible base for seeing Levoča and surrounding towns if you have a car. Otherwise, skip the modern, industrial city. From the adjacent train and bus stations the central pedestrian square, Nám sv Egídia, is a five-minute walk south on Alžbetina.

### Information

**City Information Centre** ( ☎ 7721 700; www.poprad .sk; Nám sv Egídia 15; ☾ 8am-6pm Mon-Fri, 9am-noon Sat Jul-Aug, 8.30am-5pm Mon-Fri, 9am-noon Sat Sep-Jun) Has information about the Tatras and can help with accommodation.

**Sinet** (Nám sv Egídia 28; per hr 40Sk; ☾ 9am-9pm Mon-Sat, from 1pm Sun). Internet and email available.

### Sleeping

The old Germanic village of Spišská Sobota, 2km northeast of the centre, is now a Poprad adjunct. There are more than 10 lodging options on or near its medieval square.

**Hotel Sobota** ( ☎ 4663 121; www.hotelsobota.sk; Kežmarská 15; s/d 1750/2200Sk; Ⓟ ⓧ ⓧ ⌷ ) One of the newer lodging options; it has great slate and timber construction. It's near the road connecting Kežmarok and Levoča.

### Eating

Numerous restaurants and cafés line Nám sv Egídia.

**Pizzeria Utopia** ( ☎ 7732 222; Dostojevského 23; pizzas 100-200Sk) For eclectic antiques and pizza head south across the E18 to Utopia. Salami, blue cheese and corn is an interesting combination, don't you think?

### Getting There & Away

Bus 12 travels between the Poprad city centre and **Poprad-Tatry International airport** ( ☎ 7763 875;

www.airport-poprad.sk; Na Letisko 100), 5km west of the centre. The only flights that use this airport are the ones to and from London (see p928).

Intercity (IC) or Eurocity (EC) trains are the quickest way to get in and out of Poprad; four a day run to Bratislava (420Sk, 4¼ hours) and Košice (154Sk, 1¼ hours). For more on the electric trains that traverse the 13km or so to the High Tatras resorts, see p805.

To cities in Western and Central Slovakia, trains are generally better than buses (quicker, comparable cost). For more on transferring to the High Tatras resorts by bus, see p805. To get to Poland, you can take a bus from Poprad to Tatranska Javorina (58Sk, 1¼ hours, four daily), near the border at Lysá Poľana. Walk across to the buses waiting to take you to Zakopane.

## KEŽMAROK

☎ 052 / pop 12,740

Snuggled beneath the broody peaks of the High Tatras, Kežmarok may not seem dramatic, but it is a truly pleasant place. The numerous architecturally distinct churches, the pocket-sized old town square with resident castle, all the ice-cream shops…

Ever since it was colonised by Germans back in the 13th century, Kežmarok has been treading a subtly different path from the rest of the country. The residents even declared themselves an independent republic, albeit infinitesimally, in 1918. Though the Germanic settlers moved on, they left behind something of their character on the town buildings. On the second weekend in July, the **European Folk Craft Market** attracts artisans from all across the country to demonstrate and sell their wares. Plenty of food and drink to be had then too.

### Orientation & Information

Kežmarok is 14km east of Tatranská Lomnica and 16km northeast of Poprad – easy day-tripping distances. The bus and train stations are side by side, northwest of the old town, just across the Poprad River, via Dr Alexandra, to the main square, Hlavné nám.

The extremely useful **Kežmarok Information Agency** ( ☎ 4524 047; www.kezmarok.net; Hlavné nám 46; ☾ 8am-noon & 1-5pm Mon-Fri, 9am-2pm Sat, 9am-2pm Sun Jun-Sep) stocks heaps of brochures and souvenirs. The staff can help with info about the Tatras too. One of the best bookstore map selections in the country is at **Alter Ego** ( ☎ 4525 432; Hlavné nám 3).

## Sights

The huge red-and-green, 1894 pseudo-Moorish **New Evangelical Church** (cnr Toporcerova & Hviezdoslavovo; ⏰ 10am-noon & 2-4pm May-Sep) dominates the south end of town. Next door, the **Old Wooden Evangelical Church** (⏰ 10am-noon & 2-4pm Mon-Sat May-Sep) was built in 1717 without a single nail and has an amazing interior of carved and painted wood. A 30Sk ticket covers entry to both.

The wooden altars in the 15th-century Gothic **Basilica of the Holy Cross** (Bazilika sv Kríža; Nám Požárnikov; donation 10Sk; ⏰ 9am-5pm Mon-Fri Jun-Sep) were supposedly carved by students of Master Pavol of Levoča. Small, mansionlike **Kežmarok Castle** (☎ 4522 618; Hradné nám 45; adult/student 60/30Sk; ⏰ 9am-noon & 1-5pm Tue-Sun May-Sep) dates back to the 15th century and is now a museum with local history, archaeology and period furniture exhibits. Entry from October to April is with a tour that leaves on the hour from 8am to 3pm, Monday to Friday.

## Sleeping & Eating

**Penzión U Jakubu** (☎ 4526 314; www.penzionujakuba .sk; Starý trh 39; d 880-1190Sk) An authentic, folksy Slovakness pervades this *penzión* and restaurant. Take a seat at a big wooden bench table near the open fire and be waited on by servers in area folk dress. Remember to call a day ahead if you want a whole roast pig. Rooms are simply dressed in pine.

Sidewalk cafés abound in the pedestrian area around Hlavné nám. There are no fewer than six *cukráreň* serving pastries and ice cream, or you could stop at the tables on the square run by **Pizza Classica** (☎ 4523 693; cnr Hviezdoslavova & Hlavné nám; pizzas 90-170Sk).

## Getting There & Away

Buses are the way to get around locally – they run hourly to/from Poprad (22Sk, 30 minutes) and every 1½ hours to/from Tatranská Lomnica (22Sk, 30 minutes). From Monday to Friday, there are three buses a day to Červený Kláštor (58Sk, 1" hours, only one on Saturday and Sunday).

## PIENINY NATIONAL PARK

☎ 052

Gently bubbling water flows between impressive 500m-tall sheer cliffs: the 21 sq km **Pieniny National Park** (Pieninský Národný Park) was created to protect the 9km **Dunajec Gorge**. The park combines with a similar one on the Polish side of the river and extends between the Slovak village of Červený Kláštor and Szczawnica, Poland. River rafting is the main attraction here, but there are also hiking trails and an ancient monastery. Pick up VKÚ's 1:25,000 *Pieninský Národný Park* map (sheet No 7) for detailed exploring.

At the mouth of the gorge is the fortified **Red Monastery** (Červený Kláštor; ☎ 4822 955; adult/student 50/25Sk; ⏰ 9am-5pm May-Oct). Built in the 14th century, it's now used as a park administrative centre and museum with a collection of statuary and old prints of the area. Two kilometres west of the monastery is a small **information centre** (☎ 4822 122; Rte 543; www.pieniny .sk; ⏰ 9am-5pm May-Oct).

There are two departure points along Rte 243 for a **river float trip** (adult/child 250/100Sk; ⏰ daylight May-Oct) on a *plte* (shallow, flat-bottom wood rafts): one opposite the monastery, and another 1km upriver west of the village. A raft may wait to set out until it has as many passengers as possible (capacity 12). Don't be expecting white-water thrills – the Dunajec is a rather sedate 1½-hour experience terminating near the Slovak village of Lesnica.

To return to Červený Kláštor you can hike back the way you came, roughly southwest, along the river-side trail through the gorge, in a little over an hour. It's an interesting walk even if you don't do water. Or, walk 500m southeast of the river to Chata Pieniny in Lesnica. The hiker's lodge rents out bicycles (one way 100Sk) and runs a shuttle bus (50Sk) to take you the 22km over-mountain distance by road. Follow the yellow trail north of Lesnica (1.5km) and you reach a pedestrian border crossing into Poland for tourists, open from 9am to 4pm from May to October.

## Sleeping & Eating

Cheap and cheerful **Chata Pieniny** (☎ 4397 530; www.chatapieniny.sk; Lesnica; dm 280Sk) is an old log lodge with two- to six-bed rooms at the terminus of the raft trip. There's a restaurant, a minimarket and bike rental available. It's located 500m south of the river landing terminus, at the far north end of Lesnica.

Copious *privaty* and *zimmer frei* ('private', or 'free' room in Slovak and German respectively) and *pension* signs line the one long road in Červený Kláštor. The not-so-youthful **Hotel Pltník** (☎ 4822 525; www.hotelpltnik.sk; s/d 720/870Sk; P) also has camping (per person/tent 60/50Sk) in the big river-front field next door.

SLOVAKIA

Food stalls stand between the monastery and the river launch.

## Getting There & Away

Getting here is a challenge unless you have a car. Buses run to Červený Kláštor from Poprad (89Sk, 1⅓ hours) three times a day Monday to Saturday and once on Sunday. From Košice (152Sk, 3″ hours) there's one direct afternoon bus, otherwise you have to change in Stará Ľubovňa (120Sk, 2″ hours, five daily) for the connecting service to Červený Kláštor (40Sk, 35 minutes, six daily).

## LEVOČA

☎ 053 / pop 14,604

Medieval walls stand stolid and defensive, protecting the age-old centre from onslaught. Thank goodness no hyper-mart developer is getting in here. Levoča is one of the few Slovak cities to have her ancient old town defences largely intact. The pride of Slovakia's religious art collection, an 18m-high altar carved by renowned artist Master Pavol of Levoča, resides within the centre square's Church of St Jacob.

In the 13th century the king of Hungary invited Saxon Germans to colonise the eastern frontiers of his kingdom as a protection against Tatar incursions. Levoča was one of the main towns comprising what came to be known as the Spiš region.

## Orientation & Information

Levoča is on the main E50 motorway between Poprad (28km) and Košice (94km). The centre is 1km north of the train and bus stations. Both banks and post are on the small main square, Nám Majstra Pavla.

**Levonet Internet Café** (Nám Majstra Pavla 38; per hr 80Sk; ☺ 10am-midnight) Check your email.

**Tourist information office** (☎ 4513 763; www .levoca.sk; Nám Majstra Pavla 58; ☺ 9am-5pm Mon-Sat, 10am-2pm Sun May-Oct, 9am-4.30pm Mon-Fri Nov-Apr) Ask staff for the free photocopied map they keep under the counter if you want one.

## Sights

The spindles-and-spires **Church of St Jacob** (Chrám sv Jakuba; ☎ 4512 347; www.chramsvjakuba.sk; adult/student 50/30Sk; ☺ 11.30am, 1, 2, 3 & 4pm Tue-Sat Sep-Jun, 11am-5pm Mon, 9am-5pm Tue-Sat Jun-Aug), built in the 14th and 15th centuries, elevates your spirit with its soaring arches, precious art and rare furnishings. Everyone comes to see the splen-

did golden Gothic altar (1517) created by Master Pavol of Levoča. On it he carved and painted representations of the Last Supper and the Madonna and Child. (This Madonna's face appears on the 100Sk banknote.) Buy tickets at the **cashier** (kasa; ☺ 11am-5pm) inside the **Municipal Weights House** across the street from the north door. Once inside, drop a 5Sk coin in the machine at the back for a recorded description in English.

The square is choc-a-bloc with Gothic and Renaissance eye candy. No 20 is the **Master Pavol Museum** (☎ 4513 496; adult/student 40/20Sk; ☺ 9am-5pm) dedicated to the city's most celebrated son. The 15th-century **town hall** (rad-nica) houses a lacklustre **Spiš Museum** (☎ 4512 449; adult/student 50/20Sk; ☺ 9am-5pm). The adjacent 16th-century **cage of shame** is for naughty boys and girls.

From town you can see the **Church of Marián-ska hora**, 2km north, where the largest Catholic pilgrimage in Slovakia takes place in early July.

## Sleeping

**Recreačné Zariadenie** (☎ 4512 705; www.rz-levoca .web2001.cz; Levočská Dolina; per person/tent 85/70Sk, 2-bed hut 380Sk; ℗) A good camping option, Recreačné Zariadenie is 5km northwest of the centre and bikes can be rented. Relax in the sauna after all that pedalling.

**Oáza** (☎ 4514 511; www.ubytovanieoaza.sk; Nová 65; per person 300Sk) Two-bed rooms with shared bathroom, and four-bed rooms with bathroom and kitchen, are just what the budget doctor ordered. There's a big garden (with lawn, caged chickens and vegetables) between the two parts of the house.

On the main square, choose between the self-catering friendly apartments (with a new lift) at **Penzión U Leva** (☎ 4502 311; www.uleva.sk; Nám Majstra Pavla 24; s/d 1100/2000Sk; ℗) or the swishy luxury of **Hotel Satel** (☎ 4512 943; www.hotelsatel .com; Nám Majstra Pavla 55; s/d 1765/2730Sk; ℗) in a 14th-century building.

## Eating

**Vegetarián** (☎ 4514 576; Uhoľná 137; mains 45-90Sk; ☺ 10am-3.15pm Mon-Fri) Wholesome smells and a no-fuss menu make this basic veggie haunt a hit.

**Reštaurácia u Janusa** (☎ 4514 592; Klaštorská 22; mains 70-120Sk) Choose from all the fried pork favourites at this, the locals' pick for best Slovak food.

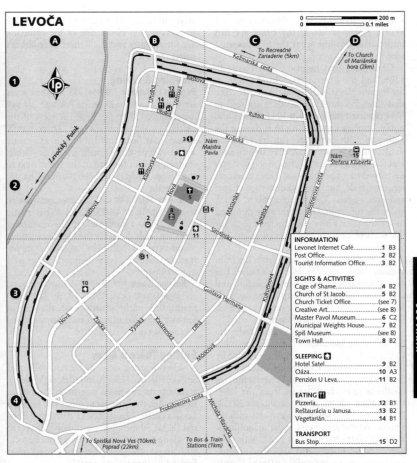

**LEVOČA**

| INFORMATION | |
| --- | --- |
| Levonet Internet Café | 1 B3 |
| Post Office | 2 B2 |
| Tourist Information Office | 3 B2 |

**SIGHTS & ACTIVITIES**
Cage of Shame...............4 B2
Church of St Jacob...........5 B2
Church Ticket Office.......(see 7)
Creative Art...............(see 8)
Master Pavol Museum.........6 C2
Municipal Weights House.....7 B2
Spiš Museum...............(see 8)
Town Hall..................8 B2

**SLEEPING**
Hotel Satel................9 B2
Oáza......................10 A3
Penzión U Leva............11 B2

**EATING**
Pizzeria..................12 B1
Reštaurácia u Janusa.......13 B2
Vegetarián................14 B1

**TRANSPORT**
Bus Stop..................15 D2

SLOVAKIA

**Pizzeria** ( ☎ 0905396528; Vetrová 4; pizzas 100-160Sk) For such a smoky, nameless place, the pizza's really not bad.

### Getting There & Away

Bus travel is pretty practical in the area as there are frequent services to Spišské Podhradie (22Sk, 20 minutes, 11 daily) and to Poprad (40Sk, 30 minutes, 21 daily), which has onward train connections. Two to five buses a day wend their way to/from Košice (128Sk, two hours). Buses also run to Spišská Nová Ves (18Sk, 20 minutes, every 30 minutes), where you can switch to the main Bratislava to Košice train line. The local bus stop at Nám Štefana Kluberta is a little closer to town than the station, and most routes stop there.

## SPIŠSKÉ PODHRADIE
☎ 053

Slovakia's most grandiose castle sits above a bedraggled little town (big village). Not much reason to come here except for Spiš Castle and the Spiš Chapter ecclesiastical settlement on either side.

### Sights

From the motorway you catch glimpses of eerie outlines and stony ruins crowning the ridge on the eastern side of Spišské Podhradie. Can it really be that big? Indeed, **Spiš Castle** (Spišský hrad; ☎ 4541 336; www.spisskyhrad.com in Slovak; adult/student 100/60Sk; ☺ 9am-6pm May-Oct, by appointment Nov-Apr), among the largest in Eastern Europe, spreads over more than

4 hectares. In 1993 it was added to Unesco's World Heritage list. If the ruins are this impressive, imagine what the fortress once was.

Chronicles first mention Spiš Castle in 1209, and the central residential tower, at the highest elevation, is thought to date from that time. From here defenders are said to have repulsed the Tatars in 1241. Rulers and noble families kept adding to it during the 15th and 16th centuries. But by 1780 the site had already lost its military significance and was largely deserted after much of it was destroyed in a fire that year. Few structures remain whole, but there's a cistern, a chapel and a rectangular Romanesque palace, which holds the museum. Descend to the dungeon to see the meaty bits – it's incredible to see the torture devices the human mind has thought up.

The castle is a good hike up from the train station, 1km south of Spišské Podhradie's bus stop. Cross at the tracks near the station and follow the yellow markers up to the castle. If you're driving or cycling, the access road is off the Prešov highway east of town.

A kilometre west of Spišské Podhradie sits the still active **Spiš Chapter** (Spišská Kapitula), a 13th-century Catholic complex encircled by a 16th-century wall. Charming Gothic houses line the single street running between the two medieval gates. Buy tickets from the **information office** ( ☎ 0907388411; adult/student 20/10Sk; ☼ 11.15am-2.45pm), where you can also pick up a guide. At the upper end is the magnificent **St Martin's Cathedral**, built in 1273, with twin Romanesque towers and a Gothic sanctuary. Inside are several trifold painted Gothic altars from the 15th century that are quite impressive. On either side of the cathedral are the **seminary** and the Renaissance **bishop's palace** (1652).

## Sleeping & Eating

**Penzión Podzámok** ( ☎ 4541 755; www.penzionpod zamok.sk; Podzámková 28, Spišské Podhradie; s/d with shared bathroom 300/650Sk; P ♨ ) A view of the castle in your own backyard. Three family houses have been cobbled together to create a 42-bed guesthouse with meals available. Podzámok is at the end of the street next to the bridge, halfway between the Spiš Chapter and Castle.

**Spišsky Salaš** ( ☎ 4541 202; www.spisskysalas.sk; Levočská cesta 11; s/d 420/800Sk; P ) What rustic fun! Dig into a lamb stew in the restaurant and then settle down for the night in a simple wood-panelled room. The log cabin complex is on the road to Spisšké Podhradie, 3km west of Spiš Chapter.

**Kolping House** ( ☎ 0905790097; www.hotelkolping .sk; Spišská Kapitula 15; s/d 1100/1600Sk; P ☐ ) A romantic little outfit actually inside the walls of Spišská Kapitula; antiques and reproductions fill the rooms and restaurant.

## Getting There & Away

A railway line connects Spišské Podhradie and Spišské Vlachy (12Sk, 10 minutes, eight daily), a station on the main line from Poprad to Košice. Relatively frequent buses run to/from Levoča (22Sk, 20 minutes, 11 daily) and Poprad (55Sk, 50 minutes, eight daily). If you're travelling to Spiš Chapter by bus from Levoča, you can get off one stop before the main town Spišské Podhradie, at Kapitula.

---

**TOP FIVE FORTRESSES**

Castles and ruins abound in Slovakia. Pick up a national map, look for the ruin symbols and start hiking. You may find only a hearth, or you may find a room's outlines, but you're sure to have a good work-out and great views once you reach the crest. Here are the top-five formal castle sights to tour:

▪ This was the big one; the ruins of **Spiš Castle** (p809) spread out for what seems like forever.

▪ Walt Disney couldn't have invented a dreamier sight than **Bojnice Castle** (p798).

▪ **Devín Castle** (p795) has stood at the intersection of Slovakia, Austria and Hungary for a millennium.

▪ Be led by torch light by a medieval guide on a night tour of **Trenčín Castle** (p796)

▪ Climb up the tower of **Bratislava Castle** (p789) and you're at the highest vantage point in the old town.

# SLOVENSKÝ RAJ

☎ 053

Rumbling waterfalls, steep gorges, sheer rockfaces, thick forests and hilltop meadows: **Slovenský raj** (Slovak Paradise; www.slovenskyraj.sk; admission 20Sk) is a national park for the passionately outdoorsy. Easier trails exist, but the one-way, ladder- and chain-assist ascents are the most dramatic. You cling to a metal rung headed straight up a precipice while an icy waterfall splashes and sprays a metre away, that's after you've scrambled horizontally across a log ladder to cross the stream down below. Pure exhilaration.

## Orientation & Information

The nearest town of any size is the unattractive but almost unavoidable Spišská Nová Ves, 23km southeast of Poprad. The main trailheads on the northern edge of the national park are at Čingov, 5km west of Spišská Nová Ves and Podlesok, 1km southwest of Hrabušice. There are lodgings and eateries near northern trailheads, but for full town services, go into Spišská Nová Ves or Hrabušice. Dedinky, at the south end of the park, is a regular village with pub, supermarket, a lake and houses. Before you go trekking, make sure to buy VKÚ's 1:25,000 *Slovenský raj* hiking map (No 4), available at many tourist offices and bookshops countrywide.

### EMERGENCY

**Mountain Rescue Service** (Horská Služba; emergency ☎ 183 00)

### INTERNET ACCESS

**Internet Klub** ( ☎ 4414 402; Letná 4, Spišská Nová Ves; per hr 50Sk; ☺ 9am-9pm)

**Ascona Café** (Hlavná 99, Hrabušice; per hr 25Sk; ☺ 1pm-midnight Sun-Thu, to 3am Fri & Sat)

### MONEY

It's best to procure money before you get to the park unless you're planning to stop in Spišská Nová Ves, where there's an ATM at the train station and at banks on the main square.

### TOURIST INFORMATION

Your lodging place is usually your best source of information; orientation maps are posted near trailheads. **Tourist Information Centre** ( ☎ 4428 292; www.slovenskyraj.sk; Letná 49, Spišská Nová Ves; ☺ 8am-5pm Mon-Fri, 9.30am-1.30pm Sat Jun-Sep, 8am-4.30pm Mon-Fri Oct-May) Hit-or-miss help with area accommodation and info.

**Tourist information** ( ☎ 4299 854; Hlavná, Hrabušice; ☺ 8am-6pm Jul & Aug, 8am-4pm Mon-Fri Sep-Jun) Small, summertime office.

## Sights & Activities

Trails that include a one-way *roklina* (gorge) take at least a half day: the shortest, **Zejmarska' Gorge** hike on a blue trail, starts at Biele Vody (25 minutes northeast of Dedinky on the red trail). The physically fit can run, clamber and climb up in 50 minutes; others huff and puff up in 90 minutes. To get back, you can follow the green trail down to Dedinky, or there's a **chairlift** (adult/student 30/15Sk; ☺ 9am-5pm) that, if it's working, goes on the hour.

From Čingov a green trail leads up the **Hornád River Gorge** to **Letanovský mlyn** (1½ hours), from there the blue trail continues along the river to the base of the green, one-way, technically aided **Kláštorisko Gorge** hike (one hour). At **Kláštorisko chata** ( ☎ 4493 307; cabins per person 250Sk), there's a restaurant and small cabins (book ahead to make sure you have a place). From Kláštorisko you can follow another green trail back along the ridge towards Čingov. Allow at least six hours for the circuit, lunch at Kláštorisko included.

From Podlesok, an excellent day's hike heads up the **Suchá Belá Gorge** (with several steep ladders), then east to Kláštorisko on a yellow then red trail. From here, take the blue trail down to the Hornád River, then follow the river gorge upstream to return to Podlesok. Six to seven hours.

Six kilometres west of Dedinky is **Dobšinská Ice Cave** (Dobšinská Ľadová Jaskyňa; ☎ 7881 470; adult/student 150/130Sk; ☺ 9am-4pm Tue-Sun Jun-Aug, 9.30am-2pm Tue-Sun May & Sep). The frozen formations are most dazzling in May, before they start to melt. Tours leave every hour or so.

## Sleeping & Eating

Surrounding towns also have private rooms and pensions (a lot of which are listed at www.slovenskyraj.sk); those below are closer to the trails. All the park's lodgings have restaurants. From May to September there are food stands near the Podlesok trailhead parking lot; a Bila supermarket sits next to the bus station in Spišska Nová Ves.

**Autocamp Podlesok** ( ☎ 4299 165; slovrajbela@stonline .sk; Podlesok; per person/tent 60/60Sk; huts per person 230Sk; Ⓟ ) Big, big, big. Pitch a tent in the field or

SLOVAKIA

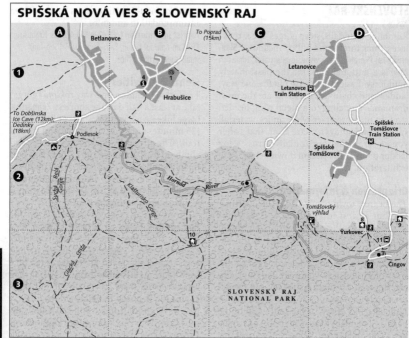

## SPIŠSKÁ NOVÁ VES & SLOVENSKÝ RAJ

choose from the A-frames, small huts or cottages with two to 12 beds and a bathroom. It's a 2km walk from Hrabušice.

**Autocamping Tatran** ( ☎ 4297 105; www.durkovec.sk; per person/tent 80/60Sk, dm 220Sk, 2-person hut with shared bathroom 190Sk; P 🖭 ) Tents crowd together in the pasture surrounded by tiny huts, a big dormitory and multiroom rental houses with satellite TV (2500Sk). Tromp 2km west of the Čingov bus stop.

**Hotel Flora** ( ☎ 4491 129; www.hotelfloraslovenskyraj .sk; Čingov; s/d 750/1200Sk; P ) A renovation made the lobby and restaurant of this mountain hotel fabulous: stone fireplace, leather chairs, big windows. Food's good too. Pity the rooms didn't come along for the ride. It's 1km before the village.

**Penzión Pastierňa** ( ☎ 058-798 1175; Dedinky 42; per person from 300Sk; P ) Small wooden guesthouse at the edge of Dedinky, near the forest and green trailhead.

### Getting There & Around

You may want to consider springing for a car in Košice; connections aren't great. A few buses run directly from Poprad to Dedinky (53Sk, 1¼ hours, three daily) and to Hrabušice (25Sk, 40 minutes, five on weekdays, one on weekends). Other than that, Spišska Nová Ves is the main transfer point for the Slovenský raj region; most buses go in the morning. There's a bus service to/from Poprad (40Sk, 45 minutes, eight daily), Levoča (18Sk, 20 minutes, every half hour) and Košice (117Sk, two to three hours, two daily).

From Spišska Nová Ves, two buses a day run to Hrabušice (22Sk, 35 minutes), two to the trailheads of Čingov (10Sk, 12 minutes) and three to Dedinky (53Sk, one hour).

## BARDEJOV

☎ 054 / pop 33,400

All steep roofs and flat fronts, each main-square Gothic-Renaissance burgher's house is set apart by its particular pastel hue and intricate paint-and-plaster details. It may as well be the 15th century, this town has been so enthusiastically well preserved (there's always some scaffolding signalling upkeep somewhere). Unesco thought so too, adding it to the World Heritage list in 2000. Today the quiet square is the tourist draw, but there's

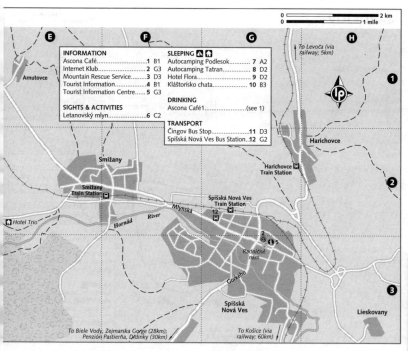

**INFORMATION**
Ascona Café............................1 B1
Internet Klub.........................2 G3
Mountain Rescue Service.........3 D3
Tourist Information.................4 B1
Tourist Information Centre.......5 G3

**SIGHTS & ACTIVITIES**
Letanovský mlyn.....................6 C2

**SLEEPING**
Autocamping Podlesok............7 A2
Autocamping Tatran...............8 D2
Hotel Flora............................9 D2
Kláštorisko chata..................10 B3

**DRINKING**
Ascona Café1....................(see 1)

**TRANSPORT**
Čingov Bus Stop....................11 D3
Spišská Nová Ves Bus Station..12 G2

also an excellent icon museum that sheds light on this region's eastern-facing religion. A couple of kilometres north of town in Bardejovské Kúpele there's a hot spring spa inviting you to take a cure, and an open-air village museum waiting to be explored. Wooden churches in the area reflect the Carpatho-Rusyn heritage that the area shares with neighbouring parts of the Ukraine and Poland.

## History
Bardejov received its royal charter in 1376, and grew rich on trade between Poland and Russia. After an abortive 17th-century revolt against the Habsburgs, Bardejov's fortunes declined. In late 1944 heavy WWII fighting took place at the Dukla Pass on the Polish border, 54km northeast of Bardejov, near Svidník (preserved WWII Soviet and German tanks still sit on the roadside and there's a military museum).

## Orientation
The main square, Radničné nám, is a 600m walk southwest of the bus and train station. Some old town walls still encircle the city, enter through the gate off Slovenská at Baštová.

## Information
**ČSOB** (Radničné nám 7) Bank and ATM.
**Golem Internet Café** (Radničné nám 25; per hr 25Sk; 9am-11pm Mon-Fri, 1-11pm Sat & Sun)
**Main post office** (Dlhý rad 14)
**Tourist information centre** ( ☎ 4744 003; www
.e-bardejov.sk; Radničné nám 21; 9am-5.30pm Mon-
Fri, 11.30am-3.30pm Sat & Sun May-Sep) Info, souvenirs
and guide service.

## Sights
There are two branches of the **Šariš Museum**
( ☎ 4724 966; www.muzeumbardejov.sk; adult/student
40/20Sk; 8am-noon & 12.30-4pm Tue-Sun) Housing
altarpieces and a historical collection, the **town
hall** (radnica) was built in 1509 and was the
first Renaissance building in Slovakia. More
than 130 dazzling icons from the 16th to 19th
century make up the **Icon Exposition** (Expozícia ikony;
Radničné nám 27). Originally they decorated Greek
Catholic and Orthodox churches east of here.

The interior of the 15th-century **Basilica of
St Egídius** (Bazilika Sv Egídia; adult/student 30/20Sk; tower
40/20Sk; 10am-3pm Mon-Fri, to 2pm Sat) is packed
with no less than 11 Gothic altarpieces, built
from 1460 to 1510.

**SLOVAKIA**

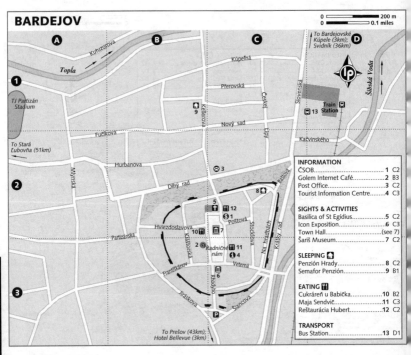

## Sleeping & Eating

Ask at the information office about private rooms (from 300Sk a night).

**Penzión Hrady** ( ☎ 0903211865; www.penzionivana.sk; Stocklova 8; s/d/tr 495/750/880Sk; P ) Want your hair cut? There's a salon across the hall in this busy building. Basic rooms, basic prices.

**Penzión Semafor** ( ☎ 0905830984; www.penzion semafor.sk; Kellerova 13; s/d 700/900Sk, ste 800/1100Sk; P ) If the large, bright doubles are good, the 'apartments' (bigger rooms) are even better. All share a communal kitchen in this family-run guesthouse.

**Hotel Bellevue** ( ☎ 4728 404; www.bellevuehotel.sk; Mihalov 2503; s/d 2600/1900Sk; P ✕ ☼ 🖳 🕮 ) This hotel on a hill is as close as the town comes to swank. From here you have a view from above, cherrywood beds, a pool and a full-service restaurant. It's 3km south of the city; take bus 8 from the train station.

**Reštaurácia Hubert** (Radničné nám 4; mains 100-169Sk; ☼ 10am-10pm Mon-Fri, 11am-3pm Sat & Sun) Game dishes and other meaty fare top the list in this cellar restaurant.

On the main square **Cukráreň u Babička** (Radničné nám 49; cakes 30-100Sk), back in a Renais-

sance arcade, serves pastries and cakes like your Slovak grandma used to make, and **Maja Sendvič** ( ☎ 091941064; Radničné nám 15; sandwiches 40-50Sk; ☼ 8am-8pm Mon-Thu, 8am-midnight Fri, 3-11pm Sat & Sun) has baguette sandwiches to go.

## Getting There & Away

Buses run between Bardejov and Košice (100Sk, 1¾ hours, eight daily) and to/from Poprad (135Sk, 2½ hours, 12 daily).

## AROUND BARDEJOV

Three short kilometres to the north, with frequent local bus connections, is the parklike spa town of **Bardejovské Kúpele**. If you want to book a service (mineral bath 200Sk, 15-minute massage 170Sk), you have to go in person to the **Spa House** (Kúpelny dom; ☎ 4774 225; ☼ 8am-noon & 1-5pm Mon-Sat) at the top of the main pedestrian street. Across the way is the **Museum of Folk Architecture** (Múzeum ľudovej Architektúry; ☎ 4722 070; adult/student 40/20Sk; ☼ 9am-5pm Tue-Sun, to 3pm Oct-Apr). One of the nail-less wooden churches is among the many traditional buildings moved to this *skansen* (open-air village museum). Peer into the simple dwellings and see how rural folk lived. If you have a car, park in the lot by the bus station at the base of the village and walk up; the whole place is pedestrian-only.

Buy a *Wooden Churches Around Barde-jov* booklet at the tourist information centre (p813) in Bardejov if you want to explore more of the area's Eastern vernacular architecture.

# KOŠICE

☎ 055 / pop 235,006

Wander among the midday work crowd down the long town square, crane your neck to admire the massive Cathedral of St Elizabeth then head underground to explore the ancient city's archaeology. Come evening, gather with the rest of Košice on the benches near the musical fountain. With so many people out and about, Slovakia's second city has a real sense of cohesion and community that's missing in the capital. You get the feeling if you sat down for a beer at one of the many street festivals, you might actually make friends. Old town buildings range from 12th-century Gothic to 20th-century Art Nouveau. Why not spend a day or two and check it out?

## History

Košice received its city coat of arms in 1369 and for many years was the eastern stronghold of the Hungarian Kingdom. Transylvanian prince Ferenc Rákóczi II had his headquarters at Košice during the Hungarian War of Independence against the Habsburgs (1703–11). On 5 April 1945 the Košice Government Program – which made communist dictatorship in Czechoslovakia a virtual certainty – was announced here. Today US Steel girders form the backbone of the city; you can't miss the company's influence – from the flare stacks to the brand new ice-hockey stadium it sponsored.

## Orientation

The adjacent bus and train stations are just east of the old town. A five-minute walk along Mlynská brings you into Hlavná, which broadens to accommodate the squares of Nám Slobody and Hlavné nám.

## Information

### BOOKSHOPS

**Art Forum** ( ☎ 6232 677; Mlynská 6) Coffee-table pictorials and fiction in English, some even by Slovak authors.

**BP Press** (Hlavná 102; ☉ 7am-8pm Mon-Fri, 8am-8pm Sat & Sun) Foreign magazines and newspapers.

### EMERGENCY

**Police station** ( ☎ 159; Pribinova 6)

### INTERNET ACCESS

**City Information Centre** ( ☎ 6258 888; Hlavná 59; per hr 30Sk; ☉ 9am-6pm Mon-Fri, 9am-1pm Sat)
**Net Club** (Hlavná 9; per hr 50Sk; ☉ 9am-10pm) Fast connections.

### MEDICAL SERVICES

**Fakultná Nemocnica L Pasteura** ( ☎ 6153 111; Rastislavova 45) Hospital.

### MONEY

**Ľudová Banka** (Mlynská 29) ATM and exchange; between the centre and transport stations.

### POST

**Main post office** (Poštová 18)

### TOURIST INFORMATION

The train station and airport also have information stands.
**Municipal Information Centre** (MIC; ☎ 16 168; www.mickosice.sk) Tesco Department Store (Hlavná 111; ☉ 8am-8pm Mon-Fri, 8am-4.30pm Sat); Dargov Department Store (Hlavná 2; ☉ 8am-7pm) Small and personal, with a vibrant staff and tonnes of knick-knacks for sale.
**City Information Centre** ( ☎ 6258 888; www.kosice .sk; Hlavná 59; ☉ 9am-6pm Mon-Fri, 9am-1pm Sat) Large and busy; books galore. Runs information stands at the airport and train station with the same hours.

## Sights

The dark and brooding 14th-century **Cathedral of St Elizabeth** (Dóm sv Alžbety; ☎ 0908667093; adult/student 70/35Sk; ☉ 1-5pm Mon, 9am-5pm Tue-Fri, 9am-1pm Sat) wins the prize for sight most likely to grace your Košice postcard home. You can't miss Europe's easternmost Gothic cathedral dominating the square. Below the church a **crypt** contains the tomb of Duke Ferenc Rákóczi, who was exiled to Turkey after the failed 18th-century Hungarian revolt against Austria. Don't forget to climb the church's **tower** for city views. To the south of the cathedral is the 14th-century **St Michael's Chapel** (adult/student 30/15Sk; ☉ 1-5pm Mon, 9am-5pm Tue-Fri, 9am-1pm Sat).

Get lost in the mazelike passages and tunnels of the **archaeological excavations** ( ☎ 6228 393; adult/child 25/10Sk; ☉ 10am-6pm Tue-Sun), discovered

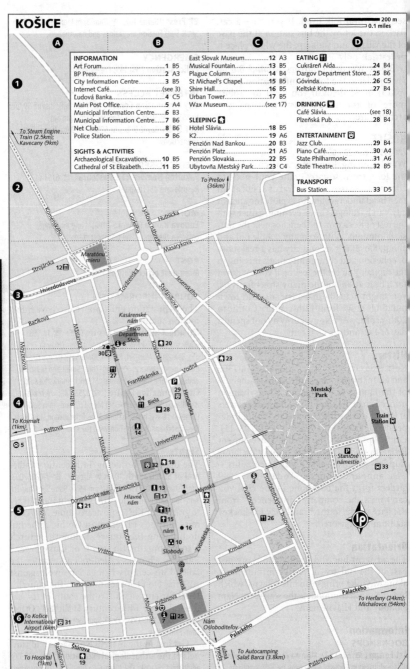

# KOŠICE

| | | |
|---|---|---|
| 0 | | 200 m |
| 0 | | 0.1 miles |

**INFORMATION**
Art Forum..........................1 B5
BP Press...........................2 A3
City Information Centre.......3 B5
Internet Café.................(see 3)
Ľudová Banka....................4 C5
Main Post Office.................5 A4
Municipal Information Centre..6 B3
Municipal Information Centre..7 B6
Net Club...........................8 B6
Police Station.....................9 B6

**SIGHTS & ACTIVITIES**
Archaeological Excavations.....10 B5
Cathedral of St Elizabeth.......11 B5

East Slovak Museum..............12 A3
Musical Fountain...................13 B5
Plague Column.....................14 B4
St Michael's Chapel...............15 B5
Shire Hall..........................16 B5
Urban Tower........................17 B5
Wax Museum...................(see 17)

**SLEEPING**
Hotel Slávia........................18 B5
K2..................................19 A6
Penzión Nad Bankou..............20 B3
Penzión Platz......................21 A5
Penzión Slovakia..................22 B5
Ubytovňa Mestský Park...........23 C4

**EATING**
Cukráreň Aida.....................24 B4
Dargov Department Store........25 B6
Góvinda............................26 C5
Keltské Krčma.....................27 B4

**DRINKING**
Café Slávia....................(see 18)
Plzeňská Pub......................28 B4

**ENTERTAINMENT**
Jazz Club..........................29 B4
Piano Café.........................30 A4
State Philharmonic................31 A6
State Theatre......................32 B5

**TRANSPORT**
Bus Station........................33 D5

To Steam Engine
Train (2.5km);
Kavecany (9km)

To Prešov
(36km)

Komenského
Tyršovo nábrežie
Gorkého
Hutnícka
Masarykova
Strojárska
Maratónu
mieru
Kmeťová
Hviezdoslavova
Továrenská
Jesenského
Svätoplukova
Bačíkova
Štefánikova
Kasárenské
nám
Tesco
Department
Store
Kováčska
Vodná
Mestský
Park
Mlynská
Františkánska
Biela
Hmčiarska
Univerzitná
Poštová
To Košmalt
(1km)
Baštová
Hradbová
Zámočnícka
Hlavné
nám
Mlynská
Pribišova
Dominikánske nám
Alžbetina
Bočná
nám
Slobody
16
Vrátna
Timonova
Roosveltova
Kmaňová
Zvonárska
Puškinova
Protifašistických bojovníkov
Staničné
námestie
Train
Station
To Herľany (24km);
Michalovce (54km)
Palackého
To Košice
International
Airport (6km)
Pribinova
Nám
Osloboditeľov
To Hospital
(1km)
Štúrova
Štúrova
Palackého
Južná trieda
To Autocamping
Salaš Barca (3.8km)
Patárkova
To Prešov
Mäsiarska
Mäsiarska
Moyzesova
Moyzesova

SLOVAKIA

during building work in 1996. These are the buried remains of medieval Košice: defence chambers, fortifications and waterways.

To check out the **Urban Tower** (built in the 14th century, rebuilt in the 1970s) you have to buy entry to the cheesy **Wax Museum** (Múzeum voskových figurín; ☎ 6232 534; www.waxmuseum.sk; Hlavná 3; adult/student 120/80Sk; ❂ noon-4pm Tue-Sun).

Don't miss the intriguing gold treasure in the basement vault of the **East Slovak Museum** (Východoslovenské múzeum; ☎ 6220 309; Hviezdoslavovo 3; adult/student 40/20Sk; ❂ 9am-5pm Tue-Sat, 9am-1pm Sun). A secret stash of 2920 gold coins, dating from the 15th to 18th centuries, was discovered during the renovation of the house at Hlavná 68 in 1935. Anyone have a shovel?

Young and old gather on the benches in front of the **musical fountain** by the 1899 **State Theatre** (right).

North of the theatre is a large baroque **plague column** from 1723. The 1945 Košice Government Program was proclaimed from the 1779 **Shire Hall** (Župný dom; Hlavná 27); today there's a minor art gallery inside.

## Sleeping

For available accommodation, the City Information Centre puts out a booklet that includes summer dorms and private rooms (both from 300Sk).

**Kosmalt** ( ☎ 6423 572; www.kosmalt.sk; Kysucká 16; s/d 590/630Sk; ▢ ℗ ) It's usually possible to find a room in this big apartment-block hostel with common game room, bar and restaurant. Antique elevators, tolerable rooms. Take tram 6 from the train/bus station to the Kino Družba stop.

**Penzión Slovakia** ( ☎ 7289 820; www.penzionslovakia .sk; Orlia 6; s 950-1150Sk, d 1350-1750) This small city guesthouse has loads of charm. Named after Slovak towns, the rooms have wood-panelled ceilings, skylights and midcentury mod furnishings in the apartments. Rosto Steakhouse grill restaurant, downstairs, is worth visiting in its own right.

**Penzión Nad Bankou** ( ☎ 6838 221; www.penzion nadbankou.holiday.sk; Kováčska 63; s/d 1000/1400Sk; ℗ ) Whitewashed walls and pine furniture characterise the simple pension 'above a bank'. Through the owners you can arrange a light-aeroplane ride for 1950Sk.

**Hotel Slávia** ( ☎ 6224 395; www.hotelslavia.sk; Hlavná 63; s 2100-3050Sk, d 2700-3900Sk; ℗ ❂ ▢ ) Colourful mosaic murals are the icing on this 1902 Art Nouveau cake. The flourish continues

inside with serpentine, flower-shape lights and candy-coloured pastels.

Other options:

**Ubytovňa Mestský Park** ( ☎ 6333 904; www.uby tovna-ke.sk; Mestský Park 13; dm 220Sk) Workers hostel, mostly male guests.

**K2** ( ☎ 6255 948; Štúrova 32; s/d with shared bathroom 350/700Sk) Hostel with bed-only singles and doubles that book up fast.

**Penzión Platz** ( ☎ 6223 450; www.platz.sk; Dominikánske nám 23; r 1500-1800Sk) It's a modular veneer world behind the pretty plaster façade.

## Eating & Drinking

**Dargov Department Store** (Hlavná 2; mains 20-80Sk; ❂ 7am-7pm Mon-Fri, 9am-5pm Sat, 9am-3pm Sun) The ground-floor cafeteria serves hot dishes – sausages, stuffed cabbage rolls – as well as sandwiches and salads. There's a supermarket too.

**Góvinda** ( ☎ 6200 428; Puškinova 8; mains 80-120Sk ❂ noon-7pm Mon-Sat) Dive in to divine vegetarian Indian food at this small Hare Krishna eatery.

**Keltské Krčma** (Celtic Pub; ☎ 6225 328; Hlavná 80; mains 160-300Sk; ❂ 10am-11.30pm Mon-Thu, to 1am Fri & Sat, 3-11.30pm Sun) Vaulted ceilings, ancient-looking masks and wood booths create a scene conducive to leisurely eating or drinking Celt style. The eclectic menu includes Slovak pork in an apricot sauce, English roast beef and Mexican enchiladas.

**Plzeňská Pub** ( ☎ 6220 402; Hlavná 92; ❂ noon-midnight Mon-Thu, to 1am Fri-Sun) Czech beer on tap and roast pork and dumplings in the kitchen. Eat it in the beer garden out back.

Drink your coffee or cocktail in turn-of-the-20th-century style at **Café Slaviá** ( ☎ 6233 190; Hotel Slaviá, Hlavná 63; ❂ 7am-11pm) or indulge in a creamy cake with your java down the street at **Cukráreň Aida** ( ☎ 6256 649; Hlavná 81; snacks 30-100Sk; ❂ 8am-10pm). Ice cream for breakfast, yum.

## Entertainment

The monthly publication *Kam do Mesta* (www.kamdomesta.sk) lists in Slovak the whats, wheres and whens of Košice's entertainment scene.

**State Theatre** (Štátne Divadlo Košice; ☎ 6221 231; www.sdke.sk; Hlavná 58; box office ❂ 9am-5.30pm Mon-Fri, 10am-1pm Sat) This 1899 neobaroque theatre stages operas, ballets and dramas from September to May.

**State Philharmonic Košice** (Štátna Filharmónia Košice; ☎ 6224 514; www.sfk.sk; Moyzesova 66) The city's principal orchestra has extra performances in May during the spring music festival.

SLOVAKIA

DJs spin house most nights at both at the **Jazz Club** ( ☎ 6224 237; Kováčska 39; 🕙 11am-midnight Mon-Thu, 11am-2am Fri, 4pm-2am Sat, 4pm-midnight Sun) and at the **Piano Café** ( ☎ 0915517339; Hlavná 92; 🕙 10am-midnight Mon-Thu, 10am-1am Fri, 3pm-1am Sat, 3pm-midnight Sun). But each occasionally has live jazz.

## Shopping

Wander onto the alleylike Hrnčiarska for some truly unique shopping. Along this 'craftsman' street there's a potter's shop, an iron-works master, a herbalist and a gemstone artist, among others.

## Getting There & Away

### AIR

**Košice International airport** (KSC; ☎ 6221 093; www.airportkosice.sk) is about 6km southwest of the centre. **Sky Europe** ( ☎ reservations 02-4850 4850; www.skyeurope.com) has two or three daily flights to/from Bratislava (one hour) that may set you back as little as 500Sk oneway with tax, if you book ahead. **Czech Airlines** (ČSA; ☎ 6782 490; www.czechairlines.com) has three daily flights to and from Prague. For more on getting to Košice from outside Eastern Europe see (p928)

### BUS

Buses wend their way to/from Levoča (117Sk, 2½ hours, two daily), Bardejov (98Sk, 1¾ hours, eight daily) and Poprad (134Sk, 2½ hours, four daily). Buses also travel to Uzhhorod in Ukraine (140Sk, 2½ hours) at least once a day (twice from Tuesday to Sunday) and to Nowy Targ in Poland (180Sk, four hours) Thursday and Saturday. A bus goes from Košice to Miskolc (120Sk, two hours), in Hungary, on Wednesday, Friday and Saturday.

### CAR

There are several big international chain car rental representatives at the airport, but **Alimex** ( ☎ 7290 100; www.alimex.sk; Košice International airport) is cheaper, especially if you're willing to drive around with adverts painted on the car (as little as 699Sk per day, unlimited kilometres).

### TRAIN

Express trains run to/from Poprad (154Sk, 1¼ hours, up to 10 daily) and Žilina (316Sk, 2¾ hours, 14 daily). If you're commuting all the way to/from Bratislava, an IC or EC train (518Sk, 5½ hours, four daily) is your

best bet; otherwise you could crawl along for more than seven hours with no dining car. For domestic schedules visit www.zsr.sk.

A sleeper train leaves Košice every morning for Kyiv in Ukraine (913Sk, 22½ hours), stopping at Čop (193Sk, 2½ hours), 14km from Uzhhorod. Two trains (one overnight) a day head for Prague in the Czech Republic (1140Sk, 11 hours), two for Budapest in Hungary (967Sk, four hours) and three to Kraków in Poland (844Sk, 6½ hours).

## Getting Around

Transport tickets (12Sk, one zone) are good for buses and trams in most of the city; buy them from newsstands and public transport kiosks and validate on board. Bus 23 between the airport and the train station requires a two-zone ticket (19Sk).

# SLOVAKIA DIRECTORY

## ACCOMMODATION

For every season there is a price: May to September is considered tourist season, but prices top out around the Christmas/New Year and Easter holidays. From October to April, rates drop dramatically (10% to 50%). We quote tourist season prices. Reviews in this chapter are ordered according to price. There's a tourist tax of 30Sk.

For more lodging options in Bratislava, see www.lonelyplanet.com. Note that nonsmoking rooms are not yet common outside the capital.

## Camping

Most camping grounds open from May to September and are often accessible on public transport. Many have a restaurant and assorted cheap cabins. Wild camping is generally prohibited in national parks.

## Hostels

Outside Bratislava there are no backpacker-style hostels in Slovakia. Student dormitories throughout the country open to tourists in July and August. If you're looking for cheap sleeps outside those months, *ubytovňa* is the word to know. These are hostels for workers (in cities) or Slovak tourists (near natural attractions) that usually have basic, no-nonsense shared-bathroom singles and doubles or bunks.

## Private Rooms, Pensions & Hotels

Tourist towns usually have private rooms for rent; look for signs reading '*privát*' or '*zimmer frei*' (from 1100Sk in Bratislava, 300Sk elsewhere). Information offices may have lists of renters.

Pensions are family-run B&Bs, or bigger inns, that have fewer services but more character than hotels. Outside the capital, hotels are often still institutional, communist leftovers. At both, breakfast is usually either included in the rate or can be added on for 80Sk to 200Sk.

## ACTIVITIES

Slovakia is one of Eastern Europe's best areas for hiking: see the Malá Fatra (p798), High Tatras (p801) and Slovenský raj (p811). There's also excellent rock climbing and mountain biking in the High Tatras. See the Starý Smokovec section (p803).

The country has some of Europe's cheapest ski resorts. The season runs from December to April in the High Tatras and Malá Fatra. Ski hire starts at 299Sk per day.

## BUSINESS HOURS

Restaurants nationwide are generally open from 10am to 10pm. Stand-alone shops open around 9am and close at 5pm or 6pm weekdays and at noon on Saturday. The local *potraviny* (supermarket) hours are from 6.30am or 7am until 5pm or 6pm Monday to Friday and from 7am to noon on Saturday. Big-name chain grocery and department stores (Tesco, Billa etc) have longer hours, typically until 9pm for downtown branches and 24 hours for suburban hyper-markets.

Bank hours are open from about 8am to 5pm Monday to Thursday, and until 4pm Friday. Post offices work from about 8am to 7pm Monday to Friday and until 11am Saturday.

Most museums and castles are closed on Monday. Many tourist attractions outside the capital open only from May to September.

## DANGERS & ANNOYANCES

Crime is low compared with the West, but pickpocketing does happen. Just be aware. Never leave anything on the seat of an unattended vehicle, even a locked one; apparently that's just advertising that you don't want it any more.

## DISABLED TRAVELLERS

Slovakia is behind many EU countries in terms of facilities for the disabled. Few hotels and restaurants have ramps or barrier-free rooms.

**Slovak Union for the Disabled** (Slovenský zväz tělesně postihnutých; ☎ 02-6381 4478; www.sztp.sk) is fighting to change the status quo.

## EMBASSIES & CONSULATES
### Slovak Embassies & Consulates

**Australia** ( ☎ 02 6290 1516; www.slovakemb-aust.org; 47 Culgoa Circuit, O'Malley, Canberra, ACT 2606)

**Austria** ( ☎ 01-318 905 5200; www.vienna.mfa.sk; Armbrustergasse 24, 1-1190 Wien)

**Canada** ( ☎ 613-749 4442; www.ottawa.mfa.sk; 50 Rideau Terrace, Ottawa, Ontario K1M 2A1)

**Czech Republic** ( ☎ 233 113 051; www.praha.mfa.sk; Pod Hradbami 1, 160 00 Praha 6)

**France** ( ☎ 01-44 14 56 00; www.amb-slovaquie.fr; 125 Rue de Ranelagh, 75016 Paris)

**Germany** ( ☎ 030-8892 6 200; www.botschaft-slowakei .de; Fredrichstrasse 60, Berlin 10707)

**Hungary** ( ☎ 01-460 9010; www.budapest.mfa.sk; Stéfania út 22-24, H-1143 Budapest XIV)

**Ireland** ( ☎ 01-660 0012; www.dublin.mfa.sk; 20 Clyde Rd, Ballsbridge, Dublin 4)

**UK** ( ☎ 020-7313 6470; www.slovakembassy.co.uk; 25 Kensington Palace Gardens, London W8 4QY)

**USA** ( ☎ 202-237 1054; www.slovakembassy-us.org; 3523 International Court NW, Washington, DC 20008)

### Embassies & Consulates in Slovakia

Australia and New Zealand do not have embassies in Slovakia; the nearest are in Vienna and Berlin respectively. The following are all in Bratislava (area code ☎ 02).

**Austria** (Map p790; ☎ 5443 1443; www.embassy austria.skwww.mzv.cz/bratislava/; Ventúrska 10)

**Czech Republic** (Map p790; ☎ 5920 3303; Hviezdoslavovo nám 8)

**France** (Map p790; ☎ 5934 7111; www.france.sk; Hlavné nám 7)

**Germany** (Map p790; ☎ 5920 4400; www.german embassy.sk; Hviezdoslavovo nám 10)

**Ireland** (Map p790; ☎ 5930 9611; bratislava@iveagh .irlgov.ie; Carlton Savoy Bldg, Mostová 2)

**Poland** (Map p787; ☎ 5441 3174; Hummelova 4)

**UK** (Map p790; ☎ 5998 2000; www.polskevelvys lanectvo.sk; Panská 16)

**USA** (Map p790; ☎ 5443 0861; www.britishembassy.sk; www.usembassy.sk; Hviezdoslavovo nám 4)

## FESTIVALS & EVENTS

During summer months folk festivals take place all over Slovakia. In late June or early

July folk dancers and musicians from all over Slovakia gather at the biggest, the **Východná Folklore Festival** (www.obec-vychodna.sk in Slovak), 32km west of Poprad. The two-week **Bratislava Music Festival** (Bratislavské hudobné slānosti; ☎ 02-5443 4546; www.bhsfestival.sk in Slovak) is held in late September to early October, and the **Bratislava Jazz Days** (Bratislavských jazzových dnī'; ☎ 02-5293 1572; www .bjd.sk) swings one weekend in September. The **Slovak Spectator** (www.slovakspectator.sk) newspaper lists events countrywide.

## HOLIDAYS

**New Year's & Independence Day** 1 January
**Three Kings Day** 6 January
**Good Friday & Easter Monday** March/April
**Labour Day** 1 May
**Victory over Fascism Day** 8 May
**Cyril & Methodius Day** 5 July
**SNP Day** 29 August
**Constitution Day** 1 September
**Our Lady of Sorrows Day** 15 September
**All Saints' Day** 1 November
**Christmas** 24 to 26 December

## INTERNET RESOURCES

The **Slovak Tourism Board's website** (www.slova kiatourism.sk) boasts about the country's attractions. **Slovakia Document Store** (www.panorama.sk) contains links to a wealth of Slovakia-related stuff; including books you can buy from abroad. **What's On Slovakia** (www.whatsonslovakia .com) lists events. You can check on the news from Slovakia at www.slovensko.com, get the low-down on exhibits nationwide at www .muzeum.sk and find yourself at the Slovak map site www.kompas.sk.

## MONEY

Slovakia's currency is the Slovak crown, or Slovenská koruna (Sk), containing 100 halier (hellers). There are coins of 50 hellers, and one, two, five and 10 crowns (Sk). Banknotes come in denominations of 20, 50, 100, 200, 500, 1000 and 5000 crowns.

Almost all banks have exchange desks and there are usually branches in or near a town's old town square. ATMs are quite common even in smaller towns, but shouldn't be relied upon in villages. Main banks include the **Všeobecná úverová banka** (VUB; General Credit Bank; www.vub.sk) and the **Slovenská sporiteľňa** (Slovak Savings Bank; www.slsp.sk).

In Bratislava, credit cards are widely accepted. Elsewhere, Visa and MasterCard are accepted at most hotels, at some shops and at higher category restaurants (if you announce before requesting the bill that you plan to pay with credit).

If you stay in hostels, eat your meals in local pubs and take local transport, and you can expect to spend €25 to €45 a day in Bratislava (€20 to €30 elsewhere). Double this amount if you are looking to bed down in pensions and dine in smarter eateries. Some businesses quote prices in euros; prices in this chapter reflect the quotes of individual businesses.

## POST

Poste restante sent to Bratislava (c/o Poste restante, 81000 Bratislava 1), can be picked up at the Main Post Office (p788) and will be kept for one month.

## TELEPHONE
### Phone Codes

Slovakia's country code is ☎ 421. When dialling from abroad, you need to drop the zero on city area codes and mobile phone numbers. To dial internationally from inside Slovakia, dial ☎ 00, the country code and the number.

Mobile phone numbers are often used for business and generally start with ☎ 09. If you are calling a Slovak mobile phone from abroad, drop the initial zero.

### Phonecards

Most payphones require *telefónna karta* (telephone cards), which you can purchase from newsagents, for local calls. International phone cards, like **EZ Phone** (www.ezcard.sk; per min to UK & USA 2Sk) can also be bought there. Both of these cards are easy to mistake for mobile phone credit, so pay attention to what you're buying.

## TOURIST INFORMATION

The **Association of Information Centres of Slovakia** (AiCES; ☎ 16 186; www.aices.sk) is an extensive network of city information centres. There's no Slovakiawide information office; your best bet is to go online to the **Slovak Tourist Board** (www .slovakiatourism.sk).

---

**EMERGENCY NUMBER**

▪ Ambulance, Fire, Police ☎ 112

## VISAS

Slovakia joined the EU in May 2004. Citizens of other EU countries, Australia, New Zealand, Canada, Japan and the US can enter visa-free for up to 90 days. South Africans do need a visa. For a full list, see www.mzv .sk, under Ministry and then Travel. If you do require a visa, it must be bought in advance – they are not issued on arrival.

# TRANSPORT IN SLOVAKIA

## GETTING THERE & AWAY

### Air

Bratislava's small airport receives flights from more than 20 cities across the Continent. **Czech Airlines** (ČSA; ☎ 02-5296 1042; www.czechairlines .com) flies to Prague three times per day. **Slovak Airlines** ( ☎ 02-4870 4870; www.slovakairlines.sk) flies to Moscow weekly in conjunction with Aeroflot. **SkyEurope Airlines** ( ☎ 02-4850 4850; www .skyeurope.com) connects Bratislava a couple of times a week to Split, Zadar and Dubrovnik in Croatia, Sofia and Burgas in Bulgaria, and Bucharest in Romania.

For more on getting to Slovakia from outside Eastern Europe, see the Regional Directory chapter (p928).

Vienna's international airport is just 60km from Bratislava, and is served by a vast range of international flights. Buses connect to Bratislava hourly.

### Land

#### BUS

**Eurolines** ( ☎ 02-5556 7349; www.eurolines.sk) runs buses between Bratislava and Prague (410Sk, four hours, three daily) and Bratislava and Budapest (570Sk, 3½ hours, one daily). Other international lines heading east do so from Košice (p818).

For more on getting to Bratislava by bus from further afield see the Regional Directory chapter (p930).

#### CAR & MOTORCYCLE

As well as your vehicle's registration papers, you need a 'green card', which shows you are covered by at least third-party liability insurance. Your vehicle must display a nationality sticker and carry a first-aid kit and warning triangle.

### TRAIN

Direct trains connect Bratislava with Prague (655Sk, 4½ hours, six daily), Budapest (486Sk, three hours, seven daily) and Vienna (297Sk, one hour, 30 daily). Night departure trains link Bratislava with Moscow (2738Sk, 32½ hours, one daily) and Warsaw (1410Sk, 10½ hours, one daily). A daily train to Kyiv (1913Sk, 21 hours, one daily) passes through Košice on its way from Budapest.

### River

For more on the boats that link Bratislava with Vienna and Budapest from April to September, see p794.

## GETTING AROUND

### Bicycle

Roads are often narrow and potholed and in towns cobblestones and tram tracks can prove dangerous. Theft's a problem, so a lock is a must. You can hire bikes in popular biking areas like the High Tatras. The cost of transporting a bike by rail is usually 10% of the train ticket.

### Bus

National buses run by **Slovenská autobusová doprava** (SAD; www.eurolines.sk) are comparably priced to trains, but less convenient for the bigger cities in this chapter. Buses are quite useful in East Slovakia, however. To search for schedules, go to www.busy.sk; it's in Slovak, but is decipherable if you remember *odkiaľ* means 'from', *kam* means 'to', and *vyhľadať* means 'search' (click it a second time after the error-looking message comes up). When looking at bus schedules in terminals, beware of the footnotes (many fewer buses go on weekends). It's helpful to know that *premáva* means 'it operates' and *nepremáva* means 'it doesn't operate'.

### Car & Motorcycle

#### DRIVING LICENCE

All foreign driving licences with photo ID are valid in Slovakia.

#### HIRE

Both Bratislava and Košice airports have several international and local car rental agencies.

#### ROAD RULES

In order to use Slovakia's motorways (denoted by green signs) all vehicles must have a motorway sticker (*nálepka*), which should be displayed in the windscreen. Rental cars

**SLOVAKIA**

come with them. You can buy stickers at border crossings, petrol stations or Satur offices (100Sk for 15 days, 600Sk for a year, both for vehicles up to 1.5 tonnes).

Parking restrictions are eagerly enforced with bright orange tyre boots. Always buy a ticket, either from a machine, or from the attendant wandering around with a waist pack, and put it on your dashboard.

## Local Transport

City buses and trams operate from around 4.30am to 11.30pm daily. Tickets are sold at public transport offices and at newsstands. In Bratislava, some stops have ticket-vending machines. Validate tickets in the red machines on board or you could face a fine of up to 1400Sk.

## Train

**Slovak Republic Railways** (Železnice Slovenskej Republiky or ŽSR; ☎ 18 188; www.zsr.sk) provides a cheap and efficient rail service. Most of the places covered in this chapter are on or near the main railway line between Bratislava and Košice.

# Slovenia

It's a tiny place – there's no doubt about that – with a surface area of just over 20,000 sq km and only 2 million people. But 'good things come in small packages', and never was that old chestnut more appropriate than in describing Slovenia (Slovenija), an independent republic bordering Italy, Austria, Hungary and Croatia.

Slovenia has been dubbed a lot of different things by its PR machine – 'Europe in Miniature', 'The Sunny Side of the Alps', 'The Green Piece of Europe' – and they're all true. Slovenia has everything, from beaches, snowcapped mountains, hills awash in grapevines and wide plains blanketed in sunflowers, to Gothic churches, baroque palaces and Art Nouveau civic buildings. Its incredible mixture of climates brings warm Mediterranean breezes up to the foothills of the Alps, where it can snow in summer. And with more than half of its total area covered in forest, Slovenia truly is one of the 'greenest' countries in the world. And in recent years it really has become Europe's activities playground.

Among Slovenia's greatest assets, though, are the Slovenes themselves – welcoming, generous, multilingual and broad-minded.

## FAST FACTS

- **Area** 20,273 sq km
- **Capital** Ljubljana
- **Currency** euro (€); A$1 = €0.58; ¥100 = €0.67; NZ$1 = €0.47; UK£1 = €1.44; US$1 = €0.78
- **Famous for** mountain sports, Lipizzaner horses, ruby red Teran wine
- **Official Language** Slovene; English, Italian and German widely spoken
- **Phrases** *dober dan* (hello), *živijo* (hi), *prosim* (please), *hvala* (thank you), *oprostite* (excuse me), *nasvidenje* (goodbye)
- **Population** 2 million
- **Telephone Codes** country code ☎ 386; international access code ☎ 00; ☎ toll free ☎ 080
- **Visas** not required for most nationalities; see p856

## HIGHLIGHTS

- Experience the architecture, hilltop castle, green spaces and vibrant nightlife of **Ljubljana** (p827), Slovenia's 'Beloved' capital.
- Be astounded at the impossibly picture-postcard setting of **Bled** (p838): the lake, the island, the hilltop castle as backdrop.
- Get outdoors in the majestic mountain scenery at **Bovec** (p843), arguably the country's best outdoor-activities centre.
- Explore theThe series of karst cave at **Škocjan** (p846) that look straight out of Jules Verne's *A Journey to the Centre of the Earth*.
- Swoon in the romantic Venetian port of **Piran** (p849), with great restaurants, and the nearby resort of **Portorož** (p852).

## ITINERARIES

- **Three days** Enjoy a long weekend in Ljubljana, sampling the capital's museums and nightlife, with an excursion to Bled.
- **One week** Spend a couple of days in Ljubljana, then head northward to unwind in Bohinj or romantic Bled beside idyllic mountain lakes. Depending on the season take a bus or drive over the hair-raising Vršič Pass into the valley of the vivid blue Soča River and take part in some extreme sports in Bovec or Tolmin before returning to Ljubljana.
- **Two weeks** As above, adding a trip to the coast – Koper and, of course, Piran – via Škocjan or perhaps a journey to both Postojna and Predjama.

## CLIMATE & WHEN TO GO

The ski season lasts mainly from December to March, though avalanche risks can keep the Vršič Pass closed as late as May. Lake Bled freezes over in winter, but the short coastline has a mild, almost Mediterranean climate. April is often wet, but accommodation is cheaper then, and the flower-carpeted meadows and forests are at their scenic best. May and June are warmer, but during summer hotel prices start to rise, peaking in August, when rooms can be hard to come by at any price in certain parts of the country. Moving into autumn, warm September days are calm and ideal for hiking and climbing, while October and November can be damp.

### HOW MUCH?

- **100km by bus/train** €9/5.50
- **Bicycle rental (one day)** €4.7020 to €5.45
- **Bottle of ordinary/quality Slovenian wine** €4.20/8.35
- **Cup of coffee in a café** €0.85
- **Ski pass (one day)** €20.20

### LONELY PLANET INDEX

- **Litre of petrol** €1 to €1.05
- **Litre of water** €0.6045 to €0.70
- **Half-litre of local beer** €0.9575 to €1.10 (shop), €1.70 to €2.30 (bar)
- **Souvenir T-shirt** € 10€8.35 to €12.50
- **Street snack (burek)** €1.90 to €2.2050

## HISTORY

Slovenes can make a credible claim to have invented democracy. By the early 7th century their Slavic forebears had founded the Duchy of Carantania based at Krn Castle (now Karnburg in Austria). Ruling dukes were elected by ennobled commoners and invested with power before ordinary citizens. This model was noted by the 16th-century French political theorist Jean Bodin, whose work was a key reference for Thomas Jefferson when writing the American Declaration of Independence. Carantania (later Carinthia) was fought over by Franks and Magyars from the 8th to 10th centuries, and later divided up among Austro-Germanic nobles and bishops, who protected themselves within ever-multiplying castles. By 1335 Carantania and most of present-day Slovenia, with the exception of the Venetian-controlled coastal towns, were dominated by the Habsburgs.

Indeed, Austria ruled what is now Slovenia until 1918, apart from a brief but important interlude when Napoleonic France claimed the area among its half-dozen 'Illyrian Provinces' (1809–13) and made Ljubljana the capital. Though he razed many castles, Napoleon proved a popular conqueror, as his relatively liberal regime de-Germanised the education system. Slovene was taught in schools for the first time, leading to a blossoming of national

SLOVENIA

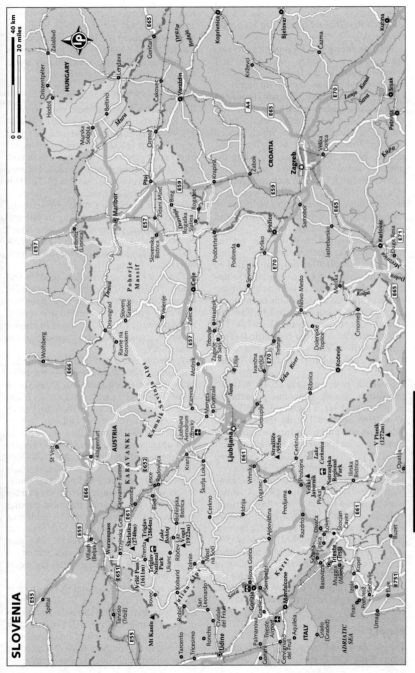

**SLOVENIA**

consciousness. In tribute, Ljubljana still has a French Revolution Square (Trg Francoske Revolucije).

Fighting during WWI was particularly savage along the Soča Valley – what would later become known as the Isonzo Front, which was occupied by Italy then dramatically retaken by German-led Austrian-Hungarian forces. Many fighters' tunnels are still visible around Kobarid (p844). WWI ended with the collapse of Austria-Hungary, which handed western Slovenia to Italy as postwar reparations. Northern Carinthia, including the towns of Beljak and Celovec (now Villach and Klagenfurt), voted to stay with Austria in a 1920 plebiscite. What little was left of Slovenia joined fellow south (jug) Slavs in forming the Kingdom of Serbs, Croats and Slovenes, later Yugoslavia.

Nazi occupation in WWII was for the most part courageously resisted by Slovenian partisans, though after Italy capitulated in 1943 the anti-partisan Slovenian Domobranci (Home Guards) were active in the west and, in a bid to prevent the communists from gaining political control in liberated areas, began supporting the Germans. The war ended with Slovenia regaining Italian-held areas from Piran to Bovec, but losing Trst (Trieste) and part of divided Gorica (Gorizia).

Slovenia, with only 8% of the national population, was the economic powerhouse of Tito's postwar Yugoslavia, producing up to 20% of the GDP. By the 1980s the federation was becoming increasingly Serb-dominated, and Slovenes, who already felt taken for granted economically, feared losing their political autonomy. After free elections and careful planning, Slovenia broke away from Yugoslavia on 25 June 1991. A 10-day war that left 66 people dead followed; rump Yugoslavia swiftly signed a truce in order to concentrate on bashing Croatia instead. Slovenia was admitted to the UN in May 1992 and in May 2004, together with nine other 'accession' countries, became a member of the EU. In January 2007 Slovenia became the first of these 10 new EU states to adopt the euro, which replaced the tolar as the national currency.

## PEOPLE

The population of Slovenia is largely homogeneous. Some 83% is ethnic Slovene, with the remainder being Croats, Serbians, Bosnians and Roma; there are also small, long-term enclaves of Italians and Hungarians, who have special deputies looking after their interests in Parliament. Slovenes are ethnically Slavic, typically multilingual and extroverts.

## ARTS

Far and away Slovenia's best-loved writer is the Romantic poet France Prešeren (1800–49), whose statue commands Ljubljana's most central square (p832). Prešeren's patriotic yet humanistic verse was a driving force in raising Slovene national consciousness. Fittingly a stanza of his poem Zdravljica (A Toast) is now the national anthem.

Many of Ljubljana's most characteristic architectural features, including its idiosyncratic recurring pyramid motif, were added by celebrated Slovenian architect Jože Plečnik (1872–1957), who cut his professional teeth working on Prague's Hradčany Castle.

Slovenia has some excellent modern and contemporary artists, including Rudi Skočir, whose Klimt-with-muscles style reflects a taste for Viennese Art Nouveau that continues to permeate day-to-day Slovenian interior design. A favourite sculptor-cum-designer is Oskar Kogoj.

Postmodernist painting and sculpture has been more or less dominated since the 1980s by the multimedia group Neue Slowenische Kunst (NSK) and the artists' cooperative Irwin. It also spawned the internationally known industrial-music group Laibach, whose leader, Tomaž Hostnik, died tragically in 1983 when he hanged himself from a kozolec (see the boxed text, p841), the traditional Slovenian hayrack. Slovenia's vibrant music scene embraces rave, techno, jazz, punk, thrash-metal and chanson (torch songs from the likes of Vita Mavrič); the most popular rock band in Slovenia at present is Siddharta. There's also a folk-music revival: listen for the groups Katice and Katalena, who play traditional Slovene music with a modern twist. Terra Folk is the quintessential world music band.

One of the most successful Slovenian films in recent years was Damjan Kozole's Rezerni Deli (Spare Parts; 2003) about the trafficking of illegal immigrants through Slovenia from Croatia to Italy by a couple of embittered misfits living in the southern town of Krško, site of the nation's only nuclear power plant.

## ENVIRONMENT

Slovenia is amazingly green; indeed, 57% of its total surface area is covered in forest. It is home to some 3200 plant species – some 70 of which are endemic. Triglav National Park (p838) is particularly rich in indigenous flowering plants. Living deep in karst caves, the endemic 'living fossil' *Proteus anguinus* is a blind salamander that can survive for years without eating (see the boxed text, p845).

## FOOD & DRINK

It's relatively hard to find such archetypal Slovenian foods as *žlikrofi* ('ravioli' filled with cheese, bacon and chives) served with *bakalca*, a lamb-based goulash, *mlinci* (corn pancakes) often served with goose and *ajdovi žganci z ocvirki* (buckwheat porridge with the savoury pork crackling/scratchings). An inn (*gostilna* or *gostišče*) or restaurant (*restavracija*) more frequently serves pizza, *rižota* (risotto), *klobasa* (sausage), *zrezek* (cutlet/steak), *golaž* (goulash) and *paprikaš* (piquant chicken or beef 'stew'). Fish (*riba*) is usually priced by the *dag* (100gdecagram or 0.1kg). Freshwater trout (*postrv*) generally costs half the price of other sea fish, though grilled squid (*lignji na žaru*) doused in garlic butter is a ubiquitous bargain at around €6.25 per plate.

Also common are Balkan favourites, such as *cevapčiči* (spicy meatballs of beef or pork), *pleskavica* (meat patties) and *ražnjiči* (shish kebabs). Add €1.50 to €2.10 for the *krompir* (potatoes).

You can snack cheaply on takeaway pizza slices or slabs of *burek* (€1.90 to €2.50), flaky pastry sometimes stuffed with meat but more often cheese or even apple. Alternatives include *štruklji* (cottage-cheese dumplings) and *palačinke* (thin sweet pancakes).

Some restaurants have bargain-value *dnevno kosilo* (four-course lunch menus), including *juha* (soup) and *solata* (salad), for around €6.25. This can be less than the price of a cheap main course, and usually one option will be vegetarian.

Tap water is safe to drink; people drink it everywhere. Distinctively Slovenian wines (*vino*) include peppery red Teran made from Refošk grapes in the Karst region and Cviček, a dry light red – almost rosé – wine from eastern Slovenia. Slovenes are justly proud of their top vintages, but cheaper bar-standard 'open wine' (*odprto vino*) sold by the decilitre (0.1L) are often pure rot-gut.

---

**TOP FIVE CAFÉS**

- **Café Teater**, Piran (p852)
- **Kavarna Cacao**, Portorož (p852)
- **Kavarna Zvezda**, Ljubljana (p835)
- **Loggia Café**, Koper (p849)
- **Slaščičarna Šmon**, Bled (p840)

---

Beer (*pivo*), whether *svetlo* (lager) or *temno* (dark), is best on draught (*točeno*).

There are dozens of kinds of *žganje* (fruit brandy) available, including *češnovec* (made with cherries), *sadjavec* (mixed fruit), *brinjevec* (juniper), *hruška* (pears, also called *viljamovka*) and *slivovka* (plums).

*Na zdravje!* (Cheers!).

# LJUBLJANA

☎ 01 / pop 254,200

Ljubljana is by far and away Slovenia's largest and most populous city. It is also the nation's political, economic and cultural capital. In many ways, though, the city whose name almost means 'beloved' (*ljubljena*) in Slovene does not feel like an industrious municipality of national importance but a pleasant, self-contented town with responsibilities only to itself and its citizens. You might think that way, too, especially in spring and summer when café tables fill the narrow streets of the Old Town and street musicians entertain passers-by on Čopova ul and Prešernov trg. Then Ljubljana becomes a little Prague without the heavy crowds or a Paris without the attitude. The Slovenian capital may lack the grandeur or big-name attractions of those two cities, but the great museums and galleries, atmospheric bars and varied, accessible nightlife make it a great place to visit and stay awhile.

## HISTORY

If Ljubljana really was founded by Jason and the Golden Fleece–stealing Argonauts as the city would have you believe, they left no proof of their stay. However, legacies of the Roman city of Emona – remnants of walls, dwellings and early churches – can still be seen throughout the city. Ljubljana more or less took its present form as Laibach under the Austrian Habsburgs,

# LJUBLJANA

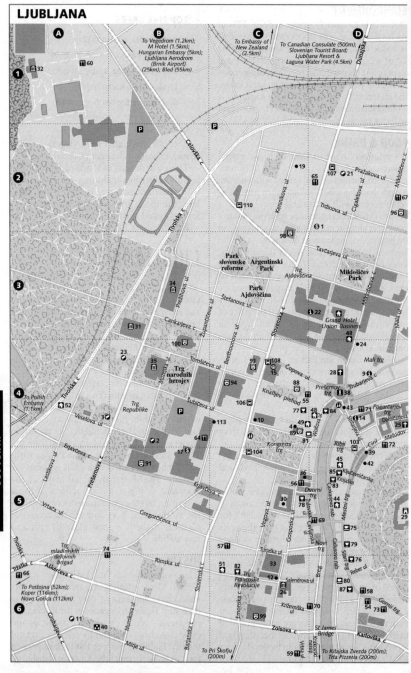

To Vegedrom (1.2km);
M Hotel (1.5km);
Hungarian Embassy (5km);
Ljubljana Aerodrom
(Brnik Airport)
(25km); Bled (55km)

To Embassy of
New Zealand
(2.5km)

To Canadian Consulate (500m);
Slovenian Tourist Board;
Ljubljana Resort &
Laguna Water Park (4.5km)

To Polish
Embassy
(1.1km)

To Postojna (52km);
Koper (116km);
Novo Gorica (112km)

To Pri Škofju
(200m)

To Kitajska Zvezda (200m);
Trta Pizzeria (200m)

SLOVENIA

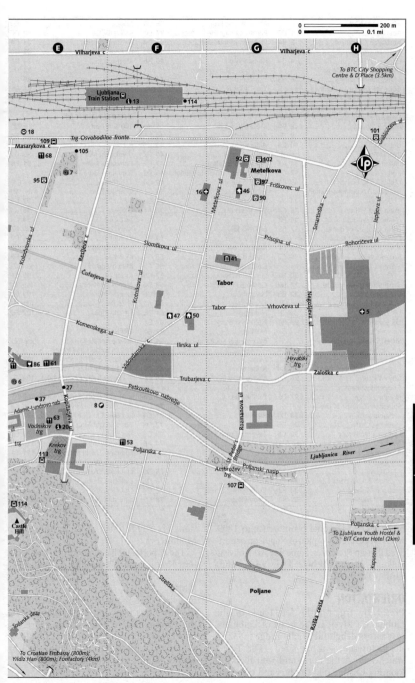

but it gained regional prominence in 1809, when it became the capital of Napoleon's short-lived Illyrian Provinces. Some fine Art Nouveau buildings filled up the holes left by a devastating earthquake in 1895.

## ORIENTATION

Prešernov trg, on the left bank of the Ljubljanica River, is the heart of Ljubljana. Just across delightful Triple Bridge (p832) is the picturesque – if bite-sized – Old Town, which follows the north and west flanks of looming Castle Hill. The bus and train sta-

tions are 800m north of Prešernov trg up Miklošičeva c.

The airport, Ljubljana Aerodrom, is at Brnik near Kranj, some 27km north of Ljubljana.

### Maps

Excellent free maps, some of which show the city's bus network, are available from the various tourist offices. The more detailed 1:20,000-scale *Mestni Načrt Ljubljana* (Ljubljana City Map; €7.05) published by Kod & Kam is available at newsstands and bookshops.

# INFORMATION

## Bookshops

**Geonavtik** ( ☎ 252 70 27; www.geonavtik.com, in Slovene; Kongresni trg 1; ☷ 8.30am-8.30pm Mon-Fri, 8.30am-4pm Sat) Stocks Lonely Planet guides and books about Slovenia.

**Kod & Kam** ( ☎ 200 27 32; www.kod-kam.si; Trg Francoske Revolucije 7; ☷ 9am-8pm Mon-Fri, 8am-1pm Sat) Map specialist.

## Internet Access

Web connection is available at virtually all hostels and hotels, the **Slovenian Tourist Information Centre** (right; €1.05 per half-hour) and **STA Ljubala café** (right; €1.05 per 20 minutes), as well as the following:

**Cyber Café Xplorer** ( ☎ 430 19 91; Petkovškovo nabrežje 23; per 30min/hr/5hr €2.40/4/11; ☷ 10am-10pm Mon-Fri, 2-10pm Sat & Sun) Ljubljana's best internet café, with 10 superfast computers and wi-fi.

**DrogArt** ( ☎ 438 72 70; Kolodvorska ul 20; per 15min/hr free/€1.70; ☷ 10am-6pm Mon-Fri) Opposite the train station.

**Portal.si Internet Kotiček** ( ☎ 090 42 30; Trg OF 4; per hr €3.75; ☷ 7am-8.30pm) Located in the bus station.

## Laundry

Washing machines are available, even to non-guests, at the **Celica Hostel** ( ☎ 230 97 00; www.hostel celica.com; Metelkova ul 8) for €5 per load, including washing powder. Commercial laundries, including **Chemo Express** ( ☎ 251 44 04; Wolfova ul 12; ☷ 7am-6pm Mon-Fri), charge from €3.75 per kg.

## Left Luggage

**Bus station** (Trg OF 4; per day €1.80; ☷ 5am-9.30pm)
**Train station** (Trg OF 6; per day €2.10; ☷ 24hr) Coin lockers on platform No 1.

## Ljubljana Card

The excellent-value Ljubljana Card (€12.50), valid for three days (72 hours) and available from the tourist offices, offers free admission to many museums, unlimited city bus travel, and discounts on organised tours, accommodation and restaurants, hire cars etc.

## Medical Services

**Clinic – Emergency Medical Assistance Clinic** (Klinični Centre – Urgenca; ☎ 232 30 60; Bohoričeva ul 9; ☷ 24hr)
**Medical Centre** (Zdravstveni Dom Center; ☎ 472 37 00; Metelkova ul 9; ☷ 7.30am-7pm) For nonemergencies.

## Money

There are ATMs at every turn, including in both the train and bus stations, where you'll also find **bureaux de change** ( ☷ 6am-10pm) that will change cash for no commission but not travellers cheques.

**Abanka** ( ☎ 471 81 00; Slovenska c 50; ☷ 9am-5pm Mon-Fri, 9am-noon Sat)
**Nova Ljubljanska Banka** ( ☎ 425 01 55; Trg Republike 2; ☷ 8am-6pm Mon-Fri) Headquarters of the nation's biggest bank.

## Post

**Main post office** (Slovenska c 32; ☷ 8am-7pm Mon-Fri, 8am-1pm Sat) Holds poste restante for 30 days.
**Post office branch** (Trg OF 5; ☷ 7am-9pm Mon-Fri, 7am-6pm Sat) Due west of the train station.

## Toilets

Two convenient public toilets (€0.20) are in the **Plečnikov podhod**, the underpass/subway below Slovenska c linking Kongresni trg with Plečnikov trg, and on **Hribarjevo nabrežje** below Pločnik (p836) on Prešernov trg.

## Tourist Information

**Ljubljana Tourist Information Centre** (TIC; ☎ 306 12 15; www.ljubljana-tourism.si) Stritarjeva ul (Kresija Bldg, Stritarjeva ul; ☷ 8am-9pm Jun-Sep, 8am-7pm Oct-May); Train Station ( ☎ 433 94 75; Trg OF; ☷ 8am-10pm Jun-Sep, 10am-7pm Oct-May)
**Slovenia Tourist Information Centre** (STIC; ☎ 306 45 76; www.slovenia-tourism.si; Krekov trg 10; ☷ 8am-9pm Jun-Sep, 8am-7pm Oct-May) Internet and bicycle hire also available.

## Travel Agencies

**Erazem** ( ☎ 430 55 37; www.erazem.net; basement, Miklošičeva c 26; ☷ 10am-5pm Mon-Fri, 10am-1pm Sat Jun-Sep, noon-5pm Mon-Fri Oct-May) Popular with backpackers and students. Staff make flight and train bookings, and sell ISIC, ITIC and IYTC cards.
**STA Ljubljana** ( ☎ 439 16 90; www.staljubljana.com, in Slovene; 1st fl, Trg Ajdovščina 1; ☷ 10am-1pm & 2-5pm Mon-Fri) Offers discount airfares for students and its café has internet access.

# SIGHTS

**Ljubljana Castle** crowns a wooded hill that forms the city's focal point. It's an architectural mish-mash, including fortified walls dating from the early 16th century, a 1489 chapel and a 1970s concrete café. Admission to the central courtyard and some north-facing ramparts is free, but there are even better 360-degree views from

---

**LJUBLJANA IN TWO DAYS**

Begin your first day at **Ljubljana Castle** (p831) to get an idea of the lay of the land. After a sea-food lunch at **Ribca** (p835), explore the Old Town then cross the Ljubljanica via St James Bridge and walk north along bust-lined Vegova ul to **Kongresni trg** and **Prešernov trg** (below). Over a fortifying libation at **Pločnik** (p836), plan your evening: low key at **Jazz Club Gajo** (p837), raucous at **Funfactory** (p836) or **D'Place** (p836), or alternative at one of the **Metelkova** (p836) venues.

On your second day check out some of the city's excellent **museums** and **galleries** (p831), and then stroll through **Park Tivoli** (below) to the **Museum of Contemporary History** (below) before returning to dine at **Aska in Volk** (p835) in the Old Town.

---

the 19th-century **Belvedere** (adult/student & senior €3.30/2; ☺ 9am-9pm May-Sep, 10am-6pm Oct-Apr); admission includes a visit to the Virtual Museum, a 20-minute 3-D video tour of Ljubljana and its history. The fastest way to reach the castle is via the new **funicular** (not yet open at the time of writing), which ascends from Vodnikov trg, though you can also take the hourly **tourist train** (adult/child €2.50/1.70; ☺ 9am-9pm mid-Jun–Sep, 11am-6pm Apr–mid-Jun, 9am-7pm Oct, 11am-3pm Nov-Mar) from Prešernov trg. You can also reach it on foot in about 15 minutes from the Old Town.

Central Prešernov trg is dominated by the salmon pink **Franciscan Church of the Annunciation** (1660; ☺ 6.40am-12.30pm & 3-8pm) and the **Prešeren monument** (1905), in honour of the national poet France Prešeren. Furtively observing Prešeren from a terracotta window at Wolfova ul 4 is a bust of his unrequited love (and poetic inspiration), Julija Primic. Wander north of the square to admire the fine **Art Nouveau buildings** along Miklošičeva c, including the **Grand Hotel Union Executive** (p834) at No 1, built in 1905, and the colourful **former Cooperative Bank** (1922) at No 8.

Leading southward from Prešernov trg is the small but perfectly formed **Triple Bridge**; prolific architect Jože Plečnik (p826) added two side bridges to the original span (1842) in 1931 to create something truly unique. The recently renovated baroque **Robba Fountain** stands before the Gothic **Town Hall** (1718) in **Mestni trg**, the 'City Sq', that leads into two more: **Stari trg** (Old Sq) and **Gornji trg** (Upper Sq), which has become something of a centre for Slovenian fashion boutiques. The squares wind picturesquely around the castle bluff and are sprinkled with inviting cafés and restaurants.

East of the Triple Bridge, the 18th-century **Cathedral of St Nicholas** (☺ 10am-noon & 3-6pm) is filled with pink marble, white stucco, gilt and a panoply of baroque frescoes. Behind the cathedral is a lively open-air **market** (p835)

selling both foodstuffs and dry goods, the magnificent riverside **Plečnik Colonnade** and the **Dragon Bridge** (Zmajski Most; 1901), a span guarded by four of the mythical creatures that have become the city's mascots.

The grand if rather pompous main building of **Ljubljana University** (Kongresni trg 12) was the regional parliament (1902) under Habsburg rule. The more restrained **Philharmonic Hall** (Filharmonija; Kongresni trg 10) dates from 1898 and is home to the Slovenian Philharmonic Orchestra, founded in 1701. South of the university building is the **National and University Library** (Gosposka ul 14; ☺ 8am-8pm Mon-Fri, 9am-2pm Sat), Plečnik's masterpiece completed in 1941, and its stunning **main reading room**. Diagonally opposite is the excellent **City Museum** ( ☎ 241 25 00; www.mm-lj.si; Gosposka ul 15; adult/child €2.10/1.25; ☺ 10am-6pm Tue-Sun), which focuses on Ljubljana's history and culture. The reconstructed Roman street in the basement is worth a visit in itself.

Of several major galleries and museums west of Slovenska c, the best are the impressive **National Gallery** ( ☎ 241 54 34; www.ng-slo.si; Prešernova c 24; adult/student & senior €2.90/4.20, free admission 2-6pm Sat & 1st Sun of month; ☺ 10am-6pm Tue-Sun), which contains the nation's historical art collection; the vibrant and inspiring (but outwardly drab) 1940s **Modern Art Museum** ( ☎ 241 68 00; www.mg-lj.si; Cankarjeva cesta 15; adult/student & senior €4.20/2.10; ☺ 10am-6pm Tue-Sun); and the fascinating **Museum of Contemporary History** ( ☎ 300 96 10; www.muzej-nz.si; Celovška c 23; adult/student €2.10/1.25; ☺ 10am-6pm Tue-Sat) in **Park Tivoli**, with its imaginative look at 20th-century Slovenia, via the milk carton. The latter museum also plunges you unexpectedly into a WWI trench.

The **National Museum** ( ☎ 241 44 04; www.narmuz-lj.si; Muzejska ul 1; adult/student & senior €4.60/3.35, admission 1st Sun of month free; ☺ 10am-6pm Fri-Wed, 10am-8pm Thu) occupies an elegant 1888 building. It has rich archaeological and coin collections, but at the time of writing only temporary exhibitions and the natural history section were accessible, while the main galleries were closed for a protracted renovation.

The **Slovenian Ethnographic Museum** ( ☎ 300 87 45; www.etno-muzej.si; Metelkova ul 2; adult/student/senior €3.35/2.10; 🕑 10am-6pm Tue-Sun), housed in the 1886 Belgian Barracks on the southern edge of Metelkova (see Metelkova Mesto, p836), has a permanent collection on the 3rd floor with traditional Slovenian trades and crafts – everything from beekeeping and blacksmithing to glass-painting and pottery making – and some excellent exhibits directed at children. Temporary exhibits are on the 1st and 2nd floors.

## TOURS

A two-hour guided **walking tour** (adult/student & senior €6.25/2.90; 🕑 10am daily Apr-Sep, 11am Fri-Sun Oct Mar) in English and organised by the TIC departs from the **Town Hall** (Mestni trg 1) year-round. Ask the TIC about its cycle, boat and balloon tours.

## SLEEPING

Ljubljana is not overly endowed with accommodation choices, especially at the midrange level, but things are changing. In fact, the following selection includes the lion's share of central budget and midrange options available at the time of research. The tourist offices have comprehensive details of other hotels further out in the suburbs, of similarly inconvenient private rooms and of the half-dozen other central top-end hotels.

### Budget

**Ljubljana Resort** ( ☎ 568 39 13; www.ljubljanaresort.si; Dunajska c 270; camp sites per adult €7.10-12.10, per child €5.30-9.10; 🕑 year-round; 🖳 🐾 ) It's got a pretty grandiose name, but wait till you see the facilities at this attractive seven-hectare camping ground-cum-resort 5km north of the city centre. Along with a 62-room hotel (singles/doubles from €54.25 to €75.10) and five chalets (rooms €75.10), there's

the Laguna water park (open from June to September), with outdoor swimming pools, fitness studio with sauna, and badminton and volleyball courts. Take bus 8 to its terminus or the more frequent bus 6 (stop Ježica).

**Dijaški Dom Tabor** ( ☎ 234 8840; www2.arnes.si /~ssljddta4; dm/s/d €10/26/38; 🕑 late Jun-late Aug; ✗ ) From sometime in June until to August five colleges open their dormitories *(dijaški dom)* to foreigner travellers, but only this 300-bed one, a 10-minute walk southeast of the bus and train stations, is really central. Enter from Kotnikova ul.

**Ljubljana Youth Hostel** ( ☎ 548 00 55; www.yh -ljubljana.com; Litijska c 57; dm HI member/nonmember €16.50/17.50; 🖳 ) This HI-affiliated hostel has six rooms with shared facilities at the BIT Center Hotel (below). While not in the most central location, 3km east of the city centre, the hostel is easily reached on bus 5, 9 or 13 (stop Emona). A boon is the attached sports centre (open 7am to 11pm), where guests get a 50% discount.

**Alibi Hostel** ( ☎ 251 12 44; www.alibi.si; Cankarjevo nabrežje 27; dm/d €20/60; ✗ 🐾 🖳 ) This unbelievably well-situated 110-bed hostel is changing the face of budget accommodation in Ljubljana. It's right on the Ljubljanica in the former headquarters of the British Council, and has brightly painted, airy dorms with six to 12 wooden bunks and five doubles on four floors.

### Midrange

**Vila Veselova** ( ☎ 059-926 721, 041-678 000; www.v-v .si; Veselova ul 14; dm €20-25, d/tr €70/90; ✗ 🐾 🖳 ) This very attractive freestanding villa, with its own garden and 40 beds in the centre of the museum district, offers mostly hostel accommodation in three rooms with four to eight beds, but a double and an apartment with en suite facilities make it an attractive midrange option. Some rooms face Park Tivoli across busy Tivolska c.

**BIT Center Hotel** ( ☎ 548 00 55; www.bit-center.net; Litijska c 57; s/d/tr €34/50/54; 🖳 ) The Bit Center

**SLOVENIA**

---

**AUTHOR'S CHOICE**

**Celica Hostel** ( ☎ 230 97 00; www.hostelcelica.com; Metelkova ul 8; dm €17, s/d/w cell €44/46/57, 4-to 5-bed room per person €24, 6-to 7-bed room per person €19; 🅿 ✗ 🖳 ♿ ) This stylishly revamped former prison (1882) in Metelkova has 20 designer 'cells', complete with original bars, both rooms and apartments with three to seven beds, and a packed-full, popular 12-bed dorm. The ground floor is home to three cafés (set lunch €3 to €5.25; open 7.30am to midnight): a traditional Slovenian *gostilna*, a Western-style café (with two internet stations) and the Oriental Café, with cushions, water pipes and shoes strictly outside. Celica has become such a landmark that there are guided tours daily at 2pm.

offers one of the best-value deals in Ljubljana, although at 3km east of the city centre (bus 5, 9 or 13 to Emona stop), it's a bit far from the action. Its 33 rooms are spartan but bright and comfortable.

**Park Hotel** ( ☎ 300 25 00; www.hotelpark.si; Tabor 9; s €39-55, d €48-71; ✕ ▢ ) A partial face-lift inside and out has made this 145-room tower-block hotel an even better-value midrange choice in central Ljubljana. Pleasant, well-renovated standard rooms are bright and unpretentiously well equipped. Cheaper rooms have en suite toilet but share showers. Students with ISIC cards get a 10% discount.

**Hotel Emonec** ( ☎ 200 15 20; www.hotel-emonec.com; Wolfova ul 12; s €53, d €60-70, tr €83; ✕ ▢ ) The décor is simple and coldly modern at this 26-room hotel, but everything is spotless and you can't beat the central location – only steps away from Prešernov trg at the back of a courtyard.

**Pri Mraku** ( ☎ 421 96 00; www.daj-dam.si; Rimska c 4; s €60-74.50, d €95-112, tr €116-125; ✕ ✕ ▢ ) Although it calls itself a *gostilna*, the 'At Twilight' is really just a smallish hotel (36 rooms) in an old building with no lift. Almost opposite the Križanke on Trg Francoske Revolucije, it's ideally located for culture vultures. Only some rooms have air-con.

**M Hotel** ( ☎ 513 70 00; www.m-hotel.si; Derčeva ul 4; s €62-83, d €95-115; ✕ ▢ &) This hotel 2km northwest of the city center and set back from noisy Celovška c (bus 1, 5, 8 or 15 to Kino Šiška stop) is not much to look at from the outside, but the 154 rooms are comfortable and airy, with all the basic mod-cons.

## Top End

**Grand Hotel Union Executive** ( ☎ 308 1270; www.gh -union.si; Miklošičeva c 1; s €149-179, d €159-212, ste €350- 420; ✕ ✕ ▢ ▨ ) This 187-room hotel, the Art Nouveau southern wing of a two-part hostelry, was built in 1905 and remains the most desirable address for visitors to Ljubljana. It has glorious public areas, including a cellar restaurant, Unionska Klet, which moves to the Unionski Vrt (Union Garden) restaurant in summer. Guests can use the indoor swimming pool, sauna and fitness centre on the 8th floor of adjacent Grand Hotel Union Business.

## EATING

The Old Town has plenty of appealing restaurants, though the choice of bona fide restaurants isn't quite as overwhelming as that of cafés. For cheaper options, try the dull but functional snack bars around the bus and train stations and both on and in the shopping mall below Trg Ajdovščina.

## Restaurants

**Kitajska Zvezda** ( ☎ 425 88 24; Hrenova ul 19; entrées €1.50-2.45, mains €5-6.45; ⏱ 11am-11pm) If you're looking for a fix of rice or noodles, try the 'Chinese Star' on the river just south of the Old Town. Szechuan dishes, including the *ma po doufu* (tofu with garlic and chilli), are quite good.

**Vegedrom** ( ☎ 513 26 42; Vodnikova c 35; soups & salads €2.10-3.35, dishes €4.20-9.80; ⏱ 9am-10pm Mon-Fri, noon-10pm Sat) This appealing, if somewhat pricey, vegan restaurant is at the northeastern edge of Park Tivoli. The platters for two are good value at €17.50 to €20.90, and there's a salad bar.

**Cantina Mexicana** ( ☎ 426 93 25; Knafljev prehod 3; entrées €2.70-3.75, mains €7.10-13.80; ⏱ 11am-midnight Sun-Thu, 11am-1am Fri & Sat) The capital's most stylish Mexican restaurant has an eye-catching red and blue exterior, and hacienda-like décor, sofas and lanterns inside. The fajitas (€7.50 to €11.70) are great.

**Harambaša** ( ☎ 041-843 106; Vrtna ul 8; dishes €2.70- 4; ⏱ 10am-10pm Mon-Fri, noon-10pm Sat, noon-6pm Sun) Here you'll find authentic Bosnian – Sarajevan to be precise – cuisine served at low tables in a charming modern cottage atmosphere, with quiet Balkan music and a lively crowd.

**Yildiz Han** ( ☎ 426 57 17; Karlovška c 19; entrées €2.70-5, mains €6.90-10.20; ⏱ noon-midnight Tue-Sun) If Turkish is your thing, head for this mum and dad–run restaurant, which features belly dancing and/or live Turkish music on Friday night.

**Gostilna Pri Pavli** ( ☎ 425 92 75; Stari trg 1; entrées €4.10-5.40, mains €5.80-10.85; ⏱ 8am-11pm) A wonderful holdover from the socialist era, 'Paula's Place' is an attractive, country-style inn in an enviable location that has managed to retain its old-school style and prices. The Farmer's Feast (€22.10) is a two-person feast.

**Pri Škofju** ( ☎ 426 45 08; Rečna ul 8; entrées €4.20-6.25, mains €4.60-13.35; ⏱ 8am-midnight Mon-Fri, noon-midnight Sat & Sun) This wonderful little place in tranquil Krakovo south of the city centre serves some of the best prepared local dishes and salads in Ljubljana, with an ever-changing menu. Set lunches are a snip at €5 to €6.70.

**Julija** ( ☎ 425 64 63; Stari trg 9; entrées €5-7.50, mains €7.50-15.85; ⏱ 8am-midnight Mon-Thu & Sat, 8am-1am Fri, 10am-11pm Sun) Julija serves decent risotto and pasta dishes either outside on the pavement terrace or in a Delft-tiled backroom behind a café decorated with 1920s prints.

**Taverna Tatjana** ( ☎ 421 00 87; Gornji trg 38; entrées €5-8.35, mains €8.35-20.90; ☷ 5pm-midnight) Looking like an old-world wooden-beamed cottage pub with a nautical theme, this is actually a rather exclusive fish restaurant with a lovely (and protected) back courtyard for the warmer months.

**Sokol** ( ☎ 439 68 55; Ciril Metodov trg 18; entrées €4.10-9.50, mains €5.80-11.20; ☷ 7am-11pm Mon-Sat, 10am-11pm Sun) In this old vaulted house, traditional Slovenian food is served on heavy tables by costumed waiters. Pizza is available if traditional dishes like *obara* (veal stew; €5.40) and Krvavica sausage with cabbage (€5.80) don't appeal.

**Pri Vitezu** ( ☎ 426 60 58; Breg 18-20; entrées €6.70-14.20, mains €11.70-20;, ☷ noon-11pm Mon-Sat) Located directly on the left bank of the Ljubljanica, 'At the Knight' is the place for a special meal (Mediterranean-style grills and Adriatic fish dishes), whether in the vaulted cellar dining rooms or adjoining wine bar.

**Ali Baba** ( ☎ 230 17 87, 051-234 066; Poljanska c 11; mains €7.10-7.75; ☷ 7am-11pm Mon-Fri, 10am-10pm Sat) Carpets and low brass tables decorate this cosy little restaurant, whose Iranian and Indian dishes are popular with journalists and students.

**Aska in Volk** ( ☎ 251 10 69; Gornji trg 4; mains €7.10-13.80; ☷ noon-10pm Sun-Thu, noon-11pm Fri & Sat) The 'Lamb and Wolf', which takes its name from a Bosnian novel, is a very stylish choice for South Slav specialities, including roast lamb.

Like most European capitals today, Ljubljana is awash in pizzerias, where pizza routinely costs €4 to €6.50. The pick of the crop includes **Foculus Pizzeria** ( ☎ 251 56 43; Gregorčičeva ul 3; ☷ 10am-midnight Mon-Fri, noon-midnight Sat & Sun), which boasts a vaulted ceiling painted with spring and autumn leaves; **Trta** ( ☎ 426 50 66; Grudnovo nabrežje 21; ☷ 11am-10.30pm Mon-Fri, noon-10.30pm Sat), on the right bank of the Ljubljanica; and **Mirje** ( ☎ 426 60 15; Tržaška c 5; ☷ 10am-10pm Mon-Fri, noon-10pm Sat), southwest of the city centre, which does some excellent pasta dishes, too.

## Quick Eats

**Delikatesa Ljubljanski Dvor** ( ☎ 426 93 27; Kongresni trg 11; pizza slices €1.20-1.70; ☷ 9am-midnight Mon-Sat) Locals queue for huge, bargain slices of pizza, salads and grilled vegetables sold by weight, and braised veggies to take away or eat on the spot.

**Nobel Burek** (Miklošičeva c 30; burek €1.90, pizza slice €1.50; ☷ 24hr) This round-the-clock hole-in-the-wall serves Slovenian-style fast food.

**Paninoteka** ( ☎ 059-018 445, 041-529 824; Jurčičev trg 3; soups & toasted sandwiches €2.10-3.35; ☷ 8am-1am Mon-Sat, 9am-11pm Sun) Healthy sandwich creations on a lovely little square by the river.

**Hot Horse** Trubarjeva c 31 (snacks & burgers €2.50-3.35; ☷ 8am-1am Mon-Sat, noon-1am Sun) Park Tivoli branch (Park Tivoli; ☷ 24hr) These two places exist to supply Ljubljančani with a favourite treat: horse burgers. The branch in Park Tivoli is just down the hill from the Museum of Contemporary History (p832).

**Ribca** ( ☎ 425 15 44; Adamič-Lundrovo nabrežje 1; dishes €2.70-6.70; ☷ 7am-4pm Mon-Fri, 7am-2pm Sat) This basement seafood bar below the Plečnik Colonnade in Pogačarjev trg serves tasty fried squid, sardines and herrings to hungry market-goers.

### Self-Catering

Handy supermarkets and convenience stores include **Mercator** (Slovenska c 55; ☷ 7am-9pm) and, opposite the train and bus stations, **Noč in Dan** ( ☎ 234 79 62; Trg OF 13; ☷ 24hr), a variety store open 'Day and Night'. The **Maximarket supermarket** ( ☎ 476 68 00; basement, Trg Republike 1; ☷ 9am-9pm Mon-Fri, 8am-5pm Sat) below the department store of that name has the largest selection of food and wine in the city centre, as well as a bakery.

The open-air **market** (Pogačarjev trg & Vodnikov trg; ☷ 8am-6pm Mon-Fri, 6am-5pm Sat Jun-Sep, 6am-4pm Mon-Sat Oct-May) opposite the cathedral sells mostly fresh fruit and vegetables.

## DRINKING

Few cities have central Ljubljana's concentration of fabulously inviting cafés and bars, the vast majority with outdoor seating.

### Cafés & Teahouses

**Kavarna Zvezda** ( ☎ 421 90 90; Kongresni trg 4 & Wolfova ul 14; ☷ 7am-11pm Mon-Sat, 10am-8pm Sun) The Star Café is celebrated for its shop-made cakes, especially *skutina pečena* (€2), an eggy cheesecake.

**Café Antico** ( ☎ 425 13 39; Stari trg 17; ☷ 10am-midnight Mon-Sat, 11am-10am Sun) With Frescoed ceilings and retro-style furniture, this is *the* place for a quiet tête-à-tête over a glass of wine.

**Čajna Hiša** ( ☎ 421 24 44; Stari trg 3; ☷ 9am-11pm Mon-Fri, 9am-3pm & 6-10pm Sat) If you take your cuppa seriously, come here; the appropriately named 'Teahouse' offers a wide range of green and black teas and fruit tisanes for €1.60 to €3.15 a pot, and sells the leaves, too.

**Le Petit Café** ( ☎ 426 14 88; Trg Francoske Revolucije 4; ☷ 7.30am-11pm Sun-Thu, 9am-midnight Fri & Sat) Just opposite the Križanke, this pleasant, studenty place offers great coffee and a wide range of breakfast goodies (€2.90 to €4.20).

**Kafeterija Lan** (Gallusovo nabrežje 27; ☺ 9am-midnight Mon-Thu, 9am-1am Fri & Sat, 10am-1am Sun) This little greener-than-green café-bar on the river below Cobbler Bridge is something of a hipster-gay magnet.

**Slaščičarna Pri Vodnjaku** ( ☎ 425 07 12; Stari trg 30; ☺ 8am-midnight) For all kinds of chocolate of the ice cream and drinking kind, the 'Confectionery by the Fountain' will surely satisfy – there are 32 different flavours (€0.85 per scoop), as well as teas (€1.50) and fresh juices (€1.05 to €3.35)

## Pubs & Bars

**Pločnik** (Prešernov trg 1; ☺ 7am-1am Apr-Oct) This roped-off café-bar on the southern side of Prešernov trg, with the distinctive name of 'Pavement', is one of the most popular places for a drink if you just want to sit outside and watch the passing parade. There's often live music.

**Maček** ( ☎ 425 37 91; Krojaška ul 5; ☺ 9am-1am) *The* place to be seen on a sunny summer afternoon, the 'Cat' is Pločnik's rival on the right bank of the Ljubljanica. Happy hour is between 4pm and 7pm daily.

**Cutty Sark** ( ☎ 425 14 77; Knafljev prehod 1; ☺ 9am-1am Mon-Sat, noon-1am Sun) A pleasant and well-stocked nautically themed pub in the courtyard behind Wolfova ul 6, the Cutty Sark is a congenial place for a *pivo* or glass of *vino*.

**Dvorni Bar** ( ☎ 251 12 57; Dvorni trg 1; ☺ 8am-1am) This wine bar is an excellent place to taste Slovenian vintages; it stocks 100 varieties, and frequently schedules promotions and wine tastings.

**Pr'skelet** ( ☎ 252 77 99; Ključavničarska ul 5; ☺ 10am-3am) OK, it might be something of a one-joke wonder, but you'll shake, rattle and roll at this skeleton-themed basement bar, where cocktails are two for one throughout the day.

**Salon** ( ☎ 439 87 64; Trubarjeva c 23; ☺ 9am-1am Mon & Tue, 9am-3am Wed-Sat, 10am-1am Sun) Salon is a dazzling designer-kitsch cocktail bar featuring gold ceilings, faux leopard armchairs, heavy burgundy and gold drapes, and excellent cocktails (€4.20 to €6.25) and shooters (€3.75 to €4.20).

**Žmavc** ( ☎ 251 03 24; Rimska c 21; ☺ 7.30am-1am Mon-Sat, 8am-1am Sun) A super-popular student hang-out west of Slovenska c, with comic-strip scenes and figures running halfway up the walls. It's owned by the same people who run the Vila Veselova (p833).

## ENTERTAINMENT

The free quarterly magazine **Ljubljana Life** (www .ljubljanalife.com) has practical information and listings. It's distributed free at the airport and in hotels and the tourist offices.

*Where to? in Ljubljana*, available from the tourist offices, lists cultural and sporting events.

## Nightclubs

**D'Place** ( ☎ 040-626 901; www.club-dplace.com, in Slovene; Šmartinska c 152; ☺ 10pm-6am Thu-Sat) This new club, with different themed evenings (eg hip-hop and R 'n' B on Saturday), has been making quite a splash since it's recent opening. It's in the Kolosej multiplex cinema at BTC City Shopping Centre.

**Funfactory** ( ☎ 428 96 90; Jurčkova c 224; ☺ 9pm-dawn Thu-Sat) Ljubljana's biggest club is hidden in a shopping centre opposite the Leclerc Hypermarket (take bus 3 to the end) in the far southeastern suburbs

**Global** ( ☎ 426 90 20; www.global.si, in Slovene; Tomšičeva ul 2; ☺ 9am-5am5pm Mon-Sat) This retro cocktail bar on the 6th floor of the Nama department store becomes a popular dance venue nightly and attracts a chi-chi crowd. Take the bouncer-guarded lift in the passageway linking Cankarjeva ul and Tomšičeva ul.

**Klub K4** ( ☎ 438 03 04; www.klubk4.org; Kersnikova ul 4; ☺ 10pm-4am) This evergreen club in the basement of the Student Organisation of Ljubljana University (Študentska Organizacija Univerze Ljubljani; ŠOU) features rave-electronic music Friday and Saturday, with other styles of music on weeknights, and a popular gay and lesbian night on Sunday. It closes when the university breaks up.

**Bacchus Center Club** ( ☎ 241 82 44; Kongresni trg 3; ☺ 10pm-5am Mon-Sat) This place has something for everyone (it also has a restaurant and bar-lounge) and attracts a mixed crowd.

**As Pub** ( ☎ 425 88 22; Knafljev prehod 5a; ☺ 7am-3am Wed-Sat) DJs transform this candlelit basement bar, hidden beneath an incongruously upmarket fish restaurant, into a pumping, crowd-pulling nightclub four nights a week.

**Metelkova Mesto** (Metelkova ul; www.metelkova .org) 'Metelkova Town', an ex-army garrison taken over by squatters after independence, is now a free-living commune – a miniature version of Copenhagen's Christiania. In this two-courtyard block, half a dozen idiosyncratic venues hide behind gaily tagged doorways, coming to life generally after midnight Thursday to Saturday. Entering the main 'city gate' from Masarykova c, the building to the right houses Gala Hala, with live bands and club nights, Channel Zero (punk, hardcore) and 100% Mizart. Easy to miss in the first building to the left are Klub Tiffany for gay men and Klub Monokel for lesbians. Beyond the first courtyard to the southwest, well-hidden Klub Gromka (folk, live concerts) is beneath the body-less heads. Next door is Menza pri Koritu (performance) and the idiosyncratic Čajnica pri Mariči (psycho-blues). Cover charges and midweek openings are rare but erratic for all Metelkova venues.

## Live Music

### ROCK, POP & JAZZ

**Orto Bar** ( ☎ 232 16 74; www.orto-bar.com; Grabol-ičeva ul 1; ✆ 6pm-4am Mon-Thu, 6pm-5am Fri & Sat, 6pm-2am Sun) A popular bar for late-night drinking and dancing with occasional live music, Orto is just five minutes' walk from Metelkova.

**Jazz Club Gajo** ( ☎ 425 32 06; www.jazzclubgajo.com; Beethovnova ul 8; ✆ 11am-2am Mon-Fri, 7pm-midnight Sat & Sun) Gajo is the city's premier venue for live jazz, and attracts both local and international talent, usually midweek or on Friday at 8.30pm (jam sessions at 8.30pm Monday).

### CLASSICAL

**Cankarjev Dom** ( ☎ 241 71 00; www.cd-cc.si, in Slovene; Prešernova c 10) Ljubljana's premier cultural and conference centre has two large auditoriums (the Gallus Hall has perfect acoustics) and a dozen smaller performance spaces offering a remarkable smorgasbord of performance arts. The ticket office ( ☎ 241 72 99; open 11am to 1pm and 3pm to 8pm Monday to Friday, 11am to 1pm Saturday and one hour before performance) is in the subway below Maximarket supermarket on the opposite side of Trg Republike.

**Philharmonic Hall** (Filharmonija; ☎ 241 08 00; www.fil harmonija.si; Kongresni trg 10) Head on down to the attractive Philharmonic Hall for classical concerts.

**Opera House** ( ☎ 241 17 40; www.opera.si; Župančičeva ul 1) Opera and ballet are performed at the neo-Renaissance 1882 Opera House.

**Križanke** ( ☎ 241 60 00, 241 60 26; Trg Francoske Revolucije 1-2) Hosts events of the Ljubljana Summer Festival (p854) in what was a sprawling monastic complex dating back to the 13th century.

## Cinema

**Kinoteka** ( ☎ 434 25 20; www.kinoteka.si, in Slovene; Miklošičeva c 28) The 'Slovenian Cinematheque' screens archival art and classic films.

**Kino Dvor** (Court Cinema; ☎ 434 25 44; www.kinodvor .si, in Slovene; Kolodvorska ul 13; ✆ 6pm, 8pm & 10pm) Kinoteka's sister-cinema shows more contemporary films.

## GETTING THERE & AWAY

The shedlike **bus station** ( ☎ 234 46 01, information 090 42 30; www.ap-ljubljana.si; Trg OF 4; ✆ 5.30am-10.30pm Mon-Sat, 8am-8pm Sun) opposite the train station has bilingual info-phones, and its timetable is useful once you get the hang of it. Frequent buses serve Bohinj (€8, two hours, 86km, hourly) via Bled (€6.15, 1¼ hours, 57km). Most buses to Piran (€11.70, three hours, 140km, up to seven daily) go via Koper (€10.75, 2½ hours, 122km, up to 11 daily) and Postojna (€5.75, one hour, 53km, up to 24 daily). All bus services are much less frequent on weekends.

Ljubljana's **train station** ( ☎ 291 33 32; www.slo -zeleznice.si; Trg OF 6; ✆ 5am-10pm) has daily services to Koper (€7.30 to €8.70, 2½ hours, 153km, four times daily). Alternatively take the Sežana-bound train (5.55am) and change (rapidly – you've got seven minutes!) at Divača (1¾ hours). For international services, see p857.

## GETTING AROUND

The cheapest way to **Ljubljana Aerodrom** (LJU; www.lju-airport.si) at Brnik is by city bus from stop 28 (€3.70, 50 minutes, 27km) at the bus station. These run hourly from 6.10am to 8.10pm Monday to Friday; on the weekend there's a bus at 6.10am and then one every two hours from 9.10am to 7.10pm. A **private airport van** ( ☎ 04-252 63 19, 041-792 865) also links Trg OF near the bus station with the airport up to 10 times daily between 5.20am and 10.30pm (€8, 30 minutes).

You can park on the street (€0.40 to €0.50 per hour) in Ljubljana, though not always easily in the museum area and near Metelkova. Once you've found a space it's generally most efficient to walk.

Ljubljana has an excellent network (21 lines) of city buses; the main lines operate every five to 15 minutes from 3.15am to midnight. However, the central area is perfectly walkable, so buses are really only necessary if you're staying out of town. Buy little metal tokens (žetoni; €0.80) in advance from newsstands, or pay €1.25 on board.

**Ljubljana Bike** ( ☎ 051-441 900; per 2hr/day €0.85/4.20; ⊙ 8am-8pm Apr-Oct) has bikes available from some 10 locations around the city, including the train station, the STIC office (p831), the Celica Hostel (p833) and at the at the start of Miklošičeva c.

# JULIAN ALPS

The Julian Alps – named in honour of Caesar himself – form Slovenia's dramatic northwest frontier with Italy. Triglav National Park, established in 1924, includes almost all of the alps lying within Slovenia. The centrepiece of the park is, of course, Mt Triglav (2864m), Slovenia's highest mountain, but there are many other peaks here reaching above 2000m, as well as ravines, canyons, caves, rivers, streams, forests and alpine meadows. Along with an embarrassment of fauna and flora, the area offers a wide range of adventure sports at very affordable prices.

## KRANJ
☎ 04 / pop 34,850

Situated at the foot of the Kamnik-Savinja Alps, with the snow-capped peak of Storžič (2132m) and others looming to the north, Kranj is Slovenia's fourth-largest city. The attractive Old Town, perched on an escarpment above the confluence of the Sava and Kokra Rivers, barely measures 1km by 250m.

The frequent weekday buses between Kranj and Ljubljana Aerodrom at nearby Brnik make it possible to head straight from the plane to the Julian Alps without diverting to the capital. While waiting for your onward bus to Bled or Kranjska Gora, have a look at the Old Town, starting with the Art Nouveau **former post office** (Maistrov trg), a 600m walk south

from the bus station past the eyesore 87-room **Hotel Creina** ( ☎ 281 75 00; www.hotel-creina.si; Koroška c 5; s/d €60/80; ⚙ 🖳 ), the only game in town and where most airline crews stay while overnighting in Slovenia. Most places of interest are along just three south-bound pedestrianised streets – Prešernova ul, Tavčarjeva ul and Tomišičeva ul – two of which lead to the **Church of St Cantianus**, with impressive frescoes and stained glass. Another 300m further south, the Old Town dead-ends behind the Serbian Orthodox **Plague Church**, built during a time of pestilence in 1470, and a 16th-century **defence tower**. **Mitnica** ( ☎ 040-678 778; Tavčarjeva ul 35; ⊙ 7am-11pm Mon-Wed, 7am-1am Thu, 7am-3am Fri & Sat), a lovely café-bar in the basement of a 16th-century toll house with a huge terrace backing on to the river, is just the place to relax in Kranj on a warm afternoon.

From Kranj it's an easy excursion to **Škofja Loka**, whose main square, **Mestni Trg**, is one of Slovenia's most beautiful and whose fine **Loka Castle** (Grajska pot 13) contains a decent **ethnographical museum** ( ☎ 517 04 00; adult/child €2.90/2.10; ⊙ 9am-6pm Tue-Sun Apr-Oct, 9am-5pm Sat & Sun Nov-Mar). Buses depart hourly from Kranj (€2.10, 25 minutes, 13km).

## BLED
☎ 04 / pop 5250

With its emerald-green lake, picture-postcard church on an islet, medieval castle clinging to a rocky cliff, and some of the highest peaks of the Julian Alps and the Karavanke as backdrops, Bled seems too to good to be true, designed, it would seem, by some god of tourism. As it is Slovenia's most popular destination it can get pretty crowded in summer, but it's small, convenient and a delightful base from which to explore the mountains.

---

**HIKING MT TRIGLAV**

The Julian Alps offer some of Europe's finest hiking. In summer some 167 mountain huts (planinska koča or planinski dom) operate, none more than five hours' walk from the next. These huts get very crowded, especially on weekends, so booking ahead is wise. If the weather turns bad, however, you won't be refused refuge.

At €20 per person in a private room or half that amount in a dormitory in a Category I hut (Category II huts charge €13.35 and €7.50 respectively), the huts aren't cheap, but as they serve meals you can travel light. Sturdy boots and warm clothes are indispensable, even in midsummer. Trails are generally well marked with a white-centred red circle, but you can still get lost and it's very unwise to trek alone. It's best to engage the services of a qualified (and licensed) guide.

The tourist offices in Bled, Bohinj, Kranjska Gora and Bovec all have lots of hiking information, sell maps in a variety of useful scales and can help book huts in their regions.

## Information

**3glav adventures** ( ☎ 041-683 184, 041-819 636; www.3glav-adventures.com; Ljubljanska c 1; ☼ 9am-7pm Apr-Oct)

**À Propos Bar** ( ☎ 574 40 44; Bled Shopping Centre, Ljubljanska c 4; per 15/30/60min €1.25/2.10/4.20; ☼ 8am-midnight) Offers internet access.

**Gorenjska Banka** (C Svobode 15; ☼ 9-11.30am & 2-5pm Mon-Fri, 8-11am Sat) In the Park Hotel shopping complex.

**Kompas** ( ☎ 572 75 00; www.kompas-bled.si; Bled Shopping Centre, Ljubljanska c 4; ☼ 8am-7pm Mon-Sat, 8am-noon & 4-8pm Sun Jul & Aug, 8am-7pm Mon-Sat, 8am-noon & 4-7pm Sun Sep-Jun) Rents private rooms and bicycles.

**Tourist Information Centre Bled** ( ☎ 574 11 22; www .bled.si; C Svobode 10; ☼ 8am-10pm Mon-Sat, 10am-10pm Sun Jul & Aug, 8am-8pm Mon-Sat, 10am-6pm Sun Jun & Sep,

8am-7pm Mon-Sat, 9am-5pm Sun Oct & Mar-May, 9am-5pm Mon-Sat, 9am-2pm Sun Nov-Feb)

## Sights

On its own tiny island, the baroque **Church of the Assumption** ( ☼ 8am-dusk) is Bled's icon. Getting there by a piloted **gondola** (pletna; ☎ 041 293 424) is the archetypal tourist experience. Gondola prices (return per person €10) are standard from any jetty, and you'll stay on the island long enough to ring the 'lucky' bell; all in all, it's a 1½-hour trip. Ordinary row-yourself boats for three to four people cost €10.50 per hour.

Perched atop a 100m-cliff, **Bled Castle** ( ☎ 578 05 25; Grajska c 25; adult/student/child €5/4.60/3.10; ☼ 8am-8pm May-Oct, 8am-5pm Nov-Apr) is the perfect backdrop to a lake view. One of many access

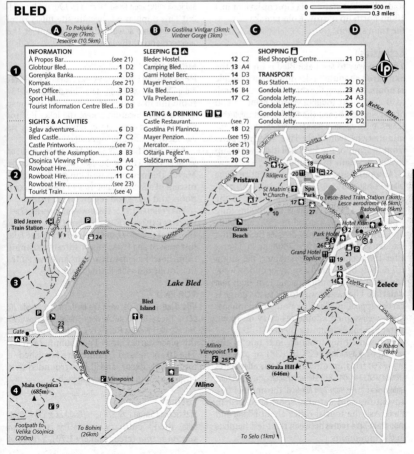

**BLED**

0 — 500 m
0 — 0.3 miles

SLOVENIA

footpaths leads up from behind the Bledec Hostel (right). Admission includes entry to the **museum collection** as well as **Castle Printworks**. The fabulous views are 'free' if you have a meal or sunset beer on the superbly situated terrace of the Castle Restaurant (opposite).

A short distance southeast of Bled and well served by bus (€1.70, 15 minutes, 7.5km, half-hourly), the town of **Radovljica** appears at first glance to be an amorphous, modern sprawl. However, it has a particularly delightful square called **Linhartov trg** in its Old Town, where there's a restored, painted **manor house**, an interesting **gallery** and the fascinating **Beekeeping Museum** ( ☎ 532 05 20; Linhartov trg 1; adult/student €2.10/1.90; ☼ 10am-1pm & 3-6pm Tue-Sun May-Oct, 10am-noon & 3-5pm Wed, Sat & Sun Mar, Apr, Nov & Dec). The square starts 400m southeast of Radovljica bus station via Gorenjska c or just 100m north up narrow Kolodvorska ul from the train station.

## Activities

The best way to see Lake Bled is on foot; the 6km stroll shouldn't take more than a couple of hours, including the short (but steep) climb to the brilliant **Osojnica viewing point**. If you prefer, jump aboard the **tourist train** (adult/child €2.50/1.70; ☼ 9.30am-9.30pm May–mid-Oct) for the 45-minute twirl around the lake, which departs from in front of the **Sport Hall** (Ljubljanska c 5) up to 20 times daily in summer.

A popular and easy walk is to **Vintgar Gorge** (adult/student/child €2.90/2.50/2.10; ☼ 8am-7pm late Apr-Oct) some 4km from the town centre to the northwest. The highlight is the 1600m-long wooden walkway, erected in 1893 and continually rebuilt, that criss-crosses the swirling Radovna River for the first 700m or so. Thereafter the scenery becomes tamer, passing a tall railway bridge and a spray-spouting weir, and ending at the anticlimactic 13m-high **Šum Waterfall**. The easiest way to get to the gorge is via the appealing Gostilna Vintgar, an inn just three well-signed kilometres away on quiet, attractive roads from the Bledec Hostel.

For something tougher, join one of the **rafting** or **kayaking** (€23 to €38) or **paragliding** (€70) trips on offer from **3glav adventures** ( ☎ 041-683 184, 041-819 636; www.3glav-adventures.com; Ljubljanska c 1; ☼ 9am-7pm Apr-Oct), the number one adventure- and extreme-sport specialist in Bled. Ask the tourist office about **hiking** and **mountain-bike routes** between road-less hamlets in the mountains.

## Sleeping

### BUDGET

Private rooms are offered by dozens of homes in the area. Both Kompas (p839) and **Globtour Bled** ( ☎ 575 13 00; www.globtour-bled.com; Ljubljanska c 7; ☼ 8am-8pm Mon-Sat, 8am-noon & 4-8pm Sun Jul & Aug, 8am-7pm Mon-Fri, 9am-2pm Sat Sep-Jun) in the Hotel Krim have extensive lists, with prices for singles/doubles starting at €20/30.

**Bledec Hostel** ( ☎ 574 52 50; Grajska c 17; HI members/nonmembers high season dorm €17.5/20, low season €15.50/18, d high season €23.50/26, low season €21.50/24; ☒ ▣ ) This well-organised hostel has four-bed dorms with private bathrooms, a bar and an inexpensive restaurant. Laundry (€8.35 per load €8.35) and internet access (€2.10 per half-hour €2.10) are available.

**Camping Bled** ( ☎ 575 20 00; www.camping.bled.si; Kidričeva c 10c; adult €8.50-11, child €6-7.70; ☼ Apr–mid-Oct) This popular 6.5-hectare site fills a rural valley behind a waterside restaurant at the western end of the lake.

### MIDRANGE

**Mayer Penzion** ( ☎ 574 10 58; www.mayer-sp.si; Želeška c 7; d/q €70/90, apt €65-75; ☒ ▣ ) This delightful 13-room inn in a renovated 19th-century house is in a quiet location above the lake. Even if you're not staying here, have a meal at its excellent restaurant (opposite).

**Garni Hotel Berc** ( ☎ 576 56 58; www.berc-sp.si; Pod Stražo 13; s €40, d €65-70; ☒ ▣ ) Just opposite the Mayer, this new purpose-built *penzion*, reminiscent of a Swiss chalet, has 15 rooms on two floors and gets good reviews from readers.

**Vila Prešeren** ( ☎ 578 08 00; www.vila.preseren.s5.net; Kidričeva c 1; s lake view €58-64, park view €50-55, d lake view €78-88, park view €67-72, ste €112-154) Facing the lake just west of Spa Park, this positively charming mini-hotel has just six rooms and two suites in a lovely old villa dating from 1865.

### TOP END

**Vila Bled** (579 15 00; www.vila-bled.com; C Svobode 26; s €130-150, d €170-190, ste lake view €210-240, park view €190-210; ▣ ☙ ) Now a Relais & Chateaux property, this place started life as Tito's summer retreat. The 10 rooms and 20 suites are furnished in retro 1950s décor, and it is surrounded by a large park and has its own beach.

## Eating

**Slaščičarna Šmon** ( ☎ 574 16 16; Grajska c 3; ☼ 7.30am-9pm) Bled's culinary speciality is *kremna snežna rezina* (cream cake; €1.70), a layer of vanilla custard topped with whipped cream and sandwiched neatly between two layers of flaky pastry, and this is the place to try it.

**Gostilna Pri Planincu** ( ☎ 574 16 13; Grajska c 8; entrées €4.20-8, mains €5.85-15; ☣ noon-10pm) 'At the Mountaineers' is a homey pub-restaurant just down the hill from the Bledec Hostel, with simple Slovenia mains and grilled Balkan specialities, like *čevapčiči* (spicy meatballs of beef or pork; €5.65) and tasty *pljeskavica z kajmakom* (Serbian-style meat patties with mascarpone-like cream cheese; €6.25).

**Ostarija Peglez'n** ( ☎ 574 42 18; C Svobode 19a; entrées €4.60-7.50, mains €6.25-16.25; ☣ 11am-midnight) Our new favourite restaurant in Bled, the 'Iron Inn' is just opposite the landmark Grand Hotel Toplice, with fascinating retro décor and serving some of the best fish dishes in town.

**Mayer Penzion** ( ☎ 574 10 58; www.mayer-sp.si; Želeška c 7; entrées €7-8, mains €9.20-18.80; ☣ 5pm-midnight Tue-Fri, noon-midnight Sat & Sun) The restaurant at this delightful inn (above) serves such tasty Slovenian fare such as sausage, trout, roast pork and *skutini štruklji* (cheese curd pastries). The list of Slovenian wines is a cut above.

**Castle Restaurant** ( ☎ 579 44 24; entrées €5-10.85, mains €10.85-18.80; ☣ 10am-10pm) You can't beat the views from this place and the wine list – all Slovenian – is exceptional.

You'll find a **Mercator** (Ljubljanska c 4; ☣ 7am-7pm Mon-Sat, 8am-noon Sun) at the eastern end of Bled Shopping Centre.

## Getting There & Away

Frequent buses to Bohinj (€3.50, one hour, 26km, hourly), Ljubljana (€6.10, 1¼ hours, 57km, hourly) and Radovljica (€1.70, 15 minutes, 7.5km, half-hourly) use the central bus station.

Bled has no central train station. Trains to Bohinjska Bistrica (€1.45, 20 minutes, 18km, seven daily) and Nova Gorica (€5.05, 2¼ hours, 79km, seven daily) use little Bled Jezero train station, which is 2km west of central Bled – handy for the camping ground but little else. Trains for Ljubljana (€3.90 to €5.30, 55 minutes, 51km, up to 17 daily) use Lesce-Bled train station, 4km to the east of town.

## BOHINJ

☎ 04 / pop 5260

Bohinj, a larger and much less-developed glacial lake 26km to the southwest, is a world apart from Bled. Triglav itself is visible from the lake and there are activities galore – from kayaking and mountain biking to trekking up Triglav via one of the southern approaches.

**Bohinjska Bistrica**, the area's largest village, is 6km east of the lake and useful mainly for its train station. The main tourist hub on the lake is **Ribčev Laz**, at the lake's eastern end. Its miniscule commercial centre contains a supermarket, post office with ATM and the obliging **Tourist Information Centre Bohinj** ( ☎ 574 60 10; www.bohinj.si; Ribčev Laz 48; ☣ 8am-8pm Jul & Aug, 8am-6pm Mon-Sat, 9am-3pm Sun Sep-Jun), which changes money, sells **fishing licences** (€25 to €50.50 per day) and can help with accommodation. Central **Alpinsport** ( ☎ 572 34 86; www.alpinsport.si; Ribčev Laz 53; ☣ 9am-7pm Jun-Aug, 10am-6pm Sep-May) organises a range of activities, and hires kayaks, canoes, bicycles and other equipment from a kiosk near the stone bridge. Next door is the **Church of St John the Baptist**, which contains splendid 15th- and 16th-century frescoes, but is undergoing a protracted renovation.

A nearby village called **Stara Fužina** has an appealing little **Alpine Dairy Museum** ( ☎ 572 30 95;

**SLOVENIA**

---

### A NATIONAL ICON

Nothing is as Slovenian as the *kozolec*, the hayrack seen almost everywhere in the country, except on the far northeastern plain and in the Karst region. Because the ground in Alpine and hilly areas can be damp, wheat and hay are hung from racks, allowing the wind to do the drying faster and more thoroughly.

Until the late 19th century the *kozolec* was looked upon as just another tool to make a farmer's work easier and the land more productive. Then the artist Ivan Grohar made it the centrepiece of many of his impressionist paintings, and the *kozolec* became as much a part of the cultural landscape as the physical one. Today it has become virtually a national icon.

There are many different types of Slovenian hayracks: single ones standing alone or 'goat hayracks' with sloped 'lean-to' roofs, parallel and stretched ones and double hayracks (*toplarji*), often with roofs and storage areas on top. Simple hayracks are not unknown in other parts of Alpine central Europe, but *toplarji*, decorated or plain, are unique to Slovenia.

Stara Fužine 181; adult/child €1.70/1.25; 11am-7pm Tue-Sun Jul & Aug, 10am-noon & 4-6pm Tue-Sun Jan-Jun, Sep & Oct). Just opposite is a cheesemonger called **Planšar** ( 572 30 95; Stara Fužina 179; 10am-8pm Tue-Sun Jun-Oct, 10am-8pm Sat & Sun Dec-May), which specialises in home-made dairy products: hard Bohinj cheese, a soft, strong-tasting cheese called *mohant*, cottage cheese, curd pie, sour milk and so on. Just 2km east is **Studor**, a village famed for its *toplarji*, the double-linked hayrack with barns or storage areas at the top, some of which date from the 18th and 19th centuries.

Depending on the season, **Tourist boats** ( 041-434 986; adult/child one-way €6.25/4.60, return €7.45/5.45; 10am-6pm) depart from the pier just opposite the Alpinsport kiosk every half-hour to an hour, terminating 15 minutes later at the Ukanc jetty at the lake's far western west end. Just 300m up from the Ukanc jetty and 5km west of Ribčev Laz, a **cable car** (adult/child return €10/7; every 30min 7am-7pm Jul & Aug, 8am-6pm Sep-Jun) will whisk you up a vertical kilometre to 1540m; from here, paths continue up **Mt Vogel**.

## Sleeping

**Private rooms** (per person €9.20-15.10) are available through the tourist office.

**Penzion Rožič** ( 572 33 93; rozic@siol.net; Ribčev Laz 42; per person €20-25; ) This unpretentious chalet-style guesthouse with 20 rooms and a popular restaurant is just 200m east of the tourist office.

**Hotel Bellevue** ( 572 33 31; www.alpinum.net; Ribčev Laz 65; s €39-52, d €55-89; ) The shabby, 59-room Bellevue has a beautiful (if somewhat isolated) location on a hill about 800m south of the Hotel Jezero. Whodunit fans take note: Agatha Christie stayed here for three weeks in 1967. Thirty-eight of the rooms are in the unattractive Savica Annexe.

**Hotel Jezero** ( 572 91 00; www.bohinj.si/alpinum /jezero; Ribčev Laz 51; s €52-86, d €69-141; ) This recently renovated 63-room place is the closest hotel to the lake, just opposite the stone bridge in Ribčev Laz. It has a lovely indoor swimming pool, two saunas and a fitness centre.

**Autokamp Zlatorog** ( 572 34 82; www.alpinum .net; Ukanc 2; per person €5.85-10; May-Sep) This pine-shaded 2.5-hectare camping ground accommodating 500 guests is on the lake at its western end.

## Getting There & Around

Buses run regularly from Ukanc to Ljubljana (€8.50, two hours, 91km, hourly) via Ribčev

Laz, Bohinjska Bistrica and Bled (€4, one hour, 34km), with six extra buses daily between Ukanc and Bohinjska Bistrica (€2.20, 20 minutes, 12km). Buses headed as far as Ukanc are marked to 'Bohinj Zlatorog'. From Bohinjska Bistrica, passenger trains to Novo Gorica (€4.50, 1½ hours, 61km, up to seven daily) make use of a century-old tunnel under the mountains that provides the only direct option for reaching the Soča Valley. In addition there are six daily auto trains (*avtovlaki*) to Podbrdo (€7.10, eight minutes, 7km) and Most na Soči (€10.85, 25 minutes, 28km).

# KRANJSKA GORA

04 / pop 1420

Kranjska Gora, lying in the Sava Dolinka Valley that separates the Karavanke range of mountains from the Julian Alps, is the largest and best-equipped ski resort in the country. It's at its most perfect under a blanket of snow, but its surroundings are wonderful to explore in warmer months as well. There are endless possibilities for hiking and mountaineering in Triglav National Park on the town's southern outskirts, and few travellers will not be impressed by a trip over the Vršič Pass (1611m), the gateway to the Soča Valley.

As ski resorts go, compact Kranjska Gora is relatively cute and sits right beside the ski lifts. There are world record-setting ski jumps 4km west at Planica. Needless to say, there are a lot of places offering ski tuition and equipment hire, including **ASK Kranjska Gora Ski School** ( 588 53 00; www.ask-kg.com; Borovška c 99a) in the same building as SKB Banka.

Borovška c, 400m south of where buses arrive and depart, is the heart of the village, with the endearing **Liznjek House** ( 588 19 99; Borovška 63; adult/child €2.30/1.70; 10am-8pm Tue-Sat, 10am-5pm Sun May-Oct & Dec-Mar), an 18th-century museum house with a good collection of household objects and furnishings peculiar to this area of Gorenjska province. At its western end is the **Tourist Information Centre Kranjska Gora** ( 588 17 68; www.kranjska-gora.si; Tičarjeva c 2; 8am-7pm Mon-Sat, 9am-6pm Sun Jun-Sep & mid-Dec–Mar, 8am-3pm Mon-Fri, 9am-6pm Sat, 9am-1pm Sun Apr, May, Oct–mid-Dec).

## Sleeping & Eating

Accommodation costs peak from December to March and in midsummer. April is the cheapest time to visit, though some hotels close for renovations and redecorating at this time. **Private rooms** (s €15.50-20.50, d €21-35) can be arranged through the tourist office and **Globtour** ( ☎ 582 02 00; www.globtour-kranjskagora.com; Borovška c 92; ⊗ 9am-7pm daily Jul, Aug, Dec-Mar, 9am-7pm Mon-Sat Sep-Nov & Apr-Jun).

**Hostel Nika** ( ☎ 588 10 00; zvone.oreskovic@s5.net; Čičare 2; dm €11, s/d €16/28; ⊠ 🖳 ) This somewhat institutional hostel, with 66 beds in a large village, is about 800m northeast of the town centre and just across the main road from the TGC Shopping Centre.

**Hotel Miklič** ( ☎ 588 16 35; www.hotelmiklic.com; Vitranška ul 13; s €45-66, d €70-112; ⊠ 🖳 ) This pristine *penzion* south of the town centre is surrounded by luxurious lawns and flowerbeds, and boasts an excellent restaurant. It's definitely a cut above most other accommodation options in Kranjska Gora.

**Hotel Kotnik** ( ☎ 588 15 64; hotel@hotel-kotnik.si; Borovška c 75; s €48-62, d €56-84; ⊠ ) If you're not into big high-rise hotels with hundreds of rooms, choose this charming, bright yellow property. It has 15 cosy rooms, a great restaurant and pizzeria, and it couldn't be more central.

**Gostilna Pri Martinu** ( ☎ 582 03 00; Borovška c 61; entrées €4.20-5.85, mains €5.85-10; ⊗ 10am-11pm) This atmospheric tavern-restaurant in an old house opposite the fire station is one of the best places in town to try local specialities, such as venison, trout and *telečja obara* (veal stew,; €3.75).

## Getting There & Away

Buses run hourly to Ljubljana (€8.50, two hours, 91km) via Jesenice (€3, 30 minutes, 23km), where you should change for Bled (€2.60, 20 minutes, 16km). There are just two direct departures to Bled (€4.90, one hour, 40km) on weekdays at 9.15am and 1.10pm. A service to Bovec (€5.50, two hours, 46km) via the spectacular Vršič Pass departs daily in July and August, and on Saturday and Sunday in June and September.

## SOČA VALLEY

The region of the Soča Valley stretches from Triglav National Park to Nova Gorica. It is dominated by the 96km-long Soča River coloured a deep – almost artificial – turquoise. The valley has more than its share of historical sights, but most people come here for rafting, hiking and skiing.

### Bovec

☎ 05 / pop 1650

The effective capital of the Soča Valley, Bovec has a great deal to offer adventure-sports en-

thusiasts. With the Julian Alps above, the Soča River below and Triglav National Park at the back door, you could spend a week hiking, kayaking, mountain biking and, in winter, skiing at Mt Kanin, Slovenia's highest ski station, without ever doing the same thing twice.

The compact village square, **Trg Golobarskih Žrtev**, has everything you need. There are cafés, a hotel, the extremely helpful **Tourist Information Centre Bovec** ( ☎ 384 19 19; www.bovec .si; Trg Golobarskih Žrtev 8; ⊗ 9am-8pm daily Jul & Aug, 9am-5pm Mon-Fri, 9am-noon & 4-6pm Sat, 9am-noon Sun Sep-Jun) and a handful of adrenaline-raising adventure-sports companies, including: **Avantura** ( ☎ 041-718 317; bovecavantura@hotmail.com); **Soča Rafting** ( ☎ 389 62 00; www.socarafting.si); **Outdoor Freaks** ( ☎ 389 64 90, 041-553 675; www.freakoutdoor .com); **Sport Mix** ( ☎ 389 61 60, 031-871 991; traft@siol .net); and **Top Extreme** ( ☎ 330 00 90, 041-620 636; www .top.si). Following are just some of the activities on offer:

**Canyoning** Two hours at Sušec costs €33.70 to €39.

**Hydrospeed** Like riding down a river on a boogie board; you'll pay €30 to €35 for an 8km ride.

**White-water rafting** Available only from April to October, it costs around €27 to €37 for a 10km trip, €34.60 to €40 for 21km.

**Kayaking** A guided 10km paddle costs from €30 per person, or two-day training courses from €77.

**Caving** A trip costs from €25.50 per person with guide.

In winter you can take a tandem paraglider flight (ie as a passenger accompanied by a qualified pilot) from the top of the Kanin cable car, 2000m above the valley floor. AThe cost of a flight costs from €100; ask the Avantura agency for details.

**Private rooms** (per person €12-25) are easy to come by in Bovec, and the tourist office and other agencies have hundreds on their lists.

Camping facilities are generally better in Kobarid, but **Kamp Polovnik** ( ☎ 388 60 69; www.camp -polovnik.com; adult/child €6.70/4.80; ⊗ Apr-Oct) about 500m southeast of the town centre is in an attractive setting and much more convenient.

The 103-room **Alp Hotel** ( ☎ 388 60 40; www.bovec .net/hotelalp; Trg Golobarskih Žrtev 48; s €37-48, d €57.50-78; ⊠ 🖳 ) is fairly good value and as central as you are going to find in Bovec.

**Dobra Vila** ( ☎ 389 64 00; www.dobra-vila-bovec.com, Mala Vas 112; s/d €55/72; 🖳 ) is a positive stunner of a 12-room boutique hotel housed in the former telephone exchange building. It has its own small cinema, library and vine cellar, as well as a fabulous restaurant.

SLOVENIA

## Kobarid

☎ 05 / pop 1250

Some 21km south of Bovec, quaint Kobarid (Caporetto in Italian) lies in a broad valley on the west bank of the Soča River. Although it's surrounded by mountain peaks higher than 2200m, Kobarid feels more Mediterranean than alpine, and the Italian border at Robič is only 9km to the west.

On the town's main square is the extreme-sports agency, **XPoint** ( ☎ 388 53 08, 041-692 290; www.xpoint.si; Trg Svobode 6; ☽ 9.30am-5pm Apr-Oct), which can organise rafting, canyoning, canoe-ing and paragliding in Kobarid and Tolmin, 16km to the southeast. The **Tourist Informa-tion Centre Kobarid** ( ☎ 380 04 90; www.lto-sotocje .si; Gregorčičeva ul 8; ☽ 9am-8pm Mon-Fri, 9am-12.30pm & 3.30-8pm Sat & Sun Jul & Aug, 9am-12.30pm & 1.30-7pm Mon-Fri, 9am-1pm Sat Sep-Jun) is next door to the award-winning **Kobarid Museum** ( ☎ 389 00 00; Gregorčičeva ul 10; adult/student/child €4/2.90/2.10; ☽ 9am-6pm Mon-Fri, 9am-7pm Sat & Sun Apr-Oct, 10am-5pm Mon-Fri, 10am-6pm Sat & Sun Nov-Mar), devoted almost entirely to the Isonzo (Soča) Front of WWI (p826), which formed the backdrop to Ernest Hemingway novel's *A Farewell to Arms*. A free pamphlet titled *The Kobarid Historical Walk* outlines a 5km-long route that will take you past remnant WWI troop emplacements to the impressive Kozjak Stream Waterfalls.

The oldest camping ground in the Soča Valley, **Kamp Koren** ( ☎ 389 13 11; www.kamp-koren.si; Drežniške Ravne 33; per person €6.50-8.50; ☽ mid-Mar–Oct) is a small, one-hectare site, with wheelchair access, about 500m north of Kobarid on the left bank of the Soča River and just before the turnoff to Drežniške Ravne, a lovely village with traditional farmhouses.

The welcoming little **Apartma-Ra** ( ☎ 389 10 07; apartma-ra@siol.net; Gregorčičeva ul 6c; per person €15-25; ✂ ✂ ) between the museum and Trg Svobode is entirely nonsmoking. Some rooms have terraces, and bicycles are available for hire to guests for €6/9 per half-/full day.

In the centre of Kobarid you'll find two of Slovenia's best provincial restaurants, both of which specialise in fish and seafood: the incomparable **Topli Val** ( ☎ 389 93 00; Trg Svobode 1; entrées €7.50-10.85, mains €6.75-25; ☽ noon-10pm) and **Kotlar** ( ☎ 389 11 10; Trg Svobode 11; entrées €5.40-10.40, mains €6.25-16.70; ☽ noon-11pm Thu-Mon).

### Getting There & Away

Weekday buses from Bovec via Kobarid go to Novo Gorica (€5.75, 1½ hours, 55km, five daily) and to Ljubljana (€6.95, three hours, 130km, up to four daily) passing Most na Soči train station for Bled and Bohinj. A bus crosses over the spectacular Vršič Pass to Kranjska Gora (€6.65, three hours, 68km) daily in July and August.

## Novo Gorica

☎ 05 / pop 12,600

Novo Gorica is a green university town strad-dling the Italian border. When the town of Gorica, capital of the former Slovenian prov-ince of Goriška, was awarded to the Italians after WWII, the new socialist government in Yugoslavia set itself to building a model town on the eastern side of the border. They called it 'New Gorica' and erected a chain-link bar-rier between the two towns. This mini-'Berlin Wall' was pulled down to great fanfare in 2004, leaving the anomalous Piazza Transalp-ina (Trg z Mozaikom) straddling the border right behind Novo Gorica train station, where you'll now find the rather esoteric **Museum of the Border** ( ☎ 333 44 00; admission free; ☽ 1-5pm Mon-Fri, 9am-7pm Sat, 10am-7pm Sun).

With no barrier remaining, there's really nothing to stop you wandering across to the Italian side, where the Italian bus 1 will whisk you to Gorizia train station. However, this is still not a *legal* border crossing and won't become one until Slovenia joins the Schengen Convention. Meanwhile EU citizens may use a less direct shuttle bus (€1, 25 minutes, hourly) between the two train stations, or cross on foot at the **Gabrielle border crossing** ( ☎ 8am-8pm), some 500m south at the end of Erjavčeva ul, which becomes Via San Gabriele in Italy.

Other passport-holders are expected to use the 24-hour **Rožna Dolina-Cassa Rosa border cross-ing**. That's reached by half-hourly buses (any number) from Novo Gorica bus station, or by walking 20 minutes south from the train sta-tion: follow the railway line through the cycle tunnel, from where you immediately cross the tracks on a footbridge and continue along Ul Pinka Tomažiča and Pot na Pristavo. From Cassa Rosa take Italian bus 8 northbound along its convoluted route, which loops back to Gorizia bus/train stations.

The helpful **Tourist Information Centre Nova Gorica** ( ☎ 333 46 00; www.novagorica-turizem.com; Bev-kov trg 4; ☽ 8am-8pm Mon-Fri, 9am-1pm Sat & Sun Jul & Aug, 8am-6pm Mon-Fri, 9am-1pm Sat & Sun Sep-Jun) is in the lobby of the Kulturni Dom (Cultural House).

Novo Gorica's only inexpensive accommodation option, **Prenočišče Pertout** ( ☎ 330 75 50, 041-624 452; www.prenociscepertout.com; Ul 25 Maja 23; s/d/tr €22.50/36/48), is a five-room B&B in Rožna Dolina, south of the town centre and scarcely 100m northeast of the Italian border.

The Italian restaurant **Marco Polo** ( ☎ 302 97 29; Kidričeva ul 13; entrées €5.85-12.50, mains €7.50-1500; 🕑 11am-11pm Sun-Thu, 11am-midnight Fri & Sat, noon-midnight Sun), 250m east of the tourist office, is one of the town's best places to eat, serving both pizza (€3.75 to €6.25) and more ambitious dishes, and with a delightful back terrace.

Buses travel hourly between Novo Gorica and Ljubljana (€10.35, 2½ hours, 116km) via Postojna (€5.75, one hour, 53km), and up to six times daily to Bovec (€7.30, two hours, 77km) via Kobarid (€5.75, 1½ hours, 55km).

Trains link Novo Gorica with Bohinjska Bistrica (€4.50, 1½ hours, 61km, up to seven daily) and Bled or via Sežana and Divača to Postojna and Ljubljana (€7.30, 3½ hours, 153km, up to six daily).

# KARST & COAST

Slovenia's short coast (47km) on the Adriatic is not renowned for its fine beaches, though the southernmost resort of Portorož has some decent ones. Three important towns full of Venetian Gothic architecture – Koper, Piran and Izola – are the drawing card here and will keep even the most indefatigable of sightseers busy. En route from Ljubljana you'll cross the Karst, a huge limestone plateau and a land of olives, ruby-red Teran wine, *pršut* (air-dried ham), old stone churches and deep subterranean caves. In fact, Slovenia's two most famous caverns – theme park–like Postojna and awesome Škocjan – are here.

## POSTOJNA
☎ 05  /  pop 8670

Slovenia's most popular natural tourist attraction, **Postojna Cave** ( ☎ 700 01 00; www.postojnska-jama .si; adult/student/child €16.65/12.50/13.80; 🕑 tours hourly 9am-6pm May-Sep, 10am, noon, 2pm & 4pm Apr & Oct, 10am, noon & 2pm Mon-Fri, 10am, noon, 2pm & 4pm Sat & Sun Nov-Mar) is about 2km northwest of the town of Postojna. The 5.7km-long cavern is visited on a 1½-hour tour, but about 4km of it is covered by an electric train. The remaining 1700m is on foot. Inside, impressive stalagmites and stalactites stretch almost endlessly in all directions, as do the chattering crowds who pass them. The tour culminates with a quick encounter (in a tank) with the endemic *Proteus anguinus* (below). Dress warmly or rent a woollen cape (€2); even on summer days it's only 10°C (50°F) inside the cave.

Close to the cave's entrance is the **Proteus Vivarium** (adult/student/child €5/3.50/2.90; 🕑 8.30am-6.30pm May-Sep, 9.30am-4.30pm Apr & Oct, 9.30am-2.30pm Mon-Fri, 9.30am-4pm Sat & Sun Nov-Mar), a speliobiological research station with a video introduction to underground zoology. A 45-minute tour then leads you into a small, darkened cave to peep at some of the shy creatures you've just learned about. Don't expect monsters

---

**THE HUMAN FISH**

*Proteus anguinus* is one of the most mysterious creatures in the world. A kind of salamander, but related to no other amphibian, it is the largest known permanent cave-dwelling vertebrate. The blind little fellow lives hidden in the pitch black for up to a century and can go for years without food. It was discovered by the 17th-century Slovenian polymath Janez Vajkard Valvasor, who named it after the protector of Poseidon's sea creatures in Greek mythology and the Latin word for 'snake'.

*Proteus anguinus* is 25cm to 30cm long and is a bundle of contradictions. It has a long tail fin that it uses for swimming, but can also propel itself with its four legs (the front pair have three small 'fingers' and the back have two 'toes'). Though blind, *Proteus anguinus* has an excellent sense of smell and is sensitive to weak electric fields in the water. It uses these to move around in the dark, locate prey and communicate. It breathes through frilly, bright-red gills at the base of its head when submerged, but also has rudimentary lungs for breathing when outside the water. The human-like skin has no pigmentation whatsoever, but looks pink in the light due to blood circulation.

The question that scientists have asked themselves for three centuries is: how do they reproduce? The salamander's reproduction has never been witnessed in a natural state, and they haven't been very cooperative in captivity. It is almost certain that they hatch their young from eggs and don't reach sexual maturity until the (almost human) age of 16 or 18 years.

of the deep; most are so minuscule you can hardly see them.

Predjama, a village 9km northwest of Postojna, consists of half a dozen houses, an inn, a mock-medieval jousting course and the remarkable **Predjama Castle** ( ☎ 751 60 15; adult/student/child €5/3.50/2.90; ☺ 9am-7pm May-Sep, 10am-6pm Apr & Oct, 10am-4pm Nov-Mar), which actually appears to grow out of a yawning cave. The partly furnished interior boasts costumed wax mannequins, one of which dangles from the dripping rock-roofed torture chamber. Beneath are stalactite-adorned **caves** (adult/student/child €5/3.50/2.90, cave & castle combination ticket €9/6.30/5.20), which lack Postojna's crowds but also much of its grandeur.

## Sleeping & Eating

Lots of houses in Postojna rent out **private rooms** (per person €13.90-15.80). Your best contact is **Kompas Postojna** ( ☎ 721 14 80; info@kompas-postojna.si; Titov trg 2a; ☺ 8am-8pm Mon-Fri, 9am-1pm Sat Jun-Aug, 8am-7pm Mon-Fri, 9am-1pm Sat May, Sep & Oct, 8am-5pm Mon-Fri, 9am-1pm Sat Nov-Apr).

**Hotel & Hostel Sport** ( ☎ 720 622 44; www.sport-hotel .si; Kolodvorska c 1; dm €13-15, s €34-38, d €43-56; ☒ ▢ ) This recent arrival, with 37 spic-and-span and very comfortable rooms, including 40 hostel beds, is just 300m north of the centre of Postojna. True to its name, it can arrange all sorts of activities, including mountain-biking trips in nearby Notranjska Regional Park.

**Pizzeria Minutka** ( ☎ 720 36 25; Ljubljanska c 1; pizza €4.20-5.85; ☺ 10am-11pm) A pizzeria with a terrace, Minutka is a favourite with locals and is just south of the Hotel & Hostel Sport.

## Getting There & Away

Buses from Ljubljana to Koper, Piran or Novo Gorica all stop in Postojna (€5.75, one hour, 54km, half-hourly). The train is less useful, as the train station is 1km east of town near the bypass (ie 3km from the caves).

As close as you'll get by local bus from Postojna to Predjama (€1.70, 15 minutes, 9km, five daily Monday to Friday) and during the school year only is Bukovje, a village about 2km northeast of Predjama. A taxi from Postojna, including an hour's wait at Predjama Castle, will cost €25, which staff at Kompas Postojna can arrange.

## ŠKOCJAN CAVES

☎ 05

The immense **Škocjan Caves** ( ☎ 763 28 40, 708 21 10; www.park-skocjanske-jame.si; Škocjan 2; adult/student/child

€10.85/7.50), a Unesco World Heritage site since 1986, are far more captivating than the larger one at Postojna, and for many travellers a visit here will be one of the highlights of their trip to Slovenia – a page right out of Jules Verne's *A Journey to the Centre of the Earth*. With relatively few stalactites, the attraction is the sheer depth of the awesome underground chasm, which you cross by a dizzying little footbridge. To see this you must join a shepherded two-hour walking tour, involving hundreds of steps and ending with a rickety funicular ride. Tours depart hourly from 10am to 5pm from May to September, and 10am, 1pm and 3.30pm in April, May and October, and 10am and 1pm Monday to Saturday, and 10am, 1pm and 3pm Sunday from November to March.

The nearest town with accommodation is **Divača** (population 1300), 5km to the northwest. Here **Gostilna Malovec** ( ☎ 763 02 00; Kraška 30a; s/d €20/40) has a half-dozen basic but comfortable renovated rooms in a building beside its popular restaurant (entrées €3.35 to €5.85, mains €5 to €9.10; open 7am to 10pm). For something a bit more, well, 21st century, cross the road to **Orient Express** ( ☎ 763 30 10; Kraška c 67; pizza €5-10.85; ☺ 11am-11pm Sun-Fri, 11am-2am Sat), a lively pizzeria and pub.

Buses from Ljubljana to Koper and the coast stop at Divača (€7.60, 1½ hours, 82km, half-hourly), as do trains (€5.90, 1½ hours, 104km, hourly). Staff at both the train station and at helpful **Kraški Turist** ( ☎ 041-573 768; kraskiturist@gmail.com; ☺ 8am-5pm Apr-Oct) next to the small café at the station can provide you with a photocopied route map for walking to the caves. Alternatively, Kraški Turist has bicycles for hire (€1.25/8.35 per hour/day) and can arrange transport for around €5 per person.

## LIPICA

☎ 05 / pop 130

Lipica is where Austrian Archduke Charles, son of Ferdinand I, established a stud farm to breed horses for the Spanish Riding School in Vienna in 1580.

The snow-white beasties are still bred here at the **Lipica Stud Farm** ( ☎ 739 15 80; www.lipica.org; Lipica 5; adult/student from €7/3.50), which offers equestrian fans a variety of tours, as well as rides and lessons. Tour times are too complex and varied to list here, please contact the farm for details.

The 68-room **Hotel Maestoso** ( ☎ 739 15 80; www .lipica.org; s €53-68, d €82-106; ▢ ☖ ) has excellently appointed modern rooms looking over the golf links–like landscape.

## KOPER

☎ 05 / pop 23,270

By far the largest town on the Slovenian coast, Koper (Capodistria in Italian) is a workaday port city that at first glance scarcely seems to give tourism a second thought. Yet its central core is delightfully quiet, quaint and much less touristy than its ritzy cousin Piran, 17km down the coast.

Koper grew rich as a key port trading salt, and was the capital of Istria under the 15th- and 16th-century Venetian Republic. At that time it was an island commanding a U-shaped bay of saline ponds, something hard to imagine now, given the centuries of land reclamation that have joined it very firmly to the mainland.

### Orientation

The joint bus and train station is 1.4km southeast of central Titov trg. To walk into town, just head north along Kolodvorska c in the direction of the cathedral's distinctive campanile (bell tower). Alternatively, take bus 1, 2 or 3 to Muda Gate.

### Information

**Banka Koper** (Kidričeva ul 14; ☽ 8.30am–noon & 3-5pm Mon-Fri, 8.30am-noon Sat)

**Kompas** ( ☎ 663 05 82; Pristaniška ul 17; ☽ 8am-7.30pm Mon-Fri, 8am-1pm Sat) Has private rooms.

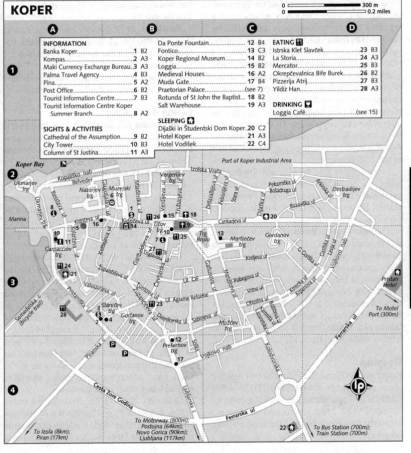

## KOPER

0 _____ 300 m
0 _____ 0.2 miles

**INFORMATION**
Banka Koper.................................1 B2
Kompas........................................2 A3
Maki Currency Exchange Bureau..3 A3
Palma Travel Agency....................4 B3
Pina.............................................5 A2
Post Office...................................6 B2
Tourist Information Centre...........7 B3
Tourist Information Centre Koper
   Summer Branch.......................8 A2

**SIGHTS & ACTIVITIES**
Cathedral of the Assumption.......9 B2
City Tower..................................10 B3
Column of St Justina..................11 A3

Da Ponte Fountain....................12 B4
Fontico......................................13 C3
Koper Regional Museum...........14 B2
Loggia.......................................15 B2
Medieval Houses.......................16 A2
Muda Gate................................17 B4
Praetorian Palace..................(see 7)
Rotunda of St John the Baptist..18 B2
Salt Warehouse.........................19 A3

**SLEEPING** 🏠
Dijaški in Študentski Dom Koper.20 C2
Hotel Koper...............................21 A3
Hotel Vodišek...........................22 C4

**EATING** 🍴
Istrska Klet Slavček....................23 B3
La Storia....................................24 A3
Mercator....................................25 B3
Okrepčevalnica Bife Burek........26 B2
Pizzerija Atrij.............................27 B3
Yildiz Han..................................28 A3

**DRINKING** 🍷
Loggia Café..........................(see 15)

**Maki Currency Exchange Bureau** (Pristaniška ul 13; 7.30am-7.30pm Mon-Fri, 7.30am-1pm Sat)

**Palma Travel Agency** ( ☎ 663 36 60; Pristaniška ul 21; 8am-7pm Mon-Fri, 8am-noon Sat) Can arrange private rooms.

**Pina** ( ☎ 627 80 72; Kidričeva ul 43; adult/student per hr €3.75/1.25; 9am-9pm Mon-Fri) Central internet café with 10 terminals.

**Tourist Information Centre** main branch ( ☎ 664 64 03; tic@koper.si; Praetorian Palace, Titov trg 3; 8am-9pm Jul & Aug, 9am-5pm Sun Sep-Jun); summer branch ( ☎ 663 20 10; Ukmarjev trg 7; 8am-9pm Jul & Aug)

## Sights

The greatest attraction of Koper is aimless wandering. You change centuries abruptly passing through the **Muda Gate** (1516). Continue north past the **Da Ponte Fountain** (Prešernov trg), erected in 1666, and up Župančičeva ul and Čevljarska ul, the narrow commercial artery, to reach Titov trg. This fine central square is dominated by the 1480 **City Tower** attached to the part-Gothic, part-Renaissance **Cathedral of the Assumption**. The renovated 15th-century **Praetorian Palace** (Titov trg 3; admission free) contains the town hall, with exhibits on the 1st floor and an old pharmacy and the tourist office on the ground floor. Opposite, the splendid 1463 **Loggia** is now an elegant yet affordable café (opposite). To the east of it is the circular Romanesque **Rotunda of St John the Baptist**, a baptistery dating from the second half of the 12th century.

Several more fine façades face **Trg Brolo**, a wide, peacefully Mediterranean square to the southeast. One is the shield-dotted **Fontico** that started life as a grain warehouse in the late 14th century.

The **Koper Regional Museum** ( ☎ 663 35 70; Kidričeva ul 19; adult/child €1.70/1.25; 10am-6pm Tue-Fri, 9am-1pm Sat & Sun) is inside the Belgramoni-Tacco Palace and contains an Italianate sculpture garden. Kidričeva ul also has a few appealing **medieval houses** with beamed overhangs. It leads west into Carpacciov trg, the former fish market with a 15th-century **salt warehouse** and a stone **Column of St Justina**, topped with a statue of St Justina and dating from 1571.

## Sleeping

Kompas (p847) and the Palma Travel Agency (above) can arrange **private rooms** (s €12.50-14.60, d €20.85-25) and **apartments** (apt for 2 €29.20-35.40, apt for 4 €43.80-54.20). Most rooms and apartments are in the new town beyond the train station, however.

**Motel Port** ( ☎ 639 32 60; motel.port@siol.net; Ankaranska c 7; dm €14, rm for up to 3/4 €46/65; ) Hidden on the top floor of a Mondrianesque shopping centre south of the Old Town, this place has excellent en suite rooms, but its location beside a truck terminal results in a deep traffic rumble and the mainly male, lorry-driver clientele may discourage single women.

**Dijaški in Študentski Dom Koper** ( ☎ 662 62 50; www.d-dom.kp.edus.si, in Slovene; Cankarjeva ul 5; dm €15; late Jun-late Aug; ) In summer this relatively central student dormitory becomes a hostel. Try to arrive early, as it gets booked up fast.

**Hotel Vodišek** ( ☎ 639 24 68; www.hotel-vodisek.com; Kolodvorska c 2; s/d/tr €40/60/75; ) This tiny hotel, with 32 reasonably priced rooms is in a shopping centre halfway between the Old Town and the train and bus stations. TheIt has wheelchair access, and use of bicycles is free for guests.

**Hotel Koper** ( ☎ 610 05 00; www.terme-catez.si; Pristaniška ul 3; s €60, d €100-110; ) This pleasant, 65-room property on the very edge of the historic Old Town is the only central hotel in Koper. RatesIt has wheelchair access, and rates include entry to Aquapark at the Hotel Žusterna.

## Eating & Drinking

**Okrepčevalnica Bife Burek** ( ☎ 271 347; Kidričeva ul 8; snacks €1.50-2.10; 7am-10pm) Buy good-value *burek* and pizza slices here and enjoy them at Titov trg for a take-away snack.

**Yildiz Han** ( ☎ 626 14 60; Pristaniška ul 2; entrées €2.70-5, mains €6.90-10.20; noon-midnight) 'Star House', a branch of a similarly named establishment in Ljubljana, has all our Turkish favourites, including *sigara böreği* (filo parcels filled with cheese) and *yaprak dolmasi* (stuffed vine leaves), as well as kebabs.

**Istrska Klet Slavček** ( ☎ 627 67 29; Župančičeva ul 39; dishes €3.35-10.85; 7am-10pm Mon-Fri) This 'Istrian Cellar', situated in the 18th-century Carli Palace, is one of the most colourful places for a meal in the Old Town. Filling set lunches go for less than €10, and there's Malvazija and Teran wine drawn straight from the barrel.

**Pizzerija Atrij** ( ☎ 626 28 03; Triglavska ul 2; pizza €4.20-6.05; 9am-10pm Mon-Fri, 10am-10pm Sat) This popular pizzeria down an alleyway no wider than your average quarterback's shoulder spread has a small back garden.

**La Storia** ( ☎ 031-769 079; Pristaniška ul 3; entrées €4.80-6.70, mains €5-10; 11am-9pm Mon-Fri, noon-5pm Sat & Sun) This Italian-style trattoria in the same building as the Hotel Koper focuses on pasta dishes and salads, and has outside seating in the warmer months. The salad bar (small/large €2.30/3.35) is good value.

**Mercator** (Titov trg 2; 7am-8pm Mon-Fri, 7am-1pm Sat, 8am-noon Sun) This small supermarket branch in the Old Town also opens on weekends.

**Loggia Café** ( 621 32 13; Titov trg 1; 7.30am-10pm Mon-Sat, 10am-10pm Sun) This lovely café in the exquisite 15th-century Loggia is the best vantage point for watching the crowds on Titov trg.

## Getting There & Away

Buses run to Piran (€2.60, 30 minutes, 18km) half-hourly on weekdays and every 40 minutes on weekends. Up to 15 buses daily run to Ljubljana (€10.35, 1¾ to 2½ hours, 120km), though the train is more comfortable, with IC services (€8.70, 2¼ hours) at 5.55am and 2.45pm, and local services (€7.30, 2½ hours) at 10.03am and 7.12pm.

Buses to Trieste (€3, one hour, 23km, up to 13 daily) run along the coast via Ankaran and Muggia on weekdays only. Destinations in Croatia include Rijeka (€7.60, two hours, 84km, 10.10am Monday to Friday), Rovinj (€11.10, 129km, three hours, 3.55pm daily July and August) via Poreč (€8, two hours, 88km), plus two or three to Poreč only, notably at 8.30am Monday to Friday.

## IZOLA

☎ 05 / pop 10,425

Overshadowed by much-more genteel Piran, Izola (Isola in Italian) is bypassed by most foreign visitors and, frankly, the locals don't seem to give a damn. This also-ran place does have a certain Venetian charm, a few narrow old streets, and some nice waterfront bars and restaurants. Ask the helpful **Tourist Information Centre Izola** ( 640 10 50; tic.izola@izola .si; Sončno nabrežje 4; 9am-9pm Mon-Sat, 10am-5pm Sun Jun-Sep, 8am-7pm Mon-Fri, 8am-5pm Sat Oct-May) about private rooms, or in summer check out the 174-bed **Dijaški Dom Izola** ( 662 1740; branko .miklobusec@guest.arnes.si; Prekomorskih Brigad ul 7; dm from €20; Jul & Aug; ) which overlooks the marina and offers about the cheapest beds you'll find within striking distance of Piran. Because of the lack of tourists Izola is a good place to enjoy a seafood meal, especially at **Ribič** ( 641 83 13; Veliki trg 3; entrées €4.20-8.75, mains €8-17.50; 8am-1am), a venue much loved by locals. Out in Izola's industrial suburbs, **Ambasada Gavioli** ( 641 8212; www.ambasada-gavioli.com; Industrijska c; midnight-6am Sat) remains Slovenia's

top nightrave club, featuring a procession of international star DJs.

Frequent buses between Koper (€1.70, 15 minutes, 6km) and Piran (€1.70, 20 minutes, 9.5km) go via Izola, and there's a catamaran service to Venice (p857).

## PIRAN

☎ 05 / pop 4050

Everyone's favourite town on the Slovenian coast, picturesque little Piran (Pirano in Italian) sits on the tip of a narrow peninsula, the westernmost point of Slovenian Istria. Strunjan Bay is to the north; Piran Bay and Portorož, Slovenia's largest beach resort, lie to the south. Piran's Old Town is a gem of Venetian Gothic architecture and is full of narrow streets. In summer the town gets pretty overrun by tourists, but in April or October it's hard not to fall in love with the winding Venetian-Gothic alleyways and tempting seafood restaurants. It's thought that the town's name comes from the Greek word for fire *(pyr)*. In ancient times fires were lit at Punta, the very tip of the peninsula, to guide ships to the port at Aegida (now Koper).

## Orientation

Buses from everywhere except Portorož arrive at the bus station, just a 300m stroll along the portside Cankarjevo nabrežje from central Tartinijev trg. Be warned that a car is an encumbrance, not a help in Piran. Vehicles are stopped at a tollgate 200m south of the bus station, where the sensible choice is to use the huge Fornače car park (€0.80/7.70 per hour/day €0.80/7.70). You could take a ticket and drive on into the town centre (first hour free, then €2.70 per hour) but old Piran is so small, parking is so limited and its alleyways so narrow (mostly footpaths) that you're likely to regret it.

## Information

**Banka Koper** (Tartinijev trg 12; 8.30am-noon & 3-5pm Mon-Fri, 8.30am-noon Sat)

**Cyber Point Piran** ( 671 00 22; http://cyberpoint .ksop-cscp.si, in Slovene; 4th fl, Študentek Bldg, Župančičeva ul 14; per hr €4.20; 1-9pm Mon-Fri) Internet access on five terminals.

**Maona Tourist Agency** ( 673 45 20; www.maona .si; Cankarjevo nabrežje 7; 9am-7pm Mon-Fri, 10am-1pm & 5-7pm Sat, 10am-1pm Sun) Unstintingly helpful travel agency can organise anything from private rooms to activities and cruises.

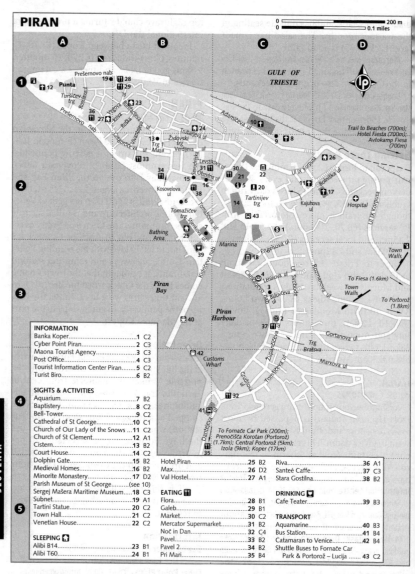

**PIRAN**

GULF OF TRIESTE

Piran Bay

Piran Harbour

Customs Wharf

SLOVENIA

**Tourist Information Center Piran** ( ☎ 673 02 20; www.piran.si; Tartinijev trg; ⏰ 9am-1.30pm & 3-9pm mid-Jun–mid-Sep, 10am-5pm mid-Sep–mid-Jun) Located in the impressive Town Hall.

## Sights & Activities

Piran is continuously watched over by the **Cathedral of St George** (Adamičeva ul 2). If time weighs on your hands, visit the attached **Parish Museum of St George** ( ☎ 673 34 40; admission €1; ⏰ 11am-5pm), which contains church plate, paintings and a lapidary. The cathedral's freestanding **bell tower** (1608) was clearly modelled on the campanile at San Marco's Basilica in Venice, and its octagonal **baptistery** dating from the mid-17th century has imaginatively recycled a 2nd-century Roman sarcophagus for use as a baptismal font. The **Minorite Monastery** ( ☎ 673 44 17; Bolniška ul 20) on the way down to Tartinijev trg has a delightful cloister, and in the **Church of Our Lady of the Snows** almost opposite is a superb 15th-century arch painting of the Crucifixion. The **Sergej Mašera Maritime Museum** ( ☎ 671 00 40; Cankarjevo nabrežje 3; adult/student €2.50/2.10; ☼ 9am-noon & 6-9pm Tue-Sun Jul & Aug, 9am-noon & 3-6pm Tue-Sun Sep-Jun) has 2000-year-old Roman amphorae beneath the glass ground floor, and lots of impressive antique ships' models and ex-voto offerings upstairs.

One of Piran's most eye-catching structures is the red 15th-century **Venetian House** (Tartinijev trg 4), with its tracery windows and stone lion relief. When built this would have overlooked Piran's inner port, which was filled to form Tartinijev trg in 1894. The square is named in honour of the violinist and composer Giuseppe Tartini (1692–1770), who was born in what is now the house at Tartinijev trg 7 and whose **statue** stands in the middle of the square. The square is dominated to the north by the porticoed 19th-century **Town Hall**, which houses the tourist office, and to the west by the **Court House**. The **Aquarium** ( ☎ 673 25 72; Kidričevo nabrežje 4; adult/child €2.50/1.70; ☼ 10am-noon & 2-7pm late Mar–mid-Jun, Sep–mid-Oct, 9am-10pm mid-Jun–Aug), south of the square along the harbour, has a tremendous variety of sea life packed into its two-dozen tanks.

Behind the market north of Tartinijev trg, **medieval homes** have been built into an ancient defensive wall along Obzidna ul, which passes under the 15th-century **Dolphin Gate**. **Trg 1 Maja** (1st May Sq) may sound like a socialist parade ground, but in fact it's one of Piran's most attractive squares, with a **cistern** dating from the late 18th century. Rainwater from the surrounding roofs flowed into it through the fish borne by the two stone putti in the back.

Punta, the historical 'snout' of Piran, still has a **lighthouse**, but today's is small and modern. Just behind it, however, the round, serrated tower of 18th-century **Church of St Clement** evokes the ancient beacon from which Piran likely got its name.

Most water-related activities take place in Portorož, but if you want to give diving a go, **Subnet** ( ☎ 673 22 18; www.sub-net.si; Prešernovo nabrežje 24; shore/boat dive €25/40; ☼ 9am-noon & 2-6pm Sun-Fri, 9am-noon & 2-7pm Sat) organises shore and boat-guided dives, gives PADI open-water courses (around €150) and hires equipment. Don't expect Red Sea–style coralcorals in these parts,

though. The most unusual underwater sight hereabouts is the wreck of a WWII seaplane in Portorož Bay.

## Sleeping

**Private rooms** (s €15.85-25, d €23-35) and **apartments** (apt for 2 people €36.30-44.20, for 4 €56-72) are available through Maona Tourist Agency (p849) and the **Turist Biro** ( ☎ 673 25 09; www.turistbiro-ag.si; Tomažičeva ul 3; ☼ 10am-1pm & 4-7pm Mon-Fri, 10am-1pm Sat & sun), opposite the Hotel Piran.

**Avtokamp Fiesa** ( ☎ 674 62 30, 031-487 255; autocamp .fiesa@siol.net; adult €8.35-10, child €2.50; ☼ May-Sep) The closest camping ground to Piran is at Fiesa, 4km by road but less than 1km if you follow the coastal trail east of the Cathedral of St George. It's tiny and becomes very crowded in summer.

**Val Hostel** ( ☎ 673 25 55; www.hostel-val.com; Gregor-čičeva ul 38a; with/without HI card €20/24 Jun-Aug, €18/23 Sep-May; ✗ 🖳 ) This central partially renovated hostel has 22 rooms, with shared shower, free internet access, kitchen and washing machine. It's a great favourite with backpackers.

**Alibi B14** ( ☎ 031-363 666; www.alibi.si; Bonifacijeva ul 14; per person €20-25; ✗ 🖳 ) The most welcome arrival on the budget/midrange accommodation scene in Piran in years is this upbeat and colourful four-floor party hostel, with six rooms, each with four to six beds, kitchenette and bath. It's in ancient townhouse on a narrow street, and there's a washing machine and free internet access.

**Alibi T60** (Trubarjeva ul 60; per person €30; ✗ 🎮 🖳 ) Even better is Alibi B14's sister-hostel, the more subdued Alibi T60, to the east, with a fully equipped double on each of its five floors. The top room's view terrace view is priceless. Reception is at Alibi B14.

**Hotel Fiesa** ( ☎ 671 22 00; www.hotel-fiesa.com; Fiesa 57; s €53-70, d €75-98) Although not in Piran itself, this 22-room hotel overlooking the sea near the Avtokamp Fiesa camping ground is one of the most atmospheric places to stay in the area.

**Max** ( ☎ 673 34 36, 041-692 928; www.maxpiran.com; Ul IX Korpusa 26; s/d €50/60; ✗ 🖳 ) Piran's most romantic accommodation option has rooms, each named rather than numbered, in a delightful, very pink townhouse just down from the cathedral.

**Hotel Piran** ( ☎ 676 21 00; www.hoteli-piran.si; Stjenk-ova ul 1; s €57-84, d €70-123, ste €131-181; ✗ 🎮 🖳 ) The Hotel Piran has 80 rooms and 10 apartments, and is right on the water.

## Eating & Drinking

One of Piran's attractions is its plethora of fish restaurants, especially along Prešernovo nabrežje, though don't expect any bargains. Virtually all charge around €6.25 for a plate of grilled squid and from €33.40 per kg for fish.

**Pavel** ( ☎ 674 71 01; Gregorčičeva ul 3; ⏲ 11am-11pm) This fish restaurant – the granddaddy of them all – and its sister-eatery nearby, **Pavel 2** ( ☎ 674 71 02; Kosovelova ul 1; ⏲ 11am-midnight), cater to the tourist trade and are somewhat overpriced; expect to pay about €25 per person with house wine.

**Flora** ( ☎ 673 12 58; Prešernovo nabrežje 26; pizza €3.35-5.85; ⏲ 8am-1am Jul & Aug, 10am-10pm Sep-Jun) The terrace of this simple pizzeria east of the Punta lighthouse has uninterrupted views of the Adriatic.

**Pri Mari** ( ☎ 673 47 35, 041-616 488; Dantejeva ul 17; entrées €3.75-8.30, mains €6.25-14.60; ⏲ noon-10pm Tue-Sat, noon-6pm Sun) This very stylish restaurant south of the bus station makes an ambitious (and successful) attempt at combining Mediterranean and Slovenian food. Service is slow, so go with time on your hands.

**Stara Gostilna** ( ☎ 673 31 65; Savudrijska ul 2; entrées €4.20-7, mains €5.85-14.60; ⏲ 9am-11pm) This delightful bistro in the Old Town serves both meat and fish dishes, and offers some of the best and most welcoming service in town.

**Riva** ( ☎ 673 22 25; Gregorčičeva ul 43; entrées €5-8.30, mains €5-16.60; ⏲ 9am-midnight) Our new favourite (and very classy) seafood restaurant on Prešernovo nabrežje has the best sea views, décor and a pizzeria (pizza €4.20 to €5.40) next door for ichthyphobes.

**Galeb** ( ☎ 673 32 25; Pusterla ul 5; meals from €14.60; ⏲ 11am-4pm & 6pm-midnight Wed-Mon) This excellent family-run restaurant is east of the Punta lighthouse. It's totally nonsmoking.

**Santeé Caffe** ( ☎ 051-309 980; Cankarjevo nabrežje 11; sandwiches from €1.25, salads €4.20; ⏲ 7am-midnight) The hyperfriendly Santeé Caffe has sandwiches (€1.25 to €3.10) and salads (€4.20), and walls painted in colours as vivid as its excellent ice creams.

**Café Teater** ( ☎ 041-638 933; Stjenkova ul 1; ⏲ 7am-3am Mon-Fri, 9am-3am Sat & Sun) Anyone who's anyone in Piran can be found at this café, with a waterfront terrace and antique furnishings.

There's an outdoor **market** (Zelenjavni trg; ⏲ 7am-2pm Mon-Sat) in the small square behind the Town Hall. There's a small **Mercator** (Levstikova ul 3; ⏲ 7am-8pm Mon-Fri, 7am-1pm Sat, 8-11am Sun) supermarket in the Old Town, and a **Noč**

**in Dan** ( ☎ 671 57 52; Tomšičeva ul 41; ⏲ 7am-midnight) branch opposite the bus station.

## Getting There & Away

From the bus station buses run every 30 to 40 minutes to Koper (€2.60, half-hour, 18km) via Izola, while five daily (Monday to Friday only) head for Trieste (€4.60, 1¾ hours, 36km) and up to eight daily to Ljubljana (€11.70, 2½ to three hours, 140km) via Divača and Postojna.

From Tartinijev trg, shuttle buses (€1) travel to Portorož–Lucija (bus 1) and Portorož via Strunjan (bus 3).

Piran and Izola despatch catamarans to Venice (p857) at least once a week.

## PORTOROŽ
☎ 05 / pop 2800

Portorož (Portorose in Italian), Slovenia's biggest resort, can be a bit honky-tonk, especially along Obala, the main drag, but it isn't all bad. Its sandy beaches are the largest on the coast and are relatively clean, there are pleasant spas and wellness centres where you can take the waters or cover yourself in curative mud, and the list of other activities is endless. At the same time the vast array of accommodation options makes Portorož a useful fall back if everything's full in nearby Piran. Full listings are available at the **Tourist Information Centre Portorož** ( ☎ 674 02 31; www.portoroz.si; Obala 16; ⏲ 9am-1.30pm & 3-9pm mid-Jun–mid-Sep, 10am-5pm mid-Sep–mid-Jun). Just off the main road between Piran and the centre of Portorož, the unusually upmarket, summer-only hostel **Prenočišča Korotan** ( ☎ 674 5400; www.sd.upr.si/sdp/prenocisca; Obala 11; s/d/tr €29/41/55; ⏲ Jul & Aug; ▯ ) in Korotan has en suite rooms and its internet computers are open to nonguests year-round. Most of Portorož is high-rise city. For something on a more human scale, check out the lovely 48-room **Hotel Marco** ( ☎ 617 40 00; www.hotel-marko.com; Obala 28; s €54-83, d €67-104), with lovely gardens and just opposite the beach.

The pleasant cantina **Papa Chico** ( ☎ 677 93 10; Obala 26; entrées €3.75-5.45, mains €4.60-8.75; ⏲ 9am-2am Mon-Sat, 10am-2am Sun) serves 'Mexican fun food' (go figure), including fajitas (€7.50 to €9.20).

The über-designer café **Kavarna Cacao** ( ☎ 674 10 35; Obala 14; ⏲ 8am-3am) wins the award as the most stylish on the coast, with a fabulous terrace.

There are dozens of decent pizzerias all along Obala, but the place of choice is **Pizzeria Figarola** ( ☎ 674 22 00; Obala 14a; pizza €5.65-7.50; ⏲ 10am-10pm), with a huge terrace just up from the main pier, serving pizza and pasta dishes.

Every 20 minutes, shuttle bus 1 (€1) from Piran trundles right along Obala to Lucija, passing by Prenočišča Korotan.

# SLOVENIA DIRECTORY

## ACCOMMODATION

Accommodation listings throughout this guide have been ordered by price – from the cheapest to the most expensive. Very, very roughly, budget accommodation means a double room under €50, midrange is €51 to €100 and top end is anything over €101.

Camping grounds generally charge per person, whether you're in a tent or caravan. Rates always include hot showers. Almost all sites close from mid-October to mid-April. Camping 'rough' is illegal in Slovenia, and this is enforced, especially around Bled. Seek out the Slovenian Tourist Board's *Camping in Slovenia.*

Slovenia's growing stable of hostels includes Ljubljana's trendy Celica and the Alibi hostels found both in the capital and at Piran. Throughout the country there are student dorms moonlighting as hostels in July and August. Unless stated otherwise hostel rooms share bathrooms. They typically cost €13 to €21; prices are at their highest in midsummer, when it can sometimes be difficult to find accommodation at any price.

Tourist information offices can help you access extensive networks of private rooms, apartments and tourist farms, or they can recommend private agencies that will. Such accommodation can appear misleadingly cheap if you carelessly overlook the 30% to 50% surcharge levied on stays of less than three nights. Also beware that many such properties are in outlying villages with minimal public transport, and that the cheapest one-star category rooms with shared bathroom are actually very rare, so you'll often pay well above the quoted minimum. Depending on the season you might save a little money by going directly to any house with a sign reading *sobe* (rooms).

Guesthouses, known as a *penzion, gostišče,* or *prenočišča,* are often cosy and better value than full-blown hotels, some of which are unattractive if well-renovated socialist-era holdovers. Nonetheless it can be difficult to find a double room in a hotel for under €50. Beware that locally listed rates are usually quoted per person assuming double occupancy. A tourist tax – routinely €0.65 to €1 per person and a hefty single-occupancy supplement – often lurk in the footnotes. Unless otherwise indicated, room rates include en suite toilet, shower with towels and soap, and breakfast.

## ACTIVITIES

Slovenia is a very well-organised place for all outdoor activities.

### Extreme Sports

Several areas specialise in adrenaline-rush activities, the greatest range being available at Bovec, famous for white-water rafting, hydro-speed, kayaking and canyoning – ie sliding down and through waterfalls and gullies in a neoprene wetsuit with the assistance of a well-trained (and licensed) guide. Bovec is also a great place for paragliding; in winter you ascend Mt Kanin (below) via ski lift and then jump off. Gliding costs are very reasonable from Lesce near Bled. Scuba diving from Piran is also good value.

### Hiking

Hiking is extremely popular, with the **Alpine Association of Slovenia** (www.pzs.si) counting some 55,000 members and Ljubljančani flocking in droves to Triglav National Park on weekends. There are around 7000km of waymarked paths, and in summer 167 mountain huts offer comfortable trailside refuge. Several shorter treks are outlined in the Sunflower Guide *Slovenia* (www.sunflowerbooks.co.uk), now in its 2nd edition.

### Skiing

Skiing is a Slovenian passion, with slopes particularly crowded over the Christmas holidays and early in February; see **Slovenia – Official Travel Guide** (www.slovenia-tourism.si/skiing) for much more information.

Just west of Maribor in eastern Slovenia (the country's second-largest city) is a popular choice and the biggest downhill skiing area in the country. Although relatively low (336m to 1347m), it's easily accessible, with very varied downhill pistes and relatively short lift queues.

Kranjska Gora (up to 1291m) has some challenging runs, and the world record for ski-jumping was set at nearby Planica. Above Lake Bohinj, Vogel (up to 1800m) is particularly scenic, as is Kanin (up to 2300m) above Bovec, which can have snow as late as May. Being relatively close to Ljubljana, Krvavec (up to 1970m), northeast of Kranj, can have particularly long lift queues.

## Other Activities

Mountain bikes are available for hire from travel agencies at Bovec, Bled and Bohinj. The hire season is usually limited to May to October, however.

The Soča River near Kobarid and the Sava Bohinjka near Bohinj are great for fly-fishing (season April to October). Licences (per day €5, catch and release €34) are sold at tourist offices and certain hotels.

Spas and wellness centres are very popular in Slovenia; see **Slovenia Spas** (www.terme-giz.si) for more information. Most towns have some sort of spa complex, and hotels often offer free or bargain-rate entry to their guests. One of the most celebrated spa towns in the country is Rogaška Slatina, close to the Croatian border about 40km east of Celje.

## BUSINESS HOURS

All businesses post their opening times (delovni čas) on the door. Many shops close Saturday afternoons. Sundays are still 'holy'; although a handful of grocery stores open, including some branches of the ubiquitous Mercator chain. Most museums close on Monday. Banks often take lunch breaks from 12.30pm to 2pm and only a few open on Saturday morning.

Restaurants typically open for lunch and dinner until at least 10pm, and bars until midnight, though they may have longer hours on the weekend and shorter ones on Sunday.

## EMBASSIES & CONSULATES
### Slovenian Embassies & Consulates

Slovenian representations abroad are fully listed on **Government of the Republic of Slovenia – Ministry of Foreign Affairs** (www.mzz.gov.si) and include the following embassies:**Australia** ( ☎ 02-6243 4830; vca@gov.si; 6th fl, St George's Bldg, 60 Marcus Clarke St, Canberra ACT 2601)

**Austria** ( ☎ 01-586 13 09; vdu@gov.si; Nibelungengasse 13, A-1010 Vienna)

**Canada** ( ☎ 613-565 5781; vot@gov.si; Ste 2101, 150 Metcalfe St, Ottawa K2P 1P1)

**Croatia** ( ☎ 01-63 11 000; vzg@gov.si; Savska c 41, 10000 Zagreb)

**Hungary** ( ☎ 01-438 5600; vbp@gov.si; Cseppkő út 68, 1025 Budapest)

**Ireland** ( ☎ 01-670 5240; vdb@gov.si; 2nd fl, Morrison Chambers, 32 Nassau St, Dublin 2)

**Italy** ( ☎ 06-80 914 310; vri@gov.si; Via Leonardo Pisano 10, 00197 Rome)

**Netherlands** ( ☎ 070-310 86 90; vhg@gov.si; Anna Paulownastraat 11, 2518 BA Den Haag)

**UK** ( ☎ 020-7222 5400; vlo@gov.si; 10 Little College St, London SW1P 3SH)

**USA** ( ☎ 202-667 5363; vwa@gov.si; 1525 New Hampshire Ave NW, Washington, DC 20036)

### Embassies & Consulates in Slovenia

Following are among the embassies and consulates in Ljubljana:**Australia** Consulate ( ☎ 01-425 42 52; 12th fl, Trg Republike 3; 🕑 9am-1pm Mon-Fri)

**Austria** Embassy ( ☎ 01-479 07 00; Prešernova c 23; 🕑 8am-noon Mon-Thu, 8-11am Fri) Enter from Veselova ul.

**Canada** Consulate ( ☎ 01-430 35 70; Dunajska c 22; 🕑 9am-noon Mon-Fri)

**Croatia** Embassy ( ☎ 01-425 62 20; Gruberjevo nabrežje 6; 🕑 10am-1pm Mon-Fri)

**Hungary** Embassy ( ☎ 01-512 18 82; ul Konrada Babnika 5; 🕑 9am-noon Mon, Wed & Fri)

**Ireland** Embassy ( ☎ 01-300 89 70; Poljanski nasip 6; 🕑 9am-12.30pm & 2.30-4.30pm Mon-Fri)

**Italy** Embassy ( ☎ 01-426 21 94; Snežniška ul 8; 🕑 9-11am Mon-Fri)

**Netherlands** Embassy ( ☎ 01-420 14 61; Poljanski nasip 6; 🕑 9am-noon Mon-Fri)

**New Zealand** Consulate ( ☎ 01-580 30 55; Verovškova ul 57; 🕑 8am-3pm Mon-Fri)

**South Africa** Consulate ( ☎ 01-200 63 00; Pražakova ul 4; 🕑 3-4pm Tue)

**UK** Embassy ( ☎ 01-200 39 10; 4th fl, Trg Republike 3; 🕑 9am-noon Mon-Fri)

**USA** Embassy ( ☎ 01-200 55 00; Prešernova c 31; 🕑 9-11.30am Mon-Fri)

## FESTIVALS & EVENTS

Major cultural and sporting events are listed under 'Events' on the website of the **Slovenian Tourist Board** (www.slovenia-tourism.si) and in the STB's annual Calendar of Major Events in Slovenia. Among the most important and/or colourful are **Kurentovanje** (www.kurentovanje.net) in Ptuj, a 'rite of spring' celebrated for 10 days up to Shrove Tuesday (February or early March) and the most popular Mardi Gras celebration in Slovenia; the three-day **Ski Jumping World Cup Championships** (www.planica.info) at Planica near Kranjska Gora in March; **Druga Godba** (www.druga godba.si), a festival of alternative and world music at the Križanke in Ljubljana in late May/early June; the **Festival Lent** (http://lent.slov enija.net), a two-week extravaganza of folklore and culture in Maribor's Old Town in late June/early July; the **Ljubljana Summer Festival** (www.festival-lj.si), the nation's premier cultural event (music, theatre and dance) held from early July to late August; **Rock Otočec** (www.rock -otocec.com), a three-day rock concert in early

July at Prečna airfield, 5km northwest of Novo Mesto and Slovenia's biggest open-air rock concert; the **Cows' Ball** at **Bohinj** (www.bohinj.si), a zany weekend of folk dance, music, eating and drinking in September to mark the return of the cows from their high pastures to the valleys; and the **Ljubljana Marathon** (http://maraton .slo-timing.com) in late October.

## GAY & LESBIAN TRAVELLERS

The typical Slovenian personality is quietly conservative but deeply self-confident, remarkably broad-minded and particularly tolerant. **Roza Klub** ( ☎ 01-430 47 40; Kersnikova ul 4) in Ljubljana is made up of the gay and lesbian branches of ŠKUC (Študentski Kulturni Center or Student Cultural Centre).

**GALfon** ( ☎ 01-432 40 89; ☽ 7-10pm) is a hotline and source of general information for gays and lesbians. The websites of **Slovenian Queer Resources Directory** (www.ljudmila.org/siqrd) and **Out in Slovenia** (www.outinslovenija.com) are both extensive and partially in English.

## HOLIDAYS

Slovenia celebrates 14 holidays (praznjiki) a year. If any of the following fall on a Sunday, then the Monday becomes the holiday.

**New Year** 1 & 2 January
**Prešeren Day** (Slovenian Culture Day) 8 February
**Easter & Easter Monday** March/April
**Insurrection Day** 27 April
**Labour Days** 1 & 2 May
**National Day** 25 June
**Assumption Day** 15 August
**Reformation Day** 31 October
**All SaintsSaints' Day** 1 November
**Christmas Day** 25 December
**Independence Day** 26 December

## INTERNET ACCESS

There is internet access in towns and cities throughout the county but most cyber-cafés usually have only a handful of terminals. In some places you may have to resort to the local library, school or university. Be advised that Slovenian keyboards are neither qwerty nor azerty but qwertz, reversing the y and z keys, but otherwise following the Anglophone norm.

## INTERNET RESOURCES

The website of the **STB** (www.slovenia-tourism.si) is tremendously useful, as is that of **Mat'Kurja** (www.matkurja.com), a directory of Slovenian web

resources. Most Slovenian towns and cities have a website accessed by typing www.town name.si or www.townname-tourism.si. Especially good are **Ljubljana** (www.ljubljana-tourism .si) and **Piran-Portorož** (www.portoroz.si).

## LANGUAGE

Closely related to Croatian and Serbian, Slovene (slovenščina) is written in the Latin alphabet and consonants are generally pronounced as in English, with some notable exceptions: c=ts, č=ch, and j=y (though a 'j' is silent at the end of a word), š=sh and ž=zh (as the 's' in 'pleasure'). On toilets an 'M' (Moški) indicates 'men', and 'Ž' (Ženske) is 'women'. Virtually everyone in Slovenia speaxks at least one other language; restaurant menus and ATMs are commonly in Italian, German and English, as well as Slovene. See the Language chapter (p944) for key phrases and words.

## MONEY

Slovenia exchanged its 15-year-old currency, the tolar (SIT), for the euro in January 2007, the first of the 10 so-called accession countries that joined the EU in 2004 to do so. Exchanging cash is simple at banks, major post offices, travel agencies and menjalnice (bureaux de change), although some of the latter don't accept travellers cheques. Prices listed in this chapter are in euros, for the most part converted from prices quoted in tolars at the time of research, so expect some slight variations. Major credit and debit cards are accepted almost everywhere, and ATMs are ubiquitous.

## POST

Local mail costs €0.20 for up to 20g, while an international airmail stamp costs €0.45. Poste restante is free; address it to and pick it up from the main post office at Slovenska c 32, 1101 Ljubljana.

## TELEPHONE

Public telephones require a phonecard (telefonska kartica or telekartica), available at post offices and some newsstands. The cheapest card (€3, 25 unit) gives about 20 minutes' calling time to other European countries. Most locals have a mobile phone; SIM cards with around €4 credit are available for €12 from **SiMobil** (www.simobil.si) and €15.40 from **Mobitel** (www.mobitel.si). In fact, even certain businesses only quote mobile

**SLOVENIA**

---

**EMERGENCY NUMBERS**

- Police ☎ 113
- Ambulance ☎ 112
- Fire brigade ☎ 112
- Road emergency or towing ☎ 1987

---

numbers, identified by the prefix 031, 040, 041 and 051.

## TOILETS

Toilets are free in restaurants, but usually incur a €0.20 charge at bus stations and other public sites.

## TOURIST INFORMATION

The Ljubljana-based **Slovenian Tourist Board** ( ☎ 01-589 18 40; www.slovenia-tourism.si; Dunajska c 156) has dozens of tourist information centres (TICs) in Slovenia and branches in a half-dozen cities abroad; see its 'Representations of STB Abroad' on its website for details. Request its free *Next Exit: Guide to Slovenia's Byways*, which contains coupons for 5% to 15% savings on various hotels, activities and sights, including the Škocjan Caves.

## VISAS

Citizens of virtually all European countries, as well as Australia, Canada, Israel, Japan, New Zealand and the USA, do not require visas to visit Slovenia for stays of up to 90 days. Holders of EU and Swiss passports can enter using a national identity card.

Those who do require visas (including South Africans) can get them at any Slovenian embassy or consulate (see p854) for up to 90 days. They cost €35 regardless of the type or length of validity. You'll need confirmation of a hotel booking plus one photo, and may have to show a return or onward ticket.

## WOMEN TRAVELLERS

Travelling as a single woman in Slovenia is no different from travelling in most Western European countries. If you can handle yourself in the very occasional less-than-comfortable situation, you'll be fine.

In the event of an emergency call the **police** ( ☎ 113) any time or the **SOS Helpline** ( ☎ 080-11 55; www.drustvo-sos.si; ☻ noon-10pm Mon-Fri, 6-10pm Sat & Sun).

# TRANSPORT IN SLOVENIA

## GETTING THERE & AWAY
### Air

Slovenia's only international airport receiving regular scheduled flights is **Ljubljana Aerodrom** (LJU; www.lju-airport.si) at Brnik, 27km north of Ljubljana. From its base here, the Slovenian flag-carrier, Adria Airways, serves up to two-dozen European destinations depending on the season. Adria flights can be remarkably good value, but with the inauguration of easyJet and Wizzair flights between the Slovenian capital and London, most British visitors are now weekend visitors on budget airlines. Adria flights include useful connections to Pristina (Kosovo), Ohrid (Macedonia) and Tirana (Albania). Flight frequency drops in winter.

The following airlines travel to and from Slovenia:

**Adria Airways** (code JP; ☎ 01-231 33 12; www.adria -airways.com)
**Air France** (code AF; ☎ 01-244 34 47; www.airfrance .com) Daily flights to Paris (CDG).
**Austrian Airlines** (code OS; ☎ 01-202 01 22; www.aua .com) Multiple daily flights to Vienna.
**ČSA Czech Airlines** (code OK; ☎ 04-206 17 50; www .csa.cz) Flights to Prague.
**easyJet** (code EZY; ☎ 04-206 16 77; www.easyjet.com) Low-cost flights to London Stansted.
**JAT Airways** (code JU; ☎ 01-231 43 40; www.jat.com) Daily flights to Belgrade.
**LOT Polish Airlines** (code LO; ☎ 04-202 01 22; www .lot.com) Flights to Warsaw.
**Malév Hungarian Airlines** (code MA; ☎ 04-206 16 76; www.malev.hu) Daily flights Budapest.
**Turkish Airlines** (code TK; ☎ 04-206 16 80; www.turkish airlines.com) Flights to Istanbul.
**Wizz Air** (code W6; ☎ 04-206 19 81; www.wizzair.com) Budget flights to London Luton and Brussels (Charleroi).

An alternative budget option to Slovenia, especially if you want to concentrate on the coast, is **Ryanair** (www.ryanair.com), which links London Stansted with **Ronchi dei Legionari airport** (www.aeroporto.fvg.it) at Trieste. Trieste may (still) be in Italy but it's much closer to Koper, Piran and the Soča Valley than Ljubljana's airport at Brnik. From the Trieste airport terminal there is a daily bus (single/return €15/25) at 2.40pm to Koper (1½ hours, 56km), Izola (two hours, 61km), Portorož and Piran (2½ hours, 69km). Check **Terravision**

**Airport Bus Transfer** (www.lowcostcoach.com) for this service.

## Land

### BUS

International bus destinations from Ljubljana include Frankfurt (€80, 12½ hours, 777km, 7.30pm Sunday to Friday, 9.30pm Saturday) via Munich (€35.40, 6¾ hours, 344km); Sarajevo (€35.65, 9½ hours, 570km, 7.15pm Monday, Wednesday and Friday); Split (€34.20, 10½ hours, 528km, 7.40pm daily) via Rijeka (€11.43, 2½ hours, 136km); and Zagreb (€13.20, 2¾ hours, 154km, 2.30am, 7.30am and 8pm).

There are regular buses on weekdays only between Trieste and Koper (see p849) plus a direct year-round Ljubljana–Trieste service (€11.50, 2½ hours, 105km, 6.25am Monday to Saturday), with an additional departure at 8.15am on Saturday between June and mid-October.

### TRAIN

Ljubljana–Vienna trains (€57, 6¼ hours, 385km, twice daily) via Graz (€30, 200km, 3½ hours) are expensive, although SparSchiene fares as low as €29 apply on certain trains at certain times. Otherwise save money by going first to Maribor (€7.30 to €12.30, 2½ hours, 156km, up to two dozen daily), where you can buy a Maribor–Graz ticket (€11, 1¼ hours, three daily) and then continue on domestic tickets from Graz to Vienna (€13.50, 2¾ hours, 201km). Similar savings apply via Jesenice and Villach and/or Klagenfurt.

Three trains depart daily from Ljubljana for Munich (€66, 6½ hours, 405km). The 8.17pm departure has sleeping carriages available.

Ljubljana–Venice trains (€25, four hours, 244km) depart at 1.47am (via Trieste; €15, 99km), 10.28am and 4.16pm. It's cheaper to go first to Novo Gorica (€7.30, three hours, 153km, six daily), walk to Gorizia and then take an Italian train to Venice (€7.90, 2¼ hours).

For Zagreb there are eight trains daily from Ljubljana (€11.90, two hours, 154km) via Zidani Most. Several trains from the capital serve Rijeka (€11.40, two hours, 136km) via Postojna.

Ljubljana–Budapest trains (€58.60, 8¾ hours, 451km, three daily) go via Ptuj and Hodoš; there are Budapest Spezial fares available for as low as €39 on certain trains at certain times. The 9.05pm train to Thessaloniki (€83.80, 25 hours, 1159km, one daily) goes via Belgrade (€39.40, 10 hours, 535km).

Seat reservations, compulsory on trains to and from Italy and on InterCity (IC) trains, cost €3, but it is usually included in the ticket price.

## Sea

From Piran **Venezia Lines** (☎ 05-674 70 29; www .topline.si) catamarans sail to Venice (one way/ return €49/60.50, 2¼ hours) from May to mid-September. The **Prince of Venice** (☎ 05-617 80 00; portoroz@kompas.si) catamaran from nearby Izola also serves Venice (€42 to €67, 2½ hours) from mid-April to September. Both operate between once and four times a week, generally returning the same evening.

## GETTING AROUND

Trains are usually cheaper but less frequent than buses. Be advise that the frequency on both forms of transport drops off very significantly on weekends and during school holidays.

## Bus

It's worth booking long-distance buses ahead of time, especially for travel on Friday afternoon. If your bag has to go in the luggage compartment below the bus, it will cost €1.25 extra. The online bus timetable, **Avtobusna Postaja Ljubljana** (www.ap-ljubljana.si), is extensive, but generally only for buses that use Ljubljana as a hub.

## Car & Bicycle

Hiring a car is recommended, and can even save you money as you can access cheaper out-of-centre hotels and farm or village homestays. Daily rates usually start at €45/245 per day/week, including unlimited mileage, collision-damage waiver and theft protection. Unleaded 95-octane petrol (*bencin*) costs €1.03 to €1.05 per litre, with diesel at €0.98. You must keep your headlights illuminated throughout the day.

Bicycles are available for hire at some train stations, tourist offices, travel agencies and hotels. You'll find mountain bikes easiest to hire in Bovec, Bled and Bohinj.

## Hitching

Hitchhiking is fairly common and legal, except on motorways and a few major highways. Even young women hitch in Slovenia, but it's

**SLOVENIA**

never totally safe and Lonely Planet doesn't recommend it.

## Train

The national railway, **Slovenske Železnice** (Slovenian Railways; ☎ 01-291 33 32; www.slo-zeleznice.si) has a useful online timetable that's easy to use. Buy tickets before boarding or you'll incur a €2.10 supplement. Be aware that InterCity

(IC) trains carry a surcharge of €1.40 to €1.70 on top of standard quoted fares.

A useful and very scenic rail line from Bled Jezero station via Bohinjska Bistrica near Lake Bohinj cuts under the mountains to Most na Soči (for Kobarid), then down the Soča Valley to Nova Gorica. Cars are carried through the tunnel section on a special auto train (*avtovlak*).

# Ukraine Україна

The West cheered heartily for Ukraine's mutiny in orange – the flashiest 'colour revolution' by far – and a rousing sense of rebellion and thirst for change still lingers in the air here. You can feel it when you're in the awesome, frenetic capital – Kyiv, where peaceful but passionate protests break out at the drop of a hat, and where citizens flaunt bold fashions and fresh attitudes as they smoke, drink, dance and sing wherever and whenever they want. You can see it along the resort-speckled coasts Odesa and Crimea, where reconstructions and renovations are turning the run-down architectural pearls of the Black Sea into eye-catching beauties, ready and eager for your business. And you can hear it in the super-nationalistic western region, where the purest strains of the Ukrainian language are spoken with zeal under the Gothic eaves of Old World cafés.

It's an exciting time to be here, to bear witness to it all. And they *want* you here. Ever since this hulking giant of a country broke through the chains of repression and corruption, it's been striking poses and flexing its muscles at the West. Visas are no longer required for most Westerners, so there's no good reason you shouldn't accept the invitation and take your explorations to the very edges of Eastern Europe.

## FAST FACTS

- **Area** 603,700 sq km
- **Capital** Kyiv (Kiev)
- **Currency** hryvnia (hry); €1 = 6.44hry; US$1 = 5.05hry; UK£ = 9.47hry; A$1 = 3.82hry; ¥100 = 4.51hry; NZ$1 =3.12hry
- **Famous for** Orange Revolution, poisoned president, Chornobyl, football striker Andriy Shevchenko
- **Official Language** Ukrainian
- **Phrases** Doh-brih dyen (hello), *ya nih rah-zoo-mee-yu* (I don't understand), *dya-koo-yoo* (thanks)
- **Population** 46.5 million
- **Telephone codes** country code ☎ 38; international access code ☎ 8+ 10
- **Visa** required for Australians and New Zealanders, arrange in advance ($80-290), see p904

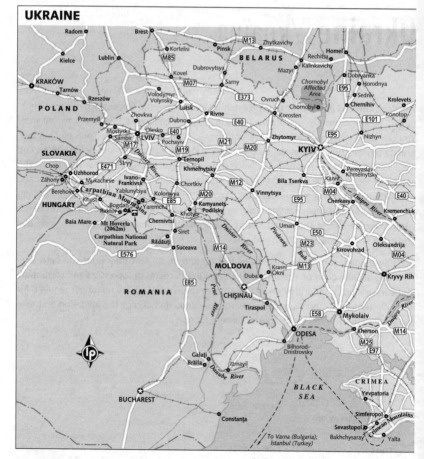

**UKRAINE**

## HIGHLIGHTS

- Cover all bases in **Kyiv** (p865), where religious landmarks and wild nightlife peacefully coexist.
- Lose the map and lose yourself in the winding, narrow, cobblestone alleys and gorgeous Old World buildings of **Lviv** (p874) that are best explored aimlessly and on your own.
- Warm your buns where so many locals do – in **Odesa** (p885), the hotbed of Ukrainian hedonism.
- Take the longest, most stunning trolley-bus ride in the world to the palace-lined, horseshoe coast of **Yalta** (p895).
- Take a detour to little, undiscovered **Kamyanets-Podilsky** (p883), set on a tower-

ing island of rock and surrounded by a deep ravine. This place is begging to be an epic movie backdrop.

## ITINERARIES

- **One week** Split your time evenly between Kyiv and Lviv (if you want to chill) or Odesa (if you want to party).
- **Two weeks** Spend five days in Kyiv, two in Lviv, then choose a week in Odesa or Crimea, making Yalta your base.

## CLIMATE & WHEN TO GO

Inland Ukraine enjoys a relatively moderate continental climate. The hottest month, July, averages 23°C, while the coldest, January, is literally freezing. Along the coast, Yalta and

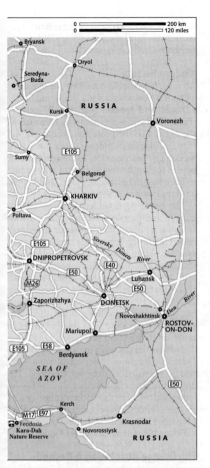

Odesa enjoy a marginally subtropical climate and are much milder in winter. See climate charts on p912.

Near Odesa and in Crimea, tourism is at its peak from June to August, and accommodation is priciest then. The country basically comes to a halt during the first two weeks of May for a series of holidays, making a visit then both interesting and frustrating. For weather and crowds, mid-April to late May is the best bet.

## HISTORY
### Kyivan Rus
In 882 Oleh of Novgorod – of the Varyagi (a Scandinavian civilisation) – declared himself ruler of Kyiv. The city prospered and grew into a large, unified Varyagi state that, during its peak, stretched between the Volga River, the Danube River and Baltic Sea. By the 11th and 12th centuries, the Varyagi state began to splinter into 10 rival princedoms. When prince of Suzdal Andriy Bogolyubov sacked Kyiv in 1169, followed by the Mongols 70 years later, the end of the Varyagi era was complete.

Prince Roman Mstyslavych regained control of Kyiv in 1203 and united the regions of present-day western, central and northern Ukraine. There was a period of relative prosperity under his dynamic son, King Danylo, and grandson Lev. During this time, much of eastern and southern Ukraine came under the control of the Volga-based, Mongol Golden Horde. Its empire was emasculated, however, in the 14th century by the Black Death, as well as by the growing military strength of Russian, Polish and Lithuanian rulers.

### Cossacks & Russian Control
By the turn of the 15th century, the uncontrolled steppe in southern Ukraine began to attract runaway serfs, criminals, Orthodox refugees and other outcasts from Poland and Lithuania. Along with a few semi-independent Tatars, the inhabitants formed self-governing militaristic communities and became known as *kazaki* (Cossacks), from the Turkic word meaning 'outlaw, adventurer or free person'. Ukrainian Cossacks eventually developed the self-ruling Cossack Hetmanate, which to some degree reasserted the concept of Ukrainian self-determination.

In 1648 Hetman Bogdan Khmelnytsky (aided by Tatar cavalry) overcame the Polish rulers at the battle of Pyliavtsi. He was forced to engage in a formal but controversial military alliance with Muscovy in 1654, but in 1660 a war broke out between Poland and Russia over control of Ukraine. This ended with treaties that granted control over Kyiv and northern Ukraine to Russia and territory to the west of the Dnipro River to the Poles.

During the course of the 18th century Russia expanded into southern Ukraine and also gained most of Western Ukraine from Poland, except for the far west, which went to the Habsburg Empire.

### The Early 20th Century
Following WWI and the collapse of tsarist power, Ukraine had a chance – but failed – to gain independence. Civil war broke out and

UKRAINE

---

**HOW MUCH?**

- **Kyiv metro ride** 50 kopeks
- **Bottle of Medoff vodka** 25hry
- **Cup of brewed coffee** 7hry
- **Ticket to opera in Kyiv** 20hry
- **Ticket to football game at Dynamo stadium (Kyiv)** 15hry

**LONELY PLANET INDEX**

- **Litre of petrol** 3.10hry
- **Litre of bottled wate**r 2hry
- **Half-litre Chernihivsky beer** 4hry
- **High-quality matryoshka (stacking doll)** 50hry
- **Street snack** (*Kyivska perepichka* – **meat roll**) 4hry

---

exploded into anarchy: six different armies vied for power, and Kyiv changed hands five times within a year. Eventually Ukraine was again divided between Poland, Romania, Czechoslovakia and Russia. The Russian part became a founding member of the USSR in 1922, but Stalin looked upon Ukraine as a laboratory for testing Soviet restructuring while at the same time stamping out 'harmful' nationalism. Consequently, in 1932–33 he engineered a famine that killed millions of Ukrainians.

The Soviet Red Army rolled into Polish Ukraine in September 1939. The Germans attacked in 1941 and by the year's end controlled virtually all of Ukraine. Kharkiv and Kyiv were retaken by the Red Army, however, two years later. An estimated six million Ukrainians died in WWII, which left most of the country's cities in ruin. After the war, the USSR kept the territory it had taken from Poland in 1939.

## Modern History

After the failed Soviet counter-coup in August 1991, the Verkhovna Rada (Supreme Council) met, and speaker Stanyslav Hurenko's memorable announcement was recorded by the *Economist* for posterity: 'Today we will vote for Ukrainian independence, because if we don't we're in the shit.' In December, some 84% of the population voted in a referendum to back that pragmatic decision, and Leonid Kravchuk was elected president.

The economy floundered, things seemed chaotic and people were largely dissatisfied with the results of their move for independence. Finally, the hryvnia, Ukraine's currency, was introduced in 1996, and a process of privatisation kick-started the economy. It wasn't until 1997, under President Leonid Kuchma, that inflation fell from an inconceivable 10,000% to 10%. The economy strengthened but not enough: the hryvnia felt the ripple effects hard from the 1998 Russian financial crisis, dipping 51% in value.

Presidential elections in October 1999 saw President Kuchma reelected in what were widely regarded as dubious elections. His credibility shrivelled further due to his relationship with former prime minister and money-launderer Pavel Lazarenko, as well as his alleged association with the shocking murder of gadfly journalist Georgy Gongadze.

## The Orange Revolution & Beyond

Kuchma knew he wouldn't be able to run in the October 2004 presidential elections, so he

---

**LOSE OR DIE**

During WWII, when Kyiv was occupied by Nazi Germany, the members of the talented Dynamo soccer team were challenged to a public match with a team of German soldiers. The Ukrainians formed a team called Start, and despite physical weakness brought on by the occupation, they started off ahead. At half-time German officers came into the locker room and commanded them to let up. Nevertheless, Start continued to play hard, and before the game finished the referee blew the whistle and called it off (with a score of 4-1).

The Germans reshuffled their players, and Start was offered another chance to lose. Instead they won. Next, Start was matched with a Hungarian team – and won again. Finally, the enraged Germans challenged Start to a match against their finest, undefeated team, Flakelf. When the *'Übermensch'* of Flakelf lost, the Nazis gave up – and proceeded to arrest most of the Start players. They were executed at Babyn Yar (p870). There is a monument to them at Dynamo Stadium in Kyiv, and their story inspired the movie *Victory,* starring Sylvester Stallone and Pele.

got his crony Viktor Yanukovych to run for him instead. But both the international press and Ukrainian public were all about Viktor Yushchenko, who was poisoned a week before elections, allegedly by political foes, turning his ruggedly handsome face into…just *rugged*. A great media story.

Because no-one carried more than 50% of the votes in the first round of elections, a run-off was scheduled for November 21. The official results of this run-off had Yanukovych – who still had close ties with the reigning government and media – ahead by 3%, but exit polls showed Yushchenko ahead by 11%. Something was rotten in the state of Ukraine, and by the next day, about 500,000 people had peacefully gathered on Kyiv's maydan Nezalezhnosti (Independence Square), bearing flags, setting up tents, chanting, singing and having a good time. Kyiv citizens took into their homes complete strangers, hosted out-of-towners, and the media reported a marked drop in city crime during the span of the protest. The world was watching, and officials had no choice but to annul the run-off results.

But the protesters stayed on, sometimes numbering over a million and often withstanding freezing temperatures, until 26 December 2004, when a second run-off took place under intense international scrutiny. Yushchenko won with 52% and was inaugurated 23 January 2005. He chose lovely, powerful and crafty Yuliya Timoshenko (also known as 'the Gas Princess' and 'Glamour Girl of the Orange Revolution') as his prime minister – a real 'beauty and the beast' story – but ended up firing her under pressure from his associates. But she's not going down without a fight, and plans to get her job back, come hell or high water.

As the saying goes, revolutions eat their children. Since Yushchenko's victory, his popularity has declined, with allegations of corruption, bad press about his obnoxious son and a Russian oil crisis. The country is impatient for improvement, and it seems no one can satisfy it.

## PEOPLE

Ukraine's population of 46,500,000 has been steadily declining since independence. About 66% live in urban areas such as Kyiv, Kharkiv, Dnipropetrovsk, Odesa and Donetsk. Some 78% are Ukrainian and another 17%

are ethnic Russians. The remainder includes Belarusians, Moldovans, Bulgarians, Poles, Hungarians, Romanians, Tatars and Jews. Almost all of the country's Tatar population (less than 250,000) lives in Crimea (see p892).

## RELIGION

Almost 97% of Ukrainians are Christian, and most of those follow some sort of orthodoxy.

Orthodoxy in Ukraine has a complex history of its own, but basically, central and southern Ukraine mostly follow the Ukrainian Orthodox Church (UOC; with a Moscow patriarch), while the rest of the country follows the Ukrainian Autocephalous Orthodox Church (UAOC; with a Kyiv patriarch). To make matters more confusing, the UOC split in 1992, with a breakaway new church called the Ukrainian Orthodox Church of Kyiv and All-Ukraine, which recognises the Kyiv patriarch.

But wait, there's more. The Uniate Church, which is also referred to as the Ukrainian-Greek Catholic Church, follows Orthodox worship and ritual but recognises the Roman pope as its leader. Uniate priests are the only Catholic priests in the world allowed to marry.

There are some very small Jewish minorities in all cities, while Muslim communities, primarily Tatars, live in Crimea.

## ARTS

Many Ukrainians believe that to understand their heritage you must appreciate the significance of Taras Shevchenko, who was punished by exile in 1847 for his satirical poems about Russian oppression. Arguably the most talented and prolific Ukrainian writer of the early 20th century was Ivan Franko, whose scholarly and moving works shed light on the issues plaguing Ukrainian society. He was, of course, imprisoned by the Russians. Lesia Ukrainka, a wealthy young woman whose frail health kept her indoors writing moody poetry, could be considered the Emily Dickinson of Ukraine.

In the cinema world, Aleksandr Dovzhenko's 1930 silent film *Earth* is considered by some critics to be one of the most significant films of all time. The most notable contemporary Ukrainian director (although she was born in a part of Romania that's now in Moldova) is Kira Muratova. Her absurdist, cruel style and fascination with the repulsive have earned her films much critical acclaim, if not a huge fan base.

The art of creating *pysanky* (brightly coloured, detailed eggshells), is uniquely Ukrainian. During Easter you will be able to find some for sale (great souvenirs but hard to pack safely), and there are year-round wooden-egg samples for purchase.

Okean Elzy (www.okeanelzy.com) is one of the country's bigger music sensations. The well-respected rock group sounds a little like the Clash and has a charismatic lead singer.

# ENVIRONMENT

The largest country wholly within Europe, Ukraine has a topography consisting almost completely of steppe: gently rolling, partially wooded plains, bisected by the Dnipro River. The only serious mountains are the Carpathians, in the west, and the Crimeans, in the south. A central belt of fertile, thick, humusrich soil in Ukraine spawned the term *chernozem* (meaning 'black earth') and is what gave the country the nickname 'the breadbasket of Europe'.

Visitors don't come for rare-wildlife watching, but there is a good amount of diversity including elk, deer, wild boars, brown bears and wolves. Lots of geese and ducks, and

---

**CHORNOBYL**

*And the third angel sounded, and there fell a great star from heaven, burning as it were a lamp, and it fell up on the third part of the rivers, and upon the fountains of waters; And the name of the star is called Wormwood: and the third part of the waters became wormwood; and many men died of the waters, because they were made bitter.*

From Revelations 8:10-11

Chornobyl means 'wormwood'.

On 26 April 1986 reactor No 4 at Chornobyl nuclear power station, 100km north of Kyiv, exploded and nearly nine tons of radioactive material (90 times as much as in the Hiroshima bomb) spewed into the sky. An estimated 4.9 million people in northern Ukraine, southern Belarus and southwestern Russia were affected. Some people – especially the elderly, who cannot conceive of the dangers of this invisible stuff called radiation – have refused to leave, and even live off the small gardens they've planted by their homes. Undoubtedly the most tragically affected were the young and unborn children. For more information about the situation and how to help, visit www.childrenofchornobyl.org, and watch the Oscar-winning documentary *Chernobyl Heart*.

Western monitors now conclude that radioactivity levels at Chornobyl are negligible, so organised tours of the site and surrounding 'ghost' villages have started to pop up. But visiting Chornobyl should not be a frivolous undertaking. Firstly, although the half-life of the thyroid-attacking iodine isotopes is long past, the dangerous plutonium ones will not decompose for another 20,000 or so years. (Although tour agencies may claim they won't go to plutonium affected areas, it's hard to imagine how an explosion of radioactive particles could be contained into certain zones). Secondly, the cement 'sarcophagus' that was built over the still-burning reactor is crumbling and unstable. Before jumping into a decision to take extreme tourism to the subatomic level, do your own research.

If you do decide to go, the standard price for a six-hour visit is about $180. SAM Travel (p867) is a long-established company that organises trips. If you opt to play it safe and eschew Chornobyl itself, do pay a visit to the riveting Chornobyl Museum (p869) in Kyiv.

small furry mammals such as rabbits and muskrats, can be seen from trains. Ukraine has a few national parks, the most significant of which is the Carpathian National Natural Park (p882).

In addition to the destructive Soviet industrialisation of the countryside, Ukraine still suffers from the effects of Chornobyl (Chernobyl in Russian), the worst nuclear accident in history (see p864).

## FOOD & DRINK

Some tasty Ukrainian dishes are *varenyky* (traditional dumplings made with rolled dough), *borshch* (beet soup) and *holubtsi* (stuffed cabbage rolls). Chicken Kiev *(kotleta po-Kyivsky)*, is a deep-fried butter-stuffed ball of chicken.

Crimea produces sweet wines, and champagne from around Odesa is surprisingly palatable. The most popular Ukrainian beers are Slavutych, Chernihivsky and Obolon.

Vegetarians can have a hard time outside Kyiv. Here's how to say 'I am a vegetarian (male/female)' – 'ya vyeh-gyeh-tah-ree-*ahn*-yets/-ka'.

# KYIV КИЇВ

☎ 044 / pop 2.66 million

The click of stilettos on cobblestones, the woosh of expensive cars barrelling down the boulevards, the dizzying aromas from ethnic restaurants and stylish cafés, and the eye-catching advertisements cleverly squeezed into every available space: This is the new, postrevolutionary Kyiv. It's flashy, fast and ready for action – and set amid the monumental Stalinist architecture and glorious gilded onion domes that have been pulling in tourists long before anyone even heard of a colour revolution.

Every last citizen here is feeling their free-market oats – from the babushkas hawking home-baked goods on the street to the high-level investors opening up more enterprises than a poor guidebook author can keep up with. That said, the ancient city – believed to be at least 1500 years old – is far less overwhelming and more laid-back than Moscow and St Petersburg.

Explore the Caves Monastery, where the mummified bodies of revered monks still receive the prayers and kisses of believers. Do some prime souvenir shopping on steep, winding Andriyivsky uzviz. Catch a awe-inspiring glimpse of the gargantuan steel Soviet woman on the banks of the gentle Dnipro River. Take a leisurely stroll down vul Khreshchatyk to maydan Nezalezhnosti, the nerve centre of the Orange Revolution, and celebrate the country's victory with a Ukrainian beer at one of the city's many happening nightclubs. This is Kyiv. Vive la revolución!

## ORIENTATION

Kyiv's main street is vul Khreshchatyk, which heads northeast towards maydan Nezalezhnosti, the main square and centre of the Orange Revolution. On weekends Khreshchatyk is closed to traffic, and citizens flood the street.

The area north of the Old Town from around St Andrew's Church to Kontraktova ploscha is Podil, the historic merchants' quarter and river port.

Across the river, on the more working-class 'left' (east) bank, are a cluster of islands hugged by beaches and parkland.

## INFORMATION

### Bookshops

**Baboon** ( ☎ 234 1503; vul Bohdana Khmelnytskoho 39; ◑ 9am-2am; Ⓜ Universitet) A hipster bookstore-restaurant that for once has an English-language literature selection, which includes stuff other than *A Tale of Two Cities* and *Jane Eyre* and a used-book section. Decent food, espresso and live shows on weekend nights, when the place gets packed.

### Internet Access

Just next to the post office's main entrance is a 24-hour place charging 10hry per hour.

### Laundry

There are no self-service laundries, but hotel floor maids will do a good job for a reasonable rate. Many apartment rentals offer a washing machine.

### Left Luggage

Possible for a small fee at the train and bus stations. Also, your hotel will hold it for you for several hours, usually for free.

### Medical Services

**American Medical Centre** ( ☎ 490 7600, emergency ☎ 461 9595; www.amcenters.com; vul Berdychivsta 1; Ⓜ Lukyanivska) Handles routine and emergency medical and dental. Staff speak English.

UKRAINE

# CENTRAL KYIV

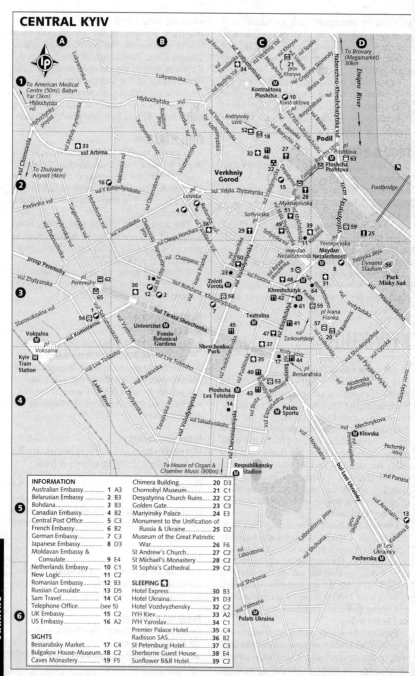

UKRAINE

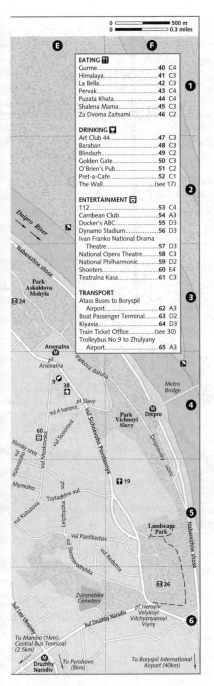

## Money

Both ATMs and exchange booths signposted обмін валют (*obmin valyut)* are ubiquitous. Rates offered by exchange booths in hotels are not necessarily worse. Larger banks will cash traveller cheques and give cash advances on credit cards.

## Post & Telephone

**Central post office** ( ☎ 065; vul Khreshchatyk 22; 🕒 8am-9pm Mon-Fri, to7pm Sun; Ⓜ Khreshchatyk) Has a 24-hour phone office.

## Travel Agencies

There are no tourist information centres, but there are plenty of travel agencies, which do city tours as well as day trips to the Chornobyl Exclusion Zone (p864). Two of the most reliable and popular are:

**New Logic** ( ☎ 206 3322; vul Mykhaylivska 6a; Ⓜ Maydan Nezalezhnosti) Popular for weekend city sightseeing tours.

**Sam Travel** ( ☎ 287 5019; vul Chervonoarmiyska 34; Ⓜ Ploscha Lva Tolstoho) A popular choice for Chornobyl.

## SIGHTS
### Caves Monastery

Rolling across 28 hectares of wooded slopes above the Dnipro River, the **Caves Monastery** ( ☎ 290 3071; vul Sichnevoho Povstannya 21; adult/child incl map 16/8hry; 🕒 upper lavra 9.30am-6pm, lower lavra sunrise-sunset, caves 8.30am-4.30pm), also known as the Kyiv-Pechersk Lavra, deserves at least a half-day. It is the single most popular tourist site in the city, a highlight of visiting Ukraine and arguably the spiritual heart of the Ukrainian people.

The two sets of **caves** are a few minutes' walk southeast of the cathedral and through the southern gate; buy a candle at a kiosk on the way. Inside the caves, dozens of niches contain glass-topped coffins holding the blanketed bodies of the monks; believers kneel and pray at the coffins, and kiss the glass tops as well.

The **excursion bureau** ( ☎ 291 3171) is on the left just past the entrance but unofficial guides lingering offer better two-hour tours in English for just 50hry per small group.

The museums and churches inside the preserve have extra admission fees (3hry to 6hry each) and are open daily from about 10am to 5pm. Most museums are rather esoteric; the only one that is interesting for anyone is the Museum of Microminiatures.

# KYIV METRO

UKRAINE

Legend:
- Svyatoshyno-Brovarska line
- Kurenivsko-Chervonoarmiyska line
- Syretsko-Pecherska line
- Transfer station

Svyatoshyno-Brovarska line:
- Akademmistechko / Академмістечко
- Zhytomyrska / Житомирська
- Svyatoshyn / Святошин
- Nyvky / Нивки
- Beresteyska / Берестейська
- Shulyavska / Шулявська
- Politekhnichny Instytut / Політехнічний Інститут
- Vokzalna / Вокзальна
- Universytet / Університет
- Teatralna / Театральна
- Khreshchatyk / Хрещатик
- Arsenalna / Арсенальна
- Dnipro / Дніпро
- Hydropark / Гідропарк
- Livoberezhna / Лівобережна
- Darnytsya / Дарниця
- Chernihivska / Чернігівська
- Lisova / Лісова

Kurenivsko-Chervonoarmiyska line:
- Heroyiv Dnipra / Героїв Дніпра
- Minska / Мінська
- Obolon / Оболонь
- Petrivka / Петрівка
- Tarasa Shevchenka / Тараса Шевченка
- Kontraktova pl / Контрактова пл
- Poshtova pl / Поштова пл
- Maydan Nezalezhnosti / Майдан Незалежності
- Pl Lva Tolstoho / Пл Льва Толстого
- Respublikansky Stadion / Республіканський Стадіон
- Palats Ukraïna / Палац Україна
- Lybidska / Либідська

Syretsko-Pecherska line:
- Dorohozhychi / Дорогожичі
- Lukyanivska / Лук'янівська
- Zoloti Vorota / Золоті Ворота
- Palats Sportu / Палац Спорту
- Klovska / Кловська
- Pecherska / Печерська
- Druzhby Narodiv / Друзби Народів
- Vydubychi / Видубичі
- Slavutych / Славутич
- Osokorky / Осокорки
- Pozniaky / Позняки
- Kharkivska / Харківська

**KYIV IN TWO DAYS**

Muse over mummies at the **Caves Monas-tery** (p867), then scoot to the nearby **Mu-seum of the Great Patriotic War** (right) and **Rodina Mat** (right).

Imagine 1 million orange-clad protesters at maydan Nezalezhnosti, preferably on a weekend, when Khreshchatyk is pedestrian-only. Move on to **St Sophia's Cathedral** (below) and **Andriyivsky uzviz** (below). Catch a live show at **Art Club 44** (p871) or go dancing at **Caribbean Club** (p872).

## St Sophia Cathedral Complex

The city's oldest standing church is **St Sophia's Cathedral** (Sofiysky Sobor; ☎ 278 2083; Sofiyivska plo-scha; grounds 1hry, adult/child 11/4hry; bell tower 3hry; 10am-5.30pm Fri-Tue, to 4.30pm Wed, grounds 8.30am-8pm; Ⓜ Maydan Nezalezhnosti). Built from 1017 to 1031 and named after Hagia Sofia (Holy Wisdom) Cathedral in Istanbul, its Byzantine plan and decoration announced the new religious and political authority of Kyiv. Prince Yaroslav himself is buried here. Perhaps most memorable aspect of a visit is the cathedral's interior, where there are 11th-century mosaics and frescoes.

## Andriyivsky Uzviz

Your visit to Kyiv wouldn't be complete without a walk along steep, cobblestoned Andriyivsky uzviz (Andrew's Descent), one of the oldest streets in town. Avoid the incline by taking the **funicular** (tickets 50 kopeks; 6.30am-11pm; Ⓜ Poshtova Ploscha) to the top of the hill, where you'll find the **St Michael's Monastery**, with its seven-cupola, periwinkle cathedral. Further down the street is the gorgeous baroque **St Andrew's Church** (admission 4hry), built in 1754 in St Petersburg. Across from St Andrew's, up a small flight of stairs and on the ground before the National Museum of Ukrainian History are the **Desyatynna Church ruins**. Prince Volodymyr ordered it built in 989 and used 10% of his income for it, hence the name (*desyatyn* means 'one-tenth'). In 1240 it collapsed under the weight of people who took refuge on its roof during a Tatar siege.

From here, take souvenir stall–lined Andriyivsky uzviz down the hill to start your descent into the realm of *matryoshkas* (stacking dolls) and McLenin T-shirts.

## Museums

For most people the following are the most interesting museums; little is posted in English.

**Chornobyl Museum** ( ☎ 470 5422; provulok Khoryva; admission 5hry; 10am-6pm Mon-Fri, to 5pm Sat, closed last Mon of month; Ⓜ Kontraktova Ploscha) This artistic and moving display is a must-see.

**Bulgakov House-Museum** ( ☎ 416 3188; Andriyivsky uzviz 13; admission 3hry; 10am-5pm Thu-Tue; Ⓜ Kontraktova Ploscha) The beloved author of *The Master & Margarita* lived here in the early 20th century, and his home has been turned into a museum. It's often booked in advance with tour groups.

**Pyrohovo** ( ☎ 226 5542; vul Chervonopraporna; admission 10hry; 10am-4pm Thu-Tue) This outdoor museum holds 17th- to 20th-century wooden cottages, churches, farmsteads and windmills. Take *marshrutka* (minibus) 24, trolleybus 11 or bus 27 from the Lybidska metro station; the entrance is hard to miss. A taxi will cost about 50hry each way.

**Museum of the Great Patriotic War** ( ☎ 295 9452; vul Sichnevoho Povstannya 44; admission 4hry; 10am-4pm Tue-Sun) features triumphant displays of Soviet heroism. Visible from miles around is **Rodina Mat** (Defence of the Motherland Monument), a 62m-high titanium statue of a valiant woman with shield and sword.

## Other Sights

Originally erected in 1037 but reconstructed in 1982, the **Golden Gate** (Zoloti Vorota; vul Volodymyrska 40A; Ⓜ Zoloti Vorota) was the original entrance into Old Kyiv. It has long been closed for repairs that don't seem to be taking place, but a glimpse from the street is interesting (notice the chapel at the top).

The very Gaudí-like **Chimera Building** (vul Bankova 10; Ⓜ Khreshchatyk), with its demonic-looking animals and gargoyles, is probably

**TOP FIVE REASONS TO HAVE HEALTH INSURANCE IN KYIV**

| Affliction | Culprit |
| --- | --- |
| 3rd-degree burn | Molten butter explosion from chicken Kiev |
| Broken nose | Metro door face-slam |
| Busted assbone | Marble stairs in winter |
| Charley horse leg cramp | Karate chop from Metro turnstile |
| Chest puncture wound | Stiletto love, baby |

UKRAINE

the weirdest building in the city. It was constructed at the beginning of the 20th century by architect Vladislav Gorodetski, an eccentric genius who made it his home.

The baroque, 18th-century **Mariyinsky Palace** (vul Hrushevskoho 5; M Arsenalna) is surrounded by a lovely park with great city views, but entrance to the palace is not allowed.

The **Bessarabsky Market** (ploscha Bessarabska; M Lva Tolstoho) is a large covered place that sells for the most part produce, meats and honey; it can make for nice photos.

The metal-rainbow **Monument to the Unification of Russia & Ukraine** ( M Maydan Nezalezhnosti) offers excellent vistas of the city along the Dnipro; there's also a good viewpoint at Mariyinsky Palace (above).

Just outside metro Dorohozhychi is **Babyn Yar**, the location of a WWII execution site and mass grave used by Nazis. Over 100,000 Kyiv citizens – mostly Jews – were murdered here from 1941 till 1943. Actually, the monument is in the wrong spot. A small marble monument nearby marks the actual place of execution. See also the boxed text on p862.

## SLEEPING

If you're staying in Kyiv for more than a few days, you may find it more worthwhile to book an apartment online with one of many reputable companies. Tried and true are **Teren Plus** ( ☎ 428 1010; www.teren.kiev.ua) and **UA Apartments** ( ☎ 205 9292; www.uaapartments.com). Rates start at around US$40.

The follow listings show high-season, weekday rates; weekends are cheaper in Kyiv.

### Budget

**St Petersburg** ( ☎ 279 7364; s-peter@i.kiev.ua; bulvar Tarasa Shevchenka 4; s 294-343hry, d 381-572hry, s with shared bathroom 143-165hry, d with shared bathroom 172-196hry, tr with shared bathroom 237-270hry) Staffed by relatively friendly women who are happy to have a job where they can watch trashy TV between customers, St Petersburg's rooms are worn down, but some have a little charm or have remodelled bathrooms. The shared bathrooms are clean and turn the place into an incredible bargain, but the place may be bought up soon.

A good deal is hard to find, and that includes **IYH Kiev** ( ☎ 331 0260; www.hihostels.com.ua; vul Artema 52A, bldg 2, 5th fl; dm 117hry). Rooms are new and simple; no kitchen. Wi-fi (not free) and a computer are planned for the near future. A detailed map is on the website. **IYH Yaroslav**

( ☎ 331 0260; www.hihostels.com.ua; vul Yaroslavska 10; dm 110-130hry) is easier to find and in Podil.

### Midrange

**Sherborne Guest House** ( ☎ 295 8832; www.sherbornehotel.com.ua; provulok Sichneviy 9; ste 364-936hry; M Arsenalna) Each cosy apartment in this building differs in décor and layout (many have slanted ceilings). On-site staff are helpful and speak English, and the prices are great.

**Hotel Express** ( ☎ 239 8995; www.expresskiev.com; bulvar Tarasa Shevchenka 38/40; s 236-600hry, d 834hry, ste 1282-1627hry; 🗙 🖳; M Universitet) There's nothing Soviet left about even the lowest-priced rooms with shared bathroom (there are only a few, and you'll have to request them specifically), which are by far the best deal – so-called improved rooms hardly differ.

**Hotel Ukraina** ( ☎ 279 0266; www.ukraine-hotel .kiev.ua; vul Instytutska 4; s 335-490hry, d 450-560hry, ste 450-990hry; M Maydan Nezalezhnosti) Location is the best reason to stay in this Stalinist Hotel overlooking the cradle of the Orange Revolution, maydan Nezalezhnosti. The staff aren't thrilled to be at work, and service with a smile isn't likely, but they aren't rude either. Count the number of women on staff with bright-red dyed hair.

**Sunflower B&B Hotel** ( ☎ 279 3846; www.sunflowerhotel.kiev.ua; vul Kostolna 9-41; d 610-712hry; 🗙 🖳; M Maydan Nezalezhnosti) The yellow, Western-standard rooms are spacious and quiet, with light-wood floors and comfortable beds. You'll also get free in-room DSL and continental breakfast (with a warm pastry), delivered, on request, on a cart by English-speaking staff. There are only a few rooms (all doubles, some with kitchens), so book in advance.

### Top End

**Hotel Vozdvyzhensky** ( ☎ 531 9900; www.vozdvyzhensky .com; vul Vozdvyzhenska 60; s 750-1380hry, d 990-1800hry, ste 1560-2100hry; 🗙 🗙 🖳; M Poshtova Ploscha) Catering mostly to foreign couples, Vozdvyzhensky exudes confidence and style. The minimalist Western-standard rooms themselves are not so impressive, but beds look and feel fantastic. Apart from flooring, standard and superior rooms hardly differ.

If money is no object, you won't be disappointed by **Radisson SAS** ( ☎ 492 2200; www.kiev .radissonsas.com; vul Yaroslaviv Val 22; s 1872-2195hry, d 1872-2324hry, ste 2582-5486hry; 🗙 🗙 🖳; M Zoloti Vorota) or **Premier Palace** ( ☎ 537 4500; www.premier-palace.com; bulvar Tarasa Shevchenka 5-7/29; s 2175-2485hry, d 2610-2740hry, ste 2795-9315hry; 🗙 🗙 🖳 🗙; M Teatralna).

UKRAINE

# EATING

If this list isn't long enough, stop by a fancy hotel for a copy of *Gourmet Guide* (although it focuses on pricier places) or the *Kyiv Business Directory*, on sale outside the Central Post Office. Also see www.chicken.kiev.ua/eng.

**Shalena Mama** (Crazy Mama; ☎ 234 1751; vul Tereshchenkivska; mains 15-50hry; ⏲ 24hr; Ⓜ Teatralna) It's all an homage to the Rolling Stones, and clear by the Thai-Western menu, where every dish is named for a song: Angie, Sympathy for the Devil, you name it.

**Pervak** (☎ 235 0952; vul Rognidynska 2; mains 25-65hry; ⏲ 11am-last customer; Ⓜ Ploscha Lva Tolstoho) Soviet style is super-hip at Pervak, which serves high-quality Ukrainian food and has a popular and fun bar scene, as well as live music. Old Soviet black-and-white talkies play on screens throughout the restaurant.

**La Bella** (☎ 279 2701, vul Pushkinska 7; mains 30-75hry; Ⓜ Teatralna) Even real Italians will enjoy the simple, thin-crust, oven-fired pizzas here, and the pasta is done right too (try the spaghetti carbonara). The large place hasn't caught on yet and is usually very quiet.

**Mambo** (☎ 522 8224; bulvar Druzhby Narodov; mains 30-100hry; ⏲ noon-2am; Ⓜ Lybidska) If you are yearning for some good Latin food (possibly more like Mexican–American) and tasty steaks, Mambo is well worth the trip. Outdoor seating, live world music, and good service round out the dining experience. From the metro, walk to Druzhby Narodov, go left, and it's about 150m down on the left, after Hotel Druzhba.

**Za Dvoma Zaitsami** (☎ 279 7972; Andriyivsky uzviz 34; mains 45-130hry; ⏲ 11am-11pm) Here's a precious little restaurant for a precious little street. The décor is Ukrainian kitsch, and the food, which is surprisingly delicious for such an obvious tourist trap, focuses on rabbit. (The name

means 'chasing two hares' and was named for a popular Soviet film).

**Gurme** (vul Chervonoarmiyska 12; mains 5-10hry; ⏲ 10am-8pm; Ⓜ Ploscha Lva Tolstoho) and **Puzata Khata** (☎ 246 7245; vul Baseyna 1/2A; mains 5-15hry; ⏲ 8am-11pm; Ⓜ Teatralna) are both cheap, popular cafeteria-style places; the food isn't spectacular but isn't bad either.

# DRINKING
## Cafés

There are so many cafés that you won't struggle to find a good cup of joe with decent atmosphere. **Pret-a-Cafe** (☎ 425 1297; Andriyivsky uzviz 10A; ⏲ 11am-11pm; Ⓜ Kontraktova Ploscha) is stylish and makes a welcome respite from souvenir shopping on the *uzviz*. Try the chocolates. Also, the bookshop Baboon (p865) has good espresso.

## Bars

**Art Club 44** (☎ 229 4137; vul Khreshchatyk 44; cover varies; Ⓜ Teatralna) Lots of beer, booze and food (try the pea soup) at this locally famous live-concert venue.

**Baraban** (☎ 229 2355; vul Prorizna 4A; ⏲ 11am-11pm; Ⓜ Maydan Nezalezhnosti) It's not readily apparent why this small, smoky place ('The Drum' in English) is so recommended; it has a history of cool clientele (journalists and the like). It's hard to find (in the back of a courtyard).

**Blindazh** (☎ 228 1511; Mala Zhytomirska 15; Ⓜ Maydan Nezalezhnosti) This dive bar is decked out with war paraphernalia and Soviet-era posters (one has been changed so that a pipe-smoking Stalin proclaims 'We Shall Overcome Cottonmouth'). The Doors, Kino and other music associated with wartime is played. People come for the moody atmosphere and inexpensive libations, not for the food, which makes army rations seem preferable.

**The Wall** (Stina; ☎ 235 8045; Bessarabsky ploscha 2; Ⓜ Teatralna) It's easy to miss this smoky place on the back side of the Bessarabsky Market. Look for the red sign over the door.

**Golden Gate** (☎ 235 5188; vul Zolotovoritska 15; Ⓜ Zoloti Vorota) and **O'Brien's Pub** (☎ 229 1584; vul Mykhailivska 17A; Ⓜ Maydan Nezalezhnosti) are two Irish-style pubs popular with expats.

# ENTERTAINMENT
## Nightclubs

Inventive small concerts are held at Art Club 44 (above) and Baboon (p865). The following are some fun clubs that don't focus on gambling and stripping (which are well marketed

---

**AUTHOR'S CHOICE**

**Himalaya** (☎ 270 5437; vul Khreshchatyk 23; mains 15-60hry; Ⓜ Khreshchatyk) This may be the only restaurant in the world that actually has *improved* with time. The Indian food here is great, and the raised location along Khreshchatyk is great for scoping the main-street scene. If you can't enter from Khreshchatyk, go through the huge arch just north of the restaurant, walk uphill, take the first right, and go about 100m.

UKRAINE

and need no review here). Most charge a cover that varies (probably 20hry to 50hry) depending on what's up.

**112** ( ☎ 230 9633; vul Chervonoarmiyska 5, Arena Complex; ◔ 9pm-4am; Ⓜ Ploscha Lva Tolstoho) This sequel to long-time party club 111 (now closed) is the number-one spot for expats and those who want to meet them.

**Carribean Club** ( ☎ 235 5222; vul Kominternu 4; ◔ 4pm-last customer Mon-Fri, from 6pm Sat & Sun; Ⓜ Ploscha Lva Tolstoho) Kyiv's premier Latin disco; great dancers strut their stuff.

**Docker's ABC** ( ☎ 278 3456; vul Zankovetskoyi 15/4A; ◔ 24hr; Ⓜ Khreshchatyk) By day a café-bar, Docker's is best once the sun goes down, when it opens up as a popular nightclub.

**Shooters** ( ☎ 254 2024; vul Moskovska 22; ◔ 24hr; Ⓜ Ploscha Lva Tolstoho) Wild, sexy and welcoming; staff wear kilts for some reason.

## Performing Arts

If you're looking for something a little more refined, you're also in luck – there's plenty of performing arts, and you won't have to blow your budget. Tickets can be purchased in advance at the **Teatralna Kasa** (vul Khreshchatyk 21; Ⓜ Khreshchatyk). Same-day tickets can be purchased at the venue.

**National Opera Theatre** ( ☎ 234 7165; www.opera.com.ua; vul Volodymyrska 50; Ⓜ Zoloti Vorota) Performances at this lavish opera house are a grandiose affair.

**Ivan Franko National Drama Theatre** ( ☎ 279 5921; ploscha Ivana Franka 3; Ⓜ Khreshchatyk) Highly respected performances.

**National Philharmonic** ( ☎ 228 1697; www.filarmonia.com.ua; Volodymyrska uzviz 2; Ⓜ Maydan Nezalezhnosti) Housed in a beautiful white building. Inside is a phenomenal organ.

**House of Organ & Chamber Music** ( ☎ 268 3186; vul Chervonoarmiyska 75; Ⓜ Palats Ukraina) Classical concerts are held in the cool Gothic St Nicholas' Church.

**Dynamo Stadium** ( ☎ 229 0209; vul Hrushevskoho 3; Ⓜ Maydan Nezalezhnosti) Ukraine's most beloved stadium, named after Ukraine's most beloved football team.

## SHOPPING

Without a doubt, the place to shop for souvenirs is along Andriyivsky uzviz. Western-style malls and shopping centres are fast becoming ubiquitous in the town centre, even though the number of people who can shop there hasn't quite justified the sheer quantity of them.

---

**WORTH A TRIP**

It's a pricey taxi ride (100hry each way), but if you get a group together, it's worth a trip to ride out to the Kyiv suburb of Brovary to the **Megamarket** ( ☎ 200 1400; vul Kyivska 316; 60-80hry), where there's a huge shopping centre with a place for carting. You get your own helmet and coveralls, the cars are fast, the track is gnarly, and beer and snacks are served in the upstairs bar while you wait your turn. There's a climbing wall too.

---

## GETTING THERE & AWAY
### Air

The **Boryspil international airport** ( ☎ 490 4777; www.airport-borispol.kiev.ua) is 35km from central Kyiv. All international flights use Terminal B; Terminal A is used for daily flights to Lviv and Odesa.

Most domestic flights and some charters to other CIS countries arrive and leave from **Zhulyany Airport** ( ☎ 242 2308; www.airport.kiev.ua, in Ukrainian); it's conveniently close to the centre (about 8km away). There are regular flights to Ivano-Frankivsk, Lviv, Odesa, Simferopol and Uzhhorod.

From Kyiv, there are weekday-only flights to/from Lviv (525hry, 1½ hours) and several daily flights to/from Odesa (525hry, one hour).

**Kiyavia** ( ☎ 490 4902; vul Horodetskoho 4; www.kiyavia.com) works well for booking domestic flights; offices are all over the place.

### Bus

Almost all long-distance buses, including Autolux, use the **Central Bus Terminal** ( ☎ 265 0430; ploscha Moskovska 3; Ⓜ Lybidska). To get there from Lybidska metro station, take minibus 457 (1.50hry), trolleybus 4, 11 or 12, or tram 9 or 10 one stop.

Trains are more comfortable than buses. If it must be bus, try the privately owned **Autolux** (www.autolux.ua), which goes between Kyiv and Ivano-Frankivsk, Lviv, Odesa, Simferopol and Uzhhorod. All routes stop at Boryspil Airport and the Kyiv train station. The website allows for online booking.

From Kyiv, state-run buses go to Odesa (55hry to 60hry, 8½ hours, 21 daily), Simferopol (105hry, 16 hours, one daily), Lviv (55hry, 11 hours, six daily), Kamyanets-Podilsky (57hry, 12 hours, two daily), Ivano-

Frankivsk (75hry, 11 hours, five daily) and Uzhhorod (88hry, 14 hours, two daily).

## Train

The modern **train station** ( ☎ 005; ploscha Vokzalna 2) is located right next to the Vokzalna metro station. Foreigners must go to windows No 40 or 41; to get there, use the main escalator, walk forward to the end of the station, and go right. The **train ticket office** ( ☎ 050; bulvar Tarasa Shevchenka 38/40; ☺ 8am-7pm Mon-Fri, to 6pm Sat & Sun), next to the Hotel Express, is usually less hectic for ticket purchase. For non-CIS destinations, go to Hall No 1, down a hallway on the left as you enter the main area.

Trains from Kyiv go to Uzhhorod, (*kupeyny/platskartny* 62/42hry, 17 hours, four daily), Ivano-Frankivsk (52/32hry, 13 hours, two daily), Kamyanets-Podilsky (32/22hry, 12 hours, one daily), Lviv (44/26hry, 10 hours, six daily), Odesa (60/44hry, 15 hours, five daily), Sevastopol (62/41hry, 17 hours, two daily) and Simferopol (*kupeyny* 56hry to 79hry, *platskartny* 38hry, 15 hours, one daily).

For more information about train travel, see p906. For definitions of the train classes given above, see p938.

## GETTING AROUND
### To/From the Airport

The usual way to Boryspil airport (10hry, 45 minutes) is on an **Atass bus** ( ☎ 296 7367). Buses depart from the bus stop at ploscha Peremohy (4am to midnight) and from the train station (5am to 3.30am) every 15 to 30 minutes, although they leave once an hour until 6am. At Boryspil, buses arrive/depart from in front of the international terminal. A taxi will set you back about 100hry.

**Autolux** (www.autolux.ua) buses also travel between Boryspil and Kyiv's main bus and train stations (35 mins); you can book on the website.

To get to Zhulyany airport, take trolleybus 9 from ploscha Peremohy (40 minutes) or a taxi (about 40hry for a 20-minute ride).

## Boat

At the **Boat Passenger Terminal**, near metro Poshtova Ploscha, boats leave when full for rides lasting 1½ to 3½ hours, from April to November and starting about 10am (adult 20hry to 40hry, child 10hry to 20hry). Beer and snacks are sold on board. The whole thing is thoroughly unorganised. Currently there are no long-distance Dnipro boat trips.

## Public Transport

Kyiv's metro is clean, efficient, reliable and easy to use, especially if you read Cyrillic. Trains run frequently between around 6am and midnight on all three lines. Single-ride tokens (*zhetony*) cost 50 kopeks and are sold at entrances; there are also token-vending machines that only sometimes work.

Tickets for buses, trams and trolleybuses cost 50 kopeks and are sold at street kiosks or directly from the driver or conductor. Minibuses (*marshrutki*) cost 1hry to 1.50hry; pay the driver upon entering.

## Taxi

Catching a taxi from the train station, on ploscha Peremohy and outside hotels, inevitably incurs a higher price, so try to find one elsewhere on the street. From the train station to the centre may cost 30hry. Try to look for newer, official-looking cars, which are more likely to have a meter and hence won't rip you off. Catching metered cabs on the street is rare. By phone, try **FM Taxi** ( ☎ 502 0502), which has a standard, metered rate of 15hry for the first 4km, then 1.50hry per kilometre. You can also flag down a private car and negotiate a price if you speak the language.

# WESTERN UKRAINE

It doesn't get more Ukrainian than this. Nowhere in the country are the people so passionate about their original culture and language than in Western Ukraine. Here, countless monuments and references to Cossacks, dissidents and other patriots vouch for Ukrainian pride, and speaking Russian is just plain gauche. The region wasn't annexed by the USSR until 1939, and somehow escaped bombing during WWII, so both the architecture and the attitudes have, for the most part, managed to avoid the Soviet influence, leaving it with a relaxed, Central European look and feel.

Strangely enough, Western Ukraine is still largely undiscovered by foreign visitors – and not for want of attractions. The city of Lviv is an unpolished gem, and the motley architecture and sooty beauty of its Old Town was enough for Unesco to deem it a World

UKRAINE

Heritage site in 1998. Even many Ukrainians don't really know about little Kamyanets-Podilsky, an ancient town perched on a island of rock in the middle of a deep ravine – but visit it once, and you'll never forget it. And let's not forget the Carpathian Mountains, where hiking, biking and skiing adventures in remote, almost untouched locales are relatively inexpensive and easily arranged.

Before travelling between this region and Odesa, read the boxed text on p891.

## LVIV ЛЬВІВ

**☎ 032 (7 digits), 0322 (6 digits) / pop 745,000**

Gorgeous and glorious, Lviv knows it's next up on the list of hot new Eastern European destinations. And with an English-speaking service industry, new youth hostels and quality hotels, and the only tourist information centre in the country, it's just waiting to be adored by you.

The Old Town, a Unesco World Heritage site, is jam-packed with ornate churches and historic buildings in a mishmash of styles ranging from rococo to baroque and Renaissance to Gothic. Wandering through the seemingly endless network of narrow cobblestone alleys, and cowering under the piercing stares of hidden gargoyles and sudden statues, Lviv's atmosphere of mystery is absolutely enticing. If you're not already a photographer, artist or writer, this city and its secrets will inspire you to become one.

### Information

**Central post office** (☎ 065; vul Slovatskoho 1; 🕑 8am-8pm Mon-Fri, 8am-4pm Sat, 9am-3pm Sun) The telephone office around the corner is open 7am to 11pm daily.

**Internet Klub** (☎ 722 738; vul Dudaeva 12; per hr 4hry; 🕑 24hr) Has about a dozen computers with a relatively speedy connection, as well as cheap international calls.

**Khuru Books** (☎ 722 550; ploscha Mitskevycha; 🕑 10am-6pm Mon-Fri, to 3pm Sat) Weirdly compartmentalised, with separate sections having separate entrances. At least one section has local maps and guides; another section has some novels in English.

**Oschadnyy Bank** (☎ 272 793; vul Sichovykh Striltsiv 9) Full banking services, including Western Union; cashes traveller cheque.

**Tourist information centre** (☎ 975 767; www.tourism.lviv.ua; vul Pidvalna 3; 🕑 10am-1pm & 2-6pm Mon-Fri) English-speaking staff arranges city tours and day trips in many languages. They have plans of moving back to the *ratusha* (town hall) on ploscha Rynok.

### Sights

In addition to doing the walking tour (below) and checking out some museums, make a point of visit the **Lychakiv Cemetery** (vul Mechnikova; admission 4hry; 🕑 9am-5pm Mon-Fri), and bring a camera – it's one of the loveliest cemeteries in Eastern Europe. If you get on tram 7 at the stop on vul Pidvalna, it arrives right in front of the cemetery five stops later (if you get confused, ask for the *klad*-bee-sheh).

There are loads of museums in town, the **National Museum** (☎ 742 280; prospekt Svobody 20; admission 14hry; 🕑 10am-6pm Sat-Thu) features 15th- to 19th-century icons and works by Ukrainian artists. The interior of the building itself is impressive as well.

The **Arsenal Museum** (☎ 721 901; vul Pidvalna 5; admission 3hry; 🕑 10am-5pm Thu-Tue) has chronologically arranged weaponry from around the world, as well as some English-language city guidebooks for sale.

There are two branches of the **Museum of Ethnography & Historic Artefacts** (☎ 727 808; ploscha Rynok 10 & prospekt Svobody 15; admission 2hry; 🕑 10am-5.30pm Tue-Sun). Both buildings hold exhibits on farm culture and village life in the Carpathians, including furniture, woodcarvings, ceramics and farming implements.

The **Lviv History Museum** (☎ 720 671; 🕑 10am-6pm Thu-Tue) is split among three collections surrounding ploscha Rynok, at No 4, 6 and 22.

The **Pharmacy Museum** (☎ 722 041; vul Drukarska 2; admission 1.50hry; 🕑 10am-6pm Mon-Fri, to 4pm Sat & Sun) is in the back of a functioning pharmacy that dates back to 1735. Pay the pharmacists to open it up for you, and walk into a world of containers, drawers and other gadgets for herbs and tinctures and salves. You can buy a small bottle of medicinal 'iron wine'.

The **Museum of Folk Architecture & Rural Life** (☎ 718 017; vul Chernecha Hora 1; adult/child 1.50/0.75hry; 🕑 11am-7pm Tue-Sun Apr-Oct, to 6pm Nov-Mar) is a large park that holds over a hundred old wooden homes and churches. Take tram 7 four stops from vul Pidvalna, continue in same direction and turn left on vul Krupyarska (Крупярська), and follow the signs.

### Walking Tour

This 5km tour starts at ploscha Rynok (Market Square), the hub of political and commercial life during the Middle Ages. In 1998 it was declared a Unesco World Heritage site. The town hall *(ratusha)*, which takes up the majority of space in the square, was

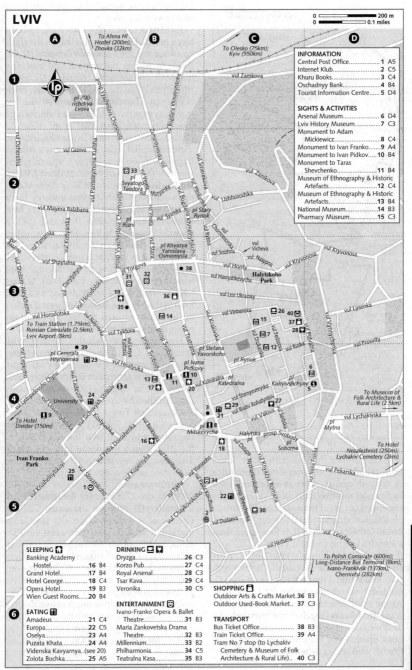

# LVIV

0 ————— 200 m
0 ————— 0.1 miles

**INFORMATION**

| | |
|---|---|
| Central Post Office............................**1** A5 | |
| Internet Klub....................................**2** C5 | |
| Khuru Books.....................................**3** C4 | |
| Oschadnyy Bank................................**4** B4 | |
| Tourist Information Centre..................**5** D4 | |

**SIGHTS & ACTIVITIES**

| | |
|---|---|
| Arsenal Museum.................................**6** D4 | |
| Lviv History Museum..........................**7** C3 | |
| Monument to Adam Mickiewicz.........**8** C4 | |
| Monument to Ivan Franko...................**9** A4 | |
| Monument to Ivan Pidkov.................**10** B4 | |
| Monument to Taras Shevchenko........**11** B4 | |
| Museum of Ethnography & Historic Artefacts...................................**12** C4 | |
| Museum of Ethnography & Historic Artefacts...................................**13** B4 | |
| National Museum.............................**14** B3 | |
| Pharmacy Museum...........................**15** C3 | |

**SLEEPING** 🛏

| | |
|---|---|
| Banking Academy Hostel......................**16** B4 | |
| Grand Hotel....................................**17** B4 | |
| Hotel George..................................**18** C4 | |
| Opera Hotel....................................**19** B3 | |
| Wien Guest Rooms..........................**20** B4 | |

**EATING** 🍴

| | |
|---|---|
| Amadeus.........................................**21** C4 | |
| Europa............................................**22** C5 | |
| Oselya............................................**23** A4 | |
| Puzata Khata...................................**24** A4 | |
| Videnska Kavyarnya........(see 20) | |
| Zolota Bochka.................................**25** A5 | |

**DRINKING** 🍺 🍷

| | |
|---|---|
| Dryzga............................................**26** C3 | |
| Korzo Pub.......................................**27** C4 | |
| Royal Arsenal..................................**28** C3 | |
| Tsar Kava........................................**29** C4 | |
| Veronika.........................................**30** C5 | |

**ENTERTAINMENT** 🎭

| | |
|---|---|
| Ivano-Franko Opera & Ballet Theatre...............................**31** B3 | |
| Maria Zankovetska Drama Theatre...............................**32** B3 | |
| Millennium.....................................**33** B2 | |
| Philharmonia..................................**34** C5 | |
| Teatralna Kasa................................**35** B3 | |

**SHOPPING** 🛍

| | |
|---|---|
| Outdoor Arts & Crafts Market.........**36** B3 | |
| Outdoor Used-Book Market............**37** C3 | |

**TRANSPORT**

| | |
|---|---|
| Bus Ticket Office.............................**38** B3 | |
| Train Ticket Office...........................**39** A4 | |
| Tram No 7 stop (to Lychakiv Cemetery & Museum of Folk Architecture & Rural Life)...**40** C3 | |

**UKRAINE**

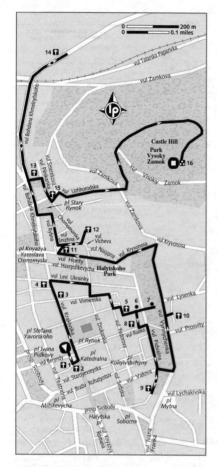

originally built in the 14th century, but it has been rebuilt several times since then: once in the 16th century when it was demolished by fire and most recently in 1851. From the southwest corner of the square, walk south to ploscha Katedralna, where you can't miss the **Roman Catholic Cathedral (1)**. It took more than a hundred years to build (1370–1480) and therefore a few different styles (Gothic, Renaissance, baroque) are apparent. On the north side, you'll find a relief of Pope Jean Paul II, erected to commemorate his 2001 Lviv visit. At the southeastern corner of the cathedral is the 1617 **Boyim Chapel (2)**, the burial chapel of a wealthy Hungarian merchant family. Look up, and you'll see an atypical statue of Christ, who seems to be mournfully observ-

ing the mess we wretched sinners have made of this world.

Head back toward ploscha Rynok, and go a block north of it onto Krakivska; on the right, you'll see the 1363 **Armenian Cathedral (3)**. Go inside to admire the atypical and evocative frescoes. Continue north to vul Lesi Ukrainky, where you'll find the late-17th-century, twin-bell towered **Transfiguration Church (4)**, the first in the city to revert to Ukrainian Catholic after independence. Turn east onto vul Lesi Ukrainky then right onto Drukarska, left onto Virmenska, and right onto Fedorova. Almost immediately on your left is a square, where you'll see the 1745–64 **Dominican Church & Monastery (5)**, distinguished by its large dome and its rococo, baroque and classical features. Just a bit further east is the arched façade of the **Royal Arsenal (6)**. Built between 1639 and 1646, it once held weapons to be used in wars against the Turks; it now holds the city's archives. The statue here is of Federov, a 16th-century monk who brought printing to Ukraine (perhaps why there's an outdoor used-book market here as well). Cross vul Pidvalna and head toward the 1554–56 **Gunpowder Tower (7)**. Over the last four centuries the bottom 2m of the tower have slowly become covered in soil.

Head back across Pidvalna, turning south at the Royal Arsenal, to one of the most memorable moments of the tour. To your right, you'll find the **Assumption Church & Three Saints Chapel (8)**. The church (1591–1629) is easily distinguished by the 65m-high, triple-tiered Kornyakt Bell Tower (1572–78). The Three Saints Chapel (1578–91) is nestled beneath the tower and built into the north side of the church, in a wonderful little courtyard. Together, the two structures are considered to be the historic centre of the city.

Continue south on Pidvalna for about 200m to the 17th-century **Bernardine Church & Monastery (9)**, now the Ukrainian Catholic Church of St Andrew – a major Lviv landmark. Go back the way you came on Pidvalna, turning right onto vul Valova and then left onto vul Vynnychenka. Head north about 200m to the 1644 **St Mary Carmelite Monastery (10)**. Some fragments of its original defensive walls can still be seen. Walk back to Vynnychenka, and continue north about 300m to Kryvonosa, where you'll turn left. Continue west on this street, which turns into vul Honty, for about 400m. On your right, up a small set of steps, is the tiny 18th-century stone church, the **Church of Maria Snizhna (11)**. After the church, turn right onto Snizhna, pass vul Rybna, and on your left, through a cast-iron gate, is the **Nunnery of the Benedictines (12)**. Note the detailed, crown-like stone carving at the top of the tower. Return to the corner of Rybna and head north on that street, through ploscha Stary Rynok (Old Market Square), then up Bohdana Khmelnytskoho to the green-domed **St Nicholas Church (13)**. Dating from the 13th century and remodelled in the 16th century, its Old Rus Quarter is an excellent example of early Byzantine architecture.

Continue north, and when you reach the railway tracks go through the underground passageway then continue north for about 100m to the **Church of Good Friday (14)**. It was originally built in the 13th century, but was reconstructed in the mid-17th century. If you can get inside, there is a beautiful 17th-century iconostasis.

Go back the way you came, under the tracks. Make a left just past St Nicholas Church, then a right onto Pylnykarska. When you get to ploscha Stary Rynok, make a left, and you'll see the humble little brick-and-stone church of **St John the Baptist (15)**, built in 1260.

Take Uzhhorodska, the road just south of the church, for about 200m, cross Zamkova and then veer left up a road that leads to the **High Castle (16)**. At the top of the hill (the wind can be strong), you'll have an all-inclusive view of what you've seen up close – although you may have to squint through some trees.

## Sleeping
### BUDGET
Unlike Kyiv, Lviv is starting to see more good low-cost accommodation options.

**Banking Academy Hostel** ( ☎ 296 5734; www.hi hostels.com.ua; vul Kopernyka 14; dm 120hry) The only bummer about this awesome new hostel is that at least for now, it's only open July and August. Reception is open 9am to 6pm daily, so give notice if you will arrive later.

**Afena** ( ☎ 296 5834; www.hihostels.com.ua, vul Khymychna 49A; dm 120hry) This is another good HI hostel option. It's not quite as central (linked by buses), but it's open year-round.

**Hotel Nezalezhnist** ( ☎ 757 214; fax 754 561; vul Tershakivtsiv 6a; s/d 120/130hry, d with shared bathroom 80hry) Nezalezhnist is Soviet-style, but with sunshine and church views. Some rooms here even have

a spot of personality…leopard-print blankets on the beds. Hot water is only available from 7am to 11am, so set your alarm clock if you plan on a relaxing shower in the morning. From the train station, take tram 9a to the end of the line, walk east on Pekarska, go right on Tershakivtsiv and walk 100m.

### MIDRANGE
**Hotel George** ( ☎ 725 952; www.georgehotel.com.ua; ploscha Mitskevycha 1; s/tw 319/388hry, s/tw with shared bathroom 154/187hry) In a way, the George is almost as grand as the Grand – but it's a weary sort of grandeur, and little fuss is made over it. The rooms with shared bathrooms are a super-duper deal. Staff speak some English and are good-humoured.

**Wien Guest Rooms** ( ☎ 444 314; www.wienhotel .lviv.ua; prospekt Svobody 12; s 330-520hry, d 360-550hry, ste 650-700hry; 🗷 🖳 ) Hidden from view, deep behind Videnska Kavyarnya (p878), little Wien doesn't get any street traffic. Nevertheless, its 20 freshly renovated, cosy rooms host a steady stream of people in the know. The kind and English-speaking reception, tasteful and elegant décor, and totally agreeable pricing are what make it so successful.

**Hotel Dnister** ( ☎ 974 317; www.dnister.lviv.ua; vul Mateika 6; d 400-800hry, ste 1000-1500hry; 🗷 🖳 ) Don't judge the Dnister by its Soviet-style cover. True, its 1970s brown-and-yellow exterior makes it look like a large rectangular bumblebee, but inside is a totally different tale. Take a trip to the top-floor restaurant, where the glorious panoramic city view blows the one from Castle Hill out the water.

### TOP END
**Grand Hotel** ( ☎ 724 042; www.ghgroup.com.ua; prospekt Svobody 13; s 530-630hry, d 795-885hry, ste 975-1590hry; 🗷 🖳 🗷 ) With a long history as the classiest joint in town, the Grand is the proud peacock of Lviv hotels. What you're paying for, and paying for well, is the history and, as the name implies, the grandeur of the place. Where the lustre fades is in service, which does the job but can leave you cold.

**Opera Hotel** ( ☎ 225 9000; www.hotel-opera.lviv.ua; prospekt Svobody 45; s 420-520hry, d 620-780hry, ste 920-1520hry; 🗷 🖳 ) Making its big debut in 2005, the Opera is the new kid in town. Whereas the décor and ambience are more modern than one would expect, service harkens back to the good old days: we even got a curtsy from the maid.

UKRAINE

## Eating

In addition to these listings, there are several good outdoor cafés on the east side of prospekt Svobody.

**Puzata Khata** ( ☎ 240 3265; vul Sichovykh Striltsiv; mains 5-15hry; ☒ 8am-11pm) This popular cafeteria-style chain serves up Ukrainian staples, and unlike the one in Kyiv, there is plenty of seating.

**Europa** ( ☎ 725 862; prospekt Shevchenka 14; mains 12-30hry; ☒ 8am-11pm Mon-Fri, 10am-10pm Sat & Sun) Small, cosy and relatively quiet, Europa is a good place for a filling meal of Ukrainian food. Only the TV is a drawback to the ambience, but if the weather's nice, there is a small amount of sidewalk seating.

**Zolota Bochka** ( ☎ 727 804; vul Doroshenka 38; mains 15-35hry; ☒ 10am-10pm) Locals recommend this humble little eatery for its simple Ukrainian food.

**Oselya** ( ☎ 272 1601; vul Hnatyuka 11; mains 5-50hry) It's lined with kitschy Ukrainian décor from floor to ceiling, but can be deserted, making one wonder whether the place is open. However, it usually is, delivering honest-to-goodness Ukrainian and central European cuisine.

**Videnska Kavyarnya** ( ☎ 722 021; www.wientkaffe .lviv.ua; prospekt Svobody 12; mains 8-60hry; ☒ 10am-11pm) One of many popular restaurants with spring and summer sidewalk seating; this one offers billiards inside, Ukrainian cuisine and an English-language menu – although the bizarro translation ('veal' translated as 'teleooze'?) may make the Ukrainian menu more helpful.

**Amadeus** ( ☎ 978 022; ploscha Katedralna 7; mains 30-100hry; ☒ 11am-11pm) This small, bistro-like restaurant is perfect for romance, with meals like risotto or fondue for two. The food (regional and European cuisine) is scrumptious. There's no TV; the music is lilting and at a mild volume – sometimes there is live accordion music.

## Drinking

There are plenty of little bars to discover in town too, and most restaurants have good beer on tap. The numerous summertime sidewalk cafés along the east side of prospekt Svobody are a great place to sit under an umbrella and sip on a Ukrainian tap beer.

**Korzo Pub** ( ☎ 296 7092; vul Brativ Rohatyntsiv 10; ☒ noon-midnight Sun-Thu, to 2am Fri & Sat) Bars are thin on the ground in Lviv, and this is the closest the city has to an Irish pub. There's food (not great), and sometimes a happy hour from 6pm on Thursday. Expats and locals alike come here.

**Tsar Kava** ( ☎ 720 093; ploscha Rynok 27; ☒ 9am-10pm) A little gem of a sweet shop, whose coffee and pastries are popular with the refined folk. It's tucked away behind the Roman Catholic Cathedral – a very cool location.

**Veronika** ( ☎ 297 8128; prospekt Shevchenka 21; ☒ 10am-midnight) The choice of gorgeous pastries and chocolates brought tears to this guidebook writer's eyes and had her singing Elvis Costello out on the café's summer terrace. There's also downstairs seating.

## Entertainment

For a perfect evening, enjoy a drink at one of the cafés and a performance at the beautiful **Ivano-Franko Opera & Ballet Theatre** ( ☎ 728 562; prospekt Svobody 28; tickets 40-300hry) or the **Philharmonia** ( ☎ 741 086; vul Chaykovskoho 7; tickets 30-90hry). If you speak Ukrainian, see a play at the well-respected **Maria Zankovetska Drama Theatre** ( ☎ 720 762; vul Lesi Ukrainky 1). Tickets are sold on site or at the **teatralna kasa** ( ☎ 233 3188; prospekt Svobody 37; ☒ 11am-2pm & 5-7pm).

**Millennium** ( ☎ 230 3591; prospekt Vyacheslava Chornovola 2; admission 15-40hry; ☒ 9pm-late Tue-Sun) boasts four bars, a disco and billiards, as well as hookah rentals. Women are admitted free on Tuesday and Wednesday.

## Shopping

Souvenirs and gifts of all sorts – including T-shirts that say, in Ukrainian, 'Thank God I'm not a Muscovite' (only using a more derogatory term for them) – are sold at the **outdoor arts and crafts market** ( ☒ morning-sunset), off prospekt Svobody. If you're into old books, there's a quirky **outdoor used-book market** ( ☒ morning-sunset) by the Royal Arsenal.

## Getting There & Away
### AIR

The **Lviv airport** ( ☎ 692 112; www.avia.lviv.ua) is about 9km west of the centre. It's small and basic (no ATM or currency exchange). There

---

**AUTHOR'S CHOICE**

**Dyzga** (vul Virmenska 35) Come admire the local graffiti artists and check out some paintings at this café-cum-arts-centre. It's super chilled-out, attracting bohemian, alternative types. Caffeine and alcohol are both served.

are mostly domestic flights, and the main international flights are via Vienna on Austrian Airlines. Word has it you should make sure you have more than 30 minutes to transfer in Vienna – no matter what the airline says – if you want your baggage to arrive at your final destination the same time you do.

From Kyiv, there are weekday-only flights to/from Lviv (525hry, 1½ hours).

### BUS

Lviv has eight bus terminals, but only one is of use to most travellers – the **long-distance bus terminal** ( ☎ 632 473; vul Stryiska 271), about 8km south of the city centre. Advance tickets for public buses to Ivano-Frankivsk (20hry, three hours, hourly) and Kyiv (65hry, nine hours, three daily), as well as international destinations (see p904), are sold at the **bus ticket office** ( ☎ 971 108; vul Teatralna 26; ☽ 9am-2pm & 3-6pm); it's easy to walk past the place, which is also a CD shop – look for the 'каса' sign. Bus information (not in English) can be had at ☎ 004 until 8pm.

Privately run **Autolux** (www.autolux.com.ua) also operates from the long-distance terminal, sending nice, modern buses regularly to Kyiv and other cities; see the website for details.

### TRAIN

The **train station** ( ☎ 353 360, 261 906; ploscha Dvirtseva) is 1.75km west of the city centre. Tickets can also be obtained from the **train ticket office** ( ☎ 748 2068; vul Hnatyuka 20; ☽ 8am-8pm Mon-Fri, to 6pm Sat & Sun, closed 2-3pm); have your passport (or a copy of it) ready, and be prepared to stand in line, especially in spring and summer. Each window closes for ten minutes an hour. For train information (not in English), call ☎ 005.

From Lviv, there are trains to Kyiv (kupeyny/platskartny 47/29hry, 10 hours, four daily), Odesa (45/29hry, 12 hours, two daily) Uzhhorod (18/11hry, seven hours, four daily), Ivano-Frankivsk (16/10hry, 2½ hours, one daily) and Simferopol (67/44hry, 25 hours, one daily).

### Getting Around

Unless you're going somewhere off the map provided here, walking is the best option. *Marshrutka* 95 links the airport and the centre, as does trolleybus 9 from the university building on vul Universytetska. A taxi there will cost from 25hry to 35hry.

Tram 1 or 9, or *marshrutka* 66, 67 or 68 link the train station with prospekt Svobody and ploscha Rynok.

*Marshrutka* 71 and 180 from prospekt Svobody or trolleybus 5 from ploscha Petrushevycha go to the long-distance bus terminal.

There are multitudes of *marshrutki* marked Центр (Centre), and any of these should traverse the main part of prospekt Svobody.

## UZHHOROD УЖГОРОД
☎ 03122 (5 digits), ☎ 0312 (6 digits)
**pop 110,000**

The pretty, quiet Transcarpathian town of Uzhhorod (Uzhgorod in Russian) is the southern gateway to the Ukrainian section of the Carpathian Mountains. It's split in half by the Uzh River, which separates the New and Old Towns. There's a split in population too, as Uzhhorod is home to both a pronounced and poor Roma population and a conspicuous nouveau-riche contingent. It's an ideal staging post for anyone travelling to/from Slovakia or Hungary but is probably too far off the beaten track for other travellers.

### Information

Banks, exchange offices and ATMs are easy to find in the town centre. For internet access, try **Planeta I-Net** (naberezhnaya Nezalezhnosti 1; per hr 2hry; ☽ 24hr), which is poorly run by a bunch of rowdy boys. There are other options, but it's the easiest to locate – right at the end of the pedestrian bridge on the centre side of the river.

### Sights

The 16th-century **Uzhhorod Castle** (vul Kapitulna; adult/child 5/2hry, grounds only 1hry; ☽ 9am-5pm Tue-Sun) is on a hill 400m northeast of the main square. It has a museum, but best is the sweeping view of the region from its grounds. If you have trouble finding it, ask for the *zamok*. Across from the castle is the open-air **Museum of Folk Architecture & Rural Life** (adult/child 4/1hry; ☽ 10am-5pm Wed-Mon). Transcarpathian abodes, tools and crafts are on display.

Downhill from the castle is the twin-towered, yellow 1640 **cathedral** (vul Kapitulna).

You can explore the ruins of the **Nevitsky Zamok** (Bride-to-Be Castle), 12km from the city (taxi 50hry return). The castle was first mentioned in chronicles in the 14th century, and rumour has it villagers used to hide women during enemy attacks. Views from the castle are jaw-dropping.

## Sleeping & Eating

**Hotel Svitanok** ( ☎ 643 852; www.tok-svitanok.uzhgorod
.ua; vul Koshytska 30; s 133-164hry, d 102-322hry, d/tr with
shared bathroom 84/117hry) It used to be the cheapest
place in town, but Svitanok has been remodelled (in a sort of tacky way). Now only the
cheapest rooms make it worthwhile.

**Hotel Uzhhorod** ( ☎ 35 060; hotel@email.uz.ua; ploscha Khemlnitskoho 2; s 119-239hry, d 189-239hry, ste 199-
370hry; ✷ ) This remodelled Soviet monster
knows the meaning of service (chocolates
on your pillow in the pricier rooms) and is a
good choice if staying at Atlant. It's a pleasant
10-minute walk along the river to the centre
of town.

**Atlant** ( ☎ 614 095; www.hotel-atlant.com; ploscha
Koryatovicha 27; s 120hry, d 165-200hry, ste 225-310hry; ✷ )
These modern rooms are as sweet as can be
and awesome value – especially the singles,
which are on the top floor (no lift) and have
skylights and slanted ceilings. It's a small place
though; book ahead if you can.

**Cafe Da Da** ( ☎ 32 346; vul Kapitulna 5; mains 3-20hry;
⏲ 7am-10pm) Funky-arty-bohemian is what
it is, just down the hill from the Uzhhorod
Castle. Not much serious food here – mostly
snacks and beverages.

**Kaktus Kafe** ( ☎ 32 515; vul Korzo 7; mains 8-25hry;
⏲ 10am-11pm) Probably the most popular hang-
out in town, this smoky, noisy joint is full of
beer- and coffee-drinkers. The theme is decidedly Wild West upstairs; downstairs it seems
to be Aztec. The food is pretty good, but the
service can be slow.

**Delfin** ( ☎ 614 963; Kyivskaya naberezhnaya 3; mains 8-
45hry, ⏲ 11am-11pm) Locals consider this one of
the better restaurants in town. European and
Ukrainian dishes are served, but it's known
for its grilled meats and rooftop terrace.
You can find it at the end of the pedestrian
bridge on the non-centre side of the river
(you'll have to go upstairs once you get to
the building).

## Getting There & Away

The bus and train stations are across the street
from each other. A **taxi** ( ☎ 051) within Uzhhorod will set you back 5hry or 6hry.

### BUS

Twice-daily buses go from the **bus terminal**
(prospekt Svobody) to Ivano-Frankivsk (42hry, 10
hours) and Lviv (34hry, four hours). You can
also get very cheap, uncomfortable buses to
Slovakia and Hungary here (see p904).

### TRAIN

The newly built Uzhhorod train station is fab.
One building is for local electric trains only.

Trains go to Kyiv (*kupeyny/platskartny*
62/45hry, 19 hours, two daily), Lviv (25/18hry,
eight hours, one daily), and Odesa (65/48hry,
12 hours, one daily).

## IVANO-FRANKIVSK
## ІВАНО-ФРАНКІВСЬК

☎ 03422 (5 digits), 0342 (6 digits) / pop 204,000
If the type of storefronts within its tranquil
pedestrian precinct are any indication, reading, eating pizza and drinking coffee must
be the favourite pastimes of the people of
Ivano-Frankivsk. Although it's theoretically
the traditional cultural and economic capital
of the Carpathian region, there's little to see
and do. Nevertheless it's a spacious, relaxed
and well-manicured city, and it works great
as a jumping-off point for adventures into the
mountains or visits to the traditional villages
of the Hutsuls (p882).

### Information

Currency exchanges, ATMs and Western
Unions are common at banks and are easily found along the pedestrian zone of vul
Nezalezhnosti. Bookshops seem to be everywhere, too.

**Central post office** ( ☎ 231 041; vul Sichovych Striltsiv
13A)

**Bukinist** ( ☎ 23 828; vul Nezalezhnosti 19; ⏲ 10am-
6pm Mon-Fri, to 2pm Sat) Friendly staff and local maps.
There are two bookstores under the white columns here;
Bukinist is the smaller one, with the far-right corner
entrance.

**Internet Centre** ( ☎ 552 580; vul Nezalezhnosti 5; per
hr 7hry; ⏲ 24hr) Not well-marked; between the bank and
the casino. Calls here are cheaper than at Ukrtelecom.

**Nadiya Tours** ( ☎ 537 042; nadia@utel.net.ua; vul
Nezalezhnosti 40) In Hotel Nadiya; does Carpathian tours.

**Tourist Information Centre** (ploscha Rynok 4;
⏲ 11am-4pm Mon-Fri) In the Town Hall; lots of pamphlets
(none of them particularly useful) and a couple of maps.

**Ukrtelecom** ( ⏲ 7am-11pm) Domestic and international
phone office; across from the post office.

### Sights

Don't miss the **Art Museum** ( ☎ 30 039; ploscha Sheptytsky 8; admission 3hry; ⏲ 11am-6pm Tue-Sun). Housed
in the 1672–1703 **Parish Church** (also known
as the Church of the Blessed Virgin Mary),
this peaceful museum focuses on religious
art and icons.

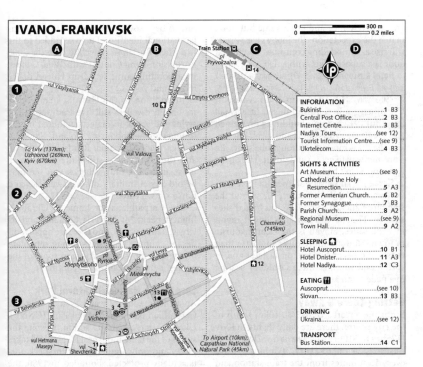

# IVANO-FRANKIVSK

Ploscha Rynok is dominated by the **Town Hall** (built in 1695, but totally redone in 1929–32 in a boring constructivist style with some Art Deco elements), which houses the two-storey **Regional Museum** ( ☎ 22 326; ploscha Rynok 4A; adult/child 60/40 kopeks; ☼ 10am-5pm Tue-Sun), covering a broad range of exhibits. (Look for the beautiful old faded *pysanky*.)

Diagonally opposite the Art Museum and Parish Church is the resorted baroque **Cathedral of the Holy Resurrection** (ploscha Sheptytsky 22), a Ukrainian Greek Catholic church. If you happen to be around during Catholic Easter, you'll be probably see an orange-neon Христос Воскрес! (Christ has Risen!) sign inside – which looks pretty out of place with the beautiful iconography that surrounds it.

East of the square is the 1742–62 **former Armenian Church** (vul Virmenska 6) with its attractive baroque façade and rounded bell towers.

During the city's Nazi occupation (1941–42), almost the entire Jewish population of Ivano-Frankivsk was wiped out. Around the corner from the entrance to a **former synagogue** is a memorial to 27 Ukrainians killed by Germans during WWII. There is no mention of the city-wide genocide. The synagogue itself is now a faded, salmon-coloured travel agency, bearing just a single Star of David on high as testament to its original purpose.

## Sleeping & Eating

Nadiya and Auscoprut have decent restaurants (Nadiya's restaurant is called Ukraina), and vul Nezalezhnosti has several dining options.

**Hotel Dnister** ( ☎ 23 533; vul Sichovykh Striltsiv 12; s/d with shared bathroom 50/80hry, d 150-300hry) Dnister has decent staff but depressing rooms, and the shared bathrooms could use a little scrubbing. There is no hot water after midnight, and even when there is hot water you'll have to let it run for about 10 minutes before it starts to warm up.

**Hotel Nadiya** ( ☎ 53 775; www.nadia.if.ua; vul Nezalezhnosti 40; s 120-270hry, d 300-340hry, ste 390hry) The grand white marble lobby might make you think the rooms cost a fortune here, but it's not the case. Formerly a more Soviet-style place called Hotel Ukraina, Nadiya is getting a makeover from the ground up, but so far only the ground really shows it. The rooms are relatively nice and good value but don't match the expectations the lobby gives. Prices will rise as remodelling continues. Right next door is a supermarket with a deli.

**Hotel Auscoprut** ( ☎ 23 401; auscoprut@ivf.ukrpack .net; vul Gryunvaldska 7/9; s 180-320hry, d 240-400hry, ste 450-550hry; 🖭 ) Auscoprut is an Austrian-Ukrainian joint venture housed in a small beautiful 1912 baroque building with stained glass. Staff are professional and speak English, and the lift is modern, although the stairs are a prettier way to get up and down. The onsite restaurant isn't bad.

**Slovan** ( ☎ 712 594; vul Shashkevicha 4; mains 10-37hry; 🕙 11am-midnight) With yummy pizzas and the standard Chicken Kiev, as well as bold dishes such as Tijuana chicken and stewed rabbit in wine sauce, Slovan is the clear favourite in town. Staff are more eager to please than most. The décor borders on tasteful and in spring and summer there's outdoor seating in a pedestrian area.

### Getting There & Away

From the **airport** ( ☎ 598 348), 10km south of the city centre, there are daily flights to Kyiv (125hry to 510hry), by **Kyiavia** (www.kiyavia.com). Buses 21, 24 and 65 (1hry, 30 minutes) leave every 15 minutes from the train station and go to the airport.

The train station and bus station are conveniently right next to each other, on ploscha Privozksalna.

There are trains to Kyiv (*kupeyny/platskartny* 51/29hry, 14 hours, one daily), Lviv (21/15hry, 3½ to seven hours, two daily), Odesa (44/30hry, 21 hours, odd dates), and Uzhhorod (25/18hry, 11 hours, odd dates), as well as *kupeyny* only trains to Simferopol (85hry, 33 hours) in summer.

Buses from Ivano-Frankivsk go to Kyiv (66hry to 70hry, 12 hours, four daily), Lviv (16hry to 19hry, 3½ hours, 20 daily) and Uzhhorod (35hry, nine hours, four daily). There is also a single daily bus that goes straight to Kyiv's Boryspil airport (90hry, 12 hours).

## CARPATHIAN MOUNTAINS

One of the least-developed areas in all of Europe is the easternmost section of the Carpathian Mountains, which cut through the lower corner of Western Ukraine. Among the undulating ridges lives a cluster of various ethnic groups, including the Hutsuls, who, despite their clear Romanian ties, have turned out to be a source of pride to the Ukrainian national identity. (Fuel was added to the fire when Ruslana Lyzhychko won the 2004 Eurovision Song Contest with *Wild Dances*, incorporating some sexed-up Hutsul dance moves and vocals.)

In addition to the Hutsuls, many other mountain dwellers still live traditional lifestyles and speak in dialects coloured by the tongues of neighbouring Poland, Slovakia, Hungary and Romania. Roads are still bad, and the economy is still quite poor, so in most areas, the only vehicles you see may be old Soviet military off-road vehicles and horse-drawn carts.

The Carpathians are home to Ukraine's highest peak, Mt Hoverla (2062m) and its largest national park, and there are opportunities for camping, homestays, hiking, mountain biking and most of all skiing in some of the wildest natural areas on the continent.

### Carpathian National Natural Park

About 45km south of Ivano-Frankivsk lies the Carpathian National Natural Park (CNNP), Ukraine's largest at 503 sq km. Despite the status of the land, industrial logging still takes place, and only about 25% of the park area is actually protected. Founded in 1980, the CNNP shelters wolves, brown bears, lynx, bison and deer. Hutsuls still live in the park, and the country's highest peak, Mt Hoverla (2062m), is here as well. Wild camping is allowed, although you have to pay an entrance fee (adult/child 6/2hry). Fires are also prohibited, although this is largely ignored.

**Yaremche** is a tourist Hutsul village, with lots of folk crafts on sale and several 'Hutsul' restaurants. It is probably the most obvious place for a home base, as it's easy to reach and makes a good staging point for a Mt Hoverla ascent. From Ivano-Frankivsk, there are dozens of buses and *marshrutki* to Yaremche (7hry, 1½ hours). There is a good range of accommdations, from rented rooms and cottages to hotels. You can book in advance via their websites.

### Snow Sports

The area is still largely undeveloped, but Ukraine's small collection of ski resorts offers one European-standard resort and several inexpensive options, with both hotel and homestay accommodation on site or nearby. Rentals are no problem, although except for

Bukovel, the equipment might be older. The season lasts usually until early May. You can arrange package ski trips through **Piligrim** (www.piligrim.lviv.ua) and **Lviv Ecotour** (www.lviveco tour.com), or book your own accommodation online through www.skiukraine.info, which also provides transport details. Homestays can be arranged in advance via **Rural Green Tourism** (www.greentour.com.ua/en/orders).

**Bukovel** ( ☎ 0342 559 546; www.bukovel.com; lift tickets 100-11hry, rentals 55-65hry), not far from Ivano-Frankivsk, is Ukraine's newest resort and meets European standards. Lines are rarely longer than five minutes for the modern chairlifts, and night skiing, snow machines, a ski school, a medical centre and new rental equipment are all on offer. Accommodation in cottages is pricey, but you'll get a 9% discount for advance booking, and there are some more economical triples as well. Cheaper accommodation can be found in Yarmeche, 30km away, which has buses to/from the resort. **Transfers** ( ☎ 38-050 373 3251; fax 38-0342 559 389; natalia@bukovel .info) from Ivano-Frankivsk start at 190hry. Hint: last we heard, lift tickets could be shared with a buddy while you take a break.

Just 120km from Lviv, **Slavske** ( ☎ 38 0322 42 242; www.slavsko.com.ua, in Ukrainian; lift tickets 50-100hry), called Slavsko in Russian, is the most popular and easiest to reach. There are four mountains here, making up the country's greatest variety of slopes. The downside? There's only one chairlift (the rest are tows), large moguls can be a problem, rentals are not-so-new and there are sometimes long lines on weekends and holidays. If you're willing to fork out 100hry though, you'll get VIP status and go right to the front. Three well-priced **hotels** (www.skiukraine.info) are nearby, and at the train station, people offer cottages for rent. There are at least three daily trains between Uzh-horod and Kyiv that stop in Slavsko.

A favourite for hardcore skiers and snow-boarders, **Drahobrat** ( ☎ 03132-42 009; www.ski.lviv .ua/drahobrat; 4hry per lift) is the tallest, longest slope (base at 1300m, elevation drop up to 350m). As such, it gets the most snow and long-est season but has more inclement weather. Since it's hard to get to (a two- to three-hour bus or car ride), it's worthwhile only if you stay a few days. There are only tow lifts, but slopes are well groomed, and lines are not much of a problem. Take a bus or taxi from Ivano-Frankivsk train station to Yasinya. At the bottom of the road in Yasinya, old Soviet

vehicles wait to take you 18km to the resort (80hry to 120hry per car). Homestays aren't available, but well-priced accommodation can be booked online (www.skiukraine.info).

Since it used to be a Soviet training base for Olympic skiiers, **Tysovets** (www.skiukraine.info /resorts/tysovets.shtml; lift tickets 60hry, rentals 40-90hry) is still run by the Ministry of Defence, so don't be surprised if you see uniformed soldiers shovelling snow. Everything is dirt cheap here, and slopes are nice and wide, but the facili-ties are pretty run-down. There's one single-chairlift; the rest are tows that are slow enough to create lines on weekends. Take the train to Skole, on the Kiev–Uzhhorod line, and hire a driver to take you 32km to the resort (80hry to 100hry). There is a separate bunny slope next to the parking lot; day passes for that cost a separate 60hry. There are hotels on site, which can be booked via www.skiukraine.info.

# KAMYANETS-PODILSKY
## КАМ'ЯНЕЦЬ-ПОДІЛЬСЬКИЙ
☎ 03849 / pop 100,000

It's a mystery why Kamyanets-Podilsky has gotten so little attention for so long. Unless you later get hit over the head with something hard and heavy, the arresting sight of the fortressed hamlet, perched high on a tower-ing island of rock above the lush Smotrych River canyon, will stay with you for the rest of your life.

## History
The Old Town is broken into different quar-ters, and under the medieval Magdeburg Law, the main settlers – Ukrainians, Poles, Arme-nians and Jews – each occupied a different one. In the town's heyday, during the inter-war period, there were five Roman Catholic churches, 18 Orthodox churches and a Jewish community of 23,500 served by 31 prayer houses. During WWII the Germans used the Old Town as a ghetto, and an estimated 85,000 people died there. Intensive fighting and air raids destroyed some 70% of the old town, and only 13 churches survived.

## Orientation & Information
The fortified Old Town is accessible by two bridges. The western bridge takes you to the castle and the eastern bridge heads to the New Town. The road (partially called vul Star-obulvarna) between the two bridges passes ploscha Virmenskyi (old town square).

UKRAINE

Many hotels offer internet access, but we've yet to find an internet café.

**Avaal Bank** ( ☎ 23 344; vul Starobulvarna 10) Changes money, cashes travellers cheques and gives credit card cash advances.

**Post & phone office** (vul Soborna 9)

## Sights & Activities

The walk across the bridge to the Old Town is probably one of the best parts of visiting Kamyanets-Podilsky. Once you're there, the main sight is the **old castle** (vul Zamkova; admission 4hry; �9am-6pm), which was originally built of wood in the 10th century but reconstructed of stone some 500 years later. On the north side of the courtyard is the **Ethnographic Museum** (admission 3hry; �9am-5pm), not a big deal. Behind the castle, to the west, is the **new castle**, a series of earth ramparts and 17th-century stone walls.

The faded salmon-coloured **Dominican Monastery & Church** (ploscha Virmenskyi) features a tall bell tower. It was founded in the 14th century but was expanded in baroque style in the 18th century. In a park just to the north is the 14th-century **Town Hall**, currently under reconstruction.

Another 500m further the north is the 16th-century **Cathedral of SS Peter & Paul** (vul Tatarska). About two minutes' walk further north is the 16th-century **Porokhovi Gate** and the seven-storey, stone **Kushnir Tower**.

If you're game, you can arrange for a **bungee jump** 54m into the canyon from rickety old 'Running Deer' bridge. Contact **Bungee Jumping** ( ☎ 8-067 906 6713, 294 0099, 262 0977; bungee@kp.rel.com.ua; s/tandem 200/400hry) or Filvarky Centre ( ☎ 34 024, 33 606; www.filvarki.km.ua/en/index.html; vul Lesi Ukrainki 99), which does jumps as well as **hiking and biking tours**.

## Sleeping

**Hotel Ukraina** ( ☎ 32 300, 39 148; vul Lesi Ukrainky 32; d 44hry, ste 1000-180hry) It feels lonely inside this hotel, which used to be the city favourite – long, long ago. Now, reception seems surprised to see anyone walking through the door. It's fair value though, with a cosier feel than the others and an attempt at cheer in décor. There is no lift or restaurant.

**Hotel Smotrich** ( ☎ 30 392, 30 322; vul Soborna 4; d 80hry) It's a large Soviet-style place, but only two floors are serviced. Rooms have yet to see the sweet touches of Western remodelling, but some have pretty views of the Old Town.

**Filvarky Centre** ( ☎ 34 024, 33 606; www.filvarki.km.ua/en/index.html; vul Lesi Ukrainki 99; s 70-80hry, d 95-125hry, ste 120-260hry) In a peaceful location near a park, Filvarky is a hotel 'complex' set apart from the action and offers a bit more to do – billiards, sauna, tanning, tennis and massage – plus it arranges bungee jumps and cycling tours.

**Gala Hotel** ( ☎ 28 106; www.hotelcomplex-gala.com.ua; vul Lesi Ukrainki 84; d 200hry) This new kid on the block is not far from the western, pedestrian bridge that leads to the rock island. It's good value – even more so if you have three or four people, as rooms with a fold-out couch are just 220hry.

**Hetman** ( ☎ 067-588 2215; www.hetman.mkc.com.ua; Polski rynok 8; d 350-400hry, ste 450-500hry) Also new, the Hetman has the lucky status of being the only hotel in the Old Town and is housed in a renovated building dating back to 1735.

## Eating

**Gostinny Dvir** (vul Trotiyska 1; mains 5-10hry) Probably the best joint in the Old Town, and great for a heavy, meaty, stick-to-your-ribs feast. If you don't eat flesh though, let them know, and they should be able to work something out for you.

**Pizza Chelantano** (vul Knyaziv Koriatorychiv; pizzas from 5hry) Like everywhere in Ukraine, this pizza chain is popular with the young crowd. Mayonnaise salads and *blini* (pancakes), as well as espresso drinks, can be ordered here too. Look for the plastic palm tree.

**Kafe Pid Bramoyu** (shashlik & mains 3-20hry) On the bridge and overlooking the castle and canyon, the view here is outstanding, but the lazy staff needs bucking up.

## Getting There & Away

The train station is 1.3km north of the bus terminal. A taxi into town should be about 6hry, or you can take bus 1 into the new or old Town. The only direct trains are to/from Kyiv (*kupeyny/platskartny* 32/22hry, 12 hours, one daily) and Odesa (*platskartny* 25hry, 16 hours) on odd dates only.

The **bus terminal** (vul Koriatovychiv) is 500m east of the new town, and about 1km from the bridge that leads into the Old Town. There are direct bus services to/from Kyiv (57hry, 12 hours, two to four daily), but if you can get to Chernivtsi (easily reached by train or bus from all over), there are another three buses from there (14hry, 2½ hours).

A taxi ride within the town costs from 4hry to 6hry. Once in town, things are all pretty walkable though.

# ODESA ОДЕСА

☎ 0482 (6 digits), 048 (7 digits) / pop 1.01 million

It's a whirlwind of dust and cars, a cacophony of construction and celebration, a bubbling melting pot of ethnicities and lifestyles. It's part industrial port city and part summer getaway, where people come in hordes to laze on beaches and stroll through leafy streets lined with ornate architecture. It's raw and real, and it shoulders with nonchalance the extremes of decay and luxury.

Yes, Odesa is decadent. But it's not segregated. Here, cultures don't clash, they click. Stately townhouses mix with slums, nouveau riche bump elbows with bums – and it's all as natural as can be. Look at the street names and you'll see what you're dealing with: Jewish Street, Bulgarian Street, French Street, Italian Boulevard…who *doesn't* have an accent here? With all these varied tongues lashing, it's no wonder the lively Odesan patter is a wellspring of hip Russian slang. And then there's the joking. When you live in a city this wild, you better learn to laugh about it. Odesans do; they seem to have a hereditary talent for brassy wisecracks and snappy witticisms, and their sense of humour is legendary in the Russian-speaking world.

To see the reckless driving, the neglected gorgeous buildings and litter-lined gutters, you'd hardly think Odesans are proud of their city. Think again. With a rich history as a crossroads of cultures, languages and trade, Odesa has always had a glamorous, cosmopolitan status. During Soviet times,

Odesa was *the* place to see and be seen, to work off that collective farmer's tan, to kick back drinks and kick-dance your ass off as the full moon rises above the big Black Sea. Now, long after the iron curtain has dropped, Russians and Ukrainians are free to summer within their means instead of within their government's restrictions. They can go anywhere they want, but they still want Odesa. It's crazy and cool, a culture all its own and – to Odesans at least – it's the centre of the universe. Which leads to the famous local attitude: 'I'm from Odesa. Who the hell are *you*?'

## HISTORY

Before it became part of the Russian empire, modern-day Odesa was, among others, a part of the Greek empire, the Roman empire, and the Golden Horde. In the second half of the 15th century, the Turks founded a settlement named Hadjibey here, building a fortress around it.

Meanwhile, Catherine the Great was eyeing the place, imagining it as 'the St Petersburg of the South' and in 1789, her dutiful lover, General Potemkin, captured the fortress for her. In 1815, things really began to boom when the city became a duty-free port, and a huge demand for labour arose. Newcomers were encouraged with free land and a five-year tax-free status, and soon the city became a refuge – 'Odesa Mama' – for runaway serfs, criminals, renegades and dissidents.

Odesa was the crucible of the early 1905 workers' revolution, with a local uprising and the mutiny on the battleship *Potemkin Tavrichesky*. And between 1941 and 1944, Odesa sealed its reputation as one of Stalin's 'hero' cities, when partisans sheltering in the city's catacombs (see p889) during WWII put

---

### THE JOKE'S ON YOU

*A lost tourist in Odesa stops a local to ask where vul Derybasivska is. The Odesan immediately smiles and says 'Where are you from?' The tourist says he's from Zhitomir. The Odesan exclaims 'What a co-incidence, my grandmother came from there!' and launches into an drawn-out account of his family's history, how they struggled during the war, how they could barely feed their children… It goes on for half an hour before the tourist loses his patience and repeats his question.*

*'Jesus Christ,' says the Odesan. 'Would you stop wasting my time? We're standing on Derybasivska!'*

On that note, you may as well entirely disregard the street signs posted on poles on corners – they are usually twisted to point the wrong way.

**UKRAINE**

# ODESA

**BLACK SEA**

Map labels:
- prov Kordenko
- To Simferopol (508km)
- vul Prymorska
- vul Sofiyivska
- vul Kinna
- bul Mystetstv
- Mother-in-Law Bridge
- Boat Passenger Terminal
- 32
- 11
- vul Tolhova
- 5
- vul Shchepkina
- prov Nekrasova
- Voyeny spusk
- vul Preobrazhenska
- vul Sabaneyev Mist
- 9
- Richelieu Statue
- Potemkin Steps
- vul Prymorska
- prov Mayakovskoho
- pl Yekaterynynska
- 14
- Pushkin Statue
- Dumska pl
- vul Pasteyra
- vul Dvoryanska
- vul Sadova
- 1
- 22
- vul Chaykovskoho
- City Garden
- 24
- vul Havanna
- vul Lanzheronivska
- 8
- Tamozhenna pl
- 23
- 25
- 20
- 4
- 13
- 26
- vul Derybasivska
- Polsky spusk
- 27
- 16
- pl Soborna
- pl Hretska
- vul Hretska
- Devolanovsky spusk
- vul Yuriya Oleshy
- vul Kanatna
- vul Koblevska
- vul Tolstoho
- vul Nizhynska
- pl Very Kholodnoyi
- vul Bunina
- vul Yekaterynynska
- vul Rishelievska
- 10
- vul Pushkinska
- vul Polska
- vul Novoseltskoho
- vul Zhukovskoho
- 15
- vul Kuznechna
- pr Oleksandrivsky
- vul Preobrazhenska
- vul Tyraspilska
- 21
- vul Evreyska
- 2
- vul Marazliyevska
- vul Troyitska
- vul Uspenska
- vul Uspenska
- Staro-Bazarny skver
- vul Bazarna
- vul Yekaterynynska
- vul Rishelievska
- vul Bazarna
- To Long-Distance Bus Station & Autolux (2.2km); Nerubayske Catacombs (12km)
- Bolshaya Arnautska vul
- 3
- Bolshaya Arnautska vul
- Staroportofrankivska vul
- vul Mechnikova
- vul Mala Arnautska
- 12
- vul Shmidta
- vul Kanatna
- vul Bohdana Khmelnytskoho
- vul Kuybysheva
- vul Panteleymonivska
- vul Heneralə Vatutina
- vul Pryvozna
- 31
- vul Panteleymonivska
- vul Myasoyidovska
- pl Pryvokzalna
- 19
- Italyansky bul
- Italyansky bul
- vul Yampilskoho
- vul Mechnikova
- vul Novoshchipny Ryad
- 6
- vul Matrska
- vul Bolgarska
- Train Station
- pl Kulykovo Pole
- vul Pyrohovska
- To Airport (12km)
- vul Lazareva
- Park Ilicha
- vul Vodoprovodna
- pl Starosinna
- To Arkadia (6km); Lanzheron Beach
- vul Starosinna

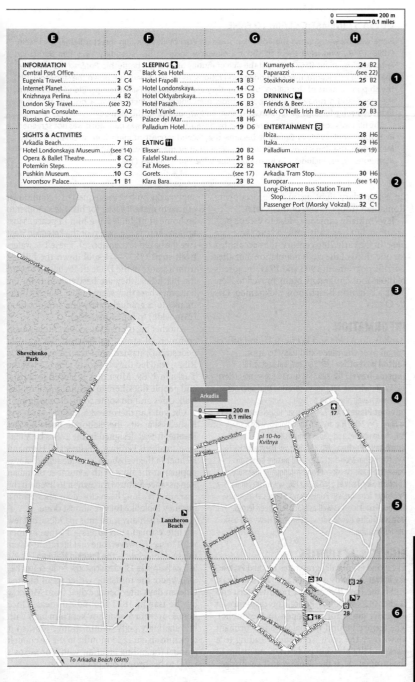

INFORMATION
Central Post Office.........................**1** A2
Eugenia Travel..............................**2** C4
Internet Planet.............................**3** C5
Knizhnaya Perlina.........................**4** B2
London Sky Travel.....................(see 32)
Romanian Consulate......................**5** A2
Russian Consulate.........................**6** D6

SIGHTS & ACTIVITIES
Arkadia Beach..............................**7** H6
Hotel Londonskaya Museum......(see 14)
Opera & Ballet Theatre..................**8** C2
Potemkin Steps............................**9** C2
Pushkin Museum..........................**10** C3
Vorontsov Palace.........................**11** B1

SLEEPING
Black Sea Hotel............................**12** C5
Hotel Frapolli ..............................**13** B3
Hotel Londonskaya.......................**14** C2
Hotel Oktyabrskaya......................**15** D3
Hotel Pasazh................................**16** B3
Hotel Yunist.................................**17** H4
Palace del Mar..............................**18** H6
Palladium Hotel............................**19** D6

EATING
Elissar.........................................**20** B2
Falafel Stand................................**21** B4
Fat Moses....................................**22** B2
Gorets......................................(see 17)
Klara Bara....................................**23** B2

Kumanyets...................................**24** B2
Paparazzi.................................(see 22)
Steakhouse .................................**25** B2

DRINKING
Friends & Beer..............................**26** C3
Mick O'Neills Irish Bar...................**27** B3

ENTERTAINMENT
Ibiza...........................................**28** H6
Itaka...........................................**29** H6
Palladium.................................(see 19)

TRANSPORT
Arkadia Tram Stop.......................**30** H6
Europcar...................................(see 14)
Long-Distance Bus Station Tram
  Stop.........................................**31** C5
Passenger Port (Morsky Vokzal).....**32** C1

---

**ODESA'S CINEMATIC CLAIM TO FAME**

Fame was showered upon the Potemkin steps (below) by Russian film director Sergei Eisenstein (1898–1948), who used them to shoot a massacre scene in his legendary 1925 film *Battleship Potemkin*. The silent B&W epic told the tale of mutiny aboard the battleship *Potemkin Tavrichesky*, sparked off by meagre, maggot-ridden food rations. As local Odesans run down the steps towards the ship in support of the sailors' uprising, they are fired on by Tsarist troops. Blood spills down the steps, and a runaway pram, baby inside, methodically bounces down; a brilliant trick that induces strong feelings of tension, suspense and impotence in the viewer.

The film was considered too provocative by the authorities and was banned. It was not screened in Europe until 1954. In Britain it became the second-longest-running ban in cinema history. Meanwhile, the film's most spellbinding scene (that of the runaway pram) has been 'borrowed' numerous times, including in Brian de Palma's *The Untouchables* (1987).

---

up a legendary fight against the occupying Romanian troops (allies of the Nazis).

Jews initially came to Odesa to escape persecution, but tragically suffered the same fate here. In the early 20th century, they accounted for one-third of the city's population, but after horrific pogroms in 1905 and 1941, hundreds of thousands emigrated. Many moved to New York's Brighton Beach, now nicknamed 'Little Odesa'.

## INFORMATION

Banks with ATMs and Western Union offices are all over the place and easy to spot.

**Central post office** ( ☎ 266 467; vul Sadova10)

**Eugenia Travel** ( ☎ 220 554; janna@eugen.intes.odesa .ua; vul Rishelevska 23) English-speaking staff arranges tours and travel; prices can be high.

**Internet Planet** ( ☎ 724 2177; vul Rishelevska 58; per hr 6hry; ☽ 24hr) Hip and air-conditioned, with a snack bar, cheap phones and photo exhibits.

**Knizhnaya Perlina** ( ☎ 358 404; vul Derybasivska 14; ☽ 10am-6pm Mon-Sat) Maps and picture books on Odesa; the basic classics of English-language literature.

**London Sky Travel** ( ☎ 729 3196; www.lst.com.ua; Sea Passenger Terminal, vul Primorskaya 6) Does visas, tours and hotel bookings, as well as Black Sea speed ferries.

**Odessa Globe** (www.odessaglobe.com) News and basic city information.

## SIGHTS & ACTIVITIES

Everyone eventually gravitates toward **Prymorsky bulvar**, a shady promenade. At southeast end is the **Town Hall**, and the northwestern end is the 1826 **Vorontsov Palace**, the residence of a former governor (not open to the public). The terrace behind the palace offers brilliant views over the port. To the left, leading to a park and the pleasing pedestrian extension of the promenade, is the 'Mother-in-Law Bridge,'

supposedly built at the request of a communist official to make it easier for his wife's mother to go home at night, leaving him in peace. Most famous here is the sweep of the **Potemkin Steps** (see the boxed text on above). These 192 waterfront steps (1837–41) spill down the hillside from a statue of the Duke de Richelieu toward the Black Sea; they are best viewed from the bottom, where they seem higher than they are, thanks to a gradual narrowing from bottom (21m wide) to top (13m wide).

Another big tourist hot spot is Odesa's main commercial street, **vul Derybasivska** (mostly pedestrian), named after the Frenchman De Ribas, who led the capture of Odesa from the Turks in 1789. Most of it is closed to traffic, and people flock here to stroll alongside sidewalk cafés and do some souvenir shopping.

On vul Lanzheronivska, facing down vul Rishelevska, sits the elaborate **Opera & Ballet Theatre**. It was designed in the 1880s by Viennese architects Ferdinand Fellner and Hermann Helmer in the Habsburg baroque style that was popular at the time, with a number of Italian Renaissance features thrown in to liven up the ensemble. It's long been closed for renovations, but they look like they're almost done.

There are many museums in Odesa, but few are interesting to foreigners – it's the city they want to see. However, one that literature-lovers might appreciate is the **Pushkin Museum** ( ☎ 251 034; vul Pushkinska 13; admission 4hry; ☽ 10am-5pm Tue-Sun), where the romantic writer spent his first Odesan days after being exiled from Moscow by the tsar in 1823 for radical ideas. Once here, Governor Vorontsov kept him busy with humiliatingly petty administrative jobs, so it took him an entire 13 months to stir up enough scandal (including an affair with Vorontsov's wife) to be thrown out of Odesa too.

The Hotel Londonskaya (p890) is gorgeous (worth a look around no matter what) and has a small, 3rd-floor **Hotel Londonskaya Museum** (Primorsky bulvar 11; admission free; ⏲ 24hr) showing photographs and memorabilia of famous people who have stayed there over the years.

A trip to the **Nerubayske catacombs** (see boxed text, below) is a highlight, especially if you've never done a tour of this type of underground passageway before.

The beaches are a big draw for Russians and Ukrainians, but apart from the club scene during the summer at **Arkadia Beach**, foreigners aren't going to think much of the rather unattractive coast. To get there, take tram 5 down lovely, sanatoria-lined **Frantsuzskii bulvar** to the end of the line. **Lanzheron Beach** is closer to the centre and a bit more family oriented, with a dilapidated fun fair.

## SLEEPING

During summer it's pretty easy to arrange a private room in the home of one of the older ladies hanging around the train station. Expect to pay 40hry to 70hry per person per day including meals, and try in advance to figure out its location and proximity to public transport.

From June to August it's highly recommended that you book hotels in advance. Prices here are for the high season; from September to May, rooms, particularly at pricier hotels, can be as much as 50% less.

### Budget

**Hotel Pasazh** ( ☎ 728 5500/01/02; passage@londred.com; vul Preobrazhenska 34; s 65-175hry, d 100-225hry, ste 325hry; 🖳 ) Dilapidated? Yes, but it's in a beautiful old central building (which might soon close for renovations), and it has the lowest prices you'll find. Pasazh does offer one touch of modernity: a good internet centre (open 9am to midnight, 7hry per hour).

**Hotel Yunist** ( ☎ 738 0404; yunist@te.net.ua; vul Pionerska 32; s & d 130-429hry; 🖳 ) Being in a monolith away from the centre has its advantages – that's right, views! Cheaper options share a bathroom with the neighbouring room. Take tram 5 or *marshrutka* 194 or 195 down lovely Frantsuzskii bulvar, and ask to get off at 'Sanitoria Rossiya'. Gorets (p890) is around the corner.

### Midrange

**Hotel Oktyabrskaya** ( ☎ 728 8863; info@oktyabrskaya .od.ua; vul Kanatna 31; s 200-300hry, d 150-300hry, ste 400-700hry; 🕃 ) In an elegant, worn building, Hotel Oktyabrskaya thankfully evokes only a little of the proletariat revolution its name refers to. Think red marble walls, polished old parquet floors, wide, banistered staircases, and soaring ceilings. Rooms waver between tacky and cute, differing mostly in hue. It's a fantastic deal.

**Black Sea Hotel** (Chornoye More Hotel; ☎ 300 904; blacksea@bs-hotel.com.ua; vul Rishelevska 59; s 350hry, d 450-500hry, ste 600-800hry; 🕃 🖳 🕃 ) People choose

---

### THE ODESA UNDERGROUND

The limestone below Odesa is riddled with more than 1000km of catacombs (so some buildings in the city are literally sinking). They weren't used as cemeteries, but were formed by Cossacks and other residents who mined the land for the limestone, which was used to build the city. The resulting network of tunnels turned out to be a great place for smugglers, revolutionaries and fugitives throughout history.

One network of tunnels in Nerubayske, 12km northwest of Odesa, sheltered a group of partisans during WWII. This event is explained at the **Museum of Partisan Glory** (admission 6hry; ⏲ 9am-4pm), which includes a fascinating, flashlight tour of the catacombs, with exhibits showing what life was like for the underground fighters who hid and lived here when they weren't derailing Nazi trains or otherwise thwarting the fascists.

You can just show up in Nerubayske in a taxi (80hry return trip), but you may have to rustle up staff to open the doors if they're not expecting you, and tours will be in Russian only. In summer, Russian-language tour guides tout trips from the train station. If you don't know Russian, it's still interesting to visit, but Eugenia Travel (opposite) and other agencies do tours in English and other languages (about 125hry).

Keep in mind that it will be dark and close in the catacombs (claustrophobes beware), as well as chilly – no matter how warm the day is. Each year at least one person wanders into a catacomb entrance they discover around Odesa and never comes out. Don't be one of them. Stick to the tour.

partially remodelled Chornoye More out of convenience (near the train station), but you could luck out and get a view of the silver and yellow Panteleymonovsky Church, whose recent facelift was clearly done with a more devoted hand.

**Hotel Frapolli** ( ☎ 356 801; frapolli@te.net.ua; vul Derybasivska 13; s/d/ste 316-669hry, d 474-827hry, ste 827-1143hry; 🍴 🖳 ) The location is primo but the vacuous, standardised rooms are completely starved of any imaginative elements. Anyway, you can stoke up on visual input from your in-room PC with pay-by-the-hour internet access, or take a meal in the hotel's glass-covered sidewalk restaurant and feast your eyes on what walks by.

**Palladium Hotel** ( ☎ 728 6651; welcome@hotel-palladium.com.ua; Italyansky bulvar 4; d 488-746hry, ste 1050-1394hry; 🍴 🖳 ) Architecturally, Palladium looks like someone put a bank and a Roman coliseum into a teleportation device and pressed 'Go'. Rooms are appointed in pastels, with minimalist décor (a Schiele print here, an orchid there) and fine-textured carpets. Bonus: as a guest, you'll get free admission to both Itaka and Palladium nightclubs.

## Top End

**Hotel Londonskaya** ( ☎ 738 0110; www.londred.com; Primorsky bulvar 11; s 594-740hry, d 756-902hry, ste 1134-3348hry; 🗙 🍴 ) Ever since the magnificent Londonskaya opened its doors in the mid-19th century, it has been attracting members of the cultural elite. Last refurbished in the early 1990s, the hotel could use some refreshment (smudged walls and furniture showing signs of wear). Nevertheless, with iron-lace balustrades, stained-glass windows, crystal chandeliers, parquet flooring and an inner courtyard, the Londonskaya oozes grand Regency charm.

**Palace del Mar** ( ☎ 301 900; www.palace-del-mar.od.ua; provulok Khrustalny 1; d 1155-2420hry, ste 2613-4050hry; 🍴 🖳 🖳 ♿ ) Set apart from Arkadia beach's thumping summer nightlife, Palace del Mar feels like an 1930s European estate. Rooms vary in size according to price but otherwise are similar: spacious, minimalist, yet warm design (with fuzzy white wall-to-wall carpet and light colours) beautiful beds, and bathrooms with all the niceties. You will take your meals in a sunny dining hall whose *coup de grâce* is an unforgettably stunning stained-glass ceiling. Staff are professional, gracious and ready to smile. You will feel special.

## EATING

On the corner of vul Preobrazhenska and Troyitska, there's a great cheap falafel stand (5hry to 6hry).

**Kumanyets** ( ☎ 376 946; vul Havana 7; mains 20-50hry) This is a full-on Ukrainian-themed restaurant with down-home country dishes. Friendly staff wear kitschy costumes with nary a tic of irony.

**Elissar** ( ☎ 496 498; vul Derybasivska 18; mains 10-60hry) If *shashlik* is no longer 'ethnic' enough for you, never fear. Elissar offers tasty Lebanese dishes – including *labneh* (yogurt cheese) – in addition to its European menu. The footpath seating is perfect, and if you're cold, they'll give you a wool blanket.

**Klara Bara** ( ☎ 200 331; vul Deribasivska; mains 30-65hry) Tucked away in a quiet corner of the city garden, this modern ivy-covered café and restaurant has a cosy atmosphere. It serves European fare with Thai touches, plus brilliant Turkish coffee.

**Steakhouse** ( ☎ 287 775; vul Derybasivska 20; mains 30-135hry) Meat and potatoes are what it's all about at this super-stylish eatery with hot staff and an open kitchen. The coffee drinks are yummy and artistically presented. Make sure you drink enough to pay a visit to the surprising bathrooms. Bonus: free wi-fi.

**Fat Moses** ( ☎ 714 4774; vul Yekaterynynska 8/10; mains 15-45hry) This cosy, unpretentious bistro-style joint has an eclectic menu of includes souvlaki, Hungarian goulash and Jamaican chicken.

**Paparazzi** ( ☎ 348 070; vul Yekaterynynska 8; mains 40-55hry) Next door to Fat Moses, this more fashionable outlet is loved for its stone-grilled meats.

**Gorets** ( ☎ 358 938; vul Pionerska 32; mains 10-60hry) It doesn't warrant a special trip, but if you've decided to take tram 5 down Frantsuzskii bulvar for a joyride – or if you're staying at Hotel Yunist – the *shashlik* here are tasty.

## DRINKING

**Friends & Beer** (Druzya i Pivo; ☎ 769 1998; vul Derybasivska 9) This recreated charming USSR-era living room is proof that 'Retro Soviet' doesn't have to mean political posters and constructivist art.

**Mick O'Neills Irish Bar** ( ☎ 268 437; vul Deribasovskaya 13; 🕑 24hr) Two storeys of wooden railings and all the trappings of pub décor (paper money from all over the world, billiards, pinball machines) set the scene for this restaurant and hangout.

## ENTERTAINMENT

Odesa has dozens of clubs, ranging from the flirty to the seriously sleazy. Striptease performances are common, even at the more respectable end of the spectrum. Door prices range from 10hry to 50hry.

**Ibiza** ( ☎ 777 0205; Arkadia beach; ☺ summer) A white, free-form open cave structure and a fun pick-up joint.

**Itaka** ( ☎ 349 188; Arkadia beach; ☺ summer) This seaside amphitheatre tips a nod to Odesa's Greek name with columns and statues right out of ancient Athens.

**Palladium** ( ☎ 728 6566; Italyansky bulvar 4) Flashy new Palladium shares ownership with Itaka and is the city's best year-round club. Multiple levels, a crazy design and gorgeous clientele make it hot hot hot.

## GETTING THERE & AWAY

### Air

The Odesa **airport** ( ☎ 006, 658 186, 213 576) is located about 12km southwest of the city centre. For ticketing, try **Kiyavia** ( ☎ 276 259), at the train station. From Kyiv, there are several daily flights to/from Odesa (525hry, one hour).

### Train

The **train station** ( ☎ 273 357; ploscha Pryvokzalna) is a big busy place. Tickets for future dates or with non-CIS destinations must be purchased at the **Service Centre** ( ☺ 7am-9.30pm), which can be found inside the station; look for the sign 'Сервисний Центр'. To find it from the main entrance of the station, go right and walk to the end, turn left past the pharmacy and look for the signed double doors. Once you're there, go to **window 5** ( ☺ 8am-7pm) for non-CIS destinations. All other windows will be able to help with train tickets for future dates.

Trains from Odesa head to Kyiv (*kupeyny/platskartny* 60/50hry, 11 hours, three daily), Uzhhorod (55/35hry, 20 hours, one daily), Lviv (59/42hry, 12 hours, one daily) and Simferopol (45/27hry, 13 hours). On odd dates there are *platskartny*-only trains to Kamyanets-Podilsky (25hry, 16 hours); on even dates there are daily trains to Ivano-Frankivsk (48/32hry, 21 hours).

### Bus

The **long-distance bus station** ( ☎ 004; vul Kolontaevskaya 58) is 3km southwest of the city centre. To get to the bus station, from ploscha Pryvokzalna take tram 5 (heading away from

---

### AVOIDING MOLDOVA

It used to be possible, when travelling by train or bus between Western Ukraine and Odesa, that you might pass a bit through Moldova, which requires a visa for entrance. We've been assured this is no longer the case, but to be on the safe side, when buying a ticket, ask: 'Ts-ey id-e cher-ez Mol-do-vu?' (Does this go through Moldova?) or point to this: Цей іде через Молдову? And if it does…wait for the next one.

---

Arkadia) to the end of the line. Once or twice a day, buses leave from Odesa for Sevastopol (73hry, 13 hours), Simferopol (70hry to 80hry, 12 hours) and Yalta (70hry, 15 hours), and there are eight or more daily buses to Kyiv (45hry to 60hry, eight hours). From the same terminal, **Autolux** (www.autolux.com.ua) runs modern, comfortable private buses to Kyiv, Boryspil airport and other Ukrainian destinations.

### Sea

From the **passenger port** (vul Primorskaya), there are regular ferries to Istanbul and Varna (p932) and to other Ukrainian Black Sea destinations, such as Yalta and Sevastopol (see London Sky Travel, p888).

## GETTING AROUND

From the airport, Bus 129 goes to the train station; bus 101 goes between the airport and ploscha Hretska, in the centre, southwest of vul Deribasivska.

From the train station, bus 137 and 146 go to ploscha Hretska (a 20-minute walk). Bus 155 and 109, and trolleybus 4 and 10, go up vul Pushkinska before curving around to vul Suvorova past the passenger port and the foot of the Potemkin Steps.

Tram 5 goes between the train and long-distance bus stations. To get to the latter, take the tram away from Arkadia to the end of the line. Walk to the front of the tram and take the first street right, then look for the coaches down this street.

Taxis in Odesa charge incredibly high prices. Hotels will say a taxi from the airport should cost 25hry, but you're more likely to pay three times that, as the taxi drivers are stubborn when it comes to fleecing tourists. When taking a taxi from your hotel, ask the front desk to call one for you, and ask them to agree on a price over the phone. You're more likely to pay the right price that way than if you just flag one down from in front of the hotel by yourself. **Elit-Taxi** ( ☎ 371 030) has reliable service.

Rental cars for use in the city only can be arranged through **Europcar** ( ☎ 777 4011; www .europcar.ua; Primorsky bulvar 11; ☽ 9am-5pm Mon-Fri, 10am-2pm Sat) in the Hotel Londonskaya.

# CRIMEA КРИМ

Astounding landscape, enchanting palaces, a fascinating past and warm climes…sound good? It is good. No wonder this peninsula has had such a hot-potato history, fought over by the Greeks, Khazars, Tatars, Mongols, Huns, Genoese, Ottomans and Russians. It's a long haul from Kyiv, but if you can make it down this far south, you'll feel as if you've been to two completely different countries. And in a way, you have, since the Crimea is an autonomous republic, with its own constitution, legislature and government.

Today, most visitors to the 'Russian Riviera' concentrate on Yalta and its nearby attractions, although Bakhchysaray is well worth an overnight, and the inland cities of Sevastopol and Simferopol exude a little charm of their own. The more adventurous take advantage of the rare hiking opportunities in the soaring, little explored Crimean Mountains.

## History

The blunder-strewn, stalemated Crimean War of 1854–56 was a classic clash of imperial ambitions. Much to the chagrin of its rival empires, Russia wanted to take over the faltering Turkish Empire, and when Tsar Nicholas I sent troops into the Ottoman provinces of Moldavia and Wallachia (ostensibly to protect the Christians there), the British and French assembled in Varna (now in Bulgaria) to protect Istanbul. Both sides lost about 250,000 soldiers in the war, many from bad medical care – to which British nurse Florence Nightingale drew attention.

As soon as the 1860s, however, Crimea became a chic leisure spot when Russia's imperial family built a summer estate at Livadia, on the outskirts of Yalta (the same palace later used for the post-WWII Yalta Conference of Churchill, Stalin and Roosevelt).

During the civil war that followed the Russian revolution (p696), Crimea was one of the last 'white' bastions. The Germans occupied the peninsula for three years during WWII and Crimea lost nearly half its inhabitants, and then the population was drained once again by Stalin (see the boxed text, below).

Throughout the Soviet era, millions came each year to Crimea, attracted by the warmth, beauty, beaches and mountain air. In 1954 Khrushchev transferred control of the peninsula to Ukraine, but the inhabitants of the Autonomous Republic of Crimea have more in common with Russia, and have been working to make Russian the official language – even trying to return the land to Russian rule.

## SIMFEROPOL СІМФЕРОПОЛЬ
☎ 0652 / pop 340,000

With a glut of exhaust-spewing *marshrutki* honking to get around each other, the capital of the Autonomous Republic of Crimea definitely looks, sounds and smells like the regional transport hub it is. Attractions are minimal, so most visitors are only in town for a short spell before they head further south to the Black Sea coast or to nearby Bakhchysaray

---

### CRIMEA'S TATAR POPULATION

On 18 May 1944 Stalin accused Crimea's Tatars of collaborating with the Nazis, and deported the entire Muslim population to Central Asia and Siberia. The Tatar language was banned and all traces of the culture were obliterated. Crimea was repopulated with Ukrainians, Russians, Bulgarians and Germans. It is estimated that more than 46% percent of the Tatars died during deportation.

Since the late 1980s, about 260,000 Tatars have returned to their lost homeland and have been trying to re-establish themselves and their culture. It hasn't been easy. Few speak their Turkic mother tongue and many still live in poor, slumlike conditions with no water or electricity. However, the Ukrainian government has started giving money to the cause of the returning deportees, and conditions are improving. You will probably see new Tatar homes being constructed in the foothills.

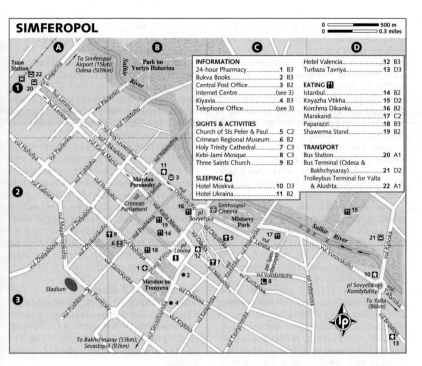

# SIMFEROPOL

0 — 500 m
0 — 0.3 miles

| INFORMATION | | |
|---|---|---|
| 24-hour Pharmacy | 1 | B3 |
| Bukva Books | 2 | B3 |
| Central Post Office | 3 | B2 |
| Internet Centre | (see 3) | |
| Kiyavia | 4 | B3 |
| Telephone Office | (see 3) | |

| SIGHTS & ACTIVITIES | | |
|---|---|---|
| Church of Sts Peter & Paul | 5 | C2 |
| Crimean Regional Museum | 6 | B2 |
| Holy Trinity Cathedral | 7 | C3 |
| Kebi-Jami Mosque | 8 | C3 |
| Three Saints Church | 9 | B2 |

| SLEEPING | | |
|---|---|---|
| Hotel Moskva | 10 | D3 |
| Hotel Ukraina | 11 | B2 |

| | | |
|---|---|---|
| Hotel Valencia | 12 | B3 |
| Turbaza Tavriya | 13 | D3 |

| EATING | | |
|---|---|---|
| Istanbul | 14 | B2 |
| Knyazha Vtikha | 15 | D2 |
| Korchma Dikanka | 16 | B2 |
| Marakand | 17 | C2 |
| Paparazzi | 18 | B3 |
| Shawerma Stand | 19 | B2 |

| TRANSPORT | | |
|---|---|---|
| Bus Station | 20 | A1 |
| Bus Terminal (Odesa & Bakhchysaray) | 21 | D2 |
| Trolleybus Terminal for Yalta & Alushta | 22 | A1 |

(p898). Don't worry if you'll be here a day or two – you can easily spend a few highly pleasant hours off the main streets, strolling along peaceful pedestrian avenues. In recent years, a lot of money has been spent on renovating the city, which you'll see in the rowdy construction areas and freshly painted façades.

## Information

**24-hour Pharmacy** ( ☎ 546 911; prospekt Kirova 22)
**Bukva Books** ( ☎ 273 153; vul Sevastopilska 6; ✆ 9am-8pm Mon-Fri, to 7pm Sat, to 6pm Sun) Offers a small selection of English-language classics and several Crimea-related maps.
**Central post office** ( ☎ 272 255; vul Rozy Lyuxemburg 1) Also has an ATM, telephone office and internet centre (2hr to 3hr per hour), all with 24-hour access (post office has typical hours).

## Sights

The attractions of Simferopol aren't going to leave much of an impression. Most enjoyable during a visit is a tranquil walk along the Salhir River, which is dotted with willow trees. Also, strolling the pedestrian zone of vul Pushkina makes for good window-shopping

and people-watching, especially because there are benches to rest on along the way.

**Three Saints Church** (vul Hoholya 16), **Holy Trinity Cathedral** (vul Odeska 12) and **Church of Sts Peter & Paul** (vul Oktyabrska) are three Orthodox churches in town and worth a gander because of the ornate mosaic iconography on the façades. East of the centre, up the quaint vul Kurchatova, is the restored 1502 **Kebi-Jami Mosque**, overlooking a sort of slummy neighbourhood repopulated by Tatars. It was reconstructed in the 17th century and is the oldest building in the city.

The town's **Crimean Regional Museum** ( ☎ 276 347; vul Hoholya 14; admission 6hry; ✆ 9am-5pm Wed-Mon) features a geology room with mastodon jaws, a natural history (read: taxidermy) room, a Christian history room, and a WWII history room.

## Sleeping

**Hotel Moskva** ( ☎ 237 520; fax 239 795; vul Kyivska 2; s 100-190hry, d 222hry, ste 290-500hry) You'd almost have to be a masochist to stay at the haggard Soviet extravaganza that is Hotel Moskva. Curmudgeonly staff sit at reception, just

UKRAINE

waiting to be difficult. Rooms are passable but don't make up for the rude service; they really push the suites too.

**Turbaza Tavriya** ( ☎ 638 914; vul Bespalova 21; s 115-170hry, d 160-240hry) This tranquil, hill-side place is a bit far from the centre, but not much further than similarly priced Hotel Moskva, which it beats by a long, long, long shot. It consists of two buildings; one has been fully renovated, the other partially so (no lift or in-room phone, but otherwise, rooms are similar to the other building's). *Marshrutki* 15 and 17 go here from ploscha Sovyetska. It's popular, and rightfully so; call ahead if possible.

**Hotel Valencia** ( ☎ 510 606; www.valencia.crimea.ua; vul Odeska 8; s 101hry, d 202-353hry, ste 303-580hry; ✖ ) An odd hotel fusion of Crimea and Spain. Cheerful and professional staff work at the hotel and its good restaurant and rooms (each one different) are a great value. There are only a few though, so book in advance if you can.

**Hotel Ukraina** ( ☎ 510 165; jscukrcomp@crimea.com; vul Rozy Lyuxemburg 7; s 260-370hry, d 420-480hry, ste 800hry) Talk about covering all bases. In your first five seconds here, you'll think you've entered a five-star hotel, with a very chi-chi façade and lobby (fanciful doormen, a pianist, gold-painted frippery etc) Service seems four-starrish, and the hastily remodelled but Western-style rooms rank at about three stars.

## Eating

Several restaurants with outdoor seating line vul Ushinskoho.

**Paparazzi** (vul Hoholya 5; mains 25-100hry; ✖ 8am-last customer) Surround yourself with pop culture, a hipster interior, and a wide-ranging menu (even foie gras) as you compete with your friends in an electronic darts tournament.

**Istanbul** ( ☎ 527 862; vul Horkoho 5; mains 10-30hry; ✖ 11am-11pm) As one of many cellar-style restaurants in Simferopol, this Turkish place has a small, not very Turkish menu, although it is a dependable place for quality *shashlik* (there are some veggie options as well). Seating is at picnic tables, and Turkish music videos are played.

**Marakand** ( ☎ 524 698; vul Vorovskoho 17; mains 5-9hry; ✖ 9am-11pm Mon-Sat) Here's an authentic Central Asian–style open-air tea house and restaurant, where you can get *plov* (meat and rice), *manty* (large meat-filled dumplings) and *shashlik* (shish kebab) grilled over an open fire before your eyes. The local Muslim

community hangs out here, drinking tea and chewing over debates; in spring, you can see a small waterfall nearby.

**Korchma Dikanka** ( ☎ 290 608; vul Ushinskoho 2/46; mains 10-25hry; ✖ 9-5am) With murals, costumed staff, wooden tables and typical Ukrainian food, this central and popular eatery is thankfully not too loud with the Russian pop music it plays. In addition to *varenyky*, *pelmeni* and *blini*, you can sample *holubtsi*.

**Knyazha Vtikha** ( ☎ 251 020; vul Turgeneva 35; mains 20-40hry; ✖ noon-midnight) Talk about all-out with the Ukrainian folk theme. In warm months you can dine outside in your own little hut. Inside, live music is played. To find it, walk along the north bank of the river until it makes a sharp left, then look for the white building with shutters and cars out front.

**Shawarma stand** (cnr of vul Karla Marksa & vul Pushkina; 5-10hry; ✖ 11am-9pm) Grab a quick hot meal from this popular stand.

## Getting There & Around

**Simferopol airport** (SIP; ☎ 006, 295 516; www.airport .crimea.ua) is 15km northwest of the town centre and accessible by trolleybus 9 (50 kopeks, 30 minutes) and *marshrutki* 49, 50, 98, 113 and 115 (1hry, 20 minutes), which ply bulvar Lenina.

For local transport around town, *marshrutki* are the way to go – in fact, the city is clogged with them, so walking is another good option. See p730 for information on flagging one down.

There are two places to catch buses, the **bus station** ( ☎ 252 560), which is next to the trains station, and the **bus terminal** ( ☎ 275 211), which is near Hotel Moskva. The one on vul Gagarina, at the end of bulvar Lenina and next to the train station, is in a small pink building behind the McDonald's. From here, dozens of *marshrutki* leave for destinations around Crimea (except Bakhchysaray), including two to Yalta (19hry, two hours, four hourly) and to Sevastopol (19hry, two hours, four hourly). The bus terminal on vul Kyivska, by Hotel Moskva, has regular buses and microbuses to Odesa (70hry to 80hry, 12 hours, four daily) and Bakhchysaray (6hry, one hour, seven daily), as well as to other destinations around Crimea, including Sevastopol (20hry, two hours, 20 daily).

The **train station** ( ☎ 005, 243 418, 242 350) is at the end of bulvar Lenina. Most trains to/from Simferopol are very busy, especially from June to August, so book your tickets as early as possible. To Kyiv, (*kupeyny/platskartny* 75/42hry, 15 hours) there are at least two daily, and once-daily trains leave for Lviv (75/50hry, 26 hours) and Odesa (41/27hry, 15 hours). See p904 for information on getting to Minsk, Moscow and St Petersburg from here.

From 5am to 8pm, the world's longest – and slowest! – trolleybus ride leaves from the **trolleybus terminal** (vul Gagarina), next to the train station, for Yalta (11hry, 2½ hours, every 20 minutes), stopping in Alushta. It's not the most time-efficient method of transport, but it's definitely a novelty. The views along the way are spectacular, but if you don't want to dawdle, the Yalta-bound *marshrutki* take the same route and zip by the trolleys.

## YALTA ЯЛТА
☎ 0654 / pop 81,000
Once you start to descend the craggy Crimean Mountains toward the sparkling Black Sea, you'll soon realise that the journey itself is one of the greatest aspects of a visit to the seaside resort town of Yalta, a vacation hot spot for more than 200 years.

In town, you'll find a lively waterfront promenade, lined with tiny flashing casinos, touristy restaurants, touts beseeching you to touch their monkey while they take your picture, and desperate artists offering to draw an unflattering caricature of you. In fact, especially after recent renovations, Yalta seems like a caricature of itself – sort of a painted-up, exaggerated version of what a resort town is supposed to look like. Some people love Yalta, and some think it's silly, but everyone is impressed once they turn their back on the waterfront and gaze up at that grand amphitheatre of mountains cupping the coast. That, as well as the nearby attractions – historic palaces, lush botanical gardens, cable-car rides up to staggering cliffs –are what makes Yalta the popular destination it always has been and always will be.

## Information
**Aval Bank** (ploscha Lenina) Booth No 14 of the post office handles Western Union and cash advances.
**Central post office** ( ☎ 312 073; ploscha Lenina 1; �---- 8am-8pm)
**Internet Centre** (vul Ekaterynynska 3; per hr 5hry; �---- 9am-10pm) Ten slow computers run by bratty

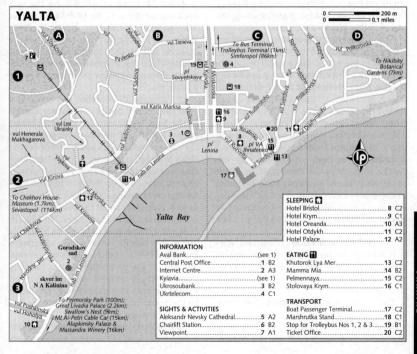

**YALTA**

0 _____ 200 m
0 _____ 0.1 miles

*Yalta Bay*

| SLEEPING 🛏 | |
|---|---|
| Hotel Bristol.................................... 8 | C2 |
| Hotel Krym..................................... 9 | C1 |
| Hotel Oreanda.............................. 10 | A3 |
| Hotel Otdykh................................ 11 | C2 |
| Hotel Palace................................. 12 | A2 |

| INFORMATION | |
|---|---|
| Aval Bank.................................(see 1) | |
| Central Post Office........................1 | B2 |
| Internet Centre..............................2 | A3 |
| Kyiavia.....................................(see 1) | |
| Ukrosoubank.................................3 | B2 |
| Ukrtelecom...................................4 | C1 |

| SIGHTS & ACTIVITIES | |
|---|---|
| Aleksandr Nevsky Cathedral.........5 | A2 |
| Chairlift Station.............................6 | B2 |
| Viewpoint......................................7 | A1 |

| EATING 🍴 | |
|---|---|
| Khutorok Lya Mer........................13 | C2 |
| Mamma Mia.................................14 | B2 |
| Pelmennaya..................................15 | C2 |
| Stolovaya Krym.............................16 | C1 |

| TRANSPORT | |
|---|---|
| Boat Passenger Terminal...............17 | C2 |
| Marshrutka Stand.........................18 | C1 |
| Stop for Trolleybus Nos 1, 2 & 3....19 | B1 |
| Ticket Office................................20 | C2 |

**UKRAINE**

post-teen gamers. But unlike at Ukrtelecom, you won't have trouble getting a computer. Go through the gate and take the door on the left.

**Ukrosoubank** (naberezhnaya imeni Lenina 5) Western Union and outdoor 24-hour ATM.

**Ukrtelecom** (vul Moskovska 9; per hr 5hry; ☉ 24hr) Internet and phone calls; computer access often requires a long wait.

## Sights

### CITY CENTRE

The **promenade**, naberezhnaya imeni Lenina, stretches past numerous piers, palm trees, restaurants, boutiques and souvenir stalls to **Prymorsky Park**, where there are some carnival-type rides. It starts at **ploscha Lenina**, the centre of activity. Here there are plenty of benches for people-watching under the shadow of a statue of Lenin. The former Soviet leader gawks at the McDonald's across the way as if it were the devil himself. In spring and summer a chess teacher who specialises in teaching children hangs out here; even if you opt out of a lesson, it's fun to watch the kids play with him.

Although swimming isn't an option along the promenade, you can descend to a few short lengths of beach, which is all rocks – most of them flat and perfect for skipping along the placid, rather plain waterfront.

Anton Chekhov was a crafty short-story writer and one of the most esteemed playwrights in the world. He wrote *The Cherry Orchard* and *Three Sisters* in what is now the **Chekhov House-Museum** ( ☎ 394 947; vul Kirova 112; adult/student 15/8hry; ☉ 10am-5pm Wed-Sun, Tue-Sun Jun-Sep), the small estate where he suffered from, and eventually died of, tuberculosis. Take *marshrutki* 6 or 8 (not 8a), which go by every 15 minutes from the west side of vul Kyivska; ask for 'dom mu-*zyey che*-kho-va'. At the stop, cross the street and go down some stairs to the museum area. Included in the price of admission is a tour (in Russian only) from women who are obviously passionate about the place, and the grounds are lovely.

The 1903 **Aleksandr Nevsky Cathedral** (vul Sadova 2) is a beautiful example of neo-Byzantine architecture. The architect was Nikolai Krasnov, who designed many palaces on Crimea's southern coast.

There is a mediocre **chairlift** (10hry return; ☉ 10am-5pm Apr-Sep) Buy your ticket, step into a big dented bucket, and you're off, swinging above dilapidated rooftops to a bizarre pseudo-Greek temple and **viewpoint**, called Darsan. The boarding point is behind naberezhna Lenina 17, along vul Kirova.

### OTHER SIGHTS

Many travellers hang in Yalta not because they're into the resorty Yalta vibe, but because it makes an excellent base from which to see Crimea's spectacular historic and natural sights. We've just listed the basics (in order of spectacularness), but if you've time, there is much more to discover along the coast. See p898 for information on getting to these places. And don't forget a day trip to Bakhchysaray (p898) is possible.

Get a picnic lunch and a bottle of wine and find a secluded spot to enjoy them in the Alupka palace-park complex, 16km southwest of Yalta. The setting is peaceful and beautiful, and the majestic **Alupkinsky Palace** (adult/child 20/10hry; ☉ 9am-4pm, longer in summer), built for Count Mikhail Vorontsov, is quite impressive. It happens to be where Churchill stayed during the Yalta Conference. The palace grounds and park are free; only the interior requires paid admission.

About 1km east of Alupka, on the way back toward Yalta, is the **Mt Ai-Petri cable car** (kanatnaya doroga; return trip 40hry; ☉ 11am-3pm, hr vary greatly). It's a truly dizzying ride across the foothills and up the mountain's sheer face, during which you overlook the coast and the sea. At the summit, there are expansive views inland, too.

In February 1945 Stalin, Roosevelt and Churchill shaped the face of postwar Europe at the Yalta Conference in the **Great Livadia Palace** ( ☎ 315 579; admission adult/child 15/7hry; ☉ 10am-4pm Thu-Tue), 3km southwest of central Yalta. Included in the price is a one-hour Russian-language tour, although you're welcome to stroll through on your own. It features photos and memorabilia about this historic event, as well as displays about the palace's original owner, the last Russian emperor, Nicholas II. He spent just four seasons here with his family before they (the Romanovs) were all arrested by the Bolshevik revolutionaries and eventually shot. If you go by *marshrutka*, carefully cross the street where it stops for you, and make your descent. Go down stairs on the left by the orange building. You'll eventually find it if you keep descending.

The **Nikitsky Botanical Gardens** (adult/child 6/3hry; ☉ 8am-6pm) are worth a visit for their beauty and views. Tumbling down 3 sq km of hillside to the sea, they are home to 28,000 species, including 2000 rose types, a 500-year-old yew tree and a 1000-year-old pistachio tree.

Fifty metres in the opposite direction from the bus stop at Alupka, and back up the road down which you came, is the **Massandra winery** ( ☎ 721 198; admission 20hry; ☼ tours Tue-Sat May-Nov, Tue, Thu & Sat rest of year). Here you can participate in a tasting tour of Crimean wines, although dry wine lovers will be disappointed. Between May and November, tours kick off at 11.30am, 12.30pm, 3pm, 4pm and 5pm. The rest of the year there are tours at 11.30am and 3pm, and at 11.30am on Saturday.

Possibly the most internationally famous landmark on the peninsula is the cliff-side castle known as the **Swallow's Nest** (Lastochkino Gnizdo; admission 2-8hry; ☼ 8am-6pm Tue-Sun). Honestly, although it looks great on a postcard or a travel brochure, the Swallow's Nest is weirdly small, unimpressive and fake-looking. From the castle-like building, you may see dolphins frolicking (or is it a feeding frenzy?) in the distance. Be prepared for a lot of stairs (which start next to the Kodak stand).

## Sleeping

Hotel prices fluctuate seasonally, peaking in July and August and during the new year season, when reservations for all hotels are recommended. We've listed the highest rates. Many hotel rooms have air-conditioning in their pricier rooms, but hot water can be spotty here and throughout Crimea. Yalta is crawling with hotels; the ones reviewed here are most central.

Also, women hang around the main bus terminal offering private rooms (see p902). There are signs all over town with phone numbers of people offering rooms; look for variations containing the words 'сдам, жильё, квартира'.

**Hotel Krym** ( ☎ 271 701; baza@hotelkrim.yalta.crimea .ua; vul Moskovska 1/6; s 40-55hry; d 90-250hry; tr & q 105-345hry; ❄ ) You'll have to step up the charm to crack a smile from the staff at Hotel Krym, designed by architect Krasnov (who also did the Livadia Palace, among others). But you can't beat the prices or the location (expect noise, especially in summer). The cheaper rooms for each category have a shared bathroom, and the priciest doubles and triples have air-conditioning.

**Hotel Otdykh** ( ☎ 353 069; www.yalta-otdyh.com; vul Drazhynskoho 14; s 160-335hry, d 220-490hry; ❄ ) Once a 19th-century brothel for visiting government dignitaries, Hotel Otdykh perches high on the oldest street in town, removed from the main hustle and bustle (although the 1st and 2nd floor get some street noise). Rooms have sea views and are sunny in the mornings, and on Sunday you can hear church bells. Staff speak some English, a so-so set breakfast is included (although otherwise, the restaurant is good), and discounts are given for longer stays.

**Hotel Bristol** ( ☎ 271 603; www.hotel-bristol .ua; vul Ruzvelta 10; d 120-180hry, ste 240-280hry; ✗ ❄ ) Service seems to have declined over the years at Hotel Bristol, which once seemed to aspire to a greater stature. But prices have declined as well, and the large, chintzy Western-style rooms (many with big bathtubs) are good value. Breakfast is included.

**Hotel Palace** ( ☎ 324 380; fax 230 492; vul Chekhova 8; s/d 450/550hry; ❄ ) It's true – the building has a palatial quality, with a pretty marble staircase (no lift) decorated with interesting Crimean art on the walls to make the time pass as you trudge up and down. The spacious rooms often have large balconies (great for watching fireworks) with sea views, and the bathrooms are remodelled. It's become overpriced, but in the off season it could be good value.

**Hotel Oreanda** ( ☎ 274 250; www.hotel-oreanda .com; naberezhna imeni Lenina 35/2; s 1155-1345hry, d 1695-2055hry; ✗ ❄ ▯ ▮ ) The Oreanda offers great service and most of the luxuries you would expect in a top Western European city hotel (large rooms, in-room internet access, two pools, a Turkish bath…) Not surprisingly, it is overpriced, but if you're ready to splash out, this is the place.

## Eating

The waterfront walkway is dotted with several cute little places to eat, and there are many well-signed super-cheap cafeterias (Столовая) around town as well. One is **Stolovaya Krym** (mains 5hry; ☼ 8am-7pm), associated with the budget hotel next door.

**Pelmennaya** ( ☎ 323 932; vul Sverdlova 8; mains 6-12hry; ☼ 10am-8pm) Not far from Hotel Otdykh, this hole-in-the-wall place is great for a quick hot bite with Yalta's working class. *Pelmeni*, of course, is the main offering, but *blini* and a few other dishes can be had here too.

**Mamma Mia** ( ☎ 234 372; naberezhnaya imeni Lenina 15; mains 23-55hry; ☼ 10am-8pm, summer till last customer)

This cellar-like restaurant has pop music that doesn't fit with the yummy thin-crust pizzas, which you can cover with another crust for 3hry more. But wait, there's more – spaghetti, ravioli and risotto too, as well as meats and fish. You can watch the puffy-hatted pizzaman bake your pie in the red-hot oven while you debate whether the restaurant's mascot is really Mamma or actually Uncle Guido in drag.

**Khutorok Lya Mer** ( ☎ 271 815; vul Sverdlova 9; mains 25-95hry; ☽ 11-2am) This place is decked out like a wooden ship, but the menu (available in English) strangely features more meat than fish, such as the daring bulls' balls with horseradish. There's an eclectic wine list with Crimean, Georgian and Aussie selections. Book ahead to make sure you get a seaview table.

### Getting There & Away

There are no trains or flights to Yalta. However, if you plan to take a train or plane from Simferopol and want to get your ticket while in Yalta, there is a two-storey **ticket office** ( ☽ 8am-7pm). It's sort of strangely located. First find the Pelmennaya restaurant. Take the stairs between it and the next building; the office is on the right. The first floor charges 10hry more for 'better' service. A branch of **Kiyavia** ( ☎ 325 943; ploscha Lenina) is in booth No 13 at the post office.

Trolleybuses to/from Simferopol (p895) start/finish at the **trolleybus terminal** (vul Moskovskaya). Opposite that is the **bus terminal** where buses leave for Bakhchysaray (25hry, 2½ hours, thrice daily) – the 11am departure is most prudent for a day trip. Half-hourly buses go to Sevastopol (20hry, two hours) and Simferopol (20hry, two hours). The daily Odesa-bound bus (90hry, 14 hours) departs at 4.50pm. If you happen to be jetting off to Chişinău in Moldova (see p506), a daily bus leaves at 2.05pm (130hry, 18½ hours), stopping in Odesa (100hry) at 3.30am.

There is a **boat passenger terminal** (morskoy vokzal; ☎ 320 094; vul Ruzvelta 5), but it seems to be deserted. However, it is possible to reach Odesa on London Sky Travel's speed ferry (see p888) as well as Istanbul and Varna (p891).

### Getting Around

A trolleybus ride is 50 kopeks. *Marshrutki* within the town are 1hry. Taxis within the town are relatively expensive (7hry to 10hry), and drivers are not particularly eager for your business (hard to bargain). They hang out around hotels and busy intersections, lazily playing chess, backgammon or *durak* (a popular card game) on benches designated specifically for them. What a life. **Avka-Trans Taxis** ( ☎ 231 085, 8-067 563 0444) are metered and cost half as much around town. They're often found at the intersection of vul Ruzvelta and naberezhna Lenina.

To get to/from the terminals, take trolleybus 1, 2 or 3 along vul Moskovskaya/Kyivskaya; most *marshrutki* along those streets also go to/from the terminals.

Just off vul Moskovska, there is a *marshrutka* stand where these minibuses go to sights just outside of Yalta. *Marshrutki* 27 and 32 (3.50hry) stop at Livadia, Swallow's Nest, and the Mt Ai-Petri cable car, stopping and turning around at Alupka (where Massandra Winery is). *Marshrutka* 34 goes to Nikitsky Gardens (3hry).

## BAKHCHYSARAY БАХЧИСАРАЙ
☎ 06554 / pop 33,000

There are three great reasons to make it out to this tattered old town: the remarkably well-preserved Khan's Palace, dating back to the 16th century; the still-working Uspensky Monastery, built into sheer cliff walls; and the 6th-century cave city of Chufut-Kale. Many locals but few foreigners make it out this way, which is a shame as the attractions and vistas here are some of the most unforgettable on the peninsula.

Once the capital of the Crimean khanate (a spin-off from the Golden Horde), Bakhchysaray (bakh-chee-sah-*rai*) is a dusty, run-down place 33km southwest of Simferopol and about 64km northwest of Yalta. It's split into a new town and old town, where all the great sights are located (old town is known both as *stary gorod* or *starosel'ye*).

### Sights

The remarkable **Khan's Palace** (Khansky Palats; www.hansaray.iatp.org.ua; vul Lenina 129; adult/student & child 16/8hry; ☽ 9am-5.30pm Jul-Aug, to 4.30pm Wed-Mon May, Jun, Sep & Oct, to 4.30pm Thu-Mon Nov-Apr) was built by Russian and Ukrainian slaves in the 16th century and has been relatively well maintained since it was spared destruction by Catherine the Great in the 18th century.

Even visitors who have had enough of visiting churches and monasteries will not regret visiting the **Uspensky Monastery** (admission free). Built into the side of a cliff (note the frescoes high up above on the cliff walls!), the working monastery has such a lovely and romantically devout feel, you may even consider signing up for monkhood yourself. The water there is said to have miraculous healing properties, and you'll see visitors filling their plastic Coca-Cola bottles with the stuff. Look across to the opposite cliffs for wild peacocks – you're likely to hear their persistent calls before you see them.

Next up is the 6th-century cave city of **Chufut-Kale** (admission free). It's a 1.5km uphill walk (much of it shady) – along the way you'll see the entrance to a Dervish and Muslim cemetery that is in ruins; only a couple of tombstones are still legible. Chufut-Kale, a honeycomb of caves and structures where people took refuge for hundreds of years, is an exciting and breathtaking place to explore. Although the joint entrance to the Uspensky Monastery and Chufut-Kale looks a bit touristy, the 1.5km uphill (but shady) walk to the cave city ensures it's not too overrun with people. Although you might see people asking you to pay for entrance, just ignore them. It's free.

### Sleeping & Eating

If you get stuck in town, or if you have fallen in love and want to stick it out another day or two, **Prival** ( ☎ 47 846, 52 270; fax 47 235; vul Shmidta 43; www.prival.crimea.com; dm 30hry, d 180-200hry, 2- to 4-person cottages 180-400hry) offers breathtaking vistas of the limestone cliffs, a sauna, pool, Jacuzzi, a tennis court, a restaurant…Cheap triples and quads are available too. It's a well-signed 0.5km from the entrance to the Khan's Palace. You can just show up, but keep in mind that it gets booked up from time to time with large groups.

### Getting There & Around

Enjoying all three sights as a day trip from Yalta is nearly impossible without a car. If, like many, you've made Yalta your Crimean home base and want to see everything in Bakhchysaray from there, consider making two trips or staying the night.

Because buses and trains connect Bakhchysaray with Simferopol and Sevastopol super frequently and until the evening, it's more feasible to conquer all three attractions as a day trip from one of those cities. The bus from Yalta leaves at 11am (23hry, 2½ hours) and returns at 4pm. Consider buying

your return ticket in advance if you're taking this bus, which is small and often full. You can also catch a train to Kyiv (*kupeyny/platskartny* 55/44hry, 17 hours, two daily) if you so desire.

All stop at the train and bus stations (located together); ask for the 'vag-*zal*.' Once there, take any *marshrutka* (1hry) marked Старосельє and ask for *khansky palats*. Having visited the palace, you can stick out your hand for a *marshrutka* to take you further up the road to Uspensky Monastery and Chufut-Kale – they are all going that way now, and you get off at the end of the line, when the *marshrutka* turns around. Walk up the paved path to the monastery, and keep walking to get to Chufut-Kale.

Buses to Sevastopol (7hry, one hour, every 40 minutes) run until 7pm and buses to Simferopol (5hry, one hour, every 20 minutes) run until 5pm. Trains are another option: the last one to Simferopol (3hry, 45 minutes, eight daily) leaves at 9.30pm; the last to Sevastopol (3hry, seven daily, 1½ hours) leaves at 9.45pm.

## SEVASTOPOL СЕВАСТОПОЛЬ
☎ 0692 / pop 328,000

Do you love a man in a uniform? Are you fascinated with all things Crimean War–related? If you've answered 'yes' to either of these questions, a visit to Sevastopol is a must. Otherwise, it's not particularly rife with things to do or sights to see – but the look and feel of Sevastopol does stand out among other Crimean cities. It dons a characteristic civic pride, and its whitewashed buildings, litterless streets, polite population and sharply dressed officers combine to form a pleasant impression of a city that is, so to say, in shipshape.

### History

Modern Sevastopol (see-va-*stope*-all in Russian) has an attractive appearance, but it was a different story when the city was making international headlines during the Crimean War. After 349 days of bombardment by the British, French and Turks in 1854–55, it lay devastated by the time of its defeat. Arriving 10 years later, Mark Twain still felt moved to remark, 'In whatsoever direction you please, your eye scarcely encounters anything by ruin, ruin, ruin!'

History repeated itself in 1942, when the city fell to the Germans after a brutal 250-day

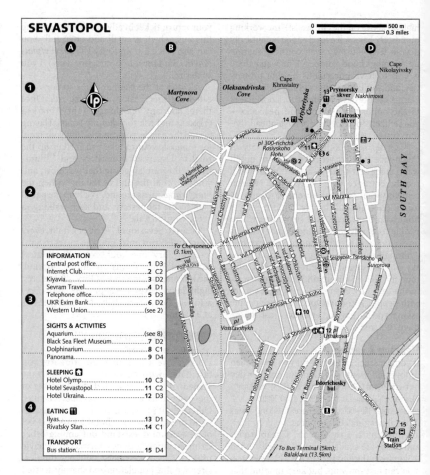

**SEVASTOPOL**

0 — 500 m
0 — 0.3 miles

siege. Stalin promptly proclaimed it a 'hero city' for holding out so long. Today only 10 buildings in town date from before 1945. As a military centre, Sevastopol was a 'closed' city (no tourists allowed) until 1996, and Russia has a lease on the port until 2019.

## Information

There are 24-hour ATMs along prospekt Nakhimova and vul Bolshaya Morskaya.

**Central post office** ( ☎ 544 881; vul Bolshaya Morskaya 21; ⏰ 9am-7pm Mon-Fri, to 2pm Sat) Internet access available too.

**Internet club** (vul Mayakovskogo 4; club ⏰ 24hr) About 10 not-slow computers.

**Kiyavia** ( ☎ 542 829; vul Lenina 13; ⏰ 9am-2pm & 3-7pm Mon-Fri) Plane tickets.

**Sevram Travel** ( ☎ 555 878, 550 829; office@sevram .com; Office 63, Palace of Childhood, prospekt Nakhimova 4) City tours with Crimean War specialists in English and other languages. Located in the building's eastern rotunda.

**Telephone office** ( ⏰ 9am-10pm) Near the post office.

**UKR Exim Bank** (prospekt Nakhimova 15; ⏰ 9am-4.30pm Mon-Fri) Offers ATM and credit-card advances.

**Western Union** (vul Mayakovskogo 4; ⏰ 9am-6pm Mon-Fri, 10am-4pm Sat & Sun) Same building as the internet club.

## Sights

The major Crimean War sight in town is the **Panorama** (Istorichesky bulvar; admission 12hry; ⏰ 10am-5pm Tue-Sun), a massive painting with 3D elements depicting the defence of Sevastopol. The **Black Sea Fleet Museum** ( ☎ 542 289; vul Lenina 11;

admission 15hry; ☿ 10am-5pm Wed-Sun, closed last Fri of month) provides colourful displays about the controversial Russian fleet; no English assistance is on hand. The Crimean War and naval history aside, the ruins of the ancient Greek city of **Chersonesus** (admission 10hry; ☿ 9am-7pm) are fun to explore. Founded in 422 BC, Chersonesus (Khersones locally) is the spot where Volodymyr the Great was famously baptised as a Christian in AD 989, thus launching what would become the Russian Orthodox Church. Except at the height of summer, when some *marshrutki* go there, a taxi (10hry) is the only option. Get your hotel to call.

Sevastopol is known for its **Dolphinarium** (☎ 559 955; naberezhnaya Kornilova 2; admission 18hry; ☿ 10am-4.30pm Tue-Sun) and adjacent **Aquarium** (☎ 543 892; adult/child 6/3hry; ☿ 9am-7pm); conditions for the animals were not particularly uplifting. It's doubtful, but perhaps that's what's being improved.

### Sleeping

**Hotel Sevastopol** (☎ 466 400; fax 466 409; prospekt Nakhimova 8; s 50-205hry, d 80-330hry, tr 108-435hry) In a palatial, historic (no lift) building, Hotel Sevastopol exudes a sort of weary grandeur with Soviet accents. Bathrooms have water heaters, but they are small – so you can count on a hot two-minute shower.

**Hotel Ukraina** (☎ 542 127; fax 545 378; vul Hoholya 2; s 170-390hry, d 260-480hry) With a sort of awkward, hot-pink attempt at sleek style (throw pillows on the common room floors?), Ukraina is definitely a step above Hotel Sevastopol in service. The rooms have a brighter look, with shinier floors and slightly better furniture, but even the higher-priced rooms have that Soviet feel one only learns to love with time.

**Hotel Olymp** (☎ 455 758, 455 789; www.olymphotel .com; vul Kulakova 86; s/d 550/700hry; ▣ ▨ ▨) On a peaceful residential street and in a hopeful-looking new yellow building, Hotel Olymp stands out from the standard Sevastopol offerings. The faux-Greek motifs are a trifle chintzy, but there's a pool and sauna, and staff at this new hotel are eager to make the place successful, so you should sense that in the service.

### Eating

Cafés and restaurants abound in the main waterfront area. In the peaceful park surrounding the Panorama are several other decent eateries.

**Rivatsky Stan** (☎ 557 278; Harbour; mains 25-85hry; ☿ 11-3am) This is possibly the best seafood restaurant in Crimea, although it also serves delicious poultry, meat, lip-smacking salads and even frog's legs and snails. Its wooden deck on the waterfront is a lovely spot for a drink at dusk, although when cruise ships are in, they obscure some of the view.

**Ilyas** (☎ 544 766; prospekt Nakhimova 2; mains 10-25hry; ☿ 9am-11pm) You'll want a table by the window here, especially at midday when the harbour shimmers all they way out to the fort. The seafood isn't as spectacular, so you might prefer the Tatar menu of *shashlik*, *pilaf*, *manty* (large minced-lamb dumplings), *bureks* and samosas.

### Getting There & Around

The bus station and train station are within visible walking distance of each other. Any *marshrutka* (1.50hry, pay on exit) or trolleybus from the stations will take you to the centre (prospekt Nakhimova).

From the **bus terminal** (vul Vokzalna), you can catch a ride to Simferopol (17hry, two hours, 32 daily), Yalta (20hry, two hours, 20 daily) and Bakhchysaray (11hry, one hour, 22 daily). Once-daily buses to Odesa (73hry, 13 hours) are available for hardcore kopek-pinchers who can sleep in a chair.

From the Sevastopol **train station** (vul Portovaya), there are only trains to Kyiv (*kupeyny/platskartny* 60/40hry, 17 hours, twice daily) and international trains to Moscow, St Petersburg and Minsk, but many more trains leave from nearby Simferopol (p894).

# UKRAINE DIRECTORY

## ACCOMMODATION

Book travel and accommodation well in advance if you'll be anywhere in the country during the May 1 holidays. Know that some hotels actually charge a certain percentage for the 'service' of advance booking.

Organised camping grounds are rare anywhere in Ukraine and are usually at least 10km from the city centre. Wild camping is allowed, although you have to pay an entrance fee (adult/child 6/2hry). Fires are also prohibited, although this is largely ignored.

Hostels are just starting up in Ukraine, check www.hihostels.com.ua/en for information on top of what's provided in this book.

Most budget hotels are unsightly Soviet monstrosities built in the 1960s and '70s. Rooms are often well-worn with outdated furniture, but are reasonably comfortable, clean and cheap. Many hotels have cheaper rooms with a shared bathroom. Readers have reported foot fungus to be a problem in the country, so wear flip-flops (thongs) in shared showers. Hot water can be an issue at some budget hotels, especially in Odesa and in Crimea.

Midrange hotels or more expensive rooms in budget hotels may have more polite staff and remodelled, Western-style bathrooms.

Top-end hotels usually meet most Western standards of service and aesthetics.

Private rooms in family homes are a popular option in Crimea and Odesa, especially in the summer. Look for people with signs around their necks reading кімнати (*kimnaty*, Ukrainian) or комнаты (*komnaty*, Russian), both of which mean 'rooms'. Before deciding, however, always check the exact location and proximity to public transport. The cost ranges from 45hry to 80hry per person per night.

## ACTIVITIES

Hiking opportunities are richest in the Carpathian National Natural Park (p882) and around Crimea (p892). Before arrival, try to buy the *Hiking Guide to Poland & Ukraine*, by Tim Burford, which describes different hikes around Ukraine. Available in Kyiv are the detailed Topograficheskaya Karta maps, though hiking trails are poorly marked on the maps or not at all. The virtually untouched slopes of the Carpathians are starting to become popular for snow sports (p882) between November and May. Bungee jumping in Kamyanets-Podilsky (p883) is now an option for the very brave.

## BUSINESS HOURS

Official working hours are 9am (or 10am) to 5pm (or 6pm) Monday to Friday, with an hour-long break anywhere between noon and 2pm. Shops often open until about 8pm on weekdays and all day Saturday. Most bars and restaurants tend to open from 10am until 11pm or midnight; nightclubs stay open later.

## EMBASSIES & CONSULATES
### Ukrainian Embassies & Consulates

**Australia** ( ☎ 02-6230 5789; www.ukremb.info; Level 12, George Centre, 60 Marcus Clarke St, Canberra 2601)
**Belarus** ( ☎ 017-283 1990; fax 283 1980; vul Staravilenska 51, Minsk)

**Canada** Ottawa ( ☎ 613-230 8015, www.ukremb.ca; 311 Metcalfe St); Toronto ( ☎ 416-763 3114, fax 763 2323) 2120 Bloor St West)
**France** ( ☎ 01-43 06 07 37; fax 43 06 02 94; 21 ave de Saxe, Paris)
**Germany** ( ☎ 4930-2888 7116; www.botschaft-ukraine .de; Albrechtstrasse 26, Berlin)
**Hungary** Budapest ( ☎ 1-422 4120; emb_hu@mfa.gov .ua; 77 Stefania ut, Magyarorszag); Nyiregyhaza ( ☎ 42-50 67 43; gc_hu@mfa.gov.ua; Rakoczi ut 1, Pf 190)
**Ireland** ( ☎ 01 668 5189; emb_ie@mfa.gov.ua; 16 Eglin Rd, Ballsbridge Dublin)
**Japan** ( ☎ 813-5474 9770; 5474 9772; 3-15-6 Nishi Azabu, Minato-ku, Tokyo)
**Netherlands** ( ☎ 3170-362 60 95; www.oekraine .com/core/embassy; 76 Zeestraat, The Hague)
**Moldova** ( ☎ 3732-58 21 51; emb_md@mfa.gov.ua; 17 Vasile Lupu str, Chișinău)
**Poland** Warsaw ( ☎ 022-625 01 27; emb_pl@mfa.gov .ua; 7 Aleja Szucha); Gdansk ( ☎ 4858-346 06 90; gc_plg@ mfa.gov.ua; ul Jaskowa Dolina 44); Kraków ( ☎ 4812-429 29 36; gc_kra@mfa.gov.ua; ul Krakówska 41)
**Romania** Bucharest ( ☎ 01-211 69 86; emb_ro@mfa.gov .ua; Calea Dorobantilor nr 16); Suceava ( ☎ 40230-531 345; gc_ro@mfa.gov.ua; Mihaj Vitjazu 48)
**Russia** ( ☎ 495-229 1079; emb_ru@mfa.gov.ua; Leontevsky pereulok 18, Moscow)
**Slovakia** ( ☎ 7-5441 26 51; fax 7-5441 26 51; Radvanska 35, Bratislava)
**UK** ( ☎ 020-7243 8923; www.ukremb.org.uk; 78 Kensington Park Rd, London)
**USA** Washington DC ( ☎ 202-333-7507/08/09; www .ukraineinfo.us; 3350 M St NW); New York ( ☎ 212-371-5690; www.ukrainesf.com; 240 E 49th St); Chicago ( ☎ 312-642-4388; www.ukrchicago.com; 10 E Huron St); San Fransisco ( ☎ 415-398-0240; www.ukrainesf.com; 530 Bush St, Ste 402)

### Embassies & Consulates in Ukraine

The following are in Kyiv unless otherwise noted.

**Australia** ( ☎ /fax 044-235 7586; vul Kominternu 18/137; Ⓜ Vokzalna)
**Belarus** ( ☎ 044-537 5200; ukraine@belembassy.org; vul Kotsyubynskoho 3; Ⓜ Universitet)
**Canada** ( ☎ 044-270 7144; www.kyiv.gc.ca; vul Yaroslaviv val 31)
**France** ( ☎ 044-278 8728; www.ambafrance.kiev.ua; vul Reitarska 39)
**Germany** ( ☎ 044-247 6800; www.german-embassy .kiev.ua; vul Khmelnytskoho 25; Ⓜ Zoloti Vorota)
**Japan** ( ☎ 044-490 5500; www.ua.emb-japan.go.up; Muzeyny prov 4, 7th fl; Ⓜ Maydan Nezalezhnosti)
**Moldova** ( ☎ 044-280 7721; moldoukr@sovamua.com; vul Sichnevoho Povstannya 6; Ⓜ Arsenalna)

UKRAINE

**Netherlands** ( ☎ 044-490 8200; nlambkie@ukrpack.net; Kontraktova ploscha 7; Ⓜ Kontraktova Ploscha)
**Romania** Kyiv ( ☎ 044-234 5261; romania@iptelecom.net .ua; vul Kotsyubynskoho 8; Ⓜ Universitet); Odesa ( ☎ 0482-23 62 98; konsulro@tm.odessa.ua; vul Pastyora 21, Odesa)
**Russia** Kyiv ( ☎ 044-294 7936; embrus@public.icyb.kiev .ua; vul Kutuzova 8; Ⓜ Pecherska); Odesa ( ☎ 0482-22 22 32; consul.rf.od@farlep.net; vul Kanatanaya 83); Lviv ( ☎ 0322-69 20 36; consrus@lviv.gu.net; vul Patona 7A)
**UK** ( ☎ 044-490 3600; www.britemb-ukraine.net; vul Desyatynna 9)
**USA** ( ☎ 044-490 0000; www.usemb.kiev.ua; vul Y Kotsyubynskoho 10)

## FESTIVALS & EVENTS

**International Labour Day** (1 May) is always a big deal no matter where you are in the former Soviet Union; bigger cities have fireworks, concerts and other performances. On 24 August, **Independence Day**, each city in Ukraine hosts a festival and parade. On April Fool's Day (1 April), Odesa celebrates **Humourina**, a huge street carnival centred around comedy. In Kamyanets-Podilsky, there's a national hot-air balloon competition, complete with stunts, in mid-May; in September is the 'Tournament of Knights', complete with jousting and sword-fighting.

## HOLIDAYS

**New Year's Day** 1 January
**Orthodox Christmas** 7 January
**International Women's Day** 8 March
**Orthodox Easter (Paskha)** April
**Labour Day** 1-2 May
**Victory Day** 9 May
**Constitution Day** 28 June
**Independence Day** 24 August
**Catholic Christmas** 25 December

## GAY & LESBIAN TRAVELLERS

Homosexuality is legal in Ukraine, but few people are very 'out' here. Looking gay doesn't raise eyebrows – some straight men can look quite gay – nor do acquaintances mind it if they know you're queer. However, you rarely, if ever, see displays of affection between two gay men or two lesbians on the street, and it may create hostility.

## LANGUAGE

Ukrainian was adopted as the sole official language at independence. However, apart from the west, many Ukrainians (especially in the south), prefer to speak Russian. A hy-brid of the two languages, called Surzhyk, is spoken in Kyiv and other major cities. In the Carpathians, some people living outside of city centres speak a Ukrainian dialect that is influenced by Polish, Slovak and Russian; they usually understand Russian, but it may be difficult to understand their accent.

## MONEY

The hryvnia (hry) is divided into 100 units, each called a kopek. In addition to the new one-hryvnia coins, kopek coins come in denominations of one, two, five, 10, 25 and 50 kopeks, while there are one, two, five, 10, 20, 50, 100 and 200 hryvnia notes.

The only things you can legally pay for in foreign currency (usually US dollars) are international flights and foreign visas. Although many hotels give prices in US dollars or euros, you will still be paying in hryvnia.

ATMs and foreign-exchange offices (euros and US dollars only) are easily found even in small cities in Ukraine, and Western Union seems to have a desk in most banks. Exchanging money on the black market is unnecessary and illegal. Avoid bringing travellers cheques – they're hard to change.

## POST

Normal-sized letters or postcards cost 3hry to anywhere outside Ukraine by ordinary mail or a bit more for express service. Domestic services take three days to a week; international takes a week to 10 days. There are offices of DHL and FedEx in many cities.

## TELEPHONE

Every city and large town has a telephone centre (many open 24 hours), usually near the central post office. To make interstate or international calls, pay in advance at the counter inside the telephone centre (you'll get change for unused time). Avoid using public phone booths, which require specific phonecards and are a hassle. Operator assistance can be reached 24 hours at ☎ 8-191/2/3/4; English is possible but problematic.

---

**EMERGENCY NUMBERS**

- Ambulance ☎ 03
- Fire brigade ☎ 01
- Police ☎ 02

UKRAINE

When dialling Ukraine from abroad, dial the country code ( ☎ 380), the city code (without the first zero) and then the number. To call overseas from Ukraine, dial ☎ 8 (wait for a tone, then) 10, followed by the country code, city code and number. You can reach an AT&T operator by dialling ☎ 8-100-11 and an MCI operator by dialling ☎ 8-100-13.

For interstate calls within Ukraine, dial ☎ 8, wait for a tone, then the city code (with its first zero) and number – there should always be a 10-digit combination. If a telephone number has seven digits, use the first two digits of the area code, but if the telephone number has five/six digits use the first four/three digits of the area code.

## Mobile Phones

To dial a local mobile-phone number within Ukraine, you must always prefix it with an ☎ 8, as if calling another town. Common codes for mobiles include ☎ 050 and ☎ 067.

European GSM phones usually work in Ukraine, but check with your operator. If you're going to be making several calls, it makes more sense to buy a local prepaid SIM card (from 37hry). Try **Golden Telecom** ( ☎ 490 5000; www.goldentel.com; Sofiyvska 1a, Kyiv). The main network operators **Kyivstar** ( ☎ 466 0466; www.kyivstar.net; Sichnevoho Povstannia 24, Kyiv) and **UMC** ( ☎ 500 0500; www.umc.com.ua; Leiptsyzka 15). Recharge cards are sold absolutely everywhere.

## VISAS

For stays of up to 90 days, visas are no longer required for EU, US, Swiss, Canadian and Japanese citizens. Australians, Israelis, New Zealanders and South Africans still need them. Point-of-entry visas are not issued. Comprehensive information about application forms and fees can be found at www.ukremb.info.

# TRANSPORT IN UKRAINE

## GETTING THERE & AWAY
### Air

Most international flights use Kyiv's **Boryspil international airport** (KBP; ☎ 490 4777; www.airport-borispol.kiev.ua). Odesa receives some international flights from nearby countries; Lviv does too but not as many. Simferopol gets some only in summer. There's no departure tax in the Ukraine.

Ukraine's international airline carriers are **AeroSvit** ( ☎ 235 8710; www.aerosvit.com) and **Ukraine International Airlines** ( ☎ 461 5050; www.flyuia.com).

The following are the main international airlines with offices in Kyiv. Complete airline information, including flight schedules, can be found in the quarterly *Kyiv Business Directory* (sold outside Kyiv's central post office).

**Aeroflot** (code SU; ☎ 245 4359; www.aeroflot.com)
**Air Baltic** (code BT; ☎ 238 2668; www.airbaltic.com)
**Air France** (code AF; ☎ 496 3575; www.airfrance.com)
**Austrian Airlines** (code OS; ☎ 230 0020; www.aua.com)
**British Airways** (code BA; ☎ 585 5050; www.ba.com)
**Czech Airlines** (code OK; ☎ 281 7449; www.czechairlines.com)
**Delta** (code DL; ☎ 246 5656; www.delta.com)
**El Al** (code LY; ☎ 230 6993; www.elal.co.il)
**Estonian Air** (code OV; ☎ 289 0520; www.estonian-air.ee)
**Finnair** (code AY; ☎ 247 5777; www.finnair.com)
**KLM** (code KL; ☎ 490 2490; www.klm.com)
**LOT Polish Airlines** (code LO; ☎ 246 5620; www.lot.com)
**Lufthansa** (code LH; ☎ 490 3800; www.lufthansa.com)
**Malév Hungarian Airlines** (code MA; ☎ 490 7342; www.malev.hu)
**South African Airways** (code SA; ☎ 490 6501; www.flysaa.com)
**Swiss International Airlines** (code LX; ☎ 490 6500; www.swiss.com)
**Transaero** (code UN; ☎ 296 7870; www.transaero.ru)
**Turkish Airlines** (code TK; ☎ 490 5933; www.thy.com)

## Land
### BUS

Buses are far slower, less frequent and less comfortable than trains for long-distance travel.

From the Kyiv central bus station there are buses to Chişinău (59hry to 70hry, 9½ hours, four daily) and Moscow (97hry to 115hry, 20 hours, one daily), as well as some nonregular buses to Minsk (88hry, 12½ hours).

From Lviv, there are buses to Poland: Warsaw (85hry, 11 hours, four daily), Kraków (75hry, two daily, nine hours) and Przemyszl (30hry, three hours, 11 daily).

From Uzhhorod, there are one or two daily buses to the Slovak cities of Košice (29hry, three hours) and Michalovce (15hry, two hours), and to the Hungarian city of Nyiregyhaza (30hry, three hours).

From Ivano-Frankivsk, you can get to Chişinău (23hry to 60hry, 14 hours, once daily), Warsaw (125hry, 14 hours, three daily),

Kraków (108hry, 10 hours, daily except Tuesday), Prague (284hry, 24 hours, daily except Monday and Thursday) and Brno (244hry, 21 hours, daily except Tuesday).

From Odesa, there are nine daily buses to Chişinău (15hry to 25hry, seven hours).

From Yalta, there is one bus a day to Chişinău (180hry, 19 hours).

### CAR & MOTORCYCLE

Always drive across official border stations to avoid complications. Foreign drivers must have an International Driving Permit and must sign a declaration that they will be leaving the country with the car by a given date (no more than two months later). You'll also need vehicle insurance valid for the former Soviet Union. Policies bought at the border often prove useless, so buy beforehand.

### TRAIN

Most cities have two stations located right next to each other. The one for regular trains (that is, those listed in this book) is referred to as ЖД (zhe-*deh*), the abbreviation for 'railway.' The other, Пріміські, is for local electric trains that go to smaller villages not covered here.

To be safe, try to get tickets a day in advance; if you're travelling during the New Year or May holidays, or going to Odesa or Crimea anytime in summer, get tickets as early as possible.

The entire country is well-connected by train to many places in Russia, and less so to major places in Belarus. The following trains leave from Kyiv.

| Destination | Cost kupeyny/platskartny (hry) |
|---|---|
| Belgrade | 570/- |
| Brest | 104/68 |
| Budapest | 535/- |
| Chişinău | 195/105 |
| Kraków | 360/- |
| Minsk | 102/66 |
| Moscow | 230/180 |
| Prague | 530/- |
| Sofia | 445/- |
| St Petersburg | 398/168 |
| Warsaw | 340/- |

### Sea

**London Sky Travel** ( ☎ 38-048 729 3195; www.lst.com .ua), in Odesa, has twice-weekly speed ferries between Varna and Odesa (eight hours,

twice weekly); it has an office at the Odesa passenger port.

## GETTING AROUND

### Air

In Kyiv, there are several offices of **Kiyavia** ( ☎ 056, 490 4949; www.kiyavia.com; vul Horodetskoho 4; Ⓜ Khreshchatyk). Tickets within the CIS can be booked by email through Kiyavia but must be picked up in person.

Domestic airlines include **Ukraine International Airlines** ( ☎ 461 5050, Kyiv; www.flyuia.com) and **Aerosvit** ( ☎ 235 8710, Kyiv; www.aerosvit.com), which have flights between Kyiv, Lviv, Odesa, Simferopol and Ivano-Frankivsk. In Kyiv, virtually all domestic flights arrive at and depart from **Zhulyany Airport** ( ☎ 242 2309; 92 Provitroflotsky prospekt). In winter, flights on smaller planes are sometimes delayed or cancelled.

### Bicycle

Despite zero biking infrastructure, cycling is becoming more popular in Ukraine, even as a means of intracity travel. City roads are too congested and crumbling to make riding in them really enjoyable, but in Kyiv, you'll see people doing it anyway, and there are a few places to get away. The website www.tryukraine .com/travel/cycling.shtml is a good resource.

### Boat

In Odesa, **London Sky Travel** ( ☎ 38-048 729 3195; www.lst.com.ua) offers high-speed ferries between Odesa, Sevastopol and Yalta.

### Bus

Travelling around the country by train is often far quicker and more comfortable than by bus. Most public buses are decrepit, but a few private bus companies, such as **Autolux** (www.autolux.com.ua), offer comfortable services between points in Crimea, Kyiv, Odesa and Lviv. Schedules and price information are available on the website.

Larger cities often have several *avtovokzal* (bus terminals) but only one normally handles long-distance routes of interest to travellers. Tickets can be bought one or two days in advance at the major bus terminal and sometimes at separate ticket offices in the city centres.

### Car & Motorcycle

To drive a private or rented vehicle to and around Ukraine you'll need an International

Driving Permit and acceptable insurance. Ukraine participates in the Green Card System (p934), so procure one in advance, as border guards have been known to sell useless policies.

Drive on the right. Unless otherwise indicated, speed limits are 60km/h in towns, 90km/h on major roads and 110km/h on highways. Speed traps are common and traffic police often wave you down without obvious reason. Fines for speeding start at 40hry but most officers are open to negotiation (meaning you pay less – 20hry – but don't get an official receipt).

It's a criminal offence to drive after consuming alcohol or without wearing a seat belt. Legally you must always carry a fire extinguisher, first-aid kit and warning triangle.

**Avis** (www.avis.com), **Europcar** (www.europcar.com) and **Hertz** (www.hertz.com.ua) have offices in Ukraine, including Kyiv, Lviv, Odesa, Simferopol and Yalta. Rental starts at 275hry a day (for a weekly hire). Check insurance and hire conditions carefully.

## Local Transport

Cheap but crowded trolleybuses, trams and buses operate in all cities and major towns. Tickets can be bought on board and *must* be punched to be validated – look for others doing this to see how.

The fare for any given *marshrutka* (see p730) is displayed prominently at the front inside each bus; payment is usually taken upon entry but sometimes upon exit. To stop a *marshrutka*, simply hold out your hand and it will stop. Jump in, sit down, pass cash to the driver (a human chain operates if you are not sitting close enough) and then call out *'ostanovee-tyes po-zha-lusta!'* when you want to get out and the driver will pull over.

Although it's often possible to hire an official taxi in larger towns, private taxis are a popular and surprisingly safe alternative, but difficult if you don't speak Ukrainian or Russian. Negotiate a price before you get in, and never get into a car if there's already a passenger.

## Train

Train travel is normally frequent, cheap and efficient. An overnight train is an economical way to get around, and most services are timed to depart at dusk and arrive in the morning (after dawn). For information on train classes and terminology, see p937.

If you will be travelling during the 1 May holidays, book tickets in advance.

# Regional Directory

## CONTENTS

The regional directory gives general overviews of conditions and information that apply to the whole of Eastern Europe. Given the vast size of the region, this has meant some generalisation, so for specifics on any given topic, see the relevant Directory for the country you require information on.

## ACCOMMODATION

As a rule, for each accommodation listing we have used the currency you are most likely to be quoted a price in. This means that for some hotels we give hotel prices in local currency, others are listed in euros or US dollars.

In Eastern Europe, as in the rest of Europe, the cheapest places to rest your head are camping grounds, followed by hostels and student accommodation. Guesthouses, pensions, private rooms and cheap hotels are also good value. Self-catering flats in the city and cottages in the countryside are worth considering if you're in a group, especially if you plan to stay put for a while. Eastern Europe remains relatively undeveloped in accommodation terms and in many places these options simply won't exist. Things are changing though, and nearly every country now has a decent hostel in its capital and a growing hotel market.

The concept of a B&B remains a somewhat mysterious one in most countries of Eastern Europe, where you stay either in a hotel or hostel. Central Europe and some of the Balkan countries have a long tradition of homestays, although breakfast is not always included. In Russia, Belarus, Ukraine and Moldova people sometimes let out rooms, but this is nowhere as homely as a British B&B or even a Hungarian pension.

See the Directory sections in the individual country chapters for an overview of local accommodation options. During peak holiday periods accommodation can be hard to find and, unless you're camping, it's advisable to book ahead where possible. Even some camping grounds can fill up, particularly popular ones near large towns and cities.

Hostels and cheap hotels in popular tourist destinations, such as Prague, Budapest and Kraków, fill up very quickly – especially the well-run ones in desirable or central neighbourhoods. It's a good idea to make reservations as many weeks ahead as possible – at least for the first night or two. A two- or three-minute international phone call to book a bed or room is a more sensible use of time than wasting your first day in a city searching for a place to stay.

---

**BOOK ACCOMMODATION ONLINE**

For more accommodation reviews and recommendations by Lonely Planet authors, check out the online booking service at www.lonelyplanet.com. You'll find the true, insider lowdown on the best places to stay. Reviews are thorough and independent. Best of all, you can book online.

If you arrive in a country by air, there is often an accommodation-booking desk at the airport, although it rarely covers the lower strata of hotels. Tourist offices often have extensive accommodation lists, and the more helpful ones will go out of their way to find you something suitable. In most countries the fee for this service is very low and, if the accommodation market is tight, it can save you a lot of running around.

The accommodation options in each city or town are listed according to price range. Starting with budget options, then midrange and top end, we try to include a balanced representation of what's available in each place. Of course, in some cities there's a lack of budget accommodation and too many top-end places to list, or vice versa. Within these subsections, the accommodation options are listed in ascending price order.

## Camping

The cheapest way to go is camping, and there are many camping grounds throughout the region, although as cities make up such a large proportion of the region's attractions, you'll often find there simply aren't any camp sites. Those that exist are usually large sites intended mainly for motorists, though they're often easily accessible by public transport and there's almost always space for backpackers with tents. Many camping grounds in Eastern Europe rent small on-site cabins, bungalows or caravans for double or triple the regular camping fee. In the most popular resorts all the bungalows will probably be full in July and August. Some countries, including Albania and Belarus, have yet to develop any camping grounds at all.

The standard of camping grounds in the rest of Eastern Europe varies from country to country. They're unreliable in Romania, crowded in Hungary (especially on Lake Balaton) and Slovenia, and variable in the Czech Republic, Poland, Slovakia and Bulgaria. Croatia's coast has nudist camping grounds galore (signposted 'FKK', the German acronym for 'naturist'); they're excellent places to stay because of their secluded locations, although they can be a bit far from other attractions.

Camping grounds may be open from April to October, May to September, or perhaps only June to August, depending on the category of the facility, the location and demand. A few private camping grounds are open year-round. In Eastern Europe you are sometimes allowed to build a campfire (ask first). Camping in the wild is usually illegal; ask local people about the situation before you pitch your tent on a beach or in an open field.

## Farmhouses

'Village tourism', which means staying at a farmhouse, is highly developed in Estonia, Latvia, Lithuania and Slovenia, and popular in Hungary. In these it's like staying in a private room or pension, except that the participating farms are in picturesque rural areas and may offer nearby activities such as horse riding, kayaking, skiing and cycling. It's highly recommended.

## Guesthouses & Pensions

Small private pensions are now very common in parts of Eastern Europe. Priced somewhere between hotels and private rooms, pensions typically have less than a dozen rooms and sometimes a small restaurant or bar on the premises. You'll get much more personal service at a pension than you would at a hotel at the expense of a wee bit of privacy. If you arrive at night or on a weekend when the travel agencies assigning private rooms are closed, pensions can be a lifesaver. Call ahead to check prices and ask about reservations – someone will usually speak some halting English, German or Russian.

## Homestays & Private Rooms

Homestays are often the best and most authentic way to see daily life in Eastern Europe. It's perfectly legal to stay with someone in a private home (although in countries such as Russia, where visa registration is necessary, you'll have to pay a travel agency to register your visa with a hotel). Any travel agency can register you at a hotel they have an understanding with if you're staying with friends, there's nothing strictly illegal or dangerous about doing this.

Staying with Eastern European friends will almost certainly be a wonderful experience, thanks to the full hospitality the region is justly famous for. Make sure you bring some small gifts for your hosts – it's a deeply ingrained cultural tradition throughout the region.

In most Eastern European countries, travel agencies can arrange accommodation in private rooms in local homes. In Hungary you can get a private room almost anywhere, but in the other countries only the main tourist centres have them. Some 1st-class rooms are like mini apartments, with cooking facilities and private bathrooms for the sole use of guests. Prices are low but there's often a 30% to 50% surcharge if you stay less than three nights. In Hungary, the Czech Republic and Croatia, higher taxation has made such a deal less attractive than before, but it's still good value and cheaper than a hotel.

People will frequently approach you at train or bus stations in Eastern Europe offering a private room or a hostel bed. This can be good or bad – it's impossible to generalise. Just make sure it's not in some cardboard-quality housing project in the outer suburbs and that you negotiate a clear price. Obviously, if you are staying with strangers like this, you shouldn't leave your valuables behind when you go out; certainly don't leave your money, credit cards or passport.

You don't have to go through an agency or an intermediary on the street for a private room. Any house, cottage or farmhouse with '*zimmer frei*', '*sobe*' or '*szoba kiadó*' displayed outside is advertising the availability of private rooms (these examples are in German, Slovene and Hungarian); just knock on the door and ask if any are available.

## Hostels

Hostels offer the cheapest (secure) roof over your head in Eastern Europe, and you don't have to be a youngster to take advantage of them. Most hostels are part of the national Youth Hostel Association (YHA), which is affiliated with the Hostelling International (HI, www .hihostels.com) umbrella organisation.

Hostels affiliated with HI can be found in most Eastern European countries. A hostel card is seldom required, though you sometimes get a small discount if you have one. If you don't have a valid HI membership card, you can buy one at some hostels.

To join HI you can ask at any hostel or contact your local or national hostelling office. There's a very useful website at www.iyhf.org, with links to most HI sites.

At a hostel, you get a bed for the night plus use of communal facilities, often including a kitchen where you can prepare your own meals. You may be required to have a sleeping sheet – simply using your sleeping bag is often not allowed. If you don't have a sleeping sheet, you can sometimes hire one for a small fee.

Hostels vary widely in their character and quality. The hostels in Poland tend to be ex-

tremely basic but they're inexpensive and friendly. In the Czech Republic and Slovakia many hostels are actually fairly luxurious 'junior' hotels with double rooms, often fully occupied by groups. Many Hungarian hostels outside Budapest are student dormitories open to travellers for six or seven weeks in summer only. In Budapest and Prague a number of privately run hostels now operate year-round and are serious party venues. The hostels in Bulgaria are in cities, resort and mountain areas.

There are many available hostel guides with listings, including the 'bible', HI's *Europe*. Many hostels accept reservations by phone, fax or email, but not always during peak periods (though they might hold a bed for you for a couple of hours if you call from the train or bus station). You can also book hostels through national hostel offices.

## Hotels

At the bottom of the bracket, cheap hotels may be no more expensive than private rooms or guesthouses, while at the other extreme they extend to beautifully designed boutique hotels and five-star hotels with price tags to match. Categorisation varies from country to country and the hotels recommended in this book accommodate every budget. We have endeavoured, where possible, to provide a combination of budget, midrange and top-end accommodation in each city or town. Where the full gauntlet of price ranges isn't available, we simply make a note of what is.

Single rooms can be hard to find in Eastern Europe, where you are generally charged by the room and not by the number of people in it; many local people still refuse to believe that anyone would actually take to the road alone. The cheapest rooms sometimes have a washbasin but no bathroom, which means you'll have to go down the corridor to use the toilet and shower. Breakfast may be included in the price of a room or be extra – and mandatory.

## University Accommodation

Some universities rent out space in student halls in July and August. This is quite popular in the Baltic countries, Croatia, the Czech Republic, Hungary, Macedonia, Poland, Slovakia and Slovenia. Accommodation will sometimes be in single rooms (but is more commonly in doubles or triples), and cooking facilities may be available. Inquire at the college or university, at student information services or at local tourist offices.

## ACTIVITIES

### Canoeing & Kayaking

Those travelling with folding kayaks will want to launch them on the waterways surrounding Poland's Great Masurian Lakes district (p608), the Soča River in Slovenia (p843), the Vltava River in the Czech Republic (p292) and Latvia's Gauja River (p430). Special kayaking and canoeing tours are offered in these countries, as well as in Croatia (p241).

### Cycling

Along with hiking, cycling is the best way to really get close to the scenery and the people, keeping you fit in the process. It's also a good way to get around many cities and towns and to see remote corners of a country you wouldn't ordinarily get to.

The hills and mountains of Eastern Europe can be heavy going, but this is offset by the abundance of things to see. Physical fitness is *not* a major prerequisite for cycling on the plains of eastern Hungary, but the persistent wind might slow you down. Popular holiday cycling areas in Eastern Europe include the Danube Bend in Hungary (p410), most of eastern Slovakia (p804), the Karst region of Slovenia (p846), and the Curonian Spit (p464) and Palanga (p460) in western Lithuania. The valleys of Maramureş (p663) in northern Romania are a great place for a cycling tour. Most airlines will allow you to put a bicycle in the hold for a surprisingly small fee. Alternatively, this book lists possible places where you can hire one.

See Bicycle in the Transport in Eastern Europe section (p932) for more information on bicycle touring, and the individual country chapters and destination sections for rental outfits as well as routes and tips on places to go.

### Hiking

There's excellent hiking in Eastern Europe, with well-marked trails through forests, mountains and national parks. Public transport will often take you to the trailheads; chalets or mountain huts in Poland, Bulgaria, Slovakia, Romania and Slovenia offer dormitory accommodation and basic meals. In this book we include information about hiking in the High Tatras of Poland (p575) and Slovakia (p803), the Malá Fatra of Slovakia (p800), the Bucegi (p640) and Făgăraş Ranges (p652) in Romania's Carpathian Mountains, the Rila Mountains of Bulgaria (p148) and the Julian Alps of Slovenia (p838), but there are many other hiking areas that are less well known, including the Bieszczady in Poland (p576) and the Risnjak and Paklenica National Parks in Croatia (p240). The best months for hiking are from June to September, especially late August and early September when the summer crowds will have largely disappeared.

### Horse Riding

Though horse riding is possible throughout Eastern Europe, the sport is best organised – and cheapest – in Hungary, whose people, it is said, 'were created by God to sit on horseback'. The best centres are on the Great Plain, though you'll also find riding schools in Transdanubia and northern Hungary (see p405) for more information. Horse riding is also very popular (and affordable) in the Baltic countries, the Czech Republic, Poland and Slovenia.

### Sailing

Eastern Europe's most famous yachting area is the passage between the long, rugged islands off Croatia's Dalmatian coast (p218). Yacht tours and rentals are available, although this is certainly not for anyone on a budget. If your means are more limited, the Great Masurian Lakes of northeastern Poland (p608) are a better choice, as small groups can rent sailing boats by the day for very reasonable rates. Hungary's Lake Balaton (p385) is also popular among sailing enthusiasts.

### Skiing

Eastern Europe's premier skiing areas are the High Tatras of Slovakia (p804) and Poland (p575); the Carpathians near Braşov in Romania (p645) and Yablunytsia in Ukraine (p882); Borovets (p150) in the Rila Mountains near Sofia; Pamporovo (p157) in the Rodopi Mountains in Bulgaria and Slovenia's Julian Alps (p838). The Bosnian capital Sarajevo (p115), which hosted the 1984 Winter Olympics, is a growing place for skiing and you'll find some of the best-value slopes in Europe within an hour of the city. The skiing season generally lasts from early December to late March, though at higher altitudes it may extend an extra month either way. Snow conditions can vary greatly from year to year and region to region, but January and February tend to be the best (and busiest) months. Snowboarding is especially popular in Slovakia, as is cross-country skiing in the Czech Republic and Ukraine.

## Thermal Baths & Saunas

There are hundreds of thermal baths in Eastern Europe open to the public. The most affordable are in the Czech Republic, Hungary and Slovenia, as well as along the Black Sea in Romania. Among the best are the thermal lake at Hévíz (p390), the Turkish baths of Budapest (p364), the spa town of Harkány (p394) in Hungary and the *fin-de-siécle* spas of Karlovy Vary (Karlsbad; p285) in the Czech Republic.

The Baltic countries are famous for the proliferation of saunas – both the traditional 'smoke' variety and the clean and smokeless modern sauna. The traditionalist will find many opportunities to take in an old-style sauna in Lithuania. Another must for lovers of heat and sweat is the traditional Russian *banya* (p710) where you can be beaten into cleanliness with birch twigs!

## White-Water Rafting

This exciting activity is possible in summer on two of Eastern Europe's most scenic rivers: the Tara River in Montenegro (p537) and the Soča River in Slovenia (p843). Rafting on the Dunajec River along the border of Poland and Slovakia is fun, but it's not a white-water experience.

## BUSINESS HOURS

Eastern Europe tends to have similar working patterns to Western Europe and North America. Saturdays and Sundays are usually days off, although only banks and offices are shut – most shops, restaurants and cafés are open everyday of the week.

Banks are usually open from 9am to 5pm Monday to Friday, often with an hour or two off for lunch. During the hot summer months, some enterprises will shut for two or three hours in the early afternoon, reopening at 3pm or 4pm and working into the evening when it's cooler. See the Directory of whichever country you are in for more specific detail.

## CHILDREN

Successful travel with young children requires planning and effort. Don't try to overdo things; even for adults, packing too much into the time available can cause problems. And make sure the activities include the kids as well – balance that morning at Budapest's Museum of Fine Arts with a performance at the Puppet Theatre. A good resource is Lonely Planet's *Travel With Children* by Cathy Lanigan and Maureen Wheeler.

Include children in the trip planning; if they've helped to work out where you will be going, they will be much more interested when they get there. In Eastern Europe most car-rental firms have children's safety seats for hire at a small cost, but it is essential that you book them in advance. The same goes for highchairs and cots (cribs); they're standard in many restaurants and hotels but numbers are limited. The choice of baby food, infant formulas, soy and cow's milk, disposable nappies (diapers) and the like can be as great in the supermarkets of many Eastern European countries as it is back home, but the opening hours may be quite different to what you are used to.

## CLIMATE CHARTS

The weather in Eastern Europe can be fairly extreme at times, but very rarely enough to prevent travel. It's a fascinating place to visit any time of year – even during the icy winter (and that's particularly icy in the Baltic countries, Russia and Ukraine) when the cities take on a magical frosty charm. July and August can be uncomfortably hot in the cities and throughout the Balkans, but this is the time when the alpine areas such as the High Tatras, the Carpathians and the Rila Mountains are best to visit, not to mention the beaches. All in all, May, June and September are the best times to visit from a climatic point of view, as nowhere will be too warm or too cool.

## COURSES

Apart from learning new physical skills by doing something like a ski course in Slovenia or horse riding in Hungary, you can enrich your mind with a variety of structured courses in Eastern Europe, on anything from language to alternative medicine. Language courses are often available to foreigners through universities or private schools, and are justifiably popular, as the best way to learn a language is in the country where it's spoken.

In general, the best sources of information are the cultural institutes maintained by many European countries around the world. Failing that, you could try national tourist offices or embassies. Student exchange organisations, student travel agencies, and organisations such as HI can also put you on the right track.

REGIONAL DIRECTORY

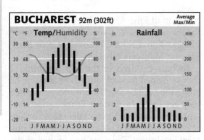

**BUCHAREST** 92m (302ft)

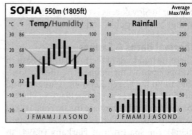

**SOFIA** 550m (1805ft)

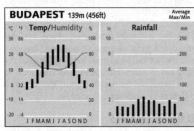

**BUDAPEST** 139m (456ft)

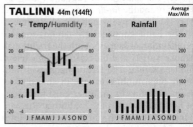

**TALLINN** 44m (144ft)

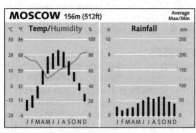

**KYIV** 179m (587ft)

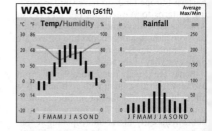

**TIRANA** 89m (292ft)

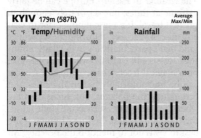

**MOSCOW** 156m (512ft)

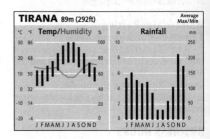

**WARSAW** 110m (361ft)

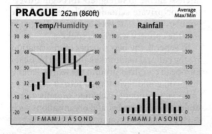

**PRAGUE** 262m (860ft)

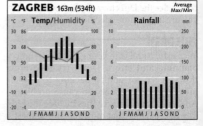

**ZAGREB** 163m (534ft)

## CUSTOMS

While there's no problem with bringing in and taking out personal effects, be aware that antiques, books printed before 1945, crystal glass, gemstones, lottery tickets, philatelic materials, precious metals (gold, silver, platinum), securities and valuable works of art may still have to be declared in writing or even accompanied by a 'museum certificate' (available from the place of purchase) in many Eastern European countries. There may also be restrictions on the import/export of local currency, although the amounts allowed these days are actually quite large.

Throughout most of Eastern Europe, the usual allowances for tobacco (eg 200 to 250 cigarettes, but a lung-busting 1000 cigarettes in Belarus), alcohol (2L of wine, 1L of spirits) and perfume (50g) apply to duty-free goods purchased at airports or on ferries. Customs checks are pretty cursory and you probably won't even have to open your bags, but don't be lulled into a false sense of security.

## DANGERS & ANNOYANCES

Eastern Europe is as safe – or unsafe – as any other part of the developed world. If you can handle yourself in the big cities of Western Europe, North America or Australia, you'll have little trouble dealing with the less pleasant side of Eastern Europe. Look purposeful, keep alert and you'll be OK.

Some locals will regale you with tales of how dangerous their city is and recount various cases of muggings, break-ins, kidnappings etc, often involving Roma or popular scapegoats (most Eastern Europeans will tell you horror stories about the Romanians and Albanians). Bosnia and Kosovo have an unusual form of danger – land mines. It's the only time Lonely Planet will ever advise you *not* to venture off the beaten track.

Low-level corruption is disappearing fast as the back-scratching system, so common during the communist regimes, claims its rightful place in the dustbin of history. Do *not* pay bribes to persons in official positions, such as police, border guards, train conductors, ticket inspectors etc, although be aware that these very anachronistic systems still exist in Belarus, Moldova and Transdniestr. If corrupt cops want to hold you up because some obscure stamp is missing from your documentation or on some other pretext, just let them and consider the experience an integral part of your trip. Insisting on calling your embassy is always a good move; if the situation is brought to the attention of the officer's superiors, they will, unsurprisingly, get in trouble.

Don't worry at all if you're taken to the police station for questioning as you'll have a unique opportunity to observe the quality of justice in that country from the inside, and more senior officers will eventually let you go (assuming, of course, you haven't committed a real crime). If you do have to pay a fine or supplementary charge, insist on a proper receipt before turning over any money; this is now law in Hungary, for example, where traffic police were once notorious for demanding (and getting) 'gifts' from motorists guilty of some alleged infraction. Russia is still a hot bed of corrupt officials. In some cases a $50 bill will often end an unpleasant situation. In all of this, try to maintain your cool, as any threats from you will only make matters worse.

### Drugs

Always treat drugs with a great deal of caution. There are a lot of drugs available in the region, but that doesn't mean they are legal. The continual fighting in the former Serbia and Montenegro in the 1990s forced drug traffickers to seek alternative routes from Asia to Western Europe, sometimes crossing through Hungary, Slovakia, the Czech Republic and Poland. Now EU members, these countries do not look lightly upon drug abuse.

### Scams

A word of warning about credit cards: fraudulent shopkeepers have been known to make several charge-slip imprints with your credit card when you're not looking and then simply copy your signature from the authorised slip. There have also been reports of these unscrupulous people making quick and very hi-tech duplicates of credit or debit card information with a machine. If your card leaves your possession for longer than you think necessary, consider cancelling it.

Now that most Eastern European currencies have reached convertibility, the days of getting five times the official rate for cash on the streets of Warsaw and Bucharest are well and truly over. Essentially, there is no longer a black market in most countries of this region; anyone who approaches you offering such a deal (an uncommon occurrence these days) is your average, garden-variety thief.

## Theft

Theft is definitely a problem in Eastern Europe, and the threat comes from both local thieves and fellow travellers. The most important things to guard are your passport, other documents, tickets and money – in that order. It's always best to carry these next to your skin or in a sturdy leather pouch on your belt. Train-station lockers or luggage-storage counters are useful to store your luggage (but not valuables) while you get your bearings in a new town. Be very suspicious of people who offer to help you operate your locker. Carry your own padlock for hostel lockers.

You can lessen the risks by being wary of snatch thieves. Cameras or shoulder bags are great for these people, who sometimes operate from motorcycles or scooters and slash the strap before you have a chance to react. A small day-pack is better, but watch your rear. Be very careful at cafés and bars; loop the strap around your leg while seated. While it makes pickpocketing harder, carrying a backpack on your front will both let everyone know you are a tourist (and one who thinks everyone is a thief) as well as make you look like a prize idiot. Far better is to keep all valuables inside pockets and only have things you could stand to lose in easily accessible pockets.

Pickpockets are most active in dense crowds, especially in busy train stations and on public transport during peak hours. A common ploy in the Budapest and Prague metros has been for a group of well-dressed young people to surround you, chattering away while one of the group zips through your pockets or purse.

Be careful even in hotels; don't leave valuables lying around in your room.

Parked cars containing luggage or other bags are prime targets for petty criminals in most cities, and cars with foreign number plates and/or rental agency stickers attract particular attention. While driving in cities, beware of snatch thieves when you pull up at the lights – keep doors locked and windows rolled up high.

In case of theft or loss, always report the incident to the police and ask for a statement. Otherwise your travel-insurance company won't pay up.

## Violence

Though it's unlikely that travellers will encounter any violence while in Eastern Europe, skinheads and neo-Nazis have singled out the resident Roma, blacks and Asians as scapegoats for their own problems, while foreigners have been attacked in Hungary and the Czech Republic. Avoid especially run-down areas in cities and *never* fight back. These people can be extremely dangerous. Russian neo-Nazis have developed a charming tradition of seeking out fights with nonwhite people on Hitler's birthday (20 April). People of non-European origin should exercise caution if they are in Moscow or St Petersburg on this date. In fact the situation in Russia had soured considerably at the time of research, with an extraordinary amount of violence against ethnic minorities, particularly in St Petersburg. While we don't discourage nonwhite people from visiting, we do urge a great deal of caution; avoid the suburbs, travel with friends and don't go out at night alone.

## DISABLED TRAVELLERS

Eastern Europe can be very unpredictable when it comes to facilities for the disabled. The golden rule is never to expect much and you won't be disappointed, which is not exactly encouraging. Most major museums and sites have disabled access, although there are still exceptions. However, hotels outside the top bracket and public transport are still universally poor, and it's fair to say that access for the disabled has not been a priority in the region's past two decades of rapid reform.

If you have a physical disability, get in touch with your national support organisation (preferably the travel officer if there is one) and ask about the countries you plan to visit. They often have complete libraries devoted to travel, with useful things like access guides, and they can put you in touch with travel agencies who specialise in tours for the disabled. The **Royal Association for Disability & Rehabilitation** (Radar; ☎ UK 020-7250 3222, fax 7250 0212; www.radar.org.uk; 12 City Forum, 250 City Rd, London EC1V 8AF) is a very helpful association and sells a number of publications for the disabled.

## DISCOUNT CARDS
### Camping Card International

The Camping Card International (CCI) is a camping ground ID valid for a year. It can be used instead of a passport when checking in to camping grounds and includes third-party insurance. As a result, many camping grounds will offer a small discount (usually 5% to 10%)

if you have one. CCIs are issued by automobile associations, camping federations and, sometimes, on the spot at camping grounds. The CCI is also useful as it can sometimes serve as a guarantee, so that you don't have to leave your passport at reception.

## Hostel Cards

No hostels in Eastern Europe require that you be a hostelling association member, but they sometimes charge less if you have a card. Some hostels will issue one on the spot or after a few days' stay, though this might cost a bit more than getting it at home.

## International Student, Youth & Teacher Cards

An International Student Identity Card (ISIC), a plastic ID-style card with your photograph, provides discounts on many forms of transport (including airlines and local transport), cheap or free admission to museums and sights, and inexpensive meals in some student cafeterias and restaurants. If you're under 26 but not a student, you are eligible to apply for an International Youth Travel Card (IYTC, formerly GO25), issued by the Federation of International Youth Travel Organisations, or the Euro26 card (the latter card may not be recognised in Albania, Moldova, Romania, Serbia and Montenegro). Both go under different names in different countries and give much the same discounts and benefits as an ISIC. An International Teacher Identity Card (ITIC) identifies the holder as an instructor and offers similar deals. All these cards are issued by student unions, hostelling organisations or youth-oriented travel agencies.

## Senior Cards

Many attractions offer reduced-price admission for people over 60 or 65 (sometimes as low as 55 for women). Make sure you bring proof of age. For a fee of around €20, European residents aged 60 and over can get a Railplus Card as an add-on to their national rail senior pass. It entitles the holder to train-fare reductions of around 25%.

Check before you leave home about age-related travel packages and discounts (on car hire, for instance) through organisations and travel agencies that cater for senior travellers. See p937 for one such organisation, Saga Holidays. Start hunting at your local senior citizens' advice bureau.

## DVDS

DVDs are sold throughout Eastern Europe, and the further east you go, the less likely they are to be licensed. This can result in great bargains for those who don't mind buying pirated copies, but you should also realise that unlicensed DVDs are illegal in most countries, although you're unlikely to be caught bringing a few cheap DVDs home. In general, DVDs sold in Eastern Europe will be Region 2 DVDs, which mean that unless you have a multiregion DVD player, they will not play in North America (Region 1) or anywhere where Region 2 is not the norm. Even if a film has had its title and cover translated into a local language, if the original was English (and often even if it wasn't) there will usually be the option to watch the DVD in English, but check before you buy.

## ELECTRICITY

Eastern European countries run on 220V, 50Hz AC; check the voltage and cycle (usually 50Hz) used on your appliances. Most appliances set up for 220V will quite happily handle 240V without modification (and vice versa). It's preferable to adjust your appliance to the exact voltage if you can (some modern battery chargers and radios will do this automatically). Don't mix 110/125V with 220/240V without a transformer, which will be built in if the appliance can, in fact, be adjusted.

Several countries outside Europe (the USA and Canada, for instance) have 60Hz AC, which will affect the speed of electric motors even after the voltage has been adjusted, so CD and tape players (where motor speed is all-important) will be useless. But appliances such as electric razors, hairdryers, irons and radios will work fine.

Plugs in Eastern Europe are the standard round two-pin variety, sometimes called the 'europlug'. If your plugs are of a different design, you'll need an adapter.

## EMBASSIES & CONSULATES

See the individual country chapters for the addresses of embassies and consulates both in Eastern Europe and in your home country.

It's important to realise what your embassy can and cannot do to help if you get into trouble while abroad. Generally speaking, it won't be much help in emergencies if the trouble you're in is remotely your own fault. Remember that you are bound by the laws of the country you are visiting.

In genuine emergencies you might get some assistance, but only if other channels have been exhausted. For example, if you need to get home urgently, a free ticket back is exceedingly unlikely – the embassy would expect you to have insurance. If you have all your money and documents stolen, it might assist with getting a new passport, but a loan for onward travel is almost always out of the question.

## GAY & LESBIAN TRAVELLERS

Eastern Europe has an unpredictable reaction to homosexuality in all its forms. While gay and lesbian sex is legal in all countries covered by this book, this is often far more to do with governments earning kudos with the EU than an open-minded approach to sexual minorities. Whether or not this is the case where you are travelling, public displays of affection are still best avoided. Despite this, things are slowly changing – Latvia, Hungary, Poland and Russia have all had gay pride events in the past few years, but marchers have been outnumbered on most occasions by antigay protesters, and they have usually ended in arrests on both sides. Many gays and lesbians in Eastern Europe actually oppose such parades as they often provoke the majority into taking an antigay stance, whereas for the most part few heterosexuals are even aware of the gay and lesbian population.

Most Eastern European capitals have lively, if small, gay scenes, usually centred around one or two bars and clubs. Exceptions to this rule are Tirana, Skopje, Sarajevo and Chişinău where there is nothing gay- or lesbian-specific that is accessible to visitors. Outside large population centres, gay and lesbian life is almost nonexistent.

Good resources for gay travellers include websites such as www.gaydar.com and www.gay.com. Listings are given wherever possible in the individual country sections.

## HOLIDAYS

Eastern Europe's school calendar is nothing unusual – children get the summer months off (usually July and August) as well as breaks for Easter and Christmas. Even in countries with a large Muslim population, such as Bosnia and Hercegovina, and Albania, these dates are generally followed – a hangover from communist times. See the relevant country's Directory for details of local public holidays and festivals.

## INSURANCE

A travel-insurance policy to cover theft, loss and medical problems is a good idea. The policies written by STA Travel and other student travel organisations are usually good value. Some policies offer lower and higher medical expense options, so check the fine print.

Some insurance policies will specifically exclude 'dangerous activities', which can include scuba diving, motorcycling and even trekking. Some even exclude entire countries.

You may prefer a policy that pays doctors or hospitals directly rather than you having to pay on the spot and claim later. If you have to claim later make sure you keep all documentation. Some policies ask you to call back (reverse charges) to a centre in your home country where an immediate assessment of your problem is made. Check that the policy covers ambulances and an emergency flight home. For more information on health insurance, see p940.

For details on car insurance, see p934.

Worldwide cover to travellers from over 44 countries is available online at www.lonelyplanet.com/travel_services.

## INTERNET ACCESS

With a few exceptions, almost any decent-sized town in Eastern Europe has internet access. Connections may be slow, internet 'cafés' may not serve coffee or any other drinks, and sometimes you'll be limited to a monitor in a dark, smelly room full of teenage boys playing war games – but one way or another you'll never be far from your email account, even in less developed nations such as Albania or Moldova. Indeed, in some more developed cities, internet cafés can be a social hub and a great way of meeting locals as well as travellers. Make sure you have a web-based email account so you can pick up email on the road without your own laptop.

If you are carrying your laptop with you, the good news is that wi-fi has taken off in Eastern Europe. The Baltics are particularly good – Tallinn alone has over 300 wi-fi spots, most of them free. It's increasingly common for any high-standard or boutique hotel to have wi-fi in the rooms. Sadly, most business hotels charge for this service, while as a rule boutique hotels are more likely to offer it for free. Whenever a café, hotel or bar has wi-fi, we make a note of it in reviews.

# MAPS

Bringing a good regional map will make things a great deal easier if you are planning a long trip taking in more than a couple of countries. There's a huge range available but we recommend *Eastern Europe,* produced by Latvian publishers Jana Seta, and *Eastern Europe,* from Freytag and Berndt.

In general, buying city maps in advance is unnecessary, as nearly all large towns produce them locally for a fraction of the price you'll pay at home. However, maps of Eastern European capitals and other major towns are widely available from travel bookshops if you want a particularly detailed map in advance.

# MONEY

Things have simplified in Eastern Europe these days, with no real worries about 'soft' and 'hard' currencies. The main problem you'll face is constant currency changes as you flit between the crown, zloty, rouble, lei, lev, lek, dinar and various other national currencies. There is no longer any particular desire to change for 'hard' currency (long gone are the days where hoteliers would slash the rates if you paid in US dollars) and the convertibility of almost all Eastern European currencies makes them a stable and reliable way to carry cash. The euro remains the easiest currency to change throughout the region, particularly in light of the US dollar's weakness over the past few years.

With the accession of half of the region to the EU, there's a move for some countries to adopt the euro themselves. While countries have to meet complex economic criteria, it's pretty certain that at least four of them will have adopted it by 2010. On the other hand some countries such as Poland are sceptical about the common currency and have not set a target for entry.

## ATMs & Credit Cards

The hassle of trying to change travellers cheques at the weekend and rip-off *bureaux de change* is a thing of the past in most parts of Eastern Europe, with the arrival of ATMs that accept most credit and cash cards. Nearly all Eastern European countries have plenty of ATMs, and not only in the capital city. Check the specific situation in each country's chapter before banking on this.

As purchase tools, credit cards are still not as commonly used as in Western Europe but they're gaining ground: especially Amex,

Visa and MasterCard. You'll be able to use them at upmarket restaurants, shops, hotels, car-rental firms, travel agencies and many petrol stations.

Cash or debit cards, which you use at home to withdraw money directly from your bank account or savings account, can be used throughout Eastern Europe at those ATMs linked to international networks like Cirrus and Maestro. The major advantage of using ATMs is that you don't pay commission charges to exchange money and the exchange rate is usually at a better interbank rate than that offered for travellers cheques or cash exchanges. Bear in mind that if you use a credit card for purchases, exchange rates may have changed by the time your bill is processed, which can work out to your advantage or disadvantage.

Charge-card companies like Amex, and to a lesser extent Diners Club, have offices in most countries in Eastern Europe and they can generally replace a lost card within 24 hours. That's because they treat you as a customer of the company rather than of the bank that issued the card. Their major drawback is that they're not widely accepted off the beaten track. Charge cards may also be hooked up to some ATM networks. Credit and credit/debit cards like Visa and MasterCard are more widely accepted because they tend to charge merchants lower commissions.

If you choose to rely on plastic, go for two different cards – this allows one to be used as backup in the case of loss, or more commonly, because a certain bank will accept one credit card and not another for no discernable reason. Better still is a combination of credit card and travellers cheques so you have something to fall back on if an ATM swallows your card or the banks in the area won't accept it (a not uncommon occurrence). There are also a couple of tricky scams involving credit cards; see p913.

## Cash

This is, of course, the easiest way to carry money, but if you lose it, that's it. The two most favoured currencies throughout Eastern Europe are the euro and the US dollar. However, it is perfectly easy to exchange virtually any other major world currency in big cities, but you are inevitably at the mercy of the exchange office and their rates. Far better is to change your money into euros or US dollars before you leave home and you'll have no problems whatsoever.

## Moneychangers

Shop around, never stop at the first place you see, and if you happen to be in a tourist area you can rest assured you'll be offered crappy rates everywhere. So don't bother shopping around, just leave for a less-touristed neighbourhood. Examples are around the Charles Bridge in Prague or the Old Town Square in Kraków. Borders, airports and train stations are typically places where rates aren't great but many people change money out of necessity. One alternative, certainly at airports and train stations, is to withdraw local currency from an ATM.

## Tipping

Tipping practices vary from country to country, and often differ from place to place. Rurally, you'll find some people astonished if you give them a good tip, while employees at fashionable restaurants in big cities will be miffed if you don't. See the individual country chapters for specific advice, but in general rounding the bill up or adding a maximum of 10% is the norm. Porters at luxury hotels will expect a few euros for their trouble, but it's up to you at less-smart places.

## Travellers Cheques

The main idea of using travellers cheques rather than cash is the protection they offer from theft, though they have lost their once-enormous popularity as more and more travellers – including those on tight budgets – withdraw cash through ATMs as they go along.

Banks usually charge from 1% to 2% commission to change travellers cheques (up to 5% in Bulgaria, Estonia, Latvia, Lithuania and Romania). Their opening hours are sometimes limited. In the individual chapters, we recommend the most efficient banks of each country.

The privately owned exchange offices in Albania, Bulgaria, Poland, Romania and Slovenia change cash at excellent rates without commission. Not only are their rates sometimes higher than those offered by the banks for travellers cheques, but they stay open much longer hours, occasionally even 24 hours. However, do take care in Belarus, the Czech Republic, Estonia, Hungary, Latvia, Lithuania, Moldova, Slovakia and Ukraine, as some big moneychangers take exorbitant commissions unless you cash a small fortune with them. Before signing a travellers cheque or handing over any cash always check the commission and rate.

Amex and Thomas Cook representatives cash their own travellers cheques without commission, but both give poor rates of exchange. If you're changing more than US$20, you're usually better off going to a bank and paying the standard 1% to 2% commission to change there.

## Western Union

If all goes horribly wrong – your money, travellers cheques and credit cards are all stolen – don't despair. While it's a terrible (and highly unusual) situation, as long as you know the phone number of a friend or relative back home, they will be able to wire money to you anywhere in Eastern Europe via Western Union (WU). We don't bother listing WU representatives in this guide, as there are literally thousands of them. Just look for the distinctive yellow and black sign, and if you're somewhere remote, ask the person sending you the money to ask WU for the nearest office to you. The sender is then given a code that they communicate to you. You take the code to the nearest office, along with your passport, to receive your cash.

# PHOTOGRAPHY & VIDEO

Film and camera equipment is available everywhere in Eastern Europe, but shops in the larger places offer a wider choice. Avoid buying film at tourist sites in Europe, such as the Castle District in Budapest or by Charles Bridge in Prague. It may have been stored badly or reached its sell-by date. It will certainly be more expensive than in normal photography shops.

Eastern Europe was once notorious for its photographic restrictions – taking shots of anything 'strategic' such as bridges or train stations was strictly forbidden. These days local officials are much less paranoid, but you need to use common sense when it comes to this issue; photographing military installations, for example, is never a good idea anywhere in the world. Most importantly, have the courtesy to ask permission before taking close-up photos of people.

In most countries, it is easy to obtain video tapes in large towns and cities, but make sure you buy the correct format. It is usually worth buying at least a few at home at the start of your trip.

Be aware that museums often demand that you buy permission to photograph or video their displays. Do this when you buy your tickets if you think you will get snap happy, as you'll have to retrace your steps if you don't – no laughing matter in the enormous Hermitage in St Petersburg.

Anyone using a digital camera should check that they have enough memory to store your snaps – two 128MB cards will probably be enough. If you do run out of memory space your best bet is to burn your photos onto a CD. Even if you don't have your laptop with you, an increasing number of processing labs now offer this service.

To download your pics at an internet café you'll need a USB cable and a card reader. Some places provide a USB on request but be warned that many of the bigger chain cafés don't let you plug your gear into their computers, meaning that it's back to plan A – the CD.

## POST

Details of post offices are given in the information sections of each city or town in the individual country chapters, and postage costs given in the country Directory. Both efficiency and cost vary enormously. There seem to be no set rules, but EU-accession countries are likely to be faster, more reliable and more expensive than the non-EU states. Don't send anything back home from Russia, Ukraine, Belarus or Moldova unless you can deal with its possible loss, although in practice things are quite reliable.

Poste restante (having letters sent to you care of local post offices) is unreliable, not to mention an increasingly unnecessary communication method in the 21st century. If you desperately need something posted to you, do your research – find a friend of a friend who could receive the mail at their address, or ask nicely at a hotel you plan to stay at. You can also have mail sent to you at Amex offices as long as you have an Amex card or are carrying its travellers cheques. When you buy Amex cheques, ask for a booklet listing all its office addresses worldwide. Amex will forward mail for a small fee, but what it won't do is accept parcels, registered letters, notices for registered letters, answer telephone inquiries about mail or hold mail longer than 30 days.

To send a parcel from Eastern Europe you usually have to take it unwrapped to a main post office. Parcels weighing over 2kg often must be taken to a special customs post office. They will usually wrap the parcels for you. They may ask to see your passport and note the number on the form. If you don't have a return

address within the country put your name care of any large tourist hotel to satisfy them.

## SOLO TRAVELLERS

Travelling alone is a unique experience. There are a huge number of advantages – you do exactly what you want to do, see what you want to see and are more likely to meet locals and socialise with people you'd otherwise never speak to. However, it can also be lonely and less fun when things get frustrating or don't work out. Backpacking and hostel culture is well adapted to people travelling alone, and hostels are great places to meet others. Indeed, you may find you'll spend a few days here and there with others you've met in hostels and who are heading in your direction, or keen to share the cost of a day trip or two. The best advice for solo travellers, therefore, is to head for your nearest hostel if you feel like some company. Most big cities in Eastern Europe have expat bars (usually the ubiquitous Irish pubs) if you are missing a slice of ersatz-home.

## TELEPHONE

Telephone service has improved throughout the region in a very short time. Cities in Eastern Europe have a huge number of call centres – increasingly the domain of entrepreneurs who offer discounted rates, although there are also the state-run call centres, which are often in the same building as the main post office. Here you can often make your call from one of the booths inside an enclosed area, paying the cashier as you leave. Public telephones are almost always found at post offices. Local telephone cards, available from post offices, telephone centres, newsstands or retail outlets, are popular everywhere in the region. In fact, in many countries they have become the norm.

There's a wide range of local and international phonecards. For local calls you're usually better off with a local phonecard.

To call abroad from a landline you simply dial the international access code for the country you are calling from (most commonly ☎ 00 in Eastern Europe, but ☎ 8/wait for tone/10 in Russia, Belarus, Moldova and Ukraine). From a mobile phone simply dial +, the country acccess code, the city code and the local number. See individual country chapters for each country's international access number, for example +7 for Russia.

To make a domestic call to another city in the same country in Eastern Europe dial the area code with the initial zero and the number. Area codes for individual cities and regions are provided in the country chapters.

## Mobile Phones

Like being in some horribly saccharine mobile phone commercial, today you'll see farmers travelling by horse and cart chatting on their mobiles in rural Romania, while old grannies selling sunflower seeds on a quiet Moscow side street write text messages to their grandchildren. The expansion of mobile phones has been nothing short of breathtaking in the region and this can be great for travellers too. If you plan to spend more than a week or so in one country, seriously consider buying a SIM card to slip into your phone (check with your provider at home before you leave that your handset has been unlocked). SIM cards can cost as little as €10 and can be topped up with cards available at supermarkets and any mobile phone dealers. Alternatively, if you have roaming, your phone will usually switch automatically over to a local network. This can be expensive if you use the phone a great deal, but can be very useful for ad hoc use on the road.

## Phone Codes

Every country's international dialling code and international access code is given in the Fast Facts section at the beginning of each chapter. Every town has its local or area code within the country listed directly underneath its chapter heading.

## TIME

Eastern Europe spans three time zones. Greenwich Mean Time (GMT) is five hours ahead of New York, eight hours ahead of Los Angeles and 10 hours behind Sydney. Thus, at noon in New York, it's 6pm in Warsaw, 7pm in Minsk and 8pm in Moscow.

**Central European Time (GMT+1 hour)** Albania, Bosnia and Hercegovina, Croatia, Czech Republic, Hungary, Macedonia, Montenegro, Poland, Serbia, Slovakia and Slovenia.

**Eastern European Time (GMT+2 hours)** Belarus, Bulgaria, Estonia, Kaliningrad, Latvia, Lithuania, Moldova, Romania and Ukraine.

**Moscow Time (GMT+3 hours)** Moscow and St Petersburg.

All countries employ daylight savings. Clocks are put forward an hour usually on the last Sunday in March. They are set back one hour on the last Sunday in September.

## TOURIST INFORMATION

The provision of tourist information varies enormously. While countries that have successfully realised their potential as holiday destinations have developed a network of excellent Tourist Information Centres (TICs), there are still many countries that take little or no interest in the economic benefits tourism can bring. Among the best prepared are Slovenia, Croatia, the Czech Republic, Hungary, Poland and Bulgaria, many of which have tourist offices abroad as well as throughout the country. Countries in the latter category are (unsurprisingly) Ukraine, Belarus and Moldova. Russia is similarly badly organised, although there are now two TICs in St Petersburg, although they're hardly dynamic. However, it's a start and things look set to improve. The Baltic countries, Montenegro, Albania and Macedonia fall in a middle category of places actively trying to encourage tourism, but whose efforts remain rather obscure at the moment. See individual country entries for details of TICs locally.

## VISAS & DOCUMENTS
### Copies

The hassles created by losing your passport can be considerably reduced if you have a record of its number and issue date or, even better, photocopies of the relevant data pages. A photocopy of your birth certificate can also be useful.

Also note the serial numbers of your travellers cheques (cross them off as you cash them) and take photocopies of your credit cards, air ticket and any other travel documents. Keep all this emergency material separate from your passport, cheques and cash, and leave extra copies with someone you can rely on at home. Add some emergency money (eg €50 to €100 in cash) to this separate stash as well. If you do lose your passport, notify the police immediately to get a statement, and contact your nearest consulate (listed in the Directory sections of individual destination chapters).

### Passport

Your most important travel document is your passport, which should remain valid until well after you return home. If it's just about to expire, renew it before you travel. Some countries insist that your passport remain valid for a specified period (usually three months) beyond the expected date of your departure from that country. In practice, this is rarely checked.

## SPONTANEITY VS PLANNING AHEAD

Visa regulations vary throughout Eastern Europe; for most countries you won't need a visa at all, while for others obtaining a visa is a trial of skill, patience and planning. This table outlines visa requirements for those countries requiring a visa at the time of writing (whether a visa is available on arrival and whether it can be obtained on arrival by citizens of the countries listed); see individual country chapters for more detail. Be aware, however, that visa regulations can and do change, so you should always check with the individual embassies or a reputable travel agency before travelling.

| | Visa on arrival | EU citizens | US citizens | Canadian citizens | Australian citizens | NZ citizens |
|---|---|---|---|---|---|---|
| Albania | No* | No | No | No | No | No |
| Belarus | Yes** | Yes | Yes | Yes | Yes | Yes |
| Macedonia | Varies | No | No | Yes | Yes | No |
| Moldova | Varies | No | No | No | Yes | Yes |
| Romania | No | No | No | No | Yes | Yes |
| Russia | No | Yes | Yes | Yes | Yes | Yes |
| Ukraine | No | No | No | No | Yes | Yes |

\* Compulsory €10 entry fee payable on arrival.
\*\* Visa invitation still required in advance.

Once you start travelling, carry your passport (or a copy of it) at all times and guard it carefully. Camping grounds and hotels sometimes insist that you hand over your passport for the duration of your stay, which is very inconvenient, we suggest you avoid such establishments or offer to pay upfront. If you've paid upfront, anyone insisting they keep your passport for longer than one night to register it is up to no good.

## Visas

A visa is a stamp in your passport or a separate piece of paper permitting you to enter the country in question and stay for a specified period of time. A decade ago a trip through Eastern Europe could take up several pages of your passport, whereas today you'll be lucky to even get an entry stamp in many cases. EU and US citizens now only need a visa for Russia and Belarus, while Australians and New Zealanders don't have it quite so easy. See the Directory of each individual country for specific requirements for entry and check the table Spontaneity vs Planning Ahead.

When you do need a visa, you can sometimes get it at the border or at the airport on arrival, but not always, especially if you're travelling by train or bus and the procedure is likely to hold up others. Check first with the embassies or consulates of the countries you plan to visit; otherwise you could find yourself stranded at the border. With a valid passport and visa (if required) you'll be able to visit most Eastern European countries for up to three (and sometimes even six) months, provided you have some sort of onward or return ticket and/or 'sufficient means of support'.

In line with the Schengen Agreement, there are no longer strict passport controls at the borders between most EU countries, but procedures between EU and non-EU countries can still be fairly thorough. For those who do require visas, it's important to remember that these will have a 'use-by' date, and you'll be refused entry after that period has elapsed.

Consulates sometimes issue visas on the spot, although some levy a 50% to 100% surcharge for 'express service'. If there's a choice between getting a visa in advance and on the border, go for the former option if you have the time. They're often cheaper in your home country and this can save on bureaucratic procedure.

Decide in advance if you want a tourist or transit visa. Transit visas, usually valid for just 48 or 72 hours, are often cheaper and issued faster, but it's usually not possible to extend a transit visa or change it to a tourist visa.

The visa form may instruct you to report to police within 48 hours of arrival. If you're staying at a hotel or other official accommodation (camping ground, hostel, private room arranged by a travel agency etc), this should be taken care of for you. If you're staying with friends, relatives or in a private room, you're supposed to register with the police yourself. During the communist days these regulations were strictly enforced, but things are pretty casual in most countries nowadays. However, consult the Visa section in the relevant country's Directory for full information. Russia is one country, for example, where not registering your visa can cause big problems.

## WOMEN TRAVELLERS

Frustrating though it is, women travellers continue to face more challenging situations when travelling than men do. If you are a woman traveller, especially a solo woman, you may find it helpful to understand the status of local women to better understand the responses you elicit from locals. Hopes of travelling inconspicuously, spending time alone and absorbing the surroundings are often thwarted by men who assume a lone woman desires company, or who seemingly find it impossible to avert their penetrating gaze. Bear in mind that most of this behaviour is harmless, more often than not. Hopefully, the more women that travel, whether alone, in pairs or in groups, the less unwanted attention lone female travellers in the region will attract.

Despite feminism's grip on many European countries, women remain under-represented in positions of power, in both governmental and corporate spheres. Despite exciting progress to elevate the status of women in recent years, the percentage of women in the upper management levels of institutions still leaves a lot to be desired. In many areas, you may notice the glut of women in low-paid, menial jobs.

In Muslim countries, where conservative conceptions of the largely house-bound role of women still tend to prevail, women travelling alone or with other women will certainly be of interest or curiosity to both local men and women. Unmarried men rarely have contact with women outside their family unit, which is why many men in, for example, Albania and Bosnia and Hercegovina, may afford travelling women so much attention. In such areas, women travelling with a male companion will often experience the opposite, and may need to pinch themselves as a reminder that yes, they actually exist.

## WORK

With the massive expansion of the EU in recent years, EU citizens at least have free reign to work in many countries in the region. However, with unemployment still a problem throughout the region, Eastern European countries aren't always keen on handing out jobs to foreigners. Outside the EU the paperwork involved in arranging a work permit can be almost impossible, especially for temporary work.

That doesn't prevent enterprising travellers from topping up their funds occasionally, and they don't always have to do this illegally. If you do find a temporary job in Eastern Europe, though, the pay is likely to be abysmally low. Do it for the experience – not to earn your fortune – and you won't be disappointed. Teaching English is the easiest way to make some extra cash, but the market is saturated in places like Prague and Budapest. You'll probably be much more successful in less popular places like Sofia and Bucharest.

If you play an instrument or have other artistic talents, you could try working the streets. As every Peruvian pipe player (and his fifth cousin) knows, busking is fairly common in major Eastern European cities like Prague, Budapest and Ljubljana. Some countries may require municipal permits for this sort of thing. Talk to other street artists before you start.

There are several references and websites that publicise specific positions across Eastern Europe. Transitions Abroad publishes *Work Abroad: The Complete Guide to Finding a Job Overseas* and the *Alternative Travel Directory: The Complete Guide to Work, Study and Travel Overseas* as well as a colour magazine, *Transitions Abroad*. Its website lists paid positions and volunteer and service programmes. **Action Without Borders** (www.idealist.org) and **Go Abroad** (www.goabroad.com) list hundreds of jobs and volunteer opportunities.

*Work Your Way Around the World* by Susan Griffith gives good, practical advice on a wide range of issues. The publisher, **Vacation Work** (www.vacationwork.co.uk), has many other useful titles, including *The Directory of Summer Jobs Abroad,* edited by David Woodworth. *Working Holidays* by Ben Jupp (Central Bureau for Educational Visits & Exchanges in the UK) is another good source, as is *Now Hiring! Jobs in Eastern Europe* by Clarke Canfield (Perpetual Press).

## Volunteer Work

Organising a volunteer work placement is a great way to gain a deeper insight into local culture. If you're staying with a family, or working alongside local colleagues, you'll probably learn much more about life here than you would if you were travelling through the country.

In some instances volunteers are paid a living allowance, sometimes they work for their keep and other programmes require the volunteer to pay.

Several websites can help you search for volunteer work opportunities in Eastern Europe. The **Coordinating Committee for International Voluntary Service** (www.unesco.org/ccivs) is an umbrella organisation with over 140 member organisations worldwide. It's useful if you want to find out about your country's national volunteer placement agency. Check www.serve yourworld.com and www.transitionsabroad .com and search for vacancies and other volunteering opportunities in Eastern Europe.

# Transport in Eastern Europe

# GETTING THERE & AWAY

The revolution in cheap air travel, so long confined to Western Europe, has well and truly spread to the east of the continent, opening up the region as never before. Given low prices for accommodation and getting around, it has traditionally been the prohibitive airfare that has put travellers off. Now there truly is no excuse if you're coming from Europe, and even if you're coming from much further afield, it's now much cheaper to connect to almost any region of Eastern Europe from a major Western European hub.

While it may be environmentally unsustainable, there are over 2000 low cost air routes criss-crossing Europe at the moment, run by 50 budget airlines serving almost 300 airports. There has never been a better time to take advantage of these bargains and explore Europe's fastest-changing region.

Some travellers choose alternatively and get to Eastern Europe by train – a far more exciting, atmospheric and environmentally friendly way to enter the region than flying. Particularly thrilling of course is to approach Eastern Europe from Asia on the mythical trans-Siberian, trans-Mongolian or trans-Manchurian express trains. Not as pumped full of kudos perhaps, but still fun (not to mention cheaper and quicker), is taking the train from Western Europe over the psychological boundary between East and West that still exists, despite EU enlargement.

There are many ferry services operating in the Baltic Sea linking Scandinavia and Germany with countries such as Poland, Lithuania, Latvia and Estonia. Other routes cross the Adriatic from Italy to Slovenia, Croatia, Macedonia and Albania. This is a truly old-world way to travel, and lots of fun as well. Of course, bus, bicycle and car are also popular ways to enter the region – whichever method you choose you'll find some helpful, practical information in the relevant sections in this chapter. Flights, tours and rail tickets can be booked online at www.lonelyplanet.com/travel_services.

## ENTRY REQUIREMENTS

All countries obviously require travellers to have a valid passport, preferably with a good window between the time of departure and the passport's expiration date. Increasingly, EU travellers from countries that issue national identity cards use these to travel within the EU, although it's impossible to use these as the sole travel documents outside the EU.

Visas are another thing to consider. Countries may require some nationalities to buy a document that allows entry to the country between certain dates. Visas are sometimes free, sometimes available at the border for a price, and sometimes only available in advance and with considerable bureaucratic wrangling. Wherever you are going, be clear on the visa requirements and plan on getting them in advance to save yourself headaches. See the Directory for each country for visa information.

## AIR

Moscow, Prague, Budapest and Warsaw are the region's best-connected air hubs; all have trans-Atlantic flights as well as plenty of flights from Western Europe. With the exception of Moscow, all have plenty of budget airlines serving them. Other smaller hubs are Rīga, Timişoara, Zagreb, St Petersburg, Kyiv and

## CLIMATE CHANGE & TRAVEL

Climate change is a serious threat to the ecosystems that humans rely upon, and air travel is the fastest-growing contributor to the problem. Lonely Planet regards travel, overall, as a global benefit, but believes we all have a responsibility to limit our personal impact on global warming.

## FLYING & CLIMATE CHANGE

Pretty much every form of motorised travel generates $CO_2$ (the main cause of human-induced climate change) but planes are far and away the worst offenders, not just because of the sheer distances they allow us to travel, but because they release greenhouse gases high into the atmosphere. The statistics are frightening: two people taking a return flight between Europe and the US will contribute as much to climate change as an average household's gas and electricity consumption over a whole year.

## CARBON OFFSET SCHEMES

Climatecare.org and other websites use 'carbon calculators' that allow travellers to offset the level of greenhouse gases they are responsible for with financial contributions to sustainable travel schemes that reduce global warming – including projects in India, Honduras, Kazakhstan and Uganda.

Lonely Planet, together with Rough Guides and other concerned partners in the travel industry, support the carbon offset scheme run by climatecare.org. Lonely Planet offsets all of its staff and author travel.

For more information check out our website: www.lonelyplanet.com.

Bratislava, all of which have regular flights to many European cities. Most of the small hubs also have budget airline connections, although as a rule the further east you go the fewer there are.

## Airports & Airlines

Eastern Europe is covered in international airports. The biggest in the region is Moscow's Sheremetyevo airport, the hub of transport behemoth (and butt of many a joke) Aeroflot and its many 'baby' flots – the privatised parts of the company now making up innumerable strangely-named regional airlines.

### THINGS CHANGE

The information in this chapter is particularly vulnerable to change. Check directly with the airline or a travel agent to make sure you understand how a fare (and ticket you may buy) works and be aware of the security requirements for international travel. Shop carefully. The details given in this chapter should be regarded as pointers and are not a substitute for your own careful, up-to-date research.

Other significant regional airlines are ČSA (Czech Airlines), whose hub is in Prague's Ruzyně airport, Malév (Hungarian Airlines), based in Budapest and LOT Polish Airlines, based in Warsaw.

## Air Routes

### ALBANIA

Albania's international flight provision is improving slowly. Recently British Airways added a daily flight from London Gatwick to Tirana's Mother Teresa airport, making the country far more accessible to long-haul travellers. There are also connections to Athens, Bologna, Cologne, Frankfurt, Istanbul, Milan, Rome, Turin, Venice, Vienna and Zurich.

### BELARUS

Minsk-2 is the only airport that takes international flights (at least from non-CIS places). Foreign airlines include Czech Airlines, Austrian Airlines and Lufthansa. Belavia is the Belarusian airline, which has direct flights to Vienna (daily, shared with Austrian Airlines), Paris (Tuesday and Friday), Shannon (Thursday), Berlin (Thursday and Sunday), London (Wednesday and Sunday) and Frankfurt

---

## FLYING TO EASTERN EUROPE ON THE CHEAP

Invaluable travellers website www.flycheapo.com is a great resource to see which budget airlines fly where. Schedules change almost every week, so it's always best to check online, but look out for some of the following airlines that provide the biggest selection of flights to/from Eastern Europe:

**Air Berlin** (www.airberlin.com)
**Alpi Eagles** (www.alpieagles.com)
**Blue Air** (www.blueair-web.com)
**Bmibaby** (www.bmibaby.com)
**Carpatair** (www.carpatair.com)
**Condor** (www.condor.com)
**DBA** (www.flydba.com)
**EasyJet** (www.easyjet.com)
**Germania Express** (www.gexx.de)
**Germanwings** (www.germanwings.com)
**Norwegian Air Shuttle** (www.norwegian.no)
**Ryanair** (www.ryanair.com)
**SkyEurope Airlines** (www.skyeurope.com)
**Smart Wings** (www.smartwings.net)
**Wizz Air** (www.wizzair.com)

---

(Wednesday and Sunday). Czech Airlines has direct flights to/from Stockholm thrice weekly.

### BOSNIA & HERCEGOVINA

Austrian Airlines, Czech Airlines and Lufthansa connect Sarajevo to the world via the intercontinental hubs of Vienna, Prague and Frankfurt. There are also flights to Istanbul and Zurich. No discount airlines fly into Bosnia and Hercegovina yet, but a cheap flight to Zagreb or Dubrovnik and a bus trip could be an option.

### BULGARIA

Bulgaria's main international hub is at Sofia, but there are also a huge number of (mainly chartered) international flights to Varna and Burgas, the gateways for popular Black Sea resorts. Sofia is connected to Amsterdam, Berlin, Frankfurt, Lisbon, London, Milan, Paris and Rome by a number of carriers including national airline Bulgaria Air and also British Airways and Lufthansa. Wizz Air has just commenced four flights weekly from London to Sofia, and two flights a week to Burgas.

### CROATIA

Zagreb is connected to most European capitals as well as Frankfurt, Munich, Hamburg, Stuttgart, Cologne, Istanbul and Damascus. Dubrovnik has direct flights to Brussels, Glasgow, London (Gatwick), Manchester, Hannover, Frankfurt, Cologne, Stuttgart, Munich and Vienna. Split has direct flights to London, Frankfurt, Munich, Cologne, Manchester and Rome. Rijeka is directly connected to London (Luton), Hannover, Cologne, Stuttgart and Munich. Pula has nonstop flights to Manchester, London (Gatwick), Glasgow and Edinburgh. Note that there are no direct flights from North America to Croatia.

### CZECH REPUBLIC

As the major gateway city to the region, Prague has a huge number of international flights, lots of no-frills airlines connecting to it. Prague's Ruzyně airport has links to all Western European capitals as well as Beirut, Cairo, Dubai, Jeddah, Kuwait, Montreal, New York, Riyadh, Seoul, Tbilisi, Tel Aviv and Yerevan.

### ESTONIA

The national carrier Estonian Air links Tallinn with some 20 cities in Europe and Russia, and at reasonable prices. Destinations include Berlin, Copenhagen, Frankfurt, Helsinki and London. Copterline (www.copterline.ee) runs helicopter flights between Helsinki and Tallinn's Copterline Terminal.

### HUNGARY

Big international carriers fly in and out of Budapest's Ferihegy 2, with main destinations including all major Western European capitals, the USA and Canada. Malév is the Hungarian national airline. Low-cost airlines such as easyJet, Wizz Air, SkyEurope and Air Berlin use Ferihegy 1 airport, a few kilometres down the road. Ryainair flies to Balaton airport from the UK and Ireland. Alternatively, Vienna's Schwechart airport is only about three hours from Budapest by bus or train and often has less expensive international airfares.

### LATVIA

Rīga airport is scrviced by direct flights from dozens of Western European cities, including Amsterdam, Berlin, Brussels, Copenhagen, Dublin, Frankfurt, Glasgow, Helsinki, London and Stockholm. Flagship carrier Air Baltic serves some 30 cities, while the recent arrival of budget airlines Ryanair, easyJet and Norwegian Air Shuttle has made it easier and cheaper than ever to visit Rīga.

## LITHUANIA
Vilnius is well connected throughout Europe with direct flights to most major cities including Amsterdam, Berlin, Brussels, Copenhagen, Dublin, Frankfurt, Helsinki, London, Moscow and Stockholm. Budget airlines Ryanair and Wizz Air now have regular flights linking Kaunas with about 10 cities in Western Europe, while local budget provider Lithuanian Airlines serves 15 Western European cities. Air Baltic is another option, it has services to about a dozen destinations in Western Europe.

## MACEDONIA
Macedonia has two international airports, Skopje's Petrovec and the much smaller Ohrid airport. From Skopje there are regular flights to Berlin, Dusseldorf, Frankfurt, Istanbul, Hamburg, Milan, Rome, Vienna and Zurich, while Ohrid has services to Vienna and Zurich.

## MOLDOVA
Moldova's only international airport is the originally named Chişinău international. Air Moldova is the national carrier. While most of Moldova's international flights are within Eastern Europe, Air Moldova has direct service to Athens and Vienna. Aerotour has three flights weekly to Amsterdam and Rome, two weekly flights to Paris and one or two flights daily to Istanbul and Vienna. Though no budget airlines connect Chişinău directly with Western Europe, Carpatair flies to Timişoara in Romania from where it connects with many major European cities.

## MONTENEGRO
Apart from holiday charter flights, Montenegro is not well served by international airlines; this may change with independence. Currently Adria and Austrian Airlines are the only regional airlines serving Western Europe, with flights to London and Vienna respectively. European discount airlines have yet to fly to Montenegro and currently Dubrovnik and Split (Croatia) are the nearest airports.

## POLAND
Warsaw is the major destination for most foreign airlines, though Katowice, Kraków,

Gdańsk, Poznań and Wrocław have flights to several European cities. National carrier LOT and all major European carriers fly to Warsaw. Apart from Europe, LOT connects Warsaw directly to Chicago, New York, Toronto and Tel Aviv. A recent development is the rapid growth of discount airline flights between Polish and British cities, and Dublin, in response to Poles' ability to work freely in the UK and Ireland as EU citizens. Ryanair is at the forefront of UK–Poland flights, often servicing major Polish cities daily from London, and less frequently from other centres. Other discount airlines frequently linking Western Europe and Poland include Wizz Air, SkyEurope, easyjet and Centralwings. SAS flies daily to Copenhagen.

## ROMANIA
Romania has a surprisingly good array of connections to Western Europe, mainly thanks to budget airline Carpatair, which has its hub in Timişoara and flies to Dusseldorf, Frankfurt, Milan, Munich, Paris, Rome and Venice among others. Bucharest is the other big hub, where budget Blue Air link it to Barcelona, Istanbul, Lyon, Milan, Paris and Valencia. Wizz Air has just started flights between Bucharest and London. Other flights on national carrier Tarom and foreign airlines link Bucharest to most Western European capitals and throughout the Middle East.

---

### ONLINE TICKETS

Some recommended air-ticket websites include those listed below. They usually levy a booking fee on any flights bought, but even if you don't buy through them, they can be very useful for checking that the flight prices offered to you by other travel agents are the best ones available. E-tickets are increasingly common with scheduled airlines, so often you won't even need a ticket, meaning you can complete your booking in minutes and print out your reference number.

www.ebookers.com
www.expedia.com
www.opodo.com
www.flybudget.com
www.statravel.com

## RUSSIA

Moscow is a huge air hub with three international airports, but it's all but ignored by budget flights. Germania Express, which flies to Moscow daily from several airports in Germany for reasonable (but not bargain) fares is one exception. Moscow is linked to nearly every European capital city as well as Bangkok, Beijing, Beirut, Damascus, Dubai, Hanoi, Hong Kong, Mumbai, Seoul, Tehran, Tokyo and Ulan Bator in Asia and the Middle East; Havana, Los Angeles, New York, San Francisco, Seattle, Toronto and Washington in the Americas and with Cairo and Luanda in Africa.

St Petersburg is not as well connected with long-haul flights but has excellent connections with Western Europe including London, Paris, Frankfurt, Helsinki, Copenhagen, Rome and Vienna. Budget flights on Norwegian Air Shuttle connect it to Oslo, Germanwings to Cologne and Wind Jet from Bologna.

Kaliningrad has no international connections outside Eastern Europe.

## SERBIA

Serbia is well served by regional airlines that pick up at intercontinental hubs. Travellers from Australasia can fly to Dubai and pick up a JAT flight to Belgrade or fly with Lufthansa via Frankfurt or Austrian Air via Vienna. Travellers from North America would pick up regional connecting flights in London or Frankfurt. Serbia remains ignored by budget airlines. At present Germanwings flies to Belgrade and Prishtina from Cologne, as well as to Prishtina from Hamburg and Stuttgart. The national carrier, JAT, connects Belgrade to all major European cities as well as to Beiruit, Cairo, Dubai, Lanaca, Tel Aviv and Tripoli. For information on Prishtina airport and flying into Kosovo, see p779.

## SLOVAKIA

Bratislava's MR Štefánika airport is a growing European hub. Low-cost SkyEurope is headquartered there and flies to 22 European cities, including Amsterdam, Athens, Copenhagen, Paris, London and Rome. For long-haul flights to/from Australia and the Americas, you'll need to fly into Vienna's Schwechat airport (VIE), 60km west in Austria. A regular one-hour bus ride connects the two. There are also twice-weekly flights between Poprad and London. From Košice international airport, Austrian Airlines flies to Vienna several times a day. Air Slovakia very occasionally connects Košice to Birmingham in England, to Amritsar in India, to Larnaca in Cyprus, and to Tel Aviv. National carrier Slovak Airlines only connects Bratislava to Brussels and Moscow.

## SLOVENIA

For a little country, Slovenia's Brnik airport near Ljubljana is surprisingly well connected throughout Europe, notably on Adria Airways, which serves Amsterdam, Brussels, Copenhagen, Dublin, Frankfurt, Istanbul, London, Manchester, Munich, Paris, Vienna and Zürich direct. EasyJet has low-cost flights from London and Wizz Air connects it to Brussels. Several other low-cost carriers serve a selection of nearby airports just across the Italian and Austrian borders.

## UKRAINE

Kyiv's Boryspil airport is the major destination for most foreign airlines that come to Ukraine. Foreign airlines that serve Kyiv include Air Canada, Air France, British Airways, KLM, Lufthansa, Swiss, El Al, Northwest, Austrian Airlines and SAS. Ukraine International Airlines has direct flights to several destinations (sometimes partnering with a foreign airline), including Amsterdam (daily), Berlin (five weekly), Brussels (four weekly), Dusseldorf (three weekly), London (daily), Paris (daily), Vienna (dozens weekly), Zürich (daily). Aerosvit has direct flights to New York (six weekly) and Toronto (Sunday only).

---

### THE KOSOVO PUZZLE

While Kosovo is still legally part of Serbia, it is administered separately by the UN and Serbia has no immigration facilities at Kosovan border crossings with Albania, Macedonia or Montenegro. However, there are also no borders on the boundary between Kosovo and Serbia either (as they are officially one country), so if you arrive overland in Kosovo from any country other than Serbia you will be there without a Serbian entry stamp in your passport. This means that you will have to leave Kosovo via Albania, Macedonia or Montenegro and then enter Serbia 'legally' via Macedonia or Montenegro if you want to carry on into Serbia proper.

## LAND
### Border Crossings

With the advent of the EU, border crossing in the region has never been simpler. Even candidate members, Bulgaria and Romania, have cleaned up their acts, with polite and efficient staff checking you on entry and exit, and levels of harassment falling hugely over recent years.

The region can be entered from all sides with no problem at all. Some of the major routes are from Germany and Austria into the Czech Republic, into Bulgaria from Turkey or Greece, into Slovenia from Italy and Austria and into Russia from Finland.

The only time real complications while crossing borders are likely to arise is when crossing between Kosovo and Serbia (opposite) and when crossing between Russia and Belarus (below).

For details of overland transport into individual countries refer to the Transport sections in the individual country chapters.

### Bus

Never a great option for long-distance travel, buses have recently been undercut even by airlines in prices. However, not all places are served by budget airlines and so buses are always a useful fall-back and reliably cheap. Major gateway cities to the region by bus from Western Europe include Budapest, Prague, Warsaw and Ljubljana, among others.

#### ALBANIA

Buses to Thessaloniki (10 hours) go daily from Tirana, and three times a week to Athens (24 hours).

#### BULGARIA

From Sofia there are bus services to Greece and Turkey: Athens (12 to 13 hours, one or two daily), Thessaloniki (six to seven hours, two to six daily) and Istanbul (eight to 10 hours, nine daily).

#### CZECH REPUBLIC

Prague's main international bus station is ÚAN Praha Florenc. From Prague there are daily buses to and from Amsterdam (15 hours), Frankfurt (8½ hours), London (20 hours), Geneva (15 hours), Paris (15 hours), Salzburg (7½ hours) and Vienna (five hours).

#### HUNGARY

Buses run from Budapest to Vienna (3½ hours, four daily), Frankfurt (15 hours, four weekly) via Munich (nine hours), Paris (22 hours, four weekly), London (26 hours, daily) and, finally, Rome (15 hours, six weekly) via Florence (11 hours).

#### LATVIA

Buses serve various cities in Western European countries, including Berlin (€43, daily), Amsterdam (€90) and London (€115, four weekly).

#### LITHUANIA

There are regular buses to/from a handful of Western European cities, including Berlin (€63), Munich (€77), Amsterdam (€95), London (€115) and Dublin (€150).

#### MACEDONIA

From Skopje buses travel to Thessaloniki (three hours, three weekly) and on to Athens.

---

**CROSSING INTO RUSSIA: WARNING**

Travellers have reported problems with entering Russia from Ukraine and Belarus. As there is often no border control (particularly between Belarus and Russia) and Ukrainians and Belarusians entering Russia don't need to have their passports stamped, travellers don't get a migration card when entering, or their passports aren't stamped on entry. Without a stamp in your passport showing you've entered Russia, hotels won't register your visa. And when leaving you again face problems for not having a migration card. Some travel agencies recommend that you fly into Russia from Belarus and Ukraine instead of taking the train, until this gets sorted out.

In addition to problems with train travel, flying to Moscow's Domodedovo airport from Minsk can be problematic, as you don't go through customs. There is no problem flying between Ukraine and Russia.

If you do not receive a migration card when entering Russia, contact your embassy immediately upon arrival to find out how to get one. If you do not receive an entry stamp, go to the local OVIR (Visa and Registration) office in Russia and bring a full supply of patience.

### POLAND

From Warsaw there are regular buses to and from Amsterdam (20 hours, five weekly), Cologne (20½ hours, daily); London (27 hours, four weekly), Paris (24 hours, daily), Rome (28 hours, four weekly) and Vienna (13 hours, five weekly). Schedules and fares for a range of other destinations can be found (in English) at www.eurolinespolska.pl.

### RUSSIA

There are regular buses between the Finnish capital, Helsinki, and St Petersburg (eight hours, four to six daily).

### SLOVAKIA

Eurolines (www.eurolines.sk) connects Bratislava by bus with many major European cities including Hamburg (18½ hours, Wednesday), London (23 hours, five weekly), Paris (20 hours, three weekly) and Vienna (one hour, hourly).

### SLOVENIA

Buses to Ljubljana arrive from various German cities including Frankfurt (12½ hours, daily) via Munich (6½ hours). Monday to Saturday there are buses from Koper to Trieste in Italy (one hour, up to 13 daily).

## Car & Motorcycle

Travelling by car or motorcycle gives you an immense amount of freedom and is generally worry-free in Eastern Europe. Travelling by car between EU states is no problem at all, but trickier to non-EU members. Some insurance packages (especially those covering rental cars) do not include all European countries; for example hiring a car in Italy and driving it to Croatia will cause problems unless you have the correct insurance stamp (ask the agency to insure you for wherever you plan to travel). Due to high theft levels and terrible roads, Albania remains something of a no-go area for many, although the roads have been improving steadily and criminality declining slowly. Russia, Belarus and Ukraine still remain tediously difficult places to drive into – border controls can take a long time and bribes are often the order of the day.

## Hitching

See the section under Hitching in Getting Around, p936.

## Train

There are numerous routes into Eastern Europe by train, most of these from Western Europe. The big railway hubs in Eastern Europe are Prague, Budapest, Bucharest, Belgrade and Moscow. Albania is unique in Eastern Europe, having no international train services at all.

### AUSTRIA

Services from Vienna include Budapest (3½ hours, five daily), Prague (4½ hours, six daily), Belgrade (11 hours, daily), Brno (1½ hours, daily) Bucharest (14 hours, daily), as well as Ljubljana (6¼ hours, daily) via Graz. From Salzburg there are also services such as that to Prague (eight hours, daily).

### FINLAND

From Finland there are connections between Helsinki and St Petersburg (6 hours, two daily) and an overnight train to Moscow (16 hours, daily). From here you can connect throughout the region, although there are no direct trains to elsewhere in Eastern Europe from Finland.

### GERMANY

Germany is great for connecting by train to Eastern Europe. The numerous routes include Berlin to Prague (five hours, seven daily), Frankfurt to Prague (7½ hours. one daily), Munich to Budapest (7½ hours, two daily), Munich to Ljubljana (6¾ hours, three daily), as well as Munich to Belgrade (17 hours, daily).

### GREECE

Services to Eastern Europe include the daily service from Athens to Sofia (16½ hours), one daily service from Thessaloniki to Belgrade (16 hours) and a daily train runs between Skopje and Thessaloniki (five hours).

### ITALY

Northern Italy is well connected to the central European capitals. Routes include Venice to Budapest (16 hours, one overnight train daily), Venice to Prague (14¾ hours, one daily) and Venice to Ljubljana (four hours, three daily) via Trieste, and Rome to Prague (20 hours, 4 weekly).

### TURKEY

One of the main routes into Eastern Europe is the Istanbul–Sofia train (14½ hours, daily), the overnight Istanbul–Bucharest train (17 to

---

**TOP FIVE UP-AND-COMING EASTERN EUROPEAN HOTSPOTS**

- **Lviv, Ukraine** (p874) – Possibly 'The New Prague', this delightful medieval old town near Poland in newly visa-free Ukraine is our top tip, although go soon, as word is already well and truly out.
- **Veliko Târnovo, Bulgaria** (p162) – Bulgaria's most beautiful city is just waiting for a cheap airline to connect it to Western Europe. Be glad that hasn't happened yet…
- **Chişinău, Moldova** (p506) – Newly visa-free Moldova's fun capital draws those searching for adventure, cheap wine and good nights out.
- **Sarajevo, Bosnia & Hercegovina** (p106) – The exciting Bosnian capital is no longer synonymous with war, but with fun, cultural events and great day trips to the beautiful countryside.
- **Wrocław, Poland** (p584) – Beautiful architecture, a student vibe and excellent nightlife has made people sit up and take notice of Wrocław. You should too if the crowds in Kraków get too much.

---

19 hours, daily) and the daily Belgrade train (26 hours, daily).

### ELSEWHERE

There are also connections from Switzerland, the Netherlands and France. For example: Zürich to Budapest (12½ hours, one overnight train daily), Basel to Prague (10 hours, daily), Amsterdam to Prague (15 hours, change in Berlin) and Paris to Prague (15 hours, change in Frankfurt or Cologne).

From Asia, there are of course the trans-Siberian, trans-Manchurian and trans-Mongolian express trains, which connect Moscow to the Russian far east, Ulan Bator (Mongolia) and Beijing. Central Asian cities such as Tashkent, Almaty and Dushanbe are also regularly connected by long-distance trains to and from Moscow. Moscow is so well connected to the rest of the region that travelling on from here is easy.

## SEA

The expansion of budget airlines into Eastern Europe has made travelling by sea into the region far less attractive. Before the budget revolution a cheap flight to Italy, Greece or Finland followed by a boat connection to the West Balkans or Estonia was a good budget way of arriving in the region, but it's rather unnecessary these days. However, it's still atmospheric and exciting to travel by boat and not expensive. All the following prices are for a seat only – cabins (when available) quickly send the price soaring.

### GREECE

There's a daily boat (several daily in summer) from Corfu to Saranda in Albania (one hour).

### ITALY

Regular boats from several companies connect Italy with Croatia, Slovenia, Montenegro and Albania. This is a popular way to enter the region, as the Balkans are still quite badly served by cheap flights.

Companies servicing routes between Italy and Eastern Europe include the following.

**Adriatica di Navigazione** (www.adriatica.it) Operates ferry services to Durrës from Bari (8½ to 12 hours, daily).

**Agemar** (www.agemar.it) Operates a luxury car ferry complete with swimming pool to Durrës from Trieste (24 hours, three weekly).

**Azzurra Lines** (www.azzurraline.com) Sails from Bari to Kotor (nine hours, weekly in summer).

**Montenegro Lines** (www.montenegrolines.net) Sails to Bari (nine hours, three weekly) and Ancona (11 hours, twice weekly in summer).

**Jadrolinija** (www.jadrolinija.hr) Croatia's national boat line runs car ferries from Ancona to Split (nine or 10 hours, six weekly) and Zadar (six to eight hours, daily), and also a route from Bari to Dubrovnik (eight hours, six weekly).

**SEM** (www.sem-marina.hr) Connects Ancona and Split (nine hours), continuing on to Stari Grad (Hvar, 12 hours). Ferrys leave twice daily Saturday to Monday and daily on other days.

**SNAV** (www.snav.com) Has a fast car ferry that links Pescara and Ancona with Split (4½ hours, daily) and Pescara with Hvar (3½ hours, daily).

**Venezia Lines** (www.venezialines.com) Runs a weekly boat from Venice to Pula (three hours, four weekly) and six other Istrian coastal towns (from 2¼ hours, mid-April to late September).

### SCANDINAVIA

Even during the cold winter months, ferries plough the Gulf of Finland connecting Helsinki with Tallinn and Rīga with Stockholm, as well as the wide open Baltic, linking Gdańsk and Gdynia with Sweden and Denmark.

The companies plying this area include the following.

**Polferries** (www.polferries.pl) Offers services between Gdańsk and Nynäshamn (18 hours) in Sweden every other day in summer (less frequently from October to April). It also has services from Świnoujście to Ystad (seven hours, daily) in Sweden, to Rønne (5½ hours, Saturdays) and to Copenhagen (11 hours, five weekly), both in Denmark.

**Stena Line** (www.stenaline.pl) Operates between Gdynia and Karlskrona (11 hours, daily) in Sweden.

**Tallink** ( ☎ Helsinki 09 228 311; www.tallink.fi) Does a fast Helsinki–Tallinn route (1¾ hours, at least six daily) as well as a new Stockholm to Rīga service.

**Viking Line** ( ☎ Helsinki 09 123 577; www.vikingline.fi) Sails its luxury *Rosella* daily in both directions between Helsinki and Tallinn (three hours, twice daily).

### TURKEY

There are twice-weekly ferries between Odesa and Istanbul. See www.ukferry.com for details.

# GETTING AROUND

## AIR

The major Eastern European cities are connected by a schedule of regular flights and with the advent of low-cost airlines, there's serious price competition with trains and even buses. Particularly well-connected regional airports are Moscow, St Petersburg, Prague, Budapest, Warsaw, Rīga, Timişoara and Zagreb.

Many countries offer domestic flights, although, again, unless you are in a particular rush, there's rarely a need to take these. Russia is the exception – flying from either Moscow or St Petersburg to Kaliningrad saves you the trouble of getting a double-entry Russian visa (by boat or land, you are given an exit stamp, thus invalidating your single-entry visa).

## BICYCLE

A tour of Eastern Europe by bike may seem a daunting prospect but help is at hand. The **Cyclists' Touring Club** (CTC; ☎ 0870 873 0060; www.ctc .org.uk; Parklands, Railton Rd, Guildford, Surrey GU2 9JX) is based in the UK and offers its members an information service on all matters associated with cycling (including maps, cycling conditions, itineraries and detailed routes). If the club is not able to answer your questions the chances are they will know someone who can.

The key to a successful bike trip is to travel light. What you carry should be largely determined by your destination and type of trip. Even for the shortest and most basic trip it's worth carrying the tools necessary for repairing a puncture. You might want to consider packing spare brake and gear cables, spanners, Allen keys, spare spokes and strong adhesive tape. Before you set off, ensure that you are competent at carrying out basic repairs. There's no point in loading up with equipment that you haven't got a clue how to use. Always check your bike thoroughly each morning and again at night when the day's touring is over. Take a good lock and always use it when you leave your bike unattended.

The wearing of helmets is not compulsory but is certainly advised.

A seasoned cyclist can average about 80km a day but this depends on the terrain and how much weight is being carried. Don't overdo it – there's no point burning yourself out during the initial stages.

One major drawback to cycling in Eastern Europe is the disgusting exhaust fumes put out by Eastern European vehicles, especially buses and trucks. You'll often find yourself gasping in a cloud of blue or black smoke as these vehicles lumber along quiet country roads. Likewise, roads in the south Balkans, particularly Albania, Bosnia and Hercegovina, Serbia, Macedonia and Montenegro can be terrible, not to mention the risk of landmines and unexploded ordinance Bosnia and Hercegovina and Kosovo.

### Hire

Except for in a few of the more visited regions, it can be difficult to hire bikes in most of Eastern Europe. The best hunting grounds are often camping grounds and resort hotels during the summer months. See the country chapters for more details.

### Purchase

For major cycle tours, it's best to have a bike you're familiar with, so consider bringing your own (see the following section) rather than buying on arrival. If you can't be bothered with the hassle then there are places to buy in Eastern Europe (shops selling new and second-hand bicycles or you can check local papers for private vendors), but you'll need a specialist bicycle shop for a machine capable of withstanding touring. CTC can provide members with a leaflet on purchasing.

## Transporting a Bicycle

If you want to bring your own bicycle to Europe, you should be able to take it on the plane. You can either take it apart and pack all the pieces in a bike bag or box, or simply wheel it to the check-in desk, where it should be treated as a piece of check-in luggage. You may have to remove the pedals and turn the handlebars sideways so that it takes up less space in the aircraft's hold; check all this with the airline well in advance, preferably before you pay for your ticket. If your bicycle and other luggage exceed your weight allowance, ask about alternatives or you may find yourself being charged a fortune for excess baggage.

Within Europe, bikes can usually be transported as luggage subject to a fairly small supplementary fee. If it's possible, book your tickets in advance.

## BOAT

Eastern Europe's massive rivers, myriad canals, lakes and seas provide rich opportunities for boat travel, although in almost all cases these are very much pleasure cruises rather than particularly practical ways to get around. Boat travel is usually far more expensive than the equivalent bus or train journey, but that's not necessarily the point. Below, the authors of this book have chosen their favourite boat trips, a great chance to sit back and drink in some wonderful scenery. For details of getting to Eastern Europe by boat see p931.

## BUS

Buses are a viable alternative to the rail network in most Eastern European countries. Generally they tend to complement the rail system rather than duplicate it, though in some countries – notably Hungary, the Czech Republic and Slovakia – you'll almost always have a choice.

In general, buses are slightly cheaper and slower than trains; in Russia, Poland, Hungary, the Czech Republic and Slovakia they cost about the same. Buses tend to be best for shorter hops such as getting around cities and reaching remote rural villages. They are often the only option in mountainous regions. The ticketing system varies in each country, but advance reservations are rarely necessary. It's always safest to buy your ticket in advance at the station, but on long-distance buses you usually just pay upon boarding.

The only company covering the majority of the region is **Eurolines** (www.eurolines.com). See also the individual country chapters for more details about long-distance buses.

## CAR & MOTORCYCLE

Travelling with your own vehicle allows increased flexibility and the option to get off the beaten track. Cars can be inconvenient in city centres when you have to negotiate strange one-way systems or find somewhere to park in the narrow streets of old towns. Also, theft from vehicles is a problem in many parts of the region – never leave valuables in your car.

### Driving Licence & Documentation

Proof of ownership of a private vehicle should always be carried (a Vehicle Registration

**TRANSPORT IN EASTERN EUROPE**

---

### FIVE GREAT BOAT JOURNEYS IN EASTERN EUROPE

- **Budapest–Bratislava (Hungary/Slovakia, p409)** From one gorgeous capital to another, this journey takes in the magnificent Danube Bend, Szentendre and lovely Esztergom with its grand cathedral.

- **Split–Dubrovnik (Croatia, p246)** The dramatic, stunning Croatian coastline can be cruised down on this great day trip. Some ferries stop at Mljet as well as Hvar and Korčula.

- **Lake Bled (Slovenia, p839)** Extremely touristy, but a cruise on Slovenia's lovely Lake Bled should not be missed.

- **Moscow–St Petersburg (Russia, p715)** This charming trip through the canals of Russia takes in lots of beautiful villages and is a slow and relaxing way to travel between the country's two biggest cities.

- **Lake Balaton (Hungary, p385)** Don't miss a pleasure cruise on Hungary's biggest lake, a beautiful haven of peace and tranquillity.

Document for British-registered cars) when touring Europe. An EU driving licence is acceptable for driving throughout most of Eastern Europe, as are North American and Australian ones. But to be on the safe side – or if you have any other type of licence – you should obtain an International Driving Permit (IDP) from your local motoring organisation. You'll need a certified Russian translation for driving in Russia; so find a translation agency that can notarise their translation for you. Always check which type of licence is required in your chosen destination before departure.

## Fuel & Spare Parts

The problems associated with finding the right kind of petrol (or petrol of any kind without special coupons) are all but over in Eastern Europe. Fuel prices still vary considerably from country to country and may bear little relation to the general cost of living; relatively affluent Slovenia, for example, has very cheap fuel while the opposite is true in inexpensive Hungary. Savings can be made if you fill up in the right place. Russia is the cheapest – then Romania, which has prices half those of neighbouring Hungary. Motoring organisations in your home country can give more details.

Unleaded petrol of 95 or 98 octane is now widely available throughout Eastern Europe, though maybe not at the odd station on back roads, or outside main cities in Russia. To be on the safe side in Russia, bring a 20L can to carry an extra supply, especially if your car is fitted with a catalytic converter, as this expensive component can be ruined by leaded fuel. Unleaded fuel is usually slightly cheaper than super (premium grade). Look for the pump with green markings and the word *Bleifrei*, German for 'unleaded'. Diesel is usually significantly cheaper in Eastern Europe.

Good quality petrol is easy to find in the Baltics, but stations seem to be placed somewhat erratically. Several may be within a few kilometres of each other and then there may not be any for incredibly long stretches. Make sure you fill up your tank wherever possible – especially if you are travelling off the main highways.

The embracing of western-made cars throughhout the region has meant that spare parts for western cars are widely available from garages and spare parts dealerships. This is less the case in Belarus, Moldova and Ukraine, and of course in more rural areas throughout the region.

## Hire

Hiring a car is now a relatively straightforward procedure. The big international firms will give you reliable service and a good standard of vehicle. Prebooked rates are generally lower than walk-in rates at rental offices, but either way you'll pay about 20% to 40% more than in Western Europe. However, renting from small local companies is nearly always cheaper. Bear in mind that many companies will not allow you to take cars into certain countries. Russia, Belarus, Moldova and Albania all regularly feature on forbidden lists – there's usually a way around this, but check in advance with the car hire firm you're planning to use.

You should be able to make advance reservations online. Check out the following websites.

**Avis** www.avis.com
**Budget** www.budget.com
**Europcar** www.europcar.com
**Hertz** www.hertz.com

If you're coming from North America, Australia or New Zealand, ask your airline if it has any special deals for rental cars in Europe, or check the ads in the weekend travel sections of major newspapers. You can often find very competitive deals.

Although local companies not connected with any chain will usually offer lower prices than the multinationals, when comparing rates beware of printed tariffs intended only for local residents, which may be lower than the prices foreigners are charged. If in doubt, ask. The big chain companies sometimes offer the flexibility of allowing you to pick up the vehicle from one place and drop it off at another at no additional charge.

## Insurance

Third-party motor insurance is compulsory throughout Europe. For non-EU countries make sure you check the requirements with your insurer. For further advice and more information contact the **Association of British Insurers** ( ☎ 020-7600 3333; www.abi.org.uk).

In general you should get your insurer to issue a Green Card (which may cost extra), an internationally recognised proof of insurance, and check that it lists all the countries you intend to visit. You'll need this in the event of an accident outside the country where the vehicle is insured. The European Accident Statement is available from your insurance company and is copied so that each party at an accident can record information for insurance purposes. The Association of British Insurers has more details. Never sign accident statements you cannot understand or read – insist on a translation and sign that only if it's acceptable.

If the Green Card doesn't list one of the countries you're visiting and your insurer cannot (or will not) add it, you will have to take out separate third-party cover at the border of the country in question. This will probably be the case for Bulgaria and almost certainly for Russia. Note that the Green Card is also not accepted in the Baltic countries and you should allow extra time at borders to purchase insurance. Delays can sometimes last several hours.

Taking out a European breakdown assistance policy, such as the Five Star Service with **AA** ( ☎ UK 0870 550 0600) or the Eurocover Motoring Assistance with **RAC** ( ☎ UK 0800 550 055; www.rac.co.uk), is a good investment. Non-Europeans might find it cheaper to arrange for international coverage with their own national motoring organisation before leaving home. Ask your motoring organisation for details about free and reciprocal services offered by affiliated organisations around Europe.

Every vehicle travelling across an international border should display a sticker that shows the country of registration. It's compulsory to carry a warning triangle almost everywhere in Europe, which must be displayed in the event of a breakdown. Recommended accessories are a first-aid kit (this is compulsory in Croatia, Slovenia and Serbia and Montenegro), a spare bulb kit and a fire extinguisher (compulsory in Bulgaria). Contact the RAC or the AA for more information.

## Road Rules

Motoring organisations are able to supply their members with country-by-country information on motoring regulations, or they may produce motoring guidebooks for general sale.

According to statistics, driving in Eastern Europe is much more dangerous than in Western Europe. Driving at night can be particularly hazardous in rural areas as the roads are often narrow and winding, and

you may encounter horse-drawn vehicles, cyclists, pedestrians and domestic animals. In the event of an accident you're supposed to notify the police and file an insurance claim. If your car has significant body damage from a previous accident, point this out to customs upon arrival and have it noted somewhere, as damaged vehicles may only be allowed to leave the country with police permission.

Standard international road signs are used throughout all of Eastern Europe. You drive on the right-hand side of the road throughout the region and overtake on the left. Keep right except when overtaking, and use your indicators for any change of lane and when pulling away from the kerb. You're not allowed to overtake more than one car at a time, whether they are moving or stationary.

Speed limits are posted, and are generally 110km/h or 120km/h on motorways (freeways), 100km/h on highways, 80km/h on secondary and tertiary roads and 50km/h or 60km/h in built-up areas. Motorcycles are usually limited to 90km/h on motorways, and vehicles with trailers to 80km/h. In towns you may only sound the horn to avoid an accident.

Everywhere in Eastern Europe the use of seat belts is mandatory and motorcyclists (and their passengers) must wear a helmet. In most countries, children under 12 and intoxicated passengers are not allowed in the front seat. Driving after drinking *any* alcohol is a serious offence – most Eastern European countries have a 0% blood-alcohol concentration (BAC) limit (0.02% in Poland).

Throughout Eastern Europe, when two roads of equal importance intersect, the vehicle coming from the right has right of way unless signs indicate otherwise. In many countries this rule also applies to cyclists, so take care. On roundabouts (traffic circles) vehicles already in the roundabout have the right of way. Public transport vehicles pulling out from a stop also have right of way. Stay out of lanes marked 'bus' except when you're making a right-hand turn. Pedestrians have right of way at marked crossings and whenever you're making a turn. In Europe it's prohibited to turn right against a red light even after coming to a stop.

It's usually illegal to stop or park at the top of slopes, in front of pedestrian crossings, at bus or tram stops, on bridges or at level crossings. You must use a red reflector warning triangle when parking on a highway (in an emergency). If you don't use the triangle and another vehicle hits you from behind, you will be held responsible.

Beware of trams (streetcars) as these have priority at crossroads and when they are turning right (provided they signal the turn). Don't pass a tram that's stopping to let off passengers until everyone is out and the doors have closed again (unless, of course, there's a safety island). Never pass a tram on the left or stop within 1m of tram tracks. A police officer who sees you blocking a tram route by waiting to turn left will flag you over. Traffic police administer fines on the spot (always ask for a receipt).

## HITCHING

Hitching is never entirely safe in *any* country, and we don't recommend it. Travellers who decide to hitch should understand that they are taking a small but potentially serious risk. People who do choose to hitch will be safer if they travel in pairs and let someone know where they plan to go.

Also, as long as public transport remains cheap in Eastern Europe, hitchhiking is more for the adventure than the transport. In Russia, Albania, Romania and occasionally times Poland, drivers expect riders to pay the equivalent of a bus fare. In Romania traffic is light, motorists are probably not going far, and almost everywhere you'll face small vehicles overloaded with passengers. If you want to give it a try, though, make yourself a small, clearly written cardboard destination sign, remembering to use the local name for the town or city ('Praha' not 'Prague', or 'Warszawa' not 'Warsaw'). Don't try to hitch from the city centres; city buses will usually take you to the edge of town. Hitchhiking on a motorway (freeway) is usually prohibited; you must stand near an entrance ramp. If you look like a Westerner your chances of getting a ride might improve.

Women will find hitchhiking safer than in Western Europe, but the standard precautions should be taken: never accept a ride with two or more men, don't let your pack be put in the boot (trunk), only sit next to a door you can open, ask drivers where they are going before you say where you're going etc. Don't hesitate to refuse a ride if you feel at all uncomfortable, and insist on being let out at the first sign of trouble. Best of all, try to find a travelling companion (although three people will have a very hard time getting a lift).

Travellers considering hitching as a way of getting around Eastern Europe may find the following websites useful. For general facts, destination-based information and rideshare options visit www.bugeurope.com. The useful www.hitchhikers.org connects hitchhikers and drivers worldwide.

## LOCAL TRANSPORT

Public transport in Eastern Europe has been developed to a far greater extent than in Western Europe. There are excellent metro networks in Moscow, St Petersburg, Warsaw, Prague, Kyiv, Minsk, Budapest and Bucharest. It is a great way to cover distances for a small flat fare.

One form of transport (both city- and nation-wide) that doesn't exist in Western Europe is the shared minibus (*marshrutka* in the former Soviet Union, *furgon* in the Balkans). These quick but cramped minibuses are used throughout Eastern Europe as a form of both intercity and city transport. St Petersburg would cease to function without them, and it's also the most likely way you'll travel between mountain towns in Albania.

Trolleybuses are another phenomenon of the one-time Soviet block. Despite their slowness, they are very environmentally friendly (being powered by electricity and having no emissions in the city) and can be found throughout the former Soviet Union, including the world's longest trolleybus route (see p895) running between Simferopol and Yalta in Ukraine.

Trams are popular throughout Eastern Europe and vary hugely in their speed and modernity. Those in Russia are borderline antiques that seem to derail on a daily basis, while Prague's fleet of sleek trams have everything from electronic destination displays to pickpockets.

## TOURS

A package tour is worth considering only if your time is very limited or you have a special interest such as skiing, canoeing, sailing, horse riding, cycling or spa treatments. Cruises on the Danube are an exciting and romantic way to see Europe's most famous river, although they tend to be on the expensive side. Most tour prices are for double occupancy, which means singles have to share a double room with a stranger of the same sex or pay a supplement to have the room to themselves.

Probably the most highly experienced British company in booking travel to Eastern

Europe is **Regent Holidays** ( ☎ 0117-921 1711, fax 0117-925 4866; www.regent-holidays.co.uk; 15 John St, Bristol BS1 2HR). Their comprehensive fly/drive, individual tours and group tours take in everything from a two-week Hanseatic Baltic Tour to city breaks in Minsk and tours of Albania.

Other recommended travel agents in the UK include **Baltic Holidays** ( ☎ 0870 757 9233; www .balticholidays.com; 40 Princess St, Manchester M1 6DE) who exclusively run tours of the Baltic region, including weekend city breaks, activity holidays, cycling tours and organise independent travel (including the inevitable stag and hen dos).

**Exodus** ( ☎ 0870 240 5550; www.exodus.co.uk) and **Exploreworldwide** ( ☎ 0870 333 4001; www.exploreworld wide.com) are also recommended.

In Australia you can obtain a detailed brochure outlining dozens of upmarket tours (including to Russia) from the **Eastern Europe Travel Bureau** ( ☎ 02-9262 1144; www.eetbtravel.com; Level 5, 75 King St, Sydney, NSW 2000) and tours of the Balkans are organised by **Eastern Europe Holidays** ( ☎ in Australia 0400 994 265; www.e-europeholidays.com; 18 Jauncey Court, Charnwood, ACT 2615).

A general Australian tour operator that includes Eastern Europe and is generally good value is **Intrepid Travel** ( ☎ 1300 360 887; www.intrepid travel.com).

Young revellers can party on Europe-wide bus tours. **Contiki** ( ☎ in London 020-8290 6422; www .contiki.com) and **Top Deck** (www.topdecktravel.co.uk) offer either camping or hotel-based bus tours for the 18-to-35 age group. See Top Deck's website for multiple agents in the UK, US, Canada, Australia and New Zealand. The duration of Contiki's tours that include Eastern Europe or Russia are 22 to 46 days. Another young people's coach tour company to look out for is **Beetroot Backpackers** (www.beetroot.org), a great way to see Russia, run by Russian specialists and highly recommended by some travellers.

For people aged over 50, **Saga Holidays** ( ☎ 0800 096 0074; www.sagaholidays.com; Saga Bldg, Middelburg Sq, Folkestone, Kent CT20 1AZ) offers holidays ranging from cheap coach tours to luxury cruises (and has cheap travel insurance).

National tourist offices in most countries offer trips to points of interest. These may range from one-hour city tours to excursions of several days' duration into regional areas. They are often more expensive than going it alone, but are sometimes worth it if you are pressed for time. A short city tour will give you a quick overview of the place and can be a good way to begin your visit.

## TRAIN

Trains are the most atmospheric, comfortable and fun way to make long overland journeys in Eastern Europe. All major cities are on the rail network, and it's perfectly feasible for train travel to be your only form of intercity transport. Overnight trains also have the benefit of saving you a night's accommodation. It's a great way to meet locals – and it's not unusual to be invited to stay for a night or two with people who shared your cabin.

**TRANSPORT IN EASTERN EUROPE**

---

### FIVE GREAT TRAIN RIDES IN EASTERN EUROPE

■ **Moscow–St Petersburg (Russia, p730)** The overnight sleeper train won't afford you great views of flat central Russia, which is fairly dull even during the daytime, but pitch up in the dining car at midnight and drink vodka with your fellow passengers for a truly fun train trip.

■ **Septemvri–Bansko (Bulgaria, p151)** This train clanks along a narrow gauge through the valley where the Rila and Rodopi Mountains meet. Get ready for some lovely mountain scenery and some chain-smoking shepherds jumping on and off the train.

■ **Belgrade–Bar (Serbia & Montenegro, p780)** Take the day train on this charming route that passes through the Moraca canyon north of Podgorica.

■ **Gdynia–Hel (Poland, p604)** This gentle train ride along the Hel peninsula stops at a number of sleepy villages on the way, then as the peninsula narrows towards its destination you get alternating views of the Baltic Sea on one side and the Gulf of Gdańsk on the other.

■ **Elbasan–Pogradec (Albania, p74)** This trip, made with decades-old Italian trains with no electricity, takes you through lovely scenery as you wend your way slowly to Lake Ohrid through the valleys and over the rivers of Albania. Hang on to your bag when you go through the pitch-black tunnels!

When travelling overnight (nearly always the case when going between countries) you'll get a bed reservation included in the price of your ticket, although you may have to pay a few euros extra for the bedding once on board. Each wagon is administered by a steward or stewardess who will look after your ticket and – crucially, if you arrive during the small hours – who will make sure that you get off at the correct stop. Each wagon has a toilet and washbasin at either end, although their state of cleanliness can vary massively. Be aware that toilets may be closed while the train is at a station and a good half-hour before you arrive in a big city, so go to the toilet while you can. In general trains run like clockwork, and you can expect to arrive pretty much to the timetabled minute.

If you plan to travel extensively by train, it might be worth getting hold of the *Thomas Cook European Timetable,* which gives a complete listing of train schedules and indicates where supplements apply or where reservations are necessary. It is updated monthly and is available from **Thomas Cook** (www.thomascook .com) outlets in the UK. In Australia, look for it in a Thomas Cook outlet or one of the bigger bookstores, which can order in copies if they don't have any in stock. Elsewhere you'll have to order through www.raileurope.com.

If you intend to stick to one or a handful of countries it might be worthwhile getting hold of the national timetable(s) published by the state railway(s). A particularly useful online resource for timetables in Eastern Europe is the DeutscheBahn website at www.bahn.de, in German. Train fares in US and Canadian dollars and schedules for the most popular routes in Europe, as well as information on passes, can be found on www.raileurope.com. For fares in UK pounds go to www.raileurope.co.uk.

## Classes

Throughout Eastern Europe there exists a similar system of classes on trains as there is in Western Europe. Short trips, or longer ones that don't involve sleeping on the train, are usually seated like a normal train – benches (on suburban trains) or aeroplane-style seats (on smarter intercity services).

There are generally three classes of sleeping accommodation on trains – each country has a different name for them, but for the sake of simplicity, we'll call them 3rd, 2nd and 1st class.

Third-class accommodation is not available everywhere, but it's the cheapest way to sleep, although you may feel your privacy has been slightly invaded. The accommodation consists of six berths in each compartment (in the former Soviet Union this is called *platskartny;* there are no compartments as such, just one open carriage with beds everywhere).

Second class (known as *kupeyny* in the former Soviet Union) has four berths in a closed compartment. If there are a couple of you, you will share your accommodation with two strangers. However, if there are three of you, you'll often not be joined by anyone.

First class, or 'SV' in the former Soviet Union, is a treat, although you are paying for space rather than décor or unsurly service in most countries. Here you'll find two berths in a compartment, usually adorned with plastic flowers to remind you what you've paid for.

## Costs

While it's reasonable, train travel is pricier than bus travel in some countries. First-class tickets are double the price of 2nd-class tickets, which are in turn approximately twice the price of 3rd-class tickets.

## Reservations

It's always advisable to buy a ticket in advance. Seat reservations are also advisable but only necessary if the timetable specifies one is required. Out of season, reservations can be made pretty much up to an hour before departure, but never count on this. On busy routes and during the summer, always try to reserve a seat several days in advance. For peace of mind, you may prefer to book tickets via travel agencies before you leave home, although this will be more expensive than booking on arrival in central Europe. You can book most routes in the region from any main station in central Europe.

## Safety

Be aware that trains, while generally extremely safe, can attract petty criminals. Carry your valuables on your person at all times – don't even go to the bathroom without taking your cash, wallet and passport. If you are sharing a compartment with others, you'll have to decide whether or not you trust them. If there's any doubt, be very cautious about leaving the compartment. At night, make sure your door is locked from the inside. If you have a compartment to yourself, you can ask the steward/ess to lock it while you go to the dining car or go for a wander outside when the train is stopped. However, be aware that most criminals strike when they can easily disembark from the train, and – in a tiny minority of cases – the stewards have been complicit.

In the former Soviet Union, the open-plan 3rd-class accommodation is by far the most vulnerable to thieves.

## Train Passes

Not all countries in Eastern Europe are covered by rail passes, but passes do include a number of destinations and so can be worthwhile if you are concentrating your travels around the region. They may also be useful for getting to or from neighbouring countries. These are available online or through most travel agents.

Of the countries covered in this book, Eurail passes are valid only in Hungary, so it's not a good pass to have for travel here; check out the excellent summary of available passes and their pros and cons at www.seat61.com/Railpass.htm.

### BALKAN FLEXIPASS

The new Balkan Flexipass includes Bulgaria, Romania, Greece, Serbia, Montenegro, Macedonia and European Turkey. This pass is available to anyone not resident in the above countries and is valid for 1st-class travel only (not a bad thing at all considering the quality of 2nd-class in these countries). In the USA, **Rail Europe** (www.raileurope.com) charges US$197 for five days of 1st-class travel within one month; extra rail days (maximum five) are also available. The Balkan Flexipass can also be bought via **RailChoice** (www.railchoice.co.uk) in the UK for £69/117 under 26s/over 26s for five days unrestricted travel over a month.

### EURODOMINO

There is a Eurodomino pass for each of the countries covered by the InterRail pass, and they are probably only worth considering if you're concentrating on a particular region. Adults (travelling 1st or 2nd class) and people aged under 26 can opt for three- to eight-days' travel within one month. Note that Eurodomino passes are only for people who've been resident in Europe for six months or more.

### EUROPEAN EAST PASS

The European East Pass can be purchased by anyone not permanently resident in Europe (including the UK). The pass is valid for travel in Austria, Hungary, Czech Republic, Slovakia and Poland, with benefits such as discounted Danube river trips with DDSG Blue Danube.

This pass is sold in North America, Australia and the UK. Within the USA, **Rail Europe** (www.raileurope.com) charges US$124/172 for five days of 1st-/2nd-class travel within one month; extra rail days (maximum five) cost US$29/23 each.

The European East Pass can also be bought via **RailChoice** (www.railchoice.co.uk), which charges UK£124 (2nd class) for five days plus approximately an extra UK£15 per extra day of validity.

### INTERRAIL

These passes are available to European residents of more than six months' standing (passport identification is required), although residents of Turkey and parts of North Africa can also buy them. Terms and conditions vary slightly from country to country, but when travelling in the country where you bought the pass, there is only a discount of about 50% on normal fares. The InterRail pass is split into zones. Zone D is the Czech Republic, Slovakia, Poland, Hungary and Croatia; G includes Slovenia; and H is Bulgaria, Romania, Serbia, Montenegro and Macedonia.

The normal InterRail pass is for people under 26, though travellers over 26 can get the InterRail 26+ version. The price for any single zone is UK£145/223 for those aged under 26/26 and over for 16 days of travel. Two-zone passes are valid for 22 days and cost UK£205/295, and the all-zone Global Pass is UK£285/405 for one month of travel.

### NATIONAL RAIL PASSES

If you're intending to travel extensively within either Bulgaria, the Czech Republic, Hungary or Romania, you might be interested in their national rail passes. You'll probably need to travel extensively to recoup your money but they will save you the time and hassle of buying individual tickets that don't require reservations. You need to plan ahead if you intend to take this option, as some passes can only be purchased prior to arrival in the country concerned. Some national flexipasses, near-equivalents to the Eurodomino passes (left), are only available to non-Europeans. See www.raileurope.com for details.

# Health

## CONTENTS

Travel health largely depends on your predeparture preparations, your daily health care while travelling and how you handle any medical problem that does develop. Eastern Europe is generally an exceptionally safe place to visit from a medical point of view, with no tropical diseases and an extensive, if sometimes basic, healthcare system throughout the region.

# BEFORE YOU GO

Prevention is the key to staying healthy while abroad. A little preplanning, particularly for pre-existing illnesses, will save trouble later: see your dentist before a long trip, carry spare contact lenses or glasses, and take your optical prescription with you. Bring medications in their original, clearly labelled, containers, along with a signed and dated letter from your physician describing your medical conditions and medications, including generic names. If carrying syringes or needles, be sure to have a physician's letter documenting their medical necessity.

## INSURANCE

In 2004 the European Health Insurance Card (EHIC) was introduced for all EU citizens, replacing the E111 form that was previously necessary to receive free or reduced-price treatment. With large numbers of Eastern European countries now EU members, this is a very useful card to have, although it will not cover you for nonemergencies or emergency repatriation.

Others should find out if there is a reciprocal arrangement for free medical care between their country and the country visited. If you do need health insurance, strongly consider a policy that covers you for the worst possible scenario, such as an accident requiring an emergency flight home. Find out if your insurance plan will make payments directly to providers or reimburse you later for overseas health expenditures. The former option is generally preferable, as it doesn't require you to pay out-of-pocket expenses in a foreign country.

## RECOMMENDED VACCINATIONS

The World Health Organization (WHO) recommends that all travellers should be covered for diphtheria, tetanus, measles, mumps, rubella and polio, regardless of their destination. Since most vaccines don't produce immunity until at least two weeks after they're given, visit a physician at least six weeks before departure.

## INTERNET RESOURCES

The WHO's publication *International Travel and Health* is revised annually and is available on line at www.who.int/ith/. Some other useful websites include the following.

**www.mdtravelhealth.com** Travel health recommendations for every country, updated daily.

**www.fitfortravel.scot.nhs.uk** General travel advice for the layperson.

**www.ageconcern.org.uk** Advice on travel for the elderly.

**www.mariestopes.org.uk** Information on women's health and contraception.

## FURTHER READING

'Health Advice for Travellers' (currently called the 'T7.1' leaflet) is an annually updated leaflet by the UK's Department of Health, available free in post offices. It contains some general information, legally required and recommended vaccines for different countries and information on reciprocal health agreements. Lonely Planet's *Travel with Children* includes advice on travel health for younger children. Other recommended references include *Travellers' Health* by Dr Richard Dawood and *The Traveller's Good Health Guide* by Ted Lankester.

# IN TRANSIT

## DEEP VEIN THROMBOSIS (DVT)

Blood clots may form in the legs during plane flights, chiefly because of prolonged immobility. The longer the flight, the greater the risk. The chief symptom of DVT is swelling or pain of the foot, ankle, or calf, usually but not always on just one side. When a blood clot travels to the lungs, it may cause chest pain and breathing difficulties. Travellers with any of these symptoms should immediately seek medical attention.

To prevent the development of DVT on long flights you should walk about the cabin, contract the leg muscles while sitting, drink plenty of fluids and avoid alcohol and tobacco.

## JET LAG & MOTION SICKNESS

To avoid jet lag (common when crossing more than five time zones) try drinking plenty of nonalchoholic fluids and only eating light meals. On arrival, get exposure to sunlight and readjust your schedule (for meals, sleep and so on) as soon as possible.

Antihistamines such as dimenhydrinate (Dramamine) and meclizine (Antivert, Bonine) are usually the first choice for treating motion sickness. A herbal alternative is ginger.

# IN EASTERN EUROPE

## AVAILABILITY & COST OF HEALTH CARE

Good basic health care is readily available and for minor illnesses pharmacists can give valuable advice and sell over-the-counter medication. They can also advise when more specialised help is required and point you in the right direction. The standard of dental care is usually good, however it is sensible to have a dental check-up before a long trip.

Medical care is not always readily available outside of major cities but embassies, consulates and five-star hotels can usually recommend doctors or clinics. In some cases, medical supplies required in hospital may need to be bought from a pharmacy and nursing care may be limited. Note that there can be an increased risk of hepatitis B and HIV transmission via poorly sterilised equipment.

In general health-care costs are still relatively low in Eastern Europe, and tend to be more expensive in EU member states than in non-EU member states, but bear in mind that in most non-EU member states for anything more than a doctor's consultation you'll probably want to go to a private clinic, and therefore comprehensive health insurance is essential.

## INFECTIOUS DISEASES
### Poliomyelitis

Poliomyelitis is spread through contaminated food and water, and its vaccine is one of those given in childhood and should be boosted every 10 years, either orally (a drop on the tongue) or as an injection.

### Rabies

Spread through bites or licks on broken skin from an infected animal, it is always fatal unless treated promptly. Animal handlers should be vaccinated, as should those travelling to remote areas where a reliable source of postbite vaccine is not available within 24 hours. Three injections are needed over a month. If you have not been vaccinated, you will need a course of five injections starting 24 hours or as soon as possible after the injury. If you have been vaccinated, you will need fewer injections and have more time to seek medical help.

### Tickborne Encephalitis

Spread by tick bites, tickborne encephalitis is a serious infection of the brain and vaccination is advised for those in risk areas who are unable to avoid tick bites (such as campers, forestry workers and walkers). Two doses of vaccine will give a year's protection, three doses up to three years'. Anyone walking in the Baltics and Russia for any length of time should consider vaccination, as cases have been steadily rising.

### Typhoid & Hepatitis A

Both of these diseases are spread through contaminated food (particularly shellfish) and water. Typhoid can cause septicaemia; hepatitis A causes liver inflammation and jaundice. Neither is usually fatal but recovery can be prolonged. Typhoid vaccine (typhim Vi, typherix) will give protection for three years. In some countries, the oral vaccine Vivotif is also available. Hepatitis A vaccine (Avaxim, VAQTA, Havrix) is given as an injection; a single dose will give protection for up to a year, and a booster after a year gives 10 years' protection. Hepatitis

A and typhoid vaccines can also be given as a single dose vaccine, hepatyrix or viatim.

## TRAVELLER'S DIARRHOEA

To prevent diarrhoea, only eat fresh fruits or vegetables if cooked or peeled; be wary of dairy products that might contain unpasteurised milk. Eat food which is hot through and avoid buffet-style meals. If a restaurant is full of locals the food is probably safe.

If you develop diarrhoea, be sure to drink plenty of fluids, preferably an oral rehydration solution (eg dioralyte). A few loose stools don't require treatment, but if you start having more than four or five stools a day, you should start taking an antibiotic (usually a quinolone drug) and an antidiarrhoeal agent (such as loperamide). If diarrhoea is bloody, persists for more than 72 hours or is accompanied by fever, shaking, chills or severe abdominal pain you should seek medical attention.

## ENVIRONMENTAL HAZARDS
### Heat Exhaustion & Heatstroke

Heat exhaustion occurs after excessive fluid loss with inadequate replacement of fluids and salt. Symptoms include headache, dizziness and tiredness. Dehydration is already happening by the time you feel thirsty – aim to drink sufficient water to produce pale, diluted urine. To treat heat exhaustion, replace lost fluids by drinking water and/or fruit juice, and cool the body with cold water and fans. Treat salt loss with salty fluids such as soup or Bovril, or add a little more table salt to foods than usual.

Heat stroke is much more serious, resulting in irrational and hyperactive behaviour and eventually loss of consciousness and death. Rapid cooling by spraying the body with water and fanning is ideal. Emergency fluid and electrolyte replacement by intravenous drip is recommended.

### Insect Bites & Stings

Mosquitoes are found in most parts of Europe. They may not carry malaria but can cause irritation and infected bites. Use a DEET-based insect repellent.

Bees and wasps cause real problems only to those with a severe allergy (anaphylaxis). If you have a severe allergy to bee or wasp stings carry an 'epipen' or similar adrenaline injection.

Sand flies are found around the Mediterranean beaches. They usually cause only a nasty itchy bite but can carry a rare skin disorder called cutaneous leishmaniasis.

Bed bugs lead to very itchy, lumpy bites. Spraying the mattress with crawling-insect killer after changing the bedding will get rid of them.

Scabies are tiny mites that live in the skin, particularly between the fingers. They cause an intensely itchy rash. Scabies is easily treated with lotion from a pharmacy; other members of the household also need treatment to avoid spreading scabies between asymptomatic carriers.

### Snake Bites

Avoid getting bitten – do not walk barefoot or stick your hand into holes or cracks. Half of those bitten by venomous snakes are not actually injected with poison (envenomed). If bitten by a snake, do not panic. Immobilise the bitten limb with a splint (eg a stick) and apply a bandage over the site firmly, similar to a bandage over a sprain. Do not apply a tourniquet, or cut or suck the bite. Get the victim to medical help as soon as possible so that antivenin can be given if necessary.

### Water

Tap water may not be safe to drink so it is best to stick to bottled water or boil water for 10 minutes, use water purification tablets or a filter. Do not drink water from rivers or lakes as it may contain bacteria or viruses that can cause diarrhoea or vomiting. St Petersburg is a particular hotspot for dangerous water – NEVER drink from the tap here. Brushing your teeth with tap water is very unlikely to lead to problems, but use bottled water if you want to be ultrasafe.

## TRAVELLING WITH CHILDREN

All travellers with children should know how to treat minor ailments and when to seek medical treatment. Make sure the children are up to date with routine vaccinations, and discuss possible travel vaccines well before departure, as some vaccines are not suitable for children less than one year old.

In hot, moist climates any wound or break in the skin is likely to let in infection. The area should be cleaned and kept dry.

Remember to avoid contaminated food and water. If your child has vomiting or diarrhoea, lost fluids and salts must be replaced. It may be helpful to take rehydration powders for reconstituting with boiled water.

Children should be encouraged to avoid and mistrust any dogs or other mammals because of the risk of rabies and other diseases. Any bite, scratch or lick from a warm-blooded, furry animal should immediately be thoroughly cleaned. If there is any possibility that the animal is infected with rabies, immediate medical assistance should be sought.

## WOMEN'S HEALTH

Emotional stress, exhaustion and travelling through different time zones can all contribute to an upset in the menstrual pattern. If using oral contraceptives, remember some antibiotics, diarrhoea and vomiting can stop the pill from working and lead to the risk of pregnancy – remember to take condoms with you just in case. Time zones, gastrointestinal upsets and antibiotics do not affect injectable contraception.

Travelling during pregnancy is usually possible but there are important things to consider. Always seek a medical check-up before planning your trip. The most risky times for travel are during the first 12 weeks of pregnancy and after 30 weeks. Antenatal facilities vary greatly between countries and you should think carefully before travelling to a country with poor medical facilities or where there are major cultural and language differences from home.

Illness during pregnancy can be more severe so take special care to avoid contaminated food and water and insect and animal bites. A general rule is to only use vaccines, like other medications, if the risk of infection is substantial. Remember that the baby could be at serious risk if you were to contract infections such as typhoid or hepatitis. Some vaccines are best avoided (eg those that contain live organisms). However there is very little evidence that damage has been caused to an unborn child when vaccines have been given to a woman very early in pregnancy, before the pregnancy was suspected.

Take written records of the pregnancy with you. Ensure your insurance policy covers pregnancy delivery and postnatal care, but remember insurance policies are only as good as the facilities available. Always consult your doctor before you travel.

## SEXUAL HEALTH

Emergency contraception is most effective if taken within 24 hours after unprotected sex. The International Planned Parent Federation (www.ippf.org) can advise about the availability of contraception in different countries.

When buying condoms, look for a European CE mark, which means they have been rigorously tested, and then keep them in a cool dry place or they may crack and perish. Safe condoms are available throughout the region.

HEALTH

# Language

## CONTENTS

This language guide offers basic vocabulary to help you get around Eastern Europe. For more extensive coverage of the languages included in this guide, pick up a copy of Lonely Planet's *Eastern Europe Phrasebook* or *Baltic Phrasebook*.

Some of the languages in this chapter use polite and informal modes of address (indicated by the abbreviations 'pol' and 'inf' respectively). Use the polite form when addressing older people, officials or service staff.

## ALBANIAN

### PRONUNCIATION

Written Albanian is phonetically consistent and pronunciation shouldn't pose too many problems for English speakers. Each vowel in a diphthong is pronounced and the **rr** is trilled. However, Albanian possesses certain letters that are present in English but rendered differently. These include:

| ë | often silent; at the beginning of a word it's like the 'a' in 'ago' |
| c | as the 'ts' in 'bits' |
| ç | as the 'ch' in 'church' |
| dh | as the 'th' in 'this' |
| gj | as the 'gy' in 'hogyard' |
| j | as the 'y' in 'yellow' |
| q | between 'ch' and 'ky', similar to the 'cu' in 'cure' |
| th | as in 'thistle' |
| x | as the 'dz' in 'adze' |
| xh | as the 'j' in 'jewel' |

### ACCOMMODATION

| hotel | hotel |
| camping ground | kamp pushimi |
| | |
| Do you have any rooms available? | A keni ndonjë dhomë të lirë? |
| a single room | një dhomë më një krevat |
| a double room | një dhomë më dy krevat |
| How much is it per night/person? | Sa kushton për një natë/njeri? |
| Does it include breakfast? | A e përfshin edhe mëngjesin? |

### CONVERSATION & ESSENTIALS

| Hello. | Tungjatjeta/Allo. |
| Goodbye. | Lamtumirë. |
| | Mirupafshim. (inf) |
| Yes. | Po. |
| No. | Jo. |
| Please. | Ju lutem. |
| Thank you. | Ju falem nderit. |
| That's fine. | Eshtë e mirë. |
| You're welcome. | S'ka përse. |
| Excuse me. | Me falni. (to get past) |
| | Më vjen keq. (before a request) |

---

### EMERGENCIES – ALBANIAN

| Help! | Ndihmë! |
| Call a doctor! | Thirrni doktorin! |
| Call the police! | Thirrni policinë! |
| Go away! | Zhduku!/Largohuni! |
| I'm lost. | Kam humbur rrugë. |

---

| I'm sorry. | Më falni, ju lutem. |
| Do you speak English? | A flisni anglisht? |
| How much is it? | Sa kushton? |
| What's your name? | Si quheni ju lutem? |
| My name is ... | Unë quhem .../Mua më quajnë ... |

## SHOPPING & SERVICES

| | |
|---|---|
| **a bank** | një bankë |
| **chemist/pharmacy** | farmaci |
| **the ... embassy** | ... ambasadën |
| **the market** | pazarin |
| **newsagency** | agjensia e lajmeve |
| **the post office** | postën |
| **the telephone centre** | centralin telefonik |
| **the tourist office** | zyrën e informimeve turistike |
| **What time does it** | Në ç'ore hapet/mbyllet? |
| **open/close?** | |

## TIME, DAYS & NUMBERS

| | |
|---|---|
| **What time is it?** | Sa është ora? |
| **today** | sot |
| **tomorrow** | nesër |
| **in the morning** | në mëngjes |
| **in the afternoon** | pas dreke |

| | |
|---|---|
| **Monday** | e hënë |
| **Tuesday** | e martë |
| **Wednesday** | e mërkurë |
| **Thursday** | e ënjte |
| **Friday** | e premte |
| **Saturday** | e shtunë |
| **Sunday** | e diel |

| | |
|---|---|
| **1** | një |
| **2** | dy |
| **3** | tre |
| **4** | katër |
| **5** | pesë |
| **6** | gjashtë |
| **7** | shtatë |
| **8** | tetë |
| **9** | nëntë |
| **10** | dhjetë |
| **100** | njëqind |
| **1000** | njëmijë |

## TRANSPORT

| | |
|---|---|
| **What time does** | Në ç'orë niset/arrin ...? |
| **the ... leave/arrive?** | |
|   **boat** | barka/lundra |
|   **bus** | autobusi |
|   **tram** | tramvaji |
|   **train** | treni |

| | |
|---|---|
| **I'd like ...** | Dëshiroj ... |
|   **a one-way ticket** | një biletë vajtje |
|   **a return ticket** | një biletë kthimi |

| | |
|---|---|
| **(1st/2nd) class** | klas (i parë/i dytë) |
| **timetable** | orar |
| **bus stop** | stacion autobusi |

---

### SIGNS – ALBANIAN

| | |
|---|---|
| **Hyrje** | Entrance |
| **Dalje** | Exit |
| **Informim** | Information |
| **Hapur** | Open |
| **Mbyllur** | Closed |
| **E Ndaluar** | Prohibited |
| **Policia** | Police |
| **Stacioni I Policisë** | Police Station |
| **Nevojtorja** | Toilets |
|   **Burra** | Men |
|   **Gra** | Women |

---

### Directions

| | |
|---|---|
| **Where is ...?** | Ku është ...? |
| **Go straight ahead**. | Shko drejt. |
| **Turn left.** | Kthehu majtas. |
| **Turn right.** | Kthehu djathtas. |
| **near/far** | afër/larg |

# BULGARIAN

Bulgarian uses the Cyrillic alphabet and it's definitely worth familiarising yourself with it (see p961).

## ACCOMMODATION

**camping ground**
къмпингуване     kâmpinguvane

**guesthouse**
пансион     pansion

**hotel**
хотел     khotel

**private room**
стоя в частна квартира   stoya v chastna kvartira

**youth hostel**
общежитие     obshtezhitie

**single room**
единична стая     edinichna staya

**double room**
двойна стая     dvoyna staya

**Do you have any rooms available?**
Имате ли свободни стаи?
imateh li svobodni stai?

**How much is it?**
Колко струва?
kolko struva?

**Is breakfast included?**
Закуската включена ли е?
zakuskata vklyuchena li e?

## EMERGENCIES – BULGARIAN

**Help!**
Помош!     *pomosh!*
**Call a doctor!**
Повикайте лекар!     *povikayte lekar!*
**Call the police!**
Повикайте полиция!     *povikayte politsiya!*
**Go away!**
Махайте се!     *mahayte se!*
**I'm lost.**
Загубих се.     *zagubih se*

## CONVERSATION & ESSENTIALS

**Hello.**
Здравейте.     *zdraveyte*
**Hi.**
Здрасти. (inf)     *zdrasti*
**Goodbye.**
Довиждане.     *dovizhdane*
Чао. (inf)     *chao*
**Yes.**
Да.     *da*
**No.**
Не.     *ne*
**Please.**
Моля.     *molya*
**Thank you.**
Благодаря.     *blagodarya*
Мерси. (inf)     *mersi*
**I'm sorry.**
Съжалявам.     *sâzhalyavam*
**Excuse me.**
Извинете ме.     *izvinete me*
**I don't understand.**
Аз не разбирам.     *az ne razbiram*
**What's it called?**
Как се казва това?     *kak se kazva tova?*
**How much is it?**
Колко струва?     *kolko struva?*

## SHOPPING & SERVICES

**the bank**
банката     *bankata*
**the church**
църквата     *tsârkvata*
**the hospital**
болницата     *bolnitsata*
**the market**
пазара     *pazara*
**the museum**
музея     *muzeya*
**the post office**
пощата     *poshtata*

**the tourist office**
бюрото за туристи-     *byuroto za turisticheska*
ческа информация     *informatsiya*

## TIME, DAYS & NUMBERS

**What time is it?**    Колко е часът?    *kolko e chasât?*
**today**    днес    *dnes*
**tonight**    довечера    *dovechera*
**tomorrow**    утре    *utre*
**in the morning**    сутринта    *sutrinta*
**in the evening**    вечерта    *vecherta*

**Monday**    понеделник    *ponedelnik*
**Tuesday**    вторник    *vtornik*
**Wednesday**    сряда    *sryada*
**Thursday**    четвъртък    *chetvârtâk*
**Friday**    петък    *petâk*
**Saturday**    събота    *sâbota*
**Sunday**    неделя    *nedelya*

| | | |
|---|---|---|
| **0** | нула | *nula* |
| **1** | едно | *edno* |
| **2** | две | *dve* |
| **3** | три | *tri* |
| **4** | четири | *chetiri* |
| **5** | пет | *pet* |
| **6** | шест | *shest* |
| **7** | седем | *sedem* |
| **8** | осем | *osem* |
| **9** | девет | *devet* |
| **10** | десет | *deset* |
| **20** | двайсет | *dvayset* |
| **100** | сто | *sto* |
| **1000** | хиляда | *hilyada* |

## TRANSPORT

**What time does the ... leave/arrive?**
В колко часа заминава/пристига ...?
*v kolko chasa zaminava/pristiga ...?*
  **city bus**
  градският автобус    *gradskiyat avtobus*
  **intercity bus**
  междуградският    *mezhdugradskiyat*
   автобус    *avtobus*
  **plane**
  самолетът    *samolehtât*
  **train**
  влакът    *vlakât*
  **tram**
  трамваят    *tramvayat*

**arrival**    пристигане    *pristigane*
**departure**    заминаване    *zaminavane*
**timetable**    разписание    *razpisanie*

---

### SIGNS – BULGARIAN

| Вход | Entrance |
| --- | --- |
| Изход | Exit |
| Информация | Information |
| Отворено | Open |
| Затворено | Closed |
| Забранено | Prohibited |
| Полицейско Управление | Police Station |
| Тоалетни | Toilets |
| Мьже | Men |
| Жени | Women |

---

**Where is the bus stop?**
Къде е автобусната спирка?
*kâde e avtobusnata spirka?*

**Where is the train station?**
Къде е железопътната гара?
*kâde e zhelezopâtnata gara?*

**Where is the left-luggage office?**
Къде е гардеробът?
*kâde e garderobât?*

## Directions

| straight ahead | направо | *napravo* |
| --- | --- | --- |
| left/right | ляво/дясно | *lyavo/dyasno* |

**Please show me on the map.**
Моля покажете ми на картата.
*molya pokazhete mi na kartata*

# CROATIAN & SERBIAN

## PRONUNCIATION

The writing systems of Croatian and Serbian are phonetically consistent: every letter is pronounced and its sound will not vary from word to word. With regard to position of stress, only one rule can be given: the last syllable of a word is never stressed. In most cases the accent falls on the first vowel in the word.

Serbian uses both the Cyrillic and Roman alphabet, so it's worth familiarising yourself with the latter (see p961). Croatian uses a Roman alphabet.

The principal difference between Serbian and Croatian is in the pronunciation of the vowel 'e' in certain words. A long 'e' in Serbian becomes 'ije' in Croatian (eg *reka*, *rijeka* (river), and a short 'e' in Serbian becomes 'je' in Croatian, eg *pesma*, *pjesma*

(song). Sometimes, however, the vowel 'e' is the same in both languages, as in *selo* (village). There are also a number of variations in vocabulary between the two languages. We haven't marked these differences in pronunciation in the following words and phrases, but you'll still be understood, even with a Croatian lilt to your language. Where significant differences occur, we've included both, with Croatian marked (C) and Serbian marked (S).

## ACCOMMODATION

**hotel**
| *hotel* | хотел |
| --- | --- |

**guesthouse**
| *privatno prenoćište* | приватно преноћиште |
| --- | --- |

**youth hostel**
| *omladinsko prenoćište* | омладинско преноћиште |
| --- | --- |

**camping ground**
| *kamping* | кампинг |
| --- | --- |

**Do you have any rooms available?**
*Imate li slobodne sobe?*
Имате ли слободне собе?

**How much is it per night/per person?**
*Koliko košta za jednu noć/po osobi?*
Колико кошта за једну ноћ/по особи?

**Does it include breakfast?**
*Da li je u cijenu uključen i doručak?*
Да ли је у цену укључен и доручак?

**I'd like ...**
| *Želim ...* | Желим ... |
| --- | --- |

**a single room**
| *sobu sa jednim krevetom* | собу са једним креветом |
| --- | --- |

**a double-bed room**
| *sobu sa duplim krevetom* | собу са дуплим креветом |
| --- | --- |

## CONVERSATION & ESSENTIALS

**Hello.**
| *Zdravo.* | Здраво. |
| --- | --- |

**Goodbye.**
| *Doviđenja.* | Довиђења. |
| --- | --- |

**Yes.**
| *Da.* | Да. |
| --- | --- |

**No.**
| *Ne.* | Не. |
| --- | --- |

**Please.**
| *Molim.* | Молим. |
| --- | --- |

**Thank you.**
| *Hvala.* | Хвала. |
| --- | --- |

**You're welcome.** (as in 'don't mention it')
| *Nema na čemu.* | Нема на чему. |
| --- | --- |

LANGUAGE

## EMERGENCIES – CROATIAN & SERBIAN

**Help!**
| | |
|---|---|
| *Upomoć!* | Упомоћ! |

**Call a doctor!**
| | |
|---|---|
| *Pozovite (lekara (S)/* | Позовите лекара! |
| *liječnika! (C)* | |

**Call the police!**
| | |
|---|---|
| *Pozovite miliciju (S)/* | Позовите милицију! |
| *policiju (C)!* | |

**Go away!**
| | |
|---|---|
| *Idite!* | Идите! |

**I'm lost.**
| | |
|---|---|
| *Izgubljen/Izgubljena* | Изгубио/Изгубила сам |
| *sam se. (m/f)* | сам се. (m/f) |

| | | |
|---|---|---|
| **Excuse me.** | | |
| *Oprostite.* | Опростите. | |
| **Sorry.** (excuse me, forgive me) | | |
| *Pardon.* | Пардон. | |
| **Do you speak English?** | | |
| *Govorite li engleski?* | Говорите ли енглески? | |
| **How much is it ...?** | | |
| *Koliko košta ...?* | Колико кошта ...? | |
| **What's your name?** | | |
| *Kako se zovete?* | Како се зовете? | |
| **My name is ...** | | |
| *Zovem se ...* | Зовем се ... | |

## SHOPPING & SERVICES

**I'm looking for ...**
| | |
|---|---|
| *Tražim ...* | Тражим ... |
| **a bank** | |
| *banku* | банку |
| **the ... embassy** | |
| *... ambasadu* | ... амбасаду |
| **the market** | |
| *pijacu* | пијацу |
| **the post office** | |
| *poštu* | пошту |
| **the tourist office** | |
| *turistički biro* | туристички биро |

## TIME, DAYS & NUMBERS

| | | |
|---|---|---|
| **What time is it?** | *Koliko je sati?* | Колико је сати? |
| **today** | *danas* | данас |
| **tomorrow** | *sutra* | сутра |
| **in the morning** | *ujutro* | ујутро |
| **in the afternoon** | *popodne* | поподне |

| | | |
|---|---|---|
| **Monday** | *ponedjeljak* | понедељак |
| **Tuesday** | *utorak* | уторак |
| **Wednesday** | *srijeda* | среда |
| **Thursday** | *četvrtak* | четвртак |

## SIGNS – CROATIAN & SERBIAN

| | |
|---|---|
| **Ulaz/Izlaz** | Entrance/Exit |
| **Улаз/Излаз** | |
| **Informacije** | Information |
| **Информације** | |
| **Otvoreno/Zatvoreno** | Open/Closed |
| **Отворено/Затворено** | |
| **Slobodne Sobe** | Rooms Available |
| **Слободне Собе** | |
| **Nema Slobodne Sobe** | Full/No Vacancies |
| **Нема Слободне Собе** | |
| **Milicija (S)/Policija (C)** | Police |
| **Милиција** | |
| **Stanica Milicije (S)/** | Police Station |
| **Policije (C)** | |
| **Станица Милиције** | |
| **Zabranjeno** | Prohibited |
| **Забрањено** | |
| **Toaleti (S)/Zahodi (C)** | Toilets |
| **Тоалети** | |

| | | |
|---|---|---|
| **Friday** | *petak* | петак |
| **Saturday** | *subota* | субота |
| **Sunday** | *nedjelja* | недеља |

| | | |
|---|---|---|
| **1** | *jedan* | један |
| **2** | *dva* | два |
| **3** | *tri* | три |
| **4** | *četiri* | четири |
| **5** | *pet* | пет |
| **6** | *šest* | шест |
| **7** | *sedam* | седам |
| **8** | *osam* | осам |
| **9** | *devet* | девет |
| **10** | *deset* | десет |
| **100** | *sto* | сто |
| **1000** | *hiljadu (S)* | хиљаду |
| | *tisuću (C)* | |

## TRANSPORT

**What time does the ... leave/arrive?**
| | |
|---|---|
| *Kada ... polazi/dolazi?* | Када ... полази/долази? |
| **boat** | |
| *brod* | брод |
| **bus (city)** | |
| *autobus (gradski)* | аутобус (градски) |
| **bus (intercity)** | |
| *autobus (međugradski)* | аутобус (међуградски) |
| **train** | |
| *voz (S)/vlak (C)* | воз |
| **tram** | |
| *tramvaj* | трамвај |

LANGUAGE

**one-way ticket**
*kartu u jednom pravcu*   карту у једном правцу
**return ticket**
*povratnu kartu*   повратну карту
**1st class**
*prvu klasu*   прву класу
**2nd class**
*drugu klasu*   другу класу

## Directions
**Where is the bus/tram stop?**
*Gdje je autobuska/tramvajska stanica* (S)/*postaja* (C)?
Где је аутобуска/трамвајска станица?
**Can you show me (on the map)?**
*Možete li mi pokazati (na karti)?*
Можете ли ми показати (на карти)?

**Go straight ahead.**
*Idite pravo naprijed.*   Идите право напред.
**Turn left.**
*Skrenite lijevo.*   Скрените лево.
**Turn right.**
*Skrenite desno.*   Скрените десно.
**near**
*blizu*   близу
**far**
*daleko*   далеко

# CZECH

## PRONUNCIATION
Many Czech letters are pronounced as per their English counterparts. An accent lengthens a vowel and the stress is always on the first syllable. Words are pronounced as written, so if you follow the guidelines below you should have no trouble being understood. When consulting indexes on Czech maps, be aware that **ch** comes after **h**.

| | |
|---|---|
| **c** | as the 'ts' in 'bits' |
| **č** | as the 'ch' in 'church' |
| **ch** | as in Scottish *loch* |
| **ď** | as the 'd' in 'duty' |
| **ě** | as the 'ye' in 'yet' |
| **j** | as the 'y' in 'you' |
| **ň** | as the 'ni' in 'onion' |
| **ř** | as the sound 'rzh' |
| **š** | as the 'sh' in 'ship' |
| **ť** | as the 'te' in 'stew' |
| **ž** | as the 's' in 'pleasure' |

## ACCOMMODATION
| | |
|---|---|
| **hotel** | *hotel* |
| **guesthouse** | *penzión* |
| **youth hostel** | *ubytovna* |
| **camping ground** | *kemping* |
| **private room** | *privát* |
| **single room** | *jednolůžkový pokoj* |
| **double room** | *dvoulůžkový pokoj* |
| **Do you have any rooms available?** | *Máte volné pokoje?* |
| **Does it include breakfast?** | *Je v tom zahrnuta snídaně?* |

## CONVERSATION & ESSENTIALS
| | |
|---|---|
| **Hello/Good day.** | *Dobrý den.* (pol) |
| **Hi.** | *Ahoj.* (inf) |
| **Goodbye.** | *Na shledanou.* |
| **Yes.** | *Ano.* |
| **No.** | *Ne.* |
| **Please.** | *Prosím.* |
| **Thank you.** | *Děkuji.* |
| **That's fine/You're welcome.** | *Není zač/Prosím.* |
| **Sorry.** | *Promiňte.* |
| **I don't understand.** | *Nerozumím.* |
| **What's it called?** | *Jak se to jmenuje?* |

## SHOPPING & SERVICES
| | |
|---|---|
| **How much is it?** | *Kolik to stojí?* |
| **the bank** | *banka* |
| **the chemist** | *lékárna* |
| **the church** | *kostel* |
| **the market** | *trh* |
| **the museum** | *muzeum* |
| **the post office** | *pošta* |
| **the tourist office** | *turistické informační centrum (středisko)* |
| **travel agency** | *cestovní kancelář* |

## TIME, DAYS & NUMBERS
| | |
|---|---|
| **What time is it?** | *Kolik je hodin?* |
| **today** | *dnes* |
| **tonight** | *dnes večer* |
| **tomorrow** | *zítra* |

LANGUAGE

## SIGNS – CZECH

| Vchod | Entrance |
|---|---|
| Východ | Exit |
| Informace | Information |
| Otevřeno | Open |
| Zavřeno | Closed |
| Zakázáno | Prohibited |
| Policie | Police Station |
| Telefon | Telephone |
| Záchody/WC/ Toalety | Toilets |

| | |
|---|---|
| in the morning | ráno |
| in the evening | večer |

| | |
|---|---|
| Monday | pondělí |
| Tuesday | úterý |
| Wednesday | středa |
| Thursday | čtvrtek |
| Friday | pátek |
| Saturday | sobota |
| Sunday | neděle |

| | |
|---|---|
| 1 | jeden |
| 2 | dva |
| 3 | tři |
| 4 | čtyři |
| 5 | pět |
| 6 | šest |
| 7 | sedm |
| 8 | osm |
| 9 | devět |
| 10 | deset |
| 100 | sto |
| 1000 | tisíc |

## TRANSPORT

| | |
|---|---|
| What time does the ... leave/arrive? | Kdy odjíždí/přijíždí ...? |
| boat | loď |
| city bus | městský autobus |
| intercity bus | meziměstský autobus |
| train | vlak |
| tram | tramvaj |

| | |
|---|---|
| arrival | příjezdy |
| departure | odjezdy |
| timetable | jízdní řád |
| Where is the bus stop? | Kde je autobusová zastávka? |
| Where is the station? | Kde je nádraží? |
| Where is the left-luggage office? | Kde je úschovna zavazadel? |

### Directions

| | |
|---|---|
| Where is it? | Kde je to? |
| left | vlevo |
| right | vpravo |
| straight ahead | rovně |

| | |
|---|---|
| Please show me on the map. | Prosím, ukažte mi to na mapě. |

# ESTONIAN

## ALPHABET & PRONUNCIATION

The letters of the Estonian alphabet: **a b d e f g h i j k l m n o p r s š z ž t u v õ ä ö ü**.

| | |
|---|---|
| a | as the 'u' in 'cut' |
| b | similar to English 'p' |
| g | similar to English 'k' |
| j | as the 'y' in 'yes' |
| š | as 'sh' |
| ž | as the 's' in 'pleasure' |
| õ | somewhere between the 'e' in 'bed' and the 'u' in 'fur' |
| ä | as the 'a' in 'cat' |
| ö | as the 'u' in 'fur' but with rounded lips |
| ü | as a short 'you' |
| ai | as the 'ai' in 'aisle' |
| ei | as in 'vein' |
| oo | as the 'a' in 'water' |
| uu | as the 'oo' in 'boot' |
| öö | as the 'u' in 'fur' |

## CONVERSATION & ESSENTIALS

| | |
|---|---|
| Hello. | Tere. |
| Goodbye. | Head aega/Nägemiseni. |
| Yes. | Jah. |
| No. | Ei. |
| Excuse me. | Vabandage. |
| Please. | Palun. |
| Thank you. | Tänan/Aitäh. (inf) |
| Do you speak English? | Kas te räägite inglise keelt? |

## SHOPPING & SERVICES

| | |
|---|---|
| Where? | Kus? |
| How much? | Kui palju? |
| bank | pank |
| chemist | apteek |
| currency exchange | valuutavahetus |
| market | turg |
| toilet | tualett |

## TIME, DAYS & NUMBERS

| | |
|---|---|
| today | täna |
| tomorrow | homme |

| Monday | esmaspäev |
| Tuesday | teisipäev |
| Wednesday | kolmapäev |
| Thursday | neljapäev |
| Friday | reede |
| Saturday | laupäev |
| Sunday | pühapäev |

| 1 | üks |
| 2 | kaks |
| 3 | kolm |
| 4 | neli |
| 5 | viis |
| 6 | kuus |
| 7 | seitse |
| 8 | kaheksa |
| 9 | üheksa |
| 10 | kümme |
| 100 | sada |
| 1000 | tuhat |

## TRANSPORT

| airport | lennujaam |
| bus station | bussijaam |
| port | sadam |
| stop (eg bus stop) | peatus |
| train station | raudteejaam |
| bus | buss |
| taxi | takso |
| train | rong |
| tram | tramm |
| trolleybus | trollibuss |

| ticket | pilet |
| ticket office | piletikassa/kassa |
| soft class/deluxe | luksus |
| sleeping carriage | magamisvagun |
| compartment (class) | kupee |

# HUNGARIAN

## PRONUNCIATION

The pronunciation of Hungarian consonants can be simplified by pronouncing them more or less as in English; the exceptions are listed below. Double consonants **ll**, **tt** and **dd** aren't pronounced as one letter as in English but lengthened so you can almost hear them as separate letters. Also, **cs**, **zs**, **gy** and **sz** (consonant clusters) are separate letters in Hungarian and appear that way in telephone books and other alphabetical listings. For example, the word *cukor* (sugar) appears in the dictionary before *csak* (only).

| | |
| --- | --- |
| **c** | as the 'ts' in 'hats' |
| **cs** | as the 'ch' in 'church' |
| **gy** | as the 'j' in 'jury' |
| **j** | as the 'y' in 'yes' |
| **ly** | as the 'y' in 'yes' |
| **ny** | as the 'ni' in 'onion' |
| **r** | like a slightly trilled Scottish 'r' |
| **s** | as the 'sh' in 'ship' |
| **sz** | as the 's' in 'set' |
| **ty** | as the 'tu' in British English 'tube' |
| **w** | as 'v' (found in foreign words only) |
| **zs** | as the 's' in 'pleasure' |

Vowels are a bit trickier, and the semantic difference between **a**, **e** or **o** with and without an accent mark is great. For example, *hát* means 'back' while *hat* means 'six'.

| | |
| --- | --- |
| **a** | as the 'o' in hot |
| **á** | as in 'father' |
| **e** | short, as in 'set' |
| **é** | as the 'e' in 'they' with no 'y' sound |
| **i** | as in 'hit' but shorter |
| **í** | as the 'i' in 'police' |
| **o** | as in 'open' |
| **ó** | a longer version of **o** above |
| **ö** | as the 'u' in 'burst' without the 'r' sound |
| **ő** | a longer version of **ö** above |
| **u** | as in 'pull' |
| **ú** | as the 'ue' in 'blue' |

ü   similar to the 'u' in 'flute'; purse your lips tightly and say 'ee'

ű   a longer, breathier version of **ü** above

## ACCOMMODATION

| | |
|---|---|
| hotel | *szálloda* |
| guesthouse | *fogadót* |
| youth hostel | *ifjúsági szálló* |
| camping ground | *kemping* |
| private room | *fizetővendég szoba* |
| Do you have rooms available? | *Van szabad szobájuk?* |
| How much is it per night/person? | *Mennyibe kerül éjszakánként/ személyenként?* |
| Does it include breakfast? | *Az ár tartalmazza a reggelit?* |
| single/double room | *egyágyas/kétágyas szoba* |

## CONVERSATION & ESSENTIALS

| | |
|---|---|
| Hello. | *Szia/Szervusz.* (inf/pol) |
| Good afternoon/day. | *Jó napot kivánok.* (pol) |
| See you later. | *Viszontlátásra.* |
| Goodbye. | *Szia/Szervusz.* (inf/pol) |
| Yes. | *Igen.* |
| No. | *Nem.* |
| Please. | *Kérem.* |
| Thank you. | *Köszönöm.* |
| Sorry. | *Sajnálom.* |
| Excuse me. | *Bocsánat.* (to get past) |
| | *Elnézést.* (to get attention) |
| What's your name? | *Hogy hívják?* (pol)/ *Mi a neved?* (inf) |
| My name is ... | *A nevem ...* |
| I don't understand. | *Nem értem.* |
| Do you speak English? | *Beszél angolul?* |
| What's it called? | *Hogy hívják?* |

## SHOPPING & SERVICES

| | |
|---|---|
| Where is ...? | *Hol van ...?* |
|   a bank | *bank* |
|   a chemist | *gyógyszertár* |
|   the market | *a piac* |
|   the museum | *a múzeum* |
|   the post office | *a posta* |
|   a tourist office | *idegenforgalmi iroda* |
| How much is it? | *Mennyibe kerül?* |
| What time does it open? | *Mikor nyit ki?* |
| What time does it close? | *Mikor zár be?* |

---

### EMERGENCIES – HUNGARIAN

| | |
|---|---|
| Help! | *Segítség!* |
| Call a doctor! | *Hívjon egy orvost!* |
| Call an ambulance! | *Hívja a mentőket!* |
| Call the police! | *Hívja a rendőrséget!* |
| Go away! | *Menjen el!* |
| I'm lost. | *Eltévedtem.* |

## TIME, DAYS & NUMBERS

| | |
|---|---|
| What time is it? | *Hány óra?* |
| today | *ma* |
| tonight | *ma este* |
| tomorrow | *holnap* |
| in the morning | *reggel* |
| in the evening | *este* |
| Monday | *hétfő* |
| Tuesday | *kedd* |
| Wednesday | *szerda* |
| Thursday | *csütörtök* |
| Friday | *péntek* |
| Saturday | *szombat* |
| Sunday | *vasárnap* |
| 1 | *egy* |
| 2 | *kettő* |
| 3 | *három* |
| 4 | *négy* |
| 5 | *öt* |
| 6 | *hat* |
| 7 | *hét* |
| 8 | *nyolc* |
| 9 | *kilenc* |
| 10 | *tíz* |
| 100 | *száz* |
| 1000 | *ezer* |

## TRANSPORT

| | |
|---|---|
| What time does the ... leave/arrive? | *Mikor indul/érkezik a ...?* |
|   boat/ferry | *hajó/komp* |
|   city bus | *helyi autóbusz* |
|   intercity bus | *távolsági autóbusz* |
|   plane | *repülőgép* |
|   train | *vonat* |
|   tram | *villamos* |
| Where is ...? | *Hol van ...?* |
|   the bus stop | *az autóbuszmegálló* |
|   the station | *a pályaudvar* |
|   the left-luggage office | *a csomagmegőrző* |

LANGUAGE

### SIGNS – HUNGARIAN

| | |
|---|---|
| **Bejárat** | Entrance |
| **Kijárat** | Exit |
| **Információ** | Information |
| **Nyitva** | Open |
| **Zárva** | Closed |
| **Tilos** | Prohibited |
| **Rendőrőr-** | Police Station |
| **Kapitányság** | |
| **Toalett/WC** | Toilets |
| **Férfiak** | Men |
| **Nők** | Women |

| | |
|---|---|
| **arrival** | *érkezés* |
| **departure** | *indulás* |
| **timetable** | *menetrend* |

### Directions

| | |
|---|---|
| **(Turn) left.** | *(Forduljon) balra.* |
| **(Turn) right.** | *(Forduljon) jobbra.* |
| **(Go) straight ahead.** | *(Menyen) egyenesen elore.* |
| **Please show me on the map.** | *Kérem, mutassa meg a térképen.* |
| **near/far** | *közel/messze* |

# LATVIAN

## ALPHABET & PRONUNCIATION

The letters of the Latvian alphabet: **a b c č d e f g ģ (Ġ) h i j k ķ l ļ m n ņ o p r s š t u v z ž**.

| | |
|---|---|
| **c** | as the 'ts' in 'bits' |
| **č** | as the 'ch' in 'church' |
| **ģ** | as the 'j' in 'jet' |
| **j** | as the 'y' in 'yes' |
| **ķ** | as the 'tu' in 'tune' |
| **ļ** | as the 'lli' in 'billiards' |
| **ņ** | as the 'ni' in 'onion' |
| **o** | as the 'a' in 'water' |
| **š** | as the 'sh' in 'ship' |
| **ž** | as the 's' in 'pleasure' |
| **ai** | as in 'aisle' |
| **ei** | as in 'vein' |
| **ie** | as in 'pier' |
| **ā** | as the 'a' in 'barn' |
| **ē** | as the 'e' in 'where' |
| **ī** | as the 'i' in 'marine' |
| **ū** | as the 'oo' in 'boot' |

## CONVERSATION & ESSENTIALS

| | |
|---|---|
| **Hello.** | *Labdien/Sveiki.* |
| **Goodbye.** | *Uz redzēšanos/Atā.* |

### EMERGENCIES – LATVIAN

| | |
|---|---|
| **Help!** | *Palīgā!* |
| **I'm ill.** | *Es esmu slims/slima.* (m/f) |
| **I'm lost.** | *Es esmu apmaldījies/ apmaldījusies.* (m/f) |
| **Go away!** | *Ejiet projam!* |
| **Call ...!** | *Izsauciet ...!* |
| **a doctor** | *ārstu* |
| **an ambulance** | *ātro palidzību* |
| **the police** | *policiju* |

| | |
|---|---|
| **Yes.** | *Jā.* |
| **No.** | *Nē.* |
| **Excuse me.** | *Atvainojiet.* |
| **Please.** | *Lūdzu.* |
| **Thank you.** | *Paldies.* |
| **Do you speak English?** | *Vai jūs runājat angliski?* |

## SHOPPING & SERVICES

| | |
|---|---|
| **bank** | *banka* |
| **chemist** | *aptieka* |
| **currency exchange** | *valūtas maiņa* |
| **hotel** | *viesnīca* |
| **market** | *tirgus* |
| **post office** | *pasts* |
| **toilet** | *tualete* |

| | |
|---|---|
| **Where?** | *Kur?* |
| **How much?** | *Cik?* |

## TIME, DAYS & NUMBERS

| | |
|---|---|
| **today** | *šodien* |
| **yesterday** | *vakar* |
| **tomorrow** | *rīt* |

| | |
|---|---|
| **Sunday** | *svētdiena* |
| **Monday** | *pirmdiena* |
| **Tuesday** | *otrdiena* |
| **Wednesday** | *trešdiena* |
| **Thursday** | *ceturtdiena* |
| **Friday** | *piektdiena* |
| **Saturday** | *sestdiena* |

| | |
|---|---|
| **0** | *nulle* |
| **1** | *viens* |
| **2** | *divi* |
| **3** | *trīs* |
| **4** | *četri* |
| **5** | *pieci* |
| **6** | *seši* |
| **7** | *septiņi* |
| **8** | *astoņi* |
| **9** | *deviņi* |

LANGUAGE

**SIGNS – LATVIAN**

| | |
|---|---|
| **Ieeja** | Entrance |
| **Izeja** | Exit |
| **Informācija** | Information |
| **Atvērts** | Open |
| **Slēgts** | Closed |
| **Smēķet Aizliegts** | No Smoking |
| **Policijas Iecirknis** | Police Station |
| **Maksas Tualetes** | Public Toilets |
| Sieviešu | Women |
| Vīriešu | Men |

| | |
|---|---|
| **10** | *desmit* |
| **11** | *vienpadsmit* |
| **12** | *divpadsmit* |
| **100** | *simts* |
| **1000** | *tūkstots* |

## TRANSPORT

| | |
|---|---|
| **airport** | *lidosta* |
| **train station** | *dzelzceļa stacija* |
| **train** | *vilciens* |
| **bus station** | *autoosta* |
| **bus** | *autobuss* |
| **port** | *osta* |
| **taxi** | *taksometrs* |
| **tram** | *tramvajs* |
| **stop** (eg bus stop) | *pietura* |
| **departure time** | *atiešanas laiks* |
| **arrival time** | *pienākšanas laiks* |
| **ticket** | *biļete* |
| **ticket office** | *kase* |

# LITHUANIAN

## ALPHABET & PRONUNCIATION

The letters of the Lithuanian alphabet: **a b c č d e f g h i / y j k l m n o p r s š t u v z ž**. In some circumstances the **i** and **y** are interchangeable.

| | |
|---|---|
| **c** | as 'ts' |
| **č** | as 'ch' |
| **y** | between the 'i' in 'tin' and the 'ee' in 'feet' |
| **j** | as the 'y' in 'yes' |
| **š** | as 'sh' |
| **ž** | as the 's' in 'pleasure' |
| **ei** | as the 'ai' in 'pain' |
| **ie** | as the 'ye' in 'yet' |
| **ui** | as the 'wi' in 'win' |

**EMERGENCIES – LITHUANIAN**

| | |
|---|---|
| **Help!** | *Gelėbkite!* |
| **I'm ill.** | *Aš sergu.* |
| **I'm lost.** | *Aš paklydęs/paklydusi.* (m/f) |
| **Go away!** | *Eik šalin!* |
| **Call ...!** | *Iššaukite ...!* |
| a doctor | *gydytoją* |
| an ambulance | *greitąją* |
| the police | *policiją* |

Accent marks above and below vowels (eg ā, ė and į) all have the general effect of lengthening the vowel:

| | |
|---|---|
| **ā** | as the 'a' in 'father' |
| **ę** | as the 'e' in 'there' |
| **į** | as the 'ee' in 'feet' |
| **ų** | as the 'oo' in 'boot' |
| **ū** | as the 'oo' in 'boot' |
| **ė** | as the 'e' in 'they' |

## CONVERSATION & ESSENTIALS

| | |
|---|---|
| **Hello.** | *Labas/Sveikas.* |
| **Goodbye.** | *Sudie/Viso gero.* |
| **Yes.** | *Taip.* |
| **No.** | *Ne.* |
| **Excuse me.** | *Atsiprašau.* |
| **Please.** | *Prašau.* |
| **Thank you.** | *Ačiū.* |
| **Do you speak English?** | *Ar kalbate angliškai?* |

## SHOPPING & SERVICES

| | |
|---|---|
| **bank** | *bankas* |
| **chemist** | *vaistinė* |
| **currency exchange** | *valiutos keitykla* |
| **hotel** | *viešbutis* |
| **market** | *turgus* |
| **post office** | *paštas* |
| **toilet** | *tualetas* |
| **Where?** | *Kur?* |
| **How much?** | *Kiek?* |

## TIMES, DAYS & NUMBERS

| | |
|---|---|
| **today** | *šiandien* |
| **tomorrow** | *rytoj* |
| **Monday** | *pirmadienis* |
| **Tuesday** | *antradienis* |
| **Wednesday** | *trečiadienis* |
| **Thursday** | *ketvirtadienis* |
| **Friday** | *penktadienis* |

LANGUAGE

SIGNS – LITHUANIAN

| | |
|---|---|
| Įėjimas | Entrance |
| Išėjimas | Exit |
| Informacija | Information |
| Atidara | Open |
| Uždara | Closed |
| Nerūkoma | No Smoking |
| Patogumai | Public Toilets |

| | |
|---|---|
| Saturday | šeštadienis |
| Sunday | sekmadienis |

| | |
|---|---|
| 1 | vienas |
| 2 | du |
| 3 | trys |
| 4 | keturi |
| 5 | penki |
| 6 | šeši |
| 7 | septyni |
| 8 | aštuoni |
| 9 | devyni |
| 10 | dešimt |
| 100 | šimtas |
| 1000 | tūkstantis |

## TRANSPORT

| | |
|---|---|
| airport | oro uostas |
| bus station | autobusų stotis |
| port | uostas |
| train station | geležinkelio stotis |
| stop (eg bus stop) | stotelė |
| bus | autobusas |
| taxi | taksi |
| train | traukinys |
| tram | tramvajus |

| | |
|---|---|
| departure time | išvykimo laikas |
| arrival time | atvykimo laikas |
| ticket | bilietas |
| ticket office | kasa |

# MACEDONIAN

There are 31 letters in the Macedonian Cyrillic alphabet and it's well worth familiarising yourself with it (see p961). Stress usually falls on the third syllable from the end in words with three syllables or more. If the word has only two syllables, the first is usually stressed. There are exceptions, such as new borrowings and other foreign loan words – eg литература 'li·te·ra·tu·ra', not 'li·te·ra·tu·ra' (literature).

## ACCOMMODATION

**hotel**

| | |
|---|---|
| хотел | hotel |

**guesthouse**

| | |
|---|---|
| приватно сметување | privatno smetuvanje |

**youth hostel**

| | |
|---|---|
| младинско | mladinsko |
| преноќиште | prenočište |

**camping ground**

| | |
|---|---|
| кампинг | kamping |

**Do you have any rooms available?**
Дали имате слободни соби?
*dali imate slobodni sobi?*

**How much is it per night/per person?**
Која е цената по ноќ/по особа?
*koja e cenata po noč/po osoba?*

**Does it include breakfast?**
Дали е вкључен pојадок?
*dali e vključen pojadok?*

**a single room**
соба со еден кревет
*soba so eden krevet*

**a double room**
соба со брачен кревет
*soba so bračen krevet*

**for one/two nights**
за една/два вечери
*za edna/dva večeri*

## CONVERSATION & ESSENTIALS

**Hello.**

| | |
|---|---|
| Здраво. | zdravo. |

**Goodbye.**

| | |
|---|---|
| Приатно. | priatno. |

**Yes.**

| | |
|---|---|
| Да. | da. |

**No.**

| | |
|---|---|
| Не. | ne. |

**Excuse me.**

| | |
|---|---|
| Извинете. | izvinete. |

**Please.**

| | |
|---|---|
| Молам. | molam. |

**Thank you.**

| | |
|---|---|
| Благодарам. | blagodaram. |

**You're welcome.**

| | |
|---|---|
| Нема зошто/ | nema zošto/ |
| Мило ми е. | milo mi e. |

**Sorry.**

| | |
|---|---|
| Опростете ве молам. | oprostete ve molam. |

LANGUAGE

## EMERGENCIES – MACEDONIAN

**Help!**
Помош! *pomoš!*
**Call a doctor!**
Повикајте лекар! *povikajte lekar!*
**Call the police!**
Викнете полиција! *viknete policija!*
**Go away!**
Одете си! *odete si!*
**I'm lost.**
Јас загинав. *jas zaginav.*

---

**Do you speak English?**
Зборувате ли *zboruvate li*
англиски? *angliski?*
**What's your name?**
Како се викате? *kako se vikate?*
**My name is ...**
Јас се викам ... *jas se vikam ...*

## SHOPPING & SERVICES

**bank**
банка *banka*
**chemist/pharmacy**
аптека *apteka*
**the embassy**
амбасадата *ambasadata*
**the market**
пазарот *pazarot*
**newsagents**
киоск за весници *kiosk za vesnici*
**the post office**
поштата *poštata*
**stationers**
книжарница *knižarnica*
**the telephone centre**
телефонската *telefonskata*
централа *centrala*
**the tourist office**
туристичкото биро *turističkoto biro*

**How much is it?**
Колку чини тоа? *kolku čini toa?*
**What time does it open/close?**
Кога се отвора/затвора? *koga se otvora/zatvora?*

## TIME, DAYS & NUMBERS

| | | |
|---|---|---|
| **What time is it?** | Колку е часот? | *kolku e časot?* |
| **today** | денес | *denes* |
| **tomorrow** | утре | *utre* |
| **morning** | утро | *utro* |
| **afternoon** | попладне | *popladne* |

| | | |
|---|---|---|
| **Monday** | понеделник | *ponedelnik* |
| **Tuesday** | вторник | *vtornik* |
| **Wednesday** | среда | *sreda* |
| **Thursday** | четврток | *četvrtok* |
| **Friday** | петок | *petok* |
| **Saturday** | сабота | *sabota* |
| **Sunday** | недела | *nedela* |

| | | |
|---|---|---|
| **0** | нула | *nula* |
| **1** | еден | *eden* |
| **2** | два | *dva* |
| **3** | три | *tri* |
| **4** | четири | *četiri* |
| **5** | пет | *pet* |
| **6** | шест | *šest* |
| **7** | седум | *sedum* |
| **8** | осум | *osum* |
| **9** | девет | *devet* |
| **10** | десет | *deset* |
| **100** | сто | *sto* |
| **1000** | илада | *ilada* |

## TRANSPORT

**What time does the next ... leave/arrive?**
Кога доаѓа/заминува идниот ...?
*koga doagja/zaminuva idniot ...?*

**boat**
брод *brod*
**city bus**
автобус градски *avtobus gradski*
**intercity bus**
автобус меѓуградски *avtobus megjugradski*
**train**
воз *voz*
**tram**
трамвај *tramvaj*

**timetable**
возен ред *vozen red*
**bus stop**
автобуска станица *avtobuska stanica*

LANGUAGE

**train station**
железничка станица    *zheleznička stanica*

**I'd like ...**
Сакам ...
*sakam ...*
   **a one-way ticket**
   билет во еден правец    *bilet vo eden pravec*
   **a return ticket**
   повратен билет    *povraten bilet*
   **1st class**
   прва класа    *prva klasa*
   **2nd class**
   втора класа    *vtora klasa*

**I'd like to hire a car/bicycle.**
Сакам да изнајмам кола/точак.
*sakam da iznajmam kola/točak.*

## Directions
**Where is ...?**
Каде је ...?    *kade je ...?*
**Go straight ahead.**
Одете право напред.    *odete pravo napred.*
**Turn left/right.**
Свртете лево/десно.    *svrtete levo/desno.*
**near/far**
блиску/далеку    *blisku/daleku*

# POLISH

## PRONUNCIATION
Written Polish is phonetically consistent, which means that the pronunciation of letters or clusters of letters doesn't vary from word to word. The stress almost always falls on the second-last syllable.

## Vowels
**a**   as the 'u' in 'cut'
**e**   as in 'ten'
**i**   similar to the 'ee' in 'feet' but shorter
**o**   as in 'lot'
**u**   a bit shorter than the 'oo' in 'book'
**y**   similar to the 'i' in 'bit'

There are three vowels unique to Polish:

**ą**   a nasal vowel sound like the French *un*, similar to 'own' in 'sown'
**ę**   also nasalised, like the French *un*, but pronounced as 'e' in 'ten' when word-final
**ó**   similar to Polish **u**

## Consonants
In Polish, the consonants **b**, **d**, **f**, **k**, **l**, **m**, **n**, **p**, **t**, **v** and **z** are pronounced more or less as they are in English. The following consonants and clusters of consonants sound very different to their English counterparts:

**c**   as the 'ts' in 'its'
**ch**   similar to the 'ch' in the Scottish *loch*
**cz**   as the 'ch' in 'church'
**ć**   much softer than Polish **c** (as 'tsi' before vowels)
**dz**   similar to the 'ds' in 'suds' but shorter
**dź**   as **dz** but softer (as 'dzi' before vowels)
**dż**   as the 'j' in 'jam'
**g**   as in 'get'
**h**   as **ch**
**j**   as the 'y' in 'yet'
**ł**   as the 'w' in 'wine'
**ń**   as the 'ny' in 'canyon' (as 'nee' before vowels)
**r**   always trilled
**rz**   as the 's' in 'pleasure'
**s**   as in 'set'
**sz**   as the 'sh' in 'show'
**ś**   as **s** but softer (as 'si' before vowels)
**w**   as the 'v' in 'van'
**ź**   softer version of **z** (as 'zi' before vowels)
**ż**   as **rz**

## ACCOMMODATION
**hotel**   *hotel*
**youth hostel**   *schronisko młodzieżowe*
**camping ground**   *kemping*

**Do you have any**   *Czy są wolne pokoje?*
   **rooms available?**
**Does it include**   *Czy śniadanie jest wliczone?*
   **breakfast?**

**single room**   *pokój jednoosobowy*
**double room**   *pokój dwuosobowy*
**private room**   *kwatera prywatna*

## CONVERSATION & ESSENTIALS

| | |
|---|---|
| **Hello.** | *Cześć.* (inf) |
| **Hello/Good morning.** | *Dzień dobry.* |
| **Goodbye.** | *Do widzenia.* |
| **Yes/No.** | *Tak/Nie.* |
| **Please.** | *Proszę.* |
| **Thank you.** | *Dziękuję.* |
| **Excuse me/Sorry.** | *Przepraszam.* |
| **I don't understand.** | *Nie rozumiem.* |
| **What's it called?** | *Jak to się nazywa?* |

## SHOPPING & SERVICES

| | |
|---|---|
| **the bank** | *bank* |
| **the chemist** | *apteka* |
| **the church** | *kościół* |
| **the city centre** | *centrum miasta* |
| **the market** | *targ/bazar* |
| **the museum** | *muzeum* |
| **the post office** | *poczta* |
| **the tourist office** | *informacja turystyczna* |

| | |
|---|---|
| **How much is it?** | *Ile to kosztuje?* |
| **What time does it open/close?** | *O której otwierają/zamykają?* |

## TIME, DAYS & NUMBERS

| | |
|---|---|
| **What time is it?** | *Która jest godzina?* |
| **today** | *dzisiaj* |
| **tonight** | *dzisiaj wieczorem* |
| **tomorrow** | *jutro* |
| **in the morning** | *rano* |
| **in the evening** | *wieczorem* |

| | |
|---|---|
| **Monday** | *poniedziałek* |
| **Tuesday** | *wtorek* |
| **Wednesday** | *środa* |
| **Thursday** | *czwartek* |
| **Friday** | *piątek* |
| **Saturday** | *sobota* |
| **Sunday** | *niedziela* |

| | |
|---|---|
| **1** | *jeden* |
| **2** | *dwa* |
| **3** | *trzy* |
| **4** | *cztery* |
| **5** | *pięć* |
| **6** | *sześć* |
| **7** | *siedem* |
| **8** | *osiem* |
| **9** | *dziewięć* |
| **10** | *dziesięć* |
| **20** | *dwadzieścia* |
| **100** | *sto* |
| **1000** | *tysiąc* |

---

### SIGNS – POLISH

| | |
|---|---|
| **Wejście** | Entrance |
| **Wyjście** | Exit |
| **Informacja** | Information |
| **Otwarte** | Open |
| **Zamknięte** | Closed |
| **Wzbroniony** | Prohibited |
| **Posterunek Policji** | Police Station |
| **Toalety** | Toilets |
| **Panowie** | Men |
| **Panie** | Women |

## TRANSPORT

| | |
|---|---|
| **What time does the ... leave/arrive?** | *O której godzinie przychodzi/odchodzi ...?* |
| **plane** | *samolot* |
| **boat** | *statek* |
| **bus** | *autobus* |
| **train** | *pociąg* |
| **tram** | *tramwaj* |

| | |
|---|---|
| **arrival** | *przyjazd* |
| **departure** | *odjazd* |
| **timetable** | *rozkład jazdy* |

| | |
|---|---|
| **Where is the bus stop?** | *Gdzie jest przystanek autobusowy?* |
| **Where is the station?** | *Gdzie jest stacja kolejowa?* |
| **Where is the left-luggage office?** | *Gdzie jest przechowalnia bagażu?* |

### Directions

| | |
|---|---|
| **straight ahead** | *prosto* |
| **left** | *lewo* |
| **right** | *prawo* |
| **Please show me on the map.** | *Proszę pokazać mi to na mapie.* |

# ROMANIAN

## PRONUNCIATION

Until the mid-19th century, Romanian was written in the Cyrillic alphabet. Today Romanian employs 28 Latin letters, some of which bear accents. At the beginning of a word, **e** and **i** are pronounced 'ye' and 'yi', while at the end of a word **i** is virtually silent. At the end of a word **ii** is pronounced 'ee'. Word stress is usually on the second last syllable.

| | |
|---|---|
| **ă** | as the 'a' in 'ago' |
| **î** | as the 'i' in 'river' |

**EMERGENCIES – ROMANIAN**

| | |
|---|---|
| Help! | Ajutor! |
| Call a doctor! | Chemaţi un doctor! |
| Call the police! | Chemaţi poliţia! |
| Go away! | Du-te!/Pleacă! |
| I'm lost. | Sînt pierdut. |

| | |
|---|---|
| **c** | as 'k', except before **e** and **i**, when it's as the 'ch' in 'chip' |
| **ch** | always as the 'k' in 'king' |
| **g** | as in 'go', except before **e** and **i**, when it's as in 'gentle' |
| **gh** | always as the 'g' in 'get' |
| **ş** | as 'sh' |
| **ţ** | as the 'tz'in 'tzar' |

## ACCOMMODATION

| | |
|---|---|
| hotel | hotel |
| guesthouse | casa de oaspeţi |
| youth hostel | camin studentesc |
| camping ground | camping |
| private room | cameră particulară |
| single room | o cameră pentru o persoană |
| double room | o cameră pentru două persoane |
| | |
| Do you have any rooms available? | Aveţi camere libere? |
| How much is it? | Cît costă? |
| Does it include breakfast? | Include micul dejun? |

## CONVERSATION & ESSENTIALS

| | |
|---|---|
| Hello. | Bună. |
| Goodbye. | La revedere. |
| Yes. | Da. |
| No. | Nu. |
| Please. | Vă rog. |
| Thank you. | Mulţumesc. |
| Sorry. | Iertaţi-mă. |
| Excuse me. | Scuzaţi-mă. |
| I don't understand. | Nu înţeleg. |
| What's it called? | Cum se cheamă? |

## SHOPPING & SERVICES

| | |
|---|---|
| How much is it? | Cît costă? |
| | |
| the bank | banca |
| the chemist | farmacistul |
| the city centre | centrum oraşului |
| the ... embassy | ambasada ... |
| the market | piaţa |
| the museum | muzeu |
| the post office | poşta |
| the tourist office | birou de informatii turistice |

**SIGNS – ROMANIAN**

| | |
|---|---|
| Intrare | Entrance |
| Ieşire | Exit |
| Informaţii | Information |
| Deschis | Open |
| Inchis | Closed |
| Nu Intraţi | No Entry |
| Staţie de Poliţie | Police Station |
| Toaleta | Toilets |

## TIME, DAYS & NUMBERS

| | |
|---|---|
| What time is it? | Ce oră este? |
| today | azi |
| tonight | deseară |
| tomorrow | mîine |
| in the morning | dimineaţa |
| in the evening | seară |
| | |
| Monday | luni |
| Tuesday | marţi |
| Wednesday | miercuri |
| Thursday | joi |
| Friday | vineri |
| Saturday | sîmbătă |
| Sunday | duminică |
| | |
| 1 | unu |
| 2 | doi |
| 3 | trei |
| 4 | patru |
| 5 | cinci |
| 6 | şase |
| 7 | şapte |
| 8 | opt |
| 9 | nouă |
| 10 | zece |
| 100 | o sută |
| 1000 | o mie |

## TRANSPORT

| | |
|---|---|
| What time does the ... leave/arrive? | La ce oră pleacă/soseşte ...? |
| boat | vaporul |
| bus | autobusul |
| train | trenul |
| tram | tramvaiul |
| plane | avionul |
| | |
| Where is the bus stop? | Unde este staţia de autobuz? |
| Where is the station? | Unde este gară? |
| Where is the left-luggage office? | Unde este biroul pentru bagaje de mînă? |

| arrival | *sosire* |
| departure | *plecare* |
| timetable | *mersul/orar* |

### Directions

| straight ahead | *drept înainte* |
| left | *stînga* |
| right | *dreapta* |
| Please show me on the map. | *Vă rog arătaţi-mi pe hartă.* |

# RUSSIAN

## THE CYRILLIC ALPHABET

The Russian Cyrillic alphabet, with Roman-letter equivalents and common pronunciations, is shown on the chart on p961.

## PRONUNCIATION

The sounds of **а**, **о**, **е** and **я** are 'weaker' when the stress in the word does not fall on them, eg in вода (*voda*, water) the stress falls on the second syllable, so it's pronounced 'va-DA'. The vowel **й** only follows other vowels in so-called diphthongs, eg **ой** 'oy', **ей** 'ey/yey'. Russians usually print **ё** without the dots, a source of confusion in pronunciation.

The 'voiced' consonants **б**, **в**, **г**, **д**, **ж** and **з** are not voiced at the end of words or before voiceless consonants. For example, хлеб (bread) is pronounced 'khlyep'. The **г** in the common adjective endings '-его' and '-ого' is pronounced 'v'.

## ACCOMMODATION

| hotel | гостиница | *gastinitsa* |
| room | номер | *nomer* |
| breakfast | завтрак | *zaftrak* |

**How much is a room?**
Сколько стоит номер?   *skol'ka stoit nomer?*

## CONVERSATION & ESSENTIALS

**Hello.**
Здравствуйте.   *zdrastvuyte*
**Good morning.**
Доброе утро.   *dobraye utra*
**Good afternoon.**
Добрый день.   *dobryy den'*
**Good evening.**
Добрый вечер.   *dobryy vecher*
**Goodbye.**
До свидания.   *da svidaniya*

### UKRAINIAN

Because of Ukraine's history of domination by outside powers, the language was often considered inferior or subservient to the dominant languages of the time – Russian in the east, Polish in the west. Today, the Ukrainian language is slowly being revived, and in 1990 it was adopted as the official language. Russian is understood everywhere by everyone, and it still remains the principal language travellers will need.

### Alphabet & Pronunciation

Around 70% of the Ukrainian language is identical or similar to Russian and Belarusian. The Cyrillic alphabet chart opposite covers the majority of letters used in the Ukrainian alphabet. Ukrainian has three additional letters not found in Russian, **i**, **ï**, and **є**, all of which are neutral vowel sounds (the Russian letter **о** is often replaced by a Ukrainian **i**). The Ukrainian **г** usually has a soft 'h' sound. The Ukrainian alphabet doesn't include the Russian letters **ё**, **ы** and **э**, and has no hard sign, **ъ**, although it does include the soft sign, **ь**. These differences between the two languages are sometimes quite simple in practice: for example, the town of Chernigov in Russian is Chernihiv in Ukrainian. Overall, Ukrainian is softer sounding and less guttural than Russian.

The **-я** *(-ya)* ending for nouns and names in Russian (especially in street names) is dropped in Ukrainian, and the letter **и** is transliterated as *y* in Ukrainian, whereas in Russian it's transliterated as *i*, eg a street named *Deribasovskaya* in Russian would be *Derybasivska* in Ukrainian.

**Bye!**
Пока! (inf)   *paka!*
**How are you?**
Как дела?   *kak dila?*
**Yes.**
Ла.   *dat*
**No.**
Нет.   *net*
**Please.**
Пожалуйста.   *pazhalsta*
**Thank you (very much).**
(Большое) спасибо.   *(bal'shoye) spasiba*
**Pardon me.**
Простите/Пожалуйста.   *prastite/pazhalsta*

# THE CYRILLIC ALPHABET

| CYRILLIC | ROMAN | PRONUNCIATION |
|---|---|---|
| А а | a | as in 'father'; also as in 'ago' when unstressed in Russian |
| Б б | b | as in 'but' |
| В в | v | as in 'van' |
| Г г | g | as in 'go' |
| Ѓ ѓ | gj | as the 'gu' in 'legume' (Macedonian only) |
| Д д | d | as the 'd' in 'dog' |
| Е е | ye | as in 'yet' when stressed; as in 'year' when unstressed (Russian) |
|  | e | as in 'bet' (Bulgarian); as in 'there' (Macedonian) |
| Ё ё | yo | as in 'yore' (Russian only) |
| Ж ж | zh | as the 's' in 'measure' |
| З з | z | as in 'zoo' |
| S s | zj | as the 'ds' in 'suds' (Macedonian only) |
| И и | i | as the 'ee' in 'meet' |
| Й й | y | as in 'boy' |
| Ј ј | j | as the 'y' in 'young' (Macedonian only) |
| К к | k | as in 'kind' |
| Ќ ќ | kj | as the 'cu' in 'cure' (Macedonian only) |
| Л л | l | as in 'lamp' |
| Љ љ | lj | as the 'lli' in 'million' (Macedonian only) |
| М м | m | as in 'mat' |
| Н н | n | as in 'not' |
| Њ њ | nj | as the 'ny' in 'canyon' (Macedonian only) |

| CYRILLIC | ROMAN | PRONUNCIATION |
|---|---|---|
| О о | o | as the 'a' in 'water' when stressed; as the 'a' in 'ago' when unstressed (Russian); as in 'hot' (Bulgarian & Macedonian) |
| П п | p | as in 'pick' |
| Р р | r | as in 'rub' (but rolled) |
| С с | s | as in 'sing' |
| Т т | t | as in 'ten' |
| У у | u | as in 'rule' |
| Ф ф | f | as in 'fan' |
| Х х | kh | as the 'ch' in 'Bach' (Russian) |
|  | h | as in 'hot' (Macedonian) |
| Ц ц | ts | as in 'bits' |
| Џ џ | dz | as the 'j' in 'judge' (Macedonian only) |
| Ч ч | ch | as in 'chat' |
| Ш ш | sh | as in 'shop' |
| Щ щ | shch | as 'shch' in 'fresh chips' (Russian) |
|  | sht | as the '-shed' in pushed' (Bulgarian) |
| Ъ ъ | â | as the 'a' in 'ago' (Bulgarian only) |
| ъ | | 'hard' sign (Russian only) |
| Ы ы | y | as the 'i' in 'ill' (Russian only) |
| ь | | 'soft' sign (Russian only) |
| Э э | e | as in 'end' (Russian only) |
| Ю ю | yu | as the word 'you' |
| Я я | ya | as in 'yard' |

**LANGUAGE**

---

**No problem/Never mind.**

Ничего.      *nichevo* (literally, 'nothing')

**Do you speak English?**

Вы говорите      *vy gavarite*
по-английски?      *pa angliyski?*

**What's your name?**

Как вас зовут?      *kak vas zavut?*

**My name is ...**

Меня зовут ...      *minya zavut ...*

## SHOPPING & SERVICES

**How much is it?**

Сколько стоит?      *skol'ka stoit?*

**bank**

банк      *bank*

**market**

рынок      *rynak*

**pharmacy**

аптека      *apteka*

**post office**

почтам      *pochta*

**telephone booth**

телефонная будка      *tilifonnaya budka*

## TIME, DATE & NUMBERS

**What time is it?**

Который час?      *katoryy chas?*

**today**

сегодня      *sivodnya*

**tomorrow**

завтра      *zaftra*

**am/in the morning**

утра      *utra*

## EMERGENCIES – RUSSIAN

**Help!**

| На помощь!/ | na pomashch'!/ |
| Помогите! | pamagite! |

**I'm sick.**

| Я болен./Я больна. | ya bolen (m)/ya bal'na (f) |

**I need a doctor.**

| Мне нужен врач. | mne nuzhin vrach |

**hospital**

| больница | bal'nitsa |

**police**

| милиция | militsiya |

**I'm lost.**

| Я заблудился. | ya zabludilsya (m) |
| Я заблудилась. | ya zabludilas' (f) |

---

## SIGNS – RUSSIAN

| Вход | Entrance |
| Выход | Exit |
| Открыто | Open |
| Закрыто | Closed |
| Справки | Information |
| Касса | Ticket Office |
| Больница | Hospital |
| Милиция | Police |
| Туалет | Toilets |
| Мужской (М) | Men |
| Женский (Ж) | Women |

---

**pm/in the afternoon**

| дня | dnya |

**in the evening**

| вечера | vechira |

| 0 | ноль | nol' |
| 1 | один | adin |
| 2 | два | dva |
| 3 | три | tri |
| 4 | четыре | chityri |
| 5 | пять | pyat' |
| 6 | шесть | shest' |
| 7 | семь | sem' |
| 8 | восемь | vosim' |
| 9 | девять | devit' |
| 10 | десять | desit' |
| 11 | одиннадцать | adinatsat' |
| 100 | сто | sto |
| 1000 | тысяча | tysyacha |

## TRANSPORT

**What time does the ... leave?**

В котором часу прибывает ...?
f katoram chasu pribyvaet ...?

**What time does the ... arrive?**

В котором часу отправляется ...?
f katoram chasu atpravlyaetsa ...?

**bus**

| автобус | aftobus |

**fixed-route minibus**

| маршрутное такси | marshrutnaye taksi |

**steamship**

| пароход | parakhot |

**train**

| поезд | poyezt |

**tram**

| трамвай | tramvay |

---

**pier/quay**

| причал/пристань | prichal/pristan' |

**train station**

| железно дорожный | zhilezna darozhnyy |
| (ж. д.) вокзал | vagzal |

**stop** (bus/trolleybus/tram)

| остановка | astanofka |

**one-way ticket**

| билет в один конец | bilet v adin kanets |

**return ticket**

| билет в оба конца | bilet v oba kantsa |

**two tickets**

| два билета | dva bilety |

**soft or 1st-class** (compartment)

| мягкий | myahkiy |

**hard or 2nd-class** (compartment)

| купейный | kupeyny |

**reserved-place or 3rd-class** (carriage)

| плацкартный | platskartny |

### Directions

**Where is ...?**

| Где ...? | gde ...? |

**to/on the left**

| налево | naleva |

**to/on the right**

| направо | naprava |

**straight on**

| прямо | pryama |

**Can you show me (on the map)?**

pakazhite mne pazhalsta (na karte)
Покажите мне, пожалуйста (на карте).

# SLOVAK

## PRONUNCIATION

In Slovak words of three syllables or less the stress falls on the first syllable. Longer words generally also have a secondary accent on the third or fifth syllable. There are thirteen vowels (**a**, **á**, **ä**, **e**, **é**, **i**, **í**, **o**, **ó**, **u**, **ú**, **y**, **ý**), three semi-vowels (**l**, **ľ**, **r**) and five diphthongs (**ia**, **ie**, **iu**, **ou**, **ô**). Letters and diphthongs that may be unfamiliar to native English speakers include the following:

| | |
|---|---|
| **c** | as the 'ts' in 'its' |
| **č** | as the 'ch' in 'church' |
| **dz** | as the 'ds' in 'suds' |
| **dž** | as the 'j' in 'judge' |
| **ia** | as the 'yo' in 'yonder' |
| **ie** | as the 'ye' in 'yes' |
| **iu** | as the word 'you' |
| **j** | as the 'y' in 'yet' |
| **ň** | as the 'ni' in 'onion' |
| **ô** | as the 'wo' in 'won't' |
| **ou** | as the 'ow' in 'know' |
| **š** | as the 'sh' in 'show' |
| **y** | as the 'i' in 'machine' |
| **ž** | as the 'z' in 'azure' |

## ACCOMMODATION

| | |
|---|---|
| **hotel** | hotel |
| **guesthouse** | penzion |
| **youth hostel** | mládežnícka ubytovňa |
| **camping ground** | kemping |
| **private room** | privat |
| **single room** | jednolôžková izba |
| **double room** | dvojlôžková izba |

| | |
|---|---|
| **Do you have any rooms available?** | Máte voľné izby? |
| **How much is it?** | Koľko to stojí? |
| **Is breakfast included?** | Sú raňajky zahrnuté v cene? |

## CONVERSATION & ESSENTIALS

| | |
|---|---|
| **Hello.** | Ahoj. |
| **Goodbye.** | Dovidenia. |
| **Yes.** | Áno. |
| **No.** | Nie. |
| **Please.** | Prosím. |
| **Thank you.** | Ďakujem. |
| **Excuse me.** | Prepáčte mi. |
| **I'm sorry.** | Ospravedlňujem sa. |
| **I don't understand.** | Nerozumiem. |
| **What's it called?** | Ako sa do volá? |

## SHOPPING & SERVICES

| | |
|---|---|
| **How much is it?** | Koľko to stojí? |

| | |
|---|---|
| **the bank** | banka |
| **the chemist** | lekárnik |
| **the church** | kostol |

| | |
|---|---|
| **the city centre** | stred (centrum) mesta |
| **the market** | trh |
| **the museum** | múzeum |
| **the post office** | pošta |
| **the tourist office** | turistické informačné centrum |

## TIME, DAYS & NUMBERS

| | |
|---|---|
| **What time is it?** | Koľko je hodín? |
| **today** | dnes |
| **tonight** | dnes večer |
| **tomorrow** | zajtra |
| **in the morning** | ráno |
| **in the evening** | večer |

| | |
|---|---|
| **Monday** | pondelok |
| **Tuesday** | utorok |
| **Wednesday** | streda |
| **Thursday** | štvrtok |
| **Friday** | piatok |
| **Saturday** | sobota |
| **Sunday** | nedeľa |

| | |
|---|---|
| **1** | jeden |
| **2** | dva |
| **3** | tri |
| **4** | štyri |
| **5** | päť |
| **6** | šesť |
| **7** | sedem |
| **8** | osem |
| **9** | deväť |
| **10** | desať |
| **100** | sto |
| **1000** | tisíc |

## TRANSPORT

| | |
|---|---|
| **What time does the ... leave/arrive?** | Kedy odchádza/prichádza ...? |
|   **boat** | loč |
|   **city bus** | mestský autobus |
|   **intercity bus** | medzimestský autobus |
|   **plane** | lietadlo |
|   **train** | vlak |
|   **tram** | električka |

| | |
|---|---|
| **arrival** | príchod |
| **departure** | odchod |
| **timetable** | cestovný poriadok |

| | |
|---|---|
| **Where's the bus stop?** | Kde je autobusová zastávka? |
| **Where's the station?** | Kde je vlaková stanica? |
| **Where's the left-luggage office?** | Kde je úschovňa batožín? |

### Directions

| | |
|---|---|
| **left** | vľavo |
| **right** | vpravo |
| **straight ahead** | rovno |
| **Please show me on the map.** | Prosím, ukážte mi to na mape. |

# SLOVENE

## PRONUNCIATION

Slovene pronunciation isn't difficult. The alphabet consists of 25 letters, most of which are very similar to English. It doesn't have the letters 'q', 'w', 'x' and 'y', but you will find ê, é, ó, ò, č, š and ž. Each letter represents only one sound, with very few exceptions. The letters **l** and **v** are both pronounced like the English 'w' when they occur at the end of syllables and before vowels. Though words like *trn* (thorn) look unpronounceable, most Slovenes (depending on dialect) add a short vowel like an 'a' or the German 'ö' in front of the 'r' to give a Scot's pronunciation of 'tern' or 'tarn'. Here is a list of letters specific to Slovene:

| | |
|---|---|
| **c** | as the 'ts' in 'its' |
| **č** | as the 'ch' in 'church' |
| **ê** | as the 'a' in 'apple' |
| **e** | as the 'a' in 'ago' (when unstressed) |
| **é** | as the 'ay' in 'day' |
| **j** | as the 'y' in 'yellow' |

| | |
|---|---|
| **ó** | as the 'o' in 'more' |
| **ò** | as the 'o' in 'soft' |
| **r** | a rolled 'r' sound |
| **š** | as the 'sh' in 'ship' |
| **u** | as the 'oo' in 'good' |
| **ž** | as the 's' in 'treasure' |

## ACCOMMODATION

| | |
|---|---|
| **hotel** | hotel |
| **guesthouse** | gostišče |
| **camping ground** | kamping |

| | |
|---|---|
| **Do you have a ...?** | Ali imate prosto ...? |
| **bed** | posteljo |
| **cheap room** | poceni sobo |
| **single room** | enoposteljno sobo |
| **double room** | dvoposteljno sobo |

| | |
|---|---|
| **How much is it ...?** | Koliko stane ...? |
| **per night/person** | za eno noč/osebo |
| **for one/two nights** | za eno noč/za dve noči |

| | |
|---|---|
| **Is breakfast included?** | Ali je zajtrk vključen? |

## CONVERSATION & ESSENTIALS

| | |
|---|---|
| **Hello.** | Pozdravljeni. (pol) |
| | Zdravo/Živio. (inf) |
| **Good day.** | Dober dan! |
| **Goodbye.** | Nasvidenje! |
| **Yes.** | Da/Ja. (inf) |
| **No.** | Ne. |
| **Please.** | Prosim. |
| **Thank you (very much).** | Hvala (lepa). |
| **You're welcome.** | Prosim/Ni za kaj! |
| **Excuse me.** | Oprostite. |
| **What's your name?** | Kako vam je ime? |
| **My name is ...** | Jaz sem ... |
| **Where are you from?** | Od kod ste? |
| **I'm from ...** | Sem iz ... |

## SHOPPING & SERVICES

| | |
|---|---|
| **Where is the/a ...?** | Kje je ...? |
| **bank/exchange** | banka/menjalnica |
| **embassy** | konzulat/ambasada |
| **post office** | pošta |
| **telephone centre** | telefonska centrala |
| **tourist office** | turistični informacijski urad |

| SIGNS – SLOVENE | |
|---|---|
| **Vhod** | Entrance |
| **Izhod** | Exit |
| **Informacije** | Information |
| **Odprto** | Open |
| **Zaprto** | Closed |
| **Prepovedano** | Prohibited |
| **Stranišče** | Toilets |

| | |
|---|---|
| **3** | *tri* |
| **4** | *štiri* |
| **5** | *pet* |
| **6** | *šest* |
| **7** | *sedem* |
| **8** | *osem* |
| **9** | *devet* |
| **10** | *deset* |
| **100** | *sto* |
| **1000** | *tisoč* |

## TIME, DAYS & NUMBERS

| | |
|---|---|
| **today** | *danes* |
| **tonight** | *nocoj* |
| **tomorrow** | *jutri* |
| **in the morning** | *zjutraj* |
| **in the evening** | *zvečer* |

| | |
|---|---|
| **Monday** | *ponedeljek* |
| **Tuesday** | *torek* |
| **Wednesday** | *sreda* |
| **Thursday** | *četrtek* |
| **Friday** | *petek* |
| **Saturday** | *sobota* |
| **Sunday** | *nedelja* |

| | |
|---|---|
| **1** | *ena* |
| **2** | *dve* |

## TRANSPORT

| | |
|---|---|
| **What time does ... the leave/arrive?** | *Kdaj odpelje/pripelje ...?* |
| boat/ferry | *ladja/trajekt* |
| bus | *avtobus* |
| train | *vlak* |

| | |
|---|---|
| **timetable** | *spored* |
| **train station** | *železniška postaja* |
| **bus station** | *avtobusno postajališče* |
| **one-way (ticket)** | *enosmerna (vozovnica)* |
| **return (ticket)** | *povratna (vozovnica)* |

| | |
|---|---|
| **Can you show me on the map?** | *A mi lahko pokažete na mapi?* |

**LANGUAGE**

Also available from Lonely Planet:
*Eastern Europe Phrasebook*

# Behind the Scenes

## THIS BOOK

*Eastern Europe* is part of Lonely Planet's Europe series, which includes *Western Europe*, *Mediterranean Europe*, *Central Europe*, *Scandinavian Europe* and *Europe on a Shoestring*. Lonely Planet also publishes phrasebooks to these regions.

This guidebook was commissioned in Lonely Planet's London office, and produced by the following:

**Commissioning Editor** Will Gourlay, Tashi Wheeler
**Coordinating Editors** Craig Kilburn, Rosie Nicholson, Alison Ridgeway
**Coordinating Cartographer** Valentina Kremenchutskaya
**Coordinating Layout Designer** Jacqui Saunders, Cara Smith
**Managing Editor** Bruce Evans
**Managing Cartographer** Mark Griffiths
**Assisting Editors** Carolyn Boicos, Jackey Coyle, Peter Cruttenden, Charlotte Harrison, Victoria Harrison, Helen Koehne, Shawn Low, Kate McLeod, Alan Murphy, Sally O'Brien, Kristin Odijk
**Assisting Cartographers** Owen Eszeki, Matthew Kelly, Jody Whiteoak
**Cover Designer** Pepi Bluck
**Colour Designer** Yvonne Bischofberger
**Project Managers** Ray Thomson, Glenn van der Knijff, Eoin Dunlevy
**Language Content Coordinator** Quentin Frayne

**Thanks to** Fiona Buchan, David Burnett, Helen Christinis, Sally Darmody, Jennifer Garrett, Mark Germanchis, Trent Holden, Trent Paton, Celia Wood

## THANKS

**Tom Masters (Coordinating Author)** Thanks to all the authors working with me on this book, especially to Patrick who worked overtime to split Serbia and Montenegro when the latter inconveniently voted to become a separate country just days before deadline. Thanks also to all in house at Lonely Planet for huge efforts on the briefing, editing, mapping and design of this book. In Russia thanks to Zurab Zaalishvili in Moscow and to Simon, Olga and Grish Patterson in St Petersburg for loads of local help and advice. Thanks also to everyone else with whom I've shared Eastern European adventures in the past year or two, particularly Jess, Craig, Jules and Warren for a maddening trans-Baltic adventure chasing Harry Enfield across Eastern Europe in an oversized jeep. Unforgettable stuff – another teapot of vodka anyone?

**Brett Atkinson** Thanks to Tomáš and Kateřina for overwhelming me with hospitality (long may the chicken fly, and see you in Enzed guys). Hi and thanks to Greg and the crew in Olomouc, and to Oldřiška in Český Krumlov. In LP'ville, thanks to Judith Bamber and Janine Eberle for their support and giving me this opportunity. To Will Gourlay, Sarah Johnstone and Tom Masters, thanks for answering my questions with grace. *Dobrý den* and *děkuji* to all the tourism offices around the Czech Republic that provided me with information, often meeting me halfway with the challenges of language. Back in New Zealand, thanks to Mum and Dad for their unconditional support, and love and special thanks to Carol – my partner in travel

---

### THE LONELY PLANET STORY

The story begins with a classic travel adventure: Tony and Maureen Wheeler's 1972 journey across Europe and Asia to Australia. There was no useful information about the overland trail then, so Tony and Maureen published the first Lonely Planet guidebook to meet a growing need.

From a kitchen table, Lonely Planet has grown to become the largest independent travel publisher in the world, with offices in Melbourne (Australia), Oakland (USA) and London (UK). Today Lonely Planet guidebooks cover the globe. There is an ever-growing list of books and information in a variety of media. Some things haven't changed. The main aim is still to make it possible for adventurous travellers to get out there – to explore and better understand the world.

At Lonely Planet we believe travellers can make a positive contribution to the countries they visit – if they respect their host communities and spend their money wisely. Every year 5% of company profit is donated to charities around the world.

adventures and life. Long may the adventures continue.

**Greg Bloom** Starting in Kaliningrad (where information is scarcest), a hearty thanks to Andry Naoumtchouk for all the help both on the ground and in cyberspace. I owe you several pivos, my friend. In Latvia, thanks to Karlis Celms, Rūta Šteinberga and Marty Zaprauskis for the inside scoop on Rīga. A special nod to Marty for helping me sift through the capital's intractable hotel scene, and to Rūta for setting me straight on blue cows and such things during write-up. In Lithuania, a big thanks to Tony Pappa for the tips and the crazy Wednesday night out in Vilnius, and to Bernie ter Braak for some quality bar and club education. Thanks to Gabija Thomson for arranging my Vilnius tour, to friendly Kristina Markeviciute in the Vilnius tourist office, and to Rimas for rescuing my brokendown ass in (quite literally) the middle of Europe. Last but not least, thanks to all the helpful peeps in the Rīga, Kaunas, Liepāja and Sigulda tourist offices.

**Peter Dragicevich** *Blagodaram* to Ivica in Skopje and *ju falem nderit* to Ilir and Gent in Tirana for being friendly faces along the way and great sources of local knowledge. Thanks to Lonely Planet veterans Richard Plunkett and Vesna Maric for pointing this newbie in the right direction and to Tim Benzie for getting me on the road. Special thanks to Ben Preston and Adrienne Wong Preston for your ongoing support and Islington knowledge, and answering panicked calls about missing luggage. Ditto to Kurt Crommelin for keeping me chipper with phonecalls and Kate Bush. Many thanks to Pip Judson-Steel, Miranda Playfair and Jack Dragicevich for your advice on the manuscript. Last but not least a big *hvala ljepa* to my Dad, my greatest supporter and supplier of chocolate fish.

**Lisa Dunford** Dearest Saša, what would I have done without you and your family, Fero, Šimon, Sara and Mom & Dad Augustin – thank you doesn't seem to cover it. You are a true friend. To Magda, and your son, Martin: you've been helping me as long as I can remember. You're in my thoughts. Olga, Easter breakfast with champagne was magnificent. Thanks too to the Lonely Planet readers like the students I met on the train to Velky Meder, to the random strangers who tolerated my Slovak and put me on the right bus, and to the Lonely Planet editors, copy editors and cartographers who made all this possible. Oh, and Billy, you're the best travelling companion ever; ICAU.

**Steve Fallon** A number of people assisted in the research and writing of the Slovenia chapter, in particular my two dear friends and fonts-of-all-knowledge, Verica Leskovar and Tatjana Radovič at the Ljubljana Tourist Board. Others to whom I'd like to say *najlepša hvala* for assistance, sustenance and/or inspiration along the way include Valburga Baričević of Hoteli Piran; Tjaša Borštnik of the Ljubljana Tourist Board; Jelena Dašič of the Bovec Tourist Information Centre; Majda Rozina Dolenc of the Slovenian Tourist Board, Ljubljana; Marino Fakin of Slovenian Railways, Ljubljana; Darjono Husodo and Maja Tratar-Husodo of the Antiq Hotel, Ljubljana; Aleš Hvala of the Hvala hotel, Kobarid; Lado Leskovar of Unicef and RTV, Ljubljana; Vojko Anzeljc and Tone Plankar at the Ljubljana bus station; Aleksander Riznič of Radio Odeon, Črnomelj; Petra Stušek of the Ljubljana Tourist Board; Eva Štravs of the Bled Tourist Information Centre; Brigita Zorec of Ljubljana Aerodrom; and Olga Žvanut of Slovenian Railways, Ljubljana. As always, my efforts here are dedicated to my partner, Michael Rothschild, an 'honest' man at last.

**Patrick Horton** Authors are always indebted to the folk on the ground who provide not only the nitty gritty but help an author's understanding of a country. In Serbia I must thank Nikola Vrzic for his work, careful driving and companionship, and Naim Shala likewise in Kosovo. Thanks to Tim Clancy in Sarajevo for some interesting behind the scenes revelations and to the staff at the Ljubičica for the coffee, loza and information. In all three countries big thanks go to dedicated tourist office staff who were prepared to answer copious questions on the most mundane but important matters. Endless thanks to my partner Christine without whose support none of this would be really possible.

**Steve Kokker** Back in Lonely Planet land, thanks to Tom Masters and map meister Mark Griffiths. In Estonia, Anne Kurepalu was as always an immense help, and Marco Partel a great companion for car trips. Thanks in general to the kind, creative people in this small, chilly country I've been blessed to have in my life. Final, eternal gratitude to Dagmar, without whose guidance I might never have found my true way here in the land of my ancestors.

**Vesna Maric** As always, my first and biggest thanks go to Rafael for making everything more fun. Then, thanks to Gabriel for his kindness and desire to dine at the Gay Hussar. Thanks to Réka Kocics for meeting me on a wintry night in Sopor, and to Daniel Robinson for providing me with a contact.

Big thanks go to Tom Masters, the Great Coordinator, for all the help, and to Will Gourlay and the editors. Thanks to my mother for making it on the train, and to Philip Roth for making me laugh while I waited for four hours at a train station. Thanks also to the Hungarian-only speaking railway worker in Sopor who was happy to help despite impossible communication and made my life easier.

**Jeanne Oliver** Jeanne sends a huge *hvala* to Nena Komarica and Andrea Petrov of the Croatian National Tourist Board for their unstinting assistance. Maja Molovčić was most helpful in Dubrovnik and Ivo Tomić was warm and welcoming. Thanks also to Alen Karabaić in Krk for his knowledge of the island and Stanka Kraljević in Korčula. At home, thanks to Marie-Rose Aubert for looking after the cats and *bisoux* to John.

**Leif Pettersen** Foremost thanks goes to Catalina Papuc for her tireless efforts and assistance when I came a whisker away from being vanquished by Romanian bureaucracy. In Chişinău, Marina Vozian's telephone resourcefulness and Vitale Eremia's speedy and detailed emails saved my behind. I'm in eternal debt to Tanya Tsurcan whose tenacity, wit and flirting skills got me into, and more importantly out of, Transdniestr. In Suceava, Ciprian Slemcho rescued me before I could seriously consider pushing my car off a bridge and Tatiana Hostiuc's vast knowledge of Bucovina and careful detail contributed mightily to the Moldova chapter. The lovely Daniela at Info Litoral Tourist Information Centre in Mamaia gave me hours of her time (and incessant follow-up emails) as we discussed the entire Black Sea coast. Thanks to Katie Mardis in Minneapolis for moral support, ad hoc fact checking and pertinent highlights from *People* magazine. In London, I'm indebted to Fiona Buchan and Will Gourlay for holding my hand though my first LP assignment and pacifying various nervous breakdowns triggered by ceaseless car trouble, snow storm delays and bureaucratic impasses. Finally, special thanks to Robert Reid whose advice and cool confidence provided balance to the chaos and snowballing exhaustion that engulfed us.

**Robert Reid** Thanks to Fiona Buchan for signing me up, Tom Masters for keeping me in line, and to Leif Pettersen for splitting Romania's broad being with me. So many people in Buglaria and Romania selflessly gave time to help with fares, times – or to just show family pics while the line builds up behind me (eg Shumen, Bulgaria, bus station), but particular nods go to Assen of Sofia and Lorenziu of Fagaras.

**Tim Richards** *Dziękuję bardzo* to the extremely helpful Polish tourist office staff who let me bend their ears on all matters involving their cities: especially Tom in Kraków; Agnieszka, Joanna and Monika in Warsaw; Karolina in Łódź; Bożena in Wrocław; Antoni in Lublin; Joanna in Zakopane; Maciej in Toruń; Monika in Poznań; Ewa in Szczecin; and Anna in Giżycko. Amy Doidge and her colleagues at the Australian Embassy in Warsaw also provided useful assistance, as did Aussie expat Darren Haines-Powell. Thanks to my former teaching colleagues Magda Fijałkowska and Ewa Bandura for their friendship across the years and continents, and to new friend Gosia Grabarczyk for that home-cooked dinner! Thanks (and continuing prosperity) to 'paj' manufacturer Beata Zielińska in Gdynia; and to the barstaff at U Szkota in Gdańsk, who kept the *goldwasser* coming when it was needed. Thanks also to the PKP staff who keep Poland's trains running on time, no matter what the weather. A final thanks to the elderly gentleman who talked with me in Polish and German at a tram stop below Wawel Castle, about his experiences as a slave labourer for the Nazi regime: it's personal stories like his that make travel so enlightening.

**Wendy Taylor** Thanks to my friends and family back home, especially my mom, Pat Moran, my best one, Matthew Wood, and my sister and her guy, Sandy Taylor and Jason Linder, who provided me with the space and light to finish this project. David Hamilton and Rob Gala did a million little favours for me in Ukraine, making my life and work much easier. In Belarus, Valeria Klitsunova and I spent an unforgettable day together in her wonderful outdoor interactive museum, Dudutki, drinking *samogon* and talking life and politics in Belarus. No one gave me more help, support, and incredible adventures than Inna Bukshtynovich, my dear friend and partner in crime. Finally, I'd like to acknowledge all of the amazing Belarusians who, despite the world's ignorance of their situation, are risking their livelihoods to live in a country that isn't controlled by force and fear.

## OUR READERS

Many thanks to the travellers who used the last edition and wrote to us with helpful hints, useful advice and interesting anecdotes:

**A** Stephen Akehurst, Ruth Alban, Andrew Ambrosius, Yiannis Andreopoulos, Rault Morgane, Luitgard Anthony, James Appleyard, Achilleas Askotis **B** Sanda Bajgoric, Gokhan Balci, Attie Balogh, Andrea Barbati, John Barton, Chris Begley, Daniel Berry, Asmund Bertelsen, Pere Bilbeny, Elias Bizannes, Kate Bland, Petr Bohac, Lee Bone, Philippe Boss, Anthony Botterley,

Peter Bradbury, Daniel Bralich, Per Bråmå, Jean Brasille, Robert Brocklehurst, Alan & Lesley Brown, Geoff Brown, Oliver Buckley, Les Burke **C** Simon Campbell, Gerard Casamiquela, Yoav Caspin, Jacqueline Catherall, Alexander Cellmer, Ryan Chaplin, John Chapman, Sanieel Chung, Jemetha Clark, Ron Clough, Cristina Ramos Colas, Mark Cooper, Dan Coplan, Robert Cosgrove, Columba Cryan, Oliver Cumming, Grant Cura, Michael Cwach **D** Dianne Davis, Camiel de Leeuw, Sjoerd de Vries, Eduardo Delgado, Johan Dittrich Hallberg, Darren Downs, Noel Duffin, Euan Duncan, Sarah Dyer **E** Michael Eckett, Kjersti Engehaugen, Kerstin Eriksson **F** Natalie Faber, Silvano Fait, Fernando Ferreira Lima, Mitchel Fidel, Martin Fiedler, Jim Fitzpatrick, Val Fomov, Sylvio Franco Amaral, Geer Furtjes **G** Patrick Gallagher, Marco Germani, Christopher Getz, Cora Gilbey, Anders Glette, Sarah Goldsmith, Jack Gore, Elvira Gottardi, Riley Graebner, Bowden Granville, James Green, Brendan Griffin, Laura Grignani, Joanne Grimwood, Michael Groth, Pierre Grumpay, Martin Grznar, Nargiz Gurbanova **H** Dianne Haines, Kræn Hansen, David Harper, Cheryl Harris, Jacqui Harris, Kay Harrison, Diana Hebditch, Michael Hensen, Richard Hey, John Hill, Nele Hollo, Susan Howard, Nam Seok Hwang **J** Vicky Janssens, Amelia Jenkinson, Fiona Johnson, Melissa Johnson, Tommy Johnson, Alex Johnstone, Ask Jørgensen **K** Matthias Kalwitzki, Martina Kamenikova, Austin Kinsella, Christian Kirsch, Melissa Kluger, Leylli Knur, Jan Kotuc, Sven Kropf, Natalia Kudimova **L** Zev la Mont, Ilona Lablaika, Melissa Lane, Megan Layne, Frantisek Lengal, Christopher Lobash, Karen Locke, Thomas Lohr, David & Melissa Lonergan, Jane Lowson, Peter Lowthian, Jim Lum **M** Jay & Carolyn MacInnes, Jan Macutek, Nick Mahieu, Jacob Majarian, Stephen Mak, Bojan Manusev, David Marchant, Mirek Marut, Valeria Marzullo, Michael & Beatrix Mathew, Olexandr Melnyk, Francesca Meloni, Brian Michaels, Cynthia Milton, Mike Mimirinis, Marjanka Mingels, Paul Mollatt, Steve Moore, Karin Moosberger, Catherine Moss, Elaine Muir, Janice Munden, Beth Mylius **N** Robin & Carol Nance, Raluca Nemtanu, Rebecca Newton, Wolfgang Niebel, Mick Nishikawa **O** Carolyn Orcutt, Jeroen Overduin **P** Kirsten Paul, Mike Payne, Maarten Peeters, Stjepan Perkovic, Ameet Pinto, Karen Playfair, Jeanette Pohlman, Thijs Polfliet, Pam Poole **R** Tracy Radisich, Doug Rand, Michael Raue, Timothy Reilly, Wilfried Rekowski, Johan Rhodin, Jorge Ribeiro, Kyle Richardson, Simon Robertson, Andoni Rodelgo, Sven Roeben, Eva Romo, Tim Rooth, Gregory Rose, Armin Rosencranz, Stephen Rott, David Route, Bruce Rumage, Hannes Rutqvist, Johanna Rydelius **S** Cyriel Schenk, Josef Schmidt, Jason Schock, Hugh Scrine, David Siegel, Juuk Slager, Tanya Smith, Wendy Smith, Manuela Sonderegger, Balázs Sonnevend, Graham Stagg, Maarten Stam, Charlie Steel, Reni Stoll, John Streets, Theo Sudomlak, Richard Szmola **T** Steve Taylor, Bruce Thomson, Adam Thorn, Anders Thorsell, Daystan Tiller, Fab Tomlin, Anna Travali, Zoran Tuntev, Denise Turcinov, Sam Turvey, Gillian Twigg, Donald Tyson **U** Michael Unger, Gail Upperton, Rahel Uster **V** Rob Vaessen, Monique van den Broek, Puteshestvuem van Krem, Wendy van Lubek, Vesna Velkovrh Bukilica, Michael Veraya, Kristian Vestergaard, Rimas VisGirda, Sini Vlaisavljevic **W** Eric Wagensonner, Jan Wasserman, Kelly Weiss, Philipp Wendtland, Jonas Wernli, Joachim Whaley, Jonathan Wheatley, Katie & Geoff Whitehouse, Mavis Whitfield, Flora Whittall, Jonathan Wickens, Nils Wiemer, Caroline Williams, Elizabeth Williams, Ruth Willmott, David Wright, Alishia Wurgler **Z** Sarah Zarrow, Maria Zavala, Gilbert & Cynthia Zimmer

## ACKNOWLEDGMENTS

Many thanks to the following for the use of their content:

Map data contained in colour highlights map © Mountain High Maps 1993 Digital Wisdom, Inc.

# Index

**000** Map pages
**000** Photograph pages

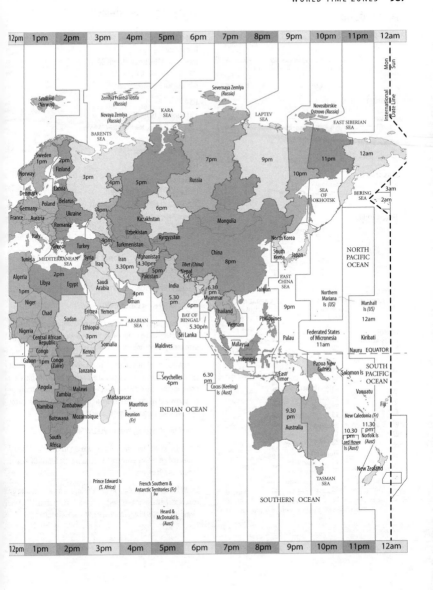

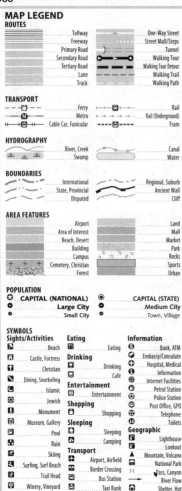

## MAP LEGEND

**ROUTES**

Tollway · One-Way Street · Freeway · Street Mall/Steps · Primary Road · Tunnel · Secondary Road · Walking Tour · Tertiary Road · Walking Tour Detour · Lane · Walking Trail · Track · Walking Path

**TRANSPORT**

Ferry · Rail · Metro · Rail (Underground) · Cable Car, Funicular · Tram

**HYDROGRAPHY**

River, Creek · Canal · Swamp · Water

**BOUNDARIES**

International · Regional, Suburb · State, Provincial · Ancient Wall · Disputed · Cliff

**AREA FEATURES**

Airport · Land · Area of Interest · Mall · Beach, Desert · Market · Building · Park · Campus · Rocks · Cemetery, Christian · Sports · Forest · Urban

**POPULATION**

⊙ **CAPITAL (NATIONAL)** · ◉ CAPITAL (STATE)
● **Large City** · ● Medium City
● Small City · ○ Town, Village

**SYMBOLS**

**Sights/Activities**
Beach · Castle, Fortress · Christian · Diving, Snorkeling · Islamic · Jewish · Monument · Museum, Gallery · Pool · Ruin · Skiing · Surfing, Surf Beach · Trail Head · Winery, Vineyard · Zoo, Bird Sanctuary

**Eating**
Eating

**Drinking**
Drinking · Café

**Entertainment**
Entertainment

**Shopping**
Shopping

**Sleeping**
Sleeping · Camping

**Transport**
Airport, Airfield · Border Crossing · Bus Station · Taxi Rank · Parking Area

**Information**
Bank, ATM · Embassy/Consulate · Hospital, Medical · Information · Internet Facilities · Petrol Station · Police Station · Post Office, GPO · Telephone · Toilets

**Geographic**
Lighthouse · Lookout · Mountain, Volcano · National Park · Pass, Canyon · River Flow · Shelter, Hut · Waterfall

## LONELY PLANET OFFICES

### Australia
Head Office
Locked Bag 1, Footscray, Victoria 3011
☎ 03 8379 8000, fax 03 8379 8111
talk2us@lonelyplanet.com.au

### USA
150 Linden St, Oakland, CA 94607
☎ 510 893 8555, toll free 800 275 8555
fax 510 893 8572
info@lonelyplanet.com

### UK
72-82 Rosebery Ave,
Clerkenwell, London EC1R 4RW
☎ 020 7841 9000, fax 020 7841 9001
go@lonelyplanet.co.uk

## Published by Lonely Planet Publications Pty Ltd
ABN 36 005 607 983

© Lonely Planet Publications Pty Ltd 2007

© photographers as indicated 2007

Cover photograph: Dubrovnik at evening, Johanna Huber/4 Corners Images. Many of the images in this guide are available for licensing from Lonely Planet Images: www.lonelyplanetimages.com.